What's in a Dictio

guide word — guide word

entry word

wal·lop (wol′əp) *Informal.* **1** hit very hard. **2** a very hard blow: *The wallop knocked him out.* **3** defeat thoroughly. **4** **walloping,** very big. 1, 3 *v.,* 2 *n.,* 4 *adj.*

definition

example

wal·low (wol′ō) **1** roll around in something: *The pigs wallowed in the mud. The boat wallowed helplessly in the stormy sea.* **2** let yourself enjoy something so much that it is actually disgusting: *to wallow in self-pity.* **3** the act of wallowing. **4** a place where an animal wallows: *There used to be many buffalo wallows on the prairies.* 1, 2 *v.,* 3, 4 *n.*

part(s) of speech

wall·pa·per (wol′pā′pər) **1** paper printed with a coloured pattern, for decorating and covering walls. **2** decorate with this paper. 1 *n.,* 2 *v.*

wal·nut (wol′nut′) **1** a rather large, almost round nut with a bumpy shell and a division between its two halves. It is good to eat. **2** the tree it grows on, whose wood is often used for making furniture. *n.*

illustration with extra information in the caption

Walruses dive to great depths to catch clams from the ocean floor with their long curving tusks. Apart from humans, their only enemies are polar bears and killer whales.

plural form

wal·rus (wol′rəs) a large sea mammal of the arctic regions, like a seal but with rough, wrinkled skin and long tusks. *n., pl.* **wal·rus** or **wal·rus·es.**

waltz (wolts) **1** a smooth, gliding dance with a slow one-two-three beat. **2** a piece of music for such a dance. **3** do this dance. 1, 2 *n.,* 3 *v.*

wam·pum (wom′pəm) beads made from shells, which eastern First Nations people used to use for money, for decoration, in ceremonies, or in wampum belts. In a wampum belt, the beads were arranged in patterns which told a story. *n.*

feature box

> **WORD HISTORY........ wampum**
>
> **Wampum** comes from an Algonquian language called Narraganset. The original word was *wampompeag,* meaning "strings of white."

adjective forms

wan (won) pale, weak, or tired-looking: *a wan smile.* *adj.,* **wan·ner, wan·nest.** —**wan′ly,** *adv.*

pronunciation

wand (wond) a thin rod: *a magician's wand.* Some scanners have a wand you pass over the bar code. *n.*

related word

wan·der (won′dər) **1** go here and there without any special goal: *We wandered through stores without buying anything.* **2** leave the right spot or the right way; stray: *The dog wandered off and got lost.* *v.* —**wan′der·er,** *n.*

wane (wān) become gradually smaller: *The moon wanes after it has become full. Her interest in the subject has waned.* *v.,* **waned, wan·ing.**

on the wane, growing less; waning: *The power of the president was on the wane.*

verb forms

wan·gle (wang′gəl) *Informal.* manage to get, by tricks or persuasion: *She wangled an invitation to the party.* *v.,* **wan·gled, wan·gling.**

idiom

want (wont) **1** wish for; wish: *The child wants his dinner. She wants to become an engineer.* **2** something desired or needed: *He is a man of few wants and leads a simple life.* **3** lack; need: *That plant wants water (v.). The plant died for want of water (n.).* 1, 3 *v.,* 2, 3 *n.*

want for, lack; be without: *She has never wanted for friends.*

want ad (wont′ ad′) *Informal.* a notice in a newspaper that someone is looking for a job, a car, a person to hire, an apartment, etc.

want·ing (won′ting) lacking; missing or not good enough: *Two pieces were wanting from the puzzle. The stranger was wanting in politeness.* *adj.*

wan·ton (won′tən) wild or reckless; ignoring good sense and reason: *a wanton attack, a wanton mood.* *adj.*

Each year, the males of this species grow antlers that may span almost 2 m.

Canadianism

wap·i·ti (wop′i tē) the North American elk, a large member of the deer family with long branched antlers. *n., pl.* **wap·i·ti** or **wap·i·tis.**

pronunciation guide

a bat	e bed	i bid	o pot	u cup	th thin
ā cake	ē me	ī bite	ō go	ü rude	TH then
ä bar	ə about	ər over	ô for	u̇ put	zh measure

Collins Gage Canadian *Junior* Dictionary

Collins

THOMSON NELSON

Australia Canada Mexico Singapore Spain United Kingdom United States

THOMSON NELSON™

Previous edition published under the title Gage Canadian Junior Dictionary, copyright © 2000

Printed and bound in Canada
1 2 3 4 09 08 07 06

School distribution by **Nelson, a division of Thomson Canada Limited**
1120 Birchmount Road, Toronto, Ontario, M1K 5G4
www.nelson.com

Trade distribution by
HarperCollins Canada
2 Bloor Street East,
Toronto, ON M4W 1A8
www.harpercollins.ca

Collins is one of the world's leading reference publishers. The **Collins Word Web** contains 125 million words of Canadian English and grows at over 1.5 million words per month.

Gage represents a 40-year tradition of Canadian dictionary making. Today, Gage is the reference division of **Thomson Nelson**, Canada's foremost educational publisher.

Page Design: ArtPlus Ltd.

Database: Total Graphics

Library and Archives Canada Cataloguing in Publication

Collins Gage Canadian junior dictionary
ISBN-13: 978-0-17-632531-2
ISBN-10: 0-17-632531-X
Previous ed. published under title: Gage Canadian Junior Dictionary
ISBN 0-7715-1997-4

1. English language—Dictionaries, Juvenile.

PE1628.5.C65 2006 j423 C2006-901182-6

Editorial and Production

Director of Publishing
Bev Buxton

General Manager, Literacy and Reference
Kevin Martindale

Director of Publishing, Literacy and Reference
Joe Banel

Publisher, Supplementary Literacy and Reference
David Friend

Executive Managing Editor, Development
Darleen Rotozinski

Senior Program Manager, Supplementary Literacy and Reference
Ann Downar

Assistant Editor
Lisa Peterson

Production Manager
Cathy Deak

Design Director
Ken Phipps

Cover Design
Peter Papayanakis
Jan John Rivera

Compositor
Zenaida Diores

Printer
Transcontinental Printing

Editorial Team, Original Edition

Joe Banel
Eileen Brett
Chelsea Donaldson
Ann Downar
Jan Harkness
Anna Kress
T. K. Pratt
Darleen Rotozinski
Debbie Sawczak
Tom Shields
Fraser Sutherland
Carol Waldock

Original *Gage Junior Dictionary* Author Team: W.S. Avis, R.J. Gregg, M.H. Scargill

Consulting Editor

T. K. Pratt
Professor Emeritus of English
University of Prince Edward Island

Reviewers and Consultants

Joan Alexander
Team Leader, Curriculum Services
St. Albert PSSD 6, Alberta

Pauline Allen
Teacher
School District 18, New Brunswick

Halina Bartley
Principal
Kawartha Pine Ridge DSB, Ontario

Sid Bentley
Religions Teacher
Surrey, British Columbia

Marc Bookbinder
UJA Federation
Toronto, Ontario

Faye Brownbridge
Language Coordinator
Calgary RCSSB 1, Alberta

Erin Campbell
Kingswood Elementary
Hammonds Plains, Nova Scotia

John Cassano
Language Consultant
The Education Centre, Ontario

Dr. Sandra Clarke
Professor of Linguistics
Memorial University of Newfoundland

Cam Colville
Assistant Principal
Edmonton Public SB, Alberta

Diana Cruise
Consultant
Interlake SD 21, Manitoba

Robert Cutting
Teacher
Durham SDSB, Ontario

Patricia Delgaty
Curriculum Adviser
Toronto DSB, Ontario

Nancy Dixon
Vice Principal
School District 12, New Brunswick

Vernon Douglas
Native Education Advisor
Toronto DSB, Ontario

Veronica Dyck, Gary Robson, Helen Settee
Native Education Directorate
Department of Education and Training
Manitoba

Gillian Federico
Consultant
Religious Education/Family Life
Dufferin-Peel CDSB, Ontario

Wanda Gibbons
Teacher,
Westwind SD 74, Alberta

Jeanne Godfrey
Program Consultant
Greater Essex County DSB, Ontario

Ruby Gosse
Fairview Heights Elementary School
Halifax, Nova Scotia

Gloria Gustafson
Consultant
Coquitlam SD 43, British Columbia

David Hodgkinson
Former Language Consultant
Waterloo Region DSB, Ontario

Helen Hohmann
Consultant
Edmonton Catholic Schools, Alberta

Thayyiba Ibrahim
Islam Society of North America
Ontario

Eddie Ing
Howard Public School
Toronto, Ontario

Brinder Jauhal
Former Language Consultant
Toronto DSB, Ontario

Rebecca Kudloo
Development Officer
Keewatin Divisional Board
of Education
Nunavut

Nathalie Lachance
Métis National Council,
Ottawa

Martin MacDonald
Programming, Professional
Development
Strait Regional SB, Nova Scotia

Sister Dorothy Moore
Mi'kmaq Services Division
Department of Education and Culture
Nova Scotia

Looee Okalik
Inuit Tapirisat of Canada
Ottawa

Teresa Paoli
Teacher
Toronto CDSB, Ontario

Joanne Pelletier
Program Coordinator
Urban Native Teacher Education
Saskatchewan

Wendy Phillips
Teacher
School District 38, British Columbia

Linda Reid
Curriculum Coordinator
Thames Valley DSB, Ontario

Liz Rose
Department of Education
Northwest Territories

Laura Rudland
District Resource Teacher,
First Nations
Vancouver SB, British Columbia

Margaret Ryall
Program Specialist
Avalon East SB, Newfoundland

Martha Sanger
Former Teacher
Avalon East SB, Newfoundland

D. Greg Stafford
Richardson Elementary
Delta, British Columbia

Ed Swain
Métis National Council
Ottawa

Larry Trafford
Executive Assistant,
Religious Education
OECTA, Ontario

Lynda Tysowski
Consultant
Saskatoon SB 13, Saskatchewan

Gerald Woodman
Co-ordinator
Religious Education/Family Life
Dufferin-Peel CDSB, Ontario

Literacy Consultants, Appendix

James Coulter
Project Leader, Middle Years Adolescent
Literacy Project
Toronto DSB, Ontario

Ruth McQuirter Scott
Professor
Faculty of Education, Brock University
St. Catharines, Ontario

Contents

A Challenge

There are features in this dictionary that you may not have seen in a dictionary before. Can you find the following?

1. A word that first came into the English language in Canada.
2. Two words that are often confused with each other.
3. An activity that helps you pronounce words correctly.
4. A picture that tells you how tall a grizzly bear is.
5. A situation where "for good" doesn't have to be a good thing.
6. The Roman numeral for eight.
7. The correct places to use capital letters.

You can find out even more by doing the activities on pages 7 to 19. Try them!

1. There's one on page 340, **humidex**. You can find more of these words by looking for a picture of a tiny red maple leaf.
2. There's **accept** and **except**, on page 23. You can find more of these words by looking for boxes titled CONFUSABLES. There are also different boxes that tell you about grammar, using words, word families, and word history. Just open the dictionary almost anywhere!
3. There's one on page 15. You can find more activities to help you improve your dictionary skills on pages 7 to 19.
4. Look at page 71. You can find many other pages with pictures and captions that give you detailed information about animals, plants, ships, people, etc. If you want to know more, use an encyclopedia or the Internet to look up key words from the captions.
5. There's one on page 303. You can find more of these phrases that have special meanings (they're called idioms) on almost every page of this dictionary.
6. Look at page 788. You can find many more useful facts about numbers, Canada, abbreviations, countries of the world, etc. by looking at pages 773–800.
7. Look at page 802. You can find more information about grammar and using words in the rest of the pages of this *Mini-Guide*.

Getting to Know Your Dictionary

This dictionary contains facts about nearly 30 000 entry words that you are most likely to use when you speak, write, listen, or read. The following pages provide information and activities that will help you to find and use these words.

Looking Up a Word You Can't Spell

How do you look up a word you can't spell?

Suppose, for example, that you want to find the spelling and meaning of a word that you heard as **kaos**. You look up **kaos** in the dictionary, and there's no such word. So, use the chart *Common Spellings of English Sounds*, shown on pages 8 and 9. Here's what to do.

- Look at the first column (*Sound*) and find *k*.
- Look to the right and you can see some possible spellings for the sound *k* at the *beginning of a word*: **c**oat, **ch**emistry, **k**ind, **qu**ick, **qu**ay. This means the word you heard could be *caos*, *chaos*, *kaos* (no good, you've tried that), *qaos*, or *quaos*. Check these out, and you will find the word *chaos*.

For some words, you may have to go to the other columns for *middle of word* or *end of word* spellings.

It also helps to know the symbols used for sounds. Here they are. The symbol ə is called the schwa (pronounced shwȧ).

a	b**a**t	e	b**e**d	i	b**i**d	o	p**o**t	u	c**u**p	th	**th**in
ā	c**a**ke	ē	m**e**	ī	b**i**te	ō	g**o**	ü	r**u**de	ᴛʜ	**th**en
ȧ	b**a**r	ə	**a**bout	ər	ov**er**	ȯ	f**o**r	u̇	p**u**t	zh	mea**s**ure

TRY IT

Use the *Common Spellings of English Sounds* chart on pages 8 and 9 to find the spellings of words that sound like these.

1. sī′əns
2. shō fər′
3. ō′shən
4. ə kwīr′
5. nā′bər
6. thrü

Common Spellings of English Sounds

Sound	Beginnings of words	Middles of words	Ends of words
a	and, aunt	hat, plaid, half, laugh	—
ā	age, aid, eight	face, fail, straight, payment, gauge, break, vein, neighbour	say, weigh, bouquet, they, café, matinée
ȧ	art	barn, bazaar, heart	hurrah
b	bad	table, rabbit	rub, ebb
ch	child	cappuccino, richness, nature, watching, question	much, catch
d	do	lady, ladder	red, used
e	any, aerial, air, end	many, said, says, let, bread, leopard, friend, bury	—
ē	equal, eat, either	metre, team, need, receive, people, keyhole, machine, believe	algae, quay, acne, flea, bee, key, Métis, loonie, pity
f	fat, phone	after, coffee, often, laughter, gopher	roof, sniff, cough, half, epitaph
g	go, ghost, guess	ago, giggle, catalogues	bag, egg, rogue
h	help, who	ahead	—
i	enamel, in	message, been, pin, sieve, women, busy, build, hymn	—
ī	aisle, aye, either, eye, ice, island	height, line, align, might, buying, type	aye, eye, lie, high, buy, sky, dye
j	gem, jam	educate, badger, soldier, adjust, tragic, exaggerate, enjoy	bridge, rage, hajj
k	coat, chemistry, kind, quick, quay	record, account, echo, lucky, acquire, looking, liquor, extra	back, seek, walk, tuque
l	land, llama	only, follow	coal, fill
m	me	coming, climbing, summer	calm, hum, comb, solemn
n	gnaw, knife, nut	miner, manner	sign, man, inn
ng	—	ink, finger, singer	bang, tongue
o	all, almond, author, awful, encore, honest, odd, ought	watch, palm, taut, taught, sawed, hot, bought	Ottawa, paw

Common Spellings of English Sounds

Sound	Beginnings of words	Middles of words	Ends of words
ō	open, oath, own	George, sewn, home, boat, folk, brooch, soul, flown	chateau, sew, potato, toe, though, blow
ȯ	order, oar	born, board, floor, mourn	—
oi	oil, oyster	boil, boyhood	boy
ou	hour, out, owl	bound, drought, howl	plough, now
p	pen	paper, supper	up
r	run, rhythm	parent, hurry	bear, burr
s	cent, psychology, say, science, sword	decent, loosen, muscle, massive, answer, extra	nice, marvellous, miss, lax
sh	chauffeur, sure, shirt	ocean, machine, special, unsure, conscience, nauseous, tension, issue, mission, nation	cache, wish
t	ptarmigan, tell, Thomas	doubtful, later, latter	doubt, crashed, bit, mitt
th	thin	toothache	bath
ᴛʜ	then	mother	smooth, bathe
u	oven, up	come, does, flood, trouble, cup	—
ü	ooze	neutral, move, food, group, rule, fruit	threw, shoe, caribou, through, blue
u̇	—	wolf, good, should, full	—
yü	Europe, use, you, Yukon	beauty, feud, duty	queue, few, cue, you
v	very	over	of, love
w	will, wheat, one	choir, quick, twin	—
y	young	opinion, canyon	—
z	xylophone	raisin, scissors, exact, lazy, dazzle	has, maze, buzz
zh	—	measure, division	mirage
ə	alone, essential, oblige, upon	spaghetti, fountain, moment, pencil, bottle, criticism, button, cautious, circus	sofa
ər	early, urge	salary, term, learn, first, word, journey, turn, syrup	liar, deter, stir, actor, fur, burr, measure

Fast Find

How do you find a word quickly? Here are two strategies to use.

Alphabetical Order

The entry words in the *Collins Gage Canadian Junior Dictionary* are in alphabetical order:

A B C D E F G H I J K L M N O P Q R S T U V W X Y Z

Whenever you want to look up a word in the dictionary, decide if the first letter of the word comes in the first third of the alphabet (A to F, which has blue tabs) or the middle third (G to Q, which has red tabs) or the last third (R to Z, which has green tabs). Then **try to open the dictionary near the right part.**

TRY IT

Which third of the dictionary would you turn to if you were looking up each of the following entry words?

1. empty
2. shark
3. portfolio
4. literature

Words in the dictionary with the **same first** letter are also arranged alphabetically according to the **second letter**. Here are some **c** words, in alphabetical order: case, cease, chain, coal, cry, cycle.

When the **first two letters** are the same, words are alphabetized by the **third letter**, and so on: chair, cheer, chief, choice, choose, chum.

TRY IT

1. Arrange the following words in alphabetical order to make sentences.
   - me followed black dog a yesterday
   - clawed cat a big David
   - four wrestling them were of
   - brothers truck Al's chairs in can't their carry
2. Find the two entry words between which your name would go.

Guide Words

At the top of each page of the dictionary are two words. For example:

additional 27 **admission**

These words are called **guide words.** The guide word on the left is the first entry word to appear on the page; the guide word on the right is the last. All the entry words on that page will fall between the two guide words alphabetically. **Looking at guide words helps you find the entry that you want more quickly.**

TRY IT

By looking at the guide words shown for page 27, decide which of the following will appear as entry words on page 27:

admire, adjective, addition, adopt, advantage, adjust, adequate, adult

Definitions

A definition explains the meaning of a word. If a word has more than one definition, each definition is given a different number. Usually the most common meaning is given first. For example, **belly** has three definitions:

bel·ly (bel′ē) 1 the part of the body which contains the stomach and intestines; abdomen. 2 the bulging part of anything, or the hollow in it: *the belly of a ship.* 3 swell out; bulge: *The sails bellied in the wind.*

TRY IT

Do you know the meanings of the words in italics below? Look up each word in the dictionary and write down the definition that makes sense.

1. My brother and his friends play in a *band.*
2. I must *enter* the information in the computer.
3. The firefighter directed a *jet* of foam at the burning airplane.
4. Please don't turn down the corner of the *page.*

Examples

Many definitions are followed by one or more examples, printed in italics. Examples show how the word is used in sentences or phrases. Look at the entry for **deep**.

deep (dēp) 1 going far down, far back, or far in: *a deep well, a deep forest* (*adj.*). *They talked deep into the night. Dig deep* (*adv.*). 2 low: *a deep voice.* 3 needing or showing a lot of understanding: *Her poetry is very deep.*

TRY IT

Write your own example sentences for the following definitions.

1. **block** (def. 3) stop or prevent:...
2. **bottom** (def. 1) the deepest or lowest part:...
3. **head** (def. 5) the chief person; leader:...
4. **patch** (def. 4) a small area:...

With a partner, check your examples to make sure they fit the definitions and make good sense. Then compare them with the examples in the dictionary. In each case, decide whether your example, your partner's example, or the one in the dictionary is best. Be prepared to say why.

Root Words

Sometimes a word you want to look up is not a main entry. In such cases, you should find the root word of the one you want to look up.

Related Words

Some entries in the dictionary are in the same paragraph as a main entry.

col·o·ny (kol′ə nē) 1 a territory ruled by a powerful country far away which has **colonized** it, or taken it by force and sent people to live there: *England had many colonies in Africa and Asia.* 2 a group of people who go to live there from the conquering country, and who set up towns and farms. These people are also called **colonists.** 3 a number of people of one country, faith, or occupation living as a group: *There are several Doukhobor colonies in Saskatchewan.* 4 a group of animals or plants of one kind, living or growing together: *We found two colonies of ants under the steps.* *n., pl.* **col·o·nies.** —**co·lo′ni·al** (kə lō′nē əl), *adj.* —**col′o·ni·za′tion,** *n.*

Here you can see the words **colonized**, **colonists**, **colonial**, and **colonization.** They are related to the word **colony**, that is, they all come from the same root.

Word family boxes are another place to find words related to a main entry. Read more about them on p. 19.

Endings

Sometimes a word you want to look up is a different form of a main entry. Again, you should **find the root word** of the one you want to look up.

- **Verb forms** made by simply adding *-ed* or *-ing* to the root word are not given as entries in the dictionary. If you look for *watched* or *watching* you will find only the root word **watch.** You will find entries like **magnified**, **magnifying**, where the spelling of the root word **magnify** has changed.
- **Adjective forms** made by simply adding *-er* or *-est* to the root word are not given as entries in the dictionary. If you look for *smaller* or *smallest* you will find only the root word **small.** You will find entries like **happier**, **happiest**, where the spelling of the root word **happy** has changed.
- **Plural forms** made by simply adding *-s* or *-es* to the root word are not given as entries in the dictionary. If you look for *cars* or *buses* you will find only the root word **car** or **bus.** You will find entries like **hobbies**, where the spelling of the root word **hobby** has changed.

TRY IT

Write down the main entry word you would look up to find each word in italics.

1. Marilou is *giving* me chocolates for my birthday.
2. We made an *agreement* about sharing the work.
3. I was *terrified* by that movie.
4. There were several *children* in the park.
5. Lynn Johnston is a famous *cartoonist.*
6. We saw the *funniest* clown at the party!
7. I find that game *babyish.*
8. I've been to three *parties* this month.

Idioms

Suppose you read the sentence *Michael asked his sister to lend a hand with the snow shovelling*. You know the meaning of *lend*. But what about *lend a hand*? You will find this phrase explained at the end of the entry for **lend**:

lend (lend) 1 let someone have for a while: *Will you lend me your bike for an hour? Banks lend money to people for various purposes.* 2 give; add: *That lace curtain lends a certain charm to the window.* *v.*, **lent, lend·ing.**
—**lend′er,** *n.*
lend a hand, help: *They lent a hand with the dishes.*

Lend a hand is an idiom. It has a special meaning that you could not guess from the meanings of the separate words. Michael does not want his sister to lend him one of her hands!

TRY IT

Rewrite each of the following sentences, using an idiom in place of the words in italics. The key word of the correct idiom is in parentheses ( ) after each sentence.

1. After he has heard a song once, he can play it *without reading the music.* (**ear**)
2. She is a sensible person, and her ideas are always *practical.* (**earth**)
3. My mother gave me a *scolding* for being late for supper. (**piece**)
4. The job won't take long if we all *do our part.* (**pitch**)

Pronunciation

The way a word sounds is shown in parentheses ( ) immediately after the entry word. Since English words are often not pronounced the way they are spelled, the pronunciations are marked using special symbols.

Pronunciation Symbols

Below is a pronunciation key. You will find a copy of this on the right hand pages of the dictionary. The symbol ə is called the schwa (pronounced shwȧ). Consonant sounds that are written with ordinary letters are not included in this key.

a	**bat**	e	**bed**	i	**bid**	o	**pot**	u	**cup**	th	**thin**
ā	**cake**	ē	**me**	ī	**bite**	ō	**go**	ū	**rude**	ᴛʜ	**then**
ȧ	**bar**	ə	**about**	ər	**over**	ȯ	**for**	u̇	**put**	zh	**measure**

TRY IT

1. Pronounce each of the following words, and look carefully at the special vowel symbols used.

   game (gām) **put** (pu̇t) **yolk** (yōk) **hurt** (hərt)
   war (wȯr) **mark** (mȧrk) **view** (vyū) **line** (līn)
   town (toun) **leap** (lēp) **toy** (toi) **zoom** (zūm)

2. Say each of the following words aloud. Then write them down, underlining the syllables that are pronounced with a schwa.

   bottom, buffalo, corral, button, gorilla, command

3. Use the pronunciation key to write down the pronunciation for each of the following words. Say each word aloud to yourself, then put down one symbol for each sound that you hear.

   climb, creep, forge, great, learn, leave, love, pale, stones, thick, then, write

   When you have finished, look up these words in the dictionary and check the pronunciations you have written.

Stress

In most words of two or more syllables, one syllable is spoken with more force, or stress, than any of the others. The stressed syllable is shown by a heavy raised mark (′) placed after it. For example, in these words the stress is on the first syllable:

cotton (kot′ən), **nephew** (nef′yū), **paper** (pā′pər).

In the following words the stress is on the second syllable:

delight (di līt′), **excite** (ek sīt′), **prefer** (pri fər′).

TRY IT

Say each of the words that follow and decide which is the stressed syllable. Then copy the pronunciation of each word and add the stress mark.

decide (di sīd)	survive (sər vīv)	terrible (ter ə bəl)
pattern (pat ərn)	image (im ij)	pursue (pər sū)

In addition to the main stress, many words have one or two syllables with a lighter stress. This is shown by means of a lighter mark (′) placed after the syllable. Say the following examples and listen for the lighter stress:

demonstrate (dem′ən strāt′) **hippopotamus** (hip′ə pot′ə məs)

The main stress is called **primary stress** and the lighter is **secondary stress.**

Part-of-Speech Labels

Words like *noun, adjective,* and *verb* are names for parts of speech. The eight parts of speech used in the dictionary, together with their abbreviations, are listed below.

noun	*n.*	pronoun	*pron.*
verb	*v.*	preposition	*prep.*
adjective	*adj.*	conjunction	*conj.*
adverb	*adv.*	interjection	*interj.*

TRY IT

Look up the following words and write which part of speech they are.

1. basic	3. munch	5. ouch	7. unless
2. cape	4. often	6. toward	8. who

Entry words found inside a definition do not have a label showing their part of speech. In the entry below, **bossy** is not a noun or verb; those labels refer only to **boss**, the main entry word.

boss (bos) *Informal.* 1 the one in charge; a person who hires workers or tells them what to do. 2 give orders to: *He likes to boss people. Don't boss me around!* A person who does this is **bossy.** 1 *n.*, 2 *v.*

Usage Labels

Informal and Slang

Some words are labelled *Informal.* These words are all right to use in ordinary speech, written conversation, or a letter to a friend, but not in formal writing.

Some words are labelled *Slang.* These words are not yet considered part of the general language. Slang may be all right to use in ordinary speech but should not be used in written work.

Canadianisms

The entry ✱ **outport** is labelled with a tiny red maple leaf. This means that the word or meaning is used mainly in Canada or that it first came into the English language in Canada. Such words are called *Canadianisms.*

TRY IT

Look up the following Canadianisms in the dictionary. Then write a sentence for each one.

1. bateau
2. break-up
3. lobstick
4. muskeg
5. slapshot
6. toonie
7. tuque
8. umiak

Feature Boxes

There are five kinds of feature boxes in the *Collins Gage Canadian Junior Dictionary.* They are titled **Word History**, **Using Words**, **Confusables**, **Word Family**, and **Grammar Check.** These boxes give extra information about one or more of the entry words above them. See pages 18-19 for descriptions of these feature boxes.

Word History

These feature boxes tell about the history of words.

TRY IT

Look up the *Word History* boxes for the following and read the box. Then answer the question.

1.	decathlon	How many events are in a decathlon?
2.	digit	What is another English word that comes from the Latin *dicitus*?
3.	engine	From which language did this word come into English?
4.	geography	What is an English word that begins with *geo*, meaning "the study of shapes and solids"?

Using Words

These boxes give advice on how to use a particular word. Some boxes will tell about words that have similar, but not identical, meanings; other boxes explain when it is (or is not) all right to use a particular word.

TRY IT

Look up the *Using Words* boxes for the following, and write an example sentence to illustrate the information in the box.

1. data 2. interested 3. less 4. real

Confusables

These boxes highlight words that can get confused with one another, often because they are spelled, or sound, almost the same.

TRY IT

Choose the correct word from inside the parentheses that will complete the sentence. If you are unsure which word to use, look up the *Confusables* box for that word.

1. (Lay, Lie) down on the bed and have a rest.
2. I (new, knew) that trick was not (new, knew)!
3. The (principal, principle) of the school is in her office.
4. That dog over (there, their, they're) belongs to (there, their, they're) son.

Word Family

Words that are built from similar building blocks are all related by their meaning as well as their spelling, and can be thought of as a family. A word family can be:

- words that all contain a certain root: *heartbeat, hearten, heartfelt,* and so on.
- words that all use a certain prefix or suffix: *misbehave, misdeed, mistreat,* and so on.
- compounds that are all made by joining a certain word with others: *tea bag, teacup, teapot, tea towel,* and so on.

Word Family boxes may show any of these kinds of families.

TRY IT

Find answers to the following questions in the *Word Family* boxes that contain the words in italics.

1. What does astronomy have to do with an *astrolabe*?
2. What is a *bedstead*?
3. What's the difference between *hard-headed* and *hard-hearted?*
4. If there is a *round table* of six people, who is allowed to speak?

Grammar Check

Important information about grammar, writing, or punctuation is highlighted in the *Grammar Check* boxes. If you need more detailed information, look at the *Grammar and Usage Mini-Guide* at the end of the dictionary.

TRY IT

Find answers to the following questions in the *Grammar Check* boxes for the words in italics.

1. Write today's *date* in five different ways.
2. Write a sentence using the words *good* and *well* correctly.
3. What are two examples of irregular *past tense* verbs?
4. What is one way to avoid *repetition* in your writing?

Aa

a or **A** (ā) 1 the first letter of the English alphabet, or any speech sound that it stands for. The sound of *a* in *mat* is different from the sound of *a* in *mate.* 2 the first thing in a list. 3 in music: **a** a note. On a keyboard it is the white note between G and B. **b** a scale or key that has A as its home note. *n., pl.* **a's** or **A's.**

A *symbol for* ampere or amperes.

Aardvark is from an old Dutch word meaning "earth pig." The animal does have a long snout, but is not like a pig in any other way.

aard•vark (ȧrd′vȧrk′) an animal from southern Africa that eats ants and termites which it catches with its long sticky tongue. Aardvarks have ears like a donkey and strong claws that they use to dig up anthills. *n.*

a•back (ə bak′)
taken aback, taken by surprise; startled and confused: *She was taken aback when her friend burst into tears.* *adv.*

ab•a•cus (ab′ə kəs) a frame with rows of beads that slide along wires or grooves, used for counting. *n., pl.* **ab•a•cus•es** or **ab•a•ci** (ab′ə sī′ *or* ab′ə sē′).

a•ban•don (ə ban′dən) 1 give up completely: *They finally abandoned the idea as hopeless.* 2 leave a place, person, or thing without planning to come back; desert: *The sailors had to abandon their sinking ship.* *v.*
—a•ban′doned, *adj.*
with abandon, without holding back.

a•bashed (ə basht′) a little ashamed: *The boy was abashed when we pointed out his mistake.* *adj.*

ab•bey (ab′ē) the building or buildings where a group of monks (under the rule of an **abbott**) or nuns (under the rule of an **abbess**) live. *n., pl.* **ab•beys.**

ab•bre•vi•ate (ə brē′vē āt′) make a word or phrase into a shorter form: *We can abbreviate the word Doctor to Dr.* *v.,* **ab•bre•vi•at•ed, ab•bre•vi•at•ing.**

ab•bre•vi•a•tion (ə brē′vē ā′shən) a short form, such as *Ont.* for *Ontario* or *MP* for *Member of Parliament.* *n.*
▶ See the Grammar and Usage Mini-Guide.

ab•di•cate (ab′də kāt′) give up a position of authority or responsibility: *When the king abdicated, his daughter became queen.* *v.,* **ab•di•cat•ed, ab•di•cat•ing.**
—ab′di•ca′tion, *n.*

ab•do•men (ab′də mən) 1 the part of the body that contains the stomach, the intestines, and other important organs; the belly. 2 the last of the three parts of an insect's body. *n.* **—ab•dom′i•nal** (ab dom′ə nəl), *adj.*

ab•duct (ab dukt′) take a person away by force or trickery; kidnap. *v.* **—ab•duc′tion,** *n.*
—ab•duc′tor, *n.*

Ab•e•na•ki (ab′ə nak′ē) 1 a First Nations people living in southern Québec. 2 their language, which belongs to the Algonquian family. 3 having to do with these people or their language. 1, 2 *n.,* 3 *adj.*

ab•hor (ab hȯr′) hate; think of as disgusting and horrible: *Some people abhor snakes.* *v.,* **ab•horred, ab•hor•ring.** **—ab•hor′rent,** *adj.*

a•bide (ə bīd′) 1 put up with; tolerate: *He cannot abide untidiness.* 2 stay; remain: *Our friendship will abide forever.* *v.,* **a•bid•ed, a•bid•ing.**
abide by, **a** accept and act on: *We will have to abide by their rules.* **b** keep: *Will you be able to abide by your promise?*

a•bid•ing (ə bī′ding) unending; lasting: *We hope for an abiding peace.* *adj.*

a•bil•i•ty (ə bil′ə tē) 1 power to do or act: *A horse has the ability to pull heavy loads.* 2 skill or talent: *She has great ability as a hockey player.* *n., pl.* **a•bil•i•ties.**

ab•ject (ab′jekt) that destroys a person's dignity: *The people in that remote village were living in abject poverty. Abject fear showed on the coward's face.* *adj.*
—ab•ject′ly, *adv.*

a•blaze (ə blāz′) 1 on fire: *He set the whole building ablaze* (*adv.*). 2 bright or glowing: *The great hall was ablaze with lights* (*adj.*). *adv. or adj.*

a•ble (ā′bəl) 1 having power or skill: *Little kids are able to walk, but they're not able to drive.* 2 skilful; competent: *She is an able teacher.* *adj.,* **a•bler, a•blest.**
—a′bly, *adv.*

ab•nor•mal (ab nȯr′məl) very different from what is normal or ordinary, especially in a bad way: *The drug produced an abnormal thirst.* *adj.*
—ab•nor′mal•ly, *adv.*

a•board (ə bȯrd′) on board; on, in, onto, or into a ship, train, bus, aircraft, etc.: *All the passengers went aboard (adv.). They went aboard the ship (prep.).* *adv. or prep.*
all aboard, a conductor's call telling passengers to enter a train, bus, etc. that is about to start.

a•bode (ə bōd′) a home. *n.*

a•bol•ish (ə bol′ish) do away with; put an end to: *I wish that we could abolish war.* *v.* **—ab′o•li′tion,** *n.*

a•bom•i•na•ble (ə bom′ə nə bəl) disgusting; hateful: *Kidnapping is an abominable act. What abominable weather—rainy, windy, and cold.* *adj.*

abominable snowman (ə bom′ə nə bəl snō′ man′) a humanlike monster supposed to live in the Himalayas, a mountain range in Asia.

ab•o•rig•i•nal (ab′ə rij′ə nəl) having to do with people who first lived in a country, or their descendants. In Canada, the aboriginal peoples are the First Nations, the Inuit, and the Métis. This word is often spelled **Aboriginal.** *adj.* ► See Appendix.

A shield and a boomerang (wooden throwing stick) were traditionally used by Aborigines in Australia.

Ab•o•rig•i•ne (ab′ə rij′ə nē′) one of a group of people who are the first ones known to have lived in Australia. *n.*

a•bound (ə bound′) **1** be plentiful: *Fish abound in the ocean.* **2** be well supplied or filled: *The ocean abounds with fish.* *v.*

a•bout (ə bout′) **1** having to do with: *a story about horses.* **2** nearly; almost: *He has about finished his work.* **3** around: *Look about and tell me what you see.* **1** *prep.,* **2, 3** *adv.*
about to, on the point of; going to; ready to: *The plane is about to take off.*

a•bove (ə buv′) **1** overhead; in a higher place: *The sky is above.* **2** over: *The moon was directly above the house. Can you hear above the noise?* **3** more than: *The cost of repairs is not likely to be above $500. She is above average in height.* **4** above zero on a temperature scale: *The high today is five above.* **5** having too much dignity or honour for: *I am above cheating. Her behaviour is above reproach.* 1, 4 *adv.,* 2, 3, 5 *prep.*

a•breast (ə brest′) side by side: *The soldiers marched three abreast.* *adv.*
abreast of or **abreast with,** up to date with: *Read the newspapers to keep abreast of what is going on.*

a•bridge (ə brij′) shorten something written or printed; condense: *The story had to be abridged because it was too long for the magazine.* *v.,* **a•bridged, a•bridg•ing.**
—a•bridg′ment or **a•bridge′ment,** *n.*

a•broad (ə brod′) **1** outside your own country, especially overseas: *He spent a year abroad, mostly in Norway.* **2** out and about; going around: *They travelled by night because fewer enemy patrols were abroad then. There is a rumour abroad that the mayor is resigning.* **3** far and wide: *The news of his arrival spread abroad.* *adv.*

a•brupt (ə brupt′) **1** sudden: *Her speech came to an abrupt end.* **2** very steep or sharp: *an abrupt angle. The road made an abrupt rise up the hill.* **3** gruff; rude; blunt: *He had an abrupt way of speaking.* *adj.*
—a•brupt′ly, *adv.* **—a•brupt′ness,** *n.*

ab•scess (ab′ses) a pocket of pus in some part of the body. An abscess results from an infection and often makes a painful red lump on the skin. *n.*

ab•sent (ab′sənt *for 1–3,* ab sent′ *for 4*) **1** away; not in the expected place: *Three members of the class were absent.* **2** lacking; not existing: *Trees are almost absent in some parts of the Prairies.* **3** absent-minded: *He said "Yes" in an absent way and kept on reading.* **4** keep oneself away: *She absented herself from the meeting because she had another appointment.* 1–3 *adj.,* 4 *v.*
—ab′sent•ly, *adv.* **—ab′sence,** *n.*

ab•sen•tee (ab′sən tē′) a person who is away. *n.*

ab•sent–mind•ed (ab′sənt mīn′did) forgetting or not noticing because your mind is on something else: *I'm so absent-minded! I went to the fridge and put in my books instead of my lunch!* *adj.* **—ab′sent-mind′ed•ly,** *adv.*
—ab′sent-mind′ed•ness, *n.*

a bat	e bed	i bid	o pot	u cup	th thin
ā cake	ē me	ī bite	ō go	ū rude	ᴛʜ then
ä bar	ə about	ər over	ȯ for	u̇ put	zh measure

ab·so·lute (ab′sə lūt′) **1** complete; perfect: *absolute silence, absolute ignorance, absolute justice.* **2** certain; unquestionable; positive: *Don't say anything unless you have absolute proof that she stole your money.* *adj.*
—ab′so·lute′ly, *adv.*

A sponge is a sea creature. Its skeleton is springy and full of holes, so it can absorb a lot of water. Divers collect sponges and sell them, for people to use in washing and cleaning.

ab·sorb (ab zôrb′) **1** take in and hold moisture, light, or heat: *A sponge absorbs water.* Something that absorbs a lot is **absorbent.** **2** take into one's mind and remember: *We can't absorb so much information at once.* **3** take up all the attention and interest of: *The puzzle has absorbed him for hours.* Anything very interesting is **absorbing.** *v.* **—ab·sorp′tion,** *n.*

ab·stain (ab stān′) choose not to do or use something: *Most athletes abstain from smoking.* *v.*
—ab′sti·nence (ab′ stə nəns), *n.*

ab·stract (ab′strakt) **1** thought of apart from any particular object or actual thing; not concrete: *A sugar cube is a real thing; the idea or quality of sweetness is abstract.* **2** hard to understand: *Her reasoning was so abstract that I gave up trying to follow it.* **3** having to do with a style of art that tries to express ideas or feelings by showing certain qualities or parts of real things instead of the real things themselves. An abstract painting doesn't look like a picture of anything. *adj.*
—ab·stract′ly, *adv.* **—ab·stract′ness,** *n.*

ab·surd (ab zərd′ *or* ab sərd′) plainly not true or sensible; foolish; ridiculous: *Expecting a baby to eat without making a mess is absurd.* *adj.*
—ab·surd′ly, *adv.* **—ab·surd′i·ty,** *n.*

a·bun·dant (ə bun′dənt) more than enough; very plentiful: *There are abundant oil reserves in Alberta.* *adj.*
—a·bun′dant·ly, *adv.* **—a·bun′dance,** *n.*

a·buse (ə byūz′ *for 1, 3, and 5,* ə byūs′ *for 2, 4, and 6*) **1** use wrongly: *The officer abused his authority by arresting a harmless onlooker.* **2** a wrong use: *the abuse of a privilege.* **3** treat badly: *to abuse a child.* **4** bad treatment: *abuse of a helpless prisoner.* **5** use harsh, insulting language to: *The angry captain abused the crew at the top of his voice.* **6** harsh, insulting language.
1, 3, 5 *v.,* **a·bused, a·bus·ing;** 2, 4, 6 *n.*
—a·bu′sive (ə byū′ siv), *adj.*

a·bys·mal (ə biz′məl) very bad: *Harold had an abysmal record for attendance.* *adj.*

a·byss (ə bis′) a very deep crack or hole; chasm. *n.*

AC, A.C. or **a.c.** *abbreviation for* alternating current.

ac·a·dem·ic (ak′ə dem′ik) **1** having to do with school or schoolwork: *Linda's academic program included math, science, and computer studies.* **2** someone who teaches or does research at a university: *Ms. Wu had been an academic before she went into business.* **3** completely unrelated to practical things: *Let's not waste time discussing academic questions.* 1, 3 *adj.,* 2 *n.*

a·cad·e·my (ə kad′ə mē) a school, especially a private one or one giving special training in a certain subject: *a dance academy.* *n., pl.* **a·cad·e·mies.**

A·ca·di·a (ə kā′dē ə) that part of old French Canada which included present-day Nova Scotia and New Brunswick: *Acadia was a French colony from 1604 to 1713.* *n.* **—A·ca′di·an,** *n., adj.*

ac·cel·er·ate (ak sel′ə rāt′) go or cause to go faster; speed up: *The engineer accelerates a train by turning on more power.* *v.* **—ac·cel′er·a′tion,** *n.*

ac·cel·er·a·tor (ak sel′ə rā′tər) the pedal that the driver presses to make a car, truck, etc. go faster. *n.*

ac·cent (ak′sent; *sometimes,* ak sent′ *for 4 and 5*) **1** a special way of pronouncing words: *She speaks with a Canadian accent.* **2** emphasis or stress on a particular syllable of a word: *In the word "abundant," the accent is on the second syllable.* **3** a mark (such as ′ or ′) showing the stress on a syllable, as in *a bun′*dant. **4** mark with an accent. **5** pronounce with an accent or stress: *Is the word "harass" accented on the first or second syllable?* **6** **accents,** *pl.* extras or trim in a different colour: *The room was decorated in blue, with yellow accents.* 1–3, 6 *n.,* 4, 5 *v.*

ac·cept (ak sept′) 1 take what is offered or given: *He accepted our gift.* 2 agree to or believe; say yes to: *She accepted his proposal. She refused to accept our story of what had happened.* 3 tolerate: *We cannot accept this kind of behaviour.* 4 welcome; approve: *He was soon accepted by his new classmates.* *v.* **—ac·cept′a·ble,** *adj.* **—ac·cept′ance,** *n.*

> **CONFUSABLES ..... accept**
>
> **accept** means "receive": *Will you accept this prize?*
> **except** means "other than": *Everyone smiled, except me.*

ac·cess (ak′ses) 1 the right to approach, enter, or use: *All children have access to the library during the afternoon.* 2 a way of reaching a place: *A ladder was the only access to the attic.* 3 reach a place or get at something: *You can access the computer files if you have the password.* 1, 2 *n.,* 3 *v.* **—ac·ces′si·ble,** *adj.*

ac·ces·so·ry (ak ses′ə rē) 1 something extra that is added because it is useful or attractive: *He bought a mirror and some other accessories for his bicycle. This leather belt is the perfect accessory to my jeans.* 2 a person who helps another commit a crime, without actually taking part in it: *The person who drives the getaway car for a bank robber is an accessory.* *n., pl.* **ac·ces·so·ries.**

ac·ci·dent (ak′sə dənt) something that happens unexpectedly and by chance. It is sometimes a bad thing but not always: *He was hurt in a car accident. Their meeting was an accident.* *n.*
by accident, by chance; not on purpose: *I dropped it by accident.*

ac·ci·den·tal (ak′sə den′təl) 1 happening unexpectedly or by chance: *They had searched for months, but the actual discovery of the treasure was accidental.* 2 in music, a sign showing a change in a single note; a sharp (♯), a flat (♭), or a natural (♮). 1 *adj.,* 2 *n.* **—ac′ci·den′tal·ly,** *adv.*

ac·claim (ə klām′) 1 show approval publicly by cheering, clapping, praising, etc.: *The crowd acclaimed the firefighter for rescuing two people from the burning house.* 2 a shout or other show of approval: *The actor was received with great acclaim.* 3 🍁 elect someone to office when there is no other candidate: *She was acclaimed mayor.* 1, 3 *v.,* 2 *n.*

ac·cla·ma·tion (ak′lə mā′shən) a shout of welcome or show of approval by a crowd: *The winning team received the acclamation of the people.* *n.*
by acclamation, a 🍁 as the only candidate in an election: *Since no one else was running for office, Mr. Kress was elected by acclamation.* b with a great majority by an oral vote, rather than by ballot.

ac·com·mo·date (ə kom′ə dāt′) 1 hold; have room for; lodge: *This big bedroom will easily accommodate both girls. Can you accommodate a group of five for two weeks?* 2 give what is wanted; help out: *He wanted change for five dollars, but I could not accommodate him.* Someone who willingly does a favour is **accommodating.** *v.,* **ac·com·mo·dat·ed, ac·com·mo·dat·ing.**

ac·com·mo·da·tions (ə kom′ə dā′shənz) room; a place to stay: *This hotel has accommodations for 100 people.* *pl.n.*

ac·com·pa·ny (ə kum′pə nē) 1 go along with: *May we accompany you on your walk? Smoke accompanies fire.* 2 in music, play or sing along with to make a richer or stronger sound: *She accompanied him on the guitar.* *v.,* **ac·com·pa·nied, ac·com·pa·ny·ing.** **—ac·com′pa·ni·ment,** *n.*

ac·com·plice (ə kom′plis) a person who helps another to commit a crime: *Without an accomplice to open the door, the thief could not have got into the building so easily.* *n.*

ac·com·plish (ə kom′plish) carry out; complete: *Did you accomplish your purpose? He can accomplish more in a day than any other worker on the farm.* *v.*

ac·com·plished (ə kom′plisht) expert; skilled: *an accomplished dancer, an accomplished liar.* *adj.*

ac·com·plish·ment (ə kom′plish mənt) 1 the act of doing or carrying out successfully: *The accomplishment of her plan took three weeks.* 2 something done with knowledge and skill: *The teacher was proud of his student's accomplishments.* 3 skill or talent: *She was a girl of many accomplishments, including swimming, skiing, and painting.* *n.*

ac·cord (ə kȯrd′) 1 agree: *Their account of the accident accords with yours.* 2 agreement: *The two friends were in complete accord.* 1 *v.,* 2 *n.* **—ac·cord′ance,** *n.*
of one's own accord, without being asked: *He is old enough now to go to bed of his own accord.*

according (ə kȯr′ding)
according to, a in agreement with: *She came according to her promise.* b going by; based on: *Sort these according to colour. According to this book, a tiger is really a big cat.* *adj.*

ac·cord·ing·ly (ə kȯr′ding lē) 1 in agreement with something stated: *These are the rules. You can act accordingly or leave the club.* 2 therefore: *He was too sick to stay. Accordingly, we sent him home.* *adv.*

a bat	e bed	i bid	o pot	u cup	th thin
ā cake	ē me	ī bite	ō go	ū rude	TH then
ä bar	ə about	ər over	ȯ for	u̇ put	zh measure

ac•cor•di•on (ə kôr′dē ən) a musical instrument with bellows, buttons, and a keyboard. The sound is made by opening and closing the bellows while the melody and chords are played on the keys and buttons. *n.*

ac•count (ə kount′) **1** a report or explanation: *The newspaper published an account of the trial. He could give no acceptable account of his absence.* **2** an arrangement with a bank or company for saving money or paying for things. **3** the amount of money owed or saved under this kind of agreement. **4** Usually, **accounts,** *pl.* an ongoing record of money received and spent: *My parents do our family's accounts on our computer.* *n.*
account for, **a** give a reason or explanation for: *He couldn't account for the strange message.* **b** tell what has happened to: *The club treasurer has to account for all the money received. Have all the passengers been accounted for?*
of little (or **no**) **account,** not important.
on account, **a** on credit, with regular payments: *She bought the coat on account.* **b** as part payment: *If you accept five dollars on account, I can pay the rest next week.*
on account of, because of: *The game was put off on account of rain.*
on no account, under no circumstances: *On no account should you tell him everything.*
on someone's account, for someone's sake: *Don't wait on my account.*
take into account or **take account of,** make allowance for; consider: *When planning a vacation, you have to take travelling time into account.*

ac•count•ant (ə koun′tənt) a person who looks after or checks business accounts. *n.*
—ac•count′ing, *n.*

ac•cu•mu•late (ə kyū′myə lāt′) collect little by little: *He accumulated a fortune by hard work. Dust had accumulated during the weeks we were gone.* *v.,* **ac•cu•mu•lat•ed, ac•cu•mu•lat•ing.**
—ac•cu′mu•la′tion, *n.*

ac•cu•rate (ak′yə rit) exactly right; correct: *Accurate timing is important in track and field competitions.* *adj.* **—ac′cu•rate•ly,** *adv.*
—ac′cu•ra•cy (ak′yər ə sē), *n.*

ac•cuse (ə kyūz′) say that someone has done something wrong: *They accused him of being a liar. The woman was accused of speeding.* *v.,* **ac•cused, ac•cus•ing.**
—ac•cus′er, *n.* **—ac•cus′ing•ly,** *adv.*
—ac′cu•sa′tion, *n.*

ac•cus•tomed (ə kus′təmd) usual: *By Monday he was back in his accustomed place.* *adj.*
accustomed to, used to; in the habit of: *She was accustomed to hard work.*

ace (ās) **1** a playing card with one spot: *In most card games, the ace is the highest card in a deck.* **2** an expert: *Peter is an ace at basketball.* **3** *Informal.* do something perfectly or extremely well: *Stella aced the math test.* 1, 2 *n.,* 3 *v.,* **aced, ac•ing.**

ac•e•tate (as′ə tāt′) **1** a substance made by treating cellulose with an acid. It is used for making plastics, varnishes, etc. **2** something made from this substance, such as a transparency for an overhead projector. *n.*

ache (āk) **1** an ongoing pain, such as an earache, headache, or toothache. **2** feel this kind of pain: *My back aches.* **3** *Informal.* wish very much: *During the hot days we ached to go swimming.* 1 *n.,* 2, 3 *v.,* **ached, ach•ing.**

a•chieve (ə chēv′) **1** get done: *I achieved very little today.* **2** reach a difficult goal by one's own efforts: *She achieved fame as a swimmer.* *v.,* **a•chieved, a•chiev•ing.**
—a•chieve′ment, *n.*

ac•id (as′id) **1** a chemical that works against bases. Acids eat away at metal or flesh. **2** sour or bitter; sharp and biting: *Rhubarb has an acid taste. His acid remarks hurt my feelings.* **3** a harsh or bitter quality: *There was acid in his voice as he replied.* 1, 3 *n.,* 2 *adj.*
—a•cid′ic, *adj.*

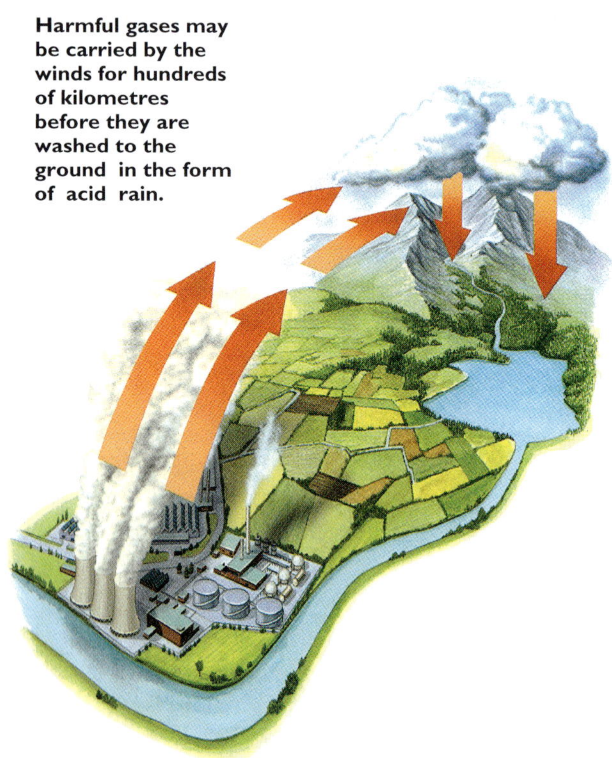

acid rain (as′id rān′) rain or snow that is polluted by acids formed in the air after waste chemicals are released into the air by factories, cars, power plants, etc.

ac•knowl•edge (ak nol′ij) **1** admit or recognize: *He acknowledges his faults. She was acknowledged to be the best player on the team.* **2** show that one has received or noticed something: *She acknowledged the gift with a pleasant letter.* *v.,* **ac•knowl•edged, ac•knowl•edg•ing.** **—ac•knowl′edg•ment** or **ac•knowl′edge•ment,** *n.*

ac•ne (ak′nē) a very pimply condition of the skin, common among teenagers. It results when the skin's oil-producing glands become clogged. *n.*

a•corn (ā′kôrn) the nut of an oak tree. *n.*

a•cous•tics (ə kū′stiks) the qualities of a room that affect whether you hear a sound badly or well. The size and shape of a room affect its acoustics. *n.* **—a•cous′tic,** *adj.*

ac•quaint (ə kwānt′) make familiar: *"Let me acquaint you with the facts," she said.* *v.*
be acquainted with, have personal knowledge of people or things: *I have heard about your friend, but I am not acquainted with him.*

ac•quaint•ance (ə kwān′təns) **1** a person known to you but not a close friend: *The actor had many acquaintances but few friends.* **2** knowledge or experience of someone or something: *I have some acquaintance with computers, but I'm no expert.* *n.*

ac•quire (ə kwīr′) gain or get: *In a few years she acquired a store of her own.* *v.,* **ac•quired, ac•quir•ing.**

ac•qui•si•tion (ak′wə zish′ən) **1** the act of acquiring: *He spent many years in the acquisition of knowledge.* **2** something acquired: *Our most recent acquisition is a colour printer.* *n.*

ac•quit (ə kwit′) declare not guilty: *The jury acquitted the man accused of stealing.* *v.,* **ac•quit•ted, ac•quit•ting.** **—ac•quit′tal,** *n.*
acquit yourself, do your part; perform: *The players acquitted themselves well on the soccer field.*

a•cre (ā′kər) a non-metric unit for measuring land area, equal to about 0.4 hectares. *n.*

a•cre•age (ā′kər ij) **1** the number of acres: *What is the acreage of the farm?* **2** a piece of land of several acres: *She bought a small acreage north of town.* *n.*

ac•rid (ak′rid) sharp, bitter, or stinging: *Smoke feels acrid in your mouth and nose. I was hurt by your acrid comments.* *adj.*

ac•ro•bat (ak′rə bat′) a person who can dance on a rope or wire, swing on a trapeze, turn handsprings, and so on. *n.* **—ac′ro•bat′ic,** *adj.* **—ac′ro•bat′ics,** *pl.n.*

ac•ro•nym (ak′rə nim′) a word made up of the first letters of the full name of something: *DOS is an acronym for Disk Operating System.* *n.*

a•cross (ə kros′) **1** from one side to the other: *What is the distance across?* (*adv.*). *She drew a line across the page* (*prep.*). **2** on the other side of; beyond: *The woods are across the river.* 1, 2 *prep.,* 1 *adv.*
come across, find: *We come across hard words in some books.*

NORTH
EAST
WEST
SOUTH

an acrostic of NEWS

a•cros•tic (ə kros′tik) a poem or piece of writing in which the first or last letter of each line spells out a word if you read them one after another. *n.*.

a•cryl•ic (ə kril′ik) **1** a clear, tough plastic made from an acid. It is used in sheet form instead of glass and also for making paint, rubber, and glue. **2** a kind of paint made with this plastic as a base. **3** a painting done with this paint: *We bought one of her acrylics.* **4** a strong, lightweight fibre made from a related acid and used especially for yarn, fabrics, and carpets. *n.*

act (akt) **1** something done; a deed: *an act of kindness.* **2** do something: *The firefighters acted quickly and saved the house.* **3** behave: *to act like a fool.* **4** perform in a play, musical, etc.: *My brother is acting the part of the hero in our school play. He acts very well.* **5** a main division of a play or opera: *This play has three acts.* **6** one of several performances on a program: *The magician's act was good.* **7** a law or decree. An Act of Parliament is a law that has been passed by Parliament. **8** phony behaviour: *He seems pleasant, but that's just an act.* **9** do the work of: *This thick, folded towel can act as a sponge. While the principal was gone, the vice principal acted for her.* 1, 5–8 *n.,* 2–4, 9 *v.*
act on, **a** follow or obey: *to act on someone's advice.* **b** affect or influence: *Yeast acts on dough, making it rise.*
act out, actions, as in pantomime: *In charades one player acts out a word and the others guess it.*
act up, *Informal.* **a** behave badly: *He's acting up because he didn't get his way.* **b** be troublesome: *The knee I hurt last summer is acting up again.*

a bat	e bed	i bid	o pot	u cup	th thin
ā cake	ē me	ī bite	ō go	ū rude	ꟻH then
ä bar	ə about	ər over	ô for	ů put	zh measure

ac•tion (ak′shən) 1 the process of doing something; acting: *The quick action of the lifeguard saved the child.* 2 something done; an act: *Giving food to the dog was a kind action.* 3 battle: *My grandparents know someone who was wounded in action in the Second World War.* *n.*
take action, begin to act, especially in order to stop or oppose something: *The government took action to prevent forest fires.*

ac•ti•vate (ak′tə vāt′) make active: *You can activate dried yeast by mixing it with warm water.* *v.,* **ac•ti•vat•ed, ac•ti•vat•ing.**

ac•tive (ak′tiv) 1 acting or working: *an active volcano. This old mine is no longer active.* 2 doing or moving a lot; lively: *She was a very active child.* *adj.* **—ac′tive•ly,** *adv.*

ac•tiv•ist (ak′tə vist) someone who works hard to make changes in society: *Karen was an activist for animal rights.* *n.* **—ac′tiv•ism′,** *n.*

ac•tiv•i•ty (ak tiv′ə tē) 1 the state of being active; movement; liveliness: *The kitchen hummed with activity as they prepared the dinner.* 2 an action: *The suspect's activities were being closely watched by the police.* 3 something to do, usually planned: *outdoor activities, classroom activities.* *n., pl.* **ac•tiv•i•ties.**

ac•tor (ak′tər) 1 a person who acts on the stage, in movies, or on television or radio. Some people use the word **actress** for a girl or woman. 2 any person who does something or takes part in something. *n.*

ac•tu•al (ak′chū əl) real; existing as a fact: *What she told us was not a dream but an actual happening.* *adj.* **—ac′tu•al•ly,** *adv.*

ac•u•punc•ture (ak′yə pungk′chər) a way of relieving pain or disease by inserting special needles into particular parts of the body: *Lillian trained in acupuncture when she lived in China.* *n.*

a•cute (ə kyūt′) 1 sharp and severe: *A cavity in a tooth can cause acute pain.* 2 keen: *Dogs have an acute sense of smell.* *adj.* **—a•cute′ly,** *adv.* **—a•cute′ness,** *n.*

acute angle (ə kyūt′ ang′gəl) an angle less than 90°.

ad (ad) *Informal.* advertisement. *n.*

AD *abbreviation for* the Latin words *anno Domini,* meaning "in the year of our Lord," that is, after the birth of Jesus Christ. Look up CE.

ad•age (ad′ij) a well-known saying, or proverb. *n.*

ad•a•mant (ad′ə mənt) firm; unyielding: *Columbus was adamant in refusing his sailors' requests to turn back.* *adj.*

Adam's apple (ad′ əmz ap′əl) the lump in the front of the neck, formed by the larynx.

a•dapt (ə dapt′) 1 make fit or suitable: *Good writers adapt their words to the age and interests of their readers.* 2 change one's behaviour so as to fit in with a new situation: *He has adapted well to his new school.* 3 change a thing so as to use it in a new way: *The farmer can adapt her barn for use as a garage.* *v.* **—a•dapt′a•ble,** *adj.* **—ad′ap•ta′tion,** *n.*

a•dap•ter or **a•dap•tor** (ə dap′tər) any device that lets something fit where it was not made to fit, or that lets it be used in a new way. *n.*

add (ad) 1 put together: *When you add 4 and 2 and 3, you have 9.* 2 go on to say; say further: *She said goodbye and added that she had enjoyed her visit.* *v.*
add to, a put with: *She added sugar to her tea.* b make greater: *The fine day added to our pleasure.*

ad•dend (ad′end) a number to be added to another number. *n.*

This adder, with a black zigzag pattern on its back, is Europe's only poisonous snake.

ad•der (ad′ər) 1 any of various poisonous snakes of different sizes, found in Europe, Asia, Africa, and Australia. 2 any of several small, harmless snakes of North America. *n.*

ad•dict (ad′ikt) 1 a person who is dependent on a harmful drug, such as heroin. An addict is controlled by the drug and cannot normally stop taking it. 2 a person who is devoted to a habit or practice: *She is an Internet addict.* *n.* **—ad•dict′ed,** *adj.* **—ad•dic′tion,** *n.*

ad•di•tion (ə dish′ən) 1 the adding of numbers or things: *2 + 2 = 4 is a simple addition. The addition of flour will thicken gravy.* 2 something added: *Workers are building an addition to this house.* *n.*
in addition or **in addition to,** besides: *In addition to the money, the girls received free lunches for their work.*

ad·di·tion·al (ə dish′ə nəl) added; extra; more: *We will need additional help to get all these decorations up.* *adj.* **—ad·di′tion·al·ly,** *adv.*

ad·di·tive (ad′ə tiv) a substance that is added to food in small amounts to improve, colour, or preserve it: *Chocolate bars are full of additives.* *n.*

ad·dress (ə dres′; *also* ad′res *for 1 and 3*) **1** the house number, street name, and other details that tell where someone lives or where a piece of mail is going: *Send the letter to this address.* **2** write on an envelope or package the information that shows where it is going: *Please address this letter for me.* **3** the code label telling exactly where a piece of information is stored in a computer's memory, or where a site is on the Web. **4** a formal speech: *The Prime Minister gave an address over radio and television.* **5** speak to: *The safety officer addressed the students. Address the judge as "Sir" or "Madam."* **6** deal with; do something about: *to address a problem.* 1, 3, 4 *n.,* 2, 5, 6 *v.*

a·dept (ə dept′) very skilful; expert: *He is adept with his hands and makes many beautiful crafts.* *adj.* **—a·dept′ly,** *adv.* **—a·dept′ness,** *n.*

ad·e·quate (ad′ə kwit) enough; good enough, high enough, strong enough, etc.: *Her wages are adequate to support her family.* *adj.* **—ad′e·quate·ly,** *adv.* **—ad′e·quate·ness,** *n.*

ad·here (ad hēr′) **1** stick; cling: *Mud adheres to shoes.* **2** follow closely or firmly: *He adhered to his plan.* *v.,* **ad·hered, ad·her·ing.**

ad·he·sive (ad hē′siv) **1** sticky; used for sticking: *adhesive tape.* **2** any substance used to stick things together. Glue is an adhesive. 1 *adj.,* 2 *n.*

a·dieu (ə dyū′) goodbye. *interj. or n., pl.* **a·dieus** or **a·dieux** (ə dyūz′).

ad·ja·cent (ə jā′sənt) next; adjoining: *The house adjacent to ours has just been sold.* *adj.*

ad·jec·tive (aj′ik tiv) a word describing a person, place, or thing. In the sentence *Her little dog is hungry,* the words *little* and *hungry* are adjectives that describe the noun *dog.* Other examples of adjectives are *warm, heavy, noticeable, hectic, thoughtful,* and *happy.* *n.*

> **Grammar Check . . . . adjective**
>
> Try to use adjectives that are clear, not vague:
> *The meal they served was* ***mouthwatering*** is more expressive than *The meal they served was* ***nice***.

ad·join (ə join′) be next to; be side by side: *Saskatchewan adjoins Manitoba. We have adjoining desks.* *v.*

ad·journ (ə jərn′) **1** stop business until next time: *The meeting adjourned at ten o'clock.* **2** move somewhere else: *Let's adjourn to the basement where it's cooler.* *v.* **—ad·journ′ment,** *n.*

ad·just (ə just′) **1** change so as to fit, look, sound, or work better: *to adjust a radio dial. You can adjust this chair to different heights.* **2** get used to; adapt: *The boy from Winnipeg soon adjusted to life in Montréal.* *v.* **—ad·just′a·ble,** *adj.* **—ad·just′ment,** *n.*

ad lib (ad′ lib′) *Informal.* **1** making it up as you go along: *Did they have a script, or did they do their skit ad lib?* **2** **ad-lib,** make up as one goes along; improvise: *I had forgotten my thank-you speech at home so I had to ad-lib it.* **3** **ad-lib,** not prepared ahead of time; improvised: *an ad-lib speech.* 2 *v.,* **ad-libbed, ad-lib·bing;** 3 *adj.*

ad·min·is·ter (ad min′i stər) **1** manage the affairs of; direct: *A principal administers a school.* **2** give; apply: *A doctor administers medicine to sick people. Judges administer justice.* *v.*

ad·min·is·tra·tion (ad min′i strā′shən) **1** the managing of a business, school, or country: *The administration of a big business takes skill in dealing with people.* **2** the group of people who do this managing: *The principal is part of the administration of a school.* **3** the act of giving out or applying: *Volunteers handled the administration of aid to the flood victims.* *n.*

ad·mi·ra·ble (ad′mə rə bəl) **1** worth admiring: *Terry Fox had an admirable character.* **2** very good: *Our family doctor is taking admirable care of my baby sister.* *adj.* **—ad′mi·ra·bly,** *adv.*

ad·mi·ra·tion (ad′mə rā′shən) **1** a feeling of wonder, pleasure, and approval: *I am full of admiration for your bravery.* **2** a person or thing that is admired: *Her talent in painting was the admiration of all her friends.* *n.*

ad·mire (ad mīr′) **1** look at with wonder and pleasure: *We all admired Jordan's beautiful clay sculpture.* **2** think highly of: *Everyone admires her brave deeds.* *v.,* **ad·mired, ad·mir·ing.** **—ad·mir′er,** *n.*

ad·mis·sion (ad mish′ən) **1** the act of allowing someone to enter: *admission of immigrants into Canada.* **2** the right to enter: *Everyone who finishes elementary school has admission to high school.* **3** the price of entering: *Admission to the show is seven dollars.* **4** the act of admitting that something is true: *We appreciate your honest admission of the mistake.* *n.*

a bat	e bed	i bid	o pot	u cup	th thin
ā cake	ē me	ī bite	ō go	ū rude	ᴛʜ then
ä bar	ə about	ər over	ô for	u̇ put	zh measure

Adobe

Adobe was a common building material used by Incas and pueblo Native Americans. The illustration shows how bricks were made. A similar method is still used today.

Step 3
The finished bricks are used to build houses.

Step 2
When dry, the bricks are removed from the mould and set to bake in the sun.

Step 1
Clay is mixed with water and straw, then scooped into a brick-shaped mould.

ad•mit (ad mit′) 1 say that something is real or true; confess: *He admits now that he was wrong.* 2 allow to enter: *This ticket will admit you to the play.* *v.,* **ad•mit•ted, ad•mit•ting.** **—ad•mit′ted•ly,** *adv.*

ad•mit•tance (ad mit′əns) the right to enter: *She gained admittance to the meeting.* *n.*

ad•mon•ish (ad mon′ish) warn or advise a person about his or her behaviour: *The officer admonished me for biking without my helmet.* *v.* **—ad′mo•ni′tion,** *n.*

a•do (ə dū′) action; stir; fuss; trouble: *The family made much ado about the wedding.* *n.*

a•do•be (ə dō′bē) 1 a kind of brick made from clay mixed with straw and dried in the sun: *Adobe has been used for thousands of years to build houses.* 2 a building made of such bricks. *n.*

ad•o•les•cent (ad′ə les′ənt) 1 a person who is no longer a child but not yet an adult. 2 between about 12 and 18 years old: *an adolescent boy.* 3 having to do with people of this age: *adolescent behaviour.* 1 *n.,* 2, 3 *adj.* **—ad′o•les′cence,** *n.*

a•dopt (ə dopt′) take as your own: *I liked your idea and adopted it. The Kazowskis have adopted a baby girl.* *v.* **—a•dop′tion,** *n.*

a•dor•a•ble (ə dȯ′rə bəl) *Informal.* cute; attractive; delightful: *an adorable child.* *adj.* **—a•dor′a•bly,** *adv.*

a•dore (ə dȯr′) 1 respect and love deeply: *She adores her mother.* 2 *Informal.* like very much: *I just adore that movie.* *v.,* **a•dored, a•dor•ing.** **—ad′o•ra′tion,** *n.*

a•dorn (ə dȯrn′) add beauty to; decorate: *He adorned his room with posters.* *v.* **—a•dorn′ment,** *n.*

a•drift (ə drift′) drifting; floating without being guided: *They floated adrift in a lifeboat for three days* (*adv.*). *The lost children were adrift in the fairground* (*adj.*). *adj. or adv.*

a•droit (ə droit′) skilful: *Monkeys are adroit climbers. A good teacher is adroit at asking questions.* *adj.* **—a•droit′ly,** *adv.* **—a•droit′ness,** *n.*

a•dult (ə dult′ *or* ad′ult) 1 mature; full-grown; grown-up: *the adult members of the family. An adult frog looks very different from a tadpole.* 2 a grown-up person, animal, or plant. 1 *adj.,* 2 *n.*

ad·vance (ad vans′) **1** move forward: *The excited crowd advanced toward the city centre.* **2** forward movement; progress: *Our advance through the checkout line was very slow.* **3** help forward: *to advance the cause of peace.* **4** loan: *My parents gave me an advance of ten dollars toward my new video game (n.). They advanced me the money (v.).* 1, 3, 4 *v.,* **ad·vanced, ad·vanc·ing;** 2, 4 *n.* **—ad·vance′ment,** *n.*
in advance, **a** in front. **b** ahead of time: *They paid their rent in advance.*
make advances on or **toward,** approach.

ad·van·tage (ad van′tij) something that helps a person to succeed or win: *A good education is always a great advantage.* *n.* **—ad′van·ta′geous** (ad′vən tā′jəs), *adj.*
be to someone's advantage, be useful to someone: *It would be to your advantage if you learned to use a computer.*
take advantage of, **a** make good use of: *She took advantage of the confusion to slip out of the room unnoticed.* **b** use or treat unfairly: *People take advantage of his good nature by making him do all the work.*

ad·vent (ad′vent) **1** coming or arrival: *The first green buds marked the advent of spring.* **2** **Advent,** the four weeks leading up to Christmas. *n.*

ad·ven·ture (ad ven′chər) **1** an experience that is exciting because it is unusual, difficult, or dangerous: *The trip to Whitehorse was an adventure for us.* **2** take part in this kind of experience: *a summer of adventuring in the far north.* 1 *n.,* 2 *v.,* **ad·ven·tured, ad·ven·tur·ing.** **—ad·ven′tur·er,** *n.* **—ad·ven′tur·ous** or **ad·ven′ture·some,** *adj.*

ad·verb (ad′vərb) a word that is used with a verb or an adjective to give information about time, place, manner, degree, or circumstance. In the sentence *She walked rapidly,* the word *rapidly* is an adverb describing the way she walked. In the sentence *They are very happy,* the word *very* is an adverb describing how happy they are. Other examples of adverbs are *soon, easily, here, possibly,* and *extremely.* *n.*

Grammar ✓Check . . . . adverb

Many adverbs are made by adding *-ly* to an adjective: *sad**ly**, quick**ly**, clear**ly**.* Sometimes the spelling is a little different: *happ**ily**, eas**ily**, miserab**ly**.*

ad·ver·sar·y (ad′vər ser′ē) a person, group, or thing that you are fighting or competing against: *The tennis player defeated his adversary.* *n., pl.* **ad·ver·sar·ies.**

ad·verse (ad vərs′ *or* ad′vərs) unfavourable: *adverse conditions, adverse criticism. The hot weather had an adverse effect on his health.* *adj.*

ad·ver·si·ty (ad vər′sə tē) trouble; difficulty; hardship: *The Depression was a time of adversity for many Canadians.* *n., pl.* **ad·ver·si·ties.**

ad·ver·tise (ad′vər tīz′) **1** let people know about: *We put a notice in the newspaper to advertise the yard sale.* **2** praise the good qualities of something so people will want to buy it: *to advertise a new kind of cereal. Toymakers advertise regularly on TV.* *v.,* **ad·ver·tised, ad·ver·tis·ing.**
advertise for, let people know that you need or want something: *He advertised for a job.*

ad·ver·tise·ment (ad′vər tīz′mənt *or* ad vər′tis mənt) a public announcement or notice, especially one trying to persuade people to buy: *The store has an advertisement in the newspaper.* *n.*

ad·vice (ad vīs′) an opinion given to someone about what that person should do: *The doctor's advice is to get a good rest.* *n.*

CONFUSABLES . . . . . . advice

advice is the noun: *I gave him advice.*
advise is the verb: *I advised him.*

ad·vis·a·ble (ad vī′zə bəl) wise; sensible; suitable: *It's not advisable for him to go while he is sick.* *adj.*

ad·vise (ad vīz′) **1** tell someone what he or she should do: *He advised me to keep my money in the bank.* **2** tell; warn: *We were advised of the dangers before we began our trip.* *v.,* **ad·vised, ad·vis·ing.** **—ad·vis′er** or **ad·vi′sor,** *n.*

ad·vo·cate (ad′və kāt′ *for 1,* ad′və kit *for 2*) **1** speak in favour of; support: *She advocates longer recesses.* **2** a person who speaks in favour of something; supporter: *They are strong advocates of recycling.* 1 *v.,* **ad·vo·cat·ed, ad·vo·cat·ing;** 2 *n.*

adze (adz) **1** an axe whose blade is set across the handle, for chipping out wood: *Adzes were used by First Nations peoples in British Columbia, to shape canoes from cedar trees.*

ae·on (ē′on *or* ē′ən) a less common spelling of **eon.**

a bat	e bed	i bid	o pot	u cup	th thin
ā cake	ē me	ī bite	ō go	ū rude	ꟸH then
ä bar	ə about	ər over	ô for	ù put	zh measure

aer·i·al (er′ē əl) 1 a radio or television antenna. 2 having to do with the air or with aircraft. An aerial photograph is one taken from high in the air. Aerial roots are roots that grow in the air instead of the ground. 1 *n.*, 2 *adj.*

aer·o·bics (er ō′biks) very active exercise that helps your heart and lungs and increases the amount of oxygen your body uses: *She put on a tape to listen to while she did aerobics.* *n.* **—aer·o′bic,** *adj.*

aer·o·dy·nam·ic (er′ō dī nam′ik) able to travel fast because it is shaped so that the air can easily pass around it while it is moving. Racing cars are aerodynamic. *adj.*

aer·o·gram (er′ə gram′) a pre-stamped form that you can write a letter on and then fold, seal, and address to be sent by air mail. It does not need an envelope, and you cannot put anything inside it. *n.*

aer·o·nau·tics (er′ə not′iks) the science of building and flying aircraft. *n.*

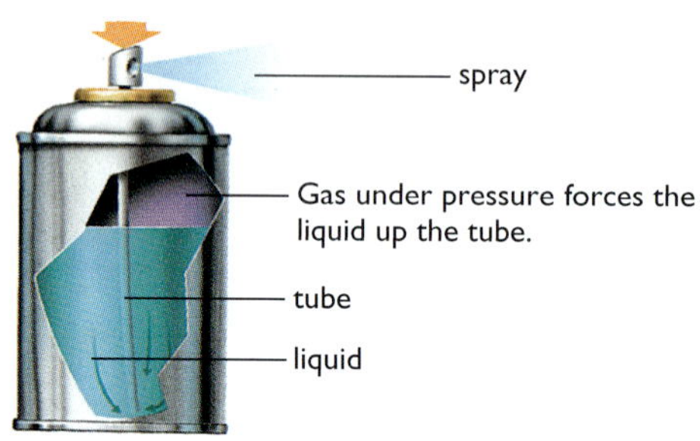

aer·o·sol (er′ə sol′) a spray can, or the mist or foam it sprays out. The paint, shaving cream, or other substance inside is mixed with a gas under pressure. Pressing the button lets the mixture shoot out through a tiny opening. The gas part then escapes into the atmosphere. *n.*

aer·o·space (er′ə spās′) 1 the earth's atmosphere and the space beyond it. 2 the science of building and operating airplanes, rockets, missiles, and other spacecraft. *n.*

aes·thet·ic (es thet′ik) having to do with beauty or the appreciation of beautiful things: *They liked the museum's Web page from an aesthetic point of view, but decided that it gave too little information.* *adj.*

a·far (ə fär′) far; far away; far off: *I saw them from afar.* *adv.*

af·fa·ble (af′ə bəl) easy to talk to; courteous and pleasant: *Our principal is a very friendly and affable woman.* *adj.*

af·fair (ə fer′) 1 anything to be done; a matter of business: *The Prime Minister has many affairs to look after.* 2 any thing or happening: *The party on Saturday was a disappointing affair.* *n.*

af·fect[1] (ə fekt′) cause a change in; influence: *The amount of rain affects the growth of crops.* *v.*

CONFUSABLES ...... affect

affect means "influence": *Did that affect you?*

effect means "result": *It had no effect on me.*

Notice that **affect** is a verb; **effect** is usually a noun.

af·fect[2] (ə fekt′) pretend to have or feel: *He affected a great knowledge of computers, but he hardly knew how to use a keyboard.* *v.* **—af·fect′ed,** *adj.*

af·fec·ta·tion (af′ek tā′shən) a fake or unnatural way of acting or talking, to impress people: *His rough talk is just an affectation; he's really very kind.* *n.*

af·fec·tion (ə fek′shən) a friendly feeling; love: *The father's affection for his baby was easy to see.* *n.* **—af·fec′tion·ate** (ə fek′shə nit), *adj.*

af·fil·i·ate (ə fil′ē āt′ *for 1,* ə fil′ē it *for 2*) 1 link one person or group with another: *Our school choir is affiliated with the local choir association.* 2 a person or group that is linked with another. 1 *v.,* **af·fil·i·at·ed, af·fil·i·at·ing;** 2 *n.* **—af·fil′i·a′tion,** *n.*

af·firm (ə fərm′) declare firmly: *She affirmed that the signature was genuine.* *v.*

af·firm·a·tive (ə fər′mə tiv) showing agreement; saying yes: *an affirmative answer.* *adj.* **—af·firm′a·tive·ly,** *adv.*

in the affirmative, with a word or statement meaning yes: *She replied in the affirmative when asked if she would like to go bowling.*

af·flict (ə flikt′) cause pain to; trouble very much: *All his life he was afflicted with poor health.* *v.* **—af·flic′tion,** *n.*

af·flu·ent (af′lū ənt) rich. *adj.* **—af′flu·ence,** *n.*

af·ford (ə fôrd′) 1 have enough money, time, or strength for something: *Can we afford to upgrade our computer system? You can't afford to waste so much time.* 2 give: *Reading this story will afford real pleasure.* *v.* **—af·ford′a·ble,** *adj.*

af·front (ə frunt′) 1 insult openly and purposely: *The girl affronted the bus driver by making a face at him.* 2 an open insult: *To be called a coward is an affront.* 1 *v.,* 2 *n.*

af·ghan (af′gan) a crocheted or knitted blanket or shawl. 1 *n.,* 2 *adj.*

a·field (ə fēld′) away; away from home: *He wandered far afield in foreign lands.* *adv.*

> **WORD HISTORY........afield**
>
> In Old English, people used the prefix *a-* to make an adjective or an adverb out of almost anything. *Blaze* was used to make *ablaze*, and *sleep* became *asleep*. We still have lots of those words in modern English. Some of them are on this page. Can you think of others? Try making some up.

a·flame (ə flām′) 1 in flames; on fire. 2 as if on fire; excited: *Your words have set my heart aflame (adv.).* **Afire** has the same meanings. *adj. or adv.*

a·float (ə flōt′) floating on the water or in the air: *White, fluffy dandelion seeds were afloat on the summer breeze (adj.).* *adv. or adj.*

a·foot (ə fu̇t′) going on; in progress: *Preparations for dinner were afoot in the kitchen (adj.).* *adv. or adj.*

a·fraid (ə frād′) 1 frightened; feeling fear: *She is not afraid of snakes.* 2 sorry: *I'm afraid I must ask you to leave now.* *adj.*

a·fresh (ə fresh′) again: *to start afresh.* *adv.*

Af·ri·ca (af′rə kə) a large continent south of Europe. It has the Atlantic Ocean to the west and the Indian Ocean to the east. The equator runs through the middle of Africa. —**Af′ri·can,** *n. or adj.*

Aft is only one of the directions on a boat — here are some others.

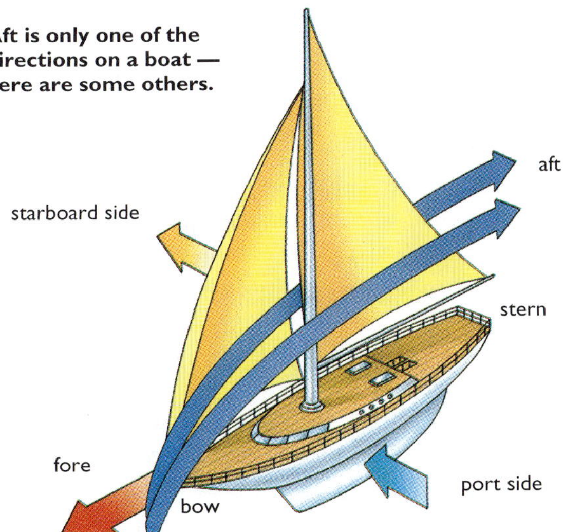

aft (aft) to or at the back of a ship, boat, aircraft, or spacecraft. *adv.*

af·ter (af′tər) 1 following some other person, thing, or time: *Kim is after me in line (prep.). Put it away after you use it (conj.). Let's work now—we can play after (adv.).* 2 considering; because of: *After all her help, how can you ignore her like that (prep.)? This is a pretty disappointing mark, after I studied so hard (conj.)!* 3 chasing or looking for: *What is he after? That dog is always after our cat.* 1–3 *prep.,* 1 *adv.,* 1, 2 *conj.*

af·ter·life (af′tər līf′) life after death. *n.*

af·ter·math (af′tər math′) result: *The aftermath of war is hunger and disease.* *n.*

af·ter·noon (af′tər nün′) the time from noon to evening. *n.*

af·ter·thought (af′tər thot′) 1 a thought that comes after you have already finished planning. 2 something that shows a lack of planning. *n.*

af·ter·ward (af′tər wərd) later: *The bud was small at first, but afterward it became a large flower.* **Afterwards** is another form. *adv.*

a·gain (ə gen′ *or* ə gān′) another time; once more: *Come again to play. Say that again.* *adv.*

a·gainst (ə genst′ *or* ə gānst′) 1 in opposition to: *He spoke against the suggestion.* 2 on: *Rain beats against the window.* 3 in defence from: *A fire is a protection against cold.* 4 in preparation for: *Squirrels store up nuts against the winter.* *prep.*

ag·ate (ag′it) 1 a stone with coloured stripes or cloudy colours. 2 a marble that looks like this stone, used in games. *n.*

age (āj) 1 how old a person or thing is, was, or will be: *the age of ten. Turtles live to a great age.* 2 a certain time in a person's life or in history: *old age, the information age.* 3 Usually, **ages,** *pl., Informal.* a long time: *I haven't seen you for ages.* 4 make or become old: *He is aging fast. Worry ages a person.* 1–3 *n.,* 4 *v.,* **aged, ag·ing** or **age·ing.**
of age, old enough to have full rights and responsibilities under the law.

a·ged (ā′jid *for 1,* ājd *for 2*) 1 old; having lived a long time: *The aged woman had many grandchildren.* 2 that has been left for a time, to improve the flavour: *aged cheese, aged wine.* *adj.*

a bat	e bed	i bid	o pot	u cup	th thin
ā cake	ē me	ī bite	ō go	ū rude	ŦH then
ä bar	ə about	ər over	ȯ for	u̇ put	zh measure

a·gen·cy (ā′jən sē) 1 a company or group that helps people with something or does business for them: *a rental agency. The Human Rights Commission is a government agency.* 2 the place where this kind of group has its office: *We walked down to the agency together.* *n., pl.* **a·gen·cies.**
through the agency of, with the help of; by means of: *Through the agency of friends she was set free.*

a·gen·da (ə jen′də) 1 a notebook for writing down what needs to be done: *a homework agenda.* 2 a list of things to be done or discussed: *the agenda for a meeting.* *n.*

a·gent (ā′jənt) 1 a person or company that acts for another: *You can get an agent to find a buyer for your house.* 2 anything that accomplishes some purpose: *Yeast is an important agent in the making of bread.* *n.*

ag·gra·vate (ag′rə vāt′) 1 make worse: *His bad temper was aggravated by his headache.* 2 annoy; irritate. *v.,* **ag·gra·vat·ed, ag·gra·vat·ing.** —**ag′gra·va′tion,** *n.*

ag·gres·sive (ə gres′iv) 1 likely to start a quarrel; attacking: *an aggressive person, aggressive behaviour.* 2 active; energetic; forceful: *The police began an aggressive campaign against speeding.* *adj.* —**ag·gres′sor,** *n.* —**ag·gres′sion,** *n.*

a·ghast (ə gast′) struck with surprise or horror: *The children were aghast at the visitor's bad manners.* *adj.*

ag·ile (aj′īl *or* aj′əl) moving or thinking quickly and easily: *An acrobat has to be agile. Tasi is such an agile thinker that she never loses an argument.* *adj.* —**ag′ile·ly,** *adv.* —**a·gil′i·ty** (ə jil′ə tē), *n.*

ag·i·tate (aj′ə tāt′) 1 move or shake: *The slightest wind will agitate the leaves of some trees.* 2 disturb or upset; excite: *She was very agitated by the news of her brother's accident.* 3 keep talking or writing about something you want changed: *They were agitating for a later bedtime.* *v.,* **ag·i·tat·ed, ag·i·tat·ing.** —**ag′i·ta′tion,** *n.*

ag·i·ta·tor (aj′ə tā′tər) 1 a person who keeps talking or writing about something, hoping that it will be changed. 2 a device for shaking or stirring: *Most washers have an agitator in the centre for swishing the laundry around in the water.* *n.*

a·glow (ə glō′) glowing: *The tree was aglow with lights (adj.). A smile set his face aglow (adv.).* *adj. or adv.*

ag·nos·tic (ag nos′tik) a person who believes that human beings cannot know anything about God or an afterlife. *n.*

a·go (ə gō′) gone by; in the past: *I met her two years ago. Huge herds of bison lived on the plains of Canada long ago.* *adv.*

ag·o·niz·ing (ag′ə nī′zing) very painful or difficult: *an agonizing decision.* *adj.*

ag·o·ny (ag′ə nē) very great suffering of body or mind: *the agony of a toothache.* *n., pl.* **ag·o·nies.**

a·gree (ə grē′) 1 have the same opinion: *I agree with you that math is fun.* 2 be alike or in harmony: *Your story agrees with mine.* 3 arrange: *We agreed to have supper together.* 4 consent: *She agreed to our plan.* *v.,* **a·greed, a·gree·ing.** —**a·gree′ment,** *n.*
agree with, have a good effect on; suit: *This food does not agree with me; it makes me sick.*

a·gree·a·ble (ə grē′ə bəl) 1 pleasant; pleasing: *The boy had an agreeable manner.* 2 willing: *If my mother is agreeable, we could go to the park this afternoon.* *adj.* —**a·gree′a·bly,** *adv.*

ag·ri·cul·ture (ag′rə kul′chər) farming; the raising of crops and farm animals. *n.* —**ag′ri·cul′tur·al,** *adj.*

a·ground (ə ground′) on the shore; on the bottom in shallow water: *The ship ran aground and stuck in the sand (adv.).* *adv. or adj.*

a·head (ə hed′) 1 in front; before: *They told me to walk ahead.* 2 farther on: *Jim was ahead of his class in reading.* 3 winning in a race or game: *The Maple Leafs shot ahead 3 to 1.* *adv.*
get ahead, succeed: *You need a good education to get ahead.*
go ahead, **a** begin or continue: *Go ahead with your work.* **b** it's all right; you may do it: *Want to try it? Go ahead!*

a·hoy (ə hoi′) a call used especially by sailors to attract attention or to greet someone. *interj.*

aid (ād) 1 help or support: *The flood victims were aided by people from all over Canada (v.). I can walk now with the aid of a crutch (n.).* 2 a thing or person that helps: *Pictures are often used as teaching aids.* 1 *v.,* 1, 2 *n.*

aide (ād) assistant; helper: *He works as a nurse's aide.* *n.*

AIDS (ādz) acronym for a very serious disease caused by a virus that keeps a person's body from fighting infections. Its full name is **Acquired Immune Deficiency Syndrome.** *n.*

ai·ki·do (ī kē′dō *or* ī′kēdō′) a system of self-defence first used in Japan. It uses no weapons. *n.*

ail (āl) 1 be the matter with: *What ails the child?* 2 be sick: *She had been ailing for a week.* *v.* —**ail′ing,** *adj.*

ai·ler·on (ā′lə ron′) the movable part at the back of an airplane's wing nearest the tip. Ailerons help to keep an airplane level while it is flying. *n.*

ail·ment (āl′mənt) an illness or sickness. *n.*

aim (ām) 1 point or direct a gun, a throw, words, etc. at someone or something: *I aimed at the target but missed. Her questions were aimed at the younger children.* 2 the act or skill of pointing or directing at something: *His aim was so poor that he missed the target.* 3 try or plan: *I aim to be the best goalie in the league.* 4 goal; purpose: *Her aim was to make at least one new friend.* 1, 3 *v.,* 2, 4 *n.*

aim·less (ām′lis) without aim or purpose: *He had gone on an aimless walk but happened to meet some friends.* *adj.*

ain't (ānt) *Informal.* 1 am not; are not; is not. 2 have not; has not.

air (er) 1 the mixture of gases that surrounds the earth, which we breathe. Air is made up of nitrogen, oxygen, hydrogen, and other gases. 2 the sky: *Birds fly in the air.* 3 put out in the air; let air through: *We aired the blankets outside on the line.* 4 **a** make known: *Don't air your troubles too often.* **b** broadcast on the radio or TV: *to air a program.* 5 a melody or tune. 6 a way; a look or manner: *He had the air of a child who was afraid.* 1, 2, 5, 6 *n.,* 3, 4 *v.*
in the air, going around: *Wild rumours were in the air.*
on the air, broadcasting or being broadcast on radio or TV.
put on airs, act fancy; show off.
up in the air, *Informal.* uncertain; undecided: *Our plans for the trip are still up in the air.*

Word Family.......... air

aircraft: any machine that can travel through the air
airfield: the landing field of an airport
airline: a company that offers regular flights
airliner: a large aircraft for passengers
airplane: a flying machine with fixed wings and a motor
airport: a place where aircraft regularly land and take off
airspace: the part of the air that is above a country and is said to belong to it
airstrip: a temporary runway

air bag (er′ bag′) in a car, a special built-in bag that pops out and fills with air in an accident: *When she crashed into a tree only an air bag kept her from being killed.* *n.*

The first controlled and powered flight was made when this airplane, the Wright brothers' *Flyer*, became airborne in 1903.

air·borne (er′bôrn′) in or carried through the air: *airborne seeds. The plane is now airborne.* *adj.*

air conditioning (er′ kən dish′ ə ning) a system of treating the air in buildings, cars, etc. to control its temperature and moisture and to free it from dust. —**air′ con·di′tion·er.** —**air′-con·di′tion,** *v.* —**air′-con·di′tioned,** *adj.*

air force (er′ fôrs′) the branch of a country's armed forces that uses aircraft. Canada's air force is called **Air Command.**

air·lock (er′lok′) a small, airtight room used for moving between two places that have different air pressure. The pressure in the airlock can be gradually adjusted while the person waits inside it. Both a spacecraft and a submarine can have airlocks. *n.*

air mail (er′ māl′) 1 mail sent by aircraft. 2 the system of sending mail by aircraft. —**air′-mail′,** *v.*

air mass (er′ mas′) a large layer of air with a certain temperature and a certain amount of moisture. It may travel a great distance, affecting the weather wherever it goes: *A cold air mass moved down from Hudson Bay.*

air·ship (er′ship′) a kind of aircraft shaped something like a long, oval balloon. It is filled with a gas that keeps it up in the air. The equipment for steering and moving the airship is attached to the bottom on the outside. **Dirigible** is another word for this craft. *n.*

air·tight (er′tīt′) 1 so tight that no air can get in or out. 2 unbeatable; with no weaknesses: *airtight logic.* *adj.*

air·waves (er′wāvz′) the radio waves in the air that carry radio and TV signals: *The news was announced over the airwaves.* *pl.n.*

a bat	e bed	i bid	o pot	u cup	th thin
ā cake	ē me	ī bite	ō go	ū rude	ᴛʜ then
ä bar	ə about	ər over	ô for	ů put	zh measure

air•way (er′wā′) 1 a route for airplanes. 2 a passage for air to flow through. *n.*

air•y (er′ē) 1 light; carefree: *an airy tune, airy laughter.* 2 breezy; with air moving through it: *a large, airy room.* *adj.,* **air•i•er, air•i•est.**

aisle (īl) a walkway between rows of seats in a church or theatre, between shelves in a store, etc. *n.*

a•jar (ə jär′) slightly open: *Leave the door ajar (adj.). A breeze blew the door ajar (adv.).* *adv. or adj.*

a•kim•bo (ə kim′bō) with the hands on the hips and the elbows bent outward. *adv. or adj.*

a•kin (ə kin′) 1 belonging to the same family; related: *Peaches are akin to apricots.* 2 alike: *The friends are akin in their love of video games.* *adj.*

al•a•bas•ter (al′ə bas′tər) a smooth, white stone. Alabaster is often carved into ornaments and vases. *n.*

a•larm (ə lärm′) 1 sudden fear when you become aware of danger: *The deer darted off in alarm.* 2 make uneasy; frighten: *The breaking of a branch under my foot alarmed the deer.* 3 a warning of danger or a call to action: *They heard the alarm and ran to help.* 4 a bell or other thing that makes a noise to warn or waken people. 1, 3, 4 *n.,* 2 *v.*

alarm clock (ə lärm′ klok′) a clock that can be set to ring or beep at a certain time, especially to wake people up.

a•las (ə las′) an exclamation of sorrow, grief, regret, pity, or dread. *interj.*

The large surface area of the wings of the albatross (on the right) allows this bird to glide for hours. The wings of the vulture (on the left) are broader, but equally useful for soaring.

al•ba•tross (al′bə tros′) a large black, brown, or white ocean bird found especially in the southern hemisphere. It has very long, narrow wings, a hooked beak, and webbed feet. *n.*

Al•ber•ta (al bər′tə) the western Canadian province between British Columbia and Saskatchewan. *n.* —**Al•ber′tan,** *n.*

al•bi•no (al bī′ nō) an animal or plant without the usual amount of pigment in its body tissues. A person who is an albino has pink skin and eyes and white hair. *n.*

al•bum (al′bəm) 1 a book with blank pages for holding things like photographs or stamps. 2 a collection of songs on CD, tape, or record. *n.*

WORD HISTORY...... album

Album is from the Latin *albus* meaning "white." The pages of an album are blank, or white, so that you can put whatever you want on them.

al•bu•men (al byū′mən *or* al′byə mən) egg white. *n.*

al•che•my (al′kə mē) the unscientific chemistry of the Middle Ages. Alchemy was concerned mainly with finding a way to turn ordinary metals into gold and producing something that would cure all diseases and make people live forever. *n.* —**al′che•mist,** *n.*

al•co•hol (al′kə hol′) a colourless liquid in beer, wine, whisky, gin, and other strong drinks. Alcohol acts as a drug. *n.*

al•co•hol•ic (al′kə hol′ik) 1 having to do with alcohol: *alcoholic drinks.* 2 a person who is addicted to alcohol. This addiction is called **alcoholism.** 1 *adj.,* 2 *n.*

al•cove (al′kōv) a small room or space opening off a larger room. *n.*

al•der (ol′dər) a deciduous tree similar to the birch, found especially in cool, wet parts of the northern hemisphere. *n.*

ale (āl) a kind of beer, made from malt and hops. *n.*

a•lert (ə lərt′) 1 wide awake and aware of what's going on: *The dog was alert, noticing every sound.* 2 a warning signal. 3 warn; make someone aware of a problem: *I saw someone shoplifting and alerted the store owner.* 1 *adj.,* 2 *n.,* 3 *v.* —**a•lert′ness,** *n.*
on the alert, watchful; ready at any instant for what is coming: *A security guard must be on the alert.*

al•fal•fa (al fal′fə) a plant with deep roots, leaves like clover, and bluish-purple flowers. Alfalfa is used as a food for horses and cattle. *n.*

al•gae (al′jē) a name for simple plants like seaweeds that grow in water and make their own food. Some algae form a scum on the top of ponds. *pl.n.*

al•ge•bra (al′jə brə) a branch of mathematics that uses letters and other symbols to stand for numbers and how they are used. Combined with regular numbers, these symbols are used to solve mathematical problems. *n.*

Al•gon•quin (al gong′kwin) **1** a First Nations people living in eastern Ontario and Québec. **2** their language. **3** having to do with these people or their language. 1, 2 *n.*, 3 *adj.*

a•li•as (ā′lē əs) a false name; other name: *The spy's real name was Harrison, but she sometimes went by the alias of Lee.* *n., pl.* **a•li•as•es.**

al•i•bi (al′ə bī′) **1** a claim made by an accused person that he or she was somewhere else when a crime was committed. **2** *Informal.* any excuse. *n., pl.* **al•i•bis.**

> **WORD HISTORY........alibi**
>
> **Alibi** is Latin for "somewhere else." Traditionally, the language of law was Latin, so this word often came up when lawyers were defending their clients: *The accused could not have stolen the money. She was somewhere else at the time.* It was eventually lifted straight into English as a noun: *She had an alibi.*

al•ien (ā′lē ən) **1** a being from outer space. **2** a person who is not a citizen of the country he or she is living in. **3** strange or unfamiliar; completely unknown: *an alien language. Unkindness is alien to her nature.* 1, 2 *n.*, 3 *adj.*

al•ien•ate (āl′yə nāt′) **1** cause a person to lose interest or become unfriendly: *Her bad temper is alienating her friends.* **2** cause a person to feel that he or she does not belong: *When I first came to Canada I felt alienated because I could not speak the language.* *v.,* **al•ien•at•ed, al•ien•at•ing.** **—al′ien•a′tion,** *n.*

a•light[1] (ə līt′) **1** get down; get off: *to alight from a horse, to alight from a train.* **2** land: *The bird alighted on our window sill.* *v.,* **a•light•ed** or **a•lit, a•light•ing.**

a•light[2] (ə līt′) on fire; lighted up: *Holger set the candles alight (adv.). Her face was alight with happiness (adj.).* *adv. or adj.*

a•lign (ə līn′) **1** bring into a straight line: *We aligned the chairs in front of the stage.* **2** bring into co-operation with others: *They aligned themselves with the peace movement.* *v.* **—a•lign′ment,** *n.*

a•like (ə līk′) the same: *These twins are very much alike (adj.). Joel and his father walk alike (adv.).* *adj. or adv.*

al•i•men•ta•ry canal (al′ə men′tə rē kə nal′) the parts of the body that food passes through as it is being digested. The mouth, stomach, and intestines are part of the alimentary canal.

al•i•mo•ny (al′ə mō′nē) money paid by a person to support his or her wife or husband (or former wife or husband) when they are separated or divorced. *n.*

a•lit (ə lit′) a past tense and past participle of **alight[1]:** *A bird alit on the window sill.* *v.*

a•live (ə līv′) **1** living: *Was the snake alive or dead?* **2** active; lively; brisk. *adj.*
alive to, noticing; paying attention to: *He waited in the dark, alive to every sound.*
alive with, full of; swarming with: *The streets were alive with people.*
look alive! hurry up! be quick!

al•ka•li (al′kə lī′) a chemical that works against acids. Alkalis dissolve in water, and strong ones can burn flesh. Lye and ammonia are alkalis. Soil or anything else that contains an alkali is **alkaline.** *n.*

all (ol) **1** the whole amount or number of: *all children, all the cars. The mice ate all the cheese.* **2** everyone or everything: *To all a good night. All is well.* **3** completely; entirely: *He was all tired out.* 1 *adj.*, 2 *pron.*, 3 *adv.*
all at once, suddenly: *All at once, the cat pounced.*
all but, almost; nearly: *All but dead from hunger, she struggled on.*
at all, in any way or at any time: *They refused to work at all.*
in all, altogether: *There were 100 people in all.*

Al•lah (al′ə *or* ȧ′lə) in the Muslim religion, God. *n.*

al•lege (ə lej′) claim without proof: *This man alleges that his watch has been stolen.* *v.,* **al•leged, al•leg•ing.**

al•le•giance (ə lē′jəns) loyalty; faithfulness: *Her allegiance to Canada never wavered.* *n.*

al•ler•gy (al′ər jē) sickness or discomfort such as sneezing or itching caused by something that is harmless to most people: *He has an allergy to strawberries and gets a rash when he eats them.* *n., pl.* **al•ler•gies.** **—al•ler′gic** (ə lər′jik), *adj.*

a bat	e bed	i bid	o pot	u cup	th thin
ā cake	ē me	ī bite	ō go	ū rude	ᴛʜ then
ȧ bar	ə about	ər over	ȯ for	u̇ put	zh measure

al•ley¹ (al′ē) 1 a narrow back street in a city or town. 2 a building where people can go bowling. *n., pl.* **al•leys.**

al•ley² (al′ē) a glass marble used in games. *n., pl.* **al•leys.**

al•li•ance (ə lī′əns) 1 an agreement to help each other: *The two countries formed an alliance to try to reduce pollution.* 2 the people or nations that make the agreement. *n.*

al•lied (ə līd′) 1 united by agreement: *allied nations, allied armies.* 2 connected; related: *Cutting and pasting are allied activities. adj.*

An alligator kills by pulling its prey under water and drowning it.

al•li•ga•tor (al′ə gā′tər) a large scaly, thick-skinned reptile that has big teeth, short legs, and a long body and tail. American alligators live in wet areas in warm places like Florida. *n.*

al•lit•er•a•tion (ə lit′ə rā′shən) the use of a connected series of words that begin with the same sound. *Example: Powerful panthers pushed past pigs.* **—al•lit′er•ate′,** *v.*

al•lot (ə lot′) 1 divide up and give a share: *The profits from the sale were allotted equally to each group that took part.* 2 give or assign: *You should allot three weeks for working on this project. v.,* **al•lot•ted, al•lot•ting.**

CONFUSABLES ...... allot

allot means "distribute": *He allotted the cash for food.*

a lot means "many" or "much": *a lot of snowflakes*

Notice that **allot** is one word, but **a lot** is two words!

al•low (ə lou′) 1 let; permit: *Mrs. Jha does not allow her children to go swimming alone. Dogs are allowed in this park.* 2 give; let have: *She is allowed one hour a day on the family computer.* 3 set aside for a certain purpose: *We ought to allow an extra hour in case of delays. v.* **allow for,** take into consideration: *I made the dress a little large to allow for shrinking when it was washed.*

al•low•ance (ə lou′əns) an amount given or set aside: *Angelo gets a weekly allowance. My mom's company gives her a travelling allowance for business trips. n.* **make allowance for,** take into account; allow for: *You must make allowance for the wishes of others.*

al•loy (al′oi *for 1,* ə loi′ *for 2*) 1 a mixture of two or more metals. Alloys are often harder, lighter, and stronger than the pure metals. Brass is an alloy of copper and zinc. 2 mix, especially with something less valuable or not as good. 1 *n.,* 2 *v.*

all right (ol′ rīt′ *for 1, 3, and 4,* ol′ rīt′ *for 2*) 1 satisfactory: *The work was not excellent, but it was all right.* 2 yes: *"Will you come with me?" "All right."* 3 in good health; well: *He said he was feeling all right.* 4 in a satisfactory way: *The engine seemed to be working all right.*

all–round (ol′ round′) able to do many things; useful in many ways: *an all-round athlete. adj.*

al•lude (ə lūd′) refer to indirectly; mention in passing: *Do not ask Dad to buy that trampoline; don't even allude to it. v.,* **al•lud•ed, al•lud•ing. —al•lu′sion** (ə lū′zhən), *n.*

al•lure (ə lūr′) 1 fascinate; attract or charm: *the alluring possibility of a trip to New Zealand.* 2 attraction; fascination: *the allure of the sea.* 1 *v.,* **al•lured, al•lur•ing;** 2 *n.*

al•ly (ə lī′ *for 1,* al′ī *for 2*) 1 join with another for support in a conflict: *Canada allied itself with several other countries in World War II.* 2 a person or group on the same side as another in a conflict: *Gloria is my friend and ally.* 1 *v.,* **al•lied, al•ly•ing;** 2 *n., pl.* **al•lies.**

al•ma•nac (ol′mə nak′ *or* al′mə nak′) a book giving information about the expected weather, the sun, moon, stars, tides, and holidays for one year. It often contains other facts as well. *n.*

al•might•y (ol mī′tē) 1 having all power. 2 **the Almighty,** a name some people use for God. 1 *adj.,* 2 *n.*

al•mond (om′ənd, ol′mənd, *or* am′ənd) a sweet, oval nut with a light-coloured shell. It is a seed found inside the fruit of a tree grown in warm regions. *n.*

al•most (ol′mōst) nearly: *We're almost there; the house is at the end of this block. adv.*

alms (omz *or* olmz) money or gifts to help the poor. *pl. or sing.n.*

a•loft (ə loft′) high up: *They threw the ball aloft (adv.). There was Jill, aloft in the crow's-nest, looking for the distant shore (adj.). adv. or adj.*

a•lone (ə lōn′) without any other people or things: *She is alone in the treehouse (adj.). One boy can do this work alone (adv.). You alone understand how I feel (adj.). adv. or adj.*
leave alone, not bother; not meddle with: *Please leave my jigsaw puzzle alone.*

a•long (ə long′) **1** from one end of something to the other: *Trees are planted along the street.* **2** further; onward: *Move along quickly.* **3** with oneself: *He took his dog along.* 1 *prep.,* 2, 3 *adv.*
all along, the whole time: *He was here all along.*
along with, as well as: *She paid for all the food, along with everything else.*

a•long•side (ə long′sīd′) by the side of something or someone: *The boat was alongside the dock (prep.). It was tied up alongside (adv.). adv. or prep.*

a•loof (ə lüf′) **1** away; apart: *One boy stood aloof from the others.* **2** not very warm or friendly toward others: *She was rather aloof and no one could get to know her.* 1 *adv.,* 2 *adj.* **—a•loof′ness,** *n.*

a•loud (ə loud′) **1** loud enough to be heard; not in a whisper: *I read the story aloud to the others.* **2** loudly; in a loud voice: *He groaned aloud with pain. adv.*

al•pac•a (al pak′ə) a South American grass-eating animal with long, soft, silky hair or wool that is used to make clothing. The alpaca is a kind of llama. *n.*

al•pha•bet (al′fə bet′) the set of letters used in writing a language, especially as arranged in a familiar order: *The English alphabet has twenty-six letters. "D" is the fourth letter of the alphabet. n.* **—al′pha•bet′i•cal** (al′fə bet′ə kəl), *adj.*

al•pha•bet•ize (al′fə bə tīz′) arrange in **alphabetical order,** the order of the alphabet. *v.,* **al•pha•bet•ized, al•pha•bet•iz•ing.**

al•read•y (ol red′ē) before this time; by this time; even now: *You are half an hour late already. The baby has already broken her new toy. adv.*

CONFUSABLES ..... already

already means "by this time": *No, he's already gone.*
all ready means "completely ready": *I'm all ready to go.*

al•so (ol′sō) too; in addition: *This dress is prettier than the other one; it is also cheaper. adv.*

al•tar (ol′tər) **1** a table or stand in the most sacred part of a church or temple, used for ceremonies. **2** a raised outdoor place built of earth or stone, for making sacrifices or offerings to gods. *n.*

al•ter (ol′tər) change: *If this coat is too big, I can alter it to fit you. Since her summer on the farm, her whole outlook has altered. v.* **—al′ter•a′tion,** *n.*

al•ter•nate (ol′tər nāt′ *for 1,* ol′tər nit *for 2 and 3*) **1** follow each other by turns, first one and then the other: *Squares and circles alternate in this row:* □○□○□○□ *Lucy and her brother will alternate in setting the table.* **2** every other: *I clean my room on alternate days because I don't have time every day.* **3** a person chosen to take someone's place if necessary; a substitute. 1 *v.,* **al•ter•nat•ed, al•ter•nat•ing;** 2 *adj.,* 3 *n.* **—al′ter•nate•ly,** *adv.*

alternating current (ol′tər nā′ting kər′ənt) an electric current that reverses its direction many times per second.

al•ter•na•tive (ol tər′nə tiv) **1** a choice: *We had the alternative of going to a movie or renting a video. Steve took the second alternative and rented* Star Wars. **2** giving a choice: *Some English words have alternative spellings. I have an alternative recipe that uses no eggs.* 1 *n.,* 2 *adj.*

al•though (ol ꜩHō′) in spite of the fact that: *Although it had rained all morning, they went on the hike. conj.*

al•tim•e•ter (al tim′ə tər *or* al′tə mē′tər) an instrument for measuring height above the earth, used in aircraft and so on. *n.*

al•ti•tude (al′tə tyūd′ *or* al′tə tūd′) **1** height above the earth or above sea level: *What altitude did the airplane reach? The altitude of Banff, Alberta is 1380 m.* **2** a high place: *At some altitudes the snow never melts. n.*

al•to (ol′tō *or* al′tō) **1** in music, the range of notes that a girl or woman with a low voice can sing. **2** having this range of notes: *an alto voice, an alto recorder.* **3** a singer or instrument with this range, or the part written for it in a song: *We have six altos in our choir. You play the alto.* 1, 3 *n., pl.,* **al•tos;** 2 *adj.*

al•to•geth•er (ol′tə geꜩH′ər) **1** completely; entirely: *The house was altogether destroyed by fire.* **2** all included: *Altogether there were ten books on the shelf. adv.*

CONFUSABLES .... altogether

altogether means "completely": *She's altogether mean.*
all together means "co-operatively": *Sing all together!*

a bat	e bed	i bid	o pot	u cup	th thin
ā cake	ē me	ī bite	ō go	ū rude	ꜩH then
à bar	ə about	ər over	ò for	ù put	zh measure

a·lu·mi·num (ə lū′mə nəm) a silver-white, very light and strong metal that does not tarnish easily. It is used to make cans, foil, and many other things. *n.*

al·ways (ol′wiz *or* ol′wāz) every time; all the time: *Night always follows day. Christine is always animated.* *adv.*

Alz·hei·mer's disease (olts′hī mərz də zēz′) a very serious disease of unknown cause that affects older people and gradually gets worse. Alzheimer's disease makes people become confused and lose their memory.

a.m. or **A.M.** *abbreviation for* the time from midnight to noon: *Classes begin at 9 a.m.*

WORD HISTORY........ a.m.

a.m. stands for the Latin words *ante meridiem,* meaning "before noon."

p.m. stands for the Latin words *post meridiem,* meaning "after noon."

a·mass (ə mas′) collect; pile up: *The miser amassed a fortune.* *v.*

am·a·teur (am′ə chər) **1** a person who does something for pleasure, not for money or as a job: *Only amateurs used to take part in the Olympics.* **2** a person without much skill: *You can tell this haircut was given by an amateur—what a mess!* **3** made or done by amateurs: *an amateur play.* 1, 2 *n.,* 3 *adj.* **—a′ma·teur′ish,** *adj.*

a·maze (ə māz′) surprise or impress very much: *She was so amazed by the surprise party that she couldn't think of a thing to say.* *v.,* **a·mazed, a·maz·ing.** **—a·maze′ment,** *n.*

am·bas·sa·dor (am bas′ə dər) **1** a representative of the highest rank sent by one government to another. An ambassador lives in a foreign country and speaks and acts on behalf of his or her government. **2** a person who represents an organization, or who stands up for something in words and actions wherever he or she goes: *Sonja is an ambassador for people with disabilities.* *n.*

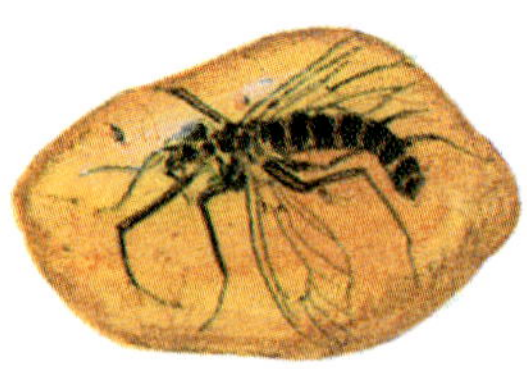

This piece of amber contains the body of an insect, preserved almost perfectly.

am·ber (am′bər) a brownish yellow substance like glass, often used in jewellery. It is the fossilized resin of pine trees that grew long ago. *n.*

am·bi·dex·trous (am′bə dek′strəs) able to use both hands equally well. *adj.*

am·big·u·ous (am big′yū əs) having more than one possible meaning. The sentence *After Ted hit Hari, he ran away* is ambiguous because you can't tell who ran away. *adj.*

am·bi·tion (am bish′ən) **1** a goal that a person wants very much to reach: *Her ambition was to be a great writer.* **2** a strong desire for fame or success: *Ambition is what kept him working.* *n.*

am·bi·tious (am bish′əs) **1** very eager to succeed: *My ambitious sister is training very hard in tae kwon do. "I must win!" she keeps saying.* **2** that can only be done by someone eager to succeed, because it is so difficult: *Build a deck in an afternoon? That's a pretty ambitious plan!* *adj.*

am·ble (am′bəl) **1** go with an easy, slow pace. When a horse ambles, it lifts first the two legs on one side and then the two on the other side. **2** an easy, slow pace in walking. 1 *v.,* **am·bled, am·bling;** 2 *n.*

am·bu·lance (am′byə ləns) a van, boat, or aircraft equipped to carry sick or wounded people. *n.*

am·bush (am′bu̇sh) **1** a surprise attack from a hiding place. **2** the attackers who are hiding or the place where they hide. **3** attack in this way: *A group of bandits ambushed the travellers on the trail through the woods.* 1, 2 *n.,* 3 *v.*

a·men (ā′men′ *or* ȧ′men′) in some religions, a word said to end a prayer, meaning "may it be so." *interj.*

a·mend (ə mend′) **1** change: *The rules for hockey have been amended many times.* **2** change for the better; correct: *It is time you amended your poor table manners.* *v.* **—a·mend′ment,** *n.*

a·mends (ə mendz′)
make amends for, make up for: *She promised to make amends for not doing her homework.* *n.*

am·e·thyst (am′ə thist) a purple type of quartz, used for jewellery. *n.*

a·mi·a·ble (ā′mē ə bəl) good-natured and friendly: *I like Joan. She is an amiable girl.* *adj.* **—a′mi·a·bly,** *adv.*

a·mid (ə mid′) in the middle of; surrounded by: *The little church stood unharmed amid the rubble of the bombed village.* *prep.*

USING WORDS .... amid/among

Use **amid** for things that cannot be counted: *amid the laughter, amid the darkness, amid the fog.*

Use **among** with a plural noun: *among the ruins, among the trees, among the people.*

a·mid·ships (ə mid′ships) in or toward the middle of a ship. *adv.*

a·miss (ə mis′) wrong; not the way it should be; out of order: *Something is amiss; Larry has not eaten for days* (*adj.*). *adv. or adj.*
take amiss, take the wrong way: *Rick had not meant to be rude to his mother, but she took his answer amiss.*

am·mo·nia (ə mōn′yə) **1** a colourless gas with a strong smell. **2** water with this gas dissolved in it. Ammonia is useful for cleaning. *n.*

am·mu·ni·tion (am′yə nish′ən) **1** bullets, bombs, and anything else that can be shot or thrown as a weapon. **2** anything that can be used to fight or argue against a person or idea: *In our attack on smoking, our main ammunition was information about lung cancer.* *n.*

am·ne·sia (am nē′zhə) loss of memory, caused by brain injury, disease, or shock: *She had amnesia for several weeks after the car accident.* *n.*

a·moe·ba (ə mē′bə) a very small animal having only one cell (def. 3). Amoebas are so small that they can be seen only with a microscope. *n., pl.* **a·moe·bas** or **a·moe·bae** (ə mē′bē *or* ə mē′bī).

a·mong (ə mung′) **1** surrounded by: *a house among the trees.* **2** a part of; one of: *Canada is among the largest countries of the world. His brothers were among the crowd.* **3** giving some to each of: *We divided the grapes among us.* *prep.*
among ourselves, yourselves, or **themselves,** together; as a group: *The children quarrelled among themselves. They agreed among themselves to have a party.*

USING WORDS . . . among/between

Use **among** when more than two people or things are involved: *They divided the work among the four of them.*

Use **between** when there are just two: *Bo and I had only three dollars between us.*

a·mount (ə mount′) **1** quantity: *No amount of coaxing would make the dog leave its master.* **2** the total: *What is the amount of the bill for the groceries?* **3** add up; be equal: *The loss from the flood amounts to a million dollars. Keeping what belongs to another amounts to stealing.* 1, 2 *n.,* 3 *v.*

USING WORDS . . amount/number

Use **amount** when talking about things that can be measured: *Our class ate a huge amount of ice cream at the picnic.*

Use **number** when talking about things that can be counted: *Our class ate a large number of hot dogs at the picnic.*

am·pere (am′pēr) an SI unit for measuring electric current. About one ampere of current is needed to produce 100 watts of electric power. The ampere is one of the seven base units in the SI. *Symbol:* A *n.*

am·phib·i·an (am fib′ē ən) **1** an animal that lives both on land and in water. Frogs are amphibians. **2** a vehicle able to travel across land or water. **3** an aircraft that can take off or land on either land or water. *n.*
—am·phib′i·ous, *adj.*

Some ancient Roman amphitheatres are still standing.

am·phi·the·a·tre (am′fə thē′ə tər) **1** a round or oval building with rows of seats rising all around an open space in the middle, called an arena. **2** a theatre, sports arena, lecture hall, etc. arranged the same way. **Amphitheater** is another spelling. *n.*

am·ple (am′pəl) **1** more than enough; plenty: *We'll be gone all day, so take an ample supply of food.* **2** big; roomy: *This house has ample closets.* *adj.*
—am′ply, *adv.*

am·pli·fy (am′plə fī′) make stronger, louder, fuller, etc. *When sound is amplified, it can be heard over a greater distance. You can amplify your description by giving more details.* An **amplifier** makes sound louder by strengthening electrical impulses. *v.,* **am·pli·fied, am·pli·fy·ing.**

am·pu·tate (am′pyə tāt′) to cut off a body part in a medical operation: *The man's leg was so badly crushed in the accident that it had to be amputated.* *v.,* **am·pu·tat·ed, am·pu·tat·ing.** **—am′pu·ta′tion,** *n.*

Am·rit·sar (ȧm rit′sȧr) the location of the **Golden Temple,** the centre of the Sikh religion. *n.*

a·muse (ə myūz′) **1** cause to laugh or smile: *Her tricks did not amuse the babysitter!* **2** keep pleasantly interested; entertain: *The new game amused the children for hours.* *v.,* **a·mused, a·mus·ing.**

a **bat**	e **bed**	i **bid**	o **pot**	u **cup**	th **thin**
ā **cake**	ē **me**	ī **bite**	ō **go**	ū **rude**	ᴛʜ **then**
ȧ **bar**	ə **about**	ər **over**	ȯ **for**	ů **put**	zh **measure**

a·muse·ment (ə myūz′mənt) 1 enjoyment; pleasure; being amused: *We showed our amusement by laughing.* 2 anything that amuses; entertainment, such as a game, a show, or a ride. An **amusement park** has many of these. *n.*

an·a·con·da (an′ə kon′də) a huge olive-green snake that kills its prey by squeezing it so it cannot breathe. The anaconda is the largest snake in the world. It lives near water in hot, humid areas of South America. *n.*

an·a·gram (an′ə gram′) a word or phrase that can be made by changing around the letters in another word or phrase. *Example: silent* and *listen.* *n.*

an·a·logue (an′ə log′) giving or handling information through moving parts instead of just numbers. An analogue watch is one with hands that move around a dial. The opposite of analogue is **digital.** *adj.*

a·nal·o·gy (ə nal′ə jē) 1 a similarity in certain details or features between two things that otherwise seem quite different: *There is an analogy between a bird's wings and a dog's front legs.* 2 a comparison between two things so as to bring out this kind of similarity: *She drew an analogy between a pump and the human heart.* *n., pl.* **a·nal·o·gies.**

an·a·lyze or **an·a·lyse** (an′ə līz′) 1 examine all the parts or features of: *Many people have tried to analyze success. You analyze a sentence by explaining the form and use of every word in it.* 2 separate something into its parts: *A chemist can analyze water into two gases, hydrogen and oxygen.* *v.,* **an·a·lyzed, an·a·lyz·ing.**

a·nal·y·sis (ə nal′ə sis) the act or the result of analysing something: *The chemist made an analysis of the medicine to find out what it was made of. Careful analysis of our plan showed that some changes should be made.* *n., pl.* **a·nal·y·ses** (ə nal′ə sēz′).

an·ar·chy (an′ər kē) 1 the lack of any system of government or law. 2 a state of extreme disorder and confusion among people. *n.*

a·nat·o·my (ə nat′ə mē) 1 the structure of an animal or plant: *The anatomy of an earthworm is much simpler than that of a person.* 2 the science of the structure of animals or plants: *Anatomy is a part of biology.* *n.*

an·ces·tor (an′ses tər) a person, animal, or thing of the past that another is directly descended from. Your great-grandparents are your ancestors; the mammoth is the ancestor of the elephant. You can even say that the typewriter is the ancestor of the computer. *n.* —**an·ces′tral,** *adj.*

an·chor (ang′kər) 1 a heavy object, often made of metal, that is fastened to a ship or boat by a long chain or rope. When dropped into the water, it keeps the boat from drifting. 2 hold or stay in place by dropping an anchor: *to anchor a ship. The ship anchored in the bay.* 3 fix firmly: *Pegs anchored the tent to the ground.* 4 anything that makes a person feel secure: *Her faithful friend was her anchor during hard times.* 5 the main announcer on a news program. 1, 4, 5 *n.,* 2, 3 *v.*

an·cient (ān′shənt) 1 of times long past: *The ancient Egyptians built pyramids.* 2 very old: *An ancient house stood on the corner.* 3 **the ancients,** people who lived very long ago. 1, 2 *adj.,* 3 *n.*

an·droid (an′droid) a robot that looks like a human. *n.*

an·ec·dote (an′ik dōt′) a short story about some interesting incident or event: *Many anecdotes are told about Sir John A. Macdonald.* *n.*

a·ne·mi·a (ə nē′mē ə) a sickness caused when the blood does not have enough red blood cells or does not carry enough oxygen. A person who has anemia is usually pale and weak, and gets tired quickly. **Anaemia** is another spelling. *n.* —**a·ne′mic,** *adj.*

an·e·mom·e·ter (an′ə mom′ ə tər) a machine that measures the speed of wind. *n.*

a·nem·o·ne (ə nem′ə nē) a plant with slender stems and white flowers that bloom in early spring. *n.*

an·es·thet·ic (an′əs thet′ik) a drug that causes the body to lose all or part of its ability to feel. Anesthetics are used by doctors so that patients will feel no pain during operations. A **general anesthetic** puts a person to sleep. A **local anesthetic** just numbs a certain area of the body. **Anaesthetic** is another spelling. *n.*

a·new (ə nyū′ *or* ə nū′) 1 again; once more: *He made so many mistakes that he had to begin his work anew.* 2 in a new way: *We arranged the furniture anew.* *adv.*

an·gel (ān′jəl) 1 an immortal, heavenly being. In some religions angels are messengers and servants of God. 2 a person who is very good, kind, innocent, or beautiful. *n.* —**an·gel′ic** (an jel′ik), *adj.*

an·gel·fish (ān′jəl fish′) a small tropical fish with a very deep, flat body and long fins. The black and silver South American angelfish lives in fresh water and is often kept in aquariums. Most other angelfish are brightly coloured saltwater fish. *n., pl.* **an·gel·fish** or **an·gel·fish·es.**

an·ger (ang′gər) 1 the feeling you have toward someone who has done something very wrong to you or another person on purpose: *In a moment of anger, I wanted to hit my brother.* **2** fill with this feeling: *The girl's disobedience angered her parents.* 1 *n.,* 2 *v.*

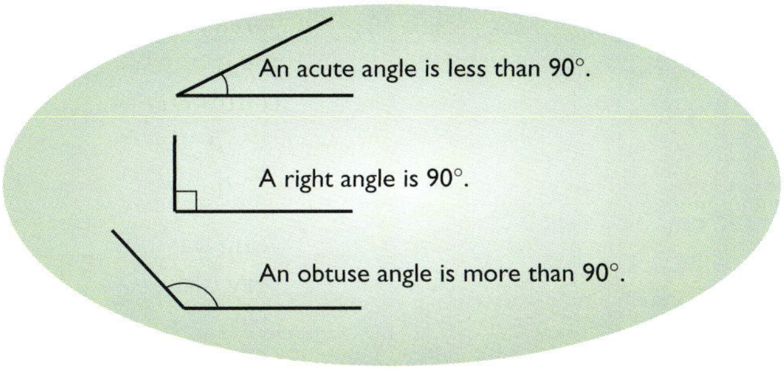

an·gle¹ (ang′gəl) **1** two straight lines or surfaces that meet, and the space between them. **2** a point of view: *From any angle the job was excellent.* **3** move, place, turn, or bend at an angle: *He angled the table across the corner of the room.* **4** slant toward a certain point of view: *Consuelo angled the story so as to make herself look better.* 1, 2 *n.,* 3, 4 *v.,* **an·gled, an·gling.**

an·gle² (ang′gəl) **1** fish with a hook and line. **2** try to get something by using tricks or schemes. *v.,* **an·gled, an·gling.** —**an′gler,** *n.*

An·glo·phone or **an·glo·phone** (ang′glə fōn′) especially in a bilingual or multilingual country, such as Canada, a person whose first or main language is English. *n.*

This Anglo-Saxon battle helmet is decorated with silver and gold.

An·glo–Sax·on (ang′glō sak′sən) **1** the name of a people who controlled England until the Norman Conquest in 1066. The ancestors of the Anglo-Saxons came from what is now northern Germany. **2** their language, Old English. **3** having to do with the Anglo-Saxons or their language. **4** a person of English descent. 1, 2, 4 *n.,* 3 *adj.*

an·go·ra (ang gȯ′rə) the long, silky hair of the **Angora rabbit** or the **Angora goat.** It is made into yarn and used to make clothes. *n.*

an·gry (ang′grē) **1** feeling or showing anger: *I was angry when she borrowed my bicycle without asking. My friend's angry words hurt my feelings.* **2** stormy: *an angry sky.* *adj.,* **an·gri·er, an·gri·est.** —**an′gri·ly,** *adv.*

an·guish (ang′gwish) very great pain or grief: *He was in anguish until the doctor set his broken leg.* *n.*

an·gu·lar (ang′gyə lər) **1** having angles or sharp corners: *an angular piece of rock.* **2** thin and bony; not plump: *A tall, angular figure approached them.* *adj.*

an·i·mal (an′ə məl) **1** a living thing that is not a plant. Unlike most plants, most animals can move from one place to another and are unable to make their own food. **2** any creature other than a human. **3** any four-footed creature. **4** a person with no manners. *n.*

an·i·mate (an′ə māt′ *for 1 and 2,* an′ə mit *for 3*) **1** make lively: *His funny stories animated the whole party.* **2** make into a movie using cartoons, clay figures, etc. instead of real actors, animals, and things: *Disney's* Bambi *is an animated classic.* **3** living. Plants and animals are animate. 1, 2 *v.,* **an·i·mat·ed, an·i·mat·ing.** 3 *adj.* —**an′i·mat′ed,** *adj.* —**an′i·ma′tion,** *n.*

an·i·mism (an′ə miz′əm) belief that each creature, thing, or natural event has its own spirit. *n.*

an·i·mos·i·ty (an′ə mos′ə tē) very strong dislike; hostile attitude or action: *The speaker's insults stirred up the animosity of the crowd.* *n.*

A·nish·i·na·be (ə nish′ ē nȧ′be) **1** a First Nations people living in the region around Lake Superior. **2** their language. **3** having to do with these people or their language. 1, 2 *n.,* 3 *adj.*

an·kle (ang′kəl) the joint that connects the foot with the leg. *n.*

an·nex (ə neks′ *for 1,* an′eks *for 2*) **1** take and add to the property you already have: *The U.S. tried to annex Canada in 1812.* **2** something added; an added part: *We are building an annex to the school.* 1 *v.,* 2 *n.* —**an′nex·a′tion,** *n.*

an·ni·hi·late (ə nī′ə lāt′) destroy or wipe out completely: *The hurricane annihilated three villages.* *v.,* **an·ni·hi·lat·ed, an·ni·hi·lat·ing.** —**an·ni′hi·la′tion,** *n.*

a bat	e bed	i bid	o pot	u cup	th thin
ā cake	ē me	ī bite	ō go	ū rude	ᴛʜ then
ȧ bar	ə about	ər over	ȯ for	u̇ put	zh measure

an·ni·ver·sa·ry (an′ə vər′sə rē) the yearly return of a certain date when people celebrate or remember something special that happened in an earlier year: *Tomorrow is their wedding anniversary.* *n., pl.* **an·ni·ver·sa·ries.**

an·nounce (ə nouns′) make known publicly: *The principal has announced that there will be no school this afternoon.* *v.,* **an·nounced, an·nounc·ing.** —**an·nounce′ment,** *n.*

an·nounc·er (ə noun′sər) in radio or television, a person who introduces programs, reads news, etc. *n.*

an·noy (ə noi′) bug; bother; irritate; make angry: *The baby annoys his sister by pulling her hair.* *v.* —**an·noy′ance,** *n.* —**an·noy′ing,** *adj.*

an·nu·al (an′yū əl) **1** coming once a year: *Your birthday is an annual event.* **2** for a year: *Ms. Kuzak's annual income is $45 000.* **3** living only one year or season: *Corn and beans are annual plants.* **4** a plant that lives only one year or season. 1–3 *adj.,* 4 *n.* —**an′nu·al·ly,** *adv.*

a·noint (ə noint′) put oil or ointment on, especially in a ceremony: *The archbishop anointed the new king.* *v.*

anon. *abbreviation for* anonymous.

a·non·y·mous (ə non′ə məs) **1** of unknown name: *The author of this poem is anonymous.* **2** by a person whose name is not known or given: *an anonymous letter, an anonymous poem.* *adj.*

an·o·rak (an′ə rak′) **1** an Inuit waterproof hooded coat made of animal skins, used when kayaking. The lower edge of an anorak can be fastened tightly around the opening in the kayak. Today anoraks are made of other waterproof material. **2** any hooded, medium-length coat or jacket. *n.*

an·o·rex·i·a (an′ə reks′ē ə) an eating disorder. People with anorexia stop eating because they are afraid of getting fat. **Anorexia nervosa** is the full name. *n.* —**an′o·rex′ic,** *adj. or n.*

an·oth·er (ə nuᴛʜ′ər) **1** one more: *Drink another glass of milk* (*adj.*). *She ate one apple and then asked for another* (*pron.*). **2** a different: *Borrowing is OK, but stealing is another thing altogether.* **3** a different one; someone or something else: *I don't like this book; give me another.* 1, 2 *adj.,* 1, 3 *pron.*

an·swer (an′sər) **1** speak, write, or act in return: *I asked him a question, but he would not answer. We knocked on the door and Cory answered.* **2** whatever is said or done in return: *I could barely hear your answer. A nod was her only answer.* **3** a solution to a problem: *We have found the answer at last!* 1 *v.,* 2, 3 *n.*
answer back, reply in a rude, saucy way.
answer for, take the responsibility for; give an explanation for: *You must answer for what you have done.*
answer to, correspond to: *This person answers to the description.*

In an ant colony there are different chambers that the ants use to lay eggs and bring up their young.

ant (ant) a small insect that lives in tunnels in the ground or in wood. Ants live together in large groups or communities called colonies. *n.* —**ant′like′,** *adj.*

an·tag·o·nism (an tag′ə niz′əm) a feeling of being enemies; conflict or hostility: *During the argument, John's antagonism showed plainly in his voice.* If you make someone your enemy, you **antagonize** that person. *n.* —**an·tag′o·nis′tic,** *adj.*

an·tag·o·nist (an tag′ə nist) one who fights or competes against another; an opponent: *The knight defeated each antagonist who came against him.* *n.*

ant·arc·tic (an tärk′tik *or* an tär′tik) **1** at, near, or having to do with the South Pole: *an antarctic weather station, antarctic wildlife.* **2 the Antarctic, a** the region around the South Pole. **b** the Antarctic Ocean. 1 *adj.,* 2 *n.*

Antarctic Circle (an tärk′tik sər′kəl) an imaginary line around the earth 66½° south of the equator, that marks off the south polar region.

Antarctic Ocean (an tärk′tik ō′shən) the ocean of the south polar region.

ant·eat·er (an′tē′tər) an animal that eats ants and termites, which it catches with its long, sticky tongue. *n.*

an·te·lope (an′tə lōp′) **1** a swift, grazing animal that looks like a deer but is related to goats and cattle and does not shed its horns. Most kinds live in the grasslands of Africa. **2** a swift, grazing animal from North America that looks like an antelope, but is different; the pronghorn. *n., pl.* **an·te·lope** or **an·te·lopes.**

an·ten·na (an ten′ə) **1** a feeler on the head of an insect, lobster, etc. **2** in radio or television, a rigid wire or set of wires often placed high in the air to send or receive electrical signals. The signals carry the sound and pictures for a program. *n., pl.* **an·ten·nae** (an ten′ē *or* an ten′ī) for 1, **an·ten·nas** for 2.

an·them (an′thəm) a song of praise, devotion, or patriotism. "O Canada" is the national anthem of Canada. A church anthem has words from the Bible. *n.*

an·ther (an′thər) the part of the stamen of a flower that produces the pollen. *n.*

ant·hill or **ant hill** (ant′hil′) a heap of dirt piled up by ants around the entrance to their underground nest. *n.*

an·thol·o·gy (an thol′ə jē) a book that is a collection of poems, stories, or other writings by a number of different authors: *I have a big anthology of Canadian literature.* *n., pl.* **an·thol·o·gies.**

an·thra·cite (an′thrə sīt′) a type of hard, shiny coal that burns with very little smoke or flame. *n.*

an·thro·pol·o·gy (an′thrə pol′ə jē) the science that deals with the origin, development, customs, and beliefs of human beings. *n.* **—an′thro·pol′o·gist,** *n.*

anti– *a prefix meaning* against. *Anti-aircraft* missiles are for fighting "against aircraft." *Antigravity* means "against gravity."

an·ti·bi·ot·ic (an′tē bī ot′ik) a drug that can kill microbes that cause disease. Penicillin is an antibiotic. *n.*

an·ti·bod·y (an′tē bod′ē) a substance produced in the blood that fights disease-causing microbes and poisons. *n., pl.* **an·ti·bod·ies.**

an·tic·i·pate (an tis′ə pāt′) **1** expect; look forward to: *She had anticipated a good vacation in the mountains; but when the time came, she was sick.* **2** do something before someone else does: *The Chinese anticipated the Europeans' discovery of gunpowder.* **3** think of and prepare for in advance: *The nurse anticipated all the patient's wishes.* *v.,* **an·tic·i·pat·ed, an·tic·i·pat·ing.** **—an·tic′i·pa′tion,** *n.*

an·tics (an′tiks) funny actions and tricks: *The clown amused us by his antics.* *pl.n.*

an·ti·dote (an′tē dōt′) something that acts against a poison, disease, or other bad thing; a remedy: *Milk is an antidote for some poisons. A hug is a good antidote for a bad mood.* *n.*

an·ti·freeze (an′tē frēz′) a substance added to a liquid to lower its freezing point. Ethylene glycol is used as an antifreeze in car radiators because it prevents the water in the radiator from freezing. *n.*

an·tip·a·thy (an tip′ə thē) strong dislike: *He felt an antipathy toward snakes.* *n.*

an·ti·quat·ed (an′tə kwā′tid) old-fashioned; out of date: *Most science books written 20 years ago are now antiquated.* *adj.*

an·tique (an tēk′) **1** of times long ago: *This antique chair was made in 1750.* **2** something made long ago: *That carved chest is a genuine antique.* 1 *adj.,* 2 *n.*

an·tiq·ui·ty (an tik′wə tē) **1** oldness; great age: *That vase is of such antiquity that its exact age can only be guessed at.* **2** the early ages of history: *Moses and Cleopatra are two great figures of antiquity.* **3** an ancient object or custom. *n., pl.* **an·tiq·ui·ties.**

an·ti–Sem·i·tism (an′tē sem′ə tiz′əm) the reasonless hatred of Jews. *n.* **—an′ti-Se·mit′ic** (an′tē sə mit′ik), *adj.*

an·ti·sep·tic (an′tə sep′tik) **1** a substance that kills germs and prevents infection: *Iodine is a common antiseptic.* **2** preventing infection: *an antiseptic ointment.* 1 *n.,* 2 *adj.*

an·ti·so·cial (an′tē sō′shəl) **1** going against the generally accepted rules of how people act toward one another: *Spreading disease, stealing, and murder are antisocial acts.* **2** not wanting the company of other people; not sociable: *He's a bit antisocial, so he doesn't like parties.* *adj.*

an·ti·tox·in (an′tē tok′sən) a substance formed in the body that protects a person against poison made by infection or disease. *n.*

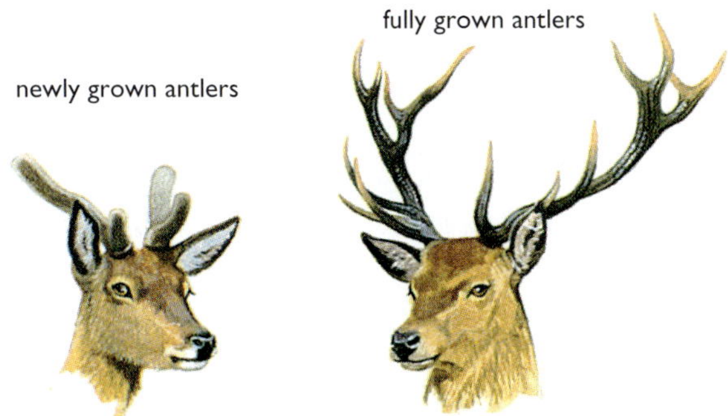

Male deer lose their antlers every winter, and grow a new set in the spring.

ant·ler (ant′lər) **1** the solid horn of a deer, elk, moose, etc. **2** a branch of such a horn. *n.*

a bat	e bed	i bid	o pot	u cup	th thin
ā cake	ē me	ī bite	ō go	ū rude	ᴛʜ then
ä bar	ə about	ər over	ô for	u̇ put	zh measure

an·to·nym (an′tə nim′) a word that means the opposite of another word. *Hot* is an antonym of *cold*. *n.* ▶ See the *Grammar and Usage Mini-Guide.*

Grammar Check . . . . antonym

Many antonyms are made by adding *dis-*, *un-*, or *mis-*: *approve* and ***dis****approve*, *friendly* and ***un****friendly*, *understand* and ***mis****understand*.

an·vil (an′vəl) an iron block on which metals such as iron are hammered and shaped while hot and soft. *n.*

anx·i·e·ty (ang zī′ə tē *or* angk sī′ə tē) **1** uneasy thoughts; fear or worry: *Parents feel anxiety when their children are sick.* **2** eager desire: *Her anxiety to succeed made her work hard.* *n., pl.* **anx·i·e·ties.**

anx·ious (angk′shəs) **1** full of uneasy thoughts, fear, or worry: *The week of the flood was an anxious time for all of us.* **2** wishing very much; eager: *She was anxious to finish her homework before the game started.* *adj.* —**anx′ious·ly,** *adv.*

an·y (en′ē) **1** one or more out of many, no matter which: *Any book will do (adj.). I'm getting rid of these videotapes—take any that you like (pron.).* **2** some (used in questions and with **not, never,** etc.): *Do you have any fresh fruit (adj.)? No, I don't have any (pron.).* **3** every: *Any child knows that.* **4** at all; even a little: *If she leans over any farther, she'll fall. Has the sick child improved any?* 1–3 *adj.,* 1, 2 *pron.,* 4 *adv.*

Word Family. . . . . any

anybody or **anyone**: any person
anyplace or **anywhere**: in, at, or to any place

an·y·how (en′ē hou′) **1** in any case; even so: *I wouldn't get it finished anyhow, even if I worked all day.* **2** no matter how: *It is wrong anyhow you look at it.* **3** at least: *We must have waited an hour anyhow; maybe two.* **4** *Informal.* carelessly: *We had a hard time sorting the papers, because he had just piled them up anyhow.* *adv.*

an·y·more (en′ē mȯr′) these days or any longer (used in questions or with **not, never,** etc.): *That book is not available anymore. Who walks to work anymore?* *adv.*

an·y·thing (en′ē thing′) **1** any thing: *Have you had anything to eat?* **2** at all: *Is your skateboard anything like mine?* 1 *pron.,* 2 *adv.*

an·y·time (en′ē tīm′) at any time: *Feel free to drop in anytime.* *adv.*

an·y·way (en′ē wā′) in any case: *I am coming anyway, no matter what you say.* *adv.*

a·or·ta (ā ȯr′tə) the main artery that carries the blood from the left side of the heart to all parts of the body except the lungs. *n., pl.* **a·or·tas** or **a·or·tae** (ā ȯr′tē *or* ā ȯr′tī).

a·part (ə pärt′) **1** to pieces; in pieces; in separate parts: *Krista took the watch apart to see what made it tick.* **2** away from each other: *Keep the dogs apart.* **3** to one side; aside: *He stood apart from the others.* *adv.*
apart from, besides; except for: *Apart from that one mistake, we did a very good job.*

a·part·heid (ə pärt′hīt) a system that used to be in South Africa, where blacks had fewer rights than whites and were forced to live in separate areas and go to their own schools, restaurants, etc. *n.*

a·part·ment (ə pärt′ mənt) a self-contained set of rooms to live in, in a house or larger building. *n.*

ap·a·thy (ap′ə thē) a lack of feeling, interest, or desire: *The miser heard the beggar's story with apathy. Your laziness and apathy are annoying.* *n.*

ape (āp) **1** an animal like a monkey, but with no tail. Apes are able to stand almost erect and to walk on two feet. Chimpanzees, gorillas, orangutans, and gibbons are apes. **2** a person who imitates or mimics. **3** imitate; mimic: *The girl aped the movie star's hairstyle.* 1, 2 *n.,* 3 *v.,* **aped, ap·ing.** —**ape′like′,** *adj.*

ap·er·ture (ap′ər chər) an opening or hole. A camera has a small aperture for letting in light. *n.*

a·pex (ā′peks) the highest point; peak: *The apex of a triangle is the vertex opposite to the base.* *n., pl.* **a·pex·es** or **a·pi·ces** (ā′pə sēz′ *or* ap′ə sēz′).

a·phid (ā′fid *or* af′id) a very small insect that lives by sucking juices from plants. *n.*

a·piece (ə pēs′) each; for each one: *These apples are 12 cents apiece.* *adv.*

a·pol·o·get·ic (ə pol′ə jet′ik) **1** saying you are sorry: *They sent us an apologetic note explaining their mistake.* **2** sounding as if you expect others to disapprove of your works or actions: *He answered the principal in an apologetic voice.* *adj.* —**a·pol′o·get′i·cal·ly,** *adv.*

a·pol·o·gize (ə pol′ə jīz′) say you are sorry; make an apology: *She apologized for hurting my feelings.* *v.,* **a·pol·o·gized, a·pol·o·giz·ing.**

a·pol·o·gy (ə pol′ə jē) **1** words saying you are sorry for an offence, fault, or accident; words asking pardon: *I owe you an apology for forgetting to phone.* **2** a weak substitute: *One cracker is a poor apology for breakfast.* *n., pl.* **a·pol·o·gies.**

a·pos·tro·phe (ə pos′trə fē) a sign (') used: **1** to show that one or more letters have been left out, as in *o'er* for *over, aren't* for *are not.* **2** to show the possessive forms of nouns, as in *Shanti's book, the lions' den.* **3** to form certain plurals, especially of letters: *There are two o's in "apology."* *n.*

Grammar Check . . . . apostrophe

An apostrophe has two main uses.
- In contractions, to show that some letters are missing: *can't (cannot), she's (she is or she has), '99 (1999).*
- To show possession, for example in singular: *Sulu's cat, Ross's jacket, Archimedes' bath* in plural: *the Ranganathans' house, the girls' bicycles, the men's washroom.*

ap·pal or **ap·pall** (ə pol′) fill with horror and dismay: *She was appalled when she saw the river had risen to the doorstep. We are appalled at the thought of nuclear war.* *v.,* **ap·palled, ap·pal·ling.**

ap·pa·ra·tus (ap′ə rat′əs) tools, equipment, or machinery used for a certain activity. *n., pl.* **ap·pa·ra·tus** or **ap·pa·ra·tus·es.**

ap·par·el (ə per′əl) **1** clothing: *Does this store sell women's apparel?* **2** clothe; dress up: *Horseback riders, colourfully apparelled, formed part of the parade.* 1 *n.,* 2 *v.,* **ap·par·elled** or **ap·par·eled, ap·par·el·ling** or **ap·par·el·ing.**

ap·par·ent (ə per′ənt) **1** obvious; easy to see or understand: *The rockiness of the Canadian Shield is very apparent. It is quite apparent that cold water takes longer to reach boiling point.* **2** seeming; that appears to be: *The apparent thief was innocent; we found the real thief later.* *adj.* —**ap·par′ent·ly,** *adj.*

ap·pa·ri·tion (ap′ə rish′ən) **1** a ghost: *The apparition, clothed in white, glided from behind a tombstone.* **2** the appearance of something strange or unexpected. *n.*

ap·peal (ə pēl′) **1** ask for help, support, sympathy, etc.: *The children appealed to their mother when they were in trouble.* **2** a request for help, support, sympathy, etc.: *an appeal for forgiveness.* **3** be interesting, attractive, or enjoyable: *That painting appeals to me.* **4** a quality that interests or attracts people: *Television has little appeal for Hannah.* 1, 3 *v.,* 2, 4 *n.*

ap·pear (ə pēr′) **1** be seen; come in sight: *One by one the stars appear.* **2** seem; look: *The apple appeared sound on the outside, but it was rotten inside.* **3** be presented to the public: *His latest book appeared a year ago. Celine Dion will appear on TV tonight.* *v.*

ap·pear·ance (ə pē′rəns) **1** the act of appearing: *His appearance in the doorway was welcomed with shouts.* **2** the outward look of anything: *The appearance of the old stone house made us think it was empty.* *n.*
keep up appearances, act as if everything is normal when it's not.

ap·pease (ə pēz′) satisfy: *A good dinner will appease your hunger. The mayor appeased the angry crowd by promising to lower taxes.* *v.,* **ap·peased, ap·peas·ing.**

ap·pend (ə pend′) add to a larger thing; attach as an extra part: *A list of books for further reading is appended to the chapter.* *v.*

ap·pend·age (ə pen′dij) something attached to a larger thing. A tail is an appendage. *n.*

ap·pen·di·ci·tis (ə pen′də sī′tis) an inflammation of the appendix (def. 2). *n.*

ap·pen·dix (ə pen′diks) **1** an extra part added at the end of a book. **2** a small part attached to the large intestine. *n., pl.* **ap·pen·dix·es** or **ap·pen·di·ces** (ə pen′də sēz′).

a bat	e bed	i bid	o pot	u cup	th thin
ā cake	ē me	ī bite	ō go	ū rude	ᴛʜ then
ä bar	ə about	ər over	ô for	ù put	zh measure

ap·pe·tite (ap′ə tīt′) 1 a desire for food: *Since he had no appetite, they had to coax him to eat.* 2 desire: *Amy has a great appetite for adventure.* *n.*

ap·pe·tiz·ing (ap′ə tī′zing) giving an appetite to people who see or smell it: *appetizing food.* *adj.*

ap·plaud (ə plod′) 1 show approval by clapping hands, shouting, etc.: *The audience at the concert applauded all the old songs.* 2 approve; praise: *My parents applauded my decision to continue piano lessons.* *v.*

ap·plause (ə ploz′) 1 approval shown by clapping hands, shouting, etc.: *The applause for the singer's good performance was deafening.* 2 approval; praise. *n.*

Red Delicious apple

There are over 1800 named varieties of apple today, and more are being developed.

ap·ple (ap′əl) the firm, round fruit of a tree grown in temperate regions. Apples are usually red, yellow, or green on the outside. *n.*

ap·ple·sauce (ap′əl sos′) apples cut in pieces, cooked with sugar and water until soft, and then mashed. *n.*

ap·pli·ance (ə plī′əns) a machine, especially an electric one that does one particular task. Vacuum cleaners, washing machines, refrigerators, etc. are household appliances. *n.*

ap·pli·cant (ap′lə kənt) a person who applies for a job, help, etc.: *Are you an applicant for this job?* *n.*

ap·pli·ca·tion (ap′lə kā′shən) 1 a formal request: *I have put in my application for art camp.* 2 the act of using; a way of using: *The application of what you have just learned will help you solve new problems.* 3 the act of applying or putting on: *the application of paint to a house.* 4 continued effort or concentration: *Improving your spelling will take some real application.* 5 a computer program that does a particular kind of work: *a word-processing application.* *n.*

ap·ply (ə plī′) 1 put on: *He applied two coats of paint to the table.* 2 use: *I know the rule but I don't know how to apply it.* 3 be useful or suitable; fit: *This question doesn't apply to me.* 4 ask formally: *She applied for a job.* 5 set to work and stick to it: *She applied herself to her music.* *v.,* **ap·plied, ap·ply·ing.**

ap·point (ə point′) choose for a certain job or purpose: *Mr. Leclerc was appointed postmaster. We met at the appointed place and time.* *v.*

ap·point·ment (ə point′mənt) 1 an arrangement to see or meet someone at a certain place and time: *I have an appointment at four o'clock.* 2 the choice of someone for a certain job or position: *The appointment of Lucia as president pleased her friends.* 3 the job or position that the person is chosen for. *n.*

ap·praise (ə prāz′) judge the value, worth, or quality of: *The ring has been appraised at $600. The coach appraises each player's skill.* *v.,* **ap·praised, ap·prais·ing. —ap·prais′al,** *n.*

ap·pre·ci·a·ble (ə prē′sh ə bəl) enough to be noticed and measured: *When he was ill, he suffered an appreciable loss of weight.* *adj.*

ap·pre·ci·ate (ə prē′shē āt′) 1 think highly of; value; enjoy: *Almost everybody appreciates good food.* 2 be thankful for: *We appreciate your help.* 3 recognize: *Everyone can appreciate the danger of war. A musician can appreciate small differences in sounds.* *v.,* **ap·pre·ci·at·ed, ap·pre·ci·at·ing. —ap·pre′ci·a′tion,** *n.*

ap·pre·ci·a·tive (ə prē′ shə tiv) aware of how valuable or good something is and enjoying it: *an appreciative audience.* *adj.*

ap·pre·hend (ap′ri hend′) seize; arrest: *The thief was apprehended and put in jail.* *v.*

ap·pre·hen·sion (ap′ri hen′shən) 1 fear of what might happen; uneasiness: *The roar of the hurricane filled us with apprehension.* 2 the act of finding and catching; an arrest: *the apprehension of a thief.* *n.*

ap·pre·hen·sive (ap′ri hen′siv) fearful; anxious: *The captain was apprehensive for the safety of the passengers during the storm.* *adj.* **—ap′pre·hen′sive·ly,** *adv.* **—ap′pre·hen′sive·ness,** *n.*

ap·pren·tice (ə pren′tis) 1 a person who is learning a trade by working under someone already skilled at it. 2 set to work as an apprentice: *My father was apprenticed to a printer.* 1 *n.,* 2 *v.,* **ap·pren·ticed, ap·pren·tic·ing. —ap·pren′tice·ship,** *n.*

ap·proach (ə prōch′) 1 come near: *They quietly approached the crib and looked down at the sleeping baby. Winter is approaching.* 2 go and talk to: *We decided to approach the neighbours about their noisy parties.* 3 the act of coming near: *the approach of night.* 4 a way of reaching a place or person: *The approach to the house was a narrow path. Our best approach to the manager was by letter.* 5 go about dealing with something: *How would* *you approach this problem?* **6** a way of dealing with something: *a new approach to mathematics.* 1, 2, 5 *v.,* 3, 4, 6 *n.*

ap·proach·a·ble (ə prō′chə bəl) **1** able to be approached: *The fishing camp was approachable from the south only.* **2** easy to go and talk to: *She looks stern but is really very friendly and approachable.* *adj.*

ap·pro·pri·ate (ə prō′prē it *for 1,* ə prō′prē āt′ *for 2*) **1** suitable; proper: *Jeans and a sweater are appropriate clothes for the hike.* **2** take for yourself: *You can't just appropriate other people's belongings without asking.* 1 *adj.,* 2 *v.,* **ap·pro·pri·at·ed, ap·pro·pri·at·ing.** **—ap·pro′pri·ate·ly,** *adv.* **—ap·pro′pri·ate·ness,** *n.*

ap·prove (ə prūv′) **1** think or say that something is good: *The teacher looked at the student's work and approved it. I'm not sure I approve of what you want to do.* **2** give permission for: *Our parents approved our plans for the weekend.* *v.,* **ap·proved, ap·prov·ing.** **—ap·prov′al,** *n.*

ap·prox·i·mate (ə prok′sə mit *for 1,* ə prok′sə māt′ *for 2*) **1** nearly correct: *The approximate distance of the Olympic marathon is 42 km; the exact distance is 42.195 km.* **2** come or be near to: *Your story approximates the truth, but you did exaggerate a bit.* 1 *adj.,* 2 *v.,* **ap·prox·i·mat·ed, ap·prox·i·mat·ing.** **—ap·prox′i·mate·ly,** *adv.* **—ap·prox′i·ma′tion,** *n.*

ap·ri·cot (ap′rə kot′ *or* ā′prə kot′) a sweet, juicy, pale-orange fruit, like a peach but smaller. *n.*

A·pril (ā′prəl) the fourth month of the year. April has 30 days. *n.*

April Fools' Day (ā′pril fūlz′ dā′) April 1, a day when people fool one another with tricks and practical jokes. A person who gets fooled on this day is called an **April fool.**

a·pron (ā′prən) a garment worn over the front part of the body to protect the clothes: *A carpenter's apron has pockets for nails.* *n.*

apt (apt) **1** likely: *A careless person is apt to make mistakes.* **2** suitable or fitting: *His apt reply showed that he had understood the question very well.* **3** quick to learn: *an apt pupil.* *adj.* **—apt′ly,** *adv.* **—apt′ness,** *n.*

apt. *abbreviation for* apartment. *pl.* **apts.**

ap·ti·tude (ap′tə tyūd′ *or* ap′tə tūd′) a natural ability: *Alexander Graham Bell had a great aptitude for inventing things.* *n.*

a·quar·i·um (ə kwer′ē əm) **1** a pond, tank, or glass bowl in which living fish, water animals, and water plants are kept. **2** a building used for showing collections of living fish, water animals, and water plants: *For our field trip we visited the aquarium.* *n., pl.* **a·quar·i·ums** or **a·quar·i·a** (ə kwer′ē ə).

a·quat·ic (ə kwot′ik *or* ə kwat′ik) having to do with water: *Water lilies are aquatic plants. Swimming and sailing are aquatic sports.* *adj.*

The most famous aqueducts were built by the Romans. Some are still in use today.

aq·ue·duct (ak′wə dukt′) **1** a large trough or pipe for bringing water from a distance. **2** the bridgelike structure that supports it. *n.*

Ar·ab (er′əb) **1** any of a people who came originally from the Arabian Peninsula in southwestern Asia, and now live throughout the Middle East and northern Africa: *The language of the Arabs is Arabic.* **2** having to do with the Arabs: *the Arab countries.* 1 *n.,* 2 *adj.*

A·ra·bi·an (ə rā′bē ən) **1** of or having to do with the Arabian Peninsula in southwestern Asia: *the Arabian desert.* **2** having to do with Arabs or their culture. **3** a breed of horse that originally came from the Arabian Peninsula. It is very swift and graceful. 1, 2 *adj.,* 3 *n.*

Ar·a·bic numerals (er′ə bik nyū′mə rəlz) the figures 1, 2, 3, 4, 5, 6, 7, 8, 9, 0.

ar·a·ble (er′ə bəl) fit for farming: *There is little arable land on the side of that mountain.* *adj.*

a·rach·nid (ə rak′nid) any of a group of small animals that have eight legs and two body parts. Like insects, arachnids have hard outer coverings; spiders, scorpions, mites, and ticks are arachnids. *n.*

ar·bi·trar·y (àr′bə trer′ē) based only on what a person feels like doing at the time; not going by any rule or law: *A good judge tries to be fair and does not make arbitrary decisions.* *adj.*

a bat	e bed	i bid	o pot	u cup	th thin
ā cake	ē me	ī bite	ō go	ū rude	ᴛʜ then
à bar	ə about	ər over	ò for	ù put	zh measure

ar·bi·trate (är′bə trāt′) 1 decide how a dispute between other people should be settled: *Who will arbitrate between us?* 2 settle a dispute by agreeing to follow the decision of a judge, umpire, or committee: *When the two nations agreed to arbitrate their dispute, war was avoided.* *v.,* **ar·bi·trat·ed, ar·bi·trat·ing.** —**ar′bi·tra′tion,** *n.*

ar·bour or **ar·bor** (är′bər) a shaded place formed by vines or other plants growing on a frame. *n.*

arc (ärk) 1 part of a circle. 2 a curved line or path: *The football followed a graceful arc as it sailed between the goal posts.* 3 the stream of bright light or sparks that you can see when an electric current jumps across a gap. 4 move in an arc: *The shooting star arced across the heavens.* 1–3 *n.,* 4 *v.* —**arc′like,** *adj.*

ar·cade (är kād′) 1 a passageway with an arched roof. 2 any covered passageway: *Some buildings have arcades with small stores along either side.* 3 a place where people can pay to play video games. *n.*

arch[1] (ärch) 1 a curved structure that forms the top of a doorway, window, bridge, or tunnel. 2 bend into an arch; curve: *The wind arched the trees over the path.* 3 the part of the bottom of the foot between the ball and the heel: *Fallen arches cause flat feet.* 1, 3 *n.,* 2 *v.*

arch[2] (ärch) 1 chief; main: *When the arch rebel was caught the revolt died down.* This word is also often used to form compounds, such as **archbishop** and **archenemy.** 2 playfully mischievous: *Nikki gave her mother an arch look and ran off.* *adj.*

ar·chae·ol·o·gy (är′kē ol′ə jē) the study of the life and customs of ancient times by digging up and examining the buried remains of cities, homes, monuments, etc.: *The archaeology student was excited to find pieces of tools and pottery at the dig.* **Archeology** is another spelling. *n.* —**ar′chae·ol′o·gist,** *n.*

ar·cha·ic (är kā′ik) old and no longer used: *"Varlet" is an archaic word for "rascal."* *adj.*

arch·er·y (är′chə rē) the practice or art of shooting with bows and arrows. *n.* —**arch′er,** *n.*

ar·chi·pel·a·go (är′kə pel′ə gō′) 1 a sea with many islands in it. 2 the islands themselves: *The islands in the Arctic Ocean north of Canada are called the Canadian Archipelago.* *n., pl.* **ar·chi·pel·a·gos** or **ar·chi·pel·a·goes.**

ar·chi·tect (är′kə tekt′) a person who designs buildings. *n.*

ar·chi·tec·ture (är′kə tek′chər) 1 the science and art of designing buildings. 2 a special style or manner of building: *Greek architecture made use of many pillars.* *n.*

ar·chive (är′kīv) Usually, **archives,** *pl.* a collection of public records or historical papers: *The Public Archives of Canada are in Ottawa.* *n.*

arch·way (ärch′wā′) an entrance or passage under an arched or curved roof. *n.*

arc·tic (ärk′tik *or* är′tik) 1 at, near, or having to do with the North Pole: *the arctic fox.* 2 **the Arctic,** **a** the region around the North Pole. **b** the Arctic Ocean. 1 *adj.,* 2 *n.*

arctic char or **Arctic char** (ärk′tik chär′) a food fish of the salmon and trout family found throughout the Arctic.

Arctic Circle (ärk′tik sər′kəl) an imaginary line around the earth that marks off the north polar region. It is 66½° north of the equator.

Arctic Ocean (ärk′tik ō′shən) the ocean of the north polar region.

ar·dent (är′dənt) very enthusiastic; eager: *She is an ardent Roughriders fan.* *adj.* —**ar′dent·ly,** *adv.*

ar·dour or **ar·dor** (är′dər) warmth of feeling; eagerness; great enthusiasm. *n.*

ar·du·ous (är′jū əs *or* är′dyū əs) hard to do; taking a lot of effort; difficult: *an arduous climb.* *adj.*

ar·e·a (er′ē ə) 1 a surface or space: *The playing area was marked off with white lines.* 2 a part or region: *The Rocky Mountain area is the most mountainous in Canada.* 3 the size of a surface: *The area of this floor is 9 m².* *n.*

area code (er′ēə kōd′) a three-digit number standing for a particular area served by a telephone system. When making long-distance calls between areas, people must dial this code: *The area code for all of Prince Edward Island is 902.*

a·re·na (ə rē′nə) 1 a building for indoor sports: *There is a basketball game at the arena tonight.* 2 in ancient times, a space where contests or shows took place: *Roman slaves fought with lions in the arena.* 3 anything thought of as a place of conflict: *The arena of politics.* *n.*

aren't (ärnt) are not.

ar·gue (är′gyū) 1 talk with someone who disagrees, sometimes angrily, trying to prove you are right: *He argued with his brother about who should wash the dishes.* 2 give reasons for or against something: *Laura argued for camping instead of staying in hotels.* 3 try to prove by reasoning: *Galileo argued that the world moved around the sun.* *v.,* **ar·gued, ar·gu·ing.**

ar·gu·ment (är′gyə mənt) 1 a talk, sometimes angry, between people who disagree and want to prove they are right: *We had an argument about who won the card game.* 2 a reason or set of reasons offered for or against something: *My argument for getting a new computer was not convincing to my mother.* *n.*

ar·id (er′id) dry and lifeless: *Desert lands are arid.* *adj.* **—ar′id·ly,** *adv.*

a·rise (ə rīz′) 1 rise up; get up. 2 come into being; come about: *Problems can arise in doing the simplest jobs.* *v.,* **a·rose, a·ris·en** (ə riz′ən)**, a·ris·ing.**

ar·is·toc·ra·cy (er′i stok′rə sē) 1 people of high rank. Usually this has to do with being born into a noble family and having a title such as earl or duchess. But it can also mean all the smartest, best educated, or richest people. 2 government or control by these people. *n., pl.* **ar·is·toc·ra·cies.**

a·ris·to·crat (ə ris′tə krat′) a person who belongs to the aristocracy. *n.* **—a·ris′to·crat′ic,** *adj.*

a·rith·me·tic (ə rith′mə tik) the use of addition, subtraction, multiplication, and division. *n.*

ark (ärk) 1 in the Bible, the large boat in which God saved Noah, his family, and a pair of each kind of animal from the Flood. 2 a chest or box that the ancient Jews kept certain holy things in, especially the two flat pieces of stone with the Ten Commandments written on them. Nowadays a similar box holds the Torah scrolls in a synagogue. *n.*

arm[1] (ärm) 1 the part of your body between your shoulder and your hand. 2 something shaped or used like an arm: *the arm of a chair, an arm of the sea.* *n.*
—arm′less, *adj.* **—arm′ful′,** *n.*
an arm and a leg, *Informal.* a lot of money: *These skates cost me an arm and a leg.*
twist someone's arm, *Informal.* put strong pressure on someone: *I had to twist his arm to get him to come at all.*

arm[2] (ärm) 1 **arms,** *pl.* weapons: *Arms may be used for defence or attack.* 2 provide with weapons of any kind: *"Arm yourselves and be ready to fight," said the leader. Each lawyer entered court armed with facts.*
3 gather or put on weapons: *The soldiers armed for battle.*
4 **arms,** *pl.* a design used as a symbol of a family, government, etc. 1, 4 *n.,* 2, 3 *v.*
take up arms, use weapons for attack or defence: *The settlers took up arms against the invaders.*
up in arms, very angry; in rebellion: *The students were up in arms when their class trip was cancelled.*

ar·mad·a (är mä′də *or* är mad′ə) a fleet of warships or warplanes. *n.*

Most armadillos live in South America but one kind lives as far north as the southern United States.

ar·ma·dil·lo (är′mə dil′ō) a small burrowing animal with armourlike coverings and strong claws. *n., pl.* **ar·ma·dil·los.**

ar·ma·ment (är′mə mənt) 1 war equipment and supplies: *The two nations agreed to reduce their armaments.* 2 the act or process of preparing for war. 3 the weapons on a warship, warplane, tank, etc. *n.*

arm·chair (ärm′cher′) a chair with sidepieces to rest your arms or elbows on. *n.*

armed forces (ärmd′ fôr′siz) all the groups that fight for one country in a war, including those on land (the army), at sea (the navy), in the air (air force), and in space.

ar·mi·stice (är′mə stis) an agreement to stop fighting a war. *n.*

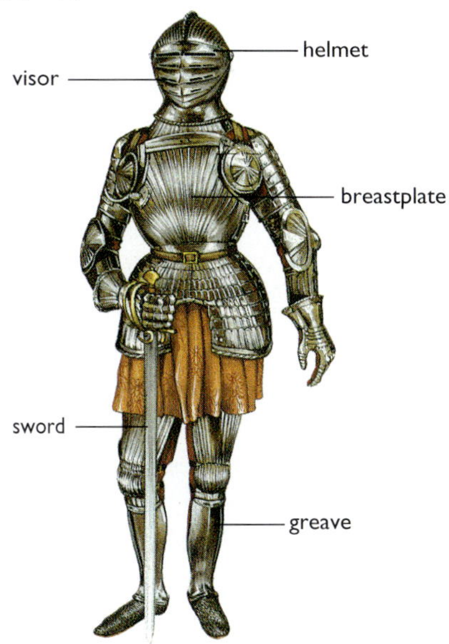

ar·mour or **ar·mor** (är′mər) 1 a suit, often of metal, that soldiers used to wear for protection. 2 any protective covering: *The steel plates of a warship and the scales of a fish are armour.* *n.* **—ar′moured** or **ar′mored,** *adj.*

a bat	e bed	i bid	o pot	u cup	th thin
ā cake	ē me	ī bite	ō go	ü rude	ᴛʜ then
ä bar	ə about	ər over	ô for	ů put	zh measure

ar•mour•y or **ar•mor•y** (är′mə rē)
1 🍁 **armouries,** *pl.* the place where the reserve part of the army has offices and does training exercises. 2 a place where weapons are kept. *n., pl.* **ar•mour•ies** or **ar•mor•ies.**

arm•pit (ärm′pit′) the hollow under the arm at the shoulder. *n.*

ar•my (är′mē) 1 a very large group of soldiers trained and armed for war. 2 a very large number of anything: *an army of ants. n., pl.* **ar•mies.**

a•ro•ma (ə rō′mə) a pleasant smell, especially of food or certain plants: *the aroma of fresh apple pie. n.* **—ar′o•mat′ic** (er′ə mat′ik), *adj.*

a•rose (ə rōz′) the past tense of **arise:** *She arose from her chair. v.*

a•round (ə round′) 1 in a circle: *spin around (adv.). The moon revolves around the earth (prep.).*
2 approximately; about: *around six o'clock, around five dollars. It was around here that I lost the key.* 3 avoiding an object or a hassle with something: *to swerve around a pothole. Can we work around that problem somehow? We plan our day around the baby's schedule.* 1–3 *prep.,* 1 *adv.*

a•rouse (ə rouz′) 1 awaken. 2 excite; stir up: *The report aroused my curiosity. v.,* **a•roused, a•rous•ing.**

ar•range (ə rānj′) 1 put in order; set up: *The room is arranged for a party.* 2 plan: *Can you arrange to be here by six o'clock?* 3 rewrite music for certain instruments or voices: *This music for the violin is also arranged for the piano. v.,* **ar•ranged, ar•rang•ing. —ar•range′ment,** *n.*

ar•ray (ə rā′) 1 display: *an array of beautiful handicrafts (n.). The dinosaur bones were arrayed on a table (v.).* 2 variety: *She used an array of tools for the job.* 3 clothes: *bridal array.* 4 dress or decorate: *She was arrayed in her best uniform.* 5 regular arrangement: *a square array of numbers.* 1–3, 5 *n.,* 1, 4 *v.*

ar•rest (ə rest′) 1 catch and take to jail or court: *The police arrested the bank robber as he ran down the street.* 2 stop: *Filling a tooth arrests decay.* 3 catch and hold: *Our attention was arrested by the sound of a shot.* 4 the capture of a person by the police: *the arrest of a burglar.* 1–3 *v.,* 4 *n.*

ar•riv•al (ə rī′vəl) 1 arriving; coming: *She's waiting for the arrival of the train.* 2 a person or thing that arrives: *The new arrivals were made welcome. n.*

ar•rive (ə rīv′) 1 come to a particular place: *We arrived in Fredericton a week ago.* 2 come: *The day of the party has arrived. v.,* **ar•rived, ar•riv•ing.**
arrive at, come to; reach: *We have arrived at a decision.*

ar•ro•gant (er′ə gənt) very conceited and bossy. *adj.* **—ar′ro•gant•ly,** *adv.* **—ar′ro•gance,** *n.*

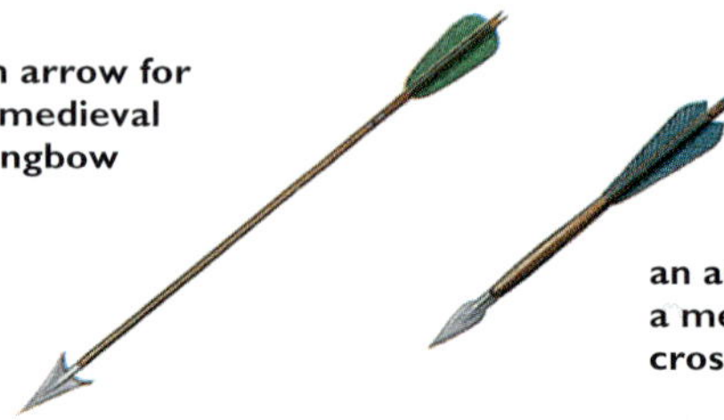

ar•row (er′ō) 1 a thin stick with a pointed tip and feathers at the other end. An arrow is made to be shot from a bow. 2 anything shaped like this, such as a sign (→) used to point to something. *n.*

ar•row•head (er′ō hed′) the head or tip of an arrow, especially a separately made piece of stone or metal. *n.*

ar•se•nal (är′sə nəl) a building for storing or making weapons and ammunition. *n.*

ar•se•nic (är′sə nik) a greyish-white, tasteless powder that is very poisonous. *n.*

ar•son (är′sən) the crime of setting fire to a building or other property on purpose. *n.* **—ar′son•ist,** *n.*

art[1] (ärt) 1 drawing, painting, or sculpture: *He is studying art and music.* 2 a branch of learning or a skill, thought of as having more to do with creativity or imagination than rules: *the art of cooking, the art of making friends. Writing stories is an art; grammar is a science.* 3 a clever trick. *n.*

art[2] (ärt) an old or poetic form meaning "are." "Thou art" means "You are." *v.*

ar•ter•y (är′tə rē) 1 any of the tubes that carry blood from the heart to all parts of the body. 2 a main transportation route: *Yonge Street is one of the main arteries of Toronto. n., pl.* **ar•ter•ies.**

ar•te•sian well (är tē′zhən wel′) a deep well made by drilling, from which water gushes up without being pumped.

art•ful (ärt′fəl) crafty or clever: *That cheat uses artful tricks to get people's money away from them. adj.* **—art′ful•ly,** *adv.* **—art′ful•ness,** *n.*

ar•thri•tis (är thrī′tis) any disease affecting the joints of the body, making them stiff, swollen, and painful. *n.*

The black widow spider is an arthropod that is poisonous to humans.

ar·thro·pod (är′thrə pod′) one of a very large group of animals, including insects and spiders, that have no backbone and have legs and bodies made up of joined segments. About three-quarters of all animal species are arthropods. *n.*

ar·ti·choke (är′tə chōk′) a plant with a thick, ball-shaped green flower that is cooked and eaten as a vegetable. *n.*

ar·ti·cle (är′tə kəl) **1** a piece of writing in a magazine, newspaper, or book: *This newspaper has a good article on gardening.* **2** a thing of a specific kind: *Bread is an important article of food.* **3** one of the words *a, an,* and *the,* which usually come before nouns: *a book, an egg, the small boy.* *n.*

ar·tic·u·late (är tik′yə lit *for 1,* är tik′yə lāt′ *for 2 and 3*) **1** using words well to express ideas: *You have written an articulate letter. She is an articulate speaker.* **2** express clearly in words: *He could not articulate his feelings of anger.* **3** pronounce: *Some sounds are hard to articulate.* 1 *adj.,* 2, 3 *v.,* **ar·tic·u·lat·ed, ar·tic·u·lat·ing.**

ar·ti·fact (är′tə fakt′) anything made by humans: *The archaeologist discovered several Stone-Age artifacts.* *n.*

ar·ti·fi·cial (är′tə fish′əl) **1** made by humans; not natural: *artificial flowers, artificial ice.* **2** put on or pretended; phony: *an artificial voice.* *adj.*
—ar′ti·fi′cial·ly, *adv.*

artificial respiration (är′tə fish′əl res′pə rā′shən) a way of getting a person to breathe normally again by forcing air in and out of the person's lungs.

ar·til·ler·y (är til′ə rē) **1** big guns mounted on wheels. **2** the part of an army that uses them. *n.*

ar·ti·san (är′tə zən *or* är′tə zan′) a person skilled in a trade or craft. Carpenters and weavers are artisans. *n.*

art·ist (är′tist) **1** a person who has skill in any of the fine arts, such as sculpture, music, or literature. **2** a person who does any work with skill, creativity, and good taste. *n.* **—ar·tis′tic,** *adj.* **—ar′tist·ry,** *n.*

art·less (ärt′lis) natural and straightforward: *Small children ask many artless questions.* *adj.*
—art′less·ly, *adv.* **—art′less·ness,** *n.*

art·work (ärt′wərk′) pictures and other material used in a book, magazine, bulletin board display, etc. *n.*

as (az) **1** to the same degree; equally: *Beth is as tall as Ann.* **2** in the role or position of: *Malik will act as teacher today.* **3** while: *They sang as they worked.* **4** in the same way that: *Treat others as you wish them to treat you.* **5** because: *We should get going, as it is quite late.* 1 *adv.,* 2 *prep.,* 3–5 *conj.*
as for, about. **As for** is used to contrast someone or something with one already mentioned: *We're leaving now; as for Sonia, she'll have to come on her own.*
as if or **as though,** as it would be if: *The car looked as if it had been driven on rough roads.*
as it were, to use a figure of speech: *This noble act is another note, as it were, in the song of your life.*
as of, beginning on: *As of March 31, the library will be closed for repairs.*
as to, about; regarding: *We have no information as to the cause of the riot.*

USING WORDS ...... as/like

As is often confused with **like**.

In comparisons, use **as** when a whole clause follows, complete with its own subject and verb:
She worked ***as she never did before***.

Use **like** if just a noun follows, with or without adjectives:
She worked ***like a horse***.

as·bes·tos (as bes′təs *or* az bes′təs) a greyish-white mineral found in the form of fibres. Because it will not burn, it was once used to make things fireproof. Breathing its dust, however, damages the lungs. *n.*

a bat	e bed	i bid	o pot	u cup	th thin
ā cake	ē me	ī bite	ō go	ū rude	ᴛʜ then
ȧ bar	ə about	ər over	ȯ for	u̇ put	zh measure

as·cend (ə send′) go up; rise; climb: *He watched the airplane ascend higher and higher. Few people ascend such high mountains.* *v.* —**as·cent,** *n.*

as·cer·tain (as′ər tān′) find out: *He phoned home to ascertain if his father had arrived.* *v.*

as·cribe (ə skrīb′) think of as caused by or belonging to: *Friendliness is one of the qualities often ascribed to Canadians.* *v.,* **as·cribed, as·crib·ing.**

ash[1] (ash) what is left after something has been thoroughly burned: *We cleaned the ashes out of the fireplace.* *n.*

ash[2] (ash) a kind of shade tree that is valued for its tough, springy wood. *n.*

a·shamed (ə shāmd′) **1** feeling shame; very sorry or uncomfortable because you or someone close to you has done something wrong or silly: *I was ashamed that I had been rude to them. She was ashamed of her brother's foolishness.* **2** unwilling because of shame: *He was ashamed to tell his mother he had failed.* *adj.*

a·shore (ə shôr′) on or to the shore: *The sailor had been ashore for months. I rowed the boat ashore.* *adv.*

ash·tray (ash′trā′) a container for the ashes of cigarettes, cigars, and pipes. *n.*

A·sia (ā′zhə) the largest continent, attached to Europe but usually thought of separately. The Ural mountains are the dividing line. *n.*

a·side (ə sīd′) to one side: *Move the table aside.* *adv.*

ask (ask) **1** try to find out from someone by a question: *Ask him how old he is.* **2** try to get by words: *Ask her to sing. Ask for what you want.* **3** invite: *She asked ten friends to the party.* *v.*

a·skance (ə skans′) with doubt or disapproval: *The students looked askance at the suggestion of having classes on Saturday.* *adv.*

a·skew (ə skyū′) out of the proper position: *The wind blew her hat askew (adv.). The bottom line of printing is askew (adj.).* *adv. or adj.*

a·sleep (ə slēp′) **1** sleeping: *The cat is asleep.* **2** into sleep: *The tired boy fell asleep.* **3** numb: *My foot is asleep.* 1, 3 *adj.,* 2 *adv.*

asp (asp) a small poisonous snake from Egypt, held sacred by the ancient Egyptians: *They say that Cleopatra died after being stung by an asp.* *n.*

as·par·a·gus (ə sper′ə gəs) a plant whose long, tender green shoots are used for food. *n.*

as·pect (as′pekt) **1** one side, part, or view of something: *We must consider all the aspects of this plan.* **2** a look or appearance: *The judge has a solemn aspect.* *n.*

as·pen (as′pən) a kind of poplar tree whose leaves tremble and rustle in the slightest breeze. *n.*

as·phalt (as′folt *or* ash′folt) a black substance, heated and mixed with crushed rock, which is used for paving. A roller packs it down and smooths it while it is still hot and soft. *n.*

as·pire (ə spīr′) have a hopeful desire for something; seek: *Kayla aspired to be captain of the team. Scholars aspire after knowledge.* *v.,* **as·pired, as·pir·ing.** —**as′pi·ra′tion,** *n.*

As·pi·rin (as′pə rin) *a trademark for* a pill used to relieve the pain or fever of headaches, colds, etc. *n.*

The North African wild ass is probably the ancestor of the donkey.

ass (as) **1** a wild animal like a donkey. **2** an old or poetic word for "donkey." *n.*

as·sail (ə sāl′) attack violently: *The older kids assailed our snow fort.* An attacker is an **assailant.** *v.*

as·sas·si·nate (ə sas′ə nāt′) murder a politically important person. The murderer is called an **assassin.** *v.,* **as·sas·si·nat·ed, as·sas·si·nat·ing.** —**as·sas′si·na′tion,** *n.*

as·sault (ə solt′) attack: *They made an assault on the enemy camp (n.). You have assaulted my friend (v.)!* *n. or v.*

as·sem·ble (ə sem′bəl) **1** gather together: *Assemble all the ingredients first. We assembled in the gym.* **2** put together; build: *This model car is easy to assemble.* *v.,* **as·sem·bled, as·sem·bling.**

as•sem•bly (ə sem′blē) **1** a gathering of people; a meeting: *The principal called an assembly of the students for Monday morning.* **2** the action of putting parts together: *The label reads, "Some assembly required."* **3** anything made up of parts fitted together: *the tail assembly of an aircraft.* *n., pl.* **as•sem•blies.**

assembly line (ə sem′blē līn′) a row of workers or machines for assembling something, such as a car, in a factory. Each one does part of the work and passes it to the next, until the product is finished.

assembly member (ə sem′blē mem′bər) in Prince Edward Island, a member of the Legislative Assembly who is not a councillor.

as•sent (ə sent′) **1** agree: *Everyone assented to the plan to sponsor a child.* **2** agreement: *She gave a nod of assent.* 1 *v.,* 2 *n.*

as•sert (ə sərt′) **1** declare; state firmly: *Luc asserts that he will go no matter what.* **2** speak up and insist on a right, a claim, etc.: *Assert your independence.* *v.* **—as•ser′tion,** *n.* **—as•ser′tive,** *adj.*
assert yourself, put yourself forward; make others notice you and listen to you.

as•sess (ə ses′) decide on the value, worth, or importance of: *The staff will assess the need for new playground equipment. We have assessed your work and found it excellent.* *v.* **—as•sess′ment,** *n.*

as•set (as′et) **1** something valuable: *The ability to get along with people is an asset.* **2** **assets,** *pl.* property: *Her assets include a house, a car, bonds, and jewellery.* *n.*

as•sign (ə sīn′) **1** give a share or task: *The camp director assigned a job to each cabin. The captain assigned two soldiers to guard the gate.* **2** fix or set: *The judge assigned a day for the trial.* *v.* **—as•sign′ment,** *n.*

as•sim•i•late (ə sim′ə lāt′) **1** absorb; digest: *She does so much reading that she cannot assimilate it all. The human body will not assimilate sawdust.* **2** become like the surrounding people or things: *Newcomers to Canada are not forced to assimilate.* *v.,* **as•sim•i•lat•ed, as•sim•i•lat•ing.**

as•sist (ə sist′) **1** help: *She assisted her mother with the yard work. She assisted in the scoring of the goal.* **2** in some sports, the credit given to a player who helps score a goal, put an opponent out, etc. **3** an act of helping: *With an assist from me, you can soon climb that fence.* 1 *v.,* 2, 3 *n.* **—as•sist′ance,** *n.*

as•sist•ant (ə sis′tənt) **1** a helper; an aid. **2** helping; assisting: *an assistant teacher.* 1 *n.,* 2 *adj.*

as•so•ci•ate (ə sō′shē āt′ *for 1 and 2,* ə sō′shē it *for 3 to 5*) **1** connect in thought: *We associate camping with summer.* **2** join as a companion or friend; keep company: *She associates only with people interested in sports.* **3** a companion or partner: *I am one of his associates on this project.* **4** joined in some work or activity: *We are an associate company of Smartgreen, Inc. and will service their products.* **5** working together with more senior people in the same kind of job: *He is associate editor of the school newspaper.* 1, 2 *v.,* **as•so•ci•at•ed, as•so•ci•at•ing;** 3 *n.,* 4, 5 *adj.*

as•so•ci•a•tion (ə sō′sē ā′shən) **1** a group of people joined together for some common purpose; a society: *Artists in the local Arts Association share a studio and gallery.* **2** a connection or relationship: *Anna and Jo enjoyed a close association over many years. There is a clear association between campfires and marshmallows.* *n.*

as•sort•ment (ə sôrt′mənt) a collection of various kinds: *an assortment of candies.* *n.* **—as•sort′ed,** *adj.*

as•sume (ə süm′) **1** take for granted; suppose: *Eva assumed that the bus would be on time.* **2** take: *to assume a responsibility, to assume the blame. Queen Elizabeth assumed the throne in 1953.* **3** to fake or put on: *Jake assumed a know-it-all attitude. I assumed ignorance of the fight.* *v.,* **as•sumed, as•sum•ing.**

as•sump•tion (ə sump′shən) **1** the act of taking for granted: *Abdul ordered us around with an assumption of authority.* **2** something taken for granted: *We thought we would win the prize, but this assumption proved incorrect; we lost!* *n.*

as•sur•ance (ə shü′rəns) **1** a statement meant to make a person more sure: *Sara gave me many assurances that she would not tell my secret.* **2** certainty; sure knowledge: *We have the assurance of final victory.* **3** self-confidence: *Hours of practice gave me assurance in reciting.* *n.*

as•sure (ə shür) **1** make sure: *The man assured himself that the bridge was safe before crossing it.* **2** tell positively: *The captain of the ship assured the passengers that there was no danger.* *v.,* **as•sured, as•sur•ing.**

as•sured (ə shürd′) sure; certain: *You may be assured that we are OK.* *adj.* **—as•sur′ed•ly** (ə shü′rid lē), *adv.*

as•ter•isk (as′tə risk) a star-shaped mark (*) used in printing and writing to call attention to something. *n.*

a bat	e bed	i bid	o pot	u cup	th thin
ā cake	ē me	ī bite	ō go	ū rude	ᴛʜ then
ä bar	ə about	ər over	ô for	ü put	zh measure

Asteroid

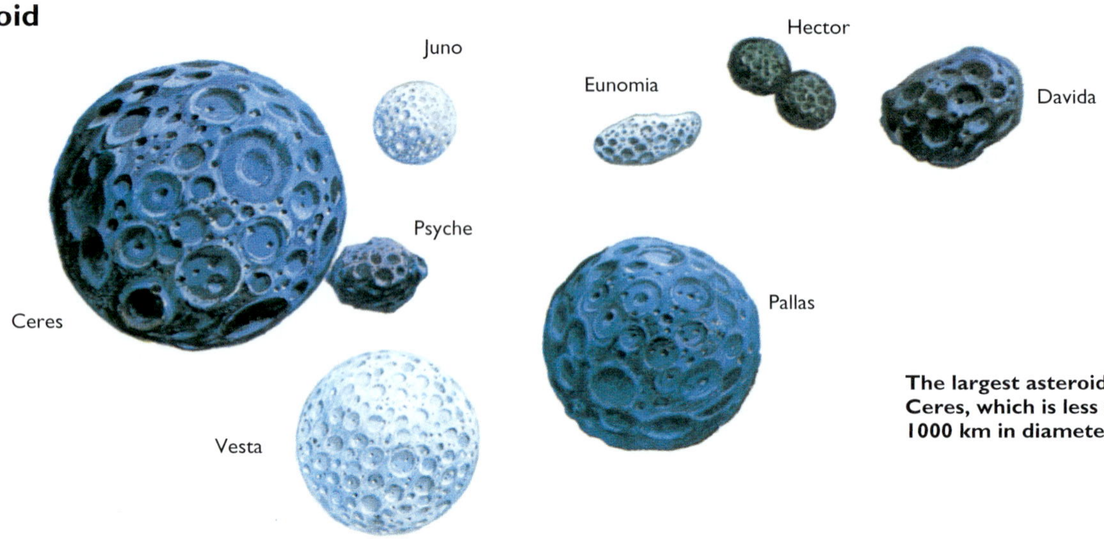

The largest asteroid is Ceres, which is less than 1000 km in diameter.

a·stern (ə stərn′) **1** at or toward the rear of a ship: *The captain went astern.* **2** backward: *The ship moved slowly astern.* **3** behind: *Some yachts tow small boats astern.* *adv.*

as·ter·oid (as′tə roid′) any of the many very small celestial bodies that revolve around the sun, mainly between the orbits of Mars and Jupiter. *n.*

Word Family........ aster-/astro-

Words beginning with **aster** or **astro** all have to do with stars. These words come from the Greek words *aster* and *astron*, both meaning "star."
astrolabe: an instrument that uses the stars to find directions in navigation
astrology: the supposed influence of stars and planets
astronaut: a crew member on a spacecraft

asth·ma (az′mə) a long-term disease that causes coughing and difficulty in breathing. *n.* **—asth·mat′ic** (az mat′ik), *adj. or n.*

a·stir (ə stər′) in motion; up and about: *Even at midnight the whole town was astir.* *adj.*

as·ton·ish (ə ston′ish) surprise very much; amaze: *The magic trick astonished the little girl.* *v.* **—as·ton′ish·ment,** *n.* **—as·ton′ish·ing,** *adj.*

as·tound (ə stound′) fill with wonder; amaze: *We were astounded by the beauty of Niagara Falls.* *v.* **—as·tound′ing,** *adj.*

a·stray (ə strā′) off the right path or out of the right way: *The trail was poorly marked and we went astray.* *adv.*

a·stride (ə strīd′) with one leg on each side of: *Moira sat astride her horse.* *prep.*

as·tro·nom·i·cal (as′trə nom′ə kəl) **1** extremely large or great, like the numbers used to describe distances between stars: *an astronomical price.* **2** having to do with astronomy: *an astronomical telescope.* *adj.*

as·tron·o·my (ə stron′ə mē) the science that deals with the sun, moon, planets, stars, and other bodies in space. *n.* **—as·tron′o·mer,** *n.*

as·tute (ə styūt′ *or* ə stūt′) shrewd; clever: *He was an astute chess player.* *adj.* **—as·tute′ly,** *adv.* **—as·tute′ness,** *n.*

a·sun·der (ə sun′dər) an old or poetic word for "apart": *torn asunder.* *adv.*

a·sy·lum (ə sī′ləm) **1** refuge or shelter: *Many refugees from warring countries have found asylum in Canada.* **2** a place where mentally ill people used to stay in order to receive care. *n.*

ate (āt) the past tense of **eat:** *Jan ate his dinner an hour ago.* *v.*

a·the·ist (ā′thē ist) a person who believes that there is no God. *n.* **—a′the·is′tic,** *adj.* **—a′the·ism′,** *n.*

ath·lete (ath′lēt) a person who is active and skilled in sports: *Baseball players and swimmers are athletes.* *n.* **—ath·let′ic** (ath let′ik), *adj.*

athlete's foot (ath′lēts fůt′) a skin disease of the feet, caused by a fungus. It causes red, itchy sores.

At·lan·tic (at lan′ tik) 1 the ocean east of North and South America, stretching to Europe and Africa. 2 having to do with the Atlantic Ocean: *the Atlantic coast, Atlantic air routes.* 1 *n.,* 2 *adj.*

Atlantic Provinces (at lan′tik prov′in siz) Newfoundland, Prince Edward Island, Nova Scotia, and New Brunswick.

at·las (at′ləs) a book of maps. *n.*

WORD HISTORY........ atlas

The word **atlas** comes from the name *Atlas*, a character in Greek myth. The first map books used to have a picture of him holding up the world with his shoulders and hands. According to the story, he was punished in this way for rebelling against the gods.

ATM *abbreviation for* automated teller machine, a machine that lets you take out or put in money in your bank account.

at·mos·phere (at′məs fēr′) 1 the layer of air that surrounds the earth. 2 mental and moral surroundings; surrounding influence: *a friendly atmosphere. He lived in an atmosphere of poverty.* 3 the air in any given place: *The atmosphere in the cave was damp.* *n.*
—at′mos·pher′ic (at′məs fer′ik), *adj.*

a·toll (at′ol *or* ə tol′) a ring-shaped coral island or reef formed on top of land in the ocean. The pool in the centre is called a lagoon. *n.*

at·om (at′əm) 1 the smallest part of an element, that still has all its special characteristics. An atom of an element can react with other substances, without being forever changed. Atoms are made up of protons, neutrons, and electrons. 2 the tiniest bit: *There is not an atom of truth in his whole story.* *n.* **—a·tom′ic** (ə tom′ik), *adj.*

atomic bomb (ə tom′ik bom′) a bomb that splits atoms to cause a horrific explosion. **Atom bomb** is another name for it.

atomic energy (ə tom′ik en′ər jē) the energy, or power, that holds atomic nuclei together, also called **nuclear energy.** Some elements can be made to release this energy, either slowly in a nuclear reactor or very violently in a bomb.

a·tone (ə tōn′) make up for wrong behaviour: *Allen atoned for his unkindness to Joanna by sharing his snack with her.* *v.,* **a·toned, a·ton·ing.** **—a·tone′ment** *n.*

a·top (ə top′) on the top of: *atop a hill.* *prep.*

a·tri·um (ā′trē əm) 1 either of the two upper chambers of the heart, which receive blood from the veins. 2 a high hall or court in a large building, often with a skylight. *n., pl.* **a·tri·a** (ā′trē ə) or **a·tri·ums.**

a·tro·cious (ə trō′shəs) extremely bad: *an atrocious crime, atrocious weather, atrocious spelling.* *adj.*
—a·tro′cious·ly, *adv.*

a·troc·i·ty (ə tros′ə tē) an extremely cruel or wicked act: *the atrocities of war.* *n., pl.* **a·troc·i·ties.**

at·tach (ə tach′) 1 fasten or connect: *Julia attached a rope to her sled.* 2 write at the end: *The signers attached their names to the petition.* *v.* **—at·tach′ment,** *n.*
be attached to, like very much: *She is very attached to her cousin.*

at·tack (ə tak′) 1 use force, words, or weapons to hurt or fight: *The dog attacked with its teeth bared. The newspapers attacked the new prime minister.* 2 start on something energetically: *to attack a problem.* 3 an act of attacking: *The attack of the enemy took the town by surprise. Her speech was an attack on greed.* 4 act harmfully on: *Some bacteria attack tooth enamel.* 5 the sudden beginning of sickness, pain, etc.: *an attack of malaria, an attack of remorse.* 1, 2, 4 *v.,* 3, 5 *n.*

at·tain (ə tān) reach: *Grandmother has attained the age of 80. James attained his goal.* *v.*

at·tain·ment (ə tān′mənt) 1 the act of attaining or reaching: *the attainment of our goals.* 2 an accomplishment or ability: *Leonard Cohen is a Canadian of varied attainments; he is a poet, a composer, and a singer.* *n.*

at·tempt (ə tempt′) 1 try: *I will attempt to get better grades.* 2 a try; an effort: *They made an attempt to bike across Canada.* 1 *v.,* 2 *n.*

at·tend (ə tend′) 1 be present at: *I attend school.* 2 give care and thought: *Attend to your lesson.* 3 go or come along with: *Three ladies attended the princess. Success often attends hard work.* *v.*

at·tend·ance (ə ten′dəns) 1 the act of attending: *Attendance at all classes is required.* 2 the number of people present: *The attendance at the meeting was over 200.* *n.*

at·tend·ant (ə ten′dənt) 1 a servant who follows a ruler or noble wherever he or she goes: *the prince's attendants.* 2 a person whose job is to help or serve: *a flight attendant on a plane.* *n.*

a bat	e bed	i bid	o pot	u cup	th thin
ā cake	ē me	ī bite	ō go	ü rude	ᴛʜ then
ä bar	ə about	ər over	ô for	u̇ put	zh measure

at·ten·tion (ə ten′shən) 1 care and thought: *The students gave the teacher their full attention.* 2 notice: *A sudden movement caught my attention.* 3 **attentions,** *pl.* acts of kindness: *My friend received many attentions, such as visits, cards, and flowers, when she was sick.*
4 **Attention!** a command to stand straight and still.
1–3 *n.,* 4 *interj.*
at attention, straight and still: *The soldier stood at attention at the door.*
pay attention, watch or listen carefully.

at·ten·tive (ə ten′tiv) 1 listening or watching carefully: *Attentive students learn the most.* 2 polite and thoughtful toward others: *Our attentive host tried to make us feel at home.* *adj.* —**at·ten′tive·ly,** *adv.*

at·tic (at′ik) a room or space just below the roof of a house. *n.*

At·tik·a·mek (ə tik′ə mek′) 1 a First Nations people living in southwestern Québec. 2 their language, a dialect of Cree. 3 having to do with these people or their language. 1, 2 *n.,* 3 *adj.*

at·tire (ə tīr′) 1 clothes of a special kind: *swimming attire, evening attire.* 2 clothe; dress: *He was attired in a full military uniform.* 1 *n.,* 2 *v.,* **at·tired, at·tir·ing.**

at·ti·tude (at′ə tyūd′ *or* at′ə tūd′) 1 way of thinking, acting, or feeling: *I like your helpful attitude.* 2 a position of the body: *Ken stood in the attitude of a boxer ready to fight.* *n.*

at·tor·ney (ə tər′nē) 1 a person who has legal power to act for another. 2 a lawyer. *n., pl.* **at·tor·neys.**

Attorney General (ə tər′nē jen′ ə rəl) the chief law officer of Canada or of a Canadian province. The Attorney General is a member of the Cabinet. *n., pl.* **Attorneys General** or **Attorney Generals.**

at·tract (ə trakt′) 1 pull or draw to itself: *A magnet attracts iron.* 2 be interesting and pleasing to: *Bright colours attract children.* *v.* —**at·trac′tion,** *n.* —**at·trac′tive,** *adj.*

at·trib·ute (ə trib′yūt *for 1,* at′rə byūt′ *for 2*) 1 think of as belonging to or caused by: *We attribute courage to heroes. She attributes her success to hard work.* 2 a quality or characteristic: *Patience is an attribute of a good teacher.* 1 *v.,* **at·trib·ut·ed, at·trib·ut·ing;** 2 *n.*

auc·tion (ok′shən) 1 a public sale in which each thing is sold to the person who offers the most money for it. 2 sell at an auction. 1 *n.,* 2 *v.*

au·da·cious (o dā′shəs) 1 bold; daring: *an audacious rescue attempt.* 2 too bold; rude: *an audacious request for money.* *adj.*

au·dac·i·ty (o das′ə tē) 1 boldness: *He had the audacity to go to the party without being invited.* 2 a rude remark or act. *n., pl.* **au·dac·i·ties.**

au·di·ence (od′ē əns) 1 the people watching or listening to something: *The audience cheered the cabinet minister's speech.* 2 the readers of something published: *This newspaper has a wide audience.* 3 a chance to be heard; an interview: *The Prime Minister granted an audience to the inventor.* *n.*

Word Family........... audi-

Words beginning with **audi** all have to do with sound. These words come from the Latin word *audire,* meaning "hear."
audible: able to be heard
audition: a hearing to test ability
auditor: a listener or examiner
auditorium: a large room for an audience

au·di·o (od′ē ō) having to do with sound that is recorded or broadcast: *audio equipment, the audio part of a movie.* *adj.*

au·ger (og′ər) a tool having a spiral blade like a corkscrew, for drilling holes. *n.*

aug·ment (og ment′) increase: *Jila bought some stamps to augment her collection.* *v.*

au·gust (o gust′) inspiring reverence and admiration; majestic: *The people were silent in the august presence of their chief.* *adj.*

Au·gust (og′əst) the eighth month of the year. August has 31 days. *n.*

Auks are found only in the northern hemisphere. Like penguins they stand upright, and dive underwater to catch fish.

auk (ok) a diving sea bird with short wings that it uses mainly as paddles: *Auks are found in arctic regions.* *n.*

aunt (ant *or* ont) 1 the sister of a person's father or mother. 2 the wife of a person's uncle. *n.*

au•ral (ȯ′rəl) having to do with hearing: *I have an aural defect, so I use a hearing aid.* *adj.* **—au′ral•ly,** *adv.*

au•ror•a bor•e•al•is (ȯ rȯ′rə bȯ′rē al′is) streamers of coloured light in the northern sky at night; the northern lights. In the southern hemisphere, a similar thing can be seen in the southern sky. It is called the **aurora australis.**

aus•pi•cious (o spish′əs) favourable; hopeful: *Our hockey team's easy win in its first game was an auspicious start to the season.* *adj.* **—aus•pi′cious•ly,** *adv.*

aus•tere (o stēr′) 1 strict and stern. 2 very simple and bare: *The tall, plain columns stood against the sky in austere beauty.* *adj.* **—aus•ter′i•ty** (o ster′ə tē), *n.*

au•then•tic (o then′tik) genuine; real: *authentic Inuit carvings.* *adj.*

au•thor (oth′ər) 1 a person who writes books: *Barbara Smucker is a famous Canadian children's author.* 2 the inventor or creator of something. *n.*

au•thor•i•ta•tive (ə thȯr′ə tā′tiv) 1 having authority; deserving to be believed or obeyed: *authoritative guidelines. This is the authoritative statement of an expert.* 2 commanding: *In authoritative tones the police officer shouted, "Keep back!"* *adj.*

au•thor•i•ty (ə thȯr′ə tē) 1 the right to command, judge, or act: *Parents have authority over their children. A police officer has the authority to arrest careless drivers.* 2 a person or group who has this right: *Who are the authorities in charge of building permits?* 3 a source of correct or reliable information: *A good dictionary is an authority on the meaning of words.* *n., pl.* **au•thor•i•ties.**

au•thor•ize (oth′ə rīz′) 1 give someone the authority or the right: *The Prime Minister authorized her to make the decision.* 2 approve: *This dictionary authorizes the two spellings "traveller" and "traveler."* *v.,* **au•thor•ized, au•thor•iz•ing.**

au•tism (ot′iz əm) a disorder that makes it hard for a person to understand words and to communicate, even though the person may be very intelligent. Autism can be mild or severe and affects people in many different ways. *adj.* **—au•tis′tic,** *adj.*

au•to•crat (ot′ə krat′) a leader who makes all the rules and decisions himself or herself without asking or caring what anyone else thinks, and then forces them on everyone. *n.* **—au′to•crat′ic,** *adj.*

Word Family .... **auto-**

Words beginning with **auto** all have to do with self. These words come from the Greek word *auto,* meaning "self."

autobiography: a person's life written by that person
autograph: a signature, especially as a souvenir; to sign
automate: set up something to be done by machines like robots, instead of by people
automation: automatic controls in machines
automobile: a car (a vehicle with its own engine)
automotive: having to do with cars, trucks, etc.
autopsy: an examination of a dead body to see for oneself what caused that person to die

au•to•mat•ic (ot′ə mat′ik) 1 working by itself: *an automatic lock, an automatic pump.* 2 done without thought or attention: *Breathing and swallowing are usually automatic.* 3 something with parts that work by themselves, such as a car whose motor changes gear by itself. 1, 2 *adj.,* 3 *n.* **—au′to•mat′i•cal•ly,** *adv.*

au•tumn (ot′əm) the season between summer and winter; fall. *n.*

aux•il•ia•ry (og zil′ə rē *or* og zil′yə rē) 1 helping; assisting: *Some sailboats have auxiliary engines.* 2 a person, group, or thing that helps: *A microscope is a useful auxiliary to the human eye.* 1 *adj.,* 2 *n., pl.* **aux•il•ia•ries.**

auxiliary verb (og zil′ə rē vərb) a kind of verb used along with the main verb in a sentence to show the time of the action and certain other things. *Examples: be, have, will.* In the sentence *I will take my camera along,* the auxiliary verb *will* shows that the action (the main verb *take*) is in the future.

Grammar ✓ *Check* .... **auxiliary verb**

Here are some examples of auxiliary verbs.

- *I will take my camera with me.* Here the auxiliary verb **will** shows that the action (*take*) is in the future.
- *We are eating supper.* Here the auxiliary verb **are** helps to show that the action (*eat*) is going on right now.
- *Have you read this book?* Here the auxiliary verb **have** helps to show that the action (*read*) happened sometime in the past.
- *The CD was stolen.* Here the auxiliary verb **was** helps to show that the action (*steal*) is not something the CD did, but something that happened to the CD.

a bat	e bed	i bid	o pot	u cup	th thin
ā cake	ē me	ī bite	ō go	ū rude	ᴛʜ then
ä bar	ə about	ər over	ȯ for	u̇ put	zh measure

a•vail (ə vāl′) help; be useful: *Money will not avail you now. Talk will not avail without work.* *v.*
avail yourself of, take advantage of; use: *He availed himself of the opportunity to learn French.*
of no avail, useless: *Arguing is of no avail now.*
to no avail, without results: *I complained, but to no avail.*

a•vail•a•ble (ə vā′lə bəl) there for people to use or get: *The saw is not available at the moment; Bryony is using it. Some tickets are still available.* *adj.*

av•a•lanche (av′ə lanch′) the sudden sliding of a large mass of snow, ice, dirt, or rocks down the side of a mountain. *n.*

av•a•rice (av′ə ris) a greedy desire for money. *n.* —**av′a•ri′cious** (av′ə rish′əs), *adj.*

av•a•tar (av′ə tȧr′) a made-up name, imaginary personality, or graphic image that a person uses to identify himself or herself in a chat room on the Internet. It protects the person's privacy and often gives a false impression of what he or she is like. *n.*

Ave. *abbreviation for* avenue.

a•venge (ə venj′) get revenge for: *The knight avenged the insult by defeating his enemy in a duel.* *v.,* **a•venged, a•veng•ing.** —**a•veng′er,** *n.*
avenge yourself or **be avenged,** get revenge for a wrong done to you: *The robber swore to avenge himself on those who betrayed him.*

av•e•nue (av′ən yü′) a wide street. *n.*

av•er•age (av′ə rij) **1** in arithmetic, the quantity found by adding up several other quantities and then dividing the sum by the number of quantities: *The average of 3, 10, and 5 is 6.* **2** find the average of: *Will you average those numbers for me?* **3** obtained by averaging: *The average temperature for the week was 22°C.* **4** have, be, or do as an average: *The cost of their lunches averaged $15 a week. She averages six hours of work a day.* **5** the usual sort or amount: *The amount of rain this year has been below average.* **6** usual; ordinary: *average ability.* 1, 5 *n.,* 2, 4 *v.,* **av•er•aged, av•er•ag•ing;** 3, 6 *adj.*

a•ver•sion (ə vər′zhən) **1** a strong dislike: *Some people have an aversion to snakes.* **2** a thing or person that is disliked: *Nicknames are my pet aversion.* *n.*

a•vert (ə vərt′) **1** prevent; avoid: *The driver averted an accident by a quick turn of the steering wheel.* **2** turn away; turn aside: *She averted her eyes from the car wreck.* *v.*

a•vi•ar•y (ā′vē er′ē) a caged area where birds are kept. *n., pl.* **a•vi•ar•ies.**

a•vi•a•tion (ā′vē ā′shən) the designing, making, and flying of aircraft. *n.*

a•vi•a•tor (ā′vē ā′tər) a person who flies an aircraft; pilot. *n.*

av•id (av′id) enthusiastic: *He is an avid reader.* *adj.*

Avocados are sometimes called avocado pears, because of their shape.

av•o•ca•do (av′ə kȧ′dō) a tropical fruit shaped like a pear, with a thin, dark green skin and a very large seed. Avocados are good to eat. *n.*

av•o•ca•tion (av′ə kā′shən) a hobby or sideline: *She is a lawyer, but writing short stories is her avocation.* *n.*

a•void (ə void′) keep away from; keep from doing or having: *Avoid the really muddy area at the back of the schoolyard. We avoided driving through large cities on our trip.* *v.* —**a•void′a•ble,** *adj.* —**a•void′ance,** *n.*

a•wait (ə wāt′) wait for: *We eagerly await your coming. Many pleasures await you on your trip.* *v.*

a•wake (ə wāk′) **1** wake up; arouse: *We awoke from a sound sleep. The alarm clock awoke me.* **2** roused from sleep; not asleep: *Wanda is always awake early.* **3** on the alert; watchful: *Our government is awake to that danger.* 1 *v.,* **a•woke, a•wak•ing;** 2, 3 *adj.*

a•wak•en•ing (ə wā′kə ning) **1** the act of waking up or becoming aware and interested: *an awakening to danger.* **2** waking up or reviving: *the sounds of the awakening birds.* 1 *n.,* 2 *adj.*

a•ward (ə wȯrd′) **1** give to a deserving person, group, etc.: *A medal was awarded to the woman who saved the child.* **2** a prize for excellence: *His dog won the highest award.* 1 *v.,* 2 *n.*

a•ware (ə wer′) knowing; realizing; conscious: *I was too sleepy to be aware how cold it was. He is not aware of his danger.* *adj.* —**a•ware′ness,** *n.*

a·way (ə wā′) 1 at or to some other place; in another direction: *Get away from the fire (adv.). The sailor was far away from home (adj.). She looked sad and turned away (adv.).* **Away** is used with many verbs that have to do with getting rid of something or using it up: *to give away something, to take away pain, to while away the time.* 2 without stopping: *I worked away at my writing.* 1–3 *adv.,* 1 *adj.*

USING WORDS ...... away

Away is used with many verbs that have to do with getting rid of something (*give away a book, take away pain*), using up something (*pass away the time*), or of something gradually disappearing (*The noise died away.*). See how many more examples you can think of.

awe (o) 1 great wonder and fear or reverence: *We feel awe when we gaze up at high mountains.* 2 fill with wonder and fear or reverence: *The size and beauty of the mountains awed us.* 1 *n.,* 2 *v.,* **awed, aw·ing.**

awe·some (os′əm) causing awe: *The great fire was an awesome sight. adj.*

aw·ful (of′əl) 1 *Informal.* very bad, great, ugly, etc.: *Your room is in an awful mess.* 2 an older word for "awesome." *adj.* —**aw′ful·ly,** *adv.*

a·while (ə wīl′ *or* ə hwīl′) for a short time: *She stayed awhile. adv.*

awk·ward (ok′wərd) 1 clumsy; not graceful in movement or shape: *Seals are very awkward on land, but are graceful in the water.* 2 hard to use or manage: *The handle of this cup has an awkward shape.* 3 embarrassing: *He asked me an awkward question. adj.* —**awk′ward·ly,** *adv.* —**awk′ward·ness,** *n.*

awl (ol) a pointed tool used for making small holes in leather or wood. *n.*

awn·ing (on′ing) a piece of canvas, plastic, or other material spreading outward from the top of a window or door for protection from the sun or rain. *n.*

a·woke (ə wōk′) the past tense of **awake:** *She awoke at seven. v.*

a·wry (ə rī′) 1 crooked or out of place: *Her hat was blown awry by the wind.* 2 wrong: *Our plans have gone awry (adv.). I knew something was awry as soon as I saw the open window (adj.). adv. or adj.*

axe (aks) a tool for chopping wood. *n., pl.* **ax·es.**

ax·is (ak′sis) 1 an imaginary or real line going through an object, on which the object turns or seems to turn: *The earth's axis is an imaginary line through the North and South Poles.* 2 either of the lines that you start with in making a graph. One is vertical, the other is horizontal. *n., pl.* **ax·es** (ak′sēz).

ax·le (ak′səl) a bar or shaft that a wheel or pair of wheels turns on. *n.*

aye[1] or **ay** (ā) a poetic word for "always"; ever: *Peace shall reign forever and aye. adv.*

aye[2] or **ay** (ī) 1 yes: *Aye, aye, sir.* 2 a "yes" vote or voter: *The ayes won when the vote was taken.* 1 *adv.,* 2 *n.*

a·zal·ea (ə zāl′yə) a bush with funnel-shaped flowers. Azaleas come in a variety of colours. *n.*

Bb

b or **B** (bē) **1** the second letter of the English alphabet, or the speech sound that it stands for. The sound of *b* is heard twice in *baby.* **2** the second thing in a list. **3** in music: **a** a note. On a keyboard it is the white note between A and C. **b** a scale or key that has B as its home note. *n., pl.* **b's** or **B's.**

bab·ble (bab′əl) **1** talk too much, too fast, or in a way that cannot be understood: *She babbled on and on about her great adventure.* **2** foolish talk or talk that cannot be understood: *A confused babble filled the room.* **3** a soft flowing or rippling sound: *the babble of a brook.* **4** make this sound: *The little brook babbled over the stones.* 1, 4 *v.,* **bab·bled, bab·bling;** 2, 3 *n.*

babe (bāb) a poetic word for "baby." *n.*

This is a mandrill, which belongs to the same family as baboons, but is more brightly coloured.

ba·boon (bə bün′) a kind of large, fierce monkey with a doglike face and a short tail. Baboons live in the rocky hills of Africa and the Arabian peninsula. *n.*

ba·by (bā′bē) **1** a very young child or animal: *Some babies cry a lot.* **2** the youngest: *Six-year-old Simon is the baby of the family.* **3** very small or young: *a baby bird.* **4** suitable for a baby: *baby shoes, baby talk.* **5** a person who acts like a baby: *Don't be a baby.* **6** treat like a baby: *to baby a sick child.* **7** handle very carefully: *to baby a new car.* 1, 2, 5 *n., pl.* **ba·bies;** 3, 4 *adj.,* 6, 7 *v.,* **ba·bied, ba·by·ing.** —**ba′by·ish,** *adj.*

baby carriage (bā′bē ker′ij) a light carriage used for wheeling a baby around. **Baby buggy** is an informal name for it.

ba·by-sit (bā′bē sit′) take care of a child while the parents are busy or away from home. *v.,* **ba·by-sat, ba·by-sit·ting.** —**ba′by-sit′ter,** *n.*

baby tooth (bā′bē tüth′) one of the first set of teeth of a child or young animal, which fall out to make room for the permanent teeth.

bach·e·lor (bach′ə lər) an unmarried man. *n.*

back (bak) **1** the part of a person's body opposite to the chest; the upper part of an animal's body: *She turned her back to the wind.* **2** the side of anything opposite or behind the front: *the back of the room, the back of a rug.* **3** opposite or behind the front: *the back seat of a car.* **4** the part of a chair or chesterfield that supports the back of a person sitting down. **5** move in reverse; move backward: *She backed her car into the driveway.* **6** behind in space or time: *a back issue of a magazine* (*adj.*), *to walk back three steps* (*adv.*). *Years back this land was all in farms* (*adv.*). **7** to the place or person that something or someone came from: *Put the book back. I gave the money back.* 1, 2, 4 *n.,* 3, 6 *adj.,* 5 *v.,* 6, 7 *adv.*
back and forth, first one way and then the other: *He paced back and forth impatiently.*
back down, give up a claim: *When I challenged her to prove it, she backed down.*
back off, stop attacking.
back out, *Informal.* decide not to do something after all: *He was going to come on the trip, but he backed out.*
back up, a move backward. **b** support: *If you tell your dad what happened, I'll back you up.* **c** copy from a computer onto a disk. **d** plug up so that liquid collects and overflows: *The drain is backed up.*
behind someone's back, secretly and with a mean purpose: *He seemed to be a good friend but then I found out he was talking about me behind my back.*
get off someone's back, *Informal.* stop nagging or criticizing someone: *I finally told him if he didn't get off my back I wouldn't help him at all.*
get someone's back up, *Informal.* make or become angry and stubborn: *She was only joking, so don't get your back up.*
go back on, *Informal.* **a** fail to live up to: *to go back on your word.* **b** not be faithful or loyal to: *He went back on his friends.*
in back of, behind: *The garden is in back of the house.*

back bacon (bak′ bā′kən) bacon cut from the back of the pig rather than the sides: *Back bacon has little fat and tastes like ham.*

back•board (bak′bȯrd′) **1** a board above and behind the basket on a basketball court. **2** any other board that forms the back of something or acts as a support. *n.*

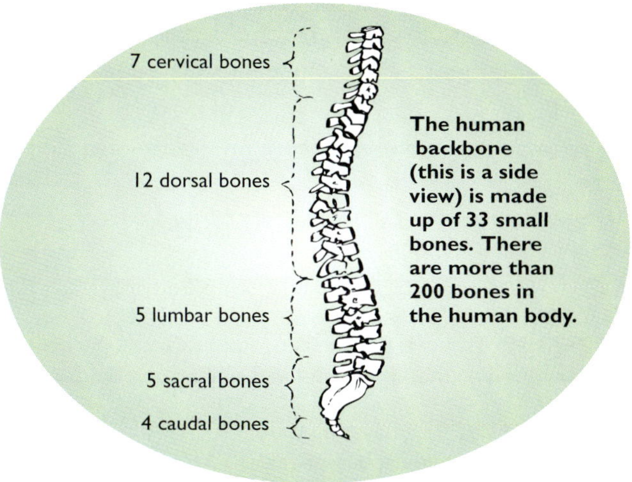

The human backbone (this is a side view) is made up of 33 small bones. There are more than 200 bones in the human body.

back•bone (bak′bōn′) **1** the spine; a series of small bones along the middle of the back in humans and many other animals. **2** the main strength or support: *She is the backbone of the organization.* **3** the courage to stand up for what you think is right. *n.*

back•fire (bak′fīr′) **1** explode too soon or in the wrong place. **2** have an unexpected bad result: *His plan backfired, and instead of getting rich he lost all his money.* **3** a fire set to stop a prairie or forest fire by burning off the area in front of it. 1, 2 *v.,* **back•fired, back•fir•ing;** 3 *n.*

back•gam•mon (bak′gam′ən *or* bak′gam′ən) a game for two people who move pieces on a special board according to the throw of dice. *n.*

back•ground (bak′ground′) **1** the back part of a picture, scene, or pattern: *The cottage stands in the foreground with the mountains in the background. The material had pink flowers on a white background.* **2** all the things that lead up to or explain something: *We studied the background to the news.* **3** upbringing or heritage; experience and training: *a farming background. Gita's background is Hindu.* *n.*
in the background, out of sight; not in clear view: *The shy boy kept in the background.*

back•hoe (bak′hō′) a very large machine for digging ditches, with a seat for the driver: *They used a backhoe to dig a trench for water pipes going into the house.* *n.*

back•log (bak′log′) **1** a number of things to be done or dealt with: *The office had a backlog of orders still waiting to be filled.* **2** become a backlog: *Our assignments backlogged because we were away from school for a week.* 1 *n.,* 2 *v.,* **back•logged, back•log•ging.**

back•pack (bak′pak′) **1** a light cloth or leather bag for schoolbooks, food, or other equipment, with straps for carrying it on your back. Bigger backpacks for hiking or bike trips are attached to a light metal frame for support. **2** travel while carrying all your belongings in such a bag: *They backpacked 200 km last summer.* 1 *n.,* 2 *v.* **—back′pack•ing,** *n.*

back to back (bak′tə bak′) **1** with the backs against each other or close together and the fronts or faces turned in opposite directions: *We placed the chairs back to back.* **2** *Informal.* one after the other: *We saw three videos back to back.* **—back′-to-back′,** *adj.*

back•up (bak′up′) **1** a person, group, or thing available for support or as a replacement: *If Plan A fails, we have Plan B as a backup.* **2** in computer systems, a copy of important programs or data stored on a disk in case the originals are destroyed or lost. *n.*

back•ward (bak′wərd) **1** toward the back or toward an earlier time: *He looked backward (adv.). She gave him a backward look (adj.).* **2** with the back first; with the last part first: *a backward somersault (adj.). Count backward from 100 (adv.).* **Backwards** is another form for the adverb (defs. 1 and 2). **3** slow in development: *He seemed a bit backward as a child, but by the end of high school he was doing very well.* 1–2 *adv.,* 1–3 *adj.* **—back′ward•ness,** *n.*

USING WORDS .... backward

You can use **backward** and **backwards** as adverbs:
Niko tumbled backward over his own gym bag.
Niko tumbled backwards over his own gym bag.
But use only **backward** as an adjective:
Niko took a backward tumble over his own gym bag.

back•wa•ter (bak′wot′ər) **1** a stretch of still water that is held back or is not part of the current: *The beaver dam had caused a backwater to form behind it.* **2** a place that seems dull or dead: *The quiet little town was often referred to as a backwater.* *n.*

back•woods (bak′wu̇dz′) forests or wild regions far away from towns. *pl.n.*

a bat	e bed	i bid	o pot	u cup	th **thin**
ā cake	ē me	ī bite	ō go	ū rude	ᴛʜ **then**
ȧ bar	ə about	ər over	ȯ for	u̇ put	zh measure

back·yard or **back yard** (bak′yärd′) a yard behind a house: *She grows vegetables in her backyard.* **in your own backyard,** where you live or work: *We have a lot of talented people right here in our own backyard.* *n.*

ba·con (bā′kən) salted and smoked meat from the back and sides of a pig. *n.*

bac·te·ri·a (bak tē′rē ə) very tiny and simple living things that are like plants in some ways and like animals in other ways. They can only be seen through a microscope and are found everywhere, in the air, soil, water, and in the bodies of all plants and animals. Some bacteria in our bodies help us digest; others make us sick. *pl.n., sing.* **bac·te·ri·um.** —**bac·te′ri·al,** *adj.*

bad (bad) **1** not good; wrong, harmful, etc.: *Cheating is bad. Smoking is bad for your lungs.* **2** severe; serious: *A bad thunderstorm delayed the airplane.* **3** rotten; spoiled: *a bad egg.* **4** sorry or sick: *I feel bad about losing your baseball. He felt so bad he had to lie down.* *adj.,* **worse, worst.** —**bad′ness,** *n.* **not bad,** *Informal.* pretty good.

bade (bad *or* bād) a past tense of **bid:** *She bade me a friendly farewell.* *v.*

badge (baj) something worn on a piece of clothing to show that a person belongs to a certain school, organization, occupation, etc. Police officers wear badges. *n.*

badg·er (baj′ər) **1** an animal of the weasel family with long, coarse grey fur, a wide, heavy body, and long front claws for digging. Badgers live in burrows; in Canada, they are found especially on the Prairies. **2** nag or pester: *He's been badgering his sister to let him come along.* 1 *n.,* 2 *v.*

bad·lands (bad′landz′) a region of barren land marked by ridges, gullies, and unusual rock formations, as found in southwestern Saskatchewan and southeastern Alberta. The skeletons of prehistoric animals have been found in the badlands. *n.*

bad·ly (bad′lē) **1** in a bad manner: *She sings badly.* **2** *Informal.* very much: *We badly need that money.* *adv.*

bad·min·ton (bad′min tən) a game for either two or four players who use light racquets to hit a shuttlecock back and forth over a high net. *n.*

baf·fle (baf′əl) be too hard for a person to figure out: *This puzzle baffles me.* *v.,* **baf·fled, baf·fling.** —**baf′fle·ment,** *n.*

bag (bag) **1** a container made of paper, plastic, cloth, leather, etc. that can be pulled together or folded over to close at the top: *Fresh fruit is often sold in plastic bags.* **2** a purse or suitcase. **3** put into a bag or bags: *We bagged the cookies for the bake sale.* **4** bulge: *These pants bag at the knees (v.). When I'm tired I have bags under my eyes (n.).* **5** *Informal.* manage to get, win, etc.: *Look at the stuffed lion I bagged at the fall fair.* 1, 2, 4 *n.,* 3–5 *v.,* **bagged, bag·ging.** —**bag′ful′,** *n.*

ba·gel (bā′gəl) a firm, doughnut-shaped bread roll. *n.*

> **WORD HISTORY........ bagel**
>
> **Bagel** comes from the Yiddish word *beygel*, which originally meant "ring."

bag·gage (bag′ij) the bags, suitcases, etc. packed with belongings that a person takes when travelling. *n.*

bag·gy (bag′ē) hanging loosely: *The clown had baggy pants.* *adj.,* **bag·gi·er, bag·gi·est.**

bag·pipes (bag′pīps′) a musical instrument that looks like a cloth bag with wooden pipes sticking out of it. You blow air into the bag through one of the pipes, and play the notes with your fingers on another pipe. *pl.n.*

Ba·hai (bə hī′) **1** a religion based on the teachings of **Baha Ullah** (bə hä′ ū lä′), a prophet of Persia and the author of a holy book called the Kitab-i-Aqdas. He taught that all people are united under God regardless of their religion. **2** a follower of this religion. **3** having to do with this religion or its followers. 1, 2 *n.,* 3 *adj.* —**Ba·ha′ism,** *n.*

bail¹ (bāl) **1** money paid to free an arrested person until he or she is tried in court: *The man gave bail for his son, who was accused of setting fire to a barn.* **2** get someone out of jail by paying this money: *He bailed out his son.* 1 *n.,* 2 *v.*

bail² (bāl) scoop water out of the bottom of a boat. *v.* **bail out, a** drop from an airplane by parachute: *When the plane caught fire, the pilot bailed out.* **b** drop out of some activity that you think is likely to fail.

bail·ey (bā′ lē) See the picture and caption at **keep** on page 381. *n.*

Bai·sak·hi (bī sä′kē) a festival of the Sikh religion, held on April 13. It celebrates the day that the first five Sikhs were baptized and the five symbols of the Sikh faith were adopted. *n.*

bait (bāt) **1** food used to attract fish or other animals in order to catch them: *Worms are often used as bait in fishing.* **2** put bait on a hook or in a trap.

3 anything used to trick someone into doing something. 4 do or say things to a person just to get a reaction: *He was determined not to get angry because he knew they were only baiting him.* 1, 3 *n.*, 2, 4 *v.*

bake (bāk) 1 cook by dry heat in an oven: *to bake bread. Cookies bake quickly.* 2 dry or harden by heat: *to bake bricks or china.* *v.*, **baked, bak·ing.**

bak·er (bā′kər) a person who makes and sells bread, pies, cakes, etc. *n.*

baker's dozen (bā′kərz duz′ən) thirteen: *We counted the fish and found we had caught exactly a baker's dozen.*

bak·er·y (bā′kə rē) a baker's shop; a place where bread, cakes, etc. are made or sold. **Bake shop** is another name. *n., pl.* **bak·er·ies.**

bake sale (bāk′ sāl′) a sale of homemade baked goods to raise money.

baking powder (bā′king pou′dər) a white powdered mixture of baking soda and other chemicals, put in tea biscuits, cakes, etc. to make them rise.

baking soda (bā′king sō′də) a white powder used in baking, medicine, cleaning, etc. **Bicarbonate of soda** is the scientific name.

bal·a·clav·a (bal′ə klȧ′və) a knitted cap that covers most of your head and neck: *We put on balaclavas before we went skiing.* *n.*

bal·ance (bal′əns) 1 steadiness: *He lost his balance and fell off the ladder.* 2 keep or put in a steady condition or position: *Can you balance a loonie on its edge?* 3 a condition where different things are the same in amount or importance: *A balance of work and play is healthy.* 4 keep things equal in amount or importance. 5 compare the value, importance, etc. of: *She balanced a trip to the Rockies against missing most of the soccer season.* 6 an instrument for weighing something. It looks like a bar with a pan hanging from each end, supported in the middle like a seesaw. 7 place two things opposite each other on scales or in your hands to see which is heavier. 8 the part that is left over; the remainder: *I'll pay five dollars now and the balance later on.* 1, 3, 6, 8 *n.*, 2, 4, 5, 7 *v.*, **bal·anced, bal·anc·ing.**
in the balance, undecided: *The result was in the balance until the last moment.*

bal·co·ny (bal′kə nē) 1 an outside platform with an entrance from an upper floor of a building. 2 an upper level of seats in a theatre or hall. *n., pl.* **bal·co·nies.**

bald (bold) 1 without hair on the head. 2 bare: *a bald mountaintop.* 3 plain: *The bald truth can be hard to take.* *adj.* **—bald′ly,** *adv.* **—bald′ness,** *n.*

The bald eagle isn't really bald — it has white feathers on top of its head. This bird lives only in North America. It is the national emblem of the United States.

bald eagle (bold′ ē′gəl) a large, powerful North American bird, with white feathers on its head, neck, and tail.

bale (bāl) 1 a large bundle of hay, straw, or cotton. 2 make into bales; tie in large bundles: *We watched the big machine bale hay.* A **baler** is a machine that does this. 1 *n.*, 2 *v.*, **baled, bal·ing.**

bale·ful (bāl′fəl) evil; harmful: *The wicked witch gave the children a baleful glance.* *adj.* **—bale′ful·ly,** *adv.*

balk (bok) hang back, not wanting to go through with something: *My horse balked at the third jump. Vito balked at doing the dishes.* *v.*

ball[1] (bol) 1 a round or oval object that is thrown, kicked, knocked, bounced, or batted around in a game. 2 a game where you use a ball. 3 anything round or roundish; something that looks like a ball: *a ball of string, the ball of your thumb. The earth is a ball.* 4 in baseball, a ball pitched too high, too low, or not over the plate, and which the batter does not swing at. *n.*

ball[2] (bol) 1 a large, formal party with dancing. 2 *Informal.* a very good time; a lot of fun: *We had a ball at camp.* *n.*

a bat	e bed	i bid	o pot	u cup	th thin
ā cake	ē me	ī bite	ō go	ū rude	ᴛʜ then
ȧ bar	ə about	ər over	ȯ for	u̇ put	zh measure

Balloons and Airships

What's the difference between a balloon and an airship? A balloon can be guided upward or downward, but cannot be steered in any other direction. An airship can be steered, using some type of engine.

a simple hot-air balloon

Below is a drawing of the first successful airship. It flew in 1852, powered by a steam engine.

a hot-air balloon made by the Montgolfier brothers in 1783

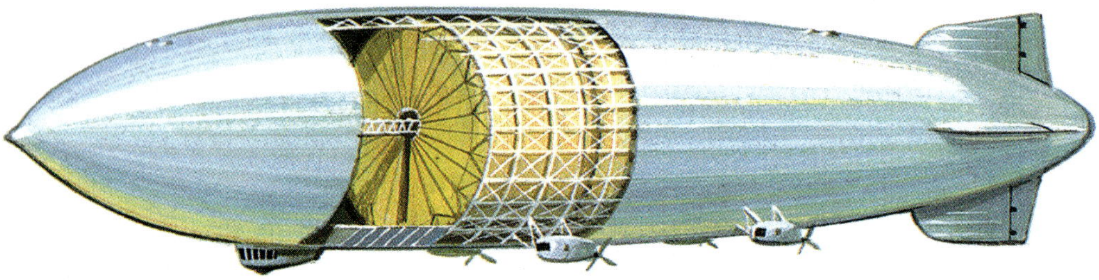

The airship Graf Zeppelin flew around the world in 1929.

bal•lad (bal′əd) a simple poem that tells a story, often put to music. *The Wreck of the Edmund Fitzgerald* is a ballad by Canadian **balladeer** Gordon Lightfoot. *n.*

bal•last (bal′əst) **1** something heavy carried in a ship to steady it, or in a balloon to control how high it rises. **2** the gravel or crushed rock used in making the bed for a road or railway track. *n.*

ball bearing (bol′ ber′ing) **1** a ring that has a groove all the way around the inside with little metal balls rolling around in it, so that a rod going through the ring can turn easily. **2** one of the little metal balls.

bal•le•ri•na (bal′ə rē′nə) a female ballet dancer. *n., pl.* **bal•le•ri•nas.**

bal•let (bal′ā) **1** an artistic dance that usually tells a story or expresses a mood, performed on stage by one or more dancers. **2** the art of creating or performing ballets: *He is studying ballet.* *n.*

ball hockey (bol′ hok′ē) hockey played with a tennis ball on pavement. **Road hockey** is another name for it.

bal•loon (bə lūn′) **1** a little rubber bag filled with air or a gas lighter than air, used as a toy or decoration. **2** a very large cloth bag filled with hot air or light gas, so that it will rise and float. It may have a basket underneath for passengers, and can be used as a signal, advertisement, etc. **3** swell out like a balloon: *The sails of the boat ballooned in the wind.* 1, 2 *n.,* 3 *v.*

bal•lot (bal′ət) **1** a piece of paper for writing down or checking off your vote. When you are done someone collects it or you put it in a **ballot box.** **2** the total number of votes. **3** vote or decide by using ballots. 1, 2 *n.,* 3, *v.,* **bal•lot•ed, bal•lot•ing.**

ball•point pen (bol′point′ pen′) a pen with a small metal ball for its writing point. The movement and pressure of writing make the ball turn against a cartridge of very thick ink, so that some ink is transferred to the paper.

ball·room (bol′rüm′) a large room for dancing. *n.*

balm (bom *or* bȧm) **1** a sweet-smelling oil obtained from certain kinds of trees, used to heal or to lessen pain. **2** anything that heals or soothes: *My mother's kind words were a balm to my hurt feelings.* *n.*

balm·y (bom′ē *or* bȧ′mē) mild; soft; gentle: *a balmy breeze.* *adj.,* **balm·i·er, balm·i·est.**

ba·lo·ney (bə lō′nē) **1** nonsense or foolishness: *Karl thought that his uncle's story about the fish he caught was a lot of baloney.* **2** another spelling of **bologna,** a kind of sausage. *n.*

bal·sa (bol′sə) a tropical American tree with wood that is light and soft. *n.*

bal·sam (bol′səm) a sticky substance obtained from certain trees. It is also short for **balsam fir,** an evergreen tree that gives this substance. *n.*

bam·boo (bam bü′) a treelike tropical grass with a stiff, hollow, woody stem that has hard, thick joints: *She bought a fishing rod made of bamboo.* *n., pl.* **bam·boos.**

bam·boo·zle (bam bü′zəl) *Informal.* **1** cheat or trick: *He was bamboozled into trading his best baseball cards for a cheap bike lock.* **2** puzzle or confuse: *The computer manual had me completely bamboozled.* *v.,* **bam·boo·zled, bam·boo·zling.**

ban (ban) **1** make a rule against; forbid: *Smoking is banned on buses.* **2** a rule against something: *There is a ban on parking in this street.* 1 *v.,* **banned, ban·ning;** 2 *n.*

ba·nan·a (bə nan′ə) a long, curved tropical fruit with a yellow peel and firm, creamy flesh: *Bananas grow in large bunches.* *n.*

band¹ (band) **1** a group travelling or acting together: *a band of robbers, a band of wild dogs.* **2** form a group: *The children banded together to buy a present for their teacher.* **3** a group of musicians: *Dmitri sings and plays keyboards for a rock band.* **4** 🍁 a group of First Nations people living on a reserve and officially recognized as a unit by the government. A single First Nation may be divided into many bands. 1, 3, 4 *n.,* 2 *v.*

band² (band) **1** a strip of colour, or of some material such as metal, cloth, or rubber: *a blue rug with bands of grey. The oak box was strengthened with bands of iron. Put an elastic band around that package.* **2** put a band on: *Scientists often band birds' legs in order to identify them later.* **3** in radio broadcasting, a particular range of wavelengths or frequencies. 1, 3 *n.,* 2 *v.*

band·age (ban′dij) **1** a strip of cloth or other material for covering a wound or injury. **2** put a bandage on. 1 *n.,* 2 *v.,* **band·aged, band·ag·ing.**

Band–Aid (ban′dād′) *a trademark for* a small bandage made of a soft pad attached to the middle of a piece of tape. *n.*

ban·dan·a (ban dan′ə) a large, coloured handkerchief. **Bandanna** is another spelling. *n.*

ban·dit (ban′dit) a robber. *n.*

ban·dy (ban′dē) toss casually around or back and forth: *We bandied around some names for our new cat.* *v.,* **ban·died, ban·dy·ing.**

bang (bang) **1** a sudden loud noise: *She popped a balloon, and the bang scared me.* **2** hit, close, etc. with a sudden loud noise: *The baby was banging the pan with a spoon. The door banged shut.* **3** a violent, noisy blow: *She gave the drum a bang.* 1, 3 *n.,* 2 *v.*

bangs (bangz) a fringe of hair on the forehead: *I have short hair and bangs.* *pl.n.*

ban·ish (ban′ish) send away, especially as a punishment: *She was banished from the game because she was always cheating.* *v.* **—ban′ish·ment,** *n.*

ban·is·ter (ban′i stər) the handrail of a staircase together with its row of supports. *n.*

ban·jo (ban′jō) a stringed musical instrument played with the fingers or a pick. *n., pl.* **ban·jos** or **ban·joes.**

bank¹ (bangk) **1** a long pile or heap: *There was a bank of snow over a metre deep.* **2** pile up; heap up: *The ploughs banked the snow by the side of the road.* **3** the ground beside a river. **4** a shallow place in water; a shoal. The Grand Banks are shallow places in the Atlantic off Newfoundland. **5** the tilting of an airplane when turning in the air. **6** tilt when turning: *The pilot banked the airplane steeply. The airplane banked as it turned south.* **7** cover a fire with ashes so that it will burn slowly. 1, 3–5 *n.,* 2, 6, 7 *v.*

bank² (bangk) **1** a place for saving or borrowing money. **2** do business at a bank: *My mother banks at the branch near her office.* **3** a supply of anything, used and refilled as needed: *a food bank.* 1, 3 *n.,* 2 *v.*
bank on, depend on: *I can bank on Kurt to help me.*

bank³ (bangk) a row or tight group of things: *a bank of switches, a bank of machines.* *n.*

a bat	e bed	i bid	o pot	u cup	th thin
ā cake	ē me	ī bite	ō go	ū rude	ᴛʜ then
ȧ bar	ə about	ər over	ȯ for	ů put	zh measure

bank account (bangk′ ə kount′) 1 an arrangement for putting your money in a bank until it is needed. 2 the sum of money kept in a bank by a person or company: *My bank account is very low right now.*

bank·er[1] (bang′kər) a person or company that manages a bank. *n.* —**bank′ing,** *n.*

✱ **bank·er[2]** (bang′kər) 1 someone who fishes off the Grand Banks. 2 a fishing boat of the Grand Banks: *The crowd cheered as the banker came into port.* *n.*

bank·rupt (bangk′rupt) 1 a person declared unable to pay his or her debts. A court divides the property of a bankrupt among the people that he or she owes money to. 2 unable to pay debts. 3 make bankrupt: *Their last business deal bankrupted them.* 1 *n.,* 2 *adj.,* 3 *v.* —**bank′rupt·cy** (bangk′rəp sē), *n.*

WORD HISTORY...... bankrupt

Bankrupt comes originally from the Italian word *bancarotta* = "bank" + "broken."

ban·ner (ban′ər) 1 flag: *a school banner.* 2 outstanding: *a banner year for Canada at the Olympics.* 1 *n.,* 2 *adj.*

✱ **ban·nock** (ban′ək) a flat, round cake made of flour, salt, and water, especially if cooked over an open fire. Sometimes baking powder is added. *n.*

ban·quet (bang′kwit) a formal dinner or a feast, often with speeches: *The teachers had a banquet for the principal when she retired.* *n.*

ban·tam (ban′təm) 1 a small, brightly coloured type of chicken: *a bantam rooster.* 2 in sports, a class for players under 15 years: *a bantam hockey league.* *n.*

ban·ter (ban′tər) 1 playful teasing; joking: *She didn't mind her friends' banter about her freckles.* 2 talk in a joking or teasing way. 1 *n.,* 2 *v.*

bap·tize (bap′tīz *or* bap tīz′) 1 in Christian churches, to dip under water or sprinkle with water as a sign of washing away sin. 2 give a first name to a person when he or she is baptized; christen: *The baby was baptized Daniel.* *v.,* **bap·tized, bap·tiz·ing.** —**bap′tism,** *n.*

bar (bär) 1 a long, narrow piece of something: *an iron bar, a bar of soap, a bar of chocolate.* 2 close or block by putting a bar or something else across: *He bars the doors every night. The way out was barred by chairs.* 3 anything that blocks the way: *His bad temper was a bar to making friends.* 4 exclude; forbid: *All talking is barred during a study period.* 5 except; excluding: *She is the best student, bar none.* 6 stripe: *a chicken with barred feathers* (*v.*). *The flag had a blue bar on each side of a yellow centre* (*n.*). 7 in music, a unit of rhythm, from one **bar line** to another: *The accent falls on the first note of each bar.* 8 the whole group of practising lawyers: *After passing his law examinations, he was called to the bar.* 9 a place where alcoholic drinks are served. 10 a store counter where certain articles are sold: *a snack bar, a cosmetic bar.* 1, 3, 6–10 *n.,* 2, 4, 6 *v.,* **barred, bar·ring;** 5 *prep.*

barb (bärb) 1 a point sticking out and back from the main point. A fish-hook has a barb on it. 2 a nasty remark. 3 put barbs on. 1, 2 *n.,* 3 *v.* —**barbed,** *adj.*

bar·bar·i·an (bär ber′ē ən) 1 in ancient times, a person belonging to a tribe thought to be uncivilized: *Rome was conquered by barbarian peoples.* 2 not civilized; rude, savage, or ignorant. 1 *n.,* 2 *adj.* —**bar·bar′ic** (bär ber′ ik), *adj.*

bar·ba·rous (bär′bə rəs) so harsh as to be unfit for civilized people: *Torturing people is barbarous.* *adj.* —**bar′ba·rous·ly,** *adv.*

bar·be·cue (bär′bē kyū′) 1 a grill or open fireplace for cooking food over coals or over an open flame. 2 an outdoor meal prepared on a barbecue. 3 roast food over coals or open flame, or in the spicy sauce often used for this. 1–2 *n.,* 3 *v.,* **bar·be·cued, bar·be·cu·ing.**

USING WORDS .... barbecue

You may sometimes see this word written *barbeque,* with a *q.* This is incorrect spelling. Don't use it.

barbed wire (bärbd′ wīr′) heavy wire with short, sharply pointed pieces of wire twisted around it. Barbed wire is used mainly for fences.

bar·ber (bär′bər) a person whose business is cutting hair and shaving or trimming beards. *n.*

bar·bi·can (bär′bə kan′) See the picture at **castle** on page 118. *n.*

bar code (bär′ kōd′) a series of printed lines of different widths that a machine can read to show how much something costs or where it is supposed to go. Bar codes can be printed on cans and boxes in a supermarket, on library books, and on envelopes sent in the mail.

bard (bärd) a poet and singer, especially of long ago: *The bard sang his own poems to the music of his harp.* *n.*

bare (ber) 1 without any clothing, decoration, furniture, or anything extra: *bare legs, bare branches,*

bare walls, the bare facts. 2 make bare; uncover or show: *The dog bared its teeth.* 1 *adj.*, **bar•er, bar•est;** 2 *v.*, **bared, bar•ing.** —**bare′ness,** *n.*
with your bare hands, without tools or weapons: *He can break bricks with his bare hands.*

bare•back (ber′bak′) without a saddle; on a horse's bare back: *to ride bareback (adv.), a bareback rider (adj.).* *adv. or adj.*

bare•foot (ber′fůt′) without shoes or socks on: *A barefoot child played in the puddles (adj.). If you go barefoot, watch out for broken glass (adv.).* *adj. or adv.*

bare•ly (ber′lē) 1 only just; hardly: *He has barely enough money to live on.* 2 in a rather bare style: *The room was furnished barely but neatly.* *adv.*

bar•gain (bär′gən) 1 an agreement to trade or exchange: *Let's make a bargain: I'll do your chores if I can borrow your bike.* 2 try to get a good price or make a good trade: *For ten minutes I stood bargaining with the farmer for her vegetables.* 3 something good for a low price: *These skates are a bargain at $15.* 1, 3 *n.*, 2 *v.*
bargain for, expect; be ready for: *We expected rain, but the hail was more than we bargained for.*
into the bargain, besides; also: *I can't come; I've got piano lessons, and a pile of homework into the bargain.*

barge (bärj) 1 a large, flat-bottomed boat for carrying loads. 2 move clumsily like a barge: *He barged around the room, knocking things over.* 1 *n.*, 2 *v.*, **barged, barg•ing.**
barge in, *Informal.* enter rudely without an invitation.

bar graph (bär′ graf′) a chart showing bars of different lengths in order to compare different amounts: *The longer the bar, the greater the amount it stands for.*

bar•i•tone (ber′ə tōn′) 1 a male voice with a medium range. 2 a singer with this range, or the part of a song written for it. *n.*

Bark is dead wood. It is waterproof, so it protects the living wood inside.

bark[1] (bärk) the tough outside covering of the trunk, branches, and roots of trees. *n.*

bark[2] (bärk) 1 the short, sharp sound a dog makes, or a sound like it, such as a cough. 2 make this sound: *The dog barked.* 3 speak sharply. 1 *n.*, 2, 3 *v.*

bar•ley (bär′lē) a grain used for food and for making malt. *n.*

bar mitz•vah (bär′mits′və) 1 a ceremony that formally brings a boy into the Jewish religious community. 2 a boy who has reached the age of thirteen, the age of religious responsibility.

barn (bärn) a farm building for hay, grain, machinery, and animals. *n.*

bar•na•cle (bär′nə kəl) a small saltwater animal with a shell. It attaches itself to undersea things like rocks, the bottoms of ships, and docks. *n.*

barn•yard (bärn′yärd′) the yard around a barn for farm animals. *n.*

ba•rom•e•ter (bə rom′ə tər) 1 an instrument that measures the pressure of the air and shows likely changes in the weather. 2 anything else that reports or measures changes: *Newspapers are often called barometers of public opinion.* *n.* —**bar′o•met′ric** (ber′ə met′rik), *adj.*

bar•on (ber′ən) in the Middle Ages, a person who held lands or property directly from the sovereign. *n.*

bar•racks (ber′əks) 1 a building or group of buildings for soldiers to live in. 2 a local office or training centre of the Royal Canadian Mounted Police. *n.*

bar•ra•cu•da (ber′ə kū′də) a fish found in warm seas, with long, pointed jaws and strong, sharp teeth. *n.*, *pl.* **bar•ra•cu•da** or **bar•ra•cu•das.**

bar•rage (bə räzh′) a heavy attack with gunfire or words or any other weapon: *The lawyer met a barrage of questions from reporters as she left the courtroom.* *n.*

bar•rel (ber′əl) 1 a container with round, flat ends and curved sides, made of boards held together by hoops. 2 the metal tube of a gun. 3 move with speed and force; rush: *Late for class, he barrelled along the hallway.* 1, 2 *n.*, 3 *v.*

bar•ren (ber′ən) 1 not producing anything: *A desert is barren.* 2 **the Barrens,** a barren stretch of land in northern Canada, west of Hudson Bay. It is also called the **Barren Ground** or **Barren Lands.** 1 *adj.*, 3 *n.*

a bat	e bed	i bid	o pot	u cup	th thin
ā cake	ē me	ī bite	ō go	ū rude	ᴛʜ then
ä bar	ə about	ər over	ȯ for	ů put	zh measure

bar•rette (bə ret′) a hair clip. *n.*

bar•ri•cade (ber′ə kād′) 1 a rough wall for defence, made quickly from whatever is around. 2 block or obstruct with a barricade: *Tory barricaded the doorway with chairs to keep Zack out.* 1 *n.,* 2 *v.,* **bar•ri•cad•ed, bar•ri•cad•ing.**

bar•ri•er (ber′ē ər) something that blocks the way or separates: *Shyness can be a barrier to making friends. A barrier separated the two tennis courts.* *n.*

bar•ter (bär′tər) trade instead of using money to buy or sell: *He bartered a computer game for some CDs* (*v.*). *Barter is still used in some marketplaces* (*n.*). *v. or n.*

ba•salt (bā′ solt) a hard, dark-coloured volcanic rock. *n.*

base[1] (bās) 1 the part that something rests on; the bottom: *The machine rests on a wide base of steel.* 2 a headquarters or main centre: *an army base. This company has its base in Fredericton.* 3 build or rest something on a foundation: *Base your arguments on fact.* 4 a main ingredient: *This dog food has a meat base.* 5 in baseball, any of the four stations that players run to at the corners of the diamond-shaped field. 6 in arithmetic, the number that is the starting point for a numbering system: *The base of the decimal system is ten.* 7 a chemical that works against acids. Bases dissolve in water, and strong ones can burn flesh. **Alkali** is another word for base. 1, 2, 4–6 *n.,* 3 *v.,* **based, bas•ing.**
based on, following; judging by or depending on: *Based on the weather forecast, I advise you to take an umbrella!*

base[2] (bās) 1 mean and selfish; low; cowardly: *To betray a friend is a base thing to do.* 2 not very valuable, compared to something else: *Iron and lead are base metals; gold and silver are precious metals.* *adj.,* **bas•er, bas•est.**

base•ball (bās′bol′) 1 a game played with a bat and ball by two teams of nine players each, on a field with four bases. 2 the ball used in this game. *n.*

base•board (bās′bȯrd′) 1 a strip of wood trim around the walls of a room at the bottom. 2 a board forming the base of anything: *We glued our model onto a wooden baseboard.* *n.*

base•ment (bās′mənt) the lowest storey of a building, partly or completely below ground; cellar. *n.*

ba•ses[1] (bā′sēz) plural of **basis.** *n.*

bas•es[2] (bā′siz) plural of **base**[1]**.** *n.*

bash•ful (bash′fəl) shy and awkward around strangers: *The little child was too bashful to say hello.* *adj.* **—bash′ful•ly,** *adv.* **—bash′ful•ness,** *n.*

ba•sic (bā′sik) forming the base or starting point: *Addition, subtraction, multiplication, and division are the basic operations of arithmetic.* *adj.* **—ba′si•cal•ly,** *adj.*

ba•sin (bā′sən) 1 a wide, shallow bowl used especially to hold water for washing. 2 a low place in land, usually containing water, such as the Annapolis Basin in Nova Scotia. 3 all the land drained by a river and the streams that flow into the river: *the St. Lawrence basin.* *n.*

ba•sis (bā′sis) the fact, idea, feeling, etc. that something is built on: *The basis of their friendship was their interest in hockey.* *n., pl.* **ba•ses** (bā′sēz).

bask (bask) warm oneself pleasantly: *The seals enjoyed basking in the sun.* *v.*

bas•ket (bas′kit) 1 a container made of twigs, strips of wood, plastic, or metal, etc. woven together: *a clothes basket, a wastepaper basket, a fruit basket.* 2 **a** the ring and net used as a goal in basketball. **b** a score made in basketball by tossing the ball through this net. *n.*

bas•ket•ball (bas′kit bol′) 1 a game played with a large, round ball by two teams, usually of five players each. The players try to toss the ball through a ring into a net shaped like a basket but open at the bottom. 2 the ball used in this game. *n.*

bass[1] (bās) 1 the range of notes sung by the lowest male voice. 2 having this range: *a bass singer.* 3 a singer or instrument with such a range, or the part of a song written for it. 1, 3 *n., pl.* **bass•es** (bās′iz); 2 *adj.*

bass[2] (bas) a fish found in both fresh and salt water, used for food. *n., pl.* **bass** or **bass•es.**

bass clef (bās′ klef′) in music: 1 the symbol that shows that the notes on a staff are below middle C. 2 a staff having the bass clef symbol. A note on the fourth line from the bottom is the F below middle C.

bass drum (bās′ drum′) a large drum that can be hit on both sides and makes a deep sound.

bas•soon (bə sün′) in music, a wind instrument with a double reed, a wooden tube, and a curved metal mouthpiece. It has a deep sound. *n.*

baste[1] (bāst) drip or pour melted fat or butter or a sauce on meat as it is roasting: *He basted the turkey to brown it and keep it moist.* *v.,* **bast•ed, bast•ing.**

baste[2] (bāst) sew temporarily with long, loose stitches: *I basted the seam before sewing it on the machine.* *v.,* **bast•ed, bast•ing.**

bat[1] (bat) 1 a specially shaped wooden stick or club, used to hit the ball in baseball, cricket, etc. 2 hit with a bat; hit: *He bats well. I batted the balloon over to him with my hand.* 1 *n.,* 2 *v.,* **bat·ted, bat·ting.**
at bat or **up to bat,** taking a turn batting.
go to bat for someone, support or stand up for someone.
not bat an eyelash, show no surprise at all: *When I dyed my hair green, nobody batted an eyelash!*
right off the bat, right away.

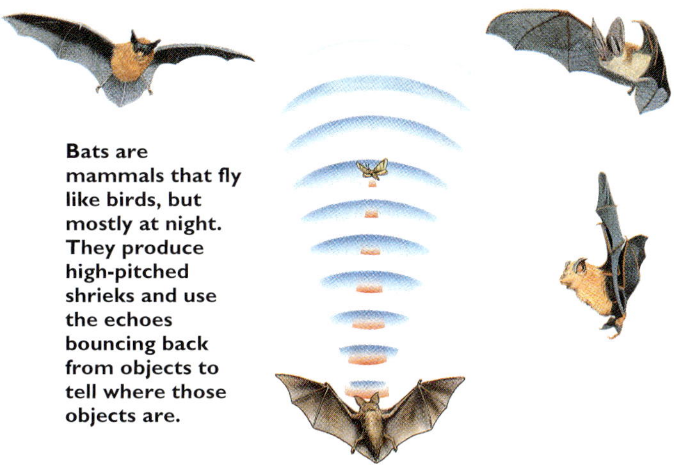

Bats are mammals that fly like birds, but mostly at night. They produce high-pitched shrieks and use the echoes bouncing back from objects to tell where those objects are.

bat[2] (bat) a flying animal that resembles a mouse with skinlike wings. Bats fly at night and feed mostly on insects. They find their way by the echo from the sound they make. *n.* —**bat′like′,** *adj.*

batch (bach) a quantity of anything made or handled as one lot or set: *a batch of cookies, a batch of mail.* *n.*

🍁 **ba·teau** (ba tō′) a light, flat-bottomed riverboat: *Bateaux were used to carry freight and passengers between Montréal and Kingston.* *n., pl.* **ba·teaux** (ba tōz′).

bath (bath) 1 a washing of the body. 2 the water for a bath: *Your bath is ready.* 3 a tub, a room, or other place for bathing: *The cabin had no bath, so we built one.* 4 give a bath to: *Mother baths the baby every day.* 1–3 *n., pl.* **baths** (baᴛʜz); 4 *v.*

bathe (bāᴛʜ) 1 take a bath: *He bathes every morning.* 2 give a bath to: *We bathe our dog regularly.* 3 put water or other liquid on something to wash or soothe it: *Bathe your feet if they are tired. The doctor told her to bathe her eyes with the lotion.* 4 cover or surround: *The valley was bathed in sunlight.* *v.,* **bathed, bath·ing.** —**bath′er,** *n.*

bathing suit (bā′ᴛʜing sūt′) a garment worn for swimming.

bath·robe (bath′rōb′) a loose robe worn when going to and from a bath or when relaxing. *n.*

bath·room (bath′rūm′) a room with a toilet, a sink, and often a bath or shower. A room with toilets in a public building is usually called a **washroom.** *n.*

bath·tub (bath′tub′) a tub to take a bath in. *n.*

ba·tik (bə tēk′) 1 the art of making designs on cloth by dyeing only part at a time, protecting the rest with a coating of melted wax which is later removed. 2 a design made in this way. *n.*

bat mitz·vah (bȧt′ mits′və) a Jewish girl who has reached the age of 12, the age of religious responsibility.

ba·ton (bə ton′) 1 a light, hollow metal rod twirled as an art: *She marched ahead of the band, twirling a baton.* 2 a stick used by the leader of a band or choir to keep time and direct the performance. 3 a stick passed from runner to runner in a relay race. *n.*

bat·tal·ion (bə tal′yən) 1 a large group of soldiers. 2 any large group organized to act together: *A battalion of volunteers helped to rescue the flood victims.* *n.*

bat·ter[1] (bat′ər) hit again and again so as to bruise, damage, or break: *The firefighter battered down the door with a heavy axe.* *v.* —**bat′tered,** *adj.*

bat·ter[2] (bat′ər) a thick liquid mixture made by beating together flour, milk, eggs, etc. Pancakes and muffins are made from batter. Other things are often coated in batter and deep-fried. *n.*

bat·ter[3] (bat′ər) the player whose turn it is to bat in baseball, cricket, etc. *n.*

battering ram (bat′ər ing ram′) a war machine consisting of a long, thick pole carried by many soldiers, once used for breaking down the walls or gates of enemy castles and towns.

bat·ter·y (bat′ə rē) 1 a container holding materials that produce electricity by chemical action. A watch battery is tiny, round, and flat, while a flashlight battery is long and tube-shaped. A car battery is a large, heavy box with smaller batteries inside it: *Most flashlights work on two batteries.* 2 any set of things or people acting together: *A battery of loudspeakers blared through the hall.* *n., pl.* **bat·ter·ies.**

bat·tle (bat′əl) 1 fight or struggle: *a battle with enemy soldiers, a battle of words, the battle against poverty* (*n.*). *Our team is battling for first place in the league* (*v.*). 2 war: *His wounds were received in battle.* 1, 2 *n.,* 1 *v.,* **bat·tled, bat·tling.**

a bat	e bed	i bid	o pot	u cup	th **thin**
ā cake	ē me	ī bite	ō go	ū rude	ᴛʜ **then**
ȧ bar	ə about	ər over	ȯ for	u̇ put	zh measure

bat·tle–axe (bat′ə laks′) a kind of axe once used as a weapon of war. *n., pl.* **bat·tle-ax·es.**

bat·tle·field (bat′əl fēld′) a place where a battle is fought or has been fought. *n.*

bat·tle·ment (bat′əl mənt) a low wall for defence at the top of a castle tower or wall, with spaces to shoot through. *n.*

baux·ite (bok′sīt) a claylike mineral. We get aluminum from it. *n.*

WORD HISTORY....... bauxite

Rocks and minerals are often named after the places they were found. Bauxite is named after a place called Les Baux in France.

What South American places are **amazonite** and **andesite** named after?

bawl (bol) **1** *Informal.* cry loudly: *The small boy bawled whenever he hurt himself.* **2** yell or make a loud noise: *The sergeant bawled out a command.* **3** a loud cry: *the bawl of a calf.* 1, 2 *v.*, 3 *n.*
bawl out, scold: *He bawled me out for losing a computer file.*

bay¹ (bā) a part of a sea or lake reaching into the land, such as Hudson Bay or the Bay of Fundy. *n.*

bay² (bā) a space, area, platform, etc. used for a special purpose: *The truck backed up to the loading bay of the warehouse.* *n.*

bay³ (bā) howl or bark: *The hunters heard the distant bay of the hounds* (*n.*). *Dogs sometimes bay at the moon* (*v.*). *n. or v.*
at bay, a forced to face an enemy when escape is impossible: *The deer stood at bay on the edge of the cliff.* **b** being kept away or fought off: *The movie star's bodyguard held the reporters at bay.*

bay⁴ (bā) a small evergreen tree with smooth, shiny leaves. Bay leaves are used for flavouring food. **Laurel** is another name for this tree. *n.*

bay⁵ (bā) **1** reddish brown: *a bay horse* (*adj.*). **2** a reddish brown horse. 1, 2 *n.*, 1 *adj.*

bay·o·net (bā′ə net′) **1** a blade for piercing or stabbing, attached to the end of the barrel of a rifle. **2** pierce or stab with a bayonet. 1 *n.*, 2 *v.*, **bay·o·net·ed, bay·o·net·ing.**

bay window (bā′ win′dō) a large window or set of windows that stick out from a wall, forming extra space in a room.

ba·zaar (bə zär′) **1** a market. **2** a sale, especially of used or homemade things, held to raise money. *n.*

BB gun (bē′bē gun′) a gun that shoots small, round metal balls called **BBs,** which can cause serious injury.

BCE *abbreviation for* before the Common Era, the time since the birth of Jesus Christ. For times after Jesus Christ was born, **CE** is used: *From 20 BCE to 50 CE is 70 years.*

beach (bēch) **1** an almost flat shore of sand or little stones at the edge of a lake or ocean. **2** pull up on the shore: *to beach a canoe.* 1 *n.*, 2 *v.*

bea·con (bē′kən) **1** a fire or light used as a signal to guide or warn: *The beacon in the window guided him through the blizzard to the house.* **2** a tall tower for a signal light; lighthouse. *n.*

bead (bēd) **1** a bit of glass, plastic, clay, etc. with a hole through it, so that it can be strung on a thread with others like it. **2 beads,** *pl.* **a** a necklace of beads: *She wore her new beads to the party.* **b** a string of beads used in saying prayers. **3** a tiny ball, drop, or bubble: *beads of sweat.* *n.* **—bead′ed,** *adj.* **—bead′like′,** *adj.*

bead·y (bē′dē) small, round, and shiny: *That bird has beady eyes.* *adj.,* **bead·i·er, bead·i·est.**

beak (bēk) **1** the horny mouth of a bird. **2** anything like this, such as the mouth of some turtles. **3** *Slang.* a person's mouth or nose. *n.*

beak·er (bē′kər) **1** a glass container with a wide top and a little spout, used in laboratories. **2** a large cup or glass. *n.*

beam (bēm) **1** a large, long piece of wood, concrete, or steel used to support buildings. **2** a ray or rays of light: *The beam from the flashlight made the cat's eyes shine.* **3** send out rays of light; shine. **4** look or smile brightly: *Her face beamed with delight.* **5** a radio signal. **6** broadcast by radio: *to beam programs to the Northwest Territories.* 1, 2, 5 *n.*, 3, 4, 6 *v.*

bean (bēn) **1** a smooth, rather flat seed used as a vegetable: *pork and beans.* **2** the long pod containing these seeds: *When young and fresh, green or yellow beans are good eaten raw.* **3** any seed shaped like a bean: *Coffee beans are seeds of the coffee plant.* *n.*

bean·bag (bēn′bag′) a small bag partly filled with dried beans or pellets, used to toss in play. A **beanbag chair** is a very large, specially shaped beanbag for sitting in. *n.*

bean curd (bēn′ kərd′) another name for **tofu,** a food made of ground cooked soybeans. It looks a bit like cheese and is very high in protein.

Bears in Canada

Bears are carnivorous (meat-eating) but they also eat roots, berries, and honey.

bear[1] (ber) **1** carry: *Ships came from faraway places, bearing wonderful foods. That ice is too thin to bear your weight.* **2** endure: *She can't bear the noise.* **3** produce fruit: *This tree bore a lot of apples last year.* **4** give birth to: *Women bear children. That woman has borne four boys. I was born on June 4.* *v.,* **bore, borne** or **born, bear·ing.** **—bear'a·ble,** *adj.* **—bear'er,** *n.*
bear down, a press or push down: *Don't bear down so hard with the marker or you'll ruin the tip.* **b** try hard; work seriously: *You'll have to bear down if you expect a better mark next term.* **c** come quickly and dangerously nearer and nearer: *They paddled furiously when they saw the ship bearing down on them.*
bear on, have an effect on; have something to do with: *The answer did not bear on the question.*
bear out, show or prove that something is true.
bear up, stay brave and hopeful during a hard time.
bear with, be patient with.

bear[2] (ber) **1** a large, heavy animal with fur, a very short tail, and large, flat paws. The **brown bear, black bear,** and **polar bear** are all found in Canada. **2** a grouchy person. *n.*
a bear for punishment, someone who loves challenges and hard work.

beard (bērd) **1** the hair growing on a man's chin and cheeks. **2** something that looks like this, such as the tuft of hair on a goat's chin, or the hairs on the head of a wheat plant. *n.*

bear·ing (ber'ing) **1** a person's way of standing, sitting, or moving: *The dancer had a graceful bearing.* **2** connection in thought or meaning: *Your question has no bearing on the problem.* **3 bearings,** *pl.* **a** a description of a person's exact position: *The pilot radioed her bearings.* **b** knowledge of where you are: *Without a guide in the bush, we would soon have lost our bearings.* *n.*

Bear·lake (ber'lāk') **1** a First Nations people living around the southwestern end of Great Bear Lake in Northwest Territories. **2** their language, which belongs to the Athapascan family. **3** having to do with these people or their language. 1, 2 *n.,* 3 *adj.*

beast (bēst) **1** any animal except a human, especially a four-footed animal. **2** a cruel or very rude person. *n.*

a bat	e bed	i bid	o pot	u cup	th thin
ā cake	ē me	ī bite	ō go	ū rude	ᴛʜ then
à bar	ə about	ər over	ò for	ü put	zh measure

beast·ly (bēst′lē) terrible or terribly: *Watch out, I'm in a beastly mood (adj.). It's beastly cold out there today (adv.).* *adj.,* **beast·li·er, beast·li·est,** *or adv.*

beat (bēt) **1** hit hard, again and again: *The cruel rider beat his horse.* **2** make a sound by hitting or being hit, especially according to a rhythm: *The drums beat loudly. The rain beats on the window.* **3** the sound made in this way: *We heard the beat of a drum.* **4** in music: **a** a single unit of time: *three beats to a measure.* **b** the rhythm: *a song with a fast beat.* **5** move in and out, back and forth, up and down, etc.: *The bird beat its wings. Her heart beat fast with joy.* **6** win against: *Their team beat ours by a huge score.* **7** stir thoroughly: *to beat eggs.* **8** the area regularly patrolled by a police officer. **9** *Informal.* tired; worn out: *"I'm beat," he said, flopping into a chair.* 1, 2, 5–7 *v.,* **beat, beat·en, beat·ing;** 3, 4, 8 *n.,* 9 *adj.*
off the beaten path, where few people go.

beau (bō) a humorous word for "boyfriend." *n., pl.* **beaus** or **beaux** (bōz).

beau·ti·ful (byū′tə fəl) very pleasing to see, hear, experience, or think about: *a beautiful picture, beautiful music, a beautiful dream.* **Beauteous** (byü′tē əs) is a poetic word for this. *adj.* —**beau′ti·ful·ly,** *adv.*

beau·ti·fy (byū′tə fī) make beautiful: *Flowers beautify a garden. We beautified the room with paintings.* *v.,* **beau·ti·fied, beau·ti·fy·ing.** —**beau′ti·fi·ca′tion,** *n.*

beau·ty (byū′tē) **1** the quality that pleases in a person, flowers, music, pictures, etc.: *That painting captures the beauty of the forest. There is beauty in a kind act.* **2** something beautiful: *the beauties of nature.* **3** a beautiful woman. *n., pl.* **beau·ties.**

The beaver uses its strong teeth to cut down trees for building dams and lodges. The front teeth never wear out because they keep growing throughout the beaver's life.

bea·ver (bē′vər) a soft-furred animal with a broad, flat tail and feet adapted to swimming. It is a Canadian symbol. *n.*

be·came (bi kām′) the past tense of **become:** *The seed became a plant.* *v.*

be·cause (bi kuz′) **Because** is used to tell the reason for something: *Most children play tag because they enjoy it. Because we were very late, we ran.* *conj.*
because of, by reason of; on account of: *We did not go because of the rain.*

beck (bek)
at someone's beck and call, having to carry out every little wish or command of someone: *A waiter is at the beck and call of people in a restaurant.* *n.*

beck·on (bek′ən) signal with the hand or head: *He beckoned me to follow.* *v.*

be·come (bi kum′) **1** **Become** is used to talk about a change: *It is becoming colder. He became a father last year.* **2** seem proper for; suit; look good on: *That white dress becomes you.* *v.,* **be·came, be·come, be·com·ing.**
become of, happen to: *What has become of the box of candy?*

be·com·ing (bi kum′ing) fitting; suitable: *Burping at a banquet is not very becoming.* *adj.* —**be·com′ing·ly,** *adv.*

bed (bed) **1** anything to sleep or rest on. **2** put to bed or go to bed: *She bedded her horse down with straw. The hikers bedded down in sleeping bags under the stars.* **3** the bottom or base of something: *a muddy stream bed. They set the post in a bed of concrete.* **4** a piece of ground for planting a garden: *We have a large bed of roses.* **5** a layer: *a bed of coal.* 1, 3, 4, 5 *n.,* 2 *v.,* **bed·ded, bed·ding.**

Word Family.......... bed

bedbug: an insect found in beds
bedclothes: sheets, blankets, quilts, etc.
bedding: sheets, blankets, quilts, etc.
bedroll: rolled-up blankets or sleeping bag
bedroom: a room used for sleeping in bed
bedside: the side of a bed
bedspread: a cover spread over a bed
bedstead: the framework of a bed
bedtime: the usual time for going to bed

bed·lam (bed′ləm) uproar; confusion: *When the home team won, there was bedlam in the arena.* *n.*

be·drag·gled (bi drag′əld) wet, messy or dirty, and hanging limp: *She tried to comb her bedraggled hair.* *adj.*

bed·rid·den (bed′rid′ən) having to stay in bed; not able to be up and around: *I was bedridden with the flu for two days.* *adj.*

bed•rock (bed′rok′) the solid rock beneath the soil and looser rocks. *n.*

bee[1] (bē) an insect with four wings that lives in large groups and makes honey and wax. Female bees can sting. *n.*
a bee in your bonnet, something you are always thinking and talking about: *Dad has a bee in his bonnet about messy countertops.*

bee[2] (bē) a gathering for work and fun: *a quilting bee, a spelling bee.* *n.*

beech (bēch) a tree with smooth, grey bark and glossy leaves. It bears a sweet nut that is good to eat, and its wood is often used for furniture. *n.*

beef (bēf) **1** the meat from a steer, cow, or bull, used for food. **2** *Slang.* complain: *Some people are always beefing.* **3** *Slang.* a complaint.
beef up, *Informal.* make stronger, heavier, etc. 1, 3 *n.,* 2 *v.*

beef•steak (bēf′stāk′) a slice of beef for broiling or frying. *n.*

beef•y (bē′fē) **1** strong; solid; heavy. **2** like beef: *a beefy taste.* *adj.,* **beef•i•er, beef•i•est.**

The honey and wax that bees produce can be gathered more easily if the bees can be trained to live in a manufactured beehive.

bee•hive (bē′hīv′) **1** a hive or house for bees. **2** a busy, crowded place: *The shopping centre is a beehive in December.* *n.*

bee•line (bē′līn′)
make a beeline for, head straight toward something: *As soon as we enter a toy store, Mark makes a beeline for the board game section.* *n.*

beep (bēp) **1** a short, sharp sound made by a machine. It is often a signal: *A beep from the microwave told us that our dinner was ready.* **2** make or cause to make this sound: *Someone was beeping the horn outside.* 1 *n.,* 2 *v.*

beep•er (bē′pər) a small portable device that makes a beeping sound to let you know you should phone somebody, take a pill, etc. A beeper is controlled by radio waves: *She had just fallen asleep when her beeper sounded.* *n.*

beer (bēr) **1** an alcoholic drink made from malt, water, yeast, and hops. **2** a soft drink made from roots or plants, such as root beer or ginger beer. *n.*

🍁 **beer parlour** or **parlor** (bēr′ pȧr′lər) a room in a hotel or tavern where beer is sold.

bees•wax (bēz′waks′) the wax made by bees, which they use to build their honeycomb. *n.*

beet (bēt) the round, red, sweet root of a leafy plant, eaten as a vegetable. White beets are a source of sugar. *n.*

bee•tle (bē′təl) an insect with two pairs of wings—the hard, shiny front pair protects the soft flying pair. *n.*

be•fall (bi fol′) an old or poetic word for "happen"; happen to: *Whatever befalls, you can count on me. An accident must have befallen them.* *v.,* **be•fell, be•fall•en, be•fall•ing.**

be•fit (bi fit′) be fit for; be proper or suitable for: *Wear clothes that befit the occasion.* *v.,* **be•fit•ted, be•fit•ting.**

be•fore (bi fȯr′) **1** earlier than something else: *We always play games before the bell rings (conj.). The main course comes before dessert (prep.). Come at five o'clock, not before (adv.).* **2** in the past: *He has never been late before.* **3** in front or ahead of someone or something: *The door opened and a little girl stood before me (prep.). Their guide went before to see if the road was safe (adv.).* **4** rather than: *I'll give up the trip before I go with them (conj.). I'd take ice cream before candy (prep.).* 1, 3, 4 *prep.,* 1–3 *adv.,* 1, 4 *conj.*

be•fore•hand (bi fȯr′hand′) ahead of time: *We got everything ready beforehand.* *adv.*

be•friend (bi frend′) act as a friend to; help: *The police officer befriended the lost boy.* *v.*

beg (beg) **1** ask people to give you food, clothes, or money as a gift: *The old man said that he had no way to live except by begging.* **2** ask humbly or with all your heart: *He begged his sister to forgive him.* *v.,* **begged, beg•ging.**
beg off, escape from a promise, duty, etc. by asking: *Although he had promised to go biking with me, he begged off because of a headache.*

a bat	e bed	i bid	o pot	u cup	th thin
ā cake	ē me	ī bite	ō go	ū rude	ᴛʜ then
ȧ bar	ə about	ər over	ȯ for	u̇ put	zh measure

be•gan (bi gan′) the past tense of **begin:** *Snow began to fall early in the evening.* *v.*

beg•gar (beg′ər) **1** a person who lives by begging. **2** make poor; bring to poverty: *Your wasteful spending will beggar you.* 1 *n.*, 2 *v.*

be•gin (bi gin′) start: *to begin work. I began reading the book yesterday. The program began two years ago.* *v.*, **be•gan, be•gun, be•gin•ning.**

be•gin•ner (bi gin′ər) a person learning to do something for the first time: *You skate well for a beginner.* *n.*

be•gin•ning (bi gin′ing) **1** a start: *Make a good beginning.* **2** the first part: *I enjoyed this book from beginning to end.* **3** the first cause; the source: *One wrong decision was the beginning of all my problems.* **4** first: *This is the beginning lesson of the spelling book.* **5** just starting: *a beginning student.* 1–3 *n.*, 4, 5 *adj.*

be•gone (bi gon′) an old word for "go away": *"Begone!" cried the prince.* *interj.*

be•gun (bi gun′) the past participle of **begin:** *The work was begun on Monday. It has begun to rain.* *v.*

be•half (bi haf′)
on behalf of or **in behalf of,** in support of; for: *I am speaking on behalf of my friend.* *n.*

be•have (bi hāv′) **1** act: *She behaved very politely the whole time.* **2** be good: *"Behave, or I'll take you home," said her mother. Did you behave yourself?* *v.*, **be•haved, be•hav•ing.**

be•hav•iour or **be•hav•ior** (bi hāv′yər) **1** a way of acting; actions: *His sulky behaviour turned everyone off.* **2** what a plant, substance, body, etc. does or what happens to it according to the laws of nature: *the behaviour of water when heated.* *n.*

be•head (bi hed′) cut off the head of. *v.*

be•held (bi held′) the past tense and past participle of **behold:** *We beheld a strange and frightening scene. Never before had he beheld such beauty.* *v.*

be•hind (bi hīnd′) **1** at or toward the back of someone or something: *Stand behind me (prep.). They walked along, the dog following behind (adv.).* **2** *Informal.* rear end; seat: *He fell on his behind.* **3** supporting: *Her friends are behind her.* **4** late; later than someone or something else: *The buses are behind today (adv.). This puppy is behind the others in its growth (prep.).* 1, 3, 4 *prep.*, 1, 4 *adv.*, 2 *n.*

be•hold (bi hōld′) an old or poetic word for "see" or "look at": *They wanted to behold the sunrise. Behold the king!* *v.*, **be•held, be•hold•ing.** —**be•hold′er,** *n.*

be•ing (bē′ing) **1** a person; a living creature: *Men, women, and children are human beings.* **2** life; existence: *This world came into being long ago.* *n.*

be•lat•ed (bi lā′tid) late: *She suddenly remembered that her friend's birthday had been the day before, so she sent a belated birthday card.* *adj.* —**be•lat′ed•ly,** *adv.*

belch (belch) **1** burp. **2** throw out with force: *The volcano belched fire and smoke.* 1, 2 *v.*, 1 *n.*

bel•fry (bel′frē) a tower for a bell or bells. *n.*, *pl.* **bel•fries.**
have bats in the belfry, be a little crazy.

be•lief (bi lēf′) **1** what someone thinks is true; opinion: *It was once common belief that the world was flat.* **2** the action of accepting something as true: *Belief did not come easily—his story was so strange.* **3** religious faith; creed: *All are welcome here, regardless of belief.* *n.*

be•lieve (bi lēv′) **1** think something is true or real: *We all believe that the earth is round. Do you believe in ghosts?* **2** think somebody tells the truth: *My friends believe me.* **3** have faith; trust: *I'll believe in you, Cas, no matter what.* *v.*, **be•lieved, be•liev•ing.** —**be•liev′er,** *n.* —**be•liev′a•ble,** *adj.*

be•lit•tle (bi lit′əl) put down; try to make someone or something seem unimportant: *Jealous people belittled the explorer's great discoveries.* *v.*, **be•lit•tled, be•lit•tling.**

A bell is made by pouring molten metal between a solid core mould and an outer mould in the shape of a bell.

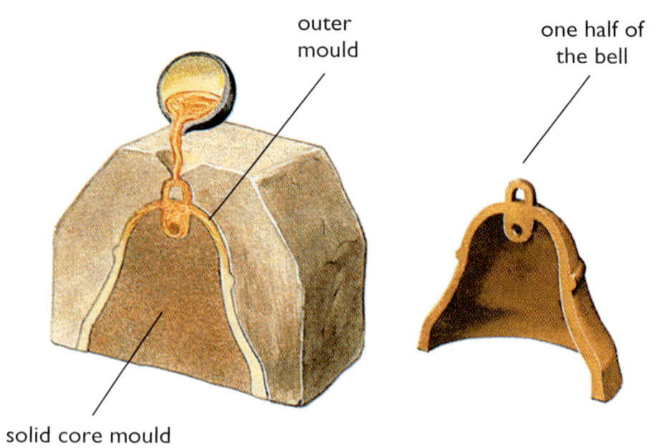

bell (bel) **1** a hollow metal object that rings when it is struck. It is often shaped like an upside-down cup. **2** the stroke or sound of a bell: *Our teacher dismissed us before the last bell.* **3** a bell-shaped part of something, such as the end of a trumpet. **Bell bottoms** are pants that flare out at the bottom. *n.*

belle (bel) a beautiful woman or girl, especially the most beautiful one: *She was the belle of the ball.* *n.*

bel·lig·er·ent (bə lij′ə rənt) **1** ready to fight or quarrel: *They get belligerent if you disagree with them.* **2** at war: *belligerent nations.* *adj.*
—bel·lig′er·ent·ly, *adv.* **—bel·lig′er·ence,** *n.*

bel·low (bel′ō) **1** roar as a bull does. **2** shout in a deep, loud voice: *The lifeguard bellowed to the swimmers to stay near the shore.* **3** the sound of either of these. 1, 2 *v.,* 3 *n.*

bel·lows (bel′ōz) a tool for blowing air, that people use to make a fire burn stronger. It was like a box that was wider at one end than the other and had sides made of a soft material. When you pressed the top and bottom together, the sides folded up and the air inside was pushed out through a small opening at the narrow end. The folding part of an accordion is also called a bellows. *pl. or sing.n.*

bel·ly (bel′ē) **1** the part of the body which contains the stomach and intestines; abdomen. **2** the bulging part of anything, or the hollow in it: *the belly of a ship.* **3** swell out; bulge: *The sails bellied in the wind.* 1, 2 *n., pl.* **bel·lies;** 3 *v.,* **bel·lied, bel·ly·ing.**

belly button (bel′ē but′ən) *Informal.* navel.

be·long (bi long′) **1** have a proper place: *That file belongs in this folder.* **2** be accepted: *Right away, they made me feel that I belonged.* *v.*
belong to, a be the property of: *Does this cap belong to you?* **b** be a part of or be a member of: *She belongs to the local swim club.*

be·long·ings (bi long′ingz) things that belong to a person. *pl.n.*

be·lov·ed (bi luv′id *or* bi luvd′) **1** loved very much; precious. **2** a person who is loved. 1 *adj.,* 2 *n.*

be·low (bi lō′) **1** in or to a lower place or part: *From the airplane we could see the fields below.* **2** lower than; under: *My brother's room is below mine. No one got below 9 out of 15 on the quiz.* **3** below zero on a thermometer: *That morning it was ten below.* 1 *adv.,* 2 *prep.,* 3 *adj.*

belt (belt) **1** a strip of leather, cloth, etc. worn around the body to tighten or hold up clothing, to hold tools, or as a decoration. **2** any broad strip or band; an area or region: *a belt of trees. The wheat belt is where wheat is grown.* **3** an endless band joining parts in a motor, so that when one moves, so does the other. A belt moves the fan in a car. **4** put a belt around. **5** *Informal.* hit suddenly and hard: *The bully belted me in the jaw.* **6** a hard, sudden hit. 1–3, 6 *n.,* 4–5 *v.*
belt out, sing loudly.

be·lu·ga (bə lū′gə) a small white whale that lives in the Arctic and as far south as the Gulf of St. Lawrence. Like some other whales, the beluga is an endangered species. *n.*

bench (bench) **1** a long seat, usually of wood or stone. **2** a worktable used by a carpenter or other worker: *He worked at his bench in the basement.* **3** a judge or a group of judges sitting in a law court: *Bring the prisoner before the bench.* **4** the position of being a judge: *The lawyer was appointed to the bench.* *n.*

bend (bend) **1** turn or curve out of a straight line: *The strong man bent the iron bar as if it were rubber. The branch began to bend as I climbed along it.* **2** a turn or curve: *a sharp bend in the road.* **3** direct: *Our steps were bent toward home now. She bent her mind to her homework.* **4** bow; stoop: *She bent to pick up a stone.* 1, 3, 4 *v.,* **bent, bend·ing;** 2 *n.*
around the bend, *Informal.* crazy: *Her knuckle-cracking nearly drove me around the bend.*
bend over backward, try very hard for someone else: *We bent over backward to make him feel at home.*

be·neath (bi nēth′) **1** below. **2** not good enough for: *The proud girl thought washing dishes was beneath her.* 1 *adv.,* 1, 2 *prep.*

ben·e·fac·tor (ben′ə fak′tər) a person who has helped others through gifts or actions. *n.*

USING WORDS ...... benefactor

A **benefactor** helps others: *Benefactors donate clothing and supplies to homeless shelters every year.*

A **patron** sponsors or supports a specific person or cause: *Our theatre is very lucky to have such a generous patron.*

A **humanitarian** tries to help humankind in general: *A group of humanitarians helped the community rebuild their homes after an earthquake struck their village.*

ben·e·fi·cial (ben′ə fish′əl) helpful: *Sunshine is beneficial to plants.* *adj.* **—ben′e·fi′cial·ly,** *adv.*

a bat	e bed	i bid	o pot	u cup	th thin
ā cake	ē me	ī bite	ō go	ū rude	ᴛʜ then
à bar	ə about	ər over	ȯ for	u̇ put	zh measure

ben•e•fit (ben′ə fit) **1** a good, helpful thing or result: *One of the benefits of exercise is fitness.* **2** be good for: *Rest will benefit a sick person.* **3** be helped; receive good: *How will we benefit from the new rules?* **4** a concert, show, etc. done to raise money. **5** **benefits,** *pl.* money from the government to help people who need it. 1, 4, 5 *n.,* 2, 3 *v.,* **ben•e•fit•ed** or **ben•e•fit•ted, ben•e•fit•ing** or **ben•e•fit•ting.**

be•nev•o•lent (bə nev′ə lənt) kind: *Helping at the food bank is a benevolent act.* *adj.*
—be•nev′o•lent•ly, *adv.* **—be•nev′o•lence,** *n.*

bent (bent) **1** a past tense and past participle of **bend:** *He bent the wire. You have bent the frames of my glasses!* **2** not straight; curved; crooked: *a bent branch.* **3** a habit or talent: *You have a bent for drawing.* 1 *v.,* 2 *adj.,* 3 *n.*
bent on, determined to do something: *She is bent on becoming a pilot.*
bent out of shape, *Slang.* angry.

Be•oth•uk (bē oth′ək) a First Nations people that used to live in Newfoundland. None are alive today. *n.*

be•queath (bi kwēth′) give or leave something to someone who comes after you: *The father bequeathed the farm to his daughter. My mom bequeathed her sense of humour to me.* *v.*

be•reaved (bi rēvd′) suffering from the death of someone: *The bereaved relatives and friends comforted one another.* *adj.*

be•reft (bi reft′)
bereft of, left without: *Bereft of hope and friends, the old man led a wretched life.* *adj.*

be•ret (bə rā′) a soft, round cap of wool, felt, etc., with no brim or visor. *n.*

Many berries, such as strawberries and currants, are used for food.

ber•ry (ber′ē) a small, juicy fruit that has two or more seeds. *n., pl.* **ber•ries.**

ber•serk (bər zərk′)
go berserk, go into a frenzy: *Paul went berserk when he learned the bus had left without him.* *adj. or adv.*

berth (bərth) **1** a place to sleep on a ship, train, or aircraft. **2** a place for a ship to stay in a harbour. *n.*

be•seech (bi sēch′) a poetic or formal word for "ask earnestly" or "beg": *I beseech you to stop fighting.* *v.,* **be•sought, be•seech•ing.**

be•set (bi set′) attack or surround on all sides: *beset by doubts. In the swamp we were beset by mosquitoes.* *v.,* **be•set, be•set•ting.**

be•side (bi sīd′) by the side of; near; close to: *Grass grows beside the creek.* *prep.*
beside oneself, out of one's mind: *He was beside himself with worry over his lost dog.*
beside the point, not related to the question or topic.

be•sides (bi sīdz′) **1** also; more than that; moreover: *He didn't want to quarrel; besides, he had come to enjoy himself.* **2** in addition to: *Others came to the picnic besides our own family.* 1 *adv.,* 2 *prep.*

be•siege (bi sēj′) **1** surround and try to capture, often for a long time: *The Greeks besieged the city of Troy for ten years.* **2** overwhelm with requests, questions, etc.: *The gold medallist was besieged with requests for her autograph.* *v.,* **be•sieged, be•sieg•ing.**

be•sought (bi sot′) the past tense and past participle of **beseech.** *v.*

best (best) **1** most excellent: *Who does the best work (adj.)? We want only the best (n.).* **2** in the most excellent way: *Who reads best?* **3** favourite; closest: *your best friend.* **4** the most you can do or give: *I did my best to explain.* **5** beat; defeat: *Our team was bested in the final game.* 1, 3 *adj.,* 2 *adv.,* 1, 4 *n.,* 5 *v.*
at best, under the most favourable circumstances: *Summer is at best rather short.*
get the best of, beat; defeat.
make the best of, do as well as possible with: *Try to make the best of a bad job.*
the best part of, most of: *He worked on his project for the best part of the day.*

be•stow (bi stō′) give something valuable to someone: *The Governor General bestowed a medal on the boy who rescued the baby.* *v.*

bet (bet) **1** promise to give something to someone you disagree with if that person is right and you are wrong: *I bet you a quarter I will pass this test.* **2** a promise of this kind: *I made a bet that I would pass.* **3** the money or thing promised: *A quarter is not much of a bet.*

4 be very sure: *I bet they'll be late.* 1, 4 *v.,* **bet, bet·ting;** 2, 3 *n.*
a safe bet, something you can be sure of.

be·tide (bi tīd′)
woe betide, something bad will happen to: *Woe betide the person who hurts my little brother!* *v.,* **be·tid·ed, be·tid·ing.**

be·tray (bi trā′) **1** be unfaithful or disloyal to: *She betrayed her friends by breaking her promise. The traitors betrayed their country.* **2** show; reveal: *His smile betrayed his amusement. You betrayed our secret.* *v.*
—be·tray′al, *n.*

be·troth (bi trōᴛʜ′) an old or poetic word for "promise" or "engage to marry": *The prince and his true love were betrothed.* *v.* **—be·troth′al,** *n.*

bet·ter (bet′ər) **1** more desirable or of higher quality: *We need a better computer than this.* **2** in a more excellent way: *I will plan better next time.* **3** improved in health: *Are you feeling better?* **4** improve: *Good coaching helped us better our score.* **5** a person or thing that is more desirable or excellent: *Which is the better of the two books?* 1, 3 *adj.,* 2 *adv.,* 4 *v.,* 5 *n.* **—bet′ter·ment,** *n.*
better off, in a better condition: *We're better off now that Mom has a job.*
get the better of, beat; defeat: *The tortoise got the better of the hare.*
had better, should: *I had better go before it rains.*

USING WORDS ...... better

In informal speech, people often say **better** instead of **had better**: *I better go before it rains.*

Always use **had better** in formal language: *You had better be careful in your choice of words.*

be·tween (bi twēn′) **Between** is used: **1** to talk about a space, time, or amount that has two things as its boundaries: *between the house and the barn, between three and four o'clock, between five and ten dollars (prep.). We watched the moon until a cloud came between (adv.).*
2 to talk about a comparison, choice, activity, or connection that involves two things or people: *an argument between a brother and sister. You can choose between this video and that one. Jess and I went fishing; between us we caught nine fish. There is now a road between Nova Scotia and Prince Edward Island.* 1, 2 *prep.,* 1 *adv.*
▶ See the entry for **among.**
between a rock and a hard place, forced to choose one of two bad things or situations.
between you and me, as a secret: *Let's keep this between you and me.*

be·twixt (bi twikst′) an old-fashioned word for "between." *prep. or adv.*
betwixt and between, in the middle; neither one nor the other.

bev·el (bev′əl) **1** a sloping edge: *The edge of the plate-glass mirror has a bevel.* **2** cut a square edge to make it slope: *The edges of the board have been bevelled with a plane.* 1 *n.,* 2 *v.,* **bev·elled** or **bev·eled, bev·el·ling** or **bev·el·ing.**

bev·er·age (bev′ə rij) a drink. Milk, tea, coffee, juice, and pop are beverages. *n.*

be·wail (bi wāl′) complain or be sad about: *The little girl was bewailing the loss of her toy truck.* *v.*

be·ware (bi wer′) be careful; be on your guard: *Beware! Falling rock. Beware of strangers.* *v.*

be·wil·der (bi wil′dər) confuse completely; fill with uncertainty: *The little boy was bewildered by the noise of the crowd.* *v.* **—be·wil′der·ment,** *n.*

be·witch (bi wich′) **1** put under a spell: *The wicked fairy bewitched the princess, and made her fall into a long sleep.* **2** charm; delight very much: *The cute toddler bewitched us all.* *v.*

be·yond (bi yond′) **1** past: *It is an hour beyond the time I should have gone. She lives beyond the edge of town.* **2** out of the reach of: *He was beyond medical help. The meaning of this story is beyond me.* **3** more than: *The price was beyond what he could pay. Our success was beyond our wildest hopes.* *prep.*

bi·as (bī′əs) **1** a tendency to favour one side too much: *The writer's bias was easy to recognize.* **2** to influence unfairly. 1 *n.,* 2 *v.,* **bi·ased** or **bi·assed, bi·as·ing** or **bi·as·sing.** ▶ See the *Grammar and Usage Mini-Guide.*

WORD HISTORY .... bias

Bias comes from the French word *biais* meaning "slant," and that is the original meaning of the English word. You can see how it grew to refer to *a slanted way of looking at something.*

bi·ased or **bi·assed** (bī′əst) favouring one side too much; giving or having an unbalanced view: *She was biased where her children were concerned.* *adj.*

a bat	e bed	i bid	o pot	u cup	th thin
ā cake	ē me	ī bite	ō go	ū rude	ᴛʜ then
ä bar	ə about	ər over	ô for	u̇ put	zh measure

bib (bib) 1 a piece of cloth or plastic covering a baby's chest and fastened around the neck to protect the clothes during meals. 2 the part of an apron or overalls above the waist. *n.*

Bi·ble (bī′bəl) 1 the book of sacred writings of the Christian religion; the **Old Testament** and the **New Testament.** The New Testament is the part written after Jesus Christ's birth. 2 **bible,** a highly respected book on any subject. *n.* —**bib′li·cal** (bib′lə kəl), *adj.*

bib·li·og·ra·phy (bib′lē og′rə fē) a list of books, articles, etc. about a certain subject or by a certain author. *n., pl.* **bib·li·og·ra·phies.**

Grammar Check . . . . bibliography

A **bibliography** is a list of all the works used in a project, or in research.

Place it on a separate page at the end of the paper.

All bibliography entries should include:
- the name of the author(s)
- the title of the work
- the publisher's name, with the date and place

Arrange the entries alphabetically, by author's name.

For more details, see the *Grammar and Usage Mini-Guide.*

bi·car·bo·nate of soda (bī kär′bə nit əv sō′də) a white powder used in cooking, medicine, etc. **Baking soda** is the usual name for it.

bi·ceps (bī′seps) the large muscle at the front of the upper arm, used to bend the elbow. *n., pl.* **bi·ceps** or **bi·ceps·es.**

bick·er (bik′ər) argue about things that don't matter: *The cousins bickered all afternoon.* *v.*

bi·cus·pid (bī kus′pid) a double-pointed tooth for grinding. A human adult has eight bicuspids, two before each set of molars. *n.*

bi·cy·cle (bī′sə kəl) 1 a vehicle with two wheels, one behind the other, that support a light metal frame with handlebars and a seat. You ride it by pushing two pedals with your feet. A bicycle is often called a **two-wheeler.** 2 ride a bicycle. 1 *n.,* 2 *v.,* **bi·cy·cled, bi·cy·cling.**

WORD HISTORY....... bicycle

Bicycle is one of many words in English that use the prefix **bi-**. This prefix comes from Latin and means "two." In **bicycle** it is joined to **cycle**, from the Greek *kyklos* meaning "wheel." A bicycle has two wheels!

There are several other bi- words in this dictionary that have to do with *two.* See if you can find them.

bid (bid) 1 offer to pay a certain price: *First she bid five dollars for the tablecloth. He then bid six dollars.* 2 an offer: *My bid was seven dollars.* 3 wish; tell: *His friends came to bid him goodbye.* 4 a try: *The prisoner made a bid for freedom.* 5 an old or poetic word for: **a** command: *Do as I bid you.* **b** invite: *The king bade the nobles stay for the feast.* 1, 3, 5 *v.,* **bid, bid·ding** (for def. 1); **bade** or **bid, bid·den, bid·ding** (for defs. 3, 5); 2, 4 *n.* —**bid′ding,** *n.*

bide (bīd)
bide one's time, wait for a good chance: *If you bide your time, you can probably get a shot past the goalie.* *v.,* **bid·ed** or **bode, bid·ed, bid·ing.**

bi·en·ni·al (bī en′ē əl) 1 lasting two years. 2 a plant that lives two years: *Carrots and onions are biennials.* 1 *adj.,* 2 *n.*

bi·fo·cals (bī fō′kəlz) glasses with two-part lenses, the higher part for seeing things far away and the lower part for seeing things close up. *pl.n.*

big (big) 1 large: *a big room, a big book. An elephant is a big animal.* 2 older or grown up: *my big brother. You are a big girl now.* 3 important: *This is big news.* *adj.,* **big·ger, big·gest.** —**big′ness,** *n.*
big deal! *Informal.* So what? It's not important!

Big·foot (big′fu̇t′) according to legend, a very large, hairy, humanlike creature that is supposed to live wild in the mountains of the Pacific Coast: *They claimed they had seen Bigfoot during a hiking trip.* **Sasquatch** is another name for this creature. *n.*

big·horn (big′hôrn′) a greyish-brown wild sheep of the Rocky Mountains. *n., pl.* **big·horn** or **big·horns.**

big·ot (big′ət) a prejudiced person. Someone who treats people with contempt or decides they are inferior without even knowing them, because they are different in some way. *n.* —**big′ot·ed,** *adj.* —**big′ot·ry,** *n.*

bike (bīk) *Informal.* bicycle. A **mountain bike** or **all-terrain bike** (ATB) has wide tires with deep tread, and nearly straight handlebars. A **BMX bike** has similar tires but high, V-shaped handlebars with a bar connecting them across the middle. *n. or v.,* **biked, bik·ing.**

bi·ki·ni (bə kē′nē) 1 a two-piece swimsuit for women and girls. 2 tight, hip-hugging underpants or men's swimming trunks. *n.*

bile (bīl) a bitter, yellowish liquid produced by the liver to aid digestion. *n.*

bi·lin·gual (bī ling′gwəl) 1 able to speak two languages. 2 🍁 **a** able to speak both English and French.

b using or serving speakers of both English and French: *bilingual courts, a bilingual hospital.* *adj.*

bil·ious (bil′yəs) **1** bad-tempered: *a bilious mood.* **2** disgusting: *a bilious green colour.* *adj.*

bill[1] (bil) **1** a paper showing how much is owed or paid: *The garage sent my parents a bill for repairing our car. You can't return this to the store without the bill.* **2** send someone a notice showing how much they owe: *The telephone company bills its customers each month.* **3** a piece of paper money: *a five-dollar bill.* **4** a poster advertising something. **5** announce or advertise: *The movie* Ruby's Quest *has been billed as the summer's best hit.* **6** a planned law to be discussed and voted on by a lawmaking body. In Canada, a bill becomes an act if it gets a majority vote in Parliament. 1, 3, 4, 6 *n.,* 2, 5 *v.*
fill the bill, *Informal.* be just what is needed.
foot the bill, *Informal.* pay the bill.

bill[2] (bil) the horny part of the jaws of a bird; a beak. *n.*

bill·board (bil′bȯrd′) a large outdoor sign displaying an advertisement. *n.*

bil·liards (bil′yərdz) a game played with balls on a special table. A long stick called a cue is used to hit the balls. *n.*

bil·lion (bil′yən) a thousand million (1 000 000 000). *n. or adj.*

bill of fare (bil′əv fer′) a menu.

bill of rights (bil′əv rīts′) a statement of human rights and basic freedoms.

bil·low (bil′ō) **1** a big wave or cloud: *the billows of the Atlantic. Billows of smoke rose from the chimney.* **2** rise or roll in great waves or clouds: *The sea billowed as the wind grew stronger.* **3** swell out; bulge: *Their skirts billowed in the wind.* 1 *n.,* 2, 3 *v.*

bil·ly goat (bil′ē gōt′) a male goat.

bin (bin) a large box for holding loose things like potatoes, toys, bulk foods, etc. *n.*

bi·na·ry (bī′nə rē) having to do with two. In math, the **binary system** uses only two digits, 0 and 1. *adj.*

binary digit (bī′nə rē dij′it) either of the digits 0 or 1, that are the basic unit of information in computers. You can think of a light switch with 0 as *off* and 1 as *on.* **Binary digit** is often shortened to **bit.**

bind (bīnd) **1** tie: *She bound the package with a strong cord. Shared memories bind us together.* **2** wrap in a bandage: *The nurse will bind your cut.* **3** hold by a promise, duty, law, etc.: *Signing this agreement binds you to keep it.* **4** fasten sheets of paper into a book with a cover. **5** make loose materials stick together: *Tar is used to bind gravel.* **6** put a border on to decorate or prevent from fraying. Leftover pieces of carpet are bound and sold as rugs. *v.,* **bound, bind·ing.**

bind·er (bīn′dər) **1** a cover with metal rings in it for holding loose sheets of paper together. **2** a machine that cuts stalks of grain and ties them into bundles using a strong, coarse string called **binder twine.** *n.*

bind·ing (bīn′ding) **1** the covering of a book. **2** a strip protecting or decorating an edge. Binding is sometimes used on the seams of clothing. **3** holding someone to a promise, duty, etc.: *If you signed the agreement, it is binding.* 1, 2 *n.,* 3 *adj.*

bin·go (bing′gō) a game where you cover the numbers on your card as they are called out by a caller, until you have covered five in a straight line. Then you yell, "Bingo!" *n.*

bi·noc·u·lars (bə nok′yə lərz) an instrument that makes objects seem bigger and closer when you look through it. Binoculars are like two small telescopes fastened together, one for each eye. *pl.n.*

bio– *a prefix meaning* life or living things. A *biography* is the story of someone's life. *Biology* is the study of living plants and animals.

bi·o·de·grad·a·ble (bī′ō di grā′də bəl) able to be broken down by a natural process, such as by the action of bacteria: *The paper wrappers were biodegradable so she added them to the compost.* *adj.*

bi·og·ra·phy (bī og′rə fē) the written story of a person's life. *n., pl.* **bi·og·ra·phies.** **—bi·og′ra·pher,** *n.* **—bi′o·graph′i·cal** (bī′ə graf′ə kəl), *adj.*

a bat	e bed	i bid	o pot	u cup	th thin
ā cake	ē me	ī bite	ō go	ū rude	ᴛʜ then
ä bar	ə about	ər over	ȯ for	ů put	zh measure

Birds

bi•ol•o•gy (bī ol′ə jē) the science of living things; the study of plants (botany) and animals (zoology). *n.* **—bi•ol′o•gist,** *n.* **—bi′o•log′i•cal** (bī′ə loj′ə kəl), *adj.*

bi•o•mass (bī′ō mas′) the total amount of living organisms in a certain area. *n.*

bi•ome (bī′ōm) a large area with a distinct climate, vegetation, etc. *n.*

bi•on•ic (bī on′ik) **1** having to do with an artificial body part that strengthens or replaces a natural one and works electronically: *a bionic arm.* **2** in science fiction, having superhuman powers given by this kind of body part. *adj.*

bi•o•sphere (bī′ə sfēr′) the parts of the earth and its atmosphere that plants and animals can live in: *Some scientists worry that our biosphere is shrinking.* *n.*

birch (bərch) a deciduous tree with pale, smooth bark that often peels off easily in thin layers. Its hard wood is used to make furniture. *n.*

bird (bərd) **1** an animal that lays eggs and has wings, two legs, and a body covered with feathers. Most birds can fly. A **bird of prey,** such as a hawk or owl, is one that eats other birds or small animals. **2** the plastic object you hit with a racquet in badminton; shuttlecock. *n.*

birth (bərth) **1** the act or fact of being born: *the birth of a baby.* **2** a beginning: *the birth of a nation.* *n.*

birth•day (bərth′dā′) **1** the day that a person is born or something begins. **2** the yearly return of this day, often celebrated: *Tomorrow is my birthday; I will be 12 years old.* *n.*

birth•mark (bərth′mark′) a spot or mark on the skin that was there at birth. *n.*

birth•place (bərth′plās′) the place where a person was born or something started: *Kingston, Ontario, was the birthplace of hockey.* *n.*

birth•right (bərth′rīt′) the rights enjoyed by a person because of some fact about his or her birth, such as being the oldest child or being born in a free country. *n.*

bi•sect (bī sekt′) in mathematics, divide something into two equal parts. *v.*

bish•op (bish′əp) **1** a person in charge of a church district. **2** one of the pieces in the game of chess. *n.*

Bison

Huge herds of American bison, more commonly known as buffalo, once roamed the plains, but Europeans killed them in such great numbers that by 1889 there were only 500 left. Today, buffalo are a protected species.

bi•son (bī′zən) a large, shaggy, grass-eating wild animal of the North American prairies. **Buffalo** is another name for it. *n., pl.* **bi•son.**

bis•tro (bēs′trō) a small restaurant where simple meals are served: *We found a wonderful bistro in Montréal. n., pl.* **bis•tros.**

bit[1] (bit) **1** part of a tool for drilling. **2** the part of a bridle that goes in the horse's mouth. *n.*

bit[2] (bit) **1** a small piece or amount: *bits of broken glass. Could I have a bit of your orange? I am a bit tired.* 2 a short time: *Why don't you stay for a bit? n.*

bit[3] (bit) the past tense of **bite:** *He bit into the apple. v.*

bit[4] (bit) the basic unit of information in computers; short for **binary digit.** *n.*

bitch (bich) a female dog or wolf. *n.*

bite (bīt) **1** grab, cut into, or cut off with the teeth: *She bit the carrot. Don't bite your fingernails.* **2** the act of biting: *The dog gave a bite or two at the bone.* **3** a piece bitten off; mouthful: *I ate a bite of the cookie.* **4** a light meal; snack: *Can you stay and have a bite with us?* **5** sting: *words that bite. A mosquito bit me. The sharp wind bit our faces.* **6** a wound made by biting or stinging: *Don't scratch your mosquito bite.* 1, 5 *v.,* **bit, bit•ten, bit•ing;** 2–4, 6 *n.*
bite the bullet, bravely face something very difficult.
bite the dust, fall dead, be defeated, or come to an end.

WORD HISTORY.... bite the bullet

The expression **bite the bullet** comes from the days when wounded soldiers used to have surgery on the battlefield with no anesthetic. They were given a bullet to bite on to keep them from crying out in pain.

bit•ter (bit′ər) **1** having a sharp, unpleasant taste: *bitter medicine.* **2** full of pain, disappointment, anger, or grief: *a bitter defeat, a bitter cry. The death of his father was a bitter loss.* **3** very cold: *a bitter wind. adj.* **—bit′ter•ly,** *adv.* **—bit′ter•ness,** *n.*

bit•tern (bit′ərn) a wading bird that lives in marshes and has a booming call. *n.*

biv•ou•ac (biv′ū ak′) **1** a camp without tents or with very small tents: *The mountaineers made a bivouac for the night in a cave.* **2** make camp in this way: *They bivouacked near the creek.* 1 *n.,* 2 *v.,* **biv•ou•acked, biv•ou•ack•ing.**

bi•zarre (bə zär′) extremely strange or odd: *The bizarre scarecrow was dressed in slippers, raincoat, and a woman's hat. adj.*

blab (blab) tell secrets; talk too much. **Blabber** is another word for this. *v.,* **blabbed, blab•bing.** **—blab′ber•mouth′,** *n.*

black (blak) **1** the colour of coal or soot. Black is the darkest colour; pure black reflects no light. **2** very dark: *The room was black as night.* **3** a person with African ancestors. **4** having to do with people who have African ancestors: *a black Trinidadian.* **5** very dirty. **6** very sad or angry: *It was a black day for all of us. She gave me a black look.* 1, 3 *n.,* 1, 2, 4–6 *adj.* **—black′ish,** *adj.*
black out, a become unconscious; faint: *I don't know what happened after that, because I blacked out.* **b** darken completely. **c** keep from being published or broadcast: *The local TV station blacked out the hockey game.*
in the black, not in debt. In the account books of a business, amounts are written in red if they are debts; otherwise they are written in black. **—black′ly,** *adv.* **—black′ness,** *n.*

black and blue (blak′ən blū′) badly bruised.

a bat	e bed	i bid	o pot	u cup	th **thin**
ā cake	ē me	ī bite	ō go	ū rude	ᴛʜ **then**
ä bar	ə about	ər over	ô for	u̇ put	zh measure

black and white (blak ən wīt *or* hwīt) **1** writing; print: *You can read it right there in black and white.* **2** a colour scheme that shows everything only as black, white, or some shade of grey: *They used to film everything in black and white.* —**black-and-white,** *adj.*

black•ber•ry (blak′ber′ē) the small, black or dark purple fruit that grows on some bushes and vines: *Blackberries are sweet and juicy.* *n., pl.* **black•ber•ries.**

black•bird (blak′bərd′) any bird whose male is mainly black. The cowbird, grackle, and red-winged blackbird are all blackbirds. *n.*

black•board (blak′bȯrd′) a dark, smooth surface for writing or drawing on with chalk. *n.*

black•en (blak′ən) make or become black, dark, or dirty: *Slush from traffic blackened the snow. The sky blackened and soon it began to rain.* *v.*

black–eyed Su•san (blak′īd′ sū′zən) a yellow daisy with a black centre.

black•fly (blak′flī′) a tiny black fly whose bite is itchy and painful.

black•head (blak′hed′) a pore in the skin plugged with dirt, dead cells, and oil. *n.*

black hole (blak′ hōl′) an area in space with such strong gravity that nothing caught in it can escape, not even light. Some scientists believe it results from the collapse of a star.

black ice (blak′ īs′) ice that forms on roads and sidewalks, so thin that it is invisible or looks like wet pavement.

black•mail (blak′māl′) **1** the act of trying to get money or some other advantage from a person by saying that if he or she does not give what is asked, you will tell his or her secrets. **2** get or try to get money, etc. from someone in this way. 1 *n.,* 2 *v.* —**black′mail′er,** *n.*

WORD HISTORY..... blackmail

Blackmail comes from Old English *mal*, meaning money. Farmers would pay so that their cattle would not be stolen.

black•out (blak′out′) **1** a short spell of blindness or unconsciousness. **2** a power failure: *The storm caused a blackout in our neighbourhood.* **3** the act of holding back news or other information: *Sports blackouts are used to boost ticket sales.* *n.*

black•smith (blak′smith′) a person who works with and makes things out of iron: *Blacksmiths can mend tools and make horseshoes.* *n.*

black•top (blak′top′) asphalt; pavement. *n.*

black widow (blak′ wid′ō) a spider found in warm areas of the world. The female is black with a red hourglass-shaped spot on its underside. Its bite is very poisonous.

WORD HISTORY..... black widow

The **black widow** spider gets its name from its colour and from the fact that the female often eats the male after mating.

blad•der (blad′ər) **1** a soft, thin bag in the body that receives urine from the kidneys. **2** any bag that holds liquids or air. *n.*

blade (blād) **1** the cutting part of anything like a knife or sword: *My mother's vegetable knife has a very sharp blade.* **2** a sword, especially in poems or stories. **3** a leaf of grass. **4** the flat, wide part of a leaf or of anything else: *the blade of a paddle, the shoulder blade.* **5** *Informal.* go inline skating. 1–4 *n.,* 5 *v.*

blame (blām) **1** say that something bad or wrong was caused by: *We blamed the fog for our accident. We blamed our accident on the fog.* **2** the act of saying this about someone or something: *Carelessness deserves the blame for many mistakes.* **3** criticize: *I don't blame you for feeling a little jealous–I would too.* 1, 3 *v.,* **blamed, blam•ing;** 2 *n.*
be to blame, deserve to be blamed: *Each person said somebody else was to blame.*

blame•less (blām′lis) not deserving to be criticized for anything. *adj.* —**blame′less•ly,** *adv.* —**blame′less•ness,** *n.*

blanch (blanch) **1** turn white or pale: *The camper blanched with fear when he saw the bear coming.* **2** loosen the skins of raw vegetables, nuts, etc. by putting them first in boiling water and then in cold water. *v.*

bland (bland) **1** without any strong flavour or spice; dull: *Baby food has a bland taste.* **2** almost too smooth and polite in speaking. *adj.*

blank (blangk) **1** a space left empty or to be filled in: *Leave a blank after each word.* **2** not written or printed on: *blank paper.* **3** with spaces left for filling in: *Here is a blank form for you to fill in.* **4** an empty place: *My mind was a blank for hours after the accident.*

5 without interest or meaning; empty: *a blank look on someone's face.* 1, 4 *n.*, 2, 3, 5 *adj.* —**blank′ly,** *adv.* —**blank′ness,** *n.*
draw a blank, try to think of something and fail.

blan·ket (blangk′it) 1 a soft, heavy covering of wool or other material to keep people or animals warm. 2 anything like a blanket: *A blanket of snow covered the ground.* 3 cover with a blanket or anything like a blanket: *Apple blossoms blanketed the ground.* 1, 2 *n.*, 3 *v.*

blare (bler) 1 make a loud, harsh sound: *The trumpets blared, announcing the start of the parade.* 2 a loud, harsh sound: *The blare of the car horn startled me.* 1 *v.*, **blared, blar·ing;** 2 *n.*

blast (blast) 1 a strong, sudden rush of wind or air: *the icy blasts of winter.* 2 the sound made by blowing a horn or trumpet. 3 make by blowing up with dynamite, etc.: *They blasted a tunnel through the rock.* 4 an explosion: *The blast made our house shake.* 5 *Slang.* a fun and exciting time: *We had a blast at the Halloween party.* 1, 2, 4, 5 *n.*, 3 *v.*
blast off, take off, as a rocket does: *Make ready to blast off.*

blast–off (blast′of′) the moment of taking off: *All the parts of a rocket are checked carefully before blast-off.* *n.*

bla·tant (blā′tənt) obvious and very wrong: *a blatant lie.* *adj.* —**bla′tant·ly,** *adv.*

blaze[1] (blāz) 1 a bright flame, light, or display: *the blaze of a campfire, a blaze of colours, the blaze of the noon sun.* 2 burn or shine brightly: *A fire was blazing in the fireplace. The house blazed with lights at Diwali.* 3 burst out in anger: *She blazed at the insult.* 4 violent outburst: *a blaze of temper.* 1, 4 *n.*, 2, 3 *v.*, **blazed, blaz·ing.**

blaze[2] (blāz) 1 a mark made on a tree by cutting off some of its bark in order to mark a path. 2 mark a tree or a path in this way: *The hunters blazed a trail through the bush.* 3 a white mark on an animal's forehead. 1, 3 *n.*, 2 *v.*, **blazed, blaz·ing.**

blaz·er (blā′zər) a jacket like a suit coat but not forming part of a suit. *n.*

bleach (blēch) 1 whiten by chemicals or sunlight: *We bleached the stains out of the shirt. Bleached bones lay on the desert.* 2 a chemical used to whiten. 1 *v.*, 2 *n.*

bleach·ers (blē′chərz) the rows of seats at outdoor games such as baseball and football. *pl.n.*

bleak (blēk) 1 bare and empty: *the bleak, rocky peak of a high mountain.* 2 harsh; dreary; dismal: *A prisoner's life is bleak.* *adj.* —**bleak′ly,** *adv.* —**bleak′ness,** *n.*

blear·y (blēr′ē) dim; blurred: *Her eyes were bleary from crying.* *adj.*, **blear·i·er, blear·i·est.**

bleat (blēt) 1 the sound made by a sheep, goat, or calf, or a sound like it. 2 make this sound. 1 *n.*, 2 *v.*

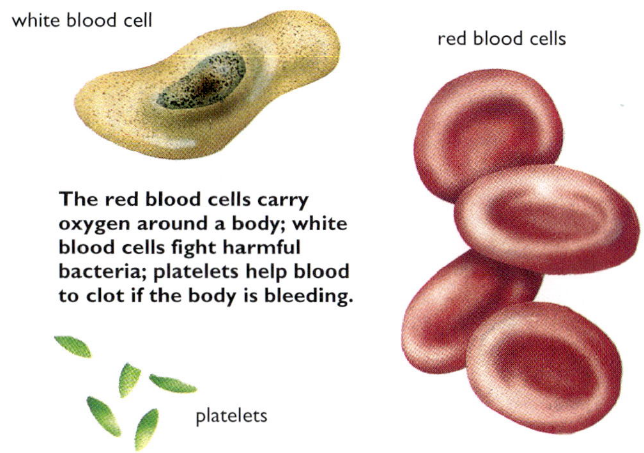

The red blood cells carry oxygen around a body; white blood cells fight harmful bacteria; platelets help blood to clot if the body is bleeding.

bleed (blēd) 1 lose blood: *This cut is bleeding.* 2 take blood from: *Doctors used to bleed people when they were sick.* 3 lose sap, juice, etc. from a surface that has been cut or scratched: *The injured elm is bleeding.* 4 feel pity, sorrow, or grief: *His heart bled for the children who had lost their parents.* *v.*, **bled** (bled), **bleed·ing.**

blem·ish (blem′ish) 1 a mark or other thing that keeps something from being perfect: *A pimple is a blemish on a person's skin.* 2 spoil something by making a mark on it: *One bad deed can blemish a good reputation.* 1 *n.*, 2 *v.*

blend (blend) 1 mix so thoroughly that the different things cannot be picked out or separated: *Their voices blend beautifully in that song. Blend these ingredients for the cake.* 2 lead into each other by very gradual changes: *The colours of the rainbow blend into one another.* 3 a mixture: *This coffee is a blend of three varieties.* 1, 2 *v.*, 3 *n.*

bless (bles) 1 cause good things and experiences to come to someone: *Our grandparents have blessed our family in many ways.* 2 ask God to give good things and experiences to: *The minister blessed the little children.* 3 make holy: *The bishop blessed the new church.* *v.*, **blessed** or **blest, bless·ing.**

bless·ed (bles′id *or* blest) 1 holy; sacred. 2 happy; sent or helped by God: *The birth of a baby is often called a blessed event.* *adj.*

a bat	e bed	i bid	o pot	u cup	th thin
ā cake	ē me	ī bite	ō go	ū rude	ᴛʜ then
ä bar	ə about	ər over	ô for	ů put	zh measure

bless·ing (bles′ing) 1 a prayer of thanks or of dedication. 2 a wish for happiness and success: *When she left home, she received her parents' blessing.* 3 something good given by God; anything that makes people happy: *Peace is a great blessing.* *n.*

blew (blü) the past tense of **blow:** *All night long the wind blew.* *v.*

blight (blīt) 1 any disease that causes parts of plants to wither and die: *The apple crop was wiped out by blight.* 2 anything that causes ruin or unhappiness. 3 cause to wither and die; ruin: *Rain blighted our hopes for a picnic.* 1, 2 *n.*, 3 *v.*

blimp (blimp) an oval aircraft like a long balloon, full of gas that keeps it up in the air: *Blimps are often used to display advertisements.* *n.*

blind (blīnd) 1 not able to see: *The person with the white cane is blind.* 2 make unable to see: *The bright lights blinded me for a moment.* 3 without thought or good sense: *blind fury, a blind guess.* 4 take away the power to understand or judge: *His prejudices blinded him.* 5 done without the help of sight, using only instruments: *The pilot made a blind landing.* 6 a window covering, heavier and stiffer than a curtain, that can be closed by pulling it down or sideways. A **Venetian blind** is made of strips going across; a vertical blind has strips going up and down. 7 hard to see; hidden: *We were warned about the blind curve on the highway.* 8 a hiding place for a hunter, wildlife photographer, etc. 1, 3, 5, 7 *adj.*, 2, 4 *v.*, 6, 8 *n.* **—blind′ly,** *adv.* **—blind′ness,** *n.*

blind alley (blīnd′ al′ē) a dead end.

blind·fold (blīnd′fōld′) 1 cover the eyes of: *The robbers blindfolded and tied up the cashier.* 2 something covering the eyes: *They used a scarf for a blindfold.* 3 with the eyes covered: *I can walk a straight line blindfold.* 1 *v.*, 2 *n.*, 3 *adj. or adv.*

blink (blingk) 1 close and open the eyes quickly: *to blink your eyes. She blinked at the sudden light.* 2 flicker or flash on and off: *A little flashlight blinked in the darkness.* *v.*

blip (blip) 1 an image on a radar screen. 2 a small change or interruption in the normal pattern of something. *n.*

bliss (blis) very great happiness; perfect joy: *For Marci, a day at the beach is pure bliss.* *n.* **—bliss′ful,** *adj.* **—bliss′ful·ly,** *adv.*

blis·ter (blis′tər) 1 a little bubble filled with watery liquid, that forms on the skin because of burning or rubbing: *My new shoes are making blisters on my heels.* 2 a bubble on painted wood or some other surface. 3 make or get blisters: *All that shovelling blistered his hands. People often blister when they get sunburned.* 1, 2 *n.*, 3 *v.*

blithe (blīᴛʜ) happy and cheerful. *adj.*

bliz·zard (bliz′ərd) a violent, blinding snowstorm, usually with temperatures of –10°C or colder. *n.*

bloat (blōt) swell; puff up. *v.*

blob (blob) a small, soft drop or lump: *Blobs of wax covered the candlestick.* *n.*

block (blok) 1 a solid piece of wood, stone, ice, etc. with straight sides: *The child loved to play with blocks.* 2 fill up so no one can get through: *The country roads were blocked with snow.* 3 stop or prevent: *to block traffic.* 4 anything that stops or prevents something else: *writer's block, a mental block.* 5 **a** in a city or town, a space surrounded by streets. **b** the distance between two streets: *Walk one block east.* 6 a number of similar things joined together and forming a unit: *a block of tickets, an office block.* 1, 4–6 *n.*, 2, 3 *v.*

block·ade (blok ād′) 1 something designed to stop people from getting through: *The protesters put up a blockade on the road.* 2 block up; obstruct; put something in the way: *We blockaded the doorway with chairs.* 1 *n.*, 2 *v.*, **block·ad·ed, block·ad·ing.**
run the blockade, to sneak past the blockade.

block and tackle (blok′ən tak′əl) a set of pulleys and ropes used to lift or pull heavy loads.

block·head (blok′hed′) a stupid person; fool. *n.*

blog (blog) 1 a website where users can enter their ideas or opinions for others to read. The full name is **weblog.** 2 write such an entry. 1 *n.*, 2 *v.*
—blog′ger, *n.* **—blog′ging,** *n.*

blond (blond) 1 light in colour: *blond hair, blond furniture.* 2 having light-coloured hair. 3 a man or boy with light hair. **Blonde** is the form for a woman or girl. 1, 2 *adj.*, 3 *n.* **—blond′ness,** *n.*

blood (blud) 1 the red liquid flowing through your body, that shows when you get a cut. Blood flows through veins and arteries, or **blood vessels,** carrying oxygen and digested food to all parts of the body and taking away waste. 2 family; birth: *She is of royal blood.* *n.*
bad blood, anger because of a disagreement: *There was bad blood between them.*
in cold blood, cruelly and on purpose.
make your blood boil, make you very angry.
make your blood run cold, terrify you.

blood bank (blud′ bangk′) a supply of blood that hospitals can use for patients, given by **blood donors.**

blood·y (blud′ē) 1 bleeding or covered with blood: *a bloody nose, a bloody bandage.* 2 with much killing: *a bloody battle.* *adj.,* **blood·i·er, blood·i·est.**

Word Family.......... blood

These words come from the Old English word *blod.*

bloodcurdling: terrifying
bloodshed: the shedding of blood; killing
bloodshot: of eyes, red and sore, tinged with blood
bloodstain: a mark or stain left by blood
bloodstream: the blood flowing through a living body
bloodsucker: a leech or other animal that sucks blood
bloodthirsty: eager to kill

bloom (blüm) 1 a flower. 2 have flowers; open into a flower: *Many plants bloom in spring.* 3 be full of health and beauty: *She was blooming with happiness.* 4 a look of health and beauty: *A year of country living brought the bloom back to their cheeks.* 5 the powdery coating on some leaves and fruits such as grapes and plums. 1, 3, 5 *n.,* 2, 4 *v.*
in bloom, opened into flowers: *The roses are in bloom now.*

Blossoms are a fruit tree's reproductive organs.

blos·som (blos′əm) 1 a flower, especially on a fruit tree: *apple blossoms.* 2 have flowers; open into flowers. 3 develop: *He blossomed into an excellent actor.* 1 *n.,* 2, 3 *v.*
in blossom, with flowers on: *a cherry tree in blossom.*

blot (blot) 1 stain or spot: *an ink blot on a piece of paper (n.). Dirty fingerprints blotted the new paint job (v.).* 2 dry or soak up with paper, a cloth, etc.: *I blotted the spill with a paper towel.* 1 *n.,* 1, 2 *v.,* **blot·ted, blot·ting.** —**blot′ter,** *n.*
blot out, a cover up: *She blotted out her mistake with black marker.* **b** wipe out; destroy.

blotch (bloch) 1 a large, unevenly shaped spot. 2 make large spots on: *The ugly curtains were bright orange blotched with pink.* *n.* —**blotch′y,** *adj.*

blouse (blouz) a shirt for women and girls, usually worn tucked in. *n.*

blow¹ (blō) 1 a hard hit; a knock; stroke: *I got a blow to the head from a falling branch.* 2 something that causes hurt or loss; a severe shock: *His mother's death was a great blow to him.* *n.*
come to blows, start fighting.

blow² (blō) 1 move air in a stream: *The fan was blowing in my face. The wind blew gently. Blow your nose.* 2 make a sound using a strong stream of air: *to blow a horn. The whistle blew.* 3 carry or move by a stream of air: *The papers blew away. The breeze is blowing the leaves all over the yard.* 4 explode, burst, burn out, or ruin in some other way: *to blow a fuse or a tire. The dynamite blew the wall to bits. That one mistake blew the whole project.* 5 pant; puff: *The horse was blowing after the race.* 6 an act of blowing: *One blow of the whistle means stop; two blows means go.* 1–5 *v.,* **blew, blown, blow·ing;** 6 *n.* —**blow′er,** *n.*
blow out of the water, *Slang.* be far better than; defeat totally.
blow over, a pass by or over: *The storm has blown over.* **b** be forgotten: *After a while the big fuss blew over.*
blow someone away or **blow someone's mind,** *Slang.* amaze or shock someone.
blow up, a explode. **b** fill with air: *to blow up a balloon.* **c** *Informal.* get very angry: *Mom blew up at me for getting tar on the rug.* Other expressions for this are **blow your top, blow your stack.** **d** start: *A storm suddenly blew up.* **e** enlarge: *We blew the photo up into a poster.*

blow·gun (blō′gun′) a tube that a person can blow darts through. *n.*

blow·hole (blō′hōl′) 1 a hole for breathing in the top of the head of some sea mammals, such as whales. 2 a hole in the ice where whales, seals, etc. come to breathe. *n.*

blown (blōn) the past participle of **blow²:** *The wind has blown the clouds away.* *v.*

blow·out (blō′out′) 1 the bursting of a tire. 2 *Slang.* a big party or celebration. *n.*

blow·torch (blō′tôrch′) a small gas torch that shoots out a very hot flame, used to melt metal and burn off paint. *n.*

a bat	e bed	i bid	o pot	u cup	th thin
ā cake	ē me	ī bite	ō go	ü rude	ᴛʜ then
ä bar	ə about	ər over	ô for	u̇ put	zh measure

blow·up (blō′up′) 1 an explosion. 2 an explosion of anger or a quarrel. 3 an enlargement of a photograph: *There's a blowup of our class picture on the wall.* *n.*

blub·ber (blub′ər) the fat of some sea mammals, such as whales. *n.*

bludg·eon (bluj′ən) 1 a short, heavy club. 2 hit with a heavy club. 1 *n.*, 2 *v.*

blue (blū) 1 the colour of the clear sky in daylight. 2 sad: *I felt blue when my best friend moved away.* 3 **the blue,** a the sky or air: *He vanished into the blue.* b the sea: *The ship sailed far over the blue.* 4 **the blues,** *pl.* a *Informal.* a sad feeling: *Rainy days give me the blues.* b sad folk or jazz music. 1, 3, 4 *n.*, 1, 2 *adj.*, **blu·er, blu·est.** **—blue′ness,** *n.* **—blu′ish,** *adj.*
a blue streak, very much or very fast: *When Morgan came home from camp, he talked a blue streak for two days, telling us about it.*
once in a blue moon, very rarely: *Once in a blue moon she phones me up.*
out of the blue, completely unexpectedly: *Their visit came out of the blue.*

blue·ber·ry (blū′ber′ē) a small, round, blue berry that is good to eat and grows on a small bush. *n., pl.* **blue·ber·ries.**

blue·bird (blū′bərd′) a small North American songbird. The male has bright blue feathers. *n.*

blue·bot·tle (blū′bot′əl) a large fly having a shiny blue body. *n.*

blue jay or **blue·jay** (blū′jā′) a noisy, chattering North American bird with a crest and a blue back. *n.*

🍁 **Blue·nose** (blū′nōz′) 1 the name given to a famous boat built in Nova Scotia. It was a special kind of sailboat called a **schooner.** The *Bluenose* sailed from 1921 to 1946 and was the fastest sailing boat in the North Atlantic fishing fleets. 2 a nickname for a Nova Scotian. *n.*

blue·print (blū′print′) 1 a building plan shown in white outlines on a blue background. 2 a detailed plan for doing anything. *n.*

bluff¹ (bluf) 1 a high, steep cliff. 2 🍁 a line or clump of trees on the flat prairie: *The farmhouse was sheltered from the wind by a bluff.* 3 honest in a rough but good-natured way: *Don't be put off by his bluff manner.* 1, 2 *n.*, 3 *adj.*

bluff² (bluf) 1 pretend to be confident in order to get others to respect you or do what you want: *She bluffed her way through the interview.* 2 a show of pretended confidence: *She's not that brave; it's all a bluff.* 3 a threat that cannot be carried out. 1 *v.*, 2, 3 *n.* **—bluff′er,** *n.*

blun·der (blun′dər) 1 a stupid mistake. 2 make a stupid mistake. 3 move or act blindly or clumsily: *Carl stumbled around, blundering into furniture in the dark.* 1 *n.*, 2, 3 *v.* **—blun′der·er,** *n.*

blun·der·buss (blun′dər bus′) a short gun with a wide muzzle, once used to shoot a short distance. *n.*

blunt (blunt) 1 not sharp; dull: *a blunt knife.* 2 make less sharp: *You will blunt the scissors if you use them to cut twigs.* 3 giving your opinion without being careful of the feelings of others: *blunt criticism.* 1, 3 *adj.*, 2 *v.* **—blunt·ly,** *adv.* **—blunt′ness,** *n.*

blur (blər) 1 make fuzzy in form or outline: *Mist blurred the hills.* 2 make unable to see clearly: *Tears blurred my eyes.* 3 an unclear image: *The photo of Nina running was just one big blur.* 1, 2 *v.*, **blurred, blur·ring;** 3 *n.* **—blur′ry,** *adj.*

blurb (blərb) a short description or advertisement for a book, video, etc., often printed on the cover or box: *After reading the enthusiastic blurbs she decided to buy the book.* *n.*

blurt (blərt) say suddenly or without thinking: *He blurted out the secret.* *v.*

blush (blush) 1 a reddening of the skin when you are embarrassed or excited. 2 turn red in the face: *He was so shy that he blushed every time he was spoken to.* 3 be ashamed: *I blushed at my sister's bad table manners.* 4 a rosy colour: *The blush of dawn showed in the east.* 1, 4 *n.*, 2, 3 *v.*

blus·ter (blus′tər) 1 storm or blow noisily and violently: *The wind blustered around the house.* 2 talk loudly, roughly, and arrogantly: *When he was excited and angry, he blustered a great deal.* 3 loud, rough, arrogant talk: *We get tired of his angry bluster.* 1, 2 *v.*, 3 *n.* **—blus′ter·y,** *adj.*

B.N.A. Act *abbreviation for* **British North America Act,** the act of Parliament that joined Ontario, Québec, Nova Scotia, and New Brunswick into the Dominion of Canada in 1867. Ever since 1981, it has been called the **Constitution Act** of 1867.

bo·a (bō′ə) 1 a non-poisonous snake that kills its prey by coiling around it so it cannot breathe. Two kinds of boa are the **boa constrictor** and the **anaconda.** 2 a long scarf of fur or feathers, worn by women around the neck or shoulders. *n.*

Boats

an Egyptian sailing vessel

a Phoenician sailing vessel, used by traders

Boats are usually small, open vessels. Until the invention of the steam engine, boats had to be propelled by oars, paddles, poles, or sails.

boar (bôr) a male pig or a wild pig. *n.*

board (bôrd) **1** a wide, thin piece of wood used for building, etc.: *We used pine boards to make the shelves.* **2** cover with boards: *We boarded up the broken window.* **3** a flat piece of wood used for some special purpose: *a snowboard, a diving board.* **4** 🍁 **the boards,** *pl.* the wooden guard fence surrounding the ice of a hockey rink. **5** 🍁 in hockey, push an opposing player into the boards: *He was given a penalty for boarding.* **6** meals provided for pay: *She charges $75 a week for board.* **7** give or get regular meals, or room and meals, for pay: *A university student boards at our house.* **8** a group of people managing something; council: *a school board.* **9** get on a bus, plane, etc.: *We board the school bus at the corner every day.* **10** go snowboarding. 1, 3, 4, 6, 8 *n.,* 2, 5, 7, 9, 10 *v.* —**board′er,** *n.*

on board, on a train, aircraft, etc.: *When everybody was on board, the plane took off.*

boarding school (bôr′ding skūl′) a school with buildings where students live during the school year.

board·walk (bôrd′wok′) a sidewalk made of boards, usually on a waterfront: *She liked to stroll along the boardwalk early in the morning.* *n.*

boast (bōst) **1** talk too proudly; brag: *She boasts about her new computer.* **2** something said too proudly; bragging words: *I don't believe his boast that he will win every race.* **3** have something to be proud of: *Our team boasts a perfect record so far.* 1, 3 *v.,* 2 *n.* —**boast′er,** *n.* —**boast′ful,** *adj.*

boat (bōt) **1** a vessel for travelling on water, such as a motorboat, a rowboat, or a sailboat. **2** use a boat; go in a boat. 1 *n.,* 2 *v.*

boat·house (bōt′hous′) a building for sheltering boats. *n.*

boat·swain (bō′sən *or* bōt′swān′) an officer on a ship who is in charge of the lifeboats, anchors, ropes, hull, and rigging. *n.*

USING WORDS .... boatswain

Sailors away at sea for a long time developed their own way of speaking. Many words to do with boats, like **boatswain,** are spoken a lot differently from the way they look. With the word **boatswain**, the spelling finally came to match the pronunciation: **bosun**. Look up **gunwale** and **mainsail** and check out the pronunciation.

a bat	e bed	i bid	o pot	u cup	th thin
ā cake	ē me	ī bite	ō go	ū rude	ᴛʜ then
à bar	ə about	ər over	ȯ for	ů put	zh measure

bob¹ (bob) 1 move up and down with short, quick motions: *The duckling bobbed up and down on the waves.* 2 a short, quick motion up and down: *a bob of the head.* 1 *v.,* **bobbed, bob·bing;** 2 *n.*

bob² (bob) 1 a short haircut. 2 to cut short. 3 a float on a fishing line. 1, 3 *n.,* 2 *v.,* **bobbed, bob·bing.**

bob·bin (bob′ən) a reel or spool for holding thread or yarn. *n.*

bob·by pin (bob′ē pin′) a hairpin that is a thin strip of metal folded tightly in half.

The bobcat is active mainly at night, using its keen eyesight and hearing to track down the small animals it eats.

bob·cat (bob′kat′) a wild cat closely related to the Canada lynx but having a longer tail, shorter ears, and smaller paws. *n.*

bob·o·link (bob′ə lingk′) a common North American songbird that lives in fields and meadows. The male has a white back and black underside. *n.*

WORD HISTORY..... bobolink

The word **bobolink** was originally an imitation of the sound that this bird makes.

Several other birds are named for the sound of their call: bobwhite, chickadee, cuckoo. Do you know any other bird names like these? Where would you look for more?

bob·sled (bob′sled′) 1 a long closed-in sled with a steering wheel and brakes. 2 ride or coast on a bobsled. Bobsledding is an Olympic sport. 1 *n.,* 2 *v.,* **bob·sled·ded, bob·sled·ding.**

bob·white (bob′wīt′ *or* bob′hwīt′) a North American bird with a reddish back and striped sides. *n.*

bode (bōd) be a sign of: *Dark clouds boded rain.* *v.,* **bod·ed, bod·ing.**
bode well, be a good sign.

bod·i·ly (bod′ə lē) 1 of the body; in the body. 2 in person: *The man we thought was dead walked bodily into the room.* 3 as one group; as a whole: *The audience rose bodily to cheer the pianist.* 1 *adj.,* 2, 3 *adv.*

bod·y (bod′ē) 1 all the material that makes up a person, animal, or plant: *This girl has a strong, healthy body.* 2 the main part of a person or animal, not including the head, arms, or legs: *He has a short body and long legs.* 3 the main part of anything. 4 a group or mass: *The entire student body went to the play. A lake is a body of water.* 5 *Informal.* a person: *What can one body do?* 6 a dead person; corpse: *The body was found by the police.* 7 thickness or fullness: *This shampoo is supposed to add body to your hair.* *n., pl.* **bod·ies.**

bod·y·check (bod′ē chek′) in hockey: 1 the act of bumping into the player who has the puck. 2 check a player in this way. 1 *n.,* 2 *v.*

bod·y·guard (bod′ē gärd′) a person or group of people who guard someone: *A bodyguard goes with the Prime Minister all the time.* *n.*

bog (bog) 1 an area of wet, soft, spongy ground; a marsh. 2 **bog down,** get stuck in anything: *I bogged down in my science project and asked the teacher for help.* 1 *n.,* 2 *v.,* **bogged, bog·ging.** —**bog′gy,** *adj.*
get bogged down, get stuck.

bo·gus (bō′gəs) not real; counterfeit; fake: *The cashier refused the bogus twenty-dollar bill.* *adj.*

boil¹ (boil) 1 make or be so hot that bubbles form and steam or vapour rises: *Water boils at 100°C. Boil some water for tea.* 2 hold a liquid that is doing this: *A kettle was boiling on the stove.* 3 cook in a boiling liquid: *We boil the eggs four minutes.* 4 be very excited or stirred up: *to boil with anger.* 5 a boiling condition: *Bring the mixture to a boil.* 1–4 *v.,* 5 *n.*
boil down, a make less by boiling: *Boil down the sauce to half the amount.* **b** shorten by getting rid of unimportant parts: *He boiled down his notes to a list of the main facts.*

boil² (boil) a red, painful swelling on the skin: *Boils are caused by infection.* *n.*

boil·er (boi′lər) a large tank for heating liquids, especially so that the steam can be used to heat a building or run an engine. *n.*

bois·ter·ous (boi′stə rəs) noisy and rough in a cheerful way: *a boisterous game, a boisterous child.* *adj.* —**bois′ter·ous·ly,** *adv.* —**bois′ter·ous·ness,** *n.*

bold (bōld) 1 brave; daring: *bold deeds. The bold voyageurs travelled thousands of kilometres by canoe.* 2 rude: *The bold little boy made faces at us as we passed.*

3 sharp and clear: *The mountains stood in bold outline against the sky.* *adj.* —**bold′ly,** *adv.* —**bold′ness,** *n.*

bo·le·ro (bə ler′ō) 1 a very short, loose jacket worn open in front. 2 a lively Spanish dance, or the music for it. *n., pl.* **bo·le·ros.**

bo·lo·gna (bə lō′nē *or* bə lō′nə) a large, mildly flavoured sausage made from finely ground meat: *Jerry often had fried bologna for lunch.* **Baloney** is another spelling. *n.*

bol·ster (bōl′stər) 1 a long, firm pillow for a bed. 2 support: *Her hopeful words bolstered our courage.* 1 *n.,* 2 *v.*

bolt (bōlt) 1 an object like a screw but with a flat end instead of a point. It is meant to go right through the things it is holding together and stick out the other side, where a nut (def. 2) is screwed onto the end to keep it in place. 2 a sliding lock for a door, gate, etc. 3 fasten with a bolt: *Bolt the doors. The two metal plates are bolted together.* 4 a short arrow with a thick head. Bolts were shot from crossbows. 5 a stroke of lightning. 6 run away suddenly: *The horse bolted.* 7 a sudden running away: *to make a bolt for safety.* 8 a roll of cloth. 9 swallow food quickly without chewing: *Don't bolt your food.* 1, 2, 4, 5, 7, 8 *n.,* 3, 6, 9 *v.*
a bolt from the blue, something completely unexpected.
bolt upright, stiff and straight: *Awakened by a noise, he sat bolt upright in bed.*

bomb (bom) 1 a container filled with explosive that is set off by a fuse or by hitting something. 2 attack with bombs. 3 *Slang.* drive very fast or with a lot of noise: *bombing down the highway on her motorbike.* 1 *n.,* 2, 3 *v.*

bom·bard (bom bȧrd′) 1 attack with bombs or big guns, or anything that can be thrown. 2 direct many questions, remarks, etc. at: *She bombarded me with suggestions.* *v.* —**bom·bard′ment,** *n.*

bom·bar·dier[1] (bom′bə dēr′ *or* bom′bə dēr′) a soldier who manages big guns or who aims and drops bombs from a plane. *n.*

Bom·bar·dier[2] (bom′bə dēr′ *or* bom bȧrd′yā) *a trademark for* a large vehicle for travelling over snow and ice, usually with tracked wheels. *n.*

WORD HISTORY......Bombardier

This vehicle was named after Armand **Bombardier** (1908-1964), the Canadian who invented it.

bomb·er (bom′ər) an airplane used to drop bombs on the enemy in war. A **bomber jacket** is a short coat in the same style as those worn by bomber pilots. *n.*

bomb·proof (bom′prūf′) safe from bombs. *adj.*

bo·nan·za (bə nan′zə) a rich mass of ore in a mine, or any other source of great riches or profit: *My uncle said his store is turning out to be a bonanza.* *n.*

bond (bond) 1 anything that ties or unites: *a bond of love between sisters.* 2 start to love or feel close to someone: *Dad has not bonded with our new puppy yet.* 3 stick together: *This glue bonds wood in ten minutes.* 4 a certificate you can buy from a government or private company which promises to pay back the money you paid plus interest. Buying bonds is like lending money to the government or company that sells them. 5 a written agreement that a person will pay a certain sum of money if he or she fails to do a job properly. 1, 4, 5 *n.,* 2, 3 *v.*

bond·age (bon′dij) slavery. *n.*

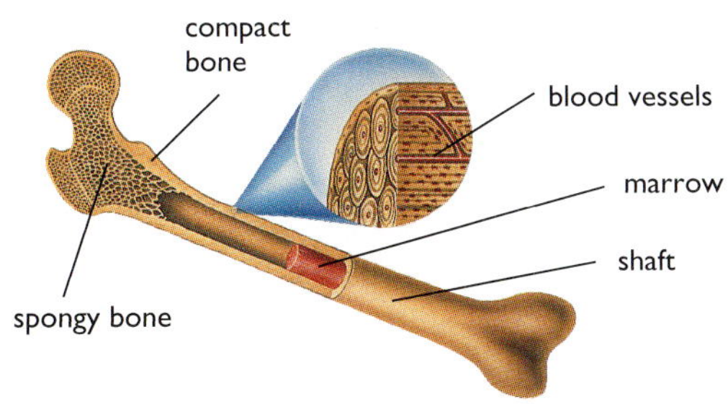

bone (bōn) 1 one of the pieces of the skeleton of an animal. 2 take the bones out of: *We boned the fish before eating it.* 1 *n.,* 2 *v.,* **boned, bon·ing.** —**bone′less,** *adj.* —**bon′y,** *adj.*

bon·fire (bon′fīr′) a large fire built outdoors: *We warmed ourselves around the bonfire.* *n.*

WORD HISTORY........bonfire

This word was originally *bonefire*, that is, a funeral fire for burning dead bodies.

bon·go (bong′gō) one of a pair of small connected drums, one slightly larger than the other, that are played with the hands. Bongos are usually held between the knees. *n., pl.* **bon·gos** or **bon·goes.**

bon·net (bon′it) a cap for baby girls, covering the top and back of the head and tied under the chin, with a wide frill around the face. Bonnets were also worn by older girls and women long ago. *n.*

a bat	e bed	i bid	o pot	u cup	th thin
ā cake	ē me	ī bite	ō go	ū rude	TH then
ȧ bar	ə about	ər over	ȯ for	u̇ put	zh measure

bo·nus (bō′nəs) something given free, as an extra: *The last question on the quiz is a bonus.* *n.*

boo (bü) **1** a sound made to show disapproval or to frighten: *Their suggestion was greeted with loud boos* (*n.*). *He jumped from behind the door and shouted, "Boo!"* (*interj.*). **2** make such a sound. 1 *n., pl.* **boos;** 1 *interj.,* 2 *v.,* **booed, boo·ing.**

boo·by trap (bü′bē trap′) a trick set up to surprise a person.

book (bu̇k) **1** a number of pages bound together, for reading or for writing in: *a homework book, a story book.* **2** a number of flat things fastened together along one side like a book: *a book of matches, tickets, or cheques.* **3** in some card games, a set of cards that belong together and that you try to collect or win. **4** reserve; ask for something ahead of time: *We booked a table at the restaurant.* 1–3 *n.,* 4 *v.*

Word Family.......... **book**

bookcase: shelves for holding books
bookend: a support at the end of a row of books
booklet: a little book
bookmobile: a travelling library van
bookshop/bookstore: a store that sells books
bookstall/bookstand: a stand for selling books

book·keep·er (bu̇k′kē′pər) a person who keeps a record of money going in and out of a business. *n.* —**book′keep·ing,** *n.*

book·worm (bu̇k′wərm′) **1** any of various insects that eat away at the bindings or pages of books: *The librarian was concerned about silverfish in her collection, one of the worst bookworms.* **2** somebody who loves to read: *All the kids in that family were bookworms.* *n.*

boom¹ (büm) **1** a deep, hollow sound like the roar of thunder: *the boom of a bass drum.* **2** make this sound: *The big man's voice boomed above the rest.* **3** a sudden rapid growth in business, population, etc.: *There has been a boom in computer sales in the last few years.* **4** grow rapidly: *Their business is booming.* 1, 3 *n.,* 2, 4 *v.*

boom² (büm) **1** any long pole or beam, like the one stretching out the bottom of a sail or the one that lifts and carries the load on a crane. **2** in logging: **a** a chain, cable, or other barrier in the water, used to keep the logs from floating away. **b** a large raft of logs being towed over water. *n.*

boom·er·ang (bü′mə rang′) a curved flat piece of wood used as a weapon by the native people of Australia. One kind of boomerang can be thrown so that it will return to the thrower if it misses its target. *n.*

boor (bür) a person with very bad manners. *n.*

boost (büst) **1** a push that helps a person up or forward: *She gave her friend a boost over the wall.* **2** lift or push from below or behind. **3** increase: *The store has boosted its prices.* 1 *n.,* 2, 3 *v.*

boot¹ (büt) **1** a strong outer covering for the foot and ankle and often, the whole lower leg. **2** kick: *She gave the ball a boot* (*n.*). *I booted the can off the sidewalk* (*v.*). **3 boot up,** start the operating system of a computer, usually by turning the computer on. 1, 2 *n.,* 2, 3 *v.*
give someone the boot, send someone away or fire a worker in an unkind way.
too big for your boots, too proud of yourself.
you can bet your boots, you can be very sure.

boot² (büt)
to boot, besides; as well: *She is a hard worker, and very talented to boot.* *n.*

boot·ee (bü′tē) a baby's soft shoe. *n.*

booth (büth) a closed-in or partly closed-in space for a certain purpose. Public telephones are often in booths, and a market has booths where people show and sell their things. Some restaurant tables are in booths for more privacy. *n., pl.* **booths** (büᴛʜz *or* büths).

boo·ty (bü′tē) things taken or won from an enemy or stolen by robbers: *The pirates fought over the booty taken from the merchant ship.* *n.*

bor·der (bȯr′dər) **1** a boundary separating two provinces, states, countries, etc.: *We reached Detroit by crossing the border at Windsor.* **2** form a boundary with: *Manitoba borders Ontario.* **3** an edge, or a strip on the edge: *The tablecloth had a lace border.* **4** put around the edge of: *a rose garden bordered with ferns.* 1, 3 *n.,* 2, 4 *v.*
border on, a touch at the border; be next to: *Canada borders on the United States.* **b** be very much like: *His behaviour bordered on insanity.*

bore¹ (bȯr) **1** make someone tired and uninterested: *The TV show bored me so much I turned it off. I was bored by the idea of spending another day weeding the garden.* **2** a very dull, uninteresting person or thing: *Washing dishes is a bore.* 1 *v.,* **bored, bor·ing;** 2 *n.* —**bor′ing,** *adj.* —**bore′dom,** *n.*

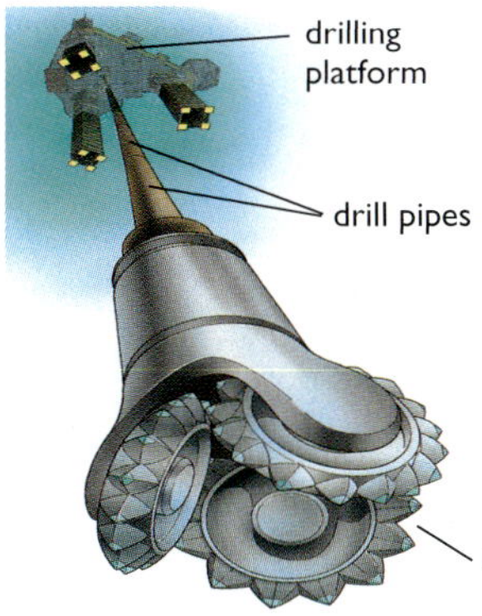

This is a seabed view of a rotary drill bit used to bore for oil. The drill pipes contain several channels. Mud pumped down one channel cools and lubricates the boring bit and forces drilled rock up through another channel.

bore² (bôr) 1 make a hole or tunnel through something: *A drill can bore through wood or cement.* 2 the hollow space inside a pipe, a tube, or a gun barrel: *He cleaned the bore of his rifle.* 3 the distance across this space: *a pipe with a bore of 5 cm.* 1 *v.,* **bored, bor·ing;** 2, 3 *n.*

bore³ (bôr) the past tense of **bear¹:** *She bore her troubles bravely.* *v.*

born (bôrn) 1 a past participle of **bear¹:** *He was born on May 17, 1990.* 2 by birth; by nature: *a born athlete.* 1 *v.,* 2 *adj.*

borne (bôrn) a past participle of **bear¹:** *I have borne it as long as I can. She has borne three children.* *v.*

bor·row (bô′rō) 1 get something from another person with the understanding that it must be returned: *Are you finished with that book you borrowed from me?* 2 take and use as one's own: *The word "toboggan" was borrowed from the Abenaki language.* *v.*
—bor′row·er, *n.*

CONFUSABLES ..... borrow

borrow means "get." When you borrow something, you **get** it from someone: *Saito wants to borrow Janna's bicycle.*

lend means "give." When you lend something, you **give** it to someone for a time: *Janna was happy to lend her bicycle to Saito.*

bos·om (bu̇z′əm *or* bū′zəm) 1 the upper front part of the human body, especially of a woman. 2 the heart, thoughts, affections, etc.: *He kept the secret in his bosom.* *n.*
bosom buddy, a very close friend.

boss (bos) *Informal.* 1 the one in charge; a person who hires workers or tells them what to do. 2 give orders to: *He likes to boss people. Don't boss me around!* A person who does this is **bossy.** 1 *n.,* 2 *v.*

bot·a·ny (bot′ə nē) the science of plants. *n.*
—bot′a·nist, *n.* **—bo·tan′i·cal** (bə tan′ə kəl), *adj.*

botch (boch) do a bad job of something: *They tried to load the new software, but they botched it.* *v.*

both (bōth) two, when only two are thought of; the one and the other: *Both blouses are white (adj.). Both belong to her, and they are both new (pron.). She was both strong and healthy (conj.).* *adj., pron., conj.*

both·er (boᴛʜ′ər) 1 worry; fuss; trouble or extra work: *What a lot of bother about nothing.* 2 spend the effort, time, or worry; take the trouble: *Don't bother to write it down, I'll remember it.* 3 a person or thing that causes worry, fuss, or trouble: *A stuck zipper is such a bother.* 4 annoy or make uncomfortable: *The flies are bothering me.* 1, 3 *n.,* 2, 4 *v.*
be bothered, spend the effort, time, or worry: *I can't be bothered redrawing this; it'll have to do as it is.*

bot·tle (bot′əl) 1 a container for holding liquids, usually made of glass or plastic, with a narrow top and no handles. 2 put into bottles. 1 *n.,* 2 *v.,* **bot·tled, bot·tling.**
bottle up, hold in; keep back: *He bottled up his anger and said nothing.*

bot·tle·neck (bot′əl nek′) a place, condition, or thing that makes going forward difficult or slow: *a bottleneck in traffic. Lack of co-operation was the bottleneck in our project.* *n.*

bot·tom (bot′əm) 1 the deepest or lowest part: *the bottom of a tree, the bottom of a hill, the bottom of my heart.* 2 the underside or the floor of something: *the bottom of the sea. The bottom of that glass is wet.* 3 the root or starting point: *We must get to the bottom of the mystery.* 4 lowest: *the bottom branch of a tree, bottom prices.* 1–3 *n.,* 4 *adj.* **—bot′tom·less,** *adj.*

bough (bou) one of the main branches on a tree: *The children built a treehouse in the boughs of a beech tree.* *n.*

bought (bot) the past tense and past participle of **buy:** *We bought apples from the farmer. I have bought some new markers.* *v.*

bouil·lon (bu̇l′yən) a clear, thin soup made by boiling meat or vegetables. **Bouillon cubes** are made from the material left after all the water from the soup is boiled off. If you add boiling water to the cube, you have soup again. *n.*

a bat	e bed	i bid	o pot	u cup	th thin
ā cake	ē me	ī bite	ō go	ū rude	ᴛʜ then
à bar	ə about	ər over	ô for	u̇ put	zh measure

boul·der (bōl′dər) a large rock. *n.*

boul·e·vard (bůl′ə vård′) 1 a wide street. 2 the strip of grass between a sidewalk and a curb, or the strip dividing a road into two lanes with one-way traffic on each side. *n.*

bounce (bouns) 1 fly into the air after hitting a surface, like a ball: *to bounce up and down on the bed.* 2 cause to do this: *Bounce the ball to me.* 3 one act of hitting a surface and flying back or up: *I caught the ball on the first bounce.* 4 come or go noisily, cheerfully, energetically, etc.: *She bounced out of the room.* 5 *Informal.* be sent back by the bank because there is too little money in the person's account to cover it: *Your cheque bounced.* 1, 2, 4, 5 *v.,* **bounced, bounc·ing;** 3 *n.*
bounce something off someone, *Informal.* get someone's opinion on a thing before trying it.

boun·cy (boun′sē) 1 cheerful and full of energy: *A week after the accident, she was as bouncy as ever.* 2 that bounces or makes things bounce: *a bouncy surface.* *adj.,* **boun·ci·er, boun·ci·est.**

bound¹ (bound) the past tense and past participle of **bind:** *I bound the rope tightly around the tree. We are bound together by our common interests.* *v.*
bound to, sure to; certain to: *It's bound to rain soon.*

bound² (bound) leap; jump: *The mountain goats bounded from rock to rock (v.). With one bound the deer disappeared into the woods (n.).* *v. or n.*

bound³ (bound) 1 a boundary or limit: *the farthest bounds of the earth. Keep your spending within bounds.* 2 form the boundary of; limit: *The country was bounded by the sea on two sides.* 1 *n.,* 2 *v.* **—bound′less,** *adj.*
out of bounds, outside the area allowed by rules, custom, or law: *She kicked the ball out of bounds. The river is out of bounds for us.*

bound⁴ (bound) going; on the way: *Where are you bound? I am bound for home.* *adj.*

USING WORDS . . . . . . bound⁴

This word **bound** often appears in compounds with *north, south, east, west: northbound.* When **bound** follows some other word, or a place name, the combination is usually spelled as two words: *The ship was outward bound from St. John's to Bermuda. For our trip this summer, we are Alberta bound.*

bound·a·ry (boun′də rē) a line that divides two areas or forms the edge or limit of something: *Lake Ontario forms part of the boundary between Canada and the United States. Rules are boundaries for behaviour.* *n., pl.* **bound·a·ries.**

boun·ti·ful (boun′tə fəl) 1 more than enough: *We have a bountiful supply of tomatoes.* 2 generous; given or giving freely: *bountiful gifts, bountiful friends.* **Bounteous** (boun′tē əs) is a more poetic word. *adj.* **—boun′ti·ful·ly,** *adv.* **—boun′ti·ful·ness,** *n.*

boun·ty (boun′tē) 1 generosity, or something generously provided: *We live off the bounty of the earth.* 2 a reward for capturing a criminal, or for killing an animal thought to be harmful. *n., pl.* **boun·ties.**

bou·quet (bū kā′ *or* bō kā′) 1 a bunch of flowers. 2 fragrance: *The perfume has a delicate bouquet.* *n.*

bout (bout) 1 a contest: *The Flames had another bout with the Oilers last night.* 2 a spell; a time of sickness, effort, or difficulty: *I have just had a long bout of the flu.* *n.*

bow¹ (bou) 1 bend the body or lower the head in greeting, respect, etc.: *The man bowed to his dance partner. I bow my head to pray.* 2 the act of doing this: *She answered his bow with a curtsy.* 3 cause to stoop; bend: *I was bowed down by the heavy backpack.* 4 give in: *We cannot bow to their every wish.* 1, 3, 4 *v.,* 2 *n.*
bow out of something, decide not to participate.

bow² (bō) 1 a knot with a loop or loops, often for decoration: *a bow of ribbon.* 2 a weapon for shooting arrows, made from a length of springy wood bent by a tight string joining the ends. 3 a light wooden rod with a flat band of horsehairs stretched between the two ends, for playing a violin, cello, etc. *n.* **—bow′like,** *adj.*

bow³ (bou) the front part of a ship, boat, or aircraft. *n.*

bow·el (bou′əl) 1 intestine. 2 **bowels,** *pl.* the deep, inner part of anything: *Miners dig for coal in the bowels of the earth.* *n.*

bow·er (bou′ər) a shelter of leafy branches or vines. *n.*

bowl¹ (bōl) 1 a hollow, rounded dish, usually without handles. 2 a hollow rounded part of something: *the bowl of a spoon.* *n.* **—bowl′ful′,** *n.* **—bowl′-like′,** *adj.*

bowl² (bōl) 1 play the game of bowling. 2 roll along a surface: *Our car bowled merrily along.* 3 throw the ball to the batter in the game of cricket. *v.* **—bowl′er,** *n.*
bowl over, a knock over: *The force of the wind nearly bowled him over.* **b** *Informal.* make helpless and confused: *I was bowled over by the bad news.*

bowl·ing (bō′ling) an indoor game where you roll a heavy ball down a lane at bottle-shaped wooden pins in order to knock them down. It is played in a **bowling alley.** *n.*

bow·sprit (bou′sprit′) a pole sticking out from the front, or bow, of a ship, with ropes attached to help steady sails and masts. *n.*

box[1] (boks) **1** a usually rectangular container, with or without a lid, made of wood, metal, cardboard, etc. to pack or put things in. **2** pack in a box. **3** a closed-in space for one or more persons: *a theatre box, a sentry box.* 1, 3 *n.,* 2 *v.*

box[2] (boks) **1** punch: *A box on the jaw hurts* (*n.*). *He boxed me in the shoulder* (*v.*). **2** fight with the fists as a sport: *My sister and I would box in the basement to practise our skills.* 1 *n.,* 1, 2 *v.*

box·car (boks′kär′) a railway freight car that is closed on all sides. *n.*

box·ing (bok′sing) the sport of fighting with fists using padded **boxing gloves,** according to special rules. *n.* **—box′er,** *n.*

box office (boks′ of′is) the place where tickets are sold in a theatre, hall, etc.

boy (boi) **1** a male child. **2** *Informal.* an exclamation of surprise, admiration, pleasure, scorn, etc.: *Boy, is it hot!* 1 *n.,* 2 *interj.* **—boy′hood′,** *n.* **—boy′ish,** *adj.*

boy·cott (boi′kot′) **1** refuse to buy or have anything to do with, as a way of showing you don't agree with something: *to boycott products that harm the environment. The neighbourhood boycotted the store when the owner raised his prices too much.* **2** the act or practice of boycotting: *The boycott lasted two weeks.* 1 *v.,* 2 *n.* **—boy′cot′ter,** *n.*

boy·sen·ber·ry (boi′zən ber′ē) a purple berry that tastes like a raspberry. *n., pl.* **boy·sen·ber·ries.**

bra (brä) **1** a piece of underwear worn by women to support the breasts. The full word is **brassiere** (brə zēr′). **2** a plastic or leather cover for the front end of a sports car. *n.*

brace (brās) **1** something that holds parts in place; a support: *We used a log as a brace for the leaning wall.* **2 braces,** *pl.* **a** a special set of wires worn on your teeth to straighten them. **b** an old word for suspenders. **3** make firm or steady by supporting: *I braced my foot on a rock and pulled hard on the rope.* **4** a pair; couple: *a brace of ducks.* **5** a crank-shaped handle for holding and turning a drill bit. 1, 2, 4, 5 *n.,* 3 *v.,* **braced, brac·ing.**

brace·let (brās′lit) a band or chain worn around the wrist or arm. *n.*

brack·en (brak′ən) a large fern or field of ferns. *n.*

brack·et (brak′it) **1** an L-shaped support sticking out from a wall, used to hold up a shelf, etc. **2** support with a bracket. **3** any of these signs, ( ), [ ], or { }, used around words or numbers to separate them from others. **4** put in brackets. 1, 3 *n.,* 2, 4 *v.*

brack·ish (brak′ish) slightly salty. *adj.*

brag (brag) talk very proudly: *He bragged about his new computer.* *v.,* **bragged, brag·ging.**

braid (brād) **1** a band or cord formed by weaving together three or more strands of hair, ribbon, straw, etc.: *a navy vest trimmed with gold braid. She wore her hair in braids.* **2** weave or twine three or more strands of hair, ribbon, straw, etc. together: *She can braid her own hair.* 1 *n.,* 2 *v.*

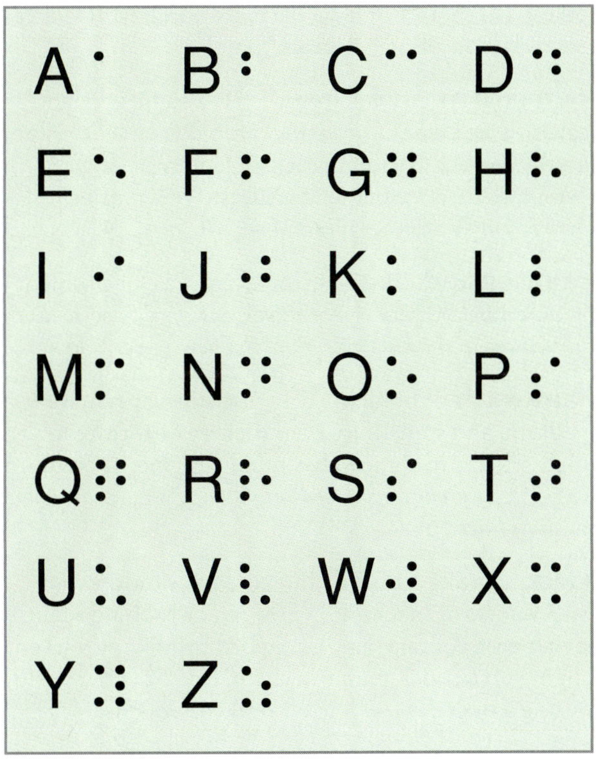

braille or **Braille** (brāl) a system of writing and printing for blind people. The letters in braille are made of raised dots and you read by feeling them. *n.*

a bat	e bed	i bid	o pot	u cup	th thin
ā cake	ē me	ī bite	ō go	ū rude	ᴛʜ then
ä bar	ə about	ər over	ȯ for	ů put	zh measure

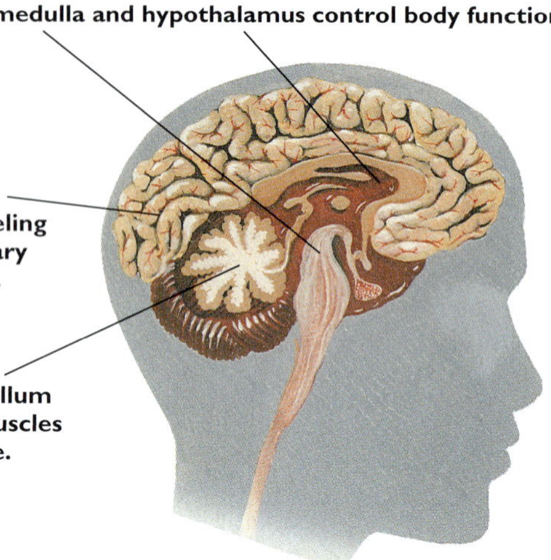

brain (brān) **1** the mass of nerve cells inside the skull or head of humans and animals, used in feeling and thinking. **2** Often, **brains,** *pl.* intelligence: *A dog has more brains than a worm.* **3** *Informal.* a very smart person: *Angela is a brain in math.* **4** kill by smashing the skull of: *The trapper brained the injured wolf with a large stone.* 1–3 *n.,* 4 *v.* **—brain′y,** *adj.*

brain·storm (brān′stȯrm′) **1** a sudden bright idea: *Patty had a brainstorm that proved to be the answer to our problem.* **2** try to solve a problem by having a meeting where everyone shares ideas: *We brainstormed all morning but nothing useful resulted.* 1 *n.,* 2 *v.*

brain·teas·er (brān′tē′zər) a puzzle or problem that you must be very clever to solve: *Karen liked to do the brainteasers in the kids' section of the newspaper.* *n.*

brain·wash (brān′wosh′) use strong persuasion, repetition, and sometimes even trickery or torture to replace what is in somebody's mind with new thoughts or ideas: *They were brainwashed into buying a new car when they didn't need one.* *v.*

brake (brāk) **1** something used to slow down or stop a vehicle or machine by pressing or rubbing against a moving part. A brake may be applied by moving a lever, stepping on a pedal, pulling a chain, etc. **2** slow or stop by using a brake. 1 *n.,* 2 *v.,* **braked, brak·ing.**

bram·ble (bram′bəl) a shrub with thin, drooping branches covered with prickles: *Blackberry and raspberry bushes are brambles.* *n.*

bran (bran) the brown covering of a grain of wheat, rye, etc., often separated from the main part of the kernel when the grain is ground into flour. *n.*

branch (branch) **1** part of a tree that grows out from the trunk. **2** a division; part: *a branch of a river, a branch of a family. Geometry is a branch of mathematics.* **3** divide into branches: *The road branches at the bottom of the hill.* 1, 2 *n.,* 3 *v.*
branch out, a put out branches. **b** become involved in more different things.

brand (brand) **1** a certain kind, made by a particular company: *Do you like this brand of peanut butter?* **2** Usually, **brand name,** a name or mark that a company uses to distinguish its products from the products of other companies; trademark. **3 a** a mark made by burning the skin with a hot iron: *Ranchers put brands on their cattle and horses to show who owns them.* **b** the hot iron used for this. **4** mark by burning the skin with a hot iron. **5** a mark of disgrace. **6** give a disgraceful label to: *He has been branded as a traitor.* **7** a piece of wood that is burning. 1–3, 5, 7 *n.,* 4, 6 *v.*

bran·dish (bran′dish) shake or wave in a threatening manner: *The knight drew his sword and brandished it at his enemy.* *v.*

brand–new (brand′nyū′ *or* brand′nū′) very new; as new as if just made: *a brand-new bicycle.* *adj.*

brash (brash) loud, hasty, or rude: *The brash TV crew pushed through the crowd.* *adj.*

brass (bras) **1** a yellow metal made of copper and zinc. **2** anything made of brass. **3** the metal wind instruments, such as trumpets and trombones, in a band or orchestra. They are usually made of brass. *n.*

brat (brat) an annoying child. *n.* **—brat′ty,** *adj.*

brave (brāv) **1** able to face danger or difficult things even though you are afraid: *Brave Miranda stood up to the bully.* **2** face something difficult without giving up: *The early explorers braved much danger.* 1 *adj.,* **brav·er, brav·est;** 2 *v.,* **braved, brav·ing.** **—brave′ly,** *adv.* **—brav′er·y,** *n.*

bra·vo (brȧ′vō) a cry meaning "well done! excellent!": *The teacher wrote "Bravo!" on my perfect test paper (interj.). At the end of our play we heard many bravos from the audience (n.).* *interj. or n., pl.* **bra·vos.**

brawl (brol) **1** a noisy fight involving several people: *The hockey game turned into a brawl after one player pushed another.* **2** have a fight like this. 1 *n.,* 2 *v.* **—brawl′er,** *n.*

brawn (bron) strong muscles: *Football requires brains as well as brawn.* *n.* **—brawn′y,** *adj.*

bray (brā) **1** the loud, harsh cry made by a donkey, or a noise like it. **2** make this noise: *The man brayed with laughter.* 1 *n.,* 2 *v.*

bra•zen (brā′zən) **1** not caring at all how rude or wrong your behaviour is: *The brazen girl told lie after lie.* **2** made of brass. *adj.* —**bra′zen•ly,** *adv.* —**bra′zen•ness,** *n.*

Brazil nuts are good to eat. They have a very hard, thick shell that is difficult to crack.

Bra•zil nut (brə zil′ nut′) a large, three-sided nut that grows on a tropical South American tree.

breach (brēch) **1** a broken place; a gap: *There is a breach in the dam where the earth washed away.* **2** break through: *The enemy's fierce attack finally breached our defence.* **3** the act of breaking a law, promise, friendship, etc.: *Quitting now would be a breach of duty. There was never a breach between the two friends.* 1, 3 *n.,* 2 *v.*

bread (bred) **1** a food made of flour mixed with milk or water and, often, yeast. It is baked or fried in various shapes. **2** food; livelihood: *How will you earn your daily bread?* **3** cover with bread crumbs before cooking: *to bread chicken before frying it.* 1, 2 *n.,* 3 *v.*

bread•fruit (bred′frūt′) a large, round, starchy fruit grown in the islands of the Pacific Ocean. When baked, it tastes a bit like bread. *n.*

breadth (bredth) how broad a thing is; the distance across; width: *He has travelled the length and the breadth of this land.* *n.*

break (brāk) **1** come apart or cause to come apart; crack; burst: *The plate broke into pieces when it fell on the floor. I broke my pencil.* **2** stop working or cause to stop working: *Her radio broke. I broke my watch by overwinding it.* **3** a broken place; crack: *a break in the wall.* **4** fail to keep; act against: *to break a promise, to break the law.* **5** force one's way: *The man broke out of the locked room. A thief broke into the house.* **6** stop or interrupt something: *to break a habit. The bushes broke her fall, so she was not hurt. Let's break for lunch.* **7** a short stop or interruption: *The coach told us to take a five-minute break.* **8** train; tame: *to break a colt.* **9** come or start: *Day is breaking. The storm broke within ten minutes.* **10** *Slang.* chance; opportunity: *Finding the money was a lucky break.* 1, 2, 4–6, 8, 9 *v.,* **broke, brok•en, break•ing;** 3, 7, 10 *n.* —**break′a•ble,** *adj.*
break away, a start before the signal: *The excited horse broke away at a fast gallop.* **b** get ahead of others in a race or contest.
break down, a stop working: *The car's engine broke down.* **b** give way; collapse: *Our snow fort broke down when we tried to put a roof on it.* **c** begin to cry: *She broke down when she heard the bad news.* **d** separate into parts: *Big projects can be broken down into small jobs.*
break even, *Informal.* finish with the same amount one started with; not win or lose: *She had hoped to sell the lemonade at a profit, but she could only break even.*
break in, a train or use until comfortable: *to break in a new pair of shoes, to break in a new worker.* **b** enter by force: *The thieves broke in through the cellar.* **c** interrupt: *He broke in with a funny remark while I was talking.*
break off, a stop suddenly: *He broke off in the middle of a sentence.* **b** stop being friends: *She broke off with the old crowd.*
break out, a start suddenly; begin: *War broke out.* **b** have pimples, rashes, etc. on the skin: *Strawberries make me break out.*
break the news, tell the bad news: *The police had to break the news to the injured girl's parents.*
break up, a scatter: *The fog is breaking up.* **b** end: *The Student Council broke up their meeting early.*
break with, stop being friends with: *He broke with me after our fight.*

break•down (brāk′doun′) **1** a failure to work: *Everything stopped because of a breakdown in the machinery.* **2** a loss of health: *He had a mental breakdown from working too hard.* **3** the separation of something into its parts: *We made a breakdown of the trip costs, including gas, food, motels, and activities.* *n.*

break•er (brā′kər) a wave that breaks into foam on the shore. *n.*

break•fast (brek′fəst) **1** the first meal of the day. **2** eat breakfast: *They breakfasted at 7:30 a.m.* 1 *n.,* 2 *v.*

break–in (brā′k in′) burglary. *n.*

break•neck (brāk′nek′) likely to cause a broken neck; very dangerous: *The car travelled at breakneck speed.* *adj.*

break•through (brāk′thrū′) a new, important discovery: *The Salk vaccine was a breakthrough in treating polio.* *n.*

break–up or **break•up** (brā′k up′) **1** the end of a friendship, marriage, or partnership. **2** 🍁 especially in the North, the breaking of the ice on a river or lake, the sign of the coming of spring: *We stood on the bridge and watched the break-up. They plan to start work on the new road after break-up.* *n.*

a bat	e bed	i bid	o pot	u cup	th thin
ā cake	ē me	ī bite	ō go	ū rude	ᴛʜ then
ä bar	ə about	ər over	ò for	u̇ put	zh measure

break·wa·ter (brāk′wot′ər) a wall or barrier built to break the force of waves. *n.*

breast (brest) **1** either of the two milk-producing glands on a woman's chest. **2** the upper front part of the body; the chest. **3** the heart: *He felt a joy deep within his breast.* *n.*
make a clean breast of, confess completely: *When he was asked about the broken window, he made a clean breast of it.*

breast·bone (brest′bōn′) the thin, flat bone in the front of the chest that the ribs are attached to. *n.*

breast·plate (brest′plāt′) a piece of armour for the chest. *n.*

breath (breth) **1** air taken into the lungs and let out again: *Hold your breath a moment.* **2** the act of taking in air and letting it out: *She took a deep breath.* **3** moisture from breathing: *You can see your breath on a very cold day.* **4** a slight movement in the air: *There was not a breath of wind.* *n.*
catch your breath, **a** gasp; pant. **b** stop for rest: *The hikers sat down on a rock to catch their breath.*
lose your breath, have a hard time breathing, from effort or shock, etc.
take a person's breath away, amaze or thrill a person.
under your breath, in a whisper: *She was talking under her breath so we couldn't hear her.*

breathe (brēᴛʜ) **1** take air into the lungs and let it back out. **2** stop for rest after hard work or exercise: *At last we have time to breathe.* **3** whisper: *He breathed a warning in my ear.* **4** give a feeling of: *His enthusiasm breathed new life into the team.* *v.,* **breathed, breath·ing.**

breath·er (brē′ᴛʜər) a short rest. *n.*

breath·less (breth′lis) **1** panting or gasping: *Running upstairs very fast made him breathless.* **2** holding one's breath because of fear, interest, excitement, etc.: *The beauty of the scenery left her breathless.* *adj.* **—breath′less·ly,** *adv.* **—breath′less·ness,** *n.*

breath·taking (breth′tā′king) thrilling; exciting: *a breathtaking ride on a roller coaster.* *adj.*

bred (bred) the past tense and past participle of **breed:** *He bred cattle for market. I was born and bred right here in The Pas.* *v.*

breech·es (brich′iz *or* brēch′iz) loose pants that end just below the knee, where they are tightly fastened around the leg. They were worn in earlier times. *pl.n.*
too big for your breeches, thinking much too proudly of yourself.

breed (brēd) **1** have babies: *Rabbits breed rapidly.* **2** raise: *The farmer breeds cattle and pigs for market.* **3** cause: *Careless driving breeds accidents.* **4** kind; sort: *Terriers and spaniels are breeds of dog.* 1–3 *v.,* **bred, breed·ing;** 4 *n.*

breed·ing (brē′ding) **1** the raising of animals or plants, especially to develop better kinds: *The farmer kept cattle for breeding.* **2** upbringing; training: *Politeness is a sign of good breeding.* *n.*

breeze (brēz) **1** a light, gentle wind. **2** *Informal.* move along easily or quickly: *She breezed through her homework.* 1 *n.,* 2 *v.,* **breezed, breez·ing.**

breez·y (brē′zē) **1** with light winds blowing: *a breezy day.* **2** light-hearted; cheerful: *We like his breezy, joking manner.* *adj.,* **breez·i·er, breez·i·est.**

breth·ren (breᴛʜ′rən) an old or poetic plural of "brother." *n.*

brev·i·ty (brev′ə tē) shortness; briefness: *The brevity of the clown's visit disappointed the children.* *n.*

brew (brū) **1** make a drink by boiling and soaking something to draw out the flavour: *to brew tea. Your tea is brewing.* **2** a drink that is brewed: *She gave me a brew made from herbs.* **3** plan; plot: *Those kids whispering in the corner are brewing some mischief.* **4** begin to form: *Dark clouds show that a storm is brewing.* 1, 3, 4 *v.,* 2 *n.*

bribe (brīb) **1** a gift offered to someone in order to get that person to do something wrong: *The thief offered the police a bribe to let him go.* **2** a reward for doing something you don't want to do: *Don't tell me she needs a bribe to tidy her room!* **3** give a bribe to: *He bribed another student to help him cheat.* 1, 2 *n.,* 3 *v.,* **bribed, brib·ing.** **—brib′er·y** (brī′bə rē), *n.*

Bricks are usually laid in horizontal layers known as courses. Different patterns are called bonds.

brick (brik) **1** a block of hard clay, used for building: *It took three loads of bricks to build the wall.* **2** anything shaped like a brick: *a brick of ice cream.* **3** cover or line with bricks: *They bricked the inside of the well.* 1, 2 *n.,* 3 *v.*
brick in or **up,** close or fill up with bricks: *The old doorway was bricked up by the workers.*

bride (brīd) a woman just married or about to be married. *n.* **—brid′al,** *adj.*

bride·groom (brīd′grūm′) a man just married or about to be married. *n.*

brides·maid (brīdz′mād′) a woman who stands with the bride at a wedding. *n.*

bridge[1] (brij) **1** something built over a river, road, etc. so that people can get across. **2** make or form a bridge over: *A stone arch bridged the canal. The hikers bridged the stream with a log.* **3** the platform above the deck of a ship for the officer in command. **4** the upper, bony part of the nose, or the part of a pair of glasses that fits over it. **5** the piece of wood that the strings are stretched over on a guitar or violin body. 1, 3–5 *n.,* 2 *v.,* **bridged, bridg·ing.**

bridge[2] (brij) a card game for two teams of two players each, played with 52 cards. *n.*

bri·dle (brī′dəl) **1** the part of a horse's harness that fits over the head and holds the bit in the horse's mouth. **2** put a bridle on. **3** anything that holds back or controls. **4** hold back; control: *Bridle your temper.* 1, 3 *n.,* 2, 4 *v.,* **bri·dled, bri·dling.**

brief (brēf) **1** short: *a brief visit, a brief letter.* **2 briefs,** *pl.* underpants. **3** a report giving background information about a court case, official request, plan, etc. **4** give detailed information to: *On our way to the wedding reception Mom briefed us on proper manners.* 1 *adj.,* 2, 3 *n.,* 4 *v.* **—brief′ly,** *adv.* **—brief′ness,** *n.*

briefcase (brēf′kās′) a flat case, usually made of leather and with a handle, for carrying papers and books: *Hannah got a new briefcase for her birthday.* *n.*

bri·er (brī′ər) a thorny or prickly plant or bush, especially the wild rose. **Briar** is another spelling.

bri·gade (bri gād′) **1** a large group of soldiers; part of an army. **2** any group of people organized for some job: *A fire brigade puts out fires.* **3** 🍁 a **fur brigade,** a group of canoes or dog sleds that used to carry furs to a trading post. *n.*

brig·and (brig′ənd) in the old days, a person who attacked and robbed travellers on country roads. *n.*

bright (brīt) **1** giving or having much light: *a bright star, a bright day. A new copper pot is bright.* **2** vivid; deep but not dark: *bright yellow, bright green.* **3** smart: *A bright person learns quickly.* **4** cheerful or happy: *a bright smile. There is a bright outlook for the future.* *adj.* **—bright′ly,** *adv.* **—bright′ness,** *n.* **—bright′en,** *v.*

bril·liant (bril′yənt) **1** very bright: *brilliant colours, brilliant sunshine, a brilliant student.* **2** showing or having great ability: *a brilliant performance. He is a brilliant musician.* *adj.* **—bril′liance,** *n.*

brim (brim) **1** the edge of a cup, glass, bowl, etc.: *I filled my glass to the brim.* **2** fill to the brim; be full to the brim: *The barrel is brimming with water after the heavy rain.* **3** the projecting edge of something: *The hat's wide brim shaded her eyes from the sun.* 1, 3 *n.,* 2 *v.,* **brimmed, brim·ming.**

brine (brīn) salty water: *Some pickles are kept in brine.* *n.* **—brin′y,** *adj.*

bring (bring) **1** carry to another place or person: *Bring me a clean plate, please. The bus brought us home from school.* **2** cause to come: *What brings you into town today?* **3** persuade; convince: *I can't bring myself to eat worms.* *v.,* **brought, bring·ing.**

bring about, cause; cause to happen: *The flood was brought about by a heavy rain.*

bring forth, a give birth to or result in. **b** take out and show: *He reached into his pocket and brought forth a strange little box.*

bring off, do or get successfully: *She brought off a perfect mark in science.*

bring on, cause to start: *I think my headache was brought on by lack of sleep.*

bring out, a show clearly: *His paintings bring out the vastness of the North.* **b** offer to the public: *Every year car makers bring out new models.*

bring someone around, a revive someone who is unconscious. **b** win over to an idea or plan; convince: *At first they thought we were nuts but we brought them around eventually.*

bring someone to, revive someone who is unconscious: *He blacked out when he hit the floor, but they soon brought him to.*

bring up, a care for and train a child: *They brought up four children.* **b** suggest or mention: *Please don't bring that up at the table!* **c** vomit.

bring up short, a stop suddenly: *The rider brought his horse up short at the high fence.* **b** scold sharply: *She was brought up short for her rude remarks.*

CONFUSABLES ...... bring

bring means "carry to": *Bring me a bag from the car.*
take means "carry away": *Take the dog out to the park.*

a bat	e bed	i bid	o pot	u cup	th thin
ā cake	ē me	ī bite	ō go	ū rude	ᴛʜ then
ä bar	ə about	ər over	ô for	ů put	zh measure

brink (bringk) a dangerous edge: *the brink of the cliff. His business is on the brink of ruin.* *n.*

brisk (brisk) quick and active; lively and sharp: *a brisk walk, a brisk "Hello!"* *adj.* —**brisk′ly,** *adv.* —**brisk′ness,** *n.*

bris·tle (bris′əl) 1 the short, stiff hair of some animals or plants: *Brushes are often made of the bristles of hogs.* 2 show anger or fear. Some animals do this by raising the hairs on their necks: *The dog growled and bristled. I bristled at their mean remarks.* 1 *n.,* 2 *v.,* **bris·tled, bris·tling.**
bristle with, be full of or covered with individual things: *The harbour bristled with sailboats.*

bris·tol·board (bris′təl bòrd′) a heavy, stiff, very smooth cardboard used for printing, drawing, and painting.

Brit·ish Co·lum·bi·a (brit′ish kə lum′bē ə) the westernmost province of Canada. —**Brit′ish Co·lum′bi·an,** *n.*

British North America Act (brit′ish nòrth′ ə mer′ə kə akt′) the act of Parliament that in 1867 created the Dominion of Canada by the union of Ontario, Québec, Nova Scotia, and New Brunswick. The other six provinces joined the confederation as follows: Manitoba, 1870; British Columbia, 1871; Prince Edward Island, 1873; Alberta, 1905; Saskatchewan, 1905; and Newfoundland, 1949. Since 1981, the British North America Act has been called the **Constitution Act** of 1867.

brit·tle (brit′əl) hard but very easily broken. Thin glass and dead twigs are brittle. *adj.* —**brit′tle·ness,** *n.*

broach (brōch) 1 begin to talk about: *She broached the subject of a party to her parents.* 2 open by making a hole: *to broach a barrel of cider.* *v.*

broad (brod) 1 wide: *a broad road.* 2 with lots of variety or freedom to choose: *a broad range of styles, broad views in education, a person with broad experience.* 3 not detailed: *Give us a broad summary of the book.* 4 clear; full: *The theft was made in broad daylight.* *adj.* —**broad′ly,** *adv.*

broad·cast (brod′kast′) 1 send out by radio or television: *Her speech will be broadcast tonight.* 2 a radio or television program. 3 let everyone know: *He broadcast that story all over town.* 4 scatter seed, etc. over an area by hand. 1, 3, 4 *v.,* **broad·cast, broad·cast·ing;** 2 *n.* —**broad′cast′er,** *n.*

broad·en (brod′ən) make or become broader: *The river broadens at its mouth. Travel can broaden a person's thinking.* *v.*

broad·loom (brod′lūm′) 1 wall-to-wall carpeting: *The workers are here to install the broadloom.* 2 put wall-to-wall carpeting in: *We broadloomed the basement.* 1 *n.,* 2 *v.*

broad–minded (brod′mīn′did) respecting customs and ideas that are different from your own. *adj.*

broad·side (brod′sīd′) 1 a heavy attack or blow from one source: *In his speech the Leader of the Opposition delivered a broadside to the Prime Minister.* 2 squarely on the side, or with the side turned toward something: *The other car hit mine broadside. The ship drifted broadside to the wharf.* 1 *n.,* 2 *adv.*

bro·cade (brō kād′) rich, heavy cloth with raised designs woven into it, often with gold or silver threads. *n.*

broc·co·li (brok′ə lē) a vegetable with green stems and flower heads. *n.*

bro·chure (brō shūr′) a booklet, often with pictures, that advertises something or gives information: *I sent for a brochure on Nunavut; we may go there this summer.* *n.*

broil (broil) 1 cook something directly over the fire or heat on a rack, or under the heat in a pan: *to broil steaks.* 2 be or make very hot: *We broiled in the hot sun.* *v.*

broil·er (broi′lər) 1 a pan or rack for broiling. 2 a young chicken for broiling. *n.*

broke (brōk) 1 the past tense of **break:** *She broke a toy.* 2 *Informal.* without money: *We can't eat out because we're broke.* 1 *v.,* 2 *adj.*

bro·ken (brō′kən) 1 the past participle of **break:** *The window was broken by a ball.* 2 not smooth: *broken ground.* 1 *v.,* 2 *adj.*

bron·chi (brong′kī) the two main branches of the windpipe, one going to each lung. The bronchi together with all the smaller tubes branching off are called the **bronchial tubes.** *pl.n.*
—**bron′chi·al** (brong′kē əl), *adj.*

bron·chi·tis (brong kī′tis) a disease with a lot of coughing, caused by irritation of the lining of the bronchial tubes, the tubes that carry air to the lungs. *n.*

bron·co (brong′kō) a western pony, often wild or only partly tamed. *n., pl.* **bron·cos.**

WORD HISTORY.......bronco

Bronco came into English from the Spanish word *bronco*, meaning "rough" or "rude."

Brontosaurus

The *brontosaurus* is part of the *sauropod* group of dinosaurs, which were the largest animals that have ever lived on land. Some were as long as 24 metres. *Brontosaurus* is more correctly known as *apatosaurus*. You can do a search for *brontosaurus* on the Internet to find out how this confusion of names happened.

***Stegosaurus* was also a plant eater. The bony plates along its back helped protect it from flesh-eating dinosaurs like *allosaurus*.**

bron·to·saur·us (bron′tə sȯr′əs) a huge plant-eating dinosaur with a long neck, a long tail, and a small head. It walked on all four legs. It is sometimes called a **longneck.** *n.*

bronze (bronz) **1** a yellowish or reddish brown alloy made of copper and tin. A medal made of bronze is often the prize for a person who comes third in a contest. **2** make or become brown: *The sailor was bronzed from the sun.* 1 *n.,* 2 *v.,* **bron·zed, bronz·ing.**

brooch (brōch) a pin worn on the clothes as a decoration. *n.*

brood (brūd) **1** a group of baby birds hatched and cared for together: *a brood of chicks.* **2** *Informal.* all the children in a family: *They brought their whole brood along to the party.* **3** sit on eggs in order to hatch them: *Don't disturb that hen; she's brooding.* **4** think a long time about something serious or sad: *He brooded over his lost dog.* 1, 2 *n.,* 3, 4 *v.* **—brood′y,** *adj.*

brook (bru̇k) a natural stream of water smaller than a river; creek. *n.*

broom (brūm) a brush for sweeping, with a long handle called a **broomstick.** *n.*

broth (broth) a thin soup made from the water that meat, fish, or vegetables have been boiled in. *n.*

broth·er (bruᴛʜ′ər) **1** a son of the same parents: *My parents had me first, then my brother.* **2** a man or boy that has a close relationship or something in common with another person. **3** a monk. *n.*
—broth′er·ly, *adj.*

broth·er·hood (bruᴛʜ′ər hu̇d′) **1** the closeness between brothers. **2** a group of men linked by their common aim, belief, or work. *n.*

broth·er–in–law (bruᴛʜ′ər in lȯ′) **1** the brother of a person's husband or wife. **2** the husband of a person's sister. *n., pl.* **broth·ers-in-law.**

a bat	e bed	i bid	o pot	u cup	th thin
ā cake	ē me	ī bite	ō go	ū rude	ᴛʜ then
ä bar	ə about	ər over	ȯ for	u̇ put	zh measure

brought (brot) the past tense and past participle of **bring:** *She brought her lunch yesterday. Have you brought your skates?* *v.*

brow (brou) **1** the forehead: *a wrinkled brow.* **2** the arch of hair over the eye; an eyebrow. **3** the top of a slope or cliff: *Our house is on the brow of the hill.* *n.*

brown (broun) **1** the colour of coffee, cinnamon, or chocolate. **2** make or become brown: *Brown the onions in hot butter.* 1 *n. or adj.,* 2 *v.* —**brown′ish,** *adj.*

brown·ie (brou′nē) **1** a small square of rich, chewy chocolate cake often containing nuts. **2** in stories, a good-natured, helpful elf or fairy. *n.*

browse (brouz) **1** look casually for something interesting in a book or computer file, on the Web, or in a store. **2** a casual look here and there: *Have a browse through the catalogue before choosing.* **3** feed on the tender parts of trees and bushes: *The deer moved through the woods, browsing on young shoots and leaves.* 1, 3 *v.,* **browsed, brows·ing;** 2 *n.*

bruise (brūz) **1** an injury that doesn't break the skin but leaves a dark, sore spot. **2** a soft spot on a fruit or vegetable where it has been pressed or dropped. **3** cause or get bruises: *I bruised my leg when I fell on the step. Peaches bruise easily.* **4** hurt: *His harsh words bruised our feelings.* 1, 2 *n.,* 3, 4 *v.,* **bruised, bruis·ing.**

brunch (brunch) a meal that is eaten in late morning and combines breakfast and lunch: *We met for brunch at the new restaurant.* *n.*

bru·nette (brū net′) a woman or girl having dark hair. *n.*

brunt (brunt) the main force or violence: *The island felt the brunt of the hurricane.* *n.*

brush[1] (brush) **1** a tool for cleaning, tidying your hair, or painting. A brush is made of bristles, hair, or wires fastened into a stiff back or handle. **2** use a brush on: *She brushed her hair until it was shiny.* **3** brushing; a rub with a brush: *He gave his puppy a good brush.* **4** wipe away: *The child brushed the tears from his eyes.* **5** touch lightly in passing: *Her jacket got dirty when she brushed against the car door.* **6** a light touch in passing: *Give the desk a brush with the cloth.* **7** a short fight or quarrel: *The protesters had a brush with the police.* **8** the bushy tail of an animal, especially of a fox. 1, 3, 6–8 *n.,* 2, 4, 5 *v.*
brush up on something, study; review: *I need to brush up on my French before the test.*

brush[2] (brush) Sometimes, **brushwood:** **1** branches broken or cut off. **2** small trees or bushes growing rather thickly together. *n.*

brusque (brusk) a little rude, or almost rude: *Saying "I don't like it" was rather brusque; he could have said "No, thank you."* *adj.*

Brus·sels sprouts (brus′əlz sprouts′) a vegetable that looks like tiny cabbages. They grow in a cluster around a stalk.

bru·tal (brū′təl) extremely harsh or cruel: *a brutal winter. The pirates were brutal in battle.* *adj.* —**bru′tal·ly,** *adv.* —**bru·tal′i·ty** (brū tal′ə tē), *n.*

brute (brūt) **1** an animal without power to think. **2** a very cruel or stupid person. **3** without thought or without feeling: *the brute forces of nature.* 1, 2 *n.,* 3 *adj.*

bub·ble (bub′əl) **1** a very thin, round shell of liquid or solid with air or gas inside: *soap bubbles. I like breaking the bubbles in packing material.* **2** a ball of air in a liquid or solid: *Sometimes there are bubbles in ice or glass.* **3** have or make bubbles; send up or rise in bubbles: *Water bubbled up between the stones.* **4** something shaped like a bubble. 1, 2, 4 *n.,* 3 *v.,* **bub·bled, bub·bling.** —**bub′bly,** *adj.*
bubble over, talk enthusiastically: *The campers bubbled over with ideas for the canoe trip.*

bubble gum (bub′əl gum′) chewing gum that can be blown up to form a large bubble.

buc·ca·neer (buk′ə nēr′) pirate. *n.*

buck[1] (buk) a male animal such as a deer, hare, rabbit, kangaroo, or antelope. *n.*

buck[2] (buk) **1** jump into the air with the back arched and come down with the front legs stiff: *Her horse began to buck, but she stayed on.* **2** throw by bucking: *The rider was bucked off by the bronco.* **3** an act of bucking. **4** work against: *The swimmer bucked the current with strong strokes.* 1, 2, 4 *v.,* 3 *n.*
buck up, *Informal.* cheer up.

buck[3] (buk) *Slang.* dollar. *n.*

buck·et (buk′it) **1** a large, rounded container with a flat bottom and an arched handle, used for carrying liquids, sand, etc.; a pail. **2** the part of a digging machine that holds the dirt. *n.*

buck·le (buk′əl) **1** a catch or clasp to hold together two loose ends of a belt or strap. **2** fasten with a buckle: *He buckled his belt.* **3** bulge, kink, wrinkle or give way under heavy strain or pressure: *The heavy snowfall caused the roof of the arena to buckle.* 1 *n.,* 2, 3 *v.,* **buck·led, buck·ling.**
buckle down, begin to work hard: *She buckled down to her homework.*

buck•skin (buk′skin′) **1** a kind of strong, soft, yellowish leather made from the skins of deer or sheep. **2 buckskins,** *pl.* clothing made of buckskin. *n.*

buck•wheat (buk′wēt′ *or* buk′hwēt′) a plant with brown, three-sided seeds and white flowers. The seeds are fed to animals or ground into flour. Honey is made from the nectar of the flowers. *n.*

If the covering of a bud is pulled back, the tightly packed leaves or flower petals can be seen.

bud (bud) **1** a small swelling on a plant stem that will grow into a flower, leaf, or branch. **2** a partly opened flower or leaf. **3** grow buds: *The rosebush has budded.* 1, 2 *n.,* 3 *v.,* **bud•ded, bud•ding.**
in bud, in the time or condition of budding: *The pear tree will soon be in bud.*

Bud•dha (bůd′ə *or* bū′də) **1 the Buddha,** the title of a great Indian philosopher and teacher who lived in the 500s BCE and founded Buddhism. The name means "Enlightened One." **2** in Buddhism, anyone who has achieved true and full understanding; someone who is freed from suffering and from the cycle of being reborn again and again. *n.*

Bud•dhism (bůd′iz əm *or* bū′diz əm) the religion founded by Siddhartha Gautama, the Buddha, in the 500s BCE. It teaches that people can free themselves from suffering and discontent and reach true understanding by following the **Eightfold Path,** the directions for living. Each soul is born over and over again until it reaches that goal. *n.* —**Bud′dhist,** *adj.* or *n.*

bud•dy (bud′ē) **1** *Informal.* a close friend. **2** a partner in a **buddy system,** where people work or play together in pairs so that each person can watch out for and help his or her partner. *n., pl.* **bud•dies.**

budge (buj) move or give way even a little: *The stone was so heavy that we could not budge it.* *v.,* **budged, budg•ing.**

budg•et (buj′it) **1** a plan showing how much money will probably be received and how it will be spent during a given time: *They've increased the music budget at our school.* **2** make a plan for spending: *I budget my allowance.* 1 *n.,* 2 *v.,* **budg•et•ed, budg•et•ing.**

budg•ie (buj′ē) a small, brightly coloured Australian parakeet, popular as a pet. **Budgerigar** (buj′ə rə gär′) is the full name. *n.*

buff[1] (buf) **1** dull yellow. **2** polish, especially with leather. 1 *n.,* 2 *v.*
in the buff, naked.

buff[2] (buf) *Informal.* a fan or enthusiast: *a hockey buff, a theatre buff.* *n.*

buf•fa•lo (buf′ə lō′) **1** a large North American wild animal closely related to cattle. It has a big, shaggy head, a hump, and very strong front legs. Great herds of buffalo used to graze on the plains. **Bison** is another name for it. **2** a large horned animal from Asia or Africa, related to cattle. The Asian water buffalo is tame but the wild water buffalo of Africa is fierce and dangerous. *n., pl.* **buf•fa•loes, buf•fa•los,** or **buf•fa•lo.**

buff•er (buf′ər) **1** something that softens or absorbs the force of something: *They planted some trees as a buffer against wind and snow.* **2** in science, a substance that keeps the acid level in a solution about the same even when an acid or alkali is added. *n.*

buf•fet[1] (bə fā′) **1** a low cabinet with a flat top, for holding dishes, silver, and table linen. **2** a meal at which guests serve themselves from food laid out on a table. *n.*

buf•fet[2] (buf′it) **1** knock, strike, or hurt: *The waves buffeted us.* **2** a knock, stroke, or hurt: *The boat withstood the buffets of the waves.* 1 *v.,* **buf•fet•ed, buf•fet•ing;** 2 *n.*

bug (bug) *Informal.* **1** any insect or a creature somewhat like an insect. Ants, flies, spiders, beetles, and mosquitoes are all bugs. It is not a scientific label. **2** a disease germ: *the flu bug.* **3** a problem in a machine or computer program: *a bug in the fire alarm system.* **4** a person who is very interested in something: *a camera bug.* **5** annoy; bother: *His grumbling bugs me.* **6** a very small hidden microphone. **7** hide a small microphone in: *This room is bugged.* 1–4, 6 *n.,* 5, 7 *v.,* **bugged, bug•ging.** —**bug′gy,** *adj.*

a bat	e bed	i bid	o pot	u cup	th thin
ā cake	ē me	ī bite	ō go	ū rude	TH then
ä bar	ə about	ər over	ȯ for	ů put	zh measure

bug·bear (bug′ber′) 1 a scary imaginary thing. **Bugaboo** is another word for this. 2 a difficult thing: *Tidying her room has always been a bugbear for Narya.* *n.*

bug·gy (bug′ē) 1 a light open carriage pulled by one or more horses. It has a wide, benchlike seat or seats for passengers. 2 a baby carriage. 3 something with wheels, usually small, for transporting things or people. A grocery cart may be called a buggy. A **lunar buggy** is a small vehicle used on the moon. *n., pl.* **bug·gies.**

bu·gle (byū′gəl) a musical instrument like a small trumpet. Bugles are sometimes used in the army for sounding calls and orders. *n.* **—bu′gler,** *n.*

build (bild) 1 make by putting materials together: *It took us a whole year to build our cottage. Birds build nests.* 2 the way in which something is put together: *An elephant has a heavy build.* 1 *v.,* **built, build·ing;** 2 *n.*

build·ing (bil′ding) 1 something built, especially something with walls and a roof. Barns, houses, sheds, factories, and hotels are all buildings. 2 the business or work of making houses, stores, bridges, ships, etc. *n.* **—build′er,** *n.*

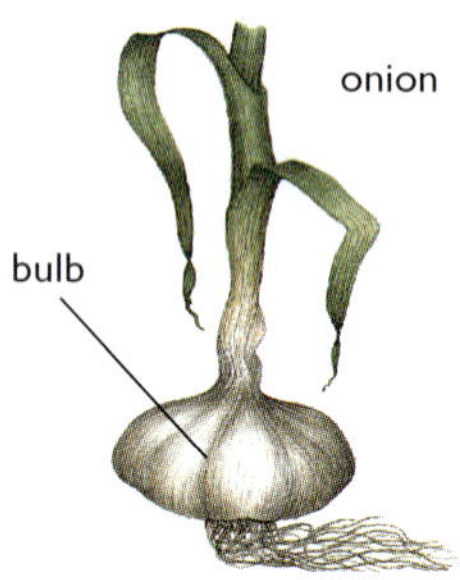

It is not difficult to see where the light bulb got its name.

bulb (bulb) 1 a round underground bud or stem from which certain plants grow. Onions, tulips, and lilies grow from bulbs. 2 an electric light made of glass. It has a rounded body and a narrow neck with metal around the bottom for screwing it into a special base. 3 a rounded part at the end of something: *the bulb of a thermometer.* *n.* **—bulb′ous,** *adj.*

bulge (bulj) 1 swell outward: *His pockets bulged with apples and candy.* 2 an outward swelling: *There was a bulge where she was holding the kitten under her jacket.* 1 *v.,* **bulged, bulg·ing;** 2 *n.*

bu·lim·i·a (bə lē′mē ə) an eating disorder. People with bulimia eat too much food and then try to get rid of it by vomiting or taking laxatives. *n.* **—bu·lim′ic,** *adj. or n.*

bulk (bulk) 1 large size, thickness, or heaviness: *An elephant has bulk.* 2 the largest part: *The oceans form the bulk of the earth's surface.* *n.* **—bulk′y,** *adj.*

in bulk, a in large amounts. **b** loose in bins, not in packages. Food set out for sale in this way is called **bulk food.**

bull (bu̇l) 1 the adult male of cattle. 2 the male of other large adult animals, such as the buffalo, moose, whale, elephant, or seal. *n.*

bull·doz·er (bu̇l′dō′zər) a powerful tractor with a wide steel blade attached to its front. It is used to move dirt, rocks, etc., and to clear and level ground for building. *n.*

bul·let (bu̇l′it) a piece of metal made to be shot from a rifle, pistol, or other small gun. *n.*

bul·le·tin (bu̇l′ə tən) 1 a short news report. 2 a regular newsletter, such as one published by a club, church, etc. for its members. *n.*

bulletin board (bu̇l′ə tən bȯrd′) a board where people can put up notices, display artwork, etc.

bull·fight (bu̇l′fīt′) a fight between men with weapons and a bull in front of spectators in an arena. Bullfights are illegal in many countries. *n.* **—bull′fight′er,** *n.*

bull·frog (bu̇l′frog′) a large frog of North America that makes a loud, croaking noise. *n.*

bull·ock (bu̇l′ək) a young bull, an ox, or a steer. *n.*

bull's–eye (bu̇l′zī′) the centre of a target: *Robin Hood's arrows always hit the bull's-eye.* *n.*

bul·ly (bu̇l′ē) 1 a person who teases, frightens, or hurts smaller or weaker people. 2 frighten into doing something by rough talk or threats: *He was bullied into giving away his candy.* 1 *n., pl.* **bul·lies;** 2 *v.,* **bul·lied, bul·ly·ing.**

bul·rush (bu̇l′rush′) a tall, slender plant that grows in wet places. **Cattail** is another name for it. *n.*

bul·wark (bu̇l′wərk) 1 anything that protects or defends: *A free press and free speech are bulwarks of democracy.* 2 Usually, **bulwarks,** *pl.* the part of a ship's side that sticks up above the deck level like a wall or railing. *n.*

bum[1] (bum) *Informal.* 1 a lazy or good-for-nothing person; loafer. 2 get (food, money, etc.) by begging from other people: *She tried to bum a ride.* 1 *n.,* 2 *v.,* **bummed, bum·ming.**

bum around, loaf around; do nothing: *He spent his whole summer bumming around.*

bum[2] (bum) *Informal.* rear end; seat. *n.*

bum•ble•bee (bum′bəl bē′) a large bee with a thick, hairy body, usually having yellow and black bands. *n.*

bump (bump) **1** push or hit against something solid: *Craig bumped into me. The heavy bag of books kept bumping my leg.* **2** a blow or knock: *The bump made the lamp fall over.* **3** move or proceed with bumps: *Our car bumped along the rough road.* **4** a raised place: *She has a bump on her head from getting hit by a baseball. Try to avoid the bumps in the road.* **5** *Informal.* move a person or thing out of the original position, usually in order to make room for someone or something else: *Their win bumped our team from second place to third in the tournament.* 1, 3 *v.,* 2, 4 *n.* **—bump′y,** *adj.*

bump•er (bum′pər) **1** the bar or bars of rubber or metal across the front and back of a vehicle that protect it from damage if it is bumped. **2** a similar strip of rubber protecting a boat or dock. **3** unusually large: *The farmer raised a bumper crop of wheat last year.* 1, 2 *n.,* 3 *adj.*

bun (bun) a small, round piece of bread dough that has been baked. Buns are often sweet. *n.*

bunch (bunch) **1** a group of things of the same kind joined together: *a bunch of grapes, a bunch of flowers.* **2** *Informal.* any group or large amount: *a bunch of friends, a bunch of junk.* **3** come or bring together in a bunch: *The sheep were all bunched in one corner of the field. We have bunched the flowers for you to carry home.* 1, 2 *n.,* 3 *v.*

bun•dle (bun′dəl) **1** a number of things tied or wrapped together: *We recycled several bundles of old clothing.* **2** wrap or tie together; make up into a bundle: *We bundled our newspapers for the blue box pickup.* **3** send away in a hurry: *They bundled Ramie off to the hospital in an ambulance.* 1, 2 *n.,* 3 *v.,* **bun•dled, bun•dling.**
bundle up, dress warmly.

bun•ga•low (bung′gə lō′) a one-storey house. *n.*

WORD HISTORY...... bungalow

The word **bungalow** came into English from the Hindi word *bangla,* meaning "belonging to Bengal." Part of the former country of Bengal is now *Bangladesh,* which means "Bengal nation."

bun•gee cord (bun′jē kôrd′) a stretchable cable that is used to fasten loads on vehicles, etc. **Bungee jumping** is a sport where people jump from high places wearing a harness with a bungee cord attached, which pulls them back before they can land.

bun•gle (bung′gəl) spoil by doing or making in a clumsy way: *He tried to make a toy boat, but bungled the job.* *v.,* **bun•gled, bun•gling.** **—bun′gler,** *n.*

bun•ion (bun′yən) an enlargement of the first joint of the big toe, causing the toe to be bent inward. *n.*

bunk (bungk) **1** a bed set against a wall like a shelf, or joined in a frame to another one above or below it. The two together are called **bunkbeds.** **2** sleep in a bunk or makeshift bed: *We bunked in an old barn.* 1 *n.,* 2 *v.*

bun•ny (bun′ē) a cute name for a rabbit. *n., pl.* **bun•nies.**

Bun•sen burner (bun′sən bər′nər) a small gas burner that produces a very hot blue flame, used in laboratories.

bunt (bunt) **1** hit lightly; especially, in baseball, hit a ball so it goes to the ground and rolls only a short distance. **2** a hit made in this way. 1 *v.,* 2 *n.*

buoy (boi *or* bū′ē) **1** an anchored object floating on the water as a warning or guide. Buoys mark hidden rocks or shallows, show the safe areas for swimming or boating, etc. **2** something that floats, used in the water to keep a person from sinking; a life preserver. **3 buoy up, a** hold up; keep from sinking: *Kendra's life jacket buoyed her up until rescuers came.* **b** support or encourage: *Hope buoys us up when things go wrong.* 1, 2 *n.,* 3 *v.*

buoy•ant (boi′ənt) **1** able to float: *A cork is buoyant in water; a stone is not.* **2** able to keep things afloat: *It's easier to float in the Dead Sea because its salty water is more buoyant.* **3** light-hearted; cheerful and hopeful: *Tsvi's buoyant attitude kept our spirits up.* *adj.*
—buoy′an•cy, *n.*

bur•den (bər′dən) **1** a heavy load: *a burden of firewood, a burden of debts.* **2** put a burden on; load: *The mule was burdened with heavy bags of grain. She was burdened with worries.* 1 *n.,* 2 *v.* **—bur′den•some,** *adj.*

bu•reau (byū′rō) **1** the office of a certain kind of business: *We asked about the plane fares at a travel bureau.* **2** dresser; a chest of drawers. *n., pl.* **bu•reaus.**

bur•ger (bər′gər) *Informal.* hamburger: *I ordered a burger and fries.* *n.*

–burger a word element used to form the name of various foods similar to a hamburger, as in *fishburger, cheeseburger.*

a bat	e bed	i bid	o pot	u cup	th thin
ā cake	ē me	ī bite	ō go	ū rude	TH then
ä bar	ə about	ər over	ô for	ů put	zh measure

bur·glar (bər′glər) a person who breaks into a house or other building to steal. *n.* **—bur′glar·y,** *n.* **—bur′glar·ize′,** *v.*

bur·i·al (ber′ē əl) the act of putting a dead body in a grave, in a tomb, or in the sea; burying. *n.*

bur·lap (bər′lap) rough, loose, heavy cloth. Burlap is mainly used for making sacks. *n.*

bur·ly (bər′lē) big and strong; muscular. *adj.,* **bur·li·er, bur·li·est.** **—bur′li·ness,** *n.*

burn (bərn) **1** be on fire: *The campfire burned all night.* **2** set on fire; destroy or be destroyed by fire: *They burn wood in the fireplace. Please burn those old papers.* **3** hurt or mark with fire, heat, or acid: *He burned his hand on the hot iron. You can burn designs in wood with this set.* **4** an injury caused by fire, heat, or an acid: *The burn on her arm healed quickly. That cigarette burn ruined the carpet.* **5** feel hot: *burning with fever.* **6** make or be excited with anger, eagerness, etc.: *to burn with fury, burning with enthusiasm.* **7** give light: *Lamps were burning in every room.* 1–3, 5–7 *v.,* **burned** or **burnt, burn·ing;** 4 *n.*
burn down, a destroy or be destroyed completely by fire: *The barn burned down.* **b** burn more slowly and with less flame: *By midnight the fire began to burn down.*
burn out, a burn until it is used up: *This bulb has burned out.* **b** work too hard for too long, so that you lose the interest and energy needed to continue: *Take a rest this summer or you will burn out.* **Burnout** is the noun: *Avoid burnout.*
burn up, a use up: *This car burns up a lot of gasoline.* **b** *Informal.* make angry: *Their teasing burns me up.*

burn·er (bər′nər) the part of a stove, furnace, etc. where the flame or heat is produced.
on the back burner, not being dealt with because other things are more urgent. *n.*

bur·nish (bər′nish) polish; shine: *The metal was burnished till it glistened.* *v.*

bur·noose (bər nūs′ *or* bər′nūs) a long cloak with a hood, traditionally worn by Arabs. It is also spelled **burnous.** *n.*

burnt (bərnt) a past tense and past participle of **burn:** *I burnt my finger. This toast is burnt.* *v.*

burp (bərp) **1** let air up from the stomach, often with a noise. **2** cause to do this: *to burp a baby.* **3** the act or sound of letting air up from the stomach. 1, 2 *v.,* 3 *n.*

burr (bər) a prickly seedcase or flower of some plants. Burrs stick to cloth and fur. *n.*

bur·ro (bər′ō *or* bůr′ō) a small donkey, especially one used to carry loads. *n., pl.* **bur·ros.**

WORD HISTORY.......burro

Burro comes from the Spanish *burro,* which in turn came from Latin *burricus,* meaning "small horse."

bur·row (bər′ō) **1** a hole dug in the ground by an animal for shelter: *Rabbits live in burrows.* **2** dig a burrow: *Rabbits have burrowed in the ground near the river.* **3** search with the hands: *She burrowed through the pile of clothes looking for the lost ring.* 1 *n.,* 2, 3 *v.*

burst (bərst) **1** break open; break out or fly apart suddenly with force: *The balloon burst with a bang.* **2** move, act, or change suddenly or with force: *to burst into tears. Don't burst into the room without knocking.* **3** be very full: *bursting with enthusiasm. The barns were bursting with grain.* **4** a sudden outbreak or increase: *There was a burst of laughter when the clown fell down. He won the race with a burst of speed.* 1–3 *v.,* **burst, burst·ing;** 4 *n.*

bur·y (ber′ē) **1** put in a hole in the ground and cover with soil: *The girls buried the dead bird.* **2** put away; cover up; hide: *The squirrels buried nuts under the fallen leaves.* *v.,* **bur·ied, bur·y·ing.**
bury yourself in something, let your attention be completely taken up with one thing.

bus (bus) a large vehicle with seats inside for many passengers. *n., pl.* **bus·es** or **bus·ses.**

bush (bůsh) **1** a woody plant smaller than a tree, with many separate branches starting at or near the ground. **2** forest or wild country: *He disliked towns after living in the bush for many years.* **3** the tree-covered part of a farm: *They went to the bush to get firewood.* *n.*
beat around the bush, take a long time to get to the point: *Tell me the truth right away and don't beat around the bush.*

bushed (bůsht) *Informal.* very tired. *adj.*

bush·el (bůsh′əl) **1** a nonmetric measure of volume for grain, fruit, vegetables, etc., usually equal to about 36 L. **2** a basket holding a bushel: *We bought a bushel of apples.* *n.*

🍁 **bush pilot** (bůsh′ pī′lət) someone who flies planes mostly in the bush country of the far north.

bush·y (bůsh′ē) **1** spreading out like a bush; growing thickly: *a bushy beard.* **2** overgrown with bushes: *a bushy area.* *adj.,* **bush·i·er, bush·i·est.**

busi·ness (biz′nis) **1** work: *A carpenter's business is building with wood.* **2** a matter; affair: *The whole business sounds pretty silly to me.* **3** trade; buying and selling: *This store does a lot of business in summer.* **4** a company that does buying and selling, along with all of its property: *They sold their bakery business for $500 000.* **5** the right to know or act; responsibility: *My personal life is not your business. She had no business telling you off like that.* *n.*
mind your own business, stay out of the affairs of others.
mean business, *Informal.* be serious: *When my mother's voice gets quiet like that, she means business!*

busi·ness·like (biz′nis līk′) organized; showing good control of things: *She ran her store in a businesslike manner.* *adj.*

busi·ness·per·son (biz′nis pər′sən) a man or woman who works for or operates a business. Businessperson can be used in place of **businessman** or **businesswoman:** *Sally joined other businesspeople for lunch on Fridays.* *n., pl.* **busi·ness·peo·ple.**

bust[1] (bust) **1** a statue of a person's head, shoulders, and chest. **2** the breasts of a woman. *n.*

bust[2] (bust) *Slang.* **1** break: *I busted the zipper on this gym bag.* **2** arrest: *They were busted for shoplifting.* *v.*

bus·tle (bus′əl) **1** hurry around busily: *The children bustled to get ready for the party.* **2** noisy or excited activity: *There was a lot of bustle as we packed for our camping trip.* 1 *v.,* **bus·tled, bus·tling;** 2 *n.*

bus·y (biz′ē) **1** working; active; having plenty to do: *Mother is a busy person.* **2** full of work or activity: *Main Street is a busy place. Holidays are a busy time.* **3** make busy; keep busy: *The bees busied themselves at making honey.* **4** in use: *I tried to phone her, but her line was busy.* 1, 2, 4 *adj.,* **bus·i·er, bus·i·est;** 3 *v.,* **bus·ied, bus·y·ing.** **—bus′i·ly,** *adv.*

bus·y·bod·y (biz′ē bod′ē) a nosey person who interferes in the affairs of others. *n., pl.* **bus·y·bod·ies.**

butch·er (bu̇ch′ər) **1** a person whose work is killing animals to be sold for food, or the person who cuts up animals and sells their meat. **2** kill animals for food: *Cattle, sheep, and pigs are butchered at the abattoir.* **3** kill needlessly or cruelly. **4** do very badly: *He butchers that song by singing it so fast and loud.* 1 *n.,* 2–4 *v.*

but·ler (but′lər) the head male servant in a household. *n.*

butt[1] (but) **1** the thicker end of anything: *the butt of a gun.* **2** the end that is left; a stub or stump: *the butt of a cigarette.* *n.*

butt[2] (but) a target, especially of teasing or laughter: *That braggart was the butt of many jokes.* *n.*

butt[3] (but) hit with the head: *A goat butts.* *v.*
butt in, *Informal.* **a** meddle; interfere. **b** enter the middle of a line-up instead of going to the end.
butt out, *Informal.* **a** mind your own business. **b** put out a cigarette.

butte (byūt) a steep, flat-topped hill standing alone. *n.*

but·ter (but′ər) **1** the yellowish fat obtained by churning cream or whole milk. **2** put butter on: *Please butter my bread.* **3** a spread that is like butter: *peanut butter, honey butter.* 1, 3 *n.,* 2 *v.*

but·ter·cup (but′ər kup′) a common plant with small, bright yellow flowers shaped like cups. *n.*

The female butterfly lays its eggs on a leaf.

An egg hatches into a caterpillar.

A fully grown caterpillar spins a belt of silk and ties itself to a twig. It sheds its skin and becomes a pupa.

Inside the case of silk, the pupa changes into a butterfly. This process is called metamorphosis.

but·ter·fly (but′ər flī′) an insect with a slender body and four large, often brightly coloured wings. *n., pl.* **but·ter·flies.**

a bat	e bed	i bid	o pot	u cup	th thin
ā cake	ē me	ī bite	ō go	ū rude	ᴛʜ then
ä bar	ə about	ər over	ȯ for	u̇ put	zh measure

but·ter·milk (but′ər milk′) the sour, fat-free liquid left after butter has been made from cream. Milk can also be changed to buttermilk artificially. *n.*

but·ter·scotch (but′ər skoch′) candy made from brown sugar and butter. *n.*

butter tart (but′ər tärt′) a rich, sweet tart with a firm or runny filling made from butter, brown sugar, syrup, raisins, etc.

but·tocks (but′əks) rear end; seat. *pl.n.*

but·ton (but′ən) **1** a little piece of metal, plastic, etc. sewn on clothing and other things, to hold parts together or to decorate. **2** fasten with buttons: *We buttoned our coats when the rain began.* **3** a small part that is pushed or turned to make something work: *Push that button to start the machine.* 1, 3 *n.,* 2 *v.*

but·ton·hole (but′ən hōl′) **1** the hole or slit you put a button through. **2** *Informal.* stop someone and force him or her to listen, as if holding the person by a buttonhole: *Let's leave before he buttonholes us.* 1 *n.,* 2 *v.,* **but·ton·holed, but·ton·hol·ing.**

but·tress (but′ris) **1** a support built against a wall. **2** any support or prop. **3** support and strengthen: *Buttress your argument with examples.* 1, 2 *n.,* 3 *v.*

buy (bī) **1** get by paying a price: *You can buy a bag of chips for a dollar.* **2** *Informal.* a bargain: *That jacket was a real buy.* 1 *v.,* **bought, buy·ing;** 2 *n.* —**buy′er,** *n.*

CONFUSABLES ...... buy

buy means "purchase": *Where did you buy those boots?*

by means "beside": *Put your boots by the door.*

buzz (buz) **1** a loud humming like the sound made by flies or bees: *the buzz of a mosquito, the buzz of conversation.* **2** make a steady humming sound: *This radio buzzes when you turn it on.* **3** *Slang.* a very short haircut, done with clippers. **4** *Slang.* give someone this haircut. **5** *Informal.* call, using a buzzer: *Just buzz me if you need help.* 1, 3 *n.,* 2, 4, 5 *v.*

buz·zard (buz′ərd) a kind of hawk or vulture. *n.*

buzz·er (buz′ər) a button or switch that makes a buzzing sound as a signal: *a door buzzer.* *n.*

bye or **'bye** (bī) *Informal.* goodbye. **Bye-bye** is another form. *interj.*

by–e·lec·tion (bī′ə lek′shən) an extra election held in one riding because the person already elected has quit or died. *n.*

by·gone (bī′gon′) past: *The Romans lived in bygone days.* *adj.*
let bygones be bygones, let the past be forgotten.

by–law (bi′lo′) a law made by a city, company, club, etc.: *Our city has a by-law to control the height of buildings.* *n.*

by·pass (bī′pas′) **1** a way that goes around or to one side of something, such as a highway that goes past or around a city instead of through it, or a tube added to a vein to carry blood around a blockage. **2** go past or around: *We bypassed Huntsville on our way to North Bay.* **3** ignore a rule, person, etc. in order to get something done faster or more easily: *We bypassed the assistant manager and went directly to the manager with our complaint.* 1 *n.,* 2, 3 *v.*

by–prod·uct (bī′prod′əkt) something produced in making or doing something else: *Buttermilk is a by-product of making butter.* *n.*

by·road (bī′rōd′) a side road. *n.*

by·stand·er (bī′stan′dər) a person who stands near or watches but does not take part: *Innocent bystanders are often hurt in street fights.* *n.*

byte (bīt) a unit of computer memory, made up of eight bits. One letter or number keyed in on a computer takes one byte of memory. *n.*

by·way (bī′wā′) a side path or road; a way that is not often used. *n.*

Cc

c or **C** (sē) 1 the third letter of the English alphabet, or any speech sound that it stands for. The *c* in *cat* is different from the *c* in *city.* 2 the third thing in a list. 3 in music: **a** a note. On a keyboard it is the white note between B and D. Middle C is the C about halfway down the keyboard of a piano. **b** a scale or key that has C as its home note. *n., pl.* **c's** or **C's.**

C 1 the Roman numeral for 100. 2 *symbol for* Celsius.

cab (kab) 1 a car that can be hired with a driver for a short trip; taxi: *We phoned for a cab to take us to the airport.* 2 the closed-in part of a truck where the driver sits. *n.*

cab·bage (kab′ij) a vegetable with thick leaves closely wrapped to form a round head. *n.*

cab·in (kab′ən) 1 a small, roughly built house. 2 a room to sleep in on a ship. 3 the part of an aircraft where the passengers sit. *n.*

cab·i·net (kab′ə nit) 1 a piece of furniture with shelves or drawers to hold dishes, medicines, etc. 2 a group of advisers for a government leader. 3 🍁 Usually, **Cabinet,** **a** a group of advisers to the prime minister. Each member, or **cabinet minister,** is in charge of a government department and is chosen from the majority party in parliament. **b** a similar group of advisers to a provincial premier. *n.*

🍁 **cabin fever** (kab′in fē′vər) a feeling of being depressed and restless because you've been kept inside for a long time: *After two days of steady rain we began to get cabin fever.* *n.*

ca·ble (kā′bəl) 1 a thick electric cord containing a bundle of wires protected from each other by insulation: *A cable connects the printer to our computer.* 2 *Informal.* short for **cable television:** *Do you have cable?* 3 another word for a telegram sent across the ocean by wires laid under the water. It is also called a **cablegram.** 4 send a telegram in this way: *Susan cabled her sister in England.* 5 a strong, thick rope, usually made of wires twisted together: *The truck used a cable for towing the car.* 1–3, 5 *n.,* 4 *v.,* **ca·bled, ca·bling.**

cable car (kā′bəl kär′) a vehicle that moves when the cable it is attached to is pulled by a motor. Cable cars are used to carry people up and down steep hills, etc.

cable TV (kā′bəl tē′vē′) a system that picks up programs from various TV stations through a very high antenna and sends them by electric cable to the TV sets of people who pay for it. A TV set that is hooked up to cable TV does not need an antenna. The full name for this system is **cable television.**

ca·boose (kə büs′) a small car on a freight train, usually the last car, where the train staff can work, rest, and sleep. *n.*

ca·ca·o (kə kā′ō) a tropical American tree. Cocoa and chocolate are made from its seeds. *n., pl.* **ca·ca·os.**

cache (kash) 1 a place to hide things. 2 🍁 a storing place for food, furs, etc.: *The trappers made a cache to keep their food safe from bears and other animals.* 3 the things hidden or stored in a cache: *The police found a cache of stolen jewels.* 4 hide or store in a cache. 1–3 *n.,* 4 *v.,* **cached, cach·ing.**

cack·le (kak′əl) 1 the shrill, broken sound that a hen makes after laying an egg, or any sound like this. 2 make this sound; talk or laugh with this sound: *After each joke he cackled with amusement.* 1 *n.,* 2 *v.,* **cack·led, cack·ling.**

The spines of a cactus protect it from being eaten by desert animals in search of water.

cac·tus (kak′təs) a plant with a thick stem that is soft, moist and spongy inside, usually having prickles but no leaves. Most cactuses grow in dry, hot regions. *n., pl.* **cac·tus·es** or **cac·ti** (kak′tī).

cad·die or **cad·dy** (kad′ē) 1 a person who helps a golf player by carrying the clubs, finding lost balls, etc. 2 help a golf player in this way. 1 *n.,* 2 *v.,* **cad·died, cad·dy·ing.**

a bat	e bed	i bid	o pot	u cup	th thin
ā cake	ē me	ī bite	ō go	ü rude	ᴛʜ then
ä bar	ə about	ər over	ȯ for	u̇ put	zh measure

ca·dence (kā′dəns) **1** rhythm; beat: *the steady cadence of a march.* **2** a rising and falling sound: *She speaks with a pleasant cadence.* *n.*

ca·det (kə det′) a person training to be an officer in the armed forces. *n.* —**ca·det′ship,** *n.*

ca·fé (ka fā′) a small, informal restaurant that serves light meals, coffees and teas, pastries, etc. *n.*

caf·e·te·ri·a (kaf′ə tē′rē ə) an eating place, usually inside another building such as a school, hospital, workplace, etc., where customers serve themselves. *n.*

caf·feine (kaf ēn′) a drug found in coffee, chocolate, cola, and tea. *n.*

cage (kāj) **1** a frame or box closed in with wires or bars, for keeping animals in. **2** put or keep in a cage: *After the lion was caught, it was caged.* 1 *n.,* 2 *v.,* **caged, cag·ing.**

ca·hoots (kə hüts′)
in cahoots, working secretly with somebody, especially to do something wrong: *The police thought that the two strangers were in cahoots.* *n.*

cairn (kern) a pile of stones heaped up as a memorial, tomb, or landmark. *n.*

cake (kāk) **1** a baked mixture of flour, sugar, eggs, and other things: *a layer cake, a sponge cake, a fruit cake.* **2** any small, flat mass of food fried on both sides: *fish cake.* **3** a solid, shaped mass: *a cake of soap, a cake of maple sugar.* **4** harden into a solid mass: *Mud cakes as it dries.* 1–3 *n.,* 4 *v.,* **caked, cak·ing.**
take the cake, a win first prize; be the best. **b** be the worst or last in a series of annoying things.

ca·lam·i·ty (kə lam′ə tē) serious trouble or hardship, or an event causing this: *Calamity may come to anyone. The newspaper reported fires, floods, and other calamities.* *n., pl.* **ca·lam·i·ties.**

cal·ci·um (kal′sē əm) a substance that is part of bones and teeth, milk, chalk, and certain other things. *n.*

cal·cu·late (kal′kyə lāt′) **1** use math in order to find out something: *She calculated how much wood she would need for a treehouse.* **2** plan carefully or cleverly; do on purpose: *That remark was calculated to hurt my feelings.* *v.,* **cal·cu·lat·ed, cal·cu·lat·ing.**
—**cal′cu·la′tion,** *n.*

WORD HISTORY....... calculate

Calculate comes from the Latin word *calculus*, which means "pebble." People once used pebbles for counting.

cal·cu·la·tor (kal′kyə lā′tər) a little electronic machine that calculates. It has a keypad and a tiny screen. *n.*

ca·lèche (kə lesh′) a light, two-wheeled, one-horse carriage for two passengers, with a top that can be folded down and a seat in front for the driver: *We had a calèche ride in Québec City.* *n.*

cal·en·dar (kal′ən dər) **1** a chart showing the months of the year, with the days numbered and arranged in weeks. **2** a list or schedule: *What's on the calendar of events for this year's carnival?* *n.*

calf[1] (kaf) a baby cow, bull, moose, elephant, whale, seal, etc. *n., pl.* **calves.**

calf[2] (kaf) the thick, fleshy part of the leg below the knee. *n., pl.* **calves.**

ca·liph (kā′lif *or* kal′if) a traditional title of the leader of the worldwide Islamic community. There is no caliph at the present time. *n.*

call (kol) **1** shout: *He called from downstairs* (*v.*). *I heard the child's call for help* (*n.*). **2** the special cry of an animal or bird: *the call of a moose.* **3** make this cry: *The loons called to each other across the lake.* **4** command or ask to come: *She called her dog with a loud whistle.* **5** a command to come or bring: *Every farmer in the neighbourhood answered the firefighters' call for volunteers.* **6** order to happen: *to call a meeting.* **7** name; describe as: *His pals call him Speedy. Are you calling me a liar?* **8** visit or stop: *The rabbi called at our house yesterday* (*v.*). *We made a call at the travel agency to pick up our tickets* (*n.*). **9** to telephone: *Call me at this number.* **10** the act of phoning: *a long-distance call.* **11** end; stop: *The ball game was called because of rain.* 1, 3, 4, 6–9, 11 *v.,* 1, 2, 5, 8, 10 *n.* —**call′er,** *n.*
call attention to something, make people notice.
call for, a stop someplace and get. **b** need or demand: *This recipe calls for two eggs.*
call into question, raise doubts about.
call it a day, stop work or some other activity.
call off, a cancel: *We called off our trip.* **b** order to stop attacking: *Call off your dog.*
call on, a visit. **b** ask: *She called on her friends for help.*
call up, a bring to mind: *This place calls up childhood memories.* **b** telephone.
on call, ready or available: *There are doctors on call day and night.*

cal·lig·ra·phy (kə lig′rə fē) the art of beautiful writing using special pens or brushes. *n.*
—**cal·lig′ra·pher,** *n.*

call·ing (kol′ing) a person's main life work: *The teacher took great pleasure in his calling.* *n.*

cal·li·per or **cal·i·per** (kal′ə pər) Usually, **callipers,** *pl.* a tool used to measure the thickness of something. *n.*

cal·lous (kal′əs) **1** hard; hardened: *Going barefoot makes the soles of your feet callous.* **2** unfeeling: *How callous to watch people suffer without trying to help them.* *adj.* **—cal′lous·ly,** *adv.* **—cal′lous·ness,** *n.*

cal·lus (kal′əs) a hard, thickened place on the skin. *n., pl.* **cal·lus·es.**

calm (kom *or* kȧm) **1** quiet; still; peaceful; steady: *a calm sea, a calm voice.* **2** quietness; stillness; steadiness or peacefulness. **3** make calm; become calm: *Dale quickly calmed the crying baby. The sea calmed.* 1 *adj.,* 2 *n.,* 3 *v.* **—calm′ly,** *adv.* **—calm′ness,** *n.*

cal·o·rie (kal′ə rē) a unit measuring the energy value of foods, equal to about four kilojoules: *An orange has about 100 calories.* *n., pl.* **cal·o·ries.**

calve (kav) give birth to a calf. *v.,* **calved, calv·ing.**

calves (kavz) plural of **calf**[1] and **calf**[2]. *n.*

ca·lyp·so (kə lip′sō) a style of Caribbean music used for light-hearted songs. Calypso has a fast, strong rhythm with the accent falling on the offbeat. *n.*

ca·lyx (kā′liks) the outer leaves that surround a flower bud. The individual leaves are called sepals. *n., pl.* **ca·lyx·es** or **cal·y·ces** (kal′ə sēz).

cam (kam) a mechanism that changes circular motion into linear motion. *n.*

cam·bi·um (kam′bē əm) the layer of soft, growing tissue between the bark and the wood of growing trees and shrubs. New bark and wood grow from here. *n.*

cam·cord·er (kam′kôr′dər) a small video camera and recorder combined in one machine. *n.*

came (kām) the past tense of **come:** *I came to school too early this morning.* *v.*

cam·el (kam′əl) a large, four-legged desert animal with wide, cushioned feet and either one or two humps on its back. The humps store fat which the camel's body turns into water and energy. Camels are used to carry riders and burdens in the desert because they can go a long time without drinking water. *n.*

cam·er·a (kam′ə rə) a machine for making photos, movies, or TV images, or for recording videos. *n.*

cam·ou·flage (kam′ə flȧzh′) **1** an outward appearance that makes a person, animal, or thing blend in with its surroundings to keep it from being noticed: *The white fur of a polar bear is a natural camouflage in the snowy Arctic.* **2** give a false appearance in order to hide; disguise: *The girls used branches to camouflage their fort in the woods. The boy camouflaged his embarrassment by laughing.* 1 *n.,* 2 *v.,* **cam·ou·flaged, cam·ou·flag·ing.**

camp (kamp) **1** a place in the outdoors used for staying overnight, often with a tent, a trailer, or a small, rough shelter: *Our camp was hidden in the bush.* **2** make a camp; choose a place and set up tents or a sleeping area, make a fire, and so on: *We decided to camp by the river the first night.* The spot where you do this is called a **campsite.** A **campground** is a park with a lot of campsites in it. **3** live in a camp (*often used with* **out**): *We camped out all summer.* **4** an organized program of activities like sports, art, hiking, computer learning, music, or other things, happening during vacation time. Such a camp can be held anywhere, with people staying overnight or going home every evening. 1, 4 *n.,* 2, 3 *v.* **—camp′ing,** *n.*
break camp, pack up tents and equipment: *We broke camp early in the morning to return home.*
make camp, set up a camp; set up tents, etc.: *We hiked until sunset, then made camp beside a creek.*

cam·paign (kam pān′) **1** a series of connected activities, such as fund-raising activities, battles in a war, attempts to convince someone, etc., with a certain goal in mind: *The hospital had a campaign to raise money.* **2** take part or serve in a campaign: *The candidates campaigned for votes.* 1 *n.,* 2 *v.*

camp·er (kam′pər) **1** a person who camps or who goes to a camp (def. 4). **2** a vehicle equipped for camping, such as a trailer or a special van. Campers often have built-in beds, cupboards, etc. *n.*

camp·fire (kamp′fīr′) **1** a fire in a camp for warmth or cooking. **2** a social gathering around an outdoor fire. *n.*

a bat	e bed	i bid	o pot	u cup	th thin
ā cake	ē me	ī bite	ō go	ū rude	ᴛʜ then
ȧ bar	ə about	ər over	ȯ for	u̇ put	zh measure

cam·phor (kam′fər) a white substance with a strong odour and a bitter taste, used to make mothballs and medicines. *n.*

cam·pus (kam′pəs) the grounds and buildings of a college, university, or school. *n.*

can¹ (kan) an auxiliary verb used: **1** to say that a person or thing has the power or ability to do something: *My new model train can go very fast. I can't see because you're standing in my way.* **2** to say that someone is allowed to do something: *You can cross the street here. You can leave at four o'clock.* *v.,* past tense **could.**

USING WORDS . . . . can/may

In careful English, some people don't use **can** to mean "be allowed to." For example, they insist that *Can I go?* means *Am I able to go?* and *May I go?* means *Am I allowed to go?*

In informal language, people use **can** for both.

can² (kan) **1** a metal container, sometimes with a cover or lid but usually sealed in one piece so that a special tool is needed to open it: *an oil can, a pop can, a can of fruit.* **2** preserve food by putting in airtight cans or jars: *These peaches are ready to be canned.* 1 *n.,* 2 *v.,* **canned, can·ning.**
can of worms, something very complicated and hard to deal with.

Canada Day (kan′ə də dā′) July 1st, Canada's national holiday. Canada became a nation on July 1, 1867.

Canada goose (kan′ə də gūs′) a large wild goose of North America. It has a black head and neck, a white throat, and a brownish-grey body.

Canada jay (kan′ə də jā′) a North American bird having black and grey feathers. It is also known as the **whisky-jack.** It has many nicknames, including **lumberjack, moosebird,** and **camp robber.**

Ca·na·darm (kan′ə därm′) a special mechanical arm that extends out from a spacecraft so it can move things around in space. It is built in Canada. *n.*

Ca·na·di·an (kə nā′dē ən) **1** a person born in Canada or living there. **2** having to do with Canada or its people. 1 *n.,* 2 *adj.*

Canadian Charter of Rights and Freedoms (kə nā′dē ən chär′tər əv rīts ənd frē′dəmz) a part of our constitution that lists and explains what rights and freedoms we have as Canadian citizens.

Canadian Forces (kə nā′dē ən fôr′siz) the armed forces of Canada, including the army, navy, and air force.

Ca·na·di·an·ism (kə nā′dē ə niz′əm) **1** an expression, such as *muskeg* or *caribou,* or custom that is unique to Canada. **2** loyalty to Canada and to the Canadian way of life. *n.*

Canadian Shield (kə nā′dē ən shēld′) an area of ancient rock encircling Hudson Bay and covering nearly half the mainland of Canada. The Canadian Shield is rich in gold, copper, nickel, and iron.

ca·nal (kə nal′) **1** a waterway dug across land for ships or small boats to go through, or to carry water to places that need it. **2** a tube or passageway in the body or in a plant for carrying food, liquid, etc.: *The food that we eat goes through the alimentary canal.* *n.*

ca·nar·y (kə ner′ē) **1** a small, yellow songbird. **2** light yellow. 1, 2 *n., pl.* **ca·nar·ies;** 2 *adj.*

WORD HISTORY . . . . canary

The word **canary** comes from the Latin word for "dog." What does a bird have to do with a dog? Well, this bird was first seen in the Canary Islands, and one of these islands got its name from the Latin *canares,* meaning "dogs." It seems that sailors named this island after the packs of large dogs that lived on it.

can·cel (kan′səl) **1** do away with; stop the plans for something: *He cancelled his order for the books. The walkathon was cancelled because of the rain.* **2** cross out; mark, stamp, or punch something so that it cannot be used again: *The post office cancels the stamp on a letter that is mailed.* *v.,* **can·celled** or **can·celed, can·cel·ling** or **can·cel·ing.** **—can′cel·la′tion,** *n.*
cancel out, balance or match something opposite so that both can be ignored: *The bus ticket you borrowed from me cancels out the loonie I owe you.*

can·cer (kan′sər) **1** a very harmful disease. Abnormal body cells multiply quickly and spread, destroying the healthy tissues and organs of the body. **2** any evil or harmful thing that tends to spread: *the cancer of hatred.* *n.*

can·de·la·bra (kan′ də lab′ rə) a candle holder that has two or more branches: *Ruth's mother set the candelabra in the middle of the table.* *n.*

can·did (kan′did) **1** speaking honestly and openly. **2** taken without the person knowing or posing: *candid photographs of famous movie stars.* *adj.*
—can′did·ly, *adv.*

can·di·date (kan′də dāt′) a person trying to be elected, get a job, or pass a special exam: *There are four candidates running for mayor in the local elections.* *n.*

To make handmade candles, the wicks are dipped over and over again into melted wax.

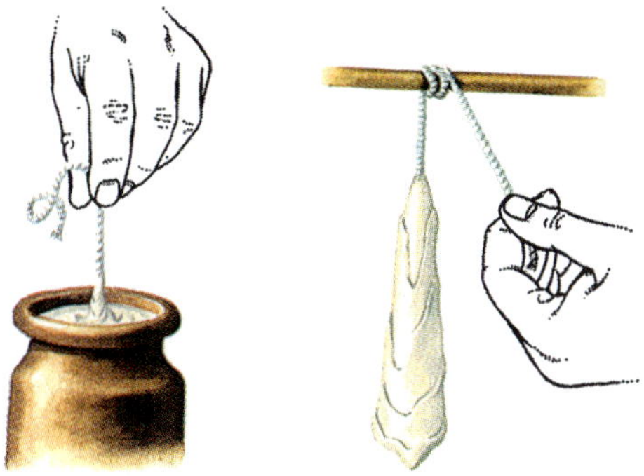

can·dle (kan′dəl) a stick of wax with a string in it called a wick, burned to give light: *She had ten candles on her birthday cake. When the power went off during the storm, we had to use candles.* *n.*
not hold a candle to, be not nearly as good as: *That story can't hold a candle to the one Mikhail wrote.*

Word Family......... **candle**

candlelight: the light from a candle
candlelit: lit by the light from a candle
candlepower: the strength of a light, measured in candelas
candlestick: a holder for a candle

can·dour or **can·dor** (kan′dər) honesty and openness in speaking: *He gave his opinion with complete candour.* *n.*

can·dy (kan′dē) **1** a food made with sugar or syrup and flavouring: *We need sugar, milk, chocolate, and walnuts to make that kind of candy.* **2** a piece of this: *Take a candy from the box.* **3** harden into sugar: *This honey has candied.* **4** cook in sugar; preserve by boiling in sugar: *candied apricots.* 1, 2 *n., pl.* **can·dies;** 3, 4 *v.,* **can·died, can·dy·ing.**

cane (kān) **1** a stick used to lean on in walking: *I had to use a cane until my twisted ankle got better.* **2** beat with a cane. **3** a long jointed stem, or a plant having such stems, such as sugar cane or bamboo. 1, 3 *n.,* 2 *v.,* **caned, can·ing.**

ca·nine (kā′nīn) **1** like a dog; having to do with dogs. **2** a dog or any member of the dog family such as a wolf or fox. **3** one of the four pointed teeth next to the incisors. 1 *adj.,* 2, 3 *n.*

can·is·ter (kan′i stər) a small box or can with a lid, especially one used for flour, sugar, coffee, or tea. *n.*

can·ker (kang′kər) **1** a sore in the mouth. **2** any bad thing that destroys by slowly eating away. *n.*

canned (kand) **1** preserved by being put in airtight cans or jars: *canned fruit.* **2** *Informal.* recorded so it can later be played in a performance or show instead of using the real thing: *canned music, canned laughter.* *adj.*

can·ni·bal (kan′ə bəl) **1** a person who eats human flesh: *Tribes of cannibals once lived on islands in the south Pacific Ocean.* **2** an animal that eats others of its own kind: *Many fish are cannibals.* *n.*

can·non (kan′ən) a big gun fixed to the ground or mounted on a carriage, especially the old-fashioned type that fired large **cannonballs** of iron or steel. *n., pl.* **can·non** or **can·nons.**

can·not (kə not′) can not.

ca·noe (kə nū′) **1** a light, narrow boat having pointed ends, moved with a paddle. **2** paddle a canoe; go in a canoe. 1 *n., pl.,* **ca·noes;** 2 *v.,* **ca·noed, ca·noe·ing.** —**ca·noe′ist,** *n.*

can·on (kan′ən) **1** a law of a church. **2** a rule or standard for judging something by: *the canons of good taste.* **3 a** a list of books of the Bible accepted by the Christian church as being inspired by God. **b** the list of saints recognized by a church. **4** a member of the Christian clergy who has certain duties in a cathedral. *n.*

can·o·py (kan′ə pē) a rooflike covering above a bed, throne, entrance to a building, etc.: *Many animals live in the shade of the forest canopy.* *n., pl.* **can·o·pies.**

can't (kant) cannot.

can·ta·loupe (kan′tə lōp′) a kind of sweet, juicy melon with rough, greyish skin and orange flesh. **Muskmelon** is another word for it. *n.*

can·tan·ker·ous (kan tang′kə rəs) hard to get along with; quarrelsome and bad-tempered. *adj.*

can·ta·ta (kən tȧ′tə *or* kən tat′ə) a set of songs with words telling a story like an opera, but intended to be performed without scenery or action. *n.*

can·teen (kan tēn′) **1** a small container for carrying water or other drinks, often flat and with a cover of cloth or leather. **2** a place in a factory, school, camp, army base, etc. where food, drinks, and other things are sold or given out. *n.*

a bat	e bed	i bid	o pot	u cup	th thin
ā cake	ē me	ī bite	ō go	ū rude	ᴛʜ then
ȧ bar	ə about	ər over	ȯ for	u̇ put	zh measure

can·ter (kan′tər) 1 a horse's running pace, faster than a trot but slower than a gallop. 2 run at this pace: *The horse cantered across the field.* 1 *n.,* 2 *v.*

can·ti·lev·er (kan′tə lē′vər *or* kan′tə lev′ər) 1 a large beam that is fastened at one end only and extends outward from there to support something else such as a bridge or balcony. 2 build with cantilevers: *Our balcony is cantilevered; theirs is supported by pillars.* 1 *n.,* 2 *v.*

cantilever bridge (kan′tə lē′vər brij′) a bridge made of two cantilevers, whose projecting ends meet in the middle.

can·tor (kan′tər) a Jewish man who leads the congregation in prayer, usually in a songlike manner. *n.*

🍁 **Ca·nuck** (kə nuk′) *Informal.* a Canadian. *n.*

can·vas (kan′vəs) 1 a strong, rough cloth made of cotton, flax, or hemp, used to make tents, sails, casual shoes, etc. 2 a piece of this cloth for painting a picture on, especially in oil paints. 3 a picture painted on canvas: *The artist exhibited her best canvases at the fair.* *n.*

can·vass (kan′vəs) 1 go around asking for subscriptions, votes, orders, etc.: *We canvassed the neighbourhood for contributions to UNICEF.* 2 an attempt to get subscriptions, votes, orders, etc.: *We did a canvass of the district.* 1 *v.,* 2 *n.*

can·yon (kan′yən) a narrow valley with high, steep sides, usually with a stream at the bottom. *n.*

cap (kap) 1 a soft, close-fitting covering for the head, especially one with a visor. 2 anything like a cap, such as the lid of a bottle. 3 the highest part; the top. 4 cover the top of, with a cap or something else: *He capped the bottle. Whipped cream capped the dessert.* 5 match one thing with something as good or better: *Karl capped the teacher's joke with one of his own.* 6 a tiny amount of explosive in a covered dot on a strip of paper, especially for using with a **cap gun.** When struck, the cap explodes with a loud crack. 1–3, 6 *n.,* 4, 5 *v.,* **capped, cap·ping.**

ca·pa·bil·i·ty (kā′pə bil′ə tē) ability or power: *This computer system has scanning capability.* *n., pl.* **ca·pa·bil·i·ties.**

ca·pa·ble (kā′pə bəl) able or fit to do something; skilled and efficient: *Saroj is a very capable organizer—she planned a great party!* *adj.* **—ca′pa·bly,** *adv.*
capable of, **a** able or likely to do: *You are capable of excellent work if you try.* **b** open to; ready for: *a statement capable of being misunderstood.*

ca·pa·cious (kə pā′shəs) large and roomy: *a capacious closet.* *adj.*

ca·pac·i·ty (kə pas′ə tē) 1 the amount a room or container can hold: *The capacity of this can is 4 L. This room has a seating capacity of 100 people.* 2 the ability to learn or do: *Vinh has a great capacity for practical jokes!* 3 the position or relation: *I am here in the capacity of an adviser.* *n., pl.* **ca·pac·i·ties.**

cape¹ (kāp) an outer garment without sleeves, falling loosely from the shoulders. *n.*

cape² (kāp) a point of land stretching out into the water. *n.*

ca·per (kā′pər) 1 skip or jump around in a playful way. 2 a playful leap or jump. 3 a prank; trick. 1 *v.,* 2, 3 *n.*

ca·pil·lar·y (kə pil′ə rē *or* kap′ə ler′ē) a very tiny, thin tube joining the end of an artery to the beginning of a vein. *n., pl.* **cap·il·lar·ies.**

cap·i·tal¹ (kap′ə təl) 1 the city where the government of a country, province, or state is located: *Victoria is the capital of British Columbia.* 2 Also, **capital letter,** an upper-case letter like A, G, or Y: *A capital is used at the beginning of a sentence or a proper name.* 3 important; leading: *The invention of the telephone was a capital step forward in communication.* 4 punishable by death: *Murder is a capital crime in many countries.* 5 money or property, especially in business: *A great deal of capital is needed to set up a factory.* 1, 2, 5 *n.,* 3, 4 *adj.*

Grammar Check .... capital letter

When writing English, you should always give a capital letter to the first word in a sentence. Look in the *Grammar and Usage Mini-Guide* for more rules on capitalizing letters.

cap·i·tal² (kap′ə təl) the top part of a column or pillar. *n.*

cap·i·tal·ism (kap′ə tə liz′əm) an economic system in which private individuals own land, businesses, factories, and other kinds of property and pay workers to make things or provide services for profit. Another name for this is **free enterprise.** In some other systems, the government owns all property and pays all workers. *n.*

cap·i·tal·ist (kap′ə tə list) 1 a person whose money and property are used in carrying on business. 2 *Informal.* a rich person. *n.*

cap·it·al·ize (kap′ə tə līz′) write or print with a capital: *You forgot to capitalize the first letter of the name.* *v.,* **cap·i·tal·ized, cap·i·tal·iz·ing.** **—cap′i·tal·i·za′tion,** *n.*
capitalize on, take advantage of: *We capitalized on the unexpected good weather by going on a picnic.*

cap·puc·ci·no (kap′ə chē′nō) a mixture of hot Italian coffee and steamed milk, often topped with powdered cinnamon or cocoa and whipped cream. *n.*

ca·pri·cious (kə prish′əs) likely to change suddenly without reason; changeable; fickle: *capricious weather. adj.* —**ca·pri′cious·ly,** *adv.* —**ca·pri′cious·ness,** *n.*

cap·size (kap′sīz *or* kap sīz′) overturn; turn bottom side up: *The little boat capsized. Rough waves capsized the canoe. v.,* **cap·sized, cap·siz·ing.**

cap·stan (kap′stən) a thing like a large, upright spool, used for winding in long, heavy ropes, anchor chains, etc. Capstans may be turned by hand or by machinery. *n.*

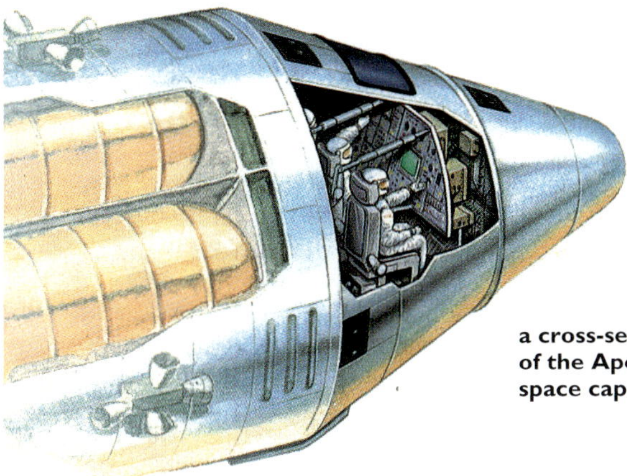
a cross-section of the Apollo space capsule

cap·sule (kap′səl) **1** a small case or covering: *Medicine in capsules is easy to swallow.* **2** the front section of a rocket, made to carry instruments, astronauts, etc. into space. In flight the capsule can separate from the rest of the rocket and go into orbit or be brought back to earth. **3** a dry seedcase that opens when ripe. *n.*

cap·tain (kap′tən) **1** a leader; chief: *I was proud that the coach chose me to be captain of the swim team.* **2** an officer in the armed forces, ranking next above a lieutenant. **3** a commander of a ship or pilot of an aircraft. **4** lead or command as captain: *Barbara will captain the team.* 1–3 *n.,* 4 *v.*

cap·tion (kap′shən) an explanation or title for a picture or cartoon. *n.*

cap·ti·vate (kap′tə vāt′) completely hold a person's attention and interest: *The children were captivated by the puppet show. v.,* **cap·ti·vat·ed, cap·ti·vat·ing.**

cap·tive (kap′tiv) **1** a person or animal taken and held by force, skill, or trickery: *The army brought back many captives.* **2** taken and held; captured: *The captive wolf missed its mate.* 1 *n.,* 2 *adj.* —**cap·tiv′i·ty,** *n.*

cap·tor (kap′tər) a person who takes or holds a prisoner. *n.*

cap·ture (kap′chər) **1** take by force, skill, or trickery: *Three enemy soldiers were captured during the raid.* **2** an act of capturing; the fact of capturing or being captured: *The capture of this ship took place on July 6.* **3** anything taken in this way: *My first capture in the chess game was just a pawn.* **4** attract and hold: *The detective story captured the girl's attention.* 1, 4 *v.,* **cap·tured, cap·tur·ing;** 2, 3 *n.*

car (kår) **1** a motorized passenger vehicle used on roads: *They made the trip by car.* **2** any vehicle that moves on more than two wheels, such as a railway car or streetcar. **3** anything that carries passengers, such as the basket on a hot air balloon: *an elevator car, a cable car, bumper cars. n.* —**car′ful′,** *n.*

Word Family........... **car**

carload: the amount a car can carry
car pool: taking turns to drive others to work/school
carport: a roofed shelter for cars
car-sick: nauseous from being in a moving car
carwash: a place where vehicles are machine washed

car·a·ga·na (ker′ə gan′ə) a shrub with small, light green leaves growing in pairs along a stem. People in the prairies use it for hedges, windbreaks, etc. Caraganas grow well in dry climates. *n.*

car·a·mel (ker′ə məl *or* kår′məl) **1** sugar browned or burned over heat, used for colouring and flavouring. **2** a sauce or chewy candy flavoured with this sugar. *n.*

car·at (ker′ət) a unit of mass for precious stones, equal to 200 mg. *n.*

car·a·van (ker′ə van′) **1** a group of people travelling together in separate vehicles or on separate animals: *A caravan of Arab merchants and camels moved across the desert.* **2** the vehicles or animals used by such a group. **3** a large vehicle that you can live in on a long trip. *n.*

car·a·way (ker′ ə wā′) a plant that yields fragrant, tasty seeds which are used to flavour food. *n.*

a bat	e bed	i bid	o pot	u cup	th thin
ā cake	ē me	ī bite	ō go	ū rude	ᴛʜ then
å bar	ə about	ər over	ȯ for	ů put	zh measure

car·bo·hy·drate (kär′bō hī′drāt) a substance, such as sugar or starch, made up of carbon, hydrogen, and oxygen. Carbohydrates give our bodies energy. *n.*

car·bon (kär′bən) a substance that is found along with other substances in all plants and animals. Diamonds are pure carbon; charcoal is impure carbon. *n.*

car·bon·ate (kär′bə nāt′) add carbon dioxide to produce bubbles and fizz: *Many soft drinks are carbonated.* *v.,* **car·bon·at·ed, car·bon·at·ing.**

carbon dating (kär′bən dāt′ing) a method of finding out the age of very old objects by measuring how much of a certain form of carbon remains in them. Carbon dating is done on objects that were once plants or animals, or things made from them. Because scientists know how fast this form of carbon disappears over time, they can figure out the object's age.

carbon di·ox·ide (kär′bən dī ok′sīd) a gas that has no colour or smell and is present in the atmosphere. The air you breathe out contains carbon dioxide. Plants absorb carbon dioxide from the air and use it to make plant tissue.

carbon mon·ox·ide (kär′bən mə nok′sīd) a poisonous gas that has no colour or smell. It is present in car exhaust fumes.

car·bu·re·tor (kär′bə rā′tər) a part in some gasoline engines that mixes gasoline with air to make an explosive mixture. *n.*

car·cass (kär′kəs) the body of a dead animal: *They saw vultures feeding on the carcass of a lion.* *n.*

card¹ (kärd) **1** a small, rectangular piece of stiff paper, thin cardboard, or plastic: *a credit card, a business card, a playing card, a score card.* **2** **cards,** *pl.* a game played with a set of playing cards: *She enjoys cards.* **3** a piece of stiff paper, usually folded, with a message or greeting and a picture or design, given on a special occasion: *a birthday card, a Valentine card.* **4** a small board with electronic circuits on it that can be added to a computer to allow it to do certain things: *a sound card.* **5** *Informal.* a funny person: *She's really a card.* *n.*

a card up your sleeve, a secret plan or advantage saved until it is needed: *I'm not beaten yet; I still have a card up my sleeve.*

in or **on the cards,** sure to happen: *It was in the cards that it would rain; nothing has gone right all day.*

put your cards on the table, be completely honest about your plans and goals: *We finally came to an agreement after we had both put our cards on the table.*

card² (kärd) **1** a wire brush or other tool with teeth. **2** clean or comb with such a tool: *Wool must be carded to smooth it out before it is spun.* 1 *n.,* 2 *v.*

card·board (kärd′bôrd′) a fairly thick kind of stiff paper used for making cards, cartons, boxes, etc. *n.*

car·di·ac (kär′dē ak′) having to do with the heart. A **cardiac pacemaker** keeps the heartbeat steady. A **cardiac arrest** is a stopping of the heart, or a heart attack.

car·di·gan (kär′də gən) a sweater that opens down the front. *n.*

car·di·nal (kär′də nəl) **1** a North American songbird. The male has bright red feathers marked with grey and black. **2** very important; main: *Patience is a cardinal requirement for parents.* **3** bright, rich red. 1, 3 *adj.,* 2–4 *n.*

cardinal number (kär′də nəl num′bər) any of the numbers that show quantity and are used in ordinary counting. One, two, three, four, five, six, fifteen, forty-eight, eight hundred, etc. are cardinal numbers.

cardinal points (kär′də nəl points′) the four main directions of the compass; north, south, east, and west.

care (ker) **1** feel strong interest: *He cares about music.* **2** serious attention to what you are doing; thoughtful effort: *A good cook works with care.* **3** love and respect shown by giving what someone needs: *Your child will have the best of care.* **4** watchful keeping and protection: *The wallet was left in Rajiv's care.* **5** like; wish: *A cat does not care to be caged.* **6** worry: *to be burdened with care. He was always a care to his parents.* 2–4, 6 *n.,* 1, 5 *v.,* **cared, car·ing.**

care for, **a** like: *I don't care for her.* **b** want or wish: *I don't care for any dessert, thanks.* **c** watch over and give what is needed: *The nurse will care for him during the night.*

in care of, at the address or in the charge of: *Send it in care of the secretary. Symbol:* c/o

take care, be careful: *Take care on the icy path or you will slip.*

take care of, **a** watch over and give what is needed: *A babysitter takes care of children.* **b** deal with: *My mother will take care of this bill.* **c** be careful with: *Take care of your money.*

ca·reen (kə rēn′) **1** tip to one side; tilt: *The ship careened in the strong wind.* **2** rush along with a bobbing, leaning movement: *The waitress careened among the tables, balancing a heavy tray on one hand.* *v.*

ca·reer (kə rēr′) **1** an occupation or profession: *She chose law for her career.* **2** the path or movement of a person or thing through life; lifetime: *The school's Junior*

Caribou and Moose

The caribou is the reindeer of North America. Unlike most deer, both males and females have antlers. Caribou grow over 1 m tall at the shoulder, and vary in colour from white to brown.

The moose is the largest deer. Males can be over 2 m tall and weigh over 800 kg.

Opera Club had a short career. **3** rush along wildly: *The driverless truck careered down the hill.* 1, 2 *n.,* 3 *v.*

care•free (ker′frē′) without worry; light-hearted; happy. *adj.*

care•ful (ker′fəl) **1** thinking about what you say and do; watchful; cautious; paying attention: *Be careful crossing the street. She was careful of the feelings of others.* **2** done with thought or effort: *careful work.* *adj.* —**care′ful•ly,** *adv.* —**care′ful•ness,** *n.*

care•giv•er (ker′giv′ər) someone who looks after children, sick people, or anyone else that needs help. *n.*

care•less (ker′lis) **1** not thinking or caring about what you say or do: *One careless step may cost a life.* **2** done without enough thought or effort; sloppy: *careless work.* *adj.* —**care′less•ly,** *adv.* —**care′less•ness,** *n.*

ca•ress (kə res′) **1** touch or stroke gently and lovingly. **2** a gentle, loving touch. 1 *v.,* 2 *n.*

care•tak•er (ker′tā′kər) a person who takes care of a building, property, etc.; janitor. *n.*

car•go (kär′gō) the load carried on a ship, aircraft, truck, etc.: *a cargo of wheat.* *n., pl.* **car•goes** or **car•gos.**

Car•ib•be•an (ker′ə bē′ən *or* kə rib′ē ən) of or having to do with the Caribbean Sea, between North and South America, or the islands in it. *adj.*

🍁 **car•i•bou** (ker′ə bū) a North American reindeer. They live in great herds on the tundra. *n., pl.* **car•i•bou** or **car•i•bous.**

WORD HISTORY....... caribou

Caribou comes from an Algonquian word *xalibu* meaning "one that paws or scratches." The deer paws through snow to reach the grass underneath.

car•il•lon (ker′ə lon′) a set of bells for playing melodies: *There is a carillon in the Peace Tower in Ottawa.* *n.*

car•i•ole (ker′ē ōl′) **1** a small one-horse carriage. **2** a covered cart. **3** 🍁 a one-horse sleigh. **4** 🍁 a dogsled that can carry one person lying down: *The sick trapper was brought to the trading post in a cariole.* **5** 🍁 ride or carry in a cariole. 1–4 *n.,* 5 *v.,* **car•i•oled, car•i•ol•ing.**

car•nage (kär′nij) the killing of a great number of people. *n.*

car•na•tion (kär nā′shən) a fragrant flower very often used for bouquets, as a decoration, or for pinning to your clothes. *n.*

car•ni•val (kär′nə vəl) **1** a fair or a travelling show with rides, food, games, etc. **2** a program of events celebrating a particular sport, season, etc.: *There were many amazing ice sculptures at the winter carnival.* **3** in some Roman Catholic cultures, a time of feasting and celebration just before Lent. During Lent, many Christians give up certain foods or activities to remind them of Jesus Christ's suffering. *n.*

car•ni•vore (kär′nə vôr′) any animal that feeds mainly on flesh rather than plants; a meat-eater. Cats, dogs, etc. are carnivores. *n.* —**car•niv′o•rous,** *adj.*

car•ol (ker′əl) **1** a song or hymn of joy: *Christmas carols.* **2** sing carols: *On Christmas Eve we went carolling.* 1 *n.,* 2 *v.,* **car•olled** or **car•oled, car•ol•ling** or **car•ol•ing.** —**car′ol•ler** or **car′ol•er,** *n.*

a bat	e bed	i bid	o pot	u cup	th thin
ā cake	ē me	ī bite	ō go	ū rude	ᴛʜ then
ä bar	ə about	ər over	ô for	ů put	zh measure

car•ou•sel (ker′ə sel′) **1** a merry-go-round. **2** at an airport, a platform that turns around and around, where arriving passengers can pick up their baggage. The baggage slides down a chute onto the platform. *n.*

carp¹ (kärp) criticize; complain. *v.*

carp² (kärp) a fish that lives in calm areas of rivers, lakes, streams, and ponds. *n.*

A carpenter at work in medieval times would have tools very similar to those in use today. The design of some tools like hammers or chisels has changed very little over time.

car•pen•ter (kär′pən tər) a worker who builds the wooden parts of houses, barns, ships, etc. *n.* **—car′pen•try,** *n.*

car•pet (kär′pit) **1** Sometimes, **carpeting,** a heavy, woven covering for floors and stairs. **2** anything thought of as being like this: *a carpet of fallen leaves.* **3** cover the floor or ground with a carpet: *Let's carpet the bedrooms. Dandelions carpeted the ground.* 1, 2 *n.,* 3 *v.*

car•riage (ker′ij) **1** a horse-drawn vehicle with wheels that was common before cars were invented. **2** anything with wheels used to move or carry people or things, usually by pushing it: *a baby carriage, a gun carriage.* **3** a person's way of holding the head and body, of walking and moving: *She has a graceful carriage.* *n.*

car•ri•er (ker′ē ər) **1** a person, company, or thing that takes goods, packages, and messages from one place to another. **2** a person or animal that carries disease germs without getting sick, but can still pass the disease on to others. *n.*

car•ri•on (ker′ē ən) dead, rotting flesh: *Vultures live on carrion.* *n.*

car•rot (ker′ət) a long, tapering, orange root that is used as a vegetable. *n.*

car•ry (ker′ē) **1** take from one place or time to another: *Buses carry passengers. This story will carry your thoughts back to last year.* **2** support the weight of; hold up: *Those pillars carry the roof.* **3** hold the body and head in a certain way: *This boy carries himself well.* **4** keep in stock; have for sale: *Our store carries children's clothing.* **5** cover the distance: *Will your voice carry to the back of the room?* **6** in adding, transfer a ten from one column to the next. **7** win a vote, battle, game, etc. *v.,* **car•ried, car•ry•ing.**
carried away, so full of strong feeling that you can't act or speak reasonably: *Arguing for your own opinion is fine, but don't get carried away.*
carry on, a do; manage: *She carries on a successful business.* **b** keep going; continue: *Carry on reading from where we left off.* **c** *Informal.* behave or talk wildly or foolishly: *Oh, stop whining and carrying on!*
carry out, do; get done; complete: *She carried out her job well.*

car•ry•all (ker′ē ol′) a large bag or basket. *n.*

cart (kärt) **1** a vehicle, often with only two wheels, used to carry loads by pushing or pulling: *a baggage cart, a shopping cart. In India I rode in a cart pulled by oxen.* **2** carry in a cart: *Cart away this rubbish.* **3** *Informal.* carry something, or travel, in a way that is bothersome: *carting all over town in the heat. I don't want to cart this backpack around all day.* 1 *n.,* 2, 3 *v.*
put the cart before the horse, get things backward.

car•ti•lage (kär′tə lij) a tough, elastic substance forming parts of the skeleton; gristle. The tip of the nose is made of cartilage and skin. *n.*

car•ton (kär′tən) a cardboard box. Those containing drinks are usually tall, coated with wax, and equipped with a spout for pouring. *n.*

car·toon (kȧr tün′) **1** a sketch or drawing showing persons, things, or events in alight-hearted way. **2** a comic strip. **3** a movie or TV show made from drawings rather than photographs: *Her favourite cartoon comes on at 4:00.* *n.* —**car·toon′ist,** *n.*

car·tridge (kȧr′trij) container for ink, gunpowder, film, etc., specially made as a removable part that fits into some larger thing such as a pen, machine, camera, etc. *n.*

cart·wheel (kȧrt′wēl′ *or* kȧrt′hwēl′) **1** the wheel of a cart. **2** a sideways somersault, made with the arms and legs stretched out stiffly like the spokes of a wheel. *n.*

carve (kȧrv) **1** cut; make by cutting: *to carve a statue out of wood.* **2** decorate with figures or designs cut on the surface: *a jewel box with a beautifully carved lid.* **3** cut into slices or pieces: *Grampa carved the roast at the table.* *v.,* **carved, carv·ing.** —**carv′er,** *n.*

cas·cade (ka skād′) **1** a small waterfall. **2** anything like this: *a cascade of ruffles down the front of a blouse.* **3** form a cascade: *Flowering vines cascaded over the balcony.* 1, 2 *n.,* 3 *v.,* **cas·cad·ed, cas·cad·ing.**

case[1] (kās) **1** any special condition or circumstance: *What would you do in this case?* **2** an instance or example: *We agreed that every case of cheating should be punished.* A **case study** is a story or situation that can be studied as a good example of something: *Our trip to Florida was a case study in poor vacation planning!* **3** a person who has a disease or injury; patient: *The more severe burn cases are sent to the big hospital in the city.* **4** a matter for a law court to decide: *The case will be brought before the court tomorrow.* **5** the reasons or arguments for or against something. *n.*
in any case, anyhow; no matter what happens: *In any case, you should prepare for the worst.*
in case, so as to be ready for what might happen: *Here's an umbrella in case it rains. Keep it just in case.*
in case of, if there is: *In case of fire walk, don't run.*
on someone's case, *Slang.* nagging or criticizing someone.

case[2] (kās) **1** anything to hold or cover something: *Put the knife back in its case.* **2** a box: *There is a big case of books in the hall.* *n.*

case·ment (kās′mənt) a window with hinges on the side, like a door. *n.*

cash (kash) **1** money that can be paid right away. Coins, paper money, and money paid by a bank card are all forms of cash. Cheques and credit cards are not. **2** change into cash; give or get cash for: *The bank cashed my $20 cheque. I can't give you your allowance till I cash my paycheque.* **3** *Informal.* a counter with a cash register in a store, restaurant, etc.: *Please pay at the cash.* 1, 3 *n.,* 2 *v.*

cash·ew (kash′ū) a small, kidney-shaped nut that is good to eat. It grows on a tree in tropical America. *n.*

cash·ier (ka shēr′) a person in charge of money in a store, bank, or any business. *n.*

cash·mere (kash′mēr) a fine, soft wool used in making sweaters, shawls, etc. *n.*

cash register (kash′ rej′ə stər) a machine used in stores for holding money and adding up the amount to be paid by the customer. Usually it prints out the sale on a little slip of paper which the customer keeps as a receipt.

ca·si·no (kə sē′nō) a place where people try to win money by gambling. *n., pl.* **ca·si·nos.**

cask (kask) barrel. *n.*

cas·ket (kas′kit) **1** coffin. **2** a small, fancy box or chest, used to hold jewels, letters, etc. *n.*

cas·se·role (kas′ə rōl′) **1** food cooked in a dish in the oven and served in the same dish. Usually it contains mixed ingredients and can be a meal in itself. **2** the oven dish that this kind of food is cooked and served in. *n.*

cas·sette (kə set′) an audiotape or videotape inside a small, flat, sealed plastic case. You put the whole case in the tape recorder or VCR. *n.*

cast (kast) **1** throw: *to cast a stone. The thieves were cast into jail.* **2** throw one end of a fishing line out into the water. **3** a throw; the distance a thing is thrown: *The fisher made a long cast with his line.* **4** shape by pouring or squeezing into a mould to harden: *Metal is first melted and then cast.* **5** something, such as a statue, made by this method: *A cast of Sir Wilfrid Laurier was set up as a monument.* **6** a plaster support used to keep a broken bone in place while it is mending: *He had his arm in a cast for more than a month.* **7** choose for a part in a play: *Ben was cast as Long John Silver in the school play.* **8** the actors in a play: *The cast was listed in the program.* **9** form or appearance: *Her face had a gloomy cast.* **10** a faint tinge: *a white dress with a pink cast.* 1, 2, 4, 7 *v.,* **cast, cast·ing;** 3, 5, 6, 8–10 *n.*
cast about, look around; search: *We cast about for some way to get up the cliff.*
cast a ballot, vote.
cast down, a lower: *His head was cast down in shame.* **b** discourage: *I was cast down by the bad news.*
cast off, a untie a boat or raise its anchor. **b** make the last row of stitches in knitting.

a bat	e bed	i bid	o pot	u cup	th thin
ā cake	ē me	ī bite	ō go	ü rude	ᴛʜ then
ȧ bar	ə about	ər over	ȯ for	u̇ put	zh measure

Castle

To invade a heavily fortified castle, all kinds of siege machinery were needed: powerful catapults that hurled stones, giant siege towers, and ladders to scale the castle walls.

cas·ta·net (kas′tə net′) a small wooden or plastic rhythm instrument made up of two parts which you hold in your hand and click together, especially to accompany dancing. *n.*

cast·a·way (kas′tə wā′) 1 a shipwrecked person. 2 a person who doesn't seem to belong anywhere. *n.*

caste (kast) 1 one of the ranked social classes that Hindus are born into by tradition. In earlier times, Hindus were not allowed to marry someone from another caste, and some castes had fewer rights than others. 2 any ranked social group. 3 any system of distinct ranked classes or groups. *n.*

cast iron (kast′ ī′ərn) a hard, brittle form of iron made by melting iron and pouring it into a mould to harden. **—cast′-i′ron,** *adj.*

cas·tle (kas′əl) 1 a large building or fort of medieval times, protected against attack by thick walls, towers, heavy gates, drawbridge, moat, etc. 2 any huge, beautiful home. 3 another name for the **rook** in chess, a piece that looks like a castle tower. *n.*

cast·off (kas′tof′) something that has been thrown away or put aside as no longer useful: *You can use those gloves to work in the garden; they're castoffs.* *n.*

cas·tor oil (kas′tər oil′) a yellow oil taken from the beans of a tropical plant, used as a strong laxative.

cas·u·al (kazh′ū əl) 1 not planned: *a casual visit, a casual meeting in the mall.* 2 careless; without much thought or method: *a casual remark, a casual attempt at something.* 3 relaxed and informal: *casual clothes.* *adj.,* **—cas′u·al·ly,** *adv.* **—cas′u·al·ness,** *n.*

cas·u·al·ty (kazh′ū əl tē) a person injured or killed in an accident or war: *The car was a wreck, but there were no casualties.* *n., pl.* **cas·u·al·ties.**

cat (kat) 1 a small, tame, furry meat-eating animal with short ears, a tail, long whiskers, and soft paws with claws that can be drawn in. 2 any animal of the group that includes cats, lions, tigers, leopards, etc. *n.* **—cat′like,** *adj.*
let the cat out of the bag, tell a secret: *It was supposed to be a surprise party, but he let the cat out of the bag.*
rain cats and dogs, rain very hard.

cat·a·logue (kat′ə log′) 1 a list of things in a collection, with notes or descriptions and sometimes pictures: *a book catalogue in a library, a sales catalogue from a store.* 2 make a list of; enter in the proper place in a list: *She catalogued all the insects in her collection.* 1 *n.,* 2 *v.,* **cat·a·logued, cat·a·logu·ing.**

cat·a·ma·ran (kat′ə mə ran′) 1 a boat with two hulls or floats joined side by side by a frame. 2 🍁 a large, roughly built sled for hauling lumber, etc. *n.*

cat·a·pult (kat′ə pult′) 1 a large weapon used in ancient times for shooting stones, arrows, etc. 2 slingshot. 3 a device for launching an airplane from the deck of a ship. 4 throw or be thrown as if from a catapult: *I stopped my bike so suddenly that I was catapulted over the handlebars.* 1–3 *n.,* 4 *v.*

cat·a·ract (kat′ə rakt′) **1** a large, steep waterfall. **2 cataracts,** *pl.* an eye disease. The lens of the eye becomes cloudy, causing faulty vision or blindness. *n.*

ca·tas·tro·phe (kə tas′trə fē) a sudden great disaster; a terrible event: *A big earthquake or flood is a catastrophe. It was a catastrophe for the town when the mine closed and the workers lost their jobs.* *n.*

cat·call (kat′kol′) **1** a shrill yell or whistle to express scorn and disapproval: *The premier's excuses for not doing more about pollution were met with catcalls.* **2** make catcalls at someone: *They catcalled the speaker.* 1 *n.,* 2 *v.*

catch (kach) **1** grab and hold something moving; seize; trap; capture: *to catch a ball, to catch someone's attention. The police caught the thief.* **2** take; get: *to catch fire, to catch a cold. Did you catch what he said? You have just five minutes to catch your train.* **3** notice; discover: *You thought I wouldn't catch that mistake! She caught me stealing a cookie.* **4** be the catcher in baseball: *She catches for our school team.* **5** the act of catching: *She made a fine catch with one hand.* **6** something on a door, lid, etc. to hold it closed. **7** *Informal.* a hidden meaning or difficulty; trick: *There's a catch to that question; think about it carefully.* **8** anything that is caught: *We went fishing and ate the catch for lunch.* 1–4 *v.,* **caught, catch·ing;** 5–8 *n.*
catch on, *Informal.* **a** get the idea; understand: *They caught on when I gave an example.* **b** become popular: *That new song is sure to catch on.*
catch sight of, notice; become aware of; see: *The dog suddenly caught sight of the cat.*
catch up, a come up level with or pass a person or thing going the same way: *Our dog ran to catch up with us.* **b** make up for lost time, missed work, etc.
caught up in something, very involved or interested.

catch·er (kach′ər) in baseball, the player who stands behind the batter to catch the ball thrown by the pitcher. *n.*

catch·ing (kach′ing) likely to spread from one person to another. *adj.*

catch·y (kach′ē) attractive; easy to remember: *a catchy tune.* *adj.,* **catch·i·er, catch·i·est.**

cat·e·go·ry (kat′ə gôr′ē) one division in a system for grouping things: *The two main categories of books are fiction and non-fiction.* *n., pl.* **cat·e·go·ries.** —**cat′e·gor·ize′,** *v.*

ca·ter (kā′tər) **1** provide food or supplies: *She runs a restaurant and also caters for weddings and parties.* **2** provide what is needed or wanted: *The new magazine caters to children who are interested in crafts.* *v.*

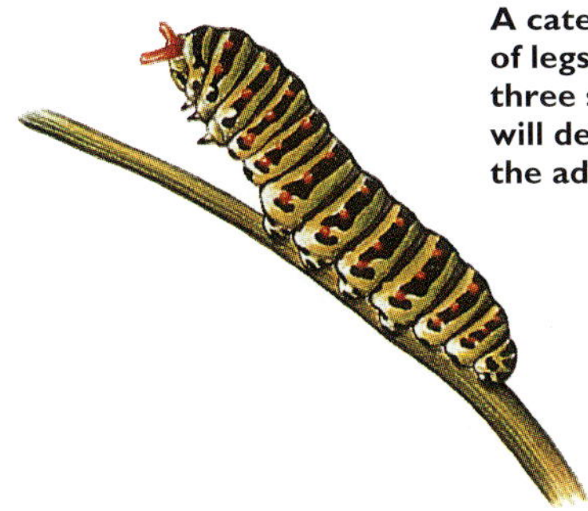

A caterpillar has three pairs of legs (attached to its first three segments) that later will develop into the legs of the adult insect.

cat·er·pil·lar (kat′ər pil′ər) **1** the larva or wormlike form that later turns into a butterfly or moth. **2** Often, **caterpillar tractor,** a tractor that can travel over rough land on wheels that run inside two endless belts of linked steel plates. *n.*

cat·fish (kat′fish′) a fish with long, slender feelers around its mouth, like a cat's whiskers. *n., pl.* **cat·fish** or **cat·fish·es.**

cat·gut (kat′gut′) the dried and twisted intestines of sheep or other animals, used for violin strings and racquet strings. *n.*

ca·the·dral (kə thē′drəl) a large or important church, especially the home church of a bishop. *n.*

Cath·o·lic (kath′ə lik′) **1** having to do with the Christian church led by the Pope. The full name is **Roman Catholic. 2** a member of this church. **3 catholic,** including all people; very broad; universal: *Music has a catholic appeal.* 1, 3 *adj.,* 2 *n.* —**Ca·thol′i·cism′** (kə thol′ə siz′əm), *n.*

cat·kin (kat′kin) a soft, fuzzy, pointed cluster of flowers of the willow, poplar, or birch tree. *n.*

cat·nap (kat′nap′) a short nap or doze. *n.*

cat·nip (kat′nip) a plant that looks like mint, with scented leaves that cats like. *n.*

cat·tail (kat′tāl′) a tall marsh plant with long, tube-shaped, furry brown spikes; bulrush. *n.*

cat·tle (kat′əl) cows, bulls, steers, and oxen. *pl.n.*

🍁 **cat–train** (kat′trān′) a series of large sleds pulled by a **caterpillar tractor.** Cat-trains are used in the North for hauling goods over the frozen muskeg in winter. *n.*

cat·walk (kat′wok′) a high, narrow place to walk, as on a bridge. *n.*

a bat	e bed	i bid	o pot	u cup	th thin
ā cake	ē me	ī bite	ō go	ū rude	TH then
ä bar	ə about	ər over	ô for	u̇ put	zh measure

caught (kot) the past tense and past participle of **catch:** *He caught the ball. The mouse was caught in a trap.* *v.*

caul·dron (kol′drən) a large pot, kettle, or boiler: *Maple syrup may be boiled down to sugar in a cauldron.* *n.*

WORD HISTORY...... cauliflower

Cauliflower comes from the Latin word *cauliflora*, from *caulis* "cabbage" + *floris* "flower." Names for this vegetable in some other languages can also be translated "flower cabbage": *Blumenkohl* in German, and *bloemenkool* in Dutch.

cau·li·flow·er (kol′ē flou′ər) a vegetable that has a solid, white head with a few leaves around it. *n.*

caulk (kok) fill up a seam, crack, or joint with a special rubbery substance called **caulking** so that it will not leak; make watertight: *We had to caulk the seams of our boat again this spring.* *v.*

cause (koz) **1** a person, thing, or event that makes something else happen: *The flood was the cause of much damage.* **2** make happen; make do something; bring about: *The fire caused much damage. A loud noise caused me to jump back.* **3** a reason or occasion for action: *The hero's return was a cause for celebration. You have no cause to complain.* **4** an important goal or movement shared by many people: *World peace is a worthy cause.* 1, 3, 4 *n.,* 2 *v.,* **caused, caus·ing.**

cause·way (koz′wā′) a raised road or path built across wet ground or shallow water. *n.*

WORD HISTORY...... causeway

In case you were wondering what **causeway** has to do with **cause**, the answer is, nothing. Here's the chain:

causeway comes from an Old English word *causey*, which comes from an old Norman French word *caucie*, which comes from the Latin word *calciata*, "paved way," which comes from the Latin word *calx*, "limestone," which is what the Romans used for paving roads. Whew!

cau·tion (kosh′ən) **1** taking care to be safe; avoiding risks: *Use caution in crossing streets.* **2** a warning: *Be sure to read the caution on the label.* **3** warn; urge to be careful: *The police officer cautioned us against playing in the street.* 1, 2 *n.,* 3 *v.* —**cau′tious,** *adj.* —**cau′tious·ly,** *adv.*

cav·al·cade (kav′əl kād′) **1** a procession of people riding on horses, in carriages, or in cars. **2** a series of scenes or events: *a cavalcade of sports.* *n.*

cav·a·lier (kav′ə lēr′) **1** in medieval times, a knight or gentleman who rode a horse. **2** any polite gentleman. **3** too casual; careless; offhand: *a cavalier reply to a serious question, a cavalier attitude toward others.* 1, 2 *n.,* 3 *adj.*

cav·al·ry (kav′əl rē) soldiers who fight on horseback or, nowadays, those who operate tanks and other armoured land vehicles. *n., pl.* **cav·al·ries.**

cave (kāv) **1** a hollow space underground: *He found four caves in the side of the hill.* **2 cave in, a** fall in; sink: *The weight of the snow caused the roof of the arena to cave in.* **b** *Informal.* give in: *Mom finally caved in and bought the video we wanted.* 1 *n.,* 2 *v.,* **caved, cav·ing.** —**cave′-in′,** *n.*

cav·ern (kav′ərn) a large cave. *n.* —**cav′ern·ous,** *adj.*

cav·i·ar (kav′ē är′) the eggs of a fish, usually a sturgeon, preserved in salt and served in small amounts as a special treat: *She loved caviar but couldn't afford to buy it.* *n.*

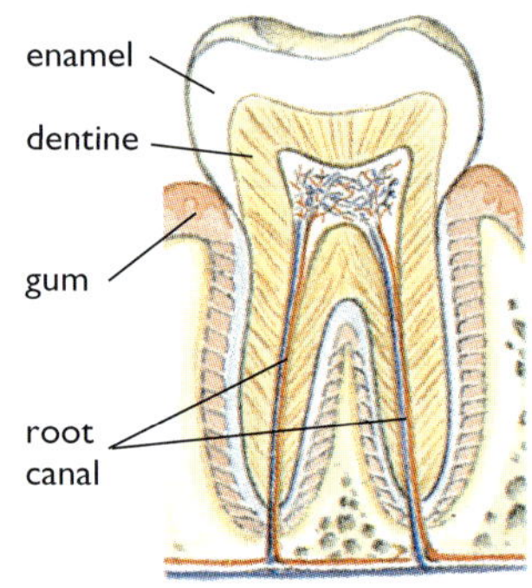

Dental decay is a complex process. Bacteria in the mouth digest the starch and sugar in food, and produce an acid. This acid dissolves the tooth enamel, causing a cavity.

cav·i·ty (kav′ə tē) a hole; a hollow place: *Cavities in teeth are caused by decay.* *n., pl.* **cav·i·ties.**

ca·vort (kə vôrt′) leap around friskily: *A horse cavorts when it feels excited.* *v.*

caw (ko) **1** the harsh cry made by a crow or raven. **2** make this cry. 1 *n.,* 2 *v.*

CBC *abbreviation for* the Canadian Broadcasting Corporation, a radio and TV network supported by the federal government.

cc or **c.c.** *abbreviation for* cubic centimetre(s). The SI symbol is cm^3.

CD (sē′dē′) *abbreviation for* compact disc, a small round plate with sounds, pictures, or words digitally stored on it in very tiny pits. A laser beam inside a compact disc player or computer finds the information on the disc and transmits it.

Cdn. *abbreviation for* Canadian.

CD–ROM (sē′dē′rom′) a compact disc on which huge amounts of information can be stored and later read or used on a computer. For example, CD-ROMs can be used to play games, or to let you look up things in an encyclopedia. *n., pl.* **CD-ROMs.**

CE *abbreviation for* Common Era, the period of history since the birth of Jesus Christ. **CE** is used for times after Christ was born. **BCE** is used for times before Christ was born: *From 200 BCE to 500 CE is 700 years.*

cease (sēs) stop: *The music ceased suddenly.* *v.,* **ceased, ceas·ing.** —**cease′less,** *adj.*

ce·dar (sē′dər) a tree that bears cones and has scalelike leaves, such as the **western red cedar** or the **eastern red cedar.** Cedars are valued for their tough, fragrant wood. *n.*

cede (sēd) give up; surrender; hand over to another: *France ceded Canada to Britain after the defeat of Montcalm in 1759.* *v.,* **ced·ed, ced·ing.**

ce·dil·la (sə dil′ə) a mark like a comma under the letter *c* in certain words that come from French, to show that the *c* has the sound of *s. Example:* façade. *n.*

🍁 **CE·GEP** (sā zhep′) a college in Québec that prepares students for university or for training in a particular kind of work. *n., pl.* **CE·GEPs.**

ceil·ing (sē′ling) **1** the inside top covering of a room. **2** a limit on how high something can go: *That plane has a ceiling of 12 km. The government put a ceiling on rent increases.* *n.*

cel·e·brate (sel′ə brāt′) have a joyful time; do special things to mark a particular day, season, or event: *to celebrate Canada Day with fireworks. The people celebrated when the war ended.* *v.,* **cel·e·brat·ed, cel·e·brat·ing.** —**cel′e·bra′tion,** *n.*

cel·e·brat·ed (sel′ə brā′tid) famous; often talked about: *Charles Dickens was a celebrated author.* *adj.*

ce·leb·ri·ty (sə leb′rə tē) **1** a famous person: *I collect autographs of celebrities.* **2** fame; being famous. *n., pl.* **ce·leb·ri·ties.**

cel·er·y (sel′ə rē) a vegetable with long, crisp stalks which are eaten raw or cooked. *n.*

ce·les·tial (sə les′chəl) **1** having to do with the sky: *The sun, moon, planets, and stars are celestial bodies.* **2** heavenly; very good or beautiful: *celestial music.* *adj.*

cell (sel) **1** a small room in a prison, convent, or monastery. **2** any small, hollow place: *Bees store honey in the cells of a honeycomb.* **3** a very small unit of living matter, made up of jellylike protoplasm with a very thin membrane or wall around it. All living things are made of cells. The human body has blood cells, nerve cells, skin cells, etc. **4** a small battery. *n.*

cel·lar (sel′ər) an underground storage room, usually under a building. *n.*

cel·lo (chel′ō) the second largest instrument of the modern violin family, with a low, rich tone. When played, it rests upright on the floor between the knees of the player, who is seated. *n., pl.* **cel·los.** —**cel′list,** *n.*

cel·lo·phane (sel′ə fān′) a clear, crinkly plastic packaging material, made from cellulose. CDs, etc. are wrapped in cellophane. *n.*

cell·phone (sel′ fōn′) a phone without any wires attached to it that you can carry around with you. A cellphone works by sending radio signals within a certain area, and then passing them on to other areas through a special computer. **Cellular phone** is the full name.

cel·lu·loid (sel′yə loid′) a stiff, transparent plastic used for photographic film. *n.*

cel·lu·lose (sel′yə lōs′) a substance that forms the walls of plant cells; the woody part of trees and plants, used to make paper, plastics, etc. *n.*

Cel·si·us (sel′sē əs) the name of a scale for measuring temperature. On this scale water freezes at 0° and boils at 100°. **Centigrade** is another name for it. *adj.*

Cel·tic (kel′tik *or* sel′tik) the name of a people including the Irish, Highland Scots, Welsh, and Ancient Britons. They are the **Celts.** *adj.*

ce·ment (sə ment′) **1** a fine, grey powder made by burning clay and limestone. It becomes hard when mixed with water. Sand or gravel is added to the mixture to make concrete. **2** any soft substance that hardens to make things stick together: *rubber cement.* **3** fasten together or make firm with, or as if with, cement: *to cement a broken cup. Their many shared adventures cemented their friendship.* **4** pour or spread concrete for: *The workers were cementing the sidewalk.* 1, 2 *n.,* 3, 4 *v.*

cem·e·ter·y (sem′ə ter′ē) a place for burying the dead; graveyard. *n., pl.* **cem·e·ter·ies.**

a bat	e bed	i bid	o pot	u cup	th thin
ā cake	ē me	ī bite	ō go	ū rude	ŧʜ then
ä bar	ə about	ər over	ô for	ù put	zh measure

cen•sor (sen′sər) 1 a person whose job is to examine books, news reports, movies, and so on, and to change them if necessary to make sure they contain nothing that could be too harmful or politically dangerous. 2 examine and make changes as needed; take out unacceptable parts: *All letters from the battlefront were censored. Two scenes in the movie had been censored.* 1 *n.,* 2 *v.* —**cen′sor•ship,** *n.*

cen•sure (sen′shər) 1 an expression of disapproval; criticism: *Censure is sometimes harder to take than punishment.* 2 criticize: *His employer censured him for being late.* 1 *n.,* 2 *v.,* **cen•sured, cen•sur•ing.**

cen•sus (sen′səs) an official count of the people of a country or district. *n.*

cent (sent) a coin of Canada and many other countries: *There are 100 cents in one dollar. Symbol:* ¢ *n.*

cen•taur (sen′tȯr) in Greek myths, a monster that had the head, arms, and chest of a man, and the body and legs of a horse. *n.*

cen•ten•ni•al (sen ten′yəl) 1 a hundredth anniversary: *Canada celebrated its centennial in 1967.* 2 having to do with 100 years or a hundredth anniversary: *a centennial project.* 1 *n.,* 2 *adj.*

centi– *an SI prefix meaning* hundredth; $^1/_{100}$ A centimetre is one hundredth of a metre. The prefix **centi-** can be used with other units too, such as *gram* or *litre.*

cen•ti•me•tre (sen′tə mē′tər) a measure of length equal to one hundredth of a metre. *Symbol:* cm *n.*

The word centipede comes from Latin words meaning "a hundred feet." These creatures don't really have one hundred feet. There are similar animals called millipedes. How many feet do you think they are supposed to have?

cen•ti•pede (sen′tə pēd′) a small wormlike animal with a long, flat body and many pairs of legs. *n.*

cen•tral (sen′trəl) 1 having to do with the centre: *The sun is central in the solar system. The park is in the central part of town. We shop at a central market.* 2 main; most important: *What is the central idea in this story?* *adj.* —**cen′tral•ly,** *adv.*

Central America (sen′trəl ə mer′ə kə) the narrow area of land joining North and South America and containing several countries. —**Central American.**

cen•tre (sen′tər) 1 in math, a point inside a circle or sphere that is the same distance away from all the points on the circumference or surface. 2 the middle point or part: *the centre of a room.* 3 a place with a lot of coming and going and other activity; a main point: *Victoria is a centre of tourism.* 4 put in the middle: *Centre the table on the stage.* 5 or **be centred,** have as a main location or main focus: *About 50 loggers are centred at this camp. All his hopes centred on winning.* **Center** is another spelling. 1–3 *n.,* 4, 5 *v.,* **cen•tred, cen•tring.**

cen•tu•ry (sen′chə rē) a period of 100 years, especially from one "round" hundred to the next in a particular system of counting years: *From 1800 to 1900, or from 1824 to 1924, is a century.* *n., pl.* **cen•tu•ries.**

USING WORDS ...... century

The name of a century is almost always one more than the number of its hundred: 1867 is in the 19th century, 1967 is in the 20th century, and so on.

But what about, for example, the year 1900? Is it the first year of the 20th century, or the last year of the 19th? People have agreed that it should be the last year of the 19th century.

So, what date is the beginning of the 21st century? Yes, that's right, if December 31, 2000 is the last day of the 20th century, then January 1, 2001 is the first day of the 21st century.

ce•ram•ic (sə ram′ik) 1 having to do with pottery, earthenware, porcelain, etc.: *a ceramic vase, ceramic tiles.* 2 **ceramics,** *pl.* a the art of making pottery, earthenware, etc.: *We're learning ceramics in art class.* b earthenware things: *I saw some beautiful ceramics at the craft show.* 1 *adj.,* 2 *n.*

ce•re•al (sē′rē əl) 1 any grass that produces a grain used as food: *Wheat, rice, corn, oats, and barley are cereals.* 2 food made from the grain, especially breakfast food: *Granola is my favourite cereal.* *n.*

ce•re•bral pal•sy (sə rē′brəl pol′zē *or* ser′ə brəl pol′zē) a disease caused by damage to the brain before or during birth. Cerebral palsy makes it hard for a person to control body movements or speech.

cer•e•mo•ni•ous (ser′ə mō′nē əs) very formal, fussy, or polite. *adj.*

cer•e•mo•ny (ser′ə mō′nē) 1 a special form or set of acts to be done on special occasions such as weddings, funerals, graduations, etc.: *A rabbi performed the marriage ceremony.* 2 a very polite, formal, or fussy way of doing anything: *The manager welcomed us with a great deal of*

ceremony. Ramona makes such a ceremony of getting ready for bed. *n., pl.* **cer·e·mo·nies.** **—cer′e·mo′ni·al,** *adj.*
stand on ceremony, be very stiff and formal: *The premier does not stand on ceremony but always makes people feel comfortable and relaxed.*

cer·tain (sər′tən) 1 sure: *It is certain that 3 and 2 do not add up to 6.* 2 definite but not named; some: *Certain plants will not grow in this country.* *adj.* **—cer′tain·ly,** *adv.* **—cer′tain·ty,** *n., pl.* **cer′tain·ties.**

cer·tif·i·cate (sər tif′ə kit) a written statement that may be used as proof of some fact: *a birth certificate. A teaching certificate proves that you are a trained teacher.* *n.*

cer·ti·fy (sər′tə fī′) declare, in speech or writing, that something is true or meets a certain standard. Doctors certify that a person is really dead and manufacturers may certify the safety of their products. A **certified cheque** is one guaranteed to be good because the money to cover it has already been set aside by the bank. *v.,* **cer·ti·fied, cer·ti·fy·ing.** **—cer′ti·fi·ca′tion,** *n.*

ces·sa·tion (se sā′shən) the fact of having ceased; a pause; stop: *a cessation of fighting.* *n.*

CFCs chemicals that have been used to cool refrigerators and to make the mixture inside spray cans shoot out through the tiny opening. When CFCs escape as gases into the atmosphere, they destroy the ozone layer that helps protect us from harmful rays of the sun. The full name for CFCs is **chlorofluorocarbons** (klôr′ə flôr′ə kär′bənz).

chafe (chāf) 1 rub: *This stiff collar chafes my neck.* 2 make or become angry: *His sister's teasing chafed him. He chafed at the teasing.* *v.,* **chafed, chaf·ing.**

chaff[1] (chaf) 1 the stiff, strawlike bits around the grains of wheat, rye, or oats. It is removed by threshing. 2 something worthless. *n.*

chaff[2] (chaf) 1 tease good-naturedly: *Her friends chaffed her about her forgetfulness.* 2 good-natured teasing: *She didn't mind their chaff.* 1 *v.,* 2 *n.*

cha·grin (shə grin′) a feeling of disappointment, failure, or humiliation: *He felt chagrin because he did not get a prize.* *n.* **—cha·grined′,** *adj.*

chain (chān) 1 a series of links or rings joined together. It can be used for connecting or keeping things in place, or for decoration: *The anchor was attached to a heavy steel chain. We hung coloured paper chains around the room.* 2 any series of things linked together: *a mountain chain, a chain of events, a restaurant chain.* 3 Often, **chains,** *pl.,* anything that keeps a person from being free: *the chains of poverty.* 4 fasten or keep captive with a chain. 1–3 *n.,* 4 *v.*

Word Family.......... chain

chain letter: a letter sent on to other people
chain reaction: a series of things each caused by the one before
chain saw: a power saw with teeth in a looped chain
chain store: a group of stores run by one company

chair (cher) 1 a single seat with a back and, sometimes, arms. 2 a leadership position at a university: *Professor Ferreira occupies the chair of Astronomy.* 3 a short form of **chairperson, chairman,** or **chairwoman.** *n.*

chair·per·son (cher′pər′sən) the person in charge of a meeting, committee, council, etc. In some places, the official title is **chairman. Chairperson, chairman,** and **chairwoman** are all sometimes shortened to **chair.** *n.*

cha·let (sha lā′) a house in the countryside or forest with a very steep roof that hangs over quite far on each side: *They rent a chalet on weekends during the winter.* *n.*

chal·ice (chal′is) a cup; goblet, especially one used in ceremonies. *n.*

chalk (chok) 1 a soft, white or grey limestone, made up mostly of very tiny bits of sea shell. 2 a material like this used to make sticks for writing on a chalkboard. 3 mark, write, or draw with chalk. 1, 2 *n.,* 3 *v.* **—chalk′y,** *adj.*
chalk up, score: *Our team chalked up 20 points.*

chalk·board (chok′bôrd′) a board with a smooth, hard surface for writing or drawing on with chalk. *n.*

chal·lenge (chal′ənj) 1 invite someone to compete or take risk: *They challenged me to a race.* 2 an invitation to compete or take a risk: *This mountain climber sees every peak as a challenge.* 3 ask someone to identify himself or herself or to give an explanation, proof, etc.: *The security guard challenged us at the gate. Jorg challenged my claim that city life was boring.* 4 demand real effort from: *I think this assignment will challenge you.* 5 something that demands real effort: *Memory work is a challenge for Marta.* 1, 3, 4 *v.,* **chal·lenged, chal·leng·ing;** 2, 5 *n.* **—chal′leng·ing,** *adj.* **—chal′leng·er,** *n.*

a bat	e bed	i bid	o pot	u cup	th thin
ā cake	ē me	ī bite	ō go	ū rude	ᴛʜ then
ä bar	ə about	ər over	ȯ for	u̇ put	zh measure

cham·ber (chām′bər) **1** a room for a special purpose. **2** a group of lawmakers, or the hall where they meet. Parliament has two chambers, the Senate and the House of Commons. **3** any closed-in space in the body of an animal or plant, or in a machine: *The heart has four chambers.* *n.*

cham·ber·lain (chām′bər lin) the person who manages the household of a ruler or of a great noble. *n.*

The chameleon can move its eyes independently of each other. Its tongue shoots out at lightning speed, to a length greater than its body.

cha·me·le·on (kə mē′lē ən) **1** a lizard that can change the colour of its skin to match its surroundings. **2** a changeable or fickle person. *n.*

cham·ois (sham′ē) **1** a piece of soft leather for polishing. **2** a small mountain goat of Europe and southwestern Asia. Very soft leather is made from its skin. *n., pl.* **cham·ois** (sham′ēz).

cham·pi·on (cham′pē ən) **1** the winner of a major contest or tournament: *an Olympic champion.* **2** first; best in a contest: *a champion runner.* **3** a person who fights or speaks up for something: *a great champion of peace.* **4** fight or speak up for: *She championed the environment.* 1, 3 *n.*, 2 *adj.*, 4 *v.*
—cham′pi·on·ship, *n.*

chance (chans) **1** an opportunity or possibility: *a chance to make some money. There is a chance that the sick child will get well.* **2** fate; luck: *We didn't plan to meet; it happened by chance.* **3** happen: *She chanced to notice a coin on the sidewalk.* **4** risk: *He took a chance when he swam the river.* **5** unplanned; accidental: *a chance visit.* 1, 2, 4 *n.*, 3 *v.*, **chanced, chanc·ing;** 5 *adj.*
—chanc′y, *adj.*
chance upon or **on,** happen to find or meet: *I chanced upon an old friend.*
on the off chance, in case some unlikely thing happens: *It was a working day, but I stopped by anyway on the off chance that she was home.*
stand a chance, have even the least possibility or hope: *We don't stand a chance of winning without Lauren.*

chan·cel·lor (chan′sə lər) **1** a high official in the government of certain countries. **2** the highest official in some universities. *n.*

chan·de·lier (shan′də lēr′) a light fixture that hangs from a ceiling and has branches for individual lights. *n.*

change (chānj) **1** make different; become different: *She changed the rules when we complained. He has changed a lot over the years.* **2** the act, fact, or result of this: *Don't be afraid of change. There has been a change in plans.* **3** shift; switch: *to change clothes, to change seats, to change direction* (*v.*). *The change from farming to city life was hard* (*n.*). **4** get or give smaller units of money for: *Can you change a ten-dollar bill?* **5** smaller units of money given for a larger one: *I need change for a twenty.* **6** the money you get back when you give more than a thing costs: *If the bread is $1.50 and you pay with a toonie, you'll get 50¢ change.* **7** coins: *a five-dollar bill and some change.* 1, 3, 4 *v.*, **changed, chang·ing;** 2, 3, 5–7 *n.*
—change′a·ble, *adj.* **—change′less,** *adj.*
change hands, pass from one person to another: *During the sale a lot of money changed hands.*
change of heart, a complete change in your character or in the way you feel about something.

chan·nel (chan′əl) **1** a body of water joining two larger bodies of water: *The English Channel lies between the North Sea and the Atlantic Ocean.* **2** the bed of a stream, river, etc., or any passage for water or other liquid. **3** the route taken by something: *The information came through secret channels.* **4** a TV or radio station. **5** form or cut a passageway: *The river had channelled its way through the rock.* **6** a path on the Internet to information that appeals to people who have a particular interest. 1–4, 6 *n.*, 5 *v.*, **chan·nelled** or **chan·neled, chan·nel·ling** or **chan·nel·ing.**

chant (chant) **1** a song where several syllables or words are sung to one note: *Chants are used in some religious services.* **2** sing in this way. **3** say words over and over to a steady beat: *We chanted, "Go, team, go!"* **4** something said in this way. 1, 4 *n.*, 2, 3 *v.*
—chant′er, *n.*

chant·ey (shan′tē *or* chan′tē) a song once sung by sailors in rhythm with their work. The usual spelling is **shanty.**

cha·os (kā′os) very great confusion; complete disorder: *The tornado left chaos behind it.* *n.*
—cha·ot′ic (kā ot′ik), *adj.*

chap[1] (chap) make or become cracked and rough: *My lips chap in very cold weather.* *v.*, **chapped, chap·ping.**

chap² (chap) *Informal.* a fellow; a man or boy. *n.*

cha·pa·ti (chə pȧ′ tē) a thin, flat bread like a pancake, usually made of whole-wheat flour: *We ordered vegetable curry and a couple of chapatis.* *n., pl.* **cha·pa·tis.**

chap·el (chap′əl) a small place for Christian worship, either a separate building or a special room inside a building: *The airport has a chapel in it for travellers.* *n.*

chap·er·one (shap′ə rōn′ *or* shap′ ə rōn′) **1** an adult who supervises children or young people at a social event like a dance or party. **2** supervise people at this kind of event: *Mr. Suggett and Mrs. Donato are going to chaperone for the grade 6 dance.* 1 *n.,* 2 *v.,* **chap·er·oned, chap·er·on·ing.**

chap·lain (chap′lən) a member of the clergy serving a hospital, prison, university, etc. *n.*

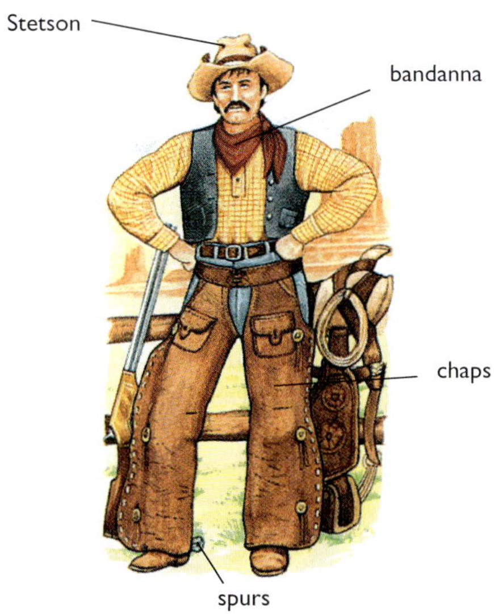

chaps (shaps *or* chaps) backless leggings of tough leather, worn by a cowboy or cowgirl to protect the pants when riding. *pl.n.*

chap·ter (chap′tər) **1** a main division of a book. **2** a local branch of an organization. *n.*

char¹ (chȧr) burn until black. *v.,* **charred, char·ring.**

char² (chȧr) a freshwater fish from northern waters, belonging to the salmon and trout family. It is good to eat. *n.*

char·ac·ter (ker′ik tər) **1 a** nature; kind; sort: *I heard sounds of a very strange character.* **b** special quality or atmosphere that makes something unique and interesting: *This old house has a lot of character.* **2** moral nature or strength: *She is a woman of character, honest and courageous.* **3** a person in a movie, play, or story. **4** an especially unusual or interesting person: *The retired sea captain was a character in the village.* **5** any symbol used in writing, printing, or computing, including letters, numerals, punctuation marks, math symbols, etc. *n.*

char·ac·ter·is·tic (ker′ik tə ris′tik) **1** that makes a certain person or thing different from others: *Bananas have their own characteristic smell.* **2** a special quality or feature: *The characteristic I like best in him is his cheerfulness. An elephant's trunk is its most noticeable characteristic.* 1 *adj.,* 2 *n.*

char·ac·ter·ize (ker′ik tə rīz′) **1** describe the special qualities or features of: *I would characterize our teacher as a very friendly person.* **2** distinguish; mark out: *Her taste in clothes is characterized by bright colours and casual styles.* *v.,* **char·ac·ter·ized, char·ac·ter·iz·ing.**

cha·rade (shə rād′) **1** a word represented by a picture or an action, etc. **Charades** is a game where people act out a word, phrase, etc. for others who try to guess it. **2** an action that is very obviously phony: *That apology was just a charade.* *n.*

char·coal (chȧr′kōl′) a form of carbon produced from wood by a special burning process. It is black and can be used for drawing with as well as for fuel and in filters. *n.*

charge (chȧrj) **1** ask as a price: *They charge two dollars for eggs.* **2** price: *a charge for delivery.* **3** treat as a debt to be settled later; pay for with a **charge card** or a **charge account:** *Please charge this to my account.* **4** rush forward, especially to attack: *The angry bull charged* (*v.*). *The captain led the charge against the enemy* (*n.*). **5** accuse: *The officer charged me with speeding.* **6** accusation: *She pled guilty to the charge in court.* **7** give someone a duty: *We were charged with tidying the rec room.* **8** a duty or an order: *You have carried out your charge very well.* **9** a person or thing someone is taking care of: *The babysitter never took her eyes off her young charges.* **10** care or safekeeping: *All their belongings were left in our charge.* **11** give or get a supply of electrical energy: *to charge a battery.* **12** a supply of electrical energy: *Plug it in to restore the charge.* **13** thrill or amusement: *He gets a real charge out of learning new skateboarding stunts.* 1, 3–5, 7, 11 *v.,* **charged, charg·ing;** 2, 4, 6, 8–10, 12, 13 *n.*
in charge, in the position of leadership or responsibility: *The adults left a teenager in charge. Who's in charge of intramural sports?*

charg·er (chȧr′jər) a war horse. *n.*

a bat	e bed	i bid	o pot	u cup	th thin
ā cake	ē me	ī bite	ō go	ū rude	ᴛʜ then
ȧ bar	ə about	ər over	ȯ for	u̇ put	zh measure

The chariot is the ancestor of all modern wheeled vehicles. It could be pulled by two, three, or four horses.

char·i·ot (cher′ē ət) a two-wheeled horse-drawn vehicle of ancient times. *n.*

char·i·ta·ble (cher′ə tə bəl) 1 generous and kind, both in helping those who need it and in judging people's behaviour: *It was very charitable of you to ignore that nasty remark I made.* 2 working to help others, not to make money: *The Salvation Army is a charitable organization.* *adj.* —**char′i·ta·ble·ness,** *n.* —**char′i·ta·bly,** *adv.*

char·i·ty (char′ə tē *or* cher′ə tē) 1 gifts or work to help people in need. 2 a group that does work or collects gifts for people in any kind of need: *She gives money to the United Way and to other charities.* 3 kindness in helping and judging other people. *n., pl.* **char·i·ties.**

char·ley horse (chàr′lē hôrs′) *Informal.* a stiffness or cramp in a muscle, especially of the leg or arm.

charm (chàrm) 1 the quality that makes a person or thing delightful or fascinating: *We were impressed by the dancer's grace and charm.* 2 delight and fascinate: *The children were charmed by the sailor's tales of adventure.* 3 a small ornament worn on a necklace, bracelet, etc. 4 anything supposed to have magic power to help or harm people. 5 protect or act on by magic or as if by magic: *a charmed life. His grandchildren's laughter charmed away the old man's troubles.* 1, 3, 4 *n.,* 2, 5 *v.* —**charm′ing,** *adj.*

chart (chàrt) 1 information arranged in a table, graph, diagram, etc. 2 a sailor's map showing the coastlines, sailing routes, and dangerous places of an ocean. 3 make a chart of: *to chart the course of a ship, to chart a patient's progress.* 1, 2 *n.,* 3 *v.*

char·ter (chàr′tər) 1 a document granting certain rights, to citizens, or to companies or individuals who want to do special kinds of business: *All Canadian banks must have charters from the federal government.* 2 give a charter to. 3 hire a bus, plane, etc. for private use. 1 *n.,* 2, 3 *v.*

chase (chās) 1 follow or run after in order to catch: *The cat chased the mouse. The dog chased the stick I threw.* 2 the act of going after in order to catch: *The thieves were caught after a brief chase.* 3 drive away; shoo: *to chase away flies.* 4 go somewhere in a rush: *I have to chase downtown for a meeting at 3 p.m.* 1, 3, 4 *v.,* **chased, chas·ing;** 2 *n.*

chasm (kaz′əm) a deep opening in the earth. *n.*

chas·sis (shas′ē *or* chas′ē) the frame that supports the body of a car, plane, etc. *n., pl.* **chas·sis** (shas′ēz *or* chas′ēz).

chaste (chāst) 1 pure; morally good and decent. 2 not too fancy in taste or style; simple. *adj.*

chas·ten (chā′sən) 1 make more careful, humble, etc.; subdue: *The fright they got chastened them.* 2 use loving discipline to teach. *v.*

chas·tise (chas tīz′) 1 punish. 2 criticize or tell off severely: *The coach chastised the players for being late.* *v.,* **chas·tised, chas·tis·ing.**

chat (chat) 1 easy, familiar talk: *We had a pleasant chat about old times.* 2 talk in an easy, familiar way: *We sat chatting by the fire after supper.* 3 have a discussion by computer in a **chat room.** 1 *n.,* 2, 3 *v.,* **chat·ted, chat·ting.**

chat room (chat′ rūm′) an Internet site where a group of people interested in some subject can converse online by typing on their computer keyboards. Since all the people taking part are sharing the connection, your message appears on all their screens as you type, and any of them can instantly reply. Another spelling is **chatroom. Chat site** and **chat line** are other words for this; a **chat group** can also be people using the chat room.

chat·ter (chat′ər) 1 talk fast and foolishly or make meaningless noise. A person who talks too much is a **chatterbox.** 2 rapid, foolish talk that goes on and on, or a sound like this. 3 rattle together: *Cold makes your teeth chatter.* 1, 3 *v.,* 2 *n.* —**chat′ter·er,** *n.*

chat·ty (chat′ē) 1 fond of friendly, familiar talk. 2 written in a friendly, casual style: *a chatty letter.* *adj.,* **chat·ti·er, chat·ti·est.**

chauf·feur (shō fər′ *or* shō′fər) a person who drives a car for someone rich or famous: *The president of the bank has a chauffeur.* *n.*

cheap (chēp) 1 with a low price, or low prices: *cheap clothing, a cheap grocery store* (*adj.*). *We sold the car cheap to get rid of it* (*adv.*). 2 not worth very much; poor quality: *cheap novels, cheap jewellery.* 3 stingy; not generous; mean: *a cheap thing to do. They were too cheap to give even a small tip to the waiter.* 1–3 *adj.,* 1 *adv.* **—cheap′ness,** *n.* **—cheap′ly,** *adv.* **—cheap′en,** *v.*

cheat (chēt) 1 trick someone; do something unfair or dishonest: *The peddler cheated me out of ten cents change.* 2 a person who is not honest or fair and tries to trick others. 3 a trick. 1 *v.,* 2, 3 *n.*

check (chek) 1 look or listen to see if something is true, or to make sure something is OK: *Check that you have everything packed. Check your answers before handing in your paper.* 2 the act of doing this: *During one of his routine safety checks he found a loose bolt. Run a spell check on this computer file before printing it.* 3 Often, **check mark,** a mark like this [✔] to show that something has been looked at and is OK. 4 the bill in a restaurant. 5 give to some official person for safekeeping: *to check baggage at the airport before boarding.* 6 the place to do this: *The coat check is over there.* 7 stop or hold back: *She started to say something rude, but checked herself just in time.* 8 something that stops or holds back: *Stiff fines act as a check on speeding.* 9 in hockey, slow down or stop the player who has the puck, using your stick or your body. 10 a pattern of little squares: *a sports shirt in a blue check.* 11 in chess, the position of the king when it is standing where an enemy piece could take it. **Check mate** means there is no safe square for the king to move to. 1, 5, 7, 9 *v.,* 2–4, 6, 8, 10, 11 *n.*
—checked, *adj.* **—check′er,** *n.*
check in, a arrive and register at a hotel, etc. **b** go to an airline counter to hand over your baggage and get your boarding pass before flying.
check off, mark something on a list to show that it has been taken care of or is correct.
check on or **check up on,** find out about in order to see if there is some problem: *The police were checking up on her.*
check out, a leave a hotel or motel, etc. and pay your bill: *We checked out of the hotel at noon.* **b** in a store, take your purchases to the cashier and pay for them: *It took a long time to check out.*
in check, held back, controlled: *He managed to keep his temper in check.*

> *Word Family*.......... **check**
>
> **checklist**: a complete list of items for checking
> **checkup**: a complete examination

check•er (chek′ər) 1 mark in a pattern of squares of different colours, like a chessboard: *The wall was checkered with blue and white tiles.* 2 one of the 12 flat, round pieces used in the game of **checkers.** Checkers is played by two people on a **checkerboard** marked with 64 squares of two alternating colours. 1 *v.,* 2 *n.*

check•out (chek′out′) 1 the counter where you pay for your things in a store: *I went to the express checkout.* 2 Usually, **checkout time,** the latest that you can leave a hotel, campground, etc. without paying for another day: *Checkout time is 11 a.m.* *n.*

🍁 **chee•cha•ko** (chē chok′ō) a newcomer: *It took the cheechako many months to learn the ways of the Yukon.* *n.*

cheek (chēk) 1 either side of the face below the eye. 2 disrespectful talk or behaviour: *That's enough of your cheek!* *n.* **—cheek′y,** *adj.* **—cheek′i•ly,** *adv.*

cheep (chēp) 1 make a noise like a young bird; chirp; peep. 2 a young bird's cry. 1 *v.,* 2 *n.*

cheer (chēr) 1 a shout of encouragement and support or praise: *Give three cheers for the birthday girl!* 2 give shouts of encouragement or praise: *The boys cheered loudly. Everyone cheered our team.* 3 good spirits; hope; gladness: *The warm fire and good food brought cheer to our hearts again.* 4 make glad; comfort: *Our visit cheered the sick boy.* 1, 3 *n.,* 2, 4 *v.*
—cheer′ful, *adj.* **—cheer′y,** *adj.* **—cheer′less,** *adj.* **—cheer′i•ly,** *adv.*
cheer up, make or become happier: *Cheer up, perhaps we'll win the next game.*

cheer•lead•er (chēr′lē′dər) a person who leads a group in organized cheering, especially at high-school or college athletic events: *The cheerleaders spent weeks practising the school yells.* *n.*

cheese (chēz) a solid food made from the curds of milk. *n.*

cheese•burg•er (chēz′bər′gər) a hamburger with a slice of cheese melted on top of the meat. *n.*

cheese•cloth (chēz′kloth′) a thin, very loosely woven cotton cloth. It used to be for wrapping freshly made cheese. *n.*

a bat	e bed	i bid	o pot	u cup	th thin
ā cake	ē me	ī bite	ō go	ū rude	ŦH then
ä bar	ə about	ər over	ô for	ù put	zh measure

Cheetah

All cats stalk slowly and then pounce, but cheetahs can also chase their prey, at speeds over 100 km/h. It is the fastest animal over short distances.

chee•tah (chē′tə) a long-legged animal of the cat family, thought to be the fastest mammal on earth. It has a small head, long tail, and a reddish yellow coat with black spots: *Cheetahs are found in Africa and Asia.* *n.*

chef (shef) a skilled cook, especially in a restaurant. *n.*

chem•i•cal (kem′ə kəl) **1** having to do with the science of chemistry: *a chemical compound, chemical reactions, chemical research.* **2** a substance made or used in a laboratory. It may come from nature, such as crude petroleum or minerals, or from other substances already made in a laboratory: *Plastics, drugs, and insecticides are chemicals.* **3** having to do with any of these substances or materials: *Chemical preservatives, chemical pollution, the chemical industry.* 1, 3 *adj.,* 2 *n.*

chem•is•try (kem′i strē) the science that studies the simple substances (elements) that everything in the world is made of and how they combine and act. *n.* **—chem′ist,** *n.*

cheque (chek) a small form you can fill out and sign and give instead of cash. It tells the bank to take money from your account and pay it to whomever you have named: *She pays her bills by cheque.* *n.*

cher•ish (cher′ish) **1** hold dear; treasure and care for: *Cherish your friends.* **2** keep in mind; cling to: *The old woman cherished the hope of her son's return.* *v.*

cher•ry (cher′ē) **1** a small, round, juicy red fruit with a hard seed or stone in its centre. It grows on a tree. **2** bright red: *cherry lips* (*adj.*). *n., pl.* **cher•ries;** *adj.*

cher•ub (cher′əb) **1** an angel, especially one pictured as a child with wings. **2** a beautiful or good child. *n., pl.*

chess (ches) a game played by two people, each with 16 pieces, or **chessmen,** that can be moved in special ways on a **chessboard.** The board has 64 squares of two alternating colours, and each player has a king and queen, 2 rooks, 2 knights, 2 bishops, and 8 pawns. *n.*

chest (chest) **1** the upper front part of the body, containing the ribs, lungs, heart, etc. **2** a large box with a hinged lid: *a linen chest, a tool chest.* **3** a piece of furniture with drawers. *n.*

🍁 **ches•ter•field** (ches′tər fēld′) a long, covered seat with a back and arms; a sofa. *n.*

chest•nut (ches′nut) **1** a sweet nut with a prickly outer shell. It grows on a tree. **2** deep reddish brown: *chestnut hair* (*adj.*). **3** a horse of this colour. 1, 3 *n.,* 2 *adj.*

chew (chū) **1** crush or grind with the teeth: *Some meat is hard to chew.* **2** an act of chewing: *Don't gobble your food—give each mouthful six chews.* **3** something for chewing, especially chewy candy: *licorice chews.* 1 *v.,* 2, 3 *n.*

chewing gum (chū′ing gum′) candy meant to be chewed without swallowing. It is sticky and stretchy.

chew•y (chū′ē) needing much chewing; becoming soft and sticky when chewed; not crunchy: *a chewy caramel candy.* *adj.*

chic (shēk) fashionable or stylish. *adj.*

chick (chik) a baby chicken or other bird. *n.*

chick·a·dee (chik′ə dē′) a small bird with black, white, and grey feathers. *n.*

chick·en (chik′ən) 1 a hen or rooster, especially a young one. 2 the meat of a chicken, used as food. 3 *Slang.* a timid person; a coward. 4 *Slang.* cowardly; timid: *The bully said I was too chicken to be part of his gang.* A less slang word for this is **chicken-hearted.** 1–3 *n.*, 4 *adj.*

chicken pox (chik′ən poks′) a very contagious disease that gives you a fever and a rash.

chick pea (chik′ pē′) a vegetable like a green pea but bigger and light-yellow. Chick peas grow in pods on a plant that originally came from Asia.

chick·weed (chik′wēd′) a weed with small white flowers. Its leaves and seeds are eaten by birds. *n.*

chic·o·ry (chik′ə rē) a plant with blue, daisylike flowers. Its leaves are used in salads and its roots are used as a substitute for coffee. Chicory is a common weed in many parts of Canada. *n.*

chide (chīd) scold; criticize: *Dad chided me for ripping my new shirt.* *v.*, **chid·ed** or **chid, chid·ing.**

chief (chēf) 1 the top leader: *a police chief.* The chief of a First Nations band is elected by the people and speaks for them in dealings with the government. 2 leading; in authority; at the top: *the chief engineer of a building project.* 3 most important; main: *the chief reason.* 1 *n.*, 2, 3 *adj.* **—chief′ly,** *adv.*
in chief, mainly; chiefly.

child (chīld) 1 a young boy or girl, especially one up to the early teens. 2 a son or daughter: *He has three grown-up children.* *n.*, *pl.* **chil·dren.** **—child′hood,** *n.*

child·birth (chīld′bərth′) the act or process of giving birth to a child. *n.*

child·ish (chīl′dish) 1 acting like a very young child when in fact you are older and should know better: *How childish to make such a fuss over a little thing like that!* 2 normal for a child: *childish trust.* A more usual word for this meaning is **childlike.** *adj.* **—child′ish·ly,** *adv.* **—child′ish·ness,** *n.*

chil·i (chil′ē) 1 the spicy dried pod of a kind of red pepper, used for seasoning. The pods grow on a tropical bush. 2 short for **chili con carne** (chil′ē kən kȧr′nē), hamburger cooked with chilies or chili powder, kidney beans, and tomatoes. *n.*, *pl.* **chil·ies.**

chill (chil) 1 unpleasant coldness: *There was a sharp chill in the air.* 2 unpleasantly cold: *a chill wind.* 3 make cold: *We chilled the pop in the fridge.* 4 a sudden coldness of the body with shivering: *She was very sick with chills and fever.* 1, 2, 4 *n.*, 3 *v.* **—chill′y,** *adj.*

chime (chīm) 1 **chimes,** *pl.*, a set of bells tuned to the musical scale, usually played by hammers or simple machinery. 2 ring out musically: *The bells chimed at midnight.* 3 the musical sound of bells or a sound like it: *We heard the chime of the clock every hour.* 1, 3 *n.*, 2 *v.*, **chimed, chim·ing.**
chime in, *Informal.* break into or join in a conversation: *"The island? Oh, take us with you!" cried the girls. "Me too! Me too!" little Max chimed in.*

chim·ney (chim′nē) 1 an upright tubelike structure that lets in a draft for a fireplace and carries the smoke out through the roof. It must be cleaned by a special worker called a **chimney sweep.** 2 a glass tube placed around the flame of a lamp. *n.*, *pl.* **chim·neys.**

Chimpanzees use twigs to pull insects out of rotten logs. This makes them tool-using animals, just like humans.

chim·pan·zee (chim′pan zē′ *or* chim pan′zē) an intelligent ape of Africa. The name is often shortened informally to **chimp.** *n.*

chin (chin) 1 the bottom of the face at the front. 2 **chin yourself,** hang by the hands from a bar and pull yourself up until your chin is even with the bar or above it. 1 *n.*, 2 *v.*, **chinned, chin·ning.**

chi·na (chī′nə) a fine, delicate white pottery made of clay baked by a special process, first used in China. **Porcelain** is another name for it. It is used especially for dishes, but also for knick-knacks, vases, etc.: *We set the table with the best china when great-grandma comes.* *n.*

chin·chil·la (chin chil′ə) a South American rodent that looks a bit like a fat squirrel, valued for its very soft, whitish grey fur. *n.*

chink[1] (chingk) 1 a narrow opening; crack: *The arrow entered a chink in the knight's armour.* 2 fill in a crack: *The cracks in the walls of the cabin were chinked with mud.* 1 *n.*, 2 *v.*

chink[2] (chingk) 1 a sound like glasses or coins striking against one another. 2 make such a sound. 1 *n.*, 2 *v.*

a bat	e bed	i bid	o pot	u cup	th thin
ā cake	ē me	ī bite	ō go	ū rude	ᴛʜ then
ȧ bar	ə about	ər over	ȯ for	ů put	zh measure

chi·nook (shi nůk′) a warm winter wind that blows from the west across the Rocky Mountains into Alberta. When a chinook blows, the temperature can rise 15°C in an hour. *n.*

chip (chip) **1** a small, thin piece cut or broken off: *wood chips, dried banana chips.* **2** a place where a small piece has broken off: *One of the new plates has a chip on the edge.* **3** cut or break off in small pieces: *He chipped off the old paint. Handle these cups gently because they chip easily.* **4** potato chip: *We ate the whole bag of chips.* **5** french fry: *fish and chips.* **6** in electronics, a small, flat piece of silicon with many tiny electric circuits on it. Chips are used a lot in computers, often to add memory. **7** in games, a round, flat piece of plastic used as a counter. 1, 2, 4–7 *n.,* 3 *v.,* **chipped, chip·ping.**
a chip off the old block, *Informal.* someone who looks like his or her parent.
a chip on your shoulder, *Informal.* a feeling that you are always being treated unfairly.
chip in, *Informal.* give a share: *If we all chipped in, we'd have enough money for pizza.*

Chip·e·wy·an (chip′ə wī′ən) **1** a First Nations people living in northern Manitoba and Saskatchewan and in the Northwest Territories. They belong to the Dene nation. **2** their language, which belongs to the Athapascan family. **3** having to do with these people or their language. 1, 2 *n.,* 3 *adj.*

chip·munk (chip′mungk) a small, striped North American ground squirrel. *n.*

WORD HISTORY..... chipmunk

The word **chipmunk** comes from an Algonquian word meaning "one who descends trees headfirst." In Ojibwa the word is *atchitamon.*

chirp (chərp) **1** the short, sharp sound made by certain small birds and insects. **2** make this sound: *Crickets and sparrows chirp.* 1 *n.,* 2 *v.*

chis·el (chiz′əl) **1** a tool with a steel cutting edge at the end of a strong blade: *Chisels are used for shaping wood, stone, or metal.* **2** cut or shape with a chisel. Facial features that seem sharp and angular are often described as **chiselled.** 1 *n.,* 2 *v.,* **chis·elled** or **chis·eled, chis·el·ling** or **chis·el·ing.**

chiv·al·ry (shiv′əl rē) **1** the qualities of an ideal knight in the Middle Ages; bravery, honour, protection of the weak, respect for women, and fairness to enemies. These qualities were upheld by a code of rules for knights. **2** courtesy, especially of men toward women. *n.* **—chiv′al·rous,** *adj.*

chives (chīvz) the long, slender leaves of a plant that looks like green onion. They are often chopped and sprinkled on soups or salads. *pl.n.*

chlor·ine (klôr ēn′) a chemical element often added to things to bleach or disinfect them. City tap water and paper pulp are usually **chlorinated.** At normal temperatures chlorine is a greenish yellow, bad-smelling, poisonous gas. *n.* **—chlor′in·ate′,** *v.*

chlor·o·form (klôr′ə fôrm′) **1** a colourless liquid with a sweetish smell, used to dissolve rubber, resin, etc. and as an anesthetic. **2** kill or put an animal to sleep with chloroform. 1 *n.,* 2 *v.*

chlor·o·phyl or **chlor·o·phyll** (klôr′ə fil′) the green colouring matter of plants. It changes carbon dioxide, water, and sunlight into food for the plant. *n.*

chock–full (chok′fůl′) as full as can be; completely full. *adj.*

choc·o·late (chok′lit) **1** a dark brown substance used as a food or flavouring and made by roasting and grinding cacao seeds. It is usually mixed with sugar and has a strong, rich flavour. **2** a drink or candy made with chocolate and sugar. *n.*

choice (chois) **1** the act of choosing: *Be careful in your choice of friends.* **2** the person or thing chosen: *This story was the judges' choice.* **3** a chance to choose: *We had no choice; we had to stay home.* **4** a variety to choose from: *a wide choice of vegetables in the market.* **5** excellent; of fine quality: *The choicest fruit had the highest price.* 1–4 *n.,* 5 *adj.,* **choic·er, choic·est.**

choir (kwīr) an organized group of singers: *a school choir, a church choir.* *n.*

choke (chōk) **1** make or be unable to breathe because the windpipe is being squeezed or blocked: *The smoke almost choked the firefighters. He choked when some food stuck in his throat.* **2** the act or sound of choking: *We heard a choke behind us.* **3** put out a fire by cutting off the air supply. **4** a valve that reduces the supply of air to a gasoline engine. **5** clog; plug: *Sand is choking the river.* 1, 3, 5 *v.,* **choked, chok·ing;** 2, 4 *n.*
choke back, hold back; keep in: *He choked back his angry words.*
choke down, swallow something with difficulty.
choke off, put an end to; stop: *The rock slide choked off our water supply.*
choke up, be or cause to be about to cry: *I choked up when she got to the sad part of her story.*

choke·cher·ry (chōk′cher′ē) a North American shrub or small tree of the same family as plums, cherries, and peaches. It has small, black or dark-red fruit that is good to eat but sour when raw. The seeds and leaves are poisonous. *n., pl.* **choke·cher·ries.**

chol·er·a (kol′ə rə) a serious, infectious disease of the stomach and intestines that can kill. Cholera is marked by vomiting and cramps and is caused by drinking impure water. *n.*

cho·les·ter·ol (kə les′tə rol′) a chemical fatty substance made by the body and found in foods such as milk and meat. Scientists believe that some forms of it may cause heart disease: *Her doctor advised her to cut down on cholesterol.* *n.*

chomp (chomp) **1** bite or chew noisily: *They chomped their way through two bags of potato chips.* **2** a big bite: *I thought that dog was going to take a chomp out of my leg.* 1 *v.,* 2 *n.*

choose (chüz) pick out from different possibilities; decide what you want to have or do: *Choose the cake you like best. You have chosen wisely. She chose to rest.* *v.,* **chose, cho·sen, choos·ing.**

choos·y (chü′zē) *Informal.* very fussy about choosing; hard to please: *She's very choosy when renting a video.* *adj.,* **choos·i·er, choos·i·est.**

chop[1] (chop) **1** cut by hitting with something sharp: *to chop wood with an axe. Don't chop down so many trees.* **2** cut into small pieces: *to chop up cabbage.* **3** a cutting blow. **4** a slice of meat attached to a piece of rib: *pork chops for supper.* 1, 2 *v.,* **chopped, chop·ping;** 3, 4 *n.*

chop[2] (chop) the jaw, especially the fleshy covering of an animal's jaw: *The dog licked its chops.* *n.*
lick your chops, *Slang.* look forward to something really enjoyable: *The children looked at all the presents, licking their chops.*

chop·per (chop′ər) **1** a tool or machine for chopping. **2** *Informal.* helicopter. *n.*

chop·py (chop′ē) **1** jerky: *a choppy ride.* **2** forming short, uneven, broken waves: *The lake is choppy today.* *adj.,* **chop·pi·er, chop·pi·est.**

Chopsticks are used especially by Chinese, Japanese, and Korean people.

chop·sticks (chop′stiks′) a pair of light, thin sticks used together in one hand, something like tongs, for picking up food. *pl.n.*

chor·al (kôr′əl) **1** having to do with a choir or chorus: *a choral society, a choral hymn.* **2** done out loud by a group, sometimes as a performance: *choral reading, choral speaking.* *adj.*

chord[1] (kôrd) three or more notes of music sounded at the same time in harmony. *n.*

chord[2] (kôrd) in mathematics, a straight line connecting two points on a curve. *n.*
touch a chord in someone, draw a response from deep inside a person: *Their story touched a sorrowful chord in him.*

chore (chôr) **1** an odd job; a minor task, especially one that must be done daily: *Feeding the chickens is one of the chores on a farm.* **2** a task that is tiresome or irritating: *I found the work quite a chore.* *n.*

cho·re·og·ra·phy (kô′rē og′rə fē) the arranged movements of a dance. *n.* **—cho′re·o·graph′,** *v.,* **—cho′re·og′ra·pher,** *n.*

WORD HISTORY...... chortle

Chortle was made up by Lewis Carroll, the author of *Alice in Wonderland*. He took bits of the words **ch**uckle and sn**ort**.

Try to make your own new word from bits and pieces of other words!

chor·tle (chôr′təl) **1** chuckle and snort at the same time: *He chortled as he read the comic strip.* **2** a combined chuckle and snort. 1 *v.,* 2 *n.*

chor·us (kôr′əs) **1** a group of singers, sometimes together with dancers. **2** a song sung by many singers together: *The opera ended with a splendid chorus.* **3** the part of a song that is repeated after each verse. **4** sing or speak all at the same time: *The birds chorused around me.* **5** something said by many at the same time: *My announcement was followed by a chorus of cheers.* **6** a short, modern religious song. 1–3, 5, 6 *n.,* 4 *v.*
in chorus, all together at the same time: *The children sang "O Canada" in chorus.*

chose (chōz) the past tense of **choose:** *She chose the red jeans.* The past participle is **chosen:** *Have you chosen a book from the library?* *v.*

chow (chou) *Informal.* **1** food or a meal: *After we went skating we had some chow.* **2 chow down,** eat heartily; have a meal: *to chow down on a big plate of spaghetti.* 1 *n.,* 2 *v.*

a bat	e bed	i bid	o pot	u cup	th thin
ā cake	ē me	ī bite	ō go	ū rude	ᴛʜ then
ä bar	ə about	ər over	ô for	ü put	zh measure

chow·der (chou′dər) a thick soup or stew, often made of clams or fish with potatoes, onions, etc. *n.*

Christ (krīst) 1 the Messiah; the deliverer foretold by the ancient Hebrew prophets. 2 Jesus of Nazareth, regarded by Christians as the Son of God and the true Messiah. *n.*

chris·ten (kris′ən) 1 baptize a child as a Christian. 2 give a first name, or **Christian name,** to a person at baptism: *The child was christened Yvette.* 3 give a name to anything. *v.*

Chris·ti·an·i·ty (kris′chē an′ə tē) the religion that accepts Jesus of Nazareth as the Son of God and the true Messiah foretold by the ancient Hebrew prophets. *n.* —**Chris′tian** (kris′chən), *adj. or n.*

Christ·mas (kris′məs) the yearly celebration of the birth of Christ. In most Christian churches, Christmas is on December 25, but from **Christmas Eve** (Dec. 24) to Jan. 6 is thought of as **Christmastime.** *n.*

Christmas tree (kris′məs trē′) an evergreen tree, such as a spruce or pine, or an imitation of one, hung with decorations at Christmastime.

chro·mi·um (krō′mē əm) a shiny, hard, brittle metal that does not rust or become dull easily. It is used to make stainless steel. *n.*

chro·mo·some (krō′mə sōm′) any of the tiny rod-shaped bodies that appear in the nucleus of a plant or animal cell when it divides. Chromosomes carry the genes that pass on inherited characteristics. *n.*

chron·ic (kron′ik) 1 of a disease, lasting a long time: *chronic bronchitis.* 2 constant; habitual: *a chronic liar, a chronic smoker.* *adj.*

chron·i·cle (kron′ə kəl) 1 a history or story that tells events in the order of their happening. 2 write or tell the story of. 1 *n.,* 2 *v.,* **chron·i·cled, chron·i·cling.** —**chron′i·cler,** *n.*

chron·o·log·i·cal (kron′ə loj′ə kəl) arranged according to the order in which things happened: *The teacher asked them to put together a chronological list of the events.* *adj.*

chrys·a·lis (kris′ə lis) 1 the covering that protects a caterpillar while it changes into a butterfly. 2 the butterfly in this stage. **Pupa** is the other name for this. *n.*

chry·san·the·mum (krə san′thə məm) a plant having ball-shaped flowers with many long, thin petals. It blooms in the fall. *n.*

chub·by (chub′ē) round and plump: *chubby cheeks.* *adj.,* **chub·bier, chub·bi·est.**

chuck (chuk) 1 throw; toss: *He chucked his boots in a corner.* 2 throw out; abandon; scrap. 3 pat; tap: *She chucked her nephew good-naturedly under the chin.* 4 *Informal.* in the West, food. *v.*

chuck·le (chuk′əl) 1 laugh quietly: *Mom chuckled as she watched us trying to give the dog a bath.* 2 a soft laugh; quiet laughter. 1 *v.,* **chuck·led, chuck·ling;** 2 *n.*

chuck·wag·on (chuk′wag′ən) in the West, a wagon that carries food and cooking equipment for cowhands, harvest hands, etc. The **chuckwagon race** is a traditional event at rodeos and stampedes in western Canada. *n.*

chug (chug) 1 a short, loud, puffing sound: *the chug of a steam engine.* 2 make this sound or move with this sound. 1 *n.,* 2 *v.,* **chugged, chug·ging.**

chum (chum) *Informal.* 1 a friend. 2 be friends: *Tom and Anook have chummed for years.* 1 *n.,* 2 *v.,* **chummed, chum·ming.** —**chum′my,** *adj.*

chunk (chungk) a thick piece or lump: *a chunk of wood, bread, etc.* *n.*

chunk·y (chung′kē) *Informal.* 1 like a chunk; short and thick. 2 heavy and solidly built: *a chunky little girl.* 3 containing chunks, as of meat or potatoes: *chunky soup.* *adj.,* **chunk·i·er, chunk·i·est.**

church (chərch) 1 a building for public Christian worship: *We walked past the church.* A cemetery next to a church is often called a **churchyard.** 2 a service of public worship: *Church starts at 10 a.m.* 3 Usually, **Church,** an organization of Christians with the same beliefs, led by people who have religious authority; denomination: *She is a member of the Presbyterian Church.* 4 **the Church,** all Christians. *n.*

churn (chərn) 1 a container or machine for turning cream into butter by beating and shaking. 2 beat and shake cream, etc. in a churn. 3 move or seem to move as if beaten and shaken: *The water churns in the rapids. My stomach is churning.* 1 *n.,* 2, 3 *v.*

chute (shūt) 1 a sloping trough for dropping or sliding things down to a lower level. There are chutes for carrying mail, dirty clothes, garbage, etc. A toboggan slide is also called a chute. 2 rapids in a river; waterfall. *n.*

ci·ca·da (sə kā′də) a large insect with transparent wings. The male cicada makes a buzzing sound in hot, dry weather. *n.*

ci·der (sī′dər) the juice pressed out of apples for use as a drink or to make vinegar. *n.*

ci·gar (sə gär′) a tight, fat roll of dried tobacco leaves for smoking. *n.*

cig·a·rette (sig′ə ret′ *or* sig′ə ret′) a small roll of finely cut tobacco wrapped in a thin sheet of paper, for smoking. *n.*

cinch (sinch) **1** a strong band or belt, usually of leather, for fastening a saddle or pack on a horse. **2** fasten on with a cinch; bind firmly. **3** *Informal.* something easy: *Making brownies is a cinch.* 1, 3 *n.,* 2 *v.*

cin·der (sin′dər) **1** a small, rough piece of something burnt. **2** a small piece of coal or wood that is still burning or glowing, but without a flame. **3** **cinders,** *pl.* ashes. *n.*

cin·e·ma (sin′ə mə) **1** a movie theatre. **2** movies as an art form: *His interest in cinema began in art and drama classes.* *n.*

cin·na·mon (sin′ə mən) a spice made of the inner bark of a tree that grows in the East Indies. It is light reddish brown. *n.*

cin·quain (sing′ kān) a poem or a verse of poetry that has five lines. *n.*

ci·pher (sī′fər) secret writing; code: *She sent me a note in cipher.* *n.*

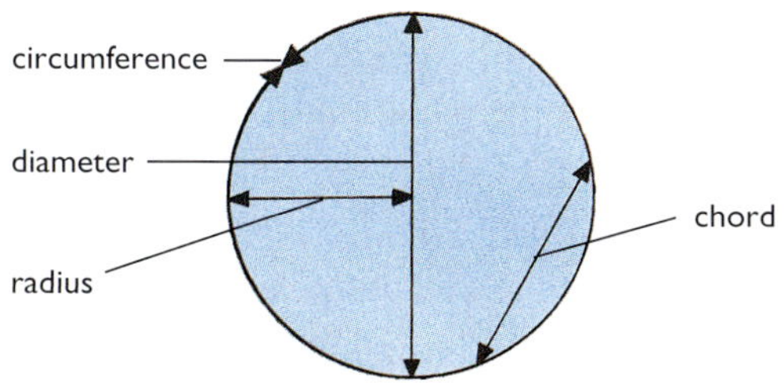

cir·cle (sər′kəl) **1** an exactly round shape. Every point on the curved line of a circle is the same distance from the centre. **2** a ring; something like a circle or part of one: *a circle of cloud around the moon. The girls danced in a circle.* **3** move around in a circle: *The airplane circled before it landed.* **4** form a circle around; surround: *A ring of highways circled the city.* **5** draw a circle around: *Circle the answer you think is correct.* **6** a group of people held together by the same interests: *the family circle, a circle of friends.* **7** in aboriginal culture, a symbol for the way that nature, culture, the community, the Creator, and the individual are all related and touch one another in a process that goes on forever. 1, 2, 6, 7 *n.,* 3–5 *v.,* **cir·cled, cir·cling.**

cir·cuit (sər′kit) **1** movement in a circle around something: *It takes a year for the earth to make its circuit of the sun.* **2** the complete path followed by an electric current. A **circuit breaker** is a switch that automatically breaks the circuit when the current is too strong. **3** a route followed regularly, with several stops: *a bookmobile's circuit.* *n.*

circuit board (sər′kit bȯrd′) a thin, flat board with a set of connections or switches mounted on it to run a piece of electronic or electrical equipment. There are circuit boards inside a computer.

cir·cu·lar (sər′kyə lər) **1** forming a circle: *a circular driveway, glasses with circular lenses.* **2** a letter, notice, or advertisement sent to each of a number of people. 1 *adj.,* 2 *n.*

cir·cu·late (sər′kyə lāt′) go or send around; pass from person to person or place to place: *to circulate a rumour. Blood circulates in our veins.* *v.,* **cir·cu·lat·ed, cir·cu·lat·ing.**

cir·cu·la·tion (sər′kyə lā′shən) **1** the act of going or sending around; circulating: *Opening the windows increases the circulation of air in a room.* **2** the movement of the blood from the heart through the body and back to the heart. **3** the number of copies of a newspaper, magazine, etc. that are sent out during a certain time. *n.*

cir·cu·la·to·ry (sər′kyə lə tȯr′ē) having to do with circulation. Arteries and veins are parts of the **circulatory system** of the human body. *adj.*

cir·cum·fer·ence (sər kum′fə rəns) **1** the boundary line of a circle. Every point in the circumference of a circle is at the same distance from the centre. **2** the distance around a circle or anything round: *The big tree had a circumference of 3 m.* *n.*

cir·cum·flex (sər′kəm fleks′) a mark (^) used over a vowel in certain languages. There is a circumflex in the French word *hôtel.* *n.*

cir·cum·nav·i·gate (sər′kəm nav′ə gāt′) sail completely around: *Magellan's ship circumnavigated the earth.* *v.,* **cir·cum·nav·i·gat·ed, cir·cum·nav·i·gat·ing.**

cir·cum·stance (sər′kəm stans′) **1** one of a set of facts or events that influence something: *The place, the weather, and other circumstances made the picnic a great success.* **2** a fact or event, especially an accidental one: *It was a lucky circumstance that she found her money.* **3** **circumstances,** *pl.* a person's condition with regard to money: *Now that she has a job, her circumstances have improved.* *n.*

a bat	e bed	i bid	o pot	u cup	th thin
ā cake	ē me	ī bite	ō go	ū rude	ᴛʜ then
ä bar	ə about	ər over	ȯ for	ů put	zh measure

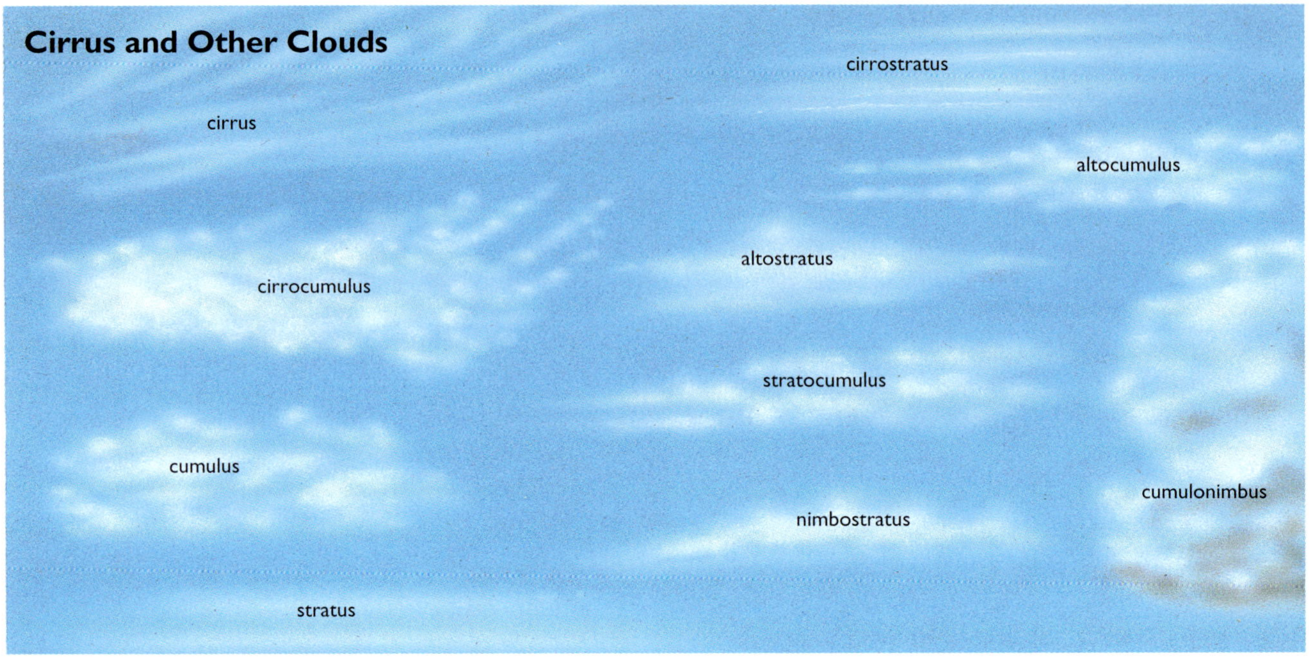

cir•cum•vent (sər′kəm vent′) 1 defeat or get the better of by clever action: *The planned bank robbery was circumvented by the police.* 2 avoid by going around: *We can circumvent the heavy traffic by taking this route.* *v.*

cir•cus (sər′kəs) 1 a travelling company of acrobats, clowns, jugglers, etc. who put on shows for the public: *The circus is in town.* 2 *Informal.* a very lively but disorderly scene: *Our place was a circus that last night as we rushed to get ready for the trip.* 3 in ancient Rome, a large, usually oval stadium with tiers of seats around it, used for chariot races, etc. *n.*

cir•rus (sir′əs) a thin, curling, wispy cloud very high in the air. Cirrus clouds are so high that the water in them has frozen into ice crystals. *n., pl.* **cir•ri** (sir′ī *or* sir′ē).

cis•tern (sis′tərn) a tank or reservoir for storing water. *n.*

cit•a•del (sit′ə dəl) a fortress, especially one in a city: *Halifax has a famous citadel.* *n.*

cite (sīt) 1 quote or mention as an example: *He cited the Qur'an and Shakespeare to support his statement.* 2 mention publicly as an example of outstanding behaviour. *v.,* **cit•ed, cit•ing.** **—ci•ta′tion,** *n.*

cit•i•zen (sit′ə zən) 1 a member of a state or nation, with certain rights and duties. A person can be a citizen of a country by birth, or become one by going through certain procedures. 2 an inhabitant of a city or town. *n.* **—cit′i•zen•ship,** *n.*

cit•rus fruits (sit′rəs frūts′) lemons, limes, oranges, grapefruit, etc. *n.*

cit•y (sit′ē) 1 a large town: *Montréal is one of the largest cities in Canada.* 2 the people living in a city: *The whole city celebrated when the Blue Jays won the World Series.* *n., pl.* **cit•ies.**

city hall (sit′ē hol′) the headquarters of the government of a city: *The mayor's office is in the city hall.*

civ•ic (siv′ik) 1 having to do with a city or cities in general. 2 having to do with citizenship: *Obeying the laws, voting, and paying taxes are civic duties.* *adj.*

civ•ics (siv′iks) the study of the duties, rights, and privileges of citizens. *n.*

civ•il (siv′əl) 1 having to do with citizens: *civil rights.* **Civil disobedience** is disobedience to the law by citizens as a way of protesting against the government. 2 not connected with the army or the church: *civil defence, a civil marriage ceremony.* 3 polite: *It's hard to be civil when you are angry.* *adj.* **—ci•vil′i•ty** (sə vil′ə tē), *n.*

ci•vil•ian (sə vil′yən) 1 a person who is not in the army or police force. 2 having to do with civilians: *Soldiers often wear civilian clothes when on leave.* 1 *n.,* 2 *adj.*

civ•i•li•za•tion (siv′ə lī zā′shən) 1 a people with a well-developed political and social system and a culture that includes arts and sciences: *The archaeologists found the remains of an ancient civilization.* 2 *Informal.* all the conveniences of modern life, or any place where these are available: *After a month of camping in the wilderness, it was good to get back to civilization.* 3 the condition of being civilized. *n.*

civ·i·lized (siv′ə līzd′) 1 having a well-developed political and social system, with a culture that includes arts and sciences. 2 polite; well-mannered. *adj.* **—civ′i·lize′,** *v.*

civil service (siv′əl sər′vis) the whole organized group of workers who do the day-to-day work in government offices. Individually they are **civil servants.**

civil war (siv′əl wȯr′) a war between two groups of citizens of one nation.

clack (klak) 1 make a short, sharp sound: *The needles clacked as I knitted.* 2 a short, sharp sound: *the clack of heels on the tile floor.* 1 *v.,* 2 *n.*

clad (klad) a past tense and past participle of **clothe:** *He was clad all in green.* *v.*

claim (klām) 1 say that something belongs to you: *Does anyone claim this pencil?* 2 a right to expect something: *She has a claim on us because she gave us a place to live.* 3 deserve; require: *The care of the garden claims much time.* 4 say firmly; declare as a fact, with or without proof: *He claims he's an expert.* 1, 3, 4 *v.,* 2 *n.*
lay claim to, claim as your own: *She laid claim to the books in the hallway.*
stake your claim, choose and claim an area of land, living space, etc.

clam (klam) 1 a shellfish with a soft body and a hinged double shell, living in sand along the seashore or at the edges of lakes and rivers. Some clams are good to eat. 2 go out after clams; dig for clams. 1 *n.,* 2 *v.,* **clammed, clam·ming.**
clam up, *Informal.* stop talking all of a sudden: *He had been chatting happily, but clammed up as soon as I mentioned the accident.*

clam·bake (klam′bāk′) a picnic where clams are baked or steamed. *n.*

clam·ber (klam′bər) climb, using both hands and feet; scramble: *The boys clambered up the steep hill.* *v.*

clam·my (klam′ē) cold and damp: *The walls of the cave were clammy.* *adj.,* **clam·mi·er, clam·mi·est.**

clam·our or **clam·or** (klam′ər) 1 a loud noise, especially of voices; confused shouting. 2 make a loud noise, especially to complain or ask for something: *The children were clamouring for a picnic.* 1 *n.,* 2 *v.* **—clam′or·ous,** *adj.*

clamp (klamp) 1 a device for holding things tightly together: *She used a clamp to hold the joint until the glue dried.* 2 set or hold something firmly and tightly, with or without this device: *Clamp the two pieces together while the glue is drying. The dog clamped its jaws on my pant leg.* 1 *n.,* 2 *v.*
clamp down on, forbid or punish strictly: *The police are clamping down on drunk driving.*

clan (klan) a group of families descended from one ancestor. In First Nations, Scottish, and many other cultures, the clan was an important unit in the way a society was traditionally organized. Different cultures may trace the descent through the mother or through the father, and may have a special emblem for each clan, such as an animal among First Nations peoples or a particular pattern of plaid among the Scots. *n.*

clang (klang) 1 the loud, harsh ringing sound of metal striking metal: *the clang of the fire bell.* 2 make such a sound: *The fire bells clanged.* 1 *n.,* 2 *v.*

clank (klangk) 1 a sound like the rattle of a heavy chain. 2 make such a sound: *The sword clanked against the armour.* 1 *n.,* 2 *v.*

clap (klap) 1 a sudden, sharp, loud noise, such as a single burst of thunder or the sound of the hands struck together. 2 hit the palms of your hands together: *When the show was over, we all clapped.* 3 strike with a quick blow: *He clapped his friend on the back.* 1 *n.,* 2, 3 *v.,* **clapped, clap·ping.**
clap eyes on, *Informal.* look at; see.

clap·per (klap′ər) 1 the movable part inside a bell that strikes and rings the outer part. 2 a clacky-sounding noisemaker: *We had horns and clappers at the party.* *n.*

clar·i·fy (kler′ə fī′) make something clear: *Mo's explanation clarified her answer.* *v.,* **clar·i·fied, clar·i·fy·ing. —clar′i·fi·ca′tion,** *n.*

clar·i·net (kler′ə net′) a wind instrument, usually wooden, with a single reed. *n.*

clar·i·on (kler′ē ən) 1 clear and sharp. 2 a trumpet with clear, sharp tones. 1 *adj.,* 2 *n.*

clar·i·ty (klar′ə tē *or* kler′ə tē) clearness. *n.*

clash (klash) 1 a loud, harsh sound like that of two hard things running into each other or of metal striking metal. 2 hit with a clash: *In my haste, I clashed the pots against the stove.* 3 a strong disagreement; a conflict: *a clash of opinion.* 4 be out of harmony; go badly together: *Your tie clashes with your shirt.* 1, 3 *n.,* 2, 4 *v.*

a bat	e bed	i bid	o pot	u cup	th thin
ā cake	ē me	ī bite	ō go	ū rude	ᴛʜ then
ä bar	ə about	ər over	ȯ for	u̇ put	zh measure

clasp (klasp) **1** a fastener with a hook or catch of some kind: *This suede belt has a gold clasp.* **2** fasten together with a clasp. **3** hold tightly with the hand or the arms: *Rahel clasped her new puppy in her arms. He clasped a coin in his hand.* **4** a firm grasp: *He gave my hand a warm clasp.* 1, 4 *n.,* 2, 3 *v.*

class (klas) **1** a group of students taught together. **2** the time spent by such a group together with their teacher: *In today's art class we did papier mâché.* **3** a rank of society: *People who owned land used to be thought of as the upper class.* **4** any group of people or things thought of together because they are the same in some way. In science, mammals are a class of animals; they all feed their babies with their own milk. **5** put in a class; classify: *Names of people, places, and things are all classed as nouns.* **6** a level of service or quality: *First class is the most costly way to travel.* **7** elegance and good style; good character: *to dress with class. Your public apology showed real class.* **—class′y,** *adj.* 1–4, 6, 7 *n.,* 5 *v.*

clas·sic (klas′ik) **1** a book or artistic work of the highest rank or quality: *The book* Alligator Pie *is a classic.* **2** very typical or very excellent; used as a perfect example of its kind: *a classic example of clear, attractive handwriting.* **3** simple and elegant: *a classic white tablecloth.* 1 *n.,* 2, 3 *adj.*

clas·si·cal (klas′ə kəl) recognized over time as being of high artistic excellence: *She likes classical music.* *adj.*

clas·si·fy (klas′ə fī′) put in groups or classes; group in some way. In the post office, mail is classified according to where it is going. **Classified ads** in a newspaper are arranged according to what they are offering or asking for. *v.,* **clas·si·fied, clas·si·fy·ing.**
—class′i·fi·ca′tion, *n.*

class·mate (klas′māt′) a member of the same class in school. *n.*

class·room (klas′rūm′) a room in which classes are held. *n.*

clat·ter (klat′ər) **1** a loud rattling noise: *the clatter of dishes.* **2** move or fall with a loud rattling noise: *The wagon clattered over the stones.* 1 *n.,* 2 *v.*

clause (kloz) **1** any combination containing a subject and a verb. The sentence *He arrived before we left* has two clauses: *He arrived* is a **main clause** that could stand alone as a sentence, and *before we left* is a **subordinate clause** that adds information. **2** a single requirement or point in a law or any other written agreement: *There is a clause in our lease contract that says we may not keep a dog in this building.* *n.*

Nails and claws are made of hard skin, like animals' horns.

claw (klo) **1** a sharp, hooked nail on the toe of a bird or animal: *The chicken scratched the earth with its claws.* **2** anything shaped or used like a claw. The part of a hammer used for pulling nails is the claw. **3** scratch, tear, or pull with claws or fingernails: *The kitten was clawing the screen door.* 1, 2 *n.,* 3 *v.*

clay (klā) a sticky kind of earth that can be easily shaped when wet and hardens when dried or baked. Bricks and dishes are made from various kinds of clay. *n.*

clean (klēn) **1** not dirty at all; not stained or polluted: *clean clothes, clean air.* **2** liking to be clean: *Cats are thought to be clean animals.* **3** make clean: *to clean a room.* **4** smooth and even; neat and trim: *The clean lines of his new car.* **5** honest; legal and fair: *a clean victory.* **6** drug-free. **7** completely; totally: *I clean forgot about the invitation.* 1, 2, 4–6 *adj.,* 3 *v.,* 7 *adv.*
—clean′ly, *adv.* **—clean′ness,** *n.*
clean out, a make clean by emptying: *Clean out your desk.* **b** empty; use up: *The girls cleaned out a whole box of cookies.* **c** *Slang.* leave a person without money: *Buying that chocolate bar cleaned me right out.*
clean up, a make clean by removing dirt, junk, etc.: *to clean up the yard.* **b** *Informal.* finish; complete: *I finally got that job cleaned up.* **c** *Slang.* make money; profit: *We really cleaned up on the bake sale.*
clean up your act, *Informal.* start behaving, working, etc. better.
come clean, tell the truth. Another expression for this is **make a clean breast of it.**

clean·li·ness (klen′lē nis) cleanness as a habit: *Personal cleanliness was very important to him.* *n.*

cleanse (klenz) make thoroughly clean and pure. *v.,* **cleansed, cleans·ing.**

cleans·er (klenz′ər) a powder or liquid used in household cleaning to get rid of stains, odours, and germs. *n.*

clear (klēr) **1** not cloudy, misty, or hazy: *a clear morning.* **2** easy to see through; transparent: *clear glass.* **3** easily heard, seen, or understood; plain; distinct: *a clear voice, a clear outline, a clear explanation. It is clear that it is going to rain.* **4** clean or empty; not blocked or cluttered: *a clear countertop, clear drains, a clear pathway, a clear view.* **5** make or become clear: *Clear your desk. The sky cleared.* **6** all the way, without pausing or slowing: *The bullet went clear through the door.* **7** get over or past without touching: *The jumper cleared the hurdle.* **8** give or get permission for: *I can probably go, but I have to clear it with my parents first.* **9** make as total profit: *We cleared $400 on the sale.* 1–4 *adj.,* 5, 7, 8, 9 *v.,* 6 *adv.* —**clear′ly,** *adv.* —**clear′ness,** *n.*

clear off or **away, a** remove, making a clear space: *He cleared away the dishes.* **b** leave: *I cleared off as soon as I saw them coming.*

clear out, a make clear by throwing out or emptying: *to clear out a cupboard.* **b** *Informal.* go away; leave: *We cleared out as soon as the show was over.*

clear up, make or become clear: *The weather will clear up soon. Clear up this mess. Your explanation has cleared everything up.*

clear–cut (klēr′kut′ *for 1,* klēr′ kut′ *for 2*) **1** clear and distinct; not vague: *a clear-cut image, clear-cut ideas.* **2** cut down all the trees in an area. 1 *adj.,* 2 *v.,* **clear-cut, clear-cutting.** —**clear′cut′ting,** *n.*

clear•ing (klēr′ing) an open space of cleared land in a forest. *n.*

cleat (klēt) **1 cleats,** *pl.* a set of raised bars or points designed to prevent slipping. The points on the sole of a soccer shoe and the crosswise bars on a ramp are cleats. **2** a T-shaped piece of wood or other material on to a boat, dock, stage scenery, etc., used for securing ropes. You wind the rope around the ends of the cleat. *n.*

cleav•er (klē′vər) a chopper with a heavy blade and a short handle, used by a butcher for cutting through meat or bone. *n.*

clef (klef) a symbol in music indicating the pitch of the notes on a staff. *n.*

clench (klench) **1** close tightly together: *to clench one's teeth, a clenched fist.* **2** grasp firmly: *He clenched my arm.* **3** a tight grip: *I felt the clench of his hand on my arm.* 1, 2 *v.,* 3 *n.*

cler•gy (klər′jē) the people specially trained and chosen to lead religious organizations. Ministers, priests, and rabbis are members of the clergy. *n., pl.* **cler•gies.**

cler•i•cal (kler′ə kəl) **1** having to do with a clerk or clerks: *She has a clerical job in a large office.* **2** having to do with the clergy: *clerical robes, clerical duties.* *adj.*

clerk (klərk) **1** a salesperson in a small store or shop. **2** a worker in an office or bank who files records, copies letters, keeps accounts, etc. *n.*

clev•er (klev′ər) **1** bright; quick to learn and good at coming up with solutions, ideas, plans, tricks, etc.: *She is the cleverest person in our class.* **2** showing this kind of ability: *a clever trick, a clever answer.* *adj.* —**clev′er•ly,** *adv.* —**clev′er•ness,** *n.*

cli•ché (klē shā′) a word, phrase, or idea that has been used too much and has lost most of its power: *She tried her best to write without clichés.* *n., pl.* **cli•chés.**

click (klik) **1** a short, sharp sound: *We heard the click as she turned the key in the lock.* **2** make such a sound: *We heard a key click in the lock.* **3** *Slang.* get along well: *We clicked from the start.* 1 *n.,* 2–4 *v.*

cli•ent (klī′ənt) customer; anyone buying goods, services, or advice. *n.*

cliff (klif) a steep, high wall of rock or earth: *Great cliffs overhung the canyon.* *n.*

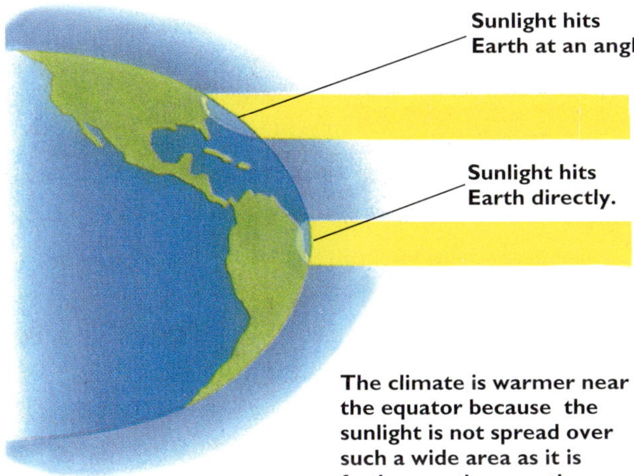

cli•mate (klī′mit) **1** the kind of weather patterns a place usually has. **2** a part of the world where a certain kind of weather is usual: *The doctor ordered him to go to a drier climate.* *n.*

cli•max (klī′maks) the highest point of interest; the most exciting part: *Shooting the rapids was the climax of our canoe trip.* *n.*

climb (klīm) **1** go up, especially step by step or bit by bit: *to climb a hill, to climb a ladder. The price of food has climbed during the past year.* **2** the act of going up: *Our climb took two hours.* **3** go in any direction with the help of the hands: *to climb down a rope. She climbed under the fence.* 1, 3 *v.,* 2 *n.*

a bat	e bed	i bid	o pot	u cup	th thin
ā cake	ē me	ī bite	ō go	ū rude	ᴛʜ then
ä bar	ə about	ər over	ô for	ů put	zh measure

clinch (klinch) 1 settle; make something certain: *A deposit of $50 clinched the bargain.* 2 hold on tight to each other, as in boxing or wrestling. 3 a tight hold on each other: *The referee broke the hockey players' clinch.* 4 bend down the point of a nail after hammering it in, for a firmer hold. 1, 2, 4 *v.,* 3 *n.*

cling (kling) 1 hold tightly: *The child clung to his father. They cling to their hope of a happier future.* 2 stick; be attached: *A vine clings to the wall.* *v.,* **clung, cling·ing.** —**cling′y,** *adj.*

clin·ic (klin′ik) 1 a place where people can get medical treatment without having to stay overnight. It can be part of a hospital or in a separate building: *They have the latest equipment in the eye clinic.* 2 a special session held to deal with certain problems, teach certain skills, etc.: *a soccer clinic.* *n.*

clink (klingk) 1 a light, sharp, ringing, like the sound of glasses hitting together. 2 make a sharp, ringing sound: *The spoons and glasses clinked.* 1 *n.,* 2 *v.*

clip[1] (klip) 1 cut or cut out with shears, scissors, or clippers: *to clip your nails. I'm going to clip this recipe and save it.* 2 the act of clipping: *His hair needs a clip at the back.* 3 a short portion from a movie or video: *a film clip.* 4 a fast speed: *We rode through the village at quite a clip.* 5 *Informal.* hit or punch sharply: *The boxer clipped his opponent on the jaw.* 6 *Informal.* a sharp blow or punch. 1, 5 *v.,* **clipped, clip·ping;** 2–4, 6 *n.*

clip[2] (klip) 1 a fastener that works by squeezing, such as a paper clip. 2 fasten loose things together with this kind of fastener: *to clip papers together.* 1 *n.,* 2 *v.,* **clipped, clip·ping.**

clip art (klip′ ärt′) pictures or designs stored in a computer program or on a compact disc that can be copied and used: *She found an excellent picture of a dinosaur in the clip art.* —**clip′-art′,** *adj.*

clip·board (klip′bôrd′) a small board with a strong spring clip at one end for holding papers while you write on them. *n.*

clip·per (klip′ər) 1 Often, **clippers,** *pl.* a tool for cutting: *hair clippers, a nail clipper.* 2 a sailing ship built for speed: *Clippers from Nova Scotia used to sail all over the world.* *n.*

clip·ping (klip′ing) a piece cut out of a newspaper, magazine, etc. *n.*

clique (klēk) a small group of friends who won't let others join them. *n.*

cloak (klōk) 1 a loose outer garment usually without sleeves. 2 cover with a cloak. 3 anything that covers or hides: *He won my trust under the cloak of friendship and then let me down.* 4 hide: *She cloaked her evil purpose with friendly words.* 1, 3 *n.,* 2, 4 *v.*

cloak·room (klōk′rūm′) a room in a public building, where coats, hats, etc. can be left for a time. *n.*

This clock's pendulum controls its speed.

This ship's chronometer, of the early 1700s, is run by a slowly unwinding spring.

clock (klok) 1 an instrument for measuring and showing time, made to be hung on a wall or set on a desk, etc. but not for wearing on the body. 2 measure or record the time of; time: *The coach clocked the three girls to see who was the fastest runner.* 1 *n.,* 2 *v.*
around the clock, all day and all night.
turn the clock back, behave and think the way people used to.
working against the clock, racing to get something done in time.

clock radio (klok′ rā′dēō) a radio with a built-in clock that can be set to turn the radio on or off automatically at a certain time. Many people use clock radios to wake them up in the morning.

clock·wise (klok′wīz′) in the direction in which the hands of a clock move: *a clockwise movement* (*adj.*). *Turn the lid clockwise to tighten it* (*adv.*). The opposite direction is **counter-clockwise.** *adv. or adj.*

clock·work (klok′wərk′) the machinery of a clock, or any machinery that works the same way. Wind-up toys are run by clockwork. *n.*
like clockwork, very smoothly and regularly: *The launching of the rocket went off like clockwork.*

clod (klod) 1 a lump of earth. 2 a rude, thoughtless person. *n.*

clod·hop·per (klod′hop′ər) a large, heavy boot or shoe. *n.*

clog (klog) 1 block or become blocked by filling up; plug up: *Leaves clogged the drain. The drain clogged with leaves.* 2 a shoe or sandal with a wooden sole. 1 *v.,* **clogged, clog·ging;** 2 *n.*

clois·ter (kloi′stər) 1 a covered walk along the wall of a building, with a row of pillars on the open side. A cloister is often built around the courtyard of a monastery, church, or college building. 2 a convent or monastery. 3 a quiet place shut away from the world. 4 shut away in a quiet place: *She spent months cloistered in her office, writing a book.* 1–3 *n.,* 4 *v.*

clone (klōn) 1 to copy a plant or animal in every detail by taking a cell from it and developing it in a laboratory: *Everyone was amazed when scientists were able to clone a sheep.* 2 a person or thing that is, or seems to be, an exact copy of another: *In the science fiction story, the girl has her clone do all her work. The TV show was so successful that many clones of it appeared.* 1 *v.,* **cloned, clon·ing;** 2 *n.*

close[1] (klōz) 1 shut: *Close the door. The sleepy child's eyes are closing.* 2 get rid of an opening by filling it in or bringing the edges together: *to close a gap. The cut has closed.* 3 finish; end: *to close a meeting, to close a business deal (v.). She spoke at the close of the meeting (n.).* 1–3 *v.,* **closed, clos·ing;** 3 *n.*
close down, stop working or doing business.
close in, come near and surround on all sides: *The thief gave up when the police closed in. The hunters closed in on the moose.*
close on, catch up to someone in a race.

close[2] (klōs) 1 near: *close to home.* 2 with little space between: *a close fit. They followed close behind me.* 3 nearly equal: *The race was a close contest.* 4 stifling; stuffy: *With the windows shut, the room was hot and close.* 5 stingy: *He was close with his money.* *adj.,* **clos·er, clos·est.** **—close′ly,** *adv.* **—close′ness,** *n.*
close up, from a very short distance away: *to look at something close up, to photograph someone close up.* A more formal expression for this is **at close range** or **at close quarters.**

closed–cap·tioned (klōzd′ kap′shənd) broadcast on television with captions underneath the pictures so that people who are deaf can follow the words. *adj.* **—closed cap·tion·ing.**

clos·et (kloz′it) 1 a small room or large cupboard for storing things: *Hang your coat in the closet.* 2 shut up in a room for a private talk: *She was closeted with the lawyer for over an hour.* 1 *n.,* 2 *v.*

close–up (klōs′up′) a picture taken at close range: *That's a good close-up of the flowers.* *n.*

clot (klot) 1 a blob of thickened liquid: *A clot of blood formed in the cut.* 2 form into clots: *Bleeding s tops when the blood clots.* 1 *n.,* 2 *v.,* **clot·ted, clot·ting.**

cloth (kloth) 1 material made from wool, silk, linen, cotton, or other fibre: *Cloth is used to make clothes, curtains, sheets, etc.* 2 a piece of this, used for a special purpose: *a polishing cloth.* *n.*

clothe (klōᴛʜ) 1 put clothes on; dress. 2 provide clothes for: *It costs quite a bit to clothe a family of six.* 3 cover or wrap as if with clothes: *The trees are clothed in green leaves. He clothed his simple ideas in fancy words.* *v.,* **clothed** or **clad, cloth·ing.**

clothes (klōz *or* klōᴛʜz) the things that people wear; shirts, dresses, pants, etc. **Clothing** is another word for it. *pl.n.*

clothes·line (klōz′līn′ *or* klōᴛʜz′līn′) a string, wire, etc. to hang clothes on in order to dry or air them. The clothes may be clipped on with a **clothespin** or **clothespeg.** *n.*

cloud (kloud) 1 a white or grey mass in the sky, made up of very tiny drops of water or ice particles: *A cloud hid the sun and rain began to fall.* 2 a mass of smoke or dust in the air. 3 anything thought of as bringing darkness or dimness: *a cloud of gloom.* 4 cover or fill with a cloud; darken or dim: *The sky clouded over. The mist clouded our view. Her face clouded with anger.* 1–3 *n.,* 4 *v.* **—cloud′less,** *adj.*

cloud·burst (kloud′bərst′) a short, sudden, very heavy rainfall. *n.*

cloud·y (klou′dē) not clear: *a cloudy sky, a cloudy mixture, cloudy thinking.* *adj.,* **cloud·i·er, cloud·i·est.** **—cloud′i·ly,** *adv.* **—cloud′i·ness,** *n.*

clout (klout) 1 hit hard: *She finally got so tired of his teasing that she clouted him.* 2 a hard blow; a hit: *The bully gave me a clout on the head.* 3 *Informal.* power and influence: *He has no clout, because nobody respects him.* 1 *v.,* 2, 3 *n.*

clove (klōv) 1 **cloves,** *pl.* a strong, fragrant spice made from the dried flower buds of a tropical tree. It is used with sweet things. 2 one section of a garlic bulb. *n.*

a bat	e bed	i bid	o pot	u cup	th thin
ā cake	ē me	ī bite	ō go	ū rude	ᴛʜ then
ä bar	ə about	ər over	ô for	ů put	zh measure

clo·ver (klō′vər) a plant with leaves made up of three small leaflets each. It has sweet-smelling rounded heads of red or white flowers and is grown as food for horses and cattle. *n.*
in clover, *Informal.* enjoying a life of pleasure and luxury without work or effort.

clo·ver·leaf (klō′vər lēf′) a series of ramps or roads where two highways meet, arranged so that traffic can move from one highway to the other without crossing in front of other traffic. *n.*

clown (kloun) **1** a person in a costume who makes people laugh with a show full of tricks and jokes: *The clowns in the circus were very funny.* **2** act like a clown; play tricks and jokes; act silly. **3** a person with bad manners that make him or her look foolish: *That clown does not know how to behave.* 1, 3 *n.,* 2 *v.*

club (klub) **1** a heavy stick of wood, thick at one end, used as a weapon. **2** a special stick used in some games to hit a ball: *golf clubs.* **3** beat or hit with a club or something similar. **4** a group of people joined together for some special purpose: *a tennis club, a birdwatching club.* **5** the building where they meet, also sometimes called a **clubhouse.** **6** **clubs,** *pl.* a series of playing cards marked with one or more black designs shaped like this: ♣ 1, 2, 4–6 *n.,* 3 *v.,* **clubbed, club·bing.**
club together, unite for some special purpose: *The children clubbed together to collect items for recycling.*

cluck (kluk) **1** the sound a hen makes when calling her chicks. **2** make such a sound. 1 *n.,* 2 *v.*

clue (klū) something that helps to solve a mystery or problem: *The police could find no clues to help them solve the crime.* *n.*

clump (klump) **1** a group set very close together: *a clump of trees.* **2** walk with a heavy, clumsy, noisy step: *The pirate clumped along on his wooden leg.* **3** the sound of such walking. 1, 3 *n.,* 2 *v.*

clum·sy (klum′zē) **1** always bumping into things, dropping things, etc. Someone who is clumsy with words is always saying the wrong thing. **2** not well-shaped or well-made: *a clumsy drawing, a clumsy apology.* *adj.,* **clum·si·er, clum·si·est.** **—clum′si·ly,** *adv.*

clung (klung) the past tense and past participle of **cling:** *The child clung to her father. The burrs had clung to my sweater.* *v.*

clus·ter (klus′tər) **1** a number of things of the same kind growing or grouped close together: *a cluster of grapes, a little cluster of houses.* **2** be in a bunch; gather in a group: *The students clustered around their teacher.* 1 *n.,* 2 *v.*

clutch (kluch) **1** grasp tightly: *The frightened boy clutched his big sister's hand.* **2** a tight grasp: *The eagle flew away with a rabbit in its clutch.* **3** a part of a car that puts it in gear or out of gear. The car must be in gear for the motor to be able to turn the wheels. 1 *v.,* 2, 3 *n.*
clutch at, grasp eagerly for; try to seize or take hold of: *She clutched at the branch, but missed it and fell.*

clut·ter (klut′ər) **1** too many things taking up space; things everywhere. **2** fill or cover with things: *His desk was all cluttered with books and papers.* 1 *n.,* 2 *v.*

cm *symbol for* centimetre or centimetres.

co– *a prefix meaning:* **1** with; together. *Co-operate* means "work together." **2** fellow; joint, as in *co-traveller, co-worker.*

Co. *abbreviation for* company. *Bramie and Co.* means "Bramie and Company."

c.o. or **c/o** *abbreviation for* in care of, used in addressing mail.

coach (kōch) **1** a bus that travels between cities. **2** a passenger car of a railway train. **3** in the old days, a large, closed, horse-drawn carriage with seats inside and often on top, driven by a **coachman.** Coaches carried passengers along a regular route, stopping for meals and fresh horses. **4** a person who trains athletes: *a football coach.* **5** a person who helps anyone learn or practise anything. **6** train or teach; help along: *He got his mom to coach him in math.* 1–5 *n.,* 6 *v.*

co·ag·u·late (kō ag′yə lāt′) change from a liquid to a thickened mass; thicken; clot: *Cooking coagulates the white of an egg. Blood coagulates when exposed to air.* *v.,* **co·ag·u·lat·ed, co·ag·u·lat·ing.**

coal (kōl) **1** a black mineral formed in the earth from partly decayed plants that have been under great pressure for a long time: *Coal is mined for use as a fuel.* **2** a small piece of wood, coal, etc., burning or glowing: *We wrapped the potatoes in foil and put them among the coals to bake.* *n.*

co·a·li·tion (kō′ə lish′ən) an agreement between different political parties to work together for a limited time and for a special purpose. If, in an election, no party wins a majority of seats in the House of Commons, two parties may form a coalition together in order to carry on government. *n.*

coal oil (kōl′ oil′) a thin oil for use in some kinds of stoves and lanterns where there is no electricity. It is made from petroleum and is also called **kerosene.**

coarse (kȯrs) **1** made up of fairly large bits. Coarse gravel has bigger stones than fine gravel. Coarse cloth is made with heavy, thick fibres. **2** rough; not delicate, elegant, or fine: *coarse food, coarse language. adj.,* **coars•er, coars•est. —coarse′ly,** *adv.* **—coarse′ness,** *n.* **—coars′en,** *v.*

coast (kōst) **1** the land along the sea; seashore: *Many ships were wrecked on the rocky coast.* **2** move along without using effort or power: *to coast downhill on a bike or snowboard.* 1 *n.,* 2 *v.* **—coast′al,** *adj.*

coast•er (kō′stər) **1** something that slides down a hill, such as a sled that you ride. **2** a little mat of cardboard, cork, plastic, etc. that you put a glass or bottle on to protect the surface underneath. *n.*

coast guard (kōst′ gȧrd′) a government agency that helps people in trouble at sea or on the Great Lakes and breaks ice in the North.

coast•line (kōst′līn′) the outline of a coast: *the rugged coastline of Newfoundland. n.*

coat (kōt) **1** a piece of clothing with sleeves, worn over other clothes. **2** the fur or hair of an animal. **3** Sometimes, **coating,** a thin layer: *a coat of paint.* **4** cover with a thin layer: *to coat a floor with varnish. This pill is coated with sugar.* 1–3 *n.,* 4 *v.*

coat of arms (kōt′ əv ȧrmz′) a design containing symbols that stand for the special things about a noble family, a government, a city, etc. In the Middle Ages, each knight or lord had his own coat of arms.

coax (kōks) persuade by soft words and gentle ways: *She coaxed the shy newcomer to join the game. I coaxed a smile from the baby. v.*

cob (kob) **1** the central part of an ear of corn, that the kernels grow on. **2** a strong horse with short legs, often used for riding. *n.*

co•balt (kō′bolt) a silver-white metal used in making steel, paint, etc. *n.*

cob•ble (kob′əl) **1** repair shoes. **2** put together clumsily: *He used toilet rolls and cereal boxes to cobble together a model castle. v.,* **cob•bled, cob•bling.**

cob•bler (kob′lər) **1** a person who fixes shoes; shoemaker. **2** a baked fruit dessert with a crumb crust on top. *n.*

cob•ble•stone (kob′əl stōn′) a rounded stone used in earlier times for paving. You can still find some streets paved with cobblestones. *n.*

An Indian cobra may grow to nearly 2 m long. A king cobra may grow to over 5 m — it is the longest poisonous snake known.

co•bra (kō′brə) a very poisonous snake of tropical Asia and Africa. An excited cobra can flatten its neck so that its head looks like a hood. *n.*

WORD HISTORY....... cobra

The word **cobra** came into English from Portuguese. The full name was *cobra de capelle,* meaning "snake with a hood."

Why don't cobwebs just get blown away or washed away? Spider silk is made up of protein. It cannot be dissolved in water, and is the strongest natural fibre known.

cob•web (kob′web′) an old spider's web that has trapped a lot of dust. *n.*

a bat	e bed	i bid	o pot	u cup	th thin
ā cake	ē me	ī bite	ō go	ū rude	ᴛʜ then
ȧ bar	ə about	ər over	ȯ for	u̇ put	zh measure

cock¹ (kok) 1 a rooster; a male chicken or the male of other birds. 2 a tap used to turn the flow of a liquid or gas on or off. 3 the hammer of a gun. 4 pull back the hammer of a gun, ready to fire: *They heard a click as the pirate cocked his pistol.* 1–3 *n.,* 4 *v.*
cock of the walk, the most powerful person in a group.

cock² (kok) turn or tilt upward or to one side: *The little bird cocked its head at me.* *v.*
cock your ears, listen carefully for a sound.

cock·a·too (kok′ə tū′) a large, mainly white parrot of Australia and south Asia. It has a crested head and a short tail. Don't confuse it with the **cockatiel,** a smaller bird from the same area, with a long tail and a yellow head. *n., pl.* **cock·a·toos.**

cock·le (kok′əl) a small shellfish that is good to eat and has a heart-shaped shell. *n.*
warm the cockles of a person's heart, please and encourage someone very much: *His kind welcome warmed the cockles of my heart.* This expression is now mostly used as a funny exaggeration.

cock·pit (kok′pit′) the place where the pilot sits in an aircraft. *n.*

cock·roach (kok′rōch′) an insect with long feelers and a long, flat, shiny body. Cockroaches are household pests in some areas. *n.*

cock·y (kok′ē) *Informal.* saucy and a bit conceited. *adj.,* **cock·i·er, cock·i·est.**

co·coa (kō′kō) 1 a reddish brown powder made from unsweetened chocolate (def. 1) by pressing out most of the fat. 2 a drink made from this powder, with sugar and milk or water. *n.*

co·co·nut (kō′kə nut′) the large, round, brown, hard-shelled seed of a tree called the **coconut palm.** Coconuts have a thick white lining inside and a white liquid in the centre called **coconut milk.** Both are good to eat. *n.*

co·coon (kə kūn′) 1 a silky covering spun for itself by the larva of certain insects such as the ant and the moth. The cocoon protects the larva while it is changing into an adult. 2 stay or keep inside a small cozy place: *cocooned in his warm sleeping bag.* Today many people work at home instead of an office, rent videos and have food delivered instead of going out to movies and restaurants, do their banking at home by computer, etc. We call this **cocooning.** 1 *n.,* 2 *v.*

cod (kod) a food fish of the cold parts of the northern Atlantic Ocean. It has soft fins, a long body, and a small, square tail. **Cod-liver oil** is a vitamin-rich oil taken from the livers of cod. *n., pl.* **cod** or **cods.**

C.O.D. or **c.o.d.** *abbreviation for* cash on delivery; collect on delivery, meaning you don't pay for the thing you ordered until it arrives at your home.

cod·dle (kod′əl) treat with extra tenderness; pamper: *to coddle a sick child.* *v.,* **cod·dled, cod·dling.**

code (kōd) 1 any system of symbols to stand for information. Ordinary writing is a well-known code, but a code can also be secret writing, a set of special flags, labels, or hand signals, or beeps like the **Morse code.** A computer program is also a code. 2 change or translate into a code, or assign a code symbol to: *to code a message. These exercises are coded according to difficulty: red means easy, blue means hard.* 3 any collection of laws or rules: *the criminal code, a moral code.* 1, 3 *n.,* 2 *v.,* **cod·ed, cod·ing.**

co–ed (ko′ ed′) short for **co-educational,** putting boys and girls or men and women together in the same school or class. Public schools in Canada are co-educational, but many private schools are not. *adj.*

co·ef·fi·cient (kō′ə fish′ənt) in mathematics, the number or symbol put before an unknown quantity to multiply it. For example, in the expression 3*x*, the coefficient of *x* is 3.

co·erce (kō ərs′) force or use extreme pressure on: *The victim was coerced into handing over all his money.* *v.,* **co·erced, co·erc·ing.** —**co·er′cion,** *n.* —**co·er′cive,** *adj.*

A coffee plant is usually six to eight years old before it bears a full crop of berries.

cof·fee (kof′ē) 1 a dark brown drink or flavouring made from the roasted and ground beans of a tall shrub that grows in the tropics. 2 the beans, especially when roasted and ground: *a bag of coffee.* *n.*

cof·fer (kof′ər) a box, chest, or trunk used to hold money or valuable things. *n.*

cof·fin (kof′ən) a box for burying a dead body. *n.*

cog (kog) one of a series of teeth on the edge of a **cogwheel.** They fit into the grooves on another cogwheel so that one wheel turns the other. *n.*

co•her•ent (kō hēr′ənt) making sense because the ideas hold together well: *Elsie made a coherent argument about assigning less homework.* *adj.*
—co•her′ence, *n.*

coil (koil) **1** wind around and around in a series of circles to form a pile, a tube, or a curl: *The sailor coiled the rope so it would not take up much space. The snake coiled around a branch.* **2** a series of such circles, or just one of the circles: *The coil of hose was hung on the wall. One coil of the rope was smaller than the others.* **3** one or two wires wound around a metal core again and again. Coils are used in various machines to make or charge an electric current. 1 *v.,* 2, 3 *n.*

coin (koin) **1** a piece of metal stamped by a government for use as money. Loonies are coins.
2 metal money: *Coin has been in use for thousands of years.* **3** make money by stamping metal; mint.
4 make up or invent a new word or phrase. 1, 2 *n.,* 3, 4 *v.* **—coin′age,** *n.*
coin money, *Informal.* get rich fast: *She is coining money in the oil business.*

co•in•cide (kō′in sīd′) **1** happen at the same time or be in the same spot: *The working hours of the two men coincided. Our placements in September coincided; we were both assigned to the same class.* **2** agree: *Her opinion coincides with mine.* *v.,* **co•in•cid•ed, co•in•cid•ing.**

co•in•ci•dence (kō in′sə dəns) the chance happening of two or more things together in such a way as to seem remarkable or especially appropriate: *My cousin was born on the same day as I was. Isn't that a coincidence?* *n.*

coke (kōk) the black substance left after coal has been heated in an oven with almost no air in it. Coke is used as a fuel and gives a lot of heat with little smoke and no fumes. *n.*

co•la (kō′lə) any pop flavoured with kola nuts, the fruit of a tree related to the cacao tree. *n.*

col•an•der (kol′ən dər) a bowl with many small holes in it, used to drain off liquids from foods. *n.*

cold (kōld) **1** a lot less warm than your body: *Snow and ice are cold.* **2** not warm or hot enough: *This coffee is cold. My feet are cold.* **3** coldness; chilly weather; low temperature: *the cold of winter.* **4** a common sickness that causes a stuffy or runny nose and, sometimes, a cough or a sore throat. **5** unfriendly: *a cold greeting.* **6** without any preparation, warm-up, or practice: *Because I arrived late, I had to give my speech cold.* 1, 2, 5 *adj.,* 3, 4 *n.,* 6 *adv.* **—cold′ly,** *adv.* **—cold′ness,** *n.*
catch cold, become sick with a cold.
cold comfort, something that is supposed to be comforting but isn't.
have or **get cold feet,** be or become nervous or afraid.
in cold blood, without caring or feeling sorry at all.
leave someone cold, hold no interest for someone.
out cold, unconscious.
throw or **pour cold water on,** put down or discourage: *Not to pour cold water on your idea, but I think it's far too expensive.*

Word Family........... **cold**

There are many expressions that use the word **cold**. Here are a few.
cold cash: money, in coins or bills
cold cream: a white, oily cream for skin care
cold cuts: slices of various cooked meats
give the cold shoulder: be deliberately unfriendly
cold snap: a sudden spell of cold weather
cold sore: a group of small blisters near the mouth
break out in a cold sweat: sweat from fear or shock

cold–blood•ed (kōld′blud′id) **1** having blood that is about the same temperature as the air or water around the animal: *Turtles are cold-blooded.* **2** with no feelings; cruel: *a cold-blooded murderer.* *adj.*

cole•slaw (kōl′slȯ′) a salad of sliced raw cabbage. *n.*

col•i•se•um (kol′ə sē′əm) a large building or stadium for games, contests, etc. *n.*

col•lage (kə lȧzh′) a picture or design made by pasting different items on a background. *n.*

col•lapse (kə laps′) **1** break down suddenly: *The little folding chair collapsed when my uncle sat down on it. Their business collapsed after the first year.* **2** a breakdown: *She is suffering from a nervous collapse. Heavy flooding caused the collapse of the bridge.* **3** fold or push together: *to collapse a telescope.* 1, 3 *v.,* **col•lapsed, col•laps•ing;** 2 *n.*

col•lar (kol′ər) **1** the part of a coat, a dress, or a shirt that fits around the neck. **2** a band around a pet's neck. **3** seize by the collar; capture: *The police officer collared the thief.* 1, 2 *n.,* 3 *v.*

a bat	e bed	i bid	o pot	u cup	th thin
ā cake	ē me	ī bite	ō go	ū rude	TH then
ȧ bar	ə about	ər over	ȯ for	u̇ put	zh measure

col•lar•bone (kol′ər bōn′) the bone going from the front of your neck to either shoulder. *n.*

col•league (kol′ēg) a fellow student or fellow worker: *The doctor asked her colleague to examine the patient.* *n.*

col•lect (kə lekt′) **1** gather together or pick up; go around and get: *to collect money for charity. The teacher collected the tests. The bus driver collected our tickets.* **2** come together in one place, increasing all the time: *A crowd soon collects at the scene of an accident. Drifting snow collects behind fences.* **3** look for, get, and keep, as a hobby: *Aaron collects stamps and coins.* **4 collect yourself,** get control of your thoughts and feelings. *v.* —**col•lec′tor,** *n.* —**col•lec′tion,** *n.*
call collect, make a phone call that is to be paid for by the person you call. The call is a **collect call.**
calm and collected, not confused, nervous, or upset.

col•lec•tive (kə lek′tiv) of a group; as a whole group together: *Keeping the neighbourhood clean is our collective responsibility.* *adj.* —**col•lec′tive•ly,** *adv.*

Grammar Check .. collective noun

- A collective noun refers to a group of people or things, but is singular in form: *The basketball team was chosen early in September. This bunch of flowers smells beautiful.*
- There are many special collective nouns that go with certain groups of animals: *a gaggle of geese, a troop of monkeys, a pride of lions.* Can you think of any others? (A good thesaurus will have a list.)

col•lege (kol′ij) **1** a school you can go to after high school. It is usually smaller and more practical or job-oriented than a university. Some colleges teach only one kind of subject, like art or business. **2** one of several divisions within a university. **3** an organization that controls which people get to do a certain kind of work, such as teaching or medicine, and tries to make sure they follow certain rules. *n.*

col•le•giate (kə lē′jit) **1** 🍁 a high school. **2** having to do with high-school or college students. 1 *n.,* 2 *adj.*

col•lide (kə līd′) hit something; run into each other; crash: *In running around the corner, he collided with another boy. The two skaters collided.* *v.,* **col•lid•ed, col•lid•ing.** —**col•li′sion** (kə lizh′ən), *n.*

col•lie (kol′ē *or* kō′lē) a large, long-haired dog with a long pointed nose and a bushy tail. Collies came originally from Scotland where they were trained to look after sheep. *n.*

co•logne (kə lōn′) a sweet-smelling liquid like perfume, but with a much weaker scent. *n.*

WORD HISTORY...... cologne

The word **cologne** is a short form of the French *eau de cologne,* meaning "water from Cologne." The city of Cologne in Germany is where cologne was first made.

In German, the city is called Köln, and the perfume is called *Kölnisch Wasser,* which also means "water from Cologne."

co•lon¹ (kō′lən) a punctuation mark (:) used after a sentence or heading to show that an explanation, example, list, long quotation, etc. follows. *Example: I have been in three countries: Canada, the United States, and Pakistan.* *n.* ▶ See the *Grammar and Usage Mini-Guide.*

Grammar Check .... colon

You often see a **colon** just before a list:

Party decorations: Elen, Jacques, Strother.

Please bring the following: snacks, a soft drink, two balloons, and a pair of socks.

These shapes all have four sides: square, rectangle, parallelogram, kite, rhombus, and quadrilateral.

co•lon² (kō′lən) the lower part of the large intestine. *n., pl.* **co•lons.**

col•on•nade (kol′ə nād′) a row of columns, or pillars, evenly spaced. *n.*

col•o•ny (kol′ə nē) **1** a territory ruled by a powerful country far away which has **colonized** it, or taken it by force and sent people to live there: *England had many colonies in Africa and Asia.* **2** a group of people who go to live there from the conquering country, and who set up towns and farms. These people are also called **colonists.** **3** a number of people of one country, faith, or occupation living as a group: *There are several Doukhobor colonies in Saskatchewan.* **4** a group of animals or plants of one kind, living or growing together: *We found two colonies of ants under the steps.* *n., pl.* **col•o•nies.** —**co•lo′ni•al** (kə lō′nē əl), *adj.* —**col′o•ni•za′tion,** *n.*

Word Family......... colony

colonial: belonging to a colony
colonist: a settler in a colony
colonize: set up a colony
colonization: the process of setting up a colony

Colour

Sunlight looks colourless, but it is a mixture of colours. If you shine light into a glass prism, the light breaks into a rainbow of colours, called a spectrum.

When the three primary light colours are mixed together, the result is many different colours, including white.

When the three primary paint colours are mixed together, the result is many different colours, including black.

col•our or **col•or** (kul′ər) **1** red, yellow, blue, or any combination of them: *She never wears colours, but always dresses in black or white. The colour you get from mixing yellow and blue is green.* **2** give colour to; put colour on: *Colour the sky blue.* **3** draw or fill in pictures or designs with crayons, markers, etc.: *He can sit and colour for hours.* **4** a paint, stain, or dye. **5** become red in the face; blush: *He coloured when his mistake was mentioned.* **6** an interesting quality: *Add some details to the story to give it some colour.* **7** twist the facts to give a wrong idea: *The dishonest journalist coloured her report of the debate.* **8 the colours,** the flag of a nation, organization, etc.: *I carried the colours in the parade.* 1, 4, 6, 8 *n.*, 2, 3, 5, 7 *v.* —**col′our•ful** or **col′or•ful,** *adj.* —**col′our•less** or **col′or•less,** *adj.*
people of colour, people with brown or black skin.
show your true colours, show yourself as you really are: *In the fight, the bully showed his true colours and ran away.*
with flying colours, with great success; triumphantly: *You all passed the test with flying colours.*

USING WORDS .... colour

Colour is the spelling used by most Canadians, but in many places the spelling **color** is preferred.

This also happens with other words, for example: **favour** and **favor**, **honour** and **honor**, **labour** and **labor**, **odour** and **odor**.

col•our–blind or **col•or–blind** (kul′ər blīnd′) unable to see certain colours or tell them apart. *adj.* —**col′our blind′ness.**

col•our•ing or **col•or•ing** (kul′ə ring) **1** the pattern or amount of colour that a person or thing has: *Some animals have protective colouring to keep them from being noticed by their enemies.* Another word for this is **coloration.** **2** a substance used to give or add colour: *There is colouring in margarine.* *n.*

co•los•sal (kə los′əl) huge; gigantic; enormous: *a colossal explosion, a colossal mistake.* *adj.*

colt (kōlt) a young horse, donkey, etc., especially a male horse under four or five years old. *n.*

col•umn (kol′əm) **1** a slender, upright structure; pillar. **2** anything narrow and tall or long like a column: *A column of smoke rose from the fire. I added up the column of figures. The children lined up in two columns at the bus stop.* **3** a narrow division of a page reading from top to bottom, kept separate by lines or blank spaces: *This page has two columns.* **4** a piece of writing on a certain subject or by a certain writer, that appears regularly in a newspaper or magazine: *She writes a sports column.* *n.*

a bat	e bed	i bid	o pot	u cup	th thin
ā cake	ē me	ī bite	ō go	ū rude	ᴛʜ then
ä bar	ə about	ər over	ô for	ů put	zh measure

co·ma (kō′mə) a condition caused by a serious illness or injury. A person in a coma is unconscious and cannot think, speak, or respond to other people: *After his accident Kumar was in a coma for two weeks.* *n.*

comb (kōm) **1** a narrow, short piece of plastic, wood, metal, etc. with teeth, used to tidy the hair or hold it in place. A similar tool is used to clean and untangle wool or flax. **2** use a comb on: *I comb my hair after washing it.* **3** search thoroughly: *We combed the neighbourhood for our lost dog.* **4** the thick, red, fleshy piece on the head of chickens and some other birds: *A rooster has a larger comb than a hen has.* **5** honeycomb (def. 1). 1, 4, 5 *n.*, 2, 3 *v.*

com·bat (kom′bat) **1** fight against: *Doctors combat disease.* **2** fighting; battle: *The soldier was wounded in combat.* 1 *v.*, **com·bat·ted** or **com·bat·ed, com·bat·ting** or **com·bat·ing;** 2 *n.*

com·ba·tant (kom′bə tənt *or* kəm bat′ənt) a fighter, especially a soldier who takes part in actual fighting. *n.*

com·bi·na·tion (kom′bə nā′shən) **1** the action or result of combining things: *The combination of flour and water makes paste. The colour purple is a combination of red and blue.* **2** a series of numbers you follow to open a certain kind of lock: *He forgot the combination to his bicycle lock.* *n.*

A combine cuts and threshes grain in one operation.

com·bine (kəm bīn′ *for 1,* kom′bīn *for 2 and 3*) **1** join together; unite: *The two classes combined to lead the assembly. A healthy lifestyle combines work and play.* **2** a machine used in harvesting. **3** use a combine: *We combined the wheat last week.* 1, 3 *v.*, **com·bined, com·bin·ing;** 2 *n.*

com·bust (kəm bust′) catch on fire and burn: *Oily rags may combust if left lying around.* *v.*
—**com·bus′ti·ble,** *adj.* —**com·bus′tion,** *n.*

come (kum) **1** move toward the person speaking or writing, or the place where that person is, was, or will be: *Come over here. Come with me. They're coming to our party.* **2** arrive or happen: *The train comes at noon. Hard times came that summer.* **3** reach: *The dress comes to her knees.* **4** be made or sold: *This sweater comes in white and yellow.* *v.*, **came, come, com·ing.**

come about, happen: *The crash came about by accident.*
come across, meet or find by chance: *He came across a dollar in the street.*
come along, improve; progress: *She is coming along well.*
come around, a visit. **b** revive after being unconscious. **c** be persuaded; give in.
come between, cause unfriendly feelings in: *Don't let your differences of opinion come between you.*
come by, a visit. **b** get: *How did you come by that black eye?*
come down on, scold; criticize: *Don't come down too hard on him; it was a mistake.*
come forward, volunteer: *She came forward when someone was needed to do the job.*
come from, a be born in or live in: *That boy comes from a rich family. I come from Manitoba.* **b** be caused by: *Accidents come from carelessness.*
come in, a enter. **b** begin; be brought into use: *Steamboats came in after the invention of the steam engine.*
come into, a enter. **b** inherit: *His wife came into a lot of money.*
come off, a take place; happen: *When is the final game going to come off?* **b** turn out: *The concert came off well.*
come off it! *Informal.* You must be kidding!
come on, a progress: *How is your project coming on?* **b** meet by chance; find: *The hunters came on a herd of deer in the bush.* **c** make an entrance onto the stage: *The villain comes on in the second act.*
come out, a be revealed or told: *It finally came out that the whole thing was a lie.* **b** result; turn out; end up: *How did the ball game come out?* **c** be offered to the public: *The new CD is coming out next week.* **d** show up: *How many boys came out for baseball?* **e** make your opinion known: *She came out strongly against the new rule.*
come out with, a say: *He comes out with the funniest things!* **b** produce for the public: *The store has come out with a new catalogue.*
come over, a visit. **b** happen to; influence: *I don't know what came over me; I began to see spots everywhere.*
come through, a experience; survive: *She has come through a lot.* **b** do or give what you promised: *They said they'd help us, but they never came through.* **c** be given by some authority: *Has your loan come through yet?*
come to, a amount to; total: *The bill comes to five dollars.* **b** revive after being unconscious.
come up, arise; start or be mentioned: *The question is sure to come up in class. A storm came up.*
come upon, meet or find by chance: *We came upon two friends at the mall this morning.*
come up with, provide; produce, especially as a solution to a problem: *She always came up with the right answer.*

have something coming, deserve something; have something owed to you.
see something coming, expect something.

co•me•di•an (kə mē′dē ən) a person who makes people laugh, especially one who does this for a living. *n.*

com•e•dy (kom′ə dē) a funny movie, play, or show with a happy ending. *n., pl.* **com•e•dies.**

come•ly (kum′lē) an old or poetic word for "pretty." *adj.,* **come•li•er, come•li•est.** —**come′li•ness,** *n.*

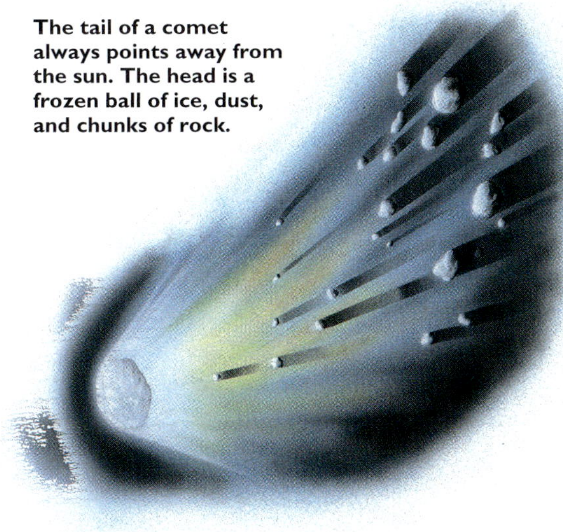

The tail of a comet always points away from the sun. The head is a frozen ball of ice, dust, and chunks of rock.

com•et (kom′it) a bright body in space that has a starlike centre and a usually cloudy tail. Comets move around the sun like planets, but their orbit is long and oval. *n.*

com•fort (kum′fərt) **1** take away or lessen someone's sadness or disappointment: *His kind words comforted the sobbing child.* **2** any person or thing that makes trouble or sadness easier to bear: *to bring comfort to a suffering family. My sister is a great comfort to me.* **3** freedom from hardship: *to have enough money to live in comfort.* **4** something pleasant or convenient that makes life comfortable: *the comforts of home.* 1 *v.,* 2–4 *n.*

com•fort•a•ble (kum′fər tə bəl) **1** relaxed; feeling no pain, hardship, or anxiety: *The warm fire made him feel comfortable after a cold day outdoors.* **2** that lets you feel relaxed: *a comfortable chair, a comfortable atmosphere. adj.* —**com′fort•a•bly,** *adv.*

com•fort•er (kum′fər tər) a padded or quilted covering for a bed. *n.*

com•ic (kom′ik) **1** having to do with comedy or funny things: *A clown is a comic actor.* **2** a comedian. **3** a cartoon drawing. A series of them attached in a row and all telling one joke or story is a **comic strip,** and a whole booklet of them is a **comic book.** A newspaper may have a page or section of them, called the **comics.** 1 *adj.,* 2, 3 *n.*

com•i•cal (kom′ə kəl) funny: *The clown's actions were comical. adj.*

com•ma (kom′ə) a punctuation mark (,), usually used where a pause would be made in saying a sentence out loud. *n.* ▶ See the *Grammar and Usage Mini-Guide.*

com•mand (kə mand′) **1** order; tell: *The officer commanded the man to stop.* **2** an order or instruction: *He obeyed the officer's command. Key in the command to copy this file onto your computer, please.* **3** have authority over; be the boss of: *Who commands this ship?* **4** authority; power or control: *to take command. The captain is in command.* **5** the ability to use well: *She has a good command of the English language.* **6** deserve and get: *Her firm manner commands respect.* 1, 3, 6 *v.,* 2, 4, 5 *n.* —**com•mand′ment,** *n.* —**com•mand′ing,** *adj.*

com•man•do (kə man′dō) **1** a soldier who makes quick, daring raids on enemy territory and does close-range fighting. **2** a group of such soldiers. *n., pl.* **com•man•dos** or **com•man•does.**

com•mem•o•rate (kə mem′ə rāt′) honour the memory of: *The new stamp commemorates the end of the war. v.,* **com•mem•o•rat•ed, com•mem•o•rat•ing.** —**com•mem′o•ra′tion,** *n.*

com•mence (kə mens′) begin; start: *The play will commence at eight o'clock. v.,* **com•menced, com•menc•ing.**

com•mence•ment (kə mens′mənt) **1** a beginning; start. **2** a graduation ceremony. *n.*

com•mend (kə mend′) **1** praise: *Honesty is a virtue that everyone commends.* **2** hand over for safekeeping: *She commended the child to her aunt's care. v.* —**com′men•da′tion,** *n.*

com•ment (kom′ent) **1** a note or remark: *The teacher had written helpful comments on my homework.* **2** make a note or remark: *Everyone commented on my new haircut. The article commented on the election.* 1 *n.,* 2 *v.*

com•men•ta•tor (kom′ən tā′tər) a person who talks about the news, sports, etc. on radio or television, especially while these events are going on: *a sports commentator, a fashion-show commentator. n.*

a bat	e bed	i bid	o pot	u cup	th thin
ā cake	ē me	ī bite	ō go	ū rude	ᴛʜ then
ä bar	ə about	ər over	ô for	ù put	zh measure

com·merce (kom′ərs) trade; business; buying and selling in large amounts between different countries or people. *n.*

com·mer·cial (kə mər′shəl) **1** having to do with buying and selling, or with advertising by businesses: *a commercial TV station. Toronto is a commercial centre.* **2** an advertisement on radio or TV between programs or during a program: *The movie was interrupted by many commercials.* 1 *adj.*, 2 *n.* —**com·mer′cial·ly,** *adv.*

com·mis·sion (kə mish′ən) **1** a reward for selling something, which is part of a salesperson's pay: *She gets a commission of ten percent on every dishwasher she sells.* **2** ask somebody to do a specific piece of work: *to commission a painting from an artist. The club commissions one of its members to buy supplies.* **3** the piece of work someone is asked to do. **4** a chosen group of people given the authority to do certain things: *The Prime Minister appointed a commission to look for solutions to unemployment.* **5** the act of committing: *the commission of a crime.* 1, 3–5 *n.*, 2 *v.*
in commission or **out of commission,** working or not working: *This pop machine is out of commission again.*

com·mis·sion·er (kə mish′ə nər) **1** a member of a commission (def. 4). **2** an official in charge of some department of a government: *a police commissioner.* *n.*

com·mit (kə mit′) **1** hand over for safekeeping: *The sick man committed himself to the doctor's care. The judge committed the thief to prison.* **2** do (usually something wrong): *A person who steals commits a crime.* **3 commit yourself,** make a firm statement one way or the other: *When I asked if she agreed, she refused to commit herself, and only said "Maybe." I have committed myself now and must keep my promise.* **4** devote; set aside: *a large sum of money has been committed to this project.* *v.*, **com·mit·ted, com·mit·ting.** —**com·mit′ment,** *n.*
commit to memory, memorize or learn by heart.

com·mit·tee (kə mit′ē) a group of people chosen to do some special thing: *The student council appointed a committee of four members to plan the banquet.* *n.*

com·mod·i·ty (kə mod′ə tē) anything that is bought and sold: *Groceries are commodities.* *n., pl.* **com·mod·i·ties.**

com·mon (kom′ən) **1** shared, done, or given by all: *common knowledge, a common effort. In the Middle Ages, villagers grazed their animals on a common pasture.* **2** ordinary; usual; familiar: *a common weed. Snow is common in most of Canada.* **3** without high rank or position: *the common people. A common soldier is a private.* **4 Commons,** short for the **House of Commons,** the group of elected people who make laws in the government. 1–3 *adj.*, 4 *n.* —**com′mon·ly,** *adv.*
in common, shared: *You and I have many interests in common.*

common denominator (kom′ən di nom′ə nā′tər) **1** a number that is a multiple of all the denominators of a group of fractions. A common denominator of ½, ⅔, and ¾ is 12 because these three fractions can also be expressed as $^{6}/_{12}$, $^{8}/_{12}$, and $^{9}/_{12}$. **2** a quality, opinion, etc. shared by all the people or things in a group: *Interest in their community was the common denominator that brought the people of the neighbourhood together.*

com·mon·er (kom′ə nər) a person who is not a noble; one of the common people. *n.*

common multiple (kom′ən mul′tə pəl) a number that can be divided by two or more other numbers without a remainder: *12 is a common multiple of 2, 3, 4, and 6; they all go into 12 with no remainder.*

com·mon·place (kom′ən plās′) **1** ordinary; not new or interesting: *The plot of the story was very commonplace.* **2** an ordinary or everyday thing or remark: *Today television is a commonplace. "Have a nice day" is a commonplace.* 1 *adj.*, 2 *n.*

common sense (kom′ən sens′) good sense in everyday situations; practical knowledge: *Vijay loved to dream, but he also had a lot of common sense.*

com·mon·wealth (kom′ən welth′) **1 the Commonwealth,** short for **the Commonwealth of Nations,** a large group of countries that have been under British rule. Many, like Canada, are now independent. The nations in the Commonwealth try to help each other in many different ways. **2** any group of nations, states, etc. united by some common bond or interest. **3** the people who make up a nation; citizens of a state. *n.*

com·mo·tion (kə mō′shən) confusion; noise or disturbance: *His voice could hardly be heard above the commotion.* *n.*

com·mune¹ (kom′yūn) a group of families living together, sharing everything and often working together on a farm or in some other business that they all own. *n.*

com·mune² (kə myūn′) share deepest thoughts and feelings with someone, understanding each other completely. *v.*, **com·muned, com·mun·ing.**

com·mu·ni·ca·ble (kə myū′nə kə bəl) that can be passed along to others; contagious: *Chicken pox is a communicable disease.* *adj.*

com•mu•ni•cate (kə myū′nə kāt′) **1** share ideas or information by talking, writing, pictures, sign language, or any other way: *He and his cousin communicate by e-mail.* **2** get in touch with; get through to: *It was impossible to communicate with my family during the storm.* **3** pass along; transfer: *A stove communicates heat to a room.* *v.*, **com•mu•ni•cat•ed, com•mu•ni•cat•ing.**

com•mu•ni•ca•tion (kə myū′nə kā′shən) **1** the act of sharing ideas or information: *Computers have made communication easier.* **2** the information or ideas shared; a letter, message, etc.: *The communication came in time to allow her to change her plans.*
3 **communications,** *pl.* a system of communicating by telephone, radio, TV, satellites, etc. *n.*

com•mun•ion (kə myūn′yən) **1** the sharing and understanding of deepest thoughts and feelings.
2 **Communion,** a Christian ceremony with bread and wine that celebrates Jesus' last supper with his disciples before he died on the cross. *n.*

com•mu•nism (kom′yə niz′əm) an economic and social system in which the government owns all property, business, and industry. *n.* **—com′mu•nist,** *n. or adj.*

com•mu•ni•ty (kə myū′nə tē) **1** any district, town, or neighbourhood, or the people living there: *This lake provides water for six communities.* **2** a group of people living together or sharing a certain purpose or interest: *a community of monks. The arts community includes all artists.* **3** a group of animals and plants sharing a particular environment in a natural balance, depending on each other for food, protection, etc. *n., pl.* **com•mu•ni•ties.**

community centre (kə myū′nətē sen′tər) a large building used by a community for sports meetings, shows, parties, etc.

community college (kə myū′nə tē kol′ij) a place where students go after finishing high school in order to learn special skills, often in a program that takes two years to complete. Community colleges also offer courses for people who want to go to school part-time or at night.

com•mute (kə myūt′) travel a long way every day from your home in one community or town to your job or school in another: *She commutes to work by train every day.* *v.*, **com•mut•ed, com•mut•ing.** **—com•mut′er,** *n.*

com•pact[1] (kom′pakt *for 1, 2, and 3,* kəm pakt′ *for 4*) **1** neatly fitting a lot into a small space or short time: *a compact kitchen, a compact speech.* **2** a small case with face powder and a mirror in it. **3** a small car. **4** press or squeeze something together into a smaller space or shorter time. A **garbage compactor** compacts garbage so it takes up less room. 1, 2 *adj.,* 3, 4 *n.* **—com•pact′ly,** *adv.* **—com•pact′ness,** *n.*

com•pact[2] (kom′pakt) an agreement to do something. *n.*

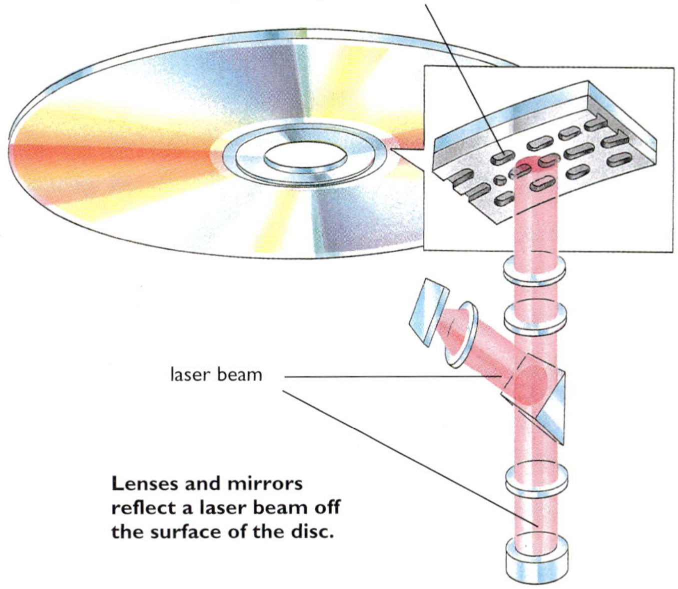

compact disc (kom′pakt disk′) a small round plate with sounds, pictures, or words digitally stored on it in very tiny pits. A laser beam inside a **compact disc player** or computer finds the information on the disc and transmits it. It is changed back into images or sounds so you can hear it or see it. *Abbreviation:* CD

com•pan•ion (kəm pan′yən) **1** a person who goes or stays with another; someone who shares in what another is doing: *a travelling companion. Her twin sister was her dearest companion.* **2** mate; matching part of a pair: *I can't find the companion to this mitt.* *n.* **—com•pan′ion•ship′,** *n.*

WORD HISTORY...... companion

From the Latin *com* "together" + *panis* "bread," a **companion** was a person you shared a meal with.

com•pan•ion•a•ble (kəm pan′yə nə bəl) nice to be with. *adj.*

a bat	e bed	i bid	o pot	u cup	th thin
ā cake	ē me	ī bite	ō go	ū rude	ᴛʜ then
ä bar	ə about	ər over	ô for	ů put	zh measure

com·pan·ion·way (kəm pan′yən wā′) a stairway leading from the deck of a ship to the rooms below. *n.*

com·pa·ny (kum′pə nē) **1** a business; a group of people who own or work for a business. **2** companions or companionship: *You are known by the company you keep. The dog provided the man with company during the long winters.* **3** guests or visitors: *Let's clean up—company's coming!* **4** any group of people acting or travelling together. *n., pl.* **com·pa·nies.**
keep someone company, go or stay with someone so he or she won't feel lonely.
part company, separate: *The hikers parted company at the gate.*

com·pa·ra·ble (kəm per′ə bəl *for 1,* kom′pə rə bəl *for 2*) **1** able to be compared: *A fire is comparable with the sun; both give light and heat.* **2** about equal when compared: *That store sells a comparable stereo for a much lower price.* *adj.*

com·par·a·tive (kəm per′ə tiv) **1** that compares: *a comparative study of bees and wasps.* **2** compared to other people or things: *Things were not perfect, but she lived in comparative comfort.* **3** the second degree of comparison of adjectives and adverbs. Taller is the comparative of tall. More quickly is the comparative of quickly. ▶ See the *Grammar and Usage Mini-Guide.* 1, 2 *adj.,* 3 *n.* **—com·par′a·tive·ly,** *adv.*

com·pare (kəm per′) **1** find out or point out how people or things are alike and how they are different: *Compare the jackets for quality, style, and price before choosing.* **2** be considered like or equal to: *Artificial light cannot compare with daylight.* *v.,* **com·pared, com·par·ing.** **—com·par′i·son,** *n.*
beyond compare, without an equal; most excellent: *Her voice is beyond compare.*

com·part·ment (kəm pärt′mənt) a separate division or section of anything: *That tool box has several compartments for holding different things.* *n.* **—com·part′ment′al·ized′,** *adj.*

In a magnetic compass like this, the needle is fixed to a pivot and is free to swing round. It always points north and south when at rest. The earth acts like a big magnet.

com·pass (kum′pəs) **1** an instrument for showing directions, with a magnetized needle that points to the North Magnetic Pole, which is near the North Pole. **2** an instrument for drawing circles and for measuring. **3** the limit or range: *Some questions are beyond the compass of human knowledge.* *n.*

com·pas·sion (kəm pash′ən) a feeling of wanting to help a person who is suffering: *The doctor was full of compassion for the badly burned child.* *n.* **—com·pas′sion·ate,** *adj.*

com·pat·i·ble (kəm pat′ə bəl) **1** going well together; agreeing; in harmony: *My two cats are always fighting; they are just not compatible. That wallpaper is very compatible with our new carpet.* **2** able to be used with a certain system, such as a computer system, without special changes: *This game is compatible with both Macintosh and IBM.* *adj.*

com·pel (kəm pel′) force: *to compel obedience. Heavy rain compelled us to go inside.* *v.,* **com·pelled, com·pel·ling.**

com·pen·sate (kom′pən sāt′) **1** give someone what is fair in exchange for work, damage, loss, etc.: *We will compensate you for the broken window.* **2** balance out; make up for: *Skill sometimes compensates for lack of strength.* *v.,* **com·pen·sat·ed, com·pen·sat·ing.** **—com′pen·sa′tion,** *n.*

com·pete (kəm pēt′) **1** try to do better than someone else: *The two girls competed with each other in every subject.* **2** take part in a contest: *to compete in the finals.* *v.,* **com·pet·ed, com·pet·ing.**
—com′pe·ti′tion (kom′pə tish′ən), *n.*
—com·pet′i·tive (kəm pet′ə tiv), *adj.*
—com·pet′i·tor, *n.*

com·pe·tent (kom′pə tənt) able; skilled: *A competent welder is highly paid. Dr. Ho is competent to treat tropical diseases.* *adj.*

com·pile (kəm pīl′) collect and bring together information into one list, report, file, book, etc.: *She compiled all her notes for the report. This encyclopedia was compiled by many experts.* *v.,* **com·piled, com·pil·ing.** **—com′pi·la′tion** (kom′pə lā′shən), *n.*

com·pla·cent (kəm plā′sənt) having or showing the attitude that you don't need to improve in any way: *Let's not be complacent; we still have a long way to go in learning to recycle. The winner's complacent smile annoyed some people.* *adj.* **—com·pla′cent·ly,** *adv.* **—com·pla′cen·cy,** *n.*

com·plain (kəm plān′) say that something is wrong: *to complain about the food, to complain to the police. He complained of sore feet.* *v.* **—com·plaint′,** *n.*

com·ple·ment (kom′plə mənt *for 1,* kom′plə ment′ *for 2*) **1** a thing or amount that makes something complete: *The team now has its full complement of players.* **2** make something complete: *Our different ideas complement one another.* 1 *n.,* 2 *v.* —**com′ple·men′ta·ry** (kom′plə men′tə rē), *adj.*

CONFUSABLES . . . complement

complement means "complete": *The shoes perfectly complemented the rest of the outfit.*

compliment means "praise": *She complimented me on my choice of shoes.*

You can remember the difference by thinking:
compl**e**ment has an **e** inside, like compl**e**te
compl**i**ment has an **i** inside, like pra**i**se.

complementary colours or **colors** (kom′plə men′tə rē kul′ərz) **1** two colours of light that produce white light when mixed. Red and blue-green are complementary light colours. **2** two colours of paint that produce black when mixed. Blue and orange are complementary paint colours.

com·plete (kəm plēt′) **1** with all the parts: *a complete set of tools.* **2** supply whatever part is missing: *She completed her set of tools by buying a cordless drill.* **3** absolute; total: *complete surprise, a complete mess.* **4** finish: *Have you completed your chores?* **5** finished; done: *My homework is complete.* 1, 3, 5 *adj.,* 2, 4 *v.,* **com·plet·ed, com·plet·ing.** —**com·plete′ly,** *adv.* —**com·plete′ness,** *n.* —**com·ple′tion,** *n.*

comp·lex (kom′pleks *or* kom pleks′ *for 1 and 2,* kom′pleks *for 3 and 4*) **1** made up of a number of parts. A **complex sentence** has more than one clause. **2** hard to understand: *The directions for assembling the swing set were so complex that we couldn't follow them.* **3** a group of related or connected buildings, parts, etc.: *The new complex includes a library, a gallery, and a theatre.* **4** an abnormally tense or anxious attitude to a particular thing: *Will you stop talking about my haircut? You're giving me a complex!* 1, 2 *adj.,* 3, 4 *n.* —**com·plex′i·ty,** *n.*

com·plex·ion (kəm plek′shən) **1** the colour and quality of the skin, especially of the face. **2** general character; nature: *The arrival of two newcomers changed the whole complexion of the group.* *n.*

com·pli·cat·ed (kom′plə kā′tid) hard to understand or deal with because of too many related details, parts, connections, problems, choices, etc.: *This game is hard to learn because the rules are so complicated.* *adj.* —**com′pli·cate′,** *v.* —**com′pli·ca′tion,** *n.*

com·pli·ment (kom′plə mənt *for 1,* kom′plə ment′ *for 2*) **1** something good said about a person; something said in praise. **2** praise; say nice things about: *We complimented him on the good job he had done on the newsletter.* 1 *n.,* 2 *v.*

with someone's compliments, as a gift from someone: *Help yourself to tea and cookies in the hotel lounge, with our compliments.*

com·pli·men·ta·ry (kom′plə men′tə rē) **1** expressing a compliment; praising. **2** given free: *We received two complimentary tickets to the ball game.* *adj.*

com·ply (kəm plī′) obey or follow a request, command, or rule: *Dad said to come in for supper, and we complied. A patient should comply with the doctor's orders.* *v.,* **com·plied, com·ply·ing.**

com·po·nent (kəm pō′nənt) **1** one of the parts that something is made up of: *The monitor is an important component of a computer system.* **2** forming a part of something: *The component parts of a knife are the blade and the handle.* 1 *n.,* 2 *adj.*

com·pose (kəm pōz′) **1** make up: *to compose a song or a story, to compose a list. The group was composed of three grown-ups and four children.* **2** **compose yourself,** calm down; pull yourself together: *Try to stop crying and compose yourself before the doctor sees you.* *v.,* **com·posed, com·pos·ing.**

Word Family **. . . . . compose**

composed: calm, quiet
composer: a person who composes, especially music
composure: calmness, self-control

com·pos·ite (kom′pə zit *or* kəm poz′it) **1** made up of various parts; compound: *The photographer made a composite picture by putting together parts of several others.* **2** something made up of various parts: *This picture is a composite of three different photos.* A **composite number** is a number with more than two factors. For example, 8 is a composite number with four factors: 1, 2, 4, and 8. 1 *adj.,* 2 *n.*

com·po·si·tion (kom′pə zish′ən) **1** the make-up of anything: *The composition of this candy includes sugar, chocolate, and milk.* **2** the putting together of a whole. Writing sentences, making pictures, and setting type in printing are all forms of composition. **3** something composed, such as a piece of music, writing, etc. *n.*

a bat	e bed	i bid	o pot	u cup	th thin
ā cake	ē me	ī bite	ō go	ū rude	ᴛʜ then
ä bar	ə about	ər over	ô for	ů put	zh measure

com·post (kom′pōst) **1** a mixture of leaves and other parts of plants that decays and is added to soil to make it healthier for growing things: *Suzy added some banana peels to the compost heap.* **2** to make compost out of plant material: *Do you compost? Yes, we compost all our garden waste.* 1 *n.,* 2 *v.*

com·pound (kom′pound *for 1, 2, and 4,* kəm pound′ *for 3*) **1** having more than one part. A clover leaf is a **compound leaf.** "Spacecraft" is a **compound word.** A **compound sentence** is actually two sentences joined by a conjunction. **2** a mixture, especially one where every molecule has more than one kind of atom in it: *Water is a compound of hydrogen and oxygen.* **3** mix; combine: *The pharmacist compounds the medicines that the doctor orders.* **4** a group of homes and sometimes other buildings inside a fenced or walled area, forming a little community. 1 *adj.,* 2, 4 *n.,* 3 *v.*

compound eye (kom′pound ī′) the kind of eye most insects have. It is made up of many separate little eyes, each forming a part of the whole image the insect sees.

com·pre·hend (kom′pri hend′) **1** understand: *If you can use a word correctly, you comprehend it.* **2** include; contain: *His report comprehended all the facts.* *v.* **—com′pre·hen′sion,** *n.*

com·pre·hen·sive (kom′pri hen′siv) that deals with everything or nearly everything: *a comprehensive test. The board of education made a comprehensive study of the need for new schools.* *adj.*

com·press (kəm pres′ *for 1,* kom′pres *for 2*) **1** squeeze together into less space or less time: *Paper is compressed into bales for recycling. Air that has been compressed has a great deal of force when suddenly released.* **2** a hot or cold cloth pad, often with medicine on it, put on a part of the body to soothe, stop bleeding, bring down a fever, etc. 1 *v.,* 2 *n.* **—com·pres′sion,** *n.* **—com·press′or,** *n.*

com·prise (kəm prīz′) include: *Our school council comprises six students and one teacher.* *v.,* **com·prised, com·pris·ing.**

com·pro·mise (kom′prə mīz′) **1** settle a quarrel by agreeing that each side will go along with part of what the other one wants: *I wanted to invite twenty friends to my party, but my parents wanted only four, so we compromised and had ten.* **2** an agreement like this: *They both wanted the apple; their compromise was to share it.* **3** lay open to danger or shame: *to compromise public safety. You will compromise your good name if you go along with such a dishonest trick.* 1, 3 *v.,* **com·pro·mised, com·pro·mis·ing;** 2 *n.*

com·pul·sion (kəm pul′shən) force; the act of compelling or being compelled, either by others or by a feeling inside: *He takes his medicine only by compulsion.* *n.* **—com·pul′sive,** *adj.*

com·pul·so·ry (kəm pul′sə rē) required: *In Ontario, seat belts are compulsory.* *adj.*

com·pute (kəm pyūt′) figure out by arithmetic; calculate, often with the aid of a computer: *It took some time to compute the cost of our trip.* *v.,* **com·put·ed, com·put·ing.** **—com′pu·ta′tion,** *n.*

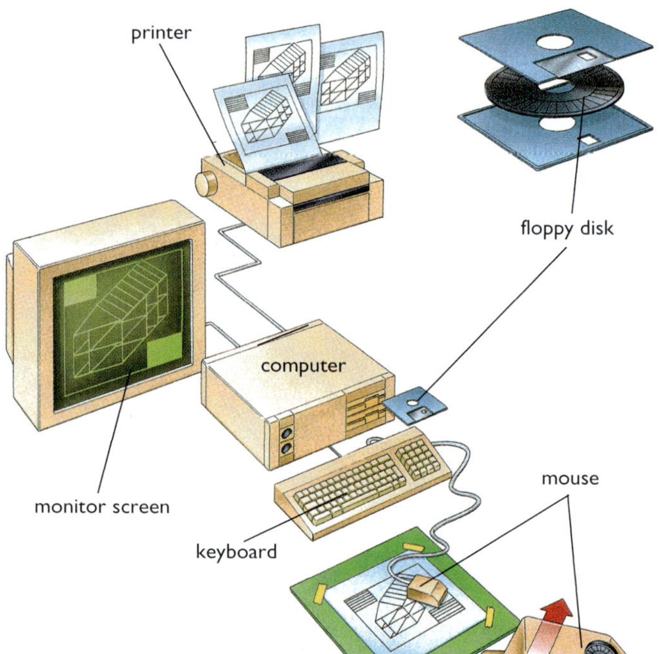

Charles Babbage (1792-1871) spent much of his life developing calculating machines. He is respected as a computing pioneer.

com·put·er (kəm pyū′tər) an electronic machine that can process all kinds of information at very high speeds and store it for later use. It runs according to a set of instructions called a program. With a computer you can write, calculate, draw, design, compose music, play games, do research, and keep track of things. Computers can also run other machines. *n.*

com·rade (kom′rad) a companion and friend; partner. *n.*

con¹ (kon) a reason against. The **pros and cons** of a question are the arguments for and against it. *n.*

con² (kon) *Slang.* **1** trick; swindle: *He was conned into buying a baseball card that was worthless* (*v.*). *The whole thing was just a con, but I fell for it* (*n.*). **2 con artist,** a swindler. 1 *v.,* **conned, con·ning;** 1, 2 *n.*

con·cave (kon kāv′ *or* kon′kāv) curved like the inside of a bowl. *adj.*

con·ceal (kən sēl′) hide: *She concealed the ball behind her back.* *v.* **—con·ceal′ment,** *n.*

con·cede (kən sēd′) **1** admit; admit as true: *He conceded that our idea was better.* **2** allow a person to have; grant: *She conceded us the right to walk across her land.* *v.,* **con·ced·ed, con·ced·ing.**

con·ceit (kən sēt′) too much pride in yourself and your ability to do things: *In his conceit, the track star thought that no one could outrun him.* *n.*
—con·ceit′ed, *adj.*

con·ceiv·a·ble (kən sē′və bəl) imaginable: *We should take every conceivable precaution against fire.* *adj.*

con·ceive (kən sēv′) **1** imagine; think up; form an idea of: *Sir Sandford Fleming conceived the method of Standard Time, dividing the world into 24 time zones. She couldn't conceive of a person not liking chocolate.* **2** become pregnant with: *to conceive a child.* *v.,* **con·ceived, con·ceiv·ing.**

con·cen·trate (kon′sən trāt′) **1** bring or come together to one place: *A magnifying glass concentrates the rays of light on a single spot. The population of Canada is concentrated in the southern regions.* **2** pay close attention: *He concentrated on his reading so that he would understand the story.* **3** make stronger, especially by boiling off some of the water. **4** a substance made stronger in this way: *a bottle of lemon juice concentrate.* 1–3 *v.,* **con·cen·trat·ed, con·cen·trat·ing;** 4 *n.*
—con′cen·tra′tion, *n.*

con·cen·tric (kən sen′trik) having the same centre. Concentric circles are different-sized circles with the same centre, like the ones around a bull's-eye. *adj.*

con·cept (kon′sept) a thought; a general notion or idea: *the concept of truth. Freedom and equality are basic concepts of democracy.* *n.*

con·cep·tion (kən sep′shən) **1** a way of imagining or thinking about something: *Your conception of the problem is different from mine.* **2** the fact of becoming pregnant. *n.*

con·cern (kən sərn′) **1** worry: *The father's concern over his sick child kept him awake all night* (*n.*). *I didn't want to concern you with the details of the accident* (*v.*). **2** have to do with; be the business of; affect, involve, or interest: *This letter concerns only me.* **3** business; affair; interest or interests: *How I spend my money is my concern, not yours.* **4** a business company; firm. 1, 2 *v.,* 1, 3, 4 *n.*
concern oneself, be concerned.
of concern, of importance; of interest: *a matter of concern.*

con·cerned (kən sərnd′) **1** interested; caring: *Some concerned citizens met to discuss the proposed dump.* **2** involved; affected: *All those concerned in the school play must attend the dress rehearsal.* **3** worried: *We are quite concerned about his poor health.* *adj.*

con·cern·ing (kən sər′ning) about: *The police officer asked many questions concerning the accident.* *prep.*

con·cert (kon′sərt) a performance by one or more musicians or singers. *n.*
in concert, all together: *The rebel groups acted in concert to seize the building.*

con·cer·ti·na (kon′sər tē′nə) a musical instrument like a small accordion, but with round instead of rectangular ends. *n.*

con·cer·to (kən cher′tō) a piece of music for one or more main instruments, such as a violin, piano, etc., backed up by an orchestra. *n., pl.* **con·cer·tos.**

con·ces·sion (kən sesh′ən) **1** the act of conceding or giving in: *As a concession, Mom let me stay up an hour longer.* **2** land or space given to a person or company to carry on business, such as land for a mining company or space for a hot dog stand. **3** 🍁 **a** mainly in Ontario and Québec, a block of farmland within a township. **b** a road marking off one of these blocks. **Concession road** is the full name for it. *n.*

conch (kongk *or* konch) a shellfish with a large, spiral shell. *n.*

con·cil·i·ate (kən sil′ē āt′) win someone over who is angry: *She conciliated her angry little sister with a cookie.* *v.,* **con·cil·i·at·ed, con·cil·i·at·ing.**

con·cise (kən sīs′) saying a lot in few words; short but full of information: *He gave a concise report of the meeting.* *adj.*

a bat	e bed	i bid	o pot	u cup	th thin
ā cake	ē me	ī bite	ō go	ū rude	TH then
à bar	ə about	ər over	ò for	ů put	zh measure

con·clude (kən klüd′) 1 finish; end: *She concluded her speech with a funny story.* 2 figure out or decide by reasoning: *From the clues we found, we concluded that the thief must have left in a hurry.* *v.*, **con·clud·ed, con·clud·ing.** —**con·clu′sion,** *n.*
jump or **leap to conclusions,** decide something is true without looking at all the related facts.

con·clu·sive (kən klü′siv) decisive; definite: *a conclusive victory. The evidence against the burglar was conclusive.* *adj.*

con·coct (kən kokt′) prepare or cook up; put together: *to concoct a plan or story, to concoct a meal.* *v.* —**con·coc′tion,** *n.*

con·course (kon′kôrs) 1 a large, open area where crowds gather or wait: *We met in the concourse of the railway station.* 2 a running, flowing, or coming together: *The fort was built at the concourse of two rivers.* *n.*

con·crete (kon′krēt *for 1,* kon′krēt *or* kon krēt′ *for 2)* 1 a mixture of cement, water, and sand or gravel that hardens as it dries. Concrete is used for foundations, sidewalks, dams, bridges, etc. 2 existing as an actual physical object, not merely as an idea or quality: *A painting is concrete; its beauty is abstract.* 1, 2 *adj.*

concrete poem (kon′krēt pō′əm) a poem arranged in the form of a picture.

con·cur (kən kər′) agree: *The judges all concurred in their choice of the winning entry.* *v.*, **con·curred, con·cur·ring.**

con·cus·sion (kən kush′ən) an injury to the brain from a blow or fall or other shock: *She suffered a severe concussion in the accident.* *n.*

con·demn (kən dem′) 1 say that a person or act is very bad or wrong: *We condemn cruelty and cruel people.* 2 cause to suffer some punishment; doom: *The murderer was condemned to prison.* 3 declare not safe for use: *This old bridge has been condemned.* *v.* —**con′dem·na′tion** (kon′dem nā′shən), *n.*

con·dense (kən dens′) 1 change from a gas or a vapour to liquid by cooling. If steam touches cold surfaces, it condenses into water droplets called **condensation.** 2 reduce the volume of by getting rid of some of the water: *Milk is condensed before it is canned.* 3 put into fewer words: *A long story can sometimes be condensed into a few sentences.* *v.*, **con·densed, con·dens·ing.** —**con′den·sa′tion** (kon′den sā′shən), *n.*

con·de·scend (kon′di send′) 1 come down graciously to the level of someone of lower rank: *The princess condescended to eat with the beggars.* 2 grant someone a favour in a proud, snobbish way, as if that person were very low and the favour very great: *Cynthia condescended to answer my "Hi!" with a nod.* 3 lower oneself to do something considered wrong: *He would not condescend to cheating.* *v.* —**con′de·scend′ing,** *adj.*

con·di·tion (kən dish′ən) 1 the state a person or thing is in; good shape or bad shape: *The condition of his health kept him from doing heavy work. The accident victim is in poor condition.* 2 put in good condition: *Exercise conditions your muscles.* 3 something that another thing depends on or hinges on: *Ability and effort are conditions of success. You can go, but only on the condition that an adult goes along.* 4 teach by experience; accustom: *This dog has been conditioned to expect food when it obeys a command.* 1, 3 *n.*, 2, 4 *v.*

con·di·tion·al (kən dish′ə nəl) depending on something else: *"You may go if the sun shines" is a conditional promise.* *adj.*

con·di·tion·er (kən dish′ə nər) a lotion or cream used to improve the condition of the hair, skin, etc. *n.*

con·do·min·i·um (kon′də min′ē əm) an apartment or townhouse owned rather than rented by the people living in it. The individual apartments or townhouses are joined together in one big building which often has facilities like a pool, playground, or parking garage that all the people living there own together. **Condominium** is often shortened to **condo,** *pl.* **condos.** *n.*

The Andean condor is the world's largest flying bird. It can reach heights of over 4000 m, gliding upward in rising air currents.

con·dor (kon′dôr) a large vulture with a featherless neck and head. Condors live on high mountains in South America and California. *n.*

con·duct (kon′dukt *for 1,* kən dukt′ *for 2–5*) **1** actions; behaviour: *Their rude conduct was inexcusable. He won a medal for good conduct.* **2** **conduct yourself,** act or behave in a certain way: *She must learn how to conduct herself in a restaurant.* **3** carry out; do: *We are conducting some experiments with baking soda.* **4** direct; lead: *to conduct an orchestra. Mr. Vos conducted us through the museum.* **5** be a channel for; transmit: *Metals conduct heat and electricity.* 1 *n.,* 2–5 *v.* **—con·duc′tion,** *n.*

con·duc·tiv·i·ty (kon′duk tiv′ə tē) the ability to carry heat, sound, or electricity. *n.*

con·duc·tor (kən duk′tər) **1** the leader of a choir or orchestra. **2** the person in charge of passengers on a train, or the driver of a streetcar or bus. **3** anything that transmits heat, sound, or electricity: *Copper is a good conductor of electricity.* *n.*

cone (kōn) **1** a solid object that has a flat, round base and narrows evenly to a point at the other end. **2** anything shaped like a cone: *an ice-cream cone, the cone of a volcano.* **3** the part that carries seeds on evergreen trees like pine, spruce, etc. *n.*

con·fed·er·a·cy (kən fed′ə rə sē) a group of people, states, countries, etc. joined together for a special purpose, especially against another group or against the law. *n., pl.* **con·fed·er·a·cies.**

con·fed·er·ate (kən fed′ə rit *for 1, 3,* kən fed′ə rāt′ *for 2*) **1** a person joined with others for a special purpose, often a bad one; accomplice: *The thief had three confederates.* **2** join together: *Newfoundland confederated with Canada in 1949. Four provinces of Canada confederated in 1867—Nova Scotia, New Brunswick, Québec, and Ontario.* **3** joined together for a special purpose; allied: *confederate nations.* 1, 2 *v.,* **con·fed·er·at·ed, con·fed·er·at·ing;** 3 *adj.*

con·fed·er·a·tion (kən fed′ə rā′shən) **1** the act of joining together in a league or alliance: *a plan for the confederation of the colonies.* **2** a group of countries, states, etc. joined together for some purpose. **3** 🍁 **Confederation,** **a** the union of Ontario, Québec, Nova Scotia, and New Brunswick in 1867: *The 100th anniversary of Confederation was in 1967.* **b** Canada, thought of as a group of united provinces: *Six other provinces have joined Confederation since 1867—Manitoba, British Columbia, Prince Edward Island, Alberta, Saskatchewan, and Newfoundland.* *n.*

con·fer (kən fər′) **1** talk something over together: *The prime minister conferred with the premiers about creating more jobs.* **2** give; award: *Diplomas are conferred on students at graduation.* *v.,* **con·ferred, con·fer·ring.**

con·fer·ence (kon′fə rəns) a meeting to discuss a particular subject. It can be for a few minutes, or last for several days with people giving presentations on the subject. In a **conference call,** several people talk together on separate phones. *n.*

con·fess (kən fes′) **1** admit; own up: *He confessed to eating all the cake. When the police questioned the prisoner, she confessed.* **2** in some Christian churches, tell your sins to a priest. *v.* **—con·fes′sion,** *n.*

con·fet·ti (kən fet′ē) tiny bits of coloured paper, traditionally thrown at weddings. *n.*

> **WORD HISTORY......confetti**
>
> **Confetti** means "candies" in Italian. People used to throw candies at weddings and carnivals—much better than bits of paper!

con·fide (kən fīd′) **1** tell as a secret: *He confided his troubles to his brother.* **2** **confide in,** **a** tell a secret to: *She always confides in her sister.* **b** trust: *to confide in the truth.* *v.,* **con·fid·ed, con·fid·ing.**

con·fi·dence (kon′fə dəns) **1** firm belief or trust: *We have no confidence in a liar.* **2** firm belief in yourself and your abilities: *She went at her work with confidence.* **3** something told as a secret: *I would not betray a confidence.* *n.* **—con′fi·dent,** *adj.*

con·fi·den·tial (kon′fə den′shəl) **1** to be treated as a secret: *The detective made a confidential report.* **2** trusted with secret matters: *a confidential assistant.* *adj.*

con·fine (kən fīn′ *for 1 and 2,* kon′fīnz *for 3*) **1** keep within limits; restrict: *I confine myself to two videos a week.* **2** keep in; shut in: *confined in a jail cell. Confine your pet or keep it on a leash.* **3** Usually, **confines,** *pl.* a boundary; border; limit: *These people have never been beyond the confines of their own valley.* 1, 2 *v.,* **con·fined, con·fin·ing;** 3 *n.* **—con·fine′ment,** *n.*

con·firm (kən fərm′) **1** say or show that something is true or correct: *The experiment confirmed our hypothesis; it turned out as we expected. The premier confirmed the rumour of an election.* **2** make definite or certain: *The travel agent said the reservation has been confirmed.* **3** in some Christian churches, bring someone into full membership by a ceremony where the person declares his or her faith publicly. *v.* **—con′fir·ma′tion,** *n.*

a bat	e bed	i bid	o pot	u cup	th thin
ā cake	ē me	ī bite	ō go	ū rude	ᴛʜ then
ä bar	ə about	ər over	ȯ for	u̇ put	zh measure

con·firmed (kən fərmd′) settled; habitual: *a confirmed bachelor.* *adj.*

con·fis·cate (kon′fə skāt′) seize by authority; take away something that a person is not allowed to have: *The customs officer confiscated the smuggled cigarettes.* *v.,* **con·fis·cat·ed, con·fis·cat·ing.**

con·flict (kon′flikt *for 1,* kən flikt′ *for 2*) **1** a fight, struggle, clash, or disagreement: *A conflict arose over what colour to paint our kitchen. I have a conflict in my schedule; piano and swimming are on the same night.* **2** disagree; clash; be out of harmony: *conflicting opinions.* 1 *n.,* 2 *v.*

con·form (kən fȯrm′) act in agreement with; follow a pattern or standard: *Players must conform to the rules of the league. You don't have to conform to the latest fad.* *v.*

con·front (kən frunt′) face, especially boldly or in some kind of conflict: *to confront a difficult problem, to confront a bully. We confronted the girls with the damage they had caused.* *v.*
—con′fron·ta′tion (kon′frən tā′shən), *n.*

con·fuse (kən fyūz′) **1** mix up; throw into disorder; bewilder: *So many people talking to me at once confused me.* **2** be unable to tell apart; mistake one thing for another: *People often confuse this boy with his twin brother.* *v.,* **con·fused, con·fus·ing.** **—con·fu′sion,** *n.*

con·geal (kən jēl′) make or become firm rather than fluid, as water when it freezes to ice, or blood when it clots. People even talk about plans congealing. *v.*

con·ge·ni·al (kən jēn′yəl) well matched with your tastes and interests; easy to feel comfortable with: *a congenial roommate, congenial work.* *adj.*

con·gest·ed (kən jes′tid) plugged up: *a congested nose, streets congested with traffic.* *adj.* **—con·ges′tion,** *n.*

con·glom·er·ate (kən glom′ə rit *for 1 and 2,* kən glom′ə rāt′ *for 3*) **1** rock made up of waterworn boulders, pebbles, etc. held together by a natural cementing material. **2** a huge company made up of a lot of different smaller companies joined together. **3** form a mass of mixed things stuck together. 1, 2 *n.,* 3 *v.,* **con·glom·er·at·ed, con·glom·er·at·ing.**

con·glom·er·a·tion (kən glom′ə rā′shən) a mixed-up mass of various things or people: *There was such a conglomeration of things in the room that he didn't know what to clean up first.* *n.*

con·grat·u·late (kən grach′ə lāt′) say how glad you are about someone's happiness or good fortune: *I congratulated my friend on her success.* *v.,* **con·grat·u·lat·ed, con·grat·u·lat·ing.**
—con·grat′u·la·to′ry, *adj.*

con·grat·u·la·tion (kən grach′ə lā′shən) **1** the act of congratulating: *to write a note of congratulation.* **2** **congratulations,** *pl.* an expression of pleasure at someone else's happiness or good fortune: *Congratulations! You won!* 1, 2 *n.,* 2 *interj.*

con·gre·gate (kong′grə gāt′) come together into a crowd or mass; assemble: *The people of Rome congregated in St. Peter's Square to see the Pope.* *v.,* **con·gre·gat·ed, con·gre·gat·ing.**

con·gre·ga·tion (kong′grə gā′shən) **1** coming together into a crowd or mass; assembling: *There was a congregation of bees around the hive.* **2** a gathering of people or things, especially for worship. *n.*

con·gress (kong′gris) a meeting or gathering, especially a meeting of elected people to discuss some subject or to pass laws. The national lawmaking body of the United States is called the **Congress.** *n.*

con·gru·ent (kong′grū ənt *or* kən gru′ənt) **1** in math, exactly the same in size and shape, so that all parts match: *These triangles are not congruent; one is bigger than the other.* **2** agreeing; in harmony. *adj.*
—con′gru·ence, *n.*

con·i·cal (kon′ə kəl) cone-shaped; like a cone: *The wizard wore a conical hat.* *adj.*

con·i·fer (kon′ə fər) a cone-bearing tree. Conifers are typically evergreens with needles. Pine, spruce, cypress, hemlock, fir, and larch are conifers. *n.*
—co·nif′er·ous (kə nif′ə rəs), *adj.*

con·jec·ture (kən jek′chər) guess: *She thinks weather forecasts are mostly conjecture (n.). Would you care to conjecture on the outcome of the World Series (v.)?* *n.* or *v.*, **con·jec·tured, con·jec·tur·ing.**

con·junc·tion (kən jungk′shən) **1** connection: *A severe illness in conjunction with the hot weather has left the baby very weak.* **2** in grammar, a word used to connect clauses, phrases, or words. In the sentence *They ate their sandwiches and apples but they were too tired to jog or swim,* the words *and, but,* and *or* are conjunctions. Other examples of conjunctions are: *though, if, when, since, because,* and *unless.* *n.*

con·jure (kon′jər) **1** cause to appear by magic, or as if by magic: *The wizard used a spell to conjure a dragon. Grandma conjured up a bag of toys from the attic.* **2** bring images to someone's mind: *Her song conjured up memories of my old home.* *v.*, **con·jured, con·jur·ing.**

con·nect (kə nekt′) **1** join or fasten; put together: *to connect pipes. This cable connects the keyboard to the computer.* **2** link or relate: *We usually connect spring with sunshine and flowers.* *v.* **—con·nec′tion,** *n.* **—con·nec′tor,** *n.*

Grammar ✓Check .. connecting words

Use **connecting words** to link your ideas. This will make your writing flow easily from one idea to the next. Here are some useful connecting words and phrases: *afterward, although, as if, as long as, as much as, as soon as, even if, even though, first, firstly, in addition to, in order that, in spite of, provided that, similarly, since, so that.*

con·ning tower (kon′ing tou′ər) a small tower on a submarine, used as an exit and as a lookout.

con·nois·seur (kon′ə sər′) a person who is an expert judge of art, food, music, etc.: *Sandra's mother was a connoisseur of fine furniture.* *n.*

con·note (kə nōt′) make you feel or think of something more than just the basic meaning: *To Louisa "summer" connotes freedom and excitement.* *n.* **—con′no·ta′tion** (kon′ə tā′shən), *n.* **—con′no·ta′tive** (kon′ə tā′tiv), *adj.*

con·quer (kong′kər) **1** get something by fighting for it and winning: *to conquer new territory.* **2** overcome or defeat; be victorious over someone or something: *to conquer an enemy, to conquer a bad habit.* *v.* **—con′quer·or,** *n.*

con·quest (kon′kwest *or* kong′kwest) **1** the act of conquering or the thing conquered: *the conquest of a country.* **2** the thing conquered: *Her latest conquest is the Olympic gold medal in figure skating.* *n.*

con·quis·ta·dor (kən kwis′tə dôr′ *or* kən kis′tə dôr′) one of the Spanish conquerors who came to South America and the southern parts of North America in the 1500s to look for gold. The conquistadors conquered the Indian civilizations of Mexico and South America in their search for treasure. *n.*

con·science (kon′shəns) a sense of right and wrong: *The boy's conscience prompted him to return the book he had stolen.* *n.*

con·sci·en·tious (kon′shē en′shəs) **1** careful to do what your conscience tells you is right; wanting to do your best. **2** done carefully and seriously: *conscientious work.* *adj.* **—con′sci·en′tious·ly,** *adv.*

con·scious (kon′shəs) **1** knowing; realizing; aware: *She was not conscious of my presence in the room.* **2** awake; able to feel: *When he became conscious again, he asked what had happened.* **3** done knowingly: *a conscious error.* *adj.* **—con′scious·ly,** *adv.*

con·scious·ness (kon′shəs nis) **1** the state of being conscious; awareness: *The injured man did not regain consciousness for two hours. People and animals have consciousness; plants and stones do not.* **2** all of a person's thoughts and feelings that he or she is aware of having. Many events of your early childhood are no longer part of your consciousness. *n.*

con·se·crate (kon′sə krāt′) set apart, especially for a holy or noble purpose: *to consecrate a church. His life was consecrated to music.* *v.*, **con·se·crat·ed, con·se·crat·ing.** **—con′se·cra′tion,** *n.*

con·sec·u·tive (kən sek′yə tiv) following one right after another: *Monday, Tuesday, and Wednesday are consecutive days. We stayed up late for three consecutive nights.* *adj.* **—con·sec′u·tive·ly,** *adv.*

con·sent (kən sent′) **1** agree; give approval or permission: *My mother has consented to the birthday sleepover.* **2** agreement; permission: *You can't go without your parents' consent.* 1 *v.*, 2 *n.*

con·se·quence (kon′sə kwens′) **1** result: *The consequence of her fall was a broken leg.* **2** importance: *That little mistake is of no consequence.* *n.*
suffer the consequences, accept what happens because of your action: *If you do your work carelessly, you'll have to suffer the consequences.*

a bat	e bed	i bid	o pot	u cup	th thin
ā cake	ē me	ī bite	ō go	ū rude	TH then
ä bar	ə about	ər over	ô for	ů put	zh measure

con•se•quent (kon′sə kwənt) resulting; following as an effect: *His illness and consequent absence put him behind in his work.* *adj.*
—**con′se•quent•ly,** *adv.*

con•ser•va•tion (kon′sər vā′shən) the protection and careful management of something, especially the environment, so that it will not be wasted or wrecked. A **conservation area** is an area of land kept free of housing and industry and taken care of by government, so that people can enjoy it as a park for many years to come. *n.* —**con′ser•va′tion•ist,** *n.*
—**con′ser•va′tion•ism′,** *n.*

con•serv•a•tive (kən sər′və tiv) **1** not liking change or risk; preferring what is familiar and safe, both in behaviour and in ideas: *She is adventurous, while her sister is conservative.* **2** a person who does not like change or risk. **3 Conservative,** **a** a member of a conservative political party. **b** in Canada, a member of the Conservative Party. 1, 3 *adj.,* 2, 3 *n.*

Conservative Party (kən sər′və tiv pär′tē) one of the main political parties of Canada.

con•serve (kən sərv′) use and manage something carefully so that it will not be wasted or wrecked: *We should conserve our natural resources. Conserve your strength for the end of the race.* *v.,* **con•served, con•serv•ing.**

con•sid•er (kən sid′ər) **1** think about in order to decide: *Take time to consider the problem.* **2** think of as: *I consider myself a Canadian.* **3** allow for; take into account: *This watch runs very well, if you consider how old it is. A kind person considers the feelings of others.* *v.*

Word Family......... **consider**

considerable: quite a lot
considerate: thinking of others and their feelings
considering: taking into account

con•sid•er•a•tion (kən sid′ə rā′shən) **1** careful thought about something before making a decision: *Please give full consideration to my question.* **2** something to be considered: *Price and quality are two considerations in buying anything.* **3** thoughtfulness for others and their feelings: *The girl's consideration for her father was in sharp contrast with her sister's rudeness.* **4** money or other payment: *I'll cut your grass for a small consideration.* *n.*
in consideration of, **a** because of: *In consideration of his wife's poor health, he moved to a milder climate.* **b** in return for: *She gave him a present in consideration of his helpfulness.*
take into consideration, allow for; take into account: *The judge took the boy's age into consideration.*

con•sist (kən sist′)
consist in, be; mean: *Good listening consists in giving your full attention and respect.*
consist of, be made up of: *A week consists of seven days.* *v.*

con•sist•en•cy (kən sis′tən sē) **1** a degree of firmness or thickness: *Jam must be of the right consistency to spread easily without dripping.* **2** keeping to the same ideas, standards, etc.: *To be fair you must enforce the rule with consistency.* **3** harmony; agreement: *There was little consistency between what she said and what she did.* *n., pl.* **con•sist•en•cies.**

con•sist•ent (kən sis′tənt) **1** keeping to the same ideas, standards, and habits: *He was always consistent in giving his best effort.* **2** harmonious; in agreement: *Biking without a helmet is not consistent with safety.* *adj.*

con•so•la•tion (kon′sə lā′shən) **1** comfort. **2** a comforting person, thing, or event. A **consolation prize** is often given to those in a competition who tried hard but did not win. *n.*

con•sole[1] (kən sōl′) comfort. *v.,* **con•soled, con•sol•ing.**

con•sole[2] (kon′sōl) **1** a control panel of buttons, switches, dials, etc. **2** a cabinet made to stand on the floor and to contain a built-in television set, stereo system, etc. **3** the keyboard, stops, and pedals of an organ. *n.*

con•sol•i•date (kən sol′ə dāt′) **1** unite; combine: *The three towns were consolidated under a single regional government.* **2** make solid or firm; strengthen: *The review helped us consolidate what we had learned in the unit.* *v.,* **con•sol•i•dat•ed, con•sol•i•dat•ing.**

con•so•nant (kon′sə nənt) **1** a speech sound made by completely or partly blocking your breath with your lips, tongue, or teeth. All languages have both consonants and vowels. The first and last sounds in "tab" are consonants. **2** a letter standing for such a sound. In English, the consonants are *b, c, d, f, g, h, j, k, l, m, n, p, q, r, s, t, v, w, x, y, z.* *n.*

con•sort (kon′sôrt *for 1,* kən sôrt′ *for 2*) **1** a husband or wife, especially of a queen or king. **2** keep company; associate: *It is unwise to consort with criminals.* 1 *n.,* 2 *v.*

con•spic•u•ous (kən spik′yū əs) noticeable or impossible to ignore; attracting attention: *a conspicuous hairstyle, a sign in a conspicuous location. Canada has played a conspicuous part in the work of the United Nations.* *adj.* —**con•spic′u•ous•ly,** *adv.*

Constellations

The Babylonians named many constellations after animals whose shapes they saw in the patterns of the stars.

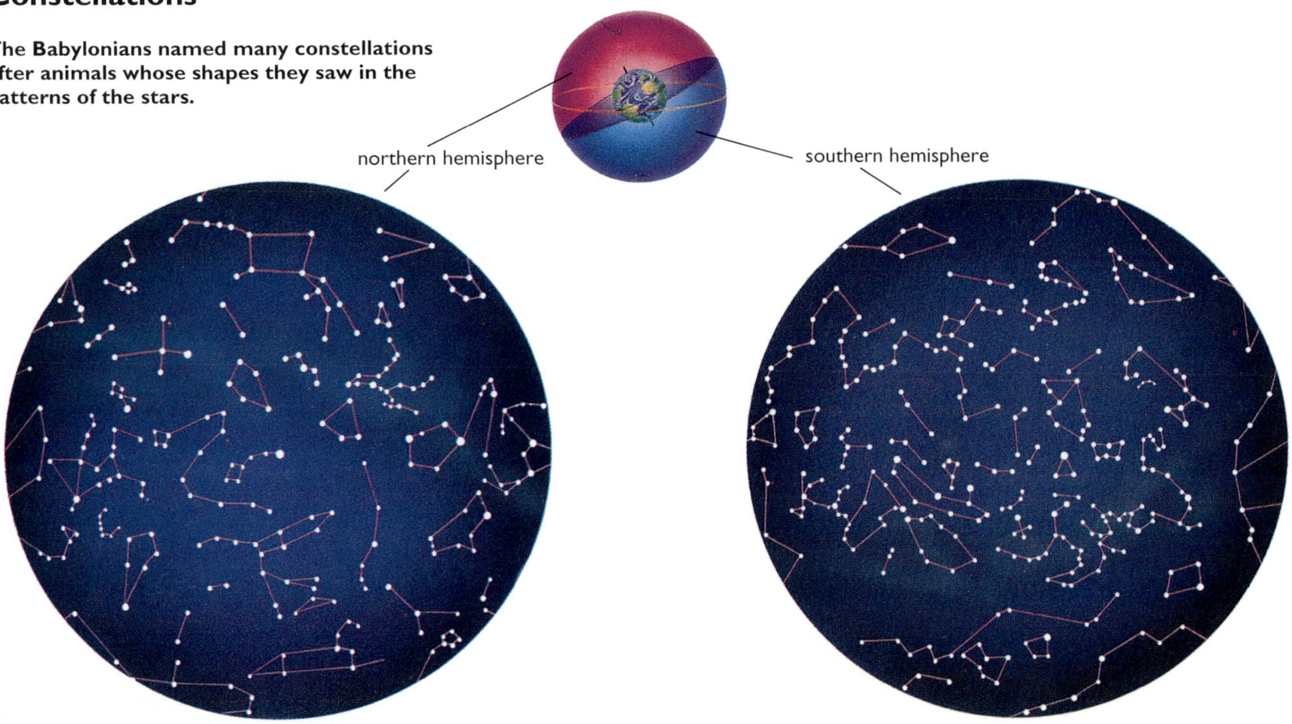

con·spir·a·cy (kən spēr′ə sē) 1 a secret plot with others to do something wrong: *a conspiracy to overthrow the government.* 2 the group of people involved in making the plot: *All those in the conspiracy were punished.* *n., pl.* **con·spir·a·cies.** —**con·spir′a·tor** (kən spēr′ə tər), *n.*

con·spire (kən spīr′) 1 plan secretly with others to do something wrong; plot: *A gang of thieves conspired to steal the jewels.* 2 act together: *All things conspired to make my birthday a happy one.* *v.,* **con·spired, con·spir·ing.**

con·sta·ble (kon′stə bəl) a low-ranking police officer. *n.*

con·stant (kon′stənt) 1 not changing: *If you keep walking due north, your direction is constant.* 2 never stopping: *three days of constant rain. A clock makes a constant ticking sound.* 3 faithful; loyal. *adj.* —**con′stant·ly,** *adv.* —**con′stan·cy,** *n.*

con·stel·la·tion (kon′stə lā′shən) a group of stars: *The Big Dipper is the easiest constellation to find.* *n.*

con·ster·na·tion (kon′stər nā′shən) dismay; paralysing terror: *To their consternation the train rushed toward the burning bridge.* *n.*

con·sti·pa·tion (kon′stə pā′shən) a condition in which bowel movements are delayed or difficult. *n.* —**con′sti·pat′ed,** *adj.*

con·stit·u·en·cy (kən stich′ū ən sē) 1 a voting district. Each constituency elects one person to speak for the people of that constituency in parliament. **Riding** is another word for constituency. 2 the voters in the district: *A member of parliament must listen to his or her constituency.* *n., pl.* **con·stit·u·en·cies.**

con·stit·u·ent (kən stich′ū ənt) 1 a part of a whole; ingredient: *Sugar is the main constituent of candy.* 2 needed to make up a whole: *Flour, liquid, salt, and yeast are constituent parts of bread.* 3 a voter in a constituency: *The Member of Parliament received many letters from her constituents.* 1 *adj.,* 2, 3 *n.*

con·sti·tute (kon′stə tyūt′ *or* kon′stə tūt′) make up; form: *Seven days constitute a week.* *v.,* **con·sti·tut·ed, con·sti·tut·ing.**

con·sti·tu·tion (kon′stə tyū′shən *or* kon′stə tū′shən) 1 a person's physical or mental nature or make-up: *He has a very healthy constitution.* 2 the basic rules and principles that a country, town, or organization is run by. The Canadian Charter of Rights and Freedoms is part of Canada's constitution and was added by the **Constitution Act, 1982.** *n.* —**con′sti·tu′tion·al,** *adj.*

a bat	e bed	i bid	o pot	u cup	th **thin**
ā cake	ē me	ī bite	ō go	ū rude	ᴛʜ **then**
ä bar	ə about	ər over	ȯ for	u̇ put	zh measure

con·strain (kən strān′) force: *She was constrained to accept her boss's decision or leave her job.* *v.*

con·straint (kən strānt′) **1** a fact or feature that limits what you can do: *coping with the constraints of a very small budget.* **2** a feeling of not being at ease; embarrassed awkwardness: *We felt a little constraint with the new teacher for the first day or so.* **3** force: *He didn't want to do it; he was acting under constraint.* *n.*

con·strict (kən strikt′) squeeze; narrow: *The collar was too tight and constricted the dog's neck.* *v.*

con·stric·tor (kən strik′tər) any snake that kills its prey by squeezing the prey in its coils. Boas and pythons are constrictors. *n.*

con·struct (kən strukt′) build: *to construct a bridge. Sentences are constructed of words.* *v.* **—con·struc′tion,** *n.*

construction paper (kən struk′shən pā′pər) a type of thick coloured paper with a texture like felt, used for cutting and pasting and other art projects.

con·struc·tive (kən struk′tiv) building up so as to improve; helpful: *People appreciate constructive suggestions.* *adj.*

con·sul (kon′səl) **1** an officer sent by the government of one country to look after its business interests in a city of another country and to help any of his or her fellow citizens living there. The consul's office is called a **consulate.** **2** a top leader of the ancient Roman republic. There were two consuls at a time. *n.*

con·sult (kən sult′) **1** get information or advice from: *You can consult persons, books, or maps to find out what you wish to know.* **2** talk something over: *He is consulting with his lawyer.* **3** consider; think of when making decisions: *A good teacher consults the interests of the class.* *v.* **—con′sul·ta′tion** (kon′səl tā′shən), *n.*

con·sult·ant (kən sul′tənt) somebody who is paid to give advice on a subject: *a medical consultant, a computer consultant.* *n.*

con·sume (kən sūm′) **1** eat or drink up: *We consumed a whole cake at the birthday party.* **2** use up or spend: *She consumes much of her time in reading. This machine consumes too much electricity.* *v.,* **con·sumed, con·sum·ing.** **—con·sum′a·ble,** *adj.* **—con·sump′tion** (kən sump′ shən), *n.*

con·sum·er (kən sū′mər) **1** an ordinary person who buys and uses food, clothing, or anything grown or made by producers. Things we buy go from farms or factories to wholesale distributors, then to retail stores, and finally to us—the consumers. **2** an organism that feeds on other organisms. *n.*

con·tact (kon′takt) **1** the condition of touching: *This lotion may sting; avoid contact with the eyes.* **2** a connection for communication: *The control tower lost contact with the pilot.* **3** get in touch with; touch: *Contact me as soon as you hear any news. Don't let your fingers contact the hot light bulb.* **4** *Informal.* short for **contact lens,** a thin, curved plastic lens to correct eyesight, worn on the front of the eyeball: *He has worn contacts for years.* **5** a person you know and can get in touch with for help or advice: *I have a contact in an advertising firm who might be able to make the posters for us.* 1, 2, 4, 5 *n.,* 3 *v.*

con·ta·gious (kən tā′jəs) passed on to others through contact; easily spread from one person to another: *Chicken pox is contagious. She has a contagious joy.* *adj.*

con·tain (kən tān′) **1** have inside; hold; include: *My wallet contains money. Books contain information.* **2** keep in or hold back; control feelings: *He managed to contain his anger when they insulted him. She was so excited, she could hardly contain herself.* *v.*

con·tain·er (kən tā′nər) a box, can, jar, etc. used to put something in: *We bought some small plastic containers for freezing raspberries.* *n.*

con·tam·i·nate (kən tam′ə nāt′) make unclean or impure; pollute or mix with something unwanted: *Flies can contaminate food.* *v.,* **con·tam·i·nat·ed, con·tam·i·nat·ing.** **—con·tam′i·na′tion,** *n.*

con·tem·plate (kon′təm plāt′) **1** look at or think deeply about something for a long time: *She contemplated the photo for ten minutes before putting it away. Marc found a peaceful spot to sit and contemplate.* **2** have in mind; consider as a possible plan; intend: *We are contemplating a trip to Europe.* *v.,* **con·tem·plat·ed, con·tem·plat·ing.** **—con′tem·pla′tion,** *n.*

con·tem·po·rar·y (kən tem′pə rer′ē) **1** of today; modern: *contemporary music.* **2** a person living at the same time as another: *Queen Victoria and Louis Riel were contemporaries.* 1 *adj.,* 2 *n., pl.* **con·tem·po·rar·ies.**

con·tempt (kən tempt′) the feeling that a person or thing deserves no respect; scorn: *He has contempt for tattletales.* *n.*

con·tempt·i·ble (kən temp′tə bəl) deserving contempt or scorn: *Cheating her own family was a contemptible thing for her to do.* *adj.*

con·temp·tu·ous (kən temp′chū əs) full of contempt; scornful: *They are contemptuous of anyone who is different from them.* *adj.*
—con·temp′tu·ous·ly, *adv.*

con·tend (kən tend′) **1** struggle: *The Arctic explorers had to contend with extreme cold, hunger, and loneliness.* **2** compete: *Five runners were contending in the first race.* **3** say that something is true even though others disagree; argue: *Columbus contended that the earth was round.* *v.*

con·tent[1] (kon′tent) **1** Usually, **contents,** *pl.* what is contained in anything; all things inside: *An old chair, a desk, and a bed were the only contents of the room.* **2** the actual ideas in something written or spoken, rather than how the person expressed them: *The content of your report is excellent, but it is rather messy and the spelling needs work.* **3** the amount contained: *Cream has a high fat content.* *n.*

con·tent[2] (kən tent′) **1** satisfied; happy: *They were content with just a short holiday. Then they were content to stay home.* **Contented** means much the same thing. **2** satisfy; please: *When he's in a bad mood, nothing contents him. She had to content herself with a plain slice of bread.* **3** contentment; satisfaction. Used mostly in **to your heart's content,** as much as you want: *Go ahead and play to your heart's content.* 1 *v.,* 2 *adj.,* 3 *n.* **—con·tent′ment,** *n.*
—con·tent′ed·ly, *adv.*

con·ten·tion (kən ten′shən) **1** argument or dispute: *Doing the dishes was a major source of contention till we got a dishwasher.* **2** a statement or point that someone argues for: *Columbus's contention that the earth was round proved to be true.* *n.*

con·test (kon′test *for 1,* kən test′ *for 2 and 3*) **1** any activity that has winners and losers. A game or race is a contest; school is not a contest. **2** to dispute; argue or fight against: *She promised to contest the court's unfavourable decision.* **3** try to win; compete for: *The two athletes contested the championship.* 1 *n.,* 2, 3 *v.*
no contest, *Slang.* easily; so easily that there is really no competition: *Our team will win, no contest!*

con·test·ant (kən tes′tənt) a person who takes part in a contest: *My mother was a contestant in a quiz show.* *n.*

con·text (kon′tekst) the whole text, conversation, environment, or situation surrounding a word, sentence, event, or act. Knowing the context makes a thing easier to understand. *n.* **—con·tex′tu·al,** *adj.*

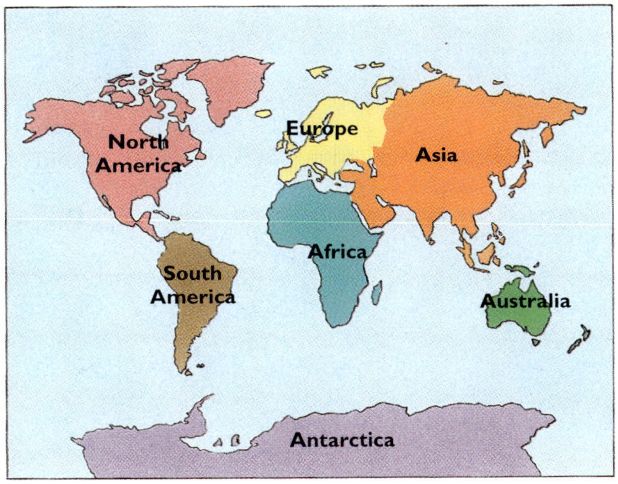

con·ti·nent (kon′tə nənt) **1** one of the seven great masses of land on the earth, including North America, South America, Europe, Africa, Asia, Australia, and Antarctica. **2 the Continent,** the mainland of Europe. *n.* **—con′ti·nent′al,** *adj.*

Continental Divide (kon′tə nen′təl də vīd′) the great ridge of the Rocky Mountains in North America: *The Continental Divide separates streams flowing toward the Pacific from those flowing toward the Atlantic.*

continental shelf (kon′tə nen′təl shelf′) the submerged shelf of land that borders most continents and ends in a steep slope to deep water.

con·tin·u·al (kən tin′yū əl) repeated many times; very frequent: *Ballet dancing requires continual practice.* *adj.* **—con·tin′u·al·ly,** *adv.*

CONFUSABLES .... continual

continual means "often repeated": *I'm sick of the continual ringing of that phone!*

continuous means "without interruption": *There was continuous rain for the whole weekend.*

con·tin·ue (kən tin′yū) **1** keep up; keep on; go on: *We continued playing until supper. The road continues for quite a distance in this direction.* **2** go on again after stopping: *The play will continue after the intermission. He ate lunch and then continued his work.* *v.,* **con·tin·ued, con·tin·u·ing.** **—con·tin′u·a′tion,** *n.*

a bat	e bed	i bid	o pot	u cup	th thin
ā cake	ē me	ī bite	ō go	ū rude	ᴛʜ then
à bar	ə about	ər over	ȯ for	ů put	zh measure

con·ti·nu·i·ty (kon′tə nyū′ə tē *or* kon′tə nū′ə tē) a sense of being a smoothly connected whole: *The story lacked continuity because there were too many unrelated events.* *n.*

con·tin·u·ous (kən tin′yū əs) going on without any break or stop: *a continuous line, a continuous sound. Instead of two half-hour sessions with a break in between, we worked for one continuous hour.* *adj.*
—con·tin′u·ous·ly, *adv.*

con·tort (kən tôrt′) twist out of shape: *The clown contorted his face.* *v.* **—con·tor′tion,** *n.*

con·tour (kon′tūr) **1** the outline of something: *The contour of the Atlantic coast of Canada is very irregular. Give us the general contours of your plan.* **2** build or shape with a particular outline: *a gracefully contoured sailing ship. This car has seats contoured to fit the body.* **3** mark with contour lines: *to contour a map.* 1 *n.,* 2, 3 *v.*

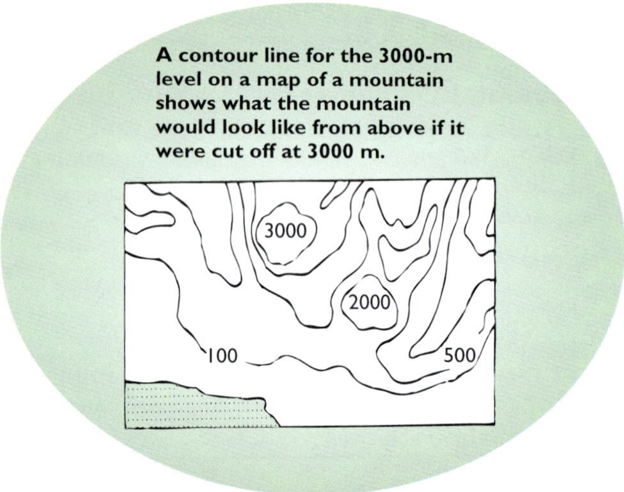

A contour line for the 3000-m level on a map of a mountain shows what the mountain would look like from above if it were cut off at 3000 m.

contour map (kon′tūr map′) a map showing high and low places on the earth's surface by means of **contour lines.** Contour lines show the outline of physical features as seen from above, by joining all the points that are at a certain height.

con·tra·band (kon′trə band′) **1** that people are not allowed to have: *Chewing gum and electronic pets are contraband items in our classroom.* **2** things that people are not allowed to have; often, smuggled articles: *Customs officials went through each bag looking for drugs and other contraband.* 1 *adj.,* 2 *n.*

con·tract (kən trakt′ *for 1 and 4,* kon′trakt *for 2,* kon′trakt *or* kən trakt′ *for 3*) **1** shrink or draw together; make or become shorter: *Pulling the drawstring contracts the opening of this cloth bag. Wool fibres contract in hot water.* **2** an agreement, especially a written agreement that the law requires a person to keep: *All professional hockey players sign contracts each year, agreeing to play for a certain salary.* **3** make an agreement of this kind; agreement: *The builder contracted to build a new house for a certain price.* **4** get; catch a disease: *to contract a cold.* 1, 3, 4 *v.,* 2 *n.*

con·trac·tion (kən trak′shən) **1** a shortened form: It's *is a contraction of "it is."* ▶ See the *Grammar and Usage Mini-Guide.* **2** the process or result of contracting: *Cold causes the contraction of liquids, gases, and metals, while heat causes expansion.* *n.*

Grammar *Check* ... contraction

Contractions combine two words, leaving out one or more letters. An apostrophe shows where letters are missing:
can't is a contraction of can*not*
she's is a contraction of she *is* or she *has*
it's is a contraction of it *is*

Notice that **it's** is not possessive:
Look at the tiger. ***It's*** *licking* ***its*** *paw.*

con·trac·tor (kon′trak tər *or* kən trak′tər) a person or company that agrees to furnish materials or to do a piece of work for a certain price. *n.*

con·tra·dict (kon′trə dikt′) say the opposite of: *She contradicts everything I say. It is rude to contradict a guest. The two reports contradict each other.* *v.*
—con′tra·dic′tion, *n.* **—con′tra·dic′to·ry,** *adj.*

con·trap·tion (kən trap′shən) device; gadget: *They invented a crazy contraption for removing the shells from boiled eggs.* *n.*

con·tra·ry (kon′trer ē) **1** opposite; totally different or in complete disagreement: *Your reckless driving is contrary to the rules of the road.* **2** the opposite. **3** refusing to do what others want, just out of bad temper. 1, 3 *adj.,* 2 *n., pl.* **con·tra·ries.**
on the contrary, instead, the opposite is true: *She didn't go straight home; on the contrary, she stopped at three different stores and even visited a friend.*
to the contrary, opposite to what has just been said: *They claim I am lazy, but the facts are to the contrary.*

con·trast (kon′trast *for 1 and 2,* kən trast′ *for 3 and 4*) **1** a great and obvious difference: *the contrast between black and white.* **2** anything that shows obvious differences next to something else: *Black hair is a sharp contrast to light skin.* **3** compare so as to show their differences: *In our science class we contrasted flies and bees.* **4** show an obvious difference: *The black and gold contrast well in that design.* 1, 2 *n.,* 3, 4 *v.*

con·trib·ute (kən trib′yūt) 1 give money or help: *Will you contribute to our fundraising drive? Everyone contributed suggestions for the class trip.* 2 write articles, stories, etc. for a newspaper or magazine. *v.,* **con·trib·ut·ed, con·trib·ut·ing.** **—con′tri·bu′tion,** *n.* **—con·trib′u·tor,** *n.*
contribute to, help cause: *Poor food contributed to the child's illness.*

con·trite (kon′trīt *or* kən trīt′) truly sorry after doing something wrong: *The boy was contrite after he had yelled at his little sister.* *adj.*

con·trive (kən trīv′) 1 invent; design: *He contrived a new kind of engine.* 2 manage by clever arrangement: *They contrived to get there all at the same time.* *v.,* **con·trived, con·triv·ing.** **—con·triv′ance,** *n.*

con·trol (kən trōl′) 1 power over something: *He has no control over my decision. The rebels are in control of the capital.* 2 have power over; run: *A ship's captain controls the ship and its crew.* 3 hold back or keep in; check; keep within limits: *to control a forest fire, to control a fever, to control your anger.* 4 anything that controls something else: *a control against price increases, the controls of a plane.* 5 a standard used for comparison, to test the results of a scientific experiment. One sample in the experiment gets the "special" treatment, while the other, the control, does not. Then the two are compared and you come to a conclusion. 1, 4, 5 *n.,* 2, 3 *v.,* **con·trolled, con·trol·ling.** **—con·trol′la·ble,** *adj.*

control tower (kən trōl′ tou′ər) at an airfield, the building where the people sit who give orders for planes to take off and land.

con·tro·ver·sial (kon′trə vər′shəl) tending to arouse argument: *controversial questions, a controversial politician.* *adj.*

con·tro·ver·sy (kon′trə vər′sē) an argument, especially a public one involving many people and points of view: *The building of the new highway was delayed by months of controversy about it.* *n., pl.* **con·tro·ver·sies.**

co·nun·drum (kə nun′drəm) a riddle or puzzling problem. *n.*

con·va·lesce (kon′və les′) gradually get better after illness: *Kula will have to convalesce for three weeks after her operation.* *v.,* **con·va·lesced, con·va·lesc·ing.** **—con′va·les′cence,** *n.* **—con′va·les′cent,** *adj. or n.*

con·vec·tion (kən vek′shən) the transfer of heat from one place to another by the movement of heated particles of a gas or liquid. A forced-air furnace system heats a room by convection. *n.*

con·vene (kən vēn′) 1 come together for some work or activity: *Parliament convenes at least once a year.* 2 call together: *The principal convened the staff for an emergency meeting.* *v.,* **con·vened, con·ven·ing.**

con·ven·ience (kən vēn′yəns) 1 the fact of being convenient: *The convenience of frozen foods makes them popular for busy households.* 2 comfort; advantage: *Many provincial parks have camping for the convenience of tourists.* 3 anything handy or easy to use; something that saves trouble or work: *This sofa bed is a great convenience. It will be a convenience if we can meet at my house this time.* *n.*
at someone's convenience, at whatever time or place is most convenient for someone: *Pick me up at your convenience.*

con·ven·ient (kən vēn′yənt) easy to do, use, reach, schedule, etc.: *a convenient storage closet, a convenient plan, a convenient time or place.* *adj.* **—con·ven′ient·ly,** *adv.*
convenient to, *Informal.* near; easy to reach from: *The library is convenient to my apartment.*

con·ven·or or **con·ven·er** (kən vē′nər) a person who is responsible for calling people together for meetings or activities and often acts as their chairperson: *My mother is convenor for the Hospital Volunteer Association.* *n.*

con·vent (kon′vent) 1 a group of women, called nuns, who live together and devote their lives to worship and to serving others. 2 the building or buildings they live in. *n.*

con·ven·tion (kən ven′shən) 1 a meeting, usually large and often lasting for days, to discuss some topic or make decisions: *A political party holds a convention to choose a new leader.* 2 a particular custom or practice approved by common agreement: *Using the right hand to shake hands is a convention.* 3 this kind of custom or agreement in general: *to dress according to convention.* *n.*

con·ven·tion·al (kən ven′shə nəl) 1 depending on conventions; customary: *"Good morning" is a conventional greeting.* 2 too ordinary and predictable; not original. *adj.*

con·verge (kən vərj′) to come from different directions and meet at a particular point: *The lines converged at the bottom of the page. Every winter tourists converge on Québec City for the Carnival.* *v.* **—con·ver′gent,** *adj.* **—con·ver′gence,** *n.*

a bat	e bed	i bid	o pot	u cup	th thin
ā cake	ē me	ī bite	ō go	ū rude	ᴛʜ then
à bar	ə about	ər over	ȯ for	ů put	zh measure

con·ver·sa·tion (kon′vər sā′shən) friendly talk: *Grandpa and I had a long conversation about life on the farm.* *n.*

con·verse (kən vərs′) talk with someone informally: *We conversed at the table between bites of pizza.* *v.,* **con·versed, con·vers·ing.**

con·vert (kən vərt′ *for 1,* kon′vərt *for 2*) **1** change; turn: *to convert from one faith to another. These machines convert pulp into paper. One last effort converted defeat into victory.* **2** a person who has changed over to a certain faith. 1 *v.,* 2 *n.* **—con·ver′sion,** *n.*

con·vert·er (kən vər′tər) a device that turns one thing into another or gives something a different form. A converter may turn one kind of electrical current into another, or allow a television set to receive more channels than it was designed to. *n.*

con·vert·i·ble (kən vər′tə bəl) **1** able to be converted: *A loonie is convertible into ten dimes.* **2** a car with a roof that can be folded down or removed. 1 *adj.,* 2 *n.*

con·vex (kon veks′ *or* kon′veks) curved like the outside of a ball. *adj.*

con·vey (kən vā′) **1** carry from one place to another: *A bus conveys passengers from the train to the boat. A wire conveys an electric current.* **2** communicate: *The painting conveyed a sense of peace.* *v.*

con·vey·ance (kən vā′əns) vehicle: *cars, buses, and other conveyances.* *n.*

con·vey·or (kən vā′ər) a machine that carries things from one place to another by means of a moving belt (**conveyor belt**) or a series of rollers: *A conveyor belt carried the boxes of groceries out to the pickup area.* *n.*

con·vict (kən vikt′ *for 1,* kon′vikt *for 2*) **1** prove or declare to be guilty: *The evidence convicted the guilty person. The jury convicted the prisoner of murder.* **2** a person serving a prison sentence for some crime. 1 *v.,* 2 *n.*

con·vic·tion (kən vik′shən) **1** the act of proving or declaring guilty; convicting: *The trial resulted in the conviction of the prisoner.* **2** a firm belief: *Stand by your personal convictions.* *n.*

con·vince (kən vins′) make a person believe something or agree to something; persuade firmly: *Your encouragement has convinced me that I can do it.* *v.,* **con·vinced, con·vinc·ing. —con·vinc′ing,** *adj.* **—con·vinc′ing·ly,** *adv.*

con·voy (kon′voi) **1** go with in order to protect; escort: *Warships convoy merchant ships in time of war.* **2** an escort; people or vehicles going along for protection: *a police convoy for a parade or funeral.* **3** the people or supplies that are being protected. 1 *v.,* 2, 3 *n.*

con·vulse (kən vuls′) **1** shake or twist violently: *An earthquake convulsed the island. Rage convulsed his face.* **2** throw into fits of laughter: *The comedian's jokes convulsed the audience.* *v.,* **con·vulsed, con·vuls·ing. —con·vul′sion,** *n.* **—con·vul′sive,** *adj.*

coo (kū) **1** the soft, murmuring sound made by doves or pigeons. **2** make this sound, or a soft sound like this: *The baby cooed happily in her crib.* 1 *n., pl.,* **coos;** 2 *v.,* **cooed, coo·ing.**

cook (ku̇k) **1** prepare food using heat: *We cooked our sausages over an open fire. Let the meat cook slowly.* **2** a person who prepares food. 1 *v.,* 2 *n.* **—cook′er·y,** *n.*

Word Family.......... cook

cookbook: a book of recipes
cookery: the art of cooking
cookhouse: a place for cooking, especially at a mine or a logging camp
cookout: cooking and eating a meal outside

cook·ie (ku̇k′ē) a small, sweet, more or less flat cake, usually fairly crisp or crunchy. *n., pl.* **cook·ies.**

cool (kūl) **1** somewhat cold; feeling more cold than hot to the body: *We sat in the shade where it was cool.* **2** not excited or nervous; calm. **3** unfriendly or uninterested: *a cool greeting.* **4** *Slang.* stylish or excellent. **5** a cool part, place, or time: *the cool of the evening.* **6** make or become cool: *We cooled the pop in the stream.* 1–4 *adj.,* 5 *n.,* 6 *v.*
cool down, a lose enthusiasm. **b** practise or exercise after the main activity. The noun or adjective is **cool-down:** *cool-down exercises.*

cool·er (kū′lər) a container that cools food or drinks or keeps them cool. *n.*

coop (kūp) **1** a small cage or pen for chickens, rabbits, etc. **2** shut up in a small place: *The children were cooped up indoors because of the rain.* 1 *n.,* 2, 3 *v.*

coop·er (kū′pər) especially in the old days, a maker of barrels, tubs, casks, etc. *n.*

co–op·er·ate (kō op′ə rāt′) work together: *The children co-operated in keeping the playroom neat.* *v.,* **co-op·er·at·ed, co-op·er·at·ing. —co-op′er·a′tion,** *n.*

co–op·er·a·tive (kō op′ə rə tiv) 1 willing to work together with others: *The work got done very quickly because everyone was so co-operative.* 2 done or made together: *a co-operative effort.* 3 Usually shortened to **co-op** (kō′op), a business owned and run by all the people who regularly use it, so that they all share in the costs and profits. A co-op can be a farm, store, nursery school, housing project, art or craft studio, or just about any other kind of business. 1, 2 *adj.*, 3 *n.*

co–or·di·nate or **co·or·di·nate** (kō ȯr′də nit *for 1 and 2,* kō ȯr′də nāt′ *for 3 and 4*) 1 a Usually, **co-ordinates,** *pl.*, things that match or form a set, such as matching pants and top. b Usually, **coordinates,** *pl.*, the two numbers that tell where a point is on any kind of grid or graph, such as lines of latitude and longitude. 2 equal or matching. 3 make different parts work together smoothly: *to co-ordinate your arms and legs in swimming, to co-ordinate the efforts of a team.* 4 match: *the curtains are co-ordinated with the bedspread.* 1 *n.*, 2 *adj.*, 3, 4 *v.*, **co-or·di·nat·ed, co-or·di·nat·ing.** —**co-or′di·na′tion,** *n.*

cop (kop) *Informal.* police officer. *n.*

cope (kōp) manage in a difficult situation: *He said he just couldn't cope anymore. Is she strong enough to cope with the extra work?* *v.*, **coped, cop·ing.**

co–pi·lot (kō′pī′lət) a pilot who flies with another pilot. *n.*

co·pi·ous (kō′pē əs) plentiful; abundant: *There was a copious supply of wheat in the elevators.* *adj.* —**co′pi·ous·ly,** *adv.*

cop·per (kop′ər) 1 a reddish brown metal that is easily shaped into wire or sheets and resists tarnish. Copper is a good conductor of electricity. 2 a one-cent piece: *I found a copper on the sidewalk.* *n.*

copse (kops) a number of small trees or bushes growing together. *n.*

cop·y (kop′ē) 1 anything made to be just like another: *We printed 400 copies of the newsletter. This chair is an exact copy of that one.* 2 make or do the same as: *She copied her friend's painting. Adam copies his big brother's way of talking.* 3 written material ready to be printed in a newspaper, magazine, or book. 1, 3 *n.*, *pl.* **cop·ies;** 2 *v.*, **cop·ied, cop·y·ing.** —**cop′i·er,** *n.*

cop·y·right (kop′ē rīt′) 1 a special right to copy, given by law to an author, composer, artist, etc., meaning that no one else can sell, print, publish, or copy that person's work without his or her permission. It only lasts for a certain number of years; Shakespeare's plays are not under copyright, so anyone can produce them on stage without paying a fee. 2 protect a piece of work by getting a copyright. 1 *n.*, 2 *v.*

cor·al (kȯr′əl) a hard, red, pink, or white substance built up in shallow, warm seas from the skeletons of tiny sea animals. Coral is often used in making jewellery. *n.*

cor·bel (kȯr′bəl) a stone or wooden bracket that sticks out from a wall and helps support its weight. *n.*

cord (kȯrd) 1 a thick, strong string; a very thin rope. 2 a small insulated cable with a plug on the end and electric wires running through it, used to plug in a lamp or other electrical appliance. 3 a cordlike part of an animal body: *spinal cord, vocal cords.* 4 cloth with ridges on it such as corduroy. 5 **cords,** *pl.* corduroy pants. 6 a measure of cut firewood. A standard cord is a stack 8 feet long, 4 feet high, and 4 feet deep. It is equal to about 3.5 m^3. *n.* —**cord′less,** *adj.*

cor·di·al (kȯr′dē əl *or* kȯr′jəl) 1 warm; friendly: *a cordial welcome.* 2 an alcoholic fruit drink. 1 *adj.*, 2 *n.* —**cor′di·al·ly,** *adv.* —**cor′di·al′i·ty,** *n.*

cor·dil·le·ra (kȯr di le′rə) a chain of parallel mountain ranges. *n.*

cor·don (kȯr′dən) 1 a barrier set up by those in authority to keep people out of a place: *A cordon surrounded the collapsed building.* 2 **cordon off,** put a barrier around, by authority: *The display of famous paintings was cordoned off.* *n.*

cor·du·roy (kȯr′də roi′) thick cloth with a ridged pattern. *n. or adj.*

🍁 **corduroy road** (kȯr′də roi′ rōd′) a road made of logs laid crosswise, often across low, wet land. The logs are like the ridges on corduroy.

core (kȯr) 1 the central part of anything. The core of an apple contains the seeds. The earth's core is made of molten iron and is about 6760 m across. 2 take out the core of: *to core apples.* 1 *n.*, 2 *v.*, **cored, cor·ing.**

a bat	e bed	i bid	o pot	u cup	th thin
ā cake	ē me	ī bite	ō go	ū rude	ᴛʜ then
ä bar	ə about	ər over	ȯ for	u̇ put	zh measure

cork (kôrk) 1 the light, thick, outer bark of a tree called the **cork oak.** Cork is used for bottle stoppers, floats for fishing lines, and notice boards. 2 a bottle stopper made of cork. 3 stop up with a cork: *Fill these bottles and cork them carefully.* 1, 2 *n.,* 3 *v.*

cork•screw (kôrk′skrü′) 1 a tool used to pull corks out of bottles. 2 shaped like a corkscrew; spiral: *The plane did a corkscrew dive.* 1 *n.,* 2 *adj.*

cor•mo•rant (kôr′mə rənt) a large black sea bird with a long neck and a pouch under its beak for holding captured fish. *n.*

corn¹ (kôrn) yellowish kernels that grow in rows along a thick, woody core called a **cob** on a tall grass plant. **Sweet corn** is cooked and eaten as a vegetable; **field corn** is not as sweet and juicy and is used to feed farm animals. *n.*

corn² (kôrn) a hardened, thickened area on the skin of a toe. It is caused by rubbing or pressure and can be quite painful. *n.*

cor•ne•a (kôr′nē ə) the transparent outside coating on the front of the eyeball. The cornea covers the iris and the pupil. *n.*

corned beef (kôrnd′ bēf′) beef preserved with strong salt water or dry salt.

cor•ner (kôr′nər) 1 the place where two lines or surfaces meet: *the corner of a room, the corner of Main St. and Queen St.* 2 drive around corners: *Cornering on a motorbike is tricky.* 3 a tough spot: *His enemies had driven him into a corner.* 4 force into a corner or into a tough spot: *The lawyer cornered her with a direct question. I finally cornered our dog and got the leash on him.* 5 an out-of-the-way place, unknown to most people: *The money was hidden in odd corners all over the house. These things were not done in a corner; we all saw what went on.* 1, 3, 5 *n.,* 2, 4 *v.*

cor•ner•stone (kôr′nər stōn′) 1 a block of stone placed at the corner of a building to hold two walls together, especially a large one near the bottom with a date or motto carved into it. There is often a ceremony when the cornerstone is laid. 2 the most important part of something because everything else depends on it: *The teacher said that practice was the cornerstone to becoming a good musician.* *n.*

cor•net (kôr net′ *or* kôr′nit) an instrument like a small trumpet. *n.*

corn•meal (kôrn′mēl′) dried corn that has been ground up.

corn•starch (kôrn′stärch′) a starchy flour made from corn, used to thicken sauces, gravy, etc. *n.*

cor•nu•co•pi•a (kôr′nyə kō′pē ə) a curved horn overflowing with fruits and vegetables, used as a symbol of a good harvest at Thanksgiving. It is also called a **horn of plenty.** *n.*

corn•y (kôr′nē) *Slang.* too ordinary, simple, or unsophisticated: *corny jokes. That movie has a corny plot.* *adj.,* **corn•i•er, corn•i•est.**

co•rol•la (kə rol′ə) the petals of a flower. *n.*

cor•o•na•tion (kôr′ə nā′shən) the ceremony of crowning a king or queen. *n.*

cor•o•ner (kôr′ə nər) a government official, usually a doctor, whose job is to look into any death that is not clearly due to natural causes. *n.*

cor•po•ral punishment (kôr′pə rəl pun′ish mənt) physical punishment such as spanking. *adj.*

cor•po•ra•tion (kôr′pə rā′shən) a group of people recognized as a unit by the government. A corporation can be a business, a charity, a town council, or any other organization. *n.*

corps (kôr) 1 a section of the army. 2 a group of people who do a certain kind of work together as a team: *A hospital has a corps of nurses. You and I are part of the clean-up corps for the banquet.* *n., pl.* **corps** (kôrz).

corpse (kôrps) the dead body of a human being. *n.*

cor•pu•lent (kôr′pyə lənt) fat: *a corpulent gentleman.* *adj.* **—cor′pu•lence,** *n.*

cor•pus•cle (kôr′pus əl *or* kôr′pə səl) a blood cell. Red corpuscles carry oxygen from the lungs to various parts of the body; some white corpuscles destroy disease germs. *n.*

cor•ral (kə ral′) 1 a fenced area for horses, cattle, etc. 2 drive into or keep in a corral. 3 surround and keep from escaping: *My friends corralled me in the hall and tried to make me sign up for intramurals.* 1 *n.,* 2, 3 *v.,* **cor•ralled, cor•ral•ling.**

cor•rect (kə rekt′) 1 right; proper: *the correct answer, correct manners.* 2 point out or fix the mistakes in: *She always corrects my French. Correct any errors before you hand in your paper.* 3 discipline in order to improve: *The parent corrected the child.* 1 *adj.,* 2, 3 *v.* **—cor•rect′ly,** *adv.* **—cor•rec′tion,** *n.* **—cor•rec′tive,** *adj.*

Costume

cor•re•spond (kôr′ə spond′) **1** agree or match in some way: *His friendly manner corresponded with what we had heard about him. The arms of a human being correspond to the wings of a bird.* **2** exchange letters: *They rarely saw each other but they corresponded for many years.* *v.* **—cor′re•spond′ence,** *n.*

cor•ri•dor (kôr′ə dôr) a long hallway with rooms opening off from it: *My mother's office is at the end of the corridor.* *n.*

cor•rode (kə rōd′) eat away gradually; rust: *The car body is beginning to corrode.* *v.,* **cor•rod•ed, cor•rod•ing. —cor•ro′sion,** *n.* **—cor•ro′sive** (kə rō′siv), *adj.*

cor•ru•gate (kôr′ə gāt′) give a wavy surface to; make wrinkles in: *The shack had a roof of corrugated iron. Some boxes are made of corrugated cardboard.* *v.,* **cor•ru•gat•ed, cor•ru•gat•ing.**

cor•rupt (kə rupt′) **1** influenced by bribes; dishonest: *a corrupt judge.* **2** bribe; influence by bribes: *He failed in his attempt to corrupt the police officer.* **3** twist, pollute, or make bad. **4** twisted; no longer good or pure: *a corrupt mind.* 1, 4 *adj.,* 2, 3 *v.* **—cor•rup′tion,** *n.*

cor•sage (kôr säzh′) a flower or tiny bouquet worn on a woman's dress. *n.*

cor•set (kôr′sit) a stiff, close-fitting undergarment women used to wear around the waist and hips to have a slimmer figure. *n.*

cos•met•ics (koz met′iks) make-up; creams, lotions, powders, etc. for beautifying the skin or hair. *pl.n.*

cos•mic (koz′mik) **1** having to do with the whole universe: *Cosmic forces produce stars and meteors.* **2** huge; vast. *adj.*

cosmic rays (koz′mik rāz′) extremely powerful streams of particles from outer space that enter the earth's atmosphere at very high speeds.

cos•mo•naut (koz′mə not′) astronaut. *n.*

cos•mos (koz′mos) the whole universe thought of as following a plan of organization. *n.*

cost (kost) **1** the price: *The cost of this toy was $18.* **2** the loss or sacrifice: *The poor fox escaped from the trap at the cost of a leg.* **3** carry a price of: *This toy costs $18.* **4** require: *This project has cost much time and effort.* 1, 2 *n.,* 3, 4 *v.,* **cost, cost•ing. —cost′ly,** *adj.*
at all costs or **at any cost,** no matter what must be done: *They had to catch the next boat at all costs, or lose their last chance to escape.*

cos•tume (kos′chūm *or* kos′tyūm) **1** dress belonging to another time or place, or representing a character, for acting or pretending: *In our play the actors wore medieval costumes. I made a clown costume for Halloween.* **2** a style of dress: *Everyone wore the national costume of their home country.* *n.*

a bat	e bed	i bid	o pot	u cup	th thin
ā cake	ē me	ī bite	ō go	ū rude	ᴛʜ then
ä bar	ə about	ər over	ô for	ů put	zh measure

cot (kot) a narrow bed, especially a folding one made of canvas stretched on a frame. *n.*

cot·tage (kot′ij) a small wooden house used for holidaying away from the city, in the forest or in the country. Some can be used all year around, but most are for summer only. A cottage is often by a lake. *n.*

cottage cheese (kot′əj chēz′) a soft, white cheese made from the curds of sour milk.

cot·ton (kot′ən) **1** cloth made from the soft, white fluff around the seeds of a plant that grows in warm places. Cotton is popular for clothes. **2** Usually, **cotton wool,** this fluff spun into soft balls, wads, or sheets and used for various purposes, including gentle cleaning of the skin. *n.* **—cot′ton·y,** *adj.*

cotton candy (kot′ən kan′dē) a light, fluffy mass of candy made by spinning melted sugar in a special machine.

cot·ton·tail (kot′ən tāl′) a common North American wild rabbit, which has brownish or greyish fur and a fluffy tail with a white underside. *n.*

cot·y·le·don (kot′ə lē′dən) the first simple leaf, or pair of leaves, to grow from a seed. *n.*

couch (kouch) **1** a sofa or chesterfield. **2** put in words; express: *His thoughts were couched in beautiful language.* 1 *n.,* 2 *v.*

The cougar is known by many names: puma, mountain lion, panther, etc. The Maliseet name for the cougar is *pitwal*, which means "the long-tailed one."

cou·gar (kū′gər) a large, usually sand-coloured wildcat found in many parts of North and South America, with short, black ears and a very long, black-tipped tail; mountain lion: *Cougars usually hunt at night.* *n.*

cough (kof) **1** clear your throat by forcing air from the lungs suddenly with a short, harsh noise. **2** the act or sound of coughing: *He heard a cough outside the room.* **3** a sickness that makes you cough: *She is at home with a bad cough.* 1 *v.,* 2, 3 *n.*
cough up, a get something out of the throat or lungs by coughing. **b** *Slang.* give: *One crook tried to keep more than his share of the money, but the others made him cough up.*

cough drop (kof′ drop′) a small candy that has medicine in it to soothe your throat or stop you coughing.

could (ku̇d) the past tense of **can**[1] used: **1** to make a request more polite: *Could you lend me some money?* **2** to express something that would be possible under certain conditions: *She could be prime minister if she wanted to.* *v.*

could·n't (ku̇d′ənt) could not.

✱ **cou·lee** (kū′lē) a deep ravine or gulch, especially on the prairies. The water flowing in a coulee usually dries up in summer. *n.*

cou·lomb (kū′lom) an SI unit for measuring the amount of an electrical charge. One coulomb is the charge created by a current of one ampere flowing for one second. *Symbol:* C *n.*

coun·cil (koun′səl) **1** a group of leaders called together to give advice and help make decisions about something: *the student council, an arts council, a council of war.* **2** a small group of people elected to govern a city, town, village, etc. *n.*

coun·cil·lor or **coun·ci·lor** (koun′sə lər) **1** an elected member of the council of a town, village, etc. **2** ✱ in Prince Edward Island, a member of the Legislative Assembly elected by the property owners. *n.*

coun·sel (koun′səl) **1** advice: *A wise person gives good counsel.* **2** give advice to; advise: *She counsels high school students.* **3** the lawyer or group of lawyers that give advice to a person in a court case: *He acted as counsel for the defence.* 1, 3 *n.,* 2 *v.,* **coun·selled** or **coun·seled, coun·sel·ling** or **coun·sel·ing.**
hold or **take counsel,** talk something over; discuss together: *The stranded travellers held counsel to decide what they should do next.*

CONFUSABLES ..... counsel

counsel means "adviser" or "advice" or "advise":
She acted as defence counsel.
Elders give counsel to younger people.
The confused person was counselled by her friend.
council means "a group of advisers": *the town council*

coun·sel·lor or **coun·sel·or** (koun′sə lər) 1 a person who gives advice; adviser. 2 lawyer. 3 a person who supervises at a summer camp. *n.*

count (kount) 1 name numbers in order: *The child can count to ten.* 2 find out exactly how many there are: *He counted the pups to make sure they were all there.* 3 the act or result of doing this: *Let's do a careful count of the votes. The exact count is 5170.* 4 include or be included in a total: *Let's not count that game. All our tests and projects count toward our final grade.* 5 have an influence; matter; be worthwhile: *Make every moment count.* 6 consider; think of: *She counts herself lucky to have good health.* 1, 2, 4–6 *v.,* 3 *n.*
count for, be worth: *His strength counted for little against theirs.*
count in, *Informal.* include: *Count me in for the party!*
count off, divide into equal groups by counting: *Count off in fours from the left.*
count on, a depend on; rely on: *Can I count on you to help?* **b** plan on; expect: *Count on spending at least an hour on this job.*
count out, a *Informal.* leave out of the plans: *If you go skiing, count me out.* **b** declare a fallen boxer the loser when he cannot get up after ten seconds have been counted: *He was counted out in the third round of the fight.*

count·down (kount′doun′) the minutes and seconds leading up to an event, especially the last ten seconds as they are called out. *n.*

coun·te·nance (koun′tə nəns) face: *a noble countenance, an angry countenance.* *n.*

count·er[1] (koun′tər) 1 a long, flat surface, often with cupboards or shelves underneath, in a kitchen, workshop, or store. A counter in a home is for working or eating at; in a store or restaurant it is where you get served or pay for things. 2 a small, round, flat disk, often used to keep score in card games. *n.*

coun·ter[2] (koun′tər) 1 **counter to,** against: *She acted counter to her solemn promise.* 2 respond by speaking or acting against: *He countered my proposal with one of his own.* 1 *adv.,* 2 *v.*

counter– *a prefix meaning:* 1 against, as in "counteract." 2 in return, as in "counterattack." 3 corresponding, as in "counterpart."

coun·ter·act (koun′tə rakt′) work against: *She took a cold shower to counteract her sleepiness.* *v.*

coun·ter·clock·wise (koun′tər klok′wīz′) in the direction opposite to the way the hands of a clock move. *adv. or adj.*

coun·ter·feit (koun′tər fit) 1 copy something valuable in order to deceive: *He was sent to prison for counterfeiting $20 bills.* 2 a copy that someone pretends is the real thing, in order to cheat; a fake: *This $20 bill is a counterfeit.* 3 not genuine: *a counterfeit stamp.* 4 fake; pretend: *She counterfeited interest in order to be polite.* 1, 4 *v.,* 2 *n.,* 3 *adj.*

coun·ter·part (koun′tər pärt′) a person or thing resembling another in some way: *Our principal met with her counterparts at a principals' conference.* *n.*

count·less (kount′lis) too many to count: *the countless stars.* *adj.*

coun·try (kun′trē) 1 nation; the land belonging to a nation: *the country of France. We crossed the border into another country.* 2 the open land away from towns and cities; farmland: *He likes the country better than the city.* 3 a region or area of land of a certain kind or lying in a certain direction: *the hill country, the north country.* 4 a style of music that developed from the old folk music of white people in the southern United States. Modern country music has spread throughout North America. *n., pl.* **coun·tries.**

coun·try·side (kun′trē sīd′) land outside cities and towns, especially when you think of it as being full of natural beauty: *The countryside looked splendid in the fall.* *n.*

coun·ty (koun′tē) a division of a country, province, or state. The government of a county may look after schools, certain roads, fire departments, nursing homes, etc. The county form of municipal government is used in Nova Scotia, New Brunswick, Québec, Ontario, and Alberta. *n., pl.* **coun·ties.**

cou·ple (kup′əl) 1 two people or two things that go together; a pair. A husband and wife are a couple; so are the partners in a dance. 2 **a couple of,** *Informal.* two; or a few: *A couple of minutes later, she phoned again.* 3 join together: *Heavy rains coupled with low temperatures ruined the crops.* 1, 2 *n.,* 3 *v.,* **cou·pled, cou·pling.**

cou·plet (kup′lit) two lines of poetry that rhyme and have the same rhythm. *n.*
Example: And then my heart with pleasure fills,
And dances with the daffodils.

cou·pling (kup′ling) a device for joining things together, such as railway cars or parts of machinery. *n.*

a bat	e bed	i bid	o pot	u cup	th thin
ā cake	ē me	ī bite	ō go	ū rude	ᴛʜ then
ä bar	ə about	ər over	ò for	ù put	zh measure

cou·pon (kū′pon) a slip of paper that lets you get something free or for less money than the usual price. *n.*

cour·age (kər′ij) the strength of mind to control fear and act firmly in the face of danger or difficulties. *n.* —**cou·ra′geous** (kə rāj′əs), *adj.*

cou·reur de bois (kū rər′də bwȧ′) in history, a French or Métis fur trader or woodsman in the North or Northwest. Radisson and Groseilliers were coureurs de bois. *pl.* **cou·reurs de bois** (kū rər′də bwȧ′).

cour·i·er (kər′ē ər) a person or company that delivers letters and packages, especially when extra speed or careful handling is required: *They sent the diskettes by courier.* *n.*

course (kôrs) **1** a series of classes or lessons in some subject at a college, university, or other school: *My cousin is taking a computer course this summer.* **2** a part of a meal served at one time: *The first course was chicken soup.* **3** an area marked out for a game or sport: *a golf course, a race course.* **4** flow or run: *Blood courses through your veins.* **5** a route or a plan of action; a way to go: *Our course was straight to the north. The only sensible course was to call the police.* **6** the going on of something: *the course of events. She gets little rest in the course of her daily work.* 1–3, 5, 6 *n.,* 4 *v.,* **coursed, cours·ing.**
in due course, in a reasonable time; after a while: *I know he will be here in due course.*
of course, a as anyone would expect; naturally: *Of course it will rain on the weekend.* **b** certainly; without question: *Of course I'll do it.*

court (kôrt) **1** a place marked off for a game: *a tennis court, a handball court.* **2** a short street that has a dead end or forms a circle: *Our house is on York Court.* **3** a place where trials are held and justice is administered by judges: *The prisoner was brought to court for trial.* **4** a king, queen, or other ruler, his or her family, followers, etc., and the place where they live and work. **5** try to win the favour or love of someone. 1–4 *n.,* 5 *v.*
hold court, lead a gathering or meeting, especially as a ruler, to hear people's opinions and make plans.

Word Family........... court

courtier: an attendant at the court of a monarch
courtly: with manners fit for a monarch's court
courtship: a time of wooing, or romantic friendship, before marriage

cour·te·ous (kər′tē əs) polite. *adj.*

cour·te·sy (kər′tə sē) **1** politeness; thoughtfulness for others. **2** a considerate or polite act: *The girl's courtesies were much appreciated.* *n., pl.* **cour·te·sies.**
by courtesy of or **through the courtesy of, a** with the permission or approval of: *The poem is included in that book by courtesy of the author.* **b** as a gift of: *Refreshments are provided in the lounge, by courtesy of the airline.*

court·house (kôrt′hous′) a building where courts of law are held. Inside a courthouse there are **courtrooms.** *n.*

court–mar·tial (kôrt′mȧr′shəl) **1** a court or trial for soldiers accused of breaking army laws. Army officers act as the judges. **2** try by such a court. 1 *n., pl.* **courts-mar·tial;** 2 *v.,* **court-mar·tialled** or **court-mar·tialed, court-mar·tial·ling** or **court-mar·tial·ing.**

court·yard (kôrt′yȧrd′) a space enclosed by walls, in or near a large building: *Two big buses stood in the courtyard of the hotel.* *n.*

cous·cous (kūs′kūs) small white pellets made from wheat that soften and swell when they are steamed over a stew of meat or vegetables. Couscous is popular in North Africa. *n.*

WORD HISTORY..... couscous

The word **couscous** comes originally from the Arabic *kaskasa*, meaning "grind" or "pound."

Notice how **couscous** repeats the first syllable. Many languages have words that do something like this to show a repeated action. In English, examples are singsong, or wiggle-waggle. Can you think of other words like this?

cous·in (kuz′ən) the son or daughter of a person's uncle or aunt. **First cousins** have the same grandparents; **second cousins** have the same great-grandparents; and so on for third and fourth cousins. *n.*

cove (kōv) a small, sheltered bay; an inlet on the shore. *n.*

cov·e·nant (kuv′ə nənt) **1** a solemn agreement between two or more people or groups: *the covenant of marriage, an international covenant to fight child poverty.* **2** agree solemnly to do certain things: *These nations have covenanted to reduce pollution.* 1 *n.,* 2 *v.*

cov·er (kuv′ər) **1** be, or put something, over or around a person or thing so as to keep warm, protected, or hidden: *He covered the sleeping child with his coat. Snow covered the ground.* **2** anything that protects or hides: *Put covers on your school books.*

Covered wagons

Pioneers travelling westward across North America carried all their possessions in covered wagons like these.

3 protection; shelter: *We took cover in an old cabin during the storm. The refugees travelled under cover of darkness.* **4** go through or over: *We covered 400 km on the first day of our trip. This test covers the last unit in math.* **5** report on events for a newspaper, etc.: *He covered the meetings of city council.* **6** be enough for; provide for: *This money will cover the cost of a hamburger for each of us.* 1, 4–6 *v.,* 2, 3 *n.* —**cov′er·ing,** *n.*
cover for, a take someone's place when they can't be there: *Miss D'Angelo often covers for our teacher.* **b** give an excuse or explanation for another person so he or she will not get into trouble.
cover up, hide or conceal, especially something wrong: *She tried to cover up her guilt.*

cov·er·alls (kuv′ə rolz′) a one-piece suit, made of strong cloth, worn over shirt and pants to protect them. Mechanics wear coveralls. *pl.n.*

covered wagon (kuv′ərd wag′ən) a large wagon with an arched canvas cover that can be taken off. Covered wagons were pulled by horses or oxen and were used to haul goods on long trips.

cov·er·let (kuv′ər lit) a bedspread. *n.*

cov·et (kuv′it) want something very much, especially something that belongs to another person; be greedy for. *v.* —**cov′et·ous,** *adj.*

cow¹ (kou) **1** the adult female of cattle. Milk comes from cows. **2** the female of other large adult mammals such as the buffalo, moose, whale, elephant, or seal. *n.*

cow² (kou) make afraid; frighten: *Don't let his threats cow you.* *v.*

cow·ard (kou′ərd) a person who lacks the courage to face danger or difficulty. *n.* —**cow′ard·ice** (kou′ər dis), *n.* —**cow′ard·ly,** *adj.*

cow·bell (kou′bel′) a bell hung around a cow's neck so that its sound will indicate where the cow is. *n.*

cow·boy (kou′boi′) a man who looks after cattle on a ranch and out on the range. *n.*

cow·catch·er (kou′kach′ər) a metal frame on the front of a locomotive, streetcar, etc., intended to clear the tracks of anything in the way. *n.*

cow·er (kou′ər) crouch in fear or shame: *The frightened dog whimpered and cowered under the table.* *v.*

cow·girl (kou′gərl′) a woman who looks after cattle on a ranch and out on the range. *n.*

cow hand (kou′ hand′) a cowboy or cowgirl.

cow·hide (kou′hīd′) the hide of a cow, made into leather. *n.*

🍁 **Cow·i·chan** (kou′i chən) **1** a member of a First Nations people living mainly in the southern part of the Fraser River Valley in British Columbia. The Cowichan people are known for their sweaters knitted with symbolic designs in them. **2** their Salishan language. **3** having to do with these people or their language. 1, 2 *n.,* 3 *adj.*

cowl (koul) the hood on a cloak or shawl, like the ones some monks wear. *n.*

cow·lick (kou′lik′) a small tuft of hair that will not lie flat. *n.*

🍁 **cow·punch·er** (kou′pun′chər) *Informal.* a cowboy or cowgirl. *n.*

a bat	e bed	i bid	o pot	u cup	th thin
ā cake	ē me	ī bite	ō go	ū rude	ᴛʜ then
ä bar	ə about	ər over	ô for	ů put	zh measure

cow·slip (kou′slip) a North American marsh plant with bright yellow flowers that bloom in early spring. **Marsh marigold** is another name for it. *n.*

coy (koi) shy and modest, or pretending to be. *adj.* —**coy′ly,** *adv.*

coy·ote (kī ō′tē, kī′ōt, *or* kī′ūt) a North American wild animal related to the dog. It is most common on the prairies, has yellowish grey fur, and is noted for the way it howls at night. *n., pl.* **coy·otes** or **coy·ote.**

co·zy or **co·sy** (kō′zē) having a warm, comfortable, friendly or homey atmosphere; snug: *This is a cozy little apartment!* *adj.,* **co·zi·er** or **co·si·er, co·zi·est** or **co·si·est.** —**co′zi·ly** or **co′si·ly,** *adv.* —**co′zi·ness** or **co′si·ness,** *n.*

crab[1] (krab) a shellfish with eight legs, two claws, and a wide, flat shell. Many crabs are good to eat. *n.*

crab[2] (krab) *Informal.* **1** a grouchy person. **2** be always complaining or finding fault: *Stop crabbing about the food.* 1 *n.,* 2 *v.,* **crabbed, crab·bing.**

crab apple (krab′ ap′əl) a small, sour apple used in making jelly. Crab apple trees have masses of white, pink, or purple flowers in spring.

crab·by (krab′ē) *Informal.* grouchy. *adj.,* **crab·bi·er, crab·bi·est.**

crab·grass (krab′ gras′) a coarse grass that spreads rapidly.

crack (krak) **1** a split made by breaking without separating into parts: *There is a crack in this cup.* **2** break without separating into parts: *You have cracked the window.* **3** a narrow opening: *There were cracks between the boards of the old floor.* **4** *Informal.* break; break down; break into: *to crack a safe, to crack a code. After days of questioning, he finally cracked.* **5** a sudden, sharp noise: *the crack of a whip.* **6** make or cause to make a sudden, sharp noise: *The whip cracked. He cracked the whip.* **7** of a person's voice, change suddenly and sharply because of hoarseness, emotion, etc.: *Her voice cracked when she spoke.* **8** *Informal.* a joke or a sarcastic remark: *What do you mean by that crack?* **9** expert: *a crack shot.* 1, 3, 5, 8, 9 *n.,* 2, 4, 6, 7 *v.*
crack a joke, tell a joke or say something funny.
crack down on, start to punish strictly: *The police are cracking down on speeders.*
crack up, a *Informal.* send or go into fits of laughter: *I crack up every time I hear that joke. This TV show always cracks her up.* **b** *Informal.* have a nervous breakdown. **c** *Informal.* praise: *The book is not what it's cracked up to be.*
get cracking, hurry up and start.

cracked (krakt) **1** broken. **2** *Informal.* crazy. *adj.*

crack·er (krak′ər) **1** a thin, crisp biscuit or wafer: *a soda cracker, a graham cracker.* **2** a small paper roll used as a party favour. When you pull it apart, it makes a loud bang. There is often a toy or message inside. *n.*

crack·le (krak′əl) **1** make slight, sharp sounds: *A fire crackled on the hearth.* **2** a slight, sharp sound, such as paper makes when it is crumpled. 1 *v.,* **crack·led, crack·ling;** 2 *n.*

cra·dle (krā′dəl) **1** a baby's little bed, usually on rockers or swinging on a frame. **2** hold or rock as in a cradle: *She cradled the sleepy child in her arms.* **3** the place where anything begins its growth: *The area around the Mediterranean Sea is sometimes called the cradle of civilization.* **4** a supporting frame that something can be laid in, such as the part of a phone that holds the receiver. 1, 3, 4 *n.,* 2 *v.,* **cra·dled, cra·dling.**

This cradleboard is held by a strap going around the mother's head, leaving her hands free to work.

cra·dle·board (krā′dəl bôrd′) a framework of wood, leather, and cloth that First Nations mothers used to use for carrying their babies on their backs. *n.*

craft (kraft) **1** artistic skill: *These totem poles show the craft of the people who carved them. Carpentry is a craft.* **2** a piece of work done with artistic skill: *Each summer at camp we do a craft; this year we each made a leather wallet.* **3** clever trickery: *He got all their money from them by craft.* **4** a boat, ship, or aircraft: *There is a strange craft at the dock.* **5** make by hand with artistic skill: *to craft a vase from clay.* 1–4 *n., pl.* **crafts** *for 1 and 2,* **craft** *for 4;* 5 *v.*

craft·er (kraf′tər) a person who practises a craft. A crafter may be called a **craftsman** or a **craftswoman.**

craft·y (kraf′tē) tricky; sly: *The crafty thief escaped by disguising himself as a waiter.* *adj.,* **craft·i·er, craft·i·est.** —**craft·i·ly,** *adv.*

crag (krag) a steep, rugged or sharp rock rising above others. *n.* —**crag′gy,** *adj.*

cram (kram) 1 pack tightly; stuff: *She crammed all her clothes into the bag. The hall was crammed with many people.* 2 *Informal.* study a lot of material in a short time: *He had to cram for two weeks to catch up on his work.* *v.,* **crammed, cram·ming.**

cramp (kramp) 1 shut into a small space: *The two of us were cramped in the telephone booth.* 2 a sudden pain in the abdomen or the muscles: *The swimmer was seized with a cramp. I had cramps from mild food poisoning.* 3 limit; restrict: *His work was cramped by the very short time he could spend on it.* 1, 3 *v.,* 2 *n.*

cran·ber·ry (kran′ber′ē) a firm, sour, dark red berry that grows on trailing vines or short shrubs in marshes. Cranberries are used in making sauce and jelly. *n., pl.* **cran·ber·ries.**

crane (krān) 1 a large machine with a long, swinging arm, for lifting and moving very heavy things. 2 a large grey or white wading bird with long legs and neck and quite a long bill. The **sandhill crane** is common in Canada. 3 stretch your neck as a crane does: *She craned her neck to see over the crowd.* 1, 2 *n.,* 3 *v.,* **craned, cran·ing.**

cra·ni·um (krā′nē əm) the skull, especially the part that encloses the brain. *n.* **—cra′ni·al,** *adj.*

crank (krangk) 1 a handle that must be turned in a circle in order to get a machine going: *the crank of a pencil sharpener.* 2 work or start by turning a crank: *He had to crank the old Model T car to start it.* 3 *Informal.* an odd person; a person who has strange ideas or habits. A **crank call** is a phone call made by such a person to a stranger, with no proper reason. 4 *Informal.* a grouchy person. 1, 3, 4 *n.,* 2 *v.*
crank up, *Informal.* increase, especially by turning a dial: *Crank up the volume. Can you crank the heat up a bit?*

crank·y (krang′kē) grumpy; irritable: *The baby has been cranky all morning.* *adj.,* **crank·i·er, crank·i·est.**

cran·ny (kran′ē) a small, narrow opening; a crack: *There were many nooks and crannies in the wall.* *n., pl.* **cran·nies.**

crash (krash) 1 a sudden, loud noise like many dishes falling and breaking. 2 make such a noise; fall, hit, or break with such a noise: *The thunder crashed. The dishes crashed to the floor. The car crashed through the gates.* 3 an accident where a vehicle slams into something or falls violently to the ground: *a plane crash. No one was injured in the car crash.* 4 fail or break down suddenly: *My computer crashed again in the middle of a game.* 5 a sudden failure or breakdown. 6 *Informal.* sleep or relax after working hard or being awake for a long time. 1, 3, 5 *n.,* 2, 4, 6 *v.*
crash a party, *Informal.* go to a party without being invited.

crass (kras) rude, gross, stupid, or too cheap: *She thought it was pretty crass of him to come to the party when he wasn't invited.* *adj.*

crate (krāt) 1 a large wooden box, used to pack furniture, glass, fruit, etc. for transport or storage. 2 pack in a crate. 3 a junky old car. 1, 3 *n.,* 2 *v.,* **crat·ed, crat·ing.**

cra·ter (krā′tər) 1 the opening at the top of a volcano. 2 a big bowl-shaped hole in the surface of the earth, moon, or other planet. *n.*

crave (krāv) long for; desire very strongly: *A starving person craves food.* *v.,* **craved, crav·ing.** **—crav′ing,** *n.*

crawl (krol) 1 move as a worm or bug does. 2 move on hands and knees: *Babies crawl. We crawled through a hole in the wall.* 3 move slowly: *The traffic crawled on the icy roads.* 4 a slow movement: *The traffic was moving at a crawl.* 5 swarm with crawling things: *The ground was crawling with ants.* 6 feel creepy: *My skin crawled at the eerie sounds.* 7 a fast way of swimming, using overarm strokes and a continuous kicking motion. 1–3, 5, 6 *v.,* 4, 7 *n.* **—crawl′er,** *n.* **—crawl′y,** *adj.*

cray·fish (krā′fish′) a freshwater animal that looks like a small lobster. *n., pl.* **cray·fish** or **cray·fish·es.**

cray·on (krā′on *or* krā′ən) 1 a stick or pencil of coloured wax, oil pastel, chalk, or charcoal for drawing or colouring. 2 draw or colour with a crayon. 1 *n.,* 2 *v.*

craze (krāz) 1 a short-lived, extreme enthusiasm for one thing: *Every year he has a new craze; this year it's model ships.* 2 make crazy: *crazed with pain.* 1 *n.,* 2 *v.,* **crazed, craz·ing.**

cra·zy (krā′zē) 1 out of one's mind; insane. 2 *Informal.* very eager or enthusiastic: *crazy about cats.* 3 with no order or pattern: *crazy paving, a crazy quilt.* *adj.,* **cra·zi·er, cra·zi·est.** **—cra′zi·ly,** *adv.* **—cra′zi·ness,** *n.*

creak (krēk) 1 squeak loudly: *Door hinges creak when they need oiling.* 2 a creaking noise. 1 *v.,* 2 *n.* **—creak′y,** *adj.*

a bat	e bed	i bid	o pot	u cup	th thin
ā cake	ē me	ī bite	ō go	ū rude	ᴛʜ then
à bar	ə about	ər over	ò for	ù put	zh measure

cream (krēm) **1** the yellowish part of milk that contains the fat. Cream rises to the top when milk that is not homogenized is allowed to stand. Butter is made from cream. **2** a smooth, rich mixture like cream: *ice cream, face cream.* **3** make into a smooth mixture like cream: *to cream butter and sugar together for a cake.* **4** yellowish white. **5** **the cream,** the best part of anything: *the cream of the crop. The cream of the class entered the science competition.* 1, 2, 5 *n.,* 3 *v.,* 4 *adj.* —**cream′y,** *adj.*

cream·er·y (krē′mə rē) a place where butter and cheese are made. *n., pl.* **cream·er·ies.**

crease (krēs) **1** a fold or wrinkle, or the line left by it: *Pants are pressed with creases down the front.* **2** make or get creases in. **3** in hockey and lacrosse, a small rectangular area marked off in front of a goal. 1, 3 *n.,* 2 *v.,* **creased, creas·ing.**

cre·ate (krē āt′) **1** make, especially something original or artistic: *She has created an amazing sculpture.* **2** cause: *Do not create a disturbance.* *v.,* **cre·at·ed, cre·at·ing.**

cre·a·tion (krē ā′shən) **1** the act of creating. **2** something created; especially, the universe, thought of as something created by God: *Is this story your own creation? In all of creation, there is no one like you.* *n.*

cre·a·tive (krē ā′tiv) having the power to create; inventive; imaginative or original: *a creative person, creative ideas.* *adj.* —**cre′a·tiv′i·ty** (krē′ā tiv′ə tē), *n.*

cre·a·tor (krē ā′tər) **1** a person who creates. **2** **the Creator,** God. *n.*

crea·ture (krē′chər) any living person or animal. *n.*

crèche (kresh *or* krāsh) **1** a model showing the baby Jesus in the manger, with Mary and Joseph and, often, other figures: *Crèches are displayed in many homes, churches, etc. at Christmas.* **2** a nursery for babies and toddlers. *n.*

cred·i·ble (kred′ə bəl) believable: *a credible explanation, a credible politician.* *adj.* —**cred′i·bil′i·ty,** *n.*

CONFUSABLES .... credible

credible means "believable": *She spoke so calmly that we all thought her explanation quite credible.*
creditable means "bringing praise": *Your good work lately has earned you a creditable term report.*
credulous means "too ready to believe": *He told his little brother there was a monster under the bed, and the credulous little boy ran away, yelling.*

cred·it (kred′it) **1** belief; faith or trust: *I don't put much credit in that story.* **2** believe something is true; trust: *It's hard to credit such a strange explanation.* **3** praise; honour: *The person who does the work should get the credit.* **4** the privilege of borrowing money: *He had no trouble getting credit for his purchase.* **5** the amount of money in an account or added to an account: *She had a credit of $5000 in her savings account.* **6** add to an account as a deposit: *The bank credited $100 to my account.* **7** reputation for paying debts, measured by a **credit rating:** *If you pay your bills on time, your credit will be good.* 1, 3, 4, 5, 7 *n.,* 2, 6 *v.*
do credit to or **be a credit to,** bring honour to: *His quick action did credit to his courage.*
give someone credit for, say or believe that someone has some good quality or has done some good thing: *Give her credit for some intelligence and let her try the job herself.* A similar expression is **credit someone with.**
on credit, on a promise to pay later: *She bought a new computer on credit.*

cred·it·a·ble (kred′ə tə bəl) bringing praise or honour: *a creditable performance.* *adj.*

credit card (kred′it kärd′) an identification card that gives a person the right to buy things on credit.

cred·i·tor (kred′ə tər) a person that someone owes money to. *n.*

credit union (kred′it yūn′yən) an association that people can belong to which holds their money in savings accounts and loans it out to members at good rates of interest. It is like a bank that is owned by its customers.

cred·u·lous (krej′ə ləs) too ready to believe; gullible: *He was too credulous and was often fooled.* *adj.*

Cree (krē) **1** a large First Nation spread across Canada. The Cree can be divided into three main groups according to where they live and what dialect they speak: the **Plains Cree** in central Alberta and Saskatchewan, the **Woodland Cree** in northern Saskatchewan and Manitoba, and the **Swampy Cree** around Hudson and James Bays. **2** their language, which belongs to the Algonquian family. **3** having to do with these people or their language. 1, 2 *n.,* 3 *adj.*

creed (krēd) a set of beliefs or principles, or a statement that summarizes them: *to recite a creed in church. Buddhism and Judaism are two ancient creeds. It was his creed that work should come before play.* *n.*

creek (krēk *or* krik) **1** a small freshwater stream. **2** a narrow bay running inland for some distance from the sea. *n.*

creep (krēp) 1 crawl. 2 move slowly and unnoticeably: *The hunter crept silently through the woods.* 3 grow along the ground or over a wall by means of clinging stems: *Ivy creeps.* 4 *Informal.* a nasty or scary character. 5 **the creeps,** *Informal.* an eerie or scary feeling: *That place gives me the creeps.* 1–3 *v.,* **crept, creep·ing;** 4, 5 *n.* **—creep′y,** *adj.*

cre·mate (kri māt′) burn a dead body to ashes. *v.,* **cre·mat·ed, cre·mat·ing.** **—cre·ma′tion,** *n.*

cre·nel (kre′nəl) the low part of the top of a battlement. The **merlon** is the high part. *n.* **—cren′·el·la′tion,** *n.*

crepe or **crêpe** (krāp) 1 cloth or rubber that has a crinkled surface. Black crepe cloth is a traditional sign of mourning at deaths. Crepe rubber is used for the soles of shoes and boots. 2 Usually, **crepe paper,** thin, crinkly, coloured paper used to make party decorations such as streamers. 3 a large, very thin pancake. *n.*

crept (krept) the past tense and past participle of **creep:** *The dog crept under the bed. Night had crept up on us without our noticing.* *v.*

cre·scen·do (krə shen′dō) something that gradually becomes louder, such as a sound or part of a piece of music. *n.*

As the new moon moves through the first quarter of its orbit, a crescent moon is seen, followed by a half moon, then a full moon. The sequence continues in reverse order, waning instead of waxing, until the moon is new again.

cres·cent (kres′ənt) 1 the shape of the moon as seen from the earth in its first or last quarter. 2 anything that curves in a similar way, such as a street. *n.*

cress (kres) a plant with peppery-tasting leaves used on sandwiches or in salad. The most familiar kind is watercress. *n.*

crest (krest) 1 a tuft of feathers, or a growth of skin, on the head of a bird or animal. 2 a symbol standing for a family or clan. Among some First Nations peoples, it was the image of a certain animal; among Europeans it was a **coat of arms,** a design combining different symbols linked to the family's history: *The knight wore his family's crest on his shield.* 3 the symbol or logo of a team, school, or other organization, often worn on a jacket or sweater. 4 the top of a hill or wave. 5 reach the highest point: *The river crests in the spring. We crested the hill and admired the view.* 1–4 *n.,* 5 *v.* **—crest′ed,** *adj.*

crest·fall·en (krest′fol′ən) very disappointed; discouraged: *She came home crestfallen because she had not made the team.* *adj.*

cre·vasse (krə vas′) a deep, often wide crack in the ice of a glacier. *n.*

crev·ice (krev′is) a narrow crack: *Tiny ferns grew in crevices in the stone wall.* *n.*

crew (krū) 1 a group of people working together, such as the sailors on a ship, or a team of construction workers. 2 a gang; mob: *The boys on that street are a rough crew.* *n.*

crib (krib) 1 a baby's small bed with high, barred sides. 2 a rack or bin for grain, corn, etc. on a farm. *n.*

crick·et¹ (krik′it) a black insect related to the grasshopper: *On a summer evening crickets can often be heard chirping merrily.* *n.*

crick·et² (krik′it) an outdoor game played by two teams of eleven players each, with ball, bats, and wickets. *n.*

crime (krīm) 1 a deed that is against the law: *Murder is a crime.* 2 an unacceptable act or situation: *It is a crime to waste good food.* *n.*

crim·i·nal (krim′ə nəl) 1 a person who has committed a crime. 2 illegal or unacceptable: *a criminal offence. It is criminal to charge such high prices!* 3 having to do with crime: *criminal law, a criminal lawyer.* 1 *n.,* 2–3 *adj.*

crimp (krimp) to press something into small, even folds or waves. You can crimp cloth, paper, hair, the edge of a pie crust, etc. *v.*

cringe (krinj) 1 shrink from danger or pain; crouch in fear: *The dog cringed at the sight of the whip.* 2 try to get favour by acting timid, slavish, and pitiful. *v.,* **cringed, cring·ing.**

a bat	e bed	i bid	o pot	u cup	th thin
ā cake	ē me	ī bite	ō go	ū rude	ᴛʜ then
ä bar	ə about	ər over	ȯ for	ů put	zh measure

crin•kle (kring′kəl) **1** make or become full of small wrinkles: *His shirt was crinkled from being stuffed in his knapsack.* **2** a small wrinkle. **3** the noise of paper being crumpled up. **4** make this noise: *The dry leaves crinkled under our feet.* 1, 4 *v.,* **crin•kled, crin•kling;** 2, 3 *n.*

crip•ple (krip′əl) damage; weaken: *The ship was crippled by the storm.* *v.,* **crip•pled, crip•pling.**

> **USING WORDS . . . . cripple**
>
> A creature that is lame or unable to move in its usual way can be called **crippled**: *The crippled deer could not escape from the pack of dogs.*
>
> It is rude to use the word **cripple** about a person. Instead, use **person with a disability**.

cri•sis (krī′sis) **1** a turning point; a moment or event that decides which way things will turn out. **2** a time of danger; emergency: *England faced a crisis during the Battle of Britain.* *n., pl.* **cri•ses** (krī′sēz).

crisp (krisp) **1** firm and stiff but breaking or snapping easily and sharply: *Dry toast is crisp. Fresh celery is crisp.* **2** fresh; sharp and clear: *The air was cool and crisp.* **3** clear, firm, and to the point in speaking: *a crisp manner.* *adj.*

criss•cross (kris′kros′) **1** with crossed lines; crossed; crossing: *Plaids have a crisscross pattern (adj.). He laid the sticks crisscross in the fireplace (adv.).* **2** move or lie across in different directions: *Buses and cars crisscross the city. Little cracks crisscrossed the wall.* 1 *adj. or adv.,* 2 *v.*

cri•te•ri•on (krī tē′rē ən) a rule or standard for making a judgment about something: *Entries to the art contest will be judged on various criteria, including originality.* *n., pl.* **cri•te•ri•a.**

crit•ic (krit′ik) **1** an expert who makes thoughtful judgments of the good and bad points of something, often as his or her job: *a film critic, a restaurant critic.* **2** a person who criticizes or finds fault: *She was such a constant critic that the other girls did not like her.* *n.*

crit•i•cal (krit′ə kəl) **1** quick to criticize others: *A critical person is hard to work with.* **2** most important; key: *Timing is critical in this game.* **3** having to do with judgments based on thorough knowledge and careful examination: *critical thinking, a critical analysis. She knows enough to make a critical judgment.* **4** urgent or dangerous: *in critical condition, in critical need. The situation is critical.* *adj.*

crit•i•cism (krit′ə siz′əm) **1** negative remarks; the act of finding fault. **2** the making of thoughtful judgments; the work of a critic (def. 1). *n.*

crit•i•cize (krit′ə sīz′) blame; find fault with: *Do not criticize him until you know all the facts.* *v.,* **crit•i•cized, crit•i•ciz•ing.**

cri•tique (krə tēk′) **1** an explanation of why something, such as a book or a painting, is good or bad: *I read a critique of that new movie that pans it completely.* **2** a well-thought-out piece of criticism; a suggestion for improvement: *She offered some valuable critiques of my work.* **3** thoughtfully say what the strong and weak points of something are: *We critiqued each other's oral presentations.* 1, 2 *n.,* 3 *v.,* **cri•tiqued, cri•tiqu•ing.**

crit•ter (krit′ər) *Informal.* any living creature. *n.*

croak (krōk) **1** a deep, hoarse sound made by a frog or crow. **2** make this sound. **3** *Informal.* complain; grumble. **4** *Slang.* die. 1 *n.,* 2–4 *v.*

cro•chet (krō shā′) **1** a kind of needlework done using a single needle with a hooked end, called a **crochet hook:** *I am trying to learn crochet so I can make a vest.* **2** make things in this way. 1 *n.,* 2 *v.,* **cro•cheted** (krō shād′), **cro•chet•ing** (krō shā′ing). **—cro•chet′er** (krō shā′ər), *n.*

crock (krok) a pot or jar made of baked clay. As a group, things made of baked clay are called **crockery.** *n.*

When a crocodile closes its mouth, its fourth lower tooth is still visible. When an alligator closes its mouth, all of its teeth are hidden.

crocodile

alligator

croc•o•dile (krok′ə dīl′) a large reptile, closely related to the alligator, but faster moving and having a narrower snout. Crocodiles live mainly in the rivers and marshes of the warm parts of Africa, Asia, Australia, and America. *n.*

cro•cus (krō′kəs) **1** a small garden plant with white, yellow, or purple flowers that bloom in early spring. **2** 🍁 a small wildflower of the Prairies that bears one large mauve flower in early spring. The crocus is the provincial flower of Manitoba. *n.*

crois·sant (krə sont′) a flaky bread roll that is shaped in a curve. *n.*

cro·ny (krō′nē) a buddy; chum. *n., pl.* **cro·nies.**

crook (kru̇k) **1** a person who cheats people; a swindler. **2** the curved or bent part of anything: *the crook of a hockey stick.* **3** a shepherd's hooked stick. *n.*

crook·ed (kru̇k′id) **1** not straight; bent; curved; twisted: *a crooked stick.* **2** dishonest: *a crooked person. adj.*

croon (krün) hum or sing quietly and tenderly: *The father was crooning to his baby. v.*

crop (krop) **1** plants of one kind, grown in order to be used, especially as food: *Wheat is the main crop of the Prairie provinces. The cotton crop in the U.S. was very poor this year.* **2** bite off, clip, or cut until short: *The horse's tail was cropped. The sheep had cropped the grass.* **3** a baglike part of a bird's food passage, where food is prepared for digestion. **4** a short whip with a loop instead of a lash: *a riding crop.* 1, 3, 4 *n.,* 2 *v.,* **cropped, crop·ping.**
crop up, appear or happen unexpectedly: *All sorts of difficulties cropped up.*

crop–dust·ing (krop′dus′ting) the spraying of chemicals on growing crops, usually from a plane that flies low, in order to kill weeds or harmful insects. *n.* **—crop′-dust′er,** *n.*

crop rotation (krop′ rō tā′ shən) a system of planting a crop in a different field in consecutive years.

cro·quet (krō kā′) an outdoor game where players use mallets to knock balls through small wire arches. *n.*

cro·quette (krō ket′) a small patty, stick, or ball of ground meat or fish, chopped vegetables, etc. It is rolled in bread crumbs and then fried. *n.*

cross (kros) **1** any thing, design, or mark shaped like a + or an ×: *I've made a little cross where you have to sign your name.* **2** draw a line through or across: *In writing you cross the letter "t." Cross my name off your list. He crossed out the wrong word.* **3** put, go, or lie across something or across each other: *to cross your arms, to cross a bridge. The two highways cross at Paisley.* **4** mix breeds of animals or plants: *A new plant is sometimes made by crossing two others.* **5** the act or result of this mixing: *A mule is a cross between a horse and a donkey.* **Crossbreed** is another form for defs. 4 and 5. **6** a stick or post with another one across it like a + or an ×. The ancient Romans punished criminals by hanging them on a cross. **7 the Cross,** the cross Jesus died on. It is the symbol of the Christian faith. **8** make the sign of a cross on or over a person or thing: *The priest crossed himself.* **9** angry or grumpy. **10** act or speak against: *If anyone crosses him, he gets very angry.* 1, 5, 6, 7 *n.,* 2–4, 8, 10 *v.,* 9 *adj.* **—cross′ing,** *n.* **—cross′ly,** *adv.* **—cross′ness,** *n.*
cross someone's path, meet someone.
cross your mind, come into your mind: *Telling a lie never crossed her mind.*

Word Family.......... **cross**

crossbar: a bar or stripe going crosswise
crossbones: two bones shown under a skull, to mean death or danger
cross-legged: with one leg folded over the other
crosspiece: a piece of wood or metal placed across
crosswalk: a street crossing for people walking
crosswise: across
crossword: a puzzle with words crossing each other

cross·bow (kros′bō′) a medieval weapon. It had a bow fixed across a thick wooden stick with a groove along the middle to direct an arrow. *n.*

cross–check (kros′ chek′) **1** check again or check against another source: *to check and cross-check a list.* **2** in hockey or lacrosse, check a player illegally by holding your stick in both hands and pushing it in front of his or her face or body. **3** the act of cross-checking. 1, 2 *v.,* 3 *n.*

cross–coun·try (kros′ kun′trē) **1** across open country instead of on a track: *a cross-country race.* **2** going across a country: *a cross-country tour. adj.*

cross–ex·am·ine (kros′ eg zam′ən) question closely to test whether a person is telling the truth, especially in a trial: *The first witness for the prosecution was cross-examined by the defence for two hours. v.,* **cross-ex·am·ined, cross-ex·am·in·ing.**

cross–eyed (kros′ īd′) with one eye or both eyes turned in toward the nose. *adj.*

cross reference (kros′ ref′rəns) an instruction in one part of a book, index, etc. to look in another part for more information.

cross·road (kros′rōd′) **1** a road that crosses another or that runs across between two others. **2 crossroads, a** a place where roads cross: *At the crossroads, turn left.* **b** a point where an important choice must be made: *This is a crossroads in my life. n.*

a bat	e bed	i bid	o pot	u cup	th thin
ā cake	ē me	ī bite	ō go	ü rude	ᴛʜ then
ä bar	ə about	ər over	ô for	u̇ put	zh measure

cross section (kros′ sek′shən) 1 the act of cutting anything across. To slice a tomato, you make a series of cross sections. 2 the surface that such a cut makes or would make: *The picture shows a cross section of a log.* 3 a sample; a small number of people or things chosen to stand for a whole group: *They interviewed a cross section of the community.*

crotch (kroch) the place where anything divides into two parts or branches: *the crotch of a pair of pants. The nest was in the crotch of a tree.* *n.*

crotch•et•y (kroch′ə tē) stubborn and unreasonable about odd little things: *Wendy's father was often crotchety before he had breakfast, insisting that the window shades be exactly halfway down and the radio volume set to between 2 and 3.* *adj.,* **crotch•et•i•er, crotch•et•i•est.** **—crotch′et•i•ness,** *n.*

crouch (krouch) 1 stoop low with bent legs like an animal ready to spring, or like a person hiding or ducking. 2 a crouching position. 1 *v.,* 2 *n.*

croup (krūp) an illness that causes a cough and difficult breathing, especially in children. *n.*

crou•ton (krū′ton) a small cube of bread toasted or fried until it is crisp and served in soup or salad. *n.*

crow[1] (krō) 1 the loud cry of a rooster. 2 a happy sound made by a baby. 3 make either of these sounds. 4 celebrate with boastful pride: *They crowed about their victory for weeks.* 1, 2 *n.,* 3, 4 *v.*

crow[2] (krō) a big black bird with a harsh cry. *n.*
as the crow flies, in a straight line.
eat crow, be forced to do something humiliating.

crow•bar (krō′bär′) a strong bar of iron or steel used to lift things or pry them apart. *n.*

crowd (kroud) 1 a large number of people, animals, or things together: *A crowd gathered to hear the street musician.* 2 *Informal.* a group of friends, followers, etc.: *the "in" crowd.* 3 gather, move, or squeeze close together in large numbers: *to crowd around the door, to crowd into a building. Shoppers crowded the store.* 1, 2 *n.,* 3 *v.*
crowd out, force someone or something out by taking up all the room.

crown (kroun) 1 a head covering of precious metal and jewels, worn by a ruler. 2 the position and power of a ruler. 3 put a crown on, especially on a new ruler. 4 to honour; reward: *Her hard work was crowned with success.* 5 the top; the highest part: *the crown of a hat, the crown of a mountain.* 6 be on top of: *A fort crowns the hill.* 7 the part of a tooth that shows above the gum, or an artificial substitute for it. 8 a former British coin. 1, 2, 5, 7, 8 *n.,* 3, 4, 6 *v.*

✱ **Crown corporation** (kroun′ kôr pə rā′shən) a company owned and run by the government of Canada or one of the provinces to serve the public. The CBC and the St. Lawrence Seaway Authority are Crown corporations.

✱ **crown land** (kroun′ land′) in some Commonwealth countries, land that is owned by the government: *Some crown lands in Canada are set aside as provincial and national parks.*

crow's–feet (krōz′ fēt′) wrinkles at the outer corners of a person's eyes. *pl.n.*

crow's–nest or **crows–nest** (krōz′ nest′) on a ship, a lookout platform near the top of a mast. *n.*

cru•cial (krū′shəl) very important: *Proper eating habits are crucial to good health.* *adj.*

cru•ci•fy (krū′sə fī′) 1 kill by nailing or tying the hands and feet to a cross, as the ancient Romans did to criminals. 2 criticize publicly and very severely: *The newspapers crucified the mayor for his careless remark about housing.* *v.,* **cru•ci•fied, cru•ci•fy•ing.** **—cru′ci•fix′ion** (krū′ sə fik′shən), *n.*

crude (krūd) 1 in a natural or raw state, before being refined or prepared for use: *crude oil.* 2 rough: *a crude shelter made out of a box, crude manners.* *adj.,* **crud•er, crud•est.** **—cru′di•ty,** *n.*

cru•el (krū′əl) 1 eager to hurt others; unkind or hardhearted: *a cruel master.* 2 causing great pain or suffering: *a cruel war, a cruel disease.* *adj.* **—cru′el•ty,** *n.*

cruise (krūz) 1 sail, drive, or walk around from place to place: *to cruise along the coast in a yacht. Police cars cruised the streets.* 2 a trip from place to place with or without a special destination: *We went for a cruise on the Great Lakes last summer.* 1 *v.,* **cruised, cruis•ing;** 2 *n.* **—cruis′er,** *n.*

crumb (krum) 1 a very small piece broken from bread, cake, etc.: *You left crumbs all over the floor!* 2 a little bit: *a crumb of comfort.* *n.*

crum•ble (krum′bəl) 1 break up or fall apart into small pieces or crumbs: *The cookie crumbled when I picked it up. The old wall was crumbling away at the edges.* 2 a fruit dessert with a layer of crumbs on top. *v.,* **crum•bled, crum•bling.** **—crum′bly,** *adj.*

crum•ple (krum′pəl) 1 crush together: *She crumpled the letter into a ball.* 2 wrinkle badly: *Her shirt*

Crystals

snowflakes

Snowflakes and diamonds are two examples of crystals. The material in a crystal is arranged in a regular pattern. All snowflakes, for example, are six-sided symmetrical crystals.

was crumpled from sleeping in it. **3** collapse: *He crumpled to the floor in a faint.* *v.,* **crum·pled, crum·pling.**

crunch (krunch) **1** crush or chew noisily: *He crunched the celery.* **2** the act or sound of crunching. **3** make this sound: *The hard snow crunched under our feet.* 1, 3 *v.,* 2 *n.* **—crunch′y,** *adj.*

cru·sade (krū sād′) **1 Crusade,** any one of the Christian campaigns between 1096 and 1272 to win the Holy Land back from the Muslims by force. **2** a strong, enthusiastic movement for or against something: *the crusade against poverty.* **3** take part in a crusade: *to crusade for freedom.* 1, 2 *n.,* 3 *v.,* **cru·sad·ed, cru·sad·ing. —cru·sad′er,** *n.*

crush (krush) **1** squeeze or press so hard as to break, flatten, bruise, or wrinkle: *The horse's hooves crushed the flowers. His hat was crushed when I sat on it.* **2** thoroughly defeat or discourage: *The enemy was crushed. He was crushed by her refusal to marry him.* **3** a mass of people crowded close together: *There was a terrific crush at the football game.* 1, 2 *v.,* 3 *n.*

crust (krust) **1** the hard outside layer of anything. Bread and pies have a crust. So does the earth. Snow sometimes forms a crust thick enough to walk on. **2** cover with a crust or form a crust: *By the next day the snow had crusted over.* 1 *n.,* 2 *v.* **—crust′y,** *adj.*

crus·ta·cean (krus stā′shən) an animal that has a hard shell, five pairs of legs, and lives mostly in water. Crabs, lobsters, and shrimps are crustaceans. *n.*

crutch (kruch) **1** a support designed to help an injured person walk. **2** anything that gives support or makes up for a weakness. *n.*

crux (kruks)
the crux of the matter, the most important point about something being discussed: *She thought the need to work harder was the crux of the matter.* *n.*

cry (krī) **1** shed tears of sadness or pain, often with a noise. **2** a fit of tears. **3** shout or call out loudly: *He cried, "Help!"* **4** a loud call; a shout: *We heard the drowning man's cry for help.* **5** a call or noise made by an animal: *a gull's cry, the cry of a wolf.* 1, 3 *v.,* **cried, cry·ing;** 2, 4, 5 *n., pl.* **cries.**

crypt (kript) an underground room, especially one under a church that was used as a burial place. *n.*

cryp·tic (krip′tik) very puzzling or with a secret meaning: *I couldn't understand her cryptic remarks.* *adj.* **—cryp′ti·cal·ly,** *adv.*

crys·tal (kris′təl) **1** a clear, transparent mineral that looks like ice. It is a kind of quartz. **2** a piece of crystal, cut to a certain shape. **3** clear glass of very fine quality: *wine glasses of crystal.* **4** the glass over the face of a watch. **5** one of the regularly shaped pieces, with angles and flat surfaces, that make up many solid substances: *crystals of snow, sugar crystals.* *n.* **—crys′tal·line** (kris′tə līn′ *or* kris′tə lēn′), *adj.*

crys·tal·lize (kris′tə līz′) **1** form into crystals: *Water crystallizes to form snow.* **2** take a definite shape: *Our vague ideas crystallized into a clear plan.* *v.,* **crys·tal·lized, crys·tal·liz·ing.**

a bat	e bed	i bid	o pot	u cup	th thin
ā cake	ē me	ī bite	ō go	ū rude	ᴛʜ then
ä bar	ə about	ər over	ô for	ů put	zh measure

cub (kub) a young bear, fox, wolf, lion, etc. *n.*

cub·by·hole (kub′ē hōl′) a small, enclosed space. *n.*

cube (kyūb) 1 a solid with six square faces or sides, all equal. 2 cut or shape into cubes: *to cube beets.* 3 the product when a number is used three times as a factor. The cube of 5 is 125; that is, 5 × 5 × 5 = 125. 1, 3 *n.,* 2 *v.,* **cubed, cub·ing.**

cu·bic (kyū′bik) 1 shaped like a cube. 2 having length, width, and thickness. A cubic metre is the volume of a cube whose edges are each 1 m long. *adj.*

cu·bi·cle (kyū′bə kəl) a small room or compartment. Public washrooms are usually divided into cubicles. *n.*

The pyramid builders of Egypt over 5000 years ago used the cubit as a unit of measurement.

cu·bit (kyū′bit) an ancient unit for measuring length, equal to about 45 to 55 cm. It was based on the length of a person's forearm from the elbow to the tip of the middle finger. *n.*

cuck·oo (kū′kū) a bird whose call sounds much like its name. The common European cuckoo lays its eggs in the nests of other birds instead of hatching them itself. North American cuckoos build their own nests and have a call less like their name. *n., pl.* **cuck·oos.**

cuckoo clock (kū′kū klok′) a clock with a toy bird that pops out of a little door and cries "Cuckoo!" to mark the hours or quarter hours.

cu·cum·ber (kyū′kum bər) a long, fleshy green vegetable eaten raw, often in salad, or used to make pickles. It grows on a vine. *n.*
cool as a cucumber, completely calm and relaxed.

cud (kud) food that has been brought up into the mouth from the first and second stomachs of cattle, deer, camels, and similar animals, to be chewed before being swallowed again. *n.*

cud·dle (kud′əl) 1 hold close and lovingly in your arms or lap: *She was cuddling the little kittens.* 2 lie close and comfortably; curl up: *The two puppies cuddled together in front of the fire.* *v.,* **cud·dled, cud·dling.**

cudg·el (kuj′əl) 1 a short, thick stick used as a weapon; club. 2 beat with a cudgel. 1 *n.,* 2 *v.,* **cudg·elled** or **cudg·eled, cudg·el·ling** or **cudg·el·ing.**
cudgel your brains, try very hard to think.

cue[1] (kyū) 1 a hint or signal to do or say something: *When she sits down, that's your cue to come on stage. A chord on the organ was the cue for everyone to stand.* 2 give someone a cue: *I'll cue you when it's your turn to speak.* 1 *n.,* 2 *v.,* **cued, cu·ing.**
on cue, exactly when expected.
take your cue from someone, copy someone; follow someone's lead.

cue[2] (kyū) a long stick used for hitting the ball in the game of billiards or pool. *n.*

> **WORD HISTORY..... cue**
>
> Both meanings of the word **cue** came from the French word *queue,* meaning "a tail." The pool cue is tail-shaped. The cue for an actor comes at the tail end of another actor's speech.

cuff[1] (kuf) a separate piece or a turned-up fold at the end of a sleeve or a pant leg. *n.*
off the cuff, without preparation: *I can't answer that off the cuff.*

cuff[2] (kuf) 1 hit with a paw or with the back of the hand. 2 a hit like this. 1 *v.,* 2 *n.*

cuff link (kuf′ lingk′) a device for linking together the open ends of a fancy shirt cuff.

cui·sine (kwə zēn′) a style or method of cooking: *French cuisine, vegetarian cuisine, stir-fry cuisine.* *n.*

cull (kul) 1 pick out; select: *Perhaps you can cull some ideas from these books.* 2 select and kill some members of an animal population, either because they are sick or because the size of the population is upsetting the natural balance. *v.*

cul·mi·nate (kul′mə nāt′) reach a climax or an end: *The action of the play culminates in a dramatic rescue. The Canada Day celebration culminated in a fireworks display.* *v.,* **cul·mi·nat·ed, cul·mi·nat·ing.**
—**cul′mi·na′tion,** *n.*

cu·lottes (kū lots′ *or* kyə lots′) women's and girls' pants with very wide legs that make them look like a skirt. *pl.n.*

cul·prit (kul′prit) the guilty person: *Have they found the culprit who did the graffiti?* *n.*

cul·ti·vate (kul′tə vāt′) **1** prepare and use land to raise crops: *This whole area is cultivated because it is so fertile.* **2** raise plants: *to cultivate roses.* **3** dig around growing plants to kill weeds, etc.: *to cultivate the soil.* **4** improve; develop by steady effort or practice: *Reading cultivates your imagination.* *v.,* **cul·ti·vat·ed, cul·ti·vat·ing.** **—cul′ti·va′tion,** *n.*

cul·ti·va·tor (kul′tə vā′tər) a tool or machine used to loosen the ground and destroy weeds. *n.*

cul·ture (kul′chər) **1** way of life; the customs, values, traditions, and beliefs of a nation or people at a certain time: *the culture of the ancient Vikings. Respect for differences is part of Canadian culture.* **2** the literature, music, and art of a nation or people. **3** a controlled growth of viruses, bacteria, etc. in a laboratory, for scientific study or for use as a medicine. **4** the raising of honey bees, silkworms, and certain other creatures that provide things useful to humans. *n.* **—cul′tur·al,** *adj.*

cul·vert (kul′vərt) a pipe or ditch that allows water to run under a road or railway. *n.*

cum·ber·some (kum′bər səm) hard to manage; clumsy; troublesome: *long, cumbersome sentences.* *adj.*

cu·mu·la·tive (kyū′myə lə tiv) built up from many things added together over time: *The cumulative effect of so many little annoyances finally made him lose his temper.* *adj.*

cu·mu·lus (kyū′myə ləs) a piled-up, rounded mass of white cloud with a flat bottom. *n., pl.* **cu·mu·li** (kyū′myə lī′ *or* kyū′myə lē′).

cu·ne·i·form (kyū′ nē ə fȯrm′) an ancient writing system using wedge-shaped characters cut in clay or carved on stone. *n.*

cun·ning (kun′ing) **1** crafty; clever; sly: *a cunning spy.* **2** cleverness; slyness: *She used all her cunning to plan a way of escape.* 1 *adj.,* 2 *n.*

cup (kup) **1** a small container to drink from, usually with a handle on the side. **2** a traditional measure of volume used especially in cooking, equal to about 250 mL. **3** anything shaped like a cup. **4** shape like a cup: *She cupped her hands to catch the ball.* **5** an ornamental cup given to the winner of a contest; trophy. 1–3, 5 *n.,* 4 *v.,* **cupped, cup·ping.** **—cup′ful′,** *n.*
your cup of tea, the thing you like: *Camping in the rain is not my cup of tea.*

cup·board (kub′ərd) a closet or cabinet with shelves. *n.*

cup·cake (kup′kāk′) a small cake baked in a tin shaped like a cup. *n.*

cur (kər) a worthless dog; mongrel. *n.*

cu·ra·tor (kyə rā′tər *or* kyū′rā tər) the person in charge of a museum, library, etc.: *The curator of an art museum knows a lot about paintings.* *n.*

curb (kərb) **1** a raised border of concrete or stone along the edge of a street. **2** hold in check; restrain: *We must curb our spending if we want to save enough for a trip.* 1–3 *n.,* 4 *v.*

curd (kərd) **1** the thick part of milk that separates from the watery part when the milk sours. Cheese is made from curds. **2** form into curds. 1 *n.,* 2 *v.*

cur·dle (kər′dəl) form into curds: *Milk curdles when it is kept too long.* *v.,* **cur·dled, cur·dling.**
curdle your blood, fill you with horror.

cure (kyūr) **1** make well again: *The sick child was soon cured.* **2** get rid of: *to cure a cold, to cure a bad habit.* **3** something that gets rid of disease or any other problem: *a cure for sore eyes, a cure for laziness.* **4** preserve bacon or other meat by drying, smoking, or salting it. 1, 2, 4 *v.,* **cured, cur·ing;** 3 *n.* **—cur′a·ble,** *adj.*

cur·few (kər′fyū) a rule that says you must be home by a certain time every night. In some places, especially where there is war or other danger, the government sets a curfew for all the people, including adults. *n.*

WORD HISTORY..... curfew

The word **curfew** comes from Anglo-French *covrir* meaning "to cover" and *feu*, meaning "fire." In the Middle Ages, a bell would signal that it was time to put out candles and lamps, and cover the fires.

cu·ri·os·i·ty (kyū′rē os′ə tē) **1** eager desire to know: *Curiosity got the better of her, and she read her sister's diary.* **2** a strange, rare object: *One of his curiosities was a drinking cup made from the horn of a bull.* *n., pl.* **cu·ri·os·i·ties.**

a bat	e bed	i bid	o pot	u cup	th thin
ā cake	ē me	ī bite	ō go	ū rude	ᴛʜ then
ä bar	ə about	ər over	ȯ for	u̇ put	zh measure

Ocean currents

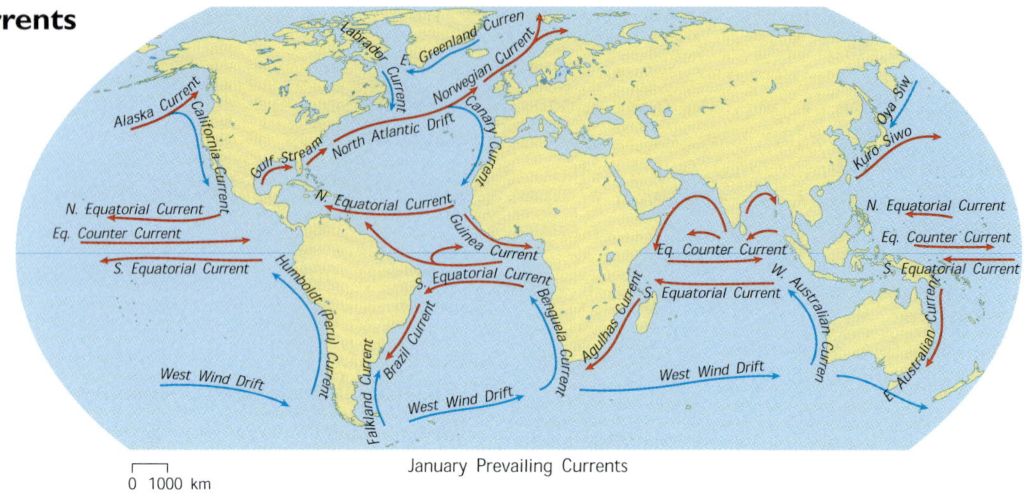

January Prevailing Currents

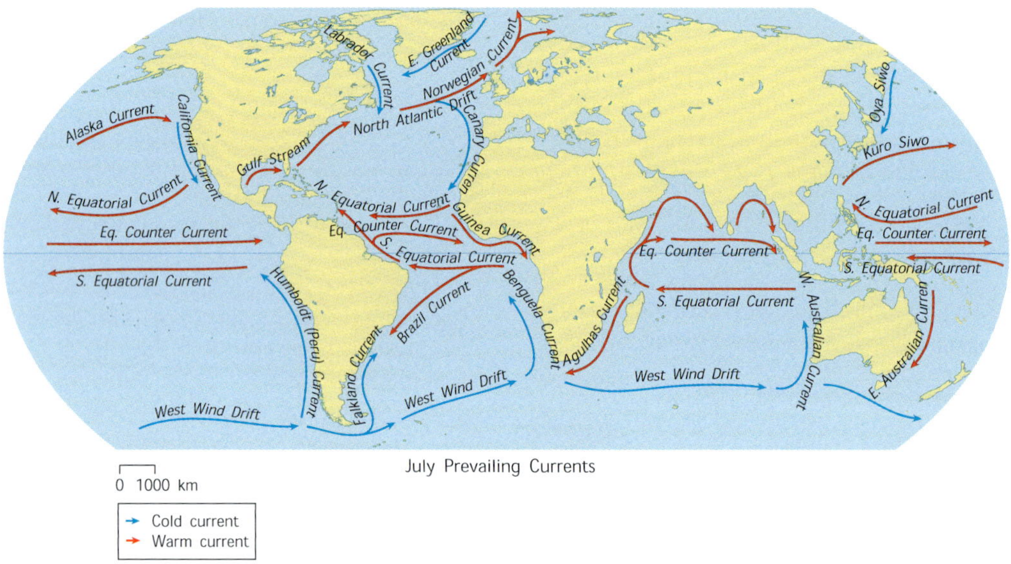

July Prevailing Currents

cu·ri·ous (kyū′rē əs) **1** eager to know: *Small children are very curious and ask many questions.* **2** strange; odd; unusual: *a curious old book.* *adj.*

curl (kərl) **1** twist or roll into rings or coils: *My mother has to curl her hair, but mine curls naturally.* **2** a curled lock of hair, or anything else that is curled. **3** play the game of curling; slide a stone down the ice in this game. 1, 3 *v.*, 2 *n.* —**curl′y,** *adj.*
curl up, lie down or sit in a comfortable, relaxed position, with the legs tucked up: *curled up in a big chair. She curled up by the fire with a book.*

curl·er (kər′lər) **1** a person who plays the game of curling. **2** a little roll or tube for winding hair on to make it curl. *n.*

curl·i·cue (kər′li kyū′) a fancy twist or curl, such as in handwriting or a design. *n.*

curl·ing (kər′ling) a game played on ice with large, round stones, called **curling stones,** that are slid toward a target at the end of the rink. *n.*

cur·rant (kər′ənt) **1** a small, sour, red or black berry, used for jam, wine, etc. It grows on a bush. **2** a small raisin made from certain sorts of small, sweet grapes: *Currants are often used in puddings, cakes, and buns.* *n.*

cur·ren·cy (kər′ən sē) **1** the money of a particular country: *Canadian currency cannot be used in Mexico.* ▶ See Appendix. **2** the fact of being current (def. 3). *n., pl.* **cur·ren·cies.**

cur·rent (kər′ənt) **1** a flow or stream that has some force: *ocean currents, a current of air.* **2** the flow of electricity through a wire, etc. **3** up to date; of the present time: *current fashions, the current month. Do you have the current issue of* Maclean's *magazine?* 1, 2 *n.*, 3 *adj.*

cur·ric·u·lum (kə rik′yə ləm) what is taught in the different subjects or courses at a school, college, or university. *n., pl.* **cur·ric·u·lums** or **cur·ric·u·la.** —**cur·ric′u·lar,** *adj.*

cur·ry¹ (kər′ē) rub and clean a horse with a very stiff brush called a **curry comb.** *v.,* **cur·ried, cur·ry·ing.**
curry favour, seek favour by flattery, attention, etc.

cur·ry² (kər′ē) 1 food cooked with a spicy, dark orange sauce or powder. 2 prepare food with curry sauce or curry powder: *curried lamb.* 1 *n., pl.* **cur·ries;** 2 *v.,* **cur·ried, cur·ry·ing.**

curse (kərs) 1 ask a god or other powerful spirit to bring trouble to: *He cursed his enemy solemnly.* 2 the special words said when doing this. 3 bring trouble to a person or thing. 4 a source of trouble: *My bad temper is a curse to me.* 5 swear; use bad language. 6 bad language: *Their talk was full of curses.* 1, 3, 5 *v.,* **cursed, curs·ing;** 2, 4, 6 *n.*
cursed with, troubled by.

cur·sive (kər′siv) written in a smoothly flowing way with the letters joined together. *Example: This is cursive writing.* *adj.*

cur·sor (kər′sər) a mark on a computer screen, showing where the next character will be placed. *n.*

curt (kərt) short and rude; abrupt: *Her curt answer made him angry.* *adj.* —**curt′ly,** *adv.* —**curt′ness,** *n.*

cur·tain (kər′tən) 1 a piece of cloth or other material hung at a window or in a doorway for shade, privacy, or decoration. 2 a hanging screen that separates the stage of a theatre from the part where the audience is. 3 **curtain off,** close off with a curtain: *We curtained off a space in the corner for storage.* 4 anything that covers or hides: *a curtain of fog.* 1, 2, 4 *n.,* 3 *v.* —**cur′tained,** *adj.*

curtain wall (kər′tən wol) the wall or part of the wall that enclosed a castle.

curt·sy or **curt·sey** (kərt′sē) 1 a bow made by women and girls, done by bending the knees and lowering the body slightly. 2 make a curtsy. 1 *n., pl.* **curt·sies** or **curt·seys;** 2 *v.,* **curt·sied** or **curt·seyed, curt·sy·ing** or **curt·sey·ing.**

curve (kərv) 1 a line that has no straight part. 2 bend into a line with no straight part. 3 something with a rounded or bending shape: *a curve in the road.* 4 in baseball, a ball thrown with a spin so that it swerves in flight. 1, 3, 4 *n.,* 2 *v.,* **curved, curv·ing.** —**cur′va·ture** (kər′və chər), *n.*
throw someone a curve, confuse a person with something unexpected.

cush·ion (ku̇sh′ən) 1 a soft pillow or pad used to sit, lie, or kneel on. Sofas have cushions. 2 anything soft: *a cushion of moss.* 3 lessen the painful or bad effect of something: *The straw cushioned her fall from the barn loft. The support of friends cushioned his disappointment.* 1, 2 *n.,* 3 *v.*

cuss (kus) *Informal.* curse. *v. or n.*

cus·tard (kus′tərd) a baked or boiled pudding made of eggs, milk, and sugar. *n.*

cus·to·di·an (kə stō′dē ən) 1 a caretaker; janitor. 2 a guardian or keeper: *In a democracy, all citizens are the custodians of freedom.* *n.*

cus·to·dy (kus′tə dē) safekeeping; charge; care: *Parents have the custody of their young children.* *n., pl.* **cus·to·dies.**
in custody, in prison; in the charge of the police.

cus·tom (kus′təm) 1 the usual way of doing things, whether for one person or a whole nation: *It was her custom to rise early. He found it hard to adjust to the customs of his new country.* 2 **customs,** *pl.* **a** the office at a seaport, airport, or border crossing where passports and imported goods are checked. **b** taxes paid to the government on things brought in from a foreign country. *n.* —**cus′tom·ar·y,** *adj.* —**cus′tom·ar′i·ly,** *adv.*

USING WORDS...... custom

The words **custom** and **habit** have similar meanings, but they are used in different situations.

A **custom** is a way of doing things that a person, or a group of people, always follows: *It is a custom among many people to eat turkey at Thanksgiving.*

A **habit** is something a person does without thinking: *Brushing your teeth becomes a habit.*

cus·tom·er (kus′tə mər) 1 a person who buys. 2 *Informal.* a person: *a rough customer.* *n.*

cut (kut) 1 open, shape, carve, or divide with something sharp: *to cut a loaf of bread, to cut a hole in a box. Terry cut a design into the wooden block.* 2 hurt with something sharp, by accident: *Vibha cut her finger on the broken glass.* 3 make lower or shorter: *We will have to cut expenses. Our ice time was cut by 15 minutes.*

a bat	e bed	i bid	o pot	u cup	th thin
ā cake	ē me	ī bite	ō go	ū rude	ᴛʜ then
à bar	ə about	ər over	ȯ for	u̇ put	zh measure

4 go by a more direct way: *Let's cut through the woods and get ahead of the others.* **5** change direction suddenly: *She had to cut to the right to avoid the oncoming car.* **6** sting painfully: *The cold wind cut me to the bone. Ivan was cut by their harsh criticism.* **7** the act of cutting, or its result: *a cut in pay, a cut across the field. Make two little cuts in the cardboard. I'll put a bandage on that cut.* **8** a piece of meat: *an expensive cut of beef.* **9** the shape or style of something: *I don't like the cut of this coat. Hervé got a crew cut at the barber's.* **10** *Informal.* skip without permission: *You'll get into trouble if you cut class.* 1–6, 10 *v.,* **cut, cut·ting;** 7–9 *n.*

cut and run, leave in a hurry.

cut back, a cut the ends of branches to encourage new growth: *The lilac bush needs to be cut back.* **b** spend, use, or eat less.

cut both ways, have advantages and disadvantages.

cut corners, try to save time, money, effort, etc. by not doing something thoroughly.

cut down, a make something fall by cutting: *to cut down a tree.* **b** lower: *to cut down the noise.*

cut in, butt in: *She cut in before the speaker had finished.*

cut it, be good enough: *I'm sorry, but your excuse just doesn't cut it.*

cut off, a remove by cutting: *He cut off the fat before broiling the steak.* **b** stop the supply of: *They cut off our hydro.* **c** go right in front of another car when driving, causing the other driver to slam on the brake. **d** interrupt. **e** block: *to cut off someone's escape.*

cut out, a take out by cutting: *May I cut out this picture?* **b** *Informal.* stop: *Cut out the fighting! Cut it out!*

cut out for, suited to: *I'm just not cut out for this work.*

cut short, cause to end suddenly.

cut teeth, have teeth grow through the gums: *Babies are sometimes cranky when they are cutting teeth.*

cut up, a cut into small pieces. **b** *Informal.* show off or clown around.

cute (kyūt) *Informal.* **1** good-looking, sweet, and lovable: *a cute baby.* **2** clever in an annoying way. *adj.,* **cut·er, cut·est.**

cu·ti·cle (kyū′tə kəl) the skin around the base of a fingernail or toenail. *n.*

cut·lass (kut′ləs) a short, heavy, slightly curved sword. *n.*

cut·ler·y (kut′lə rē) knives, forks, and spoons for table use. *n.*

cut·let (kut′lit) a slice of meat for broiling or frying: *a veal cutlet.* *n.*

cut·off (kut′of′) **1** an exit on a highway. **2 cutoffs,** *pl.* shorts made by cutting off the legs of pants.

cut·out (kut′out′) a shape or design to be cut out: *Some books for children have cutouts.* *n.*

cut·ter (kut′ər) **1** a person, tool, or machine that cuts. **2** a small horse-drawn sleigh. **3** a small sailboat with one mast. *n.*

cut·ting (kut′ing) **1** a small shoot cut from a plant to grow a new plant. **2** an article cut from a newspaper. **3** sharp; painful; stinging: *a cutting remark, a cutting wind.* **4** a way cut through a hill: *a railway cutting.* 1, 2, 4 *n.,* 3 *adj.*

cut–up (kut′up′) *Slang.* a person who shows off or plays tricks. *n.*

cy·ber·bul·ly (sī′bər bŭ′lē) a person who harasses someone by e-mail, text messaging, or other electronic means of communication. *n., pl.* **cy·ber·bul·lies.**

cy·ber·space (sī′bər spās′) computer networks, especially the Internet, thought of as a "place" where information, sounds, pictures, etc. exist apart from any particular computer. Cyberspace is not an actual place. *n.*

Word Family.......... cyber-

Words beginning with **cyber** all have to do with computers or the Internet.
cyberart: art created by computers on the Internet
cybernetics: the study of comparing living systems with machine systems
cyborg: short for **cyb**ernetic **org**anism, a creature that is part living and part mechanical

cy·cle (sī′kəl) **1** any process or action that keeps repeating itself in the same order, like the seasons of the year. **2** a complete set or series: *She went through a whole cycle of auditions to get the part.* **3** all the stories or legends told about a certain hero or event: *The Arthurian cycle relates the adventures of King Arthur and his knights.* **4** ride a bicycle. 1–3 *n.,* 4 *v.,* **cy·cled, cy·cling.** **—cy′clist,** *n.*

cy·clone (sī′klōn) a severe windstorm caused when winds move in a spiral toward a centre of low air pressure. Hurricanes and typhoons are cyclones. *n.*

cyl·in·der (sil′ən dər) **1** a hollow or solid body shaped like a roller or tube. **2** a tubelike part in an engine. The piston is pushed up and down inside it by little explosions, making other parts move that are attached to the end of it. *n.* **—cy·lin′dri·cal** (sə lin′drə kəl), *adj.*

cym·bal (sim′bəl) one of a pair of brass plates that you strike together to make a ringing sound. A cymbal can also be struck with a drumstick, hammer, or wire brush. *n.*

cyn·ic (sin′ik) somebody who thinks that people behave the way they do only for selfish reasons, even when they do good things. *n.* —**cyn′i·cal,** *adj.* —**cyn′i·cism,** *n.*

Different varieties of cypress trees grow in North America, Europe, and Asia, but none are native to Canada.

cy·press (sī′prəs) an evergreen tree or shrub with hard wood and small scaly leaves. There are many varieties of cypress. *n.*

cyst (sist) a baglike growth in an animal or plant, usually with fluid in it and no outside opening. Cysts often occur on a person's skin when an oil gland becomes blocked. *n.*

cy·to·plasm (sī′tō plaz′əm) the living matter around the nucleus of a plant or animal cell. *n.*

czar (zȧr) a Russian emperor. Tsar is another spelling. *n.*

cza·ri·na (zȧ rē′nə) a Russian empress or the wife of a Russian emperor. Tsarina is another spelling. *n.*

Dd

d or **D** (dē) 1 the fourth letter of the English alphabet, or the speech sound that it stands for. The sound of *d* is heard in *day* and *hard.* 2 the fourth thing in a list. 3 in music: **a** a note. On a keyboard it is the white note between C and E. **b** a scale or key that has D as its home note. 4 the Roman numeral for 500. *n., pl.* **d's** or **D's.**

dab (dab) 1 put something on, or wipe it off, with quick, light touches: *I dabbed some lotion on the burn. He dabbed at the smudged mirror with a cloth.* 2 a small blob: *dabs of butter, a dab of paint.* 1 *v.,* **dabbed, dab·bing;** 2 *n.*

The two main types of duck are dabbling ducks and diving ducks. Dabbling ducks feed on the surface of the water, and diving ducks go underwater for food. These shoveller ducks are dabblers.

dab·ble (dab′əl) 1 put in and out of water; splash: *We dabbled our feet in the pool.* 2 do only as a hobby, not in a very serious way: *to dabble at painting, to dabble in politics.* *v.,* **dab·bled, dab·bling.**

dad·dy (dad′ē) *Informal.* father. **Dad** is a shorter form. *n., pl.* **dad·dies.**

dad·dy–long·legs (dad′ē long′legz′) a small spiderlike creature with eight very long, thin bent legs. *n., pl.* **dad·dy-long·legs.**

daf·fo·dil (daf′ə dil′) a plant with long, slender leaves and yellow or white trumpet-shaped flowers that bloom in spring. Daffodils are grown from bulbs. *n.*

daft (daft) silly; crazy: *Go out in this blizzard? Don't be daft!* *adj.*

dag·ger (dag′ər) a small knife with a short pointed blade. *n.*

dahl (dȧl) split dried lentils, cooked with spices and eaten with rice and curry. Lentils are a little like small peas or beans and can be yellow, orange, or brown. *n.*

dai·ly (dā′lē) 1 lasting or covering a day: *a daily supply.* 2 coming or happening once a day: *a daily visit* (*adj.*). *Her strength is increasing daily* (*adv.*). 3 a newspaper printed every day. 1, 2 *adj.,* 2 *adv.,* 3 *n., pl.* **dai·lies;** 3 *adv.*

dain·ty (dān′tē) 1 small, delicate, and pretty: *The violet is a dainty spring flower.* 2 overly fussy, elegant, or fine in manners or tastes: *He took dainty sips of his mineral water.* 3 good to eat; delicious: *dainty morsels.* 4 a fancy treat: *chocolate truffles and other dainties.* 1–3 *adj.,* **dain·ti·er, dain·ti·est;** 4 *n., pl.* **dain·ties.** **—dain′ti·ly,** *adv.*

dair·y (der′ē) 1 a place where milk and cream are made into butter and cheese. 2 a place where milk and milk products are sold. 3 having to do with milk, butter, cheese, etc.: *dairy products. A dairy farmer raises milk cows.* 1, 2 *n., pl.* **dair·ies;** 3 *adj.*

da·is (dā′is) a raised platform at the end of a hall or large room: *The king's throne stood on a dais.* *n.*

dai·sy (dā′zē) a plant that has flowers with a yellow centre and many white or pink raylike petals. *n., pl.* **dai·sies.**

Dakota (də kō′tə) 1 a First Nations people living in the southern Prairies, also called the **Sioux.** 2 their language, which belongs to the Siouan family. 3 having to do with these people or their language. 1, 2 *n.,* 3 *adj.*

dale (dāl) an old or poetic word for "valley." *n.*

dal·ly (dal′ē) 1 play or toy with: *He dallied with the idea of going to Dimitri's place, but finally decided to stay home.* 2 dawdle; waste time: *She was late because she dallied along the way.* *v.,* **dal·lied, dal·ly·ing.**

dam (dam) 1 a wall built to hold back the water of a stream, creek, river, etc. 2 hold back by building a dam: *Beavers had dammed the stream.* 1, 2 *n.,* 3 *v.,* **dammed, dam·ming.**

dam·age (dam′ij) 1 injury or harm that makes something less beautiful or useful: *The accident did very little damage to the car.* 2 injure or harm in this way; break or hurt: *I damaged my thumb when I hit it with the hammer.* 3 **damages,** *pl.* money paid by law to make up for some harm done to a person or to his or her property: *The other driver asked for $5000 damages.* 1, 3 *n.,* 2 *v.,* **dam·aged, dam·ag·ing.**

damn (dam) 1 say that something is extremely bad;

condemn: *The new movie was damned by the reviewers.* **2** curse or send to hell. **3** prove the guilt of a person: *damning evidence.* *v.*

damp (damp) **1** slightly wet; moist: *This house is damp in rainy weather.* **2** moisture: *I felt the damp in the night air.* **3** allow less air to flow through a fire, so it dies down a little. Fireplaces have an adjustable plate for this, called a **damper.** **4** a poisonous, explosive gas in mines. 1 *adj.,* 2, 4 *n.,* 3 *v.* **—damp′ness,** *n.*

damp·en (dam′pən) **1** make moist or slightly wet: *I dampened the cloth to wipe the table.* **2** cast a gloom over; depress; discourage: *The bad news dampened our spirits.* To **put a damper on** means the same thing. *v.*

dam·sel (dam′zəl) an old or poetic word for "maiden" or "young girl." *n.*

dance (dans) **1** move in time with music: *They can dance very well.* **2** the art of moving in time with music. **3** a special set of steps for dancing: *The waltz is a well-known dance.* **4** a party where people dance. **5** one round of dancing: *May I have the next dance?* **6** jump up and down; move in a lively or graceful way: *See that boat dancing on the water.* **7** cause to dance; lead by dancing: *He danced his partner across the ballroom floor.* 1, 6, 7 *v.,* **danced, danc·ing;** 2–5 *n.* **—danc′er,** *n.*

Young dandelion leaves are good to eat, in salads.

dan·de·lion (dan′dē lī′ən) a very common weed with bright yellow flowers that look like pompoms. *n.*

dan·druff (dan′drəf) small flakes of dead skin that come off the scalp. *n.*

dan·dy (dan′dē) **1** *Informal.* excellent; first-rate: *Everything is just dandy.* **2** *Informal.* anything very good or special in some way: *That last question was a dandy!* **3** a man who is very fussy about his appearance. 2, 3 *n., pl.* **dan·dies;** 1 *adj.*

dan·ger (dān′jər) **1** a chance of harm; risk: *A mountain climber's life is full of danger.* **2** anything that may cause harm: *Hidden rocks are a danger to ships.* *n.* **—dan′ger·ous,** *adj.*
in danger of, likely to do or have: *The old bridge is in danger of collapsing. The sick woman is in danger of dying.*

dan·gle (dang′gəl) hang and swing loosely: *The curtain cord dangles. The boy dangled the toy in front of his baby sister.* *v.,* **dan·gled, dan·gling.**

dank (dangk) damp and musty: *The cave was dark, dank, and chilly.* *adj.*

dap·per (dap′ər) neat and trim; smartly dressed. *adj.*

dap·pled (dap′əld) spotted: *a dappled horse.* *adj.*

dare (der) **1** be bold enough to do or face something risky: *I wouldn't dare dive from the high board. The explorer dared the perils of the Barren Ground.* **2** challenge: *I dare you to jump* (*v.*). *I took his dare and jumped* (*n.*). Someone who is reckless enough to take almost any dare is a **daredevil.** 1, 2 *v.,* **dared, dar·ing;** 2 *n.*
I dare say, probably: *I dare say she's heard it all before.*

dar·ing (der′ing) **1** boldness; the courage to take risks. **2** bold; fearless. 1 *n.,* 2 *adj.*

dark (dȧrk) **1** without much light: *a dark, moonless night. It turned out to be a dark, cloudy day.* **2** close to black in colour: *dark eyes.* **3** nightfall: *He can't stay out after dark.* **4** sad or bad: *We have come through some dark times.* **5** darkness: *She's not afraid of the dark.* **6** hidden; secret: *a dark plot.* 1, 2, 4, 6 *adj.,* 3, 5 *n.* **—dark′ly,** *adv.* **—dark′ness,** *n.* **—dark′en,** *v.*
in the dark, without information.

dar·ling (dȧr′ling) **1** a very dear person; someone much loved. **2** very dear; much loved. 1 *n.,* 2 *adj.*

darn[1] (dȧrn) mend by weaving rows of thread or yarn across a hole, using a large needle. *v.*

darn[2] (dȧrn) *Informal.* a word used to express annoyance, anger, surprise, etc.: *Darn! The window's frozen shut* (*interj.*). *How do you use this darn thing* (*adj.*)? *Don't drive so darn fast* (*adv.*). *interj., adj., adv., or n.*

dart (dȧrt) **1** a small pointed weapon for throwing or shooting. **2** **darts,** *pl.* a game where you throw small darts at a round board that has two small rings in the centre, with twenty numbered sections arranged like pizza slices around them. **3** move or send suddenly and quickly: *I darted a warning glance at him. The deer saw us and darted away.* **4** a tapered seam designed to make a garment fit better. 1, 2, 4 *n.,* 3 *v.*

a bat	e bed	i bid	o pot	u cup	th thin
ā cake	ē me	ī bite	ō go	ü rude	ᴛʜ then
ȧ bar	ə about	ər over	ȯ for	u̇ put	zh measure

dash (dash) **1** rush: *They dashed by in a hurry* (*v.*). *We made a dash for safety* (*n.*). **2** a short race: *the 50-m dash.* **3** a mark (—) used in writing to show a break in thought or to stand for missing letters or words. ▶ See the *Grammar and Usage Mini-Guide.* **4** smash: *He dashed the bowl to bits on a rock. Our hopes were dashed.* **5** splash: *The artist dashed some green paint on the canvas to represent a distant forest.* **6** a small amount: *Put in just a dash of pepper.* **7** energy; spirit; liveliness: *She certainly has a lot of dash.* 1, 4, 5 *v.*, 2, 3, 6, 7 *n.*
dash off, do, make, write, etc. quickly: *Mauro dashed off an e-mail to his friend.*

dash•board (dash′bȯrd′) a panel with controls, gauges, radio, etc. below the front window inside a car or other vehicle. *n.*

dash•ing (dash′ing) **1** full of energy and spirit; lively. **2** smart-looking; handsome: *The soldiers wore dashing uniforms.* *adj.*

da•ta (dā′tə *or* dat′ə) information: *She is gathering data on Emily Carr for her essay on Canadian painting.* *n.*

USING WORDS .... data

In general everyday English, the word **data** is usually treated as a singular noun: *The data we collected is in this notebook.*

In formal English, the word **data** is treated as plural: *Analyse the data that have been collected.*

da•ta•base (dā′tə bās′ *or* dat′ə bās′) a large amount of information stored in a computer program that lets you arrange it in different ways and easily find what you want. **Data base** is another spelling. *n.*

date¹ (dāt) **1** the day, month, or year when something happens or is made: *The date of their wedding was September 30, 1980.* **2** mark the date on: *Please date your letter.* **3** find out the date of: *The scientist was unable to date the fossil.* **4** an appointment for a certain time. **5** go out with someone who is, or may become, a boyfriend or girlfriend. **6** the person that someone like this goes out with: *Who is your date for the school dance?* 1, 4, 6 *n.*, 2, 3, 5 *v.*, **dat•ed, dat•ing.**
bring up to date, provide with the newest information: *The bank teller brought my account book up to date. Bring us up to date on your family's news.*
date from, belong to a certain period of time: *This old house dates from the 1780s.*
date yourself, show how old you must be by your words, actions, etc.
out of date, out of style; old-fashioned: *That dress looks out of date.* **Dated** means the same thing.
to date, up to the present time: *There have been no replies to date.*
up to date, a modern; in style. **b** based on or giving the newest information: *Is this report up to date?* The spelling before a noun is **up-to-date.**

Grammar✓Check .... date

A date can be written in different ways.

- You put a comma between the day, the day of the month, and the year: I was born on Wednesday, August 17, 1994.
- You put a comma between the day of the month and the year: My sister was born on February 4, 2003.
- You don't put a comma in dates like June 2003 or 30 June 2003.
- When you write a date using just numbers, the correct Canadian style is Year-Month-Day. So 30 June 2003 would be written 03-06-30.
- Dates that show on computers are often done in the U.S. style, as Month/Day/Year. So 30 June 2003 would show as 06/30/03.

date² (dāt) the sweet fruit of a kind of palm tree. *n.*

daub (dob) **1** smear something on, thickly or in blobs. **2** a smear or sticky blob of something: *daubs of paint.* 1 *v.*, 2 *n.*

daugh•ter (dot′ər) **1** a girl or woman in relation to either or both of her parents. **2** a girl or woman thought of as coming from a particular place or time or influenced by some force: *a daughter of France, a daughter of the '60s.* **3** a result of something thought of as a person: *Dishonesty is the daughter of fear.* *n.*

daugh•ter–in–law (dot′ə rin lo′) the wife of a person's son. *n., pl.* **daugh•ters-in-law.**

daunt (dont) frighten; discourage: *Danger did not daunt the journalist.* A **dauntless** person is not easily frightened. *v.*

daw•dle (dod′əl) waste time: *Don't dawdle over your work.* *v.*, **daw•dled, daw•dling.**

dawn (don) **1** the beginning of day; the first light in the eastern sky. **2** the beginning: *before the dawn of history.* **3** begin; appear: *The day dawned bright and clear. A new era of peace is dawning.* 1, 2 *n.*, 3 *v.*
dawn on someone, finally become clear to a person: *It dawned on me that this was not Art, but Art's brother.*

Day, Month, and Year

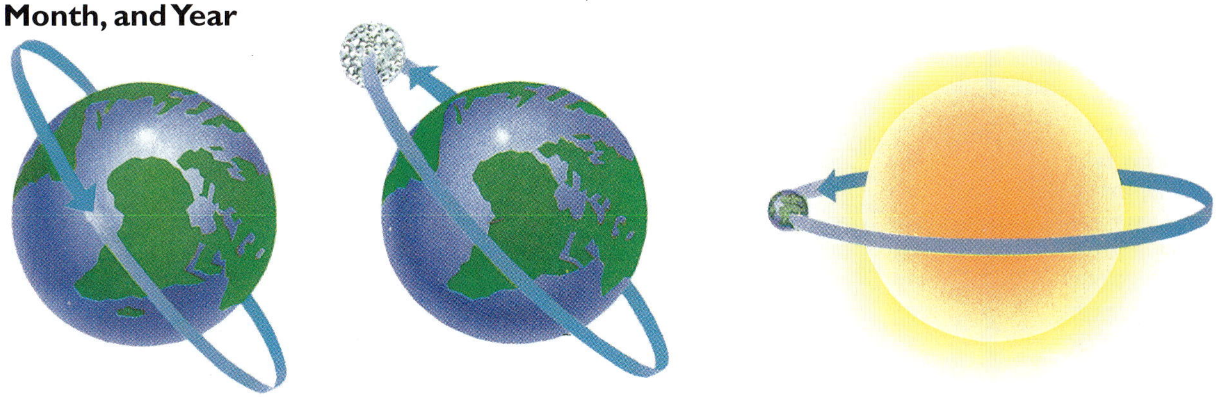

In one day (24 hours) the earth spins once.

In one lunar month (28 days) the moon travels once around the earth.

In one solar year (365.25 days) the earth travels once around the sun.

day (dā) **1** the time of light between sunrise and sunset: *Owls sleep during the day.* **Daytime** means the same thing. **2** the 24 hours that the earth takes to turn on its axis. **3** the part of the day spent working, in school, travelling, etc. rather than relaxing: *She works an eight-hour day. Wednesday is a long day for me.* **4** a period of history: *the present day, in days of old.* *n.*
call it a day, *Informal.* stop work: *I'm tired; let's call it a day.*
win the day, be the winner: *The debate is over; our side has won the day.*

day·break (dā′brāk′) the first light of day. *n.*

day care (dā ′ker′) the care of babies and preschool children outside the home during the day: *Parents want reliable day care.* *n.* —**day′-care′,** *adj.*

day·dream (dā′drēm′) **1** think for a long time about things that are nice but not practical: *He spent a whole hour just daydreaming.* **2** a spell of doing this. 1 *v.,* 2 *n.*

day·light (dā′līt′) **1** the light of day: *Artificial light is not as good for the eyes as daylight.* **2** dawn; daybreak: *We were up at daylight.* *n.*

daylight–saving time (dā′līt sā′ving tīm′) time that is one hour ahead of standard time, giving more daylight in summer evenings. Clocks are set ahead one hour in the spring and back one hour in the fall. Two o'clock daylight-saving time is one o'clock standard time.

daze (dāz) **1** confuse; bewilder: *The child was dazed by the sudden noise and bright lights.* **2** a confused state of mind; bewilderment: *He was wandering around in a daze after the accident.* 1 *v.,* **dazed, daz·ing;** 2 *n.*

daz·zle (daz′əl) **1** hurt the eyes with too bright a light, or bewilder with quick-moving lights: *To look straight at the sun dazzles the eyes.* **2** overwhelm with skill, beauty, etc.: *The pianist's performance dazzled the audience.* **3** a painful or bewildering brightness: *the dazzle of car headlights.* 1, 2 *v.,* **daz·zled, daz·zling;** 3 *n.*

DC, D.C., or **d.c.** *abbreviation for* direct current, the kind of electrical current produced by batteries.

DDT an odourless, powerful poison for killing insects. It can no longer be used for this in Canada because it is harmful to people and to the environment.

de– *a prefix meaning:* **1** the opposite or reverse of. *Decode* means "do the opposite of coding." **2** down. *Depress* means "press down." **3** away, off. *Derail* means "cause to go off the rails."

Word Family.......... de-

The prefix **de** can be used to show the opposite of a verb. Here are some examples.

deactivate: switch off, stop
de-ice: remove the ice
deforest: cut down the trees

dead (ded) **1** no longer alive: *The flowers in my garden are dead.* **2** without human, animal, or plant life: *a dead planet.* **3** without force, power, spirit, feeling, activity, etc.: *This old battery is dead. Without Mr. Malik the school seemed kind of dead.* **4** complete or perfect: *dead silence, a dead certainty.* **5** completely: *You were dead wrong that time.* **6** directly; straight: *Walk dead ahead.* **7** the time when there is the least life stirring: *the dead of night.* 1–4 *adj.,* 5, 6 *adv.,* 7 *n.*
dead to something, not aware of something or not interested in it.
dead to the world, fast asleep.

a bat	e bed	i bid	o pot	u cup	th thin
ā cake	ē me	ī bite	ō go	ū rude	ᴛʜ then
à bar	ə about	ər over	ȯ for	u̇ put	zh measure

Word Family........... dead

deadbeat: a lazy person
deadbolt: a lock that can only be opened with a key
deadline: the latest possible time to do something
deadpan: with no expression on one's face
deadwood: useless people or things

dead•en (ded′ən) lessen the force or sharpness of: *Some medicines are given to deaden pain. Thick walls deadened the sound.* *v.*

dead end (ded′ end′) **1** a street or passage closed at one end so that there is only one way in or out. **2** a point in a discussion, plan, etc. where no more progress can be made: *This idea is a dead end; let's try something else.*

dead•lock (ded′lok′) **1** a position of being unable to act or continue because of disagreement: *The employers and strikers were at a deadlock.* **2** bring or come to such a position: *The talks were deadlocked for weeks.* 1 *n.*, 2 *v.*

dead•ly (ded′lē) **1** causing or likely to cause death: *a deadly disease, deadly poison.* **2** like death: *deadly paleness.* **3** lasting till death: *deadly enemies, a deadly hatred.* *adj.*, **dead•li•er, dead•li•est.**

deaf (def) not able to hear. *adj.* **—deaf′en,** *v.* **—deaf′ness,** *n.*
be deaf to or **turn a deaf ear to,** ignore; not respond to: *They were deaf to our cries for help.*

deal (dēl) **1 deal with,** **a** have to do: *Arithmetic deals with numbers.* **b** take care of; settle: *I'll let you deal with this.* **c** cope with; bear: *I can't deal with so much stress.* **2** act: *Deal fairly with everyone.* People's **dealings** are their actions toward others. **3** carry on business; buy and sell: *This store deals in toys and games.* **4** *Informal.* a bargain: *We got a good deal on our new car.* **5** give: *She dealt the nail a hard blow with the hammer.* **6** give out; distribute: *In card games, one player deals the cards to the others.* **7** the act of giving out, or the thing given: *I lost the first round of cards because I got such a rotten deal.* 1–3, 5, 6 *v.*, **dealt, deal•ing;** 4, 7 *n.* **—deal′er,** *n.* **—deal′er•ship,** *n.*
a good deal or **great deal,** a lot: *A great deal of her money is spent on software.*
a square deal, fair and honest treatment.

dear (dēr) **1** much loved; precious: *His sister is very dear to him.* **2** a darling; someone who is much loved: *"Come here, my dear," she said.* **3** expensive; costing a lot: *Fresh fruit is dear in winter.* **4** an exclamation of surprise, trouble, etc.: *Oh, dear! I spilled it!* 1, 3 *adj.*, 2 *n.*, 4 *interj.* **—dear′ly,** *adv.*

dearth (dərth) shortage; lack: *There was a dearth of vegetables after the drought.* *n.*

death (deth) **1** the act of dying; the ending of life in human beings, animals, or plants: *She faced death with courage.* **2** any ending that is like dying: *the death of an empire.* *n.* **—death′less,** *adj.*
at death's door, about to die.
put to death, kill.
sign the death warrant of: cause or lead to the death of.
to death, **a** until dead: *to bleed to death.* **b** extremely: *bored to death.*
to the death, to the absolute end of your strength: *to fight to the death.*

death•ly (deth′lē) **1** like death or likely to cause death: *a deathly paleness* (*adj.*). **2** extreme; extremely: *deathly hot* (*adv.*). *adj.* or *adv.*

de•base (di bās′) **1** lessen the value of: *debased coinage.* **2** dishonour; lessen the dignity of: *You debase yourself by cowardly actions.* *v.*, **de•based, de•bas•ing.**

de•bate (di bāt′) **1** consider; think about reasons for and against: *I am debating getting my hair cut really short.* **2** argue or discuss both sides of a subject logically: *We debated whether to go or stay.* **3** a discussion of reasons for and against: *There was a debate about who should be captain.* 1, 2 *v.*, **de•bat•ed, de•bat•ing;** 3 *n.*

debit card (deb′it kärd′) a plastic card that lets you pay for things by directly subtracting the amount from your bank account when you slide it through a card reader in a store: *We used a debit card to buy the videos.*

de•bris (də brē′) scattered bits; rubbish: *The street was covered with debris from the explosion.* *n.*

debt (det) **1** something owed to another: *He used his allowance to pay his debt to Luisa.* A person who owes something is a **debtor.** **2** the condition of owing something to someone: *to get out of debt. She is in debt $2000 to the car dealer.* *n.*

de•bug (dē bug′) **1** find and remove mistakes, especially in a computer program. **2** find and remove hidden microphones in a room. *v.*, **de•bugged, de•bug•ging.**

deca– *an SI prefix meaning* ten; 10. A *decagram* is ten grams. The prefix **deca-** can also be used with other metric units, such as *metre* or *litre. Symbol:* da

dec•ade (dek′ād) a period of ten years. *n.*

de•can•ter (di kan′tər) a glass bottle with a stopper, used for serving wine or liquor. *n.*

de·cath·lon (di kath′lon) an athletic competition with ten running, jumping, and throwing events, won by the person with the highest total of points. A person who competes in the decathlon is a **decathlete.** *n.*

> **WORD HISTORY..... decathlon**
>
> The prefix *deca* means "ten" in Latin. So a **dec***athlon* is made up of ten events. A ***bi****athlon* has two events. How many events are in a ***pent****athlon*?

de·cay (di kā′) **1** become rotten; decompose: *The fallen apples began to decay.* **2** a rotting condition: *The decay in the tree trunk had not proceeded very far.* **3** a loss of strength, goodness, or beauty: *the decay of a civilization.* **4** lose strength, goodness, or beauty. **5** in a radioactive substance, the break-up of atoms as their nuclei send out particles and rays. As its atoms are changed, the substance actually turns gradually into other substances, one after another. The process ends with a substance that is no longer radioactive. Uranium, for example, eventually turns to lead. **6** go through this process. 1, 4, 6 *v.,* 2, 3, 5 *n.* **—dec′a·dent** (dek′ə dənt), *adj.*

de·cease (di sēs′) death: *His decease was sudden.* *n.* **—de·ceased′,** *adj.*

de·ceit (di sēt′) the act or habit of lying, pretending, or cheating; trickery; dishonesty. *n.* **—de·ceit′ful,** *adj.*

de·ceive (di sēv′) make someone believe something that is false; trick or mislead: *They got in trouble for trying to deceive the police.* *v.,* **de·ceived, de·ceiv·ing.**

De·cem·ber (di sem′bər) the twelfth and last month of the year. December has 31 days. *n.*

de·cent (dē′sənt) **1** proper and right: *a decent burial. The decent thing to do is apologize.* **2** not vulgar or obscene: *decent language.* **3** honest, good, sincere, etc.: *They are decent people.* **4** fairly good; adequate: *a decent wage. I get decent marks at school.* *adj.* **—de′cen·cy,** *n.*

de·cep·tion (di sep′shən) the act of deceiving; lies or trickery. *n.* **—de·cep′tive,** *adj.*

deci– *an SI prefix meaning* one-tenth; $^{1}/_{10}$. A *decimetre* is one-tenth of a metre. The prefix **deci-** can also be used with other metric units, such as *gram* or *litre. Symbol:* d

dec·i·bel (des′ə bel′) a unit for measuring the loudness of a sound. *n.*

de·cide (di sīd′) **1** make a choice; make up your mind: *He decided to be a nurse. Mother decided in favour of a small car.* **2** settle; cause one side or the other to win out: *decide the question by tossing a coin.* *v.,* **de·cid·ed, de·cid·ing.**

de·cid·ed (di sī′did) **1** definite; clear: *The home team had a decided advantage.* **2** making definite choices and sticking with them: *Sali was a very decided person.* *adj.* **—de·cid′ed·ly,** *adv.*

In cooler climates, broad-leaved trees are deciduous, shedding their leaves in the fall. A typical broad-leaved tree has spring flowers, which later develop into fruits. The leaves of deciduous trees have many shapes.

de·cid·u·ous (di sij′ū əs) **1** falling off at a particular season or stage of growth: *deciduous leaves, deciduous horns.* **2** shedding leaves at a certain time each year: *Maples, poplars, and most oaks are deciduous trees.* *adj.*

dec·i·mal (des′ə məl) **1** based on or having to do with the number 10: *The metric system is a decimal system of measurement.* **2** a numeral with a dot separating the ones column from the tenths column. The numeral $23^{6}/_{10}$ can be expressed as the decimal 23.6. **Decimal fraction** is another name for such a numeral. **3** the dot in such a numeral: *Put the decimal between the ones and the tenths.* This dot is also called the **decimal point.** 1 *adj.,* 2, 3 *n.*

de·ci·pher (di sī′fər) **1** manage to figure out something that is not clear: *I can't decipher this poor handwriting.* **2** decode; put into ordinary language: *The spy deciphered the secret message.* *v.*

a bat	e bed	i bid	o pot	u cup	th thin
ā cake	ē me	ī bite	ō go	ū rude	ᴛʜ then
ȧ bar	ə about	ər over	ȯ for	u̇ put	zh measure

de·ci·sion (di sizh′ən) 1 the act of deciding or choosing; making up your mind: *Too many choices make a decision difficult.* 2 what is chosen, or a statement telling what someone has decided: *They disagreed with our decision.* 3 firmness; determination: *She is a woman of decision; she makes up her mind what to do and then does it.* *n.*
make a decision, reach a decision, or **come to a decision,** decide.

de·ci·sive (di sī′siv) 1 having a clear result; settling something beyond question: *a decisive victory.* 2 showing firmness or determination: *a decisive answer.* *adj.*

CONFUSABLES .....decisive

decisive means "firm": *Our basketball team won a decisive victory.*
decided means "definite": *Her height gave her a decided advantage in basketball.*

deck (dek) 1 the floor on a ship. A ship can have decks at different levels, like the floors of a building. 2 a platform or floor like this: *a sun deck.* 3 a pack of playing cards. 4 decorate: *The room was decked with flowers.* 5 *Slang.* knock someone down. 1–3 *n.*, 4, 5 *v.*
clear the deck, prepare for action.
decked out, dressed up.
hit the deck, a drop to the ground. **b** prepare for action.
stack the deck, a arrange a pack of cards so as to cheat. **b** arrange things unfairly for or against someone.

de·clare (di kler′) 1 announce publicly or officially: *Parliament has declared a national holiday.* 2 say openly or strongly: *The boy declared that he was innocent.* 3 let government authorities know as required by law. Travellers returning to Canada must declare to the customs officers what they have bought abroad. Taxpayers have to declare their income every year. *v.*, **de·clared, de·clar·ing.** —**dec′la·ra′tion,** *n.*

de·cline (di klīn′) 1 refuse politely: *The man declined my offer of help. They invited her, but she declined to go.* 2 get lower, weaker, or worse: *With too little food, his strength had begun to decline. The number of school-age children in the neighbourhood is declining.* 3 a lowering or weakening of something: *the decline of the sun at dusk, a decline in prices.* 1, 2 *v.*, **de·clined, de·clin·ing;** 3 *n.*

de·code (dē kōd′) translate a coded message into ordinary language: *I sent Ari a secret in code, and he decoded it.* *v.*, **de·cod·ed, de·cod·ing.** —**de·cod′er,** *n.*

de·com·pose (dē′kəm pōz′) 1 decay; rot or become rotten: *Fruit decomposes quickly in hot weather.* 2 break down into a simpler arrangement of parts. A prism decomposes sunlight into a rainbow of colours. Radioactive substances decompose into non-radioactive ones over time. *v.*, **de·com·posed, de·com·pos·ing.** —**de′com·po·si′tion** (dē′kom pə si′shən), *n.*

de·com·pos·er (dē′kəm pō′zər) a very tiny organism that breaks down the cells of dead plants and animals into simpler parts. A decomposer may be a fungus or a bacterium. *n.*

dé·cor or **de·cor** (dā kôr′) the way a room or building is decorated: *Only the kitchen had modern décor.* *n.*

dec·o·rate (dek′ə rāt′) 1 add things to make beautiful: *We decorated the windows with coloured lights.* 2 paint or paper a room, house, etc. 3 give a badge, ribbon, or medal to as a reward for heroism: *The general decorated the soldier for his brave act.* *v.*, **dec·o·rat·ed, dec·o·rat·ing.** —**dec′o·ra′tion,** *n.* —**dec′o·ra·tive** (dek′ə rə tiv), *adj.*

dec·o·ra·tor (dek′ə rā′ tər) a person who decorates. An **interior decorator** plans and arranges the furnishings of homes, offices, and other buildings. *n.*

de·coy (dē′koi *for 1 and 2,* di koi′ *for 3*) 1 a bird or other animal, real or artificial, used to lure others into a trap or within shooting range. 2 any person or thing used to lure someone into danger. 3 act as a decoy; lure into danger by a trick. 1, 2 *n.*, 3 *v.*

de·crease (di krēs′ *for 1,* dē′krēs *for 2*) 1 make or become less: *to decrease prices. Hunger decreases as you eat.* 2 a lessening: *At night there is a decrease in temperature.* 1 *v.*, **de·creased, de·creas·ing;** 2 *n.*

de·cree (di krē′) 1 an official decision or order; law: *A government decree set the date of Thanksgiving Day.* 2 decide or order by authority: *The government decreed that the election would take place July 8.* 1 *n.*, 2 *v.*, **de·creed, de·cree·ing.**

de·crep·it (di krep′it) weak, worn out, or falling apart because of age: *Our old car was getting pretty decrepit.* *adj.* —**de·crep′i·tude′,** *n.*

ded·i·cate (ded′ə kāt′) 1 set apart or give over to some person or purpose: *These gardens are dedicated to the memory of Lucy Maud Montgomery. He dedicated his life to looking after the poor.* 2 address a book or other piece of work to someone as an honour to that person: *She dedicated her first novel to a teacher who had encouraged her to write.* *v.*, **ded·i·cat·ed, ded·i·cat·ing.**

Deer

There are more than 60 kinds of deer, living in many parts of the world, and in all climates. The largest deer is the moose (North America), which can grow to over 2 m tall and weigh over 800 kg. The smallest deer is the pudu (South America), which can grow to only 30 cm tall and weigh about 9 kg.

ded·i·ca·tion (ded′ə kā′shən) 1 the act of dedicating something, often with a ceremony; the words used to dedicate something. 2 whole-hearted interest, effort, or loyalty: *All his co-workers admired his dedication and team spirit.* *n.* **—ded′i·cat′ed,** *adj.*

de·duce (di dyūs′ *or* di dūs′) figure out by logic: *After looking at the evidence, the inspector deduced the cause of the fire.* *v.,* **de·duced, de·duc·ing.** **—de·duc′tion,** *n.* **—de·duc′tive,** *adj.*

de·duct (di dukt′) take away; subtract. *v.* **—de·duc′tion,** *n.* **—de·duct′i·ble,** *adj.*

deed (dēd) 1 an action, especially a remarkable one: *a brave deed, evil deeds.* 2 a paper that proves you are the owner of a property. 3 give property to someone by putting his or her name on the deed: *He deeded his house to his daughter.* 1, 2 *n.,* 3 *v.*

deem (dēm) think; believe; consider: *The captain deemed it unwise to sail in such weather.* *v.*

deep (dēp) 1 going far down, far back, or far in: *a deep well, a deep forest (adj.). They talked deep into the night. Dig deep (adv.).* 2 low: *a deep voice.* 3 needing or showing a lot of understanding: *Her poetry is very deep.* 4 strong; intense: *deep feelings, a deep sleep.* 5 **the deep,** the sea. 1–4 *adj.,* 1 *adv.,* 5 *n.* **—deep′ly,** *adv.* **—deep′en,** *v.*
deep down, in your heart: *He acts happy, but deep down he is sad.*
in deep, very involved in a risky or dangerous situation.

deep–fry (dēp′ frī′) fry something in enough oil to cover it. *v.,* **deep-fried, deep-fry·ing.**

deer (dēr) a wild, swift, cud-chewing animal with long, slender legs and small split hooves. The male has antlers. The elk, caribou, moose, reindeer, and white-tailed deer are all different kinds of deer. Leather made from the hide of a deer is **deerskin.** *n., pl.* **deer.**

a bat	e bed	i bid	o pot	u cup	th thin
ā cake	ē me	ī bite	ō go	ū rude	ᴛʜ then
à bar	ə about	ər over	ȯ for	u̇ put	zh measure

def. *abbreviation for* definition.

de•face (di fās′) spoil the appearance of: *Do not deface the desks by carving in them.* *v.,* **de•faced, de•fac•ing.** **—de•face′ment,** *n.*

default (di folt′) **1** something that happens automatically unless you do something to change it: *On the computer, saving files to the c:\ directory was the default.* **2** having to do with something automatic like this: *The default screen colour is blue; do you want to change it?* **3** do or go back to the automatic thing: *If you don't choose a colour, it defaults to blue.* **4** fail to do something you are supposed to: *When his business went bankrupt he defaulted on his loan.* 1 *n.,* 2 *adj.,* 3, 4 *v.*
win by default, win a game or contest because an opponent did not play.

de•feat (di fēt′) **1** beat; win a victory over: *to defeat the enemy in battle, to defeat another team in basketball.* **2** make useless; undo: *to defeat someone's plans.* **3** the act of defeating or of being defeated: *a crushing defeat.* 1, 2 *v.,* 3 *n.*

de•fect (dē′fekt *for 1,* di fekt′ *for 2*) **1** a flaw or fault; something wrong or imperfect: *This jacket was cheap because of a slight defect in one sleeve. A bad temper was his only character defect.* **2** leave your own country without permission in order to escape to one where there is more freedom. 1 *n.,* 2 *v.* **—de•fec′tive** (di fek′tiv), *adj.*

de•fence (di fens′ *for 1, 2, and 4,* dē′fens *for 3*) **1** the act of defending or protecting: *The armed forces are responsible for the defence of the country.* **2** anything that defends, guards, or protects: *The city wall was a defence against attack. Your best defence against their lies is the truth.* **3** in games, the group of players defending a goal: *Our hockey team has a good defence.* **4** in a court trial, the accused person (or **defendant**) together with his or her lawyer or lawyers: *a witness for the defence.* **Defense** is another spelling. *n.* **—de•fence′less,** *adj.*

de•fend (di fend′) **1** guard from attack or harm; protect. **2** speak up for someone or something being criticized: *The newspapers defended the mayor's action.* *v.* **—de•fend′er,** *n.* **—de•fen′si•ble,** *adj.*

de•fen•sive (di fen′siv) **1** defending; ready to defend; intended to defend: *A shield is a defensive weapon.* **2** the position or attitude of defence: *After two shots on our goal, the other team returned to the defensive.* 1 *adj.,* 2 *n.*
on the defensive, quick to defend or explain your actions, even when no one is accusing you: *They have been criticized so much that they are always on the defensive.*

de•fer[1] (di fər′) put off; postpone: *The test was deferred because so many students were sick.* *v.,* **de•ferred, de•fer•ring.** **—de•fer′ment,** *n.*

de•fer[2] (di fər′) politely give in to someone else: *She deferred to her sister's wishes.* When you do this, you show **deference** (def′ə rəns). *v.,* **de•ferred, de•fer•ring.**

de•fi•ant (di fī′ənt) openly refusing to obey; challenging authority: *The angry prisoners shouted a defiant answer to the guard.* *adj.* **—de•fi′ance,** *n.*

de•fi•cient (di fish′ənt) weak or lacking; not enough, or not good enough: *Their diet was deficient in vitamin C.* *adj.* **—de•fi′cien•cy,** *n.*

de•fine (di fīn′) **1** explain the meaning of: *A dictionary defines words.* **2** describe in detail, so as to set the limits of: *Together we came up with a set of rules to define proper classroom behaviour.* **3** make something what it is: *Your life is defined by the choices you make.* **4** cause to stand out by contrast: *The city's skyline was clearly defined against the prairie sky.* *v.,* **de•fined, de•fin•ing.**

def•i•nite (def′ə nit) **1** clear and firm; positive: *a definite answer. She was very definite about the time of the accident. Is it definite that we are going?* **2** exactly stated or defined; specific: *a definite area, a definite number of players.* *adj.* **—def′i•nite•ly,** *adv.*

definite article (def′ə nit är′tə kəl) the word **the.**

def•i•ni•tion (def′ə nish′ən) **1** an explanation of the meaning: *I looked up the definition of "taut" in the dictionary.* **2** clarity; distinctness; exactness: *This photo is blurry; it lacks definition.* *n.*

de•flate (di flāt′) **1** let the air or gas out of something: *Vlad deflated the balloon.* **2** take away someone's confidence or pride: *Sarah felt deflated after losing the match.* **3** change the rules for buying and selling in a country so that prices fall: *The government deflated the currency.* *v.,* **de•flat•ed, de•flat•ing.** **—de•fla′tion** (di flā′shən).

de•flect (di flekt′) turn aside in a different direction: *The ball popped out of the catcher's glove and was deflected into the stands.* *v.*

de•fog (dē fog′) clear the mist from a window, lens, mirror, etc. *v.,* **de•fogged, de•fog•ging.** **—de•fog′ger,** *n.*

de•form (di fôrm′) give an abnormal form or shape to: *Shoes that are too tight deform the feet.* *v.* **—de•form′i•ty,** *n.*

de•fraud (di frod′) cheat; take money, rights, etc. away from by trickery: *The fake company defrauded its customers of all their savings.* *v.*

deft (deft) skilful; nimble; moving quickly and expertly: *A violinist's fingers must be deft.* *adj.*

de·fy (di fī′) 1 refuse to obey or submit to; resist boldly: *If you defy the law, you must take the consequences.* 2 be too hard, strong, great, etc. for: *some feelings defy explanation.* 3 dare: *The Arctic explorers defied the extreme cold in order to reach their goal.* *v.*, **de·fied, de·fy·ing.**

de·gen·er·ate (di jen′ə rāt′ *for 1,* di jen′ə rit *for 2 and 3*) 1 become bad or worse: *After the sick girl was in bed for a week, her condition suddenly degenerated.* 2 bad: *a degenerate criminal.* 3 someone who has become bad: *We joked that Mandy was a degenerate because she hardly ever did her homework.* 1 *v.*, **de·gen·er·at·ed, de·gen·er·at·ing;** 2 *adj.*, 3 *n.*

de·grade (di grād′) 1 rob of dignity; dishonour; humiliate: *Such cruel treatment degrades people.* 2 lower the value of: *Any bruises will degrade the apple crop.* *v.*, **de·grad·ed, de·grad·ing.**
—deg′ra·da′tion (deg′rə dā′shən), *adj.*

de·gree (di grē′) 1 a step in a scale; a stage in a process: *The colour changed by degrees from light blue to dark purple.* 2 the amount or extent: *Her interest depends on the degree of risk—the riskier, the better!* 3 a unit for measuring temperature. *Symbol:* ° 4 a unit for measuring an angle or an arc of a circle. *Symbol:* ° 5 rank: *A princess is a lady of high degree.* 6 a title given to a student by a university or college for successfully completing a certain course of studies: *a Bachelor of Arts degree, a Master of Science degree.* *n.*

WORD HISTORY..... degrees Celsius

Canada uses the Celsius scale for temperature. This scale was named after Anders Celsius (1701-1744), a Swedish astronomer, who invented it. It is sometimes referred to as the **centigrade** scale, from the Latin *centum* "a hundred" + *gradus* "degree."

de·hy·drate (dē hī′drāt) lose or take away water or moisture; dry out: *Milk can be dehydrated to form a powder. We get thirsty in hot weather because our bodies dehydrate when we sweat.* *v.*, **de·hy·drat·ed, de·hy·drat·ing.** **—de′hy·dra′tion,** *n.*

deign (dān) stoop so low as; be so humble as: *Those snobs would never deign to speak to us.* *v.*

de·i·ty (dē′ə tē) 1 a god or goddess: *Jupiter was the chief of the ancient Roman deities.* 2 the state or fact of being a god or goddess: *The ancient Egyptians believed in the deity of their rulers.* *n., pl.* **de·i·ties.**

de·ject·ed (di jek′tid) sad; discouraged: *The defeated runner wore a dejected frown.* *adj.*

deke (dēk) *Slang.* in hockey: 1 draw a player out of position by faking a play. 2 a play made in this way. 1 *v.*, **deked, dek·ing;** 2 *n.*

WORD HISTORY....... deke

Deke is short for *decoy*. Deking in hockey is similar to what a decoy does to other animals: it tricks them into going to the wrong place at the wrong time!

de·lay (di lā′) 1 put something off till later: *They had to delay the party for a week.* 2 be late or make late because of a stop or slowdown on the way: *The storm delayed the bus for two hours.* 3 the act of delaying; a stopping or waiting: *We can afford no further delay.* 1, 2 *v.*, 3 *n.*

de·lec·ta·ble (di lek′tə bəl) very delicious: *We had a delectable sundae after the movie.* *adj.*

del·e·gate (del′ə git *for 1,* del′ə gāt′ *for 2 and 3*) 1 a person chosen to act for a group; a representative: *Each country sent two delegates to the trade conference.* A group of delegates is a **delegation.** 2 choose or send a person to act for others: *The class delegated Stan to buy the flowers.* 3 give up a task, right, or responsibility to someone else: *The provinces have delegated some of their rights to the federal government.* 1 *n.*, 2, 3 *v.*, **del·e·gat·ed, del·e·gat·ing.**

de·lete (di lēt′) erase or take out anything written, printed, filmed, or recorded: *He deleted the last sentence from his composition. Do not delete any of the files on this disk.* *v.*, **de·let·ed, de·let·ing.** **—de·le′tion,** *n.*

deli (del′ē) a place where different kinds of cheese, cold meats, and salads are sold: *We stopped at the deli to pick up some potato salad.* **Delicatessen** (del′ə kə tes′ən) is the full name for it. *n., pl.* **del·is.**

de·lib·er·ate (di lib′ə rit *for 1 and 2,* di lib′ə rāt′ *for 3*) 1 intended; done on purpose; thought over beforehand: *That excuse was a deliberate lie.* 2 slow, careful, and with firm purpose: *The fashion show model walked with deliberate steps.* 3 think over or discuss carefully; consider: *Parliament was deliberating the question of raising taxes.* 1, 2 *adj.*, 3 *v.*, **de·lib·er·at·ed, de·lib·er·at·ing.** **—de·lib′er·ate·ly,** *adv.* **—de·lib′er·a′tion,** *n.*

a bat	e bed	i bid	o pot	u cup	th thin
ā cake	ē me	ī bite	ō go	ū rude	ᴛʜ then
ä bar	ə about	ər over	ô for	ů put	zh measure

del•i•ca•cy (del′ə kə sē) 1 a food that is considered a special treat: *Your home-made pecan cookies are a real delicacy.* 2 the fact of being delicate. *n., pl.* **del•i•ca•cies.**

del•i•cate (del′ə kit) 1 gentle; graceful; mild; soft: *delicate movements, delicate colours, delicate fragrance.* 2 easily hurt or broken; not tough: *A spider's web is very delicate. Frank is a delicate child.* 3 needing or showing care, skill, or tact: *a delicate situation, delicate handling.* 4 finely tuned; sensitive: *delicate instruments, a delicate sense of smell. adj.*

del•i•ca•tes•sen (del′ə kə tes′ən) a store that sells sausages, cold meats, smoked fish, cheeses, salads, pickles, etc., often imported ones. *n.*

WORD HISTORY..... delicatessen

This word is taken straight from the German *delikatessen*, meaning "delicacies." We think of "deli" food as being different from regular food.

de•li•cious (di lish′əs) very pleasing or satisfying; delightful, especially to taste or smell: *a delicious cake, the delicious warmth of the fire. adj.* **—de•li′cious•ly,** *adv.*

de•light (di līt′) 1 great pleasure; joy: *She took great delight in trying new things.* 2 something that gives great pleasure: *Dancing is his delight.* 3 please greatly: *The music delighted the audience.* 4 find great pleasure: *Children delight in surprises.* 1, 2 *n.,* 3, 4 *v.* **—de•light′ed,** *adj.* **—de•light′ful,** *adv.*

de•lin•quent (di ling′kwənt) 1 not doing what is required by law or duty, especially as a habit. 2 a person who is like this; offender; criminal. 1 *adj.,* 2 *n.* **—de•lin′quen•cy,** *n.*

de•lir•i•ous (di lir′ē əs) out of your senses for a short time; raving: *delirious with excitement. The fever had made him delirious. adj.* **—de•lir′i•um,** *n.*

de•liv•er (di liv′ər) 1 carry something to the proper place or person: *Moina delivers newspapers every morning.* 2 give; present or produce: *to deliver a speech. These trees deliver 60 L of maple syrup.* 3 strike; throw: *The fighter delivered a hard blow.* 4 give birth to or help in the birth of: *The doctor delivered the baby at noon.* 5 set free; save from evil or trouble: *They were delivered from slavery.* The noun that goes with this meaning is **deliverance;** for meanings 1 to 4, the noun is **delivery.** *v.* **—de•liv′er•er,** *n.*

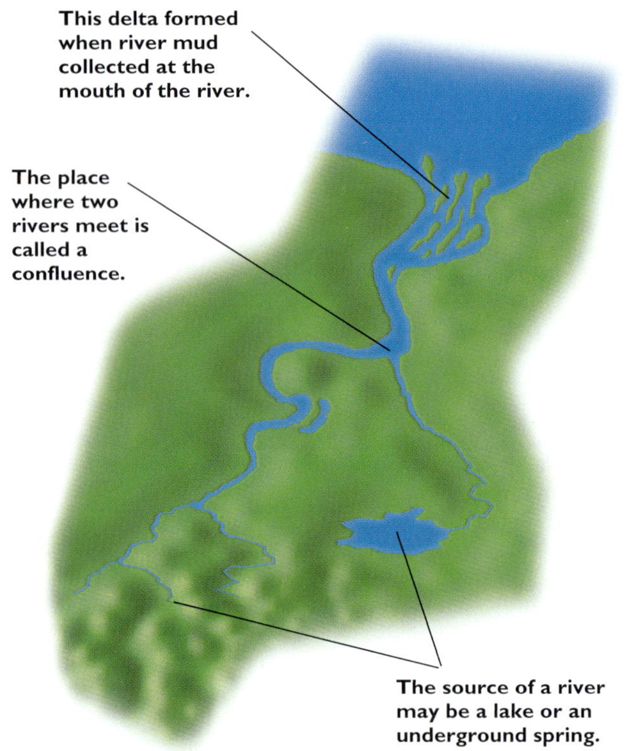

del•ta (del′tə) the deposit of earth and sand that collects at the mouth of some rivers. It is usually shaped like a triangle, with little branches of the river flowing out toward the triangle's wide end. Part of Vancouver is on the delta of the Fraser River. *n.*

de•lude (di lūd′) mislead; deceive: *If he thinks he can get out of the job, he's deluding himself! v.,* **de•lud•ed, de•lud•ing. —de•lu′sion,** *n.*

del•uge (del′yūj) 1 a heavy fall of rain, a great flood, or anything thought of as a flood: *The deluge washed away the bridge. Most stores have a deluge of orders in December.* 2 to flood: *Water deluged our cellar when the big pipe broke. The movie star was deluged with requests for her autograph.* 1 *n.,* 2 *v.,* **del•uged, del•ug•ing.**

de•luxe or **de luxe** (də luks′) of top quality; with all the best features. *adj.*

de•mand (di mand′) 1 ask for as a right; ask for firmly and expect to get: *The prisoner demanded a trial. The police officer demanded to see Dad's licence.* 2 call for; require; need: *Training a puppy demands patience.* 3 a claim or request that cannot be ignored; a need: *Their mother had many demands on her time. The supply of apples was greater than the demand.* 1, 2 *v.,* 3 *n.*
in demand, wanted or needed: *Computer skills are very much in demand.*

de•mand•ing (di man′ding) tough; requiring a lot of effort, skill, patience, etc.: *a demanding boss. The job was a demanding one, but it was interesting.* *adj.*

de•mean•our or **de•mean•or** (di mē′nər) behaviour; manner; the way a person acts and looks: *He has a quiet, modest demeanour.* *n.*

de•mer•it (di mer′it) **1** a mark against a person's record for bad behaviour or poor performance: *She already has three demerits on her driver's licence.* **2** a fault or disadvantage. *n.*

de•moc•ra•cy (di mok′rə sē) **1** a system of government where the people choose their own leaders, where all citizens have equal rights, and where certain basic freedoms are protected by law. Some of these are the freedom of religion, freedom of speech, freedom to own property, and freedom to travel. **2** a country, state, or community that has such a system: *Canada is a democracy.* *n., pl.* **de•moc•ra•cies.** **—dem′o•crat′ic** (dem′ə krat′ik), *adj.* **—dem′o•crat′i•cal•ly,** *adv.*

de•mol•ish (di mol′ish) tear down; destroy: *The barbarians demolished the fortress. One counterexample demolishes a whole theory.* *v.* **—dem′o•li′tion** (dem′ə lish′ən), *n.*

de•mon (dē′mən) **1** an evil spirit; devil; fiend. **2** *Informal.* a person who has great energy, vigour, or skill: *She's a demon on the soccer field.* *n.* **—de•mon′ic** (di mon′ik), *adj.* **—de′mo•ni′a•cal** (dē′mə nī′ə kəl), *adj.*

dem•on•strate (dem′ən strāt′) **1** show or prove: *Can you demonstrate that hot air rises? Mom demonstrated the proper way to shovel snow. He demonstrates his love by giving to others.* **2** advertise a product by using it in front of people while giving an explanation. The actual product used for this is called a **demo:** *The computer salesperson demonstrated the software. We got this radio cheap because it was a demo.* **3** take part in a parade, rally, etc. to express an opinion about something: *An angry crowd demanding more police protection demonstrated in front of the city hall.* *v.,* **dem•on•strat•ed, dem•on•strat•ing.** **—dem′on•stra′tion,** *n.*

de•mon•stra•tive (di mon′strə tiv) **1** showing your feelings freely and openly: *The girl's demonstrative greeting embarrassed her shy brother.* **2** a grammar term for a word that points out. The words *this* and *that* are demonstratives; they are demonstrative pronouns and also demonstrative adjectives. 1, 2 *adj.,* 2 *n.*

de•mor•al•ize (di môr′ə līz′) make sad and discouraged: *My low score after studying so hard for the test demoralized me.* *v.,* **de•mor•al•ized, de•mor•al•iz•ing.**

de•mote (di mōt′) put back to a lower position: *The manager was demoted because the department had lost so much money.* *v.,* **de•mot•ed, de•mot•ing.** **—de•mo′tion,** *n.*

de•mure (di myūr′) quiet, modest, and proper, or pretending to be: *a demure young lady.* *adj.*

den (den) **1** a wild animal's home; lair: *The bear's den was in a cave.* **2** a room, usually small and cozy, for doing quiet things: *Sabine was reading in the den, curled up in an armchair.* **3** a hideout or hangout, especially for criminals. *n.*

Dene (den′ā) **1** a large First Nation of the western Northwest Territories that includes many different groups, all with languages that belong to the Athapascan family. Their homeland is called **Denendeh.** **2** having to do with these people or their language. 1 *n.,* 2 *adj.*

De•ne–thah (den′ā tȧ′) **1** First Nations people living in British Columbia. **2** their language. **3** having to do with these people or their language. 1, 2 *n.,* 3 *adj.*

de•ni•al (di nī′əl) **1** the act of saying that something is not real or true: *He continued to fear monsters under the bed, in spite of my firm denial of their existence.* **2** the act of turning away from or giving up: *The traitors felt no guilt about the denial of their country.* **3** refusal: *The principal's denial of our request seemed unfair.* *n.*

den•im (den′əm) **1** a heavy, coarse cotton cloth, used for jeans and other casual clothes. **2** **denims,** *pl.* clothes made of this cloth. *n.*

de•nom•i•na•tion (di nom′ə nā′shən) **1** a group of religious congregations that all agree about certain things. Different denominations can still belong to the same basic faith. The Presbyterians and the Baptists are two Christian denominations. **2** a class or kind of units: *Canadian coins come in six denominations: 1¢, 5¢, 10¢, 25¢, $1, and $2.* **3** a name. *n.*

de•nom•i•na•tor (di nom′ə nā′tər) the number below the line in a fraction, which tells how many parts the whole has been divided into: *In ¾, 4 is the denominator, and 3 is the numerator.* *n.*

a bat	e bed	i bid	o pot	u cup	th thin
ā cake	ē me	ī bite	ō go	ū rude	TH then
ȧ bar	ə about	ər over	ȯ for	u̇ put	zh measure

de•note (di nōtʹ) mean; be the sign of: *A fever usually denotes sickness. The sign ✓⁺ on your paper denotes very good work.* *v.,* **de•not•ed, de•not•ing.**

de•nounce (di nounsʹ) speak out strongly against: *The judge denounced people who drive carelessly.* *v.,* **de•nounced, de•nounc•ing.**

dense (dens) **1** closely packed together; thick: *a dense forest, a dense fog, dense population.* **2** stupid; slow to understand. *adj.,* **dens•er, dens•est.**

den•si•ty (denʹsə tē) **1** the fact of being closely or thickly packed together: *The density of the forest made it hard to see very far ahead.* **2** the amount of matter in a unit of volume, or the amount spread over a unit of area: *Lead has greater density than wood, because a cubic metre of lead has more mass than a cubic metre of wood. The population density of Calgary is about 540 people for every square kilometre.* *n., pl.* **den•si•ties.**

dent (dent) **1** a place where a surface has been pushed inward by being hit or pressed: *There's a dent in the left front fender of our car where another car backed into it.* **2** get or make a dent: *The blow from the hammer dented the table. Soft wood dents easily.* 1 *n.,* 2 *v.*

den•tal (denʹtəl) having to do with the teeth or with dentists: *Proper dental care is important for healthy teeth. When is my next dental appointment?* *adj.*

dental floss (denʹtəl flosʹ) a thin, strong, smooth thread used to remove plaque and food particles from between your teeth.

den•tine (denʹtēn) the hard, bony material beneath the enamel of your teeth. It forms the main part of a tooth. **Dentin** is another spelling. *n.*

den•tist (denʹtist) a person who is qualified to take care of people's teeth. *n.* **—denʹtist•ry,** *n.*

den•tures (denʹchərz) a set of artificial teeth made and fitted for people who no longer have their own teeth: *Grandpa liked his new dentures.* **False teeth** is another name for them. *pl.n.*

de•nun•ci•a•tion (di nunʹsē āʹshən) a strong public statement against something: *The speaker began with a denunciation of racist attitudes.* *n.*

de•ny (di nīʹ) **1** say that something is not real or true: *The prisoner denied the accusation. The city officials deny that there is a flu epidemic.* **2** turn away from; give up: *I cannot deny my best friend.* **3** refuse: *Our request was denied.* *v.,* **de•nied, de•ny•ing.**

de•o•dor•ant (dē ōʹdə rənt) a substance that destroys or hides unpleasant odours. To **deodorize** a place is to get rid of the smell in it. *n.*

de•part (di pȧrtʹ) **1** go away; leave: *The train departs at 6:15 p.m.* **2** change: *She departed from her usual way of doing things.* **3 the departed,** the person who has died. *v.* **—de•parʹture** (di pȧrʹchər), *n.*

de•part•ment (di pȧrtʹmənt) a separate part of a whole; special branch; section. A **department store** sells many different kinds of things arranged in separate sections of the store. A **fire department** is a branch of a city government in charge of fighting and preventing fires. *Abbreviation:* dept. *n.*

de•pend (di pendʹ) **1** be a result of; be controlled or influenced by: *The success of our sports day depends partly on the weather. Health depends on good food.* **2** get support; need the help of: *Children depend on their parents for food, clothing, and shelter.* **3** rely; trust: *You can depend on this piece of advice.* A person or thing that can be trusted is **dependable.** *v.*
that depends or **it depends,** it will be based on certain other things which may not be settled or known yet: *"Can we go to the movies tomorrow?" "That depends," answered Mother.*

de•pend•ant (di penʹdənt) a person who looks to someone else for food, clothing, and shelter: *If you have no dependants to support, you pay more income tax.* *n.*

de•pend•enc•y (di penʹden si) addiction. *n.*

de•pend•ent (di penʹdənt) **1** depending; possible only if something else takes place: *Good crops are dependent on the right kind of weather.* **2** trusting or needing another person or thing for support: *A baby monkey is dependent on its parents.* *adj.*
—de•pendʹence, *n.*

de•pict (di piktʹ) show in art, photos, or words; portray: *This painting and that poem both depict the beauty of the sunset.* *v.* **—de•picʹtion,** *n.*

de•plete (di plētʹ) reduce until there is too little: *The spell of very cold weather greatly depleted the animals' food supply.* *v.,* **de•plet•ed, de•plet•ing.**
—de•pleʹtion, *n.*

de•plore (di plôrʹ) think or say that some action or situation is very bad or sad: *We deplore the practice of child labour.* *v.,* **de•plored, de•plor•ing.**
—de•plorʹa•ble, *adj.*

de•port (di pôrtʹ) **1** send a person out of the country, usually back to the country he or she came from. The action is called **deportation.** **2 deport yourself,** behave in a certain way: *The boys were trained to deport themselves like gentlemen.* Your **deportment** is your behaviour. *v.*

de·pose (di pōz′) put out of some position of authority; remove from a throne: *The king was deposed by the revolution.* *v.*

de·pos·it (di poz′it) **1** put something somewhere and leave it there: *She deposited her bundles on the table. The flood deposited a layer of mud in the streets.* **2** the material left somewhere by natural means: *a deposit of sand and mud at a river mouth, deposits of coal in the earth.* **3** put money into an account. **4** money put into an account: *a deposit of $50.* **5** a payment of part of the price of something. You pay a deposit if you rent something, in case you ruin it or fail to return it. You also pay a deposit on an item if you want a store to set it aside for you. **6** pay part of the price of something. 1, 3, 6 *v.,* 2, 4, 5 *n.* **—de·pos′i·tor,** *n.*

de·pot (dē′pō *or* dep′ō) **1** a bus or railway station. **2** a storehouse; warehouse. *n.*

de·press (di pres′) **1** make sad or gloomy, or cause to lose interest in life: *Rainy weather always depresses me. She was so depressed she couldn't get out of bed.* **2** press down: *to depress a key on a keyboard.* **3** slow down or weaken: *a depressed economy. Some medicines depress the action of the heart.* *v.* **—de·pressed′,** *adj.* **—de·pres′sing,** *adj.*

de·pres·sion (di presh′ən) **1** low spirits; loss of interest in life: *Finding a good friend cured the boy's depression.* **2** the action of pressing down: *Depression of the gas pedal makes a car speed up.* **3** a low place; hollow: *Water filled the depressions in the ground.* **4** a time when the economy is extremely weak, with high unemployment. **The (Great) Depression** took place in the 1930s. *n.*

de·prive (di prīv′) take away from; keep from having or doing something, especially something badly wanted or needed: *The barking dog deprived us of sleep.* *v.,* **de·prived, de·priv·ing.** **—dep′ri·va′tion** (dep′rə vā′shən), *n.*

dept. *abbreviation for* department.

depth (depth) **1** the distance from the surface to the bottom, or from front to back: *the depth of a hole, the depth of a lake. The depth of our playground is 90 m.* **2** the fact of being deep: *It was a hole of great depth. The philosopher was noted for the depth of her understanding.* **3** the deepest part of anything: *in the depths of the forest, in the depths of despair.* *n.*
out of your depth, a in water so deep that you cannot touch the bottom. **b** facing something you cannot understand or cope with.

dep·u·ty (dep′yə tē) **1** a person chosen to do the work or take the place of another: *A deputy minister is an assistant to a minister of the cabinet.* **2 Deputy,** in Québec, a member of the National Assembly. *n., pl.* **dep·u·ties.**

de·rail (dē rāl′) cause a train to go off the rails. *v.* **—de·rail′ment,** *n.*

de·rive (di rīv′) **1** get; obtain: *She derives much pleasure from her books. The English word "enter" is derived from the French word "entrer."* **2** make new words by adding suffixes or prefixes. From *kind* we can derive *kinder, kindness,* and *unkind.* *v.,* **de·rived, de·riv·ing.** **—der′i·va′tion** (der′ə vā′shən), *n.*

der·mis (dər′mis) skin. The **epidermis** is the thin outer layer of the skin. A **dermatologist** is a doctor specializing in skin diseases.

de·rog·a·to·ry (di rog′ə tȯr′ē) putting down or belittling others: *No derogatory remarks will be tolerated in this classroom.* *adj.*

Huge derricks (or cranes) are needed to build skyscrapers. Smaller derricks can be raised to the tops of these buildings, to complete the work.

der·rick (der′ik) **1** a machine for lifting and moving heavy objects, with a long, movable arm that sticks out sideways from an upright post or frame. **2** a towerlike framework over an oil well, gas well, etc., which holds the drilling and hoisting machinery. *n.*

a bat	e bed	i bid	o pot	u cup	th thin
ā cake	ē me	ī bite	ō go	ū rude	ᴛʜ then
ä bar	ə about	ər over	ȯ for	ü put	zh measure

Desert areas

Deserts are not necessarily hot — the polar regions are deserts. Most deserts are rocky, not sandy. Sand covers only 11% of the Sahara Desert, in Africa.

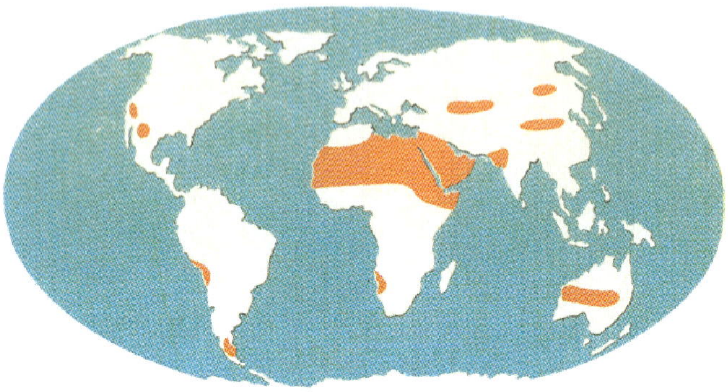

Camels are ideally suited for making long journeys across deserts. They can go for days without eating or drinking, living off the fat stored in their humps.

de•scend (di send′) go or come down: *They slowly descended the stairs. The temperature descended from 10°C to 5°C overnight.* *v.*
be descended from, have as ancestors; be the child, grandchild, great-grandchild, etc. of: *He is descended from Scottish settlers on Prince Edward Island.*
descend on, a make a sudden attack on: *The wolves descended on the sheep and killed them.* **b** arrive suddenly in great numbers: *Many tourists descended on the town during the exhibition.*

de•scend•ant (di sen′dənt) a person born of a certain family or group; a child, grandchild, great-grandchild, etc.: *She is a descendant of German settlers.* *n.*

de•scent (di sent′) **1** the act of coming or going down: *the descent of a balloon.* **2** a downward slope: *We climbed down a steep descent.* **3** a family line; ancestors: *I can trace my descent back 200 years to a family in Japan.* *n.*

de•scribe (di skrīb′) tell what a person, place, thing, or event is like; give details that help others imagine what you are talking or writing about. *v.,* **de•scribed, de•scrib•ing. —de•scrip′tion** (di scrip′shən), *n.* **—de•scrip′tive,** *adj.*

des•ert[1] (dez′ərt) **1** a region with very little water and not much plant or animal life: *The Sahara Desert is a great, sandy region in northern Africa.* **2** with no people on it: *Robinson Crusoe was shipwrecked on a desert island.* 1 *n.,* 2 *adj.*

de•sert[2] (di zərt′) go away and leave; abandon; forsake; run away from duty: *The dog was deserted by its owner. The guard deserted his post.* *v.* **—de•sert′er,** *n.* **—de•ser′tion,** *n.*

de•serve (di zərv′) have a right to; be good or bad enough for; be worthy of: *This well-researched project deserves a high mark. The vandals deserve to be punished.* *v.,* **de•served, de•serv•ing.**

de•sign (di zīn′) **1** a drawing, plan, or sketch used as a pattern for making something: *a design for a machine, a dress design.* **2** an artistic arrangement of shapes and colours; pattern: *wallpaper with leafy designs.* **3** the way something is built, styled, or laid out: *The design of these shoes makes them very comfortable.* **4** make a first sketch or outline of; figure out how a thing will work or what it will look like: *to design a dress, to design a tree fort.* **5** the art of doing this kind of planning. **6** intend for a certain purpose: *That remark was designed to stir up trouble.* 1–3, 5 *n.,* 4, 6 *v.*
by design, on purpose.

des•ig•nate (dez′ig nāt′) **1** mark out; point out; show: *Red lines on this map designate main roads.* **2** name: *Kalpra was designated team captain.* *v.,* **des•ig•nat•ed, des•ig•nat•ing. —des′ig•na′tion,** *n.*

de•sign•er (di zī′nər) **1** a person who comes up with ideas for new styles in clothes or furniture, new kinds of equipment, etc., and creates the patterns for making them. **2** created by a person who is well-known for this kind of work: *designer glasses, designer jeans.* 1 *n.,* 2 *adj.*

de•sir•a•ble (di zī′rə bəl) worth wanting or having; pleasing: *My parents don't consider snakes to be desirable pets.* *adj.* **—de•sir′a•bil′i•ty,** *n.*

de·sire (di zīr′) 1 wish for; long for: *A miser desires money more than anything else.* 2 a wish; a longing: *Her greatest desire was to become a writer.* 1 *v.,* **de·sired, de·sir·ing;** 2, 3 *n.* —**de·sir′ous,** *adj.*

de·sist (di sist′ *or* di zist′) stop: *He kept laughing although he had been asked several times to desist.* *v.*

desk (desk) a piece of furniture with a flat or gently sloping top on which to write, draw, use a computer, or rest books, papers, etc. It usually has drawers or other storage space. *n.*

desk·top (desk′top′) 1 so small and easily handled that it can be used on a desk or work table: *desktop computer, desktop printer.* 2 done with equipment that fits on a desk. **Desktop publishing** is done with an ordinary computer rather than a big printing press. 3 on a computer, the screen that comes up showing that it is ready to be used after you have turned it on. The desktop shows the different programs and drives that you can open. 1, 2 *adj.,* 3 *n.*

des·o·late (des′ə lit *or* dez′ə lit *for 1 and 2,* des′ə lāt′ *or* dėz′ə lāt′ *for 3*) 1 empty or lifeless: *desolate land, a desolate house.* 2 very sad; comfortless: *The hungry, lonely child was desolate.* 3 make empty and barren or sad and comfortless: *The volcano desolated the surrounding land. We were desolated to hear that our friends were going away.* 1, 2 *adj.,* 3 *v.,* **des·o·lat·ed, des·o·lat·ing.** —**des′o·la′tion,** *n.*

de·spair (di sper′) 1 a hopeless feeling that nothing good can happen: *Despair filled them as they felt the boat sinking.* 2 a person or thing that causes this feeling: *The wicked ruler was the despair of her people.* 3 lose hope; give up: *The doctors despaired of saving the child's life.* 1, 2 *n.,* 3 *v.*

des·per·ate (des′pə rit) 1 almost hopeless: *The situation is desperate. She would have to be desperate before she asked for help.* 2 reckless or violent because there is no hope: *a desperate criminal.* 3 wanting or needing very badly: *She was desperate for affection. After a week of being cooped up in the cabin, he was desperate to go outside.* 4 urgent: *in desperate need of help.* *adj.*

des·per·a·tion (des′pə rā′shən) a feeling that your only choice is to do something reckless: *When he saw that the stairs were on fire, he jumped out of the window in desperation.* *n.*

de·spic·a·ble (di spik′ə bəl) so bad or mean that it is disgusting: *Taking away the baby's toy was despicable.* *adj.* —**de·spic′a·bly,** *adv.*

de·spise (di spīz′) look down on; scorn; have absolutely no respect for: *Most people despise a traitor.* *v.,* **de·spised, de·spis·ing.**

de·spite (di spīt′) in spite of: *The children went for a walk despite the rain.* *prep.*

de·spond·ent (di spon′dənt) completely discouraged and hopeless; depressed: *The losers were despondent.* *adj.* —**de·spond′en·cy,** *n.*

des·pot (des′pot *or* des′pət) 1 an absolute ruler: *In ancient times many rulers were despots.* 2 any person who uses power to get his or her own way: *Their boss was a despot in the office.* *n.*

des·sert (di zərt′) a sweet course served at the end of a meal: *Pie, cake, puddings, and ice cream are common desserts.* *n.*

des·ti·na·tion (des′tə nā′shən) where a person or thing is going: *The traveller's destination was Iqaluit.* *n.*

des·tine (des′tən) 1 cause by fate: *The letter was destined never to reach us.* 2 intend; set apart for a purpose: *She was destined by her parents to take over the family business.* *v.,* **des·tined, des·tin·ing.**
destined for, headed for; bound for: *a plane destined for Korea. You are destined for stardom.*

des·ti·ny (des′tə nē) one's lot or fortune; what happens, or will happen, to a person or thing in the end, often thought of as something that has to be that way: *It was her destiny to become a national hero. He struggled in vain against his destiny.* *n., pl.* **des·ti·nies.**

des·ti·tute (des′tə tyūt′ *or* des′tə tūt′) without necessities such as food, clothing, shelter: *A destitute family needs help.* *adj.* —**des′ti·tu′tion,** *n.*
destitute of, without: *The cruel ruler was destitute of pity.*

de·stroy (di stroi′) 1 wreck or ruin: *Some pets destroy furniture.* 2 kill or put an end to: *A heavy rain destroyed all hope of a picnic. Forest fires destroy many trees every year.* The act or result of destroying is **destruction,** and a person or thing that destroys is **destructive.** *v.*

de·tach (di tach′) unfasten; remove; separate: *She detached a charm from her bracelet.* *v.*

de·tached (di tacht′) 1 separate from others: *A detached house is not stuck together with others in a row.* 2 not emotionally involved: *They asked her to settle the argument because they knew she would remain calm and detached.* *adj.*

a bat	e bed	i bid	o pot	u cup	th thin
ā cake	ē me	ī bite	ō go	ū rude	ᴛʜ then
ä bar	ə about	ər over	ô for	ů put	zh measure

de•tach•ment (di tach′mənt) 1 separation. 2 lack of emotional involvement: *He watched the scene with cool detachment.* 3 a smaller unit or group of workers, police, soldiers, etc. out of a larger force: *Some detachments of the RCMP have only one or two officers.* *n.*

de•tail (dē′tāl *or* di tāl′) 1 a small or particular thing or fact: *All the details of getting ready for the birthday party were left to the children.* 2 attention to small things; thoroughness; fineness; fussiness. 3 tell even the small and unimportant parts: *The new boy detailed to us everything he had seen in his travels.* 4 a small group chosen for some special duty: *The captain sent a detail of ten soldiers to guard the bridge.* 5 choose for special duty: *Police were detailed to hold back the crowd watching the parade.* 1, 2, 4 *n.,* 3, 5 *v.* **—de′tailed,** *adj.*
go into detail, describe or discuss each small part or fact: *Don't go into detail—we don't have time.*
in detail, part by part; with all the details: *She described the inside of the airplane in detail.*

de•tain (di tān′) 1 hold back; delay: *I was detained by the heavy snowstorm.* 2 keep from leaving; force to stay: *The police detained the suspect for questioning. I was detained after class for throwing chalk.* *v.*

de•tect (di tekt′) discover; notice; find: *Could you detect a strange smell in the room?* *v.* **—de•tect′a•ble,** *adj.* **—de•tec′tion,** *n.* **—de•tec′tor,** *n.*

de•tec•tive (di tek′tiv) a person who works for the police force or some other employer to find out things that others are trying to keep secret. *n.*

de•ten•tion (di ten′shən) the act of detaining someone or forcing someone to stay in a place: *A jail is for the detention of arrested persons. The students' behaviour resulted in a detention at recess.* *n.*

de•ter (di tər′) discourage; hinder: *The extreme heat deterred us from going downtown.* Something that deters people is a **deterrent.** *v.,* **de•terred, de•ter•ring.**

de•ter•gent (di tər′jənt) a chemical substance other than soap, used for cleansing: *dish detergent.* *n.*

de•te•ri•o•rate (di tē′rē ə rāt′) go bad or get worse: *Machinery will deteriorate if it is not given good care.* *v.,* **de•te•ri•o•rat•ed, de•te•ri•o•rat•ing.** **—de•te′ri•o•ra′tion,** *n.*

de•ter•mi•na•tion (di tər′mə nā′shən) 1 the quality of not giving up; firmness in carrying out a purpose: *Mahendra's determination took him through the difficulties he met.* 2 the act of deciding or finding out something. *n.*

de•ter•mine (di tər′mən) 1 make up your mind very firmly; decide: *She determined to become the best scout in her troop.* 2 find out for sure: *A diver was hired to determine the position of the sunken wreck.* 3 be the deciding fact in bringing about a certain result: *Your age determines what category you are in for track and field.* *v.,* **de•ter•mined, de•ter•min•ing.**

de•ter•mined (di tər′mənd) having or showing a mind firmly made up: *a determined look on her face. The determined explorers pushed on in spite of the storm.* *adj.*

de•ter•min•er (di tər′mə nər) in grammar, a specifying word such as *the, a, her,* or *this,* used before a noun or before an adjective followed by a noun. *n.*

de•test (di test′) hate: *I detest cockroaches.* *v.* **—de•test′a•ble,** *adj.*

de•tour (dē′tūr) 1 a roundabout way instead of the usual direct way: *We took a detour through the park on our way home.* 2 use a roundabout way; make a detour: *We detoured around the flooded part of the highway.* 1 *n.,* 2 *v.*

de•tract (di trakt′) take away beauty, value, etc. from: *The frame is so ugly it detracts from the painting.* *v.*

det•ri•men•tal (det′rə men′təl) damaging; harmful: *Lack of rest is detrimental to your health.* *adj.*

dev•as•tate (dev′ə stāt′) 1 destroy: *The long war devastated much of Europe.* 2 make someone feel deeply disappointed or hurt. *v.,* **dev•as•tat•ed, dev•as•tat•ing.** **—dev′as•ta′tion,** *n.*

de•vel•op (di vel′əp) 1 grow and mature; cause to grow and mature: *Plants develop from seeds. Reading develops your imagination.* 2 come to be or have: *Fog developed overnight. He's developed a cold.* 3 work out; come up with: *They've developed their own secret language.* 4 build new houses, factories, tourist attractions, stores, playgrounds, etc. in some area: *They have developed the old downtown.* 5 come to have more industry, more technology, more people living in cities, and a more stable form of government: *a developing nation.* 6 treat a photographic plate or film with chemicals so that the picture shows: *I took the film in to be developed.* *v.*

de•vel•op•ment (di vel′əp mənt) 1 the act or process of developing. 2 a happening: *We heard news of strange developments.* 3 a group of buildings put up by the same company: *The new housing development includes a school and a park.* *n.*

de•vi•ate (dē′vē āt′) turn aside from a way, rule, standard, etc.: *She never deviated from the truth in telling her story.* *v.,* **de•vi•at•ed, de•vi•at•ing.** **—de′vi•a′tion,** *n.*

de•vice (di vīs′) 1 a tool or machine: *A can opener is a device for opening cans.* 2 a plan; a scheme or trick: *By some device she got past the guards unnoticed.* *n.* **leave someone to his or her own devices,** leave someone to do as he or she pleases.

CONFUSABLES ...... device

device is a noun: *A can opener is a useful device.*

devise is a verb: *She devised a really complicated plan to avoid doing her work.*

dev•il (dev′əl) 1 **the Devil,** according to some people, the chief evil spirit, or Satan. 2 any evil spirit. 3 a person who is wicked, reckless, mischievous, etc. 4 prepare food with hot spices: *devilled ham, devilled eggs.* 1–3 *n.,* 4 *v.,* **dev•illed** or **dev•iled, dev•il•ling** or **dev•il•ing.** —**dev′il•ish,** *adj.*

de•vise (di vīz′) think up; come up with; invent: *The boys are trying to devise some scheme for earning the money for their trip.* *v.,* **de•vised, de•vis•ing.**

de•void (di void′)
devoid of, totally without: *devoid of sense.* *adj.*

de•vote (di vōt′) set apart or give up for a particular person or thing: *She devoted all her spare time to sports. The museum devotes two floors to animal exhibits.* *v.,* **de•vot•ed, de•vot•ing.**

de•vot•ed (di vō′tid) very loyal; faithful: *a devoted friend.* *adj.*

de•vo•tion (di vō′shən) 1 a deep, steady love; a feeling of loyalty: *the devotion of a father to his child.* 2 the fact of being set apart for some special person or thing: *the devotion of much time to study.* 3 **devotions,** *pl.* worship, prayers, or meditation. *n.*

de•vour (di vour′) eat something up quickly and completely: *The wolves devoured the caribou. Fire devoured the forest. He devours four books a week.* *v.*

de•vout (di vout′) 1 truly committed to your religion. 2 whole-hearted: *devout thanks.* *adj.*

dew (dyū *or* dū) moisture from the air that collects in small drops of water (**dew drops**) on cool surfaces during the night: *In the morning there were drops of dew on the grass and flowers.* *n.* —**dew′y,** *adj.*

Dew•ey decimal system (dyū′ē des′ə məl sis′təm) a system of arranging books in a library by assigning numbers to them based on what they are about.

dex•ter•ous (dek′stə rəs) showing great skill with the hands or the mind: *With dexterous movements, she tied the boat to the pier.* *adj.* —**dex•ter′i•ty** (dek ster′ə tē), *n.*

di•a•be•tes (dī′ə bē′tis *or* dī′ə bē′tēz) a disease that causes the body to produce a lot of urine. In the most common kind of diabetes, the digestive system is unable to absorb normal amounts of sugar and starch. *n.* —**di′a•bet′ic** (dī′ ə bet′ik), *adj. or n.*

di•a•bol•i•cal (dī′ə bol′ə kəl) devilish; very wicked: *The police discovered a diabolical plot to poison the drinking water.* *adj.* —**di′a•bol′i•cal•ly,** *adv.*

di•a•dem (dī′ə dem′) a crown. *n.*

di•ag•nose (dī′əg nōs′) figure out what the illness or problem is: *The doctor diagnosed the child's disease as measles.* When you have figured it out, you have made a **diagnosis.** *v.,* **di•ag•nosed, di•ag•nos•ing.**

di•ag•o•nal (dī ag′ə nəl) 1 a straight line joining any two corners that are not next to each other in a figure with four or more sides. 2 slanting, like a diagonal: *a diagonal stripe in a candy cane.* 1 *n.,* 2 *adj.* —**di•ag′o•nal•ly,** *adv.*

A diagram of a diamond shows the structure of the crystal rather than its beautiful sparkle.

di•a•gram (dī′ə gram′) 1 a drawing meant to explain something. It can be a graph or chart, or it can be a picture of a thing, showing all the parts and how they work. 2 show something in this kind of drawing. 1 *n.,* 2 *v.,* **di•a•grammed** or **di•a•gramed, di•a•gram•ming** or **di•a•gram•ing.**

a bat	e bed	i bid	o pot	u cup	th thin
ā cake	ē me	ī bite	ō go	ū rude	ᴛʜ then
ä bar	ə about	ər over	ȯ for	u̇ put	zh measure

di·al (dī′əl) 1 a circle with amounts marked around the edge and a pointer that moves around it to show a measurement of some kind. The face of a clock is a dial. A thermometer may be in the form of a dial. 2 the part on a radio or television set that lets you tune in to a station. 3 the round part on many older telephones that you turn with your finger to enter each digit in the phone number you are calling. 4 enter a phone number to make a call: *She dialled her mother's office.* 1–3 *n.,* 4 *v.,* **di·alled** or **di·aled, di·al·ling** or **di·al·ing.**

di·a·lect (dī′ə lekt′) a form of a language that is spoken in a certain place. The dialect of English spoken in Australia is different from the one spoken in Canada. *n.*

di·a·logue (dī′ə log′) 1 a conversation: *They had a long dialogue about their summer plans.* 2 all the talking in a story, play, movie, etc.: *That book has a good plot and realistic dialogue.* *n.* ▶ See the *Grammar and Usage Mini-Guide.*

Grammar Check ..... dialogue

You can report what people say: Jacko said that he wanted ice cream. You can also give a direct quotation: Jacko said, "I want ice cream."

Dialogue is the actual words that people say. Put dialogue in quotation marks.

Start a new paragraph when a different person is speaking. Sometimes you don't have to tell which person is speaking, because the kind of language used makes it clear.

Jacko said, "I want ice cream. You said if I was good I could, after supper."

"That's right, I did say that," Mary replied. "You may choose any flavour you like."

"Chocolate! Chocolate! I like chocolate!"

"All right, chocolate it is."

Who spoke last?

dial tone (dī′əl tōn′) the buzzing sound you hear in a telephone receiver to signal that the line is ready to be used.

di·al·y·sis (dī al′ə sis) the use of a special machine to remove harmful substances from a person's blood when the kidneys are unable to do this: *Karen went to hospital once a month for dialysis.* *n.*

di·am·e·ter (dī am′ə tər) 1 a straight line through the centre of a circle or sphere from one side to the other. 2 the length of this line; the distance through the centre: *The diameter of the earth is about 13 000 km. An extra large pizza is about 45 cm in diameter.* *n.*

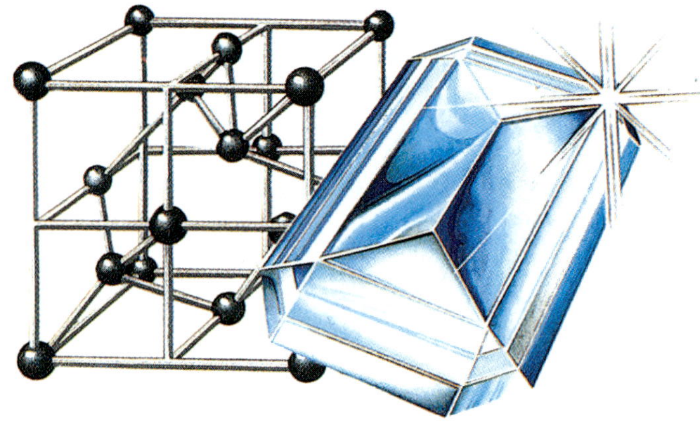

Diamonds are crystals of pure carbon. The atoms in a diamond are arranged in a dense lattice shape, which makes diamonds very hard — the hardest substance found in the world.

dia·mond (dī′mənd) 1 a clear precious stone, formed from pure carbon in crystals. Diamond is the hardest substance known. 2 a figure shaped like this: ◊ 3 the part of a baseball field inside the four lines that connect the bases. 4 a playing card with one or more red, diamond-shaped designs on it. *n.*

di·a·per (dī′pər) 1 a piece of cloth folded up, or a pad of other absorbent material, used as underpants for a baby. 2 put a diaper on. 1 *n.,* 2 *v.*

di·a·phragm (dī′ə fram′) 1 the set of muscles and tendons separating your chest from your abdomen. 2 a thin disk or cone in a piece of sound equipment that changes sound waves into electrical signals. *n.*

di·ar·rhe·a (dī′ə rē′ə) a condition that makes a person have more bowel movements than normal, with loose, soft waste: *The stomach flu gave him diarrhea.* *n.*

di·a·ry (dī′ə rē) a book for writing down what happens or what you think and feel each day. *n., pl.* **di·a·ries.**

WORD HISTORY.... diary/journal

They don't look alike, but **diary** and **journal** are related. The word **diary** comes from the Latin *diarius*, meaning "daily." The word **journal** comes through the French *journal*, from the Latin *diurnalis*, meaning "a daily portion."

dice (dīs) 1 small cubes with a different number (often shown by spots) on each side. Dice are used in games. 2 cut into small cubes: *Carrots are sometimes diced before being cooked.* 1 *pl.n.* (*sing.* **die**), 2 *v.,* **diced, dic·ing.**

dic·tate (dik′tāt *or* dik tāt′ *for 1 and 2,* dik′tāt *for 3*) **1** say or read something out loud for someone else to write or key in: *The teacher dictated the spelling list.* **2** tell others what to do: *No one is going to dictate to me.* **3** an order or rule that must be obeyed: *the dictates of a ruler, the dictates of your conscience.* 1, 2 *v.,* **dic·tat·ed, dic·tat·ing;** 3 *n.* **—dic·ta′tion,** *n.*

dic·ta·tor (dik′tā tər *or* dik tā′tər) a ruler who has total power over the people. *n.* **—dic·ta′tor·ship′,** *n.*

dic·tion·ar·y (dik′shə ner′ē) a book that lists words in alphabetical order and gives the meaning, spelling, and often the pronunciation and history of each word. *n., pl.* **dic·tion·ar·ies.**

did (did) the past tense of **do**[1]**:** *Tell us what you did yesterday.* *v.*

did·n't (did′ənt) did not.

die[1] (dī) **1** stop living; become dead. **2** get weaker or stop; come to an end: *The music died away. The motor sputtered and died.* *v.,* **died, dy·ing.**
be dying, *Informal.* want very much: *I'm just dying to hear your news. We're dying for a swim.*

die[2] (dī) a tool or machine for shaping, cutting, or stamping metal things: *Dies are used to make the threads on screws, to make coins, etc.* *n., pl.* **dies.**

die[3] (dī) a small cube with a different number on each side, used in certain games. See **dice.** *n., pl.* **dice.**
the die is cast, the decision has been made and cannot be changed.

die·sel (dē′zəl) **1** Often, **diesel engine,** an engine that burns a mixture of oil and air. This mixture is compressed so tightly that it gets hot and burns. **2** a vehicle with this kind of engine: *They drive a diesel.* **3** with or for a diesel engine: *a diesel locomotive, diesel fuel.* 1, 2 *n.,* 3 *adj.*

di·et (dī′ət) **1** the usual food and drink of a person or animal: *The diet of the giraffe is young leaves and shoots.* **2** any special choice of foods eaten to get well, stay healthy, lose or gain weight, etc.: *The doctor ordered a diet of liquids for the sick child.* **3** eat special food, especially to lose weight: *He can't eat sweets because he's dieting.* 1, 2 *n.,* 3 *v.,* **di·et·ed, di·et·ing.**

di·e·ti·tian (dī′ə tish′ən) a person trained to plan meals with the proper combination of various kinds of food: *Many hospitals and school cafeterias have dietitians.* *n.*

dif·fer (dif′ər) **1** be not the same; be different: *My answers differed from hers. We differ a lot in our interests.* **2** disagree: *They differed about how to spend the money.* *v.*

dif·fer·ence (dif′ rəns) **1** the fact of being unlike one another: *There is a difference between juice and pop.* **2** the way of being different: *The only difference between the two cars is their colour.* **3** what is left after subtracting one number from another: *The difference between 6 and 15 is 9.* **4** a disagreement: *They sat down for a talk to try to settle their differences.* *n.*

dif·fer·ent (dif′ rənt) **1** not alike; not the same: *People have different names. A car is different from a truck.* **2** separate: *We called three different times but never found her at home.* **3** unusual: *He has a very different style of dressing.* *adj.* **—dif′fer·ent·ly,** *adv.*

dif·fi·cult (dif′ə kult′) **1** hard to do or understand: *The heavy rock was difficult to move. Spelling is difficult for me.* **2** hard to get along with: *Don't be difficult—try to co-operate.* *adj.* **—dif′fi·cul′ty,** *n.*

dig (dig) **1** use a shovel, hands, claws, or snout to make a hole or to turn over ground: *to dig a hole or a tunnel. Dig around the plants to loosen the soil.* **2** get by digging: *to dig potatoes, to dig clams.* **3** poke: *Dirk gave me a dig in the ribs* (*n.*)*. The rider dug her heels into the horse* (*v.*). 1–3 *v.,* **dug, dig·ging;** 3 *n.*
dig in, *Informal.* **a** start eating with a good appetite: *"Here's your stew—dig in!"* **b** work hard: *We dug in and finished the job quickly.*
dig in your heels, be stubborn about something.
dig up, **a** get out of the ground: *to dig up treasure.* **b** find after a thorough search: *to dig up information.*

di·gest (dī jest′ *for 1 and 2,* dī′jest *for 3*) **1** change food to liquid in the alimentary canal, taking the useful parts into the blood as nourishment and getting rid of the rest. **2** think something over until you understand it clearly: *It often takes a long time to digest new ideas.* **3** a shorter, less detailed version of something written. 1, 2 *v.,* 3 *n.* **—di·gest′i·ble,** *adj.* **—di·ges′tive,** *adj.* **—di·ges′tion,** *n.*

dig·it (dij′it) **1** any of the numerals 0, 1, 2, 3, 4, 5, 6, 7, 8, 9: *The number 472 has three digits.* **2** a finger or toe. *n.*

WORD HISTORY....... digit

Digit means "finger" in Latin. It was first used in English to mean "a numeral below ten," because people counted these on their fingers.

The Latin word *digit* came from *dicitus* meaning "pointer," from which we get the English word *indicate.*

a bat	e bed	i bid	o pot	u cup	th thin
ā cake	ē me	ī bite	ō go	ū rude	ᴛʜ then
ä bar	ə about	ər over	ô for	u̇ put	zh measure

dig·it·al (dij′ə təl) giving or storing information in the form of numerals. A digital clock shows the time by numerals alone rather than by hands moving over a dial. A CD player changes the digital information on a CD back into music. *adj.*

dig·ni·fied (dig′nə fīd′) full of dignity; commanding respect; rather serious and formal: *The chief of the First Nations band has a dignified manner.* *adj.*

dig·ni·tar·y (dig′nə ter′ē) a person who has a position of honour: *the Prime Minister and other dignitaries.* *n., pl.* **dig·ni·tar·ies.**

dig·ni·ty (dig′nə tē) **1** a manner that commands respect; honour; a good kind of pride: *She spoke with such dignity that we had to listen.* **2** a serious or formal manner: *the dignity of a funeral.* *n., pl.* **dig·ni·ties.**

dike (dīk) a bank of earth built as a defence against flooding: *The dikes in Holland hold back the sea.* *n.*

di·lap·i·dat·ed (di lap′ə dā′tid) old and falling to pieces: *When all the dilapidated houses are cleared away, we can build new homes.* *adj.*

di·late (dī lāt′) make or become wider, especially an opening: *The pupil of the eye dilates in dim light.* *v.,* **di·lat·ed, di·lat·ing.** **—di·la′tion,** *n.*

di·lem·ma (di lem′ə) a situation where the only choices seem to be bad ones: *What a dilemma! I have to miss either the trip out West with my cousins, or my last chance at playing in the soccer finals.* *n.*

USING WORDS . . . . dilemma

Some people think that **dilemma** should be used when there are only two choices, because *di-* means "two."

But most people use it to mean any problem that doesn't seem to have a solution.

dil·i·gent (dil′ə jənt) hard-working; industrious: *Diligent students learn the most.* *adj.* **—dil′i·gence,** *n.*

dill (dil) a plant with spicy seeds and leaves that are used to flavour food, especially pickles. *n.*

dil·ly–dal·ly (dil′ē dal′ē) wait around; waste time. *v.,* **dil·ly-dal·lied, dil·ly-dal·ly·ing.**

di·lute (dī lüt′) make weaker or thinner by adding liquid, usually water. *v.,* **di·lut·ed, di·lut·ing.**

dim (dim) **1** not bright: *dim light.* **2** not clear: *dim eyesight. He had a dim memory of his great-grandmother.* **3** make or become dim: *This switch dims all the lights.* 1, 2 *adj.,* **dim·mer, dim·mest;** 3 *v.,* **dimmed, dim·ming.** **—dim′ly,** *adv.* **—dim′ness,** *n.* **—dim′mer,** *n.*

dime (dīm) a coin worth ten cents.
a dime a dozen, very common and easy to find or get.
stop (or **turn**) **on a dime,** stop (or turn) in a very short space. *n.*

di·men·sion (di men′shən) **1** the measurement of length, width, or thickness: *The dimensions of my room are 4.2 m by 3.1 m.* **2** Usually, **dimensions,** *pl.* size: *Pollution is a problem of enormous dimensions.* *n.*

di·min·ish (di min′ish) make or become smaller or less: *The tiger population has diminished over the years because of hunting.* *v.*

di·min·u·tive (di min′yə tiv) tiny: *A baby has diminutive hands.* *adj.*

dim·ple (dim′pəl) **1** a small hollow, usually in the cheek or chin. **2** form dimples: *Raindrops dimpled the sand. Her cheeks dimple whenever she smiles.* 1 *n.,* 2 *v.,* **dim·pled, dim·pling.**

din (din) **1** a loud, confused, continuing noise. **2** make this kind of noise. **3** say one thing over and over: *He was always dinning into our ears the importance of hard work.* 1 *n.,* 2, 3 *v.,* **dinned, din·ning.**

dine (dīn) eat dinner. *v.,* **dined, din·ing.**

din·er (dī′nər) **1** a person who is eating dinner. **2** a railway car where meals are served. **3** a restaurant, usually not very fancy and near a highway. *n.*

ding (ding) **1** Sometimes, **ding-dong,** a ringing sound. **2** make a ringing sound. **3** dent: *Someone dinged our car in the parking lot* (*v.*). *Now there's a ding in the left front fender* (*n.*). 1, 3 *n.,* 2, 3 *v.*

din·ghy (ding′ē) a small boat. *n., pl.* **din·ghies.**

din·go (ding′gō) a wild dog of Australia. *n.*

din·gy (din′jē) dim, dull, and dirty-looking: *a dingy hallway.* *adj.,* **din·gi·er, din·gi·est.** **—din′gi·ness,** *n.*

dining room (dī′ning rüm′) a room where dinner and other meals are served.

din·ner (din′ər) **1** the main meal of the day. The time for this meal is called **dinnertime,** and may be in the evening or around noon. **2** a formal meal in honour of some person or occasion: *The city officials gave the team a dinner to celebrate their victory.* *n.*

Dinosaur

pteranodon
("winged and toothless")

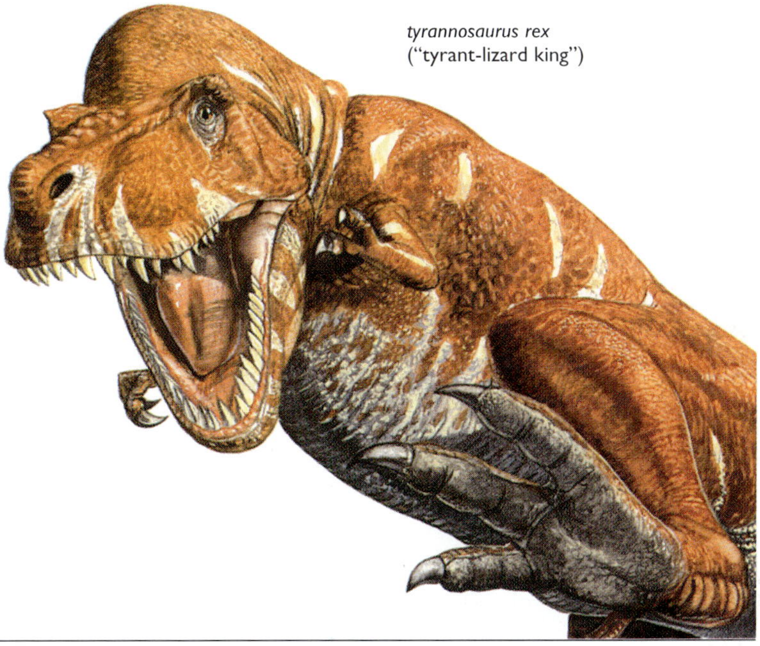

tyrannosaurus rex
("tyrant-lizard king")

The word dinosaur means "terrible lizard." There were many kinds of dinosaur, including some of the largest animals ever to have lived on Earth. About 65 million years ago, dinosaurs suddenly and mysteriously died out. Most of what we know about dinosaurs comes from bones and tracks that have been preserved as fossils in rocks.

di•no•saur (dī′nə sȯr′) an extinct creature that may have been a reptile. Some dinosaurs were bigger than elephants; others were smaller than cats. Some flew. *n.*

dip (dip) **1** put or go quickly into and then out of a liquid: *She dipped her hand into the pool. The otter dipped beneath the surface for a moment.* **2** an act of going or putting something in and out like this: *We went for a dip in the lake.* **3** put your hand or a container into something to take a little out: *to dip water out of a well. He dipped into the jar and snatched a few jelly beans.* **4** a mixture for dipping something in: *The sheep were driven through a dip to disinfect their fleece.* **5** lower and raise again quickly: *The ship's flag was dipped as a salute.* **6** go down: *The road dips into the valley.* **7** a sudden small drop: *a dip in prices, a dip in the road.* 1, 3, 5, 6 *v.*, **dipped, dip•ping;** 2, 4, 7 *n.*

diph•the•ri•a (dif thē′rē ə *or* dip thē′rē ə) a dangerous infectious disease of the throat. All Canadian children are immunized against diphtheria. *n.*

diph•thong (dif′thong′ *or* dip′thong′) a vowel sound made up of two vowels pronouned together in one syllable, such as *oi* in *noise* or *ou* in *out.* *n.*

di•plo•ma (di plō′mə) a paper given by a school or college, which says that a person has completed certain studies and has graduated. *n.*

di•plo•ma•cy (di plō′mə sē) **1** the business of keeping friendly relations between different countries. **2** skill in dealing with others in situations where they could easily become hurt or angry: *Her diplomacy made her an excellent team leader.* *n.*

dip•lo•mat (dip′lə mat′) **1** a person involved in handling the relations between his or her own country and other countries. **2** someone who is good at dealing with people and knows how to avoid hurting their feelings. *n.* **—dip′lo•mat′ic,** *adj.*

dip•per (dip′ər) a long-handled container for dipping liquids, similar to a ladle but with a bigger, deeper cup that usually has a flat bottom. The **Big Dipper** and **Little Dipper** are two groups of stars that form the outline of a container like this. *n.*

a bat	e bed	i bid	o pot	u cup	th thin
ā cake	ē me	ī bite	ō go	ū rude	ᴛʜ then
ä bar	ə about	ər over	ȯ for	ů put	zh measure

dire (dīr) causing great fear or suffering: *the dire results of a flood.* *adj.*
in dire need, in desperate or extreme need.

di·rect (də rekt′ *or* dī rekt′) 1 manage; guide: *The teacher directs the work of the class.* 2 order; command: *The police officer directed us to stop.* 3 tell or show the way: *Can you direct me to the library?* 4 point; aim: *The firefighter directed the hose at the flames. Direct your efforts toward a goal.* 5 put the address on a letter, package, etc. 6 without a break or turn; straight: *A bee makes a direct flight home to the hive (adj.). The airplane goes to Winnipeg direct (adv.).* 7 honest; clear and plain: *a direct answer.* 1–5 *v.,* 6, 7 *adj.,* 6 *adv.* **—di·rect′ly,** *adv.*

direct current (də rekt′ kər′ənt) an electric current that flows in only one direction. The current from all batteries is direct current.

di·rec·tion (də rek′shən *or* dī rek′shən) 1 the way that something points, faces, or travels: *"What direction are we driving—north or south?" Our school is in one direction and the post office is in another.* 2 knowing or telling what to do, how to do, where to go, etc.; an instruction: *Can you give me directions to the lake?*
3 guidance; management: *The school is under the direction of the principal.* 4 an order or command. *n.*

direct object (di rekt′ ob′jikt *or* dī′ rekt ob′jikt) a noun, a pronoun, or a phrase with a noun in it that completes the meaning of a verb by telling who or what received the action. *Example: the puck* in *She hit the puck into the net.*

di·rec·tor (də rek′tər *or* dī rek′tər) a manager; a person who directs, especially the leader of an organization or someone who directs a play or movie. *n.*

di·rec·to·ry (də rek′tə rē *or* dī rek′tə rē) a list of names, phone numbers, and addresses. *n., pl.* **di·rec·to·ries.**

dirge (dərj) a sad song for a funeral. *n.*

dir·ig·i·ble (də rij′ə bəl *or* dir′ə jə bəl) a craft shaped like a long, oval balloon filled with a gas that keeps it up in the air. The equipment for steering it and moving it forward are attached to the outside. A dirigible is a kind of **airship.** *n.*

dirt (dərt) 1 mud, dust, or earth: *a shovel full of dirt.*
2 a stain, smudge, or other mark that is not wanted.
3 *Slang.* a information; news. b bad rumours. *n.*

dirt bike (dərt′ bīk′) a small motorcycle made for riding over rough ground. It is not permitted on roads.

dirt·y (dər′tē) 1 not clean: *Children playing in the mud get dirty.* 2 hurtful; not nice: *a dirty trick, a dirty joke.* 3 stormy; rough: *dirty weather.* 4 get dirt on: *Don't dirty your new shirt.* 1–3 *adj.,* **dirt·i·er, dirt·i·est;** 4 *v.,* **dirt·ied, dirt·y·ing.**

dis– *a prefix meaning* the opposite or the reverse. *Disadvantage* is the opposite of *advantage. Disentangle* is the reverse of *entangle.*

Grammar Check . . . . dis-

The prefix **dis** can be used to show the opposite of the root word. Here are some examples.
disappear: vanish
disloyal: not faithful
disorganized: messy
displeased: annoyed
dissatisfied: not contented
distrust: have no confidence in

dis·a·bil·i·ty (dis′ə bil′ə tē) a lack of the usual ability in some area: *She has a learning disability. He can't walk, but he overcomes this disability by using a wheelchair.* *n., pl.* **dis·a·bil·i·ties.**

dis·a·ble (di sā′bəl) 1 do something to a thing to stop it from working: *to disable an alarm.* 2 **disabled,** having a disability: *Many disabled athletes participate in the Special Olympics.* *v.,* **dis·a·bled, dis·a·bling.**

dis·ad·van·tage (dis′əd van′tij) anything that makes it harder to succeed or to enjoy something: *His shyness was a disadvantage in making new friends.* *n.* **—dis′ad·van′taged,** *adj.*
at a disadvantage, in a more difficult position: *A poor night's sleep put her at a disadvantage for the big race.*
to someone's disadvantage, likely to hurt a person's chance of success: *It's to your own disadvantage to cheat.*

dis·a·gree (dis′ə grē′) 1 fail to agree; be different: *Your story disagrees with theirs.* 2 have different opinions: *Doctors sometimes disagree about treatment.*
3 have a bad effect; be harmful: *Eggs disagree with him.* *v.,* **dis·a·greed, dis·a·gree·ing.** **—dis′a·gree′ment,** *n.*

dis·a·gree·a·ble (dis′ə grē′ə bəl) not pleasant; hard to put up with: *a disagreeable person, a disagreeable task.* *adj.*

dis·ap·pear (dis′ə pēr′) 1 go out of sight: *The little dog disappeared down the road.* 2 go out of existence; come to an end: *When spring comes, the snow disappears.* *v.* **—dis′ap·pear′ance,** *n.*

dis·ap·point (dis′ə point′) make a person sad by not turning out as he or she hoped and expected: *The news that Grandma could not come disappointed the whole family.* *v.* **—dis′ap·point′ment,** *n.*

dis·ap·prove (dis′ə prüv′) think or say that something is wrong: *My parents disapprove of smoking.* *v.,* **dis·ap·proved, dis·ap·prov·ing.** **—dis′ap·prov′al,** *n.*

dis·arm (di sårm′) **1** take weapons away from: *The police captured the bandits and disarmed them.* **2** reduce the number of soldiers and weapons: *More nations are starting to disarm.* This process is called **disarmament. 3** get rid of someone's anger or fear: *His smile could disarm even his worst enemies.* **4** make harmless: *The soldiers disarmed the big bomb.* *v.*

dis·ar·ray (dis′ə rā′) mess; confusion: *The whole house was in disarray after the frantic search for her pet snake.* *n.*

dis·as·ter (də zas′tər) an event that causes much suffering or loss; a terrible happening: *floods, fires, wars, and other disasters.* *n.* **—dis·as′trous,** *adj.*

dis·band (dis band′) break up; separate: *The rock group disbanded after the drummer died.* *v.*

dis·be·lief (dis′bi lēf′) the state of being unable or unwilling to believe: *When we saw the rabbit appear, we stared in disbelief at the magician.* *n.* **—dis′be·lieve′,** *v.*

disc (disk) **1** short for **compact disc. 2** another spelling of **disk,** any flat, thin, round object. *n.*

dis·card (di skård′ *for 1,* dis′kård *for 2*) **1** throw away: *to discard an old pair of shoes, to discard an idea.* **2** something thrown away: *That old book is a discard from the school library.* 1 *v.,* 2 *n.*

> **WORD HISTORY....... discard**
>
> This word originally came from card games; when you **discard**, you get rid of a card.

dis·cern (di sərn′) see clearly; recognize by looking or thinking carefully: *She looked where he pointed, but could discern nothing. When there are so many lies, it is hard to discern the truth.* *v.* **—dis·cern′ing,** *adj.* **—dis·cern′ment,** *n.* **—dis·cern′i·ble,** *adj.*

dis·charge (dis chårj′ *for 1–3,* dis′chårj *or* dis chårj′ *for 4, 5*) **1** release; let out; let go: *to discharge a patient from a hospital, to discharge passengers at a station. A volcano discharges steam, ashes, and lava.* **2** fire off; set off; shoot: *to discharge a gun, to discharge a bomb.* **3** take care of something you have to do: *to discharge a debt, to discharge a duty.* **4** the act of letting out, unloading, firing, etc.: *an early discharge from prison, the discharge of a load of lumber from a truck. Lightning is a discharge of built-up electricity in the air.* **5** something given off or let out: *the watery discharge from a sore.* 1–3 *v.,* **dis·charged, dis·charg·ing;** 4, 5 *n.*

dis·ci·ple (də sī′pəl) **1** a person who believes in the ideas and teachings of another person and follows them. **2** teach someone to believe and follow certain ideas faithfully. 1 *n.,* 2 *v.,* **dis·ci·pled, dis·ci·pling.**

dis·ci·pline (dis′ə plin) **1** train; teach self-control and good behaviour and stop wrong behaviour, especially by laying down certain rules and backing them up strictly: *to discipline children. She had been disciplined by a life of hardship.* **2** this process of teaching, training, and correcting: *Good discipline takes patience.* **3** the self-control, orderly behaviour, and strong character that result from this: *Her calm reaction to their insults showed real discipline.* **4** punish: *The lazy employee was severely disciplined.* **5** an area of study; a subject, such as math, languages, science, or history. 1, 4 *v.,* **dis·ci·plined, dis·ci·plin·ing;** 2, 3, 5 *n.* **—dis′ci·pli·nar′y,** *adj.*

disc jockey (disk jok′ē) a person who plays recorded music over the radio or at a dance.

dis·close (dis klōz′) uncover; let people see or know: *The lifting of the curtain disclosed beautiful scenery. The letter discloses a secret.* *v.,* **dis·closed, dis·clos·ing.** **—dis·clo′sure** (dis klō′zhər), *n.*

dis·col·our or **dis·col·or** (dis kul′ər) **1** spoil the colour of; stain: *Smoke had discoloured the building.* **2** change colour: *Some materials discolour in bright sunshine.* *v.* **—dis·col′or·a′tion,** *n.*

dis·com·fort (dis kum′fərt) **1** a feeling of not being comfortable; pain or embarrassment: *He felt some discomfort after the operation. Her discomfort increased as one by one they turned to look at her.* **2** something that causes discomfort: *Life in the Barrens has many discomforts, but also many rewards.* *n.*

dis·con·nect (dis′kə nekt′) **1** separate; unfasten: *I disconnected the cars of the model train.* **2** unplug something electric: *She disconnected the fan before trying to fix it.* *v.*

dis·con·nect·ed (dis′kə nek′tid) broken; confused: *The injured man's story was so disconnected that it was hard to tell what had happened to him.* *adj.*

dis·con·tent (dis′kən tent′) a feeling of not being satisfied with what you have and wanting something different. *n.* **—dis′con·tent′ed,** *adj.*

a bat	e bed	i bid	o pot	u cup	th thin
ā cake	ē me	ī bite	ō go	ü rude	ᴛʜ then
å bar	ə about	ər over	ȯ for	u̇ put	zh measure

dis•con•tin•ue (dis′kən tin′yū) stop something that has gone on for some time: *That TV show has been discontinued.* *v.,* **dis•con•tin•ued, dis•con•tin•u•ing.**

dis•cord (dis′kȯrd) lack of harmony, whether in music, in ideas, or in relations between people; a clash: *There was discord while all the band members tuned their instruments at the same time. Angry discord spoiled the get-together.* *n.* **—dis•cord′ant** (dis kȯr′dənt), *adj.*

dis•count (dis′kount· *sometimes* dis kount′ *for 1 and 3*) **1** take off a certain amount from a price: *The store discounts three percent on your order if you bring your own bag.* **2** the amount taken off a price: *There is a ten percent discount for seniors on Thursdays.* **3** not believe; ignore: *You have to discount a lot of what Jack tells you; he gets carried away sometimes.* 1, 3 *v.,* 2 *n.*
discount store, a store that sells its goods for less than the regular price.

dis•cour•age (di skər′ij) **1** take away someone's courage and hopes: *Don't let your failures discourage you.* **2** try to prevent by disapproving; advise against something: *My parents discourage us from eating sugary snacks.* **3** make something seem like a bad idea: *This blizzardy weather sure discourages travel.* *v.,* **dis•cour•aged, dis•cour•ag•ing.** **—dis•cour′age•ment,** *n.*

dis•cov•er (di skuv′ər) find out; see or learn about something for the first time: *On one of our hikes we discovered a cave in the woods.* *v.* **—dis•cov′er•er,** *n.* **—dis•cov′er•y,** *n.*

dis•cred•it (dis kred′it) **1** destroy belief or trust in someone or something: *New discoveries in science have discredited that old theory.* **2** a bad reputation, or the cause of it: *The young thief brought discredit to his family. The traitor was a discredit to his country.* 1 *v.,* 2 *n.*

dis•creet (di skrēt′) careful and sensible; showing thoughtfulness and good judgment: *a discreet adviser, a discreet remark.* *adj.*

dis•cre•tion (di skresh′ən) **1** the freedom to judge or choose: *It is within the principal's discretion to suspend a pupil.* **2** good judgment; care and thought: *You will need discretion to criticize his work without hurting his feelings.* *n.*
at someone's discretion, according to someone's careful decision.

dis•crim•i•nate (di skrim′ə nāt′) **1** notice the fine but important differences: *Can you discriminate between true and artificial diamonds?* **2** treat people differently when their differences don't matter: *Employers should not discriminate against any nationality when hiring.* *v.,* **dis•crim•i•nat•ed, dis•crim•i•nat•ing.** **—dis•crim′i•na′tion,** *n.*

Discus throwing was a popular event in the ancient Greek Olympic Games. Competitors get extra force behind the throw by spinning several times before releasing the discus.

dis•cus (dis′kəs) **1** a sport in which people try to throw a round heavy disc as far as they can. **2** the disc thrown in this sport. *n.*

dis•cuss (di skus′) talk over the various sides of a question: *The class discussed the problem. Dad discussed my report card with my teacher.* *v.* **—dis•cus′sion,** *n.*

dis•dain (dis dān′) **1** look down on; think of as being beneath yourself: *She disdained to wear the silly party hat.* **2** scorn; an attitude of looking down on a person or thing: *He had disdain for anyone who disagreed with him.* 1 *v.,* 2 *n.* **—dis•dain′ful,** *adj.*

dis•ease (də zēz′) sickness; illness: *Disease kills some plants each year. Chicken pox is an infectious disease.* *n.* **—dis•eased′,** *adj.*

dis•em•bark (dis′em bärk′) get out of a boat or any vehicle: *We disembarked from the ferry at Charlottetown.* *v.*

dis•fa•vour or **dis•fa•vor** (dis fā′vər) dislike; disapproval: *Mom looks with disfavour on torn jeans.* *n.*
in disfavour, viewed with dislike or disapproval: *The mayor was in disfavour with the townspeople.*

dis•fig•ure (dis fig′ər *or* dis fig′yər) spoil the beauty of: *Huge billboards disfigure the countryside.* *v.,* **dis•fig•ured, dis•fig•ur•ing.** **—dis•fig′ure•ment,** *n.*

dis•grace (dis grās′) **1** shame; a loss of respect or honour: *There is no disgrace in losing.* **2** bring shame upon: *He disgraced his family by his behaviour.* **3** something to be ashamed of: *Their unfriendly attitude to the new neighbours was a disgrace.* 1, 3 *n.,* 2 *v.,* **dis•graced, dis•grac•ing.** **—dis•grace′ful,** *adj.*
in disgrace, in a state of dishonour or shame: *The girl was in disgrace for cheating on an exam.*

dis·grun·tled (dis grun′təld) annoyed and disappointed because something has not happened as you expected: *Karen was disgruntled because the school trip was cancelled.* *adj.*

dis·guise (dis gīz′) **1** make a person look like someone else: *She disguised herself as a much older woman, using a wig, make-up, a cane, and different clothes.* **2** the clothes or actions used for this: *Her disguise also included glasses and a hat.* **3** make something seem like something else: *He disguised his hatred by pretending to be friendly.* 1, 3 *v.,* **dis·guised, dis·guis·ing;** 2 *n.*

dis·gust (dis gust′) **1** sickening dislike: *Their cruelty to the animals filled us with disgust.* **2** cause sickening dislike in: *The smell at the dump disgusted them.* **3** a feeling of being fed up. **4** make someone fed up: *Their laziness disgusted him.* 1, 3 *n.,* 2, 4 *v.* **—dis·gust′ing,** *adj.*

dish (dish) **1** a small bowl: *a dish of ice cream.* **2 dishes,** *pl.,* anything to serve food in, such as plates, bowls, cups and saucers. **3** food prepared a certain way: *Lasagna is my favourite dish.* **4** a radio or TV antenna that is shaped like a huge bowl and receives signals from communications satellites in space. It is also called a **dish antenna** or **satellite dish.** *n.* **—dish′ful′,** *n.*
dish out, give out, especially words or actions: *to dish out compliments.*
dish up, put in a dish to serve: *She asked Manish to dish up the potatoes.*

Word Family.......... dish

dishcloth: a cloth to wash dishes with
dishful: as much as a dish can hold
dishtowel: a cloth for drying dishes with
dishwasher: a machine for washing and drying dishes
dishwater: water that dishes are washed in

dis·heart·en (dis här′tən) discourage; depress: *Her long sickness was disheartening.* *v.*

di·shev·elled or **di·shev·eled** (də shev′əld) rumpled; disordered; untidy: *a dishevelled appearance, dishevelled hair.* *adj.*

dis·hon·est (di son′ist) not honest; not fair or truthful: *A person who lies, cheats, tricks people, or steals is dishonest.* *adj.* **—dis·hon′es·ty,** *n.*

dis·hon·our or **dis·hon·or** (di son′ər) **1** shame; loss of respect and dignity. **2** a person or thing that causes this: *That bully is a dishonour to his family.* **3** bring shame to; bring someone down in the eyes of others: *A dishonest police officer dishonours the entire force.* 1, 2 *n.,* 3 *v.* **—dis·hon′our·a·ble,** *adj.*

dis·il·lu·sioned (dis′i lü′zhənd) so disappointed with something that you give up on it: *Keen to take the photography course, Bernice became disillusioned halfway through it.* *adj.* **—dis′il·lu′sion·ment,** *n.*

dis·in·fect (dis′in fekt′) kill the germs in or on: *A doctor's instruments are disinfected before they are used.* A substance that kills germs is a **disinfectant.** *v.*

dis·in·te·grate (di sin′tə grāt′) break apart completely into small bits: *The explosion completely disintegrated the building. The old papers had disintegrated into a pile of dust.* *v.,* **dis·in·te·grat·ed, dis·in·te·grat·ing.**

dis·in·ter·est·ed (di sin′tris tid) without selfish motives; not acting for your own gain or taking sides: *The Olympic judges are supposed to be disinterested.* *adj.*

USING WORDS .... disinterested

The adjective *interested* has two opposites.

- If you are **disinterested** in something, you have no selfish interest: *A referee must be disinterested in the outcome of the game.*
- If you are **uninterested** in something, you have no feelings about it: *He was uninterested in watching the basketball game.*

disk (disk) **1** any flat, thin round object. **2** a thin, small, magnetic plate used for storing computer data. There are two main types: the **floppy disk** and the **hard disk.** Any part of a computer that can read data from a disk is called a **disk drive.** *n.*

diskette (di sket′) a thin, round, bendable magnetic plate for storing computer data, protected by a hard, plastic case that can't be removed. A diskette is put into a computer and taken out again every time it is used. **Floppy disk** is another name for it. *n.*

dis·like (dis līk′) **1** a feeling of not liking; a feeling against: *Dad has a dislike for the neighbour's dog.* **2** have this feeling against; not like: *She dislikes studying and would rather play football.* **3** something a person doesn't like: *Liver is one of my greatest dislikes.* 1 *n.,* 2 *v.,* **dis·liked, dis·lik·ing.**

dis·lo·cate (dis′lō kāt′) cause the bones of a joint to be shifted out of place: *He dislocated his shoulder when he fell.* *v.,* **dis·lo·cat·ed, dis·lo·cat·ing.**

a bat	e bed	i bid	o pot	u cup	th thin
ā cake	ē me	ī bite	ō go	ü rude	ᴛʜ then
à bar	ə about	ər over	ȯ for	ů put	zh measure

dis·lodge (dis loj′) force something out of a place where it is stuck: *The worker used a crowbar to dislodge a heavy stone from the wall.* *v.,* **dis·lodged, dis·lodg·ing.**

dis·loy·al (dis loi′əl) not loyal; letting down those who trust in you. *adj.* **—dis·loy′al·ty,** *n.*

dis·mal (diz′məl) dreary and gloomy: *Cold, rainy days are dismal.* *adj.*

dis·man·tle (dis man′təl) take apart: *We had to dismantle the bookcases to move them.* *v.,* **dis·man·tled, dis·man·tling.**

dis·may (dis mā′) **1** a feeling of very heavy spirits from fear or great disappointment: *The family stared in dismay at the burned remains of their house.* **2** fill with this feeling: *The thought that she might never see her friend again dismayed her.* 1 *n.,* 2 *v.*

dis·miss (dis mis′) **1** send away; let go: *The teacher dismissed the class at noon. They dismissed the cook because his cooking was awful.* **2** decide not to think about or pay attention to: *He dismissed every one of our complaints with an impatient wave of his hand.* *v.* **—dis·miss′al,** *n.*

dis·mount (dis mount′) **1** get off a horse, bicycle, etc.: *When biking, dismount to cross the street.* **2** take a thing from its base or support: *The telescopes were dismounted for shipping to another observatory.* *v.*

dis·o·be·di·ent (dis′ə bē′dē ənt) not following orders or rules; refusing to obey. *adj.* **—dis′o·be′di·ence,** *n.*

dis·o·bey (dis′ə bā′) not follow orders or rules; refuse to obey: *The student got a detention for disobeying the teacher.* *v.*

dis·or·der (di sôr′dər) **1** messiness; confusion: *The disorder in your room is shocking.* **2** lack of rules and discipline; rebellious behaviour. **3** mess up; throw into confusion: *Her thoughts were disordered by the upsetting scene.* **4** a sickness or disease: *a disorder of the stomach.* 1, 2, 4 *n.,* 3 *v.* **—dis·or′der·ly,** *adj.*

dis·or·gan·ized (di sôr′gə nīzd′) showing lack of planning; messy; not following any system. *adj.*

dis·or·i·ent (dis ôr′ē ent′) cause to become confused about the right direction, or about what is happening around you: *The hot sun so disoriented her that she could hardly find her way home.* *v.* **—dis·o′ri·en·ta′tion,** *n.* **—dis·o′ri·ent′ed,** *adj.*

dis·own (di sōn′) refuse to recognize as your own; cast off: *The mother duck disowned the Ugly Duckling. The politician disowned his former views.* *v.*

dis·par·age (di sper′ij) put down or belittle; criticize: *Klara disparaged every effort I made.* *v.,* **dis·par·aged, dis·par·ag·ing.**

dis·patch (di spach′ *for 1, 3;* dis′pach *for 2, 4*) **1** send off: *He dispatched a messenger to tell the king what had happened.* **2** a message that has been sent, especially an official one: *This dispatch has been two days on the way.* **3** finish something off: *The job was quickly dispatched. The hungry girl soon dispatched the meal.* **4** promptness in doing anything; speed: *This student works with neatness and dispatch.* 1, 3 *v.,* 2, 4 *n.*

dis·pel (di spel′) drive away and scatter: *The captain's cheerful laugh dispelled their fears.* *v.,* **dis·pelled, dis·pel·ling.**

dis·pense (di spens′) **1** give out, whether for sale or as a gift: *a machine that dispenses candy. The aid workers dispensed food and clothing to the homeless refugees.* **2** apply; carry out: *Judges and law courts dispense justice.* *v.,* **dis·pensed, dis·pens·ing.**
dispense with, a get rid of; do away with: *He dispensed with the old papers by burning them.* **b** get along without; do without: *I think I can dispense with a second dessert.*

Word Family........ **dispense**

dispensable: unnecessary
dispensary: a place where medicines are given out

dis·pens·er (di spens′ər) a machine, pump, container, etc. which lets out its contents one at a time or in measured amounts: *a drinking straw dispenser, a soap dispenser, a chocolate bar dispenser.* *n.*

dis·perse (di spərs′) scatter; go or send off in different directions: *The Mounties dispersed the rioters. The crowd dispersed when the game was over.* *v.,* **dis·persed, dis·pers·ing.**

dis·place (dis plās′) **1** take the place of; put something else in the place of: *Cars have displaced the horse and buggy.* **2** move from the original spot: *When he returned, he saw that a few of his tools had been displaced. When we dropped a rock into the beaker, it displaced 150 mL of water—the level rose from 300 mL to 450 mL.* *v.,* **dis·placed, dis·plac·ing.** **—dis·place′ment,** *n.*

dis·play (di splā′) **1** show: *He displayed his knowledge by answering all our questions* (*v.*). *A tantrum is a display of bad temper* (*n.*). **2** something specially set up or arranged for people to look at: *Grade 4 had two displays of student drawings.* 1 *v.,* 1, 2 *n.*

dis·please (dis plēz′) make angry or unhappy: *Your rude answer displeased your mother.* *v.,* **dis·pleased, dis·pleas·ing.**

dis·pleas·ure (dis plezh′ər) annoyance; disapproval; anger: *His displeasure could be heard in his angry tones.* *n.*

dis·pos·a·ble (di spō′zə bəl) **1** designed to be thrown away after use: *disposable paper cups.* **2** available for use: *disposable income.* *adj.*

The disposal of millions of tonnes of waste from homes and businesses is a growing problem. Most of the waste is buried in landfill sites, which are lined to prevent harmful liquids from leaking into nearby water supplies.

dis·pos·al (di spō′zəl) **1** the act of getting rid of something: *the disposal of garbage.* **2** a special place or device for getting rid of garbage. *n.*
at one's disposal, ready for one's use or service at any time: *She put all her books at her guests' disposal.*

dis·pose (di spōz′)
dispose of, a get rid of: *Dispose of that junk.* **b** take care of; settle: *She disposed of all our questions in five minutes.* *v.,* **dis·posed, dis·pos·ing.**

dis·posed (di spōzd′) having a particular attitude: *How were they disposed toward the plan?* *adj.*
disposed to, inclined; tending: *He is disposed to get mad at the least little thing.*

dis·po·si·tion (dis′pə zish′ən) a person's usual way of acting and thinking: *a cheerful disposition, a selfish disposition, a disposition to argue.* *n.*

dis·prove (dis prūv′) prove false: *Melanie thought she had less candy, but we soon disproved that by weighing both bags.* *v.,* **dis·proved, dis·prov·ing.**

dis·pute (di spyūt′) **1** argue or fight over: *They spent the evening disputing who would get to sleep in the top bunk.* **2** an argument or fight: *a dispute about how to load the dishwasher.* **3** question; challenge; not accept: *The neighbours disputed his right to keep a goat in the backyard of his city home.* 1, 3 *v.,* **dis·put·ed, dis·put·ing;** 2 *n.* **—dis·put′a·ble,** *adj.*

dis·qual·i·fy (dis kwol′ə fī′) keep someone from doing something because he or she does not meet certain requirements: *His weak back disqualified him for the job of moving pianos. The runner was disqualified from the race after she made three false starts.* *v.,* **dis·qual·i·fied, dis·qual·i·fy·ing.**

dis·re·gard (dis′ri gȧrd′) **1** pay no attention to; take no notice of: *Disregard that stupid remark.* **2** the act of not paying attention: *The reckless driver was arrested for her disregard of traffic laws.* 1 *v.,* 2 *n.*

dis·re·pair (dis′ri per′) a bad condition; a need of repairs: *The car was in such disrepair that it was not safe to drive.* *n.*

dis·rep·u·ta·ble (dis rep′yə tə bəl) having a bad reputation: *Don't hang around too much with that disreputable bunch.* *adj.*

dis·re·spect (dis′ri spekt′) rudeness; lack of respect: *Don't answer in that tone of disrespect.* *n.* **—dis′re·spect′ful,** *adj.*

dis·rupt (dis rupt′) disturb something so badly as to keep it from continuing normally: *A violent quarrel disrupted the game.* *v.* **—dis·rup′tion,** *n.* **—dis·rup′tive,** *adj.*

dis·sat·is·fied (dis sat′is fīd′) unhappy; not content: *When we do not get what we want, we are dissatisfied.* *adj.* **—dis·sat′is·fac′tion,** *n.*

dis·sect (di sekt′ *or* dī sekt′) **1** cut up an animal or plant in order to study it. **2** examine anything part by part; analyse. *v.* **—dis·sec′tion,** *n.*

dis·sent (di sent′) **1** disagree with most others: *Most of the class wanted to go to the planetarium, but three boys dissented.* **2** disagreement in a group. 1 *v.,* 2 *n.* **—dis·sen′sion,** *n.*

dis·si·pate (dis′ə pāt′) scatter; disappear or drive away gradually: *By morning their anger had dissipated. The sun dissipated the fog.* *v.,* **dis·si·pat·ed, dis·si·pat·ing.**

dis·solve (di zolv′) **1** mix completely with a liquid: *You can dissolve sugar in water. Sugar dissolves in water.* **2** end an agreement or partnership. **3** fade away: *My fears dissolved when she smiled.* *v.,* **dis·solved, dis·solv·ing.**

a bat	e bed	i bid	o pot	u cup	th thin
ā cake	ē me	ī bite	ō go	ū rude	ᴛʜ then
ȧ bar	ə about	ər over	ȯ for	u̇ put	zh measure

dis·so·nant (dis′ə nənt) clashing; not in harmony: *dissonant opinions, the dissonant sounds of an orchestra tuning up.* *adj.* —**dis′so·nance,** *n.*

dis·suade (di swād′) persuade not to do something: *The father finally dissuaded his son from running away.* *v.,* **dis·suad·ed, dis·suad·ing.** —**dis·sua′sion** (di swā′zhən), *n.*

dis·tance (dis′təns) **1** the space in between: *The distance from the farm to the town is 5 km.* **2** a long way: *The campground is quite a distance from the highway.* *n.* **in the distance,** a long way off: *The hikers saw a light in the distance.*

dis·tant (dis′tənt) **1** far away in space or time; not close: *stories from the distant past. We could see the distant mountains from the top of the tower.* **2** away: *The town is 5 km distant.* **3** not very friendly: *She answered him with only a distant nod.* *adj.*

dis·taste (dis tāst′) dislike: *His distaste for carrots showed clearly on his face.* *n.* —**dis·taste′ful,** *adj.*

dis·til or **dis·till** (di stil′) **1** boil a liquid to make a vapour and then cool the vapour so it condenses back into a liquid. When the liquid turns to vapour, it leaves behind any other substances that were mixed in. **2** separate by distilling: *Gasoline is distilled from crude oil.* *v.,* **dis·tilled, dis·til·ling.** —**dis′til·la′tion** (dis′tə lā′shən), *n.*

dis·tinct (di stingkt′) **1** separate; able to be noticed or thought of separately: *two distinct sounds.* **2** different: *Mice are distinct from rats.* **3** clear; easily seen, heard, or understood: *Your speech should be distinct.* *adj.* —**dis·tinct′ly,** *adv.*

dis·tinc·tion (di stingk′shən) **1** the act of making a difference: *He treated all alike, without distinction.* **2** a difference: *What is the distinction between ducks and geese?* **3** a mark or sign of honour; a fact that makes a person or thing special: *She had the distinction of being the first female astronaut.* **4** excellence: *an achievement of great distinction.* *n.*

dis·tinc·tive (di stingk′tiv) unique; special: *Skunks have a distinctive smell.* *adj.*

dis·tin·guish (di sting′gwish) **1** tell apart: *Can you distinguish real leather from fake leather?* **2** see or hear clearly: *It was too dark for her to distinguish the outline of the house.* **3** make different from others; be a special quality or feature of: *What distinguishes the elephant is its trunk.* **4** make famous; win honour for: *He distinguished himself by winning three prizes.* *v.*

dis·tin·guished (di sting′gwisht) **1** outstanding: *a distinguished artist, a medal for distinguished conduct.* **2** dignified or impressive in appearance. *adj.*

dis·tort (di stört′) **1** pull or twist out of shape: *His face was distorted with rage.* **2** give something a wrong meaning or purpose: *She distorted the facts so someone else would get the blame.* *v.* —**dis·tor′tion,** *n.*

dis·tract (di strakt′) **1** draw the attention away: *Noise distracts me from my studying. She told the children a story to distract them from their fear.* **2** **distracted,** confused and unable to cope: *So many people shouting at him at once made him distracted.* *v.* —**dis·trac′tion,** *n.*

dis·traught (di strot′) so upset that you cannot think clearly: *Martin's parents were distraught after hearing that the school bus had collided with a steetcar.* *adj.*

dis·tress (di stres′) **1** great pain, sorrow, or anxiety: *The loss of her dog caused her great distress.* **2** cause pain, anxiety, or sorrow to: *The idea of moving to another town distressed him.* **3** trouble; difficult conditions: *The Coast Guard went to help the ship in distress.* 1, 3 *n.,* 2 *v.*

dis·trib·ute (di strib′yūt) **1** give out: *She distributed the cookies among all the children.* **2** spread; scatter: *Distribute the paint evenly over the wall.* **3** divide into parts: *The students were distributed into three groups for the field trip.* *v.,* **dis·trib·ut·ed, dis·trib·ut·ing.** —**dis′tri·bu′tion** (dis′trə byū′shən), *n.*

dis·trict (dis′trikt) **1** a part of a larger area: *Northern Ontario is an important mining district in Canada. They lived in a quiet district of the city.* **2** a division of a country, province, or city marked off by the government for a special purpose: *a school district, a voting district.* *n.*

dis·trust (dis trust′) **1** put no trust in: *I didn't tell him the secret because I distrusted him.* **2** lack of trust; suspicion: *She looked sideways at the stranger with distrust.* 1 *v.,* 2 *n.* —**dis·trust′ful,** *adj.*

dis·turb (di stərb′) **1** destroy the peace, quiet, or rest of: *Heavy truck traffic disturbed the neighbourhood all day long. Do not disturb the baby; he is asleep.* **2** break in on; interrupt: *A phone call disturbed our family council.* **3** put out of order; mess up: *Someone has disturbed my shell collection.* **4** make uneasy or upset: *He was disturbed by the news of her illness.* *v.* —**dis·turb′ance,** *n.*

ditch (dich) **1** a long, narrow trench dug in the earth, often beside a road: *Ditches are usually used to carry off water.* **2** *Informal.* abandon; get rid of: *Don't ditch your old friends just because you've made new ones.* 1 *n.,* 2 *v.*

dit·to (dit′ō) 1 the same; exactly the same as appeared before. 2 a mark (″) that stands for ditto. *Example:* 6 kg beans at 90¢...$5.40
4 ″ ″ ″ ″ ...$3.60
n., pl. **dit·tos.**

dit·ty (dit′ē) a short, simple song or poem. *n., pl.* **dit·ties.**

di·van (di van′) a long, low, armless couch. *n.*

This diver is wearing a deep-sea pressure suit, a bit like a spacesuit. Air, or a mixture of gases for really deep diving, is contained in tanks on the surface. In suits like this, divers can descend to as much as 600 m.

dive (dīv) 1 jump headfirst into the water. A pool often has a **diving board** for this purpose. 2 go down fast with the front end toward the earth: *The airplane dived suddenly.* 3 the act of diving, or a certain way of diving: *The plane did a nose-dive. The jack-knife is a difficult dive.* 4 start doing something with great energy and concentration: *She dived into her research project.* 1, 2, 4 *v.,* **dived** or **dove, dived, div·ing;** 3 *n.* **—div′er,** *n.*

USING WORDS ...... dived

Dived and **dove** are both used for the past tense of *dive,* although dived is used more in formal English.

di·verge (di vərj′ *or* dī vərj′) branch off in different directions from a given point, getting further and further apart: *Their paths diverged at the corner and each went her own way.* *v.*

di·verse (di vərs′ *or* dīvərs′) showing a lot of variety: *The population of our school is very diverse.* *adj.* **—di·ver′si·ty,** *n.*

di·vert (di vərt′ *or* dī vərt′) 1 turn aside: *A ditch diverts water from the stream into the fields.* 2 distract: *The rattle diverted the baby's attention from the food.* 3 amuse; entertain. *v.* **—di·ver′sion,** *n.*

di·vide (di vīd′) 1 separate into parts: *A path divides the field. The river divides and forms two streams.* 2 in mathematics, show a number as separated into equal parts by a smaller number: *When you divide 8 by 2, the result is two equal sets of 4. Symbol:* ÷ 3 share: *The children divided the pizza.* 4 to separate in feeling, opinion, etc.; split by a disagreement: *The school was divided on the choice of a logo.* 5 a ridge of land separating the regions drained by two river systems. The Rocky Mountains are called the **Great Divide.** 1–4 *v.,* **di·vid·ed, di·vid·ing;** 5 *n.*

div·i·dend (div′ə dend′) 1 a number to be divided. 2 profits earned by a company and divided among the owners of the company. 3 **dividends,** *pl.,* rewards; advantages; benefits: *Reading brings great dividends.* *n.*

di·vine (di vīn′) 1 having to do with God or a god. 2 *Informal.* excellent; unusually good: *"Try one of our divine desserts," it said on the menu.* 3 guess; predict. 1, 2 *adj.,* 3 *v.,* **di·vined, di·vin·ing.**

diving suit (dī′ving sūt′) a waterproof suit with a helmet that is worn by a diver to work underwater. A tube attached to the helmet supplies air from a tank on the diver's back.

di·vis·i·ble (di viz′ə bəl) capable of being divided with no remainder: *12 is divisible by 4.* *adj.*

di·vi·sion (di vizh′ən) 1 the act of dividing or the fact of being divided. 2 the process of showing how many times one number is contained by another: *10 ÷ 2 = 5* is a simple division. 3 something that divides, such as a boundary line. 4 one of the parts into which a thing is divided; section: *a division of the animal kingdom, the primary division of a school.* *n.*

a bat	e bed	i bid	o pot	u cup	th thin
ā cake	ē me	ī bite	ō go	ū rude	ᴛʜ then
à bar	ə about	ər over	ȯ for	ů put	zh measure

di·vi·sor (di vī′zər) the number that another number is divided by. *n.*

di·vorce (di vôrs′) 1 the legal ending of a marriage. 2 legally end a marriage: *The judge divorced Mr. and Mrs. Ivanovitch. David's aunt divorced her husband.* 3 separate: *Learning should not be divorced from play.* 1 *n.,* 2, 3 *v.,* **di·vorced, di·vorc·ing.**

di·vulge (di vulj′ *or* dī vulj′) tell something secret: *The traitor divulged the plans to the enemy.* *v.,* **di·vulged, di·vulg·ing.**

Di·wa·li (di vä′lē) an important fall festival in the Hindu religion, celebrating the New Year. It is also called the **Festival of Lights. Divali** is another spelling. *n.*

diz·zy (diz′ē) 1 unable to keep your balance; feeling like your head is spinning: *Sometimes when I get up suddenly, I feel dizzy.* 2 confused; bewildered: *The noise and crowds of the city streets made the little boy dizzy.* 3 make dizzy: *The ride on the merry-go-round dizzied her.* 4 likely to cause dizziness: *The mountaineer climbed to a dizzy height.* 1, 2, 4 *adj.,* **diz·zi·er, diz·zi·est;** 3 *v.,* **diz·zied, diz·zy·ing.** **—diz′zi·ly,** *adv.* **—diz′zi·ness,** *n.*

dm *symbol for* decimetre or decimetres.

DNA a substance found in the cells of living things that tells the body what characteristics will be passed from one generation to the next. DNA also tells the new organism how to form all the proteins it needs to grow and develop. Its full name is **deoxyribonucleic acid.**

do (dü) 1 carry out; perform: *That's easier said than done. She did her work.* 2 make; produce: *They're doing a film about Arctic wildlife.* 3 act; behave: *You did wisely in returning the money.* 4 get along; manage: *How are they doing in their new home?* 5 be good enough: *He said any kind of paper would do.* 6 go: *We did 600 km today. This dirt bike can do 70 km/h.* 7 a party or other gathering: *There's always a do at my grandparents' on Thanksgiving.* 8 **Do** is also used in certain types of sentences as an auxiliary verb: **a** in asking questions: *Do you like milk?* **b** to emphasize a verb: *I do want to go. Do hurry, please.* **c** to stand for another verb already used: *My dog goes everywhere I do.* **d** in statements that contain **not:** *I do not think they will come.* 1–6, 8 *v.,* **does, did, done, do·ing;** 7 *n.* **—do′a·ble,** *adj.*
do away with, a put an end to; get rid of: *to do away with a rule.* **b** kill.
do in, tire out completely: *That climb did me in.*
do someone out of, get from someone by a trick: *That cheat just did me out of my lunch money.*
do up, a close, tie, or fasten: *to do up a coat.* **b** wrap: *to do up a package.* **c** clean and get ready for use: *to do up a room.*
do with, enjoy or use: *I could do with a cold pop right now.*
have to do with, a relate to: *Her stories all have to do with the future.* **b** be involved with: *I won't have anything to do with that crazy plan.*
How do you do? a formal greeting used when meeting someone for the first time.

do·cile (dō′sīl *or* dos′īl) easily managed; obedient: *a docile dog.* *adj.*

dock[1] (dok) 1 a platform built on the shore or out from shore, where boats can come alongside for loading and unloading or to be tied up or anchored. 2 come or bring alongside a dock: *The captain docked the ferry with hardly a bump. The ship will dock at 1:15.* 1 *n.,* 2 *v.*

dock[2] (dok) 1 cut short: *Dogs' tails are sometimes docked.* 2 take away part of: *The company docks the employees' wages if they come late to work.* *v.*

dock[3] (dok) the place where an accused person stands in a law court. *n.*

doc·tor (dok′tər) 1 a person who has a licence to practise medicine or perform surgery: *a medical doctor.* 2 any of certain other professionals who care for people or animals. Dentists, chiropractors, and veterinarians are doctors. 3 give medical treatment to: *Dad doctored me when I had the flu.* 4 a person who has taken the highest degree possible in a university: *Doctor of Philosophy.* 5 change something for a harmful purpose: *She doctored the enemy agent's drink. The dishonest bank clerk doctored the accounts.* 1, 2, 4 *n.,* 3, 5 *v.*

doc·trine (dok′trən) a belief that is taught or passed on: *Christian doctrine, racist doctrine.* *n.*

doc·u·ment (dok′yə mənt) 1 something written or printed that gives information, especially something official: *Show these documents to the customs officer at the border.* 2 a computer file made with ordinary writing software. 3 give or keep a record of something: *Our summer trip is documented in this big photo album.* *n.*

doc·u·men·ta·ry (dok′yə men′tə rē) a movie, show, or book that presents facts in an artistic way. If it adds some fiction for greater interest, it is called a **docudrama** (dok′yə drä′mə). *n., pl.* **doc·u·men·ta·ries.**

doc·u·men·ta·tion (dok′yə mən tā′shən) 1 a book or other printed material that explains how you use a piece of equipment: *The new computer system came with full documentation.* 2 the act of writing down information about something in an organized way. *n.*

dodge (doj) 1 move quickly to one side, especially to escape being hit or seen: *As I watched, he dodged behind the house. I dodged the ball as it came flying toward my head.*

2 a sudden movement to one side. **3** get away from or avoid by some trick: *She has dodged her chores again.* **4** *Informal.* a trick: *a clever dodge.* 1, 3 *v.,* **dodged, dodg·ing;** 2, 4 *n.* **—dodg·er,** *n.*

dodge·ball (doj′bol′) a game where players form a circle or two facing lines and try to hit other players in the centre with a large ball. *n.*

do·do (dō′dō) a large, clumsy bird not able to fly. Dodos lived on islands in the Indian Ocean, but are now extinct. *n., pl.* **do·dos** or **do·does.**

doe (dō) the female of the deer, antelope, rabbit, hare, and most other animals whose male is called a buck. *n.*

does (duz) the present tense form of **do**[1] used with *he, she, it,* or a singular noun: *Does she sing well?* *v.*

does·n't (duz′ənt) does not.

doff (dof) take off: *He doffed his hat as he entered the church.* *v.*

A bloodhound is trained to track people and animals by the scent they leave behind.

dog (dog) **1** a four-legged, mostly meat-eating animal kept as a pet or used to guard people or property, help in hunting, or lead the blind. There are many breeds of dog. **2** hunt or follow like a dog: *The police dogged the suspected thief.* 1 *n.,* 2 *v.,* **dogged, dog·ging.**
dog in the manger, a person who tries to keep others from enjoying what he or she cannot use.

Word Family.......... dog

dogcatcher: a person who rounds up stray dogs
dog-team: a group of dogs trained to pull sleds
dog-tired: very tired
dogtrot: a fairly slow running pace

dog–ear (dog′ēr′) **1** fold over the corner of a page in a book. **2** a corner of a page that is folded over. 1 *v.,* 2 *n.* **—dog′-eared′,** *adj.*

dog·ged (dog′id) stubborn; determined: *His dogged effort helped him to win the long-distance race.* *adj.*

dog·gie bag (dog′ē bag′) a bag that you use to take leftovers home after a meal in a restaurant: *The dinner was so good we asked for a doggie bag.*

dog·house (dog′hous′) a small house for a dog. *n.*
in the doghouse, *Slang.* in trouble with somebody: *She's in the doghouse with her brother because she borrowed his shirt and ripped it.*

Dog·rib (dog′rib) **1** a First Nations people living in the Northwest Territories between the Great Bear and Great Slave Lakes. They belong to the Dene Nation. **2** their language, which belongs to the Athapascan family. **3** having to do with these people or their language. 1, 2 *n.,* 3 *adj.*

🍁 **dog·sled** (dog′sled′) a sled pulled by dogs. *n.*

dog·wood (dog′wůd′) a tree or shrub often having large, white or pink flowers and red, blue, or white berries. The Pacific or western flowering dogwood is the provincial flower of British Columbia. *n.*

doi·ly (doi′lē) a small piece of lace, or paper with a lacy design, used under plates, vases, etc. *n., pl.* **doi·lies.**

do·ings (dū′ingz) actions: *Mr. Brown was deeply interested in the doings of his neighbours.* *pl.n.*

do·jo (dō′jō) a school or hall where martial arts are taught: *After school Wendy went to the dojo for her karate lesson.* *n., pl.* **do·jos.**

dol·drums (dol′drəmz) **1** certain parts of the ocean near the equator where the wind is very light or constantly shifting. Sailing ships caught in the doldrums were often unable to move for days. **2** low spirits: *The whole family was in the doldrums because of the rainy weather.* *pl.n.*

dole (dōl) **1** give in small quantities: *Mom doled out one piece of Halloween candy a day to each of us.* **2 the dole,** *Informal.* the money given by a government to help unemployed people. 1 *v.,* **doled, dol·ing;** 2 *n.*

dole·ful (dōl′fəl) sad; mournful: *The hound gave a doleful howl.* *adj.*

doll (dol) a child's toy made to look like a person. *n.*

a bat	e bed	i bid	o pot	u cup	th thin
ā cake	ē me	ī bite	ō go	ū rude	ꟸH then
ä bar	ə about	ər over	ô for	ů put	zh measure

dol·lar (dol′ər) 1 the unit of money in Canada and some other countries. *Symbol:* $ 2 a coin worth 100 cents: *He gave me four quarters for a dollar.* *n.*

WORD HISTORY........ dollar

The track of the word **dollar** goes like this. It came into English through German *daler*, from an earlier German word *thaler*. This word *thaler* is short for *Joachimsthaler*, a kind of silver coin. *Joachimsthal*, meaning "Joachim's valley" is the place in Germany where the silver for this coin was found.

dol·lop (dol′əp) *Informal.* a portion or serving of something soft or liquid: *a dollop of ice cream.* *n.*

doll·y (dol′ē) 1 a child's name for a doll. 2 a small, low platform on wheels, used to move heavy things or to lie on when repairing the underside of a car: *The fridge was moved on a dolly.* *n., pl.* **doll·ies.**

dol·phin (dol′fən) a sea mammal related to the whale and porpoise, with a snout shaped like a beak. Dolphins are very intelligent. *n.*

dolt (dōlt) a stupid person. *n.* **—dolt′ish,** *adj.*

do·main (dō mān′) 1 the area under the control of a person, government, etc.: *The Canadian domain extends from sea to sea. The rec room is the kids' domain.* 2 a field of thought and action: *Pierre Elliott Trudeau was a leader in the domain of politics.* *n.*

The bowl shape of domes is found in many religious buildings such as mosques and churches. This is St. Paul's Cathedral in London, England.

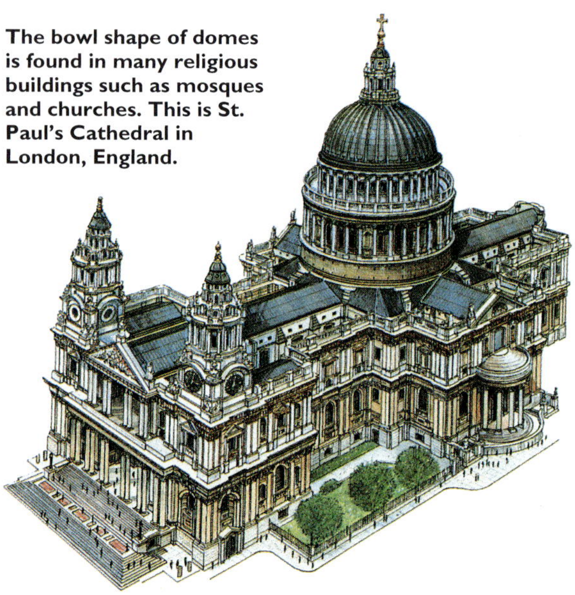

dome (dōm) 1 a large, rounded roof. 2 anything that is or seems high and rounded: *the dome of a hill, the dome of the sky.* *n.* **—domed,** *adj.*

dome fastener (dōm′ fas′ə nər) a small fastener made up of two parts, one with a little bump in the centre that snaps into a hole in the centre of the other.

do·mes·tic (də mes′tik) 1 having to do with the home or family: *domestic chores, a domestic scene.* 2 liking to do things in the home. 3 not wild; tame: *Pets are domestic animals.* To tame an animal is to **domesticate** it. 4 having to do with your own country; not foreign: *domestic news. Canadians eat a lot of domestic cheese.* 5 a household servant: *Butlers, cooks, and maids are domestics.* 1–4 *adj.,* 5 *n.*

dom·i·nant (dom′ə nənt) 1 main; controlling: *The Prime Minister was the dominant figure at the meeting. Hockey is Canada's dominant sport in winter.* 2 rising high above everything else; towering: *Dominant hills sheltered the bay.* *adj.*

dom·i·nate (dom′ə nāt′) 1 control or rule: *The boy dominated his smaller friend. Dandelions will dominate over grass if they are not kept out.* 2 rise high above; tower over: *The mountain dominates the city and its harbour.* *v.,* **dom·i·nat·ed, dom·i·nat·ing.** **—dom′i·na′tion,** *n.*

dom·i·neer·ing (dom′ə nē′ring) bossy. *adj.*

do·min·ion (də min′yən) 1 rule; control: *The British had dominion over a large part of the world.* 2 a territory under the control of a ruler or government: *The islands of St. Pierre and Miquelon are French dominions.* 3 **Dominion,** a name used for some independent countries in the Commonwealth of Nations: *The Dominion of Canada was established on July 1, 1867.* *n.*

dom·i·no (dom′ə nō′) 1 **dominoes,** *pl.* a game played with small rectangular tiles that are either blank or marked with dots on each end. You place the tiles so that matching patterns are next to each other. 2 one of the pieces used in this game. *n., pl.* **dom·i·noes** or **dom·i·nos.**

don (don) put on: *The knight donned his armour.* *v.,* **donned, don·ning.**

do·nate (dō nāt′ *or* dō′nāt) give; contribute: *Our parents donated money and books to the school library.* *v.,* **do·nat·ed, do·nat·ing.** **—do·na′tion,** *n.*

done (dun) 1 cooked; cooked enough: *Is the rice done yet?* 2 finished: *I'm not done yet.* 3 the past participle of **do**[1]**:** *Have you done all your homework?* 1, 2 *adj.,* 3 *v.*
done for, about to die.
done with, over: *I'm glad that whole business is done with.*

don•key (dong′kē) an animal related to the horse, but smaller, with larger ears, a shorter neck and mane, and smaller hooves. *n., pl.* **don•keys.**
donkey's years, a very long time: *I haven't heard that song in donkey's years.*

do•nor (dō′nər) a person who donates. *n.*

don't (dōnt) do not.

doo•dle (dū′dəl) **1** make drawings or marks of any kind while thinking of something else: *He doodled while he was talking on the telephone.* **2** a drawing or mark made absent-mindedly. 1 *v.,* **doo•dled, doo•dling;** 2 *n.*

doom (dūm) **1** a terrible fate; ruin; death: *The soldiers marched to their doom.* **2** **doomed,** headed for something bad, with no chance of escape: *prisoners doomed to die. Her plan seemed doomed to failure because everything had gone wrong from the beginning.* 1 *n.,* 2 *v.*

door (dȯr) **1** an opening in a wall for going in and out: *He just came through the door.* **Doorway** is another word for it. **2** the flat piece of wood, metal, or glass for closing this opening. It may turn on hinges or slide open and shut. **3** a part like this on a cupboard, car, etc. *n.*
darken the door of, visit.
out of doors, outside.
show someone the door, make someone leave.

Word Family.......... door

doorbell: a bell to ring for someone at the door
doorknob: a handle for opening a door
doormat: a small rug for wiping dirt off shoes
doorsill: a piece of wood, stone, or metal at the bottom of a door opening
doorstep: a step going from a door to the ground
doorstop: something that keeps a door open
door-to-door: going from one home to the next
doorway: an opening for a door

door•man (dȯr′man′) a person whose work is guarding a door and opening it for people going in or out. Some hotels have doormen. *n., pl.* **door•men** (dȯr′mən *or* dȯr′men′).

dope (dōp) *Slang.* **1** a very stupid person. **2** a habit-forming narcotic drug, such as heroin or opium. **3** give an anesthetic: *The doctor doped her before setting her broken leg.* **4** information: *What's the latest dope on the strike?* 1, 2, 4 *n.,* 3 *v.,* **doped, doping.**

dor•mant (dȯr′mənt) asleep; active: *Bears and tulip bulbs are dormant during the winter. The volcano remained dormant for years, then erupted.* *adj.* **—dor′man•cy,** *n.*

dor•mi•to•ry (dȯr′mə tȯ′rē) **1** a large sleeping room with many beds. **2** a building that is part of a boarding school, college, etc., with many small rooms in it for students to live in. **Dorm** is short for dormitory. *n., pl.* **dor•mi•to•ries.**

do•ry (dȯr′ē) a rowboat with a narrow, flat bottom and high sides, often used for ocean fishing. *n., pl.* **do•ries.**

DOS (dos) a set of basic instructions that tells a computer system how to make its parts work together. Its full name is **disk operating system.**

dose (dōs) **1** an amount of medicine to be taken at one time. The **dosage** is the size of this amount and how often you are to take it. **2** the amount of anything given as a remedy: *A good dose of praise made her feel better.* *n.*

dot (dot) **1** a small round mark: *There is a dot over each "i" in this line.* **2** mark with a dot or dots. **3** be here and there on a surface: *Boats of many kinds dotted the lake.* 1 *n.,* 2, 3 *v.,* **dot•ted, dot•ting.**
on the dot, exactly at the time mentioned: *The meeting is at five o'clock and you must be there on the dot.*

dote (dōt)
dote on, be extremely fond of someone: *The old woman dotes on her great-grandson.* *v.,* **dot•ed, dot•ing.**

dou•ble (dub′əl) **1** twice as much, as large, as strong, etc.: *The man was given double pay for working on Sunday.* **2** an amount that is twice as big as: *She earns double his pay.* **3** make or become twice as much or twice as many: *He doubled the amount of each ingredient to make more cookies. Money invested in this business will double in about ten years.* **4** in a pair: *double doors, double windows.* **5** combining two in one, especially in a surprising way: *Some words have a double meaning. The secret agent led a double life.* **6** a person or thing just like another: *The actor had a double who did all the dangerous stunts for him.* **7** fold over: *I doubled my slice of bread to make a sandwich.* **8** take another person's place: *Corrine doubled for me when I couldn't get to the meeting.* **9** in baseball, a two-base hit: *Paula hit a double in the last inning.* 1, 4, 5 *adj.,* 2, 9 *n.,* 3, 7, 8 *v.,* **dou•bled, dou•bling.** **—doub′ly,** *adv.*
double back, turn back suddenly the other way: *The fox doubled back on its track and escaped the dogs.*
double up, a draw your knees up to your chest, or bend far over at the waist: *He doubled up in pain.* **b** join another person to share a room, form a team, etc.: *When guests stayed overnight, the two brothers had to double up.*

a bat	e bed	i bid	o pot	u cup	th thin
ā cake	ē me	ī bite	ō go	ū rude	ᴛʜ then
ä bar	ə about	ər over	ȯ for	u̇ put	zh measure

Word Family..........double

Using **double** in front of a word can show something done twice. Here are some examples.

double bill: two shows in one program
double-check: check twice
double-click: click a mouse twice, quickly
double-decker: with two layers
double-digit: numbers from 10 to 99
double-header: two baseball games, same teams, same day
double-space: two line spaces between written lines

See how many more examples you can think of.

double bass (dub′əl bās′) a large stringed instrument with a very low tone, the largest member of the modern violin family.

dou·ble–cross (dub′əl kros′) *Informal.* **1** betray; cheat or play a nasty trick on: *When my friend didn't show up, I realized I had been double-crossed.* **2** an act of betrayal. 1 *v.,* 2 *n.* **—dou′ble-cross′er,** *n.*

dou·blet (dub′lit) a man's close-fitting jacket, worn in Europe from about 1400 to about 1600. *n.*

doubt (dout) **1** not believe; not be sure: *The captain doubted that the damaged ship would reach land.* **2** a feeling of being unsure: *We had doubts about which road to take.* 1 *v.,* 2 *n.* **—doubt′ful,** *adj.*
in doubt, not sure: *I'm still in doubt whether to go or stay. The outcome of the game was in doubt until the very end.*
no doubt or **without a doubt,** surely; certainly: *No doubt we will win in the end.* **Doubtless** means the same thing.

dough (dō) **1** the uncooked mixture of flour, milk, fat, and other things that bread, biscuits, pies, etc. are made of. **2** *Slang.* money. *n.* **—dough′y,** *adj.*

dough·nut (dō′nut′) a ring or roll of sweetened dough cooked in deep fat. *n.*

Doug·las fir (dug′ləs fər′) a very tall evergreen tree of western North America, with long, narrow, hanging cones and flat needles. It can grow to more than 50 m high and is one of the most important timber trees.

Douk·ho·bours or **Douk·ho·bors** (dū′kə bȯrz′) a Christian sect that started in Russia about 200 years ago. Several thousand Doukhobours left Russia in 1898 and settled in western Canada. *pl.n.*

douse (dous) **1** throw water over: *She doused her brother with a pail of water.* **2** stick in water or any other liquid: *The blacksmith doused the red-hot horseshoe to cool it.* **3** put out a fire or candle. *v.,* **doused, dous·ing.**

dove¹ (duv) a greyish bird like a pigeon that makes a soft cooing sound: *The dove is often a symbol of peace.* *n.*

dove² (dōv) a past tense of **dive:** *The diver dove deep into the water after the sunken treasure.* *v.*

dow·dy (dou′dē) **1** dressed in a dull or unstylish way: *a dowdy person.* **2** dull and unstylish: *a dowdy coat and a shapeless hat.* *adj.,* **dow·di·er, dow·di·est.**

dow·el (dou′əl) a peg that fits into matching holes in two pieces of wood so as to join them together. *n.*

down¹ (doun) **1** to or at a lower place or a lower amount: *They ran down from the top of the hill. Her fever is down to 38°C now.* **2** from an earlier time to a later time: *The story has come down through many years.* **3** along, especially along a route that leads to a lower place: *to ride down a hill, sail down a river, or walk down a street.* **4** *Informal.* a period of bad luck or unhappiness: *Her life is full of ups and downs.* **5** swallow: *He downed the juice in one gulp.* **6** on paper; in writing: *Put his name down for the clean-up crew.* **7** as a **down payment,** a part payment made right away with the promise of more later: *She paid $10 down when she bought the used bicycle.* **8** memorized: *I have my lines down for the play.* **9** not working: *Our computer is down.* **10** a chance to move a football forward. In Canadian football, a team is allowed three downs in which to move the ball forward ten yards (about 9 m). 1, 2, 6–9 *adv.,* 3 *prep.,* 5 *v.,* 4, 10 *n.*
come down with, get sick with.
down and out, going through very bad times.
down on, *Informal.* against; attacking: *He's down on anybody who doesn't like sports.*
down to the ground, through and through; all the way: *a hockey fan down to the ground.*
down with ___! get rid of ___! We don't want ___!

Word Family..........down

downhill: downward, like down the slope of a hill
downplay: make something not very important
downpour: a heavy rainfall
downsize: make something smaller
downspout: a pipe that carries rainwater from a roof to the ground
downstairs: a lower part of a building
downstream: in the direction of the current
downturn: a turn for the worse
downwind: in the direction that the wind is blowing

down² (doun) soft, fine feathers or hair: *the down on a duck or on a baby's head.* *n.* **—down′y,** *adj.*

down·cast (doun′kast′) 1 turned downward: *a shy child with downcast eyes.* 2 sad; discouraged: *He was downcast because of his failure.* **Downhearted** is another word for def. 2. *adj.*

down·fall (doun′fol′) ruin; complete failure: *the downfall of a hero, the downfall of an empire.* *n.*

down·load (doun′lōd′) move data or programs from one computer or network to another: *Mom downloaded some games for us from the Internet.* *v.*

down·right (doun′rīt′) 1 thorough; complete: *a downright lie.* 2 thoroughly; completely: *They were downright rude to me.* 3 plain; direct: *Her downright answer showed exactly where she stood.* 1, 3 *adj.,* 2 *adv.*

down·riv·er (doun′riv′ər) toward the mouth or lower part of a river: *to float downriver* (*adv.*), *a downriver settlement* (*adj.*). *adj.* or *adv.*

Down syndrome (doun′ sin′drōm) a condition that affects a person's body shape and ability to learn. People with Down syndrome are born with an extra chromosome that causes them to have shorter and heavier bodies and a fold of skin at the inner edge of their eyes. People with Down syndrome often learn more slowly.

down·town (doun′toun′) 1 the main business section of a town, especially if it is lower than the rest: *Most offices are in the downtown.* 2 to or in this part of town: *a downtown store* (*adj.*). *She goes downtown to her office* (*adv.*). 1 *n.,* 2 *adv.,* 2 *adj.*

down·ward (doun′wərd) 1 Often, **downwards,** toward a lower place: *He hurried downward toward the bottom of the hill* (*adv.*). 2 going down: *a downward slope* (*adj.*). *adv.* or *adj.*

dow·ry (dou′rē) in some cultures, the money or property that a bride brings to her husband. *n., pl.* **dow·ries.**

doze (dōz) 1 sleep lightly; be half asleep: *We found the cat dozing in the armchair.* 2 a light sleep; nap. 1 *v.,* **dozed, doz·ing;** 2 *n.*

doz·en (duz′ən) 12; a group of 12. *Abbreviation:* doz. *n., pl.* **doz·ens** or (after a number) **doz·en.**

Dr. or **Dr** *abbreviation for:* 1 Doctor: *Dr. M. H. Smith.* 2 Drive: *220 Rideau Dr., Ottawa.*

drab (drab) 1 dull; dreary-looking: *Some bright paint will make this office less drab.* 2 dull brownish grey. 1, 2 *adj.,* 2 *n.*

draft (draft) 1 a current of air. 2 a part on a woodstove, fireplace, etc. for controlling the flow of air. 3 a rough sketch or piece of writing: *He made three different drafts of his speech before he had it in final form.* ▶ See the *Grammar and Usage Mini-Guide.* 4 write out or draw, especially in rough form. 5 choose and force to do some special duty: *The teacher drafted six students to carry the tables to the gym.* People chosen in this way are **draftees.** 6 this process of choosing and forcing people, especially for the army: *During the Vietnam War, many Americans came to Canada to escape the draft.* 7 for pulling loads: *a draft horse.* 8 the depth of water needed for a ship, especially when loaded. 9 a note from one bank to another, ordering that a certain sum of money be paid to the person named. 1–3, 6, 8, 9 *n.,* 4, 5 *v.,* 7 *adj.*
—**draft′y,** *adj.*

Grammar Check .... draft

You might need to make several draft versions of a piece of writing, until it is exactly what you want.

- Make your first draft have all the ideas that you want to include. Don't worry about things like checking spelling yet.
- In your next draft, check that all the information you have is correct, and organize your ideas so that they flow from one to the next. (You may need to make another draft here.)
- In the next draft, check and fix any errors in grammar, punctuation, or spelling.
- Your final version should be clean. It should also be well written, by now!

drafts·person (drafts′pėr′sən) a person whose work is preparing exact plans, designs, or diagrams for making buildings, tools, or machinery. This work is called **drafting.** The person may also be called a **drafter.** *n., pl.* **drafts·per·sons** (drafts′pėr′sənz).

drag (drag) 1 pull or be pulled along the ground: *A team of horses dragged the big log out of the forest. Her long skirt was dragging in the dust of the street.* 2 go too slowly: *Time drags when you have nothing to do.* 3 pull a net or hook along for some purpose: *They dragged the lake bottom for remains of the sunken boat.* 4 anything that holds something else back: *A lazy player is a drag on a hockey team.* 5 *Slang.* something boring, unpleasant, or disappointing. 6 race in a vehicle. 1–3, 6 *v.,* **dragged, drag·ging;** 4–6 *n.*
—**drag′gy,** *adj.*

a bat	e bed	i bid	o pot	u cup	th thin
ā cake	ē me	ī bite	ō go	ū rude	ᴛʜ then
ä bar	ə about	ər over	ȯ for	ů put	zh measure

A traditional Chinese New Year's Day parade includes a group of people who wind down the street holding up a large dragon costume. According to an ancient belief, the dragon prevents evil spirits from spoiling the new year.

drag·on (drag′ən) in stories, a fierce, fire-breathing creature like a huge lizard with wings and claws. *n.*

drag·on·fly (drag′ən flī′) a large, harmless insect with a long, slender body and two pairs of very thin wings. It eats mosquitoes and flies. *n., pl.* **drag·on·flies.**

drain (drān) **1** let liquid flow off or out of: *to drain a cup, to drain a swamp for farmland. Set the wet dishes here to drain.* **2** take away or use up little by little: *War drains a country of its people and money.* **3** the process of draining or something that drains: *a cellar drain. Working so hard is a drain on your strength.* 1, 2 *v.,* 3 *n.* **—drain′age,** *n.*

drake (drāk) a male duck. *n.*

dra·ma (dram′ə *or* drȧ′mə) **1** a play, especially a serious one. **2** the art of writing and putting on plays: *He wants to study drama.* A **dramatist** writes plays. **3** a part of real life that has the excitement of a story: *The history of Arctic exploration is a thrilling drama.* *n.*

dra·mat·ic (drə mat′ik) **1** having to do with plays or acting. **2** full of action, suspense, or feeling: *There was a dramatic pause and then the lion leaped.* *adj.* **—dra·mat′i·cal·ly,** *adv.*

dram·a·tize (dram′ə tīz′ *or* drȧ′mə tīz′) **1** make into a play: *The class dramatized the story of Rip Van Winkle.* **2** make exciting and thrilling: *She had a way of dramatizing the stories she told the children.* *v.,* **dram·a·tized, dram·a·tiz·ing.** **—dram′a·ti·za′tion,** *n.*

drank (drangk) the past tense of **drink:** *She drank her milk an hour ago.* *v.*

drape (drāp) **1** hang with cloth falling loosely in folds: *The stage was draped with velvet. He draped the blanket over a chair.* **2 drapes,** *pl.* long, heavy curtains that are made to hang in folds. Another word for these is **draperies;** the cloth used for them is **drapery** fabric. 1 *v.,* **draped, drap·ing;** 2 *n.*

dras·tic (dras′tik) extreme; extraordinary: *drastic changes. The police took drastic measures to put a stop to drunk driving.* *adj.*

draw (dro) **1** make a picture with pen, pencil, crayon, etc.: *Draw a circle. He draws very well.* **2** attract; cause to come: *A parade always draws crowds.* **3** move: *I saw him draw back in fear. The car drew near.* **4** pull: *The horses draw the wagon. She drew the rope tight.* **5** get or take: *to draw water from a well, to draw comfort from a friend's words, to draw a breath.* **6** a game that ends in a tie. **7** a lottery: *Dean won a bike in a draw.* **8** go down to a certain depth in floating: *The big ship draws 8.5 m of water.* **9** make a draft of air to carry off smoke: *The chimney does not draw well.* 1–5, 8, 9 *v.,* **drew, drawn, draw·ing;** 6, 7 *n.* **—draw′er,** *n.*

back to the drawing board, back to the planning stage; back to the beginning.

draw a blank, try to do something, especially remember or guess, and fail completely.

draw out, a make or become long: *Rain draws out a summer day. Don't draw the story out so much.* **b** persuade to talk: *We asked the new boy about his old school to draw him out.*

draw the line, set the limit: *Joking is fine, but we draw the line at putting others down.*

draw up, a write out: *to draw up a list.* **b** stop: *The taxi drew up at the entrance.*

draw·back (dro′bak′) a disadvantage; a bad point about something: *Our trip was interesting, but the cold weather was a drawback.* *n.*

draw·bridge (dro′brij′) a bridge that can be lifted and lowered: *In old castles, drawbridges were lifted to keep out enemies. A drawbridge over a river is lifted to let boats pass.* *n.*

draw·er (drór) **1** a box that slides in and out of a dresser, desk, etc.: *She kept her shirts in the dresser drawer.* **2 drawers,** *pl.* an old-fashioned or humorous word for underpants. *n.*

draw·ing (dro′ing) **1** a picture or design done with pen, pencil, crayon, etc. **2** the making of pictures: *Drawing is taught in art classes.* *n.*

drawing room (dro′ing rūm′) a formal living room; a parlour. This word is used mostly in books.

drawl (drol) 1 talk in a slow way, stretching out the vowels of words: *He drawled a lazy answer.* 2 this way of talking: *to speak with a drawl.* 1 *v.*, 2 *n.*

drawn (dron) the past participle of **draw:** *That old horse has drawn many loads.* *v.*

draw·string (drȯ′string′) a string that runs through the top of a bag, the waist of a piece of clothing, etc., that you can pull tight: *Amy pulled the drawstring to make the sweatpants stay up.* *n.*

dread (dred) 1 look ahead to something with fear or dislike: *He dreaded the long drive home.* 2 great fear: *She hated the cold and lived in dread of winter.* 3 a poetic word for "frightening": *a dread disease.* 1 *v.*, 2 *n.*, 3 *adj.*

dread·ful (dred′fəl) terrible: *dreadful heat. A dragon is a dreadful creature.* *adj.* **—dread′ful·ly,** *adv.*

dream (drēm) 1 something you imagine while you are asleep. 2 something you hope or wish for which has only a small chance of happening: *The boy had dreams of being an astronaut.* 3 have a dream: *Last night I dreamed I was at the beach. The girl dreamed of being a famous scientist.* 4 think of something as possible; imagine: *The day seemed so bright I never dreamed there would be rain.* 1, 2 *n.*, 3, 4 *v.*, **dreamed** or **dreamt** (dremt), **dream·ing.** **—dream′er,** *n.*

dream catcher (drēm′ kach′ər) among some First Nations people, a round frame with a knotted web of strings or leather strips stretched across it, often decorated with beads and feathers. According to tradition, only good dreams can pass through the web; bad dreams get caught and disappear with the night.

dream·land (drēm′land′) a wonderful land that exists only in dreams or the imagination. *n.*
in dreamland, asleep or daydreaming.

dream·y (drē′mē) 1 like a dream; not clear; dim: *a dreamy memory.* 2 fond of daydreaming; not practical: *a dreamy person.* 3 causing dreams; soothing: *dreamy music.* *adj.*, **dream·i·er, dream·i·est.**

drear·y (drē′rē) dull and gloomy: *Without Didi, school seems very dreary.* *adj.*, **drear·i·er, drear·i·est.**

dredge (drej) 1 a machine with a scoop, or a whole series of scoops, for digging out the bottom of a harbour or channel. 2 a sort of large net, used for gathering oysters, etc. from the bottom of a river or the sea. 3 use a dredge on the bottom of a river, lake, etc. 1, 3 *n.*, 2 *v.*, **dredged, dredg·ing.**

dregs (dregz) the solid bits of matter that settle to the bottom of a liquid such as coffee or wine. *pl.n.*

drei·del (drā′dəl) a four-sided toy that spins on a point and has Hebrew letters on each side. Dreidels are often used to play a children's game during Hanukkah. *n.*, *pl.* **drei·dels** or **drei·del.**

drench (drench) wet thoroughly; soak: *We were drenched by heavy rain.* *v.*

dress (dres) 1 a piece of clothing worn by women and girls. 2 clothing: *He was wearing rather casual dress for a wedding.* 3 put clothes on: *to dress a doll. We dressed and had breakfast.* 4 wear clothes attractively: *Let me teach you how to dress.* 5 put medicine, bandages, etc. on a wound or sore: *The nurse dressed the wound every day.* 1, 2 *n.*, 3–5 *v.*, **dressed, dress·ing.**
—dress′er, *n.*
dress up, a put on your best clothes. **b** put on a costume: *She dressed up as a pirate for Halloween.*

dress·er (dres′ər) a piece of furniture with drawers for clothes and, usually, a mirror. *n.*

dress·ing (dres′ing) 1 a sauce for salad. 2 a spicy mixture of bread crumbs, spices, etc. used to stuff chickens and turkeys before cooking. **Stuffing** is another word for this. 3 medicine, bandages, etc. put on a wound or sore. *n.*

dressing gown (dres′ing goun′) a bathrobe.

dress rehearsal (dres′ ri hər′səl) the final practice of a play, with the actors wearing the costumes they will use for the actual performance.

dress·y (dres′ē) fancy; not casual: *That outfit is too dressy for a wiener roast.* *adj.*, **dress·i·er, dress·i·est.**

drew (drū) the past tense of **draw:** *He drew a picture of his mother.* *v.*

drib·ble (drib′əl) 1 flow or let flow in small amounts; trickle: *The water dribbled from the bottle.* 2 let spit drip from the mouth: *The baby dribbles on his bib.* 3 a few drops; a trickle: *All we could get out of the hose was a dribble.* 4 move a ball along by bouncing it or giving it short kicks. 1, 2, 4 *v.*, **drib·bled, drib·bling;** 3 *n.*

dribs and drabs (dribz′ ən drabz′) small amounts coming every now and then: *People arrived at the party in dribs and drabs.*

dried (drīd) the past tense and past participle of **dry:** *I dried my hands. This clay has been dried in the oven.* *v.*

a bat	e bed	i bid	o pot	u cup	th thin
ā cake	ē me	ī bite	ō go	ü rude	ᴛʜ then
ä bar	ə about	ər over	ȯ for	u̇ put	zh measure

drift (drift) **1** be carried along by currents of air or water: *A raft drifts if it is not steered.* **2** live or travel with no particular goal: *After years of drifting she bought a house and settled down.* **3** the direction of drifting: *The drift of the current is to the south.* **4** heap or be heaped up by the wind: *The wind is so strong that the snow is drifting on the highways.* **5** snow, sand, etc. heaped up by the wind: *After the heavy snow there were deep drifts in the yard.* **6** the general idea: *I caught the drift of the article, but I didn't get all the details.* 1, 2, 4 *v.*, 3, 5, 6 *n.*

drift·wood (drift′wu̇d′) wood carried along by water and washed ashore. *n.*

drill (dril) **1** a tool or machine for making holes in wood, metal, etc. **2** make a hole with this tool. **3** teach by making someone do a thing over and over: *The teacher drilled the class in arithmetic.* **4** the process of doing a thing over and over to learn it: *The gym teacher gave us plenty of drill in soccer skills.* 1, 4 *n.*, 2, 3 *v.*
know the drill, know what you are supposed to do or say because you have done it so often.

drink (dringk) **1** swallow liquid: *The children drink milk for breakfast.* **2** liquid meant to take away thirst. **3** suck up; absorb: *The dry soil drank up the rain.* **4** use alcoholic liquor: *He doesn't drink.* **5** alcoholic liquor. 1, 3, 4 *v.*, **drank, drunk, drink·ing;** 2, 5 *n.*
drink in, take in eagerly with the senses: *We sat there quietly, drinking in the beautiful scene.*

drip (drip) **1** fall or let fall in drops: *Rain drips from an umbrella.* **2** the falling of a liquid in drops: *She could hear the drip of a leaky tap somewhere.* **3** be so wet that drops fall: *My forehead was dripping with perspiration.* 1, 3 *v.*, **dripped, drip·ping;** 2 *n.*

drive (drīv) **1** operate a car, truck, etc.: *to drive a motorboat. She's learning to drive.* **2** travel or carry by car or other vehicle: *We drove to Prince Edward Island. They drove us all the way to Edmonton.* **3** a trip in a car or other vehicle: *the long drive to Grandpa's.* **4** a road, usually in street names: *Winona Drive.* **5** make go; cause to move: *He drove the cow out of the barn. Drive the nail all the way through the wood.* **6** force to work hard: *The workers complained that their boss drove them too hard.* **7** willingness to work hard; energy: *To become an Olympic athlete, you need a lot of drive.* **8** a special campaign to raise money, get new members, etc. **9** a very hard, fast hit in baseball or golf. 1, 2, 5, 6 *v.*, **drove, driv·en, driv·ing;** 3, 4, 7, 8, 9 *n.* **—driv′er,** *n.*
drive at, intend; mean: *I don't understand what you're driving at.*

drive–in (drī′vin′) a place where you can watch movies on an outdoor screen while seated in your car. *n.*

driv·el (driv′əl) stupid, meaningless talk: *I can't listen to such drivel.* *n.*

driv·en (driv′ən) the past participle of **drive:** *Mr. Carreiro has just driven past.* *v.*

drive·way (drīv′wā′) a private road leading from the street to a house or garage. *n.*

driz·zle (driz′əl) **1** rain gently, in very small drops like mist. **2** light rain that is like mist. 1 *v.*, **driz·zled, driz·zling;** 2 *n.*

The dromedary can travel at over 15 km/h, covering over 150 km in a day.

drom·e·dar·y (drom′ə der′ē) a swift Arabian camel with one hump. *n.*, *pl.* **drom·e·dar·ies.**

drone[1] (drōn) **1** a male bee. Drones do no work in the hive. **2** a lazy person. *n.*

drone[2] (drōn) **1** make a low humming sound: *Bees droned among the flowers.* **2** such a sound: *the drone of an engine.* **3** speak in a boring voice: *to drone on and on about nothing.* 1, 3 *v.*, **droned, dron·ing;** 2 *n.*

drool (drūl) **1** let spit run from the mouth. **2** spit running from the mouth. 1 *v.*, 2 *n.*

droop (drūp) **1** hang down; bend down: *These flowers are starting to droop; put them in water.* **2** the act or condition of hanging down; a bending position: *the droop of willow branches.* **3** become weak or sad: *The boy's spirits drooped when he was left out of the game. The patient drooped as his illness got worse.* 1, 3 *v.*, 2 *n.*

drop (drop) **1** fall: *The package dropped into a puddle. The temperature is dropping. His voice dropped to a whisper.* **2** let fall: *She dropped the bag.* **3** cause to fall: *She dropped her attacker with one good kick.* **4** a fall: *a drop in prices.* **5** the distance down; the length of a fall: *a drop of 10 m.* **6** a small, round blob of liquid, usually one that falls: *a drop of rain, a drop of blood.* **7** a hard round candy: *a cough drop, a lemon drop.* **8 drops,** *pl.* liquid medicine given in drops: *The doctor gave her some drops for her ear.* **9** get rid of; stop doing, using, etc.:

to drop a plan. Too bad you dropped piano lessons! Let's drop this argument. **10** let passengers out of a car, bus, etc.: *The taxi driver dropped us at the corner.* 4–8 *n.,* 1–3, 9, 10 *v.,* **dropped, drop·ping.**

a drop in the bucket, a very small amount compared with the rest.

drop by, in, or **over,** visit: *Drop over to our house tonight.*

drop off, a go to sleep: *He dropped off in his armchair.* **b** become less; decrease: *Car sales have dropped off this year.* **c** stop: *I think I'll drop off at the grocery store.* **d** let passengers out of a vehicle: *Drop me off right here.*

drop out, stop taking part; quit: *She had to drop out of the race when she twisted her ankle.*

drop–in centre (drop′in′) a place where people can come to relax, get help or information, have a coffee, play games, meet people, etc. Drop-in centres are often run by a church or a helping organization.

drop·per (drop′ər) a small glass or plastic tube with a hollow rubber bulb on one end used for sucking up liquids which can then be squeezed out in drops. *n.*

drop·pings (drop′ingz) solid waste of animals or birds. *pl.n.*

drought (drout) a long period with no rain. *n.*

drove[1] (drōv) the past tense of **drive:** *We drove downtown yesterday. v.*

drove[2] (drōv) a large group of people or animals moving along together; a crowd, herd, or flock: *People came to the lake in droves last weekend. n.*

drown (droun) **1** die under water or some other liquid because there is no air to breathe: *The man almost drowned when his boat overturned.* **2** kill by keeping under water or some other liquid. **3** be so loud or powerful as to keep something else from being heard or noticed: *The boat's whistle drowned out the girl's voice. v.*

drowse (drouz) be half asleep: *She drowsed, but did not quite fall asleep. v.,* **drowsed, drows·ing.**

drow·sy (drou′zē) sleepy: *a hot, quiet, drowsy afternoon. This music makes me drowsy. adj.,* **drow·si·er, drow·si·est. —drow′si·ly,** *adv.* **—drow′si·ness,** *n.*

drudge (druj) **1** a person who does hard, boring work for someone else. **2** do hard, boring work. 1 *n.,* 2 *v.,* **drudged, drudg·ing. —drudg′er·y,** *n.*

drug (drug) **1** a non-food substance that changes your body's functions when you eat or drink it, breathe it in, or take it through a needle. Some drugs are used as medicine. It is dangerous to abuse drugs, especially since many drugs can cause people to become addicted. **2** give drugs to, particularly drugs that are harmful or cause sleep: *The witch drugged the princess.* **3** mix harmful drugs with food or drink: *The spy drugged the guard's drink.* 1 *n.,* 2, 3 *v.,* **drugged, drug·ging.**

drug·store (drug′stôr′) a store where medicines are sold. A drugstore usually sells soft drinks, cosmetics, magazines, etc. as well as drugs. *n.*

dru·id (drū′id) a priest of the ancient religion of the Celtic peoples of the British Isles: *Helen read about some of the magic spells the druids used. n.*

Drums of various kinds are the oldest of all musical instruments.

This big kettledrum is a large shell with a single drumhead. The drummer uses the pedal to tune the drum.

drum (drum) **1** a musical instrument that you play by hitting it in time with a beat. A drum is usually a hollow cylinder with a cover stretched tight over each end. **2** play the drum. **3** keep beating or tapping with a steady rhythm: *He drummed on the table with his fingers.* **4** teach by repeating over and over: *Mom drummed it into us that if a job is worth doing, it's worth doing well.* **5** a large drum-shaped container: *an oil drum.* 1, 5 *n.,* 2–4 *v.,* **drummed, drum·ming. —drum′mer,** *n.*

drum·stick (drum′stik′) **1** a stick for beating a drum. **2** the lower part of the leg of a cooked chicken, turkey, etc. *n.*

drunk (drungk) **1** overcome by alcoholic liquor: *He was so drunk he could not stand up.* **2** a person who is in such a state. **3** showing the effects of too much alcohol: *drunk driving.* **4** the past participle of **drink:** *He had drunk all the milk.* 1, 3 *adj.,* 2 *n.,* 4 *v.*

a bat	e bed	i bid	o pot	u cup	th thin
ā cake	ē me	ī bite	ō go	ū rude	ᴛʜ then
ä bar	ə about	ər over	ô for	ů put	zh measure

drunk·ard (drung′kərd) a person who is often drunk. *n.*

drunk·en (drung′kən) **1** drunk. **2** resulting from being drunk: *a drunken quarrel.* *adj.*

dry (drī) **1** not wet: *dry leaves, a dry climate.* **2** make or become dry: *We were drying dishes. The towels soon dried in the breeze.* **3** empty: *The kettle is dry.* **4** thirsty; wanting a drink. **5** not interesting; dull: *a dry speech.* **6** funny in a quiet and clever way: *dry humour.* 1, 3–6 *adj.,* **dri·er, dri·est;** 2 *v.,* **dried, dry·ing.** **—dry′ly,** *adv.* **—dry′ness,** *n.*
dry up, a make or become completely dry: *The creek dried up last summer. The intense heat dried up the grass.* **b** be all used up.

dry cell (drī′ sel′) a type of electric cell or small battery in which the chemical that makes the current is made into a paste so it cannot spill.

dry–clean (drī′ klēn′) clean clothes, fabrics, etc. by chemicals instead of water. Clothes are dry-cleaned at a special shop. *v.* **—dry cleaner.** **—dry cleaning.**

dry dock (drī′ dok′) a sort of boxed area between two piers, built watertight so that the water may be pumped out. Dry docks are used for repairing ships. *n.*

dry·er (drī′ər) a person or thing that dries, especially a machine that uses heat or blowing air to dry things: *a clothes dryer, a hair dryer.* *n.*

du·al (dyū′əl *or* dū′əl) having two parts; double: *This piece of software has a dual purpose: learning and fun.* *adj.*

dub[1] (dub) **1** name; call: *Because of his happy nature, the boys dubbed him "Sunshine."* **2** make a man a knight by striking his shoulder lightly with a sword. *v.,* **dubbed, dub·bing.**

dub[2] (dub) **1** copy from one tape to another, or from a CD or record onto a tape: *They spent the afternoon dubbing their favourite music.* **2** make a new sound track for a movie in a different language. When people dub a movie they try to make the new sounds fit how the actors move their lips. *v.,* **dubbed, dub·bing.**

du·bi·ous (dyū′bē əs *or* dū′bē əs) **1** doubtful; uncertain: *She looked this way and that in a dubious manner.* **2** suspicious; probably bad: *a dubious scheme for making money.* *adj.*

duch·ess (duch′is) **1** the wife or widow of a duke. **2** a woman with a rank equal to that of a duke. The territory ruled or owned by a duchess or duke is called a **duchy** (duch′ē). *n.*

These goldeneye are diving ducks, going underwater for food. They are named for their yellow eyes.

duck[1] (duk) a water bird that has a thick body, a short, narrow neck, a flat bill, and short legs with webbed feet. Ducks are often raised for food and for their eggs. Their babies are called **ducklings.** *n.*

duck[2] (duk) **1** go or push out of sight for a short time, especially under water: *They ducked him and he came up sputtering. I'll just duck into the bookshop for a minute.* **2** lower your head or bend your body quickly to escape being hit or seen: *She ducked to avoid a low branch.* **3** the act of ducking. 1, 2 *v.,* 3 *n.*

duct (dukt) a tube or pipe for carrying liquid or air: *Warm air from the furnace is blown through ducts to all the rooms in a house. Tears flow from tear ducts in your upper eyelids.* *n.*

dud (dud) something that is worthless or completely uninteresting: *After taking the bike around the block, Chris decided it was a dud.* *n.*

dude (dủd *or* dyủd) **1** someone who lives in a city and spends a vacation on a ranch: *The new dude didn't even know how to ride a horse.* **2** *Slang.* a person: *Hey, dude, what's happening?* *n.*

due (dyū *or* dū) **1** that is supposed to be paid or given: *The monthly car payment is due today. Respect is due to older people.* **2** a person's right; what is owed to a person: *Politeness is his due while he is your guest.* **3** proper: *Treat your books with due care.* **4 dues,** *pl.* a fee or regular charge for membership in an organization: *Dues paid to the union go to help workers when they are on strike.* **5** expected; scheduled to come or to do something: *The train is due at noon. She is due to have her baby tomorrow.* **6** straight; directly: *due west.* 1, 3, 5 *adj.,* 2, 4 *n.,* 6 *adv.*
due to, because of: *The accident was due to carelessness.*
in due time, after a certain amount of time.

du·el (dyū′əl *or* dū′əl) **1** a formal fight to settle a quarrel. Duels used to be fought with weapons by two people in the presence of two others called seconds.

2 any contest between two people: *The two lawyers fought a duel of wits in court.* 3 take part in a duel. 1, 2 *n.*, 3 *v.*, **du•elled** or **du•eled, du•el•ling** or **du•el•ing.**

du•et (dyū et′ *or* dū et′) a piece of music for two voices or instruments. *n.*

duf•fel bag (duf′əl bag′) a large tube-shaped cloth bag used to carry clothing and personal belongings: *The campers climbed on the bus with their duffel bags.*

dug (dug) the past tense and past participle of **dig:** *The dog dug a hole in the ground. A ditch has been dug.* *v.*

dug•out (dug′out′) 1 a canoe made by hollowing out a large log. 2 a small shelter at the side of a baseball field, used by players not on the field. 3 a rough shelter made by digging into the side of a hill, trench, etc., used to protect soldiers against bullets and bombs. *n.*

duke (dyūk *or* dūk) a high-ranking nobleman. *n.*

dull (dul) 1 not sharp: *a dull knife, a dull pain.* 2 not bright or clear: *dull eyes, a dull colour, a dull day, a dull sound.* 3 slow to understand: *a dull mind.* 4 not interesting; boring: *a dull book, a dull visit.* 5 make or become dull: *Cutting that carpet dulled the scissors.* 1–4 *adj.*, 5 *v.* **—dull′ness,** *n.* **—dul′ly,** *adv.*

du•ly (dyū′lē *or* dū′lē) as it should be: *The debt was duly paid.* *adv.*

dumb (dum) 1 not speaking; unable to speak: *dumb with fright.* 2 *Informal.* stupid. *adj.* **—dumb′ly,** *adv.*

dum•found or **dumbfound** (dum′found′) amaze to the point of being unable to speak. *v.*

dum•my (dum′ē) 1 a figure of a person, used for store window displays, target practice, for putting in a car that is being crash-tested, etc. 2 *Informal.* a stupid person. 3 made to look like the real thing; pretend: *dummy swords.* 1, 2 *n.*, *pl.* **dum•mies;** 3 *adj.*

dump (dump) 1 empty out; throw down: *The truck backed up to the curb and dumped the gravel on the sidewalk. Don't just dump your books on the floor.* 2 a place where people throw garbage. 1 *v.*, 2 *n.*
down in the dumps, feeling gloomy or sad: *He was down in the dumps because his bike was broken.*
dump on, complain long and angrily to someone.

dump•ling (dump′ling) 1 a ball of dough, boiled or steamed and served with meat. 2 a similar ball that contains fruit and is served as a dessert. *n.*

dunce (duns) a stupid person. *n.*

dune (dyūn *or* dūn) a mound or ridge of loose sand heaped up by the wind. *n.*

dun•geon (dun′jən) a strong underground room in a castle, to keep prisoners in. *n.*

dunk (dungk) 1 dip something into a liquid: *to dunk doughnuts in coffee.* 2 *Informal.* push somebody into water. 3 in basketball, score by jumping up and dropping the ball through the hoop. *v.*

Dun•ne–za (dů′nə za′) 1 a First Nations people living in the Peace River Valley in Alberta. 2 their language. 3 having to do with these people or their language. 1, 2 *n.*, 3 *adj.*

du•o (dyů′ō *or* dů′o) a pair; two people who do something together: *In the last part of the movie the fearless duo broke out of jail.* *n.*, *pl.* **du•os.**

dupe (dyūp *or* dūp) 1 deceive; trick: *The stranger tried to dupe us into going with him.* 2 a person who is easily deceived or tricked. 1 *v.*, 2 *n.*, **duped, dup•ing.**

duplex (dyů′pleks *or* dů′pleks) a building with two dwellings in it, either side by side or one above the other. *n.*

du•pli•cate (dyū′plə kit *or* dū′plə kit *for 1 and 2,* dyū′plə kāt′ *or* dū′plə kāt′ *for 3*) 1 exactly alike: *We have duplicate keys for the front door.* 2 one of two things exactly alike; an exact copy: *He mailed the letter, but kept a duplicate.* 3 make an exact copy of; repeat exactly. 1 *adj.*, 2 *n.*, 3 *v.*, **du•pli•cat•ed, du•pli•cat•ing.** **—du′pli•ca′tion,** *n.* **—du′pli•ca′tor,** *n.*

du•ra•ble (dyū′rə bəl *or* dū′rə bəl) lasting a long time; tough; strong: *durable plastic, durable clothing.* *adj.* **—du′ra•bil′i•ty,** *n.*

du•ra•tion (dyə rā′shən *or* də rā′shən) the time that something lasts: *The play was of short duration. The other team was scoreless for the duration of the game.* *n.*

Dur•ga Pu•ja (dūr′gə pū′jə) an important Hindu festival in honour of Durga, the goddess of power. It lasts nine days, because Durga has nine different forms.

dur•ing (dyū′ring *or* dū′ring) while something is going on: *We played board games during the storm.* *prep.*

durum (dyů′rəm *or* dů′rəm) a hard wheat grown in the prairies. The flour in pasta is made from it. *n.*

dusk (dusk) the time just before dark; twilight: *At dusk, the lights started going on in the houses.* *n.*

a bat	e bed	i bid	o pot	u cup	th then
ā cake	ē me	ī bite	ō go	ū rude	ᴛʜ then
ä bar	ə about	ər over	ô for	ů put	zh measure

dust (dust) **1** fine, dry dirt; any fine powder: *Dust lay thick on the shelf. The ashes in the fireplace had turned to dust.* **2** brush or wipe the dust from: *My job is dusting the furniture.* **3** sprinkle with fine powder: *Dad dusted the cake with icing sugar.* 1 *n.,* 2, 3 *v.* —**dust′y,** *adj.*
bite the dust, *Slang.* **a** fall dead or wounded: *A shot rang out and one of the outlaws bit the dust.* **b** end: *Another soccer season bites the dust.*
throw dust in someone's eyes, trick or mislead a person.

Word Family.......... dust

duster: a cloth used to take the dust off things
dustpan: a kind of shovel for sweeping dust onto
dustproof: sealed against dust

dust jack·et (dust′ jak′it) a removable paper cover that fits over a book to protect it. Often it has a summary of the book or information about the author.

du·ty (dyū′tē *or* dū′tē) **1** the thing that a person is supposed to do: *It is your duty to obey the law.* **2** a feeling of having to do something because it is right. A **dutiful** person has a strong sense of duty. **3** any of the things that are part of a person's job: *One of the secretary's duties is to take care of the mail.* **4** a tax on articles brought into a country. In a **duty-free** shop you can buy goods without paying this tax on them. *n., pl.* **du·ties.**
off duty, not working.
on duty, working.

duvet (dū vā′ *or* dyū vā′) a thick but light blanket stuffed with soft material, often feathers. People usually put it in a removable cover: *The comfortable bed had a blue duvet on it.* *n.*

DVD a kind of disc, similar to a CD-ROM but able to hold a much greater amount of information, such as a whole movie. It is played on a special machine or computer drive. The full name is **digital videodisk.**

dwarf (dwôrf) **1** a person, animal, or plant much smaller than the usual size for its kind. **2** in fairy tales, a member of a short race of people, often with magic powers. **3** small for its kind: *a dwarf planet.* **4** cause to seem small: *That tall building dwarfs all those around it.* 1, 2 *n., pl.* **dwarfs** or **dwarves** (dwôrvz); 3 *adj.,* 4 *v.*

dwell (dwel) an old or poetic word for "live" or "have your home": *The princess dwelt in a beautiful castle.* *v.,* **dwelt** or **dwelled, dwell·ing.** —**dwell′er,** *n.*
dwell on, think, speak, or write about for a long time.

dwell·ing (dwel′ing) a formal or poetic word for "a home": *a two-family dwelling.* *n.*

dwin·dle (dwin′dəl) become smaller and smaller or less and less: *During the drought the supply of fresh vegetables dwindled rapidly.* *v.,* **dwin·dled, dwin·dling.**

dye (dī) **1** a substance used to colour cloth, hair, etc. **2** colour by treating with such a substance: *I dyed the T-shirt blue.* 1 *n.,* 2 *v.,* **dyed, dye·ing.**

dy·ing (dī′ing) the present participle of **die**[1]: *The woman was dying.* *adj.*

dy·nam·ic (dī nam′ik) **1** lively; energetic: *Mr. Rice is a dynamic teacher.* **2 dynamics, a** the science of energy or force in motion. **b** the way different personalities, circumstances, etc. work together or affect each other. *adj.*

dy·na·mite (dī′nə mīt′) **1** a powerful explosive often used to blow up rocks. **2** blow up with dynamite: *They had to dynamite these rocks to build the road.* **3** fantastic; exciting: *I've seen that movie—it's dynamite!* 1 *n.,* 2 *v.,* **dy·na·mit·ed, dy·na·mit·ing;** 3 *adj.*

dy·na·mo (dī′nə mō′) **1** a machine for producing electricity from some other kind of energy; generator. **2** a very energetic person. *n., pl.* **dy·na·mos.**

dy·nas·ty (dī′nəs tē *or* din′əs tē) a series of rulers who belong to the same family. *n., pl.* **dy·nas·ties.**

dys·en·ter·y (dis′ən ter′ē *or* dis′ən trē) a very serious disease of the intestines caused by consuming impure food or drink. *n.*

dys·lex·i·a (dis lek′sē ə) a disorder that makes it hard for people to read or write because they have trouble recognizing letters or words. *n.* —**dys·lex′ic,** *adj.*

Ee

e or **E** (ē) 1 the fifth letter of the English alphabet, or any sound that it stands for. The sound of *e* in *wet* is different from the sound of *e* in *equal.* 2 the fifth thing in a list. 3 in music: **a** a note. On a keyboard it is the white note between D and F. **b** a scale or key that has E as its home note. *n., pl.* **e's** or **E's.**

E or **E.** *abbreviation for* east or eastern.

each (ēch) 1 every one of a group of people or things thought of one by one: *Each boy has a crayon (adj.). Each of the girls has a book (pron.). We each have our own work to do (pron.).* 2 apiece; for one: *These pencils cost ten cents each.* 1 *adj. or pron.,* 2 *adv.*
each other, each one doing it to the other one: *"The sisters helped each other" means "Each sister helped the other."*

ea•ger (ē′gər) wanting very much; impatient to do or get something: *The team was eager for victory. Devon is eager to open his presents.* *adj.* —**ea′ger•ly,** *adv.* —**ea′ger•ness,** *n.*

Eagles belong to the same family as hawks and vultures, which all have strong curved talons. The golden eagle lives in countries in the northern hemisphere.

ea•gle (ē′gəl) a very large bird with a hooked beak, strong feet with sharp, curved claws, and keen eyesight. The chicks are called **eaglets.** Eagles nest in high places and eat small animals. *n.*
an eagle eye, the ability to see far and clearly; a sharp eye.

eagle feather (ē′gəl fə′ᴛʜ ər) among some First Nations, a feather of an eagle, which gives the person holding it the right to speak in a group. For certain other First Nations, a different object is used for this because the eagle feather is sacred and can be held only by certain individuals. Compare this with **talking stick.**

ear[1] (ēr) 1 the part of the body that people and animals hear with. 2 the ability to hear, especially small differences in sounds: *She has a good ear for music.* *n.*
be all ears, be eager to hear something.
give ear, listen. This is an old or poetic expression.
go in one ear and out the other, not really get through to the person hearing it: *She gets lots of advice, but it just goes in one ear and out the other.*
play by ear, play music without reading it.
play it by ear, decide what to do as you go along.

Word Family.......... **ear**

earache: a pain in the ear
eardrum: thin skin that stretches over the middle ear
earflap: part of a cap turned down over the ears
earlobe: the soft bit at the lowest part of the ear
earmuffs: covers to keep the ears warm
earphone: a sound receiver that fits into the ear
earplug: a plug put in the ear to keep out water or noise
earring: a piece of jewellery for the ear
earshot: the distance sound can be heard
earsplitting: painfully deafening

ear[2] (ēr) the part of certain plants that contains the grains: *an ear of corn, ears of wheat.* *n.*

ear•ly (ər′lē) 1 near the beginning: *the early years (adj.). The heroine appears early in the book (adv.).* 2 before the expected time: *an early supper (adj.). Please come early to help set up (adv.).* *adj. or adv.,* **ear•li•er, ear•li•est.**

earn (ərn) 1 get in return for work or service; be paid: *She earns $50 an hour.* 2 deserve and get; win: *Your honest answer has earned our respect.* *v.*

ear•nest (ər′nist) serious and firm about your ideas or goals; wholehearted: *an earnest campaigner for children's rights.* *adj.* —**ear′nest•ly,** *adv.* —**ear′nest•ness,** *n.*
in earnest, a serious: *We could see she was in earnest about the project.* **b** seriously; for real: *We had felt a few drops, but now it began to rain in earnest.*

a bat	e bed	i bid	o pot	u cup	th thin
ā cake	ē me	ī bite	ō go	ū rude	ᴛʜ then
à bar	ə about	ər over	ȯ for	u̇ put	zh measure

Earth

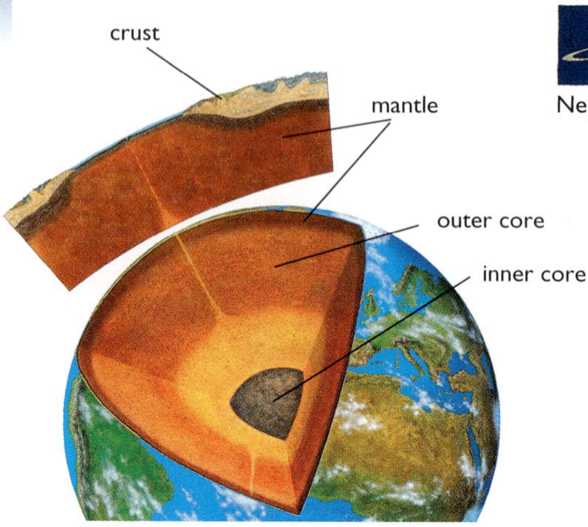

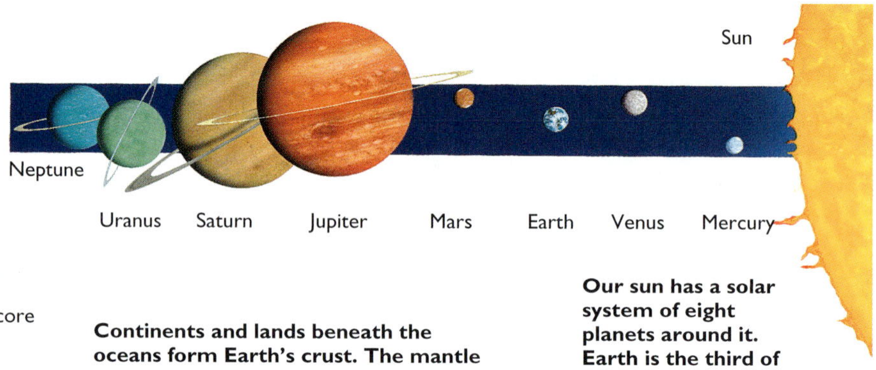

Continents and lands beneath the oceans form Earth's crust. The mantle is a thick (about 3000 km) layer of rock just below the crust. Further in, the outer core (about 2200 km thick) is made of melted iron and nickel. The ball-shaped inner core probably consists of solid iron and nickel.

Our sun has a solar system of eight planets around it. Earth is the third of the smaller inner planets and is the only planet with liquid water.

---

earn•ings (ər′ningz) money earned: *Most of our earnings went for hockey equipment.* *pl.n.*

earth (ərth) **1** the planet we live on, the third from the sun. When used as a name, this word is capitalized: *We know that Earth is round. China is on the other side of the earth.* **2** soil; dirt: *The earth in this garden is good for growing vegetables.* **3** the ground: *The arrow fell to earth 100 m away.* *n.*
down to earth, seeing things as they really are; practical.
on earth, an expression used to strengthen a question: *Why on earth would you do that?*

earth•en•ware (ər′thən wer′) **1** made of baked clay: *an earthenware jug.* **2** dishes or containers made of baked clay: *Pottery is earthenware.* 1 *adj.,* 2 *n.*

earth•ly (ərth′lē) **1** having to do with this world, and not with heaven: *The nun gave up all her earthly possessions.* **2** possible; imaginable: *That piece of junk is of no earthly use.* *adj.*

earth•quake (ərth′kwāk′) a movement of the earth's crust. Earthquakes start far below the surface and can be violent enough to destroy buildings, roads, etc. *n.*

earth•worm (ərth′wərm′) a common worm that lives in the earth. Earthworms help to loosen the soil. *n.*

ease (ēz) **1** freedom from pain, worry, hard work, etc.; comfort: *She lived a life of ease, with lots of free time and plenty of money.* **2** make less; lighten: *Some medicines ease pain. Talking to you has eased my troubles.* **3** move slowly and carefully: *He eased the big box through the door.* 1 *n.,* 2, 3 *v.,* **eased, eas•ing.**
at ease, a free from pain or trouble; comfortable: *living life at ease.* **b** with the hands behind the back, the feet apart, and the body somewhat relaxed: *The soldiers were ordered to stand at ease.*
ease up or **off,** lessen; lighten: *The rain is beginning to ease up.*
with ease, without having to try hard: *She learned to read with ease.*

ea•sel (ē′zəl) a stand for supporting a painting, chalkboard, etc. *n.*

eas•i•ly (ē′zə lē) **1** without pain or difficulty: *He solved the puzzle easily. A few hours after the operation, the patient was resting easily.* **2** by far; without question: *She is easily the best player on the field.* *adv.*

east (ēst) **1** the direction of the sunrise. **2** to or from the east: *They travelled east for two days* (*adv.*). *There was a strong east wind* (*adj.*). **3 the East, a** the eastern part of Canada or of some other country. For western Canadians, the East includes all the provinces from Ontario eastward; for Ontarians, the East means the Atlantic Provinces. **b** the countries in Asia. 1, 3 *n.,* 2 *adv. or adj.* **—east′ern,** *adj.* **—east′er•ly,** *adj.*
🍁 **back East** or **down East,** in or toward any place in the eastern part of Canada.

East•er (ēs′tər) one of the most important festivals for Christians. It begins with **Good Friday,** when they remember that Jesus died, and ends the following Sunday when they celebrate that he rose from the dead. Since it happens in April or late March, many people also celebrate the season of spring at this time. *n.*

east•ward (ēst′wərd) toward the east; east: *He walked eastward* (*adv.*). *The orchard is on the eastward slope of the hill* (*adj.*). **Eastwards** is another form for the adverb. *adv. or adj.*

Eclipse

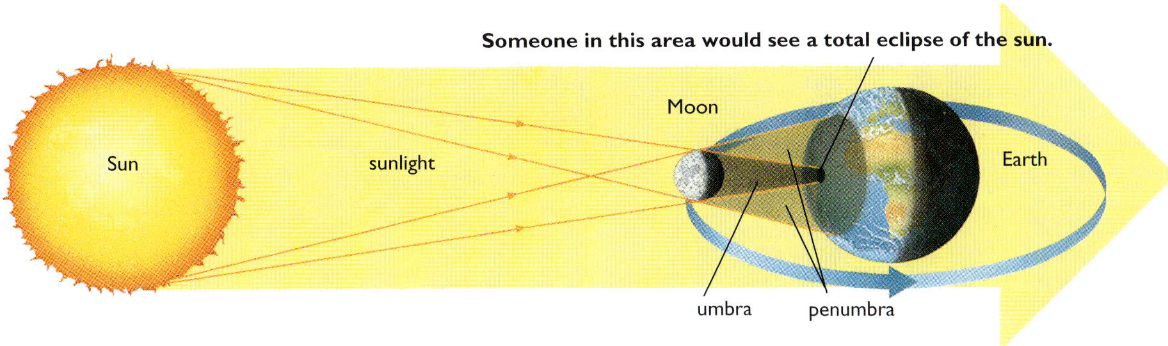

eas·y (ē′zē) 1 not hard to do: *an easy job.* 2 free from pain, hard work, trouble, or worry: *an easy life.* 3 relaxed and pleasant: *an easy manner. They started out at an easy pace.* 4 *Informal.* willing and able to go along with anything: *an easy baby. It doesn't matter to me where we go—I'm easy.* *adj.,* **eas·i·er, eas·i·est.**

eas·y·go·ing (ē′zē gō′ing) tending not to worry or get upset: *She's very easygoing and seldom gets angry.* *adj.*

eat (ēt) 1 chew and swallow: *Cows eat grass and grain.* 2 have a meal: *We ate at the Hussains' place last night.* 3 destroy, wear away, or use up: *The flames ate up the wood. The acid has eaten through the metal.* *v.,* **ate, eat·en, eat·ing.** —**eat′er,** *n.*

eaves·drop (ēvz′drop′) listen in on a private conversation. *v.,* **eaves·dropped, eaves·drop·ping.** —**eaves′drop′per,** *n.*

eaves·trough (ēvz′trof′) a gutter placed under the edge or **eaves** of a roof to catch rain water and carry it away. *n.*

ebb (eb) 1 a flowing of the tide away from the shore; the fall of the tide. 2 flow out; fall: *We waded farther out as the tide ebbed.* 3 a lessening or weakening; a low point: *Their confidence was at its lowest ebb.* 4 lessen or weaken: *His courage began to ebb as he neared the haunted house.* 1, 3 *n.,* 2, 4 *v.*

eb·on·y (eb′ə nē) a hard black wood that is often used for carving. *n., pl.* **eb·on·ies.**

ec·cen·tric (ek sen′trik) 1 out of the ordinary; strange; odd: *Singing on a public bus is rather eccentric.* 2 a person who behaves in an odd manner. 1 *adj.,* 2 *n.*

ech·o (ek′ō) 1 the repeating of a sound when sound waves are bounced back from a cliff, wall, or other surface. 2 be heard or cause to be heard again: *The hills echoed the sound of the explosion. The boom echoed through the valley.* 3 say or do what another says or does: *The little boy echoed whatever his big sister said.* 1 *n., pl.* **ech·oes;** 2, 3 *v.,* **ech·oed, ech·o·ing.**

e·clipse (ē klips′) 1 a darkening of the sun or the moon. An eclipse of the sun happens when the moon passes between the earth and the sun. An eclipse of the moon happens when the earth passes between the sun and the moon, leaving the moon in shadow. 2 cut off the light from something, making it invisible. 3 attract much more attention than another, especially by being better: *In sports she quite eclipsed her older brother.* 4 a loss of importance or fame: *The singer has suffered an eclipse.* 1, 4 *n.,* 2, 3 *v.,* **e·clipsed, e·clips·ing.**

e·col·o·gy (ē kol′ə jē) the study of the relationship of living things to their surroundings and to each other. The way in which human beings change the natural world around them is part of ecology. *n.* —**e·col′o·gist,** *n.* —**e′co·log′i·cal** (ē′kə loj′ ə kəl), *adj.*

ec·o·nom·i·cal (ek′ə nom′ə kəl *or* ē′kə nom′ə kəl) avoiding waste; cheaper or using fewer supplies: *Biking is an economical way of travelling short distances.* *adj.*

ec·o·nom·ics (ek′ə nom′iks *or* ē′kə nom′iks) the science of how people get money and other resources and how they use them. *n.* —**ec′o·nom′ic,** *adj.* —**e·con′o·mist** (i kon′ə mist), *n.*

e·con·o·mize (i kon′ə mīz′) use or spend as little as possible: *We shop at second-hand stores in order to economize.* *v.,* **e·con·o·mized, e·con·o·miz·ing.**

e·con·o·my (i kon′ə mē) 1 the system of getting and using money and other resources in any community: *The town's economy is based on mining.* 2 careful management of money and resources to avoid waste. *n., pl.* **e·con·o·mies.** —**ec′o·nom′ic** (ek′ə nom′ik), *adj.*

e·co·sys·tem (ē′kō sis′təm) all the animals and plants in one area, together with their surroundings and the ways they all live with each other. The area occupied by each ecosystem is an **ecozone.** *n.*

a bat	e bed	i bid	o pot	u cup	th thin
ā cake	ē me	ī bite	ō go	ū rude	TH then
ä bar	ə about	ər over	ô for	ů put	zh measure

ec·sta·sy (ek′stə sē) very great joy: *The little girl was in ecstasy over her brand-new tricycle.* *n., pl.* **ec·sta·sies.** —**ec·stat′ic** (ek stat′ik), *adj.*

ec·ze·ma (ek′sə mə, eg zē′mə, *or* eg′zə mə) a condition in which the skin becomes dry, red, and itchy, with a rash that oozes a watery fluid. *n.*

ed·dy (ed′ē) **1** a small whirlpool or whirlwind; water, air, or smoke swirling around. **2** swirl: *The water eddied down the drain.* 1 *n., pl.* **ed·dies;** 2 *v.,* **ed·died, ed·dy·ing.**

edge (ej) **1** the line or place where something ends; the side: *the edge of the paper, the edge of the table.* **2** the thin side that cuts: *The knife had a very sharp edge.* **3** colour or cover the edge of: *By early September the leaves were already edged with red.* **4** move sideways or little by little: *He edged his chair nearer to the fire.* **5** win a narrow victory over: *Our hockey team edged the visitors 3–2.* 1, 2 *n.,* 3–5 *v.,* **edged, edg·ing.**
on edge, nervous; tense: *Everyone was on edge during the storm.* Another word for this is **edgy.**
take the edge off, lessen the sharpness of: *A cup of herbal tea took the edge off her headache.*

edge·wise (ej′wīz′)
get a word in edgewise, get a chance to say something when others are talking. *adv.*

ed·i·ble (ed′ə bəl) fit to eat; eatable: *Not all mushrooms are edible.* *adj.*

e·dict (ē′dikt) a public order by a ruler. *n.*

ed·i·fice (ed′ə fis) a large, impressive building. *n.*

ed·it (ed′it) **1** improve the style, correct errors, check facts, etc. in something: *Edit your report at least once before handing it in.* **2** prepare an article, book, film, tape, etc. by choosing and arranging the best parts in the best way and making needed changes: *She edits the sports section of our local newspaper.* *v.* —**ed′i·tor,** *n.*

Grammar ✓Check . . . . edit

Use these editing tips to liven up your writing:
- **Vary sentence lengths.** Make some sentences short, and others long.
- **Use active verbs.** Say *The dog bit the man.* instead of *The man was bitten by the dog.*
- **Don't overuse the verb "to be."** Change *The weather is sunny...* to *The sunny weather...*

e·di·tion (i dish′ən) **1** the set of all the copies of a book, newspaper, etc. printed exactly alike and at the same time: *The first edition of* Anne of Green Gables *was printed in 1908.* **2** the form in which a book is printed: *a pocket edition, a large-print edition, a hardcover edition.* *n.*

ed·i·to·ri·al (ed′ə tȯr′ē əl) **1** an article in a newspaper or magazine, or a comment in a news broadcast, giving the person's opinion on some subject rather than just news about it. **2** having to do with editing: *editorial work.* 1 *n.,* 2 *adj.*

ed·u·cate (ej′ə kāt′) teach or train, especially in a school or with formal lessons: *She was educated at the University of Regina.* *v.,* **ed·u·cat·ed, ed·u·cat·ing.** —**ed′u·ca′tion,** *n.* —**ed′u·ca′tion·al,** *adj.* —**ed′u·ca′tor,** *n.*

Common eels can live in salt water and fresh water.

eel (ēl) a long, slippery fish shaped like a snake. *n.*

ee·rie (ē′rē) strange in a scary way; creepy; spooky: *an eerie scream.* *adj.,* **ee·ri·er, ee·ri·est.** —**ee′ri·ly,** *adv.*

ef·face (i fās′) rub out; wipe out: *The waves quickly effaced the footprints on the shore.* *v.,* **ef·faced, ef·fac·ing.**

ef·fect (i fekt′) **1** a result: *One of the effects of the storm was widespread power failure.* **2** the way something seems to your senses; a certain look, sound, etc.: *The way he has painted these racehorses creates an effect of action and speed.* **3** bring about; cause: *The year she spent overseas effected a real change in her attitude.* **4 effects,** *pl.* belongings: *They lost all their personal effects in the fire.* 1, 2, 4 *n.,* 3 *v.*
for effect, for show.
in effect, a in fact; really; going by the results: *In effect, closing the factory meant closing the town.* **b** being applied or followed: *The new rules are now in effect.*
take effect, begin to apply or work; become active: *The new prices will take effect on January 1st. The medicine took effect immediately—she was asleep in seconds.*

CONFUSABLES . . . . . . effect

effect means "result": *It had no effect on me.*
affect means "influence": *Did that affect you?*

ef·fec·tive (i fek′tiv) **1** able to cause the desired result: *These new drugs are very effective.* **2** being applied or followed; active: *That law is no longer effective.* *adj.*

ef·fer·ves·cent (ef′ər ves′ənt) 1 fizzy; giving off bubbles of gas, like pop. 2 lively; cheerful, fun-loving, and outgoing: *an effervescent personality.* *adj.*

ef·fi·cient (i fish′ənt) able to get a job done well without wasting time, energy, etc.: *If we were better organized, we'd be more efficient.* *adj.*
—ef·fi′cien·cy, *n.*

ef·fort (ef′ərt) 1 the use of energy to do something: *Climbing a steep hill takes a lot of effort.* 2 a hard try; a strong attempt: *The loser was congratulated for his fine effort.* 3 something that takes energy: *Just getting my boots on was a huge effort. We showed them our first efforts at papermaking.* 4 in science, the amount of energy needed to perform a certain amount of work. *n.*
—ef′fort·less, *adj.*

e.g. *abbreviation for* for example: *I love many different flavours of ice cream, e.g., vanilla, chocolate, and strawberry.*

egg¹ (eg) 1 a round or oval body laid by female birds, reptiles, and fish. Young hatch from them. 2 a special cell in the body of a woman or female animal that starts to develop into a baby if it is fertilized by a male sperm cell. *n.*
have egg on your face, be completely embarrassed.

Word Family.......... egg

eggnog: a drink of beaten eggs plus milk, sugar, etc.
eggplant: an egg-shaped vegetable, with a purple skin
egg roll: an egg-based pastry, filled with bits of vegetables, shrimp, etc., then deep-fried

egg² (eg)
egg on, urge by teasing, making dares, etc.: *Other boys egged him on to fight.* *v.*

egg·shell (eg′shel′) 1 the shell covering an egg. 2 very thin and easily broken, like eggshells: *eggshell china.* 3 slightly shiny when dry: *eggshell paint.* 1 *n.,* 2, 3 *adj.*

e·go (ē′gō) 1 a person's inner self; the part of your personality that knows, thinks, has feelings, and makes choices. 2 the tendency to think that you are better and more important than others. A person who thinks this way is an **egotist.** *n., pl.* **e·gos.** **—e′go·tis′tic,** *adj.*

e·gret (ē′gret *or* eg′ret) a large wading bird, usually white, found mostly in the southern United States. *n.*

ei·der·down (ī′dər doun′) 1 the soft feathers from the breast of a large sea duck called an **eider duck,** used to fill duvets. 2 a quilt stuffed with these feathers. *n.*

Eid ul–Ad·ha (ēd′ ūl ȧ′də) one of the two most important Islamic festivals. It commemorates the sacrifice of Abraham and takes place in mid-December. The other is **Eid al-Fitr** (ēd′ ul fit′rə), at the end of the month-long fast of Ramadan in the fall.

eight (āt) one more than seven; 8: *Four and four make eight (n.). I have eight coloured markers (adj.).* *n. or adj.* **—eighth,** *adj. or n.*

eight·een (āt′tēn′) eight more than ten; 18. *n. or adj.* **—eight′eenth′,** *adj. or n.*

Eight·fold Path (āt′fōld path′) in Buddhism, the way to full understanding and freedom from suffering. To follow it, your beliefs, intentions, thoughts, speech, actions, livelihood, efforts, and meditation must be right.

eighth note (ātth′nōt′) in music, a note that lasts one-eighth as long as a whole note. The symbol for it has a tail, or a line joining it to other eighth notes (♪, ♫). An **eighth rest** (𝄾) is a period of silence of the same length.

eight·y (ā′tē) eight times ten; 80. *n., pl.* **eight·ies;** *or adj.* **—eight′i·eth,** *adj. or n.*

ei·ther (ē′ᴛʜər *or* ī′ᴛʜər) 1 one or the other of two: *She can write with either hand (adj.). Choose either of us as your partner (pron.). Either come in or go out (conj.).* 2 each of two: *On either side of the river there are fields of corn.* 3 also (used with **not** or **never**): *If you do not go, I will not go either.* 1, 2 *adj.,* 1 *pron. or conj.,* 3 *adv.*

e·ject (i jekt′) 1 throw or push out; cause to come out: *The volcano ejected smoke, ashes, and lava. Push this button to eject the disk from the computer.* 2 escape from an aircraft in an emergency with an **ejection seat,** a seat that is automatically thrown out and parachuted to the ground: *The pilot ejected when the plane caught fire.* *v.*

eke out (ēk) add to or use very thriftily to make it go as far as possible: *The stranded hikers eked out their powdered milk supply by using extra water to mix it up.* *v.,* **eked out, ek·ing out.**
eke out a living, make just barely enough money to live.

e·lab·o·rate (i lab′ə rit *for 1,* i lab′ə rāt′ *for 2 and 3*) 1 very fancy or complicated: *elaborate hairdo.* 2 work out carefully and thoroughly: *The inventor spent months elaborating plans for a new engine.* 3 give more details: *Could you elaborate on your suggestion to give us a clearer idea?* 1 *adj.,* 2, 3 *v.,* **e·lab·o·rat·ed, e·lab·o·rat·ing.**

a bat	e bed	i bid	o pot	u cup	th thin
ā cake	ē me	ī bite	ō go	ū rude	ᴛʜ then
ȧ bar	ə about	ər over	ȯ for	ů put	zh measure

e•lapse (i laps′) pass; slip by: *Many hours elapsed while the boy slept.* *v.*, **e•lapsed, e•laps•ing.**

e•las•tic (i las′tik) **1** stretchy; able to return to a certain shape after being pulled or pressed out of that shape. Toy balloons, sponges, and steel springs are elastic. **2** tape or fabric woven partly of rubber threads, for sewing into clothes at the waist, cuffs, etc. so they will stretch. **3** a rubber band: *Put an elastic around the activity cards.* 1 *adj.*, 2, 3 *n.* —**e•las′tic′i•ty** (i las′tis′ə tē), *n.*

e•lat•ed (i lā′tid) very glad; joyful: *They were elated when their team won.* *adj.* —**e•la′tion,** *n.*

el•bow (el′bō) **1** the joint between the upper arm and forearm. It makes a bony point when you bend your arm. **2** something shaped like a bent arm, such as a sharp turn in a road or a curved piece of pipe. **3** push or jab with the elbow: *to elbow someone in the ribs. She elbowed her way out of the crowded elevator.* 1, 2 *n.*, 3 *v.* **at your elbow,** right next to you; close by: *When Nico did his homework his dictionary was always at his elbow.*

eld•er (el′dər) **1** older: *my elder brother.* **2** an older person: *The children showed respect for their elders.* **3** one of the leaders in a community, chosen for his or her wisdom and experience. It is often an older person, but not always. Some churches have elders; so do many First Nations communities. 1 *adj.*, 2, 3 *n.*

el•der•ber•ry (el′dər ber′ē) a very small black or dark blue berry that grows in flat clusters on a large bush. Elderberries are good to eat. *n.*, *pl.* **el•der•ber•ries.**

eld•er•ly (el′dər lē′) getting old. *adj.*

USING WORDS ..... elderly

The word **elderly** is used only to describe people, and means "past middle age and getting old": *He was an elderly man, nearly seventy.*

The word **old**, when used to describe people and animals, usually means "near the end of life": *The old dog had trouble climbing stairs.*

When **old** is used to describe things, it means "having existed for a long time": *I took a photograph of the ruins of the old castle.*

eld•est (el′dist) oldest. *adj.*

e•lect (i lekt′) **1** choose a person by voting: *The club elected a new president.* All the people who may vote are called the **electorate** (i lek′tə rit). **2** choose: *Francesca elected to spend the week with her cousins rather than go to summer camp.* *v.* —**e•lec′tion,** *n.* —**e•lec′tive,** *adj.*

e•lec•tric (i lek′trik) **1** having to do with electricity: *electric power, an electric current.* **Electrical** is another form for this meaning. **2** run or operated by electricity: *an electric train, an electric guitar.* **3** very exciting; thrilling: *The dancer gave an electric performance.* *adj.*

electric eye (i lek′trik ī′) an electric device with a small window (eye) that is sensitiveto changes in light. Electric eyes are used to run camera light meters.They can also be used to automatically open and close doors, detect movement, and count things. **Photocell** is another name for it.

electric field (i lek′trik fēld′) a force field that surrounds anything that has an electric charge.

e•lec•tri•cian (i lek′ trish′ən) a person who installs or fixes electric wiring, lights, etc. *n.*

e•lec•tric•i•ty (i lek′tris′ə tē) **1** a form of energy. With it we can produce light, heat, motion, sound, pictures, etc.: *Lightning is caused by a discharge of electricity between clouds.* **2** an electric current: *Our refrigerator is run by electricity.* *n.*

e•lec•tri•fy (i lek′trə fī′) **1** give an electric charge or current to. **2** provide with hydro service: *The tiny mountain settlement was not even electrified until last year.* **3** excite; thrill: *The final race electrified everyone in the stadium.* *v.*, **e•lec•tri•fied, e•lec•tri•fy•ing.**

e•lec•tro•cute (i lek′trə kyūt′) kill by a strong electric current. *v.*, **e•lec•tro•cut•ed, e•lec•tro•cut•ing.** —**e•lec′tro•cu′tion,** *n.*

e•lec•trode (i lek′trōd) a metal pin or terminal that allows electricity to flow in or out. *n.*

e•lec•tro•mag•net (i lek′trō mag′nit) a powerful magnet made by coiling a wire many times around an iron core and sending an electric current through it. *n.*

e•lec•tron (i lek′tron) a very tiny particle that is one of the basic building blocks of matter. It carries a negative electric charge and is found outside the nucleus of every kind of atom. *n.*

e•lec•tron•ics (i lek′tron′iks *or* ē′lek tron′iks) the science that deals with electrons in motion: *Radar, radio, television, computers, etc. are based on the principles of electronics.* *n.* —**e•lec′tron′ic,** *adj.*

e•lec•tro•stat•ic (i lek′trə stat′ik) having to do with electricity that does not flow as a current, such as the kind that gives you a shock when you touch a doorknob after walking on carpet. An electrostatic charge also makes certain fabrics cling together in dry weather. *adj.*

el•e•gant (el′ə gənt) showing good taste; beautiful in a rich, fine, classy way; graceful: *elegant furnishings, elegant manners.* *adj.* **—el′e•gance,** *n.*

el•e•ment (el′ə mənt) **1** one of the simple substances making up the whole physical universe. An element cannot be broken down into other different substances. Gold, oxygen, carbon, and tin are elements. Water is not an element, since it can be broken down into oxygen and hydrogen. **2** one of the parts of anything: *Honesty and kindness are elements of a good life.* **3 the elements,** *pl.* the weather; rain, wind, UV rays, etc.: *Keep your bike in the shed to protect it from the elements.* *n.*

el•e•men•ta•ry (el′ə men′tə rē) simple; basic: *You learn addition and subtraction in elementary arithmetic.* An **elementary school** goes up to grade five, six, or eight and can be followed by high school or junior high. *adj.*

The ears of the African elephant (shown here) are much larger than the Indian elephant's ears. Both male and female African elephants have tusks.

el•e•phant (el′ə fənt) a huge, strong animal of Africa and Asia with thick grey skin, large floppy ears, tusks, and a long flexible snout called a trunk. *n.*

el•e•vate (el′ə vāt′) raise; lift up: *He spoke from an elevated platform.* *v.,* **el•e•vat•ed, el•e•vat•ing.**

el•e•va•tion (el′ə vā′shən) **1** the height above sea level or above the earth's surface: *The elevation of Calgary is 1045 m.* **2** the act of elevating or raising something. **3** a raised place. A hill or mountain is an elevation. **4** a drawing of the front, back, or side of a structure. *n.*

el•e•va•tor (el′ə vā′tər) **1** a box like a small room that can carry people or things up and down in a building. The box is pulled up and down by cables operated by a motor. **2** a tall building for storing grain: *Elevators are a familiar sight on the prairies.* *n.*

e•lev•en (i lev′ən) one more than ten; 11. *n. or adj.* **—e•lev′enth,** *adj. or n.*
the eleventh hour, the very last minute.

elf (elf) in stories, a tiny being with magic powers who likes to play tricks. *n., pl.* **elves.** **—elf′ish,** *adj.*

el•i•gi•ble (el′ə jə bəl) able to be chosen; qualified; meeting all the requirements for something: *Only original pictures drawn by hand are eligible for the contest.* *adj.* **—el′i•gi•bil′i•ty** (el′ə jə bil′ə tē), *n.*

e•lim•i•nate (i lim′ə nāt′) **1** get rid of: *The new air filter eliminates dust.* **2** put out of a competition by defeating: *Our team was eliminated in the first round of hockey playoffs.* *v.,* **e•lim•i•nat•ed, e•lim•i•nat•ing.** **—e•lim′i•na′tion,** *n.*

e•lite or **é•lite** (i lēt′ *or* ā lēt′) **1** a group that people think have the most ability, the most money, power, status, etc.: *As top baseball and soccer player, Jay was one of the school's athletic elite. In some countries, only the elite can afford to go to university or college.* **2** high in skill, money, or power: *an elite hockey team.* 1 *n.,* 2 *adj.*

elk (elk) **1** a large North American deer. It is reddish brown with a yellowish rump patch. **2** a large deer of Europe and Asia with broad antlers. It is a smaller variety of the North American moose. *n., pl.* **elk** or **elks.**

el•lipse (i lips′) an oval with both ends alike. The path of the earth around the sun is an ellipse. *n.* **—el•lip′ti•cal,** *adj.*

elm (elm) a tall, graceful, deciduous tree with hard, heavy wood used forfurniture, hockey sticks, etc. *n.*

El Ni•ño (el nēn′yō) a warm current in the Pacific Ocean. It changes weather patterns. Look also at **La Niña.** *n.*

e•lope (i lōp′) run away to get married. *v.,* **e•loped, e•lop•ing.** **—e•lope′ment,** *n.*

el•o•quent (el′ə kwənt) using words in a powerful or beautiful way: *an eloquent speech, an eloquent storyteller.* *adj.* **—el′o•quence,** *n.*

a bat	e bed	i bid	o pot	u cup	th thin
ā cake	ē me	ī bite	ō go	ū rude	ᴛʜ then
à bar	ə about	ər over	ȯ for	ů put	zh measure

else (els) 1 other; different; instead: *That shirt is dirty—put on something else.* 2 differently: *How else can he act?* 3 more: *Is there anything else we need besides milk and bread?* 4 otherwise; if not: *Hurry, or else you'll miss the bus.* 1, 3 *adj.,* 2, 4 *adv.*
or else, *Informal.* or suffer for it; or pay a penalty: *You'd better return my bike, or else.*

else•where (els′wer′ *or* els′hwer′) in or to some other place; somewhere else. *adv.*

e•lude (i lūd′) avoid being caught or found by; slip away from: *The fox eluded the dogs.* Something hard to catch, find, or hold on to is **elusive** (i lū′siv). *v.,* **e•lud•ed, e•lud•ing.**

elves (elvz) plural of **elf.** *n.*

e•ma•ci•at•ed (i mā′sē ā′tid *or* i mā′shē ā′tid) very thin from losing too much weight: *The starving kitten was weak and emaciated.* *adj.*

e–mail (ē′māl′) 1 a system of sending messages by computer. E-mail can be sent over telephone lines or within a computer network. Its full name is **electronic mail.** 2 a message sent by this system: *We got two e-mails from Uncle Theo today.* 3 use this sytem to send a message to another person: *Sarah e-mailed me everything I needed to know.* 1, 2 *n.,* 3 *v.*

e•man•ci•pate (i man′sə pāt′) set free from slavery of any kind. *v.,* **e•man•ci•pat•ed, e•man•ci•pat•ing.** **—e•man′ci•pa′tion,** *n.*

em•balm (em bom′) treat a dead body with chemicals to keep it from decaying. *v.*

em•bank•ment (em bangk′mənt) a raised bank of earth, stone, etc. to hold back water, support a roadway, etc. *n.*

em•bar•go (em bȧr′gō) a restriction put on trade with another country, often as a way of persuading the other country to change its laws: *Canada put an embargo on South Africa until the South African government got rid of apartheid.* *n.*

em•bark (em bȧrk′) 1 board a ship, plane, train, or bus: *Passengers will embark in 15 minutes.* 2 start out: *After university, she embarked on her career.* *v.*

em•bar•rass (em ber′əs) make uncomfortable, nervous, or ashamed: *She embarrassed me by pointing out my mistake to everyone.* *v.* **—em•bar′rass•ment,** *n.*

em•bas•sy (em′bə sē) the official home and office of an ambassador and his or her staff in a foreign country: *Canada has an embassy in Paris.* *n., pl.* **em•bas•sies.**

em•bed (em bed′) stick completely into a base or surface: *The splinter was so deeply embedded in my foot that it took Dad several tries to pull it out.* *v.,* **em•bed•ded, em•bed•ding.**

em•bel•lish (em bel′ish) add details to something to make it more interesting: *Sally embellished her story about the ski trip by adding the part about the grizzly bear tracks.* *v.* **—em•bel′lish•ment,** *n.*

em•ber (em′bər) a piece of wood or coal still glowing in the ashes of a fire: *He stirred the embers to make them blaze up again.* *n.*

em•bez•zle (em bez′əl) steal the money you are supposed to be taking care of for others: *The treasurer embezzled $2000 from the company's funds.* *v.,* **em•bez•zled, em•bez•zling.**

Many countries try to find some object that uniquely represents them as an emblem on a flag or crest. Canada has the maple leaf on its crest.

em•blem (em′bləm) a symbol: *The beaver and the maple leaf are both emblems of Canada.* *n.*

em•bod•y (em bod′ē) make into something that can be seen, touched, and heard; give reality to: *A ballerina embodies gracefulness.* *v.,* **em•bod•ied, em•bod•y•ing.**

em•boss (em bos′) decorate with a design that stands out from the surface. Coins are embossed. *v.*

em•brace (em brās′) 1 hug: *The two friends embraced (v.). She gave me a warm embrace (n.).* 2 accept: *They eagerly embraced each new idea.* 3 include: *The cat family embraces lions and tigers.* 1–3 *v.,* **em•braced, em•brac•ing;** 1 *n.*

em•broi•der (em broi′dər) 1 decorate cloth with a design or pattern of stitches. 2 add imaginary details to: *He didn't exactly tell lies, but he did embroider his stories.* *v.* **—em•broi′der•y,** *n.*

em•bry•o (em′brē ō′) 1 an animal before birth or hatching: *A chicken within an egg is an embryo.* 2 an undeveloped plant within a seed. *n., pl.* **em•bry•os.**

em•er•ald (em′ə rəld) a clear, bright green precious stone. *n.*

e·merge (i mərj′) come out after being covered or hidden: *The sun emerged from behind a cloud. Many facts emerged as a result of the investigation.* *v.,* **e·merged, e·merg·ing.** —**e·mer′gence,** *n.*

e·mer·gen·cy (i mər′jən sē) **1** a serious or dangerous situation that comes up suddenly and needs quick action: *He keeps a first-aid kit in his car for emergencies.* **2** having to do with such a situation: *an emergency exit, an emergency operation on a patient.* 1 *n., pl.* **e·mer·gen·cies;** 2 *adj.*

em·i·grate (em′ə grāt′) leave your own country to settle in another. A person who does this is an **emigrant:** *Many people emigrate from countries where there is war.* *v.,* **em·i·grat·ed, em·i·grat·ing.** —**em′i·gra′tion,** *n.*

CONFUSABLES .... emigrate

emigrate means "leave": *My family emigrated from Greece to Canada in 1960.*

immigrate means "go": *My family immigrated to Canada from Greece in 1960.*

em·i·nent (em′ə nənt) high; outstanding; great or famous: *A. Y. Jackson was an eminent Canadian painter.* *adj.* —**em′i·nent·ly,** *adv.* —**em′i·nence,** *n.*

e·mir (ə mēr′) a Muslim title given to a ruler, governor, or leader of an army.

e·mis·sion (i mish′ən) **1** something that is emitted; especially, the gas or other substances released into the air by cars, factories, etc.: *The factory reduced its emissions after people living nearby began to have medical problems.* **2** the act of emitting something. *n.*

e·mit (i mit′) send out; give off: *Volcanoes emit ash. The lion emitted a loud roar.* *v.,* **e·mit·ted, e·mit·ting.**

e·mo·ti·con (i mō′tə kon′) a tiny picture that computer users make from letters and punctuation as a short way to communicate an emotion. For example, :-), a sideways smiling face, means that the person typing it is happy or has been joking. *n.*

e·mo·tion (i mō′shən) a feeling, such as joy, fear, anger, or excitement. *n.* —**e·mo′tion·less,** *adj.*

e·mo·tion·al (i mō′shə nəl) **1** having to do with the emotions. **2** stirring up the emotions: *The speaker made an emotional plea for money to help find a cure for AIDS.* **3** having strong emotions and showing them openly. *adj.* —**e·mo′tion·al·ly,** *adv.*

em·pa·thize (em′pə thīz′) imagine yourself in another person's place and feel what that person is feeling. If you can empathize with people, you have **empathy.** *v.,* **em·pa·thized, em·pa·thiz·ing.** **em′pa·thet′ic,** *adj.*

em·per·or (em′pə rər) a man who is the ruler of an empire. *n.*

em·pha·sis (em′fə sis) **1** stress; importance: *That school puts emphasis on arithmetic and reading.* **2** the special force put on particular syllables or words when speaking: *In the word "ecological," the emphasis is on the third syllable.* *n., pl.* **em·pha·ses** (em′fə sēz′).

em·pha·size (em′fə sīz′) call people's attention to; give special importance to: *In her talk at our assembly, the officer emphasized the need to follow bike safety rules.* *v.,* **em·pha·sized, em·pha·siz·ing.**

em·phat·ic (em fat′ik) forceful; firmly emphasized: *His answer was an emphatic "No!"* *adj.* —**em·phat′i·cal·ly,** *adv.*

em·pire (em′pīr) **1** a group of countries under one ruler or government: *the British Empire.* **2** any country whose ruler is called an emperor or empress: *the Japanese Empire.* **3** a very large business controlled by one person or group: *a fast-food empire.* *n.*

em·ploy (em ploi′) **1** give work and pay to: *The hotel employs a cook.* The person or company that gives the work is the **employer;** the person who is paid to do the work is the **employee.** **2** use: *He employed every argument he could think of to persuade us.* *v.*

em·ploy·ment (em ploi′mənt) **1** a job; work: *He had great difficulty finding employment.* **2** the percentage of people who have jobs: *Employment is up this month.* **3** the act of employing or using: *The artist showed amazing skill in the employment of her brushes and paint.* *n.*

em·pow·er (em pou′ər) give power or authority to: *The teacher is empowered to discipline students.* *v.*

em·press (em′pris) the wife of an emperor, or a woman who rules over an empire. *n.*

emp·ty (emp′tē) **1** with nothing in it: *The birds had gone and their nest was empty.* **2** pour out or take out all that is in a thing: *He emptied his glass quickly. Empty the sand out of the pail.* **3** become empty: *The hall emptied as soon as the concert was over.* **4** flow out: *The Fraser River empties into the Pacific Ocean.* **5** meaningless: *empty promises.* 1, 5 *adj.,* **emp·ti·er, emp·ti·est;** 2–4 *v.,* **emp·tied, emp·ty·ing.** —**emp′ti·ness,** *n.*

a bat	e bed	i bid	o pot	u cup	th thin
ā cake	ē me	ī bite	ō go	ū rude	ꟾʜ then
ä bar	ə about	ər over	ô for	ů put	zh measure

e·mu (ē′myü) an Australian bird that looks like a small ostrich. It runs very fast but cannot fly. *n.*

em·u·late (em′yə lāt′) try to imitate; follow as a model: *The little girl emulates her big sister.* *v.,* **em·u·lat·ed, em·u·lat·ing.**

e·mul·sion (i mul′shən) a mixture of two liquids that do not dissolve in each other. Very fine drops of one liquid are scattered evenly through the other. Camera film is coated with a special light-sensitive emulsion. *n.*

en·a·ble (en ā′bəl) make able to do something: *This medicine will enable him to get a good night's sleep in spite of his bad cold.* *v.,* **en·a·bled, en·a·bling.**

en·act (en akt′) make into law: *Parliament enacted a bill making* O Canada *the national anthem.* *v.* **—en·act′ment,** *n.*

e·nam·el (i nam′əl) **1** a glasslike substance melted and then cooled to make a smooth, shiny, hard coating on metal, pottery, etc. **2** a paint or varnish that forms a smooth, glossy surface when dry. **3** the outer layer of a tooth. **4** cover or decorate with enamel. 1–3 *n.,* 4 *v.,* **e·nam·elled** or **e·nam·eled, e·nam·el·ling** or **e·nam·el·ing.**

en·chant (en chant′) **1** use magic on; put under a spell: *The witch had enchanted the princess.* **2** delight: *The little children were enchanted by the puppet play.* *v.* **—en·chant′ing,** *adj.* **—en·chant′ment,** *n.*

en·cir·cle (en sər′kəl) form a circle around: *Trees encircled the pond.* *v.,* **en·cir·cled, en·cir·cling.**

en·close (en klōz′) **1** shut in on all sides; surround: *A fence encloses the schoolyard.* **2** put in an envelope or package along with something else: *A cheque was enclosed with the letter.* *v.,* **en·closed, en·clos·ing.**

en·clo·sure (en klō′zhər) **1** a closed-in place: *An enclosure for animals is sometimes called a pen.* **2** anything put in an envelope or package with something else: *He sent several newspaper clippings as enclosures with his letter.* *n.*

en·code (en kōd) put into code. *v.,* **en·cod·ed, en·cod·ing.**

en·com·pass (en kum′pəs) **1** go or reach all the way around: *The atmosphere encompasses the earth.* **2** contain: *An encyclopedia encompasses many topics.* *v.*

en·core (on′kôr) a last extra performance by a musician or other entertainer. When the audience keeps on clapping at the end of a show or concert, they are asking for an encore. *n.*

en·coun·ter (en koun′tər) **1** meet unexpectedly: *We encountered an old friend in the store.* **2** face a problem or enemy: *He encountered many difficulties before the job was done.* **3** a meeting or coming face to face: *a chance encounter, an encounter with the neighbourhood bully.* 1, 2 *v.,* 3 *n.*

en·cour·age (en kər′ij) give help or support to: *The cheers of the crowd encouraged her. High grain prices encourage farming.* *v.,* **en·cour·aged, en·cour·ag·ing.** **—en·cour′age·ment,** *n.*

en·croach (en krōch′) go beyond proper or usual limits: *Each spring the river encroached further on the farmland. A good salesperson will not encroach on the customer's time.* *v.*

en·cum·ber (en kum′bər) burden with heavy things, problems, or anything else that hinders: *Heavy packs encumbered the hikers. The country is encumbered with debt.* *v.* **—en·cum′brance,** *n.*

en·cy·clo·pe·di·a (en sī′klə pē′dē ə) a book or set of books giving information arranged alphabetically on all kinds of subjects: *She looked up "black hole" in the encyclopedia and found two pages of information.* **Encyclopaedia** is another spelling. *n.*

end (end) **1** the last part: *Tell us the end of the story.* **Ending** means the same. **2** the edge or tip of something; the place where something stops: *Those trees mark the end of their property. Every stick has two ends.* **3** bring or come to an end; stop or finish: *Let us end this fight. Their property ends here.* **4** purpose; goal: *She wanted to win and, with that end in mind, practised every day.* 1, 2, 4 *n.,* 3 *v.* **—end′less,** *adj.* **—end′less·ly,** *adv.*
at loose ends, not settled or not really knowing what to do next.
end to end, with the end of one object set next to the end of another: *Lay the dominoes end to end on the table.*
end up, finish; turn out a certain way: *He'll end up at the top of his class. It ended up that no one could come.*
go off the deep end, do something extreme; go beyond a reasonable limit with something.
hold or **keep your end up,** do your part fully in some task or project: *He was less experienced than the others, but he kept his end up very well.*
in the end, finally; at last: *Everything will turn out all right in the end.*
make ends meet, manage to afford the things you really need: *With such high rent, we can barely make ends meet.*
no end, *Informal.* very much; very many: *That dog causes no end of trouble.*
on end, a upright; straight up: *It made my hair stand on end.* **b** one after another: *It snowed for days on end.*
put an end to, stop.

These are just a few of the many species of animals that are endangered.

The giant panda is the emblem of the World Wildlife Fund, an organization that raises money for conservation programs.

en•dan•ger (en dān′jər) **1** cause danger to: *Drunk drivers endanger lives.* **2** put a species of animal or plant in danger of becoming extinct. The whooping crane is an **endangered species.** *v.* ▶ See Appendix. **—en•dan′ger•ment,** *n.*

en•dear (en dēr′) make dear: *Her kindness endeared her to all of us.* *v.* **—en•dear′ing,** *adj.* **—en•dear′ment,** *n.*

en•deav•our or **en•deav•or** (en dev′ər) try; attempt: *She endeavoured to make us feel at home* (*v.*). *He finally succeeded in his endeavour to persuade his parents* (*n.*). *v. or n.*

end of steel (end əv stēl) the end of a railway, especially going north.

en•dorse (en dôrs′) **1** approve; support: *Parents heartily endorsed the plan for new playground equipment.* **2** sign the back of a cheque, money order, etc.: *He had to endorse the cheque before the bank would cash it.* *v.,* **en•dorsed, en•dors•ing. —en•dorse′ment,** *n.*

en•dow (en dou′) give a valuable gift to someone: *The money they endowed to the school provided for a large sports program. Nature endowed her with a very scientific mind.* *v.* **—en•dow′ment,** *n.*

en•dure (en dyūr′ *or* en dūr′) **1** last; keep on without wearing away or weakening: *The Pyramids have endured for thousands of years.* **2** go through; suffer; stand: *The pioneers endured many hardships.* *v.,* **en•dured, en•dur•ing. —en•dur′ance,** *n.*

en•e•my (en′ə mē) **1** a person or group that hates, fights against, and tries to harm another: *He decided to forgive the enemy who had hurt him.* **2** anything harmful: *Frost is an enemy of flowers.* *n., pl.* **en•e•mies.**

en•er•gize (en′ər jīz′) give energy to a person or thing: *The coach's encouraging pep talk energized the team.* *v.,* **en•er•gized, en•er•giz•ing.**

en•er•gy (en′ər jē) **1** the active strength or force needed to do things: *Digging the garden took all my energy.* **2** a lively, excited, or eager manner: *She spoke with such energy that she convinced us all.* **3** the power to move, or to move other objects. Heat is a form of energy—it is the movement of the molecules of a substance. Gasoline is an important source of energy. **4 energies,** *pl.,* efforts: *Let's put all our energies into making this play a success!* *n., pl.* **en•er•gies. —en′er•get′ic** (en′ər jet′ik), *adj.* **—en′er•get′i•cal•ly,** *adv.*

en•fold (en fōld′) wrap in something soft: *She was enfolded in a shawl. A heavy fog enfolded the city.* *v.*

a bat	e bed	i bid	o pot	u cup	th thin
ā cake	ē me	ī bite	ō go	ū rude	ᴛʜ then
à bar	ə about	ər over	ô for	ů put	zh measure

en•force (en fôrs′) make sure that a rule or order is obeyed: *The police enforce traffic laws.* *v.,* **en•forced, en•forc•ing.** **—en•force′ment,** *n.*

en•gage (en gāj′) 1 involve or occupy; keep busy: *The girls were engaged in building a tree fort. That problem has engaged the town council for weeks now.* 2 **engaged,** committed to getting married: *Pierre and Anne are engaged.* 3 catch and hold: *Bright objects engage a baby's attention.* 4 fit into; lock together: *The teeth of one gear engage with those of another.* 5 hire. 6 meet in battle; attack: *The soldiers prepared to engage the enemy.* *v.,* **en•gaged, en•gag•ing.** **—en•gage′ment,** *n.*
engage in, take part in; do: *He engages in many sports.*

en•gag•ing (en gā′jing) attractive; interesting: *an engaging smile, an engaging speaker.* *adj.*

Steam engines are rarely seen now in North America but are still used in many other parts of the world.

en•gine (en′jən) 1 a machine that moves something else, especially a vehicle; a motor. It uses gasoline, steam, electricity, or some other source of energy. 2 the car that moves all the other cars in a train. *n.*

WORD HISTORY........ engine

Engine started off as the Latin word *ingenium*, meaning "a talent you are born with." When it came into French as *engin*, it meant "skill" or "cleverness," and that's what it meant when English borrowed it. It then began to mean "a clever invention," and later wound up with the meaning it has today.

en•gi•neer (en′jə nēr′) 1 a person who takes care of or runs engines. The driver of a train is an engineer. 2 a person who uses science to design roads and bridges, buildings, dams, machines, medicines, and many other kinds of useful things. This work is called **engineering.** 3 guide; manage: *She engineered the whole job from start to finish.* 1, 2 *n.,* 3 *v.*

Eng•lish (ing′glish) 1 the people of England. 2 one of the official languages of Canada. It is also spoken in many other countries. 3 having to do with this language, or with England or its people. 1, 2 *n.,* 3 *adj.*

en•grave (en grāv′) carve in a surface in an artistic way: *to engrave initials on the back of a watch. The rings were engraved with their wedding date.* A picture can be made by engraving a plate of wood, glass, metal, etc., covering the plate with ink, and then pressing it on paper or cloth. *v.,* **en•graved, en•grav•ing.**

en•gross (en grōs′) take up the full attention of: *She was engrossed in an interesting story.* *v.*

en•gulf (en gulf′) swallow up; flood; overwhelm: *The waves engulfed the boat.* *v.*

en•hance (en hans′) add to or improve: *The gardens enhanced the beauty of the house.* *v.,* **en•hanced, en•hanc•ing.** **—en•hance′ment,** *n.*

e•nig•ma (i nig′mə) something very puzzling: *He was an enigma to his neighbours; he never went out, and yet his house was always dark.* *n.* **—en′ig•mat′ic,** *adj.*

en•joy (en joi′) 1 have or use with joy; like; take pleasure in: *We enjoyed our trip to Prince Edward Island.* 2 have as an advantage or benefit: *He enjoys good health.* *v.* **—en•joy′a•ble,** *adj.* **—en•joy′ment,** *n.*
enjoy yourself, be happy; have a good time: *I enjoyed myself at the party.*

en•large (en lärj′) make or become larger: *to enlarge a photograph, to enlarge a house. That small bush will enlarge with time.* *v.,* **en•larged, en•larg•ing.** **—en•large′ment,** *n.*
enlarge on, talk or write more about: *You said your trip was "fun"—could you enlarge on that?*

en•light•en (en lī′tən) give valuable knowledge that changes the way a person thinks about something: *Her friendships with kids from many different countries enlightened her about other cultures.* *v.* **—en•light′en•ment,** *n.*

en•list (en list′) 1 get the help of; get someone to join: *The teacher enlisted several of us to set up tables in the gym. The cross-country team is enlisting new members.* 2 join the armed forces. *v.*

en•liv•en (en lī′vən) make more lively, active, or cheerful: *Her jokes enlivened the party. Bright curtains enliven a room.* *v.*

e•nor•mous (i nôr′məs) huge: *an enormous appetite, enormous dinosaurs.* *adj.*

e·nough (i nuf′) as many or as much as needed: *Are there enough seats (adj.)? I've had enough to eat (pron.). You have studied enough (adv.).* *adj., pron., or adv.*

en·quire (en kwīr′) another spelling of **inquire.** *v.,* **en·quired, en·quir·ing.** **—en·quir′y,** *n.*

en·rage (en rāj′) make very angry; make furious: *When he saw how cruelly they treated the dog, Boris was enraged.* *v.,* **en·raged, en·rag·ing.**

en·rich (en rich′) make rich or richer: *An education enriches your mind. Fertilizer enriches the soil.* *v.*

en·rol or **en·roll** (en rōl′) register; sign up: *The principal enrolled ten new students this term. She enrolled in a fitness program.* *v.,* **en·rolled, en·rol·ling.** **—en·rol′ment** or **en·roll′ment,** *n.*

en route (on rüt′) on the way: *We stopped at Gander en route from St. John's to Corner Brook.*

en·shrine (en shrīn′) **1** enclose in a shrine: *A fragment of the cross that Jesus died on is enshrined in the cathedral.* **2** keep sacred; preserve, never to be erased: *Human rights are enshrined in the Canadian constitution.* *v.,* **en·shrined, en·shrin·ing.**

en·slave (en slāv′) make into a slave; put into slavery. *v.,* **en·slaved, en·slav·ing.** **—en·slave′ment,** *n.*

en·sue (en sü′) come after; follow, usually with some connection: *In his anger he hit the man, and a fight ensued.* *v.,* **en·sued, en·su·ing.**

en·sure (en shür′) make sure or certain: *Careful planning ensured their success. Ensure that all windows are locked before you leave.* *v.,* **en·sured, en·sur·ing.**

CONFUSABLES ..... ensure

ensure means "make sure": *Proofread your work to ensure there are no mistakes.*
insure means "protect": *Before our trip we must insure our luggage against loss.*

en·tan·gle (en tang′gəl) cause to get twisted up and caught: *I managed to entangle my fishing line in the water lilies. Do not try to entangle us in your schemes.* *v.,* **en·tan·gled, en·tan·gling.** **—en·tan′gle·ment,** *n.*

en·ter (en′tər) **1** go or come in: *Open the door and let them enter. He entered the house.* **2** take part in or become a member of; sign up or register for something: *He entered the piano competition. Parents enter their children in school.* **3** write, print, or key in an item in a book, list, computer file, etc.: *Whenever I get new hockey cards, I enter the players' names in my list. Enter the e-mail address and press "Return."* *v.*
enter into, a begin to take part in: *He entered into conversation with the woman next to him on the bus.* **b** have anything to do with: *That question doesn't enter into the problem.* **c** understand and appreciate.
enter on or **upon,** begin; start: *He entered on a new career.*

en·ter·prise (en′tər prīz′) **1** a project, especially an important or adventurous one. **2** a readiness to start projects; energy in starting projects: *The successful businesswoman showed great enterprise.* People who have this quality are **enterprising.** **3** business: *He works for a wealthy enterprise in downtown Halifax.* *n.*

en·ter·tain (en′tər tān′) **1** be fun for; hold someone's interest in an enjoyable way: *The funny story entertained the children.* **2** have as a guest or guests: *He entertained ten people to dinner.* **3** take into the mind; consider: *They refused to entertain such a foolish idea.* *v.* **—en′ter·tain′er,** *n.* **—en′ter·tain′ing,** *adj.* **—en′ter·tain′ment,** *n.*

en·thral or **en·thrall** (en throl′) keep someone so interested that he or she seems to be under a magic spell: *The explorer enthralled the audience with the story of his exciting adventures.* *v.,* **en·thralled, en·thrall·ing.**

en·throne (en thrōn′) set on a throne, or in the highest position. *v.,* **en·throned, en·thron·ing.**

en·thu·si·asm (en thü′zē az′əm) lively interest and enjoyment: *The band played the piece with great enthusiasm.* *n.* **—en·thu′si·as′tic,** *adj.* **—en·thu′si·as′ti·cal·ly,** *adv.*

en·thu·si·ast (en thü′zē ast′) a person who is filled with lively interest in something: *a baseball enthusiast.* *n.*

en·tice (en tīs′) attract; lead into something by stirring up desire: *Only the promise of a reward could entice him to keep his room tidy.* *v.,* **en·ticed, en·tic·ing.** **—en·tice′ment,** *n.*

en·tire (en tīr′) whole; complete; having all the parts: *The entire house was repainted, inside and out.* *adj.* **—en·tire′ly,** *adv.*

en·ti·tle (en tī′təl) **1** give someone the right to have or do a particular thing: *The one who guesses the answer is entitled to ask the next question.* **2** give as a title; name: *The author entitled her book* Underground to Canada. *v.,* **en·ti·tled, en·ti·tling.**

a bat	e bed	i bid	o pot	u cup	th thin
ā cake	ē me	ī bite	ō go	ū rude	ᴛʜ then
à bar	ə about	ər over	ò for	ù put	zh measure

en·trails (en′trālz) the inner parts of the body of a human being or animal: *Before skinning the rabbit he removed the entrails.* *pl.n.*

en·trance[1] (en′trəns) 1 the act or the right of entering: *The actor's entrance was greeted with applause. This ticket gives you entrance to the fair.* 2 a way to get in; a doorway, gate, etc. *n.*

en·trance[2] (en trans′) delight; fill with joy; capture someone's full attention: *The boy was entranced by the beautiful music.* *v.,* **en·tranced, en·tranc·ing.**

entrant (en′trənt) a person who enters a contest. *n.*

en·tree or **ent·rée** (on trā′ *or* on′trā) the main part of a meal: *Di had chicken and rice as an entree.* *n.*

en·trench (en trench′) establish firmly: *Freedom of religion is entrenched in the Canadian Charter of Rights.* *v.*

en·tre·pre·neur (on′trə prə nər′) someone who has business ideas and is ready to risk his or her own money by starting up a business: *Duncan was a real entrepreneur; in grade two he bought and sold baseball cards and made quite a profit.* *n.*

en·trust (en trust′) 1 trust with a responsibility: *He was entrusted with the choice of colours for painting his room.* 2 hand over for safekeeping: *While travelling, they entrusted their pets to the neighbours.* *v.*

en·try (en′trē) 1 the act of entering. 2 a way to get in. 3 a word on a list, an article in an encyclopedia, a piece of data keyed into a computer file, etc.: *This dictionary entry has four definitions.* 4 something that is entered in a contest: *Anil's picture was the winning entry in the art contest.* *n., pl.* **en·tries.**

en·twine (en twīn′) twine together or twine around: *Roses and honeysuckle entwine the little cottage.* *v.,* **en·twined, en·twin·ing.**

e·nu·mer·ate (i nyū′mə rāt′ *or* i nū′mə rāt′) 1 name one by one: *The sign enumerates all the pool safety rules.* 2 🍁 put a person's name on the official list of voters: *My 18-year-old sister has been enumerated for the first time.* *v.,* **e·nu·mer·at·ed, e·nu·mer·at·ing.** —**e·nu′mer·a′tor,** *n.*

e·nun·ci·ate (i nun′sē āt′) 1 speak or pronounce words: *You must enunciate clearly to be heard by those in the back row.* 2 state formally: *The scientist has enunciated a new theory.* *v.,* **e·nun·ci·at·ed, e·nun·ci·at·ing.** —**e·nun′ci·a′tion,** *n.*

en·vel·op (en vel′əp) wrap, cover, or hide: *Fog enveloped the village.* *v.,* **en·vel·oped, en·vel·op·ing.**

en·ve·lope (en′və lōp′ *or* on′və lōp′) a folded paper cover for mailing a letter or anything flat, usually with an edge that can be stuck down to seal it. *n.*
push the envelope, *Slang.* do things that may surprise or anger some people.

en·vi·ron·ment (en vī′ərn mənt) 1 all the surrounding conditions or influences that affect the growth and development of living things: *a safe, loving environment.* 2 the earth, air, and water as the home of living things: *A polluted environment can harm wildlife.* Something that is **environment-friendly** does no harm to the environment. 3 **environs,** *pl.,* the area around a place: *Frost is predicted for Edmonton and its environs tonight.* *n.* —**en·vi′ron·men′tal,** *adj.*

en·vi·ron·men·tal·ist (en vī′rən men′tə list) a person who values the environment and works to protect it: *A group of environmentalists asked the government to set this area aside for parkland.* *n.*

en·voy (en′voi) 1 a messenger. 2 a person who represents his or her own government in another country. An envoy ranks lower than an ambassador. *n.*

en·vy (en′vē) 1 a strong feeling of wishing you had what someone else has, and being unhappy or angry that you don't: *I was filled with envy when I saw her new bicycle.* 2 feel envy toward someone or because of something: *I don't envy the rich. He envied his sister's ability to ski.* 3 the person or thing envied: *She was the envy of all her classmates.* 1, 3 *n., pl.* **en·vies;** 2 *v.,* **en·vied, en·vy·ing.** —**en′vi·a·ble,** *adj.* —**en′vi·ous,** *adj.*

en·zyme (en′zīm) a substance produced by living cells that starts or speeds up chemical changes. Enzymes control processes like blood clotting and digestion. *n.*

e·on (ē′on) a very long time; many thousands of years. *n.*

ep·ic (ep′ik) 1 a long, serious poem or story about heroic adventures and noble deeds. 2 like an epic; worth writing an epic about: *Flying over the Atlantic for the first time was an epic deed.* 1 *n.,* 2 *adj.*

ep·i·cen·tre (ep′ə sen′tər) an area above the centre of an earthquake where the shock waves begin. They spread outward from there. *n.*

ep·i·dem·ic (ep′ə dem′ik) 1 a disease that spreads quickly so that many people have it at the same time: *Six schools were closed during the measles epidemic.* 2 affecting many people at the same time; widespread: *An outbreak of flu became epidemic last winter. The wild rumours had reached epidemic proportions.* 1 *n.,* 2 *adj.*

ep·i·lep·sy (ep′ə lep′sē) a disorder of certain parts of the brain that causes people to suddenly jerk uncontrollably and lose some or all of their consciousness for a short time. *n.* **—ep′i·lep′tic,** *adj.*

ep·i·sode (ep′ə sōd′) **1** a single happening or group of happenings in real life or in a story: *The summer I spent on the farm was an important episode in my life.* **2** one show in a TV series, or a chapter in a continuing story: *We have that episode of* Road to Avonlea *on video.* *n.*

e·pis·tle (i pis′əl) a fancy word for "letter": *When I printed out her e-mail, it turned out to be a three-page epistle.* *n.*

ep·i·taph (ep′ə taf′) a short statement on a tombstone in memory of the person buried there. *n.*

e·poch (ē′pok) a period of time, especially in history or geology. *n.*

e·qual (ē′kwəl) **1** the same in amount, size, value, or importance: *Give each child an equal amount of pie. All citizens have equal rights.* **2** be the same as (in amount, size, etc.): *Two times three equals six.* The symbol for this is called an **equal sign** = **3** a person or thing with the same importance, skill, power, etc.: *In high jumping she had no equal.* **4** do just as well as; match: *He tried hard to equal her record.* 1 *adj.,* 2, 4 *v.,* **e·qualled** or **e·qualed, e·qual·ling** or **e·qual·ing;** 3 *n.*
—e′qual·ly, *adv.* **—e·qual′i·ty** (i kwol′ə tē), *n.*
—e′qual·ize′, *v.*
equal to, a the same as: *Ten dimes are equal to one dollar.* **b** strong enough for; capable of: *One person is not equal to such a task.*

e·quate (i kwāt′) say or think that two things are equal: *Don't equate doing your best with showing off.* *v.,* **e·quat·ed, e·quat·ing.**

equation (i kwā′zhən) a mathematical statement that two quantities are equal. *Example:* 4 + 5 = 9 *n.*

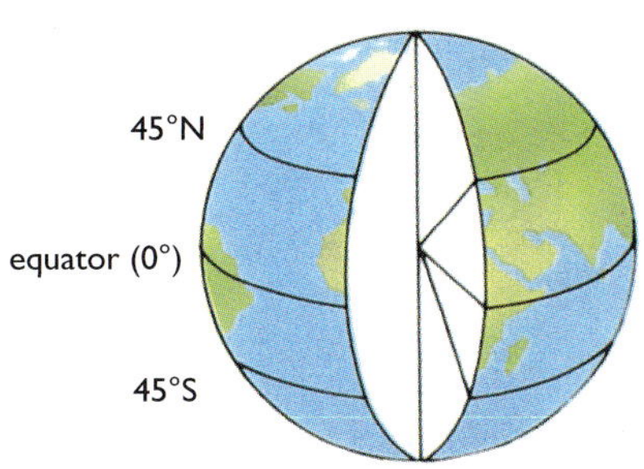

The equator is a line of latitude.

e·qua·tor (i kwā′tər) an imaginary circle around the middle of the earth, halfway between the North Pole and the South Pole: *Canada is north of the equator.* *n.*
—eq′ua·to′ri·al (ek′wə tôr′ē əl), *adj.*

e·ques·tri·an (i kwes′trē ən) **1** having to do with riding horses: *Alexa liked to watch the equestrian show at the Royal Winter Fair.* **2** someone who rides horses, especially in riding competitions. 1 *adj.,* 2 *n.*

Word Family.......... equi-

Words beginning with **equi** all have to do with being *equal.* These words come from the Latin *aequus,* meaning "equal."
equiangular: with all its angles equal
equilateral: with all its sides equal
equilibrium: balance, when opposite forces are equal
equinox: one of the two times per year, one around March 21 and one around September 22, when night and day are equally long

e·quip (i kwip′) provide with what is needed: *The camp equips each camper with craft supplies. School should equip you with research skills.* *v.,* **e·quipped, e·quip·ping.**

e·quip·ment (i kwip′mənt) what a person has or needs in order to do something: *Each player buys her own hockey equipment.* *n.*

e·quiv·a·lent (i kwiv′ə lənt) the same in amount, number, value, meaning, etc.: *Nodding your head is equivalent to saying yes* (*adj.*). *The machine will take one toonie or the equivalent in loonies, dimes, and quarters* (*n.*). *adj. or n.* **—e·quiv′a·lence,** *n.*

-er[1] *a suffix meaning:* **1** a person or thing that does some action. An *admirer* is a person who admires somebody or something. A *burner* is something that burns fuel. **2** a native or inhabitant of. A *Yukoner* is a person born in or living in the Yukon. A *villager* is a person who lives in a village.

-er[2] *a suffix meaning* more, as in *harder, slower.*

USING WORDS ..... -er/-est

Usually you can add **-er** ("more") and **-est** ("most") to adjectives and adverbs that have only one syllable: *sweeter, fastest.*

With two or more syllables, you usually use **more** and **most**: *more beautiful, most quickly.*

e·ra (er′ə *or* ē′rə) an age in history or geology: *We live in an era of space travel.* *n.*

a bat	e bed	i bid	o pot	u cup	th thin
ā cake	ē me	ī bite	ō go	ü rude	ᴛʜ then
ä bar	ə about	ər over	ô for	ů put	zh measure

Erupt

A typical volcano has a crater and a cone of solidified lava and ash. The activity takes place in the central vent through which the material erupts.

e·rad·i·cate (i rad′ə kāt′) destroy or get rid of completely: *Yellow fever has been eradicated in some countries.* *v.,* **e·rad·i·cat·ed, e·rad·i·cat·ing.**

e·rase (i rās′) **1** rub out; wipe out: *He erased the wrong answer and wrote in the right one. The blow on his head erased all memory of the accident.* **2** clear away marks or information from: *Please erase the chalkboard. I accidentally erased the whole hard drive of my computer.* *v.,* **e·rased, e·ras·ing.** —**e·ras′er,** *n.*

ere (er) an old or poetic word for "before": *They will come ere long.* *prep.*

e·rect (i rekt′) **1** standing straight up: *When a dog's ears are erect, it is a sign that it is alert.* **2** build; put up: *That building was erected 40 years ago.* 1 *adj.,* 2 *v.* —**e·rec′tion,** *n.*

er·mine (ər′mən) a weasel that is brown in summer but mostly white in winter. Its white winter fur is used for coats, to trim robes, etc. *n., pl.* **er·mines** or **er·mine.**

e·rode (i rōd′) eat away; wear away: *Water erodes soil and rock.* *v.,* **e·rod·ed, e·rod·ing.** —**e·ro′sion,** *n.*

err (er *or* ər) be wrong; make a mistake: *Everyone errs at some time or other.* *v.*

er·rand (er′ənd) **1** a trip to do something: *He has gone on an errand to the store.* **2** what you have gone to do: *She did three errands in one trip: went to the bank, bought stamps, and returned the library books.* *n.*

er·rat·ic (i rat′ik) first running or acting in one way, then in another way; totally unpredictable: *an erratic clock. His erratic manner puzzled many people.* *adj.*

er·ro·ne·ous (i rō′nē əs) mistaken; incorrect; wrong: *an erroneous belief in a flat earth.* *adj.*

er·ror (er′ər) a mistake: *The accident was caused by an error in judgment.* *n.*
in error, a wrong or mistaken: *You are in error—it's only 3:00, not 4:00.* **b** by mistake: *He got on the westbound train in error.*
the error of your ways, what you are doing wrong: *After losing all her friends, she finally saw the error of her ways.*

e·rupt (i rupt′) **1** burst forth: *to erupt into laughter. The volcano erupted and lava and ashes poured out.* **2** break out in a rash: *Your skin erupts when you have chicken pox.* *v.* —**e·rup′tion,** *n.*

es·ca·late (es′kə lāt′) grow bigger, higher, more serious, etc.: *escalating prices. Small battles can easily escalate into major wars.* *v.,* **es·ca·lat·ed, es·ca·lat·ing.**

es·ca·la·tor (es′kə lā′tər) a moving stairway: *An escalator will take you to the next floor.* *n.*

es·ca·pade (es′kə pād′) an action that is wild or full of adventure: *Shooting the rapids on a raft was a crazy escapade.* *n.*

es·cape (ə skāp′) **1** get free; get away: *The convict escaped from prison.* **2** stay free or safe from: *We all escaped the flu.* **3** an act or way of getting free: *There was no escape.* An **escape artist** entertains an audience by escaping from chains, traps, etc. **Escape velocity** is the speed needed to escape the gravitational pull of a planet. 1, 2 *v.,* 3 *n.,* **es·caped, es·cap·ing.**

es·carp·ment (e skärp′mənt) a cliff or steep slope, especially a wide one: *Hadassah and Ches hiked along the escarpment for hours.* *n.*

es·cort (es′kȯrt *for 1 and 2,* i skȯrt′ *for 3*) **1** a person or group going along with someone as a guard or to show honour: *The royal party was provided with an escort of Mounties.* **2** a man or boy who goes with a woman or girl to a party, dance, etc. **3** go with as an escort: *The police escorted the criminal to prison. Sergei escorted Cathy to the movies.* 1, 2 *n.,* 3 *v.*

–ese *a suffix meaning:* **1** the people of a country. The *Portuguese* are the people of Portugal. **2** the language of. *Burmese* is the language of Burma. **3** having to do with a certain country or its people or their language. *Japanese* art is art of Japan.

ESL *abbreviation for* English as a second language. ESL is taught to people who already speak another language but do not know English.

e·soph·a·gus (i sof′ə gəs) the tube that carries food from your mouth to your stomach. *n., pl.* **e·soph·a·gi** (i sof′ə jī).

ESP *abbreviation for* extra-sensory perception, the ability to know, without being told, what is happening somewhere else or what someone else is thinking.

es·pe·cial·ly (i spesh′ ə lē) **1** most of all; mainly; above all: *I like science, especially astronomy.* **2** more than usual; remarkably: *This was an especially busy week.* *adv.*

CONFUSABLES . . . especially

especially means "particularly": *The weather was especially cold last December.*

specially means "for one purpose": *Many movies are specially made for television.*

es·pi·o·nage (es′pē ə näzh′) spying; the use of spies: *Nations practise espionage to find out other countries' secrets.* *n.*

es·pres·so (e spres′ō) a very strong coffee, usually made in a special machine and served in small cups. *n.*

es·say (es′ā) an organized piece of writing telling what you have found out and what you think about a certain subject. An essay may be any length. *n.*

es·sence (es′əns) **1** the special quality that makes a thing what it is; the main part or parts: *The essence of good manners is kindness.* **2** a substance that has the flavour, fragrance, or effect of the plant it is taken from: *Essence of peppermint has a very strong mint flavour.* *n.*

es·sen·tial (i sen′shəl) **1** absolutely necessary; very important; basic: *Exercise is essential to good health.* **2** **essentials,** *pl.,* basic things: *Learn the essentials first; then the details.* 1 *adj.,* 2 *n.* **—es·sen′tial·ly,** *adv.*

–est *a suffix meaning* most, as in *warmest, slowest.*

es·tab·lish (i stab′lish) **1** set up a government, business, community, etc.: *An organization has been established to protect wildlife.* **2** settle in a position: *The Langs are established in their new house.* **3** cause to be accepted, followed, used, etc.: *to establish a custom, to establish a fact.* *v.* **—es·tab′lish·ment,** *n.*

es·tate (i stāt) **1** all that a person owns; property: *When the rich man died, he left an estate of 2 million dollars.* **2** a piece of land, especially a large one, owned by someone: *a big house on a beautiful country estate.* *n.*

es·teem (i stēm) **1** respect; honour: *We esteem people of good character* (*v.*). *Courage is held in esteem* (*n.*). **2** a formal word for "consider": *I esteem it a privilege to be elected president.* 1, 2 *v.,* 1 *n.*

es·ti·mate (es′tə mit *for 1 and 3,* es′tə māt′ *for 2*) **1** a judgment of an amount in round figures; a rough calculation: *He didn't know the exact length of the fish, but his estimate was 40 cm.* **2** form a judgment in round figures; calculate roughly: *We estimated that the trip would take four hours. She estimated the bike's value at $50.* **3** a formal statement of what a job will cost, made by someone willing to do the work: *We compared the painters' estimates.* 1, 3 *n.,* 2 *v.,* **es·ti·mat·ed, es·ti·mat·ing.**

es·ti·ma·tion (es′tə mā′shən) **1** opinion; judgment: *In my estimation, your plan will not work.* **2** the act or process of estimating: *Part of his job was the estimation of the value of houses.* *n.*

es·tu·ar·y (es′chū er′ē) **1** the wide mouth of a river where it flows into the sea and is affected by the tide: *The estuary of the St. Lawrence River is over 320 km long.* **2** an inlet of the sea. *n., pl.* **es·tu·ar·ies.**

etc. *abbreviation for* et cetera, a Latin expression meaning "and so on" or "and other things."

etch (ech) **1** use acid to eat a drawing or design into a metal plate, glass, etc. The plate is then covered with ink and pressed on a surface. The resulting picture is called an **etching.** **2** make a very strong impression on the mind: *The insult remains etched in my memory.* *v.*

a bat	e bed	i bid	o pot	u cup	th thin
ā cake	ē me	ī bite	ō go	ū rude	ᴛʜ then
ä bar	ə about	ər over	ȯ for	ů put	zh measure

e•ter•nal (i tər′nəl) 1 having no beginning or ending, and never changing. 2 seeming to go on forever: *Their eternal teasing nearly drove me crazy.* *adj.*

e•ter•ni•ty (i tər′nə tē) 1 all the past and all the future, including before the universe began and after it ends. 2 a period of time that seems endless: *I waited an eternity for the bus to arrive.* *n., pl.* **e•ter•ni•ties.**

e•ther (ē′thər) a colourless, strong-smelling liquid that evaporates quickly and makes you unconscious when you breathe it in. *n.*

eth•i•cal (eth′ə kəl) 1 having to do with **ethics,** or rules of right and wrong behaviour, especially in business, government, and other public activity: *ethical questions.* 2 following these rules: *It is not ethical for doctors to reveal their patients' secrets.* *adj.*

eth•nic (eth′nik) having to do with any group of people united by their customs, language, and the part of the world they are originally from. There are many different ethnic groups in Canada. The Vietnamese, the English, the Polish, and the Pakistanis are all ethnic groups. *adj.*

et•i•quette (et′ə kit) the traditional rules of politeness; manners: *Etiquette requires a man to rise when a woman enters the room.* *n.*

et•y•mol•o•gy (et′ə mol′ə jē) 1 an explanation of where a word comes from and how it has changed. 2 the part of language study that deals with this: *She is an expert in etymology.* *n., pl.* **et•y•mol•o•gies.**

eu•ca•lyp•tus (yū′kə lip′təs) a very tall tree that grows in Australia. It is valued for its wood and for the oil from its leaves, used as medicine. *n., pl.* **eu•ca•lyp•tus•es, eu•ca•lyp•ti** (yū′kə lip′tī).

eu•phe•mism (yū′fə miz′əm) a "nicer" word used instead of one that people think is harsh or unpleasant: *"Pass away" is a common euphemism for "die."* *n.*

Eur•a•sia (yu̇ rā′zhə) the largest continent, made up of Europe in the west and Asia in the east, with the dividing line at the Ural Mountains and the Black Sea. Europe is much smaller than Asia. *n.* —**Eur•a′sian,** *adj.*

Eu•rope (yu̇′rəp) the western part of the continent of Eurasia. *n.* —**Eu′ro•pe′an** (yu̇′rə pē′ən), *adj. or n.*

e•vac•u•ate (i vak′yū āt′) remove people from a dangerous place: *Firefighters evacuated the people from the burning hotel. The whole area had to be evacuated because of the poisonous fumes.* *v.,* **e•vac•u•at•ed, e•vac•u•at•ing.** —**e•vac′u•a′tion,** *n.*

e•vade (i vād′) get away from by trickery; avoid by cleverness: *to evade an embarrassing question. The thief evaded his pursuers and escaped.* *v.,* **e•vad•ed, e•vad•ing.** —**e•va′sion** (i vā′zhən), *n.* —**e•va′sive** (i vā′siv), *adj.*

e•val•u•ate (i val′yū āt′) decide how good or important something is, how much it is worth, etc.: *A group of judges will evaluate the performance of each figure skater. This old clock has been evaluated at $900.* *v.,* **e•val•u•at•ed, e•val•u•at•ing.** —**e•val′u•a′tion,** *n.*

e•vap•o•rate (i vap′ə rāt′) 1 turn from a liquid into a gas. When water dries up or turns to steam, it is evaporating. It becomes part of the air. 2 remove water from a substance by boiling. Milk is evaporated to make it thicker and sweeter. Sap is evaporated to make maple syrup. 3 disappear; fade away: *His good resolutions evaporated soon after New Year's Day.* *v.,* **e•vap•o•rat•ed, e•vap•o•rat•ing.** —**e•vap′o•ra′tion,** *n.*

eve (ēv) 1 the evening or day before some holiday or special day: *New Year's Eve.* 2 the time just before: *on the eve of an election.* 3 an old or poetic word for "evening." *n.*

e•ven (ē′vən) 1 level; flat; smooth: *Set up your tent on even ground.* 2 at the same level: *The snow is even with the window sill.* 3 staying about the same; steady: *an even speed, an even temper.* 4 equal: *She shaved off a bit of the fudge so the two pieces would be even.* 5 make even: *to even the score. I evened the edges by trimming them.* 6 amounting exactly to some round number: *Ninety-eight marbles? Throw in another two and make it an even hundred.* 7 able to be divided by 2 without a remainder: *The even numbers are 2, 4, 6, 8, etc.* 8 in fact: *He is ready, even eager, to help.* 9 although you would not expect it: *I will come even if I am tired.* 10 still; yet: *You can read even better if you try.* 1–4, 6, 7 *adj.,* 5 *v.,* 8–10 *adv.* —**e′ven•ly,** *adv.* —**e′ven•ness,** *n.*
break even, gain or get back as much as you have spent or lost: *I bought six packets of lemonade crystals but hardly sold enough lemonade to break even.*
get even, hurt someone back after he or she has hurt you.

eve•ning (ēv′ning) the last part of day and early part of night. *n.*

e•vent (i vent′) 1 anything that happens, especially something important: *everyday events. The opening of the new library was certainly an event.* 2 a contest in a sports program: *The long jump was the last event.* *n.*
in any event, in any case; anyway.
in the event, if; if there is: *In the event of rain the party will be held indoors. In the event that the roads are icy, we will not come.*

e•vent•ful (i vent′fəl) 1 full of interesting happenings: *Our day at the fall fair was highly eventful.* 2 important because of what happened: *July 1, 1867, Dominion Day, was an eventful day for Canadians.* *adj.*

e•ven•tu•al (i ven′chū əl) coming in the end: *After several failures, his eventual success was a pleasant surprise.* *adj.* —**e•ven′tu•al•ly,** *adv.*

ev•er (ev′ər) 1 at any time: *Is he ever satisfied?* 2 at all times; always: *We are ever at your service.* 3 a word to make a question or exclamation stronger: *Boy, is it ever hot! What will I ever do without you?* *adv.*
ever so, *Informal.* very: *The ocean is ever so deep.*

This evergreen ivy clings to walls, fences, tree trunks, etc. with the many tiny roots that you see growing from the stem.

ev•er•green (ev′ər grēn′) 1 having green leaves or needles throughout the year. 2 a tree, shrub, or plant that keeps its leaves or needles all year: *Pine, spruce, holly, and ivy are evergreens.* 1 *adj.,* 2 *n.*

ev•er•last•ing (ev′ər las′ting) 1 lasting forever; never stopping. 2 lasting a long time. 3 lasting too long; tiresome: *his everlasting complaints.* *adj.*

ev•er•more (ev′ər mòr′) an old or poetic word for "always," or "forever." *adv.*

eve•ry (ev′rē) 1 each one of all that there are: *Read every word on the page. Every student must come to the assembly.* 2 the greatest possible: *I have every reason to trust her. We will make every effort to help.* *adj.*
every now and then, from time to time; sometimes: *Every now and then, we have a frost that ruins the crop.* **Every so often** means the same thing.
every other, skipping one each time: *If you write on every other line, you can get only half as much on a page.*
every two hours (or **three days,** etc.), regularly, with two hours between each time: *A bus leaves every two hours.*
every which way, *Informal.* in all directions; helter-skelter: *He tripped and his books and papers flew every which way.*

eve•ry•bod•y (ev′rē bud′ē) every person: *Everybody here likes ice cream.* *pron.*

eve•ry•day (ev′rē dā′) usual; ordinary; not special: *my everyday clothes, an everyday experience.* *adj.*

eve•ry•one (ev′rē wun′) each person; everybody: *Everyone agreed to bring some food to the party.* *pron.*

eve•ry•thing (ev′rē thing′) 1 every thing; all things: *She does everything she can to help her friend.* 2 all that matters: *Money isn't everything.* *pron.*

eve•ry•where (ev′rē wer′) in or to every place: *We looked everywhere for our lost cat.* *adv.*

e•vict (i vict′) use the law to force someone renting a building or a farm, etc. to move out: *When they failed to pay the rent, they were evicted.* *v.* —**e•vic′tion,** *n.*

ev•i•dence (ev′ə dəns) 1 facts or clues showing that something is probably true: *The jam on his face was evidence that he had been eating.* 2 show clearly: *Their smiles evidenced their pleasure.* 1 *n.,* 2 *v.,* **ev•i•denced, ev•i•denc•ing.**

ev•i•dent (ev′ə dənt) easy to see or figure out; clear; plain: *From the empty carton next to her bed it was evident that she had drunk the chocolate milk.* *adj.*

ev•i•dent•ly (ev′ə dənt lē) going by what was seen or heard; it seems: *Evidently they're moving—I saw a "For Sale" sign in their yard.* *adv.*

e•vil (ē′vəl) 1 very bad; wrong; doing great harm: *an evil murderer, evil acts.* 2 a very bad thing: *racism and other evils. Slavery is a great evil.* 3 everything bad; all actions, forces, influences, etc. that cause harm: *Good shall win over evil, she believes.* 1 *adj.,* 2, 3 *n.*
—**e′vil•ly,** *adv.*

e•voke (i vōk′) call up; bring out: *This photo evokes many memories.* *v.,* **e•voked, e•vok•ing.**

ev•o•lu•tion (ev′ə lū′shən *or* ē′və lū′shən) 1 a gradual development: *The museum display showed the evolution of airplanes from the first experiments by the Wright brothers up until the present.* 2 the theory that all living things developed from a few simple forms of life over millions of years. *n.*

e•volve (i volv′) change or develop gradually: *Over the years her little computer repair business has evolved into a company that makes and sells software in many different cities.* *v.,* **e•volved, e•volv•ing.**

ewe (yū) a female sheep. *n.*

a bat	e bed	i bid	o pot	u cup	th thin
ā cake	ē me	ī bite	ō go	ū rude	ᴛʜ then
à bar	ə about	ər over	ò for	ù put	zh measure

ex– *a prefix meaning:* **1** out or away, as in *exit, export.* **2** that was, but is no longer, as in *ex-member.*

ex·act (eg zakt′) not having or making mistakes; true or correct in every detail: *an exact description, the exact amount, an exact worker. adj.* —**ex·act′ly,** *adv.*

ex·ag·ger·ate (eg zaj′ə rāt′) **1** make something out to be more than it really is; go beyond the truth: *You were exaggerating when you said there were a million cats in the backyard. The cartoon exaggerated the movie star's big eyes.* **2** make more noticeable: *Their tiredness after the long trip was exaggerated by the change in time zones. v.,* **ex·ag·ger·at·ed, ex·ag·ger·at·ing.** —**ex·ag′ger·a′tion,** *n.*

ex·alt (eg zolt′) **1** place in a high position: *She was exalted to the position of president of a huge corporation.* **2** praise; glorify; honour. *v.* —**ex′al·ta′tion,** *n.*

ex·am·i·na·tion (eg zam′ə nā′shən) **1** a careful check; inspection: *The doctor made a careful examination of my eyes.* **2** a formal test of knowledge or skill. **Exam** is a shorter form: *I passed my piano exam. n.*

ex·am·ine (eg zam′ən) **1** look at closely and carefully: *The mechanic examined the engine.* **2** test the knowledge or ability of: *The lawyer examined the witness by asking questions. v.,* **ex·am·ined, ex·am·in·ing.**

ex·am·ple (eg zam′pəl) **1** a sample; one thing given to show what the others are like: *Edmonton is an example of a busy city. The teacher did the first problem for us as an example.* **2** something to imitate or avoid imitating: *Parents should try to be a good example to their children. I hope that her suspension for fighting in the schoolyard will be an example to you all. n.*
for example, as one thing to show what I mean: *Children play many games; baseball, for example.*
make an example of, punish severely to show others the result of misbehaviour: *The judge made an example of the drunk driver by giving her a harsh sentence.*
set an example, show good behaviour for others to follow: *Yuri set a good example for his younger sister.*

ex·as·per·ate (eg zas′pə rāt′) annoy or irritate very much; make angry: *The child's endless whining exasperated his brothers. v.,* **ex·as·per·at·ed, ex·as·per·at·ing.** —**ex·as′per·a′tion,** *n.*

ex·ca·vate (ek′skə vāt′) **1** remove dirt, sand, rock, etc. to make a hole or tunnel, usually with a large digging machine called an **excavator:** *to excavate a site for the foundation of a new building.* **2** uncover by digging: *They excavated the ancient buried city. v.,* **ex·ca·vat·ed, ex·ca·vat·ing.** —**ex′ca·va′tion,** *n.*

ex·ceed (ek sēd′) go beyond; be more or greater than: *Donations exceeded $1000. v.*

ex·ceed·ing·ly (ek sē′ding lē) very; highly; unusually: *Your story is exceedingly funny! adv.*

ex·cel (ek sel′) be or do better than others; do very well: *She excels in music. v.,* **ex·celled, ex·cel·ling.**

Ex·cel·len·cy (ek′sə lən sē) a title of honour used for the Governor General, an ambassador, a bishop, etc. *n., pl.* **Ex·cel·len·cies.**

ex·cel·lent (ek′sə lənt) extremely good; much better than most others: *Excellent work deserves high praise. adj.* —**ex′cel·lence,** *n.*

ex·cept (ek sept′) **1** leaving out; other than: *He comes every day except Wednesday.* Another word for this is **excepting.** **2** leave out: *The invitation is for you all—no one is excepted.* 1 *prep.,* 2 *v.*

CONFUSABLES ..... except

except means "other than": *Everyone smiled, except me.*
accept means "receive": *Will you accept this prize?*

ex·cep·tion (ek sep′shən) **1** something left out: *She liked the songs on the tape, with two exceptions.* **2** anything that is different from the rule or the usual way: *He usually comes on time, but today is an exception. n.*
take exception, a disagree: *to take exception to an opinion.* **b** be hurt or angry: *She took exception to the remark that her jokes were stupid.*
with the exception of, except for: *With the exception of bananas, I like all fruits.*

ex·cep·tion·al (ek sep′shə nəl) unusual; out of the ordinary: *This mild weather is exceptional for January. adj.* —**ex·cep′tion·al·ly,** *adv.*

ex·cerpt (eg′zərpt *for 1,* eg zərpt′ *for 2*) **1** a passage taken from a book, speech, etc.: *The article included excerpts from the author's diary.* **2** take a passage from; quote: *He excerpted a paragraph from an article in the* Globe and Mail *for his report. 1 n., 2 v.*

ex·cess (ek ses′ *or* ek′ses) **1** the part that is too much: *Pour off the excess. He had to pay for an excess of 5 kg on his luggage before his flight.* **2** extra; more than the right amount: *After filling her son's new sandbox, Mrs. Yakuto gave the excess bags of sand to us.* 1 *n.,* 2 *adj.*
in excess of, more than: *Donations were in excess of $5000.*
to excess, too much: *He eats candy to excess.*

ex·ces·sive (ek ses′iv) going beyond reasonable limits; extreme: *She thought being grounded for a week was excessive punishment. adj.* —**ex·ces′sive·ly,** *adv.*

ex•change (eks chānj′) **1** trade for something else: *I'll take this shirt back to the store and exchange it for a bigger one.* **2** what is traded: *Ten dimes for a loonie is a fair exchange.* **3** a place where things are traded: *The used book exchange is a great place to get books without spending money.* **4** give something to each other: *to exchange ideas, to exchange glances.* **5** an arrangement where students, teachers, etc. change places with each other over a period of weeks or months as a learning experience: *My sister has gone on an exchange to Québec; her exchange partner, Lucien Dufarge from Chicoutimi, is staying at our house.* 1, 4 *v.,* **ex•changed, ex•chang•ing;** 2, 3, 5 *n.*

ex•cite (ek sīt′) **1** stir up strong feelings in: *News of the war's end excited everybody. His new snowboard excited envy among the other boys.* **2** make active and lively: *Don't excite the baby; it's her bedtime.* *v.,* **ex•cit•ed, ex•cit•ing.** **—ex•cit′a•ble,** *adj.* **—ex•cite′ment,** *n.*

ex•claim (ek sklām′) speak suddenly and with strong feeling, sometimes in a louder or higher voice than usual: *"Here you are at last!" exclaimed his mother.* *v.*

ex•cla•ma•tion (ek′sklə mā′shən) something said suddenly as the result of surprise or strong feeling. Exclamations may be interjections such as *Ouch!* or full sentences such as *What a surprise!* In writing, they always end with an **exclamation mark:** ! *n.* ▶ See the *Grammar and Usage Mini-Guide.*

Grammar Check . exclamation mark

Don't rely on an exclamation mark to make a sentence into an exclamation. The words you use must express the emotion. The exclamation mark gives emphasis: *Turn that music down at once!*

ex•clude (ek sklūd′) leave out; keep out: *Vegetarians exclude meat from their diet.* *v.,* **ex•clud•ed, ex•clud•ing.** **—ex•clu′sion,** *n.*

ex•clud•ing (ek sklū′ding) not counting: *Lower rates apply October to May, excluding weekends.* *prep.*

ex•clu•sive (ek sklū′siv) **1** only for certain people, usually the rich or famous: *an exclusive club, an exclusive private school.* **2** not shared with others: *An inventor has the exclusive right to make what he or she has invented.* *adj.* **exclusive of,** leaving out; not counting: *The label says the dress is all cotton, exclusive of trimmings.*

ex•clu•sive•ly (ek sklū′siv lē) only: *That selfish girl looks out for herself exclusively.* *adv.*

ex•crete (ek skrēt′) get rid of waste or harmful substances from the body. The body's **excretory system** uses sweat, urine, and feces as a way to get rid of wastes. *v.,* **ex•cret•ing, ex•cret•ed.** **—ex′cre•to′ry** (ek′skrə tȯr′ē), *adj.*

ex•cru•ci•ating (ek skrū′shē ā′ting) extremely painful: *This toothache is excruciating.* *adj.*

ex•cur•sion (ek skər′zhən) a trip; an outing. *n.*

ex•cuse (ek skyūz′ *for 1, 3, and 4,* ek skyūs′ *for 2*) **1** make an action seem less bad by giving reasons for it or blaming others: *She always excused her own faults.* **2** a reason given for an action to make it seem all right: *He had many excuses for coming late.* **3** be a good enough explanation for: *Sickness excuses absence from work.* **4** free someone from a duty; let off: *You are excused from washing the dishes today.* 1, 3, 4 *v.,* **ex•cused, ex•cus•ing;** 2 *n.*
excuse me, I'm sorry; something you say out of politeness after burping, sneezing, accidentally stepping on someone's toes, etc., or in order to interrupt someone.
excuse yourself, a say "excuse me": *He excused himself loudly each time he hiccupped.* **b** ask permission to leave: *I excused myself from the table.*

ex•e•cute (ek′sə kyūt′) **1** carry out; do or perform: *The nurse executed the doctor's orders. Elvis Stojko executed each figure skating move with graceful ease.* **2** punish with death according to law: *The murderer was executed.* The person who does this for a government is an **executioner** (ek′sə kyū′shə nər). *v.,* **ex•e•cut•ed, ex•e•cut•ing.** **—ex′e•cu′tion,** *n.*

ex•ec•u•tive (eg zek′yə tiv) **1** a manager in a business; person who makes decisions and then sees that they get carried out: *The president of a business is an executive.* **2** having to do with management: *The executive committee makes important decisions for the organization.* **3** having to do with the branch of government that makes laws and puts them into effect. The premier and his or her cabinet ministers are called the **Executive Council** of a provincial government. 1 *n.,* 2, 3 *adj.*

ex•empt (eg zempt′) **1** let out of doing or having something unpleasant: *The teacher exempted her from the test because she had been away from school for most of that unit.* **2** free from some duty: *School property is exempt from all taxes.* 1 *v.,* 2 *adj.*

a bat	e bed	i bid	o pot	u cup	th thin
ā cake	ē me	ī bite	ō go	ū rude	ᴛʜ then
à bar	ə about	ər over	ȯ for	u̇ put	zh measure

ex•er•cise (ek′sər sīz′) **1** activity to train and strengthen the body or mind: *Running is a form of exercise. Listening is good exercise for your mind.* **2** do or cause to do such activity: *She exercises daily. We read to exercise our imagination.* **3** a task specially designed to give practice in something: *Do the multiplication exercise on the worksheet.* **4** use; show in action: *Please exercise care in crossing the road.* **5** the act of using or putting into practice: *Keeping your temper requires the exercise of self-control.* **6** **exercises,** a set program of ceremonies, speeches, etc.: *School graduation exercises are held in June.* 1, 3, 5, 6 *n.,* 2, 4 *v.,* **ex•er•cised, ex•er•cis•ing.**

ex•ert (eg zərt′) use: *to exert your strength. No one volunteered to help, so Mom exerted her authority and ordered us to get busy.* *v.* **—ex•er′tion,** *n.*
exert yourself, make an effort; try hard: *We had to exert ourselves to get there on time.*

ex•hale (eks hāl′) breathe out: *We exhale air from our lungs.* *v.,* **ex•haled, ex•hal•ing.**

ex•haust (eg zost′) **1** tire out: *The climb up the hill exhausted us.* **2** empty or use up completely: *to exhaust a well, to exhaust the food supply, to exhaust your strength.* **3** the used steam, gases, etc. that escape from an engine: *The exhaust from an automobile engine is very poisonous.* **4** the pipe, vent, or other way of letting out the used steam, gases, etc. 1, 2 *v.,* 3, 4 *n.* **—ex•haust′ed,** *adj.* **—ex•haus′tion** (eg zos′chən), *n.*

ex•hib•it (eg zib′it) **1** show: *He exhibits a real interest in animals.* **2** put on display at a public show: *You should exhibit your roses in the flower show.* **3** something set up to show to the public: *I especially like the dinosaur exhibit at the museum.* 1, 2 *v.,* 3 *n.*

ex•hi•bi•tion (ek′sə bish′ən) **1** a large public display: *an exhibition of student art in the mall.* **2** a big fair with displays of farm animals, flowers, computers, things from around the world, etc., along with shows, rides, games, and other fun things. The **Canadian National Exhibition** happens every August in Toronto. **3** behaviour, especially bad, that everyone sees: *What an embarrassing exhibition of bad manners!* *n.*

ex•hil•a•rate (eg zil′ə rāt′) fill with energy or excitement: *The girls were exhilarated by their early morning swim. The roller coaster ride exhilarated us all.* *v.,* **ex•hil•a•rat•ed, ex•hil•a•rat•ing.** **—ex•hil′a•ra′tion,** *n.*

WORD HISTORY..... exhilarate

The prefix **ex** sometimes means "completely." For example, the word **exhilarate** comes from the Latin *ex* "completely" + *hilaris* "merry."

ex•hort (eg zôrt′) urge strongly; advise earnestly: *The speaker at the Earth Day assembly exhorted us all to reduce, reuse, and recycle.* *v.*

ex•ile (eg′zīl *or* ek′sīl) **1** force a person to leave his or her own country, often by law as a punishment: *The traitor was exiled from his country for life.* **2** a person who is forced to leave his or her own country: *She has been an exile for ten years.* **3** the experience or time of being exiled: *These stories were written by the author during his exile.* 1 *v.,* **ex•iled, ex•il•ing;** 2, 3 *n.*

ex•ist (eg zist′) **1** be or continue to be: *The world has existed a long time. A person cannot exist without air.* **2** be real: *Do fairies exist or not?* *v.* **—ex•ist′ence,** *n.*

ex•it (eg′zit *or* ek′sit) **1** a way out: *The theatre had six exits.* **2** go out: *Please exit by the side doors.* **3** the act of going out: *When the dog appeared, the cat made a hasty exit.* 1, 3 *n.,* 2 *v.*

ex•o•dus (ek′sə dəs) the act of leaving in large numbers: *Every summer there is an exodus from town.* *n.*

ex•or•bi•tant (eg zôr′bə tənt) much too high: *Six dollars is an exorbitant price for a dozen eggs.* *adj.*

Canadians consider tigers to be exotic animals because they are not native to Canada. Tigers are the largest members of the cat family, and can grow to over 3 m long.

ex•ot•ic (eg zot′ik) **1** not native to a country: *Tigers are exotic animals in Canada.* **2** unusual in a fascinating way: *exotic tales of adventures in far-off places.* *adj.* **—ex•ot′i•cal•ly,** *adv.*

ex•pand (ek spand′) **1** make or become bigger: *The balloon expanded as it was filled with air. They are expanding the highway.* **2** spread out; open out; unfold: *The bird expanded its wings. This sofa expands into a bed.* **3** write or talk in more detail: *Could you expand on that idea a little?* *v.* **—ex•pan′sion,** *n.*

ex•panse (ek spans′) a wide, unbroken area or surface: *The Pacific Ocean is a vast expanse of water.* *n.*

ex·pect (ek spekt′) 1 think that something is likely: *We expect snow in winter. I expect he'll be late again.* 2 plan: *They expect to be married in June.* 3 count on as something right and proper: *I expect you to say "Please" and "Thank you" without being reminded. A restaurant is expected to be clean.* 4 *Informal.* suppose: *I expect he's reached Fredericton by now.* *v.* **—ex′pec·ta′tion,** *n.*
be expecting, be pregnant: *My aunt is expecting.*

ex·pect·ant (ek spek′tənt) looking forward to something good: *She opened her birthday present with an expectant smile.* *adj.* **—ex·pect′ant·ly,** *adv.* **—ex·pec′tan·cy,** *n.*
expectant parents, a couple who are expecting a baby.

ex·pe·di·ent (ek spē′dē ənt) 1 useful or practical; a good idea: *It would be expedient to take an umbrella.* 2 a way of achieving something: *He tied a sheet to the balcony and escaped by this expedient.* 1 *adj.,* 2 *n.*

ex·pe·di·tion (ek′spə dish′ən) 1 a trip for a special purpose, such as exploration, trade, or war. 2 the people, ships, etc. that make such a journey: *a well-equipped expedition.* *n.*

ex·pel (ek spel′) 1 force to leave: *The violent student was expelled from school.* 2 push out: *When you burp you expel air from the stomach.* *v.,* **ex·pelled, ex·pel·ling.**

ex·pend (ek spend′) spend; use up: *A lot of time and energy has been expended on this project.* *v.* **—ex·pen′di·ture** (ek spen′də chər), *n.*

ex·pense (ek spens′) 1 the cost; the charge: *The expense of a new computer is too great for our family to afford right now.* 2 something that costs money: *Heating the house is an expense.* *n.*
at the expense of, **a** with the loss or sacrifice of: *We want peace, but not at the expense of freedom.* **b** with someone paying for it: *She travelled at her uncle's expense.* **c** with someone having to suffer or be embarrassed by it: *They had many a laugh at my expense.*

ex·pen·sive (ek spen′siv) costing a lot: *He had a very expensive bicycle; it cost $600.* *adj.*

ex·pe·ri·ence (ek spē′rē əns) 1 what happens to a person: *We had many wonderful experiences on our trip. People learn by experience.* 2 practice; knowledge gained by doing or seeing things: *Do you have any experience in this kind of work?* 3 feel; go through; have happen to you: *to experience success or failure.* 1, 2 *n.,* 3 *v.,* **ex·pe·ri·enced, ex·pe·ri·enc·ing.** **—ex·pe′ri·enced,** *adj.*

ex·per·i·ment (ek sper′ə ment′ *for 1,* ek sper′ə mənt *for 2*) 1 try something in order to see what happens, or just for the fun of doing something new and different: *He is experimenting with dyes to get different colours.* 2 something done to find out the result: *a cooking experiment. Scientists test theories by experiment.* 1 *v.,* 2 *n.* **—ex·per′i·men′tal,** *adj.*

WORD HISTORY..... experiment

The word **experiment** comes from the Latin word *experiri*, meaning "to try out." The same Latin root is in the word **experience**. You can get experience by experimenting, and you may become an **expert**!

ex·pert (ek′spərt) 1 a person who has a great deal of skill or knowledge in some special area: *This beautiful carving was obviously done by an expert.* 2 very skilled: *expert sewing, an expert drummer.* 1 *n.,* 2 *adj.*

ex·per·tise (ek′spər tēz′) special skill or knowledge: *The school is looking for a grade two teacher with expertise in music.* *n.*

ex·pire (ek spīr′) 1 run out; become worthless after a certain time limit called the **expiry date:** *You must get a new licence when your old one expires. This coupon expires in two weeks, so use it soon.* 2 die. *v.,* **ex·pired, ex·pir·ing.** **—ex′pi·ra′tion,** *n.*

ex·plain (ek splān′) 1 use words to make something clear and easy to understand; give examples; tell why and how, etc.: *The teacher explained percent to us.* 2 be the reason or excuse for: *A power failure? That explains why the clock is 40 minutes slow!* *v.* **—ex′pla·na′tion,** *n.* **—ex·plan′a·to′ry** (ek splan′ə tôr′ē), *adj.*

ex·plic·it (ek splis′it) clearly expressed, leaving nothing for people to figure out on their own: *She gave such explicit directions; we can't possibly get lost.* *adj.*

ex·plode (ek splōd′) 1 blow up with a loud noise; blow apart into pieces: *The building was destroyed when the furnace exploded. Many roads on the Canadian Shield were built by exploding the rock with dynamite.* 2 burst out noisily: *to explode with anger, to explode with laughter.* *v.,* **ex·plod·ed, ex·plod·ing.**

ex·ploit (ek′sploit *for 1,* ek sploit′ *for 2 and 3*) 1 a brave or amazing deed: *stories about the exploits of famous heroes.* 2 make good use of: *Exploit every opportunity for learning.* 3 use unfairly or selfishly: *Nations often exploited their colonies, taking the wealth and enslaving the people.* 1 *n.,* 2, 3 *v.* **—ex′ploi·ta′tion,** *n.*

a bat	e bed	i bid	o pot	u cup	th thin
ā cake	ē me	ī bite	ō go	ū rude	ᴛʜ then
ä bar	ə about	ər over	ô for	ů put	zh measure

Explorations

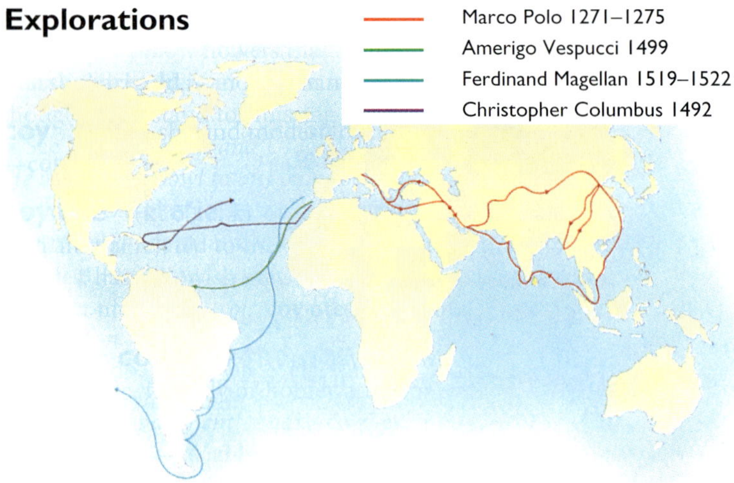

Early explorers relied on the astrolabe to calculate latitude, and the compass to show which way they were heading.

astrolabe

compass

ex·plore (ek splôr′) **1** go through a place in order to find out what is there: *Champlain explored the Ottawa River and Georgian Bay and made maps of the area. The children explored the new house from attic to cellar.* **2** find out about something by reading, trying things, asking questions, thinking, etc.: *We have been exploring Chinese culture in our class.* *v.,* **ex·plored, ex·plor·ing.** —**ex·plor′er,** *n.* —**ex′plo·ra′tion,** *n.*

ex·plo·sion (ek splō′zhən) **1** the action of blowing up or bursting with a loud noise: *The explosion of the bomb shook the whole neighbourhood.* **2** a noisy burst of laughter, anger, etc. *n.*

ex·plo·sive (ek splō′siv) **1** able to explode easily: *Gunpowder is explosive.* **2** a substance that explodes easily: *Explosives are used in making fireworks.* **3** bursting out noisily: *an explosive temper.* 1, 3 *adj.,* 2 *n.*

ex·po·nent (ek spō′nənt) in mathematics, a number written above and to the right of another number to show how many times it is used as a factor. In 10^3 the exponent is 3, meaning $10 \times 10 \times 10$. *n.*

ex·port (ek′spôrt, *also* ek spôrt′ *for 1*) **1** send things out of one country to be sold in another: *Canada exports millions of tonnes of wheat each year.* **2** the act of selling to another country: *The best products are often saved for export.* **3** something sent to another country for sale: *Oranges are an important export of Florida.* 1 *v.,* 2, 3 *n.* —**ex′por·ta′tion,** *n.*

ex·pose (ek spōz′) **1** lay open; leave without protection: *The bandage came off, exposing the wound to infection.* **2** show or make known something that was hidden; reveal: *He accidentally exposed his cards during the game. She exposed the plot to the police.* **3** allow light to reach a photographic film or plate. When you take a picture with a camera, the shutter opens and exposes the film to light coming in through the lens. *v.,* **ex·posed, ex·pos·ing.**

ex·po·si·tion (ek′spə zish′ən) a big public show or exhibition: *The Canadian National Exhibition is an exposition.* *n.*

ex·po·sure (ek spō′zhər) **1** the act of exposing or the condition of being exposed: *the exposure of a lie. Exposure to the rain has spoiled this chair.* **2** the side that is open to the sun and wind: *a house with a southern exposure.* **3** the part of a photographic film used for one picture: *This roll of film has 24 exposures.* *n.*

ex·press (ek spres′) **1** put into words: *Express your ideas clearly.* **2** show: *A smile expresses joy.* **3** fast and direct; with no stops along the way: *an express train (adj.). Send this package express to Saskatoon (adv.).* **4** a train, bus, elevator, etc. that goes from one point to another with no stops on the way: *She left on the six o'clock express.* **5** press out: *to express juice from grapes.* 1, 2, 5 *v.,* 3 *adj. or adv.,* 4 *n.* —**ex·press′i·ble,** *adj.*
express yourself, put your ideas or feelings into words: *This writer expresses herself clearly.*

ex·pres·sion (ek spresh′ən) **1** the act of putting something into words or showing it in some other way: *A hug is an expression of love.* **2** a word or group of words used as a unit: *"Chill out" is a slang expression.* **3** a look on a person's face that shows a feeling: *A grin is a happy expression.* **4** the act of using your voice to bring out the meaning or beauty of something written: *Try to read with more expression.* *n.*

ex·pres·sive (ek spres′iv) full of feeling or meaning: *He has a very expressive face.* *adj.*
expressive of, that expresses: *"Alas!" is a word expressive of sadness.*

ex·press·way (ek spres′wā′) a highway for fast driving, with few intersections: *A modern expressway runs between Calgary and Edmonton.* *n.*

ex·pul·sion (ek spul′shən) the act of expelling, or forcing out: *expulsion of air from the lungs. Expulsion from school is a punishment for bad behaviour.* *n.*

ex·qui·site (ek skwiz′ it) 1 very lovely in a delicate way: *The violet is an exquisite flower.* 2 sharp and strong: *exquisite pain, exquisite joy.* 3 excellent, superb: *She has exquisite manners.* *adj.*

ex·tend (ek stend′) 1 stretch out: *I extended my hand to the visitor.* 2 reach; continue; spread in time, space, or direction: *The beach extended for more than a kilometre in each direction.* 3 lengthen or widen: *to extend a visit, to extend your knowledge. They have extended the ski trail another 2 km.* 4 offer or give: *to extend a warm welcome to someone.* *v.*
extended family, parents and children plus grandparents, aunts, uncles, cousins, etc.

ex·ten·sion (ek sten′shən) 1 the act of stretching out, reaching, or lengthening something: *The extension of your right hand is a sign of friendship.* 2 an added part: *A new extension was built onto the school.* 3 an extra telephone added to the same line as the main one. *n.*

ex·ten·sive (ek sten′siv) far-reaching; big: *extensive changes, an extensive park.* *adj.*

ex·tent (ek stent′) 1 the size, length, amount, or degree of something; how far a thing reaches: *The extent of a judge's power is limited by law.* 2 an area: *a vast extent of prairie.* *n.*
to the extent that, as much as; in the same amount as: *You will enjoy learning only to the extent that you are interested in the subject.*

ex·te·ri·or (ek stē′rē ər) 1 the outside; the outward appearance: *I saw only the exterior of the house, not the interior. The man has a harsh exterior, but a kind heart.* 2 outer: *Skin is the exterior covering of our bodies.* 1 *n.,* 2 *adj.*

ex·ter·mi·nate (ek stər′mə nāt′) destroy completely: *This poison will exterminate rats.* *v.,* **ex·ter·mi·nat·ed, ex·ter·mi·nat·ing.** —**ex·ter′mi·na′tion,** *n.* —**ex·ter′mi·na′tor,** *n.*

ex·ter·nal (ek stər′nəl) 1 on the outside: *Don't swallow this stuff; it says, "for external use only."*
2 outside ourselves: *External influences affect our lives.*
3 **externals,** *pl.* outward appearances as opposed to real character: *Do not judge people by externals such as clothing.* 1, 2 *adj.,* 3 *n.* —**ex·ter′nal·ly,** *adv.*

ex·tinct (ek stingkt′) 1 no longer existing: *The dinosaur is an extinct animal.* 2 no longer active: *an extinct volcano.* *adj.* —**ex·tinc′tion,** *n.*

ex·tin·guish (ek sting′gwish) put out a flame, a light, etc.: *Water extinguished the fire.* *v.*

ex·tol or **ex·toll** (ek stōl′) praise highly: *The newspapers extolled the courage of the astronauts.* *v.,* **ex·tolled, ex·tol·ling.**

ex·tra (ek′strə) 1 beyond what is usual, expected, or needed: *extra work, extra clothes. Do you have an extra pencil?* 2 anything that is extra: *Her bill for extras was $30. Even the radio is an extra on this car.* 3 more than usually; especially: *extra large. He worked extra fast that afternoon.* 4 a special edition of a newspaper: *An extra announced the end of the war.* 1 *adj.,* 2, 4 *n.,* 3 *adv.*

ex·tract (ek strakt′ *for 1,* ek′strakt *for 2*) 1 take out: *to extract iron from the earth, to extract a tooth.*
2 something taken out: *I read several extracts from the poem. Vanilla extract is made from vanilla beans.* 1 *v.,* 2 *n.* —**ex·trac′tion,** *n.*

ex·tra–cur·ric·u·lar (ek′strə kə rik′yə lər) outside school or outside actual schoolwork: *The drama club was Alissa's favourite extra-curricular activity.* *adj.*

ex·traor·di·nar·y (ek strȯr′də ner′ē) very unusual; remarkable: *I say 2.5 m is an extraordinary height for a person.* *adj.* —**ex·traor′di·nar′i·ly,** *adv.*

ex·tra–ter·res·tri·al (ek′strə tə res′trē əl) 1 an alien; a being from beyond the earth: *The extra-terrestrials landed in a purple spaceship.* 2 to or from somewhere beyond the earth: *extra-terrestrial travel.* 1 *n.,* 2 *adj.*

ex·trav·a·gant (ek strav′ə gənt) 1 spending or costing more than is sensible: *They spent a whole day's pay on an extravagant dinner.* 2 beyond reasonable limits: *That is extravagant praise for a very ordinary piece of work.* *adj.* —**ex·trav′a·gance,** *n.*

ex·treme (ek strēm′) 1 beyond normal limits; going too far one way or the other: *extreme poverty, extreme wealth. The temperatures in the desert are extreme.*
2 at the very end or edge; the farthest possible: *I know the person on the extreme right of that group.* 3 something extreme; one of two things that are as far or as different as possible from each other: *Love and hate are two extremes of feeling.* 1, 2 *adj.,* 3 *n.* —**ex·treme′ly,** *adv.*
go to extremes, do or say too much of a certain thing.

a bat	e bed	i bid	o pot	u cup	th thin
ā cake	ē me	ī bite	ō go	ū rude	ᴛʜ then
ä bar	ə about	ər over	ȯ for	ů put	zh measure

Eye

When you look at something, the light rays reflected from the object are focussed upside down on the retina. Your brain has learned to interpret this as the right way up.

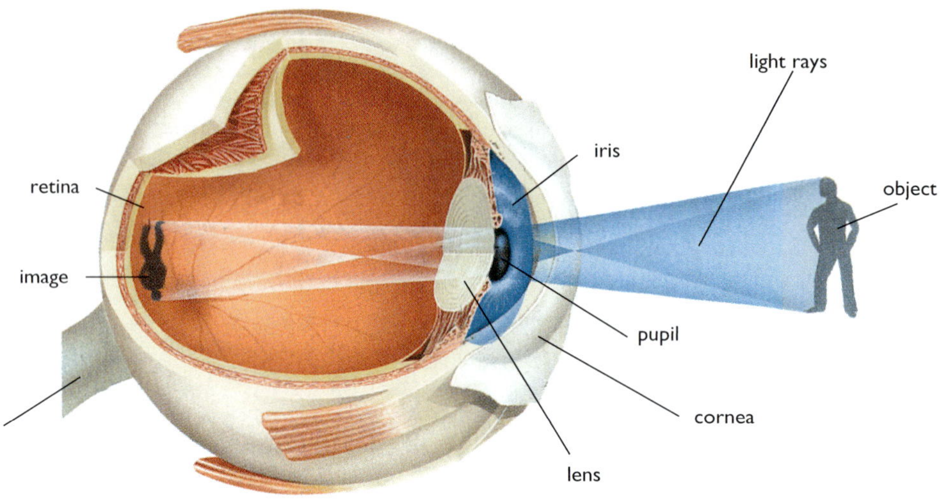

ex·trem·i·ty (ek strem′ə tē) **1** the farthest point: *Pelee Island is at the southern extremity of Canada.* **2** **extremities,** *pl.* the hands and feet. **3** an extreme action: *They were forced to the extremity of eating shoe leather to stay alive.* *n., pl.* **ex·trem·i·ties.**

ex·tri·cate (ek′strə kāt′) untangle; set free from a difficult or complicated situation: *The dog got caught in the thorn bush and had trouble extricating itself.* *v.,* **ex·tri·cat·ed, ex·tri·cat·ing.**

ex·u·ber·ant (eg zū′bə rənt) full of joyful excitement: *Åsa was exuberant when her parents announced the trip to Europe.* *adj.* —**ex·u′ber·ance,** *n.*

ex·ult (eg zult′) be very glad; speak or sing very joyfully: *The winners exulted in their victory. "A snow day! No school!" exulted Clara.* *v.* —**ex·ult′ant,** *adj.* —**ex′ul·ta′tion,** *n.*

eye (ī) **1** either of the two organs of the body that humans and animals see by. **2** the coloured part of this organ; iris: *She has brown eyes.* **3** something like an eye in some way: *the eye of a needle, the eye of a potato.* **4** a look or glance: *He let his eye rove around the room.* **5** look at: *The children eyed the stranger curiously.* 1–4 *n.,* 5 *v.,* **eyed, ey·ing** or **eye·ing.**
catch someone's eye, attract someone's attention: *The bright red scarf caught my eye.*
clap eyes on, *Informal.* see.
have an eye for, be able to recognize and judge a certain thing when you see it: *A good artist has an eye for colour.*
in the eye(s) **of,** in the opinion or view of: *In the eyes of most doctors, smoking is not worth the risk.*
keep an eye on, watch; take care of: *Keep an eye on my bike while I go into the store.*
keep an eye out for, watch for.
look someone in the eye, look straight into someone's eyes.
my eye! *Informal.* I doubt it!
see eye to eye, agree; be in agreement: *My brother and I don't usually see eye to eye when choosing TV programs.*
up to your eyes in, having more of something than you can handle: *She's up to her eyes in homework.*
with your eyes shut, very easily.

Word Family.......... eye

eyeball: the ball-shaped part of your eye
eyebrow: the bony ridge above your eye or the hair that grows on it
eyelash: one of the hairs on the eyelid
eyelid: the upper or lower fold of skin that can cover the eyeball
eyepiece: the lens you look through in a microscope
eyesight: the ability to see
eyesore: something unpleasant to look at
eyestrain: a tired condition of the eye muscles
eyewitness: a person who actually sees an action, and can give a report about it

eye·let (ī′lit) **1** a small round hole for a lace to go through, or the metal ring that is set around such a hole to strengthen it. **2** cloth that has little holes in it, with embroidery around the holes, as part of its design. *n.*

eye·tooth (ī′tūth′) an upper canine tooth. It is the third tooth from the middle on each side of the top of your mouth. *n., pl.* **eye·teeth.**
give your eyeteeth for, do or give almost anything to get: *I'd give my eyeteeth for a jacket like that!*

ey·rie (ī′rē *or* ē′rē) the nest of an eagle or other bird high on a mountain or cliff. *n.* **en·dorsed, en·dors·ing.**

Ff

f or **F** (ef) 1 the sixth letter of the English alphabet, or any sound that it stands for. The sound of *f* in *chief* is different from the sound of *f* in *of.* 2 the sixth thing in a list. 3 in music: a a note. On a keyboard it is the white note between E and G. b a scale or key that has F as its home note. c abbreviation for *forte,* "loud," on a written piece of music. Two f's (*ff*) means "very loud." 4 *abbreviation for* Fahrenheit. *n., pl.* **f's** or **F's.**

fa•ble (fā′bəl) 1 a story made up to teach a lesson. Fables are often about animals who can talk, such as "The Hare and the Tortoise." 2 any untrue story. *n.*

fab•ric (fab′rik) woven or knitted cloth. *n.*

fab•ri•cate (fab′rə kāt′) 1 build or put together: *to fabricate a machine.* 2 make up a lie: *Sharon fabricated that entire story about her Florida trip. v.,* **fab•ri•ca•ted, fab•ri•ca•ting.** —**fab′ri•ca′tion,** *n.*

fab•u•lous (fab′yə ləs) 1 incredible; amazing: *a house of fabulous size, practically a palace.* 2 *Informal.* excellent: *She makes fabulous spaghetti sauce.* 3 imaginary: *The centaur is a fabulous creature. adj.*

fa•çade (fə säd′) 1 the front of a building. 2 a fake outward appearance hiding something bad underneath: *The crook had a façade of honesty. n.*

face (fās) 1 the front part of the head. The eyes, nose, and mouth are parts of the face. 2 a look or expression of the eyes, mouth, etc. that shows a feeling: *Her face was sad.* 3 an ugly or strange look made by twisting the face: *She made a face at us.* 4 in geometry, one of the flat surfaces of a solid: *A cube has six faces.* 5 the front side of anything: *Lay the card face up.* 6 have the front turned toward: *The house faces the street. One dancer faced the other.* 7 meet; stand up to: *She had the courage to face her problems.* 8 cover the front with something, especially a different material: *That wooden house is faced with brick.* 1–5 *n.,* 6–8 *v.,* **faced, fac•ing.**
face off, in hockey, lacrosse, etc., start play by dropping or placing the puck, ball, etc. between the sticks of two players facing each other: *The referee faced off the puck at centre ice.* This act is called the **face-off.**
face to face, with faces toward each other: *The two judo experts stood face to face.*
face to face with, in the presence of: *The wounded soldiers stood face to face with death.*
face up to, meet bravely or boldly: *to face up to an enemy.*
in the face of, in the presence of: *The man showed no fear in the face of danger.*
lose face, have your pride hurt.
on the face of it, going by outward appearances: *On the face of it, this seems like a good deal—is there some trick?*
to someone's face, boldly, right in front of that person: *She repeated the gossip to the teacher's face.*

face•cloth (fās′kloth′) a cloth like a small towel, used for washing the face or body; a washcloth. *n.*

face•lift (fās′lift′) 1 an operation to make a face look younger by tightening the skin and removing wrinkles. 2 a change that makes something look newer and better: *Our basement needs a facelift. n.*

Facets reflect, bend, and break up light rays, so that the diamond sparkles.

fac•et (fas′it) 1 one of the small flat, polished surfaces of a cut gem such as a ruby or diamond. 2 any one of several different sides or views of something: *Pride was a facet of his character that we seldom saw. n.*

fa•cial (fā′shəl) 1 having to do with the face: *facial expression.* 2 a beauty treatment for the face. 1 *adj.,* 2 *n.*

fa•cil•i•ty (fə sil′ə tē) 1 Usually, **facilities,** *pl.* the space, equipment, furnishings, etc., that make an activity possible or easier: *The school has excellent lab facilities.* 2 a building or set of buildings specially designed for certain activities: *They have built a new sports facility on King Street.* 3 the ability to do something well: *facility in drawing. n., pl.* **fa•cil•i•ties.**

fact (fakt) 1 something known to be true or real: *It is a fact that the world is round. The War of 1812 is a historical fact.* 2 a statement that is supposed to be true: *We doubted their facts. n.* —**fac′tu•al** (fak′chū əl), *adj.*
in fact, actually; really: *She said she could do it when in fact she couldn't.* Other expressions that mean the same are **as a matter of fact** and **in point of fact.**

a bat	e bed	i bid	o pot	u cup	th thin
ā cake	ē me	ī bite	ō go	ū rude	ᴛʜ then
ä bar	ə about	ər over	ȯ for	ů put	zh measure

fac·tor (fak′tər) 1 one of the causes that helps bring about a result; one part of a situation: *Good soil is a factor in successful farming; enough rain is another.* 2 any of the numbers or expressions that can be multiplied together to get another number: *2 and 5 are factors of 10.* 3 separate a mathematical expression into its factors. *Example:* $2x + 6 = 2(x + 3)$. 1, 2 *n.,* 3 *v.*
factor in, include in your calculations: *When you're figuring out how much spending money you need for your trip, don't forget to factor in the cost of souvenirs.* **Factor out** means the opposite.

fac·to·ry (fak′tə rē) a place where things are manufactured: *There are a number of car factories in Ontario.* *n., pl.* **fac·to·ries.**

WORD HISTORY..... factory

Factory used to have another meaning in Canada, "trading post." That's because a trader was a factor. There are place names in Canada that still show this old meaning, like Moose Factory in Ontario.

fac·ul·ty (fak′əl tē) 1 a power of the mind or body: *At the age of 102 she still has all her faculties—good hearing, eyesight, and memory.* 2 the teachers of a college or university. *n., pl.* **fac·ul·ties.**

fad (fad) a very popular fashion or craze; something everybody is doing for a time. *n.* **—fad′dish,** *adj.*

fade (fād) 1 lose or cause to lose colour: *Those curtains have faded. Sunlight will fade some fabrics.* 2 get weaker and weaker; die away: *His fears faded when they welcomed him. The sound of the train faded in the distance.* *v.,* **fad·ed, fad·ing.** **—fade′less,** *adj.*
fade in, make or become slowly clearer and clearer: *The music fades in at the end of the scene.* **Fade out** means the opposite.

Fahr·en·heit (fer′ən hīt′) about or measured by the Fahrenheit temperature scale. On this scale, water freezes at 32°F (0°C) and boils at 212°F (100°C). It is not metric. *adj.*

fail (fāl) 1 not manage to do what you try to do; not succeed: *He tried hard to win the race, but failed.* 2 get a mark that is too low to pass a test, examination, or course in school: *She failed the spelling quiz.* 3 become too little; come to nothing: *After a long dry spell, the crops failed. When their supplies failed, the explorers died of hunger.* 4 not do: *He rarely fails to follow his parents' advice.* 5 break down: *During the storm, the boat's motor failed.* 6 disappoint; let someone down: *When I was in trouble, my friends failed me.* 7 get weaker; get close to death: *The old tree is failing.* *v.* **—fail′ure** (fāl′yər), *n.*
without fail, for sure: *She promised to come without fail.*

faint (fānt) 1 not clear; so weak, pale, fuzzy, muffled, etc. that you can hardly tell what it is: *a faint cry, a faint idea, faint colours.* 2 dizzy and wobbly: *When I saw how high up we were, I began to feel faint.* 3 fall unconscious. A person can faint from shock, fear, hunger, etc.: *He fainted at the sight of his bleeding finger.* 4 a short time of being unconscious like this. 1, 2 *adj.,* 3 *v.,* 4 *n.*

faint–heart·ed (fānt′hãr′tid) timid. *adj.*

fair¹ (fer) 1 treating everyone, including yourself, with the same strictness or kindness: *A judge must be fair.* 2 following the rules: *fair play (adj.). Play fair and don't cheat (adv.).* 3 not very good but not bad; average: *There is a fair crop of wheat this year.* 4 light-coloured: *She had fair hair and skin.* 5 clear and sunny: *The weather will be fair today.* 6 beautiful: *a fair maiden.* 1–6 *adj.,* 2 *adv.* **—fair′ly,** *adv.* **—fair′ness,** *n.*
a fair shake, fair treatment or a fair trade.
fair and square, completely fair and honest.
fair enough, an expression of agreement; fine; OK.
fairly good, fairly big, etc., pretty good, pretty big, etc. but not extremely good or extremely big: *It was fairly expensive but not more than we could pay.*
no fair! *Informal.* That is not fair!

fair² (fer) an event where people or businesses can show things for sale, sometimes with contests to see whose is the best. Often there are rides, games, food, and entertainment: *Mr. Gibson's bull won first prize at the fair. We tried out some new games and bought a better monitor at the computer fair.* The outdoor space where a fair is held is a **fairground.** Many Canadian communities have a **fall fair** every September. *n.*

fair game (fer′ gām′) 1 animals that the law allows people to hunt. 2 a person or thing that people think it is OK to criticize or make fun of: *She was fair game for political cartoonists because of her confusing speeches.*

fair·y (fer′ē) in stories, a tiny magical being, usually with wings, who can help or harm people. A **fairy tale** is a story with fairies or other magical beings in it like witches, elves, ogres, etc. *n., pl.* **fair·ies.**

faith (fāth) 1 belief without proof; trust; confidence: *We have faith in our friends.* 2 belief and trust in God: *She said that the hard times made her faith stronger.* 3 a particular religion: *He is of the Muslim faith.* *n.*
in good faith, honestly; really wanting to do the right thing: *Although her friends had done the wrong thing, they had acted in good faith.* **In bad faith** is the opposite.
keep faith, be loyal; keep your word. **Break faith** means the opposite.
keep the faith, stay true to a belief or goal.

Falcons and Kestrels

Falcons and kestrels are day-flying birds of prey, so they have excellent eyesight. They are fast fliers, swooping down from above to hit their prey with their claws. They use their large, hooked beaks for tearing flesh.

faith•ful (fāth′fəl) 1 that can be trusted; loyal: *a faithful friend, a faithful servant.* **Faithless** is the opposite. 2 giving the true facts, real meaning, etc.: *The witness gave a faithful report of what happened.* *adj.*

fake (fāk) 1 false; not the real thing: *She was caught with fake identification. This is fake leather.* 2 something that is made to look like the real thing but isn't: *The signature was a fake.* 3 make or do something that seems real but isn't: *He faked a bad cough so he could go home.* 1 *adj.,* 2 *n.,* 3 *v.,* **faked, fak•ing.** **—fak′er,** *n.*

fa•la•fel (fə lä′fəl) deep-fried balls of ground dried yellow peas eaten as a snack or meal. They are often served in a rolled-up bread wrap called a pita. *n.*

fal•con (fol′kən *or* fal′kən) a bird of prey, related to the hawk and eagle, with a hooked bill and long, strong, pointed wings for fast flying. The largest is the **gyrfalcon,** found mainly in arctic and subarctic regions. Falcons can be tamed and trained by a **falconer** to come back to their owner with whatever they have hunted. See the picture and caption on page 322. *n.*

fall (fol) 1 drop down from a higher place: *Leaves fall from the trees.* 2 trip or slip and go down: *When I first went skating, I kept falling.* 3 become lower or less: *Prices are falling.* 4 the season of the year between summer and winter; autumn. 5 happen; come: *Night falls early in winter. My birthday falls on Monday this year.* 6 start being or doing: *to fall asleep. We fell to work immediately. They fell in love.* 7 be defeated or killed: *The city fell to the enemy. Many soldiers have fallen in battle.* 8 the act or fact of falling: *a nasty fall on the steps, a fall in temperature, the fall of the Roman Empire.* 9 **falls,** *pl.* waterfall. 1–3, 5–7 *v.,* **fell, fall•en, fall•ing;** 4, 8, 9 *n.*
fall apart, a break into pieces. **b** lose control of yourself.
fall back, move backward.
fall back on, turn to as a solution or for help and support: *If plan A fails, we can fall back on plan B. In time of trouble, he knew he could fall back on his father.*
fall behind, be unable to keep up; drop back: *Before the race was half over, the slow runners had fallen a lap behind.*
fall flat, fail completely: *All his jokes fell flat.*
fall for, a fall in love with. **b** be fooled by: *She fell for our trick.*
fall in, a take a place in line: *"Fall in!" said the officer to the soldiers.* **b** meet by chance: *On our trip we fell in with some interesting people.*
fall off, become less: *Attendance at games fell off when the team kept losing.*
fall on, attack: *Thieves fell on the man and stole his money.*
fall out, quarrel; stop being friends.
fall short of, not reach; not be enough for.
fall through, fail: *His plan fell through.*
fall to, begin to do something with enthusiasm: *The hungry girls fell to as soon as they sat down at the table.*

a bat	e bed	i bid	o pot	u cup	th thin
ā cake	ē me	ī bite	ō go	ü rude	ᴛʜ then
ä bar	ə about	ər over	ô for	ů put	zh measure

fall–out (fol′out′) **1** the radioactive substance that falls to earth after a nuclear explosion. **2** the unpleasant results of anything. *n.*

fal•low (fal′ō) ploughed but with nothing planted for a season or more: *fallow land. adj.*

false (fols) **1** not true; not correct: *The witness gave a false statement.* **2** not loyal; not to be trusted: *a false friend.* **3** not real; artificial or pretended: *false teeth, false diamonds. As part of her disguise she spoke with a false accent. adj.,* **fals•er, fals•est.** **—false′ness,** *n.*
false step, a a wrong step; a stumble: *One false step and the climber would fall to her death.* **b** a mistake: *The police were waiting for the suspect to make a false step.*

false•hood (fols′hu̇d) a lie. *n.*

fal•ter (fol′tər) **1** hang back or stop for a moment; lose courage: *The horse faltered briefly but then jumped the fence after all.* **2** stumble. **3** speak with many stops and starts: *Greatly embarrassed, he faltered out his thanks. v.*

fame (fām) the fact or condition of being well-known: *Roberta Bondar achieved fame as the first Canadian woman in space. n.* **—famed,** *adj.*

WORD HISTORY........fame

Fame comes from the Latin word *fama*, meaning "talk." A person who has fame is someone that people will talk about.

fa•mil•iar (fə mil′yər) **1** known to everyone; common; everyday: *A knife is a familiar tool.* **2** known to you; that you recognize: *In all the crowd, I saw not one familiar face.* **3** well acquainted; knowing a person or thing well: *Lee is familiar with the rules. Are you familiar with my sister.* **4** too friendly, as if you were a close friend when you aren't: *His manner is too familiar; he should call the principal "Miss Das," not "Jenny." adj.* **—fa•mil′iar′i•ty** (fə mil′yer′ə tē), *n.* **—fa•mil′iar•ize′,** *v.*

fam•i•ly (fam′ə lē) **1** a group of people who are related, especially a parent or guardian, his or her partner if there is one, and their children. **2** all of a person's relatives, including aunts, uncles, grandparents, cousins, in-laws, etc. A **family tree** shows how they are all connected and who their ancestors were. **3** a group of related animals or plants or things: *Lions, tigers, and leopards belong to the cat family. French and Italian belong to the same family of languages. n., pl.* **fam•i•lies.**

family room (fam′ə lē rūm′) a room in a home that a family uses to talk, play games, or watch TV. It is usually more casual than a living room.

fam•ine (fam′ən) an extreme lack of food, with people starving: *Canada sends wheat and other food to countries where there is famine. n.*

fam•ished (fam′isht) very hungry; starving: *"Let's eat!" cried Heidi; "I'm famished!" adj.*

fa•mous (fā′məs) very well-known: *A great crowd of people greeted the famous movie star. adj.*

fan[1] (fan) **1** a thing for creating a current of air in order to cool or air a room, cool a machine, blow away smoke or dust, etc. A fan can be something flat you wave with your hand, or a machine run by a motor. **2** use a fan on; blow air on: *She fanned herself. Fan the fire to make it burn faster.* **3** anything that is flat and spread out like an open hand-held fan, wider at one end than at the other. A peacock's raised tail is often called a fan. 1, 3 *n.,* 2 *v.,* **fanned, fan•ning.**
fan out, spread out from one point: *The search party fanned out in different directions.*

fan[2] (fan) a person who likes and is very interested in a particular thing or person: *He's a baseball fan and has many books about games and players. She's a big fan of Kurt Browning.* **Fan mail** is mail received from fans. *n.*

fa•nat•ic (fə nat′ik) a person who is extreme about a certain thing: *He's such a fanatic about fresh air that he won't stay in any room with the windows closed. n.* **—fa•nat′i•cal,** *adj.* **—fa•nat′i•cism′,** *n.*

fan•ci•ful (fan′sə fəl) **1** quaint; unusual but attractive: *a fanciful decoration.* **2** using or coming from a vivid imagination: *a fanciful writer.* The Lion, the Witch, and the Wardrobe *is a fanciful story. adj.*

fan•cy (fan′sē) **1** with a lot of showy details or extra things that are meant to be beautiful or convenient: *fancy dancing, a fancy car, fancy clothes. We don't need such a fancy computer system.* **2** picture to yourself; imagine: *Fancy that!* **3** imagination: *Dragons, fairies, and giants are creatures of fancy.* **4** like; be fond of: *She fancies the idea of having a picnic.* **5** a liking: *a fancy for bright ties. They took a great fancy to each other and became close friends.* **6** of high quality: *The label on the can of pears said "Canada Grade A Fancy."* 1, 6 *adj.,* **fan•ci•er, fan•ci•est;** 2, 4 *v.,* **fan•cied, fan•cy•ing;** 3, 5 *n., pl.* **fan•cies.** **—fan′ci•ly,** *adv.* **—fan′ci•ness,** *n.*
fancy dress, costumes worn to a party.

fan•fare (fan′fer) **1** a short tune or call played on trumpets, bugles, etc.: *We heard a joyous fanfare as the bride entered.* **2** a lot of activity, talk, flashy advertising, etc. meant to draw attention to something. *n.*

Spiders are meat eaters. They have sharp, curved fangs for stabbing, then squirting poison down through a tube into the body of the prey.

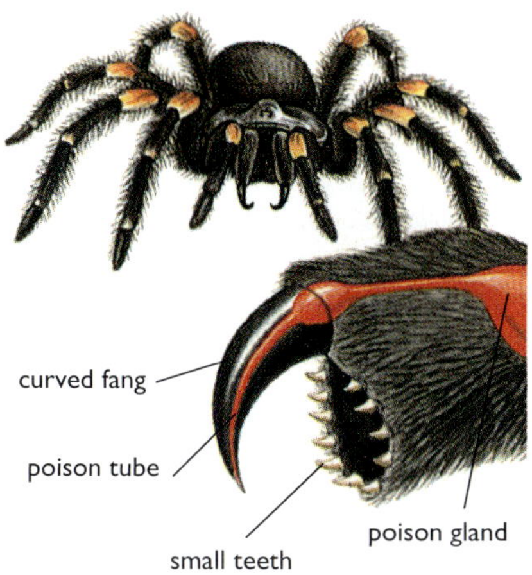

fang (fang) 1 a long, sharp front tooth of some meat-eating animals, such as tigers, wolves, etc., used to seize and hold prey. 2 a snake's hollow or grooved tooth that injects poison into its prey. *n.* —**fanged,** *adj.*

fan•ta•size (fan′tə sīz′) daydream, especially about something pleasant: *Sammy fantasized about winning a million dollars.* *v.,* **fan•ta•sized, fan•ta•siz•ing.**

fan•tas•tic (fan tas′tik) 1 *Informal.* unbelievably good: *That was a fantastic meal.* 2 very strange: *The firelight cast weird, fantastic shadows on the walls.* 3 impossible; unreal. *adj.* —**fan•tas′ti•cal•ly,** *adv.*

fan•ta•sy (fan′tə sē) 1 imagination; ideas about things or happenings that aren't real: *Spaceships were once thought to be pure fantasy.* 2 a daydream: *In one of her favourite fantasies she is a great scientist who has won the Nobel prize.* 3 **a** a story about things that could never be real: Alice in Wonderland *is a fantasy.* **b** these stories as a group: *Soren reads a lot of fantasy.* *n., pl.* **fan•ta•sies.**

far (fȧr) 1 a long way away in time or space: *to look far into the past, a trip to a far country. Mars is far from Earth.* 2 most distant: *Set it in the far corner. She lives on the far side of the hill.* 3 very much: *It is far better to go by train.* 1, 3 *adv.,* 1, 2 *adj.,* **far•ther, far•thest.**
a far cry, something completely different: *This little pool is a far cry from the Olympic one!*
by far, easily: *She was by far the better swimmer.* Another expression for this is **far and away.**
far from it, no way; by no means: *Lazy? Far from it—he works like a horse!*
so far, a to this point; to that point: *The water can only come up so far and no further.* **b** until now or then: *Our team has won every game so far this season.*
so far so good, things have been fine up till now.

far•a•way (fȧ′rə wā′) 1 distant; far away: *faraway countries.* 2 dreamy: *A faraway look in his eyes showed that he was thinking of something else.* **Far-off** is another word that means the same. *adj.*

farce (fȧrs) 1 a ridiculous situation where everything gets mixed up or is done wrong. 2 a funny play full of silly situations. *n.* —**far′ci•cal,** *adj.*

fare (fer) 1 the money that a person pays to ride in a train, car, bus, etc. 2 food: *home-cooked fare.* 3 get along; do well or poorly: *He is faring well in school. How did you fare at Grandma's?* 1, 2 *n.,* 3 *v.,* **fared, far•ing.**

Far East (fȧr′ ēst′) China, Japan, and other parts of eastern Asia.

fare•well (fer′wel′) 1 good luck; goodbye, or some other good wish said at parting: *"Farewell!" she shouted after him* (*interj.*). *They said their farewells on the station platform* (*n.*). 2 parting; last: *a farewell kiss, an actor's farewell performance.* 1 *n. or interj.,* 2 *adj.*

far–fetched (fȧr′fecht′) hard to believe; too obviously made up: *a far-fetched excuse.* *adj.*

farm (fȧrm) 1 the land, water, and buildings that someone uses to raise crops or animals. 2 use land to raise crops or animals either to eat or to sell: *Her parents farm for a living. We farm forty hectares.* 1 *n.,* 2 *v.* —**farm′er,** *n.* —**farm′ing,** *n.*
farm out, turn over to others to take care of, sometimes for money: *Whenever they go on a long trip, they farm out their five pets to various friends and neighbours.*

> *Word Family..........* **farm**
>
> **farmhouse:** a house on a farm
> **farmland:** land suitable for raising crops or animals
> **farmyard:** the yard beside the farm buildings

far–sight•ed (fȧr′sī′tid) 1 able to see faraway things better than near things. 2 looking ahead; planning wisely for the future. *adj.*

far•ther (fȧr′ᴛʜər) more far; a longer way away: *Three kilometres is farther than two* (*adj.*). *We walked farther than we meant to* (*adv.*). The matching word meaning "most far" is **farthest.** *adj. or adv.*

fas•ci•nate (fas′ə nāt′) catch and hold the attention completely by being so beautiful, exciting, unusual, etc.: *Grandpa's stories of life at sea fascinated us.* *v.,* **fas•ci•nat•ed, fas•ci•nat•ing.** —**fas′ci•na′tion,** *n.*

a bat	e bed	i bid	o pot	u cup	th thin
ā cake	ē me	ī bite	ō go	ū rude	ᴛʜ then
ȧ bar	ə about	ər over	ȯ for	u̇ put	zh measure

Fashion

Wig-wearing by both men and women became fashionable in France in the 1600s.

a French army officer's campaign wig in 1670

a wealthy Spanish woman in 1650

fas·cism (fash′iz əm) a form of government where people own their own property and businesses, etc. but everything is very strictly controlled by a very powerful leader and his or her party. *n.* —**fas′cist,** *n. or adj.*

fash·ion (fash′ən) 1 the way a thing is made or done: *The horse moved sideways in a nervous fashion.* 2 the current popular style or fad in clothes, cars, music, etc.: *They always have to follow the latest fashion.* 3 **fashions,** *pl.* stylish clothes: *This store sells women's fashions.* 4 make, shape, or form: *He fashioned a whistle out of a stick.* 1–3 *n.,* 4 *v.* —**fash′ion·a·ble,** *adj.*

fast[1] (fast) 1 quick; taking less time than you might expect: *a fast runner* (*adj.*). *Airplanes go fast* (*adv.*). 2 showing a time ahead of the real time: *That clock is fast.* 3 firm; not fading, coming apart, letting go, or giving up: *fast friends, fast colours. The boat was made fast to the dock* (*adj.*). *He held fast to the rope so he would not fall* (*adv.*). 4 tricky and smooth: *We weren't taken in by their fast talk.* 1–4 *adj.,* 1, 3 *adv.*
fast asleep, completely or fully asleep.
pull a fast one, play a trick; fool someone.

fast[2] (fast) 1 go without food for a while, especially as a spiritual exercise. 2 the fact of going without food: *The fast lasted all through Ramadan.* 1 *v.,* 2 *n.*

fas·ten (fas′ən) 1 tie, lock, or attach in any other way: *to fasten a dress, to fasten a door. The necklace fastens with a little clip.* 2 fix; direct: *The baby fastened her eyes on the colourful toy. They tried to fasten the blame on me.* *v.* —**fas′ten·er** or **fas′ten·ing,** *n.*

fast food (fast′ fūd′) food prepared quickly in a restaurant, often ready to take out: *Hamburgers are my favourite fast food.* —**fast-food,** *adj.*

fast forward (fast′ fōr′wərd) 1 a way of winding a tape or video forward very quickly without playing it. 2 **fast-forward,** **a** do this with a tape or video. **b** in a story, jump ahead to much later events.

fat (fat) 1 a white or yellow oily substance formed in the bodies of animals and also in some seeds. Fat is stored in the body for extra energy and protection from the cold, but too much of it can cause health problems. 2 big around; plump and heavy: *a fat little piglet. His father is a big, fat man.* 3 thick: *a fat book.* 1 *n.,* 2, 3 *adj.,* **fat·ter, fat·test.** —**fat′ness,** *n.* —**fat′ty,** *adj.* —**fat′ten,** *v.*
chew the fat, *Informal.* chat.

fa·tal (fā′təl) 1 causing death: *fatal accidents.* 2 causing disaster; making all the difference between success and failure: *Missing that one practice turned out to be a fatal error.* *adj.* —**fa′tal·ly,** *adv.*

fa·tal·i·ty (fə tal′ə tē) a death; a fatal accident or happening: *There were several fatalities on the highways last weekend.* *n., pl.* **fa·tal·i·ties.**

fate (fāt) 1 a power that some people believe controls what is going to happen: *They blamed their failure on fate, saying, "We just weren't meant to succeed."* 2 what happens to a particular person, group, etc., especially when thought of as being beyond human control: *History records the fate of many nations.* *n.*

fate·ful (fāt′fəl) 1 determining what is to happen; decisive: *a fateful battle that turned the whole war around.* 2 causing death or ruin; disastrous: *a fateful flood.* *adj.*

fa·ther (foTH′ər) 1 a male parent: *Her father died when she was quite young.* 2 a man who acted as leader, founder, inventor, etc.: *The* **Fathers of Confederation** *forged a new nation from the provinces of Nova Scotia, New Brunswick, Ontario, and Québec. Alexander Graham Bell was the father of the telephone.* 3 be the father of: *My uncle has fathered four children.* 4 take care of as a father does: *In* The Jungle Book, *Akela the wolf fathers Mowgli until it is time for Mowgli to return to the human village.* 5 **Father,** a title of respect used in addressing a Christian priest. 1, 2, 5 *n.,* 3, 4 *v.* —**fa′ther·ly,** *adj.* —**fa′ther·hood′,** *n.*

fa·ther–in–law (foᴛʜ′ər in lo′) the father of a person's husband or wife. *n., pl.* **fa·thers-in-law.**

fath·om (faᴛʜ′əm) 1 get to the bottom of; understand: *I can't fathom what you're driving at.* 2 an old nonmetric unit for measuring the depth of water, equal to 1.8 m. 1 *v.,* 2 *n.* **—un·fath′om·a·ble,** *adj.*

fa·tigue (fə tēg′) 1 tiredness: *She was pale from fatigue.* 2 make tired. 1 *n.,* 2 *v.,* **fa·tigued, fa·ti·guing.**

fau·cet (fos′it) a water tap. *n.*

fault (folt) 1 something that is not as it should be; a bad habit or character trait, or something not made properly: *Our dog has two faults: it eats too much, and it howls at night. A fault in the brake made it difficult to stop the bike.* 2 a cause for blame; responsibility for some problem: *It was your fault that the rabbit escaped; you left the cage open!* 3 criticize: *No one can fault your answer; it was right on.* 4 a break in the earth's crust, where the two parts have moved out of line with each other. A fault can cause earthquakes. *n.* **—fault′less,** *adj.* **—fault′y,** *adj.*
at fault, responsible; to blame: *The officer said the other driver was at fault in the accident.*
find fault with, criticize: *The teacher was always finding fault with our homework.*
to a fault, so much that it almost causes problems: *She is generous to a fault.*

faun (fon) a mythical creature like a human, but with the ears, horns, tail, and legs of a goat. *n.*

fau·na (fon′ə) all the animals of a particular region or time: *the fauna of Australia.* *n.*

fa·vour or **fa·vor** (fā′vər) 1 an act of kindness: *Will you do me a favour?* 2 show kindness to; oblige: *Favour us with a song.* 3 liking; approval: *They will look with favour on your plans.* 4 like; approve: *We favour this plan.* 5 treat better than others: *He thought the teacher favoured his twin brother.* 6 a small gift given as a souvenir at a party: *Paper hats were handed out as favours to guests at the New Year's Ball.* 1, 3, 6 *n.,* 2, 4, 5 *v.*
in favour of, a on the side of; supporting or agreeing with. **b** to the advantage of: *The referee's decision was in favour of the other team.*
in someone's favour, to someone's benefit.

fa·vour·a·ble or **fa·vor·a·ble** (fā′və rə bəl) 1 giving approval or saying yes; liking something; positive: *a favourable answer, a favourable impression of something.* 2 helpful: *A favourable wind blew the sailboat quickly to its destination.* *adj.* **—fa′vour·a·bly** or **fa′vor·a·bly,** *adv.*

fa·vour·ite or **fa·vor·ite** (fā′və rit) 1 most liked: *What is your favourite colour?* 2 a person or thing liked better than others; one liked very much: *He is a favourite with everybody.* 3 a person, horse, etc. expected to win a contest. 1 *adj.,* 2, 3 *n.*

fa·vour·it·ism or **fa·vor·it·ism** (fā′və rə tiz′əm) better treatment for some people than for others: *Good teachers show no favouritism.* *n.*

fawn[1] (fon) a deer less than a year old. *n.*

fawn[2] (fon)
fawn on someone, by flattery or slavish attention try to win someone's favour. *v.*

fax (faks) 1 a written message or picture that is sent or received by a special machine in electronic form over a telephone line. It is printed out as an exact copy of the original when it arrives. **Fax** is short for **facsimile.** 2 send a message using a fax machine. 1 *n.,* 2 *v.*

faze (fāz) *Informal.* disturb; upset; bother: *A scolding doesn't faze her at all.* *v.,* **fazed, faz·ing.**

fear (fēr) 1 a feeling that something bad is going to happen: *Fear made his heart pound as he crossed the high, narrow bridge.* 2 feel fear or worry about; be afraid of someone or something: *Our cat fears the big dog next door. I fear we won't make it in time. They feared for our safety.* 3 in formal speech and writing, be sorry or disappointed about something: *I fear I won't be able to attend your wedding.* 1 *n.,* 2, 3 *v.* **—fear′less,** *adj.*

fear·ful (fēr′fəl) 1 full of fear: *a fearful glance. She is fearful of the dark.* 2 causing fear; terrible; dreadful: *The great fire was a fearful sight.* **Fearsome** means the same. 3 *Informal.* very bad: *I have a fearful cold.* *adj.*

feast (fēst) 1 a big, rich meal, especially one prepared for many people on a special occasion: *We went to the wedding feast.* 2 eat good things; have a feast: *We feasted on fresh sweet corn and tomatoes.* 3 provide a rich meal for: *The king feasted his friends.* 1 *n.,* 2, 3 *v.*
feast your eyes on something, enjoy looking at something beautiful.

feat (fēt) a great achievement; an act of great skill, strength, or daring: *Landing on the moon was a remarkable feat.* *n.*

a bat	e bed	i bid	o pot	u cup	th thin
ā cake	ē me	ī bite	ō go	ü rude	ᴛʜ then
ä bar	ə about	ər over	ò for	u̇ put	zh measure

feath·er (feᴛʜ′ər) **1** one of the soft, light, thin coverings on a bird's body. Different kinds of feathers grow on different parts of its body. **2** put feathers on or in. 1 *n.,* 2 *v.* —**feath′er·y,** *adj.* —**feath′ered,** *adj.*
feather in your cap, something to be proud of.
feather your nest, take advantage of chances to get rich.

fea·ture (fē′chər) **1** a part of the face. The eyes, nose, mouth, chin, and forehead are features: *She has very big features.* **2** a special part or quality; something that stands out and attracts attention: *The Rockies are an outstanding feature of British Columbia.* **3** a full-length movie or main article in a magazine or newspaper. **4** offer something special; have as the main attraction: *The store was featuring radios in its fall sale. This park features several excellent hiking trails.* 1–3 *n.,* 4 *v.,* **fea·tured, fea·tur·ing.**

Feb·ru·ar·y (feb′rū er′ē *or* feb′yū er′ē) the second month of the year. February has 28 days except in leap years, when it has 29. *n., pl.* **Feb·ru·ar·ies.**

fed (fed) the past tense and past participle of **feed:** *We fed the birds yesterday. Have they been fed today?* *v.*

fed·er·al (fed′ə rəl) having to do with the central government of Canada, or of any other country made up of provinces or states that have their own separate governments but are joined together under one big one which takes over certain responsibilities for all of them. This system is called **federalism.** The **Federal Government** of Canada sits in Ottawa. *adj.*

fed·er·a·tion (fed′ə rā′shən) a group of provinces, states, or nations joined together by agreement: *Canada was formed as a federation.* *n.*

fee (fē) a charge; money paid to get something done or to enter a place: *Dentists charge a fee for fixing teeth. You have to pay a fee to get into the Royal Ontario Museum.* *n.*

WORD HISTORY........fee

Fee comes from an Old Germanic word *feoh,* meaning "cattle." The same word meant "money." Long ago, people would pay for things with cattle.

fee·ble (fē′bəl) very weak: *a feeble person, a feeble cry, a feeble attempt.* *adj.,* **fee·bler, fee·blest.** —**fee′bly,** *adv.* —**fee′ble·ness,** *n.*

feed (fēd) **1** give food to: *Dad is feeding the baby. Feed this carrot to the rabbit.* **2** eat: *The cows are feeding in the pasture. Ladybugs feed on aphids.* **3** food for animals: *Give the chickens their feed.* **4** keep supplied with whatever is needed: *You have to feed the printer with paper. Three elementary schools feed the local high school.* 1, 2, 4 *v.,* **fed, feed·ing;** 3 *n.* —**feed′er,** *n.*

feed·back (fēd′bak′) **1** reactions; opinions about whether something was good or bad: *Before the contest, Mona tried her speech out on her family so she could get their feedback.* **2** the shrieking noise that comes from a sound system when sounds amplified through a microphone go back into it. *n.*

feel (fēl) **1** touch something or notice something touching you: *Feel this piece of cloth. I felt the cool breeze.* **2** try to find by touching without seeing: *He felt in his pocket for a dime. I felt my way to the door.* **3** be; know that you are: *He feels angry. We felt tired.* **4** seem to someone touching it: *The air feels cold. Your dress feels wet.* **5** experience inside yourself: *I felt their insults very deeply.* **6** think: *If you feel you need more time to decide, just say so.* **7** the way in which something feels to the touch: *Wet soap has a greasy feel.* 1–6 *v.,* **felt, feel·ing;** 7 *n.*
feel like, *Informal.* **a** have a desire for; want: *I feel like an ice-cream cone.* **b** seem as if it is going to: *It feels like rain.* **c** seem like to the sense of touch: *The cat's fur felt like silk.*

feel·er (fē′lər) an antenna or other body part that feels. Insects have feelers. *n.*
put out feelers, ask questions or make suggestions meant to bring out the plans or opinions of others.

feel·ing (fē′ling) **1** the sense of touch; ability to feel: *After the needle there was no feeling on the right side of my mouth.* **2** a particular sensation: *There was a prickly feeling in her left foot.* **3** emotion: *Joy and anger are feelings.* **4 feelings,** *pl.,* the inward part of a person that may be hurt by words, by being left out or laughed at, etc.: *Their feelings are easily hurt. Respect people's feelings.* **5** opinion; thought: *What is your feeling about this idea?* **6** tender; sensitive: *a feeling heart.* 1–5 *n.,* 6 *adj.*

feet (fēt) plural of **foot:** *A dog has four feet.* *n.*
drag your feet, be very slow about doing something.
get to your feet, stand up.
get your feet wet, try something new: *She went to a few judo lessons just to get her feet wet, and decided she liked it.*
have your feet on the ground, be realistic and practical.
on your feet, **a** standing up. **b** able to take care of your own needs: *As soon as they were on their feet, the new couple bought a house.*

feign (fān) pretend: *Some animals feign death when in danger.* *v.*

feist·y (fī′stē) brave and full of spirit: *Jean was pretty feisty when it came to defending her rights.* *adj.,* **feist·i·er, feist·i·est.**

fe•line (fē′līn) 1 having to do with cats and other animals of the cat family. 2 any animal belonging to this group. House cats, tigers, leopards, and panthers are felines. 1 *adj.*, 2 *n.*

fell[1] (fel) the past tense of **fall:** *Snow fell all day.* *v.*

fell[2] (fel) cause to fall; cut down or knock down: *to fell a tree. One blow felled him to the ground.* *v.*

fel•low (fel′ō) 1 a name given in a friendly way to male people or animals: *That dog is a nice old fellow.* 2 sharing the same activities, feelings, conditions, etc.: *fellow citizens, fellow sufferers.* 1 *n.*, 2 *adj.*

fel•low•ship (fel′ō ship′) 1 companionship; sharing; a sense of belonging together and of understanding one another. 2 a group of people with the same interests: *She belongs to a Writers' Fellowship.* *n.*

felt[1] (felt) the past tense and past participle of **feel:** *He felt the cat's soft fur. Things are felt with the hands.* *v.*

felt[2] (felt) a kind of cloth that is not woven but made by rolling and pressing wool, hair, or fur together: *a hand puppet made of felt.* A marker with a tip made of felt may be called a **felt pen.** *n.*

fe•male (fē′māl) 1 having to do with the sex that gives birth to young or produces eggs. Cows and hens are female animals. Girls and women are also female. 2 a person or an animal belonging to this sex: *There are ten females on the school staff. Our cat is a female.* 1 *adj.*, 2 *n.*

WORD HISTORY........ female

Female and **male** both come from Latin, but they come from different words. The word **female** comes from *femella*, meaning "girl," and the word **male** comes from *masculus*, meaning "little man."

fem•i•nine (fem′ə nin) 1 having to do with women or girls or things that are supposed to be typical of them: *Sylvia hates wearing feminine clothes like dresses and skirts; Demi likes them.* 2 in some languages, such as French, a category of nouns that affects the form of adjectives and articles you put with them. In French, *tête* is feminine; you can say *la tête* but not *le tête* for "head." *adj.*

fem•i•nist (fem′ə nist) someone who believes that women should have the same rights and the same chances to do things that men have. *n.* **—fem′i•nism′,** *n.*

fence (fens) 1 something put around a yard, garden, etc. to show where it ends or to keep people or animals out or in: *Most fences are made of wood, wire, or metal.* 2 put a fence around: *Now that my baby brother can walk, we have fenced our yard.* Another form is **fence in.** 3 compete in the sport of **fencing,** fighting with long, thin swords called **foils,** that have no sharp point. 1 *n.*, 2, 3 *v.*, **fenced, fenc•ing.** **—fenc′er,** *n.*
on the fence, unable to make up your mind.

fend•er (fen′dər) 1 a curved protective covering over the wheels of a car, bike, truck, etc. to prevent mud from splashing when the vehicle is moving. 2 a guard made of plastic, rubber, rope, etc. to protect the sides of a boat; bumper. It may also be attached to the dock. *n.*

fer•ment (fər ment′) 1 go through a slow chemical change where sugar turns to alcohol and bubbles of gas are given off: *Wine is made from fermented fruit juice.* 2 cause something to go through such a change. *v.* **—fer′men•ta′tion,** *n.*

a bat	e bed	i bid	o pot	u cup	th thin
ā cake	ē me	ī bite	ō go	ū rude	ᴛʜ then
à bar	ə about	ər over	ô for	ů put	zh measure

Bracken is the world's commonest fern. It has creeping underground stems which can grow more than a metre in a year.

fern (fərn) a kind of plant that has roots, stems, and leaflike fronds, but no flowers. The tiny seeds (called spores) of the fern grow in the little brown dots on the backs of the fronds. *n.*

fe·ro·cious (fə rō′shəs) fierce; savage: *a ferocious tiger.* *adj.* **—fe·roc′i·ty** (fə ros′ə tē), *n.*

fer·ret (fer′it) **1** a long, furry animal like a weasel that is used for killing rats and driving rabbits from their holes. Some people keep ferrets as pets. **2** hunt; search: *The detectives ferreted out the criminal.* 1 *n.,* 2 *v.*

Fer·ris wheel (fer′is wēl′ *or* fer′is hwēl′) a large, round framework of steel with swinging seats that hang from its rim. It turns around and around while people ride in the seats. Ferris wheels are found at amusement parks and fairs.

fer·ry (fer′ē) **1** a boat that carries people and goods back and forth across a stretch of water. It is also called a **ferryboat.** **2** go or carry on a boat that goes back and forth: *Hundreds of visitors are ferried to Vancouver Island every day in summertime.* **3** carry back and forth or from one place to another: *Mom gets tired of ferrying us to soccer practice, ballet lessons, and friends' houses.* 1 *n., pl.* **fer·ries;** 2, 3 *v.,* **fer·ried, fer·ry·ing.**

fer·tile (fər′tīl *or* fər′təl) **1** good for growing plants: *Sand is not very fertile.* **2** able to have babies or produce fruit. **3** having a lot of original ideas; inventive: *a fertile mind.* *adj.* **—fer·til′i·ty** (fər til′ə tē), *n.*

fer·ti·lize (fər′tə līz′) **1** make soil richer by adding manure or some other fertilizer: *Farmers fertilize their land every year.* **2** cause an egg or seed to start growing into a new animal or plant by joining male and female cells. *v.,* **fer·ti·lized, fer·ti·liz·ing.** **—fer′ti·li·za′tion,** *n.*

fer·ti·liz·er (fər′tə lī′zər) manure or any other substance that can be added to soil to make it richer in plant foods. Chemical fertilizers contain nitrogen, phosporous, and potassium. *n.*

fer·vour or **fer·vor** (fər′vər) deep, warm, strong feeling; enthusiasm; earnestness: *The speaker's voice trembled as he spoke with fervour about the need to help poor children around the world.* *n.* **—fer′vent,** *adj.*

fes·ter (fes′tər) **1** form pus as a result of infection: *a festering wound.* **2** get slowly worse and more painful because it is not dealt with: *festering anger.* *v.*

fes·ti·val (fes′tə vəl) **1** a celebration, often in memory of some great happening: *Passover is an important Jewish festival.* **2** a day, week, or season of arts events, sometimes with competition among the performers: *a drama festival, a choir festival.* *n.*

fes·tive (fes′tiv) full of a spirit of celebration: *festive decorations. Her birthday was a festive occasion.* *adj.*

fes·tiv·i·ty (fes tiv′ə tē) an activity at a party or festival; something done to celebrate: *The wedding festivities lasted until late at night.* *n., pl.* **fes·tiv·i·ties.**

fes·toon (fes stūn′) **1** flowers, leaves, streamers, etc. hanging in a curve: *The flags were hung on the wall in colourful festoons.* **2** decorate with festoons: *The room was festooned with party streamers.* 1 *n.,* 2 *v.*

fet·a (fet′ə) a firm, white, crumbly cheese made from sheep's or goat's milk. *n.*

fetch (fech) **1** go and get; bring: *Please fetch my tea.* **2** be sold for: *These pears will fetch a good price.* *v.* **fetch and carry,** do boring little jobs.

fetch·ing (fech′ing) *Informal.* charming; pretty: *She wore a fetching hat.* *adj.*

Fête na·tio·nale (fet′ nas′yə nal′) a public holiday in Québec that is celebrated on June 24. **St. Jean Baptiste Day** used to be the name of this holiday.

fet·ter (fet′ər) **1** **fetters,** *pl.* chains and metal cuffs on the ankles, used in earlier times to keep prisoners from escaping. **2** put fetters on a prisoner's feet: *The spy was bound and fettered and shut in the dungeon.* 1 *n.,* 2 *v.*

fet·tu·ci·ne (fet′ə chē′nē) long, flat noodles. *n.*

fe·tus (fē′təs) a baby human, animal, or bird just before birth or hatching. Another spelling is **foetus.** *n.*

feud (fyūd) **1** a long and bitter quarrel between families or groups, often passed on from one generation to another. **2** keep up a long and bitter quarrel, especially one between families. 1 *n.,* 2 *v.*

feu·dal·ism (fyū′də liz′əm) in Western Europe during the Middle Ages, an arrangement where people worked and fought for someone richer and more powerful, called a lord, in return for the lord's protection and the use of his property. *n.* —**feu′dal,** *adj.*

fe·ver (fē′vər) 1 a body temperature that is greater than usual: *A sick person usually has a fever.* 2 an excited, restless condition: *a fever of excitement.* *n.* —**fe′vered,** *adj.* —**fe′ver·ish,** *adj.*
at fever pitch, very excited and restless.

few (fyü) not many; a small number: *There are few children who read before they are five (adj.). She was one of the lucky few who survived (n.). Many people try this, but few succeed (pron.).* *adj., n., or pron.*
quite a few, many.
few and far between, rare.

CONFUSABLES ..... fewer

fewer means "not so many," and usually refers to countable things: *There are fewer raccoons in our neighbourhood than there were last year.*

less means "not so much": *There is less damage from raccoons than there was last year.*

fi·an·cé, fi·an·cée (fē ån′sā *or* fē′ån sā′) the man (fiancé) or woman (fiancée) that someone is engaged to marry. *n.*

fi·as·co (fē as′kō) a failure; flop; disaster: *The wiener roast was a complete fiasco—not only did they forget the wieners, but it poured rain.* *n., pl.* **fi·as·cos** or **fi·as·coes.**

fib (fib) *Informal.* 1 a lie that someone thinks is small and unimportant. 2 tell such a lie: *He was fibbing when he said he had not eaten the last cookie in the box.* 1 *n.,* 2 *v.,* **fibbed, fib·bing.**

fi·bre (fī′bər) 1 one of the threadlike parts or strands that make up certain substances: *muscle fibres. Hemp fibres can be spun into rope or woven into a coarse cloth. Asbestos fibres look like little hairs.* 2 a tough part of grains, fruits, and vegetables that is not digested but helps other foods move through the digestive system. Fibre is a very important part of your diet. 3 character; nature: *A person of strong moral fibre can resist the temptation to cheat.* **Fiber** is another spelling. *n.* —**fi′brous,** *adj.*

fi·bre·glass (fī′bər glas′) a strong, light, fireproof material made from fine threads of glass. It is used for insulation, or mixed with plastic for making boats, etc. **Fiberglass** is another spelling. *n.*

fibre optics (fī′bər op′tiks) a way of carrying information, such as spoken messages or data from a computer, in the form of light along very thin wires made of glass or plastic. Huge amounts of information can be carried very quickly in this way.

fick·le (fik′əl) always changing; not dependable: *fickle fortune, a fickle friend.* *adj.*

fic·tion (fik′shən) 1 stories telling mainly of imaginary people and events. 2 anything untrue: *The report of the school burning down turned out to be a fiction.* *n.* —**fic′tion·al,** *adj.*

fic·ti·tious (fik tish′əs) 1 not real; imaginary; made-up: *Characters in stories are usually fictitious.* 2 used in order to fool others; false: *The criminal used a fictitious name.* *adj.*

fid·dle (fid′əl) 1 make aimless little movements; play nervously: *The girl fiddled with her buttons as she waited.* 2 *Informal.* violin. 3 *Informal.* play on a violin. 1, 3 *v.,* **fid·dled, fid·dling;** 2 *n.* —**fid′dler,** *n.*
fiddle around, a try things, not very seriously and not really knowing what to do: *He fiddled around with the software, trying to get the feel of it.* **b** change and mess up: *Don't fiddle around with the car radio settings!* **c** waste time: *Stop fiddling around and get to work.*
fit as a fiddle, in very good health.

fidg·et (fij′it) 1 move around restlessly because you are bored or uncomfortable: *My little brother fidgets if he has to sit still a long time.* 2 **the fidgets,** a condition of being restless or uneasy: *The long tiresome speech gave us the fidgets.* 1 *v.,* 2 *n.* —**fidg′et·y,** *adj.*

field (fēld) 1 an open stretch of land used for crops or for pasture: *a wheat field.* 2 a piece of land used for some special purpose: *a playing field, the field of battle, a landing field for aircraft.* 3 land where there is a lot of mining: *the coal fields of Alberta, the gold fields of South Africa.* 4 a large, flat area or surface: *A field of ice surrounds the North Pole.* 5 an area of special activity: *the field of politics, the field of art, the field of science.* 6 the area in which a certain force is active: *the earth's gravitational field, a magnetic field.* 7 the real world outside the classroom or laboratory. After designing a product, the manufacturer has to test it in the field, or **field-test** it. A **field trip** is a chance for students to learn things outside the classroom. 8 in baseball, stop a batted ball and throw it in. The player who does this is a **fielder.** 9 answer comments from the public: *The premier had to field many questions from news reporters.* 1–7 *n.,* 8, 9 *v.*

a bat	e bed	i bid	o pot	u cup	th thin
ā cake	ē me	ī bite	ō go	ü rude	ᴛʜ then
å bar	ə about	ər over	ȯ for	u̇ put	zh measure

field day (fēld′ dā′) 1 a day set aside for athletic contests and outdoor sports. 2 a time or triumph or great enjoyment.

field hockey (fēld′ hok′ē) a game like hockey played on a grass field with curved sticks.

field trip (fēld′ trip) a school trip that lets students learn by seeing and doing things outside the classroom.

fiend (fēnd) 1 a devil; an evil spirit. 2 a very wicked or cruel person. 3 *Informal.* a person who does a lot of something or is very good at it: *He is a fiend for work.* *n.*

fierce (fērs) 1 savage and wild; likely to attack; violent: *a fierce lion, fierce anger.* 2 *Informal.* strong; intense; extreme: *a fierce wind. The heat was fierce.* *adj.,* **fierc·er, fierc·est.** **—fierce′ly,** *adv.* **—fierce′ness,** *n.*

fier·y (fī′ə rē) 1 on fire; burning. 2 like fire; very hot or bright: *fiery red.* 3 full of spirit or strong feeling: *a fiery speech, a fiery temper.* *adj.,* **fier·i·er, fier·i·est.**

fi·es·ta (fē es′tə) a festival or celebration, especially as celebrated in Spanish-speaking countries. *n.*

fife (fīf) a small, high-pitched musical instrument like a flute: *We saw a marching band of fifes and drums.* *n.*

fif·teen (fif′tēn′) five more than ten; 15. *n. or adj.* **—fif′teenth′,** *adj. or n.*

fifth (fifth) 1 next after the 4th; last in a series of five; 5th. 2 one, or being one, of 5 equal parts: *Twenty cents is a fifth of a dollar* (*n.*). *adj. or n.*

fif·ty (fif′tē) five times ten; 50. *n., pl.* **fif·ties;** *adj.* **—fif′ti·eth,** *adj. or n.*
fifty-fifty, half-and-half.

Turkey and California are two of the world's main fig-producing areas. Much of the crop is dried, then shipped all over the world.

fig (fig) a small, soft, sweet fruit that grows on a tree in warm regions. Figs are usually eaten dried. *n.*

fight (fīt) 1 a violent struggle: *One punch can lead to a fight.* 2 a quarrel; angry argument. 3 any ongoing effort, with many problems to overcome: *the fight against racism.* 4 take part in any kind of fight: *Soldiers fight. The girls were always fighting about one thing or another. Doctors fight disease.* 5 the power or will to fight: *There is fight in the old dog yet.* 1–3, 5 *n.,* 4 *v.,* **fought, fight·ing.**
a fighting chance, the possibility of winning, but only after a long struggle.
fight it out, settle a thing by fighting till one side wins.
fight off, overcome someone or something attacking you: *to fight off an enemy. He took vitamin C to fight off a cold.*
put up a fight, resist; be ready to fight: *The hunted animal was too weary to put up a fight.*

fig·ur·a·tive (fig′yə rə tiv *or* fig′ə rə tiv) using words out of their normal meaning to add beauty or force. *Example: Her glad heart leapt and danced.* *adj.*

fig·ure (fig′ər *or* fig′yər) 1 a symbol for a number. The symbols 1, 2, 3, etc. are called figures. 2 **figures,** *pl.* arithmetic: *She was always very good at figures.*
3 *Informal.* think; imagine: *I figured it would be fun.*
4 **figure out,** think out; come to understand; find out by thinking: *I finally figured out what she meant.* 5 a number expressing size, amount, price, etc.: *They paid an astronomical figure for that pool.* 6 a shape: *Squares, triangles, circles, and other such shapes are called figures. I could see the figure of a woman against the window.* 7 a person who is noticeable in some way: *Nellie McClung was a great figure in Canadian history.* 8 be noticeable; appear: *Computers figure largely in the world of today.*
9 a chart or diagram; illustration: *Attach the bell to the handlebar as shown in Figure B.* 10 a design or pattern: *They disliked the figures on the wallpaper.*
1, 2, 5–7, 9, 10 *n.,* 3, 4, 8 *v.,* **fig·ured, fig·ur·ing.**
figure of speech, an expression using words out of their normal meaning in order to add beauty or force: *"He is a tiger on the playing field" is a figure of speech.*
figure on, *Informal.* depend on; rely on: *We are figuring on your help in setting up our computer.*

fig·ure·head (fig′ər hed′ *or* fig′yər hed′) 1 a person who is the head in name only, with no real power. 2 a statue or carving decorating the front of a ship. *n.*

figure skating (fig′ər skā′ting) the art of making graceful, dancelike movements on ice skates, usually to music. **—fig′ure-skate′,** *v.* **—fig′ure-skat′er,** *n.*

fil·a·ment (fil′ə mənt) a very fine thread. The fine wire that glows in an electric light bulb is a filament. *n.*

filch (filch) steal something small: *He filched apples from the basket.* *v.*

file[1] (fīl) 1 a set of papers kept in order, often in a folder in the drawer of a **filing cabinet:** *The doctor has a file on each patient.* 2 put away papers in order.
3 a document or other block of information stored in a

computer under a certain name: *The file "Mars.doc" is my project—don't delete it!* **4** a row of people or things one behind another: *a file of cars waiting at the lights.* **5** march or move in such a row: *The choir members filed onto the platform.* 1, 3, 4 *n.,* 2, 5 *v.,* **filed, fil·ing.**
on file, in a file; put away and kept in order: *The principal keeps all our school reports on file.*

file² (fīl) **1** a long tool with many small ridges or teeth on it. It is used to wear away hard materials or to smooth rough edges by rubbing. **2** smooth or wear away with a file. The tiny bits that come off are called **filings.** 1 *n.,* 2 *v.,* **filed, fil·ing.**

fill (fil) **1** make or become full; put or take something in until there is no room for more: *Fill this jar with jam. The bath filled with water.* **2** take up all the space in: *Furniture filled the room.* **3** spread everywhere in: *The fragrance filled the house.* **4** something that fills. Earth or rock used to level uneven land is called fill. If you **eat your fill** you eat till you are full. **5** supply what is needed for: *The pharmacist filled the doctor's prescription. The store could not fill all the orders for the video.* **6** Often, **fill in,** close an opening by putting something in: *to fill in the blanks, to fill a cavity in a tooth.* 1–3, 5, 6 *v.,* 4 *n.* **—fill′ing,** *n.*
fill in, a take somebody's place who can't be there: *Miss Vos is filling in for our usual teacher.* **b** give someone information; *I've been away; fill me in on all the news.*
fill out, a write down information asked for on a form: *to fill out a questionnaire.* **b** make or become rounder and bigger; swell. **c** make something more complete.

fil·let (fil′ət) **1** a slice of meat or fish without bones or fat. A **filet** (fi lā′) is the same thing. **2** cut into fillets. 1 *n.,* 2 *v.*

fil·ly (fil′ē) a young female horse. *n., pl.* **fil·lies.**

film (film) **1** a roll or sheet of thin material covered with a special coating and used to take photographs: *She bought two rolls of film for the camera.* **2** movie: *We saw a film about animals.* **3** make a movie of: *Steven Spielberg filmed the story of E.T.* **4** a very thin layer or coating: *a film of dust. Oil poured on water will spread and make a film.* **5** cover or become covered with a film: *Tears filmed his eyes.* 1, 2, 4 *n.,* 3, 5 *v.* **—film′y,** *adj.*

fil·ter (fil′tər) **1** a device for cleaning liquids or air by screening out dirt or other unwanted stuff. **2** any material that acts this way, such as felt, paper, charcoal, etc. **3** pass or flow slowly through a filter: *The water filters through the sand.* **4** put through a filter: *We filter this water for drinking.* **5** act as a filter for: *The charcoal filters the water.* **6** remove by a filter: *We filtered the grounds from the coffee.* 1, 2 *n.,* 3–6 *v.*

filth (filth) **1** disgusting dirt: *Filth clogged the drain.* **2** disgusting speech or thought. *n.* **—filth′y,** *adj.*

fin (fin) **1** one of the thin, movable, winglike parts of a fish's body. A fish moves the water with its fins to swim and balance itself. **2** anything shaped or used like a fin: *the tail fin of an airplane.* **3** flipper (def. 2); a sort of rubber shoe, with a piece that sticks out well past the toe, worn by divers for extra power in swimming. *n.*

fi·nal (fī′nəl) **1** at the end; closing; last: *the final chapter of a book.* **2** deciding or settling something once and for all; not to be changed or argued with: *The judge's decision is final.* **3** **finals,** *pl.* the last set in a series of games, exams, etc. A player who makes it to the finals is called a **finalist.** 1, 2 *adj.,* 3 *n.* **—fi′nal·ly,** *adv.* **—fi·nal′i·ty** (fə nal′ə tē), *n.*

fi·na·le (fə nal′ē *or* fə nȧ′lē) the last part of a piece of music or a play. *n.*

fi·nal·ize (fī′nə līz′) make final; put into a finished form, with no more changes to be made: *We haven't finalized our travel plans yet.* *v.,* **fi·nal·ized, fi·nal·iz·ing.**

fi·nance (fī′nans *or* fə nans′) **1** money matters: *The Ministry of Finance sets taxes and government spending.* **2** pay for: *She financed her daughter's way through university.* **3** **finances,** *pl.* money; funds. 1, 3 *n.,* 2 *v.,* **fi·nanced, fi·nanc·ing.** **—fi·nan′cial** (fə nan′shəl), *adj.*

Finches are found throughout the world, in wooded areas. They eat seeds, insects, and leaves. Most species have attractive songs.

finch (finch) a songbird with a short, strong, cone-shaped bill. Canaries and cardinals are finches. *n.*

a bat	e bed	i bid	o pot	u cup	th thin
ā cake	ē me	ī bite	ō go	ū rude	ᴛʜ then
ȧ bar	ə about	ər over	ȯ for	ů put	zh measure

find (fīnd) **1** notice or discover something, either by chance or while looking for it: *He found a dollar in the road. She finally found the lost mitten.* **2** manage to get: *I tried to find the courage to speak. Can you find time to do this?* **3** Often, **find out,** learn; come to know: *We found that he could not swim.* **4** experience something in a certain way: *I found the book very interesting.* **5** decide and declare: *The jury found the man guilty.* **6** something found: *The archaeologist's newest find was a buried village.* 1–5 *v.,* **found, find·ing;** 6 *n.* **—find′er,** *n.*

fine[1] (fīn) **1** very small or thin; made up of very small, thin parts: *fine sand, the fine thread of a spider web.* **2** excellent; of high quality: *Everybody praised her fine work as baseball coach.* **3** fancy; elegant; classy: *fine manners, a fine restaurant.* **4** clear and sunny: *fine weather. adj.,* **fin·er, fin·est.** **—fine′ly,** *adv.* **—fine′ness,** *n.*

fine[2] (fīn) **1** a sum of money paid as a punishment. **2** make someone pay such a sum: *The judge fined him $90 for speeding.* 1 *n.,* 2 *v.,* **fined, fin·ing.**

fin·er·y (fī′nə rē) fancy clothes, jewellery, etc. *n.*

fin·ger (fing′gər) **1** one of the five end parts of the hand, especially the four besides the thumb. The nail at the end of a finger is a **fingernail.** **2** anything shaped or used like a finger. **3** touch or handle with the fingers; use the fingers on: *to finger the keyboard of a piano.* 1, 2 *n.,* 3 *v.*

finger painting (fing′gər pān′ting) **1** a way of applying paint by using fingers, palms, or the whole hands instead of brushes. The paint used is called **finger paint.** **2** a design or picture painted in this way. **—fin′ger·paint′,** *v.*

fin·ger·print (fing′gər print′) **1** a mark left by a finger, especially one showing the skin's unique pattern of ridges: *The thief was identified by the fingerprints he left on the door.* **2** take the fingerprints of. 1 *n.,* 2 *v.*

fin·ick·y (fin′ə kē) too dainty or picky; fussy: *He's terribly finicky about his food.* *adj.*

fin·ish (fin′ish) **1** complete; bring or come to an end; get done with: *to finish a dress, to finish a meal. The game did not finish until midnight.* **2** the end: *a fight to the finish.* **3** the way a surface is made to look or feel: *a smooth finish on furniture.* **4** treat the surface of by sanding, varnishing, staining or painting, polishing, etc. 1, 4 *v.,* 2, 3 *n.*

fin·ite (fī′nīt) that has a limit; not going on forever: *The earth's water is finite.* *adj.*

fiord (fyôrd) a long, narrow sea inlet bordered by steep cliffs. **Fjord** is another spelling. *n.*

fir (fər) an evergreen tree like a spruce, with upright cones. *n.*

fire (fīr) **1** the flame, heat, and light produced by something burning: *Fire destroys many hectares of forest each summer in Canada.* **2** a mass of material burning, whether lit on purpose or by accident: *a fire in a fireplace.* **3** light a fire in a place and keep it going: *to fire a furnace.* **4** dry with heat; bake: *Clay bricks are fired to harden them.* **5** strong feeling; energy; excitement: *a heart filled with patriotic fire.* **6** stir up; excite: *Stories of adventure fire the imagination.* **7** shoot a gun or other weapon: *The hunter fired at the fleeing deer.* **8** the shooting of guns: *The enemy's fire continued all night.* **9** *Informal.* dismiss from a job. 1, 2, 5, 8 *n.,* 3, 4, 6, 7, 9 *v.,* **fired, fir·ing.**
catch fire, begin to burn: *Oily rags catch fire easily.*
fight fire with fire, answer an attack with the same kind of action.
on fire, a burning. **b** excited: *The team was on fire with the desire for victory.*
open fire, start shooting.
play with fire, meddle with something dangerous.
set fire to, cause to burn.
under fire, a being shot at. **b** being criticized: *The politician was under fire for the closing of the schools.*

Word Family........fire

fireboat: a boat with equipment to put out fires
firebomb: a bomb that starts fires
firebug: a person who crazily sets fires
firefighter: a person whose job is putting out fires
firelight: the light from a fire
fireplace: a place built to hold a fire
fireside: the space around a fire or fireplace
fire-spotter: a person whose job is to watch out for forest fires
firewood: wood for burning in a stove or fireplace

fire·arm (fī′rärm′) any gun. *n.*

fire·break (fīr′brāk′) a strip of land with the trees cut down or the soil dug and turned over to keep a forest fire or a prairie fire from spreading. *n.*

fire·crack·er (fīr′krak′ər) a paper roll containing gunpowder and a fuse. It explodes with a loud noise. *n.*

fire drill (fīr′ dril′) an exercise where people practise exactly what to do in case of fire.

fire engine (fīr′ en′jən) a truck with a pump, hoses, ladders, and other items for fighting fires. **Fire truck** is another name for it.

fire escape (fīr′ i skāp′) a special stairway or ladder used to get out of a building when it is on fire.

fire extinguisher (fīr′ ek sting′gwish ər) a container filled with chemicals that can be sprayed on a fire to put it out.

fire·fly (fīr′flī′) a small beetle that gives off flashes of light that can be seen in the dark. *n., pl.* **fire·flies.**

🍁 **fire hall** (fīr′ hol′) a building where firefighting equipment is kept or where a fire department has its offices. It is also called a **fire station.**

fire·man (fīr′mən) **1** a man who looks after the fire in a furnace, steam engine, etc. **2** a male firefighter. *n., pl.* **fire·men** (fīr′mən).

fire·proof (fīr′prūf′) **1** that will not burn, or will not burn easily: *A building made entirely of steel and concrete is fireproof.* **2** make so that it will not burn, or not burn easily: *to fireproof a mattress.* 1 *adj.,* 2 *v.*

fire·weed (fīr′wēd′) a tall plant with long spikes of purplish-pink flowers, often growing in newly burned areas. It is the floral emblem of the Yukon. *n.*

fire·works (fīr′wərks′) firecrackers, skyrockets, and so on that explode with a loud noise or beautiful display of sparks in the night sky. Canada Day and Victoria Day are often celebrated with fireworks. *pl.n.*

firm¹ (fərm) **1** hard: *a firm apple, firm ground.* **2** solid; not easily shaken or moved: *a firm support to lean on.* **3** determined, strong, and confident: *a firm voice, firm steps.* **4** not likely to change: *a firm price.* *adj.*

firm² (fərm) two or more people in business together; a company: *She works for a law firm.* *n.*

first (fərst) **1** before all others; 1st: *He is first in his class* (*adj.*). *She finished first* (*adv.*). **2** for the first time: *When I first met her, she was a child.* **3** the beginning: *I knew it from the first.* **4** rather: *"I'll never give up my farm; I'll go to jail first," she said.* 1 *adj.,* 1, 2, 4 *adv.,* 3 *n.*

at first, in the beginning: *At first he did not like school.*
first and foremost, above all; most important.
first thing, right away: *I'll do it first thing tomorrow.*
first things first, what is most important must come first.
not know the first thing about, know nothing about: *He doesn't know the first thing about camping.*

first aid (fərst′ ād′) the emergency treatment given to an injured person before a doctor comes.

first class (fərst′ klas′) **1** the highest class or best quality; the best seats, cabins, etc. on a ship, plane, or train. **2** the class of mail that includes letters and cards as opposed to magazines, large parcels, etc. **3** by this class of mail or in these seats: *to send something first class, to travel first class.* —**first′-class′,** *adj.*

first–hand (fərst′hand′) direct from the original source: *first-hand information* (*adj.*), *to hear something first-hand* (*adv.*). *adj. or adv.*

🍁 **First Nations** (fərst′ nā′shənz) communities made up of people whose ancestors lived in Canada long before the Europeans arrived. **Native people, aboriginal people,** and **Indians** are other names for these people.
▶ See Appendix.

first night (fərst′ nīt′) **1** the night when a play is first performed. **2** **First Night,** a big party with a show and family activities, held outdoors on New Year's Eve.

first person (fərst′ pər′sən) **1** in grammar, the category that includes *I, we,* and their related forms. *Me, us, mine,* and *ours* are pronouns of the first person; *am* is a form of the verb *be* in the first person. **2** a way of telling a story that makes it seem as if the author is one of the characters. A story told in first person uses *I* and *me.*

first–rate (fərst′rāt′) *Informal.* excellent; very good: *We had a first-rate meal.* *adj.*

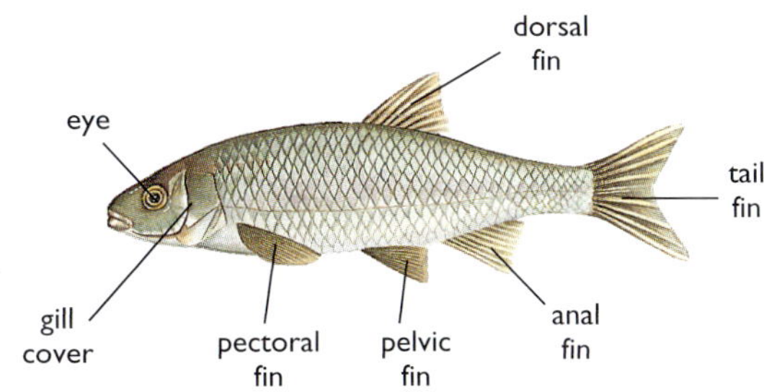

fish (fish) **1** a cold-blooded water animal with fins and a backbone. Fish have gills instead of lungs for breathing, and are usually covered with scales. **2** try to catch fish: *They have been away fishing all day.* **3** try to get or pick up something by hooking it: *She fished with a wire for her ring, which had fallen down the drain.* **4** search with the hands for something hidden, buried, etc. and pull it out: *He fished in his pockets for a match. She fished the map from the drawer.* 1 *n., pl.* **fish** or **fish·es;** 2–4 *v.*

a fish out of water, a person in uncomfortable or unfamiliar surroundings.
fish for compliments, say things that you hope will make others compliment you.

a bat	e bed	i bid	o pot	u cup	th thin
ā cake	ē me	ī bite	ō go	ū rude	ᴛʜ then
à bar	ə about	ər over	ȯ for	ů put	zh measure

fish·er (fish′ər) 1 a person, animal, or bird that catches fish. 2 an animal like a weasel, but larger and with valuable fur; marten. *n.*

fish·er·man (fish′ər mən) a person who fishes, especially one who makes a living by doing so. *n., pl.* **fish·er·men** (fish′ər mən).

fish·er·y (fish′ə rē) 1 the business or industry of catching fish and preparing them for sale. 2 a part of the sea for catching fish: *Salmon is the main catch in the Pacific fisheries. n., pl.* **fish·er·ies.**

fish flake (fish′ flāk′) a rack for drying fish.

fish–hook (fish′hu̇k′) a very sharp hook used to catch fish. It is usually barbed. *n.*

fish·pond (fish′pond′) an ornamental pool where small fish, such as goldfish, are kept. *n.*

fish stick (fish′ stik′) 1 a piece of frozen fish packaged in the form of a short rectangular stick for easy shipping and handling: *Each year, thousands of fish sticks are shipped from the Maritimes to markets in central Canada.* 2 a small piece of pre-cooked fish coated with bread crumbs or batter and kept frozen until used.

fish·y (fish′ē) 1 like a fish, especially in smell or taste. 2 *Informal.* suspicious; questionable; unlikely: *Their story sounds fishy. adj.,* **fish·i·er, fish·i·est.**

fis·sion (fish′ən) a splitting apart. The fission of atoms produces tremendous amounts of energy. *n.*

fist (fist) the hand, closed tightly: *He shook his fist at me.* A **fistfight** is a fight using the fists to punch. *n.*

fit[1] (fit) 1 be or make the proper shape and size: *This puzzle piece doesn't fit. I have to get my costume fitted for the play.* 2 make something go in or on properly: *Can you fit another book in your backpack?* 3 something that fits well or badly: *The coat was not a very good fit.* 4 be or make right for; match; suit: *The music doesn't fit the words. Fit the punishment to the crime.* 5 suitable: *Grass is a fit food for cows; it is not fit for human beings.* 6 healthy and strong: *You must exercise and eat well to stay fit.* 7 install; equip: *Their car has been fitted with a new sunroof and air conditioning.* 1, 2, 4, 7 *v.,* **fit** or **fit·ted, fit·ting;** 3 *n;* 5, 6 *adj.,* **fit·ter, fit·test.**
—fit′ness, *n.*
fit out, supply with everything needed.

fit[2] (fit) 1 a sudden, sharp attack of sickness or of strong feeling: *a fit of coughing, a fit of anger.* 2 a short period of overdoing something: *a cleaning fit. n.*
by fits and starts, starting, stopping, and starting again, on and on.

fit·ful (fit′fəl) irregular; going and then stopping for a while, and going on again: *a fitful sleep. adj.*

fit·ting (fit′ing) 1 right; proper: *It is only fitting to give Grandma the place of honour on her birthday.* 2 a session of trying on unfinished clothes to see if they will fit: *a fitting for a wedding gown.* 3 **fittings,** *pl.* furnishings; fixtures: *Desks, chairs, and files are office fittings.* 1 *adj.,* 2, 3 *n.*

five (fīv) one more than four; 5. *n. or adj.*

fix (fiks) 1 mend or repair: *to fix a broken watch.* 2 *Informal.* set right; put in order; arrange: *She fixed her hair for the photo.* 3 set or attach firmly: *The farmer fixed the post in the ground. There was a sign fixed to the door.* 4 settle; decide on: *to fix a price, to fix a date.* 5 *Informal.* a bad situation: *The boy who cried wolf got himself into a bad fix.* 1–4 *v.,* 5 *n.* **—fixed,** *adj.*

fix·ture (fiks′chər) something put in place to stay: *A toilet and sink are the usual bathroom fixtures. n.*

fizz (fiz) 1 bubble up with a hissing sound. 2 a hissing sound; bubbling: *the fizz of soda water.* 1 *v.,* 2 *n.* **—fizz′y,** *adj.*
fizz on, *Informal.* cause a strong reaction in: *I thought the story was really scary, but it didn't fizz on Teresa at all.*

fiz·zle (fiz′əl) 1 sputter weakly and then die out: *The firecracker fizzled disappointingly.* 2 a sputter; an unexciting finish. 1 *v.,* **fiz·zled, fiz·zling;** 2 *n.*

flab (flab) flesh that lacks firmness because of too much fat and not enough muscle. *n.* **—flab′by,** *adj.*

flab·ber·gast (flab′ər gast′) amaze and surprise: *I was flabbergasted that no one told me about the party. v.*

flag[1] (flag) 1 a piece of cloth with a design that stands for a country, a province, a noble family, or other group: *The Canadian flag has a red maple leaf on a white background flanked by two red bars.* 2 a brightly coloured piece of cloth hung as a decoration: *The used car lot was decorated with many flags.* 3 a piece of cloth used as a signal. A red flag is often a sign of danger, a white flag of surrender. 4 wave a flag or your arms as a signal, especially to stop: *He flagged the train before it reached the broken bridge.* 1–3 *n.,* 4 *v.,* **flagged, flag·ging.**

flag[2] (flag) get tired; grow weak: *Her horse was flagging, but she urged it on. v.,* **flagged, flag·ging.**

flag·pole (flag′pōl′) the pole that a flag is flown from. **Flagstaff** is another word for it. *n.*

flag·stone (flag′stōn′) a large, flat stone used for paving walks, patios, etc. *n.*

flail (flāl) 1 swing or beat wildly: *The angry toddler lay on the floor flailing his arms and legs.* 2 a tool with a free-swinging bar, used to thresh grain. 3 a weapon like this, used mainly in the Middle Ages. 1 *v.*, 2, 3 *n.*

flair (fler) a natural skill: *a flair for making rhymes, a flair for bargains.* *n.*

flake (flāk) 1 a small, flat, thin piece that breaks or falls apart easily: *a flake of snow, flakes of rust, corn flakes.* 2 come off in flakes: *The old paint on the gate was flaking.* 3 **fish flake,** a rack for drying fish. 4 *Informal.* a slightly weird person. 1, 3, 4 *n.*, 2 *v.*, **flaked, flak·ing.**

flam·boy·ant (flam boi′ənt) attracting attention by being a little too bright, loud, outspoken, daring, etc.: *flamboyant colours, a flamboyant person.* *adj.*

flame (flām) 1 a tongue of fire, usually bright yellow or orange. Some gases burn with a blue or green flame. 2 blaze; shoot up in flames: *The dying fire suddenly flamed brightly.* 3 a condition of burning with flames: *to burst into flame.* 4 something that suggests fire. A sweetheart is a flame; so is an angry e-mail message. 1, 3, 4 *n.*, 2 *v.*, **flamed, flam·ing.** **—flame′proof′,** *adj.*

Flamingos are found in many parts of the world, near lakes, marshes, and seas. They live in colonies. Their food is mostly shellfish and small water plants.

fla·min·go (flə ming′gō) a tropical wading bird with very long legs and neck and pink feathers. *n.*, *pl.* **fla·min·gos** or **fla·min·goes.**

USING WORDS . . . . flammable

Flammable and **inflammable** mean the same thing. In science and industry, and on warning labels, they take care to use **flammable**, so that there will be no confusion. In more poetic language, you might say, for example, that someone had an **inflammable** temper. The opposite is **non-flammable**.

flam·ma·ble (flam′ə bəl) easily set on fire. *adj.*

flank (flangk) 1 side: *the flank of an animal, the left or right flank of an army.* 2 be at the side, or both sides, of something: *A garage flanked the house. On the flag, the maple leaf is flanked by two red bands.* 1 *n.*, 2 *v.*

flan·nel (flan′əl) a soft, warm, fuzzy material made of wool. **Flannelette** is a cotton cloth like it. *n.*

flap (flap) 1 swing or sway loosely or noisily: *The sail flapped in the breeze.* 2 move something, especially wings, quickly up and down; fly by moving the wings: *The goose flapped its wings but could not rise from the ground. At last it did rise and flapped heavily away through the air.* 3 a flapping motion; a flapping noise: *We heard the flap of a bird's wings.* 4 a piece hanging or fastened at one edge only: *a flap over the top of a pocket.* 5 an upset, worried, excited condition. 1, 2 *v.*, **flapped, flap·ping;** 3–5 *n.*

flap·jack (flap′jak′) pancake. *n.*

flare (fler) 1 flame up suddenly and unsteadily: *The campfire flared when the grease spilled on it.* 2 a sudden bright flame that quickly dies. 3 a stick of something burnable that can be lit in an emergency as a signal: *The officers put flares around the smashed car.* 4 Often, **flare up,** burst into sudden action or feeling: *His temper flared up and he struck out with his fist.* 5 Sometimes, **flare out,** spread out in the shape of a bell: *This skirt flares at the bottom.* 6 a part that spreads out: *the flare of a skirt.* 1, 4, 5 *v.*, **flared, flar·ing;** 2, 3, 6 *n.* **—flare′-up′,** *n.*

flash (flash) 1 a sudden, short light or flame: *a flash of lightning.* 2 give out such a light or flame: *The light on the radio tower flashes every two seconds.* 3 come and go very suddenly and quickly: *A bird flashed by.* This sense is also used as an adjective: *a flash flood, a flash fire.* 4 a sudden, short burst of anything: *a flash of hope, a flash of temper, a flash of wit.* 5 a short, very fresh report: *a news flash.* 1, 4, 5 *n.*, 2, 3 *v.*
flash in the pan, a quick attempt or effort that looks good at first but fails or is not followed by further efforts.
in a flash, in a very short time: *It all happened in a flash.*

flash·back (flash′bak′) 1 a scene in a book, play, or movie that shows something that happened earlier in the story. 2 a sudden, very clear memory of something that happened to you in the past: *In the middle of class Karen suddenly had a flashback about last summer's vacation.* *n.*

a bat	e bed	i bid	o pot	u cup	th thin
ā cake	ē me	ī bite	ō go	ū rude	ᴛʜ then
ä bar	ə about	ər over	ô for	ů put	zh measure

flash bulb (flash′ bulb′) a bulb that gives a very bright light for an instant, used with some cameras for taking photographs indoors, in shadow, or at night.

flash cards (flash′ kärdz′) a set of cards showing letters, words, numbers, or pictures for drills in reading, arithmetic, etc. The cards are shown quickly one by one while students call out answers as fast as they can.

flash·light (flash′līt′) an electric light for carrying in your hand: *Flashlights are operated by batteries.* *n.*

flash·y (flash′ē) bright and showy so as to attract attention: *flashy clothes. adj.,* **flash·i·er, flash·i·est.**

flask (flask) **1** a glass laboratory container with a narrow neck: *Our science teacher heated the liquid in a flask so we could watch the colour change.* **2** a small glass or metal bottle with flat sides for carrying in a pocket. *n.*

flat¹ (flat) **1** smooth and level; even: *flat pavement. A tabletop is flat.* **2** horizontal; at full length: *lying flat on the ground.* **3** a flat part: *He struck his enemy with the flat of his sword.* **4** not very thick: *a fish with a flat body.* **5** clear and firm: *a flat "No."* **6** lifeless and dull; not fizzy: *a flat voice, flat food, flat pop.* **7** in music: **a** below the true pitch: *My recorder is flat.* **b** a half step below a given tone. B flat is the black note just below B. **8** the sign in music (♭) that shows this. **9** a flat tire. 1, 2, 4–7 *adj.,* **flat·ter, flat·test;** 3, 8, 9 *n.* **—flat′ly,** *adv.* **—flat′ness,** *n.* **—flat′ten,** *v.*
flat out, a clearly and firmly: *She told me flat out that she would never apologize.* **b** at top speed.
flat rate, a rate that is not by the hour, by the kilometre, etc. but fixed: *For the bikeathon, the sponsor offered me a flat rate of $10 no matter how far I went.*

> *Word Family*.......... **flat**
>
> **flatbed:** a heavy truck with no top or sides
> **flatbread:** thin bread, usually made without yeast
> **flatcar:** a railway freight car with no top or sides
> **flatfish:** a fish with a flat body and both eyes on top
> **flatfoot:** a foot with a flattened arch
> **flatland(s):** level ground with no hills or valleys
> **flatware:** knives, forks, and spoons

flat² (flat) an apartment or set of rooms on one floor of a house. *n.*

flat·ter (flat′ər) **1** try to win over or please by praise, often not true. **2** show as more beautiful or better looking than is actually the case: *This picture flatters him.* **3** surprise and please someone by how highly you think of him or her: *She was flattered that the team chose her for captain. v.* **—flat′ter·er,** *n.* **—flat′ter·y,** *n.*

flaunt (flont) show off: *She flaunts her richness by wearing the most expensive clothes.* *v.*

fla·vour or **fla·vor** (flā′vər) **1** a taste, especially one that you recognize as belonging to a specific food or spice: *This gum has a minty flavour.* **2** a special or interesting quality: *Friendship adds flavour to life.* **3** give flavour to; make more interesting: *We use spices to flavour food. He flavoured his story with funny details.* 1, 2 *n.,* 3 *v.* **—fla′vour·ing** or **fla′vor·ing,** *n.*

flaw (flo) a slight defect or fault; something less than perfect: *a flaw in a glass. His bad temper is the only flaw in his character.* *n.* **—flaw′less,** *adj.*

flax (flaks) a slender, upright plant with strong stem fibres, small, narrow leaves, and blue flowers. The seeds are used for food or oil, and the fibres are spun into linen thread for making linen cloth. *n.* **—flax′en,** *adj.*

flea (flē) a small jumping insect without wings. It feeds on blood. *n.*

flea market (flē′ mär′kit) a market selling cheap or odd items, used goods, antiques, etc.

fleck (flek) spot: *Freckles are brown flecks on the skin (n.). The bird's breast is flecked with brown (v.).* *n. or v.*

fled (fled) the past tense and past participle of **flee:** *The bully fled when a bigger student approached.* *v.*

fledg·ling or **fledge·ling** (flej′ling) **1** a young bird just able to fly. **2** any beginner. *n.*

flee (flē) run away: *The robbers tried to flee, but they were caught.* *v.,* **fled, flee·ing.**

fleece (flēs) **1** the fluffy wool that covers a sheep. **2** a warm, thick cloth used for sweat shirts and sweat pants. One side has a woolly, fuzzy surface. **3** rob by trickery; cheat: *The gamblers fleeced him of a large sum.* 1, 2 *n.,* 3 *v.,* **fleeced, fleec·ing. —fleec′y,** *adj.*

fleet¹ (flēt) a group of boats, planes, cars, etc. moving or working together or owned by one person or company: *a fleet of fishing boats, a fleet of trucks.* *n.*

fleet² (flēt) fast; swift: *a fleet horse.* *adj.*

fleet·ing (flē′ting) quickly passing away. *adj.*

flesh (flesh) **1** in a human or animal body, the softer substance that covers the bones and is covered by skin. It is made up mostly of muscles and fat. **2** the human body thought of as separate from the mind and soul: *"The spirit is willing, but the flesh is weak."* **3** the inside of a fruit or vegetable: *The McIntosh apple has crisp, juicy, white flesh.* **4** humans as a group. *n.* **—flesh′y,** *adj.*

Flightless birds

Big flightless land birds are very fast runners — ostriches can reach over 60 km/h. Like most birds that nest or feed on the ground, these birds walk and run by moving one foot forward at a time. (Birds that nest or feed in trees usually hop on both feet when on the ground.)

Penguins are also flightless, but they are excellent swimmers. Underwater, they look like they are flying, using their flippers like wings. All penguins live in the southern hemisphere, many in Antarctica.

flesh and blood, the people related to you by birth.
flesh out, **a** get fatter or more muscular. **b** add more detail to: *You need to flesh out your plan a little.*
in the flesh, **a** alive. **b** actually present, not merely thought of; in person: *There stood Leilani in the flesh.*

fleur–de–lis (flər′də lē′) **1** the iris plant or its flower. **2** the royal coat of arms of France. **3** the unofficial emblem of the province of Québec. *n., pl.* **fleurs-de-lis** (flər′də lē′ *or* flər′də lēz′).

flew (flü) the past tense of **fly**[2]: *A bird flew by.* *v.*

flex (fleks) bend: *He slowly flexed his stiff arm.* *v.*

flex·i·ble (flek′sə bəl) **1** bending easily without breaking; not stiff: *Leather, rubber, and wire are flexible materials.* **2** changing easily to fit different uses, situations, etc.: *Their plans are flexible and they can come any day.* *adj.* **—flex′i·bil′i·ty,** *n.*

flick (flik) **1** a sudden, light stroke or jerk: *The farmer drove the fly from her horse's head with a flick of her whip.* **2** strike lightly or move with a quick jerk: *He flicked the dust from his shoes with a handkerchief.* 1 *n.,* 2 *v.*

flick·er (flik′ər) **1** shine with a wavering, unsteady light: *The firelight flickered on the walls.* **2** move very quickly back and forth: *The lizard's tongue flickered in and out.* **3** a light or a movement like this: *the flicker of a candle, the flicker of an eyelash.* 1, 2 *v.,* 3 *n.*

flight (flīt) **1** the act or way of flying, or the distance or time flown: *the flight of a bird through the air.* **2** a trip in an aircraft. The servers on a plane are called **flight attendants.** **3** a group of things flying together: *a flight of airplanes, a flight of Canada geese.* **4** a set of stairs or steps. **5** a going above or beyond the ordinary: *a flight of the imagination.* **6** the act or fact of running away. *n.* **—flight′less,** *adj.*
put to flight, cause to run away.
take flight, fly away.

flight·y (flī′tē) likely to have sudden impractical ideas; not serious or reliable. *adj.,* **flight·i·er, flight·i·est.**

flim·sy (flim′zē) too light and thin; not solid or strong enough: *flimsy furniture. The flimsy wrapping paper kept tearing. What a flimsy excuse for not getting your work done!* *adj.,* **flim·si·er, flim·si·est.**

flinch (flinch) **1** pull back quickly out of fear or pain: *The toddler flinched when he touched the hot radiator.* **2** the act of pulling back like this: *She took her punishment without a flinch.* 1 *v.,* 2 *n.*

fling (fling) **1** throw forcefully or roughly: *The angry woman flung her gloves on the floor.* **2** a violent throw. **3** a carefree time of doing something fun: *We took our cousin out for one last fling before she went back to Australia.* **4** a lively Scottish dance: *the Highland fling.* 1 *v.,* **flung, fling·ing;** 2–4 *n.*
have a fling at, *Informal.* have a try at; attempt: *He had a fling at swimming across the river.*

a bat	e bed	i bid	o pot	u cup	th thin
ā cake	ē me	ī bite	ō go	ü rude	TH then
ȧ bar	ə about	ər over	ȯ for	u̇ put	zh measure

flint (flint) 1 a very hard kind of stone that makes a spark when struck against steel: *Flints are used in lighters.* 2 anything very hard: *a heart of flint.* *n.* —**flint′y,** *adj.*

flip (flip) 1 toss lightly with a quick movement of the wrist or fingers: *The girl flipped her eraser into the air.* 2 turn over quickly: *I flipped the pages of the magazine. He flipped the eggs before serving them.* 3 a quick overturning, like a somersault: *The model airplane took a flip just before it crashed.* 1, 2 *v.,* **flipped, flip·ping;** 3 *n.*
flip a coin, settle something by tossing a coin in the air and seeing which side is up when it lands.
flip out or **flip your lid,** lose control of yourself.
the flip side, the other side; the other view of something.

flip·pant (flip′ənt) disrespectful in speech or manner; not serious when you should be: *a flippant answer.* *adj.* —**flip′pan·cy,** *n.*

flip·per (flip′ər) 1 a broad, flat fin especially adapted for swimming. Seals and walruses have flippers. 2 a piece of rubber or plastic that fits onto your foot and has a broad, flat part sticking out past the toe, worn for extra power when swimming under water. *n.*

flirt (flərt) 1 play at being in love with someone; try playfully to win a person's attention and affection. 2 a person who flirts. 3 think about something, but not seriously: *She flirted with the idea of taking riding lessons.* 1, 3 *v.,* 2 *n.* —**flir·ta′tion,** *n.* —**flir·ta′tious,** *adj.*

flit (flit) fly or go lightly and quickly: *A moth flitted by. Many thoughts flitted through his mind as he lay in the sun.* *v.,* **flit·ted, flit·ting.**

float (flōt) 1 be held up by air, water, or other liquid: *A cork floats but a stone sinks.* 2 anything that stays up in water, such as a buoy. 3 move along without trying; drift; be carried by the air or water: *Dandelion seeds floated in the breeze.* 4 keep changing, usually depending on some other thing: *floating prices.* 5 a low, flat car that carries something to be shown in a parade. 6 a drink with ice cream in it: *an orange float.* 1, 3, 4 *v.,* 2, 5, 6 *n.*

flock (flok) 1 animals of one kind that feed and move around in a group, especially sheep or birds: *a flock of sparrows.* 2 a large number; a crowd: *Flocks of tourists visit this museum every year.* 3 go or stay in a group: *Sheep usually flock together.* 4 come crowding; crowd: *The children flocked around the clown.* 1, 2 *n.,* 3, 4 *v.*

floe (flō) a large mass of floating ice. *n.*

flog (flog) beat or whip hard. *v.,* **flogged, flog·ging.**

flood (flud) 1 a huge amount of water, especially when it flows over or into a place that is usually dry: *a flood in the basement. The heavy rains caused a flood in the low areas.* 2 cover or fill with water: *During the thunderstorm, our yard flooded. The attendants flood the rink before every hockey game.* 3 **the Flood,** the water that, according to some traditions, covered the whole earth long ago. 4 a great outpouring or huge amount of anything: *a flood of words, a flood of light.* 5 overwhelm with a huge amount all at once: *We were flooded with letters after our family was mentioned in the newspaper article.* 1, 3, 4 *n.,* 2, 5 *v.*
in flood, flooding; overflowing: *The river was in flood.*

flood·light (flud′līt′) a lamp that gives a broad beam of bright light: *Several floodlights were used to illuminate the stage.* *n.*

flood plain (flud′ plān) flat land bordering a river, where rich soil is left behind after the river overflows.

floor (flôr) 1 the surface or part of a room that people walk or stand on: *The floor of this room is made of wood.* 2 the flat surface at the bottom of anything: *the ocean floor, the floor of a pool.* 3 a storey of a building: *We live on the fourth floor.* 4 knock down: *Joe floored him with one blow.* 5 *Informal.* surprise or puzzle completely: *The last question on the test floored us all.* 6 the right to speak in a group or at a meeting: *She began her speech as soon as she got the floor.* 1–3, 6 *n.,* 4, 5 *v.*

flop (flop) 1 fall or move heavily or loosely: *He flopped down into a chair.* 2 twist and turn clumsily: *The fish flopped helplessly on the deck.* 3 the act or sound of flopping. 4 *Informal.* fail completely: *Our clever plan flopped.* 5 *Informal.* a complete failure: *The new play was a flop.* 1, 2, 4 *v.,* **flopped, flop·ping;** 3, 5 *n.*

flop·py (flop′ē) *Informal.* very droopy or bendy: *She bought a sun hat with a big floppy brim.* *adj.,* **flop·pi·er, flop·pi·est.**

floppy disk (flop′ē disk′) a small, thin magnetic platter used for storing computer data. It is held in a plastic case that can be put in a computer's disk drive. **Diskette** is another name for it.

flo·ra (flô′rə) all the plants of a particular region: *Arctic flora.* *n.*

flo·ral (flô′rəl) having to do with flowers: *a floral exhibit, floral decorations.* *adj.*

flo·rist (flôr′ist) the owner of a store that sells flowers, often arranged in an artistic way. *n.*

floss (flos) 1 soft, silky fluff or fibres: *Milkweed pods* *contain white floss.* **2** a strong, shiny thread made from such fibres, used for cleaning between your teeth. *n.*

floun·der[1] (floun′dər) struggle awkwardly; stumble around: *A dog floundered in the deep snow beside the road. Caley got nervous and floundered through her song.* *v.*

floun·der[2] (floun′dər) a flatfish with a wide mouth. *n., pl.* **floun·der** or **floun·ders.**

flour (flour) **1** the fine powder you get by grinding grain such as wheat. It is used a lot in baking. **2** cover with flour: *Flour the chicken legs and fry them.* 1 *n.,* 2 *v.*

flour·ish (flər′ish) **1** grow strong and healthy; do well; thrive: *Your radishes are flourishing. Their business flourished.* **2** wave: *She ran toward us, flourishing the letter* (*v.*). *With a flourish of his hands the pianist began to play* (*n.*). **3** a showy decoration; a curlicue in handwriting, a showy trill or a fancy passage in music, etc.: *a flourish of trumpets. She signs her name with a flourish.* **4** enthusiasm that is a little overdone: *The agent showed us around the house with much flourish.* 1, 2 *v.,* 2–4 *n.*

flout (flout) ignore or disobey authority in a scornful, show-off way: *The rebels flouted the laws.* *v.*

flow (flō) **1** run like water: *Blood flowed from his nose.* **2** a current; stream: *There is a constant flow of water from the spring.* **3** glide; move smoothly: *The words flowed from his mouth.* **4** any smooth, steady movement: *a flow of words.* **5** hang loosely: *Her long hair flowed down her back.* 1, 3, 5 *v.,* 2, 4 *n.*
go with the flow, relax and let things happen as they will.

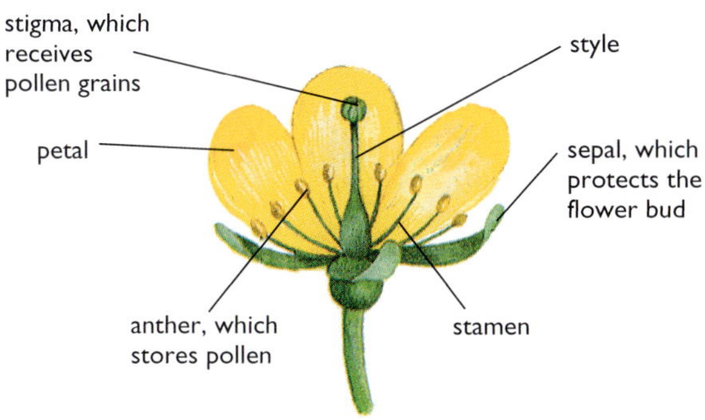

The stamens contain grains of pollen which fertilize the stigma from which a fruit forms.

flow·er (flou′ər) **1** a blossom; the part of a plant that produces the seed. It is usually colourful and sweet-smelling. Bees gather nectar from flowers. **2** a small plant with colourful blossoms: *We planted a lot of flowers this year.* **3** produce flowers; bloom. 1, 2 *n.,* 3 *v.* **—flow′er·ing,** *adj.* **—flow′er·y,** *adj.*

flow·er·pot (flou′ər pot′) a pot to hold soil for a plant to grow in. *n.*

flown (flōn) the past participle of **fly[2]:** *The flag is flown on all government buildings.* *v.*

flu (flū) influenza, an infectious disease like a very bad cold with fever, aches, and often stomach upset. *n.*

fluc·tu·ate (fluk′chū āt′) keep shifting up and down or back and forth: *The price of computers fluctuates wildly from month to month.* *v.,* **fluc·tu·at·ed, fluc·tu·at·ing.** **—fluc′tu·a′tion,** *n.*

flue (flū) a tube, pipe, etc. to let smoke or hot air escape. A chimney may have several flues. *n.*

flu·ent (flū′ənt) smooth, fast, and confident in speech or writing: *She answered us in fluent French. He was a fluent speaker.* *adj.* **—flu′en·cy,** *n.*

fluff (fluf) **1** a mass of very soft, light material: *After its bath and a rub with the towel, the puppy looked like a ball of fluff.* **2** shake up into a soft, light mass: *Fluff the pillows when you make the bed.* 1 *n.,* 2 *v.*
—fluff′y, *adj.*

flu·id (flū′id) **1** any liquid or gas; something that will flow: *Water, mercury, air, and oxygen are fluids.* **2** moving like a liquid or a gas; flowing: *The skater's fluid movements impressed the judges.* **3** changing smoothly all the time. 1 *n.,* 2, 3 *adj.*

flung (flung) the past tense and past participle of **fling:** *The girl flung a snowball at me. The paper was flung away.* *v.*

flunk (flungk) *Informal.* fail in school work: *He flunked his math test but passed all the others.* *v.*

fluo·res·cent (flůr es′ənt) giving off light when energized. A fluorescent tube has a coating inside which takes in electrical energy and gives off light. *adj.*

fluo·ride (flůr′īd *or* flôr′īd) a chemical compound that is poisonous in large quantities but helps prevent tooth decay. It is added to toothpaste and to the tap water in some cities. *n.* **—fluor′i·date′,** *v.*

flur·ry (flər′ē) **1** a light fall of snow. **2** a sudden gust of wind: *The flurry lifted off his hat and carried it away.* **3** a sudden burst of excited action or feeling: *a flurry of alarm.* 1–3 *n., pl.* **flur·ries.**

a bat	e bed	i bid	o pot	u cup	th **thin**
ā cake	ē me	ī bite	ō go	ū rude	ᴛʜ **then**
ä bar	ə about	ər over	ô for	ů put	zh **measure**

flush[1] (flush) 1 clean out with a sudden rush of water: *to flush a toilet. If you get this stuff in your eyes, flush them with clear water.* 2 a sudden rush or flow. 3 blush; glow with a rosy colour: *The girl flushed when they laughed at her* (*v.*). *The flush of sunrise was on the clouds* (*n.*). 4 cause to blush or glow: *Exercise flushed their faces.* 1, 3, 4 *v.,* 2, 3 *n.*

flush[2] (flush) 1 even; level: *The shelf is flush with the countertop.* 2 having plenty; well supplied: *After her summer job, she was flush with money.* *adj.*

flus·ter (flus′tər) confuse; make embarrassed or nervous: *He was a little flustered by all the attention.* *v.*

flute (flūt) 1 a long, slender wind instrument shaped like a tube. You play it by holding it sideways and blowing across a hole near one end. Different tones are made by opening and closing holes along the tube with your fingers or with keys. 2 make a clear, high sound like a flute. 1 *n.,* 2 *v.,* **flut·ed, flut·ing.** —**flut′ist,** *n.*

flut·ter (flut′ər) 1 wave or move back and forth quickly and lightly: *to flutter your eyelashes. The flag fluttered in the breeze.* 2 fly or fall with this kind of action: *The little bird fluttered from branch to branch. The leaf fluttered to the ground.* 3 a fluttering motion: *a flutter of the wings.* 4 a state of excitement or nervousness: *The surprise announcement caused a flutter in the crowd.* 1, 2 *v.,* 3, 4 *n.*

fly[1] (flī) 1 a common flying insect with two wings: *Houseflies, black flies, and horseflies are a great nuisance.* 2 a fish-hook with feathers, silk, tinsel, etc. on it to make it look like a fly. *n., pl.* **flies.**

fly[2] (flī) 1 move through the air with wings or a motor: *Birds fly. We heard a plane fly over.* 2 float or wave in the air: *Our flag flies every day.* 3 cause to fly: *to fly a kite.* 4 travel in an aircraft: *She is flying to Japan.* 5 go very fast: *The hours flew by.* 6 an old or poetic word for "run away." 7 an extra outer covering over a tent. 8 the zipper in the front of a pair of pants or shorts. 9 a baseball hit high into the air. 10 hit a ball high into the air: *The batter flied into left field.* 1–6, 10 *v.,* **flew, flown, fly·ing** for 1–6, **flied, fly·ing** for 10; 7–9 *n., pl.* **flies.**
fly at, attack wildly.
fly in the face of, go directly against: *This action flies in the face of the promises he made last week.*
fly off the handle, lose your temper.
let fly, shoot or throw.
on the fly, while moving; without stopping what you are doing: *We were in a rush to finish the packing, so we ate lunch on the fly.*
with flying colours or **colors,** successfully; triumphantly: *He passed the examination with flying colours.*

fly·catch·er (flī′kach′ər) a bird that catches insects while flying. There are several kinds. *n.*

fly·er or **fli·er** (flī′ər) 1 a person or thing that flies or goes very fast. 2 a sheet of paper or brochure with advertising on it. *n.*

flying buttress (flī′ing but′ris) a support for a wall, joined to the outside of the wall and slanting down to a pillar a short distance away. Flying buttresses were developed in the Middle Ages and allowed architects to make taller buildings with thinner walls than before.

flying fish (flī′ing fish′) a tropical sea fish having winglike front fins that enable it to leap through the air.

flying saucer (flī′ing sos′ər) an alien spaceship that is round and almost flat, according to some people who say they have seen one. Another name for it is **UFO** which stands for **U**nidentified **F**lying **O**bject.

FM or **F.M.** *abbreviation for* **frequency modulation,** a way of sending radio signals that makes them easier to receive. The frequency of the carrier wave is changed to match changes in the frequency of the sound.

foal (fōl) 1 a young horse or donkey; colt or filly. 2 give birth to a foal. 1 *n.,* 2 *v.*

foam (fōm) 1 a mass of very small bubbles. 2 form foam: *Pop foams if you shake it up.* 3 a spongy material made of plastic or rubber. 1, 3 *n.,* 2 *v.* —**foam′y,** *adj.*
foam at the mouth, be full of uncontrolled anger or hate.

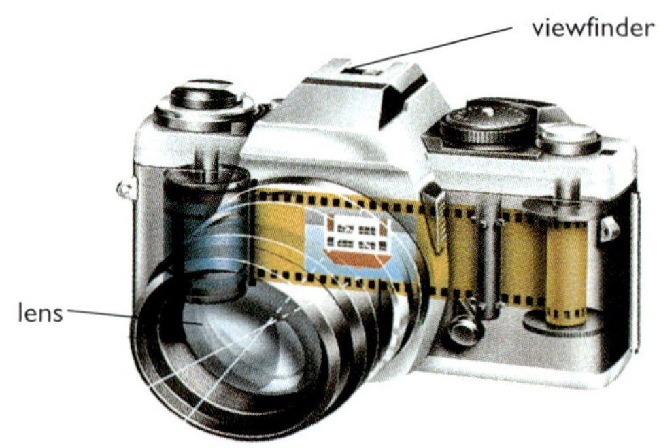

In this camera, light passes through a lens and is then focussed onto a second set of lenses.

fo·cus (fō′kəs) 1 a point where light or heat rays meet after being bounced off a mirror or bent by a lens. 2 bring rays of light, heat, etc. together at such a point: *The lens focussed the sun's rays so that they burned a hole in a piece of paper.* 3 adjust a lens, the eye, etc. so that it brings rays of light together to give a clear image:

When I'm tired I cannot focus well. Turn the little knob to focus the binoculars. **4** something that everyone is paying attention to: *The new baby was the focus of attention.* **5** concentrate: *He focussed his mind on the lesson.* 1, 4 *n., pl.* **fo·cus·es** or **fo·ci** (fō′sī); 2, 3, 5 *v.,* **fo·cus·ses** or **fo·cus·es, fo·cussed** or **fo·cused, fo·cuss·ing** or **fo·cus·ing.**
in focus, showing a sharp, clear image; well focussed. The opposite is **out of focus.**

fod·der (fod′ər) **1** rough food for horses, cattle, etc.: *Hay and cornstalks are fodder.* **2** anything thought of as supplying material for something else: *His experiences as a ship's doctor provided the fodder for many stories.* *n.*

foe (fō) enemy. *n.*

fog (fog) **1** a cloud of fine drops of water that forms just above the earth's surface; thick mist. Fog makes it hard to see very far. **2** make misty or cloudy: *Something fogged six of the pictures we took.* **3** a confused or puzzled condition: *My mind was in a fog during most of the test.* 1, 3 *n.,* 2 *v.,* **fogged, fog·ging.** **—fog′gy,** *adj.*
fog up, become covered with mist or fine drops of water: *On cold days my glasses fog up.*

fo·gey or **fo·gy** (fō′gē) an old-fashioned person. *n., pl.* **fo·geys** or **fo·gies.**

fog·horn (fog′hôrn′) a horn with a loud, deep sound, used in foggy weather to warn ships of danger: *The freighter sounded its foghorn so that other ships would not crash into it.* *n.*

foi·ble (foi′bəl) a small character weakness. *n.*

foil[1] (foil) metal that has been beaten, hammered, or rolled into a very thin sheet: *tin foil, aluminum foil.* *n.*

foil[2] (foil) outwit; prevent a person's plans from being carried out: *The hero foiled the villain.* *v.*

foist (foist) force something unwanted on a person: *I wasn't hungry but she foisted a second helping on me.* *v.*

fold[1] (fōld) **1** bend or double over on itself: *Fold the letter and put it in an envelope.* **2** a layer of something folded, or the line made by folding: *He hid the money between the folds of his towel. The old map is falling apart at the folds.* **3** bend so as to link or lock together: *to fold your arms.* **4** hug closely. **5** wrap: *He folded the gum up in a piece of paper.* **6** close because of failure: *Their typewriter repair business has folded.* 1, 3–6 *v.,* 2 *n.*

fold[2] (fōld) **1** a fenced-in area for sheep. **2** a flock of sheep kept in such an area. *n.*
come back to the fold, return to where you belong.

–fold *a suffix meaning:* **1** so many times as much. A *fourfold* increase is an increase to four times as much. **2** having so many parts or sides to it. *The reason for this is twofold* means "There are two reasons for this."

fold·er (fōl′dər) **1** a holder for papers, made of cardboard folded once. **2** a grouping of computer files together under one title in the directory. *n.*

The dried foliage of a tea plant is mixed with hot water to make the drink we call tea.

fo·li·age (fō′lē ij) the leaves of a plant. *n.*

folk (fōk) **1** people: *city folk, country folk. The Vikings were traditionally a seafaring folk.* **2 folks, a** people. **b** *Informal.* relatives, especially parents: *How are your folks?* **3** traditional; passed down for many years among the common people: *folk medicine, folk tales, folk dances.* **4** having to do with folk music: *a folk festival.* 1, 2 *n., pl.* **folk** or **folks;** 3, 4 *adj.*

folk·lore (fōk′lôr′) the legends, customs, etc. of a people, passed from generation to generation. *n.*

folk music (fōk′ myu′zik) **1** music handed down from generation to generation, like the well-known French-Canadian **folk song,** "Alouette." **2** a style of modern popular music that is similar to traditional folk music and almost always uses a non-electric guitar. Stan Rogers was a famous Canadian **folk singer.**

fol·li·cle (fol′ə kəl) a tiny opening in the skin that a hair grows out of. *n.*

a bat	e bed	i bid	o pot	u cup	th **thin**
ā cake	ē me	ī bite	ō go	ü rude	ᴛʜ **then**
ä bar	ə about	ər over	ô for	u̇ put	zh measure

fol•low (fol′ō) 1 go or come after or as a result of: *Night follows day. Follow the leader. Your headache follows directly from a lack of sleep.* 2 go along: *Follow this road.* 3 obey; act on; take as a guide: *Follow her advice.* 4 keep the eyes or attention on: *I could not follow the bird's flight.* 5 understand: *The explanation was hard to follow.* *v.*
as follows, as written out below: *Prizes are as follows.*
follow suit, **a** play a card of the same suit as the one first played by someone else. **b** do the same as another.
follow through, carry something out fully; complete: *If you start a job, you should try to follow it through.*
follow up, check on a situation again after your first action and do whatever is needed: *The doctor who treated my burn followed up every month for a year.*

fol•low•er (fol′ō ər) a person who follows the ideas or teachings of another person, a religion, etc. *n.*

fol•low•ing (fol′ō ing) 1 a group of followers or fans: *She had a large following.* 2 next: *If that was Sunday, then the following day must have been Monday.* 3 after: *Refreshments will be served following the play.* 1 *n.,* 2 *adj.,* 3 *prep.*

fol•ly (fol′ē) a foolish act or idea: *It is folly to eat so much.* *n., pl.* **fol•lies.**

fond (fond) loving; affectionate: *a fond look.* *adj.* —**fond′ly,** *adv.* —**fond′ness,** *n.*
be fond of, like: *My uncle is fond of dogs.*

fon•dle (fon′dəl) touch lovingly: *The mother fondled her baby's soft, curly hair.* *v.,* **fon•dled, fon•dling.**

fon•due (fon dū′ *or* fon dyū′) a meal where everyone dips small pieces of food, such as bread or fruit, into a pot of melted cheese or chocolate. *n.*

font (font) 1 a basin holding water for baptism. 2 a set of letters, numbers, etc. designed in the same style of type: *That's a nice font you used for your title page.* *n.*

food (fūd) 1 anything that plants, animals, or people take in to keep them alive and make them grow: *Milk and vegetables are good foods for humans.* 2 things that you eat rather than drink: *Give him food and drink.* *n.*
food for thought, something to think about.

food bank (fūd′ bangk′) a place where people with little or no money can get food very cheaply or for free.

food chain (fūd′chān′) a group of animals and plants connected by their eating habits so that each one uses another one for food. For example, people eat cattle, cattle eat grass, and grass gets nutrients from the soil.

food poisoning (fūd′ poi′zən ing) illness caused by eating food that contains harmful bacteria.

food processor (fūd′ prō′ses ər) a small machine with a fast-moving blade that chops or mixes food.

food web (fūd′web′) all the groups of plants and animals that live together and depend on each other for food. A food web is made up of many food chains.

fool (fūl) 1 a person without sense; a person who acts in a stupid or unreasonable way. 2 trick; play a joke on: *Ha ha, I fooled you! There's no quiz after all!* 3 in old times, a clown kept by a king or lord; jester. 1, 3 *n.,* 2 *v.*
fool around, **a** play around; joke or act silly. **b** waste time.
fool with, mess with; meddle with: *Who's been fooling with my stereo?*

Word Family......... **fool**

foolhardy: foolishly bold; rash
foolish: silly; unwise
foolproof: so simple that even a fool can use or do it

foot (fu̇t) 1 the end part of a leg; the part that a person or animal stands on. 2 the bottom or end of something: *the foot of a hill, the foot of a page, the foot of a bed.* 3 walk: *The boys footed the whole 20 km.* 4 a nonmetric measure of length equal to twelve inches (about 30.5 cm): 1, 2, 4 *n., pl.* **feet;** 3 *v.*
foot the bill, pay the cost: *Who'll foot the bill for this trip?*
my foot! I don't believe it! *Sick, my foot! He's faking.*
on foot, walking.
put your best foot forward, try to make a good impression.
put your foot down, act firmly or with authority.
put your foot in it, *Informal.* make a serious blunder.
put your foot in your mouth, say something that gets you into trouble.

Word Family.......... **foot**

foothill: a low hill at the foot of a mountain
footlights: a row of lights at the front of a stage
footman: a male servant, often going on a carriage to open its door
footnote: a note at the foot of a book page
footprint: the mark made by a foot
footrace: a race for runners
footsore: having sore feet from too much walking
footstool: a low stool to rest your feet on
footwear: shoes, boots, socks, etc.

foot·ball (fu̇t′bol′) 1 an outdoor game played by two teams, with each side trying to kick, throw, or carry a ball across the other team's goal line. Canadian and American football have different rules about size of field, number of players, and details of play. 2 the oval, air-filled, usually leather ball used in playing this game. 3 outside North America, soccer or a soccer ball. *n.*

foot·hold (fu̇t′hōld′) 1 a secure place to put your foot: *It was hard to climb up the cliff because there were few footholds.* 2 a firm and secure position: *It is not easy to break a habit that has gained a foothold.* *n.*

foot·ing (fu̇t′ing) 1 another word for "foothold": *The steep cliff gave us no footing.* 2 the terms of a relationship: *They are on a friendly footing with their neighbours.* 3 **footings,** *pl.* the concrete foundation of a building, wall, etc. *n.*
lose your footing, slip and fall.

foot·step (fu̇t′step′) a person's step, or the sound of it: *We heard footsteps in the hall.* *n.*
follow in someone's footsteps, do as another has done.

for·age (fôr′ij) 1 hunt or search for anything, especially food: *The children foraged in the kitchen till they found some cookies.* 2 hay, grain, or other food for horses, cattle, etc. 1 *v.,* **for·aged, for·ag·ing;** 2 *n.*

for·bid (fər bid′) not allow; make a rule against: *The teacher forbids gum in class. My dad has forbidden me to go.* *v.,* **for·bade** (fər bad′), **for·bid·den, for·bid·ding.**

for·bid·ding (fər bid′ing) not very inviting; looking rather scary, dangerous, or difficult: *The coast was rocky and forbidding.* *adj.*

force (fôrs) 1 power or strength: *The force of the wind broke the power pole.* 2 strength used against a person or thing; violence: *The rebels captured the village by force.* 3 make a person do something against his or her will: *Pressing their hands on his shoulders, they forced him to sit down.* 4 get, put, or take by force: *She forced the key out of my hand.* 5 break through: *to force a door.* 6 a group of people who work together: *the police force.* 7 **the forces,** the armed services; the army, navy, and air force. 8 in science, any cause that changes, moves, or stops an object: *the force of gravity, magnetic force.* 1, 2, 6–8 *n.,* 3–5 *v.,* **forced, forc·ing.**
force yourself, manage to do something by a great effort of willpower: *She forced herself to finish the long race.*
in force, a in use; being applied: *The old rules are still in force.* **b** in large numbers; with full strength: *The enemy attacked us in force.*

force·ful (fôrs′fəl) powerful; using a lot of energy and having a strong effect: *She is a quiet but forceful speaker.* *adj.*

for·ceps (fôr′seps) a pair of pincers or tongs used by surgeons, dentists, etc. for grabbing and holding: *Dentists use forceps for pulling teeth.* *n., pl.* **for·ceps.**

ford (fôrd) 1 a place to cross a river by walking, riding, or driving through it. 2 cross in this way: *It is shallow enough here to ford the river.* 1 *n.,* 2 *v.*

fore (fôr) 1 the front part, especially of a ship or boat. 2 at or toward the front; forward. 3 in golf, a shout of warning to people ahead who might get hit by the ball. 1 *n.,* 2 *adj. or adv.,* 3 *interj.*
bring or **come to the fore,** bring or come into an important or leading position.

fore– *a prefix meaning:* 1 front, as in *forefoot.* 2 before; beforehand, as in *foresee.*

fore·arm[1] (fôr′ärm′) the part of your arm between your elbow and your wrist. *n.*

fore·arm[2] (fôr ärm′) prepare for trouble ahead of time: *To be forewarned is to be forearmed.* *v.*

fore·bod·ing (fôr bō′ding) a feeling that something bad is going to happen: *As the storm grew worse, the travellers were filled with foreboding.* *n.*

fore·cast (fôr′kast′) 1 predict; tell what is coming: *They are forecasting a good year for business.* 2 a prediction: *What is the weather forecast for today?* 1 *v.,* **fore·cast** or **fore·cast·ed, fore·cast·ing;** 2 *n.*

fore·fa·ther (fôr′fo̤ᴛʜ′ər) an old or poetic word for "ancestor." *n.*

fore·fin·ger (fôr′fing′gər) the finger next to your thumb. *n.*

fore·front (fôr′frunt′) 1 the place of greatest importance, activity, etc.: *She was at the forefront of medical science.* 2 the part furthest to the front. *n.*

fore·ground (fôr′ground′) the part of a picture or scene nearest to the person looking at it: *The cottage is in the foreground and the hills are in the background.* *n.*

fore·hand (fôr′hand′) in tennis and other sports, a stroke made with the palm of your hand facing out. *n.*

fore·head (fôr′hed′) the part of your face above your eyes. *n.*

a bat	e bed	i bid	o pot	u cup	th thin
ā cake	ē me	ī bite	ō go	ü rude	ᴛʜ then
ä bar	ə about	ər over	ô for	u̇ put	zh measure

Forest

This mixed forest of evergreen and deciduous trees is in the Rockies. The evergreens are also called softwoods, and the deciduous trees are called hardwoods.

In the rain forest in South America, the crowns of the trees merge to form a canopy.

for•eign (fȯr′ən) 1 having to do with or coming from countries other than your own: *foreign countries, a foreign ship, foreign money.* A visitor from another country is a **foreigner.** 2 not belonging: *Sitting still all day is foreign to her nature.* *adj.*

fore•leg (fȯr′leg′) an animal's front leg. *n.*

fore•most (fȯr′mōst′) 1 first: *I am foremost in line* (*adj.*). *He stumbled and fell head foremost* (*adv.*). 2 chief; leading: *the foremost scientist.* 1, 2 *adj.*, 1 *adv.*

fore•run•ner (fȯr′run′ər) 1 a sign or warning of something to come: *Black clouds are often the forerunner of a storm.* 2 ancestor; a person or thing that comes before and is later replaced by another: *The typewriter was the forerunner of the personal computer.* *n.*

fore•see (fȯr sē′) think of, figure out, or know beforehand: *None of us brought a bathing suit because we didn't foresee that the water would be so warm.* The ability or practice of looking ahead and planning for the future is called **foresight.** *v.*, **fore•saw, fore•seen, fore•see•ing.**

fore•shad•ow (fȯr shad′ō) give a hint or sign that something is going to happen later in a story: *The part where they argued about bringing the life jackets foreshadowed the canoe accident that happened later.* *v.* **—fore•shad′ow•ing,** *n.*

for•est (fȯr′ist) a large area of land covered with trees; woods. *n.* **—for′est•ed,** *adj.*

for•est•ry (fȯ′ris trē) the science and art of planting and taking care of forests. *n.* **—for′est•er,** *n.*

fore•tell (fȯr tel′) tell beforehand; predict: *Who can foretell the future?* *v.*, **fore•told, fore•tell•ing.**

fore•thought (fȯr′thot′) 1 previous thought or consideration; planning. 2 careful thought for the future; prudence; foresight: *A little forethought will often prevent mistakes.* *n.*

for•ev•er (fə rev′ ər) 1 without ever ending or stopping: *She doesn't believe the earth will last forever.* **Forevermore** means the same. 2 always; again and again: *That dog is forever barking.* *adv.*

fore•warn (fȯr wȯrn′) warn beforehand: *We were forewarned about the storm.* *v.* **—fore•warn′ing,** *n.*

for•feit (fȯr′fit) 1 lose something or have to give it up because of your own failure to do what is required: *He forfeited his licence through careless driving.* 2 something lost or given up in this way: *to pay a forfeit.* 3 lost or given up: *Their lands were forfeit.* 1 *v.*, 2 *n.*, 3 *adj.*

for•gave (fər gāv′) the past tense of **forgive:** *She forgave my mistake.* *v.*

forge¹ (fȯrj) 1 make something false or counterfeit: *to forge someone's signature, to forge a passport.* 2 a place where metal, such as iron is heated and then shaped while it is soft. A traditional forge was a workshop with a fire in it that was kept burning very hot. 3 heat metal to a high temperature and then shape it while it is soft: *The blacksmith forged the bar of iron into a big hook.* 4 make; build or form: *They forged a strong and lasting friendship.* 1, 3, 4 *v.*, **forged, forg•ing;** 2 *n.* **—forg′er,** *n.*

forge² (fȯrj) move forward steadily: *Let's forge ahead with our plans.* *v.*, **forged, forg•ing.**

for·ge·ry (fôr′jə rē) 1 the act of forging a signature, etc.: *Forgery is a crime.* 2 a fake meant to deceive people: *The painting was a forgery.* *n., pl.* **for·ger·ies.**

for·get (fər get′) 1 fail to remember or think of: *I'm afraid I've forgotten your name.* 2 leave behind without meaning to: *I'll have to go back—I forgot my jacket.* *v.,* **for·got, for·got·ten, for·get·ting.** —**for·get′ful,** *adj.*

for·get–me–not (fər get′mē not′) a sprawling plant with many small blue or white flowers. *n.*

for·give (fər giv′) give up being angry or wanting revenge: *Please forgive my rotten behaviour.* *v.,* **for·gave, for·giv·en, for·giv·ing.** —**for·give′ness,** *n.*

for·go (fôr gō′) do without; give up: *She decided to forgo the TV show and do her homework.* *v.,* **for·went, for·gone, for·go·ing.**

for·got (fər got′) the past tense of **forget.** The past participle is **forgotten:** *She was so busy she forgot to eat her lunch. He has forgotten much of what he learned.* *v.*

fork (fôrk) 1 an eating tool with a handle and two or more long, pointed prongs. 2 a tool like this but bigger, for lifting hay, etc.; pitchfork. 3 the part of a tree, road, etc. where it divides into two parts: *When you come to the fork in the road, go left.* 4 one of the branches it divides into: *They took the left fork.* 5 divide into branches: *There is a gas station where the road forks.* 1–4 *n.,* 5 *v.*

for·lorn (fôr lôrn′) sad and miserable and with no one to turn to: *The lost kitten, a forlorn little animal, was wet and dirty.* *adj.*

form (fôrm) 1 shape: *The form of a tree appeared out of the fog (n.). The cook formed the dough into loaves (v.).* 2 come to be; develop into a certain shape: *Water forms ice at 0°C. A plan was forming in his mind.* 3 a mould or pattern: *She poured the batter into a form.* 4 make up; compose: *The provinces and territories of Canada form one country.* 5 organize; set up: *We formed a club.* 6 a kind; sort: *Heat and light are two forms of energy.* 7 a printed paper with blank spaces to be filled in: *To get a licence, you must fill out a form.* 1, 3, 6, 7 *n.,* 1, 2, 4, 5 *v.*
good form, a the elegant or proper way of behaving or of doing a certain thing: *It is not good form to burp at the table. In swimming she has good form as well as speed.* The opposite is **bad form. b** good condition; good shape: *We were in good form after a summer of hiking and canoeing.*

for·mal (fôr′məl) 1 stiff and proper; not in a relaxed, everyday style but according to strict customs or rules of politeness: *a formal introduction, a formal suit.* 2 done in the official or recognized way: *A written contract is a formal agreement to do something. She has no formal training but has learned a lot on her own.* 3 having to do only with the appearance or form of a thing, not its meaning or purpose. 4 a social event that people wear formal clothes to. 1–3 *adj.,* 4 *n.* —**for′mal·ly,** *adv.*

for·mal·i·ty (fôr mal′ə tē) 1 the fact of being formal; properness. 2 something done to follow a rule or custom: *We knew it was OK, but we asked her permission anyway just as a formality.* *n., pl.* **for·mal·i·ties.**

for·mat (fôr′mat) 1 the way in which something is presented or arranged: *book format, tape format.* 2 organize or arrange something in a certain way: *You can format your project in different ways—as an interview, a slide show, or a written assignment.* 3 prepare a disk by having the computer put the basic programs on it for recording and organizing information. Any old data on the disk is erased at the same time. 1 *n.,* 2, 3 *v.,* **for·mat·ted, for·mat·ting.**

for·ma·tion (fôr mā′shən) 1 the action of forming, making, or shaping something: *the formation of water from steam.* 2 something formed; a shape: *Stratus and cumulus are two different cloud formations.* *n.*
in formation, in a particular arrangement or order: *soldiers marching in formation.*

for·mer (fôr′mər) 1 earlier; past; old: *former times, a former student of this school.* 2 **the former,** the first of two: *When Rani is offered ice cream or pie, she always chooses the former.* 1 *adj.,* 2 *n.* —**for′mer·ly,** *adv.*

for·mi·da·ble (fôr′mə də bəl) hard to deal with; taking a lot of courage and effort: *a formidable task, a formidable enemy.* *adj.*

for·mu·la (fôr′myə lə) 1 a recipe; prescription: *a formula for making soap.* 2 a mixture for feeding a baby, made according to a recipe that includes the right amount of vitamins, minerals, fat, etc. *n.*

for·mu·late (fôr′myə lāt′) state in a clear and organized way: *Our ideas of fair treatment for all Canadians are formulated in the Canadian Charter of Rights and Freedoms.* *v.,* **for·mu·lat·ed, for·mu·lat·ing.** —**for′mu·la′tion,** *n.*

for·sake (fôr sāk′) leave; abandon or desert: *He ran away, forsaking his home and friends.* *v.,* **for·sook, for·sak·en, for·sak·ing.**

a bat	e bed	i bid	o pot	u cup	th thin
ā cake	ē me	ī bite	ō go	ū rude	TH then
ä bar	ə about	ər over	ô for	ů put	zh measure

fort (fôrt) 1 a strong building or a place surrounded by strong walls for defence against an enemy. Usually a certain number of soldiers and weapons are kept there. 2 🍁 in the early days of Canada, a trading post of the Hudson's Bay Company. *n.*
hold the fort, manage things while someone is away.

for•te (fôr′tā) 1 something that you are good at: *Cooking is Reggie's forte.* 2 in music, loud or loudly. *Symbol: f* 1 *n.,* 2 *adv.*

forth (fôrth) a somewhat formal word meaning: 1 forward; onward: *From that day forth he lived alone.* 2 out; into view: *The sun came forth from behind the clouds.* 3 away: *Go forth and seek your fortune.* *adv.*
and so forth, and so on; and the like: *We ate cake, candy, nuts, and so forth.*
back and forth, first one way and then the other.

forth•right (fôrth′rīt′) outspoken; straightforward; direct: *She was very forthright in her criticism.* *adj.*

for•ti•fy (fôr′tə fī′) 1 build forts, walls, etc.; strengthen against attack: *Many very old towns were fortified with thick stone walls.* 2 make stronger or more effective: *Breakfast cereal is often fortified with vitamins.* *v.,* **for•ti•fied, for•ti•fy•ing.** —**for′ti•fi•ca′tion,** *n.*

for•ti•tude (fôr′tə tyūd′ *or* fôr′tə tūd′) a strong, courageous spirit in facing pain, danger, or trouble. *n.*

fort•night (fôrt′nīt′) two weeks. *n.*

for•tress (fôr′tris) a large, strong, and well-protected fort. *n.*

for•tu•nate (fôr′chə nit) lucky: *a fortunate event. You were fortunate to escape without injuries.* *adj.* —**for′tu•nate•ly,** *adv.*

for•tune (fôr′chən) 1 a lot of money: *That fancy new car must have cost a fortune.* 2 what is going to happen to a person. A **fortuneteller** is someone who claims to be able to tell your fortune. 3 luck; chance; fate: *Fortune was against us; we lost.* *n.*

for•ty (fôr′tē) four times ten; 40. *n., pl.* **for•ties;** *or adj.* —**for′ti•eth,** *adj. or n.*
forty winks, a short nap.

fo•rum (fôr′əm) a gathering or a meeting place for discussing things, open to anyone who is interested. *n.*

for•ward (fôr′wərd) 1 Often, **forwards,** onward; ahead: *She strode bravely forward into the darkness.* 2 to the front: *to come forward (adv.), the forward part of a ship (adj.).* 3 send on to another place or person: *to forward a letter.* 4 in certain games, a player whose position is in the front line. 5 too bold; too quick to speak or act: *It is rude to be so forward.* 1, 2 *adv.,* 2, 5 *adj.,* 3 *v.,* 4 *n.*

This fossil is an ammonite, the hardened shell of a sea creature that became extinct. Millions of years ago, the creature died and sank to the bottom of the sea. Gradually it became covered in protective sand and other material. This slowly hardened into rock, preserving the creature's shell.

fos•sil (fos′əl) the remains of animals or plants that lived very long ago, preserved in rocks. Fossils of ferns are sometimes found in coal. Bone fossils and fossil footprints of dinosaurs have been discovered in Alberta. *n.*

fossil fuel (fos′əl fyū′əl) a fuel that results from the very slow decay of dead plants or animals over many millions of years. Coal and oil are fossil fuels.

fos•sil•ize (fos′ə līz′) 1 become a fossil. 2 completely stop changing or developing: *Over the years the business had fossilized.* *v.,* **fos•sil•ized, fos•sil•iz•ing.** —**fos′sil•i•za′tion,** *n.*

fos•ter (fos′tər) 1 help something to grow and develop: *to foster good work habits.* 2 care for as one's own for a time: *to foster a child until he or she is adopted.* 3 having to do with this kind of arrangement: *a foster child, foster parents, a foster home.* 1, 2 *v.,* 3 *adj.*

fought (fot) the past tense and past participle of **fight:** *She fought bravely against giving up. A battle was fought there.* *v.*

foul (foul) 1 very dirty or disgusting: *foul water, a foul smell.* 2 make dirty or polluted; clog: *Exhaust fumes foul the air. Hair has fouled the drain.* 3 unfair; against the rules: *to play foul (adv.), foul play (adj.).* **Foul play** can also mean dishonest or criminal behaviour. 4 in baseball, falling outside the **foul lines,** the lines that join first and third base to home plate: *to hit a foul ball (adj.).* 5 stormy: *foul weather.* 1, 3–5 *adj.,* 3, 4 *adv.,* 2 *v.*
foul up, make a mess of; bungle.

found[1] (found) 1 the past tense and past participle of **find:** *We found the treasure. The lost child was found.* 2 having to do with things discovered in nature and used in an artistic way. A found object can be made into a piece of art, or used as a musical instrument. 1 *v.,* 2 *adj.*

found² (found) set up; establish: *Québec City was founded by Champlain in 1608.* *v.* —**found′er,** *n.*

foun•da•tion (foun dā′shən) **1** the bottom of a building; the part that serves as a base for the walls: *The foundation of the house was entirely underground.* **2** the basis of a belief, idea, argument, etc.: *This report has no foundation in fact. Trust is the foundation of all friendship.* **3** the act of founding or establishing: *The foundation of King's College, Nova Scotia, took place in 1788.* **4** an organization set up to support some cause. *n.*

found•ry (foun′drē) a place where metal is melted and made into things. *n., pl.* **found•ries.**

foun•tain (foun′tən) **1** a stream or spray of water rising into the air, either naturally from the earth or through a pipe in a statue or pool used as a decoration. **2** a device that sends up a little arc of water so that people may get a drink: *a drinking fountain.* **3** source: *Your parents can be a fountain of information.* **Fount** is another form for this meaning. *n.*

fountain pen (foun′tən pen′) a pen that uses liquid ink from a container inside it. Because the ink is liquid instead of a paste, it takes some skill to write without blotting and smudging.

four (fôr) one more than three; 4: *A dog has four legs* (*adj.*). *n. or adj.* —**fourth,** *adj. or n.*
on all fours, a on all four feet. **b** on hands and knees.

four•score (fôr′skôr′) four times twenty; 80. *adj. or n.*

four•teen (fôrt′tēn′) four more than ten; 14. *n. or adj.* —**four′teenth′,** *adj. or n.*

four–wheel drive (fôr′ hwēl′ drīv′) a system in a car or truck where the power is sent to all four wheels at once, making them grip better on snow, mud, or ice.

fowl (foul) **1** any bird: *a water fowl.* **2** a large bird raised for its meat and eggs: *Chickens, ducks, geese, etc. are fowl.* *n., pl.* **fowl** or **fowls.**

red fox

Foxes are found all over the world, except in Antarctica and southeast Asia.

fox (foks) **1** a wild animal that looks like a small dog. It has pointed ears and nose and a long bushy tail. It is sometimes hunted for its fur. **2** a sly or crafty person; a trickster. *n.* —**fox′y,** *adj.*

foy•er (foi′ā) an open area just inside the entrance to a large building. *n.*

frac•tion (frak′shən) **1** one or more of the equal parts of a whole number: ½, ¼, and ¾ are fractions. **2** a very small part or amount: *He has done only a fraction of his homework. Turn it up just a fraction.* *n.*

frac•ture (frak′chər) break or crack: *a fracture in the earth's crust* (*n.*). *The boy fell from a tree and fractured his arm* (*v.*). *The X ray showed where the fracture was* (*n.*). *n. or v.,* **frac•tured, frac•tur•ing.**

frag•ile (fraj′īl *or* fraj′əl) easily broken or damaged; delicate: *Be careful; that thin glass is fragile.* *adj.*

frag•ment (frag′mənt *for 1,* frag ment′ *for 2*) **1** a broken or incomplete part: *fragments of a broken clay pot. She could only remember fragments of the story.* **2** break into bits: *Arguments among the different language groups had fragmented the country.* 1 *n.,* 2 *v.*

fra•grant (frā′grənt) sweet-smelling, like perfume or flowers: *I picked a fragrant rose.* *adj.* —**fra′grance,** *n.*

frail (frāl) not strong; weak; not able to bear much stress: *Grandma has become quite frail since her illness. Careful; that branch is frail.* *adj.* —**frail′ty,** *n.*

frame (frām) **1** a supporting structure over which something is stretched or built: *the frame of a house. The frame was all that remained of the old car left to rust in the field.* **Framework** is another word for it. **2** a person's body shape: *The wrestler had a heavy frame.* **3** the solid border that holds a thing placed into it: *a window frame, a picture frame, glasses frames.* **4** put a border or frame around: *to frame a picture. A tall figure stood framed in the doorway.* **5** one of the small pictures that make up a film or a comic strip. **6** plan or put together. **7** try to make someone appear guilty: *The real criminal tried to frame someone else.* 1, 2, 3, 5 *n.,* 4, 6, 7 *v.,* **framed, fram•ing.**
frame of mind, mood or attitude: *He woke up in an irritable frame of mind.*

fran•chise (fran′chīz) **1** the right to sell or operate something in the name of a particular business or the government: *She got a franchise from the Hot'n'Fresh pizza chain to open a store in her town.* **2** the right to vote. *n.*

Fran•co•phone or **fran•co•phone** (frangk′ə fōn′) a person whose first or main language is French, living in a bilingual or multilingual country, especially Canada. *n.*

a bat	e bed	i bid	o pot	u cup	th thin
ā cake	ē me	ī bite	ō go	ū rude	ᴛʜ then
ä bar	ə about	ər over	ô for	ů put	zh measure

frank (frangk) completely honest; openly saying just what you think or feel: *To be very frank, I find that music boring.* *adj.* —**frank′ly,** *adv.* —**frank′ness,** *n.*

frank·furt·er (frangk′fər tər) wiener. *n.*

frank·in·cense (frangk′in sens′) a resin that gives off a sweet, spicy odour when burned. It comes from trees that grow in Africa and Asia. *n.*

fran·tic (fran′tik) wild; so rushed, excited, anxious, upset, etc. that you are out of control: *He made frantic motions to stop the approaching car. The mother was frantic when her baby was stolen.* *adj.* —**fran′ti·cal·ly,** *adv.*

fra·ter·nal (frə tėr′nəl) 1 brotherly. 2 **fraternal twins,** twins that develop from two separate egg cells. They can be of opposite sexes and look different. *adj.*

fraud (frod) 1 dishonest dealing; cheating; trickery: *using counterfeit money is a form of fraud.* 2 a phony person or thing. *n.* —**fraud′u·lent** (frod′jə lənt), *adj.*

fraught (frot) loaded or filled with something bad: *Your plan is fraught with difficulty.* *adj.*

fray[1] (frā) a fight; a noisy quarrel. *n.*

fray[2] (frā) 1 separate into threads; make or become ragged or worn along the edge: *Long wear had frayed the collar and cuffs of his old shirt.* 2 wear away; rub. *v.*

freak (frēk) 1 something very strange or abnormal: *A green leaf growing in the middle of a rose would be called a freak of nature.* 2 *Slang.* someone extremely enthusiastic about a certain thing: *a health freak, a hockey freak.* 3 *Slang.* Often, **freak out,** react in an extreme way: *He freaked when I told him our family was moving.* *n.* —**freak′ish,** *adj.* —**freak′y,** *adj.*

freck·le (frek′əl) a small, light brown spot on the skin. *n.* —**freck′led,** *adj.* —**freck′ly,** *adj.*

free (frē) 1 loose; not fastened or shut up: *The hens were allowed to run free in the yard.* 2 not under the control of some other person or thing: *free speech, free nations.* 3 with no cost: *Children under 12 attend free (adv.). These tickets are free (adj.).* 4 **free of** or **free from,** without: *free from fear, air free of dust.* This meaning often occurs in compounds like *sugar-free, hassle-free.* 5 make free; allow to be free: *They had trouble freeing the boat from the weeds. The prisoner was freed early for good behaviour.* 6 not holding back: *He is always free with money. She was a little too free in telling others about her troubles.* 1–4, 6 *adj.,* **fre·er, fre·est;** 3 *adv.,* 5 *v.,* **freed, free·ing.** —**free′ly,** *adv.* —**free′dom,** *n.*
free and easy, relaxed; caring little for rules and customs: *He is pretty free and easy for a school principal.*

free·hand (frē′hand′) by hand without using instruments, measurements, etc.: *freehand drawing (adj.), to draw something freehand (adv.).* *adj. or adv.*

free verse (frē′ vėrs′) poetry that does not have a fixed rhythm or rhyme scheme.

free·way (frē′wā′) especially in the United States, a high-speed highway where no toll is charged. *n.*

freeze (frēz) 1 turn into ice: *Water freezes at 0°C.* 2 cause something to become hard and stiff by lowering the temperature to below 0°C so that all the water in it turns to ice: *We freeze meat to keep it from spoiling. In the Far North the ground is permanently frozen.* 3 feel very cold: *Turn up the heat. I'm freezing!* 4 use a drug to make a part of the body numb, usually to lessen pain: *The dentist froze my gums before filling the tooth.* 5 become motionless, usually because of fear: *The mouse froze as the snake moved toward it.* 6 stop all change or progress in something: *to freeze wages or prices. Work on the new subway has been frozen until more funds become available.* 7 the fact of freezing: *The freeze last night damaged the apple trees.* 1–6 *v.,* **froze, fro·zen, freez·ing;** 7 *n.*

freez·er (frē′zər) a refrigerator cabinet for storing food at a temperature below freezing. *n.*

🍁 **freeze–up** (frē′zup′) the time of year when the rivers and lakes freeze over; the start of winter. *n.*

freight (frāt) 1 cargo; the things carried by a ship or train: *It took a whole day to unload the freight.* A ship that carries mainly cargo is a **freighter.** 2 the system of carrying goods on a train, ship, or aircraft: *He sent the box by freight.* 3 the price paid for this. *n.*

French (french) 1 the people of France. 2 one of the official languages of Canada. It is also spoken in many other countries. 3 having to do with this language, or with France or its people. 1, 2 *n.,* 3 *adj.*

French doors (french′ dôrz′) a pair of glass doors with wood frames, leading outside or into another room.

French fries (french′ frīz′) strips of potato fried in deep fat until brown and crisp on the outside.

French horn (french′ hôrn′) a brass wind instrument that has a mellow tone.

French toast (french′ tōst′) sliced bread that is soaked in a mixture of milk and eggs and then fried, usually eaten with syrup for breakfast.

fren·zy (fren′zē) a state of being nearly crazy with pain, grief, excitement, anger, etc.: *He was in a frenzy of grief when he heard of his daughter's death. The spectators* *were in a frenzy after the home team finally scored.* *n.* **—fren′zied,** *adj.*

fre·quen·cy (frē′kwən sē) **1** how often something happens: *The flashes of light came with a frequency of three per minute. The doctors were worried by the frequency of his heart attacks.* **2** the number of times that a wave is sent through the air each second. Each radio and television station broadcasts at a different frequency. In music, the higher the frequency of vibration, the higher the pitch of the note. *n., pl.* **fre·quen·cies.**

fre·quent (frē′kwənt *for 1,* fri kwent′ *for 2*) **1** happening often: *Storms are frequent in March.* **2** go to often: *Frogs frequent ponds and marshes.* 1 *adj.,* 2 *v.* **—fre′quent·ly,** *adv.*

WORD HISTORY.....frequent

Frequent comes from the Latin word *frequens,* meaning "crowded." So, the meaning of the word **frequent** has shifted from space to time!

fresh (fresh) **1** just made or received: *fresh bread, fresh news.* **2** not frozen, canned, or pickled: *fresh corn.* **3** not salty: *There is fresh water in the Great Lakes.* **4** not tired out: *I felt much fresher after my nap.* **5** clean: *a fresh shirt, fresh air.* **6** cool: *It's a bit fresh out there this morning.* **7** *Slang.* disrespectful; too bold: *fresh talk.* *adj.* **—fresh′ness,** *n.* **—fresh′ly,** *adv.* **—fresh′en,** *v.*
be fresh out of, have just used or sold the last of: *Sorry, we're fresh out of pineapple juice.*
freshen up, do something to make, or feel, fresh: *He freshened up by taking a bath and changing his clothes.*

fresh·wa·ter (fresh′wot′ər) of or living in water that is not salty: *The pickerel is a freshwater fish.* *adj.*

fret[1] (fret) **1** worry or fuss, especially about little things: *She frets over every little mistake.* **2** a condition of worry or discontent: *Don't get in such a fret about it! Relax!* 1 *v.,* 2 *n.,* **fret·ted, fret·ting.** **—fret′ful,** *adj.*

fret[2] (fret) one of the ridges on the neck of a guitar, banjo, etc. showing where to put your fingers. *n.*

fri·ar (frī′ər) a Roman Catholic monk. Only the monks of certain orders are called friars. *n.*

fric·tion (frik′shən) **1** a rubbing of one thing against another, such as skate blades on ice, a match being struck, or the brakes on a bicycle wheel. The greater the friction, the slower or more difficult the motion becomes: *Oil reduces friction in engines.* **2** conflict; disagreement: *Political differences continued to cause friction between the two countries.* *n.*

Fri·day (frī′dā′) the day after Thursday and before Saturday. *Abbreviation:* Fri. *n.*
person Friday, a helper who does all kinds of little jobs.

fridge (frij) *Informal.* refrigerator. *n.*

friend (frend) **1** a person who knows and likes you. **2** a supporter: *a friend to the poor.* *n.* **—friend′less,** *adj.* **—friend′ship,** *n.* **—friend·ly,** *adj.*

fries (frīz) strips of potato cooked in deep fat until crisp on the outside. **French fries** is the full name. *pl.n.*

frieze (frēz) a band of decoration around a room, building, etc. A frieze may be painted or carved. *n.*

fright (frīt) **1** sudden great fear: *The boy was pale with fright when he looked over the edge of the cliff.* **2** *Informal.* a person or thing that is ugly, shocking, or ridiculous: *She looked a fright in that outfit.* *n.*
take fright, become frightened.

fright·en (frī′tən) make afraid. *v.*

fright·ful (frīt′fəl) terrible or very big: *a frightful thunderstorm, a frightful mess.* *adj.*

frig·id (frij′id) **1** very cold: *a frigid climate.* **2** very unfriendly: *a frigid stare.* *adj.*

frill (fril) **1** ruffle; a fancy, bunchy strip of lace or cloth trim on a piece of clothing, curtain, etc. **2** something extra that is nice but useless: *It was a plain house with few frills.* *n.* **—frill′y,** *adj.*

fringe (frinj) **1** a hanging border or trimming made of threads, cords, etc., either loose or tied together in small bunches: *The chesterfield had a fringe along the bottom edge.* **2** be a border for; border: *Long grass fringed the road.* 1 *n.,* 2 *v.,* **fringed, fring·ing.**

Fris·bee (friz′bē) *a trademark for* a piece of plastic shaped like a plate with a rim on it. It is thrown back and forth as a game. *n.*

frisk (frisk) **1** run and jump around playfully: *Our lively puppy frisks all over the house.* **2** search a person for hidden weapons, stolen goods, etc. by running a hand quickly over his or her clothes. *v.* **—frisk′y,** *adj.*

frit·ter[1] (frit′ər) waste little by little: *He frittered away the afternoon trying to decide what to do.* *v.*

frit·ter[2] (frit′ər) a sort of doughnut without a hole, usually containing fruit: *apple fritters.* *n.*

a bat	e bed	i bid	o pot	u cup	th thin
ā cake	ē me	ī bite	ō go	ū rude	ᴛʜ then
ä bar	ə about	ər over	ô for	ù put	zh measure

Frogs

The main power for a frog's leap comes from the strong muscles in its hips and thighs.

common tree frog

green tree frog

There are several hundred kinds of tree frog, many of which live in North America. They are usually less than 5 cm long.

friv·o·lous (friv′ə ləs) silly; not serious or sensible: *Don't waste your money on such frivolous things.* *adj.* —**friv′o·lous·ly,** *adv.*

friz·zy (friz′ē) full of tiny curls: *frizzy hair.* *adj.,* **friz′**zi·er, **friz′**zi·est.

fro (frō)
to and fro, first one way and then back again; back and forth: *A rocking chair goes to and fro.* *adv.*

frog (frog) a small, leaping animal with webbed feet that lives in water and on land: *Frogs hatch from eggs as tadpoles, living in the water till they grow legs.* *n.*
frog in your throat, *Informal.* a slight hoarseness.

frol·ic (frol′ik) **1** play around joyfully; have fun together: *The children frolicked with the puppy.* **2** a time of lively, happy play or fun. 1 *v.,* **frol·icked, frol·ick·ing;** 2 *n.* —**frol′ic·some,** *adj.*

frond (frond) the leaf of a fern or of a palm tree. *n.*

front (frunt) **1** the side, part, or end that faces forward, or the part that is at the beginning: *She spilled milk down the front of her dress. The picture is near the front of the book.* **2** the land facing a lake, an ocean, a street, etc. This sense is often in compounds: *lakefront, harbourfront.* **3** a fake surface or appearance hiding what is underneath: *a stone front on a wooden house. She turned out to be really nasty—that friendly welcome was just a front.* **4** in war, the place where fighting is going on: *The doctor spent many weeks at the front.* **5** on or in the front; at the front: *a front door.* **6** have the front toward; face: *Our house fronts on the river.* **7** the surface where two air masses meet: *The weather report says there is a cold front approaching from the northwest.* 1–4, 7 *n.,* 5 *adj.,* 6 *v.*
eyes front! look forward! direct the eyes ahead!
in front of, a closer to the front than: *Sit in front of me.* **b** in the presence or sight of: *to argue in front of guests.*

fron·tier (fron tēr′) **1** the edge of settled country, where the wild or unknown part begins: *Life can be rough on the frontier.* **2** the border between two countries. *n.*

frost (frost) **1** a condition of freezing; temperatures below 0°C: *The plants were killed by a heavy frost.* **2** moisture from the air that has frozen on a solid surface, often looking like feathery crystals of ice: *frost on the grass, frost on the windows.* **3** cover with frost. **4** cover with a sweet, creamy mixture that hardens, called **frosting** or icing: *to frost a cake.* 1, 2 *n.,* 3, 4 *v.* —**frost′y,** *adj.*

frost·bite (frost′bīt′) the freezing of some part of the body, such as the toes. *n.* —**frost′bit′ten,** *adj.*

froth (froth) **1** a mass of very small bubbles; foam: *If you shake a can of pop it turns to froth.* **2** produce foam: *An animal with rabies will froth at the mouth.* 1 *n.,* 2 *v.*

frown (froun) **1** draw your eyebrows together so that the skin between them wrinkles, showing anger or deep thought: *He frowned with annoyance.* **2** the act of frowning: *She answered him with a frown.* 1 *n.,* 2 *v.*
frown on, disapprove of: *Many people frown on gambling.*

froze (frōz) the past tense of **freeze.** The past participle is **frozen:** *The deer froze in the car headlights. The water in the pond has frozen.* *v.*

fru·gal (frū′gəl) 1 not wasting anything; using or spending as little as possible: *A frugal housekeeper never throws out leftovers.* 2 very simple and barely enough: *He ate a frugal supper of bread and milk.* *adj.*

WORD HISTORY........frugal

Did you know that **frugal** is related to fruit? It came from the Latin *frugalis*, meaning "getting the best value," which in turn is from *fruges*, which means "fruit," and also means "profit" or "value."

fruit (frūt) 1 a sweet product of a plant, used for food. Apples, berries, and grapes are fruits. 2 in science, the part of a plant that contains the seed, such as a tomato, acorn, or milkweed pod. 3 the product or result of anything, especially a good one: *Her invention was the fruit of much effort.* *n.*
—fruit′y, *adj.*

Word Family.........fruit

fruitcake: a rich cake containing dried fruit and spices
fruitful: producing a lot
fruitless: having no results; unsuccessful
fruity: tasting or smelling like fruit

frus·trate (frus′trāt) 1 defeat; keep from being successful or from coming true: *Heavy rains frustrated our plans for a picnic.* 2 fill with disappointment and anger because things have not worked out as desired. *v.,* **frus·trat·ed, frus·trat·ing.** **—frus·tra′tion,** *n.*

fry¹ (frī) 1 cook in hot fat, in a deep or shallow pan: *She is frying potatoes.* 2 a social gathering where some special fried food is served: *a fish fry.* 1 *v.,* **fried, fry·ing;** 2 *n., pl.* **fries.**

fry² (frī) 1 young fish. 2 small adult fish, such as sardines, that swim in large groups or schools. *n.*
small fry, a children: *This movie is not for small fry.* **b** people or things thought to be unimportant.

frying pan (frī′ing pan′) a shallow pan with a long handle, used for frying food.
out of the frying pan into the fire, straight from one danger or difficulty into a worse one.

ft. *abbreviation for* 1 foot or feet, a nonmetric unit of length. 2 **Ft.,** Fort, in names: *Ft. Simpson, N.W.T.*

fudge (fuj) 1 a soft candy made of sugar, milk, butter, and a flavouring such as chocolate or caramel. 2 *Informal.* not be completely honest about: *to fudge the facts.* 1 *n.,* 2 *v.,* **fudged, fudg·ing.**

fu·el (fyū′əl) 1 something burned to keep a fire going or provide power, such as wood, gas, or oil. 2 supply with fuel; keep something going: *This stove is fuelled by kerosene. Hate is fuelled by prejudice.* 1 *n.,* 2 *v.,* **fu·elled** or **fu·eled, fu·el·ling** or **fu·el·ing.**

fu·gi·tive (fyū′jə tiv) 1 a person who is running away: *The murderer became a fugitive from justice.* 2 running away: *a fugitive slave.* 1 *n.,* 2 *adj.*

–ful *a suffix meaning:* 1 full of; showing, as in *cheerful* or *careful.* 2 the amount that fills, as in *cupful.*

ful·crum (fůl′krəm *or* ful′krəm) the support on which a lever turns or rests when moving or lifting something. *n., pl.* **ful·crums** or **ful·cra** (ful′krə).

ful·fill or **ful·fil** (fůl fil′) 1 carry out or perform; do: *to fulfill a command.* 2 cause to come true: *to fulfill a promise, to fulfill a hope.* 3 satisfy a need or desire: *The house was small, but it fulfilled their needs.* *v.,* **ful·filled, ful·fill·ing.** **—ful·fill′ment** or **ful·fil′ment,** *n.*

full (fůl) 1 that can hold no more: *a full cup.* 2 complete; entire: *in full uniform. We waited a full hour.* 3 plump; round; well filled out: *a full face.* 4 with loose, wide folds or a lot of cloth: *a full skirt.* 5 squarely; directly: *The ball hit him full in the face.* 6 an old word for "very": *I know that full well.* 1–4 *adj.,* 5, 6 *adv.*
—ful′ly, *adv.*
full blast, as loud, as fast, as hot, etc. as possible; with all the power available. **Full steam** has a similar meaning.
full of, filled with: *Her room is full of toys.*
in full, to the whole amount: *paid in full.*
to the full, one hundred percent: *He enjoys life to the full.*

WORD HISTORY.....full blast

This is originally a term used about heavy industrial furnaces. A strong draft, or **blast**, of air is blown in through the bottom of the furnace to make the fire burn very hot, so it could melt metal. A furnace that was burning as hot as it could, with the strongest draft, was said to be at **full blast**.

full·fledged (fůl′flejd′) fully developed: *In no time at all they had a fullfledged business going.* *adj.*

full–grown (fůl′grōn′) adult: *a full-grown dog.* *adj.*

full moon (fůl′ mūn′) the moon seen as a whole circle.

a bat	e bed	i bid	o pot	u cup	th thin
ā cake	ē me	ī bite	ō go	ū rude	ᴛʜ then
ä bar	ə about	ər over	ȯ for	ů put	zh measure

full time (fu̇l′ tīm′) all the regular working hours in a week: *He works full time in a bank.* —**full′-time′,** *adj.*

fum·ble (fum′bəl) **1** feel or grope around clumsily; search awkwardly: *He fumbled in the darkness for the doorknob. She fumbled for words to express her thanks.* **2** handle or do awkwardly; let something drop instead of catching and holding it: *The first baseman fumbled the ball, and two runs were scored. I fumbled my speech.* **3** the act of fumbling: *After a few fumbles she got better at catching.* 1, 2 *v.,* **fum·bled, fum·bling;** 3 *n.*

fume (fyūm) **1 fumes,** *pl.* vapour, gas, or smoke, especially if harmful or strong-smelling: *The strong fumes of the acid nearly choked him.* **2** complain angrily; be angry: *He fumed about the traffic jam.* 1 *n.,* 2, 3 *v.,* **fumed, fum·ing.**

fu·mi·gate (fyū′mə gāt′) spray with poisonous fumes in order to kill bugs: *They fumigate our apartment building every year.* *v.,* **fu·mi·gat·ed, fu·mi·gat·ing.**

fun (fun) playfulness; enjoyment or entertainment; a good time: *They had a lot of fun at the party.* *n.*
in fun, as a joke; teasingly.
make fun of, laugh at.

func·tion (fungk′shən) **1** what something does or is meant to do; purpose; use: *The function of the stomach is to digest food.* **2** work; operate; act: *This table functions as my desk. This old fountain pen does not function very well.* **3** a formal gathering for some purpose: *The mayor gets invited to a lot of public functions; today she was at the opening ceremony for a new library.* 1, 3 *n.,* 2 *v.*

fund (fund) **1** a sum of money set aside for a certain purpose, often managed by a special organization: *Our school has a fund to buy books with. He works for the International Children's Relief Fund.* **2** a supply ready for use: *There is a fund of knowledge in a dictionary.* **3 funds,** *pl.* money: *She used up her allowance and is low in funds.* **4** supply the money for: *The provincial government is funding this tree-planting project.* Raising money is called **fundraising.** 1–3 *n.,* 4 *v.*

fun·da·men·tal (fun′də men′təl) **1** forming a foundation to build on; basic; essential: *a fundamental idea.* **2** a basic or essential part: *the fundamentals of mathematics.* 1 *adj.,* 2 *n.*

fu·ner·al (fyū′nə rəl) a ceremony honouring a person who has just died, often including a religious service. It may be arranged by a **funeral home,** a business that prepares dead bodies for burial or cremation and that has rooms for visiting or holding services. *n.*

fun·gi·cide (fun′jə sīd′ *or* fung′gə sīd′) a chemical that kills unwanted fungi or mould. *n.*

fun·gus (fung′gəs) a plant that has no flowers, leaves, or chlorophyl: *Mushrooms, toadstools, moulds, and mildews are fungi.* *n., pl.* **fun·gi** (fung′gī *or* fung′gē, fun′jī *or* fun′jē) or **fun·gus·es.**

fun·nel (fun′əl) **1** a cone-shaped container ending in a tube with a hole at the bottom, used for pouring something through a small opening: *He used a funnel to pour the salt into the shaker.* **2** pour through a funnel; cause to go from a wide place into a small one, or from many places into just one: *There was a jam because all the cars leaving the parking lot had to be funnelled through one exit.* **3** the smokestack or chimney on a steamship or steam engine. 1, 3 *n.,* 2 *v.,* **fun·nelled** or **fun·neled, fun·nel·ling** or **fun·nel·ing.**

fun·ny (fun′ē) **1** making you laugh: *a funny clown, a funny story.* **2** *Informal.* strange; peculiar; odd: *funny behaviour.* **3 funnies,** *pl.* the comic strip section of a newspaper. 1, 2 *adj.,* **fun·ni·er, fun·ni·est;** 3 *n.*

fur (fər) **1** the soft covering of hair on the skin of many animals. **2** Usually, **furs,** *pl.* coats, etc. made of fur: *a store that sells furs.* *n.* —**fur′ry,** *adj.*
make the fur fly, fight or work with great energy.

fu·ri·ous (fyū′rē əs) **1** wild; raging; extremely energetic: *a furious storm, furious efforts.* **2** very angry: *Dad was furious about the broken window.* *adj.*

furl (fərl) roll up: *to furl a sail, to furl a flag.* *v.*

fur·long (fər′long) a nonmetric measure of length equal to ⅛ of a mile, or about 200 m. *n.*

fur·lough (fər′lō) a long break; a time away from work, especially for a soldier or a missionary. *n.*

fur·nace (fər′nis) large metal box or cylinder with a fire in it to provide heat. A furnace in a building burns oil or natural gas and heats air or water. The hot air or water is then sent through pipes and radiators, hot-air registers, etc. There are also furnaces for melting metal. *n.*

fur·nish (fər′nish) **1** supply; provide: *to furnish a school with sports equipment. The sun furnishes heat and light.* **2** put furniture in: *to furnish a bedroom.* *v.*

fur·ni·ture (fər′nə chər) chairs, tables, beds, desks, cabinets, and other large movable objects used in homes and offices. Smaller things such as shelves, lamps, curtains, and so on, are called **furnishings.** *n.*

fur·row (fər′ō) **1** the long, narrow track dug in the soil by a plough. **2** a deep wrinkle. **3** make furrows in: *a face furrowed with age.* 1, 2 *n.,* 3 *v.*

fur·ther (fər′ᴛʜər) **1** a greater distance away: *on the further side (adj.). It was too dark to go further (adv.).* **2** more: *Do you need further help (adj.)? We will discuss the matter further tomorrow (adv.).* **3** help something toward success: *to further a plan, to further a goal.* **4** Usually, **furthermore,** besides: *I can't go; and furthermore, I don't want to.* 1, 2 *adj.,* 3 *v.,* 1, 2, 4 *adv.*

fur·thest (fər′ᴛʜist) at or to the greatest distance in space or time: *Cut down the furthest tree in the first row (adj.). Of all the family, Grandfather can remember furthest back in the past (adv.).* *adj. or adv.*

fur·tive (fər′tiv) stealthy or sneaky; secret; trying not to be seen: *He made a furtive attempt to read his sister's letter.* *adj.* —**fur′tive·ly,** *adv.*

fu·ry (fyū′rē) **1** a wild fit of anger; rage. **2** violent force or energy: *the fury of a hurricane.* *n., pl.* **fu·ries.**

fuse[1] (fyūz) **1** a part in an electric circuit, specially designed to melt if the current becomes dangerously strong. Its melting breaks the circuit. **2** melt or grow together: *The heat had fused the wires. The two stems had fused into one.* **3** blend; unite: *to fuse two different styles of art.* 1 *n.,* 2, 3 *v.,* **fused, fus·ing.** —**fu′sion,** *n.*
blow a fuse, a cause a fuse to melt and break an electric circuit. **b** lose your temper; get very angry.

fuse[2] (fyūz) a slow-burning wick attached to an explosive, giving a person time to move a safe distance away after lighting it: *Firecrackers have fuses.* *n.*
have a short fuse, have a quick temper; get angry easily.

fu·se·lage (fyū′zə läzh′ *or* fyū′zə lij) the body of an airplane. *n.*

fuss (fus) **1** a lot of bother, often about something unimportant; excited talk, activity, complaining, or worry: *There was a great deal of fuss about the lost dime.* **2** make a fuss: *Stop fussing about the time; we're only a minute late!* **3** fiddle around with something, trying to get it just right: *He spent five minutes fussing with his tie.* 1 *n.,* 2, 3 *v.*

fuss·y (fus′ē) **1** hard to please; insisting on everything being just right: *She is very fussy about colour.* **2** very fancy and detailed: *a fussy dress with bows, ruffles, and lace.* *adj.,* **fuss·i·er, fuss·i·est.**

fu·tile (fyū′tīl *or* fyū′təl) not successful; useless: *a futile attempt.* *adj.* —**fu·til′i·ty** (fyū til′ə tē), *n.*

fu·ton (fū′ton *or* fyū′ton) a mattress like a big padded cushion, often spread on a wooden frame to make a sofa or bed. Futons can be folded or rolled up. *n.*

fu·ture (fyū′chər) **1** the time to come; what is going to happen: *You cannot change the past, but you can do better in the future.* **2** coming; that will be: *future days, your future career.* **3** short for or having to do with the **future tense,** a verb form that expresses action in the future. In English it uses the auxiliary verbs **will** and **shall.** *Example: I will see you next week.* 1, 2 *n.,* 2, 3 *adj.*

fu·tur·is·tic (fyū′chə ris′tik) having to do with things as people imagine them to be far in the future: *a futuristic building design, a futuristic film.* *adj.*

fuzz (fuz) light, loose fibres or hairs that feel like short, soft fur: *Some caterpillars are covered with fuzz.* *n.*

fuzz·y (fuz′ē) **1** covered with fuzz or like fuzz: *a fuzzy teddy bear, fuzzy hair.* **2** not clear; blurry or hazy; vague and not exact: *a fuzzy outline, a fuzzy idea.* *adj.,* **fuzz·i·er, fuzz·i·est.**

Gg

g or **G** (jē) **1** the seventh letter of the English alphabet, or any speech sound that it stands for. The sound of *g* in *get* is different from the sound of *g* in *giant.* **2** the seventh thing in a list. **3** in music: **a** a note. On a keyboard it is the white note between F and A. **b** a scale or key that has G as its home note. *n., pl.* **g's** or **G's.**

g *symbol for* gram or grams.

gab (gab) *Informal.* chat; talk. *n. or v.,* **gabbed, gab·bing.** **—gab′by,** *adj.*

gab·ble (gab′əl) chatter with no sense: *to gabble foolishly* (*v.*), *such meaningless gabble* (*n.*), *n. or v.,* **gab·bled, gab·bling.**

ga·ble (gā′bəl) the end of a peaked roof, with the triangular piece of wall that it covers. *n.*

gadg·et (gaj′it) a small machine or tool, especially one that seems fancy or not necessary. *n.*

Gael·ic (gā′lik) **1** the language of the Celtic people of Scotland, Wales, or Ireland. **2** having to do with these people or their language. 1 *n.,* 2 *adj.*

gag (gag) **1** something put in or over a person's mouth to keep him or her from talking. **2** stop up someone's mouth in this way: *The bandits tied the watchman's arms and gagged him.* **3** almost vomit; choke: *The strong, horrible smell made me gag.* **4** *Informal.* a joke. 1, 4 *n.,* 2, 3 *v.,* **gagged, gag·ging.**

gai·ly (gā′lē) merrily or happily; brightly: *gaily dressed, to laugh gaily.* *adv.*

gain (gān) **1** get or win: *to gain someone's trust, to gain a clear understanding.* **2** end up with more than you started with: *I have gained two kilos this year. We gained $437 by the chocolate sale.* **3** something gained; the amount gained: *a gain in speed, a gain of ten percent.* **4** make progress; improve: *The sick child is gaining in strength.* **5** reach: *The swimmer gained the shore.* **6** of a clock or watch, run fast: *My watch gains about ten minutes a week.* 1, 2, 4–6 *v.,* 3 *n.* **—gain′ful,** *adj.*

gain on, catch up to: *The Canadian speed skater is gaining on the American.*

gait (gāt) a particular way of walking or running: *a lame gait. A gallop is one of the gaits of a horse.* *n.*

gal. *abbreviation for* gallon or gallons.

ga·la (gal′ə *or* gā′lə) **1** a festive occasion; a big party or celebration. **2** festive: *a gala dinner.* 1 *n.,* 2 *adj.*

gal·ax·y (gal′ək sē) a very large number of stars forming one system: *The Milky Way is the galaxy that contains the earth, our sun, and the other planets in our solar system.* *n., pl.* **gal·ax·ies.**

gale (gāl) **1** a very strong wind. **2** a noisy outburst: *gales of laughter.* *n.*

gall[1] (gol) **1** a bitter liquid made in the liver to help digest food. Extra gall is stored in the **gall bladder,** attached to the liver, until needed. **2** rude boldness; nerve: *She had the gall to tell us we were not invited.* *n.*

gall[2] (gol) annoy; irritate: *It galled them to be scolded about every little thing.* *v.*

gal·lant (gal′ənt) **1** noble; brave: *They made a gallant effort to save the building.* **2** very polite and charming to women. *adj.* **—gal′lant·ry,** *n.*

Galleons had square sails on two front masts, and three-cornered sails on one or two rear masts. This meant that galleons could sail into the wind.

gal·le·on (gal′ē ən) a large Spanish sailing ship used from the 1400s to the 1700s. It had several decks. *n.*

gal·ler·y (gal′ə rē) 1 a building or room where art is displayed. 2 a balcony looking down into a large room, especially the highest balcony of a theatre: *Seats in the gallery are usually the cheapest.* *n., pl.* **gal·ler·ies.**

gal·ley (gal′ē) 1 a long ship of ancient and medieval times, with oars and sails. Roman galleys were rowed by slaves. 2 the kitchen of a ship or plane. *n., pl.* **gal·leys.**

gal·li·vant (gal′ə vant′) waste time going around from place to place looking for fun or adventure. *v.*

gal·lon (gal′ən) a nonmetric measure for liquids, equal to four quarts. It is about the same as 4.5 L. *n.*

gal·lop (gal′əp) 1 the fastest run of a horse or other four-footed animal. In a gallop, all four feet are off the ground together at each leap. 2 run or ride at a gallop: *The cowgirl galloped across the field.* 3 a ride at this speed: *We went for a gallop across the prairie.* 1, 3 *n.,* 2 *v.*

gal·lows (gal′ōz) a wooden frame made of a crossbar on an upright post, used in earlier times for hanging criminals. *n., pl.* **gal·lows** or **gal·lows·es.**

ga·lore (gə lȯr′) all over the place; in plenty: *There were flowers galore in the house.* *adj.*

ga·losh (gə losh′) Usually, **galoshes,** *pl.* rubber boots worn over shoes in wet or snowy weather. *n.*

gal·va·nize (gal′və nīz′) 1 apply an electric current to. 2 stir to swift action: *The whole city was galvanized by the threat of a hurricane.* 3 cover iron or steel with a thin coating of zinc to prevent rust. This used to be done by an electrical process. *v.,* **gal·va·nized, gal·va·niz·ing.**

gam·ble (gam′bəl) 1 play games of chance where you win or lose money. 2 take a chance in hopes that things will turn out a certain way: *We hiked the extra 4 km to her house, gambling on her being home.* 3 a risky action: *Starting up a business is a gamble.* 1, 2 *v.,* **gam·bled, gam·bling;** 3 *n.* —**gam′bler,** *n.*

game (gām) 1 something done for fun or as a way of playing: *a game of catch, an action figure game, a game of tag.* 2 an activity with certain rules, where there are winners and losers: *Our team did their best to win the baseball game. My favourite game is Scrabble™.* 3 a package containing what is needed for a game, such as a board, playing pieces, or a CD-ROM: *This store sells games.* 4 a scheme or plan: *He tried to trick us, but we saw through his game.* 5 animals and birds that are hunted. A **game warden** enforces the hunting and fishing laws in an area. 6 brave; willing to dare something: *Are you game to swim the river?* 7 gamble (def. 1). 1–5 *n.,* 6 *adj.,* **gam·er, gam·est;** 7 *v.,* **gamed, gam·ing.**

gam·ma rays (gam′ə rāz′) beams of radiant energy that have short wavelengths and can pass through solid objects. Radioactive substances give off gamma rays.

gan·der (gan′dər) 1 an adult male goose. 2 *Informal.* a look: *Take a gander at this magazine.* *n.*

gang (gang) 1 a group of people involved in crime together: *a gang of thieves, a street gang.* 2 a group of people going around together or working together as a unit: *a gang of tourists. Two gangs of workers were mending the road.* *n.*

gang up on, go together as a group against someone else: *Let's gang up on that bully.*

gan·gling (gang′gling) awkwardly tall and thin. **Gangly** has the same meaning. *adj.*

gang·plank (gang′plangk′) a movable bridge used to get on and off a ship. *n.*

gan·grene (gang′grēn) the rotting of part of a living body when the blood supply is cut off by injury, infection, freezing, etc. *n.*

gang·ster (gang′stər) a member of a gang of criminals. *n.*

gang·way (gang′wā′) 1 narrow passageway, especially on a ship: *This ship has a gangway between the rail and the cabins.* 2 *Informal.* Get out of the way, please! Stand aside and make room! 1 *n.,* 2 *interj.*

gap (gap) 1 a broken place; opening: *a gap in a fence or wall.* 2 a part missing: *My diary is not complete; there are gaps in it.* 3 a pass through mountains. This sense is mostly used in place names. 4 a wide difference in opinion, lifestyle, etc.: *the generation gap.* *n.*

gape (gāp) 1 open wide: *A deep hole gaped at our feet.* 2 stare with mouth open: *The children gaped when they saw the huge birthday cake.* *v.,* **gaped, gap·ing.**

ga·rage (gə ràzh′ *or* gə raj′) 1 a place for keeping cars. 2 a place where cars are fixed; a service station. *n.*

garage sale (gə ràzh′sāl′) an informal sale of used household items, held in a private garage or driveway.

garb (gàrb) 1 clothing. 2 clothe: *garbed in white from head to toe.* 1 *n.,* 2 *v.*

gar·bage (gàr′bij) 1 waste; trash; junk to be thrown away: *Garbage is collected weekly in our city.* 2 anything worthless: *This TV show is pure garbage.* *n.*

a bat	e bed	i bid	o pot	u cup	th thin
ā cake	ē me	ī bite	ō go	ū rude	ᴛʜ then
à bar	ə about	ər over	ȯ for	u̇ put	zh measure

gar·ble (gȧr′bəl) to say or write something in a mixed up or confusing way, sometimes by leaving out or changing important facts: *Rina garbled the report of our meeting.* *v.,* **gar·bled, gar·bling.**

gar·den (gȧr′dən) 1 a piece of ground used for growing vegetables, flowers, herbs, or fruits. A **market garden** is actually a farm where vegetables are grown for sale in markets or stores. 2 take care of a garden: *She liked to garden on weekends.* 3 a park with many trees, flower beds, fountains, paths, and so on. 1, 3 *n.,* 2 *v.* **—gar′den·er,** *n.* **—gar′den·ing,** *n.*

gar·gle (gȧr′gəl) 1 move liquid around in your throat by breathing air out through the liquid without swallowing it: *She treated her sore throat by gargling with salt water.* 2 a liquid used for gargling. 1 *v.,* **gar·gled, gar·gling;** 2 *n.*

The most famous gargoyles are on Notre Dame cathedral in Paris. Gargoyles like this one decorate the Peace Tower of the Houses of Parliament in Ottawa.

gar·goyle (gȧr′goil) an ugly stone figure decorating the outside of a large older building. *n.*

WORD HISTORY..... gargoyle

The word **gargoyle** is really the same word as "gargle." These words come from an Old French word *gargole*, meaning "throat" or "waterspout." Gargoyles were originally used to decorate the end of a spout carrying rainwater from a gutter on the edge of a roof. The water would pour out of the gargoyle's mouth.

gar·ish (ger′ish) so bright that it is ugly or hurts your eyes; glaring: *garish neon signs, the garish light of an unshaded bulb.* *adj.*

gar·land (gȧr′lənd) 1 a wreath of flowers, leaves, etc. 2 decorate with garlands. 1 *n.,* 2 *v.*

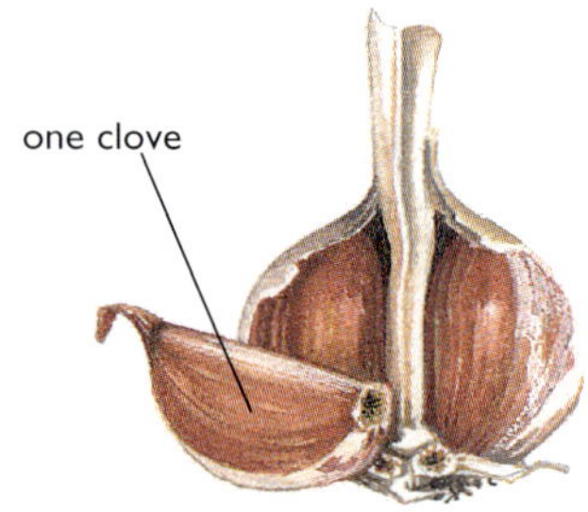

Garlic is supposed to have power to prevent some illnesses — colds, flu — and generally keep a person healthy.

gar·lic (gȧr′lik) a plant related to the onion. It grows a strong-smelling bulb that is made up of small sections called cloves. Garlic is used as a seasoning in many foods. *n.* **—gar′lick·y,** *adj.*

gar·ment (gȧr′mənt) any piece of clothing. *n.*

gar·net (gȧr′nit) a deep red semiprecious stone. *n.*

gar·nish (gȧr′nish) 1 something laid on or around food as a decoration: *a garnish of parsley.* 2 decorate food. 1 *n.,* 2 *v.*

gar·ret (ger′it) an attic; a space or room in a house just below a sloping roof. *n.*

gar·ri·son (ger′ə sən) 1 a group of soldiers stationed in a fort or town in order to defend it. 2 a town or fort where soldiers are stationed. 3 station soldiers in a fort or town to defend it. 1, 2 *n.,* 3 *v.*

gar·ter (gȧr′tər) a band or strap made of elastic and fitting around the leg to hold up a sock or a stocking. *n.*

garter snake (gȧr′tər snāk′) a small, harmless snake, brown or green with long yellow stripes on its back. Garter snakes are fairly common in North America.

gas¹ (gas) 1 vapour; any substance that is not a solid or a liquid but is like air in form. In fact, air is made up of gases. Oxygen and hydrogen are two substances that are gases at ordinary temperatures. 2 any mixture of gases that can be burned, coming from oil, coal, and other substances. Gas was once much used for lighting and is now used in some stoves and furnaces. 3 chemical vapours used for special purposes on people, animals, insects, etc.: *Laughing gas is used to lessen pain. Tear gas is sometimes used as a weapon.* 4 use such vapours on: *The police gassed the rioters.* 5 vapours made in or released from the digestive system, usually as a result of eating certain foods. 1–3, 5 *n., pl.* **gas·es;** 4 *v.,* **gassed, gas·sing.** **—gas′e·ous,** *adj.* **—gas′sy,** *adj.*

gas² (gas) 1 short for **gasoline,** the colourless liquid used as a fuel for cars, planes, tractors, etc. It comes from petroleum, and you buy it at a **gas station.**

2 supply with gasoline. 1 *n.,* 2 *v.,* **gassed, gas·sing.**
gas up, fill the tank of a motor vehicle with gasoline: *Be sure to gas up before going on a long trip.*
step on the gas, **a** push down the accelerator, or **gas pedal,** in a motor vehicle to make it go faster. **b** hurry.

gash (gash) 1 a long, deep cut or wound. 2 make a long, deep cut or wound. 1 *n.,* 2 *v.*

gasp (gasp) 1 a sudden, short breath taken in through the mouth, usually because of surprise or fear or difficulty getting enough air: *After her hard run, her breath came in gasps.* 2 breathe in in this way: *to gasp for air. He gasped in amazement at the huge icicles.* 1 *n.,* 2 *v.*

gas·tric (gas′trik) having to do with the stomach: *Gastric juices help with digestion.* *adj.*

gate (gāt) 1 a door in a fence or outside wall: *Close the gate to the backyard so the dog can't get out. The enemy soldiers broke through the castle gates.* 2 any barrier used to control the flow of people, traffic, or anything else. The barriers that go up and down at a railway crossing are often called gates. **Floodgates** control water flow. *n.*
give someone the gate, *Informal.* **a** send someone away. **b** in hockey, give a player a penalty, which puts him or her off the ice.

gate·post (gāt′pōst′) one of the posts on either side of a gate. A swinging gate is fastened to one gatepost and closes against the other. *n.*

gate·way (gāt′wā′) 1 an opening in a wall or fence with a gate across it. 2 a way in or out: *Winnipeg is known as the "Gateway to the West."* *n.*

gath·er (gaᴛʜ′ər) 1 collect; come or bring together into one place: *She gathered her books and papers and left for school. A crowd gathered at the scene of the accident.* 2 put together in the mind; figure out without being told directly: *I gathered from his tone of voice that he was very upset.* 3 pull together in folds: *The skirt is gathered at the top to fit snugly around my waist.* 4 one of the little folds made when cloth is pulled together. 1–3 *v.,* 4 *n.*

gath·er·ing (gaᴛʜ′ə ring) a meeting; a group that has come together for some purpose: *A gathering of friends welcomed the family's newly adopted daughter.* *n.*

gau·cho (gou′chō) a cowboy or herdsman in the southern plains of South America. *n.*

gaud·y (god′ē) too bright and flashy to be in good taste; cheap and showy: *The comedian wore gaudy clothes to make the audience laugh.* *adj.,* **gaud·i·er, gaud·i·est.**

gauge (gāj) 1 an instrument for measuring and showing how much: *Every car has a fuel gauge. A rain gauge is used in a weather station.* 2 measure exactly with a measuring device: *He had a special instrument to gauge the width of the metal strips.* 3 estimate; judge: *It was difficult to gauge the character of the stranger.* 4 a standard measure of the thickness or width of things like wire, railway tracks, or sheet iron. 1, 2 *n.,* 3, 4 *v.,* **gauged, gaug·ing.**

gaunt (gont) 1 very thin and bony, with sunken cheeks and eyes. 2 looking bare and gloomy; desolate; grim: *The ancient castle stood gaunt on the hilltop.* *adj.*

gaunt·let (gont′lit) 1 an iron glove that was part of a knight's armour. 2 a tough, heavy glove with a long flaring cuff, used by workers, motorcyclists, and so on to protect the hands and wrists. *n.*
throw down the gauntlet, offer a challenge. If you accept the challenge, you **take up the gauntlet.**

WORD HISTORY..... gauntlet

The word **gauntlet** means "little glove," although it's not so little! In medieval times, a knight would challenge another knight by throwing one gauntlet on the ground. If the other knight picked it up, this meant he accepted the challenge. That's where we get the expression **throw down the gauntlet**.

gauze (goz) a very thin, light cloth that is easy to see through, often used for bandages. *n.* —**gauz′y,** *adj.*

gave (gāv) the past tense of **give:** *She gave me some of her candy.* *v.*

gawk (gok) 1 *Informal.* stare rudely or stupidly: *The tourist stood gawking at the strange sights.* 2 an awkward person; clumsy fool. 1 *v.,* 2 *n.* —**gawk′y,** *adj.*

gay (gā) 1 happy and full of fun: *a gay mood.* 2 bright and lively: *gay colours.* *adj.,* **gay·er, gay·est.**

gaze (gāz) 1 look long and steadily: *We sat gazing at the fire.* 2 a long, steady look. 1 *v.,* **gazed, gaz·ing;** 2 *n.*

ga·zelle (gə zel′) a small, graceful antelope of Asia and Africa. It has large, soft eyes and a slender neck. *n.*

ga·zette (gə zet′) 1 newspaper: *the "Weekly Gazette."* 2 an official government journal containing certain public notices. *n.*

GB *abbreviation for* gigabyte, a very large unit of electronically stored information.

a bat	e bed	i bid	o pot	u cup	th thin
ā cake	ē me	ī bite	ō go	ū rude	ᴛʜ then
ä bar	ə about	ər over	ô for	ů put	zh measure

gear (gēr) 1 in a machine, a wheel with teeth that fit between the teeth on another wheel, so that one wheel turns the other. 2 one of several sets of gears that connect the motor to the wheels of a vehicle: *top gear, reverse gear.* A car in low gear moves slowly, but with a lot of power to get through mud or snow or go uphill. The lever that lets you change gears is called the **gearshift.** 3 equipment needed for some purpose, such as tools, clothing, or household goods: *She took her fishing gear on the holiday trip.* 4 adjust; design or set up to work together with something else: *The camp program is geared to the needs of disabled children.* 1–3 *n.,* 4 *v.*
gear up, a shift to a higher gear. **b** get ready to start something: *The town is gearing up for the fall fair.* **Gear down** means the opposite.
in gear, a connected to the motor. **b** working; active: *His brain is always in gear.* **Out of gear** is the opposite.

geck·o (gek′ō) a small, insect-eating lizard found in the tropics, with suction pads on its toes for climbing. Geckos sleep during the day and feed at night. *n.*

geese (gēs) plural of **goose.** *n.*

Gei·ger counter (gī′gər koun′tər) a machine that finds and measures radioactivity.

gel (jel) a very thick liquid. One kind of perfumed gel is used instead of soap in baths and showers, and another kind is used to style hair. Other gels have other uses. *n.*

gel·a·tin or **gel·a·tine** (jel′ə tən *or* jel′ə tēn′) an odourless, tasteless substance obtained by boiling the bones, hoofs, and other waste parts of animals. It is used to make glue, jelly, camera film, and other things. *n.*

gem (jem) 1 a precious stone that has been cut and polished; jewel. Diamonds and rubies are gems. 2 any excellent or precious person or thing: *You are a gem!* *n.*

gen·der (jen′dər) 1 the fact of being male or female. 2 in many languages, the grouping of nouns into classes such as masculine, feminine, neuter. In English, the marking of gender has mostly disappeared except in pronouns (*he, she, it*), but in French every noun is masculine or feminine and articles and adjectives must match the noun. This sense of gender does not necessarily have anything to do with male or female sex. 3 one of these classes of nouns. *n.*

gene (jēn) in a plant or animal cell, a tiny part of a chromosome that determines what the plant or animal will be like and how it will develop. Genes inherited from your parents determine the colour of your hair, your body shape, and so on. *n.*

ge·ne·al·o·gy (jē′nē ol′ə jē) the history of a family, tracing the line from the present family members back to their ancestors. *n.* **—ge′ne·al′o·gist,** *n.*

gen·er·al (jen′ə rəl) 1 having to do with all the people or things in a certain group. A **general election** involves all voters. A general statement about cats says something that is supposed to be true of all cats. A **general store** sells all kinds of things. 2 not detailed; rough: *a general idea; a general description.* 3 the highest officer in an army. 4 chief: *The Attorney General is the chief law officer of Canada.* 1, 2, 4 *adj.,* 3 *n.* **—gen′er·al′i·ty,** *n.* **—gen′er·al·ly,** *adv.*
in general, a mostly; as a rule: *In general, they get along fairly well together.* **b** as a whole group: *Do you mean your parents, or parents in general?*

gen·er·al·ize (jen′ə rə līz′) 1 make a general statement; say something that is supposed to be true about all the people or things in a certain group: *When she said "Kids like to eat," she was generalizing.* 2 talk vaguely, without giving details. *v.,* **gen·er·al·ized, gen·er·al·iz·ing.** **—gen′er·al·i·za′tion,** *n.*

gen·er·ate (jen′ə rāt′) make or produce: *Boiling water generates steam. The steam can generate electricity by running a generator.* *v.,* **gen·er·at·ed, gen·er·at·ing.**

gen·er·a·tion (jen′ə rā′shən) 1 the people or animals born in the same period: *Your parents belong to one generation; you belong to the following generation.* 2 one step from parent to child in a family: *The picture showed four generations—great-grandmother, grandmother, mother, and baby.* 3 the time from the birth of one generation to the birth of the next: *The Mennonites came from Europe seven generations ago.* 4 the act or process of producing: *Steam and water power are used for the generation of electricity.* *n.*

gen·er·a·tor (jen′ə rā′tər) a machine for producing electricity from other kinds of energy: *The hospital has its own generator for use in emergencies.* *n.*

ge·ner·ic (jə ner′ik) having to do with something that belongs to a whole group of similar things, rather than something that is special or unique. The word *town* is generic; the name *Moncton* is not. A generic pair of jeans is an ordinary pair with no special features and no designer name attached. *adj.*

gen·er·ous (jen′ə rəs) 1 glad to share with others; unselfish: *a generous boy.* 2 forgiving and thinking the best of others; not mean: *a generous soul.* 3 large: *a generous serving of pie.* *adj.* **—gen′er·os′i·ty,** *n.*

gen·e·sis (jen′ə sis) beginning; creation; coming into being. *n.*

Geology

There are three kinds of rock:

1. **igneous, formed from molten rock from deep inside the earth (examples are obsidian and granite)**
2. **sedimentary, which is hardened layers of sediment (examples are coal, limestone, and sandstone)**
3. **metamorphic, which is either igneous or sedimentary, changed by heat or pressure inside the earth (examples are marble and slate).**

Some rocks can be cut and polished into brilliantly flashing gemstones, like this amethyst.

ge•net•ics (jə net′iks) the study of how genes in living things pass on characteristics from one generation to another. *n.* **—ge•net′ic,** *adj.* **—ge•net′i•cist,** *n.*

ge•ni•al (jēn′yəl *or* jē′nē əl) **1** cheerful and friendly: *a genial welcome, a genial bus driver.* **2** pleasant; comforting: *genial sunshine.* *adj.*

ge•nie (jē′nē) a spirit that grants wishes: *When Aladdin rubbed his lamp, the genie obeyed Aladdin.* *n.*

gen•i•tals (jen′ə təlz) the parts of the body used for sexual intercourse. *pl.n.* **—gen′i•tal,** *adj.*

gen•ius (jēn′yəs) **1** a person who is extremely brilliant or talented: *Einstein was a genius. So was Mozart.* **2** extraordinary intelligence or talent: *a genius for acting. Shakespeare's plays display his genius.* *n., pl.* **ge•ni•us•es.**

gen•re (zhȧn′rə *or* zhȧn′ər) a particular type of writing, music, or art with its own style and rules. Rock is a musical genre; fiction is a genre of literature. *n.*

gen•tle (jen′təl) **1** light, soft, easy, or moderate; not extreme, rough, or violent: *a gentle tap, a gentle breeze, a gentle slope.* **2** kind; careful not to hurt: *a gentle heart, gentle criticism.* **3** polite and well-bred; in earlier times, high-class: *gentle manners, of gentle birth.* *adj.,* **gen•tler, gen•tlest. —gen′tle•ness,** *n.* **—gent′ly,** *adv.*

gen•tle•man (jen′təl mən) **1** a man who is honourable, polite, and considerate of others. **2** in earlier times, a man born into a family of high social standing. **3** a polite term for any man. *n., pl.* **gen•tle•men** (jen′təl mən). **—gen′tle•man•ly,** *adj.*

gen•tle•wom•an (jen′təl wu̇m′ən) in earlier times, a woman born into a family of high social standing. *n., pl.* **gen•tle•wom•en** (jen′təl wim′ən).

gen•u•ine (jen′yū ən) real; true: *genuine leather, a genuine diamond, genuine sorrow.* *adj.*

ge•nus (jē′nəs) one of the groups into which scientists classify living things. A genus is smaller than a family and larger than a species. In the two-word scientific name of a plant or animal, such as *Homo sapiens,* the first word (*Homo*) is the genus. *n., pl.* **gen•er•a** (jen′ə rə).

ge•og•ra•phy (jē og′rə fē) **1** the study of the earth's surface, climate, continents, countries, peoples, industries, and products. **2** the surface features of a particular place. *n.* **—ge•og′ra•pher,** *n.* **—ge′o•graph′i•cal** (jē′ə graf′ə kəl), *adj.*

WORD HISTORY..... geography

The word **geography** comes from the Greek words *ge* "earth" + *graphein* "describe." Similarly, **geology** is the science of the earth's crust. The word **geometry** originally referred to measuring the earth and its natural features, like mountains. Later, geometry came to mean the complete study of shapes and solids, not just their measurement.

ge•ol•o•gy (jē ol′ə jē) the science that deals with the earth's crust, the rocks and minerals that make up its different layers, and their history. *n.* **—ge•ol′o•gist,** *n.* **—ge′o•log′i•cal** (jē′ə loj′ə kəl), *adj.*

a bat	e bed	i bid	o pot	u cup	th thin
ā cake	ē me	ī bite	ō go	ū rude	ŦH then
ȧ bar	ə about	ər over	ȯ for	u̇ put	zh measure

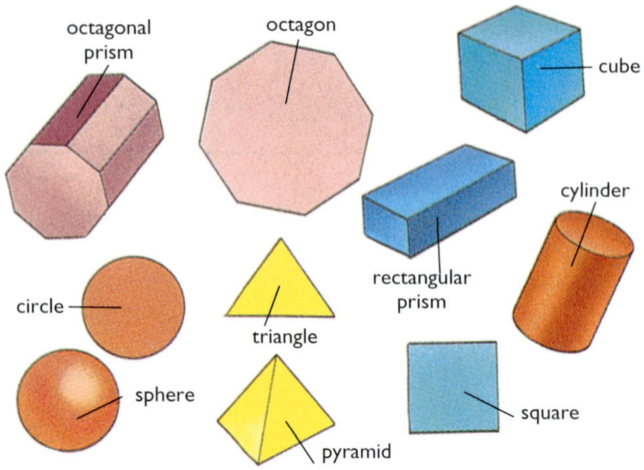

ge·om·e·try (jē om′ə trē) the branch of mathematics that measures and compares lines, angles, surfaces, and solids. *n.* —**ge′o·met′ric** (jē′ə met′rik) or **ge′o·met′ri·cal,** *adj.*

ge·o·ther·mal (jē′ō thər′məl) having to do with the internal heat of the earth: *There are geothermal hot springs on Vancouver Island. adj.*

ge·ra·ni·um (jə rā′nē əm) a common house or garden plant with showy red, pink, or white flowers. *n.*

ger·bil (jər′bəl) a small furry animal closely related to the mouse. Gerbils are often kept as pets. *n.*

germ (jərm) **1** a tiny organism you can only see with a microscope, that causes disease. Bacteria and viruses are germs. **2** the earliest form of a living thing; a seed or bud. **3** the beginning of anything: *the germ of a friendship. n.*

ger·mi·cide (jər′mə sīd′) any substance that kills disease germs. *n.*

ger·mi·nate (jər′mə nāt′) begin to grow; sprout: *In the spring, seeds germinate in the warm, moist soil. v.,* **ger·mi·nat·ed, ger·mi·nat·ing.** —**ger′mi·na′tion,** *n.*

ges·ture (jes′chər) **1** a movement of the hands or any part of the body, used to show an idea or a feeling: *She shook her fist and made other angry gestures at us.* **2** any action done mainly to send a message or make an impression: *It would be a friendly gesture to invite her, even though we know she can't come.* **3** make gestures; use gestures: *He gestured wildly at us.* Another word for this is **gesticulate.** 1, 2 *n.,* 3 *v.,* **ges·tured, ges·tur·ing.**

get (get) **1** come to have: *I got a new computer game yesterday. Where did you get that idea?* **2** go and find and bring back: *Get my glasses, please.* **3** become: *It is getting colder.* **4** cause to be, to happen, or to do: *I can't get the door open. She got her hair cut. Try to get him to come.* **5** reach; arrive: *I got to Whitehorse early last night. Your e-mail got here yesterday.* **6** begin; start: *We soon got talking about our days at camp.* **7** understand: *I don't get the point. v.,* **got, got** or **got·ten, get·ting.**

get after, nag or scold: *They're always getting after me about my messy room.*

get along, a be on good terms: *She doesn't get along with her neighbours.* **b** do well enough; manage: *We don't have a lot of money but we get along.* **c** move along; go on.

get around, a overcome a person or thing that is holding you back: *to get around the law.* **b** spread: *It doesn't take long for news to get around.* **c** go places.

get around to, find time for: *I want to read that book but I never seem to get around to it.*

get at, a reach: *We could not get at the cat in the tree without a ladder.* **b** find out: *Try to get at the truth.*

get away, a start off; leave: *We hope to get away early.* **b** escape: *The dog broke the leash and got away.*

get away with, do something bad without getting punished: *You won't get away with shoplifting.*

get back at, take revenge on; hurt someone who has hurt you. **Get even with** means the same.

get by, do well enough; manage all right: *They got by on their small salaries.*

get down, make downhearted; discourage; depress: *The hot weather was getting him down.*

get down to, start: *It's time to get down to work.*

get into, a become involved in: *We got into an argument.* **b** take an interest in; enjoy: *He really gets into languages.* **c** put on: *Get into your pyjamas.* **d** touch or open and make a mess of: *My little sister gets into everything.*

get off, escape the full punishment deserved: *The careless driver got off with just a warning.*

get on, a advance; move ahead: *It was getting on toward noon when they left.* **b** get old.

get out, a become known: *It didn't take long for the secret to get out.* **b** go places: *They don't get out much.*

get over, recover from: *He got over his illness.*

get something across, make something understood: *The teacher used a comic strip to get the idea across.*

get something over with, finish dealing with something: *As soon as we get the dishes over with, we can go biking.*

get through, a get to the end of; finish: *She always gets through her homework quickly.* **b** survive, or help survive: *to get through hard times. His friends got him through.* **c** make or get a telephone connection: *I tried to phone you, but I couldn't get through.* **d** communicate: *No one can get through to her when she's angry.*

get to, annoy; upset: *Don't let it get to you.*

get together, come or bring together; meet: *They arranged to get together at our house.*

get up, rise: *When do you get up in the morning? She got up from the chair.*

get·a·way (get′ə wā′) *Informal.* 1 the act of getting away; escape: *The bank robbers made their getaway in a fast car.* 2 the start of a race. *n.*

gey·ser (gī′zər) a natural spring that sends up fountains of hot water and steam from time to time. *n.*

Gham·bar (gum′bȧr) any of the six yearly festivals of the Zoroastrian religion which celebrate different parts of creation, such as earth, water, plants, and so on. Each Ghambar lasts about five or six days. *n.*

ghast·ly (gast′lē) horrible: *Murder is a ghastly crime.* *adj.,* **ghast·li·er, ghast·li·est.**

ghet·to (get′ō) a part of a city where people who share some characteristic, such as being poor or using a certain language, live as a group away from others. It can be because they feel stronger that way or because other communities do not welcome them. *n., pl.* **ghet·tos.**

ghost (gōst) 1 the spirit of a dead person. A ghost is supposed to live in another world and appear to living people as a pale, shadowy form. 2 a faint image; slightest suggestion: *a ghost of a smile, not a ghost of a chance.* *n.* —**ghost′ly,** *adj.*

ghost town (gōst′ toun′) a town that has been deserted by all the people who used to live there: *When the gold rush was over, the once-flourishing community became a ghost town.*

gi·ant (jī′ənt) 1 a huge person. Giants are imaginary. 2 a person or thing of great size, power, or importance. 3 huge: *a giant potato.* 1, 2 *n.,* 3 *adj.*

gib·ber·ish (jib′ər ish) something said or written that is so mixed up you can't make sense of it. *n.*

The gibbon is the smallest member of the ape family. It ranges over a wider area — India, as well as all over southeast Asia — than the other apes.

gib·bon (gib′ən) a small, long-armed ape of tropical Asia. Gibbons live in trees. *n.*

gib·lets (jib′lits) the heart, liver, and gizzard of a chicken, turkey, etc., often used to make gravy. *pl.n.*

gid·dy (gid′ē) 1 dizzy; feeling like your head is spinning: *It makes me giddy to go on a merry-go-round.* 2 causing dizziness: *They climbed to a giddy height.* 3 never serious; silly and foolish: *a giddy person, giddy laughter.* *adj.,* **gid·di·er, gid·di·est.**

gift (gift) 1 something given; present: *a birthday gift.* 2 a natural talent; a special ability: *a gift for painting.* Someone with a great deal of talent or ability is **gifted.** *n.*

gig[1] (gig) *Slang.* a job for a performer. *n.*

gig[2] (gig) a light, two-wheeled carriage drawn by one horse. *n.*

giga– *an SI prefix meaning* one billion; 1 000 000 000. A *gigametre* is one billion metres.

gig·a·byte (gig′ə bīt *or* jig′ə bīt) one billion bytes of computer memory. *Symbol:* GB

gi·gan·tic (jī gan′tik) huge; enormous: *a gigantic building project.* *adj.*

WORD HISTORY...... gigantic

The word **gigantic** comes from a Greek word *gigas*, meaning "giant."

The prefix **giga** has come to mean "one billion." You will see this prefix in words like **gigabyte**, which means "one billion bytes" of storage in a computer.

gig·gle (gig′əl) 1 laugh in a silly or nervous way: *They giggled in their embarrassment.* 2 a silly or nervous laugh. 1 *v.,* **gig·gled, gig·gling;** 2 *n.* —**gig′gly,** *adj.*

Gi·la mon·ster (hē′lə mon′stər) a poisonous lizard of the desert areas of the United States and Mexico. Its beadlike scales are black and pinkish orange.

gild (gild) cover with a thin layer of gold or something gold-coloured. The coating itself is called **gilt.** *v.*

gill (gil) one of the breathing organs of certain water animals: *Fish, tadpoles, and crabs have gills.* *n.*

gim·mick (gim′ik) a trick or clever idea that attracts attention or makes you want to buy something: *The team's latest gimmick was to include a set of miniature plastic players with every season ticket it sold.* *n.* —**gim′mick·ry,** *n.* —**gim′mick·y,** *adj.*

gin (jin) a machine for getting rid of the seeds out of the fluffy balls of the cotton plant. *n.*

a bat	e bed	i bid	o pot	u cup	th thin
ā cake	ē me	ī bite	ō go	ū rude	ᴛʜ then
ȧ bar	ə about	ər over	ȯ for	u̇ put	zh measure

gin·ger (jin′jər) the root of a tropical Asian plant. It is used as a spice, either fresh or dried and powdered. **Ginger ale** is a soft drink, **gingerbread** is a sort of cake or thick cookie, and a **gingersnap** is a thin, crisp cookie. All are made with ginger. *n.*

gin·ger·ly (jin′jər lē) very carefully and cautiously: *She gingerly picked up the hot frying pan.* *adv.*

ging·ham (ging′əm) a kind of cloth, usually cotton or part cotton, with stripes or checks. *n.*

gi·raffe (jə raf′) a large African plant-eating animal with a very long neck and legs and a spotted skin. Giraffes are the tallest living animals. *n.*

gird·er (gər′dər) a main supporting beam. Steel girders are often used to make the framework of bridges and tall buildings. *n.*

gir·dle (gər′dəl) a piece of tight, stretchy underwear that is supposed to make your figure look better. *n.*

girl (gərl) a female child. *n.* **—girl′hood′,** *n.* **—girl′ish,** *adj.*

girth (gərth) **1** the measure around anything: *a person of large girth, the girth of a tree.* **2** the strap or band that keeps the saddle in place on a horse. *n.*

GIS *abbreviation for* **geographical information system,** a computerized system used to gather and display data to do with location.

gist (jist) the basic idea: *the gist of an argument.* *n.*

Git·xsan (git′ksan) **1** a First Nations people living in central British Columbia. **2** their language. **3** having to do with these people or their language. 1, 2 *n.*, 3 *adj.*

give (giv) **1** let someone have, especially as a present: *He likes to give books to his friends.* **2** hand over or pay: *Give me that pencil. I can't give that much for a baseball glove.* **3** make a sound or movement: *She gave a loud shout.* **4** present or offer; host: *to give a concert, to give a party.* **5** provide; supply: *This tree gives apples.* **6** move, stretch, break, or bend when force is applied: *The lock gave when we kicked the door.* **7** the ability to stretch or bend: *A leather shoe has more give than a plastic one.* 1–6 *v.*, **gave, giv·en, giv·ing;** 7 *n.* **—giv′er,** *n.*
give-and-take, a situation where each one shares, co-operates, and compromises as needed.
give away, a give as a present; get rid of by giving. **b** let something be known: *His face gave away his true feelings. Don't give away our secret!*
give back, return: *Give back the book you borrowed.*
give in, let someone have his or her way in the end: *They kept asking her until she gave in.*
give off, send or put out a smell, a sound, light, heat, or anything else: *The bulb gave off a reddish glow.*
give or take, approximately, within a certain amount: *It's six o'clock, give or take a few minutes.*
give out, a hand out; pass out: *The children gave out the flyers.* **b** fail or become used up: *The food gave out during the famine. They worked until their strength gave out.*
give up, a hand over something you would rather keep: *We had to give up the kitten when the real owner was found.* **b** stop having or doing: *to give up smoking.* **c** stop trying or hoping: *I tried hard to learn tennis but I finally gave up.* **d** devote entirely: *She gave herself up to her studies.*

give·a·way (giv′ə wā′) **1** an item that is given away free: *The first day of the sale the store had a lot of giveaways.* **2** a very obvious clue: *Prue's half-closed eyes were a sure giveaway that she was very tired.* *n.*

giv·en (giv′ən) **1** stated: *You must finish the test in a given time.* **2** the past participle of **give:** *That book was given to me.* 1 *adj.*, 2 *v.*
given to, in the habit of: *Fergus is given to boasting.*

given name (giv′ən nām′) a person's first name.

giz·mo (giz′mō) any small item you can't remember the name of. *n.*

giz·zard (giz′ərd) a thick-walled part of a bird's stomach, where the food is ground up fine. *n.*

gla·cier (glā′shər) a very large mass of ice formed on land from snow. Glaciers move very slowly, often down mountainsides or along valleys. *n.* **—gla′cial,** *adj.*

glad (glad) **1** happy; joyful: *I'm glad you could come. We all cheered when we heard the glad news.* **2** very willing: *I'd be glad to help.* *adj.*, **glad·der, glad·dest.** **—glad′ly,** *adv.* **—glad′ness,** *n.* **—glad′den,** *v.*

glade (glād) a little open space in a forest. *n.*

glad·i·a·tor (glad′ē ā′tər) in ancient Rome, a slave, prisoner, or paid fighter who fought at public shows. *n.*

glam·our or **glam·or** (glam′ər) charm; a fascinating, romantic, exciting, and fashionable quality: *The glamour of being a movie star.* *n.* **—glam′or·ous,** *adj.* **—glam′or·ize′,** *v.*

WORD HISTORY..... glamour

Glamour is really the same word as **grammar**! In earlier times, *grammar* meant *Latin grammar*. So grammar was lumped together with the knowledge that only wizards ("wise persons") had. In this way, **grammar** came to be associated with magic spells (usually in Latin), and **glamour** is a kind of magical quality that holds people under a spell.

Glass

Glass is made from melting a mixture of sand, limestone, and soda ash.

To make stained glass, artists fit pieces of coloured glass together, keeping them attached by pieces of soft lead. That is why stained glass windows are sometimes called leaded windows.

In traditional glass blowing, a blob of molten glass stuck on the end of a tube is blown into a bubble. This must be shaped before it cools down.

To make crystal glass that sparkles, the limestone in the mixture is replaced by lead. That is why expensive crystal, like the drinking glasses shown here, is sometimes called lead crystal.

glance (glans) **1** look quickly: *I glanced at the clock.* **2** a quick look. **3** hit and bounce off at a slant: *The golf ball glanced off the tree trunk and went into the bushes.* 1, 3 *v.,* **glanced, glanc·ing;** 2 *n.*

gland (gland) an animal or plant organ that makes and gives out some substance: *There are sweat glands in your skin. Glands in flowers produce perfume.* *n.*

glare (gler) **1** a strong, harsh light, so bright that it hurts your eyes: *The glare from the snow blinded us.* **2** shine in this way. **3** unwanted reflection of light from the glass in a picture frame, a computer screen, etc. **4** a fierce, angry stare. **5** stare in this way: *She glared at the rude boy.* 1, 3, 4 *n.,* 2, 5 *v.,* **glared, glar·ing.**

🍁 **glare ice** (gler′ īs′) smooth, shiny ice.

glar·ing (gler′ing) bad and very obvious: *The writer made a glaring spelling mistake.* *adj.*

glass (glas) **1** a substance that can usually be seen through and breaks easily, leaving sharp edges. Glass is made by melting sand together with other materials, shaping the mixture, and then cooling it. Windows are made of glass. **2** a small container to drink out of, made of glass or other material. It has a wide opening and no handle. **3 glasses,** *pl.* eyeglasses; a pair of lenses in a frame, worn over the eyes to help them see properly. **4** an old word for a mirror or telescope. **5** cover or protect with glass: *They glassed in the porch.* 1–4 *n.,* 5 *v.* **—glass′ful′,** *n.* **—glass′y,** *adj.*

glass·ware (glas′wer′) things made of glass. *n.*

glaze (glāz) **1** coat something with a liquid that hardens to form a smooth, shiny surface. Certain foods are sometimes glazed with a sugary mixture. Earthenware is also often glazed. **2** the smooth, shiny coating or surface. **3** become glossy or glassy. When someone's eyes **glaze over** they look blank and expressionless. **4** put glass in: *to glaze a window or picture frame.* 1, 3, 4 *v.,* **glazed, glaz·ing;** 2 *n.*

gleam (glēm) **1** a flash or beam of light: *We saw the gleam of headlights through the rain.* **2** shine or glow. 1 *n.,* 2 *v.*

glean (glēn) **1** gather the grain left on the field by harvesters. **2** gather little by little: *The spy gleaned information from the soldiers' talk.* *v.*

a bat	e bed	i bid	o pot	u cup	th thin
ā cake	ē me	ī bite	ō go	ū rude	ᴛʜ then
ä bar	ə about	ər over	ô for	u̇ put	zh measure

glee (glē) playful joy; delight; merriment: *The children laughed with glee.* *n.* —**glee′ful,** *adj.*

glen (glen) a small valley. *n.*

glib (glib) using words too smoothly and easily to be sincere: *glib excuses.* *adj.,* **glib·ber, glib·best.**

glide (glīd) **1** move along smoothly, evenly, and easily: *A canoe glided through the still water.* **2** a smooth, even, easy movement. 1 *v.,* **glid·ed, glid·ing;** 2 *n.*

glid·er (glī′dər) an airplane with long wings and no engine. A regular airplane tows it high up in the sky, then sets it loose. Rising air currents keep it up. *n.*

glim·mer (glim′ər) **1** a faint, unsteady light. **2** shine with a faint, unsteady light: *The candle glimmered and went out.* 1 *n.,* 2 *v.*

glimpse (glimps) **1** a very quick or incomplete view: *I got a glimpse of the falls as our train went by.* **2** get a quick or incomplete view of: *I glimpsed something red through the keyhole.* 1 *n.,* 2 *v.,* **glimpsed, glimps·ing.**

glint (glint) gleam or flash: *the glint of a sword blade* (*n.*). *Her eyes glinted fiercely in the light* (*v.*). **Glint** is usually used of light that is reflected off something cold and hard like metal. *n. or v.*

glis·ten (glis′ən) sparkle; shine with tiny points of reflected light: *The moonlight glistened on the snow.* *v.*

glitch (glich) a small problem or defect: *A computer glitch caused the error.* *n.*

glit·ter (glit′ər) **1** sparkle; shine with a bright light reflected off something hard and smooth: *The jewel glittered in the sunlight.* **2** such a light: *There was a cold glitter in the man's eyes.* **3** the ice that coats everything outdoors after a rain that freezes. 1 *v.,* 2, 3 *n.*

gloat (glōt) gaze at or think about with a feeling of triumph or satisfaction: *The miser gloated over his gold. Don't gloat over the other team's mistakes.* *v.*

globe (glōb) **1** anything round like a ball. **2** a ball with a map of the earth or the sky on it. **3** the world. **Global** means having to do with the whole world. *n.*

glob·ule (glob′yūl) a very small ball; a tiny drop: *Globules of sweat stood out on the runner's forehead.* Informally, this word is often shortened to **glob.** *n.*

gloom (glūm) **1** deep shadow; dim light: *He could hardly see in the gloom.* **2** low spirits; sadness: *She sat there, lost in gloom.* *n.* —**gloom′y,** *adj.*

Gloos·cap (glū′skap) a trickster character in the myths of some First Nations such as the Mi'kmaq. *n.*

glo·ri·fy (glôr′ə fī′) **1** to honour or praise very highly: *singing hymns to glorify God.* **2** make a thing seem much better than it is: *Some TV shows glorify war.* *v.,* **glo·ri·fied, glo·ri·fy·ing.** —**glo′ri·fi·ca′tion,** *n.*

glo·ry (glôr′ē) **1** great praise and honour: *His victories brought him glory.* **2** something that brings great praise and honour: *Her real glory was not her beauty but her life of service to others.* **3** brightness or splendour; beauty and greatness: *We were amazed by the glory of the northern lights.* *n., pl.* **glo·ries.** —**glo′ri·ous,** *adj.*
glory in, take great pride or delight in: *Megan's parents gloried in her success as a pianist.*
in your glory, enjoying yourself to the maximum: *She's in her glory when she has a machine to tinker with.*

gloss (glos) **1** a smooth, shiny surface on anything: *Enamel paint dries with a high gloss.* **2** put a smooth shiny surface on. 1 *n.,* 2 *v.* —**gloss′y,** *adj.*
gloss over, try to make something seem OK even though it is wrong: *to gloss over a mistake.*

glos·sa·ry (glos′ə rē) a list of unusual or difficult words, with explanations: *Some schoolbooks have glossaries at the end.* *n., pl.* **glos·sa·ries.**

Grammar ✓Check ..... glossary

Giving a **glossary** is a way of explaining special or technical words without interrupting the flow of a piece of writing. Look in a math or science textbook for an example of a glossary.

glove (gluv) a covering for your hand with separate places for each finger and the thumb. A hockey glove and a baseball glove have padding to protect the hand. *n.*
fit like a glove, fit perfectly.

glow (glō) **1** a soft shine, especially from something that is red-hot or white-hot: *The glow from the burning coals gave a little light to the room.* **2** shine softly or with heat: *A lantern glowed in the window.* **3** look or feel warm and bright: *Her cheeks glowed as she danced.* **4** a bright, warm appearance or feeling: *the glow of a sunset, the glow of health on his cheeks.* 1, 4 *n.,* 2, 3 *v.*
a glowing report or **description,** a very positive one.

glow·er (glou′ər) glare; scowl: *The sullen girl glowered at her mother.* *v.*

glow–worm (glō′wərm′) an insect larva or wormlike insect that glows in the dark. *n.*

glu·cose (glū′kōs) a form of natural sugar found in fruit and other substances. *n.*

glue (glū) 1 a liquid used to stick things together. It hardens when dry. 2 stick something with glue. 1 *n.,* 2 *v.,* **glued, glu·ing.** —**glue′y,** *adj.*

glum (glum) gloomy; downhearted: *a glum look.* *adj.,* **glum·mer, glum·mest.**

glut·ton (glut′ən) 1 a greedy eater; a person who eats too much. 2 a person who never seems to have enough of something: *a glutton for cartoons.* *n.* —**glut′ton·ous,** *adj.* —**glut′ton·y,** *n.*
a glutton for punishment, someone who seems to like difficult challenges.

gnarl (nȧrl) a hard, rough lump like a knot on a stick. *n.* —**gnarl′y** or **gnarled,** *adj.*

gnash (nash) strike or grind the teeth together: *The ogres gnashed their teeth in rage.* *v.*

gnat (nat) a small, annoying fly. Most gnats bite. *n.*

gnaw (no) wear away by biting: *A mouse has gnawed right through the oatmeal box.* *v.*

gnome (nōm) in folk tales, a dwarf that lives in the earth and guards treasures of gold and jewels. *n.*

go (gō) 1 move, especially from one place to another: *He went to Labrador. The wheels go around.* 2 leave: *Don't go yet.* 3 work; run: *How do you make this thing go?* 4 get to be; become: *to go crazy.* 5 take part in; do: *to go swimming.* 6 extend; reach: *His memory goes way back.* 7 turn out; have a certain result: *How did the game go?* 8 *Informal.* make a certain sound: *The cork went "Pop!"* 9 be for a while: *to go hungry, to go naked.* 10 belong, match, or fit: *Those socks don't go with your pants. Where does this piece go?* *v.,* **went, gone, go·ing.**
a going concern, someone or something that is busy and doing well.
be going to, will: *It's going to rain soon.*
from the word "go," from the very beginning.
go about, **a** be or keep busy at: *She quietly went about her work.* **b** do; carry out, especially following some plan or method: *I'm not sure how to go about making a pizza.*
go all out, make the greatest possible effort: *They went all out to make her birthday a happy one.*
go at, attack: *The dog went at the intruder.*
go back on, **a** be unfaithful or disloyal to: *He went back on his friends.* **b** fail to keep: *She went back on her word.*
go by, **a** pass: *The hours went by slowly.* **b** be guided by; follow: *to go by the rules.* **c** be known by: *She goes by the nickname "Slim."*
go down, **a** be defeated or overthrown. **b** be accepted: *Our idea did not go down well.* **c** be swallowed: *The eggs went down easily.* **d** *Slang.* happen: *What's going down?*
go for, **a** like or be in favour of: *I don't go for sweets much.* **b** try to get. **c** attack.
go for it, *Informal.* give it your best effort.
go in for, *Informal.* **a** take part in; spend time and energy at: *She used to go in for basketball.* **b** like; approve of: *He doesn't go in for anything fancy.*
go into, **a** in arithmetic, be contained in: *3 goes into 9 three times.* **b** discuss: *Let's not go into that now.*
go it alone, act by yourself.
go off, **a** leave: *They went off to Charlottetown last night.* **b** explode; be fired: *The gun went off accidentally.* **c** turn out; happen: *Did your interview go off OK?*
go on, **a** proceed; move forward: *After a short rest, we decided to go on.* **b** start functioning: *The computer goes on when you press the button.* **c** make a fuss: *What are you going on about now?* **d** happen; take place: *Nobody seemed to know what was going on.*
go out, **a** go to parties, movies, restaurants, etc. **b** stop burning or shining: *Don't let the candle go out.* **c** date; carry on a romance: *My aunt is going out with a musician.*
go over, **a** look at carefully. **b** be accepted or appreciated: *The jokes went over very well.*
go through, **a** experience: *to go through hard times.* **b** search: *He went through his pockets to find a loonie.* **c** use up; spend; exhaust: *She went through all her money.*
go through with, complete; carry out to the end: *This plan is too risky; I refuse to go through with it.*
let go, **a** drop. **b** allow to escape; set free. **c** fail to keep in good condition: *They've really let their lawn go; it's full of weeds.* **d** fire from a job. **e** relax.
on the go, *Informal.* **a** busy or active. **b** going on; being worked on: *I already have two projects on the go.*
to go, to take out from a restaurant: *a hamburger to go.*

goad (gōd) 1 urge or push to do something: *Hunger goaded him to steal a loaf of bread.* 2 anything that urges or pushes someone to do something. 1 *v.,* 2 *n.*

goal (gōl) 1 in certain games, the space between two posts which you aim a puck or ball into. 2 the action of scoring in this way, or the points earned by doing it: *to score a goal. There were two goals by Gretzky.* 3 something you are aiming for or working toward: *His goal was to be a dancer.* *n.*

goal·ie (gō′lē) short for **goalkeeper** or **goaltender,** the player who guards the goal to keep the other team from scoring in hockey, lacrosse, and other games. *n.*

a bat	e bed	i bid	o pot	u cup	th thin
ā cake	ē me	ī bite	ō go	ū rude	ᴛʜ then
ȧ bar	ə about	ər over	ȯ for	ů put	zh measure

Goats

goat (gōt) 1 a cud-chewing animal with horns that curve backward and, usually, long hair. Goats are related to sheep but are stronger, less timid, and more active. A person who looks after goats is a **goatherd.** 2 a **mountain goat,** which is actually a kind of antelope. *n.* **get someone's goat,** *Informal.* make a person angry.

goat•ee (gō tē′) a small pointed beard that is only on the chin, not the jaws or cheeks. It looks a little like a goat's beard. *n.*

gob (gob) a wet sticky lump of something: *There was a gob of toothpaste in the sink.* *n.*

gob•ble (gob′əl) 1 eat fast and greedily. 2 the noise a turkey makes. 3 make this noise. A male turkey is called a **gobbler.** 1, 3 *v.,* 2 *n.,* **gob•bled, gob•bling.**

go–be•tween (gō′bi twēn′) a person who goes back and forth between others with messages or other things: *Don't make me a go-between in your argument—do your own talking.* *n.*

gob•let (gob′lit) a drinking glass with a base and stem, especially a fancy one. *n.*

gob•lin (gob′lən) a mischievous elf in the form of an ugly dwarf. *n.*

god (god) 1 a being that is worshipped; a being that people believe is greater and more powerful than any human. 2 a statue of a god, for praying or sacrificing to. 3 **God,** in certain religions, the maker and ruler of the universe, and the only one who is to be worshipped. 4 a person or thing that is given too much importance: *His car was a god to him.* *n.* **—god′like′,** *adj.*

god•dess (god′is) a female god. *n.*

god•ly (god′lē) worshipping, obeying, and loving God; holy. *adj.,* **god•li•er, god•li•est.**

god•par•ents (god′per′ənts) in Christianity, two people, a **godfather** and a **godmother,** who make promises when a child is being baptized. They promise to help the child to be a good Christian. The child is their **godchild,** either a **goddaughter** or a **godson.** *pl.n.*

gog•gles (gog′əlz) a pair of large, close-fitting spectacles for protecting the eyes from light or dust: *She wore goggles while welding the broken steel rod.* *pl.n.*

go•ings–on (gō′ing zon′) behaviour, especially bad: *Her parents were unhappy about the goings-on at the party.* *pl.n.*

gold (gōld) 1 a heavy, soft, yellow precious metal. It is used in jewellery, dental work, and electronics. 2 wealth; riches. 3 anything bright, beautiful, or precious: *Wheat is prairie gold.* Oil is often called **black gold.** *n.*

Word Family.......... **gold**

goldfinch: a songbird with mostly yellow plumage
goldfish: a golden orange fish kept in garden pools, or in bowls indoors
goldsmith: a person who makes jewellery, etc. of gold

gold•en (gōl′dən) 1 made of gold or shining like gold: *golden candlesticks, golden hair.* 2 very good: *golden days, a golden opportunity.* The **Golden Rule** is to treat others as you would want to be treated. *adj.*

gold·en·rod (gōl′dən rod′) a wild plant with tall clusters of small, yellow flowers that bloom in the late summer and early fall. *n.*

gold·eye (gōl′dī′) a freshwater fish found in rivers and lakes from Ontario to the Northwest Territories. Goldeye is often smoked before being sold for food. *n., pl.* **gold·eye** or **gold·eyes.**

gold rush (gōld′ rush′) a sudden movement of people to a place where gold has just been found: *The Klondike gold rush began after gold was discovered there in 1896.*

golf (golf) **1** an outdoor game played by hitting a small, hard **golfball** with different kinds of clubs. The golfer tries to hit the ball into a hole in the ground with as few strokes as possible. Usually there are 18 holes, one after another, on a **golf course.** **2** play this game: *They golf every Saturday.* 1 *n.,* 2 *v.* **—golf′er,** *n.*

gon·do·la (gon′də lə) **1** a long, narrow boat with a high peak at each end, used on the canals of Venice. The person operating it is a **gondolier** (gon′də lēr′). **2** a train car with low sides and no top, for carrying freight. **3** a sort of box for people to ride in, attached to a hot air balloon, ski lift, or Ferris wheel. **4** a broadcasting booth near the roof of a hockey arena. *n.*

WORD HISTORY..... gondola

In case you are wondering what all the definitions of **gondola** have in common, it's rocking! The word comes from the Italian *gondolare*, "to rock." Good name for a band?

gone (gon) **1** no longer there; lost, dead, used up, or moved away. **2** the past participle of **go:** *He has gone far away.* 1 *adj.,* 2 *v.*

gon·er (gon′ər) *Informal.* a person or thing that is dead, ruined, or doomed. *n.*

gong (gong) a piece of metal shaped like a disk or saucer, that makes a loud noise when you hit it. *n.*

goo (gū) something that is thick and sticky: *What's this goo you're putting in your hair?* *n.* **—goo′ey,** *adj.*

good (gůd) **1** right; doing what is right, kind, honest, fair, wise, and so on: *a good girl, good deeds.* **2** well made or well done: *a good piece of work.* **3** suitable, useful, or helpful: *a good book for children. Fresh air is good for the body.* **4** enjoyable: *Have a good time.* **5** skilled: *a good skater, good at math.* **6** real; genuine: *It is hard to tell counterfeit money from good money.* **7** not spoiled or broken; in proper condition: *a good apple. Put your weight on your good leg.* **8** that which is good: *Always look for the good in people.* **9** benefit; use: *What good is it?* 1–7 *adj.,* **bet·ter, best;** 8, 9 *n.* **—good′ness,** *n.*

a good deal, **a** a lot: *a good deal worse.* **b** a bargain.

as good as, almost; practically: *The day is as good as over.*

for good, forever; permanently: *They've left for good.*

good and, *Informal.* very: *She was good and angry.*

good for, **a** able to last for: *good for a week.* **b** worth: *a coupon good for a free ride.* **c** able to give: *He'll be good for a few dollars.* **d** congratulations to: *Good for you!*

up to no good, planning or doing something bad.

Grammar Check ..... good

Need a good way to remember how to use the words **good** and **well** correctly? Try this.

The word **good** is an adjective, so it always has a noun to describe: *a good way.*

The word **well** is an adverb, so it always has a verb to describe: *You write well.*

So, remember that using **good** and **well** correctly is *a good way to write well!*

good·bye or **good–bye** (gůd′bī′) farewell; what people say when they leave. *n.*

good–for–noth·ing (gůd′fər nuth′ing) **1** worthless; useless. **2** a person who is thought to be worthless or useless. 1 *adj.,* 2 *n.*

good–heart·ed (gůd′ här′tid) kind. *adj.*

good–look·ing (gůd′lůk′ing) handsome; attractive: *a good-looking man.* *adj.*

good·ly (gůd′lē) fairly large; considerable: *a goodly quantity.* *adj.,* **good·li·er, good·li·est.**

good–na·tured (gůd′nā′chərd) pleasant; friendly; cheerful. **Good-tempered** and **good-humoured** mean much the same. *adj.*

goods (gůdz) things that can be owned, bought, or sold: *used goods. She left all her goods to her son.* *pl.n.*

good–sized (gůd′sīzd′) fairly large: *a good-sized helping.* *adj.*

good will (gůd′ wil′) a kind, friendly attitude.

a bat	e bed	i bid	o pot	u cup	th thin
ā cake	ē me	ī bite	ō go	ü rude	ᴛʜ then
ä bar	ə about	ər over	ô for	ů put	zh measure

good·y (gu̇d′ē) *Informal.* **1** something very good to eat; treat: *There were lots of goodies at the party.* **2** an exclamation of happiness: *Are we going today? Oh, goody!* 1 *n., pl.* **good·ies;** 2 *interj.*

goo·gle (gü′gəl) *Trademark.* search for information on the Internet, using the Google search engine: *I googled* whales *and got lots of ideas for a project.* *v.*

goose (güs) **1** a domestic or wild water bird resembling a duck. It is larger and has a longer neck: *We had goose for Thanksgiving dinner.* **2** a silly person: *"What a goose you are!"* *n., pl.* **geese.**

goose·ber·ry (güs′ber′ē) a sour, greenish berry, used to make pies, tarts, jam, etc. It grows on a thorny bush. *n., pl.* **goose·ber·ries.**

go·pher (gō′fər) a small furry animal of the prairies that lives mostly underground. Gophers use their long front claws to dig tunnels. *n.*

WORD HISTORY..... gopher

Gopher comes from a French word *gaufre*, meaning "honeycomb." The name was probably given because of the gopher's habit of burrowing, making the ground like a honeycomb, and because this French word sounds like a native American word *magofer*, the name for a burrowing tortoise.

gore (gôr) wound with a horn or tusk: *The angry bull gored the bullfighter.* *v.,* **gored, gor·ing.**

gorge (gôrj) **1** a deep, narrow valley, usually steep and rocky. **2** eat too much at once: *They gorged on pizza and cookies.* 1 *n.,* 2 *v.,* **gorged, gorg·ing.**

gor·geous (gôr′jəs) very beautiful. *adj.*

go·ril·la (gə ril′ə) the largest and most powerful ape. It lives in the forests of west central Africa. *n.*

gor·y (gô′rē) bloody; full of bloodshed. *adj.,* **gor·i·er, gor·i·est.**

gos·ling (goz′ling) a young goose. *n.*

gos·pel (gos′pəl) **1** the teachings of Jesus and his first followers, written down in the first four books (the **Gospels**) of the New Testament in the Christian Bible. **2** something that is supposed to be absolutely true. *n.*

gos·sa·mer (gos′ə mər) **1** a film or thread of cobweb. **2** any very thin, light cloth or substance: *a dress of gossamer.* *n.*

gos·sip (gos′ip) **1** talk about other people and their personal lives: *Gossip is often hurtful and untrue* (*n.*). *They gossiped on the phone for hours* (*v.*). **2** a person who often talks in this way. 1, 2 *n.,* 1 *v.,* **gos·siped, gos·sip·ing.** **—gos′sip·y,** *adj.*

got (got) the past tense and a past participle of **get:** *We got our new computer yesterday. We had got tired of waiting for it.* The other past participle is **gotten:** *I haven't gotten over my cold yet.* *v.*

USING WORDS ...... got

The words **got** and **gotten** can both be used as past participles of the verb **get**: *I wish she had gotten the card in time for her birthday. I've got her present wrapped.*

Sometimes, you should try to use different wording instead of **got**. For example: *I wish she had gotten the card in time for her birthday. I've wrapped her present.*

gouge (gouj) **1** a chisel with a curved blade, used for cutting rounded grooves or holes in wood. **2** cut with a gouge or other tool; dig out. **3** a groove, deep scratch, or hole cut in a surface: *There was a long gouge in the desktop.* **4** charge an unfairly high price: *They gouged us $40 for a plate of spaghetti.* 1, 3 *n.,* 2, 4 *v.,* **gouged, goug·ing.**

gou·lash (gü′läsh) a thin stew made with meat and flavoured with mild red pepper: *beef goulash.* *n.*

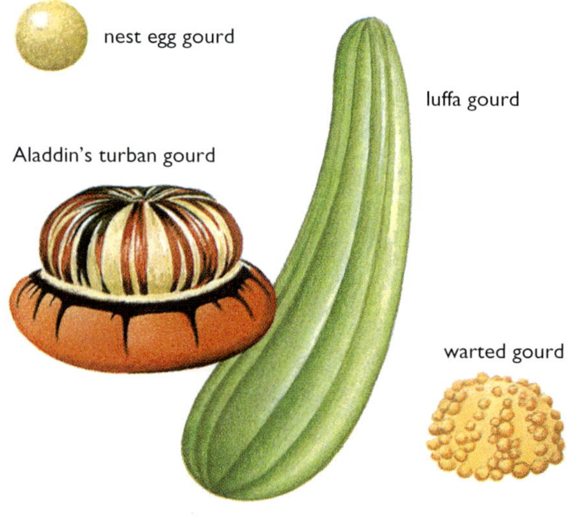

gourd (gürd *or* gôrd) a fruit like a squash. Its hard, dried shell is used as a container in some cultures. *n.*

gour·met (gūrmā′) 1 a person who knows and appreciates fine food and drink. 2 suitable for a gourmet: *a gourmet restaurant.* 1 *n.,* 2 *adj.*

gov·ern (guv′ərn) rule; control; manage: *Govern your temper. The premier and his or her cabinet govern the province. Her decisions are governed by common sense.* *v.*

gov·ern·ess (guv′ər nis) especially in earlier times, a woman who taught children in their own home. *n.*

gov·ern·ment (guv′ərn mənt) 1 the group ruling a country, province, city, etc. at any time. 2 a system of ruling: *Canada has a democratic government.* 3 rule; control. *n.* —**gov′ern·men′tal,** *adj.*

gov·er·nor (guv′ər nər) a person who rules or governs; especially under a higher government. *n.*

Governor General (guv′ərnər jen′rəl) in Canada and some other countries of the Commonwealth, the representative of the Queen or King, appointed on the advice of the Prime Minister for a five-year term.

gown (goun) 1 a woman's long formal dress. 2 a loose outer garment worn by some judges, some clergy and choir members, etc. as a symbol of their position: *Judges, some members of the clergy, and students graduating from university wear gowns.* *n.*

GPS *abbreviation for* **global positioning system,** a navigational system that lets users find their exact position by means of data received from satellites.

grab (grab) 1 take quickly and roughly; snatch: *The dog grabbed the meat and ran.* 2 the action of taking or snatching in this way: *She made a grab for the apple.* 1 *v.,* **grabbed, grab·bing;** 2 *n.*
how does that grab you? *Informal.* how do you like that?
up for grabs, *Informal.* **a** available for anyone who claims it. **b** open to negotiation; able to be won or lost.

grab bag (grab′ bag′) 1 a bag or container full of different items. You dig into it with your hand and pull out something without knowing what you will get. 2 a mixture of many different things: *The music was a real grab bag—jazz, rock, country, and classical.*

grace (grās) 1 beauty of movement: *He skated with great skill and grace.* 2 good manners and taste: *Have the grace to apologize.* 3 the favour and love of God, given freely to people. 4 a short prayer of thanks given at a meal. 5 an extra allowance of time: *The library gave him two days' grace to return the book.* 6 give grace or beauty to: *She will grace the party with her presence.* 1–5 *n.,* 6 *v.,* **graced, grac·ing.**
in someone's good graces, favoured or liked by someone.
with good grace, pleasantly; willingly: *She obeyed the order with good grace.* The opposite is **with bad grace.**

grace·ful (grās′fəl) beautiful, elegant, or tasteful: *a graceful birch tree, a graceful dance, a graceful speech of thanks.* *adj.* —**grace′ful·ly,** *adv.*

gra·cious (grā′shəs) very polite and thoughtful; generous: *a gracious host, a gracious offer.* *adj.*

gra·da·tion (grā dā′shən *or* grə dā′shən) one of a series of small changes or steps: *The chart showed the gradations of colour from red to blue. This measuring cup is marked off in gradations of 50 mL.* *n.*

grade (grād) 1 one of the divisions of a school program: *Most children enter grade one when they are six.* 2 a number or letter that shows how well a student has done: *Her grade in Music is B.* 3 a standard level of quality or value: *Grade A beef is the best in quality.* 4 give a grade to; mark: *The teacher graded the papers. Eggs are graded by size.* 5 the slope of a hill: *The car had trouble getting up the steep grade.* 6 make level; even out: *The workers graded the gravel road to get rid of the ruts.* 1, 2, 3, 5 *n.,* 4, 6 *v.,* **grad·ed, grad·ing.** —**grad′er,** *n.*

grade school (grād′ skūl′) an elementary school; a school that ends at grade five, six, or eight.

grad·u·al (graj′ū əl) slow or gentle; happening or changing little by little: *a gradual increase in sound, a gradual slope.* *adj.* —**grad′u·al·ly,** *adv.*

grad·u·ate (graj′ū āt′ *for 1 and 3,* graj′ū it *for 2*) 1 finish school, university, or college and receive a diploma or certificate: *Marya graduated from university last year.* The ceremony celebrating this is called a **graduation.** 2 a person who has graduated. 3 mark out in equal spaces: *My ruler is graduated in centimetres.* 1, 3 *v.,* **grad·u·at·ed, grad·u·at·ing;** 2 *n.*

graf·fi·ti (grə fē′tē) words and pictures that are written, drawn, or sprayed on a wall or other surface and are meant to be rude, funny, or clever. *n.*

graft (graft) 1 take a shoot from one plant and stick it in a slit in another to grow there. A shoot from an apple tree may be grafted onto a poor tree to improve the fruit. 2 take a piece of tissue from one part of a body and put it on another part. Healthy skin is often grafted onto a part where the skin has been seriously burned. 3 the shoot, bud, or tissue that has been moved. 1, 2 *v.,* 3 *n.*

a bat	e bed	i bid	o pot	u cup	th thin
ā cake	ē me	ī bite	ō go	ū rude	ᴛʜ then
ä bar	ə about	ər over	ô for	ù put	zh measure

Grain

These different types of grain are cereals, belonging to the grass family.

grain (grān) 1 a plant like wheat, oats, or corn. The seeds of these plants are used as food and may be stored in a tall building called a **grain elevator.** 2 a tiny hard bit of something like sand, sugar, or salt. 3 the smallest possible amount; tiniest bit: *a grain of truth.* 4 the little lines and markings in wood or marble: *Mahogany has a fine grain.* 5 someone's nature: *Laziness was against the grain for her.* *n.* —**grain′y,** *adj.*

gram (gram) a metric unit of mass. There are one thousand grams in a kilogram: *A nickel has a mass of about five grams. Symbol:* g *n.*

gram•mar (gram′ər) 1 the way words are put together to form sentences in a particular language. 2 the study of this. 3 the correct use of words according to the rules of a language: *Good grammar is important in formal writing.* *n.* ▶ See the *Grammar and Usage Mini-Guide.*

gram•mat•i•cal (grə mat′ə kəl) 1 having to do with grammar: *"Between you and I" is a grammatical mistake.* 2 correctly following the grammar of a particular language: *She speaks grammatical English but has a French accent.* *adj.*

gran•a•ry (gran′ə rē *or* grā′nə rē) a place or building where grain is stored. *n., pl.* **gran•a•ries.**

grand (grand) 1 big and impressive; majestic: *grand mountains, a grand palace.* 2 great and noble; heroic: *grand deeds.* 3 highest in rank: *a grand duke, the grand jury in a court.* 4 wonderful: *a grand time.* *adj.*
the grand total, the total including everything.

Grand Banks (grand′ bangks′) a shallow part, or shoal, of the ocean lying southeast of Newfoundland: *The Grand Banks have long been famous as a fishing ground.*

grand•child (grand′chīld′) the child of a person's son or daughter; a **granddaughter** or **grandson.** *n., pl.* **grand•chil•dren.**

gran•deur (gran′jər *or* grand′yər) greatness; majesty; splendour: *the grandeur of Niagara Falls.* *n.*

grand•fa•ther (grand′foᴛʜ′ər) the father of a person's father or mother. Some people call their grandfathers **grandad, grandpa,** or **grampa.** *n.*

grandfather clock (grand′foᴛʜ′ər klok′) a clock in a tall wooden case that stands on the floor. It has a pendulum that swings back and forth, moved by weights.

gran•di•ose (gran′dē ōs′) too grand and fancy; impressive but not suitable: *None of his grandiose plans ever worked out. Isn't that a rather grandiose title for such a silly little story?* *adj.*

grand•moth•er (grand′muᴛʜ′ər) the mother of a person's mother or father. Some people call their grandmothers **grandma, gramma,** or **granny.** *n.*

grand•par•ent (grand′per′ənt) a grandfather or grandmother. *n.*

grand piano (grand′ pēan′ō) a large harp-shaped piano with horizontal frame and strings.

grand•stand (grand′stand′) the sloped seating area at an athletic field, race track, or outdoor concert. Grandstands are usually sheltered by a roof. *n.*

gran•ite (gran′it) a very hard volcanic rock made up mostly of quartz and feldspar. It can be white, pink, or grey and is used for buildings and monuments. *n.*

gra•no•la (grə nō′lə) a cereal made from mixed grains, nuts, and seeds. A **granola bar** is a chewy or crunchy bar made out of granola and often fruit or chocolate chips, eaten as a snack. *n.*

grant (grant) 1 graciously give what is asked or desired: *to grant a request. Cinderella's fairy godmother granted her wish to go to the ball.* 2 admit: *I grant that you are right so far.* 3 something given, especially land or money given by the government: *She received a grant to pay for her university education.* 1, 2 *v.*, 3 *n.*
take for granted, assume that something is true or that a person will always be there, without ever thinking or wondering about it or showing that you are thankful: *Sometimes we take our parents for granted.*

gran·u·lar (gran′yə lər) made up of tiny, hard bits or grains (def. 2): *Granite is a granular rock.* *adj.*

Grape cultivation is one of the oldest human arts. Grapes are grown in vineyards, mostly in warm temperate climates.

grape (grāp) a small, round fruit that grows in bunches on a vine. Grapes can be red, purple, dark blue, or pale green; they are eaten fresh, or dried and made into raisins. *n.*

grape·fruit (grāp′frūt′) a large, pale yellow, juicy, sour fruit, related to oranges and lemons. *n.*, *pl.* **grape·fruit** or **grape·fruits.**

grape·vine (grāp′vīn′) 1 the vine that grapes grow on. 2 *Informal.* a way of spreading news among people by casual talk: *She learned through the grapevine that Mei-Ling was moving to another town.* *n.*

graph (graf) 1 a chart that uses lines, bars, sections of a circle, or rows of little pictures to stand for different amounts: *This graph shows how your weight has changed each year; that one shows how many people voted for each party in the election.* 2 show amounts in this way: *to graph the daily temperature for a week.* 1 *n.*, 2 *v.*

graph·ic (graf′ik) 1 using words to make a clear image; lifelike; vivid: *The reporter gave a graphic account of the fire.* 2 shown by a graph: *a graphic record of school attendance for a month.* 3 having to do with drawing, painting, design, etc.: *He is studying the graphic arts.*
4 **graphics,** the pictures, charts, coloured borders, etc. in something printed or in a computer display; the parts that are not words: *This computer game has great graphics, but it's boring.* 1–3 *adj.*, 4 *n.* —**graph·i·cal·ly,** *adv.*

graph·ite (graf′īt) a soft, black form of carbon used in pencils. *n.*

grap·ple (grap′əl) struggle; wrestle: *The two fighters grappled in the centre of the ring. She grappled with the problem for an hour before she solved it.* *v.*, **grap·pled, grap·pling.**

grasp (grasp) 1 take hold of tightly with your hand: *He grasped the railing to keep from falling.* 2 a tight hold. 3 the power to reach and take hold of: *Success is within her grasp.* 4 understand: *to grasp the meaning of the word.* 5 understanding: *She has a good grasp of arithmetic.* 1, 4 *v.*, 2, 3, 5 *n.*
grasp at, a try to take hold of: *The drowning man grasped at the canoe.* b accept eagerly: *He grasped at the chance to become president.*

grasp·ing (grasp′ing) greedy. *adj.*

grass (gras) 1 the green plants, with long, slender leaves and stems, that cover fields, lawns, and pastures: *Horses, cows, and sheep eat grass.* 2 any plant that has jointed stems and long, narrow leaves: *Wheat, corn, oats, rice, and sugar cane are grasses.* *n.* —**grass′y,** *adj.*

A grasshopper can make a chirping noise by rubbing its wings together.

grass·hop·per (gras′hop′ər) a winged insect with a long, thin body and long, strong legs for jumping. It is a pest that eats crops. *n.*

grass·land (gras′land′) land that is mainly covered with grass and has few trees on it. Prairies and savannas are grasslands. *n.*

grate¹ (grāt) 1 a framework of iron bars for building a fire on so that air can reach it from the bottom and the ashes can fall through. 2 iron bars or iron mesh over a prison window or over a vent in the sidewalk. It is also called a **grating.** *n.*

grate² (grāt) 1 grind off in small pieces by rubbing against a rough, sharp surface: *to grate cheese.* 2 move with a harsh, grinding sound: *The door grated on its old, rusty hinges.* 3 have an annoying or unpleasant effect: *Her rude manners grate on other people.* *v.*, **grat·ed, grat·ing.** —**grat′er,** *n.*

a bat	e bed	i bid	o pot	u cup	th thin
ā cake	ē me	ī bite	ō go	ū rude	ᴛʜ then
ä bar	ə about	ər over	ȯ for	u̇ put	zh measure

grate•ful (grāt′fəl) thankful; full of appreciation: *I am grateful for your help.* *adj.* —**grate′ful•ly,** *adv.*

grat•i•fy (grat′ə fī′) 1 make someone feel good, especially about himself or herself: *Praise is very gratifying.* 2 satisfy; give in to: *to gratify a desire.* *v.,* **grat•i•fied, grat•i•fy•ing.** —**grat′i•fi•ca′tion,** *n.*

grat•i•tude (grat′ə tyūd′ *or* grat′ə tūd′) a feeling of deep appreciation; thankfulness. *n.*

grave[1] (grāv) 1 a place to bury a dead body. Usually it is marked by a specially cut **gravestone** with the dead person's name and other information carved on it. A piece of land used for graves is a **graveyard.** 2 death: *an early grave.* *n.*

grave[2] (grāv) serious: *grave words, grave danger, a grave decision.* *adj.,* **grav•er, grav•est.** —**grave′ly,** *adv.*

grav•el (grav′əl) small pieces of rock. Gravel is often used for roads and driveways. *n.*

grav•i•tate (grav′ə tāt′) 1 settle; sink; fall: *The sand and dirt in the water gravitated to the bottom of the bottle.* 2 tend to go; be strongly attracted: *At the fair, the children gravitated to the rides.* *v.,* **grav•i•tat•ed, grav•i•tat•ing.**

grav•i•ta•tion (grav′ə tā′shən) the force or pull that makes heavenly bodies tend to move toward or around one another. The planets circle the sun because of gravitation. *n.*

grav•i•ty (grav′ə tē) 1 the natural force that causes objects to move or tend to move toward the centre of the earth, moon, planet, etc. 2 the natural force that makes heavenly bodies tend to move toward or around each other; gravitation. 3 heaviness; weight. **Zero gravity** means weightlessness. 4 seriousness: *She soon realized the gravity of the situation.* *n., pl.* **grav•i•ties.**

gra•vy (grā′vē) a sauce made from the juices that come out of meat or vegetables in cooking. *n., pl.* **gra•vies.**

WORD HISTORY...... gravy

This word is a mistake. It comes from someone thinking that an Old French word *grané* was *gravé.* The word *grané* meant "properly seasoned," coming from Latin *granum* "grain," because to season food was to put grains of spice in it.

graze[1] (grāz) 1 feed on growing grass: *Cattle were grazing in the field.* 2 put animals to feed on growing grass: *to graze a flock of sheep.* *v.,* **grazed, graz•ing.**

graze[2] (grāz) 1 lightly brush or scrape against: *The snowball grazed the top of the fence.* 2 scrape the skin from: *I fell and grazed my knee.* 3 a light scrape. 1, 2 *v.,* **grazed, graz•ing;** 3 *n.*

grease (grēs) 1 animal fat that has been melted and then cooled to a soft solid: *bacon grease.* 2 any thick, oily, slippery substance. 3 put grease on a surface to reduce friction and sticking: *to grease an engine. Grease the pan before putting in the dough.* 1, 2 *n.,* 3 *v.,* **greased, greas•ing.** —**greas′y,** *adj.*

great (grāt) 1 big; large: *a great house, a great crowd.* 2 much; more than is usual: *great pain, great kindness.* 3 important; high in rank; famous: *a great leader, a great event.* 4 *Informal.* very good: *This is great soup!* *adj.* —**great′ly,** *adv.* —**great′ness,** *n.*

Great Divide (grāt′ di vīd′) in Canada, the high ridge of land extending northwest along the Rocky Mountain range, from which rivers flow west to the Pacific Ocean or east and north to Hudson Bay and the Arctic Ocean. It is also called the **Continental Divide.**

great–grand•child (grāt′grand′chīld′) the daughter or son of a person's grandchild. The daughter of a grandchild is a **great-granddaughter** and the son is a **great-grandson.** *n., pl.* **great-grand•chil•dren.**

great–grand•par•ent (grāt′grand′per′ənt) the mother or father of a grandparent. The mother of a grandparent is a **great-grandmother** and the father is a **great-grandfather.** *n.*

great horned owl (grāt′ hȯrnd′ oul′) a large, powerful brown and white owl with large ear tufts. It hunts many different birds and small animals.

Great Lakes (grāt′ lāks′) the five large bodies of fresh water that are included in the St. Lawrence Seaway; Lakes Superior, Michigan, Huron, Erie, and Ontario.

grebe (grēb) a water bird that looks like a loon, with partly webbed feet and a pointed bill. Most grebes have crests on their heads during the nesting season. *n.*

greed (grēd) a desire to get more and more, or to get a lot in a hurry. *n.* —**greed′y,** *adj.* —**greed′i•ly,** *adv.*

green (grēn) 1 the colour of the leaves of most growing plants in summer. 2 full of living plants. 3 not ripe: *This apple is still green.* 4 not dried, cured, or seasoned to make it ready for use: *green lumber.* 5 not experienced. 6 a piece of ground covered with grass, such as the grassy area around each hole on a golf course. 7 **greens,** *pl.* leaves and stems of plants used as food. 8 not harming the environment: *green products, a green company.* 1, 6, 7 *n.,* 1–5, 8 *adj.* —**green′ish,** *adj.*

give the green light, give permission or approval.
have a green thumb, be good at growing plants.

green•horn (grēn′hȯrn′) *Informal.* a person without experience. *n.*

green•house (grēn′hous′) a building with a glass roof and glass sides, kept warm for growing plants. It is also called a **hothouse.** *n.*

greenhouse effect (grēn′hous′ i fekt′) the gradual warming of the air around the earth because of pollution. This warming changes the weather patterns on earth and can affect living things in many ways.

greet (grēt) **1** say "Hello" or "Welcome" to; say or do something when you meet a person to show that you have noticed him or her: *Mom greeted me with a kiss.* **2** receive; respond to: *His speech was greeted with cheers.* **3** meet; present itself to: *When we opened the door, the strangest sight greeted our eyes.* *v.*

greet•ing (grē′ting) **1** the act or words of a person who greets someone; a welcome. **2 greetings,** *pl.* good wishes on a special occasion: *birthday greetings.* *n.*

grem•lin (grem′lin) a small, mischievous imaginary creature people blame for little things that go wrong. *n.*

gre•nade (grə nād′) a small bomb: *The soldiers threw grenades into the enemy's trenches.* *n.*

grew (grü) the past tense of **grow:** *It grew cold last night.* *v.*

grey (grā) **1** any shade that is a mix of black and white. Ashes and storm clouds are grey. **2** dark; gloomy: *a grey day.* **3** make or become grey: *greying hair.* 1 *n.*, 1, 2 *adj.*, 3 *v.* —**grey′ish,** *adj.*

The greyhound hunts by sight instead of by scent. It is fast enough to keep the game in view, and it has no scenting ability.

grey•hound (grā′hound′) a tall, slender hunting dog with a long head. Greyhounds can run very fast. *n.*

grey jay (grā′jā′) another name for the **Canada jay,** a North American bird with black and grey feathers.

grid (grid) a system of lines or bars crisscrossing at right angles. The lines of latitude and longitude form a grid. So do the main streets of some cities. *n.*

grid•dle (grid′əl) a heavy, flat metal plate for frying bacon, pancakes, and other things on. *n.*

grief (grēf) very great sadness, usually because of losing someone or something very precious: *The boy sobbed with grief when his puppy died.* *n.*
come to grief, have trouble; fail: *Although he worked hard, his plan came to grief.*

griev•ance (grē′vəns) a reason for being angry; something that someone thinks is unfair: *The workers were told to report any grievances to the manager.* *n.*

grieve (grēv) be or make very sad: *The people grieved over the death of the princess. It grieved her that her best friend was moving overseas.* *v.*, **grieved, griev•ing.**

griev•ous (grē′vəs) causing great pain or sorrow: *grievous crimes, a grievous loss.* *adj.*

grif•fin (grif′in) an imaginary animal with an eagle's head and wings and a lion's body, hind legs, and tail. *n.*

grill (gril) **1** a framework of metal wires or bars for broiling or barbecuing food on. **2** broil or barbecue: *We grilled the fish over the charcoal.* **3** a restaurant that specializes in broiled or barbecued food. **4** question severely and persistently: *The detectives grilled the prisoner until she finally confessed.* 1, 3 *n.*, 2, 4 *v.*

grim (grim) **1** stern and harsh; fierce; frightening: *grim, stormy weather, grim fortress walls.* **2** very serious; desperate: *The situation is grim.* **3** very solemn but determined to face the worst, as people often are when they're in a desperate situation: *a grim expression. They fought on with grim resolve.* *adj.*, **grim•mer, grim•mest.**

gri•mace (grim′is) **1** a twisting of the face in fear, pain, or disgust: *a grimace caused by pain.* **2** make a face: *Ram grimaced when he tasted the sour lemon.* 1 *n.*, 2 *v.*, **gri•maced, gri•mac•ing.**

grime (grīm) dirt rubbed deeply into a surface: *the grime on a coal miner's hands.* *n.* —**grim′y,** *adj.*

grin (grin) **1** smile broadly. **2** a broad smile. 1 *v.*, **grinned, grin•ning;** 2 *n.*
grin and bear it, suffer without complaining.

a bat	e bed	i bid	o pot	u cup	th thin
ā cake	ē me	ī bite	ō go	ü rude	ᴛʜ then
ä bar	ə about	ər over	ȯ for	ů put	zh measure

grind (grīnd) 1 crush into bits or into powder: *That mill grinds coffee beans.* 2 sharpen, smooth, or wear down by rubbing on something rough: *He ground the axe on the grindstone.* 3 rub harshly together: *to grind your teeth.* 4 *Informal.* hard, dull work: *To some of us, gardening is a grind.* 5 produce with long or boring effort: *After 20 years of grinding out a weekly column for the newspaper, she decided to quit.* 1–3, 5 *v.,* **ground, grinding;** 4 *n.* **—grind′er,** *n.*

grind·stone (grīnd′stōn′) a flat, round stone set in a frame and turned by hand, foot, or a motor. It is used to sharpen tools or to smooth and polish things. *n.*

grip (grip) 1 a firm hold. 2 hold tightly: *The dog gripped the stick in its teeth.* 3 hold the interest and attention of: *An exciting story grips the reader.* 4 handle: *the grip of a suitcase.* 1, 4 *n.,* 2, 3 *v.,* **gripped, grip·ping.**

gripe (grīp) *Informal.* 1 complain: *Oh, stop griping.* 2 complaint. 1 *v.,* **griped, grip·ing;** 2 *n.*

gris·ly (griz′lē) frightful; horrible: *a grisly sight. adj.,* **gris·li·er, gris·li·est.**

grist mill (grist mil) a mill for grinding grain. **Grist** is the grain that has been ground into flour.

gris·tle (gris′əl) tough, elastic tissue found in meat: *The roast beef had too much gristle. n.*

grit (grit) 1 very fine bits of sand: *There was grit in the spinach.* 2 toughness and courage: *The fighter showed lots of grit.* 3 press tightly together. People **grit their teeth** when they are about to do something scary or difficult: *He gritted his teeth and then plunged into the cold water.* 1, 2 *n.,* 3 *v.,* **grit·ted, grit·ting.** **—grit′ty,** *adj.*

Grit (grit) *Informal.* 1 a member of the Liberal Party. 2 having to do with the Liberals. 1 *n.,* 2 *adj.*

griz·zled (griz′əld) with grey-streaked hair. *adj.*

griz·zly (griz′lē) 1 grizzled. 2 short for **grizzly bear,** a large, fierce brown bear of western North America. 1 *adj.,* **griz·zli·er, griz·zli·est;** 2 *n., pl.* **griz·zlies.**

groan (grōn) 1 a sound made down in the throat to express grief, pain, or disapproval; a deep, short moan: *We heard the groans of the wounded men.* 2 give a groan or groans. 3 be loaded or burdened: *The table groaned with food.* 1 *n.,* 2, 3 *v.*

gro·cer (grō′sər) the owner of a store that sells food and household supplies. *n.*

gro·cer·y (grō′sə rē) 1 **groceries,** *pl.* food and household supplies bought in a store. 2 having to do with food and household supplies: *our grocery bill, a grocery store. n., pl.* **gro·cer·ies.**

grog·gy (grog′ē) wobbly on your feet and unable to think clearly: *After the operation he awoke still groggy from the anesthetic. adj.*

groin (groin) the hollow at either side of your body where your thighs reach your belly. *n.*

groom (grūm) 1 short for **bridegroom,** a man about to get married or just married. 2 take care of your personal appearance: *She was brought up to groom herself carefully.* 3 feed and take care of horses; rub down and brush a horse. 4 a person who feeds and takes care of horses. 1, 4 *n.,* 2, 3 *v.*

groove (grūv) a line that has been cut or dug evenly into a surface: *My desk has a groove to hold pencils. These cupboard doors open and close by sliding in a groove at the top and bottom. n.* **—grooved,** *adj.*

grope (grōp) 1 feel around with your hands: *She groped for a flashlight when the lights went out.* 2 search with a rather helpless, bewildered feeling: *The detectives groped for some clue to the mystery. v.,* **groped, grop·ing.**

gross (grōs) 1 disgusting; vulgar: *Her manners are gross.* 2 very bad and very obvious: *gross misconduct.* 3 before anything is subtracted: *Her gross earnings were $2000, but after paying taxes on it she was left with $1600.* 4 get as the total amount: *We grossed $984 from the bikeathon, but the prize for the student who got the most pledges still has to come out of that.* 5 twelve dozen; 144. 1–3 *adj.,* 4 *v.,* 5 *n., pl.* **gross.**

gro·tesque (grō tesk′) so weird or unnatural that it is ugly or even a bit frightening: *The book was full of pictures of grotesque imaginary creatures. adj.*

grouch (grouch) *Informal.* 1 a sulky, crabby person: *Why must you be such a grouch?* 2 be sulky or crabby; complain. 1 *v.,* 2 *n.* **—grouch′y,** *adj.*

ground[1] (ground) 1 the solid surface of the earth: *Snow covers the ground.* 2 an area of land used for some purpose: *The Yukon was their favourite fishing ground.* 3 run aground; hit the bottom: *The boat grounded in shallow water.* 4 give a firm foundation to: *This class is well grounded in French. Democracy is grounded on the belief that everyone is equal.* 5 background: *a blue pattern on a white ground.* 6 connect an electric wire with the ground. 7 prevent aircraft from flying: *The planes were grounded by the fog.* 8 forbid certain outside activities of a child as a punishment: *I was grounded for a month after I stayed out too late.* 1, 2, 5 *n.,* 3, 4, 6–8 *v.*
break new ground, do or discover something new.
from the ground up, completely; thoroughly: *He learned his mother's business from the ground up.*

gain ground, make progress: *The Conservatives gained ground in the last election.* **Lose ground** is the opposite.
get off the ground, make a successful start.
stand your ground, keep your position; refuse to give in or back down: *She stood her ground no matter how much they argued with her.*

ground² (ground) the past tense and past participle of **grind:** *He ground the dried leaves to powder in his hand. The wheat was ground to make flour.* *v.*

ground·hog (ground′hog′) a small North American burrowing animal that hibernates; woodchuck. On **Groundhog Day,** February 2, the groundhog is supposed to come out of its hole to see if the sun is shining. If so, the groundhog sees its shadow and returns to its hole for six more weeks of winter. *n.*

grounds (grounz) **1** the lawns and gardens around a public building: *Smoking is not allowed on the school grounds.* **2** ground coffee beans, after they have been used. **3** a reason for saying or believing something: *What are the grounds for your complaint?* *pl.n.*

ground·wa·ter (ground′wot′ər) water that flows through the ground into springs and wells. *n.*

group (grūp) **1** a number of people or things together: *A group of children were playing tag.* **2** form into a group or into groups: *to group books by subject. On playday, younger students were grouped with older ones for each team.* 1 *n.,* 2 *v.*

group home (grūp′ hōm′) a house where people with special needs can live together and receive help.

grouse¹ (grous) a wild bird related to the chicken. It is usually brown or greyish. *n., pl.* **grouse.**

grouse² (grous) *Informal.* **1** grumble; complain. **2** complaint. **3** a person who complains; grumbler. 1 *v.,* **groused, grous·ing;** 2, 3 *n.*

grove (grōv) a group of trees standing together. *n.*

grov·el (grov′əl *or* gruv′əl) lie face downward; crawl at someone's feet; act extremely humble: *The dog grovelled before its master when he spoke harshly.* *v.,* **grov·elled** or **grov·eled, grov·el·ling** or **grov·el·ing.**

grow (grō) **1** get bigger: *Her business has grown fast.* **2** live: *Few trees grow in the desert.* **3** cause to grow; plant and care for: *We grow wheat in many parts of Canada.* **4** get naturally as a part of itself: *If this lizard loses its tail it can grow a new one.* **5** become: *It grew cold.* *v.,* **grew, grown, grow·ing.**
grow on someone, become more and more likable: *I didn't like the cat at first, but it started to grow on me.*
grow up, become full grown; become an adult.

growl (groul) **1** low rumbling like the sound that a fierce dog makes in its throat as a warning. **2** make this sound: *The dog growled at us.* **3** grumble; speak angrily: *The customers growled about the bad food.* 1 *n.,* 2, 3 *v.*

grown–up (grō′nup′) **1** fully grown; adult: *a grown-up daughter.* **2** a person who is fully grown; an adult: *The boy worked with the grown-ups.* 1 *adj.,* 2 *n.*

growth (grōth) **1** the process or the amount of growing. **2** something growing: *A thick growth of bushes covered the ground.* **3** a lump or something else that has grown abnormally: *She has a harmless growth on the back of her neck.* *n.*

As the grub grows, it sheds its skin several times before becoming a pupa.

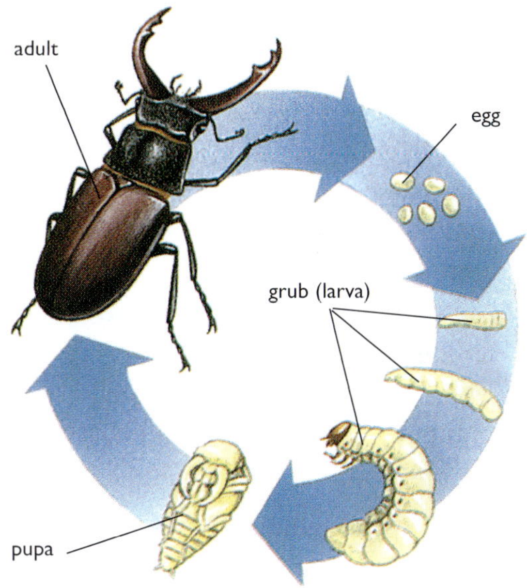

grub (grub) **1** a smooth, thick, wormlike larva of an insect, especially of a beetle. **2** dig up out of the ground: *Pigs grub for roots.* **3** to work hard: *to grub for a living.* **4** *Slang.* food. 1, 4 *n.,* 2, 3 *v.,* **grubbed, grub·bing.**

grub·by (grub′ē) dirty; grimy: *grubby hands.* *adj.,* **grub·bi·er, grub·bi·est.**

grudge (gruj) an angry feeling held against someone for a long time: *She carried a grudge against me because I won the game.* *n.*

grudg·ing·ly (gruj′ing lē) unwillingly. *adv.*

a bat	e bed	i bid	o pot	u cup	th **thin**
ā cake	ē me	ī bite	ō go	ū rude	ᴛʜ **then**
à bar	ə about	ər over	ò for	ù put	zh measure

gru·el (grū′əl) thin porridge. *n.*

gru·el·ling (grū′ə ling) very tiring; long and hard: *a gruelling cross-country race, a gruelling exam.* *adj.*

grue·some (grū′səm) causing fear or horror; horrible; frightful: *a gruesome sight.* *adj.*

WORD HISTORY..... gruesome

There used to be a word *grue*, which meant "shudder," so if something was **gruesome**, it made you shudder.

gruff (gruf) 1 low and rough-sounding: *He is a kind man with a gruff voice.* 2 rough and rather unfriendly; bad-tempered: *a gruff manner.* *adj.*

grum·ble (grum′bəl) 1 complain in a cranky way. 2 a bad-tempered complaint. 3 make a low, heavy sound like distant thunder: *My stomach was grumbling from hunger.* 1, 3 *v.*, **grum·bled, grum·bling;** 2 *n.*

grump (grump) a bad-tempered person: *What a grump! She didn't even say "Hello."* *n.* **—grump′y,** *adj.*

grunt (grunt) 1 the low, rough sound that a pig makes, or a sound like it. 2 make this sound; speak with this sound: *The sulky child grunted an apology.* 1 *n.*, 2 *v.*

gua·ca·mo·le (gwȧ′kə mō′lē) crushed avocados mixed with tomatoes, onions, and chili peppers and often used as a dip. *n.*

guar·an·tee (ger′ən tē′) 1 a promise to replace or repair something, or give the customer's money back, if the thing is not satisfactory. 2 make this kind of promise: *This company guarantees its computers for a year.* 3 promise: *I guarantee that I'll be on time* (*v.*). *Wealth is not a guarantee of happiness* (*n.*). 1, 3 *n.*, 2, 3 *v.*, **guar·an·teed, guar·an·tee·ing.**

guard (gȧrd) 1 watch over; take care that no one attacks: *The dog guards the house.* 2 keep from escaping or from doing harm: *The soldiers guarded the prisoners day and night. Guard your tongue.* 3 a person or group that guards. In some sports, a guard is a player who tries to hold back the other team from scoring. 4 something that protects: *A guard was placed in front of the fire to stop sparks.* 5 a careful watch: *A soldier kept guard over the prisoners.* 1, 2 *v.*, 3–5 *n.*
guard against, avoid or prevent by being careful: *Her mother told her to guard against getting her feet wet.*
off guard, unready; unprepared: *The pitcher was off guard when the ball was hit to him.* The opposite is **on guard.**
stand guard, do duty as a guard: *The soldier stood guard at the gate of the fort.*

guard·i·an (gȧr′dē ən) 1 someone who takes care of a person or thing. 2 a person chosen by law to take care of a child or seriously disabled person: *After the boy's parents died, his aunt became his guardian.* *n.*

guard·rail (gȧrd′rāl′) a railing used for safety. *n.*

guer·ril·la (gə ril′ə) a member of a small, independent band of soldiers who wear down the enemy by sudden raids and ambushes. Guerrillas often fight against the official army of their own country. *n.*

guess (ges) 1 have or give an opinion of something without really knowing: *She guessed at the height of the tree.* 2 an opinion formed or given in this way: *My guess is that it will rain tomorrow.* 3 get right or find out by guessing: *You have guessed the answer to the riddle!* 4 think; believe; suppose: *I guess it's OK.* 1, 3, 4 *v.*, 2 *n.*

guest (gest) a visitor. *n.*
be my guest, go ahead: *"May I use your phone?" "Be my guest."*

guide (gīd) 1 show the way; lead: *The trapper guided the hunters.* 2 a person or thing that shows the way: *Mountain climbers sometimes hire guides. Your feelings can be a poor guide for making decisions.* 3 short for **guidebook,** a book of directions and information on a particular place or thing. 1 *v.*, **guid·ed, guid·ing;** 2, 3 *n.* **—guid′ance,** *n.*

guide dog (gīd′ dog′) a dog trained to help a blind person go from place to place and avoid danger.

guide·line (gīd′līn′) a rule about the best way to do something: *When we started the job nobody gave us any guidelines.* *n.*

guild (gild) a society for people who share a certain kind of work or trade, to help each other: *the Canadian Guild of Potters.* *n.*

guile (gīl) dishonesty; tricks. *n.*
—guile′less, *adj.*

guilt (gilt) the fact, state, or feeling of having done wrong: *The evidence proved his guilt. When she saw the result of her careless act, she was overwhelmed with guilt.* *n.* **—guilt′less,** *n.* **—guilt′y,** *adj.*

guinea pig (gin′ē pig′) 1 a small, short-eared, short-tailed animal kept as a pet and for scientific experiments. It is native to South America. 2 any person or thing used for an experiment or test: *The school used our class as guinea pigs to test the new timetable.*

guise (gīz)
in the guise of, pretending to be: *in the guise of a friend.* *n.*

Guitars

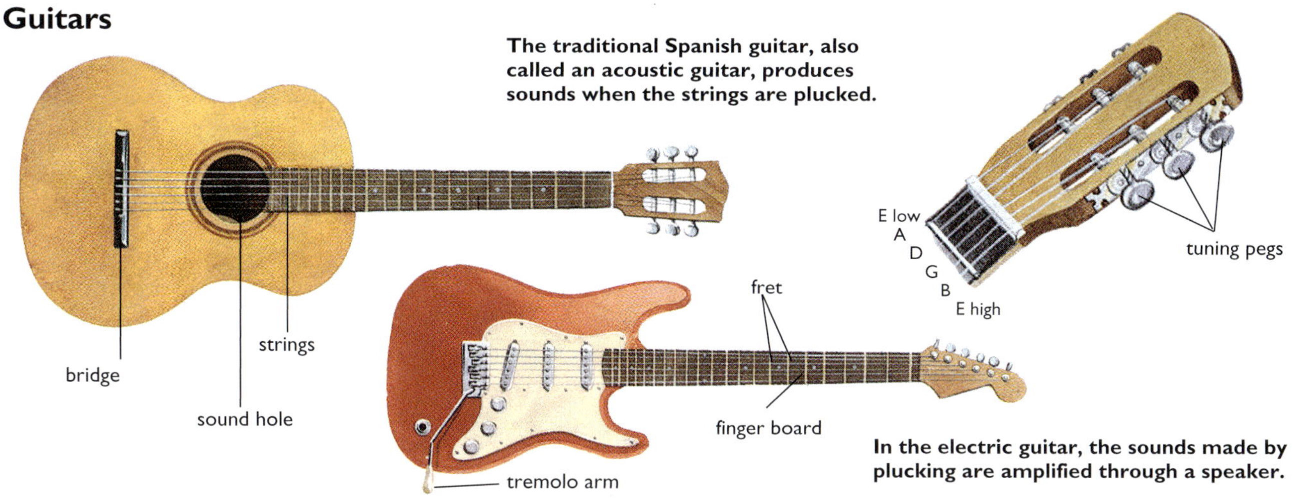

The traditional Spanish guitar, also called an acoustic guitar, produces sounds when the strings are plucked.

In the electric guitar, the sounds made by plucking are amplified through a speaker.

gui·tar (gə tȧr′) a musical instrument that usually has six strings, played with the fingers or with a pick. A **bass guitar** has four strings. *n.* —**gui·tar′ist,** *n.*

gulch (gulch) ravine; a deep, narrow valley in a dry region. It often becomes a stream bed when it rains. *n.*

gulf (gulf) **1** a large bay; part of an ocean or sea reaching far into the land: *The Gulf of St. Lawrence lies at the mouth of the St. Lawrence River, on the east coast of Canada.* **2** a very deep, wide crack or opening in the earth. **3** a wide separation: *The quarrel left a gulf between the old friends.* *n.*

gull (gul) a graceful grey-and-white bird living on or near large bodies of water. A gull has long wings, webbed feet, and a thick, strong beak. *n.*

gul·let (gul′it) another word for **esophagus,** the tube that carries food from the throat to the stomach. *n.*

gul·li·ble (gul′ə bəl) easily tricked or cheated: *The gullible reader believed everything the ad said.* *adj.*

gul·ly (gul′ē) a little valley or ditch, especially one made by flowing water: *After the storm, the newly seeded lawn was covered with gullies.* *n., pl.* **gul·lies.**

gulp (gulp) **1** swallow quickly or greedily: *Don't gulp your milk.* **2** swallow hard to control your surprise, tears, or fear: *The disappointed child gulped down a sob.* **3** a big, fast, or hard swallow. 1, 2 *v.,* 3 *n.*

gum[1] (gum) **1** a sticky juice of certain trees and plants that hardens in the air and dissolves in water. Gum is used in glue, drugs, candy, and other things. **2** a substance made of this, with sweetening and flavour, for chewing. **3** anything very sticky like gum. **4** cover or clog with something sticky. 1, 2, 3 *n.,* 4 *v.,* **gummed, gum·ming.** —**gum′my,** *adj.*

gum[2] (gum) Often, **gums,** *pl.,* the flesh around the teeth. *n.*

gum·bo (gum′bō) **1** the okra plant, including its pods, used for food. **2** soup thickened with okra pods: *chicken gumbo.* **3** soil that becomes sticky and heavy when wet, especially on the prairies. *n., pl.* **gum·bos.**

gum·drop (gum′drop′) a stiff, sugar-coated, jellylike piece of candy. *n.*

gun (gun) **1** a weapon with a metal tube for shooting bullets, shot, or cannonballs. Cannons, rifles, and pistols are guns. **2** a hand-held device shaped like a gun, for spraying or applying something: *a glue gun. He used a spray gun to paint the car.* **3** the shooting of a gun as a signal or salute: *The Governor General gets twenty-one guns as a salute.* **4** shoot with a gun: *He was gunned down by an enemy soldier.* 1–3 *n.,* 4 *v.,* **gunned, gun·ning.** —**gun′ner,** *n.*

gun for, *Informal.* try for; aim for.

gun the engine, step on the gas pedal; accelerate.

jump the gun, start too early.

stick to your guns, refuse to give in.

under the gun, being criticized or attacked.

gun·fire (gun′fīr′) the shooting of a gun or guns. *n.*

gung–ho (gung′hō′) *Informal.* very eager to do something: *Everyone was gung-ho about going to the movie.* *adj.*

gun·pow·der (gun′pou′dər) a powder that explodes when touched with fire or hammered. It is used in gun cartridges, blasting, and fireworks. *n.*

a bat	e bed	i bid	o pot	u cup	th thin
ā cake	ē me	ī bite	ō go	ū rude	ᴛʜ then
ȧ bar	ə about	ər over	ȯ for	ü put	zh measure

gun·shot (gun′shot′) **1** a shot fired from a gun, or the sound made by it. **2** the distance that a gun will shoot: *within gunshot.* *n.*

gun·wale (gun′əl) the upper edge of a ship's or boat's side. *n.*

gup·py (gup′ē) a very small, brightly coloured fish of tropical fresh water, often kept in aquariums. It comes from South America. The female guppy gives birth to live babies instead of producing eggs. *n., pl.* **gup·pies.**

gur·dwa·ra (gūr dwä′rə) a Sikh place of worship. A gurdwara usually has a yellow flag with the symbol of Sikhism on it, a circle with two swords crossed under the bottom and one sword standing upright in the middle. This symbol is called the **Khanda** (kun′də). *n.*

gur·gle (gər′gəl) **1** make the sound of bubbling, flowing water: *The stream gurgled over the stones. The baby gurgled happily.* **2** this sound. 1 *v.,* **gur·gled, gur·gling;** 2 *n.*

gu·ru (gū′rū *or* gủr′ū) **1** a Hindu teacher; a personal spiritual guide. **2** anyone that people trust to lead them or to give them expert advice: *a fitness guru.* *n.*

Guru Granth Sa·hib (gū′rū grunt′ sə hēb′) the holy book of the Sikh religion, containing the teachings of the ten Sikh gurus or prophets. It is also called the **Adi Granth.**

gush (gush) **1** pour or flow out in a sudden rush: *Water gushed from the broken pipe.* **2** speak or write with a rush of enthusiasm or exaggerated emotion. **3** a sudden rush or flow of liquid. 1, 2 *v.,* 3 *n.* **—gush′y,** *adj.*

gust (gust) a sudden, strong blast of wind: *A gust upset the small sailboat.* *n.* **—gust′y,** *adj.*

gus·to (gus′tō) hearty enjoyment: *The hungry children ate their dinner with gusto.* *n.*

gut (gut) **1 guts,** *pl. Slang.* **a** intestines. **b** courage. **2** stomach or belly. A **gut feeling** or **gut reaction** is pure emotion, not affected by reasoning. **3** remove or destroy the insides of: *They gutted the fish. The building was gutted by fire.* 1, 2 *n.,* 3 *v.,* **gut·ted, gut·ting.** **—gut′sy,** *adj.* **—gut′less,** *adj.*

gut·ter (gut′ər) **1** a ditch or low part along the side of a road to carry off water. **2** eavestrough; a trough along the edge of a roof to carry away water. *n.*

gut·tur·al (gut′ər əl) sounding harsh and coming from deep in the throat. *adj.*

guy[1] (gī) *Slang.* **1** a man or boy: *Most of the guys wore suits to the graduation.* **2** a person. *n.*

guy[2] (gī) Often, **guy rope** or **guy wire,** a rope or wire attached to something to steady it. *n.*

guz·zle (guz′əl) drink greedily; drink too much. *v.,* **guz·zled, guz·zling.**

Gwich'in (gwich′in) **1** a First Nations people living in the Northwest Territories. They belong to the Dene Nation. **2** their language, which belongs to the Athapascan family. **3** having to do with these people or their language. **Kutchin** is another form. 1, 2 *n.,* 3 *adj.*

gym (jim) **1** short for **gymnasium** (jim nā′zē əm), a building or large room equipped for indoor sports or exercise. **2** physical education as a school subject: *Ms. Khan teaches us gym.* *n.*

gym·nas·tics (jim nas′tiks) **1** exercises for developing strength, flexibility, and balance, usually done in a gymnasium on special equipment as a sport. A person who does gymnastics is a **gymnast.** **2** any very tricky or difficult moves or actions: *mental gymnastics.* *n.*

Gyp·sy (jip′sē) **1** a person belonging to a wandering race of dark-skinned, dark-eyed people who came from India in the 1400s and 1500s. Their language is called **Romany.** **2** having to do with the Gypsies. 1 *n., pl.* **Gyp·sies;** 2 *adj.*

WORD HISTORY........gypsy

Gypsy was made from the word *Egyptian.* When the gypsies first went to England in the 1500s, they were thought to come from Egypt.

gy·rate (jī′rāt) move in a circle or spiral; whirl; rotate: *A spinning top gyrates.* *v.,* **gy·rat·ed, gy·rat·ing.**

gy·ros (yē′rōs *or* jē′rōs) spiced meat roasted on a vertical skewer and then shaved off in pieces as a filling for a round, flat bread. *n.*

gy·ro·scope (jī′rə skōp′) a wheel with a heavy rim, mounted so that its axle can point in any direction. When the wheel spins, the axle will remain pointing in the same direction even if its supporting rings or outside frame is turned or tilted. Gyroscopes are used to keep ships, planes, and other things balanced. A **gyrocompass** uses a gyroscope to keep it pointing north. *n.* **—gy′ro·scop′ic** (jī′rə skop′ik), *adj.*

Hh

h or **H** (āch) 1 the eighth letter of the English alphabet, or the speech sound that it stands for. We hear the sound of *h* in *home* but not in *hour.* 2 the eighth thing in a list. *n., pl.* **h's** or **H's.**

h *symbol for* hour or hours.

ha^1 (hä *or* ha) 1 a word shouted in surprise, ridicule, or triumph: *"Ha! We have won!" shouted the team.* 2 in writing, a way of indicating laughter: *"Ha! ha! ha!" laughed the boys.* *interj.*

ha^2 *symbol for* hectare.

hab·it (hab′it) 1 a person's usual way of acting: *It is her habit to check all the doors before going to bed.* 2 an addiction: *a drug habit.* 3 a special set of clothes, such as the clothes worn for riding or the long, loose gown traditionally worn by a monk or nun. *n.*
—ha·bit′u·al (hə bich′ū əl), *adj.*

hab·it·a·ble (hab′ə tə bəl) fit to live in. *adj.*

🍁 **hab·it·ant** (hab′ə tont′ *or* ab ē tän′) a French-Canadian farmer, especially in earlier times. *n.*

hab·i·tat (hab′ə tat′) the place where an animal or plant naturally lives or grows: *The arctic coast is the habitat of polar bears.* *n.*

hab·i·ta·tion (hab′ə tā′shən) 1 a place or building to live in; home; dwelling. 2 the act of inhabiting; living in: *Is the house fit for habitation?* *n.*

hack (hak) 1 cut roughly: *She hacked the crate apart with an old axe.* 2 a rough cut. 3 a notch cut in the ice at one end of a curling rink, used as a foothold when a player throws a rock. 4 give short, dry coughs: *The boy hacked all night.* 5 a short dry cough. 6 *Slang.* handle; put up with: *I can hack anything for one day.* 7 **a** fool around on the computer using programming knowledge gained by experience. **b** break into secret computer files. 1, 4, 6, 7 *v.,* 2, 3, 5 *n.* **—hack′er,** *n.*

hack·neyed (hak′nēd) used so often in speaking or writing that it has become boring or meaningless: *a hackneyed expression.* *adj.*

hack·saw (hak′so′) a saw for cutting metal. It has a narrow, fine-toothed blade fixed in a frame. *n.*

had (had) the past tense and past participle of **have:** *She had a party. A fine time was had by all who came.* *v.*

had·dock (had′ək) a food fish of the northern Atlantic, like a cod but smaller. *n., pl.* **had·dock** or **had·docks.**

had·n't (had′ənt) had not.

hag·gard (hag′ərd) looking worn out from pain, fatigue, worry, or hunger: *The haggard faces of the rescued miners showed how they had suffered.* *adj.*

hag·gle (hag′əl) argue, especially about a price or the details of an agreement. *v.,* **hag·gled, hag·gling.**

Hai·da (hī′də) 1 a First Nations people living in the Queen Charlotte Islands. 2 their language. 3 having to do with these people or their language. 1, 2 *n.,* 3 *adj.*

hai·ku (hī′kū) a type of Japanese poem that has three lines. The first and last line have five syllables, and the second line has seven. *n., pl.* **hai·ku.**

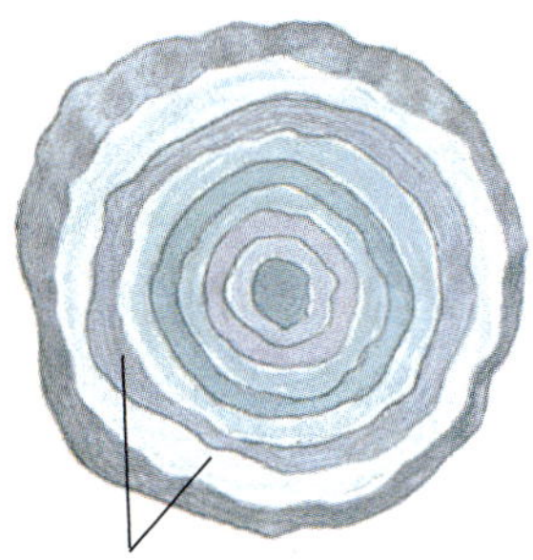

Hail is formed when raindrops in a storm cloud are repeatedly lifted by air currents, and frozen high in the cloud. When the drops are heavy enough, they fall as hailstones.

hail^1 (hāl) 1 tiny balls of ice that come down from the clouds in a shower; frozen rain: *Hail fell with such violence that it broke windows.* An individual piece of hail is a **hailstone.** 2 a shower of something like hail: *A hail of bullets met the soldiers.* 3 rain down as hail: *It sometimes hails during a thunderstorm. The angry mob hailed insults on the speaker.* 1, 2 *n.,* 3 *v.*

hail^2 (hāl) 1 cheer or praise a person or thing: *The crowd hailed the winner.* 2 Cheers! Welcome! a greeting: *Hail to the winner!* 3 call or wave to someone, either in greeting or to get him or her to notice you: *to hail a taxi. The captain hailed the passing ship.* 1, 3 *v.,* 2 *interj.*
hail from, come from: *These visitors hail from Victoria.*

a bat	e bed	i bid	o pot	u cup	th thin
ā cake	ē me	ī bite	ō go	ū rude	ᴛʜ then
ä bar	ə about	ər over	ô for	ů put	zh measure

hair (her) 1 a fine, threadlike growth from the skin of human beings and animals. 2 a mass of such growths, especially on a person's head: *Her hair is getting long.* *n.* —**hair′less,** *adj.*
get in someone's hair, be a nuisance to; annoy.
let your hair down, relax.
split hairs, make a big deal out of tiny differences.

Word Family.......... hair

hairbrush: a brush for grooming or styling your hair
haircut/hairdo/hairstyle: the way hair is arranged
hairdresser/hairstylist: a person who styles hair
hairless: bald; with no body hair at all

hair•pin (her′pin′) 1 a piece of wire folded tightly in half, used to keep a person's hair in place. 2 shaped like a hairpin; U-shaped: *a hairpin turn in a road.* 1 *n.,* 2 *adj.*

hair–rais•ing (her′rā′zing) *Informal.* so scary that it makes you feel as if your hair were standing on end: *a hair-raising story.* *adj.*

hair•y (her′ē) covered with hair: *hairy hands, a hairy ape, hairy cloth.* *adj.,* **hair•i•er, hair•i•est.**

Hai•sla (hīs′lə) 1 a First Nations people living in British Columbia. 2 having to do with these people. 1 *n.,* 2 *adj.*

hajj or **haj** (håj) the pilgrimage to Mecca, the holy city of Islam. It is a duty for Muslims to make this pilgrimage once in their lifetime. A person who has made the pilgrimage is a **hajji.** *n.*

ha•lal (hålål) permitted under Islamic religious law: *halal meats.* The opposite is **haram.** *adj.*

hale (hāl) strong and well; healthy: *The 90-year-old was still hale and hearty.* *adj.,* **hal•er, hal•est.**

half (haf) 1 one of two equal parts of something: *Half of 4 is 2. Two halves make a whole* (*n.*). *A half litre is 500 mL* (*adj.*). 2 to a half of the whole amount or degree: *a glass half full of milk.* 3 partly: *half cooked, half asleep.* 1 *n., pl.* **halves;** 1 *adj.,* 2, 3 *adv.*
half past, 30 minutes past the hour: *Half past six is 6:30.*

Word Family.......... half

half-baked: not cooked enough; not complete
half-brother: a brother related through one parent only
half-hearted: without enough enthusiasm
half-sister: a sister related through one parent only
half-time: the break between two halves of a game
half-truth: a statement that is only partly true

half–life (haf′līf′) the time it takes for any substance, especially a radioactive one, to be broken down to half its strength: *Carbon-14 has a half-life of 5730 years.* *n., pl.* **half-lives.**

half–mast (haf′mast′) a position halfway or part way down from the top of a mast or flagpole: *When the Governor General died, flags were lowered to half-mast as a mark of respect.* *n.*

half•way (haf′wā′) 1 at or to half the total distance or time: *the halfway mark* (*adj.*). *Halfway through the concert he lost his voice* (*adv.*). 2 not completely or not complete; partially or partial: *Don't just do the job halfway* (*adv.*). *We need a real solution, not just halfway measures* (*adj.*). *adv.* or *adj.*
go or **meet halfway,** in a disagreement, give in part of the way if the other person will also do so.

hal•i•but (hal′ə bət) the largest flatfish, often used as food. It lives in the North Atlantic. *n., pl.* **hal•i•but** or **hal•i•buts.**

hall (hol) 1 a narrow part in a building, with rooms opening off it: *The bathroom was at the end of a long hall.* **Hallway** is another word for this meaning. 2 a large room for holding meetings, banquets, etc.: *Our town needs a bigger hall for wedding receptions.* 3 a large public building serving some special purpose: *the Hockey Hall of Fame. The offices of the mayor and city councillors are in the city hall.* *n.*

hal•le•lu•jah (hal′ə lū′yə) in Jewish and Christian worship, a word meaning "praise the Lord!" *interj.*

Hal•low•een or **Hal•low•e'en** (hal′ə wēn′) the evening of October 31, celebrated by dressing up in costumes. Many children also go door to door, collecting candy. *n.*

ha•lo (hā′lō) 1 in pictures, a golden circle or disk of light shown over or around the head of a holy person or an angel. 2 a ring of light around a shining body such as the sun or moon. *n., pl.* **ha•los** or **ha•loes.**

hal•o•gen (hal′ə jən) a chemical element that often takes the form of a gas. In a **halogen lamp,** an electric current passes through a tube containing such a gas, producing a strong, pure white light. *n.*

halt (holt) stop: *The soldiers halted for a short rest* (*v.*). *All work came to a halt* (*n.*). *v.* or *n.*

hal•ter (hol′tər) 1 a rope or strap for leading or tying an animal. 2 Usually, **halter top,** a backless and sleeveless blouse for girls and women. It is fastened at the top and bottom by one set of ties behind the neck and another set across the lower back. *n.*

halt•ing (hol′ting) stumbling or hesitating; uncertain: *a halting apology, halting footsteps.*

halve (hav) 1 divide into two equal parts or shares: *The two girls agreed to halve expenses on their trip.* 2 cut down to half: *The new machine will halve the time and cost of doing the work by hand.* *v.,* **halved, halv·ing.**

halves (havz) plural of **half:** *Two halves make one whole.* *n.*
go halves, share equally.

ham (ham) 1 salted and smoked meat from the upper part of a pig's hind leg. 2 a person who operates his or her own short-wave radio at home as a hobby. 3 *Informal.* an actor who performs in an overdone, exaggerated style, or someone who likes to clown when people are watching. 4 Often, **ham it up,** *Informal.* clown around or overact. 1–3 *n.,* 4 *v.,* **hammed, ham·ming.**

ham·burg·er (ham′bər′gər) 1 ground beef. 2 this meat shaped into a flat patty and fried or broiled, especially when served in a split bun. This word is sometimes shortened to **burger.** *n.*

ham·let (ham′lit) a small group of houses in the country, sometimes with a post office, store, or gas station but not much else. A hamlet has no fixed boundaries, is usually smaller than a village, and does not have its own government. *n.*

ham·mer (ham′ər) 1 a tool with a heavy metal part set across the top of a long handle. It is used to drive nails and to beat metal into shape. 2 something shaped or used like a hammer, such as the part inside a piano that hits the strings when you press a key. 3 hit with a hammer: *to hammer nails. The metal was hammered into a flat sheet.* 4 pound; beat: *The angry man hammered on the door with his fist.* 1, 2 *n.,* 3, 4 *v.*
hammer and tongs, with all your force and strength: *The two girls fought hammer and tongs.*
hammer away at, a keep working hard at: *She hammered away at her homework till it was finished.* b keep nagging; badger: *He hammered away at his mother till he got what he wanted.*
hammer out, a beat into shape with a hammer. b think or talk about something until it is settled: *to hammer out a deal.*

ham·mock (ham′ək) a swinging bed made of tough cloth or netting, suspended at both ends. *n.*

ham·per¹ (ham′pər) get in the way of; hold back; hinder: *The cast on my arm hampered my efforts at getting dressed.* *v.*

ham·per² (ham′pər) a large container, often made of wickerwork, usually having a lid: *a picnic hamper, a clothes hamper.* *n.*

In their natural environment, golden hamsters live alone, and are active mostly at night.

ham·ster (ham′stər) a small, short-tailed animal of the rat family with large pouches in its cheeks, which it uses for carrying food. Hamsters can be kept as pets. *n.*

Han (hon) 1 a First Nations people living in the Yukon River valley. 2 their language. 3 having to do with these people or their language. 1, 2 *n.,* 3 *adj.*

hand (hand) 1 the end part of the arm below the wrist, including the fingers and thumb. 2 anything like a hand: *The hands of a clock show the time.* 3 a hired worker who uses his or her hands: *a farm hand, a factory hand.* 4 give with the hand; pass: *Please hand me a spoon.* 5 a part or share in doing something: *He had no hand in the matter.* 6 side: *On your left hand you will see the Parliament buildings.* 7 handwriting: *He writes in a clear hand.* 8 a measure used in giving the height of horses; the width of a hand, about 10 cm: *This horse is 18 hands high.* 9 a single round in a card game, or the cards a player holds for that round. 1–3, 5–9 *n.,* 4 *v.*
at hand, near: *The time for action is at hand.*
by hand, without machinery: *I sewed this by hand.*
from hand to mouth, without being able to put anything aside for the future: *During a drought, many pioneer families lived from hand to mouth.*
give someone a hand, a help someone. b clap for someone; applaud.
hand down, pass along to someone younger or lower in rank: *His old clothes were handed down to his younger brother. The decision was handed down by the Supreme Court.*
hand in, give something to a person who has the authority to collect it: *Hand in your bus money to the teacher.*
hand in glove, working closely together.
hand out, give out; distribute: *The storekeeper handed out free suckers.*
hand over, give up; give back: *When Mario asked for his book, I handed it over.*

a bat	e bed	i bid	o pot	u cup	th thin
ā cake	ē me	ī bite	ō go	ū rude	ᴛʜ then
ä bar	ə about	ər over	ò for	ů put	zh measure

hand to hand, close together; close up: *to fight hand to hand.*
have your hands full, have as much to do as you can manage.
in someone's hands, in someone's possession, care, or control: *The decision is no longer in my hands. Jorge left his bicycle in Leanne's hands.* The opposite is **out of someone's hands.**
lend a hand, help: *I asked my sister to lend a hand with fixing the bike.*
on hand, available; there, ready to be used or bought or to help: *There were enough people on hand to clean up the whole neighbourhood.*
on someone's hands, in someone's charge, as something that he or she is responsible for, often as a burden or nuisance: *I was left with a big mess on my hands.* The opposite is **off someone's hands:** *Let's have a yard sale and get all this old stuff off our hands.*
on the one hand, on the other hand, considering each side of the question or argument: *On the one hand, it's a great bike; on the other hand, I can't afford to buy it.*
out of hand, **a** out of control: *The angry crowd soon got out of hand.* **b** at once; without much thought: *The boy was sent to his room out of hand.*
take in hand, **a** bring under control: *Try to take your dog in hand.* **b** handle; deal with: *The principal promised to take the matter in hand.*
try your hand at, try: *After trying his hand at politics, he soon went back to business.*

Word Family......... **hand**

handball: a game played by hitting a ball with your hand, against a wall
handbill: a flyer handed out to people
handbook: a small book of directions
hand-held: about something made to be operated by holding it in your hand
handkerchief: a soft square of cloth for wiping your nose, face, or hands.
handlebars: the part of a bicycle that you hold to steer
handmade: made by hand, not by machinery
handrail: a rail used as a guard on a stair or platform, etc.
handset: a phone that has the keypad, receiver, and mouthpiece all in one unit
handshake: clasping and shaking hands with someone in friendship, or agreement
handspring: a somersault from a standing position, first onto your hands, then your feet
handstand: balancing upside down on your hands

hand•bag (hand′bag′) **1** a woman's purse, used to hold money, keys, cosmetics, and so on. **2** a small suitcase or travelling bag. *n.*

hand•craft (hand′kraft′) **1** something made skilfully by hand: *Our display of handcrafts includes quilts and wooden furniture.* **2** a trade or art requiring skill with the hands: *Basket weaving is a handcraft.* **Handicraft** is another form for both of the above. **3** make something by hand, with skill: *My grandfather handcrafted a wooden box carved with my initials.* 1, 2 *n.,* 3 *v.*

hand•cuff (hand′kuf′) **1** one of a pair of steel bracelets joined by a short chain that are fastened around the wrists of a prisoner or an arrested person. **2** put handcuffs on: *The officer handcuffed the thief.* 1 *n.,* 2 *v.*

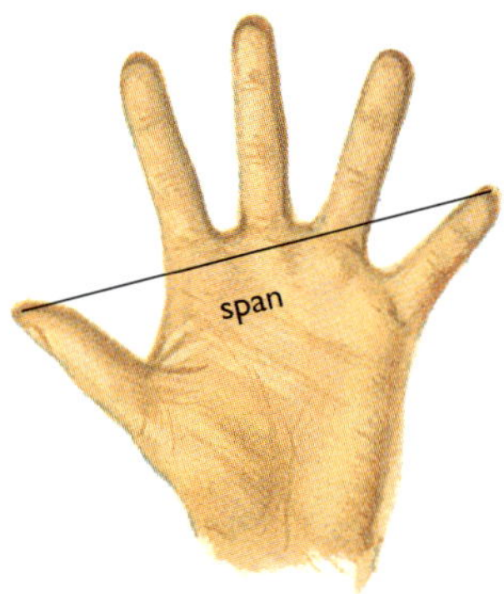

A handful is only one of the measuring units that the hand has been used for. A finger's breadth was called a digit, and two digits made an inch (about 2.5 cm). From thumb to little finger (stretched) was called a span.

hand•ful (hand′fůl′) **1** as much as the hand can hold: *a handful of candy.* **2** a small number or quantity: *Only a handful of students entered the contest.* **3** *Informal.* a person or thing that is difficult to handle or control: *That child is quite a handful.* *n., pl.* **hand•fuls.**

hand•i•cap (han′dē kap′) **1** something that puts a person at a disadvantage; hindrance: *A sore throat is a handicap to a singer.* **2** put at a disadvantage; hinder: *Tia's terrible temper handicapped her greatly.* **3** an advantage or disadvantage given to someone in a contest or game to make sure his or her chances are the same as everyone else's: *If a runner has a handicap of 5 m in a 100 m dash, it means that he has to run either 95 m or 105 m.* **4** give such a handicap to: *The Sports Committee handicapped me 5 m.* 1, 3 *n.,* 2, 4 *v.,* **hand•i•capped, hand•i•cap•ping.**

hand•i•work (han′dē wərk′) **1** work done with the hands. **2** the result of a person's action: *This mess is the handiwork of a vandal.* *n.*

han•dle (han′dəl) **1** a part of a thing used to hold it or control it with your hand. A mug, a hairbrush, and a pair of pliers all have handles. **2** touch, feel, or use with the hand: *Don't handle that until you buy it.* **3** manage; direct: *The rider handles her horses well.* **4** act or work in a certain way when driven or managed: *This car handles easily.* **5** do business in: *That store handles meat and groceries.* 1 *n.,* 2–5 *v.,* **han•dled, han•dling.**

hand·some (han′səm) 1 good-looking: *a handsome baby boy.* 2 fairly large; generous: *His aunt gave him a handsome sum of money for his birthday.* *adj.*, **hand·som·er, hand·som·est.**

hand–to–hand (hand′tə hand′) up close and using the hands: *a hand-to-hand fight.* *adj.*

hand·writ·ing (hand′rī′ting) writing done by hand. Each person's handwriting is different. *n.*

hand·y (han′dē) 1 easy to get at; close by: *Keep these instructions handy.* 2 easy to use; useful: *a handy tool.* 3 skilful with the hands: *She is handy with tools.* *adj.*, **hand·i·er, hand·i·est.**

hang (hang) 1 fasten or be fastened at the top or one side so that it can swing freely: *to hang curtains, to hang a door on its hinges. The swing hangs from a tree.* 2 kill or die by hanging with a rope around the neck. In some countries they hang murderers. 3 droop; bend down: *She hung her head in shame.* 4 the way a thing hangs: *She didn't like the hang of her new skirt.* 1–3 *v.*, **hung** (or, usually, **hanged** for 2), **hang·ing;** 4 *n.*
get the hang of, *Informal.* learn how to do: *It took me a while to get the hang of walking on stilts.*
hang around, **a** spend time in a place, not doing anything worthwhile: *He just hangs around the house all day.* **b** keep company: *She hangs around with Jody a lot.*
hang back, hesitate; be shy or doubtful about joining an activity.
hang in, keep going when things are tough: *He was tired, but hung in till the job was done.* **Hang in there** is often said to encourage someone.
hang on, **a** hold tight. **b** wait: *Hang on, I'm not quite ready.* **c** depend on: *My decision hangs on your answer.*
hang out, *Informal.* spend time, often not doing much: *to hang out at the mall. They hang out with younger kids.*
hang together, **a** stay united. **b** make sense; form a well organized whole: *This paragraph does not hang together very well.*
hang up, end a phone call.

hang·ar (hang′ər) a building for storing and working on aircraft. *n.*

hang·er (hang′ər) anything used for hanging something up: *a coat hanger.* *n.*

hang–glide (hang′ glīd′) glide through the air holding onto a large cloth-covered frame called a **hang-glider,** letting air currents lift you up and carry you along. To start off you have to jump from a high place with the hang-glider. *v.*, **hang-glid·ed, hang-glid·ing.**

hang·man (hang′man′) 1 a man who used to hang criminals who were sentenced to death by hanging. 2 a game where you guess a word by trying one letter at a time. With each incorrect letter, a line is drawn to make a picture of a person hanging from a gallows. *n.*, *pl.* **hang·men** (hang′men′).

hang·nail (hang′nāl′) a bit of skin that hangs partly loose near a fingernail. It is sometimes painful. *n.*

hank·y (hang′kē) *Informal.* handkerchief. *n.*, *pl.* **hank·ies.**

Ha·nuk·kah or **Cha·nu·kah** (hȧ′nə kə) an eight-day Jewish festival in December. Hanukkah is a feast of dedication celebrating the defeat of the ancient Greeks, who made a decree against following Jewish law and ritual in the land of Israel. Hanukkah is also called the Festival of Lights because of the eight-branched candelabra used during the holiday, in memory of the menorah lit in the ancient temple in Jerusalem. *n.*

hap·haz·ard (hap′haz′ərd) not planned or organized: *If you do the job in such a haphazard way, it will take longer.* *adj.*

hap·pen (hap′ən) 1 take place or go on, often by chance: *Nothing interesting happens here. Accidents will happen.* 2 do or experience something by chance: *I happened to sit next to a famous hockey player.* 3 be done to or go wrong with; become of: *"What happened to your arm?" "I broke it."* *v.* —**hap′pen·ing,** *n.*
as it happens, by chance; as it turns out: *As it happens, I have no money with me.*
happen on or **upon,** meet or find by chance: *She happened on a dime while looking for her ball.*

hap·py (hap′ē) 1 feeling or showing pleasure and joy; glad; contented: *a happy smile.* 2 lucky; fortunate: *By a happy coincidence we ended up in the same campground as my best friend's family!* *adj.*, **hap·pi·er, hap·pi·est.** —**hap′pi·ly,** *adv.* —**hap′pi·ness,** *n.*

hap·py–go–luck·y (hap′ē gō luk′ē) taking things easily; trusting to luck and expecting everything to be fine. *adj.*

har·ass (har′əs *or* hə ras′) keep attacking in small ways: *Stop harassing me about my untidiness.* *v.*

har·bour or **har·bor** (hȧr′bər) 1 a place of shelter for boats and ships near the shore: *Many yachts are in the harbour.* 2 any place of shelter. 3 give shelter to: *The dog's shaggy hair harbours fleas.* 4 hang on to in your mind: *Don't harbour grudges.* 1, 2 *n.*, 3, 4 *v.*

a bat	e bed	i bid	o pot	u cup	th thin
ā cake	ē me	ī bite	ō go	ū rude	ᴛʜ then
ȧ bar	ə about	ər over	ȯ for	u̇ put	zh measure

hard (härd) **1** not soft; not yielding to the touch; firm and solid: *Rocks are hard.* The **hardness** of minerals is rated from 1 to 10 on a scale called **Mohs' scale,** and is tested by scratching: a harder mineral can scratch one that is not so hard. **2** taking a lot of skill, effort, or time; difficult: *a hard job, a hard lesson, a hard person to get along with.* **3** with a lot of force or energy: *a hard wind* (*adj.*). *I tried hard to lift the log* (*adv.*). **4** tough or harsh; stern: *hard features, hard voices.* **5** severe; causing much pain, trouble, worry, etc.: *a hard winter, hard times.* 1–5 *adj.,* 3 *adv.* **—hard′ness,** *n.* **—hard′en,** *v.*
hard by, an old or poetic expression for "near": *The house stands hard by the bridge.*
hard of hearing, partly deaf.
hard up, *Informal.* needing money or anything very badly: *He is always hard up the day before he is paid. It rained all week, and we were hard up for things to do.*

Word Family.......... hard

hardcover: bound with a hard cover
hard-headed: not easily fooled; practical
hard-hearted: without pity; cruel
hard-nosed: not sentimental; practical
hardworking: usually working hard

hard–boiled (härd′boild′) **1** boiled until the inside is solid: *hard-boiled eggs.* **2** *Informal.* not easily moved by feelings; tough. *adj.*

hard copy (härd′ kop′ē) information printed out from a computer onto paper: *It's often easier to find spelling mistakes on the hard copy rather than the screen.*

hard disk (härd′ disk′) a round, flat metal plate coated with magnetic material, used inside a computer to store large amounts of data and programs. A **hard drive** holds and reads the hard disk. You cannot take the hard disk out of the computer.

hard·ly (härd′lē) **1** only just; barely: *We hardly had time to eat.* **2** not quite; not really: *I may have exaggerated, but it is hardly fair to call me a liar.* **3** probably not: *They will hardly go for a bike ride in all this rain.* *adv.*

USING WORDS ...... hardly

The words **hardly** and **scarcely** are treated as negatives, and should not have another negative with them. Instead of saying *The video showed hardly nothing that we didn't already know,* you should say *The video showed hardly anything that we didn't already know.*

Which of the following sentences is correct?
I didn't have scarcely enough money.
I scarcely had enough money

hard·ship (härd′ship) something hard to bear; a hard condition of living: *Hunger, cold, and sickness were among the hardships of pioneer life.* *n.*

hard·ware (härd′wer′) **1** articles made from metal, used to build and repair things: *Locks, hinges, nails, screws, utensils, and tools are hardware.* **2** the mechanical or electronic parts of a computer system; the computer itself, the monitor, printer, keyboard, modem, etc. but not the programs that run the system. *n.*

hard water (härd′wot′ər) water containing calcium or other minerals that make it difficult for soap to lather.

hard·wood (härd′wu̇d′) any hard, heavy wood such as oak, maple, or mahogany. Hardwood is usually from deciduous trees. *n.*

har·dy (här′dē) able to bear hard conditions; strong; tough: *Cold weather does not kill hardy plants.* *adj.,* **har·di·er, har·di·est.**

The snowshoe rabbit is really a hare. In winter, its coat turns from brown to white.

hare (her) an animal like a rabbit but larger and with longer ears and hind legs. *n.*

Hare (her) **1** a First Nations people living in the Mackenzie River valley. **2** their language, which belongs to the Athapascan family. **3** having to do with these people or their language. 1, 2 *n.,* 3 *adj.*

hark (härk) an old or poetic word for "listen." **Hearken** means the same. *v.*
hark back, go back in time: *This story harks back 20 years.*

harm (härm) **1** hurt; damage: *The accident did a lot of harm to the car* (*n.*). *The driver was not harmed in the accident* (*v.*). **2** wrong: *What harm is there in borrowing a friend's bicycle?* 1, 2 *n.,* 1 *v.* **—harm′ful,** *adj.* **—harm′less,** *adj.*

har·mat·tan (här′mə tan′) a very hot, dusty wind that blows from the Sahara desert onto the west coast of Africa. *n.*

har•mon•i•ca (här mon′ə kə) a small musical instrument with several metal reeds in a wooden frame covered with metal. You hold it across your mouth and blow into it, moving it sideways so as to make different reeds vibrate and produce different notes. The other name for it is **mouth organ.** *n.*

har•mo•ny (här′mə nē) **1** a beautiful arrangement of different colours, musical sounds, shapes, etc., so that they go well together. **2** in a song, the notes that are sung or played along with the main tune to make it sound more beautiful or interesting: *You sing the melody, I'll sing the harmony.* **3** agreement of feelings, ideas, or actions: *There was perfect harmony between the two brothers.* *n., pl.* **har•mo•nies.** **—har′mo•nize′,** *v.* **—har•mo′ni•ous** (här mō′nē əs), *adj.*

har•ness (här′nis) **1** leather fittings for a horse or other animal, which connect it to a buggy, sled, or plough or which are used in riding. **2** an arrangement of straps to fasten or hold: *a parachute harness, a rock climber's harness.* **3** put a harness on: *Harness the horse.* **4** control and put to use: *They've built dams to harness these streams for hydro-electric power.* 1, 2 *n.,* 3, 4 *v.*
in harness, at your regular work: *She was glad to get back in harness again after her long vacation.*

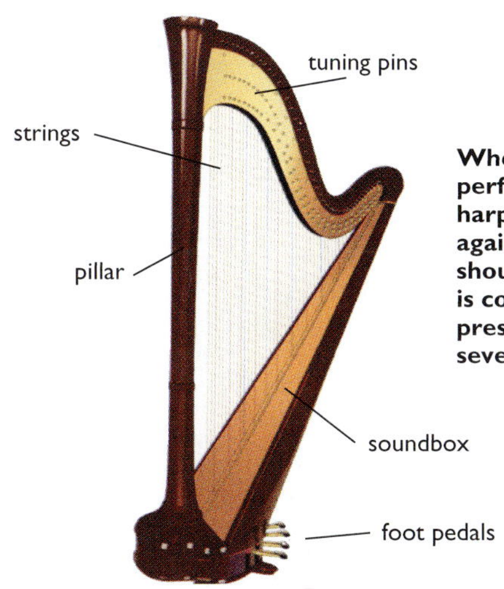

When playing, the performer tilts the harp so it rests against the right shoulder. The pitch is controlled by pressing any of the seven foot pedals.

harp (härp) **1** a triangular stringed musical instrument played with the fingers. **2 harp on,** talk about a subject very much or too much: *He kept harping on the importance of neatness.* 1 *n.,* 2 *v.* **—harp′ist,** *n.*

har•poon (här pūn′) **1** a barbed spear with a rope tied to it, for catching whales and other sea animals. It is thrown by hand or shot from a gun. **2** strike, catch, or kill with a harpoon. 1 *n.,* 2 *v.* **—har•poon′er,** *n.*

harp•si•chord (härp′sə kȯrd′) a stringed musical instrument like a piano. Because its strings are plucked rather than hit, it sounds like a harp. *n.*

harsh (härsh) **1** rough to the touch, taste, eye, or ear; sharp and unpleasant: *a harsh voice, a harsh climate.* **2** cruel or unfriendly; not gentle: *a harsh person.* *adj.*

har•um–scar•um (her′əm sker′əm) very active and noisy in a wild, reckless sort of way. *adj.*

har•vest (här′vist) **1** cut or pick ripe grain and other crops, usually in late summer or early fall: *to harvest wheat.* **2** the action or time of doing this. The full moon of late September is called the **harvest moon.** **3** the crop that is picked and gathered: *The apple harvest was small this year.* **4** the consequences: *He is reaping the harvest of his mistakes.* 1 *v.,* 2–4 *n.*
—har′vest•er, *n.*

has (haz) a present tense form of **have** used with *he, she, it,* or a singular noun: *She has my book. The child has been sick.* *v.*

hash (hash) **1** a mixture of cooked meat, potatoes, etc. chopped into small pieces and fried or baked. **2** discuss thoroughly: *They spent hours hashing out their problems.* **3** a mixture or muddle. 1, 3 *n.,* 2 *v.*
make a hash of, make a mess of; botch.

has•n't (haz′ənt) has not.

hasp (hasp) a two-part metal fastening, especially the kind on many locker doors and metal boxes, that you can put a padlock through. *n.*

has•sle (has′əl) *Informal.* **1** trouble or bother; a messy sort of problem: *Moving is just one big hassle. Do this properly now and it'll save you a lot of hassle later on.* **2** give someone a hard time; bother: *The movie star was being hassled by newspaper reporters.* 1 *n.,* 2 *v.,* **has•sled, has•sling.**

haste (hāst) rush: *All his haste was of no use; he ended up in a traffic jam.* *n.*
in haste, hurriedly.
make haste, hurry; be quick.

has•ten (hā′sən) be quick; hurry: *She hastened to explain.* *v.*

hast•y (hās′tē) **1** quick; hurried: *a hasty glance, a hasty trip to town.* **2** too quick; not well thought out: *Their hasty decision caused many problems later on.* *adj.,* **hast•i•er, hast•i•est.** **—hast′i•ly,** *adv.*

hat (hat) a covering for the head, especially one with a brim. *n.*

a bat	e bed	i bid	o pot	u cup	th thin
ā cake	ē me	ī bite	ō go	ū rude	ᴛʜ then
ä bar	ə about	ər over	ȯ for	u̇ put	zh measure

hatch¹ (hach) 1 break out as a live baby animal from the egg: *Three of the chickens hatched today. Not all eggs hatch properly.* 2 keep eggs warm until the young come out: *The heat of the sun hatches turtles' eggs.* 3 come up with an idea, especially in secret: *The robbers were hatching an evil scheme.* *v.* —**hatch′er·y,** *n.*

hatch² (hach) 1 a trapdoor in a ship's deck for loading cargo through. It leads down into the hold. 2 any similar opening. A **hatchback** is a car whose whole back end opens so you can load stuff through it. *n.*

hatch·et (hach′it) a small axe. *n.*

hate (hāt) 1 have very strong feelings against: *She hates people who are cruel to animals.* 2 strong feelings against a person or thing: *hearts full of hate.* 1 *v.,* **hat·ed, hat·ing;** 2 *n.* —**hat′er,** *n.* —**hate′ful,** *adj.*

ha·tred (hā′trid) a very strong feeling against some person or thing: *a hatred of cockroaches.* *n.*

hat trick (hat′trik′) three goals scored in a single game by the same player.

Hau·den·o·sau·nee (hou′də nō sou′nē) 1 a group of First Nations living in Ontario, Québec, and New York. 2 any of their languages. 3 having to do with these peoples or their languages. 1, 2 *n.,* 3 *adj.*

haugh·ty (hot′ē) conceited and snobby. *adj.,* **haugh·ti·er, haugh·ti·est.** —**haugh′ti·ly,** *adv.*

haul (hol) 1 pull, drag, or carry something heavy over a long distance: *The logs were hauled to the mill by horses.* 2 the act of hauling or the load hauled. 3 distance: *It is a long haul from Thunder Bay to Charlottetown.* 4 an amount received or taken: *The fishing boats made a good haul today.* 1 *v.,* 2–4 *n.*

haunch (honch) 1 the part of your body around your hip. 2 the leg and back end of an animal, used for food: *a haunch of venison.* *n.*
sit on your haunches, crouch on your feet.

haunt (hont) 1 stay or keep appearing in a place as a ghost or other spiritual force: *People say ghosts haunt that old house.* 2 go or come often to: *Our kids haunt the new skating rink. Memories of the accident haunted the victim.* 3 a place visited often: *The pool was their favourite haunt.* 1, 2 *v.,* 3 *n.* —**haunt′ed,** *adj.*

have (hav) 1 hold, own, take, eat, or experience: *What do you have in your hand? She has a big house and farm. Let's have lunch and a rest. I'm having trouble.* 2 get something done by somebody: *We had our house painted. I will have Dan wash the car for you.* 3 allow; permit: *They won't have any noise while they are reading.* 4 give birth to: *She had a baby yesterday.* 5 **Have** is also used with past participles, such as *asked, been, broken, done,* or *called,* to express completed action: *They have eaten. She had already gone. Have you called her?* *v.,* **has, had, hav·ing.**
have it in for someone, hold a bad feeling toward someone, sometimes for no particular reason.
have it out, fight or argue until something is settled: *I decided to have it out with her once and for all.*
have to (haf′ tə), must: *We have to go now; it is very late.*
I've had it, I am so annoyed or disappointed I can't take it anymore.
let someone have it, scold or punish someone severely.

ha·ven (hā′vən) a harbour; a place of shelter and safety. *n.*

have·n't (hav′ənt) have not.

hav·oc (hav′ək) very great destruction: *Tornadoes, earthquakes, and fires create widespread havoc.* *n.*
play havoc with, mess up severely; ruin.

training a hawk in the 1500s

Hunting with hawks is a sport dating back to ancient China. It was very popular in the Middle Ages. The art of training hawks is called hawking, or falconry.

hawk¹ (hok) a bird of prey with a strong, hooked beak and large, curved claws. Many hawks kill mice, grasshoppers, and other animals that damage crops. *n.*

hawk² (hok) carry things around for sale, advertising them by shouting; peddle: *He makes a living hawking cheap watches on the city streets.* *v.*

hay (hā) 1 grass or other green plants, cut and dried as food for cattle and horses. 2 cut and dry grass for hay: *The farmer is haying today.* 1 *n.,* 2 *v.*

hay fever (hā′ fē′vər) an allergy with symptoms like those of a cold. It is triggered by the pollen of ragweed and other plants.

hay•loft (hā′loft′) a floor above the stable in a barn, where hay is stored. **Haymow** (hā′mou′ *or* hā′mō′) is another name for it. *n.*

hay•stack (hā′stak′) a large pile of hay outdoors. It may also be called a **haycock** or **hayrick.** *n.*

haz•ard (haz′ərd) **1** a risk; danger: *The life of an explorer is full of hazards.* **2** take a chance with; risk: *I wouldn't hazard a journey in this snowstorm.* 1 *n.,* 2 *v.* —**haz′ard•ous,** *adj.*

haze (hāz) **1** a small amount of mist or smoke in the air: *A thin haze hung over the distant hills.* **2** vagueness or confusion. *n.* —**ha′zy,** *adj.*

ha•zel (hā′zəl) **1** a shrub whose small, roundish, light brown **hazelnuts** are good to eat. **2** greenish brown: *hazel eyes* (*adj.*). 1, 2 *n.,* 2 *adj.*

head (hed) **1** the top part of the human body, where your face and your brain are, or the same part on an animal. **2** mind; understanding: *An idea came into her head.* **3** the top, front, or rounded end of anything: *the head of a pin, the head of a line of cars, a head of cabbage.* **4** at or from the front or top: *a head wind, the head runner.* **5** the chief person; leader. **6** lead or be the head of; be the first or highest in: *to head a parade, to head a team. The common cold heads the list of childhood illnesses.* **7** chief; leading: *a head clerk.* **8** move or lead toward: *We headed for home. This road heads north.* **9** an individual person or animal: *The dinner will cost nine dollars a head. He sold fifty head of cattle.* **10** **heads,** the side of a coin with the image of a head on it: *We flipped a coin and it came up heads.* **11** the striking part of a tool: *the head of a hammer, the head of a golf club.* **12** hit with the head: *to head the ball in soccer.* 1–3, 5, 9–11 *n.,* 4, 7 *adj.,* 6, 8, 12 *v.* —**head′less,** *adj.*

be or go over someone's head, be too hard for someone to understand.
come to a head, reach a point where something must happen or something must be dealt with. You can also **bring something to a head.**
get your head around something, *Slang.* manage to fully understand something.
go to someone's head, **a** affect someone's mind or sense of balance. **b** make a person conceited: *All that attention has gone to his head.*
head off, get in front of in order to stop: *The cowhands tried to head off the stampeding herd.*
head on, with the head or front first: *The car crashed head on into the wall.*
head over heels, **a** in a somersault. **b** hastily; rashly: *She jumped head over heels into the business.* **c** completely; thoroughly: *head over heels in love.*
heads up, be careful; watch out: *Heads up! Their next batter is very good!*
lose your head, get too excited; lose your self-control.
make head or tail of, understand the least bit of: *I can't make head or tail of what she's saying, can you?*
on someone's head, someone's fault or responsibility: *It'll be on your head if this plan backfires.*
out of your head or **off your head,** *Informal.* crazy.
put heads together, discuss together to come up with ideas.
your head off, *Informal.* an extreme amount: *I laughed my head off. We worked our heads off to finish this on time.*

Word Family.......... **head**

headache: a pain in your head
headboard: a board or frame at the head of a bed
headdress: a covering or decoration for your head
headfirst: moving with your head going first
headgear: any covering for your head
headlight: a bright light at the front of a vehicle
headline: a title line over a piece of writing
headphone: an earphone held by a band over your head
headquarters: the main office
headrest: a support for your head
headroom: a clear space above
headset: a pair of earphones, often with a microphone attached
headstand: balancing upside down, by resting on your head and your hands
headstone: a marker stone set at the head of a grave
headstrong: foolishly determined to get your own way
headwaters: the sources or upper parts of a river
headway: forward movement, against wind or tide, or against a piece of work you must do

head•cheese (hed′chēz′) a spiced, jellied loaf made mainly of chopped, cooked parts of the head and feet of animals. *n.*

head•er (hed′ər) **1** a fall, dive, or plunge headfirst: *She took a header into the water.* **2** a title or line of information at the top of each page, or every other page, of something printed. *n.*

head•ing (hed′ing) **1** a title, especially of a list, column, or section of text. **2** the direction of a ship or aircraft as shown by a compass. *n.*

a bat	e bed	i bid	o pot	u cup	th thin
ā cake	ē me	ī bite	ō go	ü rude	ᴛʜ then
à bar	ə about	ər over	ò for	ù put	zh measure

head•land (hed′lənd) a high point of land jutting out into the water. **Cape** is another word for it. *n.*

head•long (hed′long′) **1** headfirst: *a headlong plunge into the sea (adj.).* **2** fast and carelessly: *to rush headlong into trouble (adv.).* *adv. or adj.*

head start (hed′ stärt′) an advantage that lets someone get ahead: *The smaller girl was given a head start. That team is playing better hockey than we are because they had a head start in practising.*

head•wind (hed′ wind′) a wind that blows against you from the front while you are moving: *It was hard work biking against the strong headwind.*

heal (hēl) make or become well and healthy again: *His cut finger healed in a few days.* *v.*

health (helth) **1** wellness; freedom from any kind of sickness or damage. **2** the condition of the body or mind: *She is in poor health.* *n.*
drink someone's health, drink a toast in someone's honour, wishing him or her health and happiness: *We all drank the bride's health.*

health card (helth kärd) a card that identifies a person as eligible for provincially funded health care.

health•y (hel′thē) **1** well and strong: *a healthy baby.* **2** giving health; good for the health: *healthy exercise, healthy food.* *adj.,* **health•i•er, health•i•est.**

heap (hēp) **1** a pile; a bunch of things thrown or lying together: *a heap of stones, a garbage heap.* **2 heaps,** *Informal.* a lot: *She was a tough teacher, but we learned heaps in her class.* **3** form into a heap: *I heaped the dirty clothes beside the washing machine.* **4** give in large amounts: *to heap insults on an enemy.* 1, 2 *n.,* 3, 4 *v.*

hear (hēr) **1** receive sounds through the ear; notice a sound: *Our old dog still hears very well. Did you hear something just now?* **2** listen thoughtfully to: *Please hear what I have to say. The judge heard the testimony of each witness.* **3** get news or knowledge: *Have you heard from your cousin in St. John's? Ling has never heard of French toast before.* *v.,* **heard** (hərd), **hear•ing.** —**hear′er,** *n.*
give someone a hearing, listen with an open mind to what someone has to say.

CONFUSABLES ..... hear

hear means "listen to": *Did you hear me?*
here means "at this place": *I've been here for hours.*

hearing aid (hēr′ing ād′) a small device worn in a person's ear to improve hearing by making sounds louder.

heark•en (härk′ən) an old or poetic word for "listen." **Hark** means the same. *v.*

hear•say (hēr′sā′) information you get from other people's talk; gossip. *n.*

hearse (hərs) a car used in funerals to carry the coffin. *n.*

A human heart beats about 70-80 times per minute, which is over 100 000 times a day.

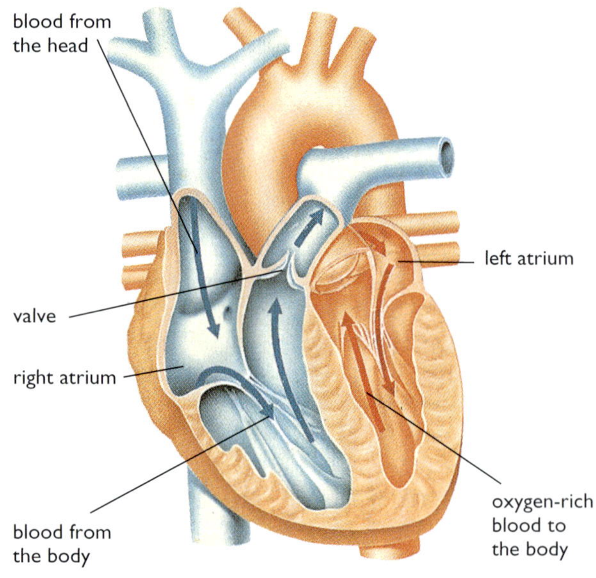

heart (härt) **1** the muscular organ in humans and other animals that pumps the blood through the body in a regular beating motion. **2** the soul; the centre of human feelings and desires: *Her heart was filled with pride when her daughter won the medal.* **3** courage; spirit: *The losing team showed plenty of heart.* **4** the middle or centre: *the heart of the city.* **5** the main or most important part: *the very heart of the matter.* **6** a figure shaped like this: ♥ *There was a big red heart on the valentine card.* **7 hearts,** *pl.* **a** the suit of playing cards marked with this figure. **b** a game where you try to get rid of cards of this suit. *n.*
after someone's own heart, pleasing someone perfectly: *Mr. Eisen's daughter was a girl after his own heart.*
at heart, in someone's deepest thoughts or feelings: *He is kind at heart, though he seems bad-tempered.*
break someone's heart, cause someone to feel great sadness or grief.
by heart, from memory.
give someone your heart, decide that you love someone. **Lose your heart to someone** means about the same.

have a heart, be kind.
have your heart in the right place, mean well; have good intentions.
heart and soul, with all your enthusiasm and energy.
heart of gold, a very kind nature.
in your heart of hearts, in your very deepest feelings and thoughts.
set your heart on, be eager and determined to have or do: *The kids have set their hearts on going to the beach today.* Also, **have your heart set on.**
take heart, be encouraged; cheer up.
take to heart, think seriously about: *She took her parents' advice to heart.*
wear your heart on your sleeve, show your feelings too plainly.
win or steal someone's heart, cause someone to love you.
with all your heart or **with your whole heart,** sincerely and completely; really meaning it.

Word Family.......... **heart**

heartbeat: one full squeeze of your heart muscle
hearten: cheer; cheer up; encourage
heartfelt: sincere; genuine
heartless: without kindness; unfeeling; cruel
heart-rending: causing great mental pain; very sad
heartsick: very depressed; very unhappy
heart-throb: a person you have a crush on
heart-to-heart: frank; open; sincere
heartwarming: able to stir up happy feelings

heart attack (härt′ ə tak′) a sudden failure of the heart to beat normally.

heart·break (härt′brāk′) very deep sadness or grief. **Heartache** is the same thing. *n.* —**heart′break′ing,** *adj.* —**heart′bro′ken** or **bro′ken-heart′ed,** *adj.*

hearth (härth) 1 the floor of a fireplace, normally including the area around it. 2 the home: *The traveller longed for his own hearth.* *n.*

heart·y (här′tē) 1 enthusiastic and sincere; full of good will or good spirits: *a hearty laugh, hearty wishes for a happy birthday.* 2 energetic and lively. 3 with plenty to eat; satisfying: *a hearty meal.* *adj.,* **heart·i·er, heart·i·est.** —**heart′i·ly,** *adv.* —**heart′i·ness,** *n.*

heat (hēt) 1 the condition of being hot; high temperature: *the heat of a fire, the heat of summer.* Heat is one form of energy. 2 make or become warm or hot: *The stove heats the room. The room is heating slowly.* 3 violence; excitement: *In the heat of the moment he said things he was sorry for later.* A **heated** argument is a rather fierce one. 4 one trial in a race: *He won the first heat, but lost the final race.* 1, 3, 4 *n.,* 2 *v.* —**heat′er,** *n.*

hea·then (hē′ᴛʜən) according to some religions, a person who does not worship the true God, or who knows nothing about God. *n., pl.* **hea·thens** or **hea·then;** *adj.*

heath·er (heᴛʜ′ər) a low shrub with small purple flowers that grows in Scotland and England. *n.*

heat shield (hēt′ shēld′) a coating or covering of special material on something to prevent it from getting hot. The nose cone of a missile or spacecraft has a heat shield to prevent it from burning up as it re-enters the earth's atmosphere at great speed.

heat·stroke (hēt′strōk′) a serious illness that results from being exposed to so much heat that your body cannot cool itself by sweating. *n.*

heave (hēv) 1 lift, throw, or pull with great effort: *She heaved the sandbags into the wagon. They heaved on the rope.* 2 give a sigh, groan, etc.; breathe heavily. 3 rise; swell; bulge: *The ground heaved during the earthquake.* 4 *Slang.* throw up. 5 an act of heaving: *With a mighty heave he got the boat into the water.* 1–4 *v.,* **heaved** or **hove, heav·ing;** 5 *n.*
heave ho! a sailors' cry when pulling up the anchor, or pulling on any rope or cable.
heave in sight, come into view. The past form **hove** is used mostly for this expression.

heav·en (hev′ən) 1 in some religions, the beautiful, joyful place where God lives and where God's people go after death. 2 Usually, **heavens,** *pl.* an old or poetic word for "sky": *Millions of stars were shining in the heavens.* *n.* —**heav′en·ly,** *adj.*

heav·y (hev′ē) 1 hard to lift or carry; weighing a lot because it has much mass: *a heavy log, heavy bricks.* 2 large or great: *a heavy rain, a heavy meal, a heavy responsibility, heavy losses.* 3 serious: *a heavy discussion, heavy reading.* 4 sad or gloomy: *a heavy heart, a heavy atmosphere.* *adj.,* **heav·i·er, heav·i·est.** —**heav′i·ly,** *adv.* —**heav′i·ness,** *n.*

heav·y–du·ty (hev′ē dyū′tē *or* hev′ē dū′tē) 1 strong and not easily damaged or worn out: *heavy-duty machinery, heavy-duty work clothes.* 2 *Informal.* very serious, important, or demanding: *a heavy-duty lecture, a heavy-duty assignment.* *adj.*

a bat	e bed	i bid	o pot	u cup	th thin
ā cake	ē me	ī bite	ō go	ū rude	ᴛʜ then
ä bar	ə about	ər over	ô for	ů put	zh measure

heck•le (hek′əl) harass and annoy a speaker by shouting out, asking bothersome questions, etc. *v.*, **heck•led, heck•ling.**

hec•tare (hek′ter *or* hek′tãr) a metric unit used to measure land area. It is equal to ten thousand square metres. *Symbol:* ha *n.*

hec•tic (hek′tik) very busy, fast-paced, or wild: *She leads a hectic life.* *adj.*

hecto– *an SI prefix meaning* one hundred; 100. A **hectometre** is one hundred metres. *Symbol:* h

he'd (hēd) **1** he had. **2** he would.

hedge (hej) **1** a thick row of bushes or small trees planted as a fence. **2** put a hedge around: *to hedge a garden.* **3** avoid giving a direct answer; answer questions in a vague way. 1 *n.*, 2, 3 *v.*, **hedged, hedg•ing.**
hedge in, surround on all sides: *The town was hedged in by mountains and a forest.*

hedge•hog (hej′hog′) a small animal of Europe with prickles on its back. When attacked, hedgehogs roll up into a bristling ball. *n.*

heed (hēd) **1** pay attention to: *Heed what I say.* **2** careful attention: *She pays heed to her clothes.* 1 *v.*, 2 *n.* —**heed′less,** *adj.*

heel[1] (hēl) **1** the back part of a person's foot, below the ankle, or the part of a sock or shoe that covers or supports it. **2** anything shaped or used like a heel, such as the end crust of a loaf of bread. **3** walk just behind the master. It is a command to a dog. **4** *Informal.* a very mean and cowardly person. 1, 2, 4 *n.*, 3 *v.*
bring to heel, tame; bring under control.
cool your heels, wait.
drag your heels, stall; act slowly or try to avoid doing something.
kick up your heels, have fun; be merry.
take to your heels, run away.

heel[2] (hēl) **1** lean over to one side; tilt; tip: *The ship heeled as it turned.* **2** the act of heeling. 1 *v.*, 2 *n.*

hef•ty (hef′tē) *Informal.* heavy or big: *That's a hefty load. They got a hefty bill for repairs.* *adj.*

heif•er (hef′ər) a young cow that has not had a calf. *n.*

height (hīt) **1** the tallness of anyone or anything; the distance from top to bottom: *My father's height is 187 cm.* **2** the distance above sea level. **3** Sometimes, **heights,** *pl.* a high point; peak: *the height of rush hour. The eagle soared above the heights.* **4** the highest degree: *Fast driving on icy roads is the height of stupidity.* *n.*

height•en (hī′tən) make or become higher, stronger, or greater; increase: *Heavy rain heightened the danger of floods.* *v.*

Heil•tsuk (hīl′tsůk) **1** a First Nations people living in British Columbia. **2** their language. **3** having to do with these people or their language. 1, 2 *n.*, 3 *adj.*

Heim•lich manoeuvre (hīm′lik mə nū′vər) a way to rescue a person who is choking on something. You close your hand over your fist on the person's stomach, then thrust inward and upward so that the object causing the person to choke is forced out.

heir (er) a person who has the right to somebody's property after the owner dies: *As the only heir, she received all of her parents' wealth when they died.* *n.*

heir•loom (er′lūm′) an article handed down from generation to generation: *This clock is a family heirloom.* *n.*

held (held) the past tense and past participle of **hold**[1]: *He held the baby. The swing is held by ropes.* *v.*

A helicopter has spinning rotor blades that provide both lift and thrust.

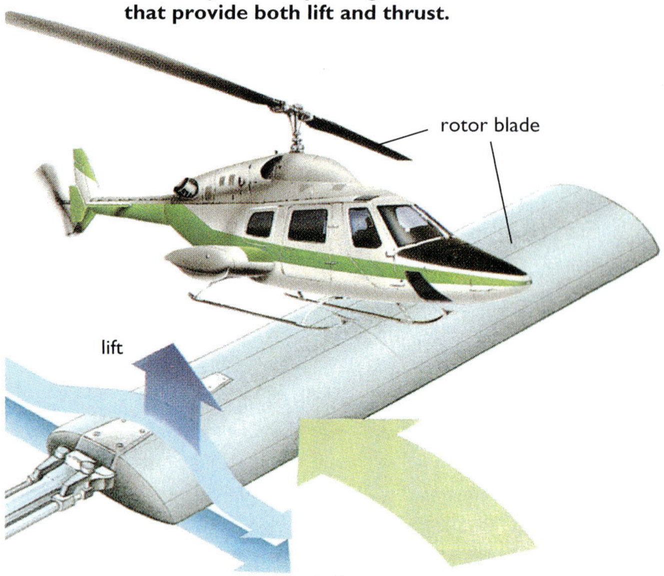

hel•i•cop•ter (hel′ə kop′tər) an aircraft that can fly up, down and sideways, and can hover in mid-air. Helicopters have overhead propellers and no wings. *n.*

hel•i•port (hel′ə pôrt′) a place for helicopters to take off and land. Heliports may be built on the tops of buildings. *n.*

he•li•um (hē′lē əm) a very light gas that will not burn, used in balloons and dirigibles to keep them floating in the air. *n.*

hell (hel) 1 in some religions, the home of the Devil and the place where wicked people are punished after death. 2 any place or time of great suffering: *The desert was hell for the lost travellers.* *n.* **—hell′ish,** *adj.*

he'll (hēl) he will.

hel·lo (hə lō′) a word used to greet people, and sometimes to express surprise or impatience. *interj. or n., pl.* **hel·los.**

helm (helm) 1 the handle or wheel used for steering a ship. 2 a position of control or guidance: *The Prime Minister is at the country's helm.* *n.*

hel·met (hel′mit) a hard covering to protect the head. You wear a helmet riding a bike or motorcycle. Knights wore helmets as part of their armour. *n.*

help (help) 1 do or give something to make a job or situation easier for someone: *Help me with my work. We helped clean up. This medicine should help your sore throat.* 2 an action, a person, or a thing that does this: *Do you need some help with the housework? Kofi was such a help when I was sick.* 3 avoid; keep from: *He cannot help falling asleep.* 4 give food to; serve with food: *Help your aunt to tea and cookies.* One serving of food is called a **helping.** 5 one or more employees: *The storekeeper treats his help well.* 1, 3, 4 *v.,* 2, 5 *n.* **—help′er,** *n.* **—help′ful,** *adj.*
help yourself, take what you wish: *Help yourself to a drink while you wait.*

help·less (help′lis) not able to help or protect yourself: *A little baby is helpless.* *adj.*
—help′less·ly, *adv.* **—help′less·ness,** *n.*

hel·ter–skel·ter (hel′tər skel′tər) in every direction, in confusion: *The sheep ran helter-skelter when the big dog came bounding toward them.* *adv.*

hem (hem) 1 a neat edge on a garment, made by folding the cloth over and sewing it down. 2 fold over and sew down the edge of: *He hemmed his new pants.* 1 *n.,* 2 *v.,* **hemmed, hem·ming.**
hem in, surround on all sides: *hemmed in by thick bush.*

hem·i·sphere (hem′əs fēr′) 1 half of a sphere or globe. 2 half of the earth's surface. North and South America are in the **western hemisphere;** Europe, Asia, and Africa are in the **eastern hemisphere.** All the countries north of the equator are in the **northern hemisphere;** the countries south of the equator are in the **southern hemisphere.** *n.*

hem·lock (hem′lok) 1 a tall evergreen tree that has short, flat needles and small cones. 2 a deadly poisonous plant that grows in wet areas. *n.*

hemp (hemp) a tall plant, originally from Asia, with tough fibres used for string, rope, and coarse cloth. *n.*

Domestic chickens are descended from Asian jungle fowl. The males have a fleshy comb and wattles at the sides of the beak.

hen (hen) 1 a female chicken: *a hen and her chicks.* 2 the female of some other birds: *a hen sparrow.* *n.*

hence (hens) 1 therefore: *We have no money, hence we cannot buy anything.* 2 an old word meaning "from now" or "from here": *Come back a week hence.* **Henceforth** means "from now on." *adv.*

her·ald (her′əld) 1 a person or thing that signals or announces the arrival of something: *The robin is the herald of spring.* 2 bring news of; announce: *The first snow heralded the arrival of winter.* 1 *n.,* 2 *v.*

her·ald·ry (her′əld rē) the study of the symbols contained in a coat of arms. *n.*

herb (hərb *or* ərb) a plant whose leaves and stems are used for medicine, seasoning, or food: *Sage, mint, and basil are herbs.* *n.*

herb·i·cide (hərb′ə sīd′) a chemical that kills unwanted plants. *n.*

herb·i·vore (hərb′ə vôr′) an animal that eats only plants. *n.* **—her·biv′o·rous** (hər biv′ə rəs)**,** *adj.*

herd (hərd) 1 a number of animals together: *a herd of cows, a herd of elephants.* 2 a large number of people. 3 form into a flock, herd, or group: *Many animals herd for protection.* 4 drive, tend, or take care of a herd: *Paul herds his uncle's sheep. The tour guide herded us into the museum.* 1, 2 *n.,* 3, 4 *v.* **—herd′er,** *n.*

a bat	e bed	i bid	o pot	u cup	th thin
ā cake	ē me	ī bite	ō go	ū rude	ᴛʜ then
ä bar	ə about	ər over	ô for	ů put	zh measure

here (hēr) 1 this place; in, at, or to this place: *Where do we go from here (n.)? Bring those things here. I live here (adv.).* 2 an answer showing that you are present when your name is read off a list. 1 *n. or adv.,* 2 *interj.*

> **Word Family.......... here**
>
> The following words are very formal ways of saying very simple things. They are often found in contracts and other legal documents.
>
> **hereby:** in this way
> **herein:** in here
> **heretofore:** until now
> **hereupon:** immediately after this
> **herewith:** with this

here•a•bouts (hē′rə bouts′) around here; about this place; near here. *adv.*

here•af•ter (hēr′ af′tər) 1 after this; in the future. 2 the life or time after death. 1 *adv.,* 2 *n.*

he•red•i•ty (hə red′ə tē) 1 the passing down of physical and mental qualities from parents to children through the genes: *His blue eyes are a result of heredity.* 2 the passing down of a right or title from parents to their children: *The new clan chief is determined by heredity. n.* —**he•red′i•tar′y** (hə red′ə ter′ē), *adj.*

here's (hērz) here is.

her•e•tic (her′ə tik) a person who holds a belief different from the accepted teaching of his or her church or other community. Such a belief is called a **heresy.** *n.* —**he•ret′i•cal** (hə ret′ə kəl), *adj.*

her•it•age (her′ə tij) the values and traditions handed on to a person from his or her ancestors: *Freedom of speech is part of Canada's heritage. n.*

her•mit (hər′mit) a person who lives his or her life completely away from other people: *The hermit had a shack on a lonely beach. n.*

hermit crab (hər′mit krab′) a crab that protects its soft stomach by living in the shell that another sea animal has cast off.

he•ro (hē′rō) 1 a person who is greatly admired for his or her courage, leadership, strength, skill, and so on. 2 the most important character in a story, play, or movie. *n., pl.* **he•roes.** —**he•ro′ic,** *adj.*

her•o•in (her′ō ən) a very harmful, habit-forming sedative drug. *n.*

her•o•ine (her′ō in) a hero who is a woman or girl. *n.*

her•o•ism (her′ō iz′əm) great courage: *an act of heroism. n.*

her•on (her′ən) a wading bird with a long neck and bill and long legs. The **great blue heron** is common in marshes and shallow waters across southern Canada. *n.*

her•ring (her′ing) a very common food fish of the northern Atlantic Ocean. It is small and silvery. *n., pl.* **her•ring** or **her•rings.**

hertz (hərts) an SI unit for measuring how often something happens per second. An alternating electric current changes direction at a speed of sixty hertz. *Symbol:* Hz *n., pl.* **hertz.**

he's (hēz) 1 he is. 2 he has: *He's broken his pencil.*

hes•i•tant (hez′i tənt) hesitating; doubtful; unsure: *She was always hesitant about asking questions. adj.*

hes•i•tate (hez′ə tāt′) stop, wait, or hold back, usually because you are not sure if you should do something: *I hesitated to ask you because you were so busy. He hesitated before asking the question. v.,* **hes•i•tat•ed, hes•i•tat•ing.** —**hes′i•ta′tion,** *n.*

hew (hyū) an old or poetic word for "chop": *to hew wood. v.,* **hewed, hewed** or **hewn, hew•ing.**

hey (hā) a word used to attract attention, or to express surprise or other feeling: *Hey, Brian! Hey, look at this! interj.*

hi (hī) *Informal.* a call of greeting; hello. *interj.*

hi•ba•chi (hi bȧ′chē) a shallow metal container like a small barbecue without a stand. It holds burning charcoal and has a grill on top for cooking food. *n., pl.* **hi•ba•chis.**

hi•ber•nate (hī′bər nāt′) spend the winter in sleep, as some snakes, bats, groundhogs, and other wild animals do. *v.,* **hi•ber•nat•ed, hi•ber•nat•ing.** —**hi′ber•na′tion,** *n.*

hic•cup (hik′up) 1 a little spasm that interrupts regular breathing and makes a sound like a click. 2 have this kind of spasm. **Hiccough** is another spelling of this word. 3 **the hiccups,** *pl.* the state of having one hiccup after another. 1, 3 *n.,* 2 *v.,* **hic•cupped, hic•cup•ping.**

hick•o•ry (hik′ə rē) a deciduous tree with egg-shaped nuts that are edible. Its tough, hard wood is used for tool handles. *n., pl.* **hick•o•ries.**

hide[1] (hīd) 1 put or keep out of sight; make something hard to find: *Hide it in this little hole behind the bricks. Clouds are hiding the sun.* 2 keep yourself out of sight: *The gopher hid in its hole.* 3 keep secret: *She hid*

her frustration. *v.,* **hid, hid·den** or **hid, hid·ing.**
hide out, stay hidden for a long time: *The robbers were hiding out in an empty building downtown.* A place where someone does this is called a **hideout.**

hide² (hīd) an animal's skin, either raw or made into leather. *n.*

hide–and–seek (hīd′ən sēk′) a children's game where some players hide and others try to find them. It is also called **hide-and-go-seek.** *n.*

hide·a·way (hī′də wā′) **1** a place of hiding. **2** a quiet, restful place away from other people: *They had a little hideaway by a lake where they went to escape the city on the weekends.* *n.*

hid·e·ous (hid′ē əs) ugly; frightful; horrible: *a hideous monster, hideous crimes.* *adj.* **—hid′e·ous·ly,** *adv.*

Early Egyptian hieroglyphics represented different objects. Later hieroglyphics, like these ones, stood for sounds rather than things.

hi·er·o·glyph·ics (hī′rə glif′iks) a system of writing that uses pictures to stand for ideas or sounds, especially the system used by the ancient Egyptians. **—hi′er·o·glyph′ic,** *adj.*

high (hī) **1** far, or reaching far, above the ground: *a high mountain, an airplane high in the air.* **2** above others in authority or power: *the high court. A general has high rank.* **3** greater, stronger, or better than average; great: *a high price, a high wind, to have a high opinion of someone. Sir Wilfrid Laurier was a person of high character.* **4** above the normal pitch: *a high voice.* **5** at or to a high place, rank, amount, pitch, etc.: *to sing high, to fly high. These pants are priced too high.* **6** happily excited: *The team felt high after winning the tournament.*
1–4, 6 *adj.,* 5 *adv.* **—high′ly,** *adv.*
high and dry, **a** up out of the water: *The whale was high and dry on the beach.* **b** alone and without help: *He has left me high and dry with all this work to do.*
high in something, having a lot of something: *Oranges are high in vitamin C.*
high noon, exactly 12:00 p.m.
high seas, the open ocean: *The high seas are outside the territory of any country.*
high spirits, happy excitement.
high time, **a** the time just before it is too late: *It was high time that he began to study.* **b** *Informal.* an exciting time at a party, etc.
on high, up above.
search high and low, look everywhere for something.

High Commissioner (hī′ kə mish′ə nər) the chief representative of one Commonwealth country in another.

high jump (hī′ jump′) an athletic contest or event where people try to jump as high as possible over a bar.

high·land (hī′lənd) Often, **highlands,** *pl.* a country or region that is higher and hillier than the rest. *n.* **—high′land′er,** *n.*

high·light (hī′līt′) **1** the most interesting or most striking part: *The highlight of our trip was the drive along the Cabot Trail.* **2** make stand out: *The new product was highlighted in all the company's brochures.* **3** a streak or patch of extra brightness or colour in something.
1, 3 *n.,* 2 *v.*

high·rise (hī′rīz′) a tall building with many storeys: *They live on the 23rd floor of a highrise downtown.* *n.*

high school (hī′ skūl′) a school attended after elementary or public school; a secondary school. In different provinces, high school begins and ends at different grades. Some provinces have junior high schools, intermediate between elementary and high schools. **—high′-school′,** *adj.*

🍁 **high·stick·ing** (hī′stik′ing) in hockey, the act of checking a player with your stick carried above the level of your shoulder. It is against the rules. *n.*

high–strung (hī′strung′) very nervous; easily excited or upset. *adj.*

high tech (hī′ tek′) the use of very modern and complicated equipment and methods in science, industry, or business. **High technology** is the full name. **—high′-tech′,** *adj.*

a bat	e bed	i bid	o pot	u cup	th thin
ā cake	ē me	ī bite	ō go	ū rude	ᴛʜ then
ä bar	ə about	ər over	ô for	ů put	zh measure

high–ten·sion (hī′ten′shən) carrying a high voltage: *high-tension wires.* *adj.*

high·way (hī′wā′) a main road or route: *We took the highway to Regina.* *n.*

high·way·man (hī′wā′mən) in former times, a man who robbed travellers on a public road. *n., pl.* **high·way·men** (hī′wā′mən).

hi·jack (hī′jak′) 1 stop a vehicle in order to steal it or its cargo, or to force the driver to go to a certain place: *The truck was hijacked on the way to the jewellery store.* 2 seize control of an aircraft in flight by threatening the crew or passengers. *v.* —**hi′jack′er,** *n.*

hike (hīk) 1 a long walk, especially one for pleasure in the forest or countryside. 2 take a long walk: *The scouts hiked in the hills.* 3 pull up or raise: *to hike prices. She hiked up her skirt so she could wade in the stream.* 1 *n.,* 2, 3 *v.,* **hiked, hik·ing.**

hi·lar·i·ous (hə ler′ē əs) 1 very funny: *The joke was hilarious.* 2 full of high spirits: *a hilarious party.* *adj.*

hill (hil) 1 a raised part of the earth's surface, smaller than a mountain. 2 a little heap or pile, such as the pile of soil made by ants. *n.* —**hill′y,** *adj.*
over the hill, *Informal.* no longer young.

hill·bil·ly (hil′bil′ē) a person who lives out in the country in a mountainous region, thought of as backward. *n., pl.* **hill·bil·lies.**

Hilts were often decorated with gold, silver, and jewels, like this one made in the 1400s.

hilt (hilt) the handle of a sword or dagger. *n.*

hind (hīnd) back; rear: *The mule kicked up its hind legs.* **Hindmost** means "furthest back"; the **hindquarters** of an animal are its rear end and back legs. *adj.*

hin·der (hin′dər) hold back or get in the way of; make hard to do: *Deep mud hindered travel. Don't hinder me from my work.* *v.* —**hin′drance,** *n.*

Hin·du (hin′dū) 1 a believer in **Hinduism,** a religion based on the worship of one God who takes many forms; the three main forms are Brahma, Vishnu, and Shiva. Krishna and Rama are forms of Shiva. 2 having to do with this religion or its followers. 1 *n.,* 2 *adj.*

hinge (hinj) 1 the joint that a door, lid, etc. is attached by so that it can move back and forth. 2 depend: *The success of the picnic hinges on the weather.* 1 *n.,* 2 *v.,* **hinged, hing·ing.**

hint (hint) 1 a slight sign; an indirect suggestion: *A small black cloud gave a hint of the coming storm.* 2 a gentle piece of advice; tip: *some helpful hints for making better pie crust.* 3 give a slight sign; suggest in an indirect way: *They hinted that they wanted their guests to leave by saying, "Do you often stay up this late?"* 1, 2 *n.,* 3 *v.*

hip (hip) 1 the bony part of the human body on each side just below the waist. 2 a similar part in animals, where the hind leg joins the body. 3 *Informal.* in style; fashionable. *n.*

hip·pie (hip′ē) someone who wants to live a simpler, more natural life than most people and believes that love and freedom are more important than work, tradition, and authority. *n.*

hip·po·pot·a·mus (hip′ə pot′ə məs) a huge, thick-skinned, plant-eating, hairless animal that lives in and around rivers in tropical Africa. Its name is often shortened informally to **hippo.** *n., pl.* **hip·po·pot·a·mus·es** or **hip·po·pot·a·mi** (hip′ə pot′ə mī).

hire (hīr) 1 agree to pay someone to do a job; give a job to: *to hire employees. We hired a teenager to cut the lawn while we were on vacation.* 2 rent something, especially together with someone's services, such as a vehicle with a driver or a banquet hall with chefs and serving staff. *v.,* **hired, hir·ing.**
hire out, give work in return for payment: *He hired out as a carpenter.*

hiss (his) 1 make a sound like the *s* in *see,* sometimes as a way of showing disapproval: *The snake hissed as we approached. The audience hissed and booed the comedian's racist jokes.* 2 such a sound: *There was a loud hiss as the water boiled over onto the hot stove.* 1 *v.,* 2 *n.*

his·to·gram (his′tə gram′) a vertical bar graph. *n.*

his·tor·ic (his tôr′ik) famous or important in history: *July 1, 1867, was a historic day for Canada.* *adj.*

his·tor·i·cal (his tôr′ə kəl) 1 of or having to do with history: *historical research.* 2 known to be true in history, or based on actual history: *a historical novel. It is a historical fact, not legend, that John Cabot sailed to Canada in 1497.* *adj.*

CONFUSABLES ..... historic

historic means "famous in history": *Halifax is a historic city.*

historical means "having to do with history": *We saw several historical museums on our trip through Nova Scotia.*

his·to·ry (his′tə rē) 1 everything that has happened in the past, especially in relation to a particular thing, nation, idea, or person: *We don't know the whole history of the earth.* 2 an account of the most important of these events: *She has written a 200-page history of our town.* 3 the study of these things: *History is my favourite subject in school.* A **historian** studies history. *n., pl.* **his·to·ries.**
make history, do something that influences future events and will always be remembered.

hit (hit) 1 come against with some force; give a blow to; strike: *She hit the ball with a bat. He hit his head against the shelf.* 2 reach; get to: *They finally hit Whitehorse at dawn.* 3 come suddenly or powerfully to: *As he stood up, a sharp pain hit him in the back. It hit me last night that we might never see each other again.* 4 a blow; stroke. 5 a popular success: *The new movie is the hit of the season.* 1–3 *v.,* **hit, hit·ting;** 4, 5 *n.* **—hit′ter,** *n.*
be hard hit, be affected deeply or painfully: *She was hard hit by the news of her classmate's accident.*
hit it off, *Informal.* agree or get along well with someone: *Gary hit it off well with Teo right away.*
hit on, come up with; discover: *We've hit on a great title for the newsletter.*

hitch (hich) 1 attach with a hook, ring, rope, or other fastener: *The farmer hitched the hay wagon to the tractor.* 2 a part used to connect two things together, such as a car and trailer. 3 move or pull with a jerk: *She hitched her chair nearer to the fire.* 4 a short, sudden pull or jerk: *The sailor gave his pants a hitch.* 5 something that goes wrong: *A hitch in their plans made them miss the train.* 6 a kind of knot used for temporary fastening, which is easy to undo. 1, 3 *v.,* 2, 4–6 *n.*

hitch·hike (hich′hīk′) travel by getting free rides from passing motorists and walking between rides: *The boys hitchhiked from Antigonish to Truro.* The verb is shortened in the phrase **hitch a ride.** *v.,* **hitch·hiked, hitch·hik·ing.** **—hitch′hik′er,** *n.*

hith·er (hiᴛʜ′ər)
hither and thither, in every direction; everywhere. *adv.*

hith·er·to (hiᴛʜ′ər tū′) a formal word meaning "up to this time." *adv.*

HIV the acronym for a virus that keeps a person's body from fighting infections, causing the disease called AIDS. HIV stands for **human immunovirus.**

hive (hīv) 1 a colony of bees, or its home. 2 a busy, crowded place: *On Saturdays the mall is a hive of activity.* 3 group together and move apart from the rest: *At camp we were hived off into groups to do separate activities.* 1, 2 *n.,* 3 *v.,* **hived, hiv·ing.**

hives (hīvz) an itchy rash, usually from an allergy: *I get hives whenever I eat strawberries.* *n.*

H.M.C.S. *abbreviation for* Her (or His) Majesty's Canadian Ship: *We toured H.M.C.S.* Haida *in the Toronto harbour.*

ho (hō) a word shouted to get someone's attention or to express surprise, joy, or pretended laughter. *interj.*

hoard (hȯrd) 1 save carefully and store up: *The squirrel hoarded nuts for the winter. The miser hoarded his money.* 2 the things stored: *Bilbo saw the dragon's hoard of jewels.* 1 *v.,* 2 *n.*

hoar·frost (hȯr′frost′) white frost; frozen dew: *The leaves were covered with hoarfrost.* *n.*

hoarse (hȯrs) talking with a rough, croaking voice: *All that shouting has made him hoarse.* *adj.,* **hoars·er, hoars·est.** **—hoarse′ness,** *n.*

hoax (hōks) 1 a made-up story meant to trick people: *The reported discovery of a computer virus was a hoax.* 2 trick with this kind of story. 1 *n.,* 2 *v.*

hob·ble (hob′əl) 1 walk with short, difficult steps; limp: *The wounded man hobbled away.* 2 a limping walk. 3 tie an animal's legs loosely so that it can move a little but not run away. 4 a rope or strap used for this. 1, 3 *v.,* **hob·bled, hob·bling;** 2, 4 *n.*

hob·by (hob′ē) something a person likes to do in his or her spare time: *Surfing the Internet is our neighbour's hobby.* *n., pl.* **hob·bies.**

hob·by·horse (hob′ē hȯrs′) 1 a stick with a horse's head, used as a toy. 2 rocking horse. 3 *Informal.* a favourite topic: *Neatness is a hobbyhorse of my dad's.* *n.*

hob·gob·lin (hob′gob′lin) something, especially something imaginary, that someone is always fearing. *n.*

hob·nail (hob′nāl′) a short nail with a large head, stuck into the soles of heavy boots or shoes to protect or reinforce them. *n.*

ho·bo (hō′bō) a homeless person who travels from town to town, taking whatever work or help can be found. A **hobo stove** is made by putting a large, open tin can over a fire built under it and using the top to cook on. *n., pl.* **ho·bos** or **ho·boes.**

a bat	e bed	i bid	o pot	u cup	th thin
ā cake	ē me	ī bite	ō go	ū rude	ᴛʜ then
ä bar	ə about	ər over	ȯ for	ů put	zh measure

hock·ey (hok′ē) **1** a game played on ice by two teams of six players wearing skates and carrying hooked sticks. Each team tries to shoot a black rubber disk, the puck, into the opposing team's goal. The full name is **ice hockey.** **2** any similar game, played on different surfaces using a ball or plastic ring instead of a puck, such as **road hockey, floor hockey,** and **field hockey.** *n.*

WORD HISTORY....... hockey

The word **hockey** probably comes from an old French word *hoquet* meaning "crook," that is, a stick with a hooked end.

hodge·podge (hoj′poj′) a jumbled mixture. *n.*

hoe (hō) **1** a tool with a small blade set across the end of a long handle, used for loosening the soil and cutting small weeds. **2** work with a hoe. 1 *n., pl.* **hoes;** 2 *v.,* **hoed, hoe·ing.**

hog (hog) **1** a pig, especially a full-grown pig raised for food. **2** a selfish, greedy person. **3** *Slang.* take more than your share of: *Don't hog the ice cream.* 1, 2 *n.,* 3 *v.,* **hogged, hog·ging.**
go hog-wild, *Slang.* go crazy; totally lose control.
go whole hog, *Informal.* do something very thoroughly; go all the way.
live high off the hog, live well; enjoy luxuries.

hog·wash (hog′wosh′) nonsense or stupid talk. *n.*

hoist (hoist) **1** raise or lift, often with ropes and pulleys: *to hoist a flag, to hoist sails, to hoist blocks of stone in building.* **2** an elevator or other machine for lifting loads: *The mechanic had our car up on a hoist and was working under it.* **3** a lift; boost: *He gave me a hoist up the wall.* 1 *v.,* 2, 3 *n.*

hold¹ (hōld) **1** keep, often in your hands or arms: *Hold my watch while I play this game.* **2** a grasp or grip: *Take a good hold of this rope.* **3** something to hang on by: *She looked for a hold on the smooth rock but couldn't find one.* **4** keep in some place or position: *This clamp holds the paper steady while I draw.* **5** contain: *This jar holds 300 mL of water.* **6** have: *Shall we hold a meeting of the club? She holds property in the city.* **7** believe; think: *People once held that the world was flat.* **8** be true; apply: *This rule holds in all cases.* 1, 4–8 *v.,* **held, hold·ing;** 2, 3 *n.* **—hold′er,** *n.*
hold back, **a** keep from letting out or expressing: *to hold back a sneeze, to hold back the truth.* **b** avoid taking part in something fully: *She was always holding back, afraid to join in.*
hold forth, talk in a preaching sort of way; lecture.
hold off, delay doing something; wait.
hold on, **a** grip: *He held on to the overturned boat till help came.* **b** continue; not stop or give up. **c** wait.
hold out, **a** last: *The water supply will not hold out much longer.* **b** keep resisting; not give in: *I managed to hold out against all their persuasion.* A **holdout** is someone who keeps resisting after everyone else has given in.
hold over, **a** keep longer than originally scheduled: *The show was so popular that it was held over for another week.* A person or thing that remains beyond the expected time is a **holdover.** **b** postpone: *The game has been held over until next week.*
hold up, **a** continue; last; endure: *He held up well under all that pressure.* **b** delay: *The accident held up the traffic.* **c** stop by force and rob.
hold with, agree with or approve of.
hold your breath, **a** stop breathing on purpose. **b** wait in suspense for something to happen.
hold your ground, keep from giving in.
hold your own, keep from being totally overshadowed or overwhelmed by somebody else's skill or power.
lay hold of, seize; grasp.

hold² (hōld) the space below a ship's deck, where cargo is kept. *n.*

hold·ing (hōl′ding) a piece of land. *n.*

hold·up (hōl′dup′) **1** the act of stopping by force and robbing. **2** delay: *The fog caused a holdup in air travel.* *n.*

hole (hōl) **1** a gap; an opening that goes right through something: *a hole in a pocket, a hole in a board.* **2** a hollow place in the ground: *a hole in the road, a gopher's hole. She hit the golf ball into the hole.* **3** a small, dark, dirty place. **4** a part where something seems to be missing in an argument, plan, or story. **5** a difficult situation. *n.* **—hol′ey,** *adj.*
hole in one, in golf, a single stroke that gets the ball right from the tee into the hole.
hole up, **a** of animals, go into a hole: *Bears hole up during winter.* **b** *Slang.* go into hiding for a time: *The gangsters holed up in an old cabin.*
in the hole, in debt.
shoot holes in, argue successfully against something. You can also **pick holes in** something.

CONFUSABLES..... hole

hole means "empty space": *There's a hole in my sock.*
whole means "entire": *I ate the whole box of cookies.*

Ho·li (hō′lē) a Hindu spring festival dedicated to the god Krishna. *n.*

hol•i•day (hol′ə dā′) 1 a day when schools and most places of work and business are closed to celebrate something: *July 1st is a holiday for all Canadians.* 2 Often, **holidays,** *pl.;* vacation; the time spent away from work or school: *She always goes to camp during the summer holidays.* *n.*

hol•ler (hol′ər) *Informal.* yell: *If you need me, just holler (v.). She let out a holler when we squirted her (n.).* *v. or n.*

hol•low (hol′ō) 1 having only air or empty space inside; not solid: *a hollow log, a hollow chocolate egg.* 2 shaped like a bowl or cup. 3 a bowl-shaped or sunken place; hole: *a hollow in the driveway.* 4 make something hollow: *He hollowed out a piece of wood to make a whistle.* 5 a small valley: *They built their house in a shady hollow.* 6 sounding as if coming from something hollow; dull: *a hollow voice, a hollow groan.* 7 sunken: *A starving person has hollow eyes and cheeks.* 8 not real or meaningful: *hollow promises, hollow joys.* 1, 2, 6–8 *adj.,* 3, 5 *n.,* 4 *v.*

hol•ly (hol′ē) a tree or shrub with shiny, sharp-pointed evergreen leaves and bright-red berries, used especially as Christmas decorations. *n., pl.* **hol•lies.**

ho•lo•caust (hol′ə kost′ *or* hō′lə kost′) the destroying of a great many things and people, especially by fire. The **Holocaust** is the planned mass murder of six million European Jews during the Second World War by the German Nazi government. *n.*

hologram (hol′ə gram′ *or* hō′lə gram′) a kind of photograph made with a laser. It changes colour and shape when you look at it from different angles. *n.*

hol•ster (hōl′stər) a leather case for a gun, usually attached to a belt. *n.*

ho•ly (hō′lē) 1 pure and perfect, with no sin. 2 belonging to God; set apart for God or a religious purpose. *adj.,* **ho•li•er, ho•li•est.**
holy of holies, the most sacred place.

hom•age (hom′ij *or* om′ij) respect; reverence; honour: *Everyone paid homage to the great leader.* *n.*

home (hōm) 1 the place where a person, family, or animal lives: *Her home is at 25 South Street. The owl made its home in our barn.* 2 at or to this place: *I want to go home.* 3 a house, townhouse, or condominium. 4 a place where a person or thing comes from, belongs, or is found: *The Canadian tundra is the home of the musk-ox.* 5 a place for people to live who need special care: *a home for senior citizens.* 1, 3–5 *n.,* 2 *adj.* **—home′less,** *adj.*
bring home to someone, make someone realize.
feel at home, feel comfortable and familiar.
hit home, a hit a target exactly: *the arrow hit home.* **b** be fully understood by someone: *He knew speeding was dangerous, but this fact didn't really hit home until he had an accident.*
home free, a in hide-and-seek, safe at home base without being tagged. **b** nearly finished and sure of success.
to write home about, remarkable: *That's nothing to write home about!*

Word Family.......... home

home-grown: grown locally
homeland: the country where you were born or live
homemade: made at home
homemaker: a person who manages things at home
homesick: sad with longing to be at home

home•ly (hōm′lē) 1 not good-looking: *He was rather a homely young man.* 2 suited to home life; simple: *homely food, homely pleasures.* *adj.,* **home•li•er, home•li•est.**

home page (hōm′ pāj′) the first file reached at an address on the World Wide Web. It has links to other files and other addresses.

home plate (hōm′ plāt′) in baseball, the base you stand beside to bat the ball. You must return there, after hitting the ball and running around the bases, in order to score.

home run (hōm run′) in baseball, a run scored on a hit that lets the batter run around all the bases without stopping. It is also called a **homer.**

home•spun (hōm′spun′) 1 spun or made at home. 2 yarn spun at home, or cloth made from it. 3 plain and simple: *homespun manners.* 1, 3 *adj.,* 2 *n.*

home•stead (hōm′sted′) 1 a farm with its buildings. 2 in the West, public land granted to a settler under certain conditions by the federal government. 3 settle and farm on such land: *Our grandfather homesteaded in Saskatchewan.* 1, 2 *n.,* 3 *v.* **—home′stead′er,** *n.*

home•ward (hōm′wərd) toward home: *We turned homeward (adv.). The ship is on a homeward course (adj.).* **Homewards** is another form for the adverb. *adv. or adj.*

a bat	e bed	i bid	o pot	u cup	th thin
ā cake	ē me	ī bite	ō go	ū rude	ᴛʜ then
à bar	ə about	ər over	ô for	ù put	zh measure

home·work (hōm′wərk′) schoolwork to be done outside of class time. *n.*
do your homework, prepare properly for something, especially by gathering background information.

home·y (hō′mē) like home; cosy and comfortable: *The old inn had a very homey atmosphere. adj.,* **hom·i·er, hom·i·est.**

hom·i·cide (hom′ə sīd′) the killing of one human being by another: *Intentional homicide is murder. n.* —**hom′i·cid′al,** *adj.*

ho·mog·e·nize (hə moj′ə nīz′) make the same throughout. The milk we buy from dairies has usually been homogenized so that the cream remains evenly mixed throughout the milk instead of rising to the top. *v.,* **ho·mog·e·nized, ho·mog·e·niz·ing.**

hom·o·graph (hom′ə graf′) a word that has the same spelling as another but a different origin and a different meaning. *Tear* meaning "a drop of water from the eye" and *tear* meaning "rip" are homographs. In this dictionary homographs are separate entries, each one identified by a small number after it. *n.*

hom·o·nym (hom′ə nim′) a homophone or homograph. Some homonyms are both, like *mail* meaning "letters" and *mail* meaning "armour." *n.*

Grammar Check . . . . homonym

Homonyms are words that have the same form, but have different meanings. For example, *a bank* can mean "a heap of something," like snow. But it can also mean "a shallow place in water," or "a place that deals with money," or "one side of a river," or "a group of something," like electric switches.

Sometimes, homonyms will sound the same, but will have different spellings, like *tale* and *tail*. Words like these are called **homophones**.

Sometimes, homonyms will look the same, but will sound different, like *lead* meaning "go in front" and *lead* meaning "a metal." Words like these are called **homographs**.

hom·o·phone (hom′ə fōn′) a word that sounds the same as another but has a different meaning and origin. *Meat* and *meet* are homophones. *n.*

Hon. *abbreviation for* Honourable, a title given to certain high officials of the government in Canada.

hone (hōn) sharpen or improve: *Over the summer we honed our canoeing skills. v.,* **honed, hon·ing.**

hon·est (on′ist) **1** fair, sincere, and truthful; not lying, pretending, cheating, or stealing: *He was an honest man.* **2** done or made fairly and truthfully: *honest profits. adj.* —**hon′est·ly,** *adv.* —**hon′es·ty,** *n.*

hon·ey (hun′ē) **1** a thick, sweet liquid that bees make out of the nectar they collect from flowers. People eat it. **2** darling; a pet name for someone you love. *n., pl.* **hon·eys.**

hon·ey·bee (hun′ē bē′) the kind of bee that makes honey and wax that can be used by people. *n.*

hon·ey·comb (hun′ē kōm′) a structure of wax containing many rows of six-sided compartments, made by bees to store honey, pollen, and their eggs. *n.*

hon·ey·dew (hun′ē dyū′ *or* hun′ē dū′) a kind of melon with a smooth, whitish skin. It is sweet and green on the inside. *n.*

hon·ey·moon (hun′ē mūn′) **1** the holiday spent together by a newly married couple. **2** have a honeymoon. 1 *n.,* 2 *v.*

hon·ey·suck·le (hun′ē suk′əl) a climbing plant with fragrant white, yellow, or red flowers. *n.*

honk (hongk) **1** the sound made by a goose or a car horn. **2** make or cause to make this sound: *to honk a horn. We honked as we drove past Pia's house.* **Honker** is a nickname for the Canada goose. 1 *n.,* 2 *v.*

hon·or·ar·y (on′ə rer′ē) having to do with a position or title that is given to someone as an honour only, without the person actually doing the work: *She received an honorary degree from Simon Fraser University in recognition of her splendid acting career. adj.*

hon·our or **hon·or** (on′ər) **1** the respect given to someone who is loved and admired. **2** show this kind of respect to: *We honour our country's dead soldiers on Remembrance Day.* **3** an act that shows this kind of respect: *The gift was a great honour.* **4** something or someone that brings this kind of respect: *She is an honour to her family and school.* **5** a high moral character: *A man of honour always keeps his promises.* **6 honours,** *pl.* a special mention or grade given to a student for having done outstanding work. **7 Honour,** a title of respect for a judge, mayor, etc.: *"Yes, your Honour." Her Honour will make a short speech.* 1, 3–7 *n.,* 2 *v.*

hon·our·a·ble or **hon·or·able** (on′ə rə bəl) **1** having, showing, or bringing honour: *an honourable achievement, an honourable burial. It was not honourable for you to cheat.* **2 Honourable,** a title given to certain officials of the government in Canada. *adj.* —**hon′our·a·bly** or **hon′or·a·bly,** *adv.*

hood (hùd) **1** a soft covering for the head and neck, either separate or as part of a coat or top: *My raincoat has* *a hood.* **2** anything shaped or used like a hood, such as the covering over a car engine. *n.* **—hood′ed,** *adj.*

-hood *a suffix meaning* the state or condition of. *Childhood* means "the condition of being a *child.*" *Likelihood* means "the condition of being *likely.*"

hoof (hūf *or* hůf) the foot of a horse, cow, deer, and some other animals, especially the hard covering on the bottom, made of something like horn. **Hoofbeats** are the sound made by the hoofs on the ground when the animal runs. *n., pl.* **hoofs** or **hooves.** **—hoofed,** *adj.*
hoof it, *Slang.* walk: *We hoofed it all the way to the arena and back.*

hook (hůk) **1** a piece of metal, wood, or other stiff material, curved or sharply bent, for catching or holding something: *a fish-hook, a clothes hook.* **2** anything curved or bent like a hook. **3** catch, fasten, or hang with a hook: *to hook a fish. Hook the bungee cord to the roof rack.* **4** make rugs or other crafts using a special hook to pull loops of cloth through a backing of coarse fabric. 1, 2 *n.,* 3, 4 *v.*
by hook or by crook, in any way at all, including trickery if necessary.
hooked on, **a** addicted to: *hooked on drugs.* **b** an enthusiastic fan of: *She was instantly hooked on the idea.*
hook up, set up an electric appliance, phone, or computer system and plug it in. The act of doing this, or something that lets you do it, is a **hookup.**
off the hook, set free from a responsibility: *You're off the hook, we found out it was Axel's fault.*
swallow something hook, line, and sinker, accept or believe something completely.

hook·y (hůk′ē)
play hooky, *Informal.* stay away from school without permission. *n.*

hooligan (hū′li gən) a noisy person who likes to fight or cause damage: *After the game some hooligans tried to knock down the goalposts.* *n.*

hoop (hūp) any large ring. The bands around a barrel are called hoops. Women used to wear hoops attached to the inside of their skirts to hold them out. A hoop can also be used as a toy. A **hoop earring** is plain, large, and ring-shaped. *n.*

hoo·ray (hə rā′) another word for **hurrah.** *interj., n., or v.*

hoot (hūt) **1** the sound that an owl makes. **2** make this sound or one like it, especially in mocking laughter or disapproval: *She hooted at my ridiculous mistake. The crowd hooted angrily at the mayor's remarks.* 1 *n.,* 2 *v.*
not give a hoot, not care: *I don't give a hoot what he says.*

hooves (hūvz *or* hůvz) a plural of **hoof.** *n.*

hop[1] (hop) **1** move by jumping on one foot, both feet, or all feet at once: *She hopped back to get her other boot, which was stuck in the snow. The bird hopped around on the lawn, chirping.* **2** jump over: *to hop a ditch.* **3** a short jump or bounce. 1, 2 *v.,* 3 *n.,* **hopped, hop·ping.**
hop on, get on quickly or with a little jump: *He hopped on the bus.* The opposite is **hop off.**
hop to it, get started right away.

hop[2] (hop) a vine with flower clusters that look like small pine cones. The ripe, dried clusters, called **hops,** are used to flavour beer and other malt drinks. *n.*

hope (hōp) **1** a feeling that something good could happen: *Her promise to help gave me hope that we could finish the job on time.* **2** wish and expect: *I hope to do well in school this year.* **3** something hoped for: *It is our hope that you will all get along together.* **4** a person or thing that gives hope: *She is the hope of the family.* 1, 3, 4 *n.,* 2 *v.,* **hoped, hop·ing.** **—hope′ful,** *adj.* **—hope′less,** *adj.*

hope·ful·ly (hōp′fůl ē) **1** in a hopeful manner: *Hearing a car in the driveway, the child ran hopefully to the door.* **2** *Informal.* I hope; we hope: *Hopefully, the weather will improve.* *adv.*

hop·per (hop′ər) **1** a sort of funnel or chute that empties into a machine such as a mixer or grinder, or into a storage bin. **2** a person or thing that hops. *n.*

hop·scotch (hop′skoch′) a children's game where you try to hop over the lines of a figure drawn on the ground and pick up an object thrown into one of the numbered squares of the figure. *n.*

horde (hȯrd) a large crowd or swarm: *hordes of grasshoppers.* *n.*

ho·ri·zon (hə rī′zən) **1** the line where the earth and sky seem to meet. **2** the limit of a person's thinking, experience, or interest: *Travel broadens your horizons.* *n.*

hor·i·zon·tal (hȯr′ə zon′təl) **1** flat; level; stretching sideways, like a floor, and not up and down like a wall. **2** a horizontal line, direction, or position: *Measure the length of the horizontal.* 1 *adj.,* 2 *n.*

hor·mone (hȯr′mōn) a substance produced in animals and plants that helps some part of their growth or function. *n.* **—hor·mo′nal,** *adj.*

a bat	e bed	i bid	o pot	u cup	th thin
ā cake	ē me	ī bite	ō go	ū rude	TH then
ä bar	ə about	ər over	ȯ for	ů put	zh measure

Horses

The different parts of a horse are called points. Together, the points of a horse make up its conformation — the way it looks.

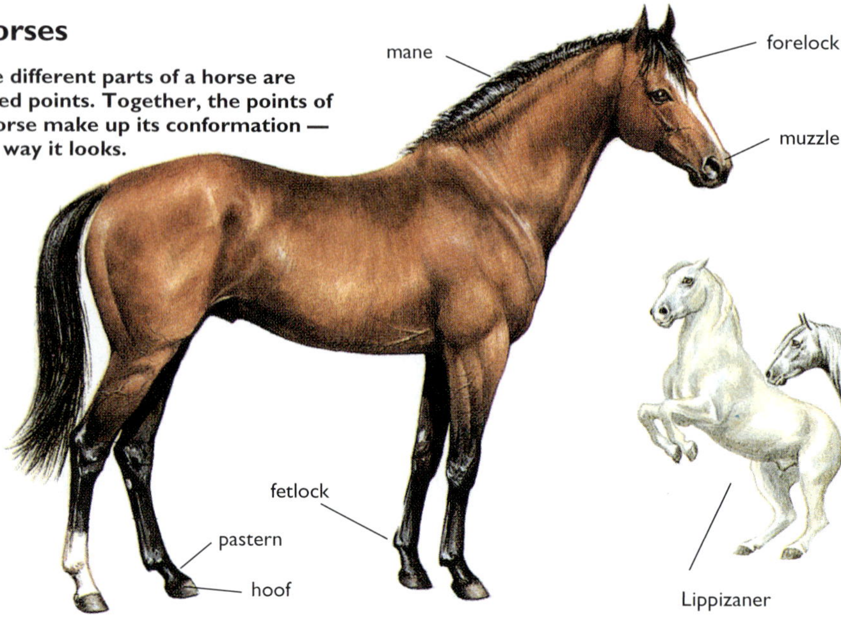

There are many different breeds of horse: some are valued for their strength, others for their speed, or their intelligence.

horn (hôrn) 1 a hard growth, usually curved and pointed, on the heads of cattle, sheep, goats, and some other animals. 2 the hard material that horns, beaks, nails, and hoofs are made of. 3 a musical instrument shaped like a tube with a flared end, played by blowing into the smaller end. The brass section of an orchestra includes several kinds of horns: *English horn, French horn.* 4 a device sounded as a warning signal: *a car horn, a bicycle horn, a foghorn.* *n.*
blow your own horn, brag about yourself.
lock horns, get into an argument or fight.

horned toad (hôrnd′ tōd′) a small lizard with a broad, flat body, short tail, and many spines.

hor•net (hôr′nit) a large wasp that can give a very painful sting. *n.*
hornet's nest, something troublesome or complicated, or something that causes arguments.

horn of plenty (hôrn′əv plen′tē) a curved horn overflowing with fruits and vegetables, used as a symbol of a good harvest at Thanksgiving. It is also called a **cornucopia.**

hor•o•scope (hôr′ə skōp′) a description of your character and your future that is based on the position of the stars and planets when you were born. It is not scientific. *n.*

hor•ri•ble (hôr′ə bəl) causing horror; frightful; shocking: *a horrible crime, a horrible disease.* **Horrific** (hôr if′ik) means about the same. *adj.*
—hor′ri•bly, *adv.*

hor•rid (hôr′id) nasty or awful. **Horrendous** (hə ren′dəs) means about the same. *adj.*

hor•ri•fy (hô′rə fī′) fill with horror: *We were horrified by the pictures of the train wreck.* *v.,* **hor•ri•fied, hor•ri•fy•ing.**

hor•ror (hôr′ər) 1 shock, fear, and disgust. 2 a very strong dislike: *Some people have a horror of snakes and spiders.* 3 something that causes feelings of shock, fear, and disgust. *n.*

horse (hôrs) 1 a large, strong, four-legged animal with solid hoofs and a mane and tail of long, coarse hair. Horses have been used from very early times for riding and carrying and pulling loads. 2 a supporting frame with legs, and often a crosspiece. A **sawhorse** is used to hold a board for sawing; a **pommel horse** has padding and handles on top and is used for gymnastics. *n.*
hold your horses, wait; be patient.
horse around, *Slang.* fool around; get into mischief.
the horse's mouth, the original source; the person who really knows: *news straight from the horse's mouth.*

horse•back (hôrs′bak′) 1 the back of a horse. 2 on the back of a horse: *to ride horseback.* 1 *n.,* 2 *adv.*

horse chestnut (hôrs′ ches′nut) a large tree with spreading branches, large leaves, and clusters of showy, white flowers. Its glossy brown nuts are poisonous. *n.*

horse•fly (hôrs′flī′) a large fly that bites people and large animals. *n., pl.* **horse•flies.**

horse•hair (hôrs′her′) the hair from the mane or tail of a horse. It used to be used a lot for stuffing sofas and chairs. *n.*

horse•man (hôrs′mən) a man who rides a horse, especially a skilled rider. *n., pl.* **horse•men** (hôrs′mən).

horse•man•ship (hôrs′mən ship′) skill in riding or managing horses. *n.*

horse•play (hôrs′plā′) rough, noisy fun. *n.*

horse•pow•er (hôrs′pou′ər) a nonmetric unit of power equal to about 746 W, used for measuring the power of a motor. *n.*

horse•shoe (hôrsh′shū′) 1 a U-shaped metal plate nailed to a horse's hoof to protect it. 2 anything shaped like a horseshoe. 3 **horseshoes,** *pl.* a game where you try to throw horseshoes over a stake 40 ft. (about 12 m) away. Horseshoes is played outdoors. *n.*

horse•wom•an (hôrs′wům′ən) a woman who rides a horse, especially a skilled rider. *n., pl.* **horse•wom•en** (hôrs′wim′ən).

hose (hōz) 1 a flexible tube for carrying any liquid a short distance: *a watering hose for the lawn, the hose of a gas pump.* 2 Usually, **hose down,** spray with a water hose. 3 an old-fashioned word for stockings or socks. Another similar word is **hosiery** (hō′zhə rē). 1 *n.,* 2 *v.,* **hosed, hos•ing;** 3 *pl.n.*

hos•pice (hos′pis) a place where people who are dying of an incurable disease can receive comfort, companionship, and pain relief. *n.*

hos•pi•ta•ble (hə spit′ə bəl) giving a warm welcome and friendly treatment to guests or strangers: *a hospitable family, a hospitable reception. adj.* **—hos′pi•ta•bly,** *adv.*

hos•pi•tal (hos′pi təl) a place where sick or injured people may be treated and cared for. *n.*

hos•pi•tal•i•ty (hos′pə tal′ə tē) friendly, generous treatment of guests or strangers. *n.*

hos•pi•tal•ize (hos′pi tə līz′) put in a hospital to be given medical care: *The cut was so bad that she had to be hospitalized. v.,* **hos•pi•tal•ized, hos•pi•tal•iz•ing.**

host[1] (hōst) 1 a person who has guests, or visitors. 2 a person who leads or runs a talk show, game show, or talent show. 3 someone who seats people in a restaurant or aircraft. 4 an animal or plant that a parasite lives in or on. 5 act as host: *to host a party.* 1–4 *n.,* 5 *v.*

host[2] (hōst) a huge number: *A host of stars glittered in the sky. n.*

hos•tage (hos′tij) a person taken and held by an enemy as a way of forcing someone to do something. If the thing is done, the hostage will be returned safe and sound; if not, he or she may be harmed or killed. *n.*

hos•tel (hos′təl) 1 a cheap place for homeless people or travellers to spend the night and get meals. 2 a home for young people who need special help. 3 a dormitory for students at a boarding school. *n.*

host•ess (hōs′tis) a host who is a woman. *n.*

hos•tile (hos′tīl *or* hos′təl) of or like an enemy; unfriendly: *a hostile army, a hostile tone. They were very hostile to our suggestion. adj.*

hos•til•i•ty (hə stil′ə tē) 1 the attitude of an enemy; unfriendliness: *He showed signs of hostility toward me.* 2 **hostilities,** *pl.* acts of war; warfare; fighting. *n., pl.* **hos•til•i•ties.**

hot (hot) 1 having, feeling, or giving a lot of heat; very warm: *a hot fire, the hot sun. The long race made the runners hot.* 2 having a sharp, burning taste: *Pepper and mustard are hot.* 3 full of strong, excited feeling: *hot with rage.* A person who gets very angry is **hot-tempered** or **hot-headed.** 4 very popular and exciting: *a hot new rock band.* 5 new; fresh: *a hot scent, a hot trail, a newspaper hot off the press.* 6 very close to what you are trying to catch or find: *The police were hot on the heels of the thieves.* 7 *Slang.* stolen. *adj.,* **hot•ter, hot•test.** **—hot′ly,** *adv.*
hot air, talk that has little importance or meaning.
hot potato, something nobody wants to talk about or get involved with because it leads to too many problems or arguments.
hot under the collar, very angry.
in hot water, in trouble.
in the hot seat, being questioned or blamed by everyone.

hot cake (hot′ kāk′) a pancake.
go or **sell like hot cakes,** be sold quickly: *The candy we made for the fall fair sold like hot cakes.*

hot dog (hot′ dog′) a wiener inside a long bun, usually served with mustard, relish, ketchup, and so on.

ho•tel (hō tel′) a place where travellers can get private rooms and restaurant meals for pay. *n.*

hot•house (hot′hous′) a greenhouse; a heated building with walls and roof of glass for growing plants in. *n.*

hot•line (hot′līn′) 1 a special telephone line that people can call to get information or talk about something. 2 a direct telephone line between the leaders of two countries that lets them talk directly when there is an urgent problem. *n.*

a bat	e bed	i bid	o pot	u cup	th thin
ā cake	ē me	ī bite	ō go	ū rude	ᴛʜ then
à bar	ə about	ər over	ô for	ů put	zh measure

Houses

Different styles of houses are influenced by climate and by available building materials.

a North American timber house

an Indonesian house built on stilts

hot•list (hot′list′) a list of frequently used websites, coded so the user can click on any name on the list to go to that site. *n.*

hot•spot (hot′spot′) a place where Internet access is available free, such as in airports or coffee shops. *n.*

hound (hound) **1** a dog, especially one of a breed used originally for hunting by scent. **2** keep on chasing or pestering: *The police hounded the thief until they caught him. She hounded me until I finally gave in.* 1 *n.,* 2 *v.*

hour (our) **1** a period of sixty minutes: *Twenty-four hours make a day. Symbol:* h **2** a time: *Our breakfast hour is seven o'clock. This is the nation's darkest hour.* **3 hours,** *pl.* the time for work, study, etc.: *Our office hours are 8:30 to 4:30.* *n.*

hour•glass (our′glas′) a device for measuring time. It takes exactly an hour for the sand in it to go from a glass bulb or container on top to one on the bottom. *n.*

hour•ly (our′lē) **1** lasting or covering an hour: *an hourly wage.* **2** coming or happening once an hour: *Give two doses of the medicine hourly (adv.). There are hourly news reports on this radio station (adj.).* *adv.* or *adj.*

house (hous *for 1–3, 5–8,* houz *for 4*) **1** a building for people to live in. **2** a building for any purpose. This meaning is often found in compounds: *an opera house, a courthouse.* **3** a family, especially a noble family: *a prince of the house of Windsor.* **4** take or put into a house; give shelter to: *Where can we house all these children?* **5** an assembly for making laws: *the House of Commons.* **6** an audience: *The singer sang to a large house.* **7** in curling, the goal or target. 1–3, 5–7 *n., pl.* **hous•es** (hou′ziz); 4 *v.,* **housed, hous•ing.** **—house′ful′,** *n.*

on the house, paid for by the owner of the business; free: *After visiting the candy factory, we were each given a box of chocolates on the house.*

house•boat (hous′bōt′) a large, flat-bottomed boat that can be used as a place to live. *n.*

house•bro•ken (hous′brō′kən) of a pet, such as a cat or dog, trained not to make a mess indoors. *adj.*

house•fly (hous′flī′) a fly that lives around and in houses, feeding on food and garbage. Houseflies can spread disease. *n., pl.* **house•flies.**

house•hold (house′hōld′) all the people living in a house; family. *n.*
household word, a word or name so famous that everyone is familiar with it.

house•keep•er (hous′kē′pər) a person who manages a home and its affairs and does the housework. *n.* **—house′keep•ing,** *n.*

House of Assembly (hous′əv ə sem′blē) the law-making body of the province of Newfoundland.

House of Commons (hous′ əv kom′ənz) **1** in Canada, the body of elected representatives who meet in Ottawa to make laws and debate questions of government. Members of Parliament belong to the House of Commons. **2** the chamber they meet in.

house•wife (hous′wīf′) a woman who manages a home and its affairs for her family. *n.*

house•work (hous′wərk′) the work to be done in a home, such as cooking and cleaning. *n.*

hous•ing (hou′zing) **1** shelter for people; homes: *That city needs more housing.* **2** a frame or case that protects the parts of a machine. *n.*

hove (hōv) a past tense of **heave:** *The ship hove into sight on the horizon.* *v.*

hov•el (huv′əl *or* hov′əl) a small, roughly built house; shack. *n.*

hov•er (huv′ər *or* hov′ər) **1** stay in one place in the air: *The hummingbird hovered in front of the flower.* **2** stay nearby, waiting or watching: *The dogs hovered around the kitchen door at mealtime.* **3** waver: *The sick man hovered between life and death.* *v.*

Hov•er•craft (huv′ər kraft′) *a trademark for* a vehicle that can travel just above the surface of water or land. It works by continuously blowing a powerful current of air out the bottom and moving along on top of it. *n.*

how (hou) **1** in what way; by what means: *How can it be done* (*adv.*)? *Tell me how it happened* (*conj.*). **2** to what degree or amount: *How tall are you? I don't know how long it will take.* **3** in what state or condition: *How is your health* (*adv.*)? *Let's see how she is* (*conj.*). **4** for what reason; why: *How is it you are late?*
1–4 *adv.,* 1, 3 *conj.*
how come, *Informal.* why: *How come you didn't call me?*
how so, why is that true?

how•ev•er (hou ev′ər) **1** but; even so; in spite of that: *We were very late for dinner; however, there was plenty left for us.* **2** no matter how: *I'll come however busy I am.* **3** a stronger version of "how" in questions: *However did you get so dirty?* *adv.*

howl (houl) **1** give a long, loud, mournful cry: *Our dog sometimes howls at night. The winter winds howled around our cabin.* **2** a long, loud, mournful cry: *the howl of a wolf.* **3** yell; shout: *It was so funny that we howled with laughter* (*v.*). *We heard a howl of pain* (*n.*). **4** *Informal.* something very funny: *The skit by Jock and Drew was a howl.* 1, 3 *v.,* 2–4 *n.*

hp *abbreviation for* horsepower.

H.R.H. *abbreviation for* Her (or His) Royal Highness.

hub (hub) **1** the central part of a wheel, often covered with a **hubcap. 2** a centre of interest or activity: *The mall is the hub of our small town.* *n.*

hub•bub (hub′ub) a loud, confused noise; an uproar: *There was a hubbub when the crowd was told to move.* *n.*

huck•le•ber•ry (huk′əl ber′ē) a small, dark-blue, edible berry similar to a blueberry. It grows on a bush. *n., pl.* **huck•le•ber•ries.**

hud•dle (hud′əl) **1** to crowd close: *The sheep huddled in a corner of the pen.* **2** crouch or curl up: *The cat huddled on the cushion.* **3** a small group of people crowded together. 1, 2 *v.,* **hud•dled, hud•dling;** 3 *n.*
go into a huddle, a in football, gather as a team to plan the next play, decide on signals, and so on. **b** *Informal.* talk things over secretly: *After the meeting, the lawyer went into a huddle with her partner.*

Hud•son Bay (hud′sən bā′) a huge inland sea in northern central Canada.

Hudson's Bay Company (hud′sənz bā′ kum′pə nē) a British trading company founded in 1670 to carry on the fur trade with the native people of North America. It played a great part in the exploration and development of Canada's Northwest.

WORD HISTORY.. Hudson's Bay Company

Hudson's Bay Company is the popular and traditional (and shorter!) name of The Company of Adventurers of England Trading into Hudson's Bay. The company's name was taken from Hudson Bay, a huge inland sea in northern Canada, named after the explorer Henry Hudson.

hue (hyū) a colour or shade: *all the hues of the rainbow.* *n.*

huff (huf) a fit of anger or sulkiness: *He walked out in a huff when he was told his dog wasn't allowed in the store.* *n.* **—huff′y,** *adj.* **—huff′i•ly,** *adv.*

hug (hug) **1** put the arms around and hold close: *Andrea hugged her new puppy.* **2** a tight clasp with the arms: *Give me a hug.* **3** keep close to: *The boat hugged the shore.* 1, 3 *v.,* **hugged, hug•ging;** 2 *n.*

huge (hyūj) extremely big: *a huge sum of money. An elephant is a huge animal.* *adj.,* **hug•er, hug•est.** **—huge′ly,** *adv.*

hulk (hulk) **1** the body of an old or wrecked ship. **2** a big, heavy person or thing. *n.* **—hulk′ing,** *adj.*

hull (hul) **1** the main body of a ship or seaplane. **2** the outer covering of a seed. **3** the green leaves at the stem of some fruits such as strawberries. **4** remove the hulls from. 1–3 *n.,* 4 *v.*

hul•la•ba•loo (hul′ə bə lū′) a loud noise or disturbance; uproar. *n.*

a bat	e bed	i bid	o pot	u cup	th thin
ā cake	ē me	ī bite	ō go	ū rude	ᴛʜ then
à bar	ə about	ər over	ȯ for	u̇ put	zh measure

hum (hum) 1 make a smooth, low sound like a bee or an electric motor: *The sewing machine hums busily.* 2 this sound: *the hum of bees, the hum of the city streets.* 3 sing with closed lips, not singing words: *She was humming a tune.* 4 *Informal.* be busy and active: *Things are humming.* 1, 3, 4 *v.,* **hummed, hum·ming;** 2 *n.*

hu·man (hyū′mən) 1 being a person; having the nature of a person: *a human creature. Men, women, and children are human beings.* 2 Usually, **human being,** a person. A being that is not a human, but resembles one, is a **humanoid.** 3 having to do with all people: *Selfishness is a human weakness. The history of Canada has great human interest.* 1, 2 *adj.,* 3 *n.* **—hu′man·ly,** *adv.*

hu·mane (hyū mān′) kind; not cruel: *A good jockey gives humane treatment to a horse. adj.* **—hu·mane′ly,** *adv.*

hu·man·i·ty (hyū man′ə tē) 1 people; all human beings: *Recent advances in medicine have helped humanity.* **Humankind** means about the same. 2 the nature of human beings; the condition of being human: *Humanity is a mixture of good and bad qualities.* 3 humane treatment; kindness: *Treat animals with humanity. n., pl.* **hu·man·i·ties.**

hum·ble (hum′bəl) 1 modest; not proud; not thinking too highly of yourself: *a humble opinion. She is a fantastic guitarist but is so humble about it—she never brags.* 2 low in position or condition; not important or fancy: *He has a humble position at the factory. They live in a humble two-room cottage.* 3 make humble. 1, 2 *adj.,* **hum·bler, hum·blest;** 3 *v.,* **hum·bled, hum·bling.** **—hum′ble·ness,** *n.* **—hum′bly,** *adv.*
eat humble pie, admit your mistakes and apologize.

hum·drum (hum′drum′) without variety; boring; dull: *a humdrum movie. adj.*

hu·mid (hyū′mid) moist; damp: *The air is very humid near the sea. adj.* **—hu·mid′i·ty,** *n.* **—hu·mid′i·fy,** *v.* **—hu·mid′i·fi′er,** *n.*

🍁 **hu·mi·dex** (hyū′mə deks′) a number scale expressed in degrees Celsius, that measures how the combination of heat and moisture in the air is likely to feel to our bodies. If the humidex is 36°C, it means that the moisture in the air makes it feel like 36°C even though the actual temperature may be less. *n.*

hu·mil·i·ate (hyū mil′ē āt′) make totally embarrassed and ashamed; destroy someone's dignity: *He was humiliated when his parents scolded him in front of us. v.,* **hu·mil·i·at·ed, hu·mil·i·at·ing.** **—hu·mil′i·a′tion,** *n.*

hu·mil·i·ty (hyū mil′ə tē) humble character; lack of pride; the attitude that you are not better or more important than others. *n.*

Hummingbirds, like bees, collect nectar from flowers.

hum·ming·bird (hum′ing bərd′) a very small, brightly coloured bird with a long, narrow bill and narrow wings. It is able to hover and fly backward as it feeds on the nectar of flowers. Hummingbird wings beat so fast that they make a humming sound. *n.*

hu·mong·ous (hyū mung′gəs) *Informal.* enormous. *adj.*

hu·mour or **hu·mor** (hyū′mər) 1 a funny quality: *The speech was full of humour and made everybody laugh.* 2 give in to someone's wishes just to keep him or her happy: *Try to humour your little brother; he's not feeling well.* 3 a state of mind; a mood or temper: *She awoke in a good humour.* 1, 3 *n.,* 2 *v.* **—hu′mor·ist,** *n.* **—hu′mor·ous,** *adj.*
sense of humour or **humor,** the ability to see the funny side of things.

hump (hump) 1 a rounded shape that sticks out: *Some camels have two humps on their backs.* 2 raise or bend up into a hump: *The cat humped its back when it saw the dog.* 1 *n.,* 2 *v.*
over the hump, past the hardest part.

hump·back (hump′bak′) 1 a large whale that has a humped back and very large front flippers. 2 another word for a **hunchback,** someone whose back is bent and forms a hump at shoulder level. 3 a kind of salmon of the Pacific Ocean. *n.* **—hump′backed′,** *adj.*

hu•mus (hyū′məs) a dark-brown or black soil formed from dead leaves and other decayed plant parts. It is very rich in nutrients for plants. *n.*

WORD HISTORY....... humus

The word **humus** comes from the Latin word *humus*, meaning "ground." So do the words **humble**, **humility**, and **humiliate**. To be humble is to be low.

hunch (hunch) **1** *Informal.* a feeling or suspicion that cannot be explained: *I had a hunch they would show up today.* **2** curl into a hump: *He sat hunched up with his chin on his knees.* 1 *n.*, 2 *v.*

hunch•back (hunch′bak′) a person with a bent back that forms a hump at the level of the shoulders. *n.* **—hunch′backed′,** *adj.*

hun•dred (hun′drəd) ten times ten; 100: *There are one hundred cents in a dollar* (*adj.*). *n.* or *adj.* **—hun′dredth,** *adj. or n.*

hung (hung) a past tense and past participle of **hang:** *He hung up his cap. Your dress has hung here all day.* *v.*
hung up on, very anxious or sensitive about: *Don't be so hung up on your looks!*

hun•ger (hung′gər) **1** a desire or need for food: *After two days without food, the caged lion roared with hunger.* **2** a strong desire for something; longing: *a hunger for books.* **3** feel a strong desire for food or anything else: *The lonely girl hungered for friends.* 1, 2 *n.*, 3 *v.* **—hun′gry,** *adj.* **—hun′gri•ly,** *adv.*
go on a hunger strike, refuse to eat until someone does what you want.

hunk (hungk) *Informal.* a big lump, piece, or slice: *a hunk of cheese.* *n.*

hunt (hunt) **1** go after wild animals to catch or kill them for food or as a sport: *to hunt deer.* **2** search; look for something for a long time: *to hunt for a lost book.* **3** the act of hunting: *Our gear for the duck hunt is all ready. I finally found my gloves after a long hunt.* 1, 2 *v.*, 3 *n.* **—hunt′er,** *n.*
hunt down, chase and catch.
hunt up, look for and find.

hur•dle (hər′dəl) **1** in a race, a barrier for people or horses to jump over. **2** a problem or difficulty. 1, 2 *n.*

hurl (hərl) throw with force or violence: *to hurl a book across the room, to hurl insults at someone.* *v.*

Hu•ron (hyū′ron) **1** a First Nations people living just north of Québec City. **2** their language. **3** having to do with these people or their language. 1, 2 *n.*, 3 *adj.*

hur•rah (hə rȧ′) **1** a shout of joy or approval: *"Hurrah!" they shouted as the team scored again* (*interj.*). *Give a hurrah for the hero* (*n.*). **Hurray** (hə rā′) is another form of the word. **2** shout hurrahs; cheer: *They hurrahed as they watched the parade go by.* 1 *interj.* or *n.*, 2 *v.*

hur•ri•cane (hər′ə kān′) a tropical storm with a violent wind and, usually, very heavy rain: *The wind in a hurricane blows over 120 km/h.* *n.*

hur•ry (hər′ē) **1** move or do something faster than usual: *to hurry supper, to hurry a sick child to the doctor. If you hurry, your work may be too sloppy.* **2** tell or force somebody to go faster: *Don't hurry the driver.* **3** the action of hurrying: *In her hurry she dropped the eggs.* 1, 2 *v.*, **hur•ried, hur•ry•ing;** 3 *n.*, *pl.* **hur•ries. —hur′ried,** *adj.* **—hur′ried•ly,** *adv.*
in a hurry, **a** trying to move or act fast: *I can't wait, I'm in a hurry!* **b** very eager to have or do as soon as possible: *We were in a hurry for school to be over.*

hurt (hərt) **1** cause pain to a person, animal, or thing; wound; injure: *The stone hurt his foot badly.* **2** suffer pain; feel pain: *My hand hurts.* **3** a cut, bruise, or other injury: *to kiss a child's hurts.* **4** damage or harm: *Will it hurt this hat if it gets wet* (*v.*)? *Not being chosen for the play was a great hurt to her pride* (*n.*). 1, 2, 4 *v.*, **hurt, hurt•ing;** 3, 4 *n.* **—hurt′ful,** *adj.*

hur•tle (hər′təl) throw or rush violently: *The train hurtled past. The driver was hurtled against the windshield when the car crashed.* *v.*, **hur•tled, hur•tling.**

hus•band (huz′bənd) the man that a woman is married to. *n.*

hush (hush) **1** make or become silent or quiet: *The wind has hushed. Can you hush those kids for me while I'm on the phone?* **2** a stopping of noise; silence; quiet. 1 *v.*, 2 *n.* **—hushed,** *adj.*
hush up, **a** be quiet. **b** tell someone to be quiet: *I tried to speak but she hushed me up.* **c** keep secret: *The whole incident was hushed up.*

husk (husk) **1** the dry outer covering of certain seeds or fruits: *to peel the husk off an ear of corn.* **2** remove the husk from: *Husk the corn.* 1 *n.*, 2 *v.*

a bat	e bed	i bid	o pot	u cup	th thin
ā cake	ē me	ī bite	ō go	ū rude	ᴛʜ then
ȧ bar	ə about	ər over	ȯ for	u̇ put	zh measure

husk·y¹ (hus′kē) 1 dry in the throat; hoarse: *A cold sometimes causes a husky cough.* 2 big and strong: *a husky young man. adj.,* **husk·i·er, husk·i·est.** —**husk′i·ness,** *n.*

husk·y² (hus′kē) a strong dog, used in the North for pulling sleds. *n., pl.* **husk·ies** or **Husk·ies.**

hus·tle (hus′əl) 1 hurry: *Mom hustled the boys off to bed. We'll have to hustle to get there by 5:00 (v.). It was a hustle to get supper ready in time (n.).* 2 push or shove roughly: *to hustle someone into a car along the street.* 3 *Informal.* use all your energy: *He had to hustle to earn enough money to support his family.* 1–3 *v.,* **hus·tled, hus·tling;** 1 *n.* —**hus′tler,** *n.*

hut (hut) a small, roughly made house: *a village of mud huts.* *n.*

hutch (huch) 1 a cage or house for rabbits. 2 a cupboard, open or with glass doors, that has shelves for dishes. It can be set on top of a separate cupboard with drawers, or built with the cupboard underneath in one piece. *n.*

Hut·ter·ite (hut′ ə rīt′) a member of a religious group that came originally from Austria and settled mainly in Alberta and Manitoba. Hutterites live in farming communities and keep to a simple, traditional lifestyle. *n.*

Hwy. *abbreviation for* highway.

hy·a·cinth (hī′ə sinth′) 1 a spring plant that grows from a bulb and has a spike of small, fragrant, bell-shaped flowers. 2 a tropical water plant with bluish-purple flowers that clogs up waterways. *n.*

hy·brid (hī′brid) 1 the offspring of two animals or plants of different kinds: *Most garden roses are hybrids.* Hybrids are produced to combine the best qualities of different kinds of plant or animal. 2 anything of mixed origin: *A word containing parts from different languages is a hybrid.* 3 produced from two different species, varieties, etc.: *A hybrid car can use two kinds of engine—electric or gasoline.* 1, 2 *n.,* 3 *adj.*

hy·drant (hī′drənt) a short, wide, capped pipe that comes up from below ground near the street. It is joined to the main water pipes below and has a place to attach a hose so the water can be used to put out fires. *n.*

WORD HISTORY..... hydrant

Words beginning with **hydr** all have to do with water. These words come from the Greek word *hydor*, meaning "water."

hy·drau·lic (hī drol′ik) 1 having to do with water or other liquids in motion. 2 working by the pressure of water or other liquid: *a hydraulic press, hydraulic brakes.* *adj.*

hy·dro (hī′drō) electric power that comes from flowing or falling water: *Niagara Falls provides hydro for many factories. The hydro was off for two hours during the storm.* The full name is **hydro-electricity** and the adjective is **hydro-electric.** *n.*

hy·dro·foil (hī′drə foil′) 1 one of a set of blades or fins attached to the hull of a boat. When moving, the boat rises on the hydrofoils, just clear of the water. Hydrofoils increase speed by reducing friction with the water. 2 a boat that has hydrofoils. *n.*

hy·dro·gen (hī′drə jən) a colourless, odourless gas that burns easily. Hydrogen, which is the lightest element, combines with oxygen to form water. *n.*

hydrogen bomb (hī′drəjən bom′) a bomb that uses the fusion of atoms to cause an explosion many times more powerful than that of an atomic bomb. It is also called an **H-bomb.**

hy·dro·plane (hī′drə plān′) 1 a motorboat that skims along on top of the water. 2 to skim along on top of water. A speeding car will hydroplane when it hits a puddle on the highway, making it harder to control. 3 an aircraft that can take off and land on water; seaplane. 1, 3 *n.,* 2 *v.,* **hy·dro·planed, hy·dro·plan·ing.**

hy·dro·sphere (hī′drō sfēr′) all the earth's water, thought of as forming part of the environment of all living things. *n.*

The spotted hyena is a powerful and aggressive animal. It hunts in packs, at night.

hy·e·na (hī ē′nə) a wild, wolflike animal of Africa and Asia. Hyenas have a cry that sounds like hysterical laughter. *n.*

hy·giene (hī′jēn) the rules of health, especially for avoiding disease by keeping clean. *n.* **—hy·gien′ic** (hī jē′nik *or* hī jen′ik), *adj.* **—hy·gien′ist** (hī jēn′ist *or* hī jen′ist), *n.*

hy·grom·e·ter (hī grom′ə tər) a device that measures the amount of moisture in the air. *n.*

hymn (him) **1** a song praising God. A **hymnal** (him′nəl) or **hymnary** (him′nə rē) is a book of hymns. **2** any song of praise. *n.*

hype (hīp) *Informal.* **1** a lot of exaggerated advertising: *There was tremendous hype for the new movie.* **2** advertise a great deal and in an exaggerated way. 1 *n.*, 2 *v.*, **hyped, hyp·ing.**

hy·per·ac·tive (hī′pər ak′tiv) having a condition that makes it hard to stay still, be quiet, or concentrate for very long. *adj.* **—hy′per·ac·tiv′i·ty,** *n.*

hy·per·bo·le (hī′pər′bə lē′) a figure of speech. In hyperbole, extravagant exaggeration is used for emphasis. *Examples: I could listen to that CD all night. That colour is so bright, I need sunglasses. n.*

hy·phen (hī′fən) a mark (-) used to join the parts of some compound words, or to divide a word at the end of a line of printing or writing. To **hyphenate** a word is to write it with a hyphen. *n.* ▶ See the *Grammar and Usage Mini-Guide.*

Grammar Check . . . . hyphen

Use hyphens in these situations.

- Words or phrases come before a noun: *Our team suffered two back-to-back losses.*
- You are writing numbers: *forty-eight; three-quarters*
- A compound word could be confusing: *mother-in-law; re-enter*
- You are adding a prefix to a proper noun: *anti-American; mid-Arctic*

hyp·no·tize (hip′nə tīz′) put into a state somewhat like sleep, called **hypnosis** (hip nō′sis). A hypnotized person cannot think or make decisions in the normal way, and carries out the suggestions of the person who has hypnotized him or her. Sometimes, a hypnotized person remembers things that he or she had forgotten. *v.,* **hyp·no·tized, hyp·no·tiz·ing.** **—hyp′no·tist,** *n.* **—hyp′no·tism′,** *n.* **—hyp·not′ic** (hip not′ik), *adj.*

hyp·o·crite (hip′ə krit′) a person who pretends to be more concerned about doing right than he or she really is. *n.* **—hyp′o·crit′i·cal,** *adj.* **—hy·poc′ri·sy** (hi pok′rə sē), *n.*

hy·po·der·mic (hī′pə dər′mik) having to do with injection under the skin: *The doctor used a hypodermic needle* (*adj.*). *n. or adj.*

hy·po·ther·mi·a (hī′pə thər′mē ə) a condition where the body temperature is greatly below normal: *People who fall into icy water can die of hypothermia. n.*

hy·poth·e·sis (hī poth′ə sis) an idea that may explain something but has not yet been proven, which can be tested by doing experiments or gathering data. To **hypothesize** is to come up with a hypothesis about something. *n.*

hy·po·thet·i·cal (hī pə thet′ə kəl) possible, but unreal or not known to be true; made up as part of a theory or argument: *Just to give a hypothetical example, suppose Sylvie decided not to brush her teeth for six weeks; what would happen? n.*

hys·ter·i·cal (hi ster′ə kəl) showing extreme lack of control; abnormally excited and unable to stop crying, screaming, or laughing: *hysterical with grief, hysterical fans at a concert.* This condition is called **hysteria** (hi stēr′ēə *or* hi ster′ē ə). *adj.* **—hys·ter′i·cal·ly,** *adv.*
go into hysterics, become hysterical.

Hz *symbol for* hertz.

Ii

i or **I** (ī) **1** the ninth letter of the English alphabet, or any speech sound that it stands for. The sound of *i* in *bit* is different from the sound of *i* in *bite.* **2** the ninth thing in a list. **3** the Roman numeral for 1. *n., pl.* **i's** or **I's.**

ibis (ī′bis) a tall wading bird of Africa and other warm regions that has a long, thin, downward-curving bill. The ancient Egyptians considered it to be sacred. *n.,* **i·bis·es** or **i·bis.**

ice (īs) **1** frozen water; water made solid by cold. **2** make cool with ice: *an iced drink.* **3** a frozen dessert, usually one made of sweetened fruit juice. **4** cover with icing: *to ice a cake.* **5** a frozen surface for skating, hockey, curling, etc. **6** in hockey, shoot a puck from your own end zone all the way past the red line at the other end of the rink. 1, 3, 5 *n.,* 2, 4, 6 *v.,* **iced, ic·ing.**

break the ice, get people feeling relaxed with each other: *The party started with a few games to break the ice.*
ice over, become covered with ice.
ice up, become clogged, filled, or covered with ice.
on thin ice, in a dangerous position.

ice age (īs′āj′) a time when much of the earth was covered with glaciers. The name of the most recent one, ending about 8000 BCE, is usually capitalized: *the Ice Age.*

ice·berg (īs′bərg′) a large mass of ice floating in the sea. About 90 percent of an iceberg is underwater. *n.*

ice·break·er (īs′brā′kər) **1** a strong ship with powerful motors, used to break a path through ice for other ships. **2** an activity that helps people in a group to feel comfortable together. *n.*

ice·cap (īs′kap′) a very large mass of ice and snow that covers a mountaintop or polar region throughout the year: *the polar icecaps. n.*

ice cream (īs′ krēm′) a frozen dessert made of cream, sweetened and flavoured.

ice cube (īs′ kjūb′) a small block of ice made in a freezer, used for making drinks or food cold.

ice field (īs′ fēld′) a huge sheet of ice covering an area of land or floating in the sea.

ice storm (īs′ stȯrm′) a storm with freezing rain that covers everything in a thin layer of ice.

Ice

Water increases in volume and decreases in density as it freezes into ice. That is why icebergs float, with about seven-eighths of their volume below the surface.

The word iceberg comes from the Dutch word *ijsberg*, meaning "mountain of ice."

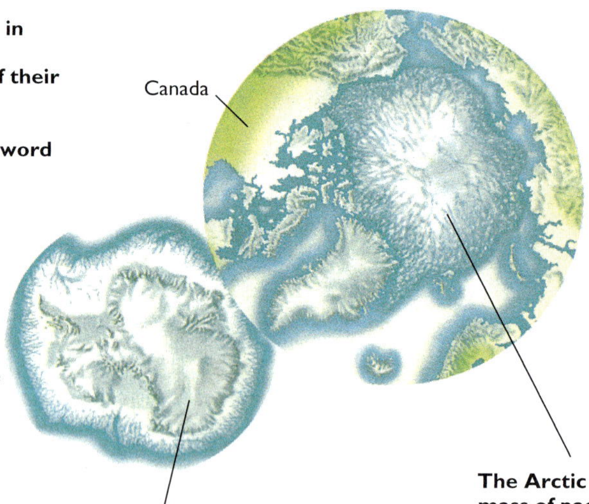

i·ci·cle (ī′sə kəl) a pointed, hanging stick of ice formed by the freezing of dripping water. *n.*

ic·ing (ī′sing) a sweet, creamy mixture used to cover cakes and so on. Another name for it is **frosting.** *n.*

i·con (ī′kon) 1 a small sign or picture on a computer screen that stands for a program or file, a group of programs or files, or a command. 2 a person or thing that is given special importance as a symbol or representative of something: *The singer, who has had a long career and many hit songs, has become an icon in the world of popular music.* 3 an image; a statue or picture. *n.* **—i·con′ic,** *adj.*

i·cy (ī′sē) 1 like ice; very cold: *an icy blast of wind.* 2 full of ice or covered with ice: *icy roads.* 3 very unfriendly: *He gave her an icy stare.* *adj.,* **i·ci·er, i·ci·est. —i′ci·ly,** *adv.* **—i′ci·ness,** *n.*

ID (ī′ dē′) *abbreviation for* **identification,** any document that can be used to prove who you are. An **ID card** shows your name, date of birth, and picture. *n.*

I'd (īd) 1 I would. 2 I had.

i·de·a (ī dē′ə) 1 a plan, picture, or thought in your mind: *I had an idea for a story.* 2 the point or purpose of something: *The idea of a vacation is to get a rest.* *n.*

i·de·al (ī dē′əl) 1 a perfect model to be followed; the best you could wish for or try to be: *Her mother is her ideal. He is a person of high ideals and strives always to be honest and kind.* 2 perfect; the best you could wish for: *The sunny clearing by the stream was ideal for our campsite.* 1 *n.,* 2 *adj.* **—i·de′al·ly,** *adv.*

i·de·al·ist (ī dē′ə list) a person who has high ideals for living and is willing to make sacrifices to follow them which may seem foolish to others. *n.* **—i′de·al·ist′ic,** *adj.* **—i·de′al·ism′,** *n.*

i·den·ti·cal (ī den′tə kəl) 1 the same: *That is the identical pen I lost.* 2 exactly alike: *The two new pennies were identical.* *adj.*

i·den·ti·fi·ca·tion (ī den′tə fə kā′shən) 1 something used to identify a person or thing, or prove who he or she is: *She showed her driver's licence as identification.* 2 the act of identifying. *n.*

i·den·ti·fy (ī den′tə fī′) 1 recognize; say or show what something is or who something is: *Can you identify each of these shapes?* 2 make the same; treat as the same: *The good ruler identified his people's welfare with his own.* 3 understand or sympathize because you have experienced the same yourself: *I can identify with your hurt at being left out.* *v.,* **i·den·ti·fied, i·den·ti·fy·ing.**

i·den·ti·ty (ī den′tə tē) who or what someone or something is: *The writer concealed his identity by signing his stories with a pen name.* *n., pl.* **i·den·ti·ties.**

id·i·om (id′ē əm) a phrase or expression whose meaning cannot be understood from the ordinary meanings of its individual words: *"How do you do?" and "catch a cold" are English idioms.* *n.* **—id′i·o·mat′ic** (id′ē ə mat′ik), *adj.*

Grammar Check ...... idiom

Idioms that contain prepositions sometimes cause trouble. Here are some to watch out for.

Don't say	say
different than,	*different to.*
try and	*try to*
be sure and	*be sure to*
off of	*off*

id·i·ot (id′ē ət) a very stupid or foolish person: *He was an idiot to behave like that.* *n.* **—id′i·ot′ic** (id′ē ot′ik), *adj.* **—id′i·o·cy** (id′ē ə sē), *n.*

i·dle (ī′dəl) 1 doing nothing; not busy or working: *idle machines, the idle hours of a holiday.* 2 lazy: *an idle good-for-nothing.* 3 foolish; not to be taken seriously: *idle fears, idle rumours.* 4 do nothing: *She spent the afternoon idling on the front porch.* 5 run slowly without being in gear: *The car idled for ten minutes while the driver stood chatting in the driveway.* 1–3 *adj.,* **i·dler, i·dlest;** 4, 5 *v.,* **i·dled, i·dling. —i′dle·ness,** *n.* **—i′dler,** *n.* **—i′dly,** *adv.*

i·dol (ī′dəl) 1 an image or other object worshipped as a god. The worship of idols is called **idolatry** (ī dol′ə trē). 2 a person or thing that is loved or admired very much: *The baby girl was the idol of her family.* *n.* **—i′dol·ize′,** *v.* **—i·dol′a·tor,** *n.*

i.e. *abbreviation for* the Latin words *id est,* meaning "that is." It is used to explain or restate something you've just said: *Please give your full name, i.e., first name, middle names if any, and family name.*

USING WORDS ...... i.e.

The abbreviation **i.e.** does NOT mean "for example."

Use **i.e.** when you want to explain something more clearly, by telling it in a different way: *I felt very hungry, i.e., I wanted something to eat right away.*

Use **e.g.** when you want to give a particular example: *I wanted to eat something sweet, e.g., a jelly doughnut.*

a bat	e bed	i bid	o pot	u cup	th thin
ā cake	ē me	ī bite	ō go	ū rude	ᴛʜ then
ä bar	ə about	ər over	ô for	ů put	zh measure

if (if) **1** supposing that; on condition that; in case: *If it rains tomorrow, we'll stay at home.* **2** whether: *I wonder if he called.* **3** although; even though: *It was a nice day, if a little windy. conj.*

if•fy (if′ē) *Informal.* uncertain: *At the moment our trip looks iffy; we may cancel it. adj.,* **if•fi•er, if•fi•est.**

The word igloo comes from the Inuktitut word *iglu*, meaning "a dwelling."

ig•loo (ig′lū) an Inuit house, especially one shaped like a dome and built of blocks of hard snow. *n.*

ig•ne•ous rock (ig′nē əs rok′) rock formed from very hot matter deep in the earth or thrown out of a volcano, hardening as it cools. Granite is an example.

ig•nite (ig nīt′) start burning: *Gasoline ignites easily. The match was ignited by scraping it against a rough stone. v.,* **ig•nit•ed, ig•nit•ing.**

ig•ni•tion (ig nish′ən) **1** the fact of starting to burn. **2** in a gasoline engine, the system of parts controlling the sparks that ignite to explode the mixture of air and gasoline in the cylinders. This starts the engine. *n.*

ig•no•rant (ig′nə rənt) **1** knowing little or nothing; without knowledge: *I had never been out of the city and felt very ignorant when I first arrived at the ranch.* **2** not knowing a particular thing: *He was ignorant of the fact that his house had burned down. adj.* **—ig′no•rance,** *n.*

ig•nore (ig nôr′) pay no attention to: *We ignored their insults. v.,* **ig•nored, ig•nor•ing.**

i•gua•na (i gwä′nə) a large plant-eating lizard with spines on its back, found in tropical America. *n.*

ill (il) **1** sick; not well: *ill with a fever.* **2** *Formal.* bad or badly: *ill deeds, ill luck* (*adj.*). *I hope you won't think ill of me for leaving early* (*adv.*). This sense often occurs in compounds: *ill-treat, ill-natured, ill-tempered.* **3** *Formal.* something evil; harm: *Poverty is a great ill.* 1, 2 *adj. or adv.,* **worse, worst;** 3 *n.* **—ill′ness,** *n.*
ill at ease, uncomfortable.

I'll (īl) I will.

il•le•gal (i lē′gəl) against the law: *It is illegal to park here. adj.* **—il•le′gal•ly,** *adv.*

il•leg•i•ble (i lej′ə bəl) very hard or impossible to read: *The smudging had made many words illegible. adj.*

il•lit•er•ate (i lit′ə rit) **1** unable to read or write: *He did not go to school and is illiterate.* **2** knowing little or nothing about a particular subject: *I'm illiterate when it comes to computers.* **3** a person who is illiterate. **4** showing a lack of education: *He writes in a very illiterate way.* 1, 2, 4 *adj.,* 3 *n.* **—il•lit′er•a•cy,** *n.*

il•log•i•cal (i loj′ə kəl) not logical. *adj.*

il•lu•mi•nate (i lū′mə nāt′) **1** light up; make bright: *The room was illuminated by four large lamps.* **2** make clear; explain: *Her detailed report illuminated the situation for us.* **3** give knowledge to: *Let me illuminate you on this matter. v.,* **il•lu•mi•nat•ed, il•lu•mi•nat•ing. —il•lu′mi•na′tion,** *n.*

il•lu•sion (i lū′zhən) **1** something that is not what it seems to be: *On some nights the moon looks twice as big as usual, but it's only an illusion.* **2** a false belief: *Many people have the illusion that riches bring happiness. n.*

il•lus•trate (il′ə strāt′) **1** provide with pictures, diagrams, maps, etc. that explain or decorate: *This book is well illustrated.* **2** make clearer by using comparisons, stories, examples, etc.: *to illustrate how the heart sends blood around the body. v.,* **il•lus•trat•ed, il•lus•trat•ing. —il′lus•tra′tion,** *n.* **—il′lus•tra′tor,** *n.*

il•lus•tri•ous (i lus′trē əs) brilliant and famous: *the illustrious Canadian artist Tom Thomson. adj.*

ill will (il′ wil′) unkind or unfriendly feelings toward someone: *I bear you no ill will.*

im– a form of the suffix **in-** used before the letters *b, m,* and *p,* as in *imbalance, immigrate, impatient.*

I'm (īm) I am.

im•age (im′ij) **1** an exact reflection or likeness: *I see my image in this mirror. She is the image of her mother.* **2** a picture or statue: *images on a Web page, a wax image of Queen Victoria in a museum.* **3** a picture in the mind: *I have a clear image of what I want.* **4** the way a person or thing is seen or thought of by other people: *Lars thinks it will ruin his image if he wears galoshes.* **5** a description in words that creates a vivid picture in your mind. The use of images is called **imagery** (im′ij rē). *n.*

i•mag•i•na•tion (i maj′ə nā′shən) the ability to form pictures in your mind or think up ideas: *The child's imagination filled the woods with talking animals. It will* *take some imagination to come up with a solution to this problem.* Something that exists only in the imagination is **imaginary;** a person or thing that shows a lot of imagination is **imaginative.** *n.*

i·mag·ine (i maj′ən) 1 see in your mind; form an idea or mental image of: *Maria likes to imagine life as a great actor.* 2 suppose; guess: *I imagine he's already left by now.* 3 believe something that isn't true: *People used to imagine the earth was flat.* *v.,* **i·mag·ined, i·mag·in·ing.** —**i·mag′i·na·ble,** *adj.*

i·mam (i mám′) a Muslim leader of prayer. *n.*

im·bal·ance (im bal′əns) a lack of proper balance between or among different things: *Acid rain causes a chemical imbalance in the lake water.* *n.*

im·be·cile (im′bə sīl *or* im′bə səl) 1 a very stupid or foolish person: *Don't be an imbecile.* 2 very stupid: *What kind of imbecile remark is that?* 1 *n.,* 2 *adj.*

im·i·tate (im′ə tāt′) 1 try to be like or act like; copy: *The little boy imitates his older brother.* 2 act like for fun: *He made us laugh by imitating a monkey.* 3 be like, especially in order to fool or deceive: *Plastic is often made to imitate wood.* *v.,* **im·i·tat·ed, im·i·tat·ing.** —**im′i·ta′tion,** *n. or adj.*

im·mac·u·late (i mak′yə lit) spotless; absolutely clean: *an immaculate kitchen.* *adj.* —**im·mac′u·late·ly,** *adv.*

im·ma·ture (im′ə chūr′) 1 not mature; childish; silly. 2 not ripe; not full-grown or developed. *adj.* —**im′ma·tu′ri·ty,** *n.*

im·meas·ur·a·ble (i mezh′ə rə bəl) too huge or deep to be measured; very great. *adj.*

im·me·di·ate (i mē′dē it) 1 coming at once, without delay: *Please send an immediate reply.* 2 closest in time or space; next: *Our immediate neighbour is Mrs. Cecutti. What are your immediate plans?* *adj.* —**im·me′di·ate·ly,** *adv.*

im·me·mo·ri·al (im′ə mȯ′rē əl) **from time immemorial,** for much longer than anyone can remember; from the earliest beginning: *From time immemorial people have expressed themselves in art.* *adj.*

im·mense (i mens′) very big; huge; vast: *An ocean is an immense body of water.* *adj.* —**im·mense′ly,** *adv.* —**im·men′si·ty,** *n.*

im·merse (i mərs′) 1 put under water or other liquid: *Do not immerse this electric beater when washing it.* 2 totally surround or involve: *immersed in French.* *v.,* **im·mersed, im·mers·ing.** —**im·mer′sion,** *n.*

im·mi·grate (im′ə grāt′) come into a country to live: *My parents immigrated to Canada in 1990.* A person who immigrates is an **immigrant.** A **landed immigrant** is recognized by the government as a possible future citizen and holds papers giving the right to stay permanently. *v.,* **im·mi·grat·ed, im·mi·grat·ing.** —**im′mi·gra′tion,** *n.*

CONFUSABLES .... immigrate

immigrate means "go": *My family immigrated to Canada from Greece in 1960.*

emigrate means "leave": *My family emigrated from Greece to Canada in 1960.*

im·mi·nent (im′ə nənt) likely to happen very soon: *The black clouds show that a storm is imminent.* *adj.* —**im′mi·nent·ly,** *adv.*

im·mo·bile (i mō′bīl *or* i mō′bəl) 1 not movable; firmly fixed. 2 not moving; motionless: *The cat lay immobile for some minutes, watching the birds.* *adj.* —**im·mo′bi·lize′,** *v.* —**im′mo·bil′i·ty** (im′ə bil′ə tē), *n.*

im·mor·al (i mȯ′rəl) wrong; wicked: *Lying and stealing are immoral.* *adj.* —**im·mor′al·ly,** *adv.* —**im′mo·ral′i·ty** (im′ə ral′ə tē), *n.*

im·mor·tal (i mȯr′təl) 1 living forever or remembered forever: *the immortal Shakespeare. A spirit is immortal.* 2 a person who lives or is remembered forever. 1 *adj.,* 2 *n.* —**im·mor′tal·ize′,** *v.* —**im′mor·tal′i·ty** (im′ȯr tal′ə tē), *n.*

im·mov·a·ble (i mū′və bəl) that cannot be moved or shaken; firmly fixed: *The great boulder was immovable.* *adj.* —**im·mov′a·bly,** *adv.*

im·mune (i myūn′) 1 not likely to be hurt or affected by something; protected from disease, poison, etc.: *Some people are immune to poison ivy; they can touch it without getting a rash.* Your **immune system** is the way your body fights disease. 2 exempt; free from some duty or from something unpleasant: *immune from taxes. No one is immune from criticism.* *adj.* —**im·mu′ni·ty,** *n.*

im·mu·nize (im′yə nīz′) protect from disease, especially by putting a small amount of a disease germ into the person's body so that the body develops the means to fight that disease: *Children are immunized against whooping cough.* *v.* —**im′mu·ni·za′tion,** *n.*

a bat	e bed	i bid	o pot	u cup	th thin
ā cake	ē me	ī bite	ō go	ū rude	ᴛʜ then
á bar	ə about	ər over	ȯ for	u̇ put	zh measure

im·p (imp) a mischievous child. *n.* **—imp′ish,** *adj.*

im·pact (im′pakt) **1** a hitting of one thing against another; collision: *The impact of the stone against the window shattered the glass.* **2** an effect or influence: *Television has a strong impact on our lives.* **3** hit; strike against. **4** *Informal.* affect: *How will the new law impact the school system?* 1, 2 *n.*, 3, 4 *v.*

im·pair (im per′) **1** damage; harm; weaken: *Poor food will impair your health.* **2 impaired, a** having a partial disability in some area. This sense is usually used in compounds: *hearing-impaired.* **b** affected by drinking alcohol: *impaired driving.* *v.* **—im·pair′ment,** *n.*

im·part (im pårt′) **1** give: *New curtains imparted an air of cheerfulness to the old house.* **2** tell: *The interviewer asked her to impart the secret of her success.* *v.*

im·par·tial (im pår′shəl) not favouring one side more than another; fair: *A judge should be impartial.* *adj.* **—im·par′tial·ly,** *adv.*

im·pa·tient (im pā′shənt) **1** not patient; not willing to spend time waiting or dealing with something: *She is impatient and is always rushing me.* **2** eager: *The horses were impatient to start the race.* *adj.* **—im·pa′tient·ly,** *adv.* **—im·pa′tience,** *n.*

im·pede (im pēd′) hinder; make more difficult: *The deep snow impeded travel.* *v.*, **im·ped·ed, im·ped·ing.**

im·ped·i·ment (im ped′ə mənt) a hindrance; something that gets in the way. *n.*

im·pending (im pen′ding) likely to happen soon (used especially of something unpleasant): *The impending test made us all a bit uneasy.* *adj.*

im·pen·e·tra·ble (im pen′ə trə bəl) **1** that cannot be entered, pierced, seen through, or passed through: *impenetrable darkness. An impenetrable thorny hedge kept the prince from reaching the castle.* **2** that cannot be understood: *an impenetrable mystery.* *adj.*

im·per·a·tive (im per′ə tiv) **1** urgently necessary: *It is imperative that this sick child stay in bed.* **2** expressing a command. *Go and brush your teeth* is an imperative sentence. **3** a command. 1, 2 *adj.*, 3 *n.*

im·per·fect (im pər′fikt) not perfect; with something wrong: *A crack in the cup made it imperfect.* *adj.* **—im·per′fect·ly,** *adv.* **—im′per·fec′tion,** *n.*

im·pe·ri·al (im pē′rē əl) **1** having to do with an empire or its ruler. **2** belonging to the old British legal standard of weights and measures: *The imperial gallon is 20 percent bigger than the U.S. gallon.* *adj.*

im·pe·ri·al·ism (im pē′rē ə liz′əm) the policy of taking over other countries and territories to build an empire. *n.* **—im·pe′ri·al·is′tic,** *adj.*

im·per·il (im per′əl) put in danger: *They imperilled their lives by going canoeing without life jackets.* *v.*, **im·per·illed** or **imper·iled, im·per·il·ling** or **im·per·il·ing.**

im·pe·ri·ous (im pē′rē əs) bossy; arrogant: *Stop ordering me around in that imperious tone.* *adj.*

im·per·son·al (im pər′sə nəl) not having, showing, or recognizing any personality or human character; without thoughts and feelings: *Some people don't like to do their banking by machine because it is so impersonal.* *adj.* **—im·per′son·al·ly,** *adv.*

impersonal pronoun (im pər′sə nəl prō′noun) any of the words *it, one, they,* or *you* when used to refer to a person or thing not identified. *Examples: It is cold today. One must do one's best. They say that next winter will be very cold. You have to be careful crossing the street.*

Grammar Check impersonal pronoun

The impersonal pronoun **one** is not used much, except in very formal writing or speech:
One must do one's best.
Instead, try using **I**, **you**, or **people**:
I must do my best.
You must do your best.
People must do their best.

im·per·son·ate (im pər′sə nāt′) pretend to be; imitate the voice, appearance, and manners of, especially in order to fool others: *The thief impersonated a police officer.* *v.*, **im·per·son·at·ed, im·per·son·at·ing.**

im·per·ti·nent (im pər′tə nənt) cheeky; smart-alecky; rude: *Enough of your impertinent remarks!* *adj.* **—im·per′ti·nence,** *n.*

im·pet·u·ous (im pech′ū əs) acting hastily, without thinking: *As soon as she heard the story, the impetuous Claudia fired off a very angry e-mail to her cousin, which she later regretted.* *adj.*

im·plant (im plant′ *for 1 and 3,* im′plant *for 2*) **1** to place something useful inside a person's body by a medical operation: *The dentist implanted an artificial tooth.* **2** something placed into a person's body in this way. **3** to put something into a person's mind so strongly that it is never forgotten: *Our dad implanted in us the idea that each person is unique and valuable.* 1, 3 *v.*, 2 *n.*

The first implements that people used were sharp flint stones. From these evolved hammers, chisels, saws, and all the power tools that we use today.

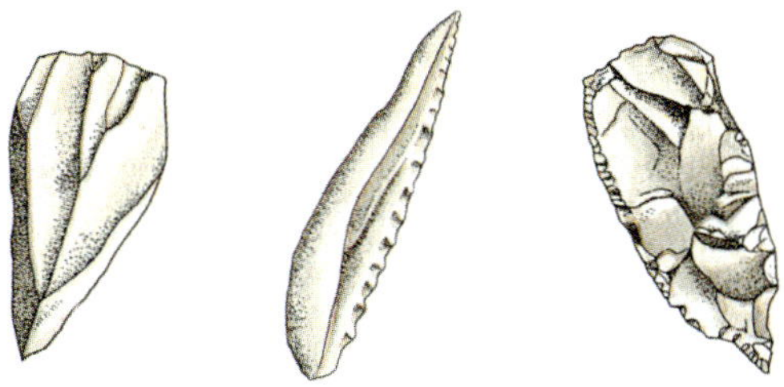

im·ple·ment (im′plə mənt *for 1,* im′plə ment′ *for 2*) 1 a piece of equipment; tool: *They keep the farming implements in that large shed.* 2 carry out; put into practice: *That's a good suggestion; we'll implement it right away.* 1 *n.,* 2 *v.* —**im′ple·men·ta′tion,** *n.*

im·pli·ca·tion (im′plə kā′shən) 1 a possible future effect or result of something: *We had to consider the implications of combining the schools.* 2 the indirect meaning of what someone has said. *n.*

im·plore (im plôr′) beg; ask earnestly: *I implore you not to do something so foolish.* *v.,* **im·plored, im·plor·ing.**

im·ply (im plī′) 1 mean something without saying it outright; express in an indirect way: *Silence often implies agreement.* 2 lead logically to an idea: *The sentence "He's doing it again" implies that he did it before.* *v.,* **im·plied, im·ply·ing.** —**im′pli·ca′tion** (im′plə kā′shən), *n.*

CONFUSABLES ...... imply

imply means "suggest": *By putting on a sad face, the speaker implied that the news was bad.*

infer means "suppose": *I inferred from the speaker's sad face that the news was bad.*

im·po·lite (im′pə līt′) not polite; rude. *adj.* —**im′po·lite′ly,** *adv.*

im·port (im pôrt′ *for 1,* im′pôrt *for 2 and 3*) 1 bring in from a foreign country for sale: *Canada imports sugar.* 2 something brought in from another country: *Rubber is a useful import.* 3 a formal word for "importance": *events of great import.* 1 *v.,* 2, 3 *n.* —**im′por·ta′tion,** *n.*

im·por·tant (im pôr′tənt) 1 that matters a lot because of the meaning, value, or results it has; worth paying attention to: *important decisions, an important occasion.* 2 famous or powerful: *The mayor is an important person in our town.* *adj.* —**im·por′tant·ly,** *adv.* —**im·por′tance,** *n.*

im·pose (im pōz′) 1 force something unpleasant on: *The judge imposed a fine of $500 on the guilty person.* 2 force your desires or your company on someone: *I don't want to impose, but I could use a ride to the mall if you're going that way.* *v.,* **im·posed, im·pos·ing.** **impose on** or **upon,** take advantage of; use in a selfish way: *to impose on the good nature of others.*

im·pos·ing (im pō′zing) impressive because of size or dignity; commanding attention: *The Peace Tower of the Parliament Buildings is an imposing structure.* *adj.*

im·pos·si·ble (im pos′ə bəl) 1 that cannot be done or be true: *an impossible story, an impossible task. It is impossible for a pig to talk.* 2 that cannot be put up with; unbearable: *an impossible person.* *adj.* —**im·pos′si·bly,** *adv.* —**im·pos′si·bil′i·ty,** *n.*

im·pos·tor (im pos′tər) a person who adopts a false name or character to trick others. *n.*

im·pov·er·ish (im pov′ə rish) make very poor: *A long war had impoverished the nation.* *v.*

im·prac·ti·cal (im prak′tə kəl) 1 involving so much time, effort, expense, and so on that it is not worth doing or using: *an impractical scheme.* 2 dreamy or out of touch with reality; having impossible goals: *She is a nice person but far too impractical to be a good leader.* *adj.*

im·press (im pres′ *for 1–4,* im′pres *for 5*) 1 fill with admiration or respect: *Her courage really impressed me.* 2 have a strong effect on someone's thoughts and feelings: *Our visit to the dump impressed us with the need to recycle more.* 3 tell someone something in a forceful way, using an urgent tone of voice, repeating it often, and so on: *Mr. Li impressed on us that we needed to practise every day.* 4 press or stamp so as to leave a mark: *The wax was impressed with the royal seal.* 5 the mark or print left by something; stamp: *All good stories carry the impress of the author's personality.* 1–4 *v.,* 5 *n.*

im·pres·sion (im presh′ən) 1 an effect produced on a person: *The big lecture seemed to make little impression on the child.* 2 an idea or notion: *I have a vague impression that I left the house unlocked.* 3 a mark made by pressing or stamping: *A dog had left the impression of its paws in the wet concrete.* *n.*

im·pres·sive (im pres′iv) causing feelings of admiration, respect, and so on; not easily forgotten: *an impressive achievement.* *adj.* —**im·pres′sive·ly,** *adv.*

a bat	e bed	i bid	o pot	u cup	th thin
ā cake	ē me	ī bite	ō go	ū rude	ᴛʜ then
ä bar	ə about	ər over	ô for	ů put	zh measure

im•print (im′print *for 1,* im print′ *for 2 and 3*) **1** a mark made by something pressed in: *the imprint of a foot in the sand.* **2** mark by pressing or stamping: *to imprint a postmark on an envelope.* **3** fix in the mind: *The scene was imprinted in her memory.* 1 *n.,* 2, 3 *v.*

im•pris•on (im priz′ən) put or keep in prison. *v.* **—im•pris′on•ment,** *n.*

im•prob•a•ble (im prob′ə bəl) not likely to happen or be true: *an improbable story.* *adj.* **—im•prob′a•bil′i•ty,** *n.*

im•promp•tu (im promp′tū) without thought or preparation beforehand: *an impromptu speech (adj.). The pianist played a few songs impromptu (adv.).* *adj. or adv.*

im•prop•er (im prop′ər) not correct; against the rules of good behaviour, grammar, tradition, common sense, etc.: *an improper sentence, improper clothing, an improper use of equipment.* *adj.* **—im•prop′er•ly,** *adv.*

improper fraction (im prop′ər frak′shən) a fraction equal to or greater than 1. *Examples:* $^3/_2$, $^{27}/_4$, $^{12}/_{12}$

im•prove (im prüv′) make or become better: *You could improve this house by finishing off the basement. His health is improving.* *v.,* **im•proved, im•prov•ing.** **—im•prove′ment,** *n.*

im•pro•vise (im′prə vīz′) **1** perform something, such as a song or skit, making it up as you go along: *He improvised a new verse for the school song at the football game.* **2** make something, not with the proper materials but with whatever happens to be around: *The girls improvised a tent out of two blankets and some long sticks.* *v.,* **im•pro•vised, im•pro•vis•ing.** **—im′pro•vi•sa′tion,** *n.*

im•pu•dent (im′pyə dənt) rude and disrespectful: *The impudent boy made a face at the bus driver.* *adj.* **—im′pu•dent•ly,** *adv.* **—im′pu•dence,** *n.*

im•pulse (im′puls) **1** a sudden, wavelike force or push: *The machine beeps with each electrical impulse.* **2** a sudden desire to do something, without thinking about why: *On an impulse he decided to throw out all his hockey cards.* *n.* **—im•pul′sive,** *adj.* **—im•pul′sive•ly,** *adv.*

im•pure (im pyůr′) **1** dirty; polluted: *The air in cities is often impure.* **2** mixed with something, especially something not as good: *The gold was slightly impure.* *adj.* **—im•pu′ri•ty,** *n.*

in (in) **In** is used with many different meanings, but its main meaning has to do with place or time: *Your snack is in the fridge; I will be back in an hour (prep.). Keep the dog in until the rain stops (adv.).*
in for, sure to get: *We are in for a storm.*
in on something, taking part; included or involved: *Are you in on the surprise party for Evan?*
ins and outs, the many different parts or details: *The manager knows all the ins and outs of the business.*

in. *abbreviation for* inch or inches.

in–[1] *a prefix meaning* not, the opposite of, or the absence of. *Inexpensive* means "not expensive." *Inattention* means "lack of attention."

in–[2] *a prefix meaning* in, into, on, upon. *Inhale* means "breathe in." *Inscribe* means "write on."

in•a•bil•i•ty (in′ə bil′ə tē) the fact of being unable: *Her inability to drive meant she had to go by bus.* *n.*

in•ac•ces•si•ble (in′ək ses′ə bəl) impossible to get to: *If there's no ramp or elevator, the second floor will be inaccessible to wheelchair users.* *adj.*

in•ac•cu•rate (i nak′yə rit) not exactly right or true: *an inaccurate report, inaccurate measurements.* *adj.* **—in•ac′cu•rate•ly,** *adv.* **—in•ac′cu•ra•cy,** *n.*

in•ac•tive (i nak′tiv) doing little or nothing; not operating or being used: *Bears are inactive during the winter. This volcano has been inactive for years.* *adj.* **—in•ac′tion,** *n.* **—in′ac•tiv′i•ty,** *n.*

in•ad•e•quate (i nad′ə kwit) not enough, or not good enough: *inadequate money for the trip. He didn't get the part because his acting was inadequate.* *adj.* **—in•ad′e•quate•ly,** *adv.*

in•ane (i nān′) silly; senseless: *inane remarks.* *adj.*

in•an•i•mate (in an′ə mit) without life: *A rock is an inanimate object.* *adj.*

in•ap•pro•pri•ate (in′ə prō′prē it) not suitable; not proper: *Jokes are inappropriate at a serious discussion.* *adj.*

in•at•ten•tive (in′ə ten′tiv) not paying attention. *adj.* **—in′at•ten′tion,** *n.*

in•au•di•ble (i nod′ə bəl) not able to be heard: *Her voice dropped to an almost inaudible murmur.* *adj.*

in•au•gu•rate (i nog′yə rāt′) mark the official opening of something or the beginning of someone's duties: *to inaugurate a new age of freedom. The new mayor was inaugurated last week. The new stadium was inaugurated with a parade and ball game.* *v.,* **in•au•gu•rat•ed, in•au•gu•rat•ing.** **—in•au′gu•ra′tion,** *n.*

in•born (in′bôrn′) born in a person; natural: *an inborn sense of rhythm.* *adj.*

Inca

The Incas of Peru built the mountain fortress-city of Machu Picchu, which was not rediscovered till 1911.

In battle, Inca soldiers used slings, bolas (stones linked by lengths of string), spears, and clubs.

Inca headdress was often elaborate.

In•ca (ing′kə) **1** a member of an aboriginal people who ruled a large empire in western South America before the Spanish conquest in the 1500s. The Incas were highly civilized, with advanced arts, sciences, and government. **2** a ruler of the Incas. *n., pl.* **In•cas.** **—In′can,** *adj.*

in•can•des•cent (in′kan des′ənt) glowing with heat; red-hot or white-hot. An **incandescent bulb** is an ordinary light bulb. It has a thin wire in it that glows when heated by the electricity flowing through it. *adj.*

in•ca•pa•ble (in kā′pə bəl) having very little skill or ability; not good at something: *The mechanic was dismissed because he was so incapable.* *adj.*
incapable of, unable to do: *A blind person is incapable of driving a car.*

in•cense[1] (in′sens) a substance that gives off a sweet-smelling smoke when burned. *n.*

in•cense[2] (in sens′) make very angry: *We were incensed at their cruelty.* *v.,* **in•censed, in•cens•ing.**

in•cen•tive (in sen′tiv) something that causes a person to want to do something; motivation, often a promised reward: *As an incentive to the students, a pizza party was promised to the class that sold the most nuts.* *n.*

in•ces•sant (in ses′ənt) never stopping; continual: *The incessant noise from the highway kept her awake all night.* *adj.* **—in•ces′sant•ly,** *adv.*

inch (inch) **1** a nonmetric measure of length; $\frac{1}{12}$ of a foot (equal to 2.54 cm). *Symbol:* " **2** move slowly or little by little: *The traffic inched along.* **1** *n.,* **2** *v.*
by inches, by small steps; gradually.
within an inch of, very near; very close to: *The house was within an inch of being burned down.*

inch•worm (inch′wərm′) the larva of a moth. It moves along slowly by first bringing the back of its body forward and then pushing ahead the front end. *n.*

in•ci•dent (in′sə dənt) a happening or event, especially a minor one. *n.*

in•ci•den•tal (in′sə den′təl) **1** happening by chance: *an incidental meeting of old friends on the street.* **2** going together with something else, but not very important: *Certain discomforts are incidental to camping.* **3** a minor thing that goes along with something else: *On our trip to Edmonton we spent $189 for meals, motel room, and gas, and $11.50 for incidentals like candy and magazines.* **1, 2** *adj.,* **3** *n.*

in•ci•den•tal•ly (in′sə den′tə lē) by the way; as a minor thing along with something else: *She mentioned incidentally that she had seen Tony at the library.* *adv.*

a bat	e bed	i bid	o pot	u cup	th thin
ā cake	ē me	ī bite	ō go	ü rude	ᴛʜ then
ä bar	ə about	ər over	ȯ for	u̇ put	zh measure

in·cin·er·ate (in sin′ə rāt′) burn to ashes. An **incinerator** is a sort of furnace for burning garbage. *n.*

in·ci·sion (in sizh′ən) a cut made in something: *The doctor made a small incision to drain the boil.* *n.*

in·ci·sor (in sī′zər) a tooth with a sharp edge for cutting; one of the front teeth. An adult human has eight incisors. *n.*

in·cite (in sīt′) spur on; cause someone to do something by stirring up feelings and desires: *The captain's example incited the other players to greater effort.* *v.,* **in·cit·ed, in·cit·ing.**

in·cli·na·tion (in′klə nā′shən) **1** tendency: *an inclination to laziness.* **2** a desire or interest: *I have absolutely no inclination to go there.* *n.*

in·cline (in klīn′ *for 1, 2, and 3,* in′klīn *for 4*) **1** have a tendency: *The men in our family incline to baldness.* **2** make favourable or willing; influence: *The concert inclined her to study music.* **3** to slope or slant; tilt: *The driveway inclines slightly.* **Inclined plane** is the scientific name for a ramp. **4** a slope; slant: *That roof has a very steep incline.* 1–3 *v.,* **in·clined, in·clin·ing;** 4 *n.*
be inclined, tend; have a desire, tendency, or interest: *I am inclined to agree with you. He was not inclined to hurry, so he took his time with everything.*

in·clude (in klūd′) **1** put or let in along with others in a total or a group: *The price includes tax. We included her in all our games.* **2** contain; be made up of: *Canada's population includes people of many different cultures.* *v.,* **in·clud·ed, in·clud·ing.** **—in·clu′sion,** *n.*

in·clu·sive (in klū′siv) including: *"Read pages 10 to 20 inclusive" means begin with page 10 and read through to the very end of page 20.* *adj.*

in·cog·ni·to (in′kog nē′tō) unannounced and in disguise: *The prince travelled incognito to avoid crowds (adv.). The famous singer made an incognito appearance (adj.).* *adv. or adj.*

in·come (in′kum) money that comes in from work, business, renting property, etc.: *Her yearly income is $40 000.* **Income tax** is a government tax calculated as a percentage of your income. *n.*

in·com·ing (in′kum′ing) **1** arriving or coming in: *incoming flights at an airport, the incoming tide.* **2** just starting a new job: *the incoming premier.* *adj.*

in·com·pa·ra·ble (in kom′pə rə bəl *or* in′kəm per′ə bəl) unlike any other; so great that it cannot be compared to others: *The beauty of the Arctic is incomparable.* *adj.*

in·com·pe·tent (in kom′pə tənt) **1** not able to do what a job requires; having very little skill: *What an incompetent builder—all the floors are uneven!* **2** an incompetent person: *There were so many incompetents in the group that the whole project failed.* 1 *adj.,* 2 *n.*

in·com·plete (in′kəm plēt′) not complete; with some parts missing. *adj.*

in·com·pre·hen·si·ble (in′kom pri hen′sə bəl) impossible to understand. *adj.*

in·con·ceiv·a·ble (in′kən sē′və bəl) impossible to imagine: *The size of the universe is inconceivable. It's inconceivable that she would ever do such a horrible thing.* *adj.*

in·con·gru·ous (in kong′grū əs) oddly different; unexpected and out of place: *The old factory looked incongruous next to the nice new houses.* *adj.*

in·con·sid·er·ate (in′kən sid′ə rit) giving no thought to other people's needs or feelings. *adj.*

in·con·sist·ent (in′kən sis′tənt) **1** not in agreement: *Leaving garbage around is inconsistent with our duty to protect the environment.* **2** not keeping to the same beliefs or ways of behaving: *He is so inconsistent; he is always changing his opinions.* **3** not always the same quality; sometimes good and sometimes not: *"Ingrid's work this term has been inconsistent," wrote the teacher.* *adj.* **—in′con·sist′ent·ly,** *adv.* **—in′con·sist′en·cy,** *n.*

in·con·spic·u·ous (in′kən spik′yū əs) not attracting people's attention; not very noticeable: *The woman's dress was an inconspicuous grey. I'm glad the spot is in an inconspicuous place.* *adj.*
—in′con·spic′u·ous·ly, *adv.*

in·con·ven·ience (in′kən vēn′yəns) **1** extra effort or trouble, or something that causes this: *The broken elevator was a real inconvenience.* **2** cause extra effort or trouble to: *Will it inconvenience you to deliver this package on your way home?* 1 *n.,* 2 *v.,* **in·con·ven·ienced, in·con·ven·ienc·ing.** **—in′con·ven′ient,** *adj.*

in·cor·po·rate (in kôr′pə rāt′) **1** make something a part of something else; work something in: *We will incorporate your suggestion into this new plan.* **2** form into a corporation according to certain laws: *When the business grew bigger, the owners incorporated it.* *v.,* **in·cor·po·rat·ed, in·cor·po·rat·ing.**

in·cor·rect (in′kə rekt′) not right; not proper; wrong. *adj.* **—in′cor·rect′ly,** *adv.*

in·crease (in krēs′ *for 1,* in′krēs *for 2*) **1** make or become more or greater: *Increase your speed as you drive onto the highway. The population of this town has increased* *every year.* **2** a gain in size, numbers, etc.: *an increase of six cents a litre, an increase in student enrolment.* 1 *v.,* **in·creased, in·creas·ing;** 2 *n.* **—in·creas′ing·ly,** *adv.* **on the increase,** increasing: *Travel is on the increase.*

in·cred·i·ble (in kred′ə bəl) hard to believe; seeming too extraordinary to be possible: *an incredible story. They gave an incredible performance at the skating finals.* *adj.* **—in·cred′i·bly,** *adv.*

CONFUSABLES .... incredible

incredible means "hard to believe": *It's incredible that anyone could swim across Lake Ontario.*

incredulous means "unbelieving": *Dad listened to our story with an incredulous smile.*

in·cred·u·lous (in krej′ə ləs) having or showing doubt about something; unbelieving; sceptical: *When she heard she had won first prize, she was incredulous.* *adj.* **—in·cred′u·lous·ly,** *adv.*

in·cre·ment (in′krə mənt) the amount of a regular increase in something: *This measuring cup is marked off in increments of 50 mL.* *n.*

in·cu·bate (ing′kyə bāt′) **1** keep eggs, bacteria, etc. warm so that they will hatch or grow. An **incubator** is a machine with a box that can be kept at a set temperature; there are different kinds for hatching eggs and growing bacteria. Another kind is used in hospitals for babies born too early. **2** stay alive and grow stronger in a person's body as a virus before actually making the person sick. Chicken pox takes about two weeks to incubate. *v.,* **in·cu·bat·ed, in·cu·bat·ing.** **—in′cu·ba′tion,** *n.*

in·cum·bent (in kum′bənt) **1** currently holding a political office: *the incumbent mayor.* **2** somebody who currently holds a political office: *The incumbent decided not to run in the next election.* 1 *adj.,* 2 *n.*

in·cur (in kər′) run into or meet with something bad; bring on yourself: *to incur an injury, to incur someone's anger.* *v.,* **in·curred, in·cur·ring.**

in·cur·a·ble (in kyū′rə bəl) not able to be cured: *an incurable disease.* *adj.*

in·debt·ed (in det′id) owing money or thanks; in debt: *We are indebted to scientists for many of our comforts.* *adj.*

in·de·cent (in dē′sənt) **1** not decent; in very bad taste; improper: *That crude remark was indecent and disrespectful.* **2** not wearing enough clothes to be seen by someone: *Don't come in; I'm indecent.* *adj.* **—in·de′cen·cy,** *n.*

in·de·ci·sive (in′di sī′siv) **1** unable to make up your mind and stick to your decision. **2** not really settling a thing: *Their victory in the first battle was indecisive and the war continued.* *adj.* **—in′de·ci′sion** (in′di sizh′ən), *n.*

in·deed (in dēd′) **1** in fact; truly: *She is hungry; indeed, she is almost starving.* **2** an expression of surprise, doubt, scorn, etc.: *Indeed! I never would have thought it.* 1 *adv.,* 2 *interj.*

in·def·i·nite (in def′ə nit) **1** not clear and specific; not exact; vague: *"Maybe" is a very indefinite answer. Anybody* and *something* are examples of **indefinite pronouns.** **2** not limited: *We have an indefinite time to finish this work.* *adj.* **—in·def′i·nite·ly,** *adv.*

indefinite article (in def′ə nit är′tə kəl) either of the articles **a** and **an.**

Grammar Check .. indefinite article

Use **a** with words that begin with a consonant: *a house, a ball.*
Use **an** with words that begin with a vowel: *an apple, an orange.*

in·del·i·ble (in del′ə bəl) that cannot be erased; permanent: *indelible ink. Three years as a soldier left an indelible impression on his memory.* *adj.*

in·dent (in dent′) **1** form notches or jags in an edge, line, border, etc.: *an indented coastline. The rim of the plate was indented.* **2** begin a line of writing or printing farther from the margin than other lines. The first line of a paragraph is often indented. *v.* **—in′den·ta′tion,** *n.*

in·de·pend·ent (in′di pen′dənt) **1** not needing, wanting, or getting help from others: *The Girl Guides encourages its members to become independent.* **2** not influenced or controlled by others: *An independent person votes as he or she pleases. Canada is an independent nation.* **3** not connected with a group. An independent candidate in an election belongs to no political party. **4** a person who is independent. 1–3 *adj.,* 4 *n.* **—in′de·pend′ent·ly,** *adv.* **—in′de·pen′dence,** *n.*

in–depth (in′depth′) thorough, detailed, and complete: *an in-depth study, in-depth research.* *adj.*

a bat	e bed	i bid	o pot	u cup	th thin
ā cake	ē me	ī bite	ō go	ū rude	ᴛʜ then
ȧ bar	ə about	ər over	ȯ for	ů put	zh measure

in·de·scrib·a·ble (in′di skrī′bə bəl) that cannot be described; beyond description: *a scene of indescribable beauty.* *adj.*

in·de·struct·i·ble (in′di struk′tə bəl) that cannot be destroyed. *adj.*

in·dex (in′deks) **1** a list of what is in a book, telling on what pages certain things are mentioned. Usually it is at the end of the book and arranged in alphabetical order. **2** some other kind of list, such as a list of things in a collection. **3** provide with an index or include in an index. **4** a sign of something, or a measure of how much: *A frown is an index of displeasure. The temperature is an index of how hot a thing is.* 1, 2, 4 *n., pl.* **in·dex·es** or **in·di·ces;** 3 *v.*

index finger (in′deks fing′gər) the finger next to the thumb; forefinger.

In·di·an (in′dē ən) **1** a person whose homeland is India. **2** having to do with India or its people: *the Indian flag.* **3** an old name for a person whose ancestors lived anywhere south of the Arctic in North or South America before the Europeans came. **4** having to do with any of these groups of people: *Ojibwa is an Indian language.* 1, 3 *n.,* 2, 4 *adj.*

USING WORDS ..... Indian

The name **Indian** came from a mistake that Christopher Columbus made. When he landed in America, he thought he had reached India, and so he called the people Indians.

Some people still use this name, and you can see it in the names of things like Indian corn. Generally it is better to use **First Nations, aboriginal people,** or **Native people.** Better still, use the exact name of the group (for example, Cree, Nisga'a) if you know it. See the map of Canada in the Appendix.

Indian corn (in′dē ən kôrn′) **1** the variety of corn first raised by the aboriginal peoples of North America: *Sweet corn, popcorn, and field corn were developed from Indian corn.* **2** corn with gold, red, purple, and brown kernels, dried and used as a fall decoration.

Indian Ocean (in′dē ən ō′shən) an ocean south of Asia. It is between Africa and Australia.

🍁 **Indian paintbrush** (in′dē ən pānt′brush′) a wild plant with showy red or orange flowerlike leaves.

Indian summer (in′dē ən sum′ər) a time of mild, dry, hazy weather in late fall.

in·di·cate (in′də kāt′) **1** point out; show; make known: *The arrow on the sign indicates the way to go. A clock indicates the time.* **2** be a sign or hint of: *Fever indicates illness.* **3** say or hint: *Our teacher indicated that a surprise quiz was possible.* *v.,* **in·di·cat·ed, in·di·cat·ing.** **—in′di·ca′tion,** *n.* **—in′di·ca′tor,** *n.*

in·di·ces (in′də sēz′) a plural of **index.** *n.*

in·dif·fer·ent (in dif′ə rənt) **1** not caring one way or the other; having or showing little interest: *Rose enjoyed the trip, but Amanda was indifferent.* **2** not mattering much: *What time we start is indifferent to me.* **3** not very good: *an indifferent hockey player.* *adj.* **—in·dif′fer·ent·ly,** *adv.* **—in·dif′fer·ence,** *n.*

in·dig·e·nous (in dij′ə nəs) **1** native; originally living or growing in a particular country, region, soil, climate, etc.: *Musk-ox are indigenous to Canada. The Inuit are an indigenous people of North America.* **2** coming from within a group's own culture or language; not borrowed: *Canada's native peoples have their own indigenous ways of dealing with crime.* *adj.*

in·di·gest·i·ble (in′də jes′tə bəl) hard or impossible for your body to digest. *adj.*

in·di·ges·tion (in′də jes′chən) a bloated, sometimes painful feeling after a meal, often with gas in your stomach or intestines: *I ate too quickly and have been suffering from indigestion as a result.* *n.*

in·dig·nant (in dig′nənt) angry at something unfair or mean: *We were indignant at the nasty rumours, which were totally untrue.* *adj.* **—in·dig′nant·ly,** *adv.* **—in′dig·na′tion,** *n.*

in·dig·ni·ty (in dig′nə tē) an injury to dignity; lack of respect or proper treatment: *William felt that being called "Billy dear" was an indignity.* *n., pl.* **in·dig·ni·ties.**

in·di·go (in′də gō′) a deep, slightly purplish blue, the second-last colour of the rainbow. *n., pl.* **in·di·gos** or **in·di·goes;** *adj.*

in·di·rect (in′də rekt′) **1** not direct; not straight: *an indirect route.* **2** not directly connected: *I broke my leg as an indirect result of the cat's running away; while chasing it, I slipped on a banana peel.* **3** not straightforward; not coming right to the point: *She would not say yes or no, but gave an indirect answer.* *adj.* **—in′di·rect′ly,** *adv.*

in·dis·creet (in′di skrēt′) not discreet; not wise and careful: *The boy's indiscreet remark embarrassed the guests.* *adj.* **—in′dis·cre′tion** (in′di skresh′ən), *n.*

in·dis·pen·sa·ble (in′di spen′sə bəl) absolutely necessary: *Air is indispensable to life.* *adj.*

Industrial Revolution

The Industrial Revolution (1750 to 1850) was made possible by the invention of steam power and of machine tools. The results were factories (the one shown below is an early textile factory), railways, and industrial towns.

the first steam engine, built in 1712 to pump water out of mines

in·dis·tinct (in′di stingkt′) not clear to the eye, ear, or mind; blurry, muffled, or confused: *an indistinct picture. We could hear an indistinct roar from a faraway waterfall.* *adj.* **—in′dis·tinct′ly,** *adv.*

in·di·vid·u·al (in′də vij′ū əl) **1** a single person, animal, or thing: *She is a very talented individual. We saw a herd of giraffes containing thirty individuals.* **2** single; separate; for one only: *A bench is for several people; chairs are individual seats.* **3** a person who acts or thinks differently from most others: *Damien has always been an individual and pays no attention to peer pressure.* **4** unique; having the special characteristics of a particular person or thing: *Each person has an individual style of handwriting.* 1, 3 *n.,* 2, 4 *adj.* **—in′di·vid′u·al′i·ty,** *n.* **—in′di·vid′u·al·ly,** *adv.*

in·di·vis·i·ble (in′də viz′ə bəl) that cannot be divided. *adj.*

in·door (in′dôr′) **1** done, found, or used inside a building: *indoor skating, an indoor rink.* **2 indoors,** inside a building: *Let's eat indoors.* 1 *adj.,* 2 *adv.*

in·duce (in dyūs′ *or* in dūs′) **1** persuade with words or by offering a reward: *Advertisements induce people to buy.* **2** cause; bring about: *This medicine induces sleep.* *v.,* **in·duced, in·duc·ing.** **—in·duce′ment,** *n.*

in·dulge (in dulj′) give in to someone's wishes or your own weaknesses; not be strict with: *We often indulge a sick person. I indulged my fondness for candy by eating a whole box.* *v.,* **in·dulged, in·dulg·ing.** **—in·dul′gent,** *adj.* **—in·dul′gence,** *n.*
indulge in, let yourself do or have, often unwisely: *to indulge in junk food, to indulge in self-pity.*

industrial arts (in dus′trē əl ärts′) a school subject that involves learning how to make things with tools and machinery.

in·dus·tri·al·ize (in dus′trē ə līz′) develop a lot of large industries in a place, especially manufacturing industries: *After the Second World War, many agricultural countries became industrialized.* *v.,* **in·dus·tri·al·ized, in·dus·tri·al·iz·ing.** **—in·dus′tri·al·i·za′tion,** *n.*

in·dus·tri·ous (in dus′trē əs) working hard and steadily: *The honey bee is a most industrious insect.* *adj.*

in·dus·try (in′dəs trē) **1** any branch of business: *the transportation industry, the publishing industry.* **2** the business of manufacturing: *He would rather be a teacher than work in industry.* **3** steady effort; hard work: *Through industry and determination the pioneer built up a successful farm.* *n., pl.* **in·dus·tries.** **—in·dus′tri·al,** *adj.*

a bat	e bed	i bid	o pot	u cup	th thin
ā cake	ē me	ī bite	ō go	ū rude	ᴛʜ then
ä bar	ə about	ər over	ô for	ü put	zh measure

in·ed·i·ble (in ed′ə bəl) not fit to eat: *Some mushrooms are inedible.* *adj.*

in·ef·fec·tive (in′i fek′tiv) not having the desired effect; of little use: *An ineffective medicine fails to cure a disease or relieve pain.* *adj.*

in·ef·fi·cient (in′i fish′ənt) unable to get things done; wasting time and energy: *an inefficient manager. A machine that uses too much power is inefficient.* *adj.* **—in′ef·fi′cient·ly,** *adv.* **—in′ef·fi′cien·cy,** *n.*

in·ept (in ept′) clumsy; not skilful: *an inept performance.* *adj.* **—in·ept′ly,** *adv.* **—in·ept′i·tude′,** *n.*

in·e·qual·i·ty (in′ē kwol′ə tē) a lack of equality; being unequal in amount, size, value, rank, etc.: *There is a great inequality between the salaries of a bank president and an office worker.* *n., pl.* **in·e·qual·i·ties.**

in·ert (in ərt′) **1** lifeless; having no power to move or act: *A stone is an inert mass of matter.* **2** inactive; sluggish. **3** unable to react chemically. *adj.*

in·er·tia (in ər′shə) **1** a tendency to stay as you are and not start changes: *The family talked about leaving, but inertia prevented them from actually doing so.* **2** a tendency of still objects to stay still and of moving objects to keep moving, unless some force interferes. *n.*

in·es·ti·ma·ble (in es′tə mə bəl) too great to be measured or estimated: *Music brings inestimable pleasure.* *adj.*

in·ev·i·ta·ble (in ev′ə tə bəl) that cannot be avoided; sure to happen: *Mistakes are the inevitable result of carelessness.* *adj.* **—in·ev′i·ta·bly,** *adv.*

in·ex·act (in′ig zakt′) not right on; close, but not the actual amount or not getting every detail right: *Five dollars is an inexact figure; it actually cost $4.89.* *adj.*

in·ex·cus·a·ble (in′iks kyū′zə bəl) that cannot be excused: *Bad manners are inexcusable.* *adj.* **—in′ex·cus′a·bly,** *adv.*

in·ex·haust·i·ble (in′ig zos′tə bəl) that cannot be worn out or used up: *inexhaustible patience.* *adj.*

in·ex·pen·sive (in′ik spen′siv) not expensive; cheap; low-priced. *adj.*

in·ex·pe·ri·enced (in′ik spē′rē ənst) without experience or practice; lacking the skill and wisdom gained by experience. *adj.*

in·ex·pli·ca·ble (in′ik splik′ə bəl) that cannot be explained: *The disappearance of the money was inexplicable.* *adj.*

in·fal·li·ble (in fal′ə bəl) **1** never wrong; never making a mistake: *Not even teachers are infallible.* **2** absolutely reliable: *an infallible recipe for spaghetti sauce.* *adj.* **—in·fal′li·bil′i·ty,** *n.*

in·fa·mous (in′fə məs) **1** causing a very bad reputation; very wicked: *an infamous act.* **2** having a very bad reputation; well-known for his or her bad deeds: *an infamous traitor.* *adj.* **—in′fa·my,** *n.*

in·fant (in′fənt) a very young baby. *n.* **—in′fan·cy,** *n.* **—in′fan·tile′,** *adj.*

in·fan·try (in′fən trē) the branch of an army made up of soldiers who fight on foot. *n., pl.* **in·fan·tries.**

in·fat·u·at·ed (in fach′ū āt′id) very much in love, but only briefly and without really knowing the person: *After the first week of school Matti wasn't infatuated with Felix any more.* *adj.* **—in·fat′u·a′tion,** *n.*

in·fect (in fekt′) **1** cause disease by letting in germs or entering as a germ: *Dirt infects an open cut. The virus has infected 20 people.* **2** influence by spreading from one to another: *The captain's courage infected the other soldiers. A computer virus has infected this disk.* *v.*

in·fec·tion (in fek′shən) **1** the entry of germs or viruses: *The cut was cleaned and bandaged to prevent infection.* **2** a disease caused by germs or viruses: *Measles is an infection that spreads from one person to another.* **3** an influence, feeling, or idea spreading from one to another: *the infection of hatred.* *n.* **—in·fec′tious,** *adj.*

in·fer (in fər′) form an opinion by noticing something and drawing your own logical conclusions: *From the wedding ring on her finger I inferred that she was married.* *v.,* **in·ferred, in·fer·ring.** **—in′fer·ence,** *n.*

in·fe·ri·or (in fē′rē ər) **1** not very good: *inferior skills, an inferior grade of coffee.* **2** lower in quality or rank than another thing or person: *This cloth is inferior to real silk. A lieutenant is inferior to a captain.* **3** a person of lower rank: *She was a good leader and generous to her inferiors.* 1, 2 *adj.,* 3 *n.* **—in·fe′ri·or′i·ty,** *n.*

in·fer·nal (in fər′nəl) **1** of hell: *infernal heat.* **2** *Informal.* a word used to describe something you are angry at: *This infernal pen won't write!* *adj.*

in·fer·no (in fər′nō) a huge fire. *n., pl.* **in·fer·nos.**

in·fest (in fest′) fill a place. This word is only used for unpleasant things: *Mosquitoes infest swamps. The house was infested with fleas.* *v.* **—in′fes·ta′tion,** *n.*

in·field (in′fēld′) **1** the part of a baseball field inside the base lines. **2** the first, second, and third base players and shortstop of a baseball team: *That team has a good infield.* *n.* —**in′field′er,** *n.*

in·fi·nite (in′fə nit) without limits; endless: *the infinite extent of space, infinite patience.* *adj.* —**in′fi·nite·ly,** *adv.* —**in·fin′i·ty** (in fin′ə tē), *n.*

in·fin·i·tive (in fin′ə tiv) the basic form of a verb. It names an action but does not show who did it or when. Infinitives are used with *to* or together with another verb. *Example: sing* in *It is fun to sing* or *She can sing.* *n.*

in·fir·ma·ry (in fər′mə rē) a place where sick or injured people are cared for in a school, camp, or other institution; sick room. *n., pl.* **in·fir·ma·ries.**

in·flame (in flām′) **1** excite very much; make violent: *Her stirring speech inflamed the crowd.* **2** make or become abnormally hot, red, sore, or swollen: *The smoke had inflamed the firefighter's eyes.* *v.,* **in·flamed, in·flam·ing.** —**in′flam·ma′tion,** *n.*

in·flam·ma·ble (in flam′ə bəl) easily set on fire: *Paper and gasoline are inflammable.* *adj.*

USING WORDS . . . . inflammable

Believe it or not, **inflammable** and **flammable** mean the same thing, "easy to set on fire." The opposite of both words is *non-flammable.*

in·flate (in flāt′) **1** fill with air or gas: *to inflate a balloon.* **2** swell or puff out: *After his success, he was inflated with pride.* **3** increase prices or currency beyond a reasonable or normal amount. **4** exaggerate: *an inflated description. Those estimates are somewhat inflated.* *v.,* **in·flat·ed, in·flat·ing.** —**in·fla′tion,** *n.*

in·flex·i·ble (in flek′sə bəl) **1** firm; not giving in or changing: *inflexible rules. No amount of argument could change her inflexible determination.* **2** not easily bent; stiff; rigid: *an inflexible rod.* *adj.*

in·flict (in flikt′) cause someone to have or suffer something bad: *to inflict a wound on a person. Mr. McRae inflicted himself on his relatives for a long visit.* *v.*

in·flu·ence (in′flū əns) **1** the power to cause certain changes in things, or to affect someone's behaviour without using force: *Since she's a known expert and also very likable, she has a lot of influence. Mountains and oceans have an important influence on climate.* **2** a person or thing that has such power: *Hon-Wah was a good influence on me.* **3** have an effect on; have power over: *The moon influences the tides. What we read influences our thinking.* 1, 2 *n.,* 3 *v.,* **in·flu·enced, in·flu·enc·ing.** —**in′flu·en′tial** (in′flū en′shəl), *adj.*

in·flu·en·za (in′flū en′zə) an infectious disease resembling a very bad cold with fever, aches, and often stomach upset. This name is usually shortened to **flu.** *n.*

in·form (in fôrm′) tell; let someone know: *Report cards inform parents about a child's progress at school.* *v.* **inform on someone,** give authorities secret information about someone who has done wrong: *The robber who was caught informed on the others who had escaped.* Someone who does this is an **informer.**

in·for·mal (in fôr′məl) **1** not formal; in a relaxed, everyday style: *an informal party.* **2** not done in the official or recognized way: *an informal vote. She got a lot of informal training in mechanics by watching her dad fix cars.* *adj.* —**in·for′mal·ly,** *adv.* —**in′for·mal′i·ty,** *n.*

in·for·ma·tion (in′fər mā′shən) **1** knowledge; facts; news: *A dictionary gives information about words.* Something that gives information is **informative** (in fôr′mə tiv). **2** words, numbers, sounds, or images, especially in connection with computer systems. *n.*

information highway (in′fər mā′shən hī′wā′) the entire system of computers, telephones, and electronic links all over the world that move words, numbers, and images from one place to another.

in·fra·red (in′frə red′) of or having to do with the long, invisible light rays just beyond the red end of the colour spectrum: *Most of the heat from sunlight and light bulbs comes from infrared rays.* *adj.*

in·fre·quent (in frē′kwənt) not happening often or coming close together: *infrequent visits. Gas stations are infrequent along this road.* *adj.* —**in·fre′quent·ly,** *adv.*

in·fu·ri·ate (in fyū′rē āt′) fill with anger; make furious: *The man was infuriated when the passing cyclist splashed him with mud.* *v.,* **in·fu·ri·at·ed, in·fu·ri·at·ing.**

–ing **1** a suffix added to a verb to form a related noun or adjective. In *Painting is a good way to relax* and *Turn off that running water, Painting* is a noun and *running* is an adjective. **2** a suffix added to a verb to make a **present participle,** which is then used with a form of **be** to make certain tenses: *We are leaving. What was she saying?*

in·ge·ni·ous (in jēn′ yəs) clever; showing creative imagination: *an ingenious device. Using his belt, a key ring, and a jack-knife, the ingenious boy found a way to fish the sandal out of the sewer.* *adj.* —**in·gen′ious·ly,** *adv.* —**in′ge·nu′i·ty** (in′jə nyū′ə tē), *n.*

a bat	e bed	i bid	o pot	u cup	th thin
ā cake	ē me	ī bite	ō go	ū rude	TH then
ä bar	ə about	ər over	ô for	ů put	zh measure

in·got (ing′gət) a mass of metal, such as gold, silver, or steel, melted and formed into a block or bar. *n.*

in·grained (in grānd′) firmly set and very hard to change or to remove: *an ingrained habit or attitude. The dirt was deeply ingrained in the fabric.* *adj.*

in·grat·i·tude (in grat′ə tyūd′ *or* in grat′ə tūd′) a lack of thankfulness; failure to be grateful. *n.*

in·gre·di·ent (in grē′dē ənt) one of the parts of a mixture: *Flour is one of the main ingredients of a cake.* *n.*

WORD HISTORY...... ingredient

An **ingredient** is "something that goes in," from the Latin *in-* meaning "in" + *gradi* "go."

in·hab·it (in hab′it) live in: *Fish inhabit the sea.* *v.* **—in·hab′i·tant,** *n.*

in·hale (in hāl′) breathe in. An **inhaler** or **inhalator** (in′hə lā′tər) is a device used for breathing in medicine. *v.,* **in·haled, in·hal·ing.**

in·her·it (in her′it) **1** get as a gift from another person after he or she dies: *Mrs. Chan's nephew inherited the farm after she died.* **2** get a physical or mental characteristic through your parents: *She inherits her red hair from her father.* *v.* **—in·her′it·ance,** *n.*

in·hib·it (in hib′it) check; stop or hold back: *Alcohol is dangerous because it inhibits your natural reflexes.* *v.* **—in′hi·bi′tion,** *n.*

in·hos·pi·ta·ble (in′ho spit′ə bəl) not hospitable; not friendly or helpful to visitors. *adj.* **—in′hos·pi·tal′i·ty** (in′hos pə tal′ə tē), *n.*

in·hu·man (in hyū′mən) without ordinary human kindness; cruel: *inhuman acts of torture.* *adj.* **—in′hu·man′i·ty,** *n.*

i·ni·tial (i nish′əl) **1** coming at the beginning; first: *His initial effort at skating was a failure.* **2** the first letter of a word: *The initials "P.E.I." stand for "Prince Edward Island."* **3** to mark or sign with your initials: *Ms. Coby A. Slofstra initialled the note "C.A.S."* 1 *adj.,* 2 *n.,* 3 *v.,* **i·ni·tialled** or **i·ni·tialed, i·ni·tial·ling** or **i·ni·tial·ing.**

Grammar Check .... initial

Some companies or organizations use their initials to form an abbreviation of their name.
Royal Canadian Mounted Police (RCMP)
Mothers Against Drunk Driving (MADD)
Canadian Broadcasting Corporation (CBC)

i·ni·ti·ate (i nish′ē āt′) **1** start something; get something going: *Charles initiated a discussion about computer games.* **2** bring in a new member by a special ceremony: *They initiated me into the Cooking Club by having me make lunch for them all.* *v.,* **i·ni·ti·at·ed, i·ni·ti·at·ing.** **—i·ni′ti·a′tion,** *n.*

i·ni·ti·a·tive (i nish′ə tiv) **1** a new thing started by someone: *One of the government's latest initiatives in water safety is a boater licensing program.* **2** the readiness and ability to start things: *A good leader has initiative.* *n.*
on someone's initiative, with that person taking the first step: *On Aldo's initiative, the students decided to raise money for library books.*
take the initiative, be the one to take the first step: *If someone takes the initiative, I know others will follow.*

in·ject (in jekt′) **1** give medicine or other liquid by needle, through the skin: *to inject insulin. They have injected her with painkiller.* **2** put in: *The win injected new enthusiasm into the team.* *v.* **—in·jec′tion,** *n.*

in·junc·tion (in jungk′shən) an order, especially by a court: *The judge gave an injunction to stop the logging immediately.* *n.*

in·jure (in′jər) do damage to; harm; hurt: *She injured her ankle while skiing. The rumours have injured his reputation.* Something that does harm is **injurious** (in jū′rē əs). *v.,* **in·jured, in·jur·ing.** **—in′ju·ry,** *n.*

in·jus·tice (in jus′tis) **1** lack of justice; unfairness: *Years of injustice had made the people angry.* **2** something unjust or unfair: *to do someone an injustice.* *n.*

ink (ingk) **1** the black or coloured liquid in a pen or printer: *Do you always write with green ink?* **2** the dark liquid squirted by a squid or octopus for protection. **3** mark or stain with ink. 1, 2 *n.,* 3 *v.* **—ink′y,** *adj.*

ink·ling (ingk′ling) a hint; a slight idea or notion: *We were lost, with no inkling where we were.* *n.*

ink·well (ingk′wel′) a container of ink that people used to keep on a desk or table. Some antique desks still have a hole for the inkwell to sit in. *n.*

in·laid (in′lād′) made of pieces set into a surface in a decorative way: *an inlaid design of light wood in dark. The box had an inlaid cover.* *adj.* **—in′lay′,** *v. or n.*

in·land (in′land′ *or* in′lənd) **1** away from the coast or the border; toward the inner part of a country: *an inland town (adj.). The source of the river is 300 km inland (adv.).* **2** the part of a country away from the border or the coast: *to travel in the inland.* **3** not foreign; going on inside a country: *inland trade.* 1, 3 *adj.,* 1 *adv.,* 2 *n.*

in–law (in′lo′) *Informal.* a relative by marriage, such as a father-in-law or sister-in-law: *They had his in-laws visiting last week.* *n.*

in·let (in′let′ *or* in′lət) 1 a narrow strip of water running from a sea, lake, etc. into the land: *The fishing village was on a small inlet.* 2 a way in. *n.*

in·line skates (in′līn′ skāts′) roller skates that have four wheels in a single row, one behind the other. **—inline skating.**

in·mate (in′māt′) a person who lives with others in the same building, especially in a prison. *n.*

inn (in) especially in earlier times, a place where travellers and others could get meals and a room to sleep in. An inn was smaller and more homelike than most modern hotels, and was run by an **innkeeper.** *n.*

in·ner (in′ər) farther or deeper inside: *an inner office. I kept my inner thoughts to myself.* *adj.*

inner ear (in′ər ēr′) the deepest part of the ear, filled with fluid. It contains the organs that control balance and that change sound into nerve impulses.

in·ner·most (in′ər mōst′) farthest or deepest: *inside the innermost depths of the mine, her innermost desire.* **Inmost** is another form of this word. *adj.*

inner tube (in′ər tyūb′) a circular rubber tube that fits inside some tires. It is pumped up with air.

in·ning (in′ing) a division of a baseball game giving each team a turn at bat. Unless a tie must be broken, there are nine innings in a game. *n.*

in·no·cent (in′ə sənt) 1 not guilty: *The robber shot at the police officer but hit an innocent bystander. The accused man was found innocent of the crime.* 2 not knowing about evil, and so not expecting it: *innocent trust.* 3 doing or meaning no harm: *an innocent prank.* *adj.* **—in′no·cent·ly,** *adv.* **—in′no·cence,** *n.*

in·no·va·tion (in′ə vā′shən) 1 something new brought in; a change in the way things are done: *The new principal made many innovations.* 2 the fact of bringing in new things or new methods: *Innovation is not always good.* *n.* **—in′no·vate′,** *v.* **—in′no·va′tive,** *adj.*

WORD HISTORY......innovation

Innovation gets its root *nov-* from the Latin *novum* meaning "new." The same root is in **novelty** (new thing) and **renovate** (make new again).

In·nu (in′ nu) 1 a First Nations People living in northern Québec. 2 their language, which belongs to the Algonquian family. 3 having to do with these people or their language. 1, 2 *n.,* 3 *adj.*

in·nu·mer·a·ble (i nyū′mə rə bəl *or* i nū′mə rə bəl) too many to count; very many: *innumerable stars.* *adj.*

in·oc·u·late (in ok′yə lāt′) put a weak or dead disease germ into a person's body so the person will develop immunity to that disease: *The doctor will inoculate the baby against whooping cough.* *v.,* **in·oc·u·lat·ed, in·oc·u·lat·ing.** **—in·oc′u·la′tion,** *n.*

in·or·gan·ic (in′ôr gan′ik) 1 not having the structure of animals and plants; not made of living matter: *Minerals are inorganic.* 2 not coming from or having anything to do with living animals and plants or their life processes. *adj.*

in–pa·tient (in′pā′shənt) someone who stays in a hospital to have treatment. An **out-patient** goes to a hospital for treatment but does not stay there. *n.*

in·put (in′pu̇t′) 1 suggestions, comments, or additional information from interested people: *We need everyone's input to plan a good trip.* 2 information fed into a computer for processing. 3 feed information into a computer. 1 *n.,* 2, 3 *v.,* **in·put, in·put·ting.**

in·quest (in′kwest) a legal inquiry to find out the cause of a death that may be the result of a crime or of a situation that could be dangerous to other people. *n.*

in·quire (in kwīr′) ask for information: *He phoned the hotel to inquire about a room.* *v.,* **in·quired, in·quir·ing.** **—in·quir′y** (in kwī′rē *or* in′kwə rē), *n.* **inquire into,** do research on; try to find out about: *She came across many old books and documents while inquiring into the history of the town.*

in·quis·i·tive (in kwiz′ə tiv) 1 curious; asking many questions: *Children are usually inquisitive.* 2 nosy: *being spied on by inquisitive neighbours.* *adj.* **—in·quis′i·tive·ly,** *adv.* **—in·quis′i·tive·ness,** *n.*

in·sane (in sān′) 1 not sane; having a severe mental illness. 2 wild or extremely foolish: *an insane plan.* *adj.* **—in·sane′ly,** *adv.* **—in·san′i·ty** (in san′ə tē), *n.*

in·sa·tia·ble (in sā′shə bəl) that cannot be satisfied: *an insatiable appetite.* *adj.*

a bat	e bed	i bid	o pot	u cup	th thin
ā cake	ē me	ī bite	ō go	ū rude	ᴛʜ then
ȧ bar	ə about	ər over	ȯ for	u̇ put	zh measure

Insects

Of all forms of life, insects are the most varied. More than 900 000 species are known. Insects are highly adaptable and can survive in all environments. No insect species has ever been wiped out by humans.

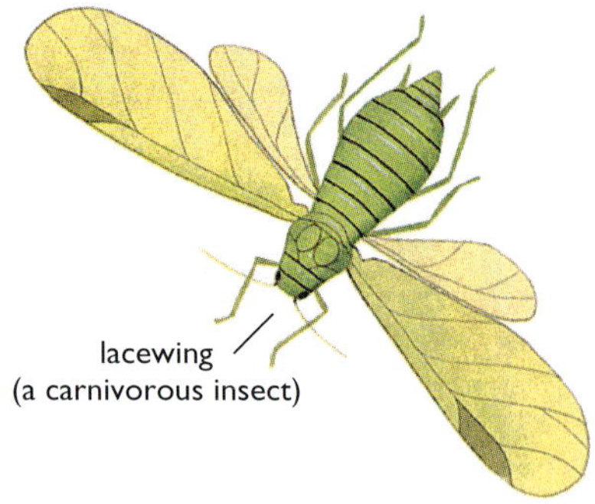

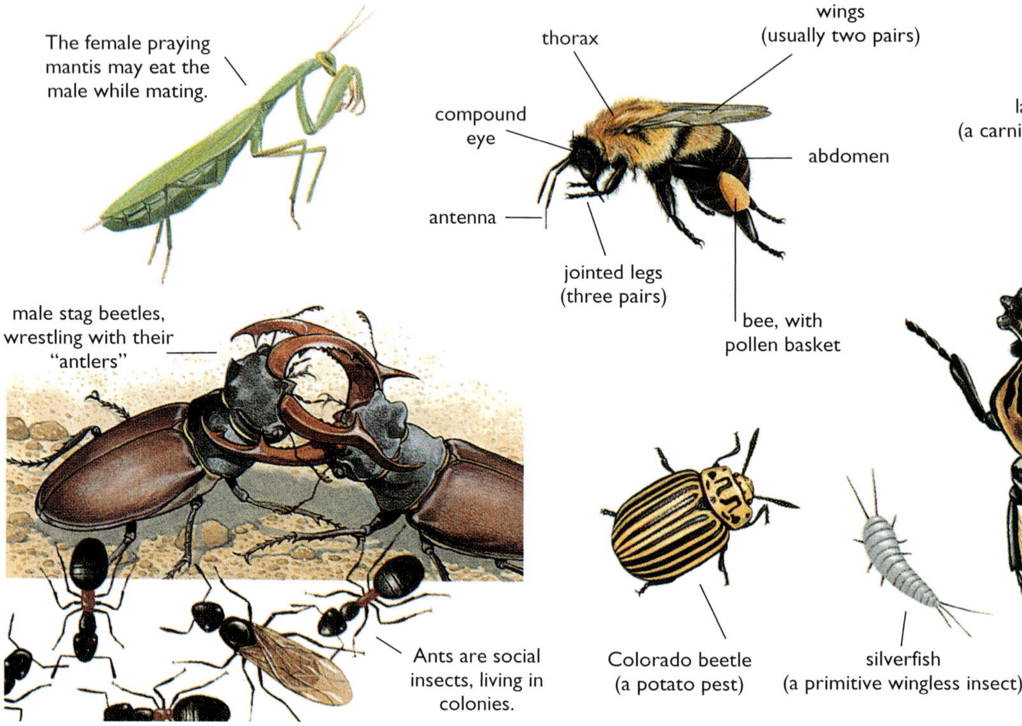

in·scribe (in skrīb′) write or engrave on: *The ring was inscribed with her name. Your words are inscribed on my memory.* *v.,* **in·scribed, in·scrib·ing.** —**in·scrip′tion,** *n.*

in·scru·ta·ble (in skrū′tə bəl) hard to figure out because no clues are given; mysterious: *We looked for the answer in her face, but her expression was completely inscrutable.* *adj.*

in·sect (in′sekt) **1** a small animal whose body is divided into three parts and has no backbone. Insects have three pairs of legs and usually one or two pairs of wings. Flies, mosquitoes, gnats, and bees are insects. **2** *Informal.* any similar small animal whose body is divided into several parts, and has several pairs of legs. Spiders and centipedes are often called insects. *n.*

in·sec·ti·cide (in sek′tə sīd′) a substance for killing insects. *n.*

in·se·cure (in′si kyūr′) **1** lacking confidence; not sure of yourself: *He felt quite insecure among all the older kids at camp.* **2** not safe or dependable; not well protected: *an insecure position, an insecure fortress.* *adj.* —**in′se·cu′ri·ty,** *n.*

in·sen·si·tive (in sen′sə tiv) not noticing or responding; not affected or influenced by: *insensitive to beauty, insensitive to pain. The insensitive girl ignored her brother's tears.* *adj.* —**in·sen′si·tiv′i·ty,** *n.*

in·sep·a·ra·ble (in sep′ə rə bəl) that cannot be separated: *The girl and her dog were inseparable.* *adj.*

in·sert (in sərt′ *for 1,* in′sərt *for 2*) **1** put in: *to insert a key into a lock, to insert a word into a sentence.* **2** something put in: *The book had an insert containing several pages of pictures.* 1 *v.,* 2 *n.* —**in·ser′tion,** *n.*

in·side (in′sīd′) **Inside** has to do with the inner part or surface of something: *The inside of the box was lined with coloured paper (n). I hope we can get an inside seat at the game (adj.). I guarded the opening to the cave while Jean went inside (adv.). The nut is inside the shell (prep.).* *n., adj., adv., prep.*
an inside job, something, usually a crime, done to an organization by an **insider,** one of its own members.
inside information, information known only to those in a certain group. Similarly, an **inside joke** is a private joke.
inside of, in less than: *We can get it done inside of a week.*
inside out, a so that the inner part is showing on the outside: *He turned his pockets inside out.* **b** completely: *I know this lesson inside out.*

in·sight (in′sīt′) deep understanding of the inner workings or the real nature of a person or thing: *We study science to gain insight into the world we live in. She has lived here a long time and has a lot of insight into Canadian culture.* *n.* —**in·sight′ful,** *adj.*

in·sig·ni·a (in sig′nē ə) the badge, logo, or other mark showing a person's rank or membership in an organization: *The general wore the insignia of the armed forces on his cap.* *n.*

in·sig·nif·i·cant (in′sig nif′ə kənt) having little importance or meaning: *an insignificant amount. Ignore their insignificant chatter.* *adj.*

in·sin·cere (in′sin sēr′) phony; speaking or acting without really meaning it. *adj.* —**in′sin·cere′ly,** *adv.* —**in′sin·cer′i·ty** (in′sin ser′ə tē), *n.*

in·sin·u·ate (in sin′yū āt′) **1** hint; suggest in an indirect way: *Although she didn't say so, she insinuated that I had lied to her.* **2** put or get in gradually and in a sneaky way: *The spy insinuated himself into the friendship of important politicians.* *v.,* **in·sin·u·at·ed, in·sin·u·at·ing.** —**in·sin′u·a′tion,** *n.*

in·sist (in sist′) do, demand, or say something and refuse to back down when others disagree with it: *He insists on biking to school in every kind of weather. Mom insists that we wash our hands before eating.* *v.* —**in·sist′ent,** *adj.* —**in·sist′ence,** *n.*

in·sole (in′sōl′) a piece of foam, leather, or other material that is shaped like a foot and fits inside a shoe to give extra comfort or protection. *n.*

in·so·lent (in′sə lənt) extremely disrespectful or rude: *His insolent remarks angered the boss.* *adj.* —**in′so·lent·ly,** *adv.* —**in′so·lence,** *n.*

in·sol·u·ble (in sol′yə bəl) **1** unable to dissolve in a liquid. **2** impossible to solve: *an insoluble problem.* *adj.*

in·som·ni·a (in som′nē ə) not being able to sleep; sleeplessness: *He suffers from insomnia.* *n.*

in·spect (in spekt′) look over carefully; examine, especially to see if there is anything wrong: *A dentist inspects my teeth twice a year.* *v.* —**in·spec′tion,** *n.*

WORD HISTORY.......inspect

Inspect, **spectacles**, and **spectator** all have to do with looking or seeing. That's because they share the Latin root *spect-* from *specare* meaning "to look."

in·spec·tor (in spek′tər) an official whose job is to inspect: *A health inspector visits all restaurants.* *n.*

in·spire (in spīr′) give someone an idea, a feeling, or a reason to do something: *Her courage inspired confidence in others. The experience inspired him to write a story.* *v.,* **in·spired, in·spir·ing.** —**in′spi·ra′tion,** *n.*

in·stall (in stol′) **1** put equipment into a building, car, or other place and make it ready for use: *to install a dishwasher.* **2** settle in a place: *The cat installed itself in the easy chair.* **3** put a person into an official position with a special ceremony: *The new judge was installed immediately.* *v.* —**in′stal·la′tion,** *n.*

in·stal·ment or **in·stall·ment** (in stol′mənt) **1** a part of a sum of money to be paid: *She has to pay the $100 in ten monthly instalments of $10.* **2** one part of a series: *a story published in six instalments.* *n.*

in·stance (in′stəns) **1** a person or thing that can be used as an example: *That rude question was an instance of bad manners.* **2** case; situation: *In this instance he decided it was best not to go along.* *n.*
for instance, as an example: *Her many hobbies include, for instance, skating and stamp collecting.*

in·stant (in′stənt) **1** a moment: *At that instant the engine stalled. He paused for an instant.* **2** immediate: *The medicine gave instant relief from pain.* **3** made quickly using a mix or kit: *instant pudding, instant potatoes.* 1 *n.,* 2, 3 *adj.* —**in′stant·ly,** *adv.*

instant messaging (in′stənt mes′ə jing) a real-time conversation on a computer network. This is often abbreviated to **IM.** Look at **text messaging** and **chat room.**

in·stan·ta·ne·ous (in′stən tā′nē əs) happening or done in an instant: *A flash of lightning is instantaneous.* *adj.* —**in′stan·ta′ne·ous·ly,** *adv.*

in·stead (in sted′) in place of some other thing or person: *She was going to stay home, but went riding instead. Instead of studying, she read a story.* *adv.*

in·sti·gate (in′stə gāt′) stir up action; get people to start something, especially something bad: *to instigate a rebellion.* *v.,* **in·sti·gat·ed, in·sti·gat·ing.**

in·stil or **in·still** (in stil′) gradually put feelings or ideas into a person's mind: *to instil knowledge. Being read to instils a love for good books.* *v.,* **in·stilled, in·still·ing.**

a bat	e bed	i bid	o pot	u cup	th thin
ā cake	ē me	ī bite	ō go	ū rude	ᴛʜ then
ä bar	ə about	ər over	ȯ for	u̇ put	zh measure

Musical Instruments

There are four kinds of musical instruments:
woodwind — clarinets, flutes, etc.
brass — French horns, trumpets, etc.
strings — guitars, violins, piano, etc.
percussion — drums, cymbals, keyboard, etc.

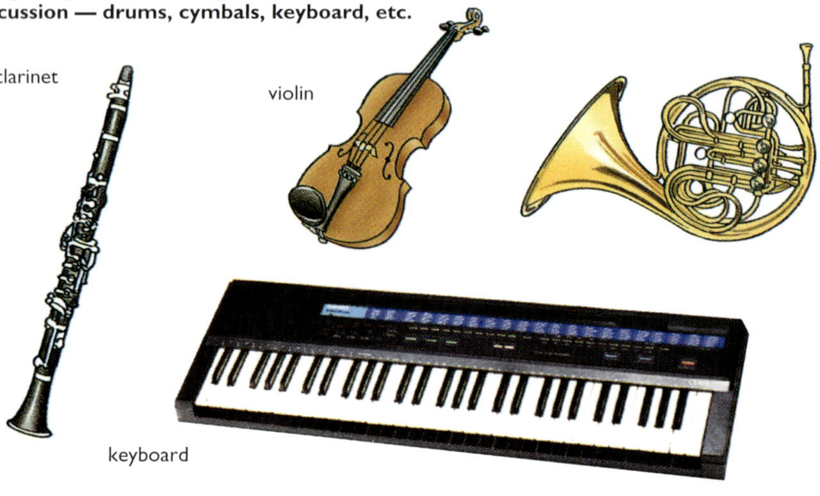

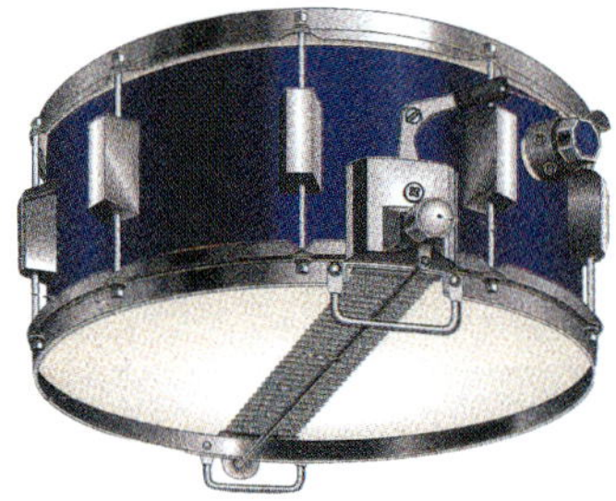

in•stinct (in′stingkt) **1** a natural ability or urge that causes animals to behave in a certain way without having to learn it or choose to do it. It is by instinct that birds fly south for the winter. **2** a natural tendency or talent: *Even as a child, the artist had an instinct for colour.* *n.* —**in•stinc′tive,** *adj.*

in•sti•tute (in′stə tyūt′ *or* in′stə tūt′) **1** an organization or society for some special purpose: *the Canadian National Institute for the Blind.* **2** the building it uses: *The recital was held at the Dance Institute.* **3** set up: *When was the Neighbourhood Watch program instituted?* 1, 2 *n.,* 3 *v.,* **in•sti•tut•ed, in•sti•tut•ing.**

in•sti•tu•tion (in′stə tyū′shən *or* in′stə tū′shən) **1 a** an organization set up to serve the public in some way, such as a church, hospital, or prison. An institution carries on its work in a building. **b** the building itself. **2** an established law or custom: *Summer camp is an institution in our family. Marriage is an institution in most cultures.* **3** the act of setting something up. *n.*

in•struct (in strukt′) **1** teach. Something that teaches you a lot is **instructive. 2** tell; give orders: *The owners of the house instructed their agent to sell it.* *v.* —**in•struc′tor,** *n.*

in•struc•tion (in struk′shən) **1** teaching or lessons: *to give instruction in music.* **2 instructions,** *pl.* orders: *Their instructions were to pick him up at seven o'clock.* **3 instructions,** *pl.* an explanation of how to do or use something: *The kit comes with instructions for building the airplane.* *n.*

in•stru•ment (in′strə mənt) **1** something used to make music, such as a trumpet, guitar, or piano. **2** a tool or machine: *a dentist's instruments.* **3** a device used to measure something, record or display information, or control part of a machine: *A thermometer is an instrument for measuring temperature.* In a vehicle, the **instrument panel** holds instruments that tell the driver the speed, the amount of fuel in the tank, the distance travelled, and other things. *n.* —**in′stru•men′tal,** *adj.*

in•suf•fer•a•ble (in suf′ə rə bəl) unbearable: *such insufferable rudeness.* *adj.*

in•suf•fi•cient (in′sə fish′ənt) not enough: *He is tired because he has had insufficient sleep.* *adj.* —**in′suf•fi′cient•ly,** *adv.*

in•su•late (in′sə lāt′) cover, pack, or line with material that will keep heat, sound, etc. in or out: *Houses, recording studios, and coolers are insulated.* *v.,* **in•su•lat•ed, in•su•lat•ing.** —**in′su•la′tion,** *n.*

in•su•lin (in′sə lin) a hormone produced by an organ called the pancreas. It helps your body to use sugar and other carbohydrates. *n.*

in•sult (in sult′ *for 1,* in′sult *for 2*) **1** treat very rudely or disrespectfully: *The rebels insulted the flag by throwing mud on it.* **2** remark or action that shows a complete lack of respect; a put-down: *To be called a dope is an insult.* 1 *v.,* 2 *n.*

in·sur·ance (in shū′rəns) 1 an arrangement made with a company to help you in times of need. You regularly pay them a certain amount, and then if your property is damaged, you need health care, or there is a death, they pay you a lot more. 2 the amount of money the company agrees to pay: *He has $250 000 life insurance, which his wife will receive if he dies first.* 3 the amount of money you pay the company: *Her car insurance is $1200 a year.* *n.* —**in·sure′,** *v.*

in·tact (in takt′) not damaged or injured and with no part missing: *The money was returned intact by the boy who found it.* *adj.*

in·take (in′tāk′) 1 an opening that lets in water, air, gas, etc.: *If you stand in front of the pool's intake, you can feel the rush of water.* 2 the process or the amount of taking in: *My daily intake of calories is about 1500.* *n.*

in·tan·gi·ble (in tan′jə bəl) 1 not able to be touched: *Light is intangible.* 2 not easily grasped by the mind; vague or hard to define: *She had that intangible quality we call charm.* *adj.*

in·te·ger (in′tə jər) a positive or negative whole number, or zero. *n.*

in·te·grate (in′tə grāt′) blend separate units or parts together into a whole: *The two schools were integrated to cut costs. Knowing English or French helps newcomers to integrate more quickly into Canadian society.* *v.,* **in·te·grat·ed, in·te·grat·ing.** —**in′te·gra′tion,** *n.*

in·teg·ri·ty (in teg′rə tē) 1 honesty and sincerity; trustworthiness: *A person of integrity is respected.* 2 completeness; wholeness: *The integrity of the country was threatened by civil war.* *n.*

in·tel·lect (in′tə lekt′) 1 the power of reasoning, knowing, and understanding: *Our actions are influenced by our intellect and our feelings.* 2 a very intelligent person; a thinker: *She was one of the great intellects of her time.* *n.*

in·tel·lec·tu·al (in′tə lek′chū əl) 1 using or having to do with the intellect: *Thinking is an intellectual process.* 2 able to think and talk intelligently about ideas; interested in ideas. 3 a person with this ability and interest; a thinker. 1, 2 *adj.,* 3 *n.*

in·tel·li·gence (in tel′ə jəns) 1 the ability to learn and think; understanding; mind: *A dolphin has more intelligence than a worm.* 2 knowledge; information: *The spy gained secret intelligence of the enemy's plans.* *n.*

in·tel·li·gent (in tel′ə jənt) able to learn and think well; quick to understand. *adj.* —**in·tel′li·gent·ly,** *adv.*

in·tel·li·gi·ble (in tel′ə jə bəl) able to be understood; clear: *My baby brother babbles a lot but hasn't said any intelligible words yet.* *adj.*

in·tend (in tend′) 1 have in mind as a goal; plan; mean to do: *We intend to go home soon. They didn't intend to hurt your feelings.* 2 mean for a particular purpose or use: *That gift was intended for you.* *v.*

in·tense (in tens′) 1 very great; very strong or deep; extreme: *intense happiness. A bad burn causes intense pain. Intense heat melts iron.* 2 always completely involved in whatever you are feeling, doing, or thinking at any time; focussed: *an intense person.* *adj.* —**in·tense′ly,** *adv.* —**in·ten′si·ty,** *n.* —**in·ten′si·fy′,** *v.*

in·ten·sive (in ten′siv) very deep, concentrated, and thorough: *intensive research. He is receiving intensive care in the hospital.* *adj.* —**in·ten′sive·ly,** *adv.*

in·tent (in tent′) 1 purpose or meaning: *The thief shot with intent to kill. What is the intent of that remark?* 2 paying complete attention; showing full concentration: *an intent look, intent on a task.* 3 determined: *I am intent on winning.* 1 *n.,* 2, 3 *adj.* —**in·tent′ly,** *adv.* **to all intents and purposes,** in every important way: *These books are to all intents and purposes the same; only the cover is different.*

in·ten·tion (in ten′shən) a purpose; plan: *He had no intention of hurting her feelings. Their intention is to spend next summer travelling.* If something is **intentional,** it is done on purpose. *n.*

inter– *a prefix meaning:* 1 back and forth; one with the other, as in *intercommunicate, interlock.* 2 between or among. *Interpersonal* means "between or among persons."

in·ter·act (in′tər akt′) 1 act on each other; have an effect on each other: *The oxygen in the air interacts with the metal to cause rust.* 2 talk and do things together. 3 communicate directly with a computer program to make things happen. *v.* —**in′ter·ac′tion,** *n.*

in·ter·ac·tive (in′tər ak′tiv) 1 with lots of talking back and forth and doing things together: *She has an interactive teaching style and likes to involve the students in discussions.* 2 describing a computer program that makes use of direct communication from the user. What the program does depends on your ongoing input. *adj.*

a bat	e bed	i bid	o pot	u cup	th thin
ā cake	ē me	ī bite	ō go	ū rude	ᴛʜ then
ä bar	ə about	ər over	ô for	ů put	zh measure

in•ter•cept (in′tər sept′) 1 take or seize on the way from one place to another: *to intercept a message.* 2 check; stop: *The bushes intercepted his fall.* *v.*

in•ter•change (in′tər chānj′ *for 1,* in′tər chānj′ *for 2 and 3*) 1 switch; exchange: *The two girls interchanged hats.* If two or more things can be used in each other's place, they are **interchangeable.** 2 the act of switching or of exchanging: *The word "team" may be turned into "meat" by the interchange of two letters. A discussion is an interchange of ideas.* 3 a place where you can get on or off a highway by using a ramp so that you don't need to cross in front of other traffic; cloverleaf. 1 *v.,* **in•ter•changed, in•ter•chang•ing;** 2, 3 *n.*

in•ter•com (in′tər kom′) a radio or telephone system that makes it possible to speak to everyone in different parts of a building or aircraft: *The principal gave us the message over the intercom.* **Intercom** is short for **intercommunication system.** *n.*

in•ter•est (in′trist *or* in′tə rest′) 1 a feeling of wanting to know, see, do, or have: *an interest in music. The baby showed no interest in eating baby food.* 2 arouse such a feeling in; make curious; catch and hold someone's attention: *A good story interests us. The sales agent tried to interest us in some new software.* 3 the power to hold someone's attention: *A boring game lacks interest.* 4 something that a person spends time and attention on: *Art and sports are her main interests.* 5 a share or part in something: *Our parents have a half interest in that farm.* 6 money paid for the use of money, usually a percentage of the amount invested, borrowed, or saved: *The interest on the loan was ten percent a year.* 1, 3–6 *n.,* 2 *v.*
in someone's interest, to someone's advantage or benefit: *It is in everyone's interest to protect the environment.*
in the interest of, with the aim of; for the sake of: *In the interest of safety, wear a bicycle helmet.*
look out for someone's interests, help or take care of someone.
of interest, interesting.

in•ter•est•ed (in′tris tid *or* in′tə res′təd) feeling or showing interest: *interested in languages. He played for an interested audience.* *adj.*

USING WORDS . . . . interested

The adjective **interested** has two opposites.

- If you are **disinterested** in something, you have no selfish interest: *A referee must be disinterested in the outcome of the game.*
- If you are **uninterested** in something, you have no feelings about it: *He was uninterested in watching the basketball game.*

in•ter•est•ing (in′tris ting *or* in′tə res′ting) arousing interest; holding someone's attention: *I think stories about travel are interesting.* *adj.*
—**in′ter•est•ing•ly,** *adv.*

in•ter•face (in′tər fās′) 1 a surface that forms a common boundary between two things: *the interface of air and water.* 2 the connection between two groups, systems, areas of study, etc.: *the interface between citizens and their government, the interface between math and science.* 3 a program or electrical device used to connect computers to each other or to machines like printers, monitors, etc. 4 meet; connect; come or bring together. 1–3 *n.,* 4 *v.,* **in•ter•faced, in•ter•fac•ing.**

in•ter•fere (in′tər fēr′) 1 clash or conflict; hinder: *I can change my plan if it interferes with your holiday. Extreme tiredness will interfere with your learning.* 2 get involved in other people's business; meddle: *This is just between Sandra and me; don't interfere!* *v.,* **in•ter•fered, in•ter•fer•ing.**

in•ter•fer•ence (in′tər fē′rəns) 1 the act of interfering, or something that interferes: *Her interference spoiled our game.* 2 in radio or TV, the interruption of the desired signal by other signals that cause poor sound or picture quality. 3 in hockey and other sports, the act of blocking an opponent in a way forbidden by the rules. *n.*

in•ter•im (in′tə rim) 1 meantime; the time between: *They couldn't leave till the rain stopped, so they played cards in the interim.* 2 for the meantime; temporary: *an interim report.* 1 *n.,* 2 *adj.*

in•te•ri•or (in tē′rē ər) 1 inside: *an interior surface* (*adj.*)*. The interior of the house was beautifully decorated* (*n.*). 2 the land away from the coast or border: *The interior of the island is sparsely populated.* 3 away from the coast or border: *interior regions.* 1, 2 *n.,* 1, 3 *adj.*

in•ter•ject (in′tər jekt′) throw in between other remarks: *Every now and then the speaker interjected a joke or story to keep us interested.* *v.*

in•ter•jec•tion (in′tər jek′shən) 1 an exclamation of surprise, pain, joy, or other feeling. Some common interjections are *Wow! Ouch!* and *Hurrah!* 2 a remark thrown in. *n.*

in•ter•lace (in′tər lās′) cross over and under each other; weave together: *Baskets are made by interlacing reeds or fibres. They held hands and their fingers interlaced.* *v.,* **in•ter•laced, in•ter•lac•ing.**

in•ter•lock (in′tər lok′) fit tightly together; lock together: *the interlocking pieces of a jigsaw puzzle.* *v.*

in·ter·lude (in′tər lüd′) 1 a pleasant break; something different that comes as an interruption: *There was an interlude of sunshine between the two showers.* 2 a piece of music played between the parts of a song, performance, etc. *n.*

in·ter·me·di·ate (in′tər mē′dē it) coming in between; midway or mid-level: *The camp has beginning, intermediate, and advanced swimming classes.* *adj.*

in·ter·mi·na·ble (in tər′mə nə bəl) endless; very long and boring. *adj.* **—in·ter′mi·na·bly,** *adv.*

in·ter·mis·sion (in′tər mish′ən) a break, especially in a show: *The band played from 7:00 to 10:00 with a short intermission at 8:30. The rain continued all day without intermission.* *n.*

in·ter·mit·tent (in′tər mit′ənt) continually stopping and starting again: *The intermittent noise of the railway trains kept him awake.* *adj.* **—in′ter·mit′tent·ly,** *adv.*

in·tern (in′tərn) a doctor receiving practical training in a hospital before going out on his or her own. *n.*

in·ter·nal (in tər′nəl) 1 inner; on the inside: *internal injuries, the internal parts of a machine.* 2 having to do with things that go on inside a country or group: *internal politics. The organization was troubled by internal squabbles.* *adj.* **—in·ter′nal·ly,** *adv.*

in·ter·na·tion·al (in′tər nash′ə nəl) between or among nations; involving more than one nation: *an international agreement. All countries are governed by international law.* *adj.* **—in′ter·na′tion·al·ly,** *adv.*

In·ter·net (in′tər net′) a huge computer network that links many smaller networks around the world. You can send and receive e-mail, find information, and shop or do banking on the Internet. Its name is often shortened to **the Net.** *n.*

in·ter·plan·e·tar·y (in′tər plan′ə ter′ē) between planets: *interplanetary gases, interplanetary travel.* *adj.*

in·ter·po·late (in tər′pə lāt′) in mathematics, insert intermediate values into a series. *v.,* **in·ter·po·lat·ed, in·ter·po·lat·ing.** **—in·ter′po·la′tion,** *n.*

in·ter·pret (in tər′prit) 1 translate a speaker's words into another language: *Juanita interpreted for us so we could converse with our Spanish visitors.* 2 understand according to your own judgment; attach a meaning to: *I'd interpret his silence as a "yes."* 3 explain the meaning of: *to interpret a coded message.* 4 perform so as to bring out the meaning or special feel of: *The actor interpreted the part of the detective with wonderful skill.* 5 work as a guide on a nature trail or at some other tourist attraction explaining things or acting out history. *v.* **—in·ter′pre·ta′tion,** *n.* **—in·ter′pret·er,** *n.*

in·ter·ro·gate (in ter′ə gāt′) ask someone a lot of detailed questions: *The lawyer took two hours to interrogate the witness.* *v.,* **in·ter·ro·gat·ed, in·ter·ro·gat·ing.** **—in·ter′ro·ga′tion,** *n.*

in·ter·rog·a·tive (in′tə rog′ə tiv) asking a question: *an interrogative sentence. When* and *where* are **interrogative adverbs** or **interrogatives.** *adj. or n.*

Grammar Check . . . interrogatives

The interrogatives **who, why, when, where,** and **what** are called **the five W's.** Reporters often think of questions using the five W's to make sure they have included all the important information.

in·ter·rupt (in′tə rupt′) 1 break in on some action and cause it to stop: *A fire drill interrupted the lesson.* 2 begin talking when someone else is talking: *It is not polite to interrupt.* *v.* **—in′ter·rup′tion,** *n.*

in·ter·sect (in′tər sekt′) cross: *Portage and Main are two streets that intersect in Winnipeg.* An **intersection** is a place where two things cross, especially streets. *v.*

in·ter·sperse (in′tər spərs′) scatter or place here and there among other things: *periods of work interspersed with play. She interspersed amusing comments throughout her story.* *v.,* **in·ter·spersed, in·ter·spers·ing.**

in·ter·stel·lar (in′tər stel′ər) among or between the stars: *the vastness of interstellar space.* *adj.*

in·ter·twine (in′tər twīn′) twist around each other: *Two vines intertwined on the wall.* *v.,* **in·ter·twined, in·ter·twin·ing.**

in·ter·val (in′tər vəl) 1 the time or space between: *There is an interval of one hour between trains. There are trees at intervals of 10 m.* 2 in music, the difference in pitch between two tones. *n.*
at intervals, a now and then: *Stir the soup at intervals.* **b** here and there: *We saw farms at intervals along the way.*

in·ter·vene (in′tər vēn′) 1 come between: *Five weeks intervene between Labour Day and Thanksgiving.* 2 get involved so as to stop, correct, or settle something: *The girls' father intervened when the argument got nasty.* *v.,* **in·ter·vened, in·ter·ven·ing.** **—in′ter·ven′tion,** *n.*

a bat	e bed	i bid	o pot	u cup	th thin
ā cake	ē me	ī bite	ō go	ū rude	ᴛʜ then
ä bar	ə about	ər over	ô for	u̇ put	zh measure

in·ter·view (in′tər vyū′) 1 a planned conversation to talk over something special or get information: *My dad had an interview with the teacher about my work. The news reporter had an interview with the premier.* 2 an exact printed report or a broadcast of such a conversation. 3 meet and talk with, especially to obtain information: *The employer interviewed six people for the job before hiring any of them.* 1, 2 *n.*, 3 *v.* **—in′ter·view′er,** *n.*

in·ter·weave (in′tər wēv′) weave together: *He interwove the different coloured threads in a beautiful design. In her book she has interwoven the stories of two families.* *v.*, **in·ter·wove, in·ter·wov·en, in·ter·weav·ing.**

in·tes·tines (in tes′tənz) two tubelike parts of the alimentary canal below the stomach. Partly digested food passes from the stomach into the **small intestine,** where it is digested further and the nutrients are absorbed by the blood. The food then goes into the **large intestine** and out of the body as waste. *n.* **—in·tes′ti·nal,** *adj.*

in·ti·mate (in′tə mit) 1 very familiar and close; known very well: *an intimate friend.* 2 gained by close personal experience; deep or thorough: *an intimate understanding of the situation.* 3 personal; private: *intimate questions, an intimate conversation.* *adj.* **—in′ti·mate·ly,** *adv.* **—in′ti·ma·cy,** *n.*

in·tim·i·date (in tim′ə dāt′) make afraid or nervous; influence by fear: *They used threats to intimidate us. We were intimidated into silence.* *v.*, **in·tim·i·dat·ed, in·tim·i·dat·ing.** **—in·tim′i·da′tion,** *n.*

in·tol·er·a·ble (in tol′ə rə bəl) unbearable; so bad that you can't stand it: *intolerable pain.* *adj.*

in·tol·er·ant (in tol′ə rənt) 1 not tolerant; not willing to accept and respect those who disagree with you. 2 unable to handle a certain substance physically: *People who are lactose intolerant have trouble digesting milk products.* *adj.*

in·to·na·tion (in′tə nā′shən) the way in which a person uses his or her voice to emphasize words or to get across the meaning: *If the sentence "She's gone" is spoken with rising intonation it becomes a question.* *n.*

in·tox·i·cate (in tok′sə kāt′) make drunk or very excited: *Too much wine intoxicates people. The team was intoxicated by victory.* *v.*, **in·tox·i·cat·ed, in·tox·i·cat·ing.**

in·tra·mu·ral (in′trə myū′rəl) involving only the people within one school or college, not from different schools: *We have intramural sports during noon hour.* *adj.*

in·trep·id (in trep′id) fearless; very brave: *The intrepid explorers were not deterred by wild animals or freezing weather.* *adj.*

in·tri·cate (in′trə kit) with many twists and turns and tiny details; complicated: *an intricate plot, an intricate design, an intricate piece of machinery.* *adj.* **—in′tri·cate·ly,** *adv.* **—in′tri·ca·cy,** *n.*

in·trigue (in trēg′) 1 secret plotting; crafty dealings: *The royal palace was filled with intrigue.* 2 stir up someone's curiosity and interest: *The book's unusual title intrigued me.* 1 *n.*, 2 *v.*, **in·trigued, in·tri·guing.**

in·tro·duce (in′trə dyūs′ *or* in′trə dūs′) 1 tell others who someone is, to help them start getting to know each other: *Introduce me to your friend.* 2 bring in: *to introduce a new subject into the conversation, to introduce a new fashion or a new rule.* 3 begin; start: *He introduced his speech with a joke.* 4 put in; insert: *The doctor introduced a long tube into the man's throat.* *v.*, **in·tro·duced, in·tro·duc·ing.** **—in′tro·duc′to·ry** (in′trə duk′tə rē), *adj.*

in·tro·duc·tion (in′trə duk′shən) 1 the act of introducing: *The introduction of steel made skyscrapers easy to build. We were waiting for an introduction to her visitor.* 2 a beginning section that leads up to the main part: *This book has a ten-page introduction by the editor.* 3 something introduced; a thing brought into use: *Television was a later introduction than radio.* *n.*

in·trude (in trūd′) barge in; come in where you aren't expected or wanted: *Do not intrude on the privacy of your neighbours.* *v.*, **in·trud·ed, in·trud·ing.** **—in·trud′er,** *n.* **—in·tru′sion,** *n.*

in·tu·i·tion (in′tyū ish′ən *or* in′tū ish′ən) 1 a way of knowing or understanding things directly without being able to explain why: *Many of his decisions are guided by intuition.* 2 something known in this way; a feeling or hunch about something: *I had an intuition that the stranger was honest.* *n.* **—in·tu′i·tive,** *adj.*

🍁 **I·nu·it** (in′ū it *or* in′yū it) 1 an aboriginal people living mainly in the arctic regions of Canada and on the northwestern coasts of Alaska. They are the original inhabitants of the Arctic. The Inuit speak two main languages, **Inuktitut** (i nůk′tə tůt′) and **Inupiat** (i nū′pē at′). These languages have different dialects and different names among the various Inuit communities. 2 having to do with these people: *Inuit traditions, Inuit art.* 1 *pl.n*, *sing.* **I·nuk** (in′ůk), 2 *adj.*

USING WORDS . . . . Inuit

In Canada, the word **Inuit,** which means "the people," should be used instead of **Eskimo.** The word **Eskimo** comes from an old Algonquian word meaning "eaters of raw flesh," and is not used by the Inuit.

Inventions

Some Great Inventions	
1440	printing press
1590	microscope
1593	thermometer
1608	telescope
1712	steam engine
1822	camera
1858	refrigerator
1876	telephone
1895	radio
1903	airplane
1925	television
1946	electronic computer
1960	laser
1979	compact disc

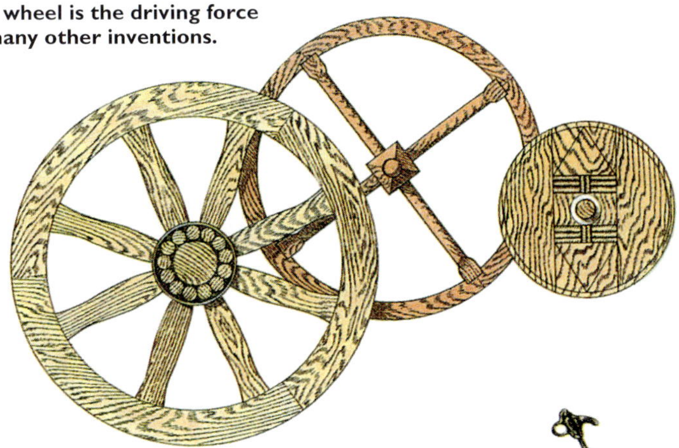

The wheel is the driving force of many other inventions.

The telescope made it possible to see and study objects in space, some of which were previously unknown.

Powered flight had been a dream since ancient times.

The zipper is only one of thousands of revolutionary inventions that we now take for granted. The zipper shown here is a very early version — inventors also keep improving their work.

in·un·date (in′ən dāt′) flood: *The river rose and inundated the valley. The newspaper office was inundated with letters from angry readers.* *v.,* **in·un·dat·ed, in·un·dat·ing.** —**in′un·da′tion,** *n.*

in·vade (in vād′) **1** enter with force or as an enemy; attack: *Soldiers invaded the country to conquer it. Disease invades the body.* **2** enter in great numbers: *Tourists invaded the city.* **3** break in on; violate: *to invade someone's privacy, to invade the rights of others.* *v.,* **in·vad·ed, in·vad·ing.** —**in·vad′er,** *n.*

in·va·lid[1] (in′və lid) a person who is weak because of sickness or injury. An invalid cannot get around and do things. *n.*

in·val·id[2] (in val′id) not valid; not acceptable; without value: *an invalid argument. Unless a cheque is signed, it is invalid.* *adj.*

in·val·u·a·ble (in val′yə bəl) priceless; very precious; more valuable than anyone can say: *Good health is an invaluable possession.* *adj.*

in·var·i·a·ble (in ver′ē ə bəl) the same every time: *When Javier painted, a huge mess was the invariable result.* *adj.* —**in·var′i·a·bly,** *adv.*

in·va·sion (in vā′zhən) **1** the act of entering by force and attacking: *There has been no invasion of England since 1066.* **2** the entry of a large number all at once: *an invasion of tourists.* **3** an intrusion or violation: *an invasion of someone's privacy.* *n.*

in·vent (in vent′) **1** make for the first time; think up something new: *Armand Bombardier invented the snowmobile when he was fifteen years old.* **2** make up; think up: *to invent an excuse.* *v.* —**in·ven′tion,** *n.* —**in·ven′tive,** *adj.* —**in·ven′tor,** *n.*

in·ven·to·ry (in′vən tȯr′ē) **1** a collection or list of things available to be sold or used: *The storekeeper had a sale to reduce his inventory. Renée has a whole inventory of excuses for different situations.* **2** make a detailed list of: *Some stores inventory their stock once a month.* **3** the process or job of making such a list or keeping it up to date: *The store is closed today for inventory.* 1, 3 *n., pl.* **in·ven·to·ries;** 2 *v.,* **in·ven·to·ried, in·ven·to·ry·ing.**
take inventory, check what you have and make a careful list of it: *The store is taking inventory this week. Jérome took inventory of all the choices open to him.*

a bat	e bed	i bid	o pot	u cup	th thin
ā cake	ē me	ī bite	ō go	ū rude	ᴛʜ then
à bar	ə about	ər over	ȯ for	u̇ put	zh measure

in·vert (in vərt′) 1 turn upside down: *He inverted the glass and the water ran out.* 2 switch the order or position of: *If you invert "I can," you have "Can I."* *v.* **—in·ver′sion,** *n.*

in·ver·te·brate (in vər′tə brit) 1 without a backbone. 2 an animal without a backbone. Worms, octopuses, and insects are invertebrates. 1 *adj.,* 2 *n.*

in·vest (in vest′) 1 buy something, such as land or shares in a company, that is expected to bring you more money in the future: *My parents have invested in Canada Savings Bonds; when they cash them in, they will get more money back than what they paid.* 2 spend for later benefit: *to invest time and energy in a worthwhile project.* *v.* **—in·vest′ment,** *n.* **—in·vest′or,** *n.*

in·ves·ti·gate (in ves′tə gāt′) look into something carefully to find out about it: *Detectives investigate crimes.* *v.,* **in·ves·ti·gat·ed, in·ves·ti·gat·ing.** **—in·ves′ti·ga′tion,** *n.* **—in·ves′ti·ga′tor,** *n.*

in·vig·or·ate (in vig′ə rāt′) fill with fresh energy: *He felt invigorated after his swim.* *v.,* **in·vig·or·at·ed, in·vig·or·at·ing.**

in·vin·ci·ble (in vin′sə bəl) impossible to defeat; unbeatable: *The tennis champion seemed invincible.* *adj.*

in·vis·i·ble (in viz′ə bəl) not visible; unable to be seen: *Germs are invisible to the naked eye. The mountain peak was invisible behind the cloud.* *adj.*

in·vite (in vīt′) 1 ask or tell someone politely to come to some place or to do something: *He invited his friends to the party. We invited her to use our pool anytime.* 2 make a polite request for: *The school newspaper invites submissions from each class.* 3 attract; tend to cause: *The story invites some questions. Carelessness invites trouble.* *v.,* **in·vit·ed, in·vit·ing.** **—in′vi·ta′tion,** *n.*

in·vit·ing (in vī′ting) attractive; tempting: *The soft bed was most inviting to the tired traveller.* *adj.*

in·voice (in′vois) 1 a detailed bill, especially for things ordered by mail or for work done by someone: *The guy who built our deck gave us an invoice, but we haven't paid it yet.* 2 put on an invoice: *Has that order been invoiced?* 1 *n.,* 2 *v.,* **in·voiced, in·voic·ing.**

in·vol·un·tar·y (in vol′ən ter′ē) 1 forced; not done by a person's own free choice; unwilling: *He was threatened until he gave involuntary consent to the plan.* 2 happening by itself, without the person planning or thinking about it: *Breathing is mainly involuntary.* *adj.* **—in·vol′un·tar′i·ly,** *adv.*

in·volve (in volv′) 1 have as a necessary part or condition: *Babysitting involves a lot of responsibility.* 2 bring into a situation, especially a complicated or unpleasant one: *Don't involve me in your argument!* 3 take up the attention of; occupy: *She was completely involved in her book.* 4 **involved,** complicated. 1–3 *v.,* **in·volved, in·volv·ing;** 4 *adj.* **—in·volve′ment,** *n.*

in·vul·ner·a·ble (in vul′nə rə bəl) unable to be hurt: *The knight was invulnerable in his armour.* *adj.*

in·ward (in′wərd) 1 toward the inside or centre: *a passage leading inward* (*adv.*), *the inward parts of the body* (*adj.*). 2 in or into the mind or soul: *to look inward* (*adv.*). *She has an inward peace* (*adj.*). **Inwards** is another form for both adverb meanings. *adv. or adj.*

in·ward·ly (in′wərd lē) in your mind or soul; not openly; secretly: *He was inwardly pleased, but he said nothing.* *adv.*

i·o·dine (ī′ə dīn′) 1 a strong-smelling chemical element in the form of greyish black crystals. Iodine is used in medicine, photography, and dye-making. The human body needs a tiny amount to stay healthy, but more than that is poisonous. 2 a poisonous brown or purple liquid containing iodine, used as an antiseptic. *n.*

An atom has a nucleus of protons (positively charged), and neutrons (no charge). Spinning around this nucleus are the electrons (negatively charged) whose gain or loss makes an ion.

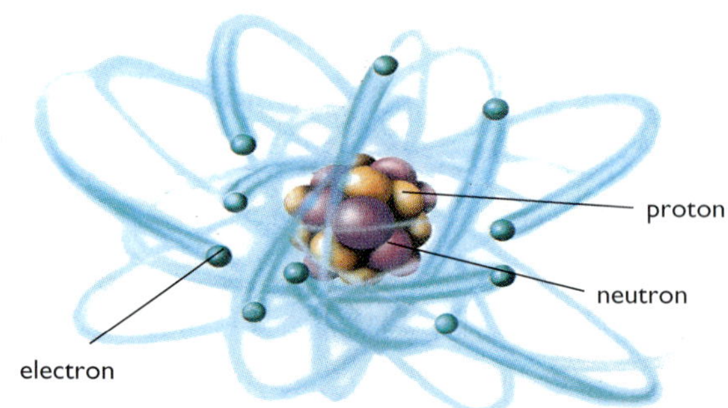

i·on (ī′on) an atom or group of atoms that has either lost or gained one or more electrons. **Positive ions** are formed by the loss of electrons; **negative ions** are formed by the gain of electrons. To **ionize** a substance is to cause it to rearrange itself into ions. *n.*

-ion a suffix that makes nouns out of verbs and adjectives. It can mean: 1 the act of. *Correction* is the act of correcting something. 2 something that does the action. A *connection* can be something that connects things. 3 something that receives the action. A *possession* is something you possess. 4 the result of action. A *reflection* is the image that results from reflecting. 5 the fact or quality of being a certain way. *Precision* is the quality of being precise. 6 something that is a certain way. A *superstition* is a belief that is superstitious.

i·on·o·sphere (ī on′ə sfēr′) a region of the earth's atmosphere above the stratosphere, containing many ions and free electrons produced by radiation from the sun and cosmic rays. Radio waves can travel long distances through the ionosphere. *n.*

IOU or **I.O.U.** (ī′ ō′ yū′) *Informal.* a piece of paper that you sign to say that you owe somebody a sum of money: *Arnie gave me an IOU for five dollars.* It means "I owe you." *n.,* **IOUs** or **I.O.Us.**

IQ or **I.Q.** (ī′ kyū′) *abbreviation for* **intelligence quotient,** a score that is supposed to measure certain kinds of intelligence according to a special test. A score of 100 is considered average.

ire (īr) anger. An angry person is **irate** (ī rāt′). *n.*

i·ris (ī′ris) **1** a plant with sword-shaped leaves and large flowers with some of the petals drooping. **2** the coloured part around the pupil of your eye. *n.*

irk (ərk) annoy; disgust; bore: *It irks us to wait for people who are always late.* *v.* **—irk′some,** *adj.*

i·ron (ī′ərn) **1** a chemical element and useful metal, from which tools, machinery, and many other things are made. Steel is made from iron. **2** an electrical appliance with a flat surface that heats up, for smoothing clothes. It used to be made of this metal. **3** smooth with an iron: *My dad irons his own shirts.* **4** some other thing made of iron or steel, such as a golf club with a metal head. **5** firm; hard; strong: *an iron constitution, an iron will.* **6** **irons,** *pl.* chains or bands of iron that used to be put on the arms and legs of prisoners. 1, 2, 4, 6 *n.,* 3 *v.,* 5 *adj.*

i·ro·ny (ī′rə nē) **1** a way of expressing something more powerfully or humorously by actually saying the opposite; sarcasm. Naming a snail "Speedy" would be irony. **2** something which is the opposite of what would be expected: *It was an amusing irony when a fake diamond was stolen instead of the real one.* *n., pl.* **i·ro·nies.** **—i·ron′ic** (ī ron′ik), *adj.* **—i·ron′i·cal·ly,** *adv.*

Ir·o·quois (ēr′ə kwȧ′) **1** in former times, a group of six First Nations spread across southern Québec and Ontario, who joined together as allies: the Mohawk, Oneida, Onondaga, Cayuga, Seneca, and Tuscarora. **2** having to do with these people. 1 *n,* 2 *adj.*

ir·ra·tion·al (i rash′ə nəl) **1** not rational; not based on any good reason: *an irrational fear of the number 13.* **2** unable to think and reason clearly: *His anger had made him irrational.* *adj.*

ir·reg·ular (i reg′yə lər) **1** not even; not smooth, straight, or steady: *irregular breathing. Nunavut has a very irregular border.* **2** not predictable; not following a set pattern or schedule: *irregular behaviour, irregular mail delivery, an irregular verb form.* **3** unusual or remarkable, especially in a disturbing way: *irregular goings-on.* *adj.* **—ir·reg′u·lar′i·ty,** *n.*

> **Grammar ✓Check . . irregular plurals**
>
> Many English words form plurals by adding **-s** or **-es**: *books, buses.*
> Some words have irregular plurals: *children, deer, moose, geese, loaves, people, men, mice, feet.*
> Can you think of any other irregular plurals?

ir·rel·e·vant (i rel′ə vənt) **1** not to the point; off the topic: *He interrupted the discussion several times with irrelevant remarks about the weather.* **2** not mattering; not meaningful or important: *As soon as he saw that his children were in danger, everything else seemed irrelevant.* *adj.* **—ir·rel′e·vant·ly,** *adv.* **—ir·rel′e·vance,** *n.*

ir·re·sist·i·ble (ēr′i zis′tə bəl) so strong or so attractive that you cannot resist: *an irresistible desire to laugh. That Black Forest cake looks irresistible.* *adj.*

ir·res·o·lute (i rez′ə lūt′) unable to make up your mind; not sure of what you want; hesitating: *An irresolute person makes a poor leader.* *adj.* **—ir·res′o·lute·ly,** *adv.* **—ir·res′o·lute·ness,** *n.*

ir·re·spon·si·ble (ēr′i spon′sə bəl) not thinking or caring enough about the consequences of your actions: *It is irresponsible to leave broken glass on the floor.* *adj.* **—ir·re·spon′si·bly,** *adv.* **—ir′re·spon′si·bil′i·ty,** *n.*

ir·rev·er·ent (i rev′ə rənt) not reverent; disrespectful, especially by poking fun at what others take seriously. *adj.* **—ir·rev′er·ent·ly,** *adv.* **—ir·rev′er·ence,** *n.*

ir·re·vers·i·ble (ēr′i vər′sə bəl) unable to be changed back to the way it was: *irreversible damage, an irreversible decision.* *adj.*

ir·ri·gate (ēr′ə gāt′) bring water to an area of land using ditches, pipes, sprinklers, etc.: *Farmers irrigate dry land to make crops grow better.* *v.,* **ir·ri·gat·ed, ir·ri·gat·ing.** **—ir′ri·ga′tion,** *n.*

a bat	e bed	i bid	o pot	u cup	th thin
ā cake	ē me	ī bite	ō go	ū rude	ᴛʜ then
ȧ bar	ə about	ər over	ȯ for	u̇ put	zh measure

ir·ri·tate (ēr′ə tāt′) 1 make impatient or angry; annoy: *The boy's silly questions irritated his mother. Flies irritate horses.* A person who is easily irritated is **irritable.** 2 make unnaturally sensitive or sore: *Some soaps irritate the skin.* *v.,* **ir·ri·tat·ed, ir·ri·tat·ing.** —**ir′ri·ta′tion,** *n.*

–ish *a suffix meaning:* 1 sort of or sort of like. *Greenish* means "sort of green." *Fallish* means "sort of like fall." 2 having to do with a particular people or their language: *Polish, Scottish.*

Is·lam (is lȧm′) the religion of Muslims, based on the Qur'an, the holy book containing God's message to the prophet Muhammad. The **five pillars of Islam** are the main religious duties of Muslims: declaring their faith, praying, giving to the poor, fasting, and pilgrimage. *n.* —**Is·lam′ic,** *adj*

is·land (ī′lənd) 1 a body of land smaller than a continent and completely surrounded by water. A person who lives on an island is an **islander.** 2 anything separate from its surroundings: *There's a traffic island at the busy intersection for people needing a place to wait while crossing.* *n.*

isle (īl) a poetic word for "island." *n.*

–ism *a suffix meaning:* 1 a system of ideas and practices. *Federalism* is the system that a federation, such as Canada, is based on. 2 an action. *Baptism* is the action of baptizing. 3 a quality or condition. *Heroism* is the quality of being heroic. 4 a disorder. *Alcoholism* is the disease of someone who is addicted to alcohol.

is·n't (iz′ənt) is not.

i·so·bar (ī′sə bȧr′) a line on a weather map connecting places that have the same average air pressure. *n.*

i·so·late (ī′sə lāt′) separate from others or from each other; keep alone: *The prison guards isolated the prisoner who had attacked his cellmate.* *v.,* **i·so·lat·ed, i·so·lat·ing.** —**i′so·la′tion,** *n.*

i·sos·ce·les (ī sos′ə lēz′) describing a triangle with two sides of equal length. *adj.*

is·sue (ish′yū) 1 one publishing of a magazine or newspaper: *Did you read the March issue of* Canadian Geographic *magazine?* 2 put out; publish: *This magazine is issued every week.* 3 something that is being discussed or that needs to be settled: *We would like to make a trip to Victoria this summer, but cost is an issue.* 4 give out: *to issue a command. Heavy boots were issued to all the workers.* 5 come or go out: *Smoke was issuing from the chimney.* 6 something that is put out or that comes out: *a new issue of postage stamps, an issue of blood from a wound.* 1, 3, 6 *n.,* 2, 4, 5 *v.,* **is·sued, is·su·ing.**
at issue, in question; to be considered or decided; likely to be affected: *What is at issue in this meeting?*
make an issue of, treat as a problem or as a matter for argument: *Do you have to make an issue of every little thing?*
take issue, disagree: *I take issue with you on that point.*

–ist *a suffix meaning:* 1 a person who does or makes. A *tourist* is a person who goes on *tours.* 2 a person with special knowledge or skill. A *biologist* is a person who knows about *biology.* A *pianist* is a person who is skilled on the *piano.* 3 one who believes in. An *idealist* is a person who believes in *idealism.*

isth·mus (is′məs) a narrow strip of land, with water on both sides, connecting two larger bodies of land: *The Isthmus of Panama connects North and South America.* *n.*

i·tal·ic (i tal′ik) 1 describing type whose letters slant to the right: *This is italic type.* 2 **italics,** *pl.* type whose letters slant to the right: *Put the title in italics.* When you put something in italics, you **italicize** it. 1 *adj.,* 2 *n.*

WORD HISTORY........italic

Italic type was introduced by printers in Venice, Italy, in the 1600s. It was named *italic* to distinguish it from the upright letters of **roman** type.

itch (ich) 1 a ticklish, prickling feeling in your skin that makes you want to scratch. 2 have or cause this feeling: *Mosquito bites itch. My finger itches.* 3 a restless, eager desire: *She always had an itch to get out and explore.* 4 have such a desire: *He was itching to find out their secret.* 1, 3 *n.,* 2, 4 *v.* —**itch′y,** *adj.*

i·tem (ī′təm) 1 an individual thing or article: *The list had twelve items on it.* 2 a piece of news: *Your new haircut has become quite an item around the school.* *n.*

i·tem·ize (ī′tə mīz′) list separately, item by item: *The storekeeper itemized the bill to show each article and its cost.* *v.,* **i·tem·ized, i·tem·iz·ing.**

it'll (it′əl) it will.

its (its) the possessive form of **it;** belonging to it: *The cat chased its tail.* *adj.*

it's (its) 1 it is: *It's my turn.* 2 it has: *It's been a beautiful day.*

CONFUSABLES....its/it's

its means "belonging to it": *The dog chased its tail.*
it's means "it is": *It's almost four o'clock.*

Ivory

Many countries are trying to protect ivory-bearing animals like elephants from being killed for their ivory tusks. Wildlife refuges, laws against hunting, and restrictions on the ivory trade may help stop the decline in the numbers of these animals.

Male Indian elephants have tusks.

Both male and female African elephants have tusks.

–ity *a suffix meaning* a condition or quality. *Sincerity* is the quality of being *sincere.*

–ive *a suffix* that makes an adjective out of a verb. *Co-operative* means "that co-operates." *Active* means "that acts."

I've (īv) I have.

i•vo•ry (ī′və rē) **1** the hard, whitish substance that the tusks of elephants and walruses are made of. Because ivory is easy to carve and can be used to make many kinds of beautiful ornaments, these animals have been overhunted. **2** creamy white. 1, 2 *n.,* 2 *adj.*

i•vy (ī′vē) **1** a climbing or trailing plant with smooth, shiny evergreen leaves. **2** any similar-looking plant, such as poison ivy. *n., pl.* **i•vies.**

–ize *a suffix* that makes a verb out of a noun or adjective. Verbs in *-ize* usually refer to actions that change the state or condition of something: *legalize* means "make something legal"; *crystallize* means "turn into crystals"; *rubberize* means "treat or coat with rubber." Other *-ize* verbs simply mean "make or do"; *apologize* means "to make an apology"; *criticize* means "to make a criticism."

Jj

j or **J** (jā) 1 the tenth letter of the English alphabet, or the sound that it stands for. 2 the tenth thing in a list. *n., pl.* **j's** or **J's.**

J *symbol for* joule, an SI unit.

jab (jab) 1 stick something pointed into; poke: *He jabbed his fork into the potato.* 2 the act of sticking with something pointed; a poke: *She gave him a jab with her elbow.* 1 *v.,* **jabbed, jab·bing;** 2 *n.*

jab·ber (jab′ər) 1 talk very fast or foolishly; chatter. 2 very fast or foolish talk; chatter. 1 *v.,* 2 *n.*

jack (jak) 1 a device for raising heavy things a short distance. It may be used to raise one end of a car in order to change a tire. 2 lift or push up with a jack: *to jack up a car.* 3 a playing card with a picture of a palace servant on it. It ranks just below a queen. 4 a spiky piece of metal or plastic used with a small rubber ball in the game of **jacks.** You try to throw the pieces up and catch them with one hand while bouncing and catching the ball with the other hand. 5 a place to plug something in, especially a phone. 1, 3–5 *n.,* 2 *v.*
jack up, *Informal.* raise prices, wages, etc.: *Stores jacked up many prices this month.*

jack·al (jak′əl) a wild dog of Asia, Africa, and southeastern Europe, with a bushy tail, a pointed nose, and usually greyish yellow or brown hair. Jackals feed mostly on animals they find dead. *n.*

jack·et (jak′it) 1 a short coat. 2 an outer covering: *a book jacket.* *n.*

jack·fish (jak′fish′) another name for the **pike,** a common Canadian fish. *n., pl.* **jack·fish** or **jack·fish·es.**

jack·ham·mer (jak′ham′ər) a noisy, powerful drill used to break up rock or cement. *n.*

jack–in–the–box (jak′in thə boks′) a toy shaped like a box with a figure inside. Turning a musical crank opens the lid, causing the figure to pop up. *n., pl.* **jack-in-the-box·es.**

jack–in–the–pul·pit (jak′ in ᴛʜə pu̇l′pit) a woodland plant having one long greenish petal that arches up over a spike of tiny flowers. *n.*

jack–knife (jak′nīf′) 1 a large, strong pocketknife. 2 fold or double up like a jack-knife: *The car and its trailer jack-knifed on the icy highway.* 3 a dive which you perform by bending to touch your toes in the air and then straightening out again before hitting the water. 1, 3 *n., pl.* **jack-knives;** 2 *v.,* **jack-knifed, jack-knif·ing.**

According to legend, the jack-o'-lantern is named after a man called Jack, who had committed many bad deeds and had to walk the earth forever, carrying his lantern.

jack–o'–lan·tern (jak′ə lan′tərn) a pumpkin hollowed out and cut to look like a face, lit up by a candle inside and used as a Halloween decoration. *n.*

jack pine (jak′ pīn′) a pine tree of North America. Jack pine cones usually stay tightly closed. They release their seeds only when there is high heat, such as in a forest fire.

jack·pot (jak′pot′) a large pool of prize money that keeps increasing until someone wins it.
hit the jackpot, have a stroke of very good luck; have great success or gain. *n.*

jack–rab·bit (jak′rab′it) a large hare of western North America, with very long ears and long back legs. *n.*

Ja·cuz·zi (jə kū′zē) *a trademark for* a large indoor bathtub that makes hot water swirl around you when you sit in it. *n.*

This finely carved jade pot was made in the 1700s, to hold brushes used in Chinese writing.

jade (jād) a hard stone, usually green or white, used for jewellery and ornaments. *n.*

jag·ged (jag′id) with sharp points sticking out; unevenly cut or torn: *We cut our bare feet on the jagged rocks.* *adj.*

jag·uar (jag′wär) a large wild cat having yellowish brown fur with black spots. Jaguars live in the jungles of Central and South America. *n.*

jail (jāl) **1** a place where people are kept locked up while waiting to be tried in court or as punishment for a minor offence. The person in charge is called a **jailer.** **2** put in jail; keep in jail. 1 *n.,* 2 *v.*

Jain (jīn) **1** a follower of the teachings and practices of **Mahavira** (mä′hə vē′rə), who lived in the 500s BCE, around the same time as Buddha. Jains believe in reincarnation and lead a very simple lifestyle. Because they are against any form of violence against any living creature, they are vegetarian. **2** having to do with the Jains or their religion. 1 *n.,* 2 *adj.* **—Jain′ism,** *n.*

jam[1] (jam) fruit boiled with sugar until it forms a thick, sweet mixture: *raspberry jam.* *n.* **—jam′my,** *adj.*

jam[2] (jam) **1** push, press, or squeeze with force: *They jammed us all into one bus. She jammed on the brakes.* **2** crush by squeezing: *I jammed my fingers in the door.* **3** block up by crowding: *The river was jammed with logs.* **Jam-packed** means "completely filled up." **4** a mass of people or things crowded together so that they cannot move freely: *a traffic jam.* **5** stick or catch so as not to work properly: *The window has jammed. The key broke off and jammed the lock.* **6** *Informal.* a tight spot or difficulty: *What a jam! I was locked out, it was pouring rain, and no neighbours were home.* **7** make music together casually or for fun: *After practising for the concert the band members jammed for a while.* 1–3, 5, 7 *v.,* **jammed, jam·ming;** 4, 6 *n.*

jan·gle (jang′gəl) **1** make a loud, clanging noise: *The pots and pans jangled in the kitchen. She jangled a bell.* **2** a loud, clanging noise: *the jangle of the alarm clock.* **3** make tense or strained: *Their continual complaints jangled her nerves.* 1, 3 *v.,* **jan·gled, jan·gling;** 2 *n.*

jan·i·tor (jan′ə tər) a person hired to clean a building and do minor repairs; caretaker. *n.*

Jan·u·ar·y (jan′yə wer′ē *or* jan′yū er′ē) the first month of the year. January has 31 days. *n.*

WORD HISTORY........ January

What do janitors have to do with January? In Latin, **janitor** meant "doorkeeper" — Janus was the Roman god of doors. He had two faces, one looking forward and one looking backward, to watch those entering and exiting. So the first month — the door to the new year — was named after him.

jar[1] (jär) a deep container made of glass or clay with a wide mouth and usually a lid: *a jar of jam, a cookie jar.* *n.*

jar[2] (jär) **1** shake something roughly: *The passengers were jarred by the bumpy ride.* **2** have a harsh, unpleasant effect on; send a shock through the ears, nerves, feelings, etc.: *The children's playful shouts jarred his nerves.* **3** clash: *We did not get on well together; our opinions always jarred.* **4** a hard shake or a shock. 1–3 *v.,* **jarred, jar·ring;** 4 *n.*

jar·gon (jär′gən) **1** language that fails to communicate because it is full of long or fancy words and very complicated sentences. **2** the technical words of a special group or profession: *medical jargon, computer jargon.* *n.*

Grammar Check .... jargon

Whether you are speaking or writing, remember to use words your audience will understand. If, for example, you are explaining a computer game to someone who has never played, you should avoid **jargon** such as "warping," or "jump block." Either find some simple English words to replace them, or explain to your audience what the technical words mean.

jas·per (jas′pər) a coloured quartz, usually with patches of red, yellow, brown, or green. It is used as a gemstone. *n.*

jaun·dice (jon′dis) **1** a condition that turns the skin and the white part of the eyes a yellowish colour, caused when the liver is not working properly. Newborn babies often have a kind of jaundice that soon goes away by itself. **2** **jaundiced,** envious or resentful about something. 1 *n.,* 2 *adj.*

jaunt (jont) **1** a short trip, especially for pleasure. **2** take a short trip. 1 *n.,* 2 *v.*

jaun·ty (jon′tē) carefree and light: *She walks with a jaunty step.* *adj.,* **jaun·ti·er, jaun·ti·est.** **—jaun′ti·ly,** *adv.*

jave·lin (jav′lin) a light spear. The **javelin throw** is a track-and-field event won by the person who throws the javelin the farthest. *n.*

a bat	e bed	i bid	o pot	u cup	th thin
ā cake	ē me	ī bite	ō go	ū rude	ᴛʜ then
ä bar	ə about	ər over	ò for	ù put	zh measure

jaw (jo) **1** Also, **jawbone**, either of two skull bones that hold your teeth and together form the framework of your mouth. The lower jaw is movable; the upper jaw is fixed. **2** the lower part of your face. **3** **jaws,** *pl.* anything that grips, swallows, or forms an opening like a mouth: *the jaws of a canyon, the jaws of a pair of pliers.* *n.*

jay (jā) a bird found in North America and Europe, related to the crow. Jays are often brightly coloured, with a crest and a long tail. They are noisy birds and make many different sounds. Two kinds of jay found in Canada are the **Canada jay** and the **blue jay.** *n.*

jay·walk (jā′wok′) *Informal.* walk across a street where there is no light or crosswalk or without paying attention to traffic. *v.* **—jay′walk′er,** *n.*

jazz (jaz) **1** a light-hearted style of music with a strong, fast, changeable rhythm, that originated among the blacks of the southern United States. Jazz musicians often make up their parts as they go along, or break into a complicated solo in the middle of a band piece. **2** **jazz up**, make fancier or more interesting. 1 *n.,* 2 *v.* **—jazz′y,** *adj.*

jeal·ous (jel′əs) **1** afraid that someone you love may prefer someone else: *When my sister sees Dad holding the new baby, she gets jealous.* **2** envious; bitter toward someone because you wish you had what that person has: *Justin is jealous of your good grades.* **3** watchful in keeping or protecting something: *She kept a jealous guard over her little sister.* *adj.* **—jeal′ous·ly,** *adv.* **—jeal′ous·y,** *n.*

jeans (jēnz) casual pants made of a strong cotton cloth called denim. *pl.n.*

Jeep (jēp) *a trademark for* a small but powerful car that can be driven on very rough land. *n.*

jeer (jēr) **1** make fun of in a very rude or unkind way: *Do not jeer at the mistakes or misfortunes of others.* **2** a mocking or insulting remark. 1 *v.,* 2 *n.*

Je·ho·vah's Wit·ness·es (jə hō′vəz wit′nis iz) a religion founded by Charles T. Russell in the United States in the 1870s. Jehovah's Witnesses believe that a person's own faith and conscience are more important than the rules of governments, and that God will soon judge the world and make it new again. **Jehovah** is one of the names of God in the Bible.

jell (jel) **1** become clear and definite: *Once we wrote them down our ideas began to jell.* **2** become a closely united group: *The student council has jelled well this year.* *v.*

jel·ly (jel′ē) **1** a food that is liquid when hot but rather firm when cold. Jelly can be made by boiling fruit juice and sugar together, by cooking bones and meat in water, or by using a stiffening ingredient like gelatin. **2** any substance like jelly: *petroleum jelly.* **3** **jellied,** prepared in or covered with jelly: *a jellied salad, jellied fruit slices.* 1, 2 *n., pl.* **jel·lies;** 3 *adj.*

jel·ly·bean or **jelly bean** (jel′ē bēn′) a small, bean-shaped candy made of jelly, coated in different colours. *n.*

Most jellyfish have long, trailing tentacles with stinging hairs on them.

jel·ly·fish (jel′ē fish′) a boneless sea animal with a saucer-shaped body that looks like it is made of jelly. *n., pl.* **jel·ly·fish** or **jel·ly·fish·es.**

jeop·ard·ize (jep′ər dīz′) put in danger; risk; endanger: *Soldiers jeopardize their lives in war.* When you jeopardize something, you put it **in jeopardy.** *v.,* **jeop·ard·ized, jeop·ard·iz·ing.**

jerk (jərk) **1** a sudden, sharp pull or twist: *She gave the cord a jerk to start the gas lawn mower.* **2** pull or twist sharply and suddenly. **3** move with many sudden, sharp bumps or stops and starts: *The old wagon jerked along.* 1 *n.,* 2, 3 *v.* **—jerk′y,** *adj.*

jer·kin (jər′kən) a short, heavy, close-fitting outer vest worn by men in the 1500s and 1600s. *n.*

jerk·y (jər′kē) strips of spiced, salted dried beef. *n.*

jer·sey (jər′zē) **1** a top or pullover made of soft, stretchy cloth knitted by machine. **2** this cloth. **3** **Jersey**, a breed of dairy cattle that give very rich milk. *n., pl.* **jer·seys.**

jest (jest) a rather formal word for "joke." *n. or v.* **in jest,** in fun; not seriously: *His words were spoken in jest.*

jest·er (jes′tər) in the Middle Ages, an entertainer hired by a ruler or noble to do tricks and make jokes. *n.*

Je·sus (jē′zəs) Jesus Christ, the central figure of the Christian religion. Christians worship him as God and as the Saviour of humankind who died and rose again. *n.*

Jewellery

Jewellery has been made since prehistoric times, when bones and teeth of animals were used. Today's jewellery is mostly made of gems and precious metals.

a brooch made in Spain, around 1400 CE

This gold ring is a fine example of Viking craftwork

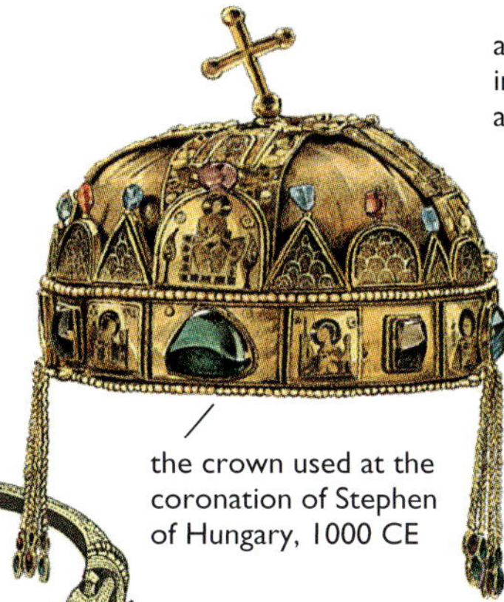

the crown used at the coronation of Stephen of Hungary, 1000 CE

a jewel probably made in the 800s, for Alfred, an English king

jet[1] (jet) 1 a stream of gas or liquid shot with force from a small opening: *A fountain sends up a jet of water.* 2 a spout or nozzle for sending out such a stream. 3 shoot out in a stream: *Water jetted from the broken pipe.* 4 an airplane driven by engines that work by forcing a powerful stream of air and gas in one direction under great pressure. This causes the plane to move very fast in the opposite direction. 1, 2, 4 *n.,* 3 *v.,* **jet·ted, jet·ting.**

jet[2] (jet) a hard, shiny black mineral used for making beads, buttons, and ornaments. *n.*

jet lag (jet′ lag′) a feeling of tiredness and confusion after travelling a long distance by plane and ending up in a very different time zone: *After the flight from India Chandra had a bad case of jet lag.*

Jet Ski (jet′ skē′) *a trademark for* a motorized craft with a ski on the bottom that lets it skim across water.

jet·ty (jet′ē) 1 a long barrier of stones or cement built out from the shore to break the force of the current or waves; it is also called a **breakwater.** 2 a long pier or dock. *n., pl.* **jet·ties.**

Jew (jū) 1 a person descended from the people of ancient Israel. 2 a person whose religion is Judaism. *n.* —**Jew′ish,** *adj.*

jew·el (jū′əl) 1 a precious stone; gem: *diamonds, rubies, and other jewels.* 2 a valuable ornament such as a brooch, ring, or necklace, made of precious metals like gold or silver and set with precious stones. Together they are called **jewellery** (jū′əl rē) and a person who makes or sells them is a **jeweller** (jū′əl ər). 3 a person or thing that is very precious. 4 make beautiful with jewels or with things like jewels: *a jewelled comb, a sky jewelled with stars.* 1–3 *n.,* 4 *v.,* **jew·elled** or **jew·eled, jew·el·ling** or **jew·el·ing.**

jib (jib) a triangular sail at the very front of a boat or ship. *n.*

jibe (jīb) *Informal.* be in harmony; agree: *There were no problems in forming the club, because they found that their ideas jibed very well.* **Jive** is another form of this word. *v.,* **jibed, jib·ing.**

jif·fy (jif′ē) *Informal.* a very short time; moment: *I'll be there in a jiffy.* *n., pl.* **jif·fies.**

jig[1] (jig) 1 a lively dance, or the music for it. 2 dance a jig. 1 *n.,* 2 *v.,* **jigged, jig·ging.**
the jig is up, it's all over; you are caught.

jig[2] (jig) 1 a fishing lure made of one or more hooks with pieces of bright metal attached. You bob it up or down or pull it through the water. 2 fish with a jig. 1 *n.,* 2 *v.,* **jigged, jig·ging.**

jig·gle (jig′əl) 1 shake or jerk slightly: *Please don't jiggle the desk when I'm trying to write.* 2 a slight shake; a light jerk. 1 *v.,* **jig·gled, jig·gling;** 2 *n.*

jig·saw (jig′so′) 1 short for **jigsaw puzzle,** a picture cut into irregular pieces that can be fitted together again. 2 a saw with a narrow blade used to make these puzzles because it can cut curves or irregular lines. *n.*

jin·gle (jing′gəl) 1 a sound like little bells ringing, or of coins or keys striking together. 2 make such a sound: *The sleigh bells jingled. He jingled the coins in his pocket.* 3 a short song with catchy words and rhythm, used in a radio or TV commercial. 1, 3 *n.,* 2 *v.,* **jin·gled, jin·gling.**

a bat	e bed	i bid	o pot	u cup	th thin
ā cake	ē me	ī bite	ō go	ū rude	ŦH then
ä bar	ə about	ər over	ȯ for	u̇ put	zh measure

jin·ja (jin′jə) a Shinto shrine, made up of an outer part called the **haiden,** and an inner part called the **hondon.** The hondon is entered only by priests. Most jinjas have a special entrance gate called a **torii** (tȯr′ē ē), made of two posts with a rafter on top that curves upward. *n.*

jinx (jingks) *Slang.* **1** a person or thing that is believed to bring bad luck: *He must be a jinx; we've lost every game since he joined the team.* **2** bring bad luck to. 1 *n.,* 2 *v.*

jit·ters (jit′ərz) *Slang.* great nervousness: *I've got the jitters about my piano recital tomorrow.* *pl.n.*
—jit′ter·y, *adj.*

job (job) **1** anything a person has to do: *It's my job to walk the dog.* **2** work done for pay; employment: *Her sister is hunting for a job.* **3** a piece of work done: *They did a lousy job painting the boat.* *n.* **—job′less,** *adj.*
on the job, at work; working.

jock·ey (jok′ē) **1** a person who rides horses in races. **2** manoeuvre so as to get an advantage: *The crews were jockeying their boats to get into the best position for the race.* 1 *n., pl.* **jock·eys;** 2 *v.,* **jock·eyed, jock·ey·ing.**
jockey for, try to get; compete for.

joc·u·lar (jok′yə lər) funny; joking: *a jocular mood.* *adj.*

jodh·purs (jod′pərz) pants that are very wide at the hips and then get much narrower and fit tightly below the knee. They are often used in horseriding. *n.*

jo·ey (jō′ē) *Informal.* in Australia, a young kangaroo. *n., pl.* **jo·eys.**

jog¹ (jog) **1** run at a slow, steady rate: *My mother goes jogging every day for exercise.* **2** a slow run. **3** shake or bump; nudge: *She jogged his elbow to get his attention.* **4** a shake, push, or nudge. 1, 3 *v.,* **jogged, jog·ging;** 2, 4 *n.* **—jog′ger,** *n.*
jog someone's memory, give someone a little reminder.

jog² (jog) **1** change direction suddenly and briefly: *The road jogs to the west just before our house and then continues north.* **2** a sudden brief change in direction: *a jog in the road.* *n.*

join (join) **1** bring or come together: *to join an island to the mainland by a bridge. The two roads join here.* **2** take part in something with others: *to join in a game. Join us for supper!* **3** become a member of: *She joined the chess club.* *v.*
join forces, a combine into one group. **b** work together.
join hands, a hold one another's hands. **b** co-operate; work together.

joint (joint) **1** the place where two parts are joined together, especially two bones that let you bend part of your body. Knees and elbows are joints. **2** make with parts connected in such a way as to allow bending or folding: *a jointed walking stick.* **3** one of the parts connected in this way: *The middle joint of my finger is about 2 cm long.* **4** involved in something together: *By our joint efforts we succeeded. My parents are joint owners of our house.* **5** *Slang.* a place or building, especially a cheap, shabby restaurant, bar, etc. **6** a large piece of meat for roasting. 1, 3, 5, 6 *n.,* 2 *v.,* 4 *adj.*
—joint′ly, *adv.*
out of joint, a out of place at the joint. **b** out of order; in bad condition. To **get your nose out of joint** is to get mad or sulky about something.

joist (joist) one of the parallel beams of wood or steel that support the boards of a floor or ceiling. *n.*

joke (jōk) **1** something said or done to make somebody laugh; something funny. **2** say or do funny things; try to make people laugh. **3** a person or thing that is laughed at or not taken seriously. 1, 3 *n.,* 2 *v.,* **joked, jok·ing.**

CONFUSABLES .... **joke**

A **joke** is something funny. It is often a story told to make someone laugh.

A **riddle** is something puzzling or hard to understand. It is often amusing as well, but not always.

jok·er (jō′kər) **1** a person who jokes a lot. **2** *Slang.* any person who has made you angry: *Who does that joker think he is?* **3** in some games, an extra playing card with a picture of a court jester on it. *n.*

jol·ly (jol′ē) **1** merry; very cheerful; full of fun. **2** *Informal.* raise a person's spirits or get him or her to do something by cheerful talk: *Maybe we can jolly her into taking us to a movie.* 1 *adj.,* **jol·li·er, jol·li·est;** 2 *v.* **jol·lied, jol·ly·ing.** **—jol′li·ty,** *n.*
get your jollies, *Slang.* get pleasure or excitement, especially in a foolish or mean way.

jolt (jōlt) **1** jerk; shock; shake: *to stop with a jolt. The bad news gave me quite a jolt* (*n.*). *The wagon jolted us when it went over the rocks* (*v.*). **2** move with a shock or jerk: *The car jolted forward.* 1, 2 *v.,* 1 *n.*

jos·tle (jos′əl) shove, push, or crowd against: *We were jostled by the impatient crowd at the entrance to the stadium.* *v.,* **jos·tled, jos·tling.**

jot (jot) 1 write briefly or quickly: *The clerk jotted down the order.* 2 a little bit; very small amount: *I don't care a jot.* 1 *n.,* 2 *v.,* **jot·ted, jot·ting.**

joule (jūl) an SI unit for measuring heat and other energy: *It takes one joule of energy to lift two golf balls through a height of one metre. Symbol:* J *n.*

jounce (jouns) shake up and down; bounce; bump; jolt: *The old car jounced along the rough road.* *v.,* **jounced, jounc·ing.**

jour·nal (jər′nəl) 1 a daily record of what happens, or of a person's thoughts and feelings. 2 a newspaper or magazine. *n.*

jour·nal·ism (jər′nə liz′əm) the work of finding out news and reporting it to the public, either in a newspaper or magazine or on radio or TV. *n.* **—jour′nal·ist,** *n.*

jour·ney (jər′nē) 1 a trip, especially a fairly long one: *a journey around the world.* 2 travel; take a trip: *We journeyed to the Yukon.* 1 *n., pl.* **jour·neys;** 2 *v.,* **jour·neyed, jour·ney·ing.**

In a joust, two knights would charge at each other and each would try to knock the other off his horse.

joust (joust *or* just) 1 a contest between two knights on horseback, armed with lances. 2 take part in one of these contests. 1 *n.,* 2 *v.* **—joust′er,** *n.*

jo·vi·al (jō′vē əl) good-natured and full of fun: *Santa Claus is pictured as a jovial old fellow.* *adj.*

> **WORD HISTORY........ jovial**
>
> **Jovial** comes from *Jove*, another name for the Roman god Jupiter. People born under the sign of the planet Jupiter were supposed to be cheerful.

jowl (joul) the flesh of the cheek and lower jaw when it hangs down. *n.*

joy (joi) 1 a deep, strong feeling of gladness or happiness: *She jumped for joy when she heard that her father had been set free.* 2 something that causes gladness or happiness: *The new baby was a joy to his parents.* *n.* **—joy′ful,** *adj.* **—joy′ous,** *adj.*

joy ride (joi′ rīd′) *Informal.* a ride in a car for fun, especially when it is driven recklessly or without the owner's permission. **—joy′-rid′ing,** *n. or adj.*

joy·stick (joi′stik′) a small upright lever that you use to control the movement of something on a computer screen, such as an icon or cursor. *n.*

Jr. *abbreviation for* Junior.

ju·bi·lant (jū′bə lənt) full of joy and showing it; rejoicing: *The people were jubilant when the war was over.* *adj.* **—ju′bi·lant·ly,** *adv.* **—ju′bi·la′tion,** *n.*

ju·bi·lee (jū′bə lē′) 1 a fiftieth anniversary: *a wedding jubilee.* 2 a joyful celebration: *a jubilee to mark the end of a war.* *n.*

Ju·da·ism (jū′dā iz′əm) the religion of the Jews, based on the teachings of Moses and the prophets as found in the Torah and Jewish Bible. Some Jews add to this the teaching of the rabbis contained in the Mishnah and Talmud, dating from 200 BCE to 50 CE. *n.*

judge (juj) 1 a government official whose job is to hear and decide cases in a law court. 2 a person chosen to settle a dispute or to decide who wins a contest. 3 do the work of a judge; settle or decide something: *to judge a criminal case, to judge an art contest.* 4 any person who tries to form an opinion of how good a thing is: *a good judge of dogs, a poor judge of poetry.* 5 form an opinion or estimate about: *to judge the quality of a piece of work, to judge the width of a doorway.* 6 blame; criticize: *You shouldn't judge him so harshly.* 1, 2, 4 *n.,* 3, 5, 6 *v.,* **judged, judg·ing.**

judg·ment or **judge·ment** (juj′mənt) 1 an opinion or estimate; a decision by any kind of judge: *In my judgment this song is better than the other one. We are still waiting to hear the judgment of the Supreme Court.* 2 the ability to form wise opinions; good sense: *She has good judgment when it comes to spending money.* 3 the act of judging. 4 criticism; blame: *Do not pass judgment on your neighbours.* A person who is quick to blame or criticize is **judgmental** (juj men′təl). *n.*

ju·di·cial (jū dish′əl) having to do with judges and courts of law: *The Attorney General is head of Canada's judicial system.* *adj.* **—ju·di′cial·ly,** *adv.*

ju·di·cious (jū dish′əs) wise; sensible; showing good judgment: *a judicious choice.* *adj.* **—ju·di′cious·ly,** *adv.*

a bat	e bed	i bid	o pot	u cup	th thin
ā cake	ē me	ī bite	ō go	ū rude	ᴛʜ then
à bar	ə about	ər over	ò for	ù put	zh measure

ju·do (jū′dō) a Japanese method of fighting without weapons by using the opponent's weight and strength against him or her. Judo is a modern form of **jujitsu.** *n.*

jug (jug) 1 a container for holding liquids. A jug usually has a handle and either a spout or a narrow neck. 2 *Slang.* jail; prison. *n.*

jug·gle (jug′əl) 1 keep several objects moving in the air at the same time by rapidly tossing them up in turn and catching them as they fall: *I can juggle three oranges at once.* 2 handle many different activities at once: *to juggle schoolwork, hockey, and trumpet lessons.* 3 change in order to cheat: *The dishonest bookkeeper juggled the accounts to hide her theft.* *v.,* **jug·gled, jug·gling.** —**jug′gler,** *n.*

jug·u·lar vein (jug′yə lər vān′) one of the two large veins in each side of the neck and head.

juice (jūs) 1 the flavourful liquid in fruits, vegetables, and meats: *the juice of a lemon, meat juices.* 2 a natural liquid in the body: *The juices of the stomach help to digest food.* *n.* —**juic′y,** *adj.*

ju·jit·su (jū jit′sū) a Japanese method of fighting without weapons by using the opponent's strength and weight against him or her. *n.*

> **WORD HISTORY........jujitsu**
>
> **Jujitsu** comes from a Japanese word *jujutsu* from *ju,* meaning "soft," and *jutsu,* meaning "art."

ju·jube (jū′jūb) a chewy candy made of fruit-flavoured gelatin. *n.*

juke·box (jūk′boks′) a machine that plays music after you select what song you want to hear and put coins in. *n.*

Ju·ly (jə lī′) the seventh month of the year. July has 31 days. *n.*

jum·ble (jum′bəl) 1 mix up or confuse: *She jumbled up everything in the drawer while hunting for her gloves.* 2 a confused mess or mix: *A jumble of boots and shoes lay in the doorway.* 1 *v.,* **jum·bled, jum·bling;** 2 *n.*

jum·bo (jum′bō) very big: *a jumbo ice-cream cone.* A **jumbo jet** carries several hundred passengers. 1 *n., pl.* **jum·bos;** 2 *adj.*

jump (jump) 1 spring up from the ground by pushing off with your feet: *Takako jumped off the porch.* 2 go over or get on something by springing in this way: *to jump a fence, to jump a train.* 3 cause to jump: *The rider jumped her horse over the stream.* 4 give a sudden jerk in surprise or fear: *I jumped when I heard the bang.* If you are nervous and easily startled, you are **jumpy.** 5 rise suddenly: *House prices have jumped.* 6 the act or fact of jumping: *a jump in prices. She crossed the room in two jumps.* 7 attack with a rush: *The robbers jumped the storekeeper.* 8 escape: *to jump ship, to jump bail, to jump prison.* 1–5, 7, 8 *v.,* 6 *n.*

have the jump on someone, be ahead of someone or have an advantage over someone.

jump at, accept eagerly and quickly: *to jump at a chance, to jump at an offer.*

jump on, *Informal.* criticize harshly. To **jump all over someone** means the same.

jump the gun, start too soon.

jump the track, leave the rails: *The train jumped the track.*

jump to conclusions, make a judgment without enough facts.

jump to it! *Informal.* be quick!

jump·er[1] (jum′pər) a person or thing that jumps. *n.*

jump·er[2] (jum′pər) a sleeveless dress, usually worn over a blouse. *n.*

jumping jack (jum′ping jak′) 1 a toy figure that can dance or jump when you pull a string or stick attached to it. 2 an exercise that imitates the movement of this toy. You throw your arms up over your head while jumping and landing with your feet outstretched; on the next jump, you bring your arms down and land with feet together again.

jump–start (jump′stârt′) 1 start a car engine whose battery is dead by giving it power from another car's battery. You connect the two batteries with special cables called **jumper cables.** 2 give something a powerful start, especially a new start to something that was failing: *The government jump-started the program by spending twice as much on it and hiring two experts to run it.* 3 a start given in this way. 1, 2 *v.,* 3 *n.*

jump·suit (jump′sūt′) a suit of clothing that combines a shirt and pants all in one piece. *n.*

junc·tion (jungk′shən) an action or place of joining or meeting: *the junction of two rivers.* A **railway junction** is a place where railway lines meet or cross. *n.*

June (jūn) the sixth month of the year. June has 30 days. *n.*

jun·gle (jung′gəl) land thickly covered with bushes, vines, and trees in a tropical climate; rain forest. The jungle is the habitat of a huge variety of living things. *n.*

jun·ior (jūn′yər) 1 having to do with younger people: *a junior tennis tournament. This is a junior*

dictionary. **2** of lower rank than some others: *the junior partner in a firm, a junior officer in the army.* **3** the younger, used after someone's name when he or she has the same name as someone older: *Walter Parker, Junior, is the son of Walter Parker, Senior.* **4** a person of lower rank. 1–3 *adj.,* 4 *n.*
be someone's junior, be younger than someone: *My sister is two years my junior.*

junior high school (jūn′yər hī′skūl′) Usually, grades seven and eight and sometimes nine; any school or division between elementary school and high school.

ju·ni·per (jū′nə pər) an evergreen shrub or tree with tiny, scalelike, overlapping leaves and small berrylike cones. *n.*

junk[1] (jungk) **1** worthless stuff; trash. **Junk food** is food that has little value for your body. **Junk mail** is advertising and other things delivered to your house that you don't want to read. **2** *Informal.* throw away as junk: *We junked the old garden chairs last fall.* 1 *n.,* 2 *v.*
—junk′y, *adj.*

junk[2] (jungk) a flat-bottomed Chinese sailing ship. *n.*

Jupiter is so huge that 1000 Earths could fit inside it. It spins faster than any of the other planets — a day lasts less than ten hours.

Ju·pi·ter (jū′pə tər) the largest planet, fifth from the sun. *n.*

ju·ris·dic·tion (jūr′is dik′shən) the right to exercise authority within a certain limited area: *The provinces have jurisdiction in the area of education. The judge said the case was outside her jurisdiction.* *n.*

ju·ry (jū′rē) a group of people, called **jurors,** chosen to listen to a case in a court of law and give a decision based on the evidence: *The question put before a jury is, "Is the prisoner guilty as charged or not?"* *n., pl.* **ju·ries.**

just (just) **1** holding to what is right; honest and fair: *a just reward, a just decision, a just ruler.* **2** exactly: *That is just a metre.* **3** very close; immediately: *a picture just above the fireplace. She arrived just after lunch.* **4** a very short time ago: *He just left.* **5** barely: *I just made it.* **6** only; merely: *just an ordinary man.* **7** *Informal.* positively: *The weather is just glorious.* 1 *adj.,* 2–7 *adv.*
just now, a very short time ago: *I saw her just now.*
just so, exactly proper and correct: *She insisted on everything being just so.*

jus·tice (jus′tis) **1** just treatment; fair dealing: *Judges should have a sense of justice.* **2** the fact of being just: *Everyone recognized the justice of her decision.* **3** a judge. It is capitalized if used as part of a name: *a panel of five justices. The case was heard by Justice Friedman.* *n.*
do justice to, a treat fairly. **b** see or show all the best or most important points of: *to do justice to a subject in a speech.* **c** show the proper appreciation for: *The crowd's weak applause did not do justice to her performance.*
do yourself justice, do as well as you really can do: *He did not do himself justice on the test.*
justice of the peace, an official with some of the same powers as a judge.

jus·ti·fy (jus′tə fī′) **1** give a good reason for: *The fine quality of the cloth justifies its high cost. Can you justify your answer?* **2** clear of blame or guilt: *She tried to justify herself by saying the whole thing was Habib's fault.* *v.,* **jus·ti·fied, jus·ti·fy·ing.** **—jus′ti·fi′a·ble,** *adj.*
—jus′ti·fi·ca′tion, *n.*

jut (jut) stick out: *a ledge jutting out from the side of the cliff. The pier juts out from the shore into the water.* *v.,* **jut·ted, jut·ting.**

jute (jūt) a strong fibre used for making rope and rough cloth. It is made from tropical plants of India and neighbouring countries. *n.*

ju·ve·nile (jū′və nīl′ *or* jū′və nəl) **1** immature: *juvenile behaviour.* **2** a young person. **3** having to do with children and young people: *a juvenile court.* 1, 3 *adj.,* 2 *n.*

jux·ta·pose (juk′stə pōz′) put two very different things side by side to create an effect: *Wendy juxtaposed drawings of flowers with her poems about war.* *v.,* **jux·ta·posed, jux·ta·pos·ing.** **—jux′ta·po·si′tion,** *n.*

Kk

k or **K** (kā) 1 the eleventh letter of the English alphabet, or the sound that it stands for. The sound of *k* in *kayak* is the same as the sound of *c* in *cat*. 2 the eleventh thing in a list. *n., pl.* **k's** or **K's.**

k *symbol for* kilo-.

K *symbol for:* 1 karat, a unit used to show how much gold there is in a mixture. Pure gold is 24 K. 2 kilobyte, a unit of computer memory. 3 Kelvin, a unit of temperature.

Kah•na•wa•ke (gȧ′nə wȧ′gē) 1 a First Nations people living near Montréal. 2 having to do with these people. 1 *n.,* 2 *adj.*

Kai•nai (kī′nī) 1 a First Nations people living in Alberta. 2 their language. 3 having to do with these people or their language. 1, 2 *n.,* 3 *adj.*

kai•ser (kī′zər) a large crusty bun often used for making sandwiches. *n.*

kale (kāl) a kind of cabbage that has loose leaves instead of a firm head. It looks like spinach. *n.*

ka•lei•do•scope (kə lī′də skōp′) a tube with an eyepiece at one end, and bits of coloured glass and two or more mirrors inside. As you look inside and turn the tube, the mirrors reflect changing coloured patterns. —**ka•lei′do•scop′ic** (kə lī′də skop′ik), *adj.*

ka•mi (kȧ′mē) the gods of Shintoism and their powers. A **kamidana** (kȧ′mē dȧ′nə) is a simple shrine inside a home, for daily worship. *pl.n.*

ka•mik (kȧ′mik) a soft, high, waterproof boot traditionally made of sealskin or caribou hide, worn in the Arctic. **Kamik** is the Inuktitut word; **mukluk** is the Yupik word for the same thing. *n.*

kan•ga•roo (kang′gə rü′) an animal of Australia and New Guinea with small forelegs and very strong hind legs, which give it great leaping power. The female kangaroo has a pouch in front to carry its young. *n., pl.* **kan•ga•roos** or **kan•ga•roo.**

Kan•i•en'•ke•ha (kan yən′kā′ha′) 1 a First Nations people living in Ontario and Québec. 2 their language. 3 having to do with these people or their language. 1, 2 *n.,* 3 *adj.*

ka•put (kə pu̇t′) *Informal.* broken or no longer working: *The washing machine is kaput; we'll have to call for repairs.* *adj.*

ka•ra (kȧr′ə) the steel bracelet worn by all baptized Sikhs. *n.*

ka•ra•o•ke (ker′ē ō′kē) the act of singing along into a microphone with a music video shown on a special machine. The sound of the original singing on the video is erased, but the words are shown to help you remember them. *n.*

kar•at (kar′ət *or* ker′ət) a unit used to state how much gold there is in a mixture. A karat is one of 24 equal parts: *An 18-karat gold ring is 18 parts pure gold and 6 parts alloy. Symbol:* K *n.*

ka•ra•te (kə rȧ′tē) a Japanese method of self-defence without weapons, using different kinds of hand or foot strokes. *n.*

kar•ma (kȧr′mə) in Hinduism, all of a person's actions, good and bad, which determine how he or she will be reborn. *n.*

Kas•ka (kȧs′kə) 1 a First Nations people living in northern British Columbia and Yukon. 2 their language. 3 having to do with these people or their language. 1, 2 *n.,* 3 *adj.*

ka•ty•did (kā′tē did′) a large, green insect that looks like a grasshopper. The male makes a sound like a cricket by rubbing its front wings together. *n.*

🍁 **kay•ak** (kī′ak) 1 an Inuit boat made of skins stretched over a light frame of wood or bone. There is an opening in the top for one person, or sometimes two people. The Inuktitut spelling of this word is **qajaaq.** 2 a similar craft made of other material. *n.* —**kay′ak•ing,** *n.* —**kay′ak•er,** *n.*

ka•zoo (kə zü′) a tube-shaped musical toy that makes a buzzing sound when you hum into one end of it. *n., pl.* **ka•zoos.**

KB *symbol for* kilobyte, a unit of computer memory.

keel (kēl) 1 the main supporting piece of wood or steel that runs along the bottom of a ship or boat. 2 **keel over,** **a** turn upside down: *The sailboat keeled over in the storm.* **b** fall over suddenly: *He keeled over in a faint.* 1 *n.,* 2 *v.*

keen (kēn) 1 sharp: *a keen blade, a keen wind, a keen sense of smell.* 2 *Informal.* enthusiastic; eager: *a keen player. adj.* —**keen′ly,** *adv.* —**keen′ness,** *n.*
keen on, enthusiastic about: *They're not keen on camping.*

A castle keep was a massive tower, built to be the strongest part of the castle. It stood in a courtyard called a bailey. Inside the keep were storerooms, rooms for soldiers, a Great Hall, and (right at the top) the lord's room.

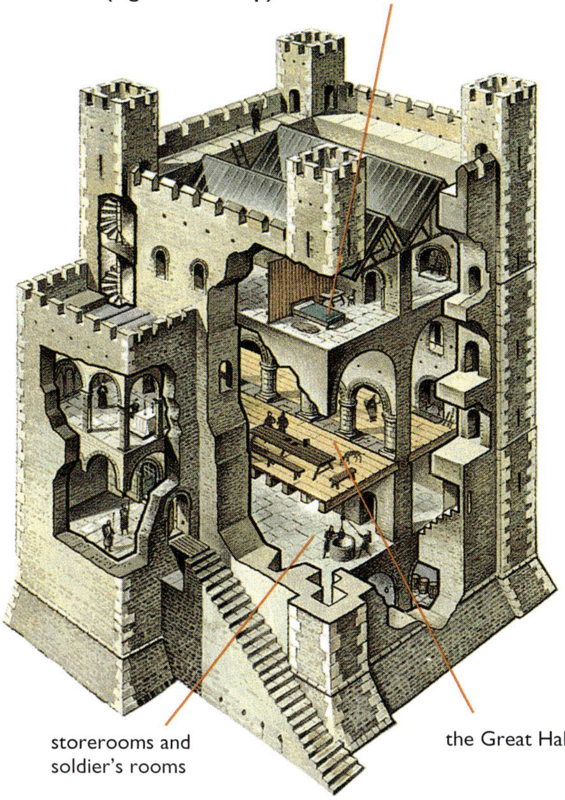

keep (kēp) 1 have or hold for a long time or forever, without letting go or giving away: *You may keep this book. They were kept in prison. Can you keep a secret?* 2 have and take care of: *My grandparents keep chickens. The bank keeps money for people.* 3 hold back; prevent: *Keep the books from falling.* 4 stay or continue; cause to stay or continue: *to keep awake, to keep working, to keep the baby warm. He kept the fire burning.* 5 delay: *What's keeping them? They should have arrived by now.* 6 be left without going bad or becoming a problem: *Butter will keep in a refrigerator. Your questions will keep until after lunch.* 7 be faithful to: *to keep a promise, to keep the rules.* 8 food and a place to sleep: *He earns his keep by doing dishes.* 9 the strongest part of a fortress or castle. 1–7 *v.,* **kept, keep·ing;** 8, 9 *n.* —**keep′er,** *n.*
for keeps, a with the agreement that the winner may keep his winnings: *to play for keeps.* **b** *Informal.* forever.
keep on, go on; continue: *The girls kept on swimming in spite of the rain.*
keep to yourself, a not do much with other people. **b** not tell to other people: *She kept the news to herself.*
keep up, a continue: *They kept up their attack until dawn.* **b** keep in good condition: *It was hard to keep up the appearance of the old boat.* **c** stay close or alongside and not fall behind: *I had to run to keep up with the bike.* **d** stay up to date: *We try to keep up with world events.*
keep up with the Joneses, do as well as your neighbour.

keep·ing (kē′ping) care; charge: *They left their dog in our keeping for the holiday. n.*
in keeping with, in agreement or harmony with: *That behaviour is not in keeping with the spirit of our school.*

keep·sake (kēp′sāk′) something kept in memory of a person or thing: *My friend gave me her picture as a keepsake when she moved away. n.*

keg (keg) a small barrel. Kegs usually hold less than 114 L. *n.*

kelp (kelp) 1 a large, tough, brown seaweed. 2 ashes of seaweed, used as a source of iodine and potassium. *n.*

kel·vin (kel′vin) 1 **Kelvin,** having to do with a scale of temperature used in science. On this scale, 0 represents the coldest possible state, equal to –273.16°C. 2 an SI unit of temperature on this scale. A difference of one kelvin is equal to a difference of one degree Celsius. The kelvin is one of the seven base units of the SI. *Symbol:* K 1 *adj.,* 2 *n.*

ken (ken) 1 the range of knowledge: *Some things are beyond our ken.* 2 a Scottish word for "know." 1 *n.,* 2 *v.*

ken·nel (ken′əl) 1 a house for a dog or dogs. 2 Often, **kennels,** *pl.* **a** a place where dogs are raised by breeders. **b** a place where dogs may be left and cared for while their owners are away. *n.*

kept (kept) the past tense and past participle of **keep:** *He kept the CD that I gave him. The juice was kept in bottles. v.*

ker·chief (kər′chif) a piece of cloth worn over your head or around your neck. *n.*

ker·nel (kər′nəl) 1 the softer part inside the hard shell of a nut or inside the stone of a fruit. 2 a grain or seed of a plant such as wheat or corn. 3 the main or central part of anything: *the kernel of an idea. n.*

a bat	e bed	i bid	o pot	u cup	th thin
ā cake	ē me	ī bite	ō go	ü rude	ᴛʜ then
ä bar	ə about	ər over	ô for	ů put	zh measure

ker•o•sene (ker′ə sēn′) a thin oil made from petroleum, used as a fuel in lanterns, camp stoves, and some engines. It is also called **coal oil.** It was invented by a Canadian, Abraham Gesner, in 1853. *n.*

ketch•up (kech′əp) a sauce used with hotdogs, French fries, and so on, made of tomatoes, onions, salt, sugar, and spices. *n.*

ket•tle (ket′əl) **1** a container with a handle and a spout, for heating water either by plugging it in or by setting it on a stove. **2** any large metal container for boiling liquids, cooking fruit, etc. *n.*

ket•tle•drum (ket′əl drum′) a drum made out of a large, hollow bowl of brass or copper, with a piece of parchment stretched over the top. *n.*

key[1] (kē) **1** a small, specially shaped piece of metal that opens and closes a lock. **2** anything shaped or used like this. **3** the answer to a puzzle or problem, or something needed in order to succeed: *the key to a secret code. Listening is the key to understanding.* **4** very important: *the key industries of a country.* **5** a chart explaining the abbreviations or symbols used in a dictionary, map, or diagram: *There is a pronunciation key at the beginning of this dictionary.* **6** one of a set of small parts pressed down by the fingers in playing a piano or operating a computer or other machine: *Don't hit the keys so hard.* **7** enter information in a computer using a keyboard: *Kareem keyed in the numbers.* **8** a scale or set of related notes in music based on a particular note called the **key note**: *a song written in the key of B flat.* **9** in basketball, the space in front of each basket, usually painted a different colour from the court. 1–3, 5, 6, 8, 9 *n., pl.* **keys;** 4 *adj.,* 7 *v.,* **keyed, key•ing.**
key up, a make very excited: *The kids are so keyed up they can't sit still.* **b** raise someone's courage or nerve: *She keyed herself up to ask for a raise.*

Word Family........... key

keychain: a chain with a ring to hang keys on
keyhole: in a lock, the hole that the key fits into
keypad: a set of keys on an electronic machine, for entering information
keystroke: one act of pressing a key on a keyboard

key[2] (kē) a low island; reef: *There are keys south of Florida.* *n., pl.* **keys.**

key•board (kē′bôrd′) **1** the set of keys on a piano, synthesizer, or computer. **2** use a keyboard. 1 *n.,* 2 *v.* **—key′board′ist,** *n.* **—key′board′ing,** *n.*

key•stone (kē′stōn′) **1** the middle stone at the top of an arch, holding the other stones or pieces in place. **2** anything on which other related parts depend: *Freedom is the keystone of our policy.* *n.*

key•word (kē′wərd′) a word used as a reference point for finding information on a computer. *n.*

kg *symbol for* kilogram or kilograms.

khak•i (kak′ē, kår′ke, *or* kå′kē) a heavy yellowish brown cloth, often used for soldiers' uniforms. *n., pl.* **khak•is.**

kib•butz (ki bu̇ts′) in Israel, a farm owned by a large group of people who live and work on it together and share the profits. *n., pl.* **kib•butz•im** (ki bu̇ts′ēm).

kick (kik) **1** hit with the foot: *Kick the ball.* **2** a blow with the foot: *The horse's kick knocked the pail over.* **3** fling one foot outward or move both feet up and down with energy: *The baby lay kicking in his crib. The dancers leapt, kicked, and spun around.* **4** Often, **kicks,** *pl. Informal.* thrill; excitement: *He gets a kick out of skiing fast. She did it just for kicks.* **5** *Informal.* something that interests a person strongly for a short time: *Tillie is on a health food kick.* 1, 3 *v.,* 2, 4, 5 *n.*
kick in, *Informal.* **a** start operating or having an effect: *It takes the medicine a while to kick in.* **b** give a share: *If we all kick in three dollars we can buy her a gift.*
kick off, a put a football into play with a kick. **b** begin: *The new TV show kicks off this fall.* The noun form for either meaning is **kickoff.**
kick out, *Informal.* send out in a humiliating or disgraceful way: *She was kicked out of the game.*
kick up, *Slang.* start; cause: *They kicked up a big fuss.*

kick•stand (kik′stand′) a lever attached to the rear of a bicycle or motorcycle that can be kicked down to hold the bike upright. You kick it up again to move the bike. *n.*

kid[1] (kid) **1** a young goat, or the leather made from its skin. **2** *Informal.* child. *n.*

kid[2] (kid) *Slang.* tease playfully; talk in a joking way: *He's only kidding.* *v.,* **kid•ded, kid•ding.**
no kidding, seriously.

kid•nap (kid′nap′) take a person by force and keep as a prisoner: *The banker's son was kidnapped and held for ransom.* *v.,* **kid•napped** or **kid•naped, kid•nap•ping** or **kid•nap•ing.** **—kid′nap′per** or **kid′nap′er,** *n.*

kid•ney (kid′nē) one of two organs that filter waste and water from the blood and pass them to the bladder as urine. A **kidney bean** is a bean shaped like a kidney, usually dark red. *n., pl.* **kid•neys.**

kill (kil) **1** cause to die: *The explosion killed her.* **2** the act of killing. **3** the animal killed in a hunt: *All the lions shared the kill.* **4** put an end to; get rid of: *to kill odours, to kill rumours.* **5** use up: *We killed an hour at the zoo.* **6** *Informal.* overcome with pain, disgust, or laughter: *My sore foot is killing me. His jokes kill me.* 1, 4–6 *v.,* 2, 3 *n.* —**kill′er,** *n.*
make a killing, *Informal.* make a lot of money.

kill·deer (kil′dēr′) a North American bird, mostly brown and white with two black bands across its white breast. It has a loud, shrill call that sounds like its name. *n., pl.* **kill·deers** or **kill·deer.**

killer whale (kil′ər wāl′) a black-and-white whale that preys on fish, seals, and even on larger whales.

kil·lick (kil′ik) a heavy stone in a box-shaped wooden frame, used as an anchor for a small boat. *n.*

kiln (kiln) a furnace or oven for burning, baking, or drying something. Limestone is burned in a kiln to make lime. Bricks and pottery are baked in a kiln. *n.*

kilo– *an SI prefix meaning* thousand. One kilowatt is a thousand watts. The prefix *kilo-* can also be used with almost any other SI unit, such as *gram* or *litre. Symbol:* k

Word Family.......... kilo

The prefix kilo means "thousand." It is added to a unit to form the name of a unit that is a thousand times as big.
kilobyte: a unit of computer memory equal to about a thousand bytes (actually 1024 bytes). *Symbol:* kB or KB
kilohertz: a unit measuring the speed of vibrations, equal to a thousand vibrations per second. *Symbol:* kHz
kilopascal: a unit of pressure. Normal air pressure is 100 kilopascals. *Symbol:* kPa
kilowatt: a unit of electrical power equal to a thousand watts. *Symbol:* kW
kilowatt-hour: a unit of electrical energy equal to one kilowatt used for one hour. *Symbol:* kWh

kil·o·gram (kil′ə gram′) an SI unit for measuring mass, equal to a thousand grams. It is often shortened to **kilo** (kē′lō). *Symbol:* kg *n.*

kil·o·me·tre (kə lom′ə tər *or* kil′ə mē′tər) a measure of length equal to a thousand metres: *It takes about 15 minutes to walk a kilometre. Symbol:* km *n.*

kilt (kilt) a pleated plaid skirt worn traditionally by men in the Scottish Highlands. *n.*

Kimonos are a traditional Japanese garment, worn by men and women. Most young people wear a kimono only on special occasions.

ki·mo·no (kə mō′nə) **1** a loose outer garment held in place by an **obi**, a wide belt or sash. **2** a loose dressing gown. *n., pl.* **ki·mo·nos.**

kin (kin) **1** family or relatives: *All our kin came to the family reunion.* **Kinsfolk** and **kindred** are more poetic words. **2** related: *My cousins are kin to me.* 1 *n.,* 2 *adj.* —**kins′man,** *n.* —**kins′wo′man,** *n.* —**kin′ship,** *n.*
kith and kin, friends and relatives.
next of kin, a person's closest living relative or relatives: *My parents are my next of kin.*

kind¹ (kīnd) friendly, caring, and helpful; doing good to others: *The kind girl offered her sweater to the shivering little boy.* **Kind-hearted** means the same. *adj.* —**kind′ness,** *n.*

kind² (kīnd) sort; variety: *He likes most kinds of candy. A viper is a kind of snake.* *n.*
kind of, *Informal.* nearly; almost; somewhat; rather: *The room was kind of dark.*
of a kind, of the same sort: *The brothers were two of a kind—easy-going and intelligent.*

USING WORDS ...... kind of

You can usually find a better choice than **kind of** to mean "somewhat." Try using *a bit, rather, quite, slightly, almost, nearly, not quite,* or *barely.*

a bat	e bed	i bid	o pot	u cup	th thin
ā cake	ē me	ī bite	ō go	ū rude	ꟻH then
ä bar	ə about	ər over	ô for	ů put	zh measure

kin•der•gar•ten (kin′dər gȧr′tən) the year of school that comes before grade one. In some places it is two years, the first year being **junior kindergarten** and the second **senior kindergarten.** *n.*

kin•dle (kin′dəl) 1 start burning: *Light a match to kindle the bonfire. This damp wood will never kindle.* **Kindling** is small pieces of wood for starting a fire. 2 stir up; arouse: *Her cruelty kindled our anger.* *v.,* **kin•dled, kin•dling.**

kind•ly (kīnd′lē) 1 good-hearted and friendly: *kindly faces, kindly people.* 2 in a kind or friendly way: *Treat your pets kindly.* 3 a formal word for "please": *Kindly pay the rent at the end of the month.* 1 *adj.,* **kind•li•er, kind•li•est;** 2, 3 *adv.* **—kind′li•ness,** *n.* **take kindly to,** like or accept: *She does not take kindly to criticism.*

kinetic energy (kə net′ik en′ər jē) the energy that an object has when it is moving.

king (king) 1 the male ruler of a nation who is not elected but inherits his position: *Richard the Lion-Hearted was a king of England.* 2 a person, animal, or thing that ranks highest in a certain group: *The lion is called the king of beasts. Ravi was the king of skateboarders.* 3 **a** in chess, the chief piece. **b** in checkers, a piece that has moved entirely across the board and can now move forward and backward. 4 a playing card with a picture of a king on it. *n.* **—king′ly,** *adj.* **—king′ship′,** *n.*

king•dom (king′dəm) 1 a country that is governed by a king or a queen. 2 one of the three divisions of the natural world. They are the animal kingdom, the plant kingdom, and the mineral kingdom. *n.*

king•fish•er (king′fish′ər) a fish-eating bird with a large crested head and a long, pointed bill. Most are brightly coloured. *n.*

king–size (king′sīz′) *Informal.* very large for its kind: *a king-size bed, a king-size sandwich.* *adj.*

kink (kingk) 1 a twist or curl in thread, rope, hair, etc. 2 form a twist or curl: *The rope kinked as he rolled it up. Don't kink the hose.* 3 pain or stiffness in a muscle. 4 an odd idea or habit. 1, 3, 4 *n.,* 2 *v.* **—kink′y,** *adj.*

ki•osk (kē′osk) a small building, usually with one or more sides open, or a stand or booth inside a building. A kiosk may be used for a newsstand, bank machine, information booth, etc. *n.*

kip•per (kip′ər) a small herring that is split, salted, dried, and smoked. *n.*

kir•pan (kēr′pun) a dagger or short sword worn by all baptized Sikhs. *n.*

kiss (kis) 1 touch with the lips as a sign of love, greeting, or respect: *a goodbye kiss* (*n.*). *She kissed the baby's cheek* (*v.*). 2 a kind of candy wrapped in a twist of paper. 1 *v.,* 1, 2 *n.*

kit (kit) 1 a set of supplies and equipment needed for a certain job or purpose: *a first-aid kit, a sewing kit.* 2 a set of parts you can put together to make something: *a radio kit.* 3 a packet of printed information: *a sales kit, a visitor's kit.* 4 the uniform and personal equipment of a soldier. *n.*

kitch•en (kich′ən) a room where food is cooked or prepared. A small one is a **kitchenette.** *n.*

kite (kīt) 1 a light frame covered with paper, cloth, or plastic and flown in the air on the end of a long string. 2 a hawk with long, pointed wings. *n.*

kit•ten (kit′ən) a young cat. **Kitty** is an informal word. *n.*

kit•ty–cor•ner (kit′ē kȯr′nər) on the diagonal; diagonally across: *The drugstore is kitty-corner from the post office.* *adj. or adv.*

Kiwis have poor eyesight, and must smell out their food (worms and grubs) with the help of nostrils at the tip of their long beaks.

ki•wi (kē′wē) 1 a bird of New Zealand that cannot fly, with shaggy feathers and a long, slender bill. The kiwi is about the size of a chicken, and is active at night. 2 a climbing plant that grows a fuzzy fruit with green flesh that tastes a bit like a strawberry. It is widely grown in New Zealand. *n.*

Kleen•ex (klē′neks) *a trademark for* a soft paper tissue that can be used like a handkerchief. *n.*

klutz (kluts) *Slang.* someone who is clumsy or does the wrong thing at the wrong time. *n.* **—klutz′y,** *adj.*

km *symbol for* kilometre or kilometres.

km/h *symbol for* kilometres per hour: *The top speed of this car is 160 km/h.*

Knights

Even though knights jousted with blunt swords and lances, many were killed or wounded in tournaments.

A knight's helmet covered his face, but the shield carried his coat of arms so that he could still be recognized in battle.

knack (nak) a special skill: *That clown has a knack for making kids laugh.* *n.*

knap·sack (nap′sak′) a leather or cloth bag with shoulder straps for carrying books, clothes, or equipment on your back. *n.*

knave (nāv) 1 an old or poetic word for "scoundrel." 2 another name for the jack in cards. *n.* **—knav′er·y,** *n.* **—knav′ish,** *adj.*

knead (nēd) 1 mix or soften by pressing and stretching, usually with your hands: *to knead bread dough, to knead clay before shaping it.* 2 massage: *The trainer kneaded the muscles of the runner.* *v.*

knee (nē) 1 the joint between your thigh and your lower leg. The bone covering the front of the joint is your **kneecap.** 2 strike with a knee: *He kneed his opponent in the thigh.* 1 *n.,* 2 *v.,* **kneed, knee·ing.**

kneel (nēl) go down or stay on your knees: *She knelt to pull a weed from the flower bed. They knelt in prayer for several minutes.* *v.,* **knelt** or **kneeled, kneel·ing.**

knew (nyū *or* nū) the past tense of **know:** *She knew the right answer.* *v.*

knick–knack (nik′nak′) a small ornament to put on a shelf or hang on a wall. *n.*

knife (nīf) 1 a tool that has a thin, flat, metal blade fastened in a handle for cutting or spreading. 2 cut or stab with a knife. 3 pierce or cut like a knife: *The wind knifed through her coat.* 1 *n., pl.* **knives** (nīvz); 2, 3 *v.,* **knifed, knif·ing.**

knight (nīt) 1 in the Middle Ages, a high-ranking man who fought for a king, queen, lord, or lady and promised to act honourably. Knights wore armour and rode horses. 2 in modern times, a man raised to an honourable rank because of great achievement or service: *A knight has the title "Sir" before his name.* 3 raise to the rank of knight: *Sir Frederick Banting was knighted in 1934 for helping to discover insulin.* 4 one of the pieces in the game of chess. It looks like a horse's head. 1, 2, 4 *n.,* 3 *v.* **—knight′hood,** *n.* **—knight′ly,** *adj.*

a bat	e bed	i bid	o pot	u cup	th thin
ā cake	ē me	ī bite	ō go	ū rude	ᴛʜ then
à bar	ə about	ər over	ȯ for	u̇ put	zh measure

Knots

The clove hitch is a quick and simple way to fasten a rope around a post or stake.

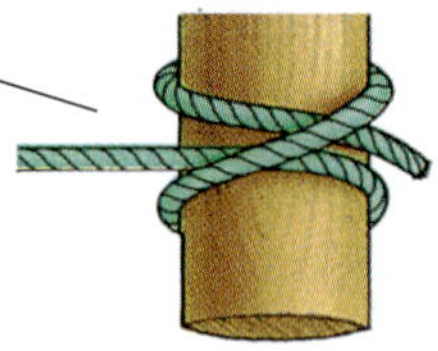

The sheepshank is a knot used to temporarily shorten a rope.

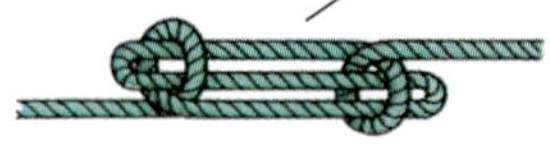

The reef knot (or square knot) is the most common knot used in tying packages. It unties easily when either free end is pulled.

The bowline is a loop knot that will not jam or slip. It is often used in lifting things.

Two half hitches is the name of a knot used to quickly fasten a rope to a post, a hook, or a ring.

knit (nit) **1** make by looping yarn or thread together in interlocking stitches, with long needles or by machine: *She is knitting a sweater. T-shirts are made of knitted cloth.* **2** join closely and firmly together: *a closely knit group of friends.* **3** grow together: *A broken bone knits as it heals.* *v.,* **knit·ted** or **knit, knit·ting.** —**knit′ter,** *n.*
knit your brows, frown.

knives (nīvz) plural of **knife.** *n.*

knob (nob) **1** the round handle on a door or drawer. **2** a round control on a radio or other machine, that you work by turning it. **3** any rounded lump. *n.* —**knob′by,** *adj.*

knock (nok) **1** hit or bump against sharply: *She knocked her head on the cupboard door.* **2** such a hit or bump: *The hard knock made her cry.* **3** make a noise by hitting with your knuckles: *I knocked on the door.* **4** make a rattling or banging noise: *That engine knocks.* **5** the sound of knocking: *The knock on the door made us all jump with surprise.* 1, 3, 4 *v.,* 2, 5 *n.*
knock around, *Informal.* **a** wander from place to place. **b** hit repeatedly; treat roughly.
knock down, a cause to fall: *You knocked down the music stand.* **Knock over** means about the same. **b** take apart: *They knocked down the bookcase and packed it in the moving van.*
knock off, *Informal.* **a** take off; deduct: *They knocked ten dollars off the price.* **b** stop: *Hey, knock off the fighting! The workers knock off at noon for lunch.*
knock out, hit so hard as to make the person unconscious.
knock together, make or put together hastily: *The girls knocked together a sort of raft out of old boards.*
knock yourself out, try your hardest: *I knocked myself out to get this fixed in time.*

knock·er (nok′ər) something to knock with, fastened on a door. *n.*

knoll (nōl) a small, rounded hill. *n.*

knot (not) **1** a fastening made by tying together pieces of rope, string, etc.: *She showed me how to make a slip knot.* **2** a tangle: *There's a knot in my shoelace.* **3** make a knot or knots in something: *to knot a thread. My hair was all knotted.* **4** a group; cluster: *There was a knot of children around the librarian.* **5** the place where a branch has grown out, which shows in a board as a small, dark, hard oval part. When it falls out it leaves a **knothole.** **6** a nonmetric measure of speed used by ships and airplanes, equal to one nautical mile per hour (1852 m/h): *This ship's usual speed is about 18 kn. Symbol:* kn 1, 2, 4–6 *n.,* 3 *v.,* **knot·ted, knot·ting.** —**knot′ty,** *adj.*

know (nō) **1** be aware; realize: *I didn't know you were here.* **2** have true information, understanding, or skill: *to know your lesson, to know how to cook. We know that 2 and 2 are 4.* **3** be familiar with: *I know her very well, but I've never met her sister. Do you know this neighbourhood?* **4** tell apart from others: *You will know him by his bright red scarf.* *v.,* **knew, known, know·ing.**
be in the know, have knowledge not shared by everyone.

know–how (nō′hou′) the knowledge or skill needed to do something: *Betty has a lot of know-how when it comes to fort-building.* *n.*

know·ing (nō′ing) **1** clever; shrewd. **2** suggesting shrewd or secret understanding: *She gave me a knowing look.* *adj.*

know·ing·ly (nō′ing lē) **1** in a knowing way: *As I casually whistled our "signal" tune, Marsha glanced at me knowingly and left the room to carry out our plan.* **2** on purpose: *to knowingly hurt someone.* *adv.*

knowl•edge (nol′ij) 1 what someone knows: *Her knowledge of whales is extensive.* A **knowledgeable** person knows a lot. 2 the fact of knowing; awareness: *The knowledge of our victory caused great joy.* *n.*

knuck•le (nuk′əl) 1 a joint in a finger. 2 the knee or hock joint of an animal used as food: *boiled pigs' knuckles.* *n.*
knuckle down, *Informal.* work hard.
knuckle under, submit; give in: *He refused to knuckle under to his enemies.*

ko•a•la (kō ȧ′lə) a grey, furry animal of Australia that looks a bit like a teddy bear and carries its young in a pouch. Koalas live in eucalyptus trees and eat the leaves. *n.*

Ko•di•ak bear (kō′dē ak′ ber′) a large brown bear that lives on the coast of British Columbia and Alaska. It is the largest meat-eating animal in the world.

ko•la nut (kō′lə nut′) a brownish seed of a tropical tree that contains caffeine and is used to flavour soft drinks.

kom•a•tik (kom′ə tik′) a large wooden dogsled used in the North, made of closely-spaced crossbars lashed to two broad runners. It has a raised bar at the back for a standing rider to hold on to. *n.*

The Komodo dragon hunts deer, pigs, and monkeys.

Ko•mo•do dragon (kə mō′dō drag′ən) a large dangerous lizard that lives on some islands of Indonesia. Up to three metres in length, it is the largest lizard in the world.

kook•a•bur•ra (kůk′ə bər′ə) an Australian kingfisher with a call that sounds like loud, harsh laughter. *n.*

Ko•ran (kō rȧn′ *or* kō ran′) another spelling for **Qur'an,** the sacred book of Islam. *n.*

ko•sher (kō′shər) 1 fit to eat according to Jewish religious law. 2 selling products that meet the requirements of Jewish law: *a kosher butcher.* 3 *Slang.* all right; proper: *It's not kosher to change the rules once the game has started.* *adj.*

kPa *symbol for* kilopascal, a unit for measuring pressure.

Ktu•na•xa (ktů nak′sə) 1 a First Nations people living in British Columbia. 2 their language. 3 having to do with these people or their language. 1, 2 *n.*, 3 *adj.*

kung fu (kung′ fū′) an ancient Chinese art of fighting in which hands and feet are used for attack and defence.

kW *symbol for* kilowatt, a unit of electric power.

Kwa•kwa•ka'•wakw (kwȧ kwȧ′ ki wȧk) 1 a First Nations people living in British Columbia. 2 having to do with these people. 1, *n.*, 2 *adj.*

Kwan•zaa (kwȧn′zə) a festival held by some black people in North America to celebrate their culture. It runs from December 26 to January 1. Another spelling is **Kwanza.** *n.*

WORD HISTORY....... Kwanzaa

Kwanzaa is a short form of *matunda ya kwanza*, meaning "first fruits of the harvest" in Swahili, an African language.

Ll

l or **L** (el) 1 the twelfth letter of the English alphabet, or the sound that it stands for. You hear the sound of *l* at the beginning and end of *lull.* 2 the twelfth thing in a list. 3 the Roman numeral for 50. *n., pl.* **l's** or **L's.**

L *symbol for* litre, a unit of volume.

la•bel (lā′bəl) 1 a slip of paper or other material attached to something to show what or whose it is, or where it is to go: *The label on the pop bottle lists the ingredients.* 2 a name used to tell what something is: *Some entries in this dictionary have the label "Slang."* 3 put or write a label on: *The bottle is labelled "Poison."* 4 describe as; call: *She labelled him a liar.* 1, 2 *n.,* 3, 4 *v.,* **la•belled** or **la•beled, la•bel•ling** or **la•bel•ing.**

lab•o•ra•to•ry (lab′rə tò′rē *or* lə bòr′ə tòr′ē) Often shortened to **lab.** 1 a place where scientific work is done: *a chemical laboratory.* 2 a place where students work on practical skills, often on their own: *a language lab, a computer lab. n., pl.* **lab•o•ra•to•ries.**

la•bo•ri•ous (lə bòr′ē əs) taking a lot of hard work: *Climbing a mountain is laborious. adj.*
—la•bo′ri•ous•ly, *adv.*

la•bour or **la•bor** (lā′bər) 1 hard work: *He was well paid for his labour.* 2 work hard: *She laboured all day in the factory.* A **labourer** does physical work for a living. 3 workers as a group separate from those who hire or manage them. 4 move slowly and heavily: *The old car laboured up the steep hill.* 5 birth pains. 1, 3, 5 *n.,* 2, 4 *v.*

Labour Day or **Labor Day** the first Monday in September, a holiday in honour of working people.

labour union or **labor union** (lā′bər yūn′yən) an organization formed by workers to make sure employers provide fair wages, safe working conditions, and so on.

Labrador retriever (lab′rə dòr′ ri trē′vər) a breed of medium-sized dog with a friendly temperament and a short, thick coat that can be black, dark brown, or yellow. It is called a **Lab** for short and was originally bred in Labrador. *n.*

lab•y•rinth (lab′ə rinth′) 1 a place that is easy to get lost in; maze. 2 another name for the inner ear. *n.*

There are several different methods of making lace by hand. This woman is making crochet lace, using very fine white silk thread and a crochet hook. She is wearing the traditional costume of the women of Brittany, a region in France. The hat is, of course, made of lace.

lace (lās) 1 a string or strip for pulling parts together, fastened by tying: *These shoes need new laces.* 2 put laces through; fasten with laces: *Lace up your shoes.* 3 see-through cloth made of threads woven loosely together in a fancy pattern. 4 trim with lace. 1, 3 *n.,* 2, 4 *v.,* **laced, lac•ing.** **—lac′y,** *adj.*

lack (lak) 1 be without: *Some guinea pigs lack tails.* 2 the condition of being without; shortage: *Lack of food had made her thin and weak.* 1 *v.,* 2 *n.*
—lack′ing, *adj.*
for lack of, in place of something that would be better but which you don't have: *For lack of proper tools we had to use Gemma's nail file to cut the strings.*

lack•a•dai•si•cal (lak′ə dā′zə kəl) not bothering to pay much attention or make much of an effort: *Cece tended to be lackadaisical about doing her homework. adj.*
—lack′a•dai′si•cal•ly, *adv.*

lac•quer (lak′ər) 1 liquid coating for wood, metal, and other surfaces that hardens into a shiny, protective layer. 2 coat with lacquer. 1 *n.,* 2 *v.*

la•crosse (lə kros′) a game played by two teams of ten players each, using a rubber ball and a stick with a net at one end. Players use the sticks to pass the ball and try to get it into the goal. *n.*

WORD HISTORY........ lacrosse

Lacrosse is really two words, *la crosse,* from Canadian French. The word *crosse* was the name of the stick used in this game.

lad (lad) a boy. **Laddie** is an affectionate form. *n.*

lad·der (lad′ər) 1 a set of steps, or **rungs,** fastened into two long sidepieces, used for climbing up or down. 2 any way to reach a higher position: *moving up on the ladder to success.* *n.*

la·den (lā′dən) loaded: *The camels were laden with bundles of silk and rice.* *adj.*

la·dle (lā′dəl) 1 a large, deep spoon with a long handle, for dipping out liquids. 2 use such a spoon to dip and serve: *The cook is ladling out the soup.* 1 *n.,* 2 *v.,* **la·dled, la·dling.**

la·dy (lā′dē) 1 a woman of high or noble rank. A **lady-in-waiting** is a high-ranking servant who acts as the personal companion of a queen or princess. 2 a woman or girl who is dignified and courteous. 3 *Informal.* any woman: *Our neighbour is a nice lady.* *n., pl.* **la·dies.** **—la′dy·ship′,** *n.*

la·dy·bug (lā′dē bug′) a small beetle with a rounded back, usually red or orange with black spots. Ladybugs eat harmful insects. *n.*

la·dy's–slip·per (lā′dēz slip′ər) 1 a wild orchid that grows in northern temperate regions. Its flower looks something like a slipper or moccasin. The pink lady's-slipper is the provincial flower of Prince Edward Island. 2 a tropical Asian flower that looks similar. *n.*

lag (lag) 1 fall behind: *The child lagged because he was tired.* 2 a delay; a gap in time between an event and its result: *There is a long lag in forwarding mail to us.* 1 *v.,* **lagged, lag·ging;** 2 *n.*

la·goon (lə gūn′) a shallow pond of fresh or salt water connected with a lake or sea but partly separated from it by ridges of sand, earth, or coral. *n.*

laid (lād) the past tense and past participle of **lay**[1]**:** *She laid down the heavy bundle. Those eggs were laid this morning.* *v.*
laid up, *Informal.* forced by illness or injury to stay indoors or in bed.

lain (lān) the past participle of **lie**[2]**:** *This bill has lain here on the table for a week.* *v.*

lair (ler) a wild animal's den or resting place. *n.*

lake (lāk) a large body of fresh water usually completely surrounded by land except where rivers come in and go out. Canada has millions of lakes. *n.*
go jump in the lake, *Slang.* take your silly ideas elsewhere.

la·ma (lȧ′mə) a Buddhist priest or monk in Tibet or Mongolia. Lamas live, work, and worship in a place called a **lamasery** (lȧ′mə ser′ē). *n., pl.* **la·mas.**

lamb (lam) 1 a young sheep or its meat. 2 give birth to a lamb or lambs: *The ewes on our farm are lambing.* 3 a gentle, innocent person. 1, 3 *n.,* 2 *v.*

lame (lām) 1 not able to walk properly for a while because of a hurt leg or foot. 2 stiff and sore: *My arm is lame from playing ball.* 3 make lame. 4 not very good or convincing: *a lame excuse.* 1, 2, 4 *adj.,* **lam·er, lam·est;** 3 *v.,* **lamed, lam·ing.** **—lame′ly,** *adv.*

la·ment (lə ment′) 1 feel or show grief or sadness about something: *to lament the dead.* 2 an expression of grief; a wail, or a sad poem or song. 3 feel sorry about; regret: *We lamented his absence.* 1, 3 *v.,* 2 *n.* **—lam′en·ta·ble,** *adj.* **—lam′en·ta′tion,** *n.*

lam·i·nate (lam′ə nāt′) 1 make by putting together different layers and binding them with glue or heat: *Plywood is made by laminating thin sheets of wood.* 2 cover with a thin layer of clear plastic using a special machine: *She had her library card laminated to protect it from wear.* *v.,* **lam·i·nat·ed, lam·i·nat·ing.**

lamp (lamp) something that gives light, usually one that can be moved around: *a desk lamp, a floor lamp. An oil lamp has a wick and burns oil.* *n.*

lam·prey (lam′prē) a water animal with a body like an eel and a large, round, sucking mouth with teeth. Many lampreys are parasites and attach themselves by their mouths to fish from which they suck blood and tissue. *n., pl.* **lam·preys.**

lance (lans) 1 a long wooden spear with an iron or steel head, like the ones carried by knights in the Middle Ages. 2 cut open with a medical blade: *The doctor had to lance the boil on my leg.* 1 *n.,* 2 *v.,* **lanced, lanc·ing.**

land (land) 1 the solid part of the earth's surface: *We stood on dry land.* A country surrounded by land is **landlocked.** 2 ground owned as property: *The farmer bought 100 hectares of land.* Someone who owns land is a **landowner.** A **landholder** may own or rent land. 3 a country or region: *desert land. Canada is a vast land.* 4 come or bring to land from the air or water: *The ship landed at the pier. The pilot landed the airplane in a field.* 5 end up: *The car landed in the ditch.* 6 *Informal.* catch; get: *to land a fish, to land a job.* 1–3 *n.,* 4–6 *v.*

land·fill (land′fil′) garbage that has been buried, sometimes letting harmful chemicals leak into the underground water supply. A **landfill site** is a piece of land where this waste is buried. *n.*

a bat	e bed	i bid	o pot	u cup	th thin
ā cake	ē me	ī bite	ō go	ū rude	ᴛʜ then
ȧ bar	ə about	ər over	ȯ for	u̇ put	zh measure

land·form (land′fôrm′) a natural physical feature on the surface of the earth, such as a mountain, valley, or ridge. *n.*

land·ing (lan′ding) **1** the act of coming to land from the air or water: *The landing was smoother than the take-off.* **Landing gear** supports a plane on land or water. A **landing strip** is a runway for small planes. **2** a platform between flights of stairs. **3** a dock or pier for unloading a ship's cargo or passengers. *n.*

land·la·dy (land′lā′dē) a woman who owns property that she rents to others. *n., pl.* **land·la·dies.** A man who owns and rents such property is called a **landlord.**

land·mark (land′märk′) **1** something familiar or easily seen that lets you figure out where you are: *That tall tower makes a good landmark.* **2** an event of outstanding importance: *The invention of the printing press was a landmark in the history of communication.* *n.*

land·scape (land′skāp′) **1** a wide view of an area of land: *The low, tree-covered hills make a beautiful landscape in fall.* **2** a piece of art showing such a view. **3** make land more beautiful by adding trees, shrubs, flowers, and so on in an artistic arrangement: *The builder landscaped the lot around the new house.* 1, 2 *n.,* 3 *v.,* **land·scaped, land·scap·ing.**

land·slide (land′slīd′) **1** the sliding down of a mass of soil or rock on a steep slope. **2** a huge majority of votes for one political party or candidate: *She was elected by a landslide.* *n.*

lane (lān) **1** a narrow road or path, especially one between hedges, walls, or fences. **2** a division of a road or racecourse, marked off for one line of traffic or one runner. **3** a strip on a bowling alley for one group playing together. *n.*

lan·gar (lung′gär) a kitchen in a Sikh temple serving free food to anyone who wishes. Eating together is an important part of Sikh religion. *n.*

lan·guage (lang′gwij) **1** human speech, spoken or written: *We can express our thoughts and feelings through language.* **2** the speech used by a nation or people group: *the French language, the Ojibwa language.* **Sign language** uses a system of hand signs instead of speech. **3** a style or kind of speech or writing: *bad language, Shakespeare's language, legal language.* *n.*

lan·guid (lang′gwid) limp and droopy; without energy: *a languid gesture. A hot, humid day makes a person feel languid.* *adj.* **—lan′guid·ly,** *adv.*

lan·guish (lang′gwish) **1** grow weak; droop: *The flowers languished from lack of water.* **2** suffer from hardship or longing: *to languish in poverty. She languished for home.* *v.*

La Ni·ña (la nen′yə) a cooling of the surface of part of the Pacific Ocean. It changes weather patterns. Look also at **El Niño.** *n.*

lank·y (lang′kē) awkwardly long and thin: *He folded his lanky body into the low armchair.* *adj.,* **lank·i·er, lank·i·est.**

lan·tern (lan′tərn) a lamp with a protective see-through case around the bulb or flame: *The campers hung a lantern over the picnic table.* *n.*

lap¹ (lap) the front part of a person sitting down, from the waist to the knees: *My cat likes to sleep on my lap.* *n.*
in the lap of luxury, surrounded by luxuries.

lap² (lap) **1** lie or place together, one partly over the other; overlap: *We lapped rows of shingles on the roof. This edge of the jacket laps over that one.* **2** one time around a track: *Who won the first lap of the race?* **3** a part of a trip, piece of work, etc.: *We woke early to start the last lap of our bike trip.* 1 *v.,* **lapped, lap·ping;** 2, 3 *n.*

lap³ (lap) **1** drink by lifting up with the tongue: *Cats and dogs lap water.* **2** move or beat gently with a light splashing sound: *Little waves lapped against the boat.* *v.,* **lapped, lap·ping.**

la·pel (lə pel′) the part of the front of a coat or jacket that is folded back just below the collar. *n.*

Lapp (lap) a member of a people living in Lapland, a region of northern Scandinavia and northwestern Russia. Their language is called **Saami.** *n.*

lapse (laps) **1** slip back; sink down: *The house lapsed into ruin. The girl's interest in the story soon lapsed.* **2** a slight mistake or slip: *a lapse of memory, a lapse of speech.* **3** a passing: *A minute is a short lapse of time.* **4** expire; end because it was not renewed: *Your driver's licence has lapsed.* 1, 4 *v.,* **lapsed, laps·ing;** 2, 3 *n.*

lap·top (lap′top′) a small portable computer that can run on batteries and fits on a person's lap. *n.*

larch (lärch) a tree with small cones and soft, short needles that turn yellow and drop off in the fall. *n.*

lard (lärd) animal fat used in cooking. *n.*

lar·der (lär′dər) a supply of food, or a place to keep it in: *The trapper's larder included flour and salt.* *n.*

large (lärj) big: *Canada is a large country. Large crowds come to see our team play.* **Largely** means "mostly." *adj.,* **larg·er, larg·est.**

at large, a free; loose: *Is the escaped prisoner still at large?* **b** as a whole; altogether: *The people at large want peace.*

lar•i•at (ler′ē ət) a long rope with a loop at one end; lasso. *n.*

lark¹ (lärk) a small, mostly brown, high-flying songbird. The **horned lark** is the only North American member of the family. *n.*

lark² (lärk) something fun; a good time: *We played tag in the pouring rain for a lark.* *n.*

lar•va (lär′və) **1** the wormlike form of an insect from the time it leaves the egg until it becomes a pupa: *A caterpillar is the larva of a butterfly or moth. Maggots are the larvae of flies.* **2** a young form of certain animals that is unlike the adult form: *A tadpole is the larva of a frog or toad.* *n., pl.* **lar•vae** (lär′vē).

lar•yn•gi•tis (ler′ən jī′tis) a sore and swollen condition of the larynx that makes talking difficult and even painful. *n.*

lar•ynx (ler′ingks) the part of your throat containing the vocal cords. *n., pl.* **la•ryn•ges** (lə rin′jēz) or **lar•ynx•es.**

la•sa•gna (lə zän′yə) a dish made with large flat noodles that are boiled and then baked with cheese, tomato sauce, and other fillings. *n.*

Laser light can perform delicate eye surgery by doing tiny welding operations.

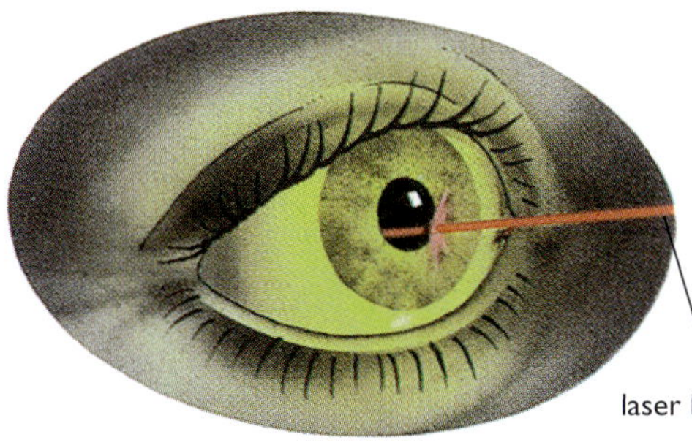

la•ser (lā′zər) a device that produces a very narrow, intense beam of light of only one colour and going in only one direction. Some laser beams are used to cut metal or to do delicate medical operations. In a **laser printer** a laser beam gives the paper an electric charge in an area that is the exact shape of the letter or other image. This makes the printer's colouring matter stick to the paper in that shape, while heat melts it on permanently. *n.*

WORD HISTORY........ laser

Laser is an acronym. It stands for **l**ight **a**mplification by **s**timulated **e**mission of **r**adiation.

lash¹ (lash) **1** whip: *The leather lash snapped in the air (n.). Do not lash the horses (v.).* **2** beat back and forth: *A lion stood still, lashing its tail.* **3** strike out violently: *The cat lashed at him angrily with its paw.* **4** a hair on the edge of your eyelid; eyelash. 1, 4 *n.,* 1–3 *v.*

lash² (lash) tie or fasten with a rope or cord: *We lashed logs together to make a raft.* *v.*

lass (las) a girl. **Lassie** is an affectionate form. *n.*

This South American gaucho (cowhand) shows how to hold a rope in the form of a lasso.

las•so (lə sū′) **1** a long rope with a loop at the end, used for catching horses and cattle: *The cowhand threw a lasso over the steer's head and pulled the animal to the ground.* **2** catch with a lasso. 1 *n., pl.* **las•sos** or **las•soes;** 2 *v.,* **las•soed, las•so•ing.**

last¹ (last) **1** at the end, after all others: *the last page of a book (adj.). Noel arrived last, half an hour late (adv.).* **2** latest; most recently: *When did you see her last?* **3** previous; the one just before this: *last week, last year (adj.). I liked this movie better than the last (n.).* **4** a person or thing that comes after all others: *She was the last in line.* **5** most unlikely: *A storm was the last thing we expected.* 1, 3, 5 *adj.,* 1, 2 *adv.,* 3, 4 *n.*
—last′ly, *adv.*
at last, at the end; after a long time; finally: *So you have come home at last.* **At long last** is even stronger.
breathe your last, die.
have the last word, be the last to speak in an argument; say something that the other person cannot answer.
see or hear the last of, be finished dealing with.
the last straw, the thing that finally makes someone lose his or her patience.

a bat	e bed	i bid	o pot	u cup	th thin
ā cake	ē me	ī bite	ō go	ū rude	ᴛʜ then
ä bar	ə about	ər over	ȯ for	ů put	zh measure

last² (last) 1 go on; continue without stopping: *The festival lasted three days.* 2 be used without wearing out or running out: *I hope these shoes last a year. How long will our money last?* *v.* —**last′ing,** *adj.*

latch (lach) 1 a fastener for a door, gate, or window. It has a small bar that falls or slides into a notch or hole. 2 fasten with a latch: *Latch the door.* 1 *n.,* 2 *v.*

late (lāt) 1 after the usual or proper time: *We had a late supper (adj.). She worked late (adv.).* 2 near the end; in the last part: *It rained late in the evening (adv.). We came home from Europe in late August (adj.).* 3 recent: *the latest news.* 4 recently dead: *The late John Candy was a great actor.* 1–4 *adj.,* **lat·er** or **lat·ter, lat·est** or **last;** 1, 2 *adv.,* **lat·er, lat·est** or **last.** —**late′ness,** *n.*
of late, lately; recently: *I haven't seen them of late.*

late·ly (lāt′lē) a little while ago; for the last little while; recently: *She has not been looking well lately.* *adv.*

la·tent (lā′tənt) hidden or undeveloped: *a latent talent. The power of a seed to grow into a plant remains latent if it is not planted.* *adj.*

lat·er·al (lat′ə rəl) sideways; on or from the side: *a lateral view of something, a lateral fin on a fish.* *adj.*

la·tex (lā′teks) 1 a milky liquid found in some plants, such as milkweeds, poppies, and some tropical trees. Rubber and chewing gum are made from different kinds of latex. 2 a mixture of rubber or plastic and water, used in paint and other products. *n.*

lathe (lāᴛʜ) a machine that holds a piece of wood or metal and spins it while a cutting tool is held against it to shape it. *n.*

lath·er (laᴛʜ′ər) 1 the foam made from soap or shampoo mixed with water. 2 make lather or put lather on: *He lathers his face before shaving. This soap lathers well.* 3 foam formed on a horse when it sweats. 1, 3 *n.,* 2 *v.*

Lat·in (lat′ən) 1 the language of the ancient Romans. 2 a native speaker of any of the languages that come from Latin. The Italians, French, Spanish, Portuguese, and Romanians are Latins. 3 having to do with Latin or the Latins. **Latin America** is the part of the western hemisphere colonized by the Spanish and Portuguese. 1, 2 *n.,* 3 *adj.*

lat·i·tude (lat′ə tyūd′ *or* lat′ə tūd′) 1 the distance north or south of the equator, measured in degrees. On maps, lines of latitude are parallel with the equator. 2 a place or region at a certain latitude: *Polar bears live in the northern latitudes.* 3 room to act or think freely: *My parents give me a lot of latitude in choosing my clothes.* *n.*

lat·ter (lat′ər) 1 later; toward the end: *the latter part of the week.* 2 **the latter,** the second of two things mentioned: *Mice and rats are similar, but the latter are bigger.* 1 *adj.,* 2 *n.*

lat·tice (lat′is) 1 a structure of crisscrossing strips with open spaces between them. 2 form into a lattice or put a lattice on: *The cook latticed strips of dough across the pie.* 1 *n.,* 2 *v.,* **lat·ticed, lat·tic·ing.**

laud (lod) to praise: *We lauded his efforts with loud cheers.* *v.* —**laud′a·ble,** *adj.*

laugh (laf) 1 make the sounds and movements that show you think something is funny: *We all laughed at the joke.* 2 the act or sound of laughing: *a hearty laugh.* 1 *v.,* 2 *n.* —**laugh′ter,** *n.* —**laugh′a·ble,** *adj.*
have the last laugh, win or turn out to be right when everyone expected the opposite.
laugh at, a make fun of; ridicule: *They laughed at me for putting my shoes on the wrong feet.* **b** pay no attention to: *She laughed at danger.*
laugh in your sleeve, laugh secretly to yourself.
laugh off, dismiss with a laugh: *She laughed off my warning about the thin ice and walked out onto the pond.*
no laughing matter, no joke; serious.

A space shuttle is launched like all other spacecraft — it is thrust into space by powerful rockets. When a shuttle returns to Earth, however, it lands like a glider.

launch¹ (lonch) 1 put a boat into the water; set afloat. 2 send up in the air: *to launch a rocket or missile.* Rockets and so on are launched from a **launching pad.** 3 start; get something going: *to launch a new business.* 4 the act of launching something: *We watched the space launch on television.* 1–3 *v.,* 4 *n.*
launch into, start something long or difficult: *Omar launched into a detailed explanation of the chart.*

launch² (lonch) an open motorboat. *n.*

laun·dry (lon′drē) 1 clothes, sheets, and so on to be washed or that have been washed. 2 the work of washing them: *I don't like doing the laundry.* 3 a place where clothes are washed and ironed. *n., pl.* **laun·dries.** —**laun′der,** *v.*

lau·rel (lȯr′əl) 1 a small evergreen tree with smooth, shiny leaves. The ancient Greeks and Romans put wreaths of laurel on the heads of people they wished to honour. 2 any tree or shrub like this, such as the **mountain laurel.** 3 **laurels,** *pl.* honour or victory. *n.*
rest on your laurels, stop trying hard because you think your past success is enough.

Lau·ren·tians (lə ren′shənz) a range of low mountains between Hudson Bay and the St. Lawrence River. *adj.*

lav·a (lav′ə *or* lȧ′və) 1 hot melted rock flowing from a volcano. 2 the rock formed when this cools and hardens. Some lavas are hard and glassy while others are light and porous. *n.*

lav·a·to·ry (lav′ə tȯ′rē) a fancy word for "washroom." *n., pl.* **lav·a·to·ries.**

lav·en·der (lav′ən dər) a small shrub with spikes of very sweet-smelling, pale purple flowers. *n.*

lav·ish (lav′ish) 1 giving or spending a lot: *The woman was lavish with her money.* 2 very big, fancy, expensive, luxurious, etc.: *lavish desserts, a lavish wedding.* 3 give a lot or too much: *The grandparents lavished gifts on the children.* 1, 2 *adj.,* 3 *v.* —**lav′ish·ly,** *adv.*

law (lo) 1 a rule made by a country, province, state, etc. for all the people who live there. 2 a system of such rules: *Canadian law, international law.* 3 the study of such a system of rules; the profession of a lawyer: *She is studying law.* 4 a statement of what always occurs under certain conditions: *Scientists study the laws of nature.* *n.*
law and order, the peaceful environment resulting from people's obedience to law.
lay down the law, use authority to insist that things will be done a certain way.
take the law into your own hands, try on your own to punish wrongdoers or make them do right.

law·ful (lof′əl) following the law or allowed by law: *a lawful arrest, lawful demands.* *adj.* —**law′ful·ly,** *adv.*

law·less (lol′is) not having or respecting any laws: *a lawless frontier town. A thief leads a lawless life.* *adj.* —**law′less·ly,** *adv.* —**law′less·ness,** *n.*

law·mak·er (lo′mā′kər) a person who helps make the laws of a country, province, etc.; legislator. *n.* —**law′mak′ing,** *adj. or n.*

lawn (lon) land covered with grass kept closely cut, especially near or around a house. A **lawn mower** is a machine with moving blades for cutting grass. *n.*

law·suit (lo′sūt′) a case in a law court to settle a dispute: *The builder did a bad job on her house, so she began a lawsuit to get her money back.* *n.*

law·yer (loi′yər) a person whose work is to give advice about the law or to speak for others in court. *n.*

lax (laks) not strict; careless: *lax behaviour. Don't let yourself become lax about doing your homework.* *adj.* —**lax′ness** or **lax′i·ty,** *n.*

lax·a·tive (lak′sə tiv) 1 a medicine that makes the bowels empty their waste. 2 causing the bowels to get rid of their waste. 1 *n.,* 2 *adj.*

lay[1] (lā) 1 place flat; put down: *Lay your books on the table.* 2 put permanently in place: *to lay bricks, to lay a new carpet.* 3 produce eggs: *Birds, fish, and reptiles lay eggs. The hens won't lay if they're upset.* 4 make ready; arrange: *I laid the table for lunch. Alberto has laid plans for a long canoe trip.* *v.,* **laid, lay·ing.**
lay aside, put away for future use; save: *I laid aside a dollar a day toward buying a bicycle.*
lay down, a declare; state: *The principal laid down the rules for the new computer lab.* **b** give; sacrifice: *to lay down your life for the cause of freedom.*
lay in, get and store up for the future: *The settlers laid in enough supplies for the winter.*
lay into, *Slang.* scold: *My parents laid into me for swearing.*
lay off, a get rid of an employee because there is not enough work: *During the slack season many workers were laid off.* The noun is **layoff. b** *Informal.* stop hassling: *Lay off the poor kid.* **c** *Informal.* stop: *Lay off the fighting!*
lay of the land, the position of hills, water, forest, etc. in an area. Some people say **lie of the land.**
lay out, a arrange; plan; mark off: *The road was laid out but not yet paved.* **b** spread out: *She laid out her sleeping bag.* **c** *Slang.* spend: *I had to lay out a lot for my new skates.* **d** knock down.
lay up, force to stay in bed because of illness or injury: *The flu laid him up for a week.*

CONFUSABLES ....lay

Lay and **lie** both mean "rest flat on a surface," but **lay** always has an object and **lie** never does: *I'm going to lay my clothes on the bed. I'm going to lie on the bed.*

a bat	e bed	i bid	o pot	u cup	th thin
ā cake	ē me	ī bite	ō go	ū rude	ŦH then
ȧ bar	ə about	ər over	ȯ for	u̇ put	zh measure

Leaves

Leaves are the food factories of green plants. They contain the green chemical chlorophyl, which reacts with water, light, and carbon dioxide to produce sugar, which feeds the plant. During this reaction, called photosynthesis, leaves release oxygen. Without this, the earth's supply of breathable air would soon be used up.

Leaves come in a great variety of shapes and textures, but they all have veins to carry food and water to the different parts of the plant.

Deciduous plants (maple trees, for example) shed all their leaves in fall, and grow a new set in spring.

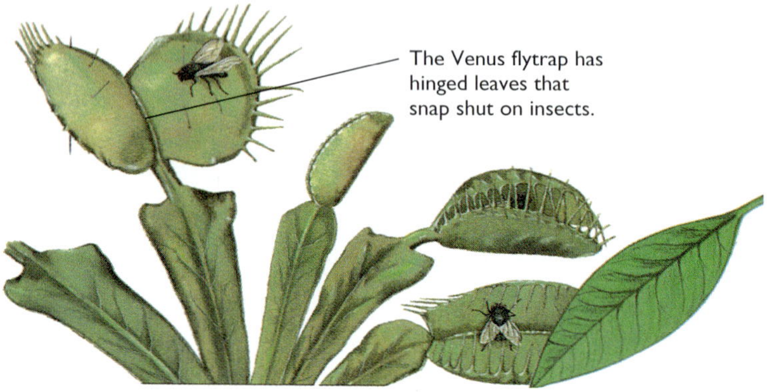

The Venus flytrap has hinged leaves that snap shut on insects.

Needleleaf plants (pine trees, for example) shed their needles and grow new ones throughout the year.

lay[2] (lā) the past tense of **lie**[2]: *After the long hike I lay down for a rest.* *v.*

lay[3] (lā) having to do with people who are not professionals in a certain field: *a lay preacher.* *adj.*

lay·er (lā′ər) 1 one thickness, level, or coating: *another layer of clothing, layers of rock, a thin layer of ice on a pond.* 2 one that lays: *Sol is an expert tile layer.* *n.*

lay·up or **lay–up** (lā′up′) in basketball, a shot on the basket at close range, often deliberately bounced off the backboard. *n.*

laze (lāz) relax in a lazy way: *It was so hot we just lazed around all afternoon.* *v.,* **lazed, laz·ing.**

la·zy (lā′zē) 1 not willing to work or be active: *She was too lazy to get up and turn off the TV.* **Lazybones** is a nickname for a lazy person. 2 moving slowly: *A lazy stream winds through the meadow.* 3 in which no one works or feels like working: *a hot, lazy afternoon.* *adj.,* **la·zi·er, la·zi·est.** **—la′zi·ly,** *adv.* **—la′zi·ness,** *n.*

lb. *abbreviation for* pound, a nonmetric unit of mass. For pounds, **lbs.** is also used.

LCD *abbreviation for* liquid crystal display, the type of electronic screen on a calculator, telephone, laptop computer, or digital watch.

leach (lēch) dissolve or lose soluble materials such as nutrients or pesticides when water is passed through. *v.* **—leach′ing,** *n.*

lead[1] (lēd) 1 show the way by going along with or in front of: *He led the horses to water.* 2 be chief of; command; direct: *A general leads an army. The conductor led the singing.* 3 be a way to: *This highway leads to Edmonton.* 4 influence; persuade: *Such actions lead us to distrust them.* 5 be first in a group: *She leads the class in spelling.* 6 the amount that someone is ahead by: *The Swiss runner had a lead of 3 m.* 7 a tip or clue: *She was not sure where to look for the information, but the librarian gave her some good leads.* 8 the main part in a play or movie. 1–5 *v.,* **led, lead·ing;** 6–8 *n.* **—lead′er,** *n.* **—lead′er·ship′,** *n.*
follow someone's lead, be guided by what someone else has done: *Other scientists followed her lead.*
it's your lead, it's your turn to go first.
take the lead, go first; lead others.

lead[2] (led) 1 a soft, heavy, bluish-grey metal which is a chemical element: *Lead is used to make car batteries.* If something is **leaden,** it is heavy or dark like lead. 2 a long, very thin piece of graphite or other substance in a pencil. 3 a heavy object tied to a line, used to find out the depth of water. It is also called a **plumb.** *n.*

leaf (lēf) 1 one of the thin, usually flat, parts of a green plant that grow along its stems or up from its roots. 2 grow leaves: *The trees along the river leaf earlier in spring than those on the hill.* 3 a sheet of paper: *Each side of the leaf of a book is a page.* 4 turn the pages: *to leaf through a book.* 5 a very thin piece or sheet of metal: *gold leaf.* 6 a flat, movable piece of a tabletop: *We put two extra leaves in the table to make it longer for the party.* 1, 3, 5, 6 *n., pl.* **leaves;** 2, 4 *v.* **—leaf′less,** *adj.* **—leaf′y,** *adj.*
in leaf, with leaves growing: *Our maple is already in leaf.*
turn over a new leaf, make a new start, trying to do or be better in the future: *I promised to turn over a new leaf in the New Year.*

leaf·let (lēf′lit) 1 a small booklet; a brochure or flyer: *advertising leaflets.* 2 a small or young leaf. *n.*

league[1] (lēg) 1 a group of teams that are all at about the same level and that play a schedule of games against each other: *a hockey league.* 2 a group of people, organizations, or nations joined together to help each other. 3 form a league. 1, 2 *n.,* 3 *v.,* **leagued, lea·guing.**
in league, working together, especially secretly: *The suspected spies were thought to be in league with the enemy.*

league[2] (lēg) an old nonmetric measure of distance equal to almost 5 km. *n.*

leak (lēk) 1 a hole or crack that is not meant to be there and that lets something in or out: *a leak in a boat, a leak in a tire.* 2 let something in or out that is meant to stay where it is: *The roof leaks and lets rain in. That pipe leaks gas.* 3 go in or out in this way: *The air leaked out.* 1 *n.,* 2, 3 *v.* **—leak′age,** *n.* **—leak′y,** *adj.*

lean[1] (lēn) 1 stand slanting, not upright; bend: *The tower of Pisa leans. Greg leaned over the table to collect the dishes.* 2 rest in a sloping or slanting position: *Lean against me. Lean the ladder against the wall.* 3 the condition of leaning; slope: *The old barn has more of a lean this year.* 4 depend: *to lean on a friend's advice.* 5 show a preference: *to lean toward mercy. Skiing is OK, but I lean more toward hockey.* 1, 2, 4, 5 *v.,* **leaned** or **leant** (lent), **lean·ing;** 3 *n.*

lean[2] (lēn) 1 with very little fat: *a lean man, a lean piece of meat.* 2 not very plentiful: *a lean harvest.* *adj.*

lean–to (lēn′tü′) 1 a small building with a sloped roof, built onto the side of a larger, higher building. 2 a rough shelter built or leaning against posts, trees, rock, etc.: *Campers have a supply of wood in a lean-to here.* *n., pl.* **lean-tos.**

leap (lēp) jump, especially high or far: *This frog can leap very high (v.). She crossed the huge puddle in one leap (n.). A sudden breeze made the flames leap up (v.).* *n.* or *v.,* **leaped** or **leapt** (lept), **leap·ing.**
by leaps and bounds, very fast: *The town grew by leaps and bounds.*

leap·frog (lēp′frog′) a game where two players take turns leaping over each other's bent back. *n.*

leap year (lēp′ yēr′) a year with 366 days, the extra day being February 29. A year is a leap year if its number can be divided exactly by four, except years at the end of a century, which must be exactly divisible by 400. Thus 1960 and 2000 are leap years, but 1900 and 1961 are not.

learn (lərn) 1 gain knowledge or skill: *He learned that salt is a mineral. We are learning about Canada's history. How did you learn to ride a bike?* 2 memorize: *to learn a poem.* *v.,* **learned, learn·ing.** **—learn′er,** *n.*

CONFUSABLES .... learn

learn means "understand": *I want to learn how to swim.*
teach means "instruct": *Can you teach me how to swim?*

learn·ing (lər′ning) 1 the process of gaining knowledge or skill: *Learning takes time.* 2 knowledge gained by study; scholarship: *a woman of great learning.* A person who has studied long and knows a lot is **learned** (lər′nid). *n.*

lease (lēs) 1 a written agreement to rent something for a certain length of time and for a certain price: *to sign a lease for a car.* 2 to rent under such an agreement: *We have leased an apartment for one year. The landlord has already leased all the apartments.* 1 *n.,* 2 *v.,* **leased, leas·ing.**

leash (lēsh) 1 a strap or chain for holding or leading an animal: *She always keeps her dog on a leash.* 2 fasten or hold with a strap or chain. 1 *n.,* 2 *v.*

least (lēst) 1 less than all others in size, amount, or importance: *He cries at the least thing (adj.). I liked that book least of all (adv.).* 2 the smallest amount or thing: *The least you can do is answer.* 1 *adj.* or *adv.,* 2 *n.*
at least, a at the lowest estimate: *The temperature was at least 35°C.* **b** still; if nothing else; in any case: *He may have been late, but at least he came.*

leath·er (leᴛʜ′ər) a material made from the skins of animals by removing the hair and then tanning them: *Her new gloves are made of leather.* *n.* **—leath′er·y,** *adj.*

leave[1] (lēv) 1 go away: *We leave tonight. Please leave the room.* 2 stop belonging to or taking part in; quit: *to leave your job. The lead singer has left the band.* 3 let stay in a certain place or condition: *We left the window open. I left a book on the table.* 4 give to someone when you die: *He left a fortune to his two daughters.* 5 give to someone else to do: *I left the driving to my sister.* 6 not do, use, take, etc.: *Leave a slice for me! I will leave my homework till tomorrow.* *v.,* **left, leav·ing.**
leave off, stop: *Continue the story from where I left off.*
leave out, not say, do, or put in: *She left out two words when she read the sentence.*

a bat	e bed	i bid	o pot	u cup	th thin
ā cake	ē me	ī bite	ō go	ū rude	ᴛʜ then
à bar	ə about	ər over	ȯ for	ů put	zh measure

leave² (lēv) 1 consent; permission: *They gave us leave to go.* 2 a time that someone spends away from work with special permission: *maternity leave. He took three months leave to look after his sick father.* *n.*
take leave of, say goodbye to.

leav•en (lev′ən) put a substance like yeast or baking powder in dough to make it rise or become lighter and puffier. Such a substance is called a **leavening agent.** *v.*

lec•ture (lek′chər) 1 a planned talk on a certain subject in front of a class or other audience. Often there is a stand called a **lectern** to hold the speaker's papers. 2 a long scolding: *My parents give me a lecture when I come home late.* 3 give a lecture. 1, 2 *n.,* 3 *v.,* **lec•tured, lec•tur•ing.** —**lec′tur•er,** *n.*

led (led) the past tense and past participle of **lead¹:** *The police officer led the children across the street. That blind woman is led by her dog.* *v.*

LED a small electrical device that gives off red or green light, usually to show whether a machine is on or off. The full name is **light-emitting diode.**

ledge (lej) a narrow shelf: *a window ledge, a ledge of rock.* *n.*

leech (lēch) 1 a sort of worm that sucks the blood of animals. It lives in ponds, quiet lakes, and slow-moving streams that are free of pollution. 2 a person who keeps trying to get what he or she can out of others, without doing anything to earn it. *n.*

leek (lēk) a vegetable related to the onion. It is larger, tube-shaped, and milder in flavour. *n.*

leer•y (lē′rē) *Informal.* wary; suspicious: *He was leery of snakes. We are leery of their advice.* *adj.*

lee•way (lē′wā′) extra time, room, material, or freedom to do something: *It should take about two hours to do this job, but give yourself a half-hour's leeway.* *n.*

left¹ (left) 1 one of two sides of any person or thing. The opposite is **right.** The 9 is on the left side of a clock; west is usually to the left on a map. In cars sold in Canada, the driver sits on the left. **Left-hand** is another form for the adjective: *on the left-hand side.* 2 Often, **Left,** a political position in favour of changing things to share power and wealth more equally in society. Also called the **left wing.** *n., adj., or adv.*
—**left′ist,** *n. or adj.*

left² (left) the past tense and past participle of **leave¹:** *The newspaper is left at our door. She left at four o'clock.* *v.*

left–hand•ed (left′han′did) 1 using the left hand more easily and readily than the right: *Charlene is left-handed.* 2 done or used with the left hand: *a left-handed pitch, left-handed scissors.* *adj.*

WORD HISTORY....... left-handed

Left came from an Old English word *lyft*, meaning "weak." For the right-handed majority, the left hand was the weaker hand. For left-handed people, of course, it's just the opposite.

leg (leg) 1 one of the parts that people and animals stand and walk on: *Dogs have four legs and human beings have two.* 2 anything shaped or used like a leg: *a table leg.* 3 one of the stages of a trip: *They were happy to be on the last leg of their long journey.* *n.*
on your last legs, about to break down or die: *I feel as if I am on my last legs, but a swim will revive me.*
pull someone's leg, *Informal.* fool someone: *We didn't really see a UFO—I was just pulling your leg.*

leg•a•cy (leg′ə sē) 1 whatever has been left to a person in the will of someone who has died.
2 something handed down from an ancestor or from anyone who came before you or influenced you: *My love of reading is a legacy from my grade one teacher.* *n., pl.* **leg•a•cies.**

le•gal (lē′gəl) 1 having to do with law or lawyers: *legal knowledge, legal advice.* 2 following the law; allowed by law: *Hunting is legal only during certain seasons.* 3 a size of paper, 22 cm by 36 cm: *For legal-size paper use the top printer tray.* *adj.* —**le′gal•ize′,** *v.*

leg•end (lej′ənd) 1 a story coming down from the past which is partly based on fact: *the legend of Robin Hood.* 2 such stories as a group. 3 on a map, a list of the symbols used and what they mean. 4 the words or caption on a coin, picture, or diagram, telling what it is. *n.* —**leg′end•ar′y,** *adj.*

leg•gings (leg′ingz) 1 tight, stretchy pants for girls or women. 2 extra outer coverings for the legs, especially ones for wearing outside in cold weather. *pl.n.*

leg•i•ble (lej′ə bəl) clear and easy to read: *make sure your handwriting is legible.* *adj.*

le•gion (lē′jən) 1 a division in the ancient Roman army, containing several thousand foot soldiers and several hundred horsemen. 2 any army. 3 a very large number: *Legions of grasshoppers destroyed the crops.* *n.*

Lenses

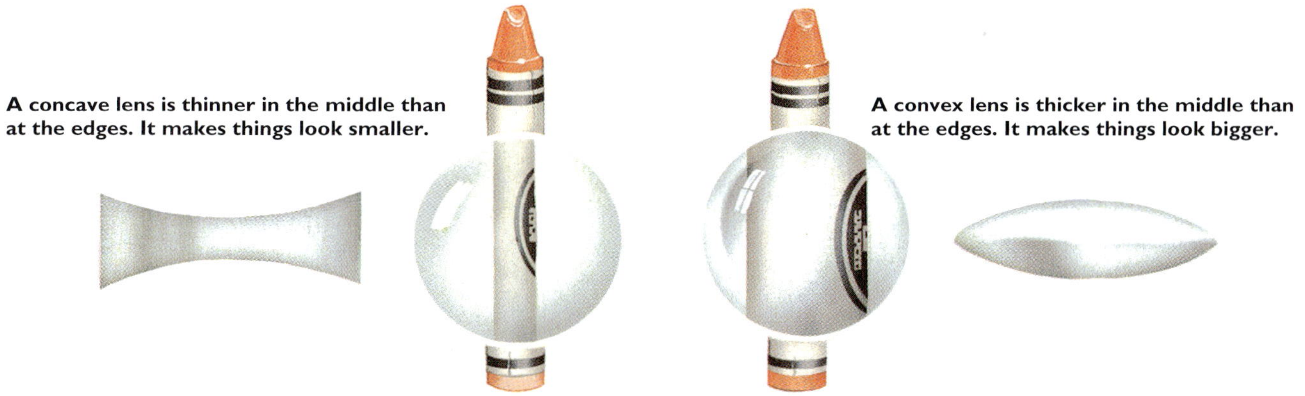

leg·is·late (lej′i slāt′) make laws: *Parliament legislates for Canada.* A law is a piece of **legislation.** *v.,* **leg·is·lat·ed, leg·is·lat·ing.** —**leg′is·la′tive,** *adj.* —**leg′is·la′tor,** *n.*

Legislative Assembly (lej′isla′tiv ə sem′blē) in Canada, the group of representatives elected to the legislature of a province or territory.

leg·is·la·ture (lej′i slā′chər) **1** a group of people with the duty and the power to make laws for a country, province, or state: *Each Canadian province has a legislature.* **2** the place where this group meets. *n.*

le·git·i·mate (lə jit′ə mit) **1** right or proper under some law or rule: *a legitimate election.* **2** allowable; acceptable: *legitimate anger. adj.* —**le·git′i·ma·cy,** *n.*

lei·sure (lezh′ər *or* lē′zhər) free time; time to relax: *He hasn't much leisure with two jobs.* A **leisure centre** is a place where people can go for recreational activities like swimming, skating, hobby groups, and so on. *n.*
at your leisure, whenever you have time.

lei·sure·ly (lezh′ər lē *or* lē′zhər lē) without hurry; relaxed: *a leisurely stroll. adj.*

lem·ming (lem′ing) a small animal related to the mouse, with greyish or brownish fur, a short tail, and furry feet. They live mostly in arctic regions. *n.*

lem·on (lem′ən) **1** a sour-tasting, light yellow fruit that grows on small trees in warm climates. You can make a drink with it called **lemonade. 2** *Informal.* something, especially a car, that gives a lot of trouble. *n.*

le·mur (lē′mər) a monkey that lives mainly in the forests of Madagascar and has a foxlike face, big eyes, soft, woolly fur, and a long bushy tail. *n.*

lend (lend) **1** let someone have for a while: *Will you lend me your bike for an hour? Banks lend money to people for various purposes.* **2** give; add: *That lace curtain lends a certain charm to the window. v.,* **lent, lend·ing.** —**lend′er,** *n.*
lend a hand, help: *They lent a hand with the dishes.*
lend itself to, be suitable for: *Our basement does not really lend itself to parties.*

length (length) **1** how long a thing is from end to end: *the length of your arm, the length of a room, 8 cm in length.* **2** the distance from one end of a pool to the other: *Swim ten lengths.* **3** how long something lasts or goes on: *the length of a visit, a speech, or a book.* **4** a long stretch or extent: *She was away for quite a length of time.* **5** a piece of anything long: *a length of wire, three lengths of copper pipe. n.* —**length′en,** *v.* —**length′y,** *adj.*
at arm's length, not closely involved.
at length, a at last; finally: *At length, after many delays, the meeting started.* **b** with all the details; fully: *She told of her adventures at length.*
go to great lengths, do extraordinary things or make great efforts to get some result: *He went to great lengths to get this finished, including working all through the night.*

length·wise (length′wīz′) in the direction of the length: *a lengthwise cut (adj.). She folded the cloth lengthwise (adv.). adv. or adj.*

len·ient (lēn′yənt) mild or merciful; not strict: *a lenient judge, a lenient punishment. adj.* —**len′ient·ly,** *adv.* —**len′ien·cy,** *n.*

lens (lenz) **1** a piece of glass or plastic that bends the rays of light passing through it, used for looking through. The lenses in a telescope make things look larger or nearer. The lenses in a pair of glasses correct a person's bad eyesight. **2** the part of the eye that directs light rays onto the retina. *n., pl.* **lens·es.**

a bat	e bed	i bid	o pot	u cup	th thin
ā cake	ē me	ī bite	ō go	ū rude	ᴛʜ then
à bar	ə about	ər over	ò for	ù put	zh measure

lent (lent) the past tense and past participle of **lend:** *I lent you my pencils. He had lent me his knife.* *v.*

len•til (len′təl) the edible seed of a plant related to the pea. It is very high in protein. *n.*

After making a kill, a leopard may drag its prey up a tree and store it there for later. Animal carcasses as heavy as 70 kg have been found, in "larders" more than 5 m above the ground.

leop•ard (lep′ərd) a large animal of the cat family native to Africa and Asia, usually with dull yellowish fur spotted with black. A **panther** is the same animal, only it is all black. *n.*

le•o•tard (lē′ə tärd′) **1** a stretchy, one-piece, close-fitting garment worn by dancers, acrobats, and so on. **2 leotards,** *pl.* tights. *n.*

lep•re•chaun (lep′rə kon′) in Irish legend, an imaginary creature that takes the form of a little old man who plays tricks on people. *n.*

lep•ro•sy (lep′rə sē) an older name for **Hansen's disease,** an infectious disease which causes sores on the skin and damages the nerves. If not treated, it can leave a person paralysed and deformed. A person with leprosy used to be called a **leper** and was often forced to stay away from other people. *n.*

less (les) **1** not as much; a smaller amount: *We had less rain this summer than last summer. Five is less than seven (adj.). Work more and talk less. She is less interested now (adv.). Put less on each plate (n.).* **2** minus: *a year less two days.* 1 *adj., adv., or n.,* 2 *prep.* **—less′en,** *v.*
more or less, a somewhat: *We are all more or less impatient.* **b** about; approximately: *The cost is $50, more or less.*

USING WORDS ..... less/fewer

Use **less** to talk about things that can't be counted, and **fewer** to talk about things that can: *We have fewer students than the other school because we have less space.*

–less *a suffix meaning:* **1** without; lacking, as in *homeless, hopeless.* **2** that does not, as in *ceaseless, tireless.*

less•er (les′ər) less important or valuable; not as great: *a lesser problem, a lesser achievement.* *adj.*

les•son (les′ən) **1** something learned or taught at one time; one basic unit of information: *I couldn't follow today's science lesson. Our math text is divided into 20 lessons.* **2** one of a series of meetings with a teacher to study a given subject or skill, often privately: *karate lessons. She is at her piano lesson.* **3** an experience that teaches you something: *The accident was a lesson to me.* *n.*

lest (lest) in order to prevent: *Be careful lest you fall from that tree.* *conj.*

let (let) **1** allow; permit: *Let the dog have this bone.* **2** allow to come or go: *Let the cat in.* **3** rent: *Mrs. Bacon lets rooms to students. The room lets for $400 a month.* **4 Let** is used in giving suggestions or certain kinds of commands: *Let's go fishing. Let everyone do his or her duty.* **5** in a math problem, suppose; assume: *Let the two lines be parallel.* *v.,* **let, let•ting.**
let down, a lower: *She let the box down from the roof.* **b** disappoint: *Don't let us down today; we're counting on you to help us.* A **letdown** is something disappointing.
let go, a allow to go free: *They let the prisoner go.* **b** dismiss an employee. **c** stop holding; drop: *Grab the rope and don't let go!*
let off, a allow to go free with little or no punishment: *The culprit was let off with a warning.* **b** fire; explode: *to let off a firecracker.*
let off steam, express feelings of anger or tension: *She let off steam by shouting.*
let on, *Informal.* let others know; reveal: *He didn't let on how surprised he was.*
let someone in on something, share a secret with someone, especially a secret plan.
let up, *Informal.* stop, pause, or get less: *I hope the rain lets up soon.* A pause in something is called a **letup.**

CONFUSABLES .... let

let means "allow": *Let me help you.*
leave means "abandon": *Leave me alone!*

le•thal (lē′thəl) able to cause death: *a lethal weapon, lethal gases.* *adj.*

leth•ar•gy (leth′ər jē) a drowsy, sluggish feeling; lack of energy: *It was very hot and we were overcome with lethargy.* *n.* **—le•thar′gic** (lə thär′jik), *adj.*

let's (lets) let us.

Levers

Levers are simple machines. They involve three things:
- **the effort — the work put into the job, such as lifting or pulling**
- **the fulcrum — the place where the lever pivots**
- **the load — the object that is to be moved.**

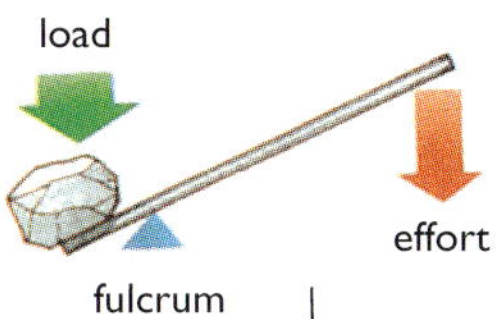

A 1st class lever has the fulcrum between the effort and the load. This crowbar, for example, is a 1st class lever. So is a seesaw.

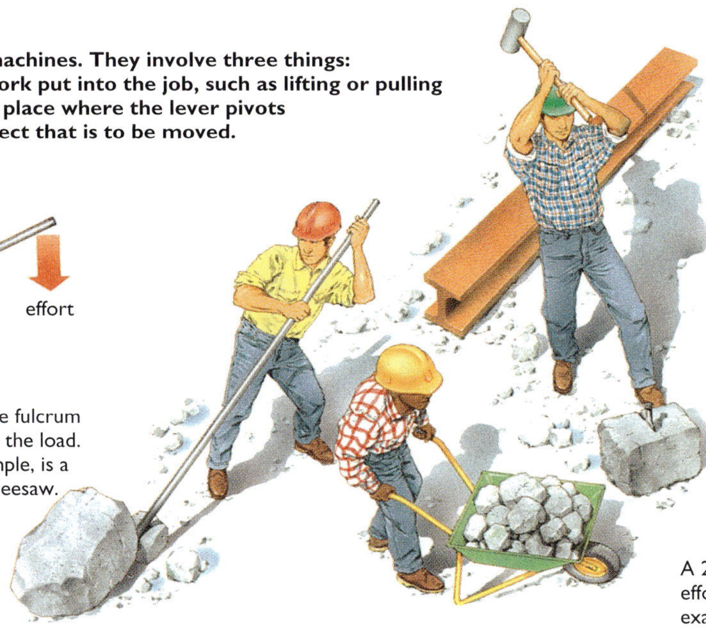

A 3rd class lever has the effort between the fulcrum and the load. A hammer is an example of a 3rd class lever. The shoulder is the fulcrum, and the load is the hammer.

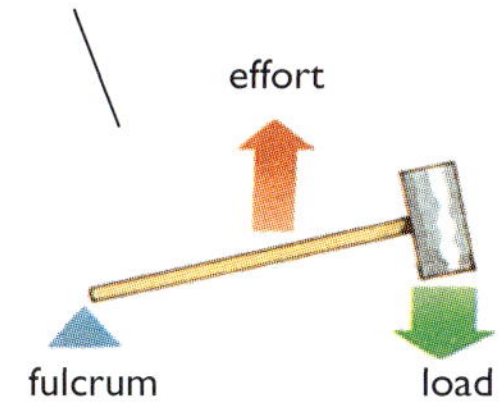

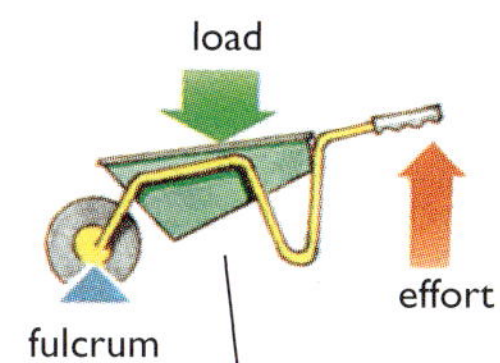

A 2nd class lever has the load between the effort and the fulcrum. A wheelbarrow is an example of a 2nd class lever.

let·ter (let′ər) **1** a written or printed message: *She told me about her vacation in Muskoka in a letter.* A **letter carrier** is a person who delivers mail for the post office. **2** a symbol or sign, used alone or combined, that stands for a speech sound; a character of an alphabet: *The word "lie" has three letters. There are 26 letters in our alphabet.* **3** to mark with letters: *a neatly lettered sign.* **4** a size of paper, 22 cm by 28 cm: *When printing out her file, she selected "letter" from the Print menu.* 1, 2, 4 *n.,* 3 *v.*
to the letter, very exactly: *I carried out your order to the letter.* **Letter-perfect** means perfect in every detail.

let·tuce (let′is) a garden plant with large, crisp, green leaves that are used in salads and sandwiches. *n.*

leu·ke·mi·a (lū kē′mē ə) a condition of the blood when it contains too many white blood cells, making the person very weak. Leukemia is a type of cancer. *n.*

lev·el (lev′əl) **1** completely flat and even, with no slope, like the surface of still water: *a level floor.* **2** of equal height; even: *The table is level with the edge of the window.* A **level crossing** is a railway crossing that is level with the road, not up on a bridge. **3** height: *The flood rose to a level of 10 m.* **4** a grade, standard, or rank: *She reached a high level of skill.* **5** an instrument for finding out whether a surface is level. **6** make flat and even: *They levelled the ground with a bulldozer.* **7** tear down: *The tornado levelled every house in the valley.* **8** aim: *The soldier levelled his rifle. That remark was levelled at me.* **9** *Informal.* steady; sensible: *a level head.* Someone sensible is **level-headed.** 1, 2, 9 *adj.,* 3–5 *n.,* 6–8 *v.,* **lev·elled** or **lev·eled, lev·el·ling** or **lev·el·ing.**
on the level, **a** on level ground: *It is easier to bike on the level.* **b** *Informal.* fair and straightforward; honest.

le·ver (lē′vər *or* lev′ər) **1** a bar for raising or moving something, supported at some point called a **fulcrum.** The advantage you get from using a lever is called **leverage** (lev′ər ij). **2** a control stick on a machine: *the gearshift lever of a car.* *n.*

lev·i·tate (lev′ə tāt′) rise or cause to rise mysteriously and float in the air, seemingly without any physical force or support: *She was so happy she almost levitated.* *v.,* **lev·i·tat·ed, lev·i·tat·ing.** —**lev′i·ta′tion,** *n.*

lev·y (lev′ē) **1** order to be paid: *The government levies taxes.* **2** money collected by authority; a fine, fee, or tax. 1 *v.,* **lev·ied, lev·y·ing;** 2 *n., pl.* **lev·ies.**

li·a·bil·i·ty (līə bil′ə tē) **1** a weakness or disadvantage: *His slowness was a liability to our team.* **2** a legal responsibility to pay something, such as the cost of someone's injury that you had some part in causing, or a debt. The **liabilities** of a business are all its debts. *n., pl.* **li·a·bil·i·ties.**

li·a·ble (lī′ə bəl) **1** likely; unpleasantly likely: *Glass is liable to break. You are liable to slip on ice.* **2** responsible under the law: *The Post Office is not liable for damage to a parcel sent by mail unless the parcel is insured.* *adj.*

a bat	e bed	i bid	o pot	u cup	th thin
ā cake	ē me	ī bite	ō go	ū rude	ᴛʜ then
à bar	ə about	ər over	ô for	ù put	zh measure

li•ai•son (lē ā′zon) **1** a communication link between people or groups that lets each one know what the other one is doing: *Kevin acted as a liaison by carrying messages back and forth.* **2** in French, the act of pronouncing a silent letter at the end of one word when the next word starts with a vowel, so that it sounds as if the two words are one long one. For example, the *n* at the end of *mon* is silent in *mon père*, but *mon ami* is pronounced (mō na mē′). *n.*

li•ar (lī′ər) a person who tells lies. *n.*

li•bel (lī′bəl) **1** something written about someone that is false and hurts his or her reputation. **2** to write something false and harmful about a person. 1 *n.*, 2 *v.*, **li•belled** or **li•beled, li•bel•ling** or **li•bel•ing.** —**li′bel•lous,** *adj.*

lib•er•al (lib′ rəl) **1** generous: *a liberal donation, a liberal supply.* **2** broad-minded; not narrow in your opinions: *a liberal thinker.* **3** eager for changes in society that will make it better, especially changes brought about by government or other authority. **4** Often, **Liberal, a** a member of a liberal political party. **b** in Canada, a member of the Liberal Party or a person who supports it. **5** not concentrating on technical skills for a certain job, but designed to broaden the mind in a general way: *a liberal education.* 1–3, 5 *adj.*, 4 *n.* —**lib′er•al′i•ty,** *n.*

WORD HISTORY........ liberal

English isn't the only language with homonyms; Latin had them too. *Liber* was an adjective meaning "free," but it was also a noun meaning "book." The first gave us **liberal** and **liberate**, the other gave us **library**.

Liberal Party (lib′rəl pär′tē) one of the main political parties of Canada.

lib•er•ate (lib′ə rāt′) set free. *v.*, **lib•er•at•ed, lib•er•at•ing.** —**lib′er•a′tion,** *n.* —**lib′er•a′tor,** *n.*

lib•er•ty (lib′ər tē) freedom: *The prisoner yearned for liberty.* *n.*, *pl.* **lib•er•ties.**
at liberty, free: *The escaped lion is still at liberty. You are at liberty to make any choice you please.*
take liberties with, a be too bold with; act too informal or friendly with someone. **b** be too loose or easy-going and not strict enough with something: *I'm afraid the author took a few liberties with the facts of the story.*

li•brar•y (lī′brer′ē) **1** a room or building where a collection of books, magazines, videos, CD-ROMs, or other material is kept for people to use or borrow: *She goes to the library every Saturday.* A **librarian** (lī brer′ē ən) takes care of the collection and signs materials out. **2** any collection of books: *My aunt has a library of history books in her living room.* *n.*, *pl.* **lib•rar•ies.**

lice (līs) plural of **louse.** *n.*

li•cence (lī′səns) **1** permission given by law to do something: *He has a licence to drive a car.* **2** the paper, card, etc. showing such permission: *The barber hung his licence on the wall.* A **licence plate** is a metal plate on a vehicle, showing that it has been registered with a government and may be used on public roads. Numbers or letters on the plate identify the vehicle. *n.*

USING WORDS . . . licence/license

Some people, especially in the United States, use **licence** for both meanings of the word, but in Canada we usually use the *-s* spelling as a verb: *The government licenses you to drive*, and the *-c* spelling as a noun: *She has a licence to practise medicine.*

li•cense (lī′səns) give a licence to; give official permission to: *to license a new driver.* *v.*, **li•censed, li•cens•ing.**

li•chen (lī′kən) a non-flowering plant that is a fungus and alga growing together. Lichens may look like moss, hair, or scaly leaves growing in patches on rocks, trees, and other hard surfaces. They can be grey, yellow, red, brown, black, or green. *n.*

lick (lik) **1** pass the tongue over: *to lick a stamp.* **2** a stroke of the tongue over something: *He gave the ice-cream cone a big lick.* **3** salt that animals can go and lick up, either in a natural deposit or as a block put out for them by a farmer. **4** *Informal.* the smallest quantity: *She didn't do a lick of work.* **5** *Informal.* beat up. **6** *Informal.* defeat or overcome: *So far we've licked every problem without help.* 1, 5, 6 *v.*, 2–4 *n.*
lick up, a eat by licking: *The cat licked up the milk.* **b** receive eagerly.

lic•o•rice (lik′ə rish) **1** the sweet-tasting, dried root of a European plant. A black substance obtained from this root is used in medicine and candy. **2** candy flavoured with this substance. *n.*

lid (lid) **1** a movable cover; top: *the lid of a jar.* **2** eyelid. *n.*

lie[1] (lī) **1** something that is not true, said in order to fool or trick someone: *Saying her friend stole it was a lie.* **2** say something untrue; tell a lie: *She finally admitted she was lying.* 1 *n.*, 2 *v.*, **lied, ly•ing.**

lie[2] (lī) **1** put or keep your body in a flat position on a surface: *to lie down on the grass, to lie in bed.*

2 rest on a surface: *The book was lying on the table.* 3 be in a certain place or condition: *to lie idle. The lake lies to the south of us.* *v.,* **lay, lain, ly·ing.**

liege (lēj) in the Middle Ages: a lord who gave protection to his vassals in return for their loyal service. *n.*

lieu·ten·ant (lef ten′ənt *or* lū ten′ənt) 1 a person who acts for someone in authority. 2 a junior officer in the armed forces. *n.*

Lieu·ten·ant–Gov·er·nor (lef ten′ənt guv′ər nər) the official head of a provincial government, appointed by the Governor General in Council for a term of five years, to represent the British monarch. *n.*

life (līf) 1 the state of being alive. People, animals, and plants have life; they can grow and reproduce. Rocks and minerals do not. **Life sciences** are the sciences that deal with living things. 2 the time of being alive, or of existing or acting: *She enjoyed a long life. Proper care extends a machine's life.* **Life span** means the same thing. 3 a person: *Five lives were lost in the fire.* 4 living things: *The desert island had almost no animal or plant life.* 5 a way of living: *a dull life, country life.* 6 spirit; vigour: *Put more life into your singing.* *n., pl.* **lives** (līvz).
—life′less, *adj.* **—life′like′,** *adj.*
for dear life, as hard as you would to save your life: *She held on for dear life.*
life and limb, physical safety and survival: *The old bridge is a danger to life and limb.*
take the life of, kill.
true to life, showing things as they are in real life.

Word Family.......... life

lifeboat: a small boat on a ship, to save people's lives if the ship sinks
lifeguard: a person who watches over swimmers to prevent drownings
lifelong: lasting someone's whole life
lifesaving: the act of saving people, usually from drowning
life-size: as big as the real person or thing
lifestyle: a person's chosen way of living
lifetime: the whole time a person is alive

life cycle (līf′ sī′kəl) all the different stages of growth and development that a plant or animal goes through from the time its life begins until it ends. Egg and tadpole are two stages in the life cycle of a frog.

life preserver (līf′ pri zėr′vər) a wide belt, jacket, doughnut-shaped tube, etc. designed to keep a person afloat in the water until rescued. One shaped like a garment with armholes is a **life jacket** or **life vest.**

life raft (līf′ raft′) an inflatable raft for saving lives in a shipwreck or in a plane crash at sea.

life–support (līf′sə pôrt′) equipment that can keep the heart pumping and the lungs breathing while a person is in a coma or otherwise unconscious. *n.*

lift (lift) 1 raise up higher or into the air; pick up: *My father gently lifted the baby from her crib.* 2 go up; be raised: *This flap lifts up to let the fresh air in. Her spirits lifted when she saw him.* 3 the act of lifting: *Do 50 leg lifts.* 4 a machine that lifts people or things: *a ski lift.* 5 the upward force created under the wing of a bird or aircraft when the pressure of the air pushing down on top is less than the pressure of the air pushing up underneath. This happens because the top of the wing is curved, so that the air passing over it has to travel farther than the air passing underneath the flat bottom. 1, 2 *v.,* 3–5 *n.*
give someone a lift, **a** help someone lift something heavy: *Could you give me a lift with this box?* **b** give someone a ride: *Mrs. Rae gave us a lift to school.* **c** cheer up or encourage: *Our friendly phone call gave him a lift.*

lift·off (lift′of′) the firing or launching of a rocket: *The liftoff took place at 3:00 p.m. yesterday.* *n.*

lig·a·ment (lig′ə mənt) a band of strong tissue that connects bones or holds parts of the body in place. *n.*

light[1] (līt) 1 that which makes it possible to see; the opposite of darkness; a form of radiant energy that the retina of the eye can see: *The sun gives light to the earth.* 2 anything that gives light, such as a lamp or a candle. 3 having light; bright: *It stays light longer on summer evenings.* 4 fill with light; make or become bright: *to light a room. The sky lights up at dawn. Her face lights up whenever she sees you.* 5 pale in colour; approaching white: *light hair, light blue.* 6 set fire to; start burning: *Let's light the candles. This match won't light.* 7 anything used to make a flame: *Give me a light to start the campfire.* 8 knowledge or understanding: *We need more light on this subject.* 9 the way a thing is thought about: *I see the matter in a different light, but we can agree to disagree.* 1, 2, 7–9 *n.,* 3, 5 *adj.,* 4, 6 *v.,* **light·ed** or **lit, light·ing.** **—light′er,** *n.* **—light′en,** *v.* **—light′ness,** *n.*
bring to light, reveal; cause to be seen or known: *Many facts were brought to light.* To **come to light** is to be revealed.
in the light of, when you think of; considering: *In the light of all these facts, what they did was right.*
shed light on, make clear; explain.

a bat	e bed	i bid	o pot	u cup	th thin
ā cake	ē me	ī bite	ō go	ū rude	ᴛʜ then
ä bar	ə about	ėr over	ô for	u̇ put	zh measure

light² (līt) **1** having little mass for its size: *Feathers are light.* **2** less than usual in mass, amount, or force: *a light rain, a light meal, light clothing, light traffic.* **3** easy to carry, endure, or do: *a light load, light work, a light punishment.* **4** moving easily; graceful: *Elvis Stojko is very light on his feet.* **5** carefree; cheerful: *a light laugh, light spirits.* **6** aiming to entertain; not serious: *light reading.* **7** low in fat or sugar: *light mayonnaise.* *adj.* **—light·ly,** *adv.* **—light′en,** *v.* **—light′ness,** *n.*
light in the head, a dizzy. **b** silly; foolish.
make light of, treat as not important.

Word Family..........light
light-headed: feeling dizzy or faint
light-hearted: happy and cheerful; playful or humorous
lightweight: not heavy or bulky

light bulb (līt′ bulb′) a glass bulb containing a short piece of very fine wire that becomes white-hot and gives off light when an electric current flows through it.

light–e·mit·ting di·ode (līt′ ē mit′ing di′ōd) a small electrical device that gives off either red or green light. Light-emitting diodes are used mainly on machines, to show whether something is on or off.

Every lighthouse can be identified by the pattern of its light flashes. This lighthouse can also be identified in daylight by its stripes.

light·house (līt′hous′) a tower with a bright light that shines far over the water. *n.*

light·ning (līt′ning) a flash of light in the sky caused by a discharge of static electricity between clouds, or between a cloud and the earth's surface. What we call thunder is the sound made by this. A **lightning rod** is a metal towerlike structure on the outside of a building. It conducts lightning into the ground to prevent fire. *n.*

light–year (līt′yēr′) the distance that light travels in one year; almost ten million kilometres. The light-year is used to measure the distance between stars. The nearest star is more than four light-years away. *n.*

like¹ (līk) **1** much the same as; similar to: *Jane looks like her sister. She can sing like a bird.* **2** *Informal.* as; as if: *He writes like you do. She acted like I was her best friend.* **3** what you would expect of; typical of: *Isn't that just like her!* **4** in the right frame of mind for doing or having: *I feel like running.* **5** the same or almost the same: *Juan's uncle promised him ten dollars if he could earn a like sum.* **6** a person or thing like another: *We shall not see her like again.* 1, 3, 4 *prep.,* 2 *conj.,* 5 *adj.,* 6 *n.*
and the like, and other things of that sort: *At the zoo we saw tigers, lions, leopards, and the like.*
like crazy, *Slang.* very much, very hard, very fast, etc.: *We worked like crazy.* Similar expressions are **like everything, like mad, like sixty,** and **like anything.**
the likes of, anyone or anything like: *This place is too fancy for the likes of you and me.*

USING WORDS ...... like
Like is often used informally instead of **as** in comparisons. In more formal language, use **as** when a clause follows: *She ran as she never did before.* Use **like** if just a noun follows, with or without adjectives: *She ran like the wind.*

like² (līk) **1** enjoy; find pleasure in: *My cat likes milk.* **2** have a friendly feeling for: *The children like their teacher.* **3** want; wish: *Come whenever you like.* **4 likes,** *pl.* what a person likes: *Mother knows all my likes and dislikes.* 1–3 *v.,* **liked, lik·ing;** 4 *n.* **—lik′a·ble,** *adj.* **—lik′ing,** *n.*
would like, a polite way of saying "want": *I would like a drink, please.*

–like *a suffix meaning:* **1** like; similar to, as in *wolflike, childlike.* **2** suited to; fit or proper for, as in *businesslike.*

like·ly (līk′lē) **1** probable; to be expected: *A likely result of this heavy rain is a flood. It is likely to snow today.* **2** probably: *I shall very likely be at home all day.* **3** seeming good, right, or true: *a likely story. Is this a likely place to fish?* 1, 3 *adj.,* **like·li·er, like·li·est;** 2 *adv.* **—like′li·hood′,** *n.*

lik·en (lī′kən) compare: *The poet likens life to a journey.* *v.*

like·ness (līk′nis) **1** the fact of being alike: *The boy's likeness to his father was striking.*

2 a picture, sculpture, or other image: *The great artist painted a likeness of the Queen.* 3 the appearance or shape: *His fairy godmother came to him in the likeness of a bird.* *n.*

like•wise (līk′wīz′) the same; in the same way; also: *Whatever I do, I expect you to do likewise.* *adv.*

li•lac (lī′lak *or* lī′lok) a tall shrub with clusters of tiny, fragrant, pale purple or white blossoms. *n.*

lilt (lilt) 1 a way of speaking in which the voice rises and falls in a light, musical way: *He talks with an Irish lilt.* 2 a lively, springing movement: *a lilt in her step.* *v.* —**lilt′ing,** *adj.*

The lily family is large. As well as lilies, it includes hyacinths, bluebells, tulips, onions, and asparagus!

wood lily

lil•y (lil′ē) 1 a plant that grows from a bulb, with leafy stems and showy, bell-shaped flowers. The **western red lily** is the provincial flower of Saskatchewan. The **white lily** is the provincial flower of Québec. 2 any of certain other plants with sweet-smelling flowers. The **water lily** grows out of the mud at the bottom of a lake or pond and has floating flowers and leaves called **lily pads.** The **lily of the valley** has tiny white flowers arranged in a row on a single stem. *n., pl.* **lil•ies.**

li•ma bean (lī′mə bēn′) a broad, flat, light green bean used for food.

limb (lim) 1 a leg, arm, or wing. 2 a large branch; bough: *They sawed the dead limb off the tree.* *n.*
out on a limb, in a risky situation.

lim•ber (lim′bər) 1 bending easily; flexible: *Willow is a limber wood. A pianist has to have limber fingers.* 2 make or become flexible; loosen up: *We did some exercises to limber up before our long run.* 1 *adj.,* 2 *v.*

lim•bo (lim′bō)
in limbo, so uncertain that no decisions can be made about it: *Our travel plans were in limbo until Mom got out of the hospital.* *n.*

lime[1] (līm) a white powder that results from burning limestone. It is used in cement and fertilizer. *n.*

lime[2] (līm) a green fruit like a lemon but smaller and even sourer. *n.*

lime•light (līm′līt′)
in the limelight, getting a lot of public attention. *n.*

lim•er•ick (lim′ə rik′) a kind of humorous poem with five lines. The first two lines rhyme with the last, and the third and fourth lines rhyme with each other. *n.*

Example:
There was a young lady named Lynn
Who was so exceedingly thin
That when she essayed
To drink lemonade
She slid down the straw and fell in.

lime•stone (līm′stōn′) a rock formed mainly from ancient shells and coral. Limestone is used for building and for making lime. *n.*

lim•it (lim′it) 1 the farthest point or edge; where something ends or must end: *the limit of a person's vision. I have reached the limit of my patience.* A **speed limit** is the highest speed allowed. 2 **limits,** *pl.* boundary; bounds: *the limits of Metropolitan Toronto.* 3 set a limit to; restrict: *We will limit the cost to $10.* 1, 2 *n.,* 3 *v.* —**lim′it•ed,** *adj.* —**lim′i•ta′tion,** *n.* —**lim′it•less,** *adj.*

lim•ou•sine (lim′ə zēn′ *or* lim′ə zēn′) a big, luxurious car, especially one driven by a paid driver. It sometimes has a pane of glass separating the passenger seats from the driver's seat. This word is often shortened to **limo** (lim′ō). *n.*

limp[1] (limp) 1 walk with difficulty because of a hurt leg or foot: *After falling down the stairs, she limped for several days.* 2 this kind of difficulty in walking: *She walked with a limp.* 1 *v.,* 2 *n.*

limp[2] (limp) not stiff or firm; hanging loosely or drooping: *The lettuce had lost its crispness and was quite limp. I am so tired I feel as limp as a rag.* *adj.*

a bat	e bed	i bid	o pot	u cup	th thin
ā cake	ē me	ī bite	ō go	ū rude	ᴛʜ then
ä bar	ə about	ər over	ȯ for	ů put	zh measure

line[1] (līn) **1** a long, narrow mark: *Draw two lines here.* **2** an edge or boundary: *That hedge marks our property line.* **3** a number of people or things coming one after another in space or time: *a line of cars. The Stuarts were a line of English kings.* **4** a row of words on a page: *a poem of 12 lines.* **5** **lines,** *pl.* **a** an actor's words in a play or movie. **b** a punishment in school where you must write the same thing over and over. **6** a rope, wire, or cord, especially for a specific purpose: *a fishing line, a measuring line, telephone lines.* **7** to mark with lines: *Please line your paper with a pencil and ruler.* **8** form a line along a road, hallway, etc.: *Cars lined the road for a kilometre.* **9** a transportation company: *a bus line, a railway line.* **10** a kind or brand of goods: *They manufacture a line of sports equipment.* **11** a branch of business; a kind of activity: *What is your line of work?* **12** a certain way of doing something: *That is a dangerous line of thought. Plan your project along these lines.* **13** 🍁in Ontario, a concession road: *He lives on Second Line.* 1–6, 9–13 *n.,* 7, 8 *v.,* **lined, lin·ing.**
draw the line, set a limit; say clearly what the difference is: *It's time to draw the line between borrowing and stealing.*
hold the line, **a** stay on the phone and wait: *Hold the line while I get my sister.* **b** keep your position without giving in to someone's attack.
in line, **a** in a line: *The children are all in line.* **b** in agreement: *This plan is in line with their ideas.* **c** behaving properly: *to keep someone in line.*
lay it on the line, state clearly what you expect or what you will do.
line up, form a line; form into a line: *People lined up to buy tickets.* A line formed by people waiting is a **lineup.**
out of line, **a** not suitable or proper: *Her last remark was out of line.* **b** not in agreement: *He's always out of line with the rest of the club members.*
read between the lines, find a hidden meaning in something said or written.
toe the line, do as you are required or expected: *If she doesn't toe the line, out she goes.*

line[2] (līn) cover the inside of something with a layer of material: *to line a jacket. The box was lined with velvet.* *v.,* **lined, lin·ing.**

lin·e·age (lin′ē ij) descent in a direct line from an ancestor: *They are proud of their dog's lineage from a North American champion.* *n.*

lin·e·ar (lin′ē ər) **1** having to do with a line or lines: *a linear drawing, a linear arrangement.* **2** strictly logical; going step by step: *linear thinking.* *adj.*

lin·en (lin′ən) **1** cloth or thread made from the fibres of the flax plant. **2** tablecloths, sheets, and towels. They were traditionally made of linen and some still are. *n.*

lin·er[1] (lī′nər) a ship or airplane belonging to a transportation company, especially one carrying passengers: *an ocean liner, a jet liner.* *n.*

lin·er[2] (lī′nər) something that acts as a lining or inside layer: *a diaper liner.* **Liner notes** are the song lyrics and other information printed on the card or booklet that lines a cassette or CD case. *n.*

lin·ger (ling′gər) stay on; go slowly, as if not wanting to leave: *Daylight lingers long in summer. She lingered after the others left.* *v.*

lin·ge·rie (lon′zhə rā′ *or* lan′zhə rē′) women's underwear, nightgowns, etc. *n.*

lin·go (ling′gō) *Informal.* the special language that goes with a certain kind of work or activity: *medical lingo, sports lingo.* *n.*

lin·guis·tics (ling gwis′tiks) the study of languages and how they work, including how the different languages show similar patterns and how they are unique. *n.* **—lin·guis′tic,** *adj.* **—lin′guist,** *n.*

lin·ing (lī′ning) a layer of material covering the inner surface of something: *the lining of a coat.* *n.*

link (lingk) **1** one ring or loop of a chain. **2** join or connect; show a connection between: *They linked arms. The article links poverty with poor health.* **3** anything that joins or connects: *a link between two ideas.* 1, 2 *n.,* 3 *v.*

linking verb (ling′king vərb) a verb that expresses no action, but links the subject of a sentence to a word or phrase that describes it. For example, *is* in *She is sad.* Other examples of linking verbs are *become* and *seem.* Some verbs with full meanings of their own can be used as linking verbs, too, like *turn* in *He turned pale.*

Grammar ✓Check . . . . linking verb

Whatever comes after a linking verb must describe the subject, which is a noun. So it could be an adjective: *I feel bad.*

It should never be an adverb: *I feel badly* is bad English!

li·no·le·um (lə nō′lē əm) a flexible, shiny material for covering floors. It is usually made of vinyl. *n.*

lin·seed (lin′sēd′) the seed of the flax plant. **Linseed oil** is used to make paint and to polish wood. *n.*

lint (lint) tiny bits of fluff that have come out of cloth. Lint collects in the **lint trap** of a clothes dryer. *n.*

Lions of the African plains live in groups (called prides) of up to thirty animals.

li·on (lī′ən) 1 a large, strong, wild cat, with a dull yellow coat, found in Africa and southern Asia. The male lion has a full, shaggy brown mane. The female is a **lioness.** 2 a person who is very brave and strong. *n.*
the lion's share, the biggest or best part.

lip (lip) 1 either one of the two soft, pinkish, movable edges of your mouth. 2 the curved-out edge of any opening: *the lip of a pitcher.* *n.*
button your lips, be quiet. **Zip your lips** means the same.
keep a stiff upper lip, be brave or firm; show no fear or discouragement.

lip reading (lip′ rē′ding) a way of understanding speech by watching the movements of a speaker's lips.

lip·stick (lip′stik′) a sort of crayon in a tube, used for colouring your lips. *n.*

lip–sync (lip′singk′) silently move your lips and often your head, hands, and body at the same time as a song is being played, so that you seem to be the one singing it. *v.,* **lip-synced, lip-sync·ing.**

liq·uid (lik′wid) 1 a substance that is not a solid or a gas; a substance that flows freely like water. 2 in the form of a liquid: *liquid soap, butter heated until it is liquid.* To **liquefy** is to change to a liquid. 3 clear, bright, or smooth like water. 1 *n.,* 2, 3 *adj.*

liquid crystal display (lik′wid kris′təl di splā′) the type of electronic screen on a calculator, telephone, laptop computer, or digital watch. *Abbreviation:* LCD

liq·uor (lik′ər) a strong alcoholic drink made by distilling, such as brandy, whisky, or rum. *n.*

lisp (lisp) 1 use a sound of *th* instead of the sound of *s* or *z* in speaking, as in "thoup" for "soup." 2 the act or sound of doing this: *He speaks with a lisp.* 1 *v.,* 2 *n.*

list[1] (list) 1 a set of similar things written or spoken one after the other: *a shopping list.* 2 make a list of; put in a list: *The winners' names are listed in the newspaper.* 1 *n.,* 2 *v.*

list[2] (list) lean to one side; tilt: *The sinking ship was listing so that water lapped its decks* (*v.*). *That sailboat has a slight list* (*n.*). *v. or n.*

lis·ten (lis′ən) 1 try to hear; pay attention to a sound: *She listened for the sound of a car. I like to listen to music.* 2 obey or follow: *If you had listened to my advice this wouldn't have happened.* *v.* **—lis′ten·er,** *n.*
listen in, **a** listen to other people's private talk: *I listened in on the extension.* **b** tune in to a station on the radio and listen: *Listen in next week for another drama.*

list·less (list′lis) seeming too tired to care about anything; not interested in doing anything: *a dull and listless mood.* *adj.* **—list′less·ly,** *adv.*

lists (lists) in the Middle Ages, a place where knights fought in tournaments. *pl.n.*

lit (lit) a past tense and past participle of **light[1]:** *Have you lit the candles? Yes, I lit them all.* *v.*

li·tchi (lē′chē) a small, round fruit that grows on a tropical tree. It has a brittle shell and is white, sweet, and juicy on the inside. **Litchi nut** is another name for it. *n., pl.* **lit·chis.**

lit·er·al (lit′ə rəl) 1 following the exact words of the original, word for word: *The French for "potato" is "pomme de terre"; the literal meaning is "apple of earth."* 2 using words in their normal or basic meaning and without exaggeration; actual. When we say *She flew down the stairs to meet them,* we do not mean *fly* in the literal sense of the word. *adj.* **—lit′er·al·ly,** *adv.*

USING WORDS ...... literally

Many people use **literally** as a way to add force to an expression: *Ricky literally tore through the house.* But this means that Ricky *actually* ripped the house in half!

Avoid using **literally** in sentences like these. Instead, choose an expression that is striking enough to get your meaning across: *Ricky raced like lightning through the house.*

a bat	e bed	i bid	o pot	u cup	th thin
ā cake	ē me	ī bite	ō go	ū rude	ᴛʜ then
ä bar	ə about	ər over	ô for	ů put	zh measure

lit·er·ate (lit′ə rit) 1 able to read and write. 2 knowing at least the basics about something: *Are you computer literate?* *adj.* —**lit′er·a·cy,** *n.*

lit·er·a·ture (lit′ə rə chər) 1 written works, such as novels, plays, and poetry, that last a long time because of their excellent style or thought: *Margaret Laurence is a famous name in Canadian literature.* Anything to do with literature is **literary.** 2 all the books and articles on a subject: *the literature of stamp collecting.* 3 printed information; brochures and so on: *We sent for some literature about New Brunswick to plan our trip there.* *n.*

CONFUSABLES ..... literary

literary means "to do with literature": *a literary journal*
literate means "able to read and write": *You're literate!*

lit·mus (lit′məs) a blue colouring matter that turns red in an acid solution and back to blue in an alkaline solution. *n.*

li·tre (lē′tər) a unit used with the SI for measuring volume or space, equal to one cubic decimetre. The litre is used for measuring liquids and other products such as ice cream and fruit, and for measuring how much a container can hold. One litre of water has a mass of one kilogram. **Liter** is another spelling. *Symbol:* L *n.*

lit·ter (lit′ər) 1 bits of garbage scattered around: *Don't leave litter on the playground.* 2 leave garbage and other things lying around; make untidy: *You have littered the room with candy wrappers, pop cans, and dirty plates.* **Litterbug** is an informal word for a person who litters. 3 the baby animals born at the same time to one mother: *a litter of puppies.* 4 fine gravel or other material used in a box to absorb the body wastes of a house cat. 5 a framework for carrying a person lying down, especially a sick or wounded person. 1, 3–5 *n.,* 2 *v.*

lit·tle (lit′əl) 1 not big or long; small or short: *An ant is little. Wait a little while.* 2 small in amount or importance: *little food, little imagination, a little problem.* 3 a small amount; a short time or distance: *to save a little for later, to move up a little* (*n.*). *He travels little* (*adv.*). 4 hardly at all; not in the least: *Little did she know what lay ahead.* 1, 2 *adj.,* **less** or **less·er, least;** or **lit·tler, lit·tlest;** 3 *n.,* 3, 4 *adv.,* **less, least.** —**lit′tle·ness,** *n.*
little by little, by small amounts; slowly; gradually.
make little of, treat as unimportant: *They made little of their troubles.*
not a little, much; very: *He was not a little upset by the accident.*
think little of, not value very much.

live[1] (liv) 1 have life; be or stay alive: *All people have an equal right to live. They managed to live through the war.* 2 last or endure: *Her memory will live forever.* 3 spend your life in a certain way: *to live well, to live a life of ease.* 4 have your home: *My aunt lives in Victoria.* *v.,* **lived, liv·ing.** —**liv′a·ble,** *adj.*
live down, cause others to forget or overlook a past mistake because of your continued good behaviour: *He is determined to live down that disgrace.*
live it up, *Informal.* enjoy lots of pleasures and luxuries.
live on, a feed or support yourself with: *They live on a small income. Birds live on seeds and insects.* **Live off** means the same. **b** endure; remain: *His spirit lives on in his works of art.*
live out, a put into practice: *to live out your ideals.* **b** survive through: *to live out a war.*
live up to, act or turn out as expected or promised: *The car has not lived up to the salesperson's description.*
live with, be satisfied with; accept.

live[2] (līv) 1 having life; living: *a live animal.* 2 burning or glowing: *live coals.* 3 carrying an electric current: *a live wire.* 4 ready to be exploded: *a live bomb.* 5 in radio or TV, broadcast while the event is going on and not from a tape or film made beforehand: *a live interview with Karen Kain.* 6 made at a public performance and not in a studio: *a live recording of a concert.* *adj.*

live·li·hood (līv′lē hůd′) a way of earning a living or supporting yourself: *Farming is their livelihood.* *n.*

live·long (liv′long′)
the livelong day, all day long. *adj.*

live·ly (līv′lē) 1 full of life, energy, and spirit; active: *A good night's sleep made us all lively again.* 2 exciting: *We had a lively time during the hurricane.* 3 bright; vivid: *lively colours.* *adj.,* **live·li·er, live·li·est.** —**live′li·ness,** *n.*

liv·en (lī′vən)
liven up, make or become more lively; brighten: *A few games would liven up this party.* *v.*

liv·er (liv′ər) 1 the large, reddish brown organ in the upper abdomen of humans and other animals with backbones. The liver makes bile, helps the body absorb food, and helps remove wastes from the blood. 2 an animal's liver used as food: *Liver is a good source of iron and vitamins.* **Liverwurst** is a spread made of ground or chopped liver, spices, and sometimes other meat. *n.*

liv·er·y (liv′ə rē) a uniform for the staff of a noble household or, in modern times, a hotel staff. *n., pl.* **liv·er·ies.**

live·stock (līv′stok′) farm animals, such as cows, horses, sheep, and pigs. *n.*

liv·id (liv′id) **1** dull bluish or greyish from a bruise: *livid marks on an arm.* **2** very pale from shock, or red with anger. **3** *Informal.* very angry: *Their insults made him livid.* *adj.*

liv·ing (liv′ing) **1** having life; alive: *a living plant.* **2** vigorous; strong; active: *a living faith.* **3** still in use: *a living language.* **4** a way of supporting yourself; livelihood: *She earns a living as a grocer.* **5** life or a way of life: *healthful living, the joy of living.* 1–3 *adj.,* 4, 5 *n.*

living room (liv′ing rūm′) a room in a house or apartment, used for relaxing and for entertaining guests.

The name of this Australian lizard is "thorny devil." The grooves in its skin channel rainwater or dew toward its mouth.

liz·ard (liz′ərd) a reptile with a long body, long tail, movable eyelids, and usually four legs. The iguana and chameleon are lizards. *n.*

lla·ma (lȧ′mə *or* lam′ə) a woolly South American animal like a camel, but smaller and without a hump. Llamas are raised for their wool, meat, and milk, and are also used to carry loads. *n., pl.* **lla·mas** or **lla·ma.**

lo (lō) an old or poetic word for "look!" *interj.*

load (lōd) **1** anything being carried: *She had a load of books in her knapsack.* **2** put something on or in a carrier of some kind: *to load a van with camping gear. The workers are loading grain into the ships.* **3** burden: *They were loaded down with debt* (*v.*). *Talking to you has taken a load off my mind* (*n.*). **4** **loads,** *pl. Informal.* a large amount: *We have loads of food here.* **5** fill; put a lot in or on: *a day loaded with fun activities.* **6** put bullets or shot in a gun. **7** put something needed into a machine: *to load film into a camera.* **8** in science, the force overcome by a machine. In the case of a lever, ramp, or pulley, the load is the mass of the object being lifted. 1, 3, 4, 8 *n.,* 2, 3, 5–7 *v.*
loaded question, a question worded so that you look bad no matter what your answer.

loaf[1] (lōf) **1** bread shaped and baked as one piece. **2** anything shaped like this: *a meat loaf.* *n., pl.* **loaves.**

loaf[2] (lōf) spend time doing nothing: *I can loaf all day Saturday.* *v.*

loam (lōm) rich, fertile soil containing decayed plant matter mixed with clay and sand. *n.*

loan (lōn) **1** anything that someone lends or borrows, especially money: *He asked his brother for a loan.* **2** lend: *Ursel loaned me her pen.* **3** the act of lending: *She asked for the loan of his pen.* 1, 3 *n.,* 2 *v.*
on loan, borrowed; loaned: *This CD is on loan from the library.*

loath (lōth) unwilling: *The little girl was loath to leave her mother.* **Loth** is another spelling, pronounced the same. *adj.*

loathe (lōᴛʜ) hate: *I loathe ketchup.* Something you hate is **loathsome.** *v.,* **loathed, loath·ing.**

loaves (lōvz) plural of **loaf**[1]. *n.*

lob·by (lob′ē) **1** a large entrance hall or waiting area: *a hotel lobby, a theatre lobby.* **2** a group that tries to influence the government: *There is a strong lobby in favour of better laws to protect the environment.* **3** try to influence the government: *to lobby for stricter gun controls.* 1, 2 *n., pl.* **lob·bies;** 3 *v.,* **lob·bied, lob·by·ing.**
—lob′by·ist, *n.*

lobe (lōb) a rounded part sticking out. The lobe of your ear is the rounded lower end. *n.*

Most lobsters have dark blue or dark green shells, which turn bright red when cooked.

lob·ster (lob′stər) a large sea crustacean with two big front claws and a muscular tail. It is good to eat. *n.*

lob·stick (lob′stik′) in the North, a spruce or pine tree trimmed of all but the top branches. Travellers often used lobsticks as landmarks. *n.*

a bat	e bed	i bid	o pot	u cup	th thin
ā cake	ē me	ī bite	ō go	ū rude	ᴛʜ then
ȧ bar	ə about	ər over	ȯ for	u̇ put	zh measure

Locks

When a Yale lock is closed, springs push a row of pins into a metal cylinder so that it cannot be turned. The notches on the lock's key push the pins free of the cylinder, so that it can be turned.

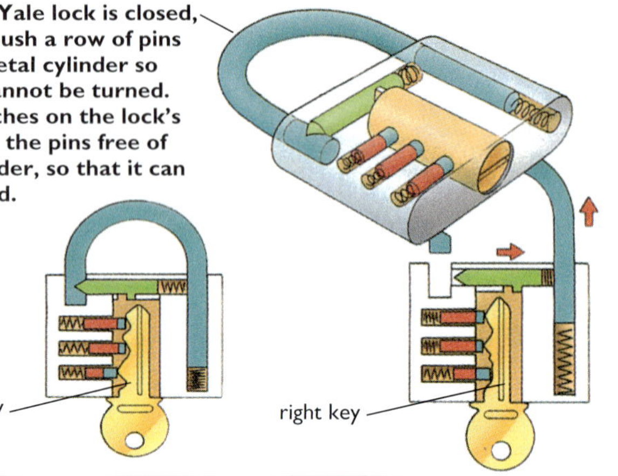

A combination lock uses numbers for a key. When the numbers are turned to the correct combination, the slots inside line up and the bolt can be pulled out.

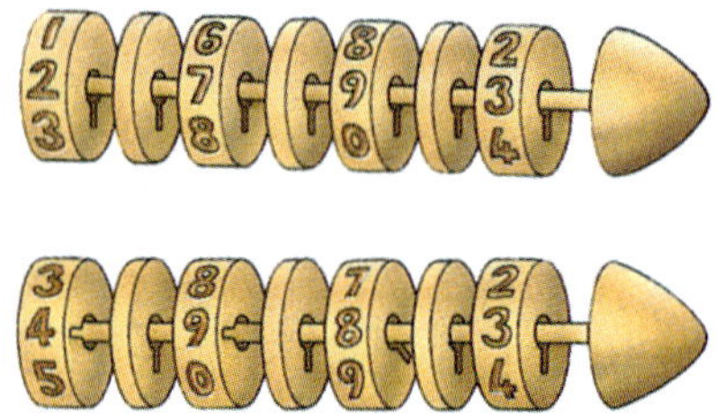

lo·cal (lō′kəl) **1** having to do with just a certain limited place or area: *the local doctor, local news.* A **locality** (lō kal′ə tē) is a neighbourhood. **2** of just one part of the body: *local anesthetic.* **3** a person who lives in a certain place and is not a visitor: *We asked one of the locals for directions.* 1, 2 *adj.,* 3 *n.* —**lo′cal·ly,** *adv.*

lo·cate (lō kāt′ *or* lō′kāt) **1** set up in a place: *Early settlers located where there was water. He located his new store in Yellowknife.* **2** find: *The search party tried to locate the crashed plane.* *v.,* **lo·cat·ed, lo·cat·ing.**
be located, be situated: *Fredericton is located on a river.*

lo·ca·tion (lō kā′shən) position; place: *The cottage was in a sheltered location.* *n.*
on location, at a place outside the movie studio: *All the outdoor scenes were shot on location.*

lock[1] (lok) **1** a device for fastening a door, lid, suitcase, etc. so that it cannot be opened without a key or a pass card. **2** fasten or shut up with a lock: *to lock a door, to lock up jewels in a safe.* **3** join, fit, snap, or hold in place: *The pieces lock securely together.* **4** a section of a canal closed off with gates so that the water level inside it can be changed by opening the gate and letting water in or out. It is a way to raise or lower ships. 1, 4 *n.,* 2, 3 *v.*
lock out, refuse to let workers work until they accept the employer's terms. The noun is **lockout.**
lock, stock, and barrel, completely.
under lock and key, locked up.

lock[2] (lok) a curl of hair. **Locks** is another word for "hair." *n.*

lock·er (lok′ər) **1** a little metal closet or cupboard that can be locked, for keeping your things in at school, at a public pool, at a train station, etc. **2** a lockable trunk or chest for personal things. *n.*

lock·et (lok′it) a necklace with a small case on it, for holding a picture of someone or a lock of hair. *n.*

lock·smith (lok′smith′) a person who makes or repairs locks and keys. *n.*

lo·co·mo·tive (lō′kə mō′tiv) **1** a railway engine. **2** any engine that goes from place to place on its own power. **Locomotion** is movement from place to place. Your **locomotor** muscles are the leg muscles that let you move from place to place. *n.*

lo·cust (lō′kəst) a sort of grasshopper. Certain kinds of locusts come in great swarms and destroy crops by eating them. *n.*

lode (lōd) a vein of metal ore: *The miners struck a rich lode of copper.* *n.*

lodge (loj) **1** a building with places to sleep, that is part of a tourist resort, hunting camp, etc.: *They run a ski lodge up in the mountains.* **2** live for a while in a rented place called a **lodging.** **3** get caught or stuck in a place; stop and go no further: *My kite lodged in the branches of a big tree.* **4** a traditional First Nations dwelling. **5** the home of a beaver or otter. **6** a club or society, one of its local branches, or the place where it meets. 1, 4–6 *n.,* 2, 3 *v.,* **lodged, lodg·ing.**
—**lodg′er,** *n.*

loft (loft) **1** an open storage space formed under a roof by a ceiling that goes partway across, making a kind of huge shelf. In a barn, it is used for hay; other lofts may be turned into studios or small apartments. A **loft bed** is a bed made like a high shelf. **2** a gallery or raised area in a church, for the choir or organ. *n.*

loft·y (lof′tē) **1** very high: *lofty mountains.* **2** noble: *lofty ideals.* *adj.,* **loft·i·er, loft·i·est.**
—**loft′i·ly,** *adv.* —**loft′i·ness,** *n.*

log (log) 1 a length of wood just as it comes from the tree. 2 cut down trees, cut them into logs, and get them out of the forest. 3 the daily record of a ship's voyage, or any other record to keep track of events: *The scientist kept a log of her observations during the year-long experiment.*
4 write something in a log. A log is kept in a **logbook.**
5 cover or do: *We logged 32 km on the first day of our bike trip.* 1, 3 *n.,* 2, 4, 5 *v.,* **logged, log·ging.** —**log′ger,** *n.*
log in, sign a book to show that you have arrived. You **log out** when you leave.
log on, start a session at a computer by keying in a password or other identification, called your **login** or **logon.** You **log off** by shutting the computer down according to a set procedure.

log·ger·head (log′ər hedz′)
at loggerheads, disagreeing with somebody and unable to settle it: *Karina and Stu were at loggerheads about whether to go to the game.* *n.*

log·ic (loj′ik) sound, careful, clear reasoning or argument that lets you reach a conclusion from facts you already know: *They were convinced by his logic.* *n.*
—**log′i·cal,** *adj.* —**log′i·cal·ly,** *adv.*

lo·go (lō′gō) a special symbol used by a company as a trademark, in advertising and so on. The publisher's logo is on the spine of this dictionary. *n.*

loin (loin) 1 Usually, **loins,** *pl.* the part of the body between the ribs and the hips. The loins are on both sides of the backbone. 2 a piece of meat from this part of an animal: *a loin of pork.* *n.*

loi·ter (loi′tər) move slowly or hang around in a place: *She loitered along the street, looking into all the store windows.* *v.*

loll (lol) 1 lie back or lean in a lazy manner: *to loll in an armchair.* 2 hang loosely or droop: *A dog's tongue lolls out in hot weather.* *v.*

lol·li·pop (lol′ē pop′) a piece of hard candy on the end of a small stick; sucker. *n.*

lone (lōn) alone; single: *The lone traveller was glad to reach home.* A **loner** is someone who spends most of his or her time alone. *adj.*

lone·ly (lōn′lē) 1 feeling sad because you are alone and longing for company or friends: *He was lonely while his brother was away.* 2 without many people around: *a lonely road, a lonely job.* **Lonesome** is another word for either meaning. *adj.,* **lone·li·er, lone·li·est.**
—**lone′li·ness,** *n.*

long[1] (long) 1 measuring far from end to end, or taking a lot of time: *a long driveway, long legs, a long story.* 2 a lot of time: *Summer will come before long (n.). I can't stay long (adv.).* 3 for the whole time mentioned: *We worked all day long.* 4 of a vowel, sounding like its name, as the *i* in *hide.* 1, 4 *adj.,* **long·er** (long′gər), **long·est** (long′gist); 2 *n.,* 2, 3 *adv.*
a long face, a sad expression.
a long shot, a try that seems unlikely to succeed: *That guess was a long shot but it turned out to be right!*
as long as or **so long as,** provided that; only if.
in the long run, over a long period of time; eventually: *The system will work out well in the long run.*
not by a long shot, by far not: *"Did she win?" "No, not by a long shot."*
the long and the short of it, the main point or points; summary: *I won't go into detail; the long and the short of it is that I can't come.*

long[2] (long) have a very deep desire: *He longed for his mother. She longed to see him.* Such a desire is a **longing.** *v.* —**long′ing·ly,** *adv.*

long–dis·tance (long′ dis′təns) 1 to do with a telephone service that connects you with somebody outside your local area: *a long-distance call (adj.),* to *call long-distance (adv.).* 2 going a long way: *a long-distance race, a long-distance runner.* 1, 2 *adj.,* 1 *adv.*

long division (long′ də vizh′ən) in arithmetic, division with numbers that have usually three or more digits, where the steps of the process are written down in full one under the other.

long·hand (long′hand′) ordinary handwriting. *n.*

long·house (long′hous′) a long, one-room dwelling of certain First Nations peoples, especially the Iroquois, in which several families of a community lived together. *n.*

lon·gi·tude (long′gə tyūd′ *or* lon′jə tyūd′) a distance east or west on the earth's surface, measured in degrees from the imaginary line running north and south through Greenwich, England. The longitude of Ottawa is about 76°W. On maps, lines running between the North and South Poles represent lines of longitude, or **meridians.** *n.* —**lon′gi·tu′di·nal,** *adj.*

CONFUSABLES .... longitude

You can remember the difference between **longitude** and **latitude** by thinking that lines of l **AT** itude are parallel to the equ **AT** or.

a bat	e bed	i bid	o pot	u cup	th thin
ā cake	ē me	ī bite	ō go	ū rude	ᴛʜ then
ä bar	ə about	ər over	ô for	ù put	zh measure

long jump (long′ jump′) an athletic contest where you try to jump as far as possible. The long jump from a running start is one of the Olympic track-and-field events. The **standing long jump** is a long jump from a standing start. It is often included in school track-and-field meets.

look (lůk) **1** try to see something; pay attention with your eyes: *Look at the pictures.* **2** search: *I looked all over for my mitts.* **3** a glance; the act of trying to see: *He took a quick look at the map.* **4** seem; appear: *She looks pale. You look like Michael J. Fox.* People or things that look the same are **look-alikes.** **5** appearance: *The deserted house had a gloomy look.* **6** **looks,** *pl.* personal appearance: *The boy has his father's good looks.* 1, 2, 4 *v.,* 3, 5, 6 *n.*
look after, take care of: *He looked after his little brother.*
look down on, think of as not very good or important.
look for, expect: *We'll look for you tonight at 6:00.*
look forward to, expect with pleasure: *We look forward to seeing you.*
look in, make a short visit: *She said she'd look in on her way back.*
look into, try to find out about.
look on, **a** watch without taking part: *The teacher did the experiment while we looked on.* **b** think of; consider: *I look on her as a very able person.*
look out, be careful; watch out: *Look out for cars as you cross the street.*
look over, examine; inspect: *The police officer looked over Dad's driver's licence.*
look to, **a** turn to for help: *I look to you for advice.* **b** pay attention to; take care of: *Look to your own problems first.*
look up, **a** find in a book: *She looked up the word in the dictionary.* **b** *Informal.* call on; visit: *Look me up when you come to town.* **c** improve: *Things are looking up.*
look up to, respect; admire.

looking glass (lůk′ing glas′) an old word for "mirror."

look·out (lůk′out′) **1** a place to keep watch from, especially a high place: *From the lookout, she could see the smoke 10 km away.* **2** a person or group whose job is to watch for something: *"Land ho!" cried the lookout to the sailors below.* **3** job; responsibility: *Don't expect me to make the invitations; that's your lookout.* *n.*

loom[1] (lūm) a frame or machine for weaving threads into cloth. *n.*

loom[2] (lūm) appear as a large, threatening shape: *An iceberg loomed through the fog.* *v.*

loon (lūn) a large, mostly black and white diving bird that nests in northern lands and has a loud, wild cry. *n.*

loon·ie (lū′nē) the Canadian one-dollar coin. It has a picture of a loon on one side. *n.*

loon·y (lū′nē) *Informal.* crazy or very foolish: *What a loony idea!* *adj.,* **loon′i·er, loon′i·est.**

loop (lūp) **1** the curved shape formed by a string, ribbon, etc. that crosses over itself or bends back on itself. **2** anything shaped like this: *The road makes a wide loop around the lake.* In handwriting, *b, g, h,* and *l* often have loops. **3** make a loop or loops in. 1, 2 *n.,* 3 *v.*
throw someone for a loop, *Informal.* surprise and confuse someone.

loop·hole (lūp′hōl′) **1** a small opening. **2** a weakness in a rule or law, letting you get away with something. *n.*

loose (lūs) **1** not firmly set or fastened: *a loose tooth, a loose thread.* **2** not tight: *loose clothing.* **3** not attached together or packaged: *loose papers, loose candy.* **Looseleaf** is loose sheets of lined paper to put in a binder. **4** free; not shut in or tied up: *The dogs are loose.* **5** not strict or exact: *a loose report of the accident.* **6** showing little attention to what is right or wrong: *loose conduct, a loose character.* *adj.,* **loos·er, loos·est.** —**loose′ly,** *adv.* —**loos′en,** *v.*

CONFUSABLES .... loose

loose means "not tight": *My tooth is loose.*
lose means "misplace": *Don't lose your scarf.*

loot (lūt) **1** stolen goods: *The burglars tried to sell their loot.* **2** rob, especially in war or during a riot or natural disaster: *Hooligans looted the jewellery store.* **3** *Informal.* goodies taken home from a party or collected at Halloween. 1, 3 *n.,* 2 *v.* —**loot′er,** *n.*

lop (lop) cut off: *to lop off branches of a tree.* *v.,* **lopped, lop·ping.**

lope (lōp) **1** run with a long, easy stride: *The coyote loped along the trail.* **2** a long, easy stride. 1 *v.,* **loped, lop·ing;** 2 *n.*

lop·sid·ed (lop′sī′did) larger or heavier on one side than the other; unevenly balanced. *adj.* —**lop′sid′ed·ly,** *adv.* —**lop′sid′ed·ness,** *n.*

lord (lôrd) **1** a ruler, master, or chief; a person who has power or authority over others. In the Middle Ages, a lord owned a lot of land and had authority over the people living on it. **2** **the Lord,** **a** in the Christian and Jewish religions, God. **b** in the Christian religion, Christ. **3** in the United Kingdom, a high-ranking nobleman: *Lord Simcoe was governor of Upper Canada.* *n.* —**lord′ly,** *adj.* —**lord′ship′,** *n.*
lord it over someone, be bossy and arrogant toward someone.

lore (lôr) knowledge; the facts and stories about a certain subject: *fairy lore, bird lore, Greek lore.* *n.*

lose (lüz) 1 not have any longer because it has been taken away from you by an accident, a death, punishment, or in any other way: *to lose a grandparent, to lose a privilege. They lost all their furniture in the fire.* 2 be unable to find; forget where something is: *to lose your way, to lose a book.* 3 fail to win: *Our team lost the game.* 4 fail to keep: *to lose your balance. I lost interest.* 5 waste or not be able to make the most of: *to lose time, to lose a chance.* 6 cause to lose: *That one mistake lost him his job.* 7 of a watch or clock, run slow: *That clock loses five minutes a day.* *v.,* **lost, los·ing.** —**los′er,** *n.*
lose out, fail to get what you could or should have got: *You lose out on a good education if you don't make any effort in school.*
lose yourself, become absorbed: *I lost myself in the story.*
lost cause, something that can never be saved, improved, or achieved: *I'm afraid changing his mind is a lost cause.*
lost in, completely absorbed by: *lost in her own thoughts.*
lost to, paying absolutely no attention to: *He was lost to their cries for help.*

loss (los) 1 the act or fact of losing or being lost: *Winning an argument is not worth the loss of a friend.* 2 the person, thing, or amount lost: *a loss of $10 000. The fire was finally put out, but her house was a total loss.* *n.*
at a loss, puzzled; not sure what to do or say: *He was at a loss for words.*

lot (lot) 1 Often, **lots,** *pl. Informal.* a great many; a great deal: *You have lots of time. I have a lot of marbles.* 2 a piece of ground marked off as a unit: *His house is between two empty lots.* 3 a number of people or things considered as a group; a collection: *This lot of oranges is not as good as the last. Those kids are a friendly lot.* 4 a method of deciding something, where each person picks blindly from a number of bits of paper or other objects, and the decision depends on who ends up with the specially marked piece: *It was settled by lot.* The process is called **drawing lots.** 5 a what you end up with by this method: *It was my lot to go first.* b your fate or fortune: *It was his lot to die in battle.* *n.*

USING WORDS .... lot

The words **a lot of** or **lots of** can be used in informal English. In everyday language you might say: *I own lots of different shoes.* But in formal English you would say: *I own a variety of shoes,* or *I own many different shoes.*

Other words that can replace **a lot** or **lots** are *numerous* or *several.*

lo·tion (lō′shən) a liquid medicine or beauty product that you put on your skin. *n.*

lot·ter·y (lot′ə rē) a game where you can win a prize of money by lot or chance. In a lottery a large number of tickets are sold, but only some of them win prizes. *n., pl.* **lot·ter·ies.**

loud (loud) 1 not quiet or soft; with a powerful sound: *a loud voice. A gun goes off with a loud bang (adj.). He blew the bugle long and loud (adv.).* 2 *Informal.* too bright or flashy: *loud clothes.* 1, 2 *adj.,* 1 *adv.* —**loud′ly,** *adv.* —**loud′ness,** *n.*
out loud, so others can hear; not to yourself or in a whisper.

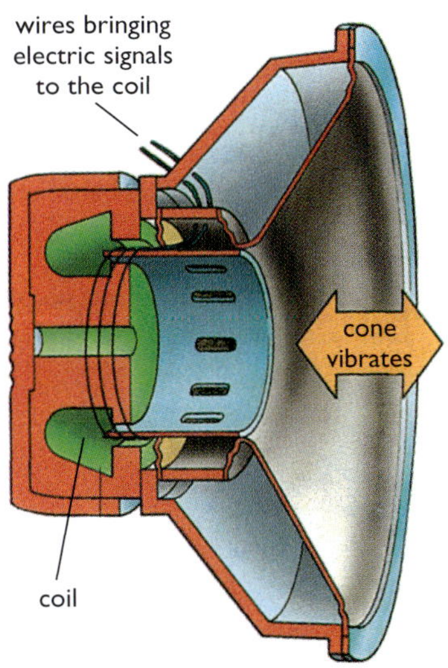

Most loudspeakers consist of a cone attached to an electromagnet. The cone is made of a special paper. As electric signals change, the coil vibrates. This makes the cone vibrate, which in turn vibrates the air, creating sound waves.

loud·speak·er (loud′spē′kər) the part of a stereo or public address system that changes the electrical signal into sound. The sound can be made louder by increasing the strength of the electrical signal. *n.*

lounge (lounj) 1 stand, sit, or lie in a relaxed, lazy way: *He lounged in an old chair.* 2 a comfortable room where people can sit and relax: *a hotel lounge.* 1 *v.,* **lounged, loung·ing;** 2 *n.*

louse (lous) 1 a small, wingless insect that makes its home in the hair or on the skin of people or other animals, causing irritation. 2 any of various similar insects that feed on animals or plants. *n., pl.* **lice.**

lous·y (lou′zē) *Informal.* bad; miserable: *I don't like that restaurant because the food is lousy.* *adj.,* **lous·i·er, lous·i·est.** —**lous′i·ly,** *adv.* —**lous′i·ness,** *n.*

a bat	e bed	i bid	o pot	u cup	th thin
ā cake	ē me	ī bite	ō go	ū rude	ᴛʜ then
ä bar	ə about	ər over	ô for	ů put	zh measure

love (luv) 1 care very much for; think of as very precious; be devoted to: *She loves her mother. I love my country.* 2 the deep, warm feeling you have toward someone or something thought of in this way: *love for your family, love for a sweetheart.* 3 like very much; take great pleasure in: *He loves music. Most kids love ice cream.* 4 a strong liking: *a love of books.* 5 a person or thing that is loved: *Come here, my love. Music is his first love.* 1, 3 *v.,* **loved, lov·ing;** 2, 4, 5 *n.* **—lov′a·ble,** *adj.* **—lov′er,** *n.* **—lov′ing·ly,** *adv.*
fall in love, begin to love.
in love, feeling love. **Lovebird** is a nickname for someone in love. A person who is so deeply in love that he or she cannot think straight is **lovesick.**
love affair, a relationship of love: *a love affair with another person, a love affair with Charlottetown.*

love·ly (luv′lē) 1 beautiful in looks or character: *a lovely sunset. She is one of the loveliest girls we know.* 2 *Informal.* very nice: *We had a lovely holiday.* *adj.,* **love·li·er, love·li·est.**

low¹ (lō) 1 not high or tall; not far above the ground, floor, or bottom: *a low bridge, a low shelf, a low jump.* 2 less than average in amount or degree: *a low temperature, a job with low pay.* 3 not powerful or important: *She rose from a low position to president of the company.* 4 in music, deep in pitch: *a low note.* 5 not loud: *a low murmur.* 6 unfavourable; bad: *We have a low opinion of cheaters.* 7 nearly used up: *Our water supply is low.* 8 in poor health or spirits: *The sick man is very low today.* 9 mean; dirty: *That was a low trick.* 10 at or to a low level, position, or amount: *The sun is sinking low. Supplies have run low.* 11 a low point or level: *Gas prices have fallen to a new low.* 1–9 *adj.,* 10 *adv.,* 11 *n.*
keep a low profile, try not to attract attention or be noticed.
lie low, *Informal.* stay hidden: *The robbers decided to lie low for a time.*
low in something, having little of something: *These crackers are low in fat.*
low tide, the time when the ocean is lowest on the shore.

low² (lō) make the sound of a cow mooing; moo. *v.*

low·er (lō′ər) 1 let down, take down, or come down: *to lower a flag. The level of the lake has lowered.* 2 lessen: *to lower the volume of the radio.* 3 less; farther down: *My marks were lower last year than this year (adj.). The boat sank lower in the water (adv.).* 1, 2 *v.,* 3 *adj.* or *adv.*

Lower Canada (lō′ər kan′ə də) an old name for the province of Québec. Lower Canada was farther down the St. Lawrence River than Upper Canada.

lower case (lō′ər kās′) letters that are not capitals. The letters *a* and *b* are in lower case; *A* and *B* are not. Capitals are called **upper case.** **—low′er-case′,** *adj.*

lowest common denominator (lō′ist kom′ən di nom′ə nā′tər) the lowest number that can be evenly divided by each denominator in a set of fractions. For the fractions ¾, ⅚, and ⅔, the lowest common denominator is 12; it can be evenly divided by 4, 6, and 3, so the fractions can be changed to 9/12, 10/12, and 8/12.

lowest terms (lō′ist tərmz′) the form of a fraction where there is no number that can be evenly divided into both the numerator and the denominator. The fraction ⅚ is in its lowest terms; the fraction 4/6 is not, because both 4 and 6 can be divided by 2, giving ⅔.

low·land (lō′lənd) land that is lower and flatter than the rest. *n.*

low·ly (lō′lē) 1 low in rank or position: *a lowly servant.* 2 humble or modest: *He had a lowly opinion of himself.* *adj.,* **low·li·er, low·li·est.**

loy·al (loi′əl) true and faithful to someone or something; supporting someone and never giving up on that person no matter what happens: *a loyal friend. During the revolution some people remained loyal to the king.* *adj.* **—loy′al·ly,** *adv.* **—loy′al·ty,** *n.*

loy·al·ist (loi′ə list) 1 a person who supports the existing government or ruler in a time of revolt. 2 🍁 **Loyalist,** a United Empire Loyalist, any of the people in the American colonies who continued to support British rule during the American Revolution. Many of them moved to Canada. *n.*

loz·enge (loz′inj) 1 a small tablet of medicine or a piece of candy: *Cough drops are sometimes called lozenges.* 2 a diamond-shaped figure or design like this: ◊ *n.*

lu·bri·cate (lū′brə kāt′) put oil or grease or another slippery substance on something to make parts move smoothly and easily. Such a substance is called a **lubricant** (lū′brə kənt). *v.,* **lu·bri·cat·ed, lu·bri·cat·ing.** **—lu′bri·ca′tion,** *n.*

luck (luk) 1 whatever seems to happen or come to a person just by accident; chance: *Luck was against the losers, even though they played better on the whole.* 2 good fortune; things going well, completely by chance: *Lots of luck to you. Her success was more than just luck.* *n.* **—luck′y,** *adj.* **—luck′i·ly,** *adv.* **—luck′less,** *adj.*
down on your luck, *Informal.* having bad luck.
in luck, having good luck; lucky: *I'm in luck today; I found a toonie.* **Out of luck** is the opposite.
luck out, *Informal.* be very lucky: *She lucked out and won $100.*

push your luck, *Informal.* take needless risks when things are going well.
try your luck, see what you can do or get: *Try your luck with this game.*

lu·di·crous (lü′də krəs) so absurd that it is funny; ridiculous: *Who would wear that ludicrous outfit?* *adj.* —**lu′di·crous·ly,** *adv.*

lug (lug) pull or carry with effort: *We lugged the heavy bags of groceries all the way home.* *v.,* **lugged, lug·ging.**

luge (lüzh) a kind of very fast, low sled that you ride lying on your back down a steep, narrow course specially made for it. The **luge race** is an Olympic event. *n.*

lug·gage (lug′ij) suitcases and so on used by a traveller to carry his or her things; baggage. *n.*

luke·warm (lük′wôrm′) **1** neither hot nor cold; slightly warm or cool. **2** showing little enthusiasm; half-hearted: *a lukewarm reaction.* *adj.*

lull (lul) **1** make or become calm or quiet: *to lull a baby to sleep, to lull someone's fears. The wind lulled.* **2** a period of calmness or quietness: *We ran home during a lull in the storm.* 1 *v.,* 2 *n.*

lul·la·by (lul′ə bī′) a song to lull a baby to sleep. *n., pl.* **lul·la·bies.**

lum·ber¹ (lum′bər) wood cut into boards or beams. A **lumberjack** cuts down trees and gets the logs to a mill; **lumbering** is the work of turning trees into lumber, and a **lumberyard** is an outdoor area for storing lumber. *n.*

lum·ber² (lum′bər) move along heavily and noisily: *The dumptruck lumbered down the road.* *v.*

lu·min·ous (lü′mə nəs) **1** having its own light; shining in the dark: *The stars are luminous. My watch has luminous numbers.* **2** bright: *luminous eyes.* *adj.*

lump (lump) **1** a solid mass of no particular shape: *a lump of coal.* **2** a swelling; a bump: *There is a lump on my head where I banged it.* **3** combine and deal with in a mass or as a whole: *We will lump all our expenses together.* **4** form into a lump or lumps: *The gravy will lump if it is not stirred.* **5** a small cube of sugar. 1, 2, 5 *n.,* 3, 4 *v.* —**lump′y,** *adj.*
in a lump, as a whole or in one amount.
lump sum, a relatively large sum of money given at one time: *She paid off the last $500 of her loan in a lump sum.*

lu·nar (lü′nər) having to do with the moon: *a lunar eclipse.* A **lunar month** is the time it takes for the moon to go once around the earth, about 29.5 days. *adj.*

lu·na·tic (lü′nə tik) **1** an insane person. **2** insane. 1 *n.,* 2 *adj.* —**lu′na·cy,** *n.*

WORD HISTORY........ lunatic

Lunatic is from *luna*, the Latin word for "moon." Insanity that came and went was thought to be caused by the phases of the moon. Some people still believe that humans and animals act strangely when the moon is full.

lunch (lunch) **1** a light meal, usually around noon. This word often occurs in compounds such as **lunchbox, lunchroom,** and **lunchtime.** A **luncheon** (lun′chən) is a fancy or formal lunch. **2** eat such a meal: *We lunched outside under a tree.* 1 *n.,* 2 *v.*

lung (lung) either of the pair of breathing organs found in the chest of humans and other air-breathing animals. The lungs bring oxygen from the air to the blood and get rid of the carbon dioxide. *n.*

lunge (lunj) **1** move or throw yourself suddenly forward: *The dog lunged at the stranger.* **2** this kind of movement; a rush or thrust: *The catcher made a lunge toward the ball.* 1 *v.,* **lunged, lung·ing;** 2 *n.*

lurch¹ (lərch) **1** lean, fall, or roll suddenly to one side; stagger: *The wounded deer lurched forward.* **2** this kind of movement. 1 *v.,* 2 *n.*

lurch² (lərch)
leave in the lurch, leave in a helpless condition or in a difficult situation: *We were counting on them to help us move, but they left us in the lurch.* *n.*

lure (lür) **1** attract; tempt; cause to come by creating a desire: *Bees are lured by the scent of flowers. They lured the rat into the trap with a piece of cheese.* **2** attraction: *the lure of the sea.* **3** anything used on purpose to attract or tempt, especially an object made to look like a fly or worm to attract fish. 1 *v.,* **lured, lur·ing;** 2, 3 *n.*

lurk (lərk) wait quietly and out of sight: *A tiger was lurking in the jungle outside the village.* *v.*

lus·cious (lush′əs) delicious; rich or juicy and full of flavour: *a luscious peach.* *adj.*

lush (lush) full of thick, healthy growth: *lush grass, lush fields.* *adj.*

lust (lust) powerful desire: *a lust for life.*

a bat	e bed	i bid	o pot	u cup	th thin
ā cake	ē me	ī bite	ō go	ü rude	ᴛʜ then
ä bar	ə about	ər over	ô for	ů put	zh measure

lus·tre (lus′tər) shine; brightness: *the lustre of pearls.* *n.* **—lus′trous,** *adj.*
lose its lustre, become less attractive.

lus·ty (lus′tē) vigorous and enthusiastic: *lusty singing.* *adj.,* **lust·i·er, lust·i·est.**

lute (lūt) a stringed musical instrument shaped a little like a guitar, used in the 1500s and 1600s. *n.*

lux·u·ry (luk′shə rē) any of the comforts and beauties of life beyond what are really necessary, especially if they are expensive: *We can't afford luxuries like banana splits and movies all the time. After two weeks surviving in the wilderness, he thought of a bed as a luxury.* *n., pl.* **lux·u·ries.** **—lux·u′ri·ous** (lug zhū′rē əs), *adj.*

-ly *a suffix meaning:* **1** in a certain way or manner. *Cheerfully* means "in a cheerful way." Many adverbs are made by adding *-ly* to an adjective. **2** like or of, as in *a ghostly shape, brotherly advice.* These *-ly* words are all adjectives. **3** of each or every, as in *daily, yearly.* These words can be used as adjectives or adverbs.

> **Grammar Check . . . . . . -ly**
>
> Watch out! The suffix **-ly** usually forms adverbs, but now and then it is used to make an adjective: *a ghostly shape, heavenly weather.*
>
> Some words ending in **-ly** can be either an adverb or an adjective: *a yearly salary* (adjective) and *We visit them yearly* (adverb).

lye (lī) a strong alkaline solution used in making soap and in cleaning. *n.*

ly·ing (lī′ing) the present participle of **lie**[1] or **lie**[2]. *v.*

lymph (limf) a nearly colourless liquid circulating through your body tissues to help remove bacteria and waste. It is like blood with white cells but no red cells. *n.*

lynch (linch) kill someone as a punishment, usually by hanging, without a proper trial: *The angry mob lynched an innocent man.* *v.*

lynx (lingks) a kind of wildcat found in North America, Europe, and Asia, with a short tail, pointed ears with long tufts of hair on them, and large paws. The two kinds of lynx found in North America are the **Canada lynx** and the **bobcat.** *n., pl.* **lynx·es** or **lynx.**

lyre (līr) an ancient stringed instrument like a small harp. *n.*

lyr·ic (lēr′ik) **1** **lyrics,** *pl.* the words for a song. **2** a short poem about the poet's own personal feelings, such as a love poem or one written like a prayer. **3** having to do with this kind of poem: *a lyric poet.* 1, 2 *n.,* 3 *adj.*

Mm

m or **M** (em) 1 the thirteenth letter of the English alphabet, or the sound that it stands for. It is the first sound in *make.* 2 the thirteenth thing in a list. 3 the Roman numeral for 1000. *n., pl.* **m's** or **M's.**

m *symbol for* metre or metres, an SI unit of distance.

ma (mȧ) *Informal.* mother. *n.*

ma'am (mam) a shortened form of **madam:** *May I help you, ma'am?* *n.*

mac·a·ro·ni (mak′ə rō′nē) pasta in the form of small tubes. Like all pasta, it is made from a flour paste and is cooked before it is eaten. *n.*

Macaws have strong hooked beaks that can open a Brazil nut easily.

ma·caw (mə ko′) a large parrot of South and Central America, with a long tail, brilliant feathers, and a harsh cry. *n.*

mace (mās) 1 a war club used in the Middle Ages. 2 a staff used as a symbol of authority. *n.*

ma·chet·e (mə shet′ē) a large, heavy knife used as a tool and weapon in South America, Central America, and the West Indies. *n.*

ma·chine (mə shēn′) 1 a device for doing work, especially one that uses fuel or electricity. Machines are made up of fixed and moving parts. Lawn mowers, cars, computers, and clothes dryers are all machines. 2 a device that lets you apply force or change its direction to reduce the amount of effort needed to do work. The **simple machines** include the lever, the ramp or inclined plane, the wedge, the wheel, the screw, and the pulley. *n.*

USING WORDS ...... machine

Machine, **engine**, and **appliance** all have similar meanings. A **machine** is any tool or device for doing work. The **engine** is usually the part of a machine that starts other parts moving. An **appliance** is a small machine for use at home, such as a toaster or a vacuum cleaner.

ma·chin·er·y (mə she′nə rē) 1 machines: *There is a lot of machinery in a car factory.* 2 the moving parts of a machine: *They opened the old grandfather clock to fix the machinery.* *n., pl.* **ma·chin·er·ies.**

machine shop (mə shēn′ shop′) a workshop where machines or parts of machines are made or repaired. A person who does this kind of work is a **machinist.**

mack·er·el (mak′ə rəl) a saltwater fish of the North Atlantic, used for food. *n., pl.* **mack·er·el** or **mack·er·els.**

mad (mad) 1 very angry: *The insults made him mad.* 2 a somewhat old-fashioned word for "crazy." A crazy person is a **madman** or **madwoman.** 3 excited; wild: *The dog made mad efforts to catch up with the car.* *adj.,* **mad·der, mad·dest.** —**mad′ly,** *adv.* —**mad′ness,** *n.* —**mad′den,** *v.*
like mad, *Informal.* furiously; very hard or fast: *I ran like mad to catch the train.*

mad·am (mad′əm) 1 a polite word used to speak to a woman: *Madam, would you like a chair?* 2 a formal title put in front of the name of a woman's official position: *Madam President, Madam Speaker.* *n.*

a bat	e bed	i bid	o pot	u cup	th thin
ā cake	ē me	ī bite	ō go	ū rude	ᴛʜ then
ȧ bar	ə about	ər over	ȯ for	u̇ put	zh measure

Magnets

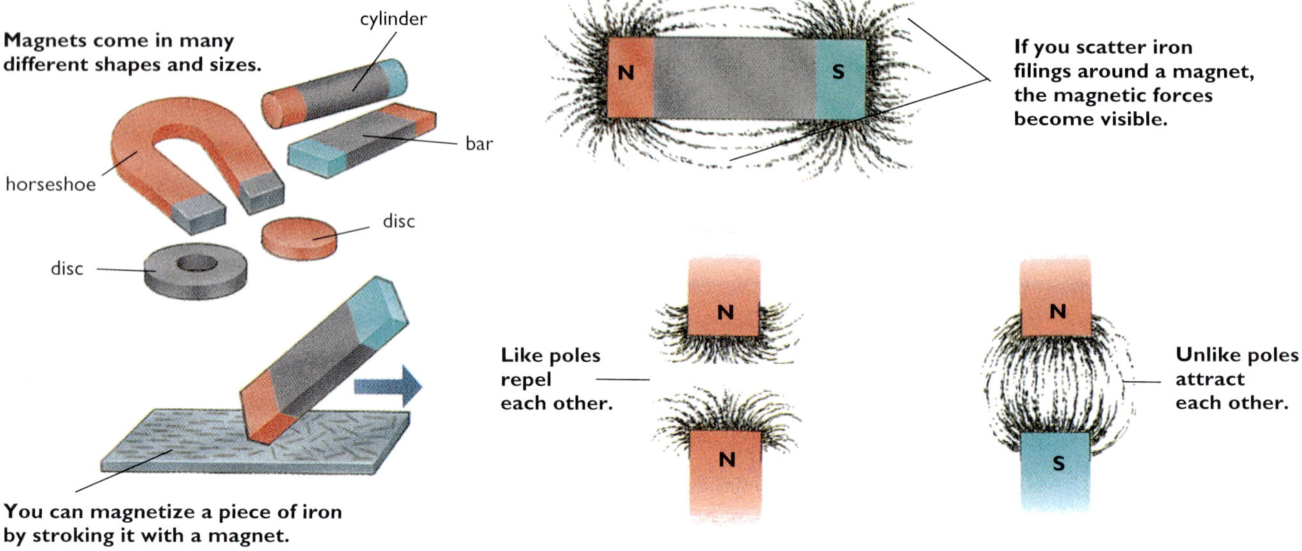

made (mād) the past tense and past participle of **make:** *I made a cake. It was made of flour, milk, butter, eggs, and sugar.* *v.*

Ma·don·na lily (mə donʹə lilʹē) a white lily that is the provincial flower of Québec.

mag·a·zine (magʹə zēnʹ *or* magʹə zēnʹ) **1** sort of booklet containing stories, pictures, news, and so on, that is published regularly. Most magazines are about a certain subject or meant for a certain audience: *a children's magazine, a sports magazine, a fashion magazine.* **2** a place for keeping ammunition or explosives. *n.*

mag·got (magʹət) the larva of a fly, like a short, fat white worm. Maggots often live in decaying matter. *n.*

mag·ic (majʹik) **1** the mysterious art of using secret powers, charms, spells, and so on to make things happen that are normally impossible: *The fairy's magic changed the brothers into swans.* **2** something that seems to be magic: *The magic of her voice charmed the audience.* The adjective is **magical:** *Grandma's attic was a magical place.* **3** the art or skill of doing tricks that seem impossible, like pulling handkerchiefs out of a person's ear. **4** having to do with magic: *a magic wand, a magic trick.* 1–3 *n.*, 4 *adj.* **—magʹi·cal·ly,** *adv.*

ma·gi·cian (mə jishʹən) a person who does magic. *n.*

mag·ma (magʹmə) the very hot liquid below the earth's crust; melted rock. Lava is formed from it. *n.*

Mag·na Car·ta (magʹnə kärʹtə) the document guaranteeing the liberties of the people of England, signed in 1215 CE.

mag·ne·si·um (mag nēʹzhəm) a light, silver-white metal that burns with a dazzling white light. It is used in fireworks and is also needed in small amounts by the human body. *n.*

mag·net (magʹnit) a piece of a metal or mineral that attracts iron and steel to it. The force of its attraction is called **magnetism** and acts within a space around the magnet called a **magnetic field.** *n.* **—mag·netʹic,** *adj.* **—magʹnet·izeʹ,** *v.*

magnetic pole (mag netʹik pōlʹ) **1** one of the two poles, or ends, of a magnet. **2 Magnetic Poles,** the two positions on the earth's surface, North and South, that a compass needle points toward. They are near the geographic North and South Poles, but not in exactly the same place.

magnetic tape (mag netʹik tāpʹ) the kind of tape used for recording sounds and images, and other information. It is a plastic ribbon coated with a substance that magnetizes easily, such as iron oxide. *n.*

mag·nif·i·cent (mag nifʹə sənt) beautiful and majestic; grand; splendid: *a magnificent palace, a magnificent view of the mountains.* *adj.* **—mag·nifʹi·cent·ly,** *adv.* **—mag·nifʹi·cence,** *n.*

mag·ni·fy (magʹnə fīʹ) **1** cause to look larger than the real size: *A microscope magnifies bacteria so that they can be seen and studied.* A **magnifying glass** is a lens that makes things look bigger. **2** show how great something really is. *v.*, **mag·ni·fied, mag·ni·fy·ing.** **—magʹni·fi·caʹtion,** *n.* **—magʹni·fiʹer,** *n.*

mag•ni•tude (mag′nə tyūd′ *or* mag′nə tūd′) **1** size or importance: *The magnitude of the crime called for a severe punishment.* **2** a measure of the brightness of a star. Stars of the **first magnitude** are the brightest. *n.*

mag•no•lia (mag nō′lē ə) a tree or shrub of North America and Asia, with large flowers that can be white, yellow, pink, or purplish. *n.*

WORD HISTORY...... magnolia

Magnolia flowers are named after Pierre Magnol (1638–1715), a French botanist.

mag•pie (mag′pī′) **1** a noisy, black-and-white bird with a long tail and short wings. **2** a person who chatters. *n.*

ma•hog•a•ny (mə hog′ə nē) a tree that grows in tropical regions. Some kinds of mahogany have beautiful, hard, dark reddish brown wood which is often used to make furniture. *n., pl.* **ma•hog•a•nies.**

maid (mād) **1** a female servant: *a kitchen maid.* **2** an old or poetic word for "girl." **3 maid of honour,** the traditional title for a woman who acts as the bride's main helper and witness in some styles of wedding. If she is married, she is often called the **matron** (mā′trən) **of honour.** *n.*

maid•en (mā′dən) **1** an old or poetic word for a young, unmarried woman or a girl. **2** first: *a ship's maiden voyage.* **3** unmarried: *a maiden aunt.* If a woman takes her husband's last name when she marries, her original last name is traditionally called her **maiden name.** 1 *n.,* 2, 3 *adj.*

mail¹ (māl) **1** letters, post cards, parcels, and so on, sent by a public delivery system. **2** this system, managed by the Post Office: *You can pay most bills by mail.* **3** send something by this system, usually by putting it in a public **mailbox** to be collected: *He mailed the letter for his mother.* The private box where you receive your mail is also a mailbox. **4** messages left on a computer or phone system: *e-mail, voice-mail.* **5** a train, boat, etc. that carries mail. 1, 2, 4, 5 *n.,* 3 *v.*

mail² (māl) armour made of tiny metal rings linked together or small, overlapping metal plates, used in medieval times. *n.*

main (mān) **1** most important; largest: *the main dish at dinner, the main street of a town, the main clause in a sentence.* **2** a large pipe that carries water or natural gas: *When the water main broke, the street was flooded.* **3** a poetic word for the open sea; the ocean. 1 *adj.,* 2, 3 *n.* **—main′ly,** *adv.*

with might and main, with all your strength or energy: *They argued with might and main.*

main•land (mān′land′) the main part of a continent or land mass; land that is not a small island or peninsula: *The Confederation Bridge links Prince Edward Island to the mainland of Canada.* *n.*

main•sail (mān′səl *or* mān′sāl′) the largest sail on a ship. *n.*

main•stream (mān′strēm) **1** the people or groups that are thought of as normal or average; the way these people think and act: *Because Katherine thought they should have more homework, she found herself out of the mainstream.* **2** usual, average, or familiar to most people: *mainstream music.* 1 *n.,* 2 *adj.*

main•tain (mān tān′) **1** keep; carry on: *to maintain good eating habits, to maintain your balance.* **2** keep in good repair: *An aircraft must be carefully maintained to be safe.* **3** pay the expenses of; provide for: *They maintain their daughter while she is at university.* **4** insist that something is true: *She maintained that she was innocent.* *v.* **—main′te•nance** (mān′tə nəns), *n.*

maj•es•ty (maj′is tē) **1** greatness, beauty, and dignity all rolled into one; an awesome quality: *We were much impressed by the majesty of the coronation ceremony.* **2 Majesty,** a title for a king, or queen: *Your Majesty, Her Majesty Queen Elizabeth.* *n., pl.* **maj•es•ties.** **—ma•jes′tic,** *adj.* **—ma•jes′ti•cal•ly,** *adv.*

ma•jor (mā′jər) **1** big or important; bigger or more important than others: *a major disaster, the major part of something.* **2** a university student's main area of study: *His major was music.* **3** have as your main area of study: *She majored in math.* **4** in music, having to do with a scale that has a whole tone between the second and third notes. Songs written in a major key generally sound brighter than songs in a minor key. **5** an officer in the armed forces. 1, 4 *adj.,* 2, 5 *n.,* 3 *v.*

ma•jor•i•ty (mə jôr′ə tē) **1** the larger number or greater part; more than half: *The majority of students passed the test.* **2** the number of votes that one side has over the other: *Since Amarjit had 18 votes to Gustav's 12, Amarjit had a majority of 6.* **3** the age when you become an adult according to the law. In some provinces people reach majority at the age of 18. *n., pl.* **ma•jor•i•ties.**

a bat	e bed	i bid	o pot	u cup	th thin
ā cake	ē me	ī bite	ō go	ū rude	ᴛʜ then
ä bar	ə about	ər over	ô for	ů put	zh measure

make (māk) 1 bring into being; create: *to make a boat, to make cookies, to make a story, to make rules.* 2 cause some result or action: *to make a noise, to make trouble. The heat made us tired. They made me go.* 3 turn one thing into something else: *I made the huge box into a playhouse.* 4 have the qualities needed for: *Birch makes a good fire. Danielle will make a good lawyer one day.* 5 do; perform: *to make an attempt, to make a mistake.* 6 get; gain: *to make a friend, to make a lot of money.* 7 amount to; add up to: *A dime, a quarter, and a nickel: that makes 40 cents.* 8 get to or get onto: *Will we make harbour before dark? She made the volleyball team.* 9 a style or brand: *What make of car is this?* 1–8 *v.,* **made, mak·ing;** 9 *n.* —**mak′er,** *n.*
be made up of, have as its parts: *Each team is made up of six players.*
make as if, pretend; act as if: *He made as if he was angry, but really he wasn't.* **Make like** is an informal version.
make believe, pretend to yourself; act out in playing: *The girl liked to make believe she was a magician.*
make do, manage with less than the best: *We had no blanket, so we had to make do with Karim's big coat.*
make fast, tie something up firmly, especially a boat: *They docked and made fast.*
make for, **a** go toward: *Make for the hills!* **b** help bring about: *Careful bike riding makes for fewer accidents.*
make it, *Informal.* **a** manage to get to a place: *We barely made it home before the rain came. I can't make it to the practice.* **b** be successful: *to make it as a singer.*
make off with, steal; take without permission: *He made off with some apples.* **Make away with** means the same.
make or break something, be the one thing that makes the difference between success and failure: *This is the game that will make or break the Canadian team.*
make out, **a** write out: *to make out a cheque.* **b** give people a certain impression: *The rumours made her out to be a snob.* **c** figure out: *I can't make out what this means.* **d** manage to see: *I can barely make out the numbers in this poor light.* **e** *Informal.* get along; manage: *How are you making out with that old printer?*
make up, **a** invent: *to make up a story.* **b** give or do in place of: *to make up for lost time.* **c** become friends again after a quarrel. **d** put paint, powder, or other cosmetics on. **e** arrange; set up: *to make up a schedule.* **f** complete; form a whole: *Seven days make up a week.*
make up your mind, decide: *I made up my mind to study harder and get better grades.*

make–be·lieve (māk′bi lēv′) 1 imagination; playful pretending: *Fairies live in the land of make-believe.* 2 imaginary; having to do with playful pretending: *a make-believe pirate ship.* 1 *n.,* 2 *adj.*

make·shift (māk′shift′) used instead of the proper thing: *We made a makeshift tent out of a blanket.* *adj.*

make–up (māk′up′) 1 powder, colour, and so on for the face, either to make it beautiful or as part of a costume. 2 the way a thing is because of the kinds of parts that make it up: *How this activity goes will depend on the make-up of the group.* *n.*

ma·lar·i·a (mə ler′ē ə) a disease that causes periods of chills, fever, and sweating. People get it from the bite of a mosquito that has already bitten someone with the disease. *n.*

male (māl) 1 belonging to the sex that can father young: *A buck is a male deer. We have a male teacher this year named Mr. Hamlen.* 2 a man, boy, or male animal. 3 having to do with males: *male interests.* 1, 3 *adj.,* 2 *n.*

mal·func·tion (mal′fungk′shən) 1 fail to work properly; break down: *They had to land the plane when one engine began to malfunction.* 2 failure to work properly. 1 *v.,* 2 *n.*

WORD HISTORY...... malfunction

The prefix **mal-** comes from the Latin *male,* meaning "badly." Some words that use this prefix are **malfunction** and **malnutrition**. What do you think **malodorous** means?

mal·ice (mal′is) a desire to hurt; spite: *She criticized us honestly, but without malice.* *n.* —**ma·li′cious,** *adj.*

ma·lig·nant (mə lig′nənt) threatening or harmful; deadly: *Cancer is a malignant growth.* *adj.* —**ma·lig′nan·cy,** *n.*

Mal·i·seet (mal′ə sēt′) 1 a First Nations people living in New Brunswick and eastern Québec. 2 their language. 3 having to do with these people or their language. 1, 2 *n.,* 3 *adj.*

mall (mol) a huge building or covered area containing many different stores. It usually has a parking lot beside it for shoppers' cars: *We spent all Saturday afternoon at the mall.* *n.*

mal·lard (mal′ərd) a common wild duck of North America, Europe, and Asia. The male mallard has a greenish-black head and a white band around its neck. *n., pl.* **mal·lards** or **mal·lard.**

mal·let (mal′it) 1 a hammer with a head made of wood or rubber. 2 a long-handled wooden hammer used to play croquet or polo. *n.*

mal·nu·tri·tion (mal′nyū trish′ən *or* mal′nū trish′ən) a condition that results from not having enough of the right kinds of food. *n.* —**mal·nour′ished** (mal nər′ isht), *adj.*

malt (molt) grain, usually barley, that is soaked in water until it sprouts and is then dried and aged. It has a sweet taste. **Malted milk** is a drink a bit like a milkshake, made with malt as one of the ingredients. *n.*

ma•ma (mum′ə *or* mȧ′mə) *Informal.* mother. *n.*

Most mammals, like this goat and its kids, give their young more protection and training than do other animals.

mam•mal (mam′əl) any warm-blooded animal with a backbone, whose babies can drink milk from their mother's body. Humans, cattle, dogs, cats, and whales are all mammals. Mammals also usually have fur or hair and are born alive instead of hatched from eggs. *n.*

mam•moth (mam′əth) **1** a large animal like an elephant, now extinct. It had a shaggy skin and long, curved tusks. **2** huge; gigantic: *Digging the St. Lawrence Seaway was a mammoth undertaking.* 1 *n.,* 2 *adj.*

man (man) **1** an adult male human being: *A man is a boy who has grown up.* **2** a somewhat old-fashioned word for "the human race": *Man has existed for thousands of years.* **3** an old or poetic word for "human being": *Death comes to all men. "No man is an island."* (John Donne) **4** one of the pieces used in playing certain games. **5** a somewhat old word for "operate" or "supply with people to operate": *A crew of ten manned the ship. They have sent up a manned space probe.* 1–4 *n., pl.* **men** (men); 5 *v.,* **manned, mann•ing.** **—man′hood′,** *n.*

USING WORDS . . . . man

Although **man** used to mean "all people," its meaning has changed over time. Nowadays, when you want to talk about all people, use words like *the human race, humanity, a human being,* or *people.*

man•age (man′ij) **1** control; make sure things run smoothly: *Nathan manages his horse well. They hired her to manage the business.* A person who manages or helps manage a business is a **manager;** all the managers together are the **management.** **2** succeed in doing or handling something difficult: *I managed to get the job done. He cannot manage such a load—give him a hand.* **3** get along: *I managed on very little money.* *v.,* **man•aged, man•ag•ing.** **—man′age•ment,** *n.* **—man′age•a•ble,** *adj.*

man-at-arms (man′ət ȧrmz′) in medieval times, a heavily armed and mounted soldier. *n., pl.* **men-at-arms.**

man•da•rin (man′də rin) **1** a small, sweet orange that has a thin, very loose peel and grows on an evergreen tree. Tangerines are mandarins. **2** **Mandarin,** the main language of modern China. *n.*

man•date (man′dāt) **1** a command or official order. **2** a direction or authority given to a government by the votes of the people in an election: *The Prime Minister said he had a mandate to increase taxes.* *n.*

man•da•to•ry (man′də tȯr′ē) required by a rule or law: *Running shoes with non-marking soles are mandatory for gym class.* *adj.*

man•di•bles (man′də bəlz) jaws, or any other pair of parts used like jaws for seizing and biting, especially the mouth parts of an insect, spider, or crustacean. *n.*

man•do•lin (man′də lin′) a musical instrument with a pear-shaped body and metal strings. *n.*

mane (mān) the long, heavy hair growing on or around the neck of a horse or lion. *n.*

mange (mānj) a skin disease of animals, resulting in scabs and loss of hair. *n.* **—man′gy,** *adj.*

man•ger (mān′jər) a box or trough in a barn for horses and cows to eat from. *n.*

man•gle (mang′gəl) **1** cut or tear roughly: *The worker's arm was badly mangled in the accident.* **2** do or play badly; ruin: *I was so nervous at the recital that I completely mangled my song.* *v.,* **man•gled, man•gling.**

man•go (mang′gō) a sweet, juicy, oval-shaped fruit that has a thick greenish peel and is orangey yellow inside. *n., pl.* **man•goes** or **man•gos.**

ma•ni•a (mā′nē ə) an unusual fondness; a craze: *She has a mania for science fiction.* *n.*

a bat	e bed	i bid	o pot	u cup	th thin
ā cake	ē me	ī bite	ō go	ū rude	ᴛʜ then
ȧ bar	ə about	ər over	ȯ for	u̇ put	zh measure

ma•ni•ac (mā′nē ak′) a person who behaves in a wild manner: *That driver is a maniac.* *n.*

man•i•cure (man′ə kyūr′) **1** a beauty treatment for the hands and fingernails: *She had a manicure at the beauty salon.* **2** to give a manicure to. People say lawns, etc. are beautifully **manicured** if they are neatly cut, with the edges carefully trimmed and so on. 1 *n.*, 2 *v.*, **man•i•cured, man•i•cur•ing.** —**man′i•cur′ist,** *n.*

man•i•fes•to (man′ə fes′tō) a public statement by a group of people, telling what they want to do and why. *n., pl.* **man•i•fes•tos** or **man•i•fes•toes.**

ma•nip•u•late (mə nip′yə lāt′) **1** handle or use, especially with skill: *to manipulate numbers. Fatima taught me how to manipulate the gears of her bike.* **2** control in a clever but unfair way: *He manipulated people to get what he wanted.* *v.*, **ma•nip•u•lat•ed, ma•nip•u•lat•ing.** —**ma•nip′u•la′tion,** *n.*

Man•i•to•ba (man′ə tō′bə) the province that lies between Ontario and Saskatchewan. *n.* —**Man′i•to′ban,** *n.*

man•i•tou (man′ə tū′) in the traditional religion of First Nations people, a spirit seen as the Creator, a force in nature, or the spirit living in all creation. **Gitchi Manitou** means "Great Spirit." *n.*

man•kind (man′kīnd′) a somewhat old or poetic word for **humankind** or the **human race.** *n.*

man•ly (man′lē) like or typical of a man: *The suit and tie gave Randall a manly appearance.* *adj.*, **man•li•er, man•li•est.** —**man′li•ness,** *n.*

man–made (man′mād′) a somewhat old word for "artificial": *a man-made lake.* *adj.*

man•ner (man′ər) **1** the way something happens or is done: *The trouble arose in a strange manner. Ms. Bergman has a kind but firm manner with students.* **2 manners,** *pl.* **a** ways of behaving toward others: *bad manners.* **b** polite behaviour: *It is nice to see people with manners.* **Mannerly** or **well-mannered** means "polite." **c** ways or customs: *Books and movies show us the manners of other times and places.* **3** kind or kinds: *We saw all manner of birds in the forest.* *n.*

ma•noeu•vre (mə nū′vər) **1** move by handling skilfully: *He manoeuvred his car through the heavy traffic.* **Maneuver** is another spelling. **2** plan skilfully; use clever, sometimes unfair methods to get what you want: *He is always manoeuvring to gain some advantage over others. She manoeuvred her mother into letting her have a party.* **3** a skilful move or clever trick: *to learn new manoeuvres on a skateboard.* **4** a planned movement of troops or warships, whether in actual battle or as a training exercise. 1, 2 *v.*, **ma•noeu•vred, ma•noeu•vring;** 3, 4 *n.*

man•or (man′ər) **1** in the Middle Ages, a large piece of land owned by a lord or lady. The owner lived on a part of it and the rest was divided among his or her peasants or serfs. **2** a large house on a large piece of property. *n.*

man•sion (man′shən) a very large, beautiful home. *n.*

man•slaugh•ter (man′slot′ər) in law, the accidental killing of a human being. *n.*

man•tel (man′təl) **1** a shelf above a fireplace. Another word for it is **mantelpiece.** **2** a decorative framework around a fireplace: *a mantel of tile.* *n.*

man•tle (man′təl) **1** an old or poetic word for a loose cloak without sleeves. **2** anything that covers like a mantle: *A mantle of snow covered the earth.* **3** the part of the earth beneath the crust and around the core. It is made up of very dense, solid rock. **4** a small, very fine netlike bag around the flame of a gas lantern. It is made of a substance that does not burn but glows very brightly when heated. *n.*

man•tra (mun′trə) in Hinduism and Buddhism, a verse from the holy writings, spoken over and over again in prayer or meditation. *n.*

man•u•al (man′yū əl) **1** done with the hands: *manual labour.* **2** operated by hand; not automatic: *This car has a manual gearshift.* **3** a book of instructions or rules; handbook: *By following the manual she was able to repair the lawn mower.* 1, 2 *adj.*, 3 *n.*

man•u•fac•ture (man′yə fak′chər) **1** make, especially by machine and in large quantities: *Paper is manufactured from wood pulp.* **2** the process of making something in this way: *Much steel is needed for the manufacture of cars.* **3** invent; make up: *The dishonest lawyer manufactured evidence.* 1, 3 *v.*, **man•u•fac•tured, man•u•fac•tur•ing;** 2 *n.* —**man′u•fac′tur•er,** *n.*

ma•nure (mə nyūr′ *or* mə nūr′) **1** animal waste, composted and put on or in the soil as fertilizer. **2** put manure in or on. 1 *n.*, 2 *v.*, **ma•nured, ma•nur•ing.**

man•u•script (man′yə skript′) a book, article, play, etc. that has not yet been published. *n.*

man•y (men′ē) a large number of people or things: *There are many parks in the city (adj.). Many had to be turned away when the theatre was full (pron.).* *adj. or pron.*, **more, most.**
a good many, a fairly large number.

Maps

Relief maps show the surface of the land, and features like rivers.

Maps of the sea bed help plot a ship's course.

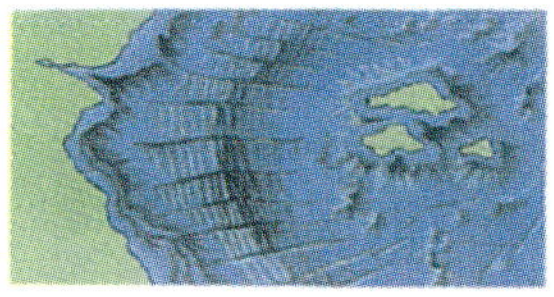

Star maps are used in navigation.

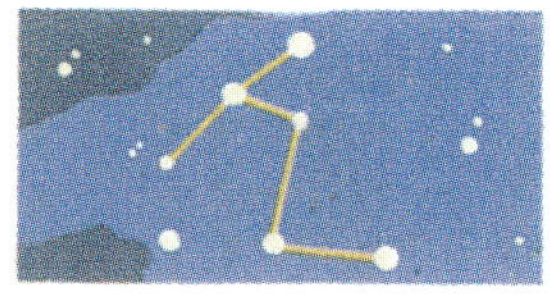

Road maps are the most commonly used maps.

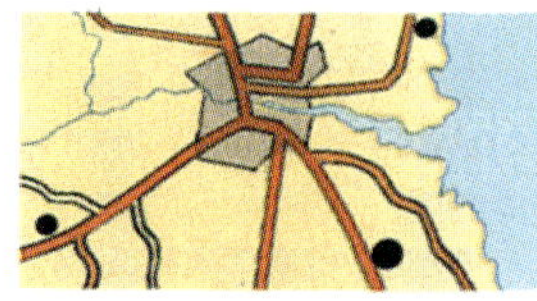

A map projection is the way geographers show the curved surface of the earth as a flat map.

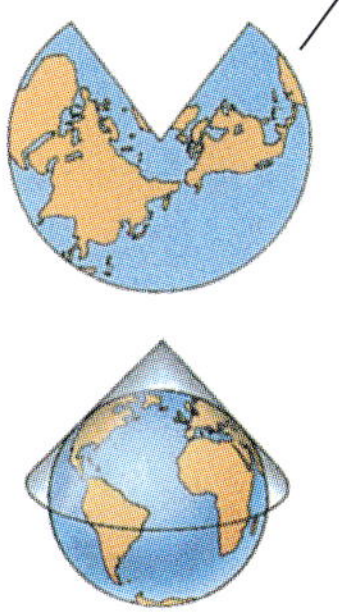

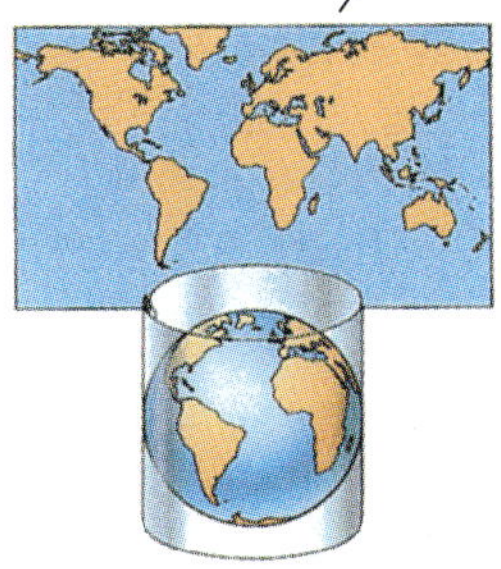

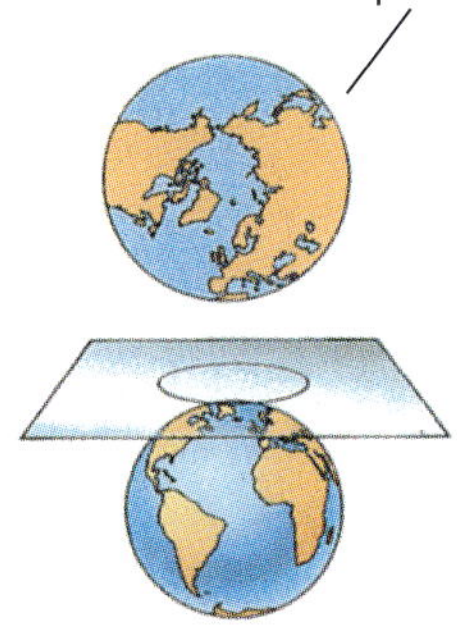

map (map) **1** a flat drawing of the earth's surface or of part of it, usually showing countries, towns, rivers, lakes, roads, mountains, and so on. **2** a drawing like this of any space, such as the sky, showing the positions of the stars, or a mall, showing where all the stores are. **3** make a map of. 1, 2 *n.*, 3 *v.*, **mapped, map·ping.**
map out, plan; arrange in detail: *Each Monday we mapped out the week's work.*

ma·ple (mā′pəl) a deciduous tree or shrub that bears seeds in winged pairs on a stalk. The **maple leaf,** an artistic version of the leaf of a sugar maple, is an emblem of Canada and appears on our flag. *n.*

maple syrup (mā′pəl sē′rəp) syrup made by boiling the sap of the sugar maple. If you boil it long enough, you end up with **maple sugar.**

ma·quette (ma ket′) a small preliminary model of a statue *n.*

mar (mȧr) spoil the beauty of: *That smudge mars the painting. Their visit was marred by an angry quarrel.* *v.*, **marred, mar·ring.**

ma·ra·ca (mə rȧ′kə) a musical instrument made of a dry, hollowed-out gourd with seeds or pebbles inside it. You shake it like a rattle. Maracas are usually played in pairs. *n.*

mar·a·thon (mer′ə thon′) **1** a foot race of 42.195 km. **2** done as a long race or in one long stretch: *a marathon swim, a marathon e-mail session.* 1 *n.*, 2 *adj.*

mar·ble (mȧr′bəl) **1** a very hard limestone, white, coloured, or streaked, that can take a beautiful polish. Marble is often used for statues and in buildings. **2** a small glass ball used in the children's game of **marbles.** You shoot your marbles at those of other players to try and knock them out of a circle. **3** to colour in imitation of the patterns in marble: *The kitchen counter top had a marbled pattern.* A **marble cake** is made by swirling different colours of batter together before baking. 1, 2 *n.*, 3 *v.*, **mar·bled, mar·bling.**

march (mȧrch) **1** to walk as soldiers do, in rhythm and with steps of the same length. **2** walk as a group for some cause, such as to raise money for charity or to make a political point: *The protesters marched down the main street carrying signs.* **3** to walk or go steadily: *Time marches on.* **4** the act or fact of marching: *the march of time, a long and exhausting march to the battlefield. Are you going on the March for Peace?* **5** a piece of music meant for marching to. 1–3 *v.*, 4, 5 *n.*

March (mȧrch) the third month of the year. March has 31 days. *n.*

mare (mer) an adult female horse, donkey, or zebra. *n.*

a bat	e bed	i bid	o pot	u cup	th thin
ā cake	ē me	ī bite	ō go	ū rude	ᴛʜ then
ȧ bar	ə about	ər over	ȯ for	u̇ put	zh measure

mar•ga•rine (mär′jə rin) a spread like butter, usually made from vegetable oils. *n.*

mar•gin (mär′jən) **1** the blank space around the writing or printing on a page: *Do not write in the margin.* **2** an extra amount; the amount beyond what is necessary; difference: *If you're coming by car, give yourself a margin of fifteen minutes in case there's a traffic jam. Bev won the vote by a wide margin.* **3** an edge or border: *the margin of a lake.* *n.*

mar•i•jua•na (mer′ə wä′nə) the dried leaves and seeds of the hemp plant, smoked like tobacco by some people. Smoking marijuana is illegal in many places. *n.*

ma•ri•na (mə rē′nə) a place along a waterfront where you can rent a boat, dock your own boat, or buy fuel and boating equipment. *n.*

WORD HISTORY........marina

Marina, **marine**, **mariner**, and **maritime** come from the Latin *mare* meaning "sea." So does the word **marinate**: the mixtures used for marinating are mostly salty, like sea water.

ma•rine (mə rēn′) **1** having to do with the sea or ocean: *Seals and whales are marine animals.* **2** having to do with boating and shipping: *marine supplies. Before you go out on Lake Superior, listen to the marine weather forecast.* **3** a U.S. soldier serving at sea, on land, and in the air. 1, 2 *adj.*, 3 *n.*

mar•i•o•nette (mer′ē ə net′) a puppet moved by strings. *n.*

mar•i•time (mer′ə tīm′) **1** having to do with the sea coast: *Halifax is a maritime city. Many maritime peoples live from fishing.* **2** having to do with shipping and sailing: *Ships and sailors are governed by maritime law.* **3 Maritimes,** *pl.* the provinces of New Brunswick, Nova Scotia, and Prince Edward Island, also called the **Maritime Provinces.** 1, 2 *adj.*, 3 *n.* **—Mar′i•tim′er,** *n.*

USING WORDS..Maritime Provinces

The **Maritime Provinces** or **Maritimes** do not include the province of Newfoundland and Labrador. The four **Atlantic Provinces** are: New Brunswick, Nova Scotia, Prince Edward Island, and Newfoundland and Labrador.

mark (märk) **1** a line, dot, smudge, stain, scratch, or scar left on one thing by another thing. **2** leave anything like this on a surface: *Be careful not to mark the table.* **3** an object, arrow, line, dot, etc. put as a guide or symbol: *the starting mark in a race, a question mark.* **4** show by means of a special symbol or label: *to mark cities on a map, to mark a trail. The ones marked with an "X" are yours.* **5** some quality or feature that tells you right away what a thing is: *She has the mark of a leader. Courtesy is a mark of good character.* **6** a letter or number to show how well a person has done: *My mark in arithmetic was B.* **7** give a grade to: *The teacher marked our projects.* **8** target: *The deer was an easy mark for the hunter as it stood in the field.* **9** an old or poetic word for "notice" or "pay attention to": *Mark how carefully he moves. Mark my words.* 1, 3, 5, 6, 8 *n.*, 2, 4, 7, 9 *v.*
—mark′ing, *n.*
make your mark, succeed; become well known.
mark off or **mark out,** make lines to show the boundaries of: *We marked out a tennis court. The hedge marks off one yard from another.*
mark time, a move the feet as if marching, but without going forward. **b** do things without really accomplishing anything.
mark up, a spoil the look of by making marks on: *Don't mark up the desks.* **b** increase the price of, especially to make a profit. To lower the price is to **mark down.** The difference in price is either a **markup** or **markdown.**

marked (märkt) **1** having a mark or marks on it: *Hand back these marked papers, please.* **2** very noticeable; very plain: *a marked difference.* *adj.*

mark•er (märk′ər) **1** a sign or object that shows where something can be found. **2** a pen with a thick, soft point that is used for drawing and colouring, writing labels or signs, and so on. *n.*

mar•ket (mär′kit) **1** a meeting of people for the purpose of buying and selling or trading: *There is a fruit and vegetable market here every Saturday.* **2** the building or open space where this happens. Another word for this is **marketplace.** **3** any store. Store names often use the short form **mart.** **4** sell or try to sell: *The farmer cannot market all of his wheat.* **5** the demand for something; all the people wanting to buy a certain thing: *There was not enough cheese to supply the market.* **6** a part of the population, or a region, containing buyers for a certain thing: *cars designed for the Canadian market. This magazine is for the student market.* 1, 2, 3, 5, 6 *n.*, 4 *v.*
in the market for something, looking for a certain thing to buy: *Colm is in the market for a DVD player.*

mar•ma•lade (mär′mə lād′) a jamlike food, made of oranges or other citrus fruit, including the peel. *n.*

ma•roon[1] (mə rün′) dark, brownish red. *adj. or n.*

ma•roon[2] (mə rün′) leave someone alone on a deserted island or in some other desolate place with no way to get anywhere else: *Pirates used to maroon people on desert islands.* *v.*

USING WORDS ...... maroon

Maroon, **desert**, and **abandon** all have similar meanings. **Maroon** means to leave a person in an isolated place. **Desert** and **abandon** both mean to go away and leave, but **desert** sometimes refers especially to soldiers or military people leaving their duty without meaning to return.

mar•row (mer′ō) a soft substance that fills the hollow centre of most bones. *n.*

mar•ry (mer′ē) **1** officially join as husband and wife: *The judge married them.* **2** take someone as husband or wife: *She married late in life. Ming planned to marry Linda.* *v.,* **mar•ried, mar•ry•ing.** —**mar′riage** (mer′ij), *n.*

The Viking probe (top left) visited Mars in 1976. At bottom left you can see Phobos, one of the two tiny moons of Mars.

Mars (mȧrz) the fourth planet from the sun, the next after Earth. *n.* —**Mar′tian** (mȧr′shən), *adj. or n.*

marsh (mȧrsh) an area of wet, muddy land that grows mostly grasses of various kinds. Marshes are sometimes partly covered with water. *n.* —**marsh′y,** *adj.* —**marsh′land′,** *n.*

mar•shal (mȧr′shəl) **1** an officer in charge of soldiers or firefighters: *a fire marshal, a field marshal.* **2** a person who arranges the order of march in a parade: *a parade marshal.* **3** arrange in proper order: *He took great care in marshalling the facts for his speech.* **4** lead in a formal, soldierly way. 1, 2 *n.,* 3, 4 *v.,* **mar•shalled** or **mar•shaled, mar•shal•ling** or **mar•shal•ing.**

marsh•mal•low (mȧrsh′mel′ō) a soft, spongy candy covered with powdered sugar. It can be white or coloured. *n.*

mar•su•pi•al (mȧr sū′pē əl) an animal that carries its young in a pouch, or **marsupium.** Kangaroos and opossums are marsupials. *n.*

mar•ten (mȧr′tən) a slender animal of the weasel family, with a long body and short legs. It lives in the northern forests of North America, Europe, and Asia, and has beautiful, valuable fur. *n.*

mar•tial (mȧr′shəl) having to do with war or fighting. Judo, karate, aikido, and tae kwan do are **martial arts. Martial law** is temporary rule by the army in a time of emergency. *adj.*

mar•tyr (mȧr′tər) **1** a person who is killed because of his or her religion or other beliefs. **2** kill a person because of his or her religion or other beliefs. **3** someone who does something hard or gives up something just to make others feel sorry or ashamed. 1, 3 *n.,* 2 *v.* —**mar′tyr•dom,** *n.*

mar•vel (mȧr′vəl) **1** something wonderful and amazing: *It is a marvel that the cat found its old home 3000 km away.* **2** be filled with wonder; be amazed: *We marvelled at the beautiful sunset.* 1 *n.,* 2 *v.,* **mar•velled** or **mar•veled, mar•vel•ling** or **mar•vel•ing.** —**mar′vel•lous** or **mar′vel•ous,** *adj.*

Marx•ism (mȧrk′siz əm) the set of ideas used by the thinker Karl Marx to explain history. Marx thought that the main thing going on in history is the struggle between the people who have power and wealth and the people who don't. *n.* —**Marx′ist,** *n. or adj.*

mas•ca•ra (ma sker′ə) a cosmetic that is used to make eyelashes look thicker and darker. *n.*

mas•cot (mas′kot) an animal, person, or thing that is supposed to bring good luck to a team or other group: *The team kept the stuffed bear as a mascot.* *n.*

mas•cu•line (mas′kyə lin) **1** having to do with men and boys: *masculine clothing, a masculine voice.* **2** in some languages, such as French, a category of nouns that affects the form of adjectives and articles you put with them. In French, the noun *nez* is masculine; you can say *le nez* but not *la nez* for "nose." *adj.*

a bat	e bed	i bid	o pot	u cup	th thin
ā cake	ē me	ī bite	ō go	ū rude	ᴛʜ then
ȧ bar	ə about	ər over	ȯ for	ů put	zh measure

mash (mash) 1 beat or crush into a soft, smooth mass: *I'll mash the potatoes.* 2 a soft, smooth mass made by crushing or beating something. 3 a warm mixture of bran and water for horses and other animals. 1 *v.,* 2, 3 *n.*

mas•jid (mus′jid) the Arabic word for a mosque, a Muslim place of worship. *n.*

Masks, like these ancient ones from North Africa, are often used in spiritual ceremonies. The face of the mask may represent a good or an evil spirit, an ancestor, an animal, a bird, and so on.

mask (mask) 1 a covering for the face, worn for disguise or for protection: *a Halloween mask, a gas mask.* 2 any disguise: *He hid his evil plans under a mask of friendship.* 3 to cover or hide with a mask or other disguise: *They were robbed by a masked man. A smile masked her disappointment.* **Masking tape** is sticky paper tape; one of its uses is to cover and protect areas around the edge of a surface that is being painted. 1, 2 *n.,* 3 *v.*

ma•son (mā′sən) a person who builds with stone, brick, or concrete. *n.* —**ma′son•ry,** *n.*

mas•quer•ade (mas′kə rād′) 1 a party or dance where everyone wears masks and costumes. 2 a disguise or a false pretence. 3 wear a costume or disguise, or pretend to be what you're not: *The king masqueraded as a beggar to find out if his people really liked him.* 1, 2 *n.,* 3 *v.,* **mas•quer•ad•ed, mas•quer•ad•ing.**

WORD HISTORY..... masquerade

English got this word from the Spanish *mascara,* meaning "mask." You can see this is also where we got our word **mascara**: make-up is a kind of mask.

mass[1] (mas) 1 a lump, heap, or blob: *a mass of dough.* 2 a large number or amount all together: *a mass of flowers. The parking lot was a solid mass of cars.* **Mass production** is the manufacture of a huge number of something at once, for example, bikes in a factory. The verb is **mass-produce.** 3 form or collect into a mass: *The snow had massed against the fence.* 4 bulk; size: *the huge mass of an iceberg.* 5 the amount of matter anything contains: *The mass of a banana is not changed by squashing it. The mass of this stone is 50 g.* On Earth, the weight of a thing due to gravity is the same as its mass. 6 **the masses,** *pl.* ordinary, common people. 1, 2, 4–6 *n.,* 3 *v.*

Mass or **mass**[2] (mas) 1 the main service of worship in the Roman Catholic Church. 2 a piece of music written for certain parts of the Mass. *n.*

mas•sa•cre (mas′ə kər) 1 the needless killing or slaughter of many people or animals. 2 kill many people or animals needlessly or cruelly. 1 *n.,* 2 *v.,* **mas•sa•cred, mas•sa•cring.**

mas•sage (mə säzh′) 1 rub the muscles and joints with firm pressure to make them less tense and stiff and to increase the circulation of the blood: *Let me massage your back for you.* 2 the action of rubbing in this way: *The massage made me feel a lot better.* A person who gives massages professionally is a **massage therapist.** 1 *v.,* **mas•saged, mas•sag•ing;** 2 *n.*

mas•sive (mas′iv) big, solid, and heavy: *The Egyptian pyramids were made of massive stone blocks.* *adj.*

mass media (mas′ mē′dē ə) all the forms of communication that reach a huge audience at once, such as television, radio, movies, newspapers, and the Internet.

mast (mast) 1 a long pole of wood or steel set upright on a ship to support the sails and ropes. The top is called the **masthead.** 2 any tall pole: *a flag mast, a TV mast.* *n.*

mas•ter (mas′tər) 1 a person who rules or commands people or things; the one in control. A **master of ceremonies** leads a program of events by announcing and introducing each one. 2 expert: *a master builder* (*adj.*), *a master at chess* (*n.*). 3 a formal title of respect for a boy: *First prize goes to Master Henry Butler.* 4 conquer or control: *to master your temper.* 5 become skilful at: *He has mastered riding a horse.* 6 main: *a master plan, a master switch.* A **master key** opens all the locks in a building. 1–3 *n.,* 2, 6 *adj.,* 4, 5 *v.* —**mas′ter•y,** *n.*

mas•ter•ly (mas′tər lē) expert; skilful: *Kurelek, a native of Alberta, was a masterly painter.* *adj.*

mas•ter•mind (mas′tər mīnd′) 1 a person who plans and organizes something complicated: *The police caught the mastermind of the bank robbery.* 2 plan and organize something complicated: *It was Ms. Lenz who masterminded the exchange between our school and one in Brandon, Manitoba.* 1 *n.,* 2 *v.*

mas·ter·piece (mas′tər pēs′) 1 anything done or made with extraordinary skill. 2 a person's greatest piece of work. *n.*

mat (mat) 1 a piece of thick material put on a floor as decoration, as a place to wipe your feet, as protection for a person doing gymnastic exercises, as a bed, etc. 2 a small piece of thick material to put under a dish, vase, lamp, etc.: *I put a mat under the hot dish to protect the table.* 3 anything thickly packed or tangled together: *a mat of weeds.* 4 pack or tangle together like a mat: *matted hair. The fur collar mats when it gets wet.* 1–3 *n.*, 4 *v.*, **mat·ted, mat·ting.**

mat·a·dor (mat′ə dôr′) a bullfighter: *The matador kills the bull with his sword.* *n.*

match¹ (mach) a very thin piece of wood or cardboard, with a mixture of chemicals stuck on the tip, that takes fire when scraped on a rough or specially prepared surface. It is also called a **matchstick.** *n.*

Word Family........ **match**

matchbook: a little folder holding rows of matches
matchbox: a little box for carrying matches
matchstick: the thin piece of wood used for a match
matchwood: little bits of wood for making matches

match² (mach) 1 be alike or go well together: *The rugs and the drapes match.* 2 find things that are alike or go together: *Match each picture with the correct word.* 3 two people or things that are alike or go well together: *Those two make a good match.* 4 be equal to in a contest: *No one could match the skill of our goalie.* 5 a person or thing equal to another in strength, skill, etc.: *Jolene is no match for Trudy at high jumping.* A person or thing that is better or greater than all others is **matchless.** 6 a game or contest: *a tennis match.* In some games, **match point** is the last point needed to win. 1, 2, 4 *n.*, 3, 5, 6 *v.*

mate (māt) 1 one of a pair: *Where is the mate to this glove?* 2 come together as a pair, male and female, to produce young: *Birds mate in the spring.* 3 the male or female animal in such a pair: *One wolf stayed in the den with the cubs while its mate went for food.* 4 a husband or wife. 5 an assistant, especially the officer who ranks just below the captain on a ship. 6 a companion or fellow worker. This meaning is often in compounds: *Doug and Barry were mates in the army. Adrienne and Josée are classmates.* 1, 3–6 *n.*, 2 *v.*, **mat·ed, mat·ing.**

ma·te·ri·al (mə tē′rē əl) 1 anything used to make something out of, especially cloth: *building materials, 3 m of striped material. Her adventures make good material for a book.* 2 having to do with matter; physical: *the material world.* 1 *n.*, 2 *adj.*

ma·te·ri·al·ize (mə tē′rē ə līz′) 1 become an actual fact: *Our plan for the party did not materialize.* 2 appear in a more concrete form: *As it approached, the shadowy figure materialized into her father.* *v.*

ma·ter·nal (mə tər′nəl) like or having to do with a mother: *a maternal hug, maternal advice.* Your **maternal grandparents** are your mother's parents. **Maternity** is the fact of being or becoming a mother. *adj.*

math·e·mat·ics (math′ə mat′iks) the study of numbers, measurement, and shapes. Arithmetic and geometry are branches of mathematics. **Math** is an informal short form. *n.* —**math′e·mat′i·cal,** *adj.* —**math′e·ma·ti′cian** (math′ə mə tish′ ən), *n.*

mat·i·née (mat′ə nā′ *or* mat′ə nā′) a play, movie, or other show in the afternoon. Another spelling is **matinee.** *n.*

mat·ter (mat′ər) 1 be important: *Nothing seems to matter when you are very sick.* 2 what physical things are made of. All matter takes up space and has mass. 3 anything that needs to be taken care of, decided, thought about, etc.: *business matters. That's a matter between you and your parents.* 1 *v.*, 2, 3 *n.*
a matter of course, something that is to be expected.
as a matter of fact, in truth; in reality.
for that matter, as far as that is concerned.
it's a matter of __, what matters in this situation is __: *It's a matter of time and money.*
no matter, **a** it's not important. **b** regardless of: *He wants a bicycle, no matter what it costs.*
the matter, wrong: *What's the matter with Emily? There's something the matter with this machine; it won't work.*

mat·ter–of–fact (mat′ər əv fakt′) plain and sticking to facts; not imaginative or fancy in style, and not concerned with how people feel about things: *a matter-of-fact report.* *adj.*

mat·tress (mat′ris) a thick, soft pad for sleeping on, used on a bed or as a bed. Mattresses can be filled with a variety of materials, and many have springs inside. An **air mattress** is filled with air. *n.*

WORD HISTORY....... **mattress**

The word **mattress** originally came from the Arabic *al matrah*, meaning "cushion."

a bat	e bed	i bid	o pot	u cup	th **thin**
ā cake	ē me	ī bite	ō go	ū rude	ᴛʜ **then**
ä bar	ə about	ər over	ô for	u̇ put	zh measure

ma·ture (mə chūr′) **1** ripe or full-grown: *Grain is harvested when it is mature. A mature frog has no tail.* **2** suitable or typical for an adult: *a mature face, mature behaviour.* **3** ripen; come or bring to full growth: *These apples are maturing fast.* **4** end or become due. This sense is for bank loans and investments that have a time limit. 1, 2 *adj.,* 3, 4 *v.,* **ma·tured, ma·tur·ing.** —**ma·tu′ri·ty** (mə chū′rə tē), *n.*

maul (mol) handle roughly: *The bear mauled the hunter very badly.* *v.*

max·i·mum (mak′sə məm) **1** the greatest possible amount: *A maximum of 12 people are allowed in this elevator.* **2** greatest possible: *The maximum score on this test is 100.* To **maximize** something is to make the most of it or make it as great as possible. 1 *n.,* 2 *adj.*

may (mā) a verb used together with a main verb: **1** to ask for or give permission: *May I have an apple? She may not leave yet.* **2** to say that something is likely or possible: *It may rain tomorrow.* **3** to express a wish: *May you have long life.* *v.,* **might.**

USING WORDS . . . . . . may

In careful English, some people prefer to use **may** instead of **can** to mean "be allowed to." That is, *Can I go?* means *Am I able to go?* and *May I go?* means *Am I allowed to go?*

In informal language, people use **can** for both.

May (mā) the fifth month of the year. May has 31 days. *n.*

Ma·ya (mȧ′yə) one of an ancient Indian people who lived in Central America and Mexico. The Mayas had a high degree of civilization from about 350 CE to about 800 CE, long before the Spanish came. *n., pl.* **Ma·yas.** —**Ma′yan,** *adj. or n.*

may·be (mā′bē) possibly or perhaps; it may be so: *Maybe Dirk knows the answer.* *adv.*

May·day (mā′dā′) a signal used internationally by ships and aircraft to call for help in an emergency. *n.*

may·flow·er (mā′flou′ər) a low-growing evergreen shrub, with pink or white flowers. It is the provincial flower of Nova Scotia. *n.*

may·on·naise (mā′ə nāz′) a thick white dressing for salads or sandwiches, made of egg yolk, oil, vinegar or lemon juice, and seasoning. **Mayo** (mā′ō) is an informal short form. *n.*

may·or (mā′ər) the person at the head of the government of a city or town. *n.*

maze (māz) a network of paths or lines that is hard to find your way through: *A guide led us through the maze of caves.* *n.*

MB *symbol for* megabyte, a unit of computer memory roughly equal to 1 000 000 bytes.

M.C. *abbreviation for* master of ceremonies, the person who leads a program involving different people or events by announcing and introducing each one. It is sometimes informally spelled **emcee.**

mead·ow (med′ō) a grassy field. *n.*

mea·gre (mē′gər) poor or scanty; with barely enough: *a meagre meal, a meagre salary.* **Meager** is another spelling. *adj.*

meal[1] (mēl) food eaten or served at any one time: *We sat down to a meal of fresh tomatoes and corn on the cob.* Breakfast, lunch, and supper are meals. *n.*

meal[2] (mēl) grain ground up, but not as fine as flour: *corn meal.* Something **mealy** is dry and powdery. *n.*

mean[1] (mēn) **1** stand for; have a certain definition: *The word "gloomy" means "sad." The green circle with a "P" in it means "Parking."* **2** be trying to say: *What do you mean?* **3** have as its result; lead to: *This means war!* **4** plan; do on purpose: *I didn't mean to break it.* **5** say truly from the heart: *He says he's sorry, but does he mean it?* **6** matter: *You mean a lot to me.* *v.,* **meant** (ment), **mean·ing.** —**mean′ness,** *n.*
mean well, have good intentions.

mean[2] (mēn) **1** cruel; unkind: *It is mean to spread lies about people.* An unkind person is informally called a **meanie.** **2** *Informal.* bad or hard to manage: *a mean horse. That's a mean cut on your arm.* **3** an old word meaning "humble" or "poor": *A peasant is of mean birth; a king is of noble birth.* **4** *Slang.* very skilful: *a mean piece of work. She is one mean basketball player.* *adj.*
no mean, very good: *Sylvie is no mean diver.*

mean[3] (mēn) **1** average: *The mean temperature for July was 18.4°C (adj.). Rainfall was 1.4 cm above the mean (n.).* **2 means, a** any object or method that can be used to do something: *A car is a means of transportation. We kept the ridge on our left and by this means finally found our way back to the camp.* **b** wealth: *a man of considerable means.* 1 *adj.,* 1, 2 *n.*
by all means, certainly: *By all means visit me one day.*
by any means, in any possible way; at any cost.
by means of, by the use of; through; with: *I found my dog by means of a notice in the paper.*
by no means, not at all: *This work is by no means easy.*
means to an end, a way of getting something done.

Meander

Curves may be found in most rivers. Over time, if the river valley is wide enough, the river will meander more and more. Big loops often become separated from the river, to create an oxbow lake.

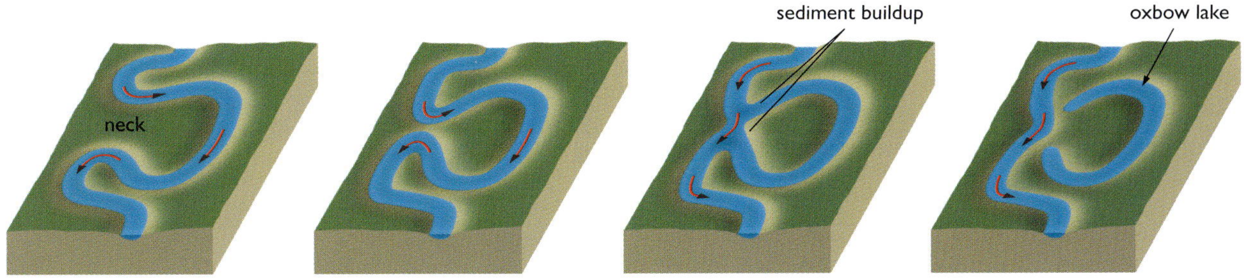

me·an·der (mē an′dər) **1** follow a winding course: *A brook meanders through the meadow.* **2** to wander aimlessly: *We meandered through the park.* *v.*

mean·ing (mē′ning) **1** the ideas expressed by something: *The meaning of that sentence is clear.* **2** result or importance: *July 1, 1867 is full of meaning for Canada.* *n.* **—mean′ing·ful,** *adj.* **—mean′ing·less,** *adj.*

mean·time (mēn′tīm′) the time between: *Aunt Helga comes on Friday; in the meantime we can get her room ready.* *n.*

mean·while (mēn′wīl′ *or* mēn′hwīl′) **1** at the same time, often in a different place: *It was a bright afternoon in Prince Albert; meanwhile, our cousins over in England were already snug in their beds.* **2** in the time or period between: *Classes finish at 12 and start again at 1:30; meanwhile we can have lunch and play soccer.* *adv.*

mea·sles (mē′zəlz) **1** a contagious childhood disease that causes a bad cold, fever, and small, red spots on the skin. **2** a similar disease that is less severe; German measles. Most Canadian children are vaccinated against both diseases. *n.*

mea·sly (mē′zlē) *Slang.* too small: *She decided to complain about her measly allowance.* *adj.,* **mea·sli·er, mea·sli·est.**

meas·ure (mezh′ər) **1** find out or show the size, amount, or mass of: *When we measured the room, we found that it was 6 m long and 4.5 m wide. This gauge measures rainfall.* **2** be of a certain size or amount: *An Olympic pool measures 50 m by 25 m.* **3** mark off, cut, pour out, etc. an exact amount of something: *Measure off 2 m of this silk. Measure out 5 kg of potatoes.* A **measuring cup** is a cup marked in millilitres or ounces for measuring volume, especially in cooking. **4** size or amount: *His waist measure is 60 cm.* **5** a certain unit, standard, or system for measuring with: *liquid measure, square measure. A metre is a measure of length.* **6** a bar of music. **7** an action that is supposed to accomplish something: *These measures are necessary for public safety.* 1–3 *v.,* **meas·ured, meas·ur·ing;** 4–7 *n.* **—meas′ure·ment,** *n.* **—meas′ure·less,** *n.* **—meas′ur·a·ble,** *adj.*
beyond measure, so great that it cannot be measured; infinite: *joy beyond measure.*
for good measure, as a little extra to make sure there will be enough.
made to measure, specially made to fit or suit a particular person; custom-made.
measure up, be good enough; meet a required standard: *The party did not measure up to her expectations.*
take measures, act; do something.

meat (mēt) **1** any animal flesh used for food. Some people do not include the flesh of fish or birds. **2** the part of anything that can be eaten: *the meat of a walnut.* **3** the main part or parts: *the meat of an argument, the meat of a book.* *n.* **—meat′y,** *adj.*

Mec·ca (mek′ə) **1** the holy city of Islam in Saudi Arabia, where the **Ka'bah** stands, the cube-shaped house of worship built by Abraham. Muslims face toward Mecca for daily prayers and have a duty to make at least one pilgrimage to Mecca. **2** **mecca,** any place that many people visit. *n.*

me·chan·i·cal (mə kan′ə kəl) **1** having to do with machinery or with the forces that cause motion: *a mechanical engineer, mechanical problems.* **2** like a machine; without life or expression: *Her dancing is very mechanical.* *adj.* **—me·chan′i·cal·ly,** *adv.*

a bat	e bed	i bid	o pot	u cup	th thin
ā cake	ē me	ī bite	ō go	ū rude	ᴛʜ then
ä bar	ə about	ər over	ô for	u̇ put	zh measure

me•chan•ics (mə kan′iks) **1** the science dealing with forces, their effects on things, and the motion they produce. **2** the technical details of how something works, especially a machine: *She understands motor mechanics very well. The mechanics of snowshoeing are not easy to master.* A **mechanic** fixes machinery. *n.*

mech•a•nism (mek′ə niz′əm) **1** one set of moving parts inside a machine, doing one specific part of the machine's work: *the braking mechanism of a bike, the steering mechanism of a car.* **2** any system of parts working together like the parts of a machine: *A reflex is a protective mechanism of your body.* To **mechanize** something is to set it up to be done by machine. *n.*

med•al (med′əl) a small piece of metal, often shaped like a coin, stamped with a design and words. A medal usually celebrates or rewards a great act: *a medal for bravery. She won the gold medal in speed skating at the Olympics.* The winner of a medal is a **medallist.** *n.*

me•dal•lion (mə dal′yən) **1** a large round medal. **2** something with a round or oval shape: *chocolate medallions.* *n.*

med•dle (med′əl) fool around with other people's things or interfere: *Don't meddle with my tools. That busybody meddles in everyone's business.* *v.,* **med•dled, med•dling.** **—med′dler,** *n.* **—med′dle•some,** *adj.*

me•di•a (mē′dē ə) a plural of **medium** (defs. 3 and 4): *Newspapers and billboards are important media for advertising. The artist used paint and other media.* *n.*

USING WORDS .... media

Media is plural, and takes a plural verb: *The media are giving daily reports on the Olympic games.*

media literate (mē′dē ə lit′ə rit) able to interpret and evaluate all the forms of communication meant for a mass audience, such as TV, newspapers, or the Internet. *adj.,* **—med′i•a lit′er•a•cy.**

me•di•an (mē′dē ən) **1** a strip of land or pavement in the middle of a road or highway, to separate traffic going in different directions. **2** the middle number of an ordered series. The median of the series 1, 3, 4, 8, 9 is 4. **3** the line that goes from one vertex or corner of a triangle to the middle of the opposite side. *n.*

med•i•cal (med′ə kəl) having to do with the science and art of medicine: *medical advice, medical supplies.* *adj.*

🍁 **med•i•care** (med′ə ker′) a government program of insurance that pays for people's medical care. *n.*

med•i•cine (med′ə sin) **1** a drug used to treat disease, lessen pain, or improve health: *They keep discovering new medicines.* **Medication** is another word for medicine. **2** the study or science of treating disease, lessening pain, and improving health: *Natasha went to university to study medicine.* *n.*
—me•dic′i•nal (mə dis′ə nəl), *adj.*
a taste of your own medicine, a chance to experience the same bad treatment you give to others.

medicine lodge (med′ə sin loj′) a building used for healing ceremonies by some aboriginal peoples. Among some First Nations of the Pacific coast, it is a place for ceremonies meant to cleanse the person's body, mind, and soul using steam. Also called a **sweat lodge.**

medicine man or **woman** (med′ə sin man′ *or* wu̇′mən) among North American aboriginal peoples, a person who uses herbs, songs, ceremonies, and traditional wisdom to heal or teach other people or to influence events. **Shaman** is another word for this person.

me•die•val (med ē′vəl *or* med′ē ē′vəl) belonging to the Middle Ages, the period from about 500 CE to about 1450 CE: *medieval customs.* **Mediaeval** is another spelling. *adj.*

WORD HISTORY .... medieval

Medieval comes from two Latin words: *medius,* meaning "middle," and *aevus,* meaning "age."

Some other words that start with *medi-* and carry the idea of "middle" or "in between" are **medium, mediate,** and **mediocre.**

me•di•o•cre (mē′dē ō′kər) not terrible but not very good: *a mediocre movie, a mediocre writer.* *adj.*
—me′di•oc′ri•ty (mē′dē ok′rə tē), *n.*

med•i•tate (med′ə tāt′) think quietly and deeply: *When she is discouraged, she meditates on all the good things in her life.* *v.,* **med•i•tat•ed, med•i•tat•ing.**
—med′i•ta′tion, *n.* **—med′i•ta′tive,** *adj.*

Med•i•ter•ra•ne•an (med′ə tə rā′nē ən) **1** a sea between Europe and Africa. **2** having to do with this sea or the countries along its shore. 1 *n.,* 2 *adj.*

me•di•um (mē′dē əm) **1** in the middle between two extremes: *a man of medium height. Do you like your boiled eggs hard, soft, or medium?* **2** something that is in the middle between two extremes: *She says life in a small town is a happy medium between city and country life.* **3** something used to carry a message or to create a piece of art: *Radio is a medium of communication. That artist's favourite medium is weaving.* **4** a substance that something can live in: *Water is the medium that fish live in.* **5** a person who is said to receive messages from the spirits of the dead to be passed on to the living. 1 *adj.,* 2–5 *n., pl.* **me·di·ums** or (for 3, 4) **me·di·a** (mē′dē ə).

med·ley (med′lē) a mixture, especially a piece of music made up of parts of different songs. *n., pl.* **med·leys.**

meek (mēk) not easily angered or quick to insist on your rights; humble and patient. *adj.* **—meek′ly,** *adv.* **—meek′ness,** *n.*

meet (mēt) **1** come face to face with something or someone coming from another direction: *Our car met another car on a narrow road.* **2** come together: *Two roads meet near the school. The club meets Tuesdays during noon hour.* **3** keep an appointment with: *Meet me at one o'clock.* **4** be introduced to: *Have you met my sister?* **5** welcome someone arriving: *We have to go to the airport to meet my cousin.* **6** satisfy: *to meet a requirement, to meet someone's needs.* **7** an event where many people gather to compete: *a swim meet.* 1–6 *v.,* **met, meeting;** 7 *n.*
meet halfway, compromise.
meet the eye, be seen by the eye: *A strange sight met my eyes. There is more to this than meets the eye.*
meet with, a get; experience: *We met with rough weather.* **b** get together with for a talk: *My parents want to meet with the teacher.*

meet·ing (mē′ting) **1** the act or fact of coming together: *He looked forward to the meeting with his sister.* **2** a planned gathering of people for some purpose: *a meeting of the computer club.* *n.*

mega– *a prefix meaning:* **1** great; large, as in *megaproject, megacity.* **2** in the SI, million; 1 000 000. A *megavolt* is one million volts. *Symbol:* M

> **USING WORDS ...... mega-**
>
> The prefix **mega-** comes from the Greek *megas*, meaning "great." It is found in **megaphone**, **megacity**, and **megabyte**. In slang English, it is freely added to all kinds of words: megarich, megastar. But watch out — too much of it is megaboring.

meg·a·byte (meg′ə bīt′) about a million bytes (actually 1 048 576) of computer memory. *Symbol:* MB

meg·a·phone (meg′ə fōn′) a large horn used outdoors to make your voice louder: *The cheerleader at the football game yelled through a megaphone.* *n.*

mel·an·chol·y (mel′ən kol′ē) **1** sad or gloomy: *A melancholy person is not very good company.* **2** sadness; a gloomy feeling: *The memory filled her with a great melancholy.* 1 *adj.,* 2 *n.*

mel·low (mel′ō) **1** ripe, juicy, and full of good flavour: *a mellow apple.* **2** soft, warm, and rich: *a violin with a mellow tone, velvet with a mellow colour.* **3** made warmer, softer, and more relaxed by the passage of time: *Later on the atmosphere at the party was very mellow.* **4** make or become mellow: *Time had mellowed his tough manner and quick temper.* 1–3 *adj.,* 4 *v.*

mel·o·dra·mat·ic (mel′ə drə mat′ik) trying too hard to be thrilling or moving; full of exaggerated feeling: *Stop being so melodramatic and just tell us what happened.* *adj.* **—mel′o·dra·mat′i·cal·ly,** *adv.*

mel·o·dy (mel′ə dē) **1** musical notes one after the other, making a tune: *He made the melody and I wrote the words for it.* **2** the main tune in a song, not the harmony. **3** any pleasant sound. *n., pl.* **mel·o·dies.** **—me·lo′di·ous** (mə lō′dē əs), *adj.*

mel·on (mel′ən) a large, juicy fruit from a vine that grows along the ground. The watermelon and cantaloupe are melons. *n.*

melt (melt) **1** change from solid to liquid by heat: *Ice becomes water when it melts.* The **melting point** of a substance is the temperature at which it turns from solid to liquid. **2** dissolve: *Sugar melts in water.* **3** change or disappear gradually: *Green melts into blue in the rainbow. As the sun came out, the clouds melted away.* **4** make soft, tender, and warm: *to melt someone's heart.* *v.*

melt·down (melt′doun′) a situation in a nuclear reactor where the system gets so hot that it makes a reaction go out of control, perhaps even causing an explosion. *n.*

mem·ber (mem′bər) a person or thing that belongs to a group: *Every member of the family helps around the house. Pluto and Venus are members of our solar system.* *n.* **—mem′ber·ship′,** *n.*

Member of Parliament (mem′bər əv pår′lə mənt) in Canada, the title of a person elected to the Federal Parliament in Ottawa. *Abbreviation:* MP
▶ See Appendix.

mem·brane (mem′brān) a thin, skinlike sheet or layer. In humans, animals, and plants, certain body parts are lined or covered with a membrane made of special tissue. A membrane protects the inside surface of your stomach, for example. *n.*

a bat	e bed	i bid	o pot	u cup	th thin
ā cake	ē me	ī bite	ō go	ü rude	ᴛʜ then
å bar	ə about	ər over	ò for	ů put	zh measure

me•men•to (mə men′tō) a small item kept as a reminder of something or somebody; souvenir: *Hans picked up a few mementos on his trip to Fredericton.* *n., pl.* **me•men•tos.**

me•mo•ri•al (mə mȯ′rē əl) **1** something made to help people remember an important event or person. It could be a statue, a coin, or even a photo album. **2** made or done to remember some person or event: *a memorial service, a memorial plaque.* 1 *n.,* 2 *adj.*

mem•o•ry (mem′ə rē) **1** the ability to remember or keep in the mind: *She has a good memory for phone numbers.* **2** something that is remembered: *His mother died when he was small; she is only a memory to him now.* **3** all that a person remembers: *My first day of school stands out in my memory.* **4** the part of a computer that stores information, measured in megabytes or gigabytes. *n., pl.* **mem•o•ries.**
in living memory, in all the time remembered by anyone alive: *the hottest summer in living memory.*
in memory of, in order to remember: *On November 11 we hold a school assembly in memory of those who died in the two World Wars.*

Word Family........ **memory**

memo: a brief reminder note. (It is short for **memorandum.**)
memoirs: a written account of the things a person remembers from his or her own life
memorable: worth remembering; unforgettable
memorize: learn by heart; learn from memory

men (men) plural of **man.** *n.*

men•ace (men′is) **1** a threat: *In dry weather forest fires are a great menace.* **2** threaten: *Floods menaced the valley every spring.* 1 *n.,* 2 *v.,* **men•aced, men•ac•ing.**

mend (mend) **1** fix; repair: *to mend a road, to mend a broken doll, to mend torn clothing.* **2** get well again: *The patient will soon mend if she gets plenty of rest.* **3** a place that has been mended: *The mend in your jacket hardly shows.* 1, 2 *v.,* 3 *n.*
mend your ways, improve your behaviour.
on the mend, getting better.

me•ni•al (mē′nē əl) having to do with small, dull jobs that don't take much skill: *In ancient Rome, slaves did all the menial tasks.* *adj.*

Men•non•ite (men′ə nīt′) a member of a Christian group that came from Europe to North America to escape persecution. Mennonites have a simple lifestyle and most refuse to go to war. The **Amish** are one kind of Mennonite. *n.*

me•nor•ah (mə nȯr′ə) **1** the eight-branched candelabra used on Hanukkah, the Jewish Festival of Lights, to remind people of the miracle of the Hanukkah story. **2** the seven-branched candelabra used in the ancient temple in Jerusalem. *n.*

men•stru•a•tion (men′strū ā′shən) the normal process that cleans the unneeded blood and tissue out of the uterus of a woman or girl who is not pregnant. Menstruation happens every month from about 12 years of age until about 50. *n.* **—men′stru•ate′,** *v.*

–ment *a suffix* added to verbs to make nouns, such as *agreement, amazement,* or *government.*

men•tal (men′təl) **1** having to do with the mind: *mental abilities, mental illness.* **2** done or made in the mind without being spoken or written down: *mental arithmetic, a mental note.* *adj.* **—men′tal•ly,** *adv.*

men•tion (men′shən) **1** talk or write about: *Did you mention food? In her letter she mentioned that her brother was sick.* **2** a short statement about: *There was mention of our band's concert in the newspaper.* 1 *v.,* 2 *n.*
don't mention it, there is no need to thank me.
make mention of, mention.

men•u (men′yū) **1** a list of the food served at a restaurant or at any meal. **2** in computer programs, a list shown on the screen so you can choose what you want to do. *n.*

mer•chan•dise (mər′chən dīs′ *for 1;* mər′chən dīz′ *for 2*) **1** goods for sale; articles bought and sold. **2** sell. 1 *n.,* 2 *v.,* **mer•chan•dised, mer•chan•dising.**

mer•chant (mər′chənt) **1** a person who buys and sells things for profit. **2** a store owner. **3** having to do with trade: *merchant ships.* 1, 2 *n.,* 3 *adj.*

mer•cu•ry (mər′kyə rē) **1** a heavy, silver-white poisonous metal that is liquid at ordinary temperatures. It is used in thermometers and barometers. **2 Mercury,** the planet nearest to the sun. *n.*

mer•cy (mər′sē) **1** kindness, especially kindness that treats people better than they deserve: *The judge showed mercy to the criminal.* **2** something to be thankful for: *It's a mercy that they arrived safely through the storm.* *n., pl.* **mer•cies. —mer′ci•ful,** *adj.* **—mer′ci•less,** *adj.*
at the mercy of, helpless against: *Without shelter we were at the mercy of the storm.*

mere (mēr) nothing else than; only: *The cut was a mere scratch. The mere sight of a dog makes him afraid.* *adj., superlative* **mer•est. —mere′ly,** *adv.*

merge (mərj) join or blend together: *Two lanes of traffic have to merge into one here. The brothers decided to merge their two businesses.* The joining of two organizations is called a **merger.** *v.,* **merged, merg·ing.**

me·rid·i·an (mə rid′ē ən) any of the imaginary lines from the North Pole to the South Pole; a line of longitude. The **prime meridian** is at 0° longitude and passes through Greenwich, England; all other meridians are a certain number of degrees east or west of that one. The meridian on the opposite side of the globe is the **International Date Line.** *n.*

me·ringue (mə rang′) **1** a mixture of egg white and sugar, beaten until stiff: *Meringue is often spread on pies, puddings, etc. and lightly browned in the oven.* **2** a small cake or shell made of this mixture. *n.*

mer·it (mer′it) **1** goodness; worth or value: *I disagree with him, but his argument has some merit.* **2** deserve: *Your work merits praise.* **3** Usually, **merits,** *pl.* actual facts or qualities, whether good or bad: *The judge will consider the case on its merits.* 1, 3 *n.,* 2 *v.*

mer·lon (mər′lən) the high part of the top of a battlement. The **crenel** is the low part. *n.*

mer·maid (mər′mād) an imaginary sea creature that is half woman, but is a fish from the waist down. *n.*

mer·ry (mer′ē) full of fun; light-hearted; happy: *a merry laugh.* **Merrymaking** is partying and having fun. *adj.,* **mer·ri·er, mer·ri·est.** **—mer′ri·ly,** *adv.* **—mer′ri·ment,** *n.*

mer·ry–go–round (mer′ē gō round′) a ride that has seats shaped like animals on a platform that goes round and round while music is played. **Carousel** is another word for it. *n.*

me·sa (mā′sə) a flat area of land raised above the land surrounding it, especially in Mexico and the southwestern United States. *n.*

mesh (mesh) **1** a network of cord, wire, or other material. A window screen is made of wire mesh. **2** one of the spaces in a network: *Seaweed was caught in the meshes of the net.* **3** fit smoothly together: *The teeth of this small gear mesh with the teeth of that big one. The two groups meshed perfectly to make one team.* 1, 2 *n.,* 3 *v.*

mes·mer·ize (mes′mə rīz′) hypnotize. *v.,* **mes·mer·ized, mes·mer·iz·ing.**

mess (mes) **1** a dirty, sloppy, or confused mass of things: *There was a mess of dirty dishes in the kitchen.* **2** an unpleasant situation full of confusion and difficulty: *How did we end up in this terrible mess?* **3** a confused or untidy condition: *Their affairs are in a mess. Don't leave your room in a mess.* **4** make a mess of; spoil: *He messed up his book by scribbling on the pages. The accident wasn't serious but it messed up our holiday.* **5** the dining room used by members of the armed forces: *I ate in the officers' mess.* 1–3, 5 *n.,* 4 *v.* **—mess′y,** *adj.* **—mess′i·ness,** *n.* **mess around,** be active without accomplishing anything. **mess with,** get into a conflict with: *Don't mess with him, he has quite a temper.*

mes·sage (mes′ij) **1** information sent from one person to another: *a message of welcome, a text message.* A **messenger** delivers messages. **2** an idea expressed by an action, a piece of art, a story, etc.: *The story contains a message of hope.* *n.*

mes·sag·ing (mes′ij ing) the sending of a message, usually by cellphone. *n.*

met (met) the past tense and past participle of **meet:** *My father met us this morning at ten o'clock. We were met at the gate by our three dogs.* *v.*

me·tab·o·lism (mə tab′ə liz′əm) the body processes that change food into energy, get rid of wastes, and cause growth. Vigorous exercise makes your body **metabolize** faster. *n.* **—met′a·bol′ic** (met′ə bol′ik)**,** *adj.*

met·al (met′əl) **1** a substance that is usually hard and shiny when solid, a good conductor of heat and electricity, and able to be made into wire or hammered into sheets. Gold, silver, copper, iron, lead, tin, and aluminum are metals. **2** an alloy or mixture of these, such as steel or brass. *n.* **—me·tal′lic** (mə tal′ik)**,** *n.*

met·a·mor·phic (met′ə mȯr′fik) **1** having to do with a change in form. **2** in geology, describing rock whose structure and texture have been changed by the action of heat or pressure. Marble is a metamorphic rock formed from limestone. *adj.*

met·a·mor·pho·sis (met′ə mȯr′fə sis) **1** the change in form that certain creatures go through as they develop into adults. Tadpoles become frogs by metamorphosis. Some insects, such as butterflies, go through **complete metamorphosis,** starting off somewhat like a worm and turning into a pupa before becoming an adult; others go through **incomplete metamorphosis,** looking just like a wingless adult when they hatch and then gaining wings later. **2** any great change. *n., pl.* **met·a·mor·pho·ses** (met′ə mȯr′fə sēz′)**.** **—met′a·mor′phose** (met′ə mȯr′fōz)**,** *v.*

a bat	e bed	i bid	o pot	u cup	th thin
ā cake	ē me	ī bite	ō go	ū rude	ᴛʜ then
ä bar	ə about	ər over	ȯ for	u̇ put	zh measure

Meteorology

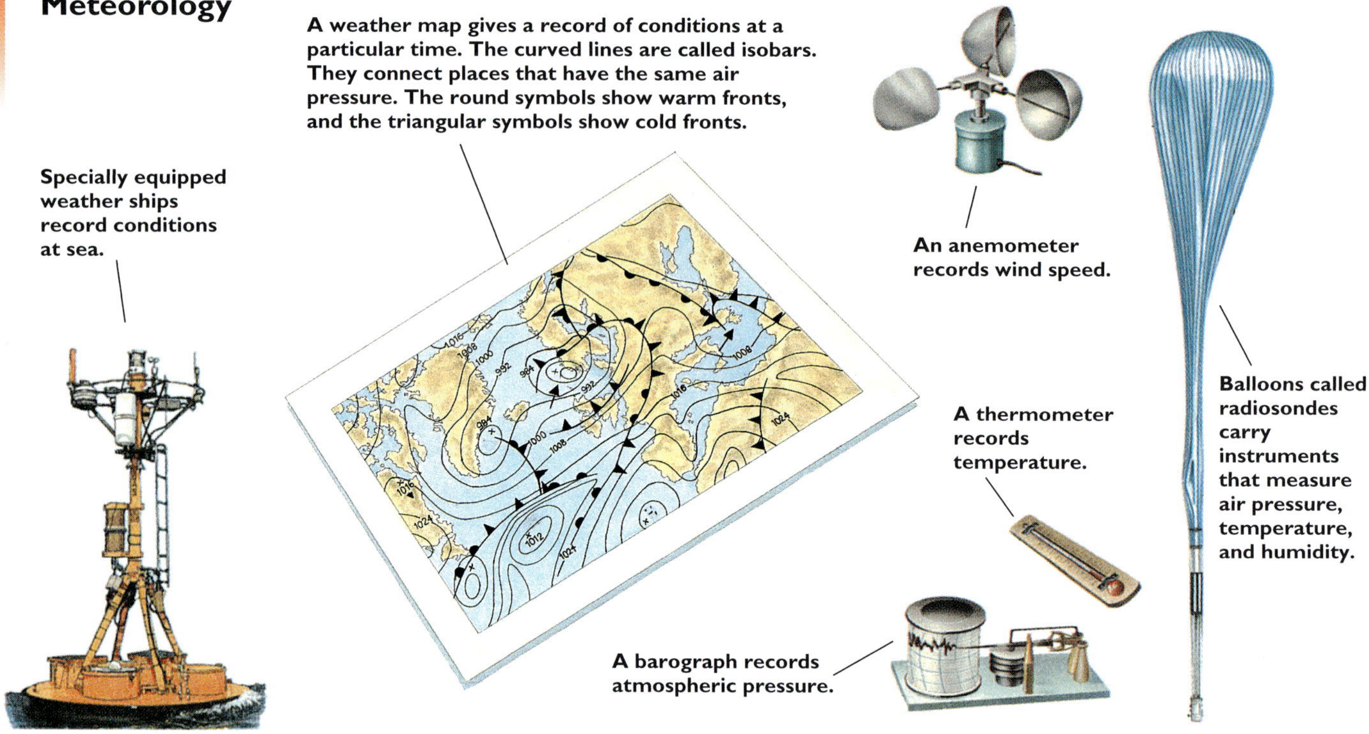

met·a·phor (met′ə fôr′) a figure of speech. In a metaphor, a word or phrase that normally means one thing is used for another thing in order to show how the two things are alike. *Examples: Fear gripped him with fingers of ice. The holidays were a merry-go-round of parties.* *n.* ▶ See the *Grammar and Usage Mini-Guide.*

> **USING WORDS .... metaphor/simile**
>
> **Metaphors** and **similes** are two ways to make comparisons.
>
> A **metaphor** talks about one thing as if it were another: *Arrows of flame shot into the air.*
> A **simile** compares two things, using *like* or *as*: *Flames shot into the air like arrows.*

me·te·or (mē′tē ər) a rock from outer space that comes speeding through the earth's air. Meteors get so hot doing this that they leave a trail of light in the night sky called a **shooting star.** Most burn up without reaching the earth; the few that last long enough to land are called **meteorites.** *n.*

me·te·or·ol·o·gy (mē′tē ə rol′ə jē) the science that deals with the atmosphere and weather. Weather forecasting is a part of meteorology. *n.* **—me′te·or·ol′o·gist,** *n.*

me·ter (mē′tər) a device that measures something and shows the amount: *a parking meter, a gas meter.* *n.*

meth·od (meth′əd) **1** a way of doing something: *a method of teaching music. Roasting is one method of cooking meat.* **2** organization in getting things done or in thinking: *If you used more method, you'd waste less time.* A person or action that follows a step-by-step, orderly procedure is **methodical** (mə thod′ə kəl). *n.*

me·tic·u·lous (mə tik′yə ləs) extremely careful about small details: *She was always so meticulous about her woodworking projects.* *adj.*

Mé·tis or **Me·tis** (mā′tē *or* mā tē′) a person who has First Nations and European ancestors. The Métis are descended from the people who settled in the Red, Assiniboine, and Saskatchewan river valleys during the 1800s. They are a distinct cultural group. *n., pl.* **Mé·tis** or **Me·tis.**

me·tre[1] (mē′tər) an SI unit for measuring length. A door is about two metres high. A **metre stick** is one metre long and is marked off in centimetres and millimetres for measuring. *Symbol:* m *n.*

me·tre[2] (mē′tər) the rhythm of poetry or music; the pattern of beats or accents on the syllables or the notes: *The metre of "Twinkle, twinkle, little star" is different from that of "One, two, buckle my shoe."* **Meter** is another spelling. *n.* **—met′ri·cal** (met′rə kəl), *adj.*

met•ric (met′rik) having to do with a system of measurement which counts by tens. The **metric system** adopted by Canada is called the **Système internationale d'unités** (**SI**) or International System of Units. It is based on the metre for length, the kilogram for mass, and the ampere for electric current.

met•ro (met′rō) *Informal.* **1** a large city together with all the smaller communities around it. Metro is short for **metropolitan.** **2** the government of such a city. **3** the subway system of Montréal. *n.*

met•ro•nome (met′rə nōm′) a small machine that can be adjusted to tick or flash a light at a certain speed. It is used by people practising musical instruments to help them keep a steady rhythm. *n.*

met•ro•pol•i•tan (met′rə pol′ə tən) having to do with a large city, together with all the smaller communities around it. A large city is a **metropolis** (mə trop′ə lis). *adj.*

met•tle (met′əl) spirit; courage. *n.*

mew (myū) **1** the sound made by a cat or kitten. **2** make this sound: *Our kitten mews when it gets hungry.* **Meow** is another word for both meanings. 1 *n.*, 2 *v.*

mez•za•nine (mez′ə nēn′) **1** a floor going part of the way across, usually between the ground floor and the second floor of a building. It is open to the floor below and can be reached by stairs. **2** in a theatre, the lowest balcony, or its front section. *n.*

mg *symbol for* milligram or milligrams.

MHA or **M.H.A.** *abbreviation for* Member of the House of Assembly. The House of Assembly is the lawmaking body of Nova Scotia or of Newfoundland and Labrador. ▶ See Appendix.

mice (mīs) plural of **mouse.** *n.*

micro– *a prefix meaning:* **1** very small, as in *micro-organism, microfilm.* **2** in the SI, one millionth: A *microsecond* is one millionth of a second. *Symbol:* µ

mi•crobe (mī′krōb) a very tiny living organism, especially a germ. *n.*

mi•cro•chip (mī′krō chip′) a tiny piece of silicon used in a computer, containing the information for one of the circuits in the computer. *n.*

mi•cro•film (mī′krō film′) a film for making very small photographs of printed material, to preserve it in a very small space. To read microfilm you need a special machine that enlarges the image and projects it on a small screen. An individual sheet of microfilm is a **microfiche** (mī′krō fēsh′). *n.*

mi•cro–or•gan•ism (mī′krō ȯr′gə niz′əm) a living thing that is too small to be seen with the naked eye. Bacteria and viruses are micro-organisms. *n.*

mi•cro•phone (mī′krə fōn′) a device that converts sound into electrical current. It can be used with other devices to make sounds louder, record them, or transmit them by telephone, radio, and so on. This word is often shortened to **mike.** *n.*

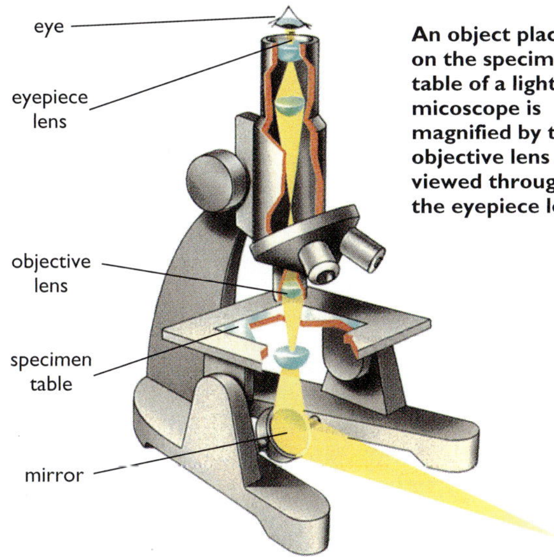

An object placed on the specimen table of a light micoscope is magnified by the objective lens and viewed through the eyepiece lens.

mi•cro•scope (mī′krə skōp′) an instrument with a combination of lenses for making small objects look bigger. It is used a lot in scientific research. Something so tiny it can only be seen through a microscope is **microscopic** (mī′krə skop′ik). *n.*

mi•cro•wave oven (mī′krō wāv′ uv′ən) an oven using electromagnetic waves to cook food. The waves go through the food and heat it by causing its molecules to vibrate.

mid (mid) middle: *mid sizes, temperatures in the mid twenties.* This word is often used in compounds, such as *midsummer, midweek, mid-April.* *adj.*

mid•day (mid′dā′) the middle of the day; noon: *at midday* (*n.*), *the midday meal* (*adj.*). *n. or adj.*

mid•dle (mid′əl) **1** halfway between two ends or sides; in the centre: *the middle house in the row.* **2** the point or part that is the same distance from each end or side; the centre: *the middle of the road. Put this around your middle.* **3** medium: *a person of middle size.* 1, 3 *adj.*, 2 *n.*

a bat	e bed	i bid	o pot	u cup	th thin
ā cake	ē me	ī bite	ō go	ū rude	ᴛʜ then
ä bar	ə about	ər over	ȯ for	u̇ put	zh measure

mid·dle age (mid′əl āj′) the time between youth and old age; from about 40 to about 60 years of age. —**mid′dle-aged′,** *adj.*

In the Middle Ages, a European town on market day was a busy place. A dancing bear (lower right) was a common entertainment for the crowds.

Middle Ages the period in European history between ancient and modern times, from about 500 CE to about 1500.

middle ear (mid′əl ēr′) a hollow space between the eardrum and the inner ear. In humans the middle ear contains three small bones that pass on sound waves from the eardrum to the inner ear.

Middle East (mid′əl ēst′) the region including Turkey, Iran, Egypt, Israel, and Saudi Arabia, and neighbouring countries.

Middle Path (mid′əl path′) in Buddhism, a good, balanced lifestyle.

middle school (mid′əl skūl′) in some provinces, a school with grades between elementary and high school, usually grades six to eight.

midg·et (mij′it) 1 a person or thing that is much smaller than the usual size. 2 very small: *a midget submarine.* 3 having to do with a sports league for young players. 1 *n.,* 2, 3 *adj.*

mid·night (mid′nīt′) twelve o'clock at night; the middle of the night. *n.*

midst (midst) the middle: *in the midst of the crowd, in the midst of supper.* *n.*
in our midst, among us: *a traitor in our midst.*

mid·way (mid′wā′ *for 1,* mid′wā′ *for 2*) 1 halfway; in the middle: *situated midway between the two towns* (*adv.*), *a midway point on the chart* (*adj.*). 2 at a fair or exhibition, the place for games, rides, and so on. 1 *adv. or adj.,* 2 *n.*

mid·wife (mid′wīf′) a trained person who helps women give birth. This work is called **midwifery** (mid wif′ə rē). *n., pl.* **mid·wives** (mid′wīvz′).

miffed (mift) *Informal.* slightly annoyed or irritated: *Denis was miffed that he wasn't invited to the party.* *adj.*

might¹ (mīt) the past tense of **may,** used to express a possibility: *It might rain tomorrow. She might not like your answer.* *v.*

might² (mīt) great power; strength: *Work with all your might.* *n.*
with might and main, with all your strength.

might·y (mī′tē) 1 strong, powerful, or great: *a mighty ruler, a mighty storm.* 2 *Informal.* very or extremely: *a mighty cold day.* 1 *adj.,* **might·i·er, might·i·est;** 2 *adv.* —**might′i·ly,** *adv.*

mi·graine (mī′grān) an extremely bad headache that causes pain behind your eyes and can result in dizziness and vomiting. It usually affects only one side of your head. *n.*

mi·grate (mī′grāt *or* mī grāt′) 1 move from one place to settle in another: *Pioneers from central Canada migrated to all parts of what are now the Prairie Provinces.* A **migrant worker** is one who goes from place to place, working wherever jobs can be found. 2 go from one region to another with the change in the seasons: *Many birds migrate to warmer regions in the winter.* *v.,* **mi·grat·ed, mi·grat·ing.** —**mi·gra′tion,** *n.* —**mi′gra·to′ry** (mī′grə tôr′ē), *adj.*

Mi'k·maw (mik′ mo) 1 a member of a First Nations people living in the Maritimes. The plural is **Mi'kmaq** (mik′mȧk). 2 their language. 3 having to do with these people or their language. 1, 2 *n.,* 3 *adj.*

mild (mīld) 1 rather warm; not harsh or severe: *a mild climate, a mild winter.* 2 not sharp or strong in taste or smell: *mild cheese.* *adj.* —**mild′ly,** *adv.*

mil·dew (mil′dyū *or* mil′dū) 1 a grey, black, or greenish fungus that appears on clothes, paper, walls, etc. when they stay damp for a long time. It can also attack plants, causing disease: *Damp clothes left in a pile will show mildew in a few days.* 2 cover or become covered with mildew. 1 *n.,* 2 *v.*

mile (mīl) 1 a measure of distance on land equal to 5280 feet (about 1609 m), called a **statute mile.** 2 a measure of about 6080 feet (1853 m) used in air and sea travel, called a **nautical mile.** *n.*

mile·age (mī′lij) **1** the distance covered or travelled by a vehicle: *What's the mileage on your car now?* **2** the distance that a vehicle can travel on a certain amount of fuel: *This little car gets good mileage.* *n.*
get a lot of mileage out of, get a lot of use or enjoyment out of.

USING WORDS ...... mileage

Distances in Canada are officially measured in kilometres, but the term *mile* still comes up in words like **mileage** and **milestone** — you can get a lot of mileage out of a good joke, and graduation is a major milestone in your life.

mile·stone (mīl′stōn′) **1** a stone set up to show the distance to a certain place. **2** an important event in the development of something: *The invention of printing was a milestone in the progress of education.* *n.*

mil·i·tant (mil′ə tənt) taking a very strong, active, outspoken stand on an issue. *adj.*

mil·i·tar·y (mil′ə ter′ē) **1** having to do with soldiers, the armed forces, or war: *military training.* **2 the military,** the armed forces; soldiers: *The military helped to control the forest fire.* 1 *adj.,* 2 *n.*

mi·li·tia (mə lish′ə) a part of the army made up of citizens who are not regular soldiers but who are trained for emergency duty. They are also called the **reserves.** *n.*

milk (milk) **1** the white liquid produced by female mammals as food for their babies. Most milk sold in stores is from cows. **2** any other whitish liquid such as the juice of some plants: *coconut milk.* **3** take milk from: *to milk a cow.* **4** take advantage of: *He was only a bit sick, but he milked it all he could to get special treatment.* 1, 2 *n.,* 3, 4 *v.* **—milk′er,** *n.* **—milk′y,** *adj.*

milk·shake (milk′shāk′) a drink made of milk, flavouring, and often ice cream, beaten together.

milk·weed (milk′wēd′) a weed with white juice in its stem that looks like milk. *n.*

Milky Way (mil′kē wā′) **1** a broad band of faint light that stretches across the sky at night. It is made up of countless stars, too far away to be seen separately without a telescope. **2** the galaxy containing these stars. The earth, the sun, and all the planets around the sun are part of the same galaxy.

mill (mil) **1** a machine for grinding or crushing: *A flour mill grinds wheat into flour. A coffee mill grinds coffee beans.* **2** a building containing a machine for grinding grain. The person running it is a **miller.** **3** grind: *to mill wheat.* **4** a building where manufacturing is done: *a paper mill.* **5** move around in a confused way: *There were many people milling around after the parade.* 1, 2, 4 *n.,* 3, 5 *v.*

mil·len·ni·um (mə len′ē əm) a period of 1000 years, especially the period from one round thousand to another in a system of counting years. *n., pl.* **mil·len·ni·a** or **mil·len·ni·ums.**

mil·let (mil′it) a grain used for food in Europe, Asia, and Africa. In North America it is grown mainly for hay. *n.*

milli– *an SI prefix meaning* thousandth. A millilitre is one thousandth of a litre. *Symbol:* m

mil·li·gram (mil′ə gram′) one thousandth of a gram. *Symbol:* mg *n.*

mil·li·li·tre (mil′ə lē′tər) one thousandth of a litre. *Symbol:* mL *n.*

mil·li·metre (mil′ə mē′tər) one thousandth of a metre. *Symbol:* mm *n.*

mil·lion (mil′yən) **1** one thousand thousand (1 000 000). **2** a very large number; very many: *He claims to have millions of friends* (*n.*). *She can always think of a million reasons for not helping with the dishes* (*adj.*). A person with a million dollars or more is a **millionaire.** *n. or adj.* **—mil′lionth,** *adj. or n.*

mil·li·pede (mil′ə pēd′) a wormlike creature with a flat body divided into many segments, each with two pairs of legs. *n.*

mil·li·sec·ond (mil′ə sek′ənd) one thousandth of a second. *Symbol:* ms *n.*

mill·stone (mil′stōn′) a huge, round, flat stone used together with another one for grinding grain. *n.*
a millstone around someone's neck, a heavy burden.

mill wheel (mil′ wēl′) a wheel that is turned by water and supplies power for a mill. A shaft attached to the wheel leads into the mill and turns the machinery.

mime (mīm) **1** a form of drama using movement and gestures but no words. **2** an actor that performs this kind of drama. **3** act out in this way: *For their skit they mimed a birthday party.* **4** gestures as a way of communicating: *They didn't know the language, so they had to use mime.* 1, 2, 4 *n.,* 3 *v.,* **mimed, mim·ing.**

a bat	e bed	i bid	o pot	u cup	th thin
ā cake	ē me	ī bite	ō go	ü rude	ŦH then
ä bar	ə about	ər over	ô for	u̇ put	zh measure

mim•ic (mim′ik) **1** copy; imitate, sometimes in order to make fun of: *Stop mimicking me. A parrot can mimic a person's voice.* **2** a person or thing that imitates. **3** resemble closely: *Some insects mimic leaves as a way of protecting themselves.* 1, 3 *v.,* **mim•icked, mim•ick•ing;** 2 *n.* —**mim′ic•ry,** *n.*

min *symbol for* minute or minutes.

This minaret was built in the 1000s, at the Jami Mosque in Simnan, Iran.

min•a•ret (min′ə ret′) a tower on a mosque, where the muezzin stands to call Muslims to prayer. *n.*

mince (mins) **1** chop up into very small pieces. **2** made with mincemeat: *mince pie.* **3** speak or move in a prissy, dainty way. 1, 3 *v.,* **minced, minc•ing;** 2 *adj.*
mince words, say something very carefully so as not to upset someone. To **mince matters** is the same thing.

mince•meat (mins′mēt′) a mixture of finely chopped apples, raisins, currants, spices, and so on, used as pie filling. In earlier times it also contained meat. *n.*

mind (mīnd) **1** the part of a person that knows, thinks, remembers, understands, decides, believes, and so on. **2** feel unhappy about; dislike or object to: *I minded very much that they didn't invite me. Some people don't mind cold weather.* **3** look after; take care of: *Please mind the baby while I make lunch.* **4** be careful about, pay attention to: *Mind the step. Mind that you come on time.* **5** obey. 1 *n.,* 2–5 *v.* —**mind′less,** *adj.*
be in two minds about something, be unable to decide.
be of one mind, have the same opinion; agree: *They were both of one mind.*
call to mind, remember or cause to remember.
give someone a piece of your mind, scold someone.
have a mind of your own, **a** have a strong will. **b** be able to think for yourself.
have a mind to, be thinking of doing: *I have a mind to watch the hockey game tonight.*
in your mind's eye, in your imagination.
keep in mind, keep one's attention on; remember. **Bear in mind** is a more formal version.
mind you, take note!
on someone's mind, filling someone's thoughts: *This problem has been on my mind lately.*
put someone in mind of, remind someone of.
set your mind on, want very much.
speak your mind, say what you really think.
to my mind, in my opinion.

mind•ful (mīnd′fəl)
mindful of, keeping in mind, remembering: *Mindful of your advice, I went slowly.* *adj.*

mine (mīn) **1** a place where people dig valuable minerals out of the earth: *a coal mine, a gold mine.* **2** dig for minerals in the earth: *to mine the Canadian Shield for nickel. They mine coal on Cape Breton Island.* **3** a rich or plentiful source: *The book was a mine of information about spacecraft.* **4** a bomb hidden under water, on the ground, or just below the ground. **5** lay this kind of bomb in: *to mine the enemy's supply route.* A **minefield** is an area where many mines have been hidden. 1, 3, 4 *n.,* 2, 5 *v.,* **mined, min•ing.** —**min′er,** *n.*

min•er•al (min′ə rəl) **1** a valuable substance that people dig out of the earth: *Iron ore and coal are minerals.* **2** in science, any natural substance that is made up of crystals and is neither plant nor animal: *Salt and sand are minerals.* According to this scientific definition, coal is not a mineral because it is made up of plant material. **3** containing or having to do with minerals: *mineral water. There are mineral deposits in the ocean floor.* 1, 2 *n.,* 3 *adj.* —**min′er•al′o•gy** (min′ə rol′ə jē), *n.*

min•gle (ming′gəl) mix: *Toni is very shy and does not mingle much with the children at school.* *v.,* **min•gled, min•gling.**

min•i (min′ē) *Informal.* **1** a miniskirt, minicomputer, or other thing that is smaller or shorter than others of its kind. **2** short for **miniature:** *mini golf.* 1 *n.,* 2 *adj.*

mini– *a prefix meaning* small or short: *miniskirt, minibus.* A **minibike** is a small motorcycle.

min•i•a•ture (min′ ə chər) **1** a small model or copy: *In the museum there is a miniature of the "Titanic."* **2** made just like the real thing only very small: *She had earrings shaped like miniature running shoes.* 1 *n.,* 2 *adj.*

min·i·mum (min′ə məm) 1 the smallest amount possible or permitted: *Try to eat a minimum of fatty foods.* 2 the lowest possible: *Eighteen is the minimum age for voting in some provinces.* The **minimum wage** is the lowest amount you can legally pay an adult worker. To **minimize** something is to make it as small or unimportant as possible. 1 *n.*, 2 *adj.*

min·is·ter (min′is tər) 1 a person in charge of a department of the government called a **ministry:** *the Minister of Finance.* 2 a recognized leader of a Christian church; a preacher or pastor. 3 serve; be helpful: *to minister to a sick person's needs.* 1, 2 *n.*, 3 *v.* —**min′is·try,** *n.*

mink (mingk) a small animal, related to the weasel, that lives in water part of the time. It has valuable brown fur. *n.*

min·now (min′ō) 1 any small freshwater fish of the carp family, often used as bait. 2 any other young, very small fish. *n.*

mi·nor (mī′nər) 1 small or not very important: *minor details, minor errors.* 2 a person who is not yet an adult according to the law. In various provinces, minors are people under 18, 19, or 21 years of age. A minor cannot vote. 3 in music, having to do with scales that have only a half step between the second and third notes. Songs written in a minor key often sound more mournful than songs in a major key. 1, 3 *adj.*, 2 *n.*

mi·nor·i·ty (mə nȯr′ə tē) 1 the smaller number or part; less than half: *The minority must often accept what the majority decides to do.* 2 Often, **minority group,** a group that differs from the main part of the population in race, religion, language, culture, etc.: *The law protects minorities from discrimination.* *n.*, *pl.* **mi·nor·i·ties.**

min·strel (min′strəl) in the Middle Ages, a singer or musician, often in a lord's household. *n.*

Mint plants come in several different flavours — this is an apple mint.

mint¹ (mint) 1 a sweet-smelling plant used for flavouring. Mint has a fresh, cool taste. 2 a piece of candy flavoured with mint. *n.*

mint² (mint) 1 a place where coins and paper money are officially made. 2 make coins or medals: *This toonie was minted in 1996.* 3 *Informal.* a lot of money: *She made a mint when she sold her house.* 1, 3 *n.*, 2 *v.*
in mint condition, in perfect condition even though it is not new: *This 20-year-old piano is still in mint condition.*

WORD HISTORY........ mint

This word **mint** is actually the cousin of **money**. Both words can be traced back to the Latin word *moneta*, meaning either "money" or "the place where money is made." Old English made this into *mynet*, meaning "coin." It later became **mint**.

mi·nus (mī′nəs) 1 less; take away: *12 minus 3 leaves 9. Symbol:* – In 12–3, 12 is the **minuend** (min′yü end′). 2 *Informal.* without: *a book minus its cover.* *prep.*

min·ute¹ (min′it) 1 one of the 60 equal periods of time that make up an hour. A minute is equal to 60 seconds. *Symbol:* min 2 a short period of time or an exact point in time: *I'll be there in a minute. The minute you see her coming, please tell me.* 3 **minutes,** *pl.* an official record of what happened at a meeting. *n.*

mi·nute² (mī nyüt′ *or* mī nüt′) 1 very small; tiny: *a minute speck of dust.* 2 going into great detail: *She gave me minute instructions about how to do my work.* *adj.*

mir·a·cle (mir′ə kəl) 1 a wonderful happening that cannot be explained by the known laws of nature, especially something that people believe was done by the power of a god. 2 any amazing and lucky event; a wonder: *It was a miracle you weren't hurt in that accident.* *n.* —**mi·rac′u·lous** (mə rak′ yə ləs), *adj.*

mi·rage (mə räzh′) 1 a trick of the light that makes a faraway scene look close and, often, upside down. This is because the actual scene is being reflected off different layers of air that have different temperatures. 2 something that seems to be there but isn't. *n.*

mir·ror (mir′ər) 1 a sheet of glass that you can see yourself in because its surface reflects light. The back of a mirror is coated with a metallic substance. 2 a true reflection or picture: *This comic strip is a mirror of everyday family life.* 3 give an exact reflection as a mirror does: *Her face mirrored her feelings.* 1, 2 *n.*, 3 *v.*

a bat	e bed	i bid	o pot	u cup	th thin
ā cake	ē me	ī bite	ō go	ū rude	ᴛʜ then
ä bar	ə about	ər over	ȯ for	ů put	zh measure

mirth (mərth) merry laughter: *Her sides shook with mirth.* *n.* —**mirth′ful,** *adj.* —**mirth′less,** *adj.*

mis– *a prefix meaning* wrong or wrongly, as in *misunderstanding, misbehave.*

Word Family.......... mis-

misbehave: behave badly. The noun is **misbehaviour**.
miscalculate: make an error in calculating
miscount: **1** count wrongly. **2** an error in counting
misdeed: wrong action
misinform: give wrong information to
misjudge: judge wrongly
mismatch: **1** match badly. **2** a bad match
mispronounce: pronounce wrongly
misspell: spell incorrectly
mistreat: treat badly

mis·cel·la·ne·ous (mis′ə lā′nē əs) made up of various kinds of things: *She had a miscellaneous collection of stones, bugs, marbles, stamps, and other things.* *adj.*

mis·chief (mis′chif) **1** playful pranks or teasing: *She looks sweet, but she's full of mischief.* **2** action that causes trouble, often without meaning it: *The child's mischief with the computer made it crash.* **3** a person who does harm or causes annoyance, often just in fun: *He was a little mischief.* *n.* —**mis′chie·vous** (mis′chə vəs), *adj.*

mi·ser (mī′zər) a person who loves money for its own sake; someone who has money, but lives poorly in order to save it and keep it. *n.* —**mi′ser·ly,** *adj.*

mis·er·a·ble (miz′ə rə bəl) **1** very unhappy: *A person who is sick is often miserable.* **2** causing trouble or unhappiness: *I have a miserable cold.* **3** poor; pitiful: *They lived in a miserable little shack.* *adj.* —**mis′er·a·bly,** *adv.*

mis·er·y (miz′ə rē) a very unhappy feeling or condition: *The thought of leaving filled him with misery. Some people live in misery, with no home or friends.* *n.*

mis·fit (mis′fit′) a person who does not seem to fit in well with other people or with his or her surroundings. *n.*

mis·for·tune (mis fôr′chən) an unlucky accident or bad luck: *She had the misfortune to break her arm.* *n.*

mis·giv·ing (mis giv′ing) an anxious or doubtful feeling: *We started hiking with some misgivings, as thunder rumbled in the distance.* *n.*

mis·guid·ed (mis gī′did) trying to be helpful or do right, but having the opposite effect: *Our misguided attempt to rescue the dog ended in disaster.* *adj.* —**mis·guid′ed·ly,** *n.*

mis·hap (mis′hap) a small accident. *n.*

mis·lay (mis lā′) put somewhere and then forget where: *My mother is always mislaying her glasses.* *v.,* **mis·laid, mis·lay·ing.**

mis·lead (mis lēd′) cause to do or believe something that is wrong: *Her cheerfulness misled us into thinking that everything was all right.* *v.,* **mis·led** (mis led′), **mis·lead·ing.**

mis·place (mis plās′) **1** put in the wrong place: *This book is on the wrong shelf; someone has misplaced it.* **2** put something somewhere and then forget where it is; lose: *I've misplaced the key.* *v.,* **mis·placed, mis·plac·ing.**

mis·read (mis rēd′) read wrongly or get the wrong meaning from: *I misread your letter and thought you weren't coming till next week.* *v.,* **mis·read** (mis red′), **mis·read·ing.**

miss¹ (mis) **1** fail to hit, find, get, meet, do, etc.: *to miss a target, to miss a train, to miss your chance.* **2** a failure to hit, etc.: *to make more misses than hits.* **3** escape or avoid: *I just missed being run over.* **4** notice the absence of: *I didn't miss my wallet till I got home.* **5** feel sad about the absence of: *He missed his mother when she went away.* 1, 3–5 *v.,* 2 *n.*

miss² (mis) **1** **Miss,** a title sometimes put before the name of a girl or an unmarried woman: *Miss Pallett.* **2** a term used to address a girl or young woman when you don't know her name: *I beg your pardon, Miss.* **3** a young unmarried woman or girl. *n.*

mis·shap·en (mis shā′pən) badly shaped; deformed. *adj.*

mis·sile (mis′īl *or* mis′əl) **1** any object that is thrown or shot, such as a stone, or arrow, or wad of paper. **2** a small rocket containing a bomb. *n.*

miss·ing (mis′ing) **1** not in the usual place: *The missing ring was found under the dresser. One of the books was missing.* **2** absent or lacking: *What's missing in my life is time to relax.* *adj.*

mis·sion (mish′ən) **1** a task or errand that someone is sent to do: *She was sent on a fact-finding mission.* **2** a goal or purpose: *Our teacher's mission in life is to turn kids on to science.* **3** a group sent out to do work for a government, to help people, or to spread a certain faith by teaching it to others: *A mission was sent to the Arctic by the Anglican Church.* A person who is part of a religious mission is a **missionary.** **4** the place where a religious mission has set up its work. *n.*

mist (mist) **1** a cloud of very fine drops of water or other liquid. Fog is thick mist. **2** cover with a mist or

spray: *Tears misted her eyes.* 1 *n.,* 2 *v.* —**mist′y,** *adj.*
mist over or **mist up,** become covered with mist: *The bathroom window has misted up.*

mis•take (mi stāk′) 1 an idea or action which you thought was right but turns out to be wrong: *Following this path was a mistake; now we're lost.* 2 not understand properly: *Don't mistake my meaning.* 3 think that a certain person or thing is someone or something else: *I mistook that stick for a snake.* 1 *n.,* 2, 3 *v.,* **mis•took, mis•tak•en, mis•tak•ing.** —**mis•tak′en•ly,** *adv.*
by mistake, without meaning to: *I took your coat by mistake—it's very much like mine.*

mis•ter (mis′tər) 1 **Mister,** the spoken form of **Mr.,** a title put before a man's name or the name of his office: *Mr. Smythe, Mr. Speaker.* 2 a term used to address any man when you don't know his name: *Excuse me, mister, you dropped something.* *n.*

Throughout the ages, people have thought that mistletoe had magical properties. Nowadays it is used as a Christmas decoration.

mis•tle•toe (mis′əl tō′) a plant with small white berries and shiny evergreen leaves, which grows as a parasite on trees. *n.*

mis•took (mis tu̇k′) the past tense of **mistake:** *I mistook you for your sister yesterday.* *v.*

mis•tress (mis′tris) a woman or girl who has ownership, control, or authority: *The dog was sitting outside the door, waiting for its mistress.* *n.*

mis•trust (mis trust′) 1 feel no confidence in; doubt: *She mistrusted her ability to do the job.* 2 a lack of trust or confidence: *Because of his mistrust of banks, he kept his money at home.* 1 *v.,* 2 *n.*

mis•un•der•stand (mis′un dər stand′) understand wrongly; give the wrong meaning to: *She misunderstood the instructions and did the wrong thing.* A **misunderstanding** can be a mistake in understanding, or a quarrel. *v.,* **mis•un•der•stood, mis•un•der•stand•ing.**

mis•use (mis yūz′ *for 1 and 2,* mis yūs′ *for 3*) 1 use for the wrong purpose or in the wrong way: *He misused my pen by stirring his tea with it.* 2 treat badly: *He misuses his sled dogs by driving them too hard.* 3 a wrong use: *Misuse of this tool could result in injury.* 1, 2 *v.,* **mis•used, mis•us•ing;** 3 *n.*

mite (mīt) 1 a very tiny spiderlike creature that lives in foods, on plants, or on humans or other animals. Some carry disease. 2 the tiniest bit: *I can't eat a mite of breakfast.* 3 anything very small: *That baby is a cheerful little mite!* *n.*

mitt (mit) 1 short for **mitten.** 2 a very thickly padded leather glove used by baseball players for catching the ball. *n.*

mit•ten (mit′ən) a covering for your hand in cold weather, with the four fingers fitting together in one part and the thumb in a separate part. *n.*

mix (miks) 1 put different things together; stir or shake up together: *Dom mixed flour and water into a paste.* 2 go or flow together: *Oil and water will not mix.* 3 a group or substance containing different kinds: *The class is a mix of students from five different countries.* 4 a product for making some kind of food, already containing most of the ingredients packaged together: *a cake mix, a gravy mix.* 5 join in with others and try to get to know them: *She finds it hard to mix with new people.*
1, 2, 4, 5 *v.,* 3 *n.* —**mix′er,** *n.*
mix up, a confuse: *I was so mixed up that I lost my way.* A confused situation is a **mixup. b** involve in some kind of trouble: *He was mixed up in a scheme to steal a car.*

mixed (mikst) 1 made up of different kinds: *mixed candy, mixed emotions.* A **mixed number** is made up of a whole number and a fraction, such as 1½. 2 including males and females: *a mixed choir.* *adj.*
mixed bag, something made up of very different parts.
mixed blessing, something good that also has a bad side.

mix•ture (miks′chər) something made by mixing: *Orange is a mixture of yellow and red.* In chemistry, a mixture is made up of ingredients that can be separated again by evaporation, distilling, etc. *n.*

mL *symbol for* millilitre or millilitres.

MLA *abbreviation for* Member of the Legislative Assembly, a title given to a person elected to the lawmaking body of most Canadian provinces and territories. ▶ See Appendix.

MNA or **M.N.A.** *abbreviation for* Member of the National Assembly. The National Assembly is the lawmaking body of Québec. ▶ See Appendix.

a bat	e bed	i bid	o pot	u cup	th thin
ā cake	ē me	ī bite	ō go	ū rude	ᴛʜ then
ä bar	ə about	ər over	ô for	u̇ put	zh measure

mo. *abbreviation for* month or months.

moan (mōn) 1 a long, low cry of pain or sadness. 2 any similar sound: *the moan of the wind.* 3 make moans. 4 complain: *She was always moaning about her luck.* 1, 2 *n.,* 3, 4 *v.*

moat (mōt) 1 a deep, wide ditch dug around a medieval castle or town and filled with water as a protection against enemies. 2 a similar ditch used to separate areas in a zoo. *n.*

mob (mob) 1 a large crowd, especially one that is excited or angry and likely to act without thinking. 2 crowd around eagerly or angrily: *The children mobbed the popcorn seller.* 1 *n.,* 2 *v.,* **mobbed, mob·bing.**

mo·bile (mō′bīl) 1 a decoration made of balanced pieces hanging from strings, so that they move if you touch them or if there is a breeze. 2 able to move around or be moved: *Now that she has a wheelchair, Sandi is mobile again.* A **mobile home** is a large trailer you can live in; a **mobile phone** is a cell phone. 3 moving; in motion. 4 quick to change from one position to another: *mobile features, a mobile mind.* *adj.* —**mo·bil′i·ty** (mō bil′ə tē), *n.*

moc·ca·sin (mok′ə sən) a style of soft shoe with the sides and bottom made from one piece of leather. Moccasins were the traditional footwear of many First Nations and Native American peoples. *n.*

mock (mok) 1 laugh at; make fun of, often by copying or imitating. 2 not real; only an imitation: *a mock battle, mock anger.* 1 *v.,* 2 *adj.* —**mock′er·y,** *n.*

mode (mōd) 1 the manner or way in which a thing is done: *Riding on a donkey is a slow mode of travel.* 2 a setting, condition, or state that goes with a certain type of activity for a machine, person, or group: *The fridge is in defrost mode right now. It takes me a while to get into school mode every morning* 3 the number that appears most often in a set of data. *n.*

mod·el (mod′əl) 1 a small but detailed version of something: *a model of the space shuttle.* 2 make or shape: *to model figures from clay.* 3 a particular style or design of a thing: *We traded in our car for a newer model.* 4 a person employed to help sell clothing or cosmetics by wearing them for people to see. 5 do this work or wear something for this purpose: *to model a dress.* 6 a person who poses for an artist or photographer. 7 a thing or person to be imitated: *Lou's neat handwriting was a model for the class.* 8 being a perfect example for others to follow: *a model child.* 9 made as an example: *a model home.* 10 a theory about how something works or how its parts are arranged: *In the old model of the solar system, the earth was at the centre.* 1, 3, 4, 6, 7, 10 *n.,* 2, 5 *v.,* **mod·elled** or **mod·eled, mod·el·ling** or **mod·el·ing;** 8, 9 *adj.*

model something on or **after,** copy in behaviour or style: *He modelled himself on his father.*

mo·dem (mō′dəm) an electronic device that uses a telephone line or cable to send information from one computer to another: *Since Radmila got a modem she has been on the Internet all the time.* *n.*

mod·er·ate (mod′ə rit *for 1,* mod′ə rāt′ *for 2 and 3*) 1 within reasonable limits; not extreme: *moderate prices, a moderate temper.* 2 make or become less extreme: *The wind is moderating. A large body of water moderates the temperature of neighbouring air masses.* 3 act as chairperson for: *All the party leaders took part in a debate on TV, moderated by a famous journalist.* A person who does this is a **moderator.** 1 *adj.,* 2, 3 *v.,* **mod·er·at·ed, mod·er·at·ing.** —**mod′er·a′tion,** *n.*

mod·er·a·tor (mod′ə rāt′ər) 1 a chairperson. 2 a person who volunteers to screen messages sent to a newsgroup or chat room. *n.*

mod·ern (mod′ərn) of the present time; of recent times: *The CD-ROM is a modern invention.* *adj.* —**mod′ern·ize′,** *v.*

mod·est (mod′ist) 1 not thinking too highly of yourself or demanding too much; humble: *In spite of the honours he received, the scientist remained a modest man.* 2 decent and respectable and not attracting a lot of attention. 3 not great or impressive: *a modest income.* *adj.* —**mod′es·ty,** *n.*

mod·i·fy (mod′ə fī′) 1 change somewhat: *New information has forced us to modify our theory.* 2 in grammar, limit the meaning of a word: *Adjectives modify nouns.* A word that modifies is a **modifier.** 3 tone down; make less severe or strong: *to modify a demand.* *v.,* **mod·i·fied, mod·i·fy·ing.** —**mod′i·fi·ca′tion,** *n.*

Grammar Check . . . . modifier

Adjectives are modifiers that describe nouns or pronouns. For example, look at the following sentence: *The small dog barked.*
Here, the adjective *small* describes the noun *dog*.

Adverbs are modifiers that describe verbs, adjectives, or other adverbs. For example, look at the following sentence: *The really small dog barked very loudly.*
Here, the adverb *really* describes the adjective *small*, the adverb *very* describes the adverb *loudly*, and the adverb *loudly* describes the verb *barked*.

mod•ule (moj′ūl) a separate unit that can be joined with others in a system, or taken away. The lunar module of a spacecraft takes the astronauts to the moon's surface while the command module stays in orbit. *n.*
—mod′u•lar, *adj.*

Mo•ham•med (mə hȧ′məd) an older spelling of **Muhammad,** the main prophet of Islam. *n.*

moist (moist) slightly wet; damp. *adj.*
—moist′en (moi′sən), *v.* **—mois′ture** (mois′chər), *n.*

mo•lar (mō′lər) a tooth with a broad, bumpy surface for grinding. Your back teeth are molars. *n.*

mo•las•ses (mə las′iz) a sweet, dark brown syrup that comes from sugar cane. *n.*

mole[1] (mōl) a dark, raised spot on the skin, present from birth. *n.*

WORD HISTORY........ molar

Molars are named after *mola*, the Latin word for "mill," because they grind food the way a mill grinds flour, or coffee, or pepper.

mole[2] (mōl) **1** a small burrowing animal that eats insects and lives underground most of the time. Moles have velvety fur, strong claws for digging, and small, weak eyes. **2** a person in a government or organization who is really a spy for a different government or organization. *n.*

When moles dig, they leave small mounds of earth on the ground, called molehills.

mol•e•cule (mol′ə kyūl′) **1** the smallest particle into which a substance can be divided without chemical change. **2** a very small particle. *n.*

mo•lest (mə lest′) bother and do harm to: *It is cruel to molest animals.* *v.*

mol•lusc or **mol•lusk** (mol′əsk) an animal with a soft body, usually protected by a shell. Most molluscs live in water or wet places. Snails, slugs, oysters, and clams are molluscs. *n.*

molt•en (mōl′tən) made liquid by great heat: *molten steel, molten lava.* *adj.*

mom (mum *or* mom) *Informal.* mother. **Mommy** is another form, used by children. *n.*

mo•ment (mō′mənt) a very short period of time or an exact point in time: *I'll be there in a moment. I started home the very moment I got your message.* Something that lasts only a moment is **momentary** (mō′mən ter′ē). *n.*
moment of truth, the moment when a person is forced to face some problem or make an important choice.

mo•men•tar•i•ly (mō′mən ter′ə lē) **1** for a moment: *He hesitated momentarily.* **2** moment by moment: *The danger was increasing momentarily.* **3** at any moment: *We are expecting them momentarily.* *adv.*

mo•men•tous (mō men′təs) very important: *a momentous decision, a momentous occasion.* *adj.*

mo•men•tum (mō men′təm) the force of a moving object. The heavier it is, and the faster it is moving, the greater the momentum, and the greater the force required to stop the object: *The bike's momentum carried it forward even after I put on the brakes.* *n.*

mon•arch (mon′ərk) **1** a king, queen, emperor, etc.; a ruler who is not elected but inherits the position and holds it for life. A country or government headed by a monarch is a **monarchy.** **2** a very large, orange-and-black butterfly that migrates from Canada to Mexico and back. *n.*

mon•as•ter•y (mon′ə ster′ē) a place where monks or nuns live together as a community according to religious rules. *n., pl.* **mon•as•ter•ies.**

Mon•day (mun′dā′) the day after Sunday. *Abbreviation:* Mon. *n.*

mon•ey (mun′ē) **1** coins and paper bills made by a national government, each with a specific value, and used to pay for things: *He has five dollars in Canadian money.* **2** wealth: *She has a lot of money.* *n., pl.* **mon•eys** or **mon•ies.**
—mon′e•tar′y (mon′ə ter′ē), *adj.*
in the money, rich.
make money, a earn or receive money. **b** become rich.

a bat	e bed	i bid	o pot	u cup	th thin
ā cake	ē me	ī bite	ō go	ū rude	ᴛʜ then
ȧ bar	ə about	ər over	ȯ for	u̇ put	zh measure

Monkeys

South American monkeys use their tails as an extra hand, to grasp tree branches. African and Asian monkeys cannot do this.

spider monkey, from South America

woolly monkey, from South America

colobus monkey, from Africa

money order (mun′ē ȯr′dər) a paper ordering that a certain amount of money be paid to a certain person. You can buy a money order at the post office or a bank and mail it to the person, who then takes it to the bank and gets the money.

mon·goose (mong′gūs) a small, slender, furry animal of Africa and Asia, used to kill rats. It is famous for its ability to kill poisonous snakes without being harmed. *n., pl.* **mon·goos·es.**

mon·grel (mong′grəl) an animal or plant of mixed breed, especially a dog. *n.*

mon·i·tor (mon′ə tər) **1** the screen that is connected to a computer, security camera, etc. **2** check or keep track of in order to control: *My parents monitor my TV watching.* **3** a device that lets you check or listen to something: *When Dad heard the baby's cries on the monitor, he went to pick her up.* **4** a student with special duties, such as cleaning the chalkboard brushes or taking attendance. **5** a large meat-eating lizard of tropical Africa, Asia, or Australia. 1, 3–5 *n.,* 2 *v.*

monk (mungk) a man who has chosen to live his life along with others according to certain religious rules. Monks pray, meditate, teach, and work to help others. *n.*

mon·key (mung′kē) **1** an animal, different from an ape, with a long tail and hands and feet adapted for climbing and grasping. **2** a mischievous child. **3** *Informal.* play; fool around; fiddle: *Don't monkey with the television set.* 1, 2 *n., pl.* **mon·keys;** 3 *v.,* **mon·keyed, mon·key·ing.**
monkey bars, a piece of playground equipment with bars for climbing on.

mon·o·gram (mon′ə gram′) a design made from a person's initials. Monograms are often used on towels, notepaper, jewellery, etc. *n.* **—mon′o·grammed,** *adj.*

mon·o·logue (mon′ə log′) **1** a long speech by one person. **2** a scene or a play for one actor, or a story made up completely of one character's thoughts or words. *n.*

mo·nop·o·ly (mə nop′ə lē) **1** a situation where one company has control of a product or service for a particular area, with little or no competition from other companies. **2** total possession or control of anything. To **monopolize** something is to have total control over it: *Don't monopolize the family computer!* *n., pl.* **mo·nop·o·lies.**

mon·o·tone (mon′ə tōn′) the same tone of voice used for a long time: *Don't read in a monotone; use more expression.* *n.*

mo·not·o·nous (mə not′ə nəs) **1** continuing in the same tone: *She spoke in a monotonous voice.* **2** boring because there is no variety: *monotonous work, monotonous meals.* *adj.*
—mo·not′o·ny (mə not′ə nē), *n.*

Word Family........ mono-

The prefix **mono-** comes from the Greek *monos,* meaning "single," or "alone."

monochrome: a piece of art done in one colour
monocle: an eyeglass for one eye
monolingual: speaking only one language
monoplane: an airplane with one set of wings
monorail: a track with a single rail, for a light train
monosyllable: a word with only one syllable

Moon

The side of the moon that faces Earth has huge flat areas called *maria* (singular *mare*). We can never see the far side of the moon from Earth, but pictures taken by spacecraft show that this far side is covered with craters and mountain ranges.

Moon rock brought back by astronauts is similar to lava rock from volcanoes on Earth.

mon·soon (mon sūn′) **1** a seasonal wind of the Indian Ocean and southern Asia. **2** the rainy season, when this wind blows from the southwest. *n.*

mon·ster (mon′stər) **1** an imaginary creature of strange appearance, especially a scary one. **2** a cruel, evil person. Something evil or very ugly is a **monstrosity** (mon stros′ə tē). **3** a huge creature or thing. *n.* **—mon′strous,** *adj.*

month (munth) **1** one of the twelve periods of time making up a year. **2** any period of about 30 days: *My birthday is one month from today.* *n.*

month·ly (munth′lē) **1** lasting or covering a month: *a monthly supply.* **2** coming or happening once a month: *a monthly meeting* (*adj.*). *This bill is paid monthly* (*adv.*). **3** a magazine published once a month. 1, 2 *adj.,* 2 *adv.,* 3 *n., pl.* **month·lies.**

mon·u·ment (mon′yə mənt) **1** something made or set up to keep a person or an event from being forgotten, especially a statue, building, or tombstone. **2** an excellent and lasting example: *The St. Lawrence Seaway is a monument of engineering.* Something very great or important is **monumental** (mon′yə men′təl). *n.*

mood (mūd) a feeling or state of mind: *I'm in the mood to play right now; I don't want to watch TV.* *n.*

mood·y (mū′dē) **1** often changing suddenly from a good mood to a bad one. **2** gloomy or sulky: *a moody silence.* *adj.,* **mood·i·er, mood·i·est.** **—mood′i·ly,** *adv.* **—mood′i·ness,** *n.*

moon (mūn) **1** a heavenly body that revolves around the earth once every 29.5 days. The moon shines in the sky at night with light reflected from the sun. **2** in some systems of measuring time without a calendar, about a month or 29.5 days. **3** the moon at any of the stages of its trip around the earth, as it appears to people: **full moon, half moon, crescent moon.** A **new moon** cannot be seen at all because it is in a position where the earth is completely blocking the sun's light. **4** a satellite of any other planet: *the moons of Jupiter.* *n.*

Word Family........ moon

moonbeam: a ray of moonlight
moonlit: lit up by the moon
moonrise: the moon's appearance above the horizon
moonstruck: dazed

moon·light (mūn′līt′) the light of the moon. A ray of moonlight is a **moonbeam.** *n.* **—moon′lit′,** *adj.*

moor[1] (mūr) put or keep a ship, boat, or seaplane in place using ropes, chains, or anchors. The ropes and so on that hold it are called **moorings.** *v.*

moor[2] (mūr) in the British Isles, open wasteland, usually hilly or high up. *n.*

a bat	e bed	i bid	o pot	u cup	th thin
ā cake	ē me	ī bite	ō go	ū rude	ᴛʜ then
à bar	ə about	ər over	ò for	ù put	zh measure

moose (mūs) a very large animal of the deer family that lives in the northern forests of North America, Europe, and Asia. The European one is a bit smaller and is called an **elk.** *n., pl.* **moose.**

mop (mop) **1** a tool that has a piece of sponge or other absorbent material fastened at the end of a long stick, used for cleaning floors. **2** clean or wipe with a mop: *to mop the floor.* **3** wipe with anything absorbent: *Mop up this puddle of milk on the table. He mopped his brow with his handkerchief.* 1 *n.,* 2, 3 *v.,* **mopped, mop·ping.**
mop of hair, hair that is thick and long.

mope (mōp) be quiet and sulky or sad. *v.,* **moped, mop·ing.**

mo·raine (mə rān′) a ridge of rocks, clay, etc. left by a glacier after being carried down a slope or pushed aside by the pressure of ice. *n.*

mor·al (mȯ′rəl) **1** having to do with character, or with the difference between right and wrong: *Whether to lie to cover up for a friend is a moral question.* **2** good and right; just; honest: *a moral act, a moral person.* **3 morals,** *pl.* standards of right and wrong: *My parents taught me good morals by their example.* **4** capable of understanding right and wrong: *An animal is not a moral being.* **5** the lesson contained in a story or an event: *The moral of the story was "Look before you leap."* 1, 2, 4 *adj.,* 3, 5 *n.* **—mo·ral′i·ty** (mə ral′ə tē), *n.*
moral support, encouragement or comfort, often given just by a person's presence.

CONFUSABLES .... moral

moral means "a lesson": *The moral of the story is, "Slow and steady wins the race."*

morale means "mental condition": *The team's morale was high after they won the tournament.*

mo·rale (mə ral′) mental condition or attitude; how much hope, courage, and enthusiasm people feel: *The morale of the team was low after its sixth defeat.* *n.*

mor·bid (mȯr′bid) **1** unhealthy or abnormal: *a morbid sense of humour. Cancer is a morbid growth.* **2** gruesome; horrible: *the morbid details of a murder.* *adj.*

more (mȯr) **1** greater in amount or number: *more heat, more children. A dozen is more than ten.* **2** further; additional: *Would you like more rice?* **3** a greater or additional amount, degree, or number: *Tell me more about your camping trip (n.). A burn hurts more than a scratch (adv.).* **4 More** is used with most adverbs and adjectives when comparing two things or ideas as in *more easily, more truly, more careful.* 1, 2 *adj.,* 3 *n.,* 3, 4 *adv.*
more or less, a somewhat: *Most people are more or less lazy.* **b** about; approximately: *The distance is 50 km, more or less.*

more·o·ver (mȯr ō′vər) also; besides; furthermore: *I don't want to go skating and, moreover, the ice is too thin.* *adv.*

morgue (mȯrg) a place, usually in a police station or hospital, where unclaimed bodies of dead people are kept until they can be identified. *n.*

Mor·mon (mȯr′mən) **1** a member of the **Church of Jesus Christ of Latter-Day Saints,** also called the Mormon Church. It was founded by Joseph Smith in the United States in 1830, and is based on the **Book of Mormon.** **2** having to do with the Mormons or their religion. 1 *n.,* 2 *adj.* **—Mor′mon·ism′,** *n.*

morn·ing (mȯr′ning) the early part of the day, ending at noon. **Morn** is a poetic short form. *n.*

mo·ron (mȯr′on) a stupid or ignorant person. *n.*

mo·rose (mə rōs′) gloomy; sulky: *"I don't care," he said in a morose voice.* *adj.*

mor·row (mȯr′ō) an old or poetic word meaning "the following day": *We expect her on the morrow.* *n.*
good morrow, an old way of saying "Good morning."

Morse code (mȯrs′ kōd′) a signalling system that uses dots and dashes or long and short sounds or flashes of light to stand for letters and numbers.

mor·sel (mȯr′səl) a small bite or piece. *n.*

mor·tal (mȯr′təl) **1** sure to die sometime. **2** a being that is sure to die sometime, especially a human. **3** causing death: *a mortal wound, a mortal illness.* **4** very great: *mortal terror, mortal enemies.* 1, 3, 4 *adj.,* 2 *n.* **—mor·tal′i·ty** (mȯr tal′ə tē), *n.* **—mor′tal·ly,** *adv.*

mor·tar (mȯr′tər) a mixture of lime or cement with sand and water, placed between bricks or stones to hold them together. It is put on wet and hardens as it dries. The square cap worn by graduating students is called a **mortarboard** because it looks like the little square board used by bricklayers to carry wet mortar on. *n.*

mort·gage (mȯr′gij) **1** a loan to buy a home or piece of land. If the loan is not paid back in time, the bank or other lender can take over the property you bought. **2** take out a loan using your property as a pledge. When you mortgage property, it means that you must give up the property if you do not repay the loan. 1 *n.,* 2 *v.,* **mort·gaged, mort·gag·ing.**

mor·ti·fy (môr′tə fī′) make extremely ashamed or embarrassed; humiliate: *I was mortified by my parents' rudeness to my friend.* *v.,* **mor·ti·fied, mor·ti·fy·ing.** —**mor′ti·fi·ca′tion,** *n.*

mo·sa·ic (mō zā′ik) 1 a picture or design made of small pieces of stone, glass, tile, etc. of different colours. 2 anything made up of many different parts where each part keeps its own particular character and adds to the beauty of the whole. A mosaic is a favourite metaphor for Canada's many cultural groups. *n.*

Mo·ses (mō′ziz) the main prophet of the Jews. God gave the Torah and taught it to the Jews through Moses. *n.*

Mos·lem (moz′ləm) an older form of **Muslim.** *n. or adj.*

mosque (mosk) a Muslim house of prayer and worship. The Arabic word often used for it is **masjid** (mus′jid). *n.*

mos·qui·to (mə skē′tō) a small, slender insect. The female mosquito sucks blood from people and animals through the skin, causing a sting that itches. *n., pl.* **mos·qui·toes** or **mos·qui·tos.**

moss (mos) very small, soft, green or brown plants that grow close together like a carpet on the ground, on rocks and trees, etc. in moist, shady places. *n.* —**moss′y,** *adj.*

most (mōst) 1 greatest in amount, degree, or number: *I have the most fun on Saturday. Blake had the most votes.* 2 the greatest amount, degree, or number: *She did most of the work* (*n.*). *This tooth hurts most* (*adv.*). 3 almost all: *Most people like ice cream.* 4 **Most** is used with many adverbs and adjectives when comparing more than two things or ideas, as in *most easily, most careful.* It is also used as a suffix with the same meaning; as in *uppermost, topmost.* 1, 3 *adj.,* 2 *n.,* 2, 4 *adv.*
at most, not more than.
for the most part, mainly; usually. **Mostly** means the same thing.
make the most of, use or deal with in the best way possible.

mo·tel (mō tel′) a roadside hotel where people travelling by car can stay overnight. Each room has an outside door leading to a parking lot. *n.*

moth (moth) a winged insect very much like a butterfly, but with a thicker body and flying mostly at night. Some moths eat holes in cloth. *n.* —**moth′proof′,** *adj. or v.*

moth·ball (moth′bol′) 1 a small white ball made of a strong-smelling chemical that is put in closets and drawers to keep moths from eating clothes that are not used very much. 2 pack away with mothballs for storage. 3 put something aside that you do not expect to use or go back to for a long time: *to mothball a project.* 1 *n.,* 2 *v.*

moth·er (muTH′ər) 1 a female parent. 2 take care of as a mother does: *She mothers her baby sister.* 3 anything thought of as like a mother: *Mother Earth, Mother Nature. Necessity is the mother of invention.* 4 the head of a community of nuns. 5 belonging to a person by birth; native: *Scotland is my mother country, and English is my mother tongue.* 1, 3, 4 *n.,* 2 *v.,* 5 *adj.* —**moth′er·hood′,** *n.* —**moth′er·ly,** *adj.*

moth·er–in–law (muTH′ə rin lo′) the mother of a person's husband or wife. *n., pl.* **mothers-in-law.**

moth·er–of–pearl (muTH′ə rəv pərl′) the hard, smooth, shiny lining of certain shells, used to make buttons and ornaments. *n.*

mo·tion (mō′shən) 1 the condition or state of moving; ongoing movement: *He swayed with the motion of the train.* **Motion sickness** is a sick feeling some people get in a moving vehicle. 2 a particular movement, especially one made as a sign or gesture: *Carson was making frantic motions for us to keep quiet.* 3 make this kind of movement: *She motioned for us to go in.* 4 a formal suggestion made in a meeting, to be voted on: *The motion to hold a Pyjama Day at school was voted down in the Student Council meeting.* 1, 2, 4 *n.,* 3 *v.*
go through the motions, do something without really meaning it or believing in it.
in motion, moving. **Motionless** means the opposite.
motion picture, a technical word for "movie."

mo·tive (mō′tiv) the desire that makes a person do something: *His motive in joining the team was a desire to make new friends.* Whatever makes you want to do something **motivates** you. *n.* —**mo′ti·va′tion,** *n.*

mo·tor (mō′tər) 1 an engine that makes a machine go. 2 run by a motor: *a motor scooter.* A **motor home** is a very large sort of van that you can live in while travelling, with a small kitchen, bathroom, and places to sleep and relax. 3 having to do with cars or other vehicles that have motors: *motor traffic.* 4 a somewhat formal word for "travel by car or other motor vehicle." A car driver is a **motorist.** 5 having to do with movement, especially of the body: *Motor nerves arouse muscles to action.* 1, 3 *n.,* 4 *v.,* 2, 5 *adj.*

a bat	e bed	i bid	o pot	u cup	th thin
ā cake	ē me	ī bite	ō go	ū rude	TH then
à bar	ə about	ər over	ò for	ù put	zh measure

mo·tor·boat (mō′tər bōt′) a boat that is propelled by a motor. *n.*

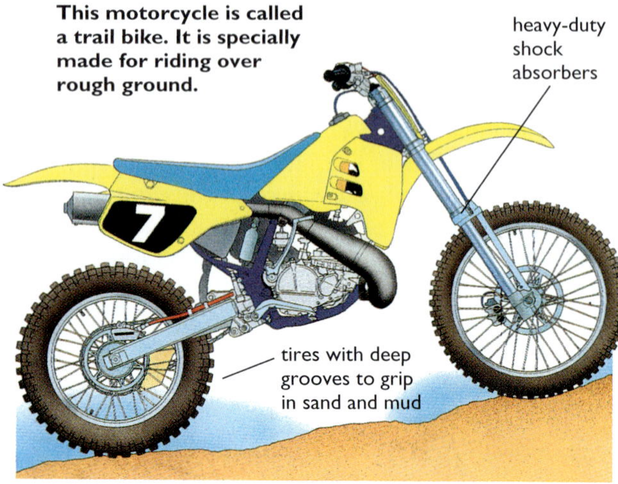

mo·tor·cy·cle (mō′tər sī′kəl) **1** a two-wheeled vehicle run by a motor. The informal word is **motorbike.** **2** travel by motorcycle. 1 *n.*, 2 *v.*, **mo·tor·cy·cled, mo·tor·cy·cling.**

mo·tor·ize (mō′tə rīz′) provide with a motor. *v.*, **mo·tor·ized, mo·tor·iz·ing.**

mot·tled (mot′əld) spotted or streaked with different colours. *adj.*

mot·to (mot′ō) a brief sentence taken as a guide for behaviour: *"Service with a smile" is that company's motto.* *n.*, *pl.* **mot·toes** or **mot·tos.**

mould[1] or **mold** (mōld) **1** a hollow form that gives its shape to a liquid allowed to harden inside it: *a jelly mould.* Many objects are made by pouring melted metal or plastic into a mould to harden. **2** to shape: *We are moulding clay into model animals. Her character was moulded by her early experiences.* 1 *n.*, 2 *v.*

mould[2] or **mold** (mōld) a growth of fungus, often fuzzy, that appears on food and some other substances when they are left too long in a warm, moist place. *n.* —**mould′y** or **mold′y,** *adj.*

mould·ing or **mold·ing** (mōl′ding) a shaped strip of wood often used around the upper and lower edges of the walls of a room, around windows and doors, and so on. *n.*

moult or **molt** (mōlt) shed the feathers, skin, etc. before a new growth. Birds and snakes moult. *v.*

mound (mound) **1** a bank or heap of earth or stones. **2** in baseball, the slightly raised ground where the pitcher stands. **3** a pile or heap of anything: *mounds of mashed potatoes.* *n.*

mount[1] (mount) **1** go up; climb: *to mount a hill, to mount the stairs.* **2** get up on: *to mount a horse, to mount a platform.* Someone who is **mounted** is on a horse: *a mounted warrior, mounted police.* **3** a horse for riding: *The jockey had an excellent mount.* **4** increase: *Excitement mounted as the holidays approached.* **5** put in position: *to mount photos in an album. The captain mounted a guard at each gate.* **6** the base that something is mounted or set on. **7** plan and begin to carry out: *to mount a campaign to raise funds.* 1, 2, 4, 5, 7 *v.*, 3, 6 *n.*

mount[2] (mount) a poetic word for "mountain," often used in names of mountains: *Mount Robson.* *n.*

moun·tain (moun′tən) **1** a very high hill: *the Rocky Mountains.* A group of connected mountains is a **mountain range.** **2** a large heap or amount of anything: *a mountain of rubbish, a mountain of difficulties.* *n.*
—**moun′tain·ous,** *adj.*
make a mountain out of a molehill, treat something unimportant as if it were very important.

mountain avens (moun′tən av′ənz) a small evergreen plant of the rose family with leathery leaves and white flowers. The mountain avens is the floral emblem of the Northwest Territories.

moun·tain·eer (moun′tə nēr′) a person who climbs mountains. *n.* —**moun′tain·eer′ing,** *n.*

mountain goat (moun′tən gōt′) a shaggy, white antelope of the Rocky Mountains, with short, black, backward-curving horns.

mountain lion (moun′tən lī′ən) another name for the **cougar,** a large, light brown wildcat of North America with black ears and a long, black-tipped tail.

moun·tain·side (moun′tən sīd′) the side of a mountain. *n.*

Mount·ie or **mount·ie** (moun′tē) *Informal.* a member of the **Royal Canadian Mounted Police,** a national police force that traditionally rode on horses. *n.*, *pl.* **Mount·ies** or **mount·ies.**

mourn (mȯrn) feel or show sadness over the death or loss of a person or thing: *She mourned her lost kitten.* *v.* —**mourn′er,** *n.* —**mourn′ful,** *adj.*
in mourning, wearing black clothes or doing other customary things to express sadness over a death.

mouse (mous) **1** a very small brownish grey animal with a pointed snout, large ears, and a long, thin tail. Mice can chew through wood, rope, or plastic. A **mousetrap** is for catching them. **2** a shy, timid person. **3** a small hand-operated device used to move the cursor and give other on-screen instructions to a computer. *n.*, *pl.* **mice.** —**mous′y,** *adj.*

mous·tache (mus′tash *or* mə stash′) another spelling of **mustache.**

mouth (mouth *for 1–3,* mouᴛʜ *for 4 and 5*) **1** the opening in the face of a person or animal, used for eating, drinking, breathing, and making sounds. **2** the lips and the surrounding area: *a pretty mouth. Use your serviette to wipe your mouth.* **3** an opening like a mouth: *the mouth of a cave. The mouth of a river is where it flows into some other body of water.* **4** say something without meaning it: *to mouth an apology.* **5** form words silently with the lips. 1–3 *n., pl.* **mouths** (mouᴛʜz); 4, 5 *v.* **—mouth′ful′,** *n.*
down in the mouth, *Informal.* in low spirits; discouraged.
have a big mouth, *Informal.* talk too much or at the wrong time.
mouth off, *Slang.* talk disrespectfully or rudely. A person who does this is **mouthy.**
the horse's mouth, the original source; the person who knows: *The news came straight from the horse's mouth.*

mouth organ (mouth′ ȯr′gən) another name for a **harmonica,** a small musical instrument played by blowing into it while moving it sideways.

mouth·piece (mouth′pēs′) **1** the part of a musical instrument that is placed in or against the player's mouth. **2** any person or publication that speaks for others. *n.*

mouth·wash (mouth′wosh′) a liquid that is swished around your mouth to make it fresher or to get rid of harmful bacteria. *n.*

mouth–wa·ter·ing (mouth′ wot′ər ing) looking or smelling so delicious that it makes your mouth water: *Judy's mother made mouth-watering apple pie.* *adj.*

move (mūv) **1** change the place or position of yourself or something else: *Move that chair closer to the window. The child moved in her sleep. The wind was moving the leaves.* **2** change your place of living or working: *We are moving to Kamloops next week.* **3** do something; act: *If you want to order at the sale price, you'd better move fast and call today.* **4** the act of moving or acting: *Our move to the country will get us away from the noise of the city. Selling that car was a smart move.* **5** the act or chance of moving a piece in chess and other games: *That was a good move. It's your move now.* **6** cause a person to act or react in a certain way: *What moved you to do this? The sad story moved her to tears.* **7** in a meeting, suggest formally: *I move that we adjourn the meeting at eight.* 1–3, 6, 7 *v.,* **moved, mov·ing;** 4, 5 *n.* **—mov·er,** *n.* **—mov′a·ble,** *adj.*
get a move on, *Slang.* hurry up.
move heaven and earth, do everything you can.
move in, move yourself, your family, and your things into a new home. **Move out** is the opposite.
on the move, moving; going someplace: *They are restless and always on the move.*

move·ment (mūv′mənt) **1** the act of moving; a change in place or position. **2** one section of a long piece of music: *The program included only the first movement of the symphony.* **3** an organized effort by a group of people for some cause: *the movement to save the environment.* **4** an emptying of the bowels. *n.*

mov·ie (mū′vē) a story or other information in the form of a series of pictures on one long piece of film, taken by a special camera and shown on a large screen. Each picture shows one tiny stage of the movements made by the people and things in the story, but the pictures are shown so fast that all the movements look smooth as in real life. Movies can have real actors or use drawings or sculptures. Another word for movie is **film.** *n.*

mov·ing (mū′ving) causing strong feelings of tenderness, pity, joy, pride, or sadness: *Our teacher read us a very moving poem on Remembrance Day.* *adj.*

mow[1] (mō) cut down grass, hay, and so on with a machine or by hand: *to mow grass. The farmers are mowing in the hayfields today.* *v.,* **mowed, mowed** or **mown, mow·ing.** **—mow′er,** *n.*
mow down, a run over with a car or other vehicle. **b** destroy at one sweep or in large numbers.

mow[2] (mou *or* mō) **1** the place in a barn where hay, grain, or straw is piled or stored. **2** a pile of hay, grain, etc. in a barn. *n.*

mox·ie (mok′sē) *Informal.* courage and determination: *It took a lot of moxie for Ivy to stay in the race after she got a cramp in her leg.* *n.*

MP or **M.P.** *abbreviation for* Member of Parliament, a title given to a person elected to the House of Commons in Ottawa. ▶ See Appendix.

mph or **m.p.h.** *abbreviation for* miles per hour.

MPP or **M.P.P.** *abbreviation for* Member of Provincial Parliament, a title given to a person elected to the lawmaking body of the province of Ontario. ▶ See Appendix.

Mr. or **Mr** (mis′tər) Mister, a title used in front of a man's name or the name of his official position: *Mr. Rosen, Mr. Speaker.*

a bat	e bed	i bid	o pot	u cup	th thin
ā cake	ē me	ī bite	ō go	ū rude	ᴛʜ then
ä bar	ə about	ər over	ȯ for	u̇ put	zh measure

Mrs. or **Mrs** (mis′iz) a title used in front of a married woman's name: *Mrs. Leung.*

ms *symbol for* millisecond.

Ms. or **Ms** (miz) a title used in front of the name of a married or unmarried woman or girl: *Ms. Melino.*

Mt. *abbreviation for* mount or mountain: *Mt. Logan.*

much (much) a lot; a great amount: *much rain, not much money* (*adj.*). *He doesn't know much. I ate too much of that cake* (*n.*). *I feel much better. This is much the same as the others* (*adv.*). *adj., adv., or n.,* **more, most.**
a bit much, unreasonable: *Not invite you? That's a bit much!*
make much of, treat as very great or important.
much as, although: *Much as I'd like to go, I know I can't.*
not much of a, not a very good: *This isn't much of a game.*
so much for, **a** enough about: *So much for my holiday, now let's hear about yours.* **b** an expression of disappointment: *So much for these boots being waterproof—my feet are soaked!*

mu·ci·lage (myū′sə lij) a kind of clear or honey-coloured glue for paper. *n.*

muck (muk) slimy, sticky mud. *n.*
—muck′y, *adj.*
muck around, *Informal.* fool around.
muck out, clean out a stall or stable.
muck up, *Informal.* mess up; wreck.

mu·cous mem·brane (myū′kəs mem′brān) the moist, slimy tissue that lines the nose, throat, and other openings of the body in contact with the air.

mu·cus (myū′kəs) a slimy substance that is produced by the mucous membranes to protect them and keep them moist. When you have a cold, mucus tends to build up in your nose and throat. *n.*

mud (mud) soft, very wet earth or sand: *The path turned to mud when it rained.* A **mudpie** is a mound of mud made by a child for fun. *n.*
clear as mud, very confusing; unclear.
your name is mud, you are in disgrace.

mud·dle (mud′əl) **1** mix up; confuse: *to muddle up the facts.* **2** act in a confused, blundering way: *to muddle through a difficulty.* **3** a mess; confusion: *Her notes were all in a muddle.* 1, 2 *v.,* **mud·dled, mud·dling;** 3 *n.*

mud·dy (mud′ē) **1** full of, covered with, or like mud: *muddy footprints, a muddy road, muddy shoes.* **2** not clear: *a muddy blue, muddy thinking.* **3** make or become muddy: *Don't muddy the water.* 1, 2 *adj.,* **mud·di·er, mud·di·est;** 3 *v.,* **mud·died, mud·dy·ing.**

mud·guard (mud′gȧrd′) a guard or shield on a vehicle, meant to stop the mud that gets splashed up or back by the moving wheels. *n.*

mues·li (myūz′lē) a mixture of grains, nuts, and dried fruit that is eaten with milk as a breakfast food. *n.*

mu·ez·zin (mū ez′in) in Islam, a crier who calls the people to prayer at certain hours of the day. *n.*

muff (muf) **1** a kind of short tube made of fur that girls and women used to use for keeping both hands warm. One hand was put in at each end. **2** *Informal.* fail to catch and hold a ball when it comes into your hands. **3** *Informal.* handle awkwardly; bungle: *My brother muffed his chance to get that job.* 1, 3 *n.,* 2, 4 *v.*

muf·fin (muf′ən) a small, round cake, often containing bran, nuts, fruit, etc. *n.*

muf·fle (muf′əl) dull or deaden a sound: *The heavy drapes helped muffle the noise of the traffic outside.* A **muffler** deadens the sound from an engine. *v.,* **muf·fled, muf·fling.**

mug (mug) **1** a large cup with a handle, used without a saucer. **2** attack and rob a passerby. **3** *Slang.* face. **4** *Slang.* make funny faces. 1, 3 *n.,* 2, 4 *v.,* **mugged, mug·ging.** **—mug′ger,** *n.*

mug·gy (mug′ē) hot and humid or stuffy: *The weather was muggy.* *adj.,* **mug·gi·er, mug·gi·est.**

Mu·ham·mad or **Mo·ham·med** (mə hȧ′məd) the prophet of Islam. Muslims believe that he is God's messenger. *n.*

🍁 **muk·luk** (muk′luk) a high waterproof boot, often made of sealskin, worn by Inuit and others in the North. *n.*

mul·ber·ry (mul′ber′ē) a small tree with raspberrylike dark red or purple fruit that is good to eat. The leaves of one kind are used for feeding silkworms. *n., pl.* **mul·ber·ries.**

mulch (mulch) **1** straw, leaves, wood shavings, etc. spread on the ground around trees or plants to protect the roots from cold or heat or keep the soil moist. **2** cover with straw, leaves, etc. **3** prepare for use as mulch. A **mulcher** is a mower that grinds up grass as it is cut and collects it in a bag attached to the mower. 1 *n.,* 2, 3 *v.*

mule (myūl) **1** an animal whose mother was a horse and whose father was a donkey. The mule looks like a horse except for its large ears, small hoofs, and tufted tail which look like a donkey's. **2** *Informal.* a stubborn person. *n.* **—mul′ish,** *adj.*

mull (mul)
mull over, think about something carefully and for a long time: *Don't decide to quit your paper route without mulling it over first.* *v.*

mul·lah (mul′ə) a leader or teacher of Islam. *n.*

mul·ti·cul·tur·al (mul′tē kul′chə rəl) having to do with a number of different cultures side by side in the same country, organization, etc.: *a multicultural city. I attend a multicultural school.* **Multiculturalism** is the practice of encouraging and celebrating this variety. *adj.*

mul·ti·eth·nic (mul′tē eth′nik′) involving many nationalities or peoples. Another word for this is **multiracial.**

mul·ti·me·di·a (mul′tē mē′dē ə) using a mixture of sound, pictures, film, and text, especially with a computer: *a multimedia encyclopedia on CD-ROM.* *n.*

mul·ti·ple (mul′tə pəl) **1** many; more than one: *a person of multiple interests.* **2** a number that can be divided by another number without a remainder: *Twelve is a multiple of three.* 1 *adj.,* 2 *n.*

mul·ti·ply (mul′tə plī′) **1** add a number to itself a certain number of times. To multiply 6 by 3 means to add 6 three times, making a total of 18. *Symbol:* × In 5 × 3 = 15, 5 is the **multiplier** and 3 is the **multiplicand** (mul′tə plə kand′); 15 is the **product.** **2** increase; become more and more: *The dangers and difficulties multiplied as we went higher up the mountain.* *v.,* **mul·ti·plied, mul·ti·ply·ing.** **—mul′ti·pli·ca′tion,** *n.*

mul·ti·syl·la·ble (mul′tē sil′ə bəl) a word with more than one syllable, such as *mul-ti-ply.* *n.* **—mul′ti·syl·lab′ic,** *adj.*

mul·ti·tude (mul′tə tyūd′ *or* mul′tə tūd′) a great many; a crowd: *a multitude of questions, a multitude of friends.* *n.*

mum[1] (mum) silent; saying nothing: *Keep mum about this; tell no one.* *adj.*

mum[2] (mum) *Informal.* short for **chrysanthemum,** a plant that blooms in late summer and fall. *n.*

mum·ble (mum′bəl) **1** speak in an unclear way, quietly or with your lips partly closed. **2** something spoken this way: *There was a mumble of protest at the umpire's decision.* 1 *v.,* **mum·bled, mum·bling;** 2 *n.*

mum·my (mum′ē) a dead body preserved from decay by the ancient Egyptian method. Egyptian mummies have lasted more than 3000 years. To preserve a body in this way is to **mummify** it. *n., pl.* **mum·mies. —mum′mi·fi·ca′tion,** *adj.*

mumps (mumps) a contagious disease that causes swelling of your neck and face, fever, and difficulty in swallowing. Most Canadian children are vaccinated against mumps. *n.*

munch (munch) chew steadily and noisily: *The horse munched its oats.* *v.*

mun·dane (mun dān′) ordinary and uninteresting: *Even the most mundane chore is fun with a friend.* *adj.*

mu·nic·i·pal (myū nis′ə pəl) having to do with the government of a city, town, or other area that has its own local government: *a municipal election. The provincial police worked with the municipal police on the case.* An area with its own municipal government is a **municipality** (myu nis′ə pal′ə tē). *adj.*

mu·ral (myū′rəl) a large picture painted on a wall, or hung in a frame that covers most of a wall. *n.*

mur·der (mər′dər) **1** the crime of killing a human being on purpose: *She was convicted of murder.* **2** kill a human being on purpose: *The gangsters murdered their enemies.* **3** do something very badly; ruin: *He murdered the song every time he tried to sing it.* **4** anything extremely difficult or unpleasant: *Pedalling up that huge hill was murder.* 1, 4 *n.,* 2, 3 *v.* **—mur′der·er,** *n.* **—mur′der·ous,** *adj.*

murk (mərk) darkness; gloom: *A light flashed through the murk of the night.* *n.* **—murk′y,** *adj.*

mur·mur (mər′mər) **1** a soft, low sound that rises and falls a little but goes on without breaks: *the murmur of the wind, the murmur of voices in another room.* **2** make a soft, low sound or speak in a soft, low voice. 1 *n.,* 2 *v.*

When you tighten the biceps muscle in your upper arm, your arm bends.

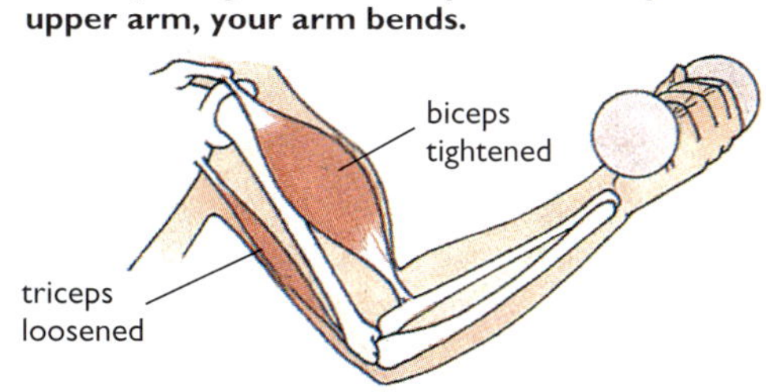

mus·cle (mus′əl) **1** the tissue in the bodies of people and animals that can be tightened or loosened so as to make the body move. **2** a bundle of such tissue that moves some particular bone or part: *You can feel the muscles in your arm.* **3** strength. *n.* **—mus′cu·lar** (mus′kyə lər), *adj.*

a bat	e bed	i bid	o pot	u cup	th thin
ā cake	ē me	ī bite	ō go	ū rude	ᴛʜ then
ä bar	ə about	ər over	ò for	u̇ put	zh measure

muse (myūz) think in a relaxed way: *He sat musing about the day's events.* *v.,* **mused, mus•ing.**

mu•se•um (myū zē′əm) a building or rooms containing a collection of old, interesting, rare, or beautiful things on display. *n.*

mush[1] (mush) **1** a soft, wet, thick mass: *The heavy rain made mush of the dirt road.* **2** corn meal boiled in water. **3** *Informal.* tender feeling expressed in a sickeningly sweet way: *Some birthday cards are pure mush.* *n.* —**mush′y,** *adj.*

mush[2] (mush) **1** a command to go forward, given to sled dogs. **2** drive a dogsled, shouting commands to the dogs: *He mushed his dog team through the blinding storm. For six days he mushed across the Barren Ground.* **3** a trip by dogsled. 1, 3 *n.,* 2 *v.*

mush•room (mush′rūm) **1** a fungus that is shaped like an umbrella and grows very fast. Some mushrooms are good to eat and some are poisonous; it takes an expert eye to tell them apart. The poisonous ones are often called **toadstools.** **2** grow rapidly: *Their business mushroomed when they opened the new store.* 1 *n.,* 2 *v.*

mu•sic (myū′zik) **1** sounds put together in beautiful or interesting arrangements, especially the sounds of singing voices or of instruments: *I like listening to music.* **2** the art of making these arrangements of sounds: *to study music. He is talented in music.* A person who writes, plays, or sings music is a **musician** (myū zish′ən). **3** an arrangement of tones written down, using notes and other symbols: *This book prints the words and music for the song.* **4** any pleasant sound: *the music of a babbling brook.* *n.*
face the music, *Informal.* meet trouble boldly or bravely.
set to music, make music to go with the words of a song.

mu•si•cal (myū′zə kəl) **1** having to do with music; like music, full of music, or good at music: *musical laughter. She is very musical and plays three instruments.* **2** a play or movie with a lot of songs in it which help to tell the story. 1 *adj.,* 2 *n.* —**mu′si•cal•ly,** *adv.*
musical chairs, a game where music plays while people walk around a group of chairs. When the music stops everyone must sit down, but there is always one chair fewer than there are people. The person without a seat is out, until finally there are only two people and one chair.

music box (myū′zik boks′) a box with a little machine in it which makes music when it is wound up.

musk (musk) a substance with a strong and lasting scent, used in making perfumes. It is obtained from the **musk deer** of Asia or made artificially. *n.*

mus•keg (mus′keg) **1** an area of bog, or soft, wet, spongy ground, made up of decaying plants, especially mosses. There are vast regions of muskeg in northern Alberta. **2** a swamp or marsh. *n.*

WORD HISTORY....... muskeg

Muskeg is from an Algonquian language related to Cree. In Cree, *muskak* means "swamp."

mus•ket (mus′kit) an old type of long-barrelled gun used before rifles were invented. A soldier armed with a musket was a **musketeer.** *n.*

musk•mel•on (musk′mel′ən) a sweet, juicy melon with a tough rind that has a netlike pattern.

musk–ox (musk′oks′) a large grazing animal of the Canadian Arctic and Greenland. It has a very long, shaggy coat and sharp horns that point outward. The wool from its coat is valued for its great warmth. *n., pl.* **musk-ox** or **musk-ox•en.**

musk•rat (musk′rat′) a water animal of North America, a little like a rat but larger and with partly webbed hind feet. Its dark brown fur is valuable. *n.*

Mus•lim (mu̇s′lim *or* muz′ləm) **1** a follower of Islam, a religion. **2** having to do with Islam or its followers. 1 *n.,* 2 *adj.*

mus•lin (muz′lən) plain cotton cloth used for dresses, curtains, sheets, and so on. It can be very fine and almost see-through, or heavy and coarse. *n.*

mus•sel (mus′əl) a mollusc with two hinged parts to its shell, like a clam. Sea mussels have dark blue shells and are used for food. *n.*

must (must) **1** a verb used together with a main verb to mean: **a** a person or thing has to do something, because it is needed or because of a rule: *You must be on time for your exam. We must eat in order to stay alive.* **b** something is probably true: *It must be time for lunch. She must have missed the bus or she would be here by now.* **2** something necessary: *Life preservers are a must when you go out in a canoe.* 1 *v.,* 2 *n.*

USING WORDS.... must have

Must have, could have, or **may have** are often mistakenly written as *must of, could of,* or *may of.* The correct way is, for example:
I must have left my knapsack at school.
Take care when using these expressions in your writing, and in your more formal speech.

mus·tache (mus′tash *or* mə stash′) the hair that grows on a man's upper lip: *The captain had a bristling, black mustache.* **Moustache** is another spelling. *n.*

mus·tang (mus′tang) a small, wild or half-wild horse of the North American plains. *n.*

mus·tard (mus′tərd) a yellow powder or paste used as a seasoning to give food a sharp, pungent taste. It is made from the seeds of a herb that grows in Europe and Asia. *n.*

mus·ter (mus′tər) **1** call or gather together for some duty or activity: *The teacher mustered a group of six students to help set up tables in the gym.* **2** a group gathered in this way, or the act of gathering. **3** work up; produce with effort: *to muster up courage.* 1, 3 *v.,* 2 *n.*
pass muster, be good enough; meet a certain standard.

must·n't (mus′ənt) must not: *The lifeguard says we mustn't swim here.* *v.*

mus·ty (mus′tē) having a damp, mouldy smell or taste: *a musty room, musty crackers.* *adj.,* **mus·ti·er, mus·ti·est.**

mu·ta·tion (myū tā′shən) **1** a change; a changed form. **2** a sudden change in the genetic structure of an animal or plant that produces a new feature or characteristic. **3** a new variety of animal or plant resulting from such a change. *n.* **—mu′tate,** *v.*

mute (myūt) **1** silent; not making any sound: *The little girl stood mute with embarrassment.* **2** unable to speak. **3** soften, deaden, or shut off the sound: *They spoke in muted tones. I always mute the TV during commercials.* **4** make less intense; soften: *muted colours.* **5** a device put on or in a musical instrument to soften the sound. 1, 2 *adj.,* 3, 4 *v.,* **mut·ed, mut·ing;** 5 *n.*

mu·ti·late (myū′tə lāt′) injure or damage badly by cutting, tearing, and so on: *The book was mutilated by someone who had torn some pages and written on others.* *v.,* **mu·ti·lat·ed, mu·ti·lat·ing.** **—mu′ti·la′tion,** *n.*

mu·ti·ny (myū′tə nē) **1** a rebellion, especially by sailors or soldiers against their officers. **2** take part in this; rebel. Someone who takes part in a mutiny is a **mutineer.** 1 *n., pl.* **mu·ti·nies;** 2 *v.,* **mu·ti·nied, mu·ti·ny·ing.** **—mu′ti·nous,** *adj.*

mutt (mut) *Informal.* a dog, especially of a mixed breed. *n.*

mut·ter (mut′ər) **1** speak low and unclearly, with lips partly closed, often in an annoyed tone.
2 complain; grumble. **3** muttered words: *We heard a mutter of discontent.* 1, 2 *v.,* 3 *n.*

mut·ton (mut′ən) the meat from a sheep. *n.*

mu·tu·al (myū′chū əl) **1** done, said, felt, etc. by two people or groups to each other: *mutual promises, mutual dislike.* **2** shared in common: *We are happy to have him as our mutual friend.* *adj.*
—mu′tu·al·ly, *adv.*

muz·zle (muz′əl) **1** the nose, mouth, and jaws of a four-footed animal. **2** a network of straps or wire for putting over an animal's mouth or head to keep it from biting, eating, barking, etc. **3** put such a covering on: *to muzzle a dog.* **4** force to keep silent about something: *The government muzzled the newspapers during the rebellion.* **5** the open front end of a gun. 1, 2, 5 *n.,* 3, 4 *v.,* **muz·zled, muz·zling.**

my·na or **my·nah** (mī′nə) a bird from Asia that can imitate human speech sounds. *n.*

myr·i·ad (mēr′ē əd) a very great number, too many to count: *There are myriads of stars (n.). We saw myriad stars that summer night (adj.).* *n. or adj.*

mys·ter·y (mis′tə rē) **1** something that is not explained or understood: *the mystery of the migration of birds.* **2** a secret; something that is hidden or unknown. **3** a story, play, etc. about strange or secret events: *My sister likes reading mysteries.* **4** secrecy; a feeling of something unknown or unexplained: *The old attic seemed full of mystery.* *n., pl.* **mys·ter·ies.** **—mys·te′ri·ous** (mi stēr′ē əs), *adj.*

mys·ti·fy (mis′tə fī′) bewilder; puzzle; perplex: *The magician's tricks mystified the audience.* *v.,* **mys·ti·fied, mys·ti·fy·ing.**

mys·tique (mi stēk′) an unexplainable quality that makes a person or thing fascinating and attractive: *For Becky, the sea always held a certain mystique.* *n.*

myth (mith) **1** a traditional story about superhuman beings such as gods, heroes, and monsters. Myths usually explain why things are the way they are. A **mythology** is a whole set of related myths: *Greek mythology, the mythology of dragons.* **2** something that many people believe but which is not true: *The idea that wealth brings happiness is a myth.* *n.* **—myth′i·cal,** *adj.*
—myth′o·log′i·cal (mith′ ə loj′ə kəl), *adj.*

Nn

n or **N** (en) 1 the fourteenth letter of the English alphabet, or the sound that it stands for. The sound is heard twice in *nine.* 2 the fourteenth thing in a list. *n., pl.* **n's** or **N's.**

N or **N.** *abbreviation for* north or northern.

na·cho (nä'chō) a crisp, deep-fried piece of tortilla, often dipped in a spicy sauce called **salsa.** *n., pl.* **na·chos.**

nag¹ (nag) 1 keep on criticizing or bugging someone to do something: *He's always nagging me about my messy room.* 2 continue to hurt or bother: *a nagging headache, nagging doubts about something.* *v.,* **nagged, nag·ging.**

nag² (nag) an old or worn-out horse. *n.*

nail (nāl) 1 a small, slender, pointed piece of metal with a flattened top, to be hammered into pieces of wood or other material to hold them together. 2 fasten with a nail or nails. 3 the hard, horny layer at the end of a finger or toe. 1, 3 *n.,* 2 *v.*
hit the nail on the head, get something exactly right.
nail down, **a** fix with nails: *The shingles were nailed down with a hammer.* **b** *Informal.* settle; make clear and certain: *Let's try and nail down the plans for this trip.*
tough as nails, very tough.

na·ive (nī ēv') simple, innocent, and too trusting because you are inexperienced. *adj.*

na·ked (nā'kid) 1 bare; with no clothes or other covering: *a naked body. The trees stood naked in the snow.* 2 with nothing to hide it or give protection from it: *a naked flame, the naked truth.* *adj.* **—na'ked·ness,** *n.*
naked eye, just the eye, with no telescope or microscope.

Na·ko·da (nə kō'də) 1 a First Nations people living in Alberta and Saskatchewan. 2 their language. 3 having to do with these people or their language. 1, 2 *n.,* 3 *adj.*

Na·ko·ta (nə kō'tə) 1 a First Nations people living in Alberta and Saskatchewan. 2 their language. 3 having to do with these people or their language. 1, 2 *n.,* 3 *adj.*

name (nām) 1 the special word or words used to refer to a particular person, animal, place, or thing: *Our dog's name is Smokey. The name of our country is Canada.* 2 give a name to: *They named the baby Kia.* 3 mention or identify by name: *Three teens were named in the report. Can you name these flowers?* 4 reputation; fame: *He made a name for himself as a writer.* 5 choose; appoint: *Jess was named captain of the team.* 1, 4 *n.,* 2, 3, 5 *v.,* **named, nam·ing.**
call names, insult by using bad names.
in the name of, **a** on the authority of; acting for: *He ordered them to stop in the name of the law.* **b** for the sake of: *We did it in the name of fairness.*

Word Family........ name

name brand: a product with a famous name
name-calling: the act of calling people insulting names
nameless: without a name, or impossible to name
namesake: either of two people with the same name

name·ly (nām'lē) that is to say: *Only two students got 100 in the test—namely, Lakshmi and Jordon.* *adv.*

nan·ny (nan'ē) 1 a person hired to take care of someone's children full time, in the children's home. 2 **nanny goat,** a female goat. *n.*

nap (nap) 1 a short sleep: *Most babies have a nap in the afternoon.* 2 take a short sleep: *Grandpa naps in his armchair.* 1 *n.,* 2 *v.,* **napped, nap·ping.**

nape (nāp) the back of your neck. *n.*

naph·tha (naf'thə *or* nap'thə) a clear liquid made from petroleum, coal tar, etc., used as fuel, paint thinner, and so on. It is highly flammable. *n.*

nap·kin (nap'kin) a piece of cloth or paper used at meals for protecting your clothes or wiping your lips and fingers; a serviette. *n.*

nar·cot·ic (när kot'ik) a drug, such as opium, that lessens pain and causes sleepiness. *n.*

nar·rate (ner'āt *or* nə rāt') 1 be the character who tells or helps tell the story in a play, novel, or film: *"Owls in the Family" is narrated by a boy named Bill.* 2 give commentary explaining what is shown in a nonfiction film or TV program: *a nature film narrated by David Suzuki.* *v.,* **nar·rat·ed, nar·rat·ing.** **—nar·ra'tion,** *n.* **—nar'ra·tor,** *n.*

nar·ra·tive (ner'ə tiv) 1 a story: *Their trip through the Far East made an interesting narrative.* 2 that tells a story: *"Hiawatha" is a narrative poem.* 1 *n.,* 2 *adj.*

nar•row (ner′ō) **1** not wide; small from side to side: *narrow ribbon, a narrow path.* **2** limited; strict: *Mosquitoes are not bugs in the narrow sense of the word.* **3** make or become narrow: *The road narrows here.* **4** close; just barely managed: *a narrow escape.* **5** not tolerant; not open to many different ideas or possibilities: *narrow views.* A person like this is said to be **narrow-minded.**
1, 2, 4, 5 *adj.,* 3 *v.* **—nar′row•ly,** *adv.*
the narrows, the narrow part of a river, valley, etc.

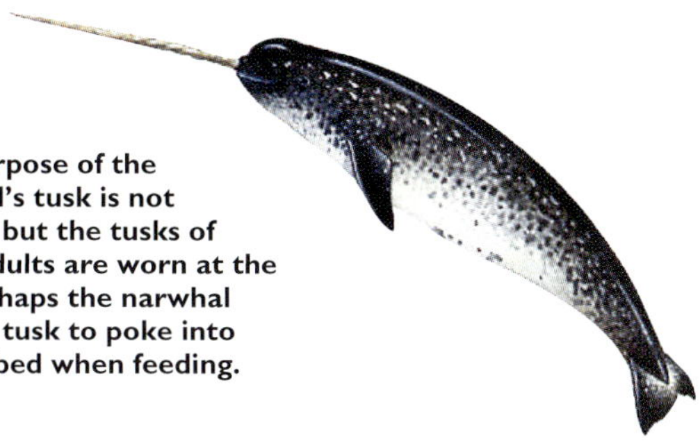

The purpose of the narwhal's tusk is not known, but the tusks of most adults are worn at the tip. Perhaps the narwhal uses its tusk to poke into the seabed when feeding.

nar•whal (när′wəl) a small whale of the arctic seas. One of the male's upper teeth grows out through its lip into a long, spiral tusk. *n.*

na•sal (nā′zəl) **1** having to do with the nose: *nasal passages, a nasal discharge.* **2** speaking or spoken through the nose: *Her voice has a nasal quality.* *adj.* **—na′sal•ize′,** *v.*

nas•ty (nas′tē) **1** very rude or unkind; mean: *That was a nasty thing to say.* **2** very unpleasant: *nasty weather, a nasty temper, a nasty smell.* *adj.,* **nas•ti•er, nas•ti•est.** **—nas′ti•ly,** *adv.* **—nas′ti•ness,** *n.*

na•tion (nā′shən) **1** a group of people occupying the same country and united under the same independent government: *The Prime Minister appealed to the nation for support of his plan.* **2** any group of people sharing the same descent, history, culture, and language: *the Inuit nation, the First Nations.* **3** several different Native people groups joined together into one by an agreement: *The Iroquois Nation included the Seneca, Mohawk, Oneida, Onondaga, Cayuga, and later the Tuscarora peoples.* *n.* **—na′tion•hood′,** *n.*

na•tion•al (nash′ə nəl) **1** having to do with a whole nation: *national laws, a national disaster.* A **national park** is land set aside by the federal government for people to enjoy. **2** a citizen of a nation: *He's a Canadian national.* A person's **nationality** is the fact of belonging to a certain nation. 1 *adj.,* 2 *n.* **—na′tion•al•ly,** *adv.*

National Assembly (nash′ənəl ə sem′blē) the lawmaking body of the provincial government of Québec. Its members are elected by the people.

na•tion•al•ism (nash′ə nə liz′əm) pride in your nation; a desire for it to grow strong and be completely free of any outside control. *n.* **—na′tion•al•ist,** *n.* **—na′tion•al•ist′ic,** *adj.*

na•tive (nā′tiv) **1** born in a certain place: *He is a native son of Canada.* **2** belonging to someone by birth: *She has native artistic ability.* **3** a person born in a certain place: *He is a native of The Pas, Manitoba.* **4** living or growing in a certain place from the very beginning, not brought or coming from elsewhere: *The Manitoba maple is native to Canada.* 1, 2, 4 *adj.,* 3 *n.*

Native people (nā′tiv pē′pəl) any of the groups of people whose ancestors lived in North America long before the Europeans arrived. The Inuit, First Nations, and Métis are all Native peoples of Canada. **Aboriginal people** or **Native Canadians** are other names for these groups. ▶ See Appendix.

nat•u•ral (nach′ə rəl) **1** made or caused by nature rather than people; found in nature: *a natural lake. Coal and oil are natural products.* **2** having to do with nature: *the natural sciences.* **Natural history** is the study of animals, plants, minerals, etc. as they exist in nature. **3** normal considering the situation; to be expected: *It was only natural for her to be angry when she heard what you did.* **4** not fake or stiff; relaxed and being your real self: *a natural manner.* **5** in music, not changed in pitch by a sharp or flat: *C natural.* *adj.*

nat•u•ral•ist (nach′ə rə list) a person who studies animals or plants in the wild. *n.*

nat•u•ral•ize (nach′ə rə līz′) give the rights of citizenship to someone from another country: *He's from Japan but is a naturalized Canadian.* *v.,* **nat•u•ral•ized, nat•u•ral•iz•ing.**

nat•u•ral•ly (nach′ə rə lē) **1** in a natural way: *Speak naturally; don't try to sound important.* **2** by nature: *naturally good with languages.* **3** of course: *My sister offered me her dessert; naturally, I took it.* *adv.*

natural number (nach′ə rəl num′bər) a whole number other than zero.

natural resource (nach′ə rəl ri zôrs′ *or* rē′zôrs) material or energy that is supplied by nature and is useful or necessary to people: *Minerals, forests, and hydro power are natural resources.*

a bat	e bed	i bid	o pot	u cup	th thin
ā cake	ē me	ī bite	ō go	ū rude	ᴛʜ then
ä bar	ə about	ər over	ô for	ů put	zh measure

na·ture (nā′chər) 1 the way things are in the universe without any human effort or activity: *Gravity is a law of nature.* 2 the outdoor world; the land and sea with their plants and animals, as opposed to the things humans have made: *the beauty of nature. I like to go camping and enjoy nature.* 3 the qualities and abilities that a person or thing is born or made with: *It is the nature of birds to build nests. Cruelty is not in her nature.* 4 sort; kind: *books of a scientific nature.* *n.*

naugh·ty (not′ē) behaving badly: *The naughty child yelled at his baby sister.* *adj.,* **naugh·ti·er, naugh·ti·est.**

nau·se·a (noz′ē ə) the feeling that you are about to throw up. *n.* —**nau′se·ate′,** *v.*

WORD HISTORY........nausea

The word **nausea** originally meant "seasickness." Like the word **nautical**, it comes from the Greek word *naus*, meaning "ship." Latin borrowed this Greek word as *navis*, giving us **navy**, **naval**, and **navigate**.

nau·se·ous (noz′e əs *or* nosh′əs) 1 feeling sick; feeling that you are about to throw up: *Keira felt nauseous riding in the car along the bumpy roads.* 2 causing nausea; sickening: *a nauseous smell.* *adj.*

nau·ti·cal (not′ə kəl) having to do with ships or sailing. A **nautical mile** is a unit for measuring distance in sea and air travel, equal to 1853.25 m. *adj.*

na·val (nā′vəl) having to do with a navy: *a naval battle, a naval officer.* *adj.*

na·vel (nā′vəl) a hollow in the middle of the surface of your abdomen, marking the place where your umbilical cord was attached before birth. The umbilical cord links an unborn baby to its mother inside her body. *n.*

nav·i·gate (nav′ə gāt′) 1 steer or manage a ship or aircraft: *Much skill is needed to navigate an airplane.* 2 sail on or over a river, sea, etc.: *Many ships navigate the St. Lawrence Seaway each year.* A body of water that is safe for ships is **navigable** (nav′ə gə bəl). 3 find your way, especially when sailing, flying, or driving: *The ancients navigated by the North Star. As a new driver, Kirk finds it hard to navigate on the superhighways.* *v.,* **nav·i·gat·ed, nav·i·gat·ing.** —**nav′i·ga′tion,** *n.* —**nav′i·ga′tor,** *n.*

na·vy (nā′vē) 1 Often, **Navy,** all the ships of war of a country, together with the people that serve on them. 2 a dark blue. 1, 2 *n., pl.* **na·vies;** 2 *adj.*

Naw Ruz (nau′ rūz′) March 21, the festival of the New Year in the Bahai and Zoroastrian religions. In Iran it is celebrated by others as well, because the calendar it is based on was traditionally used in that country for over two thousand years.

nay (nā) an old or poetic word for "no." It is still used in formal meetings to vote against something. *adv. or n.*

Na·zism (nȧt′siz əm) the belief system of a political party that led Germany before and during World War II. Its members, called **Nazis** (nȧt′sēz), thought Germany should unite all peoples of northern European descent, who they thought were better than other peoples. Then these would rule the rest of the world together under one supreme leader, Adolf Hitler. The Nazis tried to "purify" their nation by getting rid of all non-whites, Jews, and disabled people. World War II ended the Nazi Party. *n.*

N.B. or **n.b.** *an abbreviation meaning* "note," from the Latin words *nota bene* ("note well").

NDP or **N.D.P.** *abbreviation for* New Democratic Party, one of Canada's main political parties.

NE *abbreviation for* northeast or northeastern.

Ne·an·der·thal (nē an′dər thol′ *or* nē an′dər tol′) a member of an extinct group of humans who were the first to use tools. These tools were made of stone, so the time when the Neanderthals lived is called the Stone Age. *n.*

near (nēr) 1 close; not far: *They searched far and near (adv.). The post office is quite near (adj.).* 2 close to; not far from: *We live near Regina. My birthday is near Labour Day.* 3 come close to; approach: *The vacation was nearing its end.* 4 short; direct: *They took the nearest route to town.* 5 *Informal.* nearly: *He was near crazy with fright.* 1, 4 *adj.,* 1, 5 *adv.,* 2 *prep.,* 3 *v.* **near′ness,** *n.* **near at hand,** **a** within easy reach. **b** not far in the future.

near·by (nēr′bī′) near; close at hand: *They live in a nearby house (adj.). They live nearby (adv.).* *adj. or adv.*

Near East (nēr′ ēst′) the countries of southwestern Asia from Egypt to Iran.

near·ly (nēr′lē) almost: *It is nearly bedtime.* *adv.*

near–sight·ed (nēr′sī′tid) 1 not able to see far; seeing clearly only at a short distance: *Near-sighted people usually wear glasses or contact lenses.* 2 not thinking ahead; not thinking about the future. *adj.*

neat (nēt) 1 clean and tidy; in order: *a neat desk, a neat room.* 2 keeping things clean and tidy: *a neat worker.* 3 *Informal.* interesting, enjoyable, etc.: *What a neat idea! That was a neat story.* *adj.* —**neat′ness,** *n.*

The picture shows the bright central area of the Great Nebula in the constellation Orion. If a nebula doesn't show any light, and even blots out the starlight behind, it is called a dark nebula.

neb•u•la (neb′yə lə) a cloudlike cluster of gas, dust, or stars visible in the sky at night. *n., pl.* **neb•u•lae** or **neb•u•las.**

nec•es•sar•y (nes′ə ser′ē) 1 needed; required: *It is necessary to earn a living.* 2 that cannot be escaped or avoided: *A certain amount of disappointment is a necessary fact of life.* 3 something essential; something that cannot be done without: *Food, clothing, and shelter are necessaries.* 1, 2 *adj.,* 3 *n., pl.* **nec•es•sar•ies.**
—**nec′es•sar′i•ly,** *adv.*

ne•ces•si•ty (nə ses′ə tē) 1 the fact that something is necessary: *We all understand the necessity of eating.* 2 anything that cannot be done without; an essential thing: *Food and water are necessities.* *n., pl.* **ne•ces•si•ties.**

neck (nek) 1 the part of your body that connects your head with your shoulders. 2 a narrow part like a neck: *a neck of land, the neck of a bottle.* *n.*
neck and neck, equal or even in a race or contest: *The two horses ran neck and neck for a kilometre.*
neck of the woods, area; neighbourhood: *I'm going to be in your neck of the woods next week.*
risk your neck, put yourself in a dangerous position.
stick your neck out, take a risk.

neck•lace (nek′lis) a string of jewels or beads, or a chain of gold or silver, etc. worn around the neck as an ornament. *n.*

neck•tie (nek′tī′) a long, narrow band of cloth worn under a shirt collar and knotted in front so the two ends hang down, one over the other. *n.*

nec•tar (nek′tər) 1 a sweet liquid found in many flowers. Bees gather nectar and make it into honey. 2 in ancient Greek mythology, the drink of the gods. *n.*

nec•tar•ine (nek′tə rēn′ *or* nek′tə rēn′) a type of peach with no fuzz on its skin. *n.*

need (nēd) 1 be unable to do without; be without something that you must have: *I need more sleep. Plants need water.* 2 the fact of needing or the thing that is needed: *This money should be enough for all your needs. Our coach stressed the need for practice.* 3 any trouble or difficulty, especially poverty or lack of money: *a friend in need. The family's need was so great that the children did not have shoes.* 4 must; have to: *I need to go to town. You need not bother.* 1, 4 *v.,* 2, 3 *n.* —**need′ful,** *adj.*
—**need′less,** *adj.*
if need be, if it has to be.

CONFUSABLES ..... need

need means "must have": *I need a drink of water.*
knead means "press with your hands": *You knead dough to make bread.*

nee•dle (nē′dəl) 1 a very small, very slender sewing tool with a sharp point at one end and a hole, or eye, at the other to pass a thread through. Needles are made of steel nowadays. 2 a slender rod used in other crafts done with yarn, such as knitting. 3 a slender tube with a sharp point, used for putting medicine into a person's veins or taking out blood: *The doctor stuck the needle into my arm.* 4 the pointer on a compass or dial. 5 the extremely thin, pointed leaf of a pine, spruce, or fir tree. 6 *Informal.* tease: *They needled him about his pen-chewing habit.* 1–5 *n.,* 6 *v.,* **nee•dled, nee•dling.**

nee•dle•work (nē′dəl wərk′) work done with a needle, especially embroidery. *n.*

need•n't (nē′dənt) need not. *v.*

need•y (nē′dē) needing something very badly, especially money or help in coping: *a needy family.* *adj.,* **need•i•er, need•i•est.**

ne'er (ner) in poetry, never. *adv.*

a bat	e bed	i bid	o pot	u cup	th thin
ā cake	ē me	ī bite	ō go	ū rude	ᴛʜ then
à bar	ə about	ər over	ȯ for	ů put	zh measure

ne·far·i·ous (ni fer′ē əs) wicked; very bad: *the nefarious pirate Blackbeard.* *adj.*

negative (neg′ə tiv) 1 saying no: *His answer was negative.* 2 a word that says no or denies. *Won't* is a negative. 3 complaining, criticizing, and expecting the worst: *negative comments, a negative attitude.* 4 bad or harmful: *This could have a negative effect on your work.* 5 in electricity, having more electrons than protons: *a negative charge.* 6 minus; counting down from zero: *Last night we hit –2°C, the first negative temperature of the season.* 7 a piece of photographic film that shows the lighter and darker parts of the image reversed. In colour photography the negative is in complementary colours so that blue things show as yellow, green as purple, etc. Prints are made from negatives. 1, 3–6 *adj.,* 2, 7 *n.*
in the negative, saying no: *She replied in the negative.*

Grammar Check . . double negatives

When a sentence contains a negative word like *can't, won't,* or *doesn't,* be careful not to add another negative word or you may say the opposite of what you mean. *I don't want none of that soup* means *I do want some of that soup.* So, say either *I don't want any of that soup* or *I want none of that soup.*

ne·glect (ni glekt′) 1 give too little care or attention to: *She neglected her friends and lost them.* 2 leave undone; fail to do: *Don't neglect to water the plants.* 3 the act or fact of neglecting: *That bike has been ruined by neglect.* 1, 2 *v.,* 3 *n.*
—ne·glect′ful, *adj.*

neg·li·gent (neg′lə jənt) showing neglect; not showing the proper care and attention: *negligent behaviour, a negligent worker.* *adj.* **—neg′li·gence,** *n.*

ne·go·ti·ate (ni gō′shē āt′) 1 discuss in order to reach an agreement, with each side giving in on certain things: *to negotiate a price. The rebels negotiated for peace with the government.* 2 *Informal.* get past or over safely: *The car slowed down to negotiate the sharp turn.* *v.,* **ne·go·ti·at·ed, ne·go·ti·at·ing.** **—ne·go′ti·a′tion,** *n.* **—ne·go′ti·a·ble** (ni gō′shə bəl), *adj.*

neigh (nā) 1 the sound that a horse makes. 2 make such a sound. 1 *n.,* 2 *v.*

neigh·bour or **neigh·bor** (nā′bər) 1 someone who lives in the next house or nearby. 2 a person or thing that is near or next to another: *The big tree brought down several of its smaller neighbours as it fell.* 3 a fellow human being: *Be kind to your neighbour.* A **neighbourly** person is helpful and friendly. *n.*

neigh·bour·hood or **neigh·bor·hood** (nā′bər hu̇d′) an area or district of a town or city, or the people living there: *We live in a nice neighbourhood. The whole neighbourhood came to the barbecue.* *n.*
in the neighbourhood of, a near: *He lives in the neighbourhood of the mill.* b about; approximately: *The car cost in the neighbourhood of $15 000.*

neigh·bour·ing or **neigh·bor·ing** (nā′bə ring) nearby; bordering: *We could hear the children playing in the neighbouring yards.* *adj.*

neither (nē′ᴛʜər *or* nī′ᴛʜər) 1 not either: *Neither you nor I will go (conj.). Neither statement is true (adj.). Neither of the songs is any good (pron.).* 2 also not: *If you don't want to go, neither do I.* 3 nor; and not: *I don't know, neither do I care.* 1, 3 *conj.,* 1 *adj.,* 1 *pron.,* 2 *adv.*

ne·on (nē′on) 1 an element that is a colourless, odourless gas. It glows reddish orange when an electric current is passed through it. Tubes containing neon are used in electric signs. 2 very bright and with a glowing quality: *neon orange.* 1 *n.,* 2 *adj.*

neph·ew (nef′yū) the son of a person's brother or sister, or brother-in-law or sister-in-law. *n.*

Nep·tune (nep′tyūn *or* nep′tūn) a large planet, the eighth from the sun. It is so far from Earth that it cannot be seen with the naked eye. *n.*

nerve (nərv) 1 a fibre or bundle of fibres connecting the brain or spinal cord with the eyes, ears, muscles, glands, and so on. It is through the nerves that the brain controls our movements and makes use of our five senses. 2 mental strength; courage: *The diver lost his nerve and wouldn't go off the high board.* 3 **nerves,** *pl.* nervousness; anxiety. 4 *Informal.* rudeness; arrogance: *He had the nerve to tell me to get lost.* 5 work up strength and courage in: *The piano student nerved herself for the ordeal of the exam.* 1–4 *n.,* 5 *v.,* **nerved, nerv·ing.**
be a bundle of nerves, be very nervous.
get on someone's nerves, *Informal.* irritate or worry someone. Something so irritating or worrying that you can hardly stand it is **nerve-wracking** (nərv′ rak′ing).
have your nerve, be very rude: *She certainly has her nerve taking off like that.*
strain every nerve, try your hardest; concentrate totally.

nerv·ous (nər′vəs) 1 having to do with the nerves. The **nervous system** controls all the activities and functions of the body. It includes the brain, spinal cord, nerves, and sense organs. 2 tense or anxious; uneasy: *He is nervous about staying alone at night.* 3 easily excited or upset: *Don't make sudden moves or noises around this horse—it's nervous.* *adj.* **—nerv′ous·ness,** *n.*

–ness *a suffix meaning* "a quality or condition," as in *blackness* and *carefulness.*

nest (nest) 1 a bowl-shaped structure built by birds out of twigs, straw, etc. as a place to lay their eggs and protect their young. A **nestling** is a bird too young to leave the nest. 2 a place chosen or built by animals or insects for a similar purpose: *a squirrel's nest, a wasp nest.* 3 make and use a nest: *The bluebirds are nesting here now.* 4 place or fit together, each one inside the next bigger one: *a set of nesting measuring cups.* 1, 2 *n.,* 3, 4 *v.*

nes·tle (nes′əl) 1 settle or be settled comfortably and cosily: *to nestle in a big chair, a house nestling among trees.* 2 press close in love or for comfort: *A mother nestles her baby in her arms.* *v.,* **nes·tled, nes·tling.**

net[1] (net) 1 Often, **netting,** an open fabric made of string, thread, or wire, knotted together in such a way as to leave holes, evenly spaced and all the same size. 2 a piece of this, used for some special purpose: *a fishing net, a hair net, a basketball net.* 3 catch in a net: *I finally netted a fish.* 4 **the Net,** the Internet, a huge computer network linking many smaller networks worldwide. You can send and receive e-mail, find information, shop, or do banking on the Net. 1, 2, 4 *n.,* 3 *v.,* **net·ted, net·ting.**

net[2] (net) 1 having to do with the real or actual amount apart from "extras" that must be added or subtracted. A **net gain** or profit is the amount you have after all working expenses have been paid. The **net weight** of a glass jar of candy is the weight of the candy itself, without the jar. 2 to gain as a net amount: *The sale netted me a good profit.* 1 *adj.,* 2 *v.,* **net·ted, net·ting.**

The tiny hairs on a nettle are like hollow needles. If they pierce your skin and break off, poison enters the wound, and that's what stings.

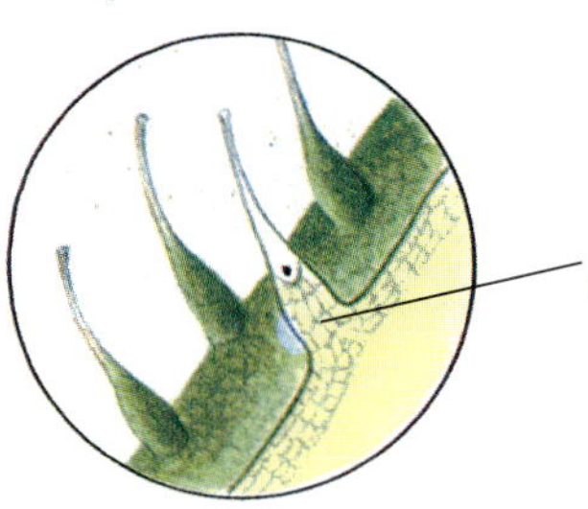

net·tle (net′əl) 1 a wild herb with sharp hairs on the leaves and stems that sting your skin when touched. 2 irritate; make angry: *Their constant teasing nettled me.* 1 *n.,* 2 *v.,* **net·tled, net·tling.**

net·work (net′wərk′) 1 a net. 2 any system of lines that cross: *a network of vines, a network of highways.* 3 a group of radio or television stations which are connected so that the same program may be broadcast by all: *the French network of the CBC.* 4 a group of computers connected by telephone lines or cables in order to share information. 5 talk to other people in your field of work and get to know them so you can help each other in different ways later on. 1–4 *n.,* 5 *v.*

neu·ron (nyūr′on *or* nūr′on) one of the cells that make up the brain, spinal cord, and nerves. **Neurology** is the study of the nervous system and its diseases. *n.* **—neur′al,** *adj.*

neu·ter (nyū′tər *or* nū′tər) do an operation on an animal to make it unable to reproduce. *v.*

neu·tral (nyū′trəl *or* nū′trəl) 1 not taking any side in a discussion or conflict: *Switzerland was neutral during the last two wars in Europe.* 2 being neither one thing nor the other and so able to go with almost any other colour. Pale grey and beige are neutral colours. 3 the position of the gears of a car, etc., when they do not give the wheels any power from the engine. To **neutralize** something is to take away its power or effect. 1, 2 *adj.,* 3 *n.* **—neu·tral′i·ty,** *n.*

neu·tron (nyū′tron *or* nū′tron) a tiny particle that is one of the basic building blocks of matter. It is found in the nucleus of every kind of atom except hydrogen. It has no electric charge. *n.*

nev·er (nev′ər) 1 not ever; at no time: *He never lies.* 2 not at all: *This coat will never do; it's far too big.* *adv.* **never mind, a** pay no attention to; forget about: *Never mind the noise.* **b** it doesn't matter; forget it.

nev·er·the·less (nev′ər ŦHə les′) however; even so: *He was very tired; nevertheless, he kept on working.* **Nonetheless** (nun′ŦHə les′) means the same. *adv.*

new (nyū *or* nū) 1 not existing or known before; just recently made, thought of, or discovered: *a new invention, a new style, a new galaxy. The detective uncovered several new facts.* 2 different from the one before: *Our class has a new teacher. They just moved; their new home is an old farmhouse.* 3 not yet familiar: *He is still new to the work. This kind of food is new to me.* 4 beginning all over again as part of a cycle: *a new year. The new moon is seen as a thin crescent.* 5 fresh: *to go on again with new courage.* *adj.* **—new′ly,** *adv.* **—new′ness,** *n.*

a bat	e bed	i bid	o pot	u cup	th thin
ā cake	ē me	ī bite	ō go	ū rude	ŦH then
ä bar	ə about	ər over	ô for	u̇ put	zh measure

CONFUSABLES .... new

new means "unused": *Do you like my new shoes?*
knew means "understood": *I knew you would say that!*

New Age (nyū′ āj′) 1 a movement whose followers believe in a more spiritual way of living and looking at the world, apart from any traditional religion. Being in tune with nature is an important part of New Age. 2 having to do with a kind of dreamy, relaxing instrumental music that often includes sounds from nature: *We spent the afternoon listening to New Age music.*

New Bruns·wick (nyū′ brunz′wik) an eastern province of Canada between Québec and Nova Scotia. **—New Bruns′wick·er.**

New Democratic Party (nyū′ dem′ə krat′ik pär′tē) a major Canadian political party begun in 1961.

New·found·land and Lab·ra·dor (nyu′fən land′ *or* nu′fən land′, lab′rə dôr′ *or* lab′rə dôr′) the easternmost province of Canada, made up of the large island of Newfoundland and a part of the mainland called Labrador, bordering Québec. **—New·found·land′er,** *n.,* **—Lab′ra·dor′i·an,** *n.*

New·found·land dog (nyū′fənd land′ dog′) a breed of shaggy, intelligent dog like a very large spaniel.

new moon (nyu′ mūn′) 1 the phase of the moon when it is directly between the earth and the sun. During this time the side of the moon facing the earth gets no sunlight, so it appears dark. 2 the very thin curved part of the moon that we see on the right side a few days later.

***Word Family*.......... new**

newborn: 1 just born **2** a baby that has just been born
newcomer: someone who has just recently arrived
newfangled: too new and unfamiliar to be any good
newly: recently; just a short time ago
newlywed: someone just recently married

news (nyūz *or* nūz) 1 information about something that has just happened or has just been found out: *The news that our teacher was leaving made us sad.* 2 a report of happenings in a newspaper, on television, radio, etc.: *We listened to the news on the radio.* *n.* **—news′y,** *adj.*
break the news, tell something, especially something surprising or hard to accept.
make the news, be considered **newsworthy,** or important enough to be reported in the news.

news·cast (nyūz′kast′ *or* nūz′kast′) a radio or television program about current events. *n.*

news·group (nyūz′grūp′ *or* nūz′grūp′) a site on the Internet where you can read information on a certain subject and also discuss it by leaving your own typed-in messages. The different users are not connected, so the communication does not happen instantly as in a chat room. Instead the messages are stored at the site and users can log on and read them anytime. *n.*

news·pa·per (nyūs′pā′pər *or* nūs′pā′pər) 1 a publication, usually printed daily or weekly, containing news stories and pictures, columns and editorials, as well as advertisements, weather reports, and comics. It is usually printed on large sheets of paper that are just folded, not stapled or bound. 2 printed sheets of this kind: *The plants were wrapped in newspaper.* *n.*

news·print (nyūs′print *or* nūs′print′) the kind of thin, unbleached, easily torn paper that newspapers are usually printed on. *n.*

news·stand (nyūz′stand′ *or* nūz′stand′) a rack or booth where newspapers and magazines are sold. *n.*

newt (nyūt *or* nūt) a small salamander that lives in water part of the time. *n.*

New Testament (nyū′ tes′tə mənt) the part of the Christian Bible that contains the life and teachings of Jesus recorded by his earliest followers, together with their own experiences and teachings.

new·ton (nyū′tən *or* nū′tən) an SI unit for measuring force. It takes about ten newtons to lift a stone of 1 kg. *Symbol:* N

New World (nyū′ wərld′) North America and South America. These continents were called the New World by early European explorers.

New Year's Day (nyū′ yērz′ dā′) January 1. The previous night, December 31, is **New Year's Eve.**

next (nekst) 1 coming right after this one or that one: *the next page, the next day.* 2 soonest or nearest: *We'll catch the next train. Stop at the next gas station.* 3 the first time after this: *When you next come, bring it.* 4 right after this: *I'm going to do my math homework next.* 1, 2 *adj.,* 3, 4 *adv.*
next door, a in the next house: *He lives next door to us.* Someone living next door is a **next-door neighbour. b** almost; very close: *What he said was next door to a lie.*
next of kin, a person's closest relatives.
next to, a beside; nearest to: *Who is the girl next to you?* **b** after someone or something else in order of rank: *Next to pizza, I like tacos best.*
next to nothing, almost nothing.

nib·ble (nib′əl) 1 eat with quick, small bites. 2 a small bite. 1 *v.,* **nib·bled, nib·bling;** 2 *n.*

nice (nīs) 1 pleasant; enjoyable: *a nice day, a nice walk.* 2 thoughtful or kind: *He was nice to us.* 3 well done; skilful: *a nice catch. Nice work, Isaac!* *adj.,* **nic·er, nic·est.** **—nice′ly,** *adv.*

niche (nēsh *or* nich) 1 a sort of shelf or space cut into a wall for a statue, vase, etc. 2 the part that an organism plays in an ecosystem. *n.*
find your niche, settle comfortably into a group, activity, situation, etc.: *It didn't take long for Chantal to find her niche in the new school.*

nick (nik) 1 a place where a small bit has been cut or broken out: *He dropped a saucer and made a nick in the edge of it.* 2 make a nick or nicks in. 1 *n.,* 2 *v.*
in the nick of time, just at the last minute.

nick·el (nik′əl) 1 a hard, silver-white metallic element. It does not corrode easily and is often used in mixtures with other metals. 2 a five-cent coin. *n.*

nick·name (nik′nām′) 1 a short form of a name, or a different name used in fun: *"The Alex" is a nickname for the Royal Alexandra Theatre.* 2 give a nickname to: *They nicknamed me "Ram" because I had an excellent memory.* 1 *n.,* 2 *v.,* **nick·named, nick·nam·ing.**

> **WORD HISTORY.......nickname**
>
> The word **nickname** used to be *ekename,* a Middle English word meaning "another name." But when people heard the words *an ekename,* it sounded like *a nekename.* Over time, *nekename* became **nickname**.

nic·o·tine (nik′ə tēn′) a strong poison contained in tobacco. It is easy to get addicted to it. *n.*

niece (nēs) the daughter of a person's brother or sister, brother-in-law or sister-in-law. *n.*

nigh (nī) an old or poetic word for "near." *adj. or adv.*

night (nīt) 1 the time between sunset and sunrise, especially when it is completely dark. This time is also called **nighttime;** the beginning of it is called **nightfall.** 2 evening; the time after work or school: *I have karate tomorrow night.* *n.*

night·gown (nīt′goun′) a loose dress worn in bed by girls and women. **Nightie** is the informal word. *n.*

night·in·gale (nīt′in gāl′) a small, reddish brown bird of Europe. The male sings sweetly at night. *n.*

night·ly (nīt′lē) 1 every night; happening every night: *her nightly routine (adj.). Performances are given nightly except on Sunday (adv.).* 2 at night; happening at night: *a nightly visit (adj.). Many animals come out only nightly (adv.).* *adj. or adv.*

night·mare (nīt′mer′) 1 a scary dream. 2 a horrible experience: *The ice storm was a nightmare.* *n.*

night·shirt (nīt′shərt′) a loose garment worn in bed. *n.*

nil (nil) nothing. *n.*

nim·ble (nim′bəl) moving quickly, easily, and skilfully: *nimble mountain goats, nimble fingers, a nimble mind.* *adj.,* **nim·bler, nim·blest.** **—nim′bly,** *adv.*

nim·bus (nim′bəs) a large dark storm cloud. *n.*

nine (nīn) one more than eight; 9: *Six and three make nine (n.).* *n. or adj.* **—ninth,** *adj. or n.*
dressed to the nines, dressed up very fancily.
on cloud nine, very happy.
the whole nine yards, *Informal.* everything.

nine·teen (nīn′tēn′) nine more than ten; 19. *n. or adj.* **—nine′teenth′,** *adj. or n.*

nine·ty (nīn′tē) nine times ten; 90. *n., pl.* **nine·ties;** *or adj.* **—nine′ti·eth,** *adj. or n.*

nin·ja (nin′jə) a medieval Japanese warrior-spy. *n.*

nip (nip) pinch or bite: *The crab nipped my toe (v.). The puppy gave the big dog a playful nip on the ear (n.)* *n. or v.,* **nipped, nip·ping.**
a nip in the air, fresh, chilly, fall-like weather. The adjective is **nippy.**
nip and tuck, *Informal.* very close, so that it is hard to tell whether a person will win, succeed, etc. or not.
nip something in the bud, stop something bad right away before it gets serious.

nip·ple (nip′əl) 1 on a human, the small raised part in the centre of either breast. 2 the mouthpiece of a baby's bottle. *n.*

nir·va·na (nər van′ə) in Buddhism, full understanding and freedom from suffering. When the soul achieves nirvana, it is not reborn anymore. *n.*

Nis·ga'a or **Nish·ga** (nish′gə) 1 a First Nations people living along the Skeena River in British Columbia. They speak a dialect of **Nass-Gitksan,** a language belonging to the Tsimshian family. 2 having to do with these people. 1 *n.,* 2 *adj.*

a bat	e bed	i bid	o pot	u cup	th thin
ā cake	ē me	ī bite	ō go	ū rude	ᴛʜ then
ä bar	ə about	ər over	ô for	ů put	zh measure

nit–pick (nit′pik′) look for the tiniest things wrong with something and fuss about them. This once referred to picking **nits,** tiny eggs of lice, out of someone's hair. *v.*

In the nitrogen cycle, nitrogen passes from air to soil, then to plants, then to animals that eat the plants, and eventually back to the air.

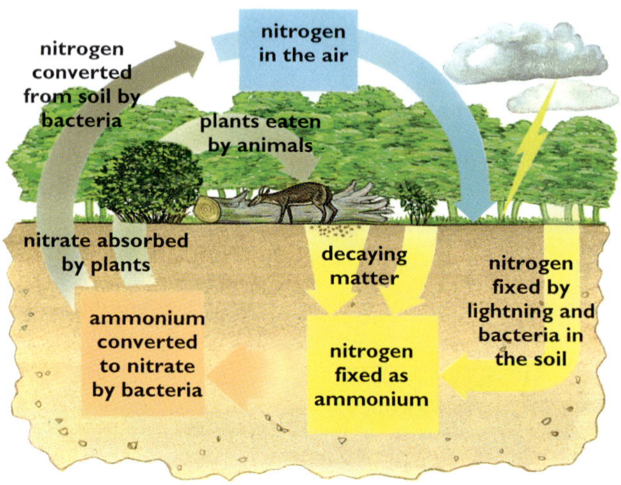

ni·tro·gen (nī′trə jən) an element which is a gas without colour, taste, or odour. It forms about four-fifths of air. *n.*

Nla·ka'·pa·mux (əng′hlo ko′pə mə) **1** a First Nations people living in British Columbia. **2** their language. **3** having to do with these people or their language. 1, 2 *n.,* 3 *adj.*

no·ble (nō′bəl) **1** high and beautiful in character; showing great courage, generosity, and so on: *a noble person, a noble deed.* **2** elegant; majestic; fine; magnificent: *Niagara Falls is a noble sight.* **3** belonging to the highest ranks of society: *a noble family.* **4** a person of very high rank. A duke is a noble; so is an earl or count. All these people as a group were called the **nobility** (nō bil′ə tē). 1–3 *adj.,* **no·bler, no·blest;** 4 *n.* **—no′ble·man** or **no′ble·wo′man,** *n.* **—no′bly,** *adv.*

no·bod·y (nō′bud′ē *or* nō′bə dē) **1** no one; no person. **2** a person of no importance. 1 *pron.,* 2 *n., pl.* **no·bod·ies.**

noc·tur·nal (nok tər′nəl) having to do with the night. A nocturnal creature, such as an owl, is active at night; a nocturnal flower is open only at night. *adj.*

nod (nod) **1** bow your head slightly and raise it again quickly, as a signal or greeting or to say "yes." **2** a nodding of the head: *He gave us a nod as he passed.* **3** let your head wobble because you are falling asleep. 1, 3 *v.,* **nod·ded, nod·ding;** 2 *n.*
nod off, fall asleep.

No·ël (nō el′) Christmas. *n.*

noise (noiz) **1** loud or harsh sound: *The noise kept me awake.* **2** any sound: *the noise of rain on the roof.* *n.* **—noise′less,** *adj.* **—nois′y,** *adj.* **—nois′i·ly,** *adv.*

WORD HISTORY........noise

Noise comes from the same root word as *nausea.* It originally meant "a loud disturbance," from the unpleasant sound made by a shipful of seasick passengers.

no·mad (nō′mad) **1** one of a group of people who move together from place to place to find pasture for their cattle or to follow the animals they hunt for food. **2** a person who is always travelling. *n.* **—no·mad′ic,** *adj.*

nom·i·nate (nom′ə nāt′) suggest someone to run in an election or to be chosen for an award: *Mrs. Wu was nominated to run for mayor.* A person who is nominated is a **nominee** (nom′ə nē′). *v.,* **nom·i·nated, nom·i·nat·ing.** **—nom′i·na′tion,** *n.*

non– *a prefix meaning* not, or the opposite of, as in *non-living* or *nonsense.*

non·cha·lant (non′shə lont′) calm and unconcerned, especially when everyone else is excited, nervous, afraid, etc.: *She remained quite nonchalant during all the excitement.* *adj.*

non–con·duc·tor (non′kən duk′tər) a substance that does not easily allow heat, electricity, or sound to pass through it: *Rubber is a non-conductor of electricity.* *n.*

none (nun) not any; not one: *We have none of that paper left. None of these is the right size.* *pron.*
none too, not at all: *They came, but none too quickly.*

USING WORDS........none

Use a singular verb with **none.** It is a singular pronoun even when it is followed by a plural noun: *None of the video clips was very interesting.*

none·the·less (nun′ᴛʜə les′) another word for **nevertheless;** even so; in spite of that: *She didn't have permission to go but she went nonetheless.*

non·fic·tion (non fik′shən) writing that has to do with facts or opinions and does not include made-up stories: *You'll find the books about the solar system in the nonfiction section.* *n.*

non·flam·ma·ble (non′flam′ə bəl) not easily set on fire; not flammable. *adj.*

non–prof•it (non′prof′it) not operated for making a profit; having to do with an organization that is not a business, such as a school, church, charity, etc. *adj.*

non–re•new•a•ble (non′ri nyū′ə bəl *or* non′ri nū′ə bəl) that cannot be replaced. Forests are a renewable resource because they will grow again; oil is a non-renewable resource because once it is taken from an oil well and used up, it is gone forever. *adj.*

non•sense (non′sens) words, ideas, or actions that are foolish or have no meaning: *It is nonsense to say that we can walk that far in an hour. Stop this nonsense and do something worthwhile.* *n.* **—non•sens′i•cal,** *adj.*

non–stop (non′stop′) with no stops: *a non-stop flight* (*adj.*), *to fly non-stop* (*adv.*). *adj.* *or* *adv.*

noo•dles (nū′dəlz) pasta made in flat strips. Pasta is made from flour and water, sometimes with egg. *pl.n.*

nook (nu̇k) a cozy little corner. *n.*

noon (nūn) twelve o'clock in the daytime; the middle of the day. **Noonday** is often used for the adjective: *the noonday sun, his noonday meal.* *n.*

> **WORD HISTORY........noon**
>
> The word **noon** comes from the Latin *nona hora,* meaning "ninth hour" (of sunlight).

no one or **no–one** (nō′wun′) no person; nobody: *No one was hurt in the car accident.*

noose (nūs) a loop in a rope, made with a slip knot that tightens as the rope is pulled. A lasso has a noose. *n.*

nor (nȯr) and also not: *I saw neither moon nor star that night. I have not been there, nor am I going.* *conj.*

> **Grammar Check .... nor**
>
> When the subject of a sentence contains **nor** or **or,** the verb agrees with the word closest to it:
> *Neither my uncles nor my father has red hair.*
> *Neither my father nor his brothers have red hair.*

norm (nȯrm) **1** the usual thing: *Mild winters are the norm for Vancouver.* **2** a rule or standard. *n.*

nor•mal (nȯr′məl) **1** usual or regular; natural; ordinary: *The normal temperature of the human body is 37°C. It's normal for children to be energetic.* **2** the usual state or level: *Rainfall was 5 cm above normal this month.* 1 *adj.,* 2 *n.* **—nor′mal•ly,** *adv.*

According to legend, Odin was the chief of the Norse gods. He owned two ravens, called Thought, and Memory. Every day he sent them out into the world to report what was going on there.

Norse (nȯrs) **1** the people and language of ancient Scandinavia, that is Norway, Sweden, and Denmark. **2** having to do with these people or their language. Many English words come from Norse words. 1 *n.,* 2 *adj.*

north (nȯrth) **1** the direction that a compass needle points in; the direction to your right as you face the setting sun. **2** to or from the north: *the north exit, a cold north wind* (*adj.*). *Drive north for 2 km* (*adv.*). **3** **North** or **the Northland,** the north part of the world or of some country: *We went canoeing in the North.* In Canada, this includes the northern parts of the provinces from Québec westward and the area to the north of them. The **Far North** is the Arctic. 1, 3 *n.,* 2 *adv.* *or* *adj.* **—north′ern** (nȯr′ᴛʜərn), *adj.* **—north′er•ly** (nȯr′ᴛʜər lē), *adj.*

North America (nȯrth′ ə mer′ə kə) the continent that contains Canada and the United States. **—North American.**

north•east (nȯr′thēst′) **1** the direction halfway between north and east. **2** a place or part that is in that direction. **3** in, to, or from the northeast: *a northeast wind* (*adj.*). *They travelled northeast* (*adv.*). 1, 2 *n.,* 3 *adj. or adv.* **—north′east′ern,** *adj.*

a bat	e bed	i bid	o pot	u cup	th thin
ā cake	ē me	ī bite	ō go	ū rude	ᴛʜ then
ä bar	ə about	ər over	ȯ for	u̇ put	zh measure

northern lights (nôr′ᴛʜərn līts′) the streamers and bands of coloured light that sometimes appear in the northern sky at night. The technical name is **aurora borealis** (ə rôr′ə bôr′ē al′is). Similar lights in the southern sky are called **aurora australis** (ə rôr′ə ə stral′is).

North Pole (nôrth′ pōl′) the northern end of the earth's axis.

North Star (nôrth′ stär′) the bright star almost directly above the North Pole.

north•ward (nôrth′wərd) toward the north; north: *He walked northward (adv.). The orchard is on the northward slope of the hill (adj.).* **Northwards** is another form for the adverb. *adv. or adj.*

north•west (nôrth′west′) **1** the direction halfway between north and west. **2** in, to, or from the northwest: *a northwest wind (adj.). They travelled northwest (adv.).* **3 the Northwest**, the northwest part of Canada or of any other country. In Canada it is the region north and west of the Great Lakes. *adj. or adv.* **—north′west′ern,** *adj.*

✱ **North West Company** (nôrth′ west′ kum′pə nē) a group of fur traders formed in Canada during the late 1700s that later became part of the Hudson's Bay Company.

✱ **North West Mounted Police** (nôrth′ west′ moun′tid pə lēs′) an old name of the Royal Canadian Mounted Police.

Northwest Territories (nôrth′west′ ter′ə tôr′ēz) a territory in the central part of Canada's North, between Yukon Territory and Nunavut. A territory is like a province but with a different form of government and fewer powers.

nose (nōz) **1** the part of the face that sticks out above the mouth and is used for breathing and smelling. **2** the sense of smell: *Most dogs have a good nose.* **3** discover by smell; smell out. **4** a part that sticks out at the front of something such as a boat or aircraft. **5** touch, push, or rub with the nose: *The cat nosed its kittens. The boat nosed along through the reeds.* **6** snoop; pry: *Who's been nosing around in my room?* 1, 2, 4 *n.,* 3, 5, 6 *v.,* **nosed, nos•ing.**
look down your nose at, treat someone as though he or she is not as good as you.
on the nose, exactly.
pay through the nose, *Informal.* pay a very high price.
poke your nose into, *Informal.* pry into; meddle in: *That gossip is always poking his nose into other people's business.*
turn up your nose at, refuse something perfectly good just because it doesn't suit you.
under someone's nose, where that person can easily see it: *I did it right under her nose and got away with it!*

nose•bleed (nōz′blēd′) a flow of blood from your nose. *n.*

nose cone (nōz′ kōn′) a protective, cone-shaped cap at the front end of a spacecraft, aircraft, or missile. It is designed to streamline the craft and protect it against the intense heat that is produced when it travels through the earth's atmosphere at very high speed.

nose–dive (nōz′dīv′) **1** a swift plunge downward with the front first, especially by an aircraft. **2** a sharp, sudden drop: *The temperature took a nose-dive yesterday.* **3** do a nose-dive: *Gas prices nose-dived overnight.* 1, 2 *n.,* 3 *v.,* **nose-dived, nose-div•ing.**

nos•ey or **nos•y** (nō′zē) too curious about other people's business. *adj.,* **nos•i•er, nos•i•est.**

nos•tal•gia (nos tal′jə) a longing for something in the past: *She thought with nostalgia of her happy childhood days on the farm.* *n.* **—nos•tal′gic,** *adj.*

nos•tril (nos′trəl) either of the two openings in your nose that let air in and out. *n.*

no•ta•ble (nō′tə bəl) **1** worth noticing; important: *a notable event, a notable writer.* **2** an important or famous person: *Many notables attended the Governor General's banquet.* 1 *adj.,* 2 *n.* **—no′ta•bly,** *adv.*

no•ta•tion (nō tā′shən) a system of written symbols: *musical notation, mathematical notation.* *n.*

notch (noch) **1** a V-shaped cut: *The lost hikers cut notches in a stick to keep track of the days.* **2** make this kind of cut in something. **3** *Informal.* a grade; step; degree: *Turn the volume up a notch.* 1, 3 *n.,* 2 *v.*

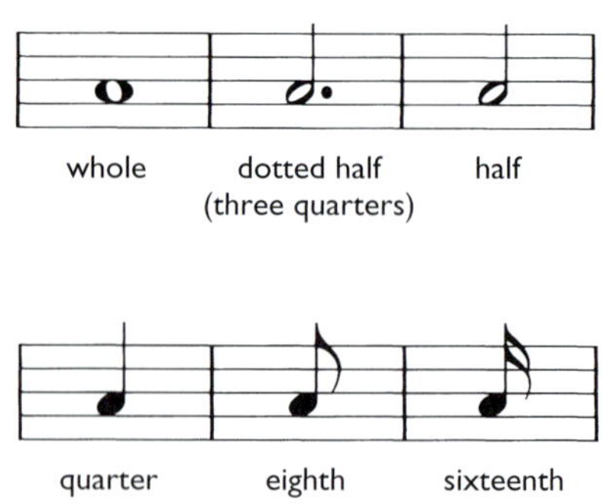

Musical notes are written on a set of lines called a staff. The shape of the note tells how long it will last — the whole note has the longest time value.

note (nōt) **1** something short written down as a message to someone or as a reminder to yourself. **2** write down as a thing to be remembered: *I noted it down on the calendar.* **3** notice; pay attention to: *Now note what I do next.* **4 a** a single musical sound: *Sing this note for me.* **b** the written sign to show the pitch and length of a musical sound. *Example:* ♪

5 a tone of voice or way of expression: *There was a note of anxiety in her voice.* 1, 4, 5 *n.,* 2, 3 *v.,* **not·ed, not·ing.**
compare notes, tell each other what you thought of something or how you experienced it.
of note, famous or important: *a person of note.*
take note, pay attention or notice: *Take note of the time, please; we must not be late.*
take notes, write downmain points as you read or listen.

note·book (nōt′bu̇k′) 1 a book with blank pages for writing in, especially for taking notes or doing assignments. 2 a small personal computer that easily fits in a briefcase or knapsack; a laptop computer. *n.*

not·ed (nō′tid) well-known; famous: *Glenn Gould was a noted musician.* *adj.*

note·pa·per (nōt′pā′pər) paper for writing letters, often decorated and with matching envelopes. *n.*

note·wor·thy (nōt′wər′ᴛʜē) worth noticing; remarkable: *The first flight across the Atlantic was a noteworthy achievement.* *adj.*

noth·ing (nuth′ing) 1 not anything: *Nothing arrived by mail. I ate nothing all morning.* 2 a thing or person of no importance: *They made all that fuss over nothing.* 3 zero. 4 not at all: *She is nothing like her sister in looks.* 1–3 *n.,* 4 *adv.*

no·tice (nō′tis) 1 attention: *A sudden movement caught his notice.* 2 see, hear, or feel and take note of: *I noticed that my purse was gone. Didn't you notice my haircut?* 3 advance information that lets a person get ready or make plans: *He gave the boss notice that he was going to quit. We can't come on such short notice.* 4 any public written message, such as a sign or an advertisement: *We saw a notice in the paper about the Kirks' new baby.* 1, 3, 4 *n.,* 2 *v.,* **no·ticed, no·tic·ing.**
—no′tice·a·ble, *adj.* **—no′tice·a·bly,** *adv.*

no·ti·fy (nō′tə fī′) let someone know that something is planned or has happened: *If anything has been stolen, notify the police.* *v.,* **no·ti·fied, no·ti·fy·ing.**
—no′ti·fi·ca′tion, *n.*

no·tion (nō′shən) 1 an idea, usually not very clear or solid: *I'm beginning to get a notion of what you mean.* 2 a sudden urge or desire: *She had a notion to visit her grandmother.* 3 **notions,** *pl.* small, useful articles for sewing, such as pins, needles, thread, etc. *n.*

no·to·ri·ous (nō tô′rē əs) well-known because of something bad: *a notorious criminal.* **Notoriety** (nō′tə rī′ə tē) is fame, whether good or bad. *adj.*

not·with·stand·ing (not′with stan′ding) a formal word meaning: 1 in spite of: *He bought it notwithstanding the price.* 2 nevertheless: *It was freezing, but we played outside notwithstanding.* 1 *prep.,* 2 *adv.*

nou·gat (nü′gət) chewy candy, often with chopped nuts and tiny pieces of fruit in it. *n.*

noun (noun) a word used to name a person, place, thing, quality, or event. In the sentence *Andrea showed great excitement when her brother arrived at the party with a new puppy,* the words *Andrea, excitement, brother, party,* and *puppy* are all nouns. *n.* ▶ See the *Grammar and Usage Mini-Guide.*

Grammar Check . . . . noun

Sometimes, a single well-chosen **noun** can replace a whole phrase. The word *skyscraper* is more impressive than *very tall building.* Try to use precise nouns as much as possible when you write.

nour·ish (nər′ish) feed well; cause to grow and be strong: *Milk is all that is needed to nourish a newborn baby. Let us nourish the hope for peace.* *v.*
—nour′ish·ment, *n.* **—nour′ish·ing,** *adj.*

no·va (nō′və) a star in a double-star system that suddenly becomes much brighter for a while. The nova's greater gravity pulls material away from the other star; when this material hits the nova, it brightens. A **supernova** is a star that becomes thousands of times brighter in an explosion that completely destroys it. *n., pl.* **no·vae** (nō′vē) or **no·vas.**

No·va Sco·tia (nō′və skō′shə) one of Canada's Atlantic provinces, east of New Brunswick.
—No′va Sco′tian.

nov·el[1] (nov′əl) new and different and therefore interesting: *The trip from Edmonton in a small plane was a novel experience for me.* *adj.*

nov·el[2] (nov′əl) a long piece of fiction; a story that fills a whole book. It is written by a **novelist.** *n.*

nov·el·ty (nov′əl tē) 1 the newness that makes a thing interesting: *After the novelty of washing dishes wore off, Gina lost interest.* 2 a new or unusual thing: *Staying up late was a novelty to the children.* 3 **novelties,** *pl.* small, cheap articles that are mildly interesting. *n., pl.* **nov·el·ties.**

No·vem·ber (nō vem′bər) the eleventh month of the year. November has 30 days. *n.*

nov·ice (nov′is) a beginner: *Novices are likely to make some mistakes.* *n.*

a bat	e bed	i bid	o pot	u cup	th thin
ā cake	ē me	ī bite	ō go	ū rude	ᴛʜ then
ä bar	ə about	ər over	ô for	u̇ put	zh measure

now (nou) 1 at this time: *He is not home now.* 2 the present; this time: *by now, until now, from now on.* 3 because of what has happened: *Now I can never believe you again.* 4 **Now** is used in many sentences to draw attention to what is being said: *Now, get to work! Drive safely, now.* 1, 3, 4 *adv.*, 2 *n.*
just now, a only a moment ago. b right at this time.
now and then, from time to time; once in a while. **Now and again** means the same.
now that, since; considering that: *Now that you mention it, I do remember.*

now·a·days (nou′ə dāz′) in these times: *Nowadays computers are everywhere.* *adv.*

no·where (nō′wer′ *or* nō′hwer′) at or to no place. *adv.*

noz·zle (noz′əl) a tip or spout on a hose, pipe, etc. that lets you control how the liquid or gas comes out: *He adjusted the nozzle so the water became a fine spray.* *n.*

nu·cle·ar (nyū′klē ər *or* nū′klē ər) 1 having to do with the nucleus of a cell, of an atom, or of anything else. A **nuclear family** is just one set of parents and their children, the "nucleus" or core of a bigger family of relatives. 2 having to do with **nuclear energy**, the energy released from the nucleus of an atom of a radioactive substance: *a nuclear reactor, the nuclear age.* *adj.*

nuclear reactor (nyū′klē ər rē ak′tər) a device for producing nuclear energy in a controlled way, rather than in an explosion as a nuclear bomb does. The energy produced by the reactor is changed into electricity.

nu·cle·us (nyū′klē əs *or* nū′klē əs) 1 a part at the centre of something: *The kitchen is the nucleus of our home.* 2 the central part of an atom, carrying a positive electric charge. Almost all nuclei consist of tiny particles called protons and neutrons. 3 a dark mass found at the centre of most living cells. It contains the material that allows the cell to grow and divide. *n.*, *pl.* **nu·cle·i** (nyū′klē ī *or* nū′klē ī) or **nu·cle·us·es.**

WORD HISTORY........nucleus

The word **nucleus** is related to the Latin word for "nut." The nucleus of something is like the central part, or kernel, of a nut.

nude (nyūd *or* nūd) 1 with no clothes on. 2 a naked figure in art. 1 *adj.*, 2 *n.* **—nu′di·ty,** *n.*
in the nude, without clothes on; naked: *They went swimming in the nude.*

nudge (nuj) 1 push or poke slightly to attract attention, etc. 2 a slight push or poke: *When he gave me a nudge, I giggled.* 1 *v.*, **nudged, nudg·ing;** 2 *n.*

nug·get (nug′it) a small chunk or lump, especially a lump of gold in its natural state. *n.*

nui·sance (nyū′səns *or* nū′səns) any troublesome, annoying thing or person: *Flies are a nuisance.* *n.*

nuke (nyūk *or* nūk) *Slang.* 1 heat or cook in a microwave oven: *We nuked the frozen pizza for lunch.* 2 destroy with nuclear weapons. *v.*, **nuked, nuk·ing.**

null (nul)
null and void, without legal force or effect; worthless. To **nullify** something is to cancel it or make it worthless.
null set, in math, an empty set. The set of whole numbers greater than 2 and less than 3 would be a null set. *adj.*

numb (num) 1 having lost the power of feeling or moving: *My fingers are numb with cold.* 2 take away the power of feeling or moving. 1 *adj.*, 2 *v.*

num·ber (num′bər) 1 the count or sum of a group of things or people: *The number of students in our class is twenty.* 2 a the idea of a certain quantity or amount; a word such as "six" or "twenty." b sometimes, a figure or symbol standing for this, such as 12 or 3. This is more formally called a **numeral.** A **number line** shows these numerals as points on a line. 3 count: *The stars were too many to number.* 4 give a number to: *The pages of this book are numbered.* 5 a number given to identify one person or thing: *a telephone number, a house number. Symbol:* # 6 amount to a certain number: *The population of our town numbers about 30 000.* 7 a quantity: *They came in great numbers.* 8 one thing in a series, such as one song in a concert or one issue of a magazine. 1, 2, 5, 7, 8 *n.*, 3, 4, 6 *v.*
a number of, several.
have someone's number, have power over a person because you know his or her weak points.
without number or **beyond number,** too many to count: *stars without number.* **Numberless** means the same.

nu·mer·al (nyū′mə rəl *or* nū′mə rəl) a figure; a symbol standing for a number. The numbers 2, 15, and 100 are Arabic numerals. II, XV, and C are Roman numerals for 2, 15, and 100. *n.* ▶ See Appendix.

CONFUSABLES.....numeral

numeral means "a figure that stands for a number": *The numeral 5 stands for five.*

number means "an amount": *The number of fingers on one hand is five.*

Nuts

The kernels of many nuts are rich in proteins and fat, and are a good, renewable food resource. Peanuts, for example, can be crushed to make peanut butter, and chestnuts can be ground to make a flour for bread.

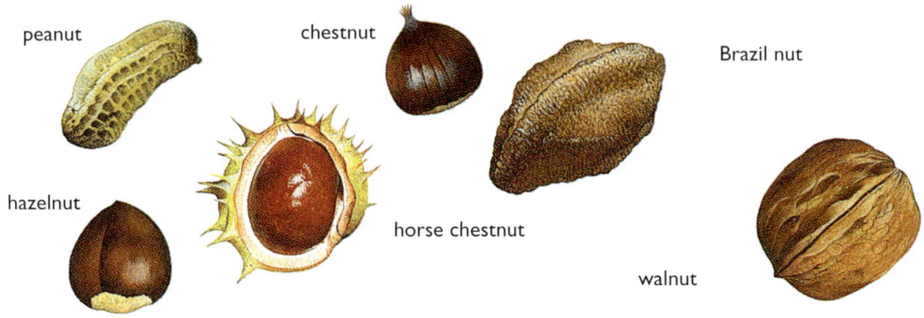

nu·mer·a·tor (nyū′mə rā′tər *or* nū′mə rā′tər) the number above the line in a fraction. In $\frac{3}{8}$, 3 is the numerator, and 8 is the denominator. *n.*

nu·mer·i·cal (nyū mer′ə kəl *or* nū mer′ə kəl) having to do with numbers. *adj.*

nu·mer·ous (nyū′mə rəs *or* nū′mə rəs) many: *The child asked numerous questions.* *adj.*

nun (nun) a woman who has chosen to live her life along with others according to certain religious rules. *n.*

Nu·na·vut (nu̇n′ə vu̇t′) a new territory east of the Northwest Territories and including most of the islands of the Arctic, which began to govern itself in 1999. *n.*

nurse (nərs) **1** a person who takes care of sick, injured, or old people: *Hospitals employ many nurses.* **2** take care of sick people or a sick person. **3** feed a baby by letting it suck milk from the breast: *Mom nurses my baby brother when he cries; he nurses every few hours.* **4** cause to grow; nourish and protect: *to nurse a plant, to nurse a secret wish.* 1 *n.*, 2–4 *v.*, **nursed, nurs·ing.**

nurs·er·y (nər′sə rē) **1** a room set apart for babies and children. **2** a place where plants are grown for sale. *n., pl.* **nurs·er·ies.**

nursery rhyme (nərs′rē rīm′) a short poem for young children: *"Humpty Dumpty sat on a wall" is the beginning of a famous nursery rhyme.*

nursery school (nərs′rē skūl′) a school for children three and four years old.

nursing home (nər′sing hōm′) a small hospital for old people who cannot look after themselves.

nur·ture (nər′chər) **1** raise; care for: *She nurtured the child as if he had been her own.* **2** the process of raising or caring for children. 1 *v.*, **nur·tured, nur·tur·ing;** 2 *n.*

nut (nut) **1** a dry fruit with a hard shell (**nutshell**) and a seed or kernel inside. Some nuts, such as walnuts and almonds, are good to eat; a **nutcracker** is a tool for cracking their shells. **2** a small piece of metal with a hole in the middle that screws on to the end of a bolt to hold it in place. **3** *Informal.* **a** someone silly or odd. **b** an enthusiastic fan: *a hockey nut.* **4** **nuts,** *Informal.* crazy: *That noise is driving me nuts. Trina is nuts about horses.* 1–3 *n.*, 4 *adj.* —**nut′ty,** *adj.*
in a nutshell, in a few words.

nut·meg (nut′meg′) a spice obtained by grating or grinding the seed of a tropical tree. *n.*

nu·tri·ent (nyū′trē ənt *or* nū′trē ənt) a substance, such as a mineral, vitamin, protein, etc., that is valuable to a living thing and forms part of its food. Nutrients give energy, maintain health, and help growth. *n.*

nu·tri·tion (nyū trish′ən *or* nū trish′ən) food; nourishment: *Good nutrition is necessary for health.* *n.* —**nu·tri′tious,** *adj.*

Nuu–chah–nulth (nu̇′chə nulth) **1** a First Nations people living mainly on Vancouver Island. **2** their language. **3** having to do with these people or their language. 1, 2 *n.*, 3 *adj.*

Nux·alk (nūks′əlk) **1** a First Nations people living in British Columbia. **2** their language. **3** having to do with these people or their language. 1, 2 *n.*, 3 *adj.*

nuz·zle (nuz′əl) poke, press, or rub with the nose: *The calf nuzzles its mother.* *v.*, **nuz·zled, nuz·zling.**

NW *abbreviation for* northwest or northwestern.

ny·lon (nī′lon) **1** an extremely strong plastic substance, used to make many things including clothing. **2** **nylons,** *pl.* pantyhose or stockings made of this. *n.*

nymph (nimf) **1** in Greek and Roman myths, a goddess of nature who lived in rivers, hills, woods, or trees. **2** an immature insect that looks like the adult but has no wings. Insects whose young become nymphs after hatching do not go through complete metamorphosis with a pupa stage the way butterflies do. *n.*

Oo

o or **O**[1] (ō) 1 the fifteenth letter of the English alphabet, or any sound that it stands for. The sound of *o* in *hope* is different from the sound of *o* in *hop*. 2 the fifteenth thing in a list. *n., pl.* **o's** or **O's.**

O[2] (ō) a word used before the name of a person or thing being called on or addressed: *O King, hear my plea! O Canada.* It is a poetic version of **oh.** *interj.*

oaf (ōf) somebody who is clumsy or rude. *n.* **—oaf′ish,** *adj.*

oak (ōk) a tree found in most parts of the world, that has nuts called **acorns** and hard, strong wood often used for building and for making furniture. *n.*

oar (ȯr) a long pole that ends in a broad, flat blade, used for rowing or steering a boat. A rowboat usually has a metal support on each side, called an **oarlock,** to hold the oar in place. *n.*

CONFUSABLES . . . . oar

oar means "paddle": *Don't drop the oar into the water.*

ore means "rock": *The miners dig for iron ore.*

o•a•sis (ō ā′sis) a spot in the desert where there is water and therefore also trees to give shade. *n., pl.* **o•a•ses** (ō ā′sēz).

oath (ōth) 1 a solemn promise to tell the truth, to be loyal, or to follow certain rules. If you break an oath, you may be punished by law. 2 a swear word. *n., pl.* **oaths** (ōᴛʜz *or* ōths).
under oath, bound by an oath: *The witness in court gave his evidence under oath.*

oats (ōts) a cereal grass whose seed is used to feed horses and to make breakfast food for people. **Oatmeal** is flattened oats that can be made into porridge. *pl.n.*

o•be•di•ent (ō bē′dē ənt) willing to obey; following orders or rules: *My dog is obedient and always comes when I call. adj.* **—o•be′di•ence,** *n.*

ob•e•lisk (ob′ə lisk) a four-sided stone pillar that gets narrower at the top and ends in a pyramid shape. The ancient Egyptians built obelisks as monuments. *n.*

o•bese (ō bēs′) so fat that it is unhealthy. *adj.* **—o•be′si•ty,** *n.*

o•bey (ō bā′) do what you are told to do; follow orders, rules, or laws: *The dog obeyed and stopped barking. A good citizen obeys the laws. v.*

o•bit•u•ar•y (ō bich′ū er′ē) a short newspaper article about the life of someone who has just died. *n., pl.* **o•bit•u•ar•ies.**

object (ob′jikt *for 1–4,* əb jekt′ *for 5 and 6)* 1 anything that can be seen or touched: *What is that black object by the fence?* 2 purpose; goal: *My object in coming here was to get her address.* The **object of the game** is what you try to do in order to win. 3 a person or thing that some feeling, thought, or action is directed at: *an object of study. Bob was the object of his dog's affection.* 4 in grammar, the person or thing that receives the action of the verb in a sentence, or that follows a preposition. In the sentence *Gilles threw the ball to his brother, ball* is the object of the verb *threw,* and *brother* is the object of the preposition *to.* 5 dislike or be against something: *Many people object to loud noise.* 6 give as a reason against something: *We were going to play outside but Dad objected that it was too wet.* 1–4 *n.,* 5, 6 *v.*

ob•jec•tion (əb jek′shən) 1 a reason given against something: *One objection to the new plan was that it would cost too much.* 2 a feeling of disapproval or dislike: *A lazy person has strong objections to working.* If you dislike or disapprove of something, you find it **objectionable.** *n.*

ob•jec•tive (əb jek′tiv) 1 a goal to work toward: *My objective this summer is to learn to use the computer.* 2 existing outside your mind as something real: *The outside world is objective; your idea of it is subjective.* 3 dealing with facts, not personal opinions or feelings; unbiassed: *Scientists must be objective in their experiments.* 4 in grammar, having to do with the object of a verb or preposition. *Me* is the objective form of *I.* 1 *n.,* 2–4 *adj.*

ob•li•gate (ob′lə gāt′) give someone the moral duty to do something: *If you promised to go, your promise obligates you to be there. v.,* **ob•li•gat•ed, ob•li•gat•ing.** **—ob′li•ga′tion,** *n.*

ob•lig•a•to•ry (ə blig′ə tȯr′ē) required: *Attendance at school is obligatory. adj.*

o•blige (ə blīj′) 1 require; force: *Drivers are obliged to stop at all red lights.* 2 do a favour for: *She obliged us by lending us her CD player.* Someone who willingly does favours or helps out is **obliging.** *v.,* **o•bliged, o•blig•ing.**

be obliged to someone, be grateful for a favour: *I am obliged to you for letting me stay at your house.*

ob·lique (ə blēk′) **1** slanting; not straight up and down or straight across: *an oblique line.* An **oblique angle** is any angle that is not a right angle. **2** not direct; not straightforward: *She made an oblique reference to her illness, but did not mention it directly.* *adj.*

ob·lit·er·ate (ə blit′ə rāt′) blot out; remove all traces of; destroy: *The heavy rain obliterated all footprints.* *v.,* **ob·lit·er·at·ed, ob·lit·er·at·ing.**

ob·liv·i·on (ə bliv′ē ən) **1** the condition of being entirely forgotten: *Many ancient cities have passed into oblivion.* **2** the condition of being unaware of what is going on: *We sat gazing at the fire in peaceful oblivion.* *n.*

ob·liv·i·ous (ə bliv′ē əs) forgetting or not noticing; unaware: *Concentrating on her Internet search, she was oblivious to her surroundings.* *adj.*

ob·nox·ious (əb nok′shəs) extremely rude: *He had few friends because he was so obnoxious.* *adj.*

o·boe (ō′bō) a wooden, tube-shaped instrument that you play by blowing through a double reed at the top. It has a very mellow tone. *n.*

ob·scene (əb sēn′) indecent and disgusting: *obscene language, obscene pictures. Their greed at every meal was obscene.* *adj.* **—ob·scen′i·ty** (əb sen′ə tē), *n.*

ob·scure (əb skyūr′) **1** hard to see, discover, or make out: *an obscure path.* **2** hard to understand; not clearly expressed: *This paragraph is a little obscure.* **3** not well-known; attracting no notice: *an obscure little village.* **4** hide or block; make unclear: *Clouds obscure the sun. The many long technical words obscured our understanding.* 1–3 *adj.,* **ob·scur·er, ob·scur·est;** 4 *v.,* **ob·scured, ob·scur·ing.** **—ob·scu′ri·ty,** *n.*

Observatories are usually built in high places, for a clear view of the sky.

ob·serv·a·to·ry (əb zėr′və tô′rē) a place for observing or studying the stars and the weather patterns. It has telescopes, measuring instruments, and so on. *n., pl.* **ob·serv·a·to·ries.**

ob·serve (əb zėrv′) **1** see and notice: *Did you observe anything strange in his behaviour?* A person who notices a lot of things is **observant. 2** watch or look at something in order to find out about it: *An astronomer observes the stars.* **3** remark; comment: *"Bad weather," the captain observed.* **4** keep; show attention to by your actions: *to observe Thanksgiving. All players must observe the rules.* *v.,* **ob·served, ob·serv·ing.** **—ob·serv′er,** *n.* **—ob′ser·va′tion,** *n.*

ob·sessed (əb sest′) always thinking about one thing, in an unhealthy way: *He is obsessed with hockey.* *n.* **—ob·ses′sion,** *n.* **—ob·ses′sive,** *adj.*

ob·so·lete (ob′sə lēt′) no longer used; out of date: *Typewriters are becoming obsolete.* *adj.*

ob·sta·cle (ob′stə kəl) something that blocks the way or makes it difficult to do something: *A tree fallen across the road was an obstacle to traffic. Not knowing the language was an obstacle in making friends.* An **obstacle course** is a route you have to follow in a race which includes fences, ditches, and other things to get over. *n.*

ob·ste·tri·cian (ob′stə trish′ən) a doctor who specializes in helping women give birth. **Obstetrics** (ob stet′riks) is the branch of medicine that deals with this. *n.* **—ob·stet′ri·cal** (ob stet′rə kəl), *adj.*

ob·sti·nate (ob′stə nit) stubborn; not giving in even when wrong: *I tried to talk her out of leaving, but she is so obstinate!* *adj.* **—ob′sti·na·cy** (ob′stə nə sē), *n.*

ob·struct (əb strukt′) block; be in the way of; hinder: *Those trees obstruct our view of the ocean. Prejudice obstructed their thinking.* *v.* **—ob·struc′tion,** *n.*

ob·tain (əb tān′) get: *We study to obtain knowledge. Where can I obtain a copy of that poster?* *v.*

ob·tuse (əb tyūs′ *or* əb tūs′) **1** greater than 90° but less than 180°: *an obtuse angle.* **2** thick-headed; stupid: *The boy was too obtuse to take the hint.* *adj.*

ob·vi·ous (ob′vē əs) so clear or plain that you can't help seeing or understanding it: *an obvious mistake.* *adj.*

oc·ca·sion (ə kā′zhən) **1** a particular time: *We have met Mr. Singh on several occasions.* **2** a special event: *Great-grandma's 90th birthday was a great occasion.* **3** a good chance; an opportunity: *The long trip gave us an occasion to get better acquainted.* **4** cause: *What's the occasion for all this fuss* (*n.*)*? Her odd behaviour occasioned a good deal of talk* (*v.*). 1–4 *n.,* 4 *v.*

on occasion, now and then; once in a while.

a bat	e bed	i bid	o pot	u cup	th thin
ā cake	ē me	ī bite	ō go	ū rude	ᴛʜ then
ä bar	ə about	ər over	ô for	ů put	zh measure

Oceans

The world's biggest ocean is the Pacific. It is twice the area of the Atlantic, and much deeper.

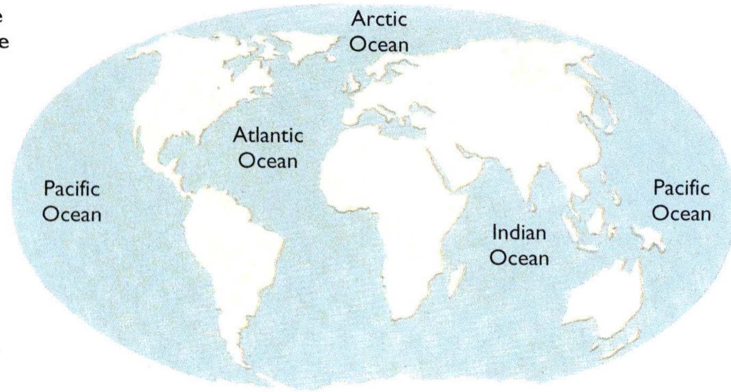

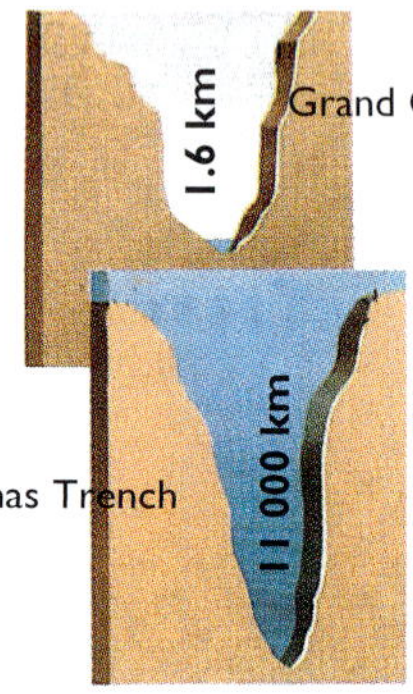

Valleys in the oceans can be very much deeper than valleys on the earth. The deepest ocean valley is the Marianas Trench — you could stack nearly 7000 Grand Canyons into it.

Ocean mountains are very tall. Mauna Kea, Hawaii, a peak that starts on the seabed, is taller than Mount Everest.

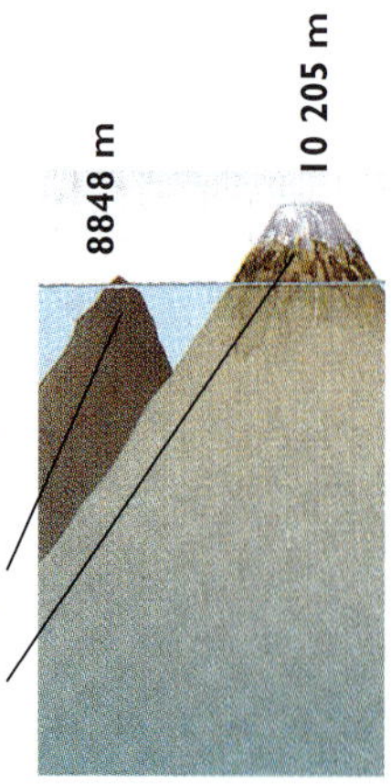

oc·ca·sion·al (ə kā′zhə nəl) happening or coming now and then: *We had fine weather all month except for an occasional shower.* *adj.* **—oc·ca′sion·al·ly,** *adv.*

oc·cu·pa·tion (ok′yə pā′shən) 1 one's business or employment; a trade: *Teaching is a teacher's occupation.* 2 the action of occupying: *the occupation of a town by the enemy, the occupation of a house by a family.* *n.*

oc·cu·py (ok′yə pī′) 1 be in; live in: *Two families occupy the house. A cat was occupying my favourite chair.* The person or thing occupying a place is the **occupant** (ok′yə pənt). 2 keep busy: *The problem continued to occupy her attention. Classes occupy the whole morning.* 3 **occupied,** **a** busy. **b** already being used by someone: *The bathroom is occupied; you'll have to wait.* 4 take over: *The enemy occupied our fort.* *v.,* **oc·cu·pied, oc·cu·py·ing.**

oc·cur (ə kėr′) 1 happen; take place: *Storms often occur in winter.* 2 be found; exist: *The letter "b" occurs twice in "bib."* 3 come to a person's mind: *He was cold but it never occurred to him to close the windows.* *v.,* **oc·curred, oc·cur·ring.** **—oc·cur′rence,** *n.*

o·cean (ō′shən) 1 the body of salt water that covers almost three-fourths of the earth's surface; the sea. The study of oceans and the creatures living in them is called **oceanography** (ō′shə nog′rə fē). 2 any of its five main divisions—the Atlantic, Pacific, Indian, Antarctic, or Arctic Ocean. *n.*
—o′ce·an′ic (ō′shē an′ ik), *adj.*

oc·e·lot (os′ə lot′) a rare spotted wildcat found from Texas to northern Argentina. *n.*

o'clock (ə klok′) a word used in telling the time when it is exactly on the hour: *It is one o'clock.*

oc·tave (ok′tiv) in music: **1** the distance of eight notes between one tone and the next tone: *From middle C to the C above is an octave.* Tones that are an octave apart are the first and last notes of a scale and sound like they "match." 2 these two tones played together. *n.*

Oc·to·ber (ok tō′bər) the tenth month of the year. October has 31 days. *n.*

Each of the octopus's eight arms has two rows of suckers which help it hold on to its prey.

oc·to·pus (ok′tə pəs) a sea animal that has a soft body and eight armlike **tentacles** with suckers on them. *n., pl.* **oc·to·pus·es** or **oc·to·pi** (ok′tə pī).

odd (od) **1** strange; unusual: *The little tree growing straight out of the side of the cliff was an odd sight.* An **oddball** is a strange person. **2** having a remainder of 1 when divided by 2: *The odd numbers are 1, 3, 5, 7, etc.* **3** occasional: *He does odd jobs around the store. We saw the odd squirrel, but no other wildlife.* **4** not matched up with a partner or set: *an odd sock in the wash.* **5** plus a few: *We still had twenty-odd kilometres to go.* **6 odds,** *pl.* **a** a difference in favour of one and against another; an advantage: *The odds are in our favour and we should win.* **b** likelihood; chance: *The odds of being hit by lightning are pretty low.* 1–5 *adj.,* 6 *pl.n.* **—odd′ly,** *adv.* **—odd′i·ty,** *n.*
at odds, quarrelling or disagreeing.
odds and ends, things left over; odd pieces; scraps.

ode (ōd) a dignified poem full of noble feeling, addressed to some person or thing. *n.*

o·di·ous (ō′dē əs) very unpleasant; hateful: *odious behaviour.* *adj.*

o·dom·e·ter (ə dom′ə tər) an instrument for measuring the distance a vehicle travels. *n.*

o·dour or **o·dor** (ō′dər) a smell: *the odour of roses, the odour of garbage.* *n.* **—o′dour·less** or **o′dor·less,** *adj.* **—o′dor·ous,** *adj.*

o'er (ȯr) in poetry, over. *prep. or adv.*

off (of) **1** away; away from the first or usual position: *to send off a letter, to drive off. Take off your coat.* **2** not on; not working, running, happening, etc.: *The power has been off all day. The trip is off—our plans fell through.* **3** free of work: *a day off.* **4** so as to leave clear: *to clean off your desk, to wipe off the counter.* **5** bad, wrong, or inaccurate: *Lack of rain made it an off year for farmers. I'm feeling a bit off—I think I'll lie down. These figures are off. His aim was off and the shot missed.* 1, 4 *adv.,* 2, 3, 5 *adj.*
be off, be on your way; leave: *I must be off now; goodbye!*
off and on, now and then: *He has been working off and on for ten months.*
off balance, not balanced. Before a noun the form is **off-balance.**
off chance, a slight chance: *I came on the off chance that I would find you here.*
off the cuff, without preparation: *It's hard to answer that off the cuff.* The adjective is **off-the-cuff:** *an off-the-cuff speech.*
off the wall, bizarre; zany. The form before a noun is **off-the-wall.**

USING WORDS .... off

Use **off** instead of the expression **off of** in sentences like this one: *Take your feet off the table.*

of·fence (ə fens′ *for 1, 2,* ō′fens *for 3*) **1** the act of breaking a law or rule: *The punishment for that offence is two years in prison.* **2** the act or fact of hurting someone's feelings or making someone angry: *I try not to cause offence. No offence was intended.* **3 a** the act of attacking or trying to score: *The team proved weak in offence.* **b** the player or players that do this on a team, or the position they play. **Offense** is another spelling for all the meanings of this word. *n.*
give offence, cause anger or hurt feelings.
take offence, become hurt or angry.

of·fend (ə fend′ *or* ō fend′) **1** hurt someone's feelings or make someone angry: *When they laughed at her accent, it offended her.* **2** break a rule; do wrong. *v.* **—of·fend′er,** *n.* **—of·fend′ing,** *adj.*

of·fen·sive (ə fen′siv) **1** hurtful or insulting; causing anger: *an offensive remark.* **2** very unpleasant: *an offensive odour.* **3** used for attack: *offensive weapons, an offensive strategy in a game.* **4** an attack: *An offensive against polio was begun when J. E. Salk developed a vaccine.* 1–3 *adj.,* 4 *n.*
take the offensive or **go on the offensive,** attack.

of·fer (of′ər) **1** hold out to be taken or refused; present: *to offer a gift. He offered a few suggestions.* **2** be willing; volunteer: *She offered to help us.* **3** give in worship: *to offer prayers, to offer sacrifices.* **4** try; attempt: *The thieves offered no resistance when arrested.* **5** the act of offering: *an offer of $190 000 for a house, many offers to help.* 1–4 *v.,* 5 *n.* **—of′fer·ing,** *n.*

off·hand (of′hand′) **1** on the spur of the moment; without thinking about it beforehand: *The carpenter could not tell offhand how much the work would cost* (*adv.*). *Her offhand remarks were often very funny* (*adj.*). **2** casual or informal: *an offhand manner.* 1 *adv.,* 1, 2 *adj.*

of·fice (of′is) **1** the room or building where a business person or professional does his or her work: *The principal's office is on the ground floor.* **2** a position with quite a lot of responsibility or authority: *The MP was appointed to the office of Minister of Defence.* **3** the people working in an office: *Half the office is on vacation.* *n.*

of·fi·cer (of′ə sər) **1** a person who commands others in the armed forces, such as a colonel, a lieutenant, or a captain. **2** a person who holds a position in the government, a church, a police force, etc.: *a police officer, a customs officer.* *n.*

a bat	e bed	i bid	o pot	u cup	th thin
ā cake	ē me	ī bite	ō go	ū rude	ᴛʜ then
ä bar	ə about	ər over	ȯ for	u̇ put	zh measure

of·fi·cial (ə fish′əl) **1** a person who holds a public position with some authority: *a high bank official. Health inspectors are government officials.* **2** belonging to such a position: *an official uniform.* **3** made or approved by the proper authority: *official town records of births and deaths, to play hockey according to official rules.* 1 *n.,* 2, 3 *adj.* **—of·fi′cial·ly,** *adv.*

off·line (of′līn′) not connected to a computer or done by computer, even though it normally is. A printer that is being repaired would be offline; if you had to write out a school project by hand because your computer was down, you would be doing your project offline. **Off-line** is another spelling. *adj. or adv.*

off·set (of′set′) make up for: *The better quality offset the higher price.* *v.,* **off·set, off·set·ting.**

off·shoot (of′shūt′) anything branching off from a main part, stem, group, etc.: *an offshoot of a plant, an offshoot of a mountain range.* *n.*

off·shore (of′shȯr′) off or away from the shore: *an offshore wind, offshore fisheries (adj.). The wind was blowing offshore (adv.).* *adv. or adj.*

off·spring (of′spring′) the young of a person, animal, or plant; descendant: *Every one of his offspring had red hair just like his own.* *n.*

off·stage (of′stāj′) **1** just behind or to the side of a stage, unseen by the audience of a play: *offstage lights (adj.). Sandy waited offstage for her cue to go on (adv.).* **2** to do with an actor's life outside the theatre: *Offstage, she is surprisingly shy (adv.).* *adj. or adv.*

of·ten (of′ən *or* of′tən) many times; frequently: *It snows often in the mountains.* **Oft** and **oftentimes** are poetic forms. *adv.*

✱ **O·go·po·go** (ō′gō pō′gō) a large snakelike monster that some people say lives in Lake Okanagan in British Columbia. *n.*

o·gre (ō′gər) in stories, a cruel giant or monster. *n.*

oh (ō) **1** a word used to express surprise, joy, grief, and other feelings: *Oh, no, my purse is gone! Oh, is that right? I was tired and, oh, how I longed to go home.* **2** a word used to call or address a person or thing: *Oh Caitlin, where are you?* **O** is the poetic form. *interj.*

oil (oil) **1** a thick, fatty, or greasy liquid that burns easily. It is lighter than water, and will not mix or dissolve in water but will dissolve in alcohol. Animal and vegetable oils, such as olive oil, are used in cooking and medicine. **2** petroleum, the thick, slippery, usually dark liquid found in the earth and used to make kerosene, gasoline, and other products, including plastic. **3** put oil on or in: *The mechanic oiled the wheels.* **4** paint made by grinding colouring matter in oil: *to paint with oils.* **5** a painting made with this paint: *an oil by a famous artist.* 1, 2, 4, 5 *n.,* 3 *v.* **—oil′y,** *adj.*
strike oil, a find oil by drilling a hole in the earth. A deposit of oil that is found and used is an **oil well. b** find something very profitable.

oil·cloth (oil′kloth′) a cloth made waterproof and glossy on one side by coating it with oil or plastic: *Oilcloth is used to cover shelves, tables, etc.* *n.*

✱ **oil sands** (oil′sandz′) a mixture of sand, clay, water, and oil, found especially in northern Alberta. Oil sands can be processed to give petroleum or oil.

oil·skins (oil′skinz′) a coat and pants for wearing in the rain, on a fishing boat, etc. made of oilcloth. *n.*

oint·ment (oint′mənt) a medicine made with oil or fat, used on the skin. **Salve** (sav) is another name for it. *n.*

OK or **O.K.** or **o·kay** (ō′kā′) *Informal.* **1** all right; acceptable: *The new schedule was OK (adj.). The car is working OK now (adv.).* **2** approve: *Get your parents to OK the plan first.* **3** approval: *The principal gave us his OK.* 1 *adj. or adv.,* 2 *v.,* **OK'd** or **O.K.'d** or **o·kayed, OK'ing** or **o·kay·ing;** 3 *n., pl.* **OK's** or **O.K.'s** or **o·kays.**

> **USING WORDS . . . . OK**
>
> **OK**, **O.K.**, and **okay** are all OK in informal speech and writing, but not suitable when you want to sound more formal. Okay?

O·ka·na·gan (ō′kə nȧ′gən) **1** a First Nations people living in southern British Columbia. **2** their language. **3** having to do with these people or their language. 1, 2 *n.,* 3 *adj.*

o·kra (ō′krə) a tall plant with sticky seed pods which are used as a vegetable and as a thickener for soups. *n.*

✱ **o·lal·lie** (ō la′lē) another name for the **salmonberry.**

old (ōld) **1** not young or new; having been or existed for some time: *old friends, an old idea, a crumbling old wall.* **2** of age; in age: *The baby is ten months old.* **3** past; no longer existing: *old civilizations.* **4** former; that became something else or was replaced: *Our old car was too small. Their home is actually an old schoolhouse!* *adj.,* **old·er** or **eld·er, old·est** or **eld·est.**
of old, of long ago: *heroes of old.*

old hand, an experienced person: *an old hand at playing chess.*
old hat, information that is already very familiar and so no longer interesting.
old school, those who believe in an older way of doing or thinking about something.

old·en (ōl′dən) a poetic word for "of long ago": *King Arthur lived in olden times.* *adj.*

old–fash·ioned (ōld′fash′ənd) following the styles or ways of an earlier time: *an old-fashioned dress, an old-fashioned housekeeper.* *adj.*

Old Testament (ōld′ tes′tə mənt) the first part of the Christian Bible, which contains the religious and social laws of the ancient Jews, a record of their history, their important literature, and writings of their prophets.

old–tim·er (ōld′tī′mər) *Informal.* a person who has lived or worked in a place or belonged to a group for a long time. *n.*

Old World (ōld′ wərld′) Europe, Asia, and Africa. The New World (North and South America) was given its name by the early European explorers.

Olive trees live longer than most other fruit trees. Some of the trees brought to North America from Spain in the 1700s are still alive.

ol·ive (ol′iv) **1** the fruit of a Mediterranean evergreen tree with grey-green leaves. Unripe green olives and ripe black olives are pickled and eaten, or pressed for their oil. An **olive branch** is a symbol of peace.
2 yellowish green or yellowish brown. 1, 2 *n.,* 2 *adj.*

O·lym·pic games (ō lim′pik gāmz′) **1** Usually, **Olympics,** *pl.,* an athletic competition held every four years in a different country, with athletes from all over the world competing. There are two years between the **Summer Olympics** and the **Winter Olympics.** The **Special Olympics** are for athletes with disabilities.
2 contests in athletics, poetry, and music, held every four years by the ancient Greeks.

om·e·lette or **om·e·let** (om′lit) eggs beaten with milk or water, cooked like a pancake, and folded over. Omelettes are sometimes filled with chopped meat, mushrooms, cheese, and so on. *n.*

o·men (ō′mən) a sign of what is to happen; an object or event that is believed to mean good or bad fortune: *Spilling salt is said to be a bad omen.* *n.*

om·i·nous (om′ə nəs) unfavourable; threatening, as if it were a sign of bad things to come: *The watchdog gave an ominous growl.* *adj.*

o·mit (ō mit′) leave out: *You omitted a word in that sentence.* *v.,* **o·mit·ted, o·mit·ting.** —**o·mis′sion,** *n.*

om·nip·o·tent (om nip′ə tənt) having all power: *an omnipotent ruler.* *adj.* —**om·nip′o·tence,** *n.*

om·nis·cient (om nish′ənt) knowing everything. One way of telling a story is with an **omniscient narrator,** a narrator who seems to know everything about every character. *adj.* —**om·nis′cience,** *n.*

om·ni·vore (om′nə vôr′) a creature that eats both plants and other animals: *Human beings are omnivores.* *n.* —**om·niv′o·rous,** *adj.*

on (on) **1** supported by something, attached to it, or covering it: *This book is on the table. There's new paint on the ceiling and fresh paper on the walls.* **2** about: *a book on animals.* **3** at the edge of: *a house on the lake. He lives on the next street.* **4** farther; longer; more: *March on. They read on for another ten pages.* **5** running, working, happening, etc.: *The race is on. All the lights are still on.* **6** right after: *They greeted us on our arrival. On completing each unit we have a test.* **7** forward in time: *later on, from that day on.* 1–3, 6 *prep.,* 4, 7 *adv.,* 5 *adj.*
and so on, and more of the same.
on and off, now and then: *It rained on and off all day.*
on and on, without stopping: *He talked on and on.*

once (wuns) **1** one time: *Read it once more.* **2** at some time in the past: *That big man was once a little baby.* **3** if ever; when; after: *Most people like to swim, once they have learned how.* 1, 2 *adv.,* 3 *conj.*
all at once, **a** suddenly: *All at once the music stopped.* **b** all at the same time.
at once, **a** immediately: *You must come at once.* **b** at the same time: *All three boys spoke at once.*
once and for all or **once for all,** finally; permanently: *Let's settle this once and for all.*
once in a while, very occasionally; now and then: *We see our cousins from Saskatchewan once in a while.*
once upon a time, long ago. This phrase is the usual beginning for a fairy tale.

a bat	e bed	i bid	o pot	u cup	th thin
ā cake	ē me	ī bite	ō go	ū rude	ᴛʜ then
ä bar	ə about	ər over	ô for	u̇ put	zh measure

one (wun) **1** the number 1: *One egg, please (adj.). I only want one (n.). One of my friends was there (pron.).* **2** a particular person or thing: *I like the ones in that box.* **3** some: *One day he'll be sorry.* **4** joined together; united: *He dreams of the day when all Canadians will be one.* **5** any person, standing for people in general: *One can easily get lost here.* 1, 2 *n.,* 1, 3, 4 *adj.,* 1, 5 *pron.* **—one′ness,** *n.* **—one·self′,** *pron.*
all one, all the same: *It's all one to me; I don't care.*
at one, in harmony: *to live at one with nature.*
one by one, one after another: *They left one by one.*
one or two, a few.

Word Family......... one

one-piece: made up of only one piece
one-shot: happening only once
one-track: thinking of only one thing
one-way: with movement in only one direction

O·nei·da (ō nī′də) **1** a First Nations people living in Ontario. **2** their language. **3** having to do with these people or their language. 1, 2 *n.,* 3 *adj.*

one–sid·ed (wun′sī′did) **1** seeing only one side of a question; biassed: *That's a very one-sided explanation.* **2** uneven; unequal: *The game was a little one-sided because the other team was so much better.* *adj.*

on·go·ing (on′gō′ing *or* on′gō′ing) continuing to happen: *an ongoing problem.* *adj.*

The bulb of an onion is made up of tightly packed layers containing a kind of oil. Cutting the onion releases fumes from this oil, and that's what makes your eyes water.

on·ion (un′yən) a vegetable that grows a thick bulb at its base. Onions are eaten raw or cooked, often as a seasoning. They have a sharp, strong smell and taste. *n.*

on·line (on′līn′) connected to or controlled by a computer: *You can do your research online using the Internet (adv.). My dad's business is finally online (adj.).* **On-line** is another spelling. *adj. or adv.*

on·look·er (on′lůk′ər) a spectator; a person who watches without taking part. *n.*

on·ly (ōn′lē) **1** existing by itself or themselves, with no other ones: *Maggie and Jan are their only children. This is the only road home.* **2** just; not as much, as big, as late, as long ago, etc. as might be expected: *He sold only two. She was in Europe only last week.* **3** and no one else; and nothing more: *Only he remained. I did it only through friendship.* **4** but: *We had camped right beside a stream, only the water was not fit to drink.* 1 *adj.,* 2, 3 *adv.,* 4 *conj.*
if only, I wish: *If only the sun would come out!*
one and only, an expression that emphasizes uniqueness.
only too, very: *She was only too glad to help us.*

USING WORDS.......... only

Be careful where you put **only** in a sentence. It should go as close as possible to the word it modifies. Look at how the meaning of the following sentence changes when **only** is moved to different positions:
Only he lifts heavy weights with his left hand.
He lifts only heavy weights with his left hand.
He lifts heavy weights with only his left hand.

on·o·mat·o·poe·ia (on′ə mat′ə pē′ə) **1** the process in many languages of making words that sound like the thing they stand for. The words *bang, click, hiss, whack,* and *buzz* are examples of onomatopoeia. **2** the use of this kind of word in speaking or writing to create a more vivid effect. *Example: a clucking, cheeping, quacking, mooing, baaing, meowing barnyard.* This description is more vivid than just *a noisy barnyard.* *n.*

On·on·da·ga (on′ən dȯ′gə) **1** a First Nations people living in southern Ontario. **2** their language. **3** having to do with these people or their language. 1, 2 *n.,* 3 *adj.*

on·set (on′set′) the beginning of some condition: *the onset of a disease, the onset of winter.* *n.*

on·shore (on′shȯr′) toward the shore: *an onshore wind (adj.). The wind was blowing onshore (adv.).* *adj. or adv.*

on·slaught (on′slot′) a vigorous attack: *The pirates made an onslaught on the ship.* *n.*

on·stage (on′stāj′) **1** on or onto the stage, where people can see: *onstage lights (adj.), to walk onstage (adv.).* **2** performing in a concert or play. *adj. or adv.*

On·tar·i·o (on ter′ē ō) a central province of Canada, between Manitoba and Québec. *n.* **—On·tar′i·an,** *n.*

on·to (on′tū) so as to be on; to a position on: *to throw a ball onto the roof, to get onto a horse, a boat driven onto the rocks.* *prep.*

on·ward (on′wərd) further forward: *an onward movement* (*adj.*). *The army marched onward* (*adv.*). **Onwards** is another form for the adverb. *adv. or adj.*

oo·dles (ū′dəlz) *Informal.* lots of something: *We put oodles of sauce on the pasta.* *pl.n.*

ooze[1] (ūz) leak little by little: *Blood oozed from her scraped knee. His courage oozed away.* *v.,* **oozed, ooz·ing.**

ooze[2] (ūz) soft mud or slime, such as at the bottom of a pond or river. *n.*

o·pal (ō′pəl) a precious stone found in many varieties and colours. Some stones even show a peculiar rainbow play of colours. *n.*

o·paque (ō pāk′) **1** not letting any light through; impossible to see through: *The opaque curtains kept the room in darkness.* **2** impossible to understand: *This author's writing is opaque.* *adj.*

o·pen (ō′pən) **1** not shut; not closed or locked: *The open windows let in the fresh air. Just walk in; the house is open.* **2** not closed in: *the open sea, an open fire.* **3** not blocked by anything: *The way is open.* In the case of water, **open** often means "not blocked by ice." **4** **the open,** wide, clear space outdoors; fresh air: *City people like to get out in the open.* **5** giving and receiving or speaking and listening freely, without holding back: *an open heart, an open mind, an open discussion.* **6** not hidden or secret: *open war, open disregard of rules.* **7** that may be entered, shared, etc. by all: *an open meeting, an open competition. The club is open to anyone who wants to join.* **8** unfilled; not taken: *The job in the bank is still open.* **9** make or become open: *to open your mouth, to open a path through the woods. The door opened easily.* **10** start or set up: *to open a new store, to open a bank account.* **11** provide an entrance or a view: *The window opens onto the garden.* 1–3, 5–8 *adj.,* 4 *n.,* 9–11 *v.* **—o′pen·ly,** *adv.*

open a person's eyes, make a person see the truth.

open out, unfold; spread out: *to open out a map.*

open question, a question that is not settled or has more than one possible answer.

open secret, something that is supposed to be secret but is known by all.

open sesame, magic words to open a door, from the story of *Ali Baba and the Forty Thieves.*

open to, **a** ready to take; willing to consider: *open to suggestions.* **b** likely to get: *open to infection.*

open up, **a** make or become completely open. **b** make a way to a place and develop it: *The early settlers opened up the West.* **c** begin talking and being friendly with others.

the open air, the outdoors: *Children like to play in the open air.* The adjective is **open-air:** *an open-air concert.*

open house (ō′pən hous′) **1** a time when a school or other institution is open for the public to visit. **2** a party or other social event that is open to all who wish to come. People come and go at any time between the beginning and end.

o·pen·ing (ō′pə ning) **1** an open space; a gap or hole: *an opening in a wall, an opening in the forest.* **2** beginning: *the opening of a new theatre* (*n.*), *the speaker's opening remarks* (*adj.*). **3** an opportunity, especially a job or position that is available: *an opening for a teller in a bank.* 1–3 *n.,* 2 *adj.*

o·pen–mind·ed (ō′pən mīn′did) willing to listen to ideas that are new or that are different from your own. *adj.*

op·er·a (op′ə rə) a play that is mostly sung, usually with costumes, scenery, and an orchestra: *"Carmen" is a popular opera.* A theatre for operas is an **opera house.** *n.*

op·er·ate (op′ə rāt′) **1** work; run: *The machinery operates night and day. This company operates three factories.* **2** have an effect: *Several causes operated to bring on the war. The medicine operated quickly.* **3** in medicine, treat the body by cutting into it in order to repair or take out some diseased or injured part: *The doctor operated on the injured man.* *v.,* **op·er·at·ed, op·er·at·ing.**

op·er·a·tion (op′ə rā′shən) **1** the act, fact, or way of working or running: *The operation of a business takes a lot of hard work.* **2** a treatment for injury or disease that involves cutting into the body to repair or take out a part: *Taking out a diseased appendix is a common operation.* **3** business; activity: *Moving is a pretty complicated operation.* **4** a planned effort by soldiers, police, secret agents, etc., to achieve some purpose; mission: *a rescue operation. "Operation Nut Fudge" was the code name of the spy mission.* **5** something done to a number or quantity in mathematics. Addition, subtraction, multiplication, and division are the four commonest operations. *n.*

in operation, running; working. Another word for this is **operational.**

op·er·a·tor (op′ə rā′tər) a skilled worker who operates a machine, especially a telephone switchboard or computer. *n.*

a bat	e bed	i bid	o pot	u cup	th thin
ā cake	ē me	ī bite	ō go	ū rude	ᴛʜ then
ä bar	ə about	ər over	ô for	ů put	zh measure

oph·thal·mol·o·gist (of′thal mol′ə jist) a doctor who treats diseases and disorders of the eye. *n.*

USING WORDS . . . ophthalmologist

An **ophthalmologist**, an **optometrist**, and an **optician** all look after people's eyes. Only an ophthalmologist can treat diseases of the eye. An optometrist tests people's eyes and prescribes glasses or contact lenses, which are then made and sold by an optician.

o·pin·ion (ə pin′yən) what a person thinks about something; a personal belief or judgment: *Learn the facts and form your own opinions. What is your opinion of her artwork?* Someone who is pushy or stubborn about his or her opinions is **opinionated** (ə pin′yə nā′tid). *n.*

o·pos·sum (ə pos′əm) a small animal that lives most of the time in trees, is active at night, and carries its young in a pouch. When frightened, it becomes unconscious and appears to be dead. *n.*

op·po·nent (ə pō′nənt) a person who is against you in a fight, game, contest, or argument: *He defeated his opponent in the election.* *n.*

op·por·tu·ni·ty (op′ər tyū′nə tē *or* op′ər tū′nə tē) a good chance to do something: *I had an opportunity to earn some money picking blueberries.* **Opportune** means "coming at a convenient time." *n., pl.* **op·por·tu·ni·ties.**

op·pose (ə pōz′) stand, act, or fight against: Many workers opposed the strike. *v.,* **op·posed, op·pos·ing.**
as opposed to, in contrast to.
opposed to, against: *I'm opposed to longer school hours.*

op·po·site (op′ə sit) 1 as far different as can be: *opposite opinions. North and south are opposite directions.* 2 a thing or person as far different as can be: *Sour is the opposite of sweet.* 3 placed face to face or back to back: *Look at the opposite page.* 4 directly across from: *opposite the church.* 1, 3 *adj.,* 2 *n.,* 4 *prep.*

op·po·si·tion (op′ə zish′ən) 1 the act or fact of standing or acting against a person or thing: *In spite of stiff opposition, they succeeded.* 2 the people on the other side in a debate or contest; especially, **Opposition,** the political party with the second largest number of members elected to Parliament. *n.*

op·press (ə pres′) 1 keep down unjustly or cruelly: *Good government does not oppress the poor.* 2 be a heavy burden on: *Fear oppresses the soul.* *v.*
—op·pres′sor, *n.* **—op·pres′sion,** *n.*
—op·pres′sive, *adj.*

opt (opt) choose or decide: *The class opted to go on a field trip.* *v.*
opt out of, choose not to take part in something.

op·ti·cian (op tish′ən) a person who makes and sells glasses and contact lenses according to the prescription of an optometrist or an ophthalmologist. *n.*

op·tics (op′tiks) the science that deals with light and seeing and the instruments that help us see. *sing.n.* **—op′ti·cal,** *adj.*

op·ti·mism (op′tə miz′əm) a hopeful attitude; a tendency to see the bright side. *n.* **—op′ti·mist,** *n.* **—op′ti·mis′tic,** *adj.*

op·ti·mum (op′tə məm) the best or most suitable for some purpose: *The greenhouse had the optimum light, temperature, and moisture for orchids* (*adj.*). *Eight hours of sleep a night is the optimum for most adults* (*n.*). *adj. or n.*

op·tion (op′shən) choice: *We have no option but to tell the truth.* Something that you may choose to do or not to do is **optional.** *n.*

op·tom·e·trist (op tom′ə trist) a person who examines eyes and recommends the kind of glasses or contact lenses needed. *n.*

–or *a suffix meaning* a person or thing that. *Actor* means "a person who acts." A *generator* is a machine that generates electricity.

or·a·cle (ȯr′ə kəl) 1 in ancient times, a message given by a god through a priest. 2 the place where the god gave messages, or the priest who received them. *n.*

o·ral (ȯr′əl) 1 spoken: *an oral quiz.* 2 having to do with your mouth: *oral hygiene.* *adj.* **—o′ral·ly,** *adv.*

Oranges probably originated in Asia. They were brought to North America by Christopher Columbus in 1493.

or·ange (ȯr′inj) 1 a round, sweet, juicy fruit related to lemons and grapefruits. It has a thick peel and grows on a small evergreen tree in warm climates. 2 the colour made by mixing red and yellow. 1, 2 *n.,* 2 *adj.*

o·rang·u·tan (ə rang′ə tan′) a large ape of the forests of south Asia. It has very long arms and reddish brown hair. Orangutans live mostly in trees and eat fruits and leaves. **Orangoutang** is another spelling. *n.*

or·a·tor (ȯr′ə tər) a person who is skilled in public speaking. The art of public speaking is called **oratory** (ȯr′ə tȯr′ē), and a formal speech is an **oration.** *n.*

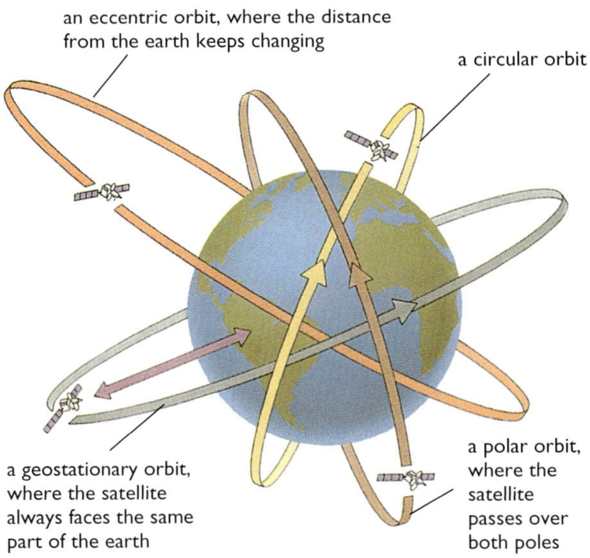

or·bit (ȯr′bit) **1** the curved path of a moon, planet, or satellite around another body in space: *the earth's orbit around the sun.* **2** travel in an orbit: *The satellite is orbiting around the earth.* 1 *n.,* 2 *v.*

or·chard (ȯr′chərd) a piece of land planted with fruit trees: *an apple orchard.* *n.*

or·ches·tra (ȯr′kis trə) **1** a large group of musicians who play together on various instruments, usually including stringed instruments. **2** the part of a theatre just in front of the stage, where the musicians sit to play. **3** the main floor of a theatre, especially the part near the front: *Buy two seats in the orchestra.* *n.* **—or·ches′tral** (ȯr kes′trəl), *adj.*

or·chid (ȯr′kid) a plant whose flower has three sepals and three petals. One petal is differently shaped and often brightly coloured. *n.*

or·deal (ȯr dēl′) a severe test or very difficult experience: *the ordeal of being lost in the snowstorm.* *n.*

or·der (ȯr′dər) **1** command: *The orders of the captain must be obeyed* (*n.*). *She ordered us to leave* (*v.*). **2** make a request for something you want to buy: *Please order dinner for me. You can order this kit from the catalogue.* **3** the request itself, or the thing requested: *We phoned in an order for a large pizza. Our order arrived 30 minutes later.* **4** the way one thing follows another: *in order of size, in alphabetical order.* **5** a condition where every part or piece is in its right place, things happen according to a regular pattern, or people act in a reasonable, organized way: *to put a room in order. There is order in nature. Let's bring some order to this situation.* **6** the condition in which laws or rules are obeyed and there is no trouble: *The police officer tried hard to keep order.* **7** put in proper condition; arrange: *to order your affairs.* **8** a title that accompanies some honour, such as a medal for bravery: *the Order of Merit, the Order of Canada.* **9** a group of people sharing certain aims, values, or rules for living: *the Franciscan order of nuns.* **10** a scientific grouping of plants or animals, bigger than a **family** and smaller than a **class.** Carnivores are an order within the class of mammals. 1, 3–10 *n.,* 2 *v.*
by order, according to an order given by an authority: *by order of the Premier.*
call to order, ask people to be quiet and pay attention: *She called the meeting to order.*
in order, **a** in the right arrangement or condition. **b** needed: *An apology is in order.*
in order to or **in order that,** having as a purpose: *She worked hard in order to win the prize. In order that everyone may have a chance, let's take turns.*
in short order, quickly: *The car was fixed in short order.*
on order, ordered but not yet received.
out of order, **a** in the wrong condition. **b** rude, unfair, or unsuitable: *That remark was out of order.*
tall order, something hard to do.
to order, just as the buyer wishes: *furniture built to order.*

ordered pair (ȯr′dərd pãr) in mathematics, two numbers given in a certain order to identify a point in a plane.

or·der·ly (ȯr′dər lē) **1** in order; following a regular arrangement, method, or system: *orderly bookshelves, an orderly mind.* **2** well behaved and following the rules: *an orderly class.* **3** a hospital worker who keeps things clean and tidy. 1, 2 *adj.,* 3 *n., pl.* **or·der·lies.**

ordinal number (ȯr′də nəl num′bər) a number that shows order or position in a series. *First, second, third, fourth* are ordinal numbers. ▶ See Appendix.

or·di·nar·y (ȯr′də ner′ē) **1** usual; common; normal: *It was an ordinary day—nothing special happened.* **2** not very good: *The story was ordinary and poorly told.* *adj.* **—or′di·nar′i·ly** (ȯr′də nər′ə lē), *adv.*
out of the ordinary, unusual; not regular.

a bat	e bed	i bid	o pot	u cup	th thin
ā cake	ē me	ī bite	ō go	ū rude	ᴛʜ then
ä bar	ə about	ər over	ȯ for	ů put	zh measure

ore (ôr) mineral or rock containing a valuable substance such as metal: *Iron ore is mined and worked to get the iron it contains.* *n.*

or·gan (ôr′gən) 1 a musical instrument with a keyboard, pedals, and pipes of different lengths. The tones are made by air blowing through the pipes. 2 a similar instrument, but with the sound produced electronically. 3 part of an animal or plant designed to perform a certain task. The eyes, heart, and lungs are human organs. Stamens and pistils are organs of flowers. *n.* **—or′gan·ist,** *n.*

or·gan·ic (ôr gan′ik) 1 having to do with the organs of the body: *an organic disease.* 2 having to do with or obtained from plants or animals rather than chemicals: *organic fertilizer.* **Organic farming** uses only organic fertilizer, and no pesticides. 3 made up of related parts that form a unit, especially one thought of as being alive in some way: *Canada is an organic whole.* *adj.*

or·gan·ism (ôr′gə niz′əm) 1 a living body with an organized structure; an individual animal or plant. 2 a system of related parts that form a unit, especially one thought of as being alive in some way: *A community may be spoken of as a social organism.* *n.*

or·gan·i·za·tion (ôr′gə nī zā′shən) 1 a group of people united for some purpose, with rules and leaders, and jobs assigned to various people. Churches, companies, and political parties are organizations. 2 the act, fact, or way of organizing: *The organization of a big picnic takes time and thought.* *n.*

or·gan·ize (ôr′gə nīz′) 1 cause to act together as a whole, with each one doing his or her part: *The general organized his soldiers into a powerful force.* 2 plan and lead; get something started: *The explorer organized an expedition to the North Pole.* 3 arrange in a system; put in order: *She organized her thoughts. He organized his stamp collection.* *v.,* **or·gan·ized, or·gan·iz·ing.**

o·reg·a·no (ə reg′ə nō) a seasoning made from the dried leaves of a herb related to mint. It is often used in Greek and Italian dishes. *n.*

o·ri·ent (ô′rē ent′) 1 figure out where you are and what you should be doing; adjust to a situation: *She used the huge tree as a landmark to orient herself. It took me a while to get oriented in my new school.* Newcomers often go through a program called **orientation** to help them become familiar with a new place, new routines, and so on. 2 face or aim a certain way: *The building is oriented north and south. The art classes are oriented toward younger children.* 3 **the Orient,** an old word for the Far East, the easternmost parts of Asia. The adjective is **Oriental.** *v.*

or·i·en·teer·ing (ôr′ē ən tēr′ing) the skill of finding your way through unfamiliar territory using a map or compass. Sometimes it is done as a sport or race, with a starting and finishing point and a series of checkpoints in between. *n.*

WORD HISTORY..... orienteering

In Latin, *orientis* meant "rising." The Orient is in the direction of the rising sun, which provides a good way to orient yourself, that is, to find out which way you are facing. So, **orienteering** is finding your way.

or·i·ga·mi (ôr′i gam′ē) the art of folding paper in the shape of various objects, without using glue or scissors. *n.*

or·i·gin (ôr′ə jin) the beginning; the starting point; where a thing or person comes from: *Nobody remembered the origin of the quarrel. The song is of Brazilian origin.* 2 the point on a graph where the *x* axis and *y* axis meet. It is usually numbered 0. *n.*

o·rig·i·nal (ə rij′ə nəl) 1 first; earliest: *The CD player has been marked down from its original price.* 2 fresh; not done or thought of before; not copied: *to come up with original ideas. She wrote an original poem.* 3 inventive; able to come up with new things: *An inventor has an original mind.* 4 anything that something else is copied or translated from: *The original of this picture is in Rome.* 1–3 *adj.,* 4 *n.* **—o·rig′i·nal·ly,** *adv.* **—o·rig′i·nal′i·ty** (ə rij′ə nal′ə tē), *n.*

o·rig·i·nate (ə rij′ə nāt′) come or bring into being; start: *to originate a new style of painting. Where did that story originate?* *v.,* **o·rig·i·nat·ed, o·rig·i·nat·ing.** **—o·rig′i·na′tor,** *n.*

o·ri·ole (ôr′ē əl *or* ôr′ē ōl′) a colourful North American songbird. The male has a black back and a yellow, orange, or reddish brown underside. *n.*

This is an example of an ornate ornament, made of gold and decorated with jewels.

or·na·ment (ôr′nə mənt *for 1,* ôr′nə ment′ *for 2*) 1 a decoration; something to add beauty: *Lace, jewels, vases, and statues are ornaments.* 2 add beauty to; decorate: *A single brooch ornamented her dress.* 1 *n.,* 2 *v.* **—or′na·men′tal,** *adj.*

or•nate (ȯr nāt′) very fancy; very highly decorated: *She liked ornate furniture.* *adj.*

or•ner•y (ȯr′nə rē) *Informal.* mean and stubborn: *an ornery person.* *adj.*

or•ni•thol•o•gy (ȯr′nə thol′ə jē) the scientific study of birds. *n.* **—or′ni•thol′o•gist,** *n.*

or•phan (ȯr′fən) **1** a child whose parents are dead. A home for the care of orphans is an **orphanage** (ȯr′fə nij). **2** make an orphan of: *A car accident orphaned her when she was five years old.* 1 *n.*, 2 *v.*

or•tho•don•tist (ȯr′thə don′tist) a dentist who specializes in straightening and adjusting teeth. *n.* **—or′tho•don′tic,** *adj.*

or•tho•dox (ȯr′thə doks′) accepted as proper or correct; agreeing with tradition or authority: *orthodox teachings in religion. The new babysitter was not very orthodox—he let us stay up till midnight.* *adj.*

Orthodox Church (or′thə doks′ chərch′) a group of Christian churches that started in eastern Europe and western Asia, led by the patriarch of Constantinople.

or•tho•pe•dic (ȯr′thə pē′dik) helping to correct or prevent problems that affect the bones and joints of the body: *orthopedic shoes, orthopedic surgery.* *adj.*

os•mo•sis (oz mō′sis) **1** the gradual process of a liquid passing through a thin piece of plant or animal tissue. Nutrients dissolved in liquid pass through cell walls by osmosis. **2** the process of learning something very gradually without being taught, just by hearing or seeing it so often: *Jackie learned French by osmosis.* *n.*

os•trich (os′trich) a large bird of Africa, the largest living bird. It can run very fast but cannot fly. *n.*

oth•er (uᴛʜ′ər) **1** remaining: *Don is here, but the other boys are at school.* **2** additional: *I have no other books with me.* **3** different or differently from this: *Come some other day (adj.). I could not do other than I did (adv.).* **4** some other person or thing: *She helps others.* 1–3 *adj.*, 3 *adv.*, 4 *pron.*
every other, every second: *We have spelling every other day.*
none other than, no one else but: *The presentation was made by none other than the Prime Minister.*
other than, apart from; except: *Other than Jimi, no one knew about it.*
the other day, night, etc. recently.

oth•er•wise (uᴛʜ′ər wīz′) **1** or else; if not: *Come at once; otherwise you will be too late.* **2** apart from that: *He is noisy, but otherwise very nice.* **3** different or differently: *It might have been otherwise (adj.) We could not do otherwise (adv.).* 1 *conj.*, 2, 3 *adv.*, 3 *adj.*

Ot•ta•wa (ot′ə wo′ *or* ot′ə wə) **1** a First Nations people living in southern Ontario. **2** their language. **3** having to do with these people or their language. 1, 2 *n.*, 3 *adj.*

ot•ter (ot′ər) a fish-eating animal of the weasel family. The otter is a good swimmer and has a long body, small ears, and webbed feet with claws. It was widely trapped for its short, thick, glossy, brown fur. *n.*, *pl.* **ot•ters** or **ot•ter.**

ouch (ouch) an exclamation of pain. *interj.*

ought (ot) a slightly more formal word for "should": *You ought to write her a thank-you note.* *v.*

ounce (ouns) **1** a nonmetric unit of weight. One ounce equals one-sixteenth of a pound (about 28 g). **2** a non-metric unit of volume for liquids, equal to about 28 mL. **3** a little bit; a very small amount: *He hadn't an ounce of strength left after moving all the furniture.* *n.*

-ous *a suffix* used to make adjectives. It can be added to nouns, as in *joyous* or *scandalous,* sometimes with minor spelling changes as in *nervous, miraculous, marvellous,* and *blasphemous.*

oust (oust) force out; drive out: *The sparrows have ousted the bluebirds from their nest.* *v.*

out (out) **1** away from a place inside: *The water rushed out. She went out to play. My dad is out right now.* **2** not in fashion or power: *That style of dress is out. The Conservatives are out—they lost the election.* **3** not burning or shining: *The fire is out.* **4** into the public or into the open, so as to be seen or heard: *Speak out. A new film has come out.* **5** completely: *tired out.* **6** to others: *Give out the books. They rent out their cottage.* **7** wrong: *Your figures are out.* **8** not allowed or not possible: *Quitting is out; you must keep trying.* **9** not in play according to the rules of a game: *That ball was out. If I touch you, you're out.* **10** from among members of a group: *Pick out something you like.* *adj. or adv.*
out of, **a** from inside: *He came out of the house.* **b** not in: *She is out of the hospital now.* **c** away from; beyond the limits of: *40 km out of Calgary. The sun faded out of sight.* **d** without: *He is out of work. We are out of coffee.* **e** from: *It is made out of tin. We picked our puppy out of that litter.* **f** because of: *I went only out of curiosity.*
out of date, too old or old-fashioned: *This software is out of date.* Before a noun, the form is **out-of-date.**
out of the way, away from where most people go; isolated. Before a noun, the form is **out-of-the-way:** *We found a motel in a little out-of-the-way place called Sharon Harbour.*

a bat	e bed	i bid	o pot	u cup	th thin
ā cake	ē me	ī bite	ō go	ū rude	ᴛʜ then
ä bar	ə about	ər over	ȯ for	ů put	zh measure

out– *a prefix meaning:* **1** outward, forth, or away, as in *outburst, outgoing.* **2** farther away; beyond some limit, as in *outfield, outlying.* **3** more than, longer than, better than, etc., as in *outlive, outnumber, outdo, outrun.*

out–and–out (out′ən out′) thorough; complete: *an out-and-out lie. adj.*

out·back (out′bak′) in Australia, the areas far away from cities and towns. *n.*

out·board motor (out′bôrd′ mō′tər) a small motor attached to the back of a boat on the outside. The motor turns a propeller which can be moved from side to side to drive the boat in any direction.

out·break (out′brāk′) a sudden burst of activity or feeling or spread of a disease: *outbreaks of rebellion, an outbreak of measles. n.*

out·build·ing (out′bil′ding) a shed, barn, outhouse or other building built near a main building. *n.*

out·burst (out′bėrst′) the act or fact of bursting forth: *an outburst of laughter, an outburst of anger. n.*

out·cast (out′kast′) **1** a person or animal shut out from home, friends, etc.: *Criminals are outcasts of society. That kitten was a tiny outcast when Jamie found it.* **2** homeless or friendless; not wanted. 1 *n.,* 2 *adj.*

out·come (out′kum′) a result; how something ends up: *the outcome of a race. n.*

out·crop·ping (out′krop′ing) a rocky part sticking up in an area that is mostly not rocky. *n.*

out·cry (out′krī′) **1** a strong protest: *The decision to close the library caused a public outcry.* **2** a sudden loud cry or scream. *n., pl.* **out·cries.**

out·dat·ed (out dā′tid) out of date; old-fashioned: *The typewriter is outdated.* **Outmoded** has a similar meaning. *adj.*

out·dis·tance (out dis′təns) leave behind in a race: *She outdistanced all the other runners and won the race. v.,* **out·dis·tanced, out·dis·tanc·ing.**

out·do (out dū′) do more or better than; surpass: *Alex can outdo everyone else in swimming. v.,* **out·did, out·done, out·do·ing.**
outdo yourself, do the most or best you've ever done.

out·doors (out′dôrz′) **1** outside in the open air; not indoors: *We can't go outdoors until it stops raining.* **2** the world outside of buildings; the open air: *Our family enjoys the outdoors.* 1 *adv.,* 2 *n.* **—out′door′,** *adj.*

out·er (ou′tər) **1** of or on the outside: *The outer door is locked.* **2** farther out; farther from the centre: *the outer suburbs of the city. adj.* **—out′er·most′,** *adj.*

outer space (ou′tər spās′) the space beyond the earth's atmosphere: *The moon, stars, and planets are in outer space. n.*

out·field (out′fēld′) in baseball, the part of the field outside the diamond or infield, or the three players who play there. *n.* **—out′field′er,** *n.*

out·fit (out′fit) **1** a matching set of clothes. **2** a special suit of clothes and gear needed for some activity: *a scuba-diving outfit.* **3** equip with everything needed for some activity, especially camping, hiking, canoeing, etc.: *He outfitted himself for camp.* An **outfitter** is a store selling this kind of equipment. **4** an organization: *What outfit does she work for?* 1, 2, 4 *n.,* 3 *v.,* **out·fit·ted, out·fit·ting.**

out·go·ing (out′gō′ing *for 1,* out′ gō′ing *for 2*) **1** going out; leaving: *outgoing cargo ships. He will replace the outgoing premier.* **2** friendly; eager to make friends: *She is very outgoing and enjoys meeting people. adj.*

out·grow (out grō′) **1** grow too big or too old for: *to outgrow clothes or toys.* **2** get rid of as you grow older: *to outgrow a babyish habit, to outgrow an allergy.* **3** grow faster or taller than: *He has outgrown his older brother. v.,* **out·grew, out·grown, out·grow·ing.**

out·growth (out′grōth′) something that grows or develops naturally from something else: *This big store is an outgrowth of the little shop she started ten years ago. n.*

out·house (out′hous′) a little building with a toilet in it, in a park or campground, at a cottage, etc. *n.*

out·ing (ou′ting) a short trip for pleasure: *On Sunday the family went on an outing to the beach. n.*

out·land·ish (out lan′dish) very strange or ridiculous: *What an outlandish idea! Everyone wore outlandish costumes to the party. adj.*

out·last (out last′) last longer than. *v.*

out·law (out′lo′) **1** a criminal. **2** make illegal: *A group of nations agreed to outlaw land mines.* **3** in earlier times, a person outside the protection of the law; outcast. **4** declare a person an outlaw. 1, 3 *n.,* 2, 4 *v.*

out·let (out′lət) **1** a way out; an opening or exit: *the outlet of a lake.* **2** a place where goods are sold, often a factory or warehouse that sells directly to consumers. **3** a chance to use or express something: *an outlet for someone's anger. He needs an outlet for his artistic talent.* **4** a place in a wall for inserting an electric plug. *n.*

out·line (out′līn′) **1** the line that shows the shape of an object: *The outline of Italy looks like a boot.* **2** draw the outer line of anything: *to outline a map of Italy.*

3 a brief plan showing how the main topics or ideas are arranged: *Make an outline before trying to write up your project.* 4 give a rough plan or summary of: *She outlined the day's activities.* 1, 3 *n.,* 2, 4 *v.,* **out·lined, out·lin·ing.**
in outline, a with only the outline shown. b with only the main features.

out·live (out liv′) live longer than, last longer than: *She outlived her older sister. That idea has outlived its usefulness.* *v.,* **out·lived, out·liv·ing.**

out·look (out′lu̇k′) 1 what you see when you look out; a view: *The room has a pleasant outlook.* 2 what seems likely to happen: *Judging by those black clouds, the outlook for our picnic is not very good.* 3 a way of thinking; attitude: *He had a gloomy outlook on life.* *n.*

out·ly·ing (out′lī′ing) far from the main centre; on the edge: *the outlying houses in the settlement.* *adj.*

out·num·ber (out num′bər) be more than: *They outnumbered us three to one.* *v.*

out·pa·tient (out′pā′shənt) a patient who goes to a hospital for medical treatment but does not have to stay overnight. One who stays overnight is an **inpatient.** *n.*

out·port (out′pȯrt′) in Newfoundland, any harbour town other than St. John's, the capital. *n.*

out·post (out′pōst′) 1 a place some distance away from an army or camp, where a small group of soldiers is placed to prevent surprise attack. 2 a settlement or village far from a major town: *an outpost in the North.* *n.*

out·put (out′pu̇t′) 1 something produced, or the amount produced: *the daily output of a car factory.* 2 the information produced by a computer. It can be displayed on the monitor, printed out, or stored on a disk. *n.*

out·rage (out′rāj′) 1 an act or situation where the rights or feelings of others are ignored or trampled on; a very great offence or insult: *Child abuse is an outrage.* 2 make very angry or offended: *The false rumours outraged the mayor.* 3 strong anger over something that is very wrong or cruel: *His letter to the newspaper expressed outrage at the premier's racist remarks.* 1, 3 *n.,* 2 *v.,* **out·raged, out·rag·ing.** **—out·ra′geous** (out rā′jəs), *adj.*

out·rig·ger (out′rig′ər) a framework ending in a float, sticking out from the side of a light boat or canoe to keep it from turning over. *n.*

out·right (out′rīt′) 1 on the spot, without delay: *You can pay for the car in monthly instalments, or buy it outright.* 2 open or openly; without holding back: *an outright refusal* (*adj.*). *We laughed outright* (*adv.*). 3 complete; thorough: *He would have to be an outright fool to do that.* 1, 2 *adv.,* 2, 3 *adj.*

out·run (out run′) run faster or farther than: *She can outrun her dad.* *v.,* **out·ran, out·run, out·run·ning.**

out·set (out′set′) beginning: *At the outset, it looked like a nice day. I was against the idea from the outset.* *n.*

out·side (out′sīd′) 1 out in the open air; outdoors: *Run outside and play.* 2 the surface that is out; the outer part: *to paint the outside of a house.* 3 on the outer surface or edge: *the outside leaves of a cabbage.* 4 out of; beyond the limits of; near but not in: *an hour outside Lethbridge. Set it outside the garage. That question is outside this discussion.* 5 *Informal.* highest; largest: *an outside estimate.* 6 the settled parts of Canada, in the eyes of those living in the North. 1 *adv.,* 2, 6 *n.,* 3, 5 *adj.,* 4 *prep.*
an outside chance, a very slight chance.
at the outside, at the most; at the limit: *I can do it in a week, at the outside.*
outside of, apart from; except for: *Outside of actually going there to help, I don't see any solution.*

out·sid·er (out′sī′dər *or* out′sī′dər) 1 a person who doesn't belong to a particular group or live in a particular area. 2 in the North, a person from the more settled parts of Canada. *n.*

out·skirts (out′skėrts′) the outer parts or edges of a town or district: *a farm on the outskirts of town.* *pl.n.*

out·smart (out smärt′) use cleverness or tricks to defeat someone: *Once the fox reached the woods it outsmarted the hunters.* *v.*

out·spo·ken (out′spō′kən) open and direct; not holding back your opinions: *an outspoken person, an outspoken criticism.* *adj.*

out·stand·ing (out stan′ding) 1 excellent; so good or skilled as to stand out from all others: *She is an outstanding basketball player.* 2 still needing to be dealt with: *outstanding debts, outstanding letters.* *adj.*

out·strip (out strip′) go much faster or do much better than: *A horse can outstrip a bike. She can outstrip most other students in computer skills.* *v.,* **out·stripped, out·strip·ping.**

out·ward (out′wərd) 1 toward the outside; away: *on our outward journey* (*adj.*). *A deck extends outward from the house* (*adv.*). **Outwards** is another form of the adverb. 2 on the surface: *He hid his sadness behind an outward cheerfulness.* 1, 2 *adj.,* 1 *adv.* **—out′ward·ly,** *adv.*

a bat	e bed	i bid	o pot	u cup	th thin
ā cake	ē me	ī bite	ō go	ū rude	ᴛʜ then
ä bar	ə about	ər over	ȯ for	u̇ put	zh measure

out·weigh (out wā′) be greater in weight, value, or importance: *The advantages of the plan outweigh its disadvantages.* *v.*

out·wit (out wit′) get the better of by being clever: *The prisoner outwitted his guards and escaped.* *v.,* **out·wit·ted, out·wit·ting.**

o·val (ō′vəl) 1 shaped like an egg or an ellipse. 2 something having this shape. 1 *adj.,* 2 *n.*

o·va·ry (ō′və rē) 1 the organ that produces eggs. Female mammals have two ovaries lying inside the body, one on either side of the uterus. The scientific name for egg is **ovum.** The plural is **ova.** 2 in a plant, the part of the flower that produces the seeds. *n., pl.* **o·va·ries.**

o·va·tion (ō vā′shən) an enthusiastic burst of applause: *The dancers received a great ovation.* *n.*

ov·en (uv′ən) a closed space that can be heated for baking and roasting food, or for drying clay. It can be part of a stove, or a separate container made of metal, brick, or other fireproof material. *n.*

o·ver (ō′vər) 1 above in place, position, or amount: *the sky over our heads. We have a captain over us. Over 20 people came.* 2 on; covering: *A smile came over her face. Put a blanket over the baby.* 3 above and to the other side: *to jump over a wall.* 4 down from an edge or from an upright position: *The ball rolled over the edge* (*prep.*). *He lost his balance and fell over* (*adv.*). 5 through: *to travel all over the province.* 6 again: *I will have to do the whole thing over. She said it over and over.* 7 ended: *The play is over.* 8 about; because of: *to fight over a toy.* 9 so as to have the other side up; upside down: *to turn over a page, to roll over.* 1–3, 5, 8 *prep.,* 4, 6, 7, 9 *adv.*
go over, get a certain reaction: *The idea went over well.*
over to, to, especially to someplace fairly close: *Can I go over to Len's house?* To **come over** is to come for a visit.
over with, finished; done.
sleep over or **stay over,** stay for the night.

over– *a prefix meaning:* 1 too; too much, too long, etc., as in *overcrowded, oversleep.* 2 extra, as in *overtime.* The prefix **over-** is also used in other senses of the word **over.** To *overflow* is to flow over the edge of a container; an *overcoat* is a coat worn over a suit jacket or blazer.

Word Family......... **over-**

overdress: dress too fancily or too formally
overestimate: think too highly of
overkill: *Slang.* too much of something
overlaid: covered with a layer of something
overreact: react too strongly; take a thing too seriously
overspend: spend too much
overuse: use too often or too much

o·ver·alls (ō′vər olz′) pants with shoulder straps attached and a part that covers the chest. You wear a shirt underneath. *pl.n.*

o·ver·bear·ing (ō′vər ber′ing) bossy; controlling: *The manager is a very overbearing person.* *adj.*

o·ver·board (ō′vər bȯrd′) from a ship or boat into the water: *Don't throw that garbage overboard.* *adv.*
go overboard, go to extremes: *She went overboard and bought way more than she needed.*

o·ver·cast (ō′vər kast′) 1 cloudy; dark; gloomy: *The sky was overcast before the storm.* 2 cover with clouds or darkness: *Clouds overcast the sky.* 3 sew over both edges of a seam with long stitches to prevent fraying. 1 *adj.,* 2, 3 *v.,* **o·ver·cast, o·ver·cast·ing.**

o·ver·coat (ō′vər kōt′) an outer coat; a coat worn over a suit jacket or blazer. *n.*

o·ver·come (ō′vər kum′) 1 conquer; defeat: *to overcome an enemy, to overcome a problem.* 2 make helpless; make unable to act or respond: *I was so overcome with disappointment that I couldn't speak.* *v.,* **o·ver·came, o·ver·come, o·ver·com·ing.**

o·ver·do (ō′vər dū′) 1 do too much: *Exercise is good, but don't overdo it.* 2 exaggerate: *The funny scenes in the play were overdone.* 3 cook too much: *These vegetables are overdone; they're all mushy.* *v.,* **o·ver·did, o·ver·done, o·ver·do·ing.**

o·ver·draw (ō′vər dro′) take more money from a bank account than you actually have in it. The privilege of overdrawing, or the amount overdrawn, is called an **overdraft.** *v.,* **o·ver·drew, o·ver·drawn, o·ver·draw·ing.**

o·ver·due (ō′vər dyū′ *or* ō′vər dū′) late; due some time ago but not yet returned, paid, etc.: *overdue library books. This bill is overdue.* *adj.*

o·ver·flow (ō′vər flō′ *for 1 and 2,* ō′vər flō′ *for 3*) 1 have or cause to have the contents flowing over the top or edge: *The bathtub is overflowing. The milk is overflowing the cup.* 2 cover; flood: *The river overflowed my garden.* 3 the act or amount of flowing over: *The overflow from the tank runs into that drain.* 1, 2 *v.,* 3 *n.*

o·ver·grown (ō′vər grōn′) 1 grown too big: *an overgrown tree.* 2 covered or filled with things that have been allowed to keep growing: *The wall is overgrown with vines.* *adj.*

o·ver·hand (ō′vər hand′) with your hand raised above your shoulder: *an overhand throw* (*adj.*), *to pitch the ball overhand* (*adv.*). *adj. or adv.*

o·ver·hang (ō′vər hang′ *for 1,* ō′vər hang′ *for 2*) 1 hang over; stick out over: *Trees overhang the street to* *form an arch of branches.* **2** something that hangs over or sticks out: *The overhang of the roof shaded the flower bed beneath.* 1 *v.,* **o•ver•hung, o•ver•hang•ing;** 2 *n.*

o•ver•haul (ō′vər hol′ *for 1,* ō′vər hol′ *for 2*) **1** examine in detail and make major repairs or improvements: *Once a year we overhaul our boat. The camp program has been completely overhauled.* **2** a thorough examination and repair job: *The mechanic is doing an overhaul on our truck.* 1 *v.,* 2 *n.*

o•ver•head (ō′vər hed′ *for 1,* ō′vər hed′ *for 2 and 3*) **1** over people's heads; above: *A helicopter flew overhead (adv.). Watch out for that overhead wire (adj.).* **2** the general expenses of running a business or organization, such as rent, hydro, phone bills, taxes, repairs, etc. **3** short for **overhead projector,** a machine that lets you project an image onto a wall or screen from a clear sheet of acetate called a **transparency.** You lay the transparency on the glass surface of the machine, which is lit from below, and the image is focussed and reflected by a lens and mirror above it. 1 *adv. or adj.,* 2, 3 *n.*

o•ver•hear (ō′vər hēr′) hear what is not meant for you: *They spoke so loudly that I couldn't help overhearing what they said.* *v.,* **o•ver•heard, o•ver•hear•ing.**

o•ver•joyed (ō′vər joid′) filled with joy; extremely glad. *adj.*

o•ver•land (ō′vər land′) on land; by land: *an overland route (adj.). We travelled overland from Winnipeg to Vancouver (adv.).* *adj. or adv.*

o•ver•lap (ō′vər lap′ *for 1 and 2,* ō′vər lap′ *for 3*) **1** cover part of the thing beside it: *Each shingle overlaps the next one.* **2** include some of the same things or the same time: *Each lesson overlaps the previous one a little to allow for some review. Our visits overlapped by two days.* **3** the part or amount that overlaps: *Allow an overlap of several centimetres.* 1, 2 *v.,* **o•ver•lapped, o•ver•lap•ping;** 3 *n.*

o•ver•load (ō′vər lōd′ *for 1,* ō′vər lōd′ *for 2*) **1** load too heavily: *to overload a boat.* **2** too great a load: *an overload of information.* 1 *v.,* 2 *n.*

o•ver•look (ō′vər lůk′) **1** fail to notice or deal with: *Here are some letters that you overlooked.* **2** pretend not to notice; excuse: *I will overlook your bad behaviour this time.* **3** have a view from above: *This high window overlooks half the city.* *v.*

o•ver•night (ō′vər nīt′) **1** during the night: *to stay overnight with a friend (adv.), an overnight storm (adj.).* **2** stay for one night: *We'll overnight in Red Deer and start again early the next morning.* An **overnight bag** is a small travel bag big enough to pack things for a one-night stay. **4** very quickly or suddenly: *His personality changed overnight.* 1, 4 *adv.,* 1 *adj.,* 2 *v.*

o•ver•pass (ō′vər pas′) a bridge over a road, railway, canal, etc. *n.*

o•ver•pow•er (ō′vər pou′ər) **1** overcome; beat: *He overpowered all his enemies. I was overpowered by the heat.* **2** be so much greater or stronger that it makes others unnoticeable: *The wind brought a horrible smell that overpowered all others. Sudden anger overpowered every other feeling.* *v.* **—o′ver•pow′er•ing,** *adj.*

o•ver•rate (ō′vər rāt′) to rate or estimate too highly: *He had overrated his strength and soon had to ask for help.* *v.,* **o•ver•rat•ed, o•ver•rat•ing.**

o•ver•rule (ō′vər rūl′) decide against someone's argument, suggestion, etc. by greater authority or power, or by vote: *My parents overruled my idea, saying it was too dangerous. We were overruled by the majority.* *v.,* **o•ver•ruled, o•ver•rul•ing.**

o•ver•run (ō′vər run′) **1** invade; take over: *Weeds had overrun the garden. The barn was overrun by rats.* **2** run or go beyond: *The speaker overran the time set for him.* *v.,* **o•ver•ran, o•ver•run, o•ver•run•ning.**

o•ver•seas (ō′vər sēz′ *for 1,* ō′vər sēz′ *for 2*) **1** across the sea; to another continent: *to travel overseas.* **2** in or to countries across the sea: *an overseas flight, overseas business.* 1 *adv.,* 2 *adj.*

o•ver•see (ō′vər sē′) supervise or manage: *to oversee a factory.* *v.,* **o•ver•saw, o•ver•seen, o•ver•see•ing. —o′ver•se′er,** *n.*

o•ver•shad•ow (ō′vər shad′ō) **1** be or seem more important than: *The boy overshadowed his older brother as a pianist.* **2** cast a shadow over. *v.*

o•ver•shoe (ō′vər shū′) a waterproof boot or covering worn over a shoe to keep the foot dry and warm. *n.*

o•ver•sight (ō′vər sīt′) a failure to notice or think of something: *Through an oversight, the kitten got no supper last night.* *n.*

o•ver•sleep (ō′vər slēp′) sleep longer than you meant to. *v.,* **o•ver•slept, o•ver•sleep•ing.**

o•ver•step (ō′vər step′) go beyond: *He overstepped the limits of politeness with that answer.* *v.,* **o•ver•stepped, o•ver•step•ping.**

a bat	e bed	i bid	o pot	u cup	th thin
ā cake	ē me	ī bite	ō go	ū rude	ᴛʜ then
ä bar	ə about	ər over	ô for	ů put	zh measure

o·ver·take (ō′vər tāk′) 1 catch up to and pass: *The blue car overtook ours.* 2 come upon suddenly or catch unprepared: *A storm overtook the children on their way home. Night overtook us while we were still looking for a campsite.* *v.,* **o·ver·took, o·ver·tak·en, o·ver·tak·ing.**

o·ver·throw (ō′vər thrō′ *for 1,* ō′vər thrō′ *for 2*) 1 destroy the power of; defeat: *The army overthrew the government.* 2 the act or fact of defeating or destroying: *the overthrow of apartheid.* 1 *v.,* **o·ver·threw, o·ver·thrown, o·ver·throw·ing;** 2 *n.*

o·ver·time (ō′vər tīm′) 1 beyond the regular hours: *overtime work (adj.). He worked overtime (adv.).* 2 time spent working beyond the regular hours: *He was paid extra for overtime.* 3 wages for this period: *I get paid overtime for Saturdays.* 4 in games, play that goes beyond the normal game time. 1 *adj. or adv.,* 2–4 *n.*

o·ver·tone (ō′vər tōn′) an attitude or point of view that comes through in a person's speaking or writing, but only in a hidden or indirect way: *The letter was polite but had angry overtones.*

o·ver·ture (ō′vər chər) 1 an attempt to start a friendship or set up an agreement: *The countries have been warring for years but are now making overtures for peace.* 2 a piece of music that introduces an opera, symphony, or other long musical composition. *n.*

o·ver·turn (ō′vər tėrn′) 1 knock down or fall down; turn upside down: *The cat overturned a vase on the shelf. The boat overturned.* 2 overthrow; defeat; destroy the power of: *The rebels overturned the government.* *v.*

o·ver·view (ō′vər vyü′) a brief summary of the main parts or ideas: *The first chapter gave an overview of Canadian history.* *n.*

o·ver·weight (ō′vər wāt′) too fat or too heavy: *He is overweight because he eats too much. We had to pay extra for our overweight baggage.* *adj.*

o·ver·whelm (ō′vər welm′ *or* ō′vər hwelm′) crush or flood; be too much for a person to handle: *Grief overwhelmed her. I am overwhelmed by your generosity.* *v.* —**o′ver·whelm′ing,** *adj.*

o·ver·work (ō′vər wėrk′) 1 too much or too hard work: *to die of overwork.* 2 work or force to work too hard or too long: *She overworks her employees.* 1 *n.,* 2 *v.*

ow (ou) an exclamation of pain. *interj.*

owe (ō) 1 have to pay; be in debt: *I owe Jessica a dollar.* 2 have a duty to be thankful or to give something: *We owe a great deal to our parents. We owe friends our trust.* *v.,* **owed, ow·ing.**

ow·ing (ō′ing) due; owed: *to pay what is owing.* *adj*
owing to, on account of; because of: *Owing to a serious illness, she was absent from school for more than a month.*

owl (oul) a bird of prey with a large flat-faced head, big eyes, and a short, hooked beak. Owls hunt mice and other small animals at night. Some owls have tufts of feathers on their heads called "horns" or "ears." *n.* —**owl′ish,** *adj.*

own (ōn) 1 have as something that belongs to you; possess: *I own many books.* 2 belonging to you; for yourself: *This is my own book. She makes her own dresses.* 3 recognize; accept: *to own someone as a friend.* 1, 3 *v.,* 2 *adj.* —**own′er,** *n.* —**own′er·ship′,** *n.*
come into your own, get the success or credit that you deserve.
hold your own, keep your position; not be forced back.
of your own, belonging to you: *I have a computer of my own now.*
on your own, **a** alone: *He lives on his own.* **b** not ruled or directed by someone else.
own up, confess; admit: *She owned up to her mistake.*

ox (oks) 1 a domestic bull with its sex glands removed, used for farm work and for beef. 2 any of the family of animals with horns and split hoofs, to which cattle, buffaloes, and bison belong. *n., pl.* **ox·en.**

ox·bow (oks′bō′) 1 a U-shaped piece of wood placed under and around the neck of an ox and attached at the top to the yoke that goes over its back. 2 a U-shaped bend in a river. *n.*

ox·cart (oks′kårt′) a cart pulled by oxen. *n.*

ox·ide (ok′sīd) a compound of oxygen and one other chemical element. *n.*

ox·i·dize (ok′sə dīz′) combine with oxygen. When a substance burns or rusts, it is oxidized. Water oxidizes some metals. *v.,* **ox·i·dized, ox·i·diz·ing.**

ox·y·gen (ok′sə jən) an element that is a colourless, odourless gas. It makes up about one-fifth of our air. Animals and plants cannot live without oxygen. Fire will not burn without oxygen. *n.*

ox·y·mo·ron (ok′sə mȯr′on) the combination of two words that seem to mean the opposite of each other. *Examples: living death, tough love, sinfully good.* *n., pl.* **ox·y·mo·rons** or **ox·y·mo·ra.** —**ox′y·mo·ron′ic** (ok′sə mə ron′ik), *adj.*

WORD HISTORY..... oxymoron

The word **oxymoron** is borrowed from Greek, where it means "very stupid thing," from *oxys*, meaning "sharp" + *moros*, meaning "stupid." Think of it as pointedly stupid, or the peak of stupidity — so stupid that you say "Ouch!" when you hear it.

Oysters and Other Molluscs

Unlike mammals, molluscs have no inner skeleton. Instead, a hard outer skeleton (a shell) protects their soft bodies.

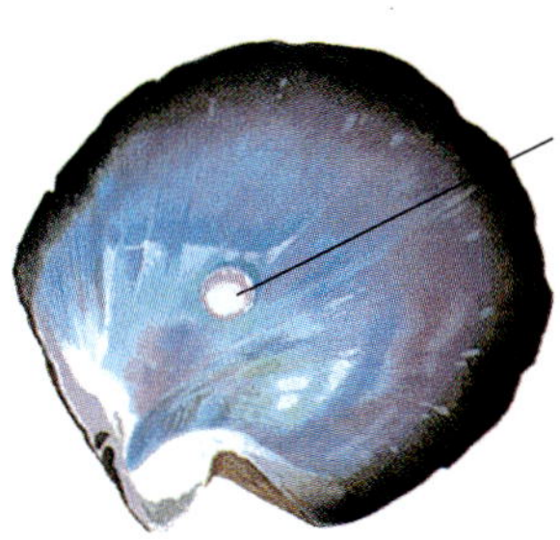

A pearl begins when a piece of grit gets inside the oyster, and irritates its soft flesh. The oyster coats the grit with material from the shell lining, many times, and this eventually forms the pearl.

Tusk shells burrow in sand.

Triton's Trumpet is a snail-like creature that is usually found clinging to rocks.

The Giant clam is the largest seashell in the world, reaching over a metre wide, and with a mass of over 250 kg.

The Philippine Nerite lives in estuary waters.

Scallops live on the seabed.

This is a Textile cone. All cones inject poison into their prey. The sting of some of the larger species can kill a person.

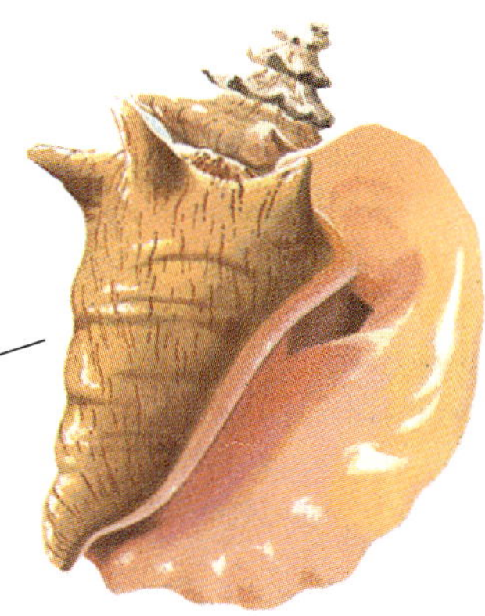

The Queen conch is a kind of sea snail. It lives in shallow tropical waters and feeds on seaweed.

oys·ter (oi′stər) a shellfish used as food. It has a rough, unevenly-shaped shell in two halves. Oysters are found in shallow water along seacoasts; some kinds yield pearls. *n.*

oz. *abbreviation for* ounce or ounces, a nonmetric unit of mass.

o·zone (ō′zōn) **1** a form of oxygen with a sharp odour. The **ozone layer** is a layer of ozone high in our atmosphere, that protects the earth from ultraviolet rays. **2** *Informal.* pure air that is refreshing. *n.*

Pp

p or **P** (pē) **1** the sixteenth letter of the English alphabet, or the sound that it stands for. We hear the sound of *p* in *pie, spot,* and *skip.* **2** the sixteenth thing in a list. *n., pl.* **p's** or **P's.**
mind your p's and q's, be careful about your manners.

p. *abbreviation for* page.

pa (pȧ) *Informal.* father. *n.*

P.A. *abbreviation for* public address system, a system of connected speakers that lets you talk into a central microphone and be heard by all the people in a building, train, open-air gathering, etc.

pace (pās) **1** a long step, or the length of such a step: *There were perhaps ten paces between me and the bear.* **2** walk with regular steps: *The tiger paced up and down its cage.* **3** a way of stepping: *The walk, trot, and gallop are some of the paces of a horse.* **4** a rate of speed; speed: *He sets a fast pace in walking.* 1, 3, 4 *n.,* 2 *v.,* **paced, pac·ing.**
keep pace with, keep up with; go as fast as.
pace off, measure in paces by walking: *We paced off the distance and found it to be 69 paces.*
set the pace, **a** set a speed that others are expected to keep up with. **b** be an example for others to follow.

pace·mak·er (pās′mā′kər) a small device placed inside the chest of a person whose heartbeat is weak or irregular. It gives tiny electrical shocks to the person's heart to help it beat regularly. *n.*

Pa·cif·ic (pə sif′ik) **1** the ocean between Asia and the Americas. **2** having to do with the Pacific Ocean: *Pacific air routes, the Pacific coast.* The **Pacific Rim** is all the countries bordering the Pacific Ocean. 1 *n.,* 2 *adj.*

WORD HISTORY........Pacific

The name **Pacific** means "peaceful," from the Latin *pacificus.* Magellan, the explorer who named this ocean in the 1500s, either thought it looked peaceful, or hoped it would be.

pac·i·fist (pas′ə fist) a person who is strongly opposed to fighting or war. *n.* —**pac′i·fism′,** *n.*

pac·i·fy (pas′ə fī′) make calm or peaceful: *We tried to pacify the man whose car we bumped into.* A **pacifier** is a rubber nipple given to a baby to suck on as a way of soothing him or her. *v.,* **pac·i·fied, pac·i·fy·ing.**

pack (pak) **1** package; a set number or amount of things sold together in one container or wrapping: *a pack of cookies, a pack of gum.* **2** put things into a container, wasting as little space as possible: *to pack books in a box, to pack groceries in bags. Pack your suitcase.* **3** a bundle of things wrapped up or tied together for carrying: *The mountaineer carried a pack on his back.* A **pack animal** is an animal used for carrying loads. **4** crowd: *A hundred kids were packed into one small room. The bus was packed.* **5** a set or group that belongs together, especially a full set of cards, or a group of animals that live or travel together: *a pack of wolves, a pack of lies. There are 52 cards in a pack.* **6** a large number of floating pieces of ice pushed together: *The ship forced its way through the pack.* **7** in Western Canada, carry, especially in a pack: *He packed his supplies into the bush.* 1, 3, 6 *n.,* 2, 4, 5, 7 *v.*
pack it in, quit.
pack off, send away: *The child was packed off to bed.*
pack rat, someone who cannot bear to get rid of anything.
pack up, gather or pack your things to leave.
send someone packing, get rid of someone.

pack·age (pak′ij) **1** a set number or amount of something packed or wrapped together for sale: *a package of candies.* **Packaging** is the paper, plastic, cardboard, etc. used to hold the items. **2** something wrapped up to be sent in the mail or given as a present. **3** put in a package. 1, 2 *n.,* 3 *v.,* **pack·aged, pack·ag·ing.**

pack·et (pak′it) a small package: *a packet of salt.* *n.*

packing snow (pak′ing snō′) snow that is just around freezing temperature and sticks together well.

pact (pakt) an agreement: *The three nations signed a peace pact.* *n.*

pad (pad) **1** a piece of something soft used for comfort, protection, or stuffing; a cushion: *Our toboggan comes with a pad to sit on.* **2** fill with something soft; stuff: *to pad a chair.* The soft material used is called **padding.** **3** a number of sheets of paper stuck together at one end for tearing off one at a time. **4** the platform that a rocket, missile, or helicopter takes off from: *The rocket rose from the pad at midnight.* **5** a cushionlike part on the bottom of an animal's foot, such as a dog's. **6** Also, **lily pad,** the large floating leaf of a water lily. **7** a surface made of foam or layers of cloth, soaked in ink for use with a rubber stamp. **8** walk softly: *A wolf padded through the woods.* 1, 3–7 *n.,* 2, 8 *v.,* **pad·ded, pad·ding.**

A paddle-steamer is propelled by two large wheels made up of the same kind of boards that are in a water wheel.

pad•dle (pad′əl) 1 a thin pole with a broad blade at one end or both ends. It is used with both hands to move a canoe, a kayak, or other small boat. 2 move a canoe or boat with one or more of these: *We paddled across the lake.* 3 play in shallow water or swim by moving your hands and feet like a dog. 4 a roundish, flat piece of wood with a handle, used to hit the ball in table tennis. 5 one of the boards on a water wheel, to push or be pushed by water. 1, 4, 5 *n.*, 2, 3 *v.*, **pad•dled, pad•dling.**

pad•dock (pad′ək) 1 a small field near a stable or house, used for exercising animals or as a pasture. 2 a pen for horses at a racetrack. *n.*

pad•dy (pad′ē) a field of rice. *n.*

pad•lock (pad′lok′) 1 a lock that can be put on and removed. It has a movable curved bar on the top; you put it through a loop on the thing you want to lock and then snap it shut. 2 fasten with such a lock. 1 *n.*, 2 *v.*

pa•gan (pā′gən) a word sometimes used by believers in one God to describe everyone else. *n. or adj.*

page[1] (pāj) 1 a sheet of paper, or one side of a sheet of paper, especially with something written or drawn on it. 2 anything thought of as a story: *The War of 1812 is an exciting page in Canadian history.* 3 turn the pages: *to page through a book.* 4 a file on the World Wide Web. The **home page** is the first file you reach at a certain Web address. 1, 2, 4 *n.*, 3 *v.*, **paged, paging.**

page[2] (pāj) 1 a boy or girl who runs errands, carries messages and so on; there are pages serving in the federal and provincial parliaments. Pages wear uniforms. 2 try to get a message to a person by announcing it on a public address system or calling the person on a pager: *The store manager paged the lost girl's father.* 3 in medieval times, a boy who served a knight as part of his training to become a knight himself. 1, 3 *n.*, 2 *v.*, **paged, pag•ing.**

pag•eant (paj′ənt) a very fancy and dignified show that often includes a parade, ceremony, or play. *n.* **—pag′eant•ry,** *n.*

pag•er (pā′jər) a beeper that a person can carry around in a pocket. When it beeps, it means the person should quickly phone someone who has been trying to reach him or her. *n.*

Pagodas originated in India from the form of Buddhist temples, and spread eastward. In China, most pagodas have an odd number of floors, and are octagonal. In Japan, they usually have only five storeys, and are square. Which country do you think this pagoda is probably in?

pa•go•da (pə gō′də) a temple that has many storeys, each one with a roof curving upward. There are pagodas in India, Japan, and China. *n.*

paid (pād) the past tense and past participle of **pay:** *I paid for my meal. Have you paid?* *v.*

pail (pāl) a round, wide container with a flat bottom and a single handle arching over the top; a bucket. *n.*

pain (pān) 1 a feeling of being hurt in your body or mind: *He had a pain in his back. The death of her kitten caused her great pain.* A **painkiller** is a drug to lessen physical pain. 2 *Informal.* a bothersome person or thing: *This zipper is such a pain—it always gets stuck.* 3 cause to suffer; give pain: *It pains me that you don't trust me.* 1, 2 *n.*, 3 *v.* **—pain′ful,** *adj.* **—pain′less,** *adj.* **on pain of,** with a certain punishment if you disobey: *The traitor was ordered to leave the country on pain of death.* **pain in the neck,** *Informal.* a bothersome person or thing. **take pains,** be careful; try hard: *She took pains to make her map accurate.* **Painstaking** is the adjective: *a painstaking piece of work.*

paint (pānt) 1 a liquid that can be put on a surface to dry as a coloured coating. Paint is made out of oil, water, or other liquid with colouring matter dissolved in it. 2 cover or decorate with paint: *to paint a ceiling.* 3 make a picture or pictures with paint: *The artist painted scenes from downtown Victoria.* A picture made with paint is a **painting.** 1 *n.*, 2, 3 *v.* **—paint′er,** *n.*

paint•brush (pānt′brush′) a brush for putting on paint. *n.*

a bat	e bed	i bid	o pot	u cup	th thin
ā cake	ē me	ī bite	ō go	ū rude	ᴛʜ then
à bar	ə about	ər over	ò for	ù put	zh measure

pair (per) 1 a set of two: *a pair of shoes, a pair of horses.* 2 arrange in sets of two; put with another to make a set of two: *His socks were neatly paired in a drawer. I was paired with Priska for the science project.* 3 a single thing made up of two parts that cannot be used separately: *a pair of scissors, a pair of jeans.* 1, 3 *n.,* 2 *v.*
pair off or **pair up,** arrange in pairs; form into pairs: *The boys and girls paired off to learn the new dance.*

CONFUSABLES .... pair

pair means "two": *A pair of blue eyes were looking at me.*
pare means "peel": *Do you know how to pare an apple?*
pear is a fruit: *I will have a pear for dessert.*

pa·ja·mas (pə jam′əz *or* pə jȧ′məz) a less common spelling of **pyjamas.**

pal (pal) a casual friend. *n.*

pal·ace (pal′is) the official home of a king, queen, or other ruler. A palace is huge, majestic, and richly furnished. *n.* —**pa·la′tial** (pə lā′shəl), *adj.*

pal·ate (pal′it) 1 the roof of your mouth. The bony part in front is the **hard palate;** the fleshy part at the back is the **soft palate.** 2 a person's sense of taste: *a flavour to please every palate.* *n.*

pale (pāl) 1 without much colour; whitish: *Are you sick? Your face is a little pale.* 2 not bright: *pale blue. The street lamp gave a pale light in the fog.* 3 turn pale: *Her face paled at the bad news.* 1, 2 *adj.,* **pal·er, pal·est;** 3 *v.,* **paled, pal·ing.**

pa·le·on·tol·o·gy (pā′lē ən tol′ə jē) the study of prehistoric plants and animals through fossils, hardened shapes left in rock. *n.* —**pa′le·on·tol′o·gist,** *n.*

pal·ette (pal′it) 1 a thin board, usually oval, with a thumb hole at one end, used by painters to mix colours on. 2 the colours used by a painter. *n.*

pal·in·drome (pal′in drōm′) a word, phrase, or sentence which reads the same backward as forward. The sentence *Madam, I'm Adam* is a palindrome. *n.*

pal·i·sade (pal′ə sād′ *or* pal′ ə sād′) a high fence of pointed posts set very close together, built especially in earlier times for protection. *n.*

palm[1] (pom) 1 the inside of your hand between your wrist and fingers. 2 hide in your hand as part of a magic trick: *The magician palmed the nickel.* 1 *n.,* 2 *v.*
palm off, get something accepted by trickery: *The book they palmed off on me turned out to have 27 pages missing.*

palm[2] (pom) a tree or shrub often found in warm climates. Many palms have a crown of large fan-shaped or featherlike leaves growing at the top of a tall trunk. From ancient times, a palm leaf has been a symbol of victory or triumph. *n.*

pal·pi·tate (pal′pə tāt′) beat very fast: *a palpitating heart.* *v.,* **pal·pi·tat·ed, pal·pi·tat·ing.**
—**pal′pi·ta′tion,** *n.*

pal·try (pol′trē) almost worthless: *a paltry sum of money.* *adj.,* **pal·tri·er, pal·tri·est.**

pam·pas (pȧm′pəz *or* pam′pəs) the wide, treeless, grassy plains of South America. *pl.n.*

pam·per (pam′pər) give all kinds of luxuries and privileges to: *That hotel really pampers its guests.* *v.*

pam·phlet (pam′flit) a small booklet or brochure: *At the community centre my mom picked up a pamphlet about swimming lessons.* *n.*

pan (pan) 1 a flat metal dish for cooking and baking, with low sides. A **frying pan** has a handle. 2 any other shallow container: *We have a plastic dishpan to wash dishes in when camping.* Gold and other metals are sometimes obtained by washing ore in pans.

3 give a bad review to a film, play, book, etc.: *They panned the new movie, saying the acting was terrible.* 1, 2 *n.,* 3 *v.,* **panned, pan·ning.**

pan for gold, wash gravel, sand, etc. in a pan to separate the gold.
pan out, *Informal.* turn out or work out: *His latest scheme panned out well.*

pan·cake (pan′kāk′) a thin, flat cake made of flour, milk, and eggs, fried in a pan. *n.*

pan·cre·as (pan′krē əs) a gland near the stomach. It produces enzymes to help digest food, and the hormone insulin to control sugar. *n.*

The giant panda is an endangered species.

You can find out about endangered species in Canada by searching the Internet.

pan·da (pan′də) **1** short for **giant panda,** a rare bear of western China. It is white with black legs, shoulders, and ears. **2** a reddish-brown animal like a raccoon, that lives in the mountains of western China and Tibet. *n.*

pan·de·mon·i·um (pan′də mō′nē əm) a lot of noise, excitement, and confusion: *When the fire started there was pandemonium as people tried to escape.* *n.*

pane (pān) a single sheet of glass in a window. *n.*

pan·el (pan′əl) **1** a strip or sheet of some material, often set off in some way from what is around it. Wooden panels may form parts of a door or wall; cloth panels may be used as parts of a dress. **2** cover or decorate with panels: *The room was panelled with oak.* **3** a group of specially chosen people brought together to discuss a question or topic: *a panel of jurors in a law court, a panel of reporters discussing the recent election on TV.* **4** a board with gauges, controls, warning lights, and so on, for operating an aircraft or other machine. **Instrument panel** or **control panel** is the full name. 1, 3, 4 *n.,* 2 *v.,* **pan·elled** or **pan·eled, pan·el·ling** or **pan·el·ing.**

pang (pang) a sudden, sharp painful feeling: *the pangs of a toothache. A pang of pity moved her heart.* *n.*

pan·ic (pan′ik) **1** a sudden fear that causes you to lose your self-control and your ability to think straight; wild fear: *There was panic when the theatre caught fire.* **2** fill or be filled with such fear: *The driver panicked when his brakes failed.* A person who panics is **panic-stricken.** 1 *n.,* 2 *v.,* **pan·icked, pan·ick·ing.** —**pan′ick·y,** *adj.*

> **WORD HISTORY........ panic**
>
> **Panic** gets its name from the ancient Greek god of woods and fields, *Pan,* who was believed to cause confusion and fear.

pan·o·ram·a (pan′ə ram′ə) **1** a wide, unbroken view: *a panorama of beach and sea.* **2** a continuously passing or changing scene: *the panorama of city life.* *n.* —**pan′o·ram′ic,** *adj.*

pan·sy (pan′zē) a garden flower with flat, velvety petals of different colours. *n., pl.* **pan·sies.**

pant (pant) **1** breathe hard and fast: *He is panting from playing soccer.* **2** a short, quick breath. 1 *v.,* 2 *n.*

pan·ther (pan′thər) a leopard or jaguar that is all black. *n.*

pan·to·mime (pan′tə mīm′) **1** the use of gestures and facial expression without words, especially as an art performed by an actor. Pantomime is usually performed in an exaggerated style. **2** a play or skit acted in this style. **3** communicate by using gestures without words: *To ask for food, I pantomimed eating.* 1, 2 *n.,* 3 *v.,* **pan·to·mim·ed, pan·to·mim·ing.** —**pan′to·mim′ist,** *n.*

pan·try (pan′trē) a large cupboard for food. In the days before refrigerators, it was often a whole small room, kept unheated. *n., pl.* **pan·tries.**

pants (pants) an outer garment for the lower part of your body, reaching from the waist roughly to the ankles and divided to cover each leg separately. A **pantsuit** is a pair of pants with matching jacket, for a woman. *pl.n.*

pan·ty·hose (pan′tē hōz′) a garment for women, like tights but made of very thin nylon. *pl.n.*

pa·pa (pä′pə) *Informal.* father; daddy. *n.*

pa·pal (pā′pəl) having to do with the Pope. *adj.*

pa·pa·ya (pə pä′yə) a large, juicy tropical fruit with a yellow-green rind. The inside is orange-yellow. *n.*

a bat	e bed	i bid	o pot	u cup	th thin
ā cake	ē me	ī bite	ō go	ū rude	TH then
ä bar	ə about	ər over	ô for	ů put	zh measure

Making Paper

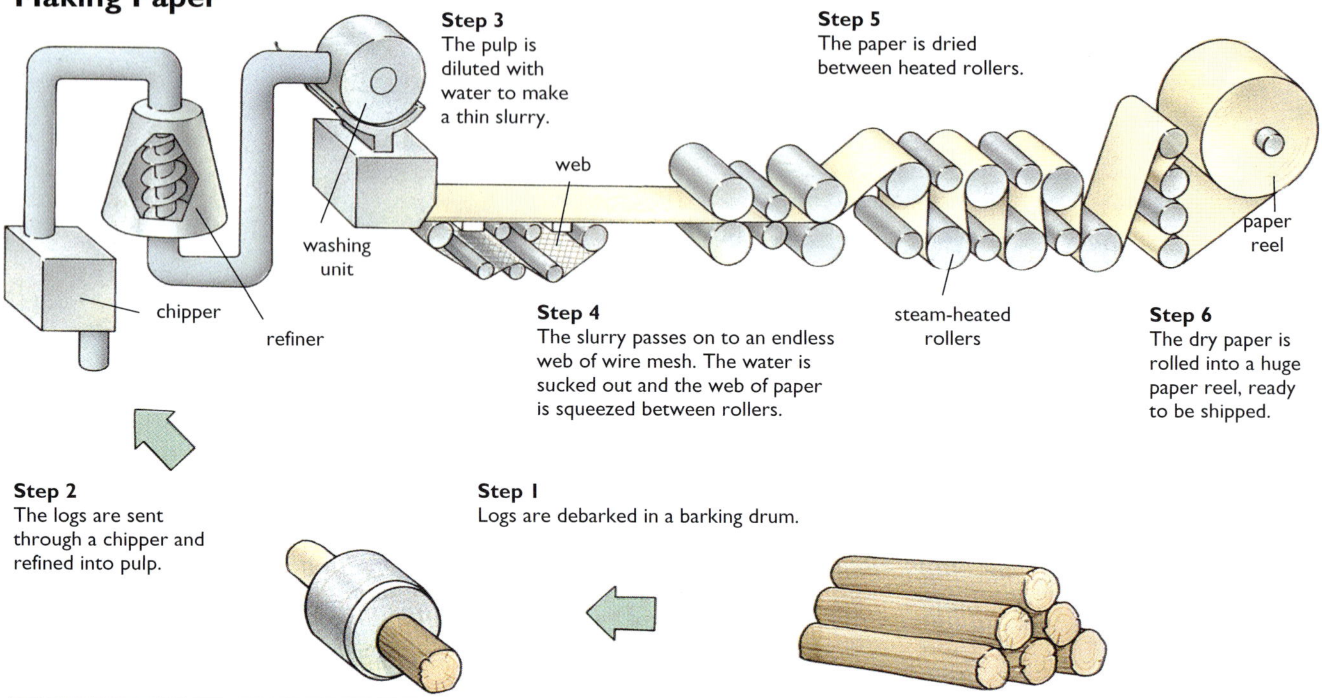

pa•per (pā′pər) **1** a material in the form of a thin sheet, used for writing and printing on, wrapping packages, and many other purposes. It is made from tiny bits of wood or cloth that have been soaked, crushed into a mushy pulp, and then rolled out flat and dried. Books and magazines are made of paper. **2** a piece or sheet of paper, especially one with writing on it: *Important papers were stolen.* **3** newspaper. **4** **papers,** *pl.* official forms telling who you are and where you are from, what rights you have, and so on: *citizenship papers.* **5** wallpaper. **6** cover with wallpaper: *to paper a room.* **7** an article or essay: *Professor Chambers has written a paper on Canadian English.* 1–5, 7 *n.,* 6 *v.* —**pa′per•y,** *adj.*
on paper, **a** in writing. **b** in theory: *His idea sounds good on paper but it won't work in practice.*

pa•per•back (pā′pər bak′) a book with paper covers. *n.*

pa•pier–mâché (pā′pər ma shā′) strips or bits of paper mixed with paste and used for modelling. Papier-mâché becomes hard and strong when dry. *n.*

pap•ri•ka (pə prē′kə *or* pap rē′kə) mild red peppers, dried and ground up and used as a spice. *n.*

pa•py•rus (pə pī′rəs) **1** a tall water plant that the ancient Egyptians, Greeks, and Romans made a kind of paper from. **2** the writing material made from this plant. **3** a piece of this material with ancient writings on it. *n., pl.* **pa•py•ri** (pə pī′rī *or* pə pī′rē).

par (pȧr) **1** equality; an equal level: *The gains and losses are about on a par. He is quite on a par with his brother in intelligence.* **2** an average or normal standard: *Her computer skills are well above par.* **3** in golf, the number of strokes set as an expert score for any one hole or for the whole course. *n.*
at par, taking one unit for another equally, without applying the exchange rate: *Some stores accept Canadian and American money at par.*

par•a•ble (per′ə bəl) a short, simple story used to teach some truth or lesson. *n.*

par•a•chute (per′ə shūt′) **1** a large piece of light, strong cloth attached to a person or thing by a set of strings and straps. When the person or thing drops from an aircraft, the parachute opens like an umbrella and lets the person or thing fall slowly and gently. **2** come or send down by a parachute: *The pilot of the burning plane parachuted safely to the ground.* 1 *n.,* 2 *v.,* **par•a•chut•ed, par•a•chut•ing.** —**par′a•chut′ist,** *n.*

pa•rade (pə rād′) **1** a march done as a show or celebration. It may include clowns and other people in costume, musical bands, and decorated vehicles called floats: *a Canada Day parade.* **2** walk proudly or do things in public to show off: *Little Meg paraded through the house in her new dress. He likes to parade his computer knowledge in front of the class.* **3** a display to show off. **4** any group of people or things coming one after another. 1, 3, 4 *n.,* 2 *v.*

par•a•dise (per′ə dīs′) heaven, or anything thought of as happy or beautiful like heaven. *n.*

par•a•dox (per′ə doks′) **1** a statement that seems to say two opposite things. *Example: "It is in giving that we receive."* **2** a person or thing that seems to be full of opposites or contradictions. *n.*

par•af•fin (per′ə fin) a white, tasteless, waxy substance, used for making candles and for sealing jars of homemade jam and so on. *n.*

par•a•graph (per′ə graf′) **1** a group of sentences all having to do with the same idea and forming a distinct part of a chapter, letter, or other piece of writing. A paragraph begins on a new line and is usually indented. **2** divide into paragraphs. 1 *n.,* 2 *v.*

Grammar Check .... paragraph

A **paragraph** should deal with only one main idea. It should have a topic sentence, that is, a sentence that gives the main idea as a statement. All the other sentences in the paragraph should relate to the topic sentence, explaining and supporting it.

par•a•keet (per′ə kēt′) a small, often brightly coloured parrot. There are many different kinds; most have slender bodies and long tails. *n.*

par•al•lel (per′ə lel′) **1** the same distance apart at every point, like the two rails of a railway track; not on an angle with each other. **2** to run in the same direction and at the same distance apart throughout the length: *The road parallels the railway.* **3** a parallel line or surface, especially a line of latitude: *The 49th parallel marks much of the boundary between Canada and the United States.* **4** a comparison or likeness: *There's an interesting parallel between this poem and that story.* **5** similar in some limited way, such as having a similar purpose or meaning, or going on at the same time: *July 1st and July 4th are parallel celebrations in Canada and the U.S.* **6** be like; be similar to: *Your version closely parallels what he told me.* 1, 5 *adj.,* 2, 6 *v.,* **par•al•leled, par•al•lel•ing;** 3, 4 *n.*

par•al•lel•o•gram (per′ə lel′ə gram′) any four-sided figure with opposite sides parallel and equal, such as a square, rectangle, or rhombus. *n.*

par•a•lyze or **par•a•lyse** (per′ə līz′) **1** take away the ability to move or feel: *His left arm was paralyzed.* **2** make powerless or helpless: *Fear paralyzed my mind.* *v.,* **par•a•lyzed** or **par•a•lysed, par•a•lyz•ing** or **par•a•lys•ing.** —**pa•ral′y•sis** (pə ral′ə sis), *n.*

par•a•med•ic (per′ə med′ik) a person who is trained to help doctors and nurses. A paramedic is often the first to treat someone who has been hurt: *Two paramedics rushed to the scene of the accident.* *n.*

par•a•mount (per′ə mount′) highest; supreme: *Safety is of paramount importance.* *adj.*

par•a•pher•nal•ia (per′ə fər nā′lē ə) personal belongings or equipment: *She leaves her hockey paraphernalia all over the house.* *pl.n.*

par•a•phrase (per′ə frāz′) **1** give the meaning in other words. **2** a version of something, using other words. 1 *v.,* **par•a•phrased, par•a•phras•ing;** 2 *n.*

par•a•site (per′ə sīt′) **1** an animal or plant that lives on or in another one, called the **host,** and gets food from it. Lice are parasites on animals; mistletoe is a parasite on oak trees. Some parasites harm their hosts. **2** a person who lives off others without giving anything in return: *The lazy man was a parasite on his family.* *n.*

par•a•sol (per′ə sol′) a light umbrella used as a sunshade. *n.*

WORD HISTORY....... parasol

Parasol comes from combining two Italian words: the verb *parare,* meaning "to shelter from" and *sole,* meaning "sun." If you know the French word for umbrella, *parapluie,* you'll notice the similarity; *pluie* means "rain."

par•a•troop•er (per′ə trū′pər) a soldier trained to be dropped by parachute from an aircraft. *n.*

par•cel (par′səl) **1** something, or a bundle of things, wrapped or tied up; a package: *I got a parcel in the mail—it was a T-shirt from Grandpa.* **2** a piece of land. **3** make into a parcel. 1, 2 *n.,* 3 *v.,* **par•celled** or **par•celed, par•cel•ling** or **par•cel•ing.**
parcel out, divide into portions and give: *They parcelled out the farm to their three grown children and retired.*

parch (parch) make or become dry or thirsty: *parched earth. The workers were parched with the heat.* *v.*

parch•ment (parch′mənt) **1** the skin of sheep or goats, prepared for use as writing material. **2** a piece of this with something written on it. **3** a kind of paper made to look like parchment. *n.*

a bat	e bed	i bid	o pot	u cup	th thin
ā cake	ē me	ī bite	ō go	ū rude	ᴛʜ then
ȧ bar	ə about	ər over	ȯ for	u̇ put	zh measure

par•don (pår′dən) **1** forgive: *Please pardon my forgetfulness.* **2** forgiveness. **3** release from punishment for a crime: *The Governor General pardoned the offender* (*v.*). *He was given a full pardon* (*n.*). 1, 3 *v.*, 2, 3 *n.*

pardon, pardon me, or **I beg your pardon,** **a** I'm very sorry. **b** I did not hear what you just said. **c** I cannot believe what you just said.

pare (per) **1** cut or trim off the outer part of: *to pare an apple.* The tool for this is called a **paring knife.** **2** cut away little by little: *to pare down expenses.* *v.*, **pared, par•ing.**

par•ent (per′ənt) **1** a father or mother. **2** anything that produces offspring or seed. **3** do the work of a parent; raise children. 1, 2 *n.*, 3 *v.* —**par′ent•ing,** *n.* —**par′ent•hood′,** *n.* —**pa•ren′tal** (pə ren′təl), *adj.*

pa•ren•the•sis (pə ren′thə sis) **1** a word, phrase, etc. inserted in a sentence to explain or add detail. **2** either of the two curved lines ( ) used to set off such an expression. *n.*, *pl.* **pa•ren•the•ses** (pə ren′thə sēz′).
► See the *Grammar and Usage Mini-Guide.*

Grammar Check . . . parentheses

Use **parentheses** to add comments or explain something within a sentence: *The hamster (we decided to call him Fred) soon became a member of the family.* Remember that the information in parentheses is extra. The sentence should still make sense when you take it away: *The hamster soon became a member of the family.*

par•ish (per′ish) **1** the area served by a church. Its people are called **parishioners** (pə rish′ə nərz). **2** in New Brunswick and Québec, a political unit similar to a township. *n.*

park (pårk) **1** a piece of land set apart for the public to enjoy. Some parks have play equipment, picnic tables, campsites, or hiking trails. Many also have the purpose of protecting and studying the natural environment. **2** leave a vehicle for a while in a certain place: *Park your car here.* A **parking lot** is a place to park many vehicles. A **parking meter** is a machine set up at a parking space, operated by a town. You put coins in and it shows how long you are allowed to park in that space. 1 *n.*, 2 *v.*

par•ka (pår′kə) a long, warm winter jacket with a hood. Parkas were originally worn by the Inuit, who made them out of fur. *n.*

par•lia•ment (pår′lə mənt) a group of people who make the laws for a country or province. In Canada, the federal Parliament includes the Queen as well as the House of Commons and the Senate. Ontario is the only province that calls its legislature a parliament. *n.* —**par′lia•men′ta•ry** (pår′lə men′tə rē), *adj.*

par•lour or **par•lor** (pår′lər) **1** in earlier times, a room in a home for receiving or entertaining guests, like a living room. **2** a business place offering a certain kind of service or refreshment: *a beauty parlour, a funeral parlour, an ice-cream parlour, a beer parlour.* *n.*

WORD HISTORY........parlour

The word **parlour** has its roots in the French word *parler,* meaning "to talk." **Parliament** comes from the same root — it's the place where things are talked over before they are made law.

par•o•dy (per′ə dē) **1** a piece of writing, art, or music that copies the style of another piece but in an exaggerated way, with changes that make it funny. **2** make fun of a piece of writing or music in this way. 1 *n.*, *pl.* **par•o•dies;** 2 *v.*, **par•o•died, par•o•dy•ing.**

pa•role (pə rōl′) **1** the privilege of leaving prison before the full term is served, with certain conditions. People let out on parole usually have to report regularly to a **parole officer.** **2** let out of prison before the full term is served: *The prisoner was paroled after serving two years of her three-year sentence.* 1 *n.*, 2 *v.*, **pa•roled, pa•rol•ing.**

par•ox•ysm (per′ək siz′əm) a sudden fit: *paroxysms of laughter, a paroxysm of coughing.* *n.*

par•rot (per′ət) **1** a tropical bird with a hooked bill and, often, brightly coloured feathers. Some parrots can imitate sounds and repeat words and sentences. **2** imitate or repeat, especially without understanding: *The small child parroted the words of the song.* 1 *n.*, 2 *v.*

pars•ley (pårs′lē) a garden plant with finely divided, fragrant leaves, used to flavour and decorate food. *n.*

pars•nip (pår′snip) a long, tapering root used as a vegetable. It looks like a white carrot. *n.*

part (pårt) **1** an amount less than the whole: *He ate part of an apple.* **2** a thing that helps to make up a whole: *car parts.* **3** a share; involvement: *They had no part in the mischief.* **4** a character in a play, or his or her words and actions: *Carly played the part of the heroine in our play. I know my part from memory.* **5** one of the voices or instruments in a piece of music, or the notes written for it: *a song for four parts. You sing the alto part.* **6** separate or divide: *A river parts the field. The friends parted in anger.* **7** a dividing line left in combing your hair.

8 comb your hair away from a dividing line. 9 partly: *I was part happy and part sad.* 1–5, 7 *n.*, 6, 8 *v.*, 9 *adv.* —**part′ing,** *n. or adj.*
do your part, do your job; do what you can do to help.
for the most part, mostly: *The attempts were for the most part unsuccessful.*
in part, partly: *Our success was due in part to your help.*
on the part of, done, thought, felt, said, etc. by: *There is a feeling on the part of some students that the rule is unfair.*
part and parcel, a necessary part: *Practising is part and parcel of learning to play the piano.*
part with, give up; let go.
play a part, be involved: *Poor road conditions played a part in the accident.*
take part, be a part of; be involved in.
take someone's part, stick up for someone in a conflict.

par·tial (pår′shəl) 1 not complete; not total: *That's only a partial answer.* 2 favouring one side unfairly: *Parents should not be partial to any one child.* *adj.* —**par′tial·ly,** *adv.* —**par′ti·al′i·ty** (pår′shē al′ə tē), *n.*
be partial to, like: *I'm partial to sports.*

par·tic·i·pate (pår tis′ə pāt′) have a share; take part; be involved: *The teacher participated in the children's games.* Someone who is involved is a **participant** (pår tis′ə pənt). *v.*, **par·tic·i·pat·ed, par·tic·i·pat·ing.** —**par·tic′i·pa′tion,** *n.*

par·ti·ci·ple (pår′tə sip′əl) in grammar, the **present participle,** which ends in *-ing,* as in *running, talking,* or the **past participle,** which ends in *-ed* for most verbs, as in *talked, closed.* Participles can be used as adjectives, as in *running water, a closed door.* They can also be used with an auxiliary verb to form various tenses, as in *I am talking, I have talked.* *n.*

par·ti·cle (pår′tə kəl) a very little bit: *I got a particle of dust in my eye.* *n.*

par·tic·u·lar (pər tik′yə lər) 1 being a certain one considered separately from others: *That particular chair is already sold.* 2 special: *This watch is of particular value to me; it belonged to my grandpa. Caring for the dog is his particular task.* 3 hard to please; wanting everything to be just right; very careful: *She is very particular; nothing but the best will do.* 4 a detail: *The work is complete in every particular.* 1–3 *adj.*, 4 *n.* —**par·tic′u·lar·ly,** *adv.*
in particular, specifically: *We drove around, not going anywhere in particular.*

par·ti·tion (pår tish′ən) 1 something that divides and separates, such as a removable wall between rooms. 2 divide into parts: *to partition a house into rooms.* 1 *n.*, 2 *v.*

part·ly (pårt′lē) to some extent; not completely: *We are partly to blame.* *adv.*

part·ner (pårt′nər) 1 a person who helps, shares, or joins with another: *Swim with a partner for safety. Who is your partner for the science project?* 2 a member of a company or firm who owns part of it and shares in all the risks and profits. *n.* —**part′ner·ship′,** *n.*

part of speech (pårt′ əv spēch′) any of the groups that words can be sorted into according to their use or function in sentences. The main parts of speech in English are noun, pronoun, adjective, verb, adverb, preposition, conjunction, and interjection. ▶ See the *Grammar and Usage Mini-Guide.*

Grammar ✓Check . . . part of speech

Many words in English can be used as more than one **part of speech.** In the sentence *I can run fast,* the word *run* is a verb. In the sentence *I am going for a run,* the same word *run* is a noun.

See if you can identify each part of speech in the following sentence: *Wow, you already know every student and teacher in Waterdown?*

par·took (pår tůk′) the past tense of **partake.** *v.*

par·tridge (pår′trij) a bird belonging to the same family as the chicken, quail, and pheasant. It is often hunted. *n., pl.* **par·tridg·es** or **par·tridge.**

part time (pårt′ tīm′) for part of the usual time: *He works part time.* —**part′-time′,** *adj.*

par·ty (pår′tē) 1 a gathering of people to have a good time together: *She had a party on her birthday.* 2 take part in such a gathering: *We partied till midnight.* 3 any group of people doing something together: *a search party. A party of four sat down at the table next to ours.* 4 an organization made up of people who share the same political ideas and who try to get their members elected: *the New Democratic Party.* 5 a person or group thought of as one unit: *The principal met with all three parties involved: the teacher, the student, and her parents.* 1, 3–5 *n., pl.* **par·ties;** 2 *v.*, **par·tied, par·ty·ing.**
third party, a person or group interested in a dispute or relationship between two others, but not actually involved or affected by it.

party line (pår′tē līn′) a telephone line shared by more than one person or family.

a bat	e bed	i bid	o pot	u cup	th thin
ā cake	ē me	ī bite	ō go	ū rude	ᴛʜ then
å bar	ə about	ər over	ȯ for	ů put	zh measure

pass (pas) **1** go by; move past: *The parade passed. We passed the big truck. The days passed quickly and so did my homesickness.* **2** go from one person, place, or condition to another: *The property passed from my grandmother to my parents. The letter carrier passed from house to house.* **3** move: *Pass your hand over the velvet and feel its softness.* **4** hand to someone: *Please pass the butter.* **5** get through successfully: *The bill passed Parliament. I passed my piano exam.* **6** approve; let through: *to pass a law.* **7** use or spend: *We passed the days happily.* **8** take place; happen: *Tell me all that has passed.* **9** a note, card, or ticket letting you in to a place: *a day pass to an amusement park. I came to school late and had to get a pass from the secretary. The reporter needed a pass to enter the armed forces base.* **10** a narrow way across a mountain range. **11** in sports, kick, throw, or shoot to another player: *He passed the puck too far ahead.* **12** in certain games, give up your chance to do something on your turn. **13** the act of passing: *to make a pass in soccer.* 1–8, 11, 12 *v.*, 9, 10, 13 *n.*
bring to pass, cause to happen.
come to pass, happen.
in passing, by the way; just as a casual remark: *She mentioned in passing that she had seen Julian.*
pass as or **pass for,** be taken or accepted as: *That stone could pass as a real diamond.*
pass away, die or come to an end.
pass on, **a** go past; keep going: *He stopped to look and then passed on.* **b** die.
pass out, **a** give out; hand out. **b** *Informal.* faint.
pass over, fail to notice; overlook; disregard: *The teacher passed over my mistake.* **Pass by** can mean the same.
pass something off, try to get people to believe something is what it isn't: *She tried to pass this off as her own work, but it is really Martin's.*
pass up, give up; say no to: *to pass up an opportunity.*

CONFUSABLES ..... passed

passed means "went by": *I passed a bookstore.* Remember, **passed** is the past tense of the verb **pass**.

past means "beyond": *I walked past your house.* **past** also means "time before": *We read about the past.* Remember, **past** is never used as a verb.

pas•sage (pas′ij) **1** a hallway, tunnel, walkway, or other narrow way. **Passageway** means the same. **2** a way through: *The explorers were looking for a passage from the Atlantic to the Pacific.* **3** the fact of passing: *the passage of time.* **4** a section from a piece of writing or music: *a passage from "Lost in the Barrens."* **5** a trip by sea: *The stowaway earned her passage by working on the ship.* *n.*

pas•sen•ger (pas′ən jər) a person who travels in any vehicle but is not the driver or part of the crew. *n.*

pass•er–by (pas′ər bī′) a person who passes by: *The robbery was seen by a passer-by who called the police.* *n., pl.* **pass•ers-by.**

pas•sion (pash′ən) **1** very strong feeling: *Love and anger are passions.* **2** a very strong liking or interest: *He has a passion for music. Cartooning is her passion.* *n.*
—**pas′sion•ate** (pash′ə nit), *adj.*
fly into a passion, become violently angry.

passion fruit (pash′ən frūt′) a small egg-shaped fruit that grows on a tropical vine and is used to make ice cream and fresh juices.

pas•sive (pas′iv) **1** not speaking out or taking firm action but just letting things happen: *passive followers. He is so passive he finds the smallest decisions difficult.* **Passive resistance** is a form of protest against a government by refusing to co-operate, going on a hunger strike, chaining yourself to a tree, etc. It is called "passive" because it is quiet and not violent. **2** in grammar, showing the subject as receiving the action rather than doing it. In *The window was fixed, was fixed* is a passive verb; although the window is the subject, it did not do the fixing. *adj.*

Grammar Check . . . passive verbs

The **passive** form of a verb gives you the option of not mentioning who or what did the action. You can use it when the doer of the action is unknown, unimportant, or obvious: *My wallet was stolen. The fire has been extinguished. The street party will be held on Saturday.*

Pass•o•ver (pas′ō′vər) a Jewish festival celebrating how the Jews were freed from slavery in ancient Egypt. According to the Bible, a destroying angel punished the Egyptians by killing the first-born son in each household, but passed over the homes of the Jews. *n.*

pass•port (pas′pôrt′) a paper or booklet giving you official permission to travel in a foreign country, under the protection of your own government. Only citizens can have passports. *n.*

pass•word (pas′wərd′) a secret word or phrase that lets you into a place, onto a computer, etc. *n.*

past (past) **1** gone by; ended: *Summer is past and fall is here. The past year was a sad one.* **2** time gone by: *Life began far back in the past.* **3** what has happened; history: *We cannot change the past. This town has an interesting past.* **4** short for or having to do with the **past tense,** a verb form showing that an act or state existed or happened before and is no longer going on. In *I had a dream last night, had* is in the past tense. **5** by; up to some point and then going on without stopping: *The bus goes past our house every hour* (*prep.*). *He saw us but walked right past* (*adv.*). **6** beyond; farther or later than: *one block past the store.* 1, 4 *adj.,* 2–3 *n.,* 5, 6 *prep.*

Grammar Check . . . . past tense

To make the **past tense** of most English verbs, add *-ed* to the root word: *aim* becomes *aimed*, *pass* becomes *passed*, *walk* becomes *walked*, and so on.

Irregular verbs form the past tense in other ways, for example *hold* becomes *held*, and *bring* becomes *brought*. If you are not sure of the past tense of a verb, check the root word in a dictionary.

The words pasta, pastry, and pâté are all related to the Greek word *pasta*, meaning something with a kind of porridgy or pastelike consistency.

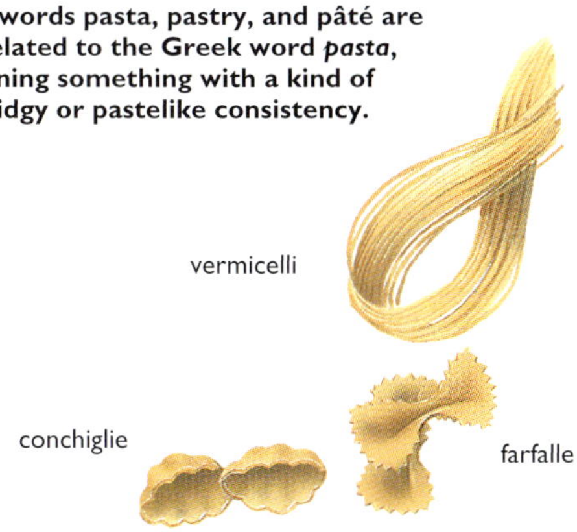

pas·ta (pȧs′tə *or* pas′tə) food made from a mixture of flour and water, such as spaghetti, macaroni, ravioli, and so on. *n.*

paste (pāst) **1** a mixture, such as flour and water, that will stick things together. **2** to stick with paste: *to paste a picture in a scrapbook.* **3** a smooth, moist mixture: *Clay and water are mixed into a paste for making pottery.* 1, 3 *n.,* 2 *v.,* **past·ed, past·ing.**

pas·tel (pas tel′) **1** a kind of soft crayon used in drawing, or a drawing made with these crayons. **2** a soft, pale shade of colour: *pastel pink* (*adj.*). *I like pastels* (*n.*). 1, 2 *n.,* 2 *adj.*

pas·teur·ize (pas′chə rīz′) heat milk, honey, etc. to a high temperature to destroy bacteria. Then it is quickly chilled to prevent changes in flavour. *v.*

pas·time (pas′tīm′) an enjoyable way to pass the time; hobby: *Games and sports are pastimes.* *n.*

pas·tor (pas′tər) a Christian minister in charge of a church. *n.*

pas·try (pās′trē) pies, tarts, and other rich baked goods, or the dough they are made from. Pastry dough is high in fat, making it flaky when baked. *n., pl.* **pas·tries.**

pas·ture (pas′chər) grassy fields where cattle, sheep, or horses can feed. *n.*

pat (pat) **1** touch or tap lightly with something flat, especially with your open hand: *Grandpa patted me on the cheek. The baker patted the dough into a flat cake.* **2** a light touch or tap like this: *a pat on the head.* **3** a small, flat mass of butter. **4** ready-made without much thought: *to give a pat answer to a difficult question.* 1 *v.,* **pat·ted, pat·ting;** 2, 3 *n.,* 4 *adj.*
have down pat or **know down pat,** *Informal.* know thoroughly: *Michael has his spelling words down pat.*
pat on the back, a compliment given as a reward.
stand pat, *Informal.* stick to your position and refuse to change: *Many people were angry with the government but the Prime Minister stood pat.*

patch (pach) **1** a piece of some material put on to fix a hole or rip, or to strengthen a weak place: *a patch for your jeans, a patch for an air mattress.* **2** put patches on; fix, protect, or decorate with a patch or patches: *The workers are patching the road with fresh asphalt.* **3** a pad worn over an injured eye to protect it. **4** a small area: *a patch of ground, a shady patch.* **5** a garden: *a strawberry patch, a vegetable patch.* 1, 3–5 *n.,* 2 *v.* —**patch′y,** *adj.*
patch up, **a** settle: *He did his best to patch up the quarrel.* **b** fix or put together hastily or for the time being: *to patch up a leaking tap.*

patch·work (pach′wərk′) **1** pieces of cloth of various colours or shapes sewn together: *a patchwork quilt.* **2** anything like this: *From the airplane, we saw a patchwork of fields and woods.* *n.*

pâ·té (pa tā′) meat ground up into a paste with spices for use as a spread. It is usually made of liver. *n.*

pat·ent (pat′ənt *for 1–3,* pā′tənt *for 4*) **1** the legal right to be the only one allowed to make or sell a new invention for a certain number of years. The government issues patents. **2** get a patent for: *The inventor patented all her inventions.* **3** protected by a patent: *patent medicines.* **4** obvious; plain: *She laughed at the patent stupidity of their plan.* 1 *n.,* 2 *v.,* 3–4 *adj.*

patent leather (pat′ənt leth′ər) leather with a very shiny, smooth surface, usually black. Patent leather was originally protected by a patent.

a bat	e bed	i bid	o pot	u cup	th thin
ā cake	ē me	ī bite	ō go	ū rude	ᴛʜ then
ȧ bar	ə about	ər over	ȯ for	u̇ put	zh measure

pa·ter·nal (pə tėr′nəl) fatherly: *paternal advice.* Your **paternal grandparents** are your father's parents. **Paternity** is the fact of being a father. *adj.*

path (path) 1 a narrow track made by people or animals walking. 2 a walkway of stone, cement, etc. 3 the line or route followed by a moving person or thing: *the path of a tornado. The ball rolled into the path of a truck.* 4 a line of action leading to some goal: *the path to success.* 5 a series of directories or memory locations searched by a computer to find a file. *n., pl.* **paths** (paтнz).

pa·thet·ic (pə thet′ik) pitiful; causing pity, either because it is so sad or because it is so badly done: *a pathetic attempt at drawing. The lost child was a pathetic sight. adj.* **—pa·thet′i·cal·ly,** *adv.*

pa·tient (pā′shənt) 1 able and willing to wait, work hard, or put up with troublesome things for a long time without complaining. 2 a person who is being treated by a doctor, dentist, etc. 1 *adj.,* 2 *n.* **—pa′tience,** *n.*

pat·i·o (pat′ē ō) a paved outdoor sitting or eating area next to a house, restaurant, etc., or in the courtyard of a hospital or mall. *n., pl.* **pat·i·os.**

pa·tri·arch (pā′trē ärk′) a father who is the head of a family or tribe, or any elderly man who commands deep respect. *n.*

pa·tri·ot (pā′trē ət) a person who loves his or her country. *n.* **—pa′tri·ot·ism′,** *n.* **—pa′tri·ot′ic** (pā′trē ot′ik), *adj.*

pa·trol (pə trōl′) 1 go around an area checking for any problems, as a guard or police officer does: *The guards patrolled the camp.* 2 the job of patrolling, the person or group doing it, or the area patrolled: *He was on patrol last night.* A **patrol car** is a car used for this by police. 1 *v.,* **pa·trolled, pa·trol·ling;** 2 *n.*

> **WORD HISTORY........ patrol**
>
> **Patrol** is from the French word *patrouiller,* meaning "to wade in mud." Soldiers patrolling an army camp had to do a lot of tramping around in muck.

pa·tron (pā′trən) 1 a regular customer. 2 someone who sponsors or supports a person, a project, or a certain kind of work: *a patron of the arts. n.* **—pa′tron·age,** *n.*

pa·tron·ize (pā′trə nīz′ *or* pat′rə nīz′) 1 be a regular customer of: *We patronize the local bookstore.* 2 support or sponsor: *Many companies patronize amateur sports.* 3 treat someone kindly but as if he or she has little skill or understanding: *Children do not like being patronized by adults. v.,* **pa·tron·ized, pa·tron·iz·ing.**

pat·ter[1] (pat′ər) 1 make soft, quick taps: *The rain pattered on the windowpane. Bare feet pattered along the hard floor.* 2 a series of soft quick taps: *the patter of rain, the patter of little feet.* 1 *v.,* 2 *n.*

pat·ter[2] (pat′ər) a stream of easy talk like that of a magician or salesperson. *n.*

pat·tern (pat′ərn) 1 any arrangement of shapes, colours, numbers, characteristics, actions, etc. that keeps repeating: *a behaviour pattern, weather patterns, the pattern in wallpaper. Do you notice a pattern in the numbers 2, 4, 8, 16, 32?* 2 a model or guide for making something: *a pattern for sewing a dress.* 3 make or design according to some model or example: *I patterned my costume after the one I saw in the store.* 1, 2 *n.,* 3 *v.*

pat·ty (pat′ē) 1 a small, flat, roundish mass of something: *a hamburger patty, a chocolate mint patty, mud patties.* 2 a hollow shell of pastry filled with meat or vegetables. *n., pl.* **pat·ties.**

paunch (ponch) a large belly. *n.*

pau·per (pop′ər) a very poor person. *n.*

pause (poz) 1 a short stop or rest: *After a short pause he went on reading.* 2 stop or cause to stop for a short time: *She paused to listen for a moment. Please pause the video while I go get a drink.* 1 *n.,* 2 *v.,* **paused, paus·ing.**

pave (pāv) cover a street, sidewalk, etc. with concrete, asphalt, flat stones, or bricks: *They are going to pave the driveway.* A paved area, or the covering used for paving, is **pavement.** *v.,* **paved, pav·ing.**
pave the way, make something easier by work done before: *Her research paved the way for later scientists.*

pa·vil·ion (pə vil′yən) 1 a light building with open sides, used for shelter or shade. 2 a large tent for entertainment or shelter. 3 a building that contains exhibits at a fair. *n.*

paw (po) 1 the foot of a four-footed animal with claws. Cats and dogs have paws. 2 strike or handle with the paws, hoofs, or feet: *The cat pawed the mouse it had caught. The horse pawed the ground, eager to be going.* 3 *Informal.* handle roughly: *The customers pawed the shirts on the bargain counter.* 1 *n.,* 2, 3 *v.*
paw the air, grab wildly at something and miss.

pawn[1] (pon) leave something with another person, called a **pawnbroker,** as a guarantee that borrowed money will be returned. If it is not, the pawnbroker may keep or sell the item: *He pawned his watch to buy food until he could get work. v.*
in pawn, being held by another person in this way: *His watch is in pawn to the man who lent him money.*

pawn[2] (pon) 1 in the game of chess, one of the eight pieces that are of lowest value and are often given up to gain some advantage. 2 an unimportant person used by somebody to gain an advantage: *The businessman used his friends as pawns in his race for power.* *n.*

pay (pā) 1 give money in exchange for goods, services, or work: *She paid $45 for the coat.* 2 the money given: *He gets his pay every Saturday.* 3 give; offer; make: *to pay attention, to pay a compliment, to pay a visit.* 4 be worth doing; bring a reward: *It pays to be patient.* 5 that you have to pay to use: *a pay phone.* 6 be punished or make up for a wrong act: *He paid for his crime in prison.* 1, 3–6 *v.,* **paid, pay·ing;** 2 *n.,* 5 *adj.* —**pay′ment,** *n.*
pay back, a return borrowed money. b give the same treatment as received: *I'll pay her back for her hospitality by inviting her to dinner.*
pay off, finish paying over time: *to pay off a debt.*
pay up, pay all that is owed.

pay·cheque (pā′chek′) a cheque paying an employee for his or her work, usually every week, every two weeks, or every month. *n.*

PC *abbreviation for:* 1 personal computer, a desktop computer used by one person at a time. 2 Progressive Conservative, having to do with one of Canada's major political parties.

pea (pē) a round seed that grows in a pod on a vine. Peas may be green, yellow, or black, and are used as a vegetable with or without the pods. *n., pl.* **peas.**

WORD HISTORY.......... pea

English used to have an old word *pease* for this vegetable. It referred to many pieces at once, like corn. But people thought the z sound showed the plural, so they started to call one individual bit of pease a **pea**.

peace (pēs) 1 freedom from war or fighting: *We are working for world peace.* **Peacetime** is time without war. 2 calmness; stillness; freedom from trouble or worry or from too much noise or activity: *peace of mind. We enjoy the peace of the country.* *n.* —**peace′ful,** *adj.*
at peace, a not fighting. b content; not upset or worried.
hold your peace, be silent; keep still.
make peace, agree to stop fighting.

peace·a·ble (pē′sə bəl) loving peace: *Peaceable people keep out of quarrels.* *adj.*

peace·keep·er (pēs′kē′pər) a soldier sent with others to a place where fighting has recently stopped, in order to try to prevent further violence. Peacekeepers are usually sent under the authority of the United Nations. *n.* —**peace′keep′ing,** *n.*

peace pipe (pēs′ pīp′) another name for the **sacred pipe** used by First Nations people in certain ceremonies.

peach (pēch) 1 a sweet, juicy, round fruit with a soft, pinkish-yellow, fuzzy skin and a rough stone or pit. It grows on a small tree. 2 yellowish pink. 1, 2 *n.,* 2 *adj.*

The peacock fans out its tail feathers (called a train) as part of its mating display. The train is about five times as long as the peacock's body.

pea·cock (pē′kok′) 1 the male **peafowl,** a large bird of southeast Asia with beautiful green, blue, and gold feathers. The peacock can spread out its tail feathers like a fan. The female is called a **peahen** (pē′hen′). 2 a person who is vain and likes showing off. *n.*

peak (pēk) 1 the pointed top of a mountain or hill: *snowy peaks.* 2 any pointed end or top: *the peak of a roof.* 3 the highest point: *at the peak of her career.* 4 reach the highest point: *The temperature peaked at 33°C.* 5 the visor or brim of a cap. 1–3, 5 *n.,* 4 *v.*

peal (pēl) 1 a loud, long sound: *a peal of thunder, peals of laughter.* 2 the loud ringing of bells. 3 a set of bells. 4 ring out loudly; ring: *The bells pealed on Sunday morning.* 1–3 *n.,* 4 *v.*

a bat	e bed	i bid	o pot	u cup	th thin
ā cake	ē me	ī bite	ō go	ū rude	ᴛʜ then
ä bar	ə about	ər over	ô for	ů put	zh measure

The peanut is more of a pea than a nut. The plant is a legume, that is, it bears fruit in the form of pods (shells) that contain one or more seeds (peanuts).

pea·nut (pē′nut′) a seed like a nut, growing in pods that ripen underground. Peanuts are used for food and cooking oil. **Peanut butter** is peanuts that have been roasted and then ground into a smooth paste. *n.*

pear (per) a sweet, juicy fruit with rounded ends, narrowing toward the stem. It grows on a small tree. *n.*

pearl (pərl) 1 a white or blue-grey gem that has a soft shine. Pearls are formed inside the shells of some oysters, clams, or similar shellfish. 2 anything that is like a pearl in shape, colour, beauty, or preciousness. 3 very pale, clear, bluish grey. 1–3 *n.,* 3 *adj.* **—pearl′y,** *adj.*

peas·ant (pez′ənt) a poor farmer, especially one who does not own the land he or she works on. *n.*

peat (pēt) a mass of partly rotted plants which can be used as fertilizer or as fuel when dried. Moss that will turn or is turning into peat is **peat moss.** *n.*

peb·ble (peb′əl) a small stone, usually worn smooth and round by water. *n.* **—peb′bly,** *adj.*

pe·can (pi kan′ *or* pē′kan) an edible nut that grows on a type of hickory tree in the southern United States and Mexico. It is shaped like an olive and has a smooth, thin reddish shell. *n.*

peck[1] (pek) 1 strike or grab with the beak: *The hen pecked corn.* 2 a stroke made with the beak: *The hen gave me a peck.* 3 make by striking with the beak: *The woodpeckers pecked holes in the trees.* 4 eat only a little, bit by bit: *She is not feeling well; she just pecks at her food.* 5 *Informal.* kiss quickly and lightly. 6 *Informal.* a light or hurried kiss: *a peck on the cheek.* 1, 3–5 *v.,* 2, 6 *n.*
pecking order, the ranking system in a group, telling who is more powerful than whom.

peck[2] (pek) 1 an old unit for measuring fruits and vegetables, equal to eight quarts or one-fourth of a bushel (about 9.1 L). 2 a great deal: *a peck of trouble.* *n.*

pe·cul·iar (pi kyūl′yər) 1 strange; odd; unusual: *We've had very peculiar weather lately; 25°C in the middle of March!* 2 belonging to one person or thing and not others; unique: *Some minerals are peculiar to the Canadian Shield.* *adj.* **—pe·cu′li·ar′i·ty** (pi kyū′lē er′ə tē), *n.*

ped·al (ped′əl) 1 a lever that you work with your foot. Cars have a pedal to operate the brakes. A bicycle has pedals to move the chain which turns the back wheel. 2 work the pedals of; move by using the pedals: *She pedalled her bicycle slowly up the hill.* 1 *n.,* 2 *v.,* **ped·alled** or **ped·aled, ped·al·ling** or **ped·al·ing.**

ped·dle (ped′əl) 1 carry from place to place and sell; sell on the street: *to peddle souvenirs, to peddle newspapers.* 2 go around giving or offering something worthless: *to peddle gossip.* *v.,* **ped·dled, ped·dling. —ped′dler,** *n.*

ped·es·tal (ped′i stəl) the decorative base that a statue, vase, floor lamp, etc. stands on. *n.*
put or **set on a pedestal,** think of someone as very high and noble; idolize: *"I don't want to be put on a pedestal," said the hockey star, "I'm just an ordinary human being."*

pe·des·tri·an (pə des′trē ən) 1 a person who goes on foot; a walker: *Pedestrians have to cross at the crosswalk.* 2 going on foot; walking: *pedestrian traffic.* 1 *n.,* 2 *adj.*

pe·di·a·tri·cian (pē′dē ə trish′ən) a medical doctor who deals with babies and children. *n.* **—pe′di·at′rics** (pē′dē at′riks), *n.* **—pe′di·at′ric,** *adj.*

ped·i·gree (ped′ə grē′) the list of the ancestors of a person or animal; a family tree. *n.*

ped·lar (ped′lər) another spelling of **peddler.** *n.*

pe·dom·e·ter (pə dom′ə tər) an instrument that records the number of steps you take so you can calculate how far you have walked. *n.*

peek (pēk) 1 look quickly or secretly: *You can't peek while you're counting in hide-and-seek.* 2 look through a small hole or crack: *I peeked through the hole in the fence.*

3 the action of peeking: *a peek through the keyhole. She had a peek at the cake in the oven.* 1, 2 *v.*, 3 *n.*

peel (pēl) 1 the skin or outer covering of a fruit or vegetable. 2 strip off the skin or something like a skin: *to peel an orange or a potato, to peel the bark off a stick. I peeled off my wet clothes.* 3 come off or take off in a thin layer: *The paint on the shed is peeling.* 1 *n.*, 2, 3 *v.*
keep your eyes peeled, *Informal.* be on the alert: *Keep your eyes peeled for a small black dog; we lost it.*

peep[1] (pēp) another word for **peek.** A **peephole** is a hole to peek through. *v. or n.*

peep[2] (pēp) 1 the short, high-pitched cry of a baby bird or chick. 2 make such a sound. 1 *n.*, 2 *v.*

peer[1] (pēr) look closely in order to see clearly: *She peered at the tag to read the price.* *v.*

peer[2] (pēr) 1 a person who is your equal in ability, age, or status: *She gets along with adults as well as with her peers.* A person or thing that stands above all others is **peerless.** The influence that people your own age have over you is called **peer pressure.** 2 in the United Kingdom, a noble, such as a duke or an earl. *n.*

peeve (pēv) *Informal.* 1 annoy: *I'm a bit peeved that she gave away my secret.* 2 an annoyance. Your **pet peeve** is something that particularly annoys you. 1 *v.*, 2 *n.* —**pee′vish,** *adj.*

peg (peg) 1 a piece of wood or metal shaped like a large, fat nail, used to fasten down a tent, hang things on, etc. A **pegboard** has evenly-spaced holes to stick pegs or hooks in for hanging things up. 2 fasten or mark with pegs: *We must peg down our tent. They pegged out the area to be dug up for a garden.* 1 *n.*, 2 *v.*, **pegged, peg·ging.**
square peg in a round hole, someone who does not fit with his or her surroundings.
take someone down a peg, lower someone's pride.

P.E.I. *abbreviation for* Prince Edward Island.

pel·i·can (pel′ə kən) a very large fish-eating water bird with a huge bill that has a pouch in the bottom for scooping up and holding food. It nests on lakes in Canada's prairies. *n.*

pel·let (pel′it) 1 a little ball of paper, hail, pet food, animal waste, etc. 2 a small piece of metal fired from a shotgun. *n.*

pell–mell or **pell·mell** (pel′mel′) in a disorganized rush: *The girls dashed pell-mell down the beach and into the waves.* *adv.*

pelt[1] (pelt) 1 throw things at: *We pelted them with snowballs.* 2 beat heavily: *The rain pelted against the window.* 3 run fast: *They came pelting after me.* *v.*

pelt[2] (pelt) the furry skin taken from a small animal such as a beaver. *n.*

pel·vis (pel′vis) the basin-shaped structure of bone at the lower end of your body, formed by the hipbones and the wedge-shaped bone at the base of the spine. *n.*

pem·mi·can (pem′i kən) lean meat that has been dried, pounded, and mixed with fat. Pemmican was the usual food of the voyageurs because it would keep for a long time. *n.*

WORD HISTORY..... pemmican

Pemmican comes from Cree *pimii*, meaning "fat," and *-kan*, meaning "prepared."

pen[1] (pen) 1 a writing instrument that uses ink. 2 write: *He penned a few lines to his father.* A **pen pal** is someone you write letters back and forth with; a **pen name** is a name used by a writer instead of his or her real name. 1 *n.*, 2 *v.*, **penned, pen·ning.**

pen[2] (pen) 1 a small, closed-in area for sheep, pigs, chickens, and so on. 2 shut in a pen or in a place that is hard to escape from: *He had me penned in a corner.* 1 *n.*, 2 *v.*, **penned, pen·ning.**

pe·nal·ize (pē′nə līz′) punish; give a penalty or disadvantage to: *to be penalized with a detention, to be penalized for highsticking in hockey. Our football team was penalized five yards.* *v.*, **pe·nal·ized, pe·nal·iz·ing.**

pen·al·ty (pen′əl tē) a punishment or disadvantage given to someone: *Her penalty for illegal parking was a fine of $20. I got a penalty for arguing with the umpire.* A **penalty shot** is a free shot given to one team in a game as a penalty against the other team. The **penalty box** is the place where hockey players wait off the ice until their penalty is over. *n.*, *pl.* **pen·al·ties.**

pen·cil (pen′səl) 1 a pointed instrument to write or draw with, usually made of wood with a long, thin piece of black or coloured material in the centre. 2 mark, write, or draw with a pencil. 1 *n.*, 2 *v.*, **pen·cilled** or **pen·ciled, pen·cil·ling** or **pen·cil·ing.**

pend·ant (pen′dənt) an ornament that hangs from a necklace or an earring. *n.*

pen·du·lum (pen′jə ləm *or* pen′dyə ləm) a weight hung from a fixed point so it can swing back and forth. Old clockworks were often timed by a pendulum. *n.*

a bat	e bed	i bid	o pot	u cup	th thin
ā cake	ē me	ī bite	ō go	ū rude	ᴛʜ then
ä bar	ə about	ər over	ô for	ů put	zh measure

pen•e•trate (pen′ə trāt′) **1** pass into or through; pierce: *The nail penetrated the board. Even where the trees were thickest, the sunshine penetrated. The smell penetrated the whole house.* **2** see into or through; understand: *to penetrate a disguise, to penetrate a mystery.* *v.,* **pen•e•trat•ed, pen•e•trat•ing.** **—pen′e•tra•ble,** *adj.*

All penguins have white feathers on the belly and black on the back. This makes good camouflage in the water — from below, the light-coloured belly is hard to see against sky or ice. From above, the dark-coloured back merges into the darkness of the seabed.

pen•guin (peng′gwin) a black and white sea bird with wings like flippers, which it uses for diving and swimming, not for flying. Penguins live in Antarctica and other cold areas of the Southern Hemisphere. *n.*

pen•i•cil•lin (pen′ə sil′ən) a very powerful **antibiotic,** a drug used to treat certain diseases and infections caused by bacteria. *n.*

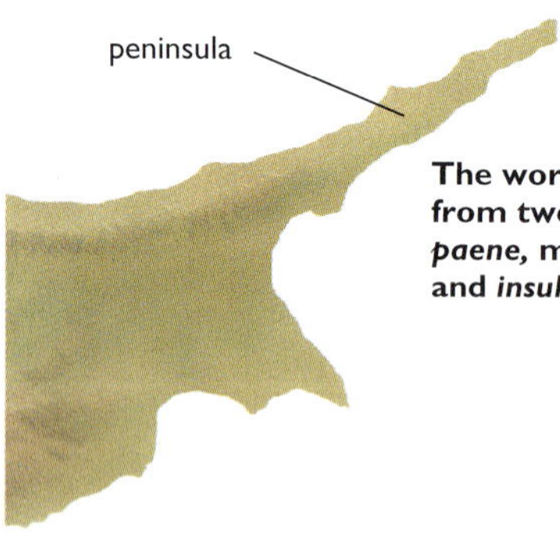

The word peninsula comes from two Latin words: *paene,* meaning "almost," and *insula,* meaning "island."

pen•in•su•la (pə nin′sə lə *or* pə nin′syə lə) a piece of land almost surrounded by water, or sticking far out into the water: *Nova Scotia is a large peninsula.* *n.*

pe•nis (pē′nis) the organ of sex and urination of a male human being or animal. *n.*

pen•i•tent (pen′ə tənt) sorry for doing wrong: *The penitent child promised never to cheat again.* *adj.* **—pen′i•tence,** *n.*

pen•i•ten•tia•ry (pen′ə ten′shə rē) a prison, especially a federal prison for people who have done serious crimes. *n., pl.* **pen•i•ten•tia•ries.**

pen•knife (pen′nīf′) a small pocketknife. *n., pl.* **pen•knives.**

pen•man•ship (pen′mən ship′) the style or skill of handwriting. *n.*

pen•nant (pen′ənt) a flag, usually long and narrow, used as a trophy, school banner, a signal flag, etc. *n.*

pen•ny (pen′ē) a cent; a copper coin of Canada and the United States. To be **penniless** is to be very poor; a **penny-pincher** is someone who hates to spend money. *n., pl.* **pennies.**

a pretty penny, a lot of money.

in for a penny, in for a pound, if you're doing it at all, you might as well go all the way.

pen•sion (pen′shən) **1** a regular payment to a person who has retired from work. Someone who gets a pension is a **pensioner.** **2** give a pension to. 1 *n.,* 2 *v.*

pen•sive (pen′siv) thoughtful in a serious or sad way: *She stared out the window with a pensive air.* *adj.*

pen•tath•lon (pen tath′lon) an athletic event with five parts that include running, jumping, and throwing. The winner is the person with the highest total of points from all the different parts. *n.* **—pen•tath′lete,** *n.*

pent•house (pent′hous′) an apartment at the top of a building. Often it is a very luxurious apartment. *n.*

pent up (pent up) shut up inside: *The child was pent up in the house all week because of illness. Let go of your pent-up feelings.*

pe•o•ny (pē′ə nē) a garden plant with large, red, pink, yellow, or white flowers. *n., pl.* **pe•o•nies.**

peo•ple (pē′pəl) **1** human beings; persons: *Ten people came.* **2** a nation; a group sharing a culture and language: *the Canadian people, Aboriginal peoples.* **3** those who are being ruled over or led by someone: *the queen and her people. The French nobles oppressed the people.* **4** fill or provide with people: *The Canadian Arctic was first peopled by the Inuit.* **5** *Informal.* family; relatives: *He spends his holidays with his people.* 1, 3, 5 *pl.n.,* 2 *sing.n., pl.* **peo•ples;** 4 *v.,* **peo•pled, peo•pling.**

pep (pep) *Informal.* **1** spirit; energy. A **pep talk** is a talk that is supposed to make people enthusiastic. **2 pep up,** fill with energy or enthusiasm; put new life into: *She did her best to pep up the dull party.* 1 *n.,* 2 *v.,* **pepped, pep•ping.** **—pep′py,** *adj.*

pep·per (pep′ər) 1 a seasoning with a hot taste, made by grinding the tiny dried fruits, called **peppercorns,** of the East Indian pepper plant. 2 a hollow green, red, orange, or yellow vegetable that is eaten raw, baked, or fried. Peppers may be sweet or hot. 3 season or sprinkle with pepper. 4 sprinkle thickly: *His face is peppered with freckles.* 5 hit with many small objects: *They peppered the enemy with bullets.* 1, 2 *n.,* 3–5 *v.* —**pep′per·y,** *adj.*

pep·per·mint (pep′ər mint′) 1 a herb whose oil is used to flavour candy and toothpaste. Peppermint is also used to make tea. 2 a candy flavoured with this oil. *n.*

pep·per·o·ni (pep′ə rō′nē) a dry, spicy sausage often sliced and used as a topping for pizza. *n.*

per (pər) for each: *He charges $20 per lesson.* **Per capita** (pər kap′ə tə) means "for each person." *prep.* **as per,** as stated or required by: *As per our agreement, I'll pay half the cost.*

per·ceive (pər sēv′) 1 be aware of through the senses; see, hear, taste, smell, or feel: *Some people are unable to perceive colour.* 2 notice and understand: *I soon perceived that I could not make him change his mind.* 3 think of: *How you react to an event depends on how you perceive it.* *v.,* **per·ceiv·ed, per·ceiv·ing.**

per·cent or **per cent** (pər sent′) a portion or fraction of some quantity, expressed in hundredths; the number of parts out of a hundred. Ten percent is one-tenth; fifty percent is half. One hundred percent is the whole amount. **Percentage** is used with an adjective instead of a number: *A large percentage of Canadians live in Ontario. Symbol:* % *n.*

WORD HISTORY........ percent

Percent is from the Latin phrase *per centum,* meaning "among a hundred." *Centum* also gave us the words **cent** and **century**.

per·cep·ti·ble (pər sep′tə bəl) that can be perceived; noticeable: *There was a barely perceptible flavour of onion in the soup.* *adj.* —**per·cep′ti·bly,** *adv.*

per·cep·tion (pər sep′shən) 1 the act, fact, or power of perceiving: *a keen perception, quick perception.* A person who perceives things clearly and quickly is **perceptive.** 2 the view or understanding you have of something: *Once we have a clear perception of the problem, we can start solving it.* *n.*

perch[1] (pərch) 1 a bar, branch, or anything else that a bird can rest on. 2 land and rest: *A robin perched on our porch railing.* 3 a rather high seat or position: *The cat looked down from its perch on top of the piano.* 4 sit or set on something high: *The village was perched on a high hill.* 1, 3 *n.,* 2, 4 *v.*

perch[2] (pərch) a small freshwater or saltwater fish used for food. There are many different kinds; most have two fins on their backs. *n., pl.* **perch** or **perch·es.**

per·chance (pər chans′) a formal or poetic word for "perhaps": *If it snows, perchance we can ski.* *adv.*

per·co·late (pər′kə lāt′) 1 drip or drain slowly through small holes or spaces: *Water percolates through sand.* 2 make coffee in a **percolator,** a pot that lets boiling water bubble up through a tube and then drip down through ground coffee, over and over. *v.,* **per·co·lat·ed, per·co·lat·ing.**

per·cus·sion (pər kush′ən) the striking of one thing against another. A **percussion instrument** is one you play by hitting it, such as a drum. *n.*

per·en·ni·al (pə ren′ē əl) 1 living more than two years: *perennial garden plants.* 2 a perennial plant: *Roses are perennials.* 3 lasting for a very long time, or always returning: *the perennial beauty of the hills, a perennial problem.* 4 lasting through the whole year: *A perennial stream does not dry up in summer.* 1, 3, 4 *adj.,* 2 *n.*

per·fect (pər′fikt *for 1, 3, and 4,* pər fekt′ *for 2*) 1 with nothing wrong or missing; completely good, right, or exact: *a perfect spelling paper, a perfect apple, a perfect circle.* 2 remove all faults from; make complete; add the finishing touches to: *to perfect an invention.* 3 absolute: *a perfect stranger.* 4 having to do with or short for **perfect tense,** any tense that uses the auxiliary *have* with the past participle of another verb, as in *He has gone* or *They had already heard.* 1, 3 *adj.,* 2 *v.,* 4 *n.* —**per′fect·ly,** *adv.*

per·fec·tion (pər fek′shən) 1 the fact of being perfect. A **perfectionist** is someone who insists on things being perfect. 2 the process of perfecting something: *The perfection of our plans will take another week.* *n.* **to perfection,** perfectly: *This pie is baked to perfection.*

per·fo·rate (pər′fə rāt′) make a hole or holes through: *The target was perforated by bullets.* A row of little holes is often made in paper as a guide for tearing. Sheets of postage stamps are perforated. *v.,* **per·fo·rat·ed, per·fo·rat·ing.** —**per′fo·ra′tion,** *n.*

a bat	e bed	i bid	o pot	u cup	th thin
ā cake	ē me	ī bite	ō go	ū rude	TH then
ä bar	ə about	ər over	ô for	ù put	zh measure

per·form (pər fôrm′) **1** do or carry out: *The diver performed a triple somersault. The surgeon performed an operation.* **2** do something to entertain others; put on a show of some kind: *Our class performed a musical play.* The **performing arts** are ones that are done in front of an audience, such as singing, acting, dancing, and so on. *v.* —**per·form′ance,** *n.* —**per·form′er,** *n.*

per·fume (pər′fyūm *or* pər fyūm′ *for 1 and 2,* pər fyūm′ *for 3*) **1** a liquid with a sweet smell, especially a liquid you put on your skin. **2** any sweet smell: *the perfume of flowers.* **3** fill with a sweet smell: *Flowers perfumed the air.* 1, 3 *n.,* 2 *v.,* **per·fumed, per·fum·ing.**

per·haps (pər haps′) maybe; possibly: *Perhaps a letter will come today. adv.*

per·il (per′əl) risk or danger: *This bridge is not safe; cross it at your peril. n.* —**per′il·ous,** *adj.*

pe·rim·e·ter (pə rim′ə tər) the outer boundary of something, or the distance around it: *the perimeter of a circle. A fence marks the perimeter of the field. n.*

pe·ri·od (pēr′yəd) **1** the dot (.) marking the end of most sentences or showing an abbreviation, as in *Mr.* or *Dec.* **2** a stretch of time: *an exciting period in Canadian history.* **3** one of the sections that a school day is divided into for different subjects, or one of three twenty-minute parts of a hockey game: *We have two art periods a week. No goals were scored in the first period.* **4** the time every month or so when a girl or woman menstruates. *n.*

Grammar Check . . . . . . period

Always use a **period** at the end of a sentence and for abbreviations such as *Mr., Mrs.,* or *Dr.* Abbreviations of companies or organizations are sometimes written without periods: CBC, NHL, YMCA.

pe·ri·od·ic (pē′rē od′ik) happening or appearing again and again, every so often: *periodic attacks of asthma. adj.* —**pe′ri·od′i·cal·ly,** *adv.*

pe·ri·od·i·cal (pē′rē od′ə kəl) **1** a magazine that appears regularly, such as every month or every week. **2** published regularly, but not daily. 1 *n.,* 2 *adj.*

pe·riph·er·al (pə rif′ə rəl) **1** having to do with an outside edge or **periphery.** When you see "out of the corner of your eye," you are using your peripheral vision. **2** any device connected to a computer to make up a computer system. Printers, monitors, mice, and disk drives are peripherals. *adj.*

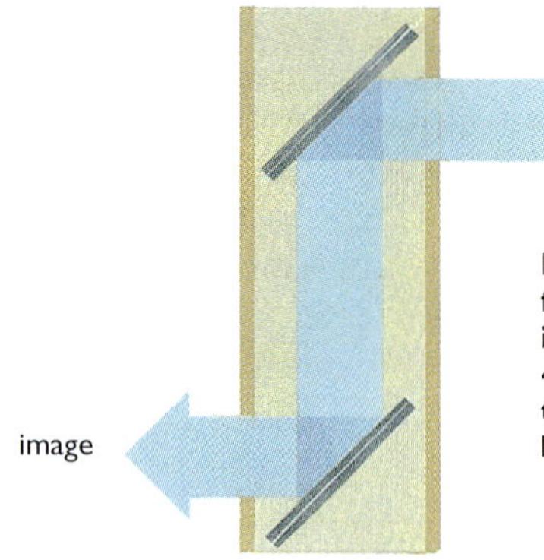

In its simplest form, a periscope is two mirrors at 45° angles, near the top and bottom of a tube.

per·i·scope (per′ə skōp′) a long tube with mirrors in it that reflect images down the tube in a way that lets you see over or around obstacles. Periscopes are used in submarines to get a view of the surface. *n.*

per·ish (per′ish) be destroyed; die: *Buildings perish in flames. Flowers perish when frost comes.* **Perishable** food is food that can spoil. *v.*

per·ju·ry (pər′jə rē) the act of telling a lie in a court of law after swearing to tell the truth. *n.*

perk (pərk) raise smartly or briskly: *The sparrow perked up its tail. v.*
perk up, brighten up; become more lively and energetic: *We all perked up after a good lunch.*

perk·y (pər′kē) cheery, bright, brisk, or saucy. *adj.*

In the Arctic winter, all moisture in the soil freezes. In summer the topsoil may thaw, but the subsoil is permanently frozen.

Oil pipelines are built above the ground, to prevent any thawing of the permafrost.

per·ma·frost (pər′mə frost′) ground that is permanently frozen. Sometimes it partly thaws in the summer: *There is permafrost in the Canadian North. n.*

per·ma·nent (pər′mə nənt) **1** lasting; meant to stay that way; not for a short time only: *a permanent change, a permanent address. My first permanent tooth came in when I was seven.* **2** short for **permanent wave,** a wave or curl put in a person's hair by a special process so as to last for a long time. **Perm** is a shortened form for this meaning. 1 *adj.,* 2 *n.* —**per′ma·nence,** *n.*

per•me•a•ble (pər′mē ə bəl) with tiny holes that let liquids or gases through: *Oxygen passes into the blood through the permeable membranes in the lungs.* *adj.*

per•me•ate (pər′mē āt′) spread through the whole of; soak into or through: *The smoke permeated the house. Water will easily permeate a cotton jacket.* *v.,* **per•me•at•ed, per•me•at•ing.**

per•mit (pər mit′ *for 1,* pər′mit *for 2*) **1** let; allow: *Permit me to explain. The law does not permit smoking in theatres.* **2** a piece of paper giving official permission to do something: *a fishing permit, a parking permit.* 1 *v.,* **per•mit•ted, per•mit•ting;** 2 *n.* **—per•mis′sion** (pər mish′ən), *n.* **—per•mis′si•ble** (pər mis′ə bəl), *adj.*

pe•ro•gy (pə rō′gē) a small pocket of dough stuffed with potato, cheese, fruit, or meat and then boiled, steamed, or fried. **Pierogy** and **pirogy** are other spellings for this food. *n., pl.* **pe•ro•gies** or **pe•ro•gy.**

per•pen•dic•u•lar (pər′pən dik′yə lər) **1** upright; standing straight up: *a perpendicular cliff.* **2** at right angles. One line is perpendicular to another when the two of them make a square corner. The floor of a room is perpendicular to the walls and parallel to the ceiling. **3** a perpendicular line, plane, or position. 1, 2 *adj.,* 3 *n.*

per•pet•u•al (pər pech′ū əl) lasting or going on forever: *the perpetual snow of the North Pole, a perpetual stream of visitors.* *adj.* **—per•pet′u•al•ly,** *adv.*

per•plex (pər pleks′) puzzle completely; bewilder: *This problem is hard enough to perplex us all.* *v.* **—per•plex′i•ty,** *n.*

per•se•cute (pər′sə kyūt′) treat someone cruelly because he or she is different or has different beliefs from most other people: *Mennonites came to North America because they were being persecuted in Europe.* *v.,* **per•se•cut•ed, per•se•cut•ing.** **—per′se•cu′tion,** *n.*

per•se•vere (pər′sə vēr′) continue steadily in doing something even though it is hard: *They persevered in their search for gold.* *v.,* **per•se•vered, per•se•ver•ing.** **—per′se•ver′ence,** *n.*

per•sim•mon (pər sim′ən) a sweet orange fruit from a tree that grows in the eastern United States. *n.*

per•sist (pər sist′) **1** continue firmly; refuse to stop or be changed: *She persisted till she had solved the difficult problem.* **2** last; stay; endure: *On some very high mountains snow persists throughout the year.* *v.* **—per•sist′ent,** *adj.* **—per•sist′ence,** *n.*

per•son (pər′sən) **1** a human being: *No one was there—not even one person.* **2** the human body or its appearance: *He kept his person neat and trim.* **3** any of the parts played by people or things in a conversation or piece of writing. The **first person** is whoever is speaking (I, me, we, us); the **second person** is the one being spoken to (you); the **third person** is anyone or anything being spoken about (he, him, she, her, it, they, them). *n.*
in person, yourself; so that you are actually physically there: *Come in person; do not write or phone.*

per•son•al (pər′sə nəl) **1** belonging to or meant for a particular person; private: *a personal letter.* **2** done with the person actually physically being there: *a personal visit.* **3** of the body or bodily appearance: *Taking baths is part of personal hygiene.* **4** rudely targeting a particular person: *personal remarks, personal insults.* *adj.*

per•son•al•i•ty (pər′sə nal′ə tē) **1** all the individual qualities that make a person unique, or different from all others; a person's attitudes, interests, style of relating to people, habits, and so on: *Their personalities are totally different but they are still best friends.* **2** the interesting or attractive qualities of a person: *Carol has a lot of personality.* **3** a well-known person: *a TV personality.* *n., pl.* **per•son•al•i•ties.**

per•son•al•ly (pər′sə nə lē) **1** in person; by actually being there or doing it yourself: *She delivered the message personally.* **2** from a person's own point of view: *Personally, I like reading better than TV.* **3** as a person: *I like him personally, but he doesn't make a very good leader.* **4** as being aimed at yourself: *She didn't mean to insult you; don't take what she said personally.* *adv.*

personal pronoun (pər′sə nəl prō′noun) a pronoun that stands for the person speaking, the person spoken to, or the person spoken about. *I, me, we, us, you, he, him, she, her, they,* and *them* are personal pronouns.

Grammar Check . . personal pronoun

When you use a **personal pronoun** to replace the name of a person or thing, be sure the pronoun you choose fits the number (singular or plural) and gender (male or female) of the noun it replaces.

Singular pronouns are *I, me, you, he, she, him, her, it.* Plural pronouns are *we, us, you, they, them.*

Mala went to the market. → *She went to the market.*
Selim went to the market. → *He went to the market.*
Lina and Joe went to the market. → *They went to the market.*
The sky was blue. → *It was blue.*

a bat	e bed	i bid	o pot	u cup	th thin
ā cake	ē me	ī bite	ō go	ū rude	ᴛʜ then
à bar	ə about	ər over	ȯ for	ů put	zh measure

per·son·i·fi·ca·tion (pər son′ə fə kā′shən) **1** a person who is a perfect example of some quality: *My sister is the personification of messiness.* **2** a figure of speech which treats a thing or quality as if it were a human being. *Examples: the brave light of dawn. The earth groans.* *n.* **—per·son′i·fy′** (pər son′ə fī′), *v.* **—per·son′i·fied′,** *adj.*

per·son·nel (pər′sə nel′) the people employed in any work, business, or service: *Hospital personnel includes nurses, doctors, cooks, etc.* *n.*

per·spec·tive (pər spek′tiv) **1** the art of making flat images look three-dimensional. **2** a mental point of view: *Adults should try to look at this problem from a child's perspective.* **3** the ability to think about things in a balanced, realistic way: *A good talk with my friend helped me get some perspective on the problem.* *n.*
in perspective, in a realistic, balanced way: *Try to see things in perspective.*

per·spire (pər spīr′) sweat: *All that hard work made us perspire.* *v.,* **per·spired, per·spir·ing.** **—per′spi·ra′tion** (pər′spə rā′shən), *n.*

per·suade (pər swād′) get someone to agree by coaxing or arguing: *I knew I should study, but he persuaded me to watch a video. We persuaded her that the whole thing was her own idea.* *v.,* **per·suad·ed, per·suad·ing.**

per·sua·sion (pər swā′zhən) **1** the act or skill of persuading: *All our persuasion was of no use; she would not come.* A person or argument with power to persuade is **persuasive** (pər swā′siv). **2** a firm belief or opinion: *He and his sister were of different political persuasions.* *n.*

per·ti·nent (pər′tə nənt) related to what is being talked about; not off the topic: *If your question is pertinent, let's hear it.* *adj.*

per·turb (pər tərb′) disturb very much: *My parents were perturbed when I got in trouble at school.* *v.*

per·vade (pər vād′) go or spread throughout; be throughout: *The fragrance of pines pervades the air.* *v.,* **per·vad·ed, per·vad·ing.**

per·verse (pər vərs′) **1** being difficult on purpose: *The perverse child did just what we told her not to do.* **2** completely opposite to what is sensible or right: *a perverse argument.* *adj.*

per·vert (pər vərt′ *for 1,* pər′vərt *for 2*) **1** twist; understand, use, or cause to go in the wrong way: *to pervert a friendly remark into an insult, to pervert your talent for humour by using it to hurt someone.* **2** a person with a twisted way of thinking or behaving. 1 *v.,* 2 *n.*

pes·ky (pes′kē) *Informal.* bothersome; annoying: *a pesky cold, pesky mosquitoes.* *adj.*

pes·si·mism (pes′ə miz′əm) a negative attitude; a tendency to look on the bad side of things. *n.* **—pes′si·mist,** *n.* **—pes′si·mis′tic,** *adj.*

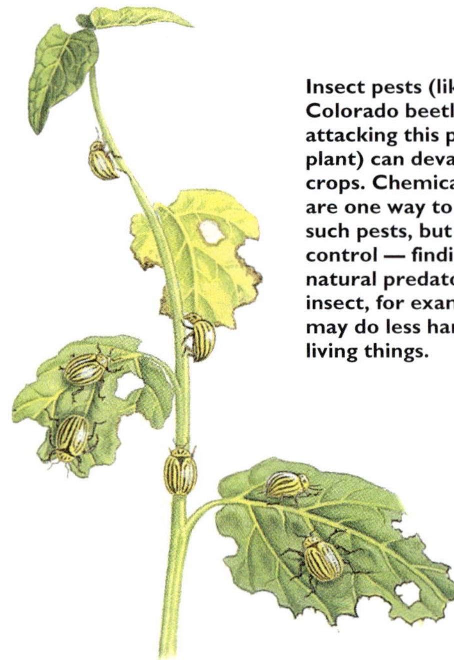

Insect pests (like the Colorado beetles attacking this potato plant) can devastate crops. Chemical pesticides are one way to control such pests, but biological control — finding a natural predator of the insect, for example — may do less harm to other living things.

pest (pest) any animal or person that causes trouble or ruins things; a nuisance. Insect pests destroy crops. *n.*

pes·ter (pes′tər) annoy; keep on bothering: *Don't pester me with foolish questions.* *v.*

pes·ti·cide (pes′tə sīd′) a chemical used to destroy plant or animal pests. *n.*

> **WORD HISTORY........pesticide**
>
> The word **pesticide** is a compound of **pest,** from the Latin *pestis,* meaning "plague," and **-cide,** from the Latin verb *caedere,* "to kill." The same verb root shows up in **genocide, homicide, insecticide,** and **suicide.**

pet (pet) **1** a tame animal kept by people so they can enjoy its company and affection. **2** treated as a pet: *a pet rabbit.* **3** favourite: *teacher's pet* (*n.*), *a pet theory about something* (*adj.*). **4** stroke or touch lovingly and gently: *to pet a kitten.* 1, 3 *n.,* 2, 3 *adj.,* 4 *v.,* **pet·ted, pet·ting.**

pet·al (pet′əl) one of the main parts of a flower. Petals usually have a colour other than green: *A rose has many petals.* *n.*

peter (pē′tər)
peter out, gradually get weaker and then stop: *By Friday our interest in the new video game had petered out.* *v.*

pe·ti·tion (pə tish′ən) 1 a letter to someone in authority from a group of people, formally asking for something: *The people on our street signed a petition asking the city council for a new sidewalk.* 2 ask formally, in writing: *They petitioned the mayor to use his influence with the city council.* 1 *n.*, 2 *v.*

pet·rel (pet′rəl) a small, often black and white sea bird with long, pointed wings. Petrels nest on land but roam far out at sea. *n.*

pet·ri·fy (pet′rə fī′) 1 slowly turn into stone by replacing animal or plant cells with mineral deposits: *We found petrified wood in the badlands of Alberta.* 2 paralyze with fear: *The hiker was petrified as the grizzly bear came near.* *v.*, **pet·ri·fied, pet·ri·fy·ing.**

pet·ro·glyph (pet′rə glif′) a carving or painting on rock, especially a prehistoric one: *On the shores of Lake Ontario are some interesting petroglyphs of animals.* *n.*

pe·tro·le·um (pə trō′lē əm) an oily liquid found below the earth's surface, formed from plant or animal material over millions of years by the pressure of rock on top of it. It burns easily and is used to make gasoline, kerosene, and other fuels as well as plastics. **Petroleum jelly** is a clear, greasy ointment made from petroleum. *n.*

pet·ty (pet′ē) 1 small or unimportant: *petty troubles, a petty official.* 2 making a big deal out of little things in a mean way. *adj.*, **pet·ti·er, pet·ti·est.**

pe·tu·ni·a (pə tyūn′ yə *or* pə tūn′yə) a common garden plant that has funnel-shaped flowers of various colours. *n.*

pew (pyū) a bench with a back, for people to sit on in a place of worship. It may be fastened to the floor. *n.*

pew·ter (pyū′tər) a metal that is a mixture of tin and copper or another metal. *n.*

phan·tom (fan′təm) 1 a ghost. 2 an image in the mind which seems to be real: *His fevered brain filled the room with phantoms from the past.* *n.*

Phar·aoh (fer′ō) a title given to the kings of ancient Egypt. *n.*

phar·ma·cy (får′mə sē) 1 a drugstore or a store counter where drugs and medicines are prepared and sold. The specially trained person who runs it is called a **pharmacist.** 2 the work or the science of preparing medicines. *n.*, *pl.* **phar·ma·cies.**

phase (fāz) 1 one of the stages of development that a person or thing goes through: *Having tantrums is a phase many toddlers go through.* 2 start or end something gradually, in stages: *to phase in a new system.* 3 any of the shapes that the moon or a planet seems to have at different times as seen from the earth. *n.*

pheas·ant (fez′ənt) a bird of Europe, Asia, and North America, related to chickens and peacocks. The male ring-necked pheasant has a long tail and brilliant feathers. *n.*, *pl.* **pheas·ants** or **pheas·ant.**

phe·nom·e·non (fə nom′ə non′ *or* fə nom′ə nən) 1 a fact, event, or process that can be observed: *Lightning is an electrical phenomenon.* 2 something or someone extraordinary or remarkable: *Naomi's great artistic talent made her quite a phenomenon in the school.* *n.*, *pl.* **phe·nom·e·na** or (especially for def. 2) **phe·nom·e·nons.** —**phe·nom′e·nal,** *adj.*

phi·lan·thro·pist (fə lan′thrə pist) a person who gives a lot of money to charitable organizations: *The philanthropist gave money to build a hospital.* *n.*

WORD HISTORY...... philanthropist

Phil- always has to do with love. It comes from the Greek *philos*, meaning "loving," and turns up in, for example, **philanthropist** ("lover of people"), and **philately** ("love of stamps").

phi·lat·e·ly (fə lat′ə lē) the hobby or science of stamp collecting. *n.* —**phi·lat′e·list,** *n.*

phil·o·soph·i·cal (fil′ə sof′ə kəl) 1 having to do with philosophy. 2 taking things calmly and reasonably. **Philosophic** is another form of the word. *adj.*

phi·los·o·phy (fə los′ə fē) 1 the study of the nature and purpose of human beings, the universe, and life; thinking that has to do with the deepest and most basic questions that people have always asked. 2 a particular set of basic ideas or beliefs about these things or about some subject, used as a guide for action: *a business philosophy, a philosophy of education. What is your personal philosophy?* *n.*, *pl.* **phi·los·o·phies.** —**phi·los′o·pher,** *n.*

phish·ing (fish′ing) trying to discover personal information by sending e-mails or instant messages that seem to be sent by a trustworthy person or business. *n.*

phlegm (flem) the thick, slimy substance in your throat and nose when you have a cold; mucus. *n.*

a bat	e bed	i bid	o pot	u cup	th thin
ā cake	ē me	ī bite	ō go	ū rude	ᴛʜ then
å bar	ə about	ər over	ȯ for	u̇ put	zh measure

phlo•em (flō′əm) the soft tissue in a plant that carries the plant's food from the part where it is produced to the part where it is stored. *n.*

pho•bi•a (fō′bē ə) an unreasonable, exaggerated fear or hatred of a particular thing: *I have a phobia of bees.* *n.*

Word Family........... phobia

Phobia is the Greek word for "fear." It is used in a lot of compound words. Here are some.
acrophobia: fear of heights
arachnophobia: fear of spiders
claustrophobia: fear of closed-in spaces
nyctophobia: fear of the dark
technophobia: fear of technology
triskadekaphobia: fear of the number 13
xenophobia: fear of strangers, or people unlike yourself

phone (fōn) short for **telephone.** *n. or v.,* **phoned, phon•ing.**

pho•net•ics (fə net′iks) the science dealing with the sounds made in speaking. Phonetic symbols stand for one sound each, no matter how the sound is spelled in ordinary letters. This dictionary uses phonetic symbols to give the pronunciations of words. *n.* **—pho•net′ic,** *adj.*

phon•ics (fon′iks) the study of how letters are used in spelling to stand for the sounds in words. Phonics is used in teaching people to read. *n.*

pho•ny or **pho•ney** (fō′nē) *Informal.* fake. *adj. or n.*

phos•pho•rus (fos′fə rəs) a solid, waxlike chemical element that can burn. One form of it glows in the dark. Phosphorus is used in matches and fertilizers; it is also necessary to the human body and is found in high-protein foods such as meat and nuts. *n.*

pho•to•cop•y (fō′tō kop′ē) **1** make a copy of something printed, written, or drawn using a machine that photographs it and then prints it out: *I photocopied my speech to send to my grandparents.* **2** a copy made in this way. 1 *v.,* **pho•to•cop•ied, pho•to•cop•y•ing;** 2 *n., pl.* **pho•to•cop•ies.** **—pho′to•cop′i•er,** *n.*

pho•to–e•lec•tric cell (fō′tō i lek′trik) an electronic device that turns something on or off whenever the light falling on it changes—for example, if the light is suddenly blocked by a person. Photo-electric cells are used to open doors automatically, set off alarms, etc.

pho•to•graph (fō′tə graf′) **1** a picture made with a camera. Light rays coming from an object are focussed by the camera's lens onto a piece of light-sensitive film inside, leaving an image on the film which can be developed into a print by a special process using chemicals. **Photo** is a shortened form. **2** take a photograph of. 1 *n.,* 2 *v.* **—pho′to•graph′ic,** *adj.*

pho•tog•ra•phy (fə tog′rə fē) the work or the skill of taking photographs. *n.* **—pho•tog′ra•pher,** *n.*

pho•to•syn•the•sis (fō′tō sin′thə sis) the process that goes on inside a plant to produce sugars from water and carbon dioxide; it happens when sunlight acts on the green substance in the plant, called chlorophyll. The sugars that are produced nourish the plant. *n.*

Photocopying

Photocopying uses the fact that static electricity attracts. The picture to be copied is beamed onto the electrostatic drum by mirrors and lenses. The charged parts attract the toner (ink dust). This is transferred to a blank sheet of paper and fixed in place by heat.

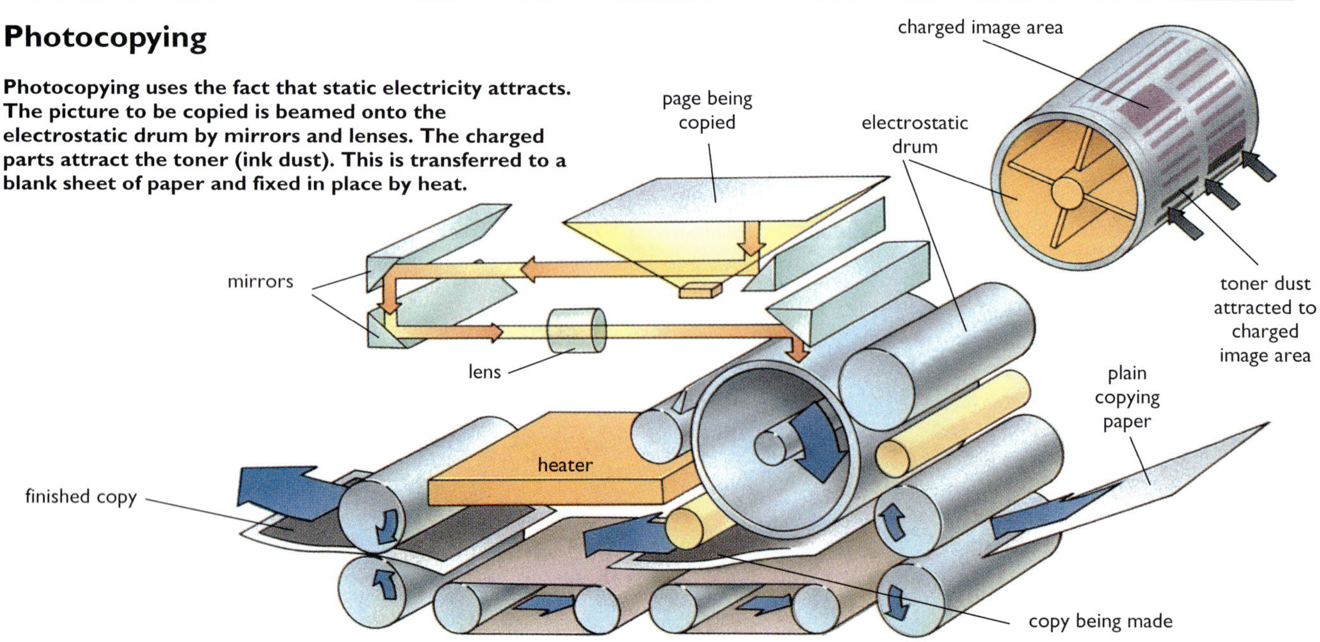

phrase (frāz) 1 a group of words used as a unit in a clause or sentence. In the sentence *He is in the house,* the words *in the house* are a prepositional phrase telling where he is. ▶ See the *Grammar and Usage Mini-Guide.* 2 a common expression: *The phrase "on pins and needles" means "anxious."* 3 express: *She phrased her criticism as politely as she could.* 1, 2 *n.,* 3 *v.,* **phrased, phras·ing.**

Grammar Check . . . . . . phrase

Phrases can be used in three main ways:
- as adjectives: *The girl with the red hair was running.* The phrase *with the red hair* describes the noun *girl.*
- as adverbs: *The girl was drawing in her book.* The phrase *in her book* describes the verb *was drawing.*
- to modify a sentence: *On second thought, I will stay home.* The phrase *on second thought* modifies the meaning of the sentence *I will stay home.*

phy·lum (fī′ləm) one of the large groupings used by scientists to sort animals. A phylum is part of a **kingdom,** and is divided in turn into **classes.** *n., pl.* **phyl·a.**

phys·i·cal (fiz′ə kəl) 1 having to do with the body: *physical strength.* 2 having to do with things that can be touched, seen, heard, etc. rather than ideas or feelings: *the physical world. The tide is a physical force.* 3 having to do with the science of physics. *adj.* **—phys′i·cal·ly,** *adv.*

physical education (fiz′ə kəl ed′jə kā′shən) a school subject teaching you how to exercise and take care of your body. **Phys ed** (fiz′ ed′) is a shortened form.

phy·si·cian (fə zish′ən) a medical doctor. *n.*

phys·ics (fiz′iks) the science that deals with matter and energy and the relationships between them. Physics includes the study of force, motion, heat, light, sound, and electricity. *n.* **—phys′i·cist** (fiz′ə sist), *n.*

phys·i·o·ther·a·py (fiz′ē ō ther′ə pē) treatment for muscles that have been damaged by disease or injury. Physiotherapy usually includes heat, massage, and special exercises. *n.* **—phys′i·o·ther′a·pist,** *n.*

phy·sique (fə zēk′) a person's body shape: *That athlete has a very muscular physique.* *n.*

pi (pī) a number equal to the circumference of any circle divided by its diameter, about 3.1416. This means that to find the circumference of a circle, you must multiply pi times the diameter of the circle. *Symbol:* π *n.*

pi·an·o (pē an′ō) a large musical instrument with strings inside it and a keyboard. When you press any key, it causes a little hammer to strike the strings, making a sound. *n., pl.* **pi·an·os.** **—pi′a·nist** (pē′ə nist), *n.*

pic·co·lo (pik′ə lō′) a small flute, sounding an octave higher than an ordinary flute. *n., pl.* **pic·co·los.**

pick¹ (pik) 1 choose: *I picked a chocolate sundae for dessert.* 2 choice: *Take your pick.* 3 pull off with your fingers: *to pick flowers. I picked the cat hairs off my sweater.* 4 use something pointed to remove things from: *to pick your teeth, to pick a bone.* 5 dig into and break up with a pointed tool: *to pick ground, to pick rocks.* 6 play a stringed instrument by plucking the strings instead of strumming them. 7 a small flat piece of plastic or other material used to pluck the strings of a musical instrument. 1, 3, 4–6 *v.,* 2, 7 *n.* **—pick′er,** *n.*
pick a lock, open a lock with something sharp.
pick apart, examine something carefully and find all the weaknesses in it: *The teacher picked apart my composition and made me rewrite it.*
pick a quarrel, start an argument on purpose.
pick at, **a** pull on something with the fingers: *The sick man picked at the blankets.* **b** eat a bit at a time: *She had no appetite and just picked at her food.*
pick on, keep being mean to someone in small ways: *He thinks the teacher picks on him.*
pick out, **a** choose from a group: *Pick out a CD you like.* **b** recognize or notice a thing separately from its surroundings: *Can you pick me out in this group picture?* **c** play one note at a time: *to pick out a tune.*
pick over, look over carefully: *to pick over vegetables before buying.*
pick someone's brains, get ideas from a person.
pick someone's pocket, steal from a person's pocket.
pick up, **a** take and lift up in your hand: *The boy picked up a stone.* **b** get by chance: *I picked up a bargain at the rummage sale.* **c** learn without being taught: *She picks up new games easily.* **d** stop and let into a vehicle: *The bus picked up passengers at every corner.* **e** *Informal.* recover; improve: *He seemed to pick up quickly after his operation.* **f** go faster. **Pick up speed** means the same. **g** receive sound waves or a radio or TV signal: *The microphone picked up our voices. Our satellite dish picks up a lot of channels.*
pick up on, notice and understand.

pick² (pik) 1 another name for a **pickaxe,** a heavy tool for breaking up rocks. It has a metal bar, sharpened at one or both ends, on a long handle. 2 a smaller pointed tool: *Ice is broken into pieces with a pick.* *n.*

a bat	e bed	i bid	o pot	u cup	th thin
ā cake	ē me	ī bite	ō go	ū rude	ᴛʜ then
ä bar	ə about	ər over	ô for	ů put	zh measure

pick•er•el (pik′ə rəl) **1** a freshwater fish with a long, narrow, pointed head, used for food. **2** another name for a **walleye,** a different fish. *n., pl.* **pick•er•el** or **pick•er•els.**

pick•et (pik′it) **1** a pointed stake or board placed upright with others to make a fence. **2** stand or walk around outside a workplace while on strike, carrying signs and trying to keep other workers or customers out: *The striking workers picketed their factory.* **3** a person doing this while on strike. Several usually stand together, forming a **picket line.** 1, 3 *n.,* 2 *v.* **—pick′et•er,** *n.*

pick•le (pik′əl) **1** a cucumber or other vegetable preserved with herbs in salt water or vinegar. **2** preserve in this way: *to pickle beets.* **3** *Informal.* a difficult situation. 1, 3 *n.,* 2 *v.,* **pick•led, pick•ling.**

pick•pock•et (pik′pok′it) a person who steals from people's pockets. *n.*

pick•up (pik′up′) **1** the act of picking something up: *the daily pickup of mail.* **2** a small microphone, especially one attached to a musical instrument. **3** a small, light truck with an open back. *n.*

pick•y (pik′ē) *Informal.* very fussy: *a picky eater. Cary thought the teacher was being overly picky when he marked the assignment. adj.,* **pick•i•er, pick•i•est.**

pic•nic (pik′nik) **1** a meal eaten outdoors and away from home. **2** eat outdoors away from home. **3** *Slang.* anything easy and fun: *Cleaning the garage was no picnic!* 1, 3 *n.,* 2 *v.,* **pic•nicked, pic•nick•ing.** **—pic′nick•er,** *n.*

pic•to•graph (pik′tə graf′) **1** a picture or symbol that stands for a word or idea. **2** a chart or graph which uses little pictures to represent quantities. For example, each little picture of a car might stand for 1000 cars. *n.*

pic•ture (pik′chər) **1** a drawing, painting, or photograph, or a printed copy of any of these: *There's a picture of Leo in the newspaper.* **2** a scene: *The trees and brook make a lovely picture.* **3** an image in your mind. **4** imagine: *It is hard to picture life a hundred years ago.* **5** a vivid description. **6** make or give a picture of: *The artist pictured a winter scene.* **7** the image on a TV screen. **8** a movie. 1–3, 5, 7, 8 *n.,* 4, 6 *v.,* **pic•tured, pic•tur•ing.** **—pic•to′ri•al** (pik tôr′ ē əl), *adj.*
be the picture of, be a perfect image of: *He was the picture of despair.*
get the picture, understand.
in the picture, involved in what is going on. The opposite is **out of the picture.**
the big picture, an understanding of something as a whole, which helps you make sense of all the details.

pic•tur•esque (pik′chə resk′) **1** pretty and interesting enough to be used as the subject of a picture: *a picturesque old mill.* **2** making a picture for the mind; vivid: *picturesque language. adj.*

pie (pī) a pastry shell with fruit, meat, or pudding in it, baked in a shallow round pan: *apple pie, chicken pie.* A **pie chart** is a chart that compares amounts by showing them as sectors of a circle, like slices of a pie. *n.*
easy as pie, very easy.
pie in the sky, a dream that will never come true.

piece (pēs) **1** one of the parts that a thing is divided or broken into: *The cup broke into pieces.* **2** a section; a small amount: *a piece of land, a piece of cloth.* **3** a single thing in a set: *This set of china has 50 pieces.* **4** a single work of art: *a piece of music, a piece of poetry.* **5** a coin: *A nickel is a five-cent piece.* **6** make or fix by joining pieces: *to piece a quilt. We pieced the broken plate back together.* 1–5 *n.,* 6 *v.,* **pieced, piec•ing.**
give someone a piece of your mind, tell someone off.
go to pieces, a fall apart; break up: *The old paper went to pieces when I picked it up.* **b** be ruined. **c** burst into tears. **d** be suddenly unable to cope.

pier (pēr) **1** a dock or walkway that stretches a long way out over the water. It may also be used to break the force of waves before they reach the shore. **2** one of the solid supports of a bridge. *n.*

pierce (pērs) **1** make a hole in or through: *A nail pierced the tire of our car.* **2** go through like something sharp: *The cold wind pierced our clothes. A hawk's cry pierced the air. v.,* **pierced, pierc•ing.**

a Gloucester Old Spot

Pigs weigh about a kilogram at birth, and usually double their mass in the first week. Fully grown, they can weigh over 200 kg.

pig (pig) a farm animal that has a long snout with a flat end, a thick body, and a short, thin tail. Pigs are raised for their meat, fat, and skin. Pork, ham, and bacon come from pigs. *n.* **—pig′gish,** *adj.*

Word Family.......... pig

piggy bank: a bank for saving coins, shaped like a pig
pig-headed: stubborn
piglet: a baby pig
pigtail: hair tied or braided into one or more loose bunches at the back

pi•geon (pij′ən) a bird with a stout body, a small head, short legs, and bluish grey or brown feathers. *n.*

pi•geon•hole (pij′ən hōl′) 1 a small box with a hole in the front, usually built in a row with others, for pigeons to nest in. 2 one of a similar set of boxes attached to a wall or forming part of a desk, to hold papers or mail. 3 put in a pigeonhole. 4 deal with quickly in your mind and then forget about it till later. 1, 2 *n.,* 3, 4 *v.,* **pi•geon•holed, pi•geon•hol•ing.**

pi•geon–toed (pij′ən tōd′) with the toes turned inward. *adj.*

pig•gy•back (pig′ē bak′) 1 on the back or shoulders: *a piggyback ride* (*adj.*), *to ride piggyback* (*adv.*). 2 carry on the back or shoulders. 1 *adj. or adv.,* 2 *v.*

pig•ment (pig′mənt) 1 a colouring matter. Paints and dyes are made with pigments. 2 a substance that colours animal and plant tissue. The colour of your hair, skin, and eyes is due to pigment in your body cells. *n.*

pig•pen (pig′pen′) 1 a pen where pigs are kept. 2 a filthy place. **Pigsty** (pig′stī′) has the same meanings. *n.*

Pii•kan•i (pē′kan i) 1 a First Nations people living in Alberta and Montana. 2 their language. 3 having to do with these people or their language. 1, 2 *n.,* 3 *adj.*

pike[1] (pīk) a large, slender freshwater fish with a head shaped like a duck's bill. It has sharp teeth. *n.*

pike[2] (pīk) a heavy spear of earlier times. *n.*

pile[1] (pīl) 1 many things lying on top of one another; stack: *a pile of dirty plates, a pile of books.* 2 a mass shaped like a hill; mound: *a pile of dirt.* 3 gather or stack into a pile; heap up: *The boys piled the blankets in a corner. The snow piled against the fences.* 4 *Informal.* a large amount: *a pile of work.* 1, 2, 4 *n.,* 3 *v.,* **piled, pil•ing.**
pile in or **out,** go in or out in a confused rush: *to pile out into the street.*
pile up, a form into a pile. **b** collect; grow into a large amount because it is being blocked or not dealt with: *Don't let your homework pile up—do it now. The traffic piled up behind the accident.* The result is a **pile-up.**

pile[2] (pīl) a heavy post supporting a bridge, dock, building, etc. *n.*

pile[3] (pīl) the thick, soft or fuzzy surface of some kinds of carpet, velvet, artificial fur, stuffed toys, etc. *n.*

pil•fer (pil′fər) steal in small quantities: *to pilfer apples from a bushel.* *v.*

The Pilgrims held a celebration when they gathered their first harvest. This event is still celebrated in the United States as Thanksgiving Day.

pil•grim (pil′grəm) 1 a person who goes on a **pilgrimage,** a journey to a sacred or holy place as a religious act. 2 any traveller or wanderer. 3 **Pilgrims,** *pl.* a group of English settlers who started the colony of Plymouth, Massachusetts in 1620. They came to escape religious persecution in England. *n.*

pill (pil) 1 medicine made up into a small tablet or capsule to be swallowed whole. 2 a person or thing that is hard to take: *Our defeat was a bitter pill.* *n.*

pil•lage (pil′ij) invade and rob: *Pirates pillaged the towns along the coast.* *v.,* **pil•laged, pil•lag•ing.**

pil•lar (pil′ər) 1 a slender, structure of stone, wood, or metal, used to support or ornament a large building. 2 anything shaped or giving support like a pillar: *a pillar of smoke. He is a pillar of the community.* *n.*

pil•low (pil′ō) 1 a bag or case filled with soft material to lay your head on when resting or sleeping. It usually has a removable cloth cover called a **pillowcase.** 2 rest as on a pillow: *He pillowed his head on a pile of leaves.* 1 *n.,* 2 *v.*

pi•lot (pī′lət) 1 a person who flies an aircraft or steers a ship. 2 be the pilot of; steer: *to pilot a ship into the harbour. She pilots her own plane.* 3 guide or lead: *The manager piloted us through the factory.* 4 done as an experiment or test: *a pilot project.* 1 *n.,* 2, 3 *v.,* 4 *adj.*

pi•men•to (pə men′tō) a sweet red pepper used as a vegetable, relish, and stuffing for green olives. *n.*

a bat	e bed	i bid	o pot	u cup	th thin
ā cake	ē me	ī bite	ō go	ū rude	ᴛʜ then
à bar	ə about	ər over	ȯ for	u̇ put	zh measure

pim·ple (pim′pəl) a small swelling of the skin, containing pus. *n.* —**pim′ply,** *adj.*

pin (pin) **1** a short, very stiff piece of wire with a point at one end and often a tiny ball at the other, used to fasten things made of cloth or paper. **2** a small piece of jewellery with a pin or clasp to fasten it to the clothing; brooch. **3** anything that holds something in place, with or without a point: *a safety pin, a bobby pin, a clothespin.* **4** fasten with a pin: *I pinned the ribbon to my shirt.* **5** hold in one position by pressing: *The fallen tree pinned him to the ground.* **6** a bottle-shaped piece of wood used in the game of bowling. 1–3, 6 *n.,* 4, 5 *v.,* **pinned, pin·ning.**
on pins and needles, anxious or in suspense: *We were on pins and needles waiting for the test results.*
pin down, a identify a person or thing for certain: *It's a strange feeling that I can't quite pin down.* **b** someone to make or keep a promise.
pin something on, *Informal.* put the blame for something on: *The police could not pin the crime on him.*

PIN (pin) a secret number that gives a person access to his or her bank account by machine, using a bank card. **Personal Identification Number** is the full name.

pin·a·fore (pin′ə fôr′) an old word for: **1** an apron worn over a dress, covering nearly all of it. **2** a jumper or sleeveless dress. *n.*

pi·ña·ta (pin yä′tə) a figure made of papier-mâché or clay, stuffed with candy and toys and hung by a string. Blindfolded children take turns hitting the piñata with a stick so it will break and let out a shower of treats. *n.*

pin·ball (pin′bol′) a game played on a machine with a small metal ball that rolls down a sloping board. The player tries to keep the ball from reaching the bottom by pulling handles on the outside of the machine. *n.*

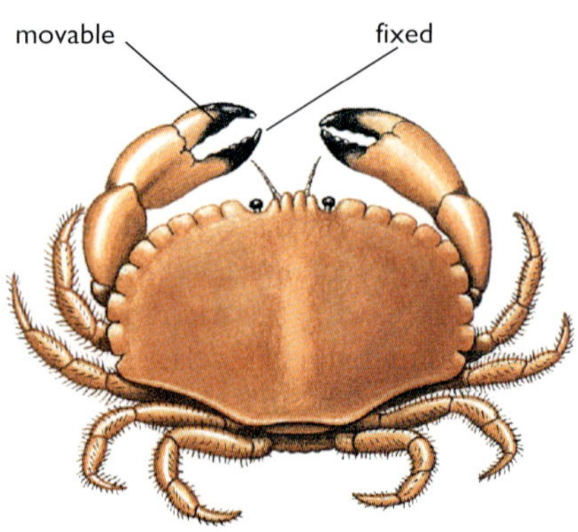

Pincers have two fingers, one fixed and the other movable.

pin·cer (pin′sər) **1 pincers,** *pl.* a hand tool like a scissors, but with jaws for gripping instead of blades. **2** a claw of a crab, lobster, etc., used to grip or pinch. *n.*

pinch (pinch) **1** squeeze hard between two surfaces, especially your thumb and forefinger: *She pinched my arm. He pinched his finger in the door. These shoes pinch my toes.* **2** a sharp pressure that hurts; a squeeze: *the pinch of tight shoes.* **3** as much as you can pick up with the tips of your finger and thumb: *a pinch of salt.* **4** *Slang.* steal: *His father caught him pinching cookies.* 1, 4 *v.,* 2, 3 *n.*
in a pinch, in an emergency or difficult situation.
pinch pennies, be very stingy with money.
take something with a pinch of salt, not take something as completely true or reliable; not take quite seriously.

pinch–hit (pinch′hit′) **1** in baseball, to bat for another player when a hit is badly needed. **2** take another's place in an emergency: *The pianist is ill and our teacher will pinch-hit for her at the concert tonight.* *v.* —**pinch′-hit′ter,** *n.*

pin·cush·ion (pin′kůsh′ən) a small cushion to stick pins in until needed. *n.*

pine¹ (pīn) an evergreen tree that has cones and long, needle-shaped leaves. Many kinds of pine are valued for tar, turpentine, and wood for furniture and building. *n.*

pine² (pīn) miss someone or long for something so much that you lose interest in everything else: *The dog was pining for my mother.* *v.,* **pined, pin·ing.**
pine away, become sick with longing or sadness.

A pineapple plant grows to a height of about a metre. The leaves have rough edges and sharp points. The single flower stem in the centre produces the fruit.

pine·ap·ple (pī′nap′əl) a large, juicy, tropical fruit that looks a little like a large pine cone. *n.*

pin·go (ping′gō) a steep mound of ice covered by peat or soil, found in tundra regions. Pingos are made when underground water keeps freezing and thawing; each time the pressure of the ice pushes up the soil. *n.*

Ping–Pong (ping′pong′) *a trademark for* table tennis. *n.*

pink (pingk) the colour made by mixing red and white; light or pale red. *n. or adj.* —**pink′ish,** *adj.*

pink·eye (pingk′ī′) a medical condition in which the eyelid becomes red, itchy, and inflamed. It is very easily spread from one person to another. *n.*

pink·ie (pingk′ē) *Informal.* your smallest finger. *n.*

pin·na·cle (pin′ə kəl) **1** peak: *a rocky pinnacle, the pinnacle of her career.* **2** a tall, slender tower or spire on a building. *n.*

pin·point (pin′point′) **1** the point of a pin. **2** something very small or sharp: *We could see a pinpoint of light through a hole in the curtain.* **3** find or aim at exactly: *to pinpoint the heart of the problem.* 1, 2 *n.*, 3 *v.*

pint (pīnt) a nonmetric unit of volume equal to half a quart (about 570 mL). **Pint-sized** means "small." *n.*

pi·o·neer (pī′ə nēr′) **1** a person who starts a new settlement or community. **2** a person who does something first, preparing the way for others. **3** take the lead in doing something new: *pioneering the exploration of outer space.* 1, 2 *n.*, 3 *v.*

WORD HISTORY........ pioneer

Pioneer comes from the French *pionnier*, meaning "foot soldier." Foot soldiers always went ahead of the rest of the army. Pioneers are those who go first.

pi·ous (pī′əs) **1** deeply religious. **2** pretending to be religious. *adj.*

pip (pip) the seed of an apple, orange, grape, etc. *n.*

This musician from Peru is playing a set of pipes called pan pipes.

pipe (pīp) **1** a tube for liquid or gas to flow through. **2** send through a pipe or pipes: *Clean water is piped into our homes.* A system of connected pipes is a **pipeline.** **3** a tube of clay, wood, etc. with a bowl at one end, for smoking tobacco. **4** a simple flute or any other tube that produces music by air flowing through it. A **pipe organ** works by forcing air through large pipes of different lengths when you press the keys or pedals. **5** **pipes,** *pl.* short for **bagpipes.** **6** play music on a pipe. **7** talk or sing in a shrill voice: *"Me too, me too!" piped two-year-old Ryan.* 1, 3–5 *n.*, 2, 6, 7 *v.*, **piped, pip·ing.** —**pip′er,** *n.*
pipe down, *Slang.* be quiet.
piping hot, very hot.

pi·ra·nha (pə rä′ nə) a freshwater fish of South America. Some kinds are meat-eaters; schools of these sometimes attack and devour human beings or large animals. *n.*

pi·rate (pī′rit) **1** a person who attacks and robs ships; a robber on the sea. **2** copy or sell a book, musical recording, piece of software, etc. without permission from the holder of the copyright. 1 *n.*, 2 *v.*, **pi·rat·ed, pi·rat·ing.** —**pi′ra·cy** (pī′rə sē), *n.*

pis·tach·i·o (pə stash′ē ō′) a small greenish nut from a tree that grows in warm climates. It is often roasted and dyed red while still in the shell. *n., pl.* **pis·tach·i·os.**

pis·til (pis′təl) the seed-bearing part of a flower. *n.*

pis·tol (pis′təl) a small, short gun held and fired with one hand. A revolver is a kind of pistol. *n.*

pis·ton (pis′tən) in an engine, a disk or short cylinder attached to a rod. It moves back and forth inside a tube or hollow cylinder, powered by the force of liquid or hot gases. *n.*

pit¹ (pit) **1** a hole in the ground, either natural or dug by people. **2** a small hollow on the surface of anything: *The hail had left little pits in the sand.* **3** mark with small pits or scars. **4** match against another thing or person in a contest: *In the first game, our team was pitted against last year's champions.* 1, 2 *n.*, 3, 4 *v.*, **pit·ted, pit·ting.**
make a pit stop, a in a car race, pull over to the side for repairs or gas. **b** stop for rest, snacks, etc. on a long trip.

pit² (pit) **1** the hard seed of a cherry, peach, plum, etc. **2** remove the pits from. 1 *n.*, 2 *v.*, **pit·ted, pit·ting.**

pi·ta (pē′tə) bread in the shape of a round, flat envelope that can be cut across the middle and stuffed with a variety of fillings. *n.*

a bat	e bed	i bid	o pot	u cup	th thin
ā cake	ē me	ī bite	ō go	ū rude	ᴛʜ then
ä bar	ə about	ər over	ô for	ù put	zh measure

pitch¹ (pich) 1 throw; toss: *I pitched the garbage in the pail.* 2 in baseball, throw to the person batting: *Shane pitched the ball to me and I swung at it* (*v.*). *That was a great pitch, Shane!* (*n.*). 3 set up a tent. 4 fall suddenly forward or backward: *He lost his balance and pitched over the cliff. The ship pitched back and forth in the storm.* 5 the highness or lowness of a sound: *A flute has a higher pitch than a tuba.* Pitch depends on the frequency of sound waves. 6 set at a certain level of highness or lowness: *The song is pitched too low for me to sing it.* 1–4, 6 *v.,* 2, 5 *n.*
pitch in, do your share of work: *All the neighbours pitched in to get the job done.*
pitch into, *Informal.* attack.

pitch² (pich) a black, sticky substance made from tar or turpentine, used in earlier times to waterproof the seams of wooden ships, cover roofs, make pavement, etc. **Pitch black** means "very black"; **pitch dark** means "very dark." Both have a hyphen before a noun. *n.*

pitch·er¹ (pich′ər) a container with a lip or spout at one side and a handle at the other, for holding and pouring out drinks. *n.*

pitch·er² (pich′ər) the player on a baseball team who pitches the ball to the batter. *n.*

pitcher plant (pich′ər plant′) an unusual plant found in bogs and similar wet areas. Pitcher plants trap and digest insects in their leaves, which are shaped like pitchers. The purple pitcher plant is the provincial flower of Newfoundland and Labrador.

pitch·fork (pich′fôrk′) a large fork with a long handle for lifting and throwing hay or straw. *n.*

pit·e·ous (pit′ē əs) filling a person with pity: *The piteous cry of a starving kitten.* *adj.*

pit·fall (pit′fol′) a hidden danger: *Life is full of pitfalls.* *n.*

pith (pith) 1 the spongy tissue forming part of certain plants. The stems of some plants have pith at the centre. Some oranges have pith between the segments. 2 the important or essential part: *the pith of a speech.* Speech or writing that is forceful and says a lot in few words is **pithy.** *n.*

pit·i·ful (pit′i fəl) 1 deserving pity: *The injured dog was a pitiful sight.* 2 deserving scorn; embarrassingly or shamefully bad: *a pitiful attempt at a joke, a pitiful coward.* **Pitiable** (pit′ē ə bəl) has the same meanings. *adj.*

pit·tance (pit′əns) a tiny sum or amount: *Gavin complained about the pittance he got for his allowance.* *n.*

pi·tu·i·tar·y gland (pə tyū′ə ter′ē *or* pə tū′ə ter′ē gland′) a small oval gland at the base of your brain. It produces hormones that help you grow and that regulate many of your body's functions.

pit·y (pit′ē) 1 sadness over another's suffering. 2 feel sorry for: *She pitied any child who was hurt.* 3 something to be sorry about: *It is a pity to spend such a beautiful day inside.* 1, 3 *n.,* 2 *v.,* **pit·ied, pit·y·ing.**
take pity on, show pity for and try to help.

piv·ot (piv′ət) 1 a shaft, pin, or point that something turns on. 2 turn on a pivot or something like a pivot: *to pivot on your heel. He leaned his chair back so it was pivoting on one leg.* 1 *n.,* 2 *v.*

piz·za (pēt′sə) a food made up of a layer of bread dough covered with spicy sauce, tomatoes, cheese, pepperoni, mushrooms, etc. and baked. A **pizzeria** (pēt′sə rē′ə) is a place where pizza is made and sold. *n.*

piz·zazz (pə zaz′) a stylish, exciting, lively quality: *The spring fashion show had lots of pizzazz.* *n.*

pkg. *abbreviation for* package.

pl. *abbreviation for* plural.

plac·ard (plak′ərd *or* plak′ård) 1 a notice put up in a public place; a poster. 2 put placards on or in: *The circus placarded the city with advertisements.* 1 *n.,* 2 *v.*

pla·cate (plə kāt′ *or* plā′kāt) sooth or satisfy; calm the anger of: *She did her best to placate the angry woman.* *v.,* **pla·cated, pla·cat·ing.**

place (plās) 1 a particular point or area in space; spot; location: *This is a good place for a picnic. Everything is back in the right place.* 2 a city or town, store, building, etc.; somewhere that has a name and a definite limit: *Montréal is an exciting place. A new haircutting place has opened up downtown.* 3 someone's home: *We all went to my place for supper after skating.* 4 a rank or position: *the third decimal place. We won first place in the contest.* 5 a point in time; a part of an event, story, or any other thing that stretches over time: *The performance went too slowly in several places.* 6 put in a particular spot or position: *to place books on a table, to place trust in someone.* 7 link someone in your mind with everything you know about him or her: *His name is familiar, but I can't place him.* 8 give to the proper person, for him or her to deal with: *to place an order, to place a newspaper ad.* 9 finish first, second, or third in a race or other contest: *He failed to place in the first race and was eliminated.* 10 duty; business: *It is not my place to criticize.* 1–5, 10 *n.,* 6–9 *v.,* **placed, plac·ing.** **—place′ment,** *n.*

go places, be successful; do well.
in place, **a** in the right place. **b** ready: *Everything is in place for the concert tomorrow night.*
in place of, instead of: *Use water in place of milk in that recipe.*
out of place, **a** not in the proper or usual place. **b** not belonging or not fitting in: *I feel out of place in a big city.*
take place, happen; occur.

plac·id (plas′id) calm; peaceful; quiet: *a placid lake, a placid temper.* *adj.*

pla·gia·rize (plā′jə rīz′) copy somebody else's work and pretend it is your own. *v.,* **pla·gia·rized, pla·gia·riz·ing.** **—pla′gia·rism′,** *n.*

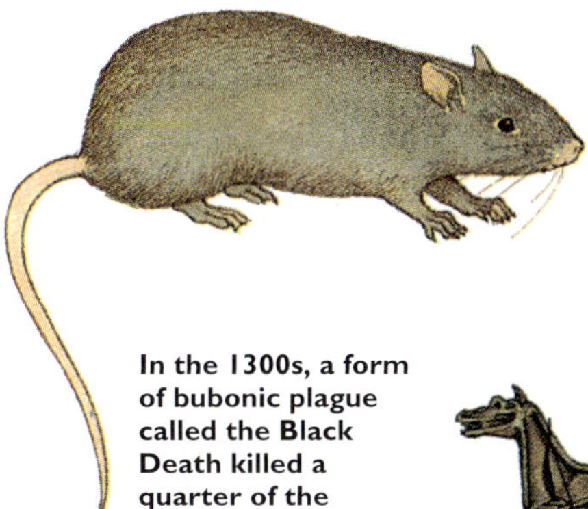

Bubonic plague is carried by rats. People become infected when they are bitten by fleas from infected rats.

In the 1300s, a form of bubonic plague called the Black Death killed a quarter of the people of Europe. The plague spread so quickly that artists pictured death in forms like this skeleton racing along on horseback.

plague (plāg) **1** any very dangerous disease that spreads rapidly. The **bubonic plague** killed many people in the Middle Ages. **2** anything that causes widespread damage or suffering: *The prairie wheat crop was destroyed by a plague of grasshoppers.* **3** cause trouble for: *The farmers have been plagued by drought.* **4** annoy; bother: *Stop plaguing me with questions.* 1, 2 *n.,* 3, 4 *v.,* **plagued, pla·guing.**

plaid (plad) **1** any cloth with a pattern of crisscross stripes. **2** a particular pattern of this kind. **3** a long piece of woollen cloth with a coloured pattern of this kind, worn over one shoulder by the Scottish Highlanders. *n.*

plain (plān) **1** clear; easy to see, hear, or understand: *The meaning is plain.* **2** simple and ordinary; not fancy: *a plain dress, plain food, plain folks.* **3** all in one solid colour: *a plain blue material.* **4** not pretty. **5** a stretch of flat land; prairie: *the western plains.* 1–4 *adj.,* 5 *n.*
plain sailing, easy progress, without problems.

plain·clothes (plān′klōz′) in ordinary clothes, not a police uniform: *a plainclothes detective.* *adj.*

plain·tive (plān′tiv) mournful; sad: *a plaintive song.* *adj.*

plan (plan) **1** an organized idea of what you are going to do in the future: *Our summer plans include a trip to the Northwest Territories.* **2** think out beforehand what you will do and how you will do it: *The prisoners planned their escape carefully.* **3** have in mind as a purpose; intend: *We are planning to go to Saskatchewan on vacation this year.* **4** a drawing or diagram to show how something is laid out: *a floor plan for a house.* 1, 4 *n.,* 2, 3 *v.,* **planned, plan·ning.** **—plan′ner,** *n.*

WORD HISTORY........ plan

We get **plan** from the Latin *planus*, meaning "flat surface," referring to a flat design of a three-dimensional building. Since this was normally drawn beforehand as a guide for builders, the word plan came to mean something that is arranged beforehand.

plane (plān) **1** short for **airplane.** **2** a flat or level surface. **3** flat; not three-dimensional: *Circles, squares, and triangles are plane figures.* **4** a standard; level: *Keep your thoughts on a high plane.* **5** a carpenter's tool with a blade for smoothing or shaping wood. **6** smooth wood with this tool. 1, 3–5 *n.,* 2 *adj.,* 6 *v.,* **planed, plan·ing.**

plan·et (plan′it) one of the large celestial bodies that move around a sun in regular paths. Mercury, Venus, Earth, Mars, Jupiter, Saturn, Uranus, and Neptune are planets in our solar system. *n.* **—plan′e·tar′y,** *adj.*
► See Appendix.

WORD HISTORY........ planet

Planet comes from Greek *planetes*, meaning "wanderer." Seen from Earth, stars don't move, but planets do.

plank (plangk) a long, flat, thick board. *n.*
walk the plank, be put to death at sea by being forced to walk off a plank sticking out from a ship's side. According to legend, pirates used to do this to their prisoners.

plank·ton (plangk′tən) the tiny animals and plants that float or drift near the surface of oceans and lakes. They provide food for fish and other water animals. *n.*

a bat	e bed	i bid	o pot	u cup	th thin
ā cake	ē me	ī bite	ō go	ü rude	ᴛʜ then
ä bar	ə about	ər over	ô for	ů put	zh measure

Plants

Without plants, there would be no life on Earth. The oxygen in the air is renewed by plants. The food we eat is either plants, or from animals that eat plants.

Some plants, like the strawberry, spread by sending out side shoots called runners. When these touch the ground, roots form, new leaves grow, and the runner can die away.

People have been changing plants for over 10 000 years. Early farmers saved seeds from their best plants, and developed bigger crops. People have produced plants more resistant to disease, and they continue to produce more varieties of many plants, like these tulips.

plant (plant) **1** a living thing that is not an animal or fungus. Trees, bushes, grass, and seaweed are all plants. **2** a living thing that has leaves, roots, and a soft stem, and is small compared to a tree or shrub: *a tomato plant, a house plant.* **3** put in the ground to grow: *Farmers plant seeds.* **4** put seeds or plants in: *He planted his garden with beans.* **5** set firmly; put; place: *She planted a kiss on my cheek. He planted his feet firmly and pulled hard.* **6** the building, machinery, tools, etc. that make up a factory: *There is an aluminum plant in Kingston.* **7** place or set something up to trap, trick, or fool someone: *to plant fake evidence at the scene of the crime.* **8** something placed or set up in this way: *That letter lying open on the desk is a plant.* 1–3, 8 *n.,* 4–7 *v.*

plan•tain (plan′tān) a starchy fruit that looks like a banana, but larger and with a green skin. Plaintains are starchier than bananas and are usually boiled or fried. *n.*

plan•ta•tion (plan tā′shən) a huge farm growing one main crop for sale: *a cotton plantation.* The work on a plantation is done by hired workers who live there. *n.*

plant•er (plan′tər) **1** a large container for growing plants indoors, on a patio, balcony, sidewalk, etc. **2** a machine for planting: *a corn planter.* **3** a person who owns or runs a plantation: *a cotton planter.* *n.*

plaque (plak) **1** a flat plate made of metal, wood, or other material, with something written on it. It may be hung on a wall as a decoration, attached to a monument for information, given as an award, etc. **2** a thin layer of saliva and bacteria that forms on your teeth. Regular brushing removes it; otherwise it hardens into tartar. *n.*

plas•ma (plaz′mə) the clear, almost colourless part of blood or lymph. The blood cells float in it. *n.*

plas•ter (plas′tər) **1** a soft mixture of lime, sand, and water that hardens in drying. It was used in old buildings to cover walls or ceilings. **Plaster of Paris** looks similar and is made of water mixed with powdered **gypsum** (jip′səm), a white mineral. It is used to make casts, cheap statues, moulds, and so on. **2** cover with plaster. **3** spread thickly with anything: *His shoes were plastered with mud.* 1 *n.,* 2, 3 *v.*

plas•tic (plas′tik) **1** a manufactured material that can be easily moulded or shaped when hot and becomes firm as it cools. Plastics are often used in place of natural substances such as leather, wood, metal, or cotton. Some common plastics are vinyl, polyester, and nylon. To **plasticize** is to coat with plastic. **2** easily moulded or shaped: *Clay, wax, and plaster are plastic substances.* **3** moulding or giving shape to materials: *Sculpture is a plastic art.* **Plastic surgery** is surgery to change the shape of a part of your body. 1 *n.,* 2, 3 *adj.*

Plas·ti·cine (plas′ti sēn′ *or* plas′ti sēn′) *trademark for* a brand of modelling clay used especially by children. *n.*

plate (plāt) 1 a dish, usually round, that is almost flat: *Our food is served on plates.* 2 the food served to one person at a meal: *It cost $60 a plate to attend the fundraising banquet.* 3 a thin, flat sheet or piece of some material; such as steel plates on the sides of a ship, or the bony plates on some reptiles. Glass plates coated with light-sensitive chemicals are used in photography; a **licence plate** with numbers or letters on it is attached to a vehicle to identify it. 4 cover with metal plates for protection. 5 cover with a thin layer of silver, gold, or some other metal: *nickel plated with gold.* 6 metal covered with a thin layer of silver or gold, or things made of this: *The tea set was made of silver plate.* 7 in baseball, the home base. 1–3, 6, 7 *n.,* 4, 5 *v.,* **plat·ed, plat·ing.**

pla·teau (plə tō′) 1 a flat area of land high above sea level. 2 a level of achievement where there is no more progress for a long time: *Our team improved rapidly and then reached a plateau.* *n., pl.* **pla·teaus** or **pla·teaux** (plə tōz′).

plate·let (plāt′lit) a very tiny plate-shaped cell in the blood. It helps the blood to thicken after bleeding starts. *n.*

plat·form (plat′fôrm) 1 a raised, level surface, usually for people to stand on: *There is a platform beside the railway track at the station. The hall has a platform for speakers.* 2 a statement of the plans and beliefs of a political party: *The platform of the new party includes lowering taxes.* *n.*

plat·i·num (plat′ə nəm) a chemical element that is a precious metal. It looks like silver, but is heavier and does not tarnish or melt easily. *n.*

plat·ter (plat′ər) a large plate for serving food. *n.*

The platypus and the spiny anteater (both Australian) are the only egg-laying mammals in the world.

plat·y·pus (plat′ə pəs) a small egg-laying water mammal of Australia. It has a rubbery snout like a duck's bill, thick fur, four webbed feet, and a broad, flat tail. *n., pl.* **plat·y·pus·es** or **plat·y·pi** (plat′ə pī′).

plau·si·ble (ploz′ə bəl) that seems true or reasonable: *His story sounded plausible to us.* *adj.*

play (plā) 1 have fun; do something for fun, such as a game or make-believe: *to play with a ball, to play tag. Let's play that this big box is a time machine.* 2 take part in a game against: *Our team played the grade six team.* 3 the act or process of playing: *She watched the puppies at play.* 4 put into the game: *to play a card. Each coach played her best goalie.* 5 a move or action in a game: *He made a good play at checkers.* 6 a story to be acted out in front of an audience. 7 act a part; act the part of: *He played Scrooge in "A Christmas Carol."* 8 produce music on an instrument or with a recording: *to play the violin, to play a CD. The radio was playing my favourite song.* 9 fool around: *Do not play with your food.* 1, 2, 4, 7–9 *v.,* 3, 5, 6 *n.,* —**play′er,** *n.*
foul play, action that is illegal or dishonest: *Police think foul play was involved in the banker's death.*
play at, do something half-heartedly; only pretend to be doing something: *She's playing at cleaning her room—I think she's just looking at all her old stuff.*
play for time, try to get an advantage by causing a delay.
play into someone's hands, act so as to give someone the advantage.
play on, take advantage of; make use of: *She played on her mother's good nature.*
play up, make the most of; make something seem as important as possible. **Play down** is the opposite.
play up to, *Slang.* try to get the favour of; flatter: *to play up to a famous person.*

Word Family........... play

play-by-play: describing all the plays in a game
playful: liking to play; not taking things too seriously
playground: a large area for play, often with swings, etc.
playmate: someone you play with
playoffs: the last games in a tournament
playpen: a box with see-through sides for a baby to play in
plaything: a toy
playtime: a time set aside for play

play·house (plā′hous′) 1 a small house for a child to play in. 2 a theatre. *n.*

play·wright (plā′rīt′) a writer of plays, also called a **dramatist.** *n.*

a bat	e bed	i bid	o pot	u cup	th thin
ā cake	ē me	ī bite	ō go	ū rude	ᴛʜ then
ä bar	ə about	ər over	ô for	ů put	zh measure

pla·za (plaz′ə) 1 a small shopping centre, especially one where each store must be entered from the outside. 2 a public square in a city or town. *n.*

plea (plē) 1 a desperate or urgent request: *The people of the flooded town made a plea for help.* 2 an answer that the accused person gives when charged in court: *a "not guilty" plea.* *n.*

plead (plēd) 1 ask urgently or humbly: *When the rent was due, the poor man pleaded for more time.* 2 speak for in a law court: *He had a good lawyer to plead his case.* 3 answer a charge in a law court: *The prisoner pleaded guilty to the charge of theft.* 4 offer as an excuse: *to plead ignorance of the law.* *v.,* **plead·ed** or **pled, plead·ing.**

pleas·ant (plez′ənt) 1 enjoyable; giving pleasure: *a pleasant swim on a hot day.* **Pleasurable** is a more formal word for this. 2 easy to get along with; friendly. 3 clear and mild: *pleasant weather.* *adj.*

please (plēz) 1 satisfy or make happy: *She finally agreed to wear the shoes to please her mother.* 2 wish: *Do what you please.* 3 a word used to ask politely for something: *Listen, please.* *v.,* **pleased, pleas·ing.**
be pleased, be happy: *He was pleased at the good news.*

pleas·ure (plezh′ər) 1 the feeling of being pleased; delight; enjoyment: *The child's pleasure in the gift was good to see.* 2 something that gives joy or delight: *It would be a pleasure to see you again.* 3 fun or relaxation; not work or business: *Is your trip for business or pleasure?* 4 wish: *I have pop or juice; what's your pleasure?* *n.*

pleat (plēt) 1 a flat, usually narrow fold made by doubling material over on itself. 2 fold or arrange in pleats: *a pleated skirt.* 1 *n.,* 2 *v.*

pledge (plej) 1 promise to give or do: *Mr. Medappa made a pledge of $50 to the hospital fund (n.). We pledge loyalty to our country (v.).* 2 bind someone by a promise: *They pledged the hearers to secrecy.* 3 something offered as a guarantee that you will give or do something: *I left my watch as a pledge to show I was coming back.* 4 offer as a guarantee. 1, 3 *n.,* 1, 2, 4 *v.,* **pledged, pledg·ing.**

plen·ti·ful (plen′ti fəl) more than enough: *Apples are cheap now because they are plentiful.* *adj.*

plen·ty (plen′tē) more than enough: *You have plenty of time to catch the train.* *n.*

pli·ers (plī′ərz) a hand tool hinged like a pair of scissors, used for bending or cutting wire, holding small objects, and so on. *sing. or pl.n.*

plight (plīt) a difficult situation. *n.*

plod (plod) 1 walk slowly and heavily; trudge: *The tired woman plodded wearily along the road.* 2 work with patience and effort, making slow progress. *v.,* **plod·ded, plod·ding.** **—plod′der,** *n.*

plop (plop) 1 the sound of a flat object striking water without a splash, or a sound like this. 2 make such a sound. 1 *n.,* 2 *v.,* **plopped, plop·ping.**

plot (plot) 1 a secret plan, especially to do something wrong: *Two men formed a plot to rob the bank.* 2 to plan secretly: *The rebels plotted against the government.* 3 the line of action in a story. A plot begins with a problem or conflict which builds up gradually to a turning point called the **climax.** After that the problem is sorted out bit by bit until it is resolved at the end. 4 a small piece of ground: *a garden plot.* 5 mark something on a map or chart: *Mom and I plotted our canoeing route on the map. The nurse plotted the patient's temperature over nine days.* 1, 3, 4 *n.,* 2, 5 *v.,* **plot·ted, plot·ting.** **—plot′ter,** *n.*

plough or **plow** (plou) 1 a farm machine used for breaking up the soil and turning it over. It has sharp blades called **ploughshares.** 2 use a plough to turn over the soil: *to plough a field.* 3 a vehicle with a blade on the front for clearing snow from roads. 4 move through anything slowly and with effort, as a plough does: *The ship ploughed through the heavy waves. Eve is ploughing through a book of 200 pages.* 1, 3 *n.,* 2, 4 *v.*

pluck (pluk) 1 pick: *to pluck flowers, to pluck the strings of a guitar. She plucked at the loose threads of her coat.* 2 pull the feathers out of a dead bird: *He was busy plucking chickens.* 3 courage: *The cat showed pluck fighting that dog.* **Plucky** means "brave." 1, 2 *v.,* 3 *n.*

plug (plug) 1 anything used to block a hole. A sink has a plug for the drain. 2 put a plug into. 3 block; clog; fill up: *Leaves are plugging the drain.* 4 a device at the end of a cord, to make an electrical connection by sticking it into an outlet in the wall. 5 *Informal.* work steadily: *She plugged away at the computer.* 6 *Informal.* advertise or recommend: *to plug a new product.* 7 *Informal.* an advertisement or recommendation. 1, 3, 6 *n.,* 2, 4, 5, 7 *v.,* **plugged, plug·ging.**
plug in, make an electrical connection by putting in a plug: *He plugged in the kettle to make tea.*

plum (plum) 1 a round, juicy fruit with a smooth skin and a stone or pit. Plums grow on a small tree and can be red, green, purple, or yellow. 2 dark bluish purple. 1, 2 *n.,* 2 *adj.*
plum pudding, a traditional Christmas dessert like a steamed cake with raisins and spices in it, often eaten with a caramel sauce.

plum·age (plū′mij) the feathers of a bird: *A parrot has bright plumage.* *n.*

plumb·ing (plum′ing) 1 the water pipes, drains,

taps, etc. in a building. **2** the work of putting these in and fixing them when needed. *n.* —**plumb′er,** *n.*

plume (plūm) **1** a large, long feather, especially one used as a decoration. **2** decorate with plumes: *a plumed hat.* **3** smooth or arrange the feathers of: *The eagle plumed its wings.* 1 *n.,* 2, 3 *v.,* **plumed, plum·ing.**
plume yourself on, be very proud of: *She plumed herself on her dancing skill.*

plum·met (plum′it) plunge; drop a long way very quickly: *to plummet into the sea.* *v.*

plump (plump) nicely rounded; fat in an attractive way: *A healthy baby has plump cheeks.* *adj.*

plun·der (plun′dər) **1** rob by force, in a large group: *The pirates entered the harbour and began to plunder the town.* **2** the things stolen in this way: *The pirates buried their plunder in a secret place.* **3** the action of robbing by force: *We must try to stop the plunder of Earth's resources.* 1 *v.,* 2, 3 *n.*

plunge (plunj) **1** throw or push with force, especially into a liquid: *to plunge your hand into water.* **2** throw suddenly or violently into a certain condition: *to plunge the world into war, to plunge the room into darkness.* **3** jump; throw yourself into something; dive: *She plunged into the river and saved the boy. He plunged into a long explanation.* **4** fall a long way very quickly or suddenly: *The aircraft plunged to earth.* **5** a sudden, fall, rush, or jump. 1–4 *v.,* **plunged, plung·ing;** 5 *n.*
take the plunge, go ahead and do something risky.

plung·er (plun′jər) a large rubber suction cup on a long stick, used for unplugging drains, toilets, etc. *n.*

plu·ral (plū′rəl *or* plər′əl) **1** the form of a word used to show that it refers to more than one. *Books* is the plural of *book. These* is the plural of *this.* **2** having to do with this form: *The usual plural ending is "-s."* 1 *n.,* 2 *adj.* —**plu′ral·ize,** *v.* ▶ See the *Grammar and Usage Mini-Guide.*

Grammar Check . . . . . . plural

Plural nouns are usually formed by adding *-s* to a singular noun: *house* becomes *houses*; *ray* becomes *rays*; *cat* becomes *cats*.

However, there are many exceptions to this rule. Here are some:

- If the word ends in **s**, **sh**, **ch**, **x**, or **z**, add -es: *buses, bushes, watches, foxes, fezes.*
- If the noun ends in a **consonant plus -y**, change the *-y* to *-i* and add -es: *ponies, candies.*
- Plurals of animal names often have no ending: *deer, moose, sheep.*
- Some nouns break all the rules: *children, geese.*

plus (plus) **1** added to: *Three plus two equals five. Symbol:* + **2** *Informal.* and also: *Good writing takes skill plus creativity* (*conj.*). *I'm very tired; plus, I have a bad cold* (*adv.*). **3** higher than: *His mark was B plus. There were thirty-plus people there.* **4** an advantage; a helpful thing: *That extra practice turned out to be a real plus for our team.* 1 *prep.,* 2 *conj. or adv.,* 3 *adj.,* 4 *n.*

plush (plush) **1** a fabric like velvet but thicker and softer. Many stuffed toys are made of plush. **2** luxurious: *a plush hotel suite.* *n.*

Plu·to (plū′tō) formerly the planet farthest from the sun, Pluto has been reclassified as a dwarf planet. *n.* ▶ See Appendix.

plu·to·ni·um (plū tō′nē əm) a radioactive metallic element. It is made from uranium in nuclear reactors and can be used to produce nuclear energy. *n.*

ply[1] (plī) a layer or strand: *three-ply rope, two-ply bathroom tissue.* *n., pl.* **plies.**

ply[2] (plī) **1** work with; use: *The rowers plied their oars.* **2** pressure someone; keep offering or asking: *to ply a person with food and drink. They plied me with questions.* **3** go back and forth regularly; shuttle: *The bus plies between the station and the hotel.* *v.,* **plied, ply·ing.**

ply·wood (plī′wu̇d′) a sheet of wood made of several thin layers glued together. *n.*

p.m. or **P.M.** *abbreviation for* the time from noon to midnight: *His birthday party lasted till 8 p.m.*

WORD HISTORY . . . . p.m.

p.m. stands for *post meridiem*, a Latin phrase meaning "after midday."

P.M. *abbreviation for* Prime Minister.

pneu·mat·ic (nyū mat′ik *or* nū mat′ik) having to do with air. A pneumatic tire contains air; a pneumatic drill is worked by air pressure. *adj.*

pneu·mo·nia (nyū mōn′yə *or* nū mōn′yə) a disease that causes the lungs to become inflamed and fill up with fluid. *n.*

P.O. *abbreviation for* Post Office, in addresses.

poach[1] (pōch) **1** cook an egg by breaking it into boiling water or into a very small pan over boiling water. **2** cook fish by simmering it in shallow water or milk. *v.*

a bat	e bed	i bid	o pot	u cup	th thin
ā cake	ē me	ī bite	ō go	ū rude	ᴛʜ then
à bar	ə about	ər over	ȯ for	u̇ put	zh measure

poach² (pōch) hunt or fish illegally, either on private land or by killing animals that are protected. *v.* —**poach′er,** *n.*

pock (pok) 1 a small scar or pit left by smallpox or chicken pox. 2 leave scars or pits or similar traces on: *Old limestone quarries pocked the landscape.* *n.* —**pock′marked′,** *adj.*

pock•et (pok′it) 1 a small pouch sewn into or onto clothing for carrying money or small things. 2 put in a pocket: *to pocket a dime.* 3 take or keep, often secretly or dishonestly: *One partner pocketed all the profits.* 4 small enough to go in a pocket: *a pocket camera.* 5 a small, definite area different from its surroundings: *a pocket of silver in the earth, farmland with a few pockets of forest left.* 1, 5 *n.,* 2, 3 *v.,* 4 *adj.*
burn a hole in your pocket, make you feel like spending: *That ten-dollar bill is burning a hole in Alan's pocket.*
out of pocket, having lost money in a transaction: *I was out of pocket $20 on the sale of my bike.*

pock•et•book (pok′it bu̇k′) 1 a small paperback book. 2 a wallet that opens and closes like a book. *n.*

pock•et•knife (pok′it nīf′) a small folding knife that can be carried in your pocket. *n., pl.* **pock•et•knives.**

pod (pod) the shell or case that the seeds of beans and peas grow in. *n.*

po•em (pō′əm) a piece of poetry. *n.*

WORD HISTORY........ poem

The word **poem** comes from the Greek *poiema*, which means "something made or composed."

po•et•ry (pō′ə trē) writing that uses words in a beautiful and unusual way. Some poetry is arranged in lines with a regular rhythm or rhyme. Poetry often uses metaphors and other colourful language, and often tells the writer's feelings about something. A **poet** is a writer of poetry; things relating to poetry are **poetic** (pō et′ik). *n.*

poin•set•ti•a (poin set′ə *or* poin set′ē ə) a Central American plant with a small flower surrounded by large red, pink, or white leaves that look like petals. Poinsettias are often used as Christmas decorations. *n.*

WORD HISTORY........ poinsettia

The poinsettia plant was named after Joel R. Poinsett, an American who discovered it in Mexico in the 1800s.

point (point) 1 a sharp end: *the point of a needle.* 2 a dot: *a decimal point.* 3 a particular place or spot: *She drew a circle around a certain point on the map.* 4 a particular moment in time, a level, or a stage in a process: *freezing point, boiling point. At that point I lost interest. She's generous, but only up to a certain point.* 5 an idea put forward in an argument or discussion: *You have mentioned an important point.* 6 a feature: *Courage and endurance were her good points.* 7 the main idea or purpose: *the point of the story. I don't see the point of all this work.* 8 aim; direct something: *Don't point your finger at me.* 9 show where something is with your finger: *He pointed the way to the village.* 10 face a certain direction: *Her toes point inward.* 11 a piece of land with a sharp end sticking out into the water, also called a **cape.** 12 a unit of scoring: *You have to be at least two points ahead to win in tennis.* 1–7, 11, 12 *n.,* 8–10 *v.* —**point′less,** *adj.*
beside the point, having nothing to do with the subject.
make a point, state an idea clearly and logically.
make a point of, insist on: *She always made a point of being on time.*
on the point of, just about to do something: *She was on the point of going out when the phone rang.*
point of view, a the position you see something from: *From this point of view the room looks smaller.* **b** a way of thinking about something: *I understand your point of view.*
point out, show or call attention to: *to point out mistakes.*
to the point, directly relating to the subject at hand: *His speech was brief and to the point.*

point–blank (point′blangk′) 1 plain and direct; in a plain and direct way: *a point-blank question* (*adj.*). *He refused point-blank* (*adv.*). 2 at very close range: *She fired point-blank at the target.* 1 *adj.,* 1, 2 *adv.*

point•ed (poin′tid) 1 having a point or points: *a pointed stick.* 2 aimed specially at someone: *a pointed remark.* 3 plain and direct: *a pointed refusal.* *adj.*

point•er (poin′tər) 1 a long stick used to point out things on a map, chalkboard, etc. 2 a hand or needle on a dial. 3 a breed of short-haired hunting dog trained to show where an animal is by standing still with its head and body pointing toward it. 4 *Informal.* hint; suggestion: *She gave him some pointers on how to improve his pitching.* *n.*

poise (poiz) 1 balance and control in standing and moving: *We admired the gymnast's poise.* 2 self-control and skill in dealing with awkward or unexpected situations. 3 keep balanced or steady: *Poise yourself on your toes.* 4 **poised,** ready to at any moment: *poised for attack.* 1, 2 *n.,* 3, 4 *v.,* **poised, pois•ing.**

Poison

The deadliest of all animals is the little golden poison-arrow frog.

The blue-ringed octopus lives in the seas around Australia. Its bite is deadly poisonous.

Spiders have fangs for squirting poison into their prey.

poi·son (poiʹzən) **1** a substance able to cause illness, death, or serious injury if taken into your body. Bleach and gasoline are poisons. **2** kill or harm with poison: *He poisoned the rats.* **3** put poison in or on: *to poison someone's food.* 1 *n.*, 2, 3 *v.* —**poiʹson·ous,** *adj.*

poison ivy (pȯiʹzən īʹvē) a woodland plant that looks like ivy and causes a painful and itchy rash on most people if they touch it. Other related plants are **poison oak** and **poison sumac.**

poke (pōk) **1** push against with something pointed; jab: *to poke a person in the ribs, to poke a fire* (*v.*), *to give someone a poke* (*n.*). **2** stick in or out; push: *She poked her head out the window.* **3** go in a slow, lazy way: *poking along the street.* **4** snoop: *Who's been poking around my desk?* 1–4 *v.*, **poked, pok·ing;** 2 *n.*

🍁 **poke·lo·gan** (pōkʹlōʹgən) a small, quiet pool or marshy place in a stream. *n.*

pok·er¹ (pōʹkər) a metal rod for stirring up a fire. *n.*

pok·er² (pōʹkər) a card game. *n.*

po·lar (pōʹlər) having to do with the North or South Pole: *It is very cold in the polar regions.* *adj.*

polar bear (pōʹlər berʹ) a large, white bear living in the arctic regions.

pole¹ (pōl) **1** a long, slender, tube-shaped piece of wood, metal, or other material: *a telephone pole, a ski pole.* **2** push or make something go with a pole: *to pole a raft down a river.* 1 *n.*, 2 *v.*, **poled, pol·ing.**

pole² (pōl) **1** either end of the earth's axis. The North Pole and the South Pole are opposite each other. **2** either of two points where opposite forces are strongest. A magnet or a battery has both a positive pole and a negative pole. *n.*

poles apart, very different; completely opposite: *Their opinions on the subject were poles apart.*

pole·star (pōlʹstärʹ) the North Star, a star that is almost directly above the North Pole. In earlier times it was often used as a guide by sailors. *n.*

pole vault a jump over a high bar using a long pole. You run with the pole and then use it to push off with. —**poleʹ-vaultʹ,** *v.*

po·lice (pə lēsʹ) **1** the people employed by a government to guard people's lives and property, preserve peace and order, and arrest lawbreakers. All these workers together are the **police force.** **2** patrol; guard or keep order in: *to police the streets.* 1 *pl.n.*, 2 *v.*, **po·liced, po·lic·ing.** —**po·liceʹ·man,** *n.* —**po·liceʹ·woʹman,** *n.*

police dog (pə lēsʹ dogʹ) a dog trained for use in police work.

police officer a member of a **police force.**

pol·i·cy¹ (polʹə sē) a plan of action; a way of doing things according to a rule you have made: *It is my policy not to lend out my CDs. The election candidate explained his party's policy.* *n.*, *pl.* **pol·i·cies.**

pol·i·cy² (polʹə sē) a written agreement about insurance, saying how much the insurance company will pay in case of damage, injury, or death. *n.*, *pl.* **pol·i·cies.**

po·li·o (pōʹlē ō) an infectious disease, caused by a virus, that often leaves muscles permanently paralyzed. The full name is **poliomyelitis** (pōʹlē ō mīʹə līʹtis). *n.*

a bat	e bed	i bid	o pot	u cup	th thin
ā cake	ē me	ī bite	ō go	ū rude	ᴛʜ then
ä bar	ə about	ər over	ȯ for	ů put	zh measure

pol·ish (pol′ish) 1 make or become smooth and shiny: *to polish silver. This leather polishes well.* 2 a substance for making things clean and shiny: *shoe polish.* 3 improve something that is already pretty good: *I want to polish my French in Québec this summer.* 4 a polished condition: *The polish of the furniture reflected our faces like a mirror. Her fine manners showed polish.* 1, 3 *v.,* 2, 4 *n.*

po·lite (pə līt′) 1 respectful and nice; showing good manners: *The polite boy gave the elderly woman his seat on the bus.* 2 high-class; elegant: *polite society.* *adj.* **—po·lite′ly,** *adv.* **—po·lite′ness,** *n.*

political party (pə lit′ə kəl pȧr′tē) an organization of people who share the same ideas about government and who try to get their members elected.

pol·i·ti·cian (pol′ə tish′ən) 1 a person who holds a government office, such as a Member of Parliament; a person who is active in politics. 2 anyone who is good at keeping people happy and avoiding quarrels while getting things done. *n.*

pol·i·tics (pol′ə tiks′) 1 the work of managing a country, province, town, etc.; the science and art of governing: *Trudeau was active in politics for many years.* 2 ideas or opinions about government: *Mom loves to discuss politics.* 3 issues of power or control in a group, including who has it or wants it and how they get it or use it. *sing. or pl.n.* **—po·lit′i·cal** (pə lit′ə kəl), *adj.*

pol·ka (pōl′kə) a lively dance, or a piece of music written for it. *n.*

polka dot (pō′kə dot′) one of many round coloured spots that form a decorative pattern on something, especially cloth. **—pol′ka-dot′ted,** *adj.*

poll (pōl) 1 the process of asking people what they think on a certain subject and then totalling the responses: *According to a recent poll, most Canadians think medicare is important.* 2 ask people questions to find out their opinion: *We polled students in grades four and five on the subject of homework.* 3 a place where votes are cast and counted in an election, also called a **polling station.** Voters can mark their ballots privately in little **polling booths** inside. 4 the number of votes cast: *The final poll at this station was 1643.* 1, 3, 4 *n.,* 2 *v.*

pol·len (pol′ən) a fine, yellowish powder made up of the male cells of flowering plants. The pollen is carried on the anthers of the flower, at the top of the stamens. *n.*

pol·li·nate (pol′ə nāt′) carry pollen from stamens to pistils of flowers so that male plant cells can join with female cells to produce fertile seed. Bees pollinate flowers. *v.,* **pol·li·nat·ed, pol·li·nat·ing.** **—pol′li·na′tion,** *n.*

pol·li·wog (pol′ē wog′) another name for a tadpole, the larva of a frog or toad. It has a short, round body, gills, and a long tail, but no legs. **Pollywog** is another spelling. *n.*

pol·lute (pə lūt′) make dirty with anything that can harm people, animals, or plants: *The exhaust from cars pollutes the air.* Substances which pollute are **pollutants** (pə lū′tənts). *v.,* **pol·lut·ed, pol·lut·ing.** **—pol·lu′tion,** *n.* **—pol·lut′er,** *n.*

po·lo (pō′lō) a game played by two teams of players on horseback, who use long-handled mallets to hit a wooden ball through the opposing team's goal. *n.*

pol·y·es·ter (pol′ē es′tər) a manufactured material commonly used to make plastics, yarns, and fabrics. *n.*

pol·y·gon (pol′i gon′) a two-dimensional figure with three or more angles and straight sides. *n.*
▶ See Appendix.

pol·y·he·dron (pol′ē hē′drən) a solid figure with four or more faces. A cube is a polyhedron with six faces. *n., pl.* **pol·y·he·drons** or **pol·y·he·dra** (pol′ē hē′drə).

Pol·y·ne·sia (pol′ə nē′zhə) a large group of islands in the Pacific Ocean, including Tahiti and Hawaii. *n.* **—Pol′y·ne′sian,** *adj. or n.*

pol·yp (pol′ip) a small water animal with a tubelike body and fingerlike tentacles around its mouth to gather in food. Polyps often grow in colonies, with their bases connected. Coral is made up of polyps. *n.*

pome·gran·ate (pom′ ə gran′it) a reddish yellow fruit with a thick skin and many seeds; each seed has tasty red pulp clinging to it. Pomegranates grow on small trees in warm regions of the world. *n.*

pomp (pomp) a splendid or grand display: *The king was crowned with great pomp.* *n.*
pomp and circumstance, lots of fancy display and formal ceremonies.

pom·pom (pom′pom) a fluffy or silky ball attached to clothing as a decoration. Tuques and clown outfits often have pompoms on them. *n.*

pom·pous (pom′pəs) trying to look or sound grand or important: *The leader of the band bowed in a pompous manner.* *adj.* **—pom·pos′i·ty,** *n.*

pon·cho (pon′chō) a large piece of material with a slit in the middle for the head to go through, sometimes with a hood. Ponchos are worn as cloaks or raincoats. *n.*

pond (pond) a body of still water, smaller than a lake. **Pond scum** is algae growing on its surface. *n.*

pon·der (pon′dər) think over carefully: *to ponder a problem.* *v.*

pon·tiff (pon′tif) another word for **pope,** the head of the Roman Catholic Church. *n.*

pon·toon (pon tūn′) one of the floating supports of a temporary bridge or a seaplane. *n.*

po·ny (pō′nē) a small horse. Most adult ponies are less than 140 cm tall at the shoulder. *n., pl.* **po·nies.**

poo·dle (pū′dəl) a breed of dog with thick, curly, woolly hair that does not shed. *n.*

pool[1] (pūl) 1 a tank of water to swim in: *Our school has a pool.* 2 a small body of water; a small pond. 3 a puddle of any liquid: *a pool of oil under a car.* *n.*

pool[2] (pūl) 1 a game played with coloured balls on a special table. The players use long sticks called **cues** to try to knock the balls into pockets at the edges of the table. 2 put things or money together for a joint purpose: *We pooled our savings to buy Dad a gift.* 3 the things or money shared in this way. In a **car pool,** each person in a group takes a turn giving the others a ride to a certain place. 1, 3 *n.,* 2 *v.*

poor (pūr) 1 not having enough money to buy the things that are considered necessary or normal to have. 2 not good: *poor health, poor soil. She is a poor reader.* 3 to be pitied; unfortunate: *Poor Rosa fell just before the end of the race.* *adj.* **—poor′ly,** *adv.*

pop[1] (pop) 1 a soft drink: *a can of pop.* 2 make a short, quick, bursting or exploding sound: *The firecrackers popped in bunches.* 3 that kind of sound: *We heard the pop of a cork.* 4 burst open with such a sound: *Popcorn was popping in the microwave.* 5 put, go, or come suddenly or quickly and easily: *to pop in for a short visit, to pop a cake in the oven. The toast popped out of the toaster.* 1, 3 *n.,* 2, 4, 5 *v.* **popped, pop·ping.**
a pop, each: *We paid $15 a pop just to get in.*
pop fly, in baseball, a hit that makes it easy to catch the ball.
pop the question, ask someone to marry you.

pop[2] (pop) short for **popular music,** a style of light music with a simple tune and a strong beat. *n.*

pop·corn (pop′kȯrn′) a kind of corn whose kernels burst open and puff out in a white mass when heated. It is eaten as a snack. *n.*

Pope or **pope** (pōp) the head of the Roman Catholic Church. *n.*

pop·lar (pop′lər) a tall, fast-growing, short-lived tree with heart-shaped leaves. Its wood is light and soft and is often used for pulp to make paper. *n.*

pop·py (pop′ē) 1 a garden plant with red, yellow, or white flowers. The tiny black seeds, called **poppyseed,** are used in cooking. 2 a red plastic poppy worn for Remembrance Day. *n., pl.* **pop·pies.**

Pop·si·cle (pop′sə kəl) *a trademark for* a long piece of fruit-flavoured ice on a small stick. *n.*

pop·u·lar (pop′yə lər) 1 liked by many people: *a popular song. He is the most popular boy in the school.* 2 that most people can appreciate, understand, afford, etc.: *popular prices, popular music, popular science.* 3 widespread among many people; of people in general: *It is a popular belief that black cats bring bad luck.* 4 by or of the people: *a government elected by popular vote.* *adj.*
—pop′u·lar′i·ty (pop′yə ler′ə tē), *n.*
—pop′u·lar·ize′, *v.*

pop·u·late (pop′yə lāt′) live in a place: *The Arctic is populated mainly by Inuit. Will humans ever populate the Moon?* *v.,* **pop·u·lat·ed, pop·u·lat·ing.**

pop·u·la·tion (pop′yə lā′shən) 1 the people of a city, country, or district, or their number: *The whole population was against the new law. The population of Montréal is in the millions.* A place with a large population is **populous** (pop′yə ləs). 2 the whole group of animals of a certain kind, especially those living in one place: *the bear population, the deer population of Algonquin Park.* *n.*

pop–up (pop′up) 1 a folding picture with parts that stand up. 2 a small window that suddenly appears on a computer screen. *n.*

por·ce·lain (pȯr′sə lin) very fine china. Teacups are often made of porcelain. *n.*

porch (pȯrch) a platform at the entrance to a building. It is usually raised and often covered, and may have low walls or a railing. **Verandah** (və ran′də) is another word for it. *n.*

Porcupines rattle their quills to warn off enemies.

por·cu·pine (pȯr′kyə pīn′) a small, slow-moving animal with sharp spines or quills on its body for protection. Porcupines are active at night. *n.*

a bat	e bed	i bid	o pot	u cup	th thin
ā cake	ē me	ī bite	ō go	ū rude	ᴛʜ then
ȧ bar	ə about	ər over	ȯ for	u̇ put	zh measure

pore¹ (pôr) a very tiny opening that fluids can pass through. There are pores in the skin of people and animals, and in the leaves of plants; sweat comes through our pores. Something that has pores is **porous.** *n.*

pore² (pôr)
pore over, study long and steadily: *We pored over a map of the Bruce Trail, planning our hike.* *v.,* **pored, por·ing.**

CONFUSABLES .... pore

pore means "study": *He pored over encyclopedias, trying to find the answer to his question.*

pour means "flow": *Water poured over the dam.*

pork (pôrk) meat from a pig. *n.*

por·nog·ra·phy (pôr nog′rə fē) writing, images, or films that show sex in an abusive or insulting way. *n.*

por·poise (pôr′pəs) **1** a small whale about 1.5 to 2.5 m long, with a black or grey back. Porpoises eat fish, squid, shrimp, etc. **2** dolphin. *n., pl.* **por·pois·es** or **por·poise.**

por·ridge (pôr′ij) a food made of oatmeal or other cereal boiled in water or milk until it thickens. *n.*

port¹ (pôrt) **1** a harbour; a place where ships and boats can take shelter from storms. **2** a town or city with a harbour where ships load and unload: *Halifax and Vancouver are important Canadian ports.* **3** the left side of a boat or aircraft when you are facing the front: *The ship was leaning a little to port.* **4** on the left side: *the port engine.* 1–3 *n.,* 4 *adj.*

port² (pôrt) a place on a computer, printer, or any other piece of hardware where you can plug in the cable from some other part of the system. *n.*

port·a·ble (pôr′tə bəl) **1** able to be carried or moved easily: *a portable stereo.* **2** a temporary building in a schoolyard, used as an extra classroom. 1 *adj.,* 2 *n.*

por·tage (pôr tázh′) **1** the act of carrying canoes, boats, supplies, etc. overland from one stretch of water to another: *We found the last portage the hardest.* **2** carry canoes, etc. in this way: *We had to portage six times.* **3** a place where you must do this: *We pitched camp at the portage.* 1, 3 *n.,* 2 *v.,* **por·taged, por·tag·ing.**

por·tal (pôr′təl) a poetic word for a gateway. *n.*

port·cul·lis (pôrt kul′is) a strong gate at the entrance to a castle. It was made of crisscrossed iron bars with sharp points at the bottom, and could be raised or lowered. *n.*

por·tent (pôr′tent) a warning of a coming event, especially something bad; a sign or omen: *The black clouds were a portent of bad weather.* *n.* **—por·tent′ous,** *adj.*

por·ter¹ (pôr′tər) **1** a person hired to carry baggage. Hotels, airports, and train stations have porters. **2** a person who sees to the needs of passengers on a train. *n.*

por·ter² (pôr′tər) a person who guards a door or entrance: *The porter let them in.* *n.*

port·fo·li·o (pôrt fō′lē ō′) **1** a folder containing examples of a student's work: *Riça's portfolio was sent to her new school when she moved.* **2** a large, flat case for large pieces of paper such as drawings by an artist or architect. **3** a collection of work by an artist, architect, photographer, etc., used by him or her as an example to show people. **4** in a group of leaders, a particular area of activity to be managed by one person. The portfolio of a cabinet minister is a department of the government, such as Finance or Health. *n., pl.* **port·fo·li·os.**

port·hole (pôrt′hōl′) an opening in a ship's side to let in light and air. *n.*

por·ti·co (pôr′tə kō′) an entrance area or walkway with a roof over it supported by pillars. *n., pl.* **por·ti·coes** or **por·ti·cos.**

por·tion (pôr′shən) **1** a measured part or share: *A portion of each school day is devoted to math.* **2** a serving of food: *This restaurant serves large portions.* **3** divide into parts or shares: *When he died, his money was portioned out among his children.* 1, 2 *n.,* 3 *v.*

port·ly (pôrt′lē) heavy, but in a dignified way: *a portly gentleman.* *adj.,* **port·li·er, port·li·est.**

por·trait (pôr′trit) **1** a posed picture of a person, especially of the face. **2** a description. *n.*

por·tray (pôr trā′) **1** show in pictures or words: *The book* Pit Pony *portrays the life of the Cape Breton coal miners.* **2** act the part of a certain character in a play or movie. *v.* **—por·tray′al,** *n.*

pose (pōz) **1** put or stay in a certain position: *He posed for an hour for his portrait.* A **poseable** toy figure has movable arms and legs. **2** a way of holding your body, especially for a picture: *That shot shows her in an attractive pose.* **3** act in order to fool people: *He posed as a rich man to impress his neighbours.* **4** a fake way of behaving: *She acts sick but that's just a pose.* **5** put forward: *to pose a question.* 1, 3, 5 *v.,* **posed, pos·ing;** 2, 4 *n.*

posh (posh) luxurious, elegant, or expensive: *To celebrate, we all got taken to a posh restaurant.* *adj.*

po•si•tion (pə zish′ən) 1 the place where a thing or person is: *I changed the position of my bed so it was right under the window.* 2 a way of being placed: *an upright position, an uncomfortable position.* 3 the place assigned to a person or thing: *Each soldier got into position to defend the fort. My position on the team is defence.* 4 a job: *He has a position in a bank.* 5 put in position; place: *I positioned myself comfortably at my desk.* 6 an opinion based on careful thought: *What is your position on this question?* 1–4, 6 *n.,* 5 *v.*

pos•i•tive (poz′ə tiv) 1 certain; sure: *I'm positive I left it right here.* 2 definite; clear: *a positive denial.* 3 full of hope, good cheer, approval, helpful ideas, etc.: *a positive attitude, positive criticism, a positive response.* 4 showing or having to do with something that is there rather than not there: *Heat is a positive thing; cold is only the absence of heat. They tested me for allergies and the result is positive.* 5 greater than zero; plus: *Positive numbers are used to count things.* 6 having an electric charge opposite to that of an electron. *adj.* —**posi′tive•ly,** *adv.*

Grammar Check . . . . . positive

Adjectives and adverbs can be written in three forms:

- **positive** (*strong, strongly*), used for regular descriptions:
  She is a strong swimmer. She swims strongly.
- **comparative** (*stronger, more strongly*), used to compare two things:
  She is the stronger of the two swimmers.
  She swims more strongly than he does.
- **superlative** (*strongest, most strongly*), used for more than two things:
  She is the strongest of all the swimmers.
  Of the whole team, she swims most strongly.

pos•sess (pə zes′) 1 have as your own: *The royal family possesses great wealth. She possessed great courage.* 2 control or influence by some powerful force or spirit: *possessed by greed. What possessed you to take such a risk? He fought like one possessed.* *v.* —**pos•ses′sor,** *n.*

pos•ses•sion (pə zesh′ən) 1 ownership; the fact of possessing: *We take possession of our new house on June 1st.* 2 something you own: *Please remove your possessions from my room. Greenland is a possession of Denmark.* *n.*

pos•ses•sive (pə zes′iv) 1 always trying or wanting to keep things or people for yourself. 2 in grammar, having to do with the form of a noun or pronoun that refers to the owner of something. *My* is the possessive form of *I* in *my books. Bird's* is the possessive form of *bird* in *a bird's wing.* ▶ See the *Grammar and Usage Mini-Guide.* 3 a word showing possession. In *the girl's horse,* the word *girl's* is a possessive. 1, 2 *adj.,* 3 *n.*

pos•si•ble (pos′ə bəl) 1 that can be chosen or done; that can happen: *We looked up possible vacation spots on the Internet. It is possible to cure tuberculosis.* 2 that can be true: *It is possible that he went.* *adj.* —**pos′si•bly,** *adv.* —**pos′si•bil′i•ty,** *n.*

pos•sum (pos′əm) short for **opossum.** *n.*
play possum, pretend to be dead or asleep.

post[1] (pōst) 1 a long, upright piece of wood, metal, or other material that supports something. This meaning is often used in compounds: *signpost, gatepost.* 2 put a notice in a public place: *The list of winners will be posted soon.* 1 *n.,* 2 *v.*

post[2] (pōst) 1 an assigned place for doing a duty: *When the fire alarm sounds, each person moves quickly to his or her post.* 2 a place far from the main settlement, where soldiers, missionaries, or traders are stationed: *a military post. The trappers brought their furs to the trading post.* 3 send to a station or post: *The captain posted guards at the door.* 4 a job or position. 1, 2, 4 *n.,* 3 *v.*

post[3] (pōst) mail: *to post a letter* (*v.*). *I shall send the package by post* (*n.*). *v. or n.* —**post′al,** *adj.*
keep someone posted, keep someone up to date on what happens.

post– *a prefix meaning* "after," as in *postscript, postpone, postdate.*

post•age (pōs′tij) the amount paid to send something by mail. *n.*

✱ **postal code** (pōs′təl kōd′) a set of letters and numbers included as part of a mailing address to speed up the sorting of mail by machines. Each code stands for a particular route or drop-off point for mail delivery. For example, the postal code of Ladysmith, B.C. is V0R 2E0.

post•card (pōst′kärd′) a card for sending a message by mail, used without an envelope. Most postcards have a picture on one side. *n.*

post•er (pōs′tər) 1 a large printed or hand-drawn advertisement put up in some public place: *There were posters all over the school announcing Pizza Day.* 2 a large printed picture or message, used for decoration. *n.*

pos•ter•i•ty (po ster′ə tē) future generations: *Our forests and waterways must be preserved for posterity.* *n.*

post•mark (pōst′märk′) 1 an official mark put on mail, showing when and where it was mailed. It also marks the stamp, showing that it has been used and cannot be used again. 2 put a postmark on. 1 *n.,* 2 *v.*

a bat	e bed	i bid	o pot	u cup	th thin
ā cake	ē me	ī bite	ō go	ū rude	ᴛʜ then
ä bar	ə about	ər over	ô for	ů put	zh measure

post office (pōst′ of′is) 1 a place where mail is handled and postage stamps are sold. 2 Often, **Post Office,** the company in charge of mail service.

post·pone (pōst pōn′) put off till later; delay: *The ball game was postponed because of rain.* *v.,* **post·poned, post·pon·ing.** **—post·pone′ment,** *n.*

post·script (pōst′skript′) a part added to the end of a letter or other piece of writing. *n.*

pos·ture (pos′chər) 1 the way you hold your body. Good posture is having your spine properly supported by the right muscles. 2 adopt a pose: *The judo instructor postured in front of us, showing us the moves.* 1 *n.,* 2 *v.,* **pos·tured, pos·tur·ing.**

pot (pot) 1 any deep container made of metal, glass, clay, etc.: *a cooking pot, a flower pot, a coffee pot.* 2 put into a pot: *We potted the young tomato plants.* 1 *n.,* 2 *v.,* **pot·ted, pot·ting.** **—pot′ful′,** *n.*
go to pot, fall gradually into ruin.

pot·ash (pot′ash′) 1 a substance containing potassium, made from wood ashes. It is used to make soap and fertilizer. 2 any of several minerals containing potassium, used in farming and industry. *n.*

po·tas·si·um (pə tas′ē əm) a chemical element that is a soft, silvery metal. It is used in combination with other chemicals to make soaps, glass, matches, fertilizers, and so on. Potassium is also necessary to the human body. Bananas are high in potassium. *n.*

po·ta·to (pə tā′tō) a round, hard, starchy vegetable that is white or yellow inside and has a thin brown, red, or whitish skin. It is a **tuber,** which means it grows as part of an underground stem. Thin slices of potato are deep-fried or baked to make **potato chips.** *n., pl.* **po·ta·toes.**

po·tent (pō′tənt) powerful; strong: *a potent medicine, a potent smell.* *adj.* **—po′ten·cy,** *n.*

po·ten·tial (pə ten′shəl) 1 possible in the future: *a potential danger.* 2 the ability to do or become something in the future: *That pianist has the potential to become a great musician.* 1 *adj.,* 2 *n.*

potential energy (pə ten′shəl en′ ər jē) the energy that something has when it is in a position that can result in motion. A coiled spring or a raised weight has potential energy; one can pop up and the other can fall.

pot·hole (pot′hōl′) a hole in a road. *n.*

po·tion (pō′shən) in stories, a drink used as a medicine or poison, or to give magic power. *n.*

pot·latch (pot′lach) a ceremony of various First Nations peoples of the West Coast, where the host gave gifts to the guests. Among the Haida, the potlatch marked special events such as the birth, marriage, or death of an important person, the raising of a new building or totem pole, and so on. It included singing, dancing, storytelling, feasting, and speeches as well as gift-giving.

pot·pour·ri (pō′pə rē′) a mixture of dried, sweet-smelling flowers and leaves kept in an open container to scent the air in a room. *n., pl.* **pot·pour·ris.**

WORD HISTORY......potpourri

Can something rotten smell sweet? Potpourri actually means "rotten pot" in French, because the plants in it are dead.

pot·ter (pot′ər) a person who makes **pottery,** that is, pots, dishes, vases, and so on out of clay. *n.*

pouch (pouch) 1 a little bag, especially of cloth or leather with a flap or drawstring to close it. 2 a fold of skin that is like a bag: *A kangaroo carries its young in a pouch. A squirrel has a pouch in each cheek.* *n.*

poul·try (pōl′trē) birds raised for their meat or eggs, such as chickens, turkeys, ducks, and geese. *n.*

pounce (pouns) 1 swoop down or jump suddenly on something and seize it: *The cat pounced on the mouse.* 2 a sudden swoop or jump like this. 1 *v.,* **pounced, pounc·ing;** 2 *n.*

pound¹ (pound) 1 a nonmetric unit of weight; 16 ounces (about 0.45 kg). *Abbreviation:* lb. 2 a unit of money in some countries, such as the United Kingdom. *Symbol:* **£** *n., pl.* **pounds** or **pound.**

pound² (pound) 1 hit hard again and again: *He pounded the door with his fist.* 2 beat hard; throb: *After a hard run your heart pounds.* *v.*

pound³ (pound) 1 a place where stray animals are taken and kept until someone claims them. 2 a place where illegally parked cars are put after being towed away. You have to pay to get your car out. *n.*

pour (pȯr) 1 flow or cause to flow in a steady stream: *I poured the milk from the jug into the cups. The crowd poured out of the arena.* 2 rain very hard. *v.*

pout (pout) 1 make a sulky face by pushing your bottom lip out and up. 2 this kind of face. 1 *v.,* 2 *n.*

🍁 **pou·tine** (pū tēn′) French fries and cheese curds covered with gravy. Poutine is a Québécois dish. *n.*

pov·er·ty (pov′ər tē) the condition of being poor: *Lack of work has caused poverty. The poverty of the soil makes the crops small.* *n.*

pow·der (pou′dər) **1** a substance in the form of dust: *powder snow, talcum powder, gunpowder, chocolate powder.* **2** turn into powder by pounding, grinding, drying, etc.: *powdered sugar.* **3** sprinkle or cover with powder. 1 *n.,* 2, 3 *v.*

pow·er (pou′ər) **1** physical strength or force: *A bulldozer has great power.* **2** ability: *power to heal, mental powers. The fairy had the power to change into different shapes.* **3** authority, control, or influence: *Parliament has the power to make laws.* **4** a person, nation, or thing with great authority or influence: *Five powers held a peace conference.* **5** energy or force that can do work, especially electricity: *water power, steam power. If the power goes off, it'll be dark.* **6** provide with energy: *a boat powered by an outboard motor.* **7** operated by a motor: *a power drill.* **Power steering** uses power from the car's motor to make steering easier. **8** the magnifying capacity of a lens. A lens with a power of ten makes things look ten times bigger than actual size. **9** the number of times a number is multiplied by itself. The expression "2 to the power of 3" is written 2^3 and is equal to 2 × 2 × 2, or 8. 1–5, 8, 9 *n.,* 6 *v.,* 7 *adj.* **—pow′er·ful,** *adj.* **—pow′er·less,** *adj.*
in power, in the position of control or authority: *the government in power.*

power plant (pou′ər plant) a building containing boilers, engines, generators, and so on, for producing electric power. It is also called a **powerhouse** or **power station.** *n.*

pow·wow (pou′wou′) **1** a gathering of First Nations people for celebration, with dancing, singing, and other social activities. **2** *Informal.* a meeting; conference. *n.*

> **WORD HISTORY...... powwow**
>
> **Powwow** is from an Algonquian word. It is related to *pauwaw*, meaning "he dreams." A medicine man was called a **powwow** because it was thought he had learned his skill from dreams.

pp. *abbreviation for* pages.

prac·ti·cal (prak′tə kəl) **1** to do with action rather than thought or theory: *practical experience. Earning a living is a practical matter.* **2** useful; convenient; well suited to what you are doing: *a practical plan. My ballerina costume isn't practical for going trick-or-treating; it isn't warm enough.* **3** having good sense: *Practical people do not spend their time and money foolishly.* *adj.*
practical joke, a trick played on someone for fun, like decorating a cake with candles that cannot be blown out. A person who does this sort of thing is a **practical joker.**

prac·ti·cal·ly (prak′ti klē) **1** in a practical way: *How can we do this more practically?* **2** *Informal.* almost; nearly: *We are practically home.* *adv.*

prac·tice (prak′tis) **1** the process of doing a thing over and over in order to get better at it: *Practice makes perfect.* **2** really doing something, as opposed to just talking or thinking about it: *It seemed like a good plan, but in actual practice it did not work.* **3** custom: *It is our practice to read together at bedtime.* **4** the business of a doctor, lawyer, or other professional: *Dr. Adams has sold her practice to a younger doctor.* **5** a period set aside for practising: *He went to hockey practice last night.* **6** a less common spelling of **practise.** 1–5 *n.,* 6 *v.*
out of practice, no longer skilled at something because you've stopped doing it: *She was out of practice at batting.*

> **CONFUSABLES..... practice**
>
> **practice** is a noun: *I have a hockey practice after school.*
>
> **practise** is a verb: *I will practise my trumpet solo until I get it right.*

prac·tise (prak′tis) **1** do a thing again and again so as to get better at it: *She practised her piano piece.* Someone who has gained skill by practising is **practised:** *a practised cook.* **2** follow or use day after day; make a habit of: *You must learn to practise patience. Practise what you preach.* **3** work at a profession: *to practise law. Is Dr. Cohen still practising in Yellowknife?* *v.,* **prac·tised, prac·tis·ing.**

prai·rie (prer′ē) **1** a large area of flat land with grass but few or no trees. **2** **the Prairies,** *pl.* the great, almost treeless plain that covers much of central and southern Manitoba, Saskatchewan, and Alberta. *n.*

prairie chicken (prer′ē chik′ən) a brown and white bird that lives on the prairies of North America. It is a type of grouse and nests on the ground.

prairie crocus (prer′ē krō′kəs) a wildflower of the prairies that blooms in spring. It is mauve and has soft, silky hairs on the stem and leaves. The prairie crocus is the provincial flower of Manitoba.

prairie dog (prer′ē dog′) a small, burrowing animal of the squirrel family. Prairie dogs live in large groups in prairie regions.

a bat	e bed	i bid	o pot	u cup	th thin
ā cake	ē me	ī bite	ō go	ū rude	ᴛʜ then
ä bar	ə about	ər over	ô for	ů put	zh measure

prairie lily (prer′ē lil′e) a North American wild lily with orange-red flowers. It is found on the prairies and in open woods from Québec to British Columbia. The prairie lily is the provincial flower of Saskatchewan.

Prairie Provinces (prer′ē prov′in siz) Manitoba, Saskatchewan, and Alberta.

praise (prāz) **1** say how good or great someone or something is: *Everyone praised the losing team for its fine effort.* **2** the words used for this: *The winner's friends heaped praise on him.* A person or thing deserving praise is **praiseworthy.** 1 *v.,* **praised, prais·ing;** 2 *n.*

prance (prans) **1** jump around on the hind legs. Horses prance when they feel lively. **2** move merrily or proudly: *The children pranced into the living room in their new Halloween costumes.* *v.,* **pranced, pranc·ing.**

prank (prangk) a playful trick: *On April Fool's Day people play pranks on each other.* *n.* **—prank′ster,** *n.*

prat·tle (prat′əl) **1** talk in a foolish or babyish way; babble. **2** foolish or babyish talk. 1 *v.,* **prat·tled, prat·tling;** 2 *n.*

Prawns are abundant in coastal waters. By day they bury themselves in sand, coming out after dark to walk and feed on the sea floor.

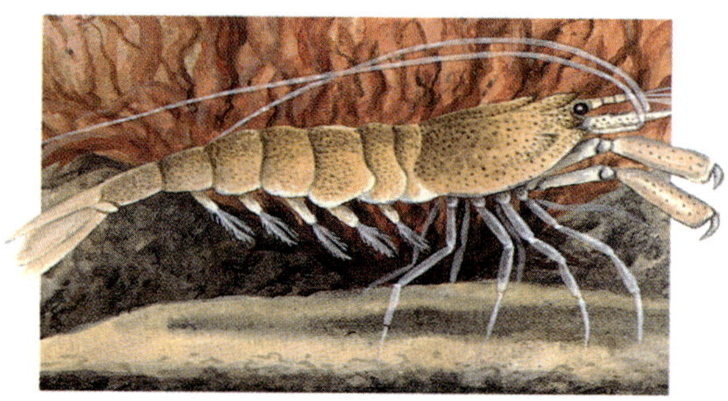

prawn (pron) a shellfish that looks like a large shrimp. *n.*

pray (prā) **1** speak to God or any spiritual being, often to ask for something: *We pray for peace.* **2** an old or poetic word for "please": *Pray come.* *v.*

CONFUSABLES .... pray

pray means "speak to God": *They pray before meals.*
prey means "victim": *The lion tracked its prey for days.*

prayer (prer) **1** the act of praying: *They knelt in prayer.* **2** the words used in praying: *a book of prayers.* **3** *Informal.* the smallest chance: *Without more practice, we haven't a prayer of winning.* *n.* **—prayer′ful,** *adj.*

praying man·tis (prā′ing man′tis) a slender insect that holds its front legs doubled up as if praying. The front legs spring forward to swiftly grab prey.

pre– *a prefix meaning* "before" in place or time, as in *prehistoric, premeditate, prepay, prepayment.*

preach (prēch) **1** speak to a group on a religious subject. **2** keep giving stern or serious advice about something: *He is forever preaching about good table manners.* *v.* **—preach′er,** *n.* **—preach′y,** *adj.*

pre·car·i·ous (pri ker′ē əs) uncertain; not safe; dangerous: *A soldier leads a precarious life. The mountain climber was in a precarious position.* *adj.*

pre·cau·tion (pri kosh′ən) something done beforehand to prevent problems: *Locking doors is a precaution against thieves.* *n.* **—pre·cau′tion·ar′y,** *adj.*

pre·cede (prē sēd′) go or come before: *A band preceded the first float in the parade.* *v.,* **pre·ced·ed, pre·ced·ing.**

prec·e·dent (pres′ə dənt) an action that may be used as a reason to do the same thing again later: *Giving you an extension on your project will set a precedent for other students.* *n.*

pre·cious (presh′əs) having great value: *Gold is a precious metal; rubies are precious stones. Every child is precious.* *adj.*

prec·i·pice (pres′ə pis) a very steep cliff. *n.*

pre·cip·i·tate (pri sip′ə tāt′) **1** bring about suddenly: *My unkind words precipitated an argument.* **2** condense; change from water vapour to snow, rain, dew, etc. **3** separate out from a solution by evaporation. When sea water evaporates, the salt precipitates; it is left behind. 1–3 *v.,* **pre·cip·i·tat·ed, pre·cip·i·tat·ing.**

pre·cip·i·ta·tion (pri sip′ə tā′shən) **1** moisture that falls in the form of rain, dew, hail, snow, etc.: *There was 10 cm of precipitation in November.* **2** the process of changing from water vapour into rain, dew, snow, etc. *n.*

pre·cise (pri sīs′) **1** exact; accurate; specific: *The precise distance was 1.73 km. What do you mean? Be more precise.* **2** careful: *precise handwriting.* *adj.* **—pre·cise′ly,** *adv.* **—pre·ci′sion** (pri sizh′ən), *n.*

pre·co·cious (pri kō′shəs) developing earlier than usual in knowledge, skill, etc.: *This precocious child already reads well at the age of four.* *adj.*

Predator

A predator, like this tiger, makes sure it approaches upwind from its prey. That is, the wind must be blowing the scent of the predator away from the prey animal. In that way, the predator can creep up to its prey undetected, until it is near enough to pounce.

pred·a·tor (pred′ə tər) an animal that lives by hunting and killing other animals for food: *Lions and hawks are predators.* *n.* **—pred′a·to′ry,** *adj.*

pred·e·ces·sor (pred′ə ses′ər *or* prē′də ses′ər) a person or thing that did a job or held a position before another: *Brian Mulroney was the predecessor of Jean Chrétien as Prime Minister.* *n.*

pre·dic·a·ment (pri dik′ə mənt) a bad, hard, or dangerous situation: *She was in a predicament when the dog chewed up her homework.* *n.*

pred·i·cate (pred′ə kit) the part of a sentence that gives the main idea about the subject. The predicate always contains a verb. In the sentence *People work, work* is the predicate. In the sentence *The school has organized a car wash,* the predicate is *has organized a car wash.* *n.*

pre·dict (pri dikt′) tell what will happen in the future: *The weather office predicts rain for tomorrow.* *v.* **—pre·dic′tion,** *n.* **—pre·dict′a·ble,** *adj.*

pre·dom·i·nate (pri dom′ə nāt′) be greater in amount, power, influence, etc.: *Art books predominate over fiction in their library.* *v.,* **pre·dom·i·nat·ed, pre·dom·i·nat·ing.** **—pre·dom′i·nant,** *adj.*

preen (prēn) **1** smooth or arrange the feathers with the beak, as a bird does. **2** try to make yourself look your best: *preening in front of the mirror.* *v.*

pre·fab·ri·cate (prē fab′rə kāt′) put parts together in advance; especially, make sections of a building beforehand so that it can be built quickly on the site. *v.,* **pre·fab·ri·cat·ed, pre·fab·ri·cat·ing.**

pref·ace (pref′is) **1** an introduction to a book or speech explaining the purpose, etc., or giving background information. **2** introduce; say or write something at the beginning: *She prefaced her speech with a few words of welcome to the audience.* 1 *n.,* 2 *v.,* **pref·aced, pref·ac·ing.**

pre·fer (pri fər′) like better; choose rather: *She prefers juice to pop. I would prefer to go home.* *v.,* **pre·ferred, pre·fer·ring.**

pref·er·a·ble (pref′ə rə bəl) better; more desirable: *She decided that going along was preferable to staying home alone.* *adj.* **—pref′er·a·bly,** *adv.*

pref·er·ence (pref′ rəns) **1** the thing preferred or chosen; what a person likes best: *My preference in ice cream is chocolate.* **2** the act or fact of favouring one above another: *A teacher should not show preference for any one of the pupils.* *n.* **—pref′er·en′tial,** *adj.*

a bat	e bed	i bid	o pot	u cup	th thin
ā cake	ē me	ī bite	ō go	ū rude	ᴛʜ then
à bar	ə about	ər over	ò for	ù put	zh measure

pre•fix (prē′fiks) **1** a syllable or word put at the beginning of a root word to change its meaning or make another word, as in *pre*historic, *un*like, *over*work. ▶ See Appendix. **2** put before: *We prefix "Mr." to a man's name.* 1 *n.,* 2 *v.*

> **Grammar ✓ Check . . . . prefix**
>
> Knowing the meaning of a **prefix** can help you to figure out what a word means. Here are some common prefixes. Look in the Appendix for more examples of prefixes.
>
> **pre-** (before) *prepay*
> **post-** (after) *postdate*
> **un-** (not) *unhappy*
> **re-** (again) *redo*

preg•nant (preg′nənt) with a baby growing inside the uterus. Human mothers are normally pregnant for nine months before giving birth. *adj.*
—preg′nan•cy, *n.*

pre•his•tor•ic (prē′his tò′rik) having to do with times before history was written down: *Fossils and stone tools tell us about prehistoric people and animals.* *adj.*

prej•u•dice (prej′ə dis) **1** a strong opinion formed about something before really knowing anything about it: *a prejudice against doctors.* **2** cause a person to form an unfair opinion in this way: *That one story has prejudiced me against all athletes.* **3** to harm or put at risk: *I don't want to prejudice my chances of winning by being tired before the race; I'm going to bed!* **Prejudicial** (prej′ə dish′əl) means "harmful." 1 *n.,* 2, 3 *v.,* **prej•u•diced, prej•u•dic•ing.** **—prej′u•diced,** *adj.*

pre•lim•i•nar•y (pri lim′ə ner′ē) **1** coming before the main business; leading to something more important: *After preliminary remarks by the principal, the school play began.* **2** a minor first step leading to the main thing: *Let's not waste too much time on the preliminaries; we have to get moving.* 1 *adj.,* 2 *n., pl.* **pre•lim•i•nar•ies.**

prel•ude (prel′yūd *or* prē′lūd) **1** a piece of music played as an introduction. **2** anything that acts as an introduction: *Our meeting at the computer show was the prelude to a long friendship.* *n.*

pre•ma•ture (prē′mə chūr′ *or* prem′ə chūr′) coming or happening too soon: *His premature arrival spoiled the surprise we had planned for him. A premature baby needs extra care at birth.* *adj.*

pre•med•i•tate (prē med′ə tāt′) think about or plan beforehand: *a premeditated crime.* *v.,* **pre•med•i•tat•ed, pre•med•i•tat•ing.**

pre•mier (prē′myər) **1** 🍁 the leader of a province: *The ten premiers attended a conference with the Prime Minister in Ottawa.* **2** the head of the government in certain other countries. **3** first in rank or quality. 1, 2 *n.,* 3 *adj.*

pre•miere (prim yer′) **1** the first public showing of a play or movie: *We went to the premiere of "Phantom of the Opera."* **2** having to do with the first time something is shown: *a premiere performance.* **3** show or be shown for the first time: *The new musical premiered in Montréal this week.* 1 *n.,* 2 *adj.,* 3 *v.,* **pre•miered, pre•mier•ing.**

prem•is•es (prem′ə siz) a house or building along with its grounds: *She asked us to keep our dog off her premises. Mom's business needs larger premises now.* *pl.n.*

pre•mi•um (prē′mē əm) **1** money paid regularly for an insurance policy: *My father pays premiums on his life insurance four times a year.* **2** something more than the ordinary price or wage: *We had to pay a high premium to get the car with special seats.* **3** a prize or reward for buying something, such as a little gift that comes with a bottle of perfume. *n.*
at a premium, wanted by many people and therefore expensive or hard to find: *Good day care is at a premium these days.*

pre•mo•lar (prē mō′lər) one of the permanent teeth in front of your molars; bicuspid. *n.*

prem•o•ni•tion (prem′ə nish′ən *or* prē′mə nish′ən) a strong feeling that something bad is about to happen: *Ned had a premonition that the car wouldn't start.* *n.*

pre•oc•cu•pied (prē ok′yə pīd′) so concerned with one thing that you can't concentrate on anything else; distracted: *She was too preoccupied with her birthday plans to do her homework.* *adj.* **—pre•oc′cu•pa′tion,** *n.*

pre•pare (pri per′) **1** make ready; get ready: *He prepared for his test by studying. They prepared a room for the new baby.* **2** make by mixing ingredients. *v.,* **pre•pared, pre•par•ing.** **—prep′a•ra′tion,** *n.* **—prep′a•ra•to′ry** (prep′ə rə tòr′ē), *adj.*

pre•pay (prē pā′) pay for something in advance. *v.,* **pre•paid, pre•pay•ing.**

prep•o•si•tion (prep′ə zish′ən) a word that is used to connect a noun to the other words in a sentence. A preposition often helps to tell the position, time, direction, cause, or purpose of something. In the sentence *The man with the ice cream for sale stands at the corner in the afternoon,* the words, *with, for, at,* and *in* are prepositions. A **prepositional phrase** is a preposition plus the noun that comes after it, such as *in the afternoon.* *n.*

pre•pos•ter•ous (pri pos′tə rəs) totally against common sense; absurd; outrageous: *It would be preposterous to shovel snow with a teaspoon.* *adj.*

pre•req•ui•site (prē rek′wə zit) something that you must do or have before you can do something else: *The water safety class was a prerequisite for all swimming lessons. Humility is a prerequisite for parents.* *n.*

pre•school (prē′skūl′) **1** having to do with children too young to go to elementary school: *preschool years. There are activities in the park for preschool children.* **2** a school for children three or four years old, separate from elementary school. 1 *adj.*, 2 *n.* **—pre′school′er,** *n.*

pre•scribe (pri skrīb′) **1** order; make into a rule: *Our school handbook prescribes certain classroom behaviour.* **2** order as medicine or treatment: *The doctor prescribed full rest for her.* A **prescription** is a note from a doctor with directions for preparing a medicine or a pair of glasses or contact lenses. *v.*, **pre•scribed, pre•scrib•ing.**

pres•ence (prez′əns) **1** the fact of being in a certain place: *His presence in the room made me nervous.* **2** the place where a person is: *The messenger was allowed to enter the king's presence.* *n.*
in the presence of, in the sight or company of: *He signed his name in the presence of two witnesses.*
presence of mind, ability to think calmly and quickly in an emergency.

pres•ent[1] (prez′ənt) **1** being in a certain place; attending: *Every member of the class was present.* **2** existing or happening now: *our present address, the present situation.* **3** now; this time: *That is enough for the present. At present she is living in the Yukon.* **4** short for or having to do with the **present tense,** a verb form used for actions or conditions that are going on now, such as *am* in the sentence *I am in school.* 1, 2, 4 *adj.*, 3, 4 *n.*

> **Grammar✓Check . . . present tense**
>
> You can express the present tense in two main ways:
> - **simple present:** *I run*, if it happens regularly.
> - **present progressive:** *I am running*, if it is happening right now.

pre•sent[2] (pri zent′ *for 1 and 3–5,* prez′ənt *for 2*) **1** give or offer, especially in a formal way: *They presented flowers to their teacher.* **2** a gift; something given: *a birthday present.* **3** do or perform in public: *to present a play. We have to present our projects orally in front of the class.* **4** put forward for others to consider: *to present a case, to present an argument.* **5** introduce a person to somebody else: *Ladies and gentlemen, may I present Mr. Dryden.* 1, 3–5 *v.*, 2 *n.* **—pres′en•ta′tion,** *n.*
present with, give: *The principal presented the top student with a plaque.*

pre•sent•a•ble (pri zen′tə bəl) fit to appear in public or to be offered to someone: *After cleaning the cellar, he had to shower and change his clothes to make himself presentable. That burnt toast is hardly presentable!* *adj.*

pres•ent•ly (prez′ənt lē) **1** at present; now: *I would check for e-mail, but I'm not presently logged on.* **2** soon: *The clock will strike presently.* *adv.*

pre•serve (pri zərv′) **1** keep from being harmed, lost, or destroyed: *to preserve the natural environment. It is important to preserve a sense of humour.* **2** prepare food to keep it from spoiling. Boiling with sugar, salting, smoking, and pickling are all ways of preserving food. Something added to food to prevent spoiling is a **preservative.** **3** Usually, **preserves,** *pl.* fruit cooked with sugar and sealed in jars: *For dessert we opened a jar of plum preserves.* **4** a place where wild animals, fish, or trees and plants are protected: *a wildlife preserve, a forest preserve.* 1, 2 *v.*, **pre•served, pre•serv•ing;** 3, 4 *n.*
—pre•ser′ver, *n.*
—pres′er•va′tion (prez′ər vā′shən), *n.*

pre•side (pri zīd′) lead, manage, or supervise: *The manager presides over the business of this store. The mayor presides at all council meetings.* *v.*, **pre•sid•ed, pre•sid•ing.**

pres•i•dent (prez′ə dənt) **1** the leader of a company, college, society, club, etc. **2** the highest officer in some governments. A government with a president is usually called a republic. *n.* **—pres′i•den•cy,** *n.*
—pres′i•den′tial (prez′ə den′shəl), *adj.*

press (pres) **1** push on something with steady force: *Press the button to ring the bell.* **2** squeeze or hug: *My grandfather pressed the baby to him.* **3** make smooth or flat with an iron: *to press clothes.* **4** keep asking or urging somebody to do something: *Because it was so stormy, they pressed us to stay overnight.* **5** a printing machine. **6** newspapers, magazines, and the people who work for them: *The results of the election were reported by the press.* A **press conference** is a meeting held with reporters to tell them about a recent event. A **press release** is an official statement or story given by a person or organization to the press, to be reported in the news. 1–4 *v.*, 5, 6 *n.*
press on, keep on going in spite of tiredness or difficulty: *The hikers pressed on through the heavy rain.*

a bat	e bed	i bid	o pot	u cup	th thin
ā cake	ē me	ī bite	ō go	ū rude	ᴛʜ then
ä bar	ə about	ər over	ô for	ů put	zh measure

press·ing (pres′ing) urgent: *pressing business.* *adj.*

pres·sure (presh′ər) **1** the force of something pressing, or the amount of this force: *The small box was flattened by the pressure of the brick on it.* **2** a burden or strain; a feeling of being rushed or weighed down: *the pressure of poverty, working under pressure.* **3** a strong influence; persuasion: *There's a lot of pressure to buy clothes that are considered cool.* A **pressure group** is a group that tries to influence the government to make certain laws. **4** try very hard to persuade; urge: *They pressured me to go along.* 1–3 *n.,* 4 *v.,* **pres·sured, pres·sur·ing.**

pres·sur·ize (presh′ə rīz′) keep the air or water pressure steady inside a closed space. The cabin of an aircraft is pressurized so people can breathe normally. *v.*

pres·tige (pres tēzh′) high status; the condition of being admired and respected by others: *The singer's prestige rose when she won a Juno award.* *n.* **—pres·ti′gious** (pres stij′əs), *adj.*

pres·to (pres′tō) quick; quickly. This word is used in music. A magician also says "Presto!" when completing a magic trick. *adj., adv., or interj.*

pre·sume (pri zūm′ *or* pri zyūm′) **1** suppose; take for granted without proving: *This coat is yours, I presume.* **Presumably** means "probably" or "I suppose." **2** be so rude as to dare: *Don't presume to tell me what to do!* **3** take advantage of someone by expecting too much: *Don't presume on his good nature by borrowing from him every week.* *v.,* **pre·sumed, pre·sum·ing.**

pre·sump·tion (pri zump′shən) **1** something not proven but taken for granted: *Since he had the stolen jewels in his pocket, the presumption was that he was the thief.* **2** rude boldness: *She had the presumption to go to the party without being invited.* *n.* **—pre·sump′tu·ous** (pri zump′chū əs), *adj.*

pre·tend (pri tend′) **1** make believe; play or act as if something is true: *Let's pretend we're pilots. They pretend to be my friends, but they aren't.* **2** claim: *I don't pretend to be a computer expert.* *v.* **—pre·tence′** or **pre′tence,** *n.*

pre·ten·tious (pri ten′shəs) trying to seem wise, great, rich, important, etc. *adj.* **—pre·ten′tious·ly,** *adv.* **—pre·ten′tious·ness,** *n.*

pre·text (prē′tekst) a fake excuse: *He skipped gym under the pretext of having a sore finger.* *n.*

pret·ty (prit′ē) **1** attractive; good-looking or nice-sounding: *a pretty face, a pretty dress, a pretty tune.* **2** fairly; quite: *It is pretty late.* 1 *adj.,* **pret·ti·er, pret·ti·est;** 2 *adv.* **—pret′ti·ly,** *adv.* **—pret′ti·ness,** *n.*

pret·zel (pret′səl) a snack made of rolled dough shaped into a knot or stick and baked till it is hard. It is usually salted on the outside. *n.*

pre·vail (pri vāl′) **1** be the most usual or strongest: *Yellow is the prevailing colour in her room. Conifers prevail in the northern forests.* **2** be the stronger; win the victory: *The knights prevailed against their foe.* *v.* **prevail upon,** a formal expression for "persuade": *Can we prevail upon you to stay for dinner?*

prev·a·lent (prev′ə lənt) widespread; common: *Colds are prevalent in winter.* *adj.* **—prev′a·lence,** *n.*

pre·vent (pri vent′) keep from doing or happening: *to prevent fire. The noise prevented him from doing his work.* *v.* **—pre·ven′tion,** *n.* **—pre·ven′tive,** *adj. or n.*

pre·view (prē′vyū′) **1** a look at something in advance: *I got a preview of the bride in her wedding dress.* **2** an advance showing of scenes from a film, TV program, etc. **3** see something ahead of time. 1, 2 *n.,* 3 *v.*

pre·vi·ous (prē′vē əs) that came before; earlier: *She did better on a previous test.* *adj.* **—pre′vi·ous·ly,** *adv.* **previous to,** before: *Previous to her arrival, I was all alone.*

This young crocodile (a predator) has become the anaconda's prey, and is being squeezed to death.

prey (prā) **1** an animal hunted or killed for food: *Mice and birds are the prey of cats.* **2** a person or thing caught or harmed by something; a victim: *to be a prey to fear, to be a prey to disease.* **3 prey on, a** hunt and kill for food: *Cats prey on mice.* **b** be a strain on; keep bothering: *The problem preys on her mind.* 1, 2 *n.,* 3 *v.*

price (prīs) **1** the amount that must be paid for a thing: *The price of this game is $29.* Something **pricey** is expensive. **2** put a price on; set the price of: *The game was priced at $29.* **3** *Informal.* find out the price of: *We priced radios at several stores before buying one.* **4** what must be done or given up in order to get or achieve a thing: *Sometimes losing a friend is the price for doing what you know is right.* 1, 4 *n.,* 2, 3 *v.,* **priced, pric·ing.** **a price on someone's head,** a reward offered for the capture of a person. **at any price,** at any cost, no matter how great: *They wanted to win at any price.*

price•less (prīs′lis) so valuable that you cannot put a price on it: *priceless paintings by famous artists.* **Without price** and **beyond price** mean the same. *adj.*

prick (prik) 1 jab with something small that has a sharp point: *I pricked myself with the needle while sewing. The thorns pricked her.* 2 the act of jabbing with a sharp point: *I felt the prick of a pin in my side.* 1 *v.,* 2 *n.*
prick up your ears, a point the ears upward: *The dog pricked up its ears.* b suddenly start listening: *He pricked up his ears when the teacher started talking about a trip.*

prick•le (prik′əl) 1 a small, sharp point, especially a thorn. 2 have a pricking or tingling feeling: *Her skin prickled when she saw the big snake.* 1 *n.,* 2 *v.,* **prick•led, prick•ling.** —**prick′ly,** *adj.*

prickly pear (prik′lē per′) a cactus of North and South America with pear-shaped fruit that is good to eat.

pride (prīd) 1 a healthy feeling that you have value and dignity; respect for yourself and a high standard for your own actions: *All the suffering they endured could not destroy their pride.* 2 too high an opinion of yourself; the belief that you are better than others. This kind of pride makes people show off, keeps them from apologizing or accepting help, and so on. 3 pleasure or satisfaction in something concerned with yourself: *to take pride in a hard job well done.* 4 something that a person is proud of: *Her granddaughter is her great pride.*
5 **pride yourself on,** be proud of: *We pride ourselves on our clean streets.* 6 a group of lions. 1–4, 6 *n.,* 5 *v.,* **prid•ed, prid•ing.**

pried (prīd) the past tense and past participle of **pry:** *She pried it open with a screwdriver.* *v.*

pries (prīz) plural of **pry**[2]. *n.*

priest (prēst) in various religions, a leader who can perform certain holy ceremonies. *n.*
—**priest′hood,** *n.* —**priest′ly,** *adj.*

prig (prig) someone who thinks he or she is better than others. *n.* —**prig′gish,** *adj.*

prim (prim) very neat and proper. *adj.,* **prim•mer, prim•mest.**

pri•ma•ry (prī′mer′ē *or* prī′mə rē) 1 first in time; first in order. The **primary grades** are the first few years of elementary school. 2 first in importance; main: *The primary reason for the party is to celebrate his birthday.* The **primary stress** in a word is the strongest; in *telephone* it is on the first syllable. *adj.* —**pri•mar′i•ly,** *adv.*

primary colour or **color** (prī′mer′ē kul′ər) one of three colours that can be mixed together to make any other colour. In painting, the primary colours are red, yellow, and blue; in light, they are red, green, and blue.

pri•mate (prī′māt) any of the order of mammals that includes human beings, apes, and monkeys. *n.*

WORD HISTORY........ primate

Prime, primary, and **primate** are all from the Latin root *primus*, meaning "first in importance." Primates are considered to rank first in the animal kingdom.

prime (prīm) 1 first in rank or order; chief: *His prime object was to make the team.* 2 top quality; best: *prime Alberta beef.* 3 the best time: *a person in the prime of life.* **Prime time** is the most popular time of day for watching TV. 4 put a special liquid on a surface before painting, to keep the paint from soaking in or to make it stick to the surface. 5 prepare a machine for starting. You prime a pump by pouring water into it. 6 give a person something to start with: *For our storywriting assignment, the teacher primed us with an exciting opening sentence.* 1, 2 *adj.,* 3 *n.,* 4–6 *v.,* **primed, prim•ing.**

prime minister (prīm′ min′ə stər) the chief minister in the federal government of Canada and in certain other governments; the head of the Cabinet.

prime number (prīm′ num′bər) a number that cannot be divided evenly by any whole number other than itself and 1. Some prime numbers are 2, 7, and 11.

prim•er (prim′ər *for 1,* prī′mər *for 2*) 1 a first book in any subject, especially reading. 2 a special liquid used to coat a surface before painting it, to keep the paint from soaking in or to make it stick to the surface. *n.*

prim•i•tive (prim′ə tiv) 1 of the earliest times; of long ago: *Primitive humans often lived in caves.* 2 very simple; not very highly developed: *She made primitive rainboots by tying a plastic bag over each shoe.* *adj.*

prince (prins) 1 the son or grandson of a king or queen, or a man who marries a queen. 2 the male ruler of certain small countries such as Liechtenstein or Monaco. Such a country is called a **principality** (prin′sə pal′ə tē). *n.* —**prince′ly,** *adj.*

Prince Ed•ward Island (prins′ ed′wərd ī′lənd) Canada's smallest province, an island in the Gulf of St. Lawrence. —**Prince Edward Islander.**

a bat	e bed	i bid	o pot	u cup	th thin
ā cake	ē me	ī bite	ō go	ū rude	ᴛʜ then
ä bar	ə about	ər over	ô for	ů put	zh measure

Printing Press

One of the greatest revolutions in communications came in the 1400s, when Johann Gutenberg invented movable type. Books could be produced more quickly and more cheaply, and became available to many more people.

In the older style of block printing, letters were carved in reverse from a piece of wood.

Gutenberg's metal type was both movable and reusable.

Prince of Wales (prins′ əv wālz′) a title given to the oldest son of the monarch of England.

prin•cess (prin′ses) 1 the daughter of a king or queen. 2 the daughter, wife, or widow of a prince. *n.*

prin•ci•pal (prin′sə pəl) 1 the head of a school. 2 most important; chief; main: *St. John's is the principal city of Newfoundland.* 3 an amount of money borrowed or invested. Interest is paid on the principal. 1, 3 *n.,* 2 *adj.* —**prin′ci•pal•ly,** *adv.*

CONFUSABLES .....principal

principal means "main," or as a noun, "head teacher": *"The principal reason for your good marks is that you studied hard," said the principal of the school.*

principle means "basic idea" or "rule": *The principle of gravity explains why we fall down instead of up.*

prin•ci•ple (prin′sə pəl) 1 a general fact, belief, or rule that something is based on: *the principles of democracy, the principle of fairness. Science is based on the principle that things can be explained.* 2 good character; honour: *Joseph Howe was a man of principle.* *n.*

print (print) 1 copy words and images onto paper using a machine, especially so as to make many copies: *Her photo was printed in all the newspapers. We got a flyer printed to advertise our garage sale.* 2 words, letters, etc. reproduced in ink by machine: *This book has clear print.* 3 make letters as they look in books instead of in cursive writing: *Print your name clearly.* 4 stamp pictures or designs on paper, cloth, or some other surface using ink, dye, or paint. It can be done by hand or by machine: *This cloth is printed with a leaf pattern.* 5 a picture or design produced in this way: *We made potato prints in art class.* 6 cloth with a design stamped on it: *We need 3 m of cotton print.* 7 a mark left by pressing into a surface: *His shoes left prints in the sand.* 8 a photograph made from a negative. 9 make a photograph from a negative by a special process. 1, 3, 4, 9 *v.,* 2, 5–8 *n.* —**print′ing,** *n.*
in print, still available from the publisher. The opposite is **out of print.**

print•er (prin′tər) a person, company, or machine that prints things. A computer system usually includes a printer. *n.*

printing press (print′ing pres′) a large machine for printing on paper by stamping it with metal type, plates, rollers, etc. that have been covered with ink.

print•out (prin′tout′) the output of a computer, produced on paper by a printer. *n.*

pri•or (prī′ər) coming before; earlier: *I can't go with you because I have a prior commitment.* *adj.*
prior to, before: *Prior to the test we had a full review.*

pri•or•i•ty (prī ȯ′rə tē) 1 a matter that needs or gets urgent attention; an important goal: *Stopping pollution should be high on our list of priorities.* 2 importance: *Fire engines have priority over other traffic. Make a list of your tasks in order of priority.* *n., pl.* **pri•or•i•ties.**

prism (priz′əm) 1 a solid with rectangular sides and two parallel end faces of the same shape and size. 2 a solid bar of clear material such as glass, usually with triangular ends. White light passing through it separates into the colours of the spectrum. *n.*

pris·on (priz′ən) 1 a building where criminals are kept locked up: *Burglars are put in prison.* 2 any place where you feel as though you have no freedom. *n.*

pris·on·er (priz′ə nər) a person who is kept in a jail or prison, or whose freedom has been taken away. *n.*
prisoner of war, a person taken by the enemy in war.

pri·vate (prī′vit) 1 meant only for a certain person or group: *a private road, a private letter.* 2 not shared with the public; personal: *the private life of a king, my private opinion.* 3 not owned by or involved in government: *a private citizen, a private school.* 4 a soldier of the lowest rank. 1–3 *adj.,* 4 *n.*
—pri′vate·ly, *adv.* **—pri′va·cy,** *n.* **—pri′va·tize′,** *v.*
in private, a not publicly: *Dad spoke to the principal in private.* b secretly: *We met in private to plan the surprise.*

priv·i·lege (priv′ə lij) a special right, advantage, or favour: *We were given the privilege of staying up late on New Year's Eve.* *n.* **—priv′i·leged,** *adj.*

🍁 **Privy Council** (priv′ē koun′səl) the group of people who advise the Governor General, made up of all those who are or were ministers in the Federal Cabinet. Members of the Privy Council are **Privy Councillors.**

prize (prīz) 1 a reward for winning a contest or given away free with something you buy: *Prizes will be given for the three best stories. Each specially marked box of cereal contains a prize.* 2 anything worth working or giving up something else for. 3 deserving a prize: *prize vegetables.* 4 treasured; valued: *This little jewel box is her prize possession.* 5 value highly: *My sister prizes her CD collection.* 1, 2 *n.,* 3, 4 *adj.,* 5 *v.,* **prized, priz·ing.**

pro[1] (prō) *Informal.* 1 professional, especially in sports: *a hockey pro (n.), pro football (adj.).* 2 an expert: *Heidi is a pro at keyboarding.* *adj. or n., pl.* **pros.**

pro[2] (prō) 1 in favour of; for. This is usually used in compounds: *She is very pro-Liberal.* 2 a reason in favour of something. The pros and cons of a question are the arguments for and against it. 1 *adv.,* 2 *n., pl.* **pros.**

prob·a·bil·i·ty (prob′ə bil′ə tē) 1 the fact of being likely or probable: *There is little probability of rain.* 2 something likely to happen: *Snow is a probability for tomorrow.* 3 the branch of mathematics that deals with the likelihood of a thing happening by chance, such as a flipped coin coming up tails. *n., pl.* **prob·a·bil·i·ties.**
in all probability, very probably.

prob·a·ble (prob′ə bəl) likely to happen or to be true: *Cooler weather is probable after this shower. Something he ate was the probable cause of his stomach ache.* *adj.* **—prob′a·bly,** *adv.*

pro·ba·tion (prō bā′shən) a trial period to see if someone can do a job properly, follow rules, keep from committing more crimes, etc. A person being tested this way is **on probation.** *n.* **—pro·ba′tion·ar′y,** *adj.*

probe (prōb) 1 search into; examine thoroughly in order to find out: *to probe the causes of a crime. I probed my feelings to figure out why I acted as I did.* 2 a thorough examination; an investigation. A government may do a probe of some organization or activity to see if a crime was committed. 3 a spacecraft carrying scientific instruments to record and report back information about planets and so on: *a lunar probe.* 4 a slender tool for exploring something. A doctor or dentist uses a probe to explore the inside of a wound or cavity. A Geiger counter has a probe to detect the amount of radioactivity in something. 1 *v.,* **probed, prob·ing;** 2–4 *n.*

prob·lem (prob′ləm) 1 a difficult question. 2 a situation that causes difficulty and needs to be fixed or put right: *Starvation is a major problem in many countries.* 3 something to be worked out in arithmetic. *n.*

pro·ce·dure (prə sē′jər) a method; a set of steps to follow for doing something: *What is the procedure for getting a book out of the library?* *n.*

pro·ceed (prə sēd′ *for 1–3,* prō′sēdz *for 4*) 1 begin to carry out an activity: *He proceeded to light the fire. Never having milked a cow before, she didn't know quite how to proceed.* 2 go on; move forward: *Please proceed with your story.* The **proceedings** are whatever is going on: *She sat down to watch the proceedings.* 3 come; follow naturally: *Each paragraph of your project should proceed smoothly from the one before.* 4 **proceeds,** *pl.,* the money from a sale, etc.: *The proceeds from the school play will be used to buy a new curtain for the stage.* 1–3 *v.,* 4 *pl.n.*

pro·cess (prō′ses *or* pros′es) 1 a set of linked actions or events leading to some result: *the process of making cloth from wool.* 2 treat or deal with by a certain method: *This cloth has been processed to make it waterproof. Your book order has not been processed yet.* 1 *n.,* 2 *v.*
in process, happening or being done: *The author has just finished one book and has another in process.*

a bat	e bed	i bid	o pot	u cup	th thin
ā cake	ē me	ī bite	ō go	ū rude	ᴛʜ then
ä bar	ə about	ər over	ô for	u̇ put	zh measure

pro·ces·sion (prə sesh′ən) a line of people, vehicles, etc., that moves forward: *A funeral procession filled the street.* *n.*
in procession, in a line and in an orderly way: *to march in procession.* A **processional** is a piece of music that a procession moves to.

pro·claim (prə klām′) make known or declare publicly and officially: *On July 1, 1867 it was proclaimed that Canada was an independent nation. The people proclaimed Arthur king.* *v.* **—proc′la·ma′tion** (prok′lə mā′shən), *n.*

pro·cras·ti·nate (prə kras′tə nāt′) keep putting something off until later: *Marie procrastinated about doing her homework.* *v.,* **pro·cras·ti·nat·ed, pro·cras·ti·nat·ing. —pro·cras′ti·na′tion,** *n.* **—pro·cras′ti·na′tor,** *n.*

prod (prod) **1** poke or jab: *to prod an animal with a stick* (*v.*), *a painful prod in the ribs* (*n.*). **2** stir up; urge on: *to prod a lazy person to action.* **3** something used to prod with. 1, 2 *v.,* **prod·ded, prod·ding;** 1, 3 *n.*

prod·i·gy (prod′ə jē) a wonder, especially a very young person who is extremely gifted. *n., pl.* **prod·i·gies.**

pro·duce (prə dyūs′ *or* prə dūs′ *for 1–4,* prod′yūs or prō′dūs *for 5*) **1** make; bring into existence: *This factory produces stoves. The tree produced hardly any apples this year.* **2** bring about; cause: *A good attitude often produces success.* **3** show; present: *Produce your ID card.* **4** be in charge of making a movie, staging a play, etc. The **producer** hires the actors and director, organizes things, pays for everything, and gets the profit. **5** fruit and vegetables: *She owns a produce market.* 1–4 *v.,* **pro·duced, pro·duc·ing;** 5 *n.* **—pro·duc′tion,** *n.*

prod·uct (prod′əkt) **1** something that is made or produced: *factory products, farm products.* **2** a result: *His poor health is the product of a poor diet.* **3** the number you get when you multiply two or more numbers together: *The product of 5 and 8 is 40.* *n.*

pro·duc·tive (prə duk′tiv) producing a lot that is worthwhile: *a productive piece of land, a productive worker, a productive discussion.* *adj.* **—prod′uc·tiv′i·ty** (prod′ək tiv′ə tē), *n.*

pro·fane (prō fān′) **1** using swearwords: *profane language.* **Profanity** (prə fan′ə tē) is another word for swearing. **2** showing complete lack of respect for holy things. **3** treat holy things with disrespect: *The soldiers profaned the church by stabling horses there.* 1, 2 *adj.,* 3 *v.,* **pro·faned, pro·fan·ing.**

pro·fess (prə fes′) **1** claim: *I don't profess to be an expert.* **2** declare openly: *He professed his love for his country.* *v.*

pro·fes·sion (prə fesh′ən) **1** an occupation requiring special education at a university, such as law, medicine, or teaching. **2** the people who work at such an occupation, seen as a community: *a member of the medical profession.* **3** an open declaration: *a profession of friendship.* *n.*

pro·fes·sion·al (prə fesh′ə nəl) **1** respectful to clients and co-workers and showing you are serious about your work: *a professional attitude.* **2** working in a profession: *A nurse is a professional person.* **3** making a living from something that others do for pleasure: *a professional baseball player, professional musicians.* **4** a person who does this. **5** done by professionals: *a professional ball game.* 1–3, 5 *adj.,* 4 *n.*

pro·fes·sor (prə fes′ər) one of the top teachers in a college or university. *n.*

pro·fi·cient (prə fish′ənt) skilled; expert: *She was very proficient in French.* *adj.* **—pro·fi′cien·cy,** *n.*

pro·file (prō′fīl) **1** a side view, especially of the human face. **2** an outline or short description: *The magazine carried an interesting profile of Susan Aglukark.* **3** make or give a profile of: *She was profiled on the music page.* 1, 2 *n.,* 3 *v.,* **pro·filed, pro·fil·ing.**

prof·it (prof′it) **1** the money gained from a business or sale, after all the costs of running it are paid: *The profit from the car wash was $213.* **2** gain money from doing business. **3** useful result; benefit: *What profit is there in worrying?* **4** get some useful result: *You can profit from your mistakes.* 1, 3 *n.,* 2, 4 *v.* **—prof′it·a·ble,** *adj.*

CONFUSABLES ...... profit

profit means "gain": *The school made a profit of $450 from the chocolate bar sale.*

prophet means "person who predicts" or "person inspired by God": *Muslims follow the teachings of the prophet Muhammad.*

pro·found (prə found′) **1** very deep; *a profound sigh, profound sorrow.* **2** showing great understanding: *profound words.* *adj.* **—pro·found′ly,** *adv.*

pro·gram (prō′gram) **1** something put on for an audience, especially a radio or TV show: *We listened to a radio program about mysteries. The graduation program included speeches, music, and an awards ceremony.* **2** an organized plan, or the actions that carry it out: *a government program to help people find work.* **3** a set of instructions for a computer, allowing it to do a certain task; a piece of software: *a word processing program.*

4 write a set of instructions for a computer so that it may perform a certain task. These instructions are written in a **programming language,** a code that the computer can recognize and deal with. **5** a list of events, performers, etc.: *a concert program, a theatre program.* 1–3, 5 *n.,* 4 *v.,* **programmed, programming.** —**pro′gram·mer,** *n.*

pro·gress (prō′gres *or* prog′res *for 1 and 2,* prə gres′ *for 3*) **1** forward movement: *the progress of science.* **2** improvement: *She made rapid progress in learning to skate.* **3** move forward or improve: *The students are progressing well in reading.* 1, 2 *n.,* 3 *v.*

pro·gres·sive (prə gres′iv) **1** modern; advanced: *a progressive nation.* **2** in favour of progress; wanting changes that will make things more modern. **3** a person who favours this kind of change. 1, 2 *adj.,* 3 *n.*

pro·hib·it (prō hib′it) **1** forbid; make a rule or law against: *Smoking is prohibited in the school.* **2** prevent: *The high price of that bike prohibits me from buying it.* *v.* —**pro·hib′i·tive,** *adj.*

pro·hi·bi·tion (prō′ə bish′ən) **1** the act of forbidding or making a rule against something. **2** laws against making or selling alcoholic drinks. *n.*

pro·ject (prō′jekt *or* proj′ekt *for 1 and 3,* prə jekt′ *for 2, 4, 5, and 6*) **1** a fairly big task or goal: *Her project for the weekend is to clean out the garage.* **2** a school assignment where you must find information about a topic on your own, organize it, and write it up. **3** stick out: *The rocky point projects far into the sea.* **4** expect or predict, based on what has happened so far: *The projected population of this town in 2020 is 60 000.* **5** cause an image to fall on a surface: *Movies are projected on a screen. The tree projects a shadow on the grass.* **6** throw or cast forward: *A catapult projects stones.* Any object that is shot or thrown, such as a rocket, stone, or bullet, is called a **projectile** (prə jek′ tīl). 1, 3 *n.,* 2, 4–6 *v.* —**pro·jec′tion,** *n.*

pro·jec·tor (prə jek′tər) a machine for showing a picture on a screen. *n.*

pro·lif·ic (prə lif′ik) producing a lot: *a prolific writer.* *adj.*

pro·logue (prō′log) a speech or piece of writing that introduces a longer work, such as a play or novel. Another spelling is **prolog.** *n.*

pro·long (prə long′) make longer; draw out; stretch: *We decided to prolong our stay for another two days. The dog uttered a prolonged howl.* *v.*

prom (prom) *Informal.* a formal dance party for students, usually held at the end of the school year. *n.*

prom·e·nade (prom′ə nād′ *or* prom′ə näd′) **1** a walk for pleasure or for show. **2** walk around or up and down for pleasure or show: *He promenaded back and forth on the ship's deck.* **3** a public place for a walk: *Toronto has a famous promenade by the lake, called the "Boardwalk."* **Promenade** is also used as the last part of a street name. 1, 3 *n.,* 2 *v.,* **prom·e·nad·ed, prom·e·nad·ing.**

prom·i·nent (prom′ə nənt) **1** well-known; important: *a prominent citizen.* **2** easy to see: *Hang the sign in a prominent place.* **3** sticking out: *a prominent chin.* *adj.* —**prom′i·nence,** *n.*

prom·ise (prom′is) **1** a firm, serious statement that you will or will not do something: *Dad kept his promise and came to watch my soccer game.* **2** state firmly that you will do or give something: *She promised to wait. They promised us $20 for the job.* **3** signs of future success: *This pupil shows promise in music.* Something that looks like it will turn out well is **promising.** 1, 3 *n.,* 2 *v.,* **prom·ised, prom·is·ing.**

prom·on·to·ry (prom′ən tȯr′ ē) a high point of land sticking out into the sea or a lake. It is also called a **headland.** *n., pl.* **prom·on·to·ries.**

pro·mote (prə mōt′) **1** raise to a higher rank or position: *Everyone in our class has been promoted to grade five.* **2** help to grow or develop: *Respect between countries will promote peace.* **3** advertise; try to create interest and support for: *to promote a new product, to promote an organization.* *v.,* **pro·mot·ed, pro·mot·ing.** —**pro·mo′tion,** *n.* —**pro·mo′tion·al,** *adj.*

prompt (prompt) **1** quick; on time and without delay: *a prompt reply.* **2** cause or inspire an action or idea: *Her curiosity prompted her to ask questions. A kind thought prompted the gift.* **3** remind someone what to do or say: *Bruno will prompt you if you forget your lines in the play.* 1 *adj.,* 2, 3 *v.* —**prompt′er,** *n.*

prone (prōn) **1** often likely; liable: *We are prone to be afraid of what we don't understand.* **2** lying face down: *He is prone on his bed.* *adj.*

prong (prong) one of the pointed ends of a fork, rake, antler, etc. *n.*

prong·horn (prong′hȯrn′) a grazing animal found on the plains of western North America. Although it looks like an antelope, it is not related. *n.*

a bat	e bed	i bid	o pot	u cup	th thin
ā cake	ē me	ī bite	ō go	ū rude	ᴛʜ then
ä bar	ə about	ər over	ȯ for	u̇ put	zh measure

pro•noun (prō′noun) a word used instead of a noun to refer to the noun without naming it. In the sentence *Taryn smiled because she was happy,* the pronoun *she* is used to refer to *Taryn* without repeating her name. Other examples of pronouns are: *it, I, yours, what, these, either.* *n.* ▶ See the *Grammar and Usage Mini-Guide.*

pro•nounce (prə nouns′) **1** make the sounds of; say: *Pronounce your words clearly.* **2** declare; make an official statement: *The doctor pronounced her cured. The judge pronounced sentence on the prisoner.* *v.,* **pro•nounced, pro•nounc•ing.** **—pro•nounce′ment,** *n.* **—pro•nun′ci•a′tion** (prə nun′sē ā′shən), *n.*

Grammar ✓Check . . . . pronounce

If you are not sure how to **pronounce** a word, check the pronunciation in the dictionary; it comes right after the main entry word. The symbols are explained at the bottom of each right-hand page.

pro•nounced (prə nounst′) definite; easily noticed: *a pronounced difference. She has very pronounced likes and dislikes.* *adj.*

pron•to (pron′tō) *Informal.* right away: *We need a fire extinguisher, pronto!* *adv.*

proof (prūf) **1** anything that shows beyond doubt the truth of something else: *Is that just your opinion or do you have proof?* **2** a photograph or piece of writing used as a test copy to check that it is all right. **3** able to resist; protected against something or keeping it out: *This house is proof against any kind of weather.* This sense is mostly used in compounds: *waterproof, fireproof.* 1, 2 *n.,* 3 *adj.*

proof•read (prūf′rēd′) read carefully in order to find and correct any mistakes. *v.,* **proof•read** (prūf′red′), **proof•read•ing.** **—proof′read′er,** *n.* ▶ See the *Grammar and Usage Mini-Guide.*

prop[1] (prop) **1** hold up by placing a support under or leaning against something: *Prop up the clothesline with a stick. Prop the ladder against the wall.* **2** a support placed under something. 1 *v.,* **propped, prop•ping;** 2 *n.*

prop[2] (prop) any object used in a play, movie, or TV scene. This word is short for **stage property.** *n.*

prop•a•gan•da (prop′ə gan′də) **1** an effort to spread certain beliefs by twisting or slanting facts or giving only part of the information. **2** the opinions spread in this way, or the material used to spread them: *racist propaganda on the Internet.* *n.*

pro•pane (prō′pān) a heavy, colourless, flammable gas used as fuel: *I have a propane stove for camping.* *n.*

pro•pel (prə pel′) drive forward; move: *to propel a boat by oars.* *v.,* **pro•pelled, pro•pel•ling.**

For boats, a propellor's blades are curved and angled to bite into the water. More blades gives extra thrust at slow speeds.

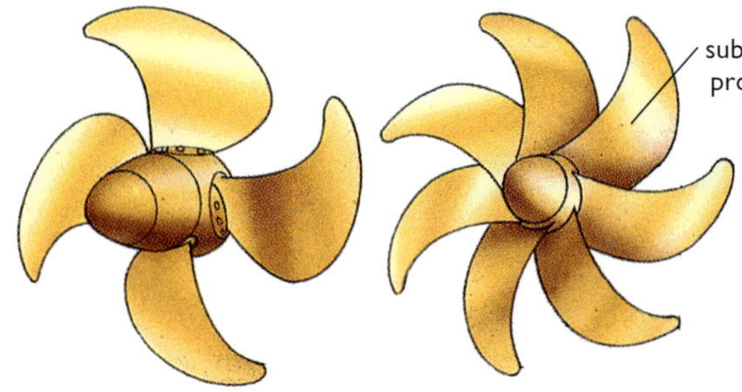

pro•pel•ler (prə pel′ər) a set of revolving blades attached to a shaft, usually as part of a boat or aircraft. When the propeller is turned by a motor, it creates enough force to move the craft forward. A fan also has a propeller, to move air. *n.*

prop•er (prop′ər) **1** correct; right; fitting: *Night is the proper time to sleep, and bed is the proper place.* **2** in the strict sense: *The population of Vancouver proper does not include the suburbs.* *adj.* **—prop′er•ly,** *adv.*

proper fraction (prop′ər frak′shən) a fraction that is less than 1.

proper noun (prop′ər noun′) a noun naming a particular person, place, or thing. *Gerald, Winnipeg,* and *Monday* are proper nouns; *boy, city,* and *day* are not. **Proper name** is another term for this.

prop•er•ty (prop′ər tē) **1** something that someone owns, especially land or buildings: *This car is the property of Mr. Gopal. Mrs. Vleer owns some property out West.* **2** a special characteristic of something: *the sudsing and cleansing properties of soap. One of the properties of iron is that it sticks to a magnet.* **3** an object used in staging a play, movie, or TV scene. The word is usually shortened to **prop** for this meaning. *n., pl.* **prop•er•ties.**

proph•et (prof′it) **1** a person who is believed to have a message from God. The things that a prophet says are called **prophecy** (prof′ə sē), and the action is **prophesying** (prof′ə sy′ing). **2** a person who tells what will happen. *n.* **—pro•phet′ic** (prə fet′ik), *adj.*

pro•por•tion (prə pôr′shən) **1** a part or share measured as a percentage or fraction: *A large proportion of British Columbia is mountainous.* **2** **proportions,** *pl.* size; dimensions: *Canada has forests of huge proportions.* **3** the relation of size or amount between things that are being compared: *Each child's allowance is in proportion to his or her age—the older you are, the more you get.*

4 a proper relation of size or amount between parts: *The legs in this drawing are out of proportion to the body; they're too short.* 5 balance the parts of something according to size: *The designs in that rug are well proportioned.* 1–4 *n.,* 5 *v.* —**pro·por′tion·ate,** *adj.*

pro·pose (prə pōz′) 1 put forward; suggest: *Mom proposed a camping trip on Cape Breton Island.* 2 intend: *I propose to save half of all I earn.* 3 make an offer of marriage. *v.,* **pro·posed, pro·pos·ing.** —**pro·pos′al,** *n.*

prop·o·si·tion (prop′ə zish′ən) 1 an offer or proposal, especially for a trade or business deal: *The tailor made a proposition to buy out his rival's business.* 2 a statement or idea: *The possibility of life on other planets is an interesting proposition.* *n.*

pro·pri·e·tor (prə prī′ə tər) owner. *n.*

pro·pri·e·ty (prə prī′ə tē) 1 properness; fitness; correctness: *I don't doubt the propriety of your decision.* 2 **proprieties,** *pl.* the customs and rules of proper behaviour: *Observe the proprieties and write a thank-you note.* *n., pl.* **pro·pri·e·ties.**

pro·pul·sion (prə pul′shən) 1 the act of propelling something, or making it move forward. 2 the force that does this: *The aircraft's jet engines provide propulsion.* *n.*

prose (prōz) the normal form of spoken or written language; language not arranged into poetry: *Stories can be told in poetry or prose.* *n.*

pros·e·cute (pros′ə kyūt′) bring before a court of law: *Reckless drivers will be prosecuted.* A **prosecutor** is a lawyer for the government who leads the case against a person accused of crimes; this side of the case is called the **prosecution.** *v.,* **pros·e·cut·ed, pros·e·cut·ing.**

pros·pect (pros′pekt) 1 something that someone expects or looks forward to: *The upcoming trip to Saskatchewan was an exciting prospect for Kazia.* 2 a person or thing that might be chosen: *My parents haven't hired a caregiver yet but they have several prospects in mind.* 3 a view or scene: *The prospect from up here is grand.* 4 to search for valuable minerals: *to prospect for gold.* A person who does this is a **prospector.** 1–3 *n.,* 4 *v.*

pro·spec·tive (prə spek′tiv) 1 probable; possible: *a prospective customer.* 2 future: *her prospective husband.* *adj.*

pros·per (pros′pər) be successful; do well, especially in making money: *Her business prospered.* A person or business that does this is **prosperous.** *v.* —**pros·per′i·ty** (pros sper′ə tē), *n.*

pros·the·sis (pros thē′sis) an artificial part of the body, such as an arm or leg, used to replace one that is missing. *n., pl.* **pros·the·ses** (pros thē′sēz).

pros·trate (pros′trāt) 1 **prostrate yourself,** kneel or lie with your face almost to the ground: *The captives prostrated themselves before the warlord, begging for mercy.* 2 make very weak or helpless; overcome: *prostrated by the heat and humidity.* 3 in either of these conditions: *prostrate with grief. He fell prostrate on the floor.* 1, 2 *v.,* **pros·trat·ed, pros·trat·ing;** 3 *adj.* —**pros·tra′tion,** *n.*

pro·tag·on·ist (prə tag′ə nist) the most important character in a story. *n.*

pro·tect (prə tekt′) keep from harm or danger; shelter; defend; guard: *Protect your skin from the sun.* *v.* —**pro·tec′tion,** *n.* —**pro·tec′tive,** *adj.* —**pro·tec′tor,** *n.*

pro·tein (prō′tēn) one of the substances needed for the growth and repair of all living tissue. Plants make their own proteins, but people and animals must eat food to get the proteins they need. Meat, fish, milk, cheese, eggs, and beans are all good sources of protein. *n.*

pro·test (prō′test *for 2,* prə test′ *for 1 and 3*) 1 say firmly that you disagree; speak up against something: *The boys protested against having to go to bed. She protested the umpire's decision.* 2 an action or statement that expresses strong disagreement: *They ignored our loud protests. They marched in protest against the hospital closings.* 3 keep claiming something is true in spite of what others say: *The accused man protested his innocence.* 1 *v.,* 2, 3 *n.*
under protest, unwillingly.

Prot·es·tant (prot′i stənt) 1 a member of certain Christian groups other than the Roman Catholic or Orthodox churches. Baptists, Presbyterians, Anglicans, Pentecostals, and many others are all Protestants. 2 having to do with these churches. 1 *n.,* 2 *adj.* —**Prot′es·tant·ism′,** *n.*

pro·to·col (prō′tə kol′) a set of rules on how to behave correctly on formal or official occasions: *Fortunately for Lucy, there was very little protocol involved in meeting the Queen.* *n.*

pro·ton (prō′ton) a tiny particle that is one of the basic building blocks of matter. It has a positive electric charge. One or more protons are found in the nucleus of every type of atom; for instance, the nucleus of a hydrogen atom has one proton and the nucleus of an oxygen atom has eight. *n.*

a bat	e bed	i bid	o pot	u cup	th thin
ā cake	ē me	ī bite	ō go	ū rude	ᴛʜ then
ä bar	ə about	ər over	ô for	ů put	zh measure

pro·to·plasm (prō′tə plaz′əm) a colourless, complex substance somewhat like egg white, that is the living part of all plant and animal cells. It is made up of **cytoplasm** and **nucleus.** *n.*

pro·to·type (prō′tə tīp′) a first version or form of something: *a hollowed log is the prototype of a modern ship.* *n.*

pro·to·zo·an (prō′tə zō′ən) a microscopic living thing made up of a single cell. *n.*

pro·trac·tor (prō trak′tər) an instrument for drawing or measuring angles. *n.*

pro·trude (prō trūd′ *or* prə trūd′) stick out: *The saucy child protruded her tongue. His huge mustache protruded on either side of his face.* *v.,* **pro·trud·ed, pro·trud·ing.** **—pro·tru′sion,** *n.*

proud (proud) 1 believing in your own worth and dignity; respecting yourself and having a high standard for your own actions: *She was too proud to give up, even though she was losing.* 2 thinking too highly of yourself; conceited: *He was too proud to admit his mistake.* 3 feeling pleasure or satisfaction in something concerned with yourself: *proud of a job well done. I am proud to call him my friend.* 4 causing feelings like this: *a proud moment.* *adj.* **—proud′ly,** *adv.*

prove (prūv) 1 show beyond doubt that something is true: *to prove a theory.* 2 turn out; turn out to be: *The book proved interesting. The boy proved to be our friend after all.* *v.,* **proved, proved** or **prov·en, prov·ing.**

prov·erb (prov′ərb) a short, wise saying used for a long time by many people. *Don't count your chickens before they hatch* is a proverb. *n.* **—pro·ver′bi·al,** *adj.*

pro·vide (prə vīd′) 1 supply; give what is needed: *Sheep provide us with wool. Parents provide for their children.* 2 take care for the future: *to provide against accident, to provide for old age.* *v.,* **pro·vid·ed, pro·vid·ing.**
provided or **provided that,** on the condition that; only if: *She will go provided her friends can go also.* *conj.*

prov·ince (prov′əns) 1 one of the ten divisions of Canada with its own government, under the Constitution Act of 1867: *Newfoundland became the tenth province on April 1, 1949.* 2 a particular area of work or activity: *It is not within the province of the principal to make such decisions.* *n.* **—pro·vin′cial** (prə vin′shəl), *adj.*

✱ **Provincial Parliament** (prə vin′shəl pär′lə mənt) the lawmaking body of Ontario.

pro·vi·sion (prə vizh′ən) 1 the act of providing: *The government is responsible for the provision of health care.* 2 something provided or supplied. 3 **provisions,** *pl.* a supply of food and drink: *They took plenty of provisions on their trip.* 4 a condition: *I'll go with the provision that you come along.* Another word for this sense is **proviso** (prə vī′zō). *n.*

pro·vi·sion·al (prə vizh′ə nəl) for the time being; temporary: *a provisional arrangement.* *adj.*

pro·voke (prə vōk′) 1 make angry: *She provoked him with her teasing.* 2 cause a person to decide to do: *What provoked you to hit him?* 3 stir up; start: *The party leader's speech provoked much discussion.* *v.,* **pro·voked, pro·vok·ing.** **—prov′o·ca′tion** (prov′ə kā′shən), *n.* **—pro·voc′a·tive** (prə vok′ə tiv), *adj.*

prow (prou) the front end of a boat or aircraft. *n.*

prow·ess (prou′is) 1 bravery; daring. 2 great skill or ability: *Her prowess as a skier was widely recognized.* *n.*

prowl (proul) 1 go around slowly and secretly, hunting for something, especially something to eat or steal: *Many wild animals prowl at night.* 2 wander: *We spent the day prowling around town.* 3 the act of prowling: *a wild animal on its nightly prowl.* 1, 2 *v.,* 3 *n.*

prox·y (prok′sē) a person with the authority to act for another. To **vote by proxy** is to let someone else vote for you according to your wishes because you are unable to be there to do it yourself. *n., pl.* **prox·ies.**

pru·dent (prū′dənt) planning carefully ahead of time; wise; taking no chances: *A prudent driver slows down in bad weather.* *adj.* **—pru′dence,** *n.*

prune[1] (prūn) a dried plum. *n.*

prune[2] (prūn) cut out useless parts from: *to prune dead branches from an apple tree. Prune your report before handing it in; it's too long.* *v.,* **pruned, prun·ing.**

pry[1] (prī) snoop and ask nosey questions: *Don't pry into other people's affairs.* *v.,* **pried, pry·ing.**

pry[2] (prī) 1 raise or move by using something as a lever: *Pry up that stone with your stick.* 2 a lever for prying: *to use a screwdriver as a pry.* 3 get with much effort: *We finally pried the secret out of him.* 1, 3 *v.,* **pried, pry·ing;** 2 *n., pl.* **pries.**

P.S. *abbreviation for:* 1 postscript, a note at the end of a letter or other piece of writing. 2 Public School.

pseu·do·nym (sū′də nim′) a name used by an author instead of his or her real name: *William Sydney Porter used O. Henry as his pseudonym.* *n.*

psy·chi·a·try (sī kī′ə trē) the branch of medicine dealing with mental illness. *n.* **—psy·chi′a·trist,** *n.* **—psy′chi·at′ric** (sī′kē at′rik), *adj.*

psy•chic (sī′kik) 1 having to do with the spirit, soul, or mind. 2 outside the known laws of science and having to do with mysterious spiritual forces: *psychic powers such as fortunetelling.* 3 a person with this kind of force or power: *The psychic had a dream about the crime which helped police to solve it.* 1, 2 *adj.,* 3 *n.*

psy•chol•o•gy (sī kol′ə jē) 1 the science that deals with the way the mind works. Psychology tries to explain why people act, think, and feel as they do. 2 the typical way of thinking and acting of an individual or group: *the psychology of crowds. I understand my brother's psychology.* *n., pl.* **psy•chol•o•gies.** —**psy•chol′o•gist,** *n.* —**psy′cho•log′i•cal** (sī′kə loj′ə kəl), *adj.*

psy•cho•path (sī′kə path′) someone who cannot understand the feelings of other people and behaves in a violent or criminal way as a form of mental illness. *n.* —**psy′cho•path′ic,** *adj.*

ptar•mi•gan (tär′mə gən) a grouse with feathered feet. It is found in mountainous and cold regions. Its feathers are mainly brown in summer and mainly white in winter. *n., pl.* **ptar•mi•gans** or **ptar•mi•gan.**

***Pterodactyls* ("winged fingers") belong to the group *pterosaurs,* that is "winged lizards." Most *pterodactyls* had long wings and little or no tail. Compare this to the *pteranodon,* shown in the dinosaur picture on page 207.**

pter•o•dac•tyl (ter′ə dak′təl) an extinct flying reptile that lived at the time of the dinosaurs. It had wings like a bat's, but much bigger—up to 12 m across.

pu•ber•ty (pyū′bər tē) the time of life when a young person becomes sexually mature and capable of producing a child. *n.*

pub•lic (pub′lik) 1 for or having to do with the people as a whole; owned or handled by the government: *public affairs, public libraries.* A **public servant** is a government employee. **Public relations** is the work of making sure the public gets the right information about your organization. 2 the people as a whole: *to inform the public.* 3 seen, heard, or known by many; not private: *a public apology, a public figure. It was a matter of public knowledge.* A **public address system** is a system of linked speakers that lets you talk into a central microphone and be heard by all the people in a building, train, open-air meeting, etc. 1, 3 *adj.,* 2 *n.* —**pub′lic•ly,** *adv.*

in public, in front of many people; openly; not in private or secret: *to stand up in public for what you believe.*

pub•li•ca•tion (pub′lə kā′shən) 1 a book, newspaper, or magazine; anything that is published: *This magazine is a weekly publication.* 2 the act or process of publishing. *n.*

pub•lic•i•ty (pə blis′ə tē) 1 public attention: *Hockey stars get a lot of publicity.* 2 advertising or information given to the public; things done to get the attention of the public: *There has been a lot of publicity about the plight of the homeless.* To give something publicity is to **publicize** it. *n.*

pub•lish (pub′lish) 1 prepare, print, and sell a book, newspaper, map, piece of music, etc. The person or company that does this is the **publisher.** 2 tell everyone about something: *Don't publish your friends' faults.* *v.*

puck (puk) a hard, black, rubber disk used in the game of hockey: *He shot the puck into the net.* *n.*

puck•er (puk′ər) 1 pull together, causing wrinkles: *to pucker your brow, to pucker your lips to kiss someone. When I yanked on the loose thread, the cloth puckered.* 2 a wrinkle caused in this way. 1 *v.,* 2 *n.*

pud•ding (pu̇d′ing) a soft, sweet, cooked food eaten for dessert. It nearly always contains milk. *n.*

pud•dle (pud′əl) a small pool of water, especially dirty water, or any other liquid: *a puddle of rain water, a puddle of oil.* *n.*

pudg•y (puj′ē) short and fat or thick: *a baby's pudgy hand.* *adj.*

a bat	e bed	i bid	o pot	u cup	th thin
ā cake	ē me	ī bite	ō go	ū rude	ᴛʜ then
ä bar	ə about	ər over	ȯ for	u̇ put	zh measure

puff (puf) 1 blow or breathe with short, quick blows: *The bellows puffed on the fire. She puffed as she climbed the stairs.* 2 a short, quick blast: *A puff of wind blew away the letter.* 3 smoke: *to puff a pipe.* 4 swell: *He puffed out his cheeks.* Something that is swollen is **puffy.** 5 a fluffy pad for putting powder on your skin, washing yourself in the shower, etc. 6 a light pastry filled with whipped cream, jam, etc.: *a cream puff.* 1, 3, 4 *v.,* 2, 5, 6 *n.* —**puff′er,** *n.*

puf•fin (puf′ən) a mostly black and white sea bird of the northern Atlantic and Pacific coasts. It has a short, triangular bill that is often brightly coloured. *n.*

pu•ja (pū′jə) Hindu worship, with prayers, offerings, and the lighting of lamps. *n.*

pull (pu̇l) 1 move something by grabbing it and bringing it toward yourself, or by bringing it along behind you as you go: *pull your socks on, to pull someone's hair, to pull a toboggan uphill.* 2 remove something in this way: *to pull weeds, to pull a tooth.* 3 move a vehicle; steer or drive: *to pull over to the side of the road, to pull into a driveway.* 4 row a boat: *Pull for the shore as fast as you can!* 5 stretch too far; strain: *to pull a muscle.* 6 the act of pulling or a force that pulls: *the pull of a magnet. The sailor gave a pull on the rope.* 7 *Informal.* do, especially something bad or annoying: *Don't pull any tricks.* 8 a handle, rope, ring, or other thing to pull by: *a bell pull, a curtain pull.* 1–5, 7 *v.,* 6, 8 *n.*
pull for, support and encourage: *We're pulling for you, Tommy!*
pull off, do successfully; manage: *That's a pretty big job; do you think we can pull it off?*
pull out, leave or quit: *If you don't like the plan, it's not too late to pull out.*
pull over, drive to the curb and stop: *She pulled over when she heard the siren.*
pull through, get through a difficult or dangerous situation.
pull together, co-operate; work as a team.
pull up, stop a vehicle: *We pulled up in front of the door.*
pull yourself together, get control of yourself.

pul•ley (pu̇l′ē) a wheel with a groove in the rim that a rope, belt, or wire can run in, making it possible to move objects by changing the direction of the pull. When you pull on the rope on one side of the pulley, it moves in the opposite direction on the other side of the pulley. A clothesline often has a pulley. *n., pl.* **pul•leys.**

pull•o•ver (pu̇l′ō′vər) a sweater that you put on by pulling it over your head. *n.*

pulp (pulp) 1 a mixture of ground-up wood, rags, or other material. Paper is made from pulp: *The pulp and paper industry is very important in B.C.* **Pulpwood** is any soft wood that is good for grinding into pulp to make paper. 2 the soft and fleshy or juicy part of any fruit or vegetable. 3 the soft inner part of a tooth, containing blood vessels and nerves. 4 any soft, wet mass. *n.* —**pulp′y,** *adj.*

pul•pit (pu̇l′pit) a raised structure in a church, that the minister stands behind when he or she preaches. *n.*

pulse (puls) 1 the beating of the arteries as the blood rushes into them after each pumping motion of the heart. 2 the rate of this beating: *The nurse took the man's pulse by holding his wrist and counting the beats.* 3 any regular, measured beat: *the pulse in music, the pulse of an engine.* 4 to beat, throb, or vibrate. **Pulsate** means the same. 1–3 *n.,* 4 *v.,* **pulsed, puls•ing.**

pul•ver•ize (pul′və rīz′) grind to powder or dust. *v.,* **pul•ver•ized, pul•ver•iz•ing.**

pu•ma (pyū′mə) another name for the **cougar,** a large wildcat of North and South America. *n.*

pum•ice (pum′is) a light stone thrown up from volcanoes, with many holes in it like a sponge. When ground into fine grains, it is used for cleaning, smoothing, and polishing. Some people use a piece of pumice as you would use a bar of soap; its slightly rough surface removes dead skin cells and improves your circulation. *n.*

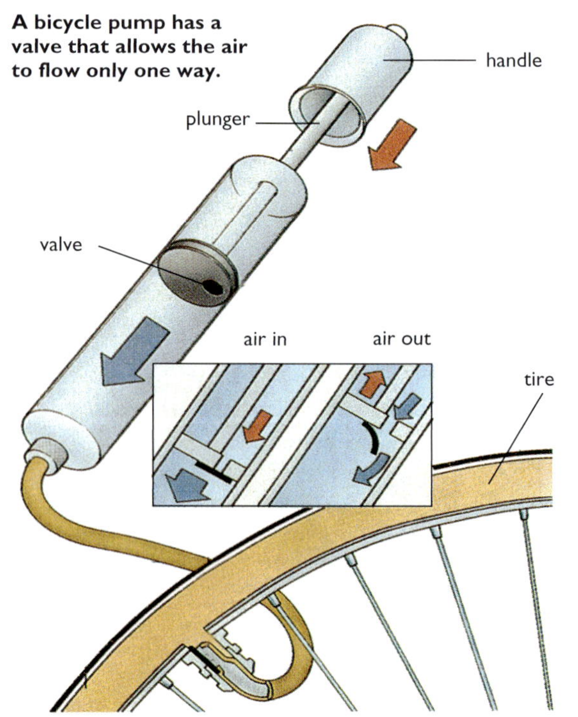

pump[1] (pump) 1 a machine for forcing liquids or gases into or out of things: *a water pump, an oil pump.*

2 move a liquid or gas by a pump: *to pump water from the well into a pail.* 3 blow air into something with a pump: *Pump up the bike tires.* 4 move up and down or back and forth, like the handle of a pump. You have to pump to keep swinging on a swing. To **pump someone's hand** is to shake hands with him or her. To **pump iron** is to lift weights. 5 *Informal.* fill with enthusiasm, energy, and excitement: *Our team was really pumped.* 6 *Informal.* get information out of; try to get information out of: *They pumped me for more details.* 1 *n.,* 2–6 *v.*

pump² (pump) a girl's or woman's low-cut shoe with no laces, straps, or other fastening: *She always wears pumps with a dress.* *n.*

pum·per·nick·el (pum′pər nik′əl) a heavy, dark, slightly sour bread made from whole grains of rye, coarsely ground. *n.*

pump·kin (pump′kin) a large, roundish, orange-yellow fruit of a trailing vine, used for making pies and sometimes soup. At Halloween, people carve a face into a hollowed-out pumpkin and put a candle inside to make a **jack-o'-lantern.** Pumpkins are a symbol of fall. *n.*

pun (pun) 1 the use of a word with two different meanings at once, for fun or to make a joke; a play on words. *Example*: *When is a door not a door? When it's a jar* (ajar). 2 make puns. 1 *n.,* 2 *v.,* **punned, pun·ning.** **—pun′ster,** *n.*

punch¹ (punch) 1 hit with the fist: *a punch in the nose* (*n.*). *She punched my arm* (*v.*). 2 press a key or button: *Punch "Enter" or "Return" to start a new line.* 3 herd or drive cattle: *He punched cows in Alberta for a living.* 4 lively power; force: *The story is OK, but it lacks punch.* 1–3 *v.,* 1, 4 *n.* **—punch′y,** *adj.*
punch in, enter information on a computer keyboard.

punch² (punch) 1 a tool for making holes through things or stamping designs into surfaces. 2 pierce a hole in: *The train conductor punches the tickets.* 1 *n.,* 2 *v.*
punch out, press out a shape that has been prestamped in paper, cardboard, plastic, etc.: *Dawn punched out the pieces of the cardboard bus and put it together.*

punch³ (punch) a drink made of different juices, pop, and so on mixed together. *n.*

punch line (punch′ līn′) the last sentence or words of a joke. The punch line is what makes it funny or surprising.

punc·tu·al (pungk′chū əl) prompt; on time: *She is always punctual for meetings.* *adj.*

punc·tu·ate (pungk′chū āt′) 1 put periods, commas, and other marks in writing to separate words into sentences, phrases, and so on so that the meaning is clear. The different marks are called **punctuation marks.** 2 interrupt now and then: *a speech punctuated with cheers.* 3 give force or emphasis to: *He punctuated his arguments by pounding the table.* *v.,* **punc·tu·at·ed, punc·tu·at·ing.** **—punc′tu·a′tion,** *n.*

punc·ture (pungk′chər) 1 a small hole made by something pointed. 2 make this kind of hole in: *A nail punctured my bicycle tire.* 1 *n.,* 2 *v.,* **punc·tured, punc·tur·ing.**

pun·gent (pun′jənt) sharp or strong in taste or smell: *a pungent pickle, the pungent smell of woodsmoke.* *adj.* **—pun′gen·cy,** *n.*

pun·ish (pun′ish) cause a person pain, loss, or discomfort for wrong behaviour: *Mom punished us by forbidding TV for a week. The law punishes crime.* *v.* **—pun′ish·a·ble,** *adj.* **—pun′ish·ment,** *n.*

punk (pungk) 1 a tough or disrespectful young person. 2 a style of loud, hard rock music often expressing violent anger. It was most popular in the early 1980s. Its fans often wore black clothes decorated with safety pins and dyed their hair bright colours. *n.*

punt (punt) 1 kick a football before it touches the ground after being dropped from the hands. 2 this kind of kick: *The punt went over the goal line.* 1 *v.,* 2 *n.*

pu·ny (pyū′nē) very small, weak, or unimportant. *adj.,* **pu·ni·er, pu·ni·est.**

pup (pup) a young dog, fox, wolf, etc. *n.*

pu·pa (pyū′pə) a stage between the larva and the adult in the development of many insects. In the pupa stage the insect stays inactive inside a case it makes for itself. To go through this stage is to **pupate.** *n., pl.* **pu·pae** (pyū′pē) or **pu·pas.**

pu·pil¹ (pyū′pəl) a student, especially one in elementary school or one taught by a private teacher: *grade three pupils, a piano pupil.* *n.*

pu·pil² (pyū′pəl) the opening in the centre of the iris of the eye which looks like a black spot. The pupil is the only place where light can enter the eye. *n.*

pup·pet (pup′it) 1 a figure made to look like a person or animal, moved by wires, strings, or your fingers. A puppet on strings is also called a **marionette.** A person who works a puppet is a **puppeteer.** 2 anybody who is completely controlled by someone else. *n.* **—pup′pet·ry,** *n.*

pup·py (pup′ē) a young dog. *n., pl.* **pup·pies.**

a bat	e bed	i bid	o pot	u cup	th thin
ā cake	ē me	ī bite	ō go	ū rude	ᴛʜ then
ä bar	ə about	ər over	ô for	ů put	zh measure

pur·chase (pər′chəs) 1 buy: *We purchased a new car.* 2 the act of buying: *The purchase of a new car can be a difficult business.* 3 the thing bought: *That canoe was a good purchase.* 1 *v.,* **pur·chased, pur·chas·ing;** 2, 3 *n.* —**pur′chas·er,** *n.*

pure (pyūr) 1 not mixed with anything else: *pure gold, pure orange juice. They won by pure luck.* 2 perfectly clean: *pure water.* 3 with no evil: *a pure life.* *adj.,* **pur·er, pur·est.** —**pure·ly,** *adv.*

> *Word Family*........... **pure**
>
> **purebred:** having ancestors from only one breed
> **purify:** make pure. **Purification** is the noun.
> **purist:** a person who insists on a strictly proper view or method
> **purity:** the quality of being pure

pu·rée (pyər ā′) 1 food put through a blender until it is completely smooth. Often it is cooked first. Sometimes water or milk and seasonings are added afterward and it is eaten as a thick soup. 2 make into a purée. 1 *n.,* 2 *v.,* **pu·réed, pu·ré·ing.**

purge (pərj) 1 get rid of anything unclean or undesirable: *The king tried to purge his land of injustice.* 2 the act of purging. 1 *v.,* **purged, purg·ing;** 2 *n.*

Pu·ri·tan (pyū′rə tən) 1 a member of a Christian group in England and the United States during the 1500s and 1600s who believed in simpler forms of worship and stricter morals. 2 of or having to do with this group. 1 *n.,* 2 *adj.*

pur·ple (pər′pəl) a colour made by mixing red and blue. *n. or adj.* —**pur′plish,** *adj.*

purple martin (pər′pəl mär′tən) a large bluish black bird of North America with a short beak and a forked tail. It is a kind of swallow.

pur·pose (pər′pəs) a goal; the reason for doing, using, or making something: *His purpose in coming was to meet my family. The purpose of a clock is to tell the time.* *n.* —**pur′pose·ful,** *adj.* —**pur′pose·less,** *adj.*
on purpose, meaning to do it; not by accident: *He tripped me on purpose.* **Purposely** means the same.

purr (pər) 1 a soft, low sound like the sound a cat makes when it is happy. 2 make this sound. 1 *n.,* 2 *v.*

purse (pərs) 1 a bag made of cloth, leather, vinyl, etc. used by a woman to carry her wallet, keys, cosmetics, and so on. It is also called a **handbag:** *She put her keys and gloves in her purse.* 2 a little pouch or case for carrying coins. 3 money prize: *A purse of $10 000 was the prize for winning the horse race.* 4 pull together in folds or wrinkles: *She pursed her lips and frowned.* 1–3 *n.,* 4 *v.,* **pursed, purs·ing.**

pur·sue (pər sū′) 1 follow in order to catch; chase: *The dogs pursued the rabbit.* 2 strive for; try to get; seek: *to pursue pleasure.* 3 carry on with: *She pursued her music studies for another year.* *v.,* **pur·sued, pur·su·ing.** —**pur·su′er,** *n.*

pur·suit (pər sūt′) 1 the act of pursuing: *The pursuit of knowledge. The pursuit of the escaped convict continued all night.* 2 a job or hobby; activity: *Fishing is one of her favourite pursuits.* *n.*

pus (pus) a thick, yellowish-white fluid that forms in infected tissue in the body. *n.*

push (pu̇sh) 1 press against something: *We pushed with all our strength, but the door did not open.* 2 move something by pressing against it: *She pushed the rock over the cliff.* 3 go or send forward by force: *We pushed through the crowd. Trees push their roots down into the ground.* 4 urge; try to persuade or force: *He pushed us to work harder.* 5 try to persuade people to buy, use, believe, do, etc.: *to push good nutrition. Our teacher really pushes neatness.* 6 the act of pushing; pushing: *Give the door a push.* 1–5 *v.,* 6 *n.*
be pushed for, have much too little of: *We're really pushed for time, so hurry.*
push around, *Informal.* treat roughly or unkindly; bully.
push for, try hard to get approval for someone or something: *The workers are pushing for higher pay.*
push off, **a** move from shore: *We pushed off in the boat.* **b** *Informal.* go away.
push your luck, take too many risks.

push–up (pu̇sh′up′) an exercise where you lie on your stomach and then push yourself up with both arms, keeping your back and legs straight and only your hands and toes on the ground. *n.*

puss (pu̇s) a cat. **Pussy** means the same. *n.*

pussy willow (pu̇s′ ē wil′ō) a small willow with short, silky, silver-white flower spikes.

put (pu̇t) 1 place, lay, set, or send; cause to be in some place or position: *I put sugar in my tea. Put away your toys. She has put the idea out of her mind.* 2 cause to be in some state or condition: *Put your room in order. The music put us to sleep.* 3 express: *The teacher puts things clearly.* 4 estimate at a certain amount: *He puts the distance at 5 km.* *v.,* **put, put·ting.**
put aside, away, or **by,** save for future use.

put down, a criticize or insult. A **putdown** is an insult or unkind criticism. **b** kill an animal that is too sick or injured to heal. **c** put an end to: *The rebellion was quickly put down.*
put forth, make or show: *to put forth buds, to put forth an effort.*
put forward, suggest.
put in, a do; spend time doing: *She always puts in a good day's work.* **b** say quickly between the remarks of others: *"Me too!" put in Tyler.* **c** dock; stop in a harbour: *The ship put in at Vancouver.* **d** give as your share: *If each person puts in $5, we can get a pizza.*
put off, a leave for some later time: *Don't put off going to the dentist.* **b** discourage; cause to lose interest.
put on, a dress or decorate yourself with: *She put on her new jeans.* **b** adopt as a pretence: *She put on an air of innocence.* A **put-on** is something done just as an act. **c** increase: *to put on weight. The driver put on speed.* **d** present on a stage; produce: *The class put on a play.*
put out, a stop something burning or shining: *to put out a fire.* **b** pay; spend. **c** make angry; offend. **d** knock out of joint: *I put out my knee when I fell.* **e** publish.
put something over on someone, fool or trick someone: *You can't put anything over on her.*
put up, a offer: *to put a house up for sale.* **b** give someone a place to stay: *We can put you up for a few days.* **c** get a person to do: *Who put you up to this?* **d** make available: *He put up the money for the car.*
put up a fuss, protest angrily against something.
put up with, bear patiently; endure.
stay put, stay in one place and not move.

putt (put) **1** in golf, make a light stroke with a special club that sends the ball a short distance. You putt when you are getting near the hole. **2** a stroke like this. 1 *v.*, 2 *n.* —**putt′er,** *n.*

put·ter (put′ər) keep busy in a rather useless way: *She likes to spend the afternoon puttering in the garden.* *v.*

putt–putt (put′put′) **1** a chugging or popping sound from an engine. **2** make this sound or move with this sound: *The motorboat went putt-putting across the lake.* 1 *n.*, 2 *v.*

put·ty (put′ē) **1** a soft mixture of powdered chalk and linseed oil, used mainly for filling holes and cracks and sealing panes of glass into window frames. It becomes firm when dry. **2** fill up or cover with putty: *He puttied the holes in the woodwork before painting it.* 1 *n., pl.* **put·ties;** 2 *v.,* **put·tied, put·ty·ing.**

puz·zle (puz′əl) **1** a design or picture cut into pieces so that people can have the fun of putting it back together. **2** be hard for someone to figure out; perplex: *Her strange answer puzzled us.* **3** try hard to figure out: *He puzzled over his arithmetic problems all evening.* **4** anything hard to figure out: *How to get all my things into one trunk is a puzzle.* 1, 4 *n.,* 2, 3 *v.,* **puz·zled, puz·zling.**
puzzle out, figure out by thinking hard: *to puzzle out the meaning of a message.*

PVC a strong plastic used to make many different things including toys. It can be rigid and coloured, or flexible and clear. **Polyvinyl chloride** (pol′ē vī′nəl klôr′īd) is the full name of this plastic.

py·ja·mas or **pa·ja·mas** (pə jam′əz *or* pə jä′məz) a loose top and matching pair of loose pants, worn for sleeping. *pl.n.*

py·lon (pī′lon) **1** an orange plastic cone used to guide traffic, block off a road, mark a dangerous spot such as an open hole, etc. **2** a tall steel framework used to carry the main electric cables across an area. **3** a post or tower for guiding aircraft pilots. *n.*

The Pyramids of Giza stand on the west bank of the Nile River. There are ten pyramids in this place, including the Great Pyramid built almost 5000 years ago.

pyr·a·mid (pēr′ə mid′) **1** a solid form with a flat base and triangular sides that meet at the top. **2 the Pyramids,** *pl.* the huge stone tombs built in this shape by the ancient Egyptians. *n.*

py·thon (pī′thon) a large snake of Asia, Africa, and Australia that kills its prey by squeezing it so it cannot breathe. Pythons are among the largest snakes. *n.*

Qq

q or **Q** (kyū) **1** the seventeenth letter of the English alphabet, or the sound that it stands for. In English words, *q* usually occurs together with *u*, as in *quick* or *quarter.* **2** the seventeenth thing in a list. *n., pl.* **q's** or **Q's.**

qt. *abbreviation for* quart or quarts, a nonmetric measure of volume.

quack[1] (kwak) **1** the sound a duck makes. **2** make this sound or one like it. 1 *n.,* 2 *v.*

quack[2] (kwak) a dishonest person who pretends to be a doctor or scientist. *n.* **—quack′er·y,** *n.*

quad·ri·lat·er·al (kwod′rə lat′ə rəl) **1** any figure with four sides and four angles. Squares, rectangles, kites, trapezoids, and rhombuses are quadrilaterals. **2** having four sides: *a quadrilateral figure.* 1 *n.,* 2 *adj.*

WORD HISTORY.......quadrilateral

Quadrilateral is a compound of the Latin roots *quadri-*, meaning "four," and *lateris*, meaning "side." Another word that uses *quadri-* is **quadrilingual**. What do you think a quadrilingual person can do?

quad·ru·ped (kwod′rə ped′) any animal with four feet. *n.*

quad·ru·ple (kwod drū′pəl *or* kwod′rə pəl) **1** four times as much or as many: *This was not a great apple harvest; last year the orchard yielded quadruple the number of apples.* **2** make or be made four times larger: *In the next game we quadrupled our score.* 1 *adj.,* 2 *v.,* **quad·ru·pled, quad·ru·pling.**

quad·ru·plet (kwod rū′plit) one of four children born at the same time from the same mother. *n.*

quaff (kwof *or* kwaf) drink in large gulps. *v.*

quag·mire (kwag′mīr′) soft, muddy ground; a boggy place. *n.*

Quail are found in many places in the world. This is the common quail of Europe, Asia, and North Africa. In North America, the quail are more colourful and slightly larger.

quail[1] (kwāl) a plump bird belonging to the same family as the pheasant, grouse, and partridge. Quails are sometimes hunted for food. *n., pl.* **quails** or **quail.**

quail[2] (kwāl) lose courage; shrink back with fear: *I quailed at the sight of the huge, angrily barking dog.* *v.*

quaint (kwānt) cute, interesting, or funny because it is strange or old: *Old photos seem quaint to us today.* *adj.*

quake (kwāk) **1** shake; tremble: *She quaked with fear.* **2** the act of shaking or trembling. **3** an earthquake. 1 *v.,* **quaked, quak·ing;** 2, 3 *n.*

qual·i·fi·ca·tion (kwol′ə fə kā′shən) **1** something about a person which makes him or her fit for a particular job or activity: *Good eyesight is a necessary qualification for a pilot.* **2** a point that limits an idea or statement: *to agree to something without qualification.* *n.*

qual·i·fy (kwol′ə fī′) **1** have or give the necessary skills or other characteristics: *She is fully qualified for the job. Do you qualify for the soccer team?* **2** limit; make less strong: *Let me qualify that statement about dogs being loyal; they're USUALLY loyal.* *v.,* **qual·i·fied, qual·i·fy·ing.**

qual·i·ty (kwol′ə tē) **1** something special about a person or object that makes it what it is: *One quality of sugar is its sweetness. She had many good qualities, including a sense of humour.* **2** a measure of how good a thing is: *These shoes are of high quality.* **3** the fact of being well-done; excellence: *Look for quality rather than quantity.* **4** well-made or well-done: *quality clothing, quality work.* 1–3 *n., pl.* **qual·i·ties;** 4 *adj.*

qualm (kwom) a sudden slight feeling of guilt, doubt, or fear: *I tried the test with some qualms. She felt some qualms at taking the last tart without asking.* *n.*

quan·da·ry (kwon′də rē) a situation where you don't know what to do or how to choose; dilemma. *n.*

quan·ti·ty (kwon′tə tē) **1** amount or number: *Equal quantities of nuts and raisins were used in the cake.* **2** a large amount or number: *The baker buys flour in quantity. She owns quantities of computer games.* *n., pl.* **quan·ti·ties.**

quar•an•tine (kwôr′ən tēn′ *or* kwôr′ən tēn′) **1** keep a person, animal, or plant away from others for a while to prevent the spread of a contagious disease: *Her pet had to be quarantined when she arrived in Canada.* **2** the practice of doing this, the place, or the length of time: *Our dog was in quarantine while it was tested for rabies.* 1 *v.,* **quar•an•tined, quar•an•tin•ing;** 2 *n.*

quar•rel (kwô′rəl) **1** an angry disagreement or argument: *The children had a quarrel over the division of the candy.* **2** argue or disagree angrily: *The children were quarrelling when their parents came home.* 1 *n.,* 2 *v.,* **quar•relled** or **quar•reled, quar•rel•ling** or **quar•rel•ing.** —**quar′rel•some,** *adj.*

quar•ry (kwô′rē) **1** a place where stone is dug, cut, or blasted out for use in building. **2** get stone from a quarry: *We watched the workers quarry a huge block of stone. Quarrying is illegal on the Niagara Escarpment.* 1 *n., pl.* **quar•ries;** 2 *v.,* **quar•ried, quar•ry•ing.**

quart (kwôrt) a nonmetric measure of volume, equal to one-fourth of a gallon or one-eighth of a peck (about 1.1 L): *a quart of berries, a quart of milk.* *n.*

quar•ter (kwôr′tər) **1** one-fourth; one of four equal parts: *a quarter of a pie. A quarter of an hour is 15 minutes.* A period of three months is called a quarter; so is each of the four phases of the moon. **2** divide into four equal parts: *to quarter an apple.* **3** one-fourth of a dollar; 25 cents, or a coin worth this amount: *Do you have change for a quarter?* **4** **quarters,** *pl.* a place to live or stay in: *to live in cramped quarters.* **5** give a place to live: *The soldiers were quartered in the town.* 1, 3, 4 *n.,* 2, 5 *v.*

quar•ter•back (kwôr′tər bak′) in football, the player who starts off right behind the centre of the line of scrimmage. The quarterback begins by receiving the ball from the centre and passing it or running with it. *n.*

quar•ter•ly (kwôr′tər lē) **1** happening or done four times a year: *a quarterly report, quarterly payments.* **2** once every three months: *The company pays its income tax quarterly.* **3** a magazine that is published four times a year. 1 *adj.,* 2 *adv.,* 3 *n., pl.* **quar•ter•lies.**

quarter section (kwôr′tər sek′shən) especially in the West, a square piece of land of 160 acres (about 65 hectares). To encourage people to go and live in the West and develop it, families who settled there in the 1800s and early 1900s were given a quarter section of land by the government.

quar•tet (kwôr tet′) **1** a group of four singers or players performing together, or the piece of music they perform. **2** any group of four. *n.*

Quartz is the main ingredient of sand. Pure quartz forms six-sided crystals that are as clear as glass.

quartz (kwôrts) a very hard mineral found in many kinds of rock. Common quartz crystals are colourless and clear. Coloured kinds of quartz include amethyst and jasper. **Quartzite** is a rock containing mostly quartz. *n.*

qua•sar (kwā′zär) a very bright object very far out in space. Quasars give off strong radio waves. *n.*

quash (kwosh) **1** reject or throw out a statement: *to quash a suggestion.* **2** use force or authority to end or crush something: *The army quashed the revolt.* *v.*

qua•ver (kwā′vər) **1** shake; tremble: *The sick man's voice quavered.* **2** sing or say in a shaky voice: *"Please don't hurt me!" quavered the prisoner.* **3** a shaking or trembling, especially of the voice. 1, 2 *v.,* 3 *n.*

quay (kē) a solid landing place where ships load and unload. *n.*

Que. *abbreviation for* Québec.

quea•sy (kwē′zē) having your stomach so upset you feel as if you might throw up: *The ride on the roller coaster made Carlos feel queasy.* *adj.,* **quea•si•er, quea•si•est.** —**quea′si•ness,** *n.*

Qué•bec (kə bek′, kwə bek′, *or* kā bek′) a large province of Canada between Ontario and New Brunswick. Its official language is French. *n.* —**Qué•beck′er,** *n.* —**Qué•bé•cois′** or **Qué•bé•coise′,** *adj. or n.*

queen (kwēn) **1** a female ruler of a nation, who has inherited her position: *Queen Elizabeth II.* **2** the wife of a king. She becomes the **queen mother** when her husband dies and one of her children takes the throne. **3** a woman judged to be first or best in some way: *the queen of his heart, a fashion queen.* **4** in a colony of bees, ants, etc., a female that lays eggs: *There is usually only one queen in a hive of bees.* **5** in chess, a piece that can move in any straight or diagonal row. **6** a playing card with a picture of a queen on it. *n.* —**queen′ly,** *adj.*

a bat	e bed	i bid	o pot	u cup	th **thin**
ā cake	ē me	ī bite	ō go	ū rude	ᴛʜ **then**
ä bar	ə about	ər over	ô for	u̇ put	zh measure

Queen Anne's lace (kwēn′ anz′ lās′) a wild plant of the parsley family that has clusters of small, lacy white flowers. **Wild carrot** is another name for it. *n.*

queen–size (kwēn′sīz′) bigger than the regular size, but smaller than king-size. A queen-size mattress is usually 152 x 203 cm. *adj.*

queer (kwēr) strange; odd; peculiar: *queer goings-on.* *adj.*

quell (kwel) put down; overcome: *The police quelled the riot.* *v.*

quench (kwench) **1** put an end to; stop: *to quench a thirst. Her sincere apology quenched my anger.* **2** drown out; put out: *Water will quench a fire.* *v.*

que·ry (kwē′rē) question: *to answer a query* (*n.*). *I would query that spelling "bridje"—shouldn't it be "bridge"* (*v.*)? *n., pl.* **que·ries;** *or v.,* **que·ried, que·ry·ing.**

quest (kwest) **1** a journey to search for something precious or a campaign to accomplish something noble or important: *a quest for inner peace, a quest to eliminate racism.* **2** go on a quest; search. 1 *n.,* 2 *v.*
in quest of, looking for.

ques·tion (kwes′chən) **1** something asked in order to get information, such as, "What time is it?" Questions always end with a **question mark.** ▶ See the *Grammar and Usage Mini-Guide.* **2** ask in order to get information: *The police questioned the witness about the accident.* **3** a matter to be talked over or considered; problem: *They were discussing an important question.* **4** doubt: *There is no question she will win* (*n.*). *I question the truth of his story* (*v.*). 1, 3, 4 *n.,* 2, 4 *v.*
—ques′tion·ing·ly, *adv.*
beyond question, not to be doubted or disputed: *His honesty is beyond question.*
call into question, raise doubts about.
out of the question, not to be considered; impossible.
without question, without a doubt: *She is without question the brightest student in the school.*

> **Grammar Check . . . question mark**
>
> Use a question mark at the end of a direct question: *When will the movie start?*
>
> You don't need to use a question mark in sentences like these: *Sarah asked when the movie would start. I wonder when the movie will start.*

ques·tion·a·ble (kwes′chə nə bəl) **1** doubtful; uncertain: *It is questionable whether he'll come.* **2** not altogether right or honest: *questionable behaviour.* *adj.*

ques·tion·naire (kwes′chə ner′) a printed set of questions used to collect information from people: *The questionnaire asked our ages, what kinds of cereal we like to eat, and what TV shows we watch.* *n.*

question period (kwes′chən pēr′yəd) a regular time in the House of Commons when government ministers must answer questions raised by other elected members.

quet·zal (ket säl′) a bird of Central America that has golden green and bright red feathers. The tail feathers of the male are very long, curved, and flowing. *n.*

queue (kyū) **1** a lineup: *There was a long queue in front of the theatre.* **2** to line up: *We had to queue up to get tickets.* 1 *n.,* 2 *v.,* **queued, queu·ing.**

quib·ble (kwib′əl) **1** a small disagreement or criticism: *We had a few quibbles with the cafeteria menu.* **2** argue about small things: *We quibbled about which flavour of gum was best.* 1 *n.,* 2 *v.,* **quib·bled, quib·bling.**

quiche (kēsh) a kind of pie with a filling of egg and cream beaten together with various other ingredients, such as ham, bacon, cheese, or spinach. It is usually eaten hot for first course. *n.*

quick (kwik) **1** fast or sudden: *a quick movement, a quick trip to the store.* Something quick is a **quickie.** **2** coming soon; prompt: *a quick reply.* **3** alert; sharp: *a quick mind, a quick ear.* **4** the tender, sensitive flesh under your nails: *The child bit his nails down to the quick.* **5** the tender, sensitive part of your feelings: *Mackenzie was cut to the quick by their harsh words.* 1–3 *adj.,* 4, 5 *n.* **—quick′ly** or **quick,** *adv.* **—quick′ness,** *n.*

quick·en (kwik′ən) **1** make or become faster: *Quicken your pace. His pulse quickened.* **2** stir up; make or become active or alive: *He quickened the hot coals into flames. Reading quickened her imagination.* *v.*

quick·sand (kwik′sand′) **1** soft, wet, deep sand that heavy things sink into: *The tractor was swallowed by the quicksand.* **2** an expanse of such sand: *There are dangerous quicksands along the shores of Lake Superior.* *n.*

qui·et (kwī′ət) **1** with little or no noise: *quiet footsteps, a quiet room.* **2** still; moving very little: *a quiet river.* **3** restful; not busy: *a quiet evening at home.* **4** not attracting a lot of attention; not bold: *quiet colours, quiet manners.* **5** stillness; freedom from noise and disturbance: *Give me some peace and quiet.* **6** make or become quiet: *The mother quieted her frightened child. The wind quieted down.* 1–4 *adj.,* 5 *n.,* 6 *v.*

Quill pens were usually made from the wing feathers of geese or swans. The tip of the shaft can be sharpened and slit to make writing easier.

quill (kwil) 1 a large, stiff feather, or its hollow stem. 2 a pen or other thing made from this. 3 a stiff, sharp spine: *A porcupine has quills on its back.* *n.*

quilt (kwilt) 1 a cover for a bed, usually made of two layers of cloth with a soft pad between, held in place by lines of stitching. The layers of cloth are often made of smaller pieces sewn together to make a pattern or picture. 2 make quilts. 3 stitch anything together in layers with a soft lining between: *a quilted bathrobe.* 1 *n.,* 2, 3 *v.*

quince (kwins) a hard, yellowish, sour fruit, used for preserves and jelly. It grows on a small tree of Asia. *n.*

quin·tet (kwin tet′) 1 a group of five singers or players performing together, or the piece of music they perform. 2 any group of five. *n.*

quin·tu·plet (kwin tup′lit, kwin tyū′plit, *or* kwin tū′plit) one of five children born at the same time from the same mother. This word is often shortened informally to **quint.** *n.*

quip (kwip) 1 a clever or funny remark. 2 say something clever or funny: *"I was so late with my assignment the teacher thought I was turning in the next one," Charley quipped.* 1 *n.,* 2 *v.,* **quipped, quip·ping.**

quirk (kwərk) a peculiar way of acting or thinking: *He writes only in green ink; it's one of his quirks.* *n.* **—quirk′y,** *adj.*

quit (kwit) 1 stop an activity: *The women quit work at five. Quit making faces at Sikander!* 2 leave or give up: *to quit a job, to quit school.* 1, 2 *v.,* **quit, quit·ting.** **—quit′ter,** *n.*
call it quits, stop or give up; quit: *The mosquitoes were so bad we decided to call it quits and go home.*

quite (kwīt) 1 completely; entirely: *We are not quite finished.* 2 pretty; rather; fairly: *It is quite hot.* *adv.*
quite a, a a real; really: *It was quite a shock. We waited quite a long time.* **b** a very remarkable: *That's quite a story!*
quite a few, a lot; many.

quiv·er[1] (kwiv′ər) 1 shake slightly; tremble: *The dog quivered with excitement.* 2 a shaking or trembling movement: *A quiver of his mouth showed that he was about to cry.* 1 *v.,* 2 *n.*

quiv·er[2] (kwiv′ər) a long case for holding arrows, which can be slung over one shoulder and carried on your back. *n.*

quiz (kwiz) 1 a short or informal test: *Each week the teacher gives us a quiz in multiplication.* 2 give such a test: *to quiz a class.* 3 ask many questions: *The lawyer quizzed the witness.* 1 *n.,* 2, 3 *v.,* **quizzed, quiz·zing.**

quiz show (kwiz′ shō′) a radio or TV program where people are given prizes for answering questions correctly.

quo·rum (kwôr′əm) the number of people that must be at a meeting in order for official decisions to be made: *The Student Council meeting couldn't start until enough people had arrived to make a quorum.* *n.*

quo·ta (kwō′tə) a set amount that is someone's share: *Each student was given a quota of chocolate bars to sell for the school. The grain elevators accept a certain quota of wheat from each farmer.* *n.*

quote (kwōt) 1 repeat the exact words of; give a passage from: *She quoted part of the Canadian Charter of Rights and Freedoms.* 2 words from another source, which someone has repeated exactly: *"To be or not to be" is a famous quote from Shakespeare.* Quotes always appear inside **quotation marks** (" ") unless they are very long. ▶ See the *Grammar and Usage Mini-Guide.* 3 mention; name: *to quote a price. The premier quoted unemployment as one of the province's main problems.* 4 a price given for something: *to compare quotes.* 1, 3 *v.,* **quot·ed, quot·ing;** 2, 4 *n.* **—quo·ta′tion,** *n.* **—quot′a·ble,** *adj.*

Grammar Check . . . quotation marks

Always use **quotation marks** at the beginning and end of somebody's exact words:"I never saw him before in my life!" cried the witness.

quo·tient (kwō′shənt) the number you get when you divide one number by another: *If you divide 26 by 2, the quotient is 13.* *n.*

Qur'an or **Ko·ran** (kü rán′) the holy book of Islam, containing God's message to Muhammad. *n.*

Rr

r or **R** (är) 1 the eighteenth letter of the English alphabet, or the sound that it stands for. The sound of *r* is heard twice in *rear.* 2 the eighteenth thing in a list. *n., pl.* **r's** or **R's.**
the three R's, reading, writing, and arithmetic.

rab•bi (rab′ī) a teacher of Jewish law and religion; a leader of a Jewish congregation. *n., pl.* **rab•bis.**

rab•bit (rab′it) a burrowing mammal with soft fur, long ears, and strong hind legs for jumping. Rabbits are smaller than hares and have shorter ears and legs. *n.*

rab•ble (rab′əl) a rude, noisy crowd; a mob: *The angry rabble threw eggs and tomatoes at the speaker.* *n.*

ra•bies (rā′bēz) a dangerous disease carried by animals. An animal with rabies is **rabid** (rab′id); it may act strangely and try to attack other animals or people that it normally wouldn't. If bitten by an animal with rabies, a person who does not get treatment may die. *n.*

Raccoons are versatile travellers. They walk like bears, with all four feet flat on the ground; they have sharp claws, which help them climb trees; and they are excellent swimmers.

rac•coon (rə kün′) a small, greyish-brown animal with a bushy, ringed tail and a dark patch around the eyes. Raccoons live in trees and are usually active at night. They are sometimes trapped for their fur. *n.*

race¹ (rās) 1 a contest to see who or what is fastest: *a horse race, a boat race.* 2 take part in this kind of contest: *Matt will race for our school at the regional track meet.* 3 try to beat in a contest of speed: *I'll race you to the gate.* 4 any close contest, such as an election. 5 run or move fast: *Race to the doctor for help. We raced through our chores so we could go out biking.* 6 cause to go fast: *Don't race the engine.* 7 a strong, fast current of water: *a mill race.* 1, 4, 7 *n.,* 2, 3, 5, 6 *v.,* **raced, rac•ing.** —**rac′er,** *n.*

race² (rās) 1 a group of living things with similar characteristics and ancestry: *the human race, the race of birds.* 2 a group of people with a certain set of physical characteristics such as skin colour, body shape, facial features, hair type, etc.: *the Asian race, the white race.* *n.* —**ra′cial** (rā′shəl), *adj.*

race•course (rās′ kôrs′) a route or track for racing. A **racetrack** is the same but usually oval in shape so it can be contained in a small area.

rac•ism (rā′siz əm) unnecessary attention paid to the colour of people's skin or where they come from; the idea that people of a certain colour are better than others. *n.* —**rac′ist,** *n. or adj.*

rack (rak) 1 a frame with bars, shelves, or pegs to hang or set things on: *a towel rack, a boot rack, a baggage rack.* 2 an instrument once used for torturing people by stretching them. 3 hurt very much: *racked with grief.* 4 a set of antlers. 1, 2, 4 *n.,* 3 *v.*
go to rack and ruin, be destroyed by neglect.
rack your brains, think as hard as you can.

rack•et (rak′it) 1 a loud, unpleasant noise. 2 *Informal.* a dishonest business scheme. The people who run it are **racketeers.** *n.*

rac•quet (rak′it) a sort of light bat ending in an oval frame with a network of strings stretched on it. Racquets are used in tennis and other games. *n.*

rac•quet•ball (rak′it bol′) a game for two or four players, who use racquets to hit a ball inside a walled court. *n.*

ra•dar (rā′där) an instrument that bounces radio waves off unseen objects to find out where they are, how fast they are moving, and in what direction. *n.*

WORD HISTORY........radar

Radar is formed from the first letters of the words "**ra**dio **d**etecting **a**nd **r**anging." Words like this are called *acronyms.* Can you think of any other acronyms?

ra•di•ant (rā′dē ənt) 1 bright; glowing; beaming: *radiant sunshine, a radiant smile.* 2 sent off in rays or waves from some source. **Radiant energy** is energy that travels in the form of rays or waves, such as heat, light, X rays, or radio waves. *adj.* —**ra′di•ance,** *n.*

ra•di•ate (rā′dē āt′) 1 give out or move out in rays or waves: *The sun radiates light and heat. Heat radiated from the woodstove.* 2 glow or shine with: *His face radiates joy.* 3 spread out from a centre: *Roads radiate from the town square.* *v.,* **ra•di•at•ed, ra•di•at•ing.**

ra·di·a·tion (rā′dē ā′shən) 1 the act or process of giving out light, heat, or other radiant energy. 2 the energy given out in this way, especially dangerous forms such as ultraviolet rays or the rays from a radioactive substance. This kind of radiation may also be used to kill harmful cancer cells. *n.*

ra·di·a·tor (rad′ē ā′tər *or* rā′dē ā′tər) 1 a device for heating a room, made up of pipes with very hot water or steam flowing through them. It is against the wall since it is attached to pipes behind the wall. 2 a device for cooling an engine. The special fluid in a car's radiator absorbs heat from the engine; the surface of the radiator, because of its shape, gives off this heat very quickly. *n.*

rad·i·cal (rad′ə kəl) 1 going to the root; very basic or deep: *Cruelty is a radical fault. If she wants to improve her marks, she must make a radical change in her work habits.* 2 extreme; favouring extreme changes or reforms. 3 a person with extreme opinions. 1, 2 *adj.*, 3 *n.* —**rad′i·cal·ly,** *adv.*

ra·di·i (rā′dē ī′) a plural of **radius.** *n.*

ra·di·o (rā′dē ō′) 1 a way to send sounds, such as music or talking, over long distances without wires. In radio, the sounds are changed into electrical signals and carried by electromagnetic waves. 2 a machine for sending or receiving sounds in this way: *I have a radio in my room.* 3 having to do with this way of sending sounds: *a radio station, radio programs.* 4 speak to someone by radio: *The pilot radioed the control tower.* 1, 2 *n., pl.* **ra·di·os;** 3 *adj.*, 4 *v.*, **ra·di·oed, ra·di·o·ing.**

ra·di·o·ac·tive (rā′dē ō ak′tiv) giving off radiant energy as a result of the break-up of atoms. This energy can harm living cells. Carbon-14 is a radioactive substance; scientists can find out how old a once-living object is by measuring how much the carbon-14 in it has disintegrated. This is called **radioactive dating.** Two other naturally radioactive substances are radium and uranium. *adj.* —**ra′di·o·ac·tiv′i·ty,** *n.*

ra·di·ol·o·gy (rā′dē ol′ə jē) the branch of medicine that uses X rays and other forms of radiation to find or treat medical problems inside the body. *n.* —**ra′di·ol′o·gist,** *n.*

radio telescope (rā′dē ō tel′ə skōp′) a kind of telescope for finding and recording radio waves coming from stars and other objects in space that go unnoticed by ordinary telescopes. It has a radio receiver and a large, dish-shaped antenna. The study of objects in space using this kind of telescope is called **radio astronomy.**

rad·ish (rad′ish) the small, crisp root of a fast-growing garden plant. The root has a red or white skin and is used in salads. *n.*

ra·di·um (rā′dē əm) a highly radioactive metal that is a chemical element. Radium is used to treat cancer. *n.*

ra·di·us (rā′dē əs) 1 any line going straight from the centre to the outside of a circle or sphere. A spoke of a wheel is a radius. 2 a circular area measured by a certain distance outward from a centre in any direction: *The explosion could be heard within a radius of 10 km.* *n., pl.* **ra·di·i** (rā′dē ī) or **ra·di·us·es.**

raf·fle (raf′əl) 1 a lottery where many people each pay a small amount for a chance to win a prize which is not money. 2 sell an article by a raffle: *They raffled off a quilt at the school bazaar.* 1 *n.*, 2 *v.*

raft (raft) 1 logs or boards fastened together to make a floating platform: *We floated down the stream on a log raft.* 2 a shallow, flat-bottomed inflatable boat: *a life raft.* 3 travel by raft; send or carry on a raft. 1, 2 *n.*, 3 *v.*

raft·er (raf′tər) a beam forming part of a roof. *n.*

rag (rag) 1 a small, torn piece of old cloth: *a polishing rag, paint rags.* 2 **rags,** *pl.* tattered or worn-out clothes: *dressed in rags.* *n.* —**rag′gy** or **rag′ged·y,** *adj.* **in rags,** torn or worn out: *Her clothes were in rags.*

rag·a·muf·fin (rag′ə muf′in) a small, dirty or ragged child. This word is often used affectionately. *n.*

rage (rāj) 1 violent anger: *Blind with rage, he stormed out of the house. She flew into a rage.* 2 talk, act, or move violently: *"Get out!" he raged. A storm is raging.* 3 what everybody wants for a short time; the fashion: *Baggy jeans were all the rage that year.* 1, 3 *n.*, 2 *v.*, **raged, rag·ing.**

rag·ged (rag′id) 1 worn or torn into rags: *ragged clothing.* 2 wearing torn or badly worn-out clothing: *a ragged beggar.* 3 not smooth and tidy; rough; uneven: *a ragged edge, a ragged lawn.* *adj.*

rag·weed (rag′wēd′) a wild plant whose greenish flowers produce a great deal of pollen in the fall, causing hay fever or an allergic reaction for some people. *n.*

raid (rād) 1 attack suddenly: *They raided the enemy camp in the night.* 2 enter and seize what is inside: *We raided the fridge for snacks after school.* 3 either of these actions: *The police made a raid on the thieves' hideout.* 1, 2 *v.*, 3 *n.*

rail (rāl) 1 a long bar of wood or metal: *a fence rail, a stair rail.* The bars laid along the ground for a train to run on are called rails. 2 railway: *We travelled by rail.* *n.*

a bat	e bed	i bid	o pot	u cup	th thin
ā cake	ē me	ī bite	ō go	ū rude	ᴛʜ then
ä bar	ə about	ər over	ô for	ů put	zh measure

Rain

Rain is part of the water cycle. Moisture in the land and sea is evaporated by the heat of the sun, forms into clouds, and eventually falls back to Earth in some form of precipitation.

Rising water vapour cools and condenses into water droplets which form into clouds. At freezing level, the droplets become ice crystals and grow into snowflakes. Most rain is formed by snowflakes melting as they fall.

A rainbow forms when sunlight shines through raindrops. Each raindrop acts as a prism, breaking the white sunlight into different colours.

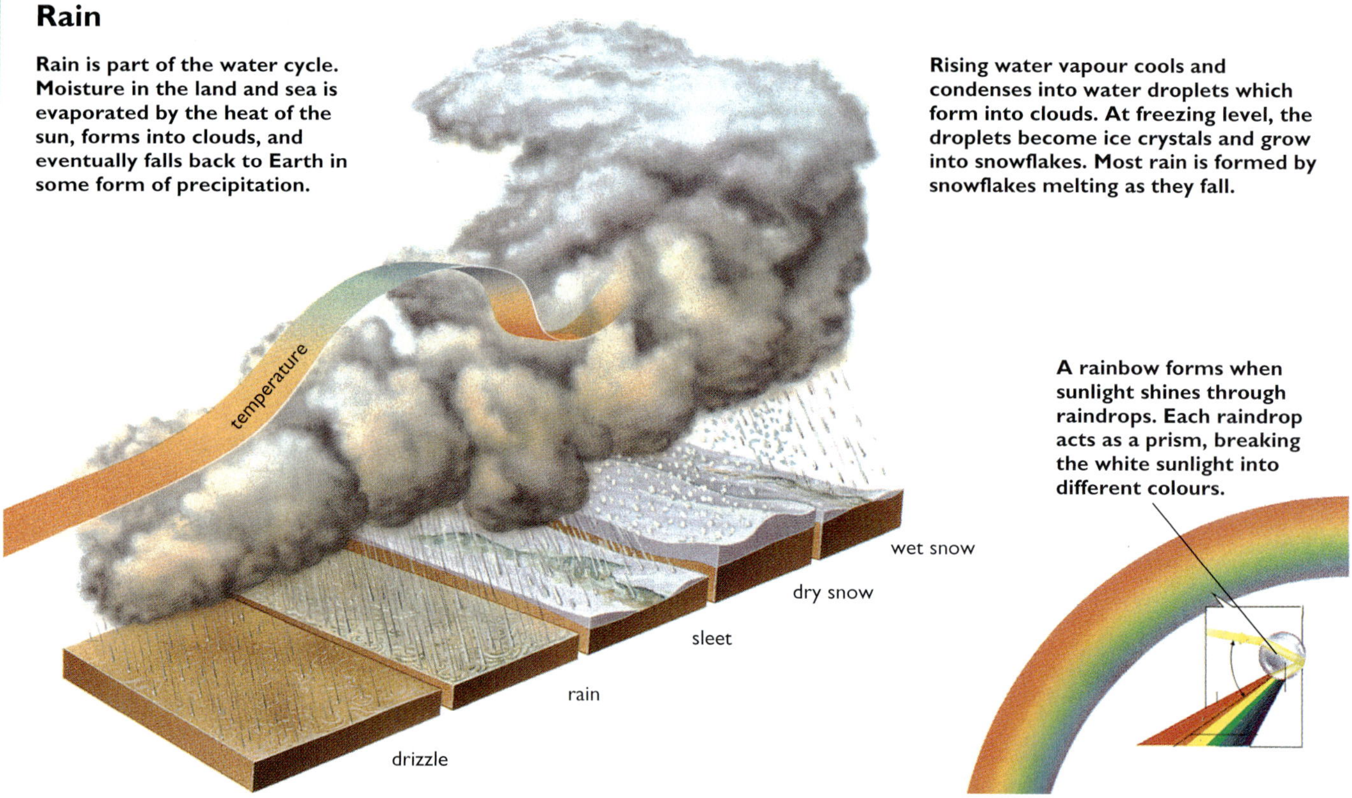

rail•ing (rā′ling) a bar or rail to hold on to for safety, on a staircase, balcony, etc. *n.*

rail•road (rāl′rōd′) 1 another word for "railway." 2 to work on a railway: *He has been railroading all his life.* 3 *Informal.* rush or pressure someone into something: *They railroaded me into signing the forms.* 1 *n.*, 2, 3 *v.*

rail•way (rāl′wā′) 1 a track with two parallel steel rails for the wheels of a train to run on. **Railroad** is another word for it. 2 a business or company that runs a system of train transportation. The tracks, stations, and the trains themselves all belong to the railway. *n.*

rain (rān) 1 water falling in drops from clouds. Rain forms when water vapour in the atmosphere condenses. 2 have rain falling: *It rained all day.* 3 fall or cause to fall like rain: *Sparks rained down from the burning roof. The tree rained blossoms on the grass.* 4 a shower of anything: *a rain of bullets.* 1, 4 *n.*, 2, 3 *v.* —**rain′y,** *adj.*

rain•bow (rān′bō′) an arch of coloured light seen in the sky when the sun shines through rain, mist, or spray. The seven colours of the rainbow are red, orange, yellow, green, blue, indigo, and violet. *n.*

rainbow trout (rān′bō trout′) a trout with black spots and a pinkish or reddish band along its sides. This freshwater fish varies so much in appearance that it has several names depending on where it lives. Two of its names are **Kamloops trout** and **steelhead.**

rain•coat (rān′kōt′) a waterproof coat worn for protection from rain. *n.*

rain•drop (rān′drop′) a drop of rain. *n.*

rain•fall (rān′fol′) 1 a shower of rain. 2 the amount of water that falls in the form of rain, sleet, or snow within a given time and area: *The yearly rainfall in Vancouver is much greater than in Regina.* *n.*

rain•for•est (rān′fȯr′ist) a large area of thick forest where it rains much of the time. Rainforests are found in tropical and temperate climates.

raise (rāz) 1 lift up, put up, set up, or send up: *to raise your hand, to raise a monument. The bus raised a cloud of dust.* 2 increase in degree, amount, price, etc.: *to raise the rent.* 3 an increase in pay: *He asked for a raise.* 4 bring up; care for and train: *to raise children.* 5 grow; breed: *The farmer raises chickens and corn.* 6 gather: *to raise money for a new science lab.* 7 mention or ask about: *The speaker raised an interesting point.* 8 cause a reaction: *A funny remark raises a laugh.* 9 bring back to life: *to raise the dead.* 1, 2, 4–9 *v.*, **raised, rais•ing;** 3 *n.*
raise the roof, *Informal.* make a big fuss or loud noise.

rai•sin (rā′zən) a sweet, dried grape. *n.*

rake (rāk) **1** a long-handled tool that has a bar at one end with teeth in it. A rake is used for smoothing the soil or gathering together loose leaves, cut grass, hay, etc. **2** move or clear with a rake: *Rake the yard. Rake the leaves off the grass.* **3** gather: *We raked up enough money to rent a canoe.* **4** scratch as a rake would: *The thorny branches raked his leg.* 1 *n.,* 2–4 *v.,* **raked, rak·ing.**
rake it in, make large amounts of money.
rake someone over the coals, scold very severely.

ral·ly (ral′ē) **1** get ready to try again with new courage: *The captain was able to rally the fleeing troops. After a bad first period, our team rallied and managed a tie.* **2** bring or come together to act or give help: *Sid rallied his classmates to clean up the school after the fair. She rallied to the side of her frightened sister.* **3** start to get better: *The sick man may rally now.* **4** the act of rallying. **5** a gathering of many people for action or to create unity and enthusiasm: *a political rally, a youth rally.* A **car rally** is a driving contest done for fun on public roads. 1–3 *v.,* **ral·lied, ral·ly·ing;** 4, 5 *n., pl.* **ral·lies.**

ram (ram) **1** a male sheep. **2** strike violently: *One ship rammed the other ship. In the dark, I rammed my head against the steel door.* **3** force: *He rammed the bolt into the wall.* 1 *n.,* 2, 3 *v.,* **rammed, ram·ming.**

RAM *abbreviation for* Random Access Memory, the part of a computer's memory where data is stored temporarily before being saved to a disk or hard drive. While in RAM, the information can be changed or erased.

Ram·a·dan (rà′mə dàn′ *or* rà′mə dàn′) in Islam, the month set aside for prayer and fasting. *n.*

ram·ble (ram′bəl) **1** wander; go walking here and there for fun: *We rambled through the woods.* **2** a walk for fun, not to go to any special place. **3** talk or write on and on with no clear connections. **4** spread or grow in different directions with no plan: *rambling vines, a rambling old house.* 1, 3, 4 *v.,* **ram·bled, ram·bling;** 2 *n.*

ram·bunc·tious (ram bungk′shəs) wild and noisy: *The babysitter said that the kids were pretty rambunctious all evening.* *adj.*

ramp (ramp) a sloping walk or roadway connecting two different levels. It may lead from a door to a sidewalk, from a road to a highway, into a parking garage, etc. *n.*

ram·page (ram′pāj) **1** a fit of wild or violent behaviour: *The elephant went on a rampage and injured its keeper.* **2** rush wildly around; behave violently. 1 *n.,* 2 *v.,* **ram·paged, ram·pag·ing.**

ram·pant (ram′pənt) growing or spreading without control: *The vines ran rampant over the fence. Disease was rampant during the famine.* *adj.*

ram·part (ram′pàrt *or* ram′pərt) a wide bank of earth, often with a wall on top, built around a fort to help defend it. *n.*

ram·shack·le (ram′shak′əl) old and falling apart; tumbledown: *ramshackle old buildings.* *adj.*

ran (ran) the past tense of **run:** *The dog ran after the cat.* *v.*

ranch (ranch) **1** a large farm with grazing land, used for raising cattle, sheep, or horses. **2** any farm used to raise one kind of animal: *a chinchilla ranch.* **3** work on a ranch; operate a ranch. 1, 2 *n.,* 3 *v.*
—ranch′er, *n.*

ran·cid (ran′sid) **1** stale: *rancid butter.* **2** tasting or smelling like stale fat or butter: *a rancid odour.* *adj.*

ran·dom (ran′dəm) happening or done by chance, with no pattern, reason, or plan: *a random choice, random acts of kindness.* *adj.*
at random, by chance; with no plan: *She took a book at random from the shelf.*

rang (rang) the past tense of **ring²:** *The phone rang.* *v.*

range (rānj) **1** a variety of possibilities within certain limits: *a range of colours to choose from, a range of prices from 5 cents to $25, students from a wide age range.* **2** vary within certain limits: *Her hobbies range from knitting to hockey.* **3** the longest distance anything can reach or travel: *the range of hearing. The range of this water gun is 15 m.* **4** a row or line of mountains. **5** be found; occur: *a plant ranging from Canada to Mexico.* **6** the area in which a certain plant or animal lives. **7** wander over; rove; roam: *Buffaloes once ranged the plains.* **8** land for grazing; ranchland; grassland. **9** a stove for cooking: *an electric range.* **10** a place to practise shooting: *a rifle range.* 1, 3, 4, 6, 8–10 *n.,* 2, 5, 7 *v.,* **ranged, rang·ing.**

rang·er (rān′jər) a person who watches over a forest, checking for fires, lost hikers, and so on from a tower. This person is usually called a **forest ranger.** *n.*

rank¹ (rangk) **1** a position that can be compared to others as higher or lower; a level: *a writer of the highest rank. He was promoted to the rank of colonel.* **2** have or give a certain position in relation to others that are higher or lower: *Brad ranked low in the test. Rank the continents in order of size.* **3** one of many rows or lines of people or things, especially soldiers. 1, 3 *n.,* 2 *v.*
the rank and file, the ordinary people in an organization as opposed to the leaders: *There was some grumbling among the rank and file.* A similar expression is **the ranks.**

a bat	e bed	i bid	o pot	u cup	th thin
ā cake	ē me	ī bite	ō go	ū rude	ᴛʜ then
à bar	ə about	ər over	ò for	ù put	zh measure

rank² (rangk) 1 large, coarse, and growing thickly: *rank weeds.* 2 having a strong, unpleasant smell or taste: *rank cigar smoke.* 3 extreme: *rank nonsense.* *adj.*

ran·kle (rang′kəl) continue to give pain: *The memory of the insult rankled in his mind.* *v.,* **ran·kled, ran·kling.**

ran·sack (ran′sak) search through thoroughly, especially to rob, and leave things in a mess: *The thief ransacked the house for jewellery.* *v.*

ran·som (ran′səm) 1 money paid to set someone free: *The robbers held the travellers as prisoners in hope of getting a ransom.* 2 buy the freedom of someone who is being held prisoner: *They ransomed the kidnapped child with a large sum of money.* 1 *n.,* 2 *v.*

rant (rant) 1 speak wildly, violently, or noisily for a long time. 2 a long, violent, noisy speech. 1 *v.,* 2 *n.*

rap¹ (rap) 1 a quick, sharp blow or knock: *a rap on the door.* 2 knock sharply; tap: *She called us to order by rapping on the table.* 1 *n.,* 2 *v.,* **rapped, rap·ping.**
take the rap, accept the punishment for something.

CONFUSABLES .... rap

rap means "knock": *I heard a rap on the door.*
wrap means "cover": *Help me to wrap the present.*

rap² (rap) 1 a kind of popular music with rhyming verses that are quickly chanted or shouted to a strong, fast beat. 2 perform rap music. 3 *Informal.* talk.
1, 3 *n.,* 2, 3 *v.,* **rapped, rap·ping.** —**rap·per,** *n.*

rape (rāp) 1 the crime of forcing someone to have sexual intercourse. 2 commit this crime on someone.
1 *n.,* 2 *v.,* **raped, rap·ing.**

rap·id (rap′id) 1 very quick; fast: *a rapid walk; a rapid worker.* 2 **rapids,** *pl.* a part of a river where the water rushes very fast over rocks that are near the surface: *The boat overturned in the rapids.* 1 *adj.,* 2 *n.*
—**rap′id·ly,** *adv.* —**ra·pid′i·ty,** *n.*

ra·pi·er (rā′pē ər) a long, two-edged sword. *n.*

rapt (rapt) lost in delight; completely absorbed: *The girls listened with rapt attention.* *adj.*

rap·ture (rap′chər) overwhelming joy: *He gazed with rapture at his newborn baby.* *n.* —**rap′tur·ous,** *adj.*

rare¹ (rer) 1 almost never found or seen; hardly ever happening: *Pelicans are rare birds in eastern Canada. Earthquakes are rare in Alberta.* 2 unusually good or great: *Edison had rare powers as an inventor.* *adj.,* **rar·er, rar·est.** —**rare′ly,** *adv.* —**rar′i·ty,** *n.*

rare² (rer) of meat, not cooked much: *a rare steak.* *adj.,* **rar·er, rar·est.**

rar·ing (rer′ing) *Informal.* very eager: *raring to go, raring for a fight.* *adj.*

ras·cal (ras′kəl) a mischievous person; a playful troublemaker. *n.* —**ras′cal·ly,** *adj.*

rash¹ (rash) done with too little thought; careless; unwise: *It is rash to cross the street without looking both ways.* *adj.*

rash² (rash) a condition where sore or itchy red spots or patches appear on the skin. It is often a reaction to something eaten or touched. *n.*

rasp (rasp) 1 make a harsh, grating sound: *The old gate rasped on its hinges.* 2 a harsh, grating sound: *a rasp in a person's voice.* 3 a coarse file with pointed teeth.
1 *v.,* 2, 3 *n.* —**rasp′ing** or **rasp′y,** *adj.*

rasp·ber·ry (raz′ber′e) 1 a small fruit that grows on a thorny bush. Raspberries are usually red or black.
2 *Slang.* a noise you make with your tongue between your lips. *n., pl.* **rasp·ber·ries.**

rat (rat) 1 a long-tailed rodent resembling a mouse, but larger and bolder. Rats are grey, black, brown, or white.
2 🍁 another word for "muskrat." 3 a person who is mean or cannot be trusted. 4 *Slang.* to tell on someone: *They ratted on me.* 1–3 *n.,* 4 *v.,* **rat·ted, rat·ting.**
—**rat′ter,** *n.*
smell a rat, suspect a trick or scheme: *I smelled a rat when none of the others showed up.*

Word Family.......... rat

rat race: a way of life that is rushed and competitive
rats!: an exclamation of annoyance or disappointment
rat-trap: a rack with a spring, to carry things on a bike
ratty: rather old and tattered; shabby

ratch·et (rach′it) an arrangement that lets something turn in one direction but not the other. It has a wheel with teeth that strike against a catch with a clicking noise. Some screwdrivers have ratchets. *n.*

rate (rāt) 1 an amount that is measured in relation to something else: *The population is growing at the rate of ten percent a year. Her rate for piano lessons is $18 per half hour.* 2 set the value or quality of something at a certain level: *He was rated one of the country's top artists.* 3 a level of quality; grade: *first rate, second rate.* 4 be judged; rank: *She rates high as a musician.* 5 *Informal.* be worthy of: *He doesn't rate. She rates the best seat in the house.*
1, 3 *n.,* 2, 4, 5 *v.,* **rat·ed, rat·ing.**
at any rate, anyway; in any case.

rate·pay·er (rāt′pā′ər) a person who pays taxes to the government of a city or town. *n.*

rath·er (raᴛʜ′ər) **1** more willingly: *I would rather go today than tomorrow.* **2** more appropriately: *This is for your parents to decide rather than for you.* **3** more correctly: *They sat up till one o'clock Monday night, or, rather, Tuesday morning.* **4** pretty; quite; more than a little: *I am rather tired.* *adv.*

rat·i·fy (rat′ə fī′) give official approval: *Parliament ratified the treaty.* *v.,* **rat·i·fied, rat·i·fy·ing.** **—rat′i·fi·ca′tion,** *n.*

rat·ing (rā′ting) a grade that measures how good or how popular something is according to some scale: *This car got a high rating for safety in crash tests.* *n.*

ra·ti·o (rā′shō) the relation of one number or quantity to another. If there are 8 sheep and 3 cows on the farm, the ratio of sheep to cows is 8 to 3 or 8:3. It would be the same ratio if there were 16 sheep and 6 cows, or 80 sheep and 30 cows: there are still 8 sheep for every 3 cows. *n., pl.* **ra·ti·os.**

ra·tion (rash′ən) **1** a fixed amount of anything, especially food, allowed for one person or family when supplies are scarce: *daily rations of sugar, a weekly ration of gas.* **2** give out supplies in strictly limited amounts when they are scarce: *Food was rationed in wartime.* 1 *n.,* 2 *v.*

ra·tion·al (rash′ə nəl) **1** sensible; reasonable; based on reason: *a rational explanation, rational behaviour.* **2** able to think and reason logically: *As children grow older, they become more rational.* *adj.*

ra·tion·ale (rash′ə nal′) a reason or set of reasons for a certain way of acting: *The rationale for this decision is that it will save us money in the long run.* To find or give reasons for an action is to **rationalize** it. *n.*

rational number (rash′ə nəl num′bər) a whole number or a fraction that does not have zero as its denominator. The numbers 2, –5, 1.2, and ½ are rational numbers.

rat·tan (rə tan′) the stems of a kind of palm tree, used for wickerwork, canes, and so on. *n.*

rat·tle (rat′əl) **1** a number of short, sharp sounds like the noise of hard things being shaken against each other: *the rattle of empty bottles.* **2** make or cause to make this noise: *The window rattled in the wind. She rattled the dishes.* A **rattletrap** is an old, broken-down car that shakes so much it rattles. **3** a baby's toy that makes a noise when it is shaken. **4** talk or say quickly and with little feeling: *She rattled off the poem from memory.* **5** *Informal.* confuse; upset: *She was so rattled that she forgot her speech.* 1, 3 *n.,* 2, 4, 5 *v.,* **rat·tled, rat·tling.**

A rattlesnake's rattle is a set of loosely interlocking segments of horn. Two to four new segments are added every year — one every time the snake sheds its skin — and some older segments fall off. Shaking its rattle is a warning that the snake is about to strike.

rat·tle·snake (rat′əl snāk′) a poisonous snake with a thick body, a broad head, and a tail that makes a rattling noise. **Rattler** is another name for it. *n.*

rau·cous (rok′əs) hoarse; harsh-sounding: *We heard the raucous caw of a crow in the cornfield.* *adj.*

rav·age (rav′ij) **1** damage greatly; destroy: *The fire ravaged many square kilometres of forest.* **2** great damage: *the ravages of war.* 1 *v.,* **rav·aged, rav·ag·ing;** 2 *n.*

rave (rāv) **1** talk wildly; be out of your mind. **2** talk with great enthusiasm: *She raved about the food.* *v.,* **raved, rav·ing.**
a rave review, very positive, enthusiastic comments about something: *The movie got a rave review in the newspaper.*

ra·ven (rā′vən) a large bird with shiny black feathers, like a crow but larger. *n.*

rav·en·ous (rav′ə nəs) very hungry: *We were ravenous after the long hike.* *adj.*

ra·vine (rə vēn′) a long, deep, narrow valley made by a river or glacier. *n.*

rav·i·o·li (rav′ē ō′lē) pasta in the form of little pockets filled with chopped meat or cheese. They are boiled in water and served with a tomato sauce. *n.*

rav·ish·ing (rav′i shing) very beautiful; enchanting: *You look ravishing in that dress.* *adj.*

a bat	e bed	i bid	o pot	u cup	th thin
ā cake	ē me	ī bite	ō go	ū rude	ᴛʜ then
ä bar	ə about	ər over	ò for	ů put	zh measure

raw (ro) 1 not cooked: *raw meat.* 2 in the natural state; not yet made into anything treated: *Raw milk has not been pasteurized.* Iron ore and logs are examples of **raw materials.** 3 damp, windy, and cold: *raw weather.* 4 with the skin rubbed off; sore: *My new shoes made a raw spot on my heel.* 5 not experienced; not trained. *adj.*
a raw deal, an unfair arrangement.

raw·hide (ro′hīd′) the untreated skin of cattle. Rawhide is used to make thongs, whips, etc. *n.*

ray[1] (rā) 1 a line or beam of light: *the rays of the sun.* 2 a line or stream of any other kind of radiant energy: *rays of heat, X rays.* 3 a slight trace; faint gleam: *a ray of hope, a ray of intelligence.* 4 a thin line or part coming out from a centre, like any of the arms of a starfish. In math, any straight line extending from a point is a ray. *n.*

Like their relatives the sharks, rays have skeletons made of flexible cartilage rather than bone.

ray[2] (rā) a fish related to the shark, with a broad, flat body and very wide fins. *n.*

ray·on (rā′on) a kind of thread or cloth made from cellulose, which comes from wood pulp and other plant materials. *n.*

raze (rāz) tear down completely: *The old school was razed and a new one built in its place.* *v.,* **razed, raz·ing.**

ra·zor (rā′zər) a tool used for shaving hair from your face or body: *an electric razor, a safety razor.* *n.*

razz (raz) *Slang.* tease somebody in a good-natured way: *We had a good time razzing Chuck about his new haircut.* *v.*

RCMP or **R.C.M.P.** *abbreviation for* Royal Canadian Mounted Police, the police force of the federal government of Canada.

Rd. *abbreviation for* road.

re– *a prefix meaning:* 1 again, as in *reappear, re-enter.* 2 in a new way, as in *redecorate, rearrange.* 3 back, as in *repay, replace.*

Word Family............ re-

The most common meaning of the prefix **re-** is "again." You can easily figure out the meaning of these words.

reappear	rearrange	rebuild	recreate
redecorate	redial	rediscover	redo
re-echo	re-elect	re-enter	refreeze
reorganize	rephrase	replay	reread
reset	rethink	retry	reunite
reuse	rewind	rewrap	rewrite

reach (rēch) 1 get to; arrive at; come to: *Your letter reached me yesterday.* 2 get close enough to touch: *I cannot reach the top of the wall.* 3 move or stretch to touch or grab something: *He reached for his flashlight. She reached out and took my arm.* 4 communicate with: *I could not reach him by phone.* 5 stretch or go all the way; extend: *Canada reaches from sea to sea.* 6 the act of reaching or the distance a person or thing can reach: *Keep it out of the baby's reach.* 7 a long stretch or extent: *the vast reaches of outer space.* 1–5 *v.,* 6, 7 *n.*

re·act (rē akt′) 1 act in response: *Dogs react to kindness by showing affection. How did she react when you said that?* 2 respond in a negative way; respond by rejecting or fighting: *An allergy is your body reacting to some substance such as cat hair. Some people really react to any kind of criticism.* 3 cause a change by a chemical process: *Acids react on metals.* *v.* **—re·ac′tion,** *n.*

read (rēd) 1 get the meaning of written or printed symbols: *We read books. The blind girl reads special raised print by touching it with her fingers.* 2 learn from written material: *We read about the customs of other lands.* 3 say written words out loud: *Please read this story to me.* 4 show by numbers, letters, or other symbols: *The thermometer reads 20°C. This plane ticket reads "From Regina to Calgary."* 5 get the meaning of; understand: *to read a person's face, to read the sky for signs of a storm.* *v.,* **read** (red), **read·ing.** **—read′a·ble,** *adj.*

CONFUSABLES .... read/reed

read means "get the meaning of": *Read the sentence.*
reed means "tall grass": *Reeds often grow in wetlands.*

CONFUSABLES ..... read/red

read is the past tense of *read*: *I read a book today.*
red is a colour: *I have red hair.*

read·er (rē′dər) 1 a person or machine that reads. 2 a book for learning and practising reading. *n.*

read·y (red′ē) 1 fit to be used or to do something right away; prepared: *Dinner is ready. We were ready to start at nine.* 2 willing: *She is ready to forgive.* 3 likely; liable: *This balloon is ready to pop at any moment.* 4 quick; prompt: *a ready answer, ready help.* 5 easily available: *ready money.* *adj.,* **read·i·er, read·i·est.** —**read′i·ly** (red′ə lē), *adv.* —**read′i·ness,** *n.*

read·y–made (red′ē mād′) made or prepared beforehand by someone else or by chance so it can be used as is: *ready-made clothes, a ready-made excuse.* *adj.*

re·al (rēl) 1 existing as a fact; not imagined or made up; actual; true: *a real place, the real reason.* 2 genuine; not fake: *real diamonds.* *adj.*

USING WORDS .... real

Real is an adjective: *real friends.*
Really is an adverb: *really happy, really well.*

In writing, be careful not to use **real** as an adverb. Write *really tall* not *real tall.*

real estate (rēl′ i stāt′) 1 land, together with anything built on it. 2 the business of buying and selling land and buildings: *She works in real estate.*

re·al·is·tic (rē′ə lis′tik) 1 like the real thing; lifelike. 2 seeing things as they really are; practical. A person who is like this is a **realist** (re′ə list). *adj.* —**re′al·ism′,** *n.*

re·al·i·ty (rē al′ə tē) 1 what exists or happens: *Don't try to hide from reality.* 2 a real thing; an actual fact: *War and disease are sad realities.* *n., pl.* **re·al·i·ties.**
in reality, really; in fact: *We thought he was joking, but in reality he was serious.*

reality TV (rē al′ə tē tē′vē′) TV programs that show how ordinary people behave in unusual situations.

re·al·ize (rē′ə līz′) 1 be aware of something and understand it: *I realized later that I had hurt his feelings.* 2 make real: *Her dream of going to Europe was finally realized.* *v.,* **re·al·ized, re·al·iz·ing.** —**re′al·i·za′tion,** *n.*

re·al·ly (rē′lē) 1 actually; truly; in fact: *She describes things as they really are.* 2 very; very much: *a really cold day. I really enjoyed that.* 3 an expression of surprise, disbelief, or disapproval: *Really! How could you do that?* 1, 2 *adv.,* 3 *interj.*

realm (relm) 1 a kingdom. 2 a region; range; extent: *The prime minister's realm of influence is very wide.* 3 a particular field of something: *the realm of poetry.* *n.*

ream (rēm) *Informal.* a great deal of written material: *I wrote reams and reams to my cousin in New Brunswick.* *n.*

reap (rēp) 1 cut grain or any other crop and gather it; harvest. 2 get as a result of action: *to reap a reward, to reap the consequences.* *v.* —**reap′er,** *n.*

rear¹ (rēr) back: *The kitchen is in the rear of the house* (*n.*). *Leave by the rear door of the bus* (*adj.*). *n. or adj.*

rear² (rēr) 1 bring up; care for and train: *to rear children.* 2 raise; lift up: *The snake reared its head.* 3 of an animal, rise on its hind legs: *The horse reared as the fire engine dashed past.* *v.*

rea·son (rē′zən) 1 an explanation for an action or happening: *The reason we go to school is to learn. Sickness is the reason for her absence.* 2 think clearly or logically: *I can't reason well when I'm so tired.* 3 the ability to think clearly. 4 discuss or argue logically: *Reason with him and try to make him change his mind.* 5 good sense; common sense: *That idea is completely contrary to reason.* 1, 3, 5 *n.,* 2, 4 *v.* —**rea′son·ing,** *n.*
stand to reason, be reasonable and sensible: *It stands to reason that he would resent your insults.*

rea·son·a·ble (rē′zə nə bəl) 1 making sense; logical; not foolish. 2 moderate; fair; decent: *a reasonable price, a reasonable amount of work. Come at a reasonable time.* *adj.* —**rea′son·a·bly,** *adv.*

re·as·sure (rē′ə shūr′) make someone feel confident and safe: *The captain's calmness during the storm reassured the passengers.* *v.,* **re·as·sured, re·as·sur·ing.** —**re′as·sur′ance,** *n.*

re·bate (rē′bāt) an amount of money taken off a price, or returned to people after they have paid it: *If you mail in three other video UPCs with your receipt, you will get a five-dollar rebate on this video.* *n.*

reb·el (reb′əl *for 1 and 2,* ri bel′ *for 3*) 1 a person who fights against authority instead of obeying: *The rebels armed themselves against the government.* 2 fighting against law or authority: *a rebel army.* 3 fight against law or authority: *Tori rebelled against the school rules and took off at recess time.* 1 *n.,* 2 *adj.,* 3 *v.,* **re·belled, re·bel·ling.** —**re·bel′lion,** *n.* —**re·bel′lious,** *adj.*

a bat	e bed	i bid	o pot	u cup	th thin
ā cake	ē me	ī bite	ō go	ū rude	ᴛʜ then
ä bar	ə about	ər over	ô for	u̇ put	zh measure

re•born (rē bôrn′) born again: *Our hopes were reborn after the team's victory.* *adj.* **—re•birth′,** *n.*

re•bound (ri bound′ *for 1,* rē′bound′ *for 2*) **1** bounce back. **2** the act of bouncing back: *You hit the ball on the rebound in handball.* **3** recover fully: *to rebound after an illness.* 1, 3 *v.,* 2 *n.*

re•buff (ri buf′) **1** reject or turn away: *My offer of help was coldly rebuffed.* **2** a rude rejection or refusal: *I was hurt by his rebuff.* 1 *v.,* 2 *n.*

re•buke (ri byūk′) **1** scold; tell someone off: *Mr. Kim rebuked Costa for throwing food on the floor.* **2** an expression of disapproval; a scolding: *Her sharp rebuke caught me off guard.* 1 *v.,* **re•buked, re•buk•ing;** 2 *n.*

re•bus (rē′bəs) a puzzle that uses pictures to suggest syllables or words. A picture of a cat on a log is a rebus for the word *catalogue.* *n.*

re•call (ri kol′ *for 1 and 3,* rē′kol′ *for 2 and 4*) **1** call back to mind; remember: *I can recall stories that my mom told me years ago.* **2** ability to remember things: *She has such good recall that she never writes anything down.* **3** call back; order back: *to recall an ambassador.* **4** an act of calling back; ordering back: *The manufacturer ordered a recall of the cars because of faulty brakes.* 1, 3 *v.,* 2, 4 *n.*

re•cap (rē′kap *for 1,* ri kap′ *for 2*) **1** a brief summary or review: *We gave Victoria a recap of what had happened while she was away.* **2** sum up or review briefly: *At the end of her presentation on space shuttles, Heather recapped the main points.* This word is a shortened form. **Recapitulation** (rē′kə pich′ə lā′shən) is the full form of the noun; the full form for the verb is **recapitulate** (rē′kə pich′ə lāt′). 1 *n.,* 2 *v.,* **re•capped, re•cap•ping.**

re•cap•ture (rē kap′chər) **1** capture again; get back. **2** bring back; recall: *The film recaptures the days of the horse and buggy.* *v.,* **re•cap•tured, re•cap•tur•ing.**

re•cede (ri sēd′) **1** move back or farther away: *The flood waters are receding. As we drove away, the village receded in the distance.* **2** slope backward: *a receding chin.* *v.,* **re•ced•ed, re•ced•ing.**

re•ceipt (ri sēt′) **1** a written statement that something has been received: *Sign the receipt for this parcel.* **2** **receipts,** *pl.* money received: *Our receipts from the garage sale were over $80.* **3** the act of receiving: *This bill must be paid immediately upon receipt.* *n.*

re•ceive (ri sēv′) **1** get something given or sent to you: *The soldier received a letter from home. I received many presents on my birthday.* **2** take and hold: *This beam receives the whole weight of the roof. A small pool receives the water from the fountain.* **3** accept or welcome; respond to: *We were warmly received at the door. His suggestion was not well received.* **4** in radio or television, change electromagnetic waves into sound or images: *Our TV receives a lot better since we got a satellite dish.* *v.,* **re•ceived, re•ceiv•ing.**

re•ceiv•er (ri sē′vər) **1** a person or thing that receives. **2** the part of a telephone that you put to your ear. **3** the part of a radio or TV set that changes electromagnetic waves into sound or images: *a radio or television receiver.* *n.*

re•cent (rē′sənt) done, made, or happening not long ago: *recent events, a recent visit.* *adj.* **—re′cent•ly,** *adv.*

re•cep•ta•cle (ri sep′tə kəl) a container or place used to put things in. Bags, baskets, and garbage bins are all receptacles. *n.*

re•cep•tion (ri sep′shən) **1** the act or manner of receiving: *Her calm reception of the bad news surprised us. We were given a warm reception on returning home.* **2** a formal party in honour of some person or occasion, with invited guests: *a wedding reception.* **3** the quality of the sound or picture on a radio or TV set. *n.*

re•cep•tion•ist (ri sep′shə nist) an office worker whose job is to welcome visitors, tell them where to go, give out information, answer phones, and so on. *n.*

re•cep•tive (ri sep′tiv) welcoming new ideas, suggestions, and information: *a receptive mind.* *adj.*

re•cess (rē′ses *for 1,* ri ses′ *for 2–5*) **1** a break from work or classes: *Our school has a fifteen-minute recess in the morning and afternoon.* **2** take a break: *Parliament has recessed for the holiday season.* **3** an inner place or part: *the recesses of a cave, the recesses of one's thoughts.* **4** a part in a wall, or other surface, set back from the rest: *This bench will fit nicely in that recess.* **5** put in a recess; set back. 1, 3, 4 *n.,* 2, 5 *v.*

re•ces•sion (ri sesh′ən) a time when most people are spending less money and many businesses are doing poorly. A recession is less severe than a depression. *n.*

rec•i•pe (res′ə pē) **1** a set of directions for making something to eat: *Please give me your recipe for oatmeal cookies.* **2** a set of directions for reaching some result: *a recipe for success.* *n.*

re•cip•i•ent (ri sip′ē ənt) a person who receives something: *All the recipients of the prizes had their names printed in the paper.* *n.*

re•cip•ro•cal (ri sip′rə kəl) **1** given or done in return: *We have a reciprocal arrangement for vacations; we look after our neighbours' pets and then they look after ours.*

To **reciprocate** is to do for someone else what that person has done for you. **2** the number that you need to multiply another number by to get 1. The reciprocal of 3 is ⅓, and the reciprocal of ⅓ is 3. 1 *adj.,* 2 *n.*

re·cit·al (ri sī′təl) **1** a public performance given by a group of music or dance students. **2** a concert by a single performer. **3** a telling of facts in detail: *a boring recital of all his experiences in the hospital.* *n.*

re·cite (ri sīt′) **1** say from memory, often in front of an audience: *He recited a Dennis Lee poem for us.* **2** tell in detail: *She recited the day's adventures.* *v.,* **re·cit·ed, re·cit·ing.** **—rec′i·ta′tion** (res′ə tā′shən), *n.*

reck·less (rek′lis) with no thought for what could happen; careless: *Reckless driving causes accidents.* *adj.*

reck·on (rek′ən) **1** *Informal.* think; suppose: *I reckon it'll snow tomorrow.* **2** calculate; figure out a total: *We reckoned that we would need five large pizzas for the whole class.* *v.*

by my reckoning, according to my calculation or estimate: *By my reckoning we are 10 km from home.*

day of reckoning, a time when you must face consequences.

reckon on, plan on; expect: *He didn't reckon on breaking his leg when he decided to try skiing.*

reckon with, **a** take into account: *We are going to have to reckon with higher prices for food.* **b** take seriously: *She is someone to be reckoned with.*

re·claim (ri klām′) **1** make poor land useful for farming or building on: *The farmer reclaimed the swamp by draining it.* **2** get by recycling: *to reclaim rubber from old tires.* **3** get back: *He had trouble reclaiming the money he had lent.* *v.* **—rec′la·ma′tion** (rek′lə mā′shən), *n.*

re·cline (ri klīn′) lean back; lie down: *The tired woman reclined on the couch.* A **recliner** is an armchair that can be adjusted to tilt back and open out into a footrest at the bottom. *v.,* **re·clined, re·clin·ing.**

rec·luse (ri klūs′ *or* rek′lūs) a person who chooses to live cut off from the world. *n.* **—re·clu′sive,** *adj.*

rec·og·nize (rek′əg nīz′) **1** realize that someone or something is the same one you saw, heard, experienced, etc. before: *You've grown so much; I scarcely recognized you.* **2** identify; pick out: *You can recognize our house by the blue door.* **3** accept or admit; agree that something is real or true: *He recognized that I was right. The new government was not recognized by the United Nations.* **4** give someone or something the praise, thanks, or reward that is deserved: *They recognized her achievement with a plaque on awards night.* *v.,* **rec·og·nized, rec·og·niz·ing.** **—rec′og·ni′tion** (rek′əg nish′ən), *n.*

re·coil (ri koil′) draw back; shrink back: *I recoiled at the sight of the huge spider.* *v.*

rec·ol·lect (rek′ə lekt′) remember. *v.* **—rec′ol·lec′tion,** *n.*

rec·om·mend (rek′ə mend′) **1** speak in favour of; suggest favourably: *The teacher recommended Dorothy for the job. Can you recommend a good computer game?* **2** advise: *The doctor recommended that she stay in bed.* *v.* **—rec′om·men·da′tion** (rek′ə men dā′shən), *n.*

rec·on·cile (rek′ən sīl′) **1** make friends again: *Liam and Kathy had a fight but were soon reconciled.* **2** make agree: *I can't reconcile their story with the facts.* **3** make someone accept a situation: *I had to reconcile myself to a long hospital stay.* *v.,* **rec·on·ciled, rec·on·cil·ing.** **—rec′on·cil′i·a′tion** (rek′ən sil′ē ā′shən), *n.*

re·con·sid·er (rē′kən sid′ər) think about something again and perhaps change your mind: *You might want to reconsider that trip—there's supposed to be a blizzard today.* *v.*

re·con·struct (rē′kən strukt′) **1** rebuild; make over: *Much of the city had to be reconstructed after the fire.* **2** imagine and describe, using the facts that you have, the exact way that something must have happened: *The police tried to reconstruct the accident, to figure out who was at fault.* *v.* **—re′con·struc′tion,** *n.*

re·cord (ri kôrd′ *for 1 and 2,* rek′ərd *for 3–8*) **1** write down or put on disk, film, CD, tape, etc. for future use: *She records her thoughts and feelings in her diary. They recorded the wedding on video.* **2** put in some permanent form; keep for remembrance: *Much information about dinosaurs is recorded in fossils.* **3** a written account, or anything that tells the story of something: *The school keeps a record of each student's progress. Theses bruises are a record of my skiing trip.* **4** the best anyone has done in a certain activity: *The record for high jumping at our school is 128 cm.* **5** the best that has been: *a record wheat crop.* **6** the reputation or past performance of a person or thing: *He has a good driving record.* **7** a thin, flat, vinyl disk with grooves on its surface that was used for storing sounds before there were CDs. It is played on a **record player.** 1, 2, 4 *v.,* 3, 5, 7, 8 *n.,* 6 *adj.* **—re·cord′ing,** *n.*

off the record, not meant to be recorded or quoted: *The Prime Minister was speaking off the record.*

on record, written down, printed, or otherwise made available: *The facts of the murder case are now on record.*

a bat	e bed	i bid	o pot	u cup	th thin
ā cake	ē me	ī bite	ō go	ū rude	ᴛʜ then
ä bar	ə about	ər over	ô for	ù put	zh measure

Recorders

Using a very sensitive and accurate tape recorder is essential in making professional recordings. The one shown at the top of the page is a reel-to-reel tape recorder, which produces very true recordings on a master tape.

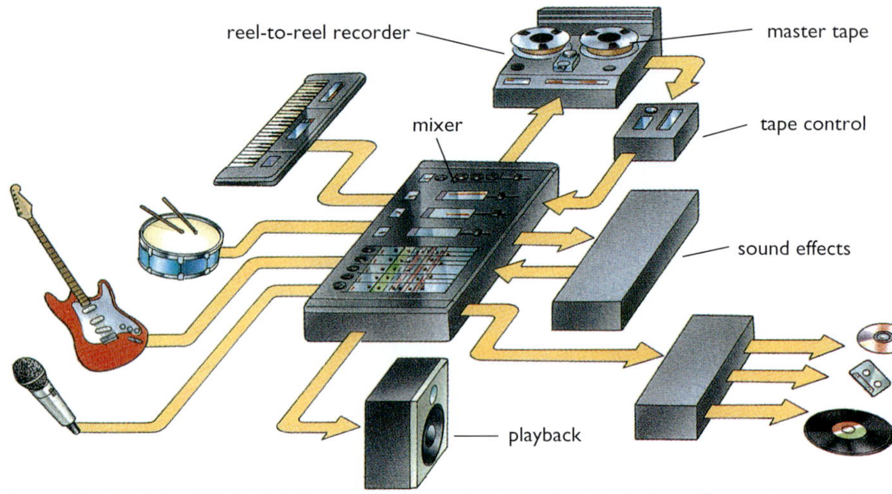

re·cord·er (ri kòr′dər) **1** a wooden musical instrument that sounds a bit like a flute. **2** a machine that records: *a tape recorder, a video recorder.* *n.*

re·count (ri kount′) tell; give an account of: *He recounted the legend of Little Bear.* *v.*

re·coup (ri kūp′) get back or make up for: *From sales at our lemonade stand we not only recouped all we had spent on supplies, but made a profit of $29.* *v.*

re·cov·er (ri kuv′ər) **1** get well again; get back to normal: *She is recovering from a cold.* **2** get back something lost or taken away: *to recover a lost wallet.* **3** make up for: *to recover lost time.* *v.* **—re·cov′er·y,** *n.*

rec·re·a·tion (rek′rē ā′shən) play or relaxation; something done for fun: *Hiking, gardening, and reading are all forms of recreation.* *n.* **—rec′re·a′tion·al,** *adj.*

rec room (rec′ rūm′) short for **recreation room,** a room in a house for playing games, relaxing, watching TV, and so on.

re·cruit (ri krūt′) **1** a new member of the armed forces or any other organization. **2** get people to join the armed forces or any other organization. **3** get people to help: *Mr. Boyko recruited six of us to carry chairs to the gym.* 1 *n.,* 2, 3 *v.*

rec·tan·gle (rek′tang′gəl) a flat, four-sided figure with four right angles. *n.*
—rec·tan′gu·lar (rek tang′gyə lər), *adj.*

rec·ti·fy (rek′tə fī′) make right; fix something that is wrong: *The storekeeper admitted his mistake and was willing to rectify it.* *v.,* **rec·ti·fied, rec·ti·fy·ing.**

re·cu·per·ate (ri kū′pə rāt′) **1** get well or get back to normal: *She has fully recuperated from her illness.* **2** get back; regain: *to recuperate stolen money.* *v.,* **re·cu·per·at·ed, re·cu·per·at·ing.** **—re·cu′pe·ra′tion,** *n.*

re·cur (ri kər′) come back or happen again; be repeated: *Leap year recurs every four years.* *v.,* **re·curred, re·cur·ring.** **—re·cur′rent,** *adj.*

re·cy·cle (rē sī′kəl) reprocess waste material, or send it to be reprocessed, so that it can be used again: *Old cars can be recycled and the steel used again. Our school recycles paper and cans.* *v.,* **re·cy·cled, re·cy·cling.**

red (red) the colour of ripe tomatoes. *n. or adj.,* **red·der, red·dest.** **—red′den,** *v.* **—red′dish,** *adj.*
in the red, *Informal.* in debt. **Red ink** means "debts."
red carpet, the warmest welcome and best treatment, especially in the phrase **roll out the red carpet.**
see red, *Informal.* become very angry.

red blood cell (red′ blud′ sel′) one of the billions of cells in the blood of humans and other animals. They carry oxygen from the lungs to the tissues of the body.

🍁 **Red Chamber** (red′ chām′bər) a name sometimes given to the Canadian Senate because of the colour of the rugs, draperies, etc. in the room where the Senate meets.

re·deem (ri dēm′) **1** cash in; exchange for cash or goods: *to redeem a coupon, to redeem an empty milk jug for 25 cents.* **2** pay off a debt: *to redeem a mortgage.* **3** **redeem yourself,** make up for something bad you have done: *After breaking the vase, he redeemed himself by vacuuming the whole house.* **4** pay to get something back: *When our car was towed, Dad had to pay $220 to redeem it from the pound.* *v.*
—re·demp′tion (ri demp′shən), *n.*
redeeming feature or **redeeming quality,** something that makes up for a lot of bad points: *Great music is the one redeeming feature of this badly acted, badly written film.*

Red Ensign (red′ en′sən) the old flag of Canada, until 1965. It was a red flag with a Union Jack in the top left corner and the national coat of arms to the right. It is still the provincial flag of Ontario.

red–hand•ed (red′ han′did) in the very act of doing something wrong: *The robber was caught red-handed.* *adj.*

red–hot (red′ hot′) very hot; so hot that it glows red: *a red-hot iron.* *adj.*

Red River cart (red′ riv′ər kärt′) a strong two-wheeled cart pulled by oxen or horses, used by pioneers in the West.

re•duce (ri dyūs′ *or* ri dūs′) 1 make less or smaller; decrease: *to reduce prices. We should try to reduce the amount of energy we use.* 2 force into a humiliating condition: *The cruel words reduced me to tears.* 3 change to a simpler form: *The chalk was reduced to powder. If you reduce the fraction* $^{15}/_{35}$ *to its lowest terms, you have* $^{3}/_{7}$. *v.*, **re•duced, re•duc•ing.** —**re•duc′tion** (ri duk′shən), *n.*

re•dun•dant (ri dun′dənt) not needed; extra. In *the two twins,* the word *two* is redundant; *twins* already carries the idea of "two." *adj.* —**re•dun′dan•cy,** *n.*

red–winged blackbird (red′wingd′ blak′bərd′) a blackbird of North America that lives around marshes and fields. The male has a scarlet patch on each wing.

red•wood (red′wůd′) a giant cone-bearing tree of the Pacific coast of North America, sometimes growing over 100 m tall and living thousands of years. Because their wood resists rot, redwoods have been cut down in large numbers in the past and there are few left. *n.*

reed (rēd) 1 any tall grass with a stiff, hollow, jointed stalk that grows in wet places. Reeds have been used for many purposes, such as weaving baskets and mats, for thousands of years. 2 a thin slice of a reed stalk in the mouthpiece of a musical instrument such as a clarinet, that makes sound when a current of air moves it. Nowadays it is made of wood, metal, or plastic instead. 3 a musical instrument with a reed. Clarinets, oboes, and saxophones are reeds, or **reed instruments.** *n.*

reef (rēf) a narrow ridge of rocks or sand just under the surface of the water: *The ship was wrecked on the hidden reef.* *n.*

reek (rēk) 1 a strong, unpleasant smell: *We noticed the reek of rotting vegetables as we entered the cottage.* 2 have a strong, unpleasant smell: *She reeked of cheap perfume.* 1 *n.*, 2 *v.*

reel¹ (rēl) 1 a frame like a spool or wheel, to wind something on such as thread, tape, film, fishing line, etc. A cassette has two little reels of tape inside it. 2 pull in by winding a reel: *She reeled in the fish.* 1 *n.*, 2 *v.*
reel off, say quickly and easily: *Eric reeled off the names of all the provinces and territories and their capital cities.*

reel² (rēl) 1 sway from a heavy blow or shock or from drunkenness; stand or walk dizzily: *The boy reeled when the ball struck him.* 2 spin; whirl: *Her mind reeled at the thought of all that needed to be done.* *v.*

reel³ (rēl) a lively dance, or a piece of music written for it. *n.*

reeve (rēv) 1 in Ontario and some western provinces, the elected leader of the government of a village or rural area. 2 in medieval times, the chief magistrate of a town or district. *n.*

re•fer (ri fər′) 1 mention or speak about: *She referred to the baseball game.* 2 have to do with: *The rule refers only to special cases.* 3 go or send to a source for information or help: *Our teacher referred to the dictionary for the spelling of a word. Let me refer you to the proper department.* 4 hand over; submit: *Let's refer the dispute to the umpire.* 5 stand for: *Does that "she" refer to Emma or to Michelle?* *v.*, **re•ferred, re•fer•ring.**

ref•er•ee (ref′ə rē′) 1 an official in certain games or sports, including hockey and soccer, who settles any disputes and watches to see that everyone plays by the rules. 2 a person who settles any kind of dispute. 3 to act as a referee. 1, 2 *n.*, 3 *v.*, **ref•er•eed, ref•er•ee•ing.**

ref•er•ence (ref′ə rəns) 1 a statement that mentions a particular thing: *In her speech about life in the future, Marilyn made several references to science fiction.* 2 a source of information: *On your "Works Cited" page, list all the references you used for your project.* 3 a description of someone's character or his or her ability to do a certain job: *Our new babysitter had excellent references from other families who had hired him.* 4 someone who can give this kind of information about another person: *He gave the Ross family as a reference.* *n.*
without reference to, regardless of; no matter what: *The law applies to everyone, without reference to race, sex, position, or income.*
with reference to, concerning; having to do with.

ref•er•en•dum (ref′ə ren′dəm) a way of deciding whether the government should do a certain thing by having the citizens themselves vote for or against it. *n.*, *pl.* **ref•er•en•dums** or **ref•er•en•da** (ref′ə ren′da).

a bat	e bed	i bid	o pot	u cup	th thin
ā cake	ē me	ī bite	ō go	ū rude	ᴛʜ then
ä bar	ə about	ər over	ȯ for	ů put	zh measure

re•fill (rē′ fil′ *for 1,* rē′fil′ *for 2*) **1** fill again. **2** the act of refilling, or something to refill with: *This restaurant offers free refills of pop.* 1 *v.,* 2 *n.*

re•fine (ri fīn′) **1** make pure: *Sugar, oil, and metals are refined before they are used.* A factory where this is done is called a **refinery. 2** make something good even better: *to refine your writing skills.* **3** teach someone proper speech and manners, elegance, and good taste. *v.,* **re•fined, re•fin•ing. —re•fine′ment,** *n.*

re•flect (ri flekt′) **1** throw back light, heat, sound, etc.: *The sidewalks reflect heat on a hot day.* **2** give back an image of: *The mirror reflects my face.* **3** reproduce or show like a mirror: *The newspaper reflected the owner's opinions.* **4** think carefully: *Take time to reflect before making important choices.* **5** make someone else look bad or good by your actions: *The dishonesty of one employee can reflect badly on the whole company.* *v.* **—re•flec′tion,** *n.* **—re•flec′tor,** *n.*

re•flex (rē′fleks) an automatic response to something. Sneezing and shivering are physical reflexes; saying "excuse me" can be a social reflex. *n.*

re•for•est (rē′fô′rist) replace trees in an area by planting new ones. *v.* **—re′for•est•a′tion,** *n.*

re•form (ri fôrm′) **1** make or become better by correcting faults: *The government wants to reform health care. The young offender promised to reform if given another chance.* **2** a change in one area that makes things better: *The new Minister of Education made many reforms.* A complete change for the better in a person's character or the way a system works is a **reformation** (ref′ər mā′shən). **3 Reform,** having to do with the Reform Party. 1 *v.,* 2 *n.,* 3 *adj.* **—re•form′er,** *n.*

re•form•a•to•ry (ri fôr′mə tôr′ē) a place where some young offenders are sent to try and help them learn better habits and attitudes. *n., pl.* **re•form•a•to•ries.**

re•fract (ri frakt′) bend a ray of light. Light is refracted when passing from one medium, such as air, into another medium that has a different density, such as water or glass. Water refracts light. *v.* **—re•frac′tion,** *n.*

re•frain[1] (ri frān′) hold yourself back from some action: *Refrain from talking during the performance.* *v.*

re•frain[2] (ri frān′) a phrase or verse that is repeated regularly in a song or poem; a chorus. *n.*

re•fresh (ri fresh′) **1** make fresh again; renew: *His swim refreshed him. Cool drinks are refreshing on a warm day. She refreshed her memory by a glance at the book.* **2** provide a welcome change. *v.* **—re•fresh′ing,** *adj.*

re•fresh•ment (ri fresh′mənt) **1 refreshments,** *pl.* food or drink: *Cake and lemonade were the refreshments at our party.* **2** the act of refreshing, or anything that refreshes: *She took a quick shower for refreshment.* *n.*

re•frig•er•ate (ri frij′ə rāt′) make or keep cold: *Milk and meat must be refrigerated to prevent spoiling.* *v.,* **re•frig•er•at•ed, re•frig•er•at•ing. —re•frig′er•a′tion,** *n.*

Inside the coils of a refrigerator there is a fluid called a refrigerant. It evaporates into a gas, absorbing heat and lowering the temperature. A pump compresses this gas, turning it back into a liquid, and the process repeats itself.

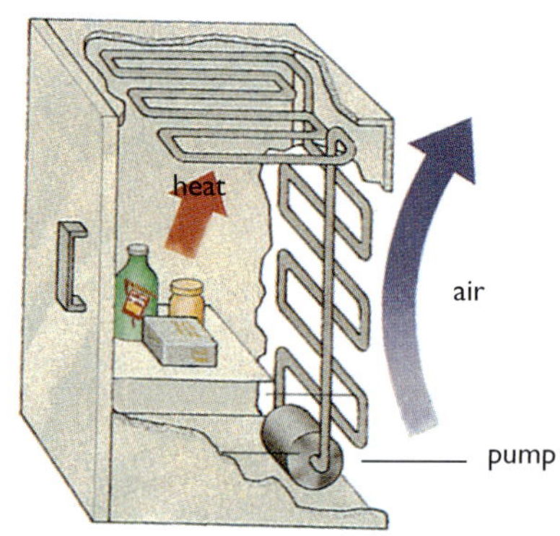

re•frig•er•a•tor (ri frij′ə rā′tər) an appliance for keeping things cold, especially food and drink. This word is often shortened informally to **fridge.** *n.*

ref•uge (ref′yūj) protection or shelter from danger or trouble; a person or thing that gives comfort and safety: *The cat took refuge in a tree. Grandma was my refuge when the other kids teased me.* *n.*

ref•u•gee (ref′yə jē′ *or* ref′yə jē′) a person who leaves his or her home in order to find refuge or safety from war, persecution, or disaster. Canada has received and helped refugees from many different countries. *n.*

re•fund (ri fund′ *for 1,* rē′fund *for 2 and 3*) **1** give back money paid for something: *If these pants do not fit, the store will refund your money.* **2** the money paid back. 1 *v.,* 2 *n.*

re•fuse[1] (ri fyūz′) say "no" to something; choose not to do or take: *He refused our suggestion. She refuses to clean her room.* *v.,* **re•fused, re•fus•ing. —re•fus′al,** *n.*

ref•use[2] (ref′yūs) garbage: *The street-cleaning department took away all refuse from the streets.* *n.*

re•fute (ri fyūt′) prove that a statement or argument is false: *Copernicus refuted the theory that the sun moves around the earth.* *v.,* **re•fut•ed, re•fut•ing.**

re·gain (ri gān′) 1 get back; recover: *to regain your health.* 2 get back to a place: *They paddled hard and regained the shore just as the first raindrops fell.* *v.*

re·gal (rē′gəl) like or having to do with a king or queen; royal: *regal power, a regal banquet.* *adj.*

re·gale (ri gāl′) entertain or delight: *The old sailor regaled the children with sea stories. We were regaled with ice cream and candy.* *v.,* **re·galed, re·gal·ing.**

re·ga·li·a (ri gā′lē ə) a ceremonial outfit including special items, such as a sceptre and crown for a queen or a headdress for a First Nations chief.

re·gard (ri gȧrd′) 1 think of; consider: *She is regarded as the best doctor in town. She always regards her patients' wishes.* 2 thoughtfulness for others; care: *Have regard for the feelings of others.* 3 good opinion; respect: *The teacher has high regard for Shanti's ability.* 4 look at; watch: *The cat regarded me anxiously when I picked up its kittens.* 5 a steady look: *He fixed his regard on a distant object.* 6 **regards,** *pl.* good wishes or an expression of esteem: *He sends his regards.* 1, 4 *v.,* 2, 3, 5, 6 *n.*
as regards, on the subject of: *As regards money, I have enough.*
in regard to or **with regard to,** concerning; about: *The teacher spoke to me in regard to being late.*

re·gard·ing (ri gȧr′ding) concerning; about: *A note was sent home regarding the class trip.* *prep.*

re·gard·less (ri gȧrd′lis) 1 in any case; no matter what: *Anyone can come, regardless of age. I told her not to go, but she went regardless.* 2 with no thought; careless: *Regardless of grammar, he said, "Him and I have went."* *adj. or adv.*

re·gat·ta (ri gat′ə) a boat race; a series of boating contests: *We had a regatta at camp; our cabin won.* *n.*

re·gen·er·ate (ri jen′ə rāt′) grow back a part that has been lost: *The lizard was able to regenerate its tail after it was cut off. The human brain is unable to regenerate destroyed brain cells.* *v.,* **re·gen·er·at·ed, re·gen·er·at·ing.** **—re·gen′er·a′tion,** *n.*

reg·gae (reg′ā) a style of music that developed in Jamaica in the mid 1970s. It is a blend of rock rhythms and traditional Caribbean folk music. *n.*

re·gime (ri zhēm′) a system of government or leadership: *Under the old regime women could not vote. Our new principal has brought in a very strict regime.* *n.*

reg·i·ment (rej′ə mənt) 1 a large unit of an army. 2 manage a group or activity by a strict system of rules: *That preschool is too regimented.* 1 *n.,* 2 *v.*

re·gion (rē′jən) a particular part of the world, a county, the body, etc.: *the Maritime region, mountainous regions, the region of the heart.* *n.*

re·gion·al (rē′jə nəl) limited to a particular region: *a regional storm.* **Regionalism** is concern for your own part of the country over and above all the rest. *adj.*

reg·is·ter (rej′is tər) 1 put your own or another person's name and other information onto an official list: *Did you register for swimming lessons yet? My parents registered me for hockey.* 2 an official list of names and other information: *All guests must sign the hotel register.* A **registry** is an office or book containing such a list, and a **registrar** is the person in charge of it. 3 pay to have a letter, package, etc. treated specially by the post office. **Registered mail** must be signed for at each stage of delivery and can be traced if it doesn't arrive.
4 anything that records. A cash register shows the amount of money placed in it or taken out of it.
5 show: *The thermometer registers 20°. Her face registered her surprise.* 6 an opening in a wall or floor with a grate covering it, to let heated or cooled air through: *I laid my mitts on the register to dry.* 7 understand or be understood properly: *I heard she was leaving, but somehow it didn't register that it was today.* 1, 3, 5, 7 *v.,* 2, 4, 6 *n.*

reg·is·tra·tion (rej′i strā′shən) 1 the act of registering, or one of the names registered. 2 the number of people registered: *Registration for camp is up to 97 so far.* *n.*

re·gret (ri gret′) 1 feel sorry about something: *We regretted our actions. I regret that I can't stay.* 2 a feeling of being sorry: *He was filled with regret for his cruelty.*
3 something that you are sorry about: *I have no regrets; I made the right choice.* 4 **regrets,** *pl.* a polite reply saying "no" to an invitation: *She sent regrets and said she'd try to come another time.* 1 *v.,* **re·gret·ted, re·gret·ting;** 2–4 *n.* **—re·gret′ful,** *adj.* **—re·gret′ta·ble,** *adj.*

reg·u·lar (reg′yə lər) 1 usual: *We will have supper at the regular time.* 2 coming, acting, or done again and again at about the same time: *regular customers, regular habits, a regular weekly visit.* 3 well-balanced; even in size, spacing, or timing: *regular teeth, regular breathing.*
4 *Informal.* thorough; complete: *a regular bore.* 5 in mathematics, having all sides and all angles equal. A square is a regular polygon. 6 a person who is a usual or steady customer, player, worker, etc. Full-time soldiers are called regulars. 1–5 *adj.,* 6 *n.* **—reg′u·lar·ly,** *adv.* **—reg′u·lar′i·ty** (reg′yə ler′ə tē), *n.*

a bat	e bed	i bid	o pot	u cup	th thin
ā cake	ē me	ī bite	ō go	ū rude	ᴛʜ then
ȧ bar	ə about	ər over	ȯ for	u̇ put	zh measure

reg·u·late (reg′yə lāt′) control by a rule, system, or special piece of equipment. Laws regulate the sale of alcohol. A thermostat regulates the temperature of a room. *v.,* **reg·u·lat·ed, reg·u·lat·ing.** **—reg′u·la′tor,** *n.*

reg·u·la·tion (reg′yə lā′shən) **1** a rule or law: *traffic regulations.* **2** the act of controlling something by a rule or system. **3** required by some rule: *Police officers wear a regulation uniform.* 1, 2 *n.,* 3 *adj.*

re·gur·gi·tate (ri gər′jə tāt′) **1** bring food back up into the mouth after it has been swallowed and partly digested. Some birds regurgitate food to give to their young. **2** give back information that you have only memorized or copied without actually understanding it or thinking it through: *"In your reports," said the teacher, "don't just regurgitate material from the textbook."* *v.,* **re·gur·gi·ta·ted, re·gur·gi·ta·ting.** **—re·gur′gi·ta′tion,** *n.*

re·hab (rē′hab) short for **rehabilitation,** the work of helping someone learn to cope and live well after a serious injury or illness, or after committing serious crimes. *n.* **—re′ha·bil′i·tate′** (rē′hə bil′ə tāt′), *v.*

re·hash (rē′hash′ *for 1,* rē hash′ *for 2*) **1** something old or familiar that is repeated or copied with only a few minor changes: *The movie was just a rehash of one made 20 years ago.* **2** repeat or copy something with only a few minor changes: *Every time someone new joined us, Carrie rehashed her story about her awful vacation.* 1 *n.,* 2 *v.*

re·hearse (ri hərs′) **1** practise for a performance: *We rehearsed our parts for the school play.* **2** tell in detail; repeat: *The child rehearsed all the day's events at the supper table.* *v.,* **re·hearsed, re·hears·ing.** **—re·hears′al,** *n.*

reign (rān) rule: *Queen Victoria reigned from 1837 to 1901* (*v.*). *Her reign lasted 64 years* (*n.*). *n. or v.*

CONFUSABLES ....reign

reign means "rule": *Queen Victoria reigned for sixty-four years.*
rain means "fall in drops": *It may rain tonight.*
rein means "strap": *Hold the reins when riding a horse.*

re·im·burse (rē′im bərs′) pay people back when they have spent their own money in order to do a job: *The school reimbursed my mom for the cloth she bought to make some of the costumes for the school play.* *v.,* **re·im·bursed, re·im·burs·ing.** **—re′im·burse′ment,** *n.*

rein (rān) **1** a long, narrow strap fastened to a bridle, for guiding and controlling a horse: *My riding teacher showed me how to hold the reins.* **2** something that gives control: *The new prime minister took the reins of government. Keep a rein on your temper.* **3** to guide and control: *He reined his horse well.* 1, 2 *n.,* 3 *v.*
give rein or **give free rein,** let move or act freely without guidance: *to give rein to your imagination.*
rein in, stop a horse by pulling the reins.

re·in·car·na·tion (rē′in kär nā′shən) in certain religions, the teaching that each individual soul is continually **reincarnated,** or born over and over again in different bodies, living a new life each time until the goal of perfection is reached. *n.*

Both male and female reindeer have antlers. In all other kinds of deer, only the male has antlers.

rein·deer (rān′dēr′) a deer with branching antlers that lives in northern regions. North American reindeer are called **caribou.** *n., pl.* **rein·deer.**

re·in·force (rē′in fôrs′) strengthen by adding people, materials, or ideas: *to reinforce an army with more soldiers, to reinforce a pair of pants by doubling cloth at the knees. Her many examples reinforced her argument.* *v.,* **re·in·forced, re·in·forc·ing.** **—re′in·force′ment,** *n.*

re·it·er·ate (rē it′ə rāt′) repeat; say or do several times: *The student did not move, though the teacher reiterated her command.* *v.,* **re·it·er·at·ed, re·it·er·at·ing.**

re·ject (ri jekt′ *for 1 and 2,* rē′jekt *for 3*) **1** refuse to accept; turn away from: *He rejected our offer of help.* **2** set aside as useless or not good enough: *All the spotted apples were rejected.* **3** something set aside like this: *The rejects were made into cider.* 1, 2 *v.,* 3 *n.* **—re·jec′tion,** *n.*

re·joice (ri jois′) be glad; be filled with joy: *Our parents rejoiced at our success.* *v.,* **re·joiced, re·joic·ing.**

re·join (rē′join′) meet or join up with again: *The detour rejoins the main route farther south. Go on; I'll rejoin you as soon as I've paid for these.* *v.*

re·lapse (rē′laps) a return to illness or to a bad habit, etc.: *He seemed to be getting over his infection but had a relapse.* *n.*

re•late (ri lāt′) **1** tell: *The traveller related her adventures.* **2** connect or be connected in some way; have to do with: *The words "better" and "best" are related to "good." We are interested in what relates to ourselves.* **3** *Informal.* behave toward others: *Put-downs are not a good way of relating.* **4** understand; feel a connection with: *He relates well to children. I can relate to her feelings of frustration—the same thing happened to me.* *v.,* **re•lat•ed, re•lat•ing.**

re•lat•ed (ri lā′tid) **1** connected in any way. **2** in the same family: *Mia and I are related; we're cousins.* *adj.*

re•la•tion (ri lā′shən) **1** a connection in thought or meaning: *That answer has no relation to the question.* **2** connections or dealings between people or groups: *The relation between parent and child is the closest in the world.* **Relationship** is the more usual word for this sense. **3** **relations,** *pl.* official dealings between nations or companies. **4** a person who belongs to the same family, more usually called a **relative.** **5** the act of telling; an account: *a simple relation of the facts.* *n.*
in relation to or **with relation to,** **a** about; concerning: *We must plan in relation to the future.* **b** compared with: *In relation to a baby, a three-year-old seems big.*

re•la•tion•ship (ri lā′shən ship′) **1** connection between ideas, things, or people. A relationship between people is what they mean to each other, how they act toward each other, and so on: *She has a close relationship with her sister. What is the relationship of clouds to rain?* **2** the exact way of being related in a family: *I don't know what their relationship is; I think he's her uncle.* *n.*

rel•a•tive (rel′ə tiv) **1** a person who belongs to the same family, such as a father, brother, aunt, cousin, etc. **2** compared to each other: *We considered the relative cost of one large versus two mediums.* **3** having meaning only in relation to something else: *East and west are relative terms; for example, Regina is east of Calgary but west of Winnipeg.* 1 *n.,* 2, 3 *adj.* **—rel′a•tive•ly,** *adv.*
relative to, **a** about; concerning: *The teacher asked me some questions relative to my project.* **b** in comparison with: *He is strong relative to his size.*

re•lax (ri laks′) **1** loosen up; make or become less stiff or tense: *Relax your muscles to rest them. After a while she relaxed and started to talk to us.* **2** take a break from work or effort; enjoy yourself: *Take a vacation and relax.* *v.* **—re′lax•a′tion,** *n.*

re•lay (rē′lā *for 1,* ri lā′ *for 2*) **1** Usually, **relay race,** a race between teams, with each person on a team going only part of the way and then tagging or passing a stick to the next one, who continues the race. **2** take and pass on: *Could you relay this message to Ms. Kumar?* 1 *n.,* 2 *v.*

re•lease (ri lēs′) **1** let go: *Release the catch and the box will open. She was released from prison.* **2** freedom or the act of giving freedom: *The end of the war brought the release of the prisoners.* **3** a form that allows something to be handed over, lets someone go, or frees someone from responsibility: *You must sign a release before the Post Office will give you the parcel.* **4** make available to the public: *to release a movie or video.* **5** something made available to the public: *His latest release is the CD "Breakaway."* **6** a device for releasing a part: *This little lever is the car's hood release.* 1, 4 *v.,* **re•leased, re•leas•ing;** 2, 3, 5, 6 *n.*

re•lent (ri lent′) become less harsh; become more merciful: *After hours of questioning the suspect, the police relented and allowed him to rest.* *v.* **—re•lent′less,** *adj.*

rel•e•vant (rel′ə vənt) important; having something directly to do with the subject; to the point: *relevant questions.* *adj.* **—rel′e•vance,** *n.*

re•li•a•ble (ri lī′ə bəl) that you can rely on or trust: *a reliable source of information.* *adj.* **—re•li′a•bil′i•ty,** *n.*

re•li•ant (ri lī′ənt) trusting or relying. If you are *self-reliant* you rely on yourself and your own abilities. *adj.* **—re•li′ance,** *n.*

rel•ic (rel′ik) something left from the past: *This ruined bridge is a relic of pioneer days.* *n.*

re•lied (ri līd′) the past tense and past participle of **rely.** *v.*

re•lief (ri lēf′) **1** something that makes a pleasing change: *The rain was a relief after such a hot, humid day.* **2** the fact of lessening or getting rid of pain or any other difficulty: *a pill for the relief of headaches.* **3** something that does this, especially help given to those who are poor or who have suffered some disaster: *Canada sent relief to the hurricane victims in Honduras.* **4** a break from work when someone else comes to take the worker's place: *This nurse is on duty from seven in the morning until seven at night, with only two hours' relief.* **5** differences between the higher and lower areas of a region. A **relief map** shows differences in height, either three-dimensionally or by using contour lines, shading, or colours. **6** a style of sculpture that has figures and designs standing out from a flat surface. *n.*
in relief, **a** standing out from a surface. **b** in contrast: *This sad scene stands in sharp relief to the funny scene in the very next chapter.*

a bat	e bed	i bid	o pot	u cup	th thin
ā cake	ē me	ī bite	ō go	ū rude	TH then
à bar	ə about	ər over	ȯ for	u̇ put	zh measure

re•lieve (ri lēv′) 1 ease someone's fear or worry: *We were so relieved when she finally showed up safe and sound.* 2 lessen or get rid of pain or suffering: *Do you have anything that will relieve a headache?* 3 set free from effort, trouble, or anything unwanted: *Your coming relieves me of the bother of writing a long e-mail. Here, let me relieve you of that heavy box.* 4 give a person on duty a break by taking his or her place. *v.,* **re•lieved, re•liev•ing.**

re•li•gion (ri lij′ən) 1 the set of beliefs a person has, whatever they are, about where the universe came from, and what the purpose of life is. 2 a set of beliefs about a being or force that is greater than humans and beyond the physical senses. Usually a religion includes teachings about right and wrong, and ceremonies that express and celebrate beliefs. Hinduism, Judaism, Christianity, and Islam are religions. 3 anything that seems to be the main focus in a person's life: *the religion of sports.* *n.*

re•li•gious (ri lij′əs) 1 having to do with religion: *religious meetings, religious books, religious differences.* 2 very interested in religion or serious about religion: *He is very religious and prays many times a day.* 3 a monk or nun. 4 strict; very careful: *We paid religious attention to the doctor's orders.* 1, 2, 4 *adj.,* 3 *n., pl.* **re•li•gious.**

re•lin•quish (ri ling′kwish) give up; let go: *The small dog relinquished its bone to the big dog. She has relinquished all hope of going to P.E.I. this summer.* *v.*

rel•ish (rel′ish) 1 a topping for hot dogs and hamburgers, made of chopped cucumbers, etc. 2 like; enjoy: *Our cat relishes cream. He did not relish the prospect of staying after school.* 3 enjoyment: *The girls played volleyball with great relish.* 1, 3 *n.,* 2 *v.*

re•luc•tant (ri luk′tənt) unwilling; slow to act because you don't want to: *I am reluctant to go out in such freezing cold weather.* *adj.* **—re•luc′tance,** *n.*

re•ly (ri lī′) depend; trust: *You can rely on me—I'll be there for you.* *v.,* **re•lied, re•ly•ing.**

re•main (ri mān′) 1 stay: *We plan to remain at the lake till September. The town remains the same year after year.* 2 be left: *A few apples still remain on the tree.* 3 **remains,** *pl.* **a** what is left: *The remains of the meal were fed to the dog.* **b** a dead body: *His remains were lowered into the grave.* 1, 2 *v.,* 3 *n.*

re•main•der (ri mān′dər) 1 the part left over; the rest: *After reading for an hour, she spent the remainder of the afternoon playing.* 2 in mathematics: **a** the number left over after subtracting one number from another. In 9 − 2, the remainder is 7. **b** the number left over after dividing one number by another. In 14 ÷ 3, the quotient is 4 with a remainder of 2. *n.*

re•mark (ri märk′) 1 say; comment: *Mom remarked that Grandpa was feeling better.* 2 a short statement; a comment: *Don't make rude remarks.* 1 *v.,* 2 *n.*

re•mark•a•ble (ri mär′kə bəl) worth noticing; unusual: *a remarkable change, a remarkable story.* *adj.* **—re•mark′a•bly,** *adv.*

rem•e•dy (rem′ə dē) 1 anything used to cure or relieve illness or to fix a problem: *Chicken soup is an old remedy for colds. A good book is the best remedy for boredom.* 3 make right; put right; cure: *A few drops of oil will remedy that bike chain problem.* 1, 2 *n.,* **rem•e•dies;** 3 *v.,* **rem•e•died, rem•e•dy•ing.**

WORD HISTORY........ remedy

The root of **remedy** is the Latin *mederi,* meaning "heal." It's the same root that gives us the words **medical** and **medicine**.

re•mem•ber (ri mem′ber) 1 call back to mind; think of again: *I can't remember that man's name. Then I remembered where I was.* 2 take care not to forget: *Remember to lock the door. Remember those who gave their lives for peace.* 3 mention a person as sending friendly greetings: *Remember me to Anh Vu when you see him.* *v.*

re•mem•brance (ri mem′brəns) 1 the act of remembering; a memory. 2 something you keep to help you remember another person, an event, or a place; souvenir: *This little china teacup is a remembrance from my great-grandmother.* *n.*

Remembrance Day (ri mem′brəns dā) November 11, the day set aside to remember and honour those killed in World Wars I and II.

re•mind (ri mīnd′) make someone remember or think of something: *This picture reminds me of a story I heard.* A **reminder** helps you remember something. *v.*

rem•in•isce (rem′ə nis′) talk about something pleasant that has happened in the past: *We listened to our grandparents reminiscing about the good old days.* *v.,* **rem•i•nisced, rem•i•nisc•ing.** **—rem′i•nis′cence,** *n.*

rem•nant (rem′nənt) a small part left over: *The fabric store often sells remnants of fabric at low prices. This town has only a remnant of its former population.* *n.*

re•mod•el (rē mod′əl) make over; change or alter: *They are remodelling the old barn into a house.* *v.,* **re•mod•elled** or **re•mod•eled, re•mod•el•ling** or **re•mod•el•ing.**

re•morse (ri mörs′) deep sorrow for having done wrong: *Andre felt remorse after being so mean to the cat.* *n.* —**re•morse′ful,** *adj.* —**re•morse′less,** *adj.*

re•mote (ri mōt′) **1** far away from a given place or time: *a remote star. Dinosaurs lived in the remote past.* **2** out of the way; far from a major centre: *Mail comes to this remote village only once a week.* **3** not closely related: *a remote relative.* **4** slight; faint: *I haven't the remotest idea what you mean.* **5** controlled from a distance: *a remote car door opener.* *adj.,* **re•mot•er, re•mot•est.**

remote control (ri mōt′ kən trōl′) **1** control of a machine or process from a distance, using a device that sends electrical impulses, radio signals, or a beam of infrared light: *Some model airplanes can be flown by remote control.* **2** the device that does this: *The TV remote control has fallen behind the couch.* This is often informally shortened to **remote.**

re•move (ri mūv′) **1** move something from a place; take off, take out, or take away: *Remove your hat.* **2** get rid of: *to remove fear or doubt.* *v.,* **re•moved, re•mov•ing.** —**re•mov′al,** *n.*

rend (rend) an old or poetic word for "rip": *A loud scream rent the silence.* *v.,* **rent, rend•ing.**

ren•der (ren′dər) **1** cause to become; make: *An accident has rendered him helpless.* **2** give; do: *to render assistance, to render a judgment in a court.* *v.*

ren•dez•vous (ron′dā vū′) **1** a planned meeting at a certain place and time. **2** a meeting place: *The big tree in the schoolyard was our favourite rendezvous.* *n., pl.* **ren•dez•vous** (ron′dā vūz′).

ren•di•tion (ren dish′ən) someone's version of a song, story, poem, etc.: *Casey can do a pretty good rendition of the "Star Wars" theme on the piano.* *n.*

re•new (ri nyū′ *or* ri nū′) **1** give or get for a new period: *We renewed our magazine subscription for another year.* **2** make new and fresh again; bring back to good condition: *Rain renews the greenness of the fields.* **3** begin again; say, do, or give again: *He renewed his efforts to move the rock.* **4** replace by new material of the same kind. A **renewable resource** is one that can keep on being used and replaced, such as a forest. *v.* —**re•new′al,** *n.*

re•nounce (ri nouns′) **1** give up: *Derek renounced candy for one month and gave the money he saved to UNICEF.* **2** cut off all ties with: *She renounced her old friends when they kept trying to involve her in shoplifting.* *v.,* **re•nounced, re•nounc•ing.**

ren•o•vate (ren′ə vāt′) make new; rebuild parts of a building and redecorate it: *to renovate a house.* *v.,* **ren•o•vat•ed, ren•o•vat•ing.** —**ren′o•va′tion,** *n.*

re•nown (ri noun′) fame: *an artist of great renown.* *n.* —**re•nown′ed,** *adj.*

rent¹ (rent) **1** pay for the privilege of using someone else's property: *We rented a canoe for our camping trip.* **2** let someone use your property for money: *He rents out several rooms.* **3** the regular payment given for this: *The rent is due on the 1st of every month.* **4** be rented: *This house rents for $1200 a month.* 1, 2, 4 *v.,* 3 *n.* —**rent′al,** *n. or adj.*
for rent, available to be rented: *That house is for rent.*

rent² (rent) **1** the past tense and past participle of **rend,** an old or poetic word meaning "rip": *He rent his cloak in despair.* **2** a tear; a torn place. 1 *n.,* 2 *v.*

re•o•pen (rē ō′pən) **1** open again: *School will reopen in September.* **2** bring up again for discussion: *The case is settled and cannot be reopened.* *v.*

re•pair (ri per′) **1** fix; put in good condition again: *She repairs cars at Canadian Tire.* **2** the job of repairing: *They are doing repairs on the school building.* **3** make up for: *How can I repair the harm done?* 1, 3 *v.,* 2 *n.*
in good repair, in good condition. The opposite is **in bad repair.**

re•pay (ri pā′) pay back: *He repaid the money he had borrowed.* *v.,* **re•paid, re•pay•ing.**

re•peal (ri pēl′) **1** do away with a law: *The racist laws of the southern United States were repealed.* **2** the action of doing away with a law: *He voted for the repeal of that law.* 1 *v.,* 2 *n.*

re•peat (ri pēt′) **1** do or say again: *to repeat an error, to repeat a question.* **2** say after someone else: *Repeat the words after me.* **3** tell to anyone else: *Promise not to repeat this.* **4** something that is repeated, or the action of repeating: *The last verse is a repeat of the first one.* 1–3 *v.,* 4 *n.* —**re•peat′ed,** *adj.* —**re•peat′ed•ly,** *adv.*

re•pel (ri pel′) **1** force back or away: *They repelled the enemy. The positive poles of two magnets repel each other.* **2** keep off or out: *a lotion to repel black flies and mosquitoes. This tent repels water.* **3** be disgusting to: *Worms repel some people.* *v.,* **re•pelled, re•pel•ling.**

WORD HISTORY........repel

Repel literally means "push back." The root is *pellere,* Latin for "push." This root is also found in **expel.**

a bat	e bed	i bid	o pot	u cup	th thin
ā cake	ē me	ī bite	ō go	ū rude	ᴛʜ then
à bar	ə about	ər over	ò for	ù put	zh measure

re·pel·lent (ri pel′ənt) 1 very unattractive: *the repellent smell of rotten eggs.* 2 anything that repels: *We sprayed insect repellent on our arms and legs.* 1 *adj.,* 2 *n.*

re·pent (ri pent′) have a change of heart; be sorry for doing wrong and decide to act differently in future: *He repented of his carelessness.* *v.* **—re·pent′ance,** *n.* **—re·pent′ant,** *adj.*

re·per·cus·sion (rē′pər kush′ən) a side effect or indirect result of something, especially an unexpected result that causes a problem: *Using pesticides to protect crops has had serious repercussions for health and for the environment.* *n.*

rep·er·toire (rep′ər twår′) all the plays, songs, parts, etc., that a theatre company, an actor, or a musician is able to perform. *n.*

rep·e·ti·tion (rep′ə tish′ən) the action of repeating, or something that is repeated: *Repetition helps learning. Any repetition of the offence will be punished.* *n.* **—rep′e·ti′tious,** *adj.* **—re·pet′i·tive** (rə pet′ə tiv), *adj.*

Grammar Check .... repetition

When you repeat words or phrases too often in your writing, the effect can be boring. Try to find synonyms (words with similar meanings) in a thesaurus.

re·place (ri plās′) 1 fill or take the place of: *Ariel replaced Urjo as team captain.* 2 get another in place of: *I will replace the cup I broke.* 3 put back; put in place again: *Replace the books on the shelves.* *v.,* **re·placed, re·plac·ing.** **—re·place′ment,** *n.*

re·plen·ish (ri plen′ish) refill; get or give a fresh supply for: *So many kids came to our door at Halloween that we soon had to replenish our bowl of candy.* *v.*

rep·li·ca (rep′lə kə) a copy; reproduction: *a replica of an original painting.* *n.* **—rep′li·cate′,** *v.*

re·ply (ri plī′) answer: *to reply to a letter* (*v.*). *She replied that she was too tired* (*v.*). *When can I expect a reply* (*n.*)? *v.,* **re·plied, re·ply·ing** or *n., pl.* **re·plies.**

USING WORDS .... reply

Reply, **retort**, and **respond** are all words you can use instead of "said."
Reply means "answer": *Janine replied to my letter.*
Retort means "give a short, sharp reply": *"That's not the point," he retorted.*
Respond can mean "react to something": *When I took my brother into the fun house, he responded by yelling.*

re·port (ri pört′) 1 tell the facts about something, especially after going and finding them out for someone: *Vic checked on the baby and reported that she was still asleep.* 2 a description or statement of facts: *a report of a traffic accident. I'm writing a report on Mexico for school.* 3 complain or speak to the authorities about: *Someone saw them dumping garbage in the field and reported them.* 4 present yourself to someone in authority: *Report for work at eight o'clock.* 5 the sound of a shot or an explosion: *the report of a gun.* 1, 3, 4 *v.,* 2, 5 *n.*

report card (ri pört′ kård′) a report sent home by a school to let parents or guardians know how a student is doing.

re·port·er (ri pör′tər) 1 a person who gathers news for a newspaper, magazine, radio station, etc. 2 a person in a court who writes down all that is said at a trial. *n.*

re·pose (ri pōz′) a formal or poetic word for "rest": *Do not disturb her repose* (*n.*). *The cat was reposing on the cushion* (*v.*). *n. or v.,* **re·posed, re·pos·ing.**

rep·re·sent (rep′ri zent′) 1 stand for; be a symbol of: *The stars on this map represent cities.* 2 speak and act for someone else: *Elected people represent us in Parliament.* 3 act the part of: *Each child will represent an animal in the play.* 4 give an image or idea of: *He represented the plan as safe, but it was not. This story represents the pioneers as brave heroes.* *v.* **—rep′re·sen·ta′tion,** *n.*

rep·re·sent·a·tive (rep′ri zen′tə tiv) 1 a person chosen to act or speak for others: *Each class elects a representative to the Student Council.* 2 having its members chosen or elected by the people: *a representative government.* 3 a typical example: *The tiger is a representative of the cat family.* 1, 3 *n.,* 2 *adj.*

rep·ri·mand (rep′rə mand′) 1 a scolding, especially a formal or official one. 2 scold, especially in a formal or official way: *The principal reprimanded the boys for smoking.* 1 *n.,* 2 *v.*

re·proach (ri prōch′) 1 criticize or blame; tell off: *My mom reproached me for being late.* 2 the act of telling someone off, or the words used: *Her stern reproach made me feel guilty.* 1 *n.,* 2 *v.* **—re·proach′ful,** *adj.*

re·pro·duce (rē′prə dyūs′ *or* rē′prə dūs′) 1 copy; produce again: *A CD player reproduces sounds. When we tried to reproduce their experiment we got a different result.* 2 produce offspring: *Most plants reproduce by seeds. People reproduce by the joining of egg and sperm.* *v.,* **re·pro·duced, re·pro·duc·ing.** **—re′pro·duc′tion,** *n.* **—re′pro·duc′tive,** *adj.*

re•prove (ri prüv′) scold; express disapproval: *to reprove a person for being rude.* *v.,* **re•proved, re•prov•ing.** **—re•proof′,** *n.*

rep•tile (rep′tīl) any member of the group of cold-blooded animals whose bodies are covered with scales or plates. Reptiles either have short legs or no legs at all. Snakes, lizards, turtles, alligators, and crocodiles are reptiles. *n.* **—rep•til′i•an** (rep til′ē ən), *adj.*

re•pub•lic (ri pub′lik) a country with an elected government which is led by a president rather than a prime minister or king or queen. The United States and Mexico are republics. *n.* **—re•pub′li•can,** *adj. or n.*

re•pug•nant (ri pug′nənt) very unattractive or distasteful: *Work is repugnant to lazy people.* *adj.*

re•pul•sive (ri pul′siv) disgusting: *Snakes are repulsive to some people.* *adj.*

rep•u•ta•ble (rep′yə tə bəl) well thought of; having a good reputation: *a reputable businessman.* *adj.*

rep•u•ta•tion (rep′yə tā′shən) **1** what people think and say about a person's character; the idea people have of someone: *Mrs. Marchese has an excellent reputation for fairness among the students.* **2** fame: *His reputation as an actor spread throughout the world.* *n.*

re•put•ed (ri pyü′tid) thought of by most people as: *Shelley is a reputed karate expert. She is reputed to be the best in the school.* *adj.* **—re•put′ed•ly,** *adv.*

re•quest (ri kwest′) **1** ask for; ask as a favour: *She requested $20 from her father.* **2** the act of asking or the thing that is asked for: *Your request for a ticket was too late. They granted my request.* 1 *v.,* 2 *n.*

re•quire (ri kwīr′) **1** need: *You will require glue and scissors for this project.* **2** order; command: *The law requires us to wear seat belts.* *v.,* **re•quired, re•quir•ing.** **—re•quire′ment,** *n.*

re•run (rē′run′) something repeated, especially a TV program that is being shown again. *n.*

res•cue (res′kyü) **1** save from danger, capture, harm, etc.: *The dog rescued the child from drowning.* **2** the action of saving a person or thing from danger, capture, harm, etc.: *a heroic rescue by two brave boys.* 1 *v.,* **res•cued, res•cu•ing;** 2 *n.* **—res′cu•er,** *n.*
come to the rescue, see someone in trouble and go to save him or her.

re•search (ri sėrch′; *for 1, also* rē′sėrch) **1** a careful search for information by studying, doing experiments, talking with people, and so on: *Medical research has done much to lessen disease.* **2** make a careful search for information: *She spent hours researching the subject on the Internet.* 1 *n.,* 2 *v.*

re•sem•ble (ri zem′bəl) be like; look like: *An orange resembles a tangerine.* *v.,* **re•sem•bled, re•sem•bling.** **—re•sem′blance,** *n.*

re•sent (ri zent′) feel insulted and angry at: *She resented being called a baby.* *v.* **—re•sent′ful,** *adj.* **—re•sent′ment,** *n.*

res•er•va•tion (rez′ər vā′shən) **1** an arrangement to save something for a certain person, such as a seat in a restaurant or plane or a room in a hotel: *We made reservations for rooms at a hotel.* **2** a doubt or concern about something, often not said out loud: *I went ahead and invited Ton even though I had some reservations about how well he would fit in.* **3** the American word for a **reserve,** land set aside for aboriginal people. *n.*

re•serve (ri zėrv′) **1** keep or set aside for some special purpose or for someone else: *Reserve some money for souvenirs on your trip. Our Saturday afternoons are reserved for family activities.* **2** something set aside for future use: *Banks must keep a reserve of money.* **3** an area of land set apart by the federal government for a First Nation to use. Most reserves were arranged as part of a treaty. **4** public land set apart for a special purpose: *a timber reserve, a wildlife reserve.* **5** hold back: *My parents agreed to reserve judgment until they had heard both sides of the story.* **6** **reserves,** *pl.* soldiers kept ready to help the main army if needed. **7** **reserved,** slow to open up to others; quiet and private. 1, 5 *v.,* **re•served, re•serv•ing;** 2–4, 6 *n.,* 7 *adj.*

res•er•voir (rez′ər vwär′) **1** a place where water is collected and stored: *This reservoir supplies the entire city.* **2** anything that holds a supply of something: *His mind was a reservoir of interesting facts.* *n.*

re•side (ri zīd′) live in a place: *This family has resided in our town for 100 years.* A person who lives in a place is a **resident** (rez′ə dənt). *v.,* **re•sid•ed, re•sid•ing.**

res•i•dence (rez′ə dəns) **1** a home; the place where a person lives. An area that has mostly homes rather than businesses or factories is **residential** (rez′ə den′shəl). **2** a building for students, nurses, etc. to live in while studying or working: *A new men's residence is being built at the university.* **3** the fact of living in a place: *Three years' residence in Canada is necessary for a person to become a citizen.* *n.*

a bat	e bed	i bid	o pot	u cup	th thin
ā cake	ē me	ī bite	ō go	ü rude	ᴛʜ then
ä bar	ə about	ėr over	ô for	ů put	zh measure

res•i•due (rez′ə dyū′ *or* rez′ə dū′) a part of some substance, left behind after cleaning, evaporation, etc.: *The spilled pop had dried up, leaving a sticky residue.* *n.*

re•sign (ri zīn′) give up a job, office, or position: *The grade four teacher resigned and moved to Nova Scotia. The MP resigned her seat in Parliament.* *v.*
resign yourself, give in without complaining, knowing you have no other choice: *I had to resign myself to a week in bed after the accident.* A person who does this is **resigned.**

res•ig•na•tion (rez′ig nā′shən) **1** the act of giving up a job or position: *Her resignation means that a new teacher must be hired.* **2** a letter that says you are doing this. **3** patient acceptance of something when there is no other choice: *She bore the pain with resignation.* *n.*

re•sil•i•ent (ri zil′yənt) **1** springing back to the original form after being bent, pressed, or stretched: *resilient moss.* **2** recovering easily from hard times: *a resilient child.* *adj.*

res•in (rez′ən) a sticky substance that flows from cone-bearing trees and some other plants. It is also made artificially and is used in medicines, varnishes, and so on. Turpentine is made from resin. *n.* **—res′in•ous,** *adj.*

re•sist (ri zist′) **1** try to fight against: *The dog resisted our efforts to give it a bath, but finally gave up and stood still.* **2** stand firm against; keep from giving in to: *I could not resist laughing. A healthy body resists disease.* *v.*

re•sist•ance (ri zis′təns) **1** the action or power of resisting: *The bank clerk made no resistance to the robbers. She has little resistance to germs and is often sick.* **2** a force that acts or fights against something: *A racing car's shape helps it overcome the resistance of the air so it can go faster.* **3** the amount of difficulty that a certain material gives to an electric current passing through it. Higher resistance means more of the current's electric energy is changed into heat. An electric stove element has a high resistance, so it gives off a lot of heat when turned on. *n.*

re•sist•ant (ri zis′tənt) resisting something, at least for a while. Fabric that is water-resistant isn't waterproof, but is not easily soaked. *adj.*

res•o•lute (rez′ə lūt′) determined; firm; bold: *a resolute attempt to climb to the top of the mountain.* *adj.*

res•o•lu•tion (rez′ə lū′shən) **1** a firm decision: *He made a resolution to get up early.* **2** a determined attitude: *Rivka faced every problem with firm resolution.* **3** the process or result of solving a problem or settling a conflict: *They argued for hours with no resolution.* **4** a measure of how clear the image is on a screen or through a lens: *This computer monitor has very high resolution.* *n.*

re•solve (ri zolv′) **1** decide firmly: *We resolved to work harder in the future.* **2** a firm decision: *He kept his resolve to stop smoking.* **3** strength not to give up; firmness or determination: *The mayor was a woman of great resolve.* To be determined is to be **resolved.** **4** settle or solve: *His answer quickly resolved the disagreement.* 1, 4 *v.,* **re•solved, re•solv•ing;** 2, 3 *n.*

res•o•nate (rez′ə nāt′) produce a full, rich, or loud sound because the vibrations keep going: *Her voice resonated through the halls.* *v.,* **res•o•nat•ed, res•o•nat•ing.** **—res′o•nance,** *n.* **—res′o•nant,** *adj.*

re•sort (ri zôrt′) **1** a place people go to spend a vacation: *There are many summer resorts in the mountains.* **2** turn to for a solution, especially when you are desperate: *Her snoring was so loud I had to resort to wearing earmuffs to bed.* **3** a person or thing turned to for a solution: *As a last resort, he decided to borrow money.* 1, 3 *n.,* 2 *v.*

re•sound (ri zound′) echo; ring: *The loon's cry resounded over the lake. The room resounded with the children's shouts.* *v.* **—re•sound′ing,** *adj.*

re•source (ri zôrs′ *or* rē′zôrs′) **1** anything you can use to solve a problem or reach a goal: *She had little money, but her other resources were a strong spirit and plenty of imagination.* **2** **natural resources,** *pl.* the things provided by nature that add to a country's wealth: *Canada's natural resources include fish, lumber, oil, and minerals.* **3** **human resources,** *pl.* the people available to work on something; staff. **4** skill in finding solutions. Someone who has this skill is **resourceful.** *n.*

re•spect (ri spekt′) **1** honour; an attitude that appreciates the value, importance, authority, and so on of a person or thing: *I have a lot of respect for my parents. Show respect for the environment by not littering.* **2** feel or show this attitude: *We respect your honesty.*
3 **respects,** *pl.* **a** actions or words that show respect: *We kept silence for one minute on Remembrance Day to pay our respects to the soldiers who died.* **b** polite greetings: *Give her my respects.* **4** a point or detail: *She is a good worker in every respect.* 1, 3, 4 *n.,* 2 *v.* **—re•spect′ful,** *adj.*
with respect to, about: *I have a few questions with respect to the new rule.* **Respecting** can have the same meaning.

re•spect•a•ble (ri spek′tə bəl) **1** worthy of respect; having a good reputation: *Respectable citizens obey the laws.* **2** good enough; decent: *a respectable income, a respectable performance. Wear something respectable.* *adj.*

re•spec•tive (ri spek′tiv) belonging to each one separately: *The classes went to their respective rooms.* *adj.*

re•spec•tive•ly (ri spek′tiv lē) in the order mentioned: *Holly and Kieran live in Moncton and Fort Simpson, respectively.* *adv.*

Respiration

Land vertebrates have lungs for respiration. Breathe in and your diaphragm contracts, increasing the space inside your chest. Breathe out and your diaphragm relaxes, reducing the space inside your chest. The air rushes out.

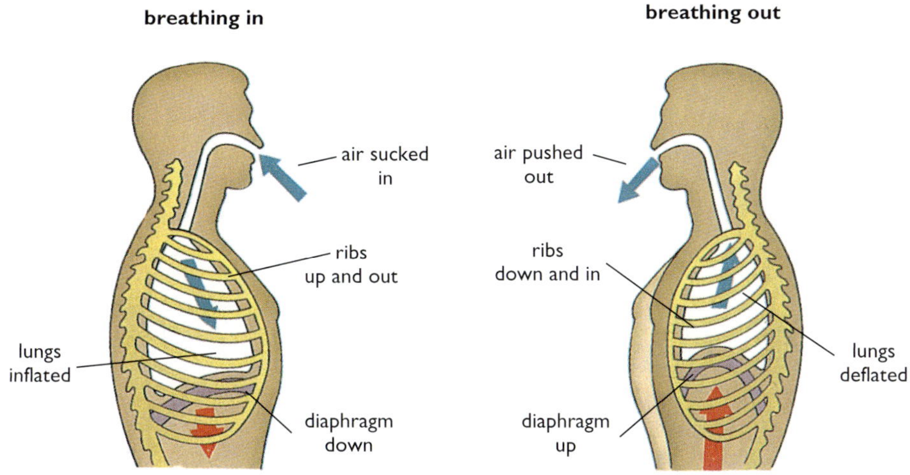

res•pi•ra•tion (res′pə rā′shən) breathing: *The nurse checked the patient's respiration.* Respiration includes all the processes that go on in a living thing to get oxygen into the cells and get rid of carbon dioxide. *n.*

res•pi•ra•to•ry (res′pə rə tôr′ē) having to do with breathing: *The lungs are respiratory organs.* *adj.*

re•splend•ent (ri splen′dənt) very bright; shining splendidly: *The queen was resplendent with jewels.* *adj.*

re•spond (ri spond′) **1** answer; reply: *He responded to the question.* **2** act as a result of something; react: *A dog responds to kindness by loving its master. She responded quickly to the medicine and was well in a few days.* *v.*

re•sponse (ri spons′) **1** an answer by word or act: *Her response to my letter came today.* **2** a reaction; a way of dealing with something or of being influenced by something: *Sweating is your body's response to heat.* A person or thing that responds quickly is **responsive.** *n.*

re•spon•si•bil•i•ty (ri spon′sə bil′ə tē) **1** the fact or quality of being responsible: *Caring for a pet teaches you responsibility.* **2** something that a person is responsible for: *Doing my homework and keeping my room tidy are my responsibilities.* *n., pl.* **re•spon•si•bil•i•ties.**

re•spon•si•ble (ri spon′sə bəl) **1** having a duty to do or to take care of something: *Students are responsible for their books. If you are going to be away, you are responsible for letting the teacher know.* **2** deserving credit or blame: *Who is responsible for this mess?* **3** trustworthy; reliable: *The class chose a responsible student to collect the money.* **4** involving serious duties: *The Prime Minister holds a very responsible position.* *adj.*

rest[1] (rest) **1** sleep or a chance to lie down or sit still for a while: *I had a good night's rest. We stopped for a little rest by the river.* **2** a break; freedom from work, worry, pain, etc.: *As a rest from her computer work, she went out and chopped wood for a while. The medicine gave the sick man a short rest from pain.* **3** have a rest or give a rest to: *to rest on the couch, to rest during your holidays. Stop and rest your horse.* **4** lean: *The ladder rested against the wall. She rested her arm on the window sill.* **5** a support; something to lean on: *a footrest.* **6** be found; lie: *In a democracy, the power rests with the people. A smile rested on the girl's lips.* **7** in music, a silence between notes, or the symbol for it. 1, 2, 5, 7 *n.,* 3, 4, 6 *v.*
—rest′ful, *adj.*
at rest, a not moving: *There was no breeze and the lake was at rest.* **b** not worried or upset: *His mind was at rest.*
come to rest, stop; land: *The ball rolled a few yards and came to rest at my feet.*

rest[2] (rest) what is left; those that are left: *The sun was out in the morning but it rained for the rest of the day. One horse ran ahead of the rest.* *n.*

res•tau•rant (res′tə ront′) a place to buy and eat a meal. *n.*

rest•less (rest′lis) **1** unable to relax; uneasy: *The dog seemed restless, as if sensing some danger.* **2** without rest or sleep: *The sick child passed a restless night.* **3** always moving: *the restless sea, restless hands.* *adj.*

re•store (ri stôr′) **1** bring back or give back: *The police restored order. The honest girl restored the money to its owner.* **2** bring back to a better condition: *The old house has been restored. He fainted, but the fresh air restored him.* *v.,* **re•stored, re•stor•ing.**
—res′to•ra′tion, *n.*

a bat	e bed	i bid	o pot	u cup	th thin
ā cake	ē me	ī bite	ō go	ū rude	ᴛʜ then
ä bar	ə about	ər over	ȯ for	u̇ put	zh measure

re•strain (ri strān′) hold back; keep under control: *She could not restrain her curiosity to see what was in the box. He restrained the excited dog when guests came.* *v.* **—re•straint′,** *n.*

re•strict (ri strikt′) keep within certain limits: *This soccer league is restricted to players 11 years old and under.* A **restricted movie** is one that only adults are allowed to watch. *v.* **—re•stric′tion,** *n.*

rest•room (rest′rūm′) a public washroom. *n.*

re•sult (ri zult′) **1** something that is caused by something else: *The result of his fall was a broken leg.* **2** the way something ends up or turns out: *The result of the game was a tie.* **3** come or happen because of: *Indigestion often results from eating too much.* **4** lead to; end up: *Eating too much often results in indigestion.* **5** a good or useful result: *We want results, not just talk. He knocked on the door, but with no result.* 1, 2, 5 *n.*, 3, 4 *v.*

re•sume (ri zūm′) **1** begin again; go on: *Resume reading where we left off.* **2** get or take again: *Those standing may resume their seats.* *v.*, **re•sumed, re•sum•ing.** **—re•sump′tion** (ri zump′shən), *n.*

re•su•mé (rez′ə mā′) a list of schools you have gone to, jobs you have held, and other things you have accomplished, that you can show to people who might hire you: *Premika spent all day working on her résumé.* *n.*

res•ur•rect (rez′ə rekt′) bring back to life: *to resurrect a ghost, to resurrect an ancient custom.* *v.* **—res′ur•rec′tion,** *n.*

re•sus•ci•tate (ri sus′ə tāt′) bring back from unconsciousness or near death; revive: *The doctor resuscitated the man who had nearly drowned.* *v.*

re•tail (rē′tāl) **1** the sale of goods in small quantities directly to the final user, as in an ordinary store: *Most stores sell at retail. She has a job in retail.* Compare this with **wholesale.** **2** having to do with this kind of selling: *a retail store, retail prices.* **3** sell at retail: *This suit retails for $210.* 1 *n.*, 2 *adj.*, 3 *v.* **—re′tail•er,** *n.*

re•tain (ri tān′) **1** keep: *Retain these instructions for future use.* **2** keep in mind; remember: *She retained the tune but not the words of the song.* A **retentive** memory remembers a lot. **3** hire for a fee: *He retained the best lawyer in the city.* *v.* **—re•ten′tion,** *n.*

re•tal•i•ate (ri tal′ē āt′) pay back someone who has done wrong to you: *If we insult people, they will retaliate.* *v.*, **re•tal•i•at•ed, re•tal•i•at•ing.** **—re•tal′i•a′tion,** *n.*

re•tard (ri tärd′) slow something; delay or hinder: *Lack of education retards progress.* A **flame retardant** is a substance that makes it harder for something to burn. *v.*

retch (rech) try to vomit when there is nothing to throw up. *v.*

ret•i•na (ret′ə nə) the layer of cells at the back of your eyeball. It is sensitive to light and receives the image of whatever you look at. *n.*

ret•i•nue (ret′ə nyū′) a group of servants and so on who travel around with a king, queen, or other important person. *n.*

re•tire (ri tīr′) **1** give up a career, either because of your age or because you want to work at something else: *Grandma retired at age 65. Mr. Gordon has retired from teaching and now farms for a living.* A person who has retired is a **retiree** (ri tī′rē′). **2** go to bed: *We retire early.* **3** go to a quieter or more private place: *She retired to her room.* A **retiring** person has a quiet, private nature. *v.*, **re•tired, re•tir•ing.** **—re•tire′ment,** *n.*

re•tort (ri tôrt′) **1** reply quickly or sharply: *"Mind your own business," he retorted.* **2** a sharp or witty reply: *"Why are your teeth so sharp?" asks Red Riding Hood. "The better to eat you with," is the wolf's retort.* 1 *v.*, 2 *n.*

re•trace (ri trās′) go back over: *We retraced our steps to where we started.* *v.*, **re•traced, re•trac•ing.**

re•treat (ri trēt′) **1** move back; go back: *Seeing the bear, the camper retreated rapidly.* **2** the act of going back or a command to go back: *The army's retreat was orderly.* **3** go away to a quiet, restful place: *He retreats to his cottage on weekends.* **4** a restful, quiet place: *Her favourite retreat was the library.* **5** a time spent away to think, relax, plan, build team spirit, pray, etc. 1, 3 *v.*, 2, 4, 5 *n.*

beat a retreat, run away: *They dropped the apples and beat a hasty retreat when the farmer shouted at them.*

re•trieve (ri trēv′) go and get; get something back: *He retrieved the ball from the creek. I showed him how to retrieve a saved file on the computer.* *v.*, **re•trieved, re•triev•ing.** **—re•triev′al,** *n.*

re•triev•er (ri trē′vər) a dog trained to go and find a hunted animal that has been killed or wounded and bring it to the hunter. *n.*

ret•ro•spect (ret′rə spekt′)
in retrospect, thinking back to something in the past, especially in a way that lets you understand it better: *In retrospect, I'd say the week I spent at camp was one of the best things that ever happened to me.* *n.*

re•turn (ri tərn′) **1** go back; come back: *When Mom returned from her trip she told us about the places she had visited.* **2** bring or send back; give or put back: *to return a book to the library. She said she liked my jacket,*

and I returned the compliment. **3** the act or fact of returning: *We look forward all winter to the return of spring.* **4** reply; answer: *"I don't care," he returned crossly.* **5** profit or reward: *The returns from the sale were over $100.* **6** a report or account: *The election returns are all in. My parents did their income tax returns last night.* **7** for the trip there and back: *a return ticket (adj.). The fare is $89 return (adv.).* 1, 2, 4 *v.*, 3, 5, 6 *n.*, 7 *adj. or adv.*
in return, as a trade; in exchange: *I'll give you this granola bar in return for your banana muffin.*

returning officer (ri tər′ning of′ə sər) the official in charge of the election process in a particular riding or voting district. He or she prepares the voters' list and the ballots and officially announces the winner.

re•un•ion (rē yūn′yən) a gathering of the members of a family, an old class, or some other group after being apart for a long time: *a family reunion in the summer.* *n.*

re•us•a•ble (rē yūz′ə bəl) able to be used more than once: *Glass bottles are reusable; plastic bottles must be recycled.* *adj.*

re•veal (ri vēl′) show or tell, especially something that was hidden: *Promise never to reveal my secret. Her smile revealed her even teeth.* When something is revealed, it is a **revelation** (rev′ə lā′shən). *v.* **—re•veal′ing,** *adj.*

rev•el (rev′əl) **1** take great pleasure: *We revel in country life.* **2** have a noisy good time: *The fans revelled in the streets when the Stampeders won the Grey Cup.* **3** a lively party. 1, 2 *v.*, **rev•elled** or **rev•eled, rev•el•ling** or **rev•el•ing;** 3 *n.* **—rev′el•ler,** *n.* **—rev′el•ry,** *n.*

re•venge (ri venj′) **1** the action of hurting or harming someone in return for having been hurt: *After Sasha teased his little sister, she knocked over his Lego™ castle in revenge.* **2** a desire to do this: *He said nothing, but there was revenge in his heart.* *n.*

rev•e•nue (rev′ə nyū′) money coming in; income: *The government gets its revenue from taxes.* *n.*

re•ver•ber•ate (ri vər′bə rāt′) echo again and again: *His loud voice reverberated across the lake.* *v.*, **re•ver•ber•at•ed, re•ver•ber•at•ing.** **—re•ver′ber•a′tion,** *n.*

rev•er•ence (rev′ə rəns) **1** deep respect, mixed with wonder, admiration, and love. **2** treat with reverence. To **revere** (ri vēr′) is the same thing. 1 *n.*, 2 *v.*, **rev•er•enced, rev•er•enc•ing.** **—rev′er•ent,** *adj.*

rev•er•ie (rev′ə rē) a daydream: *He was so lost in his reverie that he did not hear the bell ring.* *n.*

re•verse (ri vərs′) **1** the opposite: *She did the reverse of what I ordered.* **2** something turned backward: *"Reed" is the reverse of "deer."* **3** turned over or backward; opposite: *Play the reverse side of that tape. She read the numbers off in reverse order.* **4** turn the other way; turn inside out, backward, or upside down: *A mirror reverses the image of something. He reversed his sweatshirt so the fleece was on the outside.* **5** change to the opposite: *to reverse a decision.* **6** the back: *She turned the page over and continued writing on the reverse.* **7** a gear that lets a vehicle move backward: *Put the car in reverse to back out of the garage.* **8** a change to bad luck; a misfortune: *He used to be rich, but his business suffered several reverses.* 1, 2, 6–8 *n.*, 3 *adj.*, 4, 5 *v.*, **re•versed, re•vers•ing.** **—re•vers′al,** *n.* **—re•vers′i•ble,** *adj.*

re•vert (ri vərt′) go back to an earlier way, idea, etc.: *to revert to a bad habit. My thoughts reverted to the last time that I had seen her.* *v.*

re•view (ri vyū′) **1** go over something again: *Our teacher always reviews the unit with us before a test.* **2** the process of doing this: *a quick review of the main points.* **3** a description of the good and bad points about a book, play, movie, piece of work, etc.: *She wrote a review of the movie for the school newspaper.* **4** write or give such a description: *to review a book.* **5** look back on how something has gone, and decide what needs to be changed or corrected: *to review a policy.* **6** the process of doing this. 1, 4, 5 *v.*, 2, 3, 6 *n.* **—re•view′er,** *n.*

re•vise (ri vīz′) make needed changes to a piece of writing, an idea, etc.: *She revised the poem she wrote. We will have to revise our plan.* *v.*, **re•vised, re•vis•ing.** **—re•vi′sion** (ri vizh′ən), *n.*

re•vive (ri vīv′) **1** make or become conscious again: *He was nearly drowned, but we revived him.* **2** make or become fresh, strong, and lively again: *The wilting flowers revived in water. Hot soup revives a cold, tired person.* **3** bring or come back into use, fashion, etc.: *to revive an old song. Interest in medieval times is reviving.* *v.*, **re•vived, re•viv•ing.** **—re•viv′al,** *n.*

re•voke (ri vōk′) take back; cancel: *This privilege will be revoked if you abuse it.* *v.*, **re•voked, re•vok•ing.**

re•volt (ri vōlt′) **1** turn against a leader; fight against someone in authority: *The people revolted against the cruel dictator.* **2** the act or state of turning against authority: *The town is in revolt.* **3** disgust: *I was revolted by the horrible sight.* The feeling of being revolted is called **revulsion** (ri vul′shən). 1, 3 *v.*, 2 *n.* **—re•volt′ing,** *adj.*

a bat	e bed	i bid	o pot	u cup	th thin
ā cake	ē me	ī bite	ō go	ū rude	ᴛʜ then
à bar	ə about	ər over	ò for	ů put	zh measure

Rhinoceros

The rhinoceros is one of the heaviest land animals, and can weigh over three tonnes. It eats grass, leaves, and small bushes. Although this animal is not a predator, it will attack anything it feels is a threat. Since it has very poor eyesight, the rhinoceros will charge almost any moving object. It looks slow and clumsy, but can move very fast.

Notice the birds in the picture. They follow the rhinoceros around, often getting a free ride, to eat the insects stirred up by its huge feet.

rev·o·lu·tion (rev′ə lū′shən) 1 the complete overthrow of a government or political system, usually with violence. 2 a radical change: *Plastics have caused a revolution in industry.* To bring about a complete change in something is to **revolutionize** it. 3 movement in a circle around some point: *One revolution of the earth around the sun takes a year.* *n.*
—**rev′o·lu′tion·ar′y,** *adj. or n.*

re·volve (ri volv′) 1 travel or turn in a circle around a point; rotate: *The moon revolves around the earth. The wheels of a moving car revolve.* 3 have as a main focus: *His life revolves around sports.* *v.,* **re·volved, re·volv·ing.**

re·volv·er (ri vol′vər) a pistol with a revolving cylinder that holds several bullets. It can be fired several times without reloading. *n.*

re·ward (ri wȯrd′) 1 anything good that a person gets because of what he or she has done. A money reward is sometimes given for information about a crime or for returning lost property. 2 give a reward to or for: *After we raked both lawns, Dad rewarded us each with a banana split. Her kind words were rewarded with a hug.* 1 *n.,* 2 *v.*

re·ward·ing (ri wȯr′ding) bringing enjoyment and satisfaction and giving a chance to learn valuable lessons or skills: *Nursing is a rewarding profession.* *adj.*

rhe·a (rē′ə) a large South American bird that looks like the ostrich, but is smaller and has three toes instead of two. Rheas can't fly, but they can run very fast. *n.*

rheu·ma·tism (rū′mə tiz′əm) a disease that causes joints or muscles to become swollen and stiff. *n.*

rhi·noc·er·os (rī nos′ə rəs) a large, thick-skinned animal of Africa and Asia that has one or two upright horns on its snout. The name is often shortened to **rhino** (rī′nō). *n., pl.* **rhi·noc·er·os·es** or **rhi·noc·er·os.**

rho·do·den·dron (rō′də den′drən) an evergreen shrub with showy white, pink, red, or purple flowers. *n.*

rhom·bus (rom′bəs) a diamond-shaped figure with equal sides. *n., pl.* **rhom·bus·es** or **rhom·bi** (rom′bī *or* rom′bē).

rhu·barb (rū′bȧrb) a garden plant with very large leaves and thick, sour stems. The stems are cooked with a lot of sugar to make sauces and pies. The leaves are very poisonous. *n.*

rhyme (rīm) 1 sound alike in the last part. *Long* and *song* rhyme. *Go to bed* rhymes with *sleepyhead.* 2 a word or line with the same last sound as another. *Cat* is a rhyme for *mat.* 3 a short poem with some of the lines ending in the same sounds. "Humpty Dumpty" is the beginning of a famous **nursery rhyme.** 4 make rhymes: *She enjoys rhyming.* 1, 4 *v.,* **rhymed, rhym·ing;** 2, 3 *n.*

rhythm (riᴛʜ′əm) a regular pattern of beats or of repeated movements. Music has rhythm; so do ocean waves, a ticking clock, and the motion of your legs as you pedal a bicycle. *n.* —**rhyth′mic,** *adj.*

rhythm sticks (riᴛʜ′əm stiks′) pieces of wood that you strike together as a musical instrument, especially to learn about rhythm. **Rhythm blocks** is another name, depending on the shape of the wooden pieces.

rib (rib) **1** one of the bones that curve around from your backbone to your chest. Together they form the **rib cage,** which protects your heart, lungs, and other important organs. **2** something like a rib. The curved strips of wood in the frame of a wooden canoe are called ribs. An umbrella has ribs. **3** a ridge in cloth. **4** *Informal.* tease. 1–3 *n.,* 4 *v.,* **ribbed, rib·bing.**

rib·bon (rib′ən) **1** a narrow strip of silk, satin, velvet, or other smooth material used for decoration or tying: *She tied the present with ribbon.* **2** a strip like this given to the winner of a contest or to a brave soldier. **3 ribbons,** *pl.* torn pieces; shreds: *Her dress was torn to ribbons by the thorns she had come through.* *n.*

rice (rīs) a grain grown in warm, wet climates. Rice is an important food in Asia. *n.*

rich (rich) **1** having a lot of money or possessions. **2** having a lot of anything: *Canada is rich in oil and nickel. Oranges are rich in vitamin C.* **3** producing a lot: *rich soil, a rich mine.* **4** costly and beautiful: *rich dresses, rich jewels.* **5** containing a lot of fat or eggs: *a rich dessert.* **6** of colours, sounds, smells, and so on, deep, full and very pleasing: *a rich red, a rich tone.* **7 riches,** *pl.* money and valuable possessions; things that make you rich. 1–6 *adj.,* 7 *n.* **—rich′ness,** *n.*

Rich·ter scale (rik′tər skāl′) a scale for measuring the strength of an earthquake. Each whole number on the scale, beginning with 1, represents an earthquake 10 times stronger than the number before it does. An earthquake measuring 6 or more is a major one.

rick·et·y (rik′ə tē) likely to fall or break down; shaky: *a rickety old chair.* *adj.*

rick·shaw (rik′sho) a small, two-wheeled carriage pulled by a person riding a bicycle or running, used mainly in Asia. *n.*

ric·o·chet (rik′ə shā′) **1** bounce at an angle off a flat surface, often more than once: *The golf ball ricocheted off the tree trunk and into the bushes.* **2** this motion: *the ricochet of a puck off the boards.* 1 *v.,* **ric·o·cheted** (rik′ə shād′), **ric·o·chet·ing** (rik′ə shā′ing); 2 *n.*

rid (rid) make free: *They got a cat to rid the house of mice.* *v.,* **rid** or **rid·ded, rid·ding.**
be rid of, be freed from.
get rid of, get free of or do away with: *I can't get rid of this cold. I'll bet a good sleep would get rid of it.*

rid·dance (rid′əns)
good riddance, an exclamation showing you are happy that something or somebody is finally gone. *n.*

rid·den (rid′ən) the past participle of **ride:** *The horseman had ridden all day.* *v.*

rid·dle[1] (rid′əl) **1** a puzzling question or problem with a funny or surprising answer: *Example: Why did the tomato blush? Because it saw the salad dressing.* **2** any person or thing that is hard to understand or explain. *n.*

rid·dle[2] (rid′əl) **1** make many holes in: *The doorpost was riddled with termites.* **2** fill with something that ruins it: *This story is riddled with spelling mistakes.* *v.,* **rid·dled, rid·dling.**

ride (rīd) **1** sit on an animal, bicycle, or other thing and make it go. **2** be carried along by anything: *to ride on a train, to ride in a shopping cart. The eagle rides the wind.* **3** a trip on horseback, in a car, on a motorcycle, etc.: *Let's go for a ride in the country.* **4** something fun or exciting to go on while it moves, such as a roller coaster, merry-go-round, Ferris wheel, etc.: *I enjoy the rides at Canada's Wonderland.* **5** a turn on one of these: *He took two rides on the merry-go-round.* 1, 2 *v.,* **rode, rid·den, rid·ing;** 3–5 *n.* **—rid′er,** *n.*
let something ride, not do anything about it and see how it goes.
ride high, enjoy success.
ride out, get through successfully: *The small boat rode out the storm without damage.*
ride up, slide up out of place: *This sweater keeps riding up.*
take someone for a ride, *Slang.* cheat.

ridge (rij) a long, narrow raised part that slopes down on either side: *the ridge of a roof, a ridge of land, the ridges on corduroy cloth. The plough left a ridge of snow at the end of the driveway.* *n.* **—ridged,** *adj.*

rid·i·cule (rid′ə kyūl′) **1** laugh at; make fun of: *It is mean to ridicule someone's accent.* **2** words or actions that make fun of a person or thing. 1 *v.,* **rid·i·culed, rid·i·cul·ing;** 2 *n.*

ri·dic·u·lous (ri dik′yə ləs) silly; absurd; laughable: *You look ridiculous in that pig costume.* *adj.*

🍁 **rid·ing** (rī′ding) the area or community represented by a Member of Parliament or a member of a provincial legislature. Another word for a riding is **constituency** (kən stich′ū ən sē). *n.*

a bat	e bed	i bid	o pot	u cup	th thin
ā cake	ē me	ī bite	ō go	ū rude	ᴛʜ then
à bar	ə about	ər over	ȯ for	ů put	zh measure

Rid·van (rid′vən) an important festival of the Bahai religion, taking place in the spring. It lasts 12 days in honour of the 12 days that Baha Ullah spent in the Garden of Ridvan during his exile. *n.*

rife (rīf) **1** common; widespread: *Violence was rife in that neighbourhood.* **2** full of something bad: *The land was rife with rumours of war.* *adj.*

ri·fle[1] (rī′fəl) a gun with a long barrel that has spiral grooves inside which spin the bullet as it is shot. *n.*

ri·fle[2] (rī′fəl) search through and take everything of value: *Her brother had rifled her bag of Halloween goodies and it was half empty.* *v.,* **ri·fled, ri·fling.**

rift (rift) a split or break: *There's a rift in the clouds; perhaps the sun will come out soon. The quarrel created a rift between the two friends.* *n.*

rig (rig) **1** put together in a hurry or by using odds and ends: *The boys rigged up a tent with a rope and a blanket.* **2** arrange in an unfair way: *The race was rigged.* **3** the huge machine needed to get oil out of the earth. Floating oil rigs are used to get oil that is beneath the ocean floor. **4** *Informal.* any machine that seems complicated: *How do you work this rig?* **5** arrange masts, sails, and ropes on a sailing ship. The sails and ropes are called the **rigging.** 1, 2, 5 *v.,* **rigged, rig·ging;** 3, 4 *n.*
rig out, equip: *The camping trailer was rigged out with a stove, fridge, and washroom.*

right (rīt) **1** morally good; fair and just: *She did the right thing when she told the truth.* **2** in a way that is good and just: *to live right.* **3** things that are good and just: *Do right, not wrong.* **4** correct; proper: *the right answer, the right moment.* **5** correctly; properly: *I guessed right. Do the job right the first time.* **6** something that a person should be able to expect or demand: *the right to a good education. Each member of the club has a right to vote.* **7** the side opposite the left; the side that is turned east when you are facing north: *Turn to your right. The school is on the right.* **8** on or to the right: *Turn right (adv.). Our house is the fifth on the right side (adj.).* Another form of the adjective is **right-hand.** **9** exactly, completely, or directly: *Your cap is right where you left it. I looked the man right in the eye. His hat was knocked right off.* **10** make correct; fix: *to right a wrong.* **11** set upright; get back into the proper position: *The girls righted the tipped canoe.* **12** Often, **Right,** a political position in favour of keeping things the way they are or were. This position is also called the **right wing.** 1, 4, 8 *adj.,* 2, 5, 8, 9 *adv.,* 3, 6, 7, 12 *n.,* 10, 11 *v.*
—right′ly, *adv.*
by rights, according to what would be right: *You were responsible, so by rights you should be the one to apologize.*
put right, fix a problem.
put to rights, *Informal.* fix or tidy; put into proper condition, order, etc.
right away, at once; immediately: *I'll do it right away.*
right now, at this very moment: *Stop that right now!*

> **CONFUSABLES .... right**
>
> **right** means "correct": *That is the right answer.*
> **write** means "make letters": *Write with a pencil.*

right angle (rīt′ ang′əl) an angle of 90°, formed by a line perpendicular to another line, as in an "L" shape. All the angles in a square are right angles; a **right triangle** is a triangle with one right angle. **—right′-an′gled,** *adj.*

right·eous (rī′chəs) doing right; behaving justly: *a righteous man.* *adj.* **—right′eous·ness,** *n.*

right·ful (rīt′fəl) according to law or according to what is just and right: *the rightful owner of this car. This is your rightful reward.* *adj.* **—right′ful·ly,** *adv.*

right–handed (rīt′han′did) **1** using the right hand more easily and more readily than the left: *I am right-handed.* **2** done or used with the right hand: *a right-handed pitch, a right-handed scissors.* *adj.*

Right Honourable (rīt′ on′ər ə bəl) a title given to the Governor General, the Prime Minister, and certain other people in government.

right of way (rīt′ əv wā′) **1** the right to go first: *Car drivers must give fire trucks and ambulances the right of way.* **2** the right to pass over property belonging to someone else.

right whale (rīt′ wāl′) a large black whale of northern waters, with a big head and a lower lip that curves upward in a high bow on each side. The right whale used to be hunted in large numbers and is now an endangered species.

rig·id (rij′id) stiff; firm; not bending: *Hold your arm rigid. He is very rigid in his thinking.* *adj.*
—ri·gid′i·ty (rə jid′ə tē), *n.*

rig·ma·role (rig′mə rōl′) a lot of talk or activity that you put up with even though it seems unnecessary. *n.*

rig·our or **rig·or** (rig′ər) **1** harshness; toughness: *the rigour of a long, cold winter.* **2** strictness or exactness: *the rigour of scientific method.* *n.* **—rig′o·rous,** *adj.*

rile (rīl) annoy; irritate. *v.,* **riled, ril·ing.**

rim (rim) **1** an edge or border: *the rim of a wheel.* **2** be on the rim; form a rim around: *Wild flowers and grasses rimmed the pond.* 1 *n.,* 2 *v.,* **rimmed, rim·ming.**

rind (rīnd) a hard or tough outer covering. Melons and some kinds of cheese have a rind. *n.*

ring[1] (ring) 1 a thin circle of metal or other material: *a wedding ring, a key ring, a napkin ring.* 2 any circle: *The fairies danced in a ring. You can tell the age of a tree by counting the rings in a cross-section of its trunk.* 3 form a ring or circle around: *The campfire was ringed with stones.* 4 a closed-in space for races or wrestling matches, circus performances, showing livestock, etc.: *Two clowns somersaulted into the ring.* 5 a group of criminals or troublemakers acting together. 1, 2, 4, 5 *n.,* 3 *v.,* **ringed, ring·ing.**

Word Family........... ring

ringleader: the leader of a gang of wrongdoers
ringlet: a curl of hair like a tube or tight spiral
ringworm: a skin disease that looks like a ring of bumps
ringette: indoor hockey played with a ring for a puck

ring[2] (ring) 1 make a clear, bell-like sound: *The alarm is ringing.* 2 this sound: *Did you hear a ring?* 3 cause to make this sound: *Ring the bell.* 4 call by sounding a bell: *Did you ring, sir?* 5 seem to hear a sound like a bell: *My ears are ringing.* 6 echo loudly: *The room rang with shouts and laughter.* 7 a certain quality of sound: *There was a ring of sincerity in his voice.* 8 have this quality: *His words rang true.* 9 *Informal.* a phone call: *Give me a ring later.* 1, 3–6, 8 *v.,* **rang, rung, ring·ing;** 2, 7, 9 *n.*
ring up, record an amount on a cash register.

rink (ringk) 1 a sheet of ice for skating, playing hockey, or curling. A curling team is also called a rink. 2 a smooth floor for roller skating. *n.*

rinse (rins) 1 wash with clear water, especially to get rid of soap, detergent, etc.: *Rinse all the shampoo out of your hair.* 2 a wash or dip in clear water: *Give the plate a final rinse in hot water.* 3 a special liquid used in rinsing or washing: *a rinse for contact lenses, a conditioning rinse for hair.* 1 *v.,* **rinsed, rins·ing;** 2, 3 *n.*

ri·ot (rī′ət) 1 a wild, violent public disturbance by a crowd of people: *The guards stopped a riot in the prison.* 2 make this kind of disturbance. 3 a bright display: *The garden was a riot of colour.* 4 *Informal.* something very funny, or a very good time: *We had a riot at the party. That movie was a riot.* 1, 3, 4 *n.,* 2 *v.* **—ri′ot·ous,** *adj.*
run riot, a get out of control. **b** grow wildly and luxuriantly: *The weeds have run riot in our garden.*

rip (rip) 1 tear roughly: *Rip the label off this box.* 2 a torn place: *Please sew up this rip in my sleeve.* 1 *v.,* **ripped, rip·ping;** 2 *n.*
rip into, attack in words: *She ripped into me for being late.*
rip off, *Slang.* cheat: *You got ripped off—that's supposed to cost $2.50, not $3.50!* A deal that cheats you is a **rip-off.**

rip cord (rip′ kȯrd′) a cord on a parachute that you pull in order to open it after jumping from a plane.

ripe (rīp) 1 full-grown and ready to be gathered and eaten: *ripe fruit, ripe grain, ripe vegetables.* 2 fully developed; mature: *ripe cheese, a ripe age.* 3 ready: *ripe for mischief.* *adj.,* **rip·er, rip·est. —rip′en,** *v.*

rip·ple (rip′əl) 1 a very little wave: *Throw a stone into still water and watch the ripples spread in rings.* 2 a sound that seems to move like little waves: *a ripple of laughter in the crowd.* 3 make ripples or move in ripples: *A breeze rippled the quiet waters. Angry murmurs rippled through the audience.* 1, 2 *n.,* 3 *v.,* **rip·pled, rip·pling.**

rise (rīz) 1 get up from a lying, sitting, or kneeling position: *Please rise from your seat to read aloud. She rose at six every morning for breakfast.* 2 go up; reach a higher level: *The kite rose high into the air. The river rises when the ice melts. She rose from office clerk to manager.* 3 increase: *The wind is rising rapidly.* 4 an upward movement or increase: *a rise in temperature.* 5 a hill: *The house is on a rise.* 6 start; begin: *Quarrels often rise from the most minor disagreements.* 7 beginning; start: *the rise of a storm, the rise of a new problem.* 8 revolt; rebel: *The slaves rose against their masters.* 9 grow larger and lighter: *Yeast makes dough rise.* 1–3, 6, 8, 9 *v.,* **rose** (rōz), **ris·en** (riz′ən), **ris·ing;** 4, 5, 7 *n.*
give rise to, start; cause: *His strange disappearance gave rise to the fear that he might have been kidnapped.*

CONFUSABLES....... rise

rise means "go up": *If I raise my hand, my hand will rise.*
raise means "lift up": *I raise my hand.*
Notice that **raise** is always followed by a noun.

risk (risk) 1 a chance of harm or loss; danger: *He rescued the dog at the risk of his own life. Wearing a helmet lessens the risk of being hurt.* 2 take the chance of losing or damaging something: *You are risking your neck trying to climb that tree. Don't risk money in gambling.* 3 take the chance of experiencing or getting: *to risk defeat. She risked a fine of $1000 by dumping garbage there.* 1 *n.,* 2, 3 *v.*
run a risk, take the chance of harm or loss.

a bat	e bed	i bid	o pot	u cup	th thin
ā cake	ē me	ī bite	ō go	ü rude	ᴛʜ then
ä bar	ə about	ər over	ȯ for	u̇ put	zh measure

River

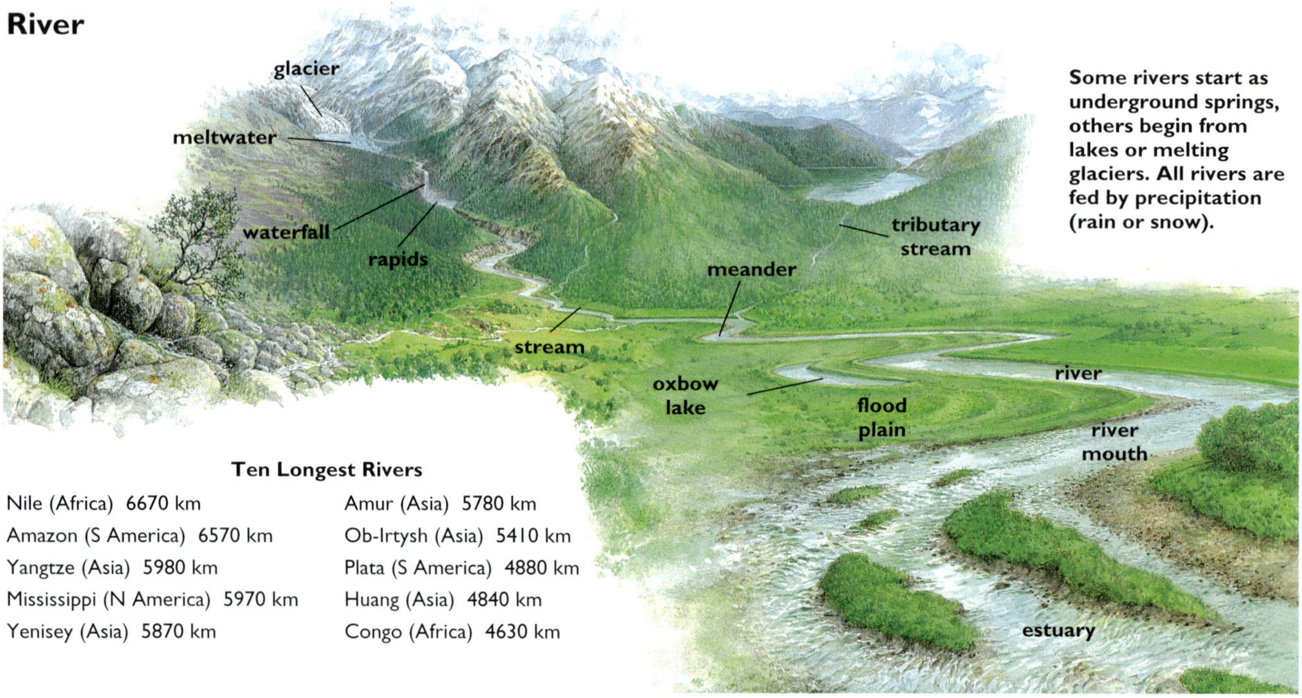

Ten Longest Rivers

Nile (Africa) 6670 km	Amur (Asia) 5780 km
Amazon (S America) 6570 km	Ob-Irtysh (Asia) 5410 km
Yangtze (Asia) 5980 km	Plata (S America) 4880 km
Mississippi (N America) 5970 km	Huang (Asia) 4840 km
Yenisey (Asia) 5870 km	Congo (Africa) 4630 km

rite (rīt) a solemn ceremony: *Most religions have rites for marriage and death.* *n.*
rite of passage, a a ceremony that a person goes through as part of becoming an adult. **b** any important event in a person's life, such as marriage or death, celebrated with a ceremony.

rit•u•al (rich′ū əl) **1** a system of rites: *The rites of baptism, marriage, and burial are parts of the ritual of most churches.* **2** an action that always involves certain steps or words done in a certain order: *Her morning ritual includes washing, dressing, and brushing her teeth.* **3** having to do with a rite or ritual: *a ritual dance.* 1, 2 *n.,* 3 *adj.* **—rit′u•al•ize′,** *v.*

ri•val (rī′vəl) **1** someone who is trying to get the same thing as another or do better than another: *The two boys were rivals for the teacher's attention.* **2** try to equal or do better than: *The stores rival each other in beautiful window displays.* **3** trying to beat another; competing: *A rival newspaper got the story first.* 1 *n.,* 2 *v.,* **ri•valled** or **ri•valed, ri•val•ling** or **ri•val•ing;** 3 *adj.* **—ri′val•ry,** *n.*
have no rival, be better than anything or anyone else.

riv•er (riv′ər) **1** a large, natural stream of water that flows into a lake or ocean. **2** anything flowing in large amounts: *rivers of lava.* A small amount flowing is a **rivulet** (riv′yə lit). *n.*

riv•er•side (riv′ər sīd′) **1** the bank of a river: *We walked along the riverside.* **2** beside a river: *a riverside path.* 1 *n.,* 2 *adj.*

riv•et (riv′it) **1** a metal bolt with a head at one end, placed through holes in pieces of metal, heavy cloth, etc. to join them together. **2** fasten with a rivet or rivets. **3** fix firmly: *Their eyes were riveted on the speaker.* 1 *n.,* 2, 3 *v.*

riv•et•ing (riv′it ing) so interesting or exciting that you cannot stop watching or listening: *The drama on TV was so riveting that we ignored four phone calls so we wouldn't miss any of it.* *adj.*

road (rōd) **1** a way made for cars, trucks, and other vehicles to travel on: *The road from here to the city is being paved.* Another word for this is **roadway. 2** a way: *the road to ruin, a road to peace.* *n.* **on the road,** travelling.

CONFUSABLES .... road

road means "route": *Follow the yellow brick road.*
rode means "did ride": *He rode home on the bus.*

road•block (rōd′blok′) something placed across a road to stop traffic: *The police set up a roadblock to stop the car thief.* *n.*

road•side (rōd′sīd′) **1** the side of a road: *Flowers grew along the roadside.* **2** beside a road: *a roadside fruit stand.* 1 *n.,* 2 *adj.*

roam (rōm) go here and there with no special plan or aim; wander: *to roam through the fields.* *v.*

roar (rôr) 1 make a loud, long, deep sound; make a loud noise: *The lions roared. The wind roared at the windows. The audience roared with laughter at the clown.* 2 a loud, long, deep sound: *the roar of the jet engines, a roar of laughter.* 1 *v.*, 2 *n.*

roast (rōst) 1 cook by heating without water; bake: *We roasted meat and potatoes.* 2 a piece of meat cooked in this way, or meant to be cooked in this way. 3 an outdoor meal with food cooked over an open fire: *a wiener roast, a corn roast.* 4 roasted: *roast beef, roast pork.* 5 make or become very hot. 1, 5 *v.*, 2, 3 *n.*, 4 *adj.*

rob (rob) 1 steal something from: *Thieves robbed the bank of thousands of dollars. Raiders robbed the village.* 2 keep someone from having or doing something good: *The disease has robbed him of his strength.* *v.*, **robbed, rob·bing.** —**rob′ber,** *n.* —**rob′ber·y,** *n.*

robe (rōb) 1 a long, loose outer garment such as the one a priest, judge, or queen wears. 2 something like this, worn over pyjamas, after a bath, etc.; a dressing gown. 3 in earlier times, a sort of heavy blanket or animal skin to wrap around yourself in a sleigh, buggy, etc.: *a buffalo robe.* 4 put a robe on; dress: *The judge was robed in black.* 1–3 *n.*, 4 *v.*, **robed, rob·ing.**

rob·in (rob′ən) 1 a North American bird with a rusty-red breast and greenish grey back. It is a kind of thrush. 2 a small European bird with an orange-red breast. *n.*

ro·bot (rō′bot) 1 any machine that works automatically or by remote control, especially one that does human tasks or is built in the shape of a human being. The science of designing robots is called **robotics** (rō bot′iks). 2 a person who acts automatically, without thinking, or who is controlled by someone else. *n.* —**ro·bot′ic,** *adj.*

ro·bust (rō bust′) strong and sturdy: *a robust person, a robust mind.* *adj.*

rock[1] (rok) 1 a large mass of stone: *The ship was wrecked on the rocks.* 2 a stone: *He threw a rock into the lake.* 3 the mass of mineral matter making up the earth's crust. 4 a heavy, roundish block used in the game of curling. 5 anything firm like a rock; a support or defence: *the rock of faith.* *n.* —**rock′y,** *adj.*
rock bottom, the very lowest point. **Rock-bottom** is the adjective: *rock-bottom prices.*

rock[2] (rok) 1 move back and forth: *The little boat rocked on the waves. I rocked the baby to sleep.* 2 shake violently: *The earthquake rocked the houses.* 3 a style of popular music with a loud, heavy beat. It developed from **rock-and-roll,** a style of popular dance music with a fast, strong beat that was fashionable in the 1950s and 1960s. 1, 2 *v.*, 3 *n.* —**rock′er,** *n.* —**rock′y,** *adj.*

rock·et (rok′it) 1 an object that can be sent at great speed through the air or into space. It is shaped like a tube that is open at one end and filled with fast-burning fuel. The burning creates quickly expanding gases that force the tube ahead at great speed. Some rockets, used as fireworks and signals, shoot high into the air and explode in a shower of sparks; others are used as weapons. Large rockets carry satellites into outer space. 2 a spacecraft, missile, etc. attached to one of these tubes. 3 rise or move extremely fast like a rocket: *The brilliant scientist rocketed to fame with her discoveries.* 1, 2 *n.*, 3 *v.*

rock garden (rok′ gär′dən) a garden full of many interesting or beautiful rocks, with plants growing over or between them. Another name for it is a **rockery.**

rocking chair (rok′ing cher′) a chair made to rock back and forth.

rocking horse (rok′ing hôrs′) a toy horse on rockers, or sometimes springs, for children to ride.

rock salt (rok′ solt′) common salt in the shape of large rocks or crystals, as it occurs in the earth. It is often used to melt ice on roads and sidewalks.

Rocky Mountains (rok′ē moun′tənz) the main system of mountains in North America, extending from the southwestern United States northward through Alberta and British Columbia all the way to Alaska. They are often called **The Rockies** for short.

rod (rod) a thin, straight bar or stick of metal or wood: *a lightning rod, a curtain rod, a fishing rod.* *n.*

rode (rōd) the past tense of **ride:** *We rode our bikes all day yesterday.* *v.*

ro·dent (rō′dənt) any mammal with a single pair of long, sharp upper front teeth that it uses for gnawing. Rats, mice, beavers, muskrats, and porcupines are all rodents. *n.*

ro·de·o (rō′dē ō) an event with shows and contests in roping cattle, riding horses and bulls, racing covered wagons, and so on. *n.*, *pl.* **ro·de·os.**

roe[1] (rō) a mass of fish eggs. *n.*

roe[2] (rō) a small reddish brown deer of Europe and Asia. The male is a **roebuck.** *n.*, *pl.* **roes** or **roe.**

a bat	e bed	i bid	o pot	u cup	th thin
ā cake	ē me	ī bite	ō go	ū rude	ᴛʜ then
ä bar	ə about	ər over	ô for	ů put	zh measure

rogue (rōg) 1 a mischievous rascal. 2 an old word for a dishonest person. *n.* —**ro′guish,** *adj.*

role (rōl) 1 an actor's part in a play, movie, etc.: *She got to play the leading role in the school play.* 2 a part played in real life: *a mother's role.* A **role model** is a person whose behaviour is an example for others to follow. *n.*

CONFUSABLES .... role

role means "part": *You will play the role of the villain.*
roll means "turn over": *Roll the ball.*

role–play (rōl′plā′) act in an imaginary situation: *In class today we will role-play going to the zoo.* *v.* —**role′–play′ing,** *n.*

roll (rōl) 1 move along by turning over and over. Wheels and balls roll. 2 wrap by turning over and over on itself or on something else: *She rolled the string into a ball. The boy rolled himself up in a blanket.* 3 something rolled up: *a roll of film, a roll of paper.* 4 a small, round bun: *a sweet roll.* 5 move on wheels: *The wagon rolled along.* 6 flatten by pressing with something shaped like a cylinder: *to roll the lawn. We rolled the dough for cookies.* 7 go in a smooth, sweeping, repeating motion: *Waves roll in on the beach. The years roll on.* 8 rise and fall, or move from side to side: *rolling countryside. The ship rolled in the waves.* 9 a side-to-side motion: *The ship's roll made many people sick.* 10 beat a drum with very fast, continuous strokes, making either a loud, rumbling sound or a soft pattering sound. 11 make a sound like this: *Thunder rolls. Can you roll your r's?* 12 the sound itself: *the roll of a drum, the roll of thunder.* 13 a list of names: *I will call the roll to find out who is absent.* 1, 2, 5–8, 10, 11 *v.,* 3, 4, 9, 12, 13 *n.*

roll•er (rō′lər) 1 any cylinder used to roll something on, such as a hair curler or the rod that a window blind or a classroom map is rolled onto. 2 a cylinder of metal, stone, wood, etc., used for smoothing, pressing, crushing, etc.: *A heavy roller was used to smooth the lawn.* *n.*

roller coaster (rō′lər kō′stər) an amusement park ride made up of a little train that moves very fast along a track that has sharp turns, loops, and steep slopes.

roller skate (rō′lər skāt′) a skate with small wheels on the bottom instead of a blade. Roller skates are used on floors, roads, sidewalks, etc. —**roller skate,** *v.* —**roll′er-skat′ing,** *n.*

rol•lick•ing (rol′i king) jolly; lively: *a rollicking time.* *adj.*

rolling pin (rō′ling pin′) a cylinder about 30 cm long, used for rolling out dough.

ro•ly–po•ly (rō′lē pō′lē) round and fat: *a roly-poly baby.* *adj.*

ROM *abbreviation for* Read Only Memory, the part of a computer's memory that cannot be erased. The ROM usually contains the basic progam that runs the computer.

Roman Catholic (ro′mən kath′ə lik) 1 a member of the Christian church that recognizes the Pope as its earthly leader. 2 having to do with this church.

ro•mance (rō mans′ *or* rō′mans) 1 a love story or love affair. 2 stories, as a group, that are full of heroes and adventure in faraway times and places. Often there is magic, mystery, or love involved. *Treasure Island, The Chronicles of Narnia,* and the stories of King Arthur are tales of romance. 3 a quality in real events that reminds you of this kind of story: *The explorer's life was filled with romance.* 4 have or try to have a love affair with: *Nick is romancing one of the grade six girls.* 1–3 *n.,* 4 *v.,* **ro•manced, ro•manc•ing.** —**ro•man′tic,** *adj.*

Roman numerals (rō′mən nyū′mə rəls) a system of numerals used by the ancient Romans, based on multiples of five. Each number is represented by a letter or combination of letters. *Examples:* XI = 10 + 1 = 11; IX = 10–1 = 9; XXI = 10 + 10 + 1 = 21. Other symbols are V for 5, L for 50, C for 100, D for 500, and M for 1000.
▶ See Appendix.

romp (romp) 1 to play in a lively, active way. 2 a time of lively, active play: *A pillow fight is a romp.* 1 *v.,* 2 *n.*

roof (rūf) 1 the top covering of a building. The highest part is called the **rooftop.** 2 something like this in shape or position: *the roof of a cave, the roof of a car, the roof of the mouth.* 3 to cover with a roof; form a roof over. A **roofer** is a person who makes or fixes roofs. 1, 2 *n.,* 3 *v.*
hit the roof or **go through the roof,** *Informal.* lose your temper.
raise the roof, *Informal.* make a disturbance; create an uproar or confusion.

rook (ru̇k) a piece in the game of chess that looks like a castle tower and can move in any straight row. It is also called a **castle.** *n.*

rook•ie (ru̇k′ē) *Informal.* a beginner. *n.*

room (rūm) 1 a part of a house, or other building, with walls of its own: *a dining room, a schoolroom.* 2 the people in a room: *The whole room laughed.* 3 space available for something: *There is room for one more in the* boat. **4** the fact of something being possible or welcome; opportunity: *There was room for improvement in his work. There is no room for that kind of talk here.* **5** rent or stay in a room: *I roomed with my cousin at Grandma's house in Nova Scotia for two weeks last summer.* **6 rooms,** *pl.* part of a house, rented by someone. 1–4, 6 *n.,* 5 *v.* **—room′ful′,** *n.*

Word Family........room

rooming house: a house with individual rooms for rent
room-mate: someone who shares a room with you
room service: the delivering of food to hotel rooms
roomy: with lots of room or space

roost (rūst) **1** a resting place for a bird. **2** rest or settle for the night on such a place. **3** a coop or small house for a group of birds. 1, 3 *n.,* 2 *v.*
rule the roost, be in control; be the boss.

roost·er (rūs′tər) a male chicken: *We have ten hens and a rooster.* *n.*

Roots anchor a plant. They are also its underground branches, supplying the plant with water and minerals from the soil.

root[1] (rūt) **1** the part of a plant that grows down into the soil and holds the plant in place. Through tiny, threadlike parts called **root hairs,** roots absorb water and nutrients for the plant; some also store these things for the plant to use later. **2** something like a root in shape, position, or use: *the root of a tooth, the roots of your hair.* **3** a cause or source: *The root of the family's problems was poverty.* **4** become fixed in the ground; send out roots and begin to grow: *Some plants root more quickly than others.* **5** have as its cause or source: *Prejudice is rooted in fear.* **6** a word part from which other words are made: *"Room" is the root of "roomy" and "roominess."* ▶ See Appendix. **7 roots,** *pl.* a person's family history, going back to long before he or she was born.
1–3, 6, 7 *n.,* 4, 5 *v.* **—root′less,** *adj.*
root out or **root up,** get rid of completely.
take root, a send down roots and begin to grow. **b** become firmly fixed: *Don't let a bad habit take root.*

root[2] (rūt) **1** dig with the snout: *Pigs like to root in gardens.* **2** search; rummage: *She rooted through the closet looking for her old shoes.* *v.*

root[3] (rūt) *Informal.* cheer someone on enthusiastically: *We are rooting for the Blue Bombers.* *v.*

root beer (rūt′ bėr′) a soft drink flavoured with the juice of the roots of certain plants. Nowadays the flavour is usually artificial.

rope (rōp) **1** a strong, thick cord made of many strands of fibre or wire twisted together. **2** tie or fasten with rope: *The climbers were roped to each other.* **3** close off with a rope: *They had roped off a section of the museum for repairs.* **4** catch a horse, calf, etc. with a lasso. **5** a number of things together on a string: *a rope of pearls.*
1, 5 *n.,* 2–4 *v.,* **roped, rop·ing. —rop′y,** *adj.*
know the ropes, *Informal.* know how something is done or managed.
rope someone in, get someone to join an activity against his or her will.
the end of your rope, the point where you are completely frustrated and feel like giving up: *Mom is at the end of her rope with trying to train our puppy.*

rose[1] (rōz) the past tense of **rise:** *The cat rose and stretched itself.* *v.*

rose[2] (rōz) **1** a sweet-smelling flower that grows on a bush with thorny stems, called a **rosebush.** Roses may be red, pink, white, or yellow. **2** pinkish red. 1, 2 *n.,* 2 *adj.*

rose·bud (rōz′bud′) the bud of a rose. *n.*

Rosh Ha·sha·nah (rōsh′ hȧ′shȧ nȧ′) the Jewish New Year, falling in late September or early October.

ros·y (rō′zē) **1** like a rose; pinkish-red. **2** bright; cheerful: *a rosy future.* *adj.,* **ros·i·er, ros·i·est.**

rot (rot) **1** decay or go bad; spoil: *So much rain will make the fruit rot.* When things rot, they break down, soften, and fall apart. Only living things, or material that comes from them, can rot. **2** the process of decaying or spoiling: *Rot had weakened the old bridge.* **3** *Slang.* nonsense; rubbish. 1 *v.,* **rot·ted, rot·ting;** 2, 3 *n.*

ro·ta·ry (rō′tə rē) **1** turning like a top or wheel; rotating. **2** a system in schools where students move to different rooms and teachers for different subjects. It doesn't usually start before grade seven. 1 *adj.,* 2 *n.*

a bat	e bed	i bid	o pot	u cup	th thin
ā cake	ē me	ī bite	ō go	ū rude	ᴛʜ then
ȧ bar	ə about	ər over	ȯ for	u̇ put	zh measure

ro·ta·te (rō′tāt *or* rō tāt′) **1** move around a centre or axis, as a wheel or the hands of a clock do; turn in a circle: *The earth rotates once every 24 hours.* **2** change in a regular order, taking turns: *Farmers rotate crops. In our house we rotate the everyday jobs like doing the dishes, walking the dog, and tidying up.* *v.,* **ro·tat·ed, ro·tat·ing.** **—ro·ta′tion,** *n.*

rote (rōt)
learn by rote, learn by repeating something over and over, without thinking and often without understanding it, until you know it from memory. *n.*

ro·tor (rō′tər) a rotating part of a machine. The blades on a helicopter are moved by a rotor. *n.*

rot·ten (rot′ən) **1** decayed; spoiled: *a rotten egg.* **2** not solid; crumbling or falling apart: *The rotten ice gave way, and he fell into the water.* **3** *Slang.* very bad: *rotten luck, to feel rotten.* *adj.* **—rot′ten·ness,** *n.*

rouge (rūzh) **1** red make-up for colouring the cheeks. **2** to colour with rouge. 1 *n.,* 2 *v.,* **rouged, roug·ing.**

rough (ruf) **1** not smooth; not level; not even: *the rough bark of oak trees, a rough ride.* **2** harsh; not easy-going or gentle: *rough manners, a rough life in camp.* **3** not polished or properly finished: *rough diamonds, a rough copy.* **4** not exact or detailed: *a rough calculation, a rough idea.* **5** *Informal.* unpleasant; hard: *He was in for a rough time.* **6** shape or sketch roughly: *to rough out a plan, to rough in the outlines of a face.* **7** wildly or violently: *Those kids play too rough for me.* 1–5 *adj.,* 6 *v.,* 7 *adv.* **—rough′ness,** *n.* **—rough′en,** *v.*
rough it, live without comforts and conveniences: *At the cottage we have to rough it a little—there's no running water, and no electricity.*
rough up, treat roughly; hurt.

CONFUSABLES ..... rough

rough means "not smooth": *Cats have rough tongues.*
ruff means "frill": *My costume has a ruff around the neck.*

rough·age (ruf′ij) the coarser parts of food that your body cannot fully digest. Because these foods move quickly through your intestines, they help other kinds of food and waste products to move along too. Bran and most raw fruits and vegetables are roughage. *n.*

rough·ly (ruf′lē) **1** approximately: *From Levis to Vancouver is roughly 5000 km.* **2** in a rough way. *adv.*

round (round) **1** shaped like a ball, ring, or cylinder; having a circle for an outline: *a round hoop.* **2** make or become roundish: *to round the edges of a table.* **3** another word for "around": *Wheels go round. Papers were scattered round the room.* **4** go or come around to the other side of: *The tires squealed as the car rounded the corner.* **5** a route that ends up where it starts from, which someone goes over and over: *The watchman was making his rounds through the building.* **6** one complete section of a game or sport: *a round in a boxing match, a round of cards.* **7** an action or set of actions that a group of people do together: *a round of applause, a round of cheers.* **8** a short song where several people or groups join in one after the other, each starting at the beginning: *"Three Blind Mice" is a round.* **9** approximate; to the nearest unit, ten, hundred, etc.: *In round numbers, 3974 would be 4000.* **10** change a number to the nearest unit, ten, hundred, etc. to make it simpler: *Round your answer to the nearest ten.* **Round off** means the same. 1, 9 *adj.,* 5–8 *n.,* 2, 4, 10 *v.,* 3 *adv., or prep.*
—round′ish, *adj.*
round out, complete: *to round out your experience by trying many different things.*
round up, bring together; gather: *to round up cattle. We rounded up enough people to do the skit.*

Word Family......... round

roundabout: not direct; not straightforward
round table: a discussion where everyone has equal say
round trip: a trip to a place and back
roundup: the act of gathering things, especially cattle
round robin: a way of scheduling games so that every team or player gets a turn against every other one

rouse (rouz) **1** wake up: *I was roused by the telephone.* **2** stir up; excite: *He was roused to anger by the insult.* *v.,* **roused, rous·ing.**

rout (rout) **1** defeat your enemies so completely that they are forced to run away or give up. **2** a complete defeat like this. 1 *v.,* 2 *n.*

route (rūt *or* rout) **1** a way to get somewhere, often by more than one road: *The route we take to Hamilton is Trafalgar Road to Highway 403, then west on 403.* **2** send by a certain route: *The bus to the United States was routed by way of Windsor, Ontario.* **3** a regular course or path always followed by a bus, a person making deliveries, etc.: *a newspaper route.* 1, 3 *n.,* 2 *v.,* **rout·ed, rout·ing.**

rou·tine (rū tēn′) **1** a set of actions done over and over and always in the same way: *Getting up and going to bed are parts of your daily routine.* **2** done often and in the same way each time; not special: *routine tasks, routine questions.* 1 *n.,* 2 *adj.* **—rou·tine′ly,** *adv.*

rove (rōv) wander or roam; travel here and there: *He loved to rove through the fields and woods.* *v.,* **roved, rov·ing.** —**rov′er,** *n.*

row[1] (rō) a line of people or things: *a row of chairs, a row of trees. The boys stood in a row against the wall.* *n.*

row[2] (rō) **1** move a boat by using oars: *We rowed to the island. Row the boat to the dock.* A boat moved with oars is called a **rowboat.** **2** a trip in a rowboat: *It's only a short row.* 1 *v.,* 2 *n.*

row[3] (rou) a noisy quarrel or fuss: *The three girls had a row over the bicycle. What's all this row about?* *n.*

row·dy (rou′dē) **1** noisy, rough, and a bit wild. **2** a person who is like this. 1 *adj.* **row·di·er, row·di·est;** 2 *n., pl.* **row·dies.**

roy·al (roi′əl) **1** having to do with kings or queens: *royal power, royal robes.* **Royal jelly** is the substance fed to queen bees in the larva stage. **2** fit for a king or queen; splendid: *They gave us a royal welcome.* **3** *Informal.* extreme; thorough: *a royal pest.* *adj.* —**roy′al·ly,** *adv.*

This is the badge of the Royal Canadian Mounted Police. The motto *Maintiens le Droit* means "Uphold the Right."

Royal Canadian Mounted Police (roi′əl kə nā′dē ən moun′tid pə lēs′) the federal police force of Canada. *Abbreviation:* RCMP

roy·al·ty (roi′əl tē) **1** a royal person; royal people: *A box in the theatre was reserved for royalty. Kings, queens, princes, and princesses are royalty.* **2** the rank or dignity of a king or queen: *The crown is the symbol of royalty.* **3** a share of the profit from a book, play, piece of music, computer program, etc. paid to the writer. *n.*

R.R. *abbreviation for:* **1** rural route: *His address is R.R. 1, Swift Current, Saskatchewan.* **2** railroad.

Rt. Hon. *abbreviation for* Right Honourable, the title given to a prime minister and certain other people.

rub (rub) **1** move your hands or some other thing back and forth against something else: *He rubbed her hands to warm them. She rubbed her hands with soap.* **2** push and press along the surface of: *The nurse rubbed my sore back.* **3** spread by rubbing: *He rubbed sunscreen onto his legs.* **4** the act of rubbing: *Give the silver a rub with this cloth.* 1–3 *v.,* **rubbed, rub·bing;** 4 *n.*
rub it in, keep making a person feel bad about something.
rub off, a take off or come off by rubbing. **b** have an influence: *My room's a mess—my sister's bad habits must be rubbing off on me.*
rub out, erase marks by rubbing with something.
rub someone the wrong way, annoy or irritate someone.

rub·ber (rub′ər) **1** a stretchy substance made from the juice of certain tropical plants or by a chemical process. Rubber is airtight, water resistant, and does not conduct electricity. **2** something made from this substance, especially an eraser for removing pencil marks. **3** a covering made of rubber that fits tightly over a shoe to keep it dry. Rubbers are sometimes called **overshoes** or **galoshes.** *n.* —**rub′ber·ize′,** *v.* —**rub′ber·y,** *adj.*

rubber band (rub′ər band′) a thin, narrow loop of rubber, used to hold things together. It is also called an **elastic** or an **elastic band.**

rubber stamp (rub′ər stamp′) **1** a stamp made of rubber, used with an ink pad for stamping signatures, dates, etc. on things. **2** *Informal.* a person or group that gives official approval to something without thinking or without any real power to refuse. —**rub′ber-stamp′,** *v.*

rub·bish (rub′ish) **1** garbage; trash: *Pick up the rubbish and burn it.* **2** nonsense: *Don't talk rubbish.* *n.*

rub·ble (rub′əl) bits of ruined buildings, bridges, etc.: *the rubble left by an earthquake.* *n.*

ru·by (rū′bē) a precious stone that is clear, hard, and red: *Real rubies are very rare.* *n., pl.* **ru·bies.**

ruck·sack (ruk′sak′) another word for knapsack, a bag with shoulder straps for carrying on your back. *n.*

ruck·us (ruk′əs) *Informal.* a noisy, confused disturbance or argument: *There was a big ruckus when they learned that the trip had been cancelled.* *n.*

rud·der (rud′ər) a flat blade attached vertically at the back end of a boat or aircraft in order to steer it. *n.*

rud·dy (rud′ē) red or reddish: *the ruddy glow of a fire.* A person with ruddy cheeks looks healthy and fresh. *adj.,* **rud·di·er, rud·di·est.**

a bat	e bed	i bid	o pot	u cup	th thin
ā cake	ē me	ī bite	ō go	ū rude	ᴛʜ then
ȧ bar	ə about	ər over	ȯ for	u̇ put	zh measure

Ruin

From a ruin you can work out what a building once looked like. The remains of the foundation of this castle ruin, for example, show the shapes of some rooms. Fireplaces and holes for beams show where each floor was.

a reconstruction based on the ruin

rude (rūd) 1 impolite or insulting; showing bad manners: *It is rude to stare at people.* 2 rough or harsh; violent: *a rude shock. Rude hands seized the man and threw him into the car.* 3 roughly made or done: *rude tools. They made a rude shelter from the branches of evergreen trees.* *adj.,* **rud·er, rud·est.** —**rude′ness,** *n.*

rue (rū) be sorry for; regret: *She will soon rue the day she insulted your mother.* This is an old or poetic word, but the related word **rueful,** meaning "sorrowful," is more common. *v.,* **rued, ru·ing.** —**rue′ful,** *adj.*

ruff (ruf) 1 a wide, stiff, high frill worn around the neck by men and women in the 1500s. 2 a growth of feathers or hairs on a bird's or animal's neck that stands out from the rest because of length, colour, etc. For example, the **ruffed grouse** is a wild chickenlike bird with a tuft of feathers on each side of its neck. *n.*

ruf·fi·an (ruf′yən) a rough, violent person. *n.*

ruf·fle (ruf′əl) 1 make rough or uneven; mess up or wrinkle: *A breeze ruffled the lake. Don't ruffle my hair; I just combed it.* 2 a frill; a strip of cloth or lace trim gathered along one edge so as to form little folds or pleats. 3 disturb; annoy or make nervous: *Nothing can ruffle her calm temper.* 1, 3 *v.,* **ruf·fled, ruf·fling;** 2 *n.*

rug (rug) 1 a heavy floor covering. 2 in earlier times, a very thick, heavy blanket to wrap yourself in on a sleigh, buggy, etc. *n.*

rug·by (rug′bē) an outdoor game played by two teams of 15 people who try to carry, pass, or kick an oval ball toward a goal. In Canada, this game is also called **rugger.** Canadian football developed from this game. *n.*

rug·ged (rug′id) 1 rough and uneven: *rugged rocks, rugged ground.* 2 sturdy and tough; able to stand up to difficulty or hard wear: *The pioneers were rugged people. These overalls are made of rugged denim.* 3 harsh; severe: *rugged weather, a rugged winter.* *adj.*

ru·in (rū′ən) 1 wreck; destroy; spoil: *The rain has ruined our snow sculpture.* 2 the fact or the cause of being destroyed: *The house had gone to ruin. You will be the ruin of me!* 3 Usually, **ruins,** *pl.* what is left of something that has been destroyed or fallen to pieces: *the ruins of an ancient city, the ruins of a brilliant career.* 1 *v.,* 2, 3 *n.* —**ru′in·ous,** *adj.* —**ru′in·a′tion,** *n.*

rule (rūl) 1 a statement of what to do and what not to do that people are expected to follow: *Obey the rules of the game.* 2 to control as a leader; be in charge; govern: *The queen ruled the country with fairness. She ruled for 30 years.* 3 the fact or time of being in control or on the throne; reign: *the rule of law. Canada became a nation during the rule of Queen Victoria.* 4 use authority to settle a question; decide: *The judge ruled against them.* A decision of this kind is a **ruling.** 5 what usually happens or is done: *Warm weather is the rule in June.* 6 another word for a **ruler** (def. 2). 7 to mark with lines: *ruled paper.* 1, 3, 5, 6 *n.,* 2, 4, 7 *v.,* **ruled, rul·ing.**
as a rule, usually; normally.
rule of thumb, something that is usually true or right, used as a general guide.
rule out, decide against; shut out: *My parents have ruled out violent TV shows. The high cost ruled out the possibility of a trip to Australia.*

rul·er (rū′lər) 1 a person who rules; a king, queen, emperor, etc. 2 a straight strip of wood, metal, or plastic marked off in units such as centimetres, for measuring or for drawing straight lines. *n.*

rum·ble (rum′bəl) 1 make a deep, heavy sound like far-off thunder. 2 this sound: *We heard the rumble of a heavy truck behind us.* 1 *v.,* **rum·bled, rum·bling;** 2 *n.*

rum·mage (rum′ij) 1 search thoroughly by moving things around: *I rummaged in my drawer for a pair of gloves.* 2 a thorough search like this. 1 *v.,* **rum·maged, rum·mag·ing;** 2 *n.*

rummage sale (rum′ij sāl′) a sale of used items held to raise money for something.

ru·mour or **ru·mor** (rū′mər) 1 a statement or story talked about as news with no proof that it is true: *The rumour spread that the grade one teacher was getting married.* 2 tell or spread as a rumour: *It was rumoured that the government was going to increase taxes.* 1 *n.,* 2 *v.*
rumour has it, people are saying: *Rumour has it that Matthew has been expelled.*

rump (rump) 1 the hind part of the body of an animal, where the legs join the back. 2 the same part of the human body; seat; rear end. *n.*

rum·ple (rum′pəl) wrinkle badly; mess up: *If you play in your good clothes, you'll rumple them.* *v.,* **rum·pled, rum·pling.**

rum·pus (rum′pəs) *Informal.* a noisy disturbance. **Ruckus** is a more usual word. *n.*

run (run) 1 go by moving your legs very quickly so that at times you have no feet on the ground. 2 go: *Vines run over the ground. The bus runs from here to Rimouski. The price of eggs can run as high as three dollars a dozen. This lease runs for two years. The well ran dry.* 3 flow: *The river runs into the sea.* Something that flows easily is **runny.** 4 have liquid flowing out: *The tap is running. My nose runs when I eat hot soup.* 5 spread: *The colour ran when the dress was washed.* 6 be a candidate in an election: *She is running for mayor.* 7 operate: *to run a machine. The dryer is not running properly.* 8 manage; be in charge of: *Who runs this business?* 9 the act of running: *to make a quick run into town, to go on a 5-km run. This play has had a six-month run in Edmonton.* 10 in baseball, the act of going around all the bases and back to home plate, or the point scored by doing this. 11 lose knitted stitches; unravel: *These pantyhose run too easily.* 12 a spot where this has happened: *a run in my pantyhose.* 13 go through: *to run a red light.* 14 publish in a newspaper, magazine, etc.: *to run an ad, to run a story.* 15 do by going somewhere: *to run an errand.* 1–8, 11, 13–15 *v.,* **ran, run, run·ning;** 9, 10, 12 *n.*
at a run, running: *The dog came at a run.*
in the long run, in the end.
in the running, having a chance to win. **Out of the running** is the opposite.
on the run, running away; trying to avoid being caught.
run across, meet by chance.
run down, a stop working: *The battery has run down.* **b** chase till caught: *The police finally ran him down in the woods.* **c** say bad things against: *She runs down everything I do.* **d** make tired or ill: *She is run down from overwork.*
run for it, run for safety.
run into, a meet by chance: *I ran into an old friend.* **b** crash into: *The truck ran into a tree.* **c** end up in: *to run into debt, to run into trouble.*
run off, a drain away: *The melting snow ran off quickly.* The noun is **runoff:** *the spring runoff.* **b** copy by machine: *Run off 50 copies of this form.* **c** run away. **d** chase away: *We ran them off our land.*
run of the mill, the ordinary kind of person or thing: *She's different from the run of the mill.* The adjective is **run-of-the-mill:** *a run-of-the-mill story.*
run out, be used up: *Our time has run out. His money soon ran out.*
run out of, use up; have no more: *We have run out of tea.*
run over, a knock down or drive over with a car: *Dad ran over my hockey net by mistake.* **b** overflow: *The coffee ran over into the saucer.* **c** go through quickly: *Please run over these figures to check my addition.*
the run of, freedom to go anywhere in a place: *We had the run of the whole neighbourhood.*

run·a·way (run′ə wā′) 1 a person or animal that runs away or runs out of control: *He found the runaway and brought her home.* 2 that has run away or run out of control: *a runaway horse, runaway spending.* 1 *n.,* 2 *adj.*

run·down (run′doun′) a brief summary: *Give me a rundown on what happened.* *n.*

run–down (run′doun′) 1 tired; sick: *The doctor said Mila was in a run-down condition.* 2 falling to pieces; partly ruined: *a run-down building.* *adj.*

rune (rūn) a letter of an alphabet used long ago in Europe, or something written in this alphabet. Runes were sometimes used as magic symbols or spells. *n.*

rung[1] (rung) the past participle of **ring**[2]**:** *The bell has rung.* *v.*

CONFUSABLES .... rung

rung means "chimed": *The bell has rung.*
wrung means "squeezed": *She wrung out the wet cloth.*

rung[2] (rung) one step of a ladder. *n.*

a bat	e bed	i bid	o pot	u cup	th thin
ā cake	ē me	ī bite	ō go	ū rude	ᴛʜ then
ä bar	ə about	ər over	ô for	ů put	zh measure

run–in (run′in′) *Informal.* a conflict; quarrel. *n.*

run•ner (run′ər) 1 a person or animal that runs: *A deer is a good runner.* 2 either of the narrow pieces with curved-up ends that a sleigh or sled slides on. 3 **runners,** *pl.* running shoes; gym shoes. 4 a long, narrow strip of carpet or cloth: *We have a runner protecting the hardwood floor in the hall. I have a flowered runner on my dresser.* 5 a slender stem that grows along the ground and takes root, producing new plants. Strawberry plants spread by runners. *n.*

run•ner–up (run′ə rup′) the person, player, or team that takes second place in a contest. *n.*

run•ning shoe (run′ing shū′) a shoe with a rubber sole, for sports or for casual wear; a gym shoe.

run–on sentence (run′on′ sen′təns) a sentence with too many clauses, especially ones not joined by the proper punctuation or connecting words.

Grammar Check . . run-on sentence

The way to fix a run-on sentence is to rewrite it as two or more sentences. For example: *The video is very good, I like it and so I've asked for it for my birthday, that way I can watch it many times.*

One possible rewrite is: *The video is very good. I like it, and so I've asked for it for my birthday. That way I can watch it many times.*

runt (runt) an animal, person, or plant which is smaller than the usual size. *n.* —**runt′y,** *adj.*

run•way (run′wā′) a long strip of level ground, usually paved, for aircraft to land and take off on. *n.*

rup•ture (rup′chər) 1 to break or burst: *a ruptured spleen. The argument ruptured their relationship.* 2 a break: *the rupture of a blood vessel, the rupture of friendly relations.* 1 *v.,* **rup•tured, rup•tur•ing;** 2 *n.*

ru•ral (rū′rəl) having to do with the country rather than the city: *She thinks rural life is healthful and quiet.* A **rural route** is a mail delivery route in the country. The abbreviation is **R.R.** *adj.*

ruse (rūz *or* rūs) a trick to fool someone. *n.*

rush[1] (rush) 1 move with speed and force: *The river rushed past.* 2 do, finish, send, etc. as fast as you can, often too fast: *She rushed to get ready. Don't rush your homework.* 3 tell or force someone else to go faster: *I won't rush you—take your time.* 4 to attack with speed and force: *The soldiers rushed the enemy's trenches.* 5 the act or fact of rushing: *the rush of city life.* In a **gold rush,** many people suddenly rush to a certain area where gold has been found. 1–4 *v.,* 5 *n.* —**rushed,** *adj.*
in a rush, rushing; trying to be fast.

rush[2] (rush) a tall grasslike plant with hollow stems, found in wet or marshy places. *n.*

rush hour (rush′ our′) the time of day when traffic is heaviest because most people are driving to or from work.

rust (rust) 1 the reddish brown or orange coating that forms on iron or steel which is exposed to moisture. 2 become covered with this coating: *The old swing set was starting to rust in the yard.* Something that will not rust is **rustproof.** 3 spoil by not being used: *Don't let your mind rust during vacation.* 4 a plant disease that spots leaves and stems. 1, 4 *n.,* 2, 3 *v.* —**rust′y,** *adj.*

rus•tic (rus′tik) belonging to the country or suitable for the country; simple, plain, and a little rough: *a rustic log cabin, rustic manners.* *adj.*

rus•tle (rus′əl) 1 the sound that papers or dry leaves make when moved against each other. 2 make or cause to make this sound: *to rustle papers. Her jacket rustled every time she moved.* 3 *Informal.* steal cattle or horses. 1 *n.,* 2, 3 *v.,* **rus•tled, rus•tling.** —**rus′tler,** *n.*
rustle up, *Informal.* **a** gather; find. **b** get ready; prepare: *The cook rustled up some food.*

rut (rut) 1 a track worn deep into the ground by wheels. 2 make ruts in: *The dirt road was badly rutted.* 3 a way of acting that has become a firm habit: *He has a different lunch every day so he won't get into a rut.* 1, 3 *n.,* 2 *v.,* **rut•ted, rut•ting.**

ru•ta•ba•ga (rū′tə bā′gə) a large, round yellow root that grows on a garden plant related to the turnip. It is eaten as a vegetable. *n.*

ruth•less (rūth′lis) showing no pity or mercy; cruel: *a ruthless tyrant.* *adj.*

rye (rī) a tough grass plant widely grown in cold regions. Its seed or grain is used to feed farm animals, or ground up into flour to make bread. *n.*

Ss

s or **S** (es) 1 the nineteenth letter of the English alphabet, or any of the sounds that it stands for. The sound of *s* in *soap* is different from the sound of *s* in *his.* 2 the nineteenth thing in a list. *n., pl.* **s's** or **S's.**

s *symbol for* second or seconds.

S or **S.** *abbreviation for* south or southern.

Sab•bath or **sab•bath** (sab′əth) in various religions, the day of the week used for rest and worship. Saturday is the Jewish Sabbath, Sunday is the Christian Sabbath, and Friday is the Muslim Sabbath. *n.*

sa•ble (sā′bəl) a small animal related to the weasel and mink. Its dark brown, glossy fur is very costly. *n.*

sab•o•tage (sab′ə täzh′) 1 block or wreck on purpose in order to hinder some activity or effort. During a war, enemy agents might sabotage the machines in a weapons factory; someone who wants a war to continue might try to sabotage a peace treaty. 2 the act or the result of doing this: *Sabotage by protesters forced the bomb factory to shut down for a time.* A person who takes part in sabotage is a **saboteur** (sab′ə tər′). 1 *v.,* **sab•o•taged, sab•o•tag•ing;** 2 *n.*

sa•bre (sā′bər) a heavy sword with one cutting edge like an ordinary knife. *n.*

sac (sak) a baglike part in an animal or plant, often containing a liquid: *the sac of a honeybee.* *n.*

sac•cha•rine (sak′ə rin) too nice or sweet. *adj.*

sack[1] (sak) a huge bag made of coarse cloth or strong paper, for holding grain, flour, potatoes, coal, and so on. *n.* **—sack′ful′,** *n.*

sack[2] (sak) 1 capture a place and take all that is valuable: *The invaders sacked the town.* 2 the act of doing this: *the sack of Rome by the barbarians.* 1 *v.,* 2 *n.*

sa•cred (sā′krid) 1 coming from God or set aside for God; holy: *a sacred building, sacred writings, sacred music.* 2 that must not be broken, forgotten, or dishonoured: *a sacred promise, a sacred memory.* *adj.*

sacred pipe (sā′krid pīp′) a pipe smoked by many First Nations people when praying as part of certain ceremonies.

sac•ri•fice (sak′rə fīs′) 1 give up something valuable for someone or something even more important: *We decided to sacrifice our March break to help out at the food bank.* 2 give or offer to a god: *The ancient Romans sacrificed oxen.* 3 the thing that is offered: *Mary and Joseph brought two doves as a sacrifice to God.* 4 the act of giving up something valuable or offering something to a god: *Sending me to camp is a sacrifice for my parents because it costs them a lot.* 1, 2 *v.,* **sac•ri•ficed, sac•ri•fic•ing;** 3, 4 *n.*
—sac′ri•fi′cial (sak′rə fish′əl), *adj.*
sell at a sacrifice, sell something for less than it is worth.

sac•ri•lege (sak′rə lij) disrespect toward anyone or anything sacred: *Robbing the mosque was a sacrilege.* *n.*

sad (sad) 1 not happy; full of sorrow: *You feel sad if your best friend moves away. The death of a pet is a sad event.* 2 *Informal.* shocking; hopeless: *a sad mess.* *adj.,* **sad•der, sad•dest.** **—sad′den,** *v.* **—sad′ness,** *n.*

sad•dle (sad′əl) 1 a seat for a rider on an animal's back. 2 anything shaped or used like a saddle, such as a bicycle seat or a ridge between two mountain peaks. 3 put a saddle on: *Saddle the horse.* 4 to burden: *They are saddled with a big house that they do not need or want.* 1, 2 *n.,* 3, 4 *v.,* **sad•dled, sad•dling.**
in the saddle, **a** in control. **b** active and working.

sa•fa•ri (sə fä′rē) a journey or hunting trip in a wild region in a hot country. *n.*

WORD HISTORY........ safari

Safari comes from the Swahili word for "journey." It was originally used specially for hunting trips in East Africa, where Swahili was the main language.

safe (sāf) 1 free from harm or danger: *a safe trip, a safe place. We feel safe with the dog in the house.* 2 careful to avoid risks: *a safe bet, safe driving.* 3 that can be trusted: *a safe guide.* 4 a box that can be locked and that is very hard to break into, used to keep valuable things in. 1–3 *adj.,* **saf•er, saf•est;** 4 *n.*
—safe′ty, *n.*

a bat	e bed	i bid	o pot	u cup	th thin
ā cake	ē me	ī bite	ō go	ü rude	ᴛʜ then
ä bar	ə about	ər over	ò for	ù put	zh measure

safe·guard (sāf′gärd′) 1 keep safe; protect: *Food laws safeguard our health.* 2 something that protects: *Keeping clean is a safeguard against disease.* 1 *v.*, 2 *n.*

safe·keep·ing (sāf′kē′ping) the fact of keeping something safe: *She put her money in the bank for safekeeping.* *n.*

safety pin (sāf′tē pin′) a pin bent back on itself to form a spring, with a guard that covers the point and prevents it from coming undone by accident.

sag (sag) 1 bend down in the middle under weight or pressure: *The planks over the hole sagged as we walked across.* 2 droop; hang weakly or loosely: *Your dress sags in the back.* 3 the fact of sagging. 1, 2 *v.*, **sagged, sag·ging;** 3 *n.* —**sag′gy,** *adj.*

sa·ga (sä′gə *or* sag′ə) a long story of adventure or heroic deeds. *n.*

sage[1] (sāj) 1 wise: *sage advice.* 2 a very wise person: *to study the writings of the sages of old.* 1 *adj.*, **sag·er, sag·est;** 2 *n.*

sage[2] (sāj) a plant whose fresh or dried greyish green leaves are often used in cooking. *n.*

sage·brush (sāj′brush′) a greyish green shrub that smells like sage, common on the dry plains of western North America. *n.*

said (sed) 1 the past tense and past participle of **say:** *He said he would come. She has said "No" every time.* 2 mentioned before: *the said sum of money.* 1 *v.*, 2 *adj.*

sail (sāl) 1 a piece of cloth that catches the wind to make a ship move on water. A boat that moves in this way is a **sailboat.** 2 take or begin a trip on water: *He sailed to England on a steamship. Her ship sails at 5:00 from Halifax.* 3 manage a boat that moves by sails: *The girls are learning to sail.* 4 move smoothly like a ship with sails: *The eagle sailed by.* 5 a trip on a boat with sails: *Let's go for a sail.* 6 something like a sail, such as the part of a windmill that catches the wind. 1, 5, 6 *n.*, 2–4 *v.* —**sail′or,** *n.*
sail into, a scold or criticize harshly and for a long time: *He sailed into me about the big mess.* b start something with enthusiasm: *She sailed into a detailed explanation.*
set sail, begin a trip by water.
under sail, moving with the sails spread out.

CONFUSABLES ....sail

sail means "travel on water": *The ship sails on Monday.*
sale means "the act of selling" or "selling for a lower price than usual": *There is a sale on at that store.*

sail·board (sāl′bȯrd′) 1 a long narrow board like a surfboard, with a sail on it. You stand on it and hold onto a horizontal bar attached to the mast, letting the wind push you as you ride the waves. 2 ride on one of these boards as a sport: *We spent two hours sailboarding on Georgian Bay.* 1 *n.*, 2 *v.* —**sail′board′ing,** *n.*

saint (sānt) 1 a holy person. 2 a person declared to be a saint by the Roman Catholic Church. These people have **Saint** in front of their names, which is usually written as **St.** 3 a person who is very humble, patient, kind, and so on. *n.* —**saint′hood,** *n.* —**saint′ly,** *adj.*

Saint Ber·nard (sānt′ bər närd′) a breed of big, powerful, friendly, brown and white dog with a large head. *n.*

sake (sāk) 1 benefit: *Don't go to any trouble for my sake.* 2 purpose; aim: *He gave in to them for the sake of peace and quiet.* *n.*

sal·ad (sal′əd) almost any dish that is served cold with a dressing. Most salads contain raw vegetables or fruits, but some also have chicken, rice, pasta, seafood, nuts, or other ingredients mixed in. At a **salad bar** you can serve yourself from many different kinds of salad. *n.*

Salamanders are amphibians, that is, they live part of their lives in water and part on land.

sal·a·man·der (sal′ə man′dər) a small lizardlike animal with smooth skin instead of scales, and no claws. *n.*

sa·la·mi (sə lä′mē) a spicy smoked sausage of pork and beef or just beef, often flavoured with garlic. It keeps for a long time. *n.*

sal·a·ry (sal′ə rē) fixed pay for regular work. Teachers and most office workers receive salaries. *n.*, *pl.* **sal·a·ries.**

sale (sāl) 1 the act of selling, or of exchanging goods for money: *The sale of their old home made them sad.* 2 a time of selling things at special low prices: *This store is having a sale on software.* 3 **sales,** *pl.* the amount sold: *This month's sales were higher than last month's.* *n.*
for sale, available for buying: *That car is for sale.*

on sale, **a** being sold at lower prices than usual: *All the winter boots are on sale now.* **b** being sold: *Tickets for the concert will be on sale here Monday.*

sales•per•son (sālz′pər′sən) a person whose job is selling something. A salesperson may also be called a **salesclerk,** a **salesman,** or a **saleswoman.** A salesperson who does not work in a store is a **sales rep,** short for **sales representative.** *n., pl.* **sales•peo•ple** (sālz′pē′pəl).

sales tax (sālz′ taks′) a tax you pay when you buy something, based on the price of whatever you bought.

Sa•lish (sā′lish) **1** a group of related First Nations peoples living in different parts of British Columbia, including the **Coast Salish,** the **Interior Salish,** and the **Straits Salish.** **2** any of their languages. **3** having to do with these people or their languages. 1, 2 *n.,* 3 *adj.*

sa•li•va (sə lī′və) the liquid produced by glands under your tongue, called the **salivary glands** (sal′i ver′ē glanz′). Saliva keeps your mouth moist, helps make food easy to swallow, and starts digestion. To **salivate** (sal′ə vāt′) is to produce a lot of saliva. *n.*

sal•low (sal′ō) pale and yellowish: *a sallow complexion, a sallow face.* *adj.*

salm•on (sam′ən) **1** a large fish with yellowish pink flesh that is often eaten as food. Salmon live in the north Atlantic and Pacific, but return to the rivers where they were born to lay their eggs. The **Atlantic, chinook, chum, coho,** and **sockeye** salmon are found in Canadian waters. **2** yellowish pink. 1, 2 *n., pl.* **salm•on;** 2 *adj.*

salm•on•ber•ry (sam′ən ber′ē) the fruit of a large, red-flowered raspberry bush of the Pacific coast. Salmonberries are yellowish pink and good to eat. *n., pl.* **sal•mon•ber•ries.**

sal•mo•nel•la (sal′mə nel′ə) a kind of bacteria sometimes found in food. It causes serious illness in people and animals. *n.*

sa•lon (sə lon′) a hairdresser's or beautician's shop. *n.*

sa•loon (sə lūn′) in the days of the wild west, a place where alcoholic drinks were sold and drunk. *n.*

salt (solt) **1** a white substance found in the earth and in sea water, used to bring out the flavour of food and to preserve it, and to melt ice and snow. **2** mix, sprinkle, or preserve with salt: *to salt cod. They ploughed and salted the roads after the snowfall.* A vehicle that spreads salt on the road is a **salter.** **3** containing salt or preserved with salt: *salt water, salt pork.* **4** a sailor: *an old salt.* **5** a chemical compound made up of an acid and a base. Baking soda is a salt. 1, 4, 5 *n.,* 3 *adj.,* 2 *v.* **—salt′y,** *adj.*

salt away, **a** pack with salt in order to preserve. **b** *Informal.* store away: *The miser salted his money away.*
salt of the earth, the best person or people: *She thinks she's the salt of the earth.*
take something with a grain of salt, not quite believe: *You have to take everything he says with a grain of salt, because he exaggerates.*
worth your salt, worthy of any respect.

salt lick (solt′ lik′) **1** a place where natural salt is found on the surface of the ground and where animals go to lick it up. **2** a block of salt put out in a pasture for horses and cattle to lick.

salt•wa•ter (solt′wot′ər) containing or having to do with salt water or the sea: *a saltwater solution, saltwater fishing.* *adj.*

sal•u•ta•tion (sal′yə tā′shən) something done or said as a greeting: *The man raised his hat in salutation. "Dear Gregory," read the salutation of the letter.* *n.*

> **Grammar Check . . . . . . salutation**
>
> Use a comma after the **salutation** of a friendly letter: *Dear Mom,*
>
> For formal letters, use a colon after the salutation: *Dear Mrs. Couloris:*

sa•lute (sə lūt′) **1** show respect in a formal manner by raising your hand to your head: *The soldier saluted the officer.* **2** show honour or appreciation with kind words, cheers, a bow, a kiss, the firing of cannons, etc.; greet warmly. **3** the act of saluting; a sign of welcome, farewell, or honour: *The principal's opening speech was a salute to the graduates.* 1, 2 *v.,* **sa•lut•ed, sa•lut•ing;** 3 *n.*

sal•vage (sal′vij) **1** save whatever is still useful from something that is being destroyed or has been destroyed: *to salvage parts from a wrecked car. Our basement was flooded, but we managed to salvage some furniture.* **2** the act of doing this. 1 *v.,* **sal•vaged, sal•vag•ing;** 2 *n.*

sal•va•tion (sal vā′shən) **1** the fact of being rescued from certain death, great danger, or trouble. This word is often used in a religious sense. **2** a person or thing that rescues like this: *The firefighters were our salvation; they stopped the forest fire before it reached our town.* *n.*

a bat	e bed	i bid	o pot	u cup	th thin
ā cake	ē me	ī bite	ō go	ū rude	ŧh then
à bar	ə about	ər over	ò for	ù put	zh measure

Samurai

Samurai warriors were part of the hereditary warrior class in Japan. This included the samurai warriors, the feudal lords (called daimyos), and the supreme war leader (called the shogun).

salve (sav) 1 healing or soothing ointment for wounds and sores. 2 put salve on. 3 something soothing: *The kind words were a salve to his hurt feelings.* 4 soothe; smooth over: *to salve a guilty conscience.* 1, 3 *n.,* 2, 4 *v.,* **salved, salv·ing.**

sal·vo (sal′vō) the firing of several cannons at the same time, as an attack or as a salute. *n.*

same (sām) 1 being this very one still or again, and not another: *We came back the same way we went.* 2 exactly alike even though they are separate items: *Her jacket and mine are the same.* 3 not changed: *He is the same kind, generous person he was as a boy.* 4 the same person or thing: *Whatever I do, he does the same.* 1–3 *adj.,* 4 *pron.* **—same′ness,** *n.*
all the same, a regardless; in spite of that. **b** of no importance: *It's all the same to me whether you go or stay.*
just the same, a in the same way. **b** in spite of that.
same here, *Informal.* I feel the same as you: *"I'm freezing!" "Same here; I forgot my mitts."*
the same, in the same manner: *"Sea" and "see" are pronounced the same.*

sa·mo·sa (sə mō′sə) a deep-fried snack made of a triangular piece of pastry wrapped around a spicy filling of meat or vegetables. *n.*

sam·ple (sam′pəl) 1 a part to show what the rest is like; one thing to show what the others are like: *We had a water sample from our well tested to see if it was safe to drink. The display samples in the store are not for sale.* 2 take a part of something to test it: *We sampled the cake and found it very good.* 1 *n.,* 2 *v.,* **sam·pled, sam·pling.**

sam·u·rai (sam′ə rī′) in medieval Japan, a professional warrior. *n., pl.* **sam·u·rai.**

sanc·tion (sangk′shən) 1 approve; say that something is all right: *Her conscience does not sanction stealing.* 2 official permission or approval: *We have the sanction of the law to play ball in this park.* 3 an action used to punish wrongdoing or force a change, as when one nation stops trading with another until the other nation agrees to change. 1 *v.,* 2, 3 *n.*

sanc·ti·ty (sangk′tə tē) 1 holiness: *the sanctity of a church.* 2 the fact of being honourable and revered and worth protecting at any cost: *the sanctity of our basic human rights.* *n., pl.* **sanc·ti·ties.**

sanc·tu·ar·y (sangk′chū er′ē) 1 a building or part of a building used for worship: *A temple is a sanctuary.* 2 a place of refuge or protection: *This island is maintained as a bird sanctuary.* *n., pl.* **sanc·tu·ar·ies.**

sand (sand) 1 tiny grains of worn-down or disintegrated rock: *the sand of the seashore, the sand of the desert.* 2 scrape, smooth, polish, or clean with sand or sandpaper. 3 spread sand over: *to sand an icy road.* 1 *n.,* 2, 3 *v.* **—sand′er,** *n.* **—sand′y,** *adj.*

san·dal (san′dəl) an open shoe made of a sole and a strap or set of straps to hold it on. There are many different styles. *n.*

sand bar (sand′ bär′) a ridge of sand in a river or along a shore, formed by the action of tides and currents.

sand·box (sand′boks′) a large box with sand in it for children to play in. *n.*

sand·pa·per (sand′pā′pər) **1** a strong paper with sand or some other rough material glued on it, used for smoothing, cleaning, or polishing. **2** to smooth, clean, or polish with sandpaper. 1 *n.,* 2 *v.*

sand·stone (sand′stōn′) a crumbly, gritty rock formed mostly of sand. It is a sedimentary rock. *n.*

sand·storm (sand′stôrm′) a windstorm that carries along clouds of sand. *n.*

sand·wich (sand′wich) **1** two or more slices of bread with a filling between them. An **open-face sandwich** is just one slice with something on top. **2** put or squeeze in between: *He was sandwiched between two big people on the bus.* 1 *n.,* 2 *v.*

WORD HISTORY........sandwich

The **sandwich** was supposedly invented by the Earl of *Sandwich* (1718–1792), so that he would not have to stop playing cards to eat his meals.

sane (sān) **1** with a healthy mind; not crazy. **2** sensible: *She has a sane attitude toward studying.* *adj.,* **san·er, san·est.** —**san′i·ty** (san′ə tē), *n.*

sang (sang) the past tense of **sing:** *He sang a solo.* *v.*

san·i·tar·y (san′ə ter′ē) clean and free of germs, so as to prevent disease: *Keep food in a sanitary place.* *adj.*

san·i·ta·tion (san′ə tā′shən) the work of keeping food and drink pure and keeping places clean and free of germs, so as to prevent disease. Disposal of garbage and government inspection of milk, meat, and other foods are important parts of sanitation. *n.*

sank (sangk) the past tense of **sink:** *The ship sank before help could reach it.* *v.*

San·ta Claus (san′tə kloz′) a character who symbolizes the spirit of Christmas giving. Santa Claus is pictured as a jolly old man with a white beard, dressed in a fur-trimmed red suit. **Saint Nicholas, Saint Nick,** and **Father Christmas** are other names for this character.

sap¹ (sap) the liquid that carries nourishment and water through a plant, as blood does in animals. Rising sap carries water and dissolved substances from the roots; sap going down carries sugar, gums, and resins. Maple sugar is made from the sap of sugar maple trees. *n.*

sap² (sap) weaken or drain gradually: *The extreme heat sapped our strength.* *v.,* **sapped, sap·ping.**

sap·ling (sap′ling) a young tree. *n.*

sap·phire (saf′īr) **1** a precious stone that is almost as hard as a diamond. Sapphires can be many different colours but the most valuable are deep blue. A red sapphire is called a ruby. **2** bright blue: *a sapphire sky* (*adj.*). 1, 2 *n.,* 2 *adj.*

sar·cas·tic (sär kas′tik) saying one thing but meaning the opposite, in an angry, hurtful, or mocking way: *"Don't rush, now!" was his sister's sarcastic comment as she waited impatiently, "Getting your coat on can be a tricky business, I know."* *adj.* —**sar′casm,** *n.*

Sar·cee (sär′sē) **1** a First Nations people living near Calgary. They used to live much further north in Alberta. **2** their language, which belongs to the Athapascan family. **3** having to do with these people or their language. 1, 2 *n.,* 3 *adj.*

sar·dine (sär dēn′) a small herring or related fish, often preserved in oil for food. *n.*
packed like sardines, very crowded, like sardines in a tin.

sa·ri (sä′rē) one of the main garments of women in India, a long piece of light cloth wound and draped around the body in a special way. *n.*

sash¹ (sash) a long, broad strip of cloth or ribbon worn for decoration around the waist, or over one shoulder and across the chest. *n.*

sash² (sash) the frame which holds the glass in a window or door: *The window sash slipped down and crushed her finger.* *n.*

Sas·katch·e·wan (sə skach′ə won′) a western province of Canada, between Alberta and Manitoba. *n.* —**Sas·katch′e·wan′i·an,** *n.*

sas·ka·toon (sas′kə tūn′) a large, sweet, purple berry that grows on a bush of the northern prairies. *n.*

Sas·quatch (säs′kwoch) according to legend, a very large, hairy, humanlike creature that is supposed to live wild in the mountains of the Pacific Coast. **Bigfoot** is another name for it. *n.*

a bat	e bed	i bid	o pot	u cup	th thin
ā cake	ē me	ī bite	ō go	ū rude	ᴛʜ then
ä bar	ə about	ər over	ô for	ů put	zh measure

sass (sas) 1 rude, disrespectful talk: *No more sass from you!* 2 talk to someone in this way: *Don't sass your mother like that.* 1 *n.*, 2 *v.* —**sass′y,** *adj.*

sat (sat) the past tense and past participle of **sit:** *Yesterday I sat in a train all day. That book has sat on the shelf for years.* *v.*

Sa·tan (sā′tən) in some religions, the main spirit of evil and the enemy of goodness; the Devil. *n.*

satch·el (sach′əl) a book bag that looks a little like a briefcase, often with shoulder straps. *n.*

sat·el·lite (sat′ə līt′) 1 a natural or artificial object that revolves around a larger heavenly body. The moon and space stations are satellites of the earth. Most artificial satellites are machines carried into space by a rocket and left in orbit to gather information, reflect communication signals for TV, telephone, etc. 2 any person, group, or nation under the control or influence of another. *n.*

sat·in (sat′ən) cloth with one very smooth, glossy side. *n.* —**sat′in·y,** *adj.*

sat·ire (sat′īr) 1 the humorous use of symbolism, exaggeration, and sarcasm to show up human foolishness and make fun of it. 2 a piece of writing that does this. *n.* —**sa·tir′i·cal** (sə tēr′ ə kəl), *adj.* —**sat′i·rist,** *n.* —**sat′i·rize′,** *v.*

sat·is·fy (sat′is fī′) 1 give enough to; fulfill a desire, hope, or demand: *He satisfied his hunger with a sandwich. This work does not satisfy the grade five requirements.* 2 make happy; please: *Are you satisfied now? After three hours of hard work, it was very satisfying to look at the clean, tidy room.* 3 convince: *The teacher was satisfied that I was telling the truth.* *v.*, **sat·is·fied, sat·is·fy·ing.** —**sat′is·fac′tion,** *n.* —**sat′is·fac′to·ry,** *adj.*

sat·u·rate (sach′ə rāt′) soak thoroughly; fill with all it can hold: *A heavy rain saturates the soil. My poor brain is saturated with information right now.* *v.*, **sat·u·rat·ed, sat·u·rat·ing.** —**sat′u·ra′tion,** *n.*

Sat·ur·day (sat′ər dā′) the day after Friday and before Sunday. *Abbreviation:* Sat. *n.*

Sat·urn (sat′ərn) the second largest planet and the sixth from the sun. Saturn is encircled by rings made up of tiny particles of matter. *n.* ▶ See Appendix.

sauce (sos) 1 a liquid served with food to make it taste better: *She likes broccoli with cheese sauce over it.* 2 fruit that has been cooked until soft and then mashed or strained: *applesauce, cranberry sauce.* *n.*

sauce·pan (sos′pan′) a small cooking pot. *n.*

sau·cer (sos′ər) 1 a very small plate meant to set a cup on. 2 anything round and shallow like a saucer. *n.*

sau·cy (sos′ē) disrespectful; smart-alecky. *adj.*, **sau·ci·er, sau·ci·est.**

sauer·kraut (sour′krout′) cabbage cut fine, salted, and pickled in vinegar. *n.*

Saul·teaux (sal′tō *or* sol′tō′) 1 a First Nations people living in Ontario, Manitoba, and Saskatchewan. 2 having to do with these people 1 *n.*, 2 *adj.*

sau·na (son′ə) 1 a steam bath. In a traditional sauna, the steam is made by pouring water over hot stones. 2 a building or room used for such baths. It is usually lined with wood. *n.*

saun·ter (son′tər) 1 walk along in a very relaxed way. 2 a stroll. 1 *v.*, 2 *n.*

Sausages may contain meat that is raw, smoked, dried, or cooked. The most famous cooked sausage is the hot dog, or Frankfurter, named after the city of Frankfurt in Germany.

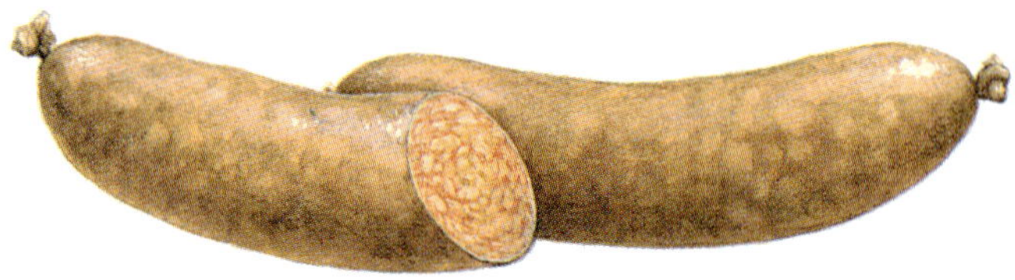

sau·sage (sos′ij) chopped meat mixed with spices and stuffed into a thin skinlike tube. *n.*

sau·té (sō tā′) fry quickly in a little fat, over high heat: *We sautéed the mushrooms for two minutes.* *v.*, **sau·téed, sau·té·ing.**

sav·age (sav′ij) 1 wild or fierce; cruel: *a savage temper, a savage winter, a savage dog.* 2 a fierce, cruel, or uncivilized person. 1 *adj.*, 2 *n.* —**sav′age·ry,** *n.*

sa·van·na (sə van′ə) 1 grassland with no trees or a scattering of trees, especially in a warm climate. 2 in the Maritimes, a swamp or a peat bog; muskeg. *n.*

save[1] (sāv) 1 make safe from harm, danger, loss, etc.; rescue: *The dog saved the boy's life. The woman saved her jewels from the fire.* 2 keep from using up or wasting; keep for later: *to save money, to save your strength. Save me some pie!* 3 prevent or avoid something by making it unnecessary: *to save work, to save trouble. Let me mail that and save you a trip to the post office.* *v.*, **saved, sav·ing.**
save for a rainy day, put something aside until you have a chance to do it or use it.

save² (sāv) except; but: *He works every day of the week save Sunday.* Sometimes **saving** has the same meaning; both words are old, poetic, or formal. *prep.*

sav•ings (sā′vingz) money saved: *He used his savings to buy a snowboard.* A **savings account** is a bank account mainly for saving money rather than paying bills. It pays higher interest than a chequing account. *pl.n. or sing.n.*

sav•iour or **sav•ior** (sāv′yər) **1** one who saves or rescues. **2 the Saviour,** in the Christian faith, Jesus Christ. *n.*

sa•vor•y (sā′və rē) a fragrant herb related to mint. Its leaves are used for seasoning food. *n.*

sa•vour or **sa•vor** (sā′vər) enjoy the taste or smell of: *He savoured every spoonful of the homemade soup.* *v.*

sa•vour•y or **sa•vor•y** (sā′və rē) **1** pleasing in taste or smell: *The savoury smell of roasting turkey greeted us as we entered the house.* **2** not sweet like dessert or candy; meant for first course. *adj.*

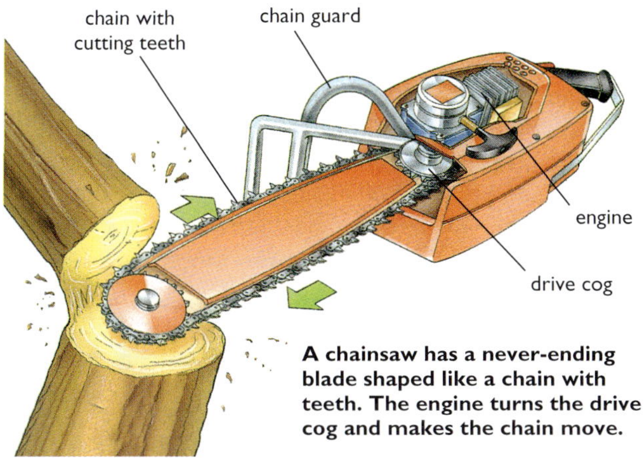

A chainsaw has a never-ending blade shaped like a chain with teeth. The engine turns the drive cog and makes the chain move.

saw¹ (so) **1** a tool for cutting, made of a thin blade with sharp teeth on the edge, and some kind of handle or frame. The blade can be long or round; some saws are run by a motor. **2** cut with a saw: *to saw wood, to saw boards from logs. Can you saw straight?* 1 *n.*, 2 *v.*, **sawed, sawed** or **sawn, saw•ing.**

saw² (so) the past tense of **see:** *I saw a robin.* *v.*

USING WORDS .... saw

Saw and **seen** are both forms of the verb see. **Saw** is the past tense and **seen** is the past participle. This means that **seen** cannot stand as a verb on its own. It needs an auxiliary verb, like *have, has, is, are, was,* or *were*: *I have seen that movie already. You were seen in the mall yesterday.*

saw•dust (so′dust′) the tiny particles of wood that you get when you saw something. *n.*

saw•horse (so′hórs′) a frame for holding wood that is being sawed. *n.*

saw•mill (so′mil′) a building where machines saw logs up into planks, strips, and so on. *n.*

sax•o•phone (sak′sə fōn′) a musical instrument that you play by blowing into it. It has a curved metal body with keys for the fingers and a reed in the mouthpiece. The name is often shortened to **sax.** *n.* —**sax′o•phon′ist** or **sax′ist,** *n.*

say (sā) **1** speak or pronounce: *Mom taught me always to say "Please" and "Thank you." My little sister cannot say her r's.* **2** put into words; tell people: *Say what you think.* **3** form an opinion; decide: *It is hard to say which shoes are better.* **4** let us suppose or guess: *You can learn to dance in, say, ten lessons.* **5** be written, or have written on it: *The label says, "Fragile."* **6** the chance to give your opinion: *Everyone will have a say before the meeting ends.* **7** authority to make a decision: *She has the final say.* 1–5 *v.*, **said, say•ing;** 6, 7 *n.*
that is to say, I mean.

say•ing (sā′ing) a wise statement that is often repeated; proverb: *"If it's worth doing, it's worth doing well" was a saying of my father's.* *n.*
go without saying, be too obvious to mention: *It goes without saying that you can stay at our place.*

scab (skab) **1** the crust that forms over a sore or wound as it heals: *A scab formed on the spot where he cut himself.* **2** a disease in animals and plants that affects the skin or surface. *n.* —**scab′by,** *adj.*

scab•bard (skab′ərd) a case for the blade of a sword, dagger, etc. **Sheath** is another word for it. *n.*

scaf•fold (skaf′əld) **1** a framework with one or more platforms for holding workers and their materials while they are working on a building or other high place. It is also called **scaffolding.** **2** a raised platform used as a base for a gallows or guillotine. *n.*

scald (skold) **1** burn with hot liquid or steam: *She scalded herself pouring the kettle.* **2** a burn caused by hot liquid or steam: *a scald on my hand.* **3** pour boiling liquid over: *Scald the dishes before drying them.* **4** heat almost to boiling: *Scald the milk.* 1, 3, 4 *v.*, 2 *n.*

a bat	e bed	i bid	o pot	u cup	th thin
ā cake	ē me	ī bite	ō go	ū rude	TH then
ä bar	ə about	ər over	ó for	ů put	zh measure

Scan

A magnetic resonance imaging (MRI) scanner is used to take many X-ray pictures, in cross section, that help in diagnosing illnesses and injuries.

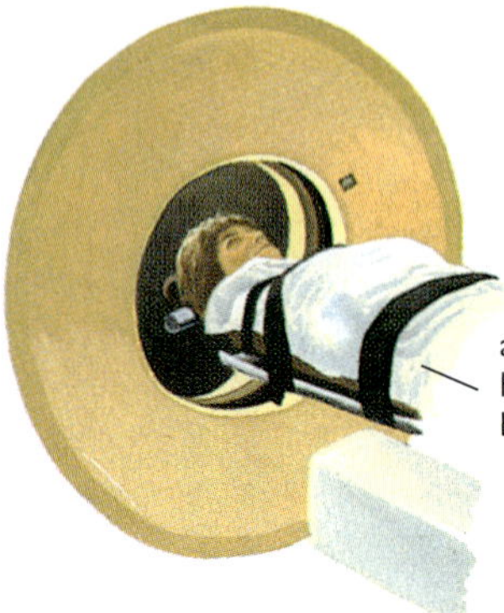

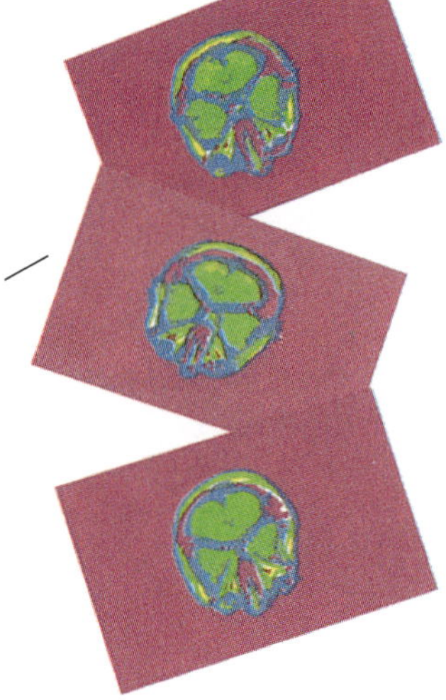

An ultrasound scanner uses pulses of ultrasonic sound waves to make a picture of organs inside a body.

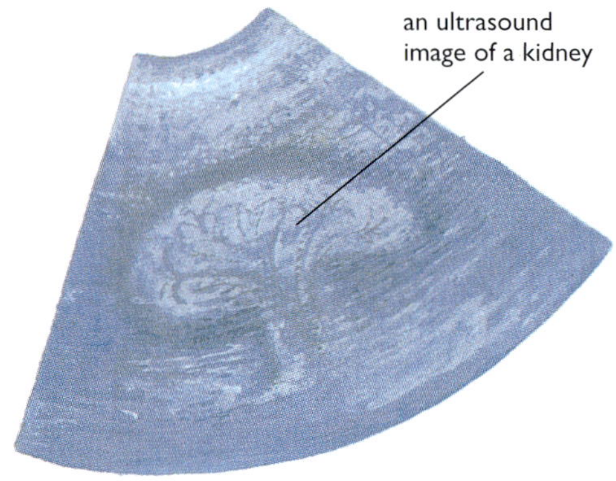

scale[1] (skāl) **1** one of the thin, flat, hard plates forming the outer covering of some fishes, snakes, and lizards. **2** a thin layer like one of these: *Scales of rust had formed on the sunken boat.* **3** remove scales from: *She scaled the fish with a sharp knife.* **4** form or come off in scales: *The old paint is scaling.* 1, 2 *n.*, 3, 4 *v.*, **scaled, scal·ing.** —**scal′y,** *adj.*

scale[2] (skāl) Often, **scales,** *pl.* an instrument for weighing, that is, measuring the mass of something: *She weighed some meat on the scales. I stepped on the doctor's scale.* *n.*

scale[3] (skāl) **1** climb: *They scaled the wall with ladders.* **2** in music, a set of tones going up or down in pitch according to a certain pattern: *She practises scales on the piano.* **3** the size of a plan, map, drawing, or model of something, compared with the real thing: *The scale of the map is one centimetre to one kilometre.* **4** a numbered line that shows this. **5** the size or amount of anything compared to other things: *Their parties are on a much larger scale than ours.* **6** a series of spaced amounts or values in order, like steps: *a pay scale for workers, a marking scale used by teachers. A thermometer has a temperature scale marked on it.* **7** change or set an amount according to this kind of system: *Camp fees are scaled to fit each family's income.* 1, 7 *v.*, **scaled, scal·ing;** 2–6 *n.*
scale down, make something smaller or less by reducing all the parts by the same amount: *I had to scale down the image before printing it out so it would fit on a page.* **Scale up** is the opposite.
to scale, made exactly according to a scale, so that a certain distance on the map, model, or drawing always equals a certain distance on the real thing. A **scale model** is made like this.

sca·lene (skā′lēn *or* skā lēn′) with three unequal sides: *a scalene triangle.* *adj.*

scal·lop (skal′əp) **1** a shellfish a bit like a clam but with a fan-shaped, ridged shell that has a wavy edge. Some kinds of scallops are harvested for the large muscle that opens and closes the shell. It is good to eat. **2** one of a set of curves that look like the wavy edge of a scallop shell: *scallops on the edge of a collar.* **3** decorate with such curves: *The edges of the pillowcases were scalloped and embroidered by hand.* **4** prepare potatoes by slicing them and baking them with a creamy sauce. 1, 2 *n.*, 3, 4 *v.*

scalp (skalp) **1** the skin on the top and back of the head that is usually covered with hair. **2** cut or tear the scalp from. 1 *n.*, 2 *v.*

scal·pel (skal′pəl) a small, light, very sharp knife that doctors use when they operate on people. *n.*

scamp (skamp) a rascal; a mischievous person, especially a child. *n.*

scam·per (skam′pər) **1** run lightly and quickly: *The mice scampered away when the cat came.* **2** run around playfully: *The dog was scampering in the yard.* *v.*

scan (skan) **1** look carefully over all of something to search or examine it: *The sailor scanned the sky for signs of a storm.* **2** glance through or look over quickly. **3** check or examine with an electronic instrument called a **scanner,** to find specific information which is then automatically entered into a computer: *The cashier scanned the cassette at the checkout to get the price.* *v.*, **scanned, scan·ning.**

scan•dal (skan′dəl) 1 something shameful that brings disgrace or shocks people: *It is a scandal that there should be so many homeless people*. 2 the disgrace, shock, or gossip that results from this. *n.* —**scan′dal•ous,** *adj.*

scan•dal•ize (skan′də līz′) shock or outrage someone by doing something thought to be wrong or improper: *She scandalized her great-grandchildren by wearing miniskirts.* *v.,* **scan•dal•ized, scan•dal•iz•ing.**

Scan•di•na•via (skan′də nāv′yə) the area including Norway, Sweden, Denmark, and sometimes Finland and Iceland. *n.* —**Scan′di•na′vi•an,** *n. or adj.*

scant (skant) 1 not enough or barely enough: *a scant supply of food.* Another word for this is **scanty.** 2 just barely: *You have a scant hour in which to pack for your trip.* *adj.* —**scant′i•ly,** *adv.*

scape•goat (skāp′gōt′) a person who is made to take the blame for something he or she did not do: *Chris came just after the children had broken the window, so they ran away quickly and left him to be the scapegoat.* *n.*

scar (skär) 1 the mark left by a cut, burn, or sore that has healed: *a small scar left by the chicken pox.* 2 any mark that shows damage or suffering: *See the scars left on the floor by your skate blades.* 3 leave a scar on: *He was scarred by the burns. The war has scarred her memory.* 1, 2 *n.,* 3 *v.,* **scarred, scar•ring.**

scarce (skers) hard to find or get; too little or too few: *Good cooks are scarce. Don't water the lawn when water is scarce.* *adj.,* **scarc•er, scarc•est.** —**scar′ci•ty,** *n.*
make yourself scarce, *Informal.* go away.

scarce•ly (skers′lē) hardly: *We could scarcely see the school through the thick fog.* *adv.*

scare (sker) 1 frighten: *The loud noise scared the baby.* 2 a fright: *You gave me a scare!* 1 *v.,* **scared, scar•ing;** 2 *n.* —**scar′y,** *adj.*
scared of, afraid of.
scare up, *Informal.* get; get together: *to scare up a few extra blankets, to scare up a meal.*

scare•crow (sker′krō′) a figure of a person, made of sticks and dressed in old clothes stuffed with straw, set in a field to frighten birds away from growing crops so they don't eat them. *n.*

scarf (skärf) a piece of silk, wool, etc. worn around the neck, shoulders, or head. *n., pl.* **scarves** (skärvz).

scar•let (skär′lit) very bright red. *n. or adj.*

WORD HISTORY........ scarlet

Scarlet is probably from an ancient Persian word *saqirlat*, meaning "rich cloth." Back then you had to be wealthy to have dyed clothes.

scat•ter (skat′ər) 1 put or throw here and there; sprinkle: Scatter sand on the icy sidewalk. Things that are few and far apart are **scattered:** *scattered snow flurries.* 2 separate and go off or send off in different directions: *The hens scattered in fright when the car honked at them.* *v.* —**scat′ter•ing,** *n.*

scat•ter•brain (skat′ər brān′) a thoughtless or absent-minded person. *n.*

scav•en•ger (skav′ən jər) 1 any creature that feeds on dead animals or other decaying matter. Vultures and jackals are scavengers. 2 a person who searches through garbage for something of value. *n.* —**scav′enge,** *v.*

scavenger hunt (skav′en jər hunt′) a game where people are sent out to find various things: *For the scavenger hunt we had to find a white stone, a feather, a tin can, an empty snail shell, and a leaf larger than a hand.*

scene (sēn) 1 a view or sight; picture: *The white sailboats in the blue water made a pretty scene.* 2 the place where something happened: *the scene of the crime, the scene of the accident.* 3 a show of bad temper in public: *The child made such a scene in the restaurant that his parents had to take him home.* 4 *Informal.* a certain environment or area of activity: *to be well-known on the music scene. What's new on the school scene?* 5 the setting of a story: *The scene of this story is Québec City in the year 1775.* 6 a particular incident in a play, movie, etc.: *I like the tornado scene in* The Wizard of Oz. 7 one of the smallest parts that a play is divided into: *The king comes to the castle in Act 1, Scene 2.* *n.*
behind the scenes, **a** out of sight of the audience. **b** not publicly; privately; secretly: *A lot of planning for the Festival was done behind the scenes.*

WORD HISTORY........ scene

Scene comes from a Greek word, *skene*, the name of the tent where actors changed their costumes.

scen•er•y (sē′nə rē) 1 the general appearance of an outdoor place; especially when it is beautiful: *We enjoyed the mountain scenery in British Columbia.* 2 the painted walls and so on used on a stage to represent places: *The grade eights made the scenery for the school play.* *n.*

a bat	e bed	i bid	o pot	u cup	th thin
ā cake	ē me	ī bite	ō go	ū rude	ᴛʜ then
ä bar	ə about	ər over	ô for	ù put	zh measure

sce•nic (sē′nik) full of the natural beauty of the outdoors: *the scenic splendours of Lake Louise, a scenic highway.* *adj.*

scent (sent) 1 smell: *The scent of roses filled the air* (*n.*). *The dog scented a rabbit and ran after it* (*v.*). 2 perfume: *She used too much scent* (*n.*). *The candle scented the whole room* (*v.*). *n. or v.*

CONFUSABLES . . . . scent

scent means "smell": *The scent of roses filled the room.*
sent means "did send": *I sent an e-mail to you yesterday.*
cent means "penny": *One hundred cents equals a dollar.*

scep•tre (sep′tər) a rod made of precious metal and decorated with jewels, held by a ruler as a symbol of royal power. **Scepter** is another spelling. *n.*

sched•ule (skej′əl *or* shej′əl) 1 a list of events and the times they are supposed to happen; a timetable. A bus schedule shows when each bus is supposed to leave or arrive; a hockey schedule shows when the different teams are going to play. 2 put something on a schedule; plan when something will happen: *Schedule the concert for late October.* 1 *n.,* 2 *v.,* **sched•uled, sched•ul•ing.**
on schedule, at the expected time: *The bus came on schedule.*

scheme (skēm) 1 a plan, especially a clever or secret one: *a scheme to cheat the government.* 2 make secret plans: *Mom is scheming to surprise Dad with a huge party on his 40th birthday.* 3 a system of connected things, parts, thoughts, etc.: *the colour scheme of a room.* 1, 3 *n.,* 2 *v.,* **schemed, schem•ing.**

schiz•o•phre•ni•a (skit′sə frē′nē ə *or* skit′sə fren′ē ə) a mental illness in which the person has powerful thoughts and feelings that do not fit with actual reality. The thoughts and feelings seem more real to the person than what is going on around him or her. *n.* —**schiz′o•phren′ic** (skit′sə fren′ik), *adj.*

schol•ar (skol′ər) a highly educated person; an expert in some field of study: *a famous Latin scholar.* *n.* —**schol′ar•ly,** *adj.*

schol•ar•ship (skol′ər ship′) 1 money given by a school, a government, or some other organization to help a good student continue studying: *He graduated from high school with such high marks that he received a scholarship.* 2 knowledge and understanding gained by study, or the depth and quality of this understanding: *The accuracy and thoroughness of her book shows excellent scholarship.* *n.*

school[1] (skūl) 1 a place for teaching and learning: *Children go to school to learn.* 2 classes: *There will be no school from December 21 to January 6.* 3 the students and their teachers: *The whole school went skating on the last day.* 4 a group of people sharing the same opinions: *the French school of painting. My Mom is of the old school that believes girls should not call up boys.* 5 train; discipline: *School yourself to control your temper.* 1–4 *n.,* 5 *v.*

***Word Family*. . . . . school**

school-age: old (or young) enough to be in school
school board: a group of schools or leaders responsible for all the schools in an area
schoolchild: a young student; a schoolboy or schoolgirl
schoolhouse: a small, house-shaped old school
schooling: the whole process of learning in school
school supplies: things that students need for school
schoolteacher: a person who teaches in a school
schoolyard: a playground around or behind a school

school[2] (skūl) a large group of the same kind of fish or water animal swimming together: *a school of mackerel, a school of porpoises.* *n.*

The Canadian dime features an image of the *Bluenose*, a well-known racing schooner from Nova Scotia.

schoon•er (skū′nər) a ship with two or more masts carrying sails set lengthways.

schwa (shwä) 1 a "loose" vowel sound like the one made by *a* in *about, e* in *towel,* or *u* in *circus.* 2 the symbol (ə) which stands for this sound. *n.*

sci•ence (sī′əns) 1 knowledge arranged in an orderly system, based on things that can be observed and tested again and again. Science tries to describe and explain what is found in nature. 2 a branch of such knowledge. Biology, chemistry, and astronomy are **natural sciences.** Agriculture and medicine are **applied sciences.** Economics is a **social science.** 3 anything studied carefully and made into a system of "laws": *the science of skateboarding. My dad has turned pancake making into a science.* *n.* —**sci′en•tif′ic,** *adj.* —**sci′en•tist,** *n.*

science fiction (sī′əns fik′shən) stories or novels that combine science and fantasy. Science fiction is usually about life in the future or in other galaxies and often makes use of the latest discoveries in science. **Sci-fi** (sī′fi′) is used as a short form.

scis·sors (siz′ərz) a tool for cutting that has two sharp blades, each with a handle, fastened together in the middle so that their edges slide against each other. *pl.n.*

scoff (skof) make fun of something to show you don't believe or respect it: *to scoff at an idea, to scoff at a law.* *v.* —**scoff′er,** *n.*

scold (skōld) talk to someone sternly and angrily about something he or she did wrong; tell off: *His mother scolded him for losing his new mitts.* *v.*

scone (skon *or* skōn) a less common name for a **tea biscuit,** a small cake that tastes a bit like bread. *n.*

scoop (skūp) **1** deep spoon or a tool like a small shovel with a short handle, used for dipping out things: *an ice cream scoop. Please use the scoop provided for each bulk food bin.* **2** the part of a digging machine that holds the dirt, rocks, and so on that are dug up. **3** dig out or pick up with a scoop, or by using your hand as a scoop: *to scoop out a kilogram of sugar, to scoop a hole in the sand. We scooped up the snow with our hands to make snowballs.* **4** a movement or process of scooping. **5** *Informal.* the latest information: *So what's the scoop on your cousin? Is he out of the hospital yet?* 1, 2, 4, 5 *n.,* 3 *v.*

scoot (skūt) *Informal.* go quickly; dart: *He scooted out the door.* *v.*

scoot·er (skū′tər) **1** a child's small vehicle made up of a board between two wheels, one in front of the other. You steer the front wheel by a tall handlebar attached to it, and stand on the board with one foot while pushing on the ground with the other. **2** a small motorcycle with a guard at the front to protect the rider's legs. **3** a sailboat with runners, for use on either water or ice. *n.*

scope (skōp) **1** the amount or range of material that a person or thing can handle: *A full history of Canada is beyond the scope of this short book.* **2** room; opportunity: *This job provides a lot of scope for creative thinking.* *n.*

scorch (skȯrch) **1** burn slightly on the outside: *The cake tastes scorched. I scorched the shirt in ironing it.* **2** a slight burn. **3** dry up; wither: *The grass was scorched by the hot sun.* A **scorcher** is a very hot day. 1, 3 *v.,* 2 *n.*

score (skȯr) **1** the number of points earned in a game, contest, or test: *The score was 9 to 2 in favour of our school.* **2** earn points in a game, contest, or test: *She scored two runs in the second inning. You score in this game by guessing the right word.* **3** a point or subject being talked about or thought about: *Don't worry on that score.* **4** cut; scratch; mark: *Use a cutting board so you don't score the countertop.* **5** the written form of a piece of music: *I can't play "O Canada" without the score.* **6** a group of twenty. This sense is found in compounds like **threescore** (60) or **fourscore** (80). **Scores** means "a large number." 1, 3, 5, 6 *n.,* 2, 4 *v.,* **scored, scor·ing.** —**score′less,** *adj.* —**scor′er,** *n.*
keep score, keep track of the points scored by each person or team. Someone who does this is a **scorekeeper.**
the score, the facts about what is going on: *Someone tell me what the score is around here.*

scorn (skȯrn) **1** look down on; have no respect at all; despise: *She scorned him because he was a sneak and a liar.* **2** reject or refuse as too low, small, or unworthy: *Now that he can read well, he scorns to look at those "baby books."* **3** a feeling that someone or something deserves no respect; contempt: *He feels scorn for students who cheat.* **4** a person or thing that is scorned or despised: *That cheat is the scorn of the school.* 1, 2 *v.,* 3, 4 *n.* —**scorn′ful,** *adj.*

Scorpions eat insects and spiders, and are most active at night.

scor·pi·on (skȯrp′yən) a small animal that lives in hot, dry areas. It has lobsterlike claws, and a poisonous stinger at the end of its coiled tail. *n.*

scot–free (skot′frē′) completely free from the expected punishment: *One gang member was jailed but the others got off scot-free.* *adj.*

scoun·drel (skoun′drəl) a bad person. *n.*

scour[1] (skour) **1** clean or polish by hard rubbing: *Scour the frying pan with cleanser.* **2** dig or clear out by the action of running water: *The stream had scoured a deep channel.* **3** the act of scouring. 1, 2 *v.,* 3 *n.*

scour[2] (skour) search all over: *They scoured the countryside for the lost child.* *v.*

a bat	e bed	i bid	o pot	u cup	th thin
ā cake	ē me	ī bite	ō go	ū rude	ᴛʜ then
ä bar	ə about	ər over	ȯ for	u̇ put	zh measure

scout (skout) **1** a person sent out to find something, such as an enemy's camp or a good path to follow. A **talent scout** looks for talented people for a sports team, modelling agency, etc. **2** act as a scout; hunt around to see what you can find: *Go and scout for firewood. They scouted out the area to find a campsite.* 1 *n.,* 2 *v.*

scowl (skoul) **1** frown angrily; make a mean face: *The angry man scowled at his neighbour.* **2** an angry frown or mean face. 1 *v.,* 2 *n.*

scram·ble (skram′bəl) **1** make your way quickly by climbing, crawling, etc.: *The girls scrambled up the steep, rocky hill.* **2** rush wildly to get something done: *We really had to scramble to get the place ready in time for our guests.* **3** struggle with others for something: *The boys scrambled to get the football.* **4** the act of scrambling: *the scramble for wealth and power. It was a scramble to finish our group project by the due date.* **5** mix up: *If you scramble the letters of "sheet," you get "these."* **Scrambled eggs** are eggs that have been beaten and then cooked in a pan. 1–3, 5 *v.,* **scram·bled, scram·bling;** 4 *n.*

Scrap metal, glass, paper, and organic waste can be recycled, so that we can use smaller amounts of natural resources.

scrap¹ (skrap) **1** a small leftover piece: *The cook gave the dog some scraps of meat. Sweep up the scraps of paper.* **2** throw out: *to scrap an idea, to scrap old furniture.* **3** break up and recycle: *They took the wrecked cars to the junkyard to be scrapped.* **4** the material to be recycled: *We sold the old stove as scrap.* **5** leftover or thrown out and available for recycling: *scrap paper, scrap lumber, scrap metal.* 1, 4 *n.,* 2, 3 *v.,* **scrapped, scrap·ping;** 5 *adj.*

scrap² (skrap) *Informal.* fight; quarrel; struggle: *He was always scrapping with his brother* (*v.*). *Our dog had a scrap with a stray cat* (*n.*). *n. or v.,* **scrapped, scrap·ping.** —**scrap′per,** *n.* —**scrap′py,** *adj.*

scrap·book (skrap′bůk′) a book to stick pictures, clippings, and other paper souvenirs in: *We made a scrapbook of our trip to Inuvik.* *n.*

scrape (skrāp) **1** rub with something sharp or rough, especially to clean it off: *Scrape your muddy shoes with this old knife. We scraped the ice off the car windows.* A tool used for scraping is a **scraper. 2** scratch or injure by rubbing against something rough: *She fell and scraped her knee on the sidewalk.* **3** the act of scraping, or the result: *a scrape on her knee.* **4** make a harsh rubbing sound: *The branch of the tree scraped against the window.* **5** a harsh rubbing sound: *the scrape of the saw.* **6** dig by scraping: *The dog scraped a hole in the sand.* **7** a difficult or dangerous situation: *Her curiosity often got her into scrapes.* 1, 2, 4, 6 *v.,* **scraped, scrap·ing;** 3, 5, 7 *n.*
scrape by or **through,** barely get through; succeed with difficulty: *I just managed to scrape through the test.*
scrape together or **scrape up,** collect with difficulty, a bit at a time: *She scraped together enough money for a guitar.*

scratch (skrach) **1** mark or cut slightly with something pointed or rough, such as nails or claws: *The screwdriver slipped and scratched the chair. The kitten scratched my hand.* **2** a mark or cut made in this way: *There are deep scratches on this desk. The scratch on my hand soon healed.* **3** rub or scrape to get rid of an itchy feeling: *Don't scratch your mosquito bites.* **4** rub with a harsh noise: *She scratched a match on the rock.* **5** the act or sound of scratching. **6** cross out or throw out: *Scratch that idea. Scratch out my name and put yours.* 1, 3, 4, 6 *v.,* 2, 5 *n.* —**scratch′y,** *adj.*
from scratch, a from the beginning: *He lost his notes and had to start his project again from scratch.* **b** without a mix: *to bake a cake from scratch.*
scratch the surface, deal with just a small part of a thing: *This article on pollution only scratches the surface.*
up to scratch, up to standard; good enough: *This work is not up to scratch.*

scratch pad (skrach′ pad′) a pad of **scratch paper,** paper for making quick notes.

scrawl (skrol) **1** write in a messy way. **2** messy handwriting. 1 *v.,* 2 *n.*

scraw·ny (skron′ē) *Informal.* too skinny: *a scrawny chicken.* *adj.,* **scraw·ni·er, scraw·ni·est.**

scream (skrēm) **1** make a loud, sharp, piercing cry: *She screamed when she saw the child fall.* **2** a loud, sharp, piercing cry. 1 *v.,* 2 *n.*

screech (skrēch) **1** cry out sharply in a high voice; shriek: *"Help! help!" she screeched.* **2** a high-pitched scream: *The woman's screeches brought the police.* 1 *v.,* 2 *n.* —**screech′y,** *adj.*

screen (skrēn) 1 a surface for displaying images by machine. Movies are shown on a screen; TVs and computer monitors have screens. 2 show on a screen: *to screen a movie.* 3 a piece of mesh or netting stretched in a frame: *Screens on the windows keep out flies. They put the sand through a screen to get the stones out of it.* 4 sift with a screen: *to screen sand.* 5 examine carefully and let only certain ones through: *Government offices screen people before hiring them.* 6 a covered frame that hides, protects, or separates: *A screen in front of the fireplace kept sparks from landing on the floor.* 7 anything that hides or protects: *A screen of trees hides our house from the road.* 8 protect or hide with a screen or as a screen does: *to screen a porch to keep out flies, to screen your face from the sun with a newspaper. The mother tried to screen her guilty son.* 1, 3, 6, 7 *n.,* 2, 4, 5, 8 *v.*

screen·play (skrēn′plā′) a story that is specially written to be performed as a movie or TV show. *n.*

screen saver (skrēn′ sā′vər) a computer program that displays a constantly changing image on the monitor if you stop using the keyboard or mouse for a while. It protects the screen from the damage caused by displaying the same image for a long time. *n.*

screw (skrū) 1 a fastening device like a nail but with a spiral ridge twisted evenly around its length and a groove in its head to fit a screwdriver into. You fasten it by turning it to the right. 2 fasten or tighten with a screw or by turning: *The carpenter screwed the hinges to the door. Screw the lid on the jar.* 3 anything that turns like a screw or looks like one, such as a simple machine that carries liquid or earth upward in its grooves. 1, 3 *n.,* 2 *v.*

screw up, *Slang.* **a** make a mess of something. **b** make a serious mistake.

screw·driv·er (skrū′drī′vər) a tool for putting in or taking out screws by turning them. *n.*

scrib·ble (skrib′əl) 1 write carelessly or hastily. 2 make meaningless marks: *The baby scribbled on the wall with crayons.* 3 something scribbled: *Erase that scribble.* 1, 2 *v.,* **scrib·bled, scrib·bling;** 3 *n.*

scribe (skrīb) a person who copied out written documents by hand in earlier times before printing was invented. *n.*

scrim·mage (skrim′ij) 1 a rough fight or struggle. 2 take part in a rough fight or struggle. 3 in football, the play that takes place when the two teams are lined up and the ball is passed from the centre to the quarterback. 1, 3 *n.,* 2 *v.,* **scrim·maged, scrim·mag·ing.**

scrimp (skrimp) try to save money by spending as little as possible: *They had to scrimp for several years in order to buy their house.* *v.*

script (skript) 1 the written version of a play or of anything to be said to an audience. A **scriptwriter** writes scripts. 2 a writing system: *Russian script, Arabic script. English is written in the roman script.* 3 handwriting, or a typeface that looks like handwriting. *n.*

WORD HISTORY........ script

Script is from the Latin *scribere*, meaning "write." All our words ending in *-scribe* come from the same root: **describe, subscribe, inscribe,** and so on.

Scrip·ture (skrip′chər) 1 the Bible, also called **the Scriptures** or **the Holy Scriptures,** *pl.* 2 **scripture,** any sacred writing. *n.*

scroll (skrōl) 1 a roll of parchment or paper with writing on it: *He slowly unrolled the scroll as he read it.* 2 move the cursor up, down, or sideways on a computer screen until the image moves, causing one part of it to go off the screen and another part to come on. 1 *n.,* 2 *v.*

scrub[1] (skrub) 1 wash or clean thoroughly by rubbing: *She scrubbed the floor with a brush and soapsuds.* 2 a thorough wash: *Give your face and hands a good scrub.* 3 remove the pollutants from gases going into the air. 1, 3 *v.,* **scrubbed, scrub·bing;** 2 *n.*

scrub[2] (skrub) low, stunted trees or shrubs. *n.*

scruff (skruf) the skin at the back of the neck. *n.*

scruf·fy (skruf′ē) dirty and messy; shabby: *This old winter coat is starting to look scruffy.* *adj.*

scrump·tious (skrump′shəs) very delicious. *adj.*

scrunch (skrunch) crumple up completely: *I scrunched the piece of foil into a tiny ball.* *v.*

scru·ple (skrū′pəl) 1 a feeling of uneasiness or doubt about what is right that keeps a person from doing something: *She has scruples about playing cards for money.* 2 feel any doubt or guilt: *A dishonest person does not scruple about cheating.* 1 *n.,* 2 *v.,* **scru·pled, scru·pling.**

scru·pu·lous (skrū′pyə ləs) 1 very careful to do what is right; honest. 2 very careful and exact: *to work with scrupulous attention to detail.* *adj.*

scru·ti·nize (skrū′tə nīz′) examine closely; inspect carefully: *The jeweller scrutinized the diamond for flaws.* *v.,* **scru·ti·nized, scru·ti·niz·ing.** —**scru′ti·ny,** *n.*

a bat	e bed	i bid	o pot	u cup	th thin
ā cake	ē me	ī bite	ō go	ū rude	ᴛʜ then
ä bar	ə about	ər over	ô for	ů put	zh measure

Scuba Diving

Scuba is an acronym of self contained underwater breathing apparatus.

The scuba (or aqualung) has a demand valve that regulates the amount of air given to the diver — the pressure inside the diver's lungs must always be equal to the pressure of the water. A diver using one tank has enough air to stay underwater for about an hour.

scu·ba diving (skū′bə dī′ving) deep diving or underwater swimming using portable breathing equipment, including one or more tanks of compressed air. *n.* —**scu′ba div′er.**

scud (skud) move rapidly: *Clouds scudded across the sky, driven by the high wind.* *v.,* **scud·ded, scud·ding.**

scuff (skuf) **1** walk without lifting your feet; shuffle. **2** make marks on something by rough use: *to scuff your shoes, to scuff a carpet.* These marks are called **scuff marks.** *v.*

scuf·fle (skuf′əl) struggle or fight but without real violence: *The children scuffled for first place in line* (*v.*). *The boy lost his hat in the scuffle* (*n.*). *n. or v.,* **scuf·fled, scuf·fling.**

scull (skul) **1** a long, narrow, light racing boat for one or more rowers. **2** one of a pair of oars used by a single rower. **3** row, especially in a race. Sculling is an Olympic event. 1, 2 *n.,* 3 *v.*

sculp·ture (skulp′chər) **1** any three-dimensional work of art. A statue is one kind of sculpture. **2** the art form that involves making three-dimensional figures. Clay, stone, papier-mâché, wood, wire, found objects, and many other materials may be used in sculpture. **3** carve or model. **Sculpt** means the same. 1, 2 *n.,* 3 *v.,* **sculp·tured, sculp·tur·ing.** —**sculp′tor,** *n.*

scum (skum) a thin layer or film on the surface of a liquid: *A scum formed on the boiling maple syrup as the impurities rose to the top. A green scum of algae floated on top of the pond.* *n.*

scur·ry (skər′ē) run quickly and lightly; scamper; hurry: *We could hear the mice scurrying back and forth in the walls.* *v.,* **scur·ried, scur·ry·ing.**

scur·vy (skər′vē) **1** a disease caused by a lack of fresh vegetables and fruits. It causes swollen and bleeding gums, extreme weakness, and bruises on the skin. Scurvy used to be common among sailors who had little to eat except bread and salt meat. **2** mean or dirty; low: *scurvy tricks, a scurvy fellow.* 1 *n.,* 2 *adj.,* **scur·vi·er, scur·vi·est.**

scut·tle (skut′əl) scamper; scurry: *The raccoon scuttled off into the woods.* *v.,* **scut·tled, scut·tling.**

scythe (sīᴛʜ) a long, curved blade on a long handle, used in some countries for cutting grain. *n.*

SE or **S.E.** *abbreviation for* southeast or southeastern.

sea (sē) **1** the salt water covering about three-fourths of the earth's surface; the ocean. **2** any large body of salt water, smaller than an ocean: *the Mediterranean Sea.* **3** a large lake of fresh water: *the Sea of Galilee.* **4** a large, heavy wave: *High seas swept away the ship's masts.* **5** a huge amount spread over a wide area: *a sea of faces.* *n.*
at sea, a out on the sea. **b** knowing or understanding nothing: *I am totally at sea when it comes to football.*
go to sea, a become a sailor. **b** begin a voyage.

Word Family.......... sea

seaboard: the part of a country near the sea
seacoast: the land along the sea
seafaring: travelling or working on the sea
seafood: fish and shellfish that you can eat
seagoing: made to go on the ocean rather than on lakes or rivers
seaman: a man who is a sailor
seaplane: a plane with floats for landing on water
seaport: a town with a harbour reachable by sea
seascape: a picture or view of the sea
seashell: the empty shell of various kinds of sea creature
seashore: the land at the very edge of the sea; beach
seasick: sick to your stomach from a ship's motion
seaside: the area by the sea
seawater: water from the sea; salt water
seaweed: any plant growing in the sea
seaworthy: able to stand storms at sea

sea bird (sē′ bərd′) any bird that spends most of its time on or near the open sea, such as gulls or puffins.

sea gull (sē′ gul′) a gull that lives on or near the sea. A gull is a type of bird.

sea horse (sē′ hȯrs′) a small saltwater fish with a horselike head and a curled tail that can hold onto things. A sea horse swims upright.

seal[1] (sēl) 1 close very tightly: *She sealed the letter. I won't say a word—my lips are sealed.* 2 a sticker or anything else used to close something. 3 the fact of being tightly closed: *The rubber strip on the door maintains a tight seal.* 4 settle once and for all: *The judge's words sealed the prisoner's fate.* 5 a piece of wax, foil, or other material with a special design stamped into it to show ownership or authority: *The official seal of Canada is attached to important government papers.* 6 the design itself, or a stamp for marking things with it. 7 mark a document with a stamp like this: *The treaty was signed and sealed by both governments.* 1, 4, 7 *v.,* 2, 3, 5, 6 *n.*

seal[2] (sēl) a meat-eating sea mammal with large flippers instead of feet. Seals usually live in cold regions. They are sometimes hunted for their skin or fur, or for their meat or blubber. *n., pl.* **seals** or **seal.**

sea level (sē′ lev′əl) the level of the surface of the sea. Mountains, flat land, ocean beds, and so on are measured as so many metres above or below sea level.

sea lion (sē′ lī′ən) a large seal of the Pacific Coast.

seal•skin (sēl′skin′) the skin of a seal, or a garment made of this. *n.*

seam (sēm) 1 the line of stitches joining two pieces sewn together: *the seams of a coat.* 2 any line where edges come together, such as between pieces of wallpaper or carpet. 3 a wrinkle, scar, or other mark like a seam: *The old sword cut had left a seam on the pirate's face.* 4 mark with wrinkles or scars: *Years of worry had seamed his brow.* 5 a thin layer of a certain kind of rock within the earth: *a seam of coal.* 1–3, 5 *n.,* 4 *v.*

CONFUSABLES .... seam

seam means "the line where parts join": *A seam runs down the side of my jeans.*

seem means "appear": *Why do you seem so sad?*

sear (sēr) 1 burn the surface of: *The hot iron seared his flesh.* 2 make hard or unfeeling: *Years of cruel treatment had seared his heart.* *v.*

search (sərch) 1 try to find; look for: *We searched for the lost kitten.* 2 look through; check or go over carefully in order to find something: *to search your pockets. The police searched the prisoner.* 3 the action of searching: *He found his book after a long search.* 1, 2 *v.,* 3 *n.*

in search of, trying to find; looking for: *They went in search of buried treasure.*

search engine (sərch′ en′jən) a computer program that retrieves data from a database or network, especially on the Internet.

search•light (sərch′līt′) a very powerful light that can throw a bright beam in any direction. *n.*

sea•son (sē′zən) 1 one of the periods of the year, marked by a certain kind of weather; spring, summer, fall, or winter. 2 any period of time marked by some special thing: *the holiday season, the hockey season.* A ticket to all the games, plays, etc. in a season is a **season ticket.** 3 add flavour to: *Season your egg with salt.* Salt, pepper, herbs, and spices are **seasonings.** 4 prepare for use by keeping for a while or by a special treatment: *Wood is seasoned for building by drying it.* **Seasoned** means "experienced" when it describes people. 1, 2 *n.,* 3, 4 *v.* **—sea′son•al,** *adj.*

in season, at the right time for picking, eating, hunting, wearing, etc.: *Strawberries are in season in June.* The opposite is **out of season.**

seat (sēt) 1 something to sit on; a place to sit. 2 the right to sit; a place in a parliament or council, a theatre or stadium, etc.: *The candidate lost his seat in the last election. She paid $30 for a seat at the show.* 3 the part of your body that you sit on, or the clothing covering it: *the seat of your pants.* 4 the part of a chair that you sit on: *This chair has a broken seat.* 5 place on a seat or lead to a seat: *He seated himself in the most comfortable chair. Please seat the guests as they arrive.* 6 have seats for: *Our school auditorium seats 1000 people.* 1–4 *n.,* 5, 6 *v.* **—seat′ing,** *n.*

seat belt (sēt′ belt′) a belt attached to the seat of a car, aircraft, etc., used to hold a person in place in case of a crash, jolt, bumps, etc.

sea urchin (sē′ ər′chin) a small sea animal with a round shell covered with movable spines.

sea•way (sē′wā′) a route that ships take over the sea or through an inland waterway connected to the sea. Ocean liners reach Thunder Bay by passing through the **St. Lawrence Seaway,** which includes the St. Lawrence River, the Welland Canal, and the Great Lakes. *n.*

a bat	e bed	i bid	o pot	u cup	th thin
ā cake	ē me	ī bite	ō go	ū rude	ᴛʜ then
ä bar	ə about	ər over	ȯ for	u̇ put	zh measure

sec. *abbreviation for* second or seconds.

se·clude (si klüd′) shut off from others: *The cottage is in a secluded spot.* *v.,* **se·clud·ed, se·clud·ing.** —**se·clu′sion,** *n.*

sec·ond[1] (sek′ənd) **1** next after the first: *the second seat from the front* (*adj.*). *I was the second to arrive* (*n.*). **2** another; other: *Napoleon has been called a second Caesar.* **3** **seconds,** a second serving of food: *She took seconds of the pie.* **4** not as good or important as first. This sense is often used in compounds such as **second-class, second-rate.** **5** an article below first quality: *These sheets are seconds and have some slight defects.* **6** support or back up a suggestion: *"Let's go for a swim." "I second that idea!"* **7** a person who supports or backs up another. 1, 2, 4 *adj.,* 1, 3, 5, 7 *n.,* 6 *v.* —**sec′ond·ly,** *adv.*
be second nature, be automatic, easy, or totally normal for someone: *Helping people is second nature for her.*
get your second wind, get a fresh burst of energy after becoming tired.
have second thoughts, have doubts. If you have no doubt about some action, you do it **without a second thought.**
on second thought, after thinking about it again.
play second fiddle, not be the leader.

sec·ond[2] (sek′ənd) **1** an SI unit for measuring time. There are sixty seconds in one minute. The second is one of the seven base units in the SI. *Symbol:* s **2** a very short time; moment. *n.*

sec·ond·ar·y (sek′ən der′ē) **1** less important than something else: *Reading fast is secondary to reading well. That is a secondary point, not the main idea.* **2** coming after something simpler or more basic. A **secondary colour** is made by mixing primary colours; **secondary school** comes after elementary school. Sawmills and steel mills are examples of **secondary industry;** they are the next stage after logging and mining. *adj.*

second class (sek′ənd klas′) **1** a standard or level of quality that is not the very best; the seats, cabins, etc. on a ship, plane, or train that are not the best. **2** the class of mail that includes magazines, parcels, and so on rather than letters and cards. **3** by this class of mail or in these seats: *to send something second class, to travel second class.* —**sec′ond-class′,** *adj.*

second hand (sek′ənd hand′) a hand on a clock or watch, showing the passing of seconds. It moves around the whole dial once in a minute.

sec·ond–hand (sek′ənd hand′) **1** not new; used already by someone else: *second-hand clothes* (*adj.*). *He bought it second-hand* (*adv.*). **2** selling used goods: *a second-hand store.* **3** coming through someone else: *second-hand information* (*adj.*). *I heard it second-hand* (*adv.*). 1–3 *adj.,* 1, 3 *adv.*

second person (sek′ənd pər′sən) **1** in grammar, the category that includes *you* and all its related forms. *Yourself, your,* and *yours* are all pronouns of the second person; *are* is the form of the verb *be* that goes with the second person. **2** a way of telling a story that makes it seem as if you are telling it to the main character.

sec·ond–rate (sek′ənd rāt′) *Informal.* not very good: *a second-rate musician.*

se·cret (sē′krit) **1** that others are not allowed to know about: *a secret plan.* **2** something that others are not allowed to know about: *Can you keep a secret? Mom's birthday gift is a secret.* **3** hidden: *a secret passageway.* **4** working in disguise or without others knowing: *secret police.* **5** a hidden explanation: *the secret of her success.* 1, 3, 4 *adj.,* 2, 5 *n.* —**se′cre·cy,** *n.* —**se′cret·ive,** *adj.*
in secret, secretly; privately; not openly.

sec·re·tar·y (sek′rə ter′ē) someone who writes letters, does paperwork, and keeps track of business details for a person or organization. *n., pl.* **sec·re·tar·ies.**

se·crete (si krēt′) produce and release a body substance: *Glands in the mouth secrete saliva.* *v.,* **se·cret·ed, se·cret·ing.** —**se·cre′tion,** *n.*

sec·tion (sek′shən) **1** a part with clear limits; division: *a pie cut into eight equal sections, the business section of a town. Our math book has a section on fractions.* **2** cut into sections; divide into sections: *to section an orange.* **3** a view of a thing as it would look if it were cut straight through: *cross section.* **4** a piece of farm land one mile square (about 259 hectares). 1, 3, 4 *n.,* 2 *v.*

sec·tor (sek′tər) **1** a distinct and clearly defined part: *Young people form one sector of society.* The part of the economy that involves government is the **public sector;** businesses are the **private sector.** **2** an area in a circle bounded by two straight lines drawn from the edge to the centre. A sector is shaped like a slice of pizza. *n.*

sec·u·lar (sek′yə lər) not sacred; not meant to be religious: *Our choir sings secular and religious music.* *adj.* —**sec′u·lar·ize′,** *v.*

se·cure (si kyür′) **1** safe against loss, attack, escape, etc.: *a secure hiding place, a secure prison cell, secure investments.* **2** sure to happen or come true: *Our victory is secure.* **3** free from worry or fear; confident: *He felt secure with his older sister around.* **4** firmly in place; not likely to break or fall: *The boards of this bridge do not look secure.* **5** make secure: *to secure your future. Secure the locks on the doors and windows.* **6** get; obtain: *to secure tickets for a play.* 1–4 *adj.,* 5, 6 *v.,* **se·cured, se·cur·ing.**

Seeds

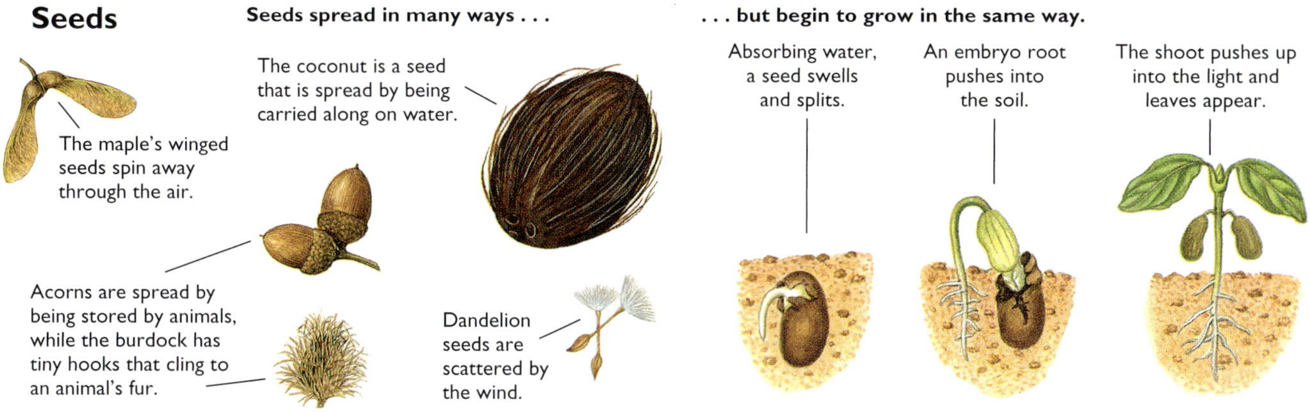

se•cu•ri•ty (si kyůr′ə tē) **1** safety or a feeling of being safe: *Locks provide security.* **2** something that secures or makes safe: *Rubber soles are a security against slipping.* **3** a group of people hired to guard or protect a place: *They called security when a fight broke out in the mall.* An individual doing this work is a **security guard.** **4** something given as a guarantee that a person will be able to pay back a loan or keep a promise. If not, he or she loses the thing: *He left his watch as security that he would come back.* *n., pl.* **se•cu•ri•ties.**

Security Council (si kyůr′ə tē koun′səl) a group of countries within the United Nations that tries to maintain international peace.

Sec•wep•emc (shə′whep mək) **1** a First Nations people living in British Columbia. **2** their language. **3** having to do with these people or their language. 1, 2 *n.,* 3 *adj.*

se•dan (si dan′) a regular car; a car that has a trunk, seats four or more people, and is not convertible. *n.*

sedan chair (si dan′ cher′) in earlier times, a covered chair carried on poles, for a rich or important person to ride in.

se•date (si dāt′) **1** quiet and dignified: *The princess was sedate out in public but harum-scarum at home.* **2** give someone a drug to lessen pain or excitement: *After the operation they sedated him so he could sleep comfortably.* 1 *adj.,* 2 *v.,* **se•dat•ed, se•dat•ing.**

sed•a•tive (sed′ə tiv) a drug that lessens pain or excitement. *n.*

sed•i•ment (sed′ə mənt) matter that settles to the bottom of a liquid and is left behind when the liquid is poured off or drains away: *Each year the Nile River overflows and deposits sediment on the land.* *n.*

sed•i•men•ta•ry (sed′ə men′tə rē) formed from layers of sediment: *Shale is a sedimentary rock.* *adj.*

se•duce (si dyūs′ *or* si dūs′) lead into wrongdoing; persuade to do wrong: *to seduce someone with a bribe.* Something very tempting is **seductive** (si duc′tiv). *v.,* **se•duced, se•duc•ing.**

see (sē) **1** notice with your eyes: *See that black cloud.* **2** be able to use your eyes: *I can't see in the dark.* **3** understand: *I see what you mean.* **4** find out: *See what time it is.* **5** take care; make sure: *See that you lock the back door.* **6** experience: *She has seen hard times.* **7** go with someone to guide or protect: *He will see you home.* **8** visit or be visited by; meet with: *to see a doctor. She is too sick to see anyone.* *v.,* **saw, seen, see•ing.**
seeing that, since: *Seeing that it's so late, I won't stay long.*
see off, say your goodbyes and watch someone leave: *We went to see Gail off at the airport.*
see through, **a** not be fooled by: *She saw through our plan.* **b** finish something long and difficult: *Don't give up; see the job through.* **c** help through a difficult time: *Janet's father saw her through her illness.*
see to, look after; take care of.

seed (sēd) **1** the part of a plant that a new plant can grow from. It contains an embryo and nutrients: *We planted seeds in the garden. Part of every crop is saved for seed.* A **seedcase** is the dry, shell-like fruit that contains seeds. A **seedling** is a young plant. **2** plant with seeds: *The farmer seeded the field with corn.* **3** produce seeds and drop them on the ground: *Dandelions seed themselves.* **4** remove the seeds from: *She seeded the grapes for the salad.* **5** the source or beginning of anything: *the seeds of trouble.* 1, 5 *n., pl.* **seeds** or **seed;** 2–4 *v.* **—seed′less,** *adj.*
go to seed, **a** produce seeds: *Dandelions go to seed when their heads turn white.* **b** gradually become run-down: *After the mines closed, the town went to seed.*

a bat	e bed	i bid	o pot	u cup	th thin
ā cake	ē me	ī bite	ō go	ū rude	ᴛʜ then
ä bar	ə about	ər over	ô for	ů put	zh measure

seed·y (sē′dē) 1 full of seeds. 2 shabby and no longer fresh: *seedy clothes.* *adj.*

Seeing Eye™ dog (sē′ing ī′ dog′) a dog trained as a guide for blind people.

seek (sēk) 1 look for: *to seek for something lost. The boys are seeking a good camping place.* 2 try to get: *He seeks your advice.* 3 try: *We sought to make peace between the two girls.* *v.,* **sought, seek·ing.**

seem (sēm) appear; look, feel, sound, etc. a certain way to a person: *This apple seemed good but it was rotten inside. I still seem to hear the music. There doesn't seem to be any problem.* *v.* **—seem′ing·ly,** *adv.*

seen (sēn) the past participle of **see:** *Have you seen Will?* *v.*

seep (sēp) ooze, trickle, or leak slowly: *Water seeps through sand.* *v.* **—seep′age,** *n.*

see·saw (sē′so′) 1 teeter-totter; a piece of play equipment made of a board supported only in the middle. People sit on the ends and move up and down. 2 play on one of these: *We were seesawing in the park.* 3 move up and down or back and forth. 1 *n.,* 2, 3 *v.*

seethe (sēᴛʜ) 1 to bubble and foam: *Water seethed under the falls.* 2 be full of strong feeling: *Lennox was seething with anger.* *v.,* **seethed, seeth·ing.**

seg·ment (seg′mənt) 1 a part cut off, marked off, or broken off; division; section: *An orange is easily pulled apart into its segments.* 2 in geometry, a part of a circle cut off by a line. *n.*

seg·re·gate (seg′rə gāt′) keep separate: *Men and women are segregated in different prisons.* *v.* **—seg′re·ga′tion,** *n.*

seine (sān) 1 a fishing net that hangs straight down in the water, with floats at the upper edge and weights at the lower. 2 fish or catch with a seine. A fishing boat that uses seines is a **seiner.** 1 *n.,* 2 *v.,* **seined, sein·ing.**

seis·mic (sīz′mik) caused by or having to do with an earthquake. A **seismograph** measures the direction, strength, and length of earthquakes. *adj.*

seize (sēz) 1 grab: *When she lost her balance, she seized his arm.* 2 capture or arrest; take by force: *The soldiers seized the city.* 3 come over suddenly: *a fever seized him.* 4 get stuck and stop working: *The engine has seized from lack of oil.* *v.,* **seized, seiz·ing.**

sei·zure (sē′zhər) 1 the action of seizing. 2 a sudden loss of control of part or all of the body. *n.*

Se·ka·ni (sə kä′nē) 1 a First Nations people living in northern British Columbia. 2 their language, which belongs to the Athapascan family. 3 having to with these people or their language. 1, 2 *n.,* 3 *adj.*

sel·dom (sel′dəm) rarely; not often: *She is seldom ill.* *adv.*

se·lect (sə lekt′) 1 choose; pick out: *His uncle let him select his own birthday present.* 2 picked as best; chosen specially: *We need a very select group of people to do this difficult job.* 1 *v.,* 2 *adj.*

se·lec·tion (sə lek′shən) 1 the act of selecting; choice: *Her selection of a library book took a long time.* 2 something selected: *The book on space travel was her selection.* 3 variety; a range of things to choose from: *The shop offered a good selection of children's books.* *n.*

self (self) 1 your own person; your own body, mind, feelings, actions, desires, and so on. This sense is usually in compounds: *Did you hurt yourself? We can take care of ourselves.* 2 the character or nature of a person: *She does not seem like her normal self.* *n., pl.* **selves.**

Word Family.......... **self**

self-addressed: with your address on
self-confident: sure of yourself; believing in yourself
self-conscious: anxious about how you appear
self-control: able to control your own actions
self-defence: the act of protecting yourself
self-denial: the act of giving up what you want
self-destruct: destroy itself suddenly
self-discipline: the ability to do what you know is right whether you feel like it or not
self-employed: working in your own small business
self-esteem: a healthy opinion of your own worth
self-explanatory: not needing any explanation
self-government: the fact of a nation or other group choosing how it will be governed
self-image: the way you think of yourself
self-important: thinking too much of yourself
self-interest: a desire to do what is good for yourself
selfish: caring too much about what you want
selfless: thinking of others instead of yourself
self-pity: an attitude of feeling sorry for yourself
self-propelled: moving under its own power
self-reliant: not expecting or wanting help
self-respect: proper pride in yourself
self-restraint: the act of keeping yourself under control, especially in speaking
self-righteous: thinking that you behave better than others
selfsame: the very same
self-satisfied: thinking that you are very good
self-serve: letting customers serve themselves
self-sufficient: independent; not needing others

self–cen·tred (self′sen′tərd) selfish; mainly caring about your own interests and affairs. **Self-centered** is another spelling. *adj.*

sell (sel) 1 exchange for money or other payment: *They are going to sell their house. The baker sells bread.* 2 be sold; get sold: *Strawberries sell at a high price in January.* 3 give away; betray: *The spy sold his country for money.* *v.,* **sold, sell·ing.**
sell off, get rid of by selling: *Before moving to Saskatchewan they sold off all their furniture.*
sell out, a sell all that you have of something: *Sorry, we've sold out of tomato soup.* **b** give up something you believe in, for some kind of gain; give in to pressure. The fact of doing this is a **sell-out.**
sell someone on something, convince someone that something is good: *You've sold me on your idea; let's do it.*
sell someone short, cheat; give someone too little.

selves (selvz) plural of **self:** *He seemed to have two selves—a friendly self and a shy self.* *pl.n.*

se·mes·ter (sə mes′tər) a school term, especially when it is half a school year: *During the first semester we concentrated on learning the multiplication tables.* *n.*

semi– *a prefix meaning* half, as in *semicircle.* A *semi-annual* magazine comes out every half year.

USING WORDS .... semi-

The prefix **semi-** is usually used with a hyphen if the next letter is a vowel: *semi-annual.*

sem·i·cir·cle (sem′ē sər′kəl) half a circle: *Set up the chairs in a semicircle.* *n.* —**sem′i·cir′cu·lar,** *adj.*

sem·i·co·lon (sem′ē kō′lən) a punctuation mark (;) that shows a break, but less of a break than a period does. *n.* ► See the *Grammar and Usage Mini-Guide.*

Grammar Check .... semicolon

You can use a **semicolon** to separate items in a list, especially if some of the items already contain commas: *On our journey we stopped in Gimli, Manitoba; Estevan, Saskatchewan; and Invermere, British Columbia.* Check the *Grammar and Usage Mini-Guide* for some other uses of a semicolon.

sem·i·fi·nal (sem′ē fī′nəl) one of the games, matches, bouts, etc. that come before the final set: *Our lacrosse team was defeated in the semifinal.* *n.*

sem·i·nar·y (sem′ə ner′ē) a school for training students to be priests, ministers, rabbis, and so on. *n., pl.* **sem·i·nar·ies.**

sem·i·pre·cious (sem′ē presh′əs) valuable, but not valuable enough to rank as gems. Amethysts and garnets are semiprecious stones; diamonds and rubies are precious stones. *adj.*

sen·ate (sen′it) 1 the upper and smaller branch of a parliament or lawmaking body. Members of the Canadian Senate are appointed by the Prime Minister, not elected. 2 any governing or lawmaking group of people: *the senate of a university.* A member of any senate is a **senator.** *n.*

send (send) 1 cause a person or thing to go from one place to another: *to send a child on an errand, to send a package by air mail. The volcano sent clouds of smoke into the air.* 2 cause to come or happen, or to be in a certain condition: *to send someone into a rage. The earthquake sent destruction to the village.* *v.,* **sent, send·ing.**
send away for something, order something by mail.
send someone packing, make someone leave.

Sen·e·ca (sen′ə kə) 1 a First Nations people living in Ontario and New York State. 2 their language. 3 having to do with these people or their language. 1, 2 *n.,* 3 *adj.*

sen·ior (sēn′yər) 1 older: *a senior member of the family.* A **senior citizen** is someone aged 65 or older. 2 a member of the graduating class of a school. 3 having to do with a graduating class: *a senior student.* 4 **Senior,** the older of two people with the same name in the same family: *John Parkhurst, Senior, is the father of John Parkhurst, Junior. Abbreviation:* Sr. 5 higher in rank or longer in service: *a senior employee.* 1, 3, 5 *adj.,* 2, 4 *n.*
be someone's senior, be older than someone: *Dave is my senior by two years.*

sen·sa·tion (sen sā′shən) 1 the action of the senses; the power to see, hear, feel, taste, smell, etc.: *A dead body is without sensation.* 2 a feeling: *He says he has a sensation of dizziness when he walks along cliffs.* 3 a lot of excitement: *The first landing on the moon caused a sensation throughout the world.* 4 a person, event, or thing that causes a lot of excitement. *n.*

sen·sa·tion·al (sen sā′shə nəl) 1 exciting and amazing: *The player's sensational catch made the crowd cheer wildly.* 2 trying to cause excitement: *a sensational newspaper story.* *adj.*

a bat	e bed	i bid	o pot	u cup	th **thin**
ā cake	ē me	ī bite	ō go	ü rude	ᴛʜ **then**
ä bar	ə about	ər over	ô for	ů put	zh measure

Senses

Through the five senses — hearing, sight, smell, taste, touch — the brain receives information about the world outside.

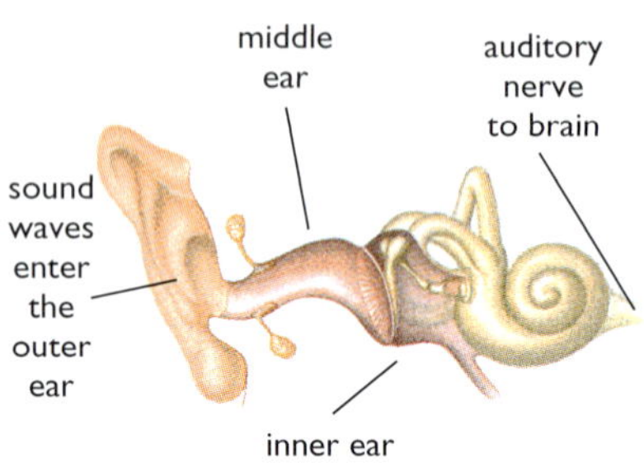

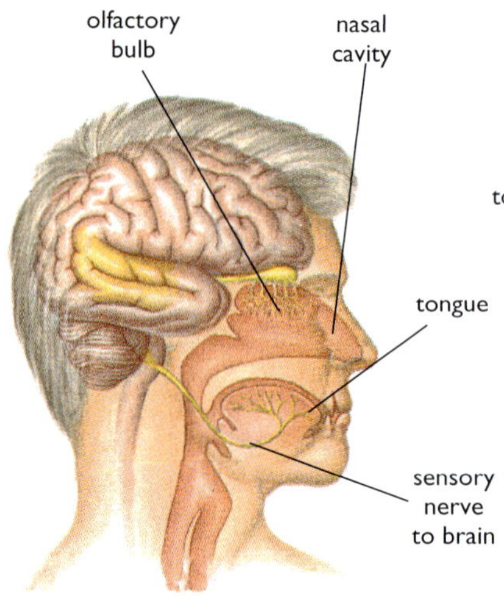

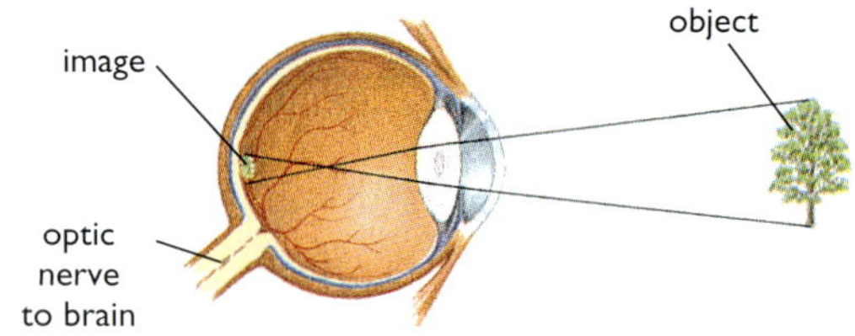

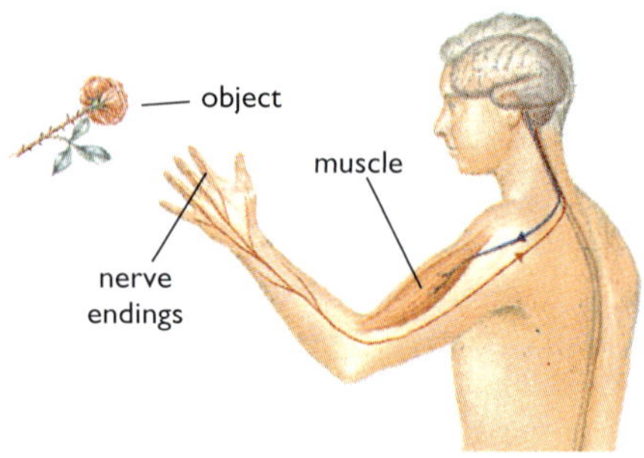

sense (sens) **1** one of the special powers of the body that allow people and animals to be aware of the world around them and of changes within themselves. The five senses are sight, smell, taste, hearing, and touch. Your eyes, ears, and so on are **sense organs.** **2** a feeling: *a sense of self-confidence.* **3** feel; understand: *My friend sensed that I was tired.* **4** an ability to judge or enjoy: *a good sense of humour, a sense of adventure. She has no sense of beauty.* **5** good judgment; wisdom or intelligence: *He had the sense to keep out of their silly argument.* **6** a meaning: *She is a friend in the truest sense of the word.* 1, 2, 4–6 *n.,* 3 *v.,* **sensed, sens·ing.** —**sen′so·ry,** *adj.*
in a sense, in a way.
lose your senses, go crazy. **Come to your senses** is the opposite.
make sense, have a meaning; be understandable: *The statement "Cow cat bless Monday" doesn't make sense.*
out of your senses, crazy.

sense·less (sens′lis) **1** unconscious: *A hard blow on the head knocked him senseless.* **2** foolish; pointless: *That was a senseless thing to do.* *adj.*

sen·si·ble (sen′sə bəl) having good sense; showing good judgment; wise: *She is much too sensible to do anything so foolish.* *adj.* —**sen′si·bly,** *adv.*

sen·si·tive (sen′sə tiv) **1** able to notice or respond to something quickly: *The eye is sensitive to light. She was sensitive to other people's feelings.* **2** easily affected or influenced: *The liquid in the thermometer is sensitive to changes in temperature.* **3** easily hurt or offended: *Don't be so sensitive; I was only teasing.* *adj.*
—**sen′si·tiv′i·ty,** *n.* —**sen′si·tize′,** *v.*

sen·sor (sen′sər) something designed to receive a certain kind of information, sometimes electronically: *a heat sensor, a motion sensor.* *n.*

sent (sent) the past tense and past participle of **send:** *They sent us a letter last week. She was sent on an errand.* *v.*

sen·tence (sen′təns) **1** a word or group of words that has a subject and a predicate. *Boys and girls* is not a sentence. *The boys and girls are here* is a sentence. ▶ See the *Grammar and Usage Mini-Guide.* **2** the punishment given to a criminal found guilty in court. **3** say what this punishment is: *The judge sentenced the bank robber to five years in prison.* 1, 2 *n.,* 3 *v.,* **sen·tenced, sen·tenc·ing.**

sen·ti·ment (sen′tə mənt) **1** any thought or belief that is based on emotion: *Admiration, patriotism, and loyalty are sentiments.* **2** tender feeling, especially if it is expressed in a rather silly, overdone way or if it blocks a person's good judgment. *n.* —**sen′ti·men′tal,** *adj.*

sen·try (sen′trē) a person, especially a soldier, stationed at a place to keep watch. **Sentinel** (sen′ti nəl) means the same. *n., pl.* **sen·tries.**
stand sentry, keep watch; guard: *We stood sentry over the sleepers.*

se·pal (sē′pəl) one of the divisions of the **calyx,** the outer covering of a flower. In many plants, the sepals make a sort of green cup at the base of the flower. *n.*

sep·a·rate (sep′ə rāt′ *for 1 and 2,* sep′rit *for 3*) **1** be between two things so as to keep them apart: *The Atlantic Ocean separates North America from Europe.* **2** come apart or take apart; divide into parts or groups: *to separate tangled strings, to separate the good apples from the wormy ones. After school we separated and went home.* **3** apart from others; not joined together; individual: *in a separate room, separate seats, separate parts of a machine.* 1, 2 *v.,* **sep·a·rat·ed, sep·a·rat·ing;** 3 *adj.* —**sep′a·rate·ly,** *adv.* —**sep′a·ra′tion,** *n.* —**sep′a·ra′tor,** *n.*

separate school (sep′ rit skūl′) a school for Catholic children in a mainly non-Catholic area, or for non-Catholic children in a mainly Catholic area. Separate schools have their own school boards and are paid for by taxes just like public schools.

sep·a·ra·tism (sep′ə rə tiz′əm) the belief, among the people of any province, that their province would be better off outside Confederation. *n.* —**sep′a·ra·tist,** *n. or adj.*

Sep·tem·ber (sep tem′bər) the ninth month of the year. September has 30 days. *n.*

sep·tic tank (sep′tik tank′) a tank that collects and holds sewage so it can be broken down by the action of bacteria. Many cottages and country homes have septic tanks because they are far from a city sewer system.

sep·ul·chre (sep′əl kər) an old or poetic word for "tomb" or "grave"; a place to put a dead body. *n.*

se·quel (sē′kwəl) 1 a complete story continuing an earlier one about the same people: *"Anne of Avonlea" is a sequel to "Anne of Green Gables" by Lucy Maud Montgomery.* 2 something that follows some earlier happening; a result: *Famine is often the sequel to war.* *n.*

se·quence (sē′kwəns) 1 a connected series: *a sequence of lessons on one subject, a sequence of numbers.* 2 the fact of coming one after another; order: *Arrange the names in alphabetical sequence.* *n.*

se·quin (sē′kwin) a very small, shiny, round object used as a decoration on clothes. *n.*

se·quoi·a (si kwoi′ə) a giant, very long-lived cone-bearing evergreen tree of California. Sequoias are protected since there are not many left. The **redwood** is one type of sequoia. *n.*

ser·e·nade (ser′ə nād′) 1 music played or sung outdoors at night, especially by a lover under his lady's window. 2 *Informal.* any piece of music played or sung for people while they are doing something else, such as eating or working. 3 sing or play to in this way. 1, 2 *n.,* 3 *v.,* **ser·e·nad·ed, ser·e·nad·ing.**

se·rene (sə rēn′) peaceful; calm: *serene happiness, a serene smile.* *adj.* —**se·ren′i·ty** (sə ren′ə tē), *n.*

serf (sərf) in medieval Europe, a poor person who farmed the land of someone rich and powerful. Serfs paid heavy fees to their landowners in return for protection and a place to live. If the land was sold, they stayed and worked for the new owner. *n.* —**serf′dom,** *n.*

se·ri·al (sē′rē əl) 1 a story presented one part at a time on TV or radio, or in a magazine or newspaper. 2 belonging to a series. A **serial number** is one of a large group of numbers used to identify many similar things, such as cars. Each car has its own number. 1 *n.,* 2 *adj.*

CONFUSABLES .... serial

serial means "arranged in a series":
The serial numbers on these tickets all start with 358.

cereal means "food made from grain":
I like cream on my cereal.

Remember that *cream* and *cereal* both start with *c*.

se·ries (sē′rēz) 1 a number of similar things in a row: *A series of rooms opened off the long hall. A series of rainy days ruined our vacation.* 2 a number of things placed in a particular order: *in an alphabetical series.* *n., pl.* **se·ries.**

se·ri·ous (sē′rē əs) 1 thoughtful; concentrating on important things: *a serious person, a serious expression on your face.* 2 not joking; really meaning what you say. 3 important; needing thought: *Choosing your life work is a serious matter.* 4 important because it may do much harm; dangerous: *The badly injured man was in serious condition.* *adj.* —**se′ri·ous·ness,** *n.*

ser·mon (sər′mən) 1 a public talk meant to teach people their religion or encourage them to live right. Ministers preach sermons in church. 2 a long, serious talk about behaviour: *The children got a sermon on table manners from their parents.* *n.* —**ser′mon·ize′,** *v.*

ser·pent (sər′pənt) an old or poetic word for a snake. *n.*

ser·rat·ed (sə rā′tid) notched like the blade of a saw; toothed: *a serrated edge.* *adj.* —**ser·ra′tion,** *n.*

se·rum (sē′rəm) 1 the clear, pale yellow, liquid part of the blood, which separates from the red clotted part if blood is allowed to stand. 2 a liquid used to prevent or cure a disease, made from the blood of an animal that has become immune to it. Polio vaccine is a serum. *n.*

serv·ant (sər′vənt) 1 in earlier times, a person who worked in someone else's private home for pay, such as a cook, housekeeper, butler, or nanny. Usually they lived in the employer's home, too, or in a separate house on the same property. 2 a person whose main goal is to be useful or helpful to someone else or to some cause: *Police officers and firefighters are public servants. She considers herself a servant of peace.* *n.*

a bat	e bed	i bid	o pot	u cup	th thin
ā cake	ē me	ī bite	ō go	ū rude	ᴛʜ then
ä bar	ə about	ər over	ô for	ů put	zh measure

serve (sərv) **1** try to be useful or helpful to someone or to some cause: *Good citizens serve their country. How can I serve you?* **2** work as an employee, paid servant, slave, etc.: *The soldier served three years in the army.* **3** wait on someone at the table; bring food to people: *The waiter served us. I helped Grandma serve the soup.* **4** be enough for: *One pie will serve six people.* **5** supply with something needed: *This library serves a town of 25 000.* **6** be useful; be what is needed: *A tree stump served as a seat.* **7** spend time in prison: *She served three years for robbery.* **8** in tennis and similar games, put the ball in play by hitting it. **9** the action of putting the ball in play in this way: *That was a good serve, Debbie!* 1–8 *v.*, **served, serv·ing;** 9 *n.* **—serv′er,** *n.*
serve someone right, be just what someone deserves: *He lost the race? It serves him right for bragging so much.*

serv·ice (sər′vis) **1** helpful or useful action for others; work done for anyone, whether for pay or not: *That family performed many services for the community. He did thirty years' service with the railway.* **2** a system meant to supply something useful or necessary: *The bus service was good.* **3** Usually, **services,** *pl.* help: *She no longer needs the services of a doctor.* **4** the fact or manner of serving food: *The service in this restaurant is excellent.* **5** a religious meeting or ceremony: *a funeral service.* **6** a department of a government: *the civil service, the armed services.* **7** duty in the army: *He was on active service during the war.* A **serviceman** or **servicewoman** is a soldier. **8** repair or keep in good shape: *The mechanic serviced our car.* **9** the act or manner of serving the ball in tennis and similar games. **10** a set of dishes: *a silver tea service.* 1–7, 9, 10 *n.*, 8 *v.*, **serv·iced, serv·ic·ing.**
at your service, ready to do what you want.
be of service, be helpful or useful.

serv·ice·a·ble (sər′vi sə bəl) useful; in good enough shape to be useful: *He wanted to buy a serviceable second-hand car.* *adj.*

service centre (sər′vis sen′tər) a place to stop next to a highway, with a gas station, restaurant, washrooms, etc.

service station (sər′vis stā′shən) a place where you can buy gas, oil, windshield washer fluid, etc. and get your car repaired.

ser·vi·ette (sər′vē et′) a napkin used at the table, especially a paper one: *He wiped his hand on his serviette.* *n.*

serv·ing (ser′ving) a portion of food served to a person at one time; helping. *n.*

ses·a·me (ses′ə mē) a plant that grows in hot parts of Asia. Its small, flat, oval, light-coloured seeds are used as food and as a source of cooking oil. *n.*

ses·sion (sesh′ən) **1** a meeting or series of meetings of a court, legislature, class, etc.: *a session of Parliament, the fall session at a university.* **2** a period of doing a certain activity: *After a long session of snow shovelling they had some hot chocolate.* *n.*
in session, meeting; going on: *School is not in session in July.*

set (set) **1** put in some place, especially carefully: *Set the box on its end. I said "Set it on the table," not "Dump it on the table!"* **2** put in some condition or relation: *to set wood on fire, to set someone free. He set the words to music.* **3** fix; arrange; choose: *We set a date for the party.* **4** control the way a machine will operate, by turning a dial, pressing a button, etc.: *to set an alarm clock, to set the volume of a radio. Set the oven temperature at 150°C.* **5** fixed or decided on beforehand: *a set time, set rules.* **6** go down in the sky: *The sun sets in the west.* **7** put a broken bone in the right position again so it can heal. **8** become firm; harden, like cement or jelly. **9** ready: *I'm all set to start.* **10** a group of things or people belonging together: *a set of dishes, a set of beliefs, a set of friends.* **11** in mathematics, any group of numbers, points, or other objects which are all the same in some specific way. The set of even numbers less than 10 includes 2, 4, 6, and 8. **12** a device for receiving or sending signals: *a TV set, a telephone handset.* **13** the scenery for a play or movie. 1–4, 6–8 *v.*, **set, set·ting;** 5, 9 *adj.*, 10–13 *n.*
set about, start doing: *Set about your work.*
set an example, be an example or model that others follow: *Set a good example for your little sister.*
set back, a stop; hinder; check: *The computer crash set me back on my project.* A **setback** is something that sets you back. **b** *Informal.* cost: *That'll set you back at least $50.*
set down, a put down. **b** put in writing.
set forth, a formal expression meaning: **a** state; declare: *to set forth a theory.* **b** start out: *We set forth on our trip.*
set in, begin: *Winter set in early.* This expression is usually used for something considered unpleasant.
set in your ways, having very firm habits.
set off, a cause to explode, ring, etc.: *to set off firecrackers, to set off an alarm.* **b** start out: *to set off for home.* **c** make more striking by contrast: *The green dress set off her red hair.* **d** mark off somehow as separate: *Use a heading to set off each section of your project.*
set on, attack or urge to attack: *The robbers set on him. She set her dogs on the robbers.*
set out, start a trip: *They set out for Steinbach yesterday.*
set straight, correct: *to set someone straight. Just to set the record straight, I did go.*
set the table, put out the dishes, cutlery, etc. for a meal.
set to, a begin: *to set to work.* **b** begin fighting: *The two boys set to.* A **set-to** is a fight.

set up, **a** build: *to set up a monument.* **b** start a business, a program, a fund, etc. **c** get things ready and in place: *to set up the gym for graduation.* **d** arrange a situation so that a certain person will get in trouble, be tricked or disappointed, or fail: *They set him up to look like a thief.* A trap like this is a **set-up.**

set your heart on, eagerly hope for something or be determined to do something: *She set her heart on winning the race.*

set·ter (set′ər) a breed of long-haired hunting dog, trained to stand still and point its nose toward any hunted animal that it scents. *n.*

set·ting (set′ing) **1** the place and time of a story. **2** the background for something; surroundings; situation: *a scenic mountain setting. It is hard to play this game in a classroom setting.* *n.*

set·tle (set′əl) **1** work out; come to an agreement about: *to settle a dispute. Have you settled on a day for the picnic?* **2** put in order; arrange: *He settled all his affairs before going on his year-long trip around the world.* **3** pay: *to settle a bill.* **4** make a home: *Our cousin plans to settle in the Yukon.* **5** set up new communities in: *The British settled Newfoundland.* People who do this are **settlers.** **6** come to rest; land: *The butterfly settled on a flower.* **7** make or get comfortable and relaxed: *The cat settled itself in the chair for a nap. Are you settled in your new job? A vacation will settle your nerves.* *v.,* **set·tled, set·tling.**

settle down, **a** live a more regular life. **b** give steady effort or attention: *She settled down to her homework.* **c** make or become calm and quiet: *"Settle down! I can't work with you two yelling and running around!"*

set·tle·ment (set′əl mənt) **1** the act of settling something. **2** a place where a permanent community has been set up: *Québec City is one of Canada's oldest settlements.* *n.*

sev·en (sev′ən) one more than six; 7. *n. or adj.* **—sev′enth,** *adj. or n.*

sev·en·teen (sev′ən tēn′) seven more than ten; 17. *n. or adj.* **—sev′en·teenth′,** *adj. or n.*

sev·en·ty (sev′ən tē) seven times ten; 70. *n., pl.* **sev·en·ties;** *or adj.* **—sev′en·ti·eth,** *adj. or n.*

sev·er (sev′ər) cut or break off: *to accidentally sever a toe with an axe, to sever a friendship. The rope severed and the swing fell down.* *v.*

sev·er·al (sev′rəl) more than two but not many; some; a few: *to eat several candies (adj.). Several are missing (pron.).* *adj. or pron.*

se·vere (sə vēr′) **1** bad or extreme; serious, heavy, difficult, or violent: *a severe headache. The storm caused severe damage.* **2** very strict; stern; harsh: *The judge was a severe-looking man. The angry principal spoke in a severe tone.* *adj.,* **se·ver·er, se·ver·est.** **—se·vere′ly,** *adv.* **—se·ver′i·ty** (sə ver′ə tē), *n.*

sew (sō) make, fix, or fasten with a needle and thread: *to sew a dress, to sew up a tear, to sew on a button.* You can sew by hand or with a **sewing machine.** *v.,* **sewed, sewn** or **sewed, sew·ing.**

CONFUSABLES .... sew

sew means "stitch with thread":
I will sew myself a dress.

so means "therefore" or "very much":
She smiled, so I smiled back. These gloves are so soft.

sow means "scatter in the ground":
The farmer sowed the seeds for next year's crop.

sew·er (sū′ər) a pipe, usually underground, to carry away **sewage,** that is, liquid waste and dirty water. *n.*

sex (seks) **1** the characteristic of being male or female: *People were admitted without regard to age or sex.* **2** the group that includes all males or all females: *The sexes are divided for some phys ed classes.* **3** the action which lets humans and animals join the two parts needed to produce a baby—the egg of the female and the sperm of the male. In humans, this action can also be an expression of love. The full name for it is **sexual intercourse,** and the parts of the body used are called **sex organs.** **4** any other activity between two people that involves these organs or goes along with sexual intercourse. *n.* **—sex′u·al** (sek′shū əl), *adj.*

sex·ism (seks′iz əm) prejudice toward women or men as a group, or attention paid to a person's sex when it does not matter. *n.* **—sex′ist,** *n. or adj.*

shab·by (shab′ē) **1** worn out: *a shabby suit.* **2** in bad repair; run-down: *a shabby old house.* **3** mean; not very honourable: *shabby treatment.* *adj.,* **shab·bi·er, shab·bi·est.** **—shab′bi·ly,** *adv.* **—shab′bi·ness,** *n.*

shack (shak) **1** a roughly built hut or cabin: *The girls made a shack in the backyard.* **2** a small house in bad shape: *There are a lot of shacks in that part of town.* *n.*

a bat	e bed	i bid	o pot	u cup	th thin
ā cake	ē me	ī bite	ō go	ū rude	ᴛʜ then
ȧ bar	ə about	ər over	ȯ for	u̇ put	zh measure

Shadow Play

You can use your hands to make different animal shapes, and perform a play which will delight younger children.

Here are a few ideas to get you started.

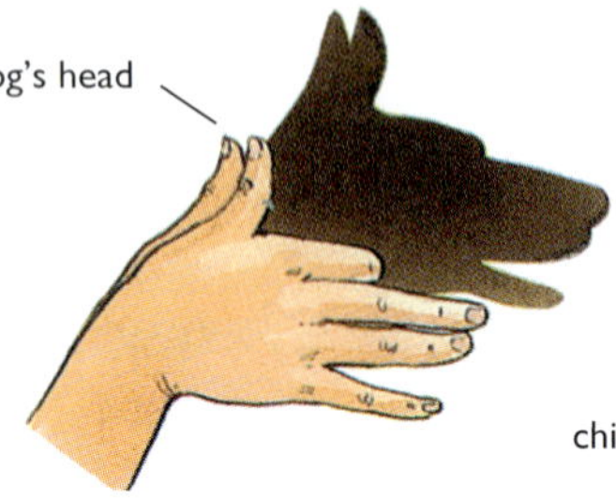

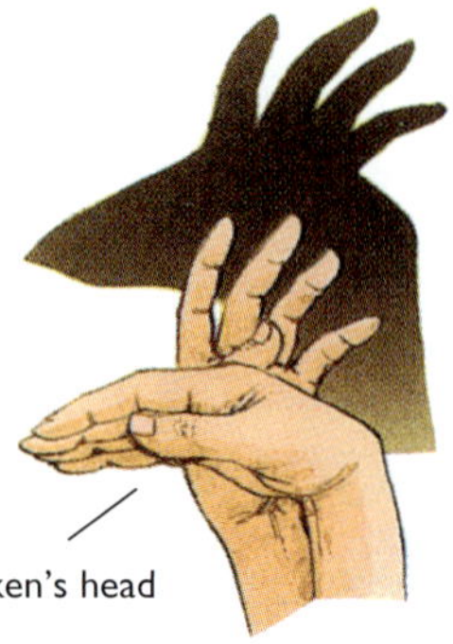

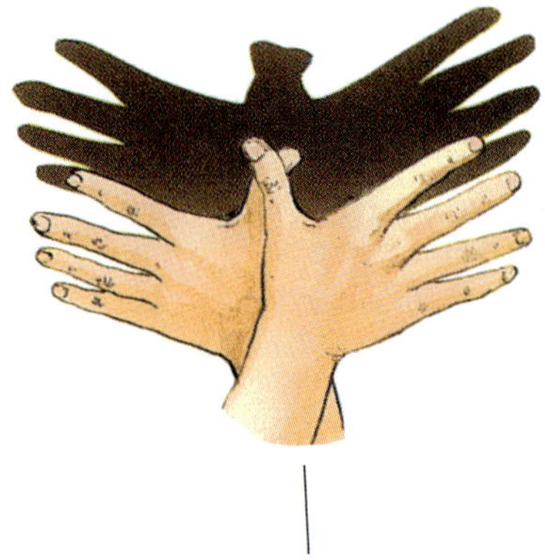

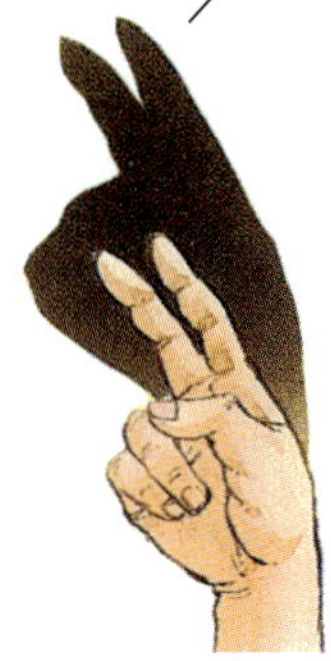

shack·le (shak'əl) **1** a metal band fastened around the ankle or wrist of a prisoner or slave and attached to a chain. **2** anything that prevents someone from acting freely. **3** put shackles on; take away the freedom of: *He was shackled by fear.* 1, 2 *n.,* 3 *v.,* **shack·led, shack·ling.**

shade (shād) **1** a place where the sun is blocked by something. It is cooler and darker in the shade: *We sat in the shade of a big tree.* **2** something that shuts out light. Windows and lamps often have shades covering them. **3** keep light from: *A big hat shades the eyes.* **4** one variety of a particular colour or one aspect of meaning: *I like all shades of blue. "Turn" is a word with many shades of meaning.* **5** in drawing and painting, make certain areas darker to imitate the effect of light and shadow and make things look more realistic. **6** a very small difference or amount; a little bit: *Your coat is a shade longer than your dress.* 1, 2, 4, 6 *n.,* 3, 5 *v.,* **shad·ed, shad·ing.**

shad·ow (shad'ō) **1** the dark shape made by some person, animal, or thing that is blocking the light: *The shadows of the houses grew longer as the sun went down.* **2** darken: *The grass is shadowed by huge oaks. Her joy was shadowed by sad memories.* **3** a faint image: *She was so worn-out, she seemed to be only a shadow of her usual self.* **4** a little bit; a slight suggestion: *There's not a shadow of doubt about his guilt.* **5** follow closely, usually secretly: *A detective shadowed the suspect.* **6** a person who follows another closely or keeps a close watch on another person's actions. 1, 3, 4, 6 *n.,* 2, 5 *v.* **—shad'ow·y,** *adj.*

shad·y (shā'dē) **1** in the shade: *a shady spot.* **2** giving shade: *a shady tree.* **3** *Informal.* not quite honest: *a shady character, a shady business deal.* *adj.,* **shad·i·er, shad·i·est.**

shaft (shaft) **1** in a machine, a bar that turns, or that holds turning parts. **2** a deep, narrow passageway that goes straight up and down: *a shaft leading into a mine, an elevator shaft.* **3** the long, straight part of anything, such as a spear, pillar, screwdriver, feather, golf club, etc. **4** a ray or beam of light. *n.*

shag·gy (shag'ē) covered with a thick, rough, untidy mass of hair, wool, etc.: *a shaggy dog.* *adj.,* **shag·gi·er, shag·gi·est.**

shake (shāk) **1** move quickly back and forth, up and down, or from side to side: *to shake a rug, to shake a pair of dice, to shake your fist angrily. The baby shook her rattle.* **2** sprinkle, throw, or scatter by this kind of movement: *He shook the snow off his clothes.* **3** tremble or cause to tremble: *He is shaking with cold. The explosion shook the earth.* **4** disturb, upset, or weaken: *His lie shook my faith in his honesty. She was badly shaken by the news.* **5** the act of shaking: *She answered with a shake of her head.* 1–4 *v.,* **shook, shak·en, shak·ing;** 5 *n.* **—shak'y,** *adj.*
shake hands, take a person's hand firmly in your own and move it up and down in greeting or agreement.
shake off, get rid of.
shake on it, seal an agreement by shaking hands.
shake up, **a** shake hard. **b** stir up. **c** disturb or upset badly: *He was very shaken up by the experience.*

shak·er (shā'kər) a container with holes in the top, which you shake upside down in order to sprinkle what's inside: *a salt shaker, a shaker for parmesan cheese.* *n.*

shale (shāl) a sedimentary rock formed from hardened clay or mud pressed together in thin layers which split easily. *n.*

shall (shal) a rather formal auxiliary verb used: **1** in questions with *I* or *we* to make a polite suggestion: *Shall we go?* **2** in an official statement of a rule: *No person shall chew gum while in class.* **3** to show future action: *I shall go tomorrow if I cannot make it today.* *v.*

shal·low (shal′ō) 1 not deep: *shallow water, a shallow dish.* 2 **shallows,** *pl.* a shallow part: *The boys splashed in the shallows of the pond.* 3 without deep thought or feeling: *a shallow mind.* 1, 3 *adj.,* 2 *n.*

sham (sham) 1 an act, just for show; pretence: *Her goodness is all a sham; really she's mean.* 2 pretended; fake: *sham anger.* 3 pretend: *He shammed sickness to get out of work.* 1 *n.,* 2 *adj.,* 3 *v.,* **shammed, sham·ming.**

sha·man (shā′mən *or* shȧ′mən) in many traditional cultures, including North American aboriginal culture, a person who uses special powers to cure illness, influence events for good or evil, etc. *n.*

sham·bles (sham′bəlz) *Informal.* confusion; mess: *The careless children made a shambles of their room.* *n.*

shame (shām) 1 an awful feeling you get when you know that you or someone close to you has done something very wrong or silly: *The child blushed with shame when she was caught stealing candy. That young man's arrest has brought shame to a fine family.* 2 give someone this feeling: *Her rudeness has shamed her parents.* Something that gives a feeling of shame is **shameful.** 3 a fact to be sorry about; pity: *It is a shame to be so wasteful. What a shame you can't come to the party!* 1, 3 *n.,* 2 *v.,* **shamed, sham·ing.**
put to shame, **a** make ashamed; disgrace. **b** be so good that others feel they have done rather poorly: *Her careful work put all the rest of us to shame.*
shame on you, you ought to feel shame.

shame·faced (shām′fāst′) showing shame and embarrassment. *adj.*

shame·less (shām′lis) caring so little about right and wrong that you are unable to feel shame; completely bold in doing wrong: *a shameless liar.* *adj.*

sham·poo (sham pü′) 1 a liquid cleanser used for washing hair, carpets, or anything else fuzzy. 2 wash hair or something else with this liquid: *We shampooed the dog.* 3 a wash of this kind: *He gave his hair a thorough shampoo.* 1, 3 *n.,* 2 *v.,* **sham·pooed, sham·poo·ing.**

sham·rock (sham′rok) a plant with a bright green leaf divided into three heart-shaped parts. It is the national emblem of Ireland. *n.*

shan't (shant) shall not.

🍁 **shan·ty**[1] (shan′tē) a roughly built hut or cabin. *n., pl.* **shan·ties.**

shan·ty[2] (shan′tē) a song sung by sailors in rhythm with the motions made during their work. *n., pl.* **shan·ties.**

shape (shāp) 1 the outline or form of a person or thing; appearance: *An apple is different in shape from a banana. A white shape stood at his bedside.* 2 give a certain form to; make: *to shape dough into balls, to shape a question.* 3 **a** condition: *What kind of shape is the car in?* **b** good condition: *The athlete exercised to stay in shape.* 1, 3 *n.,* 2 *v.,* **shaped, shap·ing.** —**shape′less,** *adj.*
shape up, **a** smarten up; change your ways and do better. **b** develop; start to look like something definite: *This is shaping up to be a beautiful weekend.*
take shape, begin to have a definite form.

shard (shȧrd) a sharp broken piece of something: *Shards from the shattered window lay on the grass.* *n.*

share (sher) 1 use or do together: *The sisters share a room. Everyone shared in making the school picnic a huge success.* 2 divide into parts, each taking a part: *Glenn shared his candy with his sister.* 3 a part belonging to one person or group: *She does more than her share of the work but doesn't always get her share of the praise.* 4 each of the parts into which the ownership of a company is divided. People who own shares in a company are **shareholders.** They get some of the company's profits and have a say in major decisions. 1, 2 *v.,* **shared, shar·ing;** 3, 4 *n.*

Sharks mostly hunt alone, but a smell or taste of blood in the water will draw a number of them to the same spot. These sharks will then go into what is called a feeding frenzy — they will attack and bite anything, including each other.

shark (shȧrk) a meat-eating fish with a skeleton made out of cartilage instead of bone. Most sharks live in the ocean. Some are large and ferocious, and can be dangerous to people. *n.*

a bat	e bed	i bid	o pot	u cup	th thin
ā cake	ē me	ī bite	ō go	ü rude	TH then
ȧ bar	ə about	ər over	ȯ for	u̇ put	zh measure

sharp (shärp) 1 having a very thin cutting edge or a fine point: *a sharp knife, a sharp pin.* 2 pointed, not rounded: *a sharp nose, a sharp corner on a box.* 3 with a sudden change of direction: *a sharp turn.* 4 very cold: *sharp weather, a sharp morning.* 5 severe; feeling like a cut or bite: *sharp words, a sharp pain.* 6 so strong that it is almost painful: *a sharp taste, a sharp desire.* 7 clear; distinct: *the sharp contrast between black and white.* 8 being aware of things quickly; alert: *sharp ears, a sharp girl. The sentry kept a sharp watch for the enemy.* 9 promptly; exactly: *Come at 1:00 sharp.* 10 in music: **a** above the true pitch: *to sing sharp (adv.).* **b** a half step above a given tone. C sharp is the black note just above C. 11 the sign (♯) that shows that a tone is to be raised a half step. 1–8, 10 *adj.,* 9, 10 *adv.,* 11 *n.* —**sharp′en,** *v.*

Word Family........... **sharp**

sharp-eyed: having very accurate vision
sharp-shooter: a person with a very good aim
sharp-tongued: saying things liable to hurt people
sharp-witted: very clever

shat·ter (shat′ər) 1 break into pieces: *A stone shattered the window.* 2 destroy or disturb greatly: *Our hopes for a picnic were shattered by the rain. She was shattered when her friend moved away.* *v.*

shave (shāv) 1 cut hair off completely with a razor: *Dad shaves every day. He shaves his beard.* 2 the act of cutting off hair with a razor. 3 cut off a very thin slice or slices: *to shave chocolate. Shave a bit off this piece of cake so it's the same size as mine.* A very thin slice of something is a **shaving.** 4 just barely touch in passing; graze: *The car shaved the pole.* 5 a narrow miss or escape: *The shot missed him, but it was a close shave.* 1, 3, 4 *v.,* **shaved, shav·ing;** 2, 5 *n.*

shawl (shol) a large piece of cloth worn around the shoulders or head. *n.*

sheaf (shēf) 1 a bundle of cut grain tied around the middle for drying, loading, and stacking: *wheat sheaves.* 2 a bundle of papers: *a sheaf of letters.* *n., pl.* **sheaves.**

shear (shēr) 1 **shears,** *pl. or sing.* a large scissors or other similar cutting instrument: *barber's shears, grass shears.* 2 cut or cut off with shears or scissors. 3 cut the wool or fleece from: *The farmer sheared the sheep.* 1 *n.,* 2, 3 *v.,* **sheared, sheared** or **shorn, shear·ing.**

sheath (shēth) 1 a case or covering for the blade of a sword or knife. 2 any covering for something sharp or long and thin, especially on an animal or plant. *n., pl.* **sheaths** (shēᴛʜz).

sheathe (shēᴛʜ) 1 put into a sheath: *He sheathed his sword.* 2 enclose in any case or covering: *a mummy sheathed in linen. The doors were sheathed in metal as protection against fire.* *v.,* **sheathed, sheath·ing.**

sheaves (shēvz) plural of **sheaf.** *n.*

shed[1] (shed) a usually one-storey building used for storing tools, farm machinery, vehicles, and so on: *a tool shed, a bike shed.* *n.*

shed[2] (shed) 1 let fall or pour out: *to shed tears. The sun sheds light on the earth. Many soldiers shed their blood for our freedom.* 2 throw off; cast aside: *The snake shed its skin. An umbrella sheds water.* *v.,* **shed, shed·ding.**
shed blood, destroy life; kill.
shed light on something, make something easier to understand or solve: *This new information may shed some light on the problem.*

she'd (shēd) 1 she had. 2 she would.

sheen (shēn) a soft brightness or shine, like that of satin or polished silver. *n.* —**sheen′y,** *adj.*

sheep (shēp) 1 a hoofed, cud-chewing animal raised for its meat, wool, and skin. There are many kinds of sheep. 2 a person who is foolish or easily led by others. *n., pl.* **sheep.**

sheep·dog (shēp′dog′) a dog trained to help guard and herd sheep. *n.*

sheep·ish (shē′pish) embarrassed, especially because you have been proven wrong about something: *a sheepish smile.* *adj.*

sheep·skin (shēp′skin′) the skin of a sheep, especially with wool on it. *n.*

sheer (shēr) 1 so thin you can almost see through it: *Her dress had long, sheer sleeves.* 2 unmixed with anything else; complete: *He fainted from sheer weariness.* 3 straight up or down; steep: *From the top of the wall, there was a sheer drop of 20 m to the water below.* *adj.*

sheet (shēt) 1 a large piece of cloth, used to sleep on or under. 2 a large, thin piece or layer of anything: *a sheet of glass, a sheet of plywood, a sheet of ice.* **Sheet metal** is metal in thin sheets. 3 a single piece of paper. **Sheet music** is music printed on loose pages. *n.*

sheik or **sheikh** (shēk *or* shāk) a chief or head of an Arab family, village, or tribe. *n.*

shelf (shelf) 1 a thin, flat piece of wood or other material fastened to a wall or into a cupboard or frame, to hold books, dishes, toys, and so on. The length of time that food will keep unrefrigerated (on a shelf in a store, for example) is its **shelf life.** 2 anything like a shelf: *a shelf of rock on the side of a cliff.* *n., pl.* **shelves.**

Seashells are the skeletons of sea creatures called molluscs. These animals look like slugs and keep their soft, boneless bodies mostly inside the protection of their shells.

shell (shel) 1 the hard outside covering of nuts, eggs, certain animals, etc.: *Oysters, turtles, and beetles all have shells.* 2 take out of a shell: *The cook is shelling peas.* 3 something like a shell; anything that is hollow or empty, or that forms the outer framework or case for something else. 4 a type of ammunition for guns. It is a cylinder containing bits of metal or explosives. 5 fire shells at: *The enemy shelled the town.* 1, 3, 4 *n.,* 2, 5 *v.*
come out of your shell, stop being shy.
shell out, *Informal.* **a** give candy to children at the door on Halloween. **b** pay out: *He shelled out $15 for the roses.*

she'll (shēl) she will.

shel·lac (shə lak′) 1 a liquid for coating wood or metal. It hardens to a smooth, shiny, finish. 2 put shellac on. 1 *n.,* 2 *v.,* **shel·lacked, shel·lack·ing.**

shell·fish (shel′fish′) a water animal with a shell but no backbone. Oysters, clams, crabs, crayfish, and lobsters are called shellfish. *n., pl.* **shell·fish** or **shell·fish·es.**

shel·ter (shel′tər) 1 protection; refuge: *We took shelter from the storm in a barn.* 2 something you can go under, into, or behind for protection: *Trees are a shelter from the sun.* 3 find or give protection: *to shelter runaway slaves. The sheep sheltered from the hot sun in the shade of the haystack.* 4 a building with beds for homeless people to use. 1, 2, 4 *n.,* 3 *v.*

shelve (shelv) 1 put on a shelf: *to shelve books.* 2 lay aside: *Plans for a new gym floor were shelved after the cutbacks.* *v.,* **shelved, shelv·ing.**

shelves (shelvz) plural of **shelf.** *n.*

shep·herd (shep′ərd) 1 a person who takes care of sheep. 2 guide or care for sheep or any other group: *to shepherd a flock. The teacher shepherded the children safely out of the burning building.* 1 *n.,* 2 *v.*

sher·bet (shər′bit) a frozen dessert made of fruit juice, sugar, and water or milk. *n.*

sher·iff (sher′if) 1 in Canada, an official whose job is to carry out certain court orders, such as forcing people out of a house when they don't pay rent and taking convicted criminals away to prison. 2 in the United States, the top police officer of a county. *n.*

she's (shēz) 1 she is. 2 she has.

shied (shīd) the past tense and past participle of **shy:** *The horse shied and threw the rider. The boy shied a stone at the tree.* *v.*

A shield was the most important personal protection a fighter had. Carried or strapped on one arm, it left the other arm free to use a weapon, usually a sword.

shield (shēld) 1 a piece of armour carried on your arm to protect your body in battle. 2 any person or thing that protects: *She held up a newspaper as a shield against the sun.* 3 protect; defend: *His friend shielded him from punishment.* 1, 2 *n.,* 3 *v.*

shift (shift) 1 change from one place or position to another: *to shift a bag from one hand to the other, to shift the blame to someone else.* 2 a change of direction, position, attitude, etc.: *a shift in the wind, a shift in a person's thinking.* 3 change gears in a car. 4 a part of a day worked by a certain group of workers, or the group of workers who work during that time: *This woman is on the night shift. My dad's shift is midnight to 8 a.m.* 1, 3 *v.,* 2, 4 *n.*
make shift, manage with what you can find: *We had no needle and thread to fix the rip so we made shift with a pin.*
shift for yourself, manage on your own.

a bat	e bed	i bid	o pot	u cup	th thin
ā cake	ē me	ī bite	ō go	ū rude	ᴛʜ then
ä bar	ə about	ər over	ô for	u̇ put	zh measure

shift·y (shif′tē) tricky; not straightforward; sly. *adj.,* **shift·i·er, shift·i·est.**

shil·ling (shil′ing) an old British silver coin that was equal to $\frac{1}{20}$ of a pound. *n.*

shim·mer (shim′ər) 1 shine faintly with a wavering light: *The moonlight shimmered on the lake.* 2 a faint gleam or shine: *the shimmer of pearls.* 1 *v.,* 2 *n.*

shin (shin) 1 the front part of your leg from your knee to your ankle. 2 climb up or down a rope, pole, etc., holding on with both your hands and your legs: *She shinned up the tree.* **Shinny** is another form for this sense. 1 *n.,* 2 *v.,* **shinned, shin·ning.**

shine (shīn) 1 give off light; be bright: *The sun is shining. Her eyes shone with happiness.* 2 the fact of giving off light: *the shine of polished silver.* 3 aim a light: *Shine the flashlight up here.* 4 make bright; polish: *to shine shoes.* The past form for this sense is always **shined.** 5 do very well; be outstanding: *She shines in math.* 1, 3–5 *v.,* **shone** or **shined, shin·ing;** 2 *n.* **—shin′y,** *adj.*
rain or shine, no matter what the weather.

shin·gle (shing′gəl) 1 a thin piece of waterproof material used to cover a roof. Rows of shingles are overlapped so no water can get between them. 2 cover with such pieces: *to shingle a roof.* 1 *n.,* 2 *v.,* **shin·gled, shin·gling.**

shin·ny[1] (shin′ē) an old word for a simple kind of ice hockey or street hockey. *n.*

shin·ny[2] (shin′ē) *Informal.* to climb a pole, rope, etc. holding on with your hands and your legs. **Shin** is another form of this word. *v.,* **shin·nied, shin·ny·ing.**

Shin·to (shin′tō) 1 a follower of the ancient religion of Japan, which includes the worship of ancestors and has many gods; the main one is **Amaterasu** (ä′mə tə rä′ sū), the sun goddess. Shintos follow a set of seven rules that require faith, hard work, and a humble, peaceful, sincere, and thankful spirit. 2 having to do with this religion. 1 *n.,* 2 *adj.* **—Shin′to·ism′,** *n.*

ship (ship) 1 a large boat, with a motor or sails, designed for ocean travel. A ship can carry people or goods. 2 a nickname for an aircraft or spacecraft. 3 send or carry from one place to another by a ship, train, or truck: *Did he ship it by express or by freight?* 4 put or take on board a ship: *They used a crane to ship the new cars aboard the freighter.* 1, 2 *n.,* 3, 4 *v.,* **shipped, ship·ping.**

–ship *a suffix meaning:* 1 the position or office of. The position of a king is called a *kingship.* 2 the quality or condition of being. *Partnership* is the condition of being a *partner. Leadership* is the quality of being a leader.

ship·load (ship′lōd′) a full load for a ship. *n.*

ship·ment (ship′mənt) 1 the act of shipping goods: *A thousand boxes of oranges were ready for shipment.* 2 a batch of goods sent at one time to a person or company: *The last two shipments are still in the warehouse.* *n.*

ship·ping (ship′ing) the business of sending things by ship, train, or truck. A person or company that does this is a **shipper.** *n.*

ship·shape (ship′shāp′) neat and trim; in good order. *adj.*

ship·wreck (ship′rek′) 1 the destruction or loss of a ship at sea, by a storm or by rocks or icebergs that it has hit: *Only two people survived the shipwreck.* 2 cause to experience a shipwreck: *The* Juliet *was shipwrecked in the storm.* 3 ruin or destroy anything: *Her life was shipwrecked by drug abuse.* 4 destruction; ruin: *Losing his job meant the shipwreck of all his plans.* 1, 4 *n.,* 2, 3 *v.*

ship·yard (ship′yärd′) a large, open place near the water where ships are built or repaired. *n.*

shirk (shərk) try to get out of doing a duty: *He lost his job because he shirked his work.* *v.* **—shirk′er,** *n.*

shirt (shərt) a garment for the whole upper part of your body. It can have short or long sleeves. *n.*
keep your shirt on, *Slang.* stay calm; keep your temper.

> **WORD HISTORY........shirt**
>
> **Shirt** comes from an Old English word *scyrte,* and **skirt** comes from a Norse word *skyrta.* Both *scyrte* and *skyrta* came originally from one word that meant "short garment."

shish ke·bab (shish′ kə bob′) chunks of meat, marinated and then cooked with mushrooms, tomatoes, onions, etc. on a skewer.

> **WORD HISTORY........shish kebab**
>
> **Shish kebab** comes from Turkish *siskebabi,* made up of *sis,* meaning "skewer" and *kebap,* meaning "roast lamb."

shiv·er (shiv′ər) 1 shake from cold, fear, or excitement: *He shivered in the icy wind* (*v.*). *A shiver of excitement ran up her spine* (*n.*). 2 **the shivers,** *pl.* a fit of shivering. 1 *v.,* 1, 2 *n.*

shoal¹ (shōl) a place in a sea, lake, or stream where the water is shallow because of a sandbank, sand bar, or other landform on the bottom: *The ship was wrecked on the shoals.* *n.*

shoal² (shōl) a large number of fish swimming together. A **school** is the same thing. *n.*

shock¹ (shok) 1 a violent surprise or sudden upsetting experience: *His death was a great shock to his family. You gave me a shock when you screamed like that.* 2 cause to feel strong surprise, horror, or disgust: *That child's bad language shocks everyone.* 3 a painful disturbance of the body caused by an electric current passing through it. 4 a condition in which certain systems in the body suddenly stop working properly as a result of severe injury or a very disturbing experience. A person in shock has low blood pressure, may have trouble breathing or responding to things going on around him or her, and may become unconscious. 5 a sudden, violent shake, blow, or crash: *The two trains collided with a terrible shock.* 1, 3–5 *n.,* 2 *v.* —**shock′ing,** *adj.*

shock² (shok) a thick, bushy mass: *He has a shock of red hair.* *n.*

shod·dy (shod′ē) 1 of poor quality: *shoddy work.* 2 mean; dishonest or unjust: *shoddy treatment.* *adj.*

shoe (shū) 1 an outer covering for a person's foot, which can be worn outside and does not go up past the ankle. 2 anything shaped or used like a shoe. 3 a horseshoe; a U-shaped piece of iron to protect a horse's hoof. 4 put shoes on: *A blacksmith shoes horses. Her feet were shod with slippers.* 1–3 *n.,* 4 *v.,* **shod, shoe·ing.**
fill someone's shoes, take someone's place.
in someone's shoes, in someone else's situation or circumstances: *I wouldn't like to be in the prisoner's shoes.*

> ***Word Family*..........shoe**
>
> **shoebox:** a cardboard box with a lid, for a pair of shoes
> **shoehorn:** a little tool for helping you get tight shoes on
> **shoelace:** the string that you tie a shoe or boot with
> **shoemaker:** a person whose work is making shoes
> **shoestring: 1** a shoelace **2** a very small budget
> **shoe tree:** a stand to put a shoe on to keep its shape

shone (shon) a past tense and past participle of **shine:** *The sun shone all last week. It has not shone since.* *v.*

shoo (shū) 1 an exclamation used to scare away hens, birds, etc. 2 scare or drive away: *Shoo those flies away from the sugar.* 1 *interj.,* 2 *v.,* **shooed, shoo·ing.**

shook (shu̇k) the past tense of **shake:** *They shook hands.* *v.*

shoot (shūt) 1 send a bullet, arrow, or other object using a weapon: *to shoot a gun, to shoot a spitball through a straw, to shoot at a target.* 2 hit with a bullet, arrow, etc.: *He shot a rabbit.* 3 send or move with force or speed: *He shot the puck into the net. A car shot past. The flames went shooting upward.* 4 take a picture with a camera: *They're shooting a movie in Charlottetown.* 5 a session of taking pictures: *a photo shoot, a film shoot.* 6 a new plant, leaf, etc. growing out; a sprout: *See the new shoots on that bush.* 7 come up or grow; sprout: *Grass was shooting up through the melting snow.* 1–4, 7 *v.,* **shot, shoot·ing;** 5, 6 *n.*
shoot the rapids, go over rapids in a canoe, raft, etc.

shooting star (shū′ting stär′) a meteor as seen when it enters the earth's atmosphere.

shop (shop) 1 a small store, especially one that sells only one kind of product: *a gift shop, a coffee shop.* It is owned by a **shopkeeper.** 2 visit stores to look at or buy things: *We shopped all morning for new coats.* 3 a place where a certain kind of service is available to customers: *a barber shop, a beauty shop.* 4 a place where things are made or repaired: *He works in a carpenter's shop.* 1, 3, 4 *n.,* 2 *v.,* **shopped, shop·ping.**
set up shop, start a business.
talk shop, talk about work. This kind of talk is called **shoptalk.**

shop·lift (shop′lift) steal from a store while pretending to be a customer. *n.* —**shop′lift′er,** *n.*

shopping centre (shop′ing sen′tər) a large block of stores under one roof, with a large parking lot. **Mall** and **shopping mall** are other words for it.

shore¹ (shôr) 1 the land at the edge of a sea, lake, etc.: *They walked along the shore.* The line where the water ends is the **shoreline.** 2 a poetic word for "land" or "country": *to travel to foreign shores.* *n.*
off shore, in or on the water, not far from the shore. The adjective is **offshore.**

shore² (shôr)
shore up, prop up; support: *They used cement blocks to shore up the sagging porch.* *v.,* **shored, shor·ing.**

shorn (shôrn) a past participle of **shear:** *The sheep had just been shorn.* *v.*
shorn of, with something beautiful or impressive taken away: *Shorn of its furniture and carpeting, the room looked like a dingy empty box.*

a bat	e bed	i bid	o pot	u cup	th thin
ā cake	ē me	ī bite	ō go	ū rude	ᴛʜ then
ä bar	ə about	ər over	ô for	u̇ put	zh measure

short (shȯrt) **1** not long or tall; measuring little from end to end, from top to bottom, or from start to finish: *a short life, a short street, short hair, a short person.* **2 shorts,** *pl.* **a** pants that end above the knees. **b** boys' or men's underpants. **3** less than what is needed: *When she gave my change, it was a dollar short. Oil is in short supply right now.* **4** speaking rather rudely because of anger: *He was so short with me that I felt hurt.* **5** suddenly or sharply: *He stopped short.* **6** a film lasting only a few minutes, coming before or after a full-length movie or TV show. **7** short for **short circuit. 8** Often, **short out,** fail because of a **short circuit. 9** of a vowel, sounding like any of the ones in *hat, bed, dig, rob,* and *sun.* 1, 3, 4, 9 *adj.,* 5 *adv.,* 2, 6, 7 *n.,* 8 *v.* **—short′en,** *v.*
cut short, end something suddenly or before it is really finished.
fall short, **a** fail to reach a target. **b** be not enough.
for short, in order to make a name or word shorter: *Robert was called Rob for short.*
in short, briefly; in summary or in a few words.
in short order, quickly.
make short work of, deal with quickly.
run short, not have enough or not be enough: *Get more butter—we've run short. The milk has run short, too.*
short for, used as a shortened form of: *"Can Lit" is short for "Canadian Literature."*
short of, **a** less than: *Nothing short of your best work will do.* **b** having too little of: *I'm short of money just now.*

short·age (shȯr′tij) a lack; too small an amount: *There is a shortage of grain because of poor crops.* **Shortfall** has a similar meaning. *n.*

short·cake (shȯrt′ kāk′) a rich sponge cake, usually served with berries or other fruit. *n.*

short–change (shȯrt′chānj′) give too little to a certain person or thing: *If you spend too much time on extra-curricular activities, you might short-change your schoolwork.* *v.,* **short-changed, short-chang·ing.**

short circuit (shȯrt′ sər′kit) an electrical circuit that accidentally bypasses the part of the main circuit that contains the resistance. As a result, too much current flows through the wiring, which may blow a fuse or cause a fire.

short–cir·cuit (shȯrt′ sər′kit) **1** have or cause a short circuit. Shortened forms of this verb are **to short** and **to short out. 2** cause something to fail: *They have short-circuited our plan!* **3** skip the proper procedure or people: *Since she knew the store owner personally, she was able to short-circuit the usual job application procedure.* *v.*

short·com·ing (shȯrt′kum′ing) a fault or imperfection: *Rudeness is a serious shortcoming.* *n.*

short·cut (shȯrt′kut′) **1** a way that is quicker or not as long. **2** take a quicker or shorter way: *We can shortcut through the field.* 1 *n.,* 2 *v.,* **short·cut, short·cut·ting.**

short·en·ing (shȯrt′ ning) fat, especially fat from plants, used in baking to make pastry, cake, etc. flaky or crumbly. **Shortbread** is a kind of thick, crumbly cookie made with a lot of fat. *n.*

short·hand (shȯrt′hand′) a method of rapid writing which uses a combination of letters and symbols to stand for sounds or syllables. *n.*

short–lived (shȯrt′ livd′) not living or lasting very long. *adj.*

short·ly (shȯrt′lē) in a short time; soon: *I will be with you shortly.* *adv.*

short–sight·ed (shȯrt′ sī′tid) **1** not able to see far. **2** not thinking ahead enough: *a short-sighted plan.* *adj.*

short·stop (shȯrt′stop′) a baseball player stationed between second and third base. *n.*

short story (shȯrt′ stȯr′ē) a short piece of fiction that has a simple plot and only a few characters.

short–tem·pered (shȯrt′ tem′pərd) tending to get angry very quickly. *adj.*

short·wave (shȯrt′wāv′) a high-frequency radio wave used to broadcast over very long distances: *If we listen in on shortwave, we can hear European radio stations.* *n.*

shot (shot) **1** the act or noise of shooting: *She made a shot on goal. The hunter's shots echoed through the woods.* **2** the distance a weapon can shoot; the range: *We were within rifle shot of the fort.* **3** a person who shoots: *She is a good shot.* **4** *Informal.* an injection: *a shot of penicillin. We get flu shots every fall.* **5** a single picture taken with a camera: *Here's a shot of you riding the camel.* **6** a heavy metal ball thrown in an athletic contest called the **shot put. 7** tiny metal balls, or one big ball, used as ammunition for a gun or cannon. **8** the past tense and past participle of **shoot:** *She shot the puck into the net. I have never shot a bow and arrow.* **9** used up, worn out, ruined, or wasted: *These old shoes are completely shot. Now the whole morning is shot.* 1–7 *n., pl.* **shots** or, for def. 7, **shot;** 8 *v.,* 9 *adj.*
a long shot, a try or a guess that is not likely to succeed.
by a long shot, by a large amount; by far.
call the shots, be the boss.
pay the shot, pay the cost.
put the shot, heave the heavy metal ball as far as you can in the athletic event called the **shot-put.**

shot·gun (shot′gun′) a gun with a long, smooth barrel, used for hunting. It fires bits of metal. *n.*

should (shůd) an auxiliary verb used: **1** in talking about duty and what is right or wrong to do: *You should learn to swim. I really should do my homework first. People should not lie.* **2** in sentences where the main idea is how the speaker feels or thinks about something: *I don't see why you should think that. It's strange that they should be so late.* **3** in a formal way, to express possible future action: *If we should decide to go, we'll call you.* **4** to say that something is probably true: *He should be there by now.* *v.*

shoul·der (shōl′dər) **1** the place where a person's arm, an animal's front leg, or a bird's wing is attached to the body. **2** lift or carry something on your shoulder: *to shoulder a heavy sack.* **3** bear a responsibility, burden, etc.: *They shouldered the main part of the work.* **4** the edge of a road, often unpaved: *Don't drive on the shoulder of the road.* **5** push with your shoulders: *He shouldered his way through the crowd.* **6** something that sticks out like a shoulder: *the shoulder of a hill.* 1, 4, 6 *n.*, 2, 3, 5 *v.*
cry on someone's shoulder, tell someone your troubles.
give someone the cold shoulder, ignore someone or be unfriendly toward him or her.
put your shoulder to the wheel, make a great effort.
straight from the shoulder, in a direct, honest way.

shoulder blade (shōl′dər blād′) the flat triangular bone sticking out in your back behind either shoulder.

should·n't (shůd′ənt) should not.

shout (shout) **1** call or speak very loudly: *The lost child shouted, "Mom!" The crowd shouted angrily.* **2** a loud call or cry: *Shouts of joy rang through the halls.* 1 *v.*, 2 *n.*
shout down, drown out or vote against by shouting: *His idea was shouted down by the others.*

shove (shuv) **1** push hard or roughly: *They shoved the door open. The people shoved to get on the crowded bus.* **2** a hard or rough push: *She gave the boat a shove that sent it far out into the water.* 1 *v.*, **shoved, shov·ing;** 2 *n.*

shov·el (shuv′əl) **1** a tool with a wide crosswise blade and a long handle, used to lift and throw loose matter: *a snow shovel.* **2** lift and throw with a shovel: *The men shovelled the sand into a cart.* **3** make with a shovel: *to shovel a path through the snow.* **4** move something fast and in large amounts, as if with a shovel: *The hungry man shovelled food into his mouth.* 1 *n.*, 2–4 *v.*, **shov·elled** or **shov·eled, shov·el·ling** or **shov·el·ing.**

show (shō) **1** let someone see something: *The little girl showed us her bike. The dog showed its teeth. Show me where you live.* **2** be visible; be seen: *The hole in his sock shows above his shoe. Anger showed in his face.* **3** guide: *Show him out.* **4** do something in front of someone to make clear how it is done: *The swimming teacher showed the children how to do the jellyfish float.* **5** something put on for people to watch or look at, such as a play, movie, exhibit, TV program, etc.: *a puppet show, a magic show, a craft show, a game show.* **6** the act of showing: *We voted by a show of hands.* **7** a false pretence or something done just to impress others: *a show of bravery. He hid his treachery by a show of friendship.* 1–4 *v.*, **showed, shown** or **showed, show·ing;** 5–7 *n.*
for show, in order to attract attention or impress people: *Some houses are furnished more for show than for comfort.*
get the show on the road, *Informal.* get started.
good show! Well done!
run the show, be in charge.
show off, **a** to show proudly: *She showed off her new dress to her friends.* **b** do or say things in order to attract attention or impress people: *That boy is always showing off.* A person who does this is a **show-off.**
show up, **a** make visible: *The bright lights showed up cracks in the plaster.* **b** stand out: *He is very tall and shows up in any crowd.* **c** *Informal.* come; be present: *The mayor showed up at the first concert.* **d** be so good that it makes others look bad: *Her excellent playing showed us all up.*

show·case (shō′kās′) **1** a glass case used to display things in a store, museum, etc. **2** anything that displays something else: *Québec City is a showcase of Canadian history.* **3** display in an attractive or impressive way: *The concert showcased the talents of many students.* 1, 2 *n.*, 3 *v.*, **show·cased, show·cas·ing.**

show·down (shō′doun′) a situation that forces two enemies to face each other honestly and settle their quarrel one way or another. *n.*

show·er (shou′ər) **1** a light or short rainfall. **2** a bath where water sprays down on you from above: *He takes a shower every morning.* **3** take a bath like this. **4** anything like a fall of rain: *a shower of hail, a shower of tears, a shower of sparks.* **5** sprinkle or fall in a shower: *The apple tree showered its blossoms on the grass. The rain showered the earth.* **6** give someone a lot of something: *Her rich aunt showered her with gifts.* **7** a party where people give gifts to someone who is about to be married, have a baby, move away, etc. 1, 2, 4, 7 *n.*, 3, 5, 6 *v.*

a bat	e bed	i bid	o pot	u cup	th thin
ā cake	ē me	ī bite	ō go	ū rude	ᴛʜ then
ä bar	ə about	ər over	ȯ for	ů put	zh measure

show·piece (shō′pēs′) something shown off as an outstanding example of its kind: *The new concert hall is a showpiece of modern architecture.* *n.*

show·room (shō′rūm′) a big room where large items like cars, furniture, etc. are displayed for sale. *n.*

show·y (shō′ē) fancy, colourful, loud, etc.; attracting attention: *a showy flower. Canadians are patrotic, but not in a showy way.* *adj.,* **show·i·er, show·i·est.**

shrank (shrangk) the past tense of **shrink:** *That skirt shrank in the wash.* *v.*

shrap·nel (shrap′nəl) pieces of metal scattered by the explosion of the container holding them. Shrapnel is used as a weapon. *n.*

shred (shred) **1** a very small piece or narrow strip torn or cut off: *The wind tore the sail to shreds.* **2** the smallest bit: *There's not a shred of evidence that he took the money.* **3** tear or cut into small pieces: *to shred secret papers.* 1, 2 *n.,* 3 *v.,* **shred·ded** or **shred, shred·ding.** **—shred′der,** *n.*

Shrews are intensely active, and must eat three times their own mass every day.

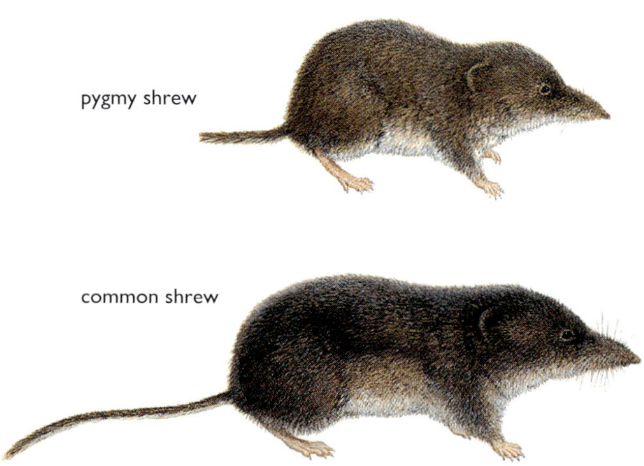

shrew (shrū) a small furry animal like a mouse, with a long snout and brownish fur. Shrews are fierce fighters and will attack animals much larger than themselves. *n.*

shrewd (shrūd) clever at making money or getting what you want, sometimes in a slightly dishonest way. *adj.* **—shrewd′ness,** *n.*

shriek (shrēk) **1** a loud, sharp, high-pitched sound: *the shriek of a whistle.* **2** make such a sound: *to shriek with terror.* 1 *n.,* 2 *v.*

shrill (shril) **1** sharp and high-pitched; piercing. **2** make a shrill sound. 1 *adj.,* 2 *v.* **—shril′ly,** *adv.*

shrimp (shrimp) a small shellfish with a long tail and a pair of antennae. The tails of some kinds of shrimp are used as food. *n., pl.* **shrimp** or **shrimps.**

shrine (shrīn) a place where holy things are kept; a saint's tomb, a box holding a holy object, or a room or building containing items used in worship. *n.*

shrink (shringk) **1** make or become smaller: *His wool sweater shrank in the wash. Shrink the picture so it fits on the page.* **2** draw back: *The dog shrank from the bear. That shy girl shrinks from meeting new people.* *v.,* **shrank, shrunk, shrink·ing.** **—shrink′age,** *n.*

shrink–wrap (shringk′ rap′) **1** a very thin, clear plastic wrapping that clings tightly to whatever it is covering. **2** wrap something in this material. Many things you buy in the store are shrink-wrapped. 1 *n.,* 2 *v.,* **shrink-wrapped, shrink-wrap·ping.**

shriv·el (shriv′əl) wither; dry up, shrink, and wrinkle: *The hot sunshine shrivelled the grass.* *v.,* **shriv·elled** or **shriv·eled, shriv·el·ling** or **shriv·el·ing.**

shroud (shroud) **1** a cloth that a dead person is wrapped in for burial. **2** something that covers or hides: *A shroud of mist hung over the city.* **3** cover or hide: *The earth is shrouded in darkness.* **4** one of the ropes running from a mast to the side of a ship. 1, 2, 4 *n.,* 3 *v.*

shrub (shrub) a bush; a small woody plant that has several branches starting at the bottom instead of a trunk: *A lilac bush is a shrub.* A number of shrubs together are called **shrubbery.** *n.*

shrug (shrug) **1** raise the shoulders to show that you don't know or don't care: *He merely shrugged and said nothing.* **2** a raising of the shoulders like this: *His only answer was a shrug.* 1 *v.,* **shrugged, shrug·ging;** 2 *n.* **shrug off,** treat something as unimportant: *She shrugged off their insults.*

shrunk (shrungk) the past participle of **shrink:** *His wool socks have shrunk.* **Shrunken** is an adjective. *v.*

shuck (shuk) **1** a husk or pod. **2** remove the husks or pods from: *to shuck corn.* 1 *n.,* 2 *v.*

shud·der (shud′ər) tremble or quiver: *He shudders at the sight of a snake* (*v.*). *A shudder of fear went through her body* (*n.*). *v. or n.*

shuf·fle (shuf′əl) **1** walk without lifting your feet: *We shuffled through the fallen leaves to hear them rustle.* **2** mix so as to change the order: *to shuffle cards.* **3** put on clumsily and hurriedly: *He shuffled on his clothes and ran out of the house.* **4** move this way and that: *to shuffle a stack of papers.* **5** the act of shuffling: *to walk with a shuffle. After a hasty shuffle of her papers, the speaker began to talk.* 1–4 *v.,* **shuf·fled, shuf·fling;** 5 *n.*

shun (shun) keep away from; avoid: *She was lazy and shunned work.* *v.,* **shunned, shun·ning.**

shunt (shunt) **1** move something aside or out of the way. **2** switch a train from one track to another. **3** a railway switch. **4** a tube inserted in a part of the body to drain away liquid: *After I got a shunt in my ear, my ear infections stopped.* *v.*

shush (shush) tell someone to be quiet: *She quickly shushed me before I could mention the surprise gift.* *v.*

shut (shut) **1** close something by putting a lid, door, etc. into place over an opening, or by bringing parts together: *He shut the door. Shut your eyes.* **2** become closed: *The drawer shut on her finger.* **3** keep from going out: *Shut the kitten in the basement.* *v.,* **shut, shut·ting.**
shut down, a close a factory or business, stop working, or stop machinery: *Shut down the photocopier. The office shuts down over holiday season.* An act of shutting down is a **shutdown. b** give a command to a computer to close its operating system before turning it off or rebooting.
shut off, a turn off; stop the flow or operation of: *Shut off the radio. Shut off the water before fixing the pipes.* **b** block the entrance to: *They've shut off the top floor.*
shut out, a keep from coming in: *The curtains shut out the light.* **b** defeat a team without allowing it to score. The noun is **shutout.**
shut up, a *Informal.* stop talking: *Nobody was listening to what I was saying, so I just shut up.* **b** close securely: *After Thanksgiving, we shut our cottage up for the winter.*

shut·ter (shut′ər) **1** a rigid cover for the outside of a window. It can be opened and closed or put on and off. **2** a sliding cover for the opening that lets light into a camera. When you take a picture, it opens and closes again very quickly. **3** cover with a shutter. 1, 2 *n.,* 3 *v.*

shut·tle (shut′əl) **1** a bus, train, airplane, etc. that runs back and forth regularly over a short distance. **2** move quickly to and fro. **3** a device that carries the thread from one side of the web to the other in weaving. 1, 3 *n.,* 2 *v.,* **shut·tled, shut·tling.**

shut·tle·cock (shut′əl kok′) the offical word for a **bird** in badminton. It is a cone made of feathers or light plastic, with a rounded rubber tip. *n.*

shy[1] (shī) **1** uncomfortable in groups or around unfamiliar people: *He is shy and dislikes parties.* **2** easily frightened away; timid: *A deer is a shy animal.* **3** step back or aside suddenly in fear: *The horse shied at the loud noise.* **4** less than; short: *This plank is 2 cm shy of what we need.* 1, 2, 4 *adj.,* **shy·er** or **shi·er, shy·est** or **shi·est;** 3 *v.,* **shied, shy·ing. —shy′ly,** *adv.* **—shy′ness,** *n.*
shy away from, avoid because of fear, uncertainty, or dislike: *This teacher shies away from using new methods.*

shy[2] (shī) throw with a sideways motion: *I shied a stone at the tree.* *v.,* **shied, shy·ing.**

SI *abbreviation for* **Système international d'unités** (International System of Units), the metric system adopted by Canada and most other nations as the official system of measurement.

sib·ling (sib′ling) a brother or sister. *n.*

sick (sik) **1** not well; having some disease or illness. **2** vomiting or about to vomit. **3** for a sick person: *Dad is on sick leave from work.* This sense is found in compounds like **sickroom, sickbed. 4** disgusting or horrible and showing a twisted sense of right and wrong: *sick crimes.* **5** stupid and not very funny: *a sick joke.* **6** suffering from sorrow or longing: *She is sick at heart.* *adj.* **—sick′en,** *v.* **—sick′en·ing,** *adj.* **—sick′ness,** *n.*
sick of, tired of; bored or fed up with: *We are sick of your complaints.*
sick to your stomach, feeling as if you have to throw up.

The sickle has been in use for thousands of years. This illustration is of a medieval harvest scene.

sick·le (sik′əl) a tool with a semi-circular blade on a short handle, used in some countries and in earlier times for cutting grass and so on. *n.*

sick·ly (sik′lē) **1** often sick; not strong and healthy. **2** causing or resulting from sickness: *a sickly climate. Her skin is a sickly yellow.* *adj.,* **sick·li·er, sick·li·est.**

a bat	e bed	i bid	o pot	u cup	th thin
ā cake	ē me	ī bite	ō go	ū rude	ᴛʜ then
à bar	ə about	ər over	ô for	ů put	zh measure

side (sīd) 1 a surface or line forming the outside of a thing: *the sides of a square, a side of a box.* 2 one of the surfaces of an object other than the front, back, top, or bottom: *There is a door at the side of the house.* 3 either of the two surfaces of paper, cloth, etc.: *Write only on one side of the paper.* 4 a particular part or area: *the side of the moon turned toward the earth, the east side of town.* 5 either the right or the left part of a person's or animal's body: *She was wounded in the side.* 6 a way of being or of looking at something: *a person's serious side, the bright side of a difficulty.* 7 any group fighting, playing, or arguing against another: *We chose sides for a game of softball. I'm on your side in this struggle.* 8 take a position in an argument: *The sisters always side with each other.* 9 a part of a family tree: *Ron is English on his mother's side.* 10 at or to one side: *a side door, a side view.* 11 not the main one but going along with it: *a side issue, a side trip, a side dish.* 1–7, 9 *n.,* 8 *v.* **sid·ed, sid·ing;** 10, 11 *adj.*
by someone's side, near someone.
on the side, along with the main dish of a meal: *A hamburger with fries on the side.*
side by side, beside one another.
take sides, support one person or group against another.

side·burns (sīd′bərnz′) hair growing down in front of the ears, especially when the chin is shaved. *pl.n.*

WORD HISTORY........sideburns

Sideburns are named for Ambrose *Burnside* (1864–1881), a U.S. general who shaved his face except in front of his ears. *Burnsides* got twisted around to become **sideburns**, because of their position on the side of the face.

side effect (sīd′ i fekt′) a result or effect of some action, medicine, etc. that goes along with the main result: *The pills stopped me sneezing but also had the side effect of making me sleepy.*

side·line (sīd′līn′) 1 in some sports, a line that marks the edge of the official playing area. 2 **sidelines,** *pl.* **a** the space just outside these lines: *We watched the game from the sidelines.* **b** a position away from the main action: *He didn't help with the clean-up but just hung around on the sidelines.* 3 a line of business that is not the main one: *The butcher sold cheese as a sideline.* *n.*

side·long (sīd′long′) to one side; toward the side: *a sidelong glance.* *adj.*

side·sad·dle (sīd′sad′əl) with both legs on the same side of the horse: *to ride sidesaddle.* *adv.*

side·step (sīd′step′) 1 step aside to avoid walking into something. 2 avoid or ignore: *to sidestep a responsibility.* *v.,* **side·stepped, side·step·ping.**

side·track (sīd′trak′) 1 cause to turn aside: *The teacher refused to be sidetracked by questions on other subjects.* 2 a topic, question, or activity that takes you away from what you are supposed to be doing. 1 *v.,* 2 *n.*

WORD HISTORY........sidetrack

The meaning of **sidetrack** comes from the world of trains. It refers to the short piece of extra railway track next to the main track, for trains that aren't being used.

side·walk (sīd′wok′) 1 a paved place to walk at the side of a street. 2 **moving sidewalk,** an indoor device like an escalator, except that it is level instead of going up or down: *A moving sidewalk led from the car rental area to the check-in counter at the airport.* *n.*

side·ways (sīd′wāz′) 1 to one side; toward one side: *to walk sideways (adv.), a sideways glance (adj.).* 2 with one side toward the front: *to stand sideways (adv.), in a sideways position (adj.).* *adv. or adj.*

si·dle (sī′dəl) move sideways, trying not to be noticed: *The little boy shyly sidled up to the visitor.* *v.,* **si·dled, si·dling.**

siege (sēj) the act of trying to capture a place by surrounding it and waiting for those inside to run out of food and surrender: *Troy was under siege for ten years.* For a picture of a **siege tower,** see the entry and caption at **castle** on page 118. *n.*
lay siege to, surround in this way: *The Greeks laid siege to Troy for ten years.*

si·es·ta (sē es′tə) a rest in the afternoon. *n.*

sieve (siv) a container with small holes that let tiny pieces and liquids pass through, but not the larger pieces: *Shaking flour through a sieve breaks up the lumps.* *n.*

sift (sift) 1 break up lumps or separate large pieces from small by shaking in a sieve: *Sift the gravel and put the larger stones in another pile.* 2 sprinkle or fall through a sieve, or as if through a sieve: *Sift sugar onto the top of the cake. The snow sifted softly down.* *v.*

sigh (sī) 1 let out a long, deep, loud breath because you are sad, tired, relieved, etc.: *Mae sighed but didn't quit until the work was done.* 2 the act or sound of sighing: *a sigh of relief.* 3 make a sound like a sigh: *The wind sighed in the treetops.* 1, 3 *v.,* 2 *n.*
sigh for, be longing for: *She often sighed for home.*

sight (sīt) 1 the ability to see: *Birds have better sight than dogs.* 2 the act or fact of seeing, or the thing that you see: *love at first sight. The sight of blood makes me faint.* 3 the distance someone can see: *Keep that car in sight. Do not swim out of sight of the lifeguard.* 4 something impressive, shocking, or unusual to see: *to go around and see the sights. She is a sight in that ugly dress.* 5 see; notice: *At last Columbus sighted land.* 6 look at a target and aim: *Gabriel sighted carefully on the balloon before throwing the dart.* 7 a way of looking at or thinking about something: *The puppy was precious in the little girl's sight.* 1–4, 7 *n.,* 5, 6 *v.*
at sight or **on sight,** as soon as you see it: *She reads music at sight.*
catch sight of, see: *I caught sight of him in the street.*
set your sights on, aim for; have as your goal.
sight unseen, without seeing it first: *He bought a used car sight unseen.*

> **CONFUSABLES .... sight**
>
> **sight** means "view": *A snowy day can be a beautiful sight.*
> **site** means "place": *The hospital will be built on this site.*

sight·ed (sīt′id) able to see. The opposite is **sightless.** *adj.*

sight·see·ing (sīt′sē′ing) the act of going around to see interesting places. *n.* —**sight′se′er,** *n.*

sign (sīn) 1 a board, large piece of paper, etc. with information or instructions on it: *The sign reads, "Keep off the grass."* 2 write your name on or in something: *to sign a cheque. The author signed a copy of her book for me.* 3 a clue that something exists or is going to happen: *There were no signs of life at the house. The robin is a sign of spring.* 4 a motion, act, mark, or object used to mean something: *a plus sign. A nod is a sign of agreement.* 5 use sign language; express in sign language: *She signed "I love you." I am learning to sign.* 1, 3, 4 *n.,* 2, 5 *v.*
sign off, in radio and TV, stop broadcasting.
sign on, accept a position by signing an agreement: *Four new people signed on with the company last year.*
sign out, sign your name to show you have borrowed something: *to sign out a book.*
sign up, sign your name to show that you want to take part or join: *Jen signed up for soccer tryouts.*

sig·nal (sig′nəl) 1 a sign given to warn someone or tell someone what to do: *A red light is a signal to stop.* 2 give a signal to: *He signalled the driver to go by waving at her.* 3 be a sign of: *A bell signals the end of the school day.* 4 a wave, current, impulse, etc. that carries sounds and images over a distance: *A TV set receives the signal and changes it back into sounds and images.* 1, 4 *n.,* 2, 3 *v.,* **sig·nalled** or **sig·naled, sig·nal·ling** or **sig·nal·ing.**

sig·na·ture (sig′nə chər) your own name written by you in your usual style. *n.*

sig·nif·i·cance (sig nif′ə kəns) 1 importance: *a matter of great significance.* 2 meaning: *She did not understand the significance of my wink.* *n.*

sig·nif·i·cant (sig nif′ə kənt) 1 important: *July 1, 1867, is a significant date for Canadians.* 2 full of hidden or special meaning: *A significant nod from his friend warned him to stop talking.* *adj.*

sig·ni·fy (sig′nə fī′) 1 mean: *A check mark signifies a right answer.* 2 express, especially in actions: *He signified his consent with a nod.* *v.,* **sig·ni·fied, sig·ni·fy·ing.**

Sign language

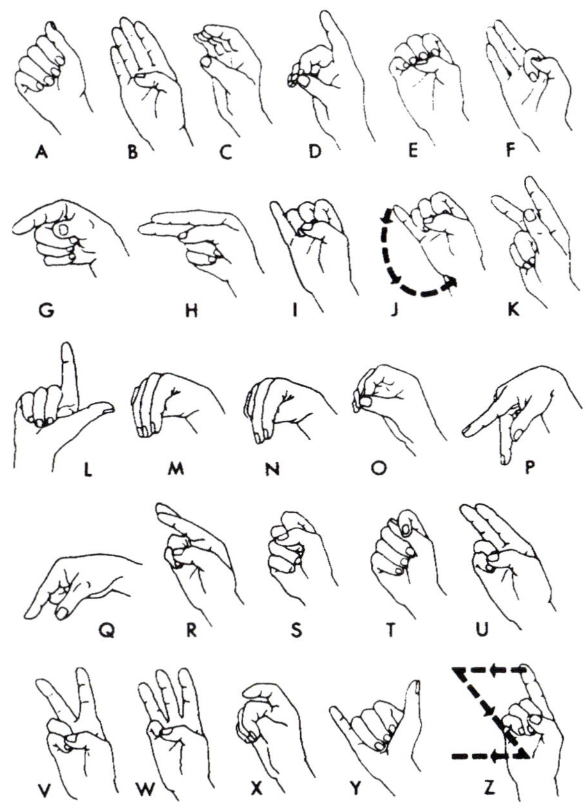

sign language (sīn′ lang′gwij) a language used by people who cannot hear, made up of hand movements instead of spoken words. **American Sign Language,** or **Ameslan** (am′ə slan′) for short, is very widely used.

a bat	e bed	i bid	o pot	u cup	th thin
ā cake	ē me	ī bite	ō go	ū rude	ᴛʜ then
ä bar	ə about	ər over	ô for	u̇ put	zh measure

sign·post (sīn′pōst′) a post with signs, notices, or directions on it. *n.*

Sikh (sēk) 1 a follower of a religion that began in India in the 1500s. It is based on the Guru Granth Sahib, a holy book containing the writings of ten great gurus or prophets. Sikhs believe in one God. 2 having to do with the Sikhs or their religion. 1 *n.,* 2 *adj.* —**Sikh′ism,** *n.*

Sik·sik·a (sik′si kə) 1 a First Nations people living in Alberta. 2 their language. 3 having to do with people or their language. 1, 2 *n.,* 3 *adj.*

si·lence (sī′ləns) 1 complete quietness; stillness: *The teacher asked for silence.* 2 make silent: *A look from Mom silenced him.* 1 *n.,* 2 *v.,* **si·lenced, si·lenc·ing.**
in silence, without speaking: *We ate our meal in silence.*

si·lent (sī′lənt) 1 quiet; still; noiseless: *a silent house.* 2 not speaking; saying little or nothing: *The stranger was silent about his early life.* 3 not spoken; not said out loud: *a silent prayer. The "l" in "folk" is a silent letter.* *adj.*

sil·hou·ette (sil′ū et′) 1 a drawing or portrait done in outline and filled in with some single colour. 2 any dark image outlined against a lighter background. 3 show in outline: *The mountain was silhouetted against the sky.* 1, 2 *n.,* 3 *v.,* **sil·hou·et·ted, sil·hou·et·ting.**

sil·i·con (sil′ə kon *or* sil′ə kən) a chemical element that is very common in the earth's crust. It is found in sand, rock, and clay. *n.*

Silk is the strongest of all natural fibres — a thread of silk can be stronger than a thread of steel. It is made from the cocoon of a moth called *Bombyx mori*. The caterpillars (silkworms) of this moth eat the leaves of the mulberry tree, until they are ready to spin their cocoons of silk.

silk (silk) 1 a fine, soft, strong fibre spun by a caterpillar called a **silkworm.** 2 the cloth made from this fibre, or similar cloth made artificially. 3 anything like silk. The yellow strands or fibres in an ear of corn are called **corn silk.** *n.* —**silk′y,** *adj.*

silk·en (sil′kən) made of silk or like silk: *silken robes, silken hair.* This is a poetic word. *adj.*

sill (sil) a flat piece of wood or stone across the bottom of a door, window, or house frame. *n.*

sil·ly (sil′ē) nonsensical; foolish; ridiculous. *adj.,* **sil·li·er, sil·li·est.** —**sil′li·ness,** *n.*

si·lo (sī′lō) a tall, round, towerlike building on a farm for keeping grain or animal feed in. The grain or feed is called **silage** (sī′lij). *n., pl.* **si·los.**

silt (silt) 1 very fine sand carried by moving water and then left on the river bottom when the current slows down: *The harbour is being choked up with silt.* 2 to fill or choke up with silt. 1 *n.,* 2 *v.*

sil·ver (sil′vər) 1 a shining, greyish white, precious metal that is a chemical element. It is used in jewellery, photography, and fancy cutlery and serving dishes. It used to be used in coins. 2 something silver, especially coins with a silvery colour, or tableware made of silver: *a handful of silver. We use the silver at special meals.* Things made of silver are called **silverware.** 3 having to do with a 25th anniversary: *a silver wedding.* 4 coat with silver or something like silver: *to silver the back of a mirror. Ice has silvered the trees.* 1, 2 *n.,* 3 *adj.,* 4 *v.* —**sil′ver·y,** *adj.*
silver lining, the brighter side of a bad situation.
the silver screen, movies in general.

sim·i·lar (sim′ə lər) 1 the same in many ways; like: *A creek and a brook are similar. This sweater is similar to the one I bought.* 2 in geometry, having the same shape but not necessarily the same size: *similar triangles.* *adj.* —**sim′i·lar′i·ty** (sim′ə ler′ə tē), *n.*

sim·i·le (sim′ə lē) a figure of speech that describes something by comparing it to another thing. *Examples: a face like marble. She was as brave as a lion.* *n.* ▶ See the *Grammar and Usage Mini-Guide.*

USING WORDS . . . simile/metaphor

Similes and **metaphors** are two ways to make comparisons.

A **simile** compares two things, using *like* or *as*: *Her voice was warm and brilliant, like sunlight.*
A **metaphor** talks about one thing as if it were another: *Her voice bathed the room in sunlight.*

sim·mer (sim′ər) 1 keep or stay just at the boiling point. 2 a cooking temperature just around the boiling point: *Keep the soup at a simmer.* 3 be just on the point

of bursting out: *He simmered with anger.* 1, 3 *v.,* 2 *n.*
simmer down, cool off or calm down: *His anger simmered down after a while.*

sim•ple (sim′pəl) **1** easy to do or understand: *a simple problem. This book is in simple language.* **2** not divided into parts. An oak leaf is a **simple leaf,** a cloverleaf is not. A sentence with only one subject and predicate is a **simple sentence.** **3** with nothing added: *the simple truth.* **4** not fancy or rich; plain: *He eats simple food and wears simple clothing.* **5** natural and sincere: *simple faith. She has a pleasant, simple manner.* **6** stupid; slow in understanding. *adj.* **sim•pler, sim•plest.** —**sim•plic′i•ty** (sim plis′ə tē), *n.* —**sim′pli•fy,** *v.*

sim•ple•ton (sim′pəl tən) fool. *n.*

sim•ply (sim′plē) **1** in a simple manner: *to dress simply. She explained the rules simply and clearly.* **2** merely; just: *The baby did not simply cry; he yelled.* **3** absolutely: *simply perfect.* *adv.*

sim•u•late (sim′yə lāt′) **1** pretend: *Some animals simulate death when attacked.* **2** imitate; make or do something artificial that copies the real thing: *simulated leather. This video game simulates the flight of an airplane.* *v.,* **sim•u•lat•ed, sim•u•lat•ing.** —**sim′u•la′tion,** *n.*

sim•ul•ta•ne•ous (sī′məl tā′nē əs *or* sim′əl tā′nē əs) done or happening at the same time. *adj.* —**si′mul•ta′ne•ous•ly,** *adv.*

sin (sin) **1** disobey God or a moral law. **2** an immoral act: *It's a sin to waste so much food.* **3** the habit of sinning: *a life of sin.* 1 *v.,* **sinned, sin•ning;** 2, 3 *n.,* —**sin′ful,** *adj.* —**sin′ner,** *n.* —**sin′less,** *adj.*

since (sins) **1** from a past time till now: *We've been up since 5:30 (prep.). She has been home only once since she went to St. John's (conj.). He caught a cold on Saturday and has been in bed ever since (adv.).* **2** at some later time between then and now: *He at first refused the offer, but has since accepted.* **3** because; in view of the fact that: *Since you're tired, you should rest.* 1 *prep.,* 1, 3 *conj.,* 1, 2 *adv.*

sin•cere (sin sēr′) free from pretence; genuine; real; honest: *a sincere apology.* *adj.,* **sin•cer•er, sin•cer•est.** —**sin•cere′ly,** *adv.* —**sin•cer′i•ty** (sin ser′ə tē), *n.*

sin•ew (sin′yū) a tough band or cord that joins muscle to bone; a tendon: *You can see the sinews in this cooked chicken leg.* *n.* —**sin′ew•y,** *adj.*

sing (sing) **1** make music with your voice: *He sings in the shower. She sang the song beautifully.* **2** make pleasant, musical sounds: *Birds sing.* *v.,* **sang, sung, sing•ing.** —**sing′er,** *n.*
sing out, call loudly; shout.

singe (sinj) burn a little, especially hair or cloth. *v.,* **singed, singe•ing.**

sin•gle (sing′gəl) **1** only one: *The spider hung by a single thread.* **2** for or involving only one; individual: *The sisters share one room with two single beds in it.* **Single combat** is a fight with only one person on each side. **3** not married: *He remained single all his life.* **4** pick out from others: *I managed to single out Mom in her old grade three class photo.* **5** draw attention to, especially by choosing for some special purpose: *The teacher knew he didn't like to be singled out, so she thanked him privately.* **6** a single thing or person, such as a one-base hit in baseball, or an unmarried person. 1–3 *adj.,* 4, 5 *v.,* **sin•gled, sin•gling;** 6 *n.* —**sin′gly,** *adv.*

single file (sing′gəl fīl′) a line of persons or things arranged one behind another: *We walked in single file along the narrow path.*

sin•gle–hand•ed (sing′gəl han′did) without help from others; working alone: *a single-handed effort.* *adj.* —**sin′gle-hand′ed•ly,** *adv.*

sin•gle–mind•ed (sing′gəl mīn′did) with one clear purpose that you work very hard to achieve: *We were single-minded about trying to win the trophy.* *adj.*

sing•song (sing′song′) **1** a way of speaking so that your voice rises and falls in a steady, boring rhythm: *Henry gave his talk in a tiresome singsong.* **2** rising and falling in this way: *a singsong voice.* 1 *n.,* 2 *adj.*

sin•gu•lar (sing′gyə lər) **1** extraordinary; unique: *Lake Louise is a sight of singular beauty.* **2** strange; unusual; odd: *The detectives were puzzled by the singular nature of the crime.* **3** referring to one: *"Car" is singular; "cars" is plural.* **4** in grammar, the form of a word used to show that one is meant: *"Ox" is the singular of "oxen."* 1–3 *adj.,* 4 *n.* —**sin′gu•lar•ly,** *adv.*

Grammar Check . . . . . . singular

Some words look plural, but are really **singular**. Here are some examples: *athletics, news, measles, mathematics,* and *mumps.*

sin•is•ter (sin′i stər) evil; threatening: *a sinister plan, a sinister look.* *adj.*

a bat	e bed	i bid	o pot	u cup	th thin
ā cake	ē me	ī bite	ō go	ū rude	ᴛʜ then
ä bar	ə about	ər over	ò for	ù put	zh measure

sink (singk) 1 go or cause to go under the surface: *The swimmer is sinking. The submarine sank two ships.* 2 go or cause to go down: *The sun is sinking in the west. She sank her voice to a whisper.* 3 go or cause to go deep into something: *to sink your teeth into a juicy apple. Let the lessons sink into your mind.* 4 a basin fixed in a certain place, with a pipe to drain it: *The dishes are in the kitchen sink.* 5 make by digging or drilling: *to sink a well.* 1–3, 5 *v.,* **sank, sunk, sink·ing;** 4 *n.*

sink·er (sing′kər) a lead weight for sinking a line or net for fishing. *n.*

si·nus (sī′nəs) an empty or hollow place in the body, especially one of the hollows in the bones of the skull that connect with the nose. The condition of inflamed sinuses is called **sinusitis** and can be very painful. *n.*

Sioux (sü) another name for the **Dakota** First Nations people. *n. or adj.*

sip (sip) 1 drink little by little: *I sipped my tea.* 2 a very small drink: *Have a sip.* 1 *v.,* **sipped, sip·ping;** 2 *n.*

This straw is acting as a siphon. If the end of the straw dips below the level of juice in the carton, the juice will flow out of the straw.

si·phon (sī′fən) 1 a bent tube for drawing liquid up over the edge of one container and down to a lower level by air pressure. 2 draw through a siphon: *He siphoned water from the rain barrel onto the garden.* 1 *n.,* 2 *v.*

sir (sər) 1 a respectful or formal title used in speaking to a man: *Excuse me, sir.* 2 **Sir,** the title of a knight: *Sir Walter Scott.* *n.*

sire (sīr) 1 in earlier times, a title of respect for a king or noble: *"I am killed, Sire!" said the messenger to Napoleon.* 2 the father of an animal: *The sire of Danger, a great racehorse, was Lightning.* 3 be the father of: *Pongo the Dalmatian sired 15 puppies.* 1, 2 *n.,* 3 *v.,* **sired, sir·ing.**

si·ren (sī′rən) a device that makes a loud wailing sound as a warning or signal: *We heard the sirens of the fire engines.* *n.*

si·roc·co (sə rok′ō) a hot, dry wind from North Africa that becomes very humid as it crosses the Mediterranean Sea. *n.*

sis·ter (sis′tər) 1 a daughter of the same parents: *I have one sister and two brothers.* 2 a woman or girl that has a close relationship or something in common with another person. 3 a nun. *n.* **—sis′ter·ly,** *adj.*

sis·ter·hood (sis′tər hu̇d′) 1 the closeness between sisters. 2 a group of women linked by their common aim, belief, or work. *n.*

sis·ter–in–law (sis′tər in lo′) 1 the sister of a person's husband or wife. 2 the wife of a person's brother. *n., pl.* **sis·ters-in-law.**

sit (sit) 1 rest on the lower part of your body, with the weight off your feet: *She sat in a chair.* 2 seat; cause to sit: *The woman sat the little boy down at the table.* 3 have a place or position: *The clock has sat on that shelf for years. He sits on several committees.* 4 perch: *The birds were sitting on the fence rail.* 5 watch children when parents are away: *She used to sit for the woman next door.* The more usual word is **babysit.** 6 hold a session: *Parliament sits next month.* *v.,* **sat, sit·ting.** **—sit′ter,** *n.*
sit down, take a seat; put yourself in a sitting position.
sit in, attend a class, meeting, etc. just to watch or listen, as a visitor: *Our class got to sit in on a Parliamentary debate.*
sit out, **a** stay out of a dance, game, etc. instead of taking part. **b** stay through; wait through: *to sit out a storm. They sat out the performance although the singing was poor.*
sit up, raise your body to a sitting position or keep yourself in this position.

si·tar (si tär′) a guitarlike musical instrument from India that has several strings, a rounded body, and a very long neck. It is played by plucking, not strumming. *n.*

WORD HISTORY........ sitar

Sitar literally means "three-stringed" in Hindi, from Persian *si,* meaning "three," and *tar,* meaning "string."

If you go back far enough, it is related to our word *guitar,* from Greek.

sit·com (sit′kom′) *Informal.* short for **situation comedy,** a TV comedy series with a separate story each time but always featuring the same characters. *n.*

site (sīt) the position or place of anything: *a battle site. The site for the new school has not yet been chosen.* *n.*

sit·ting (sit′ing) 1 one meeting or session of a court, legislature, etc. 2 a time spent in an activity that you would usually sit down for: *He read it all at one sitting. It took three sittings to finish our game of Monopoly.* *n.*

sitting room (sit′ing rūm′) another word for a living room; a room to sit and talk, relax, read, and so on.

sit·u·ate (sich′ū āt′) put in a certain place; locate: *They decided to situate the new city hall nearer to the centre of town.* *v.,* **sit·u·at·ed, sit·u·at·ing.**
be situated, be found or placed; lie, stand, or sit in a certain place: *Iqaluit is situated on Frobisher Bay.*

sit·u·a·tion (sich′ū ā′shən) a particular set of circumstances; a case or condition; state of affairs: *What would you do in the same situation? It is a scary situation to be alone and without money in a strange city.* *n.*

sit–up (sit′up′) an exercise you do by raising your body from a lying to a sitting position without using your hands to help. *n.*

six (siks) one more than five; 6: *She bought six apples (adj.).* *n. or adj.* **—sixth,** *adj. or n.*
at sixes and sevens, in confusion or disagreement.

six·teen (sik′stēn′) six more than ten; 16. *n. or adj.* **—six′teenth′,** *adj. or n.*

six·ty (sik′stē) six times ten; 60. *n., pl.* **six·ties;** *or adj.* **—six′ti·eth,** *adj. or n.*

siz·a·ble (sī′zə bəl) fairly big: *a sizable piece of property.* **Sizeable** is another spelling. *adj.*

size (sīz) 1 how big a person or thing is: *The two boys are of the same size. She was discouraged by the size of the problem.* 2 one of a set of categories based on how big or small a thing is: *a king-size bed. Drinks come in three sizes here: small, medium, and large.* 3 group according to size: *Size these nails.* 1, 2 *n.,* 3 *v.,* **sized, siz·ing.**
size up, judge; decide what a person or thing is like by looking and listening: *She sized him up pretty quickly.*

WORD HISTORY........ size

Size is actually related to an old word *assize*, which was a sort of travelling court that went from town to town settling cases. What does this have to do with bigness or smallness? Well, this court set the standards for measuring.

siz·zle (siz′əl) 1 make a hissing sound like fat that is frying or burning or liquid that hits a very hot surface. 2 a hissing sound. 1 *v.,* **siz·zled, siz·zling;** 2 *n.*

Inline skates and roller skates are both designed to be used on pavement. An inline skate has four wheels in a single row, while roller skate wheels are in two rows.

skate¹ (skāt) 1 a boot with a metal blade attached to the sole, designed for gliding over ice. It is also called an **ice skate.** 2 a **roller skate,** a boot with wheels attached to the sole, designed for rolling along on pavement.
3 glide or roll along on skates. 1, 2 *n.,* 3 *v.,* **skat·ed, skat·ing.** **—skat′er,** *n.*

skate² (skāt) a saltwater fish resembling a ray. *n.*

skate·board (skāt′bȯrd′) 1 a small, narrow board of wood or plastic, usually about 45–50 cm long, with rounded, slightly upturned ends and small wheels on the bottom. You stand on it and roll along streets, sidewalks, etc. 2 roll along on a skateboard. 1 *n.,* 2 *v.* **—skate′board′ing,** *n.* **—skate′board′er,** *n.*

skein (skān) a small bundle of yarn or thread. *n.*

skel·e·ton (skel′ə tən) 1 the bones of a body, fitted together in their natural places. 2 anything thought of as being like this, such as the framework of a building or the outline of a report; a frame: *the steel skeleton of a building.* *n.* **—skel′e·tal,** *adj.*

skep·ti·cal or **scep·ti·cal** (skep′tə kəl) tending to question or doubt things; doubtful: *Guido is skeptical about life on other planets.* A person who doubts things is a **skeptic** or **sceptic.** *adj.* **—skep′ti·cism′** or **scep′ti·cism′** (skep′tə siz′əm), *n.*

sketch (skech) 1 a rough, quick drawing. 2 an outline or short description: *Write a character sketch of Jacob Two-Two.* 3 make a sketch of; draw roughly or describe briefly. A **sketchbook** is a book with blank pages to draw in. 4 a short story or play. 1, 2, 4 *n.,* 3 *v.*

sketch·y (skech′ē) not giving enough detail; incomplete. *adj.,* **sketch·i·er, sketch·i·est.** **—sketch′i·ly,** *adv.* **—sketch′i·ness,** *n.*

a bat	e bed	i bid	o pot	u cup	th thin
ā cake	ē me	ī bite	ō go	ū rude	ŧʜ then
ä bar	ə about	ər over	ȯ for	u̇ put	zh measure

Skin

Skin has three layers:

- **the epidermis, which is contantly being rubbed away and replaced from beneath**
- **the dermis, which contains blood vessels and nerve endings**
- **subcutaneous tissue, which contains blood vessels and fat**

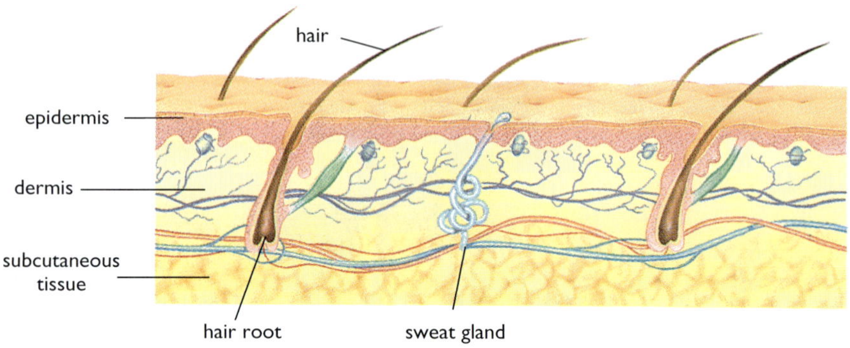

Fingerprints are unique. No two people have the same pattern of loops on their skin.

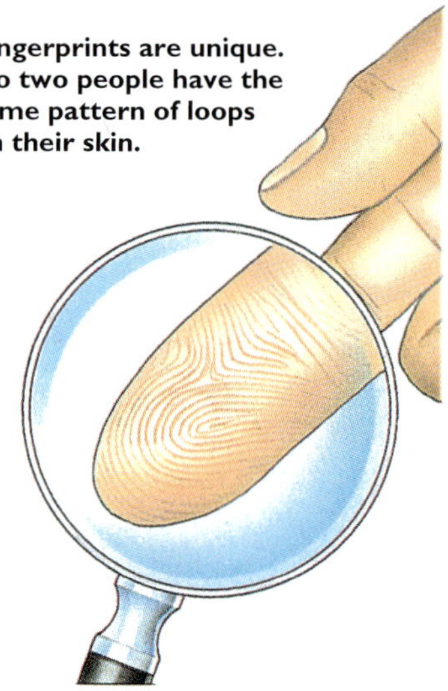

skew (skyū) slant or twist something, or change it so that it gives a false impression: *The pictures were skewed on the wall. They skewed the figures in the report to hide the fact that the company was losing money.* *v.*

skew·er (skyū′ər) **1** a long pin of wood or metal for holding a large piece of meat together while roasting, or for cooking small chunks of meat and vegetables on. **2** fasten or pierce with a skewer: *The butcher skewered the roast of beef.* 1 *n.,* 2 *v.*

ski (skē) **1** one of a pair of long, narrow pieces of wood, plastic, or metal with upturned ends, for gliding over the snow. You fasten them to your boots with special straps and use a light metal **ski pole** in each hand to balance and push yourself along. **2** glide over snow on skis. 1 *n., pl.* **skis;** 2 *v.,* **skied, ski·ing.** **—ski′er,** *n.*

skid (skid) **1** slip or slide without control: *The car skidded on the slippery road.* **2** a slipping or sliding movement like this: *The car went into a skid on the icy road.* **3** one of a pair of thick boards put under something heavy to make it easier to drag, like a sort of rough sled. **4** a flat wooden frame for piling things on to be lifted and moved by machine. 1 *v.,* **skid·ded, skid·ding;** 2–4 *n.*

skies (skīz) plural of **sky.** *n.*

skiff (skif) a small, light boat moved by oars or a single sail. *n.*

skill (skil) **1** expert ability gained by practice or knowledge: *It takes skill to tune a piano. Her skill at teaching is amazing.* **2** any activity that can be learned, such as tying shoes, catching a ball, etc. *n.* **—skil′ful** or **skill′ful,** *adj.* **—skilled,** *adj.*

skil·let (skil′it) a shallow frying pan: *He made the pancakes in a skillet.* *n.*

skim (skim) **1** take a thin layer off the top of something: *to skim milk to get cream, to skim the fat from cold soup.* **Skim milk** is milk with the cream removed. **2** move lightly over, barely touching the surface: *The pebble I threw skimmed the little waves. The skaters were skimming over the ice.* **3** read quickly and not very carefully, skipping parts here and there: *It took me an hour to skim the book.* *v.,* **skimmed, skim·ming.**

WORD HISTORY........ skim

Skim comes from the old French *escume*, meaning "scum." That is of course where we get our word scum. Scum is the stuff you skim off, so it's no surprise these two words are so closely related.

skimp (skimp) **1** save money by giving up things: *She had to skimp to send her son to university.* **2** give or use too little of: *Don't skimp the butter in this cake.* *v.*

skimp·y (skim′pē) not enough or barely enough: *a skimpy meal.* *adj.,* **skimp·i·er, skimp·i·est.** **—skimp′i·ly,** *adv.* **—skimp′i·ness,** *n.*

skin (skin) **1** the outermost layer of tissue on the body of a human or animal. **2** this part taken off a dead animal and specially treated to be used for some purpose. This sense often appears in compounds: *calfskin gloves.* **3** any thin outer covering, such as the peel of a fruit, a sausage casing, or a layer of solid matter that forms on a liquid. **4** take the skin off: *to skin a deer. He skinned his knees when he fell.* 1–3 *n.,* 4 *v.,* **skinned, skin·ning.** **by the skin of your teeth,** very narrowly; barely.

skin diving (skin′ dī′ving) swimming under water, sometimes very deep and for long periods of time, using goggles, rubber flippers, a portable breathing device, and sometimes a skin-tight rubber suit. **—skin′ div′er.**

skin·flint (skin′flint′) a very stingy person. *n.*

skin·ny (skin′ē) very thin: *a skinny child, a skinny book.* *adj.,* **skin·ni·er, skin·ni·est.**

skip (skip) **1** pass over without doing; leave out: *You may skip page 45. She skipped a grade in school.* **2** stay away from: *to skip school.* **3** *Informal.* leave in a hurry: *He skipped town to avoid meeting his enemies.* **4** leap over a turning rope again and again as a game or exercise: *We skipped all recess long.* The rope is called a **skipping rope.** **5** move along by stepping and hopping first on one foot, then on the other. **6** leap lightly and playfully: *Lambs skip in the fields.* **7** a skipping movement: *The child gave a skip of joy.* **8** send bouncing along the surface of water: *to skip stones.* 1–6, 8 *v.,* **skipped, skip·ping;** 7 *n.*

skip·per (skip′ər) the captain of a boat or ship. *n.*

skir·mish (skər′mish) **1** a small fight or battle. **2** take part in a small fight or battle. 1 *n.,* 2 *v.*

skirt (skərt) **1** a piece of women's or girls' clothing that hangs from the waist. **2** the part of a dress that hangs from the waist. **3** go around; go along the edge of: *We skirted the swamp.* 1, 2 *n.,* 3 *v.*

skit (skit) a short, usually funny play: *Our class put on a skit for the April Fool's Day assembly.* *n.*

skit·tish (skit′ish) easily excited or frightened: *The pony was skittish the first time Norah rode it.* *adj.*

skulk (skulk) move or hang around in a sneaky way, trying not to be seen: *The lion was skulking in the long grass near the zebras.* *v.*

The human skull has 22 bones in it. Eight of these bones form the cranium which protects the brain. The other 14 bones form the face and jaw. Only the jaw bone moves.

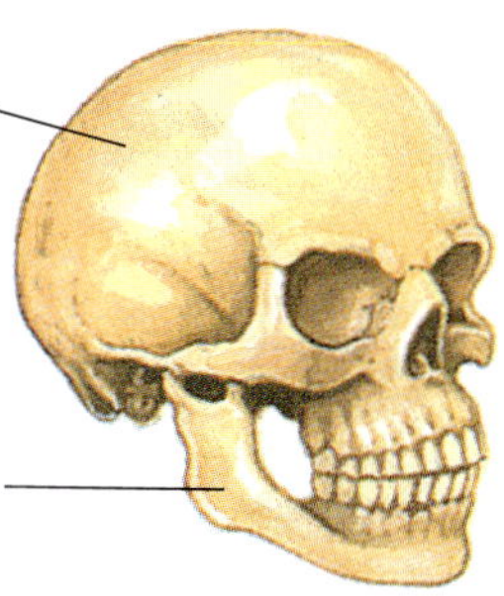

skull (skul) the bones of your head enclosing and protecting your brain and supporting your face. *n.*

skunk (skungk) a bushy-tailed animal of North America, about the size of a cat and black with white stripes along the back. When frightened, skunks spray a very strong, bad-smelling liquid at their attackers. *n.*

sky (skī) **1** the space high above the earth, looking like a great arch or dome covering the world: *clouds in the sky, a starry sky.* **2** **skies,** *pl.,* weather: *clear skies, cloudy skies.* *n., pl.* **skies.**
out of a clear sky, suddenly; unexpectedly.
praise to the skies, praise very highly.

Word Family.......... **sky**

skydiving: the sport of jumping out of a plane with a parachute that you open, halfway down
skylight: a window in a roof or ceiling
skyline: the outline of a city against the sky.
skyrocket: **1** a firework that shoots up high and then bursts into sparks **2** rise quickly, suddenly, and high
skyscraper: a very tall building
skywriting: writing in the air with smoke from a plane

slab (slab) a wide, flat, thick piece: *a slab of cheese. This walkway is made of slabs of stone.* *n.*

slack (slak) **1** not tight or firm; loose: *The rope hung slack.* **2** the part that hangs loose: *He pulled in the slack of the rope.* **3** careless: *a slack worker.* **4** slow: *The horse was moving at a slack pace. Business is slack at this season.* 1, 3, 4 *adj.,* 2 *n.* **—slack′en,** *v.*
slack off, take it easy instead of working hard.

slag (slag) the rough, hard waste left after metal is separated from ore by melting it. *n.*

slain (slān) the past participle of **slay:** *The sheep were slain by the wolves.* *v.*

slake (slāk) satisfy thirst or some other strong desire: *We slaked our thirst at the spring.* *v.,* **slaked, slak·ing.**

sla·lom (slä′ləm) **1** in skiing, a zigzag race downhill between a series of posts. **2** follow or ski on such a course. 1 *n.,* 2 *v.*

slam (slam) **1** shut hard with a bang: *He slammed the window down. The door slammed.* **2** throw, push, or hit with force: *She slammed the video down on her desk. The car slammed into a truck.* **3** *Slang.* criticize very harshly: *Critics slammed the new movie.* **4** the act or sound of slamming: *The book fell with a slam. Ignore their slams; your story's great.* 1–3 *v.,* **slammed, slam·ming;** 4 *n.*

a bat	e bed	i bid	o pot	u cup	th thin
ā cake	ē me	ī bite	ō go	ū rude	ᴛʜ then
ä bar	ə about	ər over	ô for	ů put	zh measure

slan·der (slan′dər) **1** say something false about someone in order to harm his or her reputation. **2** the action of slandering, or a statement that slanders. 1 *v.*, 2 *n.* **—slan′der·ous,** *adj.* **—slan′der·er,** *n.*

USING WORDS .... slander

In law, a person can be accused of slander by *saying* something false in order to harm someone's reputation. If a person *writes* such a statement, then that person will be accused of **libel.**

slang (slang) language not considered acceptable for use in formal speech and writing. Slang is made up mostly of new expressions or meanings that are popular for only a short time. Some words considered slang are entered in this dictionary and labelled *Slang.* *n.* **—slang′y,** *adj.*

USING WORDS .... slang words

Slang words and expressions can spice up a dialogue or a piece of informal writing by making it funny or realistic. However, not everyone understands slang (especially new slang) and it can quickly get outdated. Use it sparingly. Avoid it completely in formal writing.

slant (slant) **1** slope: *My handwriting slants to the right (v.). That roof has a very steep slant (n.).* **2** bias: *The report was heavily slanted against teenagers (v.). Those textbooks seem to have an American slant (n.).* *v. or n.*

slap (slap) **1** hit with your open hand or with something flat, making a sharp sound: *He slapped me on the back in a friendly way.* **2** put or throw with force and a sharp sound: *She slapped the book down on the table.* **3** the action or sound of slapping: *The slap of waves against the boat.* 1, 2 *v.*, **slapped, slap·ping;** 3 *n.*

slap·dash (slap′dash′) hasty and careless: *slapdash work.* *adj.*

🍁 **slap·shot** (slap′shot′) in hockey, a fast shot made with a powerful swinging stroke. *n.*

slap·stick (slap′stik′) comedy that makes you laugh mainly by using very obvious, ridiculous jokes and fast, rough action, such as people bumping into or falling over each other. 1 *n.*, 2 *adj.*

slash (slash) **1** a sweeping, powerful stroke: *the slash of a sword, the slash of rain.* **2** a long cut made by this kind of stroke; a gash. **3** make a slash in or at: *He slashed the bark of the tree with his knife. The rain slashed against the windows.* **4** reduce a great deal: *to slash prices, to slash someone's salary.* 1, 2 *n.*, 3, 4 *v.*

slat (slat) a thin, narrow piece of wood or metal. *n.*

slate (slāt) **1** a bluish grey sedimentary rock that splits easily into thin, smooth layers: *Slate was used to cover roofs in earlier times.* **2** a thin piece of this rock, used as a small chalkboard: *Children used to write on slates in school, but now they use paper.* **3** a list or schedule. **4** to schedule: *The new arena is slated to open in January.* 1–3 *n.*, 4 *v.*, **slat·ed, slat·ing.**
a clean slate, a record not spoiled by mistakes or faults: *to start again with a clean slate.*

slath·er (slaтн′ər) generously spread a thick layer of something soft: *to slather butter on bread.* *v.*

slaugh·ter (slot′ər) **1** kill an animal raised for food; butcher: *Millions of cattle are slaughtered every year.* The building where this happens is a **slaughterhouse.** **2** kill cruelly and needlessly. **3** the act of slaughtering: *the slaughter of innocent villagers, to fatten hogs for slaughter.* **4** *Slang.* defeat easily by a high score: *Their team slaughtered ours.* 1, 2, 4 *v.*, 3 *n.*

slave (slāv) **1** in earlier times, a person who was owned by someone else and could be bought and sold. A slave had to do whatever his or her master ordered, and had no rights. **2** a person who is controlled by some desire, habit, or influence: *a slave to cigarettes.* **3** a person who works very hard for someone else. **4** work like a slave: *Those parents slave for their children.* 1–3 *n.*, 4 *v.*, **slaved, slav·ing.** **—slav′er·y,** *n.* **—slav′ish,** *adj.*

slay (slā) a poetic or formal word for "kill": *Jack slew the giant.* *v.*, **slew, slain, slay·ing.**

CONFUSABLES .... slay

slay means "kill": *The knight gave a solemn promise that he would slay the dragon.*

sleigh means "sled": *Oh what fun it is to ride in a one-horse open sleigh!*

sled (sled) **1** a vehicle with ski-shaped runners on the bottom instead of wheels, for travelling or sliding on ice or snow: *Sleds pulled by dogs are used in the Far North. Kathryn flew down the snowy hillside on her sled.* **2** ride or carry on a sled. 1 *n.*, 2 *v.*, **sled·ded, sled·ding.**

sledge·ham·mer (slej′ham′ər) a large, heavy hammer, usually swung with both hands.

sleek (slēk) **1** soft, smooth, and glossy: *sleek hair.* **2** looking well-fed and well-cared-for: *a sleek cat.* **3** elegant, stylish, and streamlined: *a sleek jet plane.* *adj.*

sleep (slēp) 1 rest the body and mind: *We sleep at night.* When you sleep, your body systems slow down and you are not aware of what is going on around you. 2 rest for the body and mind: *Most adults need about eight hours of sleep a night.* 3 be in a condition like sleep: *The seeds slept in the ground all winter. The great heroes of old sleep in their graves.* 4 a state or condition like sleep. 1, 3 *v.*, **slept, sleep·ing;** 2, 4 *n.*
—**sleep′less,** *adj.* —**sleep′y,** *adj.*
—**sleep′i·ly,** *adv.*
go to sleep, begin sleeping.
in your sleep, **a** while you are sleeping: *She talks in her sleep.* **b** very easily: *I could do that test in my sleep.*
put to sleep, **a** kill a very sick or badly injured animal painlessly to end its suffering. **b** cause to fall asleep: *That music puts me to sleep.*
sleep away, spend in sleeping: *She slept away the morning.*
sleep in, **a** stay in bed later than usual: *We always sleep in on Saturday morning.* **b** sleep too long: *He was late for school because he slept in.*
sleep like a log, sleep very soundly. **Sleep like a baby** means about the same.
sleep off, get rid of by having a sleep: *His mother told him to go and sleep off his cranky mood.*
sleep on something, take time to think something over before deciding.
sleep over, spend the night at someone's house: *My mom says you can sleep over.* A party or visit that includes staying overnight is a **sleepover.**

sleep·er (slē′pər) 1 a baby's stretchy one-piece garment. 2 a railway car with small rooms for passengers to sleep in. *n.*

sleeping bag (slē′ping bag′) a zippered cloth bag for sleeping in, well padded and lined with a warm material. It is used especially when camping.

sleep·walk (slēp′wok′) walk around while asleep. *n.* —**sleep′walk′er,** *n.*

sleet (slēt) 1 partly frozen rain; snow or hail mixed with rain. 2 to rain and snow or hail at the same time: *It sleeted; then it snowed; then it rained.* 1 *n.*, 2 *v.*

sleeve (slēv) 1 the part of a piece of clothing that covers the arm: *The sleeves were too long.* 2 a tubelike part of a machine that another long part fits into. *n.*
laugh up your sleeve, laugh secretly.
up your sleeve, hidden and ready for use when needed.

sleigh (slā) 1 a vehicle with ski-shaped runners on the bottom instead of wheels, pulled over snow or ice by horses, a tractor, reindeer, etc. **Cutter** is another word for it. 2 travel in or ride on a sleigh. 1 *n.*, 2 *v.*

slen·der (slen′dər) 1 narrow or slim, especially in a graceful or elegant way: *slender hands.* 2 small; almost too small: *a slender income, a slender hope.* *adj.*

slept (slept) the past tense and past participle of **sleep:** *The baby has slept soundly for several nights.* *v.*

sleuth (slūth) *Informal.* 1 a detective. 2 find and follow clues in order to solve a mystery. 1 *n.*, 2 *v.*

slew[1] (slū) the past tense of **slay:** *According to legend, St. George slew a dragon.* *v.*

slew[2] (slū) *Informal.* a large number or amount; lot: *The new boy quickly gained a slew of friends.* *n.*

slice (slīs) 1 a thin, flat, wide piece cut from something, especially food: *a slice of bread, a slice of meat.* 2 cut into slices: *Slice the cheese.* 3 cut: *He accidentally sliced his foot with the axe. The teacher automatically slices off 10 points if the "Works Cited" page is missing from a project.* 1 *n.*, 2, 3 *v.*, **sliced, slic·ing.**
any way you slice it or **no matter how you slice it,** no matter which way you look at a situation or question.

slick (slik) 1 very smooth or slippery: *slick hair, a road slick with ice or mud.* 2 *Informal.* smooth, clever, impressive, etc. in speech or manner, often in a tricky way. 3 comb smooth, flat, and shiny with special lotion: *He wears his hair slicked back.* 4 a smooth, slippery patch or surface. An **oil slick** is a patch of spilled oil floating on the water. 1, 3, 4 *adj.*, 2 *v.*

slick·er (slik′ər) a long plastic raincoat. *n.*

slide (slīd) 1 move smoothly over a surface; slip: *The desk drawers slide in and out.* 2 move easily, quietly, or secretly: *The burglar slid behind the curtains. He slid the wallet into his pocket.* 3 slip out of control; skid: *The car slid into a hydro pole.* 4 a smooth, sloping surface for sliding, especially one set up in a playground or pool: *The children played on the slide in the park.* 5 the act of sliding, or something that slides. This sense is often in compounds: *snowslide, landslide.* 6 a small, thin sheet of glass for putting objects on in order to look at them under a microscope. 7 a small transparent photograph made of glass or film. Slides are put in a projector and shown on a screen. 1–3 *v.*, **slid, slid·ing;** 4–7 *n.*
let something slide, neglect; not bother about: *Don't let your homework slide or you'll have trouble catching up.*

a bat	e bed	i bid	o pot	u cup	th thin
ā cake	ē me	ī bite	ō go	ū rude	TH then
ȧ bar	ə about	ər over	ȯ for	u̇ put	zh measure

slight (slīt) 1 not much; not big or important; small: *a few slight errors, a slight headache.* 2 small and slim, without much muscle: *a boy of slight build.* 3 insult someone by ignoring or neglecting him or her: *She felt slighted because she was not asked to the party.* 4 this kind of insult: *When they didn't say "Hi," he took it as a slight.* 1, 2 *adj.*, 3 *v.*, 4 *n.* —**slight′ly,** *adv.*

slim (slim) 1 thin, especially in an attractive way: *a slim waist, a slim leather wallet.* 2 small; slight: *a slim chance of success.* 3 make or become thinner: *It sure slims down the newspaper when you take out all the advertising.* 1, 2 *adj.*, **slim·mer, slim·mest;** 3 *v.*, **slimmed, slim·ming.**

slime (slīm) 1 soft, sticky mud or something like it: *His shoes were covered with slime from the swamp.* 2 the slippery mucus that coats snails, slugs, fish, and so on. 3 disgusting filth. *n.* —**slim′y,** *adj.*

sling (sling) 1 a hanging loop of cloth fastened around the neck to support an injured arm or a baby. 2 hang so as to swing loosely: *His jacket was slung over one shoulder.* 3 a curved strip of leather with a string fastened to each end, for throwing stones. 4 throw hard with or without a sling. 1, 3 *n.*, 2, 4 *v.*, **slung, sling·ing.**

sling·shot (sling′shot′) a Y-shaped stick with a band of rubber between its prongs, used to shoot pebbles and so on. A slingshot is a type of catapult. *n.*

slink (slingk) move in a sneaky way: *After stealing the meat, the dog slunk away.* *v.*, **slunk, slink·ing.**

slip¹ (slip) 1 go, put, or move smoothly, quietly, easily, or quickly: *to slip a note into someone's hand. The hours slipped by.* 2 slide out of place or out of control: *The knife slipped and cut him. I slipped on the icy sidewalk.* 3 get away from; escape from: *The dog slipped its collar. Your name has slipped my mind.* 4 get weaker, worse, or less than it should be: *Your grades are slipping; study harder.* 5 the act or fact of slipping: *His broken leg was caused by a slip on the ice.* 6 Often, **slip up,** make a mistake. 7 a mistake; error: *a slip in spelling.* A **slip-up** is a little more serious. 8 a light, skirtlike piece of underwear worn under a skirt or dress. 1–4, 6 *v.*, **slipped, slip·ping;** 5, 7, 8 *n.* —**slip′page,** *n.*
give someone the slip, *Informal.* escape or get away from someone: *The deer gave the hunter the slip.*
let slip, tell without meaning to: *She let slip that we had got him a baseball and glove for his birthday.*
slip of the tongue, a mistake made in speaking.

slip² (slip) 1 a small piece of paper: *You cannot go unless your parents have signed the permission slip.* 2 a small stem cut from a plant, used to grow a new plant. *n.*

slip–knot (slip′not′) a knot made so that the rest of the rope can slip through it, forming a loop that can be made bigger or smaller. A lasso has a slip-knot in it. *n.*

slip·per (slip′ər) a light, soft shoe that is easy to slip on and off, worn indoors. *n.*

slip·per·y (slip′ə rē) 1 likely to cause slipping; hard to get a grip or foothold on: *The steps are slippery with ice. Wet soap is slippery.* 2 very tricky and hard to catch: *a slippery thief.* *adj.*, **slip·per·i·er, slip·per·i·est.**

slip·shod (slip′shod′) careless; sloppy: *slipshod work.* *adj.*

slit (slit) 1 cut along a line; make a long, straight cut in: *She used a paper knife to slit the envelope open.* 2 a long, straight, narrow cut or opening: *a slit in the side of a skirt.* 1 *v.*, **slit, slit·ting;** 2 *n.*

slith·er (sliŦH′ər) slide smoothly along while twisting or moving from side to side, as a snake does. *v.*

sliv·er (sliv′ər) a long, thin piece that has been split off, broken off, or cut off: *I want just a sliver of pie. A metal sliver got stuck in his finger.* *n.*

slob (slob) 1 *Slang.* a messy, lazy person. 2 short for **slob ice,** crushed pieces of thick ice crowded together with slush, found in many waterways in winter. *n.*

slob·ber (slob′ər) 1 let spit run out of your mouth; drool. 2 spit running out of your mouth. 1 *v.*, 2 *n.*

slo·gan (slō′gən) a word or phrase that is easy to remember, used by any group to advertise its purpose or guiding belief: *"Safety First" is our slogan.* *n.*

slop (slop) 1 spill liquid; splash: *He slopped water on me.* 2 Usually, **slops,** *pl.* liquid garbage: *the kitchen slops.* On a farm, slops are often fed to pigs. 3 a mushy or runny food that does not look appetizing. 4 *Slang.* a sloppy person. 1 *v.*, **slopped, slop·ping;** 2–4 *n.*
slop through, a splash your way through dirty liquid, muck, etc. b *Slang.* do in a careless, sloppy way: *to slop through a piece of work.*

slope (slōp) 1 go up or down at an angle; slant: *a sloping roof. The land slopes toward the sea.* 2 any line, surface, land, etc. that goes up or down at an angle: *The ball rolled down the slope.* 3 the angle formed by a slope, or the distance it covers in height: *a sharp slope. The floor of the theatre has a slope of 1 m from the back seats to the front seats.* 1 *v.*, **sloped, slop·ing;** 2, 3 *n.*

slop·py (slop′ē) 1 very wet; slushy: *sloppy ground, sloppy weather.* 2 *Informal.* careless; messy: *to use sloppy language, to do sloppy work.* *adj.*, **slop·pi·er, slop·pi·est.**

slosh (slosh) splash in slush, mud, or water: *He sloshed around in the bathtub and got the floor all wet.* *v.*

slot (slot) 1 a narrow opening or groove: *the coin slot of a pop machine, the mail slot in a door.* Any machine that you work by dropping coins in a slot is a **slot machine.** 2 make a slot in something. 3 a position in a schedule or series: *We got the 7:30 time slot for the parent-teacher interviews.* 1, 3 *n.,* 2 *v.,* **slot·ted, slot·ting.**

slot in, put a person or thing in a certain slot: *We can slot your poem in between the grade four skit and the choir.*

Sloths spend their whole lives upside down. They eat, they move along branches, they sleep, and they die — all while hanging upside down. Many sloths move so slowly that green algae grows on their fur, as though they were just another part of the forest vegetation.

sloth (sloth *or* slōth) 1 a very slow-moving animal of South America that lives in trees and eats fruits and leaves. Sloths hang upside down from branches. 2 an old or poetic word for "laziness." *n.* —**sloth′ful,** *adj.*

slouch (slouch) 1 sit, stand, walk, or move in a droopy way instead of straight and tall: *He slouched in his chair.* 2 a drooping way of standing, sitting, or walking. 3 *Informal.* someone who has little ability or doesn't get much done. 1 *v.,* 2, 3 *n.* —**slouch′y,** *adj.*

slough¹ (slū) 1 🍁 a still body of water formed by rain or melted snow: *Wild ducks nest on the prairie sloughs.* 2 a mud hole or bog. 3 🍁 a side channel of a stream or an inlet of the sea that is shallow and marshy. *n.*

slough² (sluf)

slough off, drop or cast off; get rid of something useless or burdensome: *The snake sloughed off its old skin.* *v.*

slov·en·ly (sluv′ən lē) messy, dirty, or careless in dress, work habits, and so on. *adj.*

slow (slō) 1 taking a long time; not fast or quick: *a slow journey, a slow worker.* A very slow person or thing is a **slowpoke.** 2 showing time behind the correct time: *Our clock was slow so I left late.* 3 go or cause to go less quickly: *to slow down a car. Slow down so I can catch up.* 4 not very lively: *a slow party. Business is slow in winter.* 5 not quick to learn or understand. 1, 2, 4, 5 *adj.,* 3 *v.*

Slugs have a coating of thick, sticky slime to prevent their soft bodies from drying up.

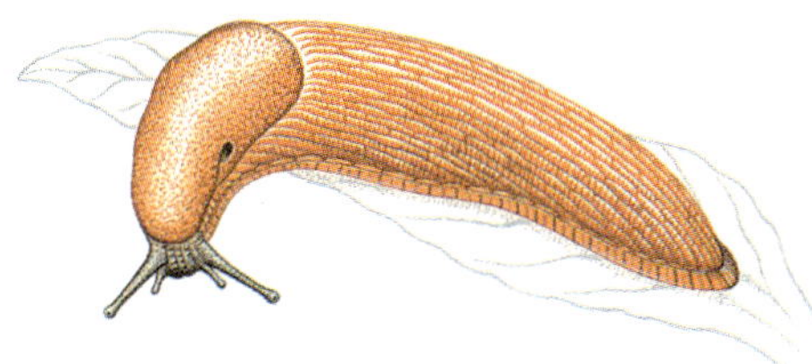

slug¹ (slug) 1 a slow-moving animal like a snail, without a shell or with only a partly developed shell. 2 a piece of metal shaped like a coin: *It is illegal to use slugs instead of coins in a slot machine.* 3 a piece of lead or other metal for firing from a gun. *n.*

slug² (slug) *Informal.* 1 hit hard with the fist, a bat, or blunt weapon. 2 a hard blow. 1 *v.,* **slugged, slug·ging;** 2 *n.*

slug·gish (slug′ish) slow; lazy or lacking energy: *a sluggish stream, a sluggish mind.* *adj.*

sluice (slūs) 1 a kind of gate or wall with a gate for holding back or controlling the flow of water: *When the water behind a dam gets too high, the sluices are opened.* 2 a long, sloping trough with water flowing through it, used to wash gold from sand, dirt, or gravel. 3 let water out or through. 4 flow or pour in a rushing stream. 1, 2 *n.,* 3, 4 *v.,* **sluiced, sluic·ing.**

slum (slum) a crowded, dirty area in a city with poor housing and social problems. *n.*

slum·ber (slum′bər) a poetic word for "sleep." *v. or n.*

slump (slump) 1 drop heavily, especially if unconscious: *He fainted and slumped to the floor.* 2 sit in a droopy way; slouch: *The bored students slumped in their seats.* 3 a time when business, work, etc. is not going as well as usual: *During her three-year slump the artist could not complete a single painting.* 1, 2 *v.,* 3 *n.*

slung (slung) the past tense and past participle of **sling:** *She slung her purse over her shoulder.* *v.*

a bat	e bed	i bid	o pot	u cup	th thin
ā cake	ē me	ī bite	ō go	ū rude	TH then
ä bar	ə about	ər over	ô for	ù put	zh measure

slunk (slungk) the past tense and past participle of **slink:** *The dog slunk off.* *v.*

slur (slər) **1** pronounce in an unclear way, especially because of tiredness, numbness, or drunkenness: *She was so sleepy she was slurring her words.* **2** an unclear pronunciation. **3** an insulting name or remark: *His slurs made her blood boil.* 1 *v.,* **slurred, slur·ring;** 2, 3 *n.*

slurp (slərp) to drink something with a loud sipping or sucking sound. *v.*

slush (slush) partly melted snow; snow and water mixed. *n.* **—slush′y,** *adj.*

sly (slī) **1** tricky and clever; crafty: *The sly cat stole the meat while the cook's back was turned. She asked sly questions.* **2** full of secret understanding: *a sly smile.* *adj.,* **sly·er** or **sli·er, sly·est** or **sli·est.** **—sly′ly,** *adv.*
on the sly, in a sly way; secretly.

smack[1] (smak) **1** slap: *She smacked his face.* **2** a loud kiss, slap, or crack. 1 *v.,* 2 *n.*
smack your lips, make a sharp sucking, licking, or popping sound with your lips, which shows you are enjoying food or else thinking about enjoying it.

smack[2] (smak) **1** have a taste, trace, or suggestion of: *The joke smacked of racism and she did not find it funny.* **2** a slight taste, trace, or suggestion: *The old sailor still has a smack of the sea about him.* 1 *v.,* 2 *n.*

small (smol) **1** not big in size, value, strength, or importance; little: *a small house, a small mistake, a small business, a small hope of success.* **2** mean; low; not noble: *Only a small mind would think of such a nasty thing to say.* **3** the slender or narrow part of your back. 1, 2 *adj.,* 3 *n.*
feel small, feel embarrassed or ashamed.
small change, a coins of little value, such as nickels, dimes, etc. **b** anything small and unimportant. **Small potatoes** means the same.
small fry, a babies or children; small or young creatures. **b** unimportant people: *He thinks himself too important to talk to small fry like us.*
small print, in an advertisement or written agreement, words in very small type giving disappointing information that makes the deal less attractive. If you don't read it you may have a nasty surprise later on, after it is too late.
small talk, conversation about unimportant things.

small letter (smol′ let′ər) the informal name for a **lower-case letter** such as *g*, not a capital like *G*.

small·pox (smol′poks′) a very serious contagious disease that causes fever, weakness, and skin sores which often leave scars shaped like little pits. Smallpox was a common disease until about 1980. Vaccination is thought to have destroyed it. *n.*

small–time (smol′tīm′) not very big, important, or famous: *a small-time movie actor.* *adj.*

smart (smárt) **1** clever; bright; showing good sense and clear thinking: *He is a smart boy. That was a smart choice.* **2** trying to be clever or funny in a disrespectful or annoying way: *That's enough of your smart remarks.* Someone who does this is a **smart aleck** (smárt′ al′ək). **3** attractive, stylish, and trim: *Sheri looks smart in her new suit.* **4** keen or sharp; lively: *We walked at a smart pace. He gave the horse a smart blow.* **5 smarts,** *pl. Informal.* intelligence; sense; cleverness: *He doesn't have the smarts to figure out our plan.* **6** feel or give sharp pain; sting: *His eyes smarted from the wind. She was still smarting from their cutting remarks.* **7** a sharp pain. 1–4 *adj.,* 5, 7 *n.,* 6 *v.* **—smart′ly,** *adv.* **—smart′ness,** *n.*

smart·en (smár′tən)
smarten up, *Informal.* start behaving or working as you are supposed to: *The teacher told the class to smarten up and quit fooling around.* *v.*

smash (smash) **1** break into pieces with violence and noise: *The boy smashed a window with a rock. The cup smashed on the floor.* **2** destroy: *to smash a person's hopes.* **3** hit violently against something; crash: *The car smashed into the tree.* **4** the act or sound of smashing: *the smash of broken glass.* **5** *Informal.* very popular; instantly successful: *a smash hit.* 1–3 *v.,* 4 *n.,* 5 *adj.*

smat·ter·ing (smat′ər ing) a small or slight amount of something, in disconnected bits: *I know only a smattering of Spanish.* *n.*

smear (smēr) **1** cover or stain by rubbing with anything sticky, greasy, or dirty: *to smear glue on paper. The baby smeared her face with jam.* **2** a messy mark left by doing this; smudge: *a smear of paint on the wall.* **3** be smudged: *Wet paint smears easily.* **4** harm a person's reputation or character: *The mayor's opponents tried to smear her by spreading bad rumours about her past.* **5** the act of trying to harm a person's reputation in this way. If it goes on for some time it is a **smear campaign.** 1, 3, 4 *v.,* 2, 5 *n.* **—smear′y,** *adj.*

smell (smel) **1** notice the scent of something with your nose: *Can you smell the smoke?* **2** breathe in on purpose to get the scent of something; sniff: *Smell this and see if you like it.* **3** the ability to do this: *Smell is keener in dogs than in people.* Smell is one of the five senses. **4** scent; odour: *the smell of burning rubber, the smell of roses.* **5** give out a smell: *The kitchen smelled of fresh bread.* **6** give out a bad smell: *That wet dog smells.* Something that smells bad is **smelly.** **7** a sniff; the act of smelling: *Have a smell of this perfume.* 1, 2, 5, 6 *v.,* **smelled** or **smelt, smell·ing;** 3, 4, 7 *n.*

smelt[1] (smelt) **1** melt ore in order to get the metal out of it. **2** purify impure metal by melting it and removing the other ingredients. *v.* —**smelt′er,** *n.*

smelt[2] (smelt) a small food fish with silvery scales. Different kinds of smelt live along northern seacoasts and in lakes. *n., pl.* **smelt** or **smelts.**

smelt[3] (smelt) a past tense and a past participle of **smell.** *v.*

smid·gen (smij′ən) a tiny amount of something: *Jerry added a smidgen of pepper to the stew.* *n.*

smile (smīl) **1** show happiness, friendliness, amusement, scorn, or mockery by a curve of the mouth: *to smile in welcome. She smiled bitterly.* **3** the act of smiling, or the expression that it makes on a person's face: *a friendly smile. Draw a smile on the clown.* 1, 2 *v.,* **smiled, smil·ing;** 3 *n.*
smile on, show favour or kindness to; give good luck to.

smirk (smərk) **1** smile in a scornful or conceited way. **2** a scornful or conceited smile. 1 *v.,* 2 *n.*

smith (smith) **1** a person who makes or shapes things out of metal. This sense is usually in compounds: *goldsmith, tinsmith.* **2** a person who makes things out of iron; blacksmith. The workshop of a smith is a **smithy.** *n.*

smith·er·eens (smiᴛʜ′ə rēnz′) *Informal.* tiny pieces; bits: *to smash a plate into smithereens.* *pl.n.*

smock (smok) a loose outer coatlike garment worn to protect clothing. *n.*

The word smog is a combination of smoke and fog.

smog (smog) a mixture of smoke, fog, and fumes that clouds the air: *Car exhaust is a source of smog.* *n.*

smoke (smōk) **1** the mixture of gases and carbon that rises in a cloud from anything burning. A **smoke detector** warns you of smoke and possible fire. **2** give off smoke: *The fireplace smokes.* **3** draw the smoke from a cigarette, pipe, or cigar into your mouth, and often your lungs, and blow it out again: *Don't smoke; it can kill you.* **4** a cigarette, or the act of smoking tobacco: *a pack of smokes, to go for a smoke.* **5** preserve and flavour meat or fish by exposing to smoke, often in a small building called a **smokehouse:** *smoked salmon, smoked ham.* 1, 4 *n.,* 2, 3, 5 *v.,* **smoked, smok·ing.** —**smok′er,** *n.* —**smok′y,** *adj.* —**smoke′less,** *adj.*
smoke out, drive out by smoke: *We tried in vain to smoke the groundhog out of its hole.*

smoke·stack (smōk′stak′) a tall chimney on a factory, big truck, or ship. *n.*

smooth (smüᴛʜ) **1** with an even surface, like glass or still water; flat and level, not bumpy or rough: *smooth stones.* **2** done or carried out evenly and easily, without problems or jerks or roughness: *the smooth movements of a dancer, a smooth voyage.* **3** without lumps: *smooth gravy.* **4** easy and flowing; pleasant and polite, often in a way that seems fake or insincere: *a smooth talker.* **5** make smooth or smoother: *She smoothed out the ball of crumpled paper and read what was on it. Her friendliness smoothed the way to an agreement.* 1–4 *adj.,* 5 *v.*
smooth away, get rid of wrinkles or difficulties.
smooth down, flatten something sticking up: *to smooth down wet hair.*
smooth over, make something seem less wrong, unpleasant, or noticeable: *The teacher tried to smooth over the argument between the two boys.*

smor·gas·bord (smôr′gəs bôrd′) a meal where you serve yourself from a large variety of meats, salads, and so on and then go and sit down to eat it. *n.*

smoth·er (smuᴛʜ′ər) **1** keep from getting air; kill by cutting off the supply of air. **2** put out flames by covering them thickly: *Smother the fire with ashes.* **3** be unable to breathe freely: *We are smothering in this stuffy room.* **4** keep back; check: *to smother a sharp reply.* *v.*

smoul·der or **smol·der** (smōl′dər) **1** burn slowly with smoke but without flames: *The fire smouldered most of the night.* **2** exist quietly, deep inside a person, barely showing: *The people's discontent smouldered for years before it broke out into open rebellion.* **3** have or show strong feeling that is kept quietly controlled inside: *The man's eyes smouldered with anger as he waited for a chance to fight back.* *v.*

smudge (smuj) **1** a dirty mark made by rubbing; a smear. **2** make this kind of mark on: *The child's drawing was smudged.* 1 *n.,* 2 *v.,* **smudged, smudg·ing.**

a bat	e bed	i bid	o pot	u cup	th thin
ā cake	ē me	ī bite	ō go	ü rude	ᴛʜ then
à bar	ə about	ər over	ô for	ů put	zh measure

smug (smug) thinking you are very good and smart; too pleased with yourself: *Her smug attitude made her unpopular.* *adj.,* **smug·ger, smug·gest.** —**smug′ly,** *adv.*

smug·gle (smug′əl) **1** bring or take things over a border secretly and against the law: *They were sent to prison for smuggling drugs into Canada.* **2** bring in or take out secretly: *He tried to smuggle his puppy into the house.* *v.,* **smug·gled, smug·gling.** —**smug′gler,** *n.*

snack (snak) a quick, light meal: *He eats a snack before going to bed.* *n.*

snack bar (snak′ bȧr′) a counter where light meals, coffee, and so on are served.

snag (snag) **1** any sharp or rough point sticking out that things can easily get caught on. **2** catch on a snag: *He snagged his coat on a nail.* **3** a pulled or broken thread in cloth where it has caught on something sharp. **4** a hidden or unexpected problem: *We had to cancel our trip because of a snag.* 1, 3, 4 *n.,* 2 *v.,* **snagged, snag·ging.**

snail (snāl) a small mollusc that has a soft body and crawls very slowly. Most snails have spiral shells on their backs that they can pull themselves back into for protection. Some snails are good to eat. *n.*

Although the cobra is a fast and poisonous snake, the mongoose can pounce so swiftly that the cobra has no time to strike with its fangs.

snake (snāk) **1** a long, slender reptile without legs. It has a scaly skin and no eyelids and moves by twisting its body back and forth in a wavy motion. Some snakes are poisonous. **2** a tricky person that you cannot trust. **3** move, wind, or curve like a snake: *The narrow road snaked through the mountains.* **4** a long, bendable metal rod used by plumbers to clear clogged drains. 1, 2, 4 *n.,* 3 *v.,* **snaked, snak·ing.** —**snak′y,** *adj.*

snap (snap) **1** a small, quick, sharp sound: *The box shut with a snap.* **2** make or cause to make a sound like this: *This wood snaps as it burns. The teacher snapped her fingers to get our attention.* **3** break suddenly or sharply: *The violin string snapped.* **4** speak quickly and sharply: *"Silence!" snapped the captain.* A **snappish** person speaks this way. **5** bite or try to bite quickly and suddenly; snatch with the teeth: *The dog snapped at the child's hand. The cat snapped up the fish.* **6** a quick, sudden bite: *The dog made a snap at a fly.* **7** move quickly and sharply: *The soldiers snapped to attention. Her eyes snapped with anger.* **8** a fastener with two parts that fit tightly together with a little click: *One of the snaps of your dress is unfastened.* It is also called a **dome fastener.** **9** a thin, crisp cookie: *a ginger snap.* **10** made or done suddenly: *a snap decision.* **11** *Informal.* short for **snapshot,** a photo taken quickly and casually. **12** take quickly with a simple camera: *to snap a picture.* **13** *Slang.* something very easy: *These cookies are a snap to make.* **14** liveliness, energy, interesting style, and so on: *This slogan needs a little more snap.* 1, 6, 8, 9, 11, 13, 14 *n.,* 2–5, 7, 12 *v.,* **snapped, snap·ping;** 10 *adj.*
cold snap, a few days of cold weather.
snap at or **snap up,** grab or seize; take eagerly: *to snap up a bargain, to snap at the chance to be in a play.*
snap out of it, get rid of a bad mood or attitude suddenly or quickly, especially by a simple decision to change.

snap·drag·on (snap′drag′ən) a garden plant with showy flowers that look something like a dragon's head. Snapdragons come in many colours. *n.*

snapping turtle (snap′ing tər′təl) a large turtle of North and Central America that lives in fresh water and has powerful, hooked jaws.

snap·py (snap′ē) *Informal.* having lots of snap; lively, smart, energetic, stylish, and so on: *a snappy design, a snappy game, a snappy sports jacket.* *adj.,* **snap·pi·er, snap·pi·est.** —**snap′pi·ly,** *adv.*
make it snappy, *Informal.* hurry up; move fast.

snap·shot (snap′shot′) a quick, casual photograph taken with a simple camera. *n.*

snare (sner) **1** a trap, especially one for catching small animals and birds: *The boys made snares to catch rabbits.* **2** catch with a snare; trap: *One day they snared a skunk.* 1 *n.,* 2 *v.,* **snared, snar·ing.**

snare drum (sner′ drum′) a small drum with wires stretched across the bottom to make a rattling sound.

snarl[1] (snȧrl) **1** growl sharply and show the teeth: *The dog snarled at the stranger.* **2** speak harshly in a nasty tone: *"Get lost!" snarled the bully.* **3** a sharp, angry growl or remark. 1, 2 *v.,* 3 *n.*

snarl[2] (snȧrl) **1** a tangle or confused mess: *She combed the snarls out of her hair.* **2** make or become tangled, confused, or messed up: *Traffic was all snarled up on account of the construction work.* A **snarl-up** is a confused mess. 1 *n.,* 2 *v.*

snatch (snach) **1** grab suddenly and roughly: *The hawk snatched the chicken and flew away.* A **purse snatcher** grabs a purse being carried by someone in a public place and runs off with it. **2** a sudden, rough grabbing movement: *The boy made a snatch at the ball.* **3** a small bit or scrap: *From time to time we heard snatches of the conversation at the next table.* 1 *v.,* 2, 3 *n.*
snatch at, **a** try to grab: *He snatched at the rail.* **b** take advantage of eagerly: *She snatched at the chance to travel.*

sneak (snēk) **1** move, bring, etc. in a quiet, secret, sly way, trying not to be noticed: *He sneaked into the kitchen and took a few cookies. We sneaked the kitten into the house.* **2** do things in a sly or secret way: *We had to do a lot of sneaking around to prepare the surprise party for Mom.* **3** a cowardly, dishonest person. **4** secret; doing things secretly, without being noticed: *a sneak thief, a sneak attack.* 1, 2 *v.,* **sneaked** or **snuck** (*Informal*), **sneak·ing;** 3 *n.,* 4 *adj.* **—sneak′y,** *adj.* **—sneak′i·ly,** *adv.*

sneak·er (snē′kər) a running shoe; a light shoe made of cloth, soft leather, or other soft material, with a flexible rubber sole. It is used for sports like tennis, or for general casual wear. *n.*

sneer (snēr) **1** show scorn or disrespect; put down or make fun of something by looks or words: *The mean girls sneered at poor Edie's clothes.* **2** a look or words like this; a put-down: *Their sneers hurt him more than sticks and stones.* **3** say in a mean, mocking way: *"Big deal!" he sneered with a curl of his lip.* 1, 3 *v.,* 2 *n.*

sneeze (snēz) **1** force air suddenly and violently through your nose and mouth without being able to help it, as a reflex: *The pepper made her sneeze. People sneeze when they have a cold or hay fever.* **2** a sudden, violent rush of air through the nose and mouth. 1 *v.,* **sneezed, sneez·ing;** 2 *n.*
sneeze at, *Informal.* look down on; treat with scorn: *Ten dollars is not a sum to be sneezed at.*

snick·er (snik′ər) **1** a little half-hidden laugh of embarrassment, disrespect, or ridicule. **2** laugh in this way: *A few kids in class snickered at Corene's accent.* **Snigger** means the same. 1 *n.,* 2 *v.*

snide (snīd) clever but in a mean or spiteful way: *a snide remark.* *adj.*

sniff (snif) **1** breathe in hard through your nose in order to clear it or smell something: *The man who had a cold was sniffing. She sniffed the medicine before taking a spoonful of it.* **2** take in through the nose with your breath: *He sniffed steam to clear his head. Sniffing glue is substance abuse.* **3** show scorn or disrespect by sniffing: *She sniffed at the present he offered her.* **4** the act or sound of sniffing: *He cleared his nose with a loud sniff. I took a sniff of fresh air.* 1–3 *v.,* 4 *n.*
sniff out, smell or snoop around and try to find.

snif·fle (snif′əl) **1** sniff again and again, as you do when you have a cold or you are trying to stop crying. **2** the act or sound of sniffling. **3** **the sniffles,** *pl. Informal.* a slight cold with a runny nose that makes you sniffle. 1 *v.,* **snif·fled, snif·fling;** 2, 3 *n.*

snip (snip) **1** cut with scissors, using small, quick strokes: *She snipped the thread.* **2** the act of cutting in this way: *With a few snips she cut out a paper doll.* **3** a small piece cut off: *Pick up the snips of cloth and thread from the floor.* 1 *v.,* **snipped, snip·ping;** 2, 3 *n.*

snipe (snīp) **1** shoot from a hidden position. A person who does this is a **sniper.** **2** make mean, cutting remarks: *He is in a bad mood and has been sniping at me all morning.* **3** a shore bird with a long bill. It is common in many parts of the world but only one kind lives in North America. 1, 2 *v.,* **sniped, snip·ing;** 3 *n., pl.* **snipe** or **snipes.**

snip·pet (snip′it) **1** a tiny piece cut from something: *snippets of cloth.* **2** a small bit of information: *We only heard snippets about their trip.* *n.*

snitch (snich) *Slang.* **1** steal something small: *Who snitched my pencil sharpener?* **2** tattle on someone: *She refused to snitch on her friends.* *v.*

sniv·el (sniv′əl) **1** cry with sniffling. **2** whine; cry in a cowardly, babyish, or fake way. *v.,* **sniv·elled** or **sniv·eled, sniv·el·ling** or **sniv·el·ing.**

snob (snob) a person who thinks he or she is too smart, too good, or too important to be bothered with most people, or to like the things most people like. *n.* **—snob′bish** or **snob′by,** *adj.* **—snob′ber·y,** *n.*

snoop (snūp) **1** sneak around trying to find out things that aren't your business; pry: *to snoop into people's private affairs.* **2** a person who does this. 1 *v.,* 2 *n.*

snoot·y (snū′tē) conceited and snobbish. *adj.,* **snoot·i·er, snoot·i·est.** **—snoot′i·ly,** *adv.* **—snoot′i·ness,** *n.*

WORD HISTORY........snooty

Snooty is from *snoot,* Scottish dialect for *snout,* or "nose," because this kind of person walks around with his or her nose in the air.

a bat	e bed	i bid	o pot	u cup	th thin
ā cake	ē me	ī bite	ō go	ü rude	ᴛʜ then
ä bar	ə about	ər over	ȯ for	ů put	zh measure

Snowmobile and Snowshoes

Armand Bombardier (1908-1964), a Canadian, invented the snowmobile when he was only fifteen years old.

In deep, soft snow, a snowmobile would not be a suitable means of transportation. Snowshoes can go where snowmobiles can't. To move around wearing snowshoes, you move your feet so that the snowshoes slide along the surface of the snow.

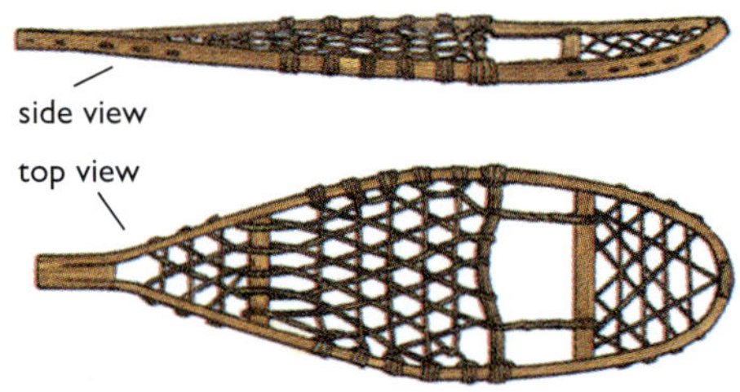

Traditionally, snowshoes are made by stretching strips of animal hide across a curved wooden frame.

snooze (snūz) *Informal.* sleep; doze; nap: *a snooze on the couch* (*n.*). *The dog snoozed in the sun* (*v.*). *n. or v.,* **snoozed, snooz·ing.**

snore (snȯr) **1** breathe with a harsh, rough sound while sleeping: *People often snore when sleeping on their backs.* **2** the act or sound of snoring. 1 *v.,* **snored, snor·ing;** 2 *n.*

snor·kel (snȯr′kəl) **1** a tube on the top of a submarine, sticking out of the water, for taking in fresh air and letting out waste air and gases. It allows the submarine to remain underwater for a long time. **2** a J-shaped tube that lets you breathe while swimming underwater near the surface. You put the curved end in your mouth, letting the straight end stick up out of the water. **3** swim underwater using a snorkel. 1, 2 *n.,* 3 *v.,* **snor·kelled** or **snor·keled, snor·kel·ling** or **snor·kel·ing.**

snort (snȯrt) **1** breathe in or out violently with a loud, harsh sound: *The horse snorted. I laughed so hard I snorted.* **2** make a sound like this: *The engine snorted as it started up.* **3** the act or sound of snorting. **4** say in a tone of scorn or disgust: *"Indeed!" snorted my aunt.* 1, 2, 4 *v.,* 3 *n.*

snout (snout) the long nose and mouth of certain animals, such as pigs, bears, and alligators. *n.*

snow (snō) **1** frozen water vapour in soft, white flakes or crystals that fall to earth in winter. **2** a fall of snow: *There were only two light snows in January.* **3** fall as snow: *It snowed all day.* 1, 2 *n.,* 3 *v.*
snow in, shut in by snow: *The town was snowed in for almost a week.*
snow under, **a** cover completely with snow. **b** *Informal.* overwhelm: *She is snowed under with work.*

snow·ball (snō′bol′) **1** a ball made of snow pressed together. **2** grow or increase very fast like a rolling snowball: *The school's enrolment has snowballed and we now have four portables.* 1 *n.,* 2 *v.*

snow–blind (snō′blīnd′) temporarily or partly blinded by the reflection of sunlight from snow or ice. *adj.* **—snow blindness.**

snow·board (snō′bȯrd′) **1** a wide plastic board with turned-up ends for sliding downhill on snow. You stand or crouch on it. **2** to ride on a snowboard. 1 *n.,* 2 *v.* **—snow′board′ing,** *n.*

snow·bound (snō′bound′) shut in by snow. *adj.*

snow·drift (snō′drift′) a bank of snow piled up by wind. *n.*

snow·fall (snō′fol′) a fall of snow, or the amount of snow that falls. *n.*

snow·flake (snō′flāk′) a small, feathery piece of snow. *n.*

snow goose (snō′ gūs′) a wild goose, white with black wing tips, that breeds in the Arctic.

snow·man (snō′man′) a figure shaped somewhat like a person, made of snow packed together. *n., pl.* **snow·men** (snō′men′).

🍁 **snow·mo·bile** (snō′mə bēl′) **1** a small, open motor vehicle seating one or two people, for travelling over snow and ice. It is moved by a looped track under the back part and steered by handlebars attached to a pair of skis under its front. **2** a much larger, closed-in vehicle similar to this, but with two tracks. It can carry several people and cargo. **3** travel by snowmobile. 1, 2 *n.,* 3 *v.,* **snow·mo·biled, snow·mo·bil·ing. —snow′mo·bil′er,** *n.*

snow·plough or **snow·plow** (snō′plou′) a vehicle for clearing snow from roads and so on. *n.*

snow·shoe (snō′shū′) 1 a light frame with strips of leather or other material stretched across it, which you strap on under each boot. Snowshoes keep your feet from sinking in deep, soft snow. 2 walk or travel on snowshoes. 1 *n.,* 2 *v.,* **snow·shoed, snow·shoe·ing.** —**snow′sho′er,** *n.*

snow·storm (snō′stȯrm′) a storm with much snow. *n.*

snow·y (snō′ē) 1 having snow or covered with snow. 2 white as snow: *snowy hair.* The **snowy owl** of Canada and the northern U.S. has mostly white feathers. *adj.,* **snow·i·er, snow·i·est.**

snub (snub) 1 treat coldly or scornfully; ignore: *She snubbed her less wealthy relatives.* 2 the act of treating someone in this way. 3 short and turned up at the tip: *a snub nose.* 1 *v.,* **snubbed, snub·bing;** 2 *n.,* 3 *adj.*

snuck (snuk) *Informal.* a past tense and past participle of **sneak:** *They snuck up on me. I have often snuck into class at the last minute.* *v.*

snuff[1] (snuf) 1 sniff: *The young hound snuffed at the track of the fox.* 2 in earlier times, powdered tobacco that was breathed up into the nose. 1 *v.,* 2 *n.*
up to snuff, *Informal.* in proper order or condition.

snuff[2] (snuf) put out a candle by cutting or pinching the burning wick. *v.*
snuff out, put an end to suddenly and completely: *The new dictator snuffed out the people's hopes for freedom.*

snug (snug) 1 comfortable, warm, and sheltered: *The cat has found a snug corner behind the stove.* 2 fitting closely: *That coat is a little too snug.* 3 neatly laid out, with just enough room: *The cabins on the boat are snug.* *adj.,* **snug·ger, snug·gest.** —**snug′ly,** *adv.*

snug·gle (snug′əl) lie or press closely against a person, animal, or thing for warmth or comfort; nestle; cuddle. *v.,* **snug·gled, snug·gling.**

so (sō) 1 to such a degree; this much or that much: *I am so excited that I can't sit still. Don't walk so fast! My head aches so!* 2 therefore: *The dog was hungry, so we fed it.* 3 in order that: *Be quiet so she can rest.* 4 also; likewise: *Pete is here; so is Jared.* 5 **So** is used: **a** to insist that a thing is true when someone else says it isn't: *"I didn't take it!" "You did so!"* **b** to refer back to something that has just been described, mentioned, or shown: *Hold your pen so. The chair is broken and has been so for a long time. If you would like to join in, please do so.* 6 **So** is also used to introduce a remark or ask for more explanation: *"So! Late again!" "Well, it was raining." "So?"* 1, 4, 5 *adv.,* 2, 3 *conj.,* 6 *interj.*
and so on, and other similar things. **And so forth** means the same but is more formal.
or so, or about that much: *It costs $15 or so.*
so-and-so, an expression to take the place of a name that is unknown, forgotten, or not mentioned.
so as to, a in order to: *Go to bed early so as to get enough sleep.* **b** in such a way as to: *The tree had fallen so as to completely block the road.*
so that, with the result or purpose that: *Hurry so that you won't be late. She had worn the wrong shoes, so that now her feet were wet and sore.*
so what? what does that matter? Who cares?

soak (sōk) 1 make very wet: *The rain soaked my clothes.* 2 leave something in water or other liquid for some purpose: *Soak the stained jeans all night before you wash them.* 3 the act of staying or leaving something in liquid: *a nice long soak in the hot tub.* 4 sink slowly into a surface: *Water soaks into the earth.* 1, 2, 4 *v.,* 3 *n.*
soaking wet, completely wet; dripping.
soak up, take in slowly; absorb: *A sponge soaks up water.*

soap (sōp) 1 a substance used for washing, especially for washing your skin. 2 rub with soap: *Soap those dirty hands well.* 1 *n.,* 2 *v.* —**soap′y,** *adj.*

soap opera (sōp′ op′ə rə) a radio or TV fiction series that is mostly about the characters' love affairs and personal problems.

soap·stone (sōp′stōn′) a heavy, soft stone that feels a bit like soap. It is often used for carving. *n.*

soar (sȯr) 1 fly very high; fly upward: *The eagle soared without flapping its wings.* 2 rise very high: *Her spirits soared at the good news. Prices are soaring.* *v.*

CONFUSABLES .... soar

soar means "fly": *An eagle can soar above the trees.*
sore means "painful": *My finger is sore.*

sob (sob) 1 cry hard with short, quick breaths: *She sobbed with pain.* 2 a tearful cry between short, quick breaths: *a loud sob.* 1 *v.,* **sobbed, sob·bing;** 2 *n.*

so·ber (sō′bər) 1 not drunk. 2 quiet; serious; solemn: *"I think we're lost," he said in a sober voice.* 3 make or become sober: *Seeing the car accident sobered us all.* 1, 2 *adj.,* 3 *v.* —**so′ber·ing,** *adj.*

a bat	e bed	i bid	o pot	u cup	th thin
ā cake	ē me	ī bite	ō go	ū rude	ᴛʜ then
ä bar	ə about	ər over	ȯ for	u̇ put	zh measure

so–called (sō′kold′) called so, but not really so: *Her so-called friend hasn't even written to her.* *adj.*

soc·cer (sok′ər) a game played between two teams of eleven people, where the players try to kick a round ball into the opponents' goal. The ball may be struck with any part of the body except the hands and arms. *n.*

so·cia·ble (sō′shə bəl) **1** liking company; friendly: *She is a sociable girl and has a lot of friends.* **2** full of friendly conversation: *a sociable evening.* *adj.*

so·cial (sō′shəl) **1** having to do with a community or society, the way it is organized, and the way people live in it: *social conditions, social problems.* The study of this is called **social science.** **2** having to do with friendships or friendly group activities: *a social club, a social event, a person's social life.* To take part in social activity is to **socialize.** **3** liking company: *She has a social nature.* **4** a party or other gathering for friendly group activities. **5** naturally living together in communities: *Ants and bees are social insects.* 1–3, 5 *adj.,* 4 *n.* **—so′cial·ly,** *adv.*

social assistance (sō′shəl ə sis′təns) the regular payments a government makes to people who are out of work, have reached a certain age, or need help.

Social Credit Party (sō′shəl kred′it pàr′tē) a Canadian political party, founded in Alberta in the 1930s. Supporters were nicknamed **Socreds** (sō′kredz′).

so·cial·ism (sō′shə liz′əm) a way of organizing a country so that many social services are under the control of an elected government, rather than privately owned. *n.* **—so′cial·ist,** *n. or adj.*

social studies (sō′shəl stud′ēz) a school subject that deals with the way people live in different parts of the world and how they lived in the past.

social work (sō′shəl wərk′) work that is meant to improve the social conditions in a community, including services such as medical clinics, family counselling, and so on. **—so′cial work′er.**

so·ci·e·ty (sə sī′ə tē) **1** all the people of a certain time and a certain part of the world, sharing certain values and customs: *Canadian society includes people from a wide variety of backgrounds.* **2** a group of people joined together by a common goal or interest: *the Canadian Cancer Society.* *n., pl.* **so·ci·e·ties.**

sock (sok) a close-fitting, knitted covering for the foot and lower leg, worn inside a shoe. *n.*

sock·et (sok′it) an opening specially designed to hold a certain thing, such as a light bulb or candle. Your eyes are in your eye sockets. *n.*

sock·eye (sok′ī′) a small salmon found in the North Pacific. It is valued for its red, oily flesh, which is sold fresh, smoked, or canned. *n., pl.* **sock·eye** or **sock·eyes.**

sod (sod) **1** a thin layer cut from the ground with grass growing on it, including the roots. **2** cover with strips of sod: *We had all the bare spots on our lawn sodded.* **3** grassy ground. 1, 3 *n.,* 2 *v.,* **sod·ded, sod·ding.**

so·da (sō′də) **1** a chemical substance containing sodium, such as **baking soda** or **sodium bicarbonate.** **2** a drink of pop with ice cream floating in it. **3** a U.S. word for "pop." *n.*

sod·den (sod′ən) completely soaked: *The earth was sodden after two days of rain.* *adj.*

so·di·um (sō′dē əm) a soft, silver-white, metal that is a chemical element. It is found only in combination with other elements; **sodium chloride** is ordinary salt. *n.*

so·fa (sō′fə) a couch or chesterfield; a long stuffed seat with a back and arms. One that folds out into a bed is a **sofa bed.** *n.*

soft (soft) **1** not hard or stiff; easy to squeeze, cut, shape, and so on: *Wet clay and wool are soft. Pine is softer than oak.* **2** very smooth; pleasant to touch; not rough or scratchy: *the soft hair of a kitten, soft silk.* **3** not harsh; not too strong, loud, or bright: *a soft spring breeze, soft music, the soft light of candles.* **4** gentle; kind; tender: *s oft words, soft eyes, a soft heart.* **5** weak and out of shape: *The athletes had become soft from lack of exercise.* *adj.*
—soft′ly, *adv.* **—soft′ness,** *n.*
—soft′en (sof′ən), *v.*
have a soft spot for, be fond of; like; care about.

Word Family.......... **soft**

softball: a game like baseball, with a larger, softer ball
soft-boiled: **1** boiled only a short time so the yolk stays liquid **2** kind; tender-hearted
softcover: with a flexible cover made of heavy paper
soft drink: any fizzy cold drink without alcohol; pop
soft-hearted: kind, gentle, and caring
soft-spoken: speaking quietly and gently
software: computer programs
soft water: water with few or no minerals in it. It makes suds easily.
softwood: the wood of most cone-bearing trees, easily cut

sog·gy (sog′ē) so wet or damp that it is soft and mushy. *adj.,* **sog·gi·er, sog·gi·est.**

Soil forms in layers called horizons. In the soil sample shown here, horizon A is rich in decomposed plants and animal matter. Horizon B is mainly particles of minerals. Horizon C is mostly rocks and bedrock.

soil[1] (soil) ground; earth; dirt: *Most plants grow best in rich soil.* *n.*
native soil, the country you were born in.

soil[2] (soil) make or become dirty: *She soiled her dress. White gloves soil easily.* *v.*

so•lar (sō′lər) having to do with the sun: *a solar eclipse.* A **solar cell** changes light energy from the sun into electrical energy. **Solar time** is measured by the earth's motion in relation to the sun. *adj.*

solar system (sō′lər sis′təm) the sun and all the planets, satellites, comets, etc. that revolve around it.
▶ See Appendix.

sold (sōld) the past tense and past participle of **sell:** *He has sold his stereo. He sold it a week ago.* *v.*

sol•der (sod′ər) **1** a metal that you can melt and use for joining or mending metal parts. **2** fasten, mend, or join with solder: *She soldered the wires together.* 1 *n.,* 2 *v.*

sol•dier (sōl′jər) a person who serves in an army, especially one who is not an officer. *n.*

sole[1] (sōl) **1** only: *He was her sole friend.* **2** shared with no one else: *We have sole rights to this piece of land.* *adj.* **—sole′ly,** *adv.*

sole[2] (sōl) the bottom surface of a foot, shoe, boot, etc. *n.*

sole[3] (sōl) a kind of flatfish which is very good to eat. *n., pl.* **sole** or **soles.**

sol•emn (sol′əm) **1** very serious: *a solemn promise, a solemn voice.* **2** formal and dignified: *a solemn procession, a solemn ceremony.* *adj.*
—so•lem′ni•ty (sə lem′nə tē), *n.*

so•lic•it (sə lis′it) **1** ask for: *to solicit someone's help.* **2** ask for donations: *The sign in the apartment lobby says "No Soliciting."* *v.*

so•lic•i•tor (sə lis′ə tər) **1** a lawyer, especially one who helps prepare cases but does not appear in court. **2** a person who asks for donations. *n.*

sol•id (sol′id) **1** not a liquid or a gas: *Water becomes solid when it freezes.* **2** a substance that is not a liquid or a gas: *Iron, wood, and ice are solids.* **3** hard; firm: *They were glad to leave the boat and stand on solid ground.* **4** strongly made or put together: *This is not a very solid table.* **5** not hollow: *a solid chocolate egg.* **6** reliable and steady: *solid support, solid citizens.* **7** unbroken: *a solid hour, a solid row of houses. The cloth is a solid blue.* **8** in mathematics, a three-dimensional figure: *A cube is a solid.* 1, 3–7 *adj.,* 2, 8 *n.* **—so•lid′i•fy′,** *v.*
—so•lid′i•ty, *n.*

sol•i•dar•i•ty (sol′ə der′ə tē) unity; support for one another; a common bond: *The week we all spent at soccer camp gave us a sense of solidarity.* *n.*

sol•i•taire (sol′ə ter′ *or* sol′ə ter′) **1** a card game you play by yourself. **2** a diamond or other gem set by itself. *n.*

sol•i•tar•y (sol′ə ter′ē) **1** alone; single; only: *A solitary rider was seen in the distance.* **2** away from people; lonely: *He leads a solitary life in his hut in the mountains.* *adj.*

sol•i•tude (sol′ə tyūd′ *or* sol′ə tūd′) the condition of being alone: *She likes company and hates solitude.* *n.*

so•lo (sō′lō) **1** a piece of music for one voice or instrument: *a piano solo. She sang three solos.* **2** by or for one voice or instrument: *a solo part.* **3** with no partner, teacher, etc.; alone: *to fly solo* (*adv.*), *a solo flight* (*adj.*). 1 *n., pl.* **so•los;** 2, 3 *adj.,* 3 *adv.* **—so′lo•ist,** *n.*

sol•stice (sōl′stis *or* sol′stis) either of the two times in the year when the sun is farthest from the equator. In the Northern Hemisphere, June 21 or 22, the **summer solstice,** is the longest day of the year and December 21 or 22, the **winter solstice,** is the shortest. *n.*

a bat	e bed	i bid	o pot	u cup	th thin
ā cake	ē me	ī bite	ō go	ū rude	ᴛʜ then
ȧ bar	ə about	ər over	ȯ for	u̇ put	zh measure

sol•u•ble (sol′yə bəl) **1** that can be dissolved: *Salt is soluble in water; oil is not.* **2** that can be solved: *This puzzle is not soluble!* *adj.* **—sol′u•bil′i•ty,** *n.*

so•lu•tion (sə lū′shən) **1** an answer; an explanation that solves a problem: *The police are seeking a solution of the crime.* **2** a mixture formed by dissolving; tea with sugar in it is a solution. The dissolved substance is called the **solute** (sol′yūt). **3** the condition of being dissolved: *Sugar can be held in solution in water.* *n.*

solve (solv) find or be the answer to; clear up or explain: *The mystery was never solved. Solve all the division problems on page 47.* *v.,* **solved, solv•ing.**

sol•vent (sol′vənt) a substance, usually a liquid, that can dissolve other substances: *Gasoline is a solvent that removes grease.* *n.*

som•bre (som′bər) gloomy; dismal: *A grey, sombre winter day. It was a sombre room with dark furniture and heavy black curtains.* **Somber** is another spelling. *adj.*

som•brer•o (som brer′ō) a broad-brimmed hat worn in Spain, Mexico, and other Spanish-speaking countries. *n., pl.* **som•brer•os.**

some (sum) **1** a certain number or amount that is not mentioned: *Some dogs are big; others are small. Drink some milk. They left the city some years ago* (*adj.*). *She ate some and threw the rest away. Some say she is a genius* (*pron.*). **2** a particular one that is not known: *Can't you find some kind person who will help you? Some other time I will stay longer.* **3** about: *Some twenty people came.* 1, 2 *adj.,* 1 *pron.,* 3 *adv.*

CONFUSABLES ....some

some means "a quantity of": *Some of us are not going to the party.*

sum means "amount" or "number": *You owe me the sum of two dollars.*

–some *a suffix meaning:* **1** tending to or liking, as in *adventuresome, meddlesome.* **2** a group of. A *foursome* is a group of four.

some•body (sum′bud′ē, sum′bod′ē, *or* sum′bə dē) **1** a person not known or not named: *Somebody took my pen.* **Someone** means the same. **2** an important person: *She thinks she's somebody because she's rich.* 1 *pron.,* 2 *n.*

some•day (sum′dā′) at some future time. *adv.*

some•how (sum′hou′) in a way not known or not described; one way or another: *I'll do it somehow.* *adv.*

some•one (sum′wun′) a person not known or not named; some person: *Someone has to lock up the house.* **Somebody** means the same. *pron.*

some•place (sum′plās′) in or to some place; somewhere. *adv.*

som•er•sault (sum′ər solt′) **1** a complete roll of your body, forward or backward, bringing your feet over your head. **2** to roll in this way. 1 *n.,* 2 *v.*

some•thing (sum′thing′) **1** a certain thing not named or not known: *I'm sure I've forgotten something.* **2** a certain amount; a little: *There is something of her father in her smile* (*n.*). *She is something like her father* (*adv.*). **3** a special or remarkable thing or person: *Wouldn't it be something if we could fly?* 1–3 *n.,* 2 *adv.*

some•time (sum′tīm′) **1** at one time or another: *Drop in sometime.* **2** at a certain point in time that is not known or named: *It happened sometime last March.* *adv.*

USING WORDS .....sometime

The words **sometime**, **sometimes**, and **some time** look like almost the same words, but they have different meanings.
Sometime means "at an unstated time": *I will see you sometime tomorrow.*
Sometimes means "at times": *I sometimes get home late if the weather is bad.*
Some time means "a period of time": *I haven't seen her for some time.*

some•times (sum′tīmz′) now and then; at times: *They come to visit sometimes.* *adv.*

some•what (sum′wut′ *or* sum′hwut′) a certain amount, worth noticing but not a lot: *He has changed somewhat since we last saw him.* *adv.*

some•where (sum′wer′ *or* sum′hwer′) in or to some place; in or to one place or another: *I must have left it somewhere.* *adv.*

son (sun) **1** a boy or man in relation to either or both of his parents. **2** a boy or man thought of as coming from a particular place or time or influenced by some force: *a native son of England, sons of liberty.* *n.*

CONFUSABLES ....son

son means "male child": *They called their son Elvis.*

sun means "star that the earth moves round": *The sun is hot today.*

Sonar

Sonar uses sound and echoes to detect objects in water. The acronym sonar is made from sound navigation and ranging. (Ranging means measuring distance.)

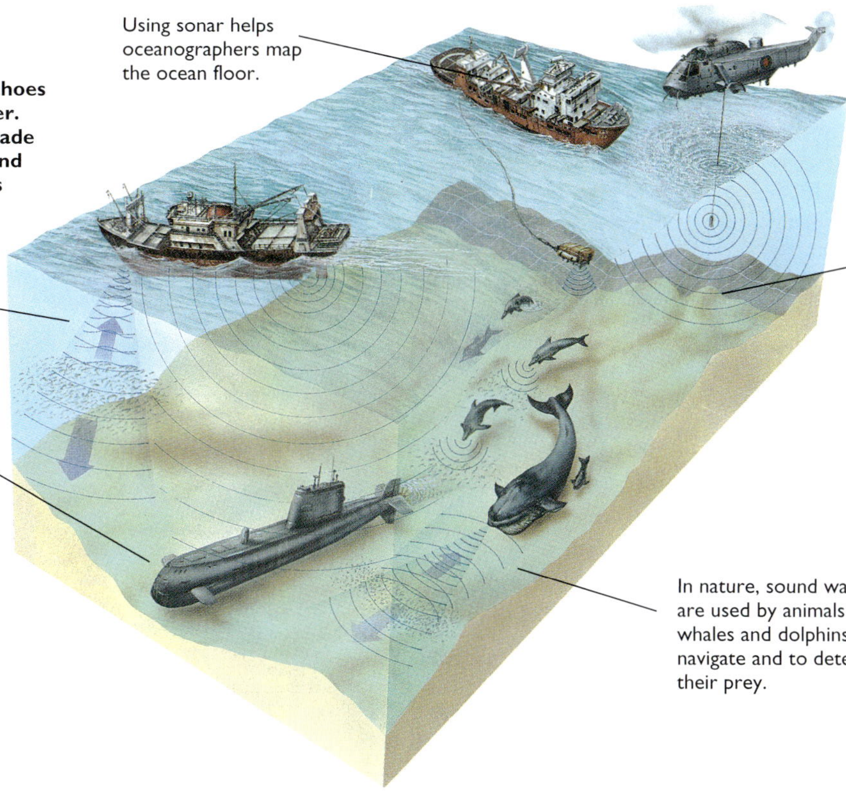

so·nar (sō′när) a device for finding objects under water by bouncing sound waves off them. *n.*

song (sông) **1** a piece of music, especially one with words for singing. **2** singing or a sound like singing: *The canary burst into song.* **3** beautiful poetry. *n.*

song·bird (sông′bėrd′) a bird that sings, especially a small perching bird such as a finch or blackbird. *n.*

sonic boom (son′ik büm′) a loud explosive sound heard by people on the ground when an aircraft travels faster than the speed of sound.

son–in–law (sun′in lo′) the husband of a person's daughter. *n., pl.* **sons-in-law.**

so·no·rous (son′ə rəs *or* sō′nə rəs) making or having a loud, full, rich sound: *a sonorous voice.* *adj.*

soon (sün) **1** in a short time; before long: *I will see you again soon.* **2** before the expected time; early: *Why have you come so soon?* **3** willingly: *I would just as soon stay home as go to a bad movie.* *adv.*
as soon as, right away when: *I'll call as soon as I arrive.*

soot (su̇t) a black, powdery substance made up mostly of carbon. It forms part of the smoke from something burning. *n.* —**soot′y,** *adj.*

soothe (süᴛʜ) **1** comfort; make calm or quiet: *The mother soothed the crying child.* A **soother** is another name for a baby's pacifier. **2** make less painful: *Heat soothed her aching muscles.* *v.,* **soothed, sooth·ing.**

sop (sop)
sop up, wipe or mop up a spill: *Please sop up that water with a cloth.*
sopping wet, soaked; drenched. *v.,* **sopped, sop·ping.**

so·phis·ti·cat·ed (sə fis′tə kā′tid) **1** modern and complicated or fashionable: *a sophisticated style of dress, sophisticated computers.* **2** experienced in worldly ways; informed and aware. **3** too elegant or clever to bother with natural, simple things and people. *adj.*

so·pran·o (sə pran′ō) **1** the highest range of notes sung by women and boys. **2** having this range: *a soprano voice.* **3** a singer or instrument with this range, or the part written for it in a song: *Our choir has eight sopranos. You play the soprano.* 1, 3 *n., pl.* **so·pran·os;** 2 *adj.*

sor·cer·y (sôr′sə rē) magic, especially harmful magic in stories; witchcraft: *The prince had been changed into a lion by sorcery.* A man who does sorcery is a **sorcerer;** a woman is a **sorceress.** *n., pl.* **sor·cer·ies.**

a **bat**	e **bed**	i **bid**	o **pot**	u **cup**	th **thin**
ā **cake**	ē **me**	ī **bite**	ō **go**	ü **rude**	ᴛʜ **then**
ä **bar**	ə **about**	ər **over**	ô **for**	u̇ **put**	zh **measure**

Sound

The loudness of sound is measured in decibels (dB). Noise louder than 140 dB can cause pain and damage hearing.

sore (sôr) 1 painful; aching or hurting: *a sore finger. Their suffering made her heart sore.* 2 a painful place on the body where the skin or flesh is broken or bruised. 3 *Informal.* angry: *She is sore at you for messing up the game.* 4 causing pain or anger: *Their defeat at the tournament is a sore subject for the team.* 1, 3, 4 *adj.,* **sor·er, sor·est;** 2 *n.* **—sore′ness,** *n.*

sore·ly (sôr′lē) a formal or poetic word for "badly" or "very much": *sorely needed. He is sorely missed.* *adv.*

sor·row (sò′rō) 1 deep sadness or regret: *She felt sorrow at the loss of her kitten.* 2 something that causes sadness; trouble or misfortune: *Her sorrows have aged her.* 3 feel or show sadness: *He sorrowed over his lost friend.* 1, 2 *n.,* 3 *v.* **—sor′row·ful,** *adj.*

sor·ry (sò′rē) 1 feeling bad about something you have done or something that has happened: *I am sorry that you are sick. We are sorry that he cannot come to the party.* 2 miserable; poor; pitiful: *The badly injured cat was a sorry sight.* *adj.,* **sor·ri·er, sor·ri·est.**
feel sorry for, have pity on: *Don't feel sorry for me; I can manage just fine.*

sort (sôrt) 1 kind; type: *What sort of work does he do? She is not the sort of person to tell tales.* 2 group things together by kinds or types; arrange in order: *Sort these cards according to their colours.* 1 *n.,* 2 *v.*
out of sorts, grumpy.
sort of, *Informal.* in a way: *In spite of her faults I sort of like her.*
sort out, a find and separate from the rest: *The farmer sorted out the best apples for eating.* **b** figure out or solve something complicated: *Can you sort out this problem?*

SOS (es′ō′es′) 1 a call for help using the letters *s o s* of the international Morse code (• • • – – –• • •), in radio communication by ships, aircraft, and so on. 2 *Informal.* any urgent call for help. *n.*

sought (sot) the past tense and past participle of **seek:** *For days she sought a safe hiding place. I have sought to do my best.* *v.*

soul (sōl) 1 the spiritual part of a person that loves, chooses, wants, and so on, thought of as separate from the body. Many religions believe that the soul lives on forever after the body dies. 2 a person: *Don't tell a soul.* 3 energy, life, or feeling: *Her singing has no soul.* *n.* **—soul′ful,** *adj.* **—soul′less,** *adj.*

sound[1] (sound) 1 what you hear: *the sound of music, the sound of thunder.* You hear sounds when vibrations strike your ear. 2 make or have a certain sound: *The wind sounds like a wolf howling. "See" and "sea" sound alike.* 3 seem: *That excuse sounds ridiculous.* 4 the part of a TV show, movie, computer game, etc. that can be heard: *Turn off the sound.* A **sound card** in a computer lets you hear sounds stored in the computer. 5 cause to be heard; cause to make a sound: *Sound the alarm! The driver sounded the horn.* 1, 4 *n.,* 2, 3, 5 *v.* **—sound′less,** *adj.*
sound out, read a word slowly by connecting the letters with their sounds one by one.

sound[2] (sound) 1 healthy: *a sound body and mind.* 2 solid and strong: *sound walls.* 3 right; reasonable: *a sound argument, sound advice.* 4 thorough; thoroughly: *a sound scolding (adj.). He was sound asleep (adv.).* 1–4 *adj.,* 4 *adv.* **—sound′ly,** *adv.* **—sound′ness,** *n.*

sound[3] (sound) measure the depth of water. *v.*
sound out, try to find out a person's thoughts or feelings about something: *They sounded out the principal on the idea of a winter carnival.*

sound[4] (sound) a long, narrow strip of water joining two larger bodies of water, reaching into the land, or separating an island from the mainland: *Queen Charlotte Sound, Howe Sound.* *n.*

sound barrier (sound′ ber′ ē ər) the sharp rise in air resistance met by an aircraft or other flying object as it nears the speed of sound (about 1200 km/h at sea level).

sound effects (sound′ i feks′) the sounds of thunder, rain, traffic, and so on, produced artificially for a play, movie, or radio or TV program.

sound·proof (sound′prūf′) **1** not letting sound pass through: *a soundproof room or ceiling.* **2** make soundproof: *Mother soundproofed the den.* 1 *adj.,* 2 *v.*

sound·scape (sound′skāp′) a combination of sounds heard in a certain environment: *the soundscape of a lively playground. The soundscape of the movie was very scary.* *n.*

sound track (sound′ trak′) a recording of the talking, music, and sound effects of a movie. **Soundtrack** is another spelling.

soup (sūp) a liquid food made by boiling meat, vegetables, and so on with seasonings. *n.*

sour (sour) **1** having a taste like vinegar or lemon juice; sharp and biting: *This green fruit is sour.* **2** spoiled: *sour milk.* **3** bad-tempered: *a sour face, a sour remark.* A grouchy person is a **sourpuss.** **4** make or become sour: *The milk soured in the heat.* 1–3 *adj.,* 4 *v.*
sour grapes, an attitude of pretending you don't want something just because you can't have it.

source (sȯrs) the person, place, or thing that something else comes from or is taken from: *We get news from many sources. Eggs are a source of protein.* *n.*

sour cream (sour′ krēm′) thick, smooth cream that has been made sour by adding certain bacteria. It is eaten with many other foods to add flavour.

sour·dough (sour′dō′) **1** dough containing active yeast. You save a bit from each baking to use for the next. Prospectors and pioneers used it for making bread so they didn't need to keep getting fresh yeast. **2** a prospector or pioneer in northwestern Canada or Alaska. *n.*

south (south) **1** the direction to your left as you face the setting sun; the direction opposite to north. **2** toward or from the south: *the south exit, a warm south wind* (*adj.*). *Drive south 40 km* (*adv.*). **3 South,** the south part of the world or of some country, especially the United States. 1, 3 *n.,* 2 *adv. or adj.*
—south′ern, *adj.* **—south′er·ly,** *adj.*

South America (south′ ə mer′ə kə) a continent in the southern half of the western hemisphere, south of North America and joined to it by a narrow piece of land. The Atlantic Ocean is on the east and the Pacific is on the west. **—South′ A·mer′i·can.**

south·east (sou′thēst′) **1** the direction halfway between south and east. **2** a place that lies in this direction. **3** of, at, in, to, toward, or from the southeast: *a southeast wind* (*adj.*). *She walked southeast* (*adv.*). 1, 2 *n.,* 3 *adj. or adv.* **—south′east′ern,** *adj.*

South Pole (south′ pōl′) the southern end of the earth's axis.

south·ward (south′wərd) toward the south; south: *He walked southward* (*adv.*). *The orchard is on the southward slope of the hill* (*adj.*). **Southwards** is another form for the adverb. *adv. or adj.*

south·west (south′west′) **1** the direction halfway between south and west. **2** a place that lies in this direction. **3** of, at, in, to, toward, or from the southwest: *a southwest wind* (*adj.*). *They walked southwest* (*adv.*). 1, 2 *n.,* 3 *adj. or adv.* **—south′west′ern,** *adj.*

sou·ve·nir (sū′və nēr′ *or* sū′və nēr′) something given or kept as a remembrance: *Our aunt bought me cowboy boots as a souvenir of my holiday in Alberta.* *n.*

sou·vla·ki (sū vlȧ′kē) cubes of meat cooked on a skewer over an open flame and then eaten on a bun or with rice and salad. *n.*

sou'·west·er (sou′wes′tər) a waterproof hat with a broad brim at the back to protect the neck. **Southwester** (south′wes′tər) is another spelling. *n.*

sov·er·eign (sov′rən) **1** above all others; supreme: *a sovereign ruler. Character is of sovereign importance.* **2** a supreme ruler; a king, queen, emperor, etc.: *Queen Victoria was the British sovereign from 1837 to 1901.* **3** not controlled by some other nation; independent: *Iceland is a sovereign state.* 1, 3 *adj.,* 2 *n.*
—sov′er·eign·ty, *n.*

sow¹ (sō) scatter or plant seeds in the ground: *to sow wheat in spring. The farmer sowed the field with corn.* *v.,* **sowed, sown** or **sowed, sow·ing.**

sow² (sou) a fully grown female pig. *n.*

soy·bean (soi′bēn′) a bean grown in many places which is very high in protein. Tofu and **soy sauce,** a dark, salty sauce used on food, are made from soybeans. *n.*

spa (spȧ) **1** a fitness resort, especially one that has mineral springs. **2** a hot tub, or any fitness club, gym, etc. with a hot tub. *n.*

a bat	e bed	i bid	o pot	u cup	th thin
ā cake	ē me	ī bite	ō go	ū rude	ᴛʜ then
ȧ bar	ə about	ər over	ȯ for	u̇ put	zh measure

Spacecraft

Spacecraft that stay in orbit around the earth are called satellites. These usually carry radio transmitters, and beam back signals gathered by the instruments on board. Many orbiting satellites provide us with information about outer space. Rosat is recording X-ray sources from dim stars. The International Ultraviolet Explorer (IUE) studies ultraviolet light from stars. The Infra-Red Astronomy Satellite (IRAS) studies infrared radiation.

space (spās) 1 the open area that stretches in all directions and contains all physical objects. The "empty" space between objects on earth is really filled with air. **Outer space** is the airless area beyond our atmosphere, where the stars and planets are. 2 a limited place or area for something; room: *This brick fits a space 20 cm by 6 cm by 10 cm. Is there space in the car for another person?* 3 a blank or empty area: *Leave a space after each name.* 4 separate by spaces: *Space your words evenly in writing.* Pressing the **space bar** on a keyboard moves the cursor one character ahead. 5 a certain distance or length of time: *The road is bad for a space of 5 km. She didn't see him for a space of two years.* 1–3, 5 *n.*, 4 *v.*, **spaced, spac·ing.**

space age (spās′ āj′) the current period of history, starting with the first trip into outer space.

space·craft (spās′kraft′) any vehicle used to fly in or probe outer space, with or without people on board. *n.*

space·ship (spās′ship′) a vehicle designed to carry people in outer space. *n.*

space shuttle (spās′ shut′əl) a spacecraft used more than once to carry people and materials from earth to a space station and back. It looks like an airplane with two rockets attached which carry it into space.

space station (spās′ stā′shən) a large, artificial earth satellite that people can live on while building or fixing spacecraft or doing experiments in outer space.

space·suit (spās′sūt′) an airtight suit that lets astronauts breathe and work in space. It protects them from radiation, supplies air, and keeps a constant safe temperature inside. *n.*

spa·cious (spā′shəs) having a lot of space; roomy: *a spacious home.* *adj.*

spade[1] (spād) a digging tool with a long handle and a flattish blade that you press into the ground with your foot; a garden shovel. *n.* —**spade′ful,** *n.*
call a spade a spade, speak plainly and honestly.

spade[2] (spād) 1 a playing card marked with one or more black figures like this: ♠ 2 **spades,** *pl.* the suit of such playing cards. *n.*

spa·ghet·ti (spə get′ē) pasta shaped into long, very thin sticks that you cook in water. *n.*

span (span) 1 reach from one side to the other: *A bridge spanned the river.* 2 the distance across, from edge to edge: *The bridge has a span of 40 m.* A bird's **wingspan** is the distance from wingtip to wingtip. 3 a length of time: *a span of 15 years.* Your **lifespan** is the length of your life. 1 *v.*, **spanned, span·ning;** 2, 3 *n.*

span·gle (spang′gəl) **1** a small piece of glittering material: *The dress was decorated with spangles.* **2** decorate with spangles: *The night sky was spangled with stars.* 1 *n.,* 2 *v.,* **span·gled, span·gling.**

span·iel (span′yəl) a gentle, affectionate breed of dog, usually of small or medium size, with long, silky hair and drooping ears. *n.*

spank (spangk) **1** strike with the open hand as a punishment. **2** a slap with the open hand as punishment. 1 *v.,* 2 *n.* **—spank′ing,** *n.*

spare (sper) **1** extra: *a spare tire* (*adj.*). *I lost my pen; do you have a spare* (*n.*)? **2** give up or make available for use: *I have no money to spare. Mom couldn't spare the computer so I had to write my story by hand.* **4** show mercy to; refrain from hurting or killing: *She spared her enemy.* **5** save someone the bother of: *I'll mail this and spare you a trip to the post office.* **6** thin; lean: *The storekeeper was a tall, spare man.* 1, 6 *adj.,* **spar·er, spar·est;** 2 *n.,* 3–5 *v.,* **spared, spar·ing.**
spare time, free time.

spar·ing (sper′ing) using as little as possible: *Be sparing with the sugar.* *adj.* **—spar′ing·ly,** *adv.*

spark (spȧrk) **1** a tiny bit of fire or burning material: *The burning wood threw off sparks.* **2** a flash given off when electricity jumps across an open space. An electric spark produced by a **spark plug** explodes the gas in a car engine. **3** a flash; gleam: *We saw a spark of light through the trees.* **4** send out sparks. **5** stir up; start or set off: *to spark a revolt.* 1–3 *n.,* 4, 5 *v.*

spar·kle (spȧr′kəl) **1** shine; glitter; flash: *The gems sparkled* (*v.*). *I like the sparkle of her eyes* (*n.*). A **sparkler** is a piece of stiff wire coated with a substance that throws off showers of sparks when lit. **2** be slightly fizzy: *sparkling drinks.* 1, 2 *v.,* **spar·kled, spar·kling;** 1 *n.*

spar·row (sper′ō) a small songbird with mostly brown and grey streaked feathers. The white-throated sparrow is common across most of Canada. *n.*

sparse (spȧrs) thinly scattered here and there: *sparse hair.* *adj.,* **spars·er, spars·est.** **—sparse′ly,** *adv.*

spasm (spaz′əm) **1** a sudden, unwanted muscle contraction, like a cramp or convulsion: *A spasm in his leg made him fall.* **2** a sudden, short spell of uncontrolled activity: *a spasm of temper, a coughing spasm.* *n.*

spat[1] (spat) a slight quarrel. *n.*

spat[2] (spat) a past tense and past participle of **spit[1]**: *The cat spat at the dog.* *v.*

spat·ter (spat′ər) **1** splash hard against a surface in blobs or large drops: *to spatter mud. Rain spattered on the sidewalk.* **2** blobs or drops splashed against something: *splatters of paint on the floor.* 1 *v.,* 2 *n.*

spat·u·la (spach′ə lə) a tool with a broad, flat blade. Spatulas are used for spreading thick substances like cake icing or putty, and for lifting flat foods like fried eggs, pancakes, or hamburgers. *n.*

spawn (spon) **1** the eggs of fish, frogs, shellfish, and so on. **2** young fish, frogs, etc. when newly hatched from these eggs. **3** produce eggs: *Salmon spawn in the rivers of British Columbia.* **4** bring into being, especially in large numbers: *The computer has spawned many useful inventions.* 1, 2 *n.,* 3, 4 *v.*

speak (spēk) **1** say words; talk: *A cat cannot speak. Speak distinctly.* **2** give a public talk: *Mr. Giani will be speaking at the graduation ceremony.* **3** tell; express; make known: *Speak the truth. Her eyes spoke her sorrow.* **4** know a language: *Do you speak French?* *v.,* **spoke, spo·ken, speak·ing.**
speak for, express the opinions of; act as speaker for: *She spoke for the group that wanted a picnic.*
speak out or **speak up,** **a** speak loudly and clearly. **b** speak boldly and publicly: *to speak out against injustice. The students all spoke up in favour of our contest idea.*
to speak of, worth mentioning: *no complaints to speak of.*

speak·er (spē′kər) **1** a person who speaks, especially to an audience. **2** **Speaker,** a person officially in charge of keeping order in a discussion: *the Speaker of the House of Commons.* **3** a device that changes the electrical signals from a radio, CD player, computer, etc. into sounds. It is also called a **loudspeaker.** *n.*

speak·er·phone (spē′kər fōn′) a telephone that has a microphone and loudspeaker in it. You can use it without having to put it next to your face, so that more than one person can use it at once. *n.*

spear (spēr) **1** a weapon with a long shaft and sharp, pointed head. **2** pierce or stab with a spear, or with any sharp thing: *She speared a wiener with the fork.* 1 *n.,* 2 *v.*

spear·mint (spēr′mint′) a kind of mint flavour that is sweeter than peppermint, used to flavour candies, toothpaste, and chewing gum. It comes from the leaves of a plant or is made artificially. *n.*

a bat	e bed	i bid	o pot	u cup	th thin
ā cake	ē me	ī bite	ō go	ū rude	ᴛʜ then
ȧ bar	ə about	ər over	ȯ for	u̇ put	zh measure

spe·cial (spesh′əl) 1 of a particular kind, different from others; for or having to do with a particular person, purpose, or thing: *This bicycle has a special frame for racing. Each animal has its own special character.* 2 singled out as more important, valuable, or remarkable than most: *a special friend, a special favourite.* 3 a product featured as a bargain in a store or restaurant: *a weekend special on stereos. The lunch special includes soup.* 4 a TV show that is not part of the regular daily or weekly programming. 1, 2 *adj.,* 3, 4 *n.* **—spe′cial·ly,** *adv.*

special effects (spesh′əl i fekts′) complicated and unusual images or sounds made for a movie, video, or TV program, usually with the help of computers. **F/X** is the abbreviation for these effects.

spe·cial·ist (spesh′ə list) a person who is an expert in only one thing: *Dr. Nakamura is a specialist in diseases of the nose and throat.* *n.*

spe·cial·ize (spesh′ə līz′) 1 be or become an expert in one particular thing: *This chef specializes in Thai food.* 2 in the theory of evolution, develop so as to suit a special purpose or environment: *A woodpecker's bill is specialized for digging insects out of trees.* *v.,* **spe·cial·ized, spe·cial·iz·ing. —spe′cial·i·za′tion,** *n.*

spe·cial·ty (spesh′əl tē) 1 something that a person is an expert in: *Computer programming is her specialty.* 2 the main product, service, or feature offered by a store, restaurant, business, etc.: *This store makes a specialty of children's clothes.* *n., pl.* **spe·cial·ties.**

spe·cies (spē′shēz *or* spē′sēz) a group of animals or plants sharing certain permanent characteristics, distinct from all other groups: *Wheat is a species of grass. The grizzly and the black bear are two species of bear.* A **threatened species** is one that is becoming rare; an **endangered species** is so rare that it will soon be extinct unless strong measures are taken. *n., pl.* **spe·cies.**

spe·cif·ic (spə sif′ik) 1 definite; exact; particular: *a specific amount, specific instructions.* 2 **specifics,** *pl.* details. *adj.* **—spe·cif′i·cal·ly,** *adv.*

spec·i·fy (spes′ə fī′) 1 mention or name definitely: *Did you specify any particular time for us to call?* 2 give specific instructions: *She delivered the paper as specified.* A list of detailed facts or instructions about something are **specifications.** *v.,* **spec·i·fied, spec·i·fy·ing.**

spec·i·men (spes′ə mən) one of a certain group of things, taken to show what the others are like; a sample: *She collects specimens of all kinds of rocks and minerals.* *n.*

speck (spek) 1 a tiny spot: *The bird looked like a speck in the distance.* 2 a tiny bit of something: *I have a speck in my eye.* *n.*

speck·le (spek′əl) 1 one of many small spots or marks: *This hen is grey with white speckles.* 2 mark with speckles: *white wallpaper speckled with blue.* 1 *n.,* 2 *v.,* **speck·led, speck·ling.**

spec·ta·cle (spek′tə kəl) 1 a remarkable sight: *The kitten and the big dog playing together made a charming spectacle. A fight is an ugly spectacle.* 2 **spectacles,** *pl.* an old-fashioned word for "eyeglasses." *n.*
make a spectacle of, display in an embarrassing way.

spec·tac·u·lar (spek tak′yə lər) 1 amazing to look at; impressive; sensational: *spectacular scenery, spectacular fireworks.* 2 an impressive show or public event: *a TV spectacular.* 1 *adj.,* 2 *n.*

spec·ta·tor (spek′tā tər) a person who looks on without taking part: *spectators at a game.* *n.*

spec·tre (spek′tər) ghost. **Specter** is another spelling. *n.* **—spec′tral,** *adj.*

spec·trum (spek′trəm) the band of colours formed when a beam of light passes through a prism, curtain of water droplets, etc., separating the different wavelengths. A rainbow has all the colours of the spectrum: red, orange, yellow, green, blue, indigo, and violet. *n., pl.* **spec·tra** (spek′trə) or **spec·trums.**

spec·u·late (spek′yə lāt′) 1 think or talk about something you can't know for sure; imagine or state possibilities: *to speculate about life on other planets.* 2 buy or sell at a big risk, hoping to profit from future price changes. *v.,* **spec·u·lat·ed, spec·u·lat·ing. —spec′u·la′tion,** *n.* **—spec′u·la′tor,** *n.*

speech (spēch) 1 the act or manner of speaking: *She just squeezed my hand—speech was unnecessary. His speech showed that he was Irish.* 2 a public talk: *The mayor made a speech after winning the election.* 3 language: *Her native speech was French.* *n.* **—speech′less,** *adj.*

🍁 **Speech from the Throne** (spēch′ frum ᴛʜə thrōn′) a general statement of a government's goals for a new session of parliament. It is read publicly by the Governor General as the Queen's or King's representative.

speed (spēd) 1 fast movement; the fact of being fast: *Speed is the cheetah's weapon.* 2 go fast or cause to go fast: *The boat sped over the water. Your help will speed the work.* 3 how fast something is moving: *high speed, low speed.* 4 a gear, setting, etc. that determines how fast a thing goes: *The blender has four speeds.* 5 drive faster than the law allows: *She was fined for speeding.* The **speed limit** is the top speed allowed. 1, 3, 4 *n.,* 2, 5 *v.,* **sped** or **speed·ed, speed·ing. —speed′y,** *adj.* **—speed′i·ly,** *adv.*
speed up, go or cause to go faster.

speed·om·e·ter (spi dom′ə tər) an instrument that shows how fast a vehicle is moving. *n.*

spell¹ (spel) **1** write or say the letters of a word: *You spelled this word wrong.* **2** write or say the letters of a word correctly and in order: *Can you spell my name?* A book of lessons about spelling is a **speller.** A **spelling bee** is a spelling contest. ▶ See the *Grammar and Usage Mini-Guide.* **3** form a word: *C-a-t spells "cat."* **4** mean: *Clouds spell rain.* *v.,* **spelled** or **spelt, spell·ing.**

Grammar ✓Check . . . . . . spelling

The **spelling** of English words can be confusing. When you have trouble remembering how to spell a word, try some of these strategies:

- Playing around with the word will help you to remember it: say it out loud, picture the letters in your head, write it down in fancy lettering.
- Think of a memory trick to help you remember hard words. For example, you can remember that *cereal* starts with *c* by remembering the sentence *I like **c**ream on my **c**ereal.*
- Make your own dictionary of words you misspell often, and check it whenever you write.
- For words with silent letters or double letters, pronounce *all* the letters in your head: *k-now, mis-spell.*
- Look for similar spelling patterns: *sight - night - fright - light; bite - kite - quite.*
- Look for a smaller word inside a big word: *argu**ment**; tra**ged**y.*

spell² (spel) **1** in stories, a word or set of words with magic power. **2** a magical effect; enchantment: *The fairy cast a spell on the prince to make him invisible.* *n.*
under a spell, controlled by a spell; enchanted: *Her story kept us under a spell.* **Spellbound** means the same thing.

spell³ (spel) a period or time of anything: *a coughing spell, a long spell of rainy weather.* *n.*

spell–check (spel′chek′) a check you run on a computer file to make sure everything is spelled correctly, using a special program called a **spell-checker.** The program is normally built into your writing software.

spend (spend) **1** pay out money: *She spent $12 on the T-shirt.* A person who spends too much money is a **spendthrift.** **2** use; use up: *to spend time or energy.* If you are **spent** you are tired. *v.,* **spent, spend·ing.**

sperm (spərm) a special cell from the body of a man or male animal that develops into a baby if it is joined with an egg cell from a female. Sperm cells contain information that determines what the new person or animal will be like. *n., pl.* **sperm.**

sperm whale (spərm′ wāl′) a large whale with a rectangular head and large teeth, often hunted in the past for its oil and blubber.

spew (spyū) flow or cause to flow out in large amounts, especially something harmful or ugly: *The volcano spewed molten lava down the mountainside. Polluted water spewed from the pipe into the lake.* *v.*

sphere (sfēr) **1** in geometry, a round solid figure bounded by a surface that is at all points equally distant from the centre. **2** an object approximately like this in form; a ball or globe. The earth is a sphere. **3** a certain area of activity or control: *This writer has a wide sphere of influence.* *n.* **—spher′i·cal** (sfer′ə kəl), *adj.*

sphinx (sfingks) a statue of a lion's body with the head of a person. There are many sphinxes in Egypt. *n.*

spice (spīs) **1** something used to flavour food, made from any part of a plant. Garlic, pepper, cinnamon, cloves, ginger, and nutmeg are common spices. **2** put spices in; season: *She spiced the eggnog with nutmeg.* 1 *n.,* 2 *v.,* **spiced, spic·ing.** **—spic′y,** *adj.*

spick–and–span (spik′ən span′) fresh, neat, and perfectly clean. *adj.*

spi·der (spī′dər) a small animal, a bit like an insect but with eight legs, two body parts, and no wings. Many spiders spin webs to catch insects for food. *n.*

spied (spīd) the past tense and past participle of **spy:** *The sailor spied land in the distance.* *v.*

a bat	e bed	i bid	o pot	u cup	th thin
ā cake	ē me	ī bite	ō go	ū rude	ᴛʜ then
à bar	ə about	ər over	ȯ for	ů put	zh measure

spig·ot (spig′ət) a spout you can open and close like a tap. *n.*

spike (spīk) **1** a large, strong nail. **2** a pointed part or piece: *Soccer players wear shoes with spikes on the soles.* **3** put spikes on or form into spikes: *He spikes his hair.* **4** pierce with a spike. 1, 2 *n.*, 3, 4 *v.*, **spiked, spik·ing.**

spile (spīl) **1** a peg plugging the small hole of a barrel or cask. **2** a spout hammered into a maple tree to draw out the sap. *n.*

spill (spil) **1** pour or let pour, fall, or splash out of a container by accident: *to spill milk, to spill salt.* **2** the fact of spilling or the material spilled: *Wipe up that spill.* **3** *Informal.* cause to fall: *The horse spilled its rider.* **4** *Informal.* a fall: *She took a bad spill on the ice.* 1, 3 *v.*, **spilled** or **spilt, spill·ing;** 2, 4 *n.*
spill the beans, let out a secret.

spin (spin) **1** turn around rapidly: *The skaters spun on the ice. The boy spun the wheels of his bicycle.* **2 a** a rapid turning: *Give the wheel a spin.* **b** a rapid turning around of an airplane as it falls. **3** feel dizzy: *My head is spinning.* **4** a short ride or drive for fun: *Get your bike and come for a spin with me.* **5** pull and twist cotton, wool, or other fibre into thread. A **spinning wheel** is a simple machine with a large wheel used for this in earlier times. **6** make a thread, web, or cocoon by giving out from the body a sticky material that hardens: *A spider spins a web.* **7** tell: *to spin a tale.* 1, 3, 5–7 *v.*, **spun, spin·ning;** 2, 4 *n.*

spin·ach (spin′ich) a plant with green leaves which are used as a vegetable. *n.*

spi·nal (spī′nəl) to do with the spine or backbone. The **spinal column** is made up of many small bones; it holds the **spinal cord,** a thick nerve coming down from the brain and branching off to all parts of the body. *adj.*

spin·dle (spin′dəl) any rod or pin that turns around or holds something that turns. *n.*

spin·dly (spin′dlē) so long and thin that it cannot support much weight: *spindly legs.* *adj.*, **spin·dli·er, spin·dli·est.**

spine (spīn) **1** backbone. **2** courage; moral strength. **3** a stiff, sharp-pointed growth on a plant or animal. Cactuses and porcupines have spines. *n.*
—spine′less, *adj.* **—spin′y,** *adj.*

spin·off or **spin–off** (spin′of′) **1** a useful side effect or by-product: *One of the spinoffs of the recycling program has been the creation of many new jobs.* **2** a movie, book, TV program, toy, etc. that purposely uses some of the same elements already used in another successful product: *This board game is a spinoff from the new movie.* *n.*

spi·ral (spī′rəl) **1** a curve that winds around and around as it goes up or down, like the stripe on a candy cane; a coil. **2** having this shape: *a spiral staircase.* **3** move in a spiral: *The flaming airplane spiralled to earth.* 1 *n.*, 2 *adj.*, 3 *v.*, **spi·ralled** or **spi·raled, spi·ral·ling** or **spi·ral·ing.**

spire (spīr) a tall, pointed top part on a tower. *n.*

spir·it (spir′it) **1** the part of a person that loves, wants, chooses, worships, and so on, thought of as separate from the body. Many religions teach that at death the spirit leaves the body and lives on forever. **2** a supernatural being such as a ghost or angel. **3** Often, **spirits,** *pl.* mood or attitude: *He is in good spirits. She took my remark in a spirit of fun.* **4** a person; personality: *She is a brave spirit. He was one of the leading spirits of the revolution.* **5** determination and enthusiasm: *Our team showed a lot of spirit.* **6** carry off secretly or mysteriously: *The painting has been spirited away.* **7** Often, **spirits,** *pl.* any strong, distilled alcoholic drink; liquor. 1–5, 7 *n.*, 6 *v.*

spir·it·ed (spir′ə tid) lively; full of energy and enthusiasm: *a spirited racehorse.* *adj.*

spir·i·tu·al (spir′i chū əl) **1** to do with the spirit rather than the body or material things. **2** religious. **3** one of the religious songs originally sung by the Blacks of the southern United States. 1, 2 *adj.*, 3 *n.*

spit[1] (spit) **1** the watery liquid produced in your mouth. The other word for it is **saliva** (sə lī′və). **2** send out this liquid, or anything else, from your mouth: *She spat on the ground. Spit out the seeds.* **3** make a hissing or spitting sound: *A cat spits when angry.* **4** rain very slightly: *It's spitting.* 1 *n.*, 2–4 *v.*, **spat** or **spit, spit·ting.**

spit[2] (spit) **1** a thin, pointed rod that large pieces of meat are roasted on. The spit turns so that the meat is cooked evenly. **2** a narrow point of land running into the water. *n.*

spite (spīt) **1** bad feeling toward someone: *She deleted his file out of spite.* **2** show bad feeling by purposely annoying someone: *He leaves his room messy to spite me.* 1 *n.*, 2 *v.*, **spit·ed, spit·ing.**
—spite′ful, *adj.*
in spite of, regardless of: *The children went to school in spite of the snowstorm.*

splash (splash) **1** cause water, mud, etc. to fly around: *The baby likes to splash in the tub.* **2** cover a surface with scattered blobs or drops: *The waves splashed*

on the beach. A passing car splashed me. **3** a blob or spot of liquid that has fallen on something: *She has splashes of paint on her smock.* **4** the act or sound of splashing: *She jumped in the pool with a loud splash.* 1, 2 *v.*, 3, 4 *n.*
make a splash, attract attention. Something that attracts a lot of attention is **splashy.**

splat·ter (splat′ər) splash; spatter. *v. or n.*

spleen (splēn) **1** a gland near the stomach that cleans and stores blood. **2** bad temper; spite. *n.*

splen·did (splen′did) **1** magnificent; glorious: *splendid jewels, a splendid victory.* **2** excellent: *a splendid chance. adj.* —**splen′dour** or **splen′dor** (splen′dər), *n.*

splice (splīs) **1** join ropes or wires by separating the ends into single strands and then weaving one into the other. **2** join pieces of film or tape by gluing the ends to a little piece that overlaps them both. **3** a joint made in either of these ways. 1, 2 *v.*, **spliced, splic·ing;** 3 *n.*

Grammar Check ...... splice

A **comma splice** happens when two sentences that ought to stand alone are joined by a comma, like this:
We really like our neighbour, he looks after our plants when we go away on holiday.
The simplest way to correct a comma splice is to use a period instead of a comma:
We really like our neighbour. He looks after our plants when we go away on holiday.

splint (splint) a rigid support made of wood, metal, etc. to hold a broken bone in place until it is treated or healed. *n.*

splin·ter (splin′tər) **1** a small, thin, sharp piece of wood, bone, glass, etc.: *She got a splinter in her hand from the rough railing.* **2** break into splinters: *The mirror splintered.* 1 *n.*, 2 *v.*

split (split) **1** break, cut, or tear into two parts: *My pants split when I bent over. She split the bagel and spread each half with jam.* **2** separate; divide: *The band split up because of an argument between the drummer and the lead singer.* **3** a division, break, tear, etc.: *There was a split in the committee over who should lead it. Frost caused a split in the rock.* **4** Often **splits,** *pl.* an exercise you do by stretching your legs out flat in opposite directions. 1, 2 *v.*, **split, split·ting;** 3, 4 *n.*
split hairs, be too fussy about minor differences: *It is splitting hairs to complain of having just 59 minutes instead of an hour in the pool.*
split second, an extremely short time, less than a second.

splotch (sploch) **1** a large, irregular spot. **2** make splotches on. 1 *n.*, 2 *v.* —**splotch′y,** *adj.*

splurge (splərj) *Informal.* **1** spend or eat more than normal on some occasion: *After eating sensibly for two weeks, he splurged one night and had two servings of pie and ice cream.* **2** an act of spending or eating more than normal: *They made a big splurge for their daughter's wedding.* 1 *v.*, **splurged, splurg·ing,** 2 *n.*

splut·ter (splut′ər) talk in a rushed, confused way, with spitting noises: *People sometimes splutter when they are excited. v.*

spoil (spoil) **1** wreck; ruin: *Rain spoiled the picnic.* A **spoilsport** is someone who spoils other people's fun. **2** turn rotten or sour: *The milk spoiled in the heat.* **3** let a person grow selfish, weak, lazy, etc. by giving in too often or making things too easy for him or her. **4 spoils,** *pl.* things taken from the enemy in war: *The soldiers carried off the spoils.* 1–3 *v.*, **spoiled** or **spoilt, spoil·ing;** 4 *n.*

spoke[1] (spōk) the past tense of **speak:** *She spoke to us about Canada's future.* The past participle is **spoken:** *Have you ever spoken to her? v.*

spoke[2] (spōk) one of the bars or stiff wires going from the centre of a wheel to the rim. *n.*

spokes·per·son (spōks′pər′sən) someone who speaks for another person or for a group: *She was the spokesperson for our class in the debate. n., pl.* **spokes·peo·ple** (spōks′pē′pəl).

sponge (spunj) **1** a kind of sea animal that attaches itself to rocks and has a light, squishy skeleton of tough, elastic material full of small holes. The skeletons of these animals are used in washing and cleaning to soak up water or other liquid. **2** an artificial thing used in the same way, made of foam rubber or similar material. **3** wipe or rub with a dampened sponge: *Sponge up the spilled water.* **4** anything like a sponge. **Sponge cake** is a very light, sweet cake full of tiny holes. **5** *Informal.* get things from others without ever paying them back: *He is always sponging off his friends.* 1, 2, 4 *n.*, 3, 5 *v.*, **sponged, spong·ing.** —**spon′gy,** *adj.*

spon·sor (spon′sər) **1** a person or group that supports or takes official responsibility for someone: *the sponsor of a person applying for immigration to Canada.* **2** a business or organization that pays the cost of a TV program or public event, using it as a chance to advertise. **3** support or pay for; act as sponsor. 1, 2 *n.*, 3 *v.* —**spon′sor·ship,** *n.*

a bat	e bed	i bid	o pot	u cup	th thin
ā cake	ē me	ī bite	ō go	ū rude	ᴛʜ then
à bar	ə about	ər over	ò for	ù put	zh measure

spon·ta·ne·ous (spon tā′nē əs) 1 acting or happening naturally and without planning or thinking beforehand; not forced: *Both sides burst into spontaneous cheers at the skilful play.* 2 happening without any noticeable cause: *a spontaneous explosion.* *adj.* —**spon′ta·ne′i·ty** (spon′tə nā′ə tē), *n.*

spook (spūk) *Informal.* 1 a ghost. Something **spooky** is weird in a scary way. 2 frighten or become frightened. 1 *n.,* 2 *v.*

spool (spūl) a cylinder of plastic, wood, or metal for winding thread, wire, etc. on. *n.*

spoon (spūn) 1 an eating tool that has a small, shallow bowl at the end of a handle. 2 pick up, take, serve, etc. with a spoon: *Spoon the applesauce into bowls.* 1 *n.,* 2 *v.* —**spoon′ful′,** *n.*

spore (spôr) a single cell that can grow into a new plant or animal without needing to join with another cell first. Ferns and fungi produce spores. *n.*

sport (spôrt) 1 a game, contest, or other activity done for fun, requiring some skill and a certain amount of physical exercise: *Baseball, skiing, and fishing are outdoor sports; basketball is an indoor sport.* 2 *Informal.* a person who joins in the fun, co-operates, and tries to be cheerful whether winning or losing: *Be a sport.* A **poor sport** does the opposite. 3 wear or possess proudly: *The town now sports a new community centre.* 4 a rather old-fashioned word for "fun" or "amusement." 1, 2, 4 *n.,* 3 *v.*

sports·plex (spôrts′pleks′) a place with a number of different areas for various kinds of sports: *The new sportsplex had a pool, skating rink, and tennis courts.* *n.*

spot (spot) 1 a mark, dot, or speck: *You have grease spots on your suit. His tie is blue with white spots.* 2 make or get spots on: *Try not to spot the tablecloth. This fabric spots easily.* 3 a place: *From this spot you can see the lake.* 4 *Informal.* pick out; find; recognize: *I spotted my sister in the crowd. The teacher spotted every mistake in my paper.* 5 watch someone doing difficult or dangerous moves, so as to be ready to help if necessary: *Spot me while I practise handsprings.* 1, 3 *n.,* 2, 4, 5 *v.,* **spot·ted, spot·ting.**
hit the spot, *Informal.* be just right; be satisfying.
in a spot, in trouble or difficulty.
on the spot, a at that very place. b at once. c in an embarrassing situation: *She put me on the spot by asking a question I could not answer.*
spot check, a a check made without warning: *The police are doing spot checks to catch drivers not wearing seat belts.* b a process of checking only a few people, places, or things chosen randomly from a whole group: *The government runs a spot check on income tax returns.*

spot·less (spot′lis) without a spot or stain; perfectly clean. *adj.*

spot·light (spot′līt′) a strong light that shines on one particular spot or person: *a spotlight in a theatre.* *n.*
in the spotlight, at the centre of attention.

spot·ty (spot′ē) 1 having spots or stains. 2 good in some parts, poor in others: *Her work was spotty.* *adj.,* **spot·ti·er, spot·ti·est.**

spouse (spous) a husband or wife. *n.*

spout (spout) 1 an opening for pouring or letting out liquid, such as a short tube, a tap, or the specially shaped rim of a container. 2 send out liquid in a stream or spray: *The fountain spouted up high. A whale spouts water when it breathes.* 3 flow out with force: *Water spouted from a break in the pipe.* 4 *Informal.* say things in a conceited way, or without thinking: *to spout useless advice.* 1 *n.,* 2–4 *v.*

sprain (sprān) 1 injure a joint or muscle by a sudden twist or wrench: *to sprain your ankle.* 2 an injury caused in this way: *a bad sprain.* 1 *v.,* 2 *n.*

sprang (sprang) a past tense of **spring:** *The tiger sprang at its prey.* *v.*

sprawl (sprol) lie or sit with your arms and legs spread out ungracefully: *The people sprawled on the beach in their bathing suits.* *v.*

The spray from a skunk can reach a distance of nearly four metres. It is foul-smelling, and the odour stays around for days.

spray[1] (sprā) 1 liquid flying through the air in a mist or small drops: *We were wet with the sea spray.* 2 send or force out liquid in this form onto a surface: *to spray paint on a wall. She sprayed us with the hose.* 3 any product you use in the form of a mist forced through a tiny hole in a container: *hair spray, deodorant spray.* The container is a **spray can, spray bottle,** or **mister.** 1, 3 *n.,* 2 *v.*

spray[2] (sprā) a small branch of some plant with its leaves, flowers, or fruit attached: *a spray of lilacs.* *n.*

spread (spred) 1 stretch out; unfold; open out: *to spread a rug on the floor. The bird spread its wings.* 2 move farther apart: *Spread out your fingers.* 3 cover a surface with a thin layer: *She spread each slice with butter. He spread icing on the cake.* 4 reach or cause to reach more and more people or places: *She spread the news. The flu spread quickly through the school.* 5 the act or the distance of spreading: *Doctors fight the spread of disease. The spread of the airplane's wings was 20 m.* 6 a top covering for a bed. 7 something to spread on bread, etc.: *Peanut butter is a spread.* 8 *Informal.* food laid out on a table; a feast. 1–4 *v.*, **spread, spread·ing;** 5–8 *n.*

spree (sprē) a time of uncontrolled activity done for enjoyment: *He went on a spending spree.* *n.*

sprig (sprig) a shoot, twig, or small branch: *a sprig of mistletoe.* *n.*

spright·ly (sprīt′lē) lively and quick: *a sprightly kitten.* *adj.*, **spright·li·er, spright·li·est.**

The springs are part of the suspension system of this all-terrain vehicle, helping to cushion the bumps and jolts. Oil in the cylinders of the shock absorbers keeps the springs from bouncing back too quickly after going over a bump.

spring (spring) 1 the season after winter, when plants begin to grow again, also called **springtime.** 2 leap or jump suddenly and lightly: *The boy sprang to his feet.* 3 a quick, sudden leap or jump. 4 a device that bounces right back to its original shape after being pulled or pressed. Mattresses have wire springs inside them. Cars have springs underneath to absorb bumps. 5 fly or cause to fly back like an elastic: *A bent branch will spring back into place.* 6 an elastic quality: *The tired girl's step had lost its spring.* 7 a stream of water flowing naturally from the earth. 8 come from some source; arise: *Your problems all spring from laziness.* 9 bring suddenly: *to spring a surprise on someone.* 1, 3, 4, 6, 7 *n.*, 2, 5, 8, 9 *v.*, **sprang, sprung, spring·ing.** —**spring′y,** *adj.*

spring a leak, crack and begin to let water through: *The boat sprang a leak.*

spring·board (spring′bȯrd′) 1 a flexible, bouncy board used to dive or jump off. 2 anything that gives a good start toward some goal: *a springboard to success.* *n.*

spring roll (spring′ rōl′) a deep-fried pastry with a finely ground filling of meat and other things. It is like an egg roll but smaller, crisper, and more tube-shaped.

sprin·kle (spring′kəl) 1 scatter in drops or tiny bits on a surface: *to sprinkle sand on an icy sidewalk. Sprinkle the flowers with water.* A **sprinkler** is a device to water a lawn or to put out fires inside a building by scattering drops. 2 a small amount scattered here and there: *a sprinkle of nuts on a cake.* 3 rain, especially just a little. 1, 3 *v.*, **sprin·kled, sprin·kling;** 2, 3 *n.*

sprint (sprint) 1 run a short way at top speed: *I had to sprint to catch up.* 2 a short, very fast run. 1 *v.*, 2 *n.*

sprock·et (sprok′it) a wheel with a set of points sticking out from the rim to fit into the links of a chain. A bicycle has a sprocket. *n.*

sprout (sprout) 1 begin to grow: *Seeds sprout. Weeds have sprouted in the garden.* 2 develop or appear quickly: *Many new hotels have sprouted up along the beach.* 3 a shoot of a plant. 1, 2 *v.*, 3 *n.*

spruce[1] (sprūs) a northern tree with cones, short needle-shaped leaves, a long, straight trunk, and scaly bark. Its soft wood is used for lumber and paper. *n.*

spruce[2] (sprūs) 1 neat; trim: *He looked very spruce in his new suit.* 2 make neat and tidy: *Spruce the place up before Gran visits. She spruced herself in front of the mirror.* 1 *adj.*, **spruc·er, spruc·est;** 2 *v.*, **spruced, spruc·ing.**

sprung (sprung) the past participle of **spring:** *New towns have sprung up.* *v.*

spry (sprī) lively; nimble: *At eighty she was as spry as ever.* *adj.*, **spry·er** or **spri·er, spry·est** or **spri·est.**

spun (spun) the past tense and past participle of **spin:** *The car skidded and spun on the ice. The thread was spun from silk.* *v.*

spunk (spungk) *Informal.* courage and spirit: *a little puppy full of spunk.* *n.* —**spunk′y,** *adj.*

a bat	e bed	i bid	o pot	u cup	th thin
ā cake	ē me	ī bite	ō go	ū rude	ᴛʜ then
ä bar	ə about	ər over	ȯ for	u̇ put	zh measure

spur (spər) 1 a pricking instrument worn on a rider's heel for urging a horse on. 2 prick with spurs: *The rider spurred her horse on.* 3 urge on; encourage to do more, go faster, try harder etc.: *Our cheers spurred the team on to victory.* 4 anything that looks or acts like a spur: *A spur of rock stuck out from the hill. Love was the spur that made him do his best.* 1, 4 *n.*, 2, 3 *v.*, **spurred, spur·ring.**
on the spur of the moment, without previous planning.

spurn (spərn) refuse proudly or scornfully: *The judge spurned the bribe.* *v.*

spurt (spərt) 1 flow or gush out suddenly with force; squirt: *Water spurted from the hose.* 2 something suddenly rushing or flowing out: *spurts of flame.* 3 a burst of effort or activity that lasts a short time: *With one final spurt she crossed the finish line.* 1 *v.*, 2, 3 *n.*

sput·ter (sput′ər) 1 make spitting or popping noises: *The firecracker sputtered and went out.* 2 talk so excitedly that you spit in doing so. *v.*

spy (spī) 1 a person who secretly watches others to find out what they are doing and planning. Governments often pay spies to do this in enemy countries. 2 keep secret watch: *He saw two men spying on him from behind a tree.* 3 catch sight of; see: *She was first to spy land in the distance.* 1 *n.*, *pl.* **spies;** 2, 3 *v.*, **spies, spied, spy·ing.**

spy·ware (spī′wār) software that tracks an Internet user's surfing habits without the user's knowledge. It can make the computer unusable. *n.*

squab·ble (skwob′əl) 1 a noisy quarrel over some little thing: *She started a squabble by making a face at her sister.* 2 take part in this kind of quarrel: *Don't squabble over three cents.* 1 *n.*, 2 *v.*, **squab·bled, squab·bling.**

squad (skwod) a small group of people organized for some special duty: *a clean-up squad.* *n.*

squad·ron (skwod′rən) a number of army planes, ships, or tanks that travel and fight together. *n.*

squal·id (skwol′id) filthy and miserable: *a squalid shack.* *adj.* —**squal′or,** *n.*

squall[1] (skwol) a short, sudden, and violent windstorm, often with rain, snow, or sleet. A **squall jacket** is a windbreaker. *n.*

squall[2] (skwol) 1 cry out harshly and loudly: *The baby squalled.* 2 a loud, harsh cry: *The parrot's squall was heard all over the house.* 1 *v.*, 2 *n.*

Squa·mish (skwom′ish) 1 a First Nations people living on the southern coast of British Columbia. 2 their language, which belongs to the Salishan family. 3 having to do with these people or their language. 1, 2 *n.*, 3 *adj.*

squan·der (skwon′dər) spend foolishly; waste: *She squanders her money on junk food.* *v.*

square (skwer) 1 a figure with four equal sides and four equal angles. 2 having this shape: *a square box.* 3 anything having this shape, or nearly this shape: *a square of chocolate.* 4 forming a 90° angle: *a square corner.* 5 an instrument shaped like a T or L, used for drawing 90° angles. 6 make square or straight: *to square a block of stone, to square a picture on a wall.* 7 multiply a number by itself: *4 squared makes 16.* The **square root** of 16 is 4. 8 having to do with units used to measure area, where each unit is equal to the area of a square with sides of the stated length. Four square centimetres, or 4 cm^2, is equal to the area of four squares which are each 1 cm × 1 cm, no matter how the squares are arranged. 9 being a certain length on each side of a square. An area four metres square is 4 m × 4 m. 10 an open, paved space in a city or town, with streets or buildings on all four sides: *The soldiers' monument is in the square opposite the city hall.* 11 to settle: *to square an account.* 1, 3, 5, 10 *n.*, 2, 4, 8, 9 *adj.*, **squar·er, squar·est;** 6, 7, 11 *v.*, **squared, squar·ing.**
a square deal, an arrangement that is fair and just.
a square meal, a meal of good, solid food.

square dance (skwer′ dans′) a folk dance for four couples arranged around a square space or in some other set form. —**square′-dance′,** *v.*

squash[1] (skwosh) 1 press until flat; crush: *The boy squashed the ball of clay.* 2 put an end to by force: *The police quickly squashed the riot.* 3 crowd; squeeze: *Can you squash one more thing into your bag?* 4 a game a bit like handball and tennis, played in a walled court with racquets and a small rubber ball. 1–3 *v.*, 4 *n.*

squash[2] (skwosh) a vegetable of several varieties that grow on vines on the ground. Pumpkins and vegetable marrows are two kinds of squash. *n.*, *pl.* **squash** or **squash·es.**

WORD HISTORY...... squash

The word for the vegetable **squash** is from an Algonquian word. The First Nations taught European settlers to eat this vegetable.

squat (skwot) 1 crouch; rest with your weight on your feet and your legs folded up underneath or in front of your body: *The campers squatted around the fire.* 2 settle without permission on land you do not own. If it is public land and you are not chased off, it eventually becomes yours. 3 short and thick: *a squat figure.* 1, 2 *v.*, **squat·ted, squat·ting;** 3 *adj.* —**squat′ter,** *n.*

squawk (skwok) 1 make a loud, harsh cry: *Chickens squawk when frightened.* 2 a loud, harsh cry. 3 complain loudly. 1, 3 *v.,* 2 *n.*

squeak (skwēk) 1 make a short, sharp, high-pitched sound: *A mouse squeaks.* 2 such a sound: *the squeak of new leather shoes.* 1 *v.,* 2 *n.*
—squeak′y, *adj.*
squeak by or **through,** barely succeed in doing something: *I just squeaked through the test.*

squeal (skwēl) 1 make a long, high-pitched sound: *A pig squeals when it is hurt.* 2 such a sound: *squeals of laughter, the squeal of brakes.* 3 *Informal.* tell on someone. 1, 3 *v.,* 2 *n.*

squeam·ish (skwē′mish) 1 having an easily upset stomach. 2 extremely careful to avoid things you think are wrong. *adj.*

squee·gee (skwē′jē) a tool with a handle, a thin rubber blade, and a sponge. It is used to spread and remove liquid, especially in cleaning windows. *n.*

squeeze (skwēz) 1 press hard on both sides or all sides: *Don't squeeze the kitten or you will hurt it.* 2 force out, in, or through by pressing: *to squeeze juice out of a lemon. She squeezed through the crowd.* 3 give way to pressure: *Sponges squeeze easily.* 4 an act of squeezing: *She gave my arm a squeeze.* 1–3 *v.,* **squeezed, squeez·ing;** 4 *n.*

squelch (skwelch) 1 silence or stop a person or thing quickly and forcefully: *One look from the teacher squelched the argument.* 2 make a squishing sound while walking in mud, water, etc. *v.*

The squid sucks water into its body, then squirts it out behind, through a narrow tube. The force of the jet can propel the squid at enormous speed.

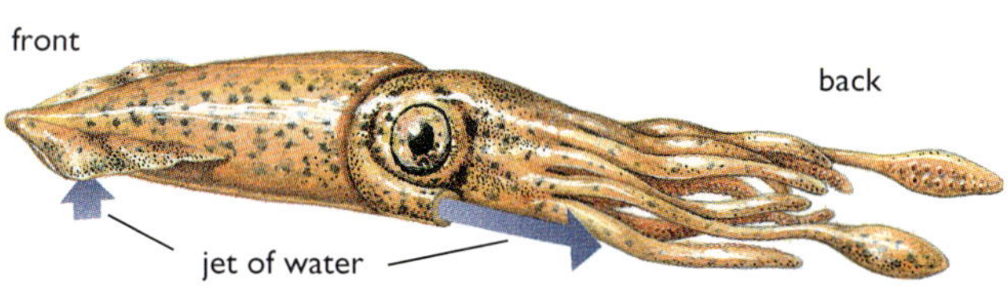

squid (skwid) a sea creature related to the octopus, having a long body, ten arms, and a pair of tail fins. Small squids are used as bait in fishing for cod. 🍁 **Squidjigging** is fishing for squid by dragging or jerking a **squidjigger,** a special set of hooks, through the water. *n.*

squig·gle (skwig′əl) a little crooked mark. *n.*

squint (skwint) 1 look with your eyes barely open, either because of bright light or because you are tensing your muscles so hard to see better. 2 a look with your eyes barely open. 1 *v.,* 2 *n.*

squire (skwīr) in medieval times, a young man of noble family who served a knight till he himself was made a knight. *n.*

squirm (skwərm) 1 wriggle; keep moving and twisting: *He squirmed restlessly in his chair.* 2 feel or act embarrassed or guilty. 3 a wriggle or twist. 1, 2 *v.,* 3 *n.*

squir·rel (skwərl) a small, furry, bushy-tailed animal with front teeth designed for gnawing. Most kinds live in trees. Squirrels are black, grey, or brown. *n.*

squirt (skwərt) 1 force liquid out through a narrow opening; be forced out in this way: *to squirt sunscreen from a tube. Water squirted from the hose.* 2 wet by shooting out liquid: *The elephant squirted me with its trunk.* 3 an act of squirting, or the liquid squirted: *She put a few squirts of ketchup on her hotdog.* 1, 2 *v.,* 3 *n.*

squish (skwish) 1 *Informal.* squash; squeeze. 2 make a soft splashing sound when walking in mud, wet shoes, etc. 3 this sound. 1, 2 *v.,* 3 *n.*
—squish′y, *adj.*

Sr. *abbreviation for* Senior.

St. *abbreviation for:* 1 Street. 2 Saint.

stab (stab) 1 stick a pointed object into: *to stab peas with a fork. He stabbed a knife into the tree trunk.* 2 hurt sharply or deeply: *The cruel words stabbed her to the heart.* 3 the act or sensation of stabbing: *Stabs of pain went up my arm.* 4 *Informal.* a try: *It was a big job but she made a stab at it.* 1, 2 *v.,* **stabbed, stab·bing;** 3, 4 *n.*

sta·ble[1] (stā′bəl) not likely to move, change, or break down; firm and steady: *a stable platform, a stable relationship, a stable economy.* *adj.* **—sta·bil′i·ty,** *n.* **—sta′bi·lize′,** *v.*

sta·ble[2] (stā′bəl) 1 a building where horses or cattle are kept and fed. 2 put or keep in a stable. 1 *n.,* 2 *v.,* **sta·bled, sta·bling.**

stac·ca·to (stə kȧ′tō) in music, played with each note breaking off sharply. *adj. or adv.*

stack (stak) 1 a pile; a number of things piled on top of each other: *a stack of books, a stack of loonies.* 2 pile or arrange in a stack: *to stack firewood.* 3 a chimney, as in *smokestack.* 1, 3 *n.,* 2 *v.*
blow your stack, lose your temper.

a bat	e bed	i bid	o pot	u cup	th thin
ā cake	ē me	ī bite	ō go	ū rude	ᴛʜ then
ȧ bar	ə about	ər over	ȯ for	u̇ put	zh measure

sta·di·um (stā′dē əm) a large, oval open space for games, concerts, and so on, with rows of seats rising around it for people to watch from. *n., pl.* **sta·di·ums** or **sta·di·a** (stā′dē ə).

staff (staf) **1** a stick, pole, or rod used as a support, as a symbol of authority, etc. A walking stick or a flagpole is a staff. A bishop carries a staff. **2** all the employees who help manage a place or a program: *Our school has a staff of twenty teachers.* **3** provide with employees. **4** in music, the five lines and the four spaces between them that the notes, rests, etc. are written on. 1, 2, 4 *n., pl.* **staves** (stāvz) or **staffs** for 1 and 4, **staffs** for 2; 3 *v.*

stag (stag) a full-grown male deer. *n.*

stage (stāj) **1** a platform for performers in a theatre, concert hall, etc. **2** the theatre; the profession of acting: *Shakespeare wrote for the stage.* **3** present on a stage: *to stage a play.* **4** plan and carry out: *to stage a protest march.* **5** fake for an audience: *It wasn't a real fight—the whole thing was staged to get our attention.* **6** one step or part in a process; a period of development: *a frog in the tadpole stage.* 1, 2, 6 *n.*, 3–5 *v.*, **staged, stag·ing.**
by or **in stages,** a little at a time; gradually: *We made the long journey in stages.*

stage·coach (stāj′kōch′) a large horse-drawn carriage used in earlier times for carrying passengers and mail over a regular route. *n.*

stage fright (stāj′ frīt′) a nervous fear of appearing in front of an audience.

stag·ger (stag′ər) **1** sway or stumble from a heavy load, weakness, or being drunk. **2** become unsteady; waver: *The troops staggered under the severe attack.* **3** shock or amaze: *We were staggered by the news of the air disaster.* **4** schedule things at different times so they don't cause a problem by happening all at once: *The doctors staggered their vacations so there was always one at the clinic.* *v.*

stag·nant (stag′nənt) **1** not flowing; standing still and therefore not fresh and clean: *stagnant air, stagnant water.* **2** not active: *During the summer, business is often stagnant.* *adj.* **—stag′nate,** *v.* **—stag·na′tion,** *v.*

stain (stān) **1** a dirty spot or mark: *He has ink stains on his shirt.* **2** leave a dirty spot on: *The tea stained the tablecloth.* **3** a sort of transparent dye used to colour or darken: *She got brown stain for the table.* **4** colour with this dye: *She stained the chair a dark green.* **Stained glass** is pieces of coloured glass arranged in a design that the light can shine through. 1, 3 *n.*, 2, 4 *v.* **—stain′less,** *adj.*

stair (ster) **1** one of a series of steps for walking from one level or floor to another. **2** Also, **stairs,** *pl.* a set of such steps, also called a **stairway** or **staircase:** *the top of the stairs.* *n.*

CONFUSABLES .... stair

stair means "step": *She climbed the stairs.*
stare means "look": *She stared at herself in the mirror.*

stake (stāk) **1** a stick or post pointed at one end for pounding into the ground. Stakes are often used as markers. **2** fasten to a stake: *to stake tomato plants so they don't fall over.* **3** mark off with stakes: *Andrew staked out a patch of ground for his garden.* **4** risk money or some valuable thing on the outcome of an event. **5** the money risked, which goes to the winner: *The gamblers played for high stakes.* **6** a share in something, which may be gained or lost; an interest: *Each of us has a stake in the future of our country.* 1, 5, 6 *n.*, 2–4 *v.*, **staked, stak·ing.**
at stake, to be won or lost; being risked: *Her job is at stake.*
pull up stakes, *Informal.* move away: *After seven years of drought, they finally pulled up stakes and left the farm.*
stake a claim, in earlier times, use stakes to mark out a piece of land which you were officially claiming as yours.

sta·lac·tite (stə lak′tīt *or* stal′ək tīt′) a hanging, icicle-shaped formation on the roof of a cave. It is formed slowly by dripping water that contains lime. *n.*

Remember the difference between stalactitites and stalagmites: stalaCtitites from the Ceiling stalaGmites from the Ground.

sta·lag·mite (stə lag′mīt *or* stal′əg mīt′) a cone-shaped formation on the floor of a cave, formed slowly by water dripping from stalactites above. *n.*

stale (stāl) **1** not fresh: *stale bread.* **2** no longer new or interesting: *a stale joke.* *adj.,* **stal·er, stal·est.**

stale·mate (stāl′māt′) **1** in the game of chess, a tie which results when a player cannot move any of his or her pieces without putting the king in check. **2** any situation where nothing further can be said or done that will do any good: *Their argument was at a stalemate.* *n.*

stalk[1] (stok) **1** the main stem of a plant. **2** any slender supporting part of a plant or animal. A flower may have a stalk. The eyes of a lobster are on stalks. *n.*

stalk[2] (stok) **1** approach or follow secretly in order to catch or attack: *The cougar stalked the deer.* **2** walk proudly with long, stiff steps: *The angry woman stalked out of the room.* *v.*

stall (stol) **1** a place in a stable for one animal. **2** a small place for selling things; booth: *Each farmer had his or her own stall at the market.* **3** any small, closed-in space for one person: *a shower stall.* **4** suddenly stop or cause to stop running, against your wish: *He stalled the engine by driving in too low a gear. The truck stalled whenever it was low on gas.* **5** *Informal.* delay, especially on purpose: *You have been stalling long enough.* **6** an act of stalling; a stop or delay: *After a few stalls the program finally got under way.* 1–3, 6 *n.,* 4, 5 *v.*

stal·lion (stal′yən) a male horse, especially one that can be used for breeding. *n.*

stal·wart (stol′wərt) strong, firm, and loyal: *a stalwart knight, a stalwart friend.* *adj.*

sta·men (stā′mən) one of the parts of a flower that carry the pollen. *n.*

stam·i·na (stam′ə nə) strength to go on under strain; endurance: *A marathon runner needs stamina.* *n.*

stam·mer (stam′ər) **1** repeat the same sound in an effort to speak. **2** say something with difficulty: *to stammer an excuse.* **3** the act or fact of stammering: *He has a nervous stammer.* 1, 2 *v.,* 3 *n.*

stamp (stamp) **1** a small piece of paper with a sticky back, put on mail to show that the postage has been paid. **2** a similar piece of paper used for various purposes. **3** put a stamp on: *to stamp a letter.* **4** something that cuts, shapes, or prints a design on a surface when pressed down hard onto it. **5** mark with such an instrument: *She stamped the papers with the date.* **6** the mark made by such an instrument: *Every textbook has the school stamp in it.* **7** bring your foot down hard: *He stamped his foot in anger.* **8** the act of stamping: *with an impatient stamp of her foot.* 1, 2, 4, 6, 8 *n.,* 3, 5, 7 *v.*

stamp out, get rid of or stop completely: *to stamp out child poverty.*

stam·pede (stam pēd′) **1** a large group of animals or people all rushing suddenly and wildly in one direction: *a buffalo stampede, a stampede of frightened people from a burning building.* **2** rush wildly in a group. **3** 🍁 a rodeo, along with the kinds of things usually found at a fair: *The Calgary Stampede began with a huge parade.* 1, 3 *n.,* 2 *v.,* **stam·ped·ed, stam·ped·ing.**

stand (stand) **1** get or stay on your feet: *We all stood when the anthem played.* **2** be or put in a certain place, especially in an upright position: *A jar of olives stood on the table. Stand the box here.* **3** bear; endure: *Those plants cannot stand cold; they die in the winter.* **4** something to put things on or in: *Leave your wet umbrella in the stand in the hall.* **5** a stall, booth, or table for a small business: *a newspaper stand, a fruit stand.* **6** a raised place where people can sit or stand: *The crowd in the stands cheered the home team.* **7** the place where a person stands; position: *The officer took his stand at the street corner.* **8** a stated opinion; a position on some question or issue: *What is your stand on the teachers' strike?* **9** stay in place; stay the same: *The rule against being late will stand.* **10** the act of standing firm: *We made a last stand against the enemy.* **11** a group of growing trees or plants: *a stand of timber.* 1–3, 9 *v.,* **stood, stand·ing;** 4–8, 10, 11 *n.*

stand behind, **a** support. **b** back up with a guarantee.
stand by, **a** support: *to stand by a friend.* **b** be ready to go or to do something, just in case: *The radio operator was ordered to stand by.* **c** watch and do nothing: *We can't just stand by while people starve.*
stand for, **a** represent; mean: *What does the abbreviation "St." stand for?* **b** be firmly in favour of; uphold: *Our school stands for fair play.* **c** *Informal.* put up with: *The teacher will not stand for anyone chewing gum in class.*
stand in, take someone's place in an emergency. A person who does this is a **stand-in.**
stand out, be very noticeable: *Certain facts stand out.*
stand up, **a** get to your feet; rise: *She stood up and left.* **b** endure; last: *This cloth will stand up under hard wear.*
stand up for, take the side of; defend: *to stand up for a friend.*
stand up to, meet or face boldly: *The young girl stood up to the bully.*
take a stand, state your beliefs publicly and firmly.

a bat	e bed	i bid	o pot	u cup	th thin
ā cake	ē me	ī bite	ō go	ü rude	ŦH then
ä bar	ə about	ər over	ô for	ù put	zh measure

Stars

stand·ard (stan′dərd) **1** a model; an accepted level of quality, size, etc., which people or things are measured or judged by: *The builder's work was not up to standard.* **2** accepted as normal or correct: *the standard rate of pay, standard spelling.* **3** a flag or other symbol of a nation, group, etc.: *The dragon was the standard of China.* 1, 3 *n.,* 2 *adj.* **—stand′ard·ize′,** *v.*

standard of living (stan′dərd əv liv′ing) the level of money and comfort that a person or community considers to be normal. Canada has a high standard of living compared to some other countries.

standard time (stan′dard tīm′) the time normally used in a region or country. Standard time is an hour behind daylight-saving time. ▶ See Appendix.

stand·ing (stan′ding) **1** rank or position: *Those two wins improved our team's standing in the league.* **2** not flowing; still: *standing water.* **3** done from a position of standing still, without a run first. The **standing long jump** is a track-and-field event. **4** the time something has lasted: *a friendship of long standing.* **5** always there to be used when needed or desired: *a standing army, a standing invitation to Sunday dinner.* 1, 4 *n.,* 2, 3, 5 *adj.*

stand·point (stand′point′) a point of view: *Try to see it from his standpoint.* *n.*

stand·still (stand′stil′) a complete stop. *n.*

stank (stangk) a past tense of **stink:** *The dead fish stank.* *v.*

stan·za (stan′zə) a verse of a poem or song: *They sang the first and last stanzas of "O Canada."* *n.*

sta·ple¹ (stā′pəl) **1** anything grown, manufactured, or traded in a place which is very important to its economy: *Wheat is the staple in Saskatchewan.* **2** important; main; used regularly: *Bread is a staple food. The weather is a staple topic of conversation.* 1 *n.,* 2 *adj.*

sta·ple² (stā′pəl) **1** a small, U-shaped piece of wire which is punched through layers of paper, cloth, etc. by a small machine called a **stapler.** The stapler bends the ends of the staple over on the other side to hold the layers together. **2** a larger U-shaped piece of metal with pointed ends, used as a fastener in building. **3** fasten with a staple or staples. 1, 2 *n.,* 3 *v.,* **sta·pled, sta·pling.**

star (stȧr) **1** a heavenly body that appears as a bright point in the sky at night and does not move. **2** a figure with five or six points like these: ★✶ * **3** mark with a star: *In this week's spelling list, the "challenge" words are starred.* **4** a famous person or top performer in anything: *a movie star, a hockey star. The violinist was the star of the concert.* **5** leading; top: *the star player on a football team, the star role in a film.* **6** be or have as the leading performer: *She has starred in many movies. There's a new movie starring Jim Carrey.* 1, 2, 4 *n.,* 3, 6 *v.,* **starred, star·ring;** 5 *adj.* **—star′dom,** *n.* **—star′ry,** *adj.* **—star′less,** *adj.*

star·board (stȧr′bərd) **1** the right side of a ship or aircraft, when facing forward. **2** on the right side of a ship or aircraft. 1 *n.,* 2 *adj.*

starch (stȧrch) **1** a white, tasteless food substance. Potatoes, wheat, rice, and sago contain a lot of starch. **2** a mixture made with this substance, used to stiffen clothes, curtains, etc., especially in earlier times. **3** stiffen with starch. 1, 2 *n.,* 3 *v.* **—starch′y,** *adj.*

stare (ster) **1** keep looking straight at something with your eyes wide open: *The little girl stared at the toys in the window.* **2** a long, direct, wide-eyed look: *He met my smile with an angry stare.* 1 *v.,* **stared, star·ing;** 2 *n.* **stare someone in the face,** be very obvious to someone: *His spelling mistake was staring him in the face.*

star·fish (stȧr′fish′) a star-shaped sea animal, not actually a fish. It is more properly called a **sea star.** *n., pl.* **star·fish** or **star·fish·es.**

stark (stärk) 1 bare and rather harsh: *the stark truth, a stark landscape.* 2 absolute or absolutely: *stark naked (adv.), living in stark poverty (adj.).* 1, 2 *adj.*, 2 *adv.*

star·light (stär′līt′) light from the stars. Something lit by stars is **starlit.** *n.*

Star of David (stär əv dā′vid) the six-pointed star often associated with the Jewish people. It appears on the flag of Israel.

start (stärt) 1 take the first steps in an activity: *to start a job, to start reading.* 2 get going or moving: *to start a machine. The train started on time.* 3 come or bring into being: *to start a fire, to start a club. How did the problem start?* 4 the beginning: *I liked her from the start.* 5 jerk; jump: *She started in surprise (v.). I awoke with a start (n.).* 6 a surprise; fright: *The sudden loud noise gave me quite a start.* 1–3, 5 *v.*, 4–6 *n.* **—start′er,** *n.*
for starters, *Informal.* as a first thing.
start in, begin a task or other activity.
start off, leave on a trip.
start out, start a trip or a major project.

star·tle (stär′təl) frighten suddenly; surprise: *The dogs loud bark startled her.* *v.*, **star·tled, star·tling.**

starve (stärv) 1 die or suffer severely from hunger. 2 weaken or kill with hunger: *That cruel man half starves his horses.* *v.*, **starved, starv·ing.** **—star·va′tion,** *n.*
be starving, *Informal.* feel very hungry: *When's lunch? I'm starving!*
starve for or **be starved for,** suffer from the lack of: *to starve for news. That child is starving for affection.*

stash (stash) 1 store something for future use, especially secretly: *Steven stashed his Halloween candy in the back corner of his closet.* 2 a supply of something stored away, especially secretly: *The teacher found a stash of bubble gum in Kelly's desk.* 1 *v.*, 2 *n.*

state (stāt) 1 say or write; express; declare: *State your opinion.* Something that is stated is a **statement.** 2 the condition of a person or thing: *He is in a state of poor health. The house is in a good state of repair.* 3 any of the three physical forms a substance can be in. The three **states of matter** are solid, liquid, and gas. 4 a country or its government. 5 one of the separate parts that some nations, such as the United States, are divided into. Each state has its own government and is similar to a province. 1 *v.*, **stat·ed, stat·ing;** 2–5 *n.*
in or **into a state,** upset; excited: *There's no need to get into a state over this.*
lie in state, lie in a coffin so as to be seen formally and publicly before being buried: *The dead king lay in state for a day in the main hall of the royal palace.*

state·ly (stāt′lē) very dignified and majestic: *Rideau Hall is a stately mansion.* *adj.*, **state·li·er, state·li·est.**

state–of–the–art (stāt′əv ᴛʜē ärt′) having to do with the best and most modern equipment, methods, or information: *state-of-the-art computer software.* *adj.*

stat·ic (stat′ik) 1 noises and other interference on radio, TV, or the telephone, caused by electrical disturbances in the air. 2 not active or changing; standing still: *Language is not static; it keeps developing.* **Static electricity** does not flow as a current but exists as a charge in an object. 3 short for **static electricity:** *This carpet produces a lot of static when the air is dry.* **Static cling** is the tendency of certain substances, like cloth, to stick together because of static electricity. 1, 3 *n.*, 2 *adj.*

sta·tion (stā′shən) 1 a building or place used for a definite purpose: *a police station. We have a craft station at the back of the classroom.* 2 a regular stopping place for a train, bus, or subway, with a platform and a building for waiting travellers. 3 a specific radio or TV frequency carrying programs by a particular company: *Every morning she listens to her favourite station.* 4 the place or equipment used by such a company for sending out or receiving programs. 5 an assigned position for duty: *The security guard took her station in the mall.* 6 give a position to; assign to a place: *He stationed himself outside the hotel. The ambassador was stationed in France.* 7 social rank: *a person of humble station.* 1–5, 7 *n.*, 6 *v.*

sta·tion·ar·y (stā′shə ner′ē) 1 standing still; not moving or changing: *A parked car is stationary.* 2 not movable or not meant to be moved. *adj.*

CONFUSABLES .... stationary

stationary means "not moving."
stationery means "writing paper."
Remember, *stationery, letter,* and *paper* all have the letters *er* in them.

sta·tion·er·y (stā′shə ner′ē) writing materials; paper, cards, and envelopes. *n.*

station wagon (stā′shən wag′ən) a car with a large space for loads right behind the back seat. It has a door at the back end which contains the rear window and opens upward.

a bat	e bed	i bid	o pot	u cup	th thin
ā cake	ē me	ī bite	ō go	ū rude	ᴛʜ then
ä bar	ə about	ər over	ô for	ù put	zh measure

sta·tis·tics (stə tis′tiks) 1 numerical facts about people, business conditions, the weather, sports, etc.: *population statistics, accident statistics, sports statistics.* 2 the science of collecting, organizing, and explaining such facts. *n.* —**sta·tis′ti·cal,** *adj.*

stat·ue (stach′ū) a three-dimensional image of a person or animal made out of stone, wood, or other solid material: *A stone statue of Louis Riel stands in the park.* *n.*

stat·ure (stach′ər) 1 a person's height. 2 high reputation: *She is a woman of stature in the arts.* *n.*

sta·tus (stat′əs *or* stā′təs) 1 a person's rank or position in society: *Slaves had very low status.* 2 present condition or state: *"What's the status of your project?" "It's almost finished."* *n.*

stat·ute (stach′ūt) a law. *n.*

staunch[1] (stonch) strong and firm; steadfast: *a staunch defence, a staunch friend.* *adj.*

staunch[2] (stonch) stop the flow of blood from a wound. *v.*

staves (stāvz) a plural of **staff:** *musical staves.* *n.*

stay (stā) 1 continue to be; keep yourself: *Stay still. The cat stayed outside all night.* 2 live for a while: *She is staying with her aunt for March break.* 3 time spent at a place: *a pleasant stay in Charlottetown.* 1, 2 *v.,* 3 *n.*

stead·fast (sted′fast′) firm and reliable; not giving up, moving, or changing: *a steadfast supporter.* *adj.*

stead·y (sted′ē) 1 firm; not swaying or shaking: *Hold the ladder steady.* 2 continuing at the same rate without stopping: *steady progress, a steady flow of visitors.* 3 not easily excited; calm: *steady nerves.* 4 make, become, or keep steady: *Steady the ladder while I climb to the roof. His hands steadied as he relaxed.* 5 that can be depended on: *a steady worker, a steady job.* 1–3, 5 *adj.,* **stead·i·er, stead·i·est;** 4 *v.,* **stead·ied, stead·y·ing.**

steak (stāk) a thick slice of meat of any kind for broiling or frying: *a beef steak, a salmon steak.* *n.*

CONFUSABLES .... steak

steak means "thick slice of meat": *to cook steak on a grill.*
stake means "pointed stick": *to put a stake in the ground.*

steal (stēl) 1 take something that does not belong to you, without permission: *Robbers stole the money.* 2 take, get, or do secretly: *to steal a glance at something.* 3 move secretly or quietly: *She stole softly out of the room.* 4 *Informal.* a great bargain: *At only $15, this coat is a steal.* 1–3 *v.,* **stole, sto·len, steal·ing;** 4 *n.*
steal someone's heart, quickly win someone's affection.
steal the show, perform so well that you become the star even though you weren't meant to be.

CONFUSABLES .... steal

steal means "take": *The thief would steal jewellery.*
steel is a metal: *This knife is made of stainless steel.*

stealth (stelth) secret, quiet, or sly action: *He obtained the letter by stealth, taking it while no one was looking.* *n.* —**stealth′y,** *adj.* —**stealth′i·ly,** *adv.*

steam (stēm) 1 water in the form of vapour or gas. Boiling water gives off steam; steam kept under pressure is a source of energy. 2 give off steam: *The cup of tea was steaming.* 3 cook, soften, or heat by steam: *to steam rice.* 4 *Informal.* **steamed,** very angry. **Steaming** can mean the same. 5 move by steam power: *The ship steamed out to sea.* 1 *n.,* 2, 3, 5 *v.,* 4 *adj.* —**steam′y,** *adj.*
let off steam, *Informal.* let out your feelings.
on your own steam, by your own effort.
run out of steam, lose your energy or enthusiasm.
steam up, fog up, or **mist up,** cover or become covered with fine water droplets when the moisture in warm air hits it: *My glasses steam up when I come in from the cold.*

Word Family.......... steam

steam engine: an engine powered by steam, especially a train engine in earlier times
steamer: a special pot that uses steam to cook food
steam iron: an iron that dampens the cloth with steam
steamroller: a heavy machine on rollers, for levelling asphalt or gravel. It used to use steam.
steamship: a ship powered by steam; also, **steamer**

steed (stēd) a poetic word for a fast horse. *n.*

steel (stēl) 1 iron mixed with carbon so that it is very hard and strong. Most tools are made from steel. 2 something made from steel. 3 make hard or strong like steel: *She steeled herself to dive into the cold water.* 1, 2 *n.,* 3 *v.* —**steel′y,** *adj.*

steel wool (stēl′ wu̇l′) fine steel threads shaped into a pad for cleaning or polishing.

steep[1] (stēp) 1 with a sharp slope; almost straight up and down: *The hill is steep.* 2 hard to accept: *a pretty steep price. That story is a bit steep if you ask me.* *adj.*

steep[2] (stēp) soak: *Pour the boiling water on the tea and let it steep for five minutes.* *v.*
steeped in, full of: *ruins steeped in history.*

stee·ple (stē′pəl) a high tower on a church: *Steeples usually have spires.* *n.*

steer¹ (stēr) 1 guide a vehicle: *to steer a car. Steer around that rock.* A **steering wheel** is a wheel the driver turns to steer a vehicle. 2 guide someone's behaviour: *They tried to steer their daughter away from trouble.* *v.*

steer² (stēr) a full grown male of cattle that has had its sex glands removed. Steers are raised for beef. *n.*

stem¹ (stem) 1 the main part of a plant, supporting the branches. A tree trunk or a cornstalk is a stem. 2 the part of a flower, fruit, or leaf that joins it to the plant or tree. 3 anything like the stem of a plant: *the stem of a wine glass.* 4 come from a source: *The difficulty stems from poor planning.* 1–3 *n.*, 4 *v.*, **stemmed, stem·ming.**

stem² (stem) stop; check; dam up: *We had to stem the flow from the burst pipe.* *v.*, **stemmed, stem·ming.**

stench (stench) a very bad smell; stink: *the stench of a garbage dump.* *n.*

sten·cil (sten′səl) 1 a thin sheet of stiff material with a pattern cut out of it. When a stencil is laid on a surface and ink or colour is spread on, the pattern is made on the surface. 2 the pattern itself. 3 mark, paint, or make with a stencil: *The walls have a stencilled border.* 1, 2 *n.*, 3 *v.*, **sten·cilled, sten·cil·ling.**

ste·nog·ra·pher (stə nog′rə fər) an office worker who takes dictation in shorthand and then types it. *n.*

step (step) 1 a movement made by lifting your foot and putting it down again in a new position, as when you walk, run, dance, etc. 2 the distance covered by doing this once: *She was three steps away from us.* 3 put your foot down: *He stepped on a bug.* 4 the sound made by doing this: *I hear steps upstairs.* 5 walk a short distance: *Step this way.* 6 **a** a place to put your foot in climbing up or down: *a ladder with six steps.* **b** **steps,** *pl.* stairs. 7 a special way of moving the feet in dancing. 8 an action: *They took steps to prevent further flooding.* 9 one part of a process: *There are three steps to making these cookies.* 1, 2, 4, 6–9 *n.*, 3, 5 *v.*, **stepped, step·ping.**
in step, **a** making your steps match the rhythm of music or of others walking with you. **b** in agreement. The opposite of both meanings is **out of step.**
keep step, **a** move in time with music or with someone else. **b** act in agreement with someone or something.
step down, resign from a position as leader.
step in, get involved in order to help solve or avoid a problem: *When the argument turned into a fist fight, our parents stepped in.*
step up, speed up or increase: *to step up production.*
watch your step, be careful.

step·fam·i·ly (step′fam′lē) people who are related by the marriage of someone with children. The children are **stepchildren** (**stepsons** or **stepdaughters**) of the new husband or wife; he or she is their **stepparent** (**stepfather** or **stepmother**). If the new husband or wife also has children from before, they are **stepbrothers** or **stepsisters** of the other children. *n., pl.* **step·fam·i·lies.**

step·lad·der (step′lad′ər) a ladder with flat steps instead of rungs and, usually, a pair of hinged legs so that it stands by itself. *n.*

steppe (step) a vast, grassy, treeless plain in southeastern Europe and Asia. *n.*

ster·e·o (ster′ē ō′) 1 a radio, CD or tape player, etc. with two or more speakers to give more lifelike sound. *n.*
in stereo, with sound from both sides.

ster·e·o·type (ster′ē ō tīp′) 1 a narrow and very unrealistic image applied unfairly to all the members of a certain group: *It is a common stereotype that wolves like to attack humans.* 2 to show or think of people according to a stereotype: *I don't like the way that movie stereotypes rich people.* 1 *n.*, 2 *v.*, **ster·e·o·typed, ster·e·o·typ·ing.** —**ster′e·o·typ′i·cal** (ster′ē ō tip′ə kəl), *adj.*

ster·ile (ster′īl *or* ster′əl) 1 free from germs: *The doctor kept her instruments sterile.* 2 unable to produce seed, offspring, crops, etc.; not fertile. 3 lifeless, dull, cold, etc.: *a sterile atmosphere.* *adj.* —**ster′i·lize′,** *v.* —**ste·ril′i·ty** (stə ril′ə tē), *n.*

ster·ling (stər′ling) 1 Often, **sterling silver,** silver that is 92.5 percent pure. 2 excellent; reliable: *a person of sterling character.* 3 British money. 1, 3 *n.*, 2 *adj.*

stern¹ (stərn) tough; strict and serious: *He was a stern master. They were given a stern warning.* *adj.*

stern² (stərn) the back end of a ship or boat. *n.*

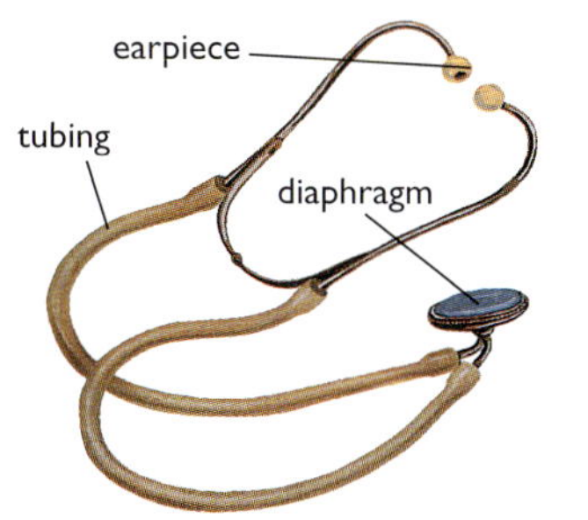

The diaphragm of the stethoscope picks up sounds inside the body. The tubing and the earpieces direct these sounds to the doctor, and help block out noise.

steth·o·scope (steth′ə skōp′) an instrument used by doctors, nurses, etc. to listen to sounds in a patient's lungs, heart, etc. *n.*

a bat	e bed	i bid	o pot	u cup	th thin
ā cake	ē me	ī bite	ō go	ū rude	ᴛʜ then
ä bar	ə about	ər over	ô for	ů put	zh measure

stew (styū *or* stū) **1** a sort of thick soup of meat and vegetables cooked slowly together in liquid: *beef stew, chicken stew.* **2** cook by slow boiling: *The cook stewed the chicken for a long time.* **3** *Informal.* worry; be upset. **4** *Informal.* a worried or upset state: *She is in a stew over her lost suitcase.* 1, 3 *v.,* 2, 4 *n.*

stew·ard (styū′ərd *or* stū′ərd) a person who manages another's property. *n.*

stick[1] (stik) **1** a long, thin piece of wood: *Put some sticks on the fire.* **2** something shaped like a stick: *a stick of candy.* **3** a thing shaped like this, meant for a special use. This sense is often in compounds: *a drumstick.* *n.*

stick[2] (stik) **1** attach or become attached: *Stick a stamp on the letter. The magnet sticks to the fridge.* **2** put: *He stuck his hand in his pocket. Don't stick your head out of the car window.* **3** jab; force something pointed into or through: *He stuck his fork into the potato. Your elbow is sticking into my ribs.* **4** extend upward or outward: *His hair sticks up at the back.* **5** be or become unable to move freely: *That door sticks—push it hard. Our car got stuck in the mud.* **6** **stuck,** faced with a problem you need help to solve. *v.,* **stuck, stick·ing.**
stick around, *Informal.* stay or wait in a place.
stick at, **a** continue without giving up: *Stick at it till it's done.* **b** hesitate at: *He sticks at nothing to get his own way.*
stick by, stay faithful: *He sticks by his friends when they are in trouble.*
stick to, stay with and not give up, back down, or quit: *to stick to a belief.*
stick up, *Slang.* rob at gunpoint. **Stick-up** is the noun.
stick up for, *Informal.* stand up for; support; defend.
stick with, **a** stay with. **b** force someone to keep or deal with: *They stuck me with the hardest job.*

stick·er (stik′ər) a label or picture with a sticky backing. *n.*

The stick insect is also known as the "walking stick."

stick insect (stik′ in′sekt) a North American insect with a long, slender body that looks like a twig.

stick·y (stik′ē) **1** that sticks: *sticky glue.* **2** hot and humid: *sticky weather.* **3** *Informal.* puzzling; difficult: *a sticky problem.* *adj.,* **stick·i·er, stick·i·est.**

sties (stīz) plural of **sty**[1] and **sty**[2]. *n.*

stiff (stif) **1** firm; hard to bend or move: *stiff cardboard.* **2** aching a little: *I'm stiff after yesterday's long hike.* **3** not relaxed or natural: *a stiff greeting.* **4** strong: *a stiff breeze, a stiff warning.* **5** hard to deal with: *a stiff test, a stiff punishment.* *adj.* —**stiff′en,** *v.*

sti·fle (stī′fəl) **1** be or make unable to breathe freely: *I am stifling in this overheated room. The smoke stifled the firefighters.* **2** keep back or put down; stop from speaking, acting, etc.: *to stifle a laugh, to stifle someone's imagination.* *v.,* **sti·fled, sti·fling.**

still (stil) **1** not moving: *Sit still. The lake is still today.* **2** silent; quiet: *The room was so still that you could have heard a pin drop.* **3** make or become calm or quiet: *The mother stilled the crying baby. The wind has finally stilled.* **4** quietness; silence: *in the still of the night.* **5** even; yet: *still better, still another reason.* **6** even so; nevertheless: *This bike is not the greatest; still, it's better than nothing.* **7** even now; even then: *Is he still here?* 1, 2 *adj.,* 3 *v.,* 4 *n.,* 5–7 *adv.* —**still′ness,** *n.*

stilt·ed (stil′tid) too stiff and unnatural: *a stilted way of speaking.* *adj.*

stilts (stilts) two poles to hold while walking, each with a support for your foot partway up, so that you are raised above the ground. Stilts are mostly for fun. *pl.n.*

stim·u·lant (stim′yə lənt) something that increases the activity of your body, such as caffeine. *n.*

stim·u·late (stim′yə lāt′) stir to thought or action: *a stimulating discussion. Praise stimulated her to try even harder.* Something that stimulates is a **stimulus.** *v.,* **stim·u·lat·ed, stim·u·lat·ing.** —**stim′u·la′tion,** *n.*

sting (sting) **1** prick with a sharp-pointed body part called a stinger. Bees, wasps, and hornets sting. **2** the wound caused in this way: *He put ointment on my bee sting to take away the pain.* **3** hurt sharply: *I was stung by their angry words. The wind stung our faces.* **4** a sharp pain: *the sting of defeat.* 1, 3 *v.,* **stung, sting·ing;** 2, 4 *n.*

sting·ray (sting′rā′) a broad, flat-bodied fish that can give severe wounds with the sharp, poisonous spines on its whiplike tail. *n.*

stin·gy (stin′jē) never wanting to spend, give, or lend what you have. *adj.,* **stin·gi·er, stin·gi·est.** —**stin′gi·ly,** *adv.* —**stin′gi·ness,** *n.*

stink (stingk) **1** a bad smell. **2** have a bad smell: *Rotten fish stinks.* **3** *Informal.* be worthless or bad: *That TV show stinks.* 1 *n.,* 2, 3 *v.,* **stank, stunk, stink·ing.** **—stink′y,** *adj.*
stink up, fill with a bad smell: *That paint stinks up the whole room.*

stir (stər) **1** mix by moving around with a spoon, fork, stick, etc.: *He stirred the sugar into his tea.* **2** move: *The wind stirs the leaves. No one was stirring in the house.* **3** produce action or strong feeling in someone: *to stir up an argument, to stir someone to greater effort. The fans were all stirred up for the final game.* **4** excitement: *The rumour caused quite a stir.* **5** the act of stirring: *She gave the mixture a good stir.* 1–3 *v.,* **stirred, stir·ring;** 4, 5 *n.*

stir–fry (stər′frī′) **1** quickly fry small pieces of food while stirring them, often in a special frying pan called a **wok.** **2** a dish or meal made in this way: *I ordered vegetable stir-fry.* 1 *v.,* **stir-fried, stir-fry·ing;** 2 *n.*

stir·rup (stər′əp *or* stēr′əp) one of a pair of foot supports that hang from a saddle. *n.*

> **WORD HISTORY........ stirrup**
>
> **Stirrup** is from Old English *stigrap*, a compound of *stige*, "climbing," and *rap*, "rope" — for climbing onto a horse.

stitch (stich) **1** one complete movement of the needle in sewing, knitting, crocheting, etc., making a loop of thread or yarn: *Take short stitches. Count the stitches in each row.* **2** a particular kind of stitch: *buttonhole stitch.* **3** sew: *He stitched the pocket to his shirt. The doctor stitched up the cut.* **4** *Informal.* the smallest bit: *The lazy boy wouldn't do a stitch of work.* **5** a sudden, sharp pain: *She got a stitch in her side from running.* 1, 2, 4, 5 *n.,* 3 *v.*

St. Jean Bap·tiste Day (sᴇɴ′ zhâɴ′ ba tēst′ dā′) another name for the **Fête nationale,** a public holiday in Québec that is celebrated on June 24.

stock (stok) **1** a supply kept on hand: *a stock of snacks. This store keeps a large stock of toys for sale.* Extra items are kept in a store's **stockroom.** **2** keep available for sale: *A bookstore stocks books.* **3** put a supply in or on: *to stock shelves with merchandise. Our fridge is well stocked with groceries.* **4** kept on hand regularly for use or sale: *That is not a stock item but we can order it for you.* **5** used all the time: *The weather is a stock subject of conversation.* **6** cattle or other farm animals; livestock. **7** water that meat or fish has been cooked in, used as a base for soups, sauces, etc. **8** family; descent: *She is of Polish stock.* **9** shares in a company, bought and sold with the help of a **stockbroker** in the **stock exchange** or **stock market.** A company's profits are divided among the owners of its stock. **10** **the stocks,** *pl.* in earlier times, a wooden frame with holes for the feet and sometimes the hands. People were placed in it in public as a punishment. 1, 6–10 *n.,* 2, 3 *v.,* 4, 5 *adj.*
in stock, available for sale in a store. The opposite is **out of stock.**
take stock, **a** find out how much stock there is on hand. **b** look at a situation and see what needs to be done.

stock·ade (stok ād′) in earlier times, a wall around a trading post, mission, settlement, etc. for defence, made of large, strong upright posts placed closely together in the ground. *n.*

stock·ing (stok′ing) a close-fitting knitted covering of nylon, cotton, wool, etc. for the foot and leg. *n.*

stock·pile (stok′pīl′) **1** keep a lot of something in reserve in case it will be needed: *Many people stockpiled flour because they thought it would become scarce.* **2** a supply of something kept in this way: *Some nations are getting rid of their stockpile of nuclear weapons.* 1 *v.,* **stock·piled, stock·pil·ing;** 2 *n.*

stock–still (stok′stil′) totally motionless. *adj.*

stock·y (stok′ē) thick and solid: *a stocky child.* *adj.,* **stock·i·er, stock·i·est.**

stock·yard (stok′yärd′) a place where cattle, sheep, hogs, and horses are collected and kept before being slaughtered or sent to market. *n.*

sto·ic (stō′ik) calm and self-controlled even when bad things happen to you: *Hilka was disappointed about losing the big race, but she was very stoic about it.* 1 *v.,* 2 *n.* **—sto′i·cal·ly,** *adv.* **—sto′i·cism′,** *n.*

stoke (stōk) stir up and feed a fire. *v.,* **stoked, stok·ing.** **—stok′er,** *n.*

stole (stōl) the past tense of **steal.** The past participle is **stolen:** *He stole the money from his brother. It was stolen years ago.* *v.*

stom·ach (stum′ək) **1** the large, muscular, baglike organ in your body that receives the food you eat and partly digests it before passing it on to the intestines. **2** the belly; the area just below your ribs at the front of your body: *He hit me in the stomach.* **3** appetite or liking: *I have no stomach for that sort of thing.* **4** put up with; bear: *I cannot stomach such an insult.* 1–3 *n.,* 4 *v.*

a bat	e bed	i bid	o pot	u cup	th thin
ā cake	ē me	ī bite	ō go	ü rude	ᴛʜ then
ä bar	ə about	ər over	ô for	u̇ put	zh measure

stomp (stomp) bring your foot down very hard. *v.*

stone (stōn) **1** a hard mineral substance that is not metal; rock: *Stone is sometimes used in building.* **2** a small piece of this: *We threw stones into the lake.* **3** a piece of rock prepared for a special purpose. This sense is often used in compounds: *a gravestone, a gemstone, a millstone.* **4** kill or chase away by throwing stones at. **5** the hard seed of a peach, plum, etc. **6** the rounded, polished, heavy piece of rock you slide down the ice in the game of curling. **7** a hard piece of matter that forms in the kidney or gall bladder, often causing pain. 1–3, 5–7 *n.,* 4 *v.,* **stoned, ston·ing.** **—ston′y,** *adj.*

Stone Age (stōn′ āj′) the period long ago when people used tools and weapons made from stone.

stone·ware (stōn′wer′) thick, heavy glazed pottery. *n.*

Sto·ney (stōnē) another name for the **Assiniboine** First Nations people. *n. or adj.*

stood (stu̇d) the past tense and past participle of **stand:** *He stood in the rain for five minutes. This building has stood here for many years.* *v.*

stool (stūl) **1** a seat without a back or arms. **2** a similar thing used to rest your feet on, or to stand on in order to reach something high. *n.*

stoop[1] (stūp) **1** bend over: *He stooped to pick up the money.* **2** a forward bend of the head and shoulders: *My uncle walks with a slight stoop.* **3** carry the head and shoulders bent forward. **4** lower yourself to do something wrong: *He stooped to cheating.* 1, 3, 4 *v.,* 2 *n.*

stoop[2] (stūp) a small, low, roofless porch. *n.*

stop (stop) **1** keep from moving, going on, doing, working, etc.: *to stop a machine. Stop that noise. I stopped the girls from teasing the cat.* **2** end; quit; no longer be moving, doing, being, etc.: *The baby stopped crying. The rain is stopping.* **3** Often, **stop off,** go to a place on the way to somewhere else: *She stopped at the bank for a few minutes.* **Stop in** and **stop by** mean the same. **4** block; plug up: *Stop the hole with this cork.* **5** the act or place of stopping: *We made a stop for lunch. Where is the bus stop?* 1–4 *v.,* **stopped, stop·ping;** 5 *n.* **—stop′page,** *n.*
put a stop to, cause to stop.
stop over, stay at a place for a short time on your way to somewhere else: *On our trip to Germany we stopped over in London, England.* A short stay like this is a **stopover.**

stop·light (stop′līt′) a traffic light or signal. *n.*

stop·per (stop′ər) a plug or cork for closing a bottle, tube, etc. *n.*

stop·watch (stop′woch′) a watch that can be stopped or started at any instant. It measures fractions of a second and is used for timing things very exactly. *n.*

store (stȯr) **1** a place where you can buy things: *a clothing store.* The person who runs it is a **storekeeper.** **2** put away to use later; keep in a place: *We stored our skis during the summer. Towels are stored in this closet.* **3** a supply that has been put away for later use: *The squirrel had a store of nuts in its nest.* 1, 3 *n.,* 2 *v.,* **stored, stor·ing.** **—stor′age,** *n.*

store·house (stȯr′hous′) a place where things are stored: *a storehouse for grain. A library is a storehouse of information.* *n.*

store·room (stȯr′rūm′) a room where things are stored. *n.*

sto·rey (stȯr′ē) a level or floor of a building: *They are now building the second storey of our new house.* *n., pl.* **sto·reys.**

There are 17 species of stork. This is the best known, the white stork. The legend that this stork brings the new baby to a home comes from the fact that the bird takes great care of its own young.

stork (stȯrk) a large, long-legged wading bird with a long neck and a long bill. *n.*

storm (stȯrm) **1** a heavy fall of rain, snow, or hail. **2** a strong wind. This sense is used mostly in compounds like *sandstorm.* **3** blow, rain, snow, hail, etc. hard. **4** a violent outburst: *a storm of complaints.* **5** rush angrily: *He stormed out angrily.* **6** attack violently: *The enemy stormed the castle.* 1, 2, 4 *n.,* 3, 5, 6 *v.* **—storm′y,** *adj.*
take by storm, seize or capture with power and speed: *The castle was taken by storm.*

storm window (stȯrm′ win′dō) an extra window outside an ordinary window, to keep out cold winds: *Dad puts the storm windows on in October each year.* A **storm door** is a strong screen door with a pane of glass that can be slid down over the screen.

sto·ry (stȯ′rē) **1** a happening or group of related happenings, told in speech or writing, shown in a play or movie, etc. It can be true or made-up: *The man told the* *story of his life. He likes stories with talking animals in them.* **2** *Informal.* a lie. *n., pl.* **sto·ries.**

CONFUSABLES .... story

A **story** tells what happened to someone or something: *Tell me the story of Robinson Crusoe.*

A **storey** is a floor of a building: *That office tower has seventy-two storeys.*

sto·ry·book (stȯ′rē bu̇k′) a book containing one or more stories, especially for children. *n.*

stout (stout) **1** fat or thick; heavy: *That boy could run faster if he weren't so stout.* **2** firm and strong: *The fort has stout walls.* **3** brave; bold: *a stout heart.* *adj.*

stove (stōv) a large device for cooking and heating. It can be electric or burn fuel such as wood or natural gas; fuel-burning stoves have a metal **stovepipe** to carry the smoke and gases to a chimney. *n.*

stow (stō) pack: *We stowed the tent in our canoe.* A person who hides on a ship, airplane, etc. to avoid paying the fare or to escape is a **stowaway** (stō′ə wā′). *v.*

strad·dle (strad′əl) sit or stand with a leg on each side of something. *v.,* **strad·dled, strad·dling.**

strag·gle (strag′əl) **1** wander in a scattered fashion: *Cows straggled along the lane.* **2** spread in an untidy, rambling way: *Vines straggled all over the yard.* *v.,* **strag·gled, strag·gling.** **—strag′gly,** *adj.*

straight (strāt) **1** without bends, curls, turns, zigzags, etc.: *a straight line, a straight path, straight hair* (*adj.*). *Walk straight* (*adv.*). **2** directly, without stopping or waiting: *Go straight home.* **3** using plain, honest language: *a straight answer* (*adj.*). *Talk straight* (*adv.*). **4** so that the facts are right: *to set the record straight. Two milks, six juices, and one water—OK, I've got it straight.* **5** not smiling or laughing: *to keep a straight face.* **6** one after another: *for three straight days* or *for three days straight.* 1, 3–6 *adj.,* 1–3 *adv.* **—straight′en,** *v.*

straight·for·ward (strāt′fȯr′wərd) clear and simple: *a straightforward answer.* *adj.*

strain¹ (strān) **1** injure or damage by too much effort, pressure, or stretching: *to strain a muscle. The heavy weight strained the rope and it broke.* **2** injury, damage, or illness caused in this way. **3** the extreme pull, effort, weight, or pressure that causes such damage: *The strain on the rope made it break. She could not bear the strain of so many sleepless nights.* **4** use to the utmost: *She strained every nerve trying to remember.* **5** pull, try, or stretch very hard: *The dog strained at its leash. He strained to hear her answer.* **6** press or pour through something that lets only liquid through it: *The cook strained the soup to remove all the lumps.* 1, 4–6 *v.,* 2, 3 *n.* **—strain′er,** *n.*

strain² (strān) **1** a group of animals or plants that form a part of a breed or variety. **2** an inherited quality: *There is a strain of artistic talent in that family.* **3** a style or manner: *He wrote in a playful strain.* **4** **strains,** *pl.* a poetic word for a melody, or part of one: *The sweet strains of an old song drifted on the air.* *n.*

strained (strānd) **1** tense because of anger or distrust: *a strained silence.* **2** the past tense and past participle of **strain.** 1 *adj.,* 2 *v.*

strait (strāt) a narrow channel connecting two larger bodies of water. *n.*

CONFUSABLES .... strait

strait means "narrow channel": *The Davis Strait.*

straight means "not bent": *straight as an arrow.*

strand¹ (strand) leave helpless in a place: *He was stranded in an unfamiliar town with no money.* *v.*

strand² (strand) **1** one of the threads, strings, or wires that are twisted together to make a rope or cable: *This is a rope of three strands.* **2** a thread or string: *a strand of hair, a strand of pearls.* *n.*

strange (strānj) **1** unusual; odd; weird: *What a strange experience!* **2** not known to someone; not familiar: *She was surrounded by strange faces. A strange cat is on our doorstep.* **3** out of place; not at home: *The poor child felt strange in the palace.* *adj.,* **strang·er, strang·est. —strange′ly,** *adv.* **—strange′ness,** *n.*

stran·ger (strān′jər) **1** a person not known, seen, or heard of before: *She is a stranger to us.* **2** a person who is new to a place or to a certain experience: *He is a stranger in Saskatoon. I am no stranger to hard work.* *n.*

stran·gle (strang′gəl) **1** kill by squeezing the throat to stop the breath: *Hercules strangled a snake with each hand.* **2** choke down; keep back: *He strangled an impulse to laugh.* *v.,* **stran·gled, stran·gling.**

strap (strap) **1** a narrow strip of tough material used to hold something together or in place: *the shoulder straps on a backpack, a leather strap around an old suitcase.* **2** fasten with a strap: *We strapped the canoe onto the roof of the car.* 1 *n.,* 2 *v.,* **strapped, strap·ping.**

a bat	e bed	i bid	o pot	u cup	th thin
ā cake	ē me	ī bite	ō go	ū rude	ᴛʜ then
ȧ bar	ə about	ər over	ȯ for	u̇ put	zh measure

strap·ping (strap′ing) *Informal.* big, strong, and healthy: *a fine, strapping boy.* *adj.*

stra·ta (strā′tə *or* strat′ə) a plural of **stratum.** *n.*

strat·e·gy (strat′ə jē) 1 the art of skilful planning and management in order to win or to reach any other goal: *Strategy is important in an election campaign.* Something that is based on strategy or very important to its success is **strategic** (strə tē′jik). 2 a particular plan to help reach a goal. *n., pl.* **strat·e·gies.**
—**strat′e·gist,** *n.*

strat·o·sphere (strat′əs fēr′) the top part of the atmosphere, from about 11 km to 50 km above the earth. *n.*

stra·tum (strā′təm *or* strat′əm) 1 a layer of rock, air, or water, especially one of several lying on top of one another. 2 a level: *people from every stratum of society.* *n., pl.* **stra·ta** or **stra·tums.**

stra·tus (strā′təs *or* strat′əs) a low grey cloud that spreads over a large area. *n.*

straw (stro) 1 the stalks or stems of grain left after drying and threshing. Straw is used for horses and cows to lie on, for making hats, and for many other purposes. 2 a thin tube made of plastic or waxed paper, used for sucking up drinks. *n.*

straw·ber·ry (stro′ber′ē) a small, juicy, red fruit that is roughly cone-shaped and good to eat. It grows on a low plant. *n., pl.* **straw·ber·ries.**

stray (strā) 1 wander: *to stray from the path. Our dog has strayed off somewhere.* 2 wandering; lost: *A stray cat is crying at the door.* 3 a wanderer; a lost animal: *That cat is a stray that we took in.* 4 scattered here and there: *There were a few stray ice fishing huts out on the frozen lake.* 1 *v.,* 2, 4 *adj.,* 3 *n.*

streak (strēk) 1 a long, thin mark or line: *He has a streak of dirt on his face.* 2 a bit of some quality: *He has a streak of humour, though he looks very serious.* 3 make long, thin marks or lines on: *The clowns streaked their faces with paint.* 4 move very fast: *She streaked past the others and crossed the finish line.* 1, 2 *n.,* 3, 4 *v.*
like a streak, *Informal.* very fast: *When the dog saw its master, it ran like a streak across the lawn to greet him.*

stream (strēm) 1 a small body of running water; a flow of liquid: *A stream runs through the park. A stream of soapy water ran down her arm.* 2 any steady flow: *a stream of light, a stream of words.* 3 flow; pour or move fast and steadily: *Tears streamed from his eyes. People streamed out of the theatre.* 1, 2 *n.,* 3 *v.*

stream·er (strē′mər) any long, narrow, flowing thing: *Streamers of ribbon hung from her hat.* *n.*

stream·line (strēm′līn′) 1 shape so as to move easily and swiftly through air or water: *to streamline an airplane.* 2 organize so as to go more smoothly and use up less time and energy: *to streamline a procedure.* *v.,* **stream·lined, stream·lin·ing.**

street (strēt) 1 a road in a city or town. 2 the people who live in the buildings on a street: *Our street is holding a neighbourhood barbecue.* *n.*
on the street, homeless. A **street person** is homeless.

street·car (strēt′kår′) a large vehicle that runs by electric power on rails on city streets. It is used for public transportation. *n.*

street·wise (strēt′wīz′) having enough knowledge and experience to avoid or deal with any trouble that might happen on the streets of a city: *Nate is streetwise enough not to play alone in the empty laneway.* *adj.*

strength (strength) the quality of being strong or tough; power; force: *the strength to lift heavy weights, the strength of a person's love, the strength of a flavour.* *n.*
—**strength′en,** *v.*
on the strength of, relying or depending on: *Dad bought the dog on the strength of our promise to take care of it.*

stren·u·ous (stren′yū əs) 1 taking a lot of effort or energy: *We had a strenuous day moving into our new house. Running is strenuous exercise.* 2 strong; vigorous: *In spite of my strenuous objections, they cut down the tree.* *adj.*

stress (stres) 1 pressure; strain: *Problems at school were causing her a lot of stress and anxiety.* Something that causes a lot of stress is **stressful.** 2 treat as important; emphasize: *The principal stressed the safety rules.* 3 emphasis; importance given to something: *My parents lay a lot of stress on sharing.* 4 greater force used in pronouncing a certain syllable in a word. In the word *hero,* the stress is on the first syllable. 5 a mark (**′**) showing this, as in *to·day***′**. Many words have two stresses, a heavy one (**′**) and a light one (′), as in *ac·cel***′**er·a′tor. 6 pronounce with a stress. The word *tomorrow* is stressed on the second syllable. 1, 3–5 *n.,* 2, 6 *v.*

stretch (strech) 1 pull or be pulled out to greater size: *Stretch this sweater a little. Rubber stretches easily.* 2 reach or spread out to the full length: *to stretch out your hand. Della got up and stretched.* 3 the act of stretching: *With a long stretch, Owen snatched the book off the shelf.* 4 continue over a certain distance or time: *The forest stretches right to the coast.* 5 an unbroken length in space or time: *A stretch of sand lay between the road and the ocean. Six months is a pretty long stretch.* 6 *Informal.* something hard to imagine, accept, etc.: *I know it's a stretch, but it's really true!* 1, 2, 4 *v.,* 3, 5, 6 *n.*
stretch the truth, exaggerate.

stretch·er (strech′ər) 1 a frame with a covering of strong cloth or other material, and either wheels or handles. It is used to carry sick, wounded, or dead people. 2 a device for stretching something: *a shoe stretcher.* *n.*

strew (strū) cover with something scattered. This verb is usually used as a past participle: *The ground was strewn with leaves.* *v.,* **strewed, strewn, strew·ing.**

strick·en (strik′ən) severely affected by any kind of trouble: *stricken with grief. Help was rushed to the fire-stricken city.* *adj.*

strict (strikt) 1 very careful, sometimes too careful, about following a rule or making others follow it: *Our teacher is strict but fair.* 2 exact; precise: *the strict sense of a word.* 3 complete; absolute: *The secret was told in strict confidence.* 4 only that and nothing else: *the strict truth.* *adj.* —**strict′ly,** *adv.*

stride (strīd) 1 walk with long steps: *The tall man strides rapidly down the street.* 2 a long step: *She crossed the brook in a single stride.* 3 a way of walking with long steps: *The child could not keep up with his father's stride.* 1 *v.,* **strode, strid·den, strid·ing;** 2, 3 *n.*
hit your stride, get up to your regular speed in an activity.
make strides, make great progress.
take in your stride, handle calmly and without difficulty: *The storm stranded her at the airport, but she took it all in her stride.*

strife (strīf) fighting: *bitter strife between rivals.* *n.*

strike (strīk) 1 hit: *The boxer struck his opponent. The car struck a fence.* 2 attack: *a strike from the air* (*n.*). *The enemy struck at dawn* (*v.*). 3 overcome by any kind of trouble or strong feeling: *They were struck with terror.* 4 occur to: *She smiled as an amusing thought struck her.* 5 make a certain impression on someone: *The idea strikes me as silly.* 6 cross out: *to strike a name off the list.* 7 a refusal to work by a group of employees, in order to force the employer to improve working conditions, pay higher wages, etc.: *There was a strike at the mine last year. They were on strike for a week.* 8 stop work for this reason: *The nurses are striking.* 9 mark time with a ringing sound: *The clock struck twelve.* 10 find gold, oil, etc. in the ground: *The miner struck gold.* 11 in baseball, a failure of the batter to make a proper hit. 12 in bowling, the act of knocking down all the pins at once. 1–6, 8–10 *v.,* **struck, struck** or **strick·en, strik·ing;** 7, 11, 12 *n.*
strike out, a cross out. b in baseball, fail to hit three times: *The batter struck out.* c cause a batter to do this: *The pitcher struck him out.*
strike up, begin: *The two boys struck up a friendship.*

strik·ing (strī′king) attracting attention; very remarkable: *There was a striking oil painting on the wall.* *adj.* —**strik′ing·ly,** *adv.*

string (string) 1 a cord, yarn, or very thin rope: *The package is tied with red string.* b a piece of this, or anything else used for tying: *a long string, apron strings.* 2 a number of things in a line or row: *a string of cars.* 3 a cord or thread with things on it: *a string of pearls.* 4 put or hang on a string: *to string beads.* 5 a length of wire for a musical instrument: *guitar strings.* 6 **strings,** *pl.* in an orchestra, violins, cellos, and other instruments with strings. They are also called **stringed instruments.** 1–3, 5, 6 *n.,* 4 *v.,* **strung, string·ing.** —**string′y,** *adj.*
pull strings, use your influence, especially secretly: *He pulled some strings to get his son on the team.*
string out, a stretch over time: *The program was strung out too long.* b arrange in a long line or row: *A dozen little towns were strung out along the highway.*
string someone along, *Informal.* fool: *They are just stringing you along with those ridiculous stories.*
string together, put one after another, especially without properly linking them: *For your report, don't just string together a bunch of facts.*

strip[1] (strip) 1 take off clothes or other covering: *to strip the peel from a banana, to strip the land of trees. He stripped down to his shorts and dived in.* 2 completely remove something from a person, place, or thing: *We stripped the fruit from the trees. The winner was stripped of his prize because he had cheated.* *v.,* **stripped, strip·ping.**

strip[2] (strip) a long, narrow, flat piece or stretch of anything: *a strip of paper, a strip of cleared land.* *n.*

stripe (strīp) 1 a long, narrow band or line of a different colour from its background: *A tiger has stripes. The uniform had a red stripe down the side of each leg.* 2 mark with stripes. 1 *n.,* 2 *v.,* **striped, strip·ing.**

strip farming (strip′ fär′ming) a way of farming that reduces soil erosion on slopes. Crops are grown in alternating strips across the slope, so that crops with weak root systems are between those with stronger root systems.

strive (strīv) 1 try hard: *Strive to succeed.* 2 fight; struggle: *The swimmer strove against the tide.* *v.,* **strove** or **strived, striv·en, striv·ing.**

strode (strōd) the past tense of **stride:** *He strode across the lawn.* *v.*

a bat	e bed	i bid	o pot	u cup	th thin
ā cake	ē me	ī bite	ō go	ū rude	TH then
ä bar	ə about	ər over	ô for	ů put	zh measure

Structure

The building of a skyscraper involves many people — architects, engineers, builders — because the structure is complex.

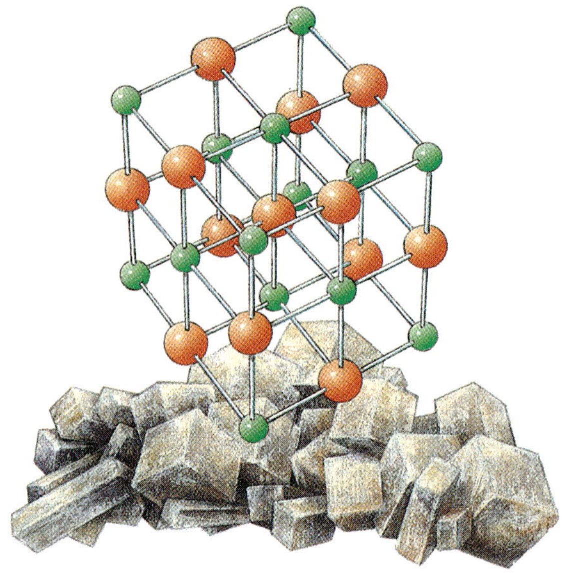

To learn about the properties of a substance, scientists use a model of its molecular structure.

stroke[1] (strōk) 1 an act of striking; a blow; a hit: *The house was hit by a stroke of lightning.* 2 a single, complete movement to be made again and again: *With each stroke of the oars we came closer to shore.* 3 a mark made by a pen, pencil, brush, etc.: *Put a stroke through that wrong word.* 4 the sound made by a clock striking: *We arrived at the stroke of three.* 5 a sudden, serious illness caused by the loss of blood to some part of the brain or by too much sun or heat. *n.*

stroke[2] (strōk) move the hand gently over; pet: *He likes to stroke his kitten.* *v.,* **stroked, strok·ing.**

stroll (strōl) 1 walk in a leisurely way. 2 a leisurely walk: *We went for a stroll in the park.* 1 *v.,* 2 *n.*

strol·ler (strō′lər) a seat on wheels for a small child to sit in, with handles for someone to push it along. *n.*

strong (strong) 1 able to do much; having great force or power: *A strong person can lift heavy things. A strong wind blew down the trees. A united nation is strong.* 2 tough; able to last, endure, resist, etc.: *a strong fort, a strong rope.* 3 having a lot of some quality: *strong perfume, strong coffee.* *adj.*

strong·hold (strong′hōld′) a fort; a well-defended place: *The guerrillas have a stronghold up in the hills.* *n.*

strove (strōv) a past tense of **strive:** *They strove to do their best in everything.* *v.*

struck (struk) the past tense and past participle of **strike:** *The clock struck four. The barn was struck by lightning.* *v.*

struc·ture (struk′chər) 1 a building; something built: *The city hall is a large stone structure.* 2 anything made of connected parts put together in an orderly way: *The human skeleton is an amazing structure.* 3 the way parts are put together or arranged: *the structure of an atom, the structure of a sentence.* 4 arrange parts according to an orderly plan. 1–3 *n.,* 4 *v.,* **struc·tured, struc·tur·ing.** **—struc′tur·al,** *adj.*

strug·gle (strug′əl) 1 make great efforts; try hard against difficulties: *The poor have to struggle for a living. The swimmer struggled against the tide. She struggled to keep back the tears.* 2 move with great effort: *The injured boy struggled to his feet.* 3 great effort; hard work: *Breaking bad habits is a struggle.* 4 fighting; a conflict: *The struggle between the two countries went on for years.* 1, 2 *v.,* **strug·gled, strug·gling;** 3, 4 *n.*

strum (strum) play by running the fingers lightly across the strings: *to strum a guitar.* *n.*

strung (strung) the past tense and past participle of **string:** *We strung the painted macaroni into a necklace. The children were strung out in a line after the teacher.* *v.*

strut (strut) walk in a proud way: *He strutted around the room in his new jacket.* *v.,* **strut·ted, strut·ting.**

stub (stub) 1 bang your toe against something by accident: *I stubbed my toe on a rock.* 2 a short piece that is left: *the stub of a pencil, the stub of a cigarette.* 3 a piece torn off and kept as a record: *a ticket stub.* 4 put out a cigarette or cigar by crushing the burning end down on a surface. 1, 4 *v.,* **stubbed, stub·bing;** 2, 3 *n.*

stub·ble (stub′əl) **1** the short stalks of grain left in the ground after the grain is cut: *The stubble hurt the children's bare feet.* **2** any short, rough growth: *There was a dark stubble of beard on his face.* *n.* —**stub′bly,** *adj.*

stub·born (stub′ərn) **1** never wanting to change or give in: *She saw that she was wrong, but was too stubborn to admit it.* **2** hard to cure or fix: *a stubborn cough.* *adj.*

stub·by (stub′ē) short and thick: *stubby fingers.* *adj.*

stuck (stuk) the past tense and past participle of **stick:** *He stuck out his tongue. I am stuck in the snowbank.* *v.*

stuck–up (stuk′up′) *Informal.* too proud; conceited; snobby. *adj.*

stud[1] (stud) **1** the head of a nail, a knob, jewel, etc. sticking out from a surface: *The belt was ornamented with silver studs.* **2** set with studs or something like studs: *The crown was studded with rubies. Stars studded the sky.* **3** one of the upright boards forming the framework of a wall in a building. 1, 3 *n.,* 2 *v.,* **stud·ded, stud·ding.**

stud[2] (stud) a male animal, especially a horse, kept for breeding. A **stud farm** raises animals for breeding. *n.*

stu·dent (styū′dənt *or* stū′dənt) **1** a person who is studying in a school, college, or university: *That high school has 3000 students.* **2** a person who likes to learn about a certain thing: *She is a student of birds.* *n.*

stud·ied (stud′ēd) **1** carefully planned; done on purpose: *What she said to me was a studied insult.* **2** the past tense and past participle of **study:** *She studied the lesson carefully.* 1 *adj.,* 2 *v.*

stu·di·o (styū′dē ō *or* stū′dē ō) **1** the workroom of an artist. **2** a place where movies, musical recordings, or radio or TV shows are made. *n., pl.* **stu·di·os.**

stu·di·ous (styū′dē əs *or* stū′dē əs) **1** liking to study; working hard at studying. **2** careful; trying hard to do a certain thing: *The clerk made a studious effort to please customers.* *adj.*

stud·y (stud′ē) **1** try to learn by reading or watching and thinking: *to study a spelling lesson, to study plant life. She is studying to be a doctor.* **2** the effort to learn in this way: *After an hour's hard study he was ready for the test.* **3** examine or consider carefully: *We studied the map to find the shortest way home.* **4** a careful examination: *The city is doing a study of homelessness.* **5** a room for reading or writing: *The rabbi was reading in his study.* 1, 3 *v.,* **stud·ied, stud·y·ing;** 2, 4, 5 *n., pl.* **stud·ies.**

stuff (stuf) **1** a substance: *What's this sticky stuff on the plate?* **2** things: *Move your stuff out of the hallway. We bought chips and stuff for the party.* **3** pack full; fill: *She stuffed her knapsack with books.* **4** force into a small space: *I stuffed my mitts into my pockets.* **5** plug up: *My nose is stuffed up with a cold.* **6** fill a food with some kind of mixture for eating: *to stuff a turkey. I love stuffed green peppers.* **7** fill the skin of a dead animal to make it look as it did when alive: *We saw many stuffed birds at the museum.* 1, 2 *n.,* 3–7 *v.*
that's the stuff! Well done!

stuff·ing (stuf′ing) **1** any material used to fill something. **2** moistened bits of bread mixed with spices, used to stuff a turkey or other bird before cooking. *n.*

stuff·y (stuf′ē) **1** lacking fresh air: *a stuffy room.* **2** too serious and dull: *a stuffy speech.* **3** blocked up: *a stuffy nose.* *adj.,* **stuff·i·er, stuff·i·est.**

stum·ble (stum′bəl) **1** trip: *She stumbled over the stool in the dark kitchen.* **2** walk, speak, or do anything in an unsteady or clumsy way: *The tired girls stumbled home. The boy stumbled nervously through his speech.* **3** an act of stumbling. 1, 2 *v.,* **stum·bled, stum·bling;** 3 *n.*
stumble on, find by chance; come across: *I stumbled on a fascinating old book in Grandma's attic.*

stump (stump) **1** what is left of a tree that has been cut down: *We sat on top of a stump.* **2** anything left after the main or important part is cut off: *The dog wagged its stump of a tail.* **3** walk in a stiff, heavy way. **4** *Informal.* be too hard for someone to answer or solve: *Our question stumped him.* 1, 2 *n.,* 3, 4 *v.*

stun (stun) **1** knock unconscious: *He was stunned by the fall.* **2** bewilder; shock; overwhelm: *She was stunned by the news.* *v.,* **stunned, stun·ning.**

stung (stung) the past tense and past participle of **sting:** *A wasp stung him. He was stung on the neck.* *v.*

stunk (stungk) the past participle of **stink:** *The garbage had stunk up the whole house.* *v.*

stun·ning (stun′ing) *Informal.* excellent; beautiful: *a stunning performance, a stunning new outfit.* *adj.*

stunt[1] (stunt) prevent from reaching full size: *Lack of proper food stunts a child.* *v.*

stunt[2] (stunt) *Informal.* an act of great daring and skill, done to entertain an audience or just for fun: *We watched Kiefer do skateboarding stunts.* A **stunt person** is hired to do stunts in a movie in place of the real actor. *n.*

a bat	e bed	i bid	o pot	u cup	th thin
ā cake	ē me	ī bite	ō go	ū rude	ᴛʜ then
à bar	ə about	ər over	ȯ for	u̇ put	zh measure

stu·pe·fy (styū′pə fī′ *or* stū′pə fī′) **1** astonish: *They worked with stupefying speed.* **2** make groggy: *stupefied by a drug.* *v.,* **stu·pe·fied, stu·pe·fy·ing.**

stu·pen·dous (styū pen′dəs *or* stū pen′dəs) amazing: *Niagara Falls is a stupendous sight.* *adj.*

stu·pid (styū′pid *or* stū′pid) not smart or sensible; showing a lack of good thinking: *a stupid idea, a stupid remark.* *adj.* —**stu·pid′i·ty,** *n.*

stu·por (styū′pər *or* stū′pər) a condition of being unable to think, feel, or act: *The injured man lay in a stupor, unable to tell what had happened.* *n.*

stur·dy (stər′dē) strong and firm: *sturdy legs, a sturdy faith.* *adj.,* **stur·di·er, stur·di·est.**

stur·geon (stər′jən) a very large food fish which has a long snout and a tough skin with rows of bony plates. Sturgeon live in fresh and salt water. *n., pl.* **stur·geon** or **stur·geons.**

stut·ter (stut′ər) **1** a speech problem where the person often repeats sounds while trying to say them, especially the first sounds in a word. **2** speak or say something in this way: *to stutter a reply.* 1 *n.,* 2 *v.*

sty[1] (stī) a pen for pigs. *n., pl.* **sties.**

sty[2] or **stye** (stī) a painful swelling on the edge of your eyelid, like a small boil. *n., pl.* **sties** or **styes.**

style (stīl) **1** a particular way of dressing, decorating, building, writing, or doing anything else. Different people prefer different styles: *This style of shoe is too fancy for me. Mr. Grigonis has a relaxed teaching style.* **2** the particular way of dressing, decorating, etc. that is popular: *That coat is out of style.* Something in the popular style is **stylish.** **3** elegance or good taste combined with creativity: *Their house is decorated with style.* **4** design or arrange in a particular style: *dresses styled in Paris. She uses a blow dryer to style her hair.* 1–3 *n.,* 4 *v.,* **styled, styl·ing.**

sty·lus (stī′ləs) a small pointed tool used to write on wax or clay tablets in ancient times. *n., pl.* **sty·li** *or* **sty·lus·es.**

Sty·ro·foam (stī′rə fōm′) *a trademark for* a light, firm plastic foam used for insulation, packaging, etc. *n.*

sub– *a prefix meaning:* **1** under or below, as in *subway, submarine, subcommittee.* **2** further, or again, as in *subdivide.* **3** near or nearly, as in *subarctic.*

sub·arc·tic (sub′ärk′tik *or* sub′är′tik) having to do with regions just south of the Arctic Circle. *adj.*

sub·di·vide (sub′də vīd′) divide again; divide a part into even smaller parts: *The book is divided into three sections; each one is subdivided into four chapters.* *v.,* **sub·di·vid·ed, sub·di·vid·ing.**

sub·di·vi·sion (sub′də vizh′ən) **1** a part of a part. **2** a piece of land divided into building lots. **3** the act of dividing a part into even smaller parts. *n.*

sub·due (səb dyū′ *or* səb dū′) **1** bring under control; overcome: *The police finally subdued the struggling thief. We subdued an urge to laugh.* **2** tone down; soften: *subdued voices, subdued light.* *v.,* **sub·dued, sub·du·ing.**

sub·ject (sub′jikt *for 1–4, and 6,* səb jekt′ *for 5 and 7*) **1** a person or thing that is being talked or thought about, written about, painted, photographed, etc.: *I tried to change the subject during our talk. She focussed the camera on the subject—a butterfly.* **2** a branch of knowledge studied in school: *Math and French are my two favourite subjects.* **3** the part of a sentence that tells what is being talked about. In the sentence *The farmer grows peaches, The farmer* is the subject. In *The peaches are picked in August, The peaches* is the subject. **4** a person under the rule of a king, queen, emperor, etc. **5** bring under some power or control: *Rome subjected all Italy to its rule.* **6** force to experience something: *We were subjected to a long lecture about neatness.* **7** under some power or rule: *a subject nation.* 1–4 *n.,* 5, 6 *v.,* 7 *adj.*
subject to, **a** under the power or authority of: *We are subject to our country's laws.* **b** likely to have: *This area is subject to heavy rains.* **c** depending on; on the condition of: *I invited Nadia over, subject to Mom's approval.*

Grammar Check . . . . subject

The **subject** usually comes at the beginning of the sentence.

- A singular subject takes a singular verb: *The cat has sharp claws.* Here, the subject (*cat*) is singular, so the verb (*has*) is singular.
- A plural subject takes a plural verb: *The cats have sharp claws.* Here, the subject (*cats*) is plural so the verb (*have*) is plural.

sub·jec·tive (səb jek′tiv) personal and found only in someone's mind: *Hanna admitted that her opinion was purely subjective; she had no actual facts to back it up.* *adj.*

sub·li·mate (sub′lə māt′ *for 1,* sub′lə mit *for 2*) **1** turn from a solid to a gas or a gas to a solid, with no liquid stage in between. Solid air fresheners work by sublimating. **2** a substance produced in this way. Snow and frost are sublimates; they are solids that form directly from water vapour in the air. 1 *v.,* **sub·li·mat·ed, sub·li·mat·ing;** 2 *n.* —**sub′li·ma′tion,** *n.*

Submarine

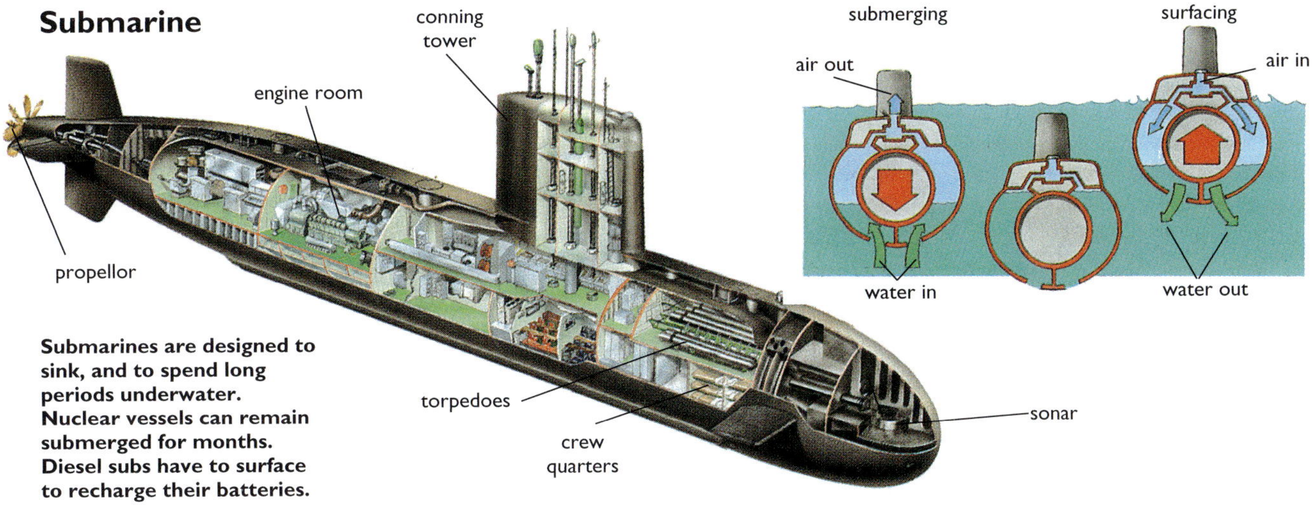

Submarines are designed to sink, and to spend long periods underwater. Nuclear vessels can remain submerged for months. Diesel subs have to surface to recharge their batteries.

sub•lime (sə blīm′) lofty; noble; majestic; grand: *Mountain scenery is often sublime.* *adj.*

sub•ma•rine (sub′mə rēn′ *or* sub′mə rēn′) **1** a boat that can go under water. **2** found or used in the ocean: *submarine plants, a submarine telephone cable.* **3** a large sandwich made with a long bun. 1, 3 *n.*, 2 *adj.*

sub•merge (səb mərj′) put under water: *A big wave submerged the raft.* *v.*, **sub•merged, sub•merg•ing.**

sub•mit (səb mit′) **1** put yourself under someone's control or authority: *We agreed to submit to camp rules.* Someone who submits easily is **submissive.** **2** hand in or send in: *I submitted a drawing to the art contest.* *v.*, **sub•mit•ted, sub•mit•ting.** **—sub•mis′sion,** *n.*

sub•or•di•nate (sə bȯr′də nit *for 1, 2, and 3,* sə bȯr′də nāt′ *for 4*) **1** in a lower rank: *Teachers are subordinate to the principal.* **2** less important; secondary. A **subordinate clause** cannot stand alone and does not contain the main idea. In the sentence *I came back as soon as I could, as soon as I could* is the subordinate clause; *I came back* is the **main clause.** **3** a person of lower rank. **4** make lower or less important than something else. 1, 2 *adj.*, 3 *n.*, 4 *v.*, **sub•or•di•nat•ed, sub•or•di•nat•ing.**

sub•scribe (səb skrīb′) **1** pay for a magazine or newspaper to be regularly delivered to you: *We subscribe to* Canadian Geographic *magazine.* **2** accept or agree: *I cannot subscribe to that idea.* *v.*, **sub•scribed, sub•scrib•ing.** **—sub•scrib′er,** *n.* **—sub•scrip′tion,** *n.*

sub•se•quent (sub′sə kwənt) coming after; later: *Subsequent events proved that she was right.* *adj.* **—sub′se•quent•ly,** *adv.*

sub•side (səb sīd′) grow less; die down: *After the rain stopped, the flood waters subsided. Her fever subsided after she took the medicine.* *v.*, **sub•sid•ed, sub•sid•ing.**

sub•si•dize (sub′sə dīz′) help pay for; support with money: *The government subsidizes hospitals.* The money given in this way is a **subsidy** (sub′sə dē). *v.*

sub•soil (sub′soil′) the layer of earth that lies just under the surface soil: *In our backyard, we have clay subsoil under a thin layer of loam.* *n.*

sub•stance (sub′stəns) **1** any material that a thing is made up of; any kind of matter: *Ice and water are the same substance in different forms.* **2** the main part of anything: *Give the substance of the speech in your own words.* **3** a solid quality: *Pea soup has more substance than water.* *n.*

substance abuse (sub′stəns ə byūz′) use of a substance, such as alcohol or drugs, in a way that damages health and interferes with a person's ability to function. *n.*

sub•stan•tial (səb stan′shəl) **1** made up of matter; physically real: *People and things are substantial; dreams and ghosts are not.* **2** solid, not light or flimsy: *something substantial to eat.* **3** fairly large: *a substantial amount of money.* *adj.* **—sub•stan′tial•ly,** *adv.*

sub•sti•tute (sub′stə tyūt′ *or* sub′stə tūt′) **1** a person or thing that takes the place of another. **2** put or act in the place of another: *We substituted honey for sugar in this recipe. She substituted for Miss Bakker, who is ill.* 1 *n.*, 2 *v.*, **sub•sti•tut•ed, sub•sti•tut•ing.** **—sub′sti•tu′tion,** *n.*

sub•ter•ra•ne•an (sub′tə rā′nē ən) underground: *A subterranean passage led from the castle to a cave.* *adj.*

a bat	e bed	i bid	o pot	u cup	th **thin**
ā cake	ē me	ī bite	ō go	ū rude	ŦH **then**
ä bar	ə about	ər over	ȯ for	u̇ put	zh measure

sub·ti·tle (sub′tī′təl) 1 an additional title of a book, article, etc. 2 words at the bottom of a movie screen, translating the dialogue for an audience that doesn't understand the original language: *The movie is in Italian with English subtitles.* 3 give a subtitle to: *"The Hobbit" is subtitled "There and Back Again."* 1, 2 *n.*, 3 *v.*, **sub·ti·tled, sub·ti·tling.**

Grammar✓Check . . . . . . subtitle

Separate a **subtitle** from the main title by a colon: *Monsters: Do They Exist?*

sub·tle (sut′əl) 1 not obvious; hard to notice, recognize, or understand right away: *a subtle odour, a subtle hint.* 2 sly; crafty; tricky: *a subtle scheme.* *adj.* **—sub′tly,** *adv.* **—sub′tle·ty,** *n.*

sub·tract (səb trakt′) take away: *Subtract 2 from 10 and you have 8. Symbol: –* *v.* **—sub·trac′tion,** *n.*

sub·tra·hend (sub′trə hend′) a number to be subtracted from another: *In 10 – 2 = 8, the subtrahend is 2.* *n.*

sub·urb (sub′ərb) a district, town, or village just outside or near a big city. *n.* **—sub·ur′ban** (sə bər′bən), *adj.*

sub·way (sub′wā′) an electric railway running mainly underground in a city. *n.*

suc·ceed (sək sēd′) 1 turn out well; do well; have or get the right result: *On her fourth try she finally succeeded. I succeeded in scoring a goal.* 2 come next after: *Chrétien succeeded Mulroney as prime minister of Canada.* The one who comes next is the previous person's **successor** (sək ses′ər). *v.*
succeed to, be the next one to have: *When he retired, his daughter succeeded to the ownership of the business.*

suc·cess (sək ses′) 1 the result that is aimed for; the fact of succeeding: *Success in school comes mostly from hard work.* 2 a person or thing that succeeds: *The school concert was a great success.* *n.* **—suc·cess′ful,** *adj.*

suc·ces·sion (sək sesh′ən) 1 a group of things happening one after another; a series: *A succession of accidents spoiled our trip.* 2 the fact, the right, or the order of coming next: *The king's oldest son was first in succession to the throne.* *n.*
in succession, one after another: *It rained several days in succession.* Things that happen one after another are **successive.**

suc·cu·lent (suk′yə lənt) juicy: *a ripe and succulent peach.* *adj.*

suc·cumb (sə kum′) give way; yield: *He succumbed to the temptation and stole a brownie.* *v.*

such (such) 1 of that kind: *Such friends are rare. School supplies include pencils, erasers, scissors, and such things.* 2 so great, so bad, so good, etc.: *He is such a liar! I had such a headache that I could hardly think straight.* 3 people or things of a certain kind: *The box contains blankets and towels and such.* 1, 2 *adj.*, 3 *pron.*
such and such, an expression for a person, place, or thing that is not named: *Every speech began, "My name is such and such and I'm going to talk about such and such."*
such as, for example: *members of the canine family, such as the wolf, fox, and jackal.*

suck (suk) 1 pull into the mouth: *to suck juice through a straw.* 2 hold in the mouth and lick: *to suck a lollipop.* 3 take in; pull in: *Plants suck up moisture from the earth.* 4 the act of sucking: *The baby took one suck at the bottle and pushed it away.* 1–3 *v.*, 4 *n.*

suck·er (suk′ər) 1 a lump of candy on a stick, for sucking or licking. 2 anything that uses a sucking action. Octopus tentacles have suckers that stick to surfaces. *n.*

suc·tion (suk′shən) the process of pulling matter into a space by sucking all the air out of the space so as to create a **vacuum.** Whatever is next to a vacuum is forced into it by the pressure of the surrounding air or liquid. Drinking through a straw works by suction. *n.*

sud·den (sud′ən) quick and without warning: *a sudden attack.* *adj.* **—sud′den·ly,** *adv.* **—sud′den·ness,** *n.*
all of a sudden, quickly and without warning.
sudden death, an extra period of play to break a tie. It ends as soon as someone scores.

suds (sudz) soapy water with bubbles and foam. *pl.n.* **—suds′y,** *adj.*

sue (sū) go to court against someone: *He sued the railway after a train killed his cow.* If you sue someone, you are starting a **suit** or **lawsuit.** *v.*, **sued, su·ing.**

suede (swād) very soft leather with a velvety fuzz on the surface. *n.*

su·et (sū′it) hard fat from certain parts of animals. *n.*

suf·fer (suf′ər) have pain, sadness, or trouble of any kind: *to suffer from headaches. He suffered a broken leg when he fell. Their business suffered greatly during the war.* *v.* **—suf′fer·ing,** *n.*

suf·fice (sə fīs′) be enough; be sufficient: *Your report doesn't need to be long; one page will suffice.* *v.*, **suf·ficed, suf·fic·ing.**

suf·fi·cient (sə fish′ənt) enough: *The poor child did not have sufficient clothing.* *adj.* —**suf·fi′cient·ly,** *adv.*

suf·fix (suf′iks) a sound or syllable put at the end of a word to change its meaning or to make another word, as *-ly* in *badly, -ness* in *goodness,* and *-ed* in *played.* *n.*
▶ See Appendix.

suf·fo·cate (suf′ə kāt′) keep from getting air; kill or die in this way: *Shutting this caterpillar in a jar will suffocate it. The parrot suffocated in the smoke-filled room.* *v.,* **suf·fo·cat·ed, suf·fo·cat·ing.** —**suf′fo·ca′tion,** *n.*

suf·frage (suf′rij) the right to vote: *Alberta granted the suffrage to women in 1916.* *n.*

To make sugar from sugar cane (or sugar beet), the sweet juice must be filtered and purified. Then the sugar solution can be evaporated to make sugar crystals.

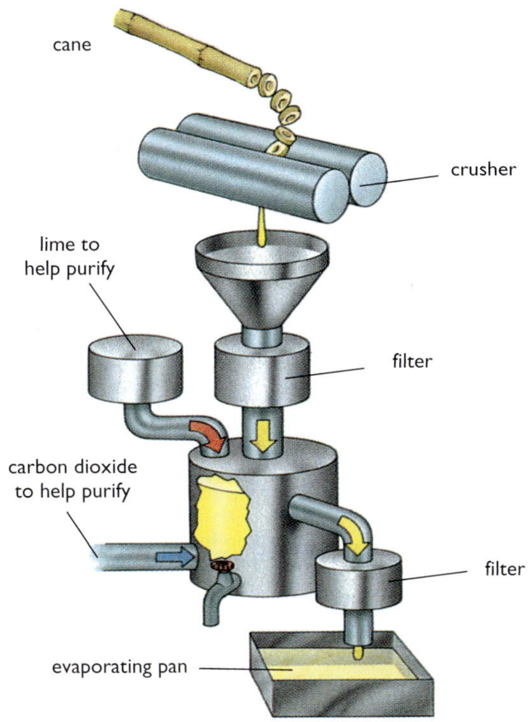

sug·ar (shu̇g′ər) **1** a sweet substance made mainly from sugar cane or sugar beets. **2** sprinkle with sugar: *sugared doughnuts.* **3** form crystals of sugar: *Honey will sugar if it is kept too long.* 1 *n.,* 2, 3 *v.*
—**sug′ar·y,** *adj.*
sugar off, make maple sugar out of maple syrup by boiling it to evaporate the water.

sugar beet (shu̇g′ər bēt′) a large beet with a white root that is a major source of sugar.

sugar cane (shu̇g′ər kān′) a very tall grass with a strong jointed stem and flat leaves, growing in warm regions. Sugar cane is one of the main sources of sugar.

sugar maple (shu̇g′ər mā′pəl) a large maple tree of eastern North America. Its sap is collected in the spring to make maple sugar and syrup, and its hardwood is used for furniture and so on. Its leaves turn bright colours in fall; a red sugar maple leaf is Canada's emblem. Many sugar maples growing together form a **sugar bush.**

sug·gest (sə jest′ *or* səg jest′) **1** offer an idea for something good to do; propose: *She suggested a swim, and we all agreed.* **2** hint at something; give people a certain idea or feeling: *Her strange smile suggested she had a secret. Bright colours often suggest warmth.* *v.*

sug·ges·tion (sə jes′chən *or* səg jes′chən) **1** the act of suggesting or the thing suggested: *The suggestion of a swim made the children jump with joy.* **2** a very small trace: *a suggestion of anger in someone's voice.* *n.*

su·i·cide (sū′ə sīd′) the act of killing yourself on purpose. *n.* —**su′i·cid′al,** *adj.*
commit suicide, kill yourself on purpose.

suit (sūt) **1** a set of clothes meant to be worn together: *a business suit, a pantsuit, a skirt suit.* **2** make or be right for: *That haircut suits your face. In writing, you have to suit the language to your reader.* **3** be acceptable or convenient to; please: *Which date suits you best? Nothing we do suits him.* **4** a case in a law court: *He started a suit against the other driver in the accident.*
5 one of the four sets of playing cards in a deck. Spades, hearts, diamonds, and clubs are the four suits. 1, 4, 5 *n.,* 2, 3 *v.*
follow suit, a follow the example of another. **b** play a card of the same suit as the one played.
suit up, put on the special clothing and so on needed for some activity: *The astronauts are suiting up for their flight.*
suit yourself, do as you please.

suit·a·ble (sū′tə bəl) right for a certain person, thing, time, or place; fitting; proper: *That fancy dress is not suitable for school.* *adj.*

suit·case (sūt′kās′) a flat, boxlike travel bag. *n.*

suite (swēt) **1** a set of connected rooms to be used by one person, family, office, etc.: *a hotel suite. The doctor's office is in Suite 305.* **2** a set of matching furniture. **3** any set of things that go together: *a suite of songs.* *n.*

suit·or (sū′tər) a man who is trying to win the love of a woman: *The princess had many suitors.* *n.*

a bat	e bed	i bid	o pot	u cup	th thin
ā cake	ē me	ī bite	ō go	ū rude	ᴛʜ then
ä bar	ə about	ər over	ô for	u̇ put	zh measure

Sun

The sun is a fiercely hot globe of burning gas, mostly hydrogen. The hydrogen atoms at the sun's centre have so much energy that they break apart. When this energy reaches the sun's surface, it is sent out into space as radiant energy in the form of heat and light — sunshine!

Some Sun Facts
The sun is a star about 150 million kilometres away.
It is over 4 600 000 000 years old.
Its diameter is roughly 1 392 000 km.
The temperature at its surface is about 5500°C.
The temperature at its centre is about 15 000 000°C.

sulk (sulk) 1 be in a bad mood and refuse to talk because you did not get your way. 2 a fit of sulking, also called **the sulks.** 1 *v.*, 2 *n.* —**sulk′y,** *adj.*

sul•len (sul′ən) 1 sulky; bad-tempered: *He becomes sullen if you dare to disagree with him.* 2 gloomy; dismal: *sullen skies.* *adj.*

sul•phur or **sul•fur** (sul′fər) a light-yellow substance that burns with a blue flame and a bad smell. Sulphur is a chemical element and is used in making matches, paper pulp, fertilizer, and other things. *n.*

sul•tan (sul′tən) the ruler of certain Muslim countries in earlier times: *Turkey was ruled by a sultan until 1922.* *n.*

sul•try (sul′trē) hot, stuffy, and humid: *We expect some sultry weather in July.* *adj.*, **sul•tri•er, sul•tri•est.**

sum (sum) 1 the total you get by adding: *The sum of 2, 3, and 4 is 9.* 2 an amount of money: *She paid a huge sum for that bicycle.* 3 an arithmetic problem: *He can do easy sums in his head.* 4 **sum up,** tell the main points of: *Sum up the story in one paragraph.* 1–3 *n.*, 4 *v.*, **summed, sum•ming.**
in sum, in short; as a summary.

su•mac or **su•mach** (shū′mak *or* sū′mak) a small tree with long clusters of red or white fruit, and leaves that turn bright red in fall. *n.*

sum•ma•ry (sum′ə rē) a brief statement giving the main points: *This history book has a summary at the end of each chapter.* To make a summary of something is to **summarize** it. *n., pl.* **sum•ma•ries.**

sum•mer (sum′ər) 1 the warmest season of the year, also called **summertime;** the season between spring and autumn. 2 pass the summer: *We summered at the seashore each year.* 1 *n.*, 2 *v.* —**sum′mer•y,** *adj.*

sum•mit (sum′it) the highest point; the top: *the summit of a mountain, the summit of a person's career.* *n.*

sum•mon (sum′ən) 1 call with authority; order to come; send for: *We summoned an ambulance. A telegram summoned her home.* An order to come or to appear somewhere is a **summons.** 2 gather up for action: *He summoned his courage and entered the deserted house.* *v.*

su•mo (sū′mō) a form of Japanese wrestling. Sumo wrestlers are tall and very big and heavy. *n.*

sump•tu•ous (sump′chū əs) luxurious; rich; magnificent: *The premier gave a sumptuous banquet.* *adj.*

sun (sun) 1 the star that the earth and the other planets revolve around. The sun lights and warms the earth. 2 the light and warmth of the sun: *The cat likes to sit in the sun.* 3 put in the light and warmth of the sun: *The swimmers sunned themselves on the beach.* 4 any star like the sun. 1, 2, 4 *n.*, 3 *v.*, **sunned, sun•ning.**

Word Family.......... sun

sunbathe: lie in the sun, for warmth or in order to tan
sunbeam: a ray of sunlight
sundial: an instrument for telling time by the position of a shadow cast by the sun
sundown: the time when the sun goes down
sunglasses: tinted glasses to protect your eyes from the sun
sunlamp: a special lamp that can tan or burn skin
sunlight: light from the sun. Things lit by it are **sunlit**.
sunny: 1 with a lot of sunshine **2** bright and cheerful
sunrise: the rising of the sun, often colouring the sky
sunroof: a window in the roof of a car
sunroom: a small room with very large windows
sunscreen: lotion to protect your skin from the sun. The most powerful kind is called **sunblock**.
sunset: the going down of the sun, often colourful
sunshade: an umbrella or awning giving shade from sun
sunshine: bright light from the sun
sunspot: a dark spot on the sun's surface, visible only by telescope
sunstroke: dangerous failure of your body's cooling system, caused by too much sun
sunup: dawn; the time when the sun rises

sun·burn (sun′bərn′) 1 a burning of the skin by the sun's rays. A sunburn is often red and painful. 2 burn the skin by the sun's rays: *He is sunburned from a day on the beach. I sunburn quickly.* 1 *n.*, 2 *v.*, **sun·burned** or **sun·burnt, sun·burn·ing.**

sun·dae (sun′dā′) a serving of ice cream with syrup, crushed fruit, nuts, etc. on it. *n.*

sun dance (sun′ dans′) a sacred dance ceremony among some First Nations peoples, held once a year by a highly respected person who had received certain gifts from the thunderbird. Only specially invited people could take part.

Sun·day (sun′dā′ *or* sun′dē) the day after Saturday and before Monday. *Abbreviation:* Sun. *n.*

sun·dry (sun′drē) 1 miscellaneous; various: *The box contained sundry items for doing crafts.* 2 **sundries,** *pl.* odds and ends; various small things. 1 *adj.*, 2 *n.*

sun·flow·er (sun′flou′ər) a tall annual plant that has big yellow flowers with brown centres. Its seeds are used as food and as a source of oil. *n.*

sung (sung) the past participle of **sing:** *Many old songs were sung at the concert.* *v.*

sunk (sungk) the past participle of **sink:** *The ship had sunk to the bottom.* *v.*

sunk·en (sung′kən) 1 that has sunk: *a sunken ship.* 2 under water: *a sunken rock.* 3 below the level of the surrounding area: *a sunken living room.* *adj.*

su·per (sū′pər) *Informal.* 1 excellent; wonderful. 2 short for **superintendent,** a manager. 1 *adj.*, 2 *n.*

su·perb (sū pərb′) magnificent; very fine; splendid: *superb scenery, a superb performance.* *adj.*

su·per·fi·cial (sū′pər fish′əl) 1 on the surface: *His burn was superficial and soon healed.* 2 not thorough; with too little thought: *You cannot understand this poem with only a superficial reading.* 3 concerned only with unimportant things, not what really matters; shallow and not serious enough: *a superficial person.* *adj.*

su·per·flu·ous (sū pər′flū əs) extra; not needed: *Don't use superfluous words.* *adj.*

su·per·hu·man (sū′pər hyū′mən) above or beyond ordinary human power: *By a superhuman effort, the driver lifted the wheel of the car off the injured pedestrian's leg.* *adj.*

su·per·im·pose (sū′pər im pōz′) put on or over something else: *A picture of Jacques Cartier was superimposed on the map of Canada.* *v.*, **su·per·im·posed, su·per·im·pos·ing.**

su·per·in·tend·ent (sū′pə rin ten′dənt) a person who oversees or manages something: *a superintendent of schools, the superintendent of an apartment building.* *n.* **—su′per·in·tend′,** *v.*

su·pe·ri·or (sə pēr′ē ər) 1 higher in quality; better; greater: *This brand of root beer is not very good; the last one we tried was superior. Your writing skills are superior to his.* 2 better than most others; excellent: *She has a superior mind.* 3 higher in position or rank: *a superior officer.* 4 a person who is higher in rank or better at something: *Respect your superiors. As a pianist, he has no superior.* 5 conceited: *The other girls disliked her superior manner.* 1–3, 5 *adj.*, 4 *n.* **—su·pe′ri·or′i·ty** (sə pēr′ē ȯr′ə tē), *n.*

su·per·la·tive (sə pər′lə tiv) 1 of the highest or greatest kind: *Hercules was a man of superlative strength.* 2 the third and strongest degree of comparison of adjectives and adverbs. *Fairest* is the superlative of "fair." *Most quickly* is the superlative of "quickly." 1 *adj.*, 2 *n.*
▶ See the *Grammar and Usage Mini-Guide.*

su·per·mar·ket (sū′pər mȧr′kit) a large grocery store that also sells small household articles. *n.*

su·per·nat·u·ral (sū′pər nach′ə rəl) above or beyond nature. Miracles and angels are considered to be supernatural. *adj.*

su·per·sede (sū′pər sēd′) take the place of an older thing which is no longer used: *Electric lighting has superseded gas lighting.* *v.*, **su·per·sed·ed, su·per·sed·ing.**

su·per·son·ic (sū′pər son′ik) 1 too high for humans to hear. 2 beyond the speed of sound (about 1200 km/h at sea level). *adj.*

su·per·sti·tion (sū′pər stish′ən) 1 fears or beliefs that have no reasonable basis at all: *As knowledge increases, superstition decreases.* 2 a particular belief or fear of this kind: *It is a common superstition that 13 is an unlucky number.* *n.* **—su′per·sti′tious,** *adj.*

su·per·vise (sū′pər vīz′) manage and direct; look after to make sure things go all right: *Examinations are supervised by teachers. A teenager supervised the younger children at the craft table.* *v.*, **su·per·vised, su·per·vis·ing.** **—su′per·vi′sor,** *n.* **—su′per·vi′sion,** *n.*

sup·per (sup′ər) the evening meal; the third main meal of the day: *We usually have supper at six o'clock.* *n.*

sup·ple (sup′əl) bending easily; flexible: *a supple birch tree, supple leather.* *adj.*, **sup·pler, sup·plest.**

a bat	e bed	i bid	o pot	u cup	th thin
ā cake	ē me	ī bite	ō go	ū rude	ᴛʜ then
ȧ bar	ə about	ər over	ȯ for	u̇ put	zh measure

sup·ple·ment (sup′lə mənt *for 1,* sup′lə ment′ *for 2*) 1 something added to complete a thing, or to make it larger or better: *a vitamin supplement. The newspaper has a supplement every Saturday.* 2 add to or complete: *He supplemented his allowance by taking a paper route.* 1 *n.,* 2 *v.* —**sup′ple·men′ta·ry,** *adj.*

sup·ply (sə plī′) 1 furnish; provide: *The school supplies books for students. He supplied us with firewood.* 2 a quantity of something ready for use: *That magazine gets its supply of paper from British Columbia. Alberta has large supplies of coal and oil.* 3 **supplies,** *pl.* the food, equipment, and so on needed for any trip, job, etc. 4 satisfy; fill: *There was just enough to supply the demand.* 1, 4 *v.,* **sup·plied, sup·ply·ing;** 2, 3 *n., pl.* **sup·plies.**

sup·port (sə pört′) 1 keep from falling; hold up: *Walls support the roof.* 2 give strength or courage to; help: *Hope supports us in trouble.* 3 provide for: *That woman supports a family of five.* 4 be in favour of; back: *He supports the local hockey team.* 5 backing; help; encouragement: *Thank you for your support.* 6 a person or thing that supports. 1–4 *v.,* 5, 6 *n.* —**sup·port′er,** *n.* —**sup·port′ive,** *adj.*

sup·pose (sə pōz′) 1 imagine a possibility: *Suppose you had three wishes; what would you wish for?* 2 guess; expect: *I suppose she will come as usual.* 3 **supposing,** if: *Supposing it rains, will we still go?* 1, 2 *v.,* **sup·posed, sup·pos·ing;** 3 *conj.*

sup·posed (sə pō′zid *for 1,* sə pōst′ *for 2*) 1 claiming or seeming to be something; accepted as true or real: *The supposed beggar was really a prince.* 2 a **supposed to,** expected to: *I was supposed to bring the cake, but I forgot.* b **not supposed to,** not allowed to: *You're not supposed to jump on the sofa.* *adj.* —**sup·pos′ed·ly** (sə pō′zid lē), *adv.*

sup·press (sə pres′) 1 put down; stop, especially by force: *to suppress a riot.* 2 keep in; hold back; cover up: *to suppress a yawn. The media were accused of suppressing important information.* *v.* —**sup·pres′sion,** *n.*

su·preme (sə prēm′) highest or greatest: *a supreme ruler, supreme courage.* The **Supreme Court** is the court with the highest authority in Canada. Each province has a similar court of its own. *adj.* —**su·prem′a·cy** (sə prem′ə sē), *n.*

sure (shůr) 1 free from doubt; certain: *Are you sure you locked the door?* 2 certain to be or to happen: *The army faced sure defeat. She is sure to win the prize.* 3 *Informal.* surely; certainly: *He sure is strong (adv.)! "Will you?" "Sure, why not (conj.)?"* 4 safe; reliable; never failing: *the sure support of a friend.* 1, 2, 4 *adj.,* **sur·er, sur·est;** 3 *adv. or conj.* —**sure′ly,** *adv.*

for sure, *Informal.* certainly; undoubtedly.
make sure or **be sure,** do not fail to do a certain thing; make it happen, or wait for it to happen: *Be sure to come early. Make sure the floor is dry.*
to be sure, of course.

sure–foot·ed (shůr′fůt′id) not liable to stumble, slip, or fall: *Mountain goats are very sure-footed.* *adj.*

surf (sərf) 1 the waves of the sea breaking on the shore: *The surf is high just after a storm.* 2 travel or ride on the crest of a wave. To do this you stand or crouch on a long, narrow board called a **surfboard.** 3 *Informal.* look for interesting material on the Internet. 1 *n.,* 2, 3 *v.* —**surf′ing,** *n.*

sur·face (sər′fis) 1 the outside of anything: *An egg has a smooth surface.* 2 the top of the ground, or of a body of water or other liquid: *The miners returned to the surface.* 3 any face or side of a thing: *A cube has six surfaces.* 4 the outward appearance: *He seems rough, but he is very kind below the surface.* 5 come to the surface: *The whale surfaced.* 1–4 *n.,* 5 *v.,* **sur·faced, sur·fac·ing.**

surface tension (sur′fis ten′shən) the way molecules in the surface of a liquid hold together, so that the area of the liquid's surface tends to shrink. Surface tension is what causes liquids to form drops. Different liquids have different amounts of surface tension.

surge (sərj) 1 move forward with force like waves, rising and falling: *The crowd surged through the streets.* 2 a powerful wave: *A surge of anger rushed over him.* 1 *v.,* **surged, surg·ing;** 2 *n.*

sur·ger·y (sər′jə rē) a medical operation to treat disease or injury: *My leg was badly broken and needed surgery.* A doctor who does surgery is a **surgeon** (sər′jən). *n.* —**sur′gi·cal,** *adj.*

sur·ly (sər′lē) bad-tempered and rude: *He grumbled a surly reply.* *adj.,* **sur·li·er, sur·li·est.** —**sur′li·ly,** *adv.* —**sur′li·ness,** *n.*

sur·mise (sər mīz′) guess: *Everyone surmised that he was guilty (v.). His guilt was a matter of surmise as there was no proof (n.).* *v.,* **sur·mised, sur·mis·ing;** or *n.*

sur·mount (sər mount′) 1 be on top of: *A statue surmounts the monument.* 2 overcome: *She had to surmount many difficulties in order to reach her goal.* *v.*

sur·name (sər′nām′) last name; family name: *Herrler is the surname of Nathan Herrler.* *n.*

sur·pass (sər pas′) 1 do better than; be greater than: *She surpasses her sister in figure skating.* 2 go beyond: *The beauty of the Arctic surpasses description.* *v.*

sur·plus (sər′pləs) 1 an extra amount, over and above what is needed: *The store gave its surplus of fresh fruit to the food bank.* 2 more than is needed; extra: *Surplus wheat is put in storage.* 1 *n.,* 2 *adj.*

sur·prise (sər prīz′) 1 something unexpected: *Such hot weather in November was quite a surprise.* 2 the feeling caused by something unexpected: *His face showed surprise at the news.* 3 be different from what was expected; astonish: *The results of the race surprised us.* 4 catch unprepared; come upon suddenly: *She surprised me in the act of stealing a cookie.* 5 unexpected: *a surprise party, a surprise visit.* 1, 2 *n.,* 3, 4 *v.,* **sur·prised, sur·pris·ing;** 5 *adj.*

sur·ren·der (sə ren′dər) 1 give up; give yourself up: *The escaped prisoner finally surrendered to the police. We had to surrender the trophy to the other team.* 2 the act of surrendering: *The pillow fight ended with Dylan's surrender amid fits of laughter.* 1 *v.,* 2 *n.*

sur·round (sə round′) shut in on every side; be all the way around: *A high fence surrounds the field. They surrounded the sick girl with every comfort.* The things or conditions that surround you are your **surroundings.** *v.*

sur·veil·lance (sər vā′ləns) a watch kept over a person: *She has been under police surveillance for several weeks.* *n.*

sur·vey (sər vā′ *for 1 and 4,* sər′vā *for 2, 3, and 5*) 1 look something over, especially something spread out: *Grandma surveyed the messy room with a stern expression.* 2 a general look; an overview: *a quick survey of the scene turned up some interesting clues.* 3 the process of finding out information about a large group of people by asking them all certain questions: *Our survey of the student body revealed that most prefer tobogganing to skating.* 4 measure an area of land for size, shape, position, boundaries, and so on. 5 a careful measurement of land, or the maplike drawing made from it. 1, 4 *v.,* 2, 3, 5 *n., pl.* **sur·veys.** —**sur·vey′or,** *n.*

sur·vive (sər vīv′) 1 live through something difficult: *The crops survived the drought.* 2 continue to exist; remain: *Statues have survived from the time of the Ancient Greeks.* 3 live longer than; remain alive after: *The old man survived his wife by three years.* *v.,* **sur·vived, sur·viv·ing.** —**sur·viv′al,** *n.* —**sur·viv′or,** *n.*

sus·cep·ti·ble (sə sep′tə bəl) likely to be influenced; easily affected: *Vain people are susceptible to flattery. Children are susceptible to many common illnesses.* *adj.*

su·shi (sū′shē) a Japanese dish made up of small amounts of cold, cooked sticky rice with pieces of raw fish or vegetables on top or in the middle. *n.*

sus·pect (sə spekt′ *for 1,* sus′pekt *for 2 and 3*) 1 have a feeling or impression that something is true, without any proof: *I suspect that some accident has delayed him. We suspected her of lying.* 2 a person who is thought to have done something wrong: *The police have arrested two suspects in connection with the bank robbery.* 3 not to be trusted: *That version of the story is suspect.* 1 *v.,* 2 *n.,* 3 *adj.*

sus·pend (sə spend′) 1 hang down by attaching to something above: *The lamp was suspended from the ceiling.* 2 hold or stay in place as if by hanging: *We saw the smoke suspended in the still air.* 3 stop or put off for a while: *They suspended building operations during the winter.* 4 bar someone from a place for a while as a form of punishment: *He was suspended from school for two days for bad behaviour.* *v.*

sus·pend·ers (sə spen′dərz) straps worn over the shoulders to hold up your pants; braces. *pl.n.*

sus·pense (sə spens′) the condition of waiting tensely to see what will happen: *The detective story kept me in suspense until the last chapter.* *n.*

sus·pen·sion (sə spen′shən) 1 a mixture containing tiny particles of a solid hanging or suspended in a gas or liquid without dissolving. A suspension has a cloudy appearance; muddy water is a suspension. 2 the act of suspending or the fact of being suspended. A **suspension bridge** is one that hangs from cables or chains between two towers. *n.*

sus·pi·cion (sə spish′ən) 1 a feeling or impression that something is the case, without any proof: *She had a suspicion that the present was for her.* 2 mistrust; the feeling that someone or something may be bad or guilty: *The small boy eyed the stranger with suspicion.* 3 a very small amount; a slight trace: *There was just a suspicion of nervousness in her voice.* *n.*
above suspicion, so honourable that you could not be suspected of wrongdoing: *The students in our class are all above suspicion.*
on suspicion, because of being suspected: *He was arrested on suspicion of robbery.*
under suspicion, suspected; believed guilty but without proof.

sus·pi·cious (sə spish′əs) 1 causing suspicion: *A man was loitering near the house in a suspicious manner.* 2 feeling or showing suspicion: *The dog is suspicious of strangers.* *adj.*

a bat	e bed	i bid	o pot	u cup	th thin
ā cake	ē me	ī bite	ō go	ū rude	ᴛʜ then
à bar	ə about	ər over	ô for	ů put	zh measure

sus·tain (sə stān′) **1** keep up; keep going: *a sustained effort. Food is needed to sustain life.* **Sustenance** (sus′tə nəns) is another word for food. **2** hold up; support: *Arches sustain the weight of the roof.* **3** suffer; experience: *She sustained a broken arm in the accident.* **4** withstand; endure without being damaged: *The sea wall sustains the shock of the waves.* *v.*

SW or **S.W.** *abbreviation for* southwest or southwestern.

swab (swob) **1** a bit of sponge, cloth, or cotton for cleansing some part of the body or putting medicine on it. **2** a mop for cleaning decks, floors, etc. **3** clean or wipe with a swab: *to swab a person's throat. Swab the decks!* 1, 2 *n.*, 3 *v.*, **swabbed, swab·bing.**

swag·ger (swag′ər) **1** walk in a bold, rude, or conceited way: *The bully swaggered into the yard.* **2** a bold, rude, conceited way of walking or acting. 1 *v.*, 2 *n.*

swal·low[1] (swol′ō) **1** use certain muscles to make something go down your throat: *Don't swallow your gum.* You can also do the action with nothing in your mouth: *She swallowed twice before starting her speech.* **2** take in and cause to disappear: *The waves swallowed up the swimmer.* **3** *Informal.* accept without questioning or protesting: *to swallow an insult. He will swallow any story.* **4** keep from expressing: *She swallowed her disappointment and smiled.* **5** the act of swallowing or an amount swallowed at one time: *a swallow of juice. He took the medicine at one swallow.* 1–4 *v.*, 5 *n.*

Every year, barn swallows migrate many thousands of kilometres, from South Africa to their traditional nesting sites in Europe.

swal·low[2] (swol′ō) a small, swift songbird with a forked tail and long, pointed wings. Anything with a shape like this bird's tail is called a **swallowtail.** *n.*

swam (swam) the past tense of **swim:** *When the boat sank, we swam to shore.* *v.*

Leaves fall into the water of shallow lakes. A layer of peat accumulates, and so a swamp is formed.

swamp (swomp) **1** wet, soft land: *The farmer will drain the swamp so that he can plant crops there.* **2** fill with water and sink: *The waves swamped the boat.* **3** overwhelm like a flood: *I am swamped with work.* 1 *n.*, 2, 3 *v.* —**swamp′y,** *adj.*

swan (swon) a large, graceful water bird with a long, slender, curving neck. Adult swans are usually pure white. *n.*

swap (swop) *Informal.* trade: *He swapped his baseball for a hockey stick (v.). It was a fair swap (n.).* *n. or v.*, **swapped, swap·ping.**

swarm (swôrm) **1** a large group of insects, animals, people, etc. moving around together: *Swarms of children were playing in the park.* **2** fly or move around in great numbers: *The mosquitoes swarmed around us.* **3** be crowded or filled with moving people or things: *The mall is swarming with last-minute shoppers.* **4** a group of bees that leave a hive and fly off together to start a new colony. **5** fly off together to start a new colony. 1, 4 *n.*, 2, 3, 5 *v.*

swat (swot) *Informal.* **1** hit sharply: *to swat a fly.* **2** a sharp hit; smack. 1 *v.*, **swat·ted, swat·ting;** 2 *n.* —**swat′ter,** *n.*

sway (swā) **1** bend or lean slowly back and forth: *He swayed and fell down in a faint. The wind swayed the trees.* **2** a movement of this kind: *the sway of a branch in the wind.* **3** change someone's opinion or feeling: *Nothing could sway him after he had made up his mind.* **4** an influence or controlling power: *They were all under the gang leader's sway.* 1, 3 *v.*, 2, 4 *n.*

swear (swer) 1 use very bad language; curse: *The pirate raged and swore when he was captured.* 2 make a solemn promise: *A witness at a trial has to swear to tell the truth.* *v.,* **swore, sworn, swear·ing.**
swear in, have someone make certain solemn promises before beginning an official job: *to swear in a jury.*
swear off, promise to give up: *to swear off smoking.*

sweat (swet) 1 give out moisture through the pores of your skin to cool your body: *We were sweating after the hard work.* 2 the moisture that comes out through your skin: *He wiped the sweat from his face.* Sweat is produced by your **sweat glands.** 3 a condition of sweating, or of anything that might make you sweat, such as anxiety or impatience: *He was in a cold sweat from fear. Don't get in such a sweat—we'll find the keys eventually.* 4 *Informal.* work very hard. 5 have drops of moisture forming on the surface: *A pitcher of ice water sweats on a hot day.* 6 drops of moisture that form on a cold surface: *The water pipes were covered with sweat.* 1, 4, 5 *v.,* 2, 3, 6 *n.,* **—sweat′y,** *adj.*

sweat·er (swet′ər) a warm outer garment for the upper body made of any stretchy, knitted material; a pullover or cardigan. *n.*

✱ **sweat lodge** (swet′ loj′) a building used by some First Nations of the Pacific coast for ceremonies meant to cleanse the person's body, mind, and soul using steam. Often these ceremonies were part of the process of becoming an adult and would lead to receiving a vision or finding a spirit guide.

sweat·shirt (swet′ shərt′) a warm, casual garment for the upper body, made of soft, fleecy, stretchy material. **Sweatpants** are made of the same material, with an elastic waist; together, the shirt and pants make a **sweatsuit.** These words can also be spelled **sweat shirt, sweat pants,** and **sweat suit.**

sweep (swēp) 1 clean or clear with a broom or brush: *The campers swept the floor of their cabin every morning.* 2 pass over with a steady movement: *His eye swept the sky, searching for signs of rain.* 3 move swiftly and powerfully: *The wind sweeps through the valley. A flood swept away the bridge.* 4 move with grace and dignity: *The dancers swept around the stage.* 5 a sweeping act or motion: *the sweep of the wind. He cut the grass with strong sweeps of his scythe.* 6 a person who cleans out chimneys. 1–4 *v.,* **swept, sweep·ing;** 5, 6 *n.* **—sweep′er,** *n.*
make a clean sweep of, remove with a single stroke or act.

sweep·ing (swē′ping) passing over a wide space or having a wide range: *a sweeping glance around the whole room, a sweeping victory, a sweeping statement.* *adj.*

sweet (swēt) 1 having a taste like sugar or honey: *Pears are much sweeter than lemons.* 2 pleasant or beautiful: *The air was sweet with the scent of roses.* 3 dear; darling. 4 kind, generous, thoughtful, etc.: *It was sweet of him to invite us.* 5 **sweets,** *pl.* candy or other sweet things. 1–4 *adj.,* 3, 5 *n.* **—sweet′en,** *v.*
sweet tooth, a liking for sweet foods.

✱ **sweet·grass** (swēt′gras′) a herb used by many First Nations people which smells sweet when dried. It is usually braided and burned to create fragrant smoke during prayer. *n.*

sweet·heart (swēt′härt′) 1 a kind, generous, thoughtful person. 2 someone you love. *n.*

sweet potato (swēt′ pə tā′tō) the sweetish, yellow-orange root of a certain vine, grown in warm areas and cooked as a vegetable. Sweet potatoes and yams are very similar.

sweet–talk (swēt′tok′) try to get someone to do something by talking as nicely as you can, making promises, and so on: *We sweet-talked Guy's father into taking us to a movie.* *v.*

swell (swel) 1 grow or make larger in size, amount, force, etc.: *Rain swelled the river. His wrist is swollen where he bumped it. The sound swelled from a murmur to a roar.* 2 the act of swelling; an increase in size, amount, force, etc.: *a swell in population.* 3 a long, unbroken wave or waves: *The boat rocked in the swell. She felt a swell of excitement.* 4 *Slang.* excellent: *That's a swell idea.* 1 *v.,* **swelled, swelled** or **swol·len** (swō′lən *or* swůl′ən), **swell·ing;** 2, 3 *n.,* 4 *adj.*
a swelled head, a conceited attitude.

swel·ter (swel′tər) suffer from heat. *v.*

swept (swept) the past tense and past participle of **sweep:** *He swept the room. It was swept clean.* *v.*

swerve (swərv) 1 turn aside suddenly: *The car swerved to avoid a hole in the road. Nothing could swerve him from doing his duty.* 2 the fact of turning aside: *The swerve of the ball made it hard to hit.* 1 *v.,* **swerved, swerv·ing;** 2 *n.*

swift (swift) 1 moving or able to move very fast: *a swift canoe.* 2 acting or happening quickly: *a swift answer.He is always swift to help when needed.* 3 a small bird with long wings. 1, 2 *adj.,* 3 *n.*

a bat	e bed	i bid	o pot	u cup	th thin
ā cake	ē me	ī bite	ō go	ū rude	TH then
ä bar	ə about	ər over	ȯ for	ů put	zh measure

swig (swig) *Informal.* **1** a big, hearty drink or swallow: *a swig of pop.* **2** drink heartily or greedily. 1 *n.,* 2 *v.,* **swigged, swig·ging.**

swim (swim) **1** move along in the water by using arms, legs, fins, etc.: *Fish swim. I like to swim in the lake.* A garment made for swimming in is a **swimsuit.** **2** swim across: *She swam the river.* **3** the act, time, or distance of swimming: *Her swim had tired her. She had had an hour's swim.* **4** be dizzy; whirl: *The heat and noise made my head swim.* 1, 2, 4 *v.,* **swam, swum, swim·ming;** 3 *n.* **—swim′mer,** *n.*
be swimming in, a be flooded or surrounded with: *The potatoes were swimming in gravy.* **b** be much too small for a piece of clothing: *He's swimming in that sweater of Dad's.*

swin·dle (swin′dəl) **1** cheat; get money from someone by a trick: *Honest storekeepers do not swindle their customers.* **2** the act of cheating in this way; a dishonest business deal. 1 *v.,* **swin·dled, swin·dling;** 2 *n.* **—swin′dler,** *n.*

swine (swīn) a less common word for "pig." *n., pl.* **swine.**

swing (swing) **1** move back and forth freely while attached to something at one or both ends: *The hammock swings. He swings his arms as he walks.* **2** move swiftly in a curve: *She swung the bat at the ball. The car swung around the corner.* **3** an act or manner of swinging: *One swing of the axe split the log. Her golf swing is very good.* **4** a seat hung from ropes or chains, that you can sit in and swing. **5** move with a free, swaying motion: *The dancers came swinging onto the stage.* **6** *Informal.* manage successfully: *I think we can swing this surprise party if we plan properly.* 1, 2, 5, 6 *v.,* **swung, swing·ing;** 3, 4 *n.*
in full swing, going on very actively: *By five o'clock the party was in full swing.*
in the swing of things, fully involved in the normal activities: *to get back into the swing of things after an illness.*

swipe (swīp) **1** a strong, sweeping stroke, especially one that misses or almost misses: *He made two swipes at the golf ball without hitting it.* **2** **swipe at,** try to hit or grab with a sweeping stroke. **3** pass a credit card or other similar card through a device that reads the card's magnetic strip. **4** *Informal.* steal: *Who swiped my disk?* 1 *n.,* 2–4 *v.,* **swiped, swip·ing.**

swirl (swərl) **1** move along with a twisting, spinning motion; whirl: *dust swirling in the air, a stream swirling over rocks.* **2** a movement like this: *the swirl of her long skirt around her ankles.* **3** a twist or curl: *a swirl of whipped cream on top of a sundae.* 1 *v.,* 2, 3 *n.*

swish (swish) **1** move fast with a light hissing or brushing sound: *The whip swished through the air. The cow swished its tail.* **2** a swishing movement or sound: *the swish of little waves on the shore.* 1 *v.,* 2 *n.*

switch (swich) **1** change; exchange: *to switch places. The boys switched hockey sweaters (v.). There's been a last-minute switch in plans (n.).* **2** a device for turning something on or off, changing a setting on a machine, etc. An electric switch works by making or breaking a connection in an electric circuit. **3** a pair of movable rails used by a train to shift from one track to another. **4** turn on or off, change, or shift by using a switch: *Switch off the light.* 1–3 *n.,* 1, 4 *v.*

switch·board (swich′bȯrd′) a board with switches, plugs, buttons, etc. for opening, closing, and combining electric circuits, especially in earlier times for telephone lines. *n.*

swiv·el (swiv′əl) **1** a fastening that allows the thing fastened to turn around freely. A **swivel chair** has a seat that can be turned around on its stand. **2** turn or swing around: *She swivelled the chair around. She swivelled her eyes in our direction.* 1 *n.,* 2 *v.,* **swiv·elled** or **swiv·eled, swiv·el·ling** or **swiv·el·ing.**

swol·len (swō′lən *or* swu̇l′ən) a past participle of **swell:** *Her ankle had swollen to twice its usual size.* *v.*

swoon (swūn) faint: *He swoons at the sight of blood (v.). She fell to the floor in a swoon (n.).* *v. or n.*

swoop (swūp) **1** come down with a rush to attack, as a hawk does: *The aircraft swooped down on the towns.* **2** a sudden, swift downward rush to attack: *With one swoop the hawk seized the mouse and flew away.* 1 *v.,* 2 *n.*

Swords may have one or two cutting edges. A curved sword, for example, has only one cutting edge.

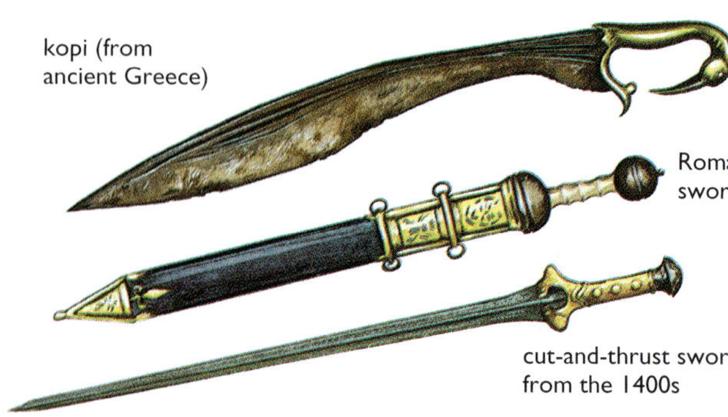

sword (sȯrd) a weapon of earlier times with a long, sharp metal blade attached to a handle. A sword is often a symbol of war. *n.*
cross swords, fight or quarrel.

sword•fish (sȯrd′fish′) a very large sea fish with a swordlike part sticking out of its upper jaw. It is often used for food. *n., pl.* **sword•fish** or **sword•fish•es.**

sworn (swȯrn) **1** the past participle of **swear:** *A solemn oath of loyalty was sworn by all the knights.* The past tense is **swore:** *She swore to tell the truth.* **2** bound or guaranteed by a solemn promise: *There were ten sworn witnesses. We have a sworn statement.* 1 *v.,* 2 *adj.*

swum (swum) the past participle of **swim:** *He had never swum before.* *v.*

USING WORDS .... swum

Swum and **swam** are both forms of the verb *swim* that are sometimes confused.
Swum is the past participle; it needs the helping verb *have: We have swum in the lake many times.*
Swam is the past tense: *I swam across the lake yesterday.*

swung (swung) the past tense and past participle of **swing:** *He swung his umbrella as he walked. The door had swung open.* *v.*

syl•la•ble (sil′ə bəl) a part of a word pronounced as a unit. A syllable is made up of a vowel alone or a vowel with one or more consonants. The words *Canadian* and *Manitoba* have four syllables; the words *do* and *stretch* have one syllable. In this dictionary, the syllables of an entry word are separated by dots. To separate a word into syllables is to **syllabify** it. *n.* **—syl•lab′ic,** *adj.*

Grammar Check ...... syllable

When you have to divide a word at the end of a line, always divide it between **syllables**: *di-vide, syl-la-bles.* Never divide proper names or words of one syllable.

sym•bi•o•sis (sim′bī ō′sis) a relationship between two different plants or animals living together, where each one depends on the other for something. For example, lichen is a symbiosis of an alga and a fungus: the alga provides the food, and the fungus provides water and protection. *n.* **—sym′bi•ot′ic** (sim′bī ot′ik), *adj.*

sym•bol (sim′bəl) anything that stands for something else: *The olive branch is the symbol of peace. The Saddledome has become a symbol of Calgary. The mark X is the symbol for multiplication.* **Symbolism** is the use of symbols. *n.* **—sym•bol′ic** (sim bol′ik), *adj.*

sym•bol•ize (sim′bə līz′) be a symbol of; stand for; represent: *A butterfly symbolizes new life.* *v.,* **sym•bol•ized, sym•bol•iz•ing.**

If you fold a symmetrical shape along its line of symmetry, the two halves will fit exactly over one another.

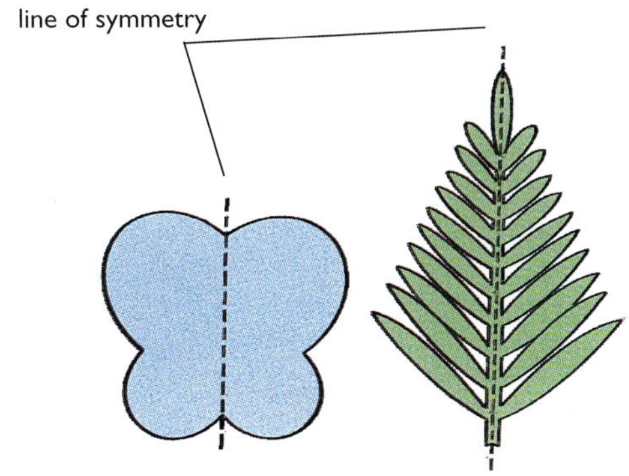

sym•me•try (sim′ə trē) **1** a balanced form or arrangement so that the parts on opposite sides of a central line or point mirror each other exactly. A maple leaf has symmetry. **2** any well-balanced arrangement of parts: *A swollen cheek spoiled the symmetry of his face.* *n., pl.* **sym•me•tries.** **—sym•met′ri•cal** (si met′rə kəl), *adj.*

sym•pa•thet•ic (sim′pə thet′ik) **1** able to understand and share the feelings of others; kind: *She told her troubles to a sympathetic friend.* **2** tending to agree: *The teacher was sympathetic to our plan but said we must ask the principal.* **3** likable: *It was an odd story because the villain was a more sympathetic character than the hero.* *adj.* **—sym′pa•thet′i•cal•ly,** *adv.*

sym•pa•thy (sim′pə thē) **1** the fact of understanding and sharing someone else's sorrow or trouble: *When I had to stop eating chocolate, my friends did too out of sympathy.* **2** agreement in feeling or opinion: *Our suggestion to order pizza had Mom's sympathy.* To show or express either kind of sympathy is to **sympathize.** *n., pl.* **sym•pa•thies.**

sym•pho•ny (sim′fə nē) **1** a long piece of music with many parts, written for an orchestra. **2** Often, **symphony orchestra,** a large orchestra with brass, woodwind, percussion, and stringed instruments: *the Vancouver Symphony.* **3** any harmonious combination: *In fall the woods are a symphony of colour.* *n., pl.* **sym•pho•nies.**

symp•tom (simp′təm) a sign of something, especially something bad: *Fever is a symptom of illness.* *n.*

syn•a•gogue (sin′ə gog′) a building used by Jews for religious worship and teaching. *n.*

a bat	e bed	i bid	o pot	u cup	th thin
ā cake	ē me	ī bite	ō go	ū rude	ᴛʜ then
ä bar	ə about	ər over	ȯ for	u̇ put	zh measure

Synthesizer

The synthesizer was invented by Robert Moog, an American physicist, in 1964. He used controlled voltage levels to produce different sounds.

The digital synthesizer, which uses a computer to create sounds, was developed in the late 1970s. Today, these are usually called keyboards.

syn·chro·nize (sing′krə nīz′) **1** cause to move or happen at exactly the same time. **Synchronized swimming** is a kind of water dance where swimmers make exactly the same moves at the same time. It is an Olympic sport. **2** make agree in time: *to synchronize all the clocks in a building.* *v.,* **syn·chro·nized, syn·chro·niz·ing.**

syn·co·pate (sing′kə pāt′) play or sing music by putting a strong accent on the beats that are normally weak. Popular music is often syncopated. *v.,* **syn·co·pat·ed, syn·co·pat·ing.** **—syn′co·pa′tion,** *n.*

syn·o·nym (sin′ə nim′) a word that means the same or nearly the same as another word: *"Little" is a synonym of "small."* *n.* **—syn·on′y·mous** (sə non′ə məs), *adj.* ▶ See the *Grammar and Usage Mini-Guide.*

Grammar ✓Check . . . . . synonym

Use a **synonym** instead of repeating a word, and you can make your writing more interesting. Find synonyms in a thesaurus.

syn·op·sis (sə nop′sis) a summary of a story. Often when a story is being continued after a break, a synopsis will be given first, telling what has happened so far. *n., pl.* **syn·op·ses**

syn·the·siz·er (sin′thə sī′zər) a computerized device, usually with a pianolike keyboard, that can imitate the sounds of all kinds of musical instruments and produce many other different sound effects. It works by generating various electric waves and combining them. *n.*

syn·thet·ic (sin thet′ik) **1** made artificially by combining chemicals: *synthetic rubber. Nylon is a synthetic fibre.* To manufacture a substance in this way is to **synthesize** it. **2** a substance manufactured in this way: *Plastic is a synthetic.* 1 *adj.,* 2 *n.*

sy·ringe (sə rinj′) a narrow tube with a squeezable rubber bulb at one end for sucking up liquid and then forcing it out in a stream. Syringes are used for cleaning wounds, injecting medicine, and so on. *n.*

syr·up (sir′əp *or* sər′əp) any sweet, sticky, thick liquid used as food or medicine: *maple syrup, cough syrup.* *n.* **—syr′up·y,** *adj.*

sys·tem (sis′təm) **1** a set of things or parts forming a whole: *a mountain system, a railway system, the digestive system.* **2** a set of ideas, practices, organizations, and so on, all resting on certain basic principles: *a system of government, a system of education.* **3** an orderly way of doing something. **4** the body as a whole: *Poor diet had weakened his system.* *n.* **—sys′tem·at′ic** (sis′tə mat′ik), *adj.* **—sys′tem·at′i·cal·ly,** *adv.*

Tt

t or **T** (tē) 1 the twentieth letter of the English alphabet, or the sound that it stands for. It is the sound at the beginning and end of the word *tot.* 2 the twentieth thing in a list. *n., pl.* **t's** or **T's.**
to a T, exactly or perfectly: *That suits me to a T.*

t *symbol for* tonne or tonnes, a metric unit of mass.

tab (tab) 1 a small flap, strap, loop, or piece attached to something: *Insert tab A into slot B. You pull this little tab to make the picture pop up.* 2 a bill to be paid in a restaurant or store. 3 a key on a keyboard which moves the cursor forward by a set distance. *n.*
keep tabs on, keep checking where someone is or what he or she is doing; keep track of.
pick up the tab, pay for something.

ta·ble (tā′bəl) 1 a piece of furniture with a smooth, flat top on legs. 2 the people seated at a table: *The whole table laughed.* 3 information presented as a list or chart: *the multiplication table. The table of contents shows what is in a book.* To put information in a table is to **tabulate** it. 4 Often, **tableland,** a flat, raised area of land; plateau. *n.*
turn the tables, reverse conditions: *Our opponents were winning, but three quick goals from our centre turned the tables on them.*

Word Family........table

tablecloth: a cloth to cover or decorate a table
tablespoon: a large spoon that holds about 15 mL
table tennis: a game played on a table with a net, small wooden bats, and a ball
tabletop: the top of a table

tableau (tab lō′) 1 a scene performed silently. 2 part of a scene where all the performers freeze in position. *n., pl* **tab·leaux** (–lō) or **tab·leaus** (–lōz)

tab·let (tab′lit) 1 a small, flat piece of medicine; pill: *vitamin tablets, sleeping tablets.* 2 a pad of writing paper. 3 a flat, rectangular piece of hard material for writing on. In ancient times people wrote on tablets of stone, wood, ivory, etc.; today you might find a metal tablet with words engraved on it, attached to a wall or statue. *n.*

ta·boo (tə bū′) forbidden by custom or tradition; banned: *That kind of language is taboo in our house. adj.*

tac·i·turn (tas′ə tərn′) not liking to talk. *adj.*

tack (tak) 1 a short nail or pin with a broad, flat head. 2 fasten with tacks: *She tacked the calendar over her desk.* 3 sail in a zigzag course against the wind: *The boat was tacking, trying to make the harbour.* 4 a course of action; strategy: *Complaining was the wrong tack to take with him; try a polite suggestion next time.* 1, 4 *n.,* 2, 3 *v.*

tack·le (tak′əl) 1 try to deal with: *to tackle a tough problem.* 2 grab or jump on someone and try to get the person down or beat him or her up. 3 in football, grab an opponent who has the ball and try to bring him or her to the ground. 4 the act of tackling. 5 equipment; gear: *fishing tackle.* 6 a set of ropes and pulleys for moving heavy things. 1–3 *v.,* **tack·led, tack·ling;** 4–6 *n.*

tack·y[1] (tak′ē) sticky. *adj.*

tack·y[2] (tak′ē) 1 *Informal.* of poor quality or appearance; shabby: *a row of tacky little houses.* 2 cheap and tasteless: *a tacky souvenir. adj.*

ta·co (tȧ′kō) a soft or crisp tortilla folded around a spicy filling of meat, grated cheese, beans, etc. *n., pl.* **tacos.**

tact (takt) a careful, thoughtful way of speaking and acting so that you won't hurt people's feelings: *If you must criticize, use tact. n.* **—tact′ful,** *adj.* **—tact′less,** *adj.*

tac·tics (tak′tiks) strategy; the methods used to get what you want or defeat an enemy: *When coaxing failed, the little boy changed his tactics and began to cry. pl.n.*

tad·pole (tad′pōl′) a very young frog or toad, at the stage when it has a tail but no legs and lives in water. *n.*

tae kwon do (tīk′ won′ dō′) a Korean system of self-defence without weapons that uses fast hand movements and powerful, leaping kicks. *n.*

taf·fy (taf′ē) a kind of chewy candy made of brown sugar, syrup, or molasses boiled down with butter. A **taffy apple** is an apple on a stick, coated with taffy. *n.*

a bat	e bed	i bid	o pot	u cup	th thin
ā cake	ē me	ī bite	ō go	ū rude	ᴛʜ then
ȧ bar	ə about	ər over	ȯ for	u̇ put	zh measure

tag[1] (tag) **1** a small piece of paper, cloth, leather, etc. tied or fastened to something, with information on it: *a price tag, a name tag. The tag inside the collar gives washing instructions.* **2** put a tag on: *All her suitcases were tagged with her name and address.* **3** *Informal.* follow or go along without being invited: *She always has to tag along with us.* 1 *n.,* 2, 3 *v.,* **tagged, tag·ging.**

tag[2] (tag) **1** a game played in a group. One person who is "It" chases the others until he or she touches one of them; then that one is "It." **2** touch someone when you are It in this game, or touch a runner in baseball before he or she reaches the base. 1 *n.,* 2 *v.,* **tagged, tag·ging.**

Tag·ish (tag′ish) **1** a First Nations people living in Yukon and British Columbia. **2** their language. **3** to do with these people or their language. 1, 2 *n.,* 3 *adj.*

Tahl·tan (tol′tan) **1** a First Nations people living in British Columbia. **2** their language. **3** to do with these people or their language. 1, 2 *n.,* 3 *adj.*

tai·ga (tī′gə) the wet forest of cone-bearing trees that grows in subarctic regions, such as northern Canada and Siberia. The taiga is just south of the tundra. *n.*

tail (tāl) **1** in certain animals, the part that sticks out or hangs down from the rear of the body. Rabbits have very short, fluffy tails. Mice have long, thin tails. **2** something like an animal's tail: *the tail of a kite.* **3** the back part of anything: *A school band formed the tail of the parade.* **4** follow close behind: *Some children tailed after the ice-cream truck.* **5** *Informal.* follow closely and secretly to watch or to prevent escape: *The police tailed the suspect for days.* **6** at or coming from the back: *a tail wind, a car's tail-lights.* **7 tails, a** the reverse side of a coin. **b** *Informal.* a coat with long tails worn on formal occasions. 1–3, 7 *n.,* 4, 5 *v.,* 6 *adj.*
on someone's tail, following someone closely.
turn tail, run away.
with your tail between your legs, afraid; humiliated: *He came up full of fight but walked off with his tail between his legs when he saw he was outnumbered.*

CONFUSABLES ....tail

tail means "end part of an animal": *a horse's tail.*
tale means "story": *a fairy tale.*

tail·gate (tāl′gāt′) **1** a hinged part at the back end of a wagon, pickup truck, station wagon, etc. that can be let down, lifted up, or removed for loading or unloading. **2** drive too close to the vehicle ahead of you. 1 *n.,* 2 *v.,* **tail·gat·ed, tail·gat·ing.**

tai·lor (tā′lər) **1** a person whose business is making or repairing clothes, especially men's clothes. **2** give a trim, elegant shape and a fine finish to: *neatly tailored lawns, a tailored suit.* **3** make specially to fit; adapt: *Tailor your speech to the interests of the audience.* 1 *n.,* 2, 3 *v.*

tail·spin (tāl′spin′) **1** a downward spin of an aircraft with the nose first. **2** a state of complete confusion or panic: *The news threw our whole family into a tailspin.* *n.*

taint (tānt) **1** spoil slightly: *tainted meat.* **2** pollute; make unclean: *food tainted by flies. Her reputation was tainted by that one lie.* **3** a stain or spot; a trace of something unclean: *No taint of dishonour ever touched her.* 1, 2 *v.,* 3 *n.*

take (tāk) **1** get and remove or keep for yourself: *Someone has taken my ruler.* **2** carry: *We take our lunch to school.* **3** reach for and hold; grab: *Take my hand.* **4** go with; cause to come along: *to take a dog for a walk. Take me to the zoo.* **5** accept: *Take my advice. I won't take such an insult.* **6** use: *to take medicine, to take a train, to take a shortcut. Take care not to fall.* **7** survive; endure: *These plants can't take frost.* **8** need; require: *It takes time and patience to learn to skate.* **9** subtract: *If you take 2 from 7, you have 5.* **10** study in school: *We are taking division now in math.* **11** get or do; give yourself; have: *to take a bath, to take delight in something. He took a holiday.* **12** make by a special method: *Please take my photograph.* **13** think of; consider: *Some animals vary a lot in size; take dogs, for instance.* **14** *Slang.* swindle; cheat: *You've been taken.* **15** the amount or number taken: *a great take of fish.* 1–14 *v.,* **took, tak·en, tak·ing;** 15 *n.*
be taken with, like very much; be very impressed by.
take after, be like; resemble: *She takes after her mother.*
take back, change your mind about something you have said or given: *I take that comment back; I didn't mean it.*
take down, write down: *Take down this phone number.*
take for, believe to be: *They took me for a spy.*
take in, a let in to your home: *to take in a stray cat.* **b** understand: *I was too sleepy to take it in properly.* **c** deceive; trick: *He was taken in by the crook's friendliness.* **d** make smaller: *to take in the waist of a skirt.* **e** include: *Greater Vancouver takes in the city and its suburbs.*
take it, assume: *I take it you're done; hand me your plate.*
taken aback, surprised and a bit confused.
take off, a leave the ground or water: *Three airplanes took off at the same time.* **b** rush away: *He took off at the first sign of trouble.*

take on, **a** hire. **b** challenge; try to deal with: *take on an opponent.* **c** start to have: *to take on an air of sadness.*
take over, take control of something, sometimes without any right to do so: *I just asked for some help—I didn't want you to take over.* The act of taking over is a **takeover.**
take someone up on, accept someone's offer: *I'll take you up on your invitation to lunch.*
take something out on someone, express your feelings by hurting someone else: *Don't take your anger out on me!*
take to, **a** develop a liking for: *She took to the new nanny right away.* **b** go to: *The frightened deer took to the woods.*
take up, **a** soak up; absorb: *A sponge takes up liquid.* **b** start doing: *She took up piano lessons in the summer.*
take your time, go at a relaxed speed.

take•off (tā′kof′) **1** the act of leaving the ground: *A plane was on the runway, ready for takeoff.* **2** *Informal.* an imitation: *Wes did a good takeoff on our teacher.* *n.*

take•out (tāk′out′) **1** food that you buy at a shop or restaurant and take away in containers to eat somewhere else: *There's no time to cook; let's get takeout for supper.* **2** a place where food is prepared and sold to be taken away: *There's a Jamaican takeout just down the street.* **3** for buying and taking it away to eat somewhere else: *takeout food.* 1, 2 *n.,* 3 *adj.*

tal•cum powder (tal′kəm pou′dər) scented powder made of a soft, white mineral called **talc** or **talcum,** for using on your skin to absorb moisture.

tale (tāl) **1** a story: *a tale of adventure.* **2** a lie. *n.*
tell tales, spread gossip.

tal•ent (tal′ənt) **1** special natural ability: *She has a talent for music.* **2** people with talent: *The show uses a lot of Canadian talent.* *n.* —**tal′ent•ed,** *adj.*

tal•is•man (tal′is mən) a good luck charm. *n., pl.* **tal•is•mans.**

talk (tok) **1** use words; speak: *The baby is learning to talk.* **2** use a language in speaking: *Can you talk French?* **3** spoken words; things that are said: *I don't like that kind of talk.* **4** a chat; conversation: *The old friends met for a good talk.* **5** an informal speech: *The coach gave us a talk about team spirit.* **6** discuss: *to talk politics.* **7** spread rumours or tell secrets: *They talked behind our backs. Mick talked and spoiled the surprise.* **8** a subject everyone is talking about: *The new principal is the talk of the school.* 1, 2, 6, 7 *v.,* 3–5, 8 *n.* —**talk′a•tive,** *adj.*
talk back, *Informal.* answer rudely or disrespectfully.
talk down to, speak to someone as if he or she were stupid or too young to understand.
talk into, persuade to do something: *We talked her into coming with us.* **Talk out of** is the opposite.
talk over, talk about something thoroughly in order to come to a decision or agreement. **Talk out** can have a similar meaning.
talk someone's ear off, talk on and on to someone. **Talk the hind leg off a donkey** has a similar meaning.
you should talk, *Informal.* you yourself do the very thing you are criticizing. **Look who's talking** means the same.

talking stick (tok′ing stik′) among some First Nations peoples, a carved stick or other object which gives the person holding it the right to speak in a group. In some cultures, an eagle feather is used for this.

talk show (tok′ shō′) a radio or TV show made up of interviews with people, discussions by experts, calls from listeners, etc.

tall (tol) **1** reaching higher than the average; measuring far from top to bottom: *Toronto has many tall buildings.* **2** *Informal.* hard to accept or believe: *a tall story. That's a pretty tall order!* *adj.*

tal•ly (tal′ē) **1** total up; count up: *to tally a score.* **2** a count or total: *She made a quick tally in her head.* **3** earn points; score: *The hockey team tallied seven goals in their last game.* **4** agree or fit with other information: *His version of what happened does not tally with what I saw.* 2, 3 *n., pl.* **tal•lies;** 1, 4 *v.,* **tal•lied, tal•ly•ing.**

The talons of eagles and other birds of prey are long and curved. The birds use them to kill by stabbing, and to carry the prey to a feeding place.

tal•on (tal′ən) the claw of a bird of prey: *Eagles have talons.* *n.*

tam•bou•rine (tam′bə rēn′) a small, shallow drum with jingling metal disks around the side, played by hitting it or shaking it. *n.*

a bat	e bed	i bid	o pot	u cup	th thin
ā cake	ē me	ī bite	ō go	ū rude	ᴛʜ then
à bar	ə about	ər over	ò for	ù put	zh measure

tame (tām) 1 of an animal, living with people and used by them as work animals, as a source of food, or as pets. 2 not afraid of people, and not attacking them: *The birds are so tame that they will eat from our hands.* 3 make or become tame: *to tame a wild horse. White rats tame easily.* 4 dull: *a tame story, a tame party.* 1, 2, 4 *adj.*, **tam·er, tam·est;** 3 *v.*, **tamed, tam·ing.**

tam·per (tam′pər) meddle; make harmful changes: *Do not tamper with the lock.* *v.*

tan (tan) 1 the brown colour of some people's skin after they have spent a lot of time in the sun: *His arms and legs had a dark tan.* 2 make or become brown from the sun: *A summer of farm work had tanned her face. I do not tan easily.* 3 make an animal's skin into leather by soaking it in a special liquid. This is done at a **tannery.** 4 light yellowish brown: *He wore tan shoes* (*adj.*). 1, 4 *n.*, 2, 3 *v.*, **tanned, tan·ning;** 4 *adj.* —**tan′ner,** *n.*

On a tandem, both riders can pedal, or one can rest while the other keeps the bicycle going.

tan·dem (tan′dəm) 1 Usually, **tandem bicycle,** a bicycle with two seats, one behind the other. 2 one behind the other: *to drive horses tandem* (*adv.*), *tandem seats* (*adj.*). 1 *n.*, 2 *adv. or adj.*
in tandem, in co-operation: *Teachers must work in tandem with parents to help students succeed.*

tan·doo·ri (tȧn dū′rē) a method of cooking that uses a small, extremely hot clay oven. It is traditional in parts of India. *n.*

tang (tang) a flavour that is a bit sharp in a pleasant way: *the tang of a grapefruit, the salty tang of sea air.* *n.* —**tang′y,** *adj.*

tan·ge·rine (tan′jə rēn′) a fruit like a small orange with a loose peel and segments that separate easily. *n.*

tan·gle (tang′gəl) 1 cause to get twisted and knotted together in a confused mass: *The kitten had tangled the ball of yarn.* 2 a confused mass: *Your hair is all in a tangle.* 1 *v.*, **tan·gled, tan·gling;** 2 *n.* —**tan′gly,** *adj.*

tank (tangk) 1 a large container for liquid or gas: *a water tank, a car's gas tank.* A **tanker** is a ship, plane, or truck with tanks for carrying liquid loads. A train car used for this is called a **tank car.** 2 put or store in a tank. 3 an armoured vehicle used in war. Tanks are mounted on tracks instead of wheels so that they can travel over rough ground. 1, 3 *n.*, 2 *v.*
tank up, put gas in a vehicle's gas tank.

tan·ta·lize (tan′tə līz′) tease by holding something desirable just out of reach, or by raising hopes that will only be disappointed: *She tantalized the hungry dog by shaking the dog food box.* *v.*, **tan·ta·lized, tan·ta·liz·ing.**

WORD HISTORY........tantalize

Tantalize comes from a Greek myth about King Tantalus. The gods once kept him standing in water up to his chin, under branches loaded with fruit. Whenever he tried to eat or drink, the fruit or water would move just out of reach.

tan·trum (tan′trəm) *Informal.* a fit of extreme bad temper. *n.*

Tao·ism (dou′iz əm) a religion that began in China, based on the teachings of Laotse who wrote the **Tao Te Ching.** Taoism teaches people to aim for harmony and balance through a humble, simple, honest, and unselfish lifestyle. *n.* —**Tao′ist,** *n.*

tap¹ (tap) 1 hit or beat lightly: *He tapped on the window. Tap out the rhythm for me.* 2 a light knock: *There was a tap at the door.* 1 *v.*, **tapped, tap·ping;** 2 *n.*

tap² (tap) 1 a device for turning a flow of liquid on and off. Most sinks have taps for hot and cold water. 2 make a hole in something to let out liquid: *They tapped the sugar maples when the sap began to flow.* 3 get or use resources from: *to tap the mineral wealth of a region.* 4 make a connection on a phone line in order to listen in secretly. 1 *n.*, 2–4 *v.*, **tapped, tap·ping.**

tap–dance (tap′ dans′) dance with very fast, loud taps of the toes and heels, using special shoes. *v.*, **tap-danced, tap-danc·ing.** —**tap′-danc′er,** *n.*

tape (tāp) 1 a strip of cloth, paper, or plastic coated with a sticky substance and used to attach things: *I fixed the torn book cover with tape.* 2 fasten or wrap with tape: *The doctor taped up the wound. He taped a note to the door.* 3 a strip of plastic that has been magnetized for recording sound, or images and sound. 4 record on this, using a special machine: *We taped the TV show so we could watch it later.* 5 a long, narrow strip of any kind of material, such as the strip stretched across the finish line in a race.

A **measuring tape,** or **tape measure,** has centimetres or inches marked on it. 1, 3, 5 *n.,* 2, 4 *v.,* **taped, tap·ing.**

tap·er (tā′pər) 1 make or become gradually smaller toward one end: *A cone tapers to a point.* 2 Usually, **taper off,** gradually grow less: *Her business tapered off as people moved away.* 3 a very thin candle. 1, 2 *v.,* 3 *n.*

tape recorder (tāp′ ri kôr′dər) a machine for recording and playing back sound on magnetized plastic audio tapes. If it is a unit combined with others in a stereo system, it is called a **tape deck.** *n.*

tap·es·try (tap′i strē) a piece of fabric with pictures or designs woven into it, used to hang on walls, cover furniture, etc. *n., pl.* **tap·es·tries.**

tape·worm (tāp′wərm′) a long, flat worm that lives as a parasite in the intestines of people and animals. *n.*

tap·i·o·ca (tap′ē ō′kə) a starchy food that comes from the root of a tropical plant called the **cassava** (kə sav′ə). Tapioca is often used to make pudding. *n.*

ta·pir (tā′pər) an animal of tropical America and southeast Asia, with hoofs and a flexible snout. It is related to the horse and rhinoceros but looks a bit like a pig. *n.*

tap·root (tap′rūt′) a single main root growing straight down. *n.*

tar (tär) 1 a thick, black, sticky substance obtained from wood or coal. It is used to cover and patch roads and to make things waterproof. **Tar paper** is heavy paper soaked in tar to make it waterproof. 2 cover or smear with tar. 1 *n.,* 2 *v.,* **tarred, tar·ring.** —**tar′ry,** *adj.*
tar and feather, in earlier times, pour heated tar on and cover with feathers as a punishment for crime.

The tarantula gets its name from Taranto, a town in southern Italy, where these spiders can be found.

ta·ran·tu·la (tə ran′chə lə) a large, hairy spider that lives mostly in warm regions. Its bite is painful but usually not serious. *n.*

tar·dy (tär′dē) late or delayed: *tardy growth. She was tardy for school four times last year.* *adj.,* **tar·di·er, tar·di·est.** —**tar′di·ness,** *n.*

tar·get (tär′git) 1 a mark for shooting at; something you aim for: *Her spitball hit the target. The target for the fundraising drive was $10 000.* 2 an object of abuse, scorn, or criticism: *His crazy ideas made him the target of many jokes.* 3 aim at; shoot for: *They're targeting the end of March for completion of the new stadium.* 1, 2 *n.,* 3 *v.*

tar·iff (ter′if) a duty or tax on goods brought in from other countries: *There is a very high tariff on imported jewellery.* *n.*

Tar·mac (tär′mak) *trademark for* a paved asphalt surface, especially a runway of an airfield. *n.*

tar·nish (tär′nish) 1 lose or cause to lose shine and develop a discoloured coating: *The brass knobs tarnished.* Some metals tarnish when exposed to air or certain chemicals. 2 the discoloured coating: *I took the tarnish off with silver polish.* 3 bring disgrace on: *All that gossip has tarnished his reputation.* 1, 3 *v.,* 2 *n.*

tar·pau·lin (tär pol′ən) a sheet of waterproof material used to protect things against the weather. *n.*

🍁 **tar sands** (tär′ sandz′) an older name for **oil sands,** a mixture of sand, clay, water, and oil. Tar sands can be processed to give petroleum or oil.

tart¹ (tärt) a piece of pastry like a tiny pie. *n.*

tart² (tärt) sharp and sour: *Some apples are tart. She made a tart reply.* *adj.*

tar·tan (tär′tən) 1 a plaid woollen cloth. 2 a particular design of plaid. Each Scottish clan has its own traditional tartan with a certain combination of colours in a certain pattern of stripes. *n.*

tar·tar (tär′tər) a hard substance that collects on teeth. *n.*

tartar sauce (tär′tər sos′) a creamy white sauce made of mayonnaise with chopped pickles and so on, usually eaten with seafood. *n.*

task (task) a piece of work; job; assignment: *Her task is to set the table.* *n.*
take to task, tell off; scold: *The teacher took me to task for not listening.*

tas·sel (tas′əl) a hanging bunch of threads or pieces of yarn, fastened together at the top end: *I have tassels on the ends of my scarf.* *n.*

a bat	e bed	i bid	o pot	u cup	th thin
ā cake	ē me	ī bite	ō go	ū rude	ᴛʜ then
ä bar	ə about	ər over	ô for	ù put	zh measure

taste (tāst) **1** the special quality of a thing which you notice with the sense organs of your mouth; flavour: *Do you like the taste of olives?* Sweet, sour, salty, and bitter are the four main tastes. **2** notice the flavour of: *I can taste almonds in this cake.* **3** have a particular flavour: *The soup tastes like onion.* Something with a lot of flavour is **tasty;** the opposite is **tasteless. 4** try the flavour of something by putting a little in your mouth: *Taste this and see if it's too sweet.* **5** a little bit; sample: *Give me a taste of the pudding. The snowstorm gave me a taste of northern winter.* **6** the ability to notice the flavour of things: *I have no taste—my tongue is still frozen from the dentist's.* **7** a liking: *Most people have a taste for sweet things.* **8** the ability to notice and enjoy what is beautiful, or to know what behaviour is appropriate in various situations: *She has excellent taste in music. That shocking joke of his showed very poor taste.* If something shows this kind of taste it is **in good taste** or **tasteful.** The opposite is **in bad taste** or **tasteless.** 1, 5–8 *n.,* 2–4 *v.,* **tast·ed, tast·ing.**

taste bud (tāst′ bud′) a special cell that is a sense organ of taste. Most taste buds are in the outer layer of your tongue.

tat·ters (tat′ərz) rags or torn pieces; ragged clothing: *children dressed in tatters. After the storm the flag hung in tatters on the mast.* *pl.n.* **—tat′tered,** *adj.*

tat·tle (tat′əl) tell what others have done wrong in order to get them into trouble. A person who does this is a **tattletale.** *v.,* **tat·tled, tat·tling.**

tat·too[1] (ta tü′ *or* tə tü′) **1** mark the skin with designs or patterns by pricking it and putting in colours: *The sailor had a ship tattooed on his arm.* **2** a mark or design like this on the skin. 1 *v.,* **tat·tooed, tat·too·ing;** 2 *n., pl.* **tat·toos.**

tat·too[2] (ta tü′ *or* tə tü′) **1** a signal on a bugle or drum. **2** a series of raps, taps, etc.: *The hail beat a loud tattoo on the windowpane.* *n., pl.* **tat·toos.**

taught (tot) the past tense and past participle of **teach:** *Miss Johannsen taught my mother. She has taught music for many years.* *v.*

taunt (tont) **1** tease in a mean way: *They taunted me because I was short.* **2** a mean, teasing remark. 1 *v.,* 2 *n.*

taut (tot) pulled very tight; tense: *a taut rope.* *adj.*

CONFUSABLES ....taut

taut means "tight": *Pull the string taut.*

taught is the past tense of "teach": *My parents taught me good manners.*

tav·ern (tav′ərn) a place where alcoholic drinks are sold and drunk. *n.*

taw·dry (tod′rē) showy and cheap. *adj.*

tax (taks) **1** money paid by people to the government to pay for roads, schools, libraries, police services, and so on. Taxes are based on how much you earn (**income tax**), own (**property tax**), and spend (**sales tax**). People who pay tax are **taxpayers. 2** make people pay a tax on something: *People who own land are taxed according to its value. Groceries are not taxed.* **3** lay a heavy burden on; be hard for: *The work taxed her strength. Reading in a poor light taxes the eyes.* 1 *n.,* 2, 3 *v.* **—tax·a′tion,** *n.*

tax·i (tak′sē) **1** Also, **taxicab,** a car with a driver who will take you where you want to go for a certain price. A meter keeps track of the fare. **2** of an aircraft, move along the ground or water: *The airplane taxied onto the runway.* 1 *n., pl.* **tax·is;** 2 *v.,* **tax·ied, tax·i·ing.**

tbsp. *abbreviation for* tablespoon or tablespoons, a nonmetric unit of volume.

tea (tē) **1** a drink made by pouring boiling water over the dried leaves of a certain shrub grown in south Asia. **2** the shrub or its dried leaves. Tea can be bought loose or in little gauze pouches called **tea bags. 3** an afternoon meal or social event where tea is served. **4** a hot drink made from herbs, meat, etc.: *peppermint tea, beef tea.* *n.*

Word Family..........tea

tea bag: a tiny gauze bag of tea leaves for making tea
tea cosy: a thick cover for a teapot, to keep it hot
teacup: a small cup with a saucer, for drinking tea
teakettle: a kettle for boiling water to make tea
teapot: a container with a spout, for making tea
teaspoon: a small spoon (about 5 mL)
tea towel: a cloth for drying dishes you have washed

teach (tēch) **1** help someone learn by explaining, showing, disciplining, and so on: *to teach someone good manners, to teach someone how to ski. The experience taught me to tell the truth.* **2** give lessons in: *She teaches music.* **3** have a job doing this, especially in a school: *She has taught for years.* *v.,* **taught, teach·ing. —teach′er,** *n.*

teak (tēk) a large tree of the East Indies with hard, yellowish brown wood used for shipbuilding, making fine furniture, etc. *n.*

Tectonics

The theory of tectonics involves seeing the crust of the earth as a number of moving plates. When one plate pushes against another, it may crumple and form mountains, or it may dip down into the earth and bring about earthquakes and volcanic activity.

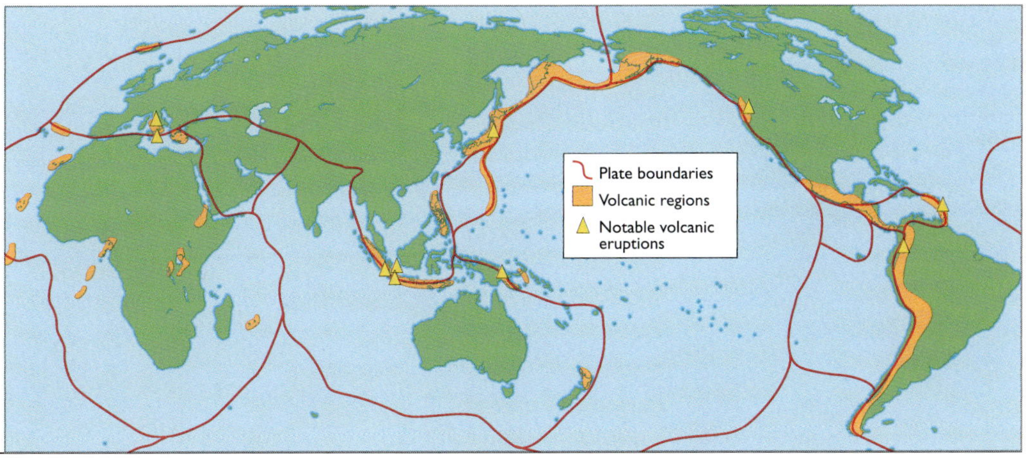

team (tēm) 1 a number of people working, playing, or acting together, especially one of the sides in a game or match: *a football team, a debating team, a clean-up team.* The people on a team are **teammates.** 2 two or more horses or other animals harnessed together to work: *He hitched up the team.* 3 join together in a team: *Everybody teamed up to decorate the gym for the party.* Effort shared by a team is **teamwork.** 1, 2 *n.,* 3 *v.*

tear[1] (tēr) a drop of salty water from your eye. **Teardrop** is another word for it. *n.* **—tear′ful,** *adj.*
in tears, crying: *The baby is in tears.*

tear[2] (ter) 1 pull or be pulled apart by force; rip: *She tore the page in half. Lace tears easily.* 2 a torn place: *She has a tear in her shirt.* 3 pull violently: *They tore the door off.* 4 cut badly: *He tore his hand on a nail.* 5 *Informal.* move very fast: *I tore up the stairs.* 1, 3–5 *v.,* **tore, torn, tear·ing;** 2 *n.*
tear down, destroy and remove something built.
tear up, tear into little pieces.
tear yourself away, leave unwillingly or with difficulty.

tease (tēz) 1 make fun of: *They teased him about his big feet.* Teasing can be playful or mean. 2 annoy by making faces, playing tricks, saying things you don't mean, etc.: *Don't tease your little sister.* 3 a person who teases. 1, 2 *v.,* **teased, teas·ing;** 3 *n.*

teat (tēt) the nipple of a female mammal, from which the young suck milk. *n.*

tech·ni·cal (tek′nə kəl) 1 having to do with the way machines work and other aspects of applied science, or with skilled trades like welding, plumbing, etc.: *Many jobs in industry require technical training.* A person skilled in this kind of work is a **technician** (tek nish′ən). 2 having to do with the special facts of a science or art, not known by most people outside that particular field: *Our art teacher uses some technical words but she always explains them first.* 3 having to do with the details of how things are done in any art, sport, or line of work. For example, technical skill in painting involves knowing the different ways to use a brush, how to mix colours, and so on. A **technician** is expert in these things. *adj.*

tech·nique (tek nēk′) 1 a way of performing the mechanical details of an art, sport, or type of work; technical skill. Scales and trills are part of piano technique; stickhandling is part of hockey technique. 2 a special method or system used to accomplish something: *a new technique for removing tonsils.* *n.*

tech·nol·o·gy (tek nol′ə jē) 1 the use of scientific knowledge for practical purposes: *computer technology, medical technology.* 2 all the systems used by the people of any society to do or get the things they need: *stone-age technology, medieval technology.* *n.*
—tech·nol′o·gist, *n.*
—tech′no·log′i·cal (tek′nə loj′ə kəl), *adj.*

tec·ton·ics (tek ton′iks) the study of the different parts of the earth's crust and how they change and move. *pl.n.* **—tec·ton′ic,** *adj.*

ted·dy bear (ted′ē ber′) a stuffed toy made to look like a bear cub. It can be called a **teddy** for short.

te·di·ous (tē′dē əs) tiring and boring. *adj.*

tee (tē) in golf: 1 the place you start from in playing each hole. 2 a short wooden or plastic peg you put the ball on for the first shot at each hole. 3 **a** Usually, **tee up,** put a golf ball on a tee. **b** Usually, **tee off,** hit the ball off the tee. 1, 2 *n.,* 3 *v.*

a bat	e bed	i bid	o pot	u cup	th thin
ā cake	ē me	ī bite	ō go	ū rude	ᴛʜ then
ä bar	ə about	ər over	ô for	ů put	zh measure

Telecommunications

Television is a large section of the telecommunications industry. Pictures and sound are converted to signals, and later decoded into the sound and images you see on your TV screen.

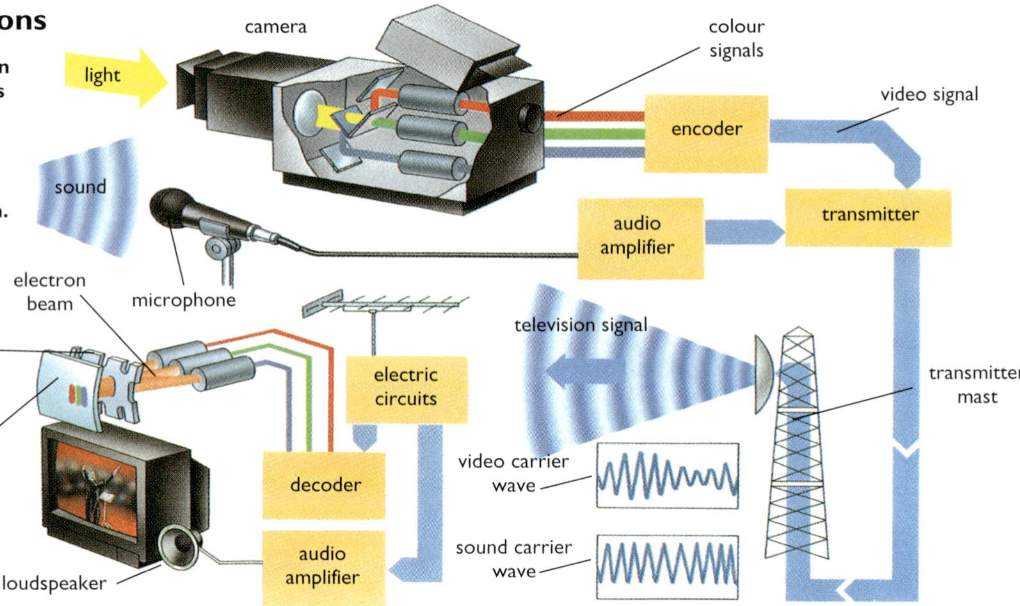

teem[1] (tēm) be filled; abound; swarm: *The swamp teemed with mosquitoes.* *v.*

teem[2] (tēm) pour; come down in torrents: *It has been teeming all afternoon.* *v.*

CONFUSABLES ....teem

teem can mean "swarm" or "pour": *The river is teeming with fish. The rain is teeming down.*

team means "people working together": *My hockey team won the tournament.*

teens (tēnz) the years of life from 13 to 19: *The high-school students were all in their teens.* **Teen years** means the same; a person of this age is a **teen** or **teenager.** *pl.n.* —**teen′age′,** *adj.*

tee•ny (tē′nē) *Informal.* tiny. **Teensy** (tēn′sē), **teeny-weeny,** and **teensy-weensy** are other forms. *adj.*

tee•pee (tē′pē) a cone-shaped tent once used by the First Nations peoples of the plains, made of animal skins or canvas over a frame of wooden poles. **Tipi** and **tepee** are other spellings. *n.*

tee•ter (tē′tər) wobble; be almost falling: *My bike teetered for a moment and then steadied.* *v.*

tee•ter–tot•ter (tē′tər tot′ər) **1** a piece of playground equipment made of a plank resting on a central support so riders can sit on the ends and move up and down; a seesaw. **2** play on this thing. 1 *n.,* 2 *v.*

teeth (tēth) plural of **tooth:** *You often show your teeth when you smile.* *n.*

by the skin of your teeth, just barely: *He escaped by the skin of his teeth.*
in the teeth of, straight against; in the face of: *We advanced in the teeth of the wind.*
lie through your teeth, tell a big lie without hesitation.
to the teeth, fully: *armed to the teeth.*

teethe (tēᴛʜ) grow teeth: *Our baby is teething.* *v.,* **teethed, teeth•ing.**

tel•e•cast (tel′ə kast′) **1** broadcast on TV. **2** a TV broadcast. 1 *v.,* **tel•e•cast, tel•e•cast•ing;** 2 *n.*

WORD HISTORY........tele-

Words beginning with **tele-** all have to do with something carried out over a distance: *tele-* means "far" in Greek. A **teleconference** is a discussion by phone with several people at once. If you **telecommute,** you do your work away from your office and send it in electronically.

tel•e•com•mu•ni•ca•tions (tel′ə kə myū′nə kā′shənz) the science and technology of sending information by computer, radio, telephone, TV, telegraph, etc. *n.*

tel•e•gram (tel′ə gram′) a message sent by special signals over wires from one station to another and then phoned or delivered to the person it is meant for. *n.*

tel•e•graph (tel′ə graf′) **1** the system of sending and receiving telegrams. **2** send a telegram: *Jodi telegraphed us from Bangladesh.* 1 *n.,* 2 *v.*

tel•e•mar•ket•ing (tel′ə mar′kə ting) the work of trying to sell things for a company by phoning possible customers in their homes. *n.* **—tel′e•mar′ket•er,** *n.*

te•lep•a•thy (tə lep′ə thē) communication without using hearing, sight, or any other physical sense; mind-reading. *n.* **—tel′e•path′ic** (tel′ə path′ik), *adj.*

tel•e•phone (tel′ə fōn′) **1** a piece of equipment for sending and receiving messages by voice. The sound is changed to electrical or radio signals which are carried by wires or through the air; you make a connection by keying or dialing the right number. **2** call someone in this way. 1 *n.,* 2 *v.,* **tel•e•phoned, tel•e•phon•ing.**

tel•e•pho•to lens (tel′ə fō′tō lenz′) a camera lens that lets you take close-ups of faraway objects.

tel•e•scope (tel′ə skōp′) an instrument with special lenses for making distant objects look closer and bigger. Telescopes are used to study the stars and planets. *n.* **—tel′e•scop′ic** (tel′ə skop′ik), *adj.*

tel•e•vise (tel′ə vīz′) broadcast on television: *to televise a baseball game.* *v.,* **tel•e•vised, tel•e•vis•ing.**

tel•e•vi•sion (tel′ə vizh′ən) **1** the system of sending and receiving pictures on a screen, along with sound, by radio waves or by cable. **2** the piece of equipment for watching these pictures, also called a **television set.** **3** the business of making programs to be broadcast in this way. **TV** is a shortened form for all the meanings of this word. *n.*

tell (tel) **1** put into words and say or write: *to tell a story. Tell the truth.* **2** let someone know something: *Don't tell my secret. One sniff told him something was burning.* **3** command: *I told you to do your work.* **4** recognize; know or notice: *I can't tell which house is yours. How can you tell the difference?* *v.,* **told, tell•ing.**
all told, altogether: *All told, 42 people showed up.*
tell me about it or **you're telling me,** *Informal.* I have experienced the very same thing.
tell off, *Informal.* scold; criticize: *His father told him off for staying out late.*
tell on, a tell what someone has done wrong: *Please don't tell on me!* **b** have a noticeable effect: *The strain was telling on his health.*
tell time, know what time it is by looking at a clock.

tell•er (tel′ər) a cashier in a bank. *n.*

tell•tale (tel′tāl′) giving away some secret; revealing: *a telltale fingerprint.* *adj.*

tem•per (tem′pər) **1** an angry state of mind: *She flew into a temper and yelled at her parents.* **2** a calm or controlled state of mind: *Try to keep your temper. He became angry and lost his temper.* **3** someone's usual state of mind: *She has a sweet temper.* **4** bring to the right condition of toughness, flexibility, etc. by mixing with something or preparing in some other special way: *to temper steel. Temper justice with mercy.* 1–3 *n.,* 4 *v.*

tem•per•a•ment (tem′prə mənt) a person's nature or make-up: *She has a nervous temperament. He has an artistic temperament.* *n.*

tem•per•a•men•tal (tem′prə men′təl) having very changeable moods; easily irritated: *The author was very temperamental and would not put up with any noise when she was writing.* *adj.*

tem•per•ate (tem′prit) **1** not very hot and not very cold: *Vancouver Island has a temperate climate.* **2** moderate; using self-control: *She spoke in a temperate manner, not exaggerating or insulting either viewpoint.* **3** moderate in using alcoholic drinks. *adj.*

tem•per•a•ture (tem′pə rə chər) **1** a measure of how hot something is: *The temperature of freezing water is 0°C.* **2** a fever. *n.*
run a temperature, have a fever.

tem•pest (tem′pist) a poetic word for "storm." *n.* **—tem•pes′tu•ous** (tem pes′chū əs), *adj.*

tem•ple[1] (tem′pəl) a building used for worship. *n.*

tem•ple[2] (tem′pəl) the flat part on either side of your head near the front. *n.*

tem•po (tem′pō) speed or pace, especially in music. *n.*

tem•po•rar•y (tem′pə rer′ē) lasting for a short time only: *The hikers made a temporary shelter out of branches.* *adj.* **—tem′po•rar′i•ly,** *adv.*

tempt (tempt) **1** make a person feel like doing something foolish or wrong: *The sight of the food tempted the hungry man to steal.* **2** appeal strongly to; attract: *The idea of a movie tempts me.* *v.* **—temp•ta′tion,** *n.* **—tempt′ing,** *adj.*
tempt Providence or **fate,** take a foolish risk; ask for trouble: *It is tempting Providence to go in that old boat.*

ten (ten) one more than nine; 10: *Five and five make ten (n.).* *n. or adj.* **—tenth,** *adj. or n.*

a bat	e bed	i bid	o pot	u cup	th thin
ā cake	ē me	ī bite	ō go	ū rude	ᴛʜ then
ä bar	ə about	ər over	ô for	ů put	zh measure

te·na·cious (tə nā′shəs) 1 holding fast: *a tenacious grip, a tenacious memory.* 2 determined; not giving up: *a tenacious fighter for human rights.* *adj.* —**te·nac′i·ty** (tə nas′ə tē), *n.*

ten·ant (ten′ənt) a person who rents land or buildings. *n.* —**ten′an·cy,** *n.*

tend[1] (tend) 1 be likely to; have a **tendency,** a certain typical or usual way of behaving: *Fruit tends to decay. She tends to talk fast.* 2 turn gradually in a certain direction: *The road tends to the south here.* *v.*

tend[2] (tend) take care of; look after: *He sometimes tends the store for his parents. A nurse tends the sick.* *v.*
tend to, see to; pay attention to: *Tend to your work.*

ten·der[1] (ten′dər) 1 not hard or tough; soft: *The meat is tender. Stones hurt the little child's tender feet.* 2 kind; gentle; loving: *tender hands, a tender heart. The mother spoke tender words to her baby.* 3 sensitive; painful; sore: *a tender wound. Cars are a tender subject with Dad since he wrecked his.* 4 young: *at the tender age of three.* *adj.* —**ten′der·ize′,** *v.*

ten·der[2] (ten′dər) 1 a formal word for "offer": *He tendered his thanks (v.). She refused his tender of marriage (n.).* 2 something offered as payment. Money is called **legal tender.** 1 *v.,* 1, 2 *n.*

ten·der·foot (ten′dər fu̇t′) *Informal.* 1 a newcomer to the pioneer life of the West, or anyone not used to rough living and hardships. 2 an inexperienced person. *n., pl.* **ten·der·feet.**

ten·don (ten′dən) a tough, strong band or cord of tissue that joins a muscle to a bone or some other part; sinew. *n.*

ten·dril (ten′drəl) 1 a threadlike part of a climbing plant that attaches itself to a surface and helps support the plant. 2 anything like this: *curly tendrils of hair.* *n.*

ten·e·ment (ten′ə mənt) a building, especially in a poor section of a city, divided into small apartments. *n.*

ten·nis (ten′is) a game played by two or four players on a special court, by hitting a ball back and forth over a net with a racquet. *n.*

ten·or (ten′ər) 1 in music, the range of notes that a man with a high voice can sing. 2 having this range: *a tenor voice, a tenor saxophone.* 3 a singer or instrument with this range, or the part written for it in a song: *We have four tenors in our choir. You play the tenor.* *n.*

tense[1] (tens) 1 stretched tight and stiff: *a tense rope.* 2 stretch tight; stiffen: *She tensed her muscles for the leap.* 3 anxious or full of suspense: *tense nerves, a tense moment.* 1, 3 *adj.,* **tens·er, tens·est;** 2 *v.,* **tensed, tens·ing.**

tense[2] (tens) in grammar, a form of the verb that shows the time of the action or state being talked about. *He obeys* is in the present tense. *He obeyed* is in the past tense. *n.* ▶ See the *Grammar and Usage Mini-Guide.*

Grammar Check . . . . . . tense

The three main **tenses** in English are:
past: *I ran, I had run, I was running*
present: *I run, I have run, I am running*
future: *I will run, I will have run, I will be running*

Don't change from one tense to another in your writing. Here is an example of this: *I was working on my project when the telephone rings.* This sentence should be rewritten in either the present tense or the past tense.

Here it is in the past tense: *I was working on my project when the telephone rang.*

Try rewriting it in the present tense.

ten·sion (ten′shən) 1 a stretched condition; tightness and stiffness: *The tension of the bowstring gives speed to the arrow.* 2 an anxious or uncomfortable feeling caused by suspense, fear, unfriendliness, etc.: *We felt some tension as we waited for our parents' reaction. There was a lot of tension between them after the fight.* *n.*

tent (tent) 1 a movable shelter made of cloth and held up by poles and ropes. 2 camp out or live in a tent: *We spent the holidays tenting in the Maritimes.* 1 *n.,* 2 *v.*

ten·ta·cle (ten′tə kəl) 1 a long, slender, flexible growth on the head or around the mouth of an animal, used to touch, hold, or move; a feeler: *An octopus has eight tentacles.* 2 anything thought of as reaching far and holding tight like an octopus's tentacle. *n.*

ten·ta·tive (ten′tə tiv) 1 done or made on a trial basis: *a tentative plan.* 2 uncertain or hesitant; not confident: *a tentative smile.* *adj.* —**ten′ta·tive·ly,** *adv.*

ten·ter·hooks (ten′tər hu̇ks′)
on tenterhooks, excited and full of suspense. *pl.n.*

tep·id (tep′id) slightly warm; lukewarm. *adj.*

ter·i·ya·ki (ter′ē yä′kē) meat cut in thin slices, soaked in soy sauce and other flavourings, and quickly broiled or barbecued. *n.*

term (tərm) 1 a word, especially a technical word belonging to a particular science, art, sport, or line of work: *medical terms. "Software" is a computer term.*

The special vocabulary of a subject is its **terminology.** 2 describe as; call: *He might be termed handsome.* 3 a set period of time: *The mayor's term of office is two years. The school year is divided into three terms.* 4 **terms,** *pl.* **a** things that are accepted as part of an agreement: *to discuss the terms of a contract.* **b** personal relations: *We are on good terms with the Smiths.* 1, 3, 4 *n.,* 2 *v.* **come to terms,** reach an agreement: *The two leaders came to terms and the dispute was settled.*

ter•mi•nal (tər′mə nəl) 1 a computer screen together with a keyboard or other input device, where a user can enter or receive information. It is connected to a central computer system or network. 2 a railway or bus station, or one of the buildings at an airport where planes load and unload. 3 a place for making an electrical connection: *the terminals of a battery.* 4 likely to end in death: *a terminal illness.* 5 being at the end: *Terminal buds grow at the end of stems.* 1, 4, 5 *adj.,* 2, 3 *n.*

ter•mi•nate (tər′mə nāt′) end: *to terminate a discussion. The school year terminates in June.* *v.,* **ter•mi•nat•ed, ter•mi•nat•ing.** —**ter′mi•na′tion,** *n.*

ter•mi•nus (tər′mə nəs) the end of a railway or bus line. *n., pl.* **ter•mi•nus•es** or **ter•mi•ni** (tēr′mə nī′).

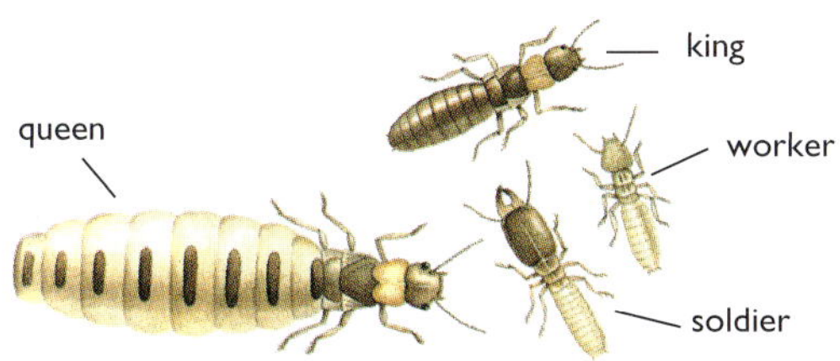

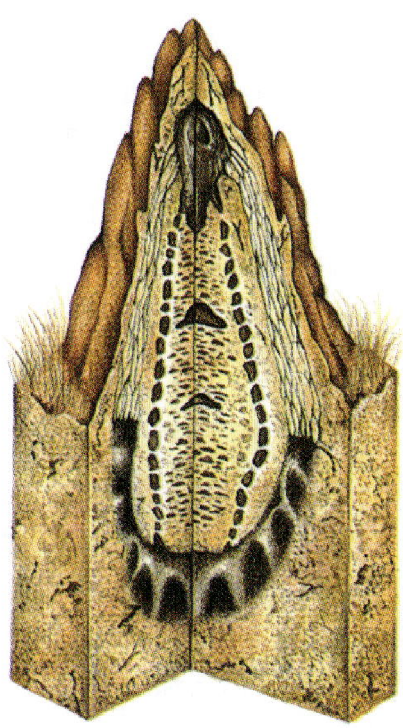

This species of termite builds a mud tower for a nest. There are many tunnels in it. Each colony of termites has a queen and a king. Thousands of workers dig the tunnels and find food and water, and soldier termites protect the colony.

ter•mite (tər′mīt) a small insect that has a soft, pale body and lives in colonies. Termites feed on wood and can be very destructive to buildings and trees. *n.*

tern (tərn) a sea bird that looks like a gull but with a more slender body and bill and a long, forked tail. *n.*

ter•race (ter′is) 1 a strip of level land set off from the land above or below it, often by a low wall. Usually it is one of a series of steplike levels on a slope. Terraces make it easier to farm hilly land; they also prevent erosion. 2 form into a terrace or terraces: *a terraced garden.* 3 a large patio adjoining a restaurant, hotel, hospital, etc. 1, 3 *n.,* 2 *v.,* **ter•raced, ter•rac•ing.**

ter•rain (tə rān′) land, especially from the viewpoint of how it looks, what grows on it, or how easy it is to travel across: *grassy terrain, rugged terrain.* *n.*

ter•rar•i•um (tə rer′ē əm) a glass container with earth, stones, etc. in it, for plants or small land animals. *n., pl.* **ter•rar•i•ums** or **ter•rar•i•a** (tə rer′ē ə).

ter•res•tri•al (tə res′trē əl) 1 having to do with the earth: *this terrestrial globe.* 2 having to do with land, not water or air: *Cows, lions, and elephants are terrestrial animals.* *adj.*

ter•ri•ble (ter′ə bəl) causing great fear; dreadful; very bad: *The terrible storm destroyed many lives.* *adj.* —**ter′ri•bly,** *adv.*

ter•ri•er (ter′ē ər) a breed of small, active, intelligent, and courageous dog originally used in hunting to chase the prey into its burrow. *n.*

ter•rif•ic (tə rif′ik) 1 causing great fear; terrifying: *A terrific earthquake shook Japan.* 2 excellent: *You have done a terrific job.* *adj.*

ter•ri•fy (ter′ə fī′) fill with great fear; frighten very much: *Terrified by the sight of the bear, he ran into the cabin.* *v.,* **ter•ri•fied, ter•ri•fy•ing.**

ter•ri•to•ry (ter′ə tô′rē) 1 an area of land, or a particular kind of land: *a large mining territory. Much territory in northern Africa is desert.* 2 land claimed or controlled by a certain person, group, government, or animal: *a salesperson's territory, the territory of a wolf pack. Baffin Island is Canadian territory.* 3 🍁 **Territory,** in Canada, a region with its own elected government but without all the powers of a province: *Yukon Territory.* *n., pl.* **ter•ri•to•ries.** —**ter′ri•to′ri•al,** *adj.*

ter•ror (ter′ər) 1 great fear: *The screams filled me with terror.* 2 a cause of great fear: *Pirates were once the terror of the sea.* *n.*

a bat	e bed	i bid	o pot	u cup	th thin
ā cake	ē me	ī bite	ō go	ū rude	ᴛʜ then
ä bar	ə about	ər over	ô for	ů put	zh measure

ter·ror·ism (ter′ə riz′əm) the use of violence to create terror, especially as a tool to force a government to agree to certain demands. *n.* —**ter′ror·ist,** *n. or adj.*

ter·ror·ize (ter′ə rīz′) 1 fill with terror: *The sight of the huge, growling dog terrorized the little child.* 2 control by causing terror: *The village was terrorized by bandits during the revolution.* *v.,* **ter·ror·ized, ter·ror·iz·ing.**

ter·ry (ter′ē) cotton cloth with tiny loops on both sides, used for towels. It is also called **terrycloth.** *n.*

terse (tərs) brief and to the point: *"No!" was my brother's terse reply when I asked him if I could use his radio.* *adj.,* **ters·er, ters·est.**

test (test) 1 a set of questions or exercises used to measure a person's knowledge or skill: *a French test, a driving test.* 2 any action done to find out the result or to prove a certain thing: *A test showed that the water from our well was pure.* 3 give a test to or do a test on; try out: *All the rides have been tested for safety.* 1, 2 *n.,* 3 *v.*
put to the test, test.

tes·ti·cle (tes′tə kəl) the organ in a man or male animal which produces sperm cells. A man has two testicles, contained in a pouch of skin called the **scrotum** (skrō′təm) under the penis. *n.*

tes·ti·fy (tes′tə fī′) 1 be proof of something: *The band's success testifies to the talent of its members.* 2 make a statement as evidence in court: *The officer testified that the driver had been speeding.* *v.,* **tes·ti·fied, tes·ti·fy·ing.**

tes·ti·mo·ny (tes′tə mō′nē) 1 a statement used for evidence or proof: *A witness gave testimony that Mr. Weber was at home all day.* 2 sign; a way of showing something: *We gave our teacher a farewell gift as a testimony of our respect and affection.* *n., pl.* **tes·ti·mo·nies.**

test tube (test′ tyūb′) a thin, tube-shaped glass container for chemicals, used in doing scientific tests and experiments. —**test′-tube′,** *adj.*

tes·ty (tes′tē) easily irritated; impatient. *adj.,* **tes·ti·er, tes·ti·est.** —**tes′ti·ly,** *adv.*

tet·a·nus (tet′ə nəs) a disease that causes muscle stiffness, violent spasms, and even death. The bacteria that cause tetanus usually enter the body through a cut or wound; in Canada, everyone is vaccinated against it. *n.*

teth·er (teᴛʜ′ər) 1 a rope or chain for fastening an animal so it can move only a certain distance. 2 fasten with a tether: *The horse is tethered to a stake.* 1 *n.,* 2 *v.*
at the end of your tether, frustrated and not knowing what to do next.

text (tekst) 1 written material: *This history book contains 300 pages of text and 50 full-page illustrations.* 2 textbook: *Get out your spelling texts.* 3 send a message by cellphone: *I'll text you later.* The full name for this process is **text messaging.** 1, 2 *n.,* 3 *v.*

text·book (tekst′bůk′) a book for regular study by students. *n.*

tex·tile (tek′stīl) a woven or knitted fabric; cloth. Cotton, rayon, and wool are textiles. *n.*

tex·ture (teks′chər) the feel of a substance as a result of the size of its parts and how they are arranged: *Flour and silk have a fine, smooth texture. Gravel and burlap have a coarse, rough texture.* *n.*

than (ᴛʜan) a word used in comparing: *I'm taller than my sister. You draw better than I do.* *conj., prep.*

USING WORDS .... than

Than and **then** are sometimes confused. **Than** is the word to use when you are comparing: *bigger than, less than.* **Then** is an adverb to do with time: *Just then, the balloon rose higher than ever.*

thank (thangk) 1 tell someone that you have noticed what he or she has given or done and that you are glad about it: *She thanked us for helping her.* 2 **thanks,** *pl.* **a** I thank you. **b** the act of thanking: *Thanks are due to all those who helped.* 1 *v.,* 2 *n.* —**thank′ful,** *adj.*
thanks to, owing to; because of: *Thanks to your efforts, we won the game.* **No thanks to** is the opposite.
thank you, the expression used to thank people: *Thank you for the lovely present.* The adjective is **thank-you:** *a thank-you note.*

thank·less (thangk′lis) 1 not likely to get thanks: *a thankless job.* 2 not feeling thankful: *The thankless girl said nothing to the neighbours who had helped her.* *adj.*

thanks·giv·ing (thangks′ giv′ing) 1 the act of thanking someone. 2 **Thanksgiving** or **Thanksgiving Day,** a holiday set apart as a time to thank God, especially for the harvest: *In Canada, Thanksgiving Day is the second Monday in October.* *n.*

that (ᴛʜat) **That** is used: 1 to point out or draw attention to a particular person, thing, or idea. If you are making a contrast between two things, use **this** for the thing closer to you and **that** for the thing farther away: *I know that girl. Let's buy this book, not that one (adj.). I like that better (pron.).* 2 to connect two clauses in a sentence: *I know that it will be fun.* 3 to show purpose or result: *He ran very fast so that he would not be late. He ran so fast*

that he was five minutes early. **4** to refer back to a person or thing in the same sentence and add information about it: *Bring the box that holds the most. She is the girl that we saw earlier. Remember the day that I met you?* **5** with an adjective or adverb to mean "so": *I cannot stay up that long.* 1 *adj.,* 2, 3 *conj.,* 1, 4 *pron.,* 5 *adv.*
that's that, *Informal.* that is settled or finished.

USING WORDS .... that

That, which, and **who** or **whom** can all be used to introduce a clause describing a noun.

Use **that** to refer to people, animals, or things: *A boy that I know broke his leg. The cat that climbed the tree got stuck. I found the nickel that I lost.*

Which is used only for things and animals, never for people. *The shoe, which fit perfectly, was made of glass.*

Who and **whom** are used for people, and sometimes for animals (especially pets): *My dog, who thinks he is human, likes to sit in the front seat of our car.*

thatch (thach) **1** straw or other bundled-up stems or leaves, used as a roof covering. **2** make or cover with thatch. 1 *n.,* 2 *v.*

that's (ᴛʜats) that is or that has.

thaw (tho) **1** melt from a frozen state; make or become free from frost: *Salt was put on the sidewalk to thaw the ice. The meat will thaw if you take it out of the freezer.* **2** a period of weather above the freezing point (0°C); a time of melting: *The spring thaw came late this year.* 1 *v.,* 2 *n.*

the·a·tre (thē′ə tər) **1** a place where plays or movies are shown. **2** the art or business of writing, acting in, or directing plays: *He would like to study theatre.* **Theater** is another spelling of this word. *n.*
—the·at′ri·cal (thē at′rə kəl), *adj.*

theft (theft) stealing: *The theft of the jewels caused much excitement. The girl was arrested for theft.* *n.*

theme (thēm) **1** a subject; topic: *Protecting the whales was the speaker's theme.* **2** an idea used again and again in different ways: *Her room is decorated using a jungle theme. The theme for the costume party was the 1950s.* **3** the main melody in a piece of music or in the sound track of a movie. **4** a melody or song associated with a particular radio or TV program, a public event, a camp or school, etc. **Theme song** is the same thing. *n.*

theme park (thēm′ pärk′) an amusement park with rides and other things to do, all designed to fit one main theme, such as jungles, outer space, fairy tales, or a time in the past: *That afternoon we went to the Canadian Pioneer theme park.*

then (ᴛʜen) **1** that time; at that time: *Grandpa talks of his childhood, and says prices were much lower then (adv.). By then it'll be over (n.). My then best friend gave it to me (adj.).* **2** after that: *The noise stopped and then began again. First comes spring, then summer.* **3** as another thing to consider: *Yes, hard work is good for you; but then, so is play.* **4** in that case; therefore: *If she broke it, then she should pay for it.* 1–4 *adv.,* 1 *n.,* 1 *adj.*

thence (thens *or* ᴛʜens) an old-fashioned or formal word meaning: **1** from that place or time: *a few years thence. She went to Italy, and thence to France.* **Thenceforth** means "from that time onward." **2** for that reason: *You didn't work; thence you will get no pay.* *adv.*

the·ol·o·gy (thē ol′ə jē) the study of religion and religious beliefs. *n., pl.* **the·ol·o·gies.** **—the′o·log′i·cal** (thē′ə loj′ə kəl), *adj.* **—the′o·lo′gian** (thē′ə lō′jən), *n.*

the·o·rize (thē′ə rīz′) come up with ideas to explain something: *We theorized that Salli probably stayed home because she was sick.* *v.,* **the·o·rized, the·o·riz·ing.**

the·o·ry (thē′ə rē) **1** a reasonable explanation which links facts but which has not itself been proved: *There are several theories about how the fire started.* **2** the ideas that guide a science or art, rather than the activity itself: *the theory of music.* **3** an idea or opinion about something. *n., pl.* **the·o·ries.** **—the′o·ret′i·cal,** *adj.*

ther·a·py (ther′ə pē) the treatment of any disease or disorder, especially without operations or after an operation has partly corrected the problem: *My knee is back to normal after weeks of therapy.* *n.*
—ther′a·pist, *n.* **—ther′a·peu′tic** (ther′ə pyū′tik), *adj.*

there (ᴛʜer) **1** that place; in, at, or to that place: *Sit there. We can't go there (adv.). We go to Hamilton first and from there to Windsor (n.).* **2** **There** is used as a placeholder for the subject in sentences where the real subject comes later: *There are three oranges left. There will come a day when you start to understand. In the palace there lived a prince.* **3** **There** is used to call attention to some thing: *There goes the bell.* **4** **There** is used to express satisfaction, triumph, comfort, etc.: *There, I've done it!* 1–3 *adv.,* 1 *n.,* 4 *interj.*

CONFUSABLES .... there

there means "in that place": *Put it down over there.*
their means "belonging to them": *Their house was robbed.*
they're means "they are": *They're arriving tomorrow.*

a bat	e bed	i bid	o pot	u cup	th thin
ā cake	ē me	ī bite	ō go	ū rude	ᴛʜ then
ä bar	ə about	ər over	ȯ for	ů put	zh measure

there•a•bouts (ᴛʜer′ə bouts′) near that place, time, or amount: *She lives on Main Street or thereabouts. He went home at five o'clock or thereabouts.* *adv.*

there•af•ter (ᴛʜer′af′tər) after that: *She won a gold medal and thereafter was considered a hero.* *adv.*

there•by (ᴛʜer′ bī′) in that way: *She had a paper route and thereby earned some spending money.* *adv.*

there•fore (ᴛʜer′fôr′) for that reason: *I was sick and therefore stayed home.* *adv.*

there•in (ᴛʜer in′) in that point: *But how to keep it secret? Ah, therein lies the difficulty!* *adv.*

there's (ᴛʜerz) there is or there has: *There's Sam! There's been a fire.*

there•up•on (ᴛʜer′ə pon′) immediately after that: *He waited till she left and thereupon ran to the window to signal his friend.* *adv.*

ther•mal (thər′məl) having to do with heat; using or giving heat: *Steaming water came from an underground thermal spring.* *adj.*

ther•mom•e•ter (thər mom′ə tər) an instrument for measuring temperature. *n.*

Ther•mos (thər′məs) *a trademark for* a special kind of bottle or jug used to keep drinks, soup, etc. hot or cold for several hours. Its sides are made of two layers with a vacuum between them.

This furnace thermostat has a coiled strip made of two metals. These expand and contract at different rates, making the coil move. The tube of mercury resting on it also moves. This breaks or completes the electric circuit which stops or starts the furnace.

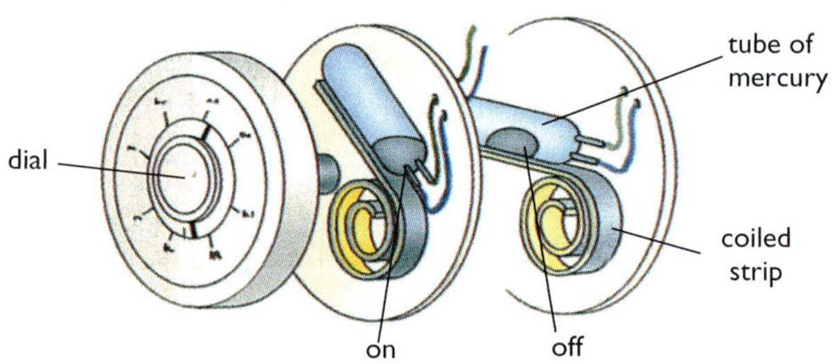

ther•mo•stat (thər′mə stat′) an automatic device for setting and controlling temperature. Furnaces and ovens have thermostats. *n.*

the•sau•rus (thə sôr′əs) a book that lists words together with their synonyms, that is, all the words that have a similar meaning. *n.*

these (ᴛʜēz) the plural of **this:** *These two problems are hard (adj.). These are my books (pron.).* *adj. or pron.*

they'd (ᴛʜād) they had or they would.

they'll (ᴛʜāl) they will.

they're (ᴛʜer) they are.

they've (ᴛʜāv) they have.

thick (thik) **1** filling a lot of space from one surface to the other; not thin: *The castle has thick stone walls.* **Thick-set** is used for people. **2** with many parts or units set close together: *thick hair, a thick forest. The sky was thick with stars.* **3** like glue or syrup; not watery; not flowing easily: *thick gravy.* **4** not clear: *The air was thick with smoke.* **5** stupid. **6** the centre; the place where the danger, activity, etc. is greatest: *in the thick of the blizzard.* 1–5 *adj.*, 6 *n.* **—thick′en,** *v.* **—thick′ly,** *adv.*
thick skin, the ability to take criticism, etc. without being hurt by it. A person with this ability is **thick-skinned.**
through thick and thin, in good times and bad: *A true friend stays loyal through thick and thin.*

thick•ness (thik′nis) **1** the fact of being thick: *The thickness of the walls shuts out all sound.* **2** how thick a thing is: *The thickness of the board is 2 cm.* **3** a layer: *The pad was made up of three thicknesses of cloth.* *n.*

thief (thēf) a person who steals, especially one who steals secretly and, usually, without using force: *A thief stole the little girl's bicycle from the yard.* To **thieve** is to steal in this way. *n., pl.* **thieves.**

thigh (thī) the part of your leg between your hip and your knee. *n.*

thim•ble (thim′bəl) a small, hard cap worn on your finger or thumb to protect it in sewing. *n.*

thin (thin) **1** filling little space from one surface to the other; not thick or fat: *thin paper, a thin person. The ice on the pond is too thin for skating.* **2** made up of parts or units that are few and far apart: *a thin population, thin hair. The actors played to a thin audience.* **3** runny; watery: *This milkshake is too thin.* **4** weak, pale, empty, etc.: *a thin colour, a thin voice. It was a thin excuse that satisfied no one.* **5** make or become thin: *to thin paint.* 1–4 *adj.,* **thin•ner, thin•nest;** 5 *v.,* **thinned, thin•ning.**
into thin air or **out of thin air,** suddenly and unexplainably, as if by magic: *She came out of thin air. It disappeared into thin air.*
thin skin, the quality of being easily hurt by criticism, etc. A person with this quality is **thin-skinned.**

thing (thing) **1** any object or substance; what you can see, hear, touch, taste, or smell: *All the things in the house were new. Put these things away.* **2** whatever is spoken or thought of; any act, fact, situation, event, or idea: *This is an important thing to understand. A strange*

thing happened. **3 things,** *pl.* **a** personal belongings: *I packed my things.* **b** life; conditions; the situation you find yourself in: *How are things?* **4** a person or animal: *I felt sorry for the poor thing.* **5** *Informal.* someone's special interest or activity: *Swimming is her thing.* *n.*
make a thing out of something, pay too much attention to something: *It was just a joke—don't make a thing out of it. He makes a thing out of keeping his desk tidy.*

think (thingk) **1** have as an idea in the mind: *"I'll go," he thought.* **2** use the mind to connect ideas, solve problems, make plans and decisions, and so on: *You must learn to think.* **3** have an opinion about something; believe: *What do you think about that suggestion? They thought it wise to leave early.* *v.,* **thought, think·ing.**
think better of, change your mind about something.
think nothing of, not hesitate to do something: *She thinks nothing of calling people up at five in the morning.*
think over, consider carefully: *Think the whole thing over before you decide.*
think the world of or **think highly of,** respect or like very much.
think through, think about something until you understand it: *If you think it through, the rule makes sense.*
think twice, think about something again and maybe change your mind: *I'd think twice about skating on that pond if I were you.*
think up, plan, invent, or discover by thinking: *We will think up a good excuse.*

third (thərd) **1** next after the 2nd; last in a series of three; 3rd. **2** one of three equal parts: *Dad divided the pizza into thirds.* 1 *adj.,* 1, 2 *n.* **—third′ly,** *adv.*

third class (thərd′ klas′) **1** the lowest acceptable standard or level of quality; the seats, cabins, etc. on a ship or train that are the cheapest. **2** the class of mail that includes advertisements and so on rather than letters or parcels. **3** by this class of mail or in these seats: *to travel third class. Send it third class.* **—third′-class′,** *adj.*

third person (thərd′ pər′sən) **1** in grammar, the category that includes *he, she, it, they,* and all their related forms. *Is* and *are* are the forms of the verb *be* that go with the third person. **2** a way of telling a story that makes it seem as if neither the author nor the listener is part of the action.

third–rate (thərd′ rāt′) *Informal.* rather bad: *a third-rate team.*

thirst (thərst) **1** a desire or need for something to drink: *The traveller in the desert suffered from thirst. She satisfied her thirst at the spring.* **2** a strong desire for anything: *a thirst for adventure.* **3** have a strong desire. 1, 2 *n.,* 3 *v.* **—thirst′y,** *adj.* **—thirst′i·ly,** *adv.*

thir·teen (thərt′tēn′) three more than ten; 13. *n. or adj.* **—thir′teenth′,** *adj. or n.*

thir·ty (thər′tē) three times ten; 30. *n., pl.* **thir·ties;** *adj.* **—thir′ti·eth,** *adj. or n.*

this (ᴛʜis) **This** is used: **1** to point out or draw attention to a particular person or thing. If you are making a contrast between two things, use **this** for the thing closer to you and **that** for the thing farther away: *This is my brother (pron.). Shall we buy this CD or that one (adj.)?* **2** with an adjective or adverb to mean "so": *I didn't think it would be this hard.* 1 *pron. or adj.,* 2 *adv.*

Thistles are often troublesome weeds. The seeds are light and easily blown over a wide area. The plant is difficult to root out — the roots are strong and any pieces left in the ground may produce another plant.

this·tle (this′əl) a wild plant with prickly stems and leaves and showy flowers. The thistle is the national flower of Scotland. *n.*

thith·er (thiᴛʜ′ər)
hither and thither, in all directions. *adv.*

thong (thong) **1** a rubber slip-on sandal. **2** a narrow strip of leather, especially one used as a fastening: *The ancient Greeks laced their sandals on with thongs.* **3** a pair of very skimpy underpants. *n.*

tho·rax (thôr′aks) **1** the second division of an insect's body, between the head and the abdomen. **2** the chest and upper back of a human. *n.*

thorn (thôrn) a sharp-pointed growth on a plant: *Roses have thorns.* *n.* **—thorn′y,** *adj.*
thorn in the flesh or **side,** a troublesome person or thing.

thor·ough (thər′ō) **1** complete: *a thorough soaking.* **2** careful; paying enough attention to all the parts or details: *a thorough search.* *adj.*
—thor′ough·ly, *adv.*

a bat	e bed	i bid	o pot	u cup	th thin
ā cake	ē me	ī bite	ō go	ü rude	ᴛʜ then
ä bar	ə about	ər over	ô for	u̇ put	zh measure

thor·ough·fare (thėr′ə fer′) a main road. *n.*
no thoroughfare, used on signs to show that walking, riding, or driving through is impossible or not allowed.

those (ᴛʜōz) the plural of **that:** *She owns that dog; the boys own those dogs (adj.). These are her books; those are mine (pron.).* *adj. or pron.*

though (ᴛʜō) **1** in spite of the fact that: *We take our medicine, though we do not like it. Though it was pouring, the girls went swimming.* **2** however; nevertheless: *I am sorry for our quarrel; you started it, though.* 1 *conj.,* 2 *adv.*
as though, as if: *You look as though you just woke up.*

thought (thot) **1** what a person thinks; an idea in someone's mind: *Tell me your thoughts.* **2** the act or power of thinking: *After careful thought, he spoke.* **3** care; concern: *Show some thought for others.* **4** the past tense and past participle of **think:** *We thought it would snow yesterday. Have you thought about this?* 1–3 *n.,* 4 *v.*

thought·ful (thot′fəl) **1** deep in thought; thinking: *She was thoughtful for a while and then replied, "No."* **2** showing careful thought: *a thoughtful argument.* **3** showing concern for the needs of others: *a thoughtful gift. It was so thoughtful of you to call.* The opposite of definitions 2 and 3 is **thoughtless.** *adj.*

thou·sand (thou′zənd) ten hundred; 1000. *n. or adj.* —**thou′sandth,** *adj. or n.*

thrash (thrash) **1** beat with a whip, belt, stick, etc. **2** move violently; toss and turn: *The feverish child thrashed around in his bed all night.* *v.*
thrash out, settle by thorough discussion: *Let's stay until we thrash out the problem.*

thread (thred) **1** extremely thin, fine string used to weave cloth or to sew: *cotton thread, nylon thread. A thread is hanging from the hem of your skirt.* **2** put a thread through: *to thread a needle, to thread beads.* **3** anything long and slender like a thread: *The spider hung by a thread.* **4** the line of thought or action that connects the parts of a story or speech: *He lost the thread of their conversation.* **5** wind in and out between things: *A cat threaded its way among the tomato plants.* **6** the ridge that winds in a spiral around a bolt, screw, pipe joint, etc.: *The thread of a nut interlocks with the thread of a bolt.* 1, 3, 4, 6 *n.,* 2, 5 *v.*

thread·bare (thred′ber′) old and worn: *a threadbare coat, a threadbare excuse.* *adj.*

threat (thret) **1** a statement of what will be done to hurt or punish: *They were frightened by the robber's threat to harm them if they shouted.* **2** a sign or cause of something bad that is likely to happen: *Those black clouds are a threat of rain. Pollution is a threat to the environment.* To be or make a threat is to **threaten;** a **threatened species** is a plant or animal that is becoming rare. *n.*

three (thrē) one more than two; 3. *n. or adj.*
the three R's, reading, writing, and arithmetic, thought of as the basics of education.

three–di·men·sion·al (thrē′ di men′shə nəl) **1** having the three dimensions of height, width, and depth: *A cube is a three-dimensional object.* **2** appearing to have depth as well as height and width: *If you look at the picture with these glasses, you get a three-dimensional image.* **Three-D** and **3-D** are short forms. *adj.*
in three-D, with three-dimensional objects or images.

three·score (thrē′skôr′) three times twenty; 60. *adj. or n.*

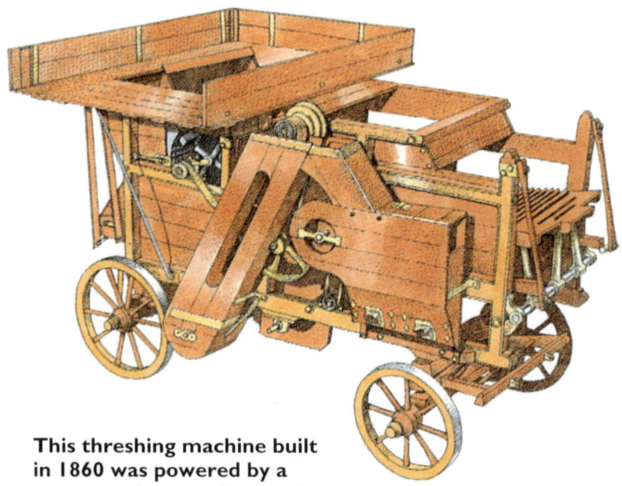

This threshing machine built in 1860 was powered by a steam engine standing at the edge of the field.

thresh (thresh) separate the seeds from wheat or other grain: *Nowadays most farmers use a machine to thresh their wheat.* *v.*

thresh·old (thresh′hōld) **1** a flat piece of wood or stone at the bottom of a door; sill. **2** a doorway or entrance to anything. *n.*

threw (thrü) the past tense of **throw:** *He threw a stone and ran away.* *v.*

CONFUSABLES ……threw

threw means "tossed": *He threw the ball.*

through means "from end to end": *It went through the kitchen window.*

thrice (thrīs) an old word meaning "three times": *He knocked thrice.* *adv.*

thrift (thrift) the habit of saving and being careful to waste nothing: *By thrift she managed to live on her small salary.* At a **thrift shop** you can buy used items very cheaply. *n.* **—thrift′y,** *adj.* **—thrift′i·ly,** *adv.*

thrill (thril) **1** a shiver of fear or excitement: *Thrills went up her spine.* **2** the pleasure of excitement: *I get a thrill from a good horror movie.* **3** give or have a rush of excitement: *Stories of adventure thrilled her. The child thrilled with joy at the sight of the birthday presents.* A very exciting, suspenseful, sometimes frightening book or movie is a **thriller.** 1, 2 *n.,* 3 *v.*

thrive (thrīv) grow strong and healthy; do well: *Most flowers will not thrive without sunshine. Her business is thriving.* *v.,* **throve** or **thrived, thrived** or **thriv·en** (thriv′ən), **thriv·ing.**

throat (thrōt) **1** the passage from your mouth to your stomach or lungs: *A bone stuck in his throat.* **2** the front of your neck: *She wore a scarf at her throat.* *n.*
jump down someone's throat, criticize or scold someone very harshly and suddenly.
lump in your throat, a feeling of being unable to swallow because of strong feelings; a feeling of being about to cry.
ram something down someone's throat, force someone to learn or accept something.

throb (throb) **1** beat fast or hard: *The long climb up the hill made her heart throb. His wounded arm throbbed with pain.* **2** a strong beat: *She felt the throb of the plane's engine.* 1 *v.,* **throbbed, throb·bing;** 2 *n.*

throne (thrōn) **1** the special chair that a king, queen, or other person of high rank sits on during ceremonies. **2** the position or power of a king, queen, etc.: *The prince will inherit the throne.* *n.*

CONFUSABLES ......throne

throne means "royal chair": *The Queen sits on her throne.*
thrown means "hurled": *The ball was thrown at the wall.*

throng (throng) **1** a huge crowd. **2** come together in one place as a huge crowd: *Fans thronged the theatre to see the famous actor. The people thronged to see the Queen.* 1 *n.,* 2 *v.*

throt·tle (throt′əl) **1** a device that controls the flow of fuel or steam to an engine. **2** choke; strangle. 1 *n.,* 2 *v.,* **throt·tled, throt·tling.**

through (thrū) **1** from end to end or out to the other side of something: *to drill holes through a board, to work through the summer* (*prep.*). *She read the book all the way through* (*adv.*). **2** between or among; between the parts of: *to walk through the trees, to slither through the grass.* **3** in many parts of: *We searched through the house.* **4** because of; out of: *The woman refused help through pride.* **5** by: *They became successful mainly through luck.* **6** completely; thoroughly: *I'm wet through.* **7** continuing without stops or dead ends: *a through train from Montréal to Vancouver, a through street.* **8** finished: *We are through school at three o'clock* (*prep.*). *I will soon be through* (*adj.*). 1–5, 8 *prep.,* 1, 6 *adv.,* 7, 8 *adj.*

through·out (thrū out′) in every part: *Canada Day is celebrated throughout Canada* (*prep.*). *The house is well built throughout* (*adv.*). *prep. or adv.*

throve (thrōv) a past tense of **thrive:** *She throve on hard work.* *v.*

throw (thrō) **1** send through the air with force: *The catcher threw the ball. The hose threw water on the flames.* **2** an act of throwing: *That was a good throw.* **3** put, send, or move carelessly or quickly: *She threw some clothes on. He threw a glance at the passing car.* **4** put suddenly into a certain condition: *to throw a person into confusion.* 1, 3, 4 *v.,* **threw, thrown, throw·ing;** 2 *n.*
throw away, a get rid of as garbage. **Throw out** means the same. **b** waste: *to throw away money.*
throw in, add as something extra for free: *They threw in a few games with our new computer system.*
throw off, a get rid of something burdensome. **b** surprise and confuse: *That remark threw me off a bit.* **c** put out of proper balance or rhythm.
throw up, *Informal.* vomit.
throw up your hands, react with helplessness or despair.
throw your voice, make your voice sound as if it is coming from somewhere else.

thrush (thrush) a songbird that usually has a brown back and a spotted breast. The robin, the bluebird, the hermit thrush, and the wood thrush are all common kinds of thrush. *n.*

thrust (thrust) **1** push with force: *He thrust his hands into his pockets. She thrust past me into the room.* **2** a forceful push: *With a quick thrust, she hid the book behind the pillow.* **3** the force that moves an object forward, such as a rocket or airplane. It is created by a powerful stream being forced out the back. This is what makes an inflated toy balloon fly around if you let go without tying it shut. **4** main purpose or direction: *the thrust of an argument.* 1 *v.,* **thrust, thrust·ing;** 2–4 *n.*

a bat	e bed	i bid	o pot	u cup	th thin
ā cake	ē me	ī bite	ō go	ū rude	ᴛʜ then
ä bar	ə about	ər over	ô for	ù put	zh measure

thud (thud) 1 a dull sound caused by a hard hit or a fall: *The book hit the floor with a thud.* 2 hit or move with a thud: *The heavy box fell and thudded on the floor.* 1 *n.,* 2 *v.,* **thud·ded, thud·ding.**

thug (thug) someone who is violent and dangerous, especially a hoodlum or robber: *A bunch of thugs jumped out of an alley and stole the woman's purse.* *n.*

thumb (thum) 1 the short, thick finger of your hand. 2 quickly turn the pages of a book or magazine: *He thumbed through the book and handed it back.* 1 *n.,* 2 *v.*
all thumbs, very clumsy.
thumbs up, a sign of approval. **Thumbs down** is the opposite.
thumb your nose at, show that you have no respect for.
under the thumb of, under the power or influence of: *We cannot let that bully keep us all under his thumb.*

thumb·tack (thum′tak′) a pin with a very broad, flat head, that you can press into a wall, notice board, etc. with your thumb. *n.*

thump (thump) 1 hit hard with something thick and heavy, making a loud, dull sound: *He thumped the table with his fist.* 2 a hard hit like this, or the sound it makes: *She gave me a friendly thump on the back. He fell with a thump.* 3 beat violently or heavily: *My heart thumped as I walked past the grizzly's den.* 1, 3 *v.,* 2 *n.*

thun·der (thun′dər) 1 the loud rumbling or crashing noise that follows a flash of lightning. Lightning heats and expands the air quickly, causing the shock wave we hear as thunder. A crash of thunder is a **thunderclap.** 2 any noise like thunder: *the thunder of the waterfall, a thunder of applause.* 3 give forth thunder or a sound like it: *It thundered, but no rain fell. The cannon thundered. He thundered a reply.* 1, 2 *n.,* 3 *v.*
—thun′der·ous, *adj.*
in thunder, an expression used to make a question stronger: *What in thunder are you doing?*

thun·der·bird (thun′dər bərd′) in the tradition of some First Nations peoples, a spiritual power that causes thunder, lightning, rain, and other natural events. The symbol for it is a huge bird, which is often found in the art of First Nations people. *n.*

thun·der·bolt (thun′dər bōlt′) 1 a flash of lightning and the thunder that follows it. 2 a great shock: *The news came as a thunderbolt.* *n.*

thun·der·cloud (thun′dər kloud′) a dark cloud that brings thunder and lightning. *n.*

thun·der·storm (thun′dər stôrm′) a storm with thunder and lightning. A **thundershower** is shorter and less severe. *n.*

thun·der·struck (thun′dər struk′) astonished; amazed: *We were thunderstruck by his idea.* *adj.*

Thurs·day (thərz′dā′) the day after Wednesday and before Friday. *Abbreviation:* Thurs. *n.*

thus (ᴛʜus) 1 therefore; based on this fact: *Thus it is obvious that they were mistaken.* 2 in this way: *He spoke thus: "Friends, Romans, countrymen."* *adv.*
thus far, so far; up to this or that point.

thwart (thwôrt) 1 defeat; keep from succeeding: *Lack of money thwarted our plans for a trip.* 2 a seat in a rowboat, or a narrow piece of wood fitted across a canoe to give added support to the sides. 1 *v.,* 2 *n.*

thyme (tīm) a small plant with sweet-smelling leaves used for seasoning. *n.*

thy·roid (thī′roid) an important gland in your neck. It produces hormones that help control your rate of growth and help change your food into energy. *n.*

ti·ar·a (tī er′ə *or* tē ȧ′rə) a band of gold, jewels, etc. worn around a woman's head like a small crown. *n.*

tick[1] (tik) 1 a light sound repeated at a regular beat, like the sound made by a clock or watch. 2 make such a sound: *The clock was ticking.* 3 of time, pass steadily: *The minutes ticked away.* 4 a small mark ✓ or / used in checking: *He put a tick beside my name.* 5 mark with a tick; check: *to tick off items on a list.* 1, 4 *n.,* 2, 3, 5 *v.*
what makes someone tick, what makes a person act in certain ways.

tick[2] (tik) 1 a tiny eight-legged animal, related to the spider, that attaches itself to humans and animals and sucks their blood. Some kinds carry serious diseases. 2 a wingless insect that lives as a parasite on animals. *n.*

tick·et (tik′it) 1 a piece of paper that lets you enter a place, take a ride, claim your baggage, win a prize, etc.: *a bus ticket, a theatre ticket, a lottery ticket.* 2 a piece of paper accusing a person of breaking a traffic law: *a ticket for speeding, a parking ticket.* 3 a piece of paper attached to something to show its price, etc. 4 put a ticket on: *All items in the store are ticketed with the price.* 1–3 *n.,* 4 *v.*

tick·le (tik′əl) 1 touch lightly, causing little shivers or wriggles that make the person laugh: *He tickled the baby's feet and she giggled.* 2 a tingling or itching feeling. 3 have a feeling like this: *My nose tickles.* 4 make someone laugh or be happy: *The story tickled him. The child was tickled with his new toys.* **Tickled pink** means "very happy." 1, 3, 4 *v.,* **tick·led, tick·ling;** 2 *n.*

tick·lish (tik′lish) 1 sensitive to tickling: *The bottoms of the feet are ticklish.* 2 requiring very careful handling: *a ticklish situation.* *adj.*

Tides and Tidal Waves

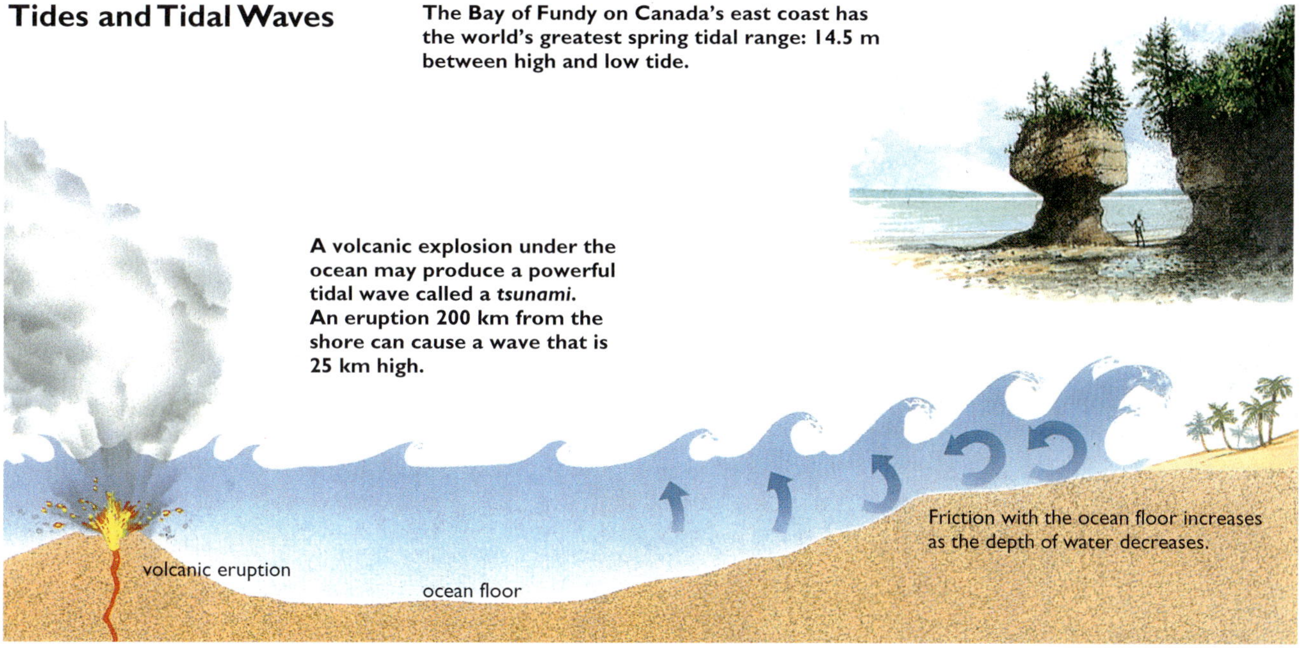

tick–tack–toe or **tic–tac–toe** (tik′tak tō′) a game for two players who take turns marking the squares of a nine-square figure, one making X's and one making O's. Each player tries to be the first to fill three squares in a row. **X's and O's** is the same thing. *n.*

tidal wave (tī′dəl wāv′) a large wave or sudden rise in the water level along a shore, caused by unusually strong winds, very high tides, or an earthquake. It can be very destructive. **Tsunami** is another name for it.

tid•bit (tid′bit′) a very enjoyable bit of food, news, etc. *n.*

tide (tīd) **1** the rise and fall of the ocean, caused by the pull of gravity from the moon and the sun. **High tide** comes about every 12 hours; **low tide** comes halfway between each high tide. **2** anything that rises and falls like the tide: *the tide of public opinion.* *n.* **—tid′al,** *adj.*
tide over, help someone through a time of need: *She said ten dollars would tide her over until payday.*

ti•dings (tī′dingz) an old or poetic word for "news": *The letter brought good tidings.* *pl.n.*

ti•dy (tī′dē) **1** neat and in order: *a tidy room.* **2** make neat; put in order: *She tidied the room.* 1 *adj.,* **ti•di•er, ti•di•est;** 2 *v.,* **ti•died, ti•dy•ing.** **—ti′di•ly,** *adv.* **—ti′di•ness,** *n.*
a tidy sum, quite a lot of money.

tie (tī) **1** fasten by making a knot or bow with string, ribbon, rope, laces, etc.: *to tie up a package, to tie your shoes. The robbers tied him to a chair.* **2** connect or attach in any way, as if by tying: *to tie ideas together. He did not want to be tied to a steady job.* **3** anything that ties or connects: *There are ties on these chair pads to fasten them to the chair. Family ties have kept him at home.* **4** a strip of cloth worn around the neck and knotted in front: *He always wears a tie to work.* **5** an equal number of points or votes for each side: *The game ended in a tie, 3 to 3.* **6** be equal in points or votes: *The two teams tied.* **7** a heavy piece of wood or iron placed crosswise under the rails of a train track to form a foundation or support. Ties are laid about 30 cm apart. **8** in music, a curved line joining two notes of the same pitch, to show that they are to be held for the total number of beats without a break. 1, 2, 6 *v.,* **tied, ty•ing;** 3–5, 7, 8 *n.*
tie up, a tie firmly or tightly into a bundle. **b** keep from getting away by tying: *Tie up your dog.* **c** delay: *The stalled truck tied up traffic for half an hour.* **d** make a person or thing unavailable by committing to some other use or activity: *His money is tied up in the business he has started. Don't tie up the phone all night! I can't go today; I'm tied up.* **e** complete: *That ties up tonight's news report.*

tier (tēr) one of a number of rows arranged one above another: *tiers of seats in a hockey arena.* *n.*

tiff (tif) a little quarrel. *n.*

ti•ger (tī′gər) a large, fierce, wild cat of Asia that has fur striped with black. The female is sometimes called a **tigress** (tī′gris). *n.*

a bat	e bed	i bid	o pot	u cup	th thin
ā cake	ē me	ī bite	ō go	ū rude	ᴛʜ then
ä bar	ə about	ər over	ô for	ů put	zh measure

tight (tīt) **1** fitting closely: *Since she gained weight, her skirt is a bit tight.* **2** firm; holding firmly: *a tight knot, a tight grip.* **3** fully stretched; tense: *Pull the rope so it is tight.* **4** not letting water, air, or gas in or out. This sense is usually in compounds: *The boat is watertight.* **5** hard to get; scarce: *Money is tight just now.* **6** *Informal.* stingy: *A miser is tight with money.* **Tight-fisted** means the same. A **tightwad** is a stingy person. *adj.* —**tight′ly,** *adv.* —**tight′en,** *v.*
sit tight, *Informal.* wait without doing anything.
sleep tight, sleep soundly.

tight·rope (tīt′rōp′) a rope stretched tight high above the ground for acrobats to perform on. *n.*

tights (tīts) a close-fitting garment for the legs and going up to the waist, worn by gymnasts and dancers. Women and girls also wear them in cold weather. *pl.n.*

tile (tīl) **1** a thin, decorative piece of baked clay, vinyl, wood, cork, etc., used for covering walls, ceilings, and floors by placing a lot of them close together. They are usually square or rectangular; tiny clay ones are used to create mosaics. **2** such squares considered together: *We have tile on the ceiling of our classroom.* **3** put tiles on or in; cover with tile: *to tile a bathroom floor.* 1, 2 *n.,* 3 *v.,* **tiled, til·ing.**

till[1] (til) **1** up to the time or place mentioned: *We played till supper (prep.). Walk till you come to a white house (conj.).* **2** before: *He didn't arrive till midnight (prep.). Don't eat till everyone's here (conj.).* **3** so long, so far, so hard, etc. that a certain result happens: *I laughed till the tears ran down my cheeks.* 1, 2 *prep.,* 1–3 *conj.*

till[2] (til) dig and plough the soil and prepare it for planting: *Farmers till the land.* *v.*

till[3] (til) a cash register or a small money box. *n.*

till·er (til′ər) a bar or handle used to turn the rudder in steering a boat. *n.*

tilt (tilt) tip; slope or slant: *Tilt your head forward. This floor tilts (v.). This table is on a tilt (n.).* *v. or n.*
full tilt, at full speed; with full force: *His car ran full tilt against the tree, but no one was hurt.*

tim·ber (tim′bər) **1** trees that have been cut down and are ready to be made into wood for building things. **2** a large piece of wood used in building; a beam or rafter. **3** trees that are growing and suitable for cutting: *Half of their land is covered with timber.* The **timber line** marks the end of the area where it is warm enough for trees to grow. **4** a word shouted when a tree that has been cut is about to fall. 1–3 *n.,* 4 *interj.*

A sundial uses shadow to record the time of day, but will not work if the sun isn't shining.

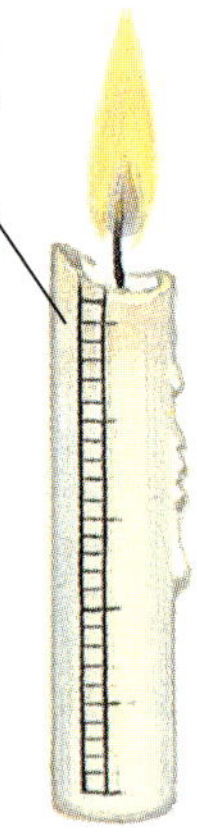

A candle burning steadily was used as a clock in medieval times, by rich people. The hours were marked on the side.

time (tīm) **1** all the seconds, hours, days, and so on that have been or ever will be; the past, present, and future. **2** a stretch of time: *A minute is a short time. He left a long time ago.* **3** a point in time: *Your arrival time is 2:45 p.m., May 8. What time is it now?* **4** the proper moment for a certain activity: *snack time.* **5** a single case of something happening or being done: *The first time I went skating, I fell five times.* **6** a way of counting time: *standard time, daylight-saving time.* **7** **times,** *pl.* conditions of life: *War brings hard times.* **8** the way someone experiences a certain event or period: *We had a good time.* **9** speed or rhythm: *march time, waltz time.* **10** measure the time of: *I timed the race with a stopwatch.* An instrument for timing things is a **timer.** **11** choose the moment for: *We timed the party to coincide with our cousins' visit.* **12** **times,** multiplied by: *Four times three is twelve. Symbol:* × The **times table** is the multiplication table. 1–9 *n.,* 10, 11 *v.,* **timed, tim·ing;** 12 *prep.*
about time, a around the right time: *It's about time to go.* **b** almost too late; already past the best time: *You're finally ready? It's about time!*
ahead of time, early.
at a time, together: *to run up the stairs two at a time.*
at times, sometimes.
behind the times, old-fashioned; out of date.
for the time being, for now.
from time to time, now and then; once in a while: *We visited her from time to time.*
in good time, not late or at the last minute.
in no time, very soon; very quickly: *We hurried and reached our companions in no time.*
in time, a after a while: *In time you will forget all this.* **b** early enough: *Will you be home in time for supper?* **c** in the right rhythm: *to march in time.*
make good time, go fairly fast.
on time, at the right time; not late.
on your own time, not during school or working hours.
pass (the) **time,** keep yourself busy; fill empty time.
time after time or **time and again,** again and again.

Word Family..........time

time-consuming: taking a lot of time
time exposure: a photo taken slowly over time
time frame: the schedule for a project
timeless: never going out of style
timely: coming at a very appropriate time
time-out: a break; a chance to rest or think
timepiece: a watch or clock
timetable: a schedule, especially for regular things like trains, buses, or classes at school

time•line (tīm′ līn′) 1 a long line meant to stand for a period of time, with the names and dates of important events marked on it in order: *The teacher drew a timeline on the board showing what went on in Canada from 1867 to the present.* 2 a schedule for completing the different parts of a project. *n.*

time zone (tīm′ zōn′) a region running from the North Pole to the South Pole with one standard of time throughout. The world is divided into 24 time zones, beginning and ending at the International Date Line.

tim•id (tim′id) easily frightened; shy: *The timid child was afraid to try anything.* *adj.* **—ti•mid′i•ty,** *n.*

tim•pa•ni (tim′pə nē′) a set of large drums played by one person in an orchestra or band. *n.*

tin (tin) 1 a soft, silver-white metal that is a chemical element. It is rustproof. **Tin foil** is a very thin sheet of tin or aluminum used for wrapping food. 2 thin sheets of other metal coated with tin. 3 any can, box, pan, etc. made of or lined with tin: *a cookie tin, a tin of soup.* *n.*
have a tin ear, have no musical ability.

tin•der (tin′dər) anything that catches fire easily, used to get a fire going. *n.*

tine (tīn) one of the sharp prongs of a fork. *n.*

tinge (tinj) 1 give a trace of some colour or quality to: *A drop of ink will tinge a cup of water. Her words were tinged with envy.* 2 a trace of some colour or quality: *There is a tinge of red in her cheeks. I like a tinge of lemon in my tea.* 1 *v.,* **tinged, tinge•ing** or **ting•ing;** 2 *n.*

tin•gle (ting′gəl) 1 have a pricking or stinging feeling, sometimes from excitement: *He tingled with delight on his first airplane trip.* 2 a pricking, stinging feeling: *The cold caused a tingle in my fingers.* 1 *v.,* **tin•gled, tin•gling;** 2 *n.* **—tin′gly,** *adj.*

tink•er (ting′kər) 1 work at casually or fool around with: *to tinker with a radio, to tinker with a new idea.* 2 long ago, a person who fixed pots and pans. 1 *v.,* 2 *n.*

tin•kle (ting′kəl) 1 make or cause to make light, ringing sounds: *The sleigh bells tinkled. The baby tinkled the little bell.* 2 light, ringing sounds: *the tinkle of sleigh bells.* 1 *v.,* **tin•kled, tin•kling;** 2 *n.*

tin•ny (tin′ē) sounding flat and dull instead of rich, bright, and clear; clinking instead of ringing. *adj.*

tin•sel (tin′səl) 1 glittering strips or threads of aluminum used as a decoration. 2 something showy but not worth much. *n.*

tin•smith (tin′smith′) a person who makes things out of tin or other light metal. *n.*

tint (tint) 1 a pale colour or slight amount of colour: *The ceiling is white with a tint of blue.* 2 colour slightly: *tinted glass.* 1 *n.,* 2 *v.*

ti•ny (tī′nē) very small; wee: *a tiny chick.* *adj.,* **ti•ni•er, ti•ni•est.**

–tion *a suffix meaning:* 1 the act or process of. *Addition* is the act or process of *adding.* 2 the condition of being. *Exhaustion* is the condition of being *exhausted.* 3 the result of. A *reflection* is the result of *reflecting.*

tip¹ (tip) 1 the end of something long or pointed: *the tips of your fingers.* 2 a small piece on the end of something: *a felt tip on a marker.* 3 put a tip on or cover at the tip: *spears tipped with steel, mountains tipped with snow.* 1, 2 *n.,* 3 *v.,* **tipped, tip•ping.**

tip² (tip) 1 slope; slant; tilt: *She tipped the table toward her.* 2 upset; overturn: *to tip a canoe.* Something that tips easily is **tippy.** *v.,* **tipped, tip•ping.**
tip your hat, raise your hat in greeting or salute.

tip³ (tip) 1 a small present of money in return for service: *He gave the taxi driver a tip.* 2 give a small present of money to: *Did you tip the waiter?* 3 a piece of secret information: *The police received a tip that led them to the criminal.* 4 a useful hint or suggestion: *tips for travellers.* 1, 3, 4 *n.,* 2 *v.,* **tipped, tip•ping.**
tip off, *Informal.* give a secret hint or warning to: *Someone tipped off the criminal and he escaped before the police arrived.* The warning is called a **tip-off.**

tip•toe (tip′tō′) 1 walk on your toes: *She tiptoed quietly up stairs.* 2 the tips of your toes: *I had to stand on tiptoe to reach it.* 1 *v.,* **tip•toed, tip•toe•ing;** 2 *n.*

ti•rade (tī′rād) a long, angry speech or piece of writing: *The teacher launched into a tirade about running in the halls.* *n.*

a bat	e bed	i bid	o pot	u cup	th thin
ā cake	ē me	ī bite	ō go	ū rude	ᴛʜ then
ä bar	ə about	ər over	ô for	ů put	zh measure

tire[1] (tīr) 1 use up someone's strength or energy: *The long walk tired her. He tires easily and often stops to rest.* A person who never seems to get tired is **tireless.** 2 make or become bored or annoyed: *She soon tired of the silly game.* Something boring or annoying is **tiresome.** *v.,* **tired, tir·ing.** —**tired,** *adj.*
tired of, bored or annoyed by.

tire[2] (tīr) 1 an air-filled rubber cover fitted around the rim of a wheel, as on a car or bicycle, to give a smooth ride. 2 a thick, solid rubber strip around a wheel. *n.*

tis·sue (tish′ū) 1 thin, soft paper that absorbs moisture easily: *toilet tissue, facial tissue.* 2 a piece or sheet of this: *There are 450 tissues in each box.* 3 a mass of similar cells forming a certain part of an animal or plant: *muscle tissue, brain tissue.* 4 Usually, **tissue paper,** very thin, crinkly wrapping paper. *n.*

tithe (tīᴛʜ) a tenth of a person's income, usually given to the church. *n.*

ti·tle (tī′təl) 1 the name of a book, poem, picture, song, etc. The title of a report or book appears on a **title page** at the front. 2 a name showing a person's rank, occupation, or condition in life. *King, Captain, Doctor, Professor, Mr.,* and *Ms.* are titles. 3 a legal right to a piece of property; ownership: *When a house is sold, the seller gives title to the buyer.* 4 the first-place position; a championship: *She won the tennis title at school.* *n.*

tit·ter (tit′ər) 1 a small nervous or embarrassed laugh: *A titter ran through the classroom.* 2 laugh in this way. 1 *n.,* 2 *v.*

Tlin·git (tling′git) 1 a First Nations people living in northwestern British Columbia. 2 their language. 3 having to do with these people or their language. 1, 2 *n.,* 3 *adj.*

A toad darts out its long, sticky tongue to capture a meal. Most toads eat insects and other small creatures.

toad (tōd) a small animal that looks like a frog, but lives mostly on land. It has rough, dry skin. *n.*

toad·stool (tōd′stūl′) an umbrella-shaped mushroom, especially a poisonous one. *n.*

toast[1] (tōst) 1 sliced bread made brown and crisp by heat. 2 heat till brown and crisp: *We toasted the hot dog buns.* A **toaster** is a machine for toasting bread. 3 heat thoroughly: *He toasted his feet in front of the fire.* 1 *n.,* 2, 3 *v.*

toast[2] (tōst) 1 take a drink and wish good fortune to someone: *We all toasted the bride and groom.* 2 the act of drinking and wishing in this way, or the words used. 3 a person with many admirers: *She used to be the toast of the town.* 1 *v.,* 2, 3 *n.*

to·bac·co (tə bak′ō) a plant whose dried leaves are smoked or chewed by some people for their stimulating effect. Tobacco is very harmful to your health and causes an extremely powerful addiction. *n.*

🍁 **to·bog·gan** (tə bog′ən) 1 a long, narrow, flat sled with its front end curved upward and no runners. It was originally used by First Nations people to haul belongings. 2 slide downhill on one of these: *We all went tobogganing in the snow on New Year's Day.* 1 *n.,* 2 *v.*

WORD HISTORY.....toboggan

Toboggan comes from the Algonquian word *tobagun*, meaning "handsled." The aboriginal peoples of North America introduced the toboggan to French settlers.

to·day (tə dā′) 1 this day: *Today is Friday (n.). How are you today (adv.)?* 2 in these times; nowadays: *Many people in the world today are starving.* 1 *n.,* 1, 2 *adv.*

tod·dle (tod′əl) walk with short, unsteady steps, as a baby does. A **toddler** is a child who has recently learned to walk. *v.,* **tod·dled, tod·dling.**

to–do (tə dū′) *Informal.* fuss: *There was a great to-do when the new puppy arrived.* *n., pl.* **to-dos.**

toe (tō) 1 one of the five end parts of your foot. The nail growing on a toe is a **toenail.** 2 touch or reach with your toes: *Toe this line.* 1 *n.,* 2 *v.,* **toed, toe·ing.**
on your toes, alert; paying attention and ready to act.
step on someone's toes, upset someone by accident.

tof·fee (tof′ē) a chewy candy made with sugar or molasses boiled down with butter, often with other flavouring added. **Taffy** is another word for it. *n.*

to·fu (tō′fū) a food very high in protein, made of ground soybeans cooked in water and then pressed into cakes. **Bean curd** is another name for it. *n.*

to·ga (tō′gə) the loose, flowing outer garment worn by citizens of ancient Rome. A toga was made of a single piece of cloth with no sleeves or armholes, covering the whole body except for the right arm. *n.*

to·geth·er (tə geᴛʜ′ər) **1** with each other: *The girls were walking together.* **2** in or into one group, mass, or unit: *The coach called the players together. I will sew these pieces together and make a dress.* **3** at the same time: *You cannot have day and night together.* **4** without a break: *He reads for hours together.* *adv.* **—to·geth′er·ness,** *n.*

tog·gle (tog′əl) **1** a switch or option that has only two settings, on and off. The "Caps Lock" function on a computer keyboard is a toggle. **2** go back and forth between two settings or positions: *The "Full Screen" option toggles on and off.* 1 *n.,* 2 *v.,* **tog·gled, tog·gling.**

toil (toil) **1** hard work; labour: *to succeed finally after years of toil.* **2** work hard: *to toil for a living.* **3** move with great effort: *Carrying heavy loads, they toiled up the mountain.* 1 *n.,* 2, 3 *v.*

toi·let (toi′lit) **1** a piece of bathroom equipment that has a bowl of water with a seat attached and a drain at the bottom to flush the bowl clean. A toilet is used to get rid of waste from the body. **2** an old word for the process of washing, dressing, combing your hair, and so on. **Toiletries** are the supplies you use for this. *n.*

to·ken (tō′kən) **1** a sign of something: *Black can be a token of mourning.* **2** something given as a keepsake: *This picture is a token of our wonderful canoe trip together.* **3** a piece of metal, plastic, etc. resembling a coin, giving a person the right to ride a bus or subway, play a video game, etc. **4** serving only as a symbol; not enough to really matter: *a token payment, a token protest.* 1–3 *n.,* 4 *adj.*

told (tōld) the past tense and past participle of **tell:** *You told me that last week. We were told to wait.* *v.*

tol·er·a·ble (tol′ə rə bəl) **1** that can be endured: *The pain has become tolerable.* **2** fairly good: *She is in tolerable health.* *adj.*

tol·er·ance (tol′ə rəns) **1** an attitude of respect and understanding toward people whose opinions or ways differ from yours. **2** willingness to put up with a lot. **3** the ability to endure something without serious effects: *a high tolerance for pain. Many birds have a low tolerance for insecticides.* *n.* **—tol′er·ant,** *adj.*

tol·er·ate (tol′ə rāt′) **1** allow; permit: *The teacher won't tolerate any disorder.* **2** bear; endure: *This plant cannot tolerate the cold.* *v.,* **tol·er·at·ed, tol·er·at·ing.**

toll[1] (tōl) **1** ring slowly with single strokes: *Bells tolled all over the country at the king's death.* **2** the sound of this. 1 *v.,* 2 *n.*

toll[2] (tōl) **1** a tax or fee paid for some right or privilege, such as using a highway or bridge or phoning long distance. **2** something paid, lost, suffered, etc.: *Car accidents take a heavy toll of human lives.* *n.*

tom·a·hawk (tom′ə hok′) a light axe used in earlier times by some First Nations people. *n.*

to·ma·to (tə mā′tō) a juicy, pulpy, usually red fruit eaten raw or cooked as a vegetable. *n., pl.* **to·ma·toes.**

tomb (tūm) a place for a dead body, often above ground. It is usually marked with a **tombstone** that has the person's name, etc. carved on it. *n.*

tom·cat (tom′kat′) a male cat. *n.*

to·mor·row (tə mȯr′ō) the day after today: *Tomorrow never comes (n.). I'm leaving tomorrow (adv.).* *n. or adv.*

tom–tom (tom′tom′) a drum, often long and narrow, usually beaten with the hands. *n.*

ton (tun) a nonmetric measure of mass equal to 2000 pounds (about 907 kg). Sometimes the expression **metric ton** is used for a **tonne** (1000 kg). *n.*

USING WORDS .... ton

When you are measuring the mass of something, it is important to use the correct unit name, **tonne**: *a tonne of wheat.*
But in expressions where the exact amount doesn't matter, use **ton**: *tons of fun.*

tone (tōn) **1** a musical sound or the sound of a voice; a sound that has pitch. **2** a certain quality of sound in a voice or instrument: *Her voice had a silvery tone. The oboe has a mellow tone.* **3** spirit; character; style: *a tone of quiet elegance. We disliked the nasty tone of her letter.* Something without spirit or character is **toneless.** **4** a shade of colour: *The room is furnished in tones of brown.* **5** **tone down,** make quieter, calmer, or less harsh. **6** a normal, healthy, firm condition: *Without exercise, muscles lose their tone.* 1–4, 6 *n.,* 5 *v.,* **toned, ton·ing.**

a bat	e bed	i bid	o pot	u cup	th thin
ā cake	ē me	ī bite	ō go	ū rude	ᴛʜ then
ä bar	ə about	ər over	ȯ for	ů put	zh measure

tongs (tongz) a tool for grabbing, holding, or lifting, made up of two long arms joined like a pair of scissors: *He picked up the hot sausage with the tongs.* *pl.n.*

tongue (tung) **1** the movable muscular organ inside your mouth. The human tongue is used for tasting and licking, etc., and for talking. **2** a language: *the English tongue.* **3** a way of speaking: *a sharp tongue, a flattering tongue.* A **tongue-lashing** is a scolding. **4** something shaped or used like a tongue: *tongues of flame.* The strip under the laces of a shoe is called a tongue. *n.*
hold your tongue, keep silent: *Please hold your tongue while I'm speaking!*
on the tip of your tongue, about to be remembered or spoken: *The name of that song is on the tip of my tongue.*

tongue twister (tung′ twis′tər) a word or phrase that is hard to say quickly. *Example: She sells seashells by the seashore.*

ton·ic (ton′ik) **1** anything that revives or gives strength, like a medicine: *The mountain air is a tonic.* **2** giving strength; bracing: *Her daily 6 a.m. run had a tonic effect.* **Tonic water** is a kind of fizzy water. 1 *n.,* 2 *adj.*

to·night (tə nīt′) the night at the end of this day; this night or evening: *I wish tonight would come* (*n.*). *Do you think it will snow tonight* (*adv.*)? *n. or adv.*

ton·nage (tun′ij) total mass of goods shipped or produced, measured in tons. A ship's tonnage is its maximum load. *n.*

tonne (tun) an SI unit for measuring mass, equal to one thousand kilograms. *Symbol:* t *n.*

ton·sils (ton′səlz) two small, oval masses of tissue on the sides of your throat, close to the root of your tongue. **Tonsillitis** (ton′sə lī′təs) is an infection that makes them red, swollen, and sore. *pl.n.*

too (tū) **1** also; besides: *The dog is hungry, and thirsty too.* **2** more than what is proper or enough: *That dress is too long. I ate too much.* **3** very: *You are too kind. I don't feel too well.* **4** indeed; most definitely, even though someone denies it: *I didn't take it. You did too!* *adv.*

CONFUSABLES ....too

too means "too much," or "also": *These problems are too hard. He stayed too.*

to means "toward": *Go to school.*

two means "one more than one": *I have two ears.*

took (tu̇k) the past tense of **take:** *She took the car an hour ago.* *v.*

tool (tūl) **1** a wrench, hammer, saw, shovel, or any other thing used with your hands to do work. This word is found in many compounds like **toolbox, toolroom,** and **toolshed.** **2** anything used to achieve some purpose: *Knowledge is a great tool.* **3** shape or engrave by hand with a tool: *tooled leather.* 1, 2 *n.,* 3 *v.*

toon·ie (tū′nē) the Canadian two-dollar coin. **Twonie** is another spelling. *n.*

toot (tūt) **1** the short, high sound of a horn, whistle, etc. **2** make or cause to make this sound: *to toot a car horn.* 1 *n.,* 2 *v.*

A child grows 20 milk (or first) teeth.
An adult human grows 32 teeth.

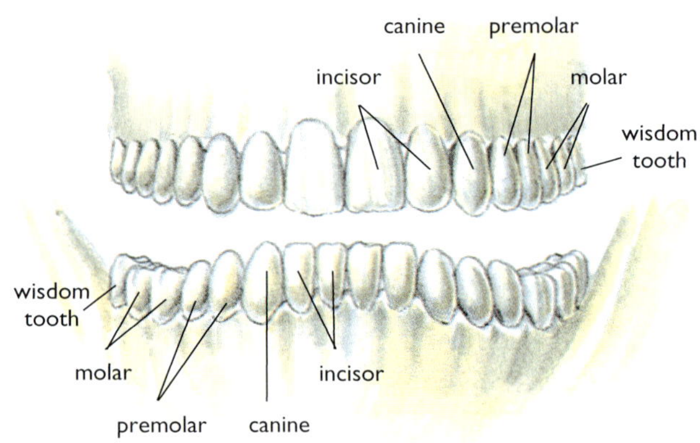

tooth (tūth) **1** one of the hard, bonelike parts in the mouth, used for biting and chewing. **2** something like a tooth. Combs, rakes, and saws have teeth. *n., pl.* **teeth.** —**toothed,** *adj.* —**tooth′less,** *adj.*
fight tooth and nail, fight fiercely.

tooth·ache (tūth′āk′) a pain in a tooth. *n.*

tooth·brush (tūth′brush′) a small, long-handled brush for cleaning your teeth. *n.*

tooth·paste (tūth′pāst′) a paste or gel for cleaning your teeth. *n.*

tooth·pick (tūth′pik′) a small, pointed stick of wood, plastic, etc. for removing bits of food from between your teeth. *n.*

top[1] (top) **1** the highest point or part: *the top of a mountain.* **2** the end or surface that faces up: *the top of the table.* **3** a piece of clothing for the upper part of your body. **4** highest, best, or greatest: *the top shelf, top marks in school, driving at top speed.* **Topmost** also has this meaning. **5** be or put something on top of: *A lone tree tops the hill. The cake was topped with fruit.*

6 reach the top of: *A grey car was just topping the hill.* **7** do higher, greater, or better than; outdo: *His story topped all the rest.* 1–3 *n.,* 4 *adj.,* 5–7 *v.,* **topped, top·ping.** —**top′less,** *adj.*

be tops, be the best.

blow your top, *Slang.* lose your temper.

off the top of your head, without preparation or careful thought.

on top of, a on. **b** in addition to: *On top of all that homework I have piano to practise.* **c** right after: *The thaw came right on top of the blizzard.* **d** in control of: *She's on top of the situation.*

top off, put a nice ending or finish to: *We topped off our meal with pie and ice cream.*

top up, fill up again: *Can I top up your water glass?*

Word Family.......... top

top-heavy: poorly balanced, with too much at the top
top-notch: of the very best quality; first-rate
topple: 1 knock down **2** fall down
top-secret: very secret
topsoil: dark surface soil suitable for growing plants in
topsy-turvy: upside down or in confusion

top² (top) a toy that spins on a point. *n.*

to·paz (tō′paz) a very hard, nearly clear mineral found in crystals of various forms and colours. Yellow topaz is used as a gem. *n.*

top·ic (top′ik) a subject that people think, write, or talk about: *The topic for your speech must be chosen by tomorrow.* *n.*

top·o·graph·ic (top′ə graf′ik) showing the surface features of an area, such as the roads, forests, railway tracks, mountains, rivers, etc. The surface features of an area are its **topography** (tə pog′rə fē). *adj.*

top·ping (top′ing) sauce or pieces of food sprinkled on top of other food to make it more interesting: *He likes nuts as a topping for ice cream. My favourite pizza topping is pepperoni.* *n.*

To·rah (tôr′ə) in the Jewish religion, the first five books of the Bible, containing the very beginning of Jewish history and the laws given to Moses by God. *n.*

torch (tôrch) **1** a flaming piece of wood used as a light to be carried around or stuck in a holder on a wall. **2** a device for producing a very hot flame, used especially to cut and weld metal by melting. *n.*

tore (tôr) the past tense of **tear²:** *She tore her dress on a nail.* The past participle is **torn:** *I've torn up the letter.* *v.*

to·ri·i (tôr′ē ē) the gate to a Shinto shrine. It is made up of two posts with a crosspiece on top that curves upward. *n.*

tor·ment (tôr ment′ *for 1 and 2,* tôr′ment *for 3*) **1** keep on causing great suffering: *Headaches tormented him.* **2** keep teasing or bullying: *Stop tormenting your brother.* **3** great suffering, or a cause of this: *That dog's endless barking is such a torment.* 1, 2 *v.,* 3 *n.* —**tor·men′tor** or **tor·ment′er,** *n.*

tor·na·do (tôr nā′dō) a violent, whirling funnel of wind extending down from dark clouds. It moves across the land, causing great damage and harm. *n., pl.* **tor·na·does** or **tor·na·dos.**

tor·pe·do (tôr pē′dō) **1** a large, cigar-shaped metal tube full of explosives. It moves through water by its own power. **2** attack or destroy a ship or submarine with torpedoes. 1 *n., pl.* **tor·pe·does;** 2 *v.,* **tor·pe·doed, tor·pe·do·ing.**

tor·rent (tôr′ənt) a violent, rushing stream: *torrents of rain, a torrent of words. The mountain torrent dashed over the rocks.* *n.* —**tor·ren′tial** (tə ren′shəl), *adj.*

tor·so (tôr′sō) the human body except for the head, legs, and arms. *n., pl.* **tor·sos.**

tor·til·la (tôr tē′yə) a thin, round, flat kind of bread, made from cornmeal or flour and fried. *n.*

tor·toise (tôr′təs) a turtle, especially a land turtle. *n., pl.* **tor·tois·es** or **tor·toise.**

tor·ture (tôr′chər) **1** the act of giving someone extreme pain. Torture used to be widely used to punish people or to force them to give information. **2** cause extreme pain or suffering: *The cat tortured the mouse.* **3** extreme pain or suffering: *She suffered torture from a toothache.* 1, 3 *n.,* 2 *v.,* **tor·tured, tor·tur·ing.**

To·ry (tôr′ē) **1** a member of a Conservative Party. **2** having to do with such a party. 1 *n., pl.* **To·ries;** 2 *adj.*

toss (tos) **1** throw lightly: *She tossed the ball to the baby.* **2** roll or bounce around: *The ship is tossed by the waves. He tossed on his bed all night.* **3** lift and turn quickly: *She tossed her head.* **4** mix lightly: *to toss a salad.* **5** throw a coin up in the air to decide something by seeing which side faces up when it lands: *to toss for first choice.* **6** an act of tossing: *A toss of a coin decided who should play first.* A **toss-up** is something that has an equal chance of turning out either way. 1–5 *v.,* 6 *n.*

a bat	e bed	i bid	o pot	u cup	th thin
ā cake	ē me	ī bite	ō go	ū rude	ᴛʜ then
ä bar	ə about	ər over	ô for	ů put	zh measure

tot (tot) a little child. *n.*

to·tal (tō′təl) **1** whole; entire: *The total cost of the house and land will be $195 000.* **2** the whole amount: *Add the different numbers to get the total.* **3** add up; add up to: *Total these figures for me. The time spent on the project totalled about eight hours.* **4** complete; absolute: *total darkness.* 1, 4 *adj.,* 2 *n.,* 3 *v.,* **to·talled** or **to·taled, to·tal·ling** or **to·tal·ing.** —**to′tal·ly,** *adv.*

tote (tōt) *Informal.* **1** carry: *I had to tote all the stuff home by myself.* **2** Usually, **tote bag,** a bag to carry personal items in. 1 *v.,* **tot·ed, tot·ing;** 2 *n.*

to·tem (tō′təm) **1** in many cultures, an animal or other natural object taken as the emblem of a clan, or group of related families. Among some First Nations peoples, the totem was thought of as the clan's ancestor. **2** an image of this animal or object, carved, painted, woven into cloth, etc. *n.*

Totem poles were a way of recording a clan's history or ancestors and could be read upward or downward. They could also be used to mark graves or land boundaries.

totem pole (tō′təm pōl′) a large upright log carved and painted with totems, traditionally erected by many of the First Nations of the northern Pacific coast.

tot·ter (tot′ər) **1** walk with shaky, unsteady steps: *The baby tottered over to the bed.* **2** wobble; shake as if about to fall: *The bowling pin tottered and fell.* *v.*

tou·can (tū′kan) a brightly coloured, fruit-eating bird with a huge beak. It is found in hot countries. *n.*

touch (tuch) **1** put the hand or some other part of your body on something: *Touch the pan to see if it's still hot.* **2** put one thing against another; be or come against: *He touched me with the ball. Your sleeve is touching the butter.* **3** the act or way of touching: *A bubble bursts at a touch. The doctor had a very gentle touch.* **4** the sense that lets a person notice things by feeling or handling them. **5** a slight amount; a little bit: *We had a touch of frost.* **6** strongly affect a person's softer feelings: *The woman's sad story touched us deeply.* Something that does this is **touching.** **7** have to do with; concern: *This matter touches your future.* **8** a special manner or quality: *The work showed an expert's touch.* 1–3, 6, 7 *v.,* 4, 5, 8 *n.*
in touch, **a** in contact or communication: *We kept in touch with her after she moved.* **b** aware of and able to respond to: *in touch with your feelings.*
touch down, land: *The plane touched down at Gander.*
touch on, mention briefly: *Our conversation touched on many subjects.*
touch up, improve by slight changes: *to touch up a photo.*

touch·down (tuch′doun′) **1** in football, the fact of holding the ball while you are on or behind the opponents' goal line. **2** the score made in this way, worth six points. **3** the landing of an aircraft or spacecraft: *From liftoff to touchdown the space flight went perfectly.* *n.*

touch football (tuch′ fůt′bol′) a game similar to football except that the person carrying the ball is touched rather than tackled.

touch–tone (tuch′ tōn′) having to do with a telephone worked by pressing buttons rather than turning a dial. Each button makes a different tone. *adj.*

touch·y (tuch′ē) very easily angered: *He is tired and very touchy this afternoon.* *adj.,* **touch·i·er, touch·i·est.** —**touch′i·ness,** *n.*

tough (tuf) **1** able to take a lot of strain or hardship; strong: *tough plastic. The pioneers were tough people.* **2** hard to cut or chew: *a tough steak.* **3** hard; difficult: *a tough assignment.* **4** with high standards; demanding a lot: *a tough teacher, tough love.* **5** rough; disorderly: *a tough neighbourhood.* **6** a rough person: *A gang of toughs attacked the officer.* 1–5 *adj.,* 6 *n.* —**tough′en,** *v.*

tou·pee (tū pā′) a wig or patch of false hair used by men to cover baldness. *n.*

tour (tūr) **1** a walk or trip through a place to see its interesting sights, often with a guide: *The children took a tour of the ship.* **2** go on such a walk or trip through a place: *to tour P.E.I. The class toured the museum.* **3** travel in order to do shows: *The band is touring with k.d. lang.* Performers who are touring are **on tour.** 1 *n.,* 2, 3 *v.*

tour·ism (tū′riz əm) **1** travelling for pleasure. People who do this are **tourists.** **2** the business of providing services for tourists. *n.*

tour·na·ment (tər′nə mənt *or* tūr′nə mənt) a set of games involving several teams or individuals: *a basketball tournament, a chess tournament.* *n.*

tour·ni·quet (tər′nə kit *or* tūr′nə kā′) a bandage tied very tightly to stop severe bleeding. *n.*

tou·sle (tou′zəl) mess up someone's hair: *She tousled his hair just to tease him.* *v.,* **tou·sled, tou·sling.**

tow (tō) 1 pull by a rope, chain, etc.: *The motorboat was towing the water skier.* A **tow truck** tows cars that can't be driven. 2 the act of towing: *Can you give me a tow? My car won't start.* 1 *v.,* 2 *n.*
in tow, a being towed: *The sailboat had a canoe in tow.* **b** following closely behind: *a man with three kids in tow.*

to·ward (tə wȯrd′) 1 in the direction of: *He walked toward the north.* 2 with respect to; about: *What is your attitude toward school?* 3 near: *It must be toward four o'clock.* 4 for the goal of: *They are saving toward a new car.* **Towards** is another form for all the meanings. *prep.*

tow·el (tou′əl) a piece of cloth or paper for wiping and drying something wet: *hand towels, dish towels.* *n.*

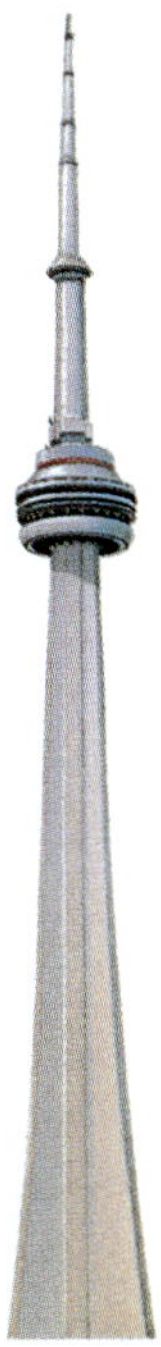

The Canadian National Tower in Toronto, Ontario, is 553 m high. When it was completed in 1976, it was the world's tallest free-standing structure.

tow·er (tou′ər) 1 a tall building or a tall part on a church, castle, or other building. 2 a tall framework used to support hydro lines, communications antennae, etc.: *a radio tower.* 3 stand very tall: *The boy towered over his baby brother.* 1, 2 *n.,* 3 *v.* **—tow′er·ing,** *adj.*

town (toun) 1 a large group of houses and other buildings, with a fixed boundary and its own government. A town is usually smaller than a city but larger than a village. 2 a city: *St. John's is a fine town.* 3 the people of a town: *The whole town celebrated.* **Townspeople** and **townsfolk** are other words for this. *n.*

town council (toun′ koun′səl) The group of elected people who run the government of a town. They have their offices in the **town hall.**

town·house (toun′hous′) a house that is attached to others in a row, each with its own street door and a small yard. *n.*

town·ship (toun′ship) 1 a part of a county with certain powers of government; municipality. A township usually contains a lot of farms and small villages. 2 in the Prairie Provinces, an area of 36 square miles (about 93 km^2), marked off when the land was originally surveyed and later divided into 36 sections. *n.*

tox·in (tok′sən) a poisonous chemical: *Factories must stop dumping toxins in the lake.* *n.* **—tox′ic,** *adj.*

toy (toi) 1 something to play with; a plaything. 2 made as a toy: *a toy airplane.* 3 play absent-mindedly: *to toy with an idea. She toyed with her beads.* 4 small; tiny: *a toy poodle.* 1 *n.,* 2, 4 *adj.,* 3 *v.*

trace (trās) 1 copy by putting your paper on top and following the lines that show through. **Tracing paper** is thin paper used for this purpose. 2 mark out; draw: *to trace letters in the sand with a stick.* 3 a sign of what has happened or been in a place; evidence left by something: *The explorer found traces of an ancient city.* 4 a very small amount: *Traces of gold were found along the creek.* 5 follow the tracks, clues, and so on left by a person or thing: *The dog traced the fox to its den.* 6 find the source of something: *to trace a phone call.* 1, 2, 5, 6 *v.,* **traced, trac·ing;** 3, 4 *n.* **—trace′a·ble,** *adj.*

tra·che·a (trā′kē ə) the windpipe. It leads from your mouth to your lungs. *n., pl.* **tra·che·ae** (trā′kē ē).

track (trak) 1 a mark left by anything that moves: *tire tracks, rabbit tracks.* 2 try to find by following the footprints, smell, etc.: *to track a bear.* 3 keep checking, recording, watching, etc.: *The teacher tracks our progress in each subject.* 4 a set of metal rails for trains or streetcars to run on: *a railway track.* 5 a path for running or racing: *We have a track behind our school for gym.* 6 the sport made up of various contests in running. 7 make footprints on or with: *Don't track up the floor; don't track that slush in here.* 8 the endless belt of linked steel treads on the bottom of a tank, bulldozer, etc. that move it forward. 1, 4–6, 8 *n.,* 2, 3, 7 *v.* **—track′less,** *adj.*
keep track of, keep remembering or checking; prevent from getting lost, forgotten, or out of control: *Keep track of what you spend.* The opposite is **lose track of.**
make tracks, *Informal.* **a** hurry. **b** run away.
off track or **off the track,** wrong; off the subject. The opposite is **on track** or **on the track.**
track down, find, especially by following clues.

a bat	e bed	i bid	o pot	u cup	th thin
ā cake	ē me	ī bite	ō go	ū rude	ᴛʜ then
ä bar	ə about	ər over	ȯ for	ů put	zh measure

track and field (trak′ ən fēld′) a group of athletic contests done on a track or in a field, including running, jumping, pole-vaulting, and throwing: *Renata doesn't play volleyball, but she's good at track and field.*

track·ball (trak′bol′) a small ball mounted in a computer mouse or keyboard, which you turn in order to control the cursor on a computer screen. *n.*

tract[1] (trakt) 1 a stretch of land or water: *a tract of desert.* 2 a system of related parts in the body: *The stomach and intestines are parts of the digestive tract.* *n.*

tract[2] (trakt) a little book or pamphlet meant to convince people of a certain point of view. *n.*

trac·tion (trak′shən) the friction between a body and the surface it moves on. Wheels slip on ice because there is too little traction. *n.*

trac·tor (trak′tər) 1 a vehicle with big tires and a powerful engine, used to pull wagons, ploughs, etc. on a farm. 2 a similar vehicle with tracks instead of wheels, used to move earth and so on at construction sites. 3 a truck with a powerful engine and a cab but no body, used to pull trailers along the highway. *n.*

trade (trād) 1 exchange: *The boys traded seats. I traded a stick of gum for a cookie* (*v.*). *That is a fair trade* (*n.*). 2 buy and sell; do business: *Some Canadian companies trade all over the world.* 3 the process of buying and selling: *Canada has trade with many foreign countries.* 4 any line of skilled work. Carpentry, plumbing, and auto mechanics are trades—you can learn them at a **trade school.** People who work at a trade are **tradespeople.** 1, 3, 4 *n.*, 1, 2 *v.*, **trad·ed, trad·ing.** —**trad′er,** *n.*
trade in, give an old thing, especially a car, as part of the payment for a new one. The old one is called a **trade-in.**
trade off, give up one good thing in order to get another: *She wondered whether to trade off free time against pocket money by getting a paper route.* A situation giving you this kind of choice is called a **trade-off.**

trade·mark (trād′märk′) 1 a picture, name, or symbol that belongs to a particular company and is put on its products, stationery, advertisements, etc. as identification. 2 anything that sets off a person or thing as unique. *n.*

trade wind (trād′ wind′) a wind blowing steadily toward the equator. North of the equator, the trade wind blows from the northeast; south of the equator, it blows from the southeast.

trading post (trā′ding pōst′) a store or station where goods can be exchanged, especially in a remote place. The Hudson's Bay Company operated many trading posts in the North.

tra·di·tion (trə dish′ən) beliefs, customs, stories, etc. from past years or generations, still held, known, or practised. *n.* —**tra·di′tion·al,** *adj.*

traf·fic (traf′ik) 1 the people, vehicles, boats, etc. coming and going along a route. 2 buy and sell illegally: *People are still trafficking in ivory.* 3 illegal buying and selling: *to stop the drug traffic.* 1, 3 *n.*, 2 *v.*, **traf·ficked, traf·fick·ing.** —**traf′fick·er,** *n.*

trag·e·dy (traj′ə dē) 1 a very sad or terrible event: *The father's death was a tragedy to his family.* 2 a serious play with an unhappy ending: *"Romeo and Juliet" is a tragedy.* *n., pl.* **trag·e·dies.** —**trag′ic** (traj′ik), *adj.*

WORD HISTORY........tragedy

The word **tragedy** has an odd origin. It is from Greek *tragoidia*, literally "goat song," from *tragos*, meaning "goat," and *oide*, "song." Nobody is quite sure where the goat comes into the meaning, though. Perhaps a goat's bleating sounds like crying?

trail (trāl) 1 a path across a wild or unsettled region: *The hikers had followed mountain trails for days.* 2 a track or smell left by a person or thing: *The dogs found the trail of the rabbit.* 3 hunt or follow by tracks, clues, or smell: *The dogs trailed the rabbit.* 4 anything that follows along behind: *The car left a trail of dust behind it.* 5 pull or be pulled along behind: *The child trailed a toy horse after her. Her dress trails on the ground.* 7 move in a long, uneven line: *children trailing home from school, vines trailing over a wall.* 1, 2, 4 *n.*, 3, 5–7 *v.*
trail off, gradually die away: *Her voice trailed off into silence.*

trail·blaz·er (trāl′blā′zər) a person who first makes a trail through an unsettled area. *n.*

trail·er (trā′lər) 1 a vehicle designed to be pulled by a car and used as a temporary home: *We have a trailer that we take to the lake every summer.* Bigger ones may be parked and used as offices, stores, classrooms, etc. 2 a large vehicle designed to be pulled along by a truck to carry goods from one place to another. *n.*

trail·ing ar·bu·tus (trā′ling är byū′təs) an evergreen vine of eastern North America that has clusters of fragrant pink or white flowers very early in spring; mayflower. It is the provincial flower of Nova Scotia.

trail mix (trāl′ miks′) a snack made up of nuts, seeds, and dried fruit: *We took some trail mix on our hike.*

train (trān) 1 a line of railway cars joined together and pulled by an engine along a track. 2 a line of people or things moving along: *A train of snowmobiles sped over the ice.* **3** part of a cloak or gown that trails behind: *The bride's wedding dress had a long train.* **4** teach by regular practice: *I was trained to say "please" and "thank you." Saint Bernard dogs were trained to hunt for travellers lost in the snow.* **5** prepare for a special kind of work, for a contest, etc.: *to train people as nurses. She is training to be a pilot. We trained for the long race by running 2 km a day.* A person being trained is a **trainee.** 1–3 *n.,* 4, 5 *v.* **—train′er,** *n.* **—train′ing,** *n.*

train of thought, connected ideas passing through your mind: *When you interrupted, I lost my train of thought.*

traipse (trāps) *Informal.* go, especially in a way that is tiring or inconvenient: *We had to traipse all over town looking for just the right pair of boots for Erik.* *v.,* **traipsed, traips·ing.**

trait (trāt) a certain quality of a person's mind or character; characteristic: *Honesty and common sense are desirable traits.* *n.*

trai·tor (trā′tər) **1** a person who betrays his or her country or ruler. **2** anyone who betrays someone else; anyone who is not loyal. *n.* **—trai′tor·ous,** *adj.*

tramp (tramp) **1** a homeless person who travels around on foot, living by begging and doing odd jobs; a hobo. **2** walk heavily: *He tramped across the floor in his heavy boots.* **3** walk steadily for a long time: *We tramped through the woods all day.* **4** the act or noise of tramping: *a long tramp in the hills. I heard the tramp of a parade.* 1, 4 *n.,* 2, 3 *v.*

tram·ple (tram′pəl) **1** crush with the feet: *The cattle broke through the fence and trampled the farmer's crops.* **2** the act or sound of tramping: *We heard the trample of many feet.* 1 *v.,* **tram·pled, tram·pling;** 2 *n.*

trample on, treat with scorn or cruelty: *The dictator trampled on the rights of his people.*

tram·po·line (tram′pə lēn′ *or* tram′pə lēn′) a tightly stretched piece of canvas or other sturdy material attached by springs to a metal frame all around the edge. It makes a very bouncy surface for jumping on. *n.*

trance (trans) **1** a state of unconsciousness a bit like sleep, only with eyes open: *I was put in a trance by the hypnotist.* **2** a dreamy, thoughtful condition that makes you forget your surroundings: *The old man sat before the fire in a trance, thinking about his boyhood.* *n.*

tran·quil (trang′kwəl) calm; peaceful; quiet: *the tranquil evening.* *adj.* **—tran·quil′li·ty,** *n.*

tran·quil·liz·er or **tran·quil·izer** (trang′kwə lī′zər) a drug used to calm people or animals down. *n.*

trans– *a prefix meaning:* **1** across, over, or through, as in *transcontinental, transatlantic.* **2** into a different place, condition, etc., as in *transform, transfusion.*

> **WORD HISTORY........trans-**
>
> *Trans* is Latin for "over," "across," or "through." Words with the prefix **trans-** all involve some idea of shift, change, or movement. Check out the ones on these pages.

trans·act (tran zakt′) do an item of business; carry on business: *to transact a sale or a bargain. He transacts business with stores all over the country.* *v.*

trans·ac·tion (tran zak′shən) **1** the carrying on of business: *She attends to the transaction of important matters herself.* **2** a single item of business: *The bank machine prints out a record of your transactions.* *n.*

Trans–Canada Highway (tranz′ kan′ə də hī′wā′) a highway that goes all the way across Canada.

tran·scribe (tran skrīb′) **1** copy in writing: *The account of the trial was transcribed from a tape recording.* The written copy is a **transcript.** **2** write in a different format: *The pronunciations in this dictionary are transcribed using special symbols.* *v.,* **tran·scribed, tran·scrib·ing.** **—tran·scrip′tion,** *n.*

> **WORD HISTORY......transcribe**
>
> **Transcribe** is made up of the prefix *trans-*, meaning "across," and the Latin *scribere*, "write." Literally, to transcribe is to carry sounds "across" into writing.

trans·fer (trans′fər; *also* trans fər′ *for 1*) **1** pass or switch from one person or place to another; change over: *Ownership of the farm was transferred from father to daughter. At Yonge Street you need to transfer from the bus to the subway.* **2** a ticket that lets you continue your journey on another streetcar, bus, train, etc. **3** a picture or design on a special material that allows it to be printed onto another surface: *Mom got me an iron-on transfer for my T-shirt.* **4** the act of transferring: *a transfer of money from one account to another.* 1 *v.,* **trans·ferred, trans·fer·ring;** 2–4 *n.* **—trans·fer′a·ble,** *adj.*

trans·fix (trans fiks′) make motionless with fear or astonishment: *They were transfixed by the sight of the huge pit that opened at their feet in the floor of the cave.* *v.*

a bat	e bed	i bid	o pot	u cup	th thin
ā cake	ē me	ī bite	ō go	ü rude	TH then
ä bar	ə about	ər over	ô for	ů put	zh measure

trans•form (trans fôrm′) 1 completely change the look of: *The blizzard transformed the bushes into glittering mounds of snow.* 2 change in nature or character: *A generator transforms mechanical energy into electricity. Her friendship has transformed him from a shy, sad person into a cheerful, outgoing one.* A **transformer** changes the voltage of an electric current so that an appliance can be used overseas. *v.* **—trans′for•ma′tion,** *n.*

trans•fu•sion (trans fyū′zhən) the process of putting blood into the veins of a person or animal to replace blood that has been lost. *n.*

trans•gress (tranz gres′) 1 sin or break a law. 2 go beyond the proper limit: *to transgress the bounds of acceptable behaviour.* *v.* **—trans•gres′sor,** *n.* **—trans•gres′sion,** *n.*

WORD HISTORY...... transgress

Transgress is from the prefix *trans-*, meaning "across" or "over," and Latin *gressus*, a form of *gradi*, meaning "to step." To transgress is to "step over the line."

tran•sit (tran′zit) 1 the process of passing or being carried from one place to another: *The goods were damaged in transit.* 2 a bus, train, or subway system in a city: *Let's go by transit and leave the car at home.* *n.*

tran•si•tion (tran zish′ən) a change; the process of passing from one condition, place, or thing to another: *He had a rough transition from city life to country life. Abrupt transitions in a story can confuse the reader.* *n.* **—tran•si′tion•al,** *adj.*

trans•late (tranz′lāt *or* tranz lāt′) 1 put into a different language or different words: *to translate a book from French into English. Translate the author's ideas into your own words.* 2 change from one condition to another: *to translate an idea into action.* *v.,* **trans•lat•ed, trans•lat•ing.** **—trans′la•tor,** *n.* **—trans•la′tion,** *n.*

trans•lu•cent (tranz lū′sənt) letting some light through, but not able to be seen through: *Frosted glass is translucent.* *adj.*

trans•mis•sion (tranz mish′ən) 1 the fact of passing or sending along: *the transmission of disease from one person to another, the transmission of radio or TV signals. E-mail has made the transmission of written messages much easier.* 2 the part of a motor vehicle that passes power from the engine to the driving axle, using a set of different gears. *n.*

trans•mit (tranz mit′) 1 send or pass along: *I will transmit your message by phone. Rats transmit disease.* 2 send out radio or TV signals carrying sounds or images: *Some radio stations transmit every hour of the day.* *v.,* **trans•mit•ted, trans•mit•ting.** **—trans•mit′ter,** *n.*

trans•par•en•cy (tran sper′ən sē) 1 a sheet of clear plastic with writing or images on it. It is used with a special machine called an **overhead projector** which shines a light from below and projects the image or writing onto a screen. 2 the fact of being transparent: *the transparency of a fly's wing, the transparency of her lies.* *n., pl.* **trans•par•en•cies.**

trans•par•ent (tran sper′ənt) 1 clear; easy to see through because it lets light through, like window glass. 2 not hiding or able to hide the truth: *a transparent excuse. You should be transparent to your friends.* *adj.*

tran•spire (tran spīr′) 1 happen: *Everything transpired exactly as she said.* 2 pass moisture through tiny openings in the surface of something, such as your skin or the leaves of plants. *v.,* **tran•spired, tran•spir•ing.** **—tran′spi•ra′tion** (tran′spə rā′shen), *n.*

trans•plant (trans plant′ *for 1 and 2,* trans′plant *for 3*) 1 plant again in a different place: *We start the flowers indoors and then transplant them to the garden.* 2 take an organ from one person or animal and put it in another: *to transplant a kidney.* 3 this process or the organ involved: *a heart transplant.* 1, 2 *v.,* 3 *n.*

tran•spond•er (tran spon′dər) a piece of radio or radar equipment that receives a signal and then sends out an answering signal automatically. On some highways which drivers must pay to use, a device at each ramp sends out a signal to an approaching car. A transponder on the car windshield sends an answering signal identifying the car, so that a bill can be sent to the owner. *n.*

trans•port (trans pôrt′ *for 1,* trans′pôrt *for 2 and 3*) 1 carry from one place to another: *Vegetables are transported from the farms to the cities.* 2 the process of carrying from one place to another: *Trucks are used for transport.* 3 a vehicle, especially a large truck, used to carry things over long distances. 1 *v.,* 2, 3 *n.*

trans•por•ta•tion (trans′pər tā′shən) the act, fact, or means of transporting or carrying people or things, especially people: *The school provided transportation to the tournament. This highway is a major transportation route.* *n.*

trans•pose (trans pōz′) 1 switch the position or order: *I accidentally transposed your initials and wrote L.A.G. instead of G.A.L.* 2 put a piece of music into a different key. *v.,* **trans•posed, trans•pos•ing.** **—trans′po•si′tion,** *n.*

trap (trap) 1 a device for catching animals, lobsters, birds, etc. 2 a trick for catching someone off guard: *The friendly conversation was a trap to make her tell the secret.* 3 catch in a trap: *The bear was trapped. The police trapped the thief by pretending they wanted to buy the stolen goods.* 4 make a living by catching animals in traps, for meat or fur: *He spent his winters trapping up north.* 5 keep water, air, or other matter from escaping. 6 any arrangement or part that does this. A clothes dryer has a lint trap in it. 1, 2, 6 *n.,* 3–5 *v.,* **trapped, trap·ping.** —**trap′per,** *n.*

trap·door (trap′dȯr′) a door in a floor or ceiling, often a secret one. *n.*

tra·peze (trə pēz′) a short bar hung by two ropes like a swing, used by acrobats in circuses. *n.*

trap·e·zoid (trap′ə zoid′) a flat, four-sided figure with two sides that are parallel and two that are not. *n.*

trap·line (trap′līn′) a series of traps set and maintained by a trapper who regularly goes over the line to remove trapped animals. *n.*

trap·pings (trap′ingz) the outward things that go along with a certain position, job, etc.: *He has all the trappings of a cowboy, but he can't even ride a horse.* *pl.n.*

trash (trash) anything worthless; junk; garbage: *Put the trash in the can.* *n.* —**trash′y,** *adj.*

trau·ma (trom′ə) 1 a serious injury or shock to the body. 2 a severe emotional shock that is very hard to get over, caused by some horrible experience. To cause someone to suffer a trauma is to **traumatize** the person. *n.* —**trau·mat′ic,** *adj.*

trav·el (trav′əl) 1 go; move along: *Sound travels in waves. The car was travelling at 80 km/h.* 2 take trips for business or pleasure; go to different places away from your home area: *She travels for a large firm. They travel every summer.* 3 the activity of taking trips and visiting places: *She loves travel.* 4 the business of planning people's trips for them, getting their tickets, and so on: *He has a career in travel.* 1, 2 *v.,* **trav·elled** or **trav·eled, trav·el·ling** or **trav·el·ing;** 3, 4 *n.* —**trav′el·ler** or **trav′el·er,** *n.*

travel agency (trav′əl ā′jən sē) a business that arranges trips for its customers by reserving their plane tickets, rental cars, hotel rooms, and so on. The person who does this is called a **travel agent.**

traveller's cheque (trav′ə lərz chek′) a special cheque that can be exchanged for foreign money and can be replaced if it is lost.

trav·erse (trə vərs′ *or* trav′ərs) pass across, over, or through: *The caravan traversed the desert.* *v.,* **trav·ersed, trav·ers·ing.**

🍁 **tra·vois** (trə vwȯ′ *or* trav′wȯ) 1 a simple vehicle without wheels, used in earlier times by the First Nations peoples of the plains. It was made of two poles tied together at one end and hitched over the neck of a dog or horse. The poles spread out at the back to hold a platform or net for carrying a load. 2 a dog sled. *n., pl.* **tra·vois.**

A trawler may also carry equipment on board to clean, process, and freeze its catch of fish.

trawl (trol) 1 a bag-shaped net dragged along the bottom of the sea to catch fish. A boat used for this is a **trawler.** 2 a rope kept afloat in the water by buoys, with many short, baited fishing lines hanging from it. 3 to fish with such a net or line. 1, 2 *n.,* 3 *v.*

tray (trā) a flat holder with a low rim around it, for carrying dishes and other things: *Our dentist keeps her instruments on a tray.* *n.*

treach·er·ous (trech′ə rəs) 1 not to be trusted; not loyal; double-crossing: *The treacherous soldier carried reports to the enemy.* **Treachery** is betraying your country or someone who trusts you. 2 very dangerous, even though it may appear safe: *Thin ice is treacherous.* *adj.*

trea·cle (trē′kəl) another word for molasses, a dark, syrupy by-product of refining sugar. *n.*

tread (tred) 1 the raised pattern on the surface of a tire or on the sole of a shoe or boot, which helps prevent slipping: *The tread on the back tires is almost gone.* 2 the part of a stair where you put your foot: *The stair treads were covered with rubber.* 3 a somewhat old-fashioned or poetic word for "walk," "step," or "trample": *Don't tread on the flower beds* (*v.*). *He walks with a heavy tread* (*n.*). 1–3 *n.,* 3 *v.* **trod, trod·den** or **trod, tread·ing.**
tread water, keep from sinking in water by slowly moving your legs as if riding a bicycle.

a bat	e bed	i bid	o pot	u cup	th thin
ā cake	ē me	ī bite	ō go	ū rude	ꟻH then
ȧ bar	ə about	ər over	ȯ for	u̇ put	zh measure

tread•mill (tred′mil′) 1 in earlier times, a machine for producing a turning motion by having a person or animal walk on the inside of a movable wheel or on a sloping, endless belt. 2 nowadays, a similar device for a person or animal to walk on as a form of exercise. 3 any tiresome or monotonous routine. *n.*

trea•son (trē′zən) the act or fact of betraying your country or ruler. *n.* **—trea′son•ous,** *adj.*

treas•ure (trezh′ər) 1 riches or valuable things stored up: *The pirates buried treasure along the coast. The palace contains art treasures.* 2 any thing or person that is loved or valued very much: *The antique silver tea set was the family's treasure.* 3 value very highly: *I treasure my friends.* 1, 2 *n.,* 3 *v.,* **treas•ured, treas•ur•ing.**

treas•ur•er (trezh′ə rər) a person in charge of the money belonging to an organization. *n.*

treas•ur•y (trezh′ə rē) 1 a place where money is kept: *The national treasury is in Ottawa.* 2 money owned by an organization: *We paid for the party out of the club treasury.* 3 a place where anything valuable is found: *This book is a treasury of information.* *n., pl.* **treas•ur•ies.**

treat (trēt) 1 act toward; handle or deal with: *He treats his baby sister gently. My father treats our new car with care.* 2 think of; consider; regard: *She treated the mistake as a joke.* 3 anything special that a person enjoys very much: *Going to the zoo is a treat to her.* 4 entertain by giving something enjoyable: *He treated his friends to ice cream.* 5 a gift like this: *"This is my treat," she said, as she paid for the movie tickets.* 6 do something to relieve or cure: *to treat a patient, to treat a disease.* 7 put through a special chemical or physical process so as to change or improve: *This cloth has been treated to make it waterproof.* 1, 2, 4, 6, 7 *v.,* 3, 5 *n.* **—treat′ment,** *n.* **—treat′a•ble,** *adj.*

trea•ty (trē′tē) 1 an agreement between nations: *Each leader signed the peace treaty.* 2 in Canada, any of the agreements made long ago between the British monarch and many groups of First Nations people. Each group gave up some of its land; in return, it received payment and certain rights, and some land was set aside for the use of that particular First Nation. The descendants of the First Nations people who made treaties are called **treaty Indians.** When Canada became an independent nation, the federal government took over these agreements. *n.,* **trea•ties.**

tre•ble clef (treb′əl klef′) in music: 1 the symbol that shows that the notes on a staff are above middle C. 2 a staff with the treble clef symbol. A note on the bottom line is the E above middle C.

Trees are the largest and oldest living things on Earth. The biggest trees are the giant redwoods, of the sequoia family. They are native to North America. Some of these trees are about 3500 years old, and are over 60 m tall.

tree (trē) 1 a large plant with a woody trunk and, usually, branches and leaves or needles on its upper part. 2 anything suggesting a tree and its branches. A **clothes tree** is a pole with hooks or bars sticking out to hang clothes on; a **family tree** is a chart of the different branches of a family, covering several generations and showing how everyone is related. *n.*
up a tree, *Informal.* in a difficult position.

tree house (trē′ hous′) a small shelter or fort built in the branches of a tree, especially one to play in.

tree•line (trē′līn′) an imaginary line marking the end of the area where trees can grow. In Canada, the tree line is the southern boundary of the Barrens.

tree•top (trē′top′) the top part of a tree: *to fly above the treetops.* *n.*

trek (trek) 1 travel slowly, especially on foot through rough country: *The settlers trekked hundreds of kilometres.* 2 a journey, especially a slow, difficult one on foot: *a long trek over the mountains.* 1 *v.,* **trekked, trek•king;** 2 *n.*

trel•lis (trel′is) a frame, usually V-shaped, of light strips of wood or metal crossing one another with spaces in between. It is used to support climbing plants. *n.*

trem•ble (trem′bəl) 1 shake slightly: *The sick woman's hands trembled. The leaves trembled in the breeze.* 2 a slight shaking: *There was a tremble in her voice as she began to recite.* 1 *v.,* **trem•bled, trem•bling;** 2 *n.*

tre•men•dous (tri men′dəs) 1 huge; very great: *a tremendous risk, a tremendous amount of money.* 2 *Informal.* excellent: *You've done a tremendous job!* *adj.*

trem·or (trem′ər) a slight shaking or trembling: *There was a nervous tremor in his voice. The earth tremor caused no damage.* *n.*

trem·u·lous (trem′yə ləs) trembling: *a tremulous voice.* *adj.*

trench (trench) **1** a ditch: *They dug a trench around the tent to carry off rainwater.* **2** a long, narrow ditch with earth thrown up in front to protect soldiers. *n.*

trend (trend) **1** a current style in fashion: *Bright colours are the trend.* Something very fashionable is **trendy;** a leader in fashion is a **trendsetter.** **2** the general direction; a tendency: *the upward trend of prices.* *n.*

trep·i·da·tion (trep′ə dā′shən) great fear. *n.*

tres·pass (tres′pas′ *or* tres′pəs) **1** go on someone's property without any right: *He put up "No Trespassing" signs to keep people off his farm.* **2** go beyond the limits of what is right, proper, or polite: *I won't trespass on your time any longer.* **3** sin. 1–3 *v.,* 3 *n.* **—tres′pass′er,** *n.*

tress·es (tres′iz) a poetic word for "hair": *golden tresses.* *pl.n.*

tres·tle (tres′əl) a framework with parts that cross over each other, used as a support for something laid on top such as a work surface or a bridge. *n.*

tri– *a prefix meaning* three, as in *triangle,* and *tricycle.*

Word Family.......... tri-

triathlon: an athletic event that combines swimming, bicycling, and running over a long distance
triennial: happening every three years
trilingual: using or able to use three languages
trilobite: a prehistoric sea creature. It had an outside skeleton divided into three sections.
trilogy: three stories which together form one long one
trimester: **1** a three-month period **2** a third of a year
trireme: a warship with three rows of oars per side

tri·al (trī′əl) **1** a court case to see if an accused person is guilty or not, based on the evidence given by witnesses. **2** the process of testing or trying out: *The engineers gave the machine another trial to see if it would work.* **3** for testing: *a trial model.* **4** something hard to bear: *Her life has been full of trials—sickness, poverty, and loss of loved ones.* 1, 2, 4 *n.,* 3 *adj.*
on trial, a being judged in a court. **b** as a test to see how things work out: *They gave him the job on trial.*

tri·an·gle (trī′ang′gəl) **1** a flat figure with three sides and three angles. **2** anything shaped like this, especially a musical instrument made of a steel rod bent into a triangle, played by hitting it. *n.*
—tri·an′gu·lar (trī ang′gyə lər), *adj.*

tribe (trīb) **1** a group of people led by a chief or council, all descended from the same ancestor. Ancient nations were divided into tribes. **2** large group: *A tribe of photographers were at the scene.* *n.* **—trib′al,** *adj.*

USING WORDS .... tribe

In the past, **tribe** has often been confused with **nation**. Aboriginal groups in Canada, such as the Mohawk or Ojibwa, are not tribes, but separate nations. It is the same for many other groups worldwide, like the Zulu nation or the Tutsi nation in Africa. A tribe is more like a big clan.

trib·u·la·tion (trib′yə lā′shən) severe hardship: *The early settlers suffered many tribulations.* *n.*

tri·bu·nal (trī byū′nəl *or* trə byū′nəl) any kind of court or place where judgments are made. *n.*

trib·u·tar·y (trib′yə ter′ē) a stream that flows into a larger stream: *The Ottawa River is a tributary of the St. Lawrence River.* *n., pl.* **trib·u·tar·ies.**

trib·ute (trib′yūt) **1** something said or done to show honour or appreciation: *Remembrance Day is a tribute to our dead soldiers.* **2** a fact that proves how good something is: *The carnival's success was a tribute to her skill as an organizer.* **3** payment made by one nation to another in return for peace or protection. *n.*

tri·cer·a·tops (trī ser′ə tops′) a dinosaur with a large, bony crest on the back of its neck, a long horn over each eye, and a smaller horn on its snout. It ate plants and walked on four legs. It is sometimes called a **threehorn.**

trick (trik) **1** something done to fool or cheat someone: *The false message was a trick to get him to leave the house.* **2** fool or cheat someone: *We were tricked into buying a poor car.* **3** a clever act of skill: *We enjoyed the magician's tricks.* **4** the key to succeeding at something, which only certain people know: *The trick to making good tea is to heat the pot beforehand.* **5** a piece of mischief; prank: *Stealing his lunch was a mean trick.* 1, 3–5 *n.,* 2 *v.* **—trick′er·y,** *n.* **—trick′ster,** *n.* **—trick′y,** *adj.*
do the trick, do just what is needed or wanted: *That new stain remover really does the trick.*
trick or treat, a phrase traditionally yelled by children collecting treats at neighbours' houses on Halloween.

a bat	e bed	i bid	o pot	u cup	th thin
ā cake	ē me	ī bite	ō go	ū rude	ᴛʜ then
ä bar	ə about	ər over	ò for	ů put	zh measure

trick·le (trik′əl) 1 flow or fall in drops or in a small, slow stream: *Tears trickled down his cheeks. The brook trickled through the valley.* 2 a small flow or stream. 1 *v.,* **trick·led, trick·ling;** 2 *n.*

tri·cy·cle (trī′sə kəl) a three-wheeled vehicle for a child, worked by pedals attached to the large single wheel in front. It is also called a **three-wheeler** or **trike.** *n.*

tried (trīd) the past tense and past participle of **try:** *I tried to call him last night. I haven't tried today yet.* *v.*

tri·fle (trī′fəl) 1 something small and unimportant: *Don't bother her with such trifles.* 2 a small amount; a little bit: *I am a trifle late.* 3 talk or act too lightly or playfully: *Don't trifle with serious matters.* 4 spend on worthless things: *She had trifled away the whole morning.* 5 a rich dessert made of sponge cake, whipped cream, custard, fruit, etc. 1, 2, 5 *n.,* 3, 4 *v.,* **tri·fled, tri·fling.**

trig·ger (trig′ər) 1 the small lever you pull back with your finger to fire a gun. 2 anything that works like a trigger or causes something else to start: *One of the triggers for asthma is dust.* 3 set off; start: *The fiery speech triggered an outburst of violence.* 1, 2 *n.,* 3 *v.*

trill (tril) 1 sing or speak with a quivering, vibrating sound: *birds trilling their songs. She trills her r's.* 2 play or sing two notes by going quickly back and forth between them. 3 the act or sound of trilling. 1, 2 *v.,* 3 *n.*

tril·li·um (tril′yəm) a plant of the lily family that has three leaves and a single white or dark red flower with three petals. The white trillium is the provincial flower of Ontario. *n.*

trim (trim) 1 make neater by cutting at the edges: *to trim a hedge, to trim someone's hair. The lumber has to be trimmed for the carpenter.* 2 tidy; in good order: *She keeps her desk neat and trim.* 3 in good condition; fit: *Exercise to stay trim.* 4 decorate: *Her white skirt was trimmed with blue ribbon.* 5 parts added as decoration: *A red blouse with yellow trim.* 1, 4 *v.,* **trimmed, trim·ming;** 2, 3 *adj.,* **trim·mer, trim·mest;** 5 *n.*

trim·ming (trim′ing) 1 material used to trim or decorate: *She bought trimming for her costume.* 2 **trimmings,** *pl.* **a** parts cut away in trimming: *Sweep up the trimmings.* **b** the extras that usually go along with something: *a turkey dinner with all the trimmings.* *n.*

trin·ket (tring′kit) any small, fancy, but not very valuable thing. *n.*

tri·o (trē′ō) 1 a piece of music for three voices or instruments. 2 a group of three people singing or playing together. 3 any group of three. *n., pl.* **tri·os.**

trip (trip) 1 a journey; the act of going someplace: *We took a trip to the Rockies. He made three trips to the kitchen for snacks.* 2 stumble or cause to stumble: *She tripped on the stairs. Emil tripped me with his hockey stick.* 3 turn on; set off: *to trip an alarm, to trip a switch.* 4 take light, quick steps; skip: *The children came tripping down the path to meet us.* 1 *n.,* 2–4 *v.,* **tripped, trip·ping.**
trip up, trick someone into making a mistake.

Tri·pi·ta·ka (trip′i tä′kə) the holy writings of the Buddhist religion. *n.*

tri·ple (trip′əl) 1 make or become three times as much or as many: *The town's population tripled in fifteen years.* 2 three times as much or as many: *She gets triple the allowance I do.* 3 including three; having three parts: *a triple bunk bed with three levels.* The **triple jump** is a track-and-field event that includes a hop, a step, and a jump. 4 in baseball, a three-base hit. 5 make a three-base hit: *He tripled in the eighth inning.* 1, 5 *v.,* **tri·pled, tri·pling;** 2, 4 *n.,* 3 *adj.* **—tri′ply,** *adv.*

tri·plet (trip′lit) 1 one of three children born at the same time from one mother. 2 any group of three. *n.*

tri·pod (trī′pod) a support or stand with three legs, such as for a camera, telescope, etc. *n.*

trite (trīt) so commonplace that it is not interesting and not very meaningful: *a trite expression, a trite story line.* *adj.,* **trit·er, trit·est.**

tri·umph (trī′umf) 1 a victory, especially after a long or difficult struggle: *The discovery of insulin is a triumph of modern medicine.* 2 gain such a victory: *In the story, good finally triumphs over evil.* 3 joy because of victory or success: *We welcomed the team home with cheers of triumph.* 4 rejoice because of victory: *They triumphed in their success.* 1, 3 *n.,* 2, 4 *v.* **—tri·um′phant,** *adj.*

triv·i·a (triv′ē ə) unimportant facts or details: *He knows all the trivia about his favourite hockey team.* *n.* **—triv′i·al,** *adj.*

WORD HISTORY........trivia

Trivialis meant "vulgar" in Latin, and was made up of *tri-*, meaning "three," and *via*, "road." It literally referred to the main intersection in town, which was where people hung out, chatting about unimportant things.

trod (trod) the past tense and a past participle of **tread:** *He trod on a tack. You have trod on my foot again.* **Trodden** is the other past participle. *v.*

troll[1] (trōl) in stories, an ugly giant or dwarf living in caves, underground, or in other dark, damp places. *n.*

troll² (trōl) fish by trailing the line behind a boat that is moving slowly: *He trolled for bass.* *v.*

trol·ley (trol′ē) **1** an electric bus that gets its power from overhead wires. **2** a cart with shelves to carry things: *a dessert trolley. The hospital orderly pushed a trolley full of cleaning supplies and fresh linen.* *n., pl.* **trol·leys.**

trom·bone (trom bōn′) a brass musical instrument with a long sliding piece for varying the tones. *n.* **—trom·bon′ist,** *n.*

troop (trūp) **1** a group of people or animals: *A troop of protesters marched to City Hall.* **2** move together in a group: *The students trooped into the gym.* **3 troops,** *pl.* soldiers: *The government sent troops to put down the revolt.* **4** a unit of cavalry in the army. 1, 3, 4 *n.,* 2 *v.*

USING WORDS ...... troop

Troop and **troupe** can both be used for a group or band of people. However, **troupe** is usually used for groups of performers, such as actors or singers. **Troop** is used to describe soldiers and other organized groups.

troop·er (trū′pər) **1** a person full of team spirit who works faithfully or endures things bravely. **2** a soldier in a cavalry regiment. **3** in the U.S., a state police officer. *n.*

tro·phy (trō′fē) **1** a statue, cup, etc. given to a winning player or team: *She kept her tennis trophy on the mantelpiece.* **2** anything taken or kept as a symbol of victory or success: *The hunter kept the lion's skin as a trophy.* *n., pl.* **tro·phies.**

trop·ics (trop′iks) the regions near the equator, between about 23½ degrees north and 23½ degrees south of it. The hottest parts of the earth are in the tropics. *pl.n.* **—trop′i·cal,** *adj.*

trop·o·sphere (trop′ə sfēr′) the lowest part of the earth's atmosphere, where clouds and winds occur. The temperature drops as you go higher. *n.*

trot (trot) **1** of horses, run lightly or slowly by lifting the right forefoot and the left hind foot at about the same time and then the other two feet in the same way. **2** run, but not fast: *The child trotted along after his mother.* **3** the motion or speed of trotting; a light easy run. 1, 2 *v.,* **trot·ted, trot·ting;** 3 *n.*

trou·ble (trub′əl) **1** problems or hard times; worry; difficulty: *That boy causes trouble for his teachers.* A person who causes trouble is a **troublemaker;** to **troubleshoot** is to figure out what is causing trouble and fix it. **2** bother; disturb: *She is troubled by headaches. It troubles me that she is so late.* **3** extra work; effort: *Don't go to any trouble for us. If she won't take the trouble to answer our letters, we'll stop writing.* **4** cause extra work or effort for yourself or another person: *Don't trouble to come to the door; I can let myself in. May I trouble you to get my coat?* 1, 3 *n.,* 2, 4 *v.,* **trou·bled, trou·bling.** **—trou′ble·some,** *adj.*

in trouble, a scolded or punished by someone in authority: *I got in trouble for being late.* **b** in difficulty.

trough (trof) **1** a long, narrow container for holding food or water for animals: *He led the horses to the watering trough.* **2** something shaped like this, such as the long, low part between two waves, or the gutter attached to a roof to carry away rainwater. *n.*

trounce (trouns) beat or defeat severely: *The home team was trounced by the visitors.* *v.,* **trounced, trounc·ing.**

troupe (trūp) a company of performers: *a circus troupe, a troupe of actors.* *n.*

trou·sers (trou′zərz) a less common word for "pants": *a pair of warm trousers.* *pl.n.*

trout (trout) a freshwater fish that people eat, belonging to the same family as salmon. The **rainbow trout** is one kind of trout. *n., pl.* **trout** or **trouts.**

trow·el (trou′əl) **1** a tool with a flat, triangular blade, used for spreading or smoothing plaster or mortar. **2** a garden tool with a curved blade like a small shovel or a scoop, used for digging up plants, loosening dirt, etc. *n.*

tru·ant (trū′ənt) **1** a student who skips school without permission. **2** a person who neglects his or her duty. **3** guilty of skipping school or neglecting a duty. 1, 2 *n.,* 3 *adj.* **—tru′an·cy,** *n.*

play truant, skip school without permission.

truce (trūs) an agreement to stop fighting for a short time: *The two armies declared a truce.* *n.*

truck (truk) **1** a large, strongly built motor vehicle for carrying heavy loads. **2** carry on a truck: *The lettuce was trucked to market.* The business of carrying goods by truck is called **trucking;** a **trucker** is one who either owns such a business or drives a truck. **3** a small vehicle, sometimes with a motor, for carrying heavy boxes and so on in a warehouse. 1, 3 *n.,* 2 *v.*

a bat	e bed	i bid	o pot	u cup	th thin
ā cake	ē me	ī bite	ō go	ū rude	ᴛʜ then
ä bar	ə about	ər over	ô for	ů put	zh measure

trudge (truj) 1 walk wearily or with effort. 2 a hard or tiring walk: *It was a long trudge up the hill.* 1 *v.,* **trudged, trudg·ing;** 2 *n.*

true (trü) 1 agreeing with the facts; not false: *It is true that 6 and 4 make 10. The story he told is true.* 2 real; genuine: *true gold, true kindness.* 3 faithful; loyal: *my truest friend, true to your promises.* 4 accurate: *a true translation.* *adj.,* **tru·er, tru·est.** **—tru′ly,** *adv.*
come true, happen as imagined; become real.
ring true, sound convincing.
yours truly, a *Informal.* I; me; myself. **b** a phrase for ending a letter, followed by the writer's name.

trum·pet (trum′pit) 1 a musical instrument made of a looped brass tube that is bell-shaped at one end and is played by blowing. It has three valves which you press with your fingers to make different notes. 2 anything shaped like a trumpet: *Some people used ear trumpets until hearing aids were invented.* 3 blow a trumpet or make a sound like a trumpet: *The elephant trumpeted in fright.* 4 tell loudly or widely: *They'll trumpet that story all over town.* 1, 2 *n.,* 3, 4 *v.* **—trum′pet·er,** *n.*

trun·dle (trun′dəl) roll along; push along, especially heavily or noisily: *The worker trundled a wheelbarrow full of cement.* *v.,* **trun·dled, trun·dling.**

trunk (trungk) 1 the main stem of a tree. 2 a closed-in compartment in the back of a car for carrying things. 3 an elephant's long, flexible nose. 4 a big metal or wooden box used for storing clothes and other things or for taking them on a long trip. 5 a body apart from the head, arms, and legs. 6 **trunks,** *pl.* very short pants worn by men for swimming and other sports. *n.*

trust (trust) 1 a firm belief in the loyalty, goodness, truthfulness, or ability of a person or thing; faith: *Trust is important between friends.* 2 have this kind of belief or faith in: *I trust her; she never lies.* Someone that can be trusted is **trustworthy.** 3 rely on; depend on: *You can trust him to find the tiniest mistake.* 4 put something into someone's care without fear: *Can I trust my pet lizard to him?* 5 hope; expect: *I trust you will soon feel better.* 6 something managed and kept safe for someone else: *The house is a trust she holds for her dead brother's children until they grow up.* 7 the duty or responsibility of taking charge of someone else's property: *Mr. Hancock will be faithful to his trust.* 1, 6, 7 *n.,* 2, 3–5 *v.* **—trust′ful,** *adj.* **—trust′ing,** *adj.*
hold in trust, manage and keep safe for another person or group: *My aunt holds the house in trust.*

trus·tee (trus tē′) 1 a person elected to a school board to speak for parents. 2 someone who manages the property or affairs of a person or organization. *n.*

trust·y (trus′tē) faithful; reliable: *my trusty old bike.* *adj.,* **trust·i·er, trust·i·est.**

truth (trüth) 1 whatever is true; whatever agrees with the facts: *Tell the truth.* 2 an important or basic fact: *scientific truths.* 3 the quality of being true: *I doubt the truth of her statement.* *n.* **—truth′ful,** *adj.*
in truth, truly; really; in fact.

try (trī) 1 make an effort to do something: *If at first you don't succeed, try, try again.* 2 test; find out about something by using it or doing it: *Try this candy and see if you like it. Try jiggling the key—that might work.* 3 an attempt: *Each person had three tries at the high jump.* 4 examine and judge in a law court: *The man was tried and found guilty of robbery.* 5 strain: *Your rudeness is trying my patience.* Something hard to put up with is **trying.** 1, 2, 4, 5 *v.,* **tried, try·ing;** 3 *n.*
try on, put on to test the fit or looks: *She tried on a hat.*
try out, a use or do as a test: *Try out this new recipe for apple pie.* **b** take a test of your skill in hopes of being chosen for something: *He tried out for the hockey team.* This test is called a **tryout.**

> **USING WORDS . . . . try**
>
> **Try and,** as in *Try and catch a fish* is fine in informal speech. In formal situations, use **try to.**

tsar (zär) another spelling of **czar,** the title of a Russian emperor. **Tsarina** is another spelling of **czarina,** a Russian empress. *n.*

Tsilh·qot'·in (tsil′kō tin) 1 a First Nations people living in British Columbia. 2 their language. 3 having to do with these people or their language. 1, 2 *n.,* 3 *adj.*

T–shirt (tē′shərt′) a light sport shirt or undershirt of a knit material, with no collar and, usually, short sleeves. *n.*

Tsim·shi·an (tsim′shē ən *or* chim′shē ən) 1 a First Nations people living in British Columbia. 2 their language. 3 having to do with these people or their language. 1, 2 *n.,* 3 *adj.*

tsp. *abbreviation for* teaspoon or teaspoons, a nonmetric unit of volume.

tsu·na·mi (tsü nä′mē) another name for a **tidal wave,** a huge ocean wave caused by very strong winds, unusually high tides, or an earthquake. Tsunamis can cause great destruction. *n., pl.* **tsu·na·mis.**

tub (tub) 1 a large, rounded open container for taking a bath in, washing clothes, and so on. A **hot tub** is a large one full of hot swirling water, big enough for several people to relax in. **2** a wide, round container for margarine, ice cream, and so on. Something shaped like a tub is **tubby.** *n.*

tu·ba (tyū′bə *or* tū′bə) a very large brass musical instrument played by blowing into it while pressing down valves to make the different notes. It has the lowest range of the brass instruments. *n.*

tube (tyūb *or* tūb) **1** a long pipe of metal, glass, plastic, etc. Tubes are mostly used to hold or carry liquids or gases. An **inner tube** is rubber and doughnut-shaped; when filled with air it is put inside a tire for extra support. The sport of sliding down a snowy slope or floating down a river on an inner tube is called **tubing. 2** anything shaped like a tube: *the bronchial tubes.* **Tube socks** are often worn for sports; some women and girls wear stretchy **tube tops. 3** a long, rounded, squeezable container with a cap for one end, for toothpaste, ointment, etc. *n.* **—tu′bu·lar** (tyū′byə lər)**,** *adj.*

tu·ber (tyū′bər *or* tū′bər) the thick part of an underground stem. A potato is a tuber. *n.*

tu·ber·cu·lo·sis (tə bər′kyə lō′sis) a contagious disease caused by bacteria. It mainly affects the lungs. It is often called **TB** for short. *n.*

tuck (tuk) **1** stick into a narrow or hidden space: *She tucked her purse under her arm. The little cottage is tucked away in the woods.* **2** make something stay in place by sticking the edge into or under something else: *Tuck your shirt in. He tucked the sheets under the mattress.* **3** a fold sewn into a piece of clothing to make it narrower. **4** candy or snacks you can get at school or camp from a little store called a **tuck shop.** 1, 2 *v.,* 3, 4 *n.*
tuck away, eat heartily: *He tucked away a big meal.*
tuck in, a cover snugly: *Mom or Dad comes every night to tuck us in.* **b** eat heartily: *As soon as the food was on the table, we all tucked in.*

Tues·day (tyūz′dā′ *or* tūz′dā′) the day after Monday and before Wednesday. *Abbreviation:* Tues. *n.*

tuft (tuft) a bunch of feathers, hair, grass, threads, etc. sticking up or sticking out: *A goat has a tuft of hair on its chin.* *n.* **—tuft′ed,** *adj.*

tug (tug) **1** pull hard: *I tugged the rope and it came loose. The child tugged at her mother's hand.* **2** a hard pull: *The baby gave my hair a tug.* **3** short for **tugboat,** a small, powerful boat used to tow ships. **4** tow by a tugboat. 1, 4 *v.,* **tugged, tug·ging;** 2, 3 *n.*

tug–of–war (tug′əv wȯr′) a contest between two teams pulling at the ends of a rope, each trying to drag the other over a line marked between them. *n.*

tu·i·tion (tyū ish′ən *or* tū ish′ən) the cost of being a student at a private school, university, or college, or for lessons from a tutor: *Her yearly tuition is $6000.* *n.*

Almost all varieties of cultivated tulips were developed from bulbs brought from Turkey in the 1500s. The name "tulip" comes from a Turkish word meaning "turban" — the overlapping petals look a bit like a turban.

tu·lip (tyū′lip *or* tū′lip) a plant that grows from a bulb and has large, cup-shaped flowers of various colours. Tulips come up in the spring. *n.*

tum·ble (tum′bəl) **1** fall with a rolling or turning movement: *The child tumbled down the stairs.* **2** a fall: *The tumble hurt him badly.* **3** roll or toss around; keep turning over: *to tumble clothes in a dryer. The sick child tumbled restlessly in his bed.* **4** do somersaults, flips, and so on. 1, 3, 4 *v.,* **tum·bled, tum·bling;** 2 *n.*

tum·ble–down (tum′bəl doun′) ready to fall down; not in good condition: *a tumble-down shack in the mountains.* *adj.*

tum·bler (tum′blər) **1** a person who does flips, somersaults, and so on. **2** a drinking glass. *n.*

tum·ble·weed (tum′bəl wēd′) a plant that dries out in the fall, breaks off from its roots, and is then blown around by the wind. The Russian thistle of the prairies is one kind of tumbleweed. *n.*

tu·mour or **tu·mor** (tyū′mər *or* tū′mər) an abnormal growth that develops on some part of the body from the tissue already there. A **benign tumour** does little or no harm, but a **malignant tumour** involves cancer. *n.*

tu·mult (tyū′mult *or* tū′mult) a violent disturbance or disorder; uproar: *We heard the tumult of the storm. The shout of "Fire!" caused a tumult in the theatre.* *n.* **—tu·mul′tu·ous,** *adj.*

tu·na (tyū′nə *or* tū′nə) a large sea fish which can grow to a length of 3 m. It is valued as food and is usually sold cooked and canned. *n., pl.* **tu·na** or **tu·nas.**

tun·dra (tun′drə) a vast, flat, treeless area in the arctic regions. The ground beneath the surface of the tundra stays frozen all year long. *n.*

a bat	e bed	i bid	o pot	u cup	th **thin**
ā cake	ē me	ī bite	ō go	ū rude	ᴛʜ **then**
à bar	ə about	ər over	ȯ for	ů put	zh measure

Tunnel

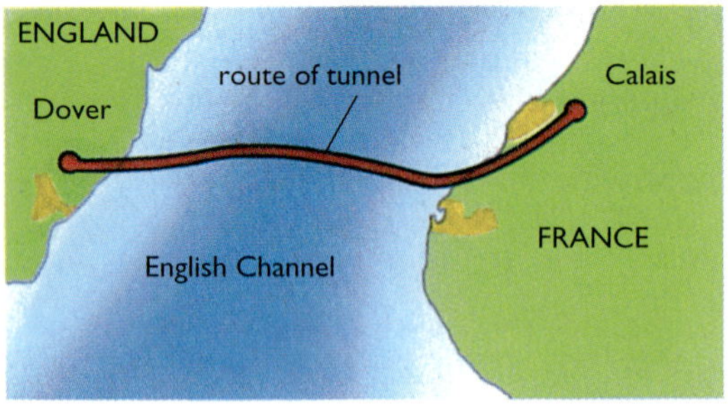

The tunnel linking England and France is nearly 50 km long. The depth of the tunnel below the ocean floor ranges from about 24 m to about 40 m.

Because this tunnel lies under the English Channel, it has been nicknamed the "Chunnel."

The tunnel is actually three tunnels — two railway and one service.

The rail tunnels are 7.5 m across. Trains can carry passengers and freight across the English Channel in about 25 minutes.

The service tunnel is 5 m across. It is used by workers to do repairs, and is also an emergency escape route.

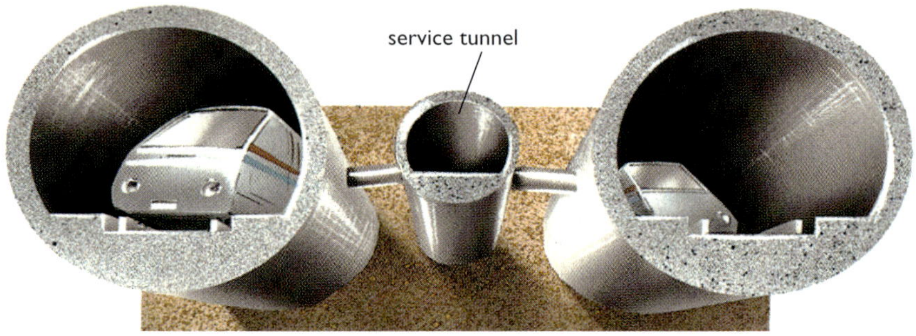

tune (tyūn *or* tūn) **1** a song apart from the words; a melody. **2** the proper pitch: *The piano is out of tune. He can't sing in tune.* **3** adjust to the proper pitch: *to tune a piano or guitar.* **4** make aware of something and able to respond to it: *Tune your heart to the needs of others.*
1, 2 *n.,* 3, 4 *v.,* **tuned, tun·ing.** —**tune′less,** *adj.*
change your tune, change your attitude and way of dealing with something.
tune in, a adjust a radio or TV set to a certain station. **b** pay attention to something and try to understand: *He is tuned in to the problems facing young people.*
tune up, put an engine, etc. into good working order. The process of doing this is a **tune-up.**

tung·sten (tung′stən) a hard, grey metal with a very high melting point. It is a chemical element and is used to make electric light bulb filaments and steel. *n.*

tu·nic (tyū′nik *or* tū′nik) a garment like a very long pullover or short gown, with or without sleeves. The ancient Greek and Roman men wore tunics; today they are worn by girls and women. *n.*

tuning fork (tyū′ning fòrk′) a small steel instrument with two prongs that always makes the same ringing tone when struck. It is used as a standard for tuning a musical instrument.

tun·nel (tun′əl) **1** any underground passageway: *a subway tunnel. Rabbits make tunnels in the earth.*
2 make a tunnel: *The workers are tunnelling under the river.* 1 *n.,* 2 *v.,* **tun·nelled** or **tun·neled, tun·nel·ling** or **tun·nel·ing.**

tu·pik (tū′pik) a tent made of animal skins, traditionally used by the Inuit as a summer home. *n.*

tuque (tūk) a knitted cap, often with a pom-pom. It can be long, like a stocking, or short. *n.*

WORD HISTORY.......tuque

Tuque is a French Canadian variation of the word *toque*, which came originally from the Basque word *tauka*, a kind of hat.

tur·ban (tər′bən) a piece of cloth wound around the head or around a cap, worn by men as part of the dress of certain cultures and religions. *n.*

tur·bine (tər′bīn) an engine or motor containing a wheel with curved blades which is turned by the force of water, steam, or gas. Turbines are used to turn the generators that produce electric power. *n.*

tur·bu·lent (tər′byə lənt) rough or stormy: *turbulent weather, turbulent water.* *adj.*
—**tur′bu·lence,** *n.*

tu·reen (tyə rēn′ *or* tə rēn′) a large, deep serving bowl with a lid, used for soup. *n.*

turf (tərf) **1** the top layer of ground along with the grass growing on it. **2** a piece of this: *We cut some turfs from a field to cover bare spots in our lawn.* **3** land; territory; an area belonging to someone. **4** cover with turf: *They turfed over the bare soil.* 1–3 *n., pl.* **turfs;** 4 *v.*
turf out, *Slang.* force to leave.

tur•key (tər′kē) a large bird with a bald head and tail feathers that can be raised like a fan. Turkeys are raised for their meat. *n., pl.* **tur•keys.**

tur•moil (tər′moil) a violent disturbance; great confusion: *Six robberies in one night put our village in a turmoil.* *n.*

turn (tərn) **1** move or cause to move around like a wheel: *The merry-go-round turned. I turned the crank three times.* **2** a motion like that of a wheel: *At each turn the screw goes in further.* **3** flip; change from one side to the other: *to turn a page* (*v.*). *Give those hamburgers a turn* (*n.*). **4** take or give a new direction: *The road turns to the north here. He turned his steps toward home.* **5** a change of direction: *Make a left turn at the lights.* **6** change so as to become: *She turned pale. The experience turned him into a different person.* A **turning point** is the moment when a major change happens. **7** move to the other side of; go around: *to turn the corner.* **8** a time or chance to do something: *It is his turn to read.* **9** a twist; bend: *Give that rope a few more turns around the tree.* **10** a change in affairs, conditions, or circumstances: *The sick man has taken a turn for the better.* **11** depend: *The success of the picnic turns on the weather.* **12** of leaves, change colour in the fall: *The maples are already turning.* 1, 3, 4, 6, 7, 11, 12 *v.,* 2, 3, 5, 8–10 *n.*
by turns, one after another.
good turn, a favour; a kind deed.
in turn, in proper order.
out of turn, at the wrong time or in a wrong way: *to speak out of turn.*
take turns, play or go one after another in proper order.
to a turn, to just the right degree: *meat done to a turn.*
turn away, a turn your back on someone. **b** send away; not let in: *They had to turn some people away.*
turn down, a refuse: *to turn down an invitation.* **b** make less bright or less loud: *Turn down the TV.* **c** fold or bend downward or put face down.
turn in, a *Informal.* go to bed: *I think I'll turn in now.* **b** hand in or hand over to someone in authority: *Turn in your test papers. The criminal turned himself in to the police.* **c** turn and go in: *Turn in at #54.*
turn loose, set free.
turn off, a shut off; switch off: *Is the tap turned off? Turn off the lights.* **b** make disgusted or uninterested. Something that does this is a **turnoff.**
turn on, a start; switch on; put on. **b** attack unexpectedly: *His dog turned on him.* **c** *Slang.* make or become excited or interested. Something that does this is a **turn-on.**
turn out, a result; end up: *How did the game turn out?* **b** be discovered: *She turned out to be a good president.* **c** end up well: *My cake didn't turn out.* **d** make; produce: *That factory turns out good shoes.* **e** put out; shut off: *Please turn out the light.* **f** come; show up; attend: *Everyone turned out for the rally.* The **turnout** at an event is the number of people who attend. **g** force to leave: *The army finally turned out the invaders.*
turn over, a give; hand over; transfer: *He turned the job over to his assistant.* **b** of an engine, start up.
turn someone's head, make someone too proud.
turn tail and run, run away in fear.
turn to, go to for help or satisfaction: *You are the only person I can turn to. He turned to video games as a way of releasing his frustration.*
turn up, a make louder or brighter. **b** appear: *He didn't turn up until six o'clock.* **c** discover: *to turn up some new information.* **d** fold or bend upward or put face up.

tur•nip (tər′nip) a plant with a large, roundish root used as a vegetable. It is yellowish inside. *n.*

turn•o•ver (tər′nō′vər) **1** a pastry made by placing jam or some other filling on one half of a piece of dough, and then folding the other half over. **2** the rate at which people leave and are replaced: *That company has had a high turnover this year.* *n.*

turn•stile (tərn′stīl′) a barrier at an entrance that lets only one person through at a time. It has a set of horizontal bars on a shaft which turns as someone goes through. *n.*

turn•ta•ble (tərn′tā′bəl) a small round platform that turns: *The diamond rings were displayed on a turntable in the store window.* A record player has a turntable to put the record on. *n.*

tur•pen•tine (tər′pən tīn′) a mixture of oil and resin from various coniferous trees, used to thin paint, clean paintbrushes, and so on. It has a very strong smell and is very poisonous and flammable. *n.*

tur•quoise (tər′koiz) a greenish-blue mineral used as a gem. *n.*

tur•ret (tər′it) a small tower, often on the corner of a building. *n.* **—tur′ret•ed,** *adj.*

tur•tle (tər′təl) a reptile with a hard shell around the main part of its body, which it can pull its head and legs into. Turtles live in fresh water, in salt water, or on land; those living on land are often called **tortoises** (tôr′təsiz). *n.*

tur•tle•neck (tər′təl nek′) a sweater with a high, stretchy, close-fitting collar that is usually folded down at the top. *n.*

a bat	e bed	i bid	o pot	u cup	th thin
ā cake	ē me	ī bite	ō go	ū rude	ᴛʜ then
ä bar	ə about	ər over	ô for	ů put	zh measure

Tus·ca·ro·ra (tus′kə rôr′ə) 1 a First Nations people living in southern Ontario. 2 their language, which belongs to the Iroquoian family. 3 having to do with these people or their language. 1, 2 *n.*, 3 *adj.*

tusk (tusk) a very long, pointed, projecting tooth. Tusks grow as a pair, one on each side of the mouth; elephants, walruses, and wild boars have them. *n.*

tus·sle (tus′əl) a struggle; scuffle; wrestle. *n. or v.*, **tus·sled, tus·sling.**

Tu·tcho·ne (tū chō′nē) 1 a First Nations people living in southern Yukon. 2 their language, which belongs to the Athapascan family. 3 having to do with these people or their language. 1, 2 *n.*, 3 *adj.*

tu·tor (tyū′tər *or* tū′tər) 1 a private teacher: *Gerrard's parents hired a tutor to help him with his math.* 2 teach privately: *Trish was tutored at home during her long illness.* 1 *n.*, 2 *v.*

tu·tu (tū′tū) a short skirt worn by ballet dancers that has many folds of thin, stiff material. It is attached to a tight-fitting top. *n., pl.* **tu·tus.**

tux·e·do (tuk sē′dō) a man's very fancy suit for special occasions: *The groom at the wedding wore a tuxedo.* It is often called a **tux** for short. *n., pl.* **tux·e·dos** or **tux·e·does.**

TV or **T.V.** *abbreviation for* television.

twang (twang) 1 a vibrating sound like the one made by a tight string that is plucked: *The bow made a twang when I shot the arrow.* 2 make or cause to make this sound: *The banjos twanged.* 1 *n.*, 2 *v.* —**twang′y,** *adj.*

tweak (twēk) 1 pinch or twist playfully, not hard: *She tweaked her little brother's ear.* 2 *Informal.* make slight changes to; adjust: *I had to tweak my story here and there before handing it in.* 3 the act of tweaking: *He gave her nose a tweak.* 1, 2 *v.*, 3 *n.*

tweed (twēd) a woollen cloth with a rough surface. Tweed is usually woven with yarns of two or more colours, and is used especially for sports jackets and blazers. *n.*

tweet (twēt) 1 the high-pitched sound made by a small bird; chirp. 2 make this sound or one like it. 1 *n.*, 2 *v.*

tweez·ers (twē′zərz) small pincers for pulling out slivers, picking up small objects, and so on. *pl.n.*

twelve (twelv) one more than eleven; 12. *n. or adj.* —**twelfth,** *adj. or n.*

twen·ty (twen′tē) two times ten; 20. *n., pl.* **twen·ties;** *adj.* —**twen′ti·eth,** *adj. or n.*

twice (twīs) two times: *We sang it twice. You took twice as much.* *adv.*

twid·dle (twid′əl) twirl or play with absent-mindedly: *to twiddle a pencil.* *v.*, **twid·dled, twid·dling.**
twiddle your thumbs, do nothing.

twig (twig) a very small branch of a tree or bush: *Dry twigs are good to start a fire with.* *n.*

twi·light (twī′līt′) 1 the faint light reflected from the sky just before the sun rises and just after it sets. 2 the period during which this light lasts, especially after sunset. *n.*

twin (twin) 1 one of two children born at the same time from the same mother. **Identical twins** are the same sex and look very much alike; **fraternal twins** may be different sexes and may not look alike. 2 one of two matching things. 3 being one of a pair of twins or matching things: *my twin sister.* A **twin bed** is a bed of the standard size for one person. It may be bought with another as a pair. 1, 2 *n.*, 3 *adj.*

twine (twīn) 1 a strong string made of two or more strands twisted together. 2 twist together: *She twined holly branches into wreaths.* 3 wind or wrap around: *The vine twines around the tree.* 1 *n.*, 2, 3 *v.*, **twined, twin·ing.**

twinge (twinj) a sudden, sharp pain: *a twinge of arthritis, a twinge of remorse.* *n.*

twin·kle (twing′kəl) sparkle; gleam; flash: *The stars twinkled (v.). My uncle Ralph has a merry twinkle in his eye (n.).* *n. or v.*, **twin·kled, twin·kling.**

twin·kling (twing′kling) a very short time; instant: *My dog was there in a twinkling when I called.* *n.*

twirl (twərl) 1 turn around fast; spin; whirl. 2 keep twisting or turning something absent-mindedly: *He twirled the ends of his mustache.* 3 a spinning movement: *a twirl in a dance.* 1, 2 *v.*, 3 *n.*

twist (twist) 1 force out of shape or place: *His face was twisted with pain. She twisted her ankle.* 2 turn; wind, especially into a spiral shape by turning one end while the other is held still or is turned in the opposite direction: *She sat nervously twisting her napkin.* 3 wind or weave together: *She twisted flowers into a wreath.* 4 have a winding shape; have many curves and bends: *The path twists in and out among the rocks.* 5 purposely give the wrong meaning to: *Don't twist my words.* 6 the act of twisting or the shape that results. 7 an odd feature or surprising change: *a mental twist. The story ends with a twist.* 1–5 *v.*, 6, 7 *n.*

twist·er (twis′tər) a tornado or whirlwind. *n.*

twitch (twich) **1** move slightly with a quick jerk: *The woman's mouth twitched as if she were about to cry.* **2** a quick, jerky, slight movement. 1 *v.,* 2 *n.*

twit·ter (twit′ər) **1** make repeated chirping sounds: *Birds begin to twitter just before sunrise.* **2** this sound. **3** an excited, trembly condition: *My nerves are in a twitter when I have to sing in public.* 1 *v.,* 2, 3 *n.*

two (tū) one more than one; 2. *adj. or n., pl.* **twos.**
in two, into two parts or pieces: *She broke the cookie in two.*
your two cents' worth, your opinion; your contribution to a discussion.

two–di·men·sion·al (tū′də men′shə nəl) having length and width but no depth; flat. Drawings are two-dimensional; carvings are three-dimensional. *adj.*

two–faced (tū′ fāst′) talking or acting one way with some people and another way with others; dishonest. *adj.*

two–way (tū′ wā′) with movement in both directions: *a two-way street, two-way traffic.* *adj.*

ty·coon (tī kūn′) a very rich and powerful leader in a certain industry or line of business: *a railway tycoon.* *n.*

ty·ing (tī′ing) the present participle of **tie:** *He is tying his shoes.* *v.*

tyke (tīk) *Informal.* a small child. *n.*

type (tīp) **1** a kind or sort: *a new type of engine. I don't like that type of dog.* **2** write using a keyboard: *She typed a letter.* A person who does this is a **typist.** **3** printed letters or figures: *a word in large type.* A particular style of printing is called a **typeface.** **4** a set of small, flat metal pieces, each with a raised, backward letter or figure on it, used in printing. Ink is spread on the pieces and they are stamped onto paper. A **typesetter** is a skilled worker who prepares the type for printing. 1, 3, 4 *n.,* 2 *v.,* **typed, typ·ing.**

type·writ·er (tīp′rī′tər) a machine with keys that you press to print letters and figures on paper. When you press a key, a piece of metal type attached to it strikes on inked ribbon against the paper. *n.*
—type′writ′ten, *adj.*

ty·phoid fever (tī′foid fē′vər) an infectious disease caused by bacteria that enter the body through polluted water, food, or milk. It causes a high fever, headaches, diarrhea, bleeding intestines, and a rash, and can be fatal.

ty·phoon (tī fūn′) a violent tropical windstorm that occurs over the western Pacific Ocean. *n.*

WORD HISTORY........ typhoon

Typhoon is from Chinese *tai fung,* meaning "big wind." But it was influenced by *typhon,* Greek for "whirlwind."

ty·phus (tī′fəs) an infectious disease that causes headaches, chills, high fever, dark red spots on the skin, and extreme weakness. Typhus is carried by lice, fleas, and ticks, and used to occur in epidemics in which many people died. *n.*

typ·i·cal (tip′ə kəl) usual or normal for a certain person or thing; showing the usual characteristics: *The typical Thanksgiving dinner includes turkey. Lateness is typical of Annique.* *adj.*

typ·i·fy (tip′ə fī′) **1** have all the usual characteristics of: *Tom Sawyer typifies the young adventurer.* **2** be a symbol of: *The dove typifies peace.* *v.,* **typ·i·fied, typ·i·fy·ing.**

ty·po (tī′pō) a small mistake made in typing or in setting type: *Darleen noticed a typo right away—"lino" instead of "lion."* The full form is **typographical error** (tī′pə graf′ə kəl er′ər). *n., pl.* **ty·pos.**

T-Rex was over 12 m tall, with sharp teeth and powerful legs — a really terrible lizard.

ty·ran·no·saur·us (tə ran′ə sôr′əs) a huge, meat-eating dinosaur that walked on its two hind legs. It had very short front legs. The full scientific name is **Tyrannosaurus Rex;** it is also called **T-Rex** for short.

ty·rant (tī′rənt) a person who uses power cruelly or unfairly and who has or seeks to have complete control over others. The rule or power of such a person is called **tyranny** (tēr′ə nē). *n.*
—ty·ran′ni·cal (tə ran′ə kəl), *adj.*

Uu

u or **U** (yū) 1 the twenty-first letter of the English alphabet, or any sound that it stands for. The *u* in *run* sounds different from the *u* in *rule.* 2 the twenty-first thing in a list. *n., pl.* **u's** or **U's.**

u·biq·ui·tous (yū bik′wə təs) everywhere, or seeming to be everywhere: *The ads for the new computer system were ubiquitous.* *adj.*

ud·der (ud′ər) the organ that produces milk in a cow or female sheep or goat, etc. It looks like a bag, with nipples for the young to drink from. *n.*

UFO *abbreviation for* **unidentified flying object,** anything seen in the sky that is unknown and might be thought to be a spaceship.

ug·ly (ug′lē) 1 unpleasant to look at or hear: *an ugly house, an ugly voice.* 2 bad, mean, or disgusting: *an ugly task, an ugly temper, ugly language.* *adj.,* **ug·li·er, ug·li·est.** —**ug′li·ness,** *n.*

U.K. *abbreviation for* **United Kingdom,** the country which includes England, Scotland, Wales, and Northern Ireland.

u·ku·le·le (yū′kə lā′lē) a small, guitarlike musical instrument with four strings. *n.*

ul·cer (ul′sər) an open sore found on the skin or on a mucous membrane inside the body, such as in the mouth or stomach. Ulcers are usually quite painful. *n.*

ul·te·ri·or (ul tēr′ē ər) hidden from others: *Watch out; he has an ulterior motive for being so nice.* *adj.*

ul·ti·mate (ul′tə mit) 1 first or last; the furthest away, the furthest back, or the furthest in the future: *the ultimate cause, our ultimate destination.* 2 greatest or best: *the ultimate solution.* *adj.* —**ul′ti·mate·ly,** *adv.*

ul·ti·ma·tum (ul′tə mā′təm) a final demand or offer, with the threat that serious action will be taken if it is rejected: *The lazy player was given an ultimatum: shape up or be dropped from the team.* *n.*

ultra– *a prefix meaning:* 1 beyond, as in *ultraviolet.* 2 extremely, as in *ultra-ambitious, ultramodern.*

ul·tra·son·ic (ul′trə son′ik) of or having to do with sound waves above the range of human hearing: *an ultrasonic dog whistle.* *adj.*

ul·tra·sound (ul′trə sound′) a way of examining tissues inside the body by sending high-frequency sound waves through the skin. The tissues inside bounce the sound waves back, but this echo changes depending on how dense the tissue is. A machine can convert the different returning sound waves into an image on a screen. Ultrasound is often used to check on an unborn baby in a woman's uterus. *n.*

ul·tra·vi·o·let (ul′trə vī′ə lit) having to do with the invisible light rays just beyond the violet part of the colour spectrum. Ultraviolet rays are present in sunlight. You can't see them but they can burn your skin. *adj.*

u·lu (ū′lū) a knife traditionally used by Inuit women, with a crescent-shaped blade and a handle of bone, ivory, or wood that fits the palm. *n.*

um·bi·li·cal cord (um bil′ə kəl kôrd′) a cordlike structure that connects an unborn human being or other animal to its mother so that it can receive food and oxygen from her body. The umbilical cord is attached to the baby's abdomen and the mother's womb, and is cut at birth. Your navel shows where it was attached.

um·brel·la (um brel′ə) a shelter from the rain or sun, made up of a light, round, folding frame of spokes covered with cloth or plastic. You hold it by a handle which sticks down from the centre. *n.*

u·mi·ak (ū′mē ak) a large, flat-bottomed boat made of skins stretched over a wooden frame, moved by paddles. Umiaks are traditionally used by Inuit women. The Inuktitut spelling of the word is **umiaq.** *n.*

um·pire (um′pīr) 1 a person who watches a game and decides whether someone has broken the rules, scored a point, etc.: *The umpire called the ball a foul.* 2 a person chosen to settle a dispute. 3 act as umpire in a game, dispute, etc. This word is often shortened formally to **ump.** 1, 2 *n.,* 3 *v.,* **um·pired, um·pir·ing.**

UN or **U.N.** *abbreviation for* **United Nations,** a worldwide organization to work toward peace and better conditions in all nations.

un– *a prefix meaning:* 1 not, as in *unfair* and *unhappily.* 2 do the opposite of, as in *untie.*

USING WORDS . . . . un-

Un- is the most common prefix in English, and the simplest in meaning. There are hundreds of *un-* words. Most are easy to figure out from the root word, and may not be entered in this dictionary; if you need information about one that is not listed, look up the root word. But a few, such as *unfurl* or *unscathed*, have roots that are rarely or never used alone. Those *un-* words are entered on these pages.

un•ac•count•a•ble (un′ə koun′tə bəl) 1 that cannot be explained: *unaccountable goings-on.* 2 not able to take responsibility: *An insane person is unaccountable for his or her actions.* *adj.*

u•nan•i•mous (yū nan′ə məs) showing complete agreement by everyone: *a unanimous vote. Her teammates were unanimous in rating her the best player.* *adj.* —**u′na•nim′i•ty** (yū′nə nim′ə tē), *n.*

un•as•sum•ing (un′ə sū′ming) modest; not trying to impress people: *The people were delighted by the prince's unassuming manner.* *adj.*

un•at•tend•ed (un′ə ten′did) with no one to take care or be in charge: *Do not leave a child unattended. A campfire left unattended can cause a disaster.* *adj.*

un•a•wares (un′ə werz′) 1 without being expected; by surprise: *The police caught the burglar unawares.* 2 without knowing: *We made the error unawares.* *adv.*

un•be•knownst (un′bi nōnst′) *Informal.* without others knowing: *He arrived unbeknownst to anyone.* *adj.*

un•born (un bôrn′) not yet born; still to come: *unborn generations.* *adj.*

un•bound•ed (un boun′did) limitless; without bounds; very great: *unbounded kindness.* *adj.*

un•bro•ken (un brō′kən) 1 not broken; whole: *There was only one unbroken cup left in the whole set.* 2 continuous; not interrupted: *I had eight hours of unbroken sleep.* 3 not tamed: *an unbroken colt.* *adj.*

un•called–for (un kold′fôr′) not necessary and not proper: *an uncalled-for remark.* *adj.*

un•can•ny (un kan′ē) so unusual that it is almost spooky: *The trees seemed to have uncanny shapes in the half darkness. She has uncanny skill in solving riddles.* *adj.*

un•chart•ed (un chär′tid) not yet mapped: *sailing in uncharted seas.* *adj.*

un•cle (ung′kəl) 1 a brother of a person's father or mother. 2 the husband of a person's aunt. *n.*

un•com•pro•mis•ing (un kom′prə mī′zing) not giving in at all; firm: *His uncompromising attitude makes him hard to deal with sometimes, but it also commands people's respect.* *adj.*

un•con•scious (un kon′shəs) 1 not conscious; not able to feel or think: *He was knocked unconscious when the car struck him.* 2 not aware: *She was unconscious of being followed.* 3 not meant; not intended: *an unconscious insult.* 4 that you feel or believe without even knowing it yourself: *He has an unconscious fear of change.* *adj.*

un•con•sti•tu•tion•al (un′kon′stə tyū′shə nəl *or* un′kon′stə tū′shə nəl) against the constitution; not allowed by the constitution. *adj.*

un•couth (un kūth′) having rude or rough manners. *adj.*

un•daunt•ed (un don′tid) not afraid; not discouraged: *The kitten was undaunted by the size of the Newfoundland dog.* *adj.*

un•de•cid•ed (un′di sī′did) 1 not settled. 2 not having your mind made up. *adj.*

un•der (un′dər) 1 below; beneath: *The book fell under the table* (*prep.*). *The swimmer went under* (*adv.*). 2 below and leading to the other side of: *The road goes under that bridge.* 3 less than: *What can you get for under a dollar?* 4 being affected or led by: *under the new rules, under such terrible conditions. We learned a great deal under her teaching.* 5 included in a particular group or category: *In this library, books on gymnastics are under sports.* 1–5 *prep.,* 1 *adv.*

under– *a prefix meaning:* 1 on the lower side; below, as in *underline, underarm.* 2 lower in rank, as in *undersecretary.* An **underling** is anyone lower in rank. 3 below normal or not enough, as in *underfed, undersized.*

un•der•age (un′dər āj′) not old enough for something. *adj.*

un•der•arm (un′dər ärm′) 1 armpit; the place underneath your arm where it joins your shoulder. 2 having to do with the armpit: *an underarm deodorant, underarm seam.* 3 underhand; with your arm starting low and then moving up: *an underarm throw* (*adj.*). *He threw the ball underarm* (*adv.*). 1 *n.,* 2, 3 *adj.,* 3 *adv.*

a bat	e bed	i bid	o pot	u cup	th thin
ā cake	ē me	ī bite	ō go	ū rude	ᴛʜ then
ä bar	ə about	ər over	ô for	ů put	zh measure

Underground

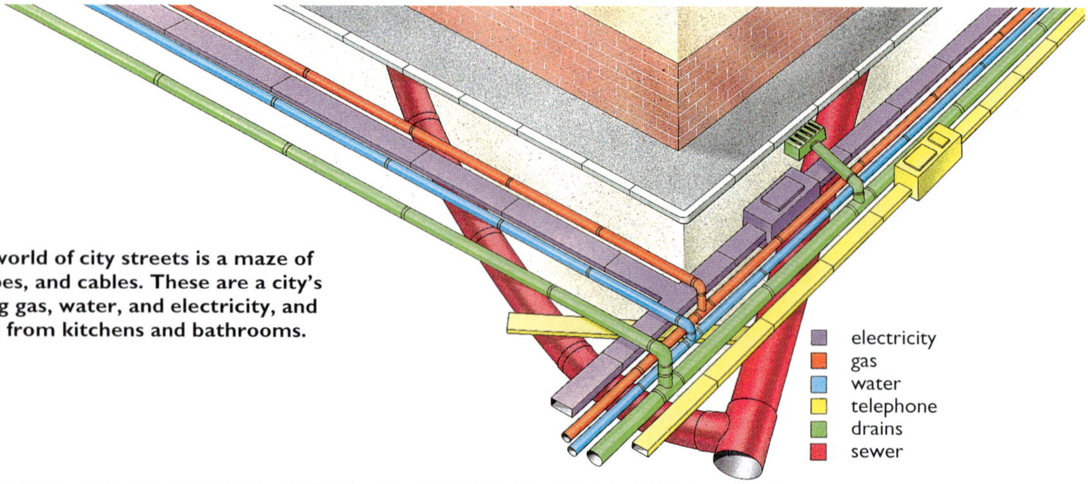

The undergound world of city streets is a maze of drains, sewers, pipes, and cables. These are a city's lifelines — bringing gas, water, and electricity, and taking away waste from kitchens and bathrooms.

un·der·brush (un′dər brush′) bushes and small trees growing at the bottom of the large trees in a forest; undergrowth. *n.*

un·der·clothes (un′dər klōz′ *or* un′dər klōᴛʜz′) clothes worn under your outer clothing; underwear. **Undergarments** are the same thing. *pl.n.*

un·der·cov·er (un′dər kuv′ər) working or done in secret: *The jeweller was an undercover man for the police.* *adj.*

un·der·cur·rent (un′dər kər′ənt) **1** a hidden and sometimes dangerous current that flows under the main current of a river: *Two people were nearly drowned when an undercurrent swept them away.* **2** a feeling that is kept partly hidden: *Although Judith was friendly enough, there was an undercurrent of anger in her manner.* *n.*

un·der·dog (un′dər dog′) someone who is getting the worst of any struggle: *We've been the underdogs for the last few years, but this year our team is going to win.* *n.*

un·der·em·ployed (un′dər em ploid′) working, but in a job that calls for much less skill and training than you have. A computer programmer with a job cleaning offices would be underemployed. *adj.*

un·der·es·ti·mate (un′dər es′tə māt′) rate a person or thing too low; expect too little of: *She lost the match because she underestimated her opponent's skill.* *v.,* **un·der·es·ti·mat·ed, un·der·es·ti·mat·ing.**

un·der·foot (un′dər fu̇t′) **1** under your feet: *The ground underfoot was soft and squishy.* **2** in the way: *That dog is always underfoot.* *adv.*

un·der·go (un′dər gō′) go through; pass through; experience: *The town is undergoing many changes as more and more people move in.* *v.,* **un·der·went, un·der·gone, un·der·go·ing.**

un·der·ground (un′dər ground′) **1** beneath the surface of the ground: *an underground cave* (*adj.*). *Miners work underground* (*adv.*). **2** secret; in hiding or in secrecy: *an underground organization* (*adj.*). *The thieves went underground after the robbery* (*adv.*). **3** a secret organization working against an unpopular government: *The French underground was active during World War II, secretly fighting the Germans who had taken over.* 1, 2 *adj. or adv.,* 3 *n.*

Underground Railroad (un′dər ground′ rāl′rōd′) during the days of slavery in the United States, a secret route used by slaves to escape to freedom in Canada.

un·der·growth (un′dər grōth′) small plants and trees growing at the bottom of the large trees in a forest. *n.*

un·der·hand (un′dər hand′) **1** secret; sly; not open or honest: *an underhand trick.* **Underhanded** is another form for this meaning. **2** with an upward movement of the hand: *an underhand pitch* (*adj.*), *to throw a ball underhand* (*adv.*). 1, 2 *adj.,* 2 *adv.*

un·der·lie (un′dər lī′) be the real cause, meaning, purpose, or feeling behind something, often hidden beneath other things: *an underlying tone of anxiety. Many factors underlie the problem of child poverty.* *v.,* **un·der·lay, un·der·lain, un·der·ly·ing.**

un·der·line (un′dər līn′) **1** draw a line under: *Underline the correct answer.* **2** draw attention to; emphasize: *His speech underlined the importance of co-operation.* **Underscore** has this meaning too. *v.,* **un·der·lined, un·der·lin·ing.**

un·der·mine (un′dər mīn′) **1** dig a hole under or wear away the foundations of: *The cliff was undermined by the waves.* **2** weaken by continually working against: *to undermine a person's efforts. Many severe colds had undermined her health.* *v.,* **un·der·mined, un·der·min·ing.**

un•der•neath (un′dər nēth′) beneath; directly under, so as to be covered: *There's a note underneath your plate (prep.). He wore a T-shirt underneath (adv.).* *prep. or adv.*

un•der•pants (un′dər pants′) a piece of underwear in the form of pants that usually reach just to the tops of your legs. *n.pl.*

un•der•pass (un′dər pas′) a road going under railway tracks or under another road. *n.*

un•der•priv•i•leged (un′dər priv′ə lijd) having fewer advantages than most people have because of poverty. *adj.*

un•der•rate (un′dər rāt′) put too low a value on or give too little importance to. **Undervalue** means the same thing. *v.,* **un•der•rat•ed, un•der•rat•ing.**

un•der•sea (un′dər sē′) beneath the surface of the sea: *an undersea cable (adj.), exploring undersea (adv.).* *adj. or adv.*

un•der•sell (un′dər sel′) **1** sell something at a lower price than someone else. Stores try to undersell each other. **2** make something seem less valuable than it really is: *Ellen tended to undersell her abilities because she was afraid of sounding conceited.* *v.,* **un•der•sold, un•der•sel•ling.**

un•der•shirt (un′dər shərt′) a collarless shirt worn next to the skin under other clothing. *n.*

un•der•side (un′dər sīd′) the surface underneath; the bottom side: *The underside of the stone was covered with ants.* *n.*

un•der•stand (un′dər stand′) **1** get the meaning of something, or see why it matters: *Now I understand your question. People listen but often do not understand.* **2** know well; know how to deal with or how something works: *A good mechanic understands cars.* **3** know by being told or by figuring it out: *I understand that he is leaving town.* **4** expect or believe something without anyone actually saying so: *It is understood that you will come.* **5** be sympathetic; be able to relate to someone's feelings and ideas: *My mother always understands when I am down.* *v.,* **un•der•stood, un•der•stand•ing.**

un•der•stand•ing (un′dər stan′ding) **1** the fact of knowing the meaning or nature of something: *a clear understanding of the problem.* **2** the meaning you get from something: *My understanding of the poem is very different from yours.* **3** intelligence; the ability to learn and know: *Einstein was a person of great understanding.* **4** kind and sympathetic: *an understanding reply.* **5** knowledge of each other's meaning and wishes: *True friendship is based on understanding.* **6** an agreement: *We have come to an understanding.* 1–3, 5, 6 *n.,* 4 *adj.*

un•der•state (un′dər stāt′) describe something so that it seems to be less than it really is: *To call this piece of work "good" would be understating the case—it's absolutely outstanding!* *v.,* **un•der•stat•ed, un•der•stat•ing.** **—un′der•state′ment,** *n.*

un•der•stud•y (un′dər stud′ē) a person who is ready to take an actor's place in an emergency. *n., pl.* **un•der•stud•ies.**

un•der•take (un′dər tāk′) **1** become involved in some project: *Don't undertake what you can't finish.* A project may be called an **undertaking.** **2** agree to do; promise: *I will undertake to feed your dogs while you are away.* *v.,* **un•der•took, un•der•tak•en, un•der•tak•ing.**

un•der•tak•er (un′dər tā′kər) a person who prepares dead bodies for burial and helps take charge of funerals; a funeral director. *n.*

un•der•tone (un′dər tōn′) **1** a low or very quiet tone: *to talk in undertones.* **2** a tint or shade, or a colour seen through other colours: *white with a faint blue undertone. There was an undertone of brown beneath all the gold and crimson of fall.* **3** a quality or feeling beneath the surface: *an undertone of sadness in the celebration.* *n.*

un•der•wa•ter (un′dər wot′ər) below the surface of the water: *underwater plants (adj.). She stayed underwater for two minutes (adv.).* *adj. or adv.*

un•der•wear (un′dər wer′) clothing worn next to the skin, under your outer clothes. **Underclothes** and **undergarments** are the same thing. **Long underwear** is underpants that go all the way down to your ankles, for cold weather. *n.*

un•der•weight (un′dər wāt′) not heavy enough. *adj.*

un•der•went (un′dər went′) the past tense of **undergo:** *Transportation underwent a great change when cars were invented.* *v.*

un•der•whelm (un′dər welm′) *Informal.* be much less than someone expected: *I am a little underwhelmed by the response to our urgent request; only one person has volunteered to help.* *v.* **—un′der•whelm′ing,** *adj.*

un•der•world (un′dər wərld′) **1** the criminal part of society. **2** in ancient myth, the place of the dead. *n.*

un•de•sir•a•ble (un′di zī′rə bəl) **1** not wanted; bad: *Too much TV can have many undesirable results.* **2** a person who is not wanted. 1 *adj.,* 2 *n.*

a bat	e bed	i bid	o pot	u cup	th thin
ā cake	ē me	ī bite	ō go	ü rude	ᴛʜ then
ä bar	ə about	ər over	ô for	ů put	zh measure

un·do (un dū′) 1 unfasten: *to undo a belt.* 2 cancel or reverse: *We shovelled the walk, but a heavy storm undid our work.* 3 ruin. *v.,* **un·did, un·done, un·do·ing.**

un·do·ing (un dū′ing) a cause of ruin: *Bankruptcy was his undoing.* *n.*

un·done (un dun′) 1 not done; not finished: *I left all my homework undone and went to a movie.* 2 the past participle of **undo:** *Your button is undone.* 1 *adj.,* 2 *v.*

un·doubt·ed (un dou′tid) accepted as being certainly true. *adj.* **—un·doubt′ed·ly,** *adv.*

un·due (un dyū′ *or* un dū′) too great or too much; more than is deserved: *A miser gives undue importance to money.* *adj.* **—un·du′ly,** *adv.*

un·earth (un ərth′) 1 dig up: *to unearth a buried city.* 2 discover; find out: *to unearth a plot.* *v.*

un·earth·ly (un ərth′lē) 1 wild; ridiculous: *They woke me at the unearthly hour of 4 a.m.* 2 not of this world; supernatural. *adj.*

un·eas·y (un ē′zē) nervous or tense; anxious: *The whole idea makes me very uneasy.* *adj.,* **un·eas·i·er, un·eas·i·est.** **—un·eas′i·ly,** *adv.* **—un·eas′i·ness,** *n.*

un·em·ployed (un′em ploid′) not having a job; looking for work: *an unemployed person.* *adj.* **—un′em·ploy′ment,** *n.*

un·e·qualled or **un·e·qualed** (un ē′kwəld) greater than any other: *unequalled speed, an unequalled success.* *adj.*

un·err·ing (un er′ing) making no mistakes; exactly right: *He shot spitballs with unerring accuracy.* *adj.*

un·e·vent·ful (un′i vent′fəl) with nothing important or unusual happening: *an uneventful day.* *adj.*

un·fair (un fer′) not fair; dishonest or against the rules; not treating people as they deserve. *adj.*

un·feel·ing (un fē′ling) 1 hard-hearted; cruel: *a cold, unfeeling person.* 2 not able to feel: *numb, unfeeling hands.* *adj.*

un·fin·ished (un fin′isht) 1 not done; not complete: *unfinished homework.* 2 rough; not polished, stained, varnished, or painted: *unfinished furniture.* *adj.*

un·flap·pa·ble (un flap′ə bəl) almost never getting upset. *adj.*

un·flinch·ing (un flin′ching) not drawing back from difficulty, danger, or pain. *adj.*

un·fold (un fōld′) 1 open the folds of; spread out: *to unfold a map.* 2 show, tell, or become clear a little at a time: *to unfold an idea to someone. The story unfolded on the stage.* 3 develop: *Buds unfold into flowers. Events are unfolding as they should.* *v.*

un·fore·seen (un′fər sēn′) not known beforehand; unexpected: *an unforeseen crisis.* *adj.*

un·for·get·ta·ble (un′fər get′ə bəl) that can never be forgotten; memorable: *an unforgettable holiday.* *adj.*

un·for·tu·nate (un fôr′chə nit) 1 bad or sad; to be regretted: *an unfortunate accident.* 2 unlucky; suffering or having trouble: *an unfortunate child.* 3 not suitable; not fitting: *The unfortunate name "Rat Trap" was chosen for the restaurant.* *adj.* **—un·for′tu·nate·ly,** *adv.*

un·found·ed (un foun′did) without any good reason or proof: *an unfounded complaint.* *adj.*

un·furl (un fərl′) spread out; shake out; unfold: *Unfurl the sail. The flag unfurled.* *v.*

un·fur·nished (un fər′nisht) without furniture: *an unfurnished apartment.* *adj.*

un·gain·ly (un gān′lē) awkward; clumsy. *adj.*

un·heard of (un hərd′ uv′) 1 never heard of; completely unknown: *Electric light was unheard of 200 years ago.* 2 outrageous; extreme: *The ticket prices were unheard of.* Either meaning is spelled **unheard-of** if it comes before a noun.

un·heed·ed (un hē′did) disregarded; unnoticed: *Her advice went unheeded.* An **unheeding** person pays no attention. *adj.*

UNICEF (yū′ni sef′) *abbreviation for* **United Nations International Children's Fund.** UNICEF is a branch of the United Nations that works to improve nutrition, health care, and education for children in developing countries. *n.*

u·ni·cel·lu·lar (yü′nə sel′yə lər) consisting of a single cell, such as in an amoeba. *adj.*

People once believed that the horn of a unicorn could be used as an antidote to poison. In medieval times, powder supposed to come from ground unicorn horn could be sold for a very high price.

u·ni·corn (yū′nə kôrn′) an imaginary animal that looks like a horse, but with a single long horn in the middle of its forehead. *n.*

u·ni·cy·cle (yū′nə sī′kəl) a vehicle made up of only a single wheel and a seat, moved by pedals. Unicycles are tricky to balance and steer, and are ridden mostly by acrobats and entertainers. *n.*

un·i·den·ti·fied flying object (un′ī den′tə fīd′ flī′ing ob′jikt) an unknown object seen in the sky that might be thought to be a spaceship. **UFO** is the short form.

u·ni·form (yū′nə fôrm′) **1** the special suit of clothes worn by the members of a certain group such as soldiers, police officers, and nurses. Some schools have their students wear uniforms; members of teams usually wear them too. **2** all alike: *All the bricks have a uniform size.* **3** always the same; not changing: *The earth turns at a uniform speed.* 1 *n.*, 2, 3 *adj.* **—u′ni·form′i·ty,** *n.* **—u′ni·form′ly,** *adv.* **—u′ni·formed′,** *adj.*

u·ni·fy (yū′nə fī′) make or form into one: *Several small states were unified into one nation.* *v.,* **u·ni·fied, u·ni·fy·ing.** **—u′ni·fi·ca′tion,** *n.*

un·ion (yūn′yən) **1** a group of workers joined together to protect and promote their interests. Unions try to make sure workers are well-paid and have good working conditions. A leader or active member of a union is a **unionist.** **2** the act or the result of uniting: *The city of Thunder Bay was formed by the union of Fort William and Port Arthur.* *n.*

Union Jack (yūn′yən jak′) the red, white, and blue flag formed by combining the crosses of St. George, St. Andrew, and St. Patrick. It used to be the flag of Canada and is still part of the flag of some provinces. It is also the flag of the United Kingdom.

u·nique (yū nēk′) **1** different from all others; being the only one of its kind: *Each fingerprint is unique.* **2** *Informal.* rare; unusual: *His style of dress is unique.* *adj.*

USING WORDS ...... unique

In formal English, a thing is either **unique** or it isn't. It can't be *more unique*, *less unique*, or *very unique*. But informally, unique is just a synonym for "unusual," so such expressions are fine. In fact, the same thing has already happened to the words *peculiar* and *singular*.

u·ni·sex (yū′nə seks′) suitable for both males and females: *unisex clothes, a unisex hairstyle.* *adj.*

u·ni·son (yū′nə sən)
in unison, a all together at the same time: *The children shouted "Happy Birthday" in unison.* **b** all voices singing the same notes: *The choir sang the first verse in unison and the second verse in parts.* *n.*

u·nit (yū′nit) **1** one whole single thing or person, especially one of the individual things that make up a group or larger thing: *The body consists of units called cells.* **2** any group of things or persons acting or thought of as one: *the family unit.* **3** a standard amount used in measuring: *A metre is a unit of length; a minute is a unit of time.* *n.*

u·nite (yū nīt′) **1** join together as one unit: *Several firms united to form one big company.* **2** bring together in one place or for one purpose: *All the tennis clubs in Edmonton will unite to plan the provincial tournament. The family was glad to be united again when the mother returned from her travels.* *v.,* **u·nit·ed, u·nit·ing.**

United Empire Loyalist (yū nī′tid em′pīr loi′ə list) any of the people who left the United States for Canada during and after the American Revolution of 1776 because they preferred to remain under British rule.

The United Nations headquarters is in the United States, in New York City. The main building, the Secretariat Building, has become well-known as a symbol of the United Nations.

United Nations (yū nī′tid nā′shənz) a worldwide organization which works to establish world peace and improve conditions in all countries. The United Nations began on October 24, 1945.

u·ni·ty (yū′nə tē) oneness; the fact of being united; harmony or connectedness: *People should live together in unity. Each paragraph must have one key idea to give it unity.* *n., pl.* **u·ni·ties.**

u·ni·ver·sal (yū′nə vər′səl) **1** applying to all the people or things in a certain category: *Food and shelter are universal human needs. Three-sidedness is a universal property of triangles.* **2** existing everywhere: *The law of gravity is universal.* *adj.* **—u′ni·ver′sal·ly,** *adv.*

u·ni·verse (yū′nə vərs′) all physical things that exist, including earth, the stars, and all of space: *Our world is only a small part of the universe.* *n.*

a bat	e bed	i bid	o pot	u cup	th thin
ā cake	ē me	ī bite	ō go	ū rude	ᴛʜ then
ä bar	ə about	ər over	ô for	ů put	zh measure

u·ni·ver·si·ty (yū′nə vėr′sə tē) a place to go after high school for studies leading to a degree. Universities offer advanced courses in general subjects such as literature, history, and science, and also often teach law, medicine, business, etc. *n., pl.* **u·ni·ver·si·ties.**

un·kempt (un kempt′) **1** not combed. **2** generally untidy in your personal appearance. *adj.*

un·known (un nōn′) **1** not known or familiar; not revealed: *an unknown country, for unknown reasons.* **2** a person or thing that is not known or familiar: *The diver descended into the unknown. The main actor in this movie is an unknown.* 1 *adj.,* 2 *n.*

un·lead·ed (un led′id) containing no lead. All cars sold in North America use unleaded gasoline. *adj.*

un·learn (un lėrn′) get rid of a habit, idea, or attitude you have learned. *adj.*

un·less (un les′) except if: *We will go unless it rains.* *conj.*

un·like (un līk′) **1** not similar; different: *The two problems are quite unlike.* **2** different from: *Unlike most birds, the penguin cannot fly.* **3** not typical of: *It is unlike her to be so quiet.* 1 *adj.,* 2, 3 *prep.*

> **USING WORDS . . . . . unlike**
>
> Watch out for dangling **unlike** phrases. Whether the phrase is at the beginning or the end of the sentence, the person or thing that is "unlike X" must be the subject. For example, *Unlike Bess, hospital food actually agreed with Sue* compares Bess to hospital food. To compare Bess with Sue, you'd need to say *Unlike Bess, Sue liked hospital food.*

un·manned (un mand′) with no people present to operate it: *an unmanned spacecraft.* *adj.*

un·nerve (un nėrv′) take away a person's confidence; make nervous or anxious: *Their stares unnerved him.* *v.,* **un·nerved, un·nerv·ing.**

un·num·bered (un num′bərd) **1** too many to count: *There are unnumbered fish in the ocean.* **2** not numbered; not counted: *The pages of this report have been left unnumbered.* *adj.*

un·ob·tru·sive (un′əb trū′səv) not attracting attention; not very noticeable: *If you must enter late, be as unobtrusive as possible so as not to disturb the others.* *adj.*

un·par·al·leled (un per′ə leld′) having no equal; greater than all others: *an unparalleled achievement.* *adj.*

un·prec·e·dent·ed (un pres′ə den′tid) never done before; never known before: *An unprecedented event took place in 1961, when a human being was launched into space.* *adj.*

un·prin·ci·pled (un prin′sə pəld) not caring much about right and wrong: *The unprincipled politician accepted a bribe.* *adj.*

un·ques·tion·a·ble (un kwes′chə nə bəl) beyond dispute or doubt; certain: *It is an unquestionable advantage to know a second language.* *adj.* —**un·ques′tion·a·bly,** *adv.*

un·rav·el (un rav′əl) **1** take apart or come apart into separate threads: *The kitten unravelled my knitting. My mitts are unravelling at the wrist.* **2** make or become clear; untangle: *to unravel a mystery.* *v.,* **un·rav·elled** or **un·rav·eled, un·rav·el·ling** or **un·rav·el·ing.**

un·re·mit·ting (un′ri mit′ing) never stopping or letting up: *After a week of unremitting drizzle, we decided to pack up and go home.* *adj.*

un·rest (un rest′) **1** anger or discontent leading almost to rebellion: *All the unrest in that country has made the government very fragile.* **2** restlessness; a lack of peace and comfort. *n.*

un·ri·valled or **un·ri·valed** (un rī′vəld) with no equal; greater than all others: *unrivalled beauty.* *adj.*

un·ru·ly (un rū′lē) hard to control; disorderly: *an unruly horse, an unruly class, an unruly lock of hair.* *adj.*

un·sa·vour·y or **un·sa·vor·y** (un sā′və rē) bad, or giving a bad impression: *Don't hang around with that unsavoury character.* *adj.*

un·say (un sā′) take back or cancel something you have said. *v.,* **un·said, un·say·ing.**

un·scathed (un skāᴛʜd′) not harmed: *Cameron walked away unscathed from the wreckage of his bike.* *adj.*

> **WORD HISTORY . . . . unscathed**
>
> **Unscathed** comes from a Viking word, *skathi,* meaning "injury." Our word *scathing,* meaning "very hurtful," is from the same source.

un·seat (un sēt′) **1** throw off: *The bronco unseated everyone who tried to ride it.* **2** remove from office: *Our previous MP was unseated in the last election.* *v.*

un·seem·ly (un sēm′lē) not proper: *His unseemly laughter annoyed the rest of the audience.* *adj.*

un·seen (un sēn′) **1** not noticed: *an unseen error.* **2** not visible: *an unseen danger.* *adj.*

un·set·tle (un set′əl) disturb; make or become unstable; shake; weaken: *The shock unsettled his mind.* *v.,* **un·set·tled, un·set·tling.**

un·set·tled (un set′əld) 1 not at peace; restless, discontented, etc. 2 not in proper condition or order: *Our house is still unsettled after our move.* 3 liable to change; uncertain: *unsettled weather.* 4 not yet dealt with or decided: *unsettled bills, an unsettled question.* 5 not inhabited: *Large parts of Canada are still unsettled.* *adj.*

un·sight·ly (un sīt′lē) ugly or unpleasant to look at: *The cluttered room was an unsightly mess.* *adj.*

un·speak·a·ble (un spē′kə bəl) 1 too great for words: *unspeakable joy, an unspeakable loss.* 2 extremely bad; so bad that it can hardly be spoken of: *That was an unspeakable thing to do!* *adj.* —**un·speak′a·bly,** *adv.*

un·strung (un strung′)
come unstrung, become completely unable to cope: *What caused her to come unstrung like that?* *adj.*

un·tapped (un tapt′) 1 not tapped to take out the liquid inside: *untapped maple trees.* 2 not used: *Canada has many untapped natural resources.* *adj.*

un·think·a·ble (un thing′kə bəl) that can hardly be imagined: *A party without her is unthinkable.* *adj.*

un·think·ing (un thing′king) thoughtless; careless: *An unthinking comment can cause a lot of trouble.* *adj.*

unthought of (un thot′ uv′) not yet imagined or considered: *Last year, the very idea of a trip to Europe was unthought of, but we have saved up a lot since then.* This is spelled **unthought-of** before a noun: *unthought-of possibilities.*

un·til (un til′) 1 up to the time or place mentioned: *It was cold from December until April* (*prep.*). *She waited until the sun had set* (*conj.*). 2 before: *She did not leave until morning* (*prep.*). *Don't move until I tell you to* (*conj.*). 3 so long or so far that: *He worked until he was too tired to do more.* 1, 2 *prep.,* 1–3 *conj.*

un·time·ly (un tīm′lē) 1 too early; too soon: *an untimely death.* 2 at a wrong time or season: *Snow in June is untimely.* *adj.*

un·to (un′tū) a formal or poetic word for "to": *Do unto others as you would have them do unto you.* *prep.*

un·told (un tōld′) 1 not told; not revealed: *an untold secret.* 2 too many to count or too great to describe: *untold millions of stars. Wars do untold harm.* *adj.*

un·used (un yūzd′) 1 not presently being used: *an unused room.* 2 never used: *We'll keep the unused paper cups for our next picnic.* *adj.*
unused to (un yūst′tū), not familiar with; not accustomed to: *I am unused to such spicy food.*

un·u·su·al (un yū′zhū əl) not common; rare; different from the ordinary: *We saw a very unusual lamp in the antique shop.* *adj.* —**un·u′su·al·ly,** *adv.*

un·veil (un vāl′) 1 take off the cloth covering a new work of art: *The Governor-General unveiled the new statue on Remembrance Day.* This happens in a formal ceremony called the **unveiling.** 2 reveal any new thing; make public in a showy way: *The city council unveiled a new plan to curb crime.* *v.*

un·war·y (un wer′ē) not cautious enough; not careful: *The pickpocket stole a wallet from the unwary shopper.* *adj.*

un·well (un wel′) sick. *adj.*

un·wield·y (un wēl′dē) hard to handle or manage; bulky, heavy, or having an awkward shape: *The armour worn by knights seems unwieldy to us today.* *adj.*

un·wind (un wīnd′) wind off; take or come off a spool, ball, etc. *v.,* **un·wound, un·wind·ing.**

un·wit·ting (un wit′ing) without knowing or intending: *She was the unwitting cause of her own failure.* *adj.* —**un·wit′ting·ly,** *adv.*

un·wor·thy (un wər′ᴛʜē) 1 not deserving: *Such a silly story is unworthy of belief.* 2 bad; shameful: *unworthy acts.* *adj.*

un·wound (un wound′) the past tense and past participle of **unwind.** *v.*

un·yield·ing (un yēl′ding) firm; not giving in: *The paralyzed man learned to walk again because of his unyielding determination.* *adj.*

up (up) 1 in or to a higher level or condition: *The bird flew up. Gas prices are up. Turn up the heat. She stayed up in the mountains several days.* 2 at or toward the top or the higher end of: *He went up the hill to get a good view. The cat is up the tree.* 3 further north: *They live up in Inuvik.* 4 toward the other end or the more northerly end of: *He lives up the road. Drive up Highway 400.* 5 above the horizon, the ground, or the surface of the water: *The sun is up. The swimmer came up for air.* 6 awake or out of bed: *The children were up at dawn.* 7 totally or thoroughly: *The paper burned up in seconds. My eraser is almost used up. Listen up.* 8 ended; over: *His time is up now.* 9 in or into being or action: *Don't stir up trouble. The engine started up. Our computer crashed, but it's up again now.* 10 *Informal.* in good spirits: *feeling up.* 11 *Informal.* a period of good luck or happiness: *Her life is full of ups and downs.* 12 *Informal.* raise: *They upped the rent.* 1, 3, 5–9 *adv.,* 2, 4 *prep.,* 10 *adj.,* 11 *n.,* 12 *v.,* **upped, up·ping.**

a bat	e bed	i bid	o pot	u cup	th thin
ā cake	ē me	ī bite	ō go	ū rude	ᴛʜ then
à bar	ə about	ər over	ô for	ù put	zh measure

on the up and up, *Informal.* **a** increasing. **b** honest.
up against, facing some kind of difficulty: *Do you know what you're up against?*
up and, *Informal.* suddenly and for no apparent reason: *She up and left.*
up and around, not in bed; active, especially after being sick or injured.
up and down, a everywhere; here and there: *We searched up and down for that thing.* **b** from top to bottom: *He looked me up and down.*
up for, a *Informal.* interested or planning to take part in: *Are you up for the party tomorrow night?* **b** running for or being tried for: *He's up for assault. She's up for president.*
up on, well informed; knowing: *She is up on all the latest computer games.*
up to, a doing or planning: *She is up to some mischief.* **b** able to do: *Do you feel up to such a long hike?* **c** *Informal.* for a certain person to do or decide: *Your story topic is completely up to you.* **d** as much as, as far as, etc.: *Read up to page 40. You can re-use it up to six times.*
what's up? *Informal.* **a** what's going on? **b** what's wrong?

up·beat (up′bēt′) cheerful and hopeful. *adj.*

up·bring·ing (up′bring′ing) a particular way of raising or teaching a child: *a very casual upbringing, a Catholic upbringing.* *n.*

UPC *abbreviation for* **Universal Product Code,** a set of small bars of different widths printed on the outside of a product. It is a code for the price and name of the product and can only be read by an electronic scanner.

up·com·ing (up′kum′ing) next; approaching: *the upcoming school year.* *adj.*

up·date (up′dāt′ *for 1,* up′dāt′ *for 2*) **1** bring up to date: *to update your wardrobe. The files are updated once a month.* **2** the act of bringing something up to date, or the new version that results: *The system performs weekly updates of all files. I bought the update for that computer program.* 1 *v.,* **up·dat·ed, up·dat·ing;** 2 *n.*

up·draft (up′draft′) an upward flow of air or other gas: *The eagle soared on an updraft.* *n.*

up·grade (up grād′ *for 1 and 2,* up′grād′ *for 3 and 4*) **1** improve the quality or performance of, often by adding or replacing something: *to upgrade a computer hard drive.* **2** promote to a higher position: *He's been upgraded to manager status.* **3** something that improves or is improved: *One recent upgrade to the family computer was a better sound card.* **4** an upward slope or hill. 1, 2 *v.,* **up·grad·ed, up·grad·ing;** 3, 4 *n.*
on the upgrade, rising; improving.

up·heav·al (up hē′vəl) a great disturbance: *Geologists say that the Rocky Mountains were formed by an upheaval of the earth's crust. The sale of the family business caused a great upheaval.* *n.*

up·hill (up′hil′) **1** up the slope of a hill; upward: *We walked uphill.* **2** sloping or going up: *an uphill trek. It is an uphill road all the way.* **3** difficult: *an uphill fight.* 1 *adv.,* 2, 3 *adj.*

up·hold (up hōld′) **1** support; agree that something was right: *The principal upheld the teacher's decision.* **2** defend; keep from being dishonoured: *We must uphold the rights of children worldwide.* *v.,* **up·held, up·hold·ing.**

up·hol·ster (up hōl′stər) provide furniture with coverings, cushions, springs, stuffing, etc. *v.*

up·hol·ster·y (up hōl′stə rē) **1** the coverings, stuffing, padding, etc. for furniture. **2** the business of stuffing and covering furniture. *n.*

up·keep (up′kēp′) maintenance; the work or the cost of keeping something in good repair: *the upkeep of a house.* *n.*

up·land (up′lənd *or* up′land′) **1** Often, **uplands,** *pl.* high land. **2** having to do with high land: *upland meadow, upland flowers.* 1 *n.,* 2 *adj.*

up·lift (up lift′ *for 1 and 2,* up′lift′ *for 3*) **1** lift up; raise: *an uplifted hand.* **2** encourage; boost mentally, socially, or morally: *Sung Li's courage and spirit uplifted us all.* **3** encouragement; a mental, social, or moral boost: *Good music gives her an uplift when she is discouraged.* 1, 2 *v.,* 3 *n.*

up·on (ə pon′) a formal or poetic word for "on": *Snow lay upon the ground.* *prep.*

up·per (up′ər) higher: *your upper lip, the upper floor, the upper range of a singer's voice.* *adj.*
upper hand, control; advantage: *During the first two periods, the visiting team had the upper hand.*

Upper Canada (up′ər kan′ə də) the name used for Ontario before 1841. Upper Canada was farther up the St. Lawrence River than Lower Canada.

upper case (up′ər kās′) capital letters. For example, the word *cat* printed in upper case would be *CAT.* —**up′per-case′**, *adj.*

WORD HISTORY.......upper case

Typesetters used to have two containers, one above the other, for the little pieces of type — that is, the bits of metal with the letters carved on them. The capital letters were in the upper tray or case, so they became the **upper case** letters.

Upper House (up′ər hous′) in a system of government where two separate branches are involved in lawmaking, the branch that has fewer members. In some countries, members of the Upper House are appointed, as in Canada; in others they are elected, as in the United States. The Upper House of the Canadian Parliament is called the **Senate. Upper Chamber** is the same thing.

Upper Lakes (up′ər lāks′) the most northerly of the Great Lakes; Lake Superior and Lake Huron and, sometimes, Lake Michigan.

up·per·most (up′ər mōst′) **1** highest. **2** with the most importance, force, or influence: *The safety of her children was uppermost in the mother's mind.* *adj. or adv.*

up·pi·ty (up′i tē) *Informal.* snobbish; acting as if you are better or more important than others. *adj.*

up·raise (up rāz′) raise; lift up: *upraised eyes.* *v.,* **up·raised, up·rais·ing.**

up·right (up′rīt′) **1** standing up straight; vertical: *an upright post. Hold yourself upright.* In an **upright piano,** the strings are vertical. **2** something standing up straight; a vertical part or piece: *The boards for the fence were nailed across the uprights.* **3** good; honest: *an upright citizen.* 1, 3 *adj.,* 2 *n.* —**up′right′ness,** *n.*

up·ris·ing (up′rī′ziŋ) a revolt; rebellion: *The revolution began with small uprisings in several towns.* *n.*

up·riv·er (up′riv′ər) toward the source or higher part of a river: *to paddle upriver (adv.), an upriver village (adj.).* *adj. or adv.*

up·roar (up′rôr′) **1** a noisy or violent disturbance: *There was an uproar when the lion escaped from the zoo.* **2** a fierce protest against something: *The prime minister's announcement caused an uproar.* *n.*

up·root (up rūt′) **1** tear up the roots of: *The storm uprooted many trees.* **2** force out of a settled position: *Famine uprooted many Irish families from their homes during the 1840s.* *v.*

up·scale (up′skāl′) posh; fancy, rich, or expensive: *an upscale neighbourhood, an upscale restaurant.* *adj.*

up·set (up set′ *for 1 to 5,* up′set′ *for 6*) **1** tip over; overturn: *He upset the milk pitcher.* **2** overthrow; defeat: *The rain upset our plans.* **3** disturb greatly; make angry, shocked, or worried: *The bad news upset him so much that he couldn't eat.* **4** cause to feel sick: *So much candy will upset your stomach.* **5** disturbed, sick, or defeated: *an upset stomach.* **6** the fact of being disturbed, defeated, or sickened: *to cause an upset in the family, tablets to relieve stomach upset.* 1, 4 *v.,* **up·set, up·set·ting;** 5 *adj.,* 6 *n.*

up·shot (up′shot′) **1** conclusion; result: *The upshot of all the delays was that we had to cancel the program.* **2** the main meaning of a message: *He rambled on for quite a while, but the upshot was that he didn't want to come.* *n.*

up·side (up′sīd′) **1** the advantage; the good part: *The blizzard caused a lot of trouble, but the upside was that we got two days off school!* **2** the upper side. *n.*
upside down, a having at the bottom what should be on top: *The slice of bread and butter fell upside down on the floor.* **b** in or into complete confusion: *The children turned the house upside down.* The form before a noun is **upside-down:** *upside-down cake.*

up·stairs (up′sterz′) **1** up the stairs: *The boy ran upstairs.* **2** on an upper floor: *She lives upstairs (adv.). There's a phone in the upstairs hall (adj.).* **3** the upper storey or storeys: *That small cottage has no upstairs.* 1, 2 *adv.,* 2 *adj.,* 3 *n.*

up·stream (up′strēm′) against the current of a stream; up toward the starting point of a stream: *It is hard to swim upstream (adv.). They stopped at an upstream camping site (adj.).* *adv. or adj.*

up·take (up′tāk′)
quick on the uptake, quick to understand and respond. *n.*

up·tight (up′tīt′) **1** angry, worried, or tense about something: *Don't get uptight; I know what I'm doing.* **2** easily worried or made angry. Uptight people have a lot of rules and are very concerned about details. *adj.*

up–to–date (up′tə dāt′) including or using the latest information, styles, and methods: *an up-to-date textbook, an up-to-date wardrobe.* *adj.*

USING WORDS . . . . . up to date

Up to date, like any other phrase that can be used as an adjective, has hyphens only if it is placed before the noun: *up-to-date methods*. Otherwise, write it as three words: *This report is not up to date.*

up·turn (up′ tərn′ *for 1,* up′tərn′ *for 2 and 3*) **1** turn upward: *their upturned faces.* **2** an upward turn: *The airplane made a sudden upturn to avoid the mountain.* **3** an improvement or increase: *Her business has taken an upturn.* 1 *v.,* 2, 3 *n.*

a bat	e bed	i bid	o pot	u cup	th thin
ā cake	ē me	ī bite	ō go	ū rude	ᴛʜ then
ä bar	ə about	ər over	ȯ for	u̇ put	zh measure

up·ward (up′wərd) 1 toward a higher place: *an upward course, an upward flight (adj.). She climbed upward till she reached the apple (adv.).* 2 above; more: *Children of twelve years and upward must pay full fare.* **Upwards** is another form of this word. 1, 2 *adv.,* 1 *adj.*
upwards of, more than: *Repairs will cost upwards of $900.*

u·ra·ni·um (yū rā′nē əm) a heavy, white, radioactive metal that is a chemical element. Uranium is a source of atomic energy. *n.*

U·ra·nus (yə rā′nəs *or* yūr′ə nəs) the third largest planet of the solar system, seventh in order from the sun. It has rings like Saturn, and many moons. *n.* ▶ See Appendix.

ur·ban (ər′bən) having to do with cities or towns: *the urban population, urban planning.* *adj.*

ur·ban·i·za·tion (ər′bən īz ā′shən) the process in which people move away from rural areas to live and work in urban areas. *n.*

ur·chin (ər′chin) a small, wild or mischievous child. *n.*

urge (ərj) 1 force or push; encourage or try to persuade: *The rider urged his horse onward with his spurs. She urged us to stay longer.* 2 a driving force or impulse; a strong desire: *The urge to travel took her to many distant places.* 1 *v.,* **urged, urg·ing;** 2 *n.*

ur·gent (ər′jənt) calling for immediate action or attention; pressing: *an urgent need for medical help, an urgent message.* *adj.* **—ur′gen·cy,** *n.*

u·rine (yūr′ən) the liquid produced by your kidneys to carry away wastes. It goes from your kidneys to your bladder, and then out of your body when you **urinate.** *n.* **—u′ri·na′tion,** *n.*

This glass scent bottle made in the shape of an urn was made around 1000 BCE.

urn (ərn) 1 a large coffee pot with a tap. 2 a large, heavy vase. *n.*

U.S.A. or **USA** *abbreviation for* **United States of America.** It is often shortened to **U.S.** or **US.**

us·age (yū′sij) 1 a way of using; treatment: *This car had rough usage.* 2 the accepted way of using words. 3 an old word for "habit" or "custom." *n.*

use (yūz *for 1–3, 7,* yūs *for 4–6*) 1 put into action or service: *We use our legs in walking. We use spoons to eat soup.* 2 eat, drink, etc. as a habit: *He does not use alcohol.* 3 take advantage of someone; treat someone like a tool: *He's not really her friend; he's just using her to impress people.* 4 the fact or manner of using: *the use of tools, a poor use of time.* 5 the purpose or point of a thing: *to find a new use for something. That thing is of no practical use. There's no use in arguing!* 6 the power, right, or privilege of using: *They gave him the use of their boat. She has lost the use of her right arm.* 7 an old word for "treat": *Use others as you would have them use you.* 1–3, 7 *v.,* **used, us·ing;** 4–6 *n.* **—us′a·ble** (yū′zə bəl), *adj.* **—us′er,** *n.*
have no use for, dislike: *We have no use for cheaters here.*
in use, being used. The opposite is **out of use.**
used to (yūst′ tū), **a** accustomed to: *Inuit are used to cold weather.* **b** formerly did: *I used to go to a different school before we moved.*
use up, use until it is all gone: *to use up all the money.*

> **USING WORDS . . . . . . used to**
>
> The expression is **used to,** not "use to," in sentences like: *We used to play tag in the park* and *I'm not used to such heat.*

used (yūzd) not new; that has belonged to someone else before: *a used car.* *adj.*

use·ful (yūs′fəl) good for some purpose; helpful: *This little pocketknife is very useful; it includes a screwdriver, scissors, and can opener.* The opposite of useful is **useless.** *adj.*

u·ser–friend·ly (yū′zər frend′lē) easy to use: *user-friendly software, a user-friendly manual.* *adj.*

ush·er (ush′ər) 1 a person who shows people to their seats in a church, theatre, etc. 2 show someone to a seat, an entrance or exit, etc.: *The host ushered his visitors to the door.* 1 *n.,* 2 *v.*

U.S.S.R. or **USSR** *abbreviation for* **Union of Soviet Socialist Republics.** It was once a huge, powerful communist country made up of 15 different nations in eastern Europe and northern Asia, including Russia. It broke up in 1992.

u•su•al (yū′zhū əl) common; normal; ordinary: *Snow is usual in most of Canada during winter.* *adj.* —**u′su•al•ly,** *adv.*
as usual, in the usual way, at the usual time or place, etc.

u•ten•sil (yū ten′səl) an everyday tool. Ladles and peelers are kitchen utensils; pens and pencils are writing utensils. *n.*

u•ter•us (yū′tə rəs) a muscular organ inside the body of a woman or female mammal that holds and nourishes a baby until birth. It is normally the size of a small pear but stretches as the baby grows. **Womb** is another word for it. *n., pl.* **u•ter•i** (yū′tə rī′ *or* yū′tə rē′).

u•til•i•ty (yū til′ə tē) **1** a company that supplies the public with a needed product or service such as natural gas, electricity, a phone system, or clean water. **2** practical usefulness: *The coat isn't very warm; she bought it more for its beauty than for its utility.* A **utility vehicle** is one used for carrying loads or equipment, such as a van or pickup truck. *n., pl.* **u•til•i•ties.**

u•ti•lize (yū′tə līz′) a formal or scientific word for "use." *v.,* **u•ti•lized, u•ti•liz•ing.**

ut•most (ut′mōst′) **1** greatest, highest, farthest, etc.; most extreme: *Sunshine is of the utmost importance to health. She walked to the utmost edge of the cliff.* **2** the extreme limit; the most that is possible: *He enjoyed himself to the utmost at camp. I will do my utmost to help you.* **Uttermost** has the same meanings. 1 *adj.,* 2 *n.*

ut•ter[1] (ut′ər) complete; total; absolute: *utter surprise, utter darkness.* *adj.* —**ut′ter•ly,** *adv.*

ut•ter[2] (ut′ər) speak or make other sounds with your mouth: *She uttered her ideas boldly. He uttered a cry of pain.* *v.* —**ut′ter•ance,** *n.*

U–turn (yū′ tərn′) a complete change in direction, especially while driving, so that you end up headed back the way you came: *Dad remembered he'd forgotten the disk and made a U-turn right in the middle of traffic.* *n.*

UV short for **ultraviolet,** having to do with the invisible light waves just beyond the violet part of the colour spectrum. UV rays can hurt your skin; the **UV index** tells you how great the danger of sunburn is on a certain day. *adj.*

Vv

v or **V** (vē) 1 the twenty-second letter of the English alphabet, or the sound that it stands for. *V* occurs twice in *vivid.* 2 the twenty-second thing in a list. 3 the Roman numeral for 5. *n., pl.* **v's** or **V's.**

va•cant (vā′kənt) 1 empty; not occupied or filled: *a vacant chair, a vacant house, a vacant space.* An empty room or apartment or an unfilled job position is a **vacancy.** 2 empty of thought or intelligence: *a vacant smile. adj.*

va•cate (vā kāt′ *or* vā′kāt) go away and leave a place empty: *They will vacate the house at the end of the month. v.,* **va•cat•ed, va•cat•ing.**

va•ca•tion (vā kā′shən *or* və kā′shən) 1 a time off work or school that lasts several days or more, often used for travelling: *She spent her vacation at the family cottage on Lake Erie.* 2 take a vacation: *We vacationed in P.E.I.* 1 *n.,* 2 *v.*

vac•ci•nate (vak′sə nāt′) protect from disease by giving the person a **vaccine,** a liquid made from weakened viruses of the disease. People can be vaccinated by mouth or by needle. *v.,* **vac•ci•nat•ed, vac•ci•nat•ing.** **—vac′ci•na′tion,** *n.*

vac•u•um (vak′yūm *or* vak′yəm) 1 a space with nothing at all in it, not even air. 2 clean with a **vacuum cleaner,** a machine that sucks up dirt: *My brother vacuumed the rugs yesterday.* 1 *n.,* 2 *v.*
live in a vacuum, live shut off from all outside influences: *Everyone has to deal with peer pressure—none of us lives in a vacuum.*

vag•a•bond (vag′ə bond′) 1 a wanderer; a person with no roots or settled home. 2 wandering: *to lead a vagabond life.* 1 *n.,* 2 *adj.*

va•gi•na (və jī′nə) the passageway in the body of a girl or woman that leads from the uterus to the outside. A baby that is being born passes through it; so does the blood that flows out during menstruation. *n.*

va•grant (vā′grənt) 1 a homeless person who lives by begging. 2 homeless. 1 *n.,* 2 *adj.* **—vag′ran•cy,** *n.*

vague (vāg) not definite or clear: *In a fog everything looks vague. His vague statement confused them. adj.,* **va•guer, va•guest.**

vain (vān) 1 too interested in yourself; always wanting to be noticed and complimented. 2 useless; unsuccessful: *I made vain attempts to reach her by telephone.* 3 meaningless or worthless; empty: *a vain boast. adj.* **—vain′ly,** *adv.*
in vain, without results or success: *The drowning man shouted in vain, for no one was near.*

> **CONFUSABLES .... vain**
>
> **vain** means "proud": *That boy is vain about his looks.*
>
> A **vane** is a device to show the way the wind is blowing: *There is a weather vane on top of the barn.*
>
> A **vein** is a tube carrying blood through your body: *Blood travels through your veins to your heart.*

vale (vāl) a poetic word for "valley." *n.*

val•e•dic•to•ri•an (val′ə dik tô r′ē ən) a student who is chosen to give a speech on behalf of his or her classmates during their graduation ceremony. The speech is called a **valedictory address.** *n.*

val•en•tine (val′ən tīn′) 1 a greeting card or small gift sent or given on **Valentine's Day,** February 14. 2 a sweetheart chosen on this day. *n.*

val•et (val ā′ *or* val′ā) a servant or a hotel worker who gives personal service and takes care of the cleaning and pressing of clothes. **Valet parking** is the service of parking guest's cars for them and bringing the car to the door again when the person leaves. *n.*

val•i•ant (val′y ənt) brave; courageous: *a valiant soldier, a valiant effort. adj.*

val•id (val′id) 1 supported by facts or authority; sound; acceptable: *a valid excuse.* 2 having force under the law: *a valid passport, a valid contract. adj.* **—va•lid′i•ty** (və lid′ə tē), *n.*

val•i•date (val′ə dāt′) 1 have something checked and put in order by the proper authorities: *We had to validate our passports before we left.* 2 show that something is right: *The results of the experiment validated our idea. v.,* **val•i•dat•ed, val•i•dat•ing.** **—val′i•da′tion,** *n.*

val•ley (val′ē) 1 low land between hills or mountains. Most large valleys have rivers running through them. 2 a wide region drained by a great river system: *the Fraser Valley. n., pl.* **val•leys.**

val•our or **val•or** (val′ər) bravery; courage. *n.*

val•u•a•ble (val′yə bəl) 1 having great value; worth a great deal: *valuable information, a valuable friend, a valuable ring. She has a valuable stamp collection.* 2 **valuables,** *pl.* things that are worth a great deal: *She keeps her jewellery and other valuables in a safe.* 1 *adj.,* 2 *n.*

val•ue (val′yū) 1 what makes a thing worthwhile, useful, or important: *the value of education, the value of milk as a food.* 2 how much a thing is worth; the proper price: *They bought the house for less than its value.* 3 rate at a certain value or price; estimate the worth of: *The land is valued at $50 000.* 4 think highly of; consider as worthwhile: *We value your suggestions.* 5 **values,** *pl.* beliefs about what is really important in life, which guide a person's choices and behaviour. 6 a bargain: *Brand-name jeans for $18—a great value!* 1, 2, 5, 6 *n.,* 3, 4 *v.,* **val•ued, val•u•ing.** —**val′ue•less,** *adj.*

valve (valv) 1 a movable part that controls the flow of a liquid or gas through a pipe by opening and closing the passage. A tap is one kind of valve; the valves of the heart control the flow of blood into and out of the heart. 2 one of the halves of the shell of a sea animal such as the oyster. *n.*

The common vampire bat has such a narrow throat that it cannot swallow solid food, only liquids. It makes a razor cut with its sharp teeth, and sucks some blood from its prey.

vam•pire (vam′pīr) 1 an imaginary creature that sucks people's blood. It is supposed to be a dead person that comes back to life at night. In the famous story, Dracula is a vampire. 2 a person who ruthlessly takes advantage of others. 3 a large bat of Central and South America that lives by sucking blood from animals. *n.*

van (van) 1 a vehicle like a small bus with side and rear doors, for carrying goods or passengers. The full name is **minivan.** 2 a closed-in truck for moving furniture, etc. *n.*

van•dal (van′dəl) a person who destroys or damages things on purpose and for no good reason. *n.* —**van′dal•ism′,** *n.* —**van′dal•ize′,** *v.*

vane (vān) 1 an object attached to the outside of a building to show which way the wind is blowing. 2 a blade, wing, or similar wide, flat part attached to a turning wheel or shaft. The vanes of a windmill are turned by the wind. *n.*

va•nil•la (və nil′ə) a sweet food flavouring and fragrance originally made from the beanlike pods of a Central American orchid plant of the same name. It is now often made artificially. *n.*

van•ish (van′ish) disappear completely, especially suddenly: *Her fears vanished at the sound of her parents' voices.* *v.*

van•i•ty (van′ə tē) 1 too much interest in yourself; a desire to be noticed and complimented all the time. 2 a lack of real value, purpose, or meaning. 3 a table or built-in counter with a mirror, in a bathroom or bedroom: *She put on her make-up in front of the vanity.* *n., pl.* **van•i•ties.**

vanity plate, a vehicle licence plate with a combination of letters or numbers specially chosen by the owner, sometimes with a special design, team logo, etc. added. Often the letters and numbers form a message.

van•quish (vang′kwish) conquer; defeat; overcome. *v.*

van•tage point (van′tij point′) 1 a position that gives you a view of something: *The second-floor window was a good vantage point for watching the parade.* 2 a person's way of looking at or thinking about something: *From Cassie's vantage point there was nothing funny about the joke.*

va•por•ize (vā′pə rīz′) change from a solid or liquid to a vapour: *The spilled gasoline vaporized quickly in the sun.* *v.,* **va•por•ized, va•por•iz•ing.** —**va′por•iz′er,** *n.*

va•pour or **va•por** (vā′pər) 1 very fine droplets of moisture that can be seen in the air as a fog or mist. You see it when you boil water or breathe outside in cold weather. 2 a gas formed from a substance that is usually a liquid or a solid: *We could smell the gasoline vapour as the gas tank of the car was being filled.* *n.*

var•i•a•ble (ver′ē ə bəl) 1 likely to change; uncertain: *variable weather conditions.* 2 that can be changed or adjusted: *This curtain rod is of variable length.* 3 something that can change: *Temperature and rainfall are variables.* In a scientific experiment, certain variables must be controlled. For example, if you are trying to find out how long it takes for sugar to dissolve in water, the variables are the amount of sugar, the amount of water, and the water temperature; you would change only one at a time to see how it affects the result. 1, 2 *adj.,* 3 *n.*

a bat	e bed	i bid	o pot	u cup	th thin
ā cake	ē me	ī bite	ō go	ū rude	ᴛʜ then
ä bar	ə about	ər over	ô for	ů put	zh measure

Vegetables

What we eat as vegetables come from different parts of plants. Vegetables can be
- **bulbs (garlic)**
- **flowers (broccoli)**
- **fruits (tomato)**
- **leaves (cabbage)**
- **roots (turnip)**
- **seeds (pea)**
- **stems (asparagus)**
- **tubers (potato).**

var•i•ant (ver′ē ənt) 1 a slightly different form or version: *We ended up using a variant of our original plan.* 2 different: *"Color" is a variant spelling of "colour."* 1 *n.,* 2 *adj.*

var•i•a•tion (ver′ē ā′shən) 1 a change: *There has been no variation in the temperature since yesterday.* 2 a different or changed form: *There are many variations of the fairy tale "Hansel and Gretel."* *n.*

var•ied (ver′ēd) of different kinds; having variety: *a varied assortment of candies.* *adj.*

va•ri•e•ty (və rī′ə tē) 1 freedom from sameness; refreshing change or difference: *Variety is the spice of life.* 2 a number of different kinds: *This shop has a variety of toys.* A **variety store** is a small store that sells a little of everything, such as groceries, books, toys, cards, small hardware, candy, gifts, drugs, etc. 3 a kind or sort: *Which variety of cake would you like?* *n., pl.* **va•ri•e•ties.**

var•i•ous (ver′ē əs) 1 several; many: *I've seen him various times but have never really spoken to him.* 2 different from one another: *Theories about pet training are many and various.* *adj.*

var•nish (vȧr′nish) 1 a clear liquid that is painted on wood and hardens into a smooth, shiny, protective coating. 2 put varnish on. 1 *n.,* 2 *v.*

var•y (ver′ē) 1 change; make or become different: *The driver can vary the speed of an automobile. The weather varies.* 2 be different from each other: *Stars vary in brightness.* *v.,* **var•ied, var•y•ing.**

vase (vāz, vȧz, *or* voz) a container used for decoration or for holding flowers. *n.*

vas•sal (vas′əl) in the Middle Ages, someone who was allowed to live under the protection of a lord or lady on his or her land. In return, the vassal promised to work and fight for the lord or lady. *n.*

vast (vast) extremely large; immense: *vast deserts. A billion dollars is a vast amount of money.* *adj.* **—vast′ly,** *adv.* **—vast′ness,** *n.*

vat (vat) a large container for liquids: *a vat of dye.* *n.*

vault[1] (volt) 1 an arched roof or ceiling. The **vault of heaven** means the sky. 2 make in the form of a vault: *The roof was vaulted.* 3 a specially protected room for safely storing valuable things. Vaults often have steel walls, ceiling, and floor and have very secure locks. 4 an underground burial room. 1, 3, 4 *n.,* 2 *v.*

vault[2] (volt) 1 to jump over by using your hands or a pole: *He vaulted the fence.* 2 a jump like this. 1 *v.,* 2 *n.*

VCR *abbreviation for* video cassette recorder, a machine for recording and playing videos.

veal (vēl) the flesh of a calf, used for food: *a veal chop.* *n.*

Ve•das (vā′dəz) the most ancient holy writings of Hinduism. *pl.n.*

veer (vēr) turn suddenly or sharply: *The wind veered to the south. The talk veered away from that touchy subject.* *v.*

veg•e•ta•ble (vej′tə bəl) 1 a part of a plant, such as the leaves, seeds, roots, or sometimes the fruit, used for food and usually eaten with the main part of the meal. Carrots, peas, tomatoes, and cabbage are vegetables. **Veggies** (vej′ēz) is an informal short form. 2 made from or having to do with plants: *the vegetable kingdom, vegetable oil.* Plant life in general is called **vegetation** (vej′ə tā′shən). 1 *n.,* 2 *adj.*

veg•e•tar•i•an (vej′ə ter′ē ən) 1 a person who eats food from plants but no meat of any kind. One who also eats no animal products such as cheese or eggs is a **vegan** (vej′ən *or* vē′gən). 2 having to do with this eating pattern: *a vegetarian diet.* 1 *n.,* 2 *adj.*

ve·he·ment (vē′ə mənt) having or showing strong feeling: *a vehement denial.* *adj.* —**ve′he·mence,** *n.*

ve·hi·cle (vē′ə kəl) 1 anything used to carry goods or people, especially something used on land. Cars, buses, trains, sleds, bicycles, and spacecraft are all vehicles. 2 anything thought of as a carrier for something else: *Language is the vehicle of thought.* *n.*

veil (vāl) 1 a piece of very thin material worn by a woman to protect or hide her face, or for decoration. 2 anything that screens or hides: *A veil of clouds hid the sun.* 3 cover with a veil: *The bride was veiled. Fog veiled the city.* 1, 2 *n.,* 3 *v.*

vein (vān) 1 one of the blood vessels or tubes that carry blood to the heart from all parts of the body. 2 one of the bundles of tubes and fibres that carry food and water through a leaf and form its main framework. 3 a rib of an insect's wing. 4 a crack or seam in rock, filled with a different mineral: *a vein of copper.* 5 a streak of different colour in wood or marble. 6 a certain tone or attitude in speech, behaviour, writing, etc.: *There is a vein of humour in these poems. If you continue in this vein you will start to lose friends.* *n.*

Vel·cro (vel′krō) *a trademark for* a type of fastener made up of two nylon strips or patches, one covered with tiny hooks and the other with loops. The fastener is closed by pressing the two surfaces together so that they lock, and opened by peeling them apart. *n.*

ve·loc·i·ty (və los′ə tē) speed; the rate of motion: *The velocity of light is nearly 300 000 km/s.* *n., pl.* **ve·loc·i·ties.**

vel·vet (vel′vit) cloth with a thick, soft, very fine fuzz on the surface, so smooth that it is almost shiny. **Velveteen** and **velour** (və lūr′) are similar types of cloth. *n.* —**vel′vet·y,** *adj.*

vend (vend) sell. A **vending machine** is one you put coins in to get candy, sandwiches, stamps, and so on. *v.* —**ven′dor,** *n.*

ve·neer (və nēr′) 1 a thin layer of fine wood or other material covering something cheaper and less attractive such as plywood. 2 cover in this way. 3 an outward appearance that hides the real character: *a veneer of honesty.* 1, 3 *n.,* 2 *v.*

ven·er·a·ble (ven′ə rə bəl) deserving respect or reverence because of age and goodness: *a venerable leader, a venerable tradition.* *adj.*

ven·er·ate (ven′ə rāt′) regard with deep respect or reverence: *Muslims venerate the prophet Muhammad.* *v.,* **ven·er·at·ed, ven·er·at·ing.** —**ven′er·a′tion,** *n.*

venge·ance (ven′jəns) revenge; punishment in return for a wrong: *He swore vengeance against the men who murdered his father.* To be **vengeful** is to want revenge. *n.*
with a vengeance, with great force or violence: *By six o'clock it was raining with a vengeance.*

ven·i·son (ven′ə sən) deer meat. *n.*

ven·om (ven′əm) 1 the poison of snakes, spiders, etc. 2 hostile, hateful feeling or words: *There was venom in his voice.* *n.* —**ven′om·ous,** *adj.*

vent (vent) 1 a hole; opening: *He used a pencil to make air vents in the box top so the frog could breathe.* 2 let out; express freely: *He vented his anger by punching his pillow.* 3 an outlet; a way out: *to give vent to frustration. Her grief found vent in tears.* 1, 3 *n.,* 2 *v.*

ven·ti·late (ven′tə lāt′) 1 let fresh air into: *to ventilate a room by opening windows.* 2 purify by fresh air; put oxygen into: *The lungs ventilate the blood.* *v.,* **ven·ti·lat·ed, ven·ti·lat·ing.** —**ven′ti·la′tion,** *n.*

ven·ti·la·tor (ven′tə lā′tər) 1 a machine or device for bringing fresh air into a closed-in space. 2 a device used by people with asthma to spray medicine through the mouth into the bronchial tubes. It is informally called a **puffer.** *n.*

ven·tri·cle (ven′trə kəl) either of the two lower chambers of the heart that receive blood and pump it into the arteries. *n.*

ven·tril·o·quist (ven tril′ə kwist) a person who can make his or her voice seem to come from another source, such as a puppet: *The ventriloquist talked almost without moving her lips.* *n.* —**ven·tril′o·quism′,** *n.*

ven·ture (ven′chər) 1 a bold or daring journey or project: *The first trip to the moon was a thrilling venture.* 2 dare; dare to say, do, or go: *to venture a timid question, to venture into the unknown. No one ventured to take on the bully.* 1 *n.,* 2 *v.,* **ven·tured, ven·tur·ing.** —**ven′ture·some,** *adj.*

ven·ue (ven′yū) the place where a public event is held, such as a concert, a conference, or a trial: *Cole missed hearing his favourite band because its venue was switched several times.* *n.*

Ve·nus (vē′nəs) the brightest planet, second in distance from the sun and coming closest to the earth. *n.* ▶ See Appendix.

a bat	e bed	i bid	o pot	u cup	th thin
ā cake	ē me	ī bite	ō go	ū rude	ᴛʜ then
ä bar	ə about	ər over	ô for	ů put	zh measure

A Venus flytrap leaf closes like a trap on any insect that lands on it. After the plant has digested the insect, the leaf opens up again. After a leaf has caught several insects this way, it dies.

Venus fly·trap (vē′nəs flī′trap′) a swamp plant of the southern United States, with hairy leaves that snap shut on insects. The plant uses the insects for nourishment. **Venus's flytrap** is another spelling.

ve·ran·da or **ve·ran·dah** (və ran′də) a raised porch on a house. *n.*

verb (vərb) a word that expresses an action or state of being. The verb *walked* in *She walked* shows an action in the past tense. The verb *is* in *She is a doctor now* shows a state of being something in the present tense. *n.* ► See the *Grammar and Usage Mini-Guide.*

USING WORDS .... verbs

A well-chosen **verb** can add a sense of action to a sentence. Use verbs that say exactly what you mean: *He went home* is not bad, but if you replace *went* with *walked, staggered, raced, trotted, drove, slunk, tottered,* or *flew,* the sentence will come alive.

ver·bal (vər′bəl) **1** in words; often, in spoken words rather than writing: *A description is a verbal picture. She made a verbal report, which we taped.* To **verbalize** something is to put it into words. **2** using language well or easily, especially spoken language: *The little boy is more verbal than his sister.* **3** made from a verb. In the sentence *We like her acting,* the word *acting* is a verbal noun. *adj.* —**ver′bal·ly,** *adv.*

ver·ba·tim (vər bā′təm) repeating the exact words of something that was spoken or written: *She copied the message verbatim.* *adv.*

ver·bi·age (vər′bē ij) a lot of extra words that are not needed: *You could improve your story by cutting some of the verbiage.* A speaker or writer who uses too many words is **verbose** (vər bōs′). *n.*

ver·dict (vər′dikt) **1** the decision of a jury in court: *The jury returned a verdict of "not guilty."* **2** any decision or judgment: *Mom's verdict on the question of a midnight swim was "No."* *n.*

verge (vərj) **1** the edge or borderline; brink: *Their business is on the verge of ruin.* **2** border: *His talk was so poorly prepared that it verged on nonsense.* 1 *n.,* 2 *v.,* **verged, verg·ing.**

ver·i·fy (ver′ə fī′) **1** prove to be true; confirm: *Noah's report of the fight was verified by two girls who had seen it happen.* **2** check: *You can verify the spelling of a word by looking it up in a dictionary.* *v.,* **ver·i·fied, ver·i·fy·ing.** —**ver′i·fi·ca′tion,** *n.*

ver·i·ly (ver′ə lē) an old or poetic word for "truly." *adv.*

ver·i·ta·ble (ver′ə tə bəl) true or real: *She's a veritable genius.* *adj.*

ver·min (vər′mən) small creatures considered to be troublesome. Fleas, lice, rats, and mice are vermin. *n.*

ver·sa·tile (vər′sə tīl′) able to do or be used for many things: *a versatile employee. The computer is a versatile tool.* *adj.* —**ver′sa·til′i·ty** (vər′sə til′ə tē), *n.*

verse (vərs) **1** poetry. **2** a line or group of lines of poetry: *Sing the first verse of "O Canada."* **3** in some holy writings, a short numbered section containing one or two sentences. *n.*

versed (vərst) having a lot of knowledge, skill, or experience in some area: *Our doctor is well versed in medicine.* *adj.*

ver·sion (vər′zhən) **1** a translation from one language to another, a rewriting, or a changed form of something: *Proofread your story, then make a corrected version. The movie version of the story is simpler than the book.* **2** a statement or description from a particular point of view: *Each of us gave our own version of the quarrel.* *n.*

ver·sus (vər′səs) against: *This year's Grey Cup game will be the Hamilton Tiger-Cats versus the Edmonton Eskimos.* *prep.*

ver·te·bra (vər′tə brə) one of the small bones of the backbone. *n., pl.* **ver·te·brae** (vər′tə brā′) or **ver·te·bras.**

ver·te·brate (vər′tə brit) **1** having a backbone. **2** any creature that has a backbone. Fish, amphibians, reptiles, birds, and mammals are all vertebrates. 1 *adj.,* 2 *n.*

ver•tex (vər′teks) **1** the point at the top of something, especially of a triangle, pyramid, cone, or similar shape. **2** the point of any angle. *n., pl.* **ver•tex•es** or **ver•ti•ces** (vər′tə sēz′).

ver•ti•cal (vər′tə kəl) **1** straight up and down. A person standing up straight is in a vertical position. **2** anything that is straight up and down. 1 *adj.,* 2 *n.*

ver•y (ver′ē) **1** much; greatly; a lot more than average: *The sunshine is very hot in July.* **2** absolute or absolutely: *in the very centre (adj.), at the very worst moment (adv.).* **3** same: *She is the very person I saw yesterday.* **4** even; mere; sheer: *The very thought of roller coasters makes me sick.* 1, 2 *adv.,* 2–4 *adj.*

ves•sel (ves′əl) **1** a ship or boat. **2** a container. Cups, bottles, and tubs are all vessels. **3** a tube carrying blood or some other fluid. Veins and arteries are blood vessels. *n.*

vest (vest) **1** a short sleeveless garment worn over a shirt or blouse. It has buttons at the front or is pulled on over your head. **2** an old word for "undershirt." **3** give someone certain powers, authority, rights, etc.: *Teachers are vested with the authority to enforce school rules.* 1, 2 *n.,* 3 *v.*

ves•ti•bule (ves′tə byūl′) a passage or hall leading from the outer door to the inside of a building; a lobby. *n.*

ves•tige (ves′tij) a last remaining bit; a trace: *A charred stump was the only vestige of the fire.* *n.*

vet (vet) *Informal.* short for **veterinarian** or **veteran.** *n.*

vet•er•an (vet′ə rən) **1** a soldier who has fought in a war: *A veteran came to speak to our school on Remembrance Day.* **2** a person with a lot of experience in a certain kind of work: *a veteran of the fire department.* **3** with a lot of experience: *a veteran farmer.* 1, 2 *n.,* 3 *adj.*

vet•er•i•nar•i•an (vet′ə rə ner′ē ən) a doctor who treats animals. *n.* **—vet′er•i•nar′y,** *adj.*

ve•to (vē′tō) **1** refuse to allow; prevent something by saying "no": *Dad vetoed our plan to buy a big snake.* **2** a decision not to allow something: *Mom added her veto to Dad's. The Senate has the power of veto over most bills passed in the House of Commons.* 1 *v.,* **ve•toed, ve•to•ing;** 2 *n., pl.* **ve•toes.**

vex (veks) **1** annoy; make angry: *It vexes her to have to wait for anyone.* **2** disturb; trouble: *vexed by doubts. This area is much vexed by storms.* *v.* **—vex•a′tion,** *n.* **—vex•a′tious,** *adj.*

VHS *a trademark for* a system to record sounds and pictures on tape. Video cassette recorders use VHS. *n.*

vi•a (vī′ə *or* vē′ə) by way of; by a route that passes through: *We travelled from Winnipeg to Saskatoon via Regina.* *prep.*

vi•a•ble (vī′ə bəl) able to stay alive, keep going, or work out well: *a viable animal or plant, a viable solution to the problem of pollution.* *adj.*

vi•a•duct (vī′ə dukt′) a long bridge supported by arches and towers, for carrying a road or railway over a valley, part of a city, etc.: *The Bloor Street viaduct connects the eastern and western parts of downtown Toronto.* *n.*

vi•al (vī′əl) a small bottle, especially one for medicine or perfume. *n.*

vibes (vībz) *Informal.* **1** a musical instrument made up of metal bars that you hit with a small hammer. Under the bars are tubes that operate by electricity to produce a vibrating sound. **Vibraphone** is the full name for this instrument. **2** a good or bad feeling that you seem to get from a person, place, or situation: *The house had good vibes and I felt at home instantly.* *pl.n.*

vi•brant (vī′brənt) full of life, warmth, energy, enthusiasm, etc.: *vibrant colours, a vibrant personality.* *adj.*

vi•brate (vī′brāt) **1** move or cause to move back and forth very fast; quiver: *A piano string vibrates and makes a sound when a key is struck.* **2** echo loudly; keep on sounding: *The clanging vibrated in his ears.* *v.,* **vi•brat•ed, vi•brat•ing.** **—vi•bra′tion,** *n.*

vice (vīs) **1** a fault; a bad habit: *He said that his horse had no vices.* **2** evil; wickedness. *n.*

vice– *a prefix meaning* next in rank; second in command. A **vice-president** is next in rank to a president, and takes the president's place when necessary. A **viceroy** does the same for a king or queen, and a **vice-principal** does the same for a principal. *n.*

vice ver•sa (vīs′ vər′sə) the other way round: *Scott blamed Harriet, and vice versa (Harriet blamed Scott).*

vi•cin•i•ty (və sin′ə tē) the area near or around a place; neighbourhood: *There are no houses for sale in this vicinity.* *n., pl.* **vi•cin•i•ties.**

vi•cious (vish′əs) **1** unusually wild or fierce: *a vicious dog.* **2** hateful; very nasty or mean: *a vicious remark.* *adj.*

a bat	e bed	i bid	o pot	u cup	th thin
ā cake	ē me	ī bite	ō go	ū rude	ᴛʜ then
à bar	ə about	ər over	ò for	ù put	zh measure

Vikings

Vikings sailed in flat-bottomed, light ships in search of wealth and land. Some places they plundered, and in some places they settled. They colonized Iceland and Greenland, and reached the shores of America.

Swords were highly valued by the Vikings, and were often richly decorated with gold and silver.

vicious circle (vish′əs sėr′kəl) two or more bad things that keep on causing each other: *It's a vicious circle: the more you scratch a mosquito bite, the more it itches, and the more it itches, the more you scratch.*

vic·tim (vik′təm) 1 a person or thing that is killed or destroyed: *victims of a disease, victims of an accident. Their small business was a victim of extremely high rents.* 2 a person badly treated by another: *the victim of a swindler.* *n.* **—vic′tim·ize′,** *v.*

🍁 **Victoria Day** (vik tôr′ē ə dā′) in Canada, a national holiday falling on the Monday before or on the 24th of May, the birthday of Queen Victoria.

vic·to·ry (vik′tə rē) success in a contest; the fact of defeating an enemy or opponent: *The game ended in a victory for our school.* A winner is called a **victor.** *n., pl.* **vic·to·ries.** **—vic·to′ri·ous** (vik tôr′ē əs), *adj.*

vict·uals (vit′əlz) an old word for "food." *pl.n.*

vid·e·o (vid′ē ō′) 1 a movie, or other images and sounds, recorded on a special magnetized tape; a **music video** shows scenes that go together with a song. You can make videos with a **video camera.** 2 the visual part, as opposed to the sound, of a film, TV show, or computer program or game. *n.*

vid·e·o·disc (vid′ē ō disk′) a disc with pictures and sounds recorded on it which can be played back on a television or computer screen using a laser device. *n.*

video game (vid′ē ō gām′) an electronic game played by controlling the action on a screen. A **video arcade** is a place where people pay to play these games.

vid·e·o·tape (vid′ē ō tāp′) 1 a wide, magnetized tape that records both sound and images for watching on a TV screen. A **video cassette** is a videotape wound inside a plastic case that cannot be opened; the machine for recording and playing back videos is a **video cassette recorder** or **VCR.** 2 to record on videotape: *Mom videotaped my tenth birthday party.* 1 *n.,* 2 *v.,* **vid·e·o·taped, vid·e·o·tap·ing.**

vie (vī) compete: *The children vied with each other to be first in line.* *v.,* **vied, vy·ing.**

view (vyū) 1 the fact of seeing; sight: *It was our first view of the ocean. A ship came into view.* 2 something seen; scene: *The view from our house is beautiful.* 3 a mental picture; idea: *This book will give you a general view of pioneer life.* 4 a way of looking at or thinking about something; opinion: *He has very sensible views on school discipline.* 5 look at: *They viewed the scene with pleasure.* 6 think of in a certain way: *She views homework with distaste.* 1–4 *n.,* 5, 6 *v.* **—view′er,** *n.*
in view of, considering; because of: *In view of the cost, my parents decided against skiing lessons.*
on view, open for people to look at: *The exhibit is on view from 9 a.m. to 5 p.m.*
with a view to, with the purpose or hope of: *She worked hard after school with a view to earning enough money for a new bicycle.*

view·point (vyū′point′) 1 your position when you are looking at something. 2 a way of looking at or thinking about something; a point of view: *A heavy rain that is good from the viewpoint of farmers may be bad from the viewpoint of tourists.* *n.*

vig·il (vij′əl) the act of staying awake or keeping watch: *All night the mother kept vigil over the sick child.* *n.*

vig·i·lant (vij′ə lənt) watchful; alert; wide-awake: *The watchdog was vigilant.* *adj.* **—vig′i·lance,** *n.*

vig·or·ous (vig′ə rəs) strong and active; energetic; forceful: *a vigorous kick. Doctors wage a vigorous war against disease.* To be vigorous is to be full of **vigour** or **vigor.** *adj.* **—vig′or·ous·ly,** *adv.*

Vi·king or **vi·king** (vī′king) one of the daring adventurers and pirates from Norway, Denmark, and Sweden who raided the coasts of Europe from the eighth to the tenth century. *n.*

vile (vīl) very bad; disgusting: *the vile deeds of a murderer. Old garbage has a vile smell.* *adj.,* **vil·er, vil·est.**

vil•la (vil′ə) a house in the country or at the seashore, especially a large and elegant one. *n.*

vil•lage (vil′ij) a group of houses and other buildings, usually in the country, and the people who live and work there. A village is smaller than a town; the people who live there are **villagers.** *n.*

vil•lain (vil′ən) 1 a very wicked person, especially in a story: *The hero eventually defeats the villain.* 2 a person or thing blamed for a particular problem: *When they studied the disease they found that impure water was the villain.* *n.* —**vil′lain•ous,** *adj.* —**vil′lain•y,** *n.*

vim (vim) lively energy; vigour: *The campers were full of vim after a good night's sleep.* *n.*

vine (vīn) any plant with a long, thin, easily bending stem that grows along the ground or that climbs by attaching itself to a wall, tree, or other support: *Grapes and pumpkins grow on vines. Ivy is a vine.* A place where grapevines are grown is a **vineyard** (vin′yərd). *n.*

vin•e•gar (vin′ə gər) a sour liquid produced by the action of bacteria on cider, wine, beer, etc. Vinegar is used to flavour and to preserve food. *n.*

vin•tage (vin′tij) 1 the wine or grapes from a certain crop: *She says 1997 was a good vintage.* 2 *Informal.* the crop of anything at some particular time: *Her car is of 1970 vintage.* 3 excellent; outstanding: *a vintage year, a vintage crop.* 4 old but still good. 1–2 *n.,* 3, 4 *adj.*

vi•nyl (vī′nəl) a tough, shiny plastic used to make floor and furniture coverings, toys, and many other things. *n.*

vi•o•la (vē ō′lə) a musical instrument similar to a violin but slightly bigger and lower in tone. *n.*

vi•o•late (vī′ə lāt′) 1 break a law, rule, agreement, promise, etc.; act contrary to: *Speeding violates the traffic laws.* 2 disturb: *The sound of the explosion violated the usual calm of early morning.* 3 treat with disrespect: *The vandals violated the church by painting on the walls.* *v.,* **vi•o•lat•ed, vi•o•lat•ing.** —**vi′o•la′tion,** *n.* —**vi′o•la′tor,** *n.*

vi•o•lent (vī′ə lənt) 1 using or showing strong, rough, hurtful force against people or things: *a violent kick, a violent person. I'm not allowed to watch violent films.* 2 very strong or severe: *a violent headache.* *adj.* —**vi′o•lence,** *n.*

vi•o•let (vī′ə lit) 1 a small woodland or garden plant with little flowers that are typically bluish purple, although some kinds have white or yellow flowers. The purple violet is the provincial flower of New Brunswick. 2 bluish purple. 1, 2 *n.,* 2 *adj.*

vi•o•lin (vī′ə lin′) a musical instrument like a tiny guitar with four strings. You play it by holding the wide end under your chin and drawing a bow across the strings. *n.* —**vi′o•lin′ist,** *n.*

vi•per (vī′pər) a poisonous snake with a pair of large, hollow fangs that carry the poison into the body of any creature bitten by the snake. *n.*

vir•gin (vər′jən) 1 a person, especially a young woman, who has never had sexual intercourse. 2 not changed, touched, spoiled, or used by humans: *virgin soil, virgin forest, virgin snow.* 1 *n.,* 2 *adj.*

vir•tu•al (vər′chū əl) 1 not strictly real but almost; real or true in a practical sense: *He is the virtual boss, even though technically he is just an ordinary employee.* 2 having reality on computer but not in a physical way. Even a laptop computer being used by someone riding on a bus can be a **virtual office.** *adj.* —**vir′tu•al•ly,** *adv.*

virtual reality (vər′chū əl rē al′ə tē) something made to seem real by computer. The computer system surrounds you with realistic sights and sounds and uses your input to make them change just as they would in real life. You usually have to wear headphones to experience virtual reality.

vir•tue (vər′chū) 1 moral goodness; good character: *She was a woman of virtue—loyal, brave, kind, and just.* 2 a particular kind of goodness: *Honesty and patience are virtues.* 3 any quality that makes a thing good or useful: *He praised the virtues of his car. There is little virtue in that medicine.* *n.* —**vir′tu•ous,** *adj.*
by or **in virtue of,** because of; on account of: *By virtue of being the oldest child, Julius gets the biggest allowance.*

vir•tu•o•so (vər′chū ō′sō) someone who is very skilled at something, especially music: *Ralf was a virtuoso on the violin.* *n., pl.* **vir•tu•o•sos** or **vir•tu•o•si** (vər′chū ō′sē).

vi•rus (vī′rəs) 1 an extremely small life form that invades cells and causes certain infectious diseases. Unlike bacteria, viruses cannot be killed by antibiotics and are so small that they can be seen only through an electron microscope. 2 anything thought of as being like this: *the virus of prejudice.* A **computer virus** is a piece of code illegally hidden in a computer program. It can destroy data and make the program malfunction, and is easily spread by copying files. *n.* —**vi′ral,** *adj.*

vi•sa (vē′zə) official permission to visit a certain country, shown by a special stamp in your passport. *n.*

a bat	e bed	i bid	o pot	u cup	th thin
ā cake	ē me	ī bite	ō go	ū rude	ᴛʜ then
à bar	ə about	ər over	ò for	ù put	zh measure

vis•cous (vis′kəs) thick and sticky like syrup or glue, so that it does not flow easily. The property of being viscous is called **viscosity** (vi skos′ə tē). *adj.*

vise (vīs) a tool with two jaws that can clamp tightly around an object to hold it in place while work is being done on it. *n.*

vis•i•bil•i•ty (viz′ə bil′ə tē) **1** the distance you can see under certain weather conditions. It is especially important for drivers: *Fog and rain decreased visibility to about 12 m.* **2** the fact of being easy to see or notice: *When walking at night, wear white for greater visibility.* *n.*

vis•i•ble (viz′ə bəl) that can be seen or noticed: *The shore was barely visible through the fog. The used car had no visible signs of wear.* *adj.* **—vis′i•bly,** *adv.*

vi•sion (vizh′ən) **1** the ability to see; the sense of sight: *People wear glasses to improve their vision.* **2** the ability to form a dream of how things could be and to plan ways of making it happen: *A leader has to have vision.* **3** a dream or plan like this, or anything seen in your imagination: *She shared her vision for Canada in the new millenium. The beggar had visions of great wealth.* *n.*

vi•sion•ar•y (vizh′ə ner′ē) **1** a person with great dreams for the future, whose ideas are far ahead of most other people's. **2** having or using such ideas or dreams: *a visionary proposal for world peace.* 1 *n., pl.* **vi•sion•ar•ies;** 2 *adj.*

vision quest (vizh′ən kwest′) a traditional part of becoming an adult in many First Nations cultures. The young person spends long periods of time fasting and meditating alone in the wilderness or visiting the sweat lodge for cleansing ceremonies, as a way of preparing to receive a vision and find his or her spirit guide. **Solo quest** is another word for this.

vis•it (viz′it) **1** go or come to see: *Would you like to visit New Brunswick? You should visit the dentist every six months.* **2** stay with someone as a guest: *I'll be visiting my aunt next week.* **3** have a friendly conversation: *We visited on the phone for 40 minutes.* **4** the act of visiting: *a visit to the principal's office. Grandma paid us a visit last week.* 1–3 *v.,* 4 *n.* **—vis′i•tor,** *n.*

vi•sor (vī′zər) **1** a part sticking out at the front of a cap to protect your eyes from bright sunlight. **2** a small movable shade attached at the top of a car windshield on the inside. **3** the movable front part of a helmet, covering your face. *n.*

vis•ta (vis′tə) **1** a scenic view: *The opening between the two rows of trees gave us a vista of the lake.* **2** a mental view: *Education should open up new vistas.* *n.*

vis•u•al (vizh′ū əl) having to do with sight or vision: *Being near-sighted is a visual defect. The teacher used diagrams and pictures as visual aids to help us learn about leaves.* *adj.*

vis•u•al•ize (vizh′ū ə līz′) form a mental picture of: *I can visualize his reaction when he hears the news.* *v.,* **vis•u•al•ized, vis•u•al•iz•ing.**

vi•tal (vī′təl) **1** having to do with or necessary to life: *Eating is a vital function. The heart is a vital organ.* **Vital statistics** include the number of births, deaths, and marriages in a population. Sometimes a person's age, size, income, and so on are jokingly called his or her "vital statistics." Heart rate, blood pressure, and temperature are **vital signs.** **2** key; very important: *Your education is vital to your future.* **3** healthy and lively: *a vital faith, a vital economy.* To give something health and strength is to **vitalize** it. *adj.*

vi•tal•i•ty (vī tal′ə tē) strength, health, and liveliness: *the vitality of a tradition. After a swim and a long sleep, she awoke with renewed vitality.* *n., pl.* **vi•tal•i•ties.**

vi•ta•min (vī′tə min) **1** one of the substances needed by the body for normal growth and health, found especially in milk and in raw fruits and vegetables. **Vitamin A,** for example, helps you fight infections; **vitamin D** makes your bones and teeth strong, while **vitamin E** keeps your skin and other tissues healthy. **2** a pill containing any of these substances. *n.*

vi•va•cious (vi vā′shəs *or* vī vā′shəs) very bright, bubbly, lively, etc.: *a vivacious smile, a vivacious personality.* *adj.* **—vi•vac′i•ty** (vi vas′ə tē), *n.*

viv•id (viv′id) **1** bright, strong, and clear: *Dandelions are a vivid yellow. I have a vivid memory of the fire.* **2** able to create clear, detailed mental images: *a vivid imagination, a vivid description.* *adj.*

vix•en (vik′sən) a female fox. *n.*

vo•cab•u•lar•y (vō kab′yə ler′ē) **1** all the words known by a person or used in a certain kind of activity: *Reading will increase your vocabulary. The vocabulary relating to computers keeps on growing.* **2** a list of words, usually arranged in alphabetical order, with their translations or meanings: *There is a vocabulary in the back of our French book.* *n., pl.* **vo•cab•u•lar•ies.**

vo•cal (vō′kəl) **1** having to do with the voice: *The tongue is a vocal organ. I like vocal music better than instrumental.* A **vocalist** is a singer, and your **vocal cords** are a pair of thin tissues deep in your throat. They produce sound when air from the lungs passes between them and makes them vibrate. **2** freely talking; making your opinions and feelings known: *He was very vocal about his disagreement with the new rule.* *adj.*

vo·ca·tion (vō kā′shən) 1 a person's main work or occupation, chosen as a lifetime career: *Teaching is her vocation.* **Vocational** training prepares you for a certain line of work such as carpentry, office work, welding, etc. 2 a strong feeling that you are meant to follow a particular career: *Since childhood she felt a vocation for flying.* *n.*

vo·cif·er·ous (və sif′ə rəs) loud and noisy; shouting; clamouring: *a vociferous person, vociferous cheers.* *adj.*

vogue (vōg) fashion: *Very bright colours are the vogue this season. That old song is in vogue again.* *n.*

voice (vois) 1 the sound that a human being makes in speaking, singing, laughing, etc.: *The voices of the children could be heard coming from the playground.* 2 the power to make such sounds: *His voice was gone because of a sore throat.* 3 a say; the right to express an opinion or choice: *We had no voice in the matter.* 4 express in words; make known: *They voiced their approval of the plan.* 5 the distinctive style of an author or a fictional character. 1–3, 5 *n.,* 4 *v.,* **voiced, voic·ing.**

give voice to, express; especially in words: *The parents wrote the school board a letter giving voice to their concerns.*

Word Family.......... **voice**

voice box: another word for **larynx**, the part of your throat containing the vocal cords
voice mail: phone messages left for a certain person, which are accessed by a password
voice-over: the narrator's part in a commercial
voiceprint: an electronic record of a voice, for ID

void (void) 1 an empty space: *The death of his dog left an aching void in Ian's heart.* 2 empty: *a heart void of any feeling.* 3 without any legal force; not valid: *The coupon is void if you don't use it by March 5.* 4 cancel; make something not count: *The cashier voided the purchase because he had rung in the wrong price.* 1 *n.,* 2, 3 *adj.,* 4 *v.*

vol·ca·no (vol kā′nō) 1 a deep hole in the earth's crust where steam, ashes, and lava are forced out. 2 a hill or mountain around this hole, built up by the material that has been forced out and has hardened. *n., pl.* **vol·ca·noes** or **vol·ca·nos.** **—vol·can′ic** (vol kan′ik), *adj.*

vole (vōl) a small animal like a mouse, but usually heavier and with short legs and tail. *n.*

vol·ley (vol′ē) 1 the act of hitting the ball back and forth over the net in volleyball: *That was a great volley—it went over ten times!* 2 hit the ball back and forth over the net: *They volleyed to see which side would serve first.* 3 a shower of stones, bullets, arrows, etc. 4 a burst or outpouring of words, shouts, cheers, etc.: *The mayor's announcement met with a volley of protests.* 5 shoot or burst out all at once: *Cannon volleyed on all sides.* 1, 3, 4 *n., pl.* **vol·leys;** 2, 5 *v.,* **vol·leyed, vol·ley·ing.**

vol·ley·ball (vol′ē bol′) 1 a game played by two teams using a large ball and a high net. Players try to hit the ball back and forth over the net with their hands without letting it touch the ground. 2 the ball used in this game. *n.*

volt (vōlt) an SI unit for measuring the pressure or force of an electric current: *This battery produces a current of six volts.* The greater the number of volts, the higher the **voltage.** *Symbol:* V *n.*

vol·ume (vol′yūm) 1 a book forming part of a set or series: *You can find what you want to know in the ninth volume of this encyclopedia.* 2 any book: *a library of five hundred volumes.* 3 the space taken up by something. For anything with a boxlike shape, you find the volume by multiplying together the height, width, and length; the answer is in cubic units: *The storeroom has a volume of 12 m³* (cubic metres). Something that takes up a lot of space is **voluminous** (və lū′mə nəs). 4 amount or loudness of sound; fullness of tone: *A pipe organ has more volume than a violin or flute.* 5 an amount; quantity: *Great volumes of smoke poured from the chimney.* *n.*

vol·un·tar·y (vol′ən ter′ē) 1 done, made, or given by your own free choice; not forced: *voluntary service. The charity is supported by voluntary contributions.* 2 done on purpose; not automatic: *Speaking and walking are voluntary; breathing is only partly voluntary.* *adj.* **—vol′un·tar′i·ly,** *adv.*

vol·un·teer (vol′ən tēr′) 1 a person who does any job or service by his or her own choice: *When the principal said she needed people to move desks to the gym, there were 12 volunteers.* 2 a person who works without pay: *In some small towns, the firefighters are volunteers.* 3 offer to do a job: *Many people volunteered for the search party. Wayne volunteered to cut up the vegetables.* 4 having to do with volunteers: *volunteer labour, a volunteer fire department.* 1, 2 *n.,* 3 *v.,* 4 *adj.*

vom·it (vom′it) 1 throw up what you have eaten. 2 the substance thrown up from your stomach. 1 *v.,* 2 *n.*

a bat	e bed	i bid	o pot	u cup	th thin
ā cake	ē me	ī bite	ō go	ū rude	ᴛʜ then
ä bar	ə about	ər over	ô for	ů put	zh measure

vo·ra·cious (və rā′shəs) **1** eating a lot; greedy for food: *a voracious appetite.* **2** very eager; always looking for more: *She is a voracious reader of mysteries.* *adj.* —**vo·rac′i·ty** (və ras′ə tē), *n.*

vote (vōt) **1** decide something by having everyone say or write down what their choice is and then doing what was chosen by the most people: *The class voted on where to go for the field trip.* **2** say what your choice is: *I voted for a trip to the candy factory.* **3** this method of making a group decision: *Each class chose its Student Council rep by vote.* **4** an individual person's choice in such a decision: *My vote was for Wilma.* **5** the right to say what your choice is and have it count: *In federal elections, we don't have the vote until we are 18 years old.* 1, 2 *v.,* **vot·ed, vot·ing;** 3–5 *n.* —**vot′er,** *n.*
take a vote, decide something by letting people vote.
vote down, reject by voting: *His suggestion was voted down by the others.*
vote in, elect; place a person in a certain job by voting: *Mr. Prasad was voted in as mayor.* The opposite is **vote out.**
vote of confidence, a in special problem situations, a vote in the House of Commons supporting the existing government. If there is a **vote of no confidence,** the government must resign and call an election. **b** any statement of support for someone.

vouch (vouch) speak up for someone or something as a guarantee; confirm: *I can vouch for the truth of the story. The principal vouched for Anita's honesty.* *v.*

vouch·er (vou′chər) a kind of ticket or coupon that can be exchanged for something, or used as proof that money has been paid: *They gave each of us two vouchers so we could get drinks.* *n.*

vow (vou) **1** a solemn promise: *a vow of secrecy, marriage vows.* **2** promise solemnly: *She vowed not to tell the secret.* 1 *n.,* 2 *v.*

vow·el (vou′əl) **1** a speech sound you make without stopping your breath at any point by the tongue, teeth, or lips. When you say *awe, oh,* or *eh,* the only sound you are making is a vowel. **2** a letter representing such a sound. There are five vowels used in writing, *a, e, i, o,* and *u*; *y* sometimes acts as a vowel too. *n.*

voy·age (voi′ij) **1** a long journey, especially by water or air: *We had a pleasant voyage to Japan. The earth takes a year to make its voyage around the sun.* **2** make or take a long journey like this: *Columbus voyaged on unknown seas.* 1 *n.,* 2 *v.,* **voy·aged, voy·ag·ing.** —**voy′ag·er,** *n.*

voy·a·geur (voi′ə zhər′ *or* vwȧ yȧ zhər′) in earlier times, a canoeist, especially a French Canadian, working and travelling for the early fur-trading companies. Through their travels the voyageurs gathered a lot of valuable knowledge about Canada and its native peoples. *n.*

WORD HISTORY........ voyageur

Voyageur is borrowed straight from French and means "traveller."

vs. *abbreviation for* versus, meaning "against" in a contest or court case: *Raptors vs. Grizzlies.*

vul·gar (vul′gər) showing poor manners, bad taste, etc.; gross; disgusting: *vulgar language.* *adj.* —**vul·gar′i·ty** (vul ger′ə tē), *n.*

vul·ner·a·ble (vul′nə rə bəl) in danger of being hurt; open to attack: *Because your head is vulnerable when you play hockey, you should wear a helmet.* *adj.* —**vul′ner·a·bil′i·ty,** *n.*
vulnerable to, likely to be hurt or influenced by: *Most people are vulnerable to ridicule.*

A vulture has no feathers on its head or neck. When it feeds from a carcass, it can put its whole head inside, without getting blood or decaying flesh stuck to it.

vul·ture (vul′chər) **1** a large, bare-headed bird of prey that eats the flesh of dead animals. **2** a greedy person who tries to profit from the misfortunes of others. *n.*

vul·va (vul′və) the folds of skin on the outside of a girl's or woman's body around the opening to the vagina. *n.*

vy·ing (vī′ing) the present participle of **vie:** *The boys were vying with each other for the teacher's attention.* *v.*

W w

w or **W** (dub′əl yū′) **1** the twenty-third letter of the English alphabet, or any sound that it stands for. The sound of *w* is heard in the word *wolf.* **2** the twenty-third thing in a list. *n., pl.* **w's** or **W's.**

USING WORDS ...... five W's

The **five W's** are **who, what, when, where,** and **why.** Reporters use the five W's to help them organize the information in their news stories. They ask questions using the 5 W's, and then answer these questions in their writing. That way they are sure they have included all the most important information.

W *symbol for* watt, an SI unit for measuring power.

W or **W.** *abbreviation for* west or western.

wack·y (wak′ē) *Informal.* odd or crazy, especially in a rather funny way. *adj.,* **wack·i·er, wack·i·est.**

wad (wod) **1** a small, thick mass of something tightly folded, rolled, or pressed together: *a wad of bubble gum, a wad of Canadian Tire money.* **2** make into a wad; press into a wad: *She wadded up the paper and threw it in the garbage.* 1 *n.,* 2 *v.,* **wad·ded, wad·ding.**

wad·dle (wod′əl) **1** walk with short steps and a swaying motion, as a duck does: *A fat porcupine waddled across the path.* **2** this way of walking. 1 *v.,* **wad·dled, wad·dling;** 2 *n.*

wade (wād) **1** walk through water or anything else that is deeper than your ankles: *We waded through the slush and snow.* **Waders** are very high waterproof boots, or pants and boots combined, used for fishing and duck hunting. **2** make way with difficulty: *I managed to wade through 13 pages.* *v.,* **wad·ed, wad·ing.** —**wad′er,** *n.*

wa·fer (wā′fər) a very thin cookie, cracker, or candy: *a soda wafer, a mint wafer.* *n.*

waf·fle[1] (wof′əl) a light, crisp, flat cake made from batter. It is cooked in a **waffle iron,** which has two hinged metal plates with a crisscross pattern on the inside. The waffle is cooked in between. *n.*

waf·fle[2] (wof′əl) act or talk in such a way as to avoid making a decision or taking a stand: *They waffled endlessly about whether to stay or go.* *v.,* **waf·fled, waf·fling.**

waft (woft) float; carry over water or through air: *The waves wafted the boat to shore. The smell of warm pie wafted upstairs.* *v.*

wag (wag) **1** move quickly from side to side: *The dog wagged its tail. Its tail wagged back and forth.* **Waggle** has a similar meaning. **2** a motion like this: *He replied with a wag of his head.* 1 *v.,* **wagged, wag·ging;** 2 *n.*

wage (wāj) **1** the pay for a certain amount of work: *Her wages are $9.50 an hour.* **2** carry on any kind of struggle or contest: *Doctors wage war against disease.* 1 *n.,* 2 *v.,* **waged, wag·ing.**

wa·ger (wā′jər) bet: *I'll wager a loonie that the Expos will win* (*v.*). *The wager was promptly paid* (*n.*). *v. or n.*

wag·on (wag′ən) a four-wheeled vehicle, especially for carrying loads. It has no power of its own and must be pulled: *a hay wagon, a toy wagon. The pioneers carried all their goods in covered wagons pulled by horses.* *n.*

waif (wāf) a homeless child or animal. *n.*

wail (wāl) **1** cry loud and long from sadness or pain: *The baby wailed.* **2** make a long, mournful sound: *The wind wailed around the old house.* **3** a cry or sound like this: *the wail of a coyote, the wail of a siren.* 1, 2 *v.,* 3 *n.*

waist (wāst) **1** the narrowest part of your body between your ribs and your hips. **2** the distance around this part, also called your **waistline.** *n.*

CONFUSABLES ...... waist

waist is a part of your body: *Let me measure your waist.*
waste means "garbage": *Put your candy wrapper in the waste basket.*

waist·coat (wāst′kōt′) an old word for a man's vest. *n.*

a bat	e bed	i bid	o pot	u cup	th thin
ā cake	ē me	ī bite	ō go	ū rude	TH then
ä bar	ə about	ər over	ô for	ů put	zh measure

wait (wāt) **1** stay in one place or do nothing until someone comes or something happens: *Let's wait for the bus in the shade. Don't order it; wait and ask Dad first.* **2** look forward to something eagerly: *They are waiting for summer holidays to start.* **3** *Informal.* delay or put off: *Can you wait dinner for us?* **4** the act or time of waiting: *We had a long wait at the doctor's office.* 1–3 *v.,* 4 *n.*
lie in wait, stay hidden, ready to attack: *Robbers were lying in wait for the travellers.*
wait on, a serve a customer. **b** work as the personal servant of a high-ranking person: *Two young men waited on the king.* This kind of servant is a **lady-in-waiting** or a **gentleman-in-waiting.**

CONFUSABLES .... wait

wait means "stop or stay till something happens": *Wait here until I get back.*

weight means "heaviness": *I could hardly bear the weight of my backpack full of books.*

wait·er (wā′tər) a man who serves people at tables in a restaurant. **Server** is another word for this. *n.*

wait·ress (wā′tris) a woman who serves people at tables in a restaurant. **Server** is another word for this. *n.*

waive (wāv) give up a right or skip the usual requirements: *The driver's test is waived if you have a licence from another country.* *v.,* **waived, waiv·ing.**

wake[1] (wāk) **1** Often, **wake up,** stop or cause to stop sleeping: *I usually wake up at dawn. The noise will wake the baby.* **Waken** means the same. **2** a gathering to pay last respects to the body of a dead person before the burial. 1 *v.,* **woke, woken, wak·ing;** 2 *n.*

wake[2] (wāk) **1** the track of waves, ripples, and foam left behind by something moving through the water. **2** a track left behind anything. *n.*
in the wake of, close behind; soon after: *Floods came in the wake of the hurricane.*

wake·ful (wāk′fəl) awake or alert. *adj.*

walk (wok) **1** go on foot: *Walk to school with me.* In walking, one foot is always on the ground. A **walker** is a frame to support someone in walking. **2** cause to walk; lead or take along while walking: *to walk your dog, to walk a bike across the street, to walk someone to the door.* **3** the act, way, or distance of walking: *Let's go for a walk. It is a short walk to the school. We knew she was happy from her bouncy walk.* **4** a route or path for walking: *I shovelled the snow off the walk. There are many pretty walks in the park.* **Walkway** means the same. **5** in baseball, let a batter go freely to first base by giving four improper pitches which are not swung at. 1, 2, 5 *v.,* 3, 4 *n.*
walk all over someone, treat someone without respect.
walk out, a leave suddenly. **b** leave a job, a meeting, etc. as a sign of protest. To do this is to stage a **walkout.**
walk someone through something, guide a person in doing something, one step at a time: *Deanna walked me through finding something on the Internet.*

walk·a·thon (wok′ə thon′) a walk taken by a group of people over a long distance, to raise money for a cause. Sponsors promise to donate a certain amount of money for every kilometre walked. *n.*

walk·ie–talk·ie (wok′ē tok′ē) a small, portable two-way radio set for talking over short distances. *n., pl.* **walk·ie-talk·ies.**

walking stick (wok′ing stik′) **1** a stick used as a support while walking. **2** a North American insect with a long, slender body that looks like a twig. **Stick insect** is another name for it.

walk·out (wok′out′) **1** the act of leaving a meeting, class, job, etc. as a sign of protest: *The factory workers are planning a walkout. The parents staged a walkout during the meeting with the school board.* **2** a wide opening with sliding glass doors in the wall of a home, leading from a room straight out to a deck, balcony, patio, etc. *n.*

wall (wol) **1** the side of a house, room, or other hollow thing. Your stomach has walls. **2** stone, brick, or other material built up to divide a space or keep people in or out: *a wall around an old city.* **3** something shaped or used like a wall: *walls of hatred. The huge wave formed a wall of water.* **4** surround or fill with a wall: *The garden is walled. Workers walled up the doorway.* 1–3 *n.,* 4 *v.*
drive someone up the wall, *Informal.* make someone nearly crazy: *His constant chatter drives me up the wall.*
off the wall, *Slang.* weird.
with your back to the wall, in a bad situation with no way out.

wal·la·by (wol′ə bē) a sort of small kangaroo. There are various kinds, some of them no larger than a rabbit. *n., pl.* **wal·la·bies** or **wal·la·by.**

wal·let (wol′it) a small, flat, folding case for carrying money, credit cards, and so on. *n.*

wall·eye (wol′ī′) a North American freshwater fish with milky eyes and brassy green sides. It is the most important freshwater fish in the Canadian economy. *n.*

wal·lop (wol′əp) *Informal.* **1** hit very hard. **2** a very hard blow: *The wallop knocked him out.* **3** defeat thoroughly. **4** **walloping,** very big. 1, 3 *v.,* 2 *n.,* 4 *adj.*

wal·low (wol′ō) **1** roll around in something: *The pigs wallowed in the mud. The boat wallowed helplessly in the stormy sea.* **2** let yourself enjoy something so much that it is actually disgusting: *to wallow in self-pity.* **3** the act of wallowing. **4** a place where an animal wallows: *There used to be many buffalo wallows on the prairies.* 1, 2 *v.,* 3, 4 *n.*

wall·pa·per (wol′pā′pər) **1** paper printed with a coloured pattern, for decorating and covering walls. **2** decorate with this paper. 1 *n.,* 2 *v.*

wal·nut (wol′nut′) **1** a rather large, almost round nut with a bumpy shell and a division between its two halves. It is good to eat. **2** the tree it grows on, whose wood is often used for making furniture. *n.*

Walruses dive to great depths to catch clams from the ocean floor with their long curving tusks. Apart from humans, their only enemies are polar bears and killer whales.

wal·rus (wol′rəs) a large sea mammal of the arctic regions, like a seal but with rough, wrinkled skin and long tusks. *n., pl.* **wal·rus** or **wal·rus·es.**

waltz (wolts) **1** a smooth, gliding dance with a slow one-two-three beat. **2** a piece of music for such a dance. **3** do this dance. 1, 2 *n.,* 3 *v.*

wam·pum (wom′pəm) beads made from shells, which eastern First Nations people used to use for money, for decoration, in ceremonies, or in wampum belts. In a wampum belt, the beads were arranged in patterns which told a story. *n.*

WORD HISTORY........wampum

Wampum comes from an Algonquian language called Narraganset. The original word was *wampompeag,* meaning "strings of white."

wan (won) pale, weak, or tired-looking: *a wan smile.* *adj.,* **wan·ner, wan·nest.** —**wan′ly,** *adv.*

wand (wond) a thin rod: *a magician's wand.* Some scanners have a wand you pass over the bar code. *n.*

wan·der (won′dər) **1** go here and there without any special goal: *We wandered through stores without buying anything.* **2** leave the right spot or the right way; stray: *The dog wandered off and got lost.* *v.* —**wan′der·er,** *n.*

wane (wān) become gradually smaller: *The moon wanes after it has become full. Her interest in the subject has waned.* *v.,* **waned, wan·ing.**
on the wane, growing less; waning: *The power of the president was on the wane.*

wan·gle (wang′gəl) *Informal.* manage to get, by tricks or persuasion: *She wangled an invitation to the party.* *v.,* **wan·gled, wan·gling.**

want (wont) **1** wish for; wish: *The child wants his dinner. She wants to become an engineer.* **2** something desired or needed: *He is a man of few wants and leads a simple life.* **3** lack; need: *That plant wants water (v.). The plant died for want of water (n.).* 1, 3 *v.,* 2, 3 *n.*
want for, lack; be without: *She has never wanted for friends.*

want ad (wont′ ad′) *Informal.* a notice in a newspaper that someone is looking for a job, a car, a person to hire, an apartment, etc.

want·ing (won′ting) lacking; missing or not good enough: *Two pieces were wanting from the puzzle. The stranger was wanting in politeness.* *adj.*

wan·ton (won′tən) wild or reckless; ignoring good sense and reason: *a wanton attack, a wanton mood.* *adj.*

Each year, the males of this species grow antlers that may span almost 2 m.

wap·i·ti (wop′i tē) the North American elk, a large member of the deer family with long branched antlers. *n., pl.* **wap·i·ti** or **wap·i·tis.**

a bat	e bed	i bid	o pot	u cup	th thin
ā cake	ē me	ī bite	ō go	ū rude	ᴛʜ then
à bar	ə about	ər over	ȯ for	ů put	zh measure

war (wôr) **1** any serious fight, especially between nations or parts of a nation: *the war between Canada and the U.S. in 1812, the war against crime.* **2** carry on a war: *to war against poverty. Germany warred against France.* 1 *n.,* 2 *v.,* **warred, war•ring.**

Word Family.......... war

- **war crime:** acts of war that are against the international code of law
- **war cry:** a slogan used in a war or any conflict
- **warfare:** the process of fighting a war
- **warlike:** quick to start or take part in wars
- **warplane:** a plane designed for use in war
- **warrior:** a person skilled or experienced in war
- **warship:** a ship designed for use in war
- **wartime:** a time when a nation is involved in war

war•ble (wôr′bəl) **1** sing or whistle like a bird. A **warbler** is a kind of small songbird. **2** a bird's song or a sound like it. 1 *v.,* **war•bled, war•bling;** 2 *n.*

ward (wôrd) **1** a division of a hospital or prison. **2** a district of a city or town, especially one that has its own representative on the town council. **3** a person placed under the care of a guardian or government. **4 ward off,** keep away or turn aside: *She warded off the blow with her arm.* 1–3 *n.,* 4 *v.*

ward•en (wôr′dən) **1** the person in charge of a prison. **2** an official who enforces certain laws or rules: *a fire warden, a park warden.* *n.*

ward•robe (wôr′drōb′) **1** a person's supply of clothes: *She is shopping for her spring wardrobe.* **2** a closet or piece of furniture for holding clothes. *n.*

ware (wer) **1** Usually, **wares,** *pl.* things for sale: *The peddler sold his wares from door to door.* **2** things made out of a certain material or for a certain purpose. This sense is usually in compounds: *silverware, cookware.* *n.*

ware•house (wer′hous′) a place where goods are kept before being delivered to stores. *n.*

warm (wôrm) **1** more hot than cold; having, giving, or holding in heat: *a warm room, a warm coat. She sat in the warm sunshine.* **2** kind, friendly, enthusiastic, etc: *a warm welcome, a warm heart.* **3** suggesting heat: *Red, orange, and yellow are warm colours.* **4** *Informal.* near what you are searching for: *You guessed wrong, but you're warm.* **5** make or become warm: *to warm a room. Her smile warms my heart.* 1–4 *adj.,* 5 *v.* **—warmth,** *n.*
warm up, a heat: *Your soup is cold; shall I warm it up for you?* **b** make or become more interested, friendly, etc. **c** practise or exercise before the main activity. The noun or adjective is **warm-up:** *warm-up exercises.*

warm–blood•ed (wôrm′blud′id) having warm blood that stays about the same temperature regardless of the surrounding air or water. Mammals and birds are warm-blooded. *adj.*

warn (wôrn) tell about something bad that may happen, or something that people need to get ready for: *The clouds warned us that a storm was coming. "The bus leaves in five minutes," she warned.* *v.*
—warn′ing, *n.*

warp (wôrp) **1** bend or twist out of shape: *This old floor has warped; it isn't level. Prejudice warps our thinking.* **2** a bend or twist: *This board has a bad warp.* 1 *v.,* 2 *n.*

war•rant (wôr′ənt) **1** a written order giving authority for something: *a warrant to search a house, a warrant for someone's arrest.* **2** justify; be a good reason for: *Nothing warrants such rudeness.* **3** a good reason: *There was no warrant for saying such a thing.* **4** guarantee: *I warrant you he'll be late just like last time.* 1, 3 *n.,* 2, 4 *v.*

war•ran•ty (wôr′ən tē) a written promise that a product is what it is supposed to be and that the manufacturer will repair or replace it if anything is wrong with it. *n., pl.* **war•ran•ties.**

war•ren (wôr′ən) a system of connected burrows where a large number of rabbits live. *n.*

wart (wôrt) **1** a small, hard, usually harmless lump on the skin, caused by a virus. **2** a fault or bad point: *We love him, warts and all.* *n.* **—wart′y,** *adj.*

wart•hog (wôrt′hog′) a wild pig of Africa that has big tusks and large growths on its face that look like warts. *n.*

war•y (wer′ē) on guard against danger or trickery; cautious: *The wary fox peeked out of its den. The man gave wary answers to all of the stranger's questions.* *adj.,* **war•i•er, war•i•est.** **—war′i•ly,** *adv.* **—war′i•ness,** *n.*
wary of, cautious about; careful about: *Be wary of gossip.*

was (wuz) a past tense of **be,** used with *I, he, she, it,* or any singular noun: *Once there was a king. I was an hour late for school yesterday.* *v.*

wash (wosh) **1** clean with water: *to wash your face, to wash out a stain.* **2** the act of washing: *This car needs a good wash.* **3** clothes that have been or will be washed: *She hung the wash on the line.* **Washing** has this meaning too. **4** carry or be carried by water or other liquid: *The wood washed up on the shore. A flood washed away the bridge.* **5** the rough, swirling water left behind a moving ship; any water with a strong current. **6** the rush or sound of moving water: *I listened to the wash of the waves against the boat.* **7** a liquid for special use, as in *mouthwash.*

8 a thin coating of colour: *He began his watercolour with a blue wash for the sky.* **9** *Informal.* be accepted or believed: *That excuse will never wash.* 1, 4, 9 *v.,* 2, 3, 5–8 *n.* —**wash′a·ble,** *adj.*
wash away, a wear away by the action of water: *The waves are washing away the cliffs.* **b** get rid of by washing: *to wash away a stain.*
wash down, a have a drink along with food to help you swallow or digest it: *They washed down the dry bread with a cup of tea.* **b** wash from top to bottom: *to wash down the walls.*
wash out, a destroy with rushing water: *The heavy rains washed out the dirt road.* **b** destroy or cause to fail. The noun for either meaning is **washout:** *The party was a complete washout.* **c** clean by washing.
wash up, a wash your hands and face, as before meals. **b** wash the dishes: *We washed up right after supper.*

Word Family.......... **wash**

washcloth: a small cloth for washing your body
washday: the day regularly set aside for doing laundry
washed-out: 1 pale; lacking colour **2** tired and weak
washroom: a room with toilet, sink, and maybe a bath
washstand: a cabinet with a basin on or in it, for washing
washtub: a large container for washing clothes by hand

wash·er (wosh′ər) **1** a person or thing that washes, especially an automatic machine for washing clothes. It is also called a **washing machine. 2** a flat ring of metal, rubber, or other material, used with a bolt or nut to make joints tight, protect surfaces, etc. *n.*

was·n't (wuz′ənt) was not.

Wasps can be divided into two main groups: social and solitary.

Social wasps live in colonies, and make communal nests, usually of paper.

Solitary wasps, like this potter wasp, usually dig nest tunnels in the ground. The potter wasp then makes its nest out of clay, lays an egg in each pot, and fills the pot with food for the developing grub.

wasp (wosp) a flying insect related to a bee, with a slender body and a powerful sting. A hornet is a type of wasp. *n.*

waste (wāst) **1** make poor use of; use something up without getting much value or benefit from it: *Don't waste time or money. We try not to waste food.* **2** the fact of wasting: *This dumb movie is a waste of money.* **3** useless material to be thrown away, such as garbage or sewage. Your body gets rid of waste after digesting food. **4** thrown away as useless: *a pile of waste lumber.* **5** wild, empty land: *a dangerous trip across the desert wastes.* **Wasteland** means the same. **6** wear down little by little; destroy or lose gradually: *The sick man's body was wasted by disease.* **7** ruin; destroy: *The soldiers wasted the fields and towns of the enemy.* 1, 6, 7 *v.,* **wast·ed, wast·ing;** 2, 3, 5 *n.,* 4 *adj.* —**waste′ful,** *adj.*
lay waste, destroy: *The invading army laid waste the countryside.*

waste·bas·ket (wāst′bas′kit) an open container for paper that is thrown away. **Wastepaper basket** is another name for it. *n.*

watch (woch) **1** look on; look at something that is going on: *to watch a hockey game, to watch someone work. Kerri watched while her aunt fixed the bike.* **2** pay attention; be very careful: *Watch that you don't drop it—it's fragile.* **3** look after; guard: *Watch the baby for a minute while I get the phone.* **4** a device for telling time, small enough to wear on your wrist or carry in your pocket. It is attached to a **watchband** or **watch chain. 5** the act or process of guarding: *She kept a careful watch to make sure he didn't escape.* **6** a period of time for guarding: *a watch in the night.* **7** a person or group acting as a guard. A man doing this is a **watchman.** 1–3 *v.,* 4–7 *n.* —**watch′ful,** *adj.*
watch for, pay close attention looking or waiting for something: *She watched for a chance to cross the street.* Another way of saying it is **be on the watch for.**
watch out, be on guard; be careful: *Watch out for cars. Watch out! The tree is falling.*
watch over or **keep watch over,** guard; protect.
watch yourself, be careful.

Word Family.......... **watch**

watchband: a band to hold a watch on your wrist
watchdog: a dog trained to guard property
watchmaker: a person who makes or fixes watches
watchtower: a tower you can stand in to watch for ships, fires, etc.
watchword: a key word or idea in a certain place or time

a bat	e bed	i bid	o pot	u cup	th thin
ā cake	ē me	ī bite	ō go	ū rude	ᴛʜ then
ä bar	ə about	ər over	ô for	u̇ put	zh measure

Water

Water is the most common substance on Earth, covering seventy percent of its surface. The bodies of all living things are mainly water. Without water, life as we know it would not be possible.

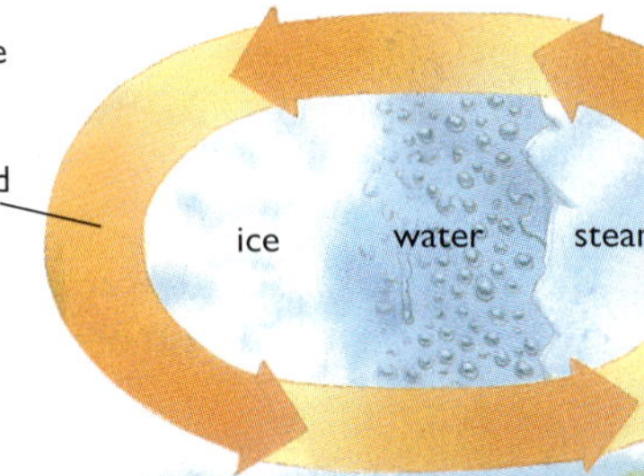

Water exists in three states. It is normally liquid, but at 0°C it changes into the solid called ice, and at 100°C it turns into the gas called steam.

When water is added, the plant embryo inside a seed bursts out and starts to grow.

Without water, there could be no plant or animal life. If this water hole in Africa dries up, the animals will die and the trees will wither.

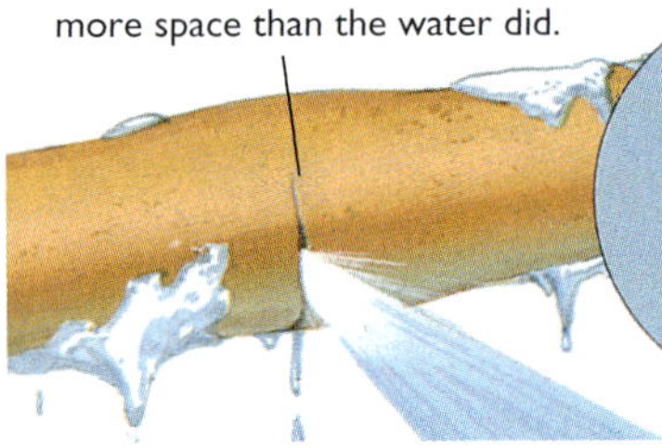
Water has the amazing property of expanding when it freezes — all other liquids contract as they cool. A frozen water pipe splits because the ice inside it needs more space than the water did.

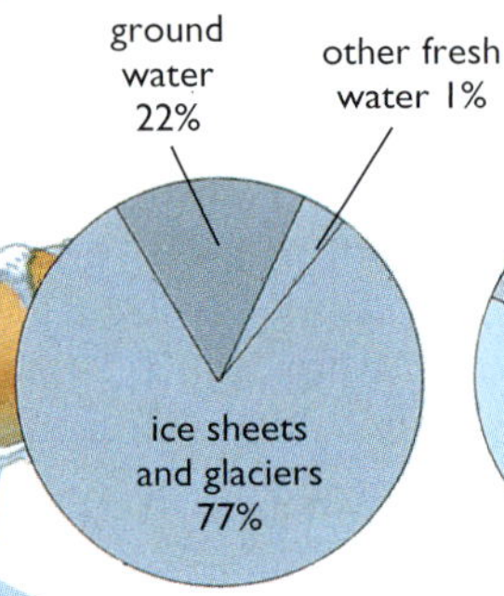

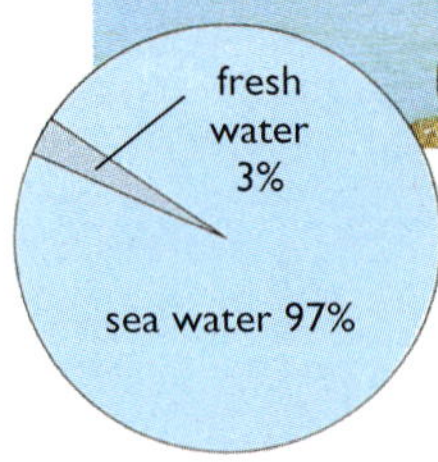

wa·ter (wot′ər) **1** the liquid that falls as rain and makes up the seas, lakes, and rivers. Pure water is clear, colourless, odourless, and tasteless. It can be converted into steam by heating it to 100°C and into ice by cooling it to 0°C. **2** sprinkle or wet with water: *to water plants.* **3** fill with water: *The smoke made my eyes water. His mouth watered when he saw the pie.* **4** supply with water: *to water horses. Our valley is watered by several brooks.* 1 *n.,* 2–4 *v.* —**wa′ter·y,** *adj.* —**wa′ter·less,** *adj.*
hold water, be logical; make sense: *That argument doesn't hold water.*
throw cold water on, discourage: *to throw cold water on someone's plans.*
tread water, keep your head above water by slowly moving your legs as if you are bicycling.
water down, a weaken a liquid by adding water. **b** soften an idea or make it simpler so it will be easier to accept or understand, weakening it in the process.

wa·ter·bed (wot′ər bed′) a bed whose mattress is a large, strong plastic bag filled with water. *n.*

water buffalo (wot′ər buf′ə lō) the common buffalo of southern Asia and the Philippines, with large, spreading horns. It is used as a work animal.

water colour or **color** (wot′ər kul′ər) **1** paint mixed with water instead of oil. **2** a picture painted with this paint. **Watercolour** is another form for both senses. —**wa′ter-col′our** or **wa′ter·col′our,** *adj.*

wa·ter·course (wot′ər kôrs′) the channel or bed of a stream: *In the summer many watercourses dry up.* *n.*

wa·ter·cress (wot′ər kres′) a small plant that grows in cool running water and has crisp, slightly peppery leaves, often used in salads. *n.*

wa·ter·fall (wot′ər fol′) a river or stream as it falls over a cliff or over large rocks. *n.*

wa·ter·fowl (wot′ər foul′) a swimming bird such as a duck or goose. *n., pl.* **wa·ter·fowl** or **wa·ter·fowls.**

wa·ter·front (wot′ər frunt′) the land at the water's edge, especially the part of a city or piece of property that is beside a river, lake, or ocean. *n.*

water lily (wot′ər lil′ē) a water plant with flat, floating leaves and showy, waxy flowers.

wa·ter–logged (wot′ər logd′) completely filled or soaked with water. *adj.*

water main (wot′ər mān′) a large pipe for carrying water through a city or town.

wa•ter•mel•on (wot′ər mel′ən) a large, juicy melon with sweet red or pink pulp and a thick, hard, green rind. *n.*

water power (wot′ər pou′ər) the power from flowing or falling water, used to work machinery and make electricity.

wa•ter•proof (wot′ər prūf′) **1** that will not let water through: *An umbrella should be waterproof.* Something that is **water-repellent** keeps water out for a while; something that is **water-resistant** is not damaged by water. **2** make waterproof: *These hiking shoes have been waterproofed.* 1 *adj.,* 2 *v.*

wa•ter•shed (wot′ər shed′) **1** a ridge of high land that divides two areas drained by different river systems. On one side, rivers and streams flow in one direction; on the other side, they flow in a different direction. **2** the region drained by one river system. **3** anything that divides people or acts as a turning point: *The issue of health care was a real watershed in the election.* *n.*

wa•ter–ski (wot′ər skē′) glide over the water on **water skis,** broad skis that carry you while you are being towed by a boat. *v.,* **wa•ter-skied, wa•ter-ski•ing.** **—wa′ter-ski′er,** *n.*

water slide or **waterslide** (wot′ər slīd′) a long slide with water flowing down it, usually ending in a swimming pool. *n.*

wa•ter•tight (wot′ər tīt′) **1** so tight that no water can get in or out: *This boat doesn't leak—all the joints and seams are watertight.* **2** impossible to misunderstand or criticize; perfect: *a watertight argument.* *adj.*

wa•ter•way (wot′ər wā′) **1** a river, canal, lake, or a system that combines them, that boats and ships can go on: *We took a cruise on the Trent-Severn waterway.* **2** a channel for water to flow in. *n.*

water wheel (wot′ər wēl′) a wheel turned by water, usually to supply power. The grindstones in flour mills used to be run by water wheels.

water wings (wat′ər wingz′) supports for a person learning to swim. You blow them up with air and put them on your arms.

wa•ter•works (wot′ər wərks′) a system of pipes, tanks, pumps, etc. for supplying a city or town with water. *sing. or pl.n.*

watt (wot) an SI unit for measuring power: *My lamp uses 100 watts; my toaster uses 1000 watts. Symbol:* W *n.*

wat•tle (wot′əl) a structure made of sticks interwoven with twigs or branches, used for fences or walls. *n.*

wave (wāv) **1** a moving ridge or swell of water: *The raft rose and fell on the waves.* **2** any movement or shape like this: *Her hair has waves.* Light, heat, and sound travel in waves. **3** a sudden increase of some condition, emotion, etc. that spreads or passes quickly: *A cold wave is sweeping over the country. The announcement brought a wave of enthusiasm.* **4** move up and down or back and forth; sway: *to wave a flag. The tall grass waved in the breeze.* **5** move your hand up and down or back and forth as a greeting or signal: *to wave goodbye. The police officer waved the speeding driver to the side of the road.* **6** the action of waving something: *a wave of the hand.* 1–3, 6 *n.,* 4, 5 *v.,* **waved, wav•ing.** **—wav′y,** *adj.*
make waves, cause excitement; upset people or attract their attention.

wave•length (wāv′length′) the distance between one peak or crest of a wave of sound, light, etc. and the next: *Radio wavelengths are measured in metres.* *n.*
on the same wavelength, sharing the same interests, opinions, feelings, and so on.

wa•ver (wā′vər) **1** tremble, flicker, or lose strength; be unsteady: *a wavering voice, a wavering light.* **2** be undecided; hesitate: *She is still wavering between staying and going.* **3** the act or fact of wavering. 1, 2 *v.,* 3 *n.*

wax[1] (waks) **1** a yellowish substance made by bees for building their honeycomb. Wax is hard when cold, but can be easily shaped when warm. **2** any substance like this. The greasy substance used to make candles is a kind of wax. **3** rub, stiffen, polish, etc. with wax or something like wax: *to wax a car.* 1, 2 *n.,* 3 *v.* **—wax′y,** *adj.*

wax[2] (waks) **1** grow bigger; increase: *The moon waxes till it becomes full, and then it wanes.* **2** a poetic word for "become": *The party waxed merry.* *v.*

wax bean (waks′ bēn′) a garden bean with long yellow pods that are eaten while young and tender.

wax paper (waks′ pā′pər) paper thinly coated with wax, used mostly for wrapping food. **Waxed paper** is another spelling.

wax•wing (waks′wing′) a small brown-and-grey bird with a crest on its head and a yellow-tipped tail, often having small, red, waxlike tips on the wings. The **cedar waxwing** is found in all provinces of Canada, the **bohemian waxwing** only in the north and west. *n.*

a bat	e bed	i bid	o pot	u cup	th thin
ā cake	ē me	ī bite	ō go	ū rude	TH then
à bar	ə about	ər over	ò for	ù put	zh measure

wax·works (waks′wərks′) a set of wax figures on display, especially lifesize figures of historical or famous people. You find them in a **wax museum.** *n.*

way (wā) **1** manner or method: *Don't talk to me in that way. Scientists are trying to find new ways to prevent disease.* **2** direction: *Look this way.* **3** point or feature; detail; respect: *This plan is better in several ways.* **4** road or path: *the way to Kelowna, a way through the forest.* **5** distance: *Mars is a long way off.* **6** a person's desire or wish: *He always get his way.* **7** habit or custom: *Ignore his teasing; that's just his way.* **8** *Informal.* far: *This is way better. Look way over there.* **9** *Informal.* condition or state: *The sick man is in a bad way.* 1–7, 9 *n.*, 8 *adv.*
by the way, as a side point while talking of other things: *By the way, how is your aunt?*
by way of, a through: *to Nova Scotia by way of the U.S.* **b** as; for: *By way of an answer he just nodded.*
come someone's way, come or happen to someone: *A surprise is coming your way.*
give way, a give in or give up. **b** break down or fall: *Several people were hurt when the platform gave way.*
go out of your way, a go someplace that does not take you closer to your real goal: *We had to go out of our way to pick Sven up.* **b** make a special effort.
in the way, blocking someone's view, path, or activities.
lead the way, go ahead of others.
make way, make room for someone or something to go through: *Make way for the fire engine.*
make your way, go: *They made their way through the bushes to the road.*
no way, *Informal.* absolutely not.
on the way, going or coming; while travelling: *We'll eat lunch on the way. He's on his way home.*
out of the way, a not blocking someone's view, path, or activities: *She wanted us out of the way before the guests arrived.* **b** far from where most people live or go. Before a noun, write **out-of-the-way.**

CONFUSABLES .... way

way means "direction": *This is the way to school.*
weigh means "find the mass of": *Weigh this box, please.*

way·far·er (wā′fer′ər) a poetic word for "traveller." *n.* **—way′far·ing,** *adj.*

way·lay (wā′lā′ *or* wā′lā′) stop or attack someone on his or her way: *Robin Hood waylaid rich travellers and robbed them. Newspaper reporters waylaid the famous actor and asked her many questions.* *v.*, **way·laid, way·lay·ing.**

way·side (wā′sīd′) **1** the edge of a road or path: *We ate lunch on the wayside.* **2** along the edge of the road or path: *We slept in a wayside inn.* 1 *n.*, 2 *adj.*

way·ward (wā′wərd) turning from the right way; disobedient or lost. *adj.*

weak (wēk) **1** that can easily be broken, hurt, or defeated with little power or force; not strong: *a weak board in a floor, a weak army, a weak law. He realized he was too weak to move the rock.* A very weak person is a **weakling.** **2** having little loudness, taste, etc.: *The tea is too weak.* **3** lacking or poor in a certain way: *The composition was weak in spelling, but otherwise quite good.* *adj.* **—weak′en,** *v.* **—weak′ly,** *adv.*

CONFUSABLES .... weak

weak means "not strong": *After her illness, she felt weak.*
week means "seven days": *She was in bed for a week.*

weak·ness (wēk′nis) **1** the condition of being weak; lack of power, force, or vigour: *Weakness kept him in bed.* **2** a weak point; a slight fault: *Putting things off is her weakness.* **3** fondness: *She has a weakness for candy.* *n.*

wealth (welth) **1** riches; money, property, or any other valuable things: *She inherited her father's wealth. Canada's wealth includes its mines and forests as well as its factories.* **2** an abundance; a large quantity: *a wealth of knowledge, a wealth of words.* *n.* **—wealth′y,** *adj.*

wean (wēn) **1** get a baby used to food other than its mother's milk. **2** get someone used to doing without something: *He tried to wean himself from cigarettes.* *v.*

weap·on (wep′ən) **1** anything designed or used to hurt or kill, such as a sword, gun, bomb, club, or knife: *The murder weapon was a gun.* **2** anything used to help you win a fight: *Medicines are used as weapons against disease.* *n.* **—weap′on·less,** *adj.* **—weap′on·ry,** *n.*

wear (wer) **1** have on your body or as part of your appearance: *to wear boots, to wear green on St. Patrick's Day. The house wore an air of sadness.* **2** clothing: *casual wear, children's wear.* **3** the fact of wearing something: *clothing for summer wear. This suit has been in constant wear for two years.* **4** damage, lessen, weaken, or change by rubbing, scraping, washing away, or hard use: *to wear a hole in your shoe. Water wore the stones smooth. The paint has worn away on the monkey bars.* **5** pass or go gradually: *It became hotter as the day wore on.* 1, 4, 5 *v.*, **wore, worn, wear·ing;** 2, 3 *n.* **—wear′er,** *n.*
wear and tear, the fact of being slowly damaged by ordinary use over time.
wear off, get weaker or disappear bit by bit over time: *This cough medicine wears off in about four hours. They were very interested at first, but their enthusiasm soon wore off.*
wear on someone, make someone bored or tired of something: *His jokes begin to wear on you after a while.*

wear out, **a** wear or use something until it is no good anymore: *This jacket is worn out. My bike is worn out.* **b** make completely tired: *That hike wore me out.* Something that tires you out quickly is **wearing.**
wear well, last a long time under hard use: *These mitts have worn well; after two winters they're still in good shape.*

CONFUSABLES ...... wear

wear means "have on your body": *I wear blue jeans.*
ware means "article for sale": *Show me your wares.*
where means "in what place": *Where are my jeans?*

wea·ry (wē′rē) **1** tired: *weary feet. He was weary of having the same food every day.* **2** make or become weary; tire: *The long climb wearied us all. They soon wearied of her excuses.* **3** causing tiredness; tiring or boring: *a weary wait.* **Wearisome** means the same. 1, 3 *adj.,* **wea·ri·er, wea·ri·est;** 2 *v.,* **wea·ried, wea·ry·ing.**

Weasels are native to every continent except Australia annd Antarctica. In winter, the fur of weasels that live in cold climates turns white.

wea·sel (wē′zəl) **1** a small, quick animal with a long, slender, furry body and short legs: *Weasels eat rats, mice, birds, and eggs.* **2** get out of doing a duty or giving a clear answer by trickiness: *Don't try to weasel out of doing the dishes!* Such behaviour is **weaselly.** 1 *n.,* 2 *v.,* **wea·selled** or **wea·seled, wea·sel·ling** or **wea·sel·ing.**

weath·er (weᴛʜ′ər) **1** the condition of the air with respect to how warm, damp, windy, or clear it is: *hot weather, rainy weather.* **2** leave outside in the sun, rain, wind, etc.: *Wood turns grey if weathered for a long time.* Something worn or toughened by the weather is **weather-beaten.** **3** go or come through something safely: *The ship weathered the storm.* 1 *n.,* 2, 3 *v.*
under the weather, *Informal.* sick: *She was under the weather and missed the cross-country meet.*
weather well, be undamaged, or even improve, by being exposed to the weather.

weath·er·proof (weᴛʜ′ər prūf′) **1** able to stand up to all kinds of weather: *They built a small weatherproof cabin to use in winter.* **2** protect against the weather: *This cream will weatherproof your boots.* 1 *adj.,* 2 *v.*

weather vane (weᴛʜ′ər vān) a device with a pointer that turns with the wind to show the direction the wind is blowing in; quite often it is shaped like a rooster and called a **weathercock.**

weave (wēv) **1** run threads or strips over and under each other to form a connected piece: *People weave thread into cloth and straw into hats. She wove a basket out of long twigs.* **2** combine parts neatly and skilfully into a whole: *The author wove three plots together into one story.* **3** go by twisting and turning: *A little stream weaves its way through the valley.* **4** a method or pattern of weaving: *Burlap is a cloth of coarse weave.* 1–3 *v.,* **wove, wo·ven, weav·ing;** 4 *n.* **—weav′er,** *n.*

web (web) **1** something woven; different strands or threads neatly connected into a unit: *A spider spins a web. His story is a web of lies.* **2** the skin joining the toes of swimming birds and certain other water animals, making them **web-footed.** **3 the Web,** short for the **World Wide Web,** a network of linked electronic files that you can access on the Internet. The files are made by individuals and organizations to give the public information about themselves. All the files that are linked under one address are a **website,** and the first file you reach at a certain address is the site's **home page.** *n.* **—webbed,** *adj.*

wed (wed) marry. **Wedlock** is a formal word for married life. *v.,* **wed·ded, wed·ded** or **wed, wed·ding.**

we'd (wēd) **1** we had. **2** we would.

wed·ding (wed′ing) **1** a marriage ceremony. **2** an anniversary of this ceremony. A **golden wedding** is the fiftieth anniversary of a marriage. *n.*

wedge (wej) **1** a piece of wood or metal with one thin end and one thick one, used to separate things or hold them tightly in place by filling the space between: *We split the logs with a hammer and wedge.* **2** something shaped like this: *We cut the big pie into ten wedges.* **3** anything that divides in some way: *Their disagreement about the game drove a wedge between the two friends.* **4** squeeze or pack tightly into a small space: *Her foot was wedged between the rocks.* 1–3 *n.,* 4 *v.,* **wedged, wedg·ing.**

Wednes·day (wenz′dā′) the day after Tuesday and before Thursday. *Abbreviation:* Wed. *n.*

wee (wē) very small; tiny. *adj.,* **we·er, we·est.**

a bat	e bed	i bid	o pot	u cup	th thin
ā cake	ē me	ī bite	ō go	ū rude	ᴛʜ then
ä bar	ə about	ər over	ȯ for	ů put	zh measure

Weight and Mass

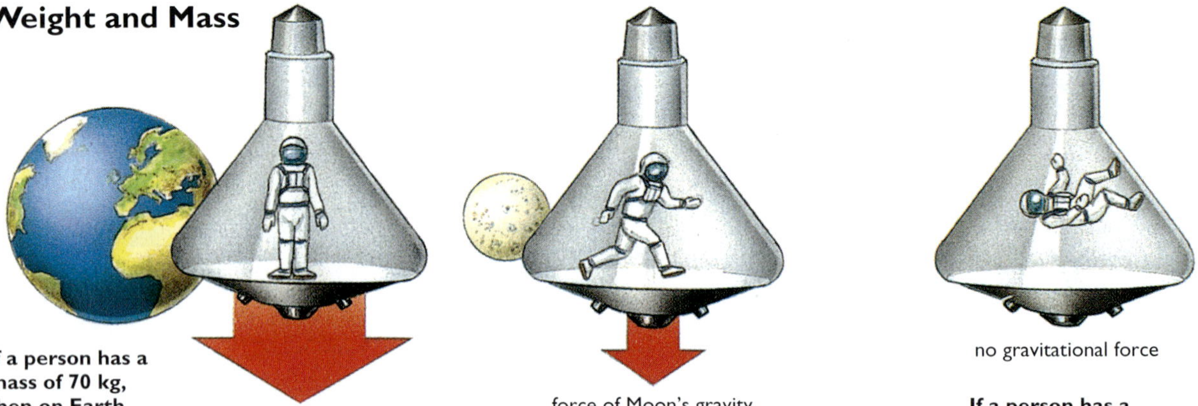

If a person has a mass of 70 kg, then on Earth that person will weigh 70 kg.

If a person has a mass of 70 kg, then on the Moon that person will weigh less than 12 kg. That's why astronauts can make huge leaps on the moon — they have muscles built to move a much heavier person!

If a person has a mass of 70 kg, then in free fall that person will be weightless.

weed (wēd) **1** a wild, unwanted, fast-growing plant: *Weeds choked out the flowers.* **2** dig weeds out: *I have to weed the garden now.* 1 *n.*, 2 *v.* —**weed′y,** *adj.*
weed out, remove as not wanted: *The weakest players were weeded out before the first game was played.*

week (wēk) **1** seven days, one after another. **2** the time from one weekend to another: *This is the last week of holidays. A school week is usually five days.* *n.*

week·day (wēk′dā′) any day of the week except Saturday and Sunday. *n.*

week·end (wēk′end′) **1** Saturday and Sunday. If the Monday or Friday is a holiday it is often included: *a weekend in the country, Easter weekend.* **2** spend a weekend: *They are weekending at the lake.* 1 *n.*, 2 *v.*

week·ly (wēk′lē) **1** lasting or covering one week: *His weekly wage is $500.* **2** coming or happening once a week: *She writes a weekly letter to her grandmother* (*adj.*). *The clerks in the store are paid weekly* (*adv.*). **3** a newspaper or magazine published once a week. 1, 2 *adj.*, 2 *adv.*, 3 *n.*, *pl.* **week·lies.**

weep (wēp) **1** cry; shed tears: *She wept for joy when she won the award.* **2** have drops of liquid forming on it or oozing out of it: *That basement wall weeps a bit.* *v.*, **wept, weep·ing.** —**weep′y,** *adj.*

wee·vil (wē′vəl) a small beetle whose larvae eat grain, flour, nuts, fruit, etc. *n.*

weigh (wā) **1** find out how heavy a thing is; find the mass (def. 5) of: *I weighed myself this morning.* **2** have a certain mass: *I weigh 45 kg.* **3** have as a measure of heaviness: *Things weigh much less on the moon than on Earth.* **4** measure out a certain amount, going by how heavy it is: *The butcher weighed out 2 kg of sausages.* **5** bend or press down with a heavy burden: *The branches of the apple tree are weighed down with fruit. The problem weighed heavily on his mind.* *v.*
weigh anchor, pull up the anchor of a ship.

weight (wāt) **1** how heavy a thing is; mass (def. 5): *The dog's weight is 20 kg.* **2** anything heavy: *A weight keeps the papers in place.* **3** an object with a certain known mass, used to weigh something else or to lift up and down as an exercise: *a fifty-gram weight. She lifts weights at the gym.* **4** load down; burden: *The elevator is weighted too heavily.* **5** influence; importance; value: *What he says carries weight with me.* 1–3, 5 *n.*, 4 *v.* —**weight′y,** *adj.*
pull your weight, do your share: *We will finish the job quickly if we all pull our weight.*

weight·less (wāt′lis) **1** very, very light: *The snow was weightless on my shoulders.* **2** free from the pull of gravity: *In outer space, all things are weightless.* *adj.* —**weight′less·ness,** *n.*

weir (wēr) a fence of sticks built across a stream to catch fish: *First Nations peoples showed European immigrants how to catch salmon in a weir.* *n.*

weird (wērd) very strange: *weird noises.* *adj.*

wel·come (wel′kəm) **1** greet in a friendly way: *to welcome a guest.* **2** receive gladly: *We welcomed the rain.* **3** a warm greeting; friendly acceptance: *You'll always have a welcome here.* **4** gladly received; good to get: *a welcome visitor, a welcome rest.* **5** allowed to do or have freely: *He is welcome to watch. You're welcome to that last cookie.* **6** an exclamation of friendly greeting: *Welcome!* 1, 2 *v.*, **wel·comed, wel·com·ing;** 3 *n.*, 4, 5 *adj.*, 6 *interj.*
you're welcome, a polite reply to the words "thank you."

weld (weld) 1 join two pieces of metal by melting the edges so they will flow into one another: *He welded the broken rod.* 2 a joint made in this way. 1 *v.,* 2 *n.* —**weld′er,** *n.* —**weld′ing,** *n.*

wel•fare (wel′fer′) 1 health, safety, and happiness: *He asked about the welfare of everyone in our family.* 2 a government program to give regular payments of money as well as free medicine and other basic things to people who need them. *n.*

well[1] (wel) 1 all right; properly; in a good way: *Is everything going well at school? The job was well done.* 2 thoroughly: *Shake the medicine well before taking it.* Senses 1 and 2 are often used in compounds: *well-fed, well-prepared, well-behaved.* 3 a lot: *The fair brought in well over a hundred dollars.* 4 in good health: *He is well.* 5 an expression used to show mild surprise, introduce a thought, or just fill in: *Well! If it isn't Mitch! Well, I'm not sure.* 1–3 *adv.,* **bet•ter, best;** 4 *adj.,* 5 *interj.*
as well, also; besides: *not only tired, but sick as well.*
as well as, in addition to; besides: *She did all my jobs as well as her own.*
might as well or **may as well,** an expression used to mean that a certain action would do no harm: *You might as well tell him—he will find out anyway.*

Word Family..........well

well-behaved: polite and co-operative
well-being: health, safety, and happiness
well-bred: well brought up; having good manners
well-known: known by many people; famous
well-meaning: done or acting with good intentions
well-off: fairly rich. **Well-to-do** means the same.
well-read: knowing a lot about books; having read a lot
well-worn: **1** often used **2** beginning to get worn out

well[2] (wel) 1 a hole dug or drilled in the ground to get water, oil, gas, etc.: *The farmer got all his water from a well.* 2 rise or fill like water in a well; gush: *A feeling of gladness welled up inside her.* 1 *n.,* 2 *v.*

we'll (wēl) we will.

welt (welt) a streak or ridge made on the skin by a hit, especially with a stick or whip. *n.*

wend (wend)
wend your way, an old or poetic expression for "go": *We wended our way home.* *v.*

went (went) the past tense of **go:** *I went home promptly after school.* *v.*

wept (wept) the past tense and past participle of **weep:** *She wept for hours. He has often wept.* *v.*

were (wər) 1 the past tense of the verb **be,** used with a plural subject: *The cookies were delicious.* 2 the form of the verb **be** used to express a wish or an unreal condition: *If I were you I wouldn't buy that. I wish she were here.* *v.*

we're (wēr) we are.

weren't (wərnt) were not.

were•wolf (wer′wůlf′ *or* wər′wůlf′) in folk tales, a person who has been changed into a wolf, or who can change into a wolf, while keeping human intelligence. *n., pl.* **were•wolves.**

Wes•ak (wes′åk) the Buddhist New Year festival, held in May.

west (west) 1 the direction of the sunset. 2 toward, from, or in the west: *a warm west wind, the west end of town* (*adj.*). *Walk west three blocks* (*adv.*). 3 **the West,** **a** the western part of Canada or of some other country; in Canada, the provinces west of Ontario. **b** the countries in Europe and America as distinguished from those in Asia. 1, 3 *n.,* 2 *adj. or adv.* —**west′er•ly,** *adj.*
🍁 **out West,** in or toward any place in the western part of Canada.

west•ern (wes′tərn) 1 toward, in, or from the west: *a western town, a western route, a western custom.* 2 a cowboy story, movie, or TV show, usually set in the 1800s. 3 having to do with this kind of story. 4 short for **western sandwich,** a sandwich filled with scrambled egg, chopped ham, peppers, and onions. A **western omelette** has similar ingredients. 1, 3 *adj.,* 2, 4 *n.*

West Indies (west′ in′dēz) a large group of islands between Florida and South America. —**West′ In′di•an.**

west•ward (west′wərd) toward the west; west: *He walked westward* (*adv.*). *The orchard is on the westward slope of the hill* (*adj.*). **Westwards** is another form for the adverb. *adv. or adj.*

wet (wet) 1 covered or soaked with water or other liquid: *wet hands, a wet sponge.* 2 not yet dry: *Don't touch the wet paint.* 3 make or become wet: *Wet the cloth before wiping the table.* 4 rainy: *wet weather.* 5 water or other liquid; rain: *Your sleeve is dragging in the wet. Come in out of the wet.* 1, 2, 4 *adj.,* **wet•ter, wet•test;** 3 *v.,* **wet** or **wet•ted, wet•ting;** 5 *n.* —**wet′ness,** *n.*
wet blanket, *Informal.* a person who has a discouraging or depressing effect: *She's really a wet blanket; she always talks about what could go wrong.*

a bat	e bed	i bid	o pot	u cup	th thin
ā cake	ē me	ī bite	ō go	ū rude	ᴛʜ then
å bar	ə about	ər over	ȯ for	ů put	zh measure

Whale

The blue whale is by far the largest animal.
The elephant is the largest land animal.
The giraffe is the tallest animal.
The ostrich is the largest bird.

wet•land (wet′land′ *or* wet′lənd) a marshy or swampy area thought of as the home of certain birds, animals, and plants, especially when protected by law. *n.*

Wet'•su•wet'•en (wət sū′wət en′) **1** a First Nations people living in British Columbia. **2** their language. **3** having to do with these people or their language. 1, 2 *n.*, 3 *adj.*

we've (wēv) we have.

whack (wak *or* hwak) *Informal.* **1** a sharp, noisy hit. **2** hit hard with a sharp noise: *The batter whacked the ball out of the park.* 1 *n.*, 2 *v.*
out of whack, wrong: *Something's out of whack here; these figures don't add up.*

> **WORD HISTORY........ wh-**
>
> A lot of words made with **wh-** imitate sounds. Many of these are slang or informal, such as **wham.** What others can you find entered in this dictionary?

whale (wāl *or* hwāl) **1** a large sea mammal shaped like a huge fish with a horizontal tail and no scales. Whales breathe air and bear live young. **2** hunt whales for their blubber, bones, and meat; **whaling** or whale hunting has endangered some species. 1 *n., pl.* **whales** or **whale;** 2 *v.,* **whaled, whal•ing.** —**whal′er,** *n.*
a whale of, *Informal.* very big, great, or good: *a whale of a car, a whale of a time.*

wharf (wôrf *or* hwôrf) a large dock where ships can load and unload. *n., pl.* **wharves** (wôrvz *or* hwôrvz) or **wharfs.**

what (wut *or* hwut) **1** a question word that usually asks for the name of a thing: *What is your favourite sport (pron.)? What day is today (adj.)?* **2** the thing or things: *I have what you want.* **3** any or anything that: *Do what you please (pron.). Take what supplies you will need (adj.).* **4** how much; how: *What does it matter?* **5** a word used to say how great or remarkable something is, or to show surprise or anger: *What a mistake (adj.)! What a good time we had (adv.)! What! Are you late again (interj.)?* 1–3 *pron.*, 1, 3, 5 *adj.*, 4, 5 *adv.*, 5 *interj.*
and what not, and all kinds of other things: *Her desk was cluttered with books, papers, pens, and what not.*
what for, why: *"I'm phoning Sue." "What for?"* The expression may be split up in a sentence: *What did you do that for?* means "Why did you do that?"
what if, what would happen if: *What if he finds out?*
what's what, *Informal.* what is going on: *That student knows what's what.*
what with, taking into account; considering: *What with school, soccer, and guitar lessons, Roop is very busy.*

what•ev•er (wət ev′ər *or* hwət ev′er) **1** any that; anything that: *Do whatever you like (pron.). Keep whatever books you want (adj.).* **2** no matter what: *Any colour whatever will do (adj.). Call, whatever happens (pron.).* Another form for senses 1 and 2 is **whatsoever.** **3** *Informal.* a stronger form of **what,** used as a question word. *Whatever do you mean (pron.)? Whatever movie can she be talking about (adj.)?* *pron. or adj.*

what's (wuts *or* hwuts) **1** what is: *What's the latest news?* **2** what has: *What's been going on here lately?*

wheat (wēt *or* hwēt) a grain plant whose seeds are used to make flour. A lot of wheat is grown in the Prairie provinces and it is one of Canada's main exports. *n.*

wheel (wēl *or* hwēl) **1** a round frame that turns on a rod through its centre. **2** anything like a wheel. A car driver uses a **steering wheel** to steer; clay is shaped on a spinning **potter's wheel.** **3** **wheels,** *pl. Informal.* a car, bike, motorbike, etc. **4** move something on wheels: *I wheeled my bicycle across the street.* **5** turn in a circle: *The rider wheeled his horse around. Gulls were wheeling in the sky.* 1–3 *n.*, 4, 5 *v.* —**wheeled,** *adj.*
the wheel, a the position of driver in a car, etc.: *Mom took the wheel when Dad got tired.* **b** the position of leader: *A company needs an organized person at the wheel.*

wheel•bar•row (wēl′ber′ō *or* hwēl′ber′ō) a small vehicle for carrying loads, with one wheel at the front. You push it with handles attached to the back. *n.*

wheel•chair (wēl′cher′ *or* hwēl′cher′) a chair mounted on wheels so that it can be pushed from behind or moved by the person sitting in it. Wheelchairs are used by people who cannot walk or cannot walk far.

wheeze (wēz *or* hwēz) 1 breathe with difficulty and with a whistling or blowing sound. 2 a breath or sound like this. 3 make a sound like this: *The old engine wheezed.* 1, 3 *v.*, **wheezed, wheez·ing;** 2 *n.*

when (wen *or* hwen) 1 a word used in questions and statements to pinpoint a time: *When do we eat (adv.)? Go when your name is called (conj.). Since when has he had a new car (pron.)?* 2 considering that: *How could we lose when we tried so hard?* 1 *adv., pron.,* 1, 2 *conj.*

whence (wens *or* hwens) a formal word meaning "from where": *Whence do you come (adv.)? There is no peace in the land whence I came (conj.).* *adv. or conj.*

when·ev·er (wə nev′ər *or* hwə nev′ər) 1 at whatever time; at any time: *Please come whenever you wish (conj.).* 2 a stronger way of asking "when?": *Whenever is he going to get here (adv.)?* *adv. or conj.*

where (wer *or* wher) 1 a word used in questions and statements to pinpoint a place: *Where do you live and where are you going (adv.)? Where did he come from (pron.)? That is the house where I was born (conj.).* 2 if: *Where there's a will, there's a way.* 1 *adv., pron.,* 1, 2 *conj.*

where·a·bouts (wer′ə bouts′ *or* hwer′ə bouts′) 1 where; near what place: *Whereabouts do you live?* 2 the place where a person or thing is: *Do you know the whereabouts of my calculator?* 1 *adv.,* 2 *n.*

where·as (wer′az *or* hwer′az) 1 but; while; on the contrary: *Some children like sports, whereas others do not.* 2 a formal word for "since": *Whereas there is need for a swimming pool in the community, we hereby request that money be made available for this project.* *conj.*

where·by (wer bī′ *or* hwer bī′) by which or according to which: *They have an arrangement whereby she teaches him computer and he teaches her French.* *conj.*

where·fore (wer′fȯr *or* hwer′fȯr) an old word for "why": *Wherefore do you weep?* *adv.*

where·up·on (wer′ə pon′ *or* hwer′ə pon′) and right after that: *The prince kissed the Sleeping Beauty, whereupon she awoke.* *conj.*

wher·ev·er (wer ev′ər *or* hwer ev′ər) 1 in or to whatever place; anywhere: *He goes wherever he wishes (conj.).* 2 a stronger way of asking "where?": *Wherever did I put my glasses (adv.)?* *conj. or adv.*

where·with·al (wer′wiᴛʜ ol′ *or* hwer′wiᴛʜ ol′) the money, supplies, or other things needed: *Has she the wherewithal to pay for the trip?* *n.*

whet (wet *or* hwet) 1 stir up; awaken: *The smell of food whetted my appetite. An exciting story whets your interest.* 2 sharpen by filing or grinding with a special stone called a **whetstone.** *v.,* **whet·ted, whet·ting.**

wheth·er (weᴛʜ′ər *or* hweᴛʜ′ər) 1 a word used with "or" in expressing a choice: *Whether we leave or stay matters very little. I don't know whether to buy it or not.* 2 if: *He asked whether there was any mail.* *conj.*

whey (wā *or* hwā) the watery part of milk that separates from the curd when milk turns sour or when cheese is made. *n.*

which (wich *or* hwich) a word used: 1 in questions and statements to single out one or more people or things from a group: *Which team won (adj.)? I don't know which shoes to wear (adj.). Of all these colours, which do you like best (pron.)?* 2 to connect a describing clause to the noun it describes in the same sentence: *Read the book which is on the desk (pron.). Stay there unless I call, in which case come right away (adj.).* *adj. or pron.*

which·ev·er (wich ev′ər *or* hwich ev′ər) any; no matter which: *Take whichever you want (pron.). Whichever side wins, I will be satisfied (adj.).* *pron. or adj.*

whiff (wif *or* hwif) 1 a slight smell: *We thought we detected a whiff of perfume in the empty room.* 2 a gust, sniff, or breath: *A whiff of fresh air cleared his head.* *n.*

while (wīl *or* hwīl) 1 a time; a space of time: *He kept us waiting a long while.* 2 during or in the time that: *While I was speaking, she took notes.* 3 although: *While I like the colour of the shirt, I hate the style.* 4 but or and: *He likes swimming while she prefers canoeing. Jonah came in second while Rhys came third.* 5 pass in some easy or pleasant way: *The children while away many afternoons on the beach.* 1 *n.,* 2–4 *conj.,* 5 *v.,* **whiled, whil·ing.**
worth your while, worth your time, attention, or effort: *Such a small matter is hardly worth our while.*

whim (wim *or* hwim) a sudden desire which has no real reason behind it and is likely to change: *Her new craze for gardening is just a whim.* *n.*

whim·per (wim′pər *or* hwim′pər) 1 cry with soft, broken sounds, as a sick child or dog does. 2 a cry like this. 1 *v.,* 2 *n.*

whim·si·cal (wim′zə kəl *or* hwim′zə kəl) full of playful, original, slightly odd ideas; full of **whimsy.** *adj.*

whine (wīn *or* hwīn) 1 make a soft, long, high-pitched complaining cry or sound: *The dog whined to go out with us.* 2 a cry or sound like this: *the whine of an engine.* 3 complain in an annoying, babyish way: *Some people are always whining about something.* 1, 3 *v.,* **whined, whin·ing;** 2 *n.* **—whin′y,** *adj.*

a bat	e bed	i bid	o pot	u cup	th thin
ā cake	ē me	ī bite	ō go	ū rude	ᴛʜ then
ȧ bar	ə about	ər over	ȯ for	u̇ put	zh measure

whin·ny (win′ē *or* hwin′ē) **1** the sound that a horse makes. **2** make such a sound. 1 *n., pl.* **whin·nies;** 2 *v.,* **whin·nied, whin·ny·ing.**

whip (wip *or* hwip) **1** any long, thin, bendable thing to hit with, usually a leather strip attached to a handle. **2** hit with a whip or in a similar way: *He whipped the horse to make it go faster. The rain whipped our faces.* **3** move quickly or suddenly: *He whipped out his wallet. I'll just whip up to the convenience store for milk.* **4** *Informal.* defeat soundly: *The mayor whipped her opponent in the election.* **5** beat cream, eggs, etc. fast until they foam. **6** stir up into a wild state: *He whipped the crowd into a frenzy.* 1 *n.,* 2–6 *v.,* **whipped, whip·ping.**
whip up, a prepare or make quickly: *She whipped up a salad for lunch.* **b** stir up: *We are trying to whip up some interest in a camera club.*

whip·lash (wip′lash′ *or* hwip′lash′) an injury to your neck from a sudden jolt that snaps your head backward and forward. *n.*

whip·poor·will (wip′ər wil *or* hwip′ər wil) a North American woodland bird whose call sounds a bit like its name. The whippoorwill is active at night or in the twilight. **Whip-poor-will** is another spelling. *n.*

whir or **whirr** (wər *or* hwər) **1** a soft buzzing noise, as of something spinning very fast: *the whir of a sewing machine.* **2** make such a noise: *The motor whirred.* 1 *n.,* 2 *v.,* **whirred, whir·ring.**

whirl (wərl *or* hwərl) **1** turn or swing round and round; spin: *The leaves whirled in the wind.* **2** a movement like this: *The dancer suddenly made a whirl.* **3** move or carry quickly: *We were whirled away in an airplane.* **4** a very busy or confused condition: *Her thoughts are in a whirl.* 1, 3 *v.,* 2, 4 *n.*

whirl·pool (wərl′pūl′ *or* hwərl′pūl′) **1** water turning round and round very fast in a funnel-shaped spiral that sucks things down: *The swimmer caught in the whirlpool had hard work to keep from drowning.* **2** a special bathtub that keeps the water moving fast by pumping it through small openings on the inside walls. The water movement is soothing for bathers. *n.*

whirl·wind (wərl′wind′ *or* hwərl′wind′) **1** a column of air blowing round and round like a small tornado. **2** very fast or rushed: *a whirlwind tour.* 1 *n.,* 2 *adj.*

whisk (wisk *or* hwisk) **1** sweep with a quick, light motion; brush: *He whisked the crumbs from the table.* **2** move quickly: *The mouse whisked into its hole. She whisked the letter out of sight.* **3** a quick, light sweeping motion. **4** a small brush or broom. **5** a wire kitchen tool for beating liquids. 1, 2 *v.,* 3–5 *n.*

whisk·er (wis′kər *or* hwis′kər) **1** Usually, **whiskers,** *pl.* the hair growing on a man's face, especially on his cheeks and chin. **2** a long, stiff hair growing near the mouth of a cat, rat, etc. **3** a tiny bit: *Move over just a whisker.* *n.* —**whis′kered,** *adj.*

whis·per (wis′pər *or* hwis′pər) **1** speak very softly, without actually using your voice. **2** make a soft, rustling sound: *The wind whispered in the pines.* **3** either of these sounds: *to talk in whispers, the whisper of skis on snow.* 1, 2 *v.,* 3 *n.*

whis·tle (wis′əl *or* hwis′əl) **1** make a clear, shrill or musical sound by forcing breath through your teeth or lips: *to whistle a tune. The boy whistled and his dog ran to him quickly.* **2** the sound made in this way. **3** an instrument for making this sound by blowing into it. **4** blow a whistle: *The police officer whistled for the traffic to stop.* 1, 4 *v.,* **whis·tled, whis·tling;** 2, 3 *n.*

whit (wit *or* hwit) the very least bit: *The sick man is not a whit better.* *n.*

white (wīt *or* hwīt) **1** the colour of fresh snow or salt, or a colour near this: *white hair* (*adj.*). *He used white for the ceiling* (*n.*). **2** a part that is white: *the white of an egg, the whites of your eyes.* **3** lighter in colour than other kinds: *white wine, white meat.* **4** light-skinned. **5** a light-skinned person. 1, 2, 5 *n.,* 1, 3, 4 *adj.,* **whit·er, whit·est.** —**whit′en,** *v.* —**whit′ish,** *adj.*

Word Family.......... **white**

white ant: another name for a termite
whiteboard: a smooth white surface for writing on with dry erasable markers
whitecap: a wave with a foaming white crest
white elephant: a useless thing that's a bother to keep
whitefish: an important freshwater food fish of the north
white gold: a silver-coloured mixture containing gold
white-hot: so hot that it glows white; extremely hot
white lie: a small lie supposedly told for a good reason
white sale: a sale of sheets, towels, and so on

white blood cell (wīt′ blud′ sel′) a white or colourless cell found in the blood and lymph of human beings and animals. White blood cells fight infection.

white·out (wī′tout′ *or* hwī′tout′) **1** a winter weather condition where blowing snow completely blocks your vision: *Many highway traffic accidents are caused by whiteouts.* **2** an arctic weather condition where the snow-covered ground and the cloudy sky blend into one shadowless mass of dazzling white, making you disoriented and temporarily blind. *n.*

white supremacy (wīt′ sə prem′ə sē) extreme racism against people who are not white. Those who practise this are called **white supremacists.**

white•wash (wīt′wosh′ *or* hwīt′wosh′) 1 a white paintlike liquid used especially in earlier times for walls, woodwork, and so on. It was made of lime and water. 2 whiten with this paint. 3 cover up the faults or mistakes in something. 1 *n.*, 2, 3 *v.*

white water (wīt′ wot′ər) rapids; rough water going over rocks. The sport of travelling over rapids in a rubber boat is called **white-water rafting. White-water canoeing** is a similar sport.

whith•er (wiᴛʜ′ər *or* hwiᴛʜ′ər) an old or poetic word meaning "to what place": *Whither shall I go?* *conj.*

whit•tle (wit′əl *or* hwit′əl) shape wood by cutting off shavings or chips with a knife; carve: *The old sailor whittled a boat in his spare time.* *v.*, **whit•tled, whit•tling.**
whittle down or **away,** cut down little by little: *We tried to whittle down our expenses.*

whiz[1] (wiz *or* hwiz) 1 a humming or hissing sound created by something moving by very fast. 2 move or rush with such a sound: *An arrow whizzed past.* 1 *n.*, 2 *v.*, **whizzed, whiz•zing.**

whiz[2] (wiz *or* hwiz) a person who is extremely good at something: *He's a whiz at languages.* *n., pl.* **whiz•zes.**

who (hū) 1 which person or people: *Who lives there? We know who told you.* 2 a word that starts a clause describing someone already mentioned in the same sentence: *The girl who waved is my best friend. My brothers, who play hockey, have a game tonight.* *pron.*
who's who, a which person is which. **b** who the important or powerful people are.

whoa (wō *or* hwō) stop!: *"Whoa there!" said the farmer to his horse.* *interj.*

who'd (hūd) 1 who would: *Who'd like to go along?* 2 who had: *She wondered who'd been there.*

who•ever (hū ev′ər) 1 any person that: *Whoever wants the book may have it.* 2 no matter who: *Whoever else goes hungry, he won't.* 3 a stronger form of "who?": *Whoever could that be, calling at this hour?* *pron.*

whole (hōl) 1 with all its parts; complete; full: *a whole set of dishes. She worked the whole day.* **Whole milk** has none of the fat removed; **whole grain** includes the tough outer part of each kernel. 2 one complete unit: *Three thirds make a whole.* 3 in one piece: *The dog swallowed the meat whole.* 4 an old or poetic word for "well"; not sick or hurt. 1, 3, 4 *adj.*, 2 *n.*
on the whole, considering everything; for the most part.

whole–heart•ed (hōl′här′tid) not holding back; giving yourself completely: *a whole-hearted effort.* *adj.*

whole number (hōl′ num′bər) a number that does not contain a fraction and is not less than zero: *0, 1, 2, 3, 15, and 106 are whole numbers;* ½, ¾, and ⅞ are fractions; *1⅜* and 2½ are mixed numbers.

whole•sale (hōl′sāl′) 1 the selling of goods in large quantities at a time, usually to storekeepers or others who will sell them again to users: *He buys at wholesale and sells at retail.* 2 having to do with this kind of selling in large quantities: *a wholesale fruit business, wholesale prices* (*adj.*). *He bought the team sweaters wholesale* (*adv.*). 3 sell in large quantities: *They wholesale these jackets at $20 each.* 1 *n.*, 2 *adj. or adv.*, 3 *v.*, **whole•saled, whole•sal•ing.** —**whole′sal′er,** *n.*

whole•some (hōl′səm) 1 good for your body, mind, or spirit: *wholesome food, wholesome movies.* 2 healthy-looking: *She has a clean, wholesome face.* *adj.*

who'll (hūl) who will.

whol•ly (hō′lē) completely: *wholly convinced.* *adv.*

whom (hūm) the form of **who** used as the object instead of the subject: *Whom do you like best? He does not know whom to believe anymore. The girl to whom I spoke is my cousin.* *pron.*

Grammar Check . . . . . . whom

In formal English, **who** is used only as the subject of a verb, just as you would use *he* or *she*: *Who went to the store? She went to the store.*

Whom is used the same way as *him* or *her*: *Whom did you meet? Did you meet him?* Always use **whom** after a preposition like *to, with, by, from,* or *of.*

whoop (hūp *or* wūp) 1 a loud, excited shout: *When land was sighted, the sailor let out a whoop of joy.* 2 shout loudly with excitement. 1 *n.*, 2 *v.*
whoop-de-do, *Slang.* **a** a big excited fuss over something. **b** so what? big deal!
whoop it up, have a lively, exciting time.

whooping cough (hū′ping kof′) a contagious disease of children and occasionally adults, with coughing fits that end in a crowlike sound. It is caused by bacteria and in Canada most children are immunized against it.

a bat	e bed	i bid	o pot	u cup	th thin
ā cake	ē me	ī bite	ō go	ū rude	ᴛʜ then
ä bar	ə about	ər over	ȯ for	u̇ put	zh measure

whooping crane (wū′ping krān′) a very large, white bird with a long neck and long legs, black wing tips, and a red patch on the face. The whooping crane, which is the tallest North American bird, is an endangered species.

whop·per (wop′ər *or* hwop′ər) *Informal.* **1** something much bigger than average: *Wow, that potato sure is a whopper!* **2** a big lie. *n.* —**whop′ping,** *adj.*

whorl (wərl *or* wȯrl, hwərl *or* hwȯrl) a circle or spiral formed by leaves around the stem of a plant, the turns of a snail shell, the lines of a fingerprint, etc. *n.*

who's (hūz) **1** who is. **2** who has.

USING WORDS .... who's/whose

who's means "who is" or "who has": *Who's going to the movie? Who's been messing around with my things?*

whose means "belonging to whom": *Whose is this shoe?* The word **whose** can also refer back to things: *The pencil, whose point kept on breaking, was driving me crazy.*

whose (hūz) the possessive form of **who** and **which;** of whom; of which: *The girl whose work got the prize is the youngest in her class. Whose book is this?* *pron.*

why (wī *or* hwī) **1** for what reason: *Why did the baby cry? That explains why he left early.* **2** an expression used to show surprise, doubt, etc. or just to fill in: *Why, the cage is empty! Why, yes, I'll be glad to.* 1 *adv.,* 2 *interj.*
why not, a way of making a suggestion: *Why don't we go swimming first?*

wick (wik) the part of an oil lamp or candle that you light, usually a piece of cord that draws up the oil or melted wax. *n.*

wick·ed (wik′id) very bad; evil: *a wicked witch, wicked deeds.* *adj.* —**wick′ed·ness,** *n.*

wick·er (wik′ər) thin, easily bent branches or twigs that can be woven together. Wicker is used to make furniture and baskets. *n.*

wick·et (wik′it) **1** a small opening where people are served at a counter, such as in a bank, etc. In some places it is protected by a window or grating. **2** in croquet, a wire arch stuck in the ground to knock the ball through. *n.*

wide (wīd) **1** reaching far, or a certain distance, from side to side; broad; not narrow: *a wide street. The door is 90 cm wide (adj.). Open your mouth wide (adv.).* **2** over a large area: *to travel far and wide.* **3** including many different things: *a wide range of experience, a wide variety.* **4** not hitting the target or goal: *a wide shot (adj.). The kick went wide (adv.).* 1, 3, 4 *adj.,* **wid·er, wid·est;** 1, 2, 4 *adv.* —**wide′ly,** *adv.* —**wid′en,** *v.*
wide awake, fully awake and alert. Before a noun it is spelled **wide-awake.**
wide of, far from: *His guess was wide of the truth. The shot was wide of the mark.*
wide open, open as far as it can go. Before a noun it is spelled **wide-open.**

wide–eyed (wīd′īd′) with the eyes wide open: *The baby gazed at the clown with wide-eyed surprise.* *adj.*

wide·spread (wīd′spred′) **1** found in many places or among many people: *a widespread belief.* **2** spread over a wide space: *widespread flooding.* *adj.*

wid·ow (wid′ō) **1** a woman whose husband is dead and who has not married again. **2** make a widow or widower of: *She was widowed when she was only thirty years old.* 1 *n.,* 2 *v.*

wid·ow·er (wid′ō ər) a man whose wife is dead and who has not married again. *n.*

width (width) **1** how wide a thing is; the distance across: *The width of the room is 3 m.* **2** a piece having a certain width: *Two widths of cloth will be enough.* *n.*

wield (wēld) hold and use; manage; control: *The soldier wielded his sword well. A writer wields a pen. The people wield the power in a democracy.* *v.*

wie·ner (wē′nər) a very plain, straight sausage. A wiener in a bun is a **hot dog.** Sometimes wieners are cooked over an outdoor fire at a **wiener roast.** *n.*

wife (wīf) the woman married to a certain man: *Frances is Donald's wife.* *n., pl.* **wives.**

wig (wig) an artificial covering of hair for the head: *The bald man wore a wig.* *n.*

wig·gle (wig′əl) **1** move with short, quick movements up and down or from side to side: *The restless child wiggled in his chair. Wiggle the handle if it gets stuck.* **2** a movement like this. 1 *v.,* **wig·gled, wig·gling;** 2 *n.* —**wig′gly,** *adj.*

wig·wam (wig′wom) one kind of home used by First Nations people from the Atlantic to the prairies. It is a framework of poles covered with bark, reed mats, or animal skins. *n.*

WORD HISTORY........ wigwam

Wigwam is the word for "house" in the language of the Ojibwa First Nation.

wild (wīld) 1 not planted or raised by people; not tame: *The coyote is a wild animal. The daisy is a wild flower.* 2 with no people living in it: *the wild regions of the North.* 3 **wilds,** *pl.* wild country. 4 violent, crazy, or out of control: *a wild rush for the ball, wild with joy, a wild storm, wild ideas.* 1, 2, 4 *adj.,* 3 *n.*
—wild′ly, *adv.*
in the wild, in a wild state: *Many animals live longer in a zoo than they would in the wild.*
wild about, *Informal.* very fond of or pleased with: *They're just wild about their new house.*
wild and woolly, a bit weird in thought or behaviour.
wild card, a a card that can be used in place of any other card in a game. **b** a team or player that is allowed into a tournament without properly qualifying. **c** something completely unpredictable.
wild goose chase, a useless search or trip.
wild West, the western United States during cowboy days.

The bobcat is a wildcat that lives in the western parts of North America, from southern Canada to Mexico.

wild•cat (wīld′kat′) 1 any small to medium-sized wild member of the cat family. The bobcat and lynx are two kinds of wildcat. 2 done without the permission of the union leaders: *a wildcat strike.* 1 *n.,* 2 *adj.*

wil•der•ness (wil′dər nis) a region with few or no people living in it. *n.*

wild•fire (wīld′fīr′)
like wildfire, very fast: *The news spread like wildfire.* *n.*

wild•flow•er (wīld′flou′ər) any flower that grows in the woods, fields, etc. without being planted. *n.*

wild•life (wīld′līf′) wild animals as a group, usually those of a particular area: *northern wildlife.* *n.*

wild rice (wīld′ rīs′) a tall North American grass that grows in wet places. It has a dark-coloured grain that can be cooked and eaten like rice.

wild rose (wīld′ rōz′) any rose that grows wild, especially a common North American rose that has large pink flowers with five petals. The wild rose is the floral emblem of Alberta.

wile (wīl) a trick to get the better of someone: *The prince was not fooled by the wiles of the witch.* *n.*

will[1] (wil) an auxiliary verb used: 1 to refer to future happenings: *The train will be late. If we leave now, we will arrive by noon.* 2 to make a polite request: *Will you please be quiet.* 3 to say what a person or thing is able to do: *This pail will hold 8 L.* 4 to refer to something that happens often: *She will read for hours at a time.* *v., past tense* **would.**

will[2] (wil) 1 a person's ability to make decisions and act on them: *A good leader must have a strong will.* 2 firm determination: *the will to live.* 3 do or cause something just by the strength of your decision: *She willed herself to stay awake.* 4 wish; desire: *What is your will, master?* 5 a legal document that states what a person wants done with his or her property after death. 6 give by a document like this: *She willed all her property to her two daughters.* 7 an attitude toward another person: *His warm smile showed his good will.* 1, 2, 4, 5, 7 *n.,* 3, 6 *v.*
at will, whenever you want: *He can hiccup at will.*
with a will, with energy and determination.

will•ful or **wil•ful** (wil′fəl) 1 determined to have your own way; stubborn: *The willful child refused to turn off the TV.* 2 done on purpose: *willful damage to property.* *adj.* **—will′ful•ly** or **wil′ful•ly,** *adv.*

will•ing (wil′ing) ready or happy to do something: *He is willing to wait. We appreciate your willing help.* *adj.* **—will′ing•ly,** *adv.* **—will′ing•ness,** *n.*

wil•low (wil′ō) a tree or shrub with tough, slender, easily bent branches and very narrow leaves. The branches of a **weeping willow** tree are very long and droopy. *n.* **—wil′low•y,** *adj.*

will•pow•er (wil′pou′ər) the ability to keep from giving in to desire: *Eileen had the willpower to turn down a second dessert.* *n.*

wilt (wilt) 1 make or become limp and drooping; wither: *Flowers wilt when they do not get enough water.* 2 lose strength or enthusiasm: *After three hours of shopping I was beginning to wilt.* *v.*

a bat	e bed	i bid	o pot	u cup	th thin
ā cake	ē me	ī bite	ō go	ü rude	ᴛʜ then
ä bar	ə about	ər over	ô for	ů put	zh measure

wil·y (wī′lē) tricky; crafty; sly: *a wily thief. The wily fox got away.* *adj.,* **wil·i·er, wil·i·est.**

win (win) **1** get victory or success in any kind of contest or battle: *The tortoise won in the end. We all hope our team will win the tournament.* **2** a success; victory: *We had five wins and no losses.* **3** get by effort, ability, or luck; gain: *to win fame, to win a trophy, to win $500 in the lottery.* 1, 3 *v.,* **won, win·ning;** 2 *n.* —**win′ner,** *n.*
win someone over, get someone to like or agree with you.

wince (wins) **1** make a face or a slight movement showing pain: *I winced when Dad pulled the sliver out of my finger.* **2** the act of wincing: *He received his booster shot without even a wince.* 1 *v.,* **winced, winc·ing;** 2 *n.*

winch (winch) a machine for lifting or pulling, which works by turning a spool with a rope or cable wound around it; the free end of the rope or cable is attached to whatever needs to be pulled or lifted. The turning is done by hand or by an engine. *n.*

wind¹ (wind) **1** moving air: *The wind bends the tree branches. This fan creates quite a strong wind.* **2** breath; the ability to breathe: *That hard fall knocked the wind out of me.* **3** put out of breath: *We were winded by the steep climb.* **4** **winds,** *pl.* all the instruments in an orchestra that are played by blowing. The full name is **wind instruments.** 1, 2, 4 *n.,* 3 *v.* —**wind′y,** *adj.*
get wind of, **a** find out about; get a hint of: *Don't let anyone get wind of our plans.* **b** smell: *The deer soon got wind of the hunter.*
get your second wind, get a burst of extra strength or energy when you are tired.
in the wind, about to happen: *An election is in the wind.*
take the wind out of someone's sails, crush someone's feelings of excitement or pride.

Word Family..........wind

windbreak: a row of trees or other barrier to stop wind
windbreaker: a light jacket
windshield: the large front window of a vehicle
windsock: a cloth tube on a pole, showing which way the wind is blowing
windstorm: a storm with a lot of wind but no rain
windsurfing: the sport of gliding over water standing on a board with a sail
wind tunnel: a narrow chamber used in experiments to see how moving air will affect an aircraft

wind² (wīnd) **1** wrap, twist, or coil something around and around something else: *to wind a scarf around your neck. The nurse wound the patient's arm with bandages.* **2** make a toy or machine go by turning some part of it: *If you wind up the toy duck by turning this knob, it walks.* A toy that works this way is a **wind-up toy.** **3** move along turning this way and that way: *A creek winds through the woods. We wound our way through the streets of the old town.* *v.,* **wound, wind·ing.**
wind down, become gradually slower or less active, as if about to quit.
wind up, **a** finish: *We hope to wind up the project today.* **b** end up: *If you try that, you'll wind up in a lot of trouble.* **c** in baseball, make practice movements just before pitching. These movements are called the **wind-up.**

wind chill (wind′ chil′) the effect of the wind in making cold air feel even colder to your skin. If there is a wind chill of −10°C, that is how the air feels because of the wind, even though the actual temperature is higher.

wind·fall (wind′fol′) **1** fruit blown down by the wind. **2** an unexpected piece of good luck. *n.*

This is a fantail windmill, built in the 1700s. The small fantail attached to the main sail kept the main sail turned toward the wind.

wind·mill (wind′mil′) a tower with large blades that turn in the wind. The blades are attached to machinery which uses their turning action to do work or to make electricity. The ones used to make electricity are also called **wind turbines** (wind′ tər′bīnz). *n.*

win•dow (win′dō) 1 an opening in a wall or roof to let in light or air. Usually there is a framed piece of glass in it called a **windowpane.** 2 a framed display area on a computer screen. You can have more than one window open on the screen at the same time, with something different happening in each. *n.*

wind•ow–shop (win′dō shop′) look at things for sale in store windows without going in and buying them. *v.,* **wind•ow-shopped, wind•ow-shop•ping.**

window sill (win′dō sil′) a piece of wood or other material across the bottom of a window. It often forms a kind of shelf.

wind•pipe (wind′pīp′) the tube that carries air from your throat to your lungs. Its scientific name is **trachea** (trā′kē ə). *n.*

wind•ward (wind′wərd) 1 facing the wind: *the windward side.* 2 the direction that the wind is blowing from: *They saw a ship to windward.* *adj.*

wine (wīn) 1 the juice of grapes, when it is fermented and contains alcohol. 2 the fermented juice of other fruits or plants: *currant wine, dandelion wine.* 3 drink wine or give wine to someone: *wining and dining.* 1, 2 *n.,* 3 *v.,* **wined, win•ing.**

wing (wing) 1 the part of a bird, insect, or bat that it uses for flying. 2 anything shaped or used like a wing: *the wings of an airplane.* A part of a building that sticks out from the main part is a wing. 3 either of the spaces to the right or left of the stage in a theatre: *The actors waited in the wings for their cues.* 4 a part of an organization. In politics, the **left wing** is the more radical group, while the **right wing** is more conservative. 5 fly: *The bird wings its way south.* 6 wound in the wing or arm: *The bullet winged the bird but did not kill it.* 1–4 *n.,* 5, 6 *v.* **—winged,** *adj.* **—wing′less,** *adj.*
take wing, fly away: *The bird took wing when I came near.*
under the wing of, under the protection of.
wing it, do something without preparing beforehand.

wing•span (wing′span′) the distance between the tips of the wings of an airplane, bird, or insect; another word for it is **wingspread.**

wink (wingk) 1 close and open one eye on purpose as a hint or signal: *Dad winked at me when Mom came in so I would stop talking about her present.* 2 twinkle or flicker: *The stars winked.* 3 an act of winking. 4 a very short time: *I'll be back in a wink.* 1, 2 *v.,* 3, 4 *n.*
forty winks, a nap.
not sleep a wink, not sleep at all.
wink at, pretend not to see something that is wrong.

win•ning (win′ing) 1 that wins: *a winning team.* 2 charming; attractive: *She has a very winning smile.* **Winsome** means the same. 3 **winnings,** *pl.* what is won; money won: *He pocketed his winnings.* 1, 2 *adj.,* 3 *n.*

win•now (win′ō) blow off the husks and bits of straw from grain. *v.*

win•ter (win′tər) 1 the coldest of the four seasons, also called **wintertime.** It comes after fall and before spring. 2 spend or cause to spend the winter: *Robins winter in the south. The ranchers wintered their cattle in the warm valley.* 1 *n.,* 2 *v.* **—win′try,** *adj.*

win•ter•green (win′tər grēn′) a small evergreen woodland plant with bright-red berries. A minty-tasting oil is made from its leaves and used as a flavouring. *n.*

win•ter•ize (win′tər īz′) prepare something for winter use. Part of winterizing a car is putting snow tires on it; a winterized cottage has plenty of insulation and some kind of heating. *v.,* **win•ter•ized, win•ter•iz•ing.**

wipe (wīp) 1 rub in order to clean or dry: *Wipe the mud off your shoes. We wiped the dishes with a towel.* 2 the act of wiping: *He gave his face a quick wipe.* 1 *v.,* **wiped, wip•ing;** 2 *n.*
wipe out, destroy completely: *The pollution in the river wiped out all the fish.*

wip•er (wī′pər) 1 a rubber blade on a metal rod attached to the windshield of a vehicle in order to clear away rain or snow. It can be turned on and off from inside. 2 any other thing or person that wipes. *n.*

wire (wīr) 1 metal in the form of a thread or a thin, bendable rod: *telephone wire.* Wire is often coated with plastic or other material. 2 a piece of this: *A wire connects these two batteries.* 3 put wires in, to carry electricity: *to wire a house.* The system of electric wires is called the **wiring.** 4 fasten with wire: *He wired the two pieces together.* 5 telegraph or telegram: *He sent a message by wire (n.). Please wire your answer at once (v.).* 1, 2, 5 *n.,* 3–5 *v.,* **wired, wir•ing.**
down to the wire, at or near the last moment or deadline.
get in under the wire, just barely meet a requirement.

wire•less (wīr′lis) using no wires. Cellphones are a means of wireless communication. *adj.*

wire•tap (wīr′tap′) 1 make a secret connection with telephone wires in order to listen in on other people's calls. 2 the act of wiretapping: *The police did a wiretap to get evidence about the smugglers.* 1 *v.,* **wire•tapped, wire•tap•ping;** 2 *n.*

a bat	e bed	i bid	o pot	u cup	th thin
ā cake	ē me	ī bite	ō go	ū rude	ᴛʜ then
ä bar	ə about	ər over	ô for	ů put	zh measure

wir·y (wī′rē) 1 like wire: *wiry bristles.* 2 strong, slim, and tough: *a wiry athlete.* *adj.,* **wir·i·er, wir·i·est.**

wis·dom (wiz′dəm) 1 knowledge and good judgment; understanding that leads to good decisions. 2 the fact of being wise. *n.*

wisdom tooth (wiz′dəm tūth′) the back tooth on either side of the upper and lower jaw. Your wisdom teeth usually come in between the ages of 17 and 25.

wise (wīz) 1 showing understanding and good judgment: *a wise judge, wise advice, wise plans.* 2 trying to be funny in a clever but disrespectful way; smart-alecky: *Enough of your wise comments!* 3 **wise up,** *Slang.* start using more sense. 1, 2, *adj.,* **wis·er, wis·est;** 3 *v.,* **wised, wis·ing.** **—wise′ly,** *adv.*
none the wiser, not having found out or learned anything: *After his long explanation we were none the wiser.*
put someone wise, inform someone.
wise to, aware of: *She's wise to our secret plan.*

–wise *a suffix meaning* in a certain way. To move *clockwise* is to move the way the hands of a clock do. *Lengthwise* means "in the direction of the length." *Healthwise* means "with regard to health."

wise·crack (wīz′krak′) *Informal.* 1 a clever remark meant to be funny, especially a disrespectful one. 2 make remarks like this. 1 *n.,* 2 *v.*

wish (wish) 1 desire; want: *You may come whenever you wish (v.). He had no wish to be famous. She got her wish (n.)* 2 say what you long for or hope for, out loud or to yourself: *He wished for a new computer and then blew out his birthday candles. I wish it were summer! We wish you luck.* 3 an expression of a desire for someone's happiness, good fortune, etc.: *Please give her my best wishes for a Happy New Year.* 1, 2 *v.,* 1, 3 *n.*
make a wish, put your wish into words.

wish·bone (wish′bōn′) the Y-shaped bone in the front of the breast in chickens and other birds. According to one custom, if two people each take one end and pull the wishbone apart while making a wish, the one who ends up with the bigger piece will get his or her wish. *n.*

wish·ful (wish′fəl) dreaming or longing for something that is not likely to happen: *His plans for spending the lottery prize were only wishful thinking.* *adj.*

wisp (wisp) a small bunch or scrap: *a wisp of hay, wisps of cloud.* *n.* **—wisp′y,** *adj.*

wist·ful (wist′fəl) longing; full of desire for something that you likely cannot have: *A child stood looking with wistful eyes at the toys in the window.* *adj.*

wit (wit) 1 the ability to be funny in a clever way: *Her wit made even the dullest events into great stories.* 2 a person with such ability: *Martin Short is a wit.* 3 **wits,** *pl.* intelligence; mind; senses: *People with quick wits learn easily. I was out of my wits with fear.* *n.* **—wit′ty,** *adj.*

witch (wich) especially in stories, a woman with evil magic power. A witch's spells and other magical activities are called **witchcraft.** *n.*

with·draw (with drо′) 1 pull back; pull away: *He quickly withdrew his hand from the hot stove.* 2 take back; remove: *to withdraw $20 from a bank account. She withdrew her racist statement and made a public apology.* 3 go away: *They withdrew from the room.* *v.,* **with·drew, with·drawn, with·draw·ing.** **—with·draw′al,** *n.*

with·drawn (with dron′) 1 the past participle of **withdraw:** *Some kids were withdrawn from class to attend an enrichment program on Tuesdays.* 2 shy; keeping to yourself a lot. 1 *v.,* 2 *adj.*

with·er (wiᴛʜ′ər) 1 cause to dry out and shrivel up: *The hot sun withered the grass and flowers.* 2 **withering,** very scornful: *He gave me a withering look.* *v.*

with·hold (with hōld′) 1 refuse to give: *to withhold permission.* 2 hold back: *Please withhold your applause till the end of the concert.* *v.,* **with·held, with·hold·ing.**

with·in (wiᴛʜ in′ *or* with in′) 1 not beyond; inside the limits of: *You don't need a passport to travel within Canada. He guessed my height within 2 cm.* 2 in or into the inner part; inside of: *X rays allow doctors to see within the body (prep.). The house has been painted within and without (adv.).* 1, 2 *prep.,* 2 *adv.*

with·out (wiᴛʜ out′ *or* with out′) 1 not having, doing, or making: *to talk without noise, to win without trying. I like tea without sugar.* 2 outside; on the outside: *The house is painted within and without.* 1 *prep.,* 2 *adv.*
do or **go without,** manage in spite of not having a certain thing: *Either cook your own supper or go without.*

with·stand (with stand′) stand against; hold out against; survive or endure: *The pioneers had to withstand many hardships. These shoes will withstand hard wear.* *v.,* **with·stood, with·stand·ing.**

wit·ness (wit′nis) 1 a person who saw something: *He started the fight in the presence of several witnesses.* 2 see: *He witnessed the accident.* 3 a person who makes a statement about what he or she has seen especially in a court of law. 4 a person who signs a document to show that another person's signature on it is genuine. 5 sign in this way: *to witness a will.* 1, 3, 4 *n.,* 2, 5 *v.*

wives (wīvz) plural of **wife.** *n.*

wiz·ard (wiz′ərd) 1 especially in stories, a man with magic power. 2 *Informal.* a very clever person; expert: *She's a wizard at word puzzles.* *n.*
—wiz′ard·ry, *n.*

wiz·ened (wiz′ənd) dried up; withered; shrivelled: *a wizened apple.* *adj.*

wob·ble (wob′əl) 1 move unsteadily back and forth; shake: *The front wheel on her bicycle wobbles.* 2 a shaky, unsteady motion. 1 *v.,* **wob·bled, wob·bling;** 2 *n.* **—wob′bly,** *adj.*

woe (wō) great sadness or trouble: *Sickness and poverty are common woes.* *n.* **—woe′ful,** *adj.*
woe betide, an expression used in warnings and threats: *Woe betide the person who dares to touch my sculptures!*

wok (wok) a bowl-shaped metal frying pan, used especially for stir-frying. *n.*

woke (wōk) the past tense of **wake[1]:** *He woke before we did.* The past participle is **woken:** *When she had woken her sister, they both had breakfast.* *v.*

wolf (wu̇lf) 1 a wild animal resembling a large dog with a bushy tail and erect ears. Wolves live in packs and are found across Canada. 2 eat greedily: *The starving cat wolfed down the food.* 1 *n., pl.* **wolves;** 2 *v.*
—wolf′ish, *adj.*
cry wolf, give a false alarm.

wol·ver·ine (wu̇l′və rēn′) a very powerful, heavily built, meat-eating mammal related to the badger and the skunk. The wolverine is found across Canada's tundra and northern forest regions. *n.*

wom·an (wu̇m′ən) an adult female human being: *A woman is a girl who has grown up.* *n., pl.* **wom·en** (wim′ən). **—wom′an·hood′,** *n.*

wom·an·ly (wu̇m′ən lē) like or typical of a woman: *womanly courage.* *adj.*

womb (wūm) another word for **uterus,** the organ inside the body of a woman or female mammal that holds and nourishes a baby until birth. It stretches as the baby grows. *n.*

won (wun) the past tense and past participle of **win:** *Which side won yesterday? We have won four games.* *v.*

CONFUSABLES .... won

won is the past tense of "win": *I won the prize!*
one means "a single thing": *That is too heavy for one person to lift.*

won·der (wun′dər) 1 be curious about; want to know; ask yourself: *I wonder what time it is. I wonder what she would like for her birthday.* 2 a strange, awesome, or surprising thing: *The pyramids are one of the wonders of the world. It is a wonder that this old car still runs.* 3 the feeling caused by something like this: *The first time the baby saw snow, she gazed at it in wonder.* **Wonderment** means the same. 4 feel wonder: *We wonder at the splendour of the stars.* 5 be surprised or astonished: *I wonder that you came at all, given this awful weather.* 1, 4, 5 *v.,* 2, 3 *n.*
no wonder, it is not surprising: *No wonder you're tired—you went to bed so late!*
work wonders, do miracles; do amazing things.

won·der·ful (wun′dər fəl) 1 excellent; very good: *We had a wonderful time at the party.* 2 causing wonder; amazing; remarkable. A more poetic word for this sense is **wondrous** (wun′drəs). *adj.*

won't (wōnt) will not.

woo (wü) try to win someone's love so he or she will marry you. This word is somewhat old-fashioned. *v.*

wood (wu̇d) 1 the hard substance forming the trunk and branches of a tree. It can be cut and used as building material or fuel: *Put some wood on the fire.* 2 **woods,** *pl.* forest; a large area with a lot of trees: *looking for flowers in the woods.* *n.* **—wood′y,** *adj.*
out of the woods, out of danger or difficulty.

***Word Family*.......... wood**

woodcraft: skills for surviving in the forest
woodcutter: someone who cuts down trees
wooded: covered with trees
woodland: a poetic word for "forest"
woodlot: a piece of property with forest on it
woodpecker: a bird with a hard, sharp bill for pecking holes in trees to get insects out
woodpile: a pile of firewood
woodshed: a small building for storing wood
woodsy: seeming to belong to the forest
woodwind: a musical instrument, not brass, played by blowing; an oboe, flute, clarinet, etc.
woodwork: the wooden parts inside a house
woodworking: the craft of making things out of wood

wood·en (wu̇d′ən) 1 made of wood. 2 stiff and not very natural; with little feeling or expression: *The actor gave a very wooden performance.* *adj.*

a bat	e bed	i bid	o pot	u cup	th thin
ā cake	ē me	ī bite	ō go	ü rude	ᴛʜ then
ä bar	ə about	ər over	ȯ for	u̇ put	zh measure

Wool

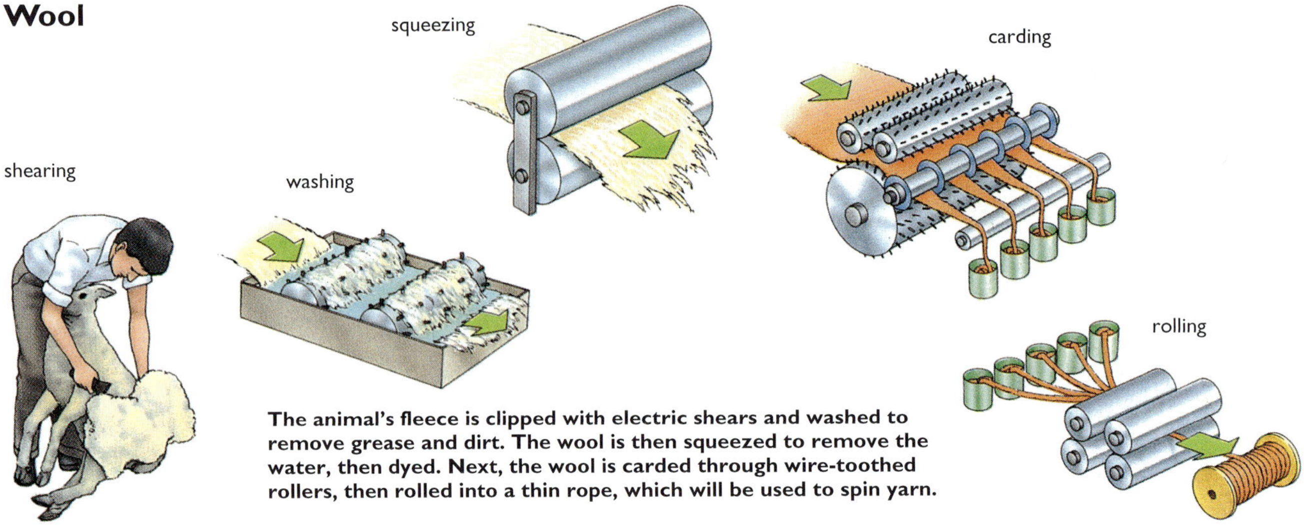

The animal's fleece is clipped with electric shears and washed to remove grease and dirt. The wool is then squeezed to remove the water, then dyed. Next, the wool is carded through wire-toothed rollers, then rolled into a thin rope, which will be used to spin yarn.

wool (wu̇l) **1** the soft, thick, curly hair of sheep and some other animals, used to make cloth and carpeting. **Woolgathering** is a humorous word for "daydreaming." **2** anything like wool. **Steel wool** comes in rolls or pads and is used for scrubbing and polishing. *n.*
—wool′len, *adj.* **—wool′ly,** *adj.*
pull the wool over someone's eyes, trick someone.

wooz·y (wü′zē) *Informal.* feeling weak and dizzy. *adj.,* **wooz·i·er, wooz·i·est.**

word (wərd) **1** a sound or group of sounds that has meaning on its own. It can be written down as a row of letters with no spaces in between, although a few words are spelled with just one letter. Sentences are made up of words. **2** a short talk or comment: *a word of advice. Can I have a word with you?* **3** a promise: *The boy kept his word.* **4** news: *Have you had any word from your cousin lately?* **5** speech: *She is honest in word and deed.* **6 words,** *pl.* angry talk; an argument: *They had words about whose fault it was.* **7** put into words: *He worded his message clearly.* 1–6 *n.,* 7 *v.* **—word′less,** *adj.*
be as good as your word, keep your promise.
by word of mouth, from what someone has said: *I found out about it by word of mouth.*
eat your words, take back what you have said.
give the word or **say the word,** order, signal, or permit someone to do something: *Don't move till I give the word.*
hang on someone's words, listen with great attention and admiration.
my word! my goodness! an expression of surprise.
take someone's word for it, believe someone.
take the words out of someone's mouth, say exactly what someone was about to say.
the last word, a the word that ends a discussion or argument. **b** the latest information. **c** the newest and best thing: *the last word in camping equipment.*
word for word, a in exactly the same words: *Repeat it word for word.* **b** one word at a time: *You can't translate word for word from one language to another.*

word·ing (wər′ding) the way something is said; the choice or use of words: *Careful wording helps make the meaning clear.* *n.*

word·play (wərd′plā′) the use of words in a creative and playful way, such as by making puns.

word processing (wərd′ prō′ses′ing) entering, editing, and printing out written material using a computer system.

word·y (wər′dē) using too many words. *adj.,* **word·i·er, word·i·est.**

wore (wôr) the past tense of **wear:** *He wore out his shoes in two months.* *v.*

work (wərk) **1** the effort of doing or making something: *It was hard work but she enjoyed it.* **2** tasks; things that must be done: *Yasoo has a lot of work to do this morning.* **3** a job which is your main duty or way of earning money; employment: *Many people are out of work.* **4** something that a person has made or achieved: *The artist calls that picture her greatest work.* **5** do things that take effort or that must be done: *We worked in the garden all day.* **6** have a paying job: *He works in a bank.* **7** do or cause to do what it is meant to do: *The plan worked. How do you work this pump?* **8** form; shape: *to work clay.* **9** cause to do work: *He works his employees long hours.* **10** move gradually or with effort: *to work something into a small space. The cork has worked loose.* **11 works,** *pl.* **a** a factory: *a steel works.* **b** the moving parts of a machine: *the works of a watch.* **c** actions; deeds: *good works.* **12** the result of force being applied to an object, with the object moving in the direction of the force. 1–4, 11, 12 *n.,* 5–10 *v.* **—work′a·ble,** *adj.*

work out, **a** plan; develop: *Work out your idea before you start writing.* **b** solve; figure out. **c** exercise: *The coach makes us work out before every game.* **d** succeed or happen; turn out as planned: *They were supposed to go to Lethbridge for Passover but it didn't work out.*
work to rule, do only what you are legally required to do and nothing more, as a protest against your employer.
work up, **a** produce with effort: *He managed to work up a smile.* **b** excite or upset: *Don't get worked up.*

Word Family...........**work**

workaholic: a person who is too devoted to work
workbench or **worktable:** a flat surface to work at
workbook: a book for doing school exercises in
workday: 1 the usual number of hours worked in a day **2** a day for working
work force: all the people who have or want paying jobs
workload: the amount of work a person has to do
workmanship: skill and care in making things
workout: a thorough session of exercise or practice
workplace: a place to work; an office, factory, shop, etc.
workroom: a room set aside for working in
worksheet: a single page for doing written work on
workshy: lazy
work station: a spot for one person to work at, such as a desk with a computer

work•er (wər′kər) **1** a person who works: *an office worker. She is a very good worker.* **2** one of the insects in a colony of bees, ants, wasps, etc. that do the work. *n.*

work•shop (wərk′shop′) **1** a room or building where things are built, made, or repaired. **2** a meeting to learn new things, share ideas and improve skills in a certain area: *Our teacher attended a music workshop on the last PD day.* *n.*

world (wərld) **1** the earth: *Airplanes can fly around the world.* **2** all people; the public: *The whole world saw it.* **3** a certain activity, group, area, etc., with all the things related to it: *the world of sports, the insect world.* **4** a great amount: *Sunshine does you a world of good.* **5** a planet, especially when thought of as inhabited. *n.*
bring into the world, give birth to or help someone give birth to. To be born is to **come into the world.**
on top of the world, very happy: *I was on top of the world when I found out I had won.*
out of this world, *Informal.* great; wonderful; fantastic: *The food was out of this world.*
think the world of, like and respect very much.

world–class (wərld′ klas′) ranking with the best in the world; deserving respect from the rest of the world: *a world-class hockey team, a world-class city.* *adj.*

world•ly (wərld′lē) having to do with or interested in this world only, rather than heaven: *worldly wealth, a worldly attitude.* *adj.,* **world•li•er, world•li•est.**

world power (wərld′ pou′ər) a country with the power to affect decisions made in many other countries.

world•view (wərld′vyū′) a person's way of looking at and understanding reality. Your worldview affects your values, choices, reactions, and so on. *n.*

World Wars (wərld′ wôrz′) two huge wars fought in Europe, Asia, Africa, and at sea. Both involved many nations, including Canada. **World War I** was from 1914 to 1918 and **World War II** was from 1939 to 1945.

world•wide (wərld′wīd′) throughout the world: *English is in worldwide use (adj.). He has travelled worldwide (adv.).* *adj. or adv.*

There are several thousand kinds of worm. Segmented worms, which have bodies made up of segments (like the rings of the clamworm shown here), are the most highly developed worms.

Clamworms live by the sea. They can grow up to 50 cm long.

worm (wərm) **1** a small animal that is long and thin and has no skeleton or legs. It moves by slithering, crawling, or wriggling. **2** the larva of an insect. **3 worms,** *pl.* a disease caused by worms in the body: *Our dog had worms, but it is fine now.* **4** a harmful computer program that spreads across a network. **5** move like a worm; crawl or wriggle: *He wormed his way under the high fence.* **6** manage to do something in a sly way or by trying again and again: *He tried to worm the secret out of me.* 1–4 *n.,* 5, 6 *v.* **—worm′y,** *adj.*
can of worms, a very complicated question or problem.

worn (wôrn) **1** the past participle of **wear:** *He has worn that suit for two years.* **2** looking old or tired: *worn rugs, a worn face.* 1 *v.,* 2 *adj.*
worn out **a** used until no longer fit for use: *Those shoes are worn out now.* **b** very tired; exhausted. The form before a noun is **worn-out.**

a bat	e bed	i bid	o pot	u cup	th thin
ā cake	ē me	ī bite	ō go	ū rude	ᴛʜ then
à bar	ə about	ər over	ô for	ù put	zh measure

wor·ry (wər′ē) 1 fearful thoughts or uneasy feelings about what might happen: *Worry kept us awake.* 2 have or cause to have these thoughts and feelings: *She will worry if we are late. The problem worried him.* A **worrywart** is a light-hearted name for someone who worries a lot. 1, *n.*, 2 *v.*, **wor·ries, wor·ried, wor·ry·ing.** —**wor′ri·er,** *n.* —**wor′ri·some,** *adj.*

worse (wərs) 1 more bad; of lower quality: *The food and the weather at camp were worse than they were last year.* 2 in a more severe, more unskilled, or more wrong way: *It is raining worse than ever today. We played even worse this time.* 3 sicker: *The patient seems worse today.* 4 someone or something that is worse: *Traffic is already bad, but we can expect even worse in an hour.* 1, 3 *adj.*, 2 *adv.*, 4 *n.* —**wor′sen,** *v.*
be none the worse for something, have no bad effects from something: *She was none the worse for her hair-raising adventure.*
for the worse, to a worse condition: *a change for the worse.*
worse off, in a worse condition: *We may be poor, but many people are even worse off.*

wor·ship (wər′ship) 1 give great honour and devotion to God, a god, or a person or thing treated like a god: *In Canada we are free to worship as we choose. Some people worship technology.* 2 this kind of honour and devotion: *the worship of God, hero worship.* 3 ceremonies or services that show this: *Join us for morning worship.* 1 *v.*, **wor·shipped** or **wor·shiped, wor·ship·ping** or **wor·ship·ing;** 2, 3 *n.* —**wor′ship·per** or **wor′ship·er,** *n.* —**wor′ship·ful,** *adj.*

worst (wərst) 1 most bad; of the lowest quality: *None of them are good, but he's the worst of the lot.* 2 in the most bad or least acceptable way: *He acts worst when he's tired.* 3 sickest: *This is the worst I've been since I got sick.* 4 the person or thing that is worst: *Yesterday was bad, but the worst is yet to come.* 1, 3 *adj.*, 2 *adv.*, 4 *n.*
at worst, under the worst conditions; if you look at it in the worst way possible.
if worst comes to worst, if the worst thing happens.

worth (wərth) 1 good or important enough for; deserving of: *Victoria is a city worth visiting.* 2 value; usefulness or importance: *Try to read books of real worth.* 3 equal in value to: *This coupon is worth a dollar.* 4 the amount you get for a certain price: *Get a dollar's worth of stamps.* 5 having property valued at: *That man is worth a million dollars.* 1, 3, 5 *adj.*, 2, 4 *n.* —**worth′less,** *adj.*

worth·while (wərth′ wīl′) worth spending time, attention, or effort on: *The film was very worthwhile—I learned a lot from it.* *adj.*

wor·thy (wər′ᴛʜē) 1 deserving: *Her courage was worthy of high praise.* 2 good; honourable: *to volunteer for a worthy cause.* *adj.*, **wor·thi·er, wor·thi·est.**

would (wůd) the past tense of **will.** It is also used: 1 to introduce a polite request: *Would you please close the window? I would like a drink, please.* 2 in sentences that express uncertainty or other feeling: *I can't imagine whose that would be. It is incredible that he would do such a thing.* 3 with **if,** to express a condition or its result: *If I knew, I would tell you. If she would just listen, we could explain.* 4 to refer to something that happened often in the past: *When I was small, I would play in the sand for hours.* *v.*

Grammar ✓Check .... would

Would is used to report what someone else has said or thought about the future. *She says Tia will never agree to it* becomes, in the past tense, *She said Tia would never agree to it.*

would·n't (wůd′ənt) would not.

wound¹ (wūnd) 1 hurt or injure, especially in a way that causes bleeding: *One shot wounded the deer.* 2 hurt someone's feelings: *His words wounded her.* 3 a hurt or injury of either kind: *The doctor sewed up the wound. The loss of his job was a wound to his pride.* 1, 2 *v.*, 3 *n.*

wound² (wound) the past tense and past participle of **wind²**: *She wound the cord around the blow dryer before packing it. It is wound too loosely.* *v.*

wove (wōv) a past tense of **weave:** *The spider wove a new web after the first was destroyed.* The past participle is **woven:** *This cloth is loosely woven.* *v.*

wow (wou) *Slang.* 1 an exclamation of delight, admiration, etc. 2 dazzle or impress: *Kim really wowed everyone with his new bike.* 1 *interj.*, 2 *v.*

wran·gle (rang′gəl) 1 argue noisily and angrily: *The children wrangled about who should sit in the front seat.* 2 a noisy, angry argument. 1 *v.*, **wran·gled, wran·gling;** 2 *n.* —**wran′gler,** *n.*

WORD HISTORY........ wr-

Originally, the **w** in words like **wrangle** was not silent; it had a *v* sound. We no longer have the combination *vr-* at the beginning of a syllable in English, except for "play" words like *vroom.* This is odd, because *vr-* is no different from *fr-* except that your voice is turned on instead of off.

wrap (rap) 1 cover by winding or folding something around: *She wrapped the leftovers in foil. Wrap a blanket around yourself.* 2 cover with paper and fasten: *Have you wrapped all the presents?* The paper or other material that something has been wrapped in is its **wrapping,** or, if it was bought that way, its **wrapper.** 3 paper for wrapping gifts: *a roll of fancy wrap.* 4 an outer covering: *Shawls, scarfs, coats, and furs are wraps.* 1, 2 *v.,* **wrapped, wrap·ping;** 3, 4 *n.*
under wraps, kept secret.
wrapped up in, devoted to; constantly thinking of: *She is wrapped up in her work.*
wrap up, **a** dress warmly. **b** finish. **c** summarize. The act of finishing or summarizing is a **wrap-up.**

wrath (rath *or* roth) an old or poetic word for "anger." *n.* **—wrath′ful,** *adj.*

wreak (rēk)
wreak havoc, cause a lot of damage, confusion, and so on: *The hurricane wreaked havoc on the city.* *v.*

wreath (rēth) 1 a ring of twigs, branches, flowers, or leaves twisted together: *The bride had a wreath of flowers in her hair.* 2 something that looks like a wreath: *wreaths of smoke.* *n., pl.* **wreaths** (rēᴛʜz).

wreathe (rēᴛʜ) surround with wreaths or something like a wreath: *The mirror was wreathed with holly. Mist wreathes the hills.* *v.,* **wreathed, wreath·ing.**

wreck (rek) 1 destroy; ruin: *to wreck a car in an accident, to wreck someone's plans.* A machine or company that tears down buildings is called a **wrecker.** 2 what is left of anything after being destroyed or badly damaged: *They are exploring the wreck of the "Titanic."* Scattered bits and pieces are called **wreckage.** 3 a person that has lost physical or mental health: *He was a wreck after the fight.* 4 the fact of being ruined or destroyed: *Heavy rains caused the wreck of many crops.* 1 *v.,* 2–4 *n.*

wren (ren) a small brown or grey songbird with a narrow beak and a short tail, often held straight up. *n.*

wrench (rench) 1 a tool with two jaws, to hold and turn nuts, bolts, and so on. An adjustable one is called a **monkey wrench.** 2 twist or pull violently: *He wrenched the knob off when he was trying to open the door. I wrenched my ankle in basketball.* 3 a violent twist or twisting pull: *She broke the branch off with a sudden wrench.* 4 something very painful or hard to do: *It was a wrench to leave our old home.* 1, 3, 4 *n.,* 2 *v.*
throw a monkey wrench into, mess up.

wrest (rest) take something by force, using a twisting, pulling motion: *He wrested the key from my hand and ran off.* *v.*

The sport of wrestling goes back more than 4000 years.

Sumo wrestlers in Japan today

wres·tle (res′əl) 1 fight by trying to throw or force the other person to the ground: *The officer wrestled the burglar to the ground.* **Wrestling** is also a sport. 2 to struggle: *I have been wrestling with this problem for an hour.* 3 the act of wrestling or struggling. 1, 2 *v.,* **wres·tled, wres·tling;** 3 *n.* **—wres′tler,** *n.*

wretch (rech) 1 a very unfortunate or unhappy person. 2 a very bad person. *n.*

wretch·ed (rech′id) 1 very unfortunate or unhappy; miserable: *I was left alone and feeling wretched. The refugees were living in wretched conditions.* 2 very bad. *adj.* **—wretch′ed·ness,** *n.*

wrig·gle (rig′əl) 1 twist and turn: *Children wriggle when they are restless. The fish wriggled out of my hand.* 2 the act of wriggling: *With one wriggle, he was under the bed.* 1 *v.,* **wrig·gled, wrig·gling;** 2 *n.*

-wright (rīt) *a suffix meaning* a maker or author of something. A *wheelwright* makes wheels. A *playwright* writes plays. *n.*

wring (ring) 1 squeeze hard while twisting, especially in order to get liquid out: *Wring out your wet towel. The hikers wrung water from their soaked clothes.* 2 get by force, effort, or persuasion: *They could not wring the secret from her.* 3 a twisting or squeezing: *Give the dishcloth a wring.* 1, 2 *v.,* **wrung, wring·ing;** 3 *n.* **—wring′er,** *n.*
wring someone's hand, shake hands very firmly and enthusiastically with someone. To **wring your hands** is to rub or squeeze them together nervously.
wring someone's heart, fill someone with deep sadness.
wring someone's neck, strangle someone.

a bat	e bed	i bid	o pot	u cup	th thin
ā cake	ē me	ī bite	ō go	ū rude	ᴛʜ then
à bar	ə about	ər over	ȯ for	u̇ put	zh measure

wrin·kle (ring′kəl) **1** a small, crooked ridge or fold; crease: *I smoothed out the wrinkles in the bedspread.* **2** make or get wrinkles: *She wrinkled her nose in disgust. This shirt will not wrinkle.* 1 *n.,* 2 *v.,* **wrin·kled, wrin·kling.** **—wrin′kly,** *adj.*

wrist (rist) the joint connecting your hand to your arm. A **wristband** is a band worn around your wrist. *n.*

wrist·watch (rist′woch′) a watch worn on a strap around your wrist. *n.*

write (rīt) **1** make letters or words with pen, pencil, chalk, etc., especially in a style that joins the letters together: *You can read and write. Write your name here.* **2** make up stories, poems, songs, and so on: *She writes for the magazine. Beethoven wrote "Ode to Joy."* **3** write a letter to someone: *I wrote Aino today.* *v.,* **wrote, writ·ten** (rit′ən), **writ·ing.** **—writ′er,** *n.* **—writ′ing,** *n.*
write down, put into writing: *He wrote down his thoughts.*
write off, a give something up as worthless: *Don't write Kala off just because you don't agree with her!* **b** report something as an expense on your income tax form so you don't have to pay tax on the money spent on it. Anything that is written off in either of these ways is a **write-off.**
write out, a put into writing. **b** write in full: *She made quick notes in the meeting and wrote out her report later.*
write up, write a description or report of: *Alicia wrote up the class trip for the school newspaper.* The piece of writing itself is called a **write-up.**

writhe (rīᴛʜ) twist this way and that way, out of control, especially from pain. *v.,* **writhed, writh·ing.**

wrong (rong) **1** not right; bad: *Stealing is wrong.* **2** not true, correct, or suitable; not what it should be: *He gave the wrong answer. I got on the wrong bus.* **3** not working well; needing to be fixed: *Something is wrong with the printer.* **4** in a bad or improper way: *You've done it all wrong.* **5** something bad or unjust: *The criminal had committed many wrongs.* **6** do something bad to; treat unjustly: *He forgave those who had wronged him.* 1–3 *adj.,* 4 *adv.,* 5 *n.,* 6 *v.* **—wrong′ful,** *adj.*
go wrong, a turn out badly: *Everything went wrong today.* **b** leave the right way: *Where did I go wrong?*
in the wrong, at fault; guilty.

wrong·do·ing (rong′dū′ing) bad actions: *The dishonest banker was guilty of wrongdoing.* *n.*

wrote (rōt) the past tense of **write:** *He wrote his mother a long letter last week.* *n.*

wrought iron (rot′ ī′ərn) a form of iron that is soft enough to be easily forged and welded, but will not break as easily as cast iron. Wrought iron is often used for decorative furniture, gates, or railings.

wrung (rung) the past tense and past participle of **wring:** *She wrung out the wet cloth and hung it up.* *v.*

wry (rī) **1** twisted; turned to one side: *She made a wry face to show her disgust.* **2** funny in a slightly sarcastic or gloomy way: *wry comments.* *adj.,* **wry·er, wry·est.**

Xx

x or **X** (eks) **1** the twenty-fourth letter of the English alphabet, or any sound that it stands for. The sound of *x* in *xylophone* is different from the sound of *x* in *box.* **2** the twenty-fourth thing in a list. **3** the Roman numeral for 10. **4** **X** is also used: **a** to indicate a target on a map. **b** to symbolize a kiss. **c** to stand for the signature of a person who cannot write. **d** for measurement in a horizontal direction on a graph. *n., pl.* **x's** or **X's.**

xe•bec (zē′bek) a small sailing ship with three masts that tilt sharply backwards. It used to be common on the Mediterranean Sea. *n.*

Xmas (kris′məs) *Informal.* a short form for **Christmas.** *n.*

X ray (eks′ rā′) **1** an invisible ray which can go through things that ordinary rays of light cannot, but which acts like visible light on photographic films or plates to produce a picture. X rays are used by dentists and doctors to find cavities, breaks in bones, etc. and to treat certain diseases. **2** a picture made by means of X rays. **—X-ray,** *v. or adj.*

X's and O's (ek′siz en ōz′) a game where two players take turns marking X and O on a chart that has nine squares. The winner is the first to mark three X's or O's in a horizontal, vertical, or diagonal line. **Tick-tack-toe** or **tic-tac-toe** is another name for this game.

xy•lem (zī′ləm) the firmer tissue in plants and trees that takes up water and minerals from the roots and supports the softer tissue, called the **phloem.** *n.*

The xylophone is a percussion instrument. It has two rows of bars arranged like a keyboard.

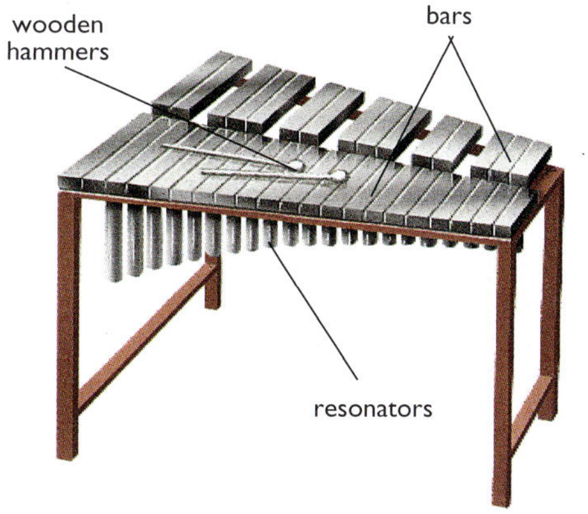

xy•lo•phone (zī′lə fōn′) a musical instrument with two rows of wooden bars of different lengths, played by hitting them with wooden hammers. *n.*

Y y

y or **Y** (wī) 1 the twenty-fifth letter of the English alphabet, or any sound that it stands for. Y is a consonant in *yes* and a vowel in *baby.* 2 the twenty-fifth thing in a list. *n., pl.* **y's** or **Y's.**

–y[1] *a suffix meaning:* 1 full of, made of, covered with, or having, as in *sunny.* 2 like or resembling, as in *watery.* 3 tending to, as in *fidgety.*

–y[2] a suffix used to show that someone or something is thought of as small and cute, or is loved, as in *doggy, dolly, Mommy.* It is also often spelled **-ie** as in **cutie.**

–y[3] *a suffix meaning:* 1 a state or quality, as in *jealousy.* 2 an activity, as in *delivery, inquiry.*

yacht (yot) 1 a sailboat that also has a motor, used for pleasure trips or for racing. 2 sail or race on a yacht. 1 *n.,* 2 *v.*

yak[1] (yak) a large, long-haired animal of central Asia, related to the North American bison, the Indian buffalo, and to cattle. Yaks are often kept by people for milk, meat, wool, and leather. They are also used as beasts of burden. *n.*

yak[2] (yak) *Slang.* talk about things that don't really matter; waste time in talking. *v.,* **yakked, yak·king.**

yam (yam) 1 the starchy root of a vine grown for food in warm countries. 2 a kind of sweet potato. *n.*

yank (yangk) *Informal.* 1 pull hard with a sudden motion: *You almost yanked my arm off!* 2 a sudden hard pull: *She gave the door a yank.* 1 *v.,* 2 *n.*

yap (yap) 1 a high-pitched, snappish bark. 2 bark in this way: *That little dog yaps at strangers.* 3 *Slang.* talk too much, especially in an irritating voice. 1 *n.,* 2, 3 *v.,* **yapped, yap·ping.** —**yap′py,** *adj.*

yard[1] (yȧrd) 1 a piece of ground near or around a building: *He is in the yard cutting grass.* 2 a piece of enclosed ground for some special purpose or business: *a chicken yard.* Both senses often appear in compounds: *schoolyard, junkyard.* *n.*

yard[2] (yȧrd) 1 a nonmetric measure of length equal to 36 inches or 3 feet (about 91 cm): *The football player ran 40 yards for a touchdown.* A **yardstick** is a measuring stick one yard long. 2 a pole fastened sideways across a boat's mast, used to support a sail. *n.*

yard sale (yȧrd′ sāl′) a sale you hold in your yard to get rid of things you no longer want: *On Saturday half the people on our street were having yard sales.*

yarn (yȧrn) 1 thick, often fuzzy thread for weaving, knitting, crocheting, and so on: *This yarn is soft enough for baby clothes.* 2 *Informal.* an entertaining story. *n.*
spin yarns, tell stories, especially by making them up as you go along.

yawn (yon) 1 open your mouth wide and breathe in deeply as a result of sleepiness or boredom. 2 the action or sound of doing this: *We heard a loud yawn behind us.* 3 open wide: *The canyon yawned beneath our feet.* 1, 3 *v.,* 2 *n.*

yd. *abbreviation for* yard or yards, a nonmetric unit of length.

ye (yē) an old form of **you,** used mostly in poetry and religion. It is the plural form of **thou.** *pron.*

yea (yā) 1 an old or poetic word for "yes" or "truly." It is still used in formal meetings to vote in favour of something. 2 a shout used in cheering: *Yea, team! Yea, we get to eat out tonight!* 1 *adv. or n.,* 2 *interj.*

year (yēr) 1 a period of time equal to 12 months or 365 days, from January 1 to December 31. Leap year has 366 days. 2 twelve months counted from any point: *I will see you again a year from today.* 3 the part of a year spent in a certain activity: *Our school year is almost ten months.* 4 the exact time taken for the earth to make one revolution around the sun, equal to 365 days, 5 hours, 48 minutes, and 46 seconds. *n.*
year in, year out, always, continuously: *He has always worked hard, year in, year out.*

year·book (yēr′bu̇k′) a book published every year, reporting what has happened during the year or what new information has been discovered. Schools and encyclopedias often publish yearbooks. *n.*

year·ling (yēr′ling) an animal one year old. *n.*

year·ly (yēr′lē) 1 once a year; in every year: *He takes a yearly trip to Charlottetown* (*adj.*). *A new volume comes out yearly* (*adv.*). 2 lasting or covering a year: *a yearly salary of $35 000, the earth's yearly revolution around the sun.* 1, 2 *adj.,* 1 *adv.*

yearn (yərn) feel a deep, strong desire: *He yearns for home.* *v.* —**yearn′ing,** *n.*

year–round (yēr′round′) throughout the year: *Our town has many summer visitors but few year-round residents (adj.). Their cottage is open year-round (adv.).* *adj. or adv.*

yeast (yēst) a substance often added to bread dough to make it light and puffy. Yeast is made up of very small fungus cells that multiply quickly wherever sugar, moisture, nutrients, and oxygen are present. It is also used to ferment beer by using up the sugar to produce alcohol. Yeast is sold as a moist blob or as little freeze-dried grains. *n.*

yell (yel) **1** shout loudly: *We yelled "Goodbye!" as the bus moved away.* **2** a loud shout. 1 *v.*, 2 *n.*

Yellowstone National Park in the United States is named after the yellow rocks that lie along the Yellowstone River. This park, established in 1872, is the oldest national park in the world.

There are many geysers and hot springs in Yellowstone Park. The most famous is Old Faithful, which spouts a plume of hot water 45 m high, about once an hour.

yel·low (yel′ō) **1** the colour of egg yolks or ripe lemons. **2** make or become yellow: *Paper yellows with age.* **3** *Informal.* cowardly. 1 *n.*, 1, 3 *adj.*, 2 *v.* —**yel′low·ish,** *adj.*

yellow jacket (yel′ō jak′it) a black wasp marked with bright yellow. It nests near the ground and often bothers picnickers.

Yel·low·knife (yel′ō nīf′) **1** a First Nations people living north of the city of Yellowknife in the Northwest Territories, between Great Bear and Great Slave Lakes. **2** their language, which belongs to the Athapascan family. **3** having to do with these people or their language. 1, 2 *n.*, 3 *adj.*

Yellow Pages (yel′ō pājiz) *a trademark for* a phone book, or part of a phone book, printed on yellow paper. It lists and advertises businesses according to the kind of work they do or what they sell.

yelp (yelp) **1** a quick, sharp bark or cry, especially from pain or excitement: *The small puppy's yelps made its owner come running.* **2** make such a bark or cry: *I yelped when the rock fell on my toe.* 1 *n.*, 2 *v.*

yes·ter·day (yes′tər dā′) **1** the day before today: *Yesterday was cold (n.). She left yesterday (adv.).* **2** the past: *The fashions of yesterday seem funny to us now.* 1, 2 *n.*, 1 *adv.*

WORD HISTORY....... yesterday

Yesterday literally means "yesterday day." It's from the Old English *geostrandaeg*, made up of *geostran*, meaning "yesterday," and *daeg*, "day."

yet (yet) **1** at this or that time, as opposed to later on. *The work is not yet finished* means it may be finished later on. **2** still: *Don't leave—it's early yet. I may win yet. It rained yet harder.* **3** but; however: *The story was strange, yet true (adv.). He has so little yet he is happy to share (conj.).* 1–3 *adv.*, 3 *conj.*
as yet, up to now: *As yet we have no news of him.*

yet·i (yet′ē) another name for the **abominable snowman,** a humanlike monster that is supposed to live in the Himalayan mountains of Asia. *n., pl.* **yet·is.**

yew (yū) a small evergreen tree with red berries. Bows for shooting arrows used to be made of a kind of yew that grows in England. *n.*

Yid·dish (yid′ish) a language that developed from a German dialect of the Middle Ages, which now also contains many Hebrew and Slavic words. It is written in Hebrew letters and is spoken especially by Jewish people of eastern and central Europe. *n.*

yield (yēld) **1** produce; bear: *This land yields good crops. Those mines yield iron ore.* **2** the amount yielded; the product: *This year's corn yield was very large.* **3** give up; give way: *I yielded to temptation and ate all the candy. The door yielded to her touch.* Something or someone that easily gives way to pressure is **yielding.** 1, 3 *v.*, 2 *n.*

yin and yang (yin′ ən yang′) in the Taoist religion, the two opposite forces that operate in the universe. The **yin** is a negative force and the **yang** is a positive force; neither will overcome the other. Some other belief systems also have yin and yang and attach different meanings to them.

yo·del (yō′dəl) **1** sing or call with a voice that changes quickly back and forth between its ordinary pitch and a much higher pitch: *The Swiss mountaineer was yodelling as we came up the valley.* **2** the act or sound of yodelling. 1 *v.*, **yo·delled** or **yo·deled, yo·del·ling** or **yo·del·ing;** 2 *n.* —**yo′del·ler** or **yo′del·er,** *n.*

a bat	e bed	i bid	o pot	u cup	th thin
ā cake	ē me	ī bite	ō go	ū rude	ᴛʜ then
ä bar	ə about	ər over	ô for	ů put	zh measure

Yoga

Yoga is intended to remove all distractions that may prevent a person from reaching a physical and mental state to live a life of the spirit. The physical training gets more and more difficult, and its aim is to bring the body under complete control.

yo·ga or **Yo·ga** (yō′gə) in the Hindu religion, a way of joining your soul with God through certain mental and physical exercises. *n.*

yo·gurt (yō′gərt) a creamy food made from milk that has had certain bacteria added to sour it and thicken it. It is often prepared with fruit or fruit flavouring. *n.*

yoke (yōk) **1** a wooden frame which fits around the necks of two work animals to fasten them together for pulling something. A **yoke of oxen** is two oxen joined by a yoke. **2** fasten animals to each other or to a vehicle with a yoke: *The farmer yoked his plough.* **3** anything that is like a yoke because it joins people together or keeps them under control. **4** a specially shaped section at the top of a garment. On a shirt or dress it covers the shoulders; on a skirt it covers the hips. 1, 3, 4 *n.,* 2 *v.,* **yoked, yok·ing.**

yolk (yōk) the yellow part of an egg. *n.*

Yom Kip·pur (yom′ ki pūr′) an annual Jewish day of fasting and atoning for sins, celebrated on the tenth day after the Jewish New Year. It falls in late September or early October.

yon·der (yon′dər) over there; within sight, but not near: *The sky is getting black yonder in the west* (*adv.*). *On yonder hill stands a ruined castle* (*adj.*). **Yon** is a short form. *adv. or adj.*

yore (yòr)
of yore, of long ago: *in days of yore, tales of yore.* *adv.*

🍁 **York boat** (yòrk′ bōt′) a type of heavy freight canoe used in earlier times. It was developed by the Hudson's Bay Company at York Factory on Hudson Bay.

you'd (yūd) **1** you had: *You'd better go quickly.* **2** you would: *You'd like this story.*

you'll (yūl) you will.

young (yung) **1** in the early part of life; not old: *A puppy is a young dog.* **2** an animal's babies: *An animal will fight to protect its young.* **3** without much experience or practice: *She was too young in the business.* 1, 3 *adj.,* **young·er** (yung′gər), **young·est** (yung′gist); 2 *n.*

young·ster (yung′stər) a child or young person: *She is a lively youngster.* *n.*

you're (yùr *or* yər) you are.

USING WORDS . . . . your

Your is possessive and is used before a noun: *Don't forget your bag.*

You're is not possessive. It is a short form of *you are*: *You're going to be late.*

youth (yūth) **1** the fact or quality of being young: *He has the vigour of youth.* **2** the time between childhood and adulthood: *She travelled a lot in her youth.* **3** a young man. **4** young people: *More jobs are needed for youth.* **5** the first or early stage of anything: *Space travel is still in its youth.* *n., pl.* **youths** (yūᴛʜz *or* yūths). **—youth′ful,** *adj.*

you've (yūv) you have.

yowl (youl) **1** a long cry of pain or sadness by an animal; a howl. **2** make this sound: *That dog is always yowling.* 1 *n.,* 2 *v.*

yo–yo (yō′yō) **1** a small, wheel-shaped toy made up of two disks joined by a peg in the middle with a long string attached to it. You hold the string and spin the toy out or reel it in by different movements of your hand, wrist, and arm. **2** always going up and down or back and forth between two extremes: *yo-yo dieting.* 1 *n., pl.* **yo-yos;** 2 *adj.*

yr. *abbreviation for* year. The usual form for "years" is **yrs.**

Yu·kon Territory (yū′kon ter′ə tòr′ē) a territory of Canada, north of British Columbia and west of the Northwest Territories.

Yule or **yule** (yūl) Christmas. **Yuletide** means the same. *n.*

yum (yum) *Informal.* an exclamation you make when enjoying food. Something that is **yummy** (*adj.*) is very good to eat. *interj.*

yup·pie or **Yup·pie** (yup′ē) *Informal.* a young, well-educated, fashionable adult who lives in a city, has a well-paying job, and likes to buy expensive things: *The yuppies next door built a new deck for their house.* The word comes from the first letters of **young urban professional.** *n.*

Zz

z or **Z** (zed) 1 the twenty-sixth and last letter of the English alphabet, or any sound that it stands for. The sound of *z* in *seizure* is different from the sound of *z* in *zoo.* 2 the twenty-sixth thing in a list. *n., pl.* **z's** or **Z's.**

Zam•bo•ni (zam bō′nē) *a trademark for* a machine used to keep the surface smooth on an ice rink. As it is driven around on the rink, it clears off the bits of ice scraped up by people's skates, and at the same time covers the surface with a new layer of ice. *n.*

za•ny (zā′nē) crazy in a funny way; wacky; ridiculous: *His zany stories make everyone laugh. adj.*

zap (zap) *Informal.* 1 hit or kill swiftly and suddenly. 2 give an electric shock to. 3 heat something in a microwave oven: *If that soup has cooled off, just zap it for 30 seconds.* 4 use a TV remote controller to keep material from being recorded onto video, or to switch channels: *If we zap all the commercials, the whole show should fit on one video. He zapped to the hockey game.* 5 the action or sound of zapping. 1–4 *v.,* **zapped, zap•ping;** 5 *n.*

zeal (zēl) eager desire or effort; whole-hearted enthusiasm: *We should all have her zeal for protecting the environment.* A person with a lot of zeal is a **zealot** (zel′ət). *n.* —**zeal′ous** (zel′əs), *adj.*

As camouflage, the zebra's stripes seem to make it more visible, not less. If, however, you think of a zebra running from a hunting lioness, all those dazzling stripes are like an optical illusion, making it difficult to judge exactly where the zebra is.

ze•bra (zē′brə) a wild animal of Africa, related to the horse and donkey, but striped with dark bands on white. *n.*

Zen (zen) a Japanese branch of Buddhism that emphasizes meditation. Often the meditation is based on a riddle or problem, and leads the person to a solution that results in greater understanding. *n.*

zen•ith (zē′nith) 1 the point in the sky that is directly overhead. 2 the highest or greatest point: *At the zenith of its power Rome controlled all of Europe. n.*

zeph•yr (zef′ər) a soft, gentle wind; a mild breeze. *n.*

ze•ro (zē′rō) 1 none; not any; nothing: *The other team's score was zero (n.). You have zero time left (adj.).* 2 the number that stands for nothing or none; the figure 0: *There are three zeros in 40 006.* 3 the point marked with a zero on any scale of measurement, such as a thermometer: *The overnight temperature will be zero.* 1–3 *n., pl.* **ze•ros** or **ze•roes;** 1 *adj.*
zero gravity, a condition in which there seems to be no gravity because its force is so weak; weightlessness.
zero hour, the exact moment set for some important event such as a space launch.

zest (zest) 1 lively enjoyment; enthusiasm: *The hungry girl ate with zest.* 2 a pleasant, interesting, lively quality: *Humour gives zest to conversation.* 3 make something more interesting or lively: *Add a few spices to zest up this stew.* 1, 2 *n.,* 3 *v.* —**zest′ful,** *adj.* —**zest′y,** *adj.*

zig•zag (zig′zag′) 1 with short, sharp turns from one side to the other: *to go in a zigzag direction (adj.). The path ran zigzag up the hill (adv.).* 2 a line or path that makes turns like this. 3 move in this way: *Lightning zigzagged across the sky.* 1 *adj. or adv.,* 2 *n.,* 3 *v.,* **zig•zagged, zig•zag•ging.**

zilch (zilch) *Slang.* nothing; zero: *I spent all morning in bed and accomplished zilch. n.*

zil•li•on (zil′yən) *Informal.* an extremely large number: *I can think of a zillion reasons why you should not buy that. n.*

zinc (zingk) a bluish-white metal that is a chemical element. It is affected very little by air and moisture and is often used as a protective coating for other metals such as iron and steel to prevent rust. It is also used in electric batteries and for many other things, and is one of the body's essential nutrients. *n.*

a bat	e bed	i bid	o pot	u cup	th thin
ā cake	ē me	ī bite	ō go	ū rude	ᴛʜ then
ä bar	ə about	ər over	ô for	ů put	zh measure

Zodiac

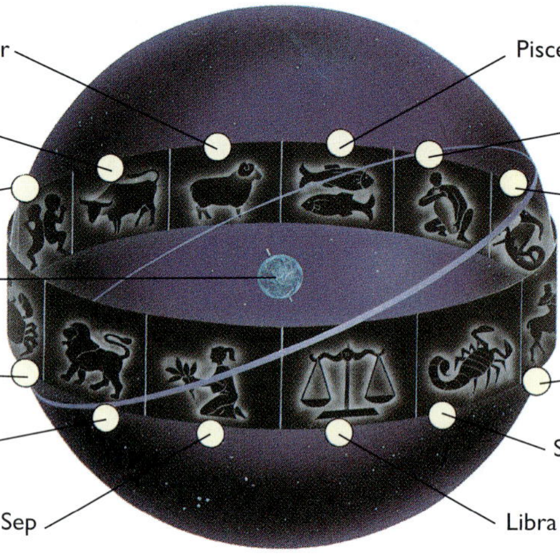

zin·ni·a (zin′yə) a garden plant with showy flowers of many colours. Zinnias originally come from Central and South America. *n.*

Zi·on·ism (zī′ə niz′əm) a movement which began in the late 1800s, to make a Jewish national state. Present-day Zionism is the support of Israel. *n.* —**Zi′on·ist,** *n. or adj.*

zip (zip) 1 fasten or close with a zipper: *He zipped up his jacket.* 2 *Informal.* go fast: *I zipped over to Duongs' on my bicycle.* 3 *Informal.* lively energy, speed, or excitement. 4 move with a sudden, short hissing sound like a flying arrow. 5 *Informal.* nothing; zero: *They paid her zip for all that work.* 1, 2, 4 *v.,* **zipped, zip·ping;** 3, 5 *n.* —**zip′py,** *adj.*

zip·per (zip′ər) 1 a sliding fastener for clothes, knapsacks, etc. with two rows of little interlocking teeth: *He has a zipper on his jacket.* 2 do up a zipper: *Zipper your coat before you go out in the cold.* 1 *n.,* 2 *v.* —**zip′pered,** *adj.*

zir·con (zər′kon) a hard mineral found in crystals of many forms and colours. Some kinds of zircon are used as gemstones. *n.*

zith·er (zith′ər) a musical instrument with 30 to 40 strings, played with the fingers and a pick (def. 7). *n.*

zo·di·ac (zō′dē ak′) an imaginary belt in the sky, forming a circle divided into 12 equal parts called signs, named after 12 groups of stars. From the viewpoint of people on earth, the sun seems to travel along this belt over the course of a year. *n.*

zone (zōn) 1 an area or section set off from others in some way: *a hospital zone, a no-parking zone.* An **ecozone** is a part of the earth with its own particular environment and plant and animal life. 2 set an area apart for a special purpose, especially in a city or town: *This area is zoned for apartment buildings.* 1 *n.,* 2 *v.,* **zoned, zon·ing.**

zoo (zū) 1 a place where wild animals are kept and shown: *We saw lions and tigers in the zoo.* 2 a place of noise and confusion. *n.*

WORD HISTORY........ zoo

Zoo is short for *zoological garden.* **Zoological** and several other words beginning with *zo-*, including **zodiac**, came from the ancient Greek word *zoion*, meaning "animal."

zo·ol·o·gy (zū ol′ə jē *or* zō ol′ə jē) the science that studies animals and animal life. Zoology is a branch of biology. *n.* —**zo·ol′o·gist,** *n.* —**zo′o·log′i·cal** (zū′ə loj′ə kəl), *adj.*

zoom (zūm) 1 move with power and speed: *The airplane zoomed through the air.* 2 the act or sound of moving in this way: *We heard the zoom of a sports car.* 3 Sometimes, **zoom in,** focus a camera on a faraway object to take a close-up with a special lens: *The next scene zooms to the eagle's nest on the cliff.* The lens used for this is a **zoom lens.** 1, 3 *v.,* 2 *n.*

Zo·ro·as·tri·an (zȯr′ō as′trē ən) 1 a follower of an ancient religion, still practised today, which teaches that the supreme God Ahura Mazda is in an unending struggle with Angra Mainyu, the spirit of evil. People are involved in this struggle and do their part by following the moral laws of God. The holy writings of this religion are called the Avesta, and the main prophet was Zoroaster. 2 having to do with this religion. 1 *n.,* 2 *adj.* —**Zo′ro·as′tri·an·ism′,** *n.*

zuc·chi·ni (zū kē′nē) a kind of dark-green squash shaped like a cucumber, which grows on a vine. It is eaten as a cooked vegetable or raw in salads. *n.*

Appendix

Provinces and Territories

	Capital	Area	Population (2001, to nearest hundred)
Newfoundland & Labrador (NL) WEBSITE www.gov.nl.ca	St. John's	405 200 km^2	512 900
Prince Edward Island (PE) WEBSITE www.gov.pe.ca	Charlottetown	5 660 km^2	135 300
Nova Scotia (NS) WEBSITE www.gov.ns.ca	Halifax	55 300 km^2	908 000
New Brunswick (NB) WEBSITE www.gov.nb.ca	Fredericton	72 900 km^2	729 500
Québec (QC) WEBSITE www.gouv.qc.ca	Québec	1 542 100 km^2	7 237 500
Ontario (ON) WEBSITE www.gov.on.ca	Toronto	1 076 400 km^2	11 410 000
Manitoba (MB) WEBSITE www.gov.mb.ca	Winnipeg	647 800 km^2	1 119 600
Saskatchewan (SK) WEBSITE www.gov.sk.ca	Regina	651 000 km^2	978 900
Alberta (AB) WEBSITE www.gov.ab.ca	Edmonton	661 900 km^2	2 947 800
British Columbia (BC) WEBSITE www.gov.bc.ca	Victoria	944 700 km^2	3 907 700
Yukon (YT) WEBSITE www.gov.yk.ca	Whitehorse	482 400 km^2	28 700
Northwest Territories (NT) WEBSITE www.gov.nt.ca	Yellowknife	1 346 100 km^2	37 300
Nunavut (NU) WEBSITE www.gov.nu.ca	Iqaluit	2 093 200 km^2	26 700
CANADA WEBSITE www.canada.gc.ca	Ottawa	9 984 700 km^2	30 007 100

Map of Canada — Provinces and Aboriginal Peoples

Main Source: Indian and Northern Affairs Canada

Map of Canada — Physical

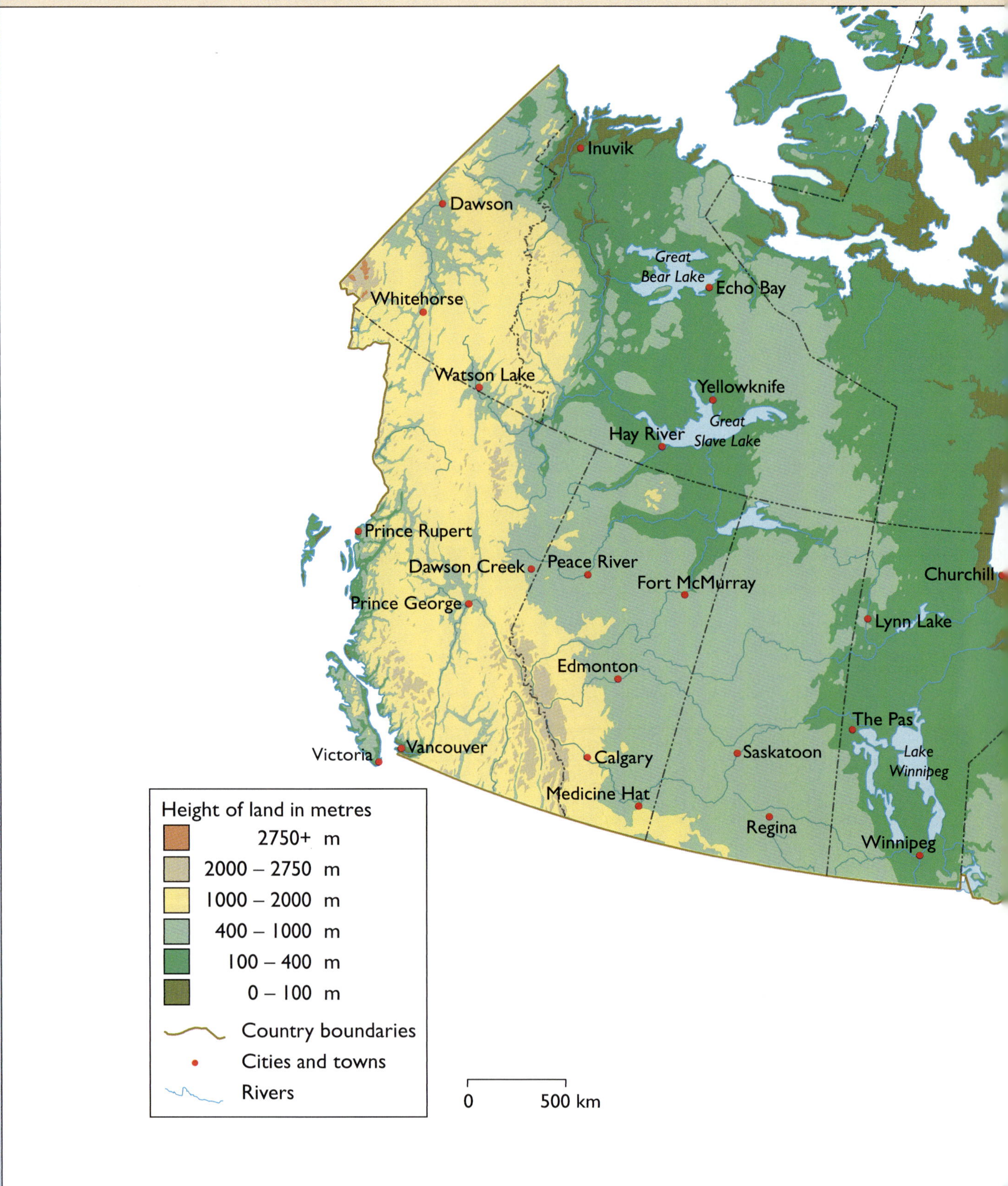

Iqaluit
Schefferville
Fort George
Sept Iles
St. John's
Moosonee
Gaspé
Channel-
Port aux Basques
Chibougamau
Charlottetown
Sydney
Thunder Bay
Moncton
Québec
Fredericton
Lake Superior
Saint John
Halifax
Sudbury
Montréal
Saulte Ste. Marie
Ottawa
Lake Huron
Toronto
Lake Ontario
Hamilton
Lake Michigan
London
St. Catharines
Lake Erie

Prime Ministers of Canada

Sir John A. Macdonald	Conservative	1867–1873, 1878–1891
Alexander Mackenzie	Liberal	1873–1878
Sir John Abbot	Conservative	1891–1892
Sir John Thompson	Conservative	1892–1894
Sir Mackenzie Bowell	Conservative	1894–1896
Sir Charles Tupper	Conservative	1896
Sir Wilfrid Laurier	Liberal	1896–1911
Sir Robert Borden	Conservative/Unionist	1911–1920
Arthur Meighen	Unionist/Conservative	1920–1921, 1926
Mackenzie King	Liberal	1921–1930, 1935–1948
Richard B. Bennett	Conservative	1930–1935
Louis St. Laurent	Liberal	1948–1957
John Diefenbaker	Progressive Conservative	1957–1963
Lester Pearson	Liberal	1963–1968
Pierre Trudeau	Liberal	1968–1979, 1980–1984
Joe Clark	Progressive Conservative	1979–1980
John Turner	Liberal	1984
Brian Mulroney	Progressive Conservative	1984–1993
Kim Campbell	Progressive Conservative	1993
Jean Chrétien	Liberal	1993–2004
Paul Martin	Liberal	2004–2006
Stephen Harper	Conservative	2006–

Titles of Elected Representatives in Canada

MHA	Member of the House of Assembly	in Newfoundland and Labrador
MLA	Member of the Legislative Assembly	in most Canadian provinces and territories
MNA	Member of the National Assembly	in Québec
MP	Member of Parliament	in the Federal Government, Ottawa
MPP	Member of the Provincial Parliament	in Ontario

Standard Time Zones Across Canada

Standard Time Zones were invented by Sir Sandford Fleming in 1878.
His system was adopted worldwide in 1884.

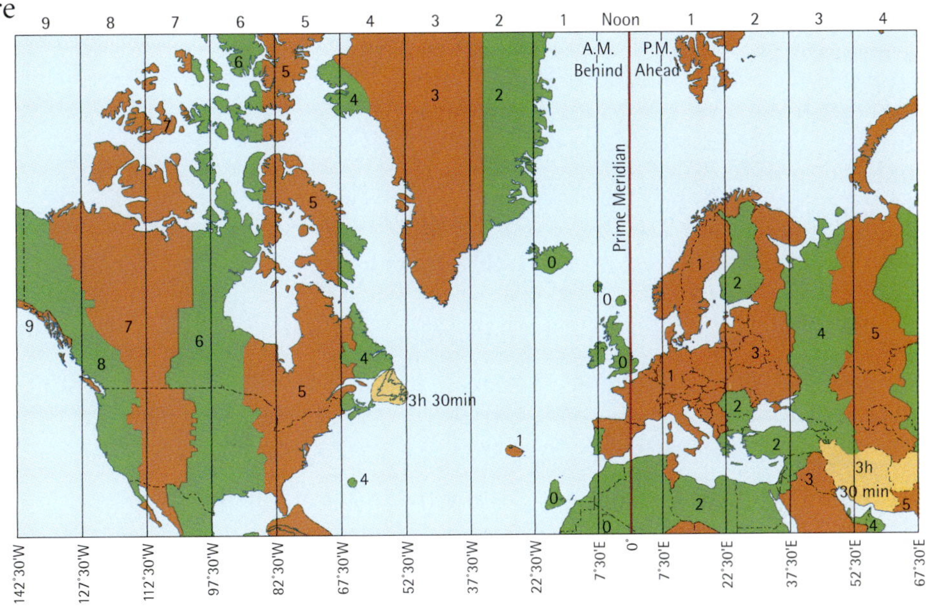

O Canada

O Canada! Our home and native land!
True patriot love in all thy sons command.
With glowing heart we see thee rise,
The True North strong and free!
From far and wide, O Canada,
We stand on guard for thee.
God keep our land glorious and free!
O Canada, we stand on guard for thee.
O Canada, we stand on guard for thee!

Ô Canada

O Canada! Terre de nos aïeux,
Ton front est ceint de fleurons glorieux!
Car ton bras sait porter l'épée,
Il sait porter la croix!
Ton histoire est une épopée
Des plus brillants exploits,
Et ta valeur, de foi trempée,
Protégera nos foyers et nos droits,
Protégera nos foyers et nos droits.

Canada's National Flag

The Maple Leaf, Canada's National Flag, was adopted by Parliament in 1964.
It must be flown daily at all federal buildings, at airports, and at all military bases inside and outside Canada.

Did You Know?—Superlative Canadian Facts

Largest City		
by area	Timmins, ON	3004 square kilometres
by population	Toronto, ON	4 264 000 people
Smallest City		
by area	L'Ile-Dorval, QC	0.18 square kilometres
by population	L'Ile-Dorval, QC	2 people
Largest Island	Baffin Island, NU	507 451 square kilometres
Northernmost Point	Cape Columbia, Ellesmere Island, NU	
Southernmost Point	Middle Island, Lake Erie, ON	
Easternmost Point	Cape Spear, NF	
Westernmost Point	Yukon-Alaska boundary	
Highest City	Kimberley, BC	1 128 metres
Highest Community	Lake Louise, AB	1 540 metres
Northernmost Ice-free Port	Stewart, BC	
Longest River	Mackenzie River, NT	4 241 kilometres
Largest Lake (totally in Canada)	Great Bear Lake, NT	31 328 square kilometres
Deepest Lake	Great Slave Lake, NT	614 metres
Highest Mountain	Mt. Logan, YT	5 959 metres
Highest Waterfall	Della Falls, BC	440 metres
Greatest Waterfall	Horseshoe Falls, ON	5 365 cubic metres/second
Longest Bridge	Confederation Bridge, NB/PE	12.9 kilometres
Longest Tunnel	Rogers Pass, BC	14.6 kilometres

Some Endangered Species in Canada

Mammals	Frogs and Reptiles	Birds
Peary Caribou	Cricket Frog	Northern Bobwhite
Woodland Caribou	Northern Leopard Frog	Whooping Crane
Marmot	Blue Racer Snake	Eskimo Curlew
Newfoundland Marten	Lake Erie Water Snake	Acadian Flycatcher
Swift Fox	Leatherback Turtle	Sage Grouse
Townsend's Mole		Barn Owl
Right Whale		Burrowing Owl
Beluga Whale	**Fish**	Spotted Owl
Wolverine	Nooksack Dace	Mountain Plover
	Salish Sucker	Piping Plover
	Aurora Trout	King Rail
	Atlantic Whitefish	Loggerhead Shrike
		Henslow's Sparrow
		Sage Thrasher
		Kirtland's Warbler
		Prothonotary Warbler
		White-headed Woodpecker

Emblems of Provinces and Territories

	Flower	Bird
Newfoundland & Labrador	Pitcher Plant	Atlantic Puffin
Prince Edward Island	Lady's Slipper	Blue Jay
Nova Scotia	Mayflower	Osprey
New Brunswick	Purple Violet	Black-capped Chickadee
Québec	Blue Flag Iris	Snowy Owl
Ontario	White Trillium	Common Loon
Manitoba	Prairie Crocus	Great Grey Owl
Saskatchewan	Western Red Lily	Sharp-tailed Grouse
Alberta	Wild Rose	Great Horned Owl
British Columbia	Pacific Dogwood	Stellar's Jay
Yukon Territory	Fireweed	Common Raven
Northwest Territory	Mountain Avens	Gyrfalcon
Nunavut	Purple Saxifrage	Rock Ptarmigan

Map of the World

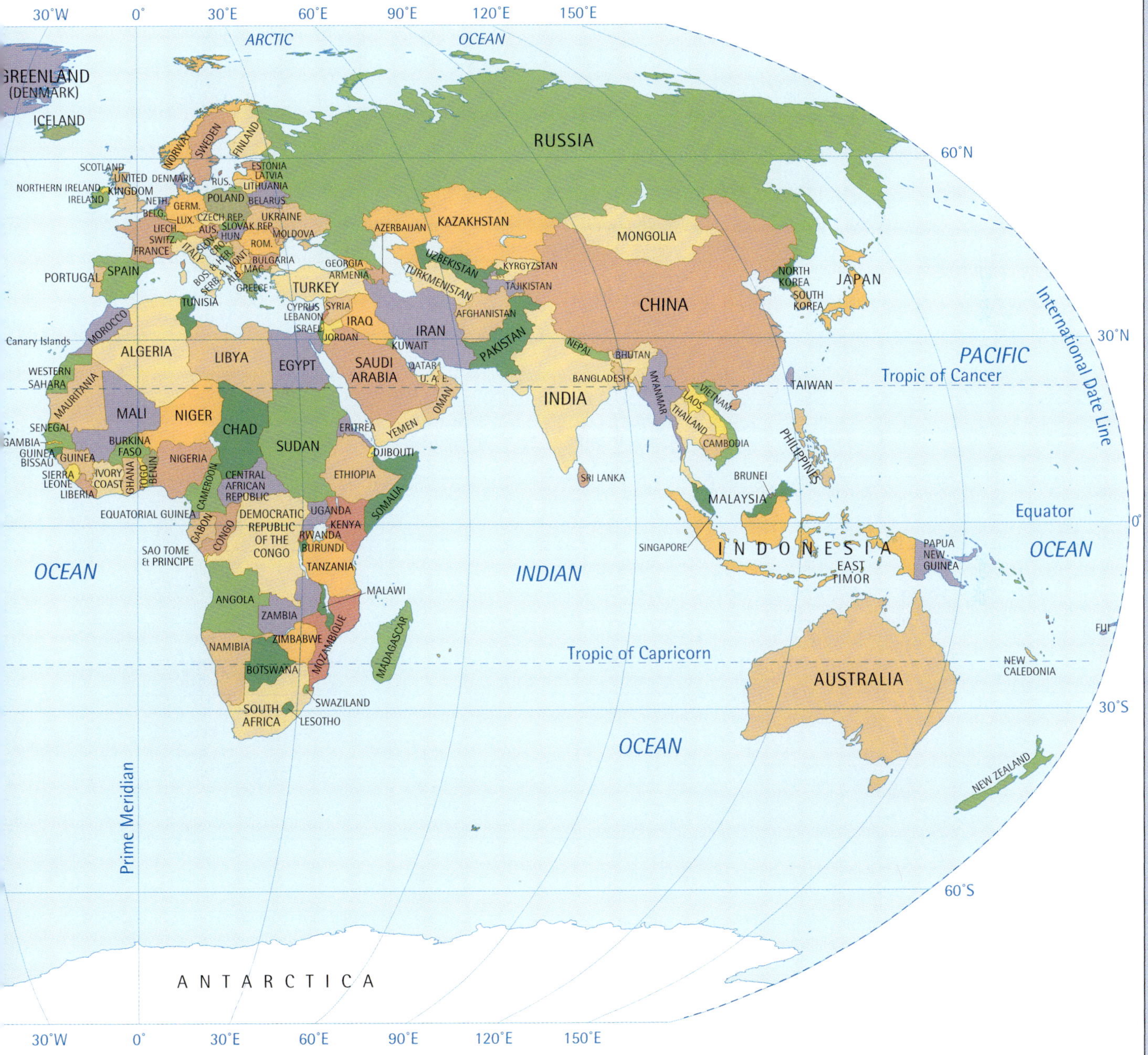
30°W
0°
30°E
60°E
90°E
120°E
150°E
ARCTIC
OCEAN
GREENLAND
(DENMARK)
ICELAND
RUSSIA
60°N
SCOTLAND
UNITED
KINGDOM
NORTHERN IRELAND
IRELAND
DENMARK
NORWAY
SWEDEN
FINLAND
ESTONIA
LATVIA
LITHUANIA
RUS.
NETH.
BELG.
GERM.
POLAND
BELARUS
LUX.
CZECH REP.
UKRAINE
LIECH.
AUS.
SLOVAK REP.
SWITZ.
HUN.
MOLDOVA
FRANCE
ROM.
ITALY
BULGARIA
MAC.
ALB.
MONT.
GREECE
PORTUGAL
SPAIN
TUNISIA
KAZAKHSTAN
MONGOLIA
AZERBAIJAN
GEORGIA
ARMENIA
UZBEKISTAN
TURKMENISTAN
KYRGYZSTAN
TAJIKISTAN
TURKEY
CYPRUS
SYRIA
LEBANON
ISRAEL
JORDAN
IRAQ
IRAN
AFGHANISTAN
PAKISTAN
KUWAIT
QATAR
U. A. E.
OMAN
YEMEN
SAUDI
ARABIA
NORTH
KOREA
SOUTH
KOREA
JAPAN
CHINA
NEPAL
BHUTAN
BANGLADESH
INDIA
MYANMAR
LAOS
VIETNAM
THAILAND
CAMBODIA
TAIWAN
PHILIPPINES
International Date Line
30°N
PACIFIC
Tropic of Cancer
Canary Islands
MOROCCO
ALGERIA
LIBYA
EGYPT
WESTERN
SAHARA
MAURITANIA
MALI
NIGER
CHAD
SUDAN
ERITREA
DJIBOUTI
SENEGAL
GAMBIA
GUINEA-
BISSAU
GUINEA
BURKINA
FASO
NIGERIA
SIERRA
LEONE
LIBERIA
IVORY
COAST
GHANA
TOGO
BENIN
CAMEROON
CENTRAL
AFRICAN
REPUBLIC
ETHIOPIA
SOMALIA
EQUATORIAL GUINEA
GABON
CONGO
DEMOCRATIC
REPUBLIC
OF THE
CONGO
UGANDA
KENYA
RWANDA
BURUNDI
TANZANIA
SAO TOME
& PRINCIPE
SRI LANKA
BRUNEI
MALAYSIA
SINGAPORE
INDONESIA
EAST
TIMOR
PAPUA
NEW
GUINEA
Equator
0°
OCEAN
INDIAN
OCEAN
MALAWI
ANGOLA
ZAMBIA
ZIMBABWE
NAMIBIA
MOZAMBIQUE
MADAGASCAR
BOTSWANA
Tropic of Capricorn
FIJI
NEW
CALEDONIA
AUSTRALIA
SWAZILAND
SOUTH
AFRICA
LESOTHO
30°S
OCEAN
NEW ZEALAND
Prime Meridian
60°S
A N T A R C T I C A
30°W
0°
30°E
60°E
90°E
120°E
150°E

Countries of the World

Country	Nationality	Adjective	Official Language	Currency
Afghanistan	Afghan	Afghan	Pushtu	afghani
Albania	Albanian	Albanian	Albanian	lek
Algeria	Algerian	Algerian	Arabic	dinar
Argentina	Argentine	Argentinian	Spanish	peso
Armenia	Armenian	Armenian	Armenian	dram
Australia	Australian	Australian	English	dollar
Austria	Austrian	Austrian	German	euro
Azerbaijan	Azerbaijani	Azerbaijani	Azerbaijani	manat
Bahamas	Bahamian	Bahamian	English	dollar
Bangladesh	Bangladeshi	Bangladeshi	Bangla	taka
Barbados	Barbadian	Barbadian	English	dollar
Belarus	Belarusian	Belarusian	Byelorussian	ruble
Belgium	Belgian	Belgian	Dutch/French	euro
Bolivia	Bolivian	Bolivian	Spanish	Boliviano
Bosnia-Herzegovina	Bosnian-Herzegovinian	Bosnian-Herzegovinian	Serbo-Croatian	dinar
Brazil	Brazilian	Brazilian	Portuguese	real
Bulgaria	Bulgarian	Bulgarian	Bulgarian	lev
Cambodia	Cambodian	Cambodian	Khmer	new riel
Canada	Canadian	Canadian	English/French	dollar
Chile	Chilean	Chilean	Spanish	peso
China	Chinese	Chinese	Mandarin Chinese	yuan
Colombia	Colombian	Colombian	Spanish	peso
Costa Rica	Costa Rican	Costa Rican	Spanish	colón
Croatia	Croat	Croatian	Serbo-Croatian	kuna
Cuba	Cuban	Cuban	Spanish	peso
Czech Republic	Czech	Czech	Czech/Slovak	koruna
Denmark	Dane	Danish	Danish	krone
Ecuador	Ecuadorian	Ecuadorian	Spanish	sucre
Egypt	Egyptian	Egyptian	Arabic	pound
El Salvador	Salvadoran	Salvadoran	Spanish	colón
Ethiopia	Ethiopian	Ethiopian	Amharic	birr
Finland	Finn	Finnish	Finnish/Swedish	euro
France	French	French	French	euro
Germany	German	German	German	euro
Ghana	Ghanaian	Ghanaian	English	cedi
Greece	Greek	Greek	Greek	euro
Guatemala	Guatemalan	Guatemalan	Spanish	quetzal
Guyana	Guyanese	Guyanese	English	dollar
Haiti	Haitian	Haitian	French	gourde
Honduras	Honduran	Honduran	Spanish	lempira
Hungary	Hungarian	Hungarian	Hungarian	forint
Iceland	Icelander	Icelandic	Icelandic	króna
India	Indian	Indian	Hindi	rupee
Indonesia	Indonesian	Indonesian	Bahasa Indonesia	rupiah
Iran	Iranian	Iranian	Farsi (Persian)	rial
Iraq	Iraqi	Iraqi	Arabic/Kurdish	dinar
Ireland, Republic of	Irish	Irish	Irish/English	euro
Israel	Israeli	Israeli	Hebrew/Arabic	shekel
Italy	Italian	Italian	Italian	euro
Jamaica	Jamaican	Jamaican	English	dollar
Japan	Japanese	Japanese	Japanese	yen
Kazakhstan	Kazakhstani	Kazakhstani	Kazakh	tenge
Kenya	Kenyan	Kenyan	English/Swahili	shilling
Korea, North	Korean	Korean	Korean	won

Country	Nationality	Adjective	Official Language	Currency
Korea, South	Korean	Korean	Korean	won
Kuwait	Kuwaiti	Kuwaiti	Arabic	dinar
Lebanon	Lebanese	Lebanese	Arabic/French	pound
Libya	Libyan	Libyan	Arabic	dinar
Lithuania	Lithuanian	Lithuanian	Lithuanian	litas
Malaysia	Malaysian	Malaysian	Malay	ringgit
Mexico	Mexican	Mexican	Spanish	peso
Morocco	Moroccan	Moroccan	Arabic	dirham
Mozambique	Mozambican	Mozambican	Portuguese	metical
Namibia	Namibian	Namibian	Afrikaans/German/English	dollar
Netherlands	Dutch	Dutch	Dutch/Frisian	euro
New Zealand	New Zealander	New Zealand	English	dollar
Nicaragua	Nicaraguan	Nicaraguan	Spanish	córdoba
Nigeria	Nigerian	Nigerian	English	naira
Norway	Norwegian	Norwegian	Norwegian	krone
Pakistan	Pakistani	Pakistani	Urdu	rupee
Panama	Panamanian	Panamanian	Spanish	balboa
Paraguay	Paraguayan	Paraguayan	Spanish	guaraní
Peru	Peruvian	Peruvian	Spanish/Quechua	nuevo sol
Philippines	Filipino	Filipino	English/Pilipino	peso
Poland	Polish	Polish	Polish	zloty
Portugal	Portuguese	Portuguese	Portuguese	euro
Romania	Romanian	Romanian	Romanian	leu
Russia	Russian	Russian	Russian	ruble
Rwanda	Rwandan	Rwandan	French/Kinyarwanda	franc
Saudi Arabia	Saudi	Saudi	Arabic	riyal
Serbia and Montenegro	Serb, Montenegrin	Serb, Montenegrin	Serbo-Croatian	dinar
Singapore	Singaporean	Singaporean	Chinese/Malay/Tamil	dollar
Slovakia	Slovak	Slovak	Slovak	koruna
Somalia	Somali	Somali	Somali	shilling
South Africa	South African	South African	See below*	rand
Spain	Spanish	Spanish	Spanish	euro
Sri Lanka	Sri Lankan	Sri Lankan	Sinhala/Tamil	rupee
Sweden	Swedish	Swedish	Swedish	króna
Switzerland	Swiss	Swiss	German/French/Italian	franc
Syria	Syrian	Syrian	Arabic	pound
Taiwan	Chinese	Chinese	Chinese	dollar
Tajikistan	Tajik	Tajikistan	Tajik	ruble
Tanzania	Tanzanian	Tanzanian	Swahili/English	shilling
Thailand	Thai	Thai	Thai	baht
Tunisia	Tunisian	Tunisian	Arabic	dinar
Turkey	Turk	Turkish	Turkish	lira
Uganda	Ugandan	Ugandan	English	shilling
Ukraine	Ukrainian	Ukrainian	Ukrainian	hryvna
United Arab Emirates	Emiri	Emirian	Arabic	dirham
United Kingdom	British	British	English/Welsh/Scottish	pound
United States	American	American	English	dollar
Uruguay	Uruguayan	Uruguayan	Spanish	peso
Uzbekistan	Uzbek	Uzbek	Uzbek	som
Venezuela	Venezuelan	Venezuelan	Spanish	bolívar
Vietnam	Vietnamese	Vietnamese	Vietnamese	dong
Zimbabwe	Zimbabwean	Zimbabwean	English	dollar

* Afrikaans, English, isiNdebele, Sepedi, Sesotho, siSwati, Xitsonga, Setswana, Tshivenda, isiXhosa, isiZulu

Air Pollution

Many different substances contribute to air pollution. These substances can be natural or manufactured. Forest fires, pollen, and dust are examples of natural pollutants. Pesticides, industrial waste, and smoke from the burning of fossil fuels are examples of manufactured pollutants. The picture below shows several types of air pollution. Can you identify which ones are natural and which ones are the result of human activities?

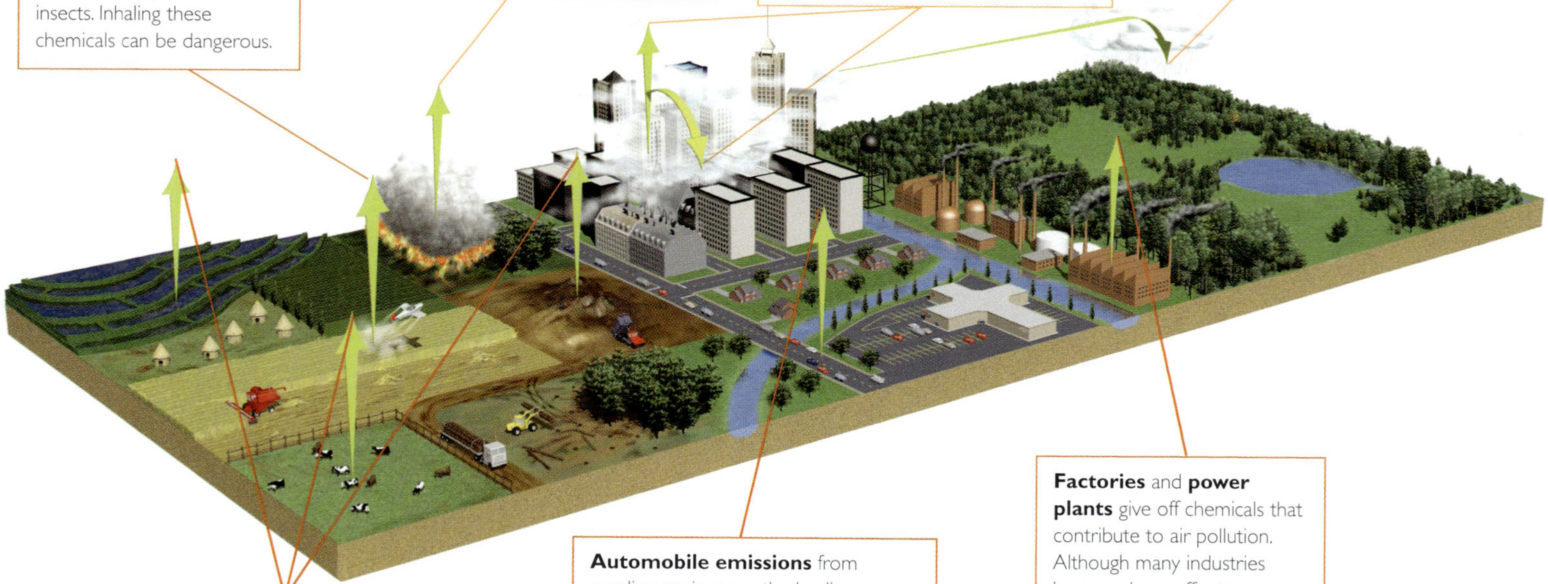

Forest fires are the only form of air pollution that can occur naturally.

Water Pollution

There are many sources of water pollution. Dumping contaminants directly into water is known as **point source pollution**. Contaminants that seep into water form **non-point source pollution**. Can you identify all of the sources of water pollution in the picture below? How many are point source and how many are non-point source?

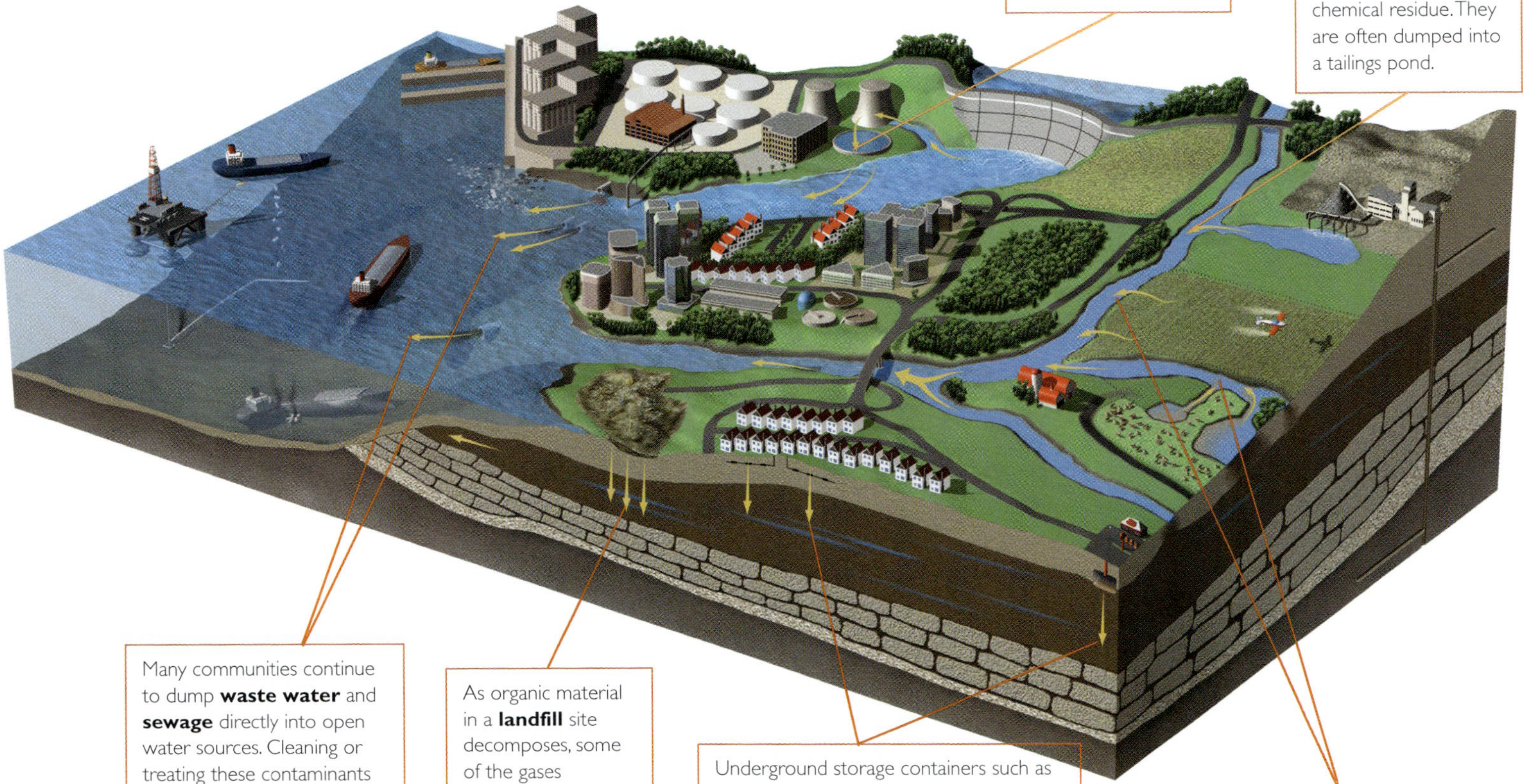

point source pollutants: waste water from households; raw sewage
non-point source pollutants: pesticides; manure from farming; seepage from oil tanks, septic tanks, and landfill.

The Solar System

In 2006, the International Astronomical Union redefined *planet* as "a celestial body that has cleared the neighbourhood around its orbit." A *dwarf planet* is a body that has **not** cleared the neighbourhood around its orbit. Since Pluto is one of many objects that occupy the same region of space, it has been reclassified from *planet* to *dwarf planet*.

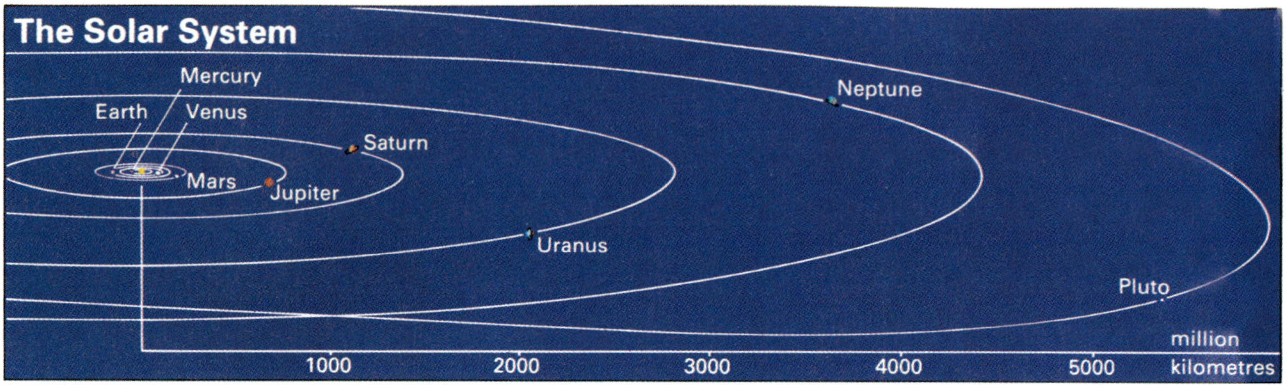

SI Units

Name	Symbol	Quantity
metre	m	length
kilogram	kg	mass
second	s	time
tonne	t	mass (= 1000 kg)

Units Used with SI

Name	Symbol	Quantity
litre	L	volume or capacity
hectare	ha	area (= 10 000 m^2)
tonne	t	mass (= 1000 kg)

SI Prefixes

Name	Symbol	Multiplying Factor	Example
giga-	G	1 000 000 000	a gigabyte (about one billion bytes)
mega-	M	1 000 000	a megavolt (one million volts)
kilo-	k	1 000	a kilometre (one thousand metres)
hecto-	h	100	a hectolitre (one hundred litres)
deca-	da	10	a decagram (ten grams)
deci-	h	0.1	a decigram (one-tenth of a gram)
centi-	c	0.01	a centimetre (one-hundredth of a metre)
milli-	m	0.001	a millilitre (one-thousandth of a litre)
micro-	m	0.000 001	a micrometre (one-millionth of a metre)
nano-	n	0.000 000 001	a nanosecond (one-billionth of a second)

Conversion Factors to Metric

1 inch	= 2.54 cm
1 yard	= 91.44 cm
1 mile	= 1.61 km
1 pound	= 0.45 g
1 gallon	= 4.55 L (U.S. 3.79 L)

Conversion Factors from Metric

1 centimetre	= 0.39 inches
1 metre	= 39.4 inches
1 kilometre	= 0.62 miles
1 kilogram	= 2.20 pounds
1 litre	= 1.76 pints

Numbers

Cardinal Number		Ordinal Number	Roman Numeral
1	one	first	I
2	two	second	II
3	three	third	III
4	four	fourth	IV
5	five	fifth	V
6	six	sixth	VI
7	seven	seventh	VII
8	eight	eighth	VIII
9	nine	ninth	IX
10	ten	tenth	X
11	eleven	eleventh	XI
12	twelve	twelfth	XII
13	thirteen	thirteenth	XIII
14	fourteen	fourteenth	XIV
15	fifteen	fifteenth	XV
16	sixteen	sixteenth	XVI
17	seventeen	seventeenth	XVII
18	eighteen	eighteenth	XVIII
19	nineteen	nineteenth	XIX
20	twenty	twentieth	XX
50	fifty	fiftieth	L
100	hundred	hundredth	C
1000	thousand	thousandth	M
1 000 000	million	millionth	M

Fractions

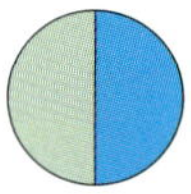

$\frac{1}{2}$ half

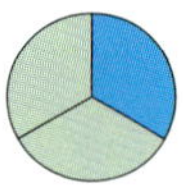

$\frac{1}{3}$ third

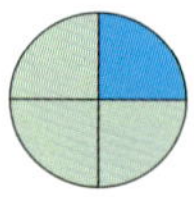

$\frac{1}{4}$ quarter

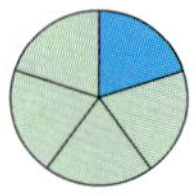

$\frac{1}{5}$ fifth

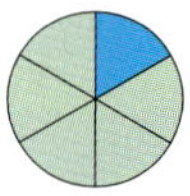

$\frac{1}{6}$ sixth

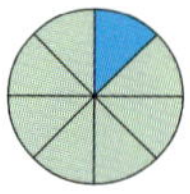

$\frac{1}{8}$ eighth

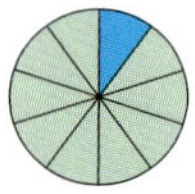

$\frac{1}{10}$ tenth

Polygons

3 angles, 3 sides
triangle

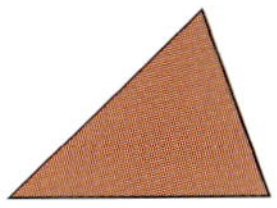

7 angles, 7 sides
septagon

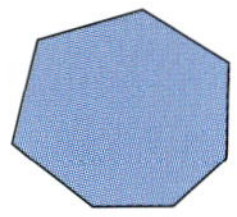

4 angles, 4 sides
quadrilateral

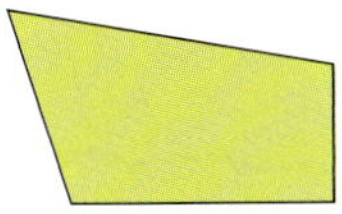

8 angles, 8 sides
octagon

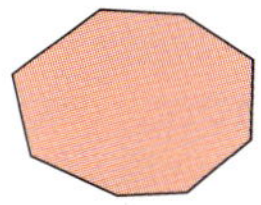

5 angles, 5 sides
pentagon

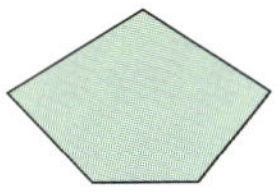

9 angles, 9 sides
nonagon

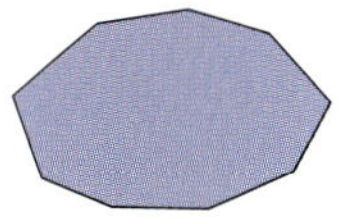

6 angles, 6 sides
hexagon

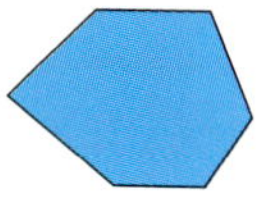

10 angles, 10 sides
decagon

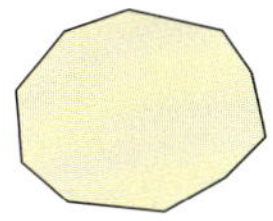

Polyhedrons

triangular prism
(3 side faces)

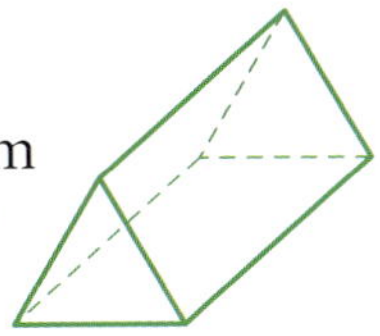

cube
(4 side faces)

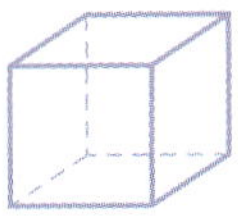

rectangular
prism
(4 side faces)

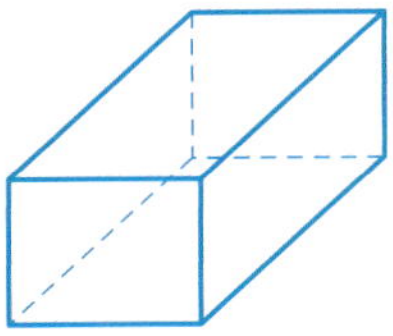

pentagonal
prism
(5 side faces)

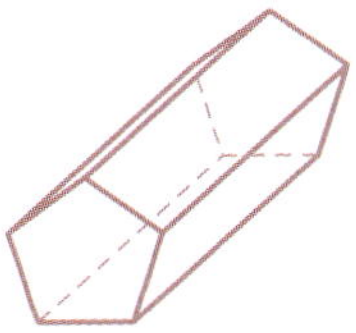

hexagonal
prism
(6 side faces)

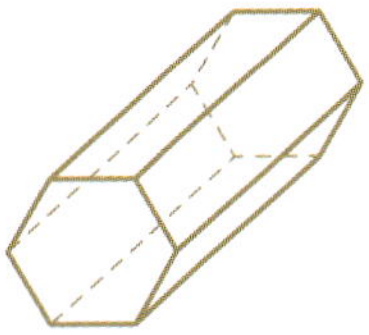

octagonal
prism
(8 side faces)

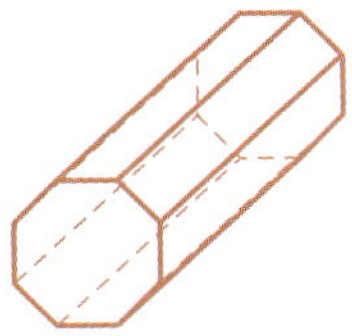

square
pyramid
(4 side faces)

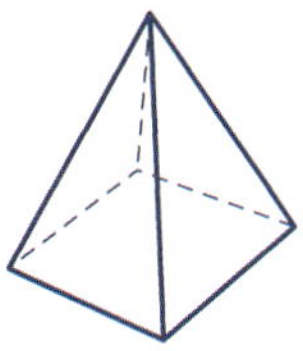

pentagonal
pyramid
(5 side faces)

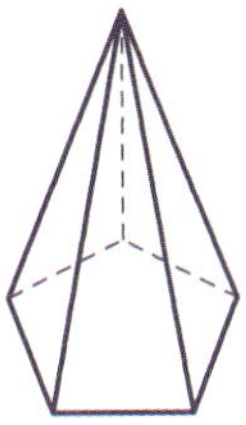

hexagonal
pyramid
(6 side faces)

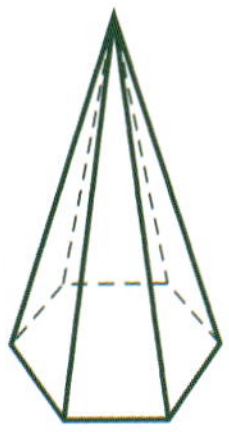

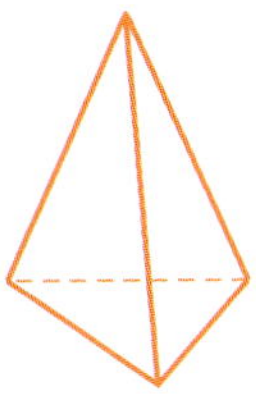

tetrahedon
(4 triangular faces)

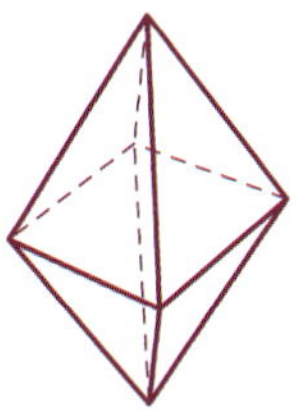

octahedron
(8 triangular faces)

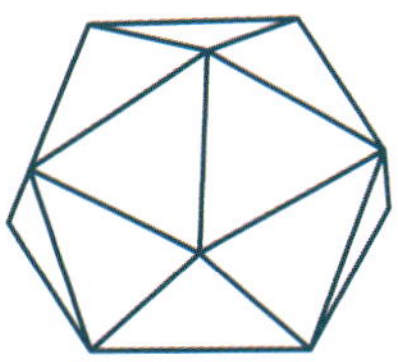

icosahedron
(20 triangular faces)

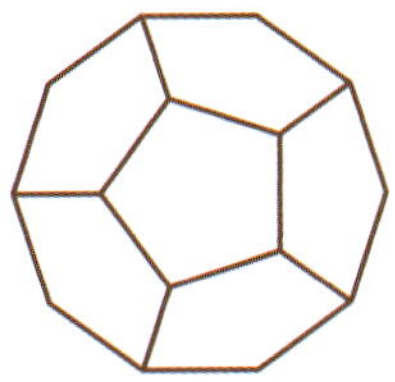

dodecahedron
(12 pentagonal faces)

Reading Strategies for Understanding Textbooks

When you pick up a textbook, you sometimes have to do many different types of reading on a single page-and that can seem like a challenge!

The trick is to learn about the special features that are built into most textbooks. Below is an example of a science text. The "think-aloud" bubbles tell you about each special feature from a student's point of view.

Heading: This tells me what the topic of this section is and what I can focus on as I read.

Photo: This gives me a visual example that tells me something new about the topic.

Caption: These words explain the photo above. The question at the end helps me see if I can apply ideas from the text.

Key Terms: These highlighted words are important for me to remember and understand.

▲ This milk bottle was taken out of the refrigerator and left on the counter. Why is it wet?

Water in the Air

Water in the air is called water vapour [VAY-puhr]. You can't see water vapour. When the ice in your glass cooled the air around it, the air became too cool to hold all of the water vapour. So some of the water vapour turned into liquid water on the outside of the glass. This did not happen to the other glass of water because it was the same temperature as the air. The process of water vapour turning into liquid water is called **condensation** [KON-den-SAY-shun].

Where does the water in a puddle go? Some of the liquid water may sink into the ground, but some turns into water vapour in the air. You can see this for yourself. Put some water in a saucer and let it sit on the counter for a few days. The water will disappear. It has changed to water vapour. The process of liquid water turning into water vapour is called **evaporation** [ih-VAP-uh-RAY-shun].

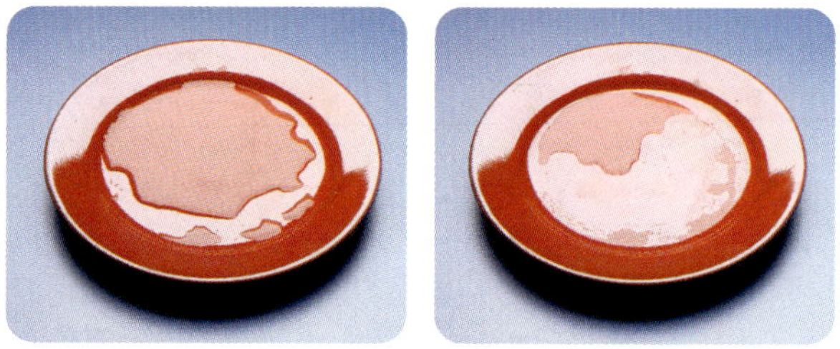

▲ Look at the two photos. The photo on the right shows how much water can evaporate from a saucer of water over a few days.

The Water Cycle

Water is recycled over and over again. We call this the **water cycle.** Warm air rises in the atmosphere. As it rises, it cools. This cooling causes some of the water vapour to condense onto tiny dust particles floating in the air to make water droplets. These water droplets form clouds. The water droplets bump into each other and form larger drops. When the drops get too big, they fall as rain, snow, or hail.

Key Terms: These words appear in the glossary, but I can also figure them out by "reading around the word." By rereading this sentence, I see that precipitation is another word for rain, snow, and hail.

Rain, snow, and hail are all called **precipitation** [prih-SIP-ih-TAY-shun].

Pronunciation Key: This shows me how to say a word I might not know.

Some precipitation evaporates in the heat of the Sun. Some of it collects in the soil, or runs into lakes and rivers. Eventually, all this water flows into the ocean or evaporates back into the air.

The Water Cycle

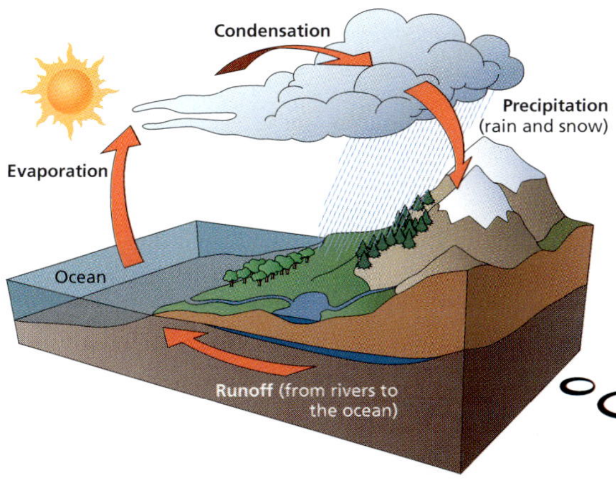

Learning Tip

Work with a partner to study this diagram. Start anywhere and follow the arrows. Explain to your partner what is happening to the water at each stage. Then have your partner explain the water cycle to you.

Text Box: Information in special boxes is usually important. This box is giving me a tip on how to learn The Water Cycle with a partner.

Diagram: Diagrams are used when a photo won't work. The labels and arrows show me how each process leads to the next one.

Check Your Understanding

1. What are two important properties of air?
2. When you cooled the water in your glass, water droplets formed on the outside of the glass. When warm air cools, water vapour condenses to form droplets of water in clouds. Use this information to explain why you can see your breath on a cold day.
3. Draw and label a diagram to show how water from the ocean could travel to a puddle in your schoolyard, then back to the ocean.

End-of Section Questions: These might be my homework! But I can also use them to find out what most important ideas in this section are. If I read them before I read the section, I will have an even better idea about what to focus on!

Reading Strategies for Understanding Unfamiliar Words

When you read, you will sometimes encounter words you don't know. This happens to even the best readers. Good readers first decide if the difficult text is important enough to know. If it is, then they use strategies that help them to figure it out. Here are some effective strategies.

Sometimes you just need to be able to say the word, then you recognize it.

To **say** the word, you can…

- look at the letters, then **sound out** the word
- say each syllable, then **slide them together**
- look for **word parts that you already know**

When you don't recognize the word even after you try to say it, you need other strategies to help you to understand it.

To **understand** the word, you can…

- **read around** the word
  - reread the sentence for clues that will help you to understand the word
  - read ahead for clues that will help you to understand the word
- **substitute another word** that makes sense
- **make a guess**, based on what you know so far
- **look at graphics** (charts, illustrations, etc.) for clues about the word
- **look for roots, prefixes, or suffixes** in the word
- think about **words that are in the same word family**
- **ask someone** about the word
- look it up in the **dictionary**

Reading Strategies for Understanding Media

Media can be any print, image, or sound that is used to carry a message. Here are some common types of media:

Print	newspaper, magazine, print ad
Image	television, movie, billboard
Sound	music, radio

Sometimes the three media types are combined (e.g., Internet websites combine print, images, and sound).

The purpose of the media and the messages they carry is usually to make money for the companies that create them. For example, the reason we have television programs is to make sure that you see the commercials!

Why is it important to be knowledgeable about media?

We are surrounded by media and media messages. Media can contain:

- **a specific point of view** → a magazine article that says violent video games make people violent
- **bias** → a TV news item that tells only one side of the story
- **a stereotype** → a movie in which all the heroes are men
- **a call to action** → a pop-up that tells you to upgrade your software

Being knowledgeable about media helps us to make our own decisions about what to think and how to respond to media messages.

Critical Questions!

- ❑ Here are some questions to think about when you are reading, listening to, or viewing media:
- ❑ Who made this media piece? What was their purpose in creating it?
- ❑ Who is it targeting? How do I know?
- ❑ How are they trying to get my attention?
- ❑ Are they trying to get me to think or act in a certain way?
- ❑ Are there stereotypes about age, race, culture, or gender?
- ❑ Whose ideas are being presented? Whose ideas are not included?

Word Study: Common Prefixes and Suffixes

Being able to recognize common prefixes, suffixes, and roots can help you understand words that you don't recognize at first.

Prefixes are added to the beginning of words, as in **pre**historic or **over**work.
Suffixes are added to the ends of words, as in bad**ly** or play**ed**.

Adding a prefix or suffix changes the meaning of the root word or makes another word.

Prefix	Meaning	Examples
SHOWS THE QUANTITY		
bi-	two	bicycle, binoculars, bisect
tri-	three	triangle, triplets, tripod
uni-	one	unicorn, unison, unite
multi-	many	multicultural, multiply
semi-	half	semicircle, semicolon, semifinal
SHOWS THE DIRECTION		
inter-	between	intermediate, international, interview
sub-	under	submarine, submerge, subway
trans-	across	transit, translate, transportation
SHOWS THE REVERSE		
dis-	opposite	disagree, disconnect, dishonest,
ir-	not	irregular, irresistible, irresponsible
un-	not	unfair, unforgettable, unlikely
un-	opposite	undress, unfurl, untie

Suffix	Meaning	Examples
MAKES AN ADJECTIVE		
-ful	full of	careful, helpful
-less	without, lacking	careless, useless
MAKES A NOUN		
-ion	the act of	immersion, revision
-tion	the condition of	attention, satisfaction
MAKES AN ADVERB		
-ly	in a way that	easily, quickly

Word Study: Common Roots

A root is a word or word part from which other words are made.

Root	Meaning	Example
aqua	water	aquarium
astr	star	astronomy
aud	to hear	audio
auto	self	autograph
bio	life	biography
dict	to speak	dictate
geo	earth	geography
graph	to write	autograph
micro	small	microscope
naut	sailor	astronaut
ped	foot	pedal
phob	fear	phobia
phon	sound	telephone
phot	light	photograph
port	to carry	transport
scope	to look at	telescope
script	to write	manuscript
spec	to look	spectator
tele	far	telephone
voc	to call	vocal

Word Building

	prefix		root		suffix		suffix
unkind	un	+	kind				
joyful			joy	+	ful		
refreshment	re	+	fresh	+	ment		
selfishly			self	+	ish	+	ly

Word Study: Confusable Words

When you read, you will sometimes encounter words you don't know.

accept/except
Will you **accept** my apology?
I remembered to thank everyone **except** you.

angel/angle
We could not see the **angel** in the stained glass window.
We were looking at the window from the wrong **angle**.

dairy/diary
I saw a herd of **dairy** cattle on my grandparents' farm.
I wrote about them in my **diary**.

dessert/desert
Strawberry shortcake is my favourite **dessert**.
Cactus plants can survive the heat of the **desert**.

it's/its
It's really funny to watch the cat chase **its** tail.

lose/loose
Be careful not to **lose** that button.
It is hanging **loose** on your jacket.

quiet/quite/quit
Please be **quiet**. It is **quite** noisy in here.
You'll have to **quit** yelling!

recipe/receipt
This **recipe** calls for maple syrup.
Would you please buy some and give me the **receipt**?

than/then
I'd rather play soccer **than** ride our bikes.
Then we could go to my place for lunch.

there/their/they're
My friends are getting **their** skateboards.
Then **they're** going to meet me over **there**.

weather/whether
The **weather** is supposed to be bad tomorrow.
Do you care **whether** we don't make the trip until next week?

where/were/we're
Where did you go for your vacation? How long **were** you gone?
We're planning to go to Calgary in May.

whose/who's
Do you know **whose** hockey bag that is?
Who's going to carry all the hockey sticks out to the bus?

your/you're
Your hat is by the door.
If you forget to wear it **you're** going to be cold.

Word Study: Overused Words

Replacing an overused word can make your writing more effective.

Instead of ...	**Try ...**
big	enormous, giant, great, huge, immense, large, massive
bad	awful, dishonest, mischievous, naughty, rotten, terrible
but	although, however, on the other hand, still, though, yet
great	amazing, delightful, excellent, fantastic, fine, superb, terrific, wonderful,
happy	cheerful, contented, delighted glad, joyful, pleased,
little	compact, miniature, minute, petite, slight, small, tiny
mad	angry, annoyed, frustrated, furious, livid
nice	considerate, decent, delightful, friendly, gentle, kind, pleasant, thoughtful, warm
pretty	attractive, beautiful, cute, elegant, fair, lovely, stunning
ran	bolted, darted, dashed, hurried, raced, rushed, sprinted
sad	dejected, depressed, gloomy, miserable, unhappy, upset
said	answered, called, cried, demanded, exclaimed, remarked, replied, responded, whispered
saw	glanced at, glimpsed, noticed, observed, spotted, watched
scared	afraid, fearful, frightened, terrified
smart	bright, brilliant, clever, gifted, intelligent, sharp, wise, witty
then	afterwards, finally, later, meanwhile, next, soon

Abbreviations

AD	in the year of our Lord	n.	noun
adj.	adjective	N	north
adv.	adverb	N.B.	nota bene (note well)
a.m.	ante meridiem (midnight to noon)	NHL	National Hockey League
anon.	anonymous	No.	number
Apr.	April	Nov.	November
Aug.	August	Oct.	October
Ave.	avenue	p. or pp.	page or pages
BC	before Christ	p.m.	post meridiem (noon to midight)
BCE	before the Common Era	prep.	preposition
CE	Common Era	pron.	pronoun
Co.	company	Prof.	professor
C.O.D.	cash on delivery	P.S.	postscript
conj.	conjunction	PTA	parent-teacher association
D.D.S.	doctor of dental surgery	RCMP	Royal Canadian Mounted Police
Dec.	December	Rd.	road
Dr.	doctor	Rev.	reverend
D.S.T.	daylight saving time	rpm	revolutions per minute
E	east	RSVP	please reply
e.g.	for example	S	south
etc.	and similar things	Sat.	Saturday
Feb.	February	Sr.	senior
Fri.	Friday	Sep.	September
i.e.	that is	S.S.	steamship
interj.	interjection	St./Ste.	saint
Jan.	January	St.	street
Jr.	junior	Sun.	Sunday
Jul.	July	TD	touchdown
Jun.	June	Thu.	Thursday
L.	lake	TOC	table of contents
Ltd.	limited	Tue.	Tuesday
Mar.	March	v.	verb
May	May	vol.	volume (of a book)
M.D.	doctor of medicine	vs.	versus (against)
Mon.	Monday	Wed.	Wednesday
Mt.	mount (mountain)	W	west

Grammar and Usage Mini-Guide

Abbreviation

An abbreviation is a shortened form of a word or phrase. Abbreviations are useful in informal writing, or in lists or tables. In formal writing, it is usually better to spell out the whole word, but a few abbreviations are acceptable in formal writing as well. They are:

- Mrs., Mr., Ms., and Dr. before someone's name
- St. for Saint in place names
- times, such as 7:00 p.m., A.D. 500

Active and Passive Voice

Active and passive voice are two ways of talking about something that happened.

- In the **active** voice, you tell who did something: *The firefighters extinguished the fire.*
- In the **passive** voice, you tell what happened, but you don't have to mention who did it: *The fire was extinguished.*

Passive voice is useful if you do not know who did something (*My purse was stolen!*), or if the doer of the action is not very important (*The room was decorated for the party.*). Otherwise, it is usually better to use the active voice.

Adjective

An adjective describes a noun or a pronoun: *loud*; *blue*; *two*. Adjectives can come before the word they describe: *a **tall** boy*. They can also come after a linking verb like *is*, *was*, or *seem*: *He is **tall**.*

Agreement of Subject and Verb

A verb should always agree with its subject.

- Singular subjects (one) take singular verbs: *John laughs loudly. Each of the games was played in the arena.*
- Plural subjects (more than one) take plural verbs: *John and Marta laugh loudly. The games were played in the arena.*

Your dictionary can help you choose the right verb form.

Adverb

An adverb describes a verb (*He ran **quickly**.*), an adjective (*a **really** dark blue car*), or another adverb (*He ran **very** quickly.*). Adverbs usually tell how, when, where, or in what manner.

Antonym

An antonym is a word that means the opposite of another word. **Hot** and **cold** are antonyms. So are **up** and **down**. Many antonyms are made by adding a prefix such as *dis-*, *mis-*, or *un-* to the word: ***dis**appear*; ***mis**understand*; ***un**roll.*

Apostrophe [']

Use an apostrophe:

- to show that something belongs to someone: *Jane's boat*
- in a contraction: *don't, can't*
- to show the plural of letters or symbols: *There are three a's in Saskatchewan and two 0's in 2008.*

Auxiliary (Helping) Verb

► See **Verb**.

Bias

Biassed language is language that talks about some group of people in an insulting way. Avoid making generalizations about men, women, racial groups, older people, or people with a disability. Mention a person's sex, race, age, or disability only if it is important to the meaning of what you are writing or saying.

Bibliography

A bibliography is a list of all the works used in a project, or in research. Place it on a separate page at the end. All bibliography entries should include the name of the author(s), the title of the work, and the publisher's name, with the date and place. Arrange the entries alphabetically, by author's name. Here are some example entries.

- *For a book:*
  Love, Ann, and Jane Drake. *Farming.* Toronto: Kids Can Press, 1996.
- *For a magazine article:*
  Jarzen, David. "Pollen Power." *Owl 22* (Mar. 1997)
- *For an Internet document:*
  [Author]. [Year]. [Title of Document]. Available: [address] [date accessed]

Capital Letter

Use capital letters for:

- the first word in a sentence: *My mother told me to be home in time for supper.*
- names of people or pets: *Jean Okalik, Sparky*
- the main words in a title: <u>*The Boy in the Drawer*</u>
- days of the week, months, and holidays: *Tuesday; September; Ramadan*
- names of companies, schools, or organizations: *Nike*; *St. Peter School*; *the United Way*

Clause

A clause is a group of words that has a subject and a verb. A sentence may have one clause (*I like watching television.*) or more than one clause (*When I have nothing better to do I like watching television, but I'd rather play hockey.*).

- A **main clause** makes a complete thought by itself: *I like watching television.*
- A **subordinate clause** does not make a complete thought by itself: *When I have nothing better to do*

► See also **Simple Sentence**; **Compound Sentence**.

Colon [:]

A colon warns you that something follows. Use colons:

- to introduce a list: *Canada has two official emblems: the maple leaf and the beaver.*
- to express time: *8:45*; *20:00*
- after the salutation of a business letter: *Dear Ms. Rosen:*

Comma [,]

A comma shows a slight pause in a sentence. Use as few commas as possible while keeping your meaning clear. You need a comma:

- between items in a series: *Jim, Walter, and Aviva sit next to each other.*
- between sentences joined by *and, or, nor, for, but, so, or yet: Rula thought hard, but no solutions came to mind.*
- between the day and the year in a date: *January 14, 2005*
- between a city and a province or country: *Ottawa, Ontario*; *Liverpool, England*
- after the salutation of a personal letter: *Dear Sam,*

Comparative

When you compare things, you can make changes to the positive form of an adjective.

- **positive** (*strong*), used for regular descriptions: *She is a strong swimmer.*
- **comparative** (*stronger*), used to compare two things: *She is the stronger of the two swimmers.*

When you compare more than two things, you use the superlative form.

- **superlative** (*strongest*), used for more than two things: *She is the strongest of all the swimmers.*

Compound Sentence

A compound sentence has two main clauses joined by a comma and *and*, *or*, *nor*, *for*, *but*, *so*, or *yet*. Each clause has its own subject and its own verb: *I want to go skating, but my skates aren't sharp.*

► See also **Simple Sentence**.

Compound Word

A compound word is a word that is made up of two other words: *chalkboard*, *weightlifter*, and handshake are compound words.

Some compound words are written as one word (*handbook*). Others are written with a hyphen (*hand-held*), and some are written as two words (*hand brake*). If you are not sure of the correct form, look the word up in a dictionary.

Conjunction

A conjunction is a word that connects other words, phrases, or clauses. The two main types of conjunctions are:

- co-ordinating conjunctions (*and, or, nor, for, but, so, yet*)
- subordinating conjunctions (*whenever, after, if, since, because, before, unless*)

Connecting Word

Use connecting words to link your ideas. This will make your writing flow from one idea to the next. Here are some useful connecting words and phrases: *afterward, although, as if, as long as, as much as, as soon as, even if, even though, first, in addition to, in order that, in spite of, similarly, since, so that.*

Contraction

A contraction is a shortened form of two words, such as *can't, won't, wouldn't.* Contractions are fine in informal writing and speech. In more formal writing, it is usually better to spell out the words: *cannot, will not, would not.*
► See also Apostrophe.

Dash (—)

A dash marks a strong break in a sentence, or emphasizes certain words: *Did you ever see the film—but no, it was made before you were born. Jack works hard—when he has to.* Sometimes, two dashes are used to set off a phrase or clause: *It wasn't until Friday—or it may have been Saturday—that I discovered the note in my backpack.* When you use dashes this way, remember to include the second dash.

Dialogue

Dialogue is conversation. To make dialogue sound like real spoken language, you can use incomplete sentences and some slang words that would not normally be acceptable in written work. Put quotation marks around each person's words and start a new paragraph every time someone starts to speak:

"Let's put a bell around the cat's neck, so we know when it is coming," said the first mouse.

"Great idea!" cried the others.

"But who," asked a small mouse from the back of the room, "will be the one to bell the cat?"

Double Negative

Using a negative word (such as *never, barely, scarcely, hardly*) in the same sentence as not makes a double negative. Avoid confusion by taking out or changing one of the two words:

Confusing: *I won't never go there again.*
Better: *I will never go there again.* OR *I won't go there again.*

Draft Version

You should make several draft versions of a piece of writing, until it is exactly what you want.

- Make your first draft have all the ideas that you want to include. Don't worry about things like checking spelling yet.
- In your next draft, check that all your information is correct, and organize your ideas so that they flow from one to the next.
- In the next draft, check and fix any errors in grammar, spelling, or punctuation.
- Your final version should be clean. Make sure you give it a title, and write your name on it.

Exclamation Mark [!]

An exclamation mark shows surprise, delight, or alarm. Avoid using too many exclamation marks, or your reader will get bored.

Too Many: *The room was a mess! Tables were overturned! The drawers had been pulled out! Clothes were everywhere! I understood immediately! The house had been robbed!!!!*

Better: *The room was a mess. Tables were overturned and the drawers had been pulled out. Clothes were everywhere. I understood immediately—the house had been robbed!*

Formal Language

Formal language is the careful language that is used in lectures, speeches, and essays. Some things that are allowed in informal speech or writing are not acceptable in formal writing. Here is a paragraph written in formal language:

Every Saturday morning, I go to the farmer's market. I buy vegetables, and I examine the goods that are for sale. Every stall contains unique treasures that catch my attention. I am never sure what I will find there.

To see the same paragraph written more informally, check the entry under **Informal Language.**

► See also **Sentence Fragment; Abbreviation.**

Homonym

Homonyms are homophones or homographs. **Homographs** are words that are **written the same** but have different meanings, such as *tear* (a drop of water from your eye) and *tear* (rip). **Homophones** are words that **sound the same** but have different meanings, such as *meat* (animal flesh) and *meet* (join up with). Words like *bank* (one side of a river) and *bank* (a place to keep money) are homophones and homographs, both at once!

Hyphen [-]

Use hyphens:

- in spelled-out numbers between 21 and 99: *twenty-six*
- in spelled-out times of the day: *the five-fifteen bus*
- to divide a word between syllables at the end of a line: *dis-satisfied*; *dissat-isfied*; *dissatis-fied*
- after some prefixes: *all-round*; *co-operate*; *ex-boyfriend*; *half-hearted*; *pre-test*; *pro-Canadian*; *re-enter*; *self-centred*
- in some compound words: *sister-in-law*; *hand-held*

► See also **Compound Word.**

Informal Language

Informal language is the language you use in everyday speech or casual writing. Here is an example of informal writing:

Every Sat. in the a.m., I head down to the farmer's market. I buy veggies, and then I check out the stuff for sale. Every stall grabs my attention with really cool things you can't find anywhere else. You just never know what you'll find there!

To see the same paragraph written more formally, check the entry under **Formal Language.**

Linking Verb

► See **Verb.**

Metaphor and Simile

Metaphors and similes are both ways of writing comparisons. A simile compares two things or ideas directly using *like* or *as*: *The icicles looked like bony fingers.* A metaphor makes the comparison indirectly, without using *like* or *as*: *Bony fingers of ice.*

Noun

A noun is a word that names a person (*boy; Jim*), place (*Canada; garden; school*), or thing (*table; river; house*). A proper noun names a specific person, place, or thing. Always capitalize a proper noun: *Jonah Allingham*; *Burnaby, B.C.*; *the Eiffel Tower.*

► See also **Subject/Verb Agreement.**

Paragraph

A paragraph is a group of sentences that tell about one main idea. The first line of a paragraph is usually indented.

A paragraph often begins with a topic sentence that tells the main idea. The other sentences in the paragraph say something about the topic sentence. Sometimes a connecting word like *next*, *therefore*, *so*, *finally*, *however*, or *then* helps to show how a sentence is connected to the rest of the paragraph.

Parentheses [()]

Use parentheses:

- to add extra comments in a sentence: *They lived happily ever after (and so did the dog).*
- to explain something or give information: *That mask (the one with the green skin) scares some people.*

Part of Speech

Every word used in a sentence belongs to one of the eight parts of speech: **noun**, **adjective**, **verb**, **adverb**, **conjunction**, **preposition**, **pronoun**, or **interjection**. A word can take on different roles, or parts of speech, in different sentences. For example, the word *run* can act as a noun (*I went on a five-kilometre run.*) or a verb (*I run fast.*) or even an adjective (*The run organizers said it was a success.*).

Period [.]

Use a period:

- at the end of a sentence: *The sky is blue.*
- after abbreviations and initials: *J.J. Cale; Mr.; St.*

Phrase

A phrase is a group of words used together in a sentence: *for the first time*; *thinking fast*; *to be a scientist* are all phrases. A phrase cannot act as a sentence or a clause on its own.

- Some phrases can act as **adjectives**: *The book* ***on the table*** *is mine.*
- Phrases can also act as **adverbs**: *We played baseball* ***after supper****.*

► See also **Clause**.

Plural

The plural form of a word shows that it talks about more than one. Nouns, pronouns, and verbs can be plural.

Plural Noun

Plural nouns usually end in *-s: houses*, *pigs*, *ideas*. However, some nouns have irregular plural forms.

- Some don't end in *-s: children, men, women, mice, geese.*
- Others have the same form for both singular and plural: *deer, moose.*
- Some words look plural, but are treated as singular: *news, measles, mathematics.*

If you aren't sure how to form the plural of a word, check the dictionary entry for the singular form of the word.

► See also **Pronoun; Subject-Verb Agreement**.

Possessive

Use possessive forms of nouns and pronouns to show belonging. Here is how to make a noun possessive:

- For most singular nouns, add *'s: Jim's idea, the cat's paw*
- For plural nouns ending in *-s*, add only an apostrophe: *the students' project, the Livakos' pet, the cars' lights*
- For plural nouns that do not end in *-s*, add *'s: children's games, people's pets, geese's feathers*

Possessive pronouns never need an apostrophe: *mine, yours, his, hers, ours, theirs.*

Prefix

A prefix is a word or syllable added to the beginning of a word to make a new word. For example, *dis-* added to *appear* makes *disappear*. Often, knowing what a prefix means can help you to figure out the meaning of a word. Here is a list of some common prefixes and their meanings:

anti- (against): *antifreeze*
multi- (many): *multicultural*
bi- (two): *bicycle*
dis- (not): *disagree*
in- (not): *inexpensive*
inter- (between; among): *international*
mis- (wrong): *misunderstand*
non- (not): *nonstop*
post- (after): *postscript*

re- (again): *reheat*
semi- (half): *semicircle*
trans- (across): *transplant*
tri- (three): *triangle*
un- (not): *unnecessary*
uni- (one): *uniform*

Preposition

A preposition is a word that shows the connection between a noun and some other word in the sentence. In the phrase *the pencil on the desk*, the preposition on connects the noun *pencil* to the word *desk*. Some words that sometimes function as prepositions are: *above, at, before, behind, by, down, for, from, in, of, on, past, since, to, under, until, with.*

Pronoun

A pronoun is a word that replaces a noun. If the noun is singular, then use a singular pronoun. If the noun is plural, use a plural pronoun. Some useful pronouns are *I, me, mine, you, yours, he, him, his, she, her, hers, it, we, us, they, them, theirs.* These are called personal pronouns. Other pronouns include words such as: *who, what, this, those, that, everyone, someone, nobody, either, neither, myself, and yourself.*

Proofreading Symbols

The following symbols may be used to mark changes on your writing.

Symbol	Meaning	Example
∧	INSERT	The house ∧ on fire. (is)
	DELETE	Rattlesnakes are are very dangerous.
≡	CAPITAL	ali may be in danger!
/	LOWER CASE	We Compost all our food scraps.
¶	NEW PARAGRAPH	So that day ended badly. ¶ The next day...
⊙	ADD PERIOD	Liu wondered which way to go ⊙
∧,	ADD COMMA	Bring your tent ∧ a sleeping bag, and a flashlight.
#	ADD SPACE	Danieland I are leaving tomorrow.
⌣	CLOSE SPACE	Chickens can't fly, but duc ks can.

Proofreading Tips

Proofreading is the last stage in the writing process, before you present your work to your audience. When you proofread, try these tips:

- Read slowly, checking each word. Sometimes it helps to start from the last word and work backward to the beginning. Use a ruler to help you keep your place.
- Make sure each sentence begins with a capital letter and has proper end punctuation.
- Check that commas, semicolons, and colons are used correctly.
- Check that all place names and proper names are spelled correctly and that they begin with a capital letter.
- Check that each paragraph is indented.
- Check for spelling errors, especially in words you often misspell. Look up any words you aren't sure of in a dictionary.

Question Mark [?]

Use a question mark at the end of a direct question: *Where is the remote?* You don't need a question mark in sentences like this: *Sasha asked where the remote was.*

Quotation Marks [“ ”]

When you write someone's exact words, put them in quotation marks: John said, *“I like school.”* You don't need quotation marks in sentences like this: *John said that he liked school.* Also use quotation marks around the titles of short stories, newspaper articles, magazine articles, and episodes of television shows.

► See also **Dialogue**.

Run-on Sentence

A run-on sentence tries to say too much. Run-ons happen when you combine two sentences into one without proper punctuation: The sky is clear we can go out to play. To fix a run-on sentence, you can do one of these things:

- Separate the sentences into two sentences beginning with a capital letter and ending with a period, question mark, or exclamation mark: *The sky is clear. We can go out to play.*
- Join the sentences with a semicolon, or with a comma and a joining word: *The sky is clear; we can go out to play.* OR *The sky is clear, so we can go out to play.*
- Join the two sentences into a single sentence: *Since the sky is clear, we can go out to play.*

Semicolon [;]

Use a semicolon:

- to separate two related sentences. When you use a semicolon like this, you tell your reader that the sentence that follows is closely connected to the one before: *I love watching television after school; it relaxes me.*
- to separate items in a list if you have already used a comma: *Walter has lived in Tokyo, Japan; London, England; and Estevan, Saskatchewan.*

Sentence Types

A sentence is a group of words that expresses a complete thought. Every sentence needs a subject and a verb. There are four kinds of sentences:

- **Declarative** sentences tell something. They end with a period: *This book is heavy.*
- **Interrogative** sentences ask a question. They end with a question mark: *Why are you so happy?*
- **Exclamatory** sentences express surprise or strong feeling. They usually end in an exclamation mark: *How beautiful the sky is tonight!*
- **Imperative** sentences give a command. They may end with a period or an exclamation mark. In imperative sentences, the subject is often not written, because it is always "you": (You) *Watch out!* (You) *Get your jacket on.*

Sentence Fragment

A sentence fragment is a group of words that is punctuated like a sentence, but is missing either a subject or a verb, or both. We use sentence fragments all the time when we speak. In informal writing, or when you are writing dialogue, they are acceptable, but in formal writing they are not:

Who won the prize? Josh. [*Josh* is a sentence fragment because it has no verb.]

I wasn't picked for the part. Never understood why. [*Never understood why* is a sentence fragment because it has no subject.]

Simile

► See **Metaphor and Simile.**

Simple Sentence

A simple sentence has one main subject and one main verb: *The camel spit at me!* *Camel* is the subject, and *spit* is the verb.

► See also **Compound Sentence.**

Spelling

The **spelling** of English words can be confusing. Here are a few rules that work most of the time. There are exceptions, though, so check in a dictionary to be sure.

- If it sounds like *me*, write *i* before *e* except after *c: piece.*
- For plurals, add *es* to words that end in *ch, s, sh,* or *x: catches, misses, wishes, boxes.*
- When adding *ing* or *ed*, double the final consonant of a verb that ends in a single vowel plus a consonant: *sitting, ripped.*

When you have trouble remembering how to spell a word, try some of these strategies:

- Playing around with the word will help you to remember it: say it out loud, picture the letters in your head, write it down in fancy lettering.
- Think of a memory trick to help you remember hard words. For example, you can remember that *cereal* starts with *c* by

remembering the sentence *I like cream in my cereal.*

- Make your own dictionary of words you misspell often, and check it whenever you write.
- For words with silent letters or double letters, pronounce *all* the letters in your head: *k-now, mis-spell*
- Look for similar spelling patterns: *sight/night/fright/light; bite/kite/quite.*
- Look for a smaller word inside a big word: *argument; tragedy.*

Subject

The subject of a sentence names the person or thing that the sentence is about. The subject is usually near the beginning of the sentence: ***Arnold*** *rode his bicycle.* ***The cat*** *scratched the screen.*

Suffix

A suffix is a syllable or letters added to the end of a word to make a new word. Adding suffixes can change adjectives to verbs, verbs to nouns, etc. Here are some common suffixes that can make different word types:

Noun suffixes:
-er, -or: *teacher, instructor*
-ment: *agreement*
-ness: *awareness*
-ship: *friendship*

Adjective suffixes:
-able: *agreeable*
-er, -est: *longer; longest*
-ful: *delightful*
-less: *fearless*

Verb suffixes:
-en: *strengthen*
-ize: *crystallize*

Adverb suffix:
-ly: *quickly*

Superlative

► See **Comparative.**

Synonym

Synonyms are words with similar meanings. *Discuss, talk,* and *chat* are synonyms. You can use synonyms to avoid repeating the same word in a passage. You can also use them to express a particular meaning. For example, in the sentence, *We chatted on the phone for over an hour,* the word *chat* is better than *talked* or *discussed,* because it tells your reader that you were talking in an easy, familiar way. Look in a thesaurus to find synonyms.

Tense

The tense of a verb tells you when the action happened. There are three main tenses in English: past, present, and future.
Do not switch from one main tense to another. For example, this passage shifts between past and present tenses:

Pedro walks up to the door. He had been waiting for this moment for the last two years. He reaches for the knocker and lets it fall. The door opens slowly, and there stood the biggest man he had ever seen.

It needs to be rewritten in either past tense or present tense. For example, here is what it would look like in present tense:

Pedro walks up to the door. He has been waiting for this moment for the last two years. He reaches for the knocker and lets it fall. The door opens slowly, and there stands the biggest man he has ever seen.

Verb

A verb is a word that tells what a person, place, or thing is or is doing.

- Most verbs are **action verbs:** *go, sleep, take, walk, run, dream.*
- **Linking verbs** link the subject to a word that describes the subject. The most common linking verbs are *is, am, are, was,* and *were*: *I am sad. That animal is an iguana.*
- An **auxiliary verb** is a verb that helps another verb. In the sentence *I have been here before,* the auxiliary verb is *have.* Some verbs that work as auxiliaries are *have, be, can,* and *will.*

► See also **Tense; Subject-Verb Agreement.**

Pronunciation Key

The pronunciation of each main entry word in this dictionary is shown after the word, in this way: **mem•o•ry** (mem′ə rē). The letters and signs used are pronounced as in the words below. The mark ′ is placed after a syllable with primary stress.

a	and, hat
ā	age, face
ȧ	art, far
b	bad, rob
ch	child, much
d	do, red
e	end, let
ē	equal, be
f	fat, if
g	go, bag
h	he, how
i	it, pin
ī	ice, five
j	jam, enjoy
k	kind, seek
l	land, coal
m	me, am
n	no, in
ng	long, bring
o	hot, rock
ō	open, go
ȯ	order, door
oi	oil, voice
ou	out, loud
p	pen, cup
r	run, car
s	say, yes
sh	she, rush
t	tell, it
th	thin, bath
ŧʜ	then, smooth, bathe
u	cup, butter
ü	rule, move
u̇	full, good
yü	use, music
v	very, love
w	will, woman
y	young, yet
z	zero, breeze
zh	seizure
ə	alone, moment, sofa
ər	early, term, measure